THE BANTAM NEW COLLEGE
GERMAN & ENGLISH DICTIONARY

The Best Low-Priced Dictionary You Can Own

With more entries than any other compact paper-bound dictionary—including thousands of new words—*The Bantam New College German & English Dictionary* is the most complete budget dictionary available today.

Whether you need it at home, the office, school, or in the library, this one indispensable, authoritative volume will prove its value over and over again, every time you use it.

THE BANTAM NEW COLLEGE DICTIONARY SERIES

John C. Traupman, Author

JOHN C. TRAUPMAN received his B.A. in German and in Latin at Moravian College and his M.A. and Ph.D. in Classics at Princeton University. He is chairman of the Department of Classical Languages at St. Joseph's University (Philadelphia). He served as president of the Philadelphia Classical Society, of the Pennsylvania Classical Association, and of the Classical and Modern Language League. He has published widely in learned journals and is the author of *The New College Latin & English Dictionary* (Bantam Books, 1966) and an associate editor of *The Scribner-Bantam English Dictionary* (Scribner's, 1977; Bantam Books, 1979).

Edwin B. Williams, General Editor

EDWIN B. WILLIAMS (1891–1975), A.B., A.M., Ph.D., Doct. d'Univ., LL.D., L.H.D., was chairman of the Department of Romance Languages, dean of the Graduate School, and provost of the University of Pennsylvania. He was a member of the American Philosophical Society and the Hispanic Society of America. Among his many lexicographical works are *The Williams Spanish and English Dictionary* (Scribner's, formerly Holt) and *The Bantam New College Spanish and English Dictionary*. He created and coordinated the Bantam series of original dictionaries—English, French, German, Italian, Latin, and Spanish.

THE BANTAM NEW COLLEGE
GERMAN & ENGLISH
DICTIONARY

JOHN C. TRAUPMAN, Ph.D.
St. Joseph's University, Philadelphia

BANTAM BOOKS
TORONTO • NEW YORK • LONDON • SYDNEY • AUCKLAND

THE BANTAM NEW COLLEGE
GERMAN & ENGLISH DICTIONARY

A Bantam Book / February 1981

2nd printing . . . . August 1983   4th printing . . December 1984
3rd printing . . . . . . June 1984   5th printing . . February 1986

ISBN 0-553-25953-9

Published simultaneously in the United States and Canada

PRINTED IN THE UNITED STATES OF AMERICA

H   14 13 12 11 10 9 8

CONTENTS

I wish to express my appreciation to the many persons on whose help I relied in researching and compiling this Dictionary. I am particularly indebted to Edwin B. Williams, Walter D. Glanze, Donald Reis, Rudolf Pillwein, and Helmut Kreitz.

J. C. T.

HOW TO USE THIS DICTIONARY

HINWEISE FÜR DEN BENUTZER

All entry words are treated in a fixed order according to the parts of speech and the functions of verbs. On the German-English side: past participle, adjective, adverb, pronoun, preposition, conjunction, interjection, transitive verb, reflexive verb, reciprocal verb, intransitive verb, impersonal verb, auxiliary verb, substantive; on the English-German side: adjective, substantive, pronoun, adverb, preposition, conjunction, transitive verb, intransitive verb, auxiliary verb, impersonal verb, interjection.

Alle Stichwörter werden in einheitlicher Reihenfolge gemäß der Wortart und der Verbfunktion behandelt. Im deutsch-englischen Teil: Partizip Perfekt, Adjektiv, Adverb, Pronomen, Präposition, Konjunktion, Interjektion, transitives Verb, reflexives Verb, reziprokes Verb, intransitives Verb, unpersönliches Verb, Hilfsverb, Substantiv; im englisch-deutschen Teil: Adjektiv, Substantiv, Pronomen, Adverb, Präposition, Konjunktion, transitives Verb, intransitives Verb, Hilfsverb, unpersönliches Verb, Interjektion.

The order of meanings within an entry is as follows: first, the more general meanings; second, the meanings with usage labels; third, the meanings with subject labels in alphabetical order; fourth, illustrative phrases in alphabetical order.

Die verschiedenen Bedeutungen sind innerhalb eines Stichwortartikels in folgender Anordnung gegeben: zuerst die allgemeinen Bedeutungen; dann die Bedeutungen mit Bezeichnung der Sprachgebrauchsebene; dann die Bedeutungen mit Bezeichnung des Sachgebietes, in alphabetischer Reihenfolge; zuletzt die Anwendungsbeispiele, in alphabetischer Reihenfolge.

Subject and usage labels (printed in roman and in parentheses) refer to the preceding entry word or illustrative phrase in the source language (printed in boldface), e.g.,

Die Bezeichnungen der Sprachgebrauchsebene und des Sachgebiets (in Antiqua und in Klammern) beziehen sich auf das vorangehende Stichwort oder Anwendungsbeispiel in der Ausgangssprache (halbfett gedruckt), z.B.

mund′tot *adj*—**j–n m. machen** (fig) silence s.o.
Pinke [′pɪŋkə] *f* (–;) (coll) dough

Words in parentheses and in roman coming after a meaning serve to clarify that meaning, e.g.,

Kursiv gedruckte Wörter in Klammern, die nach einer Bedeutung stehen, sollen diese Bedeutung illustrieren, z.B.

überschau′en *tr* look over, survey; overlook (*a scene*)

Words in parenthese and in roman type coming after or before a meaning are optional additions to the word in the target language, e.g.,	In Antiqua gedruckte Wörter in Klammern, die nach oder vor einer Bedeutung stehen, sind wahlfreie Erweiterungen des Wortes der Zielsprache, z.B.

Tanne ['tanə] *f* (-;-n) fir (tree)
Pap'rikaschote *f* (green) pepper

Meaning discriminations are given in the source language and are in italics, e.g.,	Bedeutungsdifferenzierungen sind in der Ausgangssprache angegeben und kursiv gedruckt, z.B.

überrei'zen *tr* overexcite; (*Augen, Nerven*) strain
earn [ʌrn] *tr* (*money*) verdienen; (*interest*) einbringen

Since vocabulary entries are not determined on the basis of etymology, homographs are listed as a single entry.	Da die Etymologie bei der Anführung der Stichwörter unberücksichtigt bleibt, sind gleichgeschriebene Wörter als ein und dasselbe Stichwort verzeichnet.

The entry word is represented within the entry by its initial letter followed by a period (if the entry word contains more than three letters), provided the form is identical. The same applies to a word that follows the parallels. The entry word is not abbreviated within the entry when associated with suspension points, e.g.,	Innerhalb eines Stichwortartikels wird das Stichwort (wenn es mehr als drei Buchstaben enthält) durch seinen Anfangsbuchstaben und einen Punkt angegeben, vorausgesetzt, daß die betreffende Form mit dem Stichwort identisch ist. Das Gleiche gilt für ein Wort, das nach den Vertikalstrichen steht. Wenn ein Stichwort innerhalb eines Stichwortartikels in Verbindung mit Auslassungspunkten angegeben ist, wird es nicht abgekürzt, z.B.

weder . . . noch

Parallels are used (a) to separate parts of speech, (b) to separate transitive, reflexive, reciprocal, intransitive, impersonal, and auxiliary verbs, (c) to separate verbs taking HABEN from those taking SEIN, (d) to indicate a change in pronunciation of the entry word, depending on the meaning, e.g.,	Es ist der Zweck der Vertikalstriche, (a) Wortarten voneinander zu trennen, (b) transitive, reflexive, reziproke, intransitive, unpersönliche Verben und Hilfsverben zu trennen, (c) Verben mit dem Hilfsverb HABEN von Verben mit dem Hilfsverb SEIN zu trennen, (d) verschiedene Aussprachen des Stichwortes je nach Bedeutung anzuzeigen, z.B.

bow [baʊ] *s* Verbeugung *f;* (naut) Bug *m* . . .
‖ [bo] *s* (*weapon*) Bogen *m; ...*

(e) to show change from a strong verb to a weak verb and vice versa, (f) to show a change in the case governed by	(e) den Wechsel von einem starken zu einem schwachen Verb und umgekehrt anzuzeigen, (f) den Wechsel in einem

a preposition where the entry word is a preposition, (g) to show a shift of accent, e.g.,	von einer Präposition regierten Fall anzuzeigen, wo das Stichwort selbst eine Präposition ist, (g) unterschiedliche Stellungen des Akzents anzuzeigen, z.B.

ü′bergießen *tr* . . . ‖ **übergie′ßen** *tr* . . .

The centered period in the English word on the German-English side marks the point at which the following letters are dropped before irregular plural endings are added. The centered period in the entry word on the English-German side marks the point at which the following letters are dropped before irregular plural endings are added to nouns and inflections are added to verbs. The centered period in the phonetic spelling indicates diaeresis, e.g.,	Der auf Mitte stehende Punkt im Stichwort des deutsch-englischen Teils zeigt die Stelle an, wo die nachfolgenden Buchstaben abzutrennen sind, bevor unregelmäßige Pluralendungen angefügt werden können. Der auf Mitte stehende Punkt im Stichwort des englisch-deutschen Teils zeigt die Stelle an, wo die nachfolgenden Buchstaben abzutrennen sind, bevor unregelmäßige Pluralendungen an Hauptwörter and Flexionen an Verben angefügt werden können. Der auf Mitte stehende Punkt in der Lautschrift zeigt Diärese an, z.B.

befähigt [bə′fe·ɪçt]

On the German-English and the English-German side, in the case of a transitive verb, the meaning discrimination in parentheses before the target word is always the object of the verb. On the German-English side, in the case of an intransitive verb, the meaning discrimination in parentheses before the target word is always the subject of the verb. On the English-German side, the suggested subject of a verb is prefaced by the words "said of".	Im deutsch-englischen und im englisch-deutschen Teil ist die bei transitiven Verben in Klammern vor dem Wort in der Zielsprache angegebene Bedeutungsdifferenzierung immer das Objekt des Verbs. Im deutsch-englischen Teil ist bei intransitiven Verben die vor dem Wort in der Zielsprache angegebene Bedeutungsdifferenzierung immer das Subjekt des Verbs. Im englisch-deutschen Teil stehen vor dem beabsichtigten Subjekt eines Verbs die Worte "said of."

Inflections are generally not shown for compound entry words, since the inflections have been shown where the components are entry words. However, when the last component of a compound noun on the German-English side has various inflections depending on meaning, the inflection is shown for the compound, e.g.,	Bei zusammengesetzten Stichwörtern ist die Flexion im Allgemeinen nicht angegeben, da sie unter den als Stichwörter angeführten Teilen des Kompositums angegeben ist. Falls jedoch der letzte Teil eines deutschen Kompositums je nach der Bedeutung verschieden flektiert wird, ist die Flexion für das Kompositum angegeben, z.B.

Ton′band *n* (–[e]s;∺er) . . .

German verbs are regarded as reflexive regardless of whether the reflexive pronoun is the direct or indirect object of the verb.	Deutsche Verben gelten als reflexiv ohne Rücksicht darauf, ob das Reflexivpronomen das direkte oder indirekte Objekt des Verbs ist.

On the English-German side, when the pronunciation of an entry word is not given, stress in the entry word is shown as follows: a high-set primary stress mark ′ follows the syllable that receives the primary stress, and a high-set secondary stress mark ′ follows the syllable that receives the secondary stress. When the pronunciation of an entry word *is* provided [given in brackets], a high-set primary stress mark ′ *precedes* the syllable that receives the primary stress, and a *low*-set secondary stress mark , *precedes* the syllable that receives the secondary stress.

On the German-English side, when the pronunciation of an entry word is not given, a high-set primary stress mark ′ follows the syllable of the entry word that receives the primary stress. When the pronunciation of the entry word *is* provided [given in brackets], a high-set primary stress mark ′ *precedes* the syllable that receives the primary stress. (Because opinions on the system of secondary stress in German differ widely, secondary stress marks are not employed in this Dictionary.)

Wo die Aussprache des Stichwortes im englisch-deutschen Teil nicht angegeben ist, wird die Betonung des Stichwortes folgendermaßen angedeutet: Das stärkere, obere graphische Zeichen ′ steht nach der Silbe mit dem Haupttonakzent, und das schwächere, obere Zeichen ′ steht nach der Silbe mit dem Nebentonakzent. Wo hingegen die Aussprache des Stichwortes im englisch-deutschen Teil [in eckigen Klammern] angegeben ist, steht das stärkere, obere Zeichen ′ *vor* der Silbe mit dem Haupttonakzent und das schwächere, *untere* Zeichen , *vor* der Silbe mit dem Nebentonakzent.

Wo die Aussprache das Stichwortes im deutsch-englischen Teil nicht angegeben ist, steht das starke Zeichen ′ nach der Stichwortsilbe mit dem Haupttonakzent. Wo hingegen die Aussprache des Stichwortes im deutsch-englischen Teil [in eckigen Klammern] angegeben ist, steht das starke Zeichen ′ *vor* der Silbe mit dem Haupttonakzent. (Wegen der widersprüchlichen Theorien, die die Frage des Nebentonakzents im Deutschen umgeben, wendet dieses Wörterbuch keine Nebentonakzente für die deutschen Wörter an.)

Proper nouns and general abbreviations are listed in their alphabetical position in the main body of the Dictionary.

Eigennamen und allgemeine Abkürzungen sind in den beiden Hauptteilen des Wörterbuches in alphabetischer Reihenfolge angegeben.

This Dictionary contains approximately 75,000 "entries." As entries are counted (a) nonindented boldface headwords and (b) elements that could have been set nonindented as separate headwords, too, but that for reasons of style and typography are grouped under the nonindented headwords, namely, separate parts of speech and boldface idioms and phrases.

Dieses Wörterbuch enthält ungefähr 75.000 "Stichwörter." Die folgenden Elemente gelten als Stichwörter: (a) die nicht eingerückten fettgedruckten Wörter am Anfang eines Stichwortartikels und (b) Elemente, die man auf dieselbe Weise hatte drucken können, die aber aus Stil- und Typographiegründen eingerückt wurden, nämlich die unterschiedlichen Wortarten und die fettgedruckten Redewendungen.

PART ONE

German-English

GERMAN—ENGLISH

A

A, a [ɑ] *invar n* A, a; (mus) A; **das A und O** the beginning and the end; (*das Wichtigste*) the most important thing

Aal [ɑl] *m* (–[e]s;–e) eel; (nav) torpedo

aal'glatt' *adj* (fig) sly as a fox

Aas [as] *n* (–es;–e) carrion; (sl) louse

ab [ap] *adv* off; away; down; on, e.g., **von heute ab** from today on; (theat) exit, exeunt, e.g., **Hamlet ab** exit Hamlet; **ab und zu** now and then || *prep* (*dat*) from, e.g., **ab Frankfurt** from Frankfurt; minus, e.g., **ab Skonto** minus discount

ab'ändern *tr* alter; (*völlig*) change; (*mildern*) modify; (parl) amend

Ab'änderung *f* (–;–en) alteration; change; modification; (parl) amendment

Ab'änderungsantrag *m* (parl) (proposed) amendment

ab'arbeiten *tr* work off || *ref* work hard

Ab'art *f* variety, type

ab'arten *intr* (SEIN) deviate from type

Ab'bau *m* (–[e]s;) demolition; reduction; cutback; layoff; (chem) decomposition; (min) exploitation

ab'bauen *tr* demolish; (*Maschinen, Fabriken*) dismantle; (*Steuern, Preise, Truppen*) reduce; (*Zelt*) take down; (*Lager*) break; (*Angestellte*) lay off; (chem) decompose; (min) work, exploit

ab'beißen §53 *tr* bite off || *intr* take a bite

ab'bekommen §99 *tr* (*seinen Teil*) get; (*Schmutz*) get out; (*Deckel*) get off; **du wirst was a.!** you're going to get it!

ab'berufen §122 *tr* (dipl) recall

ab'bestellen *tr* cancel

ab'betteln *tr*—**die ganze Straße a.** beg up and down the street; **j–m etw a.** chisel s.th. from s.o.

ab'biegen §57 *tr* bend, twist off; (*Gefahr*) avert; (*Plan*) thwart; **das Gespräch a.** change the subject || *intr* (SEIN) branch off; (fig) get off the track; **in e-e Seitenstraße a.** turn down a side street; **nach links a.** turn left; **von e-r Straße a.** turn off a road

Ab'bild *n* picture, image

ab'bilden *tr* represent

Ab'bildung *f* (–;–en) illustration, figure

ab'binden §59 *tr* untie; (*Kalb*) wean; (*Arm*) apply a tourniquet to; (surg) tie off || *intr* (*Zement*) set

Ab'bitte *f* apology; **A. tun wegen** apologize for

ab'bitten §60 *tr* apologize for || *intr* apologize

ab'blasen §61 *tr* blow off; (fig) call off || *intr* (mil) sound the retreat

ab'blättern *intr* (SEIN) shed leaves; (*Farben, Haut*) flake, peel

ab'blenden *tr* dim; (cin) fade out; (phot) stop down || *intr* (aut) dim the lights; (nav) darken ship; (phot) stop down the lens

Ab'blendlicht *n* (aut) low-beam lights

ab'blitzen *intr* (SEIN) be unsuccessful; **j–n a. lassen** snub s.o.

ab'blühen *intr* stop blooming || *intr* (SEIN) fade

ab'böschen *tr* slope; (*Mauer*) batter

ab'brausen *tr* hose down || *ref* shower off || *intr* (SEIN) (coll) roar off

ab'brechen §64 *tr* break off; (*Belagerung*) raise; (*Gebäude*) demolish; (*Zelt*) take down; (sport) call; **das Lager a.** break camp || *intr* (SEIN) (& fig) break off

ab'bremsen *tr* slow down; (*Streik*) prevent; (*Motoren*) (aer) rev || *intr* put on the brakes; (aer) fishtail

ab'brennen §97 *tr* burn off; (*Feuerwerk*) set off; (*Geschütz*) fire; (chem) distil out; (metal) refine; (naut) bream; **ich bin vollkommen abgebrannt** (coll) I'm dead broke || *intr* (SEIN) burn down

ab'bringen §65 *tr* (*Fleck*) remove; (*gestrandetes Schiff*) refloat; **davon a. zu** (*inf*) dissuade from (*ger*); **vom rechten Weg a.** lead astray; **vom Thema a.** throw off; **von der Spur a.** throw off the scent; **von e-r Gewohnheit a.** break of the habit

ab'bröckeln *intr* crumble; (*Farbe*) peel (off); (*Preis, Aktie*) go slowly down; (*Mitglieder*) fall off

Ab'bruch *m* (*e–s Zweiges, der Beziehungen*) breaking off; (*e–s Gebäudes*) demolition; (*Schaden*) damage; **A. des Spiels** (sport) calling of the game; **A. tun** (*dat*) harm, spoil; **auf A. verkaufen** sell at demolition value; (*Maschinen*) sell for junk

ab'brühen *tr* (culin) scald

ab'brummen *tr* (*Strafe*) (coll) serve, do || *intr* (SEIN) (coll) clear out

ab'buchen *tr* (*abschreiben*) write off; (acct) debit

ab'bürsten *tr* brush off

ab'büßen *tr* atone for; **e–e Strafe a.** serve time; **er hat es schwer a. müssen** (coll) he had to pay for it dearly

Abc [abeˈtse] *n* (–;–) ABC's

Abc'-Schütze *m* (–n;–n) pupil

ab'danken *tr* dismiss; (*pensionieren*)

retire || *intr* resign; (*Herrscher*) abdicate; (mil) get a discharge

ab'decken *tr* uncover; (*Tisch*) clear; (*Bett*) turn down; (*Vieh*) skin; (*e-e Schuld*) pay back; (mil) camouflage; (phot) mask

ab'dichten *tr* seal (off); (*Loch*) plug up; (*mit weichem Material*) pack; (naut) caulk

ab'dienen *tr* (*Schuld*) work off; (mil) serve (*one's term*)

ab'drehen *tr* twist off; (*Gas, Licht, Wasser*) turn off || *intr* turn away

ab'dreschen §67 *tr* thrash

Ab'druck *m* (-s;-e) reprint; offprint; copy; (*Abguß*) casting; (phot, typ) proof || *m* (-s;ᵘe) impression, imprint

ab'drucken *tr* print

ab'drücken *tr* (*abformen*) mold; (*Gewehr*) fire; (*Pfeil*) shoot; (*umarmen*) hug; **den Hahn a.** pull the trigger || *ref* leave an impression || *intr* pull the trigger

ab'duschen *ref* shower off

Abend ['abənt] *m* (-s;-e) evening; **am A.** in the evening; **bunter A.** social; (telv) variety show; **des Abends in the evening(s); zu A. essen** eat dinner

A'bendblatt *n* evening paper

A'bendbrot *n* supper, dinner

A'benddämmerung *f* twilight, dusk

A'bendessen *n* supper, dinner

abendfüllend ['abəntfʏlənt] *adj* full-length (*movie*)

A'bendgesellschaft *f* party (*in the evening*)

A'bendland *n* West, Occident

abendländisch ['abəntlendɪʃ] *adj* occidental

a'bendlich *adj* evening || *adv* evenings

A'bendmahl *n* supper; **das Heilige A.** Holy Communion

abends ['abənts] *adv* in the evening

Abenteuer ['abəntɔɪ·ər] *s* (-s;-) adventure; **galantes A.** love affair

a'benteuerlich *adj* adventurous; (*Unternehmen*) risky

aber ['abər] *adv* yet, however; (before adjectives and adverbs) really, indeed; **a. und abermals** over and over again; **hundert und a. hundert** hundreds and hundreds of || *conj* but || *interj*—**aber, aber!** now, now! || **Aber** *n* (-s;-s) but; **hier gibt es kein A.!** no ifs and buts

A'berglaube *m* superstition

abergläubisch ['abərglɔɪbɪʃ] *adj* superstitious

ab'erkennen §97 *tr*—**j-m etw a.** deny s.o. s.th.; (jur) dispossess s.o. of s.th.

Ab'erkennung *f* (-;-en) denial; (jur) dispossession

abermalig ['abərmalɪç] *adj* repeated

abermals ['abərmals] *adv* once more

ab'ernten *tr* reap, harvest

ab'fahren §71 *tr* cart away; (*Strecke*) cover; (*Straße*) wear out; (*Reifen*) wear down || *intr* (SEIN) depart; drive off

Ab'fahrt *f* departure

Ab'fall *m* (*der Blätter*) falling; (*Bö-*

schung) steep slope; (*von e-m Glauben*) falling away; (*von e-r Partei*) defection; (*Sinken*) drop, decrease; **Abfälle** garbage, trash; chips, shavings

ab'fallen §72 *intr* (SEIN) fall off; (*von e-r Partei*) defect; (*vom Glauben*) fall away; (*abnehmen*) decrease, fail; (*Kunden*) stay away; (sport) fall behind; **a. gegen** compare badly with; **es wird etw für dich a.** there'll be s.th. in it for you; **körperlich a.** lose weight; **steil a.** drop away

abfällig ['apfɛlɪç] *adj* disparaging

Ab'fallprodukt *n* by-product

ab'fangen §73 *tr* catch; (*Angriff*) foil; (*Brief*) intercept; (aer) pull out of a dive; (*U-Boot*) (nav) trim; (sport) catch (up with); **j-m die Kunden a.** steal s.o.'s customers

ab'färben *intr* (*Farben*) run; (*Stoff*) fade; **a. auf** (acc) stain; (fig) rub off on

ab'fassen *tr* compose, draft; (*erwischen*) catch

Ab'fassung *f* (-;-en) wording; composition

ab'faulen *intr* (SEIN) rot away

ab'fegen *tr* sweep off, whisk off

abfertigen ['apfertɪgən] *tr* get ready for sending off; (*Gepäck*) check; (*Zöllgüter*) clear; (*Kunden*) wait on; (*abweisen*) snub; (*verwaltungsmäßig*) (adm) process;

Ab'fertigung *f* (-;-en) dispatch; snub; **zollamtliche A.** clearance

ab'feuern *tr* fire; (rok) launch

ab'finden §59 *tr* (*Gläubiger*) satisfy; (*Partner*) buy off; (*entschädigen*) (für) compensate (for) || *ref*—**sich a. lassen** settle for a lump-sum payment; **sich a. mit** put up with; come to terms with

Ab'findung *f* (-;-en) satisfaction; lump-sum settlement

Ab'findungsvertrag *m* lump-sum settlement

abflachen ['apflaxən] *tr* level; (*abschrägen*) bevel || *ref* flatten out

abflauen ['apflau·ən] *intr* (SEIN) slack off; (*Interesse*) flag; (*Preis*) go down; (st. exch.) ease off

ab'fliegen §57 *intr* (SEIN) take off

ab'fließen §76 *intr* (SEIN) flow off, drain off

Ab'flug *m* takeoff, departure

Ab'fluß *m* discharge; drain, gutter, gully; **See ohne A.** lake without outlet

Ab'flußrinne *f* drainage ditch

Ab'flußrohr *n* drainpipe; soil pipe; (*vom Dach*) downspout

ab'fordern *tr*—**j-m etw a.** demand s.th. from s.o.

ab'fragen *tr*—**j-m etw a.** question s.o. about s.th.; quiz s.o. on s.th.

ab'fressen §70 *tr* eat up; crop, chew off; (*Metall*) corrode

ab'frieren §77 *intr* (SEIN) be nipped by the frost; **abgefroren** frostbitten

Abfuhr ['apfur] *f* (-;-en) removal; (*Abweisung*) (coll) cold shoulder, snub

ab'führen *tr* lead away; *(festnehmen)* arrest; (fencing) defeat ‖ *intr* cause the bowels to move

Abführmittel ['apfyrmıtəl] *n* laxative

ab'füllen *tr* (*Wein, Bier*) bottle

Ab'gabe *f* (*Auslieferung*) delivery; (*Verkauf*) sale; (*Steuer*) tax; (*Zoll*) duty; (*der Wahlstimme*) casting; (*e–s Urteils*) pronouncing; (*e–r Meinung*) expressing; (fb) pass; **Abgaben taxes, fees**

ab'gabenfrei *adj* tax-free, duty-free

abgabenpflichtig ['apgabənpflıçtıç] *adj* taxable, subject to duty

Ab'gang *m* departure; (*von e–m Amt*) retirement; (*von der Schule*) dropping out; (graduation; (*Verlust*) loss; (*Abnahme*) decrease; (gym) finish; (pathol) discharge; (pathol) miscarriage; (theat) exit; **guten A. haben sell well**

abgängig ['apgeŋıç] *adj* lost, missing; (com) marketable

Ab'gangsprüfung *f* final examination

Ab'gangspunkt *m* point of departure

Ab'gas *n* (aut) exhaust; (indust) waste gas

ab'geben §80 *tr* (*Paß*) hand over; (*Gepäck*) check; (*abliefern*) deliver; (*Schulheft*) hand in; (*Urteil*) pass; (*Meinung*) express; (*Gutachten*) give; (*Amt*) lay down; (*gute Ernte*) yield; (*Schuß*) fire; (*Wahlstimme*) cast; (*Waren*) sell, let go; (sich eignen als) act as, serve as; be cut out to be; (elec) deliver; (fb) pass; (phys) give off; **e–e Offerte a.** (jur) make an offer; **e–n Narren a.** play the fool; **er würde e–n guten Vater a.** he would make a good father; **j–m eins a.** (coll) let s.o. have it; **j–m von etw a.** share s.th. with s.o. ‖ *ref*—**sich a. mit** bother with; associate with; spend time on

abgebrannt ['apgəbrant] *adj* (coll) broke

abgebrüht ['apgəbryt] *adj* (fig) hardened

abgedroschen ['apgədro∫ən] *adj* trite, hackneyed (*Witz*) stale

abgefeimt ['apgəfaımt] *adj* cunning; out-and-out

abgegriffen ['apgəgrıfən] *adj* well-thumbed

abgehackt ['apgəhakt] *adj* jerky

abgehärmt ['apgəhermt] *adj* careworn, drawn

ab'gehen §82 *intr* (SEIN) leave, depart; (*Brief*) go off; (*Knopf*) come off; (*Schuß*) go off; (*Farbe*) fade; (*Seitenweg*) branch off; (*vom Gesprächsgegenstand*) digress, go off; (*vom rechten Wege*) stray; (*aus e–m Amt*) resign, retire; (*von der Bühne*) retire; (*von der Schule*) drop out; graduate; (com) sell; (theat) exit; **bei Barzahlung gehen fünf Prozent ab** you get a five-percent reduction for paying cash; **davon kann ich nicht a.** I must insist on it; **er geht mir sehr ab** I miss him a lot; **nicht a. von** stick to; **reißend a.** sell like hotcakes; ‖ *ref*—**sich** [dat] **nichts a.**

lassen deny oneself nothing ‖ *impers* —**es geht ihm nichts ab** he lacks for nothing; **es gehen mir zehn Dollar ab** I am ten dollars short; **es ist alles glatt abgegangen** everything went well

ab'gehend *adj* (*Post, Beamte*) outgoing; (*Zug*) departing

abgekämpft ['apgəkempft] *adj* exhausted

abgekartet ['apgəkartət] *adj* (*Spiel*) fixed; **abgekartete Sache** put-up job

abgeklappert ['apgəklapərt] *adj* hackneyed

abgeklärt ['apgəklert] *adj* mellow, wise

abgelebt ['apgəlept] *adj* decrepit

abgelegen ['apgəlegen] *adj* out-of-the-way, outlying

ab'gelten §83 *tr* meet, satisfy

abgemacht ['apgəmaxt] *adj* settled ‖ *interj* agreed!

abgemagert ['apgəmagərt] *adj* emaciated

abgemessen ['apgəmesən] *adj* measured; (*genau*) exact; (*Rede*) deliberate; (*Person*) stiff, formal

abgeneigt ['apgənaıkt] *adj* reluctant; (*dat*) averse to; **ich bin durchaus nicht a.** (coll) I don't mind if I do

Ab'geneigtheit *f* (–;) aversion

abgenutzt ['apgənutst] *adj* worn out

Abgeordnete ['apgə·ɔrdnətə] §5 *mf* delegate; (pol) representative; deputy (*member of the Bundestag*); (Brit) Member of Parliament

Ab'geordnetenhaus *n* House of Representatives; (Brit) House of Commons

abgerissen ['apgərısən] *adj* torn; (*zerlumpt*) ragged; (*ohne Zusammenhang*) incoherent, disconnected

Abgesandte ['apgazantə] §5 *mf* envoy

abgeschieden ['apgə/idən] *adj* secluded; (*verstorben*) deceased, late

Ab'geschiedenheit *f* (–;) seclusion

abgeschliffen ['apgə/lıfən] *adj* polished

abgeschlossen ['apgə/losən] *adj* isolated; (*Leben*) secluded; (*Ausbildung*) completed

abgeschmackt ['apgə/makt] *adj* tactless, tasteless; (fig) insipid

abgesehen ['apgəze·ən] *adj*—**a. davon, daß** not to mention that; **a. von** aside from, except for

abgespannt ['apgə/pant] *adj* tired out

abgestanden ['apgə/tandən] *adj* stale

abgestorben ['apgə/torbən] *adj* (*Pflanze, Gewebe*) dead; (*Glied*) numb

abgestumpft ['apgə/tumpft] *adj* blunt; (*Kegel*) truncated; (fig) dull; (*gegen*) indifferent (to)

abgetakelt ['apgətakəlt] *adj* (*Person*) seedy; (*Schiff*) unrigged

abgetan ['apgətan] *adj* settled

abgetragen ['apgətragən] *adj* threadbare

abgetreten ['apgətretən] *adj* worn-down

ab'gewinnen §52 *tr* win; **e–r Sache Geschmack a.** acquire a taste for s.th.; **e–r Sache Vergnügen a.** derive pleasure from s.th.; **j–m e–n Vorteil a.** gain an advantage over s.o.

abgewirtschaftet ['apgəvɪrt/aftət] *adj* run-down

ab'gewöhnen *tr*—**ich kann es mir nicht a.** I can't get it out of my system; **j–m etw a.** break s.o. of s.th.

abgezehrt ['apgətsert] *adj* emaciated

ab'gießen §76 *tr* pour off; (*Statue*) cast; (chem) decant; (culin) strain off

Ab'glanz *m* reflection

ab'gleiten §86 *intr* (SEIN) slip off; (an *dat*) glance off (*s.th.*); (aer, aut) skid; (st. exch.) decline

Ab'gott *m* idol

Abgötterei [apgœtə'raɪ] *f* (–;–en) idolatry; **A. treiben** worship idols; **mit j–m A. treiben** idolize s.o.

abgöttisch ['apgœtɪ/] *adj* idolatrous || *adv*—**a. lieben** idolize

Ab'gottschlange *f* boa constrictor

ab'graben §87 *tr* (*Bach*) divert; (*Feld*) drain; (*Hügel*) level

ab'grämen *ref* eat one's heart out

ab'grasen *tr* (*Wiese*) graze on; (fig) scour, search

ab'greifen §88 *tr* wear out (*by constant handling*); (*Buch*) thumb

ab'grenzen *tr* mark off, demarcate; delimit; (fig) differentiate

Ab'grund *m* abyss; precipice

abgründig ['apgryndɪç] *adj* precipitous; (fig) deep, unfathomable

ab'gucken *tr* (coll) copy, crib; (coll) pick up a habit from || *intr* (coll) copy, crib

Ab'guß *m* (sculp) cast; **A. in Gips** plaster cast

ab'hacken *tr* chop off; (*Baum*) chop down

ab'haken *tr* unhook, undo; (*in e–r Liste*) check off; (telp) take off (*the receiver*)

ab'halftern *tr* unharness; (fig) sack

ab'halten §90 *tr* hold off; (*Vorlesung*) give; (*Regen*) keep out; (*Versammlung, Parade*) hold; (**von**) keep (from)

Ab'haltung *f* (–;–en) hindrance; (*e–r Versammlung*) holding; (*e–s Festes*) celebration

ab'handeln *tr* (*Thema*) treat; (*erörtern*) discuss; **er läßt sich nichts a.** he won't come down (in price); **etw vom Preise a.** get s.th. off the price (*by bargaining*)

abhanden [ap'handən] *adv*—**a. kommen** get lost; **a. sein** be missing

Ab'handlung *f* (–;–en) essay; (*Vortrag in e–m gelehrten Verein*) paper; (*Doktorarbeit*) thesis, dissertation; (*mündlich*) discourse, discussion

Ab'hang *m* slope

ab'hängen *tr* (*vom Haken*) take off; (*e–n Verfolger*) shake off; (rr) uncouple || *intr* (telp) hang up; **a. von** depend on; be subject to (*s.o.'s approval*)

abhängig ['apheŋɪç] *adj* (*Stellung*) subordinate; (*Satz*) dependent; (*Rede*) indirect; (*Kasus*) oblique; (**von**) dependent (on), contingent (upon)

Ab'hängigkeit *f* (–;–en) dependence; (gram) subordination; **gegenseitige A.** interdependence

ab'härmen *ref* pine away; **sich a. wegen** (or **über** *acc*) fret about

ab'härten *tr* harden; (gegen) inure (to) || *ref* (gegen) become hardened (to)

ab'hauen §93 *tr* cut off; chop off || §109 *intr* (SEIN) (coll) scram, get lost

ab'häuten *tr* skin, flay

ab'heben §94 *tr* lift off; (*Rahm*) skim; (*Geld*) withdraw; (*Dividende*) collect; (*Haut*) (surg) strip off || *ref* become airborne; (**von**) contrast (with)

Ab'hebung *f* (–;–en) lifting; (*vom Bankkonto*) withdrawal; (cards) cutting

Ab'hebungsformular *n* withdrawal slip

ab'heften *tr* (*Briefe*) file; (sew) tack

ab'heilen *intr* (HABEN & SEIN) heal up

ab'helfen §96 *intr* (dat) (*e–m Unrecht*) redress; (*e–r Schwierigkeit*) remove; (*e–m Mangel*) relieve; **dem ist nicht abzuhelfen** that can't be helped

ab'hetzen *tr* drive hard, work to death; (hunt) hunt down || *ref* rush; tire oneself out

Ab'hilfe *f* remedy, redress; **A. schaffen** take remedial measures; **A. schaffen für** remedy, redress

ab'hobeln *tr* plane (down)

abhold ['aphɔlt] *adj* (dat) ill-disposed (towards), averse (to)

Abholdienst ['apholdinst] *m* pickup service

ab'holen *tr* fetch, call for, pick up

ab'holzen *tr* clear (of trees), deforest

Abhörapparat ['aphɔrapara t] *m* (mil, nav) listening device

ab'horchen *tr* overhear; (med) sound; (rad, telp) monitor

ab'hören *tr* overhear, eavesdrop on; (*Studenten*) quiz; (*Schallplatte, Tonband*) listen to; (mil) intercept; (telp) monitor

Ab'hörgerät *n* bugging device

Ab'hörraum *m* (rad, telv) control room

Ab'irrung *f* (–;–en) deviation; (opt) aberration

Abitur [abi'tur] *n* (–s;–e) final examination (*at end of junior college*); **das A. bestehen** graduate

Abiturient –in [abituri'ent(ɪn)] §7 *mf* graduate (*of a junior college*)

Abitur'zeugnis *n* diploma (*from senior high school or junior college*)

ab'jagen *tr* drive hard; **j–m etw a.** recover s.th. from s.o. || *ref* run one's head off

abkanzeln ['apkantsəln] *tr* (coll) give (*s.o.*) a good talking to

ab'kauen *tr* chew off || *ref*—**sich** [*dat*] **die Nägel a.** bite one's nails

ab'kaufen *tr*—**j–m etw a.** buy s.th. from s.o.

Abkehr ['apker] *f* (–;) turning away; estrangement; (*Verzicht*) renunciation

ab'kehren *tr* turn away, avert; (*mit dem Besen*) sweep off || *ref* turn away; become estranged

ab'klappern *tr* (coll) scour, search

ab'klatschen *tr* imitate slavishly; make an exact copy of; (*beim Tanzen*) cut in on; (typ) pull (*a proof*)

ab'klingen §142 *intr* (SEIN) (*Farbe*) fade; (*Töne*) die away; (*Schmerz*) ease off

ab'klopfen *tr* beat off, knock off; (*Teppich*) beat; (med) tap, percuss || *intr* stop the music (*with the rap of the baton*)

ab'knabbern *tr* (coll) nibble off

ab'knallen *tr* fire off; (sl) bump off

ab'knicken *tr* snap off || *intr* (SEIN) snap off

ab'knipsen *tr* pinch off, snip off; (*Film*) use up

ab'knöpfen *tr* unbutton; **j-m Geld a.** squeeze money out of s.o.

ab'knutschen *tr* (coll) pet

ab'kochen *tr* boil; (*Obst*) stew; (*Milch*) scald || *intr* cook out

ab'kommandieren *tr* detach, detail

ab'kommen §99 *intr* (SEIN) (**von**) get away (from); (*Mode*) go out of style; (naut) become afloat (again); **auf zwei Tage a.** get away for two days; **gut** (or **schlecht**) **a.** (sport) get off to a good (or bad) start; **hoch** (or **tief**) **a.** aim too high (or low); **vom Kurs a.** go off course; **vom Boden a.** become airborne; **vom Thema a.** get off the subject; **vom Wege a.** lose one's way, stray; **von der Wahrheit a.** deviate from the truth; **von e-r Ansicht a.** change one's views || **Abkommen** *n* (**-s;-**) (com, pol) agreement; (jur) settlement

abkömmlich ['apkœmlɪç] *adj*—**a. sein** be able to get away

Abkömmling ['apkœmlɪŋ] *m* (**-s;-e**) descendant, scion

ab'koppeln *tr* uncouple

ab'kratzen *tr* scratch off; (*Schuhe*) scuff up || *intr* (*sterben*) (sl) croak; (*abhauen*) (sl) beat it; **kratz ab!** drop dead!

ab'kriegen *tr* (coll) get off or out

ab'kühlen *tr, ref & intr* cool off

Abkunft ['apkunft] *f* (**-;**) lineage

ab'kürzen *tr* shorten; (*Inhalt*) abridge; (*Wort*) abbreviate; (math) reduce

Ab'kürzung *f* (**-;-en**) shortening; abridgement; abbreviation; (*kürzerer Weg*) shortcut

ab'küssen *tr* smother with kisses

ab'laden §103 *tr* unload; (*Schutt*) dump

Ab'ladeplatz *m* dump; (mil) unloading point

Ab'lage *f* (*für Kleider*) cloakroom; (*Lagerhaus*) depot, warehouse; (*abgelegte Akten*) files; (mil) dump

ab'lagern *tr* (*Wein, usw.*) age; (geol) deposit || *ref* (geol) be deposited || *intr*—**a. lassen** age, season

Ab'laß *m* (**-lasses;-lässe**) outlet, drain; (com) deduction; (eccl) indulgence

ab'lassen §104 *tr* leave off; (*Bier*) tap; (*Dampf*) let off; (*Teich, Faß*) drain; (*Waren*) sell; **etw vom Preise a.** knock s.th. off the price; **j-m etw billig a.** (com) let s.o. have s.th. cheaply || *intr* desist, stop; **a. von** let go of, give up

Ablativ ['ablatif] *m* (**-s;-e**) ablative

Ab'lauf *m* overflow; (*e-r Frist, e-s Vertrags*) expiration; (*der Ereignisse*) course; (sport) start

ab'laufen §105 *tr* (*Strecke*) run; (*Stadt*) scour; (*Schuhe*) wear out; **j-m den Rang a.** get the better of s.o.; outrun s.o. || *intr* (SEIN) run away; (*Zeit*) expire; (*ausfallen*) turn out; (com) fall due; (sport) **start**

Ab'laut *m* ablaut

Ab'leben *n* demise, decease

ab'lecken *tr* lick (off)

ab'legen *tr* (*Last, Waffen*) lay down; (*ausziehen*) take off; (*Schwert*) lay aside; (*die alte Haut*) slough; (*Karten*) discard; (*Akten, Dokumente*) file; (*Briefe*) sort; (*Namen*) drop, stop using; (*Sorgen, Kummer*) put away; (*Prüfung, Gelübde, Eid*) take; (*Predigt*) deliver; (*Gewohnheit*) give up; (*Rechenschaft*) render, give; **Bekenntnis a.** make a confession; **die Maske a.** (fig) throw off all disguise; **die Trauer a.** come out of mourning; **ein volles Geständnis a.** come clean; **Probe a.** furnish proof; **seine Fehler a.** mend one's ways; **Zeugnis a.** (für or gegen) testify (for or against) || *intr* take off one's coat or hat and coat); **bitte, legen Sie ab!** please take your things off

Ab'leger *m* (**-s;-**) (bot) shoot; (com) subsidiary; (hort) slip, cutting

ab'lehnen *tr* refuse, turn down; (*Antrag*) reject; (*Zeugen*) challenge; (*Erbschaft*) renounce; **durch Abstimmung a.** vote down

ab'lehnend *adj* negative

Ab'lehnung *f* (**-;-en**) refusal

ab'leiern *tr* recite mechanically

ab'leisten *tr* (*Eid*) take; **den Militärdienst a.** (mil) serve one's time

ab'leiten *tr* lead away; (*Herkunft*) trace back; (*Fluß, Blitz*) divert; (*Wasser*) drain off; (*Wärme*) conduct; (chem) derive; (elec) shunt; (gram, math) derive; **abgeleitetes Wort** derivative || *ref* (aus, von) be derived (from)

Ab'leitung *f* (**-;-en**) (*e-s Flusses*) diversion; (*des Wassers*) drainage; (elec, phys) conduction; (gram, math) derivation; (phys) convection

ab'lenken *tr* turn away, divert; (*Gefahr, Verdacht*) ward off; (fencing) parry; (opt, phys) deflect

Ab'lenkung *f* (**-;-en**) diversion; distraction; (opt) refraction

ab'lernen *tr*—**j-m etw a.** learn s.th. from s.o.

ab'lesen §107 *tr* read off; (*Zähler*) read; (*Obst*) pick; **es j-m vom Gesicht a., daß** tell by looking at s.o. that

ab'leugnen *tr* deny, disown; (*Glauben*) renounce

Ab'leugnung *f* (**-;-en**) denial, disavowal

ab'liefern *tr* deliver, hand over, surrender

Ab'lieferung *f* (**-;-en**) delivery; (*der Schußwaffen*) surrender

ab'liegen §108 *intr* (*Wein*) mature; (*Obst*) ripen ‖ *intr* (SEIN) be remote

ab'löschen *tr* extinguish; (*Stahl*) temper; (*Tinte*) blot; (*Kalk*) slake

ab'lösen *tr* loosen, detach; (*Posten*) relieve; (*Schuld*) discharge; (*Pfand*) redeem; (*Haut*) peel off ‖ *ref* (*bei*) take turns (at)

Ab'lösung *f* (–;–en) loosening; relief; discharge

ab'machen *tr* undo, untie; (*erledigen*) settle, arrange; (*Vertrag*) conclude; (*Rechnung*) close

Ab'machung *f* (–;–en) settlement

abmagern ['apmagərn] *intr* (SEIN) grow thin, thin down

Ab'magerung *f* (–;) emaciation

ab'mähen *tr* mow

ab'malen *tr* portray; (fig) depict

Ab'marsch *m* departure

ab'marschieren *intr* (SEIN) march off

Ab'mattung *f* (–;) fatigue

ab'melden *tr* (*Besuch*) (coll) call off; der ist bei mir abgemeldet (coll) I've had it with him; j–n bei der Polizei a. give notice to the police that s.o. is leaving town ‖ *ref* (mil) report off duty

ab'messen §70 *tr* measure (off); (*Worte*) weigh; (*Land*) survey

ab'montieren *tr* dismantle; (*Geschütz*) disassemble; (*Reifen*) take off ‖ *ref* (aer) (coll) disintegrate in the air

ab'mühen *ref* exert oneself, slave

ab'murksen *tr* (sl) do in

ab'nagen *tr* gnaw (off); (*Knochen*) pick

Ab'nahme *f* (–;–n) (*Verminderung*) (an *dat*) reduction (in), drop (in); (*des Gewichts*) loss; (*des Mondes*) waning; (*des Tages*) shortening; (*e–r Rechnung*) administering; (*e–r Rechnung*) auditing; (indust) final inspection; (surg) amputation; **A. der Geschäfte** decline in business; **A. e–r Parade** reviewing of the troops; **A. finden** be sold; **in A. geraten** decline, wane

ab'nehmen §116 *tr* take off, remove; (*Wäsche*) take down; (*Schnurrbart*) shave off; (*wegnehmen*) take away; (*Hörer*) lift, unhook; (*Strom*) use; (*Obst*) pick; (*Eid*) administer; (*Waren*) purchase; (*Rechnung*) audit; (*prüfen*) inspect and pass; (*Verband*) remove; (phot) take; (surg) amputate; **aus Berichten a.** gather from reports; **das kann ich dir nicht a.** I can't accept what you are saying; **die Parade a.** inspect the troops; **j–m die Arbeit a.** take the work off s.o.'s shoulders; **j–m die Beichte a.** hear s.o.'s confession; **j–m die Maske a.** unmask s.o., expose s.o.; **j–m die Verantwortung a.** relieve s.o. of responsibility; **j–m ein Versprechen a.** make s.o. make a promise; **j–m zuviel a.** charge s.o. too much ‖ *intr* diminish; (*Preise*) drop; (*Wasser*) recede; (*Kräfte*) fail; (*Mond*) be on the wane; **an Dicke a.** taper; **an Gewicht a.** lose weight; **an Kräften a.** lose strength ‖ **Abnehmen**

n (–s;) decrease; **im A. sein** be on the decrease

Ab'nehmer –in §6 *mf* buyer, consumer; (*Kunde*) customer; (*Hehler*) fence

Ab'neigung *f* (–;–en) (gegen, vor *dat*) aversion (to, for), dislike (of)

abnorm [ap'norm] *adj* abnormal

Abnormität [apnormı'tet] *f* (–;–en) abnormity, monstrosity

ab'nötigen *tr* (*dat*) extort (from)

ab'nutzen, ab'nützen *tr* wear out ‖ *ref* wear out, become worn out

Ab'nutzung *f* (–;–en) wear and tear; (*Abrieb*) abrasion; (mil) attrition

Ab'öl *n* (–s;–e) used oil

Abonnement [abon(ə)'mã] *n* (–s;–s) (auf *acc*) subscription (to)

Abonnements'karte *f* commutation ticket

Abonnent –in [abo'nent(ın)] §7 *mf* subscriber

abonnieren [abo'nirən] *tr* subscribe to; **abonniert sein auf** (*acc*) have a subscription to ‖ *intr* (auf *acc*) subscribe (to)

ab'ordnen *tr* delegate, deputize

Ab'ordnung *f* (–;–en) delegation

Abort [a'bort] *m* (–s;–e) toilet [a'bort] *m* (–s;–e) abortion

ab'passen *tr* measure, fit; (*abwarten*) watch for; (*auflauern*) waylay

ab'pfeifen §88 *tr* (sport) stop

ab'pflücken *tr* pluck (off)

ab'placken, ab'plagen *ref* work oneself to death, slave

ab'platzen *intr* (SEIN) come loose

Abprall ['apral] *m* rebound; (*Geschoß*) richochet

ab'prallen *intr* (SEIN) rebound; ricochet

ab'pressen *tr* extort

ab'putzen *tr* clean (off); (*polieren*) polish; (*Mauer*) roughcast, plaster

ab'raten §63 *intr*—j–m von etw a. advise s.o. against s.th.

Ab'raum *m* (–es;) rubble; (min) overburden

ab'räumen *tr* clear away; (*Tisch*) clear

ab'reagieren *tr* (*Spannung, Erregung*) work off ‖ *ref* (coll) calm down

ab'rechnen *tr* subtract; (*Spesen*) account for; (com) deduct ‖ *intr* settle accounts

Ab'rechnung *f* (–;–en) (*von Konten*) settlement; (*Abzug*) deduction; **A. halten** balance accounts

Ab'rede *f* agreement, arrangement; **in A. stellen** deny

ab'reden *intr*—j–m von etw a. dissuade s.o. from s.th.

ab'reiben *tr* rub off; (*Körper*) rub down

Ab'reise *f* departure

ab'reisen *intr* (SEIN) (nach) depart (for)

ab'reißen §53 *tr* tear off; (*Haus*) tear down; (*Kleid*) wear out ‖ *intr* (SEIN) tear off

ab'richten *tr* (*Tier*) train; (*Pferd*) break in; (*Brett*) dress

Ab'richter –in §6 *mf* trainer

ab'riegeln *tr* (*Tür*) bolt; (mil) seal off

ab'ringen §142 *tr*—j-m etw a. wrest s.th. from s.o.

ab'rinnen §121 *intr* (SEIN) run off, run down

Ab'riß *m* summary, outline; (*Skizze*) sketch

ab'rollen *tr* & *ref* unroll, unwind || *intr* (SEIN) unroll, unwind

ab'rücken *tr* push away, move back || *intr* (SEIN) clear out; (fig) dissociate oneself; (mil) march off

Ab'ruf *m* recall; **auf A.** on call

ab'rufen §122 *tr* call away; (*Zug*) call out, announce

ab'runden *tr* round off

ab'rupfen *tr* pluck (off)

ab'rüsten *tr* & *intr* disarm

Ab'rüstung *f* (–;) disarmament

ab'rutschen *intr* (SEIN) slip (off)

absacken ['apzakən] *intr* (SEIN) sink; (*Flugzeug*) pancake

Ab'sage *f* cancellation; (*Ablehnung*) refusal

ab'sagen *tr* cancel || *intr* decline; (*dat*) renounce, repudiate

ab'sägen *tr* saw off

ab'sahnen *tr* (& fig) skim (off)

Ab'satz *m* stop, pause, break; (*Zeileneinrückung*) indentation; (*Abschnitt*) paragraph; (*des Schuhes*) heel; (*der Treppen*) landing; (*Vertrieb*) market, sale(s); **ohne A.** without a break

ab'satzfähig *adj* marketable

Ab'satzgebiet *n* territory (*of a salesman*)

Ab'satzmarkt *m* (com) outlet

Ab'satzstockung *f* slump in sales

ab'saugen *tr* suck off; (*Teppich*) vacuum

Ab'saugventilator *m* exhaust fan

ab'schaben *tr* scrape off

ab'schaffen *tr* abolish, do away with; (*Mißbrauch*) redress; (*Diener*) dismiss

ab'schälen *tr* peel

ab'schalten *tr* switch off

ab'schätzen *tr* (*Wert*) estimate; (*für die Steuer*) assess, appraise

abschätzig ['apʃɛtsɪç] *adj* disparaging

Ab'schaum *m* (–[e]s;) (& fig) scum

ab'scheiden §112 *tr* part, sever; (physiol) excrete; (physiol) secrete || *intr* (SEIN) pass away, pass on

Ab'scheu *m* (–[e]s;) (vor *dat*, gegen) abhorrence (of), disgust (at)

ab'scheuern *tr* scrub off, scour; (*Haut*) scrape; (*abnutzen*) wear out

abscheu'lich *adj* atrocious

ab'schicken *tr* send away; (*Post*) mail

ab'schieben §130 *tr* shove off; deport

Abschied ['apʃit] *m* (–[e]s;–e) (*Weggang*) departure; (*Entlassung*) dismissal; (mil) discharge; **A. nehmen von** take leave of; (*e-m Amt*) resign, retire from

Ab'schiedsfeier *f* farewell party

Ab'schiedsrede *f* valediction

Ab'schiedsschmaus *m* farewell dinner

ab'schießen §76 *tr* (*Gewehr*) fire, shoot; (*Flugzeug*) shoot down; (*Panzer*) knock out; (rok) launch; **j–n a.** bring about s.o.'s downfall

ab'schinden §167 *tr* skin || *ref* slave

ab'schirmen *tr* screen (off); **(gegen)** guard (against)

ab'schlachten *tr* butcher; (fig) massacre

Ab'schlag *m* discount; (golf) tee shot; **auf A.** in part payment, on account

ab'schlagen §132 *tr* knock off; (*Baum*) fell; (*Angriff*) repel; (*Bitte*) refuse; **das Wasser a.** pass water || *intr* (golf) tee off

abschlägig ['apʃlegɪç] *adj* negative; **a. bescheiden** turn down

Ab'schlagszahlung *f* installment

ab'schleifen §88 *tr* grind off; (fig) refine, polish || *ref* become refined

ab'schleppen *tr* drag away, tow away

Ab'schleppwagen *m* tow truck

ab'schleudern *tr* fling off, catapult

ab'schließen §76 *tr* lock (up); (*Straße*) close off; (*Rechnung*) close, settle; (*Bücher*) balance; (*Vertrag*) conclude; (*Rede*) wind up; (*Wette*) wager || *ref* seclude oneself, shut oneself off || *intr* conclude

ab'schließend *adj* definitive; (*Worte*) concluding || *adv* definitively; (*schließlich*) in conclusion

Ab'schluß *m* completion; (*e–s Vertrags*) conclusion; (*Geschäft*) transaction, deal; (*Verkauf*) sale; (*Rechnungs-, Konto-, Buch-*) closing; (mach) seal

ab'schmeicheln *tr*—j-m etw a. coax s.th. out of s.o.

ab'schmelzen §133 *tr* (*Erz*) smelt; (*Schnee*) melt || *intr* (SEIN) melt

ab'schmieren *tr* copy carelessly; (coll) beat up; (aut) lubricate || *intr* (SEIN) (aer) (coll) crash

ab'schnallen *tr* unbuckle, unstrap

ab'schnappen *intr* (SEIN) (coll) stop dead; (coll) die

ab'schneiden §106 *tr* cut (off); (*Hecke*) trim; **den Weg. a.** take a shortcut; **j–m das Wort a.** cut s.o. short; **j–m die Ehre a.** steal s.o.'s good name || *intr*—gut a. do well

Ab'schnitt *m* cut, cutting; (*Teilstück*) part, section; (*im Scheckbuch*) stub; (*Kapitel*) section, paragraph; (math) segment; (mil) sector

ab'schnüren *tr* untie; (surg) ligature; **j–m den Atem a.** choke s.o.

ab'schöpfen *tr* skim off

ab'schrägen *tr* & *ref* slant, slope

ab'schrauben *tr* unscrew

ab'schrecken §134 *tr* scare off; (*abbringen*) deter

ab'schreiben §62 *tr* copy; (*Schularbeit*) crib; (*uneinbringliche Forderung*) write off; (*Literaturwerk*) plagiarize; (*Wert*) depreciate || *intr* send a refusal

Ab'schreiber **–in** §6 *mf* plagiarist

Ab'schreibung *f* (–;–en) write-off

ab'schreiten §86 *tr* pace off; (mil) review; **die Front a.** review the troops

Ab'schrift *f* copy, transcript; (com, jur) duplicate

ab'schriftlich *adj* & *adv* in duplicate

ab'schuften *ref* work oneself to death

ab'schürfen *ref*—**sich** [*dat*] **die Haut a.** skin oneself

Ab'schürfung f (-;-en) abrasion

Ab'schuß m (e-r Waffe) firing; (e-r Rakete) launching; (e-s Panzers) knocking out; (e-s Flugzeugs) downing, kill; (hunt) kill

abschüssig ['apʃʏsɪç] adj sloping; (steil) steep

Ab'schußrampe f launch pad

ab'schütteln tr shake off

ab'schwächen tr weaken; (vermindern) diminish, reduce; (Farben) tone down || ref (Preis) decline

ab'schweifen intr (SEIN) stray, digress

Ab'schweifung f (-;-en) digression

ab'schwellen §119 intr (SEIN) go down; (Lärm, Gesang) die down

ab'schwenken intr (SEIN) swerve

ab'schwören intr (dat) (dem Glauben) deny; (dem Trunk) swear off

ab'segeln intr (SEIN) set sail

absehbar ['apzebar] adj foreseeable

ab'sehen §138 tr foresee; es abgesehen haben auf (acc) be out to get || intr—a. von disregard; refrain from

ab'seifen tr soap down

abseits ['apzaɪts] adv aside; (sport) offside || prep (genit) off

ab'senden §140 tr send (off), dispatch; (Post) mail; (befördern) forward

Ab'sender –in §6 mf sender, dispatcher

Ab'sendung f (-;-en) sending, dispatching; mailing, shipping

ab'sengen tr singe off

Absentismus [apzen'tɪsmus] m (-;) absenteeism

ab'setzen tr (Betrag) deduct; (Last) set down; (entwöhnen) wean; (Beamten) remove; (König) depose; (Fallschirmtruppen, Passagiere) drop; (com) sell; (typ) set up || ref settle, set; (mil) disengage || intr stop, pause

Absetzung f (-;-en) dismissal

Ab'sicht f intention, purpose; in der A. with the intention; mit A. on purpose; ohne A. unintentionally

ab'sichtlich adj intentional || adv on purpose, intentionally

ab'sitzen §144 tr (Strafzeit) serve, do || intr (SEIN) (vom Pferde) dismount; a. lassen (chem) let settle

absolut [apzo'lut] adj

absolvieren [apzɔl'virən] tr absolve; (Studien) finish; (Hochschule) graduate from; (Prüfung) pass

abson'derlich adj peculiar, strange

ab'sondern tr separate, segregate; (Kranken) isolate; (physiol) secrete || ref keep aloof

absorbieren [apzɔr'birən] tr absorb

ab'speisen tr feed; j-n mit schönen Worten a. put s.o. off with polite words

abspenstig ['apʃpenstɪç] adj—a. machen lure away; j-m a. werden desert s.o.

ab'sperren tr shut off, block off; (Tür) lock; (Strom) cut off; (Gas) turn off

ab'spielen tr play through to the end; (Schallplatte, Tonband) play; (Tonbandaufnahme) play back || ref take place

ab'sprechen §64 tr dispute, deny; (ab-

machen) arrange; j-m das Recht a. zu (inf) dispute s.o.'s right to (inf)

ab'sprechend adj (Urteil) unfavorable; (Kritik) adverse; (tadelnd) disparaging

ab'springen §142 intr (SEIN) jump down, jump off; (Ball) rebound; (Glasur) chip; (abschweifen) digress; (aer) bail out, jump; a. von quit, desert

Ab'sprung m jump; (ins Wasser) dive; (des Balles) rebound

ab'spulen tr unwind, unreel

ab'spülen tr rinse (off)

ab'stammen intr (SEIN) (von) be descended (from); (von) be derived (from)

Abstammung f (-;-en) descent, extraction; (gram) derivation

Ab'stand m distance; (räumlich und zeitlich) interval; A. nehmen von refrain from; A. zahlen pay compensation

abstatten ['apʃtatən] tr (Besuch) pay; (Bericht) file; (Dank) give, return

ab'stauben tr dust off; (sl) swipe

ab'stechen §64 tr (töten) stab; (Rasen) cut; (Hochofen) tap; (Karten) trump || intr—gegen (or von) etwa a. contrast with s.th.

Ab'stecher m (-s;-) side trip; (Umweg) detour; (fig) digression

ab'stecken tr (Haar) unpin, let down; (Kleid) pin, fit; (surv) mark off

ab'stehen §146 intr (entfernt sein) (von) be, stand away (from); (Ohren, usw.) stick out || intr (HABEN & SEIN) (von) refrain (from)

ab'steigen §148 intr (SEIN) get down, descend; in e-m Gasthof a. stay at a hotel

ab'stellen tr (Last) put down; (Radio, Gas, usw.) turn off; (Motor) switch off; (Auto) park; (Mißstand) redress; (mil) detach, assign; a. auf (acc) gear to

Ab'stellraum m storage room

ab'stempeln tr stamp

ab'sterben §149 intr (SEIN) die off; (Pflanzen) wither; (Glieder) get numb

Abstieg ['apʃtik] m (-[e]s;) descent

ab'stimmen tr tune; (com) balance; a. auf (acc) (fig) atune (to) || intr (über acc) vote (on)

Abstinenzler –in [apstɪ'nentslər(ɪn)] §6 mf teetotaler

ab'stoppen tr stop; (sport) clock

ab'stoßen §150 tr push off; (Waren) get rid of, sell; (Schulden) pay off; (Geweih) shed; (fig) disgust, sicken; (phys) repel || ref—sich [dat] die Hörner a. (fig) sow one's wild oats || intr (SEIN) shove off

ab'stoßend adj repulsive

abstrakt [ap'strakt] adj abstract

ab'streichen tr (abwischen) wipe off; (Rasiermesser) strop; (abhaken) check off; (bact) swab; (com) deduct

ab'streifen tr (Handschuh, usw.) take off; (Haut) slough off; (Gewohnheit) break || intr (SEIN) deviate, stray

ab'streiten §86 tr contest, dispute

Ab'strich m (*beim Schreiben*) downstroke; (*Abzug*) cut; (*bact*) swab
ab'stufen tr (*Gelände*) terrace; (*Farben*) shade off
abstumpfen ['apstumpfən] tr blunt
Ab'sturz m fall; (*Abhang*) precipice; (aer) crash
abstürzen intr (SEIN) fall down; (aer) crash
ab'suchen tr (*Gebiet*) scour, comb
Ab-szeß [ap'stses] m (-szesses; -szesse) abscess
Abt [apt] m (-[e]s;ːe) abbot
ab'takeln tr unrig; (coll) sack, fire
ab'tasten tr probe; (rad) scan
Abtei [ap'tar] f (-;-en) abbey
Ab'teil n compartment
ab'teilen tr divide, partition
Ab'teilung f (-;-en) department, division; (*im Krankenhaus*) ward; (arti) battery; (mil) detachment, unit
Ab'teilungsleiter -in §6 mf department head, section head
Ab'teilungszeichen n hyphen
Äbtissin [ep'tısın] f (-;-nen) abbess
ab'tönen tr tone down, shade off
ab'töten tr (*Bakterien*) kill; (*das Fleisch*) mortify
Abtrag ['aptrak] m (-[e]s;ːe)—j-m A. leisten compensate s.o.; j-m A. tun hurt s.o.
ab'tragen §132 tr carry away; (*Gebäude*) raze; (*Kleid*) wear out; (*Schuld*) pay
abträglich ['aptreklıç] adj detrimental
ab'treiben §62 tr drive away; (*Leibesfrucht*) abort || intr (SEIN) drift away; **vom Kurs a.** drift off course
Ab'treibung f (-;-en) abortion
ab'trennen tr separate, detach; (*Glied*) sever; (*Genähtes*) unstitch
ab'treten §152 tr wear out (*by walking*); (*aufgeben*) cede, turn over || intr (SEIN) retire, resign; (theat) exit
Ab'treter m (-s;-) doormat
Ab'tretung f (-;-en) (*von Grundeigentum*) transfer; (pol) cession
ab'trocknen tr dry || intr (SEIN) dry
ab'tropfen intr (SEIN) trickle, drip
ab'trudeln intr (SEIN) go into a tailspin; (coll) toddle off, saunter off
abtrünnig ['aptrynıç] adj unfaithful; (eccl) apostate; **a. werden** defect
Ab'trünnigkeit f (-;-) desertion, defection; (eccl) apostasy
ab'tun §154 tr (*ablegen*) take off; (*beiseite schieben*) get rid of; (*töten*) kill; (*erledigen*) settle; **a. als** dismiss as; **kurz a.** make short work of; **mit e-m Achselzucken a.** shrug off
ab'urteilen tr pass final judgment on
ab'verlangen tr—j-m etw a. demand s.th. of s.o.
ab'wägen §156 tr weigh
ab'wälzen tr roll away; (*Schuld*) shift
ab'wandeln tr (*Thema*) vary; (*Hauptwort*) decline; (*Zeitwort*) (gram) conjugate
ab'wandern intr (SEIN) wander off; (*Bevölkerung*) migrate; (*Arbeitskräfte*) drift away
Ab'wanderung f (-;-en) exodus, migration

Ab'wandlung f (-;-en) variation; (*e-s Hauptwortes*) declension; (*e-s Zeitwortes*) conjugation
ab'warten tr wait for; (*Anweisung*) await; **das bleibt abzuwarten! that remains to be seen!** s-e Zeit a. bide one's time || intr wait and see
abwärts ['apverts] adv down, downwards; **mit ihm geht es a.** (coll) he's going downhill
ab'waschen §158 tr wash (off)
ab'wechseln tr & intr alternate
ab'wechselnd adj alternate
Ab'wechs(e)lung f (-;-en) variation; (*Mannigfaltigkeit*) variety; (*Zerstreuung*) diversion, entertainment
Ab'weg m wrong way; **auf Abwege führen** mislead; **auf Abwege geraten** go wrong
Ab'wehr f (-;-en) defense; (*e-s Stoßes, usw.*) warding off; (mil) counter-espionage service
ab'wehren tr ward off, avert
ab'weichen §85 intr (SEIN) deviate, diverge; (*verschieden sein*) differ
Ab'weichung f (-;-en) deviation; difference; (math) divergence
ab'weiden tr graze on
ab'weisen §118 tr refuse, turn down; (*Angriff*) repel; (*Berufung*) deny
ab'weisend adj (gegen) unfriendly (to)
Ab'weisung f (-;-en) refusal; (jur) denial; (mil) repulse
ab'wenden tr turn away, turn aside; (*Augen*) avert; (*Aufmerksamkeit*) divert; (*Krieg, Gefahr*) prevent || §140 & 120 ref (von) turn away (from)
ab'werfen §160 tr throw off; (*Bomben*) drop; (*Blätter, Geweih*) shed; (*Gewinn*) bring in, yield; (*Zinsen*) bear; (*Karten*) discard; (*Joch*) shake off
ab'werten tr devaluate
Ab'wertung f (-;-en) devaluation
abwesend ['apvezənt] adj absent, missing; (fig) absent-minded
Ab'wesenheit f (-;) absence; (fig) absent-mindedness
ab'wickeln tr unwind, unroll; (*Geschäfte*) transact; (*Schulden*) settle; (*Aktiengesellschaft*) liquidate || ref unwind; (fig) develop **sich gut a.** (com) turn out well
ab'wiegen §57 tr weigh
ab'wischen tr wipe off, wipe clean
Abwurf ['apvurf] m drop(ping); (*Bomben*) release; (*Ertrag*) yield
ab'würgen tr wring the neck of; (aut) stall
ab'zahlen tr pay off
ab'zählen tr count off
Ab'zahlung f (-;-en) payment in installments; (*Rate*) installment; **auf A.** on terms
Ab'zahlungsgeschäft n deferred-payment system
ab'zapfen tr (*Bier*) tap; (*Blut*) draw
Ab'zehrung f emaciation; consumption
Ab'zeichen n distinguishing mark; badge; (mil) decoration
ab'zeichnen tr copy, draw, sketch;

(Dokument) initial ‖ *ref* become apparent; **(gegen)** stand out (against)

Ab'ziehbild *n* decal

ab'ziehen §163 *tr* pull off; *(Kunden)* lure away; *(Reifen)* take off; *(Bett)* strip; *(vom Preise)* deduct, knock off; *(vervielfältigen)* run off; *(Abziehbild)* transfer; *(Schlüssel vom Loch)* take out; *(Rasiermesser)* strop; *(Wein)* draw; *(Truppen)* withdraw; *(Aufmerksamkeit)* divert; (arith) deduct; (phot) print; (typ) pull ‖ *intr* (SEIN) depart; *(abmarschieren)* march off; *(Rauch)* disperse

Ab'zug *m* *(e—r Summe)* deduction; *(Rabatt)* rebate, allowance; *(Skonto)* discount; *(am Gewehr)* trigger; *(Weggang)* departure; *(für Wasser)* outlet; *(für Rauch)* escape; (mil) withdrawal; (phot) print; (typ) proof sheet

abzüglich [ˈaptsyklɪç] *prep (genit* or *acc)* less, minus

Ab'zugsbogen *m* proof sheet

Ab'zugspapier *n* duplicating paper; (phot) printing paper

Ab'zugsrohr *n* drainpipe

ab'zweigen *tr* divert ‖ *intr* (SEIN) branch off

ach [ax] *interj* oh!; ah!; **ach so!** oh, I see!; **ach was!** nonsense!; **ach wo!** of course not!

Achse [ˈaksə] *f* (—;—n) axis; *(am Wagen)* axle; (mach) shaft; **auf der A.** on the move; **per A.** by truck; by rail

Achsel [ˈaksəl] *f* (—;—n) shoulder; **auf die leichte A. nehmen** make light of; **mit den Achseln zucken** shrug one's shoulders; **über die Achseln ansehen** look down on

Ach'selbein *n* shoulder blade

Ach'selgrube *f*, **Ach'selhöhle** *f* armpit

Ach'selträger **—in** §6 *mf* opportunist

acht [axt] *adj* eight; **alle a. Tage** once a week; **in a. Tagen** within a week; **über a. Tage** a week from today ‖ **Acht** *f* (—;—en) eight ‖ *f* (—;) *(Bann)* outlawry; *(Obacht)* care, attention; **in die A. erklären** outlaw; (fig) ostracize; **sich in a. nehmen vor** *(dat)* watch out for

achtbar [ˈaxtbar] *adj* respectable

achte [ˈaxtə] §9 *adj* & *pron* eight

achteckig [ˈaxtekɪç] *adj* octagonal

Achtel [ˈaxtəl] *n* (—;—) eighth *(part)*

achten [ˈaxtən] *tr (beachten)* respect; *(schätzen)* esteem; *(erachten)* consider ‖ *intr*—a. **auf** *(acc)* pay attention to; **a. darauf, daß** see to it that

ächten [ˈɛçtən] *tr* outlaw, proscribe; *(gesellschaftlich)* ostracize

ach'tenswert *adj* respectable

achter(n) [ˈaxtər(n)] *adv* aft, astern

acht'geben §80 *intr* **(auf** *acc)* pay attention *(to);* **gib acht!** watch out!

acht'los *adj* careless

Acht'losigkeit *f* (—;) carelessness

acht'sam *adj* **(auf** *acc)* cautious; **(auf** *acc)* attentive (to); **(auf** *acc)* careful (of)

Acht'samkeit *f* (—;) carefulness

achttägig [ˈaxttegɪç] *adj* eight-day; eight-day old; one-week

Ach'tung *f* (—;) attention; **(vor** *dat)* respect (for); **A.!** watch out!; (mil) attention!

ach'tungsvoll *adj* respectful; *(als Briefschluß)* Yours truly

acht'zehn *adj* & *pron* eighteen ‖ **Achtzehn** *f* (—;—en) eighteen

acht'zehnte §9 *adj* & *pron* eighteenth

achtzig [ˈaxtsɪç] *adj* eighty

achtziger [ˈaxtsɪɡər] *invar adj* of the eighties; **die a. Jahre** the eighties ‖ **Achtziger** **—in** §6 *mf* octogenarian

achtzigste [ˈaxtsɪçstə] §9 *adj* eightieth

ächzen [ˈɛçtsən] *intr* groan, moan

Acker [ˈakər] *m* (—s;‥) soil, (arable) land, field; *(Maß)* acre

Ackerbau (Ak'kerbau) *m* farming

ackerbautreibend [ˈakərbautraibənt] *adj* agricultural

Ackerbestellung (Ak'kerbestellung) *f* cultivation, tilling

Ackerland (Ak'kerland) *n* arable land

ackern [ˈakərn] *tr* & *intr* plow

addieren [aˈdirən] *tr* & *intr* add

Addiermaschine [aˈdirmaʃinə] *f* adding machine

Addition [adɪˈtsjon] *f* (—;—en) addition

ade [aˈde] *interj* farewell!; bye-bye!

Adel [ˈadəl] *m* (—s;) nobility, noble birth; *(edle Gesinnung)* noble-mindedness

ad(e)lig [ˈad(ə)lɪç] *adj* noble, titled; nobleman's ‖ **Ad(e)lige** §5 *m* nobleman ‖ §5 *f* noblewoman

A'delsstand *m* nobility

Ader [ˈadər] *f* (—;—n) vein

adieu [aˈdjø] *interj* adieu!

Adjektiv [ˈatjektif] *n* (—s;—e) adjective

Adjutant [atjuˈtant(ɪn)] §7 *mf* adjutant; *(e—s Generals)* aide(-de-camp)

Adler [ˈadlər] *m* (—s;—) eagle

Ad'lernase *f* aquiline nose

Admiral [atmiˈral] *m* (—[e]s;—e) admiral

Admiralität [atmiralɪˈtet] *f* (—;) admiralty

adoptieren [adɔpˈtirən] *tr* adopt

Adoption [adɔpˈtsjon] *f* (—;—en) adoption

Adoptiv– [adɔpˈtif] *comb. fm.* adoptive

Adressat **—in** [adreˈsat(ɪn)] §7 *mf* addressee; *(e—r Warensendung)* consignee

Adresse [aˈdresə] *f* (—;—n) address; **an die falsche A. kommen** (fig) bark up the wrong tree; **per A.** care of

adressieren [adreˈsirən] *tr* address; *(Waren)* consign

adrett [aˈdret] *adj* smart, neat

Advent [atˈvent] *m* (—s;—e) Advent

Adverb [atˈverp] *n* (—[e]s;—ien [-ɪ·ən]) adverb

Advokat **—in** [atvoˈkat(ɪn)] §7 *mf* lawyer

Affäre [aˈferə] *f* (—;—n) affair

Affe [ˈafə] *m* (—n;—n) ape, monkey; **e—n Affen haben** (sl) be drunk

Affekt [aˈfekt] *m* (—[e]s;—e) emotion; *(Leidenschaft)* passion

affektiert [afekˈtirt] *adj* affected

Affektiert'heit f (–;-en) affectation

äffen ['ɛfən] tr ape, mimic

Af'fenliebe f doting

Af'fenpossen pl monkeyshines

Af'fenschande f crying shame

Af'fentheater n farce, joke

affig ['afɪç] adj affected; (geckenhaft) foppish

Äffin ['ɛfɪn] f (–;-nen) female ape, female monkey

Afrika ['afrɪka] n (–s;) Africa

afrikanisch [afrɪ'kanɪ/] adj African

After ['aftər] m (–s;–) anus

AG, A.G., A.-G. abbr (Aktiengesellschaft) stock company

ägäisch [ɛ'gɛ·ɪ/] adj Aegean

Agende [a'gɛndə] f (–;-n) memo pad

Agent –in [a'gɛnt(ɪn)] §7 mf agent, representative; (Geheim-) secret agent

Agentur [agɛn'tur] f (–;-en) agency

aggressiv [agrɛ'sif] adj aggressive

Ägide [ɛ'gidə] f (–;-n) aegis

Agio ['aʒi·o] n (–s;-s) premium

Agitation [agɪta'tsjon] f (–;-en) agitation, rabble-rousing

Agi·tator [agɪ'tatɔr] m (–s;-tatoren [ta'torən] (& mach) agitator

agitatorisch [agɪta'torɪ/] adj inflammatory

agitieren [agɪ'tirən] intr agitate

Agraffe [a'grafə] f (–;-n) clasp

agrarisch [a'grarɪ/] adj agrarian

Ägypten [ɛ'gyptən] n (–s;) Egypt

Ägypter –in [ɛ'gyptər(ɪn)] §6 mf Egyptian

ägyptisch [ɛ'gyptɪ/] adj Egyptian

ah [ɑ] interj ah!

Ahle ['alə] f (–;-n) awl, punch

Ahn [ɑn] m (–(e)s & –en;-en) ancestor

ahnden ['andən] tr (strafen) punish; (rächen) avenge

Ahn'dung f (–;) revenge

ähneln ['ɛnəln] intr (dat) resemble

ahnen ['anən] tr have a premonition of, suspect; (erfassen) divine

Ah'nentafel f family tree

ähnlich ['ɛnlɪç] adj alike; (dat) similar (to), analagous (to): das sieht ihm ä. that's just like him; j–m ä sehen look like s.o.

Ähn'lichkeit f (–;-en) (mit) resemblance (to)

Ah'nung f (–;-en) (Vorgefühl) presentiment, hunch; (böse) misgiving; (Argwohn) suspicion; keine A. haben have no idea

ah'nungslos adj unsuspecting

ah'nungsvoll adj full of misgivings

Ahorn ['ahɔrn] m (–(e)s;-e) maple

Ähre ['ɛrə] f (–;-n) (Korn) ear; (e–r Blume) spike; Ähren lesen glean

Ais ['a·ɪs] n (–;–) (mus) A sharp

Akade·mie [akadə'mi] f (–;-mien ['mi·ən]) academy; university

Akademiker –in [aka'demɪkər(ɪn)] §6 mf university graduate

akademisch [aka'demɪ/] adj academic; university

Akazie [a'katsjə] f (–;-n) acacia

akklimatisieren [aklɪmatɪ'zirən] tr acclimate || ref become acclimated

Akkord ['akɔrt] m (–(e)s;-e) chord;

(Vereinbarung) accord; (com) settlement; im A. arbeiten do piecework

Akkord'arbeit f piecework

Akkordeon [a'kɔrde·ɔn] n (–s;-s) accordion

akkreditieren [akredɪ'tirən] tr accredit; open an account for

Akkreditiv [akredɪ'tif] n (–[e]s;-e) (Beglaubigungsschreiben) credentials; (com) letter of credit

Akkumula·tor [akumu'latɔr] m (–s; -toren ['torən]) storage battery

akkurat [aku'rat] adj accurate

Akkusativ ['akuzatif] m (–[e]s;-e) accusative (case)

Akrobat [akrɔ'bat] §7 m acrobat

Akrobatik [akrɔ'batɪk] f (–;) acrobatics

Akrobatin [akrɔ'batɪn] §7 f acrobat

Akt [akt] m (–[e]s;-e) act, action; (paint) nude; (theat) act

Akte ['aktə] f (–;-n) document; record, file; (jur) instrument; zu den Akten legen file; (fig) shelve

Ak'tendeckel m file folder

Ak'tenklammer f paper clip

Ak'tenmappe f brief case, portfolio

ak'tenmäßig adj documentary

Ak'tenschrank m file cabinet

Ak'tentasche f brief case

Ak'tenzeichen n file number

Aktie ['aktsjə] f (–;-n) stock

Ak'tienbesitzer –in §6 mf stockholder

Ak'tienbörse f stock exchange

Ak'tiengesellschaft f corporation

Ak'tieninhaber –in §6 mf stockholder

Ak'tienmakler –in §6 mf stockbroker

Ak'tienmarkt m stock market

Ak'tienschein m stock certificate

Aktion [ak'tsjon] f (–;-en) action; (Unternehmung) campaign, drive; (polizeiliche) raid; (mil) operation; Aktionen activity

Aktionär –in [aktsjɔ'ner(ɪn)] §8 mf stockholder

aktiv [ak'tif] adj active; (Bilanz) favorable; (chem) activated; (gram) active; a. werden become a member (of a student club) || Aktiv n (–s;) (gram) active voice

Aktiva [ak'tiva] pl assets; A. und Passiva assets and liabilities

Aktiv'posten m asset

aktuell [aktu'el] adj current, topical || Aktuelle pl (journ) newsbriefs

Akustik [a'kustɪk] f (–;) acoustics

akustisch [a'kustɪ/] adj acoustic(al)

akut [a'kut] adj acute

Akzent [ak'tsent] m (–[e]s;-e) accent (mark); (Nachdruck) emphasis; (phonet) stress

akzentuieren [aktsentu'irən] tr accent; (fig) stress, accentuate

akzeptieren [aktsep'tirən] tr accept

Alabaster [ala'bastər] m (–s;) alabaster

Alarm [a'larm] m (–[e]s;-e) alarm; A. blasen (or schlagen) (mil & fig) sound the alarm; blinder A. false alarm

Alarm'anlage f alarm system; warning system (in civil defense)

alarm'bereit adj on the alert

Alarm'bereitschaft *f* (state of) readiness; **in A.** on the alert

alarmieren [alar'mirən] *tr* alert; alarm

Alaun [a'laʊn] *m* (-s;-e) alum

Alaun'stift *m* steptic pencil

Albanien [al'banjən] *n* (-s;) Albania

albanisch [al'banɪʃ] *adj* Albanian

albern ['albərn] *adj* silly

Al·bum ['albʊm] *n* (-s;-ben [bən]) album

Alchimist [alçɪ'mɪst] §7 *m* alchemist

Alge ['algə] *f* (-;-n) alga; seaweed

Algebra ['algebra] *f* (-;) algebra

algebraisch [alge'bra·ɪʃ] *adj* algebraic

Algerien [al'gerjən] *n* (-s;) Algeria

algerisch [al'gerɪʃ] *adj* Algerian

Algier ['alʒir] *n* (-s;) Algiers

Alibi ['alibɪ] *n* (-s;-s) alibi

Alimente [alɪ'mentə] *pl* child support

alimentieren [alɪmen'tirən] *tr* pay alimony to; (*Kind*) support

Alkohol ['alkohol] *m* (-s;-e) alcohol

al'koholfrei *adj* non-alcoholic

Alkoholiker **-in** [alko'holikər(ɪn)] §6 *mf* alcoholic

alkoholisch [alko'holɪʃ] *adj* alcoholic

all [al] *adj* all; (*jeder*) every; (*jeder beliebige*) any; **alle beide** both (of them); **alles Gute!** take care!; (*im Brief*) best wishes; **alle zehn Minuten** every ten minutes; **alle zwei Tage** every other day; **auf alle Fälle** in any case || *indef pron* each, each one; everyone, everything; all; **aller und jeder** each and every one; **in allem** all told; **vor allem** above all, first of all

alle ['alə] *adv* all gone; **a. machen** finish off; **a. sein** be all gone; **a. werden** run low

Allee [a'le] *f* (-;-n) (tree-lined) avenue; (tree-lined) walk

Allego·rie [alego'ri] *f* (-;-rien ['ri·ən]) allegory

allegorisch [ale'gorɪʃ] *adj* allegoric(al)

allein [a'laɪn] *adj* alone || *adv* alone; only; however; no fewer than, no less than; **schon a. der Gedanke** the mere thought

Allein'berechtigung *f* exclusive right

Allein'flug *m* solo flight

Allein'handel *m* monopoly

Allein'herrschaft *f* autocracy

Allein'herrscher **-in** §6 *mf* autocrat

allei'nig *adj* (*ausschließlich*) sole, exclusive; (*einzig*) only

allein'stehend *adj* alone in the world; (*unverheiratet*) single; (*Gebäude*) detached

Allein'verkauf *m*, **Allein'vertrieb** *m* franchise

al'lemal *adv* every time; **ein für a.** once and for all

al'lenfalls *adv* if need be; (*vielleicht*) possibly; (*höchstens*) at most

allenthalben ['alənt'halbən] *adv* everywhere

al'lerart *invar adj* all kinds of

al'lerbe'ste §9 *adj* very best; **aufs a.** in the best possible manner

al'lerdings' *adv* (*gewiß*) certainly (*strong affirmative answer*); (*zugestehend*) admittedly, I must admit

al'lerer'ste §9 *adj* very first, first ... of all

Aller·gie [aler'gi] (-;-gien ['gi·ən]) allergy

allergisch [a'lergɪʃ] *adj* allergic

al'lerhand' *invar adj* all kinds of; (*viel*) a lot of || *indef pron* —**das ist a.!** that's great!; **das ist doch a.!** the nerve!

Allerhei'ligen *invar n* All Saints' Day

allerlei ['alər'laɪ] *invar adj* all kinds of || **Allerlei** *n* (-s;-s) hotchpotch; (*mus*) medley

al'lerlet'zte §9 *adj* very last, last of all; latest

allerliebste ['alər'lipstə] §9 *adj* dearest ... of all; (*Kind*) sweet

al'lermei'ste §9 *adj* most; **am allermeisten** most of all; chiefly

al'lernäch'ste §9 *adj* very next

al'lerneu'este §9 *adj* latest, newest

Allersee'len *invar n* All Souls' Day

allesamt [alə'zamt] *adv* all together

al'lezeit *adv* always

Allge'genwart *f* omnipresence

all'gemein *adj* general, universal

All'gemeinheit *f* universality; (*Öffentlichkeit*) public

Allheil'mittel *n* cure-all

Allianz [alɪ'ants] *f* (-;-en) alliance

alliieren [alɪ'irən] *ref*—**sich a. mit** ally oneself with

alliiert [alɪ'irt] *adj* allied || **Alliierte** §5 *mf* ally

alljähr'lich *adj* annual, yearly

All'macht *f* omnipotence

allmäch'tig *adj* omnipotent, almighty

allmählich [al'meliç] *adj* gradual

allnächt'lich *adj* nightly

allseitig ['alzaitiç] *adj* all-round || *adv* from all sides, on all sides

All'tag *m* daily routine

alltäg'lich *adj* daily; (fig) everyday

all'tags *adv* daily; (*wochentags*) weekdays

All'tags- *comb.fm.* everyday; (fig) commonplace

All'tagsmensch *m* common man

All'tagswort *n* (-[e]s;¨er) household word

allwissend [al'vɪsənt] *adj* omniscient

allwö'chentlich *adj & adv* weekly

allzu- *comb.fm.* all too

all'zumal *adv* one and all, all together

all'zusammen *adv* all together

Alm [alm] *f* (-;-en) Alpine meadow

Almanach ['almanax] *m* (-[e]s;-e) almanac

Almosen ['almozen] *n* (-s;-) alms

Alp [alp] *m* (-[e]s;-e) elf, goblin; (*Alptraum*) nightmare

Alp'druck *m* (-[e]s;), **Alp'drücken** *n* (-s;) nightmare

Alpen ['alpən] *pl* Alps

Alphabet [alfa'bet] *n* (-[e]s;-e) alphabet

alphabetisch [alfa'betɪʃ] *adj* alphabetical

alpin [al'pin] *adj* alpine

als [als] *adv* as, like || *conj* than; when, as; but, except; **als ob** as if

alsbald' *adv* presently, immediately

alsdann' *adv* then, thereupon

also ['alzo] *adv* so, thus; therefore, consequently; **na a.!** well then!

alt [alt] *adj* (älter ['eltər], älteste ['eltəstə] §9) *adj* old; (*bejahrt*) aged; (*gebraucht*) second-hand; (*abgestanden*) stale; (*antik*) antique; (*Sprache*) ancient || **Alt** *m* (-[e]s;-e) contralto || **Alte** §5 *m* (coll) old man; **die Alten** the ancients; **mein Alter** (coll) my husband || **Alte** §5 *f* (coll) old woman; **meine Alte** (coll) my wife

Altan [al'tɑn] *m* (-[e]s;-e), **Altane** [al'tɑnə] *f* (-;-n) balcony, gallery

Altar [al'tɑr] *m* (-[e]s;ᵉe) altar

alt′bewährt *adj* long-standing

Alt′eisen *n* scrap iron

Alt′eisenhändler *m* junk dealer

Alter ['altər] *n* (-s;-) age; (*Greisen-*) old age; (*Zeit-*) epoch; (*Dienst-*) seniority; **er ist in meinem A.** he is my age; **im A. von** at the age of; **mittleren Alters** middle-aged

altern ['altərn] *intr* (SEIN) age

Alternative [alterna'tivə] *f* (-;-n) alternative

Al′tersgrenze *f* age limit; (*für Beamte*) retirement age

Al′tersheim *n* home for the aged

Al′tersrente *f* old-age pension

al′tersschwach *adj* decrepit; senile

Al′tersschwäche *f* (feebleness of) old age

Al′tersversorgungskasse *f* old-age pension fund

Altertum ['altərtum] *n* (-s;) antiquity

altertümlich ['altərtymlɪç] *adj* ancient; (*Möbel*) antique; (*veraltet*) archaic

Al′tertumsforscher –in §6 *mf* archaeologist; (*Antiquar*) antiquarian

Al′tertumskunde *f*, **Al′tertumswissenschaft** *f* study of antiquity; classical studies

althergebracht ['alt'hergəbraxt] *adj* long-standing, traditional

alther′kömmlich *adj* ancient, traditional

Altist [al'tɪst] §7 *m* alto (*singer*)

Altistin [al'tɪstɪn] §7 *f* contralto (*female singer*)

alt′klug *adj* precocious

ältlich ['eltlɪç] *adj* elderly

Alt′meister *m* past master; (sport) ex-champion

alt′modisch *adj* old-fashioned

Alt′stadt *f* old (part of the) city

Alt′stadtsanierung *f* urban renewal

Alt′stimme *f* alto; contralto (*female voice*)

altväterlich ['altfetərlɪç], **altväterisch** ['altfetərɪʃ] *adj* old-fashioned; old-time

Alt′warenhändler –in §6 *mf* second-hand dealer

Altweibersommer [alt'vaɪbərzəmər] *m* Indian summer; (*Spinnweb*) gossamer

Aluminium [alu'minjum] *n* (-s;) aluminum

am [am] *contr* **an dem**

amalgamieren [amalga'mirən] *tr* amalgamate

Amateur [ama'tør] *m* (-s;-e) amateur

Amazone [ama'tsonə] *f* (-;-n) Amazon

Am·boß ['ambɔs] *m* (-bosses;-bosse) anvil

ambulant [ambu'lant] *adj* ambulatory || *adv*—a. **Behandelte** out-patient

Ambulanz [ambu'lants] *f* (-;-en) out-patient clinic; (*Krankenwagen*) ambulance

Ameise ['amaɪzə] *f* (-;-n) ant

Amerika [a'merika] *n* (-s;) America

Amerikaner –in [amerɪ'kɑnər(ɪn)] §6 *mf* American

amerikanisch [amerɪ'kɑnɪʃ] *adj* American

Ami ['ami] *m* (-s;-s) (sl) Yank || *f* (-;-s) American cigarette

Amme ['amə] *f* (-;-n) nurse, wet-nurse

Amnes·tie [amnes'ti] *f* (-;-tien ['ti·ən]) amnesty

amnestieren [amnes'tirən] *tr* pardon

A·mor ['amɔr] *m* (-s;-moren ['morən]) (myth) Cupid

Amortisation [amɔrtza'tsjon] *f* (-;-en) amortization

Amortisations′kasse *f* sinking fund

amortisieren [amɔrtɪ'zirən] *tr* amortize

Ampel ['ampəl] *f* (-;-n) hanging lamp; (*Verkehrs–*) traffic light

Ampere [am'per] *n* (-s;-) ampere

Amphibie [am'fibjə] *f* (-;-n) amphibian

Amphi′bienpanzerwagen *m* amphibious tank

Amphitheater [am'fite·atər] *n* (-s;-) amphitheater

Ampulle [am'pulə] *f* (-;-n) phial

Amputation [amputa'tsjon] *f* (-;-en) amputation

amputieren [ampu'tirən] *tr* amputate

Amputierte [ampu'tirtə] §5 *mf* amputee

Amsel ['amzəl] *f* (-;-n) blackbird

Amt [amt] *n* (-[e]s;ᵉer) office; (*Pflicht*) duty, function; (dipl) post; (eccl) divine service; (telp) exchange

amtieren [am'tirən] *intr* be in office, hold office; (eccl) officiate

amt′lich *adj* official

**Amts– ** *comb.fm.* official, of (an) office

Amts′antritt *m* inauguration

Amts′befugnis *f* competence

Amts′bereich *m* jurisdiction

Amts′bewerber –in §6 *mf* office seeker

Amts′bezirk *m* jurisdiction

Amts′blatt *n* official bulletin

Amts′eid *m* oath of office

Amts′enthebung *f* dismissal

Amts′führung *f* administration

amts′gemäß *adj* official || *adv* officially

Amts′gericht *n* district court

Amts′gerichtsrat *m* (official rank of) district-court judge

Amts′geschäfte *pl* official duties

Amts′gewalt *f* (official) authority

Amts′handlung *f* official act

Amts′niederlegung *f* resignation

Amts′schimmel *m* bureaucracy; (coll) red tape

Amts′siegel *n* seal of office

Amts'sprache *f* official language; (coll) officialese, gobbledygook

Amts'tracht *f* robes

Amts'träger **–in** §6 *mf* officeholder

Amts'verletzung *f* misconduct in office

Amts'weg *m*—**auf dem Amtswege** through official channels

Amts'zeichen *n* (telp) dial tone

Amulett [amu'lɛt] *n* (–[e]s;–e) amulet

amüsant [amY'zant] *adj* amusing

amüsieren [amY'zirən] *tr* amuse, entertain ‖ *ref* amuse oneself; (*sich gut unterhalten*) enjoy oneself

an [an] *adv* on; onward ‖ *prep* (*dat*) at, against, on, upon, by, to; (*Grad, Maß*) in; **an sich** per se; **an und für sich** properly speaking; **es ist an dir zu** (*inf*) it's up to you to (*inf*) ‖ *prep* (*acc*) at, on, upon, against, to

analog [ana'lok] *adj* analogous

Analo·gie [analo'gi] *f* (–;–gien ['gi·ən]) analogy

Analphabet **–in** [analfa'bet(ɪn) §7 *mf* illiterate

Analphabetentum [analfa'betəntum] *n* (–s;), **Analphabetismus** [analfabe'tɪsmus] *m* (–;) illiteracy

analphabetisch [analfa'betɪʃ] *adj* illiterate

Analyse [ana'lyzə] *f* (–;–n) analysis; (gram) parsing; **durch A.** analytically

analysieren [analy'zirən] *tr* analyze; (gram) parse

Analy·sis [a'nɑlyzɪs] *f* (–;–sen [ana'lyzən]) (math) analysis

Analytiker **–in** [ana'lytɪkər(ɪn)] §6 *mf* analyst

analytisch [ana'lytɪʃ] *adj* analytic(al)

Anämie [anɛ'mi] *f* (–;) anemia

anämisch [an'ɛmiʃ] *adj* anemic

Ananas ['ananas] *f* (–;–se) pineapple

Anarchie [anar'çi] *f* (–;) anarchy

anästhesieren [anestɛ'zirən] *tr* anesthetize

Anästheti·kum [anes'tetɪkum] *n* (–s; –ka [ka]) anesthetic

an'atmen *tr* breathe on

Anato·mie [anato'mi] *f* (–;–mien ['mi·ən]) anatomy

anatomisch [ana'tomiʃ] *adj* anatomical

an'backen §50 *tr* bake gently ‖ *intr* (HABEN & SEIN) cake on

an'bahnen *tr* pave the way for

anbandeln ['anbandəln] *intr*—**a. mit** flirt with

An'bau *m* (–[e]s;) cultivation ‖ *m* (–[e]s;–bauten) annex, new wing

an'bauen *tr* cultivate; (*Gebäudeteil*) add on

An'baufläche *f* (arable) acreage

An'baumöbel *pl* sectional furniture

An'beginn *m* outset

an'behalten §90 *tr* keep (*garment*) on

anbei [an'baɪ] *adv* enclosed (herewith)

an'beißen §53 *tr* bite into, take the first bite of ‖ *intr* nibble at the bait; (fig) bite

an'belangen *tr*—**was mich anbelangt** as far as I am concerned, as for me

an'bellen *tr* bark at

anberaumen ['anbəraumən] *tr* schedule

an'beten *tr* (& fig) worship

An'betracht *m*—**in A.** (*genit*) in consideration of, in view of

an'betteln *tr* bum, chisel

An'betung *f* (–;) worship

an'betungswürdig *adj* adorable

an'bieten §58 *tr* offer ‖ *ref* offer one's services

an'binden §59 *tr* tie (up) ‖ *intr*—**mit j–m a.** pick a quarrel with s.o.

an'blasen §61 *tr* blow at, blow on

An'blick *m* look, view, sight

an'blicken *tr* look at; (*besehen*) view; (*mustern*) eye

an'blinzeln *tr* wink at

an'brechen §64 *tr* (*Vorräte*) break into; (*Flasche, Kiste*) open ‖ *intr* (SEIN) (*Tag*) dawn; (*Nacht*) come on

an'brennen §97 *tr* light ‖ *intr* (SEIN) catch fire; (*Speise*) burn

an'bringen §65 *tr* bring, fetch; (*befestigen*) (*an acc*) attach (to): (*Bitte*) make; (*Klage*) lodge; (*Geld*) invest; (*Tochter*) marry off; (*Waren*) sell, get rid of; (*Bemerkung*) insert; (*Licht, Lampe*) install; (*Geld*) (coll) blow

An'bruch *m* break; **bei A. der Nacht** at nightfall; **bei A. des Tages** at daybreak

an'brüllen *tr* roar at

Andacht ['andaxt] *f* (–;–en) devotion; (*Gottesdienst*) devotions

andächtig ['andɛçtɪç] *adj* devout

an'dauern *intr* continue, last; (*hartnäckig sein*) persist

An'denken *n* (–s;–) remembrance; souvenir; **zum A. an** (*acc*) in remembrance of

andere ['andərə] §9 *adj & pron* other; (*folgend*) next; **ein anderer** another; another one; **kein anderer** no one else

ändern ['endərn] *tr* change; (*Wortlaut*) modify ‖ *ref* change

andernfalls ['andərn'fals] *adv* (or) else

anders ['andərs] *adj* else; (als) different (from); **a. werden** change ‖ *adv* otherwise differently

an'dersartig *adj* of a different kind

anderseits ['andər'zaɪts] *adv* on the other hand

an'derswo *adv* somewhere else

anderthalb ['andərt'halp] *invar adj* one and a half

Än'derung *f* (–;–n) change, variation; modification

Än'derungsantrag *m* amendment

anderwärts ['andər'verts] *adv* elsewhere

anderweitig ['andər'vaɪtɪç] *adj* other, further ‖ *adv* otherwise; elsewhere

an'deuten *tr* indicate, suggest; (*anspielen*) hint at, allude to; (*zu verstehen geben*) imply, intimate

an'deutungsweise *adv* by way of suggestion

an'dichten *tr*—**j–m etw a.** impute s.th. to s.o.

An'drang *m* rush; crowd; heavy traffic; (*von Arbeit*) pressure

an'drehen *tr* turn on; **j–m etw a.** palm s.th. off on s.o.

an'drohen *tr*—j—m etw a. threaten s.o. with s.th.

an'drücken *tr*—etw a. an (*acc*) press s.th. against

an'eignen *ref*—sich [*dat*] a. appropriate; (*Gewohnheit*) acquire; (*Meinungen*) adopt; (*Sprache*) master; (*widerrechtlich*) appropriate, usurp

aneinan'der together

aneinan'dergeraten §63 *intr* (SEIN) come to blows

Anekdote [anɛk'doːtə] *f* (—;—n) anecdote

an'ekeln *tr* disgust, nauseate

an'empfehlen §147 *tr* recommend

An'erbieten *n* (—s;—) offer, proposal

an'erkennbar *adj* recognizable

an'erkennen §97 *tr* (als) recognize (as); (als) acknowledge (as); (*Schuld*) admit; (*billigen*) approve; (*lobend*) appreciate; (*Anspruch*) allow; **nicht a.** repudiate, disown; (sport) disallow

An'erkennung *f* (—;—en) acknowledgement; recognition; appreciation; admission; **lobende A.** honorable mention

anfachen ['anfaxən] *tr* (*Feuer*) fan; (*Gefühle*) inflame; (*Haß*) stir up

an'fahren §71 *tr* (*herbeibringen*) carry, convey; (*anstoßen*) run into; (fig) snap at; (naut) run afoul of ‖ *intr* (SEIN) drive up; (*losfahren*) start off

An'fall *m* attack

an'fallen §72 *tr* attack, assail ‖ *intr* (SEIN) accumulate, accrue

anfällig ['anfɛlɪç] *adj* (**für**) susceptible (to)

An'fang *m* beginning, start; **von A. an** from the very beginning

an'fangen §73 *tr* & *intr* begin, start

Anfänger –in ['anfɛŋər(ɪn)] §6 *mf* beginner; (*Neuling*) novice

anfänglich ['anfɛŋlɪç] *adj* initial

an'fangs *adv* at the start, initially

An'fangsbuchstabe *m* initial (letter)

An'fangsgründe *pl* rudiments, elements

an'fassen *tr* take hold of; (*behandeln*) handle, touch ‖ *intr* lend a hand

an'faulen *intr* (SEIN) begin to rot

anfechtbar ['anfɛçtbar] *adj* debatable, questionable; (jur) contestable

An'fechtung *f* (—;—en) (eccl) temptation; (jur) challenge

an'fertigen *tr* make, manufacture

an'feuchten *tr* moisten, wet

an'feuern *tr* inflame; (sport) cheer

an'flehen *tr* implore

an'fliegen §57 *tr* (aer) approach

An'flug *m* (*Anzeichen*) suggestion, trace; (*oberflächliche Kenntnis*) smattering; (*dünner Überzug*) film; **A. von Bart** down; **leichter A. von** slight case of

an'fordern *tr* call for, demand; (mil) requisition

an'fragen *intr* (**über** *acc*, **wegen**, **nach**) ask (about *s.th.*); (**bei**) inquire (of *s.o.*)

an'fressen §70 *tr* gnaw; (*Metall*) corrode

anfreunden ['anfrɔɪndən] *ref* (**mit**) make friends (with)

an'frieren §77 *intr* (SEIN) begin to freeze; **a. an** (*acc*) freeze onto

an'fügen *tr* (an *acc*) join (to)

an'fühlen *tr* & *ref* feel

Anfuhr ['anfuːr] *f* (—;—en) delivery

an'führen *tr* lead; (*Worte*) quote; (*Grund*) adduce; (*täuschen*) take in, fool; (mil) lead, command

An'führer –in §6 *mf* leader; (mil) commander; (pol) boss

An'führung *f* quotation

An'führungszeichen *n* quotation mark

an'füllen *tr* & *ref* fill up

An'gabe *f* (*Erklärung*) statement; (*beim Zollamt*) declaration; (coll) showing off; **Angaben** data; directions; **nähere Angaben machen** give particulars; **wer hat die A.?** whose serve is it?

an'geben §80 *tr* (*mitteilen*) state; (*bestimmen*) appoint; (*anzeigen*) inform against; (*vorgeben*) pretend; (*Preis*) quote ‖ *intr* (coll) show off; (cards) deal first; (tennis) serve

An'geber –in §6 *mf* informer; (*Prahler*) show-off

angeblich ['angeblɪç] *adj* alleged

an'geboren *adj* innate, natural

An'gebot *n* offer; (*bei Auktionen*) bid; **A. und Nachfrage** supply and demand

angebracht ['angəbraxt] *adj* advisable; **es ist a. halten zu** (*inf*) see fit to (*inf*); **gut a.** appropriate; **schlecht a.** ill-timed

angegossen ['angəgɔsən] *adj*—**wie a. sitzen** fit like a glove

angeheiratet ['angəhaɪratət] *adj* related by marriage

angeheitert ['angəhaɪtərt] *adj* tipsy

an'gehen §82 *tr* charge, attack; (*Problem*) tackle; **das geht dich gar nichts an** that's none of your business; **j–n um etw a.** approach s.o. for s.th. ‖ *intr* (SEIN) begin; (*zulässig sein*) be allowable; (*leidlich sein*) be tolerable; **das geht nicht an** that won't do

an'gehend *adj* future, prospective

an'gehören *intr* (*dat*) be a member (of)

Angehörige ['angəhøːrɪgə] §5 *mf* member; **nächste Angehörigen** next of kin; **seine Angehörigen** his relatives

Angeklagte ['angəklaːktə] §5 *mf* defendant; (*wenn verhaftet*) suspect

Angel ['aŋəl] *f* (—;—n) fishing tackle; (*e–r Tür*) hinge; **aus den Angeln heben** (& fig) unhinge

an'gelangen *intr* (SEIN) (**an** *dat*, **bei**) arrive (at)

an'gelegen *adj*—**sich** [*dat*] **etw a. sein lassen** make s.th. one's business

An'gelegenheit *f* (—;—en) affair, business

angelehnt ['angəleːnt] *adj* ajar

An'gelgerät *n* fishing tackle

An'gelhaken *m* fish(ing) hook

angeln ['aŋəln] *intr* (nach) fish (for)

An'gelpunkt *m* pivot, central point

An'gelrute *f* fishing rod

angelsächsisch ['aŋəlzɛksɪʃ] *adj* Anglo-Saxon
An'gelschnur *f* fishing line
angemessen ['angəmɛsən] *adj* suitable (*ausreichend*) adequate; (*annehmbar*) reasonable; (*Benehmen*) proper; (*dat*) in keeping (with); **für a. halten** think fit
angenehm ['angənem] *adj* pleasant; **sehr a!** pleased to meet you!
angeregt ['angərekt] *adj* lively
angeschlagen ['angəʃlɑ:gən] *adj* chipped; (*Boxer*) groggy; (*mil*) hard-hit
angesehen ['angəze:ən] *adj* respected; (*ausgezeichnet*) distinguished
An'gesicht *n* countenance, face; **von A.** by sight
an'gesichts *prep* (*genit*) in the presence of; (fig) in view of
angestammt ['angəʃtamt] *adj* hereditary
Angestellte ['angəʃteltə] §5 *mf* employee; **die Angestellten** the staff
angetan ['angətɑn] (**mit**) clad (in); **a. sein von** have a liking for; **ganz danach a. zu** (*inf*) very likely to (*inf*)
angetrunken ['angətruŋkən] *adj* tipsy
angewandt ['angəvant] *adj* applied
angewiesen ['angəvi:zən] *adj*—**a. sein auf** (*acc*) have to rely on
an'gewöhnen *tr*—**j—m etw a.** accustom s.o. to s.th.
An'gewohnheit *f* (-;-en) habit
an'gleichen §85 *tr* adapt, adjust
Angler **–in** ['aŋlər(ɪn)] §6 *mf* fisher
an'gliedern *tr* link, attach; (*Gesellschaft*) affiliate
an'greifen §88 *tr* (*anfassen*) handle; (*Vorräte*) draw on, dip into; (*Körper*) affect; (*mil*) attack
an'greifend *adj* aggressive, offensive
An'greifer **–in** §6 *mf* aggressor
an'grenzen *intr* (**an** *acc*) be adjacent (to), border (on)
An'griff *m* attack
An'griffskrieg *m* war of aggression
an'griffslustig *adj* aggressive
Angst [aŋst] *f* (-;-e) fear, anxiety
ängstigen ['ɛŋstɪgən] *tr* alarm ‖ *ref* (**vor**) be afraid (of); (**um**) be alarmed (about)
ängstlich ['ɛŋstlɪç] *adj* uneasy, jittery; (*besorgt*) anxious; (*sorgfältig*) scrupulous; (*schüchtern*) timid
Angst'zustände *pl* jitters
an'haben §89 *tr* have on; **j—m etw a.** have s.th. on. s.o.; **j—m etw a. können** be able to harm s.o.
an'haften *intr* (*dat*) stick (to)
an'haken *tr* check off; (**an** *acc*) hook (onto)
an'halten §90 *tr* stop; (*Atem, Ton*) hold; ‖ *intr* stop; (*andauern*) continue, last
an'haltend *adj* continuous
An'halter *m*—**per A. fahren** hitch-hike
An'haltpunkt *m* clue, lead
An'hang *m* (-[e]s;-e) appendix; (*Gefolgschaft*) following; (*jur*) codicil
an'hängen §92 & §109 *tr* (*Hörer*) hang up; (*hinzufügen*) add on; **j—m e—e Krankheit a.** infect s.o. with a disease; **j—m e—n Prozeß a.** bring suit

against s.o.; **j—m etw a.** pin s.th. on s.o. ‖ §92 *intr* (**an** *dat*) adhere (to)
An'hänger **–in** §6 *mf* follower ‖ *m* (*Schmuck*) pendant; (*aut*) trailer
anhänglich ['anhɛŋlɪç] *adj* (**an** *acc*) attached (to), devoted (to)
Anhängsel ['anhɛŋzəl] *m* (-s;-) appendage, adjunct
an'hauchen *tr* breathe on
an'häufen *tr* & *ref* pile up
An'häufung *f* (-;-en) accumulation
an'heben §94 *tr* lift (up); (*Lied*) strike up; (*aut*) jack up
an'heften *tr* fasten; (*annähen*) stitch
an'heilen *tr* & *intr* heal up
anheim'fallen §72 *intr* (SEIN) (*dat*) devolve (upon)
anheim'stellen *tr* (*dat*) leave (to)
An'höhe *f* rise, hill
an'hören *tr* listen to, hear ‖ *ref*—**sich gut a.** sound good
Anilin [anɪ'lin] *n* (-s;) aniline
Animier'dame *f* B-girl
animieren [anɪ'mirən] *tr* encourage
Anis [a'nis] *m* (-es;-e) anise
an'kämpfen *intr* (**gegen**) struggle (against)
An'kauf *m* purchase
an'kaufen *tr* purchase
Anker ['aŋkər] *m* (-s;-) anchor; (elec) armature; **vor A. gehen** drop anchor
ankern ['aŋkərn] *intr* anchor
an'ketten *tr* (**an** *acc*) chain (to)
An'klage *f* accusation, charge; (*jur*) indictment; **A. erheben** prefer charges; **die A. vertreten** be counsel for the prosecution; **unter A. stellen** indict
an'klagen *tr* (**wegen**) accuse (of), charge (with), indict (for)
An'kläger **–in** §6 *mf* accuser; (*jur*) prosecutor
An'klageschrift *f* (bill of) indictment
an'klammern *tr* (**an** *acc*) clip (to) ‖ *ref* (**an** *acc*) cling (to)
An'klang *m* (**an** *acc*) reminiscence (of), trace (of); **A. finden** be well received, catch on
an'kleben *tr* (**an** *acc*) paste (on), stick (on) ‖ *intr* (HABEN & SEIN) stick
an'kleiden *tr* & *ref* dress
an'klingeln *tr* ring, call up ‖ *intr*—**bei j—m a.** ring s.o.'s doorbell
an'klopfen *intr* (**an** *acc*) knock (on)
an'knipsen *tr* switch on
an'knüpfen *tr* tie, attach; (*Gespräch*) start ‖ *intr* (**an** *acc*) link up (with)
an'kommen §99 *intr* (SEIN) (**in** *dat*) arrive (at); (**bei**) be well received (by); (**bei**) get a job (with); **es darauf a. lassen** take one's chances; **es kommt ganz darauf an, ob it** (all) depends on whether
Ankömmling ['ankœmlɪŋ] *m* (-s;-e) newcomer, arrival
an'kündigen *tr* announce, proclaim; **j—m etw a.** notify s.o. of s.th.
An'kündigung *f* (-;-en) announcement
Ankunft ['ankunft] *f* (-;-e) arrival
an'kurbeln *tr* crank up; **die Wirtschaft a.** prime the economy
an'lachen *tr* laugh at
An'lage *f* (*Anordnung*) plan, layout;

(Bau) construction; *(Errichtung)* installation; *(Fabrik)* plant, works; *(Garten)* park, grounds; *(Fähigkeit)* ability, aptitude *(im Brief)* enclosure; **in der A.** enclosed

An′lagekapital n invested capital; permanent assets

an′langen tr—was mich anlangt as far as I'm concerned ∥ intr (SEIN) arrive

An·laß [′anlas] m (–lasses;–lässe) occasion; *(Grund)* reason, motive; **A. geben zu** give rise to; **ohne allen A.** without any reason

an′lassen §104 tr *(Kleid)* keep on; *(Motor)* start (up); *(Wasser)* turn on; *(Pumpe)* prime; *(Stahl)* temper; **j–n hart a.** rebuke s.o. sharply ∥ ref **sich gut a.** shape up

Anlasser [′anlasər] m (–s;–) starter

anläßlich [′anleslɪç] prep *(genit)* on the occasion of

An′lauf m run, start

an′laufen §105 tr run at; *(Hafen)* put into ∥ intr (SEIN) *(Motor)* start up; *(Brille)* fog up; *(Metall)* tarnish; *(anwachsen)* accumulate; *(Schulden)* mount up; *(Film)* start, come on; **angelaufen kommen** come running up; **ins Rollen a.** (fig) get rolling; **rot a.** blush

an′legen tr (an acc) put (on), lay (on); *(Garten; Geld)* lay out; *(Kapital)* invest; *(Leitung)* install; *(Verband)* apply; *(Kolonie)* found ∥ ref—**sich a. mit** have a run-in with ∥ intr put ashore; moor

An′legeplatz m pier

an′lehnen tr (an acc) lean (against); *(Tür)* leave ajar ∥ ref (an acc) lean (against); (fig) be based (on), rely (on)

Anleihe [′anlaɪ·ə] f (–;–n) loan

an′leiten tr (zu) guide (to); **a. in** *(dat)* instruct in

An′leitung f (–;–en) guidance; *(Lehre)* instruction

an′lernen tr train, break in

an′liegen §108 intr *(passen)* fit; (an dat) lie near, be adjacent (to); **eng a.** fit tight; **j–m a.** pester s.o. ∥ **Anliegen** n (–s;–) request; **ein A. an j–n haben** have a request to make of s.o.

an′liegend adj adjacent; *(Kleid)* tight-fitting; *(im Brief)* enclosed

an′locken tr lure (on)

an′machen tr *(Licht)* switch on; *(Feuer)* light; *(zubereiten)* prepare; (an acc) attach (to)

an′malen tr paint

an′marschieren intr (SEIN) approach

anmaßen [′anmasən] ref—**sich [dat] etw a.** usurp s.th.; **sich [dat] a., etw zu sein** pretend to be s.th.

anmaßend adj arrogant

An′meldeformular n registration form

an′melden tr announce; report; *(Anspruch, Berufung)* file; *(Konkurs)* declare; *(Patent)* apply for; *(educ)* register; *(sport)* enter ∥ ref *(bei)* make an appointment (with); *(zu)* enroll (in); (mil) report in

an′merken tr note down; **j–m etw a.** notice s.th. in s.o.

an′messen §70 tr—**j–m etw a.** measure s.o. for s.th.

An′mut f (–;) charm, attractiveness

an′mutig adj charming

an′nageln tr (an acc) nail (to)

an′nähen tr (an acc) sew on (to)

annähernd [′anne·ərnt] adj approximate

An′näherung f (–;–en) approach

An′näherungsversuch m (romantic) pass; attempt at reconciliation

an′näherungsweise adv approximately

An′nahme f (–;–n) acceptance; *(Vermutung)* assumption

annehmbar [′annembar] adj acceptable

an′nehmen §116 tr accept, take; *(vermuten)* assume, suppose, guess; *(Glauben)* embrace; *(Gewohnheit)* acquire; *(Gesetz)* pass; *(Kind)* adopt; *(Arbeiter)* hire; *(Farbe, Gestalt)* take on; *(Titel)* assume; **etw als erwiesen a.** take s.th. for granted ∥ ref *(genit)* take care of

annektieren [anek′tirən] tr annex

Annexion [anɛ′ksjon] f (–;–en) annexation

Annonce [a′nõsə] f (–;–n) advertisement

annoncieren [anõ′sirən] tr advertise

anöden [a′nødən] tr bore to death

anonym [anə′nym] adj anonymous

an′ordnen tr arrange; *(befehlen)* order

an′packen tr grab hold of, seize; *(Problem)* tackle

an′passen tr fit; *(Worte)* adapt; ∥ ref (dat or an acc) adapt oneself (to)

an′passungsfähig adj adaptable

an′pflanzen tr plant, cultivate

an′pflaumen tr (coll) kid

anpöbeln [′anpøbəln] tr mob

an′pochen tr (an acc) knock (on)

An′prall m impact; *(e–s Angriffs)* brunt

an′prallen intr (SEIN) *(gegen, an acc)* collide (with), run (into)

an′preisen tr praise; **j–m etw a.** recommend s.th. to s.o.

An′probe f fitting, trying on

an′probieren tr try on

an′pumpen tr—**j–n a. um** hit s.o. for

an′quatschen tr talk the ears off

an′raten §63 tr advise, recommend

an′rechnen tr charge; **hoch a.** appreciate; **j–m etw a.** charge s.o. for s.th.

An′recht n *(auf acc)* right (to)

An′rede f address

an′reden tr address, speak to

an′regen tr stimulate; suggest

An′reiz m incentive

an′reizen tr stimulate; spur on

an′rennen §97 intr (SEIN) *(gegen)* run (into); **angerannt kommen** come running

an′richten tr *(Schaden)* cause, do; *(culin)* prepare

anrüchig [′anryçɪç] adj disreputable

an′rücken intr (SEIN) approach

An′ruf m (telephone) call

an′rufen §122 tr call; *(Gott)* invoke; *(Schiff)* hail; *(jur)* appeal to; *(mil)* challenge; *(telp)* call up

an′rühren tr touch; *(Thema)* touch on; *(mischen)* stir

An′sage f announcement

an′sagen *tr* announce; (*Trumpf*) declare
An′sager –in §6 *mf* announcer
an′sammeln *tr* gather; (*anhäufen*) amass; (*Truppen*) concentrate || *ref* gather; (*Zinsen*) accumulate
ansässig [′anzesɪç] *adj* residing; **a. werden** (or **sich a. machen**) settle || **Ansässige** §5 *mf* resident
An′satz *m* start; (*Mundstück*) mouthpiece; (*Spur*) trace; (*in e-r Rechnung*) charge; (*Schätzung*) estimate; (geol) deposit; (mach) attachment; (math) statement
an′saugen §125 *tr* suck in; (*Pumpe*) prime
an′schaffen *tr* procure; (*kaufen*) get, purchase; **Kinder a.** (coll) have kids
an′schalten *tr* switch on
an′schauen *tr* look at
an′schaulich *adj* graphic
An′schauung *f* outlook, opinion; (*Vorstellung*) perception; (*Auffassung*) conception; (*Erkenntnis*) intuition; (*Betrachtung*) contemplation
An′schauungsbild *n* mental image
An′schauungsmaterial *n* visual aids
An′schein *m* appearance
an′scheinend *adj* apparent, seeming
an′scheinlich *adv* apparently
an′schicken *ref* get ready
an′schieben §130 *tr* give (*s.th.*) a push
anschirren [′anʃɪrən] *tr* harness
An′schlag *m* (an *acc*, gegen) striking (against); (*Anprall*) impact; (*Attentat*) attempt; (*Bekanntmachung*) notice; (e–r Uhr) stroke; (e–r Taste) hitting; (*Berechnung*) calculation; (e–s Gewehrs) firing position; (*Komplott*) plot; (mach) stop (*for arresting motion*); (mus) touch; (tennis) serve; **A. spielen** play tag
An′schlagbrett *n* bulletin board
an′schlagen §132 *tr* (an *acc*) fasten (to); (*Plakat*) post; (*Gewehr*) level; (*Tasse, usw.*) chip; (*Taste*) hit; (*einschätzen*) estimate; (*Gegner*) box) have in trouble; **e–n anderen Ton a.** (fig) change one's tune || *ref* bump oneself || *intr* (*Wellen*) (an *acc*) beat against; (*Hund*) let out a bark; (*Arznei*) work
An′schlagzettel *m* notice; poster
an′schließen §76 *tr* padlock; (*anketten*) chain; (*verbinden*) connect; (*anfügen*) join; (com) affiliate; (elec) plug in || *ref* (*dat*, an *acc*) join, side with ||*intr* (*Kleid*) be tight
an′schließend *adj* (an *acc*) subsequent (to); adjacent (to) || *adv* next, then
An′schluß *m* connection; (pol) annexation, union; **sie sucht A.** (coll) she is looking for a man
An′schlußbahn *f* (rr) branch line
An′schlußdose *f* (elec) receptacle
An′schlußschnur *f* (elec) cord
An′schlußzug *m* connection, connecting train
an′schmachten *tr* make eyes at
an′schmiegen *ref* (an *acc*) nestle up (to); (*Kleid*) (an *acc*) cling (to)
anschmiegsam [′anʃmikzam] *adj* accommodating; cuddly

an′schmieren *tr* smear; (coll) bamboozle
an′schnallen *tr* buckle || *ref* fasten one's seat belt
an′schnauzen *tr* snap at, bawl out
an′schneiden §106 *tr* cut into; (*Thema*) take up
An′schnitt *m* first cut
an′schrauben *tr* (an *acc*) screw on (to)
an′schreiben §62 *tr* write down; (*Spielstand*) mark; (*dat*) charge (to): (com) write to; **etw a. lassen** buy s.th. on credit
An′schreiber –in §6 *mf* scorekeeper
An′schreibetafel *f* scoreboard
an′schreien §135 *tr* yell at
An′schrift *f* address
An′schriftenmaschine *f* addressograph
anschuldigen [′anʃʊldigən] *tr* accuse
an′schwärzen *tr* blacken, disparage
an′schwellen *tr* cause to swell; (*Unkosten, usw.*) swell || §119 *intr* (SEIN) swell up, puff up; increase
an′schwemmen *tr* wash (*s.th.*) ashore; (geol) deposit
an′sehen §138 *tr* look at; (fig) regard || **Ansehen** *n* (–s;–) appearance; (*Achtung*) reputation; (*Geltung*) prestige, authority; **von A.** by sight; of high repute
ansehnlich [′anzenlɪç] *adj* good-looking; (*beträchtlich*) considerable; (*eindrucksvoll*) imposing
An′sehung *f* (–;) —**in A.** (*genit*) in consideration of
anseilen [′anzailən] *tr* rope together
an′setzen *tr* (an *acc*) put (on), apply (to): (*zum Kochen*) put on; (*Frist, Preis*) set; (*abschätzen*) rate; (*berechnen*) charge; (*Knospen*) put forth || *intr* begin; (*fett werden*) get fat
An′sicht *f* view; (*Meinung*) opinion; **zur A.** on approval
an′sichtig *adj*—**a. werden** (*genit*) catch sight of
An′sichtspostkarte *f* picture postcard
An′sichtssache *f* matter of opinion
An′sichtsseite *f* frontal view, façade
An′sichtssendung *f* article(s) sent on approval
ansiedeln *tr* & *ref* settle
An′siedler –in §6 *mf* settler
An′siedlung *f* (–;–en) settlement
An′sinnen *n* (–s;–) unreasonable demand
an′spannen *tr* stretch; (*Pferd*) hitch up; (fig) exert, strain
An′spannung *f* (–;–en) exertion, strain
an′speien §135 *tr* spit on
an′spielen *tr* (cards) lead with || *intr* (**auf** *acc*) allude (to); (mus) start playing; (sport) kick off, serve, break
An′spielung *f* (–;–en) allusion, hint
an′spitzen *tr* sharpen (*to a point*)
An′sporn *m* spur, stimulus
an′spornen *tr* spur
An′sprache *f* (an *acc*) address (to); **e–e A. halten** deliver an address
an′sprechen §64 *tr* speak to, address; (*Ziel, Punkt*) make out; **a. als** regard as; **j–n a. um** ask s.o. for || *intr* (*dat*) appeal to, interest; (**auf** *acc*) respond (to)

an'sprechend adj appealing
an'springen §142 tr leap at || intr
(SEIN) (Motor) start (up); **angesprun-
gen kommen** come skipping along
an'spritzen tr sprinkle, squirt
An'spruch m claim; **A. haben auf** (acc)
be entitled to; **A. machen** (or **erheben**) **auf** (acc), **in A. nehmen** demand, require, claim; **große Ansprüche stellen** ask too much
an'spruchslos adj unpretentious
an'spruchsvoll adj pretentious; (wählerisch) choosy, hard to please
an'spucken tr spit on
an'spülen tr wash ashore; (geol) deposit
an'stacheln tr goad on
Anstalt ['anʃtalt] f (–;–en) institution,
establishment; **Anstalten treffen zu**
make preparations for
An'stand m (Schicklichkeit) decency;
(Bedenken) hesitation; (Einwendung)
objection; (hunt) blind
anständig ['anʃtendɪç] adj decent
An'standsbesuch m formal call
An'standsdame f chaperone
An'standsgefühl n tact
an'standshalber adv out of politeness,
out of human decency
an'standslos adv without fuss
an'starren tr stare at, gaze at
anstatt [an'ʃtat] prep (genit) instead of
an'stauen tr dam up || ref pile up
an'staunen tr gaze at (in astonishment)
an'stecken tr stick on; (Ring) put on;
(anzünden) set on fire; (Zigarette,
Feuer) light; (pathol) infect || ref
become infected
an'steckend adj infectious; (durch Berührung) contagious
An'steckung f (–;–en) infection; (durch
Berührung) contagion
an'stehen §146 intr (nach) line up
(for); (zögern) hesitate; **j–m gut a.**
fit s.o. well, become s.o.
an'steigen §148 intr (SEIN) rise, ascend; (zunehmen) increase, mount
up
an'stellen tr (an acc) place (against);
(beschäftigen) hire; (Versuch, usw.)
(Vergleich) draw; (Heizung, Radio)
turn on || ref (nach) line up (for);
sich a., als ob act as if; **stell dich
nicht so dumm an!** don't play dumb!
anstellig ['anʃtelɪç] adj skillful
An'stellung f (–;–en) hiring; job
an'steuern tr steer for
Anstieg ['anʃtik] m (–[e]s;–e) rise;
(e–s Weges) grade
an'stieren tr stare at, glower at
an'stiften tr instigate
An'stifter –in §6 mf instigator
an'stimmen tr (Lied) strike up; (Geheul) let out
An'stoß m impact; (Antrieb) impulse;
(Ärgernis) offense; (sport) kickoff;
den A. geben zu start
an'stoßen §150 tr bump against; (Ball)
kick off; (Wagen) give a push; (mit
dem Ellbogen) nudge, poke || intr
clink glasses; **a. an** (acc) adjoin; **bei
j–m a.** shock s.o.; **mit den Gläsern a.**
clink glasses; **mit der Zunge a.** lisp ||

intr (SEIN)—**mit dem Kopf a. an**
(acc) bump one's head against
an'stoßend adj adjoining
anstößig ['anʃtøsɪç] adj shocking
an'strahlen tr beam on; (fig) beam at;
(mit Scheinwerfern) floodlight
an'streben tr strive for
an'streichen §85 tr paint; (Fehler)
underline; (anhaken) check off
An'streicher m house painter
an'streifen tr brush against, graze
an'strengen tr exert; (Geist) tax; **e–n
Prozeß a.** file suit || intr be a strain
an'strengend adj strenuous, trying
An'strengung f (–;–en) exertion, effort
An'strich m (Farbe) paint; (Überzug)
coat (of paint); (fig) tinge
An'sturm m assault, charge
antarktisch [ant'arktɪʃ] adj antarctic
an'tasten tr touch, finger
An'teil m share, portion; (Quote)
quota; (st. exch.) share; **A. nehmen
an** (dat) take part in; (fig) sympathize with
an'teilmäßig adj proportional
An'teilnahme f (–;) (an dat) participation (in); (Mitleid) sympathy
Antenne [an'tenə] f (–;–n) antenna,
aerial; (ent) antenna, feeler
Antibioti·kum [antɪbi'otikum] n (–s;
–ka [ka]) antibiotic
antik [an'tik] adj ancient; classical ||
Antike f (–;–n) (classical) antiquity;
(Kunstwerk) antique
Anti'kenhändler –in §6 mf antique
dealer
Antilope [antɪ'lopə] f (–;–n) antelope
Antipa·thie [antɪpa'ti] f (–;–thien
['ti·ən]) antipathy
an'tippen tr & intr tap
Antiqua [an'tikva] f (–;) roman (type)
Antiquar –in [antɪ'kvar(ɪn)] §8 mf
antique dealer; second-hand book-
dealer
Antiquariat [antɪkva'rjat] n (–[e]s;–e)
second-hand bookstore
antiquarisch [antɪ'kvarɪʃ] adj second-
hand
Antiquität [antɪkvɪ'tet] f (–;–en) antique
Antlitz ['antlɪts] m (–es;–e) (Bib, poet)
countenance
Antrag ['antrak] m (–[e]s;⁓e) (Angebot) offer; (Vorschlag) proposal;
(Gesuch) application; (pol) motion
an'tragen §132 tr offer; (vorschlagen)
propose || intr—**a. auf** (acc) make a
motion for; propose, suggest
An'tragsformular n application form
Antragsteller –in ['antrak/telər(–ɪn)]
§6 mf applicant; (parl) mover
an'treffen §151 tr meet; find at home
an'treiben §62 tr drive on, urge on;
(Schiff) propel; (anreizen) egg on ||
intr (SEIN) wash ashore
an'treten §152 tr (Amt, Erbschaft) enter (upon); (Reise) set out on; (Mo-
torrad) start up || intr (SEIN) take
one's place; (mil) fall in; (sport)
enter
An'trieb m (–s;–e) (Beweggrund) motive; (Anreiz) incentive; (mech)
drive, impetus; **aus eigenem A.** on

one's own initiative; **neuen A. verleihen** (*dat*) give fresh impetus to

An'tritt *m* (-[e]s;-e) beginning, start; (*e-s Amtes*) entrance upon

an'tun §154 *tr* (*Kleid*) put on; **j-m etw a.** do s.th. to s.o.

Antwort ['antvɔrt] *f* (-;-en) answer

antworten ['antvɔrtən] *intr* (*auf acc*) reply (to); answer; **j-m a.** answer s.o.

an'vertrauen *tr* entrust; (*mitteilen*) tell, confide

an'verwandt *adj* related || **Anverwandte** §5 *mf* relative

an'wachsen §155 *intr* (SEIN) begin to grow; grow together; (*Wurzel schlagen*) take root; (*zunehmen*) increase

Anwalt ['anvalt] *m* (-[e]s;⁻e) attorney

An'waltschaft *f* legal profession, bar

an'wandeln *tr*—**mich wandelte die Lust an zu** (*inf*) I got a yen to (*inf*); **was wandelte dich an?** what got into you?

An'wandlung *f* (-;-en) impulse, sudden feeling; (*von Zorn*) fit

An'wärter -**in** §6 *mf* candidate; (mil) cadet, officer candidate

Anwartschaft ['anvartʃaft] *f* (-;) expectancy; (*Aussicht*) prospect

an'wehen *tr* blow on || *intr* (SEIN) drift

an'weisen §118 *tr* (*beauftragen*) instruct; (*zuteilen*) assign; (*Geld*) remit

An'weisung *f* (-;-en) instruction; assignment; (fin) money order

anwendbar ['anventbar] *adj* (*auf acc*) applicable (to); (**für, zu**) that can be used (for)

an'wenden §140 *tr* (*auf acc*) apply (to); (**für, zu**) use (for)

An'wendung *f* (-;-en) application; use

an'werben §149 *tr* recruit

an'werfen §160 *tr* (*Motor*) start up

An'wesen *n* estate, property; presence

anwesend ['anvezənt] *adj* present || **Anwesende** §5 *mf* person present; **verehrte Anwesende!** ladies and gentlemen!

An'wesenheit *f* (-;) presence

an'wurzeln *ref & intr* (SEIN) take root; **wie angewurzelt** rooted to the spot

An'zahl *f* (-;) number, quantity

an'zahlen *tr* pay down || *intr* make a down payment

an'zapfen *tr* tap

An'zeichen *n* indication, sign; (*Vorbedeutung*) omen; (pathol) symptom

Anzeige ['antsaɪɡə] *f* (-;-n) (*Ankündigung*) announcement, notice; (*Reklame*) ad; (med) advice; **kleine Anzeigen** classified ads

an'zeigen *tr* announce; notify; (*Symptome, Fieber*) show, indicate; (*bei der Polizei*) report, inform against; (*inserieren*) advertise

An'zeigenvermittlung *f* advertising agency

an'zetteln *tr* (*Verschwörung*) hatch

an'ziehen §163 *tr* pull; (& fig) attract; (*Kleid*) put on; (*e-e Person*) dress; (*Riemen, Schraube*) tighten; (*Bremse*) apply; (*Beispiele, Quellen*) quote ||

intr pull, start pulling; (*Preis*) go up; (chess) go first

An'ziehung *f* (-;-en) attraction; (*Zitat*) quotation

An'ziehungskraft *f* appeal; (& phys) attraction; (astr) gravitation

An'zug *m* suit; (mil) uniform; **in A. sein** (*Armee*) be approaching; (*Sturm*) be gathering; (*Gefahr*) be imminent

anzüglich ['antsyːlɪç] *adj* offensive; **a. werden** become personal

an'zünden *tr* set on fire; (*Feuer*) light

an'zweifeln *tr* doubt, question

apart [a'part] *adj* charming; (coll) cute

Apathie [apa'tiː] *f* (-;) apathy

apathisch [a'paːtɪʃ] *adj* apathetic

Apfel ['apfəl] *m* (-s;⁻) apple

Ap'felkompott *n* stewed apples

Ap'felmus *n* applesauce

Ap'felsaft *m* apple juice

Apfelsine [apfəl'ziːnə] *f* (-;-n) orange

Ap'feltorte *f* apple tart; **gedeckte A.** apple pie

Ap'felwein *m* cider

Apostel [a'pɔstəl] *m* (-s;-) apostle

Apostroph [apo'stroːf] *m* (-[e]s;-e) apostrophe

Apotheke [apo'teːkə] *f* (-;-n) pharmacy

Apotheker -**in** [apo'teːkər(ɪn)] §6 *mf* druggist

Apothe'kerwaren *pl* drugs

Apparat [apa'raːt] *m* (-[e]s;-e) apparatus, device; (phot) camera; (rad, telv) set; (telp) telephone; **am A.!** speaking

Appell [a'pɛl] *m* (-[e]s;-e) appeal; (mil) roll call; (mil) inspection

appellieren [apɛ'liːrən] *intr* (& jur) (**an** *acc*) appeal (to)

Appetit [ape'tiːt] *m* (-[e]s;-e) appetite

Appetit'brötchen *n* canapé

appetit'lich *adj* appetizing; (*Mädchen*) attractive

applaudieren [aplaʊ'diːrən] *tr & intr* applaud

Applaus [a'plaʊs] *m* (-es;-e) applause

Appretur [apre'tuːr] *f* (-;-en) (tex) finish

Aprikose [apri'koːzə] *f* (-;-n) apricot

April [a'prɪl] *m* (-[s];-e) April

Aquarell [akva'rɛl] *n* (-[e]s;-e) watercolor; watercolor painting

Aqua·rium [a'kvaːrjʊm] *n* (-s;-rien [ri.ən]) aquarium

Äqua·tor [ɛ'kvaːtɔr] *m* (-s;-toren ['toːrən]) equator

Ära ['ɛːra] *f* (-;Ären ['ɛːrən]) era

Araber -**in** ['araːbər(ɪn)] §6 *mf* Arab

Arabien [a'raːbjən] *n* (-s;) Arabia

arabisch [a'raːbɪʃ] *adj* Arabian; (*Ziffer*) Arabic

Arbeit ['arbaɪt] *f* (-;-en) work

arbeiten ['arbaɪtən] *tr & intr* work

Arbeiter -**in** ['arbaɪtər] *m* (-s;-) worker; **A. und Unternehmer** *pl* labor and management

Ar'beiterausstand *m* walkout, strike

Ar'beitergewerkschaft *f* labor union

Arbeiterin ['arbaɪtərɪn] *f* (-;-nen) working woman, working girl

Ar'beiterschaft *f* (–;) working class
Arbeitertum ['arbaɪtǝrtum] *n* (–s;) working class, workers
Ar'beitgeber –in §6 *mf* employer
Ar'beitnehmer –in §6 *mf* employee
arbeitsam ['arbaɪtzam] *adj* industrious
Ar'beitsanzug *m* overalls; (mil) fatigue clothes, fatigues
Ar'beitseinkommen *n* earned income
Ar'beitseinstellung *f* work stoppage
ar'beitsfähig *adj* fit for work
Ar'beitsgang *m* process; operation (*single step of a process*)
Ar'beitsgemeinschaft *f* team; (educ) workshop
Ar'beitsgerät *n* equipment, tools
Ar'beitskommando *n* (mil) work detail
Ar'beitskraft *f* labor force; Arbeitskräfte personnel
Ar'beitslager *n* work camp
Ar'beitsleistung *f* (work) quota; (*e–r Maschine, Fabrik*) output
Ar'beitslohn *m* wages, pay
ar'beitslos *adj* unemployed
Ar'beitslosenunterstützung *f* unemployment compensation
Ar'beitslosigkeit *f* unemployment
Ar'beitsmarkt *m* labor market
Ar'beitsminister *m* secretary of labor
Ar'beitsministerium *n* department of labor
Ar'beitsnachweis *m*, Ar'beitsnachweisstelle *f* employment agency
Ar'beitsniederlegung *f* walkout, strike
ar'beitsparend *adj* labor-saving
Ar'beitspause *f* break, rest period
Arbeitspferd *n* (& *fig*) workhorse
Ar'beitsplatz *m* job, place of employment
Ar'beitsrecht *n* labor law
Ar'beitsscheu *adj* work-shy, lazy
Ar'beitsschicht *f* shift
Ar'beitsstätte *f* place of employment; workshop; yard
Ar'beitsstelle *f* job, position
Ar'beitstag *m* workday
Ar'beitsvermittlung *f* employment agency
Ar'beitsversäumnis *n* absenteeism
Ar'beitszeug *n* tools
Ar'beitszimmer *n* study; workroom
archaisch [ar'çaːɪʃ] *adj* archaic
Archäologe [arçɛˑoˈloːɡǝ] *m* (–n;–n) archaeologist
Archäologie [arçɛˑolǝˈgi] *f* (–;) archaeology
Archäologin [arçɛˑoˈloːgɪn] *f* (–;–nen) archaeologist
archäologisch [arçɛˑoˈloːgɪʃ] *adj* archaeological
Architekt –in [arçɪˈtɛkt(ɪn)] §7 *mf* architect
Architektur [arçɪtɛkˈtuːr] *f* (–;–en) architecture
Ar·chiv [arˈçiːf] *n* (–[e]s;–chive ['çiːvǝ]) archives; (*für Zeitungen*) morgue
Areal [areˈaːl] *n* (–s;–e) area
Are·na [aˈreːna] *f* (–;–nen [nǝn]) arena
arg [ark] *adj* (ärger ['ɛrgǝr]; ärgste ['ɛrkstǝ] §9) bad, evil, wicked; (coll) awful; (*schlimm*) grave; (*Raucher*)

heavy ‖ Arg *n* (–s;) malice, cunning ‖ Arge §5 *m* Evil One ‖ §5 *n* evil
Argentinien [argɛnˈtiːnjǝn] *n* (–s;) Argentina
Argentinier –in [argɛnˈtiːnjɛr(ɪn)] §6 *mf* Argentinean
Ärger ['ɛrgǝr] *m* (–s;) irritation; mit j–m Ä. haben have trouble with s.o.
är'gerlich *adj* (auf *acc* or über *acc*) annoyed (at); irritating, annoying
ärgern ['ɛrgǝrn] *tr* annoy ‖ *ref* (über *acc*) be annoyed (at)
Ärgernis ['ɛrgǝrnɪs] *n* (–ses;–se) scandal, offense; (*Mißstand*) nuisance
Arg'list *f* craft, cunning
arg'listig *adj* crafty, cunning
arg'los *adj* guileless; (*nichtsahnend*) unsuspecting
Argwohn ['arkvoːn] *m* (–s;) suspicion
argwöhnen ['arkvøːnǝn] *tr* suspect
argwöhnisch ['arkvøːnɪʃ] *adj* suspicious
Arie ['aːrjǝ] *f* (–;–n) aria
Arier –in ['aːrjǝr(ɪn)] §6 Aryan
arisch ['aːrɪʃ] *adj* Aryan
Aristokrat [arɪstoˈkraːt] *m* (–en;–en) aristocrat
Aristokra·tie [arɪstokraˈtiˑ] *f* (–;–tien ['tiˑǝn]) aristocracy
Aristokratin [arɪstoˈkraːtɪn] *f* (–;–nen) aristocrat
Arithmetik [arɪtˈmeːtɪk] *f* (–;) arithmetic
Arktis ['arktɪs] *f* (–;) Arctic
arktisch ['arktɪʃ] *adj* arctic
arm [arm] *adj* (ärmer ['ɛrmǝr], ärmste ['ɛrmstǝ] §9 (an *dat*) poor in) ‖ Arm *m* (–[e]s;–e) arm; (*e–s Flusses*) branch
Armatur [armaˈtuːr] *f* (–;–en) armature; Armaturen fittings, mountings
Armatu'renbrett *n* instrument panel; (aut) dashboard
Arm'band *n* (–[e]s;–̈er) bracelet; watchband; (*Armabzeichen*) brassard
Arm'banduhr *f* wrist watch
Arm'binde *f* brassard; (med) sling
Ar·mee [arˈmeː] *f* (–;–meen ['meˑǝn]) army
Ärmel ['ɛrmǝl] *m* (–s;–) sleeve
Är'melaufschlag *m* cuff
Är'melkanal *m* English Channel
är'mellos *adj* sleeveless
Armen– [armǝn] *comb.fm.* for the poor
Ar'menhaus *n* poorhouse
Armenien [arˈmeːnjǝn] *n* (–s;) Armenia
armenisch [arˈmeːnɪʃ] *adj* Armenian
Ar'menpflege *f* public assistance
Ar'menunterstützung *f* public assistance, welfare
Ar'menviertel *n* slums
Armesün'dermiene *f* hangdog look
Arm'lehne *f* arm, armrest
Arm'leuchter *m* candelabrum
ärmlich ['ɛrmlɪç] *adj* poor, humble
arm'selig *adj* poor, wretched; (*kläglich*) paltry
Armut ['armuːt] *f* (–;) poverty
Arm'zeichen *n* semaphore
Aro·ma [aˈroːma] *n* (–s;–men [mǝn], –mata [mata]) aroma
aromatisch [aroˈmaːtɪʃ] *adj* aromatic
Arrest *m* (–[e]s;–e) arrest;

(*in der Schule*) detention; (jur) impounding, seizure

Arsch [arʃ] m (–es;¨e) (sl) ass

Arsch′backe f (sl) buttock

Arsch′kriecher m (sl) brown-noser

Arsch′lecker m (sl) brown-noser

Arsen [ar′zen] n (–s;) arsenic

Arsenal [arze′nɑl] (–s;–e) arsenal

Art [art] f (–;–en) sort, kind; nature; (*Rasse*) race, breed; species; (*Weise*) manner; (*Verfahren*) procedure; (*Muster*) model; **das ist keine Art!** that's no way to behave!

art′eigen adj true to type

arten [′artən] intr (SEIN)—a. nach take after

Arterie [ar′terjə] f (–;–n) artery

artig [′artɪç] adj (*brav*) good, well-behaved; (*höflich*) polite

Artikel [ar′tikəl] (–s;–) (com, gram, journ) article

Artillerie [artɪlə′ri] f (–;) artillery

Artillerie′aufklärer m artillery spotter

Artischocke [artɪ′ʃɔkə] f (–;–n) artichoke

Artist –in [ar′tɪst(ɪn)] §7 mf artist; (*beim Zirkus*) performer

Arznei [arts′naɪ] f (–;–en) medicine, medication, drug

Arznei′kraut n herb, medicinal plant

Arznei′kunde f, **Arznei′kunst** f pharmaceutics; pharmacology

Arznei′mittel n medication

Arzt [artst] m (–[e]s;¨e) doctor

Ärztin [′ertstɪn] f (–;–nen) doctor

ärztlich [′ertstlɪç] adj medical

As [as] n (Asses; Asse) ace ‖ n (–;–) (mus) A flat

Asbest [as′best] m (–[e]s;–e) asbestos

asch′bleich adj ashen, pale

Asche [′aʃə] f (–;–n) ash(es), cinders

Aschen– comb.fm. ash; cinder; funerary

A′schenbahn f cinder track

A′schenbecher m ashtray

Aschenbrödel [′aʃənbrødəl] n (–s;–) Cinderella; drudge

Aschermittwoch [aʃər′mɪtvɔx] m (–s; –e) Ash Wednesday

asch′fahl adj ashen, pale

äsen [′ezen] intr graze, feed

asiatisch [azi′atɪʃ] adj Asiatic

Asien [′azjən] n (–s;) Asia

Asket [as′ket] m (–en;–en) ascetic

asketisch [as′ketɪʃ] adj ascetic

Asphalt [as′falt] m (–[e]s;) asphalt

asphaltieren [asfal′tirən] tr asphalt

Asphalt′pappe f tar paper

aß[as] pret of **essen**

Assistent –in [asɪs′tent(ɪn)] §7 mf assistant

Assistenz [asɪs′tents] f (–;–en) assistance

Assistenz′arzt m, **Assistenz′ärztin** f intern

Ast [ast] m (–es;¨e) bough, branch; (*im Holz*) knot, knob

ästhetisch [es′tetɪʃ] adj esthetic(al)

Asthma [′astma] n (–s;) asthma

ast′rein adj free of knots; **nicht ganz a.** (coll) not quite kosher

Astrologe [astro′logə] m (–n;–n) astrologer

Astrologie [astrolə′gi] f (–;) astrology

Astronaut [astro′naut] m (–en;–en) astronaut

Astronom [astro′nom] m (–en;–en) astronomer

Astronomie [astrono′mi] (–;) astronomy

astronomisch [astro′nomɪʃ] adj astronomic(al)

Astrophysik [astrofy′zik] f (–;) astrophysics

Asyl [a′zyl] n (–[e]s;–e) asylum, sanctuary; (*Obdach*) shelter; **ohne A.** homeless

Atelier [ate′lje] n (–s;–s) studio

Atem [′atəm] m (–s;) breath

A′tembeklemmung f shortness of breath

A′temholen n (–s;) respiration

a′temlos adj breathless

A′temnot f breathing difficulty

A′tempause f breathing spell

a′temraubend adj breath-taking

A′temzug m breath

Atheismus [ate′ɪsmus] m (–;) atheism

Atheist –in [ate′ɪst(ɪn)] §7 mf atheist

Äther [′etər] m (–s;) ether

Athlet [at′let] m (–en;–en) athlete

Athletik [at′letɪk] f (–;) athletics

Athletin [at′letɪn] f (–;–nen) athlete

athletisch [at′letɪʃ] adj athletic

Atlantik [at′lantɪk] m (–s) Atlantic

At·las [′atlas] m (–′;) (myth) Atlas ‖ m (–lasses; –lanten [′lantən] & –lasse) atlas ‖ m (– & –lasses;–lasse) satin

atmen [′atmən] tr & intr breathe

Atmosphäre [atmo′sferə] f (–;–n) (& fig) atmosphere

atmosphärisch [atmo′sferɪʃ] adj atmospheric; **atmosphärische Störungen** (rad) static

At′mung f (–;) breathing

Atom [a′tom] n (–s;–e) atom

Atom– comb. fm. atom, atomic

Atom′abfall m fallout; atomic waste

atomar [ato′mar] adj atomic

Atom′bau m atomic structure

atom′betrieben adj atomic-powered

Atom′bombe f atomic bomb

Atom′bombenversuch m atomic test

Atom′-Epoche f atomic age

Atom′kern m atomic nucleus

Atom′müll m atomic waste

Atom′regen m fallout

Atom′schutt m atomic waste

ätsch [etʃ] interj (to express gloating) serves you right!, good for you!

Attentat [aten′tat] n (–s;–e) attempt (*on s.o.'s life*); assassination

Attentäter –in [aten′tetər(ɪn)] §6 mf assailant, would-be assassin; assassin

Attest [a′test] n (–es;–e) certificate

attestieren [ates′tirən] tr attest (to)

Attrappe [a′trapə] f (–;–n) dummy

Attribut [atrɪ′but] n (–[e]s;–e) attribute; (gram) attributive

atzen [′atsən] tr feed

ätzen [′etsən] tr corrode; (med) cauterize (typ) etch

ät′zend adj corrosive; caustic

Au [au] f (–;–en) (poet) mead, meadow

au *interj* owl, ouch!; oh!

Aubergine [ober'ʒin(ə)] *f* (-;-n) egg-plant

auch [aux] *adv* also, too; *(selbst)* even

Audienz [au'djɛnts] *f* (-;-en) audience; *(jur)* hearing

auf [auf] *adv* up; **auf und ab** up and down; **von Kind auf** from childhood on || *prep (dat)* on, upon; **auf der ganzen Welt** in the whole world; **auf der Universität** at the university || *prep (acc)* on; up; to; **auf den Bahnhof gehen** go to the station; **auf deutsch** in German; **drei aufs Dutzend** three to a dozen; **es geht auf vier Uhr zu** it's going on four; **Monat auf Monat** verging month after month passed || *interj* get up! || **Auf** *n*—**das Auf und Nieder** the ups and downs

auf'arbeiten *tr (Rückstände)* catch up on; *(verbrauchen)* use up; *(erneuern)* renovate; *(mach)* recondition || *ref* work one's way up

auf'atmen *intr* breathe a sigh of relief

aufbahren ['aufbɑrən] *tr* lay out

Auf'bau *m* (-[e]s;) construction; structure; organization; *(Anlage)* arrangement, setup; *(chem)* synthesis || *m* (-[e]s;-ten) structure; *(aer)* framework; *(naut)* superstructure

auf'bauen *tr* erect; *(Organization)* establish; *(chem)* synthesize; *(mach)* assemble || *ref*—**er baute sich vor mir auf** he planted himself in front of me; **sich** [*dat*] **e-e Existenz a.** make a life for oneself

auf'bäumen *ref* rear; *(fig)* rebel

auf'bauschen *tr* puff up; *(fig)* exaggerate

auf'begehren *intr* flare up; *(gegen)* protest (against), rebel (against)

auf'behalten §90 *tr* keep on; keep open

auf'bekommen §99 *tr* *(Tür)* get open; *(Knoten)* loosen; *(Hausaufgabe)* be assigned

auf'bereiten *tr* prepare, process

auf'bessern *tr (Gehalt)* improve, raise

auf'bewahren *tr* keep, store; **das Gepäck a. lassen** check one's baggage

auf'bieten §58 *tr* summon; *(Brautpaar)* announce the banns of; *(mil)* call up

auf'binden §58 *tr* tie up; *(lösen)* untie; **j-m etw a.** put s.th. over on s.o.

auf'blähen *tr* inflate, distend

auf'blasen §61 *tr* inflate || *ref* get puffed up

auf'bleiben §62 *intr* (SEIN) *(Tür)* stay open; *(wachen)* stay up

auf'blenden *intr* turn on the high beam

auf'blicken *intr* glance up

auf'blitzen *intr* (HABEN & SEIN) flash

auf'blühen *intr* (SEIN) begin to bloom

auf'bocken *tr* (aut) jack up

auf'brauchen *tr* use up

auf'brausen *intr* (HABEN & SEIN) bubble, seethe; *(Wind)* roar; *(fig)* flare up

auf'brausend *adj* effervescent; irascible

auf'brechen §64 *tr* break up; break open; *(hunt)* eviscerate || *intr* (SEIN) burst open; *(fortgehen)* (nach) set out (for)

auf'bringen §65 *tr* bring up; *(Geld, Truppen)* raise; *(Schiff)* capture; *(Kraft)* gather; *(Mut)* get up; *(erzürnen)* infuriate

Auf'bruch *m* departure

auf'brühen *tr* bring to a boil

auf'bügeln *tr* iron, press; refresh *(one's knowledge of s.th.)*

aufbürden ['aufbyrdən] *tr*—**j-m etw a.** saddle s.o. with s.th.

auf'decken *tr* uncover; *(Bett)* turn down; *(Tischtuch)* spread

auf'drängen *tr* force open; **j-m etw a.** force s.th. on s.o.

auf'drehen *tr* turn up; *(Uhr)* wind; *(Hahn)* turn on; *(Schraube)* unscrew; *(Strick)* untwist || *intr* *(Wagen)* increase speed; *(coll)* step on it, get a move on

auf'dringlich *adj* pushy; *(Farben)* gaudy

Auf'druck *m* print, imprint

auf'drücken *tr* impress, imprint, affix; *(öffnen)* squeeze open

aufeinan'der *adv* one after the other

Aufeinan'derfolge *f* succession; series

aufeinan'derfolgen *intr* (SEIN) follow one another

aufeinan'derfolgend *adj* successive

Aufenthalt ['aufɛnthalt] *m* (-[e]s;-e) holdup, delay; **ohne A.** nonstop

Auf'enthaltsgenehmigung *f* residence permit

Auf'enthaltsort *m (Wohnsitz)* residence; *(Verbleib)* whereabouts

Auf'enthaltsraum *m* lounge

auf'erlegen *tr* impose || *ref*—**sich** [*dat*] **die Pflicht a. zu** *(inf)* make it one's duty to *(inf)*; **sich** [*dat*] **Zwang a.** müssen have to restrain oneself

auf'erstehen §146 *intr* (SEIN) rise (from the dead)

Auf'erstehung *f* (-;) resurrection

auf'erwecken *tr* raise from the dead

auf'erziehen §163 *tr* bring up, raise

auf'essen §70 *tr* eat up

auf'fädeln *tr (Perlen)* string

auf'fahren §71 *tr (Fahrzeuge)* park; *(Geschütze)* bring up; *(Wein, Speisen)* serve up || *intr* (SEIN) rise, mount; *(im Auto)* pull up; *(in Erregung)* jump (up); *(artl)* move into position; **a. auf** *(acc)* run into

Auf'fahrt *f* ascent; *(Zufahrt)* driveway

auf'fallen §72 *intr* (SEIN) be conspicuous; **j-m a.** strike s.o.

auf'fallend, auf'fällig *adj* striking; noticeable; *(Farben)* loud, gaudy

auf'fangen §73 *tr (Ball, Worte)* catch; *(Briefe, Nachrichten)* intercept

auf'fassen *tr* comprehend; *(deuten)* interpret; *(Perlen)* string

Auf'fassung *f* (-;-en) understanding; interpretation; *(Meinung)* view

auf'finden §59 *tr* find *(after searching)*

auf'fliegen §57 *intr* (SEIN) fly up; *(Tür)* fly open; *(scheitern)* fail; **a. lassen** break up *(a gang)*

auf'fordern *tr* call upon, ask

Auf'forderung *f* (-;-en) invitation; *(jur)* summons

auf′frischen *tr* freshen up, touch up

auf′führen *tr* (*Bau*) erect; (*Schauspiel*) present; (*eintragen*) enter; (*Zeugen*) produce; (*anführen*) cite; (*mil*) post; **einzeln a.** itemize ‖ *ref* behave, act

Auf′führung *f* (-;-en) erection; performance; entry; specification; behavior

auf′füllen *tr* fill up

Auf′gabe *f* task, job; (*e-s Briefes*) mailing; (*des Gepäcks*) checking; (*e-r Bestellung*) placing; (*e-s Amtes, e-s Geschäfts*) giving up; (*educ*) homework; (*jur*) waiver; (*math* problem); (*mil*) assignment

auf′gabeln *tr* (& *coll*) pick up

Auf′gang *m* ascent; (*Treppe*) stairs; (*astr*) rise

auf′geben §80 *tr* give up; (*Amt*) resign; (*Post*) mail; (*Gepäck*) check in; (*Anzeige*) place; (*Preis*) quote; (*Arbeit*) assign; (*Telegramm*) send

auf′geblasen *adj* (*fig*) uppity

Auf′gebot *n* public notice; (*eccl*) banns; (*mil*) call-up

auf′gebracht *adj* angry, irate

auf′gedonnert *adj* (*coll*) dolled up

auf′gehen §82 *intr* (SEIN) rise; (*Tür*) open; (*Pflanzen*) come up; (*arith*) go into; **genau a.** come out exactly

auf′geklärt *adj* enlightened

auf′geknöpft *adj* (*coll*) chatty

auf′gekratzt *adj* (*coll*) chipper

Auf′geld *n* surcharge; premium

auf′gelegt *adj* (zu) disposed (to)

auf′geräumt *adj* (*fig*) good-humored

auf′geschlossen *adj* open-minded; (für) receptive (to)

auf′geschmissen *adj* (*coll*) stuck

auf′gestaut *adj* pent-up

auf′geweckt *adj* smart, bright

auf′geworfen *adj* (*Lippen*) pouting; (*Nase*) turned-up

auf′gießen §76 *tr* (auf *acc*) pour (on); (*Tee, Kaffee*) make, brew

auf′graben §87 *tr* dig up

auf′greifen §88 *tr* pick up; (*Dieb*) catch; (*fig*) take up

auf′haben §98 *tr* (*Hut*) have on; (*Tür, Mund*) have open; (*Aufgabe*) have to do

auf′hacken *tr* hoe up

auf′haken *tr* unhook

auf′halten §90 *tr* hold up; (*Tür*) hold open; (*anhalten*) stop, delay ‖ *ref* stay; (*wohnen*) live; **sich über etw a.** find fault with s.th.

Auf′hängeleine *f* clothesline

auf′hängen §92 *tr* hang up; **j-m etw a.** push s.th. on s.o.; (*Wertloses*) palm s.th. off on s.o.

auf′häufen *tr* & *ref* pile up

auf′heben §94 *tr* lift up, pick up; (*bewahren*) preserve; (*ungültig machen*) cancel; (*Gesetz*) repeal; (*ausgleichen*) cancel out, offset; (*Strafe, Belagerung*) lift; **gut aufgehoben sein** be in good hands

auf′heitern *tr* cheer up ‖ *ref* cheer up; (*Gesicht*) brighten; (*Wetter*) clear up

auf′hellen *ref* & *intr* brighten

auf′hetzen *tr* incite, egg on

auf′holen *tr* hoist; (*Verspätung*) make up for ‖ *intr* catch up

auf′horchen *intr* prick up one's ears

auf′hören *intr* stop, quit

auf′jauchzen *intr* shout for joy

auf′kaufen *tr* buy up; (*Markt*) corner

auf′klären *tr* clear up; enlighten; (*mil*) reconnoitre ‖ *ref* clear up; (*Gesicht*) light up, brighten

Auf′klärer *m* (-s;-) (aer) reconnaissance plane; (*mil*) scout

Auf′klärung *f* (-;-en) explanation; enlightenment; (*mil*) reconnaissance

Auf′klärungsbuch *n* sex-education book

Auf′klärungsspähtrupp *m* reconnaissance patrol

auf′kleben *tr* (auf *acc*) paste (onto)

auf′klinken *tr* unlatch

auf′knacken *tr* crack open

auf′knöpfen *tr* unbutton

auf′knüpfen *tr* (*lösen*) untie; (*hängen*) (*coll*) string up

auf′kochen *tr* & *intr* boil

auf′kommen §99 *intr* (SEIN) come up, rise; (*Gedanke*) occur; (*Mode*) come into fashion; (*Schiff*) appear on the horizon; **a. für** answer for; (*Kosten*) defray; **a. gegen** stand up against, cope with; **a. von** recover from ‖ **Aufkommen** *n* (-s;) rise; recovery

auf′krempeln *tr* roll up

auf′kreuzen *intr* (*coll*) show up

auf′kriegen *tr* see aufbekommen

auf′lachen *intr* burst out laughing

auf′laden §103 *tr* load up; (*Batterie*) charge ‖ *ref*—**sich** [*dat*] **etw a.** saddle oneself with s.th.

Auf′lage *f* edition, printing; (*e-r Zeitung*) circulation; (*Steuer*) tax; (*Stütze*) rest, support

auf′lassen §104 *tr* leave open; (*Fabrik, Bergwerk*) abandon

auf′lauern *intr* (*dat*) lie in wait (for)

Auf′lauf *m* gathering, crowd; (*Tumult*) riot; (*com*) accumulation; (*culin*) soufflé

auf′laufen §105 *intr* (SEIN) rise; (*anwachsen*) accrue; (*Schiff*) get stranded; (*Panzer*) get stuck

auf′leben *intr* (SEIN) revive

auf′lecken *tr* lick up

auf′legen *tr* (auf *acc*) put (on); (*Steuer*) impose; (*Hörer*) hang up; (*Buch*) publish; (*Karten*) lay on the table; (*Liste*) make available for inspection; (*Anleihe*) float; (*Faß Bier*) put on ‖ *intr* (*telp*) hang up

auf′lehnen *tr* (auf *acc*) lean (on) ‖ *ref* (auf *acc*) lean (on); (*gegen*) rebel (against)

Auf′lehnung *f* (-;-en) rebellion; resistance

auf′lesen §107 *tr* pick up, gather

auf′liegen §108 *intr* (auf *dat*) lie (on); (*zur Ansicht*) be displayed

auf′lockern *tr* loosen; (*Eintönigkeit, Vortrag*) break (up)

auf′lösbar *adj* soluble; solvable

auf′lösen *tr* untie; (*öffnen*) loosen; (*entwirren*) disentangle; (*Versammlung*) break up; (*Heer*) disband; (*Ehe*) dissolve; (*Verbindung*) sever; (*Firma*) liquidate; (*Rätsel*) solve;

(*zerlegen*) break down; dissolve; (*entziffern*) decode; **ganz aufgelöst** all out of breath

Auf'lösung *f* (–;–en) solution; disentanglement; (*e–r Versammlung, Ehe*) breakup; (*Zerfall*) disintegration; (*von Beziehungen*) severance; (com) liquidation

auf'machen *tr* open (up); (*Geschäft*) open; (*Dampf*) get up; (coll) do up (*e.g., big, tastefully*) ‖ *ref* (*Wind*) rise; (*nach*) set out (for)

Auf'machung *f* (–;–en) layout, format; (*Kleidung*) outfit

Auf'marsch *m* parade; (mil) concentration; (*zum Gefecht*) (mil) deployment

auf'marschieren *intr* (SEIN) parade; (*strategisch*) assemble; (*taktisch*) deploy

auf'merken *tr* (**auf** *acc*) pay attention (to)

aufmerksam ['aʊfmɛrkzam] *adj* (**auf** *acc*) attentive (to)

Auf'merksamkeit *f* (–;) attention

auf'möbeln *tr* (coll) dress up; (*anherrschen*) (sl) chew out; (*aufmuntern*) (coll) pep up ‖ *ref* (coll) doll up

auf'muntern *tr* cheer up

Auf'nahme *f* (–;–n) taking up; (*Empfang*) reception (*Zulassung*) admission; (*von Beziehungen*) establishment; (*Inventur*) stock-taking; (electron) recording; (phot) photograph

Auf'nahmeapparat *m* camera; recorder

Auf'nahmegerät *n* camera; recorder

Auf'nahmeprüfung *f* entrance exam

auf'nehmen §116 *tr* take up; (*erfassen*) grasp; (*Diktat*) take down; (*Gast*) receive; (*Inventar*) take; (*Geld*) borrow; (*Anleihe*) float; (*Spur*) pick up; (*Beziehungen*) establish; (*eintragen*) enter; (*durch* *Tonband, Schallplatte*) record; (geog) map out; (phot) take

auf'opfern *tr* offer up, sacrifice

auf'päpeln *tr* spoon-feed

auf'passen *intr* pay attention; look out; **paß auf!** watch out!

auf'pflanzen *tr* set up; (*Seitengewehr*) fix

auf'platzen *intr* (SEIN) burst (open)

auf'polieren *tr* polish up

auf'prägen *tr* (**auf** *acc*) (& fig) impress (on)

auf'prallen *intr* (**auf** *acc*) crash (into)

auf'pumpen *tr* pump up

auf'putschen *tr* incite; (coll) pep up

auf'putzen *tr* dress up; clean up ‖ *ref* dress up

auf'raffen *tr* pick up ‖ *ref* stand up; (fig) pull oneself together

auf'ragen *intr* tower, stand high

auf'räumen *tr* (*Zimmer*) straighten up; (*wegräumen*) clear away ‖ *intra—a. mit* do away with, get rid of

Auf'räumungsarbeiten *pl* clearance

auf'rechnen *tr* add up; (acct) balance

auf'recht *adj* upright, erect

auf'rechterhalten §90 *tr* maintain

auf'regen *tr* excite, stir up; (*unruhig machen*) disturb, upset

Auf'regung *f* (–;–en) excitement

auf'reiben §62 *tr* rub off; (*wundreiben*) rub sore; (*vertilgen*) destroy; (*Heer*) grind up; (*Kräfte*) sap; (*Nerven*) fray ‖ *ref* worry onself to death

auf'reibend *adj* wearing, exhausting

auf'reihen *tr* string, thread

auf'reißen §53 *tr* tear open; (*Straße*) tear up; (*Tür*) fling open; (*Augen*) open wide; (*zeichnen*) sketch ‖ *intr* (SEIN) split open, crack

auf'reizen *tr* provoke, incite; (*stark erregen*) excite

auf'reizend *adj* provoking, annoying; (*Rede*) inflammatory; (*Anblick*) sexy

auf'richten *tr* erect, set up; (*trösten*) comfort ‖ *ref* sit up

auf'richtig *adj* upright, sincere

Auf'richtigkeit *f* sincerity

auf'riegeln *tr* unbolt

Auf'riß *m* front view

auf'rollen *tr* roll up; (*entfalten*) unroll

auf'rücken *intr* (SEIN) advance; (**zu**) be promoted (to)

Auf'ruf *m* (*Aufschrei*) outcry; (*Aufforderung*) call; (mil) call-up

auf'rufen §122 *tr* call on; (*appellieren an*) appeal to; (*Banknoten*) call in

Auf'ruhr *m* uproar; (*Tumult*) riot

auf'rühren *tr* stir up

aufrührerisch ['aʊfryːrərɪʃ] *adj* inflammatory, rebellious; (mil) mutinous

auf'runden *tr* round out

auf'rüsten *tr & intr* arm; rearm

Auf'rüstung *f* (–;–en) rearmament

auf'rütteln *tr* wake up (*by shaking*)

auf'sagen *tr* recite; (*ein Ende machen mit*) terminate

auf'sammeln *tr* gather up

aufsässig ['aʊfzɛsɪç] *adj* hostile; (*widerspenstig*) rebellious

Auf'satz *m* superstructure; (*auf dem Tische*) centerpiece; (*Schularbeit*) essay, composition; (*in der Zeitung*) article; (golf) tee; (mil) gun sight

auf'saugen §125 *tr* suck up; absorb

auf'schauen *intr* look up

auf'scheuchen *tr* scare up

auf'scheuern *tr* scrape

auf'schichten *tr* stack (up), pile (up)

auf'schieben §130 *tr* push up; (*Tür*) push open; (*verschieben*) postpone

auf'schießen §76 *intr* (SEIN) shoot up

Auf'schlag *m* (**auf** *acc*) striking (upon), impact (on); (*an Kleidung*) cuff, lapel; (*Steuer-*) surtax; (*Preis-*) price hike; (tennis) service, serve

auf'schlagen §132 *tr* (*öffnen*) open; (*Ei*) crack; (*Karte, Ärmel*) turn up; (*Zelt*) pitch; (*Wohnung*) take up; (*Preis*) raise; (*Knie, usw.*) bruise; (*Ball*) serve ‖ *intr* (SEIN) (*Tür*) fly open; (*Flugzeug*) crash; (*Ball*) bounce; (tennis) serve

auf'schließen §76 *tr* unlock, open ‖ *ref* (dat) pour out one's heart (to) ‖ *intr* (mil) close ranks

auf'schlitzen *tr* slit open

Auf'schluß *m* information; (chem) decomposition

auf'schlußreich *adj* informative

auf'schnallen *tr* buckle; unbuckle

auf'schnappen *tr* snap up; (*Nachricht*) pick up

Auf′schneidemaschine *f* meat slicer
auf′schneiden §106 *tr* cut open; (*Fleisch*) slice ‖ *intr* (coll) talk big
Auf′schneider *m* boaster
Auf′schnitt *m*—**kalter A.** cold cuts
auf′schnüren *tr* untie, undo
auf′schrauben *tr* unscrew; (*auf acc*) screw (on)
auf′schrecken §134 *tr* startle; (*Wild*) scare up ‖ *intr* (SEIN) be startled
Auf′schrei *m* scream, yell; (fig) outcry
auf′schreiben §62 *tr* write down
auf′schreien §135 *intr* scream, yell
Auf′schrift *f* inscription; (*Anschrift*) address; (*e-r Flasche*) label
Auf′schub *m* deferment, postponement; (*Verzögerung*) delay; (jur) stay
auf′schürfen *tr* scrape; (*Bein*) skin
auf′schwellen §119 *intr* (SEIN) swell up; (*Fluß*) rise
auf′schwemmen *tr* bloat
auf′schwingen §142 *ref* (& fig) soar; **sich a., etw zu tun** bring oneself to do s.th.
Auf′schwung *m* (& fig) upswing
auf′sehen §138 *intr* look up ‖ **Aufsehen** *n* (–s;) sensation, stir
auf′sehenerregend *adj* sensational
Auf′seher –*in* §6 *mf* supervisor; (*im Museum*) guard; (*im Geschäft*) floorwalker
auf′sein §139 *intr* (SEIN) be up; (*Tür*) be open
auf′setzen *tr* put on; (*aufrichten*) set up; (*schriftlich*) compose, draft ‖ *ref* sit up ‖ *intr* (aer) touch down; (rok) splash down
Auf′sicht *f* inspection, supervision
Auf′sichtsbeamte *m*, **Auf′sichtsbeamtin** *f* inspector, supervisor
Auf′sichtsbehörde *f* control board
Auf′sichtsdame *f* floorwalker
Auf′sichtsherr *m* floorwalker
Auf′sichtsrat *m* board of trustees; (*Mitglied*) trustee
auf′sitzen §144 *intr* (SEIN) sit up; (auf *dat*) sit (on), rest (on); **j–m a.** be taken in by s.o.; **j–n a. lassen** stand s.o. up
auf′spannen *tr* stretch, spread; (*Regenschirm*) open
auf′sparen *tr* save (up)
auf′speichern *tr* store (up)
auf′sperren *tr* unlock; (*Augen, Tür*) open wide
auf′spielen *tr* strike up ‖ *ref* (mit) show off (with) ‖ *intr* play dance music
auf′spießen *tr* spear, pierce
auf′sprengen *tr* force open; (*mit Sprengstoff*) blow up
auf′springen §142 *intr* (SEIN) jump up; (*Tür*) fly open; (*Ball*) bounce; (*Haut*) chap, crack
auf′spritzen *tr* (*Farbe*) spray on; (sl) shoot up ‖ *intr* (SEIN) squirt up
auf′sprudeln *intr* (SEIN) bubble (up)
auf′spulen *tr* wind up
auf′spüren *tr* track down, ferret out
auf′stacheln *tr* goad; (fig) stir up
auf′stampfen *intr*—**mit dem Fuß a.** stamp one's foot
Auf′stand *m* insurrection, uprising

aufständisch [′auf∫tendɪʃ] *adj* insurgent ‖ **Aufständischen** *pl* insurgents
auf′stapeln *tr* stack up, pile up
auf′stechen §64 *tr* puncture; (surg) lance
auf′stecken *tr* (*Flagge*) plant; (*Haar*) pin up; (coll) give up; **j–m ein Licht a.** enlighten s.o.
auf′stehen §146 *intr* (HABEN) stand open ‖ *intr* (SEIN) stand up, get up; (*gegen*) revolt (against)
auf′steigen §148 *intr* (SEIN) climb; (*Reiter*) mount; (*Rauch*) rise; (*Gewitter*) come up; (*Tränen*) well up; **a. auf** (*acc*) get on
auf′stellen *tr* set up, put up; (*Beispiel*) set; (*Behauptung*) make; (*Wachposten*) post; (*Bauten*) erect; (*Leiter*) raise; (*Waren*) display; (*Maschine*) assemble; (als *Kandidaten*) nominate; (*Regel, Problem*) state; (*Lehre*) propound; (*Rekord*) set; (*Liste*) make out; (*Rechnung*) draw up, make out; (*Stühle*) arrange; (*Falle*) set; (*Bedingungen, Grundsätze*) lay down; (*Beweis*) furnish ‖ *ref* station oneself
Auf′stellung *f* (–;–en) erection; assertion; list, schedule; (mil) formation; (pol) nomination; (sport) lineup
auf′stemmen *tr* pry open ‖ *ref* prop oneself up
Auf′stieg *m* climb; (*Steigung*) slope; (fig) advancement
auf′stöbern *tr* ferret out; (fig) unearth
auf′stoßen §150 *tr* push open ‖ *ref*—**sich** [*dat*] **das Knie a.** skin one's knee ‖ *intr* (HABEN) belch ‖ *intr* (HABEN & SEIN) bump, touch; (*Schiff*) touch bottom ‖ *intr* (SEIN)—**j–m a.** strike s.o., cross s.o.'s mind
auf′streichen §85 *tr* (*Butter*) spread
auf′streuen *tr* (*auf acc*) sprinkle (on)
Auf′strich *m* upstroke; (*auf Brot*) spread
auf′stützen *tr* prop up
auf′suchen *tr* search for; (*nachschlagen*) look up; (*Ort*) visit; (*aufsammeln*) pick up; (*Arzt*) go to see
Auf′takt *m* upbeat; (fig) prelude
auf′tauchen *intr* (SEIN) turn up, appear; (*Frage*) crop up; (*U-Boot*) surface; (*Gerücht*) arise
auf′tauen *tr* & *intr* (SEIN) thaw
auf′teilen *tr* divide up
Auf′trag [′auftrak] *m* (–[e]s;⁼e) (*Anweisung*) orders, instructions; (*Bestellung*) order, commission; (*Sendung*) mission; **in A. von** on behalf of
auf′tragen §132 *tr* instruct, order; (*Speise*) serve; (*Farben, Butter*) put on; (*Kleidungsstück*) wear out; (surv) plot; **j–m etw a.** impose s.th. on s.o. ‖ *intr*—**dick** (or **stark**) **a.** (sl) put it on thick
Auf′traggeber –**in** §6 *mf* employer; (*Besteller*) client, customer
Auf′tragsformular *n* order blank
auf′tragsgemäß, auf′trag(s)mäßig *adv* as ordered, according to instructions
auf′treffen §151 *intr* (SEIN) strike
Auf′treffpunkt *m* point of impact
auf′treiben §62 *tr* (*Staub; Geld*) raise;

(*Wild*) flush; (*aufblähen*) distend; (*Teig*) cause to rise

auf'trennen *tr* rip, undo, unstitch

auf'treten §152 *tr* (*Tür*) kick open || *intr* (SEIN) step, tread; (*erscheinen*) appear; (*handeln*) act, behave; (*eintreten*) occur, crop up; (*pathol*) break out; (*theat*) enter || **Auftreten** *n* (-s;) appearance; occurrence; behavior; **sicheres A.** poise

Auf'trieb *m* drive; buoyancy; (aer & fig) lift; (agr) cattle drive; **j-m A. geben** encourage s.o.

Auf'tritt *m* (*Streit*) scene, row; (theat) entrance (*of an actor*); (theat) scene

auf'trumpfen *intr* play a higher trump; **gegen j-n a.** go to s.o. better

auf'tun §154 *tr & ref* open

auf'türmen *tr & intr* pile up

auf'wachen *intr* (SEIN) awaken, wake up

auf'wachsen §155 *intr* (SEIN) grow up

auf'wallen *intr* (SEIN) boil, seethe; (fig) surge, rise up

Auf'wallung *f* (-;-en) (fig) outburst

Aufwand ['aufvant] *m* (-[e]s;ꞏe) (an *dat*) expenditure (of); (*Prunk*) show

auf'wärmen *tr* warm up; (fig) drag up

Auf'wartefrau *f* cleaning woman

auf'warten *intr* (*dat*) wait on; **a. mit** oblige with, offer

Auf'wärter –in §6 *mf* attendant || *f* cleaning woman

aufwärts ['aufverts] *adv* upward(s)

Auf'wärtshaken *m* (box) uppercut

Auf'wartung *f* (-;) attendance; (*bei Tisch*) service; (*Besuch*) call; **j-m seine A. machen** pay one's respects to s.o.

Aufwasch ['aufvaʃ] *m* (-es;) washing; dirty dishes

auf'waschen §158 *tr & intr* wash up

auf'wecken *tr* wake (up)

auf'weichen *tr* soften; soak || *intr* (SEIN) become soft; become sodden

auf'weisen §118 *tr* produce, show

auf'wenden §140 *tr* spend, expend; **Mühe a.** take pains

auf'werfen §160 *tr* throw up; (*Tür*) fling open; (*Graben*) dig; (*Frage*) raise || *ref*—**sich a. zu** set oneself up as

auf'wickeln *tr* wind up; (*Haar*) curl; (*loswickeln*) unwind

auf'wiegeln ['aufviːgəln] *tr* instigate

Aufwiegler –in ['aufviːglər(ɪn)] §6 *mf* instigator

aufwieglerisch ['aufviːglərɪʃ] *adj* inflammatory

Auf'wind *m* updraft

auf'winden §59 *tr* wind up; (*Anker*) weigh || *ref* coil up

auf'wirbeln *tr* (*Staub*) raise; **viel Staub a.** (coll) make quite a stir

auf'wischen *tr* wipe up

auf'wühlen *tr* dig up; (*Wasser*) churn up; (fig) stir up

auf'zählen *tr* enumerate, itemize

auf'zäumen *tr* bridle

auf'zehren *tr* consume

auf'zeichnen *tr* make a sketch of; (*notieren*) write down, record

aufzeigen *tr* point out

auf'ziehen §163 *tr* pull up; (*öffnen*) pull open; (*Uhr*) wind; (*Saite*) put on; (*Perlen*) string; (*Kind*) bring up; (*Tier*) breed; (*Pflanzen*) grow; (*Flagge, Segel*) hoist (*Anker*) weigh; (*Veranstaltung*) arrange, organize; (coll) kid || *intr* (SEIN) approach, pull up

Auf'zucht *f* breeding, raising

Auf'zug *m* elevator; (*e-r Uhr*) winder; (*Aufmarsch*) parade, procession; (gym) chin-up; (theat) act

auf'zwingen §142 *tr*—**j-m etw a.** force s.th. on s.o.; **j-m seinen Willen a.** impose one's will on s.o.

Augapfel ['aukapfəl] *m* eyeball; (fig) apple of the eye

Auge ['augə] *n* (-s;-n) eye; (*auf Würfeln*) dot; (hort) bud; (typ) face

äugeln ['ɔɪgəln] *intr*.—**ä. mit** wink at

Augen– [augən] *comb.fm.* eye, of the eye(s), in the eye(s); visual; (anat) ocular, optic(al)

Au'genblick *m* moment, instant

au'genblicklich *adj* momentary; (*sofortig*) immediate, instantaneous

Au'genblicksmensch *m* hedonist; impulsive person

Au'genbraue *f* eyebrow

Au'genbrauenstift *m* eyebrow pencil

au'genfällig *adj* conspicuous, obvious

Au'genhöhle *f* eye socket

Au'genlicht *n* eyesight

Au'genlid *n* eyelid

Au'genmaß *n* sense of proportion; **ein gutes A. haben** have a keen eye; **nach dem A.** by eye

Au'genmerk *n* attention

Au'gennerv *m* optic nerve

Au'genschein *m* inspection; (*Anschein*) appearances; **in A. nehmen** inspect

au'genscheinlich *adj* obvious

Au'genstern *m* pupil; iris

Au'gentäuschung *f* optical illusion

Au'gentrost *m* sight for sore eyes

Au'genwasser *n* eyewash

Au'genweide *f* sight for sore eyes

Au'genwimper *f* eyelash

Au'genwinkel *m* corner of the eye

Au'genzeuge *m*, **Au'genzeugin** *f* eyewitness

–äugig [ɔɪgɪç] *comb.fm.* –eyed

August [au'gust] *m* (-[e]s & -;-e) August

Auktion [auk'tsjon] *f* (-;-en) auction

Auktio·nator [auktsjo'nator] *m* (-s; –natoren [na'torən]) auctioneeer

auktionieren [auktsjo'niːrən] *tr* auction off, put up for auction

Au·la ['aula] *f* (-;-s & –len [lən]) auditorium

aus [aus] *adv* out; **von ... aus** from, e.g., **vom Fenster aus** from the window || *prep* (*dat*) out of, from; because of

aus'arbeiten *tr* elaborate; finish || *ref* work out, take physical exercise

Aus'arbeitung *f* (-;-en) elaboration; (*schriftlich*) composition; (*körperlich*) workout; (tech) finish

aus'arten *intr* (SEIN) get out of hand; (**in** *acc*) degenerate (into)

aus'atmen *tr* exhale

aus'baden *tr* (coll) take the rap for
aus'baggern *tr* dredge
Aus'bau *m* (-[e]s;) completion; expansion, development
aus'bauen *tr* complete; (*erweitern*) expand, develop
aus'bedingen *tr* stipulate
aus'bessern *tr* repair; (*Kleid*) mend; (*Bild*) retouch
aus'beulen *tr* take the dents out of
Aus'beute *f* (*Ertrag*) output; (*Gewinn*) profit, gain
ausbeuten ['ausbɔɪtən] *tr* exploit
aus'biegen §57 *tr* bend out ‖ *intr* (SEIN) curve; (*dat*, **vor** *dat*) make way (for)
aus'bilden *tr* develop; (*lehren*) train, educate; (mil) drill ‖ *ref* train
Aus'bilder *m* (mil) drill instructor
aus'bitten §60 *ref—sich* [*dat*] **etw** a. ask for s.th.; insist on s.th.
aus'bleiben §62 *intr* (SEIN) stay out; stay away; be missing
aus'bleichen §85 *tr* & *intr* (SEIN) bleach; fade
aus'blenden *tr* (cin, rad) fade-out
Aus'blick *m* (**auf** *acc*) view (of); (fig) outlook
aus'bohren *tr* bore (out), drill (out)
aus'borgen *ref—sich* [*dat*] **etw** a. **von** borrow s.th. from
aus'brechen §64 *tr* break off ‖ *intr* (SEIN) (**aus**) break out (of)
aus'breiten *tr* & *ref* spread; extend
aus'brennen §97 *tr* burn out, gut; (*Sonne*) parch; (med) cauterize ‖ *intr* (SEIN) burn out; (*Haus*) be gutted
Aus'bruch *m* outbreak; (*e-s Vulkans*) eruption; (*e-s Gefangenen*) break-out; (*des Gelächters*) outburst
aus'brüten *tr* incubate; hatch
Ausbuchtung ['ausbʊxtʊŋ] *f* (-;-en) bulge
ausbuddeln ['ausbʊdəln] *tr* (coll) dig out
aus'bügeln *tr* iron out
Aus'bund *m* (**von**) very embodiment (of)
ausbürgern ['ausbʏrgərn] *tr* expatriate
aus'bürsten *tr* brush out
Aus'dauer *f* perseverance
aus'dauern *intr* persevere, persist
aus'dauernd *adj* persevering; (bot) perennial
aus'dehnen *tr* & *ref* stretch, expand; (*Organ*) dilate
aus'denken §66 *tr* think out; think up; **nicht auszudenken** inconceivable
aus'deuten *tr* interpret, explain
aus'dienen *intr* serve one's time
aus'dorren *intr* (SEIN) dry up; wither
aus'dörren *tr* dry up, parch
aus'drehen *tr* turn out; turn off
Aus'druck *m* expression
aus'drücken *tr* squeeze out; (fig) express
ausdrücklich ['ausdrʏklɪç] *adj* express, explicit
aus'druckslos *adj* expressionless
aus'drucksvoll *adj* expressive
Aus'drucksweise *f* way of speaking
aus'dünsten *tr* exhale, give off ‖ *intr* evaporate; (*schwitzen*) sweat

auseinan'der *adv* apart; separately
auseinan'derfallen §72 *intr* (SEIN) fall apart
auseinan'dergehen §82 *intr* (SEIN) part; (*Versammlung*) break up; (*Meinungen*) differ; (*Wege*) branch off; (*auseinanderfallen*) come apart
auseinan'derhalten §90 *tr* keep apart
auseinan'derlaufen §105 *intr* (SEIN) (*Menge*) disperse; (*Wege*) diverge
auseinan'dernehmen §116 *tr* take apart
auseinan'dersetzen *tr* explain ‖ *ref—sich mit etw* a. come to grips with s.th.; **sich mit j—m** a. have it out with s.o.; (*gütlich*) come to an understanding with s.o.
Auseinan'dersetzung *f* explanation; (*Erörterung*) discussion, controversy; (*Übereinkommen*) arrangement
aus'erkoren *adj* chosen; predestined
aus'erlesen *adj* choice ‖ §107 *tr* choose, select
aus'ersehen §138 *tr* destine
aus'erwählen *tr* pick out, choose
aus'fahren §71 *tr* (*Straße, Gleis*) wear out; (aer) let down; **den Motor** a. (coll) open it up; **die Kurve** a. not cut the corner ‖ *intr* (SEIN) drive out; (naut) put to sea; (rr) pull out
Aus'fahrt *f* departure; exit; (*Spazierfahrt*) ride, drive; (*Torweg*) gateway
Aus'fall *m* falling out; (*Ergebnis*) result; (*Verlust*) loss; (fencing) lunge; (mach) breakdown; (mil) sally
aus'fallen §72 *intr* (SEIN) fall out; (*nicht stattfinden*) fail to take place; (*ausgelassen werden*) be omitted; (*versagen*) go out of commission; (*Ergebnis*) turn out; (mil) sortie
aus'fallend *adj* aggressive, insulting
aus'fechten §74 *tr* (*Kampf*) fight; (*Streit*) settle (by fighting)
aus'fegen *tr* sweep (out)
aus'fertigen *tr* (film); (*Paß*) issue; (*Scheck*) write out; (*Schriftstück*) draw up, draft; **doppelt** a. draw up in duplicate
aus'findig *adj—a.* **machen** find out; (*aufspüren*) trace
aus'fliegen §57 *intr* (SEIN) fly out; (*wegfliegen*) fly away; (*von Hause wegziehen*) leave home; go on a trip
aus'fließen §76 *intr* (SEIN) flow out
Aus'flucht *f* evasion; **Ausflüchte machen** dodge, beat around the bush
aus'fluchten *tr* align
Aus'flug *m* trip, outing
Ausflügler ['ausflyglər] *m* (-s;-) tourist, vacationer
Aus'fluß *m* outflow; (*Eiter*) discharge; (*Ergebnis*) outcome; (*Mündung*) outlet
aus'folgen *tr* hand over
aus'forschen *tr* investigate; sound out
aus'fragen *tr* interrogate, quiz
aus'fressen §70 *tr* empty (*by eating*); (chem) corrode; (geol) erode; **was hast du denn ausgefressen?** (coll) what were you up to?
Ausfuhr ['ausfur] *f* (-;-en) export
Aus'fuhrabgabe *f* export duty
ausführbar ['ausfyrbar] *adj* feasible

aus'führen *tr* carry out; export, ship; (*Auftrag*) fill; (*darlegen*) explain

Aus'fuhrhändler –in §6 *mf* exporter

ausführlich [ˈausfyrlɪç] *adj* detailed ‖ *adv* in detail, in full

Aus'führung *f* (–ʒ–en) carrying out, performance; (*Qualität*) workmanship; (*Darlegung*) explanation; (*e-s Gesetzes, Befehls*) implementation; (*Fertigstellung*) completion; (*e-s Verbrechens*) perpetrations; (*typ*) type, model; copy

Aus'fuhrwaren *pl* exports

aus'füllen *tr* fill out; (*Zeit*) occupy; (*Lücke; Stellung*) fill

Aus'gabe *f* (*Verteilung*) distribution; (*von Geldern*) expenditure; (*von Briefen*) delivery; (*e-s Buches*) edition; (*von Aktien*) issue

Aus'gang *m* exit; (*Auslaß*) outlet; (*Ergebnis*) result; (*Ende*) close, end; (aer) gate

Aus'gangspunkt *m* starting point

Aus'gangssprache *f* source language

aus'geben §80 *tr* give out, distribute; (*Aktien; Befehl*) issue; (*Geld*) spend; (*Briefe*) deliver; (*Karten*) deal ‖ *ref*—**sich a. für** pass oneself off as

ausgebeult [ˈausgəbɔɪlt] *adj* baggy

Aus'geburt *f* figment

aus'gedehnt *adj* extensive

aus'gedient *adj* retired; (educ) emeritus

aus'gefallen *adj* (fig) eccentric, odd

aus'gefeilt *adj* (fig) flawless

aus'geglichen *adj* (*Person*) well-balanced; (*Styl*) balanced

aus'gehen §82 *intr* (SEIN) go out; (*Vorräte, Geld, Geduld*) run out; (*Haar*) fall out; (*Farbe*) fade; **a. auf** (*acc*) aim at, be bent on; **a. von** proceed from; **die Sache ging von ihm aus** it was his idea; **frei a.** get off scot-free; **gut a.** turn out well; **leer a.** come away empty-handed; **wenn wir davon a.,** daß going on the assumption that

Aus'gehverbot *n* curfew

aus'gekocht *adj* (*Lügner*) out-and-out; (*Verbrecher*) hardened

aus'gelassen *adj* boisterous

aus'geleiert *adj* trite; worn-out; (*Gewinde*) stripped

aus'gemacht *adj* settled; downright

ausgenommen *prep* (*acc*) except; **niemand a.** bar none

aus'gepicht *adj* inveterate

aus'gerechnet *adv* just, of all ...; **a. Sie!** you of all people!

aus'geschlossen *adj* out of the question, impossible

Ausgesiedelte [ˈausgəzidəltə] §5 *mf* evacuee, displaced person

aus'gestalten *tr* make arrangements for

aus'gesucht *adj* choice

aus'gezeichnet *adj* excellent

ausgiebig [ˈausgibɪç] *adj* abundant; (*ergiebig*) productive

aus'gießen §76 *tr* pour out, pour away

Aus'gleich *m* (–sʒ–e) (*Ersatz*) compensation; (*Vergleich*) compromise; (acct) settlement; (tennis) deuce

aus'gleichen §85 *tr* level, smooth out; (*Konten*) balance; (*Verlust*) compensate for ‖ *ref* cancel one another out

Ausgleichs– *comb.fm.* balancing, compensating

Aus'gleichung *f* (–ʒ–en) equalization; settlement; compensation

aus'gleiten §86 *intr* (SEIN) slip

aus'graben §87 *tr* dig out, dig up; (*Leiche*) exhume; (archeol) excavate

aus'greifen §88 *intr* reach out; **weit ausgreifend** far-reaching

Ausguck [ˈausguk] *m* (–sʒ–e) lookout

aus'gucken *intr* (nach) be on the lookout (for)

Aus'guß *m* sink; (*Tülle*) spout, nozzle

aus'haken *tr* unhook

aus'halten §90 *tr* endure, stand ‖ *intr* persevere, stick it out

aus'handeln *tr* get by bargaining

aushändigen [ˈaushɛndɪgən] *tr* hand over, surrender

Aus'hang *m* notice, shingle

Aus'hängeschild *n* (–[e]sʒ–er) sign board, shingle; (fig) front, cover

aus'harren *intr* hold out, last

aus'hauchen *tr* breathe out, exhale

aus'heben §94 *tr* lift out; (*Tür*) lift off its hinges; (*Truppen*) recruit

aushecken [ˈaushɛkən] *tr* (fig) hatch

aus'heilen *tr* heal completely ‖ *intr* (SEIN) heal up

aus'helfen §96 *intr* (dat) help out

Aus'hilfe *f* (temporary) help; (temporary) helper; makeshift

Aushilfs– *comb.fm.* temporary, emergency

Aus'hilfsarbeit *f* part-time work

Aus'hilfslehrer –in §6 *mf* substitute teacher

aus'hilfsweise *adv* temporarily

aus'höhlen *tr* hollow out

aus'holen *tr* (*ausfragen*) sound out ‖ *intr* (*beim Schwimmen*) stroke; **mit dem Arm a.** raise the arm (*before striking*); **weit a.** start from the beginning

aus'horchen *tr* sound out, pump

aus'hülsen *tr* (*Bohnen, usw.*) shell

aus'hungern *tr* starve (out)

aus'husten *tr* cough up

aus'kehlen *tr* groove

Aus'kehlung *f* (–ʒ–en) groove

aus'kehren *tr* sweep (out)

aus'kennen §97 *ref* know one's way; (*in e–m Fach*) be well versed

Aus'klang *m* end, close

aus'klappen *tr* pull out (*a fold-away bed*)

aus'kleiden *tr* line, panel; (*ausziehen*) undress ‖ *ref* undress

aus'klopfen *tr* beat the dust out of

ausklügeln [ˈausklygəln] *tr* figure out (ingeniously)

aus'kneifen §88 *intr* (SEIN) beat it

aus'knipsen *tr* (coll) switch off

ausknobeln [ˈausknobəln] *tr* figure out

aus'kochen *tr* boil out; boil clean

aus'kommen §99 *intr* (SEIN) come out, get out; (*ausreichen*) manage ‖ **Auskommen** *n* (–sʒ) livelihood

auskömmlich [ˈauskœmlɪç] *adj* adequate

aus'kosten *tr* relish

aus'kramen [ˈauskramən] *tr* (*aus Schubladen*) drag out; (fig) show off

aus'kratzen tr scratch out; (surg) curette

aus'kriechen §102 intr (SEIN) be hatched

aus'kugeln ref—sich [dat] den Arm a. dislocate the shoulder

aus'kundschaften tr explore; (mil) scout

Auskunft ['aʊskʊnft] f (-;¨e) information, piece of information

Auskunftei [aʊskʊnf'taɪ] f (-;-en) private detective agency

Aus'kunftschalter m information desk

aus'kuppeln tr uncouple; (die Kupplung) release || intr disengage the clutch

aus'lachen tr laugh at || ref have a good laugh

aus'laden §103 tr unload; (Gast) put off || intr project, jut out || **Ausladen** n (-s;) unloading; projection

Aus'lage f (von Geld) outlay; (Unkosten) expenses; (von Waren) display; (Schaufenster) display window

Aus'land n foreign country, foreign countries; im A. leben live abroad; ins A. gehen go abroad

Ausländer -in ['aʊslɛndər(ɪn)] §6 mf foreigner, alien

aus'ländisch adj foreign, alien

Auslands- comb.fm. foreign

Aus·laß ['aʊslas] m (-lasses;-lässe) outlet

aus'lassen §104 tr let out; (weglassen) omit; (Wut) (an dat) vent (on) || ref express one's opinion

Aus'lassung f omission; (Bemerkung) remark

Aus'lassungszeichen n (gram) apostrophe; (typ) caret

Aus'lauf m sailing; room to run

aus'laufen §105 intr (SEIN) run out; (Schiff) put out to sea; (Farbe) run; a. in (acc) end in; (Straße) run into

Aus'läufer m (geol) spur; (hort) runner

aus'leben tr live out || ref make the most of one's life || intr die

aus'lecken tr lick clean

aus'leeren tr empty || ref have a bowel movement

aus'legen tr lay out; (Waren) display; (erklären) construe; (Geld) advance; (Fußboden) cover (with carpeting); (Minen) lay; (Schlinge) set; falsch a. misconstrue, misinterpret

Aus'leger -in §6 mf interpreter || m outrigger; (e-s Krans) boom

aus'leihen §81 tr lend (out) || ref—sich [dat] etw a. borrow s.th.

aus'lernen intr finish one's apprenticeship; man lernt nie aus one never stops learning

Aus'lese f pick, choice

aus'lesen §107 tr pick out; (Buch) finish reading

aus'liefern tr deliver, turn over; (verteilen) distribute; (Verbrecher) extradite; j-m ausgeliefert sein be at s.o.'s mercy

aus'liegen §108 intr (SEIN) be on display

aus'löffeln tr spoon out; etw a. zu ha-

ben have to face the consequences of s.th.

aus'löschen tr (Feuer) extinguish; (Licht) put out; (Schreiben) erase

aus'losen tr draw lots for

aus'lösen tr loosen, release; (Gefangegen) ransom; (Pfand) redeem

Aus'löser m (-s;-) release

aus'loten tr (naut & fig) plumb

aus'lüften tr air, ventilate

aus'machen tr (Feuer) put out; (sichten) make out; (betragen) amount to; (Fleck) remove; (Licht) turn out; (bilden) constitute; (vereinbaren) agree upon; **es macht nichts aus** it doesn't matter

aus'malen tr paint || ref—sich [dat] etw a. picture s.th.

aus'marschieren intr (SEIN) march out

Aus'maß n measurement; dimensions; in großem A. on a large scale; (fig) to a great extent

ausmergeln ['aʊsmɛrgəln] tr exhaust

ausmerzen ['aʊsmɛrtsən] tr reject; (ausrotten) eradicate

aus'messen §70 tr measure; survey

aus'misten tr (Stall) clean; (fig) clean up

aus'mustern tr discard; (mil) discharge

Aus'nahme f (-;-n) exception

Aus'nahmezustand m state of emergency

aus'nahmslos adj & adv without exception

aus'nahmsweise adv by way of exception

aus'nehmen §116 tr take out; (Fisch, Huhn) clean; (ausschließen) exclude; (sl) clean out (of money) || ref—sich gut a. look good

aus'nutzen, aus'nützen tr utilize; (Gelegenheit) take advantage of

aus'packen tr unpack; (Geheimnis) disclose || intr (coll) unburden oneself, open up

aus'pfeifen §88 tr hiss (off the stage)

aus'plappern tr blurt out, blab out

aus'plaudern tr blab out

aus'plündern tr ransack; (coll) clean out (of money)

aus'polstern tr stuff, pad

aus'posaunen tr (coll) broadcast

aus'probieren tr try out, test

Aus'puff m (-[e]s;-e) exhaust

Aus'puffleitung f (aut) manifold

Aus'puffrohr n exhaust pipe

Aus'pufftopf m (aut) muffler

aus'pumpen tr pump out; **ausgepumpt** (coll) exhausted

aus'putzen tr (reinigen) clean out; (schmücken) adorn || ref dress up

aus'quartieren tr put out (of s.o.'s room)

aus'radieren tr erase

aus'rangieren tr (coll) scrap

aus'rauben tr rob, ransack

aus'räumen tr (Schrank) clear out; (Möbel) remove; (med) clean out

aus'rechnen tr figure out

aus'recken tr stretch || ref—sich [dat] den Hals a. crane one's neck

Aus'rede f evasion, excuse

aus'reden tr—j-m etw a. talk s.o. out

of s.th. || *ref* make excuses || *intr* finish speaking

aus′reiben §62 *tr* rub out; (mach) ream

aus′reichen *tr* suffice, be enough

aus′reichend *adj* sufficient

Aus′reise *f* departure; way out

aus′reißen §53 *tr* tear out || *ref*—er reißt sich [*dat*] dabei kein Bein aus he's not exactly killing himself || *intr* (SEIN) run away

Aus′reißer *m* runaway

aus′renken *tr* dislocate

aus′richten *tr* straighten; (in e–e Linie bringen) align; (vollbringen) accomplish; (Botschaft, Gruß) convey

aus′roden *tr* root out; (Wald) clear

aus′rollen *tr* roll out || *intr* (SEIN) (aer) taxi to a standstill

ausrotten [′ausrɔtən] *tr* root out; (Volk, Tierrasse) exterminate; (Übel) eradicate

aus′rücken *tr* (Kupplung) disengage || *intr* (SEIN) march off; run away

Aus′ruf *m* outcry; (öffentlich) proclamation; (gram) interjection

aus′rufen §122 *tr* call out; exclaim; a. als (or zum) proclaim

Aus′rufungszeichen *n* exclamation point

aus′ruhen *ref & intr* rest

aus′rupfen *tr* pluck

aus′rüsten *tr* equip, fit out; arm

aus′rutschen *intr* (SEIN) slip (out)

Aus′saat *f* sowing; (& fig) seed(s)

aus′säen *tr* sow; (fig) disseminate

Aus′sage *f* statement; (gram) predicate; (jur) affidavit

aus′sagen *tr* state || *intr* give evidence, make a statement

Aus′sagesatz *m* declarative sentence

Aus′sageweise *f* (gram) mood

Aus′satz *m* leprosy

Aussätzige [′aussɛtsɪgə] §5 *mf* leper

aus′saugen §125 *tr* suck dry; (fig) bleed white

Aus′sauger -in §6 *mf* (coll) bloodsucker

aus′schalten *tr* (Licht, Radio, Fernseher) turn off; (fig) shut out

Aus′schalter *m* circuit breaker

Aus′schank *m* sale of alcoholic drinks; (Kneipe) bar, taproom

aus′scharren *tr* dig up

Aus′schau *f*—A. halten nach be on the lookout for

aus′schauen *intr*—a. nach look out for; look like; gut schaust du aus! what a mess you are!

aus′scheiden §112 *tr* eliminate; (physiol) excrete, secrete || *intr* (SEIN) retire, resign; (sport) drop out; das scheidet aus! that's out!

Aus′scheidung *f* (-;-en) elimination; retirement; (physiol) excretion, secretion

Aus′scheidungskampf *m* elimination bout

aus′schelten §83 *tr* scold, berate

aus′schenken *tr* pour (drinks)

aus′scheren *intr* (aus) veer away (from)

aus′schiffen *tr* disembark; (Ladung) unload || *ref* disembark

aus′schimpfen *tr* scold, take to task

aus′schirren *tr* unharness

aus′schlachten *tr* cut up; (Flugzeuge, usw.) cannibalize; (ausnutzen) make the most of

aus′schlafen §131 *tr* sleep off || *ref & intr* get enough sleep

Aus′schlag *m* rash; (e–s Zeigers) deflection; den A. geben turn the scales

aus′schlagen §132 *tr* knock out; (Feuer) beat out; (Metall) hammer out; (Innenraum) line; (Angebot) refuse || *intr* bud; sprout; (Pferd) kick; (Pendel) swing; (Zeiger) move || *intr* (SEIN) turn out

aus′schlaggebend *adj* decisive

aus′schließen §76 *tr* lock out; (von der Schule) expel; (ausscheiden) exclude; (sport) disqualify

aus′schließlich *adj* exclusive, sole || *adv* exclusively, only || *prep* (genit) exclusive of

aus′schlürfen *tr* sip

aus′schmieren *tr* grease; (mit) smear (with); (fig) pull a fast one on; (mas) point

aus′schmücken *tr* adorn, decorate; (Geschichte) embellish

aus′schnaufen *intr* get one's wind

aus′schneiden §106 *tr* cut out; tief ausgeschnitten low-cut, low-necked

Aus′schnitt *m* cut up; (Zeitungs–) clipping; (Kleid–) neckline; (literarisch) extract; (geom) sector

aus′schreiben §62 *tr* write out (in full); finish writing; (ankündigen) announce; (Formular) fill out; (Rezept) make out

aus′schreiten §86 *tr* pace off || *intr* (SEIN) walk briskly

Aus′schreitung *f* (-;-en) excess

Aus′schuß *m* waste, scrap; (Komitee) committee

Aus′schußware *f* (indust) reject

aus′schütten *tr* pour out, spill; (Dividende) pay || *ref*—sich vor Lachen a. split one's sides laughing

aus′schwärmen *intr* (SEIN) swarm out; (Truppen) deploy

aus′schwatzen *tr* blab out, blurt out

aus′schweifend *adj* (Phantasie) wild; (liederlich) wild, dissolute

Aus′schweifung *f* (-;-en) excess; curve; digression

aus′schwemmen *tr* rinse out; wash out

aus′schwenken *tr* rinse

aus′schwitzen *tr* sweat out; exude

aus′sehen §138 *intr* look; nach j–m a. look out for s.o.; nach Regen a. look like rain; wie sieht er aus? what does he look like? || Aussehen *n* (-s;) look(s); appearance(s)

außen [′ausən] *adv* outside; nach a. out(wards)

außen-, Außen- *comb.fm.* external; outer; exterior; outdoor; foreign

Au′ßenaufnahme *f* (phot) outdoor shot

Au′ßenbahn *f* (sport) outside lane

aus′senden §140 *tr* send out

Au′ßenfläche *f* outer surface

Au′ßenminister *m* Secretary of State; (Brit) Foreign Secretary

Au′ßenpolitik *f* foreign policy

Au′ßenseite *f* outside

Außenseiter ['ausənzaɪtər] *m* (-s;-) dark horse, long shot; (*Einzelgänger*) loner; (*Nichtfachmann*) layman

Außenstände ['ausənʃtendə] *pl* accounts receivable

Au'ßenstelle *f* branch office

außer ['ausər] *prep* (*genit*)—a. Landes abroad ‖ *prep* (*dat*) outside, out of; except, but; besides, in addition to; **a. Hause** not at home; **a. sich sein** be beside oneself

au'ßeramtlich *adj* unofficial, private

außerdem ['ausərdem] *adv* also, besides; moreover, furthermore

au'ßerdienstlich *adj* unofficial, private; (mil) off duty

äußere ['ɔɪsərə] §9 *adj* outer, exterior, external ‖ **Äußere** §5 *n* exterior

au'ßerehelich *adj* extra-marital; (*Kind*) illegitimate

au'ßergewöhnlich *adj* extraordinary

außerhalb ['ausərhalp] *prep* (*genit*) outside, out of

äußerlich ['ɔɪsərlɪç] *adj* external, outward; (*oberflächlich*) superficial

Äu'ßerlichkeit *f* superficiality; (*Formalität*) formality; **Äußerlichkeiten** externals; formalities

äußern ['ɔɪsərn] *tr* express ‖ *ref* (über *acc*) express one's views (about); (in *dat*) be manifested (in)

au'ßerordentlich *adj* extraordinary; **außerordentlicher Professor** associate professor

äußerst ['ɔɪsərst] *adj* outermost; (fig) extreme, utmost ‖ *adv* extremely, highly ‖ **Äußerste** §5 *n* extremity, extreme(s); **aufs Ä.** to the utmost; **bis zum Äußersten** to extremes; to the bitter end

außerstande ['ausər'ʃtandə] *adj* unable

Äu'ßerung *f* (-;-en) (*Ausdruck*) expression; (*Bemerkung*) remark

aus'setzen *tr* set out, put out; (an der Küste) maroon; (*Kind*; dem Wetter) expose; (*Boot*) lower; (*Wachen*) post; (*Belohnung*) hold out, promise; (*Tätigkeit*) discontinue; **auszusetzen haben an** (*dat*) find fault with ‖ *intr* stop, halt

Aus'sicht *f* (auf *acc*) view (of); (fig) (auf *acc*) hope (of); **in A. nehmen** consider, plan

aus'sichtslos *adj* hopeless

Aus'sichtspunkt *m* vantage point

aus'sichtsreich *adj* promising

Aus'sichtsturm *m* lookout tower

aussichtsvoll *adj* promising

aus'sieben *tr* sift out; (fig) screen

aus'siedeln *tr* evacuate by force

Aus'siedlung *f* (-;-en) forced evacuation

aus'sinnen §121 *tr* think up, devise

aussöhnen ['auszøːnən] *tr* reconcile

aus'sondern *tr* (*trennen*) separate; (*auswählen*) single out; (*physiol*) excrete

aus'spähen *tr* spy out ‖ *intr* (nach) keep a lookout (for), reconnoiter

aus'spannen *tr* stretch; extend; (*Zugtiere*) unhitch ‖ *intr* relax

Aus'spannung *f* (-;) relaxation

aus'speien §135 *tr* spit out

aus'sperren *tr* lock out, shut out

aus'spielen *tr* (*Karten*) lead with; (*Preis*) play for ‖ *intr* lead off

aus'spionieren *tr* spy out

Aus'sprache *f* pronunciation; (*Erörterung*) discussion, talk

aus'sprechen §64 *tr* pronounce; (*deutlich*) articulate; (*ausdrücken*) express ‖ *ref* (über *acc*) speak one's mind (about); (für; gegen) declare oneself (for; against); **sich mit j-m über etw a.** talk s.th. over with s.o. ‖ *intr* finish speaking

Aus'spruch *m* statement

aus'spülen *tr* rinse

aus'spüren *tr* trace (down)

aus'staffieren *tr* fit out, furnish

aus'stampfen *tr* stamp out

Aus'stand *m* walkout

aus'ständig *adj* on strike, striking; (fin) in arrears, outstanding

ausstatten ['aus/tatən] *tr* furnish, equip; (*Tochter*) give a dowry to

Aus'stattung *f* (-;-en) furnishings; equipment; trousseau

aus'stechen §64 *tr* cut out; (*Auge*) poke out; (fig) outdo

aus'stehen §146 *tr* endure, stand ‖ *intr* still be expected, be overdue

aus'steigen §148 *intr* (SEIN) get out, get off

aus'stellen *tr* exhibit; (*Wache*) post; (*Quittung, Scheck*) make out; (*Paß*) issue

Aus'stellung *f* (-;-en) exhibit; issuance; criticism

Aus'stellungsdatum *n* date of issue

aus'sterben §149 *intr* (SEIN) die out

Aus'steuer *f* hope chest, dowry

aus'stopfen *tr* stuff, pad

Aus'stoß *m* (indust) output

aus'stoßen §150 *tr* knock out; (*vertreiben*) eject; (*Seufzer, Schrei, Fluch*) utter; (*Torpedo*) launch; (math) eliminate; (phonet) elide; (phys) emit

Aus'stoßrohr *n* torpedo tube

Aus'stoßung *f* (-;-en) ejection; utterance; (gram) elision

Aus'stoßzahlen *pl* (indust) production figures

aus'strahlen *tr* & *intr* radiate

aus'strecken *tr* & *ref* stretch out

aus'streichen §85 *tr* cross out; (*glätten*) smooth out; (*Bratpfanne*) grease

aus'streuen *tr* strew, scatter, spread

aus'strömen *tr* & *intr* (SEIN) pour out

aus'studieren *tr* study thoroughly

aus'suchen *tr* pick out

Aus'tausch *m* exchange

aus'tauschbar *adj* exchangeable; interchangeable

aus'tauschen *tr* exchange; interchange

Aus'tauschstoff *m* substitute

Aus'tauschstück *n* spare part

aus'teilen *tr* distribute, deal out

Auster ['austər] *f* (-;-n) oyster

aus'tilgen *tr* exterminate, wipe out

aus'toben *tr* give vent to ‖ *ref* (*Person*) let one's hair down; (*Kinder*) raise a rumpus; (*Gewitter*) stop raging

aus'tollen *ref* make a racket

Austrag ['austrak] *m* (-[e]s;)—**bis zum A. der Sache** until the matter is decided; **zum A. bringen** bring to a head; (jur) settle; **zum A. kommen** come up for a decision

aus'tragen §132 tr carry out; (Briefe) deliver; (Kleider) wear out; (Meisterschaft) decide; (Klatschereien) spread; (acct) cancel

Aus'träger m deliveryman

Australien [aus'traljən] n (-s;) Australia

Australier -in [aus'traljər(ɪn)] §6 mf Australian

aus'treiben §62 tr drive out; exorcise

aus'treten §152 tr (Feuer) tread out; (Schuhe, Treppen) wear out || intr (SEIN) step out; (Blut) come out; (coll) go to the bathroom; **a. aus** leave (school, a company, club)

aus'trinken §143 tr drink up, drain

Aus'tritt m withdrawal

aus'trocknen tr & intr (SEIN) dry up

aus'tüfteln tr puzzle out

aus'üben tr (Aufsicht, Macht) exercise; (Beruf) practice; (Pflicht) carry out; (Einfluß, Druck) exert; (Verbrechen) commit; **ausübende Gewalt** executive power

Aus'verkauf m clearance sale

aus'verkaufen tr sell out; close out

aus'wachsen §155 tr outgrow

Aus'wahl f choice, selection

aus'wählen tr select, pick out

Aus'wanderer -in §6 mf emigrant

aus'wandern intr (SEIN) emigrate

auswärtig ['ausvertɪç] adj out-of-town; (ausländisch) foreign

auswärts ['ausverts] adv outward(s); out, away from home; (außer der Stadt) out of town; (im Ausland) abroad

Aus'wärtsspiel n away game

aus'wechselbar adj interchangeable

aus'wechseln tr exchange, interchange; (ersetzen) replace

Aus'weg m way out; escape

Ausweich- comb.fm. evasive; alternate; substitute; emergency; reserve

aus'weichen §85 intr (SEIN) make way (for), get out of the way (of); (dat) evade; **a. auf** (acc) switch to

aus'weichend adj evasive

Aus'weichklausel f escape clause

Aus'weichlager n emergency store

Aus'weichstelle f passing zone

Aus'weichstraße f bypass

Aus'weichziel n secondary target

aus'weinen ref have a good cry || intr stop crying

Ausweis ['ausvais] m (-s;-e) identification (card); (com) statement

aus'weisen §118 tr expel; (aus Besitz) evict; (verbannen) banish, deport; (zeigen) show || ref prove one's identity

Aus'weispapiere pl identification papers

Aus'weisung f (-;-en) expulsion; eviction; deportation

aus'weiten tr & ref widen, expand

auswendig ['ausvendɪç] adj outer || adv outside; outwardly; by heart

aus'werfen §160 tr throw out; (Graben) dig; (Summe) allocate; (Lava) eject; (Blut, Schleim) spit up; (angl) cast

aus'werten tr evaluate; (ausnützen) utilize; (Statistik) interpret

aus'wickeln tr unwrap

aus'wiegen §57 tr weigh out

aus'wirken tr knead || ref take effect; **sich a. auf** (acc) affect; **sich** [dat] **etw bei j–m a.** obtain s.th. from s.o.

Aus'wirkung f (-;-en) effect

aus'wischen tr wipe out; wipe clean; **j–m eins a.** play a dirty joke on s.o.

aus'wittern tr season || intr weather

aus'wringen §142 tr wring out

Aus'wuchs m outgrowth; (pathol) tumor

Aus'wurf m throwing out; (fig) scum; (mach) ejection

aus'zacken tr indent; (wellenförmig) scallop

aus'zahlen tr pay out; pay off || ref— **es zahlt sich nicht aus** it doesn't pay

aus'zählen tr count out

aus'zanken tr scold

aus'zehren tr consume, waste

Aus'zehrung f (-;) consumption

aus'zeichnen tr mark, tag; (ehren) honor; (fig) distinguish

Aus'zeichnung f (-;-en) labeling; decoration, honor; distinction

aus'ziehen §163 tr pull out; (Kleid) take off; (Stelle) excerpt; (Zeichnung) ink in; (chem) extract || ref undress || intr (SEIN) set out; (aus e–r Wohnung) move out

aus'zischen tr hiss off the stage

Aus'zug m departure; moving; excerpt; (Abriß) summary; (Bib) Exodus; (chem) extract; (com) statement

aus'zugsweise adv in summary form

aus'zupfen tr pluck out

authentisch [au'tentɪʃ] adj authentic

Auto ['auto] n (-s;-s) auto(mobile)

Au'tobahn f superhighway

Au'tobus m bus

Autodidakt [autodi'dakt] m (-en;-en) self-educated person

Au'todroschke f taxi

Au'tofahrer -in §6 mf motorist

Au'tofahrschule f driving school

Au'tofahrt f car ride, drive

Au'tofalle f speed trap

Autogramm [auto'gram] n (-[e]s;-e) autograph

Autogramm'jäger -in §6 mf autograph hound

Au'tokino n drive-in movie

Au'tokolonne f motorcade

Autokrat [auto'krat] m (-en;-en) autocrat

autokratisch [auto'kratɪʃ] adj autocratic

Automat [auto'mat] m (-en;-en) vending machine; (Musik-) jukebox; (Spiel-) slot machine

Automa'tenrestaurant n automat

automatisch [auto'matɪʃ] adj automatic

Automobil [automo'bil] n (-[e]s;-e) automobile

autonom [auto'nom] adj autonomous

Autonomie [autono'mi] f (-;) autonomy

Au·tor ['autor] m (-s;-toren ['torən]) author

Autoreparatur'werkstatt *f* auto repair shop, garage
Autorin [au'torɪn] *f* (-;-nen) authoress
autorisieren [autorɪ'zirən] *tr* authorize
autoritär [autorɪ'ter] *adj* authoritarian
Autorität [autorɪ'tet] *f* (-;-en) authority
Au'toschlosser *m* automobile mechanic
Au'toschuppen *m* carport

Au'tounfall *m* automobile accident
avancieren [avã'sirən] *intr* (SEIN) advance; (zu) be promoted (to)
avisieren [avɪ'zirən] *tr* advise, notify
Axt [akst] *f* (-;ːe) ax
Azalee [atsa'leə] *f* (-;-n) azalea
Azetat [atse'tat] *n* (-s;-) acetate
Azeton [atse'ton] *n* (-s;) acetone
Azetylen [atsety'len] *n* (-s;) acetylene
azurn [a'tsurn] *adj* azure, sky-blue

B

B, b [be] *invar n* B, b; (mus) B flat
babbeln ['babəln] *intr* babble
Baby ['bebi] *n* (-s;-s) baby
Babysitter ['bebɪzɪtər] *m* (-s;-) babysitter
Bach [bax] *m* (-[e]s;ːe) brook, creek
Backe ['bakə] *f* (-;-n) cheek; jaw (*of a vise*); (mach) die
backen ['bakən] §50 (& *pret* **backte**) *tr* bake; (*in der Pfanne*) fry || (*pret* **backte**; *pp* **gebacken**) *intr* bake || §109 *intr* (HABEN & SEIN) cake; stick
Backenbart (**Bak'kenbart**) *m* side whiskers
Backenstreich (**Bak'kenstreich**) *m* slap
Backenzahn (**Bak'kenzahn**) *m* molar; **kleiner** (or **vorderer**) **B.** bicuspid
Bäcker ['beckər] *m* (-s;-) baker
Bäckerei [bekə'raɪ] *f* (-;-en) bakery
Back'fett *n* shortening
Back'fisch *m* fried fish; (fig) teenager
Back'fischalter *n* teens (*of girls*)
Back'form *f* cake pan
Back'hähnchen *n* fried chicken
Back'hendel *n* (Aust) fried chicken
Back'huhn *n* fried chicken
Back'obst *n* dried fruit
Back'ofen *m* baking oven
Back'pfeife *f* slap in the face, smack
Back'pflaume *f* prune
Back'pulver *n* baking powder
Back'stein *m* brick
Back'trog *m* kneading trough
Back'waren *pl* baked goods
Back'werk *n* pastries
Bad [bat] *n* (-[e]s;ːer) bath; bathroom; (*Badeort*) spa
Ba'deanstalt *f* public baths; public pool
Ba'deanzug *m* swim suit
Ba'dehaube *f* bathing cap
Ba'dehose *f* bathing trunks
Ba'dekappe *f* bathing cap
Ba'demantel *m* bathrobe
baden ['badən] *tr* & *ref* bathe || *intr* take a bath; **b. gehen** go swimming
Ba'deort *m* bathing resort; spa
Ba'destrand *m* bathing beach
Ba'detuch *n* bath towel
Ba'dewanne *f* bathtub
Badende ['badəndə] §5 *mf* bather
Ba'dewärter **-n** §6 *mf* lifeguard; bathhouse attendant
Ba'dezimmer *n* bathroom
baff [baf] *adj* dumbfounded

Bagage [ba'gɑʒə] *f* (-;) (fig) rabble; (mil) baggage
Bagatelle [baga'tɛlə] *f* (-;-n) trifle
Bagatel'lesache *f* petty offense
bagatellisieren [bagatelɪ'zirən] *tr* minimize, make light of
Bagger ['bagər] *m* (-s;-) dredge
baggern ['bagərn] *tr* & *intr* dredge
bähen ['be·ən] *intr* bleat
Bahn [ban] *f* (-;-en) way, path; (aer) runway; (astr) orbit; (aut) lane; (rr) railroad; (sport) course, track; (*Eis-*) (sport) rink; **auf die schiefe B.** **geraten** go astray; **B. brechen** (*dat*) pave the way (for); **mit der B.** **fahren** travel by train
bahn'brechend *adj* pioneering, epoch-making
Bahn'brecher **-in** §6 *mf* pioneer
Bahn'damm *m* railroad embankment
bahnen ['banən] *tr—***e-n Weg. b.** clear a path, open up a path
Bahn'fahrt *f* train trip
bahn'frei *adj* free on board, f.o.b.
Bahn'hof *m* railroad station
Bahn'hofshalle *f* concourse
Bahn'hofsvorsteher *m* stationmaster
Bahn'linie *f* railroad line
Bahn'schranke *f* (rr) barrier
Bahn'steig *m* (rr) platform
Bahn'strecke *f* (rr) line, track
Bahn'übergang *m* railroad crossing
Bahn'wärter *m* (rr) signalman
Bahre ['barə] *f* (-;-n) stretcher; bier
Bahr'tuch *n* pall
Bai [bar] *f* (-;-en) bay
Baiser [be'ze] *m* & *n* (-s;-s) meringue cookie
Baisse ['besə] *f* (-;-n) (com) slump
Bais'sestimmung *f* downward trend
Baissier [bes'je] *m* (-s;-s) (st.exch.) bear
Bajonett [bajo'net] *n* (-s;-e) bayonet
Bake ['bakə] *f* (-;-n) beacon
Bakterie [bak'terjə] *f* (-;-n) bacterium
Bakte'rienforscher **-in** §6 *mf* bacteriologist
Bakte'rienkunde *f* bacteriology
Balance [ba'lãsə] *f* (-;-n) balance
balancieren [balã'sirən] *tr* & *intr* balance
bald [balt] *adv* (eher ['e·ər]; **eheste** ['e·əstə]) §9 soon; (*beinahe*) nearly
baldig ['baldɪç] *adj* speedy; (*Antwort*) early

baldigst ['baldɪgst] *adv* very soon; at the earliest possible moment

Balg [balk] *m* (-[e]s;ːe) skin, pelt; (*Hülse*) shell, husk; **Bälge** bellows; **j-m den B. abziehen** fleece s.o. ‖ *m & n* (-[e]s;ːer) (coll) brat

balgen ['balgən] *ref* roll around, romp; (*raufen*) scuffle ‖ **Balgen** *m* (-s;-) (phot) bellows

Balgerei [balgə'raɪ] *f* (-;-en) scuffle

Balken ['balkən] *m* (-s;-) beam, rafter

Bal'kenwerk *n* framework

Balkon [bal'kon] *m* (-s;-e) balcony

Ball [bal] *m* (-[e]s;ːe) ball; (*Tanz*) ball

Ballade [ba'ladə] *f* (-;-n) ballad

Ballast ['balast] *m* (-[e]s;-e) ballast; (fig) drag; (coll) padding

ballen ['balən] *tr*—**die Faust b.** clench one's fist ‖ *ref* form a cluster ‖ **Ballen** *m* (-s;-) (anat) ball; (com) bale; (pathol) bunion

ballern ['balərn] *intr* (coll) bang away

Ballett [ba'let] *n* (-[e]s;-e) ballet

Ballistik [ba'lɪstɪk] *f* (-;) ballistics

Ballon [ba'lon] *m* (-s;-s) balloon

Ball'saal *m* ballroom

Ball'schläger *m* (sport) bat

Ball'spiel *n* ball game

Bal'lung *f* (-;-en) (mil) massing (of troops)

Balsam ['balzam] *m* (-s;-e) balm, balsam; (fig) balm

balsamieren [balza'mirən] *tr* embalm

balzen ['baltsən] *intr* perform a mating dance

Bambus ['bambus] *m* (-; & -ses;-se) bamboo

Bam'busrohr *n* bamboo, bamboo cane

banal [ba'nal] *adj* banal

Banane [ba'nanə] *f* (-;-n) banana

Banause [ba'nauzə] *f* (-n;-n) philistine

banausisch [ba'nauzɪʃ] *adj* narrow-minded

Band [bant] *m* (-[e]s;ːe) volume; (*Einband*) binding ‖ *n* (-[e]s;-e) bond, tie; **Bande** chains, shackles ‖ *n* (-[e]s;ːer) (e-s Hutes, usw.) band; (*Bindfaden*) string; (*zum Schmuck*) ribbon; tape; (anat) ligament; (electron) recording tape; (rad) band; **am laufenden B.** continuously

Bandage [ban'daʒə] *f* (-;-n) bandage

bandagieren [banda'ʒirən] *tr* bandage

Bande ['bandə] *f* (-;-n) band, gang, crew; (billiards) cushion

Ban'denkrieg *m* guerilla war(fare)

Ban'denmitglied *n* gangster; (mil) guerilla

Ban'denunwesen *n* gangsterism; partisan activities

bändigen ['bendɪgən] *tr* tame; (fig) subdue, overcome, master

Bandit [ban'dit] *m* (-en;-en) bandit

Band'maß *n* tape measure

Band'säge *f* band saw

Band'scheibe *f* (anat) disk

Band'scheibenquetschung *f* slipped disk

Band'wurm *m* tapeworm

bang(e) [ban(ə)] *adj* scared, anxious; (*Gefühl*) disquieting; **j-m b. machen** scare s.o. ‖ **Bange** *f* (-;) fear

Bangigkeit ['banɪçkaɪt] *f* (-;) fear

Bank [bank] *f* (-;ːe) bench; pew; (geol) layer, bed ‖ *f* (-;-en) bank

Bank'anweisung *f* check

Bank'ausweis *m* bank statement

Bank'einlage *f* bank deposit

Bankett [ban'ket] *n* (-s;-e) banquet

bank'fähig *adj* negotiable

Bank'guthaben *n* bank balance

Bank'halter –**in** §6 *mf* banker (in games)

Bankier [ban'je] *m* (-s;-s) banker

Bank'konto *n* bank account

bank'mäßig *adj* by check

bankrott [ban'rɔt] *adj* bankrupt ‖ *m* (-[e]s;-e) bankruptcy

Bank'verkehr *m* banking (activity)

Bank'wesen *n* banking

Bann [ban] *m* (-[e]s;-e) ban; (*Zauber*) spell; (eccl) excommunication

bannen ['banən] *tr* banish; (*Geister*) exorcize; (eccl) excommunicate

Banner ['banər] *n* (-s;-) banner; standard

Ban'nerträger *m* standard-bearer

Bann'fluch *m* anathema

Bann'kreis *m* spell; **in j-s B. geraten** come under s.o.'s spell

Bann'meile *f* (hist) city limits

Bann'ware *f* contraband

bar [bar] *adj* bare; (*rein*) pure, sheer; (fin) cash ‖ *adv* cash ‖ *prep* (genit) devoid of, lacking ‖ **Bar** *f* (-;-s) bar, taproom

Bär [ber] *m* (-en;-en) bear; (astr) Dipper; **j-m e-n B. aufbinden** tell s.o. a fish story

Bar- *comb.fm.* cash

Baracke [ba'rakə] *f* (-;-n) barrack; (wooden) hut

Barbar –**in** [bar'bar(ɪn)] §7 *mf* barbarian

Barbarei [barba'raɪ] *f* (-;-en) barbarism; (*Grausamkeit*) barbarity

barbarisch [bar'barɪʃ] *adj* barbarous; barbaric, primitive

bärbeißig ['berbaɪsɪç] *adj* surly

Bar'bestand *m* cash on hand

Bar'betrag *m* amount in cash

Barbier [bar'bir] *m* (-s;-e) barber

barbieren [bar'birən] *tr* shave; (fig) fleece

Barett [ba'ret] *n* (-[e]s;-e) beret

barfuß ['barfus] *adv* barefoot

barfüßig ['barfysɪç] *adj* barefooted

barg [bark] *pret* of **bergen**

Bar'geld *n* cash

barhäuptig ['barhɔɪptɪç] *adj* bareheaded

Bar'hocker *m* bar stool

Bariton ['barɪton] *m* (-s;-e) baritone

Barkasse [bar'kasə] *f* (-;-n) launch

Bärme ['bermə] *f* (-;) yeast, leaven

barmherzig [barm'hertsɪç] *adj* merciful

Bar'mittel *pl* cash

barock [ba'rɔk] *adj* baroque ‖ **Barock** *m & n* (-s) baroque; baroque period

Barometer [baro'metər] *n* (-s;-) barometer

Baron [ba'ron] *m* (-s;-e) baron

Baronin [ba'ronɪn] *f* (-;-nen) baroness

Barre ['barə] f (-;-n) bar
Barren ['barən] m (-s;-) bar; ingot; (gym) parallel bars
Barriere [bar'jerə] f (-;-n) barrier
barsch [barʃ] adj gruff, rude || **Barsch** m (-es;-e) (ichth) perch
Barschaft ['barʃaft] f (-;) cash
barst [barst] pret of **bersten**
Bart [bart] m (-[e]s;⸚e) beard; (e-r Katze) whiskers; (e-s Fisches) barb; **der B. ist ab!** the jig is up!; **sich** [dat] **e-n B. wachsen lassen** grow a beard
bärtig ['bertiç] adj bearded
bart'los adj beardless
Bar'verlust m straight loss
Basalt [ba'zalt] m (-[e]s;-e) basalt
Basar [ba'zar] m (-s;-e) bazaar
Ba•sis ['bazis] f (-;-sen [zən]) basis; (archit, math, mil) base
Baß [bas] m (Basses;Bässe) (mus) bass
Baß'geige f bass viol, contrabass
Bassin [ba'sɛ̃] n (-s;-s) reservoir; swimming pool; (naut) dock, basin
Baß'schlüssel m bass clef
Baß'stimme f bass (voice), basso
basta ['basta] interj—**und damit b.!** and that's that!
Bastard ['bastart] m (-[e]s;-e) bastard; (bot) hybrid
Bastei [bas'tar] f (-;-en) bastion
basteln ['bastəln] intr tinker
Bast'ler -in §6 mf hobbyist
bat [bat] pret of **bitten**
Bataillon [batal'jon] n (-s;-e) battalion
Batte•rie [batə'ri] f (-;-rien ['ri•ən] battery
Bau [bau] m (-[e]s;) erection, construction, building; (Bauart) structure, design; (Körper-) build; **er ist beim Bau** he is in the building trade; **er ist vom Bau** (coll) he's in the racket; **im Bau** under construction || m (-[e]s;-ten) building; **auf dem Bau** at the construction site || m (-[e]s;-e) burrow, hole; (min) mine
-bau m comb.fm. -construction, -building; -culture; -mining
Bau'abnahme f building inspection
Bau'arbeiter m construction worker
Bau'art f build; structure; type, model
Bauch [baux] m (-[e]s;⸚e) belly, stomach; (Leib) bowels; (coll) potbelly
Bauch- comb.fm. abdominal
bauchig ['bauxiç] adj bulging; convex
Bauch'klatscher m belly flop
Bauch'laden m vendor's tray
Bauch'landung f belly-landing
Bauch'redner -in §6 mf ventriloquist
Bauch'speicheldrüse f pancreas
Bauch'weh n stomach ache, bellyache
bauen ['bau•ən] tr build; erect; make, manufacture; (ackern) till; (anbauen) grow || intr build; (an dat) work (at); (auf acc) depend (on), trust
Bauer ['bau•ər] m (-s & -n;-n) farmer; (cards) jack; (chess) pawn || m (-s;-) builder || m & n (-s;-) birdcage
Bäuerchen ['bɔɪ•ərçən] n (-s;-) small farmer; (baby's) burp

Bäuerin ['bɔɪ•ərin] f (-;-nen) farmer's wife
bäuerisch ['bɔɪ•əriʃ] adj boorish
Bau'erlaubnis f building permit
bäuerlich ['bɔɪ•ərliç] adj rural
Bau'ernbursche m country lad
Bau'erndirne f country girl
Bauernfänger ['bau•ərnfɛŋər] m (-s;-) confidence man
Bau'erngut n, **Bau'ernhof** m farm
Bau'fach n architecture
bau'fällig adj dilapidated
Bau'genehmigung f building permit
Bau'gerüst n scaffold(ing)
Bau'gewerbe n building trade
Bau'gewerkschule f school of architecture and civil engineering
Bau'grundstück n building site
Bau'holz n lumber
Bau'kasten m building set
Bau'kunst f architecture
bau'lich adj architectural; structural; **in gutem baulichen Zustand** in good repair
Baum [baum] m (-[e]s;⸚e) tree; (mach) shaft, axle; (naut) boom
Bau'meister m building contractor, builder; architect
baumeln ['bauməln] intr dangle
bäumen ['bɔɪmən] ref rear
Baum'garten m orchard
Baum'grenze f timber line
Baum'krone f treetop
Baum'schere f pruning shears
Baum'schule f nursery (of saplings)
Baum'stamm m tree trunk
baum'stark adj strong as an ox
Bau'muster n model (number)
Baum'wolle f cotton
Baum'wollkapsel f cotton boll
Baum'wollsamt m velveteen
Bau'plan m ground plan
Bau'platz m building lot
Bau'rat m (-[e]s;-e) building inspector
Bausch [bauʃ] m (-[e]s;⸚e) pad, wad; (e-s Segels) bulge, belly; **in B. und Bogen** wholesale
bauschen ['bauʃən] tr, ref & intr bulge, swell
bauschig ['bauʃiç] adj puffy; baggy
Bau'schule f school of architecture and civil engineering
Bau'sparkasse f building and loan association
Bau'stahl m structural steel
Bau'stein m building stone; brick
Bau'stelle f building site; road construction
Bau'stoff m building material
Bau'techniker m construction engineer
Bau'unternehmer m contractor
Bau'unternehmung f building firm, building contractors
Bau'werk n building, edifice
Bau'wesen n building industry
Bau'zaun m hoarding
Bau'zeichnung f blueprint
Bayer -in ['baɪ•ər(in)] §6 mf Bavarian
bayerisch ['baɪ•əriʃ] adj Bavarian
Bayern ['baɪ•ərn] n (-s;) Bavaria
Bazillenträger [ba'tsiləntregər] m germ carrier

Bazil·lus [ba'tsɪlus] *m* (–;–len [lən]) bacillus

be– [bə] *insep pref*

beabsichtigen [bə'apzɪçtɪgən] *tr* intend; (**mit**) mean (by)

beach'ten *tr* pay attention to; (*merken*) note, notice; (*befolgen*) observe; (*berücksichtigen*) consider

beach'tenswert *adj* noteworthy

Beach'tung *f* (–;) attention; notice; observance; consideration

Beamte [bə'amtə] *m* (–n;–n) official

Beam'tenherrschaft *f* bureaucracy

Beam'tenlaufbahn *f* civil service career

Beamtentum [bə'amtəntum] *n* (–[e]s;) officialdom, bureaucracy

Beamtin [bə'amtɪn] *f* (–;–nen) official

beäng'stigen *tr* make anxious, alarm

beanspruchen [bə'an/pruxən] *tr* claim; (*Zeit, Raum*) require; **zu stark beansprucht werden** be worked too hard

beanstanden [bə'an/tandən] *tr* object to, find fault with; (*Waren*) reject; (*Wahl*) contest; (*Recht*) challenge

Bean'standung *f* (–;–en) objection; complaint

bean'tragen *tr* propose; (**bei**) apply for (to)

beant'worten *tr* answer

Beant'wortung *f* (–;–en) answer

bear'beiten *tr* work; (*Land*) cultivate; (*Buch, Text*) revise; (*Wörterbuch*) compile; (*für die Bühne*) adapt; (*ein Manuskript*) prepare; (*Thema; Kunden*) work on; (*Person*) try to influence; (*chem*) treat; (*Auftrag*) (*com*) handle; (*Fall*) (*jur*) handle; (*metal*) machine, tool; (*mus*) arrange

bearg'wöhnen *tr* be suspicious of

beaufsichtigen [bə'aufzɪçtɪgən] *tr* supervise; (*Arbeiten*) superintend; (*Kinder*) look after; (*educ*) proctor; **streng b.** keep a sharp eye on

beauf'tragen *tr* commission, appoint; (**mit**) entrust (with)

Beauftragte [bə'auftrɑktə] §5 *mf* representative; (*com*) agent

bebau'en *tr* cultivate; (*Gelände*) build up

beben ['bebən] *intr* (**vor**) tremble (with), shake (with); (*Erde*) quake

bebrillt [bə'brɪlt] *adj* bespectacled

Becher ['beçər] *m* (–s;–) cup, mug

bechern ['beçərn] *intr* (coll) booze

Becken ['bɛkən] *n* (–s;–) basin, bowl; (anat) pelvis; (mus) cymbal

bedacht [bə'daxt] *adj* (**auf** *acc*) intent (on); **auf alles b. sein** think of everything; **darauf b. sein zu** (*inf*) be anxious to (*inf*) || **Bedacht** *m*—**B. nehmen auf** (*acc*) take into consideration; **mit B.** deliberately, with caution

bedächtig [bə'dɛçtɪç], **bedachtsam** [bə'daxtzəm] *adj* cautious, deliberate

bedan'ken *ref*—**ich würde mich bestens b., wenn** (iron) I would be most indignant if; **sich b. bei j—m für** thank s.o. for

Bedarf [bə'darf] *m* (–[e]s;) demand; requirement; (an *dat*) need (of); **bei B.** if required; **den B. decken** meet the demand; **nach B.** as required;

seinen B. decken an (*dat*) get one's supply of

Bedarfs'artikel *pl* needs, supplies

Bedarfs'fall *m*—**im B.** in case of need

Bedarfs'güter *pl* consumer goods

Bedarfs'haltestelle *f* optional bus or trolley stop

Bedarfs'träger *m* consumer

bedauerlich [bə'dau·ərlɪç] *adj* regrettable

bedau'erlicherweise *adv* unfortunately

bedauern [bə'dau·ərn] *tr* pity, feel sorry for; regret, deplore || **Bedauern** *n* (–s;) (**über** *acc*) regret (over); (*Mitleid*) (**mit**) pity (for)

bedau'ernswert *adj* pitiful, pitiable

bedecken (bedek'ken) *tr* cover; **bedeckt** overcast

Bedeckung (Bedek'kung) *f* (–;–en) cover; escort; (mil) escort; (nav) convoy

beden'ken §66 *tr* consider; (*beachten*) bear in mind; (*im Testament*) provide for || *ref* deliberate, think a matter over; **sich e–s anderen b.** change one's mind || **Bedenken** *n* (–s;–) (*Erwägung*) consideration, reflection; (*Einwand*) objection; (*Zweifel*) doubt, scruple

bedenk'lich *adj* (*ernst*) serious, critical; (*gefährlich*) risky; (*heikel*) ticklish; (*Charakter*) questionable

bedeu'ten *tr* mean; **das hat nichts zu b.** that doesn't matter; **j—m b., daß** make it clear to s.o. that

bedeu'tend *adj* important; (*beträchtlich*) considerable

bedeutsam [bə'dɔɪtzɑm] *adj* significant; (*Blick*) meaningful

Bedeu'tung *f* (–;–en) meaning; (*Wichtigkeit*) importance

bedeu'tungsvoll *adj* significant

bedie'nen *tr* wait on, serve; (*Maschine*) operate || *ref* (*genit*) make use of; **bedienen Sie sich** help yourself || *intr* wait on people; (cards) follow suit

Bedie'nung *f* (–;) service; servants; waitresses

Bedienungs– *comb.fm.* control

Bedie'nungsanweisung *f* instructions

Bedie'nungsmannshaft *f* gun crew

bedingen [bə'dɪŋən] *tr* condition, stipulate; (*in sich schließen*) imply; **bedingt** conditioned, conditional

bedin'gungsweise *adv* conditionally

bedrän'gen *tr* press hard; (*beunruhigen*) pester; **bedrängte Lage** state of distress; **bedrängte Verhältnisse** financial difficulties

Bedrängnis [bə'drɛnnɪs] *f* (–;–se) distress; **in ärgster B.** in dire straits

bedro'hen *tr* threaten, menace

bedroh'lich *adj* threatening

bedrucken (bedruk'ken) *tr* print on; (*Stoff*) print

bedrücken (bedrük'ken) *tr* oppress

bedür'fen §69 (*genit*) require

Bedürfnis [bə'dʏrfnɪs] *n* (–ses;–se) need, requirement; (*Wunsch*) desire; **Bedürfnisse** necessities; **das dringende B. haben zu** (*inf*) have the urge to (*inf*)

Bedürf'nisanstalt *f* comfort station
bedürf'nislos *adj* having few needs
bedürftig [bə'dyrftɪç] *adj* needy; **b. sein** (*genit*) be in need of
Beefsteak ['bifstek] *n* (-s;-s) steak; **Deutsches B.** hamburger
beehren [bə'erən] *tr* honor || *ref—sich b. zu* (*inf*) have the honor of (*ger*)
beei'len *ref* hurry (up)
beein'drucken *tr* impress
beeinflussen [bə'aɪnflusən] *tr* influence
Beein'flussung *f* (-;) (*genit*) influence (on), effect (on); (*pol*) lobbying
beeinträchtigen [bə'aɪntreçtɪgən] *tr* (*Ruf*) damage; (*Wert*) detract from; (*Rechte*) encroach upon; (*Aussichten*) hurt, spoil
been'den, ben'digen *tr* end, conclude; (*Arbeit*) complete
beengen [bə'ɛŋən] *tr* confine, cramp; **sich beengt fühlen** feel cramped; (*fig*) feel restricted
beer'ben *tr—j—n b.* inherit s.o.'s estate
beerdigen [bə'erdɪgən] *tr* bury, inter
Beer'digung *f* (-;-en) burial
Beere ['berə] *f* (-;-n) berry
Beet [bet] *n* (-[e]s;-e) (agr) bed
befähigen [bə'fe·ɪgən] *tr* enable, qualify
befähigt [bə'fe·ɪçt] *adj* able, capable
Befä'higung *f* (-;-en) qualification; (*Fähigkeit*) ability
befahl [bə'fal] *pret* of **befehlen**
befahrbar [bə'farbar] *adj* (*Weg*) passable; (*Wasser*) navigable
befah'ren §71 *tr* travel; (*Meer*) sail; (*Fluß*) navigate; (*Küste*) sail along; (*Schacht*) go down into
befal'len §72 *tr* strike, attack; infest
befan'gen *adj* embarrassed; (*schüchtern*) shy; (*voreingenommen*) prejudiced; (*parteiisch*) partial
befas'sen *tr* touch, handle || *ref—sich b.* mit concern oneself with
befehden [bəfedən] *tr* make war on
Befehl [bə'fel] *m* (-s;-e) order, command; **auf B.** (*genit*) by order of
befeh'len §51 *tr* order, command; **was b. Sie?** what is your pleasure?
befehligen [bə'felɪgən] *tr* command, be in command of
Befehls'form *f* imperative mood
Befehlshaber [bə'felshabər] *m* (-s;-) (mil) commanding officer; (nav) commander in chief; **oberster B.** supreme commander
befehlshaberisch [bə'felshabərɪʃ] *adj* imperious
Befehls'stelle *f* command post
befe'stigen *tr* (an *dat*) fasten (to), attach (to); (mil) fortify
Befe'stigung *f* (-;-en) fortification
befeuchten [bə'fɔɪçtən] *tr* moisten, wet
befeu'ern *tr* (aer, naut) mark with lights; (mil) fire on, shoot at
befin'den §59 *tr* deem || *ref* be, feel || **Befinden** *n* (-s;) judgment, view; (state of) health; **je nach B.** according to taste
befindlich [bə'fɪntlɪç] *adj* present, to

be found; **all die im Hafen befindlichen Schiffe** the ships (present) in the harbor; **b. sein** happen to be
beflecken [beflek'ken] *tr* stain, taint
beflissen [bə'flɪsən] *adj* (*genit*) keen (on), interested (in) || **Beflissene** §5 *mf* (*genit*) student (of)
befohlen [bə'folən] *pp* of **befehlen**
befol'gen *tr* obey, comply with
Befol'gung *f* (-;) observance
beför'dern *tr* ship; (*spedieren*) forward; (*im Rang*) promote; (*fördern*) further
Beför'derungsmittel *n* means of transportation
befra'gen *tr* question, interrogate; poll; (*um Rat*) consult
befrakt [bə'frakt] *adj* in tails
befrei'en *tr* free; liberate; (*vom Militärdienst*) exempt; (*von e–r Aufgabe*) excuse; (*von Sorgen, e–r Last*) relieve
Befrei'ung *f* (-;-en) freeing; liberation; exemption; rescue
befremden [bə'fremdən] *tr* surprise, astonish; strike as odd || **Befremden** *n* (-s;) surprise, astonishment
befreunden [bə'frɔɪndən] *ref—sich mit etw b.* reconcile oneself to s.th.; **sich mit j—m b.** make friends with s.o.
befrieden [bə'fridən] *tr* pacify
befriedigen [bə'fridɪgən] *tr* satisfy
befrie'digend *adj* satisfactory
befristen [bə'frɪstən] *tr* set a time limit on
Befri'stung *f* (-;-en) time limit
befruchten [bə'fruxtən] *tr* (*Land*) make fertile; (*schwängern*) impregnate; (*Ei*) fertilize; **künstlich b.** inseminate; (bot) pollinate
befugt [bə'fukt] *adj* authorized
befüh'len *tr* feel, touch
Befund' *m* (-[e]s;-e) findings, facts
befürch'ten *tr* fear, be afraid of
Befürch'tung *f* (-;-en) apprehension
befürworten [bə'fyrvərtən] *tr* support; (*anraten*) recommend
begabt [bə'gapt] *adj* gifted, talented
Bega'bung *f* (-;-en) aptitude; (natural) gift, talent
Bega'bungsprüfung *f* intelligence test
begann [bə'gan] *pret* of **beginnen**
begatten [bə'gatən] *tr* mate with || *ref* copulate, mate
bege'ben §80 *tr* (*Anleihen*) float, place; (*Wertpapiere*) sell || *ref* go; occur; **es begab sich** (Bib) it came to pass; **sich an die Arbeit b.** set to work; **sich auf die Flucht b.** take to flight; **sich auf die Reise b.** set out on a trip; **sich b.** (*genit*) renounce; **sich in Gefahr b.** expose oneself to danger
Bege'benheit *f* (-;-en) event, incident
begegnen [bə'gegnən] *intr* (SEIN) (*dat*) meet, come upon; (*Schwierigkeiten, Feind*) encounter; (*Gefahr*) face
bege'hen §82 *tr* walk on; walk along; (*Verbrechen, Irrtum*) commit; (*Fest*) celebrate
Begehr [bə'ger] *m* & *n* (-s;) desire; request; (econ) demand
begehren [bə'gerən] *tr* wish for; crave;

(Bib) covet; *etw von j-m b.* ask s.o. for s.th. ‖ *intr* (**nach**) yearn (for)
begeh'renswert *adj* desirable
begehr'lich *adj* covetous
begehrt [bə'gert] *adj* in demand
begeistert [bə'gaɪstərt] *adj* enthusiastic
Begei'sterung *f* (–;) enthusiasm
Begier [bə'gir] *f* (–;) var of **Begierde**
Begierde [bə'girdə] *f* (–;-n) desire; (fleshly) appetite; eagerness; craving
begierig [bə'giriç] *adj* eager; (*Augen*) hungry; (**nach, auf** *acc*) desirous (of); **b. zu** (*inf*) eager to (*inf*)
begie'ßen §76 *tr* water; (culin) baste; **das wollen wir b.** we want to celebrate it (*by drinking*)
Beginn [bə'gɪn] *m* (–[e]s;) beginning; (*Ursprung*) origin
beginnen [bə'gɪnən] §52 *tr* & *intr* begin
beglaubigen [bə'glaubɪgən] *tr* certify, authenticate; (*Gesandten*) accredit
Beglau'bigung *f* (–;) authentication; accreditation
Beglau'bigungsschreiben *n* (dipl) credentials
beglei'chen §85 *tr* balance; (*Rechnung*) pay in full; (*Streit*) settle
begleiten [bə'glaɪtən] *tr* accompany; escort; see (*e.g., off, home*); **hinaus b.** see to the door
Beglei'ter –in §6 *mf* companion
Begleit'erscheinung *f* concomitant
Begleit'musik *f* background music
Begleit'schreiben *s* covering letter
Beglei'tung *f* (–;-en) company; escort; (*Gefolge*) retinue; (mus) accompaniment
beglück'wünschen *tr* (**zu**) congratulate (on)
Beglück'wünschung *f* (–;-en) congratulation
begnadet [bə'gnadət] *adj* highly gifted
begnadigen [bə'gnadɪgən] *tr* pardon; (pol) grant amnesty to
Begna'digung *f* (–;-en) pardon; amnesty
begnügen [bə'gnygən] *ref* (**mit**) content oneself (with), be satisfied (with)
begonnen [bə'gɔnən] *pp* of **beginnen**
begra'ben §87 *tr* bury
Begräbnis [bə'grepnis] *n* (–ses;-se) burial; funeral
Begräb'nisfeier *f* funeral
Begräb'nisstätte *f* burial place
begradigen [bə'gradɪgən] *tr* straighten; (tech) align
begrei'fen §88 *tr* touch, handle; (*verstehen*) grasp; (*enthalten*) comprise
begreif'lich *adj* understandable
begreif'licherweise *adv* understandably
begren'zen *tr* bound; limit, restrict
Begren'zung *f* (–;-en) limitation
Begriff [bə'grɪf] *m* (–[e]s;-e) idea, notion; (*Ausdruck*) term; (philos) concept; **im B. sein zu** (*inf*) to be on the point of (*ger*)
begriffen [bə'grɪfən] *adj*—**b. sein in** (*dat*) be in the process of
begrün'den *tr* found, establish; (*Behauptung*) substantiate, prove
Begrün'der –in §6 *mf* founder

Begrün'dung *f* (–;-en) establishment; proof; (*Grund*) ground, reason
begrüßen *tr* greet; welcome
begünstigen [bə'gynstɪgən] *tr* favor; (*fördern*) promote, support; (jur) aid and abet
Begün'stiger *m* (–s;–) accessory after the fact
Begünstigte [bə'gynstɪçtə] §5 *mf* (ins) beneficiary
Begün'stigung *f* (–;-en) promotion, encouragement; support, backing; (jur) aiding and abetting
begut'achten *tr* give an expert opinion on; **b. lassen** obtain expert opinion on
begütert [bə'gytərt] *adj* well-to-do
begütigen [bə'gytɪgən] *tr* appease
behaart [bə'hart] *adj* hairy
behäbig [bə'hebɪç] *adj* comfort-loving; (*beleibt*) portly
behaftet [bə'haftət] *adj* afflicted
behagen [bə'hagən] *intr* (*dat*) please, suit ‖ **Behagen** *n* (–s;) pleasure
behaglich [bə'haklɪç] *adj* pleasant; (*traulich*) snug, cozy
behal'ten §90 *tr* keep, retain; **Recht b.** turn out to be right
Behälter [bə'heltər] *m* (–s;–) container; box; (*für Öl, usw.*) tank
behan'deln *tr* treat; deal with; handle
behän'gen §92 *tr* hang; deck out
beharren [bə'harən] *intr* remain (unchanged); (**in** *dat*) persevere (in); (**auf** *dat*) persist (in), stick (to)
beharrlich [bə'harlɪç] *adj* steadfast
behau'en §93 *tr* hew
behaupten [bə'hauptən] *tr* declare, assert; (*festhalten*) maintain, retain; allege ‖ *ref* stand one's ground; (*Preise*) remain steady
behausen [bə'hauzən] *tr* lodge, house
Behau'sung *f* (–;-en) dwelling
behe'ben §94 *tr* (*Schwierigkeiten*) remove; (*Zweifel*) dispel; (*Schaden*) repair; (*Lage*) remedy; (*Geld*) withdraw; (*Schmerzen*) eliminate
beheimatet [bə'haɪmatət] *adj*—**b. sein in** (*dat*) reside in; come from
Behelf [bə'helf] *m* (–[e]s;-e) expedient; makeshift
behel'fen §96 *ref* (**mit**) make do (with)
Behelfs– *comb.fm.* temporary
behelfs'mäßig *adj* temporary, makeshift
behelligen [bə'helɪgən] *tr* bother
Behel'ligung *f* (–;-en) bother, trouble
behende [bə'hendə] *adj* agile, quick; (*gewandt*) handy; (*geistig*) smart
beherbergen [bə'herbergən] *tr* take in, put up (*as guest*)
beherr'schen *tr* (*Land*) rule; (*Sprache*) master; (*Gefühle*) control; (*überragen*) tower over; **den Luftraum b.** (mil) have air supremacy
Beherr'scher –in §6 *mf* ruler ‖ *m* master ‖ *f* mistress
beherzigen [bə'hertsɪgən] *tr* take to heart, remember
beherzt [bə'hertst] *adj* courageous
behe'xen *tr* bewitch; (fig) captivate
behilflich [bə'hɪlflɪç] *adj* helpful
behin'dern *tr* hinder; hamper; block
behor'chen *tr* overhear

Behörde [bə'høːrdə] *f* (-;-n) authority, board; *die Behörden* the authorities
behördlich [bə'hørtlɪç] *adj* official
behü'ten *tr* (*vor dat*) protect (against); **Gott behüte!** God forbid!
behutsam [bə'huːtzam] *adj* wary
bei [baɪ] *prep* (*dat*) (*Ort*) by, beside, at, with, in; (*in Anschriften*) in care of, c/o; (*Zeit, Umstände*) at, by, during, on; (*Zustände, Eigenschaften*) at, while, in; **bei mir haben** have on me; **bei meiner Ehre** upon my honor; **bei Schiller** in the works of Schiller; **bei uns** at our house; **bei weitem** by far
bei'behalten §90 *tr* retain, keep
Bei'blatt *n* supplement
bei'bringen §65 *tr* obtain, procure; (*Beweise, Zeugen*) produce; (*Arznei, Gift*) administer; (*Wunde, Niederlage, Schlag, Verluste*) inflict; **j—m die Nachricht schonend b.** break the news gently to s.o.; **j—m etw b.** teach s.o. s.th., make s.th. clear to s.o.
Beichte ['baɪçtə] *f* (-;-n) confession
beichten ['baɪçtən] *tr* (eccl) confess
Beicht'kind *n* (eccl) penitent
Beicht'stuhl *m* (eccl) confessional
beide ['baɪdə] *adj* both; two ‖ *pron* both; two; **keiner von beiden** neither of them
beiderlei ['baɪdər'laɪ] *invar adj* both kinds of
beiderseitig ['baɪdər'zaɪtɪç] *adj* bilateral; (*gemeinsam*) mutual
beiderseits ['baɪdər'zaɪts] *adv* on both sides; mutually, reciprocally ‖ *prep* (*genit*) on both sides of
beieinan'der *adv* together; **gut b. sein** (coll) be in good shape
Bei'fahrer **-in** §6 *mf* relief driver; passenger (*next to the driver*)
Bei'fall *m* approval; applause
bei'fällig *adj* approving; (*Bericht*) favorable ‖ *adv* approvingly
Bei'fallklatschen *n* clapping, applause
Bei'fallsgeschrei *n* loud cheering
Bei'fallsruf *m* cheer
Bei'film *m* (cin) second feature
bei'folgend *adj* enclosed
bei'fügen *tr* add; (*e-m Brief*) enclose
bei'fügend *adj* (gram) attributive
Bei'fügung *f* (-;-en) addition; enclosure; (gram) attributive
Bei'gabe *f* extra; funerary gift
bei'geben §80 *tr* add; assign ‖ *intr* give in; **klein b.** knuckle under
Bei'geschmack *m* taste, flavor; tinge
Bei'hilfe *f* aid; (*Stipendium*) grant; (*Unterstützung*) subsidy; allowance; (jur) aiding and abetting
bei'kommen § 99 *intr* (SEIN) (*dat*) get the better of; (*dat*) reach; **e-r Schwierigkeit** overcome
Beil [baɪl] *n* (-[e]s;-e) hatchet
Bei'lage *f* (*im Brief*) enclosure; (*e-r Zeitung*) supplement; **Fleisch mit B.** meat and vegetables
beiläufig ['baɪlɔɪfɪç] *adj* incidental; casual ‖ *adv* by the way, incidentally; **b. erwähnen** mention in passing
bei'legen *tr* add; (*Titel*) confer; (*Wichtigkeit*) attach; (*Streit*) settle; **etw**

e-m Brief b. enclose s.th. in a letter ‖ *intr* heave to
Bei'leid *n* (-s;) condolence(s)
bei'liegen §108 *intr*—e—m **Brief b.** be enclosed in a letter; **j—m b.** lie with s.o
beim *abbr* **bei dem**
bei'messen §70 *tr* attribute, impute
bei'mischen *tr* mix in
Bein [baɪn] *n* (-[e]s;-e) leg; (*Knochen*) bone; (fig) foot; **j—m ein B. stellen** trip s.o.
beinahe ['baɪnɑ·ə], [baɪ'nɑ·e] *adv* almost, nearly
Bei'name *m* appellation; (*Spitzname*) nickname
Bein'bruch *m* fracture, broken leg
Bein'schiene *f* (surg) splint; (sport) shin guard
Bein'schützer *m* (sport) shin guard
Bein'stellen *n* (sport) tripping
bei'ordnen *tr* assign, appoint (*s.o.*) as assistant; (*dat*) place (*s.th.*) on a level (with)
beipflichten ['baɪpflɪçtən] *intr* (*dat*) agree with (*s.o.*), agree to (*s.th.*)
Bei'programm *n* (cin) second feature
Bei'rat *m* (-s;⁻e) adviser, counselor; (*Körperschaft*) advisory board
beir'ren *tr* mislead
beisammen [baɪ'zamən] *adv* together
Beisam'mensein *n* (-s;) being together; gathering, reunion; **geselliges B.** social; informal reception
Bei'satz *m* addition; (*bei Legierung*) alloy; (gram) appositive
Bei'schlaf *m* sexual intercourse
bei'schließen §76 *tr* enclose
Bei'schluß *m*—**unter B. von allen Dokumenten** with all documents attached
bei'schreiben §62 *tr* write in the margin; add as a postscript
Bei'schrift *f* postscript
Bei'sein *n* (-s;) presence
beisei'te *adv* aside; **b. schaffen** remove; (coll) do (*s.o.*) in
bei'setzen *tr* bury, inter
Bei'sitzer *m* associate judge
Bei'spiel *n* example; **zum B.** for example
bei'spielhaft *adj* exemplary
bei'spiellos *adj* unparalleled
bei'spielsweise *adv* by way of example
bei'springen §142 *intr* (*dat*) come to the aid of
beißen ['baɪsən] §53 *tr & intr* bite
bei'ßend *adj* biting; stinging, pungent, acrid; sarcastic; (*Reue*) bitter
Beiß'korb *m* muzzle
Beiß'zahn *m* (anat) incisor
Beiß'zange *f* pincers, nippers
Bei'stand *m* aid, support; (*Person*) assistant
bei'stehen §146 *intr* (*dat*) stand by, back, support
Bei'steuer *f* contribution
bei'steuern *tr* contribute
bei'stimmen *intr* (*dat*) agree with
Bei'stimmung *f* (-;) approval
Bei'strich *m* comma
Beitrag ['baɪtrak] *m* (-[e]s;⁻e) contribution; (*e-s Mitglieds*) dues

bei'tragen §132 tr & intr contribute
bei'treiben §62 tr collect; (Abgaben) exact; (mil) commandeer, requisition
bei'treten §152 intr (SEIN) (dat) join; (j-s Meinung) concur in
Bei'tritt m joining; concurrence
Bei'wagen m (aut) sidecar
Bei'werk n (-[e]s) accessories
bei'wohnen intr (dat) attend; (e-m Ereignis) be witness to; (j-m) have intercourse with (s.o.)
Bei'wort n (-[e]s;⸚er) epithet; (gram) adjective
Beize ['baɪtsə] f (-;-n) corrosive; (wood) stain; (Falken-) falconry; (culin) marinade
beizeiten [baɪ'tsaɪtən] adv on time; (frühzeitig) early
beizen ['baɪtsən] tr (ätzen) corrode; (Holz) stain; (Wunde) cauterize; (hunt) go hawking
bejahen [bə'jɑ·ən] tr say 'yes' to
beja'hend adj affirmative
bejahrt [bə'jɑrt] adj aged
bekämp'fen tr fight, oppose
bekannt [bə'kant] adj known; familiar; (berühmt) well-known || Bekannte §5 mf acquaintance
Bekannt'gabe f announcement
bekannt'geben §80 tr announce
bekannt'lich adv as is well known
bekannt'machen tr announce; (Gesetz) promulgate
Bekannt'machung f (-;-en) publication, announcement; (Plakat) poster
Bekannt'schaft f (-;) acquaintance; (coll) acquaintances
bekeh'ren tr convert || ref (zu) become a convert (to)
Bekehrte [bə'kertə] §5 mf convert
beken'nen §97 tr (Sünde) confess; (zugestehen) admit; Farbe b. follow suit; (fig) put one's cards on the table || ref —sich schuldig b. plead guilty; sich zu e-r Religion b. profess a religion; sich zu e-r Tat b. own up to a deed; sich zu j-m b. stand by s.o., believe in s.o.
Bekennt'nis n (eccl) confession; (Konfession) denomination
bekla'gen tr deplore; (Tod) mourn || ref (über acc) complain (about), find fault (with)
bekla'genswert adj deplorable
Beklagte [bə'klɑktə] §5 mf defendant
beklat'schen tr applaud
bekle'ben tr paste; (mit Etiketten) label; e-e Mauer mit Plakaten b. paste posters on a wall
beklei'den tr clothe, dress; (Mauer) face, cover; (Amt) hold
beklem'men tr stifle, oppress
Beklem'mung f (-;-en) worry, anxiety; Beklemmung claustrophobia
beklommen [bə'kləmən] adj uneasy
bekom'men §99 tr get; obtain; receive; (Schnupfen) catch; (Risse) develop || intr (dat) do good; j-m schlecht b. do s.o. harm; wohl bekomm's! to your health!
bekömmlich [bə'kœmlɪç] adj digestible; (gesund) healthful; (zuträglich) wholesome

beköstigen [bə'kœstɪgən] tr board, feed || ref —sich selbst b. do one's own cooking
bekräf'tigen tr (Vorschlag) support; (bestätigen) substantiate; mit e-m Eid b. seal with an oath
bekrän'zen tr wreath, crown
bekreu'zen, bekreu'zigen ref cross oneself, make the sign of the cross
bekrie'gen tr make war on
bekrit'teln tr criticize, pick at
bekrit'zeln tr scribble on, doodle on
beküm'mern tr worry, trouble || ref (um) concern onself (with), bother (about)
beküm'mert adj (über acc) worried (about)
bekunden [bə'kundən] tr manifest, show; (öffentlich) state publicly
bela'den §103 tr load; (fig) burden
Belag [bə'lɑk] m (-[e]s;⸚) covering; coat(ing); flooring; layer; surface
bela'gern tr besiege, beleaguer
Bela'gerung f (-;-en) siege
Belang [bə'laŋ] m (-[e]s;e) importance, consequence; Belange interests
belan'gen tr (jur) sue; was mich belangt as far as I am concerned
belang'los adj unimportant
bela'sten tr load (down); (Grundstück) encumber; (fig) burden; (acct) charge; (jur) incriminate
belästigen [bə'lɛstɪgən] tr annoy, bother; (mit Fragen) pester; (unabsichtlich) inconvenience
Bela'stung f (-;-en) load; encumbrance; (fig) burden; (acct) debit; die Zeiten größter B. the peak hours
Bela'stungsprobe f (fig) acid test
Bela'stungszeuge m witness for the prosecution
belau'fen §105 ref —sich b. auf (acc) amount to, come to
belau'schen tr overhear
bele'ben tr animate; (Getränk) spike; wieder b. revive
belebt [bə'lept] adj animated, lively
Bele'bungsmittel n stimulant
Beleg [bə'lek] m (-s;-e) (Beweisstück) evidence; (Unterlage) voucher; (Beispiel) example; (jur) exhibit
bele'gen tr cover; (Platz) take, occupy; (bemannen) man; (beweisen) verify; (Vorlesung) register for; ein Brötchen mit Schinken b. make a ham sandwich; mit Beispielen b. exemplify; mit Fliesen b. tile; mit Steuern b. tax; mit Teppichen b. carpet || ref become coated
Beleg'schaft f (-;-en) crew; personnel; shift
Beleg'schein m voucher; receipt
Beleg'stelle f reference
belegt [bə'lekt] adj (Platz) reserved; (Zunge) coated; (Stimme) husky; (telp) busy; belegtes Brot sandwich
beleh'ren tr instruct || ref —sich b. lassen listen to reason
beleh'rend adj instructive
Beleh'rung f (-;-en) instruction; (Lehre) lesson; (Rat) advice; zu Ihrer B. for your information

beleibt [bə'laɪpt] *adj* stout
beleidigen [bə'laɪdɪgən] *tr* offend
belei'digend *adj* offensive
bele'sen *adj* well-read
beleuch'ten *tr* light (up), illuminate; (fig) throw light on
Beleuch'ter *m* (aer) pathfinder; (theat) juicer
Beleuch'tung *f* (-;-en) lighting, illumination; (fig) elucidation
Beleuch'tungskörper *m* lighting fixture
Belgien ['bɛlgjən] *n* (-s;) Belgium
Belgier -in ['bɛlgjər(ɪn)] §6 *mf* Belgian
belgisch ['bɛlgɪʃ] *adj* Belgian
belichten [bə'lɪçtən] *tr* (phot) expose
Belich'tung *f* (-;-en) exposure
belie'ben *intr* please || *impers* (*dat*)— wenn es Ihnen beliebt if you please || Belieben *n* (-s;) liking; es steht in Ihrem B. it's up to you; nach B. as you like
beliebig [bə'libɪç] *adj* any (you please) || *adv* as . . . as you please
beliebt [bə'lipt] *adj* favorite; (bei) popular (with)
Beliebt'heit *f* (-;) popularity
belie'fern *tr* supply, furnish
bellen ['bɛlən] *intr* bark
belob(ig)en [bə'lob(ɪg)ən] *tr* praise; commend; (mil) cite
beloh'nen *tr* reward
belü'gen §111 *tr* lie to, deceive
belustigen [bə'lʊstɪgən] *tr* amuse
bemächtigen [bə'mɛçtɪgən] *intr* (*genit*) seize, get hold of; (mil) seize
bemä'keln *tr* criticize, carp at
bema'len *tr* paint; decorate
bemängeln [bə'mɛŋəln] *tr* criticize
bemannen [bə'manən] *tr* man
Beman'nung *f* (-;-en) (nav) crew
bemänteln [bə'mɛntəln] *tr* gloss over; (*Fehler, Fehltritt*) cover up
bemei'stern *tr* master || *ref* control oneself; (*genit*) get hold of
bemerk'bar *adj* perceptible
bemer'ken *tr* notice; (*äußern*) remark
bemer'kenswert *adj* remarkable
Bemer'kung *f* (-;-en) note; remark
bemes'sen §70 *tr* measure; proportion
bemit'leiden *tr* pity, feel sorry for
bemittelt [bə'mɪtəlt] *adj* well-to-do
bemogeln [bə'mogəln] *tr* cheat
bemü'hen *tr* trouble, bother; **bemüht sein zu** (*inf*) take pains to (*inf*) || *ref* bother, exert oneself; **sich für j-n b.** intervene for s.o.; **sich um etw b.** make an effort to obtain s.th.; **sich um j-n b.** attend to s.o.; **sich zu j-m b.** go to s.o.
Bemü'hung *f* (-;-en) bother; effort
bemüßigt [bə'mysɪçt] *adj*—**sich b. fühlen zu** (*inf*) feel obliged to (*inf*)
bemu'stern *tr*—**ein Angebot b.** (com) send samples of an offer
bemuttern [bə'mʊtərn] *tr* mother
benachbart [bə'naxbart] *adj* neighboring; (*Fachgebiet*) related, allied
benachrichtigen [bə'naxrɪçtɪgən] *tr* notify; put on notice
Benach'richtigung *f* (-;-en) notification; notice
benachteiligen [bə'naxtaɪlɪgən] *tr*

place at a disadvantage, handicap; discriminate against
benebelt [bə'nebəlt] *adj* covered in mist; (fig) groggy
benedeien [bene'daɪ-ən] *tr* bless
beneh'men §116 *tr*—**j-m etw b.** take s.th. away from s.o. || *ref* behave || **Benehmen** *n* (-s;) behavior
beneiden [bə'naɪdən] *tr*—**j-n um etw b.** begrudge s.o. s.th.
benei'denswert *adj* enviable
benen'nen §97 *tr* name, term
Bengel ['bɛŋəl] *m* (-s;-) rascal
benommen [bə'nɔmən] *adj* dazed
benö'tigen *tr* need
benutz'bar *adj* usable
benut'zen, benüt'zen *tr* use, make use of
Benut'zerkarte *f* library card
Benzin [bɛnt'sin] *n* (-s;-e) gasoline
Benzin'behälter *m* gas tank
beobachten [bə'obaxtən] *tr* observe; (*polizeilich*) keep under surveillance; (med) keep under observation
Beob'achtung *f* (-;-en) observation; (*e-s Gesetzes*) observance
beor'dern *tr* order (*to go to a place*)
bepacken (bepak'ken) *tr* load (down)
bepflan'zen *tr* plant
bequem [bə'kvem] *adj* comfortable; cozy; (*Stellung*) soft; (*Raten, Lösung*) easy; (*faul*) lazy; **b. zur Hand haben** have handy
berappen [bə'rapən] *tr* (coll) shell out
bera'ten §63 *tr* (über *acc*) advise (on); discuss || *ref* & *intr* (über *acc*) confer (about), deliberate on
bera'tend *adj* advisory, consulting
beratschlagen [bə'rat/lagən] *intr* (über *acc*) consult (on); **mit j-m b.** consult s.o., confer with s.o.
berat'schlagend *adj* advisory
Bera'tung *f* (-;-en) advice; (jur, med) consultation; **in B. sein** be under consideration
Bera'tungsstelle *f* counseling center
berau'ben *tr* (*genit*) rob (of); (*genit*) dispossess (of); (*genit*) deprive (of); (*genit*) bereave (of)
berech'nen *tr* calculate, figure out; (*schätzen*) estimate; (com) charge
berech'nend *adj* calculating
Berech'nung *f* (-;-en) calculation
berechtigen [bə'rɛçtɪgən] *tr* authorize; justify, warrant; (**zu**) entitle (to)
Berech'tigung *f* (-;-en) right, authorization; justification; (**zu**) title (to)
bereden [bə'redən] *tr* talk over, discuss; **j-n zu etw b.** talk s.o. into s.th. || *ref*—**sich mit j-m über etw b.** confer with s.o. on s.th.
beredsam [bə'retzam] *adj* eloquent
beredt [bə'ret] *adj* eloquent
Bereich *m* & *n* (-[e]s;-e) region; range; (fig) field, sphere; **es fällt nicht in meinen B.** it's not within my province
bereichern [bə'raɪçərn] *tr* enrich
berei'fen *tr* cover with frost; (aut) put tires on
berei'nigen *tr* (*Streit, Konto*) settle; (*Mißverständnis*) clear up
berei'sen *tr* tour

bereit [bə'raɪt] *adj* ready

bereiten [bə'raɪtən] *tr* prepare; *(Kaffee)* make; *(Freude)* give

Bereit'schaft *f* (-;) readiness; team, squad; *(mil)* alert

bereit'stellen *tr* make available

Berei'tung *f* (-;-en) preparation; *(Herstellung)* manufacture

bereit'willig *adj* ready, willing

bereu'en *tr* rue, regret

Berg [berk] *m* (-[e]s;-e) mountain; *(Hügel)* hill; **über alle Berge sein** be off and away; **zu Berge stehen** stand on end

bergab' *adv* downhill, down the mountain

bergauf' *adv* uphill; up the mountain

Berg'bahn *f* mountain railroad

Berg'bau *m* (-[e]s;) mining

Berg'bewohner -in §6 *mf* mountaineer

bergen ['bergən] §54 *tr* rescue; *(enthalten)* hold; *(Gefahr)* involve; *(Segel)* take in; *(naut)* salvage; *(poet)* conceal; *(rok)* recover || *ref*—**in sich b.** involve

bergig ['bergɪç] *adj* mountainous

Berg'kessel *m* gorge

Berg'kette *f* mountain range

Berg'kluft *f* ravine, gully

Berg'kristall *m* rock crystal, quartz

Berg'land *n* hill country

Berg'mann *m* (-[e]s;-leute) miner

Berg'predigt *f* Sermon on the Mount

Berg'recht *n* mining law

Berg'rücken *m* ridge

Berg'rutsch *m* landslide

Berg'schlucht *f* gorge, ravine

Berg'spitze *f* mountain peak

Berg'steiger -in §6 *mf* mountain climber

Berg'steigerei *f* mountain climbing

Berg'sturz *m* landslide

Ber'gung *f* (-;-en) rescue; *(naut)* salvage; *(rok)* recovery

Ber'gungsarbeiten *pl* salvage operations

Ber'gungsschiff *n* salvage vessel; *(rok)* recovery ship

Berg'wacht *f* mountain rescue service

Berg'werk *n* mine

Berg'wesen *n* mining

Bericht [bə'rɪçt] *m* (-[e]s;-e) report

berichten [bə'rɪçtən] *tr & intr* report

Berichterstatter -in [bə'rɪçtər/tatər (ɪn)] §6 *mf* reporter; correspondent; *(rad)* commentator

Bericht'erstattung *f* (-;) reporting

berichtigen [bə'rɪçtɪgən] *tr* rectify; *(Text)* emend; *(Schuld)* pay off

berie'chen §102 *tr* sniff at; *(fig)* size up || *recip* (coll) sound each other out

Berlin [ber'lin] *n* (-s;) Berlin

Bernstein ['bern/taɪn] *m* amber

bersten ['berstən] §55 *intr* (SEIN) (vor *dat*) burst (with)

berüchtigt [bə'rʏçtɪçt] *adj* notorious

berücken (berük'ken) *tr* captivate

berücksichtigen [bə'rʏkzɪçtɪgən] *tr* *(erwägen)* consider; *(in Betracht ziehen)* make allowance for

Berück'sichtigung *f* (-;-en) consideration

Beruf' *m* (-[e]s;-e) vocation; profession; *(Gewerbe)* trade; *(Tätigkeit)* occupation; *(Laufbahn)* career

beru'fen *adj* called; authorized || §122 *tr* call; *(ernennen)* appoint; *(Geister)* conjure up || *ref*—**sich auf ein Gesetz b.** quote a law *(in support)*; **sich auf j-n b.** use s.o.'s name as a reference

beruf'lich *adj* professional; vocational

Berufs- *comb.fm.* professional; vocational

Berufs'diplomat *m* career diplomat

Berufs'genossenschaft *f* professional association; trade association

Berufs'heer *n* regular army

Berufs'schule *f* vocational school

Berufs'sportler -in §6 *mf* professional

berufs'tätig *adj* working

Beru'fung *f* (-;-en) call; vocation; appointment; *(jur)* appeal; **B. einlegen** *(jur)* appeal; **unter B. auf** *(acc)* referring to

Beru'fungsgericht *n* appellate court

beru'hen *intr* *(auf dat)* be based (on); *(auf dat)* be due (to); **e-e Sache auf sich b.** lassen let a matter rest

beruhigen [bə'ru·ɪgən] *tr* calm; appease

beru'higend *adj* soothing; reassuring

Beru'higung *f* (-;) calming; appeasement, pacification; reassurance; *(der Lage)* stabilization; **zu meiner großen B.** much to my relief

Beru'higungsmittel *n* sedative

berühmt [bə'rymt] *adj* (**wegen**) famous (for)

Berühmt'heit *f* (-;-en) renown; *(berühmte Persönlichkeit)* celebrity

berüh'ren *tr* touch; *(erwähnen)* touch on; *(wirken auf)* affect; *(Zug)* pass through || *ref* come in contact, meet

Berüh'rung *f* (-;-en) touch; contact

besä'en *tr* sow; *(bestreuen)* strew; **mit Sternen besät** star-spangled

besa'gen *tr* say; *(bedeuten)* mean

besagt [bə'zakt] *adj* aforesaid

besänftigen [bə'zenftɪgən] *tr* calm; appease || *ref* calm down

Besatz' *m* trimming

Besat'zung *f* (-;-en) garrison; occupation; army of occupation; *(aer, nav)* crew

Besat'zungsarmee *f* army of occupation

Besat'zungsbehörde *f* military government

besau'fen §124 *ref* (coll) get drunk

beschä'digen *tr* damage || *ref* injure oneself

beschaf'fen *adj*—**ich bin eben so b.** that's the way I am; **übel b. sein** be in bad shape || *tr* get, procure; *(Geld)* raise

Beschaf'fenheit *f* (-;-en) quality, property; *(Zustand)* state; *(Art)* nature; *(Anlage)* design

Beschaf'fung *f* (-;-en) procuring; *(Erwerb)* acquisition

beschäftigen [bə'ʃeftɪgən] *tr* occupy; keep busy; *(anstellen)* employ; **beschäftigt sein bei** work for *(a company)*; **beschäftigt sein mit** be busy with

beschä/men *tr* shame, make ashamed; beschämt sein be ashamed

Beschau/ *f* inspection

beschau/en *tr* look at; inspect

beschau/lich *adj* contemplative

Bescheid [bə'ʃaɪt] *m* (-[e]s;-e) answer; (*Anweisung*) instructions, directions; (*Auskunft*) information; (jur) decision; **B. hinterlassen** bei leave word with; **B. wissen** be well-informed; **j-m B. geben** (or **sagen**) give s.o. information or directions

beschei/den *adj* modest; (*Preise*) moderate; (*Auswahl*) limited; (*einfach*) simple, plain || §112 *tr* inform; (*beordern*) order, direct; (*vorladen*) summon; (*zuteilen*) allot; **abschlägig b.** turn down; **es ist mir beschieden** it fell to my lot || *ref* be satisfied

Beschei/denheit *f* (-;) modesty

bescheinigen [bə'ʃaɪnɪgən] *tr* (*Empfang*) acknowledge; (*bezeugen*) certify

Beschei/nigung *f* (-;-en) acknowledgement; certification; (*Schein*) certificate; (*im Brief*) to whom it may concern

beschei/ßen §53 *tr* (sl) cheat

beschen/ken *tr—j-n b.* mit present s.o. with

bescheren [bə'ʃerən] *tr* give gifts to

Besche/rung *f* (-;-en) distribution of gifts (*especially at Christmas*); **e-e schöne B.** (coll) a nice mess

beschicken (beschik/ken) *tr* (*mit Waren*) supply; (*Messe*) exhibit at, send exhibits to; (*Kongreß*) send delegates to; (*Hochofen*) feed, charge

beschie/ßen §76 *tr* shoot up; (mil, phys) bombard

beschimp/fen *tr* insult, call (*s.o.*) names

beschir/men *tr* shield, protect

beschla/fen *tr* (*e-e Frau*) sleep with; (*e-e Sache*) sleep on

Beschlag/ *m* (-s;-̈e) hardware; (*Huf-*) horse shoes; (*auf Fensterscheiben*) steam, vapor; (*Überzug*) thin coating; **in B. nehmen** confiscate; (*Schiff*) seize; (*Gehalt*) attach

beschla/gen *adj—b.* **in** (*dat*) well-versed in || §132 *tr* cover, coat; (*Metallverzierungen*) fit, mount; (*Pferd*) shoe || *ref* & *intr* steam up; (*Mauer*) sweat; (*Metall*) oxidize

beschlagnahmen [bə'ʃlaknamən] *tr* confiscate; (*Schuldnervermögen*) attach; (mil) requisition; (naut) seize

beschlei/chen §85 *tr* stalk, creep up on

beschleunigen [bə'ʃlɔɪnɪgən] *tr* accelerate, speed up

Beschleu/niger *m* (-s;-) accelerator

beschlie/ßen §76 *tr* end, wind up; (*sich entschließen*) decide

Beschluß/ *m* conclusion; decision; resolution; (jur) order; **unter B.** under lock and key; **zum B.** in conclusion

beschluß/fähig *adj—b.* **sein** have a quorum; **beschlußfähige Anzahl** quorum

beschmie/ren *tr* smear, coat; grease

beschmut/zen *tr* soil, dirty

beschnei/den §106 *tr* clip, trim; (fig) curtail; (surg) circumcise

beschneit [bə'ʃnaɪt] *adj* snow-covered

beschönigen [bə'ʃønɪgən] *tr* (*Fehler*) whitewash, cover up, gloss over

beschrän/ken *tr* limit

beschränkt/ *adj* limited; (*Verhältnisse*) straitened; (*geistig*) dense

beschrei/ben §62 *tr* describe; use up (*in writing*)

Beschrei/bung *f* (-;-en) description

beschrei/ten §86 *tr* walk on; **den Rechtsweg b.** take legal action

beschriften [bə'ʃrɪftən] *tr* inscribe; (*Kisten*) mark; (*mit Etikett*) label

Beschrif/tung *f* (-;-en) inscription; lettering; (*erläuternde*) caption

beschuldigen [bə'ʃuldɪgən] *tr* (*genit*) accuse (of), charge (with)

beschummeln [bə'ʃuməln] *tr* (coll) (**um**) cheat (out of)

Beschuß/ *m* test firing

beschüt/zen *tr* protect, defend

beschwat/zen *tr* gossip about; **j-n dazu b. zu** (*inf*) talk s.o. into (*ger*)

Beschwerde [bə'ʃverdə] *f* (-;-n) trouble; (*Klage, Krankheit*) complaint

beschweren [bə'ʃverən] *tr* burden || *ref* (**über** *acc*) complain (about)

beschwer/lich *adj* troublesome

beschwichtigen [bə'ʃvɪçtɪgən] *tr* appease; (*Hunger*) satisfy; (*Gewissen*) soothe

beschwin/deln *tr* (**um**) swindle (out of)

beschwingt [bə'ʃvɪŋt] *adj* lively

beschwipst [bə'ʃvɪpst] *adj* tipsy, high

beschwö/ren *tr* swear to; (*Geister*) conjure up; (*bitten*) implore, entreat

Beschwö/rungsformel *f* incantation

beseelen [bə'zelən] *tr* inspire, animate

beseelt/ *adj* animated; (*von Hoffnungen*) filled; (*Spiel*) inspired

bese/hen §138 *tr* look at; inspect

beseitigen [bə'zaɪtɪgən] *tr* eliminate, remove, clear away; (*Übel, Fehler*) redress; (*Schwierigkeit*) overcome; (*töten*) do away with; (pol) purge

Besen [ˈbezən] *m* (-s;-) broom

Be/senstiel *m* broomstick

besessen [bə'zesən] *adj* (**von**) obsessed (by); (*vom Teufel*) possessed

Beses/senheit *f* (-;-en) obsession; (*vom Teufel*) possession

beset/zen *tr* occupy; (*mit Juwelen*) set off; (*Amt, Rolle*) fill; (*Hut*) trim

besetzt/ *adj* (*Platz, Abort*) occupied; (*Stelle*) filled; (*Kleid*) trimmed, set off; (telp) busy

Besetzt/zeichen *n* (telp) busy signal

Beset/zung *f* (-;-en) decoration; (*e-r Stelle*) filling; (mil) occupation; (theat) cast

besichtigen [bə'zɪçtɪgən] *tr* view; tour; inspect; (mil) inspect, review

Besich/tigung *f* (-;-en) sightseeing; inspection; (mil) inspection, review

besie/deln *tr* colonize; populate

besie/geln *tr* seal

besie/gen *tr* defeat; (*Widerstand*) overcome; (*Gefühle*) master

besin/nen §121 *ref* consider; (auf *acc*) think (of); **sich anders b.** change one's mind; **sich e-s Besseren b.** think better of it

besinn'lich *adj* reflective

Besin'nung *f* (-;) consciousness; reflection; **j-n zur B. bringen** bring s.o. to his senses

besin'nungslos *adj* unconscious; (*unüberlegt*) senseless

Besitz' *m* (-es;-e) possession; **in B. nehmen** take possession of

bestiz'anzeigend *adj* possessive

besit'zen §144 *tr* own, possess

Besit'zer -in §6 *mf* possessor, owner

Besitz'ergreifung *f* (-;-en) occupancy; seizure

Besitz'stand *m* ownership; (fin) assets

Besitztum [bə'zɪtstum] *n* (-s;-er) possession

Besit'zung *f* (-;-en) possession, property; (*Landgut*) estate

besoffen [bə'zɔfən] *adj* (coll) soused

besohlen [bə'zolən] *tr* sole

besolden [bə'zoldən] *tr* pay

Besol'dung *f* (-;-en) pay, salary

beson'dere §9 *adj* particular, special

Beson'derheit *f* (-;-en) peculiarity; (com) specialty

beson'ders *adv* especially; separately

besonnen [bə'zɔnən] *adj* prudent; (*bedacht*) considerate; level-headed

besor'gen *tr* take care of; (*beschaffen*) procure, get; (*befürchten*) fear

Besorgnis [bə'zɔrknɪs] *f* (-;-se) concern; (*Furcht*) fear

besorg'niserregend *adj* alarming

besorgt [bə'zɔrkt] *adj* (um) worried (about), anxious (for)

Besor'gung *f* (-;-en) care; procurement; (*Auftrag*) errand; **Besorgungen machen** run errands

bespre'chen §64 *tr* discuss; (*Buch*) review; **e-e Schallplatte b.** make a recording || *ref* confer

Bespre'cher -in §6 *mf* reviewer, critic

bespren'gen *tr* sprinkle

besprit'zen *tr* splash; spray

besser ['bɛsər] *adj & adv* better

bessern ['bɛsərn] *tr* better, improve || *ref* improve

Bes'serung *f* (-;-en) improvement; **baldige B.** speedy recovery

Bes'serungsanstalt *f* reform school

Bestand' *m* (-[e]s;-e) existence; (*Vorrat*) stock, inventory; (*Kassen-*) cash on hand; (*Baum-*) stand; **B. an** (*dat*) number of; **B. an kampffähigen Truppen** effective strength; **B. haben, von B. sein** have endurance, be lasting

bestän'dig *adj* constant, steady

Bestands'aufnahme *f* inventory

Bestand'teil *m* component; ingredient

bestär'ken *tr* strengthen, fortify

bestätigen [bə'ʃtɛtɪgən] *tr* confirm; (*Zeugnis*) corroborate; (*Empfang*) acknowledge; (*Vertrag*) ratify || *ref* prove true, come true

bestatten [bə'ʃtatən] *tr* bury, inter

Bestat'tungsinstitut *n* funeral home

bestau'ben, bestäuben (bə'ʃtɔrbən) *tr* cover with dust; sprinkle; (bot) pollinate

beste ['bɛstə] §9 *adj* best; **am besten**

best (of all); auf dem besten Weg sein zu be well on the way to; **aufs b. in** the best way; **der erste b.** anybody

beste'chen §64 *tr* bribe; (fig) impress

beste'chend *adj* fascinating, charming

bestech'lich *adj* open to bribery

Beste'chung *f* (-;) bribery

Beste'chungsgeld *n* bribe

Besteck [bə'ʃtɛk] *n* (-[e]s;-e) kit; (*Tisch-*) single service; (aer, naut) reckoning, position; (med) set of instruments

bestecken (bestek'ken) *tr* stick; (culin) garnish

beste'hen §146 *tr* undergo; (*Prüfung*) pass || *intr* exist, be; (*gegen*) hold one's own (against); (*in e-r Prüfung*) pass; **b. auf** (*dat*) insist on; **b. aus** consist of; **b. in** (*dat*) consist in

beste'hend *adj* existing, extant; present

besteh'len §147 *tr* (um) rob (of)

bestei'gen §148 *tr* climb; (*Schiff*) board; (*Pferd*) mount; (*Thron*) ascend

Bestell'buch *n* order book

bestel'len *tr* order; (*Zimmer*) reserve; (*Zeitung*) subscribe to; (*ernennen*) appoint; (*Briefe*) deliver; (*Feld*) till; (*kommen lassen*) send for

Bestell'zettel *m* order slip

be'stenfalls *adv* at best

besteu'ern *tr* tax

bestialisch [bɛstɪ'jalɪʃ] *adj* beastly

Bestie ['bɛstjə] *f* (-;-n) beast

bestim'men *tr* determine; (*Zeit, Preis*) set; (*ernennen*) appoint; (*Begriff*) define; (gram) modify; (math) find; **j-n b. zu** (or **für**) destine s.o. for; talk s.o. into || *intr* decree; **b. in** (*dat*) have a say in; **b. über** (*acc*) dispose of

bestimmt' *adj* determined; definite; particular || *adv* definitely

Bestim'mung *f* (-;-en) determination; (*e-r Zeit, e-s Preises*) setting; destination; mission, goal; (*e-s Begriffs*) definition; (*Schicksal*) fate; (*Vorschrift*) regulation; (*e-s Vertrags*) provision; (gram) modifier; **mit B. nach** (naut) heading for; **seiner B. übergeben** dedicate, open

bestra'fen *tr* punish

bestrah'len *tr* irradiate; (med) give radiation treatment to

bestre'ben *ref* strive, endeavor || **Bestreben** *n* (-s;) tendency

Bestre'bung *f* (-;-en) effort

bestrei'chen §85 *tr* spread; (*mit Feuer*) rake; **mit Butter b.** butter

bestrei'ken *tr* strike

bestrei'ten §86 *tr* contest; fight; (*Ausgaben*) defray; (*Recht*) challenge; (*leugnen*) deny; **e-e Unterhaltung allein b.** do all the talking

bestreu'en *tr* (mit) strew (with)

bestricken (bestrik'ken) *tr* (fig) charm

bestücken [bə'ʃtykən] *tr* arm, equip

bestür'men *tr* storm; (fig) bombard

bestür'zen *tr* dismay

Besuch [bə'zux] *m* (-[e]s;-e) visit; (*Besucher*) visitor(s), company;

(*genit*) visit (to); **auf B. gehen** pay a visit

besu′chen *tr* visit; (*Gasthaus, usw.*) frequent; (*Schule, Versammlung*) attend; (*Kino*) go to

Besu′cher –in §6 *mf* visitor, caller

Besuchs′zeit *f* visiting hours

besudeln *tr* soil, stain

betagt [bə′takt] *adj* advanced in years

beta′sten *tr* finger, touch, handle

betätigen [bə′tɛtɪgən] *tr* set in operation; (*Maschine*) operate; (*Bremse*) apply || *ref*—**sich nützlich b.** make oneself useful; **sich politisch b.** be active in politics

betäuben [bə′tɔɪbən] *tr* deafen; stun; (*Schmerz*) deaden; (*durch Rauschgift*) drug, dope; (med) anesthetize

Betäu′bungsmittel *n* drug; painkiller; (med) anesthetic

Bete [′betə] *f* (–;–n) beet

beteiligen [bə′taɪlɪgən] *tr* (**an** *dat*, **bei**) give (*s.o.*) a share (in) || *ref* (**an** *dat*) participate (in)

Betei′ligung *f* (–;–en) participation; (*Teilhaberschaft*) partnership; (*Teilnehmerzahl*) attendance

beten [′betən] *tr & intr* pray

beteuern [bə′tɔɪ-ərn] *tr* affirm

betiteln [bə′titəln] *tr* entitle

Beton [be′tɔn] *m* (–s;) concrete

betonen [bə′tonən] *tr* (*Silbe*) stress, accent; (*nachdrücklich*) emphasize

betonieren [bətoˈnirən] *tr* cement

Betonmisch′maschine *f* cement mixer

betören [bə′tørən] *tr* infatuate

Betracht′ *m* (–[e]s;) consideration; **außer B. lassen** rule out; **es kommt nicht in B.** it is out of the question; **in B. ziehen** take into account, consider

betrachten [bə′traxtən] *tr* look at; consider

beträchtlich [bə′trɛçtlɪç] *adj* considerable

Betrach′tung *f* (–;–en) observation; consideration; meditation; **Betrachtungen anstellen über** (*acc*) reflect on

Betrag [bə′trak] *m* (–[e]s;–̈e) amount; **über den B. von** in the amount of

betra′gen §132 *tr* amount to || *ref* behave || **Betragen** *n* (–s;) behavior

betrau′en *tr* entrust

betrau′ern *tr* mourn for

Betreff [bə′trɛf] *m* (–[e]s;) (*am Briefanfang*) re; **in B.** (*genit*) in regard to

betref′fen §151 *tr* befall; (*berühren*) affect, hit; (*angehen*) concern; **betrifft** (*acc*) re; **was das betrifft as far that is concerned; was mich betrifft** I for one

betreffs [bə′trɛfs] *prep* (*genit*) concerning

betrei′ben §62 *tr* carry on; (*leiten*) manage; (*Beruf*) practice; (*Studien*) pursue; (*Maschine*) operate

betre′ten *adj* embarrassed || §152 *tr* step on; set foot on or in; (*Raum*) enter; (*unbefugt*) trespass on

betreuen [bə′trɔɪ-ən] *tr* look after

Betrieb [bə′trip] *m* (–s;–e) operation,

running; (*Unternehmen*) business; (*Anlage*) plant; (*Werkstatt*) workshop; (fig) rush, bustle; **aus dem B. ziehen** take out of service; **außer B.** out of order; **großer B.** hustle and bustle; **in vollem B.** in full swing

betriebsam [bə′tripzam] *adj* enterprising, active

Betrieb′samkeit *f* (–;) hustle

betriebs′fähig *adj* in working order

betriebs′fertig *adj* ready for use

Betriebs′ingenieur *m* production engineer

Betriebs′kosten *pl* operating costs

Betriebs′leiter *m* superintendent

Betriebs′material *n* (rr) rolling stock

Betriebs′prüfer –in §6 *mf* auditor

Betriebs′ruhe *f*—**heute B.** (public sign) closed today

Betriebs′stoff *m* fuel

Betriebs′störung *f* breakdown

Betriebs′wirtschaft *f* industrial management

betrin′ken §143 *ref* get drunk

betroffen [bə′trɔfən] *adj* shocked, stunned; (*heimgesucht*) afflicted

betrü′ben *tr* sadden, distress

betrüb′lich *adj* sad, distressing

betrübt [bə′trypt] *adj* sad, sorrowful

Betrug [bə′truk] *m* (–[e]s;) fraud, swindle; **frommer B.** white lie

betrü′gen §111 *tr* cheat, swindle

Betrügerei [bətrygəˈraɪ] *f* (–;–en) deceit, cheating

betrü′gerisch *adj* deceitful; fraudulent

betrunken [bə′trʊŋkən] *adj* drunk

Bett [bɛt] *n* (–[e]s;–en) bed

Bett′decke *f* bedspread

Bettelei [bɛtə′laɪ] *f* (–;) begging

betteln [′bɛtəln] *intr* (**um**) beg (for)

betten [′bɛtən] *tr* put to bed || *ref* **make onself a bed; bed down**

Bett′genosse *m* bedfellow

Bett′gestell *n* bedstead

Bett′himmel *m* canopy (*over a bed*)

bettlägerig [′bɛtlɛgərɪç] *adj* bedridden

Bett′laken *n* bed sheet

Bettler –in [′bɛtlər(ɪn)] §6 *mf* beggar

Bett′stelle *f* bedstead

Bettuch (**Bett′tuch**) *n* sheet

Bet′tung *f* (–;) bedding; (mil) emplacement; (rr) bed

Bett′vorleger *m* bedside rug

Bett′wäsche *f* bed linen

Bett′zeug *n* bedding

betupfen [bə′tʊpfən] *tr* dab (at); (surg) swab

beugen [′bɔɪgən] *tr* bend; (fig) humble; (gram) inflect || *ref* bend; bow

Beu′gung *f* (–;–en) bending; bowing; (gram) inflection

Beule [′bɔɪlə] *f* (–;–n) lump; (*Geschwür*) boil; (*kleiner Blechschaden*) dent

beunruhigen [bə′unru·ɪgən] *tr* make uneasy, worry, disturb

Beun′ruhigung *f* (–;–en) anxiety, uneasiness; disturbance

beurkunden [bə′urkʊndən] *tr* authenticate

beurlauben [bə′urlaubən] *tr* grant leave of absence to; (*vom Amt*) suspend; (mil) furlough; **sich b. lassen**

ask for time off || *ref* **(bei)** take one's leave (of)

beur′teilen *tr* evaluate; **(nach)** judge (by); **falsch b.** misjudge

Beute ['bɔɪtə] *f* (–;) booty, loot; **zur B. fallen** (*dat*) fall prey to

Beutel ['bɔɪtəl] *m* (–s;–) bag, pouch; purse; (billiards) pocket

beu′telig *adj* baggy

Beu′tezug *m* raid

bevölkern [bə'fœlkərn] *tr* populate

Bevöl′kerung *f* (–;–en) population

bevollmächtigen [bə'fɔlmɛçtɪgən] *tr* authorize; (jur) give (*s.o.*) power of attorney

Bevoll′mächtigte §5 *mf* authorized agent; proxy; (pol) plenipotentiary

bevor [bə'for] *conj* before; **bevor ... nicht** until

bevormunden [bə'formundən] *tr* treat in a patronizing manner

bevor′raten *tr* stock; stockpile

bevorrechtet [bə'fɔrrɛçtət] *adj* privileged

bevor′stehen §146 *intr* be imminent, be on hand; **bevorstehend** forthcoming; **j–m b.** be in store for s.o.

bevorzugen [bə'fortsugən] *tr* prefer

bevor′zugt *adj* preferential; high-priority; privileged; favorite

bewa′chen *tr* guard, watch over

bewach′sen §155 *tr* overgrow, cover

Bewa′chung *f* (–;–en) guard, custody

bewaff′nen *tr* arm

Bewaff′nung *f* (–;) armament, arms

Bewahr′anstalt *f* detention home

bewah′ren *tr* keep, preserve; **(vor** *dat)* save (from), protect (against)

bewäh′ren *tr* prove || *ref* prove one's worth; **sich nicht b.** prove a failure

Bewah′rer –in §6 *mf* keeper

bewahrheiten [bə'varhaɪtən] *tr* verify || *ref* come true

bewährt [bə'vert] *adj* tried, trustworthy

Bewah′rung *f* (–;) preservation

Bewäh′rung *f* (–;–en) testing, trial; (jur) probation

Bewäh′rungsfrist *f* (jur) probation; **j–m B. zubilligen** put s.o. on probation

Bewäh′rungsprobe *f* test

bewaldet [bə'valdət] *adj* woody

bewältigen [bə'vɛltɪgən] *tr* (*Hindernis*) overcome; (*Lehrstoff*) master

bewandert [bə'vandərt] *adj* experienced

Bewandtnis [bə'vantnɪs] *f* (–;) circumstances, situation

bewäs′sern *tr* water, irrigate

bewegen [bə'vegən] *tr* move, stir || *ref* move, stir; (*von der Stelle*) budge; (*Temperatur*) vary; (*exerzieren*) take exercise; (astr) revolve || §56 *tr* prompt, induce

Beweg′grund *m* motive; incentive

beweg′lich *adj* movable; (*behend*) agile; (*Geist*) versatile; (*Zunge*) glib

Beweg′lichkeit *f* (–;) mobility; agility; versatility

bewegt [bə'vekt] *adj* agitated; (*ergreifend*) stirring; (*Stimme*) trembling; (*Unterhaltung*) lively; (*Leben*) eventful; (*unruhig*) turbulent

Bewe′gung *f* (–;–en) movement; motion; move; (*Gebärde*) gesture; (fig) emotion; **in B. setzen** set in motion

Bewe′gungsfreiheit *f* room to move; (fig) leeway, freedom of action

bewe′gungslos *adj* motionless

beweh′ren *tr* arm; (*Beton*) reinforce

beweihräuchern [bə'vaɪrɔɪçərn] *tr* (fig) flatter; (eccl) incense

bewei′nen *tr* mourn, shed tears over

Beweis [bə'vaɪs] *m* (–es;–e) **(für)** proof (of), evidence (of)

beweisen [be'vaɪzən] §118 *tr* prove, demonstrate; (*bestätigen*) substantiate

Beweis′führung *f* argumentation

Beweis′grund *m* argument

Beweis′kraft *f* cogency, force

beweis′kräftig *adj* convincing

Beweis′last *f* burden of proof

Beweis′stück *n* exhibit

bewen′den *intr*—**es dabei b. lassen** leave it at that || **Bewenden** *n*—**damit hat es sein B.** there the matter rests

bewer′ben §149 *ref*—**sich b. um** apply for; (*kandidieren*) run for; (*Vertrag*) bid for; (*Preis*) compete for; (*Frau*) court

Bewer′ber –in §6 *mf* applicant; candidate; bidder; competitor || *m* suitor

Bewer′bungsformular *n* application form

Bewer′bungsschreiben *n* written application

bewer′fen §160 *tr* pelt; (*Mauer*) plaster

bewerkstelligen [bə'verkʃtelɪgən] *tr* manage, bring off

bewer′ten *tr* (auf *acc*) value (at), appraise (at); **b. mit fünf Punkten** give five points to (*e.g., a performance*); **zu hoch b.** overrate

Bewer′tung *f* (–;–en) valuation

bewilligen [bə'vɪlɪgən] *tr* approve, grant

Bewil′ligung *f* (–;–en) approval; permit

bewillkommnen [bə'vɪlkɔmnən] *tr* welcome

bewir′ken *tr* cause, occasion, effect

bewir′ten *tr* entertain

bewirt′schaften *tr* (*Acker*) cultivate; (*Betrieb*) manage; (*Mangelware*) ration

Bewir′tung *f* (–;) hospitality

bewitzeln [bə'vɪtsəln] *tr* poke fun at

bewog [bə'vok] *pret* of **bewegen**

bewogen [bə'vogən] *pp* of **bewegen**

bewoh′nen *tr* inhabit, occupy

Bewoh′ner –in §6 *mf* (*e–s Landes*) inhabitant; (*e–s Hauses*) occupant

bewölken [bə'vœlkən] *tr* cloud || *ref* cloud over, get cloudy

bewölkt′ *adj* cloudy, overcast

Bewöl′kung *f* (–;) clouds

bewun′dern *tr* admire

bewun′dernswert, bewun′dernswürdig *adj* admirable

bewußt [bə'vust] *adj* conscious; **die bewußte Sache** the matter in question

bewußt′los *adj* unconscious

Bewußt′sein *n* consciousness; **bei B. sein** be conscious

Bewußt′seinsspaltung *f* schizophrenia

bezah′len *tr* pay; (*Gekauftes*) pay for

Bezah'lung *f* (-;-en) payment; (*Lohn*) pay

bezäh'men *tr* tame; (fig) control

bezau'bern *tr* bewitch; (fig) fascinate

bezeich'nen *tr* (*zeichnen*) mark; (*bedeuten*) signify; (*benennen*) designate; (*kennzeichnen*) characterize; (*zeigen*) point out

bezeich'nend *adj* characteristic

Bezeich'nung *f* (-;-en) marking, mark; (*Name*) name; (*Ausdruck*) term

bezei'gen *tr* show, manifest, express

bezeu'gen *tr* attest; (jur) testify to

bezichtigen [bə'tsɪçtɪgən] *tr* accuse

bezieh'bar *adj* (*Ware*) obtainable; (*Wohnung*) ready for occupancy; (auf *acc*) referable (to)

bezie'hen §163 *tr* (*Polstermöbel*) cover; (*Wohnung*) move into; (*Universität*) go to; (*geliefert bekommen*) get; (*Gehalt*) draw; (auf *acc*) relate (to), refer (to); **das Bett frisch b.** change the bed linens; **die Stellung b.** (mil) occupy the position; **die Wache b.** (mil) go on guard duty || *ref* become overcast; **sich auf j-n b.** use s.o.'s name as a reference

Bezie'hung *f* (-;-en) relation, connection, respect; **in B. auf** (*acc*) in respect to; **in guten Beziehungen stehen zu** be on good terms with

bezie'hungslos *adj* unrelated; irrelevant

Bezie'hungssatz *m* relative clause

bezie'hungsweise *adv* respectively

Bezie'hungswort *n* [-[e]s; ̈er] (gram) antecedent

beziffern [bə'tsɪfərn] *tr* (auf *acc*) estimate (at) || *ref*—**sich b. auf** (*acc*) amount to, number

Bezirk [bə'tsɪrk] *m* (-s;-e) district, ward, precinct; (*Bereich*) sphere

Bezug' *m* (-[e]s; ̈e) cover, case; (von *Waren*) purchase; (von *Zeitungen*) subscription; (*Auftrag*) order; **Bezüge** earnings; **B. nehmen auf** (*acc*) refer to; **in B. auf** (*acc*) in reference to

bezüglich [bə'tsyklɪç] *adj* (auf *acc*) relative (to); **bezügliches Fürwort** relative pronoun || *prep* (*genit*) concerning, as to, with regard to

Bezugnahme [bə'tsuknɑmə] *f*—**unter B. auf** (*acc*) with reference to

Bezugs'anweisung *f* delivery order

bezugs'berechtigt *adj* entitled to receive || **Bezugsberechtigte** §5 *mf* (ins) beneficiary

bezwecken [bə'tsvɛkən] *tr* aim at, have in mind; (mit) intend (by)

bezwei'feln *tr* doubt, question

bezwin'gen §142 *tr* conquer; (fig) control, master

Bibel ['bibəl] *f* (-;-n) Bible

Bi'belforscher **-in** §6 *mf* Jehovah's Witness

Biber ['bibər] *m* (-s;-) beaver

Bibliothek [bɪblɪ.ə'tek] *f* (-;-en) library

Bibliothekar **-in** [bɪblɪ.ətɛ'kar(ɪn)] §8 *mf* librarian

biblisch ['biblɪʃ] *adj* biblical

bieder ['bidər] *adj* honest; (*leichtgläubig*) gullible

Bie'dermann *m* (-[e]s; ̈er) honest man

biegen ['bigən] §57 *tr* bend; (gram) inflect || *ref*—**sich vor Lachen b.** double up with laughter || *intr* (SEIN) bend; **um die Ecke b.** go around the corner

biegsam ['bikzam] *adj* flexible

Bie'gung *f* (-;-en) bend, bending; (gram) inflection

Biene ['binə] *f* (-;-n) bee

Bie'nenfleiß *m*—**mit B. arbeiten** work like a bee

Bie'nenhaus *n* beehive

Bie'nenkorb *m* beehive

Bie'nenstich *m* bee sting; (culin) almond pastry

Bie'nenstock *m* beehive

Bie'nenzucht *f* beekeeping

Bier [bir] *n* (-[e]s;-e) beer

bie'ten ['bitən] §58 *tr* offer; **b. auf** (*acc*) bid for || *ref* present itself; **das läßt er sich nicht b.** he won't stand for it

Bigamie [bɪga'mi] *f* (-;) bigamy

bigott [bɪ'gɔt] *adj* bigoted

Bigotterie [bɪgɔtə'ri] *f* (-;) bigotry

Bilanz [bɪ'lants] *f* (*acct*) balance; (acct) balance sheet

Bilanz'abteilung *f* auditing department

bilanzieren [bɪlan'tsirən] *intr* balance

Bild [bɪlt] *n* (-es;-er) picture; image; (*Bildnis*) portrait; (in *e-m Buch*) illustration; (*Vorstellung*) idea; (rhet) metaphor, figure of speech; **im Bilde sein** be in the know

Bild'band *m* (-[e]s; ̈e) picture book || *n* (-[e]s; ̈er) (telv) video tape

Bild'bandgerät *n* video tape recorder

Bild'betrachter *m* slide viewer

Bildchen ['bɪltçən] *n* (-s;-) small picture; (cin) frame

Bild'einstellung *f* (-;-en) focusing

bilden ['bɪldən] *tr* form, fashion, create; (*entwerfen*) design; (*gründen*) establish; (*Geist*) educate, develop; (*Gruppe*) constitute || *ref* form, be produced; develop; educate oneself

bil'dend *adj* instructive; **bildende Künste** fine arts, plastic arts

bil'derreich *adj* (*Buch*) richly illustrated; (*Sprache*) picturesque, ornate

Bil'derschrift *f* picture writing

Bil'dersprache *f* imagery

Bil'derstürmer *m* iconoclast

Bild'frequenz *f* camera speed

Bild'funk *m* television

bild'haft *adj* pictorial; graphic

Bildhauer ['bɪlthau.ər] *m* (-s;-) sculptor

Bildhauerei ['bɪlthau.əraɪ] *f* (-;) sculpture

Bildhauerin ['bɪlthau.ərɪn] *f* (-;-nen) sculptress

bild'hübsch *adj* pretty as a picture

Bild'karte *f* photographic map; (cards) face card

bild'lich *adj* pictorial; figurative

Bildner **-in** ['bɪldnər(ɪn)] §6 *mf* sculptor || *m* (fig) molder || *f* sculptress

Bildnis ['bɪltnɪs] *n* (-ses;-se) portrait

Bild'röhre *f* picture tube, TV tube

bildsam ['bɪltzam] *adj* plastic; (fig) pliant

Bild'säule f statue
Bild'schirm m television screen
bild'schön adj very beautiful
Bild'schriftzeichen n hieroglyph
Bild'seite f head, obverse
Bild'signal n video signal
Bild'stock m wayside shrine
Bild'streifen m filmstrip; (journ) comic strip
Bild'sucher m (phot) viewfinder
Bild'teppich m tapestry
Bild'ton'kamera f sound-film camera
Bil'dung f (-;-en) formation; shape; education, culture
Bil'dungsanstalt f educational institution
Bild'werfer m projector
Bild'werk n sculpture; imagery
Billard ['bɪljart] n (-s;) billiards
Bil'lardkugel f billiard ball
Bil'lardloch n pocket
Bil'lardstab, Bil'lardstock m cue
Billett [bɪl'jet] n (-s;-e) ticket
Billett'ausgabe f, **Billett'schalter** m ticket office; (theat) box office
billig ['bɪlɪç] adj cheap; (Preis) low; (Ausrede, Trost) poor
billigen ['bɪlɪgən] tr approve
Bil'ligung f (-;) approval
Billion [bɪl'jon] f (-;-en) trillion; (Brit) billion
bimbam ['bɪm'bam] interj ding-dong || **Bimbam** m—heiliger B.! holy smokes!
bimmeln ['bɪməln] intr (coll) jingle; (telp) ring
Bimsstein ['bɪms/taɪn] m (-s;-e) pumice stone
Binde ['bɪndə] f (-;-n) band; (Krawatte) tie; (Armschlinge) sling; (für Frauen) sanitary napkin; (med) bandage
Bin'deglied n link; (fig) bond, tie
binden ['bɪndən] §59 tr bind, tie
Bin'destrich m hyphen; mit B. schreiben hyphenate
Bin'dewort n (-[e]s;≃er) conjunction
Bind'faden m string, twine; es regnet Bindfäden it's raining cats and dogs
Bin'dung f (-;-en) binding; tie, bond, obligation; (mus) ligature
binnen ['bɪnən] prep (genit & dat) within; b. kurzem before long
Binnen— comb.fm. inner; internal; inland; domestic, home
Bin'nengewässer n inland water
Bin'nenhandel m domestic trade
Bin'nenland n inland; interior; im B. inland
Binse ['bɪnzə] f (-;-n) rush, reed; in die Binsen gehen (coll) go to pot
Bin'senwahrheit f truism
Biochemie [bɪˌoçe'mi] f (-;) biochemistry
Biogra·phie [bɪˌogra'fi] (-;-phien ['fi·ən] biography
biographisch [bɪˌo'grafɪʃ] adj biographic(al)
Biologie [bɪˌolo'gi] f (-;) biology
biologisch [bɪˌo'logɪ] adj biological
Biophysik [bɪˌofy'zik] f (-;) biophysics
Birke ['bɪrkə] f (-;-n) birch
Birma ['bɪrma] n (-s;) Burma

Birne ['bɪrnə] f (-;-n) pear; (elec) bulb; (Kopf) (sl) bean
bis [bɪs] prep (acc) (zeitlich) till, until; (örtlich) up to, to; bis an (acc) up to; bis auf (acc) except for; bis nach as far as || conj until, till
Bisamratte ['bizamratə] f (-;-n) muskrat
Bischof ['bɪʃof] m (-;≃e) bishop
bischöflich ['bɪʃøflɪç] adj episcopal
Bi'schofsamt n episcopate
Bi'schofsmütze f miter
Bi'schofssitz m episcopal see
Bi'schofsstab m crosier
bisher [bɪs'her] adv till now
bisherig [bɪs'herɪç] adj former, previous; (Präsident) outgoing
Biskuit [bɪs'kvit] m & n (-[e]s;-e) biscuit
bislang' adv till now
biß [bɪs] pret of beißen || **Biß** m (Bisses; Bisse) bite; sting
bißchen ['bɪsçən] n (also used as invar adj & adv) bit, little bit
Bissen ['bɪsən] m (-s;-) bit, morsel
bissig ['bɪsɪç] adj biting, snappish
Bistum ['bɪstum] n (-s;≃er) bishopric
bisweilen [bɪs'vaɪlən] adv sometimes
Bitte ['bɪtə] f (-;-n) request; e-e B. einlegen bei intercede with
bitten ['bɪtən] §60 tr ask || intr b. für intercede for; b. um ask for; wie bitte? I beg your pardon? || interj please!; you are welcome!
bitter ['bɪtər] adj bitter
bit'terböse adj (coll) furious
Bit'terkeit f (-;) bitterness
bit'terlich adv bitterly; deeply
Bit'tersalz n Epsom salts
Bittgang ['bɪtgaŋ] m (-[e]s;≃e) (eccl) procession
Bittsteller ['bɪt/telər] m (-s;-) petitioner, suppliant
Biwak ['bivak] n (-s;-s) bivouac
biwakieren [bɪva'kirən] intr bivouac
bizarr [bɪ'tsar] adj bizarre
blähen ['ble·ən] tr inflate, distend || ref swell || intr cause gas
blaken ['blakən] intr smolder
Blamage [bla'maʒə] f (-;-n) disgrace
blamieren [bla'mirən] tr embarrass || ref make a fool of oneself
blank [blaŋk] adj bright; (Schuh) shiny; (bloß) bare; (Schwert) drawn; (sl) broke; blanke Waffe side arms; b. ziehen draw one's sword
Blankett [blaŋ'ket] n (-s;-e) blank
blanko ['blaŋko] adv—b. lassen leave blank; b. verkaufen sell short
Blan'koscheck m blank check
Blan'kovollmacht f blanket authority
Blank'vers m blank verse
Bläschen ['blesçən] n (-s;-) small blister; small bubble
Blase ['blazə] f (-;-n) blister; bubble; (coll) gang; (anat) bladder; Blasen werfen (Farbe) blister; Blasen ziehen (Haut) blister
Bla'sebalg m pair of bellows
blasen ['blazən] tr blow; (Instrument) play || intr blow
Bla'senleiden n bladder trouble
Bläser ['blezər] m (-s;-) blower

blasiert [bla'zirt] *adj* blasé

blasig ['blazıç] *adj* blistery; bubbly

Blas'instrument *n* wind instrument

Blasphe·mie [blasfe'mi] *f* (-;-mien ['mi·ən]) blasphemy

blasphemieren [blasfe'mirən] *intr* blaspheme

Blas'rohr *n* blowpipe; peashooter

blaß [blas] *adj* pale; **keine blasse Ahnung** not the foggiest notion

Blässe ['blesə] *f* (-;) paleness, pallor

Blatt [blat] *n* (-s;ᵉer) leaf; (*Papier-*) sheet; (*Gras-*) blade

Blatter ['blatər] *f* (-;-n) pustule; **die Blattern** smallpox

blätterig ['bletərıç] *adj* leafy; scaly

blättern ['bletərn] *intr*—**in e-m Buch b.** page through a book

Blat'ternarbe *f* pockmark

Blät'terwerk *n* foliage

Blatt'gold *n* gold leaf, gold foil

Blatt'laus *f* aphid

Blatt'pflanze *f* house plant

blättrig ['bletrıç] *adj var of* blätterig

Blatt'zinn *n* tin foil

blau [blau] *adj* (& *fig*) blue; (*coll*) drunk; **blaues Auge** black eye; **keinen blauen Dunst haben** (coll) not have the foggiest notion; **mit e-m blauen Auge davonkommen** (coll) get off easy ‖ **Blau** *n* (-s;-s) blue; blueness

blau'äugig *adj* blue-eyed

Blau'beere *f* blueberry

Bläue ['blɔɪ·ə] *f* (-;) blue; blueness

bläuen ['blɔɪ·ən] *tr* dye blue

bläulich ['blɔɪlıç] *adj* bluish

blau'machen *intr* (coll) take off from work

Blech [bleç] *n* (-[e]s;-e) sheet metal; (sl) baloney; (mus) brass

Blech'büchse *f* tin can

blechen ['bleçən] *tr* (coll) pay out ‖ *intr* (coll) cough up the dough

Blech'instrument *n* brass instrument

blecken ['blekən] *tr*—**die Zähnen b.** bare one's teeth

Blei [blaɪ] *n* (-[e]s;) lead

Bleibe ['blaɪbə] *f* (-;-n) place to stay

bleiben ['blaɪbən] §62 *intr* (SEIN) remain, stay; **am Leben b.** survive; **bei etw b.** stick to s.th.; **dabei bleibt es!** that's final!; **für sich b.** keep to oneself; **sich** [*dat*] **gleich b.** never change; **und wo bleibe ich?** (coll) and where do I come in?

blei'bend *adj* lasting, permanent

bleich [blaɪç] *adj* pale ‖ **Bleiche** *f* (-;) bleaching; paleness

blei'chen *tr* bleach; make pale ‖ *intr* (SEIN) bleach; (*verblassen*) fade

Bleich'gesicht *n* paleface

Bleich'mittel *n* bleach

bleiern ['blaɪ·ərn] *adj* leaden

Blei'soldat *m* tin soldier

Blei'stift *m* pencil

Bleistiftspitzer ['blaɪʃtɪftʃpɪtsər] *m* (-s;-) pencil sharpener

Blende ['blendə] *f* (-;-n) window blind; shutter; (phot) diaphragm

blen'den *tr* blind; (*bezaubern*) dazzle

blen'dend *adj* fabulous

Blen'der *m* (-s;-) (coll) fourflusher

Blendling ['blentlıŋ] *m* (-s;-e) (*Mischling*) mongrel; (bot) hybrid

Blick [blɪk] *m* (-[e]s;-e) glance, look; (*auf acc*) view (of)

blicken [blɪk'kən] *intr* (**auf** *acc*, **nach**) glance (at), look (at); **sich b. lassen** show one's face

Blick'fang *m* (coll) eye catcher

blieb [blip] *pret of* bleiben

blies [blis] *pret of* blasen

blind [blɪnt] *adj* (**für, gegen**) blind (to); (*Spiegel*) clouded; (*trübe*) dull; (*Alarm*) false; (*Patrone*) blank; **blinder Passagier** stowaway

Blind'band *m* (-[e]s;ᵉe) (typ) dummy

Blind'boden *m* subfloor

Blind'darm *m* appendix

Blind'darmentzündung *f* appendicitis

Blind'darmoperation *f* appendectomy

Blin'denheim *n* home for the blind

Blin'denhund *m* Seeing-Eye dog

Blin'denschrift *f* braille

Blind'flug *m* blind flying

Blind'gänger *m* (mil) dud

Blind'landung *f* instrument landing

blindlings ['blɪntlıŋs] *adv* blindly

Blind'schreiben *n* touch typing

blinken ['blɪŋkən] *intr* blink, twinkle; (*Sonne*) shine; (mil) signal

Blin'ker *m*, **Blink'licht** *n* (aut) blinker

blinzeln ['blɪntsəln] *intr* blink, wink

Blitz [blɪts] *m* (-es;-e) lightning; (fig & phot) flash

Blitz'ableiter *m* lightning rod

blitz'blank *adj* shining; spick and span

Blitz'krieg *m* blitzkrieg

Blitz'licht *n* (phot) flash

Blitz'lichtaufnahme *f* (phot) flash shot

Blitz'lichtbirne *f* (phot) flash bulb

Blitz'lichtgerät *n* flash gun

Blitz'lichtröhre *f* (phot) electronic flash, flash tube

Blitz'schlag *m* stroke of lightning

blitz'schnell *adj* quick as lightning

Blitz'strahl *m* flash of lightning

Block [blɔk] *m* (-s;ᵉe) block, log; (*Stück Seife*) cake; (*von Schokolade*) bar; (*von Löschpapier*) pad; (geol) boulder; (metal) ingot; (pol) bloc

Blockade [blɔ'kadə] *f* (-;-n) blockade

Blocka'debrecher *m* blockade runner

blocken (blok/ken) *tr* (sport) block

Block'haus *n* log cabin

blockieren [blɔ'kirən] *tr* block up; (mil) blockade

Block'kalender *m* tear-off calendar

Block'schrift *f* block letters

blöd(e) ['blød(ə)] *adj* stupid, idiotic; feeble-minded; (*schüchtern*) shy

Blöd'heit *f* (-;) stupidity, idiocy

Blö'digkeit *f* (-;) shyness

Blöd'sinn *m* idiocy; nonsense

blöd'sinnig *adj* idiotic ‖ *adv* idiotically; (*sehr*) (coll) awfully

blöken ['bløkən] *intr* bleat; (*Kuh*) moo

blond [blɔnt] *adj* blond, fair ‖ **Blonde** §5 *m* blond ‖ *f* blonde

blondieren [blɔn'dirən] *tr* bleach

Blondine [blɔn'dinə] *f* (-;-n) blonde

bloß [blos] *adj* bare; (*nichts als*) mere ‖ *adv* only; barely

Blöße ['bløsə] *f* bareness; nakedness; (fig) weak point

bloß'legen *tr* lay bare
bloß'stellen *tr* expose
blühen ['blyːən] *intr* blossom, bloom; (*Backen*) be rosy; (fig) flourish
Blume ['bluːmə] *f* (-;-n) flower; (*des Weins*) bouquet; (*des Biers*) head
Blu'menbeet *n* flower bed
Blu'menblatt *n* petal
Blu'mengewinde *n* garland, festoon
Blu'menhändler –in §6 *mf* florist
Blu'menkelch *m* calyx
Blu'menkohl *m* cauliflower
Blu'menstaub *m* pollen
Blu'mentopf *m* flowerpot
Bluse ['bluːzə] *f* (-;-n) blouse
Blut [bluːt] *n* (-[e]s) blood; **bis aufs B.** almost to death; **B. lecken** taste blood; **heißes B.** hot temper
Blut'andrang *m* (pathol) congestion
blut'arm *adj* anemic
Blut'armut *f* anemia
Blut'bahn *f* bloodstream
Blut'bild *n* blood count
blut'dürstig *adj* bloodthirsty
Blüte ['blyːtə] *f* (-;-n) blossom, flower, bloom; (fig) prime
Blut'egel *m* leech
bluten ['bluːtən] *intr* bleed
Blü'tenblatt *n* petal
Blü'tenstaub *m* pollen
Blu'terguß *m* bruise
Blu'terkrankheit *f* hemophilia
Blü'tezeit *f* blooming period; (fig) heyday
Blut'farbstoff *m* hemoglobin
Blut'gerinnsel *n* blood clot
Blut'hund *m* bloodhound
blutig ['bluːtɪç] *adj* bloody
blut'jung *adj* very young, green
Blut'körperchen *n* corpuscle
Blut'kreislauf *m* blood circulation
blut'leer, blut'los *adj* bloodless
Blut'pfropfen *m* blood clot
Blut'probe *f* blood test
Blut'rache *f* blood feud
Blut'rausch *m* mania to kill
blutrünstig ['bluːtrʏnstɪç] *adj* gory
Blut'sauger *m* bloodsucker, leech
Blut'schande *f* incest
blutschänderisch ['bluːtʃɛndərɪʃ] *adj* incestuous
Blut'spender –in §6 *mf* blood donor
blut'stillend *adj* coagulant
Blut'sturz *m* hemorrhage
Bluts'verwandte §5 *mf* blood relation
Blut'übertragung *f* blood transfusion
blut'unterlaufen *adj* bloodshot
Blut'vergießen *n* (-s) bloodshed
blut'voll *adj* lively, vivid
Blut'wasser *n* lymph
Blut'zeuge *m*, **Blut'zeugin** *f* martyr
Bö [bøː] *f* (-;-en) gust, squall
Bob [bɔb] *m* (-s;-s) bobsled
Bock [bɔk] *m* (-[e]s; ⸚e) buck; ram; he-goat; (*Kutsch-*) driver's seat; (tech) horse; **B. springen** play leapfrog; **e-n B. schießen** pull a boner
bockbeinig ['bɔkbaɪnɪç] *adj* stubborn
bocken ['bɔkən] *intr* buck; (*sich aufbäumen*) rear; (*ausschlagen*) kick; (*brunsten*) be in heat; (aut) hesitate
bockig ['bɔkɪç] *adj* thickheaded
Bock'sprung *m* caper; leapfrog

Boden ['boːdən] *m* (-s;⸚) (*Erd-*) ground, soil; (*Meeres-*) bottom; (*Fuß-*) floor; (*Dach-*) attic; (*Trocken-*) loft; **B. fassen** get a firm footing; **zu B. drücken** crush
Bo'denertrag *m* (agr) yield
Bo'denfenster *n* dormer window
Bo'denfläche *f* floor space; (agr) acreage
Bo'denfliese *f* floor tile
Bodenfräse ['boːdənfrɛːzə] *f* (-;-n) Rotortiller
Bo'denhaftung *f* roadability
Bo'denkammer *f* attic
bo'denlos *adj* bottomless; (fig) unmitigated
Bo'denmannschaft *f* (aer) ground crew
Bo'denreform *f* agrarian reform
Bo'densatz *m* grounds, sediment
Bodenschätze ['boːdənʃɛtsə] *pl* mineral resources
Bo'densee *m* (-s) Lake Constance
bo'denständig *adj* native, indigenous
bog [boːk] *pret* of biegen
Bogen ['boːgən] *m* (-s;⸚) bow; (*Kurve*) curve; (*Papier-*) sheet; (*beim Schilaufen*) turn; (*beim Eislaufen*) circle; (archit) arch; (math) arc; **den B. raushaben** have the hang of it; **den B. überspannen** (fig) go too far; **e-n großen B. um j-n machen** give s.o. wide berth
Bo'genfenster *n* bow window
bo'genförmig *adj* arched
Bo'gengang *m* arcade; archway
Bo'genschießen *n* (-s) archery
Bo'genschütze *m* archer
Bo'gensehne *f* bowstring
Bohle ['boːlə] *f* (-;-n) plank
Böhme ['bøːmə] *m* (-n;-n) Bohemian
Böhmen ['bøːmən] *n* (-s) Bohemia
Bohne ['boːnə] *f* (-;-n) bean; **blaue Bohnen** bullets; **grüne Bohnen** string beans
Boh'nermasse *f* polish; floor polish
bohnern ['boːnərn] *tr* wax, polish
Boh'nerwachs *n* floor wax
Bohr- [boːr] *comb.fm.* drill, drilling, bore, boring
bohren ['boːrən] *tr* drill, bore
Bohrer *m* (-s;-) drill; (ent) borer
Bohr'insel *f* offshore drilling platform
Bohr'presse *f* drill press
Bohr'turm *m* derrick
bög ['bøːɪç] *adj* gusty; (aer) bumpy
Boje ['boːjə] *f* (-;-n) buoy
Böller ['bœlər] *m* (-s;-) mortar
böllern ['bœlərn] *intr* fire a mortar
Bollwerk ['bɔlvɛrk] *n* (-s;-e) bulwark
Bolzen ['bɔltsən] *m* (-s;-) bolt; dowel
Bombardement [bɔmbardəˈmãː] *n* (-s; -s) bombardment
bombardieren [bɔmbarˈdiːrən] *tr* bombard
Bombe ['bɔmbə] *f* (-;-n) bomb, bombshell; (coll) smash hit
Bomben- *comb.fm.* bomb, bombing; huge
Bom'benabwurf *m* bombing; **gezielter B.** precision bombing
Bom'benerfolg *m* (theat) smash hit
bom'benfest *adj* bombproof
Bom'benflugzeug *m* bomber

Bom'bengeschäft n (coll) gold mine
Bom'benpunktzielwurf m precision bombing
Bom'benreihenwurf m stick bombing
Bom'bensache f (coll) humdinger
Bom'benschacht m bomb bay
Bom'benschütze m bombardier
Bom'bentrichter m bomb crater
Bom'benzielanflug m bombing run
Bom'benzielgerät n bombsight
Bon [bõ] m (-s;-s) sales slip; (*Gut-schein*) credit note
Bonbon [bõ'bõ] m & n (-s;-s) piece of candy; **Bonbons** candy
Bonbonniere [bõbɔnɪ'erə] f (-;-n) box of candy
Bonze ['bɔntsə] m (-;-n) (coll) big shot, bigwig; (pol) boss
Boot [bot] n (-[e]s;-e) boat
Boots'mann m (-es;-leute) boatswain; (nav) petty officer
Bord [bɔrt] m (-es;e) edge; bookshelf; (naut) board, side; **an B.** aboard, on board; **von B. gehen** leave the ship
Bordell [bɔr'dɛl] n (-s;-e) brothel
Bord'karte f boarding pass
Bord'schütze m aerial gunner
Bord'schwelle f curb
Bord'stein m curb
Bord'waffen pl (aer, mil) armament
Bord'wand f ship's side
Borg [bɔrk] m (-s;) borrowing; **auf B.** on credit; on loan
borgen ['bɔrgən] tr (**von, bei**) borrow (from); loan out, lend
Borke ['bɔrkə] f (-;-n) bark
Born [bɔrn] m (-es; -e) (poet) fountain
borniert [bɔr'nirt] adj narrow-minded
Borsäure ['bɔrzɔɪrə] f (-;) boric acid
Börse ['bœrzə] f (-;-n) purse; stock exchange
Bör'senkurs m market price; quotation
Bör'senmakler –in ['bør'senmaklɐ] §6 mf stockbroker
Bör'senmarkt m stockmarket
Bör'sennotierung f (st.exch.) quotation
Bör'senpapiere pl stocks, shares, securities
Borste ['bɔrstə] f (-;-n) bristle
borstig ['bɔrstɪç] adj birstly; (fig) crusty
Borte ['bɔrtə] f (-;-n) trim; braid; (*Saum*) hem
bös [bøs] var of **böse**
bös'artig adj nasty; (*Tier*) vicious; (pathol) malignant
Böschung ['bœʃʊŋ] f (-;-en) slope; (*e-s Flusses*) bank; (rr) embankment
böse ['bøzə] adj bad, evil, nasty; angry || **Böse** §5 mf wicked person || m devil || n evil; harm
Bösewicht ['bøzəvɪçt] m (-s;-e) villain
boshaft ['boshaft] adj malicious; wicked; (*tückisch*) spiteful
bossieren [bɔ'sirən] tr emboss
bös'willig adj malicious, willful
bot [bot] pret of **bieten**
Botanik [bo'tanɪk] f (-;) botany
Botaniker –in §6 mf botanist
botanisch [bo'tanɪʃ] adj botanic(al)
Bote ['botə] m (-n;-n) messenger
Bo'tengang m errand
Botin ['botɪn] f (-;-nen) messenger

Bot'schaft f (-;-en) message, news; (*Amt*) embassy; (*Auftrag*) mission
Botschafter –in ['bot/aftɐr(ɪn)] §6 ambassador
Bottich ['bɔtɪç] m (-s;-e) tub; vat
Bouillon [bul'jõ] f (-;-s) bouillon
Bowle ['bolə] f (-;-n) punch
boxen ['bɔksən] tr & intr box
Bo'xer m (-s;-) boxer
Box'kampf m boxing match
Boykott [bɔɪ'kɔt] m (-s;-e) boycott
boykottieren [bɔɪko'tirən] tr boycott
brach [brax] pret of **brechen** || adj fallow
brachte ['braxtə] pret of **bringen**
brackig ['brakɪç] adj brackish
Branche ['brɑ̃ʃə] f (-;-n) line of business; (com) branch
Brand [brant] m (-[e]s;ːe) burning; fire; (coll) thirst; (agr) blight; (pathol) gangrene; **in B. geraten** catch fire; **in B. setzen** (or **stecken**) set on fire
Brand'blase f blister
Brand'bombe f incendiary bomb
Brand'brief m urgent letter
Brand'direktor m fire chief
branden ['brandən] intr surge, break
Brand'fackel f firebrand
brandig ['brandɪç] adj (agr) blighted; (pathol) gangrenous
Brand'mal n brand; (fig) moral stigma
brand'marken tr stigmatize
Brand'mauer f fire wall
brandschatzen ['brant/atsən] tr sack
Brand'stifter –in §6 mf arsonist
Bran'dung f (-;) breakers
Bran'dungswelle f breaker
Brand'wunde f burn
Brand'zeichen n brand
brannte ['brantə] pret of **brennen**
Branntwein ['brantvaɪn] m brandy
Brasilien [bra'ziljən] n (-s;) Brazil
Bratapfel ['bratapfəl] m baked apple
braten ['bratən] §63 tr & intr roast; (*im Ofen*) bake; (*auf dem Rost*) broil, grill; (*in der Pfanne*) fry || **Braten** m (-s;-) roast
Bra'tensoße f gravy
Brat'fisch m fried fish
Brat'huhn n broiler
Brat'kartoffeln pl fried potatoes
Brat'pfanne f frying pan, skillet
Bratsche ['brat/ə] f (-;-n) viola
Bräu [brɔɪ] m & n (-[e]s;) brew
Brauch [braux] m (-[e]s;ːe) custom
brauchbar ['brauxbar] adj useful
brauchen ['brauxən] tr need; (*Zeit*) take; (*gebrauchen*) use
Brauchtum ['brauxtum] n (-s;) tradition
Braue ['brau·ə] f (-;-n) eyebrow
brauen ['brau·ən] tr brew
Brau'er m (-s;-) brewer
Brauerei [brau·ə'raɪ] f (-;-en), **Brau'-haus** n brewery
braun [braun] adj brown; (*Pferd*) bay
Bräune ['brɔɪnə] f (-;) brown; sun tan; (pathol) diphtheria
bräunen ['brɔɪnən] tr tan; (culin) brown || ref & intr tan
bräunlich ['brɔɪnlɪç] adj brownish
Braus [braus] m (-es;) noise; revelry

Brause ['braʊzə] f (-;-n) soda, soft drink; (*Duschbad*) shower; (*an Gießkannen*) nozzle
Brau'sebad n shower
Brau'sekopf m hothead
Brau'selimonade f soda, soft drink
brau'sen tr spray, water || intr bubble; (*toben*) roar || intr (SEIN) rush
Braut [braʊt] f (-;ᵕe) fiancée; bride
Braut'ausstattung f trousseau
Braut'führer m usher
Bräutigam ['brɔɪtɪgam] m (-s;-e) fiancé; bridegroom
Braut'jungfer f (-;-n) bridesmaid; erste B. maid of honor
Braut'kleid n bridal gown
Braut'leute pl engaged couple
bräutlich ['brɔɪtlɪç] adj bridal; nuptial
Braut'schatz m dowry
Braut'werber –in §6 mf matchmaker
Braut'werbung f courting
Braut'zeit f period of engagement
Braut'zeuge m best man
brav [braf] adj well-mannered, good, honest
Brav'heit f good behavior
Bravour [bra'vʊr] f (-;) bravado
Brech'eisen n crowbar, jimmy
brechen ['brɛçən] §64 tr break; (*Papier*) fold; (*Steine*) quarry; (*Blumen*) pick; (coll) vomit; (opt) refract; die Ehe b. commit adultery || ref break; (opt) be refracted || intr (SEIN) break; (coll) vomit
Brech'reiz m nausea
Brech'stange f crowbar
Bre'chung f (-;-en) (opt) refraction
Brei [braɪ] m (-s;-e) paste; pap, gruel; zu B. schlagen beat to a pulp
breit [braɪt] adj broad, wide
breitbeinig ['braɪtbaɪnɪç] adv with legs outspread
breit'drücken tr flatten (out)
Brei'te f (-;-n) width; latitude
Brei'tengrad m degree of latitude
breit'machen ref take up (too much) room; (fig) throw one's weight around
breit'schlagen §132 tr (coll) persuade
breitschulterig ['braɪtʃʊltərɪç] adj broad-shouldered
breitspurig ['braɪtʃpʊrɪç] adj (coll) pompous; (rr) broad-gauge
breit'treten §152 tr belabor
Breit'wand f (cin) wide screen
Bremsbelag ['brɛmsbəlak] m brake lining
Bremse ['brɛmzə] f (-;-n) brake; (ent) horsefly
bremsen ['brɛmzən] tr brake; (fig) curb; (atom phys) slow down || intr brake
Brem'ser m (-s;-) brakeman
Brems'flüssigkeit f brake fluid
Brems'fußhebel m brake pedal
Brems'klotz m wheel chock
Bremsleuchte ['brɛmslɔɪçtə] f, **Brems'licht** n (aut) brake light
Brems'rakete f (rok) retrorocket
Brems'schuh m brake shoe
brems'sicher adj skidproof
Brems'spur f skid mark
Brems'wagen m (rr) caboose

Brems'weg m braking distance
Brennapparat ['brɛnaparat] m still
brennbar ['brɛnbar] adj inflammable, combustible
brennen §97 tr burn; (*Branntwein*) distil; (*Kaffee*) roast; (*Haar*) curl; (*Ziegel*) fire || intr burn; smart
Bren'ner m (-s;-) burner; distiller
Brennerei [brɛnə'raɪ] f (-;-en) distillery
Brenn'holz n firewood
Brenn'material n fuel
Brenn'ofen m kiln
Brenn'punkt m focus; im B. stehen be the focal point
Brenn'schere f curler
Brenn'schluß m (rok) burnout
Brenn'spiegel m concave mirror
Brenn'stoff m fuel
brenzlig ['brɛntslɪç] adj (*Geruch*) burnt; (*Situation*) precarious
Bresche ['brɛʃə] f (-;-n) breach; e-e B. schlagen make a breach
Brett [brɛt] n (-[e]s;-er) board; plank; (*für Bücher, Geschirr*) shelf; Bretter (coll) skis; (theat) stage; Schwarzes B. bulletin board
Bret'terbude f shack
Bret'terverschlag m wooden partition
Brett'säge f ripsaw
Brezel ['bretsəl] f (-;-n) pretzel
Brief [brif] m (-[e]s;-e) letter; Briefe wechseln correspond
Brief'ausgabe f mail delivery
Brief'bestellung f mail delivery
Briefbeschwerer ['brifbəʃverər] m (-s;-) paperweight
Brief'beutel m mail bag
Brief'bogen m piece of notepaper
Brief'bote m mailman, postman
Briefchen ['brifçən] n (-s;-) note; B. Streichhölzer book of matches
Brief'einwurf m slot in a mailbox; letterdrop; mailbox
Brief'fach n pigeonhole; post-office box
Brief'freund –in §8 mf pen pal
Brief'hülle f envelope
Brief'kasten m mailbox
Brief'klammer f paper clip
Brief'kopf m letterhead
Brief'kurs m (st.exch.) selling price
brief'lich adj written; brieflicher Verkehr correspondence || adv by letter
Brief'mappe f folder
Brief'marke f postage stamp
Brief'markenautomat m stamp machine
Brief'ordner m ring binder
Brief'papier n stationery; note paper
Brief'porto n postage
Brief'post f first-class mail
Brief'schaften pl correspondence
Brief'stempel m postmark
Brief'tasche f billfold, wallet
Brief'taube f carrier pigeon
Brief'träger m mailman, postman
Brief'umschlag m envelope
Brief'verkehr m correspondence
Brief'waage f postage scales
Brief'wahl f absentee ballot
Brief'wechsel m correspondence
briet [brit] pret of braten

Brigade [brɪˈgɑdə] f (-;-n) brigade
Briga'degeneral m brigadier general; (Brit) brigadier
Brikett [brɪˈkɛt] n (-[e]s;-s) briquette
brillant [brɪlˈjant] adj brilliant || **Brillant** m (-en;-en) precious stone (esp. diamond)
Brille [ˈbrɪlə] f (-;-n) eyeglasses; (für Pferde) blinkers; (Toilettenring) toilet seat; **B. mit doppeltem Brennpunkt** bifocals
Bril'lenbügel m sidepiece (of glasses)
Bril'lenfassung f eyeglass frame
Bril'lenschlange f cobra
bringen [ˈbrɪŋən] §65 tr bring, take; **an sich b.** acquire; **es mit sich b., daß** bring it about that; **es zu etw b.** achieve s.th.; **etw hinter sich b.** get s.th. over and done with; **etw über sich** (or **übers Herz**) **b.** be able to bear s.th.; **j-n auf etw b.** put s.o. on to s.th.; **j-n außer sich b.** enrage s.o.; **j-n dazu b. zu** (inf) get s.o. to (inf); **j-m um etw b.** deprive s.o. of s.th.; **j-n zum Lachen b.** make s.o. laugh; **unter die Leute b.** circulate
brisant [brɪˈzant] adj high-explosive
Brise [ˈbrizə] f (-;-n) breeze
Britannien [brɪˈtanjən] n (-s;) Britain
Brite [ˈbrɪtə] m (-n;-n) Briton, Britisher; **die Briten** the British
Britin [ˈbrɪtɪn] f (-;-nen) Briton, British woman
britisch [ˈbrɪtɪʃ] adj British
Broché [brɔˈʃe] n (-s;) broché; brocaded fabric
Bröckchen [ˈbrœkçən] n (-s;-) bit; morsel, crumb; fragment
bröck(e)lig [ˈbrœk(ə)lɪç] adj crumbly
bröckeln [ˈbrœkəln] tr & intr crumble
brocken [ˈbrɔkən] tr—**Brot in die Suppe b.** break bread into the soup || **Brocken** m (-s;-) piece, bit; lump; **Brocken** pl scraps, bits and pieces; **harter B.** (coll) tough job
brockenweise (brok'kenweise) adv bit by bit
brodeln [ˈbrodəln] intr bubble, simmer
Brokat [brɔˈkat] m (-[e]s;-e) brocade
Brombeere [ˈbrɔmberə] f (-;-n) blackberry
Bromid [brɔˈmit] n (-[e]s;-e) bromide
Bronchitis [brɔnˈçitɪs] f (-;) bronchitis
Bronze [ˈbrõsə] f (-;-n) bronze
Brosche [ˈbrɔʃə] f (-;-n) brooch
broschieren [brɔˈʃirən] tr stitch; brocade; **broschiert** with stapled binding
Broschüre [brɔˈʃyrə] f (-;-n) brochure
Brösel [ˈbrøzəl] m (-s;-) crumb
Brot [brot] n (-[e]s;-e) bread; loaf; **geröstetes B.** toast
Brot'aufstrich m spread
Brötchen [ˈbrøtçən] n (-s;-) roll
Brot'erwerb m livelihood, living
Brot'geber m, **Brot'herr** m employer
Brot'kasten m breadbox
brot'los adj unemployed; unprofitable
Brot'neid m professional jealousy
Brot'röster m (-s;-) toaster
Brot'schnitte f slice of bread
Brot'studium n bread-and-butter courses
Brot'zeit f breakfast

Bruch [brux] m (-[e]s;ᵘe) breaking; break, crack; breakage; (aer) crash; (geol) fault; (math) fraction; (min) quarry; (pathol) hernia; (surg) fracture; **B. machen** crash-land; **in die Brüche gehen** go to pot; **zu B. gehen** break || [brux] m & n (-s;-e) bog
Bruch'band n (-s;ᵘer) (surg) truss
Bruch'bude f shanty
brüchig [ˈbryçɪç] adj fragile, brittle
Bruch'landung f crash landing
Bruch'rechnung f fractions
Bruch'stück n fragment, chip; **Bruchstücke** (fig) scraps, snatches
bruch'stückhaft adj fragmentary
Bruch'teil m fraction; **im B. e-r Sekunde** in a split second
Bruch'zahl f fractional number
Brücke [ˈbrykə] f (-s;-n) bridge; (Teppich) small (narrow) rug; (gym) backbend
Brückenkopf (Brük'kenkopf) m bridgehead
Brückenpfeiler (Brük'kenpfeiler) m pier of a bridge
Brückenwaage (Brük'kenwaage) f platform scale
Brückenzoll (Brük'kenzoll) m bridge toll
Bruder [ˈbrudər] m (-sᵘ) brother; (Genosse) companion; (eccl) lay brother
brüderlich [ˈbrydərlɪç] adj brotherly
Brüderschaft [ˈbrydərʃaft] f (-;-en) brotherhood; fraternity
Brühe [ˈbryə] f (-;-n) broth; (Fleisch-) gravy; **in der B. stecken** be in a jam
brühen [ˈbryən] tr boil; scald
brüh'heiß adj piping hot
Brüh'kartoffeln pl potatoes boiled in broth
Brüh'würfel m bouillon cube
brüllen [ˈbrylən] tr & intr roar, bellow; (Sturm) howl; (Ochse) low; **b. vor Lachen** roar with laughter
Brummbär [ˈbrumber] m (-en;-en) grouch
brummen [ˈbrumən] tr mumble; grumble; growl || intr mumble; grumble; growl; (summen) buzz, hum; (Orgel) boom; (im Gefängnis) do time, do a stretch
brummig [ˈbrumɪç] adj grouchy
brünett [bryˈnet] adj brunet(te) || **Brünette** §5 brunette
Brunft [brunft] f (-;) rut
Brunft'zeit f rutting season
Brunnen [ˈbrunən] m (-s;-) well; (Spring-) spring
Brunnenkresse [ˈbrunənkresə] f (-;-n) watercress
Brunst [brunst] f (-;) rut, heat; (fig) ardor, passion
brunsten [ˈbrunstən] intr be in heat
brünstig [ˈbrynstɪç] adj in heat; (fig) passionate
brüsk [brusk] adj brusque
brüskieren [brusˈkirən] tr snub
Brust [brust] f (-;ᵘe) breast, chest
Brust'bein n breastbone, sternum
Brust'bild n portrait; (sculp) bust
brüsten [ˈbrystən] ref show off

Brust′fellentzündung *f* pleurisy
Brust′kasten *m*, Brust′korb *m* thorax
Brust′schwimmen *n* breast stroke
Brust′stück *n* (culin) brisket
Brust′ton *m* —im B. der Überzeugung with utter conviction
Brust′umfang *m* chest measurement; (*bei Frauen*) bust measurement
Brü′stung *f* (-;-en) balustrade
Brust′warze *f* nipple
Brust′wehr *f* breastwork
Brut [brut] *f* (-;-en) brood; (pej) scum
brutal [bru′tal] *adj* brutal
Brut′apparat *m*, Brut′ofen *m* incubator
brüten [′brytən] *tr* hatch; (fig) plan ‖ *intr* incubate; b. auf (*dat*) (fig) sit on; b. über (*dat*) brood over; pore over
brutto [′bruto] *adj* (com) gross
Brut′tosozialprodukt *n* gross national product
Bube [′bubə] *m* (-n;-n) boy; (*Schurke*) rascal; (cards) jack
Bu′benstreich *m*, Bu′benstück *n* prank; dirty trick
bübisch [′bybɪʃ] *adj* rascally
Buch [bux] *n* (-[e]s;⁼er) book; (cards) straight
Buch′besprechung *f* book review
Buchbinderei [′buxbindərar] *f* (-;-en) bookbindery; (*Gewerbe*) bookbinding
Buch′binderleinwand *f* buckram
Buch′deckel *m* book cover
Buch′drama *n* closet drama
Buch′druck *m* printing, typography
Buch′drucker *m* printer
Buch′druckerei *f* print shop; (*Gewerbe*) printing
Buche [′buxə] *f* (-;-n) beech
Buchecker [′buxekər] *f* (-;-n) beechnut
buchen [′buxən] *tr* book, reserve; (com) enter
Bücher- [byçər] *comb.fm.* book
Bü′cherabschluß *m* balancing of books
Bücherausgabe *f* circulation desk
Bü′cherbrett *n* bookshelf
Bücherei [byçə′rar] *f* (-;-en) library
Bü′cherfreund *m* bibliophile
Bü′chergestell *n* bookrack, bookcase
Bü′cherregal *n* bookshelf; bookcase
Bü′cherrevision *f* audit
Bü′cherrevisor *m* auditor; accountant
Bü′cherschrank *m* bookcase
Bü′cherstütze *f* book end
Buch′führung *f* bookkeeping, accounting
Buch′halter -in §6 *mf* bookkeeper
Buch′haltung *f* bookkeeping; accounting department
Buch′händler -in §6 *mf* book dealer
Buch′handlung *f* bookstore
Büchlein [′byçlaɪn] *n* (-s;-) booklet
Buch′macher *m* bookmaker
Buch′prüfer -in §6 *mf* auditor
Buchsbaum [′buksbaum] *m* boxwood
Buchse [′buksə] *f* (-;-n) (mach) bushing
Büchse [′byksə] *f* (-;-n) box, case; (*Dose*) can; (*Gewehr*) rifle
Büch′senfleisch *n* canned meat

Büch′senöffner *m* can opener
Buchstabe [′bux/tabə] *m* (-n;-n) letter
buchstabieren [bux/ta′birən] *tr & intr* spell
buchstäblich [′bux/tepliç] *adj* literal
Bucht [buxt] *f* (-;-en) bay
Buch′umschlag *m* book jacket
Bu′chung *f* (-;-en) booking; (acct) entry
Buckel [′bukəl] *m* (-s;-) hump; (coll) back; B. haben be hunchback; e-n B. machen arch its back
buck(e)lig [′buk(ə)lıç] *adj* hunchbacked ‖ Buck(e)lige §5 *mf* hunchback
bücken [′bykən] *tr & ref* bow (down)
Bückling [′byklıŋ] *m* (-s;-e) bow
Bude [′budə] *f* (-;-n) booth, stall; (coll) shanty; (coll) hole in the wall
Budget [by′dʒe] *n* (-s;-s) budget
Büfett [by′fe], [by′fet] *n* (-s;-s) buffet, sideboard; counter; (*Schanktisch*) bar; kaltes B. cold buffet
Büffel [′byfəl] *m* (-s;-) buffalo
Büffelei [byfə′lar] *f* (-;-en) cramming
büffeln [′byfəln] *intr* (für) cram (for)
Bug [buk] *m* (-[e]s;-e) (aer) nose; (naut) bow; (zool) shoulder, withers
Bügel [′bygəl] *m* (-s;-) handle; (*Kleider-*) coat hanger; (*Steig-*) stirrup; (*e-r Säge*) frame
Bü′gelbrett *n* ironing board
Bü′geleisen *n* iron, flatiron
Bü′gelfalte *f* crease
bü′gelfrei *adj* drip-dry
bügeln [′bygəln] *tr* iron, press
Bü′gelsäge *f* hacksaw
bugsieren [buk′sirən] *tr* tow
Buhldirne [′buldırnə] *f* (-;-n) bawd
buhlen [′bulən] *intr* have an affair; um -s Gunst b. curry favor with s.o.
Bühne [′bynə] *f* (-;-n) stage; platform
Büh′nenanweisung *f* stage direction
Büh′nenaussprache *f* standard pronunciation
Büh′nenausstattung *f*, Büh′nenbild *n* set
Büh′nenbildner -in §6 *mf* stage designer
Büh′nendeutsch *n* standard German
Büh′nendichter -in §6 *mf* playwright
Büh′nendichtung *f* drama, play
Büh′nenkünstler *m* actor
Büh′nenkünstlerin *f* actress
Büh′nenleiter -in §6 *mf* stage manager
Büh′nenstück *n* play, stage play
buk [buk] *pret* of backen
Bukarest [′bukarest] *n* (-s) Bucharest
Bulette [bu′letə] *f* (-;-n) meatball
Bulgarien [bul′garjən] *n* (-s) Bulgaria
Bullauge [′bulaugə] *n* (-s;-en) porthole
Bulldogge [′buldogə] *f* (-;-n) bulldog
Bulle [′bulə] *m* (-n;-n) bull; brawny fellow; (sl) cop ‖ *f* (-;-n) (eccl) bull
bullern [′bulərn] *intr* bubble, boil; (*Feuer*) roar; (*Sturm*) rage
Bummel [′buməl] *m* (-s) stroll
Bummelei [bumə′lar] *f* (-;-en) dawdling; loafing; sloppiness
bummelig [′buməlıç] *adj* slow; sloppy
bummeln [′buməln] *intr* loaf; dawdle; (*Autos*) crawl ‖ *intr* (SEIN) stroll

Bum′melstreik m slowdown

Bum′melzug m (coll) slow train, local

Bummler [′bumlər] m (-s;-) loafer, bum; slowpoke; gadabout

Bums [bums] m (-es;-e) thud, thump, bang ‖ interj boom!; bang!

bumsen [′bumsən] intr thud, thump, bump; (sl) have intercourse

Bums′lokal n (coll) dive, joint

Bund [bunt] m (-[e]s;-ë) union, federation; (Schlüssel-) ring; (Rand an Hose) waistband; (Ehe-) bond; (mach) flange; (mus) fret; (pol) federal government; **im Bunde mit** with the cooperation of ‖ n (-[e]s;- & -e) bunch, bundle

Bündel [′byndəl] n (-s;-) bunch, bundle; (phys) beam

Bundes- comb.fm. federal

Bun′desgenosse m ally, confederate

Bun′desgerichtshof m federal supreme court

Bun′deslade f ark of the covenant

bun′desstaatlich adj state; federal

Bun′destag m lower house

bündig [′byndıç] adj binding; (überzeugend) convincing; (treffend) succint; **b. liegen be** flush

Bündnis [′byntnıs] n (-ses;-se) agreement, pact, alliance

Bunker [′buŋkər] m (-s;-) bin; (agr) silo; (aer) air-raid shelter; (mil) bunker; (nav) submarine pen

bunt [bunt] adj colored; (mehrfarbig) multicolored; (gefleckt) dappled; (gemischt) varied, motley; (Farbe) bright, gay; (Wiese) gay with flowers; **bunter Abend** variety show; **buntes Durcheinander** complete muddle

Bunt′metall n nonferrous metal

Bunt′stift m colored pencil, crayon

Bürde [′byrdə] f (-;-n) burden

Burg [burk] f (-;-en) fortress, stronghold; citadel; castle

Bürge [′byrgə] m (-;-n) bondsman, guarantor, surety; **B. sein für** (or als **B. haften für**) stand surety for (s.o.); vouch for (s.th.)

bürgen [′byrgən] intr—**b. für** put up bail for (s.o.); vouch for (s.th.)

Bürger -in [′byrgər(ın)] §6 mf citizen; member of the middle class; commoner

Bür′gerkrieg m civil war

bür′gerlich adj civic; civil; middleclass; (nicht überfeinert) plain

Bür′germeister m mayor

Bür′gerrecht n civil rights

Bür′gerschaft f (-;) citizens

Bür′gersteig m sidewalk

Bürgschaft [′byrk∫aft] f (-;-en) security, guarantee; (jur) bail; **gegen B. freilassen** release on bail

Büro [by′ro] n (-s;-s) office

Büro′angestellte §5 mf clerk

Büro′bedarf m office supplies

Büro′klammer f paper clip

Büro′kraft f office worker; **Bürokräfte** office personnel

Bürokrat [byrə′krat] m (-en;-en) bureaucrat

Bürokra·tie [byrokra′ti] f (-;-tien [′ti·ən]) bureaucracy; (fig) red tape

bürokratisch [byrə′kratı∫] adj bureaucratic

Bursch(e) [′bur∫(ə)] m (-[e]n;-[e]n) boy, fellow; (mil) orderly; **ein übler B.** a bad egg

burschikos [bur∫ı′kos] adj tomboyish; devil-may-care

Bürste [′byrstə] f (-;-n) brush; (coll) crewcut

bürsten [′byrstən] tr brush

Bürzel [′byrtsəl] m (-s;-) rump (of bird)

Bus [bus] m (-ses;-se) bus

Busch [bu∫] m (-es;-e) bush; forest

Büschel [′by∫əl] m & n clump, bunch, cluster; (Haar-) tuft; (elec) brush

Busch′holz n brushwood

buschig [′bu∫ıç] adj bushy; shaggy

Busch′klepper m bushwacker

Busch′messer n machete

Busch′werk n bushes, brush

Busen [′buzan] m (-s;-) bosom, breast; (Bucht) bay, gulf; (fig) bosom

Bussard [′busart] m (-s;-e) buzzard

Buße [′busə] f (-n;-n) penance; (Sühne) atonement; (Strafgeld) fine

büßen [′bysən] tr atone for, pay for

Büßer -in [′bysər(ın)] §6 mf penitent

Busserl [′busərl] n (-s;-n) kiss

buß′fertig adj repentant

Bussole [bu′solə] f (-;-n) compass

Büste [′bystə] f (-;-n) bust

Bü′stenhalter m brassière, bra

Bütte [′bytə] f (-;-n) tub; vat

Butter [′butər] f (-;) butter

But′terbrot n bread and butter

But′terdose f butter dish

But′termilch f buttermilk

buttern [′butərn] butter ‖ intr make butter

byzantinisch [bytsan′tini∫] adj Byzantine

Byzanz [by′tsants] n (-′;) Byzantium

bzw. abbr (beziehungsweise) respectively

C

C, c [tze] invar n C, c;(meteor) centigrade; (mus) C

Café [ka′fe] n (-s;-s) café; coffee shop

Camping [′kempıŋ] n (-s;-s) camping

Canaille [ka′naljə] f (-;-n) scoundrel

Cäsar [′tsezar] m (-s;) Caesar

Cellist -in [t∫e′lıst(ın)] §7 mf cellist

Cello [′t∫elo] n (-s;-s) cello

Cellophan [tselo′fan] n (-s;) cellophane

Celsius [′tselzjus] centigrade

Cembalo [′t∫embalo] n (-s;-s) harpsichord

Ces [tses] n (-;-) (mus) C flat

Champagner [ʃamˈpanjər] *m* (-s;-) champagne

Champignon [ˈʃampɪnjɔ̃] *m* (-s;-s) mushroom

Chance [ˈʃɑ̃sə] *f* (-;-n) chance

Chaos [ˈkaːɔs] *n* (-;) chaos

chaotisch [kaˈoːtɪʃ] *adj* chaotic

Charak·ter [kaˈraktər] *m* (-s;-tere [ˈterə]) character; (mil) honorary rank

Charak'terbild *n* character sketch

Charak'tereigenschaft *f* trait

charak'terfest *adj* of a strong character

charakterisieren [karaktɛrɪˈziːrən] *tr* characterize

Charakteristik [karakteˈrɪstɪk] *f* (-;-en) characterization

Charakteristi·kum [karakteˈrɪstɪkum] *n* (-s;-ka [ka]) characteristic

charakteristisch [karakteˈrɪstɪʃ] *adj* (für) characteristic (of)

charak'terlich *adj* of character || *adv* in character

charak'terlos *adj* wishy-washy

Charak'terzug *m* characteristic, trait

Charge [ˈʃarʒə] *f* (-;-n) (metal) charge; (mil) rank; Chargen (mil) non-coms

charmant [ʃarˈmant] *adj* charming

Charme [ʃarm] *m* (-s;) charm, grace

Chas·sis [ʃaˈsi] *n* (-sis [ˈsi[s]]; -sis [ˈsis]) chassis

Chaus·see [ʃoˈse] *f* (-;-seen [ˈseːən]) highway

Chef [ʃɛf] *m* (-s;-s) chief, head; (com) boss; (culin) chef; C. des Generalstabs chief of staff; C. des Heeresjustizwesens judge advocate general

Chemie [çeˈmiː] *f* (-;) chemistry; technische C. chemical engineering

Chemie'faser *f* synthetic fiber

Chemikalien [çemɪˈkaljən] *pl* chemicals

Chemiker –in [ˈçemɪkər(ɪn)] §6 *mf* chemist; student of chemistry

chemisch [ˈçemɪʃ] *adj* chemical; chemische Reinigung dry cleaning

Chemotechniker –in [çemoˈtɛçnɪkər(ɪn)] §6 *mf* chemical engineer

Chiffre [ˈʃɪfər] *f* (-;-n) cipher; code; (in Anzeigen) box number

Chif'freschrift *f* code

chiffrieren [ʃɪˈfriːrən] *tr* code

China [ˈçina] *n* (-s;) China

Chinese [çiˈnezə] *m* (-n;-n;), Chinesin [çiˈnezɪn] *f* (-;-nen) Chinese

chinesisch [çiˈnezɪʃ] *adj* Chinese

Chinin [çiˈnin] *n* (-s;) quinine

Chirurg [çiˈrurg] *m* (-en;-en) surgeon

Chirurgie [çirurˈgiː] *f* (-;) surgery

chirurgisch [çiˈrurgɪʃ] *adj* surgical

Chlor [klor] *n* (-s;) chlorine

chloren [ˈkloːrən] *tr* chlorinate

Chlorid [kloˈrit] *n* (-[e]s;-e) chloride

Chloroform [kloroˈform] *n* (-s;) chloroform

chloroformieren [kloroforˈmiːrən] *tr* chloroform

Cholera [ˈkolera] *f* (-;) cholera

cholerisch [koˈleriːʃ] *adj* choleric

Chor [kor] *m* (-s;ⁱⁱe) choir; chorus

Choral [koˈral] *m* (-s;ⁱⁱe) Gregorian chant; (Prot) hymn

Chor'altar *m* high altar

Chor'anlage *f* (archit) choir

Chor'bühne *f* choir loft

Choreograph –in [koreˈoˈɡraf(ɪn)] §7 *mf* choreographer

Chor'hemd *n* surplice

Chor'stuhl *m* choir stall

Christ [krɪst] *m* (-s;) Christ || *m* (-en;-en) Christian

Christ'abend *m* Christmas Eve

Christ'baum *m* Christmas tree

Chri'stenheit *f* (-;) Christendom

Christentum [ˈkrɪstəntum] *n* (-s;) Christianity

Christin [ˈkrɪstɪn] *f* (-;-nen) Christian

Christ'kind *m* Christ child

christ'lich *adj* Christian

Christ'nacht *f* Holy Night

Chri·stus [ˈkrɪstus] *m* (-sti [sti];) Christ; nach Christi Geburt A.D.; vor Christus B.C.

Chri'stusbild *n* crucifix; picture of Christ

Chrom [krom] *n* (-s;) chromium, chrome

chromatisch [kroˈmatɪʃ] *adj* chromatic

Chromosom [kromoˈzom] *n* (-s;-en) chromosome

Chronik [ˈkronɪk] *f* (-;-en) chronicle

chronisch [ˈkronɪʃ] *adj* chronic

Chronist –in [kroˈnɪst(ɪn)] §7 *mf* chronicler

Chronolo·gie [kronoloˈgi] *f* (-;-gien [ˈɡi-ən]) chronology

chronologisch [kronoˈlogɪʃ] *adj* chronological

circa [ˈtsɪrka] *adv* approximately

Cis [tsɪs] *n* (-;-) (mus) C sharp

Clique [ˈklɪkə] *f* (-;-n) clique

Cocktail [ˈkɔktel] *m* (-s;-s) cocktail

Conferencier [kɔ̃feraˈsje] *m* (-s;-s) master of ceremony

Couch [kautʃ] *f* (-;-es) couch

Countdown [ˈkauntdaun] *m* (-s;-s) (rok) countdown

Couplet [kuˈple] *n* (-s;-s) song (in a musical)

Coupon [kuˈpɔ̃] *m* (-s;-s) coupon

Courage [kuˈraʒə] *f* (-;) courage

Courtage [kurˈtaʒə] *f* (-;-n) brokerage

Cousin [kuˈzɛ̃] *m* (-s;-s) cousin

Cousine [kuˈzinə] *f* (-;-n) cousin

Cowboy [ˈkaubɔi] *m* (-s;-s) cowboy

creme [krem] *adj* cream-colored || Creme [ˈkremə] *f* (-;) cream; custard

Crew [kru] *f* (-;) crew; (nav) cadets (of the same year)

Cut [kœt] *m* (-s;-s) cutaway

D

D, d [de] *invar n* D, d; (mus) D

da [da] *adv* there; then; in that case, **da und da** at such and such a place; **wieder da** back again ‖ *conj* since, because; when

dabei [da'baɪ] *adv* nearby; besides, moreover; at that; at the same time; (*trotzdem*) yet; **d. bleiben** stick to one's point; **d. sein** be present, take part; **d. sein zu** (*inf*) be on the point of (*ger*); **es ist nichts d.** there's nothing to it

da capo [da'kapo] *interj* encore!

Dach [dax] *n* (-[e]s;:er) roof; (fig) shelter; **unter D. und Fach** under cover

Dach′boden *m* attic

Dach′decker *m* roofer

Dach′fenster *n* dormer window; skylight

Dach′first *m* ridge of a roof

Dach′geschoß *n* top floor

Dach′gesellschaft *f* holding company

Dach′kammer *f* attic room

Dach′luke *f* skylight

Dach′organisation *f* parent company

Dach′pappe *f* roofing paper

Dach′pfanne *f* roof tile

Dach′rinne *f* rain gutter; eaves

Dach′röhre *f* downspout

Dachs [daks] *m* (-es;-e) badger; **ein frecher D.** a young whippersnapper

Dachs′hund *m* dachshund

Dach′sparren *m* rafter

Dach′stube *f* attic, garret

Dach′stuhl *m* roof framework

dachte ['daxtə] *pret* of **denken**

Dach′traufe *f* rain gutter

Dach′werk *n* roof

Dach′ziegel *m* roof tile

dadurch [da'durç] *adv* through it; thereby; by this means; **dadurch, daß** by (*ger*)

dafür [da'fyr] *adv* for it or them; in its place; that's why; therefore

Dafür′halten *n*—**nach meinem D.** in my opinion

dagegen [da'gegən] *adv* against it or them; in exchange for it or them; in comparison; on the other hand; **etw d. haben** have an objection; **ich bin d.** I'm against it

daheim [da'haɪm] *adv* at home

daher [da'her] *adv* from there; therefore; (bei Verben der Bewegung) along ‖ ['daher] *adv* that's why

dahin [da'hɪn] *adv* there, to that place; (*vergangen*) gone; (bei Verben der Bewegung) along; **bis d.** that far, up to there; until then; **es steht mir bis d.** I'm fed up with it

da′hinauf *adv* up there

da′hinaus *adv* out there

dahin′geben §80 *tr* give away; give up

dahin′gehen §82 *intr* (SEIN) walk along; pass; (*sterben*) pass away; **dahingehend, daß** to the effect that

dahingestellt [da'hɪngəʃtelt] *adj*—**d.**

sein lassen, ob leave the question open whether

dahin′leben *intr* exist from day to day

dahin′raffen *tr* carry off

dahin′scheiden §112 *intr* (SEIN) pass on

dahin′schwinden *intr* (SEIN) dwindle away; fade away; pine away

dahin′stehen §146 *impers*—**es steht dahin** it is uncertain

dahin′ten *adv* back there

dahin′ter *adv* behind it or them

dahinterher′ *adv*—**d. sein, daß** be insistent that

dahin′terkommen §99 *intr* (SEIN) find out about it; get behind the truth of it

dahin′tersetzen *tr* put (*s.o.*) to work on it

dahin′welken §113 *intr* (SEIN) fade away

dahin′ziehen §163 *intr* (SEIN) move along

Dakapo [da'kapo] *n* (-s;-s) encore

da′lassen §104 *tr* leave behind

dalli ['dalɪ] *interj*—**mach d.!** step on it!

damalig ['damalıç] *adj* of that time

damals ['damals] *adv* then, at that time

Damast [da'mast] *m* (-es;-e) damask

Dame ['damə] *f* (-;-n) lady; (*beim Tanz*) partner; (cards, chess) queen; (checkers) king; **e-e D. machen** crown a checker; **meine D.! madam!; meine Damen und Herrn!** ladies and gentlemen!

Da′mebrett *n* checkerboard

Da′menbinde *f* sanitary napkin

Da′mendoppelspiel *n* (tennis) women's doubles

Da′meneinzelspiel *n* (tennis) women's singles

Da′mengesellschaft *f* hen party

da′menhaft *adj* ladylike

Da′menhemd *n* chemise

Da′menschneider **–in** §6 *mf* dressmaker

Da′menwäsche *f* lingerie

Da′mespiel *n* checkers

damisch ['damıʃ] *adj* dopey

damit [da'mɪt] *adv* with it or them; by it; thereby; **d. hat's noch Zeit** that can wait; **es ist nichts d.** it is useless ‖ *conj* in order that, to

dämlich ['demlıç] *adj* dopey

Damm [dam] *m* (-[e]s;:e) dam; dike; embankment; causeway; breakwater; pier; (fig) barrier; (anat) perineum; **auf dem D. sein** feel up to it; **wieder auf dem D. sein** be on one's feet again

Dämmer ['demər] *m* (-s;) (poet) twilight

dammerig ['deməriç] *adj* dusky, dim

Däm′merlicht *n* dusk, twilight

dämmern ['demərn] *intr* dawn, grow light; (*am Abend*) grow dark, become twilight

Däm′merung f (-;-en) (*Morgenrot*) dawn; (*am Abend*) dusk, twilight

Dämmplatte [′dɛmplatə] f acoustical tile

Dämmstoff [′dɛm′stɔf] m insulation

Damm′weg m causeway

Dämon [′dɛmon] m (-s; Dämonen [de′monən] demon

dämonisch [dɛ′monɪʃ] adj demoniacal

Dampf [dampf] m (-[e]s;⸚e) steam; vapor; (*Angst*) (coll) fear; (*Hunger*) (coll) hunger; (vet) broken wind; **D.** dahinter machen (coll) step on it

dampfen [′dampfən] intr steam ‖ intr (SEIN) steam along, steam away

dämpfen [′dɛmpfən] tr (*dünsten*) steam; (*Lärm*) muffle; (*Farben, Gefühle, Lichter*) subdue; (*Stoß*) absorb; (*Begeisterung*) dampen; mit gedämpfter Stimme under one's breath

Dampfer [′dampfər] m (-s;-) steamer

Dämpfer [′dɛmpfər] m (-s;-) (culin) steamer, boiler; (mach) baffle; (mus) mute; (*beim Klavier*) (mus) damper; e-n D. aufsetzen (dat) put a damper on

Dampf′heizung f steam heat

Dampf′kessel m steam boiler, boiler

Dampf′maschine f steam engine

Dampf′schiffahrtslinie f steamship line

Dämp′fungsfläche f (aer) stabilizer

Dampf′walze f steam roller

Damspiel [′dam/piːl] n var of Damespiel

danach [da′nax] adv after it or them; accordingly; according to it or them; afterwards; **d.** fragen ask about it; **d.** streben strive for it; **d.** sieht er auch aus that's just what he looks like

Däne [′dɛnə] m (-n;-n) Dane

daneben [da′nebən] adv next to it or them ‖ adv in addition

dane′bengehen §82 intr (SEIN) go amiss

dane′benhauen intr miss; (fig) be wrong

Dänemark [′dɛnəmark] n (-s;) Denmark

dang [daŋ] pret of dingen

danniederliegen [da′nidərligən] §108 intr (fig) be down; **d.** an (dat) be laid up with

Dänin [′dɛnɪn] f (-;-nen) Dane

dänisch [′dɛnɪʃ] adj Danish

dank [daŋk] prep (dat) thanks to ‖ **Dank** m (-[e]s;) thanks; gratitude; **Gott sei D.!** thank God!, thank heaven!

dankbar [′daŋkbar] adj thankful; (*lohnend*) rewarding, profitable

Dank′barkeit f (-;) gratitude

danken [′daŋkən] intr (dat) thank; **danke!** thanks!; (*bei Ablehnung*) no, thanks!; **danke schön!** thank you!; **nichts zu d.!** you are welcome!

dan′kenswert adj meritorious; rewarding

dank′sagen intr return thanks

Danksagung [′daŋkzaɡuŋ] f (-;) thanksgiving

Dank′sagungstag m Thanksgiving Day

Dank′schreiben n letter of thanks

dann [dan] adv then; **d. und wann** now and then

dannen [′danən] adv—von d. away

daran [da′ran] adv on, at, by, in, onto it or them; das ist alles d.! that's great!; er ist gut d. he's well off; er tut gut d. zu (inf) he does well to (inf); es ist nichts d. there's nothing to it; ich will wissen, wie ich d. bin I want to know where I stand; jetzt bin ich d. it's my turn; nahe d. sein zu (inf) be on the point of (ger); was liegt d.? what does it matter?

daran′gehen §82 intr (SEIN) go about it; **d.** gehen zu (inf) proceed to (inf)

daran′setzen tr—alles d. zu (inf) do one's level best to (inf)

darauf [da′rauf] adv on it or them; after that; **d.** kommt es an that's what matters; gerade d. zu straight towards; gleich d. immediately afterwards; ich lasse es d. ankommen I'll risk it

daraufhin [darauf′hɪn] adv thereupon

daraus [da′raus] adv of it, from it; from that; from them; hence; **d.** wird nichts! nothing doing!; es wird nichts d. nothing will come of it

darben [′darbən] intr live in poverty

darbieten [′darbitən] §58 tr present; (theat) performance

dar′bringen §65 tr present, offer

Dardanellen [darda′nɛlən] pl Dardanelles

darein [da′rain] adv into it or them

darein′reden intr interrupt; er redet mir in alles d. he interferes in all that I do

darin [da′rɪn] adv in it or them

dar′legen tr explain; state

Dar′legung f (-;-en) explanation

Darlehe(e)n [′darlə(ə)n] n (-s;-) loan

Dar′leh(e)nskasse f loan association

Darm [darm] m (-[e]s;⸚e) intestine, gut; (*Wursthaut*) skin

Darm- comb.fm. intestinal

Darm′entzündung f enteritis

Darm′fäule f dysentery

dar′stellen tr describe; show, depict, portray; represent; mean; plot, chart; (indust) produce; (theat) play the part of

Dar′steller -in §6 mf performer

Dar′stellung f (-;-en) representation; portrayal; account, version; (indust) production; (theat) performance

dar′tun §154 tr prove; demonstrate

darüber [da′rybər] adv over it or them; (*querüber*) across it; (*betreffs*) about that; **d.** hinaus beyond it; moreover; ich bin d. hinweg I've gotten over it

darum [da′rum] adv around it or them; (*deshalb*) therefore; er weiß d. he's aware of it; es ist mir nur d. zu tun, daß all I ask is that

darunter [da′runtər] adv below it or them; among them; (*weniger*) less; **d.** leiden suffer from it; zehn Jahre und d. ten years and under

das [das] §1 def art the ‖ §1 dem adj & dem pron this, that; das und das such and such || §11 *rel pron* which, that, who

da'sein §139 *intr* (SEIN) be there; be present; exist; **es ist schon alles mal dagewesen** there's nothing new under the sun; **noch nie dagewesen** unprecedented || **Dasein** *n* (-s;) being, existence, life

Da'seinsberechtigung *f* raison d'être

daselbst [da'zɛlpst] *adv* just there; ibidem; **wohnhaft d.** address as above

dasjenige ['dasjenɪgə] §4,3 *dem adj* that || *dem pron* the one

daß [das] *conj* that; **daß du nicht vergißt!** be sure not to forget!; **daß er doch käme!** I wish he'd come; **es sei denn, daß** unless

dasselbe [das'zɛlbə] §4,3 *dem adj* & *dem pron* the same

da'stehen §146 *intr* stand there; **einzig d.** be unrivaled; **gut d.** be well-off; **wie stehe ich nun da!** how foolish I look now!

Daten ['datən] *pl* data

Da'tenverarbeitung *f* data processing

datieren [da'tirən] *tr* & *intr* date

Dativ ['datif] *m* (-s;-e) dative (case)

dato ['dato] *adv*—**bis d.** to date

Dattel ['datəl] *f* (-;-n) (bot) date

Da·tum ['datum] *n* (-s;-ten [tən]) date; **Daten** data, facts; **heutigen Datums** of today; **neueren Datums** of recent date; **welches D. haben wir heute?** what's today's date?

Daube ['daubə] *f* (-;-n) (barrel) stave

Dauer ['dau·ər] *f* (-;) length, duration; permanence; **auf die D.** in the long run; **für die D.** von **for** a period of; **von D. sein** last, endure

Dau'erauftrag *m* standing order

Dau'erbelastung *f* constant load

Dau'erertrag *m* constant yield

Dau'erfeuer *n* (mil) automatic fire

Dau'erflug *m* endurance flight

Dau'ergeschwindigkeit *f* cruising speed

dau'erhaft *adj* lasting, durable; (*Farbe*) fast

Dau'erkarte *f* season ticket; (rr) commutation ticket

Dau'erlauf *m* (long-distance) jogging

dauern ['dau·ərn] *tr*—**er dauert mich** I feel sorry for him || *intr* last, continue; **die Fahrt dauert fünf Stunden** the trip takes five hours; **es wird nicht lange d., dann** it won't be long before; **lange d.** take a long time

Dau'erplissee *n* permanent pleat

Dau'erprobe *f* endurance test

Dau'erschmierung *f* self-lubrication

Dau'erstellung *f* permanent job

Dau'erton *m* (telp) dial tone

Dau'erversuch *m* endurance test

Dau'erwelle *f* permanent wave

Dau'erwirkung *f* lasting effect

Dau'erwurst *f* hard salami

Dau'erzustand *m* permanent condition; **zum D. werden** get to be a regular thing

Daumen ['daumən] *m* (-s;-) thumb; **D. halten!** keep your fingers crossed!; **die D. drehen** twiddle one's thumbs; **über den D. peilen** (or **schätzen**) give a rough estimate of

Dau'menabdruck *m* thumb print

Dau'menindex *m* thumb index

Daune ['daunə] *f* (-;-n) downy feather; **Daunen** down

Dau'nenbett *n* feather bed

Davit ['devɪt] *m* (-s;-s) (naut) davit

davon [da'fɔn] *adv* of it or them; from it or them; about it or them; away

davon'kommen §99 *intr* (SEIN) escape

davon'laufen §105 *intr* (SEIN) run away; || **Davonlaufen** *n*—**es ist zum D.** (coll) it's enough to drive you insane

davon'machen *ref* take off, go away

davon'tragen §132 *tr* carry off; win

davor [da'for] *adv* in front of it or them; of it or them; from it or them

dawider [da'vidər] *adv* against it

dazu [da'tsu] *adv* thereto; to it or them; in addition to that; for that purpose; about it or them; with it or them

dazu'gehörig *adj* belonging to it; proper, appropriate

da'zumal *adv* at that time

dazu'tun §154 *tr* add || **Dazutun** *n*—**ohne sein D.** without any effort on his part

dazwischen [da'tsvɪʃən] *adv* in between; among them

dazwi'schenfahren §71 *intr* (SEIN) jump in to intervene

dazwi'schenfunken *intr* (coll) butt in

dazwi'schenkommen §99 *intr* (SEIN) intervene

Dazwi'schenkunft [da'tsvɪʃənkunft] *f* (-;) intervention

dazwi'schentreten §152 *intr* (SEIN) intervene

Debatte [de'batə] *f* (-;-n) debate, discussion; **zur D. stehen** be under discussion; **zur D. stellen** open to discussion

debattieren [deba'tirən] *tr* & *intr* debate, discuss

Debet ['debet] *n* (-s;) debit; **im D. stehen** be on the debit side

Debüt [de'by] *n* (-s;-s) debut

Debütantin [deby'tantɪn] *f* (-;-nen) debutante

debütieren [deby'tierən] *intr* make one's debut

Dechant [de'çant] *m* (-en;-en) (educ; R.C.) dean

dechiffrieren [deʃɪf'rirən] *tr* decipher

Deck [dek] *n* (-s;-s) deck

Deck'anstrich *m* final coat

Deck'bett *n* feather bed

Deck'blatt *n* overlay

Decke ['dekə] *f* (-;-n) cover, covering; (*Bett-*) blanket; (*Tisch-*) tablecloth; (*Zimmer-*) ceiling; (*Schicht*) layer; **mit j-m unter e-r D. stecken** be in cahoots with s.o.; **sich nach der D. strecken** make the best of it

Deckel ['dekəl] *m* (-s;-) lid, cap; (*Buch-*) cover; **j-m eins auf den D. geben** (coll) chew s.o. out

decken ['dekən] *tr* cover; (*Tisch*) set; **das Tor d.** guard the goal || *ref* coincide || *intr* cover

Deckenbeleuchtung (**Dek'kenbeleuchtung**) *f* (-;) ceiling lighting

Deckenlicht (Dek'kenlicht) n ceiling light; skylight; (aut) dome light

Deck'farbe f one-coat paint

Deck'konto n secret account

Deck'mantel m pretext, pretense

Deck'name m pseudonym; alias; (mil) code name, cover name

Deck'offizier m (nav) warrant officer

Deck'plane f awning; tarpaulin

Deckung (Dek'kung) f (-;-en) covering; protection; roofing; (box) defense; (com) security, surety; collateral

deckungsgleich (dek'kungsgleich) adj congruent

defekt [de'fekt] adj defective ‖ **Defekt** m (-[e]s;-e) defect

defensiv [defen'zif] adj defensive ‖ **Defensive** [defen'zivə] f (-;-n) defensive

definieren [defi'nirən] tr define

definitiv [defini'tif] adj (endgültig) definitive; (bestimmt) definite

Defizit ['defitsɪt] n (-s;-e) deficit

Degen ['degən] m (-s;-) sword; (poet) warrior; (typ) compositor

degradieren [degra'dirən] tr demote

Degradie'rung f (-;-en) demotion

dehnbar ['denbar] adj elastic; (Metall) ductile; (fig) vague, loose

dehnen ['denən] tr stretch; extend; expand; (Worte) drawl out; (Vokal) lengthen; (mus) sustain ‖ ref stretch out; expand

Deh'nung f (-;-en) extension; expansion; dilation; (ling) lengthening

Deich [daɪç] m (-[e]s;-e) dike; (Damm) bank, embankment

Deichsel ['daɪksəl] f (-;-n) pole

deichseln ['daɪksəln] tr (coll) manage

dein [daɪn] §2 poss adj your, thy

deinerseits ['daɪnər'zaɪts] adv on your part

deinesgleichen ['daɪnəs'glaɪçən] invar pron your own kin, your equals, the likes of you

deinethalben ['daɪnət'halbən], **deinetwegen** ['daɪnət'vegən], **deinetwillen** ['daɪnət'vɪlən] adv for your sake; because of you, on your account

deinige ['daɪnigə] poss pron yours

Dekan [de'kan] m (-s;-e) dean

deklamieren [dekla'mirən] tr & intr declaim; recite

Deklination [deklina'tsjon] f (-;-en) declension

deklinieren [dekli'nirən] tr decline

dekolletiert [dekole'tirt] adj low-necked; (Dame) bare-necked

Dekorateur [dekora'tør] m (-s;-e) decorator, interior decorator

Dekoration [dekora'tsjon] f (-;-en) decoration; (theat) scenery

dekorieren [deko'rirən] tr decorate

Dekret [de'kret] n (-[e]s;-e) decree

delikat [deli'kat] adj delicate; (lecker) delicious

Delikt [de'lɪkt] n (-[e]s;-e) offense

Delle ['delə] f (-;-n) dent; dip

Delphin [del'fin] m (-s;-e) dolphin

Delta ['delta] n (-s;-s) delta

dem [dem] §1 def art, dem adj & dem pron ‖ §11 rel pron

Demagoge [dema'gogə] m (-n;-n) demagogue

Dementi [de'menti] n (-s;-s) official denial

dementieren [demen'tirən] tr deny (officially)

dem'entsprechend adj corresponding ‖ adv correspondingly, accordingly

dem'gegenüber adv in contrast

dem'gemäß adv accordingly

dem'nach adv therefore; accordingly

dem'nächst adv soon, before long; (theat) (public sign) coming soon

demobilisieren [demobili'zirən] tr & intr demobilize

Demokrat [demo'krat] m (-en;-en) democrat

Demokra-tie [demokra'ti] f (-;-tien ['ti-ən]) democracy

Demokratin [demo'kratin] f (-;-nen) democrat

demokratisch [demo'kratiʃ] adj democratic

demolieren [demo'lirən] tr demolish

Demonstrant -in [demon'strant(ɪn)] §7 mf demonstrator

demonstrieren [demon'strirən] tr & intr demonstrate

Demontage [demon'taʒə] f (-;) dismantling

demontieren [demon'tirən] tr dismantle

demselben [dem'zelbən] §4,3 dem adj & dem pron

Demut ['demut] f (-;) humility

demütig ['demytɪç] adj humble

demütigen ['demytɪgən] tr humble; (beschämen) humiliate

De'mütigung f (-;-en) humiliation

de'mutsvoll adj submissive

dem'zufolge adv accordingly

den [den] §1 def art, dem adj & dem pron ‖ §11 rel pron whom

denen ['denən] §11 rel pron to whom

Denkarbeit ['denkarbaɪt] f (-;) brainwork

Denkart ['denkart] f var of **Denkungsart**

Denkaufgabe ['denkaufgabə] f brain twister, problem

denkbar ['denkbar] adj conceivable; (vorstellbar) imaginable

denken ['denkən] §66 tr think, consider; **was d. Sie zu tun?** what do you intend to do? ‖ ref—**bei sich (or für sich) d.** think to oneself; **denke dir e-e Zahl** think of a number; **d. Sie sich in ihre Lage** imagine yourself in her place; **sich** [dat] **etw d.** imagine s.th.; **was denkst du dir eigentlich?** what do you think you're doing? ‖ intr think; **das gibt mir zu d.** that set me thinking; **d. an** (acc) think about

denk'faul adj mentally lazy

Denk'fehler m fallacy, false reasoning

Denk'mal n (-s;-e & ⸚er) monument

Denk'schrift f (pol) memorandum

Denkungsart ['denkunsart] f way of thinking, mentality

Denk'weise f way of thinking, mentality

denk'würdig adj memorable

Denk'zettel *m—j—m* e—n D. geben teach s.o. a lesson

denn [dɛn] *adv* then; es sei denn, daß unless ‖ *conj* for

dennoch ['dɛnɔx] *adv* nevertheless, all the same, (but) still

Dentist —in [dɛn'tɪst(ɪn)] §7 *mf* dentist

Denunziant —in [denun'tsjant(ɪn)] §7 *mf* informer

denunzieren [denun'tsirən] *tr* denounce

Depesche [dɛ'pɛʃə] *f* (—;—n) dispatch

De·ponens [dɛ'ponɛns] *n* (—;-ponenzien [po'nɛntsjən]) (gram) deponent

deponieren [depo'nirən] *tr* (com) deposit

deportieren [depɔr'tirən] *tr* deport

Depot [dɛ'po] *n* (—s;—s) depot; warehouse; storage; safe; safe deposit

Depp [dɛp] *m* (—s;—e) (coll) dope

Depression [deprɛ'sjon] *f* (—;—en) depression

der [der] §1 *def art* the ‖ §1 dem adj & dem pron this, that; der und der such and such, so and so ‖ §11 rel pron who, which, that; (to) whom

der'art *adv* so, in such a way; (coll) that

der'artig *adj* such, of that kind

derb [dɛrp] *adj* coarse; tough; rude

Derb'heit *f* (—;—en) coarseness; toughness; crude joke

dereinst' *adv* some day

deren ['derən] §11 *rel pron* whose

derenthalben ['derənt'halbən], **derentwegen** ['derənt'vegən], **derentwillen** ['derənt'vɪlən] *adv* for her sake, for their sake

dergestalt ['dergə'ʃtalt] *adv* so

dergleichen ['der'glaɪçən] *invar dem adj* such; similar; of that kind ‖ *invar dem pron* such a thing; und d. and the like; und d. mehr and so on

derjenige ['derjenɪgə] §4,3 *dem adj* that ‖ *dem pron* the one; he

dermaßen [der'masən] *adv* so, in such a way

derselbe [der'zɛlbə] §4,3 *dem adj* & *dem pron* the same

derweilen ['der'vaɪlən] *adv* meanwhile

derzeit ['der'tsaɪt] *adv* at present

derzeitig ['der'tsaɪtɪç] *adj* present; then, of that time

des [dɛs] *n* (—;—) (mus) D flat

Desaster [dɛ'zastər] *n* (—s;—) disaster

Deserteur [dezɛr'tør] *m* (—s;—e) deserter

desertieren [dezɛr'tirən] *intr* (SEIN) desert

desgleichen ['dɛs'glaɪçən] *invar dem pron* such a thing ‖ *invar rel pron* the likes of which ‖ *adv* likewise

deshalb ['dɛshalp] *adv* therefore

Desinfektion [dɛsɪnfɛk'tsjon] *f* (—;—en) disinfection

Desinfektions'mittel *n* disinfectant

desinfizieren [dɛsɪnfi'tsirən] *tr* disinfect

Despot [dɛs'pot] *m* (—en;—en) despot

despotisch [dɛs'potɪʃ] *adj* despotic

Dessin [dɛ'sɛ̃] *n* (—s;—s) design

destillieren [dɛstɪ'lirən] *tr* distill

desto ['dɛsto] *adv* the; d. besser the better, all the better

deswegen ['dɛs'vegən] *adv* therefore

Detail [dɛ'taɪ(l)] *n* (—s;—s) detail; (com) retail

Detail'geschäft *n* retail store

Detail'händler —in §6 *mf* retail dealer

detaillieren [dɛta'jirən] *tr* relate in detail; specify; itemize

Detek·tiv [detɛk'tif] *m* (—s;-tive ['tivə]) private investigator; (coll) private eye

detonieren [deto'nirən] *intr* detonate; etw. d. lassen detonate s.th.

deuchte ['dɔɪçtə] *pret* of dünken

Deutelei [dɔɪtə'laɪ] *f* (—;—en) quibble

deuteln ['dɔɪtəln] *intr* (an *dat*) quibble (about), split hairs (over)

deuten ['dɔɪtən] *tr* interpret; falsch d. misinterpret ‖ *intr* (auf *acc*) (& fig) point (to)

deutlich ['dɔɪtlɪç] *adj* clear, distinct

deutsch [dɔɪtʃ] *adj* German ‖ **Deutsche** §5 *mf* German

Deu'tung *f* (—;—en) interpretation

Devise [dɛ'vizə] *f* (—;—n) motto; Devisen foreign currency

Devi'senbestand *m* foreign-currency reserve

Devi'senbilanz *f* balance of payments

Devi'senkurs *m* rate of exchange

Dezember [dɛ'tsɛmbər] *m* (—s;—) December

dezent [dɛ'tsɛnt] *adj* unobtrusive; (Licht, Musik) soft; (anständig) decent

Dezernat [detsɛr'nat] *n* (—[e]s;—e) (administrative) department

dezimal [detsɪ'mal] *adj* decimal ‖ **Dezimale** [detsɪ'malə] *f* (—;—n) decimal

Dezimal'bruch *m* decimal fraction

Dezimal'zahl *f* decimal

dezimieren [detsɪ'mirən] *tr* decimate

Dia ['di·a] *n* (—s;—s) (coll) slide

Diadem [di·a'dem] *n* (—s;—e) diadem

Diagnose [di·a'gnozə] *f* (—;—n) diagnosis

diagnostizieren [di·agnɔsti'tsirən] *tr* diagnose

diagonal [di·ago'nal] *adj* diagonal ‖ **Diagonale** *f* (—;—n) diagonal

Diagramm [di·a'gram] *n* (—[e]s;—e) diagram; graph

Diakon [di·a'kon] *m* (—s;—e & —en;—en) deacon

Dialekt [di·a'lɛkt] *m* (—[e]s;—e) dialect

dialektisch [di·a'lɛktɪʃ] *adj* dialectical

Dialog [di·a'lok] *m* (—s;—e) dialogue

Diamant [di·a'mant] *m* (—en;—en) diamond

Diapositiv [di·apozi'tif] *n* (—s;-tive ['tivə]) slide, transparency

Diät [di'ɛt] *f* (—;—en) diet (under medical supervision); Diäten daily allowance; diät leben be on a diet

Diät- comb.*fm.* dietary

diätetisch [diɛ'tetɪʃ] *adj* dietetic

dich [dɪç] §11 *pers pron* you, thee ‖ *reflex pron* yourself, thyself

dicht [dɪçt] *adj* dense; thick; heavy; leakproof; tight ‖ **Dichte** ['dɪçtə] *f* (—;—en) density

dichten ['dɪçtən] *tr* tighten; caulk; compose, write || *intr* write poetry
Dichter ['dɪçtər] *m* (-s;-) (important) writer; poet
Dichterin ['dɪçtərɪʃ] *f* (-;-nen) poetess
dichterisch ['dɪçtərɪʃ] *adj* poetic(al)
dicht'gedrängt *adj* tightly packed
dicht'halten §90 *intr* keep mum
Dicht'heit *f* (-;), **Dich'tigkeit** *f* (-;) density; compactness; tightness
Dich'kunst *f* poetry
dicht'machen *tr* (coll) close up
Dich'tung *f* (-;-en) gasket; packing; imagination; fiction; poetry; poem;
Dich'tungsring *m*, **Dich'tungsscheibe** *f* washer; gasket
dick [dɪk] *adj* thick; fat; big; (*Luft, Freunde*) close; **dicke Luft!** (coll) cheese itl; **sich d. tun** talk big || **Dicke** *f* (-;) thickness, stoutness
Dick'darm *m* (anat) colon
dickfellig ['dɪkfɛlɪç] *adj* thick-skinned
dick'flüssig *adj* viscous
Dickicht ['dɪkɪçt] *n* (-[e]s;-e) thicket
Dick'kopf *m* thick head
dickköpfig ['dɪkkœpfɪç] *adj* thick-headed
dickleibig ['dɪklaɪbɪç] *adj* stout, fat
Dick'schädel *m* thick head
dick'schädelig ['dɪkʃedəlɪç] *adj* thick-headed
die [di] §1 *def art* the || §1 *dem adj & dem pron* this, that; **die und die** such and such || §11 *rel pron* who, which, that
Dieb [dip] *m* (-[e]s;-e) thief
Dieberei [dibə'raɪ] *f* (-;-en) thievery; (*Diebstahl*) theft
Diebesbande ['dibəsbandə] *f* pack of thieves
Diebin ['dibɪn] *f* (-;-nen) thief
diebisch ['dibɪʃ] *adj* thievish || *adv*—**sich d. freuen** be tickled pink
Diebstahl ['dipʃtal] *m* (-[e]s;⸚) theft, larceny; **leichter D.** petty larceny; **schwerer D.** grand larceny
diejenige ['dijɛnɪgə] §4,3 *dem adj* that || *dem pron* the one; she
Diele ['dilə] *f* (-;-n) floorboard; (*breiter Flur*) entrance hall; **Dielen** flooring
dienen ['dinən] *intr* (*dat*) serve; **damit ist mir nicht gedient** that doesn't help me any; **womit kann ich d.?** may I help you?
Diener **-in** ['dinər(ɪn)] §6 *mf* servant
die'nerhaft *adj* servile
dienern ['dinərn] *intr* bow and scrape
Die'nerschaft *f* (-;) domestics, help
dienlich ['dinlɪç] *adj* useful
Dienst [dinst] *m* (-es;-e) service; job; employment; (adm, mil) grade; **außer D.** retired; **im. D.** on duty; **j-m e-n D. tun** do s.o. a favor
Dienstag ['dinstak] *m* (-[e]s;-e) Tuesday
Dienst'alter *n* seniority
dienstbar ['dinstbar] *adj* subservient
Dienst'barkeit *f* (-;) servitude, bondage; (jur) easement
dienst'beflissen *adj* eager to serve || *adv* eagerly

Dienst'bote *m* servant, domestic
Dienst'boteneingang *m* service entrance
Dienst'eid *m* oath of office
dienst'eifrig *adj* eager to serve || *adv* eagerly
Dienst'einteilung *f* work schedule; (mil) duty roster
Dienst'fahrt *f* official trip
dienst'frei *adj*—**d. haben** be off duty
Dienst'gebrauch *m*—**nur zum D.** for official use only
Dienst'gespräch *n* business call
Dienst'grad *m* (mil) rank, grade; (nav) rating
dienst'habend *adj* on duty
Dienst'herr *m* employer; (hist) lord
Dienst'leistung *f* service
dienst'lich *adj* official || *adv* officially; on official business
Dienst'mädchen *n* maid
Dienst'pflicht *f* official duty; compulsory military service
Dienst'plan *m* work schedule; (mil) duty roster
Dienst'sache *f* official business
dienst'tauglich *adj* fit for active service
diensttuend ['dinsttu-ənt] *adj* on duty; active; in charge
Dienst'weg *m* official channels
Dienst'wohnung *f* official residence
dies [dis] *dem adj & dem pron* var of dieses
diese ['dizə] §3 *dem adj* this || *dem pron* this one
dieselbe [di'zɛlbə] §4,3 *dem adj & dem pron* the same
Dieselmotor ['dizəlmotər] *m* diesel engine
dieser ['dizər] §3 *dem adj* this || *dem pron* this one
dieses ['dizəs] §3 *dem adj* this || *dem pron* this one
diesig ['dizɪç] *adj* hazy, misty
dies'jährig *adj* this year's
dies'mal *adv* this time
diesseits ['diszaɪts] *prep* (*genit*) on this side of
Dietrich ['ditrɪç] *m* (-s;-e) skeleton key; (*Einbrecherwerkzeug*) picklock
Differential [dɪferen'tsjal] *n* (-s;-e) (aut, math) differential
Differential- *comb.fm.* (econ, elec, mach, math, phys) differential
Differenz [dɪfe'rents] *f* (-;-en) difference
Diktaphon [dɪkta'fon] *n* (-[e]s;-e) dictaphone
Diktat [dɪk'tat] *n* (-s;-e) dictation; **nach D. schreiben** take dictation
Dik'tator [dɪk'tator] *m* (-s;-tatoren) [ta'torən]) dictator
diktatorisch [dɪkta'torɪʃ] *adj* dictatorial
Diktatur [dɪkta'tur] *f* (-;-en) dictatorship
diktieren [dɪk'tirən] *tr & intr* dictate
Dilettant **-in** [dɪle'tant(ɪn)] §7 *mf* dilettante, amateur
Diner [di'ne] *n* (-s;-s) dinner
Ding [dɪŋ] *n* (-[e]s;-e) thing; **ein D. drehen** (coll) pull a job
dingen ['dɪŋən] §109 & §142 *tr* hire

ding'fest *adj*—j—n d. machen arrest s.o.
ding'lich *adj* real
Dings [dɪŋs] *n* (-s;) (coll) thing, doo-dad, thingamajig
Dings'bums *m & n* (-;) var of **Dingsda**
Dings'da *mfn* (-s;) what-d'ye-call-it
Diözese [dɪ-ø'tseːzə] *f* (-;-n) diocese
Diphtherie [dɪfte'riː] *f* (-;) diphtheria
Dipl.-Ing. *abbr* (**Diplom-Ingenieur**) engineer holding a degree
Diplom [dɪ'ploːm] *n* (-s;-e) diploma
Diplom- *comb.fm.* holding a degree
Diplomat [dɪplo'maːt] *m* (-en;-en) diplomat
Diplomatie [dɪploma'tiː] *f* (-;) diplomacy
Diplomatin [dɪplo'maːtɪn] *f* (-;-nen) diplomat
diplomatisch [dɪplo'maːtɪʃ] *adj* diplomatic
dir [diːr] §11 *pers pron* to or for you, to or for thee || *reflex pron* to or for yourself, to or for thyself
direkt [dɪ'rɛkt] *adj* direct
Direktion [dɪrɛk'tsjoːn] *f* (-;) direction; (*Verwaltung*) management
Direk·tor [dɪ'rɛktɔr] *m* (-s;-toren ['toːrən]) director; (*e-r Bank*) president; (*e-r Schule*) principal; (*e-s Gefängnisses*) warden
Direktorat [dɪrɛkto'raːt] *n* (-[e]s;-e) directorship
Direktorin [dɪrɛk'toːrɪn] *f* (-;-nen) director; (educ) principal
Direkto·rium [dɪrɛk'toːri·um] *n* (-s;-rien [ri·ən]) board of directors; executive committee
Direktrice [dɪrɛk'triːsə] *f* (-;-n) directress, manager
Dirigent –in [dɪrɪ'gɛnt(ɪn)] §7 *mf* (mus) conductor
dirigieren [dɪrɪ'giːrən] *tr* direct, manage; (mus) conduct
Dirnd(e)l ['dɪrndəl] *n* (-s;-) girl; (*Tracht*) dirndle
Dirne ['dɪrnə] *f* (-;-n) girl; (pej) prostitute
Dis [dɪs] *n* (-;-) D sharp
disharmonisch [dɪshar'moːnɪʃ] *adj* discordant
Diskont [dɪs'kɔnt] *m* (-[e]s;-e) discount
diskontieren [dɪskɔn'tiːrən] *tr* discount
Diskothek [dɪsko'teːk] *f* (-;-en) discotheque
diskret [dɪs'kreːt] *adj* discreet
Diskretion [dɪskre'tsjoːn] *f* (-;-en) discretion
Diskussion [dɪsku'sjoːn] *f* (-;-en) discussion
diskutieren [dɪsku'tiːrən] *tr* discuss || *intr*—d. über (*acc*) discuss
disponieren [dɪspo'niːrən] *intr* (über *acc*) dispose (of)
Disposition [dɪspozi'tsjoːn] *f* (-;-en) disposition; arrangement; disposal
Distanz [dɪs'tants] *f* (-;-en) distance
distanzieren [dɪstan'tsiːrən] *tr* (mit) beat (by, *e.g.*, *one meter*) || *ref* (von) dissociate oneself (from)
distanziert' *adj* (fig) detached
Distel ['dɪstəl] *f* (-;-n) thistle
Dis'telfink *m* goldfinch

Distrikt [dɪs'trɪkt] *m* (-[e]s;-e) district
Disziplin [dɪstsi'pliːn] *f* (-;-en) discipline
disziplinarisch [dɪstsipli'naːrɪʃ] *adj* disciplinary
dito ['diːto] *adv* ditto || **Dito** *n* (-s;-s) ditto
Dividend [dɪvi'dɛnt] *m* (-en;-en), **Dividende** [dɪvi'dɛndə] *f* (-;-n) dividend
dividieren [dɪvi'diːrən] *tr* divide
Division [dɪvi'zjoːn] *f* (-;-en) division
Diwan ['diːvan] *m* (-s;-e) divan
D-Mark ['deːmark] *f* (-;-) mark (*monetary unit of West Germany*)
doch [dɔx] *adv* yet; of course
Docht [dɔxt] *m* (-[e]s;-e) wick
Dock [dɔk] *n* (-[e]s;-s & -e) dock
docken ['dɔkən] *tr & intr* (naut, rok) dock
Dogge ['dɔgə] *f* (-;-n) mastiff; **deutsche D.** Great Dane
Dog·ma ['dɔgma] *n* (-s;-men [mən]) dogma
Dohle ['doːlə] *f* (-;-n) jackdaw
Dok·tor ['dɔktɔr] *m* (-s;-toren ['toːrən]) doctor
Dok'torarbeit *f* dissertation
Dok'torvater *m* adviser (*for a doctoral dissertation*)
Dokument [dɔku'mɛnt] *n* (-[e]s;-e) document; (jur) instrument, deed
Dokumentarfilm [dɔkumɛn'tarfɪlm] *m* documentary
dokumentarisch [dɔkumɛn'tarɪʃ] *adj* documentary
Dolch [dɔlç] *m* (-[e]s;-e) dagger
Dolch'stoß *m* (pol) stab in the back
Dollar ['dɔlar] *m* (-s;-) dollar
dolmetschen ['dɔlmɛtʃən] *tr & intr* interpret
Dol'metscher –in §6 *mf* interpreter
Dom [doːm] *m* (-[e]s;-e) cathedral; dome
Domäne [dɔ'mɛːnə] *f* (-;-n) domain
Domino ['dɔmiːno] *n* (-s;-s) domino
Donau ['dɔnau] *f* (-;) Danube
Donner ['dɔnər] *m* (-s;-) thunder
Don'nerkeil *m* thunderbolt
donnern ['dɔnərn] *intr* thunder
Don'nerschlag *m* clap of thunder
Don'nerstag *m* (-[e]s;-e) Thursday
Don'nerwetter *n* thunderstorm; **zum D.!** confound it! || *interj* geez!
doof [doːf] *adj* (coll) goofy
dopen ['doːpən] *tr* dope (*a racehorse*)
Doppel ['dɔpəl] *n* (-s;-) duplicate; (tennis) doubles
Doppel- *comb.fm.* double, two, bi-, twin
Dop'pelbelichtung *f* double exposure
Dop'pelbild *n* (telv) ghost
Dop'pelbruch *m* compound fracture
Dop'pelehe *f* bigamy
Dop'pelgänger *m* double; second self
Dop'pellaut *m* diphthong
doppeln ['dɔpəln] *tr* double
Dop'pelprogramm *n* double feature
Dop'pelpunkt *m* (typ) colon
doppelreihig ['dɔpəlraɪ·ɪç] *adj* double-breasted
Dop'pelrendezvous *n* double date

dop'pelseitig *adj* reversible; (*Lungenentzündung*) double

Dop'pelsinn *m* double entendre

dop'pelsinnig *adj* ambiguous

Dop'pelspiel *n* (fig) double-dealing; (sport) double-header; (tennis) doubles

doppelt ['dɔpəlt] *adj* double; **doppelter Boden** false bottom; **ein doppeltes Spiel spielen** mit doublecross; **in doppelter Ausführung in duplicate ‖** *adv* twice; **ein Buch d. haben** have two copies of a book

Dop'pelverdiener –in §6 *mf* moonlighter

Dop'pelvokal *m* diphthong

doppelzüngig ['dɔpəltsyŋɪç] *adj* two-faced

Dorf [dɔrf] *n* (-[e]s;⸚er) village

Dorf'bewohner –in §6 *mf* villager

Dörfchen ['dœrfçən] *n* (-s;-) hamlet

Dorn [dɔrn] *m* (-[e]s;-en) thorn; tongue (*of a buckle*); (mach) pin; (sport) spike

Dorn'busch *m* briar, bramble

dornig ['dɔrnɪç] *adj* thorny

Dornröschen ['dɔrnrøsçən] *n* (-s;) Sleeping Beauty

Dörr- [dœr] *comb.fm.* dried

dorren ['dɔrən] *intr* (SEIN) dry (up)

dörren ['dœrən] *tr* dry

Dorschlebertran ['dɔrʃlebərtran] *m* (-[e]s;) cod-liver oil

dort [dɔrt] *adv* there, over there

dort'her *adv* from there

dort'hin *adv* there, to that place

dor'tig *adj* in that place, there

Dose ['dozə] *f* (-;-n) can; box

dösen ['døzən] *intr* doze

Do'senöffner *m* can opener

dosieren [do'zirən] *tr* prescribe (the correct dosage of)

Dosie'rung *f* (-;-en) dosage

Do·sis ['dozɪs] *f* (-;-sen [zən]) dose

dotieren [do'tirən] *tr* endow; **ein Preis mit 100 Mark dotiert** a prize worth 100 marks

Dotter ['dɔtər] *m & n* (-s;-) yolk

Double ['dubəl] *m & n* (-s;-s) (cin, theat) stand-in

Dozent –in [do'tsent(ɪn)] §7 (university) instructor, lecturer

Drache ['draxə] *m* (-n;-n) dragon; (*böses Weib*) battle-ax

Dra'chenfliegen *n* (-s;) hang gliding

Drachen ['draxən] *m* (-s;-) kite

Draht [drat] *m* (-[e]s;⸚e) wire; **auf D. sein** (coll) be on the beam

drahten ['dratən] *tr* telegraph, wire

draht'haarig *adj* wire-haired

Draht'hindernis *n* (mil) wire entanglement, barbed wire

drahtig ['dratɪç] *adj* wiry

draht'los *adj* wireless

Draht'seil *n* cable

Draht'seilbahn *f* cable car, funicular

Draht'zaun *m* wire fence

drall [dral] *adj* plump; (*Faden*) sturdy **‖ Drall** *m* (-s;-e) rifling

Dra·ma ['drama] *n* (-s;-men [mən]) drama

Dramatiker –in [dra'matɪkər(ɪn)] §6 *mf* dramatist, playwright

dramatisch [dra'matɪʃ] *adj* dramatic

dran [dran] *adv* var of **daran**

drang [draŋ] *pret of* **dringen ‖ Drang** *m* (-[e]s;⸚e) pressure; urge

drängeln ['drɛŋəln] *tr & intr* shove

drängen ['drɛŋən] *tr & intr* push, shove; (*drücken*) press **‖** *ref* crowd, crowd together; force one's way

Drangsal ['draŋzal] *f* (-;-e) distress, anguish; hardship

drangsalieren [draŋza'lirən] *tr* vex

drastisch ['drastɪʃ] *adj* drastic

drauf [drauf] *adv* var of **darauf**

Drauf'gänger *m* (-s;-) go-getter

drauf'gehen §82 *intr* (SEIN) (coll) go down the drain

drauflos' *adv*—**d. arbeiten an** (*dat*) work away at

drauflos'gehen §82 *intr* (SEIN)—**d. auf** (*acc*) make straight for

drauflos'reden *intr* ramble on

drauflos'schlagen §132 *intr* (auf *acc*) let fly (at)

draußen ['drausən] *adv* outside; out of doors; (*in der Fremde*) abroad

drechseln ['drɛksəln] *tr* work (*on a lathe*); (fig) embellish

Dreck [drɛk] *m* (-[e]s;-) dirt; mud; excrement; (*Abfälle*) trash

dreckig ['drɛkɪç] *adj* dirty; muddy

Dreh- [dre] *comb.fm.* revolving, rotary

Dreh'arbeiten *pl* (cin) shooting

Dreh'aufzug *m* dumb waiter

Dreh'bank *f* (-;⸚e) lathe

drehbar ['drebar] *adj* revolving

Dreh'buch *n* (mov) script, scenario

drehen ['dre·ən] *tr* turn; (*Zigaretten*) roll; (coll) wangle; (cin) shoot **‖** *ref* turn; rotate

Dreh'kreuz *n* turnstile

Dreh'orgel *f* hurdy-gurdy

Dreh'orgelspieler *m* organ grinder

Dreh'punkt *m* fulcrum; (fig) pivotal point

Dreh'scheibe *f* potter's wheel; (rr) turntable

Dreh'stuhl *m* swivel chair

Dre'hung *f* (-;-en) turn

Dreh'zahl *f* revolutions per minute

Dreh'zahlmesser *m* tachometer

drei [drai] *adj & pron* three **‖ Drei** *f* (-;-en) three; (educ) C

dreidimensional ['draidimɛnzjonal] *adj* three-dimensional

Dreieck ['drai·ɛk] *n* (-[e]s;-e) triangle

drei'eckig *adj* triangular

drei'fach *adj* threefold, triple

dreifältig ['draifɛltɪç] *adj* threefold, triple

Dreifaltigkeit [drai'faltɪçkait] *f* (-;) Trinity

Drei'fuß *m* tripod

Dreikäsehoch [drai'kezəhoç] *m* (-s;-) (coll) shrimp, runt

drei'mal *adv* three times, thrice

Drei'rad *n* tricycle

Drei'sprung *m* hop, step, and jump

dreißig ['draisɪç] *adj & pron* thirty **‖ Dreißig** *f* (-;-& -en) thirty

dreißiger ['draisɪgər] *invar adj* of the thirties, in the thirties

dreißigste ['draisɪçstə] §9 *adj & pron* thirtieth

dreist [draɪst] *adj* brazen, bold

dreistimmig ['draɪˌʃtɪmɪç] *adj* for three voices

drei'zehn *adj & pron* thirteen || Drei-zehn *f* (-;-) thirteen

drei'zehnte §9 *adj & pron* thirteenth

dreschen ['drɛʃən] §67 *tr* thresh; (coll) thrash

Dresch'flegel *m* flail

Dresch'tenne *f* threshing floor

dressieren [drɛ'sirən] *tr* train; (Pferd) break in

Dressur [drɛ'sur] *f* (-;) training

dribbeln ['drɪbəln] *intr* (sport) dribble

drillen ['drɪlən] *tr* drill; train

Drillich ['drɪlɪç] *m* (-s;-e) denim

Dril'lichanzug *m* dungarees; (mil) fatigue uniform, fatigues

Dril'lichhosen *pl* dungarees, jeans

Drilling ['drɪlɪŋ] *m* (-s;-e) triplet

drin [drɪn] *adv* var of darin

dringen ['drɪŋən] §142 *intr* (auf *acc*) press (for), insist (on); (in *acc*) pressure, urge || *intr* (SEIN) (aus) break forth (from); (durch) penetrate, pierce; (durch) force one's way (through); (in *acc*) penetrate (into), get (into); in die Öffentlichkeit d. leak out; in j-n d. press the point with s.o.; d. bis zu get as far as

drin'gend *adj* urgent; (Gefahr) imminent; (Verdacht) strong

dring'lich *adj* urgent

Dring'lichkeit *f* (-;-en) urgency; priority

Drink [drɪŋk] *m* (-s;-s) alcoholic drink

drinnen ['drɪnən] *adv* inside

dritt [drɪt] *adv*—zu d. the three of

dritte ['drɪtə] §9 *adj & pron* third; ein Dritter a disinterested person; (com, jur) a third party

Drittel ['drɪtəl] *n* (-s;-) third (part)

drittens ['drɪtəns] *adv* thirdly

dritt'letzt *adj* third from last

droben ['drobən] *adv* above; up there

Droge ['drogə] *f* (-;-n) drug

Droge·rie [drogə'ri] *f* (-;-rien ['ri·ən]) drugstore

Drogist -in [dro'gɪst(ɪn)] §7 *mf* druggist

Droh'brief *m* threatening letter

drohen ['dro·ən] *intr* (dat) threaten

dro'hend *adj* threatening; impending

Drohne ['dronə] *f* (-;-n) drone

dröhnen ['drønən] *intr* boom, roar; (Kopf, Motor) throb

Dro'hung *f* (-;-en) threat

drollig ['drolɪç] *adj* amusing, funny

Dromedar [dromə'dar] *n* (-s;-e) dromedary

drosch [droʃ] *pret* of dreschen

Droschke ['droʃkə] *f* (-;-n) cab, hackney; taxi

Drosch'kenkutscher *m* coachman

Drossel ['drosəl] *f* (-;-n) thrush; (aut) throttle

Dros'selhebel *m* (aut) throttle

drosseln ['drosəln] *tr* (coll) curb, cut; (aut) throttle; (elec) choke

drüben ['drybən] *adv* over there

Druck [drʊk] *m* (-[e]s;ⁿe) (& fig) pressure; (der Hand) squeeze; (phys)

compression, pressure || *m* (-[e]s-e) printing; print, type; (tex) print

Druck'anzug *m* (aer) pressurized suit

Druck'bogen *m* (printed) sheet

druck'dicht *adj* pressurized

Drückeberger ['drʏkəbergər] *m* (-s;-) shirker; absentee; (mil) goldbrick

drucken ['drʊkən] *tr* print

drücken ['drʏkən] *tr* press; squeeze; imprint; (Preise) lower; (cards) discard; die Stimmung d. be a kill-joy; j–m die Hand d. shake hands with s.o. || *intr* (Schuh) pinch

Druck'entlastung *f* decompression

Drucker ['drʊkər] *m* (-s;-) printer

Drücker ['drʏkər] *m* (-s;-) push button; (e-s Schlosses) latch, latch key; (e-s Gewehrs) trigger

Druckerei [drʊkə'raɪ] *f* (-;-en) print shop, press

Druckerschwärze (Druk'kerschwärze) *f* printer's ink

Druck'fehler *m* misprint

druck'fertig *adj* ready for the press

druck'fest *adj* pressurized

Druck'kabine *f* pressurized cabin

Druck'knopf *m* push button; (am Kleid) snap

Druck'knopfbetätigung *f* push-button control

Druck'luft *f* compressed air

Druckluft– *comb.fm.* pneumatic, air

Druck'luftbremse *f* air brake

Druck'lufthammer *m* jackhammer

Druck'messer *m* pressure gauge

Druck'sache *f* printed matter; Druck-sachen (com) literature

Druck'schrift *f* type; block letters; publication, printed work; leaflet

drucksen ['drʊksən] *intr* hem and haw

drum [drʊm] *adv* var of darum

Drüse ['dryzə] *f* (-;-n) gland

Drüsen– *comb.fm.* glandular

Dschungel ['dʒʊŋəl] *m* (-s;-) jungle

du [du] §11 *per pron* you, thou

Dübel ['dybəl] *m* (-s;-) dowel

Dublette [du'blɛtə] *f* (-;-n) duplicate; imitation stone

ducken ['dʊkən] *tr* (den Kopf) duck; (coll) take down a peg or two || *ref* duck

Duckmäuser ['dʊkmɔɪzər] *m* (-s;-) pussyfoot

dudeln ['dudəln] *tr* hum || *intr* hum, drone; (mus) play the bagpipe

Dudelsack ['dudəlzak] *m* bagpipe

Duell [du'ɛl] *n* (-s;-e) duel

duellieren [du·ə'lirən] *recip* duel

Duett [du'ɛt] *n* (-[e]s;-e) duet

Duft [dʊft] *m* (-[e]s;ⁿe) fragrance

duften ['dʊftən] *intr* be fragrant

duf'tend *adj* fragrant

duftig ['dʊftɪç] *adj* flimsy, dainty

dulden ['dʊldən] *tr* (ertragen) bear; (leiden) suffer; (zulassen) tolerate || *intr* suffer

duldsam ['dʊldzam] *adj* tolerant

Duld'samkeit *f* (-;) tolerance

dumm [dʊm] *adj* stupid, dumb; foolish

Dumm'heit *f* (-;-en) stupidity; foolishness; (Streich) foolish prank

Dumm'kopf *m* dunderhead

dumpf [dʊmpf] *adj* dull, muffled;

(*schwül*) muggy; (*moderig*) musty, moldy; (*Ahnung*) vague

dumpfig ['dumpfɪç] *adj* musty, moldy; muggy

Düne ['dynə] *f* (-;-n) sand dune

Dung [duŋ] *m* (-[e]s;) dung; (*künstlicher*) fertilizer

düngen ['dyŋən] *tr* manure; fertilize

Dünger ['dyŋər] *m* (-s;) var of Dung

dunkel ['duŋkəl] *adj* dark; vague; obscure || **Dunkel** *n* (-s;) darkness

Dünkel ['dyŋkəl] *m* (-s;) conceit

dün′kelhaft *adj* conceited

Dun′kelheit *f* (-;) darkness; obscurity

Dun′kelkammer *f* (phot) darkroom

Dun′kelmann *m* (-[e]s;ⁿer) shady character

dünn [dyn] *adj* thin

Dunst [dunst] *m* (-es;ⁿe) vapor, mist, haze; (*Rauch*) smoke; (*Dampf*) steam; **in D. und Rauch aufgehen** (fig) go up in smoke; **sich in (blauen) D. auflösen** vanish in thin air

dünsten ['dynstən] *tr & intr* stew; steam

dunstig ['dunstɪç] *adj* steamy; (*Wetter*) misty, hazy

Duplikat [duplɪ'kat] *n* (-[e]s;-e) duplicate; copy

Dur [dur] *invar n* (mus) major

durch [durç] *adv* throughout; **d. und d.** through and through || *prep* (*acc*) through, by, by means of

durch′arbeiten *tr* work through || *ref* (durch) work one's way (through); elbow one's way (through)

durchaus′ *adv* throughout; entirely; quite, absolutely; **d. nicht** by no means

durch′backen §50 *tr* bake through and through

durch′blättern *tr* thumb through

durch′bleuen *tr* beat up

Durch′blick *m* vista

durch′blicken *intr* be apparent; (durch) look (through); **d. lassen** intimate

durchblutet [durç'blutət] *adj* supplied with blood

durch′bohren *tr* bore through || **durchboh′ren** *tr* pierce

durch′braten §63 *tr* roast thoroughly

durchbre′chen §64 *tr* break through; (*Vorschriften*) violate; (mil) breach || **durch′brechen** *tr* cut (*a hole*); break in half || *intr* (SEIN) break through

durch′brennen §97 *tr* burn through; (*e-e Sicherung*) blow || *intr* (SEIN) run away; (*Sicherung*) blow

durch′bringen §65 *tr* get through; (*Gesetz*) pass; (*Geld*) spend; (med) pull (*a patient*) through || *ref* support oneself; **sich ehrlich d.** make an honest living

Durch′bruch *m* breakthrough; (*Öffnung*) breach, gap; (*der Zähne*) cutting

durch′denken §66 *tr* think through || **durchden′ken** *tr* think out, think over

durch′drängen *ref* push one's way through

durch′drehen *tr* grind; (*Wäsche*) put

through the wringer || *intr* (coll) go mad

durchdrin′gen §142 *tr* penetrate; pervade, imbue || **durch′dringen** *intr* (SEIN) get through; penetrate

durch′drucken *tr* (parl) push through

durchdrungen [durç'druŋən] *adj* imbued

durchei′len *tr* rush through || **durch′eilen** *intr* (SEIN) (durch) rush through

durcheinan′der *adj & adv* in confusion || **Durcheinander** *n* (-s;-) mess, muddle

durcheinan′derbringen §65 *tr* muddle

durcheinan′dergeraten §63 *intr* (SEIN) get mixed up

durcheinan′derlaufen §105 *intr* (SEIN) mill about

durcheinan′derreden *intr* speak all at once

durcheinan′derwerfen §160 *tr* throw into confusion, turn upside down

durchfah′ren §71 *tr* travel through; (*Gedanke, Schreck*) strike || **durch′fahren** §71 *intr* (SEIN) go through without stopping

Durch′fahrt *f* passage; **keine D.!** no thoroughfare

Durch′fahrtshöhe *f* clearance

Durch′fall *m* diarrhea; (coll) flop; (educ) flunk, failure

durch′fallen §72 *intr* (SEIN) fall through; (educ) flunk; (theat) flop

durch′fechten §74 *tr* fight through

durch′finden §59 *ref* find one's way

durchflech′ten *tr* interweave

durchfor′schen *tr* examine, make an exhaustive study of

Durchfor′schung *f* exploration; search; thorough research

durch′fressen §70 *tr* eat through; corrode || *ref* (bei) sponge (on); (durch) work one's way (through)

Durchfuhr ['durçfur] *f* (-;-en) transit

durchführbar ['durçfyrbar] *adj* feasible

durch′führen *tr* lead through or across; (*Auftrag*) carry out; (*Gesetz*) enforce

Durch′gang *m* passage; aisle; (fig) transition; (astr, com) transit; **D. verboten!** no thoroughfare, no trespassing

Durch′gänger *m* (-s;-) runaway

Durch′gangslager *n* transit camp

Durch′gangsverkehr *m* through traffic

Durch′gangszug *m* through train

durch′geben §80 *tr* pass on

durch′gebraten *adj* (culin) well done

durch′gehen §82 *tr* (SEIN) go through; (*durchlesen*) go over || *intr* (SEIN) go through; (*Pferd*) bolt; (*heimlich davonlaufen*) run away; abscond; (*Vorschlag*) pass

durch′gehend(s) *adv* generally; (durchaus) throughout

durchgeistigt [durç'gaistɪçt] *adj* highly intellectual

durch′greifen §88 *intr* reach through; (fig) take drastic measures

durch′greifend *adj* vigorous; drastic

durch′halten §90 *tr* keep up || *intr* hold out, stick it out

durch′hauen §93 *tr* chop through;

knock a hole through; (coll) thrash, beat

durch′hecheln tr (coll) run down

durch′helfen §96 intr (dat) (durch) help (through) || ref get by, manage

durch′kämmen tr (& fig) comb through

durch′kochen tr boil thoroughly

durch′kommen §99 intr (SEIN) come through; (durch Krankheit) pull through; (sich durchhelfen) get by; (educ) pass

durchkreu′zen tr cross; (durchstreichen) cross out; (fig) frustrate

Durch′laß ['dʊrçlas] m (–lasses; –lässe) passage; outlet; culvert

durch′lassen §104 tr let through, let pass; (Licht) transmit; (educ) pass

durchlässig ['dʊrçlesɪç] adj permeable

Durch′lässeheim m pass

durchlau′fen §105 tr run through; look through; (Schule) go through; seine Bahn d. run its course || durch′laufen §105 ref—sich [dat] die Schuhe d. wear out one's shoes || §105 intr (SEIN) run through

durchle′ben tr live through

durch′lesen §107 tr read over, peruse

durchleuch′ten tr illuminate; (Gesicht) light up; (El) test; X-ray

durch′liegen §108 ref develop bedsores || **Durchliegen** n (–s) bedsores

durchlo′chen tr punch

durch′löchern tr perforate; pierce; (mit Kugeln) riddle

durch′machen tr go through, undergo

Durch′marsch m marching through; (coll) diarrhea, runs

Durch′messer m diameter

durchnäs′sen tr soak, drench

durch′nehmen §116 tr (in der Klasse) do, have

durch′pausen tr trace

durch′peitschen tr whip soundly; (Gesetzentwurf) rush through

durchque′ren tr cross, traverse

durch′rechnen tr check, go over

Durch′reise f passage; auf seiner D. on his way through

durch′reisen intr (SEIN) travel through

Durch′reisende §5 mf transient, transit passenger

durch′reißen §53 tr tear in half || intr (SEIN) tear, break, snap

Durch′sage f special announcement

durch′sagen tr announce

durchschau′en tr (fig) see through || **durch′schauen** intr look through

durch′scheinen §128 intr shine through; show through; be seen

durch′scheuern tr rub through

durchschie′ßen §76 tr shoot through, riddle; (typ) lead || **durch′schießen** §76 intr (durch) shoot (through) || intr (SEIN) dash through

Durch′schlag m carbon copy; (Sieb) (large) strainer, separator; (elec) breakdown; (tech) punch

durchschla′gen §132 tr penetrate || **durch′schlagen** §132 tr knock a hole through; (Holz) split; (Fensterscheibe) smash; (Nagel) drive through; (Kartoffeln, Früchte) strain; (mit Kohlepapier) make a carbon copy of

|| ref fight one's way through; (sich durchhelfen) manage || intr come through; penetrate; take effect; show up || intr (SEIN) (Sicherung) blow

durch′schlagend adj effective; striking

Durch′schlagpapier n carbon paper

durch′schleichen §85 ref & intr (SEIN) creep through

durchschleu′sen tr pass (a ship) through a lock; (Passagiere, Rekruten, usw.) process; (fig) sneak (s.o.) through

durch′schneiden §106 tr cut through; cut in half || **durchschnei′den** §106 tr cut through, cut across || ref cross, intersect

Durch′schnitt m cutting through; average; cross section; der große D. der Menschen the majority of people; im D. on an average

durch′schnittlich adj average || adv on the average

Durchschnitts— comb.fm. average; mean

Durch′schnittsmensch m average person

durch′schreiben §62 tr make a carbon copy of

durch′sehen §138 tr look over, examine; (flüchtig anschauen) scan; (Papiere, Post) check || intr see through

durch′seihen tr filter; percolate

durchset′zen tr intersperse; penetrate || **durch′setzen** tr carry through; d., daß bring it about that, succeed in (ger) || ref get one's way

Durch′sicht f examination, inspection; (auf acc) view (of)

durch′sichtig adj transparent; clear

durch′sickern intr (SEIN) seep out; (Wahrheit, Gerücht) leak out

durch′sieben tr sift

durch′sprechen §64 tr talk over

durchste′chen §64 tr pierce || **durch′stechen** §64 tr (Nadel) stick through

durch′stehen §146 tr go through

durchstö′bern tr rummage through

durch′stoßen §150 tr push (s.th.) through; (Tür) knock down; (Scheibe) smash in; (Ellbogen) wear through; (mil) penetrate || **durchsto′ßen** §150 tr break through || **durch′stoßen** §150 intr (SEIN) break through

durchstrei′chen §85 tr roam through || **durch′streichen** §85 tr cross out

durchstrei′fen tr wander through

durchsu′chen tr go through, search

durch′treten §152 tr (Sohle) wear a hole in; (Gashebel) floor || intr (SEIN) go through, pass through

durchtrie′ben [dʊrç′tri:bən] adj sly

durchwa′chen tr remain awake through

durchwach′sen adj gristly

durch′wählen tr & intr dial direct

durchwan′dern tr travel or walk through || **durch′wandern** intr (SEIN) (durch) walk (through), hike (through)

durchwe′ben tr interweave

durch′weg(s) adv throughout

durchwei′chen, durch′weichen tr soak

durchwüh′len tr burrow through; (Ge-

päck, Schränke) rummage through ||
durch′wühlen *ref* burrow through;
(fig) work one's way through
durch′wursteln *ref* muddle through
durchzie′hen §163 *tr* pass through,
cross; (*Zimmer*) permeate, fill;
streak; (sew) interweave || **durch′-
ziehen** §163 *tr* pull through || *intr*
(SEIN) pass through; flow through
durchzucken (durchzuk′ken) *tr* flash
through the mind of
Durch′zug *m* passage; (*Luftzug*) draft
durch′zwängen *tr* force through || *ref*
squeeze through
dürfen [′dʏrfən] §69 *aux* be allowed;
be likely; darf ich? may I?; ich darf
nicht I must not; man darf wohl erwarten it is to be expected
durfte [′dʊrftə] *pret* of dürfen
dürftig [′dʏrftɪç] *adj* needy; poor,
wretched, miserable, scanty
dürr [dʏr] *adj* dry; (*Boden*) arid, barren; (*Holz*) dead, dry; (*Mensch*)
skinny || **Dürre** [′dʏrə] *f* (–;) dry-
ness; barrenness; leanness; drought
Durst [dʊrst] *m* (–[ə]s;) (nach) thirst
(for); D. haben be thirsty

dursten [′dʊrstən], **dürsten** [′dʏr-
stən] *intr* be thirsty; (nach) thirst
(for)
durstig [′dʊrstɪç] *adj* thirsty
Dusche [′du:ʃə] *f* (–;-n) shower
duschen [′du:ʃən] *intr* take a shower
Düse [′dy:zə] *f* (–;-n) nozzle, jet
Dusel [′du:zəl] *m* (–s;–) (coll) fluke
Düsen- *comb.fm.* jet
Dü′senantrieb *m* jet propulsion
Dü′senjäger *m* jet fighter
düster [′dy:stər] *adj* gloomy; sad; dark
|| **Düster** *n* (–s;) gloom; darkness
Dutzend [′dʊtsənt] *n* (–s;- & -e) dozen
dut′zendmal *adv* a dozen times
dut′zendweise *adv* by the dozen
Duzbruder [′du:tsbru:dər] *m* buddy
duzen [′du:tsən] *tr* say du to, be on in-
timate terms with
Dynamik [dy′na:mɪk] *f* (–s;) dynamics
dynamisch [dy′na:mɪʃ] *adj* dynamic
Dynamit [dyna′mi:t] *n* (–s;-e) dynamite
Dynamo [′dynamo] *m* (–s;-s) dynamo
Dyna·stie [dynas′ti:] *f* (–;-stien
[′sti:ən] dynasty
D′-Zug *m* through train, express

E

E, e [e] *invar n* E, e; (mus) B
Ebbe [′ebə] *f* (–;-n) ebb tide
eben [′ebən] *adj* even, level, flat; zu
ebener Erde on the ground floor ||
adv just; a moment ago; exactly
|| *interj* exactly!; that's right!
E′benbild *n* image, exact likeness
ebenbürtig [′ebənbʏrtɪç] *adj* of equal
rank, equal
ebenda [′ebən′da] *adv* right there;
(*beim Zitieren*) ibidem
ebendersel′be §4,3 *adj* self-same
ebendes′wegen *adv* for that very reason
Ebene [′ebənə] *f* (–;-n) plain; (fig)
level; (geom) plane
e′benerdig *adj* ground-floor
e′benfalls *adv* likewise, too
E′benholz *n* ebony
e′benmaß *n* right proportions
e′benmäßig *adj* well-proportioned
e′benso *adv* just as; likewise
e′bensogut *adv* just as well
e′bensoviel *adv* just as much
e′bensowenig *adv* just as little
Eber [′ebər] *m* (–s;–) boar
E′beresche *f* mountain ash
ebnen [′ebnən] *tr* level, even; smooth
Echo [′eço] *n* (–s;-s) echo
echoen [′eço-ən] *intr* echo
echt [eçt] *adj* genuine, real, true
Eck [ek] *n* (–[e]s;-e) corner; end
Eck- *comb.fm.* corner; end
Ecke [′ekə] *f* (–;-n) corner; edge
Ecker [′ekər] *f* (–;-n) beechnut
eckig [′ekɪç] *adj* angular; (fig) awkward; eckige Klammer bracket
Eck′stein *m* cornerstone; (cards) dia-
monds

Eck′stoß *m* (fb) corner kick
Eck′zahn *m* canine tooth
Eclair [e′kle:r] *n* (–s;-s) éclair
edel [′edəl] *adj* noble; (*Metall*) pre-
cious; (*Pferd*) thoroughbred; edle
Teile vital organs
e′deldenkend *adj* noble-minded
e′delgesinnt *adj* noble-minded
E′del·mann *m* (–[e]s;-leute) noble
e′delmütig *adj* noble-minded
E′delstahl *m* high-grade steel
E′delstein *m* precious stone, gem
E′delweiß *n* (–;-e) edelweiss
Edikt [e′dɪkt] *n* (–[e]s;-e) edict
Edle [′edlə] §5 *mf* noble
Efeu [′efɔ1] *m* (–s;-e) ivy
Effekt [e′fekt] *m* (–[e]s;-e) effect
Effekten [e′fektən] *pl* property; ef-
fects; (fin) securities, stocks
Effek′tenmakler –in §6 *mf* stock broker
Effekthascherei [efekthaʃə′raɪ] *f* (–;)
showiness
effektiv [efek′ti:f] *adj* effective; (*wirk-
lich*) actual
Effektiv′lohn *m* take-home pay
Effet [e′fe] *n* (–s;-s) spin, English
egal [e′ga:l] *adj* equal; all the same
Egge [′egə] *f* (–;-n) harrow
eggen [′egən] *tr* harrow
Ego [′ego] *n* (–s;) ego
Egoismus [ego′ɪsmʊs] *m* (–;) egoism
Egoist –in [ego′ɪst(ɪn)] §7 *mf* egoist
egoistisch [ego′ɪstɪʃ] *adj* egoistic
Egotist –in [ego′tɪst(ɪn)] §7 *mf* egotist
ehe [′e-ə] *adv* (Aust) anyhow, anyway
ehe [′e-ə] *conj* before || **Ehe** *f* (–;-n)
marriage; matrimony
E′hebrecher *m* (–s;–) adulterer

E′hebrecherin *f* (-;-nen) adulteress
e′hebrecherisch *adj* adulterous
E′hebruch *m* adultery, infidelity
ehedem ['e·ə'dem] *adv* formerly
E′hefrau *f* wife
E′hegatte *m* spouse
E′hegattin *f* spouse
E′hegelöbnis *n* marriage vow
E′hehälfte *f* (coll) better half
E′heleute *pl* married couple
e′helich *adj* marital; (*Kind*) legitimate
e′helos *adj* unmarried, single
E′helosigkeit *f* (-;) celibacy
ehemalig ['e·əmɑlɪç] *adj* former; ex-;
  (*verstorben*) late
ehemals ['e·əmɑls] *adv* formerly
E′hemann *m* husband
E′hepaar *n* married couple
eher ['e·ər] *adv* sooner; rather
E′hering *m* wedding band
ehern ['e·ərn] *adj* brass; (fig) unshak-
  able
E′hescheidung *f* divorce
E′hescheidungsklage *f* divorce suit
E′heschließung *f* marriage
E′hestand *m* married state, wedlock
ehestens ['e·əstəns] *adv* at the earliest;
  as soon as possible
E′hestifter –in §6 *mf* matchmaker
E′heversprechen *n* promise of mar-
  riage
Ehrabschneider –in ['erɑp/nɑɪdər(ɪn)]
  §6 *mf* slanderer
ehrbar ['erbɑr] *adj* honorable, respect-
  able
Ehr′barkeit *f* (-;) respectability
Ehre ['erə] *f* (-;-n) honor; glory
ehren ['erən] *tr* honor; **Sehr geehrter
  Herr** Dear Sir
eh′renamtlich *adj* honorary
Eh′rendoktor *m* honorary doctor
Eh′renerklärung *f* apology
eh′renhaft *adj* honorable
ehrenhalber ['erənhalbər] *invar adj*—
  Doktor e. Doctor honoris causa
Eh′renmitglied *n* honorary member
Eh′renrechte *pl*—**bürgerliche E.** civil
  rights
Eh′rensache *f* point of honor
eh′renvoll *adj* honorable, respectable
eh′renwert *adj* honorable
Eh′renwort *n* word of honor; **auf E.
  entlassen** put on parole
ehrerbietig ['erərbitɪç] *adj* respectful,
  reverent, deferential
Ehrerbietung ['erərbitʊŋ] *f* (-;), Ehrfurcht ['erfʊrçt] *f* (-;) respect, reverence; (**vor** *dat*) awe (of)
ehrfürchtig ['erfʏrçtɪç], ehrfurchtsvoll
  ['erfʊrçtsfəl] *adj* respectful
Ehr′gefühl *n* sense of honor
Ehr′geiz *m* ambition
ehr′geizig *adj* ambitious
ehrlich ['erlɪç] *adj* honest; sincere;
  fair; **j-n e. machen** restore s.o.'s
  good name
Ehr′lichkeit *f* (-;) honesty; candor
ehr′los *adj* dishonorable; (*Frau*) of
  easy virtue; infamous
Ehr′losigkeit *f* (-;) dishonesty; infamy
ehrsam ['erzɑm] *adj* respectable
Ehr′sucht *f* (-;) ambition
ehr′süchtig *adj* ambitious

Ehr′verlust *m* loss of civil rights
ehr′würdig *adj* venerable; (eccl) reverend
ei [aɪ] *interj* oh!; ah!; ei,ei! oho!; ei je!
  oh dear!; ei was! nonsense! ‖ **Ei** *n*
  (-[e]s;-er) egg
Eiche ['aɪçə] *f* (-;-n) oak
Eichel ['aɪçəl] *f* (-;-n) acorn; (cards)
  club
eichen ['aɪçən] *adj* oak ‖ *tr* gauge
Ei′chenlaub *n* oak leaf cluster
Eichhörnchen ['aɪçhœrnçən] *n* (-s;-),
  Eichkätzchen ['aɪçketsçən] *n* (-s;-)
  squirrel
Eichmaß ['aɪçmɑs] *n* gauge; standard
Eid [aɪt] *m* (-[e]s;-e) oath
Eid′bruch *m* perjury
eid′brüchig *adj* perjured
Eidechse ['aɪdeksə] *f* (-;-n) lizard
Eiderdaunen ['aɪdərdaunən] *pl* eider
  down
eidesstattlich ['aɪdəs/tatlɪç] *adj* in lieu
  of an oath, solemn
eid′lich *adj* sworn ‖ *adv* under oath
Ei′dotter *m* egg yolk
Ei′erkrem *f* custard
Ei′erkuchen *m* omelet; pancake
Ei′erlandung *f* three-point landing
Ei′erlikör *m* eggnog
Ei′erschale *f* eggshell
Ei′erstock *m* ovary
Eifer ['aɪfər] *m* (-;) zeal, eagerness
Eiferer –in ['aɪfərər(ɪn)] §6 *mf* zealot
Ei′fersucht *f* jealousy
ei′fersüchtig *adj* (auf *acc*) jealous (of)
eifrig ['aɪfrɪç] *adj* zealous; ardent
Ei′gelb *n* (-[e]s;-e) egg yolk
eigen ['aɪgən] *adj* own; of (my, your,
  etc.) own; (*dat*) peculiar (to), char-
  acteristic (of) ‖ *invar pron*—**etw
  mein e. nennen** call s.th. my own
ei′genartig *adj* peculiar; odd, queer
Eigenbrötler ['aɪgənbrøtlər] *m* (-s;-)
  (coll) lone wolf, loner; crank
Ei′gengewicht *n* dead weight
eigenhändig ['aɪgənhendɪç] *adj & adv*
  with or in one's own hand
Ei′genheit *f* (-;-en) peculiarity
Ei′genliebe *f* self-love, egotism
Ei′genlob *n* self-praise
ei′genmächtig *adj* arbitrary, high-
  handed
Ei′genname *m* proper name
Ei′gennutz *m* self-interest
ei′gennützig *adj* selfish
eigens ['aɪgəns] *adv* expressly
Ei′genschaft *f* (-;-en) quality, property; **in seiner E. als** in his capacity
  as
Ei′genschaftswort *n* (-[e]s;ˉer) adjective
Ei′gensinn *m* stubbornness
ei′gensinnig *adj* stubborn
eigentlich ['aɪgəntlɪç] *adj* actual ‖ *adv*
  actually, really
Eigentum ['aɪgəntum] *n* (-[e]s;ˉer)
  property, possession; ownership
Eigentümer –in ['aɪgəntymər(ɪn)] §6
  mf (legal) owner ‖ *m* proprietor ‖ *f*
  proprietress
eigentümlich ['aɪgəntymlɪç] *adj* odd;
  (*dat*) peculiar (to)
Ei′gentümlichkeit *f* (-;-en) peculiarity

Ei'gentumsrecht *n* ownership, title

Ei'genwechsel *m* promissory note

ei'genwillig *adj* independent; (*Stil*) original

eignen ['aıgnən] *ref* (für) be suited (to); (als) be suitable (as); (zu) be cut out (for)

Eig'nung *f* (-;-en) qualification, aptitude

Ei'gnungsprüfung *f* aptitude test

Eilbrief ['aılbrif] *m* special delivery

Eile ['aılə] *f* (-;) hurry; E. haben or in E. sein be in a hurry

eilen ['aılən] *ref* hurry (up) || *intr* be urgent || *intr* (SEIN) hurry; eilt! (*Briefaufschrift*) urgent! || *impers*—es eilt mir nicht damit I'm in no hurry about it

eilends ['aılənts] *adv* hurriedly

Eilgut ['aılgut] *n* express freight

eilig ['aılıç] *adj* quick, hurried; urgent || *adv* hurriedly; es e. haben be in a hurry

Eilpost ['aılpost] *f* special delivery

Eilzug ['aıltsuk] *m* (rr) limited

Eimer ['aımər] *m* (-s;-) bucket, pail

ein [aın] §2,1 *indef art* a, an || §2,1 *num adj* one || *adv* one; ein und aus in and out; nicht ein und aus wissen not know which way to turn || einer *indef pron & num pron* see einer

ein-, Ein- *comb.fm.* one-, single

einan'der ['aın'dər] *invar recip pron* each other; (*unter mehreren*) one another

ein'arbeiten *tr* train (for a job); (in *acc*) work (into) || *ref* (in *acc*) become familiar (with), get the hang (of)

einarmig ['aınarmıç] *adj* one-armed

einäschern ['aın'eʃərn] *tr* reduce to ashes, incinerate; (*Leiche*) cremate

ein'atmen *tr & intr* inhale

ein'äugig *adj* one-eyed

einbahnig ['aınbanıç] *adj* single-lane; single-line; one-way

Ein'bahnstraße *f* one-way street

ein'balsamieren *tr* embalm

Ein'band *m* (-[e]s;⁻e) binding; cover

ein'bauen *tr* build in, install

einbegriffen ['aınbəgrıfən] *adj* included, inclusive

ein'behalten §90 *tr* retain; (*Lohn*) withhold

ein'berufen §122 *tr* call, convene; (mil) call up, draft || **Einberufene** §5 *mf* draftee

Ein'berufung *f* (-;-en) (mil) induction

ein'betten *tr* embed

ein'beziehen §163 *tr* include

ein'bilden *ref*—sich [*dat*] etw e. imagine s.th.

ein'binden §59 *tr* (bb) bind

ein'blenden *tr* (cin) fade in

Ein'blick *m* view; (fig) insight

ein'brechen §64 *tr* break in || *intr* (SEIN) collapse; (*Nacht*) fall; (*Kälte*) set in; (*Dieb*) break in

Ein'brecher -in §6 *mf* burglar

ein'bringen §65 *tr* bring in; earn; yield

Ein'bruch *m* break-in, burglary; invasion; E. der Nacht nightfall

ein'bruchsdiebstahl *m* burglary

ein'bruchsicher *adj* burglarproof

einbürgern ['aınbyrgərn] *tr* naturalize || *ref* (fig) take root, become accepted

Ein'bürgerung *f* (-;) naturalization

Ein'buße *f* loss, forfeiture

ein'büßen *tr* lose, forfeit

ein'dämmen *tr* check, contain

ein'decken *tr* cover || *ref* (mit) stock up (on)

Eindecker ['aındekər] *m* (-s;-) monoplane

ein'deutig *adj* unequivocal, clear

eindeutschen ['aındoıt/ən] *tr* Germanize

ein'drängen *ref* squeeze in; interfere

ein'dringen §142 *intr* (SEIN) penetrate, come in; e. auf (*acc*) crowd in on; e. in (*acc*) rush into; penetrate; infiltrate; (mil) invade

ein'dringlich *adj* urgent

Eindringling ['aındrıŋlıŋ] *m* (-s;-e) intruder, interloper; gate-crasher

Ein'druck *m* imprint; impression

ein'drücken *tr* press in; crash, flatten; imprint; (*Fenster*) smash in

Ein'druckskunst *f* impressionism

ein'drucksvoll *adj* impressive

ein'engen *tr* narrow; (fig) limit

einer ['aınər] §2,4 *indef pron & num pron* one || **Einer** *m* (-s;-) (math) unit

einerlei ['aınərlaı] *invar adj* (*nur attributiv*) one kind of; (*nur prädikativ*) all the same || **Einerlei** *n* (-;) monotony

einerseits ['aınərzaıts], einesteils ['aınəstaıls] *adv* on the one hand

ein'fach *adj* single; simple || *adv* simply

einfädeln ['aınfedəln] *tr* thread; (fig) engineer

ein'fahren §71 *tr* (*Auto*) break in; (*Ernte*) bring in; (aer) retract || *ref* get driving experience; die Sache hat sich gut eingefahren it's off to a good start || *intr* (SEIN) drive in; (rr) arrive

Ein'fahrt *f* entrance; gateway

Ein'fall *m* inroad; (fig) idea; (mil) invasion

ein'fallen §72 *intr* (SEIN) fall in; cave in, collapse; (*in die Rede*) butt in; join in; e. in (*acc*) invade; j-m e. occur to s.o.; sich [*dat*] etw e. lassen take s.th. into one's head; think up s.th.; sich [*dat*] nicht e. lassen not dream of; was fällt dir ein? what's the idea?

ein'fallslos *adj* unimaginative

ein'fallsreich *adj* imaginative

Ein'falt *f* simplicity; simple-mindedness

einfältig ['aınfeltıç] *adj* (pej) simple

Ein'faltspinsel *m* sucker, simpleton

ein'farbig *adj* one-colored; plain

ein'fassen *tr* edge, trim; (*einschließen*) enclose; (*Edelstein*) set

Ein'fassung *f* (-;-en) border; mounting

ein'fetten *tr* grease

ein'finden §59 *ref* show up

ein'flechten *tr* plait; (*Haar*) braid; (fig) insert

ein'fliegen §57 *tr* (*Truppen*) fly in;

(Flugzeug) flight-test || *intr* (SEIN) fly in

ein′fließen §76 *intr* (SEIN) flow in; **e. in** *(acc)* flow into; **einige Bemerkungen e. lassen** slip in a few remarks

ein′flößen *tr* infuse, instill

Ein′fluß *m* influx; (fig) influence

ein′flußreich *adj* influential

ein′förmig *adj* monotonous

einfried(ig)en [′aɪnfriːd(ɪg)ən] *tr* enclose, fence in

ein′frieren §77 *tr* (& fin) freeze || *intr* (SEIN) freeze (up) || **Einfrieren** *n* (-s;) (fin) freeze

ein′fügen *tr* insert, fit || *ref* fit in; (in *acc*) adapt oneself (to)

ein′fühlen *ref* (in *acc*) relate (to)

Einfuhr [′aɪnfuːr] *f* (-;-en) importation; **Einfuhren** imports

ein′führen *tr* import; introduce; (in *ein Amt*) install

Ein′führung *f* (-;-en) introduction

Ein′fuhrwaren *pl* imports

Ein′fuhrzoll *m* import duty

ein′füllen *tr*—**e. in** *(acc)* pour into

Ein′gabe *f* petition; application

Ein′gang *m* entrance; entry; beginning; introduction; *(von Waren)* arrival; **Eingänge** (com) incoming goods; incoming mail; (fin) receipts

ein′geben §80 *tr* suggest, prompt; (med) administer, give

eingebildet [′aɪngəbɪldət] *adj* imaginary; self-conceited

eingeboren [′aɪngəboːrən] *adj* native; only-begotten; *(Eigenschaft)* innate || **Eingeborene** §5 *mf* native

Ein′gebung *f* (-;-en) suggestion; (höhere) inspiration

eingedenk [′aɪngədɛŋk] *adj* (genit) mindful (of)

ein′gefallen *adj (Backen, Augen)* sunken

eingefleischt [′aɪngəflaɪʃt] *adj* inveterate

ein′gefroren *adj* icebound

ein′gehen §82 *tr* (HABEN & SEIN) enter into; *(Verpflichtungen)* incur; *(Wette, Geschäft)* make; *(Chance)* take; *(Versicherung)* take out; **e-n Vergleich e.** come to an agreement || *intr* (SEIN) come in; arrive; *(aufhören)* come to an end; fizzle out; *(Stoff)* shrink; (bot, zool) die off; (com) close down; **e. auf** *(acc)* go into, consider; consent to; **e. lassen** drop, discontinue; **es geht mir nicht ein, daß** I can't accept the fact that

ein′gehend *adj* thorough

eingelegt [′aɪngəleːkt] *adj* inlaid

Eingemachte [′aɪngəmaxtə] §5 *n* (-n;) preserves

eingemeinden [′aɪngəmaɪndən] *tr (Vorort)* incorporate

eingenommen [′aɪngənɔmən] *adj* prejudiced; **von sich e.** self-conceited

eingeschnappt [′aɪngəʃnapt] *adj* (coll) peeved

eingeschneit [′aɪngəʃnaɪt] *adj* snowed in

Eingesessene [′aɪngəzɛsənə] §5 *mf* resident

Ein′geständis *n* (-ses;-se) confession

ein′gestehen §146 *tr* confess, admit

Eingeweide [′aɪngəvaɪdə] *pl* viscera; intestines; *(von Vieh)* entrails

Eingeweihte [′aɪngəvaɪtə] §5 *mf* insider

ein′gewöhnen *tr* (in *acc*) accustom (to) || *ref* (in *acc*) become accustomed (to)

eingewurzelt [′aɪngəvurtsəlt] *adj* deep-rooted

ein′gießen §76 *tr* pour in, pour out

eingleisig [′aɪnglaɪzɪç] *adj* single-track

ein′gliedern *tr* integrate; annex

ein′graben §87 *tr* bury; engrave || *ref* burrow; (mil) dig in

ein′greifen §88 *intr* take action; interfere; *(in j-s Rechte)* encroach; (mach) mesh, be in gear || **Eingreifen** *n* (-s;) interference; (mach) meshing

Ein′griff *m* interference; encroachment; (mach) meshing; (surg) operation

ein′hacken *tr*—**e. auf** *(acc)* peck at; (fig) pick at

ein′haken *tr* (in *acc*) hook (into) || *ref* —**sich bei j-m e.** link arms with s.o. || *intr* (fig) cut in

Ein′halt *m* (-[e]s;) stop, halt; **E. gebieten** *(dat)* put a stop to

ein′halten §90 *tr* stick to; *(Verabredung)* keep; *(Zahlungen)* keep up; **die Zeit e.** be punctual || *intr* stop

ein′händigen *tr* hand over

ein′hängen §92 *tr (Türe)* hang; (in *acc*) hook (into); (telp) hang up || *ref*—**sich bei j-m e.** link arms with s.o. || *intr* (telp) hang up

ein′heften *tr* sew in; baste on

ein′heimisch *adj* domestic; local; home-grown; **e. in** *(dat)* native to

einheimsen [′aɪnhaɪmzən] *tr* reap

Einheit [′aɪnhaɪt] *f* (-;-en) oneness, unity; (math, mil) unit

ein′heitlich *adj* uniform

Einheits- *comb.fm.* standard, uniform; unit; united

ein′heizen *intr* start a fire; **j-m tüchtig e.** (fig) burn s.o. up

einhellig [′aɪnhɛlɪç] *adj* unanimous

ein′holen *tr* bring in; *(Flagge)* hawl down; *(Segel)* hawl down; (im *Wettlauf)* catch up with; *(Erkundigungen)* lower, hawl down; *(im Wettlauf)* catch up with; *(Erkundigungen)* make; *(Rat, Nachricht, Erlaubnis)* get; *(Verlust)* make good; *(abholen und geleiten)* escort; *(Schiff, Tau)* tow in || *intr* shop

Ein′horn *n* (myth) unicorn

ein′hüllen *tr* wrap up; enclose

einig [′aɪnɪç] *adj* united; of one mind; **sich** *[dat]* **e. sein** be in agreement

einige [′aɪnɪgə] §9 *indef adj* & *indef pron* some

einigen [′aɪnɪgən] *tr* unite || *ref* come to terms, agree

einigermaßen [′aɪnɪgərmaːsən] *adv* to some extent; *(ziemlich)* somewhat

ein′niggehen §82 *intr* (SEIN) concur

Ei′nigkeit *f* (-;) unity; harmony; agreement

Ei'nigung f (-;-en) unification; agreement, understanding

ein'impfen tr—j—m Impfstoff e. inoculate s.o. with vaccine; j—m e., daß (fig) drive it into s.o. that

ein'jagen tr (dat) put (e.g., a scare) into

ein'jährig adj one-year-old; (bot) annual

ein'kassieren tr collect

Ein'kauf m purchase; Einkäufe machen go shopping

ein'kaufen tr purchase; e. gehen go shopping

Ein'käufer –in §6 mf shopper

Ein'kaufspreis m purchase price

Ein'kehr f—E. bei sich halten search one's conscience; E. halten stop off

ein'kehren intr (SEIN) stay overnight; (im Gasthaus) stop off, stay

ein'keilen tr wedge in

ein'kerben tr notch, cut a notch in

einkerkern ['aɪnkɛrkərn] tr imprison

einkesseln ['aɪnkɛsəln] tr encircle

ein'klagen tr sue for (a bad debt)

ein'klammern tr bracket, put in parentheses

Ein'klang m unison; accord

Ein'klebebuch n scrap book

ein'kleben tr (in acc) paste (into)

ein'kleiden tr clothe; vest; (mil) issue uniforms to

ein'klemmen tr jam in, squeeze in

ein'klinken tr & intr engage, catch

ein'knicken tr fold

ein'kochen tr thicken (by boiling); can || intr thicken

ein'kommen §99 intr (SEIN)—bei j—m um etw e. apply to s.o. for s.th. || Einkommen n (-s;) income, revenue

Ein'kommensteuer f income tax

Ein'kommensteuererklärung f income-tax return

Ein'kommenstufe f income bracket

ein'kreisen tr encircle

Einkünfte ['aɪnkʏnftə] pl revenue

ein'kuppeln tr let out the clutch

ein'laden §103 tr load; invite

Ein'ladung f (-;-en) invitation

Ein'lage f (-;-n) (im Brief) enclosure; (im Schuh) insole; arch support; (Zwischenfutter) padding; (Kapital-) investment; (Sparkassen-) deposit; (beim Spiel) bet; (culin) solids (in soup); (dent) temporary filling; (mus) musical extra

ein'lagern tr store, store up

Ein'laß ['aɪnlas] m (-lasses;) admission; admittance; (tech) intake

ein'lassen §104 tr let it, admit; (tech) (in acc) sink (into) || ref (auf acc, in acc) let oneself get involved (in)

Ein'laßkarte f admission ticket

Ein'lauf m incoming mail; (e-s Schiffes) arrival; j—m e—n E. machen give s.o. an enema

ein'laufen §105 intr (SEIN) come in, arrive; (Stoff) shrink; das Badewasser e. lassen run the bath; j—m das Haus e. keep running to s.o.'s house || ref warm up (by running)

ein'leben ref (in acc) accustom oneself (to)

Ein'legearbeit f inlaid work

Ein'legebrett n (e-s Tisches) leaf

ein'legen tr put in; (Fleisch, Gurken) pickle; (Geld) deposit; (in e-n Brief) enclose; (Film, Kassette) insert; (Veto) interpose; (Beschwerde) lodge; (Protest) enter; (Berufung) (jur) file; Busse e. put on extra buses

ein'leiten tr introduce; (Buch) write a preface to; (beginnen, eröffnen) start, open; ein Verfahren e. gegen institute proceedings against s.o.

Ein'leitung f (-;-en) introduction; initiation

ein'lenken intr (fig) give in

ein'leuchten intr be evident; (coll) sink in

ein'liefern tr deliver; (ins Gefängnis) put, commit; ins Krankenhaus e. take to the hospital

ein'lösen tr ransom; redeem; (Scheck) cash

ein'machen tr can, preserve

ein'mal adv once; (künftig) one day; auf e. suddenly; all at the same time; einmal...einmal now...now; nicht e. (unstressed) not even; (stressed) not even once

Ein'maleins' n multiplication table

ein'malig adj unique

Einmann– comb.fm. one-man

Ein'marsch m entry

ein'marschieren intr (SEIN) march in

ein'mauern tr wall in

ein'mengen ref, ein'mischen ref (in acc) meddle (with), interfere (with)

Ein'mischung f (-;-en) interference

einmotorig ['aɪnmo'toriç] adj single-engine

einmummen ['aɪnmumən] ref bundle up

ein'münden intr (in acc) empty (into); (Straßen) run (into)

Ein'mündung f (-;-en) (e-s Flusses) mouth; (e-r Straße) junction

ein'mütig adj unanimous

ein'nähen tr sew in; (Kleid) take in

Ein'nahme f (-;-n) taking; capture; (fin) receipts; Einnahmen income

ein'nehmen §116 tr take; capture; (Essen) eat; (Geld sammeln) earn; (Steuern) collect; (Stellung) fill; (sew) take in; e-e Haltung e. assume an attitude; e-e hervorragende Stelle e. rank high; j—n für sich e. captivate s.o.; j—n gegen sich e. prejudice s.o. against oneself; seinen Platz e. take one's seat

ein'nicken intr (SEIN) doze off

ein'nisten ref (in dat) settle (in); (fig) find a home (at)

Ein'öde f desert, wilderness

ein'ordnen tr put in its place; file; classify || ref fit into place; (sich anstellen) get in line; sich rechts (or links) e. get into the right (or left) lane

ein'packen tr pack up

ein'passen tr (in acc) fit (into)

ein'pauken tr—j—m etw e. drum s.th. into s.o.'s head

ein'pferchen tr pen up; (fig) crowd together

ein'pflanzen *tr* plant; implant
ein'pökeln *tr* pickle; salt
ein'prägen *tr* imprint, impress
ein'quartieren *tr* billet, quarter
ein'rahmen *tr* frame
ein'rammen *tr* ram in, drive in
ein'räumen *tr* (*Recht, Kredit*) grant; (*zugeben*) concede, admit; **e. in** (*acc*) put into
ein'rechnen *tr* include, comprise
Ein'rede *f* objection; (jur) plea
ein'reden *tr*—j–m **etw e.** talk s.o. into s.th; **das lasse ich mir nicht e.** I can't believe that || *intr*—**auf j–n e.** badger s.o.
ein'reiben §62 *tr* rub
ein'reichen *tr* hand in, file; (*Rechnung*) present; (*Abschied*) tender; (*Gesuch*) submit; (*Beschwerde, Klage*) file
ein'reihen *tr* file; rank; enroll; (*Bücher*) shelve || *ref* fall into place; fall in line
ein'reihig *adj* single-breasted
Ein'reise *f* entry
ein'reißen §53 *tr* tear; demolish || *intr* (SEIN) tear; (fig) spread
ein'renken *tr* (*Knochen*) set; (fig) set right
ein'richten *tr* arrange; establish; (*Wohnung*) furnish; (surg) set || *ref* settle down; economize, make ends meet; (**auf** *acc*) make arrangements (for); (**nach**) adapt oneself (to)
Ein'richtung *f* (–;–en) setup; establishment; furniture; equipment
Ein'richtungsgegenstand *m* piece of furniture, piece of equipment
ein'rosten *intr* (SEIN) get rusty
ein'rücken *tr* (*Zeile*) indent; (*Anzeige*) put in || *intr* (SEIN) march in; **in j–s Stelle e.** succeed s.o.; **zum Militär e.** enter military service
Ein'rückung *f* (–;–en) indentation
ein'rühren *tr* (*in acc*) stir (into)
eins [ains] *pron* one; one o'clock; **es ist mir eins** it's all the same to me ||
Eins *f* (–;–en) one; (*auf Würfeln*) ace; (educ) A
einsam ['anzam] *adj* lonely, lonesome
ein'sammeln *tr* gather; (*Geld*) collect
Ein'satz *m* insert, insertion; (*Wette*) bet; (*Risiko*) risk; (*Verwendung*) use; (*für Flaschen*) deposit; (aer) sortie; (mil) action; (mus) starting in, entry; **im E. stehen** be in action; **im vollen E.** in full operation; **unter E. seines Lebens** at the risk of one's life; **zum E. bringen** employ, use; (*Maschinen*) put into operation; (*Polizei*) call out; (mil) throw into action
ein'satzbereit *adj* combat-ready
Ein'satzstück *n* insert
ein'saugen *tr* suck in; (fig) imbibe
ein'säumen *tr* (sew) hem
ein'schalten *tr* insert; (elec) switch on, turn on || *ref* intervene
ein'schärfen *tr*—j–m **etw e.** impress s.th. on s.o.
ein'schätzen *tr* appraise, value
ein'schenken *tr* pour
ein'schicken *tr* send in
ein'schieben §130 *tr* push in; insert

ein'schießen §76 *tr* (*Gewehr*) test; (*Geld*) contribute; (*Brot in den Ofen*) shove; (fb) score || *ref* (**auf** *acc*) zero in (on)
ein'schiffen *tr & intr* embark
Ein'schiffung *f* (–;–en) embarkation
ein'schlafen §131 *intr* (SEIN) fall asleep; (*Glied*) go to sleep
ein'schläf(e)rig *adj* single (bed)
einschläfern ['am/lefərn] *tr* lull to sleep; (vet) put to sleep
Ein'schlag *m* striking; impact; explosion; (*Umschlag*) wrapper; (fig) admixture, element; (golf) putt; (sew) tuck; (tex) weft, woof
ein'schlagen §132 *tr* (*Nagel*) drive in; (*zerbrechen*) smash, bash in; (*einwickeln*) wrap; (*Weg*) take; (*Laufbahn*) enter upon; (*Pflanzen*) stick in the ground; (golf) putt; **die Richtung e.** make go in the direction of || *intr* (*Blitz*) strike; (*Erfolg haben*) be a success; **nicht e.** fail
einschlägig ['am/legɪç] *adj* relevant
Ein'schlagpapier *n* wrapping paper
ein'schleichen §85 *ref* (*in acc*) creep (into), slip (into); (*in j–s Gunst*) worm one's way
ein'schleppen *tr* tow in; (*e–e Krankheit*) bring in (*from abroad*)
ein'schleusen *tr* (*Schmuggelwaren*) sneak in; (*Spionen*) plant
ein'schließen §76 *tr* lock up; (*in e–m Brief*) enclose; (fig) include; (mil) encircle, surround
ein'schließlich *adv* inclusive(ly) || *prep* (*genit*) inclusive of
ein'schlummern *intr* (SEIN) doze off
Ein'schluß *m* encirclement; **mit E.** (*genit*) including
ein'schmeicheln *ref* (**bei**) ingratiate oneself (with)
ein'schmeichelnd *adj* ingratiating
ein'schmuggeln *tr* smuggle in
ein'schnappen *intr* (SEIN) snap shut; (fig) take offense
ein'schneidend *adj* (fig) incisive
Ein'schnitt *m* cut, incision; (*Kerbe*) notch; (geol) gorge; (pros) caesura
ein'schnüren *tr* tie up; pinch
ein'schränken *tr* (**auf** *acc*) restrict (to), confine (to); (*Ausgaben*) cut; (*Behauptung*) qualify || *ref* economize
Ein'schränkung *f* (–;–en) restriction; **ohne jede E.** without reservation
Ein'schreibebrief *m* registered letter
ein'schreiben §62 *tr* enroll; (*Brief*) register; (*eintragen*) enter; **e–n Brief e. lassen** send a letter by registered mail || *ref* register
ein'schreiten §86 *intr* (SEIN) step in, intervene; (**gegen**) take action (against)
ein'schrumpfen *intr* (SEIN) shrivel up
ein'schüchtern *tr* intimidate, overawe
Ein'schüchterung *f* (–;) intimidation
ein'schulen *tr* enroll in school
Ein'schuß *m* hit (*of a bullet*)
ein'schütten *tr* pour in
ein'segnen *tr* (*neues Gebäude*) consecrate; (*konfirmieren*) confirm
ein'sehen §138 *tr* inspect; (*Akten*) consult; (fig) realize; (mil) observe ||

Einsehen *n*—ein E. haben show (some) consideration

ein'seifen *tr* soap; (coll) softsoap

ein'seitig *adj* one-sided

ein'senden §140 *tr* send in, submit

Ein'sender –in §6 *mf* sender

ein'senken *tr* (in *acc*) sink (into)

ein'setzen *tr* insert, put in; (*Geld*) bet; (*Leben*) risk; (*Polizei*) call out; (*Truppen*) commit; (*Kräfte*) muster; (*Einfluß*) use; (*Beamten*) install; (*nennen*) appoint; (*einpflanzen*) plant; (*Artillerie, Tanks, Bomber*) employ; (*Edelsteine*) mount || *ref* (für) stand up (for) || *intr* set in, begin; (*mus*) come in

Ein'sicht *f* inspection; (fig) insight

ein'sichtig *adj* understanding

ein'sichtsvoll *adj* understanding

ein'sickern *intr* (SEIN) seep in; (mil) infiltrate

Einsiedelei [aɪnzidəˈlaɪ] *f* (-;-en) hermitage

Einsiedler –in [ˈaɪnzidlər(ɪn)] §6 *mf* hermit, recluse

einsilbig [ˈaɪnzɪlbɪç] *adj* monosyllabic; (fig) taciturn

ein'sinken §143 *intr* (SEIN) sink in; (*Erdboden*) subside

ein'sparen *intr* economize on, save

ein'sperren *tr* lock up

ein'springen §142 *intr* (SEIN) jump in; (für) substitute (for); (tech) catch

ein'spritzen *tr* inject

Ein'spritzung *f* (-;-en) injection

Ein'spruch *m* objection; (jur) appeal

einspurig [ˈaɪnʃpuːrɪç] *adj* single-track

einst [aɪnst] *adv* once; (*künftig*) someday; e. wie jezt (now) as ever

Ein'stand *m* (tennis) deuce

ein'stecken *tr* insert, put in; stick in, pocket; (*Schwert*) sheathe; (*hinnehmen*) take; (coll) lock up, jail

ein'stehen §146 *intr* (SEIN) (für) vouch (for), stand up (for); für die Folgen e. take the responsibility

ein'steigen §148 *intr* (SEIN) get in; alle e.! all aboard!

Ein'steigkarte *f* (aer) boarding pass

Ein'steigloch *n* manhole

einstellbar [ˈaɪnʃtɛlbər] *adj* adjustable

ein'stellen *tr* put in; (*Arbeiter*) hire; (*Gerät*) set, adjust; (*beenden*) stop, quit; (*Sender*) tune in on; (*Fernglas, Kamera*) focus; die Arbeit e. go on strike; etw bei j—m e. leave s.th. at s.o.'s house; in die Garage e. put into the garage; zum Heeresdienst e. induct || *ref* show up, turn up; sich e. auf (*acc*) attune oneself to

Ein'stellung *f* (-;-en) adjustment; setting; focusing; stoppage; (*der Feindseligkeiten, Zahlungen*) suspension; hiring; (aut) timing; (mil) induction; E. des Feuers cease-fire; geistige E. mental attitude

einstig [ˈaɪnstɪç] *adj* former; (*verstorben*) late; (*künftig*) future

ein'stimmen *intr* join in; e. in (*acc*) agree to, consent to

einstimmig [ˈaɪnʃtɪmɪç] *adj* unanimous

ein'studieren *tr* study; rehearse

ein'stufen *tr* classify

ein'stürmen *intr* (SEIN) (auf *acc*) rush (at); (mil) charge

Ein'sturz *m* (-es;) collapse

ein'stürzen *intr* (SEIN) collapse; e. auf (*acc*) (fig) overwhelm

einstweilen [ˈaɪnstvaɪlən] *adv* for the present; temporarily

einstweilig [ˈaɪnstvaɪlɪç] *adj* temporary

Ein'tänzer *m* gigolo

ein'tauschen *tr* trade in; e. gegen exchange for

ein'teilen *tr* divide; (*austeilen*) distribute; (*einstufen*) classify; (*Geld, Zeit*) budget; (*Arbeit*) plan

eintönig [ˈaɪntønɪç] *adj* monotonous

Ein'tönigkeit *f* (-;) monotony

Ein'topf *m*, **Ein'topfgericht** *n* one-dish meal

Ein'tracht *f* (-;) harmony, unity

einträchtig [ˈaɪntrɛçtɪç] *adj* harmonious

Eintrag [ˈaɪntrak] *m* (-[e]s;=e) entry; E. tun (*dat*) hurt

ein'tragen §132 *tr* enter, register; (*Gewinn*) bring in, yield; j—m etw e. bring down s.th. on s.o. || *ref* register

einträglich [ˈaɪntreklɪç] *adj* profitable, lucrative

Ein'tragung *f* (-;-en) entry

ein'treffen §151 *intr* (SEIN) arrive; (in Erfüllung gehen) come true

ein'treten §62 *tr* drive in; (*Geld*) collect || *intr* (SEIN) drift in, sail in

ein'treten §152 *tr* smash in || *ref*—sich [*dat*] e—n Nagel e. step on a nail || *intr* (SEIN) enter; (*geschehen*) occur; (*Fieber*) develop; (*Fall, Not*) arise; (*Dunkelheit*) fall; e. für stand up for, champion; e. in (*acc*) join, enter

Ein'tritt *m* (-s;) entry; (*Einlaß*) admittance; (*Anfang*) beginning, onset; (rok) re-entry; E. frei free admission; E. verboten no admittance

Ein'trittsgeld *n* admission fee

Ein'trittskarte *f* admission ticket

ein'trocknen *intr* (SEIN) dry up

ein'trüben *ref* become overcast

ein'tunken *tr* (in *acc*) dip (into)

ein'üben *tr* practice; train, coach

ein'verleiben *tr* incorporate

Einvernahme [ˈaɪnfɛrnaːmə] *f* (-;-n) interrogation

Ein'vernehmen *n* (-s;) agreement; sich mit j—m ins E. setzen try to come to an understanding with s.o.

einverstanden [ˈaɪnfɛrˌstandən] *adj* in agreement || *interj* agreed!

Ein'verständnis *n* agreement; approval

ein'wachsen *tr* wax || *intr* (SEIN) (in *acc*) grow (into)

Ein'wand *m* (-s;=e) objection

Ein'wanderer –in §6 *mf* immigrant

ein'wandern *intr* (SEIN) immigrate

Ein'wanderung *f* (-;) immigration

ein'wandfrei *adj* unobjectionable; (*tadellos*) flawless; (*Alibi, Zustand*) perfect; (*Quelle*) unimpeachable

einwärts [ˈaɪnverts] *adv* inward(s)

Einweg- *comb.fm.* disposable

ein'weichen *tr* soak

ein'weihen *tr* consecrate, dedicate; e. in (*acc*) initiate into; let in on

Ein'weihung *f* (-;-en) dedication; initiation

ein'weisen §118 *tr* install; (*Verkehr*) direct; **e. in** (*acc*) assign to; **j-n in seine Pflichten e.** brief s.o. in his duties; **j-n ins Krankenhaus e.** have s.o. admitted to the hospital

ein'wenden §140 *tr—etw e. gegen* raise an objection to; **nichts einzuwenden haben gegen** have no objections to

Ein'wendung *f* (-;-en) objection

ein'werfen §160 *tr* throw in; (*Fenster*) smash; (*Brief*) mail; (*Münze*) insert; (fig) interject

ein'wickeln *tr* wrap (up); (fig) trick

ein'willigen *intr* (*in acc*) agree (to)

ein'wirken *intr* (*auf acc*) have an effect (on), exercise influence (on)

Ein'wirkung *f* (-;-en) effect, influence

Ein'wohner –*in* §6 *mf* inhabitant

Ein'wurf *m* (*Schlitz*) slot; (*e-r Münze*) insertion; (*Einwand*) objection

ein'wurzeln *ref* take root

Ein'zahl *f* (-;) singular

ein'zahlen *tr* pay in; (*in e-e Kasse*) deposit

Ein'zahlung *f* (-;-en) payment; deposit

Ein'zahlungsschein *m* deposit slip

einzäunen ['aɪntsɔɪnən] *tr* fence in

Einzel ['aɪntsəl] *n* (-s;-) singles

Einzel- *comb.fm.* individual; single; isolated; detailed; retail

Ein'zelbild *n* (cin) frame; (phot) still

Ein'zelfall *m* individual case

Ein'zelgänger *m* (coll) lone wolf

Ein'zelhaft *f* solitary confinement

Ein'zelhandel *m* retail trade

Ein'zelheit *f* (-;-en) item; detail, particular; **wegen näherer Einzelheiten** for further particulars

einzellig ['aɪntsɛlɪç] *adj* single-cell

einzeln ['aɪntsəln] *adj* single; particular, individual; separate

Ein'zelperson *f* individual

Ein'zelspiel *n* singles (match)

Ein'zelwesen *n* individual

Ein'zelzimmer *n* single room; (*im Krankenhaus*) private room

ein'ziehen §163 *tr* draw in; retract; (*Flagge*) hawl down; (*Segel*) take in; (*Münzen*) call in; (*eintreiben*) collect; (mil) draft || *intr* (SEIN) move in; **e. in** (*acc*) enter; penetrate

einzig ['aɪntsɪç] *adj & adv* only; **e. darstellen** be unique || *indef pron—ein einziger* one only; **kein einziger** not a single one

ein'zigartig *adj* unique; extraordinary

Ein'zug *m* entry; moving in; (*Beginn*) start; (typ) indentation; **seinen E. halten** make one's entry

ein'zwängen *tr* (*in acc*) squeeze (into)

Eis [aɪs] *n* (-es;) ice; (*Speise-*) ice cream || ['e-ɪs] *n* (-;-s) (mus) E sharp

Eis'bahn *f* ice-skating rink

Eis'bär *m* polar bear

Eis'bein *n* (culin) pigs feet

Eis'berg *m* iceberg

Eis'beutel *m* (med) ice pack

Eis'blume *f* window frost

Eis'creme *f* ice cream

Eis'diehle *f* ice cream parlor

Eisen ['aɪzən] *n* (-s;-) iron; **altes E.** scrap iron; **heißes E.** (fig) hot potato; **zum alten E. werfen** (fig) scrap

Ei'senbahn *f* railroad; **mit der E.** by train, by rail

Ei'senbahndamm *m* railroad embankment

Ei'senbahner *m* (-s;-) railroader

Ei'senbahnknotenpunkt *m* railroad junction

Ei'senblech *n* sheet iron

Ei'senerz *n* iron ore

Ei'senhütte *f* ironworks

Ei'senwaren *pl* hardware, ironware

Ei'senwarenhandlung *f* hardware store

Ei'senzeit *f* iron age

eisern ['aɪzərn] *adj* iron; (*Fleiß*) unflagging; (*Rationen*) emergency

Eis'glätte *f* icy road conditions

eis'grau *adj* hoary

eisig ['aɪsɪç] *adj* icy; icy-cold

Eis'kappe *f* ice cap

Eis'kunstlauf *m* figure skating

Eis'lauf *m* ice skating

Eis'laufbahn *f* ice-skating rink

eis'laufen §105 *intr* (SEIN) ice-skate

Eis'läufer –*in* §6 *mf* skater

Eis'meer *n—Nördliches E.* Arctic Ocean; **Südliches E.** Antarctic Ocean

Eis'pickel *m* ice axe

Eis'schnellauf *m* speed skating

Eis'scholle *f* ice floe

Eis'schrank *m* icebox

Eis'vogel *m* kingfisher

Eis'würfel *m* ice cube

Eis'würfelschale *f* ice-cube tray

Eis'zapfen *m* icicle

Eis'zeit *f* ice age, glacial period

eitel ['aɪtəl] *adj* (*nutzlos*) vain, empty; (*selbstgefällig*) vain; || *invar adj* pure || *adv* merely

Ei'telkeit *f* (-;) vanity

Eiter ['aɪtər] *m* (-s;) pus

Ei'terbeule *f* boil, abscess

eitern ['aɪtərn] *intr* fester, suppurate

Ei'terung *f* (-;-en) festering

eitrig ['aɪtrɪç] *adj* pussy

Ei'weiß *n* (-es;-e) egg white; albumen

Ekel ['ekəl] *m* (-s;) (vor *dat*) disgust (at) || *n* (-s;) (coll) pest

ekelerregend ['ekələregənt] *adj* sickening, nauseating

e'kelhaft *adj* disgusting

ekeln ['ekəln] *impers—es eket mir* or **mich** I am disgusted || *ref* (vor *dat*) feel disgusted (at)

eklig ['eklɪç] *adj* disgusting, revolting; nasty, beastly

Ekzem [ek'tsem] *n* (-s;-e) eczema

elastisch [e'lastɪʃ] *adj* elastic

Elch [elç] *m* (-[e]s;-e) elk, moose

Elefant [ele'fant] *m* (-en;-en) elephant

Elefan'tentreiber *m* mahout

Elefan'tenzahn *m* elephant's tusk

elegant [ele'gant] *adj* elegant

Eleganz [ele'gants] *f* (-;) elegance

Elektriker [e'lektrikər] *m* (-s;-) electrician

elektrisch [e'lektrɪʃ] *adj* electric(al)

elektrisieren [elektri'zirən] *tr* electrify

Elektrolyse [elektro'lyzə] *f* (-;-) electricity

Elektrizitäts– *comb.fm.* electric, electro–

Elektro– [ɛlɛktrɔ] *comb.fm.* electrical, electro–

Elektrode [ɛlɛk'trodə] *f* (-;-n) electrode

Elek'trogerät *n* electrical appliance

Elektrizität [ɛlɛktrɪtsɪ'tet] *f* (-;) electricity

Elek·tron [ɛ'lɛktrɔn] *n* (-s;-tronen ['trɔnən]) electron

Elektronen– [ɛlɛktrɔnən–] *comb.fm.* electronic

Elektronik [ɛlɛk'trɔnɪk] *f* (-;) electronics

Elektrotechnik *f* (-;) electrical engineering

Elektrotech'niker *m* (-s;-) electrical engineer

Element [ɛle'mɛnt] *n* (-[e]s;-e) element; (elec) cell

elementar [ɛlemɛn'tɑr] *adj* elementary

Elementar'buch *n* primer

Elen ['elen] *m & n* (-s;-) elk

elend ['elənt] *adj* miserable ‖ **Elend** *n* (-[e]s;) misery; extreme poverty; **das graue E.** the blues

E'lendsviertel *n* slums

elf [ɛlf] *adj & pron* eleven ‖ **Elf** *f* (-;-en) eleven

Elfe ['ɛlfə] *m* (-n;-n), *f* (-;-n) elf

Elfenbein ['ɛlfənbaɪn] *n* (-s;) ivory

elfte ['ɛlftə] §9 *adj & pron* eleventh

Elftel ['ɛlftəl] *n* (-s;-) eleventh (*part*)

Elite [ɛ'litə] *f* (-;) elite, flower

Ellbogen ['ɛlbogən] *m* (-s;-) elbow

Ell'bogenfreiheit *f* elbowroom

Elsaß ['ɛlzas] *n* (-;) Elsace

elsässisch ['ɛlzɛsɪʃ] *adj* Alsatian

Elster ['ɛlstər] *f* (-;-n) magpie

elterlich ['ɛltərlɪç] *adj* parental

Eltern ['ɛltərn] *pl* parents; **nicht von schlechtern E.** (coll) terrific

El'ternbeirat *m* Parent-Teacher Association

El'ternhaus *n* home

el'ternlos *adj* orphaned; **elternlose Zeugung** spontaneous generation

El'ternschaft *f* parenthood

El'ternteil *m* parent

Email [e'maj] *n* (-s;), **Emaille** [e'maljə] *f* (-;) enamel

Email'geschirr *n* enamelware

Email'lack *m* enamel paint

emaillieren [ema(l)'jirən] *tr* enamel

Email'waren *pl* enamelware

emanzipieren [emantsɪ'pirən] *tr* emancipate

Embargo [ɛm'bargo] *n* (-s;-s) embargo

Embo·lie [ɛmbɔ'li] *f* (-;-lien ['li·ən]) embolism

Embry·o ['ɛmbry·o] *m* (-s;-onen ['onən]) embryo

Emigrant –in [emɪ'grant(ɪn)] §7 *mf* emigrant

Emission [emɪ'sjon] *f* (-;-en) emission; (fin) issuance; (rad) broadcasting

empfahl [ɛm'pfɑl] *pret of* **empfehlen**

Empfang [ɛm'pfaŋ] *m* (-[e]s;=e) reception; (*Erhalten*) receipt; (*im Hotel*) reception desk

empfangen [ɛm'pfaŋən] §73 *tr* receive; (*Kind*) conceive

Empfänger –in (ɛm'pfɛŋər(ɪn)) §6 *mf* receiver, recipient; addressee

empfänglich [ɛm'pfɛŋlɪç] *adj* (für) susceptible (to)

Empfängnis [ɛm'pfɛŋnɪs] *f* (-;) conception

empfäng'nisverhütend *adj* contraceptive; **empfängnisverhütendes Mittel** contraceptive

Empfäng'nisverhütung *f* contraception

Empfangs'chef *m* desk clerk

Empfangs'dame *f* receptionist; (*im Restaurant*) hostess

Empfangs'schein *m* (com) receipt

empfehlen [ɛm'pfelən] §147 *tr* recommend; **e. Sie mich** (*dat*) remember me to ‖ *ref* say goodbye

empfeh'lenswert *adj* commendable

Empfeh'lung *f* (-;-en) recommendation; (*Gruß*) compliments

empfinden [ɛm'pfɪndən] §59 *tr* feel

empfindlich [ɛm'pfɪntlɪç] *adj* sensitive; delicate, touchy; (*Kälte*) bitter; (gegen) susceptible (to)

Empfind'lichkeit *f* (-;-en) sensitivity, touchiness; susceptibility

empfindsam [ɛm'pfɪntzɑm] *adj* sensitive, touchy; sentimental

Empfind'samkeit *f* (-;-en) sensibility; sentimentality

Empfin'dung *f* (-;-en) sensation; feeling, sentiment

empfin'dunglos *adj* numb; (fig) callous

Empfin'dungswort *n* (gram) interjection

Emphysem [ɛmfy'zem] *n* (-s;) emphysema

empor [ɛm'por] *adv* up, upwards

empören [ɛm'pørən] *tr* anger, shock ‖ *ref* rebel, revolt; (mil) mutiny

empor'fahren §71 *intr* (SEIN) jump up

empor'kommen §99 *intr* (SEIN) rise up; (*in der Welt*) get ahead

Emporkömmling [ɛm'porkœmlɪŋ] *m* (-s;-e) upstart, parvenu

empor'ragen *intr* tower, rise

empor'steigen §148 *intr* (SEIN) rise

empor'streben *intr* (SEIN) rise, soar; (fig) aspire

Empö'rung *f* (-;-en) revolt; (über *acc*) indignation (at)

emsig ['ɛmzɪç] *adj* industrious, busy

Em'sigkeit *f* (-;) industry; activity

End– [ɛnt] *comb.fm.* final, ultimate

Ende ['ɛndə] *n* (-s;-n) end; ending; outcome; **letzten Endes** in the final analysis; **zu E. gehen** end; **zu E. sein** be over

enden ['ɛndən] *tr & intr* end; **nicht e. wollend** unending

End'ergebnis *n* final result, upshot

End'gerade *f* (-;) home stretch

end'gültig *adj* final, definitive

endigen ['ɛndɪgən] *tr & intr* end; **e. auf** (*acc*) (gram) terminate in

Endivie [ɛn'divjə] *f* (-;-n) endive

End'lauf *m* (sport) final heat

end'lich *adj* final; limited, finite ‖ *adv* finally, at last

end'los *adj* endless

End'runde *f* final round, finals

End'station f final stop, terminus

End'summe f sum total

End'termin m final date; closing date

En'dung f (-;-en) ending

Ener·gie [ener'gi] f (-;-gien ['gi·ən]) energy

energisch [e'nergɪʃ] adj energetic

eng [eŋ] adj narrow; tight; (Freunde) close; (innig) intimate; im engeren Sinne strictly speaking

engagieren [ãga'ziran] tr engage, hire || ref commit oneself

Enge ['eŋə] f (-;-n) narrowness; tightness; (Meer) strait; (fig) tight spot

Engel ['eŋəl] m (-s;-) angel

en'gelhaft adj angelic

eng'herzig adj stingy; petty

England ['eŋlant] n (-s;) England

Engländer ['eŋlendər] m (-s;-) Englishman; die E. the English

Engländerin ['eŋlendərɪn] f (-;-nen) Englishwoman

englisch ['eŋlɪʃ] adj English

Eng'paß m pass, defile; (fig) bottleneck

engros [ã'gro] adv wholesale

engstirnig ['eŋ'ʃtɪrnɪç] adj narrow-minded

Enkel ['eŋkəl] m (-s;-) grandson

Enkelin ['eŋkəlɪn] f (-;-nen) granddaughter

En'kelkind n grandchild

enorm [e'nɔrm] adj enormous

Ensemble [ã'sãbl(ə)] n (-s;-s) (mus) ensemble; (theat) company, cast

ent- [ent] insep pref

entarten [ent'arten] intr (SEIN) degenerate

entartet [ent'artet] adj degenerate; (fig) decadent

entäu'ßern ref (genit) divest oneself of

entbehren [ent'beran] tr lack, miss; do without; spare; dispense with

entbehr'lich adj dispensable; needless, superfluous

Entbeh'rung f (-;-en) privation, need

entbin'den §59 tr release, absolve; (Frau) deliver || intr give birth

Entbin'dung f (-;-en) dispensation; (Niederkunft) delivery, childbirth

Entbin'dungsanstalt f maternity hospital

entblät'tern tr defoliate || ref defoliate; (coll) strip

entblößen [ent'bløsən] tr bare; uncover; (mil) expose || ref strip; remove one's hat

entbren'nen §97 intr (SEIN) flare up

entdecken (entdek'ken) tr discover || ref—sich j-m e. confide in s.o.

Entdeckung (Entdek'kung) f (-;-en) discovery

Ente ['entə] f (-;-n) duck; (coll) hoax

enteh'ren tr dishonor; (Mädchen) violate, deflower

enteh'rend adj disgraceful

Enteh'rung f (-;-en) disgrace; rape

enteig'nen tr dispossess

enteisen [ent'arzen] tr defrost; deice

enter'ben tr disinherit

Enterich ['entərɪç] m (-s;-e) drake

entern ['entərn] tr (naut) board

entfachen [ent'faxen] tr kindle; (fig) provoke

entfah'ren §71 intr (SEIN) (dat) slip out (on)

entfal'len §72 intr (SEIN) (dat) slip (from); auf j-n e. fall to s.o.'s share; entfällt not applicable

entfal'ten tr unfold; display; (mil) deploy || ref unfold; develop

entfernen [ent'fernən] tr remove || ref withdraw, move away; deviate

entfernt [ent'fernt] adj distant; nicht weit davon e. zu (inf) far from (ger)

Entfer'nung f (-;-en) removal; range; distance; absence

Entfer'nungsmesser m (phot) range finder

entfes'seln tr unleash

entflam'men tr inflame || intr (SEIN) ignite; flash; (fig) flare up

entflech'ten tr disentangle; (Kartell) break up; (mil) disengage

entflie'hen §75 intr (SEIN) flee, escape; (Zeit) fly

entfremden [ent'fremdən] tr alienate

enfrosten [ent'frostən] tr defrost

entfüh'ren tr abduct; kidnap; (Flugzeug) hijack; (hum) steal

Entfüh'rer m §6 mf abductor, kidnaper; (aer) hijacker

Entfüh'rung f (-;-en) abduction; kidnaping; (aer) hijacking

entge'gen prep (dat) contrary to; in the direction of, towards

entge'gengehen §82 intr (SEIN) (dat) go to meet; (dat) face, confront

entge'gengesetzt adj contrary, opposite

entge'genhalten §90 tr hold out; point out, say in answer

entge'genkommen §99 intr (SEIN) (dat) approach; (dat) come to meet; (dat) meet halfway || Entgegenkommen n (-s;) courtesy

entge'genkommend adj on-coming; (fig) accommodating

entge'genlaufen §105 intr (SEIN) (dat) run towards; (dat) run counter to

entge'gennehmen §116 tr accept, receive

entge'gensehen §138 intr (dat) look forward to; (dat) await; (dat) face

entge'gensetzen tr put up, offer

entge'genstehen §146 intr (dat) oppose

entge'genstellen tr set in opposition || ref (dat) oppose, resist

entge'genstrecken tr (dat) stretch out (toward)

entge'gentreten §152 intr (SEIN) (dat) walk toward; (fig) (dat) confront

entgegnen [ent'gegnən] tr & intr reply

Entgeg'nung f (-;-en) reply

entge'hen §82 intr (SEIN) (dat) escape, elude; sich [dat] etw e. lassen let s.th. slip by

Entgelt [ent'gelt] n (-[e]s;) compensation, payment

entgel'ten §83 tr pay for

entgeistert [ent'garstert] adj aghast

entgleisen [ent'glarzen] intr (SEIN) jump the track; (fig) make a slip

Entglei'sung f (-;-en) derailment; (fig) slip

entglei'ten §86 intr (SEIN) (dat) slip away (from)

entgräten [ent'gretən] tr bone (a fish)

enthaaren [ent'hɑːrən] *tr* remove the hair from

Enthaa'rungsmittel *n* hair remover

enthal'ten §90 *tr* contain; comprise || *ref* (*genit*) refrain (from); **sich der Stimme e.** (parl) abstain

enthaltsam [ent'haltzəm] *adj* abstinent

Enthalt'samkeit *f* (-;) abstinence

Enthal'tung *f* (-;-en) abstention

enthär'ten *tr* (*Wasser*) soften

enthaupten [ent'haʊptən] *tr* behead

enthäuten [ent'hɔɪtən] *tr* skin

enthe'ben §94 *tr* (*genit*) exempt (from), relieve (of); (*e-s Amtes*) remove (*from office*)

enthei'ligen *tr* desecrate, profane

enthül'len *tr* unveil; reveal, expose

Enthül'lung *f* (-;-en) unveiling; (fig) exposé

enthül'sen *tr* shell; (*Mais*) husk

Enthusiasmus [ɛntuzi'asmus] *m* (-;) enthusiasm

enthusiastisch [ɛntuzi'astɪʃ] *adj* enthusiastic

entjungfern [ent'jʊŋfərn] *tr* deflower

entkei'men *tr* sterilize; (*Milch*) pasteurize || *intr* (SEIN) sprout

entkernen [ent'kɛrnən] *tr* (*Obst*) pit

entklei'den *tr* undress; (*genit*) strip (of), divest (of) || *ref* undress

Entklei'dungsnummer *f* striptease act

Entklei'dungsrevué *f* striptease show

entkom'men §99 *intr* (SEIN) (*dat*) escape (from) || **Entkommen** *n* (-s;) escape

entkor'ken *tr* uncork, open

entkräften [ent'krɛftən] *tr* weaken; (*Argument*) refute

entla'den §103 *tr* unload; (*Batterie*) discharge || *ref* (*Gewehr*) go off; (*Sturm*) break; (elec) discharge; **sein Zorn entlud sich** he vented his anger

Entla'dung *f* (-;-en) unloading; discharge; explosion; **zur E. bringen** detonate

entlang *adv* along || *prep* (*dat* or *acc* or an *dat*; or after *genit* or *dat*) along

entlarven [ent'larfən] *tr* expose

entlas'sen §104 *tr* dismiss, fire; set free; (mil) discharge

Entlas'sungspapiere *pl* discharge papers

entla'sten *tr* unburden; (*von*) relieve (of); (jur) exonerate

Entla'stungsstraße *f* bypass

Entla'stungszeuge *m* witness for the defense

entlauben [ent'laʊbən] *tr* defoliate

entlaubt' *adj* leafless

entlau'fen §105 *intr* (SEIN) (*dat*) run away (from); (*mit e-m Liebhaber*) elope

entlausen [ent'laʊzən] *tr* delouse

entledigen [ent'ledɪgən] *tr* (*genit*) release (from) || *ref* (*genit*) get rid (of), rid oneself (of)

entlee'ren *tr* empty; drain

entle'gen *adj* distant, remote

entleh'nen *tr* borrow

entlei'hen §81 *tr* borrow

entlo'ben *ref* break the engagement

entlocken (entlok'ken) *tr* elicit

entloh'nen *tr* pay, pay off

entlüf'ten *tr* ventilate

entmannen [ent'manən] *tr* castrate

entmilitarisieren [ɛntmɪlitari 'ziːrən] *tr* demilitarize

entmutigen [ent'muːtɪgən] *tr* discourage

entneh'men §116 *tr* (*dat*) take (from); (*Geld*) (aus) withdraw (from); (*dat* or aus) infer (from), gather (from)

entnerven [ent'nɛrfən] *tr* enervate

entpuppen [ent'pupən] *ref* emerge from the cocoon; **sich e. als** (fig) turn out to be

enträtseln [ent'rɛtsəln] *tr* solve; (*Schriftzeichen*) decipher

entrei'ßen §53 *tr* (*dat*) wrest (from)

entrich'ten *tr* pay

entrin'nen §121 *intr* (SEIN) escape (from)

entrol'len *tr* unroll; unfurl || *ref* unroll || *intr* (SEIN) roll down

entrüsten [ent'rystən] *tr* anger || *ref*—**sich e. über** (*acc*) become incensed at; be shocked at

Entrü'stung *f* (-;) anger, indignation

entsa'gen *intr* (*dat*) renounce, forego; **dem Thron e.** abdicate

Entsatz' *m* (-es;) (mil) relief

entschä'digen *tr* compensate; reimburse

Entschä'digung *f* (-;) compensation

Entschä'digungsanspruch *m* damage claim

entschär'fen *tr* defuse

Entscheid [ent'ʃaɪt] *m* (-[e]s;-e) (jur) decision

entschei'den §112 *tr*, *ref* & *intr* decide

entschei'dend *adj* decisive

Entschei'dung *f* (-;-en) decision

Entschei'dungsbefugnis *f* jurisdiction

Entschei'dungskampf *m* (sport) finals

Entschei'dungsspiel *n* (cards) rubber game; (sport) finals

Entschei'dungsstunde *f* moment of truth

entschei'dungsvoll *adj* critical

entschieden [ent'ʃiːdən] *adj* decided; decisive; firm, resolute

entschla'fen §131 *intr* (SEIN) fall asleep; (*sterben*) pass away, die

entschlei'ern *tr* unveil; (fig) reveal

entschlie'ßen §76 *ref* (zu) decide (on)

Entschlie'ßung *f* (-;-en) (parl) resolution

entschlossen [ent'ʃlɔsən] *adj* resolute

entschlüp'fen *intr* (SEIN) (*dat*) slip away (from); (*dat*) slip out (on)

Entschluß' *m* resolve, decision

entschlüs'seln *tr* decipher

Entschluß'kraft *f* will power

entschulden [ent'ʃʊldən] *tr* free of debt

entschuldigen [ent'ʃʊldɪgən] *tr* excuse; exculpate || *ref* apologize; **es läßt sich e.** it's excusable; **sich e. lassen** beg to be excused; **sich mit Unwissenheit e.** plead ignorance

entschul'digend *adj* apologetic

Entschul'digung *f* (-;-en) excuse; apology; **ich bitte um E.** I beg your pardon

Entschul'digungsgrund *m* excuse

entseelt [ent'zeːlt] *adj* lifeless, dead

entsen'den §140 *tr* send off

entset'zen *tr* horrify; (mil) relieve ||

ref (über *acc*) be horrified (at) || Ent-
setzen *n* (-s;) horror
entsetz′lich *adj* horrible, appalling ||
adv (coll) awfully
Entset′zung *f* (-;-) dismissal; (mil) relief
entsi′chern *tr* take (*a gun*) off safety
entsie′geln *tr* unseal
entsin′nen §121 *ref* (*genit*) recall
entspan′nen *tr & ref* relax
Entspan′nung *f* (-;) relaxation; (pol)
detente
entspre′chen §64 *intr* (*dat*) correspond
(to); (*dat*) meet, suit; (*dat*) be equivalent (to); (*dat*) answer (*a description*)
entspre′chend *adj* corresponding; ade-
quate; equivalent || *adv* accordingly
|| *prep* (*dat*) according to
entsprin′gen §142 *intr* (SEIN) rise, originate; (*entlaufen*) escape
entstaatlichen [ɛnt′ʃtɑːtlɪçən] *tr* free
from state control, denationalize
entstam′men *intr* (SEIN) (*dat*) descend
(from), originate (from)
entste′hen §146 *intr* (SEIN) originate
Entste′hung *f* (-s;) origin
entstel′len *tr* disfigure; deface; (*Tatsachen*) distort
enttäu′schen *tr* disappoint
entthronen [ɛnt′troːnən] *tr* dethrone
entvölkern [ɛnt′fœlkərn] *tr* depopulate
entwach′sen §155 *intr* (SEIN) (*dat*) outgrow
entwaff′nen *tr* disarm
entwar′nen *intr* sound the all-clear
entwäs′sern *tr* drain; dehydrate
entweder [ɛnt′veːdər] *conj*—entweder
... oder either ... or
entwei′chen §85 *intr* (SEIN) escape
entwei′hen *tr* desecrate, profane
entwen′den *tr* steal
entwer′fen §160 *tr* sketch; draft
entwer′ten *tr* (*Geld*) depreciate; (*Briefmarke*) cancel; (*Karten*) punch
entwickeln (entwik′keln) *tr* develop;
evolve; (mil) deploy || *ref* develop
Entwick′lung *f* (-;-en) development;
evolution; (mil) deployment
Entwick′lungsland *n* developing country
Entwick′lungslehre *f* theory of evolution
entwin′den §59 *tr* (*dat*) wrest (from) ||
ref extricate oneself
entwirren [ɛnt′vɪrən] *tr & ref* unravel
entwi′schen *intr* (SEIN) escape; (*dat* or
aus) slip away (from)
entwöhnen [ɛnt′vøːnən] *tr* wean; j–n e.
(*genit*) break s.o. of || *ref* (*genit*)
give up
Entwurf′ *m* (-s;⁼e) sketch; draft
entwur′zeln *tr* uproot
entzau′bern *tr* disenchant
entzie′hen §163 *tr* (*dat*) withdraw
(from), take away (from); (chem)
extract; j–m das Wort e. (parl) rule
s.o. out of order || *ref* (*dat*) shirk,
elude
Entzie′hungsanstalt *f* rehabilitation
center
entziffern [ɛnt′tsɪfərn] *tr* decipher
entzücken (entzük′ken) *tr* delight

Entzückung (Entzük′kung) *f* (-;-en)
delight, rapture
Entzug′ *m* (-[e]s;) deprivation
entzündbar [ɛnt′tsʏntbɑr] *adj* inflammable
entzün′den *tr* set on fire; (fig) inflame
|| *ref* catch fire; (pathol) become in-
flamed
Entzün′dung *f* (-;) kindling; (pathol)
inflammation
entzwei′ *adv* in two, apart
entzwei′brechen §64 *tr & intr* break in
two, snap
entzweien [ɛnt′tsvaɪ-ən] *tr* divide
Enzykli-ka [ɛn′tsʏklɪkɑ] *f* (-;-ken
[kən]) encyclical
Enzyklopä-die [ɛntsyklɔpɛ′diː] *f* (-;
-dien [′diː-ən]) encyclopedia
Enzym [ɛn′tsym] *n* (-[e]s;-e) enzyme
Epaulette [epɔ′letə] *f* (-;-n) epaulet
ephemer [efe′meːr] *adj* ephemeral
Epide-mie [epɪde′miː] *f* (-;-mien
[′miː-ən] epidemic
epidemisch [epɪ′demɪʃ] *adj* epidemic
Epigramm [epɪ′gram] *n* (-s;-e) epigram
Epik [′epɪk] *f* (-;) epic poetry
Epilog [epɪ′loːk] *m* (-s;-e) epilogue
episch [′epɪʃ] *adj* epic
Episode [epɪ′zoːdə] *f* (-;-n) episode
Epoche [e′pɔxə] *f* (-;-n) epoch
Epos [′epɔs] *n* (-; Epen [′epən]) epic
Equipage [ek(v)ɪ′pɑːʒə] *f* (-;-n) carriage; (naut) crew; (sport) team
Equipe [e′k(v)ɪp(ə)] *f* (-;-n) team;
group
er [er] §11 *pers pron* he; it
er- [er] *insep pref*
erach′ten *tr* think || Erachten *n* (-s;)
opinion; meines Erachtens in my
opinion
erar′beiten *tr* acquire (*by working*)
Erb- [ɛrp] *comb.fm.* hereditary
Erb′anfall *m* inheritance
Erb′anlage *f* (biol) gene
erbarmen [er′barmən] *tr* move to pity
|| *ref* (*genit*) pity; erbarme Dich un-
ser have mercy on us || Erbarmen *n*
(-s;) pity, mercy
erbar′menswert, erbar′menswürdig *adj*
pitiable
erbärmlich [er′bɛrmlɪç] *adj* pitiful;
wretched, miserable || *adv* awfully
erbar′mungslos *adj* pitiless
erbau′en *tr* erect; (fig) edify || *ref* (an
dat) be edified (by)
Erbau′er *m* (-s;-) builder
erbau′lich *adj* edifying
Erbau′ung *f* (-;) building; edification
Erbau′ungsbuch *n* book of devotions
erb′berechtigt *adj* eligible as heir
Erbe [′erbə] *m* (-n;-n) heir; ohne Leibliche Erben without issue *n* (-s;)
inheritance, heritage; väterliches E.
patrimony
erbe′ben *intr* (SEIN) tremble
erb′eigen *adj* hereditary
erben [′erbən] *tr* inherit
erbet′teln *tr* get (by begging)
erbeuten [er′bɔɪtən] *tr* capture
Erb′feind *m* traditional enemy
Erb′folge *f* succession
erbie′ten §58 *ref* volunteer

Erbin ['ɛrbɪn] *f* (–;-nen) heiress
erbit'ten §60 *ref*—**sich** [*dat*] **etw e.** ask for s.th., request s.th.
erbittern [ɛr'bɪtərn] *tr* embitter
Erb'krankheit *f* hereditary disease
erblassen [ɛr'blasən] *intr* (SEIN) turn pale
Erblasser –in ['ɛrplasər(ɪn)] §6 *mf* testator
erbleichen [ɛr'blaɪçən] §85 & §109 *intr* (SEIN) turn pale; (poet) die
erb'lich *adj* hereditary
Erb'lichkeit *f* (–;) heredity
erblicken (erblik'ken) *tr* spot, see
erblinden [ɛr'blɪndən] *intr* (SEIN) go blind
Erblin'dung *f* (–;) loss of sight
Erb'onkel *m* (coll) rich uncle
erbre'chen §64 *tr* break open || *ref* vomit
erbrin'gen §65 *tr* produce
Erb'schaft *f* (–;-en) inheritance
Erbse ['ɛrpsə] *f* (–;-n) pea
Erb'stück *n* heirloom
Erb'sünde *f* original sin
Erb'tante *f* (coll) rich aunt
Erb'teil *m* share (in an inheritance)
Erd– [ɛrt] *comb.fm.* earth, of the earth; geo–; ground
Erd'anschluß *m* (elec) ground
Erd'arbeiten *pl* excavation work
Erd'bahn *f* orbit of the earth
Erd'ball *m* globe
Erd'beben *n* (–s;–) earthquake
Erd'bebenmesser *m* seismograph
Erd'beere *f* strawberry
Erd'boden *m* ground, earth; **dem E. gleichmachen** raze (to the ground)
Erde ['ɛrdə] *f* (–;-n) earth; ground, soil, land; (elec) ground wire; **zu ebener E.** on the ground floor
erden ['ɛrdən] *tr* (elec) ground
erden'ken §66 *tr* think up
erdenk'lich *adj* imaginable
Erd'gas *n* natural gas
Erd'geschoß *n* ground floor
erdich'ten *tr* fabricate, think up
Erdich'tung *f* (–;-en) fabrication
erdig ['ɛrdɪç] *adj* earthy
Erd'innere §5 *n* interior of the earth
Erd'klumpen *m* clod
Erd'kreis *m* earth, world
Erd'kugel *f* globe, sphere; world
Erd'kunde *f* geography
Erd'leitung *f* (elec) ground wire
Erd'nuß *f* peanut
Erd'nußbutter *f* peanut butter
Erd'öl *n* petroleum, oil; **auf E. stoßen** strike oil
erdolchen [ɛr'dɔlçən] *tr* stab
Erd'reich *n* soil
erdreisten [ɛr'draɪstən] *ref* have the nerve, have the audacity
Erd'rinde *f* crust of the earth
erdros'seln *tr* strangle
erdrücken (erdrük'ken) *tr* crush to death
erdrückend (erdrük'kend) *adj* overwhelming
Erd'rutsch *m* land slide
Erd'schicht *f* stratum
Erd'spalte *f* fissure; chasm
Erd'teil *m* continent

erdul'den *tr* suffer
ereifern [ɛr'aɪfərn] *ref* get excited
ereignen [ɛr'aɪgnən] *ref* happen, occur
Ereignis [ɛr'aɪgnɪs] *n* (–ses;-se) event, occurrence
ereig'nislos *adj* uneventful
ereig'nisvoll *adj* eventful
Erektion [erɛk'tsjon] *f* (–;-en) erection
Eremit [ere'mɪt] *m* (–en;-en) hermit
erer'ben *tr* inherit
erfah'ren *adj* experienced || §71 *tr* find out; (*erleben*) experience; (*Pflege*) receive
Erfah'rung *f* (–;-en) experience
erfas'sen *tr* grasp; understand; include; register, list
erfin'den §59 *tr* invent
Erfin'der –in §6 *mf* inventor
erfinderisch [ɛr'fɪndərɪʃ] *adj* inventive
Erfin'dung *f* (–;-en) invention
Erfin'dungsgabe *f* inventiveness
erfle'hen *tr* obtain (by entreaty)
Erfolg [ɛr'fɔlk] *m* (–[e]s;-e) success; (*Wirkung*) result
erfol'gen *intr* (SEIN) ensue; occur
erfolg'los *adj* unsuccessful || *adv* in vain
erfolg'reich *adj* successful
Erfolgs'mensch *m* go-getter
erfolg'versprechend *adj* promising
erforderlich [ɛr'fɔrdərlɪç] *adj* required, necessary
erfor'derlichenfalls *adv* if need be
erfordern [ɛr'fɔrdərn] *tr* require
Erfordernis [ɛr'fɔrdərnɪs] *n* (–ses;-se) requirement; exigency
erfor'schen *tr* investigate; (*Land*) explore
Erfor'scher –in §6 *mf* explorer
Erfor'schung *f* (–;-en) investigation; exploration
erfra'gen *tr* ask for; find out
erfreu'en *tr* delight || *ref* (**an** *dat*) be delighted (at); **sich e.** (*genit*) enjoy
erfreulich [ɛr'frɔɪlɪç] *adj* delightful; (*Nachricht*) welcome, good
erfreut [ɛr'frɔɪt] *adj* (**über** *acc*) glad (about); **e. zu** (*inf*) pleased to (*inf*)
erfrie'ren §77 *intr* (SEIN) freeze to death; (*Pflanzen*) freeze
Erfrie'rung *f* (–;-en) frostbite
erfrischen [ɛr'frɪʃən] *tr* refresh
Erfri'schung *f* (–;-en) refreshment
erfül'len *tr* fill; fulfill; (*Aufgabe*) perform; (*Bitte*) comply with; (*Hoffnungen*) live up to || *ref* materialize
Erfül'lung *f* (–;) fulfillment; accomplishment; **in E. gehen** come true
erfunden [ɛr'fundən] *adj* made-up
ergänzen [ɛr'gɛntsən] *tr* complete; complement; (*Statue*) restore
ergän'zend *adj* complementary
ergattern [ɛr'gatərn] *tr* (coll) dig up
ergau'nern *tr*—**etw von j–m e.** cheat s.o. out of s.th.
erge'ben *adj* devoted || §80 *tr* yield; amount to; show || *ref* surrender; (*dat*) devote oneself (to); (*aus*) result (from); **sich dem Trunk e.** take to drinking; **sich e. in** (*acc*) resign oneself to
Erge'benheit *f* (–;) devotion; resignation

ergebenst [er'ge:bənst] *adv* respectfully

Ergebnis [er'ge:pnɪs] *n* (–ses;–se) result, outcome; (*Punktzahl*) score

Erge'bung *f* (–;) submission, resignation; (mil) surrender

erge'hen §82 *intr* (SEIN) come out, be published; e. lassen issue, publish; *etw* über sich e. lassen put up with s.th.; **Gnade vor Recht e. lassen** show leniency ‖ *ref* take a stroll; **sich e. in** (*acc*) indulge in; **sich e. über** (*acc*) expatiate on ‖ *impers*—es ist ihm gut ergangen things went well for him ‖ **Ergehen** *n* (–s;) state of health

ergiebig [er'gi:bɪç] *adj* productive, fertile; rich, abundant

ergie'ßen §76 *ref* flow; pour out

ergötzen [er'gœtsən] *tr* amuse ‖ *ref* (an *dat*) take delight (in)

ergötz'lich *adj* delightful

ergrau'en *intr* (SEIN) turn gray

ergrei'fen §88 *tr* seize; (*Verbrecher*) apprehend; (*Gemüt*) move; (*Beruf, Waffen*) take up; (*Maßnahmen*) take

Ergrei'fung *f* (–;) seizure

ergriffen [er'grɪfən] *adj* moved; e. von seized with

Ergrif'fenheit *f* (–;) emotion

ergrün'den *tr* get to the bottom of

Erguß' *m* discharge; (fig) flood of words

erha'ben *adj* elevated, lofty; **erhabene Arbeit** relief work; **e. sein über** (*acc*) be above

Erhalt' *m* (–es;) receipt

erhal'ten §90 *tr* get, receive; keep, keep up, maintain; conserve; (*Familie*) support; (*Gesundheit*) preserve; **Betrag dankend e.** (stamped on bills) paid; **gut e.** well preserved; **noch e. sein** survive ‖ *ref* survive; (von) subsist (on)

erhältlich [er'heltɪç] *adj* obtainable

Erhal'tung *f* (–;) preservation; maintenance; support; (*der Energie, usw.*) conservation

erhän'gen *tr* hang

erhär'ten *tr* harden; (fig) substantiate ‖ *intr* (SEIN) harden

erha'schen *tr* catch; **e-n Blick von ihr e.** catch her eye

erhe'ben §94 *tr* raise; (*erhöhen*) elevate; (*preisen*) exalt; (*Steuern*) collect; (*Anklage*) bring; (math) raise ‖ *ref* get up, rise, start; arise

erheblich [er'he:plɪç] *adj* considerable

Erhe'bung *f* (–;–en) elevation; promotion; uprising, revolt; **Erhebungen machen** make inquiries

erheitern [er'haɪtərn] *tr* amuse ‖ *ref* cheer up

erhellen [er'helən] *tr* light up; (fig) shed light on ‖ *ref* grow light(er); light up ‖ *impers*—es erhellt it appears

erhitzen [er'hɪtsən] *tr* heat; (fig) inflame ‖ *ref* grow hot; get angry

erhöhen [er'hø:ən] *tr* raise; (fig) heighten ‖ *ref* increase; be enhanced

Erhö'hung *f* (–;–en) rise

erho'len *ref* recover; relax

Erho'lung *f* (–;–en) recovery, relaxation; recreation

erho'lungsbedürftig *adj* in need of rest

Erho'lungsheim *n* convalescent home

erhö'ren *tr* (*Gebet*) hear; (*Bitte*) grant

erinnerlich [er'ɪnerlɪç] *adj*—das ist mir nicht e. it slipped my mind; soviel mir e. ist as far as I can remember

erinnern [er'ɪnern] *tr* (an *acc*) remind (of) ‖ *ref* (an *acc*) remember

Erin'nerung *f* (–;–en) recollection, remembrance; (*Mahnung*) reminder; **zur E. an** (*acc*) in memory of

Erin'nerungsvermögen *n* memory

erkalten [er'kalten] *intr* (SEIN) cool off; (fig) grow cool

erkälten [er'kelten] *ref* catch cold

Erkäl'tung *f* (–;–en) cold

erkennbar [er'kenbar] *adj* recognizable

erkennen [er'kenən] §97 *tr* make out; recognize; detect; realize; **j–n e. für** (com) credit s.o. with; **sich zu e. geben** disclose one's identity; **zu e. geben, daß** indicate that ‖ *intr*—**auf e–e Geldstrafe e.** impose a fine; **gegen j–n e.** judge against s.o.

erkenntlich [er'kentlɪç] *adj* grateful

Erkennt'lichkeit *f* (–;) gratitude

Erkenntnis [er'kentnɪs] *f* (–;–se) insight, judgment, realization, knowledge; (philos) cognition ‖ *n* (–ses; –se) decision, finding

Erker ['erkər] *m* (–s;–) (archit) oriel

Er'kerfenster *n* bay window

erklären [er'klɛ:rən] *tr* explain, account for; (*aussprechen*) state

Erklä'rer –in §6 *mf* commentator

erklär'lich *adj* explicable

Erklä'rung *f* (–;–en) explanation; statement; commentary; (jur) deposition

erklin'gen §142 *intr* (SEIN) sound; (*widerhallen*) resound

erkor (er'kor] *pret* of **erkiesen**

erkoren [er'korən] *adj* chosen

erkranken [er'kranken] *intr* (SEIN) get sick; (*Pflanzen*) become diseased

erkühnen [er'ky:nən] *ref* dare, venture

erkunden [er'kundən] *tr & intr* reconnoiter

erkundigen [er'kundɪgən] *ref* inquire

Erkun'digung *f* (–;–en) inquiry

Erkun'dung *f* (–;) reconnaissance

erlahmen [er'la:mən] *intr* (SEIN) tire; (*Kraft*) give out

erlangen [er'laŋən] *tr* reach; (*sich verschaffen*) get; **wieder e.** recover

Er-laß' [er'las] *m* (–lasses;–lässe) remission; exemption; edict, order

erlas'sen §104 *tr* release; (*Schulden*) cancel; (*Strafe*) remit; (*Sünden*) pardon; (*Verordnung*) issue; **e. Sie es mir zu** (*inf*) allow me not to (*inf*), don't ask me to (*inf*)

erläßlich [er'leslɪç] *adj* pardonable

erlauben [er'laubən] *tr* allow ‖ *ref*—**sich** [*dat*] **e. zu** (*inf*) take the liberty to (*inf*); **sich** [*dat*] **nicht e.** not be able to afford

Erlaubnis [er'laupnɪs] *f* (–;–se) permission

Erlaub'nisschein *m* permit, license

erlaucht [er'lauxt] *adj* illustrious

erläutern [er'lɔɪtərn] *tr* explain

Erläu'terung *f* (–;–en) explanation

Erle ['ɛrlə] *f* (-;-n) (bot) alder
erle'ben *tr* live to see; experience
Erlebnis [ɛr'lepnɪs] *n* (-ses;-se) experience, adventure; occurrence
erledigen [ɛr'leːdɪgən] *tr* settle; (*Post, Einkäufe, Gesuch*) attend to, take care of; **j–n e.** (coll) do s.o. in
erledigt [ɛr'leːdɪçt] *adj* (& fig) finished; (*Stellung*) open; (coll) bushed
erle'gen *tr* pay down; (*töten*) kill
erleichtern [ɛr'laɪçtərn] *tr* lighten; make easy; (*Not*) relieve, ease
Erleich'terung *f* (-;) alleviation
erlei'den §106 *tr* suffer
erler'nen *tr* learn
erle'sen *adj* choice || §107 *tr* choose
erleuch'ten *tr* light up; enlighten
erlie'gen §108 *intr* (SEIN) (*dat*) succumb (to), fall victim to
erlogen [ɛr'loːgən] *adj* false
Erlös [ɛr'løs] *m* (-es;) proceeds
erlosch [ɛr'lɔʃ] *pret* of **erlöschen**
erloschen [ɛr'lɔʃən] *pp* of **erlöschen**
erlöschen [ɛr'lœʃən] §110 *intr* (SEIN) go out; (*Vertrag*) expire; (fig) become extinct
erlö'sen *tr* redeem; free; get (*by sale*)
Erlö'ser *m* (-s;-) deliverer; (relig) Redeemer
Erlö'sung *f* (-;) redemption
ermächtigen [ɛr'mɛçtɪgən] *tr* authorize
Ermäch'tigung *f* (-;-en) authorization
ermah'nen *tr* admonish
Ermah'nung *f* (-;-en) admonition
ermangeln [ɛr'maŋəln] *intr* (genit) lack; **es an nichts e. lassen** spare no pains; **nicht e. zu** (*inf*) not fail to (*inf*)
Erman'gelung *f*—**in E.** (genit) in default of
ermä'ßigen *tr* reduce
ermatten [ɛr'matən] *tr* tire || *intr* (SEIN) tire; grow weak; slacken
Ermat'tung *f* (-;) fatigue
ermes'sen §70 *tr* judge, estimate; realize; **e. aus** infer from || **Ermessen** *n* (-s;) judgment, opinion; **nach freiem E.** at one's discretion
ermitteln [ɛr'mɪtəln] *tr* ascertain || *intr* conduct an investigation
Ermitt'lung *f* (-;-en) ascertainment; Ermittlungen investigation
Ermitt'lungsausschuß *m* fact-finding committee
Ermitt'lungsbeamte *m* investigator
Ermitt'lungsverfahren *n* judicial inquiry
ermöglichen [ɛr'møːklɪçən] *tr* enable, make possible
ermorden [ɛr'mɔrdən] *tr* murder
ermüden [ɛr'myːdən] *tr* tire || *intr* (SEIN) tire, get tired
Ermü'dung *f* (-;) fatigue
ermuntern [ɛr'muntərn] *tr* cheer up; encourage || *ref* cheer up
Ermun'terung *f* (-;) encouragement
ermutigen [ɛr'muːtɪgən] *tr* encourage
ernäh'ren *tr* nourish; (fig) support
Ernäh'rer **–in** §6 *mf* supporter
Ernäh'rung *f* (-;) nourishment; support; (physiol) nutrition
ernen'nen §97 *tr* nominate, appoint
erneuern [ɛr'nɔɪ.ərn] *tr* renew; reno-

vate; (*Gemälde*) restore; (*Öl*) change; (*Reifen*) retread; (mach) replace
erneu'ert *adj* repeated || *adv* anew
Erneu'erung *f* (-;-en) renewal; renovation; restoration; replacement
erniedrigen [ɛr'niːdrɪgən] *tr* lower; (*demütigen*) humble; (*im Rang*) degrade || *ref* humble oneself; debase oneself
ernst [ɛrnst] *adj* earnest; serious || **Ernst** *m* (-[e]s;) seriousness; **im E.** in earnest
Ernst'fall *m*—**im E.** in case of emergency; (mil) in case of war
ernst'haft *adj* earnest, serious
ernst'lich *adj* earnest; serious
Ernte ['ɛrntə] *f* (-;-n) harvest; crop
ernten ['ɛrntən] *tr* reap, harvest
ernüch'tern *tr* sober; disallusion || *ref* sober up; be disallusioned
Ero'berer *m* §6 *mf* conqueror
erobern [ɛr'oːbərn] *tr* conquer
Ero'berung *f* (-;-en) conquest
eröff'nen *tr* open; (*feierlich*) inaugurate; disclose || *ref* open; present itself; **sich j–m e.** unburden oneself to s.o.
Eröff'nung *f* (-;-en) (grand) opening; inauguration; announcement
erörtern [ɛr'œrtərn] *tr* discuss
erotisch [ɛ'roːtɪʃ] *adj* erotic
Erpel ['ɛrpəl] *m* (-s;-) drake
erpicht [ɛr'pɪçt] *adj*—**e. auf** (*acc*) keen on, dead set on, hell bent on
erpres'sen *tr* extort; (*Person*) blackmail
Erpres'sung *f* (-;-en) extortion; blackmail
erpro'ben *tr* test, try out
erquicken [ɛr'kvɪkən] *tr* refresh
erquick'lich *adj* refreshing; agreeable
erra'ten §63 *tr* guess
errech'nen *tr* calculate
erregbar [ɛr'rekbar] *adj* excitable; irritable
erregen [ɛr'reːgən] *tr* excite; cause || *ref* get excited, get worked up
Erre'gung *f* (-;) excitation; agitation; excitement; **E. öffentlichen Ärgernisses** disorderly conduct
erreichbar [ɛr'raɪçbar] *adj* reachable; available
errei'chen *tr* reach, attain; get to; (*Zug, Bus*) catch; **e., daß** bring it about that
erret'ten *tr* save, rescue
Erret'tung *f* (-;-en) rescue; (relig) Salvation
errich'ten *tr* erect; found
errin'gen §142 *tr* get; attain, achieve
errö'ten *intr* (SEIN) redden; blush
Errungenschaft [ɛr'ruŋənʃaft] *f* (-; -en) achievement; acquisition
Ersatz' *m* (-es;) substitute; replacement; compensation; (mil) recruitment
Ersatz– *comb.fm.* substitute, replacement; spare; alternative; recruiting
Ersatz'mann *m* substitute; alternate
Ersatz'stück *n*, **Ersatz'teil** *n* spare part, spare
erschaf'fen §126 *tr* create
Erschaf'fer **–in** §6 *mf* creator
Erschaf'fung *f* (-;-en) creation

erschal/len §127 intr (SEIN) begin to sound; ring out; resound

erschau/ern intr shudder

erschei/nen §128 intr (SEIN) appear; (Buch) come out, be published

Erschei/nung f (-;-en) appearance; apparition; phenomenon

erschie/ßen §76 tr shoot (dead)

Erschie/ßung f (-;-en) shooting, execution

Erschie/ßungskommando n firing squad

erschlaffen [er'ʃlafən] tr relax; enervate || intr (SEIN) relax; weaken

erschla/gen §132 tr slay; wie e. dead tired

erschlie/ßen §76 tr open up; develop; e. aus infer from; derive from || ref —sich j–m e. unburden oneself to s.o.

erschöp/fen tr exhaust; (fig) deplete

erschrak [er'ʃrak] pret of erschrecken

erschrecken (erschrek/ken) tr startle; shock || ref get scared || §134 intr (SEIN) be startled

erschreckend (erschrek/kend) adj terrifying; alarming; dreadful

erschüt/ten tr shake; upset; move deeply

Erschüt/terung f (-;-en) tremor; vibration; deep feeling; concussion

erschweren [er'veran] tr make more difficult; hamper, impede

erschwin/deln tr—etw von j–m e. cheat s.o. out of s.th.

erschwing/lich adj within one's means

erse/hen §138 tr (aus) gather (from)

erseh/nen tr long for

ersetzbar [er'zetsbar] adj replaceable

erset/zen tr replace; (Schaden) compensate for; (Kräfte) renew; j–m etw e. reimburse s.o. for s.th.; sie ersetzte ihm die Eltern she was mother and father to him

ersetz/lich adj replaceable

ersicht/lich adj evident

ersin/nen §121 tr think up

erspa/ren tr save

Ersparnis [er'ʃparnɪs] f (-;-se) (an dat) saving (in)

ersprießlich [er'ʃprislɪç] adj useful

erst [erst] adv first; at first; just; only; not until; e. recht really; e. recht nicht most certainly not

erstar/ren intr (SEIN) grow stiff; (Finger) grow numb; (Blut) congeal; (Zement) set; (fig) run cold; vor Schreck e. be paralyzed with fear

erstatten [er'ʃtatən] tr refund, repay; (Bericht) file; Meldung e. report

Erstat/tung f (-;-en) refund; reimbursement; compensation

Erst/aufführung f primiere

erstau/nen tr astonish || intr (SEIN) (über acc) be astonished (at) || Erstaunen n (-s;) astonishment; in E. setzen astonish

erstaun/lich adj astonishing

Erst/ausfertigung f original

erste ['erstə] §9 adj first; der erste beste the first that comes along; fürs e. for the time being; zum ersten, zum zweiten, zum dritten going, going, gone

erste/chen §64 tr stab

erste/hen §146 tr buy, get || intr (SEIN) rise; (Städte) spring up

erstei/gen §148 tr climb

erstel/len tr provide, supply; erect

erstens ['erstəns] adv first; in the first place

erst/geboren adj first-born

ersticken [er'ʃtɪkən] tr choke, stifle, smother; im Keim e. nip in the bud || intr (SEIN) choke; in Arbeit e. be snowed under

erstklassig ['erstklasɪç] adj first-class

Erstling ['erstlɪŋ] m (-s;-e) first-born child; (fig) first fruits

Erstlings- comb.fm. first

Erst/lingsausstattung f layette

erstmalig ['erstmalɪç] adj first

erstre/ben tr strive for

erstrecken (erstrek/ken) ref extend

ersu/chen tr request, ask

ertappen [er'tapən] tr surprise, catch

ertei/len tr give; confer; (Auftrag) place; (Audienz, Patent) grant

ertö/nen intr (SEIN) sound; resound

ertö/ten tr (fig) stifle

Ertrag [er'trak] m (-[e]s;–e) yield; proceeds; produce

ertra/gen §132 tr stand, bear

erträglich [er'treklɪç] adj bearable

ertränken [er'treŋkən] tr drown

erträu/men tr dream of

ertrin/ken §143 intr (SEIN) drown

ertüchtigen [er'tʏçtɪgən] tr train

erübrigen [er'ybrɪgən] tr save; (Zeit) spare || ref be superfluous

erwa/chen intr (SEIN) wake up

erwach/sen adj adult || §155 intr (SEIN) grow, grow up; arise || Erwachsene §5 mf adult, grown-up

erwä/gen §156 tr weigh, consider

Erwä/gung f (-;-en) consideration

erwäh/len tr choose

erwäh/nen tr mention

erwäh/nenswert adj worth mentioning

Erwäh/nung f (-;) mention

erwär/men tr warm, warm up

erwar/ten tr expect, await; etw zu e. haben be in for s.th.

Erwar/tung f (-;-en) expectation

erwar/tungsvoll adj expectant

erwecken (erwek/ken) tr wake; (Hoffnungen) raise; (Gefühle) awaken; den Anschein e. give the impression

erweh/ren ref (genit) ward off; (genit) refrain from; (der Tränen) hold back

erwei/chen tr soften; (fig) move, touch; sich e. lassen relent

erwei/sen §118 tr prove; show; (Achtung) show; (Dienst) render; (Ehre, Gunst) do || ref—sich e. als prove

erweitern [er'vaitərn] tr & ref widen; (vermehren) increase; extend, expand

Erwerb [er'verp] m (-[e]s;-e) acquisition; (Verdienst) earnings; (Unterhalt) living

erwer/ben §149 tr acquire; gain; (verdienen) earn; (kaufen) purchase

erwerbs/behindert adj disabled

Erwerbs/betrieb m business enterprise

erwerbs/fähig adj capable of earning a living

erwerbs/los adj unemployed

Erwerbs′quelle f source of income
Erwerbs′sinn m acquisitiveness
erwerbs′tätig adj gainfully employed
erwerbs′unfähig adj unable to earn a living
Erwerbs′zweig m line of business
Erwer′bung f (-;-en) acquisition
erwidern [ɛr′vɪdərn] tr reply; reciprocate, return
Erwi′derung f (-;-en) reply; return; retaliation
erwir′ken tr secure, obtain
erwi′schen tr catch; ihn hat's erwischt! (coll) he's had it!
erwünscht [ɛr′vʏnʃt] adj desired; welcome; (wünschenswert) desirable
erwür′gen tr strangle
Erz [ɛrts] n (-es;-e) ore; brass; bronze
Erz-, erz- comb.fm. ore; bronze; utterly; (fig) arch-
erzählen [ɛr′tsɛlən] tr tell, narrate
Erzäh′lung f (-;-en) story, narrative
Erz′bischof m archbishop
Erz′engel m archangel
erzeu′gen tr beget; manufacture; produce; generate
Erzeugnis [ɛr′tsɔɪknɪs] n (-ses;-se) product; produce
Erzeu′gung f (-;-en) production; manufacture
erzie′hen §163 tr bring up, rear; (geistig) educate
Erzieher [ɛr′tsiːər] m (-s;-) educator; private tutor
Erzieherin [ɛr′tsiːərɪn] f (-;-nen) educator; governess
erzieherisch [ɛr′tsiːərɪʃ] adj educational, pedagogical
Erzie′hung f (-;) upbringing; education; (Lebensart) breeding
Erzie′hungslehre f (educ) education
Erzie′hungswesen n educational system
erzie′len tr achieve, reach; (Gewinn) realize; (sport) score
Erz′lager n ore deposit
Erz′probe f assay
erzür′nen tr anger || ref get angry
erzwin′gen §142 tr force; wring, obtain by force; (Gehorsam) exact
es [ɛs] adv (as expletive) there; es gibt there is, there are || §11 pers pron it; he; she || Es n (-;-) (mus) E flat; (psychol) id
Esche [′ɛʃə] f (-;-n) ash tree
Esel [′ezəl] m (-s;-) donkey, ass
Eselei [ezə′laɪ] f (-;-en) foolish act, foolish remark
E′selsbrücke f (educ) pony
E′selsohr n dog's-ear
eskalieren [ɛska′liːrən] tr & intr escalate
Eskimo [′ɛskɪmo] m (-s;-s) Eskimo
Espe [′ɛspə] f (-;-n) (bot) aspen
eßbar [′ɛsbɑr] adj edible, eatable
Eßbesteck [′ɛsbə/tɛk] n knife, fork, and spoon
Esse [′ɛsə] f (-;-n) chimney; forge
essen [′ɛsən] §70 tr & intr eat; zu Mittag e. eat lunch || Essen n (-s;) eating; food, meal
Essenz [ɛ′sɛnts] f (-;-en) essence
Eßgeschirr [′ɛsgə/ɪr] n (-s;) tableware; table service; (mil) mess kit

Eßgier [′ɛsgir] f (-;) gluttony
Essig [′ɛsɪç] m (-s;-e) vinegar
Es′siggurke f pickle, gherkin
Es′sigsäure f acetic acid
Eßlöffel [′ɛlcefəl] m (-s;-) tablespoon
Eßnapf [′ɛsnapf] m dinner pail
Eßsaal [′ɛszɑl] m dining room
Eßstäbchen [′ɛs/tɛpçən] n chopstick
Eßwaren [′ɛsvɑrən] pl food, victuals
Eßzimmer [′ɛstsɪmər] n (-s;-) dining room
Estland [′ɛstlant] n (-s;) Estonia
Estrade [ɛs′trɑdə] f (-;-n) dais
etablieren [eta′bliːrən] tr establish
Etablissement [etablɪs(ə)′mɑ̃] n (-s; -s) establishment
Etage [e′tɑʒə] f (-;-n) floor, story
Eta′genbett n bunk bed
Eta′genwohnung f apartment
Etappe [e′tapə] f (-;-n) (Teilstrecke) leg, stage; (mil) rear echelon, rear
Etat [e′tɑ] m (-s;-s) budget
Etats′jahr n fiscal year
etepetete [etəpe′tetə] adj overly particular
Ethik [′etɪk] f (-s;) ethics
ethisch [′etɪʃ] adj ethical
ethnisch [′ɛtnɪʃ] adj ethnic
Ethnologie [ɛtnolo′giː] f (-;) ethnology
Etikett [etɪ′ket] n (-s;-e) tab, label
Etikette [etɪ′ketə] f (-;) etiquette
etikettieren [ɛtɪke′tiːrən] tr label
etliche [′ɛtlɪçə] adj & pron a few
Etui [e′tvi] n (-s;-s) case (for spectacles, cigarettes, etc.)
etwa [′ɛtva] adv about, around; perhaps; by chance; for example
etwaig [ɛt′va·ɪç] adj eventual
etwas [′ɛtvas] adj some, a little || adv somewhat || pron something; anything || Etwas n—ein gewißes E. a certain something
euch [ɔɪç] pers pron you; to you || reflex pron yourselves
euer [′ɔɪ·ər] adj your
Eukalyp·tus [ɔɪka′lʏptus] m (-;- & -ten [tən]) eucalyptus
Eule [′ɔɪlə] f (-;-n) owl
Euphorie [ɔɪfo′riː] f (-;) euphoria
euphorisch [ɔɪ′foːrɪʃ] adj euphoric
eurige [′ɔɪrɪgə] §2,5 pron yours
Europa [ɔɪ′roːpa] n (-s;) Europe
Europäer -in [ɔɪroˈpeˑər(ɪn)] §6 mf European
europäisch [ɔɪro′peˑɪʃ] adj European
Euter [′ɔɪtər] n (-s;-) udder
evakuieren [evaku′iːrən] tr evacuate
evangelisch [evan′geliːʃ] adj evangelical; Protestant
Evangelist [evange′lɪst] m (-en;-en) Evangelist
Evange·lium [evan′geljum] n (-s;-lien [ljən]) gospel
eventuell [eventu′ɛl] adj eventual || adv possibly
ewig [′eːvɪç] adj eternal; perpetual
E′wigkeit f (-s;-en) eternity
e′wiglich adv forever
exakt [e′ksakt] adj exact
Exa·men [e′ksamən] n (-s;-s & -mina [mɪna]) examination
examinieren [ɛksamɪ′niːrən] tr examine
exekutiv [ɛkseku′tif] adj executive

Exempel [ɛ'ksɛmpəl] *n* (-s;-) example; **ein E. statuieren an** (*dat*) make an example of

Exemplar [ɛksɛm'plɑr] *n* (-s;-e) sample, specimen; (*e-s Buches*) copy

exerzieren [ɛksɛr'tsirən] *tr & intr* exercise

Exil [ɛ'ksil] *n* (-s;-e) exile

Existenz [ɛksɪ'stɛnts] *f* (-;-en) existence; livelihood; personality

Existenz/minimum *n* living wage

existieren [ɛksɪs'tirən] *intr* exist

exklusiv [ɛkslu'zif] *adj* exclusive

Exkommunikation [ɛkskɔmunika'tsjon] *f* (-;-en) excommunication

exkommunizieren [ɛkskɔmunɪ'tsirən] *tr* excommunicate

Exkrement [ɛkskre'mɛnt] *n* (-[e]s;-e) excrement

exmittieren [ɛksmɪ'tirən] *tr* evict

exotisch [ɛ'ksotɪʃ] *adj* exotic

expedieren [ɛkspe'dirən] *tr* send, ship

Expedition [ɛkspedɪ'tsjon] *f* (-;-en) forwarding; (mil) expedition

Experiment [ɛkspɛrɪ'mɛnt] *n* (-[e]s; -e) experiment

experimentieren [ɛkspɛrɪmɛn'tirən] *intr* experiment

explodieren [ɛksplo'dirən] *intr* (SEIN) explode; blow up

Explosion [ɛksplo'zjon] *f* (-;-en) explosion

exponieren [ɛkspo'nirən] *tr* expose; (*darlegen*) expound, set forth

Export [ɛks'pɔrt] *m* (-[e]s;-e) export

exportieren [ɛkspɔr'tirən] *tr* export

Ex·preß [ɛks'prɛs] *m* (-presses; -presse) express

Expreß/zug *m* express train

extra ['ɛkstrɑ] *adv* extra; (coll) on purpose, for spite

Ex/trablatt *n* (journ) extra

extrahieren [ɛkstra'hirən] *tr* extract

Extrakt [ɛks'trakt] *m* (-[e]s;-e) extract; (*aus Büchern*) excerpt

extravagant [ɛkstrava'gant] *adj* luxurious; wild, fantastic

Extravaganz [ɛkstrava'gants] *f* (-;-en) luxury

extrem [ɛks'trem] *adj* extreme ‖ **Extrem** *n* (-s;-e) extreme

Exzellenz [ɛkstsɛ'lɛnts] *f* (-;-en) Excellency

exzentrisch [ɛks'tsɛntrɪʃ] *adj* eccentric

Ex·zeß [ɛks'tsɛs] *m* (-zesses;-zesse) excess

F

F, f [ɛf] *invar n* F, f; (mus) F

Fabel ['fabəl] *f* (-;-n) fable; story; (*e-s Dramas*) plot

fa/belhaft *adj* fabulous

fabeln ['fabəln] *intr* tell stories

Fabrik [fa'brik] *f* (-;-en) factory, mill

Fabrik/anlage *f* manufacturing plant

Fabrikant **–in** [fabri'kant(ɪn)] §7 *mf* manufacturer, maker

Fabrikat [fabri'kɑt] *n* (-[e]s;-e) product; brand, make

Fabrikation [fabrika'tsjon] *f* (-;) manufacture, manufacturing

Fabrikations/fehler *m* flaw, defect

Fabrikations/nummer *f* serial number

Fabrik/marke *f* trademark

fabrik/mäßig *adj* mass

Fabrik/nummer *f* serial number

Fabrik/waren *pl* manufactured goods

Fabrik/zeichen *n* trademark

fabrizieren [fabri'tsirən] *tr* manufacture

fabulieren [fabu'lirən] *tr* make up ‖ *intr* tell yarns

fabulös [fabu'løs] *adj* fabulous

Facette [fa'sɛtə] *f* (-;-n) facet

Fach [fax] *n* (-[e]s;ˉer) compartment; (*im Schreibtisch*) pigeonhole; (*Bücherbrett*) shelf; (*fig*) field, department; line, business; (educ) subject; **vom F. sein** be an expert

Fach/arbeiter *m* §6 *mf* specialist

Fach/arzt *m*, **Fach/ärztin** *f* (med) specialist

Fach/ausbildung *f* professional training

Fach/ausdruck *m* technical term

fächeln ['fɛçəln] *tr* fan

Fächer ['fɛçər] *m* (-s;-) fan

Fä/cherpalme *f* palmetto

Fach/gebiet *n* field, line; department

Fach/gelehrte §5 *mf* expert

fach/gemäß *adj* expert, professional

Fach/genosse *m* colleague

Fach/kenntnisse *pl* specialized knowledge

Fach/kreis *m* experts, specialists

fach/kundig *adj* expert, experienced

fach/lich *adj* professional; technical, specialized

Fach/mann *m* (-es;ˉer & -leute) expert, specialist

fachmännisch ['faxmɛnɪʃ] *adj* expert

Fach/schule *f* vocational school

Fachsimpelei [faxzɪmpə'laɪ] *f* (-;-en) shoptalk

fachsimpeln ['faxzɪmpəln] *intr* talk shop

Fach/werk *n* framework; specialized book

Fach/zeitschrift *f* technical journal

Fackel ['fakəl] *f* (-;-n) torch

fackeln ['fakəln] *intr* flare; (fig) hesitate, dilly-dally

Fackelschein (**Fak/kelschein**) *m* torchlight

Fackelzug (**Fak/kelzug**) *m* torchlight procession

fade ['fadə] *adj* stale; (fig) dull

Faden ['fadən] *m* (-s;ˉ) (& fig) thread; filament; (naut) fathom; **keinen guten F. lassen an** (*dat*) tear apart

Fa/denkreuz *n* crosshairs

Fa/dennudeln *pl* vermicelli

fadenscheinig [ˈfɑdənʃaınıç] *adj* threadbare

Fagott [faˈgɔt] *n* (-[e]s;-e) bassoon

fähig [ˈfɛ-ıç] *adj* capable, able

Fä′higkeit *f* (-;-en) ability; talent

fahl [fɑl] *adj* pale; faded, washed-out

fahnden [ˈfɑndən] *intr* (nach) search (for), hunt (for)

Fahn′dung *f* (-;-en) search, hunt

Fahne [ˈfɑnə] *f* (-;-n) flag; pennant; (mil) colors; (typ) galley proof

Fah′nenabzug *m* galley proof

Fah′neneid *m* (mil) swearing in

Fah′nenflucht *f* desertion

fah′nenflüchtig *adj*—f. werden desert || **Fahnenflüchtige** §5 *mf* deserter

Fah′nenmast *m* flagpole

Fah′nenträger **-in** §6 *mf* standard bearer

Fähnrich [ˈfɛnrıç] *m* (-s;-e) officer cadet; F. zur See midshipman

Fahrbahn [ˈfɑrbɑn] *f* (traffic) lane

fahrbar [ˈfɑrbɑr] *adj* passable; navigable; mobile

fahrbereit [ˈfɑrbərɑıt] *adj* in running order

Fahr′bereitschaft *f* (-;-en) motor pool

Fähre [ˈfɛrə] *f* (-;-n) ferry

fahren [ˈfɑrən] §71 *tr* haul; (lenken) drive; (Boot) **sail** || *intr* (SEIN) go; travel, drive; ride; **es fuhr mir durch den Sinn** it flashed across my mind; **f. lassen** run (a boat, train); let go; (fig) abandon, renounce; **gut f. bei** do well in; **mit der Hand f. über** (acc) run one's hand over; **rechts f.** (public sign) keep right; **was ist in ihn gefahren?** what's gotten into him?

fah′renlassen §104 *tr* let go of

Fah′rer **-in** §6 *mf* driver

Fah′rerflucht *f* hit-and-run case

Fahrgast [ˈfɑrgast] *m* passenger

Fahrgeld [ˈfɑrgelt] *n* fare

Fahrgelegenheit [ˈfɑrgəleɡənhaıt] *f* transportation (facilities)

Fahrgestell [ˈfɑrgəʃtel] *n* (-[e]s;-e) (aer) landing gear; (aut) chassis

fahrig [ˈfɑrıç] *adj* fidgety

Fahrkarte [ˈfɑrkartə] *f* ticket

Fahr′kartenausgabe *f*, **Fahr′karten-schalter** *m* ticket window

fahrlässig [ˈfɑrlesıç] *adj* negligent; **fahrlässige Tötung** involuntary manslaughter

Fahr′lässigkeit *f* (-;) negligence

Fahrlehrer **-in** [ˈfɑrlerər(ın)] §6 *mf* driving instructor

Fahrnis [ˈfɑrnıs] *f* (-;-se) movables

Fährnis [ˈfɛrnıs] *f* (-;-se) (poet) danger

Fahrplan [ˈfɑrplan] *m* schedule

fahr′planmäßig *adj* scheduled || *adv* on schedule, on time

Fahrpreis [ˈfɑrpraıs] *m* fare

Fahrprüfung [ˈfɑrpryfʊŋ] *f* driver's test

Fahrrad [ˈfɑrrad] *n* bicycle

Fahrrinne [ˈfɑrrınə] *f* channel

Fahrschein [ˈfɑrʃaın] *m* ticket

Fahrstuhl [ˈfɑrʃtul] *m* elevator; (med) wheel chair

Fahr′stuhlführer **-in** §6 *mf* elevator operator

Fahr′stuhlschacht *m* elevator shaft

Fahrstunde [ˈfɑrʃtundə] *f* driving lesson

Fahrt [fɑrt] *f* (-;-en) ride, drive; trip; **auf F. gehen** go hiking; **F. verlieren** lose speed; **freie F. haben** have the green light; **in F. kommen** pick up speed; (fig) swing into action; **in F. sein** (coll) be keyed up; (coll) be on the warpath; (naut) be under way

Fährte [ˈfɛrtə] *f* (-;-n) track, scent

Fahr′unterbrechung *f* (-;-en) stopover

Fahrwasser [ˈfɑrvɑsər] *n* navigable water; (& fig) wake

Fahrwerk [ˈfɑrverk] *n* see **Fahrgestell**

Fahrzeug [ˈfɑrtsɔık] *n* vehicle; vessel, craft

Fahr′zeugpark *m* (aut) fleet; (rr) rolling stock

fair [fer] *adj* fair

Fairneß [ˈfernes] *f* (-;) fairness

Fäkalien [feˈkaljən] *pl* feces

faktisch [ˈfaktıʃ] *adj* actual, factual

Fak-tor [ˈfaktər] *m* (-s;-toren [ˈtorən]) factor; foreman; (com) agent

Faktu-ra [fakˈtura] *f* (-;-ren [rən]) invoice

Fakultät [fakulˈtet] *f* (-;-en) (educ) department, school

falb [falp] *adj* claybank (horse)

Falke [ˈfalkə] *m* (-;-n) falcon; (pol) hawk

Fal′kenjagd *f* falconry

Falkner [ˈfalknər] *m* (-s;-) falconer

Fall [fal] *m* (-[e]s;-̈e) fall, drop; downfall; case; **auf alle Fälle** in any case; **auf keinen F.** in no case; **auf jeden F.** in any case; **gesetzt den F.** supposing; **im besten F.** at best; **im schlimmsten F.** if worst comes to worst; **von F. zu F.** according to circumstances; **zu F. bringen** (fig) ruin; (parl) defeat; **zu F. kommen** (fig) collapse

Fall′brücke *f* drawbridge

Falle [ˈfalə] *f* (-;-n) (& fig) trap; (fig) pitfall; (Bett) (coll) sack

fallen [ˈfalən] §72 *intr* (SEIN) fall, drop; (Schuß) be heard; (mil) fall in battle; **j-m ins Wort f.** interrupt s.o. || **Fallen** *n* (-s;) fall, drop; (fig) downfall

fällen [ˈfelən] *tr* (Bäume) fell; (Urteil) pass; (chem) precipitate

Fallensteller [ˈfalənʃtelər] *m* (-s;-) trapper

Fall′grube *f* trap, pit; (fig) pitfall

fällig [ˈfelıç] *adj* due; payable

Fäl′ligkeit *f* (-;-en) due date

Fall′obst *n* windfall

Fall′rohr *n* soil pipe; (e-r Dachrinne) down spout

falls [fals] *conj* in case, if

Fall′schirm *m* parachute

Fall′schirmabsprung *m* parachute jump

Fall′schirmjäger *m* paratrooper

Fall′schirmspringer **-in** §6 *mf* parachutist, sky diver

Fall′strick *m* snare

Fall′sucht *f* (pathol) epilepsy

fall′süchtig *adj* (pathol) epileptic

Fall′tür *f* trapdoor

falsch [falʃ] *adj* false; *(verkehrt)* wrong; *(unecht)* counterfeit; **falsches Spiel** double-dealing ‖ *adv* wrongly; **f. gehen** (horol) be off; **f. schreiben** misspell; **f. schwören** perjure oneself; **f. singen** sing off key; **f. spielen** cheat; **f. verbunden** wrong number ‖ **Falsch** m—**ohne F.** without guile
fälschen [ˈfɛlʃən] *tr* falsify; *(Geld)* counterfeit; *(Urkunde)* forge
Fäl′scher –in §6 *mf* forger; counterfeiter
Falsch′geld *n* counterfeit money
Falsch′heit *f* (–;–en) falsity; deceitfulness
fälschlich [ˈfɛlʃlɪç] *adv* falsely
Falsch′münzer *m* counterfeiter
Falsch′spieler –in §6 *mf* card sharp
Fäl′schung *f* (–;–en) falsification; forgery; fake
Faltboot [ˈfaltbot] *n* collapsible boat
Falte [ˈfaltə] *f* (–;–n) fold; *(Plissee)* pleat, crease; *(Runzel)* wrinkle
fälteln [ˈfɛltəln] *tr* pleat
falten [ˈfaltən] *tr* fold; wrinkle
Fal′tenrock *m* pleated skirt
Falter [ˈfaltər] *m* (–s;–) butterfly; *(Nacht–)* moth
faltig [ˈfaltɪç] *adj* creased; wrinkled
Falz [falts] *m* (–es;–e) fold; *(Kerbe)* notch; (carp) rabbet
familiär [famɪˈljer] *adj* intimate; familiar
Familie [faˈmiljə] *f* (–;–n) family
Fami′lienangehörige §5 *mf* member of the family
Fami′lienanschluß *m*—**F. haben** live as one of the family
Fami′lienname *m* last name
Fami′lienstand *m* marital status
Fami′lienstück *n* family heirloom
Fami′lienzuwachs *m* addition to the family
famos [faˈmos] *adj* excellent, swell
Fan [fɛn] *m* (–s;–s) (sport) fan
Fanatiker –in [faˈnatɪkər(ɪn)] §6 *mf* fanatic; (sport) fan
fanatisch [faˈnatɪʃ] *adj* fanatic
fand [fant] *pret* of **finden**
Fanfare [fanˈfarə] *f* (–;–n) (mus) fanfare
Fang [faŋ] *m* (–[e]s;–̈e) capture; *(Fisch–)* haul, catch; *(Falle)* trap; *(Kralle)* claw
Fang′arm *m* tentacle
Fang′eisen *n* steel trap
fangen [ˈfaŋən] §73 *tr* catch; trap; *(Ohrfeige)* get ‖ *ref* get caught ‖ **Fangen** n—**F. spielen** play catch
Fang′frage *f* loaded question
Fang′messer *n* hunting knife
Fang′zahn *m* fang; tusk
Farb– [farp] *comb.fm.* color
Farb′abzug *m* (phot) color print
Farb′aufnahme *f* color photograph
Farb′band *n* (–[e]s;–̈er) typewriter ribbon
Farbe [ˈfarbə] *f* (–;–n) color; dye; *(zum Malen)* paint; *(Gesichts–)* complexion; (cards) suit; **F. bekennen** folow suit; (fig) lay one's cards on the table
färben [ˈfɛrbən] *tr* color, dye, tint ‖

ref take on color; change color; **sich rot f.** turn red; blush
far′benprächtig *adj* colorful
Fär′ber –in §6 *mf* dyer
Farb′fernsehen *n* color television
Farb′film *m* color film
farbig [ˈfarbɪç] *adj* colored; colorful
Farb′kissen *n* ink pad
Farb′körper *m* pigment
farb′los *adj* colorless
Farb′spritzpistole *f* paint sprayer
Farb′stift *m* colored pencil; crayon
Farb′stoff *m* dye
Farb′ton *m* tone, hue, shade
Fär′bung *f* (–;–en) coloring; hue
Farm [farm] *f* (–;–en) farm
Farmer –in [ˈfarmər(ɪn)] §6 *mf* farmer
Farn [farn] *m* (–[e]s;–e) fern
Farn′kraut *n* fern
Fasan [faˈzan] *m* (–s;–e & –en) pheasant
Fasching [ˈfaʃɪŋ] *m* (–s;) carnival
Faschismus [faˈʃɪsmʊs] *m* (–;) fascism
Faschist –in [faˈʃɪst(ɪn)] §7 *mf* fascist
Faselei [fazəˈlaɪ] *f* (–;–en) drivel
Faselhans [ˈfazəlhans] *m* (–′;–e & –̈e) blabberer; scatterbrain
faseln [ˈfazəln] *intr* talk nonsense
Faser [ˈfazər] *f* (–;–n) fiber; *(im Holz)* grain; *(Faden)* thread, string
Fa′serholzplatte *f* fiberboard
fasern [ˈfazərn] *tr* unravel ‖ *ref* fray ‖ *intr* unravel
Fa′serschreiber *m* felt pen
Faß [fas] *n* (Fasses;Fässer) barrel, keg; *(Bütte)* vat, tub
Fassade [faˈsadə] *f* (–;–n) façade
faßbar [ˈfasbar] *adj* comprehensible
Faß′bier *n* draft beer
fassen [ˈfasən] *tr* *(packen)* seize; *(erwischen)* apprehend; *(begreifen)* grasp; *(Edelstein)* mount; *(enthalten können)* hold, seat; *(Essen)* (mil) draw; **e–n Gedanken f.** form an idea; **in Worte f.** put into words; **j–n bei der Ehre f.** appeal to s.o.'s honor; **Tritt fassen** fall in step ‖ *ref* get hold of oneself; **in sich f.** include; **sich f. an** *(acc)* put one's hand to, touch; **sich in Geduld f.** exercise patience; **sich kurz f.** be brief ‖ *intr* take hold; *(nach)* grab (for); **es ist nicht zu f.** is incomprehensible
Faß′hahn *m* tap, faucet
faß′lich *adj* conceivable
Fasson [faˈson] *f* (–;–en) style, cut
Fas′sung *f* (–;–en) composure; *(schriftlich)* draft; *(für Edelsteine)* setting, mounting; *(Brillenrand)* frame; *(Wortlaut)* wording; *(Lesart)* version; (elec) socket; **aus der F. bringen** upset; **außer F. sein** be beside onself
Fas′sungskraft *f* comprehension
fas′sungslos *adj* disconcerted, shaken
Fas′sungsvermögen *n* capacity; *(geistliches)* (powers of) comprehension
fast [fast] *adv* almost, nearly
fasten [ˈfastən] *intr* fast ‖ **Fasten** *n* (–s;) fasting
Fa′stenzeit *f* Lent, Lenten season
Fast′nacht *f* carnival
Fast′tag *m* day of fasting, fast day

faszinieren [fastsɪ'nirən] *tr* fascinate

fatal [fa'tɑl] *adj* disastrous; *(unangenehm)* unpleasant

fauchen ['fauxən] *intr* hiss; *(Person)* snarl; *(Katze)* spit

faul [faul] *adj* rotten; lazy; bad, nasty; *(verdächtig)* fishy; *(Ausrede, Witz)* lame, poor; (sport) foul ‖ **Faul** *n* (-s;-s) (sport) foul

Fäule ['fɔɪlə] *f* (-;) rot, decay

faulen ['faulən] *intr* rot, decay

faulenzen ['faulentsən] *intr* loaf

Faulenzer ['faulentsər] *m* (-s;-) loafer; *(Liegestuhl)* chaise lounge; *(Linienblatt)* ruled sheet of paper

Faul/heit *f* (-;) laziness

faulig ['faulɪç] *adj* rotten, putrid

Fäulnis ['fɔɪlnɪs] *f* (-;) rot; **in F.** übergehen begin to rot

Faul/pelz *m* (coll) loafer

Faust [faust] *f* (-;͏̈e) fist; **auf eigene F.** on one's own

faust/dick' *adj* (coll) whopping

Faust/handschuh *m* mitten

Faust/kampf *m* boxing match

Fäustling ['fɔɪstlɪŋ] *m* (-[e]s;-e) mitten

Faust/schlag *m* punch, blow

Favorit -in [favo'rit(ɪn)] §7 *mf* favorite

Faxen ['faksən] *pl* antics; faces; **F. machen** fool around; make a fuss; **F. schneiden** make faces

Fazit ['fɑtsɪt] *n* (-s;-e & -s) result; **das F. ziehen** sum it up

Feber ['febər] *m* (-[s];-) (Aust) February

Februar ['febru·ɑr] *m* (-[s];-e) February

fechten ['fɛçtən] §74 *intr* fence; fight; *(betteln)* beg

Feder ['fedər] *f* (-;-n) feather; pen; quill; (mach) spring; **F. und Nut** (carp) tongue and groove

Fe'derball *m* shuttlecock

Fe'derballspiel *n* badminton

Fe'derbett *n* feather bed

Fe'derbusch *m* plume

Fe'derdecke *f* feather quilt

Federfuchser ['fedərfuksər] *m* (-s;-) scribbler; hack writer

fe'derführend *adj* in charge

Fe'dergewicht *n* featherweight division

Federgewichtler ['fedərgvɪçtlər] *m* (-s;-) featherweight (boxer)

Fe'derhubtor *n* overhead door

Fe'derkernmatratze *f* innerspring mattress

Fe'derkiel *m* quill

Fe'derkraft *f* springiness; tension

Fe'derkrieg *m* paper war, war of words

fe'derleicht' *adj* light as a feather

Fe'derlesen *n*—ohne viel Federlesen(s) without much ado

Fe'dermesser *n* penknife

federn ['fedərn] *tr* fit with springs ‖ *intr* be springy; *(Vogel)* moult; (gym) bounce

Fe'derring *m* lock washer

Fe'derstrich *m* stroke of the pen

Fe'derung *f* (-;) (aut) suspension

Fe'derzug *m* stroke of the pen

Fee [fe] *f* (-;Feen ['fe·ən]) fairy

Feg(e)feuer ['feg(ə)fɔɪ·ər] *n* (-s;) purgatory

fegen ['fegən] *tr* sweep; *(Laub)* tear off ‖ *intr* (SEIN) tear along

Fehde ['fedə] *f* (-;-n) feud

Feh'dehandschuh *m* gauntlet

fehl [fel] *adj*—f. am Ort out of place ‖ **Fehl** *m* (-[e]s;-e) blemish; fault

fehl—*comb.fm.* wide of the mark; mis-, incorrectly, wrongly ‖ **Fehl**- *comb. fm.* missing; vain, unsuccessful; incorrect, wrong; faulty; negative

Fehl'anzeige *f* negative report

Fehl'ball *m* (tennis) fault

fehlbar ['felbar] *adj* fallible

Fehl'betrag *m* shortage, deficit

Fehl'bitte *f* vain request; **e-e F. tun** meet with a refusal

fehlen ['felən] *tr* miss ‖ *intr* be absent; be missing; be lacking; fail, be unsuccessful; sin, err; *(dat)* miss, e.g., **er fehlt mir sehr** I miss him very much; *(dat)* lack, e.g., **ihm fehlt die Zeit** he lacks the time; **was fehlt Ihnen?** what's wrong with you? ‖ *impers*—**es fehlte nicht viel, und ich wäre gefallen** I came close to falling

Fehler ['felər] *m* (-s;-) mistake, error; flaw, imperfection; blunder

feh'lerfrei *adj* faultless, flawless

feh'lerhaft *adj* faulty

feh'lerlos *adj* faultless, flawless

Fehl'geburt *f* miscarriage

fehl'gehen §82 *intr* (SEIN) go wrong; *(Schuß)* miss

Fehl'gewicht *n* short weight

fehl'greifen §88 *intr* miss one's hold; (fig) make a mistake

Fehl'griff *m* mistake, blunder

Fehl'leistung *f* (Freudian) slip

fehl'leiten *tr* (& fig) misdirect

Fehl'schlag *m* miss; failure, disappointment; (baseball) foul

Fehl'schluß *m* false inference; fallacy

Fehl'spruch *m* miscarriage of justice

Fehl'start *m* false start

Fehl'tritt *m* false step; (fig) slip

Fehl'wurf *m* (beim Würfeln) crap

fehl'zünden *intr* backfire

feien ['faɪ·ən] *tr*—**gefeit sein gegen** be immune to; **j-n f. gegen** make s.o. immune to

Feier ['faɪ·ər] *f* (-;-n) celebration; ceremony

Fei'erabend *m* closing time

fei'erlich *adj* solemn

Fei'erlichkeit *f* (-;-en) solemnity; **Feierlichkeiten** festivities; ceremonies

feiern ['faɪ·ərn] *tr* celebrate, observe; honor ‖ *intr* rest from work

Fei'erstunde *f* commemorative ceremony

Fei'ertag *m* holiday; holy day

feig [faɪk] *adj* cowardly

feige ['faɪgə] *adj* cowardly ‖ **Feige** *f* (-;-n) fig

Feig'heit *f* (-;) cowardice

feig'herzig *adj* faint-hearted

Feigling ['faɪklɪŋ] *m* (-s;-e) coward

feil [faɪl] *adj* for sale

feil'bieten §58 *tr* offer for sale

Feile ['faɪlə] *f* (-;-n) file

feilen ['faɪlən] tr file

feilschen ['faɪlʃən] intr (um) haggle (over), dicker (about)

Feilspäne ['faɪl/pɛnə] pl filings

fein [faɪn] adj fine; delicate; fancy

feind [faɪnt] adj hostile || **Feind** m (-[e]s;-e) enemy, foe

Feind- comb.fm. enemy, hostile; against the enemy

Feind'fahrt f (nav) operation against the enemy

Feind'flug m (aer) combat mission

Feindin ['faɪndɪn] f (-;-nen) enemy

feind'lich adj hostile

Feind'schaft f (-;-en) enmity

feind'selig adj hostile

Feind'seligkeit f (-;-en) hostility, animosity; hostile action

fein'fühlend, fein'fühlig adj sensitive

Fein'gefühl n sensitivity

Fein'heit f (-;-en) fineness, fine quality; delicacy; subtlety

Fein'mechanik f precision engineering

Feinschmecker ['faɪn/mɛkər] m (-s;-) gourmet, epicure

fein'sinnig adj sensitive; subtle

feist [faɪst] adj fat, plump

Feld [fɛlt] n (-[e]s;-er) field; panel, compartment; (checkers, chess) square; **auf dem Felde** in the field(s); **auf freiem Felde** in the open; **aufs F. gehen** go to (work in) the fields; **das F. behaupten** stand one's ground; **ins F. ziehen** take the field

Feld'bau m agriculture

Feld'becher m collapsible drinking cup

Feld'bett n army cot; camping cot

Feld'blume f wild flower

Feld'bluse f army jacket

feld'dienstfähig adj fit for active duty

Feld'flasche f canteen

Feld'geistliche m (-n;-n) army chaplain

Feld'gendarm m military police

Feld'gendarmerie f military police

Feld'geschrei n battle cry

Feld'geschütz n field gun, field piece

Feld'herr m general; commander in chief

Feld'lager n bivouac, camp

Feld'lazarett n evacuation hospital

Feld'lerche f skylark

Feld'marschall m field marshal

feld'marschmäßig adj with full field pack

Feld'messer m surveyor

Feld'meßkunst f (-;) surveying

Feld'mütze f (mil) overseas cap

Feld'postamt n army post office

Feld'schlacht f battle

Feld'stecher m field glasses

Feldwebel ['fɛltvebəl] m (-s;-) sergeant

Feld'zeichen n ensign, standard

Feld'zug m campaign

Felge ['fɛlgə] f (-;-n) rim

Fell [fɛl] n (-[e]s;-e) pelt, skin; fur; **ein dickes F. haben** be thick-skinned

Fels [fɛls] m (-es & -en;-en) rock; cliff; **zackige Felsen** crags

Fels'block m boulder

Felsen ['fɛlzən] m (-s;-) rock; cliff

fel'senfest adj firm as a rock

Fel'sengebirge n Rocky Mountains

Fel'senklippe f cliff

Fel'senriff n reef

felsig ['fɛlzɪç] adj rocky

Fenster ['fɛnstər] n (-s;-) window

Fen'sterbrett n window sill

Fen'sterflügel m casement

Fen'sterladen m window shutter

Fen'sterleder n chamois

Fen'sterplatz m (rr) window seat

Fen'sterrahmen m window frame; sash

Fen'sterrosette f rose window

Fen'sterscheibe f windowpane

Ferien ['ferjən] pl vacation; (parl) recess

Fe'rienreisende §5 mf vacationer

Fe'rienstimmung f holiday spirit

Ferkel ['fɛrkəl] n (-s;-) piglet

Ferkelei [fɛrkə'laɪ] f (-;-en) obscenity

fern [fɛrn] adj far, distant; (entlegen) remote; (weit fort) far away

Fern'amt n long-distance exchange

Fern'anruf m long-distance call

Fern'aufklärung f long-range reconnaissance

fern'bleiben §62 intr (SEIN) (dat) stay away (from) || **Fernbleiben** n (-s;) absence; absenteeism

Fern'blick m distant view, vista

Ferne ['fɛrnə] f (-;-n) distance

ferner ['fɛrnər] adj remote, distant || adv further; moreover

Fern'fahrer m long-distance trucker

Fern'fahrt f long-distance trip

Fern'gang m (aut) overdrive

Fern'geschoß n long-range missile

Fern'geschütz n long-range gun

Fern'gespräch n long-distance call; toll call

Fern'glas n binoculars

fern'halten §90 tr & ref keep away

Fern'heizung f heating from a central heating plant

Fern'kursus m correspondence course

Fern'laster m long-distance truck

fern'lenken tr guide by remote control

Fern'lenkrakete f guided missile

Fern'lenkung f (-;-en) remote control

Fern'lenkwaffe f guided missile

Fern'licht n (aut) high beam

fern'liegen §108 impers—**es liegt mir fern zu** (inf) I'm far from (ger)

Fernmelde- [fɛrnmɛldə] comb.fm. communications, signal

Fern'meldetruppen pl signal corps

Fern'meldewesen n telecommunications system

fern'mündlich adj & adv by telephone

Fern'objektiv n telephoto lens

Fernost- comb.fm. Far Eastern

fern'östlich adj Far Eastern

Fern'rohr n telescope

Fern'rohraufsatz m telescopic gun sight

Fern'ruf m telephone call; telephone number

Fern'schnellzug m long-distance express

Fern'schreiber m teletype, telex

Fernseh- [fɛrnze] comb.fm. television

Fern'sehansager -in §6 mf television announcer

Fern'sehapparat m television set

Fern'sehbildröhre f picture tube
fern'sehen §138 intr watch television
|| Fernsehen n (-s;) television
Fern'seher m (-s;-) television set;
   television viewer
Fern'sehgerät n television set
Fern'sehkanal m television channel
Fern'sehschau f television show
Fern'sehsendung f telecast
Fern'sehteilnehmer -in §6 mf tele-
   viewer
Fern'sehübertragung f telecast
Fern'sicht f view, vista; panorama
fern'sichtig adj far-sighted
Fernsprech- [fern'ʃprɛç] comb.fm. tele-
   phone
Fern'sprechauftragsdienst m answering
   service
Fern'sprechautomat m pay phone
Fern'sprecher m telephone
Fern'sprechzelle f telephone booth
fern'stehen §146 intr (dat) have no
   personal contact (with); (dat) not be
   close (to)
Fern'stehende §5 mf outsider; disinterested observer
fern'steuern tr guide by remote control
Fern'studium n correspondence course
Ferse ['fɛrzə] f (-;-n) heel
Fer'sengeld n—F. geben take to one's
   heels
fertig ['fɛrtɪç] adj finished; ready;
   (kaputt) ruined, done for
fertig-, Fertig- comb.fm. final; finished; finishing; prefabricated
fer'tigbringen §65 tr finish, get done;
   bring about; es glatt f. zu (inf) be
   capable of (ger); es nicht f., ihm das
   zu sagen not have the heart to tell
   him that
fertigen ['fɛrtɪgən] tr manufacture
Fer'tigkeit f (-;-en) skill
fer'tigrasen m sod
fer'tigstellen tr complete; get ready
Fer'tigung f (-;-en) manufacture, production; copy, draft
Fes [fes] n (mus) F flat
fesch [feʃ] adj smart, chic
Fessel ['fɛsəl] f (-;-n) fetter, bond;
   (anat) ankle; (vet) fetlock
Fes'selballon m captive balloon
fesseln ['fɛsəln] tr chain, tie; (bezaubern) captivate, arrest; (mil) contain;
   ans Bett gefesselt confined to bed,
   bedridden
fes'selnd adj fascinating, gripping;
   (Persönlichkeit) magnetic
fest [fest] adj firm; solid; tight; stationary; steady; (Preis, Kost, Einkommen, Gehalt) fixed; (Schlaf)
   sound; (mil) fortified; feste Straße
   improved road || Fest n (-es;-e)
   feast; festival
fest'backen intr (SEIN) cake (on)
fest'besoldet adj with a fixed salary
fest'binden §59 tr (an dat) tie (to)
Fest'essen n banquet
fest'fahren §71 tr run aground || ref
   come to a standstill
fest'halten §90 tr hold on to || ref (an
   dat) cling (to), hold on (to)
festigen ['fɛstɪgən] tr strengthen; con-
   solidate || ref grow stronger

Fe'stigkeit f (-;-en) firmness; steadi-
   ness; strength
Fe'stigung f (-;) strengthening; con-
   solidation; stabilization
Fest'land n continent
fest'legen tr fix, determine, set; (Anordnung) lay down; (fin, naut) tie
   up; f—n f. auf (acc) pin s.o. down on
   || ref (auf acc) commit oneself (to)
fest'lich adj festive
Fest'lichkeit f (-;-en) festivity
fest'liegen §108 intr be stranded
fest'machen tr fix; (fig) settle || intr
   (naut) moor
Fest'mahl n feast
Fest'nahme f (-;-n) arrest
fest'nehmen §116 tr arrest, apprehend
Fest'rede f ceremonial speech
Fest'saal m grand hall, banquet hall
fest'schnallen tr buckle up || ref fasten
   one's seat belt
Fest'schrift f homage volume
fest'setzen tr fix, set || ref settle down
   (in a town, etc.)
fest'sitzen intr fit tight; be stuck
Fest'spiel n play for a festive occasion;
   Festspiele (mus, theat) festival
fest'stehen §146 intr stand firm; (Tat-
   sache) be certain || impers—es steht
   fest it is a fact
fest'stehend adj stationary; (Achse)
   fixed; (Tatsache) established
feststellbar ['fest'telbar] ascertainable
Fest'stellbremse f hand brake
fest'stellen tr ascertain; (unbeweglich
   machen) lock, secure; (Tatbestand)
   find out, establish; (angeben) state;
   (Schaden) assess; (Kurs) (fin) set, fix
Fest'stellschraube f set screw
Fest'tag m feastday; holiday
Fe'stung f (-;-en) fortress
Fe'stungsgraben m moat
Fest'wagen m float
Fest'wert m standard value; (math,
   phys) constant
Fest'wiese f fairground
fest'ziehen §163 tr pull tight
Fest'zug m procession
Fetisch ['fetɪʃ] m -(e)s;-e) fetish
fett [fet] adj fat; (Boden, Milch, Ge-
   misch) rich; (Zeiten, Leben) of
   plenty || Fett n (-(e)s;-e) fat;
   (Schmalz) lard; (Pflanzen-) shorten-
   ing; (Schmier-) grease
Fett'auge n speck of fat
Fett'druck m boldface type
fetten ['fetən] tr grease, lubricate
Fett'fleck m grease spot
fettig ['fetɪç] adj fatty, greasy, oily
Fett'kloß m (coll) fatso
Fett'kohle f bituminous coal
fettleibig ['fetlaɪbɪç] adj stout
Fettnäpfchen ['fetnɛpfçən] n—bei j—m
   ins F. treten hurt s.o.'s feelings; ins
   F. treten put one's foot in it
Fett'presse f (aut) grease gun
Fett'spritze f (aut) grease gun
Fett'sucht f obesity
Fett'wanst m (sl) fatso
Fetzen ['fetsən] m (-s;-) rag; bit,
   scrap; (Aust) dishcloth; daß die F.
   fliegen violently
feucht [fɔɪçt] adj moist, damp, humid

feuchten ['fɔɪçtən] *tr* moisten, dampen
Feuch'tigkeit *f* (-;) moisture, dampness, humidity
feudal [fɔɪ'dɑl] *adj* feudal; (fig) magnificent
Feudalismus [fɔɪdɑ'lɪsmʊs] *m* (-;) feudalism
Feuer ['fɔɪ·ər] *n* (-s;-) fire
Feu'eralarm *m* fire alarm
Feu'eralarmübung *f* fire drill
feu'erbeständig *adj* fireproof
Feu'erbestattung *f* cremation
Feu'erbrand *m* firebrand
Feu'ereifer *m* enthusiasm, zeal
Feu'ereinstellung *f* cease-fire
feu'erfest *adj* fireproof
Feu'erfliege *f* firefly
feu'erflüssig *adj* molten
feu'ergefährlich *adj* inflammable
Feu'erhahn *m* hydrant, fireplug
Feu'erhaken *m* poker
Feu'erherd *m* fireplace
Feu'erkampf *m* fire fight, gun battle
Feu'erkraft *f* (mil) fire power
Feu'erleiter *f* fire ladder; (*Nottreppe*) fire escape
Feu'erlinie *f* firing line
Feu'erlöscher *m* fire extinguisher
Feu'ermelder *m* fire alarm
Feu'ermeldung *f* fire alarm
feuern ['fɔɪ·ərn] *tr* fire; (coll) fire, sack || *intr* fire, shoot
Feu'erprobe *f* ordeal by fire; acid test
Feu'ersalve *f* fusillade
Feu'erschneise *f* firebreak
Feu'erspritze *f* fire engine
Feu'erstein *m* flint
Feu'ertaufe *f* baptism of fire
Feu'erversicherung *f* fire insurance
Feu'erwache *f* firehouse
Feu'erwalze *f* (mil) creeping barrage
Feu'erwehr *f* fire department
Feu'erwehrmann *m* (-[e]s;≃er & -leute) fireman
Feu'erwerk *n* fireworks
Feu'erwerkskörper *m* firecracker
Feu'erzange *f* fire tongs
Feu'erzeug *n* cigarette lighter
Feu'erzeugbenzin *n* lighter fluid
feurig ['fɔɪrɪç] *adj* fiery; ardent
Fiasko [fɪ'ɑsko] *n* (-s;-s) fiasco
Fibel ['fibəl] *f* (-;-n) primer; (archeol) fibula
Fiber ['fibər] *f* (-;-n) fiber
Fichte ['fɪçtə] *f* (-;-n) spruce; pine
Fich'tennadel *f* pine needle
fidel [fɪ'del] *adj* jolly, cheerful
Fieber ['fibər] *n* (-s;-) fever; **das F. messen** take the temperature
fie'berhaft *adj* feverish
fieberig ['fibərɪç] *adj* feverish
fie'berkrank *adj* running a fever
fiebern ['fibərn] *intr* be feverish
Fie'berphantasie *f* delirium
Fie'bertabelle *f* temperature chart
Fiedel ['fidəl] *f* (-;-n) fiddle
Fie'delbogen *m* fiddlestick
fiel [fil] *pret* of **fallen**
Figur [fɪ'gur] *f* (-;-en) figure; (cards) face card
figürlich [fɪ'gyrlɪç] *adj* figurative
fiktiv [fɪk'tif] *adj* fictitious
Filet [fɪ'le] *n* (-s;-s) (culin) fillet

Filiale [fɪl'jɑlə] *f* (-;-n) branch
Filia'lengeschäft *n* chain store
Filigran [fɪlɪ'grɑn] *n* (-s;-e), **Filigran'arbeit** *f* filigree
Film [fɪlm] *m* (-s;-e) film; (cin) movie
Film'atelier *n* motion-picture studio
Film'empfindlichkeit *f* film speed
Film'kulisse *f* (cin) movie set
Film'leinwand *f* movie screen
Film'probe *f* screen test
Film'regisseur *m* (cin) director
Film'wesen *n* motion-picture industry
Filter ['fɪltər] *m & n* (-s;-) filter
Fil'teranlage *f* filtration plant
Fil'terkaffee *m* drip-grind coffee
Fil'termundstück *n* filter tip
filtern ['fɪltərn] *tr* filter, strain
filtrieren [fɪl'trirən] *tr* filter
Filz [fɪlts] *m* (-es;-e) felt; (coll) miser, skinflint
Filz'schreiber *m* felt pen
Fimmel ['fɪməl] *m* (-s;-) craze, fad
-fimmel *m comb.fm.* mania for
Finanz [fɪ'nɑnts] *f* (-;-en) finance
Finanz- *comb.fm.* financial, fiscal
Finanz'amt *n* internal revenue service
Finanz'ausschuß *m* (adm) ways and means committee
Finanzen [fɪ'nɑntsən] *pl* finances
finanziell [fɪnan'tsjel] *adj* financial
finanzieren [fɪnan'tsirən] *tr* finance
Finanz'minister *m* secretary of the treasury
Finanz'ministerium *n* treasury department
Finanz'wesen *n* finances
Finanz'wirtschaft *f* public finances
Findelkind ['fɪndəlkɪnt] *n* foundling
finden ['fɪndən] §59 *tr* find; **f. Sie nicht?** don't you think so? || *ref* be found; **ach, das wird sich schon f.** oh, we'll see about that; **es fanden sich there were; es findet sich it** happens, it turns out; **sich f. in** (*acc*) resign oneself to; **sie haben sich gefunden** they were united || *intr* find one's way
findig ['fɪndɪç] *adj* resourceful
Findling ['fɪntlɪŋ] *m* (-s;-e) foundling; (geol) boulder
fing [fɪŋ] *pret* of **fangen**
Finger ['fɪŋər] *m* (-s;-) finger
Fin'gerabdruck *m* fingerprint
fin'gerfertig *adj* deft
Fin'gerhut *m* thimble; (bot) foxglove
fingern ['fɪŋərn] *tr* finger
Fin'gerspitze *f* finger tip; **bis in die Fingerspitzen** through and through
Fin'gerspitzengefühl *n* sensitivity
Fin'gersprache *f* sign language
Fingerzeig ['fɪŋərtsark] *m* (-s;-e) hint
fingieren [fɪŋ'girən] *tr* feign
fingiert [fɪŋ'girt] *adj* fictitious
Fink [fɪŋk] *m* (-en;-en) finch
Finne ['fɪnə] *m* (-n;-n) Finn || *f* (-;-n) fin; (*Ausschlag*) pimple
Fin'nenausschlag *m* acne
Finnin ['fɪnɪn] *f* (-;-nen) Finn
finnisch ['fɪnɪʃ] *adj* Finnish
Finnland ['fɪnlant] *n* (-s;) Finland
finster ['fɪnstər] *adj* dark; gloomy
Finsternis ['fɪnstərnɪs] *f* (-;) darkness; gloom

Finte ['fɪntə] f (-;-n) feint; trick

Firlefanz ['fɪrləfants] m (-es;) junk; **F. treiben** fool around

Fir·ma ['fɪrma] f (-;-men [mən]) firm

Firmament [fɪrma'mɛnt] n (-[e]s;-e) firmament

firmen ['fɪrmən] tr (Cath) confirm

Fir'menschild n (com) name plate

Fir'menwert m (com) good will

Firmling ['fɪrmlɪŋ] m (-s;-e) (Cath) person to be confirmed

Fir'mung f (-;-en) (Cath) confirmation

Fir·nis ['fɪrnɪs] m (-ses;-se) varnish; **mit F. streichen** varnish

firnissen ['fɪrnɪsən] tr varnish

First [fɪrst] m (-es;-e) (archit) ridge (of roof); (poet) mountain ridge

Fis [fɪs] n (-;-) (mus) F sharp

Fisch [fɪʃ] m (-es;-e) fish

fischen ['fɪʃən] tr fish for, catch ‖ intr (nach) fish (for)

Fi'scher m (-s;-) fisherman

Fischerei [fɪʃə'raɪ] f (-;-en) fishing; fishery; fishing trade

Fi'schergerät n fishing tackle

Fisch'fang m catch, haul

Fisch'gräte f fishbone

Fisch'grätenmuster n (tex) herringbone

Fisch'händler –in §6 mf fishmonger

fischig ['fɪʃɪç] adj fishy

Fisch'kunde f ichthyology

Fisch'laich m spawn, fish eggs

Fisch'otter m & f otter

Fisch'rogen m roe

Fisch'schuppe f scale (of a fish)

Fisch'zug m (& fig) catch

fiskalisch [fɪs'kalɪʃ] adj fiscal

Fis·kus ['fɪskʊs] m (-;-kusse & -ken [kən]) treasury

Fistelstimme ['fɪstəlʃtɪmə] f falsetto

Fittich ['fɪtɪç] m (-es;-e) (poet) wing

fix [fɪks] adj (Idee, Preis) fixed; (flink) smart, sharp; **fix und fertig** all set; all in; done for; **fix und fertig mit** through with; **mach fix!** make it snappy!

fixen ['fɪksən] intr sell short

fixieren [fɪ'ksirən] tr fix, decide upon; stare fixedly at; (phot) fix

Fixier'mittel n (phot) fixer

flach [flax] adj flat, level; shallow; (Relief) low; (fig) dull

Fläche ['flɛçə] f (-;-n) surface; plain; expanse; facet; (geom) area

Flä'cheninhalt m (geom) area

Flä'chenraum m surface area

flach'fallen §72 intr (SEIN) (coll) fall flat, flop

Flach'heit f (-;) flatness; shallowness

Flach'land n lowland

Flach'relief n low relief, bas-relief

Flach'rennen n flat racing

Flachs [flaks] m (-es;-e) flax

flachsen ['flaksən] intr (coll) kid

flächse(r)n ['flɛksə(r)n] adj flaxen

Flach'zange f pliers

flackern ['flakərn] intr flicker; (Stimme) quaver, shake

Flagge ['flagə] f (-;-n) flag (esp. for signaling or identification)

Flag'genmast m flagpole

Flag'genstange f flagstaff

Flagg'schiff n flagship

Flak [flak] abbr (Flugzeugabwehrkanone) anti-aircraft gun

Flak'feuer n flak

Flakon [fla'kõ] m & n (-s;-s) perfume bottle

Flamme ['flamə] f (-;-n) flame

flammen ['flamən] intr blaze; be in flames

flam'mend adj passionate

Fla'mmenwerfer m flame thrower

Flandern ['flandərn] n (-s;) Flanders

flandrisch ['flandrɪʃ] adj Flemish

Flanell [fla'nɛl] m (-s;-e) flannel

Flanke ['flaŋkə] f (-;-n) flank

Flan'kenfeuer n (mil) enfilade; **mit F. bestreichen** enfilade

flankieren [flaŋ'kirən] tr flank

Flansch [flanʃ] m (-es;-e) flange

Flasche ['flaʃə] f (-;-n) bottle; (coll) flop; (mach) pulley

Fla'schengranate f Molotov cocktail

Fla'schenzug m block and tackle; (coll) pulley

Flaschner ['flaʃnər] m (-s;-) plumber

flatterhaft ['flatərhaft] adj fickle

flattern ['flatərn] intr flutter, flap

flau [flau] adj stale; (schwach) feeble, faint; (fade) dull, lifeless; (com) slack; (phot) overexposed; **mir ist f.** (im Magen) I feel queezy

Flaum [flaum] m (-[e]s;) down; (am Gesicht, am Pfirsich) fuzz

flaumig ['flaumɪç] adj downy, fluffy

Flause ['flauzə] f (-;-n) fib; **Flausen** funny ideas, nonsense

Flaute ['flautə] f (-;-n) (com) slack period; (naut) dead calm

fläzen ['flɛtsən] ref sprawl out

Flechse ['flɛksə] f (-;-n) (dial) sinew, tendon

Flechte ['flɛçtə] f (-;-n) plait; (bot) lichen; (pathol) ringworm

flechten ['flɛçtən] §74 tr braid, plait; (Körbe) weave

Fleck [flɛk] m (-[e]s;-e & -en) spot; blemish; (Flicken, Landstück) patch

Flecken ['flɛkən] m (-s;-) spot; piece of land; (Markt-) market town

fleckenlos (flek'kenlos) adj spotless

Fleck'fieber n spotted fever

fleckig ['flɛkɪç] adj spotty; splotchy

fleddern ['flɛdərn] tr (sl) rob

Fledermaus ['flɛdərmaus] f bat

Flegel ['flegəl] m (-s;-) flail; (coll) lout, boor

Flegelei [flegə'laɪ] f (-;-) rudeness

fle'gelhaft adj uncouth, boorish

Fle'geljahre pl awkward age

flehen ['fle·ən] intr plea; **zu j-m f.** implore s.o. ‖ **Flehen** n (-s;-) supplication

Fleisch [flaɪʃ] n (-es;) flesh; meat; **sich ins eigene F. schneiden** cut one's own throat; **wildes F.** proud flesh

Fleisch'bank f (-;-e) meat counter

Fleisch'beil n cleaver

Fleisch'beschau f meat inspection

Fleisch'brühe f broth

Flei'scher m (-s;-) butcher

Flei'scheslust f (-;) lust

Fleisch'farbe f flesh color

fleischfressend adj carnivorous

Fleisch'hacker (-s;-) *m*, **Fleisch'hauer** *m* (-s;-) butcher

fleischig ['flaɪʃɪç] *adj* fleshy; meaty

fleisch'lich *adj* carnal

Fleisch'markt *m* meat market

Fleisch'pastete *f* meat pie

Fleisch'saft *m* meat juice, gravy

Fleisch'salat *m* diced-meat salad

Fleisch'speise *f* meat course

Fleisch'spieß *m* skewer

Fleischwerdung ['flaɪʃverduŋ] *f* (-;) incarnation

Fleisch'wolf *m* meat grinder

Fleisch'wunde *f* flesh wound, laceration

Fleisch'wurst *f* pork sausage

Fleiß [flaɪs] *m* (-es;) diligence, industry; mit F. intentionally

fleißig ['flaɪsɪç] *adj* diligent, hardworking

flektieren [flɛk'tirən] *tr* inflect

fletschen ['flɛtʃən] *tr* bare (*teeth*)

Flexion [flɛk'sjon] *f* (-;-en) (gram) inflection

flicken ['flɪkən] *tr* patch, repair || **Flicken** *m* (-s;-) patch

Flick'schuster *m* cobbler

Flick'werk *n* patchwork; hotchpotch; (*Pfuscherei*) bungling job

Flick'zeug *n* repair kit

Flieder ['flidər] *m* (-s;-) lilac

Fliege ['fligə] *f* (-;-n) fly; (coll) bow tie

fliegen ['fligən] §57 *tr* fly, pilot || *intr* (SEIN) fly; (coll) get sacked; in die Luft f. blow up

Flie'genfenster *n* window screen

Flie'gengewicht *n* flyweight division

Fliegengewichtler ['fligəngəvɪçtlər] *m* (-s;-) flyweight (boxer)

Flie'gengitter *n* screen

Flie'genklappe *f*, **Flie'genklatsche** *f* fly swatter

Flie'genpilz *m* toadstool

Flie'ger *m* (-s;-) flyer

Flieger- *comb.fm.* air-force; air, aerial; flying; airman's

Flie'gerabwehr *f* anti-aircraft defense

Flie'geralarm *m* air-raid alarm

Flie'gerangriff *m* air raid

Flie'gerheld *m* (aer) ace

Flie'gerhorst *m* air base

Flie'gerin *f* (-;-nen) flyer

Flie'gerschaden *m* air-raid damage

fliehen ['fli·ən] §75 *tr* run away from; avoid || *intr* (SEIN) flee

Flieh'kraft *f* (-;) centrifugal force

Fliese ['flizə] *f* (-;-n) tile

Flie'senleger *m* tiler, tile man

Fließband ['flisbant] *n* (-[e]s;⁻er) assembly line

fließen ['flisən] §76 *intr* (SEIN) flow

flie'ßend *adj* (*Wasser*) running; (fig) fluent

Fließheck ['flishɛk] *n* (aut) fastback

Fließpapier ['flispapir] *n* blotting paper

flimmern ['flɪmərn] *intr* glimmer; glisten, shimmer; flicker

flink [flɪŋk] *adj* nimble, quick; mach mal f.! get a move on!

Flinte ['flɪntə] *f* (-;-n) shotgun; gun

Flin'tenlauf *m* gun barrel

flirren ['flɪrən] *intr* shimmer

Flirt [flɪrt] *m* (-s;-s) flirtation; boyfriend, girlfriend

flirten ['flɪrtən] *intr* flirt

Flitter ['flɪtər] *m* (-s;-) sequins; (*Scheinglanz*) flashiness

Flit'terglanz *m* flashiness

Flit'tergold *n* gold tinsel

Flit'terkram *m* trinkets

Flit'terstaat *m* flashy clothes

Flit'terwochen *pl* honeymoon

flitzen ['flɪtsən] *intr* (SEIN) flit

flocht [flɔxt] *pret of* flechten

Flocke ['flɔkə] *f* (-;-n) flake; tuft

flog [flok] *pret of* fliegen

floh [flo] *pret of* fliehen || **Floh** *m* (-s;⁻e) flea; j-m e-n F. ins Ohr setzen put a bug in s.o.'s ear

Floh'hüpfspiel *n* tiddlywinks

Flor [flor] *m* (-s;-e) bloom || *m* (-s;-e & ⁻e) gauze; (tex) nap, pile

Flor'band *n* (-[e]s;⁻er) crepe; mourning band

Florett [flo'rɛt] *n* (-s;-e) foil

florieren [flo'rirən] *intr* flourish

Floskel ['flɔskəl] *f* (-;-n) rhetorical ornament, flowery phrase

Floß [flos] *n* (-es;⁻e) raft

Flosse ['flɔsə] *f* (-;-n) fin; (aer) stabilizer

flößen ['fløsən] *tr* float

Flöte ['fløtə] *f* (-;-n) flute; (cards) flush

flöten ['fløtən] *tr* play on the flute || *intr* play the flute; f. gehen (fig) go to the dogs

flott [flɔt] *adj* afloat; brisk, lively; gay; chic, dashing

Flotte ['flɔtə] *f* (-;-n) fleet

Flot'tenstützpunkt *m* naval base

flott'gehend *adj* (com) brisk, lively

Flottille [flɔ'tɪljə] *f* (-;-n) flotilla

flott'machen *tr* set afloat; (fig) get going again

Flöz [fløts] *n* (-es;-e) (min) seam

fluchen ['fluxən] *intr* curse

Fluch [flux] *m* (-[e]s;⁻e) curse

Flucht [fluxt] *f* (-;-en) flight; escape; straight line, alignment; (*Häuser-*) row; (*Spielraum*) space, leeway; (*Zimmer-*) suite; außerhalb der F. out of line; in die F. schlagen put to flight

flüchten ['flyçtən] *ref* (an *acc*, in *acc*) take refuge (in), have recourse (to) || *intr* (SEIN) flee; escape; (vor *dat*) run away (from)

flüchtig ['flyçtɪç] *adj* fugitive; fleeting; cursory, superficial; hurried; (chem) volatile; f. sein be on the run; f. werden escape, flee

Flüch'tigkeitsfehler *m* oversight, slip

Flüchtling ['flyçtlɪŋ] *m* (-s;-) fugitive; refugee

Flücht'lingslager *n* refugee camp

Flug [fluk] *m* (-[e]s;⁻e) flight

Flug'abwehr *f* anti-aircraft defense

Flugabwehr- *comb.fm.* anti-aircraft

Flug'anschluß *m* plane connection

Flug'aufgabe *f*, **Flug'auftrag** *m* (aer) mission

Flug'bahn *f* line of flight; trajectory

Flug'blatt *n* leaflet, flyer

Flügel ['flygəl] *m* (-s;-) wing; (e-r *Doppeltür*) leaf; (mus) grand piano
Flü'geladjutant *m* aide-de-camp
Flü'gelfenster *n* casement window
Flü'gelmutter *f* wing nut
Flü'gelschlag *m* flap of the wings
Flü'gelschraube *f* thumb screw
Flü'geschraubenmutter *f* wing nut
Flü'geltür *f* folding door
Flug'gast *m* (aer) passenger
flügge ['flygə] *adj* (*Vogel*) fledged (fig) ready to go on one's own
Flug'gesellschaft *f* airline company
Flug'hafen *m* airport
Flug'hafenbefeuerung *f* airport lights
Flug'kapitän *m* captain, pilot
Flug'karte *f* plane ticket; aeronautical chart
flug'klar *adj* ready for take-off
Flug'körper *m* missile; space vehicle
Flug'leitung *f* air-traffic control
Flug'linie *f* air route; airline
Flug'meldesystem *n* air-raid warning system
Flug'motor *m* aircraft engine
Flug'ortung *f* (aer) navigation
Flug'plan *m* flight schedule
Flug'platz *m* airfield, airport
Flug'post *f* air mail
Flug'preis *m* air fare
flugs [fluks] *adv* quickly; at once
Flug'schein *m* plane ticket
Flug'schneise *f* air lane
Flug'schrift *f* pamphlet
Flug'strecke *f* flying distance
Flug'stützpunkt *m* air base
flug'tauglich, flug'tüchtig *adj* airworthy
Flug'techniker –in §6 *mf* aeronautical engineer
Flug'verbot *n* (aer) grounding
Flug'verkehr *m* air traffic
Flug'wesen *n* aviation; aeronautics
Flug'wetter *n* flying weather
Flug'zeug *n* airplane, aircraft
Flug'zeugabwehrgeschütz *n*, **Flug'zeugabwehrkanone** *f* anti-aircraft gun
Flug'zeugführer *m* pilot; **zweiter F.** co-pilot, second officer
Flug'zeugführerschein *m* pilot's license
Flug'zeuggeschwader *n* wing (*consisting of 3 squadrons of 9 planes each*)
Flug'zeugkreuzer *m*, **Flug'zeugmutterschiff** *n* seaplane tender, seaplane carrier
Flug'zeugrumpf *m* fuselage
Flug'zeugstaffel *f* squadron (*consisting of 9 planes*)
Flug'zeugträger *m* aircraft carrier
Flug'zeugwerk *n* aircraft factory
Flunder ['flundər] *f* (-;-n) flounder
Flunkerer ['fluŋkərər] *m* (-s;-) fibber
flunkern ['fluŋkərn] *intr* fib
Flunsch [fluŋʃ] *m* (-es;-e) face; **e-n F. ziehen** (or **machen**) make a face
Fluor ['flu·ər] *n* (-s;) fluorine
Fluoreszenz [flu·ɔrɛs'tsɛnts] *f* (-;) fluorescence; fluorescent light
Fluorid [flu·ɔ'rit] *n* (-[e]s;-e) fluoride
Flur [flur] *m* (-[e]s;-e) entrance hall; hallway || *f* (-;-en) open farmland; meadow; community farmland

Flur'garderobe *f* hallway closet
Fluß [flus] *m* (**Flusses; Flüsse**) river; flow; (metal) fusion; (phys) flux
flußab'wärts *adv* downstream
flußauf'wärts *adv* upstream
Fluß'bett *n* riverbed, channel
Flüßchen ['flysçən] *n* (-s;-) rivulet
flüssig ['flysɪç] *adj* liquid; fluid; (*Gelder*) ready; **f. machen** convert into cash || *adv* fluently
Flüs'sigkeit *f* (-;-en) liquid, fluid; (fig) fluency; (fin) liquidity
Flüs'sigkeitsmaß *n* liquid measure
Fluß'pferd *n* hypopotamus
flüstern ['flystərn] *tr & intr* whisper
Flü'sterparole *f* rumor
Flut [flut] *f* (-;-en) flood; waters; high tide
fluten ['flutən] *tr* flood || *intr* (SEIN) flow, pour
Flut'grenze *f* high-water mark
Flut'licht *n* floodlight
Flut'linie *f* high-water mark
Flut'wasser *n* tidewater
Flut'welle *f* tidal wave
Flut'zeit *f* flood tide, high tide
focht [foxt] *pret of* **fechten**
Focksegel ['fɔkzegəl] *n* (-s;-) foresail
fohlen ['folən] *intr* foal || **Fohlen** *n* (-s;-) foal
Folge ['fɔlgə] *f* (-;-n) sequence; consequence; succession; series; (e-s *Romans*) continuation; (e-r *Zeitschrift*) number; **die Folgen tragen** take the consequences; **in der F.** subsequently
folgen ['fɔlgən] *intr* (dat) obey || *intr* (SEIN) (dat) follow; (dat) succeed; (aus) ensue (from)
folgendermaßen ['fɔlgəndərmasən] *adv* in the following manner, as follows
fol'genschwer *adj* momentous, grave
fol'gerichtig *adj* logical, consistent
folgern ['fɔlgərn] *tr* infer, conclude
Fol'gerung *f* (-;-en) inference, conclusion
Fol'gesatz *m* (gram) result clause
fol'gewidrig *adj* inconsistent
Fol'gezeit *f*—**in der F.** in subsequent times
folglich ['fɔlklɪç] *adv* consequently
folgsam ['fɔlkzam] *adj* obedient
Foliant [fol'jant] *m* (-en;-en) folio
Folie ['foljə] *f* (-;-n) (metal) foil
Folter ['fɔltər] *f* (-;-n) torture; rack; **auf die F. spannen** put to the rack; (fig) keep in suspense
Fol'terbank *f* (-;⸚e) rack
foltern ['fɔltərn] *tr* torture
Fol'terqual *f* torture
Fol'terverhör *n* third degree
Fön [føn] *m* (-[e]s;-e) hand hair-dryer
Fond [fõ] *m* (-s;-s) background; rear, back; (culin) gravy
Fonds [fõ] *m* (-s [fõs];-s [fõs]) fund
Fontäne [fɔn'tɛnə] *f* (-;-n) fountain
foppen ['fɔpən] *tr* tease; bamboozle
Fopperei [fɔpə'raɪ] *f* (-;-en) teasing
forcieren [fɔr'sirən] *tr* force; speed up
Förderband ['fœdərbant] *n* (-;⸚er) conveyor belt

För′derer *m* (-s;-) promoter; patron

för′derlich *adj* useful; (*dat*) conducive (to)

fordern [′fordərn] *tr* demand; (*Recht*) claim; (*zum Zweikampf*) challenge; (*vor Gericht*) summon

fördern [′fœrdərn] *tr* promote, back; (*Kohle*) produce; **förderndes Mitglied** social member; **zutage f.** bring to light

For′derung *f* (-;-en) demand, claim; debt; (*zum Zweikampf*) challenge

För′derung *f* (-;-en) promotion; support; encouragement; (min) output

Forelle [fo′relə] *f* (-;-n) trout

Forke [′fɔrkə] *f* (-;-n) pitchfork

Form [form] *f* (-;-en) form; shape; mold; condition; (gram) voice; **die F. wahren** keep up appearances

formal [fɔr′mɑl] *adj* formal

Formalität [fɔrmɑlɪ′tɛt] *f* (-;-en) formality

Format [fɔr′mɑt] *n* (-[e]s;-e) size, format; distinction, stature

Formel [′fɔrməl] *f* (-;-n) formula

for′melhaft *adj* (*Wendung, Gebet*) set

formell [fɔr′mɛl] *adj* formal

formen [′fɔrmən] *tr* form, shape, mold

For′menlehre *f* morphology

Form′fehler *m* defect; flaw; (jur) irregularity

formieren [fɔr′mirən] *tr & ref* line up

–förmig [fœrmɪç] *comb.fm.* –shaped

förmlich [′fœrmlɪç] *adj* formal || *adv* virtually; literally; formally

form′los *adj* shapeless; informal; unconventional; rude; (chem) amorphous

form′schön *adj* well-shaped, beautiful

Formular [fɔrmu′lɑr] *n* (-s;-e) form, blank

formulieren [fɔrmu′lirən] *tr* formulate; word, phrase

Formulie′rung *f* (-;-en) formulation; wording

form′vollendet *adj* perfectly shaped

forsch [fɔrʃ] *adj* dashing || *adv* briskly

forschen [′fɔrʃən] *intr* do research; (nach) search (for)

For′scher **–in** §6 *mf* researcher; scholar; explorer

For′schung *f* (-;-en) research

For′schungsanstalt *f* research center

Forst [fɔrst] *m* (-[e]s;-e) forest

Förster [′fœrstər] *m* (-s;-) forester; forest ranger

Forst′fach *n* forestry

Forst′mann *m* (-es;-leute) forester

Forst′revier *n* forest range

Forst′wesen *n*, **Forst′wirtschaft** *f* forestry

fort [fɔrt] *adv* away; gone, lost; (*wetter*) on; (*vorwärts*) forward; **ich muß f.** I must be off; **in e-m f.** continuously; **und so f. and so forth** || **Fort** [fɔr] *n* (-s;-s) (mil) fort

fortan′ *adv* from now on, henceforth

Fort′bestand *m* continued existence

fort′bestehen §146 *intr* continue

fort′bewegen §56 *tr* move along || *ref* get about

fort′bilden *ref* continue one's studies

Fort′bildung *f* continuing education

fort′bleiben §62 *intr* (SEIN) stay away

Fort′dauer *f* continuance

fort′dauern *intr* continue; last

fort′fahren §71 *tr* hawl away; continue (*to say*); **f. zu** (*inf*) continue to (*inf*), go on (*ger*) || *intr* continue, go on || *intr* (SEIN) drive off, leave

Fort′fall *m* omission; discontinuation; **in F. kommen** be discontinued

fort′fallen §72 *intr* (SEIN) drop out; be omitted; be discontinued

fort′führen *tr* lead away; continue; (*Geschäft*) carry on; (*Linie*) extend

Fort′gang *m* departure; continuation; progress

fort′gehen §82 *intr* (SEIN) go away

fort′geschritten *adj* advanced; late

fort′gesetzt *adj* incessant

fort′kommen §99 *intr* (SEIN) go on, make progress; get away; **in der Welt f.** get ahead in the world || **Fortkommen** *n* (-s;-) progress

fort′lassen §104 *tr* allow to go; omit

fort′laufen §105 *intr* (SEIN) run away

fort′laufend *adj* continuing; (*Nummer*) consecutive

fort′leben *intr* live on

fort′pflanzen *tr* propagate; spread || *ref* reproduce; propagate; spread

Fort′pflanzung *f* (-;-) propagation

fort′reißen §53 *tr* tear away; **j–n mit sich f.** sweep s.o. off his feet; **sich f. lassen** be caried away

fort′schaffen *tr* remove

fort′scheren *ref* (coll) scram

fort′schreiten §86 *intr* (SEIN) progress, advance

Fort′schritt *m* progress; improvement

fort′schrittlich *adj* progressive

fort′setzen *tr* continue; resume

Fort′setzung *f* (-;-en) continuation; sequel; installment; **F. folgt** to be continued

fort′während *adj* continual; lasting, permanent || *adv* all the time, always

Fossil [fo′sil] *n* (-s;-ien [jən]) fossil

foul [faul] *adj* foul, dirty || **Foul** *n* (-s;-) (sport) foul; **ein F. begehen an** (*dat*) commit a foul against

foulen [′faulən] *tr* (sport) foul

Foyer [fwa′je] *n* (-s;-s) foyer; (*im Hotel*) lobby

Fracht [fraxt] *f* (-;-en) freight, cargo

Fracht′brief *m* bill of lading

Frachter [′fraxtər] *m* (-s;-) freighter

Fracht′gut *n* freight, goods

Fracht′raum *m* cargo compartment; cargo capacity

Fracht′stück *n* package

Frack [frak] *m* (-[e]s;e & -s) tails

Frack′schoß *m* coattail

Frage [′fragə] *f* (-;-n) question; **außer F. stehen** be out of the question; **e–e F. stellen** ask a question; **in F. stellen** call in question; **kommt nicht in F.!** nothing doing!

Fra′gebogen *m* questionnaire

fragen [′fragən] *tr* ask; **j–n f. nach** ask s.o. about; **j–n nach der Zeit f.** ask s.o. the time; **j–n f. um** ask s.o. for || *ref* wonder || *impers ref*—**es fragt sich,** ob the question is whether || *intr* ask

Fra'gesatz m interrogative sentence; **abhängiger F.** indirect question

Fragesteller ['frɑːɡə/tɛlər] m (-s;-) questioner

Fra'gewort n (-es;ⁿer) interrogative

Fra'gezeichen n question mark

fraglich ['frɑːklɪç] adj questionable

fraglos ['frɑːklɔs] adv unquestionably

Fragment [frɑˈɡmɛnt] n (-[e]s;-e) fragment

frag'würdig adj questionable

Fraktion [frɑkˈtsjoːn] f (-;-en) (chem) fraction; (pol) faction

fraktionell [frɑktsɔˈnɛl] adj factional

Fraktur [frɑkˈtuːr] f (-;-en) fracture; Gothic type, Gothic lettering; **mit j-m F. reden** talk turkey with s.o.

frank [frɑŋk] adv—**f. und frei** quite frankly

Franke ['frɑŋkə] m (-n;-n) Franconian; (hist) Frank

Franken ['frɑŋkən] m (-[e]s;-) (Swiss) franc ‖ n (-s;) Franconia

frankieren [frɑŋˈkiːrən] tr frank, put postage on

Fränkin ['frɛŋkɪn] f (-;-nen) Frank

franko ['frɑŋko] adv postage paid; **f. Berlin** freight paid to Berlin; **f. verzollt** free of freight and duty

Frank'reich n (-s;) France

Franse ['frɑnzə] f (-;-n) fringe

fransen ['frɑnzən] intr fray

Franzband ['frɑntsbɑnt] m (-[e]s;ⁿe) leather binding

Franz'branntwein m rubbing alcohol

Franzose [frɑnˈtsoːzə] m (-n;-n) Frenchman; **die Franzosen** the French

Französin [frɑnˈtsøːzɪn] f (-;-nen) Frenchwoman

französisch [frɑnˈtsøːzɪʃ] adj French

frappant [frɑˈpɑnt] adj striking

frappieren [frɑˈpiːrən] tr strike, astonish; (Wein) put on ice

fräsen ['frɛːzən] tr mill

fraß [frɑs] pret of **fressen** ‖ **Fraß** m (-es;) fodder, food; (pel) garbage

Fratz [frɑts] m (-es;-e) brat

Fratze ['frɑtsə] f (-;-n) grimace; (coll) face; **e-e F. schneiden** make a face

frat'zenhaft adj grotesque

Frau [frɑu] f (-;-en) woman; lady; wife; (vor Namen) Mrs; **zur F. geben** give in marriage

Frauen- comb.fm. of women

Frau'enarzt m, **Frau'enärztin** f gynecologist

Frau'enheld m ladykiller

Frau'enkirche f Church of Our Lady

Frau'enkleidung f women's wear

Frau'enklinik f women's hospital

Frau'enleiden n gynecological disorder

Frau'enzimmer n (pej) woman, female

Fräulein ['frɔɪlaɪn] n (-s;-) young lady; (vor Namen) Miss

frau'lich adj womanly

frech [frɛç] adj brazen; fresh, smart

Frech'dachs m smart aleck

Frech'heit f (-;-en) impudence

Fregatte [freˈɡatə] f (-;-n) frigate

frei [frɑɪ] adj free; (Feld) open; (offen) frank; **auf freien Fuß setzen** release; **auf freier Strecke** (rr) outside the station; **die freien Berufe** the professions; **freie Fahrt** (public sign) resume speed; **freies Spiel haben** have a free hand; **frei werden** (chem) be released; **ich bin so frei** thank you, I will have some; **sich frei machen** take off one's clothes ‖ **Freie** §5 n—**im Freien** out of doors; **ins Freie** out of doors, into the open

Frei'bad n outdoor swimming pool

Frei'bank f (-;ⁿe) cheap-meat counter

frei'beruflich adj freelance

Frei'betrag m allowable deduction

Frei'brief m charter; (fig) license

Freier ['frɑɪ-ər] m (-s;-) suitor

Frei'frau f baroness

Frei'gabe f release

frei'geben §80 tr release; **für den Verkehr f.** open to traffic ‖ intr—**j-m f.** give s.o. (time) off

freigebig ['frɑɪɡeːbɪç] adj generous

Frei'gebigkeit f (-;) generosity

Frei'geist m freethinker

frei'geistig adj open-minded

frei'gestellt adj optional

frei'haben intr be off

Frei'hafen m free port

frei'halten §90 tr keep open; **j-n f. pay** the tab for s.o.

Frei'heit f (-;-en) freedom; **dichterische F.** poetic license

Frei'heitskrieg m war of liberation

Frei'heitsstrafe f imprisonment

Frei'herr m baron

Frei'karte f free ticket; (theat) complimentary ticket

Frei'korps n volunteer corps

frei'lassen §104 tr release, set free

Frei'lauf m coasting

frei'legen tr lay open, expose

frei'lich adv of course

Freilicht- comb.fm. open-air

frei'machen tr (Platz) vacate; (Straße) clear; (Brief) stamp; **den Arm f.** roll up one's sleeves ‖ ref undress

Frei'marke f postage stamp

Frei'maurer m Freemason

Frei'maurerei f freemasonry

Frei'mut m frankness

frei'mütig adj frank, outspoken

frei'schaffend adj freelance

Frei'sinn m (pol) liberalism

frei'sinnig adj (pol) liberal

frei'sprechen §64 tr acquit

Frei'spruch m acquittal

frei'stehen §146 intr—**es steht Ihnen frei zu** (inf) you are free to (inf)

frei'stehend adj free-standing; (Gebäude) detached

Frei'stelle f scholarship

frei'stellen tr exempt; **j-m etw f.** leave it to s.o.'s discretion

Frei'stoß m (fb) free kick

Frei'tag m Friday

Frei'tod m suicide

Frei'treppe f outdoor stairway

Frei'wild n (& fig) fair game

frei'willig adj voluntary ‖ **Freiwillige** §5 mf (& mil) volunteer

Frei'zeichen n (telp) dial tone

Frei'zeit f spare time, leisure

Frei'zeitgestaltung f planning one's leisure time

freizügig ['frɑɪtsyːɡɪç] adj unhampered

fremd [fremt] *adj* foreign; strange; someone else's; (*Name*) assumed
fremd'artig *adj* strange, odd
Fremde ['fremdə] §5 *mf* foreigner; stranger || *f*—**aus der F.** from abroad; **in der F.** far from home; **in die F. gehen** go far from home; go abroad
Frem'denbuch *n* visitors' book
Frem'denführer –**in** §6 *mf* tour guide; (*Buch*) guidebook
Frem'denheim *n* boarding house
Frem'denlegion *f* foreign legion
Frem'denverkehr *m* tourism
Frem'denzimmer *n* guest room; spare room
Fremd'herrschaft *f* foreign domination
Fremd'körper *m* foreign body; (pol) alien element
fremdländisch ['fremtlendɪʃ] *adj* foreign
Fremdling ['fremtlɪŋ] *m* (–s;–) stranger
Fremd'sprache *f* foreign language
Fremd'wort *n* (–es;̈er) foreign word
frequentieren [frekven'tirən] *tr* frequent
Frequenz [fre'kvents] *f* (–;–en) frequency; (*Besucherzahl*) attendance
Freske ['freskə] *f* (–;–n), **Fres•ko** ['fresko] *n* (–s;–ken [kən]) fresco
Freßbeutel ['fresbɔɪtəl] *m* feed bag
Fresse ['fresə] *f* (–;–n) (sl) puss
fressen ['fresən] §70 *tr* (*von Tieren*) eat; feed on; (sl) devour; (*ätzen*) corrode, pit; (tech) freeze || **ref**—**sich satt f.** stuff oneself || *intr* (sl) eat; (an *dat*) gnaw (at)
Fresserei [fresə'raɪ] *f* (–;) gluttony
Freude ['frɔɪdə] *f* (–;–n) joy, pleasure
Freu'denbotschaft *f* glad tidings
Freu'denfeier *f*, **Freu'denfest** *n* celebration, happy occasion
Freu'denhaus *n* brothel
Freu'denmädchen *n* prostitute
freudig ['frɔɪdɪç] *adj* joyful, happy
freud'los *adj* joyless, sad
freuen ['frɔɪ-ən] *tr* please || *ref* be happy; (an *dat*) be delighted (by); (auf *acc*) look forward (to); (über *acc*) be glad (about) || *impers*—**es freut mich** I am glad
Freund [frɔɪnt] *m* (–[e]s;–e) friend; boyfriend; **F. der Musik** music lover
Freundin ['frɔɪndɪn] *f* (–;–nen) friend; girlfriend
freund'lich *adj* friendly; cheerful
Freund'lichkeit *f* (–;) friendliness
Freund'schaft *f* (–;–en) friendship
Frevel ['frefəl] *m* (–s;–) outrage; crime; sacrilege
fre'velhaft *adj* wicked
freveln ['frefəln] *intr* commit an outrage; **am Gesetz f.** violate the law
Fre'veltat *f* outrage
Friede ['fridə] *m* (–ns;), **Frieden** ['fridən] *m* (–s;) peace
Frie'densrichter *m* justice of the peace
Frie'densschluß *m* conclusion of peace
Frie'densstifter –**in** §6 *mf* peacemaker
Frie'densverhandlungen *pl* peace negotiations
Frie'densvertrag *m* peace treaty

friedfertig ['fritfertɪç] *adj* peaceable
Friedhof ['frithof] *m* cemetery
friedlich ['fritlɪç] *adj* peaceful
friedliebend ['fritlibənt] *adj* peace-loving
frieren ['frirən] §77 *intr* be cold; freeze || *impers*—**es friert mich** I'm freezing
Fries [fris] *m* (–es;–e) frieze
Frikadelle [frɪka'delə] *f* (–;–n) meatball
frisch [frɪʃ] *adj* fresh; (*kühl*) cool; (*munter*) brisk || *adv* freshly; **f. gestrichen** (public sign) wet paint; **f. zu!** on with it! || **Frische** *f* (–;) freshness; coolness; briskness
Frisch'haltepackung *f* vacuum package
Friseur [frɪ'zør] *m* (–s;–e) barber
Friseur'laden *m* barbershop
Friseur'sessel *m* barber chair
Friseuse [frɪ'zøzə] *f* (–;–n) hairdresser
frisieren [frɪ'zirən] *tr* (*Dokumente*) doctor; (aut) soup up; **j–m die Haare f.** do s.o.'s hair
Frisier'haube *f* hair dryer; hair net
Frisier'kommode *f*, **Frisier'tisch** *m* dresser
Frist [frɪst] *f* (–;–en) time, period, term; (com, jur) grace; **die F. einhalten** meet the deadline
fristen ['frɪstən] *tr*—**das Leben f. eke** out a living
Frisur [frɪ'zur] *f* (–;–en) hairstyle
frivol [frɪ'vol] *adj* frivolous
froh [fro] *adj* glad, happy, joyful
froh'gelaunt *adj* cheerful
fröhlich ['frølɪç] *adj* gay, merry
froh'locken *intr* rejoice
Froh'sinn *m* good humor
fromm [frɔm] *adj* pious, devout
Frömmelei [frœmə'laɪ] *f* (–;–en) sanctimoniousness; sanctimonious act
frommen ['frɔmən] *intr* (dat) profit
Frömmigkeit ['frœmɪçkaɪt] *f* (–;) piety
Frömmler –**in** ['frœmlər–ɪn] §6 *mf* hypocrite
Fron [fron] *f* (–;) drudgery; (hist) forced labor
frönen ['frønən] *intr* (dat) gratify
Fron'leichnam *m* Corpus Christi
Front [frɔnt] *f* (–;–en) (& mil) front
Front'abschnitt *m* (mil) sector
fror [fror] *pret* of **frieren**
Frosch [frɔʃ] *m* (–es;̈e) frog; (*Feuerwerkkörper*) firecracker; **sei kein F.!** don't be a party pooper
Frost [frɔst] *m* (–es;̈e) frost
Frost'beule *f* chilblain
frösteln ['frœstəln] *intr* feel chilly
Frosterfach ['frɔstərfax] *n* freezer compartment (*of refrigerator*)
frostig ['frɔstɪç] *adj* frosty; chilly
Frost'schutzmittel *n* antifreeze
Frottee [frɔ'te] *m & n* (–s;–s) terry cloth
frottieren [frɔ'tirən] *tr* rub down
Frottier'tuch *n* Turkish towel
Frucht [fruxt] *f* (–;̈e) fruit; foetus
fruchtbar ['fruxtbar] *adj* fruitful
frucht'bringend *adj* productive
Früch'tebecher *m* fruit cup (*as dessert*)
fruchten ['fruxtən] *intr* bear fruit; have effect; be of use

Frucht′folge *f* rotation of crops
Frucht′knoten *m* (bot) pistil
frucht′los *adj* fruitless
Frucht′saft *m* fruit juice
Frucht′wechsel *m* rotation of crops
frugal [fru′gɑl] *adj* frugal
früh [fry] *adj* early ‖ *adv* early; in the morning; **von f. bis spät** from morning till night ‖ **Frühe** *f* (–;) early morning; **in aller F.** very early
früher [′fry·ər] *adj* earlier; former ‖ *adv* earlier; sooner; formerly
frühestens [′fry·əstəns] *adv* at the earliest
Früh′geburt *f* premature birth
Früh′jahr *n*, **Frühling** [′frylɪŋ] *m* (–s; –e) spring
Früh′lingsmüdigkeit *f* spring fever
früh′reif *adj* precocious
Früh′schoppen *m* eye opener (*beer, wine*)
Früh′stück *n* breakfast; **zweites F.** lunch
frühstücken [′fry/tykən] *intr* eat breakfast
früh′zeitig *adj & adv* (too) early
Fuchs [fuks] *m* (–es;⁻e) fox; (*Pferd*) sorrel, chestnut; (educ) freshman
Fuchsie [′fuksjə] *f* (–;–n) fuchsia
fuchsig [′fuksɪç] *adj* red; (fig) furious, wild
Fuchs′jagd *f* fox hunt(ing)
fuchs′rot′ *adj* sorrel
Fuchs′schwanz *m* foxtail; (bot) amaranth; (carp) hand saw (*with tapered blade*)
fuchs′teufelswild′ *adj* hopping mad
Fuge [′fugə] *f* (–;–n) joint; (mus) fugue; **aus allen Fugen gehen** come apart; go to pieces, go to pot
fügen [′fygən] *tr* join; (*verhängen*) decree; (carp) joint ‖ *ref* give in; **es fügte sich** it so happened
fügsam [′fykzam] *adj* compliant; (*Haar*) manageable
Fü′gung *f* (–;–en) (gram) construction; **F. des Himmels, F. Gottes** divine providence; **F. des Schicksals** stroke of fate; **göttliche F.** divine providence
fühlbar [′fylbar] *adj* tangible; noticeable; **sich f. machen** make itself felt
fühlen [′fylən] *tr* feel, touch; sense ‖ *ref* feel; feel big ‖ *intr*—**f. mit** feel for (*s.o.*); **f. nach** feel for, grope for –**fühlig** [fylɪç] *comb.fm.* –feeling
Füh′lung *f* (–;) touch, contact; **F. nehmen** mit get in touch with
fuhr [fur] *pret* of **fahren**
Fuhre [′furə] *f* (–;–n) wagon load
führen [′fyrən] *tr* lead; guide; (*Artikel*) carry, sell; (*Besprechungen*) hold, conduct; (*Bücher*) keep; (*Geschäft*) run, manage; (*Krieg*) carry on; (*Sprache*) use; (*Titel*) bear; (*Truppen*) command; (*Waffe*) wield; (*Fahrzeug*) drive; (aer) pilot; **den Beweis f.** prove; **die Aufsicht f. über** (*acc*) superintend; **j-m den Haushalt f.** keep house for s.o. ‖ *ref* conduct oneself ‖ *intr* lead; (sport) be in the lead
Füh′rer –in §6 *mf* leader, guide; (aer)

pilot; (aut) driver; (com) manager; (sport) captain
Füh′rerschaft *f* (–;) leadership
Füh′rerschein *m* driver's license
Füh′rerscheinentzug *m* suspension of driver's license
Führhund [′fyrhunt] *m* Seeing Eye dog
Fuhr′park *m* (aut) fleet
Füh′rung *f* (–;–en) guidance; leadership; management; guided tour; behavior; (mil) command; (sport) lead
Füh′rungskraft *f* executive; **die Führungskräfte** management; (pol) authorities; **untere F.** junior executive
Füh′rungsschicht *f* (com) management
Füh′rungsspitze *f* top echelon
Fuhr′unternehmen *n* trucking
Fuhr′werk *n* cart, wagon; vehicle
Füllbleistift [′fylblaɪ/tɪft] *m* mechanical pencil
Fülle [′fylə] *f* (–;) fullness; abundance, wealth; (*Körper*–) plumpness
füllen [′fylən] *tr* fill ‖ *ref* fill up ‖ **Füllen** *n* (–s;–) foal, colt, filly
Fül′ler *m* fountain pen
Füll′federhalter *m* fountain pen
Füll′horn *n* cornucopia
Füllsel [′fylzəl] *n* (–s;–) stopgap; (*beim Schreiben*) padding; (culin) stuffing
Fül′lung *f* (–;–en) (Zahn–) filling; (*Tür*–) panel; (culin) stuffing
Fund [funt] *m* (–[e]s;–e) find; discovery
Fundament [funda′ment] *n* (–[e]s;–e) foundation
fundamental [fundamen′tal] *adj* fundamental
Fund′büro *n* lost-and-found department
Fund′grube *f* (fig) mine, storehouse
fundieren [fun′dirən] *tr* lay the foundations of; found; establish; (*Schuld*) fund; **fundiertes Einkommen** unearned income; **gut fundiert** well-established
fünf [fynf] *adj & pron* five ‖ **Fünf** *f* (–;–en) five
Fünf′eck *n* pentagon
fünfte [′fynftə] §9 *adj & pron* fifth
Fünftel [′fynftəl] *n* (–s;–) fifth (*part*)
fünf′zehn *adj & pron* fifteen ‖ **Fünf′zehn** *f* (–;–en) fifteen
fünf′zehnte §9 *adj & pron* fifteenth
Fünf′zehntel *n* (–s;–) fifteenth (*part*)
fünfzig [′fynfʦɪç] *adj* fifty
fünf′ziger *invar adj* of the fifties; **die f. Jahre** the fifties
fünfzigste [′fynfʦɪçstə] §9 *adj & pron* fiftieth
fungieren [fuŋ′girən] *intr* function; **f. als** function as, act as
Funk [funk] *m* (–s;) radio
Funk′amateur *m* (rad) ham
Funk′bastler –in §6 *mf* (rad) ham
Fünkchen [′fyŋkçən] *n* (–s;–) small spark; **kein F.** (fig) not an ounce
Funke [′funkə] *m* (–ns;–n), **Funken** [′funkən] *m* (–s;–) spark
funkeln [′funkəln] *intr* sparkle; (*Sterne*) twinkle
fun′kelnagelneu′ *adj* brand-new

funken ['fuŋkən] *tr* radio, broadcast || *intr* spark

Fun′ker *m* (-s;-) radio operator

Funk′feuer *n* (aer) radio beacon

Funk′leitstrahl *m* radio beam

Funk′meßanlage *f* radar installation

Funk′meßgerät *n* radar

Funk′netz *n* radio network

Funk′peilung *f* radio direction finding

Funk′spruch *m* radiogram

Funk′streifenwagen *m* squad car

Funktionär –in [fuŋktsjo′ner(ɪn)] §8 *mf* functionary

für [fyr] *prep* (*acc*) for || **Für n—das Für und Wider** the pros and cons

Für′bitte *f* intercession

Furche ['furçə] *f* (-;-n) furrow; (*Runzel*) wrinkle; (*Wagenspur*) rut

furchen ['furçən] *tr* furrow; wrinkle

Furcht [furçt] *f* (-;) fear, dread

furchtbar ['furçtbar] *adj* terrible

fürchten ['fyrçtən] *tr* fear, be afraid of || *ref* (vor *dat*) be afraid (of)

fürchterlich ['fyrçtərlɪç] *adj* terrible, awful

furcht′erregend *adj* awe-inspiring

furcht′los *adj* fearless

furchtsam ['furçtzam] *adj* timid, shy

Furie ['furjə] *f* (-;-n) (myth) Fury

Furnier [fur′nir] *n* (-s;-e) veneer

Furore [fu′rorə] *f* (-;) & *n* (-s;) stir; **F. machen** cause a stir, be a big hit

Für′sorge *f* care; welfare

Für′sorgeamt *n* welfare department

Fürsorger –in ['fyrzorgər(ɪn)] §6 *mf* social worker; welfare officer

fürsorglich ['fyrzorklɪç] *adj* thoughtful

Für′sprache *f* intercession; **F. einlegen** intercede

Für′sprecher –in §6 *mf* intercessor

Fürst [fyrst] *m* (-en;-en) prince

Fürstentum ['fyrstəntum] *n* (-s;-er) principality

Fürstin ['fyrstɪn] *f* (-;-nen) princess

fürst′lich *adj* princely

Furt [furt] *f* (-;-en) ford

Furunkel [fu′runkəl] *m* (-s;-) boil

Für′wort *n* (-[e]s;-er) pronoun

Furz [furts] *m* (-es;-e) (vulg) fart

Fusel ['fuzəl] *m* (-s;) (coll) booze

Fusion [fu′sjon] *f* (-;-en) (com) merger

Fuß [fus] *m* (-es;-e) foot; **auf freien Fuß setzen** set free; **zu Fuß** on foot; **zu Fuß gehen** walk

Fuß′abdruck *m* footprint

Fuß′ball *m* soccer; football

Fuß′bank *f* (-;-e) footstool

Fuß′bekleidung *f* footwear

Fuß′boden *m* floor; flooring

Fussel ['fusəl] *f* (-;-n) fuzz

fußen ['fusən] *intr*—**f. auf** (*dat*) be based on; rely on

Fuß′fall *m* prostration

fuß′fällig *adv* on one's knees

fuß′frei *adj* ankle-length

Fuß′freiheit *f* leg room

Fuß′gänger *m* (-s;-) pedestrian

Fuß′gelenk *n* ankle joint

Fuß′gestell *n* pedestal

–füßig [fysɪç] *comb.fm.* –footed

Fuß′knöchel *m* ankle

Fuß′leiste *f* baseboard, washboard

Füßling ['fyslɪŋ] *m* (-s;-e) foot (*of stocking, sock, etc.*)

Fuß′note *f* footnote

Fuß′pfad *m* footpath

Fuß′pilz *m* athlete's foot

Fuß′spur *f* footprint(s)

Fuß′stapfe *f* footstep

Fuß′steg *m* footbridge; footpath

Fuß′steig *m* footpath; sidewalk

Fuß′tritt *m* step; (*Stoß*) kick

futsch [fut/] *adj* (coll) gone; (coll) ruined

Futter ['futər] *n* (-s;) fodder, feed; (*e-s Mantels*) lining

Futteral [futə′ral] *n* (-s;-e) case

Fut′terkrippe *f* crib; (sl) gravy train

Fut′terkrippensystem *n* (pol) spoils system

futtern ['futərn] *intr* (coll) eat heartily

füttern ['fytərn] *tr* feed; (*Kleid, Mantel, Pelz*) line

Fut′terneid *m* jealousy

Fut′terstoff *m* lining

Fut′tertrog *m* feed trough

G

G, g [ge] *invar n* G, g; (mus) G

gab [gap] *pret of* geben

Gabardine [gabar′dinə] *m* (-s;-) (tex) gabardine

Gabe ['gabə] *f* (-;-n) gift; donation; talent; (med) dose; **milde G. alms**

Gabel ['gabəl] *f* (-;-n) fork; (arti) bracket; (telp) cradle

Ga′belbein *n* wishbone

Ga′belbissen *m* tidbit

Ga′belfrühstück *n* brunch

gabelig ['gabəlɪç] *adj* forked

gabeln ['gabəln] *tr* pick up with a fork || *ref* divide, branch off

Ga′belstapler *m* forklift

Ga′belung *f* (-;-en) fork (*in the road*)

gackeln ['gakəln], **gackern** ['gakərn], **gacksen** ['gaksən] *intr* cackle, cluck

Gage ['gɑʒə] *f* (-;-n) salary, pay

gähnen ['genən] *intr* yawn

gaffen ['gafən] *intr* gape; stare

Gala ['gala] *invar f* gala, Sunday best

galant [ga′lant] *adj* courteous; **galantes Abenteuer** love affair

Galante-rie [galantə′ri] *f* (-;-rien ['ri·ən]) courtesy; flattering word

Gala-xis [ga′laksɪs] *f* (-;-xien [ksjən]) galaxy

Galeere [ga′lerə] *f* (-;-n) galley

Gale-rie [galə′ri] *f* (-;-rien ['ri·ən]) gallery

Galgen ['galgən] *m* (-s;-) gallows

Gal′genfrist f (coll) brief respite
Gal′genhumor m grim humor
Gal′genstrick m, **Gal′genvogel** m (coll) good-for-nothing
gälisch [′gɛlɪʃ] adj Gaelic
Galle [′galə] f (-;) gall, bile; (fig) bitterness
Gal′lenblase f gall bladder
Gal′lenstein m gallstone
Gallert [′galərt] n (-[e]s;-e), **Gallerte** [ga′lɛrtə] f (-;-n) gelatine; jelly
gallig [′galɪç] adj bitter; grouchy
Gallone [ga′lonə] f (-;-n) gallon
Galopp [ga′lɔp] m (-[e]s;-s & -e) gallop; im G. reiten gallop; in gestrecktem G. at full gallop; in kurzem G. at a canter
galoppieren [galo′pirən] intr (SEIN) gallop
galt [galt] pret of gelten
galvanisieren [galvanı′zirən] tr galvanize; electroplate
Gambe [′gambə] f (-;-n) bass viol
gammeln [′gaməln] intr bum around
Gammler [′gamlər] m (-s;-) hippie
Gamsbart [′gamsbart] m goatee
gang [gan] adj—g. und gäbe customary || **Gang** m (-[e]s;ä) walk, gait; (e-r Maschine) running, operation; (im Hause) hallway; (zwischen Reihen) aisle; (Botengang) errand; (Röhre) conduit; (e-r Schraube) thread; (anat) duct, canal; (aut) gear; (box) round; (culin) course; (min) vein, lode; (min) gallery; (mus) run; außer G. setzen stop; (aut) put in neutral; erster G. low gear; es ist etw im G. there is s.th. afoot; im G. sein be in operation; be in progress; in G. bringen (or setzen) set in motion; in vollem G. in full swing
Gang′art f gait
gangbar [′ganbar] adj passable; (Münze) current; (com) marketable
Gängelband [′gɛnəlbant] n—am G. führen (fig) lead by the nose, dominate
-gänger [gɛnər] comb.fm., e.g., Fußgänger pedestrian
gängig [′gɛnɪç] adj see gangbar
Gang′schaltung f (aut) gear shift
Gangster [′gɛnstər] m (-s;-s) gangster
Ganove [ga′novə] m (-;-n) crook
Gans [gans] f (-;ᵉe) goose
Gänseblümchen [′gɛnzəblymçən] n (-s;-) daisy
Gänsehaut [′gɛnzəhaʊt] f (coll) goose flesh, goose pimples
Gänseklein [′gɛnzəklaın] n (-s;) (culin) giblets
Gänsemarsch [′gɛnzəmarʃ] m single file
Gänserich [′gɛnzərɪç] m (-s;-e) gander
ganz [gants] adj whole; all; total; intact; im ganzen in all || adv entirely, quite; g. und gar completely; g. und gar nicht not at all || **Ganze** §5 n whole; aufs G. gehen go all the way
Ganz′aufnahme f full-length photograph
Gänze [′gɛntsə] f (-;)—in G. in its entirety; zur G. entirely
Ganz′fabrikat n finished product

Ganz′leinenband m (-[e]s;ᵉe) cloth-bound volume
gänzlich [′gɛntslɪç] adj entire, total
ganz′seitig adj full-page
ganz′tägig adj full-time
gar [gar] adj (culin) well done; (metal) refined || adv quite, very; (sogar) even; gar nicht not at all
Garage [ga′raʒə] f (-;-n) garage
Garan-tie [garan′ti] f (-;-tien [′ti·ən]) guarantee
garantieren [garan′tirən] tr guarantee || intr—g. dafür, daß guarantee that
Garaus [′garaʊs] m (-;) finishing blow
Garbe [′garbə] f (-;-n) sheaf, shock
Garde [′gardə] f (-;-n) guard
Gardenie [gar′denjə] f (-;-n) gardenia
Garderobe [gardə′robə] f (-;-n) wardrobe; (Kleiderablage) cloakroom; (theat) dressing room
Gardero′benmarke f hat or coat check
Gardero′benständer m coatrack, hatrack
Garderobiere [gardərə′bjerə] f (-;-n) cloakroom attendant
Gardine [gar′dinə] f (-;-n) curtain
Gardi′nenhalter m tieback
Gardi′nenpredigt f (coll) dressing down
Gardi′nenstange f curtain rod
gären [′gerən] §78 intr ferment; bubble
Gärmittel [′germıtəl] n ferment; leaven
Garn [garn] n (-[e]s;-e) yarn; thread; snare; (fig) trap; (fig) yarn
Garnele [gar′nelə] f (-;-n) shrimp
garnieren [gar′nirən] tr garnish; trim
Garnison [garnı′zon] f (-;-en) garrison
Garnitur [garnı′tur] f (-;-en) trimming; set (of matching objects); (mach) fittings, mountings; (mil) uniform
garstig [′garstıç] adj ugly; nasty
Garten [′gartən] m (-s;ᵉ) garden
Gar′tenanlage f gardens, grounds
Gar′tenarbeit f gardening
Gar′tenarchitekt m landscape gardener
Gar′tenbau m gardening; horticulture
Gar′tenlaube f arbor
Gar′tenmesser n pruning knife
Gärtner [′gertnər] m (-s;-) gardener
Gärtnerei [gertnə′raı] f (-;-en) gardening; truck farm; nursery
Gä′rung f (-;) fermentation
Gas [gas] n (-es;-e) gas; Gas geben step on the gas
Gas′anstalt f gasworks
gas′artig adj gaseous
Gas′behälter m gas tank
gas′förmig adj gaseous
Gas′hebel m (aut) accelerator
Gas′heizung f gas heat(ing)
Gas′herd m gas range
Gas′krieg m chemical warfare
Gas′leitung f gas main
Gas′messer m gas meter
Gasse [′gasə] f (-;-n) side street; über die G. verkaufen sell takeouts
Gas′sendirne f streetwalker
Gas′senhauer m popular song
Gas′senjunge m urchin

Gast [gast] *m* (-[e]s;⁀e) guest; boarder; (com) customer; (theat) guest performer; **zu Gast bitten** invite
Gästebuch ['gɛstəbux] *n* guest book; visitors' book
Gast'freund *m* guest
gast'freundlich *adj* hospitable
Gast'freundschaft *f* hospitality
Gast'geber *m* host
Gast'geberin *f* hostess
Gast'haus *n*, **Gast'hof** *m* inn
Gast'hörer **-in** §6 *mf* (educ) auditor
gastieren [gas'tirən] *intr* (telv, theat) appear as a guest
gast'lich *adj* hospitable
Gast'mahl *n* feast; banquet
Gast'professor *m* visiting professor
Gast'rolle *f* guest performance; **e-e G. geben** pay a flying visit
Gast'spiel *n* (theat) guest performance
Gast'stätte *f* restaurant
Gast'stube *f* dining room
Gast'wirt *m* innkeeper
Gast'wirtschaft *f* restaurant
Gas'uhr *f* gas meter
Gas'werk *n* gas works
Gas'zähler *m* gas meter
Gatte ['gatə] *m* (-n;-n) husband; **Gatten** married couple
Gatter ['gatər] *n* (-s;-) grating; latticework; iron gate
Gattin ['gatın] *f* (-;-nen) wife
Gattung ['gatuŋ] *f* (-;-en) kind, type, species; family; (biol) genus
Gat'tungsname *m* generic name; (gram) common noun
Gau [gau] *m* (-[e]s;-e) district
Gaukelbild ['gaukəlbɪlt] *n* illusion
gaukeln ['gaukəln] *intr* flit, flutter; perform hocus-pocus
Gau'kelspiel *n*, **Gau'kelwerk** *n* sleight of hand; delusion
Gaul [gaul] *m* (-[e]s;⁀e) horse; nag
Gaumen ['gaumən] *m* (-s;-) palate
Gauner ['gaunər] *m* (-s;-) rogue; swindler
Gaunerei [gaunə'raı] *f* (-;-en) swindling, cheating
gaunern ['gaunərn] *intr* swindle
Gau'nersprache *f* thieves' slang
Gaze ['gazə] *f* (-;-n) gauze; cheesecloth
Gazelle [ga'tsɛlə] *f* (-;-n) gazelle
Geächtete [gə'ɛçtətə] §5 *mf* outlaw
Geächze [gə'ɛçtsə] *n* (-s;) moaning
geartet [gə'artət] *adj*—**anders g. sein** be of a different disposition
Gebäck [gə'bɛk] *n* (-s;) baked goods, cookies
geballt [gə'balt] *adj* concentrated; dense; (*Schnee*) hardened; (*Faust*) clenched; (*Stil*) succinct
gebannt [gə'bant] *adj* spellbound
gebar [gə'bar] *pret* of **gebären**
Gebärde [gə'berdə] *f* (-;-n) gesture
gebärden [gə'berdən] *ref* behave
Gebär'denspiel *n* gesticulation
gebaren [gə'barən] *ref* behave, act ‖ **Gebaren** *n* (-s;) behavior
gebären [gə'berən] §79 *tr* bear ‖ **Gebären** *n* (-s;) childbirth; labor
Gebär'mutter *f* (anat) uterus
Gebär'mutterkappe *f* diaphragm

Gebäude [gə'bɔıdə] *n* (-s;-) building
gebefreudig ['gebəfrɔıdıç] *adj* openhanded
Gebein [gə'baın] *n* (-[e]s;-e) bones; **Gebeine** bones; mortal remains
Gebell [gə'bɛl] *n* (-[e]s;), **Gebelle** [gə'bɛlə] *n* (-s;) barking
geben ['gebən] §80 *tr* give; yield; (*Gelegenheit*) afford; (*Laut*) utter; (*Karten*) deal; **Feuer g.** give (*s.o.*) a light; (mil) open fire; **viel g. auf** (*acc*) set great store by; **von sich g.** utter; throw up; (*Rede*) deliver; (chem) give off ‖ *ref* give; (*Kopfweh, usw.*) get better; **sich g. als** pretend to be; **sich gefangen g.** surrender ‖ *impers*—**es gibt** there is, there are; **es wird Regen geben** it's going to rain
Ge'ber **-in** §6 *mf* giver, donor
Gebet [gə'bet] *n* (-[e]s;-e) prayer
gebeten [gə'betən] *pp* of **bitten**
Gebiet [gə'bit] *n* (-[e]s;-e) district, territory; (*Fläche*) area; (*Fach*) line; (*Bereich*) field, sphere
gebieten [gə'bitən] §58 *tr* (*Stillschweigen*) impose; (*Ehrfurcht*) command; (*verlangen*) demand; **j-m g., etw zu tun** order *s.o.* to do *s.th.* ‖ *intr* (*über acc*) have control (over); (*dat*) control
Gebieter [gə'bitər] *m* (-s;-) master; ruler; commander; governor
Gebieterin [gə'bitərın] *f* (-;-nen) mistress; (*des Hauses*) lady
gebieterisch [gə'bitərıʃ] *adj* imperious
Gebilde [gə'bıldə] *n* (-s;-) shape, form; structure; (geol) formation
gebildet [gə'bıldət] *adj* educated
Gebirge [gə'bırgə] *n* (-s;-) mountain range, mountains; **festes G.** bedrock
gebirgig [gə'bırgıç] *adj* mountainous
Gebirgs- [gəbırks] *comb.fm.* mountain
Gebirgs'bewohner **-in** §6 *mf* mountaineer
Gebirgs'kamm *m*, **Gebirgs'rücken** *m* mountain ridge
Gebirgs'zug *m* mountain range
Ge-biß [gə'bıs] *n* (-bisses;-bisse) teeth; false teeth; (*am Zaum*) bit
gebissen [gə'bısən] *pp* of **beißen**
Gebläse [gə'blezə] *n* (-s;-) bellows; blower; (aut) supercharger
geblieben [gə'blibən] *pp* of **bleiben**
Geblök [gə'bløk] *n* (-[e]s;) bleating
geblümt [gə'blymt] *adj* flowered
Geblüt [gə'blyt] *n* (-[e]s;) (& fig) blood
geboren [gə'borən] *pp* of **gebären** ‖ *adj* born; native; **geborene nee**
geborgen [gə'bɔrgən] *pp* of **bergen** ‖ *adj* safe
Gebor'genheit *f* (-;) safety, security
geborsten [gə'bɔrstən] *pp* of **bersten**
Gebot [gə'bot] *n* (-[e]s;-e) order, command; commandment; (*Angebot*) bid
geboten [gə'botən] *pp* of **bieten** ‖ *adj* requisite; **dringend g.** imperative
Gebr. *abbr.* (**Gebrüder**) Brothers
gebracht [gə'braxt] *pp* of **bringen**
gebrannt [gə'brant] *pp* of **brennen**

Gebräu [gə'brɔɪ] n (-[e]s;-e) brew

Gebrauch [gə'braux] m (-s;ᵘe) use; usage; (Sitte) custom

gebrauchen [gə'brauxən] tr use, employ

gebräuchlich [gə'brɔɪçlɪç] adj usual; in use; (gemein) common

Gebrauchs'anweisung f directions

gebrauchs'fertig adj ready for use; (Kaffee, usw.) instant

Gebrauchs'graphik f commercial art

Gebrauchs'gut n commodity

Gebrauchs'muster n registered pattern

gebraucht [gə'brauxt] adj second-hand

Gebraucht'wagen m used car

Gebrechen [gə'breçən] n (-s;-) physical disability, infirmity

gebrech'lich adj frail, weak; rickety

gebrochen [gə'brɔxən] pp of brechen

Gebrüder [gə'brydər] pl brothers

Gebrüll [gə'bryl] n (-[e]s-) roaring; bellowing; lowing

Gebühr [gə'byr] f (-;-en) charge, fee; due, what is due; nach G. deservedly; über G. excessively; zu ermäßigter G. at a reduced rate

gebühren [gə'byrən] intr (dat) be due to || impers ref—es gebührt sich it is proper

gebüh'rend adj due; (entsprechend) appropriate || adv duly

gebüh'renfrei adj free of charge

gebüh'renpflichtig adj chargeable

gebunden [gə'bundən] pp of binden || adj bound; (Hitze) latent; (Preise) controlled; (Kapital) tied-up; g. an (acc) (chem) combined with; gebundene Rede verse

Geburt [gə'burt] f (-;-en) birth

Gebur'tenbeschränkung f birth control

Gebur'tenregelung f birth control

Gebur'tenrückgang m decline in births

gebürtig [gə'byrtɪç] adj native

Geburts'anzeige f announcement of birth; registration of birth

Geburts'fehler n congenital defect

Geburts'helfer –in §6 mf obstetrician || f midwife

Geburts'hilfe f obstetrics

Geburts'mal n birth mark

Geburts'recht n birthright

Geburts'schein m birth certificate

Geburts'tag m birthday

Geburts'tagskind n person celebrating his or her birthday

Geburts'wehen pl labor pains

Geburts'zange f forceps

Gebüsch [gə'by ʃ] n (-es;-e) thicket, underbrush; clump of bushes

Geck [gɛk] m (-en;-en) dude

geckenhaft [gɛk'kɛnhaft] adj flashy

gedacht [gə'daxt] pp of denken

Gedächtnis [gə'dɛçtnɪs] n (-ses;) memory; aus dem G. by heart; im G. behalten bear in mind; zum G. (genit or an acc) in memory of

Gedächt'nisfehler m lapse of memory

Gedächt'nisrede f memorial address

gedämpft [gə'dɛmpft] adj muffled; hushed, quiet; (Licht, Stimme) subdued; (culin) stewed

Gedanke [gə'daŋkə] m (-ns;-n) thought; notion, idea; etw in Ge-

danken tun do s.th. absent-mindedly; in Gedanken sein be preoccupied; sich [dat] Gedanken machen über (acc) worry about

Gedan'kenblitz m (iron) brain wave

Gedan'kenfolge f, Gedan'kengang m train of thought

gedan'kenlos adj thoughtless; absent-minded; irresponsible

Gedan'kenpunkt m suspension point

Gedan'kenstrich m (typ) dash

Gedan'kenübertragung f telepathy

gedank'lich adj mental; intellectual

Gedärme [gə'dɛrmə] pl intestines

Gedeck [gə'dɛk] n (-[e]s;-e) cover; table setting; menu

gedeihen [gə'daɪ·ən] §81 intr (SEIN) thrive; succeed || Gedeihen n (-s;) prosperity; success

Gedenk- [gədɛŋk] comb.fm. memorial; commemorative

gedenken [gə'dɛŋkən] §66 intr (genit) think of, be mindful of; remember; mention; g. zu (inf) intend to (inf) || Gedenken n (-s;) memory

gedeucht [gə'dɔɪçt] pp of dünken

Gedicht [gə'dɪçt] n (-[e]s;-e) poem; (fig) dream

gediegen [gə'digən] adj (Gold) solid; (Silber) sterling; (Arbeit) excellent; (Kenntnisse) thorough; (Möbel) solidly made; (Charakter) sterling; (coll) very funny

gedieh [gə'di] pret of gedeihen

gediehen [gə'di·ən] pp of gedeihen

Gedränge [gə'drɛŋə] n (-s;-) pushing; crowd; difficulties; (fb) scrimmage

gedrängt [gə'drɛŋt] adj crowded, packed; (Sprache) concise

gedroschen [gə'drɔ ʃən] pp of dreschen

gedrückt [gə'drʏkt] adj depressed

gedrungen [gə'druŋən] pp of dringen || adj compact; stocky; squat; (Sprache) concise

Geduld [gə'dult] f (-;) patience

gedulden [gə'duldən] ref wait (patiently)

geduldig [gə'duldɪç] adj patient

Geduld'spiel n puzzle

gedungen [gə'duŋən] pp of dingen

gedunsen [gə'dunzən] adj bloated

gedurft [gə'durft] pp of dürfen

geehrt [gə'ert] adj—Sehr geehrte Herren! Dear Sirs; Sehr geehrter Herr X! Dear Mr. X

geeignet [gə'aɪgnət] adj suitable, right; qualified; appropriate

Gefahr [gə'far] f (-;-en) danger; (Wagnis) risk; G. laufen zu (inf) run the risk of (ger)

gefährden [gə'ferdən] tr jeopardize

gefährlich [gə'ferlɪç] adj dangerous

gefahr'los adj safe

Gefährt [gə'fert] n (-[e]s;-e) carriage

Gefährte [gə'fertə] m (-n;-n), Gefährtin [gə'fertin] f (-;-nen) companion; spouse

Gefälle [gə'felə] n (-s;-) pitch; slope

gefallen [gə'falən] adj fallen; (mil) killed in action || §72 ref—sich g. in (dat) take pleasure in || intr please; das gefällt mir I like this; das lasse ich mir nicht g. I won't stand for this || **Gefallen** m (-;-) favor || n (-s;) (an dat) pleasure (in); **j-m etw zu G. tun** do s.th. to please s.o.; **nach G.** as one pleases; at one's descretion

gefällig [gə'fɛlɪç] adj pleasing; obliging; kind; **j-m g. sein** do s.o. a favor; **Kaffee g.?** would you care for coffee?; **was ist g.?** what can I do for you?; **würden Sie so g. sein zu** (inf)? would you be so kind as to (inf)?

Gefäl'ligkeit f (-;-en) favor

gefälligst [gə'fɛlɪçst] adv if you please; please

gefangen [gə'faŋən] pp of **fangen** || adj captive; **g. nehmen** take prisoner || **Gefangene** §5 mf captive, prisoner

Gefan'genenlager n prison camp; (mil) prisoner-of-war camp

Gefan'gennahme f (-;) capture; arrest

gefan'gennehmen §116 tr take prisoner

Gefan'genschaft f (-;) captivity; imprisonment; **in G. geraten** be taken prisoner

gefan'gensetzen tr imprison

Gefängnis [gə'fɛŋnɪs] n (-ses;-se) prison, jail; imprisonment

Gefäng'nisdirektor m warden

Gefäng'nisstrafe f prison term

Gefäng'niswärter –in §6 mf guard

Gefäß [gə'fɛs] n (-es;-e) vessel; jar

gefaßt [gə'fast] adj calm, composed; **g. auf** (acc) ready for

Gefecht [gə'fɛçt] n (-[e]s;-e) fight, battle, action

Gefechts'auftrag m (mil) objective

Gefechts'kopf m warhead

Gefechts'lage f tactical situation

Gefechts'stand m command post

gefeit [gə'faɪt] adj (gegen) immune (from), proof (against)

Gefieder [gə'fidər] n (-s;-) plumage

gefleckt [gə'flɛkt] adj spotted

geflissentlich [gə'flɪsəntlɪç] adj intentional, willful

geflochten [gə'flɔxtən] pp of **flechten**

geflogen [gə'flogən] pp of **fliegen**

geflohen [gə'flo.ən] pp of **fliehen**

geflossen [gə'flɔsən] pp of **fließen**

Geflügel [gə'flygəl] n (-s;) fowl; (Federvieh) poultry

Geflü'gelmagen m gizzard

Geflunker [gə'flʊŋkər] m (-s;) (coll) fibbing

Geflüster [gə'flʏstər] n (-s;) whisper

Gefolge [gə'fɔlgə] n (-s;-) retinue; **in seinem G.** in its wake

Gefolgschaft [gə'fɔlk/aft] f (-;-en) allegiance; followers

gefräßig [gə'frɛsɪç] adj gluttonous

Gefrä'ßigkeit f (-;) gluttony

Gefreite [gə'fraɪtə] §5 m private first class; lance corporal (Brit)

gefressen [gə'frɛsən] pp of **fressen**

Gefrieranlage [gə'frirʔanlagə] f **Ge-frierapparat** [gə'frirʔaparat] m freezer

gefrieren [gə'frirən] §77 intr (SEIN) freeze

Gefrie'rer m (-s;-) freezer; deepfreeze

Gefrier'fach n freezing compartment

Gefrier'punkt m freezing point

Gefrier'schutz m, **Gefrier'schutzmittel** n antifreeze

gefroren [gə'frorən] pp of **frieren** || **Gefrorene** §5 n ice cream

Gefüge [gə'fygə] n (-s;-) structure, make-up; arrangement; texture

gefügig [gə'fygɪç] adj pliant, pliable

Gefühl [gə'fyl] n (-[e]s;-e) feeling; feel; touch; sense; sensation

gefühl'los adj numb; callous

gefühls-, Gefühls- [gəfyls] comb.fm. of the emotions; emotional; sentimental; (anat) sensory

gefühls'betont adj emotional

Gefühlsduselei [gə'fylsduzəlaɪ] f (-;) sentimentalism, mawkishness

gefühls'selig adj mawkish

gefühl'voll adj sensitive; tender-hearted || adv with feeling

gefunden [gə'fʊndən] pp of **finden**

gefurcht [gə'fʊrçt] adj furrowed

gegangen [gə'gaŋən] pp of **gehen**

gegeben [gə'gebən] pp of **geben** || adj given; (Umstände) existing; **gegebene Methode** best approach; **zu gegebener Zeit** at the proper time

gege'benfalls adv if necessary

gegen ['gegən] prep (acc) towards; against; about, approximately; compared with; contrary to; in exchange for

gegen-, Gegen- comb.fm. anti-; counter-; contrary; opposite; back; in return

Ge'genantwort f rejoinder

Ge'genbeschuldigung f countercharge

Ge'genbild n counterpart

Gegend ['gegənt] f (-;-en) neighborhood, vicinity; region, district

gegeneinan'der adv against one another; towards one another

Ge'gengerade f back stretch

Ge'gengewicht n counterbalance; (am Rad) (aut) weight; **das G. halten** (dat) counterbalance

Ge'gengift n antidote

Ge'genkandidat –in §7 mf rival candidate

Ge'genklage f countercharge; counterclaim

Ge'genmittel n (gegen) remedy (for), antidote (against)

Ge'genrede f reply, rejoinder

Ge'gensatz m contrast; opposite, antithesis; (Widerspruch) opposition

gegensätzlich ['gegənzɛtslɪç] adj contrary, opposite, antithetical

Ge'genschlag m counterplot

ge'genseitig adj mutual, reciprocal

Ge'genstand m object, thing; subject

gegenständlich ['gegən/tɛntlɪç] adj objective; (fa) representational; (log) concrete

ge'genstandslos adj baseless; without purpose; irrelevant; (fa) non-representational

Ge'genstoß m (box) counterpunch; (mil) counterthrust

Ge'genstück n counterpart

Ge'genteil n contrary, opposite; **im G.** on the contrary

ge'genteilig adj contrary, opposite

gegenü'ber prep (dat) opposite to; across from; with regard to; compared with

gegenü'berstellen *tr* (*dat*) place opposite to; (*dat*) confront with; (*dat*) contrast with

Gegenü'berstellung *f* confrontation; comparison; (*auf e-r Wache*) line-up

Gegenwart ['gegənvart] *f* (–;) present; present time; (gram) present tense

gegenwärtig ['gegənvɛrtɪç] *adj* present, current || *adv* at present; nowadays

Ge'genwehr *f* defense, resistance

Ge'genwind *m* head wind

Ge'genwirkung *f* (auf *acc*) reaction (to)

ge'genzeichnen *tr* countersign

Ge'genzug *m* countermove

geglichen [gə'glɪçən] *pp* of **gleichen**

geglitten [gə'glɪtən] *pp* of **gleiten**

Gegner –in ['gegnər(ɪn)] §6 *mf* opponent, rival || *m* (mil) enemy

gegnerisch ['gegnərɪʃ] *adj* adverse; antagonistic; opposing; (mil) enemy

gegolten [gə'gɔltən] *pp* of **gelten**

gegoren [gə'gorən] *pp* of **gären**

gegossen [gə'gɔsən] *pp* of **gießen**

gegriffen [gə'grɪfən] *pp* of **greifen**

Gehabe [gə'habə] *n* (–s;) affectation

gehaben [gə'habən] *ref* fare; **gehab dich nicht so!** stop putting on!; **gehab dich wohl!** farewell!

Gehackte [gə'haktə] §5 *n* hamburger

Gehalt [gə'halt] *m* (–[e]s;–e) contents; capacity; standard; **G. an** (*dat*) percentage of || *n* (–[e]s;–er) salary

Gehalts'stufe *f* salary bracket

Gehalts'zulage *f* increment, raise

gehalt'voll *adj* substantial; profound

Gehänge [gə'hɛŋə] *n* (–s;–) slope; pendant; festoon; (*e-s Degens*) belt

gehangen [gə'haŋən] *pp* of **hängen**

gehässig [gə'hɛsɪç] *adj* spiteful, nasty

Gehäuse [gə'hɔɪzə] *n* (–s;–) case, box; housing; (*e-r Schnecke*) shell; (*e-s Apfels*) core

Gehege [gə'hegə] *n* (–s;–) enclosure

geheim [gə'haɪm] *adj* secret; **streng g.** top-secret

geheim'halten §90 *tr* keep secret

Geheimnis [gə'haɪmnɪs] *n* (–ses;–se) secret, mystery

geheim'nisvoll *adj* mysterious

Geheim'schrift *f* code; coded message

Geheim'tinte *f* invisible ink

Geheim'vorbehalt *m* mental reservation

Geheiß [gə'haɪs] *n* (–es;) bidding

gehen ['ge·ən] §82 *intr* (SEIN) go; walk; leave; (*Teig*) rise; (*Maschine*) work; (*Uhr*) go; (*Ware*) sell; (*Wind*) blow; **das geht nicht** that will not do; **das geht schon** it will be all right; **sich g. lassen** take it easy; **wieviel Zoll g. auf einen Fuß?** how many inches make a foot? || *impers* — **es geht mir gut** I am doing well; **es geht nichts über** (*acc*) there is nothing like; **es geht um...** is at stake; **wie geht es Ihnen?** how are you?

geheuer [gə'hɔɪ·ər] *adj* — **mir war nicht recht g. zumute** I didn't feel quite at ease; **nicht g.** spooky; suspicious; risky

Geheul [gə'hɔɪl] *n* (–s;) howling; loud sobbing

Gehilfe [gə'hɪlfə] *m* (–n;–n), **Gehilfin** [gə'hɪlfɪn] *f* (–;–nen) assistant

Gehirn [gə'hɪrn] *n* (–[e]s;–e) brains, mind; (anat) brain; **sein G. anstrengen** rack one's brain

Gehirn– *comb.fm.* brain; cerebral

Gehirn'erschütterung *f* concussion

Gehirn'schlag *m* (pathol) stroke

Gehirn'wäsche *f* brainwashing

gehoben [gə'hobən] *pp* of **heben** || *adj* (*Stellung*) high; (*Stil*) lofty; **gehobene Stimmung** high spirits

Gehöft [gə'høft] *n* (–[e]s;–e) farm

geholfen [gə'hɔlfən] *pp* of **helfen**

Gehölz [gə'hœlts] *n* (–es;–e) grove; thicket

Gehör [gə'hør] *n* (–s;) hearing; ear

Gehör– *comb.fm.* of hearing; auditory

gehorchen [gə'hɔrçən] *intr* (*dat*) obey

gehören [gə'hørən] *ref* be proper, be right || *intr* (*dat* or **zu**) belong to; (in *acc*) go into, belong in

gehörig [gə'hørɪç] *adj* proper, due; (*dat* or **zu**) belonging to || *adv* properly; duly; thoroughly

Gehörn [gə'hørn] *n* (–s;–e) horns; **Gehörne** sets of horns

gehorsam [gə'horzam] *adj* obedient || *adv* obediently; **gehorsamst** respectfully || **Gehorsam** *m* (–s;) obedience

Gehor'samverweigerung *f* disobedience

gehren ['gerən] *tr* (carp) miter

Gehrlade ['gerladə] *f* (–;–n) miter box

Gehrock ['gerɔk] *m* Prince Albert

Geh'rung *f*—**auf G., nach der G.** on the slant; **auf G. verbinden** miter

Geh'rungslade *f* (–;–n) miter box

Gehsteig ['ge·ʃtaɪk] *m* sidewalk

Gehweg ['gevek] *m* sidewalk; footpath

Gehwerk ['gevɛrk] *n* clockwork, works

Geier ['gaɪ·ər] *m* (–s;–) vulture; **zum Geier!** what the devil!

Geifer ['gaɪfər] *m* (–s;) drivel; froth, slaver, foam; (fig) venom

geifern ['gaɪfərn] *intr* slaver

Geige ['gaɪgə] *f* (–;–n) violin, fiddle

geigen ['gaɪgən] *intr* play the violin

Gei'genbogen *m* bow, fiddlestick

Gei'genharz *n* rosin

Gei'ger –in §6 *mf* violinist

geil [gaɪl] *adj* lustful, in heat; (*Boden*) rich; (*üppig*) luxuriant

Geisel ['gaɪzəl] *f* (–;–n) hostage

Geiser ['gaɪzər] *m* (–s;–) geyser

Geiß [gaɪs] *f* (–;–en) she-goat

Geißel ['gaɪsəl] *f* (–;–n) scourge

geißeln ['gaɪsəln] *tr* scourge; (fig) castigate

Geist [gaɪst] *m* (–es;–er) spirit; (*Gespenst*) ghost; (*Verstand*) mind, intellect; **im Geiste** in one's imagination; in spirit

Gei'sterbeschwörung *f* (–;) necromancy

Gei'sterstadt *f* ghost town

Gei'sterstunde *f* witching hour

geistes– [gaɪstəs] *comb.fm.* spiritually; mentally, intellectually || **Geistes–** *comb.fm.* spiritual; mental, intellectual

gei'stesabwesend *adj* absent-minded

Gei'stesanlagen *pl* natural gift

Gei'stesarbeit *f* brainwork

Gei'stesarmut *f* dullness, stupidity

Gei'stesblitz *m* brain wave; aphorism

Gei'stesflug *m* flight of the imagination

Gei'stesfreiheit *f* intellectual freedom

Gei'stesfrucht *f* brainchild

Gei'stesgegenwart *f* presence of mind

gei'stesgegenwärtig *adj* mentally alert

geistesgestört ['gaɪstəsgə/tørt] *adj* mentally disturbed

Gei'steshaltung *f* mentality

gei'steskrank *adj* insane

gei'stesschwach *adj* feeble-minded

Gei'stesstörung *f* mental disorder

Gei'stes- und Natur'wissenschaften *pl* arts and sciences

Gei'stesverfassung *f* frame of mind

gei'stesverwandt *adj* (mit) spiritually akin (to); (mit) congenial (with)

Gei'stesverwirrung *f* derangement

Gei'steswissenschaften *pl* humanities

gei'steswissenschaftlich *adj* humanistic

Gei'steszustand *m* state of mind

geistig ['gaɪstɪç] *adj* mental, intellectual; spiritual

geist'lich *adj* spiritual; (Orden) religious; (kirchlich) sacred, ecclesiastical; der geistliche Stand holy orders; the clergy || **Geistliche** §5 *m* clergyman

Geist'lichkeit *f* (-;) clergy

geist'los *adj* spiritless; dull; stupid

geist'reich *adj* witty; ingenious

Geiz [gaɪts] *m* (-es;) stinginess; avarice

geizen ['gaɪtsən] *intr*—g. mit be sparing with; nicht g. mit show freely

Geiz'hals *m* (coll) tightwad

geizig ['gaɪtsɪç] *adj* stingy, miserly

Geiz'kragen *m* (coll) tightwad

Gejammer [gə'jamər] *n* (-s;) wailing

gekannt [gə'kant] *pp* of kennen

Geklapper [gə'klapər] *n* (-s;) rattling

Geklatsche [gə'klat/ə] *n* (-s;) clapping; gossiping

Geklirr [gə'klɪr] *n* (-[e]s;) rattling

geklommen [gə'kləmən] *pp* of klimmen

geklungen [gə'kluŋən] *pp* of klingen

gekniffen [gə'knɪfən] *pp* of kneifen

gekonnt [gə'kɔnt] *pp* of können

Gekreisch [gə'kraɪ/] *n* (-[e]s;) screaming; screeching

Gekritzel [gə'krɪtsəl] *n* (-s;) scribbling

gekrochen [gə'krɔxən] *pp* of kriechen

Gekröse [gə'krøzə] *n* (-s;) tripe

gekünstelt [gə'kynstəlt] *adj* affected

Gelächter [gə'leçtər] *n* (-s;) laughter

Gelage [gə'lagə] *n* (-s;) carousing

Gelände [gə'lendə] *n* (-s;) terrain; site, lot; (educ) campus; (golf) fairway

Gelän'delauf *m* crosscountry running

Gelän'depunkt *m* landmark

Geländer [gə'lendər] *n* (-s;-) railing; guardrail; banister; parapet

gelang [gə'laŋ] *pret* of gelingen

gelangen [gə'laŋən] *intr* (SEIN) (an *acc*, in *acc*, zu) attain, reach

gelassen [gə'lasən] *pp* of lassen || *adj* composed, calm

Gelatine [ʒela'tinə] *f* (-;) gelatin

geläufig [gə'lɔɪfɪç] *adj* fluent; (gemein) common; (Zunge) glib

gelaunt [gə'launt] *adj*—gut gelaunt in good humor; zu etw g. sein be in the mood for s.th.

Geläut [gə'lɔɪt] *n* (-es;), Geläute [gə-'lɔɪtə] *n* (-s;) ringing; chimes

gelb [gelp] *adj* yellow || **Gelb** *n* (-s;) yellow

gelb'lich *adj* yellowish

Gelb'sucht *f* jaundice

Geld [gelt] *n* (-[e]s;) money; bares G. cash

Geld- *comb.fm.* money, financial

-geld *n comb.fm.* money; fee(s); tax, toll; allowance

Geld'anlage *f* investment

Geld'anleihe *f* loan

Geld'anweisung *f* money order; draft

Geld'ausgabe *f* expense; expenditure

Geld'beutel *m* pocketbook

Geld'bewilligung *f* (parl) appropriation

Geld'buße *f* fine

Geld'einlage *f* deposit

Geld'einwurf *m* coin slot

Geld'entwertung *f* inflation

Geld'erwerb *m* moneymaking

Geld'geber *m* investor; mortgagee

Geld'gier *f* avarice

Geld'mittel *pl* funds, resources

Geld'onkel *m* sugar daddy

Geld'schein *m* bank note, bill

Geld'schrank *m* safe

Geld'schublade *f* till (of cash register)

Geld'sendung *f* remittance

Geld'sorte *f* (fin) denomination

Geld'spende *f* contribution, donation

Geld'strafe *f* fine

Geld'stück *n* coin

Geld'überhang *m* surplus (of money)

Geld'währung *f* currency; monetary standard

Geld'wechsel *m* money exchange

Geld'wesen *n* financial system, finance

Gelee [ʒe'le] *m & n* (-s;-s) jelly

gelegen [gə'legən] *pp* of liegen || *adj* located; convenient; opportune; du kommst mir gerade g. you're just the person I wanted to see; es kommt mir gerade gelegen that suits me just fine; mir ist daran g. zu (inf) I'm anxious to (inf); was ist daran g.? what of it?

Gele'genheit *f* (-;-en) occasion; opportunity, chance; (com) bargain

Gelegenheits- *comb.fm.* occasional

Gele'genheitsarbeit *f* odd job

Gele'genheitskauf *m* good bargain

gele'gentlich *adj* occasional; casual; chance || *adv* occasionally || *prep* (genit) on the occasion of

gelehrig [gə'lerɪç] *adj* teachable; intelligent

gelehrsam [gə'lerzam] *adj* erudite

gelehrt [gə'lert] *adj* learned, erudite || **Gelehrte** §5 *mf* scholar

Geleise [gə'laɪzə] *n* (-s;-) rut; (rr) track; totes G. blind alley, deadlock

Geleit [gə'laɪt] *n* (-[e]s;) escort; freies (or sicheres) G. safe-conduct; j-m das G. geben escort s.o., accompany s.o.; zum G. forward

geleiten [gə'laɪtən] *tr* escort, accompany; j-n zur Tür g. see s.o. to the door

Geleit′zug *m* convoy

Geleit′zugsicherung *f* convoy escort

Gelenk [gə′leŋk] *n* (–[e]s;–e) joint

Gelenk′entzündung *f* arthritis

gelenkig [gə′leŋkıç] *adj* jointed; flexible; agile

gelernt [gə′lernt] *adj* skilled

Gelichter [gə′lıçtər] *n* (–s;) riffraff

Geliebte [gə′lıptə] §6 *mf* beloved, sweetheart

geliehen [gə′li·ən] *pp* of **leihen**

gelieren [ʒe′liːrən] *intr* jell, gel

gelinde [gə′lındə] *adj* soft; gentle, mild ‖ *adv* gently, mildly; **g. gesagt** to put it mildly

gelingen [gə′lıŋən] §142 *intr* (SEIN) succeed ‖ *impers* (SEIN)—**es gelingt mir I** succeed ‖ **Gelingen** *n* (–s;) success

gelitten [gə′lıtən] *pp* of **leiden**

gell [gel] *adj* shrill ‖ *interj* say!

gellen [′gelən] *intr* ring out; yell

gel′lend *adj* shrill, piercing

geloben [gə′loːbən] *tr* solemnly promise, vow; take the vow of ‖ *ref*—**sich** [*dat*] **g.** vow to oneself

gelogen [gə′loːgən] *pp* of **lügen**

gelt [gelt] *interj* say!

gelten [′geltən] §83 *tr* be worth; **wenig g.** mean little ‖ *intr* be valid; (*Münze*) be legal tender; (*Gesetz*) be in force; (*Grund*) hold true; (*Regel*) apply; (*Mittel*) be allowable; (*beim Spiel*) count; **g. als** or **für** have the force of; be ranked as; pass for, be considered; **g. lassen** acknowledge as correct; **j—m g.** be aimed at s.o. ‖ *impers*—**es gilt** (*acc*) be at stake; be a matter of; be worth (*s.th.*); **es gilt mir gleich, ob** it's all the same to me whether; **es gilt zu** (*inf*) it is necessary to (*inf*); **jetzt gilt's!** here goes!

Gel′tung *f* (–;) validity; value, importance; **zur G. bringen** make the most of; **zur G. kommen** show off well

Gel′tungsbedürfnis *n* need for recognition

Gelübde [gə′lɪpdə] *n* (–s;–) vow

gelungen [gə′luŋən] *pp* of **gelingen** ‖ *adj* successful; (*Wendung*) well-turned; funny

Gelüst [gə′lʏst] *n* (–[e]s;–e) desire

gelüsten [gə′lʏstən] *impers*—**es gelüstet mich nach I** could go for

gemach [gə′max] *adv* slowly, by degrees ‖ **Gemach** *n* (–[e]s;̈–er) room; apartment; chamber

gemächlich [gə′meçlıç] *adj* leisurely; comfortable

Gemahl [gə′maːl] *m* (–[e]s;–e) husband

Gemahlin [gə′maːlın] *f* (–;–nen) wife

Gemälde [gə′meːldə] *n* (–s;–) painting

gemäß [gə′meːs] *prep* (*dat*) according to

gemäßigt [gə′meːsıçt] *adj* moderate

gemein [gə′maın] *adj* common; mean, vile; **sich g. machen mit** associate with ‖ **Gemeine** §5 *m* (mil) private

Gemeinde [gə′maındə] *f* (–;–n) community; municipality; (eccl) parish

Gemein′deabgaben *pl* local taxes

Gemein′deanleihen *pl* municipal bonds

Gemein′dehaus *n* town hall

gemein′frei *adj* in the public domain

gemein′gefährlich *adj* constituting a public danger, dangerous

gemein′gültig *adj* generally accepted

Gemein′heit *f* (–;–en) meanness; dirty trick; vulgarity

gemein′hin *adv* commonly, usually

Gemein′kosten *pl* overhead

Gemein′nutz *m* public interest

gemein′nützig *adj* non-profit

Gemein′platz *m* platitude

gemeinsam [gə′maınzam] *adj* common, joint; mutual

Gemein′schaft *f* (–;–en) community; close association

gemein′schaftlich *adj* common, joint; mutual

Gemein′schaftsanschluß *m* (telp) party line

Gemein′schaftsarbeit *f* teamwork

Gemein′schaftsgeist *m* esprit de corps

Gemein′sinn *m* public spirit

gemein′verständlich *adj* popular; **g. darstellen** popularize

Gemein′wesen *n* community

Gemein′wohl *n* commonweal

Gemenge [gə′meŋə] *n* (–s;–) mixture; (*Kampfgewühl*) scuffle, melee

gemessen [gə′mesən] *pp* of **messen** ‖ *adj* deliberate; precise; dignified; **g. an** (*dat*) compared with

Gemetzel [gə′metsəl] *n* (–s;–) massacre

gemieden [gə′miːdən] *pp* of **meiden**

Gemisch [gə′mıʃ] *n* (–es;–e) mixture

Gemischt′warenhandlung *f* general store

Gemme [′gemə] *f* (–;–n) gem

gemocht [gə′mɔxt] *pp* of **mögen**

gemolken [gə′mɔlkən] *pp* of **melken**

Gemse [′gemzə] *f* (–;–n) chamois

Gemunkel [gə′muŋkəl] *n* (–s;–) gossip, whispering

Gemurmel [gə′murməl] *n* (–s;) murmur

Gemüse [gə′myːzə] *n* (–s;–) vegetable; vegetables

Gemü′sebau *m* (–[e]s;) vegetable gardening

Gemü′sekonserven *pl* canned vegetables

gemüßigt [gə′mysıçt] *adj*—**sich g. fühlen** feel compelled

gemußt [gə′must] *pp* of **müssen**

Gemüt [gə′myt] *n* (–[e]s;–er) mind; disposition; person, soul; warmth of feeling; **j—m etw zu Gemüte führen** bring s.th. home to s.o.

gemütlich [gə′mytlıç] *adj* good-natured, easy-going; (*Wohnung*) cosy

Gemüt′lichkeit *f* (–;) easy-going nature; cosiness

Gemüts′art *f* disposition, nature

Gemüts′bewegung *f* emotion

gemüts′krank *adj* melancholy

Gemüts′mensch *m* warm-hearted person

Gemüts′ruhe *f*—**in (aller) G.** in peace and quiet

Gemüts′stimmung *f* mood

Gemüts′verfassung *f* state of mind

Gemüts′zustand *m* frame of mind

gemüt′voll *adj* emotional

gen [gɛn] *prep (acc)* (poet) towards ||
Gen [gɛn] *n* (-s;-e) (biol) gene

genannt [gə′nant] *pp* of **nennen**

genau [gə′nau] *adj* exact; fussy

genau′genommen *adv* strictly speaking

Genau′igkeit *f* (-;) exactness, accuracy;
meticulousness

Gendarm [ʒã′darm] *m* (-en;-en) policeman

Gendarme·rie [ʒãdarmə′ri] *f* (-;-rien
[′ri·ən]) rural police; rural police
station

Genealo·gie [gene·alɔ′gi] *f* (-;-gien
[′gi·ən]) genealogy

genehm [gə′nem] *adj* agreeable; acceptable; *(dat)* convenient (for)

genehmigen [gə′nemigən] *tr* grant; approve; **sich** *[dat]* **etw** **g.** (coll) treat
oneself to s.th.; **genehmigt O.K.**

Geneh′migung *f* (-;-en) grant; approval; permission; permit

geneigt [gə′naikt] *adj* sloping; **(zu)**
inclined (to); *(dat)* well-disposed
(towards)

Geneigt′heit *f* inclination; good will

General [gene′ral] *m* (-[e]s;-e & -=e)
general

General′feldmarschall *m* field marshal

General′inspekteur *m* chief of the joint
chiefs of staff

Generalität [generali′tet] *f* (-;) body
of generals

General′konsul *m* consul general

General′leutnant *m* lieutenant general;
(aer) air marshal

General′major *m* major general

General′nenner *m* common denominator

General′probe *f* dress rehearsal

General′stabskarte *f* strategic map

General′vollmacht *f* full power of attorney

Generation [genera′tsjon] *f* (-;-en)
generation

generell [gene′rɛl] *adj* general, blanket

genesen [gə′nezən] §84 *intr* (SEIN) convalesce; **(von)** recover (from)

Gene′sung *f* (-;-en) convalescence

Gene′sungsheim *n* convalescent home

genetisch [ge′netiʃ] *adj* genetic

Genf [gɛnf] *n* (-s;) Geneva

Gen′forscher -in §6 *mf* genetic engineer

Gen′forschung *f* (-;) genetic engineering

genial [ge′njal] *adj* brilliant, gifted

Genick [gə′nik] *n* (-s;-e) nape of the
neck

Genick′bruch *m* broken neck

Genick′schlag *m* (box) rabbit punch

Genie [ʒe′ni] *n* (-s;-s) (man of) genius

genieren [ge′nirən] *tr* bother; embar-
rass || *ref* feel embarrassed

genießbar [gə′nisbar] *adj* edible; drinkable; (fig) agreeable

genießen [gə′nisən] §76 *tr* enjoy; eat;
drink

Genie′streich *m* stroke of genius

Genitalien [geni′taljən] *pl* genitals

Geni·tiv [′genitif] *m* (-s;-tive [′tivə])
genitive

genommen [gə′nɔmən] *pp* of **nehmen**

genoß [gə′nɔs] *pret* of **genießen**

Genosse [gə′nɔsə] *m* (-n;-n) companion, buddy; (pol) comrade

-genosse *m* *comb.fm.* fellow-, -mate

Genos′senschaft *f* (-;-en) association;
coöperative

Genossin [gə′nɔsin] *f* (-;-nen) companion, buddy; (pol) comrade

genug [gə′nuk] *invar adj* & *adv*
enough

Genüge [gə′nygə] *f—j—m* **G.** **tun** give
s.o. satisfaction; **zur G.** enough; only
too well

genügen [gə′nygən] *intr* suffice, do ||
ref—sich *[dat]* **g.** **lassen an** *(dat)* be
content with

genü′gend *adj* sufficient

genügsam [gə′nykzam] *adj* easily satisfied; frugal

genug′tun §154 *intr* *(dat)* satisfy

Genugtuung [gə′nuktu·uŋ] *f* (-;) satisfaction

Ge·nuß [gə′nus] *m* (-nusses;-nüsse)
enjoyment; pleasure; *(Nutznießung)*
use; *(von Speisen)* consumption

Genuß′mittel *n* semi-luxury *(as coffee,
tobacco, etc.)*

genuß′reich *adj* thoroughly enjoyable

genuß′süchtig *adj* pleasure-seeking

Geographie [ge·ɔgra′fi] *f* (-;) geography

geographisch [ge·ɔ′grafiʃ] *adj* geo-
graphical

Geologe [ge·ɔ′logə] *m* (-n;-n) geologist

Geologie [ge·ɔlɔ′gi] *f* (-;) geology

Geometer [ge·ɔ′metər] *m* (-s;-) surveyor

Geometrie [ge·ɔme′tri] *f* (-;) geometry

Geophysik [ge·ɔfy′zik] *f* (-;) geophysics

Geopolitik [ge·ɔpɔli′tik] *f* (-;) geopolitics

Georgine [ge·ɔr′ginə] *f* (-;-n) dahlia

Gepäck [gə′pɛk] *n* (-[e]s;) luggage

Gepäck′abfertigung *f* luggage check-in;
luggage counter

Gepäck′ablage *f* luggage rack

Gepäck′anhänger *m* tag; luggage trailer

Gepäck′aufbewahrung *f* baggage room

Gepäck′netz *n* baggage rack *(net type)*

Gepäck′raum *m* luggage compartment

Gepäck′schein *m* luggage check

Gepäck′träger *m* porter; (aut) roof
rack

Gepäck′wagen *m* (rr) baggage car

gepanzert [gə′pantsərt] *adj* armored

gepfeffert [gə′pfefərt] *adj* peppered;
(Worte) sharp; *(Preis)* exorbitant

Gepfeife [gə′pfaifə] *n* (-s;) whistling

gepfiffen [gə′pfifən] *pp* of **pfeifen**

geflogen [gə′pflogən] *pp* of **pflegen**

Gepflo′genheit *f* (-;-en) custom, practice

Geplänkel [gə′plɛŋkəl] *n* (-s;) skirmish; (fig) exchange of words

Geplapper [gə′plapər] *n* (-s;) jabber

Geplärr [gə′plɛr] *n* (-s;) bawling

Geplauder [gə′plaudər] *n* (-s;) small
talk, chat

Gepolter [gə′pɔltər] *n* (-s;) rumbling

Gepräge [gə′pregə] *n* (-s;) impression;
stamp, character

Gepränge [gə′prɛŋə] *n* (-s;) pomp

gepriesen [gə'pri:zən] *pp of* **preisen**
gequollen [gə'kvɔlən] *pp of* **quellen**
gerade [gə'ra:də] *adj* straight; even; direct; *(Haltung)* erect; *(aufrichtig)* straightforward ‖ *adv* straight; exactly; just; just now ‖ **Gerade** *f* (-n; -n) straight line; straightaway; (box) straight; **rechte G.** straight right
gerade(n)wegs [gə'ra:də(n)veks] *adv* immediately, straightaway
geradezu' *adv* downright
Geranie [ge'ra:njə] *f* (-;-n) geranium
gerannt [gə'rant] *pp of* **rennen**
Gerassel [gə'rasəl] *n* (-s;) clanking
Gerät [gə'rɛt] *n* (-[e]s;-e) device, instrument; tool; (rad, telv) set
geraten [gə'ra:tən] *pp of* **raten** ‖ *adj* successful; *(ratsam)* advisable ‖ §63 *intr* (SEIN) *(gut, schlecht, usw.)* turn out; **außer sich g.** be beside oneself; **g. an** *(acc)* come by; **g. auf** *(acc)* get into; get on to; **g. hinter** *(acc)* get behind; find out about; **g. in** *(acc)* get into, fall into; **g. nach** take after; **g. über** *(acc)* come across; **in Bewegung g.** begin to move; **in Brand g.** catch fire; **ins Schleudern g.** begin to skid; **ins Stocken g.** come to a standstill
Gerä'teschuppen *m* tool shed
Geratewohl [gə'ra:təvo:l] *n* (-s;)—**aufs G.** at random
geraum [gə'raum] *adj* considerable
geräumig [gə'rɔ:mɪç] *adj* spacious
Geräusch [gə'rɔɪʃ] *n* (-[e]s;-e) noise
gerben ['gɛrbən] *tr* tan
Gerberei [gɛrbə'raɪ] *f* (-;-en) tannery
gerecht [gə'rɛçt] *adj* just, fair; justified; **g. werden** (dat) do justice to
Gerech'tigkeit *f* (-;) justice; fairness
Gerede [gə're:də] *n* (-s;) talk; hearsay
gereichen [gə'raɪçən] *intr*—**es gereicht ihm zur Ehre** it does him justice; **es gereicht ihm zum Vorteil** it is to his advantage; **es gereicht mir zur Freude** it gives me pleasure
gereizt [gə'raɪtst] *adj* irritable; irritated
gereuen [gə'rɔɪ.ən] *tr* cause *(s.o.)* regret ‖ *ref*—**sich keine Mühe g. lassen** spare no trouble ‖ *impers*—**es gereut mich** I regret
Geriatrie [gɛrɪ.a'tri:] *f* (-;) geriatrics
Gericht [gə'rɪçt] *n* (-[e]s;-e) court; courthouse; judgment; (culin) dish; **das Jüngste G.** the Last Judgment
gericht'lich *adj* legal, judicial, court
Gerichtsbarkeit [gə'rɪçtsbarkaɪt] *f* (-;) jurisdiction
Gerichts'bote *m* (jur) bailiff
Gerichts'hof *m* law court; **Oberster G.** Supreme Court
Gerichts'medizin *f* forensic medicine
Gerichts'saal *m* courtroom
Gerichts'schreiber –in §6 *mf* (jur) clerk
Gerichts'stand *m* (jur) venue
Gerichts'verhandlung *f* hearing; trial
Gerichts'vollzieher *m* (jur) marshal
Gerichts'wesen *n* judicial system
gerieben [gə'ri:bən] *pp of* **reiben** ‖ *adj* cunning, smart
Geriesel [gə'ri:zəl] *n* (-s;) purling
gering [gə'rɪŋ] *adj* slight, trifling;

small; *(niedrig)* low; *(ärmlich)* poor; *(minderwertig)* inferior; **nicht im geringsten** not in the least
gering'achten *tr* think little of
gering'fügig *adj* insignificant
gering'schätzen *tr* look down on
Gering'schätzung *f* contempt, disdain
gerinnen [gə'rɪnən] §121 *intr* coagulate, clot; *(Milch)* curdle
Gerinnsel [gə'rɪnzəl] *n* (-s;-) clot
Gerippe [gə'rɪpə] *n* (-s;-) skeleton; *(Gerüst)* framework
gerippt [gə'rɪpt] *adj* ribbed; *(Säule)* fluted; *(Stoff)* corded
gerissen [gə'rɪsən] *pp of* **reißen** ‖ *adj* sly
geritten [gə'rɪtən] *pp of* **reiten**
gern(e) ['gɛrn(ə)] *adv* gladly; **g. haben** or **mögen** like; **ich rauche g.** I like to smoke
gerochen [gə'rɔxən] *pp of* **riechen**
Geröll [gə'rœl] *n* (-s;) pebbles
geronnen [gə'rɔnən] *pp of* **gerinnen** & **rinnen**
Gerste ['gɛrstə] *f* (-;-n) barley
Ger'stenkorn *n* grain of barley; (pathol) sty
Gerte ['gɛrtə] *f* (-;-n) switch, rod
Geruch [gə'rux] *m* (-[e]s;ˮe) smell
geruch'los *adj* odorless
Gerücht [gə'rʏçt] *m* (-[e]s;-e) rumor
geruhen [gə'ru:.ən] *intr* deign
geruhsam [gə'ru:zam] *adj* quiet; relaxed
Gerümpel [gə'rʏmpəl] *n* (-s;) junk
gerungen [gə'ruŋən] *pp of* **ringen**
Gerüst [gə'rʏst] *n* (-s;-e) scaffold; *(Tragewerk)* frame; (fig) outline
Ges [gɛs] *n* (-;-) (mus) G flat
gesamt [gə'zamt] *adj* entire, total
gesamt-, Gesamt- *comb.fm.* total, overall; all-; joint; collective
gesandt [gə'zant] *pp of* **senden**
Gesand'te §5 *mf* envoy
Gesandt'schaft *f* (-;-en) legation
Gesang [gə'zaŋ] *m* (-[e]s;ˮe) singing; song; (lit) canto
Gesang'verein *m* glee club
Gesäß [gə'zɛs] *n* (-es;-e) buttocks; (coll) behind
Geschäft [gə'ʃɛft] *n* (-[e]s;-e) business; deal, bargain; shop, store
Geschäftemacherei [gə'ʃɛftəmaxəraɪ] *f* (-;) commercialism
geschäftig [gə'ʃɛftɪç] *adj* busy
Geschäf'tigkeit *f* (-;) hustle, bustle
geschäft'lich *adj* business ‖ *adv* on business
Geschäfts'abschluß *m* contract; deal
Geschäfts'aufsicht *f* receivership
Geschäfts'bedingungen *pl* terms
geschäfts'führend *adj* managing; executive; **geschäftsführende Regierung** caretaker government
Geschäfts'führer –in §6 *mf* manager
Geschäfts'haus *n* firm; office building
Geschäfts'inhaber –in §6 *mf* proprietor
geschäfts'kundig *adj* with business experience
Geschäfts'lokal *n* business premises; *(Laden)* shop; *(Büro)* office
Geschäfts'mann *m* (-[e]s;-leute) businessman

geschäfts′mäßig *adj* business-like
Geschäfts′ordnung *f* rules of procedure; **zur G.!** point of order!
Geschäfts′reise *f* business trip
Geschäfts′schluß *m* closing time
Geschäfts′stelle *f* office; branch
Geschäfts′träger *m* agent, representative; (pol) chargé d'affaires
geschäfts′tüchtig *adj* sharp
Geschäfts′verbindung *f* business connections
Geschäfts′verkehr *m* business transactions
Geschäfts′viertel *n* business district
Geschäfts′wert *m* (com) good will
Geschäfts′zweig *m* line of business
geschah [gə′ʃa] *pret* of **geschehen**
geschehen [gə′e·ən] §138 *intr* (SEIN) happen; take place; be done; **das geschieht dir recht!** serves you right! || **Geschehen** *n* (-s;) events
Geschehnis [gə′enɪs] *n* (-ses;-se) event
gescheit [gə′aɪt] *adj* clever; bright; sensible; **er ist wohl nicht ganz g.** he's not all there
Geschenk [gə′ʃɛŋk] *n* (-[e]s;-e) gift
Geschichte [gə′içtə] *f* (-;-n) story; history; (coll) affair, thing
geschicht′lich *adj* historical
Geschichts′forscher –in §6 *mf*, **Geschichts′schreiber** –in §6 *mf* historian
Geschick [gə′ʃɪk] *n* (-[e]s;-e) fate, destiny; dexterity, skill
Geschick′lichkeit *f* (-;) skillfulness
geschickt [gə′ʃɪkt] *adj* skillful
geschieden [gə′ʃidən] *pp* of **scheiden**
geschienen [gə′ʃinən] *pp* of **scheinen**
Geschirr [gə′ʃɪr] *n* (-[e]s;-e) dishes; china; pot; (*e-s Pferdes*) harness
Geschirr′schrank *m* kitchen cabinet
Geschirrspülmaschine [gə′ʃɪrʃpylmaʃinə] *f* dishwasher
Geschirr′tuch *n* dishtowel
geschissen [gə′ʃɪsən] *pp* of **scheißen**
Geschlecht [gə′ʃlɛçt] *n* (-[e]s;-er) sex; race; family, line; generation; (gram) gender
geschlecht′lich *adj* sexual
Geschlechts′krankheit *f* venereal disease
Geschlechts′teile *pl* genitals
Geschlechts′trieb *m* sexual instinct
Geschlechts′verkehr *m* intercourse
Geschlechts′wort *n* (-[e]s;=) (gram) article
geschlichen [gə′ʃlɪçən] *pp* of **schleichen**
geschliffen [gə′ʃlɪfən] *pp* of **schleifen** || *adj* (*Glas*) cut; (*fig*) polished
geschlissen [gə′ʃlɪsən] *pp* of **schleißen**
geschlossen [gə′ʃlɔsən] *pp* of **schließen** || *adj* closed; enclosed; (*Front*) united; (*Gesellschaft*) private; (ling) close; (telv) closed-circuit || *adv* unanimously; **g. hinter j–m stehen** be solidly behind s.o.
geschlungen [gə′ʃluŋən] *pp* of **schlingen**
Geschmack [gə′ʃmak] *m* (-s;=e & =er) taste
Geschmacks′richtung *f* vogue

geschmeidig [gə′ʃmaɪdɪç] *adj* pliant; flexible; lithe; (*Haar*) manageable
Geschmeiß [gə′ʃmaɪs] *n* (-es;) vermin; rabble
geschmissen [gə′ʃmɪsən] *pp* of **schmeißen**
geschmolzen [gə′ʃmɔltsən] *pp* of **schmelzen**
Geschnatter [gə′ʃnatər] *n* (-s;) cackle
geschniegelt [gə′ʃnigəlt] *adj* spruce
geschnitten [gə′ʃnitən] *pp* of **schneiden**
geschnoben [gə′ʃnobən] *pp* of **schnauben**
geschoben [gə′ʃobən] *pp* of **schieben**
gescholten [gə′ʃɔltən] *pp* of **schelten**
Geschöpf [gə′ʃœpf] *n* (-[e]s;-e) creature
geschoren [gə′ʃorən] *pp* of **scheren**
Ge·schoß [gə′ʃɔs] *n* (-schosses; -schosse) shot; missile; shell; floor, story
Geschoß′bahn *f* trajectory
geschossen [gə′ʃɔsən] *pp* of **schießen**
geschraubt [gə′ʃraubt] *adj* affected; (*Stil*) stilted
Geschrei [gə′ʃraɪ] *n* (-[e]s;) shouting
Geschreibsel [gə′ʃraɪpsəl] *n* (-s;) scribbling, scrawl
geschrieben [gə′ʃribən] *pp* of **schreiben**
geschrien [gə′ʃri·ən] *pp* of **schreien**
geschritten [gə′ʃritən] *pp* of **schreiten**
geschunden [gə′ʃundən] *pp* of **schinden**
Geschütz [gə′ʃyts] *n* (-es;-e) gun
Geschütz′bedienung *f* gun crew
Geschütz′legierung *f* gun metal
Geschütz′stand *m* gun emplacement
Geschwader [gə′ʃvadər] *n* (-s;-) (aer) group (*consisting of 27 aircraft*); (nav) squadron
Geschwätz [gə′ʃvɛts] *n* (-es;) chatter
geschweige [gə′ʃvaɪgə]—**g. denn** let alone, much less
geschwiegen [gə′ʃvigən] *pp* of **schweigen**
geschwind [gə′ʃvɪnt] *adj* quick
Geschwin′digkeit *f* (-;-en) speed; velocity; **mit der G. von** at the rate of
Geschwin′digkeitsbegrenzung *f* speed limit
Geschwin′digkeitsmesser *m* speedometer
Geschwind′schritt *m* (mil) double time
Geschwister [gə′ʃvɪstər] *pl* brother and sister, brothers, sisters, brothers and sisters; siblings
geschwollen [gə′ʃvɔlən] *pp* of **schwellen** || *adj* turgid
geschwommen [gə′ʃvɔmən] *pp* of **schwimmen**
geschworen [gə′ʃvorən] *pp* of **schwören** || **Geschworene** §5 *mf* juror; **die Geschworenen** the jury
Geschwo′renengericht *n* jury
Geschwulst [gə′ʃvulst] *f* (-;=e) swelling; tumor
geschwunden [gə′ʃvundən] *pp* of **schwinden**
geschwungen [gə′ʃvuŋən] *pp* of **schwingen**
Geschwür [gə′ʃvyr] *n* (-s;-e) ulcer

Geselle [gə'zelə] *m* (-n;-n) journeyman; companion; lad, fellow

gesellen [gə'zelən] *ref*—**sich zu j-m** g. join s.o.

gesellig [gə'zelɪç] *adj* gregarious, sociable

Gesell'schaft *f* (-;-en) society; company; (pej) bunch; (com) company; **j-m G. leisten** keep s.o. company

Gesell'schafter -in §6 *mf* companion; shareholder; (com) partner

gesell'schaftlich *adj* social

Gesell'schaftsspiel *n* party game

Gesell'schaftswissenschaft *f* social science; sociology

gesessen [gə'zesən] *pp* of **sitzen**

Gesetz [gə'zets] *n* (-es;-e) law

Gesetz'buch *n* legal code

Gesetz'entwurf *m* (parl) bill

Gesetzes— [gəzetsəs] *comb.fm.* legal, of law, of the law

Geset'zesantrag *m*, **Geset'zesvorlage** *f* (parl) bill

gesetz'gebend *adj* legislative

Gesetz'geber -in §6 *mf* legislator

Gesetz'gebung *f* (-;) legislation

gesetz'lich *adj* legal

gesetz'los *adj* lawless

gesetz'mäßig *adj* legal; legitimate

Gesetz'sammlung *f* code of laws

gesetzt [gə'zetst] *adj* sedate; (*Alter*) mature; **g. den Fall, daß** assuming that ‖ *adv* in a dignified manner

gesetz'widrig *adj* illegal, unlawful

Gesicht [gə'zɪçt] *n* (-[e]s;-er) face; sight; eyesight; (*Aussehen*) look

Gesichts'farbe *f* complexion

Gesichts'kreis *m* horizon; outlook

Gesichts'punkt *m* point of view, angle

Gesichts'spannung *f* face lift

Gesichts'zug *m* feature

Gesims [gə'zɪms] *n* (-es;-e) molding

Gesindel [gə'zɪndəl] *n* (-s;) rabble; **lichtscheues G.** shady characters

gesinnt [gə'zɪnt] *adj* disposed; -minded

Gesinnung [gə'zɪnʊŋ] *f* (-;-en) mind; character; convictions

gesin'nungslos *adj* without definite convictions

gesin'nungsmäßig *adv* according to one's convictions

gesin'nungstreu, gesin'nungstüchtig *adj* staunch

gesittet [gə'zɪtət] *adj* polite; civilized

gesoffen [gə'zɔfən] *pp* of **saufen**

gesogen [gə'zogən] *pp* of **saugen**

gesonnen [gə'zɔnən] *pp* of **sinnen** ‖ *adj*—**g. sein zu** (*inf*) have a mind to (*inf*), be inclined to (*inf*)

gesotten [gə'zɔtən] *pp* of **sieden**

Gespann [gə'pan] *n* (-[e]s;-e) team; pair, combination

gespannt [gə'pant] *adj* stretched; tense; (*Aufmerksamkeit*) close; (*Beziehungen*) strained; **ich bin g.** (coll) I wonder, I am anxious to know

Gespenst [gə'pɛnst] *n* (-[e]s;-er) ghost, specter

gespen'sterhaft *adj* ghostly; spooky

gespenstisch [gə'pɛnstɪʃ] *adj* ghostly

gespie(e)n [gə'pi(ə)n] *pp* of **speien**

Gespiele [gə'pilə] *m* (-n;-n), **Gespielin** [gə'pilɪn] *f* (-;-nen) playmate

Gespinst [gə'pɪnst] *n* (-es;-e) yarn; (*Gewebe*) web

gesponnen [gə'pɔnən] *pp* of **spinnen**

Gespött [gə'pœt] *n* (-[e]s;) ridicule; laughing stock

Gespräch [gə'prɛç] *n* (-[e]s;-e) conversation; (telp) call; **Gespräche** (pol) talks; **G. mit Voranmeldung** person-to-person call

gesprächig [gə'prɛçɪç] *adj* talkative

gespreizt [gə'praɪtst] *adj* outspread; affected ‖ *adv*—**g. tun** act big

gesprenkelt [gə'prɛŋkəlt] *adj* spotted

gesprochen [gə'prɔxən] *pp* of **sprechen**

gesprossen [gə'prɔsən] *pp* of **sprießen**

gesprungen [gə'prʊŋən] *pp* of **springen**

Gestade [gə'tadə] *n* (-s;-) (river) bank; (sea)shore

Gestalt [gə'talt] *f* (-;-en) shape; figure; (*Wuchs*) stature

gestalten [gə'taltən] *tr* shape; form; arrange ‖ *ref* take shape; turn out

Gestal'tung *f* (-;-en) formation; development; arrangement; design

gestanden [gə'tandən] *pp* of **stehen**

geständig [gə'tendɪç] *adj*—**g. sein** admit one's guilt

Geständnis [gə'tentnɪs] *n* (-ses;-se) confession, admission

Gestank [gə'taŋk] *m* (-[e]s) stench

Gestapo [gə'tapo] *f* (-;) (**Geheime Staatspolizei**) secret state police

gestatten [gə'tatən] *tr* permit, allow

Geste ['gɛstə] *f* (-;-n) gesture

gestehen [gə'te-ən] §146 *tr* admit

Gestein [gə'taɪn] *n* (-[e]s;-e) rock

Gestell [gə'tel] *n* (-[e]s;-e) frame; rack; mounting; (coll) beanpole

Gestel'lungsbefehl *m* (mil) induction orders

gestern ['gɛstərn] *adv* yesterday; **g. abend** last evening, last night

gestiefelt [gə'tifəlt] *adj* in boots

gestiegen [gə'tigən] *pp* of **steigen**

gestikulieren [gɛstiku'lirən] *intr* gesticulate

Gestirn [gə'tɪrn] *n* (-[e]s;-e) star; (*Sternbild*) constellation

gestirnt [gə'tɪrnt] *adj* starry

gestoben [gə'tobən] *pp* of **stieben**

Gestöber [gə'tøbər] *n* (-s;-) snow flurry

gestochen [gə'tɔxən] *pp* of **stechen**

gestohlen [gə'tolən] *pp* of **stehlen**

gestorben [gə'tɔrbən] *pp* of **sterben**

gestoßen [gə'tosən] *pp* of **stoßen**

Gesträuch [gə'trɔɪç] *n* (-[e]s;) bushes, shrubbery

gestreift [gə'traɪft] *adj* striped

gestrichen [gə'trɪçən] *pp* of **streichen**

gestrig ['gɛstrɪç] *adj* yesterday's

gestritten [gə'trɪtən] *pp* of **streiten**

Gestrüpp [gə'trʏp] *n* (-[e]s;) underbrush

gestunken [gə'tʊŋkən] *pp* of **stinken**

Gestüt [gə'tyt] *n* (-[e]s;-e) stud farm

Gestüt'hengst *m* stallion, studhorse

Gesuch [gə'zux] *n* (-[e]s;-e) request; application; (jur) petition

gesucht [gə'zuxt] *adj* wanted; in demand; studied; (*Vergleich*) farfetched

Gesudel [gə'zudəl] *n* (-s;) messy job

Gesumme [gə'zumə] *n* (-s;) humming
gesund [gə'zunt] *adj* healthy; sound;
  wholesome; g. werden get well
Gesund'beter -in §6 *mf* faith healer
Gesund'brunnen *m* mineral spring
gesunden [gə'zundən] *intr* (SEIN) get
  well again, recover
Gesund'heit *f* (-;) health; auf Ihre G.!
  to your health!; G.! (God) bless you!
Gesund'heitslehre *f* hygiene
Gesund'heitspflege *f* hygiene
Gesund'heitsrücksichten *pl*—aus G.
  for reasons of health
Gesund'heitswesen *n* public health
gesungen [gə'zuŋən] *pp* of singen
gesunken [gə'zuŋkən] *pp* of sinken
Getäfel [gə'tɛfəl] *n* (-s;) wainscoting
getä'felt *adj* inlaid
getan [gə'tan] *pp* of tun
Getöse [gə'tøzə] *n* (-s;) din, noise
getragen [gə'tragən] *pp* of tragen || *adj*
  solemn
Getrampel [gə'trampəl] *n* (-s;) trample
Getränk [gə'treŋk] *n* (-[e]s;-e) drink
getrauen [gə'trau·ən] *ref* dare
Getreide [gə'traidə] *n* (-s;-) grain
Getrei'deboden *m* granary
Getrei'despeicher *m* grain elevator
getreu [gə'trɔɪ] *adj* faithful, true
getreu'lich *adv* faithfully
Getriebe [gə'tribə] *n* (-s;-) hustle and
  bustle; (adm) machinery; (aut) transmission
getrieben [gə'tribən] *pp* of treiben
getroffen [gə'trɔmən] *pp* of treffen
getrogen [gə'trogən] *pp* of trügen
getrost [gə'trost] *adj* confident
getrunken [gə'truŋkən] *pp* of trinken
Getto ['geto] *n* (-s;-s) ghetto
Getue [gə'tu·ə] *n* (-s;) fuss
Getümmel [gə'tʏməl] *n* (-s;) turmoil
getupft [gə'tupft] *adj* polka-dot
Geviert [gə'firt] *n* (-[e]s;-e) square
Gewächs [gə'veks] *n* (-es;-e) growth;
  plant
gewachsen [gə'vaksən] *adj*—g. sein
  (dat) be equal to, be up to
Gewächs'haus *n* greenhouse, hothouse
gewagt [gə'vakt] *adj* risky; off-color
gewählt [gə'velt] *adj* choice; refined
gewahr [gə'var] *adj*—g. werden (genit)
  become aware of
Gewähr [gə'ver] *f* (-s) guarantee
gewahren [gə'varən] *tr* notice
gewähren [gə'verən] *tr* grant
gewähr'leisten *tr* guarantee, ensure
Gewähr'leistung *f* (-;-en) guarantee
Gewahrsam [gə'varzam] *m* (-[e]s;)
  safekeeping, custody || *n* (-[e]s;-e)
  prison
Gewährs'mann *m* (-[e]s;﹦er & -leute)
  informant, source
Gewährs'pflicht *f* warranty
Gewalt [gə'valt] *f* (-;-en) force; violence; authority; (Aufsicht) control
Gewalt'haber *m* (-s;-) ruler; tyrant
Gewalt'herrschaft *f* tyranny
Gewalt'herrscher *m* tyrant
gewal'tig *adj* powerful; huge; (coll)
  awful || *adv* terribly
Gewalt'kur *f* drastic measure; (coll)
  crash program
gewalt'los *adj* nonviolent

Gewalt'marsch *m* forced march
Gewalt'mensch *m* brute, tyrant
gewaltsam [gə'valtzam] *adj* violent;
  forcible; drastic || *adv* by force
Gewalt'samkeit *f* (-s) violence
Gewalt'streich *m* bold stroke
Gewalt'tat *f* act of violence
gewalt'tätig *adj* violent, brutal
Gewalt'verbrechen *n* felony
Gewalt'verbrecher -in §6 *mf* felon
Gewand [gə'vant] *n* (-[e]s;﹦er) robe;
  appearance, guise; (eccl) vestment
gewandt [gə'vant] *pp* of wenden || *adj*
  agile; clever
gewann [gə'van] *pret* of gewinnen
gewärtig [gə'vertiç] *adj*—g. sein
  (genit) be prepared for
Gewäsch [gə've,] *n* (-es;) nonsense
Gewässer [gə'vesər] *n* (-s;-) body of
  water; waters
Gewebe [gə'vebə] *n* (-s;-) tissue; (tex)
  fabric
geweckt [gə'vekt] *adj* bright, sharp
Gewehr [gə'ver] *n* (-[e]s;-e) rifle
Geweih [gə'vai] *n* (-[e]s;-e) antlers
Gewerbe [gə'verbə] *n* (-s;-) trade,
  business; calling, profession; industry
Gewer'bebetrieb *m* business enterprise
Gewer'beschule *f* trade school
gewerblich [gə'verpliç] *adj* industrial;
  commercial, business
gebwerbs'mäßig *adj* professional
Gewerkschaft [gə'verk,∫aft] *f* (-;-en)
  labor union
gewerk'schaftlich *adj* union || *adv*—
  sich g. organisieren unionize
Gewerk'schaftsbeitrag *m* union dues
gewesen [gə'vezən] *pp* of sein
gewichen [gə'viçən] *pp* of weichen
Gewicht [gə'viçt] *n* (-[e]s;-e) (& fig)
  weight
gewichtig [gə'viçtiç] *adj* weighty
gewiegt [gə'vigt] *adj* experienced,
  smart, shrewd
gewiesen [gə'vizən] *pp* of weisen
gewillt [gə'vilt] *adj* willing
Gewimmel [gə'viməl] *n* (-s;) swarm;
  (Menschen-) throng
Gewimmer [gə'vimər] *n* (-s;) whim-
  pering; whining
Gewinde [gə'vində] *n* (-s;-) thread
  (of a screw); (Kranz) garland; skein
Gewinn [gə'vin] *n* (-[e]s;-e) winnings; profit; (Vorteil) advantage
Gewinn'anteil *m* dividend
Gewinn'aufschlag *m* (com) markup
Gewinn'beteiligung *f* profit sharing
gewinn'bringend *adj* profitable
gewinnen [gə'vinən] §121 *tr* win, gain;
  reach || *intr* win; make a profit;
  improve; g. an (dat) gain in; g. von
  or durch profit by
gewin'nend *adj* engaging
Gewinn'spanne *f* margin of profit
Gewinn'sucht *f* greed; profiteering
Gewinsel [gə'vinzəl] *n* (-s;) whim-
  pering
Gewirr [gə'vir] *n* (-[e]s;-e) tangle;
  entanglement; maze
gewiß [gə'vis] *adj* sure, certain || *adv*
  certainly; aber g.! of course!
Gewissen [gə'visən] *n* (-s;-) conscience

gewis'senhaft *adj* conscientious
gewis'senlos *adj* unscrupulous
Gewis'sensbisse *pl* pangs of conscience
Gewis'sensnot *f* moral dilemma
gewis'sermaßen *adv* to some extent; so to speak
Gewiß'heit *f* (–;-en) certainty
gewiß'lich *adv* certainly
Gewitter [gə'vɪtər] *n* (–s;–) thunderstorm
gewittern [gə'vɪtərn] *impers*—es gewittert a storm is brewing
Gewit'terregen *m* thundershower
gewitzigt [gə'vɪtsɪçt] *adj*—g. sein to have learned from experience
gewitzt [gə'vɪtst] *adj* bright, smart
gewoben [gə'vobən] *pp* of **weben**
gewogen [gə'vogən] *pp* of **wägen** & **wiegen** || *adj* well disposed
Gewo'genheit *f* (–;) favorable attitude
gewöhnen [gə'vønən] *tr* (an *acc*) accustom (to) || *ref* (an *acc*) get used to
Gewohnheit [gə'vonhaɪt] *f* (–;-en) habit, custom
gewohn'heitsmäßig *adj* habitual
Gewohn'heitsmensch *m* creature of habit
gewöhnlich [gə'vønlɪç] *adj* usual; normal; common, ordinary
gewohnt [gə'vont] *adj* usual; g. sein (*acc*) be used to
Gewölbe [gə'vœlbə] *n* (–s;–) vault; arch
gewölbt [gə'vœlpt] *adj* vaulted
Gewölk [gə'vœlk] *n* (–[e]s;–) clouds
gewonnen [gə'vonən] *pp* of **gewinnen**
geworben [gə'vorbən] *pp* of **werben**
geworden [gə'vordən] *pp* of **werden**
geworfen [gə'vorfən] *pp* of **werfen**
gewrungen [gə'vruŋən] *pp* of **wringen**
Gewühl [gə'vyl] *n* (–[e]s;) milling crowd
gewunden [gə'vundən] *pp* of **winden**
gewürfelt [gə'vyrfəlt] *adj* checkered
Gewürm [gə'vyrm] *n* (–[e]s;) vermin
Gewürz [gə'vyrts] *n* (–[e]s;-e) spice
Gewürz'nelke *f* clove
gewußt [gə'vust] *pp* of **wissen**
Geysir [ˈgaɪzɪr] *m* (–s;–) geyser
gezackt [gə'tsakt] *adj* jagged; (bot) serrated
gezähnt [gə'tsent] *adj* toothed; (*Rand*) perforated; (bot) dentated
Gezänk [gə'tseŋk] *n* (–[e]s;) squabbling
Gezeiten [gə'tsaɪtən] *pl* tides
Gezeiten- *comb.fm.* tidal
Gezeter [gə'tsetər] *n* (–s;) yelling
geziehen [gə'tsi·ən] *pp* of **zeihen**
geziemen [gə'tsimən] *intr* (*dat*) be proper for || *impers ref*—es geziemt sich für j-n it is right for s.o.
geziert [gə'tsirt] *adj* affected, phoney
Gezisch [gə'tsɪʃ] *n* (–es;) hissing
gezogen [gə'tsogən] *pp* of **ziehen**
Gezücht [gə'tsyçt] *n* (–[e]s;-e) riffraff
Gezwitscher [gə'tsvɪtʃ/ər] *n* (–s;) chirping
gezwungen [gə'tsvuŋən] *pp* of **zwingen** || *adj* forced; (*Stil*) labored || *adv* stiffly
Gicht [gɪçt] *f* (–;-en) gout

Giebel [ˈgibəl] *m* (–s;–) gable
Gier [gir] *f* (–;) greed
gierig [ˈgirɪç] *adj* (**nach**) greedy (for)
Gießbach [ˈgisbax] *m* torrent
gießen [ˈgisən] §76 *tr* pour; (*Blumen, usw.*) water; (metal) cast, found || *impers*—es gießt it is pouring
Gießer [ˈgisər] *m* (–s;–) foundryman
Gießerei [gisəˈraɪ] *f* (–;-en) foundry
Gieß'form *f* casting mold; (typ) matrix
Gieß'kanne *f* sprinkling can
Gift [gɪft] *n* (–[e]s;-e) poison
giftig [ˈgɪftɪç] *adj* poisonous; malicious
Gigant [gɪˈgant] *m* (–en;-en) giant
Gilde [ˈgɪldə] *f* (–;-n) guild
Gimpel [ˈgɪmpəl] *m* (–s;–) (coll) sucker
ging [gɪŋ] *pret* of **gehen**
Gipfel [ˈgɪpfəl] *m* (–s;–) top; peak
Gip'felkonferenz *f* summit meeting
Gips [gɪps] *m* (–es;-e) gypsum; plaster of Paris; (surg) cast
Gips'arbeit *f* plastering
Gips'diele *f* plasterboard
gipsen [ˈgɪpsən] *tr* plaster
Gips'verband *m* (surg) cast
Giraffe [gɪˈrafə] *f* (–;-n) giraffe
girieren [ʒɪˈrirən] *tr* endorse
Girlande [gɪrˈlandə] *f* (–;-n) garland
Giro [ˈʒiro] *n* (–s;-s) endorsement
girren [ˈgɪrən] *intr* coo
Gis [gɪs] *n* (–;–) (mus) G sharp
Gischt [gɪʃt] *m* (–es;) foam; spray
Gitarre [gɪˈtarə] *f* (–;-n) guitar
Gitter [ˈgɪtər] *n* (–s;–) grating, grille; bars; lattice; railing; trellis; (electron) grid
Git'terbett *n* baby crib
Git'ternetz *n* grid (*on map*)
Git'tertor *n* wrought-iron gate
Git'terwerk *n* latticework
Glacéhandschuhe [glaˈsehant/u·ə] *pl* (& fig) kid gloves
Gladi·ator [gladiˈɑtɔr] *m* (–s;-atoren [aˈtorən]) gladiator
Glanz [glants] *m* (–es;) shine; polish; luster; brilliance
glänzen [ˈglɛntsən] *tr* polish || *intr* shine; **durch Abwesenheit g.** be conspicuous by one's absence
glän'zend *adj* bright; glossy; polished; (fig) splendid, brilliant
Glanz'leder *n* patent leather
Glanz'licht *n* (paint) highlight
glanz'los *adj* dull; lackluster
Glanz'punkt *m* highlight
Glanz'stück *n* master stroke
glanz'voll *adj* brilliant, splendid
Glanz'zeit *f* heyday, golden age
Glas [glas] *n* (–es;-er) glass
Glaser [ˈglazər] *m* (–s;–) glazier
gläsern [ˈglɛzərn] *adj* glass; glassy
Glas'hütte *f* glassworks
glasieren [glaˈzirən] *tr* glaze; (*Kuchen*) frost, ice
glasig [ˈglazɪç] *adj* glassy; vitreous
Glas'jalousie *f* jalousie window
Glas'scheibe *f* pane of glass
Glasur [glaˈzur] *f* (–;-en) enamel (*on pots*); glaze; (culin) icing
glatt [glat] *adj* smooth; (*eben*) even; (*poliert*) glossy; (*schlüpfrig*) slippery; (*Absage*) flat; (*Lüge*) downright || *adv* smoothly; directly; entirely

Glätte ['glɛtə] *f* (—;) smoothness; slipperiness; (*Politur*) polish
Glatt'eis *n* sheet of ice; bei G. fahren drive in icy conditions
glätten ['glɛtən] *tr* smooth; smooth out || *ref* smooth out; become calm
glatt'streichen §85 *tr* smooth out
glatt'weg *adv* outright, point-blank
glattzüngig ['glatsʏŋɪç] *adj* smooth-talking
Glatze ['glatsə] *f* (—;-n) bald head
glatz'köpfig *adj* baldheaded
Glaube ['glaubə] *m* (—ns;), **Glauben** ['glaubən] *m* (—s;) belief; faith
glauben ['glaubən] *tr* believe; (*annehmen*) suppose || *intr* (*dat*) believe; g. an (*acc*) believe in; j—m aufs Wort glauben take s.o.'s word
Glau'bensbekenntnis *n* profession of faith; creed
Glau'benslehre *f* Christian doctrine
Glau'benssatz *m* dogma
gläubig ['glɔɪbɪç] *adj* believing || **Gläubige** §5 *mf* believer || **Gläubiger** –in §6 *mf* creditor
glaublich ['glauplɪç] *adj* credible
glaub'würdig *adj* credible; reliable; plausible
Glaukom [glau'kom] *n* (—s;-e) glaucoma
gleich [glaɪç] *adj* (*dat*) like; (an *dat*) equal (in); es ist mir ganz g. it's all the same to me || *adv* equally; immediately
gleichaltrig ['glaɪçaltrɪç] *adj* of the same age
gleich'artig *adj* similar, homogeneous
gleich'bedeutend *adj* synonymous
Gleich'berechtigung *f* (pol) equality
gleichen ['glaɪçən] §85 *intr* (*dat*) resemble, look like, be like
glei'chermaßen *adv* equally, likewise
gleich'falls *adv* likewise; as well
gleich'förmig *adj* uniform; regular; monotonous
gleich'gesinnt *adj* like-minded
Gleich'gewicht *n* equilibrium
gleich'gültig *adj* indifferent; es ist mir g. it's all the same to me
Gleich'heit *f* (—;-en) equality; (*Ähnlichkeit*) likeness
Gleich'klang *m* consonance; unison
gleich'kommen §99 *intr* (SEIN) (*dat*) equal; (*dat*) be tantamount to
gleich'laufend *adj* (mit) parallel (to)
gleich'machen *tr* make equal; standardize; dem Erdboden g. raze
Gleich'maß *n* regularity; evenness; balance, equilibrium; proportion
gleich'mäßig *adj* symmetrical; regular
Gleich'mut *m* equanimity, calmness
gleich'mütig *adj* calm
gleichnamig ['glaɪçnamɪç] *adj* of the same name; (phys) like
Gleichnis ['glaɪçnɪs] *n* (—ses;-se) parable; figure of speech; simile
Gleich'richter *m* (elec) rectifier
gleichsam ['glaɪçzam] *adv* so to speak; more or less, practically
gleichschenklig ['glaɪç/ɛŋklɪç] *adj* isosceles
Gleich'schritt *m*—Im G. in cadence; im G. marsch! forward, march!

gleich'seitig *adj* equilateral
gleich'setzen *tr* (*dat* or mit) equate (with)
Gleich'setzung *f* (—;), **Gleich'stellung** *f* (—;) equalization
Gleich'strom *m* direct current
gleich'tun §154 *tr*—es j—m g. emulate s.o.
Glei'chung *f* (—;-en) (math) equation
gleichviel *adv*—g. wer not matter who
gleich'wertig *adj* evenly matched
gleichwohl *adv* nevertheless
gleich'zeitig *adj* simultaneous
gleich'ziehen §163 *intr* (mit) catch up (with or to)
Gleis [glaɪs] *n* (—es;-e) (rr) track
Gleitboot ['glaɪtbot] *n* hydrofoil
gleiten ['glaɪtən] §86 *intr* (SEIN) glide; slip, slide
Gleitfläche ['glaɪtflɛçə] *f* (aer) hydroplane
Gleitflugzeug ['glaɪtfluktsɔɪk] *n* (aer) glider
Gleitschutz– *comb.fm.* skid-proof
Gleit'zeit *f* flexitime
Gletscher ['glɛt/ər] *m* (—s;-) glacier
glich [glɪç] *pret of* gleichen
Glied [glit] *n* (—[e]s;-er) limb; member; joint; link; (anat) penis; (log, math) term; (mil) rank, file
glie'derlahm *adj* paralyzed
gliedern ['glidərn] *tr* arrange; plan; divide, break down || *ref* (in *acc*) consist of
Glie'derung *f* (—;-en) arrangement; construction; division; organization
Gliedmaßen ['glitmasən] *pl* limbs
glimmen ['glɪmən] *intr* §136 & §109 *intr* glimmer; glow
Glim'mer *m* (—s;) glimmer; (min) mica
glimpflich ['glɪmpflɪç] *adj* gentle; (*Strafe*) light, lenient
glitschen ['glɪt/ən] *intr* (SEIN) slip
glitschig ['glɪt/ɪç] *adj* slippery
glitt [glɪt] *pret of* gleiten
glitzern ['glɪtsərn] *intr* glitter
global [glo'bal *adj* global
Glo-bus ['globus] *m* (–bus & –busses; –busse & –ben [bən]) globe
Glöckchen ['glœkçən] *n* (—s;-) small bell
Glocke ['glokə] *f* (—;-n) bell; (e-s *Rocks*) flare
Glockenspiel (Glok'kenspiel) *n* carillon
Glockenstube (Glok'kenstube) *f*, **Glockenturm (Glok'kenturm)** *m* belfry
Glockenzug (Glok'kenzug) *m* bell rope
Glöckner ['glœknər] *m* (—s;-) bell ringer; sexton
glomm [glom] *pret of* glimmen
Glorie ['gloriə] *f* (—;-n) glory
Glo'rienschein *m* halo
glorreich ['glorraɪç] *adj* glorious
glotzäugig ['glotsɔɪgɪç] *adj* popeyed
glotzen ['glotsən] *intr* stare, goggle
Glück [glʏk] *n* (–[e]s;) luck; fortune; happiness; auf gut G. at random; zum G. luckily
glucken ['glukən] *intr* cluck
glücken ['glʏkən] *intr* (SEIN) succeed || *impers*—es glückt mir I succeed
gluckern ['glukərn] *intr* gurgle

glück'lich adj lucky, fortunate; happy; (günstig) auspicious
glück'licherweise adv fortunately
glück'selig adj blissful; blessed; joyful
Glück'seligkeit f (–;) bliss; joy
glucksen ['glʊksən] intr gurgle; chuckle
Glücks'fall m stroke of luck; windfall
Glücks'güter pl earthly possessions
Glücks'hafen m raffle drum
Glücks'pilz m (coll) lucky dog
Glücks'spiel n game of chance
Glücks'topf m grab bag
glück'verheißend adj auspicious
Glück'wunsch m good wishes, congratulations
Glück'wunschkarte f greeting card
Glühbirne ['glyːbɪrnə] f light bulb
glühen ['glyː-ən] tr make red-hot; (metal) anneal || intr glow
glü'hendheiß' adj red-hot
Glühfaden ['glyːfadən] m filament
Glühwurm ['glyːvʊrm] m firefly
Glut [gluːt] f (–;) embers; fire; scorching heat; (fig) ardor
Glyzerin [glytsə'riːn] n (–s;) glycerine
GmbH abbr (Gesellschaft mit beschränkter Haftung) Inc.; Ltd. (Brit)
Gnade ['gnaːdə] f (–;-n) grace; favor; mercy; **von eigenen Gnaden** self-styled
Gna'denbeweis m token of favor
Gna'denbrot n—**bei j–m das G. essen** to live on s.o.'s charity
Gna'denfrist f grace, e.g., **e–e G. von zwei Monaten** two months' grace
Gna'dengesuch n plea for mercy
Gna'denstoß m coup de grâce, deathblow
gnädig ['gnɛːdɪç] adj gracious, kind; merciful; **gnädige Frau** madam; **Sehr verehrte gnädige Frau** Dear Madam
Gold [gɔlt] n (–[e]s;) gold
Gold'blech n gold foil
Gold'fink m (orn) goldfinch
goldig ['gɔldɪç] adj (coll) cute
Gold'plombe f (dent) gold filling
Gold'schmied m goldsmith
Gold'schnitt m gilt edging
Golf [gɔlf] m (–[e]s;-e) gulf; bay || n (–s;) golf
Golf'platz m golf course
Golf'schläger m golf club
Gondel ['gɔndəl] f (–;-n) gondola
Gon'delführer m gondolier
gönnen ['gœnən] tr not begrudge; allow; **j–m etw nicht g. begrudge** s.o. s.th.
Gön'ner –in §6 mf patron
gön'nerhaft adj patronizing
Gön'nerschaft f (–;) patronage
gor [goːr] pret of **gären**
Gorilla [go'rɪla] m (–s;-s) gorilla
goß [gɔs] pret of **gießen**
Gosse ['gɔsə] f (–;-n) gutter
Gote ['goːtə] m (–;-n) Goth
gotisch ['goːtɪʃ] adj Gothic
Gott [gɔt] m (–[e]s;⁻er) god; God
gottbegnadet ['gɔtbəgnaːdət] adj gifted
gott'ergeben adj resigned to God's will
Got'tesdienst m divine service; Mass
got'tesfürchtig adj God-fearing
Got'tesgabe f godsend

got'teslästerlich adj blasphemous
Got'teslästerung f blasphemy
Got'tesurteil n ordeal
gott'gefällig adj pleasing to God
Gott'heit f (–;-en) deity, divinity
Göttin ['gœtɪn] f (–;-nen) goddess
göttlich ['gœtlɪç] adj godlike, divine; (fig) heavenly
gottlob' interj thank goodness!
Gott'mensch m God incarnate
gott'selig adj godly
gott'verlassen adj godforsaken
Götze ['gœtsə] m (–n;-n) idol
Göt'zenbild n idol
Göt'zendiener –in §6 mf idolater
Göt'zendienst m idolatry
Gouvernante [guver'nantə] f (–;-n) governess
Gouverneur [guver'nøːr] m (–s;-e) governor
Grab [graːp] n (–[e]s;⁻er) grave; tomb
graben ['graːbən] §87 tr dig; burrow || **Graben** m (–s;⁻) ditch; trench; moat
Grab'geläute n death knell
Grab'gesang m funeral dirge
Grab'hügel m burial mound
Grab'inschrift f epitaph
Grab'mal n tombstone; tomb, sepulcher
Grab'stätte f burial place
Grab'stelle f burial plot
Grad [graːt] m (–[e]s;-e) degree; grade; (mil) rank
grade ['graːdə] adv var of **gerade**
Grad'einteilung f gradation
Grad'messer m graduated scale; (fig) yardstick
grad'weise adv by degrees
Graf [graːf] m (–en;-en) count; earl (Brit)
Gräfin ['grɛfɪn] f (–;-nen) countess
gräflich ['grɛflɪç] adj count's; earl's
Graf'schaft f (–;-en) county
gram [graːm] adj—**j–m g. sein** be cross with s.o. || **Gram** m (–[e]s;) grief
grämen ['grɛːmən] tr sadden, distress || ref (**über** acc) grieve (over)
grämlich ['grɛːmlɪç] adj glum; crabby
Gramm [gram] n (–s;- & -e) gram
Grammatik [gra'maːtɪk] f (–;-en) grammar
grammatisch [gra'maːtɪʃ] adj grammatical
Gran [graːn] n (–[e]s;) (fig) bit, jot
Granat [gra'naːt] m (–[e]s;-e) garnet
Granat'apfel m pomegranate
Granate [gra'naːtə] f (–;-n) (arti) shell; (mil) grenade
Granat'feuer n shelling
Granat'hülse f shell case
Granat'splitter m shrapnel
Granat'werfer m (mil) mortar
grandios [grandi'oːs] adj grandiose
Granit [gra'niːt] m (–[e]s;-e) granite
Graphik ['graːfɪk] f (–;-en) graphic arts; print; engraving; woodcut
graphisch ['graːfɪʃ] adj graphic
Graphit [gra'fiːt] m (–s;-e) graphite
Gras [graːs] n (–es;⁻er) grass
grasen ['graːzən] intr graze
Gras'halm m blade of grass
Grashüpfer ['graːshypfer] m (–s;-) grasshopper

grasig ['grɑːzɪç] *adj* grassy
Gras'mäher *m* lawn mower; grass cutter
Gras'mähmaschine *f* lawn mower
Gras'narbe *f* sod, turf
grassieren [gra'siːrən] *intr* rage
gräßlich ['grɛslɪç] *adj* grisly
Gras'weide *f* pasture
Grat [grat] *m* (-[e]s;-e) ridge; edge
Gräte ['grɛːtə] *f* (-;-n) fishbone
Gratifikation [gratɪfɪka'tsjoːn] *f* (-; -en) bonus
grätig ['grɛtɪç] *adj* full of fishbones; (*mürrisch*) crabby
gratis ['grɑːtɪs] *adv* gratis; g. und franko (coll) for free
Gratulation [gratula'tsjoːn] *f* (-;-n) congratulations
gratulieren [gratu'liːrən] *intr*—**l**—m g. zu congratulate s.o. on
grau [grau] *adj* gray; (*Vorzeit*) remote ‖ Grau *n* (- & -s;-s) gray
Grau'bär *m* grizzly bear
grauen ['grau·ən] *intr* dawn ‖ *impers* —es graut day is breaking; es graut mir vor (*dat*) I shudder at ‖ Grauen *n* (-s;) (vor *dat*) horror (of)
grau'enhaft, grau'envoll *adj* horrible
gräulich ['grɔɪlɪç] *adj* grayish
Graupe ['graupə] *f* (-;-n) peeled barley
graupeln ['graupəln] *impers*—es graupelt it is sleeting ‖ Graupeln *pl* sleet
Graus [graus] *m* (-es;) dread, horror
grausam ['grauzam] *adj* cruel; (coll) awful
Grau'schimmel *m* gray horse
grausen ['grauzən] *impers*—es graust mir vor (*dat*) I shudder at
grausig ['grauzɪç] *adj* gruesome
Graveur [gra'vøːr] *m* (-s;-e) engraver
gravieren [gra'viːrən] *tr* engrave
gravie'rend *adj* aggravating
gravitätisch [gravɪ'tɛːtɪʃ] *adj* stately
Grazie ['grɑːtsjə] *f* (-;-n) grace, charm
graziös [gra'tsjøːs] *adj* graceful
Greif [graɪf] *m* (-[e]s;-e) griffin
greifbar ['graɪfbɑːr] *adj* tangible; at hand
greifen ['graɪfən] §88 *tr* grasp; seize; (*Note*) strike ‖ *intr* (*Anker*) catch; (*Zahnrad*) engage; ans Herz g. touch deeply; an j-s Ehre g. attack s.o.'s honor; g. in (*acc*) reach into; g. nach reach for; try to seize; g. zu reach for; (fig) resort to; um sich g. grope about; (*Feuer*) spread; zu den Waffen g. take up arms
Greis [graɪs] *m* (-es;-e) old man
Greis'enalter *n* old age
grei'senhaft *adj* aged; senile
Greisin ['graɪzɪn] *f* (-;-nen) old lady
grell [grɛl] *adj* (*Ton*) shrill; (*Farbe, Kleider*) flashy; (*Licht*) glaring
Gre-mium ['greːmjum] *n* (-s;-mien [mjən]) group, body; committee; corporation
Grenze ['grɛntsə] *f* (-;-n) boundary; frontier; borderline; limit
grenzen ['grɛntsən] *intr* (an *acc*) adjoin, border (on); (fig) verge (on)
gren'zenlos *adj* limitless
Grenz'fall *m* borderline case

Grenz'linie *f* boundary line
Grenz'sperre *f* ban on border traffic; frontier barricade
Grenz'stein *m* boundary stone
Greuel ['grɔɪ·əl] *m* (-s;-) abhorrence; horror, abomination
Greu'eltat *f* atrocity
greulich ['grɔɪlɪç] *adj* horrible
Griebs ['grips] *m* (-es;-e) core
Grieche ['griçə] *m* (-n;-n) Greek
Grie'chenland *n* (-s;) Greece
Griechin ['griçɪn] *f* (-;-nen) Greek
griechisch ['griçɪʃ] *adj* Greek
Griesgram ['grisgram] *m* (-[e]s;-e) (coll) grouch
Grieß [gris] *m* (-es;-e) grit; gravel
Grieß'mehl *n* farina
griff [grɪf] *pret of* greifen ‖ Griff *m* (-[e]s;-e) grip; handle; hilt; (mus) touch
Grill [grɪl] *m* (-s;-s) grill; broiler
Grille ['grɪlə] *f* (-;-n) cricket; (fig) whim
grillen ['grɪlən] *tr* grill; broil
gril'lenhaft *adj* whimsical
Grimasse [grɪ'masə] *f* (-;-n) grimace
Grimm [grɪm] *m* (-[e]s;) anger, fury
grimmig ['grɪmɪç] *adj* furious
Grind [grɪnt] *m* (-[e]s;-e) scab
grinsen ['grɪnzən] *intr* grin
Grippe ['grɪpə] *f* (-;) grippe
grob [grop] *adj* coarse, rough; crude
Grobian ['grobjan] *m* (-s;-e) boor
gröblich ['grøplɪç] *adj* gross
grölen ['grøːlən] *intr* shout raucously
Groll [grɔl] *m* (-[e]s;) resentment
grollen ['grɔlən] *intr* rumble; (über *acc*) be resentful (about); **l**—m g. have a grudge against s.o.
Grönland ['grønlant] *n* (-s;) Greenland
Gros [grɔs] *n* (-ses;-) gross ‖ [gro] *n* (-;) bulk; (mil) main forces
Groschen ['grɔʃən] *m* (-s;-) (Aust) penny (*one hundredth of a shilling*)
groß [gros] *adj* big, large; tall; great
groß'artig *adj* grand; magnificent
Groß'aufnahme *f* (phot) close-up
groß'äugig *adj* wide-eyed
Groß'betrieb *m* big company
Großbritan'nien *n* Great Britain
Größe ['grøːsə] *f* (-;-n) size, greatness; celebrity; (astr) magnitude; (math) quantity
Groß'eltern *pl* grandparents
Groß'enkel *m* great-grandson
Groß'enkelin *f* great-granddaughter
großenteils ['grosəntaɪls] *adv* largely
Größenwahn ['grøːsənvan] *m* megalomania
Groß'grundbesitz *m* large estate
Groß'handel *m* wholesale trade; im G. kaufen buy wholesale
Großhandels- *comb.fm.* wholesale
Groß'händler –in §6 *mf* wholesaler
Groß'handlung *f* (-;-en) wholesale business
groß'herzig *adj* big-hearted
Grossist [grɔ'sɪst] *m* (-en;-en) wholesaler
groß'jährig *adj* of legal age
Groß'maul *n* bigmouth
Groß'mut *m* magnanimity

groß′mütig adj big-hearted
Groß′mutter f grandmother
Groß′onkel m great-uncle
Groß′schreibung f capitalization
Groß′segel n main sail
Groß′sprecher m braggart
großspurig ['grosʃpuːrɪç] adj pompous
Groß′stadt f large city (with over 100,000 inhabitants)
Großstädter ['grosˌʃtɛtər] m (-s;-) (coll) city slicker
Groß′tat f achievement
Groß′teil m major part
größtenteils ['grøːstəntaɪls] adv mainly
groß′tun §154 intr brag; put on the dog
Groß′vater m grandfather
Groß′wild n big game
groß′ziehen §163 tr bring up, raise
großzügig ['grosˌtsyːgɪç] adj broad-minded, liberal; generous; large-scale
grotesk [gro′tɛsk] adj grotesque
Grotte ['grotə] f (-;-n) grotto
grub [gruːp] pret of graben
Grübchen ['gryːpçən] n (-s;-) dimple
Grube ['gruːbə] f (-;-n) pit; mine
Grübelei [gryːbə′laɪ] f (-;-en) brooding
grübeln ['gryːbəln] intr brood
Gruben- [gruːbən] comb.fm. mine, miner's
Gruft [gruft] f (-;⸚e) tomb, vault
grün [gryn] adj green; **Grüne Minna** (sl) paddy wagon || **Grün** n (-s;) green
Grün′anlage f public park
Grund [grunt] m (-[e]s;⸚e) ground; land; bottom; foundation, basis; cause, ground; **auf G. von** on the strength of; **G. und Boden** property; **im Grunde genommen** after all; **in G. und Boden** outright
-grund m comb.fm. bottom of; -ground; grounds for, reasons for
Grund′anstrich m first coat
Grund′ausbildung f (mil) basic training
Grund′bedeutung f primary meaning
Grund′begriff m fundamental principle
Grund′besitz m real estate
Grund′buch n land register
grund′ehr′lich adj thoroughly honest
gründen ['gryndən] tr found; **g. auf** (acc) base on || ref (**auf** acc) be based (on)
Gründer -in ['gryndər(ɪn)] §6 mf founder
grund′falsch′ adj absolutely false
Grund′farbe f primary color
Grund′fläche f area; (geom) base
grundieren [grun′diːrən] tr prime; size
Grundier′farbe f primer coat
Grundier′schicht f primer coat
Grund′kapital n capital stock
Grund′lage f basis, foundation
grund′legend adj basic, fundamental
Grund′legung f founding, foundation
gründlich ['gryntlɪç] adj thorough
Grund′linie f (geom) base; **Grundlinien** basic features, outlines
Gründon′nerstag m Holy Thursday
Grund′riß m floor plan; outline

Grund′satz m principle
grundsätzlich ['gruntsɛtslɪç] adj basic || adv as a matter of principle
Grund′schule f primary school
Grund′stein m cornerstone
Grund′stellung f position of attention; **die G. einnehmen** come to attention
Grund′steuer f real-estate tax
Grund′stoff m raw material; (chem) element
Grund′strich m downstroke
Grund′stück n lot, property
Grund′ton m (fig) prevailing mood; (mus) keynote; (paint) ground shade
Grün′dung f (-;-en) foundation
grund′verschie′den adj entirely different
Grund′wasserspiegel m water table
Grund′zahl f cardinal number
Grund′zug m main feature; **Grundzüge** fundamentals, essentials
Grüne ['gryːnə] n—**ins G.** into the country
grün′lich adj greenish
Grün′schnabel m know-it-all
Grünspan ['gryːnʃpan] m (-[e]s;) verdigris
Grün′streifen m grass strip; (auf der Autobahn) median strip
grunzen ['gruntsən] tr & intr grunt
Gruppe ['grupə] f (-;-n) group; (mil) squad
Grup′penführer m group leader; (hist) lieutenant general (of S.S. troops); (mil) squad leader
gruppieren [gru′piːrən] tr & ref group
Gruppie′rung f (-;-en) grouping
gruselig ['gruːzəlɪç] adj creepy
gruseln ['gruːzəln] intr—j—n **g. machen** give s.o. the creeps || ref have a creepy feeling || impers—**es gruselt mir** (or **mich**) it gives me the creeps
Gruß [gruːs] m (-es;⸚e) greeting; salute; greetings, regards; **mit freundlichem Gruß, Ihr ...** Sincerely yours
grüßen ['gryːsən] tr greet; salute; **grüß Gott!** hello!; **j—n g. lassen** send best regards to s.o.
Grütze ['grytsə] f (-;-n) groats; (coll) brains
gucken ['gukən] intr look; peep
Guck′loch n peephole
Guerilla [ge′rɪlja] m (-s;-s) guerilla
Gulasch ['gulaʃ] n (-[e]s;) goulash
gültig ['gyltɪç] adj valid; legal
Gummi ['gumi] m & n (-s;-s) gum; rubber
gum′miartig adj gummy; rubbery
Gum′miband n (-[e]s;⸚er) rubber band; elastic
Gum′mibaum m rubber plant
Gum′mibonbon m & n gumdrop
gummieren [gu′miːrən] tr gum; rubberize
Gum′miknüppel m truncheon; billy club
Gummilinse f (phot) zoom lens
Gum′mimantel m mackintosh
Gum′mireifen m tire
Gum′mischuhe pl rubbers
Gum′mizelle f padded cell
Gunst [gunst] f (-;) favor, goodwill; kindness, good turn

Gunst'bezeigung f expression of good-will

günstig ['gynstɪç] adj favorable; (*Bedingungen*) easy

Günstling ['gynstlɪŋ] m (-s;-e) favorite; (pej) minion

Gurgel ['gurgəl] f (-;-n) gullet

gurgeln ['gurgəln] intr gurgle; gargle

Gurke ['gurkə] f (-;-n) cucumber

Gurt [gurt] m (-[e]s;-e) belt, strap

Gürtel ['gyrtəl] m (-s;-) girdle; belt; (geog) zone

gürten ['gyrtən] tr gird

Guß [gus] m (Gusses; Güsse) gush; (*Regen*) downpour; (*Gießen*) casting; (culin) icing; (typ) font

gut [gut] adj good; **es ist schon gut** it's all right; **mach's gut!** so long! || adv well || **Gut** n (-[e]s;^{..}er) good; possessions; estate; (com) commodity; **Güter** goods; assets

Gut'achten n (-s;-) expert opinion

gut'artig adj good-natured; (pathol) benign

gut'aussehend adj good-looking

Gut'dünken n (-s;) judgment; discretion; **nach G.** at will, as one pleases; (culin) to taste

Gute ['gutə] §5 n good; **alles G!** best of everything!; **sein Gutes haben** have its good points

Güte ['gytə] f (-;) goodness

Güter- [gytər] comb.fm. freight; property; (com) of goods

Gü'terabfertigung f freight office

Gü'terbahnhof m (rr) freight yard

gut'erhalten adj in good condition

Gü'terwagen m freight car; **geschlossener G.** boxcar; **offener G.** gondola car

Gü'terzug m freight train

gut'gelaunt adj good-humored

gut'gesinnt adj well-disposed

gut'haben §89 tr have to one's credit || **Guthaben** n (-s;-) credit balance

gut'heißen §95 tr approve of

gut'herzig adj good-hearted

gütig ['gytɪç] adj kind, good

gütlich ['gytlɪç] adj amicable

gut'machen tr—**wieder g.** make good for

gut'mütig adj good-natured

gut'sagen intr—**für j-n g.** vouch for s.o.

Gut'schein m coupon; credit note

gut'schreiben §62 tr—**j-m e-n Betrag g.** credit s.o. with a sum

Gut'schrift f credit entry; credit item

Gut'schriftsanzeige f credit note

Guts'herr m landowner

gut'tun §154 intr do good; behave

gut'willig adj willing, obliging

Gymnasiast -in [gym'nazjast(ɪn)] §7 mf high school student

Gymna·sium [gym'nazjʊm] n (-s;-sien [zjən]) high school (*with academic course*)

Gymnastik [gym'nastɪk] f (-;) gymnastics

Gynäkologe [gynɛko'logə] m (-n;-n), **Gynäkologin** [gynɛko'login] f (-;nen) gynecologist

Gynäkologie [gynɛkolo'gi] f (-;) gynecology

H

H, h [ha] invar n H, h; (mus) B

Haar [har] n (-[e]s;-e) hair; (tex) nap, pile; **aufs H.** exactly; **um ein H.** by a hair's breadth

Haar'büschel n tuft of hair

haaren ['harən] intr lose hair

Haarfärbmittel ['harferpmɪtəl] n hair dye

Haar'feder f hairspring

haar'genau adj exact, precise

haarig ['harɪç] adj hairy

haar'klein adj (coll) in detail

Haar'locke f lock of hair

Haar'nadel f hairpin

haar'scharf adj razor-sharp

Haar'schneider m barber

Haar'schnitt m haircut

Haar'spange f barrette

Haarspray ['harspre] m (-s;-s) hair spray

haar'sträubend adj hair-raising

Haar'teil m hair piece

Haar'tolle f loose curl

Haar'tracht f hairdo

Haar'trockner m, **Haar'trockenhaube** f hair dryer

Haar'wäsche f shampoo

Haar'wasser n hair tonic

Haar'wickler m curler; hair roller

Haar'zwange f tweezers

Hab [hap] invar n—**Hab und Gut** possessions

Habe ['habə] f (-;) possessions

haben ['habən] §89 tr & aux have || **Haben** n (-s;) credit side

Habe'nichts m (-es;-e) have-not

Hab'gier f greed, avarice

hab'haft adj—**h. werden** (genit) get hold of; (*Diebes*) apprehend

Habicht ['habɪçt] m (-[e]s;-e) hawk

Ha'bichtsnase f aquiline nose

Habilitation [habilɪta'tsjon] f (-;-en) accreditation as a university lecturer

habilitieren [habilɪ'tirən] ref be accredited as a university lecturer

Hab'seligkeiten pl belongings

Hab'sucht f greed, avarice

hab'süchtig adj greedy, avaricious

Hackbeil ['hakbaɪl] n cleaver

Hacke ['hakə] f (-;-n) heel; hoe; pick; pickax; hatchet; mattock

hacken ['hakən] tr hack, chop; peck || intr (nach) peck (at)

Häckerling ['hekərlɪŋ] m (-s;) chaff

Hackfleisch ['hakflaɪʃ] n ground meat

Häcksel ['heksəl] n (-s;) chaff

Hader ['hɑdər] *m* (-s;) strife ‖ *m* (-s; -n) rag

hadern ['hɑdərn] *intr* quarrel

Hafen ['hɑfən] *m* (-s;⁼) harbor; port; (fig) haven

Ha'fenamt *n* port authority

Ha'fenanlagen *pl* docks

Ha'fenarbeiter *m* longshoreman

Ha'fendamm *m* jetty, mole

Ha'fensperre *f* blockade

Ha'fenstadt *f* seaport

Ha'fenviertel *n* dock area, waterfront

Hafer ['hɑfər] *m* (-s;-) oats; **ihn sticht der H.** he's feeling his oats

Ha'fergrütze *f*, **Ha'fermehl** *n* oatmeal

Hafner ['hɑfnər] *m* (-s;-) potter

Haft [haft] *f* (-;) arrest; custody; imprisonment; **in H.** under arrest; in custody; **in prison**

haftbar ['haftbɑr] *adj* (jur) liable

Haft'befehl *m* warrant for arrest

haften ['haftən] *intr* (**an** *dat*) cling (to), stick (to); **h. für** vouch for; (jur) be held liable for; (jur) put up bail for

Haft'fähigkeit *f*, **Haft'festigkeit** *f* adhesion

Häftling ['heftlɪŋ] *m* (-s;-e) prisoner

Haft'lokal *n* (mil) guardhouse

Haft'pflicht *f* liability

haft'pflichtig *adj* (**für**) liable (for)

Haft'pflichtversicherung *f* liability insurance

Haft'richter *m* (jur) magistrate

Haft'schale *f* contact lens

Haf'tung *f* (-;-en) liability

Hag [hɑk] *m* (-[e]s;-e) enclosure; (*Hain*) grove; (*Buschwerk*) bushes

Hagedorn ['hɑgədɔrn] *m* hawthorn

Hagel ['hɑgəl] *m* (-s;) hail

Ha'gelkorn *n* hailstone

hageln ['hɑgəln] *intr* (SEIN) (fig) rain down ‖ *impers*—**es hagelt** it is hailing

Ha'gelschauer *m* hailstorm

hager ['hɑgər] *adj* gaunt, haggard

Hagestolz ['hɑgəʃtɔlts] *m* (-es;-e) confirmed bachelor

Häher ['he·ər] *m* (-s;-) (orn) jay

Hahn [hɑn] *m* (-[e]s;⁼e) rooster; (*Wasser-*) faucet; **den H. spannen** cock the gun; **H. im Korbe sein** rule the roost

Hähnchen ['hençən] *n* (-s;-) young rooster

Hah'nenkamm *m* cockscomb

Hah'nenkampf *m* cock fight

Hah'nenschrei *m* crow of the cock

Hahnrei ['hɑnraɪ] *m* (-s;-e) cuckold

Hai [haɪ] *m* (-[e]s;-e), **Hai'fisch** *m* shark

Hain [haɪn] *m* (-[e]s;-e) grove

Haiti [ha'iti] *n* (-s;) Haiti

Häkelarbeit ['hekəlarbaɪt] *f* crocheting

häkeln ['hekəln] *tr & intr* crochet ‖ **Häkeln** *n* (-s;) crocheting

Haken ['hɑkən] *m* (-s;-) hook; (*Spange*) clasp; (fig) snag, hitch

Ha'kenkreuz *n* swastika

Ha'kennase *f* hooknose

halb [halp] *adj & adv* half

halb-, Halb- *comb.fm.* half-, semi-

Halb'blut *n* half-breed

-halber [halbər] *comb.fm.* for the sake of; owing to

halb'fett *adj* (typ) bold

Halb'franzband *m* (bb) half leather

halb'gar *adj* (culin) (medium) rare

Halb'gott *m* demigod

Halbheit ['halphaɪt] *f* (-;) half-

Halb'kugel *f* hemisphere

halbieren [hal'birən] *tr* halve, bisect

Halb'insel *f* peninsula

Halb'kettenfahrzeug *n* half-track

Halb'kugel *f* hemisphere

halb'lang *adj* half-length; **halblange Ärmel** half sleeves

halb'laut *adj* low ‖ *adv* in a low voice

Halb'leiter *m* (elec) semiconductor

halb'mast *adv* at half-mast; **auf h.** at half-mast

Halb'messer *m* radius

halbpart ['halppart] *adv*—**mit j-m h. machen** go fifty-fifty with s.o.

Halb'schuh *m* low shoe

Halb'schwergewicht *n* light-heavyweight division

Halb'schwergewichtler *m* light-heavyweight

halb'stündig *adj* half-hour

halb'stündlich *adj* half-hourly ‖ *adv* every half hour

Halb'vers *m* hemistich

halbwegs ['halbveks] *adv* halfway

Halb'welt *f* demimonde

halbwüchsig ['halpvyksɪç] *adj* teenage ‖ **Halbwüchsige** §5 *mf* teenager

Halb'zug *m* (mil) section

Halde ['haldə] *f* (-;-n) slope; (*Schutt-*) slag pile

half [half] *pret* of **helfen**

Hälfte ['helftə] *f* (-;-n) half

Halfter ['halftər] *f* (-;-n) holster ‖ *n* (-s;-) halter

Hall [hal] *m* (-[e]s;-e) sound; clang

Halle ['halə] *f* (-;-n) hall; (*e-s Hotels*) lobby; (aer) hangar; (rr) concourse

hallen ['halən] *intr* sound, resound

Hal'lenbad *n* indoor pool

Hallo [ha'lo] *n* (-s;) hullabaloo ‖ *interj* (to attract attention) hey!; (telp) hello

Halm [halm] *m* (-[e]s;-e) stem, stalk; blade (*of grass*)

Hals [hals] *m* (-es;⁼e) neck; throat; **H. über Kopf** head over heels

Hals'abschneider *m* cutthroat

hals'abschneiderisch *adj* cutthroat

Hals'ader *f* jugular vein

Hals'ausschnitt *m* neckline, neck

Hals'band *n* (-[e]s;⁼er) necklace, choker; (*e-s Hundes*) collar

halsbrecherisch ['halsbreçərɪʃ] *adj* breakneck

Hals'entzündung *f* sore throat

Hals'kette *f* necklace, chain

Hals'kragen *m* collar

Hals'krause *f* frilled collar

hals'starrig *adj* stubborn

Hals'weh *n* sore throat

halt [halt] *adv* just, simply ‖ *interj* stop!; (mil) halt! ‖ **Halt** *m* (-[e]s; -e) hold; foothold; support; stability; stop, halt

haltbar ['haltbɑr] *adj* durable; tenable

halten ['haltən] §90 tr hold; keep; detain; (Rede) deliver; (Vorlesung) give; (feiern) celebrate; es h. mit do with; have an affair with; etw auf sich h. have self-respect; j–n h. für take s.o. for; viel h. von think highly of || ref keep, last; hold ones own; an sich h. restrain oneself; auf sich h. be particular about one's appearance; sich an etw h. (fig) stick to s.th.; sich an j–n h. hold s.o. liable; sich gesund h. keep healthy; sich links h. keep to the left || intr stop; last; h. auf (acc) pay attention to; h. nach head for; h. zu stick by; was das Zeug hält with might and main
Hal'ter m (-s;-) holder; rack; owner
Hal'teriemen m strap (on bus or trolley)
Hal'testelle f bus stop, trolley stop; (rr) stop
Hal'teverbot n (public sign) no stopping
-haltig [haltıç] comb.fm. containing
halt'los adj without support; helpless; unprincipled
halt'machen intr stop, halt
Hal'tung f (-;-en) pose, posture; attitude
Halte'zeichen n stop sign
Halunke [ha'luŋkə] m (-;-n) rascal
hämisch ['hemıʃ] adj spiteful, malicious
Hammel ['haməl] m (-s;-e & ꞉) wether꞉ (coll) mutton-head; (culin) mutton
Ham'melkeule f leg of mutton
Hammer ['hamər] m (-s;꞉) hammer; gavel; unter den H. kommen be auctioned off
hämmern ['hemərn] tr & intr hammer
Hämorrhoiden [hemərə'idən] pl hemorroids, piles
Hampelmann ['hampəlman] m (-[e]s; ꞉er) jumping jack
hamstern ['hamstərn] tr hoard
Hand [hant] f (-;꞉e) hand; an H. von with the help of; auf eigene H. of one's own accord; aus erster H. (bei Verkauf) one-owner; aus erster H. haben hear first-hand; aus erster H. kaufen buy directly; bei der H. at hand, handy; die letzte H. finishing touches; die öffentliche H. the state, public authorities; es liegt auf der H. it is obvious; H. ans Werk legen get down to work; H. aufs Herz! cross my heart!; Hände hoch! hands up!; H. und Fuß haben make sense; in die H. (or Hände) bekommen get one's hands on; j–m an die H. gehen lend s.o. a hand; j–m die H. drücken shake hands with s.o.; j–m etw an (die) H. geben quote s.o. a price on s.th.; j–m zur H. gehen lend s.o. a hand; unter der H. underhandedly; unofficially; von der H. weisen reject; zu Händen Herrn X Attention Mr. X; zur H. at hand, handy
Hand'arbeit f manual labor; needlework
Hand'aufheben n, **Hand'aufhebung** f show of hands

Hand'ausgabe f abridged edition
Hand'bedienung f manual control
Hand'betrieb m—mit (or für) H. hand-operated
Hand'bibliothek f reference library
hand'breit adj wide as a hand || **Hand'breit** f (-;-) hand's breadth
Hand'bremse f (aut) hand brake
Hand'buch n handbook, manual
Händedruck ['hendədruk] m handshake
Händeklatschen ['hendəklatʃən] n clapping
Handel ['handəl] m (-s;꞉꞉) trade; deal, bargain; business; affair; e–n H. eingehen conclude a deal; e–n H. treiben carry on business; H. und Gewerbe trade and industry; Händel suchen pick a quarrel; im H. sein be on the market; in den H. bringen put on the market
-handel m comb.fm. -trade, -business
handeln ['handəln] intr act; take action; proceed; gegen das Gesetz h. go against the law; gut an j–m h. treat s.o. well; h. über (acc) or von deal with; h. mit do business with; im großen h. do wholesale business || impers ref—es handelt sich um it is a matter of; darum handelt es sich nicht that's not the point
Han'delsabkommen n trade agreement
Han'delsartikel m commodity
Han'delsbetrieb m commercial enterprise; business; firm
Han'delsbilanz f balance of trade; aktive H. favorable balance of trade
Han'delsdampfer m (naut) merchantman
han'delseinig adj—h. werden mit come to terms with
Han'delsgärtner m truck farmer
Han'delskammer f chamber of commerce
Han'delsmarine f merchant marine
Han'delsmarke f trademark
Han'delsminister m secretary of commerce
Han'delsministerium n department of commerce
Han'delsplatz m trade center
Han'delsschiff n merchantman
Han'delssperre f trade embargo
händelsüchtig ['hendəlzyçtıç] adj quarrelsome
Han'delsvertrag m commercial treaty
Han'delswert m trade-in value
Han'delszeichen n trademark
Hand'exemplar n desk copy
Hand'fertigkeit f manual dexterity
Hand'fessel f handcuff
hand'fest adj sturdy; well-founded
Hand'fläche f palm of the hand
Hand'geld n advance payment; deposit
Hand'gelenk n wrist; aus (or mit) dem H. (coll) easy as pie
hand'gemein adj—h. werden come to blows
Hand'gemenge n scuffle
Hand'gepäck n hand luggage
Hand'gepäckschließfach n locker
Hand'granate f hand grenade
hand'greiflich adj tangible; obvious;

j-m etw h. machen make s.th. clear to s.o.; h. werden come to blows

Hand′griff *m* grip; handle; **keinen H. tun** not lift a finger

Hand′habe *f* (-₃-n) handle; pretext; occasion; **er hat keine H. gegen mich** he has nothing on me

hand′haben *tr* handle; (*Maschine*) operate; (*Rechtspflege*) administer; (fig) manage

-händig [hɛndɪç] *comb.fm.* -handed

Hand′karren *m* hand cart, push cart

Hand′koffer *m* suitcase; attaché case

Handlanger [′hantlaŋər] *m* (-s₃-) handyman; (pej) underling

Händler -in [′hɛndlər(ɪn)] §6 *mf* dealer, merchant; storekeeper

Hand′lesekunst *f* palmistry

Hand′leserin *f* (-₃-nen) palm reader

hand′lich *adj* handy

Hand′lung *f* (-₃-en) shop; act, action

-handlung *f comb.fm.* business; shop

Hand′lungsgehilfe *m* clerk, salesman

Hand′lungsweise *f* conduct

Hand′pflege *f* manicure

Hand′pflegerin *f* (-₃-nen) manicurist

Hand′rücken *m* back of the hand

Hand′schaltung *f* manual shift

Hand′schelle *f* handcuff

Hand′schlag *m* handshake

Hand′schreiben *n* hand-written letter

Hand′schrift *f* handwriting; manuscript; (sl) slap, box on the ear

Hand′schriftkunde *f* paleography

hand′schriftlich *adj* hand-written

Hand′schuh *m* glove

Hand′schuhfach *n* (aut) glove compartment

Hand′streich *m* (mil) raid

Hand′tasche *f* handbag, purse

Hand′tuch *n* towel; **schmales H.** (sl) beanpole

Hand′tuchhalter *m* towel rack

Hand′umdrehen *n*—**im. H. in a jiffy**

Hand′voll *f* (-₃-) handful

Hand′werk *n* craft, trade; **j-m ins H. pfuschen** (sl) stick one's nose in s.o. else's business

Hand′werker *m* craftsman

Hand′werkszeug *n* tool kit

Hand′wörterbuch *n* pocket dictionary

Hand′wurzel *f* wrist

Hand′zettel *m* handbill

hanebüchen [′hanəbyçən] *adj* (coll) incredible; (coll) monstrous

Hanf [hanf] *m* (-[e]s₃) hemp

Hang [haŋ] *m* (-[e]s₃⁼) slope; hillside; (fig) inclination, tendency

Hangar [′haŋɡor] *m* (-s₃-s) hangar

Hängebacken [′hɛŋəbakən] *pl* jowls

Hängebauch [′hɛŋəbaʊx] *m* potbelly

Hängebrücke [′hɛŋəbrykə] *f* suspension bridge

Hängematte [′hɛŋəmatə] *f* hammock

hängen [′hɛŋən] *tr* hang ‖ *ref*—**sich an j-n h.** hang on to s.o.; **sich ans Telephon h.** be on the telephone ‖ §92 *intr* hang; cling, stick

hän′genbleiben §62 *intr* (SEIN) stick; be detained, get stuck; (an *dat*) get caught (on); (educ) stay behind

Hans [hans] *m* (-′ & -ens₃) Johnny, Jack

Hans′dampf *m* (-[e]s₃-e) busybody; **H. in allen Gassen** jack-of-all trades

Hänselei [hɛnzə′laɪ] *f* (-₃-en) teasing

hänseln [′hɛnzəln] *tr* tease

Hans′narr *m* fool

Hans′wurst *m* (-es₃-e & ⁼e) clown

Hantel [′hantəl] *f* (-₃-n) dumbell

hantieren [han′tirən] *intr* (an *acc*) be busy (with); **mit etw h. handle s.th.**

hapern [′hapərn] *impers*—**bei mir hapert es an** (*dat*) (or mit) I am short of; **bei mir hapert es in** (*dat*) (or mit) I am weak in; **damit hapert's** that's the hitch

Happen [′hapən] *m* (-s₃-) morsel; mouthful; (fig) good opportunity; **fetter H.** (coll) big hawl

happig [′hapɪç] *adj* greedy; (*Preis*) steep

Härchen [′hɛrçən] *n* (-s₃-) tiny hair

Harem [′harem] *m* (-s₃-s) harem

Häre·sie [hɛrɛ′zi] *f* (-₃-sien [′zi·ən]) heresy

Häretiker [hɛ′retɪkər] *m* (-s₃-) heretic

Harfe [′harfə] *f* (-₃-n) harp

Harke [′harkə] *f* (-₃-n) rake

harken [′harkən] *tr & intr* rake

Harm [harm] *m* (-[e]s₃) harm; grief

härmen [′hɛrmən] *ref* (um) grieve (over)

harm′los *adj* harmless

Harmo·nie [harmo′ni] *f* (-₃-nien [′ni·ən]) harmony

harmonieren [harmo′nirən] *intr* harmonize

Harmoni·ka [har′monɪka] *f* (-₃-kas & -ken [kən]) accordion; harmonica

harmonisch [har′monɪʃ] *adj* harmonious

Harn [harn] *m* (-[e]s₃-e) urine; **H. lassen** pass water

Harn′blase *f* (anat) bladder

harnen [′harnən] *intr* urinate

Harn′glas *n* urinal

Harn′grieß *m* (pathol) gravel

Harnisch [′harnɪʃ] *m* (-es₃-e) armor; **in H. geraten über** (*acc*) fly into a rage over; **j-n in H. bringen** get s.o. hopping mad

Harn′leiter *m* (anat) ureter; (surg) catheter

Harn′röhre *f* urethra

harn′treibend *adj* diuretic

Harpune [har′punə] *f* (-₃-n) harpoon

harpunieren [harpu′nirən] *tr* harpoon

harren [′harən] *intr* tarry; hope; (*genit* or auf *acc*) wait (for)

harsch [harʃ] *adj* harsh ‖ **Harsch** *m* (-es₃), **Harsch′schnee** *m* crushed snow

hart [hart] *adj* hard; severe ‖ *adv*—**h. an** (*dat*) close to, hard by

Härte [′hɛrtə] *f* (-₃) hardness; severity

härten [′hɛrtən] *tr, ref & intr* harden

Hart′faserplatte *f* fiber board

Hart′geld *n* coins

hartgesotten [′hartɡəzɔtən] *adj* hard-boiled; (*Verbrecher*) hardened

hart′herzig *adj* hard-hearted

hart′köpfig *adj* thick-headed

hart′leibig *adj* constipated

Hart′leibigkeit *f* (-₃) constipation

hart′löten *tr* braze

hartnäckig ['hartnɛkɪç] *adj* stubborn
Hart'platz *m* (tennis) hard court
Harz [harts] *n* (-es;-e) resin; rosin
harzig [hartsɪç] *adj* resinous
Hasardspiel [ha'zart/pil] *n* gambling game; gamble
haschen ['haʃən] *tr* snatch, grab || *intr* (nach) try to catch, snatch (at)
Hase ['hazə] *m* (-n;-n) hare; alter H. old-timer, veteran
Ha'selnuß ['hazəlnʊs] *f* hazelnut
Hasenfuß *m* (coll) coward
Ha'senherz *n* (coll) yellow belly
Ha'senmaus *f* chinchilla
Hasenpanier ['hazənpanir] *n*—das H. ergreifen take to ones heels
ha'senrein *adj*—nicht ganz h. (fig) a bit fishy, rather shady
Ha'senscharte *f* harelip
Haspe ['haspə] *f* (-;-n) hasp
Haspel ['haspəl] *f* (-;-n) & *m* (-s;-) reel, spool; winch, windlass
haspeln ['haspəln] *tr* reel, spool
Haß *m* (Hasses;) hatred
hassen ['hasən] *tr* hate
has'senswert, has'senswürdig *adj* hateful
häßlich ['hɛslɪç] *adj* ugly; nasty
Hast [hast] *f* (-;) haste
hasten ['hastən] *intr* be in a hurry, act quickly || *intr* (SEIN) hasten, rush
hastig ['hastɪç] *adj* hasty
hätscheln ['hɛt/əln] *tr* caress, cuddle; (verzärteln) coddle, spoil
hatte ['hatə] *pret* of haben
Haube ['haubə] *f* (-;-n) cap; (aer) cowling; (aut) hood; (orn) crest
Haubitze [hau'bɪtsə] *f* (-;-n) howitzer
Hauch [haux] *m* (-[e]s;-e) breath; breeze; (Schicht) thin layer; (Spur) trace
hauch'dünn' *adj* paper-thin
hauchen ['hauxən] *tr* whisper; (ling) aspirate || *intr* breathe
Hauch'laut *m* (ling) aspirate
Haue ['hau·ə] *f* (-;-n) hoe; adze; H. kriegen get a spanking
hauen ['hau·ən] §93 *tr* hack, cut; strike; (Baum) fell; (Stein) hew || §109 *tr* beat (up) || *intr*—h. nach lash out at; um sich h. flail
Hauer ['hau·ər] *m* (-s;-) tusk
häufeln ['hɔɪfəln] *tr* hill
häufen ['hɔɪfən] *tr* & *ref* pile up
Haufen ['haufən] *m* (-s;-) pile, heap
Hau'fenwolke *f* cumulus cloud
häufig ['hɔɪfɪç] *adj* frequent || *adv* frequently
Häu'figkeit *f* (-;) frequency
Häu'fung *f* (-;-en) accumulation
Haupt [haupt] *n* (-[e]s;-er) head; top; chief, leader aufs H. schlagen vanquish
Haupt- *comb.fm.* head; chief; major; most important; prime; primary, leading
Haupt'altar *m* high altar
haupt'amtlich *adj* full-time
Haupt'bahnhof *m* main train station
Haupt'darsteller *m* leading man
Haupt'darstellerin *f* leading lady
Häuptel ['hɔɪptəl] *n* (-s;-) head
Haupt'fach *n* (educ) major

Haupt'farbe *f* primary color
Haupt'feldwebel *m* first sergeant
Haupt'film *m* (cin) feature
Haupt'gefreite §5 *m* private first class; lance corporal (Brit); seaman; airman second class
Haupt'geschäftsstelle *f* head office
Haupt'gewinn *m* first price
Haupt'haar *n* hair (on the head)
Häuptling ['hɔɪptlɪŋ] *m* (-s;-e) chief
häuptlings ['hɔɪptlɪŋs] *adv* head first
Haupt'linie *f* (rr) trunk line
Haupt'mann *m* (-[e]s;-leute) captain
Haupt'masse *f* bulk
Haupt'mast *m* mainmast
Hauptnenner ['hauptnɛnər] *m* (-s;-) (math) common denominator
Haupt'probe *f* dress rehearsal
Haupt'quartier *n* headquarters; Gro-ßes H. general headquarters
Haupt'rolle *f* leading role, lead
Haupt'sache *f* main thing; (jur) point at issue
haupt'sächlich *adj* main, principal
Haupt'satz *m* (gram) main clause; (phys) principle, law
Haupt'schalter *m* master switch
Haupt'schiff *n* (archit) nave
Haupt'schlagader *f* aorta
Haupt'schlüssel *m* master key, pass key
Haupt'schriftleiter *m* editor in chief
Haupt'spaß *m* great fun; great joke
Haupt'stadt *f* capital
Haupt'straße *f* main street; highway
Haupt'strecke *f* (rr) main line
Haupt'stütze *f* mainstay
Haupt'ton *m* primary accent
Haupt'treffer *m* first prize; jackpot
Haupt'verkehr *m* peak-hour traffic
Haupt'verkehrsstraße *f* main artery
Haupt'verkehrszeit *f* rush hour
Haupt'wort *n* (-[e]s;-er) noun
Haus [haus] *n* (-es;-er) house; ein großes H. führen do a lot of entertaining; H. und Hof house and home; öffentliches H. brothel; nach Hause home; sich zu Hause fühlen feel at home; von zu Hause from home
Haus'angestellte §5 *mf* domestic
Haus'apotheke *f* medicine cabinet
Haus'arbeit *f* housework; (educ) homework
Haus'arzt *m* family doctor
Haus'aufgabe *f* homework
haus'backen *adj* homemade; (Frau) plain; (fig) provincial
Haus'bedarf *m* household needs; für den H. for the home
Haus'brand *m* domestic fuel
Haus'bursche *m* porter
Haus'diener *m* porter
hausen ['hauzən] *intr* reside; (coll) make a mess; schlimm h. wreak havoc
Häuserblock ['hɔɪzərblɔk] *m* block of houses
Häusermakler -in ['hɔɪzərmaklər(ɪn)] §6 *mf* realtor
Haus'flur *m* entrance hall; hallway
Haus'frau *f* housewife; landlady
Haus'freund *m* friend of the family; (coll) wife's lover

Haus'gebrauch m family custom; household use

Haus'gehilfin f domestic

Haus'genosse m, **Haus'genossin** f occupant of the same house

Haus'gesinde n domestics

Haus'glocke f doorbell

Haus'halt m household; budget; **den H. führen** keep house

haus'halten §90 intr keep house; economize

Haushälter –in ['haushɛltər(ɪn)] §6 mf housekeeper

haushälterisch ['haushɛltərɪʃ] adj economical

Haus'haltsausschuß m ways and means committee

Haus'haltsgerät n household utensil

Haus'haltsjahr n fiscal year

Haus'haltsplan m budget

Haus'haltung f housekeeping; household; family budget; management

Haus'haltungslehre f home economics

Haus'herr m master of the house; landlord

Haus'herrin f lady of the house; landlady

haus'hoch' adj very high; vast

Haus'hofmeister m steward

hausieren [hau'zirən] intr—**mit etw h. peddle s.th.**; go around telling everyone about s.th.

Hausierer [hau'zirər] m (-s;-) door-to-door salesman

Haus'lehrer –in §6 mf private tutor

häuslich ['hɔɪslɪç] adj home, domestic; homey; thrifty

Häus'lichkeit f (-;) family life; home

Haus'mädchen n maid

Haus'meister m caretaker, janitor

Haus'mittel n home remedy

Haus'mutter f mother of the family

Haus'pflege f home nursing

Haus'schlüssel m front-door key

Haus'schuh m slipper

Hausse ['hose] f (-;-n) (econ, st. exch.) boom

Haus'sespekulant m (st. exch.) bull

Haussier [hos'je] m (-s;-) (st. exch.) bull

haussieren [ho'sirən] tr (fin) raise || intr (fin) go up, rise

Haus'stand m household

Haus'suchungsbefehl m search warrant

Haus'tier n domestic animal; pet

Haus'vater m father of the family

Haus'verwalter m superintendent

Haus'wesen n household

Haus'wirt m landlord

Haus'wirtin f landlady

Haus'wirtschaft f housekeeping

haus'wirtschaftlich adj domestic; household

Haus'wirtschaftslehre f home economics

Haus'zins m house rent

Haut [haut] f (-;ͤe) skin; hide; **aus der H. fahren** fly off the handle

Haut'abschürfung f skin abrasion

Haut'arzt m dermatologist

Haut'ausschlag m rash

Häutchen ['hɔɪtçən] (-s;-) membrane; pellicle; film

häuten ['hɔɪtən] tr skin || ref slough the skin

haut'eng adj skin-tight

Haut'farbe f complexion

Haut'plastik f skin graft

Haut'reizung f skin irritation

Haut'transplantation f, **Haut'verpflanzung** f skin grafting

havariert [hava'rirt] adj damaged

H'-Bombe f H-bomb

Hebamme ['hepamə] f (-;-n) midwife

Hebebaum ['hebəbaum] m lever

Hebebühne ['hebəbynə] f car lift

Hebeeisen ['hebə-aɪzən] n crowbar

Hebel ['hebəl] m (-s;-) lever

heben ['hebən] §94 tr lift, raise; (steigern) increase; (fördern) further; (aut) jack up || ref rise

Heber ['hebər] m (-s;-) siphon; (aut) jack

Hebeschiff ['hebəʃɪf] n salvage ship

Hebräer –in [he'bre-ər(ɪn)] §6 mf Hebrew

hebräisch [he'bre-ɪʃ] adj Hebrew

He'bung f (-;-en) lifting; increase; improvement; (mus, pros) stress

Hecht [heçt] m (-[e]s;-e) (ichth) pike

hechten ['heçtən] intr dive

Hecht'sprung m flying leap; jacknife dive

Heck [hɛk] n (-[e]s;-e & -s) stern; (aer) tail; (aut) rear

Heck'antrieb m (aut) rear drive

Hecke ['hɛkə] f (-;-n) hedge; brood, hatch

hecken ['hɛkən] tr & intr breed

Heckenhüpfen (Hek'kenhüpfen) n (-s;) (aer) hedgehopping

Heckenschütze (Hek'kenschütze) m sniper

Heck'fenster n (aut) rear window

Heck'licht n (aer, aut) tail light

Heck'motor m rear engine

Heck'pfennig m lucky penny

Heck'schütze m (aer) tail gunner

heda ['heda] interj hey there!

Heer [her] n (-[e]s;-e) army; host

Heeres– [herəs] comb.fm. army

Hee'resbericht m official army communiqué

Hee'resdienst m military service

Hee'resdienstvorschriften pl army regulations

Hee'resgeistliche §5 m army chaplain

Hee'resmacht f armed forces; army

Hee'reszug m (mil) campaign

Heer'lager n army camp; (pol) faction

Heer'schar f host, legion

Heer'zug m (mil) campaign

Hefe ['hefə] f (-;-n) yeast; dregs

He'feteig m leavened dough

Heft [heft] n (-[e]s;-e) haft, handle; notebook; (e-r Zeitschrift) issue

heften ['heftən] tr fasten together; sew, stitch; tack, baste; (Blick) fix || ref (an acc) stick close (to)

heftig ['heftɪç] adj violent; (Regen) heavy; (Fieber) high; **h. werden** lose one's temper

Heft'klammer f paper clip; staple

Heft'maschine f stapler

Heft'stich m (sew) tack

Heft'zwecke f thumbtack

hegen ['heːgən] *tr* (*Wild*) preserve; (*Zweifel, Gedanken*) have; **h. und pflegen** lavish care on

Hehl [heːl] *n* (-[e]s;) secret

hehlen ['heːlən] *intr* receive stolen goods

Hehʹler -in §6 *mf* fence

hehr [heːr] *adj* sublime, noble

Heide ['haɪdə] *m* (-n;-n) heathen; (Bib) gentile || *f* (-;-n) heath

Heiʹdekraut *n* heather

Heidelbeere ['haɪdəlbeːrə] *f* blueberry

Heiʹdenangst *f* (coll) jitters

Heiʹdengeld *n* (coll) piles of money

Heiʹdenlärm *m* hullabaloo

heiʹdenmäßig *adv*—**h. viel** tremendous amount of

Heiʹdenspaß *m* (coll) great fun

Heidentum ['haɪdəntum] *n* (-s;) heathendom

heidi [haɪ'di] *adj* gone; lost; **h. gehen** get lost; be all gone || *interj* quick!

Heidin ['haɪdɪn] *f* (-;-nen) heathen

heidnisch ['haɪdnɪʃ] *adj* heathen

heikel ['haɪkəl] *adj* particular, fastidious; (*Sache*) ticklish

heil [haɪl] *adj* safe, sound; undamaged || **Heil** *n* (-[e]s;) welfare, benefit; salvation || **Heil** *interj* hail!

Heiland ['haɪlant] *m* (-[e]s;) Saviour

Heilʹanstalt *f* sanitarium

Heilʹbad *n* spa

heilbar ['haɪlbar] *adj* curable

heilʹbringend *adj* beneficial, healthful

Heilbutt ['haɪlbut] *m* (-[e]s;-e) (ichth) halibut

heilen ['haɪlən] *tr* heal || *intr* (HABEN & SEIN) heal

Heilʹgehilfe *m* male nurse

Heilʹgymnastik *f* physical therapy

heilig ['haɪlɪç] *adj* holy, sacred || **Heilige** §5 *mf* saint

Heiʹligabend *m* Christmas Eve

heiligen ['haɪlɪgən] *tr* hallow

Heiʹligenschein *m* halo

Heiʹligkeit *f* (-;) holiness, sanctity

heiʹligsprechen §64 *tr* canonize

Heiligtum ['haɪlɪçtum] *n* (-[e]s;-er) sanctuary; shrine; sacred relic

Heiʹligung *f* (-;) sanctification

Heilʹkraft *f* healing power

Heilʹkraut *n* medicinal herb

Heilʹkunde *f* medical science

heilʹlos *adj* wicked; (coll) awful

Heilʹmittel *n* remedy; medicine

Heilʹmittellehre *f* pharmacology

heilsam ['haɪlzam] *adj* healthful

Heilsʹarmee *f* Salvation Army

Heilʹstätte *f* sanitarium

Heiʹlung *f* (-;-en) cure

heim [haɪm] *adv* home || **Heim** *n* (-[e]s;-e) home; (*Alters-*) old-age home

Heimat ['haɪmat] *f* (-;-en) home; hometown; homeland

heiʹmatlich *adj* native

heiʹmatlos *adj* homeless

Heiʹmatort *m* hometown, home village

Heiʹmatstadt *f* hometown, native city

heimʹbegeben §80 *ref* head home

Heimchen ['haɪmçən] *n* (-s;-) cricket

Heimʹcomputer *m* home computer

Heimʹfahrt *f* homeward journey

heimʹfinden §59 *intr* find one's way home

Heimʹgang *m* going home; passing on

heimisch ['haɪmɪʃ] *adj* local; locally-produced; domestic; **heimische Sprache** vernacular; **h. werden** settle down; become established; **sich h. fühlen** feel at home

Heimkehr ['haɪmkeːr] *f* (-;) homecoming

heimʹkehren *intr* (SEIN) return home

Heimʹkunft *f* homecoming

heimʹleuchten *intr* (sl) (*dat*) tell (*s.o.*) where to get off

heimʹlich *adj* secret

Heimʹlichkeit *f* (-;-en) secrecy; (*Geheimnis*) secret

Heimʹreise *f* homeward journey

heimʹsuchen *tr* afflict, plague

Heimʹtücke *f* treachery

heimʹtückisch *adj* treacherous

heimwärts ['haɪmverts] *adv* homeward

Heimʹweh *n* homesickness; nostalgia

heimʹzahlen *tr*—**j-m etw h.** (coll) pay s.o. back for s.th.

Heini ['haɪni] *m* (-s;) Harry; guy

Heinzelmännchen ['haɪntsəlmençən] *pl* (myth) little people

Heirat ['haɪrat] *f* (-;-en) marriage

heiraten ['haɪratən] *tr & intr* marry

Heiʹratsantrag *m* marriage proposal

heiʹratsfähig *adj* marriageable

Heiʹratsgut *n* dowry

Heiʹratskandidat *m* eligible bachelor

Heiʹratsurkunde *f* marriage certificate

Heiʹratsvermittler -in §6 *mf* marriage broker

heischen ['haɪʃən] *tr* demand; beg

heiser ['haɪzər] *adj* hoarse

heiß [haɪs] *adj* hot; (fig) ardent

heißen ['haɪsən] §95 *tr* call; ask, bid; mean || *intr* be called; **das heißt** that is, i.e.; **wie h. Sie?** what is your name?

heißʹgeliebt *adj* beloved

heiter ['haɪtər] *adj* cheerful; hilarious; serene; (*Wetter*) clear

Heiz- [haɪts] *comb.fm.* heating

Heizʹanlage *f* heating system

Heizʹapparat *m* heater

heizen ['haɪtsən] *tr* heat; **den Ofen mit Kohle h.** burn coal in the stove || *intr* give off heat; heat; turn on the heating; light the fire (or stove)

Heiʹzer *m* (-s;) boilerman; (naut) stoker; (rr) fireman

Heizʹfaden *m* (elec) filament

Heizʹkissen *n* heating pad

Heizʹkörper *m* radiator; heater

Heizʹmaterial *n* fuel

Heizʹplatte *f* hot plate

Heizʹraum *m* boiler room

Heizʹschlange *f* heating coil

Heiʹzung *f* (-;) heating; (coll) central heating; radiator

Heiʹzungskessel *m* boiler

Heiʹzungsrohr *n* radiator pipe

Held [helt] *m* (-en;-en) hero

Helʹdenalter *n* heroic age

Helʹdengedicht *n* epic

Helʹdengeist *m* heroism

helʹdenhaft *adj* heroic

Helʹdenmut *m* heroism

hel′denmütig *adj* heroic
Hel′dentat *f* heroic deed, exploit
Heldentum [′hɛldəntum] *n* (-[e]s;) heroism
Heldin [′hɛldɪn] *f* (-;-nen) heroine
helfen [′hɛlfən] *intr* (*dat*) help; **es hilft nichts** it's of no use
Hel′fer –in §6 *mf* helper
Hel′fershelfer *m* accomplice
Helikopter [helɪ′kɔptər] *m* (-s;-) helicopter
hell [hɛl] *adj* clear; bright; lucid; (*Haar*) fair; (*Bier*) light; (*Wahnsinn*, *usw.*) sheer ‖ **Helle** §5 *f* brightness; lightness; clarity ‖ *n* light; **ein Helles** a glass of light beer
hellenisch [hɛ′lenɪʃ] *adj* Hellenic
Heller [′hɛlər] *m* (-s;-) penny
hellhörig [′hɛlhørɪç] *adj* having sharp ears; **h. werden** prick up one's ears
hellicht [′hɛlɪçt] *adj*—**hellichter Tag** broad daylight
Hel′ligkeit *f* (-;-en) brightness; (astr) magnitude
hell′sehen §138 *intr* be clairvoyant ‖ **Hellsehen** *n* (-s;) clairvoyance
hell′seher –in §6 *mf* clairvoyant; (coll) mind reader
hell′sichtig *adj* clear-sighted
hell′wach *adj* wide awake
Helm [hɛlm] *m* (-[e]s;-e) helmet; (archit) dome, spire; (naut) helm
Helm′busch *m* crest, plume
Hemd [hɛmt] *n* (-[e]s;-en) shirt
Hemd′brust *f* dickey, shirt front
Hemd′hose *f* union suit
hemmen [′hɛmən] *tr* slow up; stop; **gehemmt** inhibited
Hemmnis [′hɛmnɪs] *n* (-ses;-se) hindrance
Hemmschuh [′hɛm/u] *m* (fig) hindrance; (rr) brake
Hem′mung *f* (-;-en) inhibition
hem′mungslos *adj* uninhibited
Hengst [hɛŋst] *m* (-es;-e) stallion
Henkel [′hɛŋkəl] *m* (-s;-) handle
henken [′hɛŋkən] *tr* hang (*s.o.*)
Henker [′hɛŋkər] *m* (-s;-) hangman
Henne [′hɛnə] *f* (-;-n) hen
her [her] *adv* hither, here; ago
herab [he′rap] *adv* down, downwards
herab– *comb.fm.* down; down here
herab′drücken *tr* press down; force down; **die Kurse h.** bear the market
herab′lassen §104 *ref* condescend
Herab′lassung *f* (-;) condescension
herab′sehen §138 *intr* (**auf** *acc*) look down (on)
herab′setzen *tr* put down; reduce; belittle, disparage
herab′steigen §148 *intr* (SEIN) climb down; (*vom Pferd*) dismount
herab′würdigen *tr* demean
Heraldik [he′raldɪk] *f* (-;) heraldry
heran [he′ran] *adv* near; up
heran′arbeiten *ref* (**an** *acc*) work one's way (towards)
heran′bilden *tr* (**zu**) train (as)
heran′brechen §64 *intr* (SEIN) (*Tag*) dawn, break; (*Nacht*) fall, come on
heran′gehen §82 *intr* (SEIN) go close; **h. an** (*acc*) approach, go up to
heran′kommen §99 *intr* (SEIN) come

near; **h. an** (*acc*) approach; get at; **h. bis an** (*acc*) reach as far as
heran′machen *ref*—**h. an** (*acc*) apply oneself to; approach
heran′nahen *intr* (SEIN) approach
heran′wachsen §155 *intr* (SEIN) (**zu**) grow up (to be)
heran′wagen *ref* (**an** *acc*) dare to approach
heran′ziehen §163 *tr* pull closer; call on for help; (*Quellen*) consult; (*zur Beratung*) call in; (*Pflanzen*) grow; (*Nachwuchs*) train ‖ *intr* (SEIN) approach
herauf [he′rauf] *adv* up, up here; upstairs
herauf′arbeiten *ref* work one's way up
herauf′bemühen *ref* take the trouble to come up (or upstairs)
herauf′beschwören §137 *tr* conjure up; (*verursachen*) bring on, provoke
herauf′kommen §99 *intr* (SEIN) come up
herauf′setzen *tr* raise, increase
herauf′steigen §148 *intr* (SEIN) climb up; (*Tag*) dawn
herauf′ziehen §163 *tr* pull up ‖ *intr* (SEIN) move upstairs; (*Sturm*) come up
heraus [he′raus] *adv* out, out here
heraus′bekommen §99 *tr* (**aus**) get out (of); (*Wort*) utter; (*Geld*) get back in change; (*Problem*) figure out
heraus′bringen §65 *tr* bring out; (*Wort*) utter; (*Lösung*) work out; (*Buch*) publish; (*Fabrikat*) bring out
heraus′drücken *tr* squeeze out; (*die Brust*) throw out
heraus′fahren §71 *intr* (SEIN) drive out; (*aus dem Bett*) jump out; (*Bemerkung*) slip out
heraus′finden §59 *tr* find out ‖ *ref* (aus) find one's way out (of)
heraus′fordern *tr* challenge, call on
heraus′fordernd *adj* defiant ‖ *adv* defiantly; **sich h. anziehen** dress provocatively
Heraus′forderung *f* (-;-en) challenge
heraus′fühlen *tr* sense
Heraus′gabe *f* surrender; (*e–s Buches*) publication; (jur) restitution
heraus′geben §80 *tr* surrender; give back; (*Buch*) publish ‖ *intr* (*dat*) give (*s.o.*) his change; **h. auf** (*acc*) give change for
Heraus′geber *m* publisher; (*Redakteur*) editor
heraus′greifen §88 *tr* single out
heraus′haben §89 *tr* have (*s.th.*) figured out; **er hat den Bogen heraus** (coll) he has the knack of it
heraus′halten §90 *tr* hold out ‖ *ref* (aus) keep out (of)
heraus′hängen §92 *tr & intr* hang out
heraus′kommen §99 *intr* (SEIN) come out
heraus′lesen §107 *tr* pick out; deduce; **zu viel aus e–m Gedicht h.** read too much into a poem
heraus′machen *tr* (*Fleck*) get out ‖ *ref* (*Kinder*) turn out well; (*Geschäft*) make out well
heraus′nehmen §116 *tr* take out ‖ *ref*

—sich [*dat*] **zu viel** (or **Freiheiten**) **h.** take liberties

heraus'platzen *intr* (SEIN)—**mit etw h.** blurt out s.th.

heraus'putzen *ref* dress up

heraus'reden *ref* (aus) talk one's way out (of)

heraus'rücken *tr* move out (here); (coll) (*Geld*) shell out || *intr* (SEIN) —**mit dem Geld h.** shell out money; **mit der Sprache h.** reveal it, admit it

heraus'schälen *ref* become apparent

heraus'stehen §146 *intr* protrude

heraus'steigen §148 *intr* (SEIN) (aus) climb out (of), step out (of)

heraus'stellen *tr* put out; **groß h.** give a big build-up to; **klar h.** present clearly || *ref* emerge, come to light; **sich h.** als prove to be

heraus'streichen §85 *tr* delete; (fig) praise

heraus'suchen *tr* pick out

heraus'treten §152 *intr* (SEIN) come out, step out; bulge, protrude

heraus'winden §59 *ref* extricate oneself

heraus'wirtschaften *tr* manage to save; (*Profit*) manage to make

heraus'ziehen §163 *tr* pull out

herb [herp] *adj* harsh; (*sauer*) sour; (*zusammenziehend*) tangy; (*Wein*) dry; (*Worte*) bitter; (*Schönheit*) austere || **Herbe** *f* (–;) harshness; tang; bitterness; austerity

herbei' *adv* here (*toward the speaker*)

herbei– *comb.fm.* up, along, here (*toward the speaker*)

herbei'bringen §65 *tr* bring along

herbei'eilen *intr* (SEIN) hurry here

herbei'führen *tr* bring here; cause

herbei'kommen §99 *intr* (SEIN) come up

herbei'lassen §104 *ref* condescend

herbei'rufen §122 *tr* call over; summon

herbei'schaffen *tr* bring here; procure; (*Geld*) raise

herbei'sehnen *tr* long for

herbei'strömen *intr* (SEIN) come flocking, flock

herbei'winken *tr* beckon (*s.o.*) to come over

herbei'wünschen *tr* long for, wish for

Herberge ['hɛrbɛrgə] *f* (–;–n) lodging, shelter; hostel; (obs) inn

her'beten *tr* say mechanically

Herb'heit *f* (–;), **Her'bigkeit** *f* (–;) harshness; tang; bitterness; austerity

her'bringen §65 *tr* bring here

Herbst [hɛrpst] *m* (–es;–e) autumn

herbst'lich *adj* autumn, fall

Herd [hɛrt] *m* (–[e]s;–e) hearth, fireplace; home; kitchen range; center

Herde ['hɛrdə] *f* (–;–n) herd, flock

herein [hɛ'raɪn] *adv* in, in here; **h.!** come in!

herein– *comb.fm.* in, in here (*toward the speaker*)

herein'bemühen *tr* ask (*s.o.*) to come in || *ref* trouble oneself to come in

herein'bitten §60 *tr* invite in

Herein'fall *m* disappointment, letdown

herein'fallen §72 *intr* (SEIN) fall in; **h. auf** (*acc*) fall for; **h. in** (*acc*) fall into

herein'legen *tr* fool, take in

herein'platzen *intr* (SEIN) burst in

her'fallen §72 *intr* (SEIN)—**h. über** (*acc*) fall upon, attack

her'finden §59 *ref & intr* find one's way here

Her'gang *m* background details

her'geben §80 *tr* hand over; give up || *ref*—**sich h. zu** be a party to

her'halten §90 *tr* hold out, extend || *intr*—**h. müssen** (*Person*) be the victim; (*Sache*) have to do (*as a makeshift*)

Hering ['herɪŋ] *m* (–s;–e) herring; **sitzen wie die Heringe** be packed in like sardines

her'kommen §99 *intr* (SEIN) come here; (*Wort*) originate; **wo kommst du denn her?** where have you come from? || **Herkommen** *n* (–s;–) origin; custom, tradition, convention

herkömmlich ['hɛrkœmlɪç] *adj* customary, usual; traditional, conventional

Herkunft ['hɛrkʊnft] *f* (–;) origin; birth, family

her'laufen §105 *intr* (SEIN) walk here; **hinter j–m h.** follow s.o.

her'leiten *tr* derive; deduce, infer

Her'leitung *f* (–;–en) derivation

her'machen *tr*—**viel h. von** make a fuss over || *ref*—**sich h. über** (*acc*) attack; (fig) tackle

Hermelin [hɛrmə'lin] *m* (–s;–e) ermine || *n* (–s;–e) (zool) ermine

hermetisch [hɛr'metɪʃ] *adj* hermetic

hernach' *adv* afterwards

her'nehmen §116 *tr* get; **j–n scharf h.** give s.o. a good talking-to

hernie'der *adv* down, down here

Heroin [hero'in] *n* (–s;) (pharm) heroin

Heroine [hero'in] *f* (–;–n) heroine

heroisch [he'ro·ɪʃ] *adj* heroic

Heroismus [hero'ɪsmʊs] *m* (–;) heroism

Herold ['herɔlt] *m* (–[e]s;–e) herald

Heros ['heros] *m* (–; **Heroen** [he'ro·ən]) hero

Herr [hɛr] *m* (–n;–en) lord; master; gentleman; (*als Anrede*) Sir; (*vor Eigennamen*) Mr.; (*Gott*) Lord; **meine Herren!** gentlemen!

her'reichen *tr* hand, pass

Herren– [hɛrən] *comb.fm.* man's, men's; gentlemen's

Her'renabend *m* stag party

Her'renbegleitung *f*—**in H.** accompanied by a gentleman

Her'rendoppel(spiel) *n* (tennis) men's doubles

Her'reneinzel(spiel) *n* (tennis) men's singles

Her'renfahrer *m* (aut) owner-driver

Her'renfriseur *m* barber

Her'rengesellschaft *f* male company; stag party

Her'rengröße *f* men's size

Her'rengut *n* domain, manor

Her'renhaus *n* mansion; House of Lords

Her'renhof *m* manor

Her'renleben *n* life of Riley

her'renlos *adj* ownerless

Her'renmensch *m* born leader

Her'renschnitt *m* woman's very short hairstyle

Her'renzimmer *n* study

Herr'gott *m* Lord, Lord God

her'richten *tr* arrange; get ready

Herrin ['hɛrɪn] *f* (–;-nen) lady

herrisch ['hɛrɪʃ] *adj* masterful

herr'lich *adj* splendid

Herr'lichkeit *f* (–;-en) splendor

Herr'schaft *f* (–;-en) rule, domination; mastery; control; lord, master; estate; **meine Herrschaften!** ladies and gentlemen!

herr'schaftlich *adj* ruler's; gentleman's; high-class

herrschen ['hɛrʃən] *intr* rule; prevail; exist

Herr'scher –in §6 *mf* ruler

Herrschsucht ['hɛrʃzʊçt] *f* (–;) thirst for power; bossiness

herrsch'süchtig *adj* power-hungry; autocratic; domineering

her'rühren *intr*—h. von come from, originate with

her'sagen *tr* recite, say

her'schaffen *tr* get (here)

her'stammen *intr*—h. von come from, be descended from; (gram) be derived from

her'stellen *tr* put here; (erzeugen) produce; **fabrikmäßig h.** mass-produce; **Verbindung h.** establish contact; (telp) put a call through

Her'steller *m* (–s;-) manufacturer

Her'stellung *f* (–;-en) production

Her'stellungsbetrieb *m* factory

Her'stellungsverfahren *n* manufacturing process

herüber [hɛ'rybər] *adv* over, over here, in this direction (toward the speaker)

herum [hɛ'rʊm] *adv* around; about

herum'bringen §65 *tr* bring around; (Zeit) spend

herum'drehen *tr, ref & intr* turn around

herum'fragen *intr* make inquiries

herumfuchteln [hɛ'rʊmfʊxtəln] *intr*—mit den Händen h. wave one's hands about

herum'führen *tr* show around

herum'greifen §88 *intr*—h. um reach around

herum'hacken *intr*—h. auf (dat) pick on, criticize

herum'kauen *intr* (an dat, auf dat) chew away (on)

herum'kommen §99 *intr* (SEIN) get around; h. um get around; evade

herum'lungern *intr* loaf around

herum'reiten §86 *intr* (SEIN) ride around; h. auf (dat) harp on (s.th.); pick on (s.o.)

herum'schnüffeln *intr* snoop around

herum'streichen §85 *intr* (SEIN) prowl about

herum'streiten §86 *ref* squabble

herum'treiben §62 *tr* drive around ‖ *ref* roam around, knock about

Herum'treiber *m* (–s;-) loafer, tramp

herum'ziehen §163 *tr* pull around; h. um draw (s.th.) around ‖ *ref*—sich h. um surround ‖ *intr* (SEIN) wander

around; run around; h. um march around

herunter [hɛ'rʊntər] *adv* down, down here (towards the speaker); downstairs; **den Berg h.** down the mountain; **ins Tal h.** down into the valley

herun'terbringen §65 *tr* bring down; (fig) lower, reduce

herun'tergehen §82 *intr* (SEIN) go down; (Preis, Temperatur) fall, drop

herun'terhandeln *tr* (Preis) beat down

herun'terhauen §93 *tr* chop off; (Brief) dash off; **j–m eins h.** clout s.o.

herun'terkommen §99 *intr* (SEIN) come down; come downstairs; deteriorate

herun'terlassen §104 *tr* let down, lower

herun'terleiern *tr* drone

herun'terlesen §107 *tr* (Liste) read down; rattle off

herun'termachen *tr* take down; turn down; (coll) chew out; (coll) pan

herun'terschießen §76 *tr* shoot down

herun'tersein §139 *intr* (SEIN) be run-down

herun'terwirtschaften *tr* ruin (through mismanagement)

herun'terwürgen *tr* choke down

hervor [hɛr'for] *adv* out; forth

hervor'bringen §65 *tr* bring out; engender, produce; (Wort) utter

hervor'dringen §142 *intr* (SEIN) emerge

hervor'gehen §82 *intr* (SEIN)—h. aus come from; emerge from; to have been trained at

hervor'heben §94 *tr* highlight

hervor'holen *tr* produce

hervor'kommen §99 *intr* (SEIN) come out

hervor'lugen *intr* peep out

hervor'ragen *intr* jut out; be prominent; h. über (acc) tower over

hervor'ragend *adj* prominent

hervor'rufen §122 *tr* evoke, cause; (Schauspieler) recall

hervor'stechen §64 *intr* stick out; be conspicuous; be prominent

hervor'treten §152 *intr* (SEIN) emerge; come to the fore; become apparent; (Augen) bulge; (Ader) protrude

hervor'tun §154 *ref* distinguish oneself

hervor'wagen *ref* dare to come out; **sich mit e-r Antwort h.** venture an answer

hervor'zaubern *tr* produce by magic; **ein Essen h.** whip up a meal

Herweg ['hervek] *m* way here; way home

Herz [hɛrts] *n* (–ens;-en) heart; (als Anrede) darling; (cards) heart(s); **ich bringe es nicht übers H. zu** (inf) I haven't the heart to (inf); **sich** [dat] **ein H. fassen** get up the courage; **seinem Herzen Luft machen** give vent to one's feelings

Herz– comb.fm. heart, cardiac

Herz'anfall *m* heart attack

Herz'beschwerden *pl* heart trouble

Herz'blume *f* (bot) bleeding heart

herzen ['hɛrtsən] *tr* hug, embrace

Her'zensgrund *m* bottom of one's heart

her'zensgut *adj* good-hearted

Her′zenslust *f*—**nach H.** to one's heart's content
herz′ergreifend *adj* moving, touching
Herz′geräusch *n* heart murmur
herz′haft *adj* hearty
herzig [′hɛrtsɪç] *adj* sweet, cute
–**herzig** *comb.fm.* -hearted
Herzinfarkt [′hɛrtsɪnfarkt] *m* (-[e]s; -e) cardiac infarction
herz′innig *adj* heartfelt
herz′inniglich *adv* sincerely
Herz′klappe *f* cardiac valve
Herz′klopfen *n* palpitations
Herz′kollaps *m* heart failure
herz′lich *adj* cordial; sincere ‖ *adv* very; **h. wenige** precious few
herz′los *adj* heartless
Herzog [′hɛrtsɔk] *m* (-[e]s;∹e) duke
Herzogin [′hɛrtsɔgɪn] *f* (-;-nen) duchess
Herzogtum [′hɛrtsɔktum] *n* (-[e]s;∹er) dukedom; duchy
Herz′schlag *m* heartbeat; heart failure
Herz′stück *n* heart, central point
Herz′verpflanzung *f* heart transplant
Herz′weh *n* (& fig) heartache
Hetzblatt [′hɛtsblat] *n* scandal sheet
Hetze [′hɛtsə] *f* (-;-n) hunting; hurry, rush; vicious campaign; baiting
hetzen [′hɛtsən] *tr* hunt; bait; rush; (fig) hound; **e-n Hund auf j-n h.** sic a dog on s.o. ‖ *ref* rush ‖ *intr* stir up trouble; **h. gegen** conduct a vicious campaign against ‖ *intr* (SEIN) race, dash
Het′zer –**in** §6 *mf* agitator
Hetz′hund *m* hound, hunting dog
Hetz′jagd *f* hunt; baiting; hurry
Hetz′rede *f* inflammatory speech
Heu [hɔɪ] *n* (-[e]s;) hay
Heu′boden *m* hayloft
Heuchelei [hɔɪçə′laɪ] *f* (-;-en) hypocrisy; piece of hypocrisy
heucheln [′hɔɪçəln] *tr* feign ‖ *intr* be hypocritical
Heuch′ler –**in** §6 *mf* hypocrite
heuchlerisch [′hɔɪçlərɪʃ] *adj* hypocritical
heuen [′hɔɪən] *intr* make hay
heuer [′hɔɪər] *adv* this year
heuern [′hɔɪərn] *tr* hire
Heu′fieber *n* hayfever
Heu′gabel *f* pitchfork
heulen [′hɔɪlən] *intr* bawl; (*Wind*) howl
heurig [′hɔɪrɪç] *adj* this year's ‖ **Heurige** §5 *m* new wine
Heu′schnupfen *m* (-s;) hayfever
Heuschober [′hɔɪʃobər] *m* (-s;-) haystack
Heu′schrecke *f* (-;-n) locust
heute [′hɔɪtə] *adv* today; **h. abend** this evening; **h. früh** (or **h. morgen**) this morning; **h. vor acht Tagen** a week ago today; **h. in acht Tagen** today a week
heutig [′hɔɪtɪç] *adj* today's; present-day; **am heutigen Tage** (or **der heutige Tag** or **mit dem heutigen Tag**) today
heutzutage [′hɔɪttsutagə] *adv* nowadays
Hexe [′hɛksə] *f* (-;-n) witch; hag

hexen [′hɛksən] *intr* practice witchcraft
He′xenkessel *m* chaos, inferno
He′xenmeister *m* wizard; sorcerer
He′xenschuß *m* lumbago
Hexerei [hɛksə′raɪ] *f* (-;) witchcraft
Hiatus [hɪ′atus] *m* (-;-) (& pros) hiatus
Hibis·kus [hɪ′bɪskus] *m* (-;-ken [kən]) hibiscus
hieb [hip] *pret of* **hauen** ‖ **Hieb** *m* (-[e]s;-e) blow, stroke; **Hiebe** thrashing
hieb′-undstich′fest *adj* (fig) watertight
Hieb′wunde *f* gash
hielt [hilt] *pret of* **halten**
hier [hir] *adv* here
hieran′ *adv* at (by, in, on, to) it or them
Hierar·chie [hɪˌerar′çi] *f* (-;-chien [′çi·ən]) hierarchy
hierauf′ *adv* on it, on them; then
hieraus′ *adv* out of it (or them); from this (or these)
hierbei′ *adv* near here; here; in this case; in connection with this
hierdurch′ *adv* through it (or them); through here; hereby
hierfür′ *adv* for it (or them)
hierge′gen *adv* against it
hierher′ *adv* hither, here
hier′herum *adv* around here
hierhin′ *adv* here; **bis h.** up to here
hierin′ *adv* herein, in this
hiermit′ *adv* herewith, with it
hiernach′ *adv* after this, then; about this; according to this
Hieroglyphe [hɪˌero′glyfə] *f* (-;-n) hieroglyph
hierorts [′hirɔrts] *adv* in this town
hierü′ber *adv* over it (or them); about it (or this)
hierzu′ *adv* to it; in addition to it; concerning this
hiesig [′hizɪç] *adj* local
hieß [his] *pret of* **heißen**
Hilfe [′hɪlfə] *f* (-;-n) help, aid; **zu H. nehmen** make use of
Hil′feleistung *f* assistance
Hil′feruf *m* cry for help
hilf′los *adj* helpless
hilf′reich *adj* helpful
Hilfs– [hɪlfs] *comb.fm.* auxiliary
Hilfs′arbeiter –**in** §6 *mf* unskilled laborer
Hilfs′arzt *m*, **Hilf′ärztin** *f* intern
hilfs′bedürftig *adj* needy
hilfs′bereit *adj* ready to help
Hilfs′dienst *m* help, assistance
Hilfs′gerät *n* labor-saving device
Hilfs′kraft *f* assistant, helper; (mach) auxiliary power
Hilfs′kraftbremse *f* power brake
Hilfs′kraftlenkung *f* power steering
Hilfs′lehrer –**in** §6 *mf* student teacher
Hilfs′maschine *f* auxiliary engine
Hilfs′mittel *n* aid, device; remedy; financial aid
Hilfs′quellen *pl* material; sources
Hilfs′rakete *f* booster rocket
Hilfs′schule *f* school for the mentally slow

Hilfs'truppen *pl* auxiliaries
Hilfs'werk *n* welfare organization
Hilfs'zeitwort *n* (-[e]s;ˮer) (gram) auxiliary (verb)
Himbeere ['hɪmbərə] *f* (-;-n) raspberry
Himmel ['hɪməl] *m* (-s;-) sky, skies; heaven(s); firmament; (eccl) baldachin; **ach du lieber H.!** good heavens!; **aus heiterem H.** out of the blue; **in den H. heben** praise to the skies
himmelan' *adv* skywards; heavenwards
him'melangst *invar adj*—**mir wird h.** I feel frightened to death
Him'melbett *n* canopy bed
him'melblau *adj* sky-blue
Him'melfahrt *f* ascension; assumption
Him'melfahrtstag *m* Ascension Day
Him'melreich *n* kingdom of heaven
Himmels- *comb.fm.* celestial
him'melschreiend *adj* atrocious
Him'melsgegend *f* region of the sky; point of the compass
Him'melskörper *m* celestial body
Him'melsrichtung *f* point of the compass; direction
Him'melsschrift *f* skywriting
Him'melswagen *m* (astr) Great Bear
Him'melszelt *n* canopy of heaven
himmelwärts ['hɪməlverts] *adv* skywards; heavenwards
himmlisch ['hɪmlɪʃ] *adj* heavenly, celestial; divine; (coll) gorgeous
hin [hɪn] *adv* there (*away from the speaker*); **ganz hin** (coll) bushed; (coll) quite carried away; **hin ist hin** what's done is done; **hin und her** up and down, back and forth; **hin und wieder** now and then; **vor sich hin** to oneself
hinab' *adv* down
hinan' *adv* up; **bis an etw h.** up to s.th., as far as s.th.
hinauf' *adv* up, up there; upstairs; **den Fluß h.** up the river
hinauf'reichen *tr* hand (*s.th.*) up || *intr* reach up
hinauf'schrauben *tr* (*Preis*) jack up
hinauf'setzen *tr* raise, increase
hinauf'steigen §148 *tr* (SEIN) (*Treppe, Berg*) climb || *intr* (SEIN) climb up; (*Temperatur*) rise
hinaus' *adv* out, out there; **auf viele Jahre h.** for many years to come
hinaus'beißen §53 *tr* (coll) edge out
hinaus'gehen §82 *intr* (SEIN) go out; **h. auf** (*acc*) look out over; lead to; drive at, imply; **h. über** (*acc*) exceed
hinaus'kommen §99 *intr* (SEIN) come out; **es kommt auf eins** (or **aufs gleiche**) **hinaus** it amounts to the same thing; **h. über** (*acc*) get beyond
hinaus'laufen §105 *intr* (SEIN) run out; **es läuft aufs eins** (or **aufs gleiche**) **hinaus** it amounts to the same thing
hinaus'schieben §130 *tr* push out; (*Termin, usw.*) postpone
hinaus'werfen §160 *tr* throw out; fire
hinaus'wollen §162 *intr* want to go out; **h. auf** (*acc*) be driving at; **hoch h.** aim high, be ambitious
hinaus'ziehen §163 *tr* prolong || *ref*

take longer than expected || *intr* (SEIN) go out; move out
Hin'blick *m*—**im H. auf** (*acc*) in view of
hin'bringen §65 *tr* bring (there); take (there); (*Zeit*) pass
hinderlich ['hɪndərlɪç] *adj* in the way
hindern ['hɪndərn] *tr* block; **h. an** (*dat*) prevent from (*ger*)
Hindernis ['hɪndərnɪs] *n* (-ses;-se) hindrance; obstacle
Hin'dernisbahn *f* obstacle course
Hin'dernislauf *m* (sport) hurdles
Hin'dernisrennen *n* steeplechase; hurdles
hin'deuten *intr* (auf *acc*) point (to)
hindurch' *adv* through; **den ganzen Sommer h.** throughout the summer
hinein' *adv* in, in there
hinein'arbeiten *ref*—**sich h. in** (*acc*) work one's way into
hinein'denken §66 *ref*—**sich h. in** (*acc*) imagine oneself in
hinein'geraten §63 *intr* (SEIN)—**h. in** (*acc*) get into, fall into
hinein'leben *intr*—**in den Tag h.** live for the moment
hinein'tun §154 *tr* put in
Hin'fahrt *f* journey there, out-bound passage
hin'fallen §72 *intr* (SEIN) fall down
hinfällig ['hɪnfɛlɪç] *adj* frail; (*Gesetz*) invalid
hinfort' *adv* henceforth
hing [hɪŋ] *pret* of **hängen**
Hin'gabe *f* (an *acc*) devotion (to)
hin'geben §80 *tr* give up || *ref* (*dat*) abandon oneself (to)
Hin'gebung *f* (-;) devotion
hinge'gen *adv* on the other hand
hin'gehen §82 *intr* (SEIN) go there; pass
hin'halten §90 *tr* hold out; (*Person*) keep waiting, string along; **den Kopf h.** (fig) take the rap
hinken ['hɪŋkən] *intr* limp; **der Vergleich hinkt** that's a poor comparison || *intr* (SEIN) limp
hin'länglich *adj* sufficient
hin'legen *tr* put down || *ref* lie down
hin'nehmen §116 *tr* accept; take, put up with
hin'raffen *tr* snatch away
hin'reichen *tr* (*dat*) pass to, hand to || *intr* reach; suffice
hin'reißen §53 *tr* enchant, carry away
hin'richten *tr* execute; **h. auf** (*acc*) direct towards
Hin'richtung *f* (-;-en) execution
Hin'richtungsbefehl *m* death warrant
hin'setzen *tr* put down || *ref* sit down
Hin'sicht *f* respect, way; **in H. auf** (*acc*) regarding, in regard to
hin'sichtlich *prep* (*genit*) regarding
hin'stellen *tr* put there; put down
hintan'setzen, hintan'stellen *tr* put last, consider last
hinten ['hɪntən] *adv* at the back, in the rear; **h. im Zimmer** at the back of the room; **nach h.** to the rear; backwards; **von h.** from the rear
hinter ['hɪntər] *prep* (*dat*) behind; **h. j-m her sein** be after s.o. || *prep* (*acc*) behind; **h. etw kommen** find

out about s.th., get to the bottom of s.th.

Hin′terachse f rear axle

Hin′terbacke f buttock

Hin′terbein n hind leg; **sich auf die Hinterbeine setzen** strain oneself

Hinterbliebene [ˈhɪntərblibənə] §5 mf survivor (of a deceased); **H. pl** next-of-kin

hinterbrin′gen §65 tr—j–m etw h. let s.o. in on s.th.

Hin′terdeck n quarter deck

hinterdrein [hɪntərˈdraɪn] adv after; subsequently, afterwards

hin′tere §9 adj back, rear || **Hintere** §5 m (coll) behind

hintereinan′der adv one behind the other; in succession; one after the other

Hin′terfuß m hind foot

Hin′tergaumen m soft palate, velum

Hin′tergedanke m ulterior motive

hinterge′hen §82 tr deceive

Hin′tergrund m background

Hin′terhalt m ambush

hinterhältig [ˈhɪntərhɛltɪç] adj underhanded

Hin′terhand f hind quarters (of horse)

Hin′terhaus n rear building

hinterher′ adv behind; afterwards

Hin′terhof m backyard

Hin′terkopf m back of the head

Hin′terland n hinterland

hinterlas′sen §104 tr leave behind

Hinterlas′senschaft f (–;–en) inheritance

Hin′terlauf m hind leg

hinterle′gen tr deposit

Hinterle′gung f (–;–en) deposit

Hin′terlist f deceit; trick, ruse

Hin′termann m (–[e]s;–er) instigator; wheeler-dealer; (pol) backer

Hintern [ˈhɪntərn] m (–s;–) (coll) behind

Hin′terradantrieb m rear-wheel drive

hinterrücks [ˈhɪntərʏks] adv from behind; (fig) behind one's back

Hin′tertreffen n—ins H. geraten fall behind; **im H. sein** be at a disadvantage

hintertrei′ben §62 tr frustrate

Hintertrei′bung f (–;–en) frustration

Hin′tertreppe f backstairs

Hin′tertür f backdoor

Hinterwäldler [ˈhɪntərvɛltlər] m (–s;–) hillbilly

hin′terwälderisch adj hillbilly

hinterzie′hen §163 tr evade

Hinterzie′hung f (–;) tax evasion

hinü′ber adv over, over there; across

hinun′ter adv down

hinun′tergehen §82 tr (SEIN) (Treppe) go down || intr (SEIN) go down

hinweg [hɪnˈwɛk] adv away; **über etw h.** over s.th., across s.th. || **Hinweg** [ˈhɪnvɛk] m way there

hinweg′kommen §99 intr (SEIN)—h. über (acc) get over

hinweg′sehen §138 intr—h. über (acc) look over; overlook, ignore

hinweg′setzen ref—sich h. über (acc) ignore, disregard

hinweg′täuschen tr mislead, blind

Hinweis [ˈhɪnvaɪs] m (–es;–e reference; hint; announcement

hin′weisen §118 tr—j–n h. auf (acc) point s.th. out to s.o. || intr—h. auf (acc) point to; point out

hin′werfen §160 tr throw down; (coll) dash off, jot down

hin′wirken intr—h. auf (acc) work toward(s)

hin′ziehen §163 tr attract protract || ref drag on; **sich h. an** (dat) run along; **sich h. bis zu** extend to

hin′zielen intr—h. auf (acc) aim at

hinzu′ adv there, thither; in addition

hinzu′fügen tr add

hinzu′kommen §99 intr (SEIN) come (upon the scene); be added; **es kamen noch andere Gründe hinzu** besides, there were other reasons

hinzu′setzen tr add

hinzu′treten §152 intr (SEIN) (zu) walk up (to); **es traten noch andere Gründe hinzu** besides, there were other reasons

hinzu′tun §154 tr add

hinzu′ziehen §163 tr (Arzt) call in

Hirn [hɪrn] n (–[e]s;–e) brain; brains; **sein H. anstrengen** rack one's brains

Hirn– comb.fm. brain; cerebral; intellectual

Hirn′anhang m pituitary gland

Hirn′gespinst n figment of the imagination

Hirn′hautentzündung f meningitis

hirn′los adj brainless

Hirn′rinde f (anat) cortex

Hirn′schale f cranium

hirn′verbrannt adj (coll) crazy

Hirsch [hɪrʃ] m (–es;–e) deer, stag

Hirsch′fänger m hunting knife

Hirsch′kalb n fawn, doe

Hirsch′kuh f hind

Hirsch′leder n deerskin, buckskin

Hirt [hɪrt] m (–en;–en) shepherd

–hirte [hɪrtə] m (–n;–n) –herd

Hir′tenbrief m (eccl) pastoral letter

Hirtin [ˈhɪrtɪn] f (–;–nen) shepherdess

His [hɪs] n (–;) (mus) B sharp

hissen [ˈhɪsən] tr hoist

Historie [hɪsˈtorjə] f (–;–n) history; story

Historiker –in [hɪsˈtorɪkər(ɪn)] §6 mf historian

historisch [hɪsˈtorɪʃ] adj historical

Hitze [ˈhɪtsə] f (–;–n) heat

hit′zebeständig adj heat-resistant

Hit′zeferien pl school holiday (because of hot weather)

Hit′zeschild m (rok) heat shield

Hit′zewelle f heat wave

hitzig [ˈhɪtsɪç] adj hot-tempered

Hitz′kopf m hothead

hitz′köpfig adj hot-headed

Hitz′schlag m heatstroke

hob [hop] pret of heben

Hobel [ˈhobəl] m (–s;–) (carp) plane

Ho′belbank f carpenter's bench

hobeln [ˈhobəln] tr (carp) plane

hoch [hox], (hohe [ˈho·ə] §9) adj (höher [ˈhø·ər]; höchste [ˈhøçstə] §9) high; noble; (Alter) advanced; **das ist mir zu h.** that's beyond me; **hohes Gericht!** your honor!; members of the jury!; **in höchster Not** in dire need || adv high; highly, very; (math) to the ... power || **Hoch** n (-s;-s) (*Trinkspruch, Heilruf*) cheer; (meteor) high

hoch– *comb.fm.* up; upwards; highly, very; high, as high as

hoch'achten *tr* esteem

Hoch'achtung *f* (-;) esteem; **mit vorzüglicher H., Ihr ... or Ihre ...** Very truly yours, Respectfully yours

hoch'achtungsvoll *adj* respectful || adv —h., Ihr ... or Ihre ... Very truly yours, Respectfully yours

Hoch'amt *n* (eccl) High Mass

Hoch'antenne *f* outdoor antenna

hoch'arbeiten *ref* work one's way up

hoch'aufgeschossen *adj* tall, lanky

Hoch'bahn *f* el, elevated train

Hoch'bauingenieur *m* structural engineer

hoch'bäumen *ref* rear up

Hoch'behälter *m* water tower; reservoir

Hochbeiner ['hoxbaɪnər] *m* (-s;-) (ent) daddy-long-legs

hoch'beinig *adj* long-legged

hoch'betagt *adj* advanced in years

Hoch'betrieb *m* bustle, big rush

Hoch'blüte *f* high bloom; (fig) heyday

hoch'bringen §65 *tr* restore to health; (*Geschäft*) put on its feet; **es h.** (sport) get a high score

Hoch'burg *f* fortress, citadel

hoch'denkend *adj* noble-minded

Hoch'deutsch *adj* High German

Hoch'druck *m* high pressure; (fig) great pressure; (meteor) high; **mit H.** (fig) full blast

Hoch'druckgebiet *n* (meteor) high, high-pressure area

Hoch'ebene *f* plateau

hoch'fahrend *adj* high-handed

hoch'fein *adj* very refined; high-grade

Hoch'flut *m* high tide; (fig) deluge

Hoch'form *f* top form

hochfrequent ['hoxfrekvent] *adj* high-frequency

Hoch'frequenz *f* high-frequency

Hoch'frisur *f* upsweep

Hoch'gefühl *n* elation

hoch'gemut *adj* cheerful

Hoch'genuß *m* great pleasure

Hoch'gericht *n* place of execution

hoch'gesinnt *adj* noble-minded

hoch'gespannt *adj* (*Hoffnungen*) high; (elec) high-voltage

hoch'gestellt *adj* high-ranking

Hoch'glanz *m* high polish, high gloss

Hoch'haus *n* high rise (building)

hoch'herzig *adj* generous

hoch'jagen *tr* (*Wild*) ferret out; (*Motor*) race; (coll) blow up

hochkant ['hoxkant] *adv* on end

Hoch'konjunktur *f* (econ) boom

Hoch'land *n* highlands; plateau

Hoch'leistung *f* (-;-en) high output; (sport) first-class performance

Hochleistungs– *comb.fm.* high-powered; high-capacity; high-speed; heavy-duty

Hoch'mut *m* haughtiness, pride

hoch'mütig *adj* haughty, proud

hochnäsig ['hoxnɛzɪç] *adj* snooty

Hoch'ofen *m* blast furnace

hoch'ragend *adj* towering

hoch'rappeln *ref* (coll) get on one's feet again, pick up again

hoch'rollen *tr* roll up

Hoch'ruf *m* cheer

Hoch'saison *f* height of the season

Hoch'schule *f* university, academy

Hoch'schüler –in §6 *mf* university student

Hoch'seefischerei *f* deep-sea fishing

hoch'selig *adj* late, of blessed memory

Hoch'spannung *f* high voltage

Hoch'spannungsleitung *f* high-tension line

hoch'spielen *tr* play up; put into the limelight

Hoch'sprache *f* standard language; **(die) deutsche H.** standard German

höchst *adv* see hoch

Höchst– *comb.fm.* maximum, top

Hochstapelei [hox/tapə'laɪ] *f* (-;) false pretenses; fraud

Hochstapler ['hox/taplər] *m* (-s;-) confidence man; imposter, swindler

Hoch'start *m* (sport) standing start

Höchst'belastung *f* (-;-en) maximum load; (elec) peak load

höchstens ['høçstəns] *adv* at best, at the very most

Höchst'form *f* (sport) top form

Höchst'frequenz *f* ultrahigh frequency

Höchst'geschwindigkeit *f* top speed; **zulässige H.** speed limit

Höchst'leistung *f* (-;-en) maximum output; highest achievement; (sport) record

Hoch'straße *f* overpass

Hoch'ton *m* (ling) primary stress

hoch'tönend *adj* bombastic

hochtourig ['hoxturɪç] *adj* high-revving

hoch'trabend *adj* pompous

Hoch'–und Tief'bau *m* (-[e]s;) civil engineering

hoch'verdient *adj* of great merit

Hoch'verrat *m* high treason

Hoch'verräter –in §6 *mf* traitor

Hoch'wasser *n* flood(s); **der Fluß führt H.** the river is swollen

hoch'wertig *adj* high-quality

Hoch'wild *n* big game

Hoch'würden *pl* (*als Anrede*) Reverend; **Seine H. ...** the Reverend ...

Hoch'zeit *f* wedding

hoch'zeitlich *adj* bridal; nuptial

Hoch'zeitsfeier *f* wedding ceremony; wedding reception

Hoch'zeitspaar *n* newly-weds

Hoch'zeitsreise *f* honeymoon

Hocke ['hɔkə] *f* (-;-n) crouch

hocken ['hɔkən] *ref* & *intr* squat; (coll) sit down

Hocker ['hɔkər] *m* (-s;-) stool

Höcker ['hœkər] *m* (-s;-) hump; bump

höckerig ['hœkərɪç] *adj* hunchbacked; (*Weg*) bumpy

Hockey ['hɔki] *n* (-s;) hockey

Ho'ckeyschläger *m* hockey stick

Hode ['hodə] *f* (-;-n) testicle

Ho'densack *m* (anat) scrotum

Hof [hof] *m* (-[e]s;ˇe) courtyard;

yard; barnyard; (e-s Königs) court; (astr) halo; corona; e-m Mädchen den Hof machen court a girl
Hoffart ['hofart] f (-;) haughtiness
hoffärtig ['höfertıç] adj haughty
hoffen ['höfən] tr—das Beste h. hope for the best || intr (auf acc) hope (for); auf ½-n h. put one's hopes in s.o
hoffentlich ['hofəntlıç] adv as I hope; h. kommt er bald I hope he comes soon
Hoffnung ['hofnuŋ] f (-;-en) hope
hoff'nungslos adj hopeless
hoff'nungsvoll adj hopeful; promising
Hof'hund m watchdog
hofieren [ho'firən] tr court
höfisch ['höfıʃ] adj court, courtly
höflich ['höflıç] adj polite, courteous
Höf'lichkeit f (-;-en) politeness, courtesy
Höf'lichkeitsformel f complimentary close (in a letter)
Höfling ['höflıŋ] m (-[e]s;-e) courtier
Hof'meister m steward; tutor
Hof'narr m court jester
Hof'staat m royal household; retinue
hohe ['ho·ə] adj see hoch
Höhe ['hö·ə] f (-;-en) height; altitude; (Anhöhe) hill; (mus) pitch; auf der H. in good shape; das ist die H.! that's the limit!; in der H. von in the amount of; in die H. up; in die H. fahren jump up; wieder in die H. bringen (com) put back on its feet
Hoheit ['hohart] f (-;-en) sovereignty; (als Titel) Highness
Ho'heitsbereich m (pol), **Ho'heitsgebiet** n (pol) territory
Ho'heitsgewässer pl territorial waters
Ho'heitsrechte pl sovereign rights
ho'heitsvoll adj regal, majestic
Ho'heitszeichen n national emblem
Hö'henmesser m altimeter
Hö'henruder n (aer) elevator
Hö'hensonne f ultra-violet lamp
Hö'henstrahlen pl cosmic rays
Hö'henzug m mountain range
Ho'hepriester m high priest
Hö'hepunkt m climax; height; acme
höher ['hö·ər] adj see hoch
hohl [hol] adj hollow
Höhle ['hölə] f (-;-n) cave; grotto; lair, den; hollow, cavity; socket
Höh'lenmensch m caveman
hohl'geschliffen adj hollow-ground
Hohl'heit f (-;) hollowness
Hohl'maß n dry measure; liquid measure
Hohl'raum m hollow, cavity
Hohl'saum m hemstitch
Hohl'weg m defile, narrow pass
Hohn [hon] m (-[e]s;) scorn; sarcasm; etw ½-m Hohn tun do s.th. in defiance of s.o.
höhnen ['hönən] intr jeer; sneer
höhnisch ['hönıʃ] adj scornful
hohn'sprechen §64 intr (dat) treat with scorn; defy; make a mockery of
Höker -in ['hökər(ın)] §6 mf huckster
hold [holt] adj kindly; lovely, sweet
hold'selig adj lovely, sweet

holen ['holən] tr fetch; get; (Atem, Luft) draw; h. lassen send for; sich [dat] etw h. (coll) catch s.th.
Holland ['holant] n (-s;) Holland
Holländer ['holəndər] m (-s;-) Dutchman
Holländerin ['holəndərın] f (-;-nen) Dutch woman
holländisch ['holəndıʃ] adj Dutch
Hölle ['hölə] f (-;) hell
Höl'lenangst f mortal fear
höllisch ['hölıʃ] adj hellish
Holm [holm] m (-[e]s;-e) islet; (Stiel) handle; (aer) spar; (gym) parallel bar
holp(e)rig ['holp(ə)rıç] adj bumpy
holpern ['holpərn] intr jolt, bump along; (beim Lesen) stumble
Holunder [ho'lundər] m (-s;-) (bot) elder
Holz [holts] n (-es;°er) wood; lumber; timber, trees; ins H. gehen go into the woods
Holz'apfel m crab apple
Holz'arbeit f woodwork; lumbering
Holz'arbeiter m woodworker; lumberjack
holz'artig adj woody
Holz'blasinstrumente pl wood winds
Holz'brei m wood pulp
holzen ['holtsən] tr fell; deforest; (coll) spank || intr cut wood
hölzern ['höltsərn] adj wooden; (fig) clumsy
Holzfäller ['holtsfelər] m (-s;-) lumberjack, logger
Holz'faser f wood fiber; wood pulp; grain; gegen die H. against the grain
Holz'faserstoff m wood pulp
Holzhacker ['holtshakər] m (-s;-), **Holzhauer** ['holtshau·ər] m (-s;-) lumberjack; wood chopper
holzig ['holtsıç] adj woody, wooded; (Gemüse) stringy
Holz'knecht m lumberjack
Holz'kohle f charcoal
Holz'nagel m wooden peg
Holz'platz m lumber yard
holz'reich adj wooded
Holz'schnitt m woodcut; wood engraving
Holz'schuh m wooden shoe
Holz'schuppen m woodshed
Holz'wolle f excelsior
Homi·lie ['homı'li] f (-;-lien ['li·ən]) homily
homogen [homo'gen] adj homogeneous
Homosexualität [homozeksu·alı'tet] f (-;) homosexuality
homosexuell [homozeksu'el] adj homosexual || **Homosexuelle** §5 mf homosexual
Honig ['honıç] m (-s;) honey
Ho'nigkuchen m gingerbread
ho'nigsüß adj sweet as honey
Ho'nigwabe f honeycomb
Honorar [hono'rar] n (-s;-e) fee
Honoratioren [honoratsi'oren] pl dignitaries
honorieren [hono'rirən] tr give an honorarium to; pay royalties to; (Scheck) honor
Hopfen ['hopfən] m (-s;) hops

hopp [hɔp] *interj* up!; quick!; **hopp, los!** get going!

hoppla ['hɔpla] *interj* whoops!; **jetzt aber h.!** come on!; look sharp!

hops [hɔps] *adj*—**h. gehen** go to pot; **h. sein** be done for

hopsasa ['hɔpsasa] *interj* upsy-daisy

hopsen ['hɔpsən] *intr* (SEIN) hop

Hop'ser *m* (–s;–) hop

Hörapparat ['hørap[a]raɑt] *m* hearing aid

hörbar ['hørbar] *adj* audible

hörbehindert ['hørbəhɪndərt] *adj* hard of hearing

Hörbericht ['hørbərɪçt] *m* radio report; radio commentary

horchen ['hɔrçən] *intr* listen; eavesdrop

Hor'cher –**in** §6 *mf* eavesdropper

Horch'gerät *n* sound detector; (nav) hydrophone

Horch'posten *m* (mil) listening post

Horde ['hɔrdə] *f* (–;–n) horde

hören ['hørən] *tr* hear; listen to; (*Vorlesung*) attend || *intr* hear; **h. auf** (*acc*) pay attention to, obey

Hö'rer *m* (–s;–) listener; member of an audience; student; (telp) receiver

Hö'rerbrief *m* letter from a listener

Hö'rerkreis *m* listeners

Hö'rerschaft *f* (–;–en) audience; (educ) enrollment

Hör'folge *f* radio serial

Hör'gerät *n* hearing aid

hörig ['hørɪç] *adj* in bondage || **Hörige** §5 *mf* serf, thrall

Horizont [hɔrɪ'tsɔnt] *m* (–[e]s;–e) horizon

horizontal [hɔrɪtsɔn'tal] *adj* horizontal || **Horizontale** §5 *f* horizontal line

Horn [hɔrn] *n* (–[e]s;⸚er) horn; (mil) bugle; (mus) horn, French horn

Hörnchen ['hœrnçən] *n* (–s;–) crescent roll

Horn'haut *f* (anat) cornea

Hornisse [hɔr'nɪsa] *f* (–;–n) hornet

Hornist [hɔr'nɪst] *m* (–en;–en) bugler

Horn'ochse *f* (coll) dumb ox

Horoskop [hɔrɔ'skop] *n* (–[e]s;–e) horoscope

horrend [hɔ'rent] *adj* (coll) terrible

Hör'rohr *n* stethoscope

Hör'saal *m* lecture room

Hör'spiel *n* radio play

Horst [hɔrst] *m* (–[e]s;–e) (eagle's) nest

Hort [hɔrt] *m* (–[e]s;–e) hoard, treasure; (place of) refuge; protector

Hör'weite *f*—**in H.** within earshot

Hose ['hozə] *f* (–;–n), **Hosen** ['hozən] *pl* pants, trousers; (*Unterhose*) shorts; panties; **sich auf die Hosen setzen** buckle down

Ho'senboden *m* seat (of trousers)

Ho'senklappe *f*, **Ho'senlatz** *m* fly

Ho'senrolle *f* (theat) male role

Ho'senträger *pl* suspenders

Hospitant [hɔspɪ'tant] *m* (–en;–en) (educ) auditor

hospitieren [hɔspɪ'tirən] *intr* (educ) audit a course

Hospiz [hɔs'pits] *n* (–es;–e) hospice

Hostie ['hɔstjə] *f* (–;–n) host, wafer

Hotel [ho'tel] *n* (–s;–s) hotel

Hotel'boy *m* bellboy, bellhop

Hotel'diener *m* hotel porter

Hotel'fach *n*, **Hotel'gewerbe** *n* hotel business

Hub [hup] *m* (–[e]s;⸚e) (mach) stroke

hübsch [hyp∫] *adj* pretty; handsome; (coll) good-sized

Hubschrauber ['hup∫raubər] *m* (–s;–) helicopter

huckepack ['hukəpak] *adv* piggyback

hudeln ['hudəln] *intr* be sloppy

Huf [huf] *m* (–[e]s;–e) hoof

Huf'eisen *n* horseshoe

Huf'schlag *m* hoofbeat

Hüfte ['hyftə] *f* (–;–n) hip; **die Arme in die Hüften gestemmt** with arms akimbo

Hüft'gelenk *n* hip joint

Hüft'gürtel *m*, **Hüft'halter** *m* garter belt

Hügel ['hygəl] *m* (–s;–) hill; mound

hügelab' *adv* downhill

hügelauf' *adv* uphill

hügelig ['hygəlɪç] *adj* hilly

Huhn [hun] *n* (–[e]s;⸚er) fowl; hen, chicken

Hühnchen ['hynçən] *n* (–s;–) young chicken; **ein H. zu rupfen haben mit** (fig) have a bone to pick with

Hüh'nerauge *n* (pathol) corn

Hüh'nerdraht *m* chicken wire

Hüh'nerhund *m* bird dog

Huld [hult] *f* (–;) grace, favor

huldigen ['huldɪgən] *intr* (dat) pay homage to

Hul'digung *f* (–;) homage

Hul'digungseid *m* oath of allegiance

huld'reich, huld'voll *adj* gracious

Hülle ['hylə] *f* (–;–n) cover; case; wrapper; envelope; (e–s *Buches*) jacket; (fig) cloak; **in H. und Fülle** in abundance; **sterbliche H.** mortal remains

hüllen ['hylən] *tr* cover; veil; wrap

Hülse ['hylzə] *f* (–;–n) pod, hull; cartridge case, shell case

Hül'senfrucht *f* legume

human [hu'man] *adj* humane

humanistisch [huma'nɪstɪ∫] *adj* humanistic; classical

humanitär [humanɪ'ter] *adj* humanitarian

Humanität [humanɪ'tet] *f* (–;) humanity; humaneness

Humanitäts'duselei *f* sentimental humanitarianism

Humanitäts'verbrechen *n* crime against humanity

Hummel ['huməl] *f* (–;–n) bumblebee

Hummer ['humər] *m* (–s;–) lobster

Humor [hu'mor] *m* (–s;) humor

humoristisch [humo'rɪstɪ∫] *adj* humorous

humpeln ['humpəln] *intr* (SEIN) hobble

Hund [hunt] *m* (–[e]s;–e) dog

Hündchen ['hyntçən] *n* (–s;–) small dog; puppy

Hun'deangst *f*—**e–e H. haben** (coll) be scared stiff

Hun'dearbeit *f* drudgery

Hun'dehütte *f* doghouse

Hun'dekälte *f* severe cold

Hun′demarke *f* dog tag

hun′demü′de *adj* (coll) dog-tired

hundert [′hʊndərt] *invar adj & pron* hundred ‖ Hundert *n* (−s;−e) hundred; drei von H. three percent; im H. by the hundred ‖ *f* (−;−en) hundred

hun′dertfach *adj* hundredfold

Hundertjahr′feier *f* centennial

Hun′dertsatz *m* percentage

hundertste [′hʊndərtstə] §9 *adj & pron* hundredth

Hun′deschau *f* dog show

Hun′dezwinger *m* dog kennel

Hündin [′hʏndɪn] *f* (−;−nen) bitch

hündisch [′hʏndɪʃ] *adj* (*Benehmen*) servile; (*Angst*) deadly

hunds′gemein *adj* beastly

hunds′miserabel *adj* (sl) lousy

Hunds′stern *m* Dog Star

Hunds′tage *pl* dog days

Hüne [′hynə] *m* (−n;−n) giant

hü′nenhaft *adj* gigantic

Hunger [′hʊŋər] *m* (−s;) hunger; H. haben be hungry

Hun′gerkur *f* starvation diet

Hun′gerlohn *m* starvation wages

hungern [′hʊŋərn] *intr* be hungry; go without food; h. nach yearn for ‖ *impers*—es hungert mich I am hungry

Hun′gersnot *f* famine

Hun′gertod *m* death from starvation

Hun′gertuch *n*—am H. nagen go hungry; live in poverty

hungrig [′hʊŋrɪç] *adj* hungry; (*Jahre*) lean

Hunne [′hʊnə] *m* (−n;−n) (hist) Hun

Hupe [′hupə] *f* (−;−n) (aut) horn

hupen [′hupən] *intr* blow the horn

hüpfen [′hʏpfən], hupfen [′hʊpfən] *intr* (SEIN) hop, jump

Hürde [′hʏrdə] *f* (−;−n) hurdle

Hure [′hurə] *f* (−;−n) whore

huren [′hurən] *intr* whore around

hurtig [′hʊrtɪç] *adj* nimble, swift

huschen [′hʊʃən] *intr* (SEIN) scurry

hüsteln [′hystəln] *intr* clear the throat

husten [′hustən] *tr* cough up ‖ *intr* cough; h. auf (*acc*) (coll) not give a rap about

Hut [hut] *m* (−[e]s;⁓e) hat ‖ *f* (−;) protection, care; auf der Hut sein be on guard

hüten [′hytən] *tr* guard, protect; tend; das Bett h. be confined to bed; das Haus h. stay indoors; Kinder h. baby-sit ‖ *ref* (vor *dat*) be on guard (against), beware (of); ich werde mich schön h. (coll) I′ll do no such thing

Hü′ter −in §6 *mf* guardian

Hut′krempe *f* brim of a hat

hut′los *adj* hatless

Hütte [′hytə] *f* (−;−n) hut; cabin; doghouse; glassworks; (Bib) tabernacle; (metal) foundry

Hüt′tenkunde *f*, Hüt′tenwesen *n* metallurgy

Hyäne [hy′ɛnə] *f* (−;−n) hyena

Hyazinthe [hyaˈtsɪntə] *f* (−;−n) hyacinth

Hydrant [hyˈdrant] *m* (−en;−en) hydrant

Hydraulik [hyˈdraulɪk] *f* (−;) hydraulics; hydraulic system

hydraulisch [hyˈdraulɪʃ] *adj* hydraulic

hydrieren [hyˈdrirən] *tr* hydrogenate

Hygiene [hyˈgjenə] *f* (−;) hygiene

hygienisch [hyˈgjenɪʃ] *adj* hygienic

Hymne [′hymnə] *f* (−;−n) hymn; anthem

Hyperbel [hyˈpɛrbəl] *f* (−;−n) (geom) hyperbola; (rhet) hyperbole

Hypnose [hypˈnozə] *f* (−;−n) hypnosis

hypnotisch [hypˈnotɪʃ] *adj* hypnotic

Hypothese [hflpɔˈtezə] *f* (−;−n) hypothesis

Hypochonder [hypɔˈxɔndər] *m* (−s;−) hypochondriac

Hypothek [hypɔˈtek] *f* (−;−en) mortgage

Hypothe′kengläubiger *m* mortgagee

Hypothe′kenschuldner *m* mortgagor

Hypothese [hypɔˈtezə] *f* (−;−n) hypothesis

hypothetisch [hypɔˈtetɪʃ] *adj* hypothetical

Hysterektomie [hysterɛktɔˈmi] *f* (−;) hysterectomy

Hysterie [hysteˈri] *f* (−;) hysteria

hysterisch [hysˈteriʃ] *adj* hysterical

I

I, i [i] *invar n* I, i

iah [ˈiˈɑ] *interj* heehaw!

iahen [ˈiˈɑ·ən] *intr* heehaw, bray

iberisch [ɪˈberɪʃ] *adj* Iberian

ich [ɪç] §11 *pers pron* I

ichbezogen [′ɪçbətsogən] *adj* self-centered, egocentric

Ich′sucht *f* egotism

ideal [ɪdeˈɑl] *adj* ideal ‖ Ideal *n* (−s;−e) deal

idealisieren [ɪde·ɑlɪˈzirən] *tr* idealize

Idealismus [ɪde·aˈlɪsmus] *m* (−;) idealism

Idealist −in [ɪde·aˈlɪst(ɪn)] §7 *mf* idealist

idealistisch [ɪde·aˈlɪstɪʃ] *adj* idealistic

I·dee [ɪˈde] *f* (−;−deen [ˈde·ən]) idea

Iden [ˈidən] *pl* Ides

identifizieren [ɪdɛntɪfɪˈtsirən] *tr* identify ‖ *ref*—i. mit identify with

identisch [ɪˈdɛntɪʃ] *adj* identical

Identität [ɪdɛntɪˈtɛt] *f* (−;−en) identity

Ideolo·gie [ɪde·ɔlɔˈgi] *f* (−;−gien [ˈgi·ən]) ideology

Idiom [ɪˈdjom] *n* (−s;−e) idiom, dialect, language

idiomatisch [ɪdjɔˈmɑtɪç] *adj* idiomatic

Idiosynkra·sie [ɪdjɔzynkraˈzi] *f* (−; −sien [ˈzi·ən]) idiosyncrasy

Idiot [ɪˈdjot] *m* (−en;−en) idiot

Idio·tie [ɪdjə'ti] *f* (-;-tien ['ti·ən]) idiocy

Idiotin [ɪdjotɪn] *f* (-;-nen) idiot

Idol [ɪ'dol] *n* (-s;-e) idol

idyllisch [ɪ'dylɪʃ] *adj* idyllic

Igel ['igəl] *m* (-s;-) hedgehog

Ignorant [ɪgnə'rant] *m* (-en;-en) ignoramus

ignorieren [ɪgnə'rirən] *tr* ignore

ihm [im] §11 *pers pron* (dative of er and es) (to) him; (to) it

ihn [in] §11 *pers pron* (accusative of er) him

ihnen ['inən] §11 *pers pron* (dative of sie) (to) them || **Ihnen** §11 *pers pron* (dative of Sie) (to) you

ihr [ir] §2,2 *poss adj* her; their || §11 *pers pron* (dative of sie) (to) her || **Ihr** §2,2 *poss adj* your

ihrerseits ['irərzaɪts] *adv* on her (or their) part; **Ihrerseits** on your part

ihresgleichen ['irəs'glaɪçən] *pron* the likes of her (or them); her (or their) equal(s); **Ihresgleichen** the likes of you; your equal(s)

ihrethalben ['irət'halbən] *adv* var of ihretwegen

ihretwegen ['irət'vegen] *adv* because of her (or them); for her (or their) sake; **Ihretwegen** because of you, for your sake

ihretwillen ['irət'vɪlən] *adv* var of ihretwegen

ihrige ['irɪgə] §2,5 *poss pron* hers; theirs; **Ihrige** yours

Ikone [ɪ'konə] *f* (-;-n) icon

illegal [ɪle'gal] *adj* illegal

illegitim [ɪlegɪ'tim] *adj* illegitimate

illuminieren [ɪlumɪ'nirən] *tr* illuminate

Illusion [ɪlu'zjon] *f* (-;-en) illusion

illustrieren [ɪlus'trirən] *tr* illustrate

Illustrierte [ɪlus'trirtə] §5 *f* (illustrated) magazine

Iltis ['ɪltɪs] *m* (-ses;-se) polecat

im [ɪm] *contr* in dem

Image ['ɪmɪdʒ] *n* (-s;-s) (fig) image

imaginär [ɪmagɪ'nɛr] *adj* imaginary

Im·biß ['ɪmbɪs] *m* (-bisses;-bisse) snack

Im'bißhalle *f* luncheonette

Im'bißstube *f* snack bar

Imi·tator [ɪmɪ'tator] *m* (-s;-tatoren [ta'torən]) imitator; impersonator

Imker ['ɪmkər] *m* (-s;-) beekeeper

immateriell [ɪmate'rjel] *adj* immaterial, spiritual

immatrikulieren [ɪmatriku'lirən] *tr & intr* register; sich i. lassen get registered

immens [ɪ'mens] *adj* immense

immer ['ɪmər] *adv* always; **auf i. und ewig** for ever and ever; **für i.** for good; **i. langsam!** steady now!; **i. mehr** more and more; **i. wieder** again and again; **noch i.** still; **nur i. zu!** keep trying!; **was auch i.** whatever

immerdar' *adv* (Lit) forever

immerfort' *adv* all the time

im'mergrün *adj* evergreen || **Immer·grün** *n* (-s;-e) evergreen

immerhin' *adv* after all, anyhow

immerwäh'rend *adj* perpetual

immerzu' *adv* all the time, constantly

Immobilien [ɪmo'biljən] *pl* real estate

Immobi'lienmakler –in §6 *mf* real-estate broker

immun [ɪ'mun] *adj* (gegen) immune (to)

immunisieren [ɪmunɪ'zirən] *tr* immunize

Imperativ [ɪmpera'tif] *m* (-s;-e) (gram) imperative

Imperfek·tum [ɪmper'fektum] *n* (-s; -ta [ta]) (gram) imperfect

Imperialismus [ɪmperɪ·a'lɪsmus] *m* (-;) imperialism

impfen ['ɪmpfen] *tr* vaccinate; inoculate

Impfling ['ɪmpflɪŋ] *m* (-s;-e) person to be vaccinated or inoculated

Impf'schein *m* vaccination certificate

Impf'stoff *m* vaccine

Imp'fung *f* (-;-en) vaccination; inoculation

imponieren [ɪmpo'nirən] *intr* (dat) impress

Import [ɪm'port] *m* (-[e]s;-e) import

importieren [ɪmpor'tirən] *tr* import

imposant [ɪmpo'zant] *adj* imposing

imprägnieren [ɪmpreg'nirən] *tr* waterproof; creosote

Impresario [ɪmpre'zarjo] *m* (-s;-s) agent, business manager

Impres·sum [ɪm'presum] *n* (-s;-sen [sən]) (journ) masthead

imstande [ɪm'ʃtandə] *adv—*i. sein zu (*inf*) be in a position to (*inf*)

in [ɪn] *prep* (*position*) (dat) in, at; (*direction*) (acc) in, into

Inangriffnahme [ɪn'angrɪfnamə] *f* (-;) starting; putting into action

Inanspruchnahme [ɪn'anʃpruxnamə] *f* (-;) laying claim; demands; utilization

In'begriff *m* essence; embodiment

in'begriffen *adj* included

Inbrunst ['ɪnbrunst] *f* (-;) ardor

inbrünstig ['ɪnbrynstɪç] *adj* ardent

indem [ɪn'dem] *conj* while, as; by (*ger*)

Inder –in ['ɪndər(ɪn)] §6 *mf* Indian (*inhabitant of India*)

indes [ɪn'des], **indessen** [ɪn'desən] *adv* meanwhile; however || *conj* while; whereas

Indianer –in [ɪn'djanər(ɪn)] §6 *mf* Indian (*of North America*)

Indien ['ɪndjən] *n* (-s;) India

Indio ['ɪndɪ·o] *m* (-s;-s) Indian (*of Central or South America*)

indisch ['ɪndɪʃ] *adj* Indian

indiskret [ɪndɪs'kret] *adj* indiscreet

indiskutabel [ɪndɪsku'tabəl] *adj* out of the question

individuell [ɪndɪvɪdu'el] *adj* individual

Individu·um [ɪndɪ'vidu·um] *n* (-s;-en [ən]) individual; (pej) character

Indizienbeweis [ɪn'ditsjənbəvaɪs] *m* (piece of) circumstantial evidence

Indossament [ɪndɔsa'ment] *n* (-[e]s; -e) indorsement

Indossant [ɪndɔ'sant] *m* (-en;-en) indorser

indossieren [ɪndɔ'sirən] *tr* indorse

industrialisieren [ɪndustri·alɪ'zirən] *tr* industrialize

Indus·trie [ɪndʊs'tri] *f* (-;-**trien** ['tri·ən]) industry
Industrie'anlage *f* industrial plant
Industrie'betrieb *m* industrial establishment
Industrie'kapitän *m* tycoon
industriell [ɪndʊstrɪ'el] *adj* industrial || **Industrielle** §5 *m* industrialist
ineinan'der *adv* into one another; **i. übergehen** merge
ineinan'derfügen *tr* dovetail
ineinan'dergreifen §88 *intr* mesh
ineinan'derpassen *intr* dovetail
infam [ɪn'fɑm] *adv* (coll) frightfully
Infante·rie [ɪnfantə'ri] *f* (-;-**rien** ['ri·ən]) infantry
Infanterist [ɪnfantə'rɪst] *m* (-en;-en) infantryman
infantil [ɪnfan'til] *adj* infantile
Infektion [ɪnfɛk'tsjon] *f* (-;-en) infection
Infini·tiv [ɪnfɪnɪ'tif] *m* (-s;-tive ['tivə]) infinitive
infizieren [ɪnfɪ'tsirən] *tr* infect
infolge [ɪn'fɔlgə] *prep* (genit) in consequence of, owing to; according to
infolgedes'sen *adv* consequently
Information [ɪnfɔrma'tsjon] *f* (-;-en) (piece of) information
informieren [ɪnfɔr'mirən] *tr* inform
infrarot [ɪnfra'rot] *adj* infrared || **Infrarot** *n* (-s;-) infrared
Ingenieur [ɪnʒen'jør] *m* (-s;-e) engineer
Ingenieur'bau *m* (-[e]s;) civil engineering
Ingenieur'wesen *n* engineering
ingeniös [ɪnge'njøs] *adj* ingenious
Ingrimm ['ɪngrɪm] *m* inner rage
Ingwer ['ɪŋvər] *m* (-s;) ginger
Ing'werplätzchen *n* gingersnap
Inhaber -**in** ['ɪnhabər(ɪn)] §6 *mf* owner; bearer; occupant; holder
inhaftieren [ɪnhaf'tirən] *tr* arrest
Inhalierapparat [ɪnha'lirapɑrɑt] *m* (med) inhalator
inhalieren [ɪnha'lirən] *tr* & *intr* inhale
Inhalt ['ɪnhalt] *m* (-[e]s;-e) contents; subject matter; (geom) area; volume
In'haltsangabe *f* summary; list of contents
in'haltsarm, **in'haltsleer** *adj* empty
in'haltsreich *adj* substantive; (*Leben*) full
in'haltsschwer *adj* pregnant with meaning; momentous
In'haltsverzeichnis *n* table of contents
in'haltsvoll *adj* full of meaning
inhibieren [ɪnhɪ'birən] *tr* inhibit
Initiative [ɪnɪtsja'tivə] *f* (-;-en) initiative
Injektion [ɪnjɛk'tsjon] *f* (-;-en) injection
Injektions'nadel *f* hypodermic needle
injizieren [ɪnjɪ'tsirən] *tr* inject
Inkasso [ɪn'kaso] *n* (-s;-s) bill collecting
Inkas'sobeamte *m* bill collector
inklusive [ɪnklu'zivə] *adj* inclusive || *prep* (genit) including
inkonsequent ['ɪnkɔnzekvent] *adj* inconsistent; illogical
Inkraft'treten *n* going into effect

In'land *n* (-[e]s;) home country; interior
Inländer -**in** ['ɪnlendər(ɪn)] §6 *mf* native
inländisch ['ɪnlendɪʃ] *adj* home, domestic; inland
In'landspost *f* domestic mail
Inlett ['ɪnlet] *n* (-[e]s;-e) bedtick
in'liegend *adj* enclosed
inmit'ten *prep* (genit) in the middle of, among
innehaben ['ɪnəhabən] §89 *tr* (*Amt*) hold; (*Wohnung*) occupy, own
innehalten ['ɪnəhaltən] §90 *intr* stop
innen ['ɪnən] *adv* inside; indoors; **nach i.** inwards; **tief i.** deep down
Innen- *comb.fm.* inner, internal; inside, interior; home, domestic
In'nenarchitekt -**in** §7 *mf* interior decorator
In'nenaufnahme *f* (phot) indoor shot
In'nenhof *m* quadrangle
In'nenleben *n* inner life
In'nenminister *m* Secretary of the Interior; Secretary of State for Home Affairs (Brit)
In'nenpolitik *f* domestic policy
In'nenraum *m* interior (*of building*)
In'nenstadt *f* center of town, inner city
inner- ['ɪnər] *comb.fm.* internal; intra-
innere ['ɪnərə] §9 *adj* inner, internal; inside; inward; domestic || **Innere** §5 *n* inside, interior
in'nerhalb *adv* on the inside; **i. von** within || *prep* (genit) inside, within
in'nerlich *adj* inner, inward || *adv* inwardly; mentally, emotionally
In'nerlichkeit *f* (-;-en) introspection; inner quality
innerste ['ɪnərstə] §9 *adj* innermost
innesein ['ɪnəzaɪn] §139 *intr* (SEIN) (genit) be aware of
innewerden ['ɪnəverdən] §159 *intr* (SEIN) (genit) become aware of
innig ['ɪnɪç] *adj* close; deep, heartfelt || *adv* deeply
In'nigkeit *f* (-;) intimacy; deep feeling; tender affection
Innung ['ɪnʊŋ] *f* (-;-en) guild
inoffiziell ['ɪnɔfɪtsjel] *adj* unofficial
ins *contr* in das
Insasse ['ɪnzasə] *m* (-n;-n), **Insassin** ['ɪnsasɪn] *f* (-;-nen) occupant; (*e-s Gefängnisses*) inmate; (*e-s Autos*) passenger
insbesondere [ɪnsbə'zɔndərə] *adv* in particular, especially
In'schrift *f* inscription
Insekt [ɪn'zekt] *n* (-[e]s;-en) insect
Insek'tenbekämpfungsmittel *n* insecticide
Insek'tenkunde *f* entomology
Insek'tenstich *m* insect bite
Insektizid [ɪnzekti'tsit] *n* (-[e]s;-e) insecticide
Insel ['ɪnzəl] *f* (-;-n) island
Inserat [ɪnzə'rɑt] *n* (-es;-e) classified advertisement, ad
inserieren [ɪnzə'rirən] *tr* insert || *intr* (in *dat*) advertise (in)
insgeheim [ɪnsgə'haɪm] *adv* secretly
insgemein [ɪnsgə'maɪn] *adv* as a whole; in general, generally

insgesamt [ɪnsgə'zamt] *adv* in a body, as a unit; in all, altogether

inso'fern *adv* to this extent ‖ **insofern'** *conj* in so far as

insoweit' *adv* & *conj* var of insofern

Inspek•tor [ɪn'spɛktɔr] *m* (-s;-toren ['tɔrən]) inspector

inspirieren [ɪnspɪ'rirən] *tr* inspire

inspizieren [ɪnspɪ'tsirən] *tr* inspect

Installation [ɪnstala'tsjon] *f* (-;-en) installation

installieren [ɪnsta'lirən] *tr* install

instand [ɪn'/tant] *adv*—**i. halten** keep in good condition; **i. setzen** repair

Instand'haltung *f* upkeep, maintenance

inständig [ɪn'/tɛndɪç] *adj* insistent

Instand'setzung *f* repair, renovation

Instanz [ɪn'stants] *f* (-;-en) (adm) authority; **e-e höhere I. anrufen** appeal to a higher court; **Gericht der ersten I.** court of primary jurisdiction; **Gericht der zweiten I.** court of appeal; **höchste I.** court of final appeal

Institut [ɪnstɪ'tut] *n* (-[e]s;-e) institute

instruieren [ɪnstru'irən] *tr* instruct

Instruktion [ɪnstruk'tsjon] *f* (-;-en) instruction

Instrument [ɪnstru'mɛnt] *n* (-[e]s;-e) instrument

Instrumentalist –in [ɪnstrumenta'lɪst (ɪn)] §7 *mf* instrumentalist

Insulaner –in [ɪnzu'lanər(ɪn)] §6 *mf* islander

insular [ɪnzu'lar] *adj* insular

Insulin [ɪnzu'lin] *n* (-s;) insulin

inszenieren [ɪnstse'nirən] *tr* stage

Intellekt [ɪntɛ'lɛkt] *m* (-[e]s) intellect

intellektuell [ɪntɛlɛktu'ɛl] *adj* intellectual ‖ **Intellektuelle** §5 *mf* intellectual

intelligent [ɪntɛlɪ'gɛnt] *adj* intelligent

Intelligenzler [ɪntɛlɪ'gɛntslər] *m* (-s;-) (pej) egghead

Intendant [ɪntɛn'dant] *m* (-en;-en) (theat) director

intensiv [ɪntɛn'zif] *adj* intense; intensive

–intensiv *comb.fm.*, e.g., **lohnintensive Güter** goods of which wages constitute a high proportion of the cost

interessant [ɪntɛrɛ'sant] *adj* interesting

Interesse [ɪntɛ'rɛsə] *n* (-s;-n) (an *dat*, **für**) interest (in)

interes'selos *adj* uninterested

Interes'sengemeinschaft *f* community of interest; (com) syndicate

Interessent –in [ɪntɛrɛ'sɛnt(ɪn)] §7 *mf* interested party

interessieren [ɪntɛrɛ'sirən] *tr* (für) interest (in) ‖ **ref—sich i. für** be interested in

interimistisch [ɪntɛrɪ'mɪstɪʃ] *adj* provisional

intern [ɪn'tɛrn] *adj* internal

Internat [ɪntɛr'nat] *n* (-[e]s;-e) boarding school

international [ɪntɛrnatsjo'nal] *adj* international

Internat(s)'schüler –in §6 *mf*, **Interne** [ɪn'tɛrnə] §5 *mf* boarding student

internieren [ɪntɛr'nirən] *tr* intern

Internist –in [ɪntɛr'nɪst(ɪn)] §7 *mf* (med) internist

Interpret [ɪntɛr'pret] *m* (-en;-en) interpreter; exponent

interpunktieren [ɪntɛrpuŋk'tirən] *tr* punctuate

Interpunktion [ɪntɛrpuŋk'tsjon] *f* (-; -en) punctuation

Interpunktions'zeichen *n* punctuation mark

Intervall [ɪntɛr'val] *n* (-s;-e) interval

intervenieren [ɪntɛrve'nirən] *intr* intervene

Interview ['ɪntɛrvju] *n* (-s;-s) interview

interviewen [ɪntɛr'vju·ən] *tr* interview

intim [ɪn'tim] *adj* intimate

Intimität [ɪntɪmɪ'tet] *f* (-;-en) intimacy

intolerant [ɪntɔle'rant] *adj* intolerant

intonieren [ɪntɔ'nirən] *tr* intone

intransitiv ['ɪntransitif] *adj* intransitive

intravenös [ɪntrave'nøs] *adj* intravenous

intrigant [ɪntri'gant] *adj* intriguing, scheming ‖ **Intragant** –in §7 *mf* intriguer, schemer

Intrige [ɪn'trigə] *f* (-;-n) intrigue

introspektiv [ɪntrɔspɛk'tif] *adj* introspective

Introvertierte [ɪntrɔvɛr'tirtə] §5 *mf* introvert

invalide [ɪnva'lidə] *adj* disabled ‖ **Invalide** §5 *mf* invalid

Invalidität [ɪnvalɪdɪ'tet] *f* (-;) disability

Invasion [ɪnva'zjon] *f* (-;-en) invasion

Inventar [ɪnvɛn'tar] *n* (-s;-e) inventory

Inventur [ɪnvɛn'tur] *f* (-;-en) stock taking; **I. machen** take stock

inwärts ['ɪnvɛrts] *adv* inwards

inwendig ['ɪnvɛndɪç] *adj* inward, inner

inwiefern' *adv* how far; in what way

inwieweit' *adv* var of inwiefern

In'zucht *f* inbreeding

inzwi'schen *adv* meanwhile

Ion [ɪ'ɔn] *n* (-s;-en) (phys) ion

ionisieren [ɪ·ɔnɪ'zirən] *tr* ionize

Irak [ɪ'rak] *m* (-s;) Iraq

Iraker –in [ɪ'rakər(ɪn)] §6 *mf* Iraqi

irakisch [ɪ'rakɪʃ] *adj* Iraqi

Iran [ɪ'ran] *n* (-s;) Iran

Iraner –in [ɪ'ranər(ɪn)] §6 *mf* Iranian

iranisch [ɪ'ranɪʃ] *adj* Iranian

irden ['ɪrdən] *adj* earthen

irdisch ['ɪrdɪʃ] *adj* earthly, worldly ‖ **Irdische** §5 *n* earthly nature

Ire ['ɪrə] *m* (-n;-n) Irishman; **die Iren** the Irish

irgend ['ɪrgənt] *adv*—**i. etwas** something, anything; **i. jemand** someone, anyone; **nur i.** possibly

ir'gendein *adj* some, any ‖ **ingendeiner** *indef pron* someone, anyone

ir'gendeinmal *adv* at some time or other

ir'gendwann *adv* at some time or other

ir'gendwelcher *adj* any; any kind of

ir'gendwer *indef pron* someone

ir'gendwie *adv* somehow or other

ir'gendwo *adv* somewhere or other; anywhere

ir'gendwoher adv from somewhere or other

ir'gendwohin adv somewhere or other

Irin ['ɪrɪn] f (–;-nen) Irish woman

Iris ['ɪrɪs] f (–;–) (anat, bot) iris

irisch ['ɪrɪʃ] adj Irish

Irland ['ɪrlant] n (–s;) Ireland

Iro·nie [ɪro'ni] f (–;-nien ['ni·ən]) irony

ironisch [ɪ'ronɪʃ] adj ironic(al)

irre ['ɪrə] adj stray; confused; mad; **i. werden** go astray; get confused; **i. werden an** (dat) lose faith in ‖ **Irre** §5 mf lunatic ‖ f maze; wrong track; **in die I. führen** put on the wrong track; **in die I. gehen** go astray

ir'refahren §71 intr (SEIN) lose one's way, go wrong

ir'reführen tr mislead

ir'regehen §82 intr (SEIN) lose one's way; (fig) go wrong

ir'remachen tr confuse; **j-n i. an** (dat) make s.o. lose faith in

irren ['ɪrən] intr go astray; err ‖ ref (in dat) be mistaken (about); **sich in der Straße i.** take the wrong road; **sich in der Zeit i.** misjudge the time

Ir'renanstalt f, **Ir'renhaus** n insane asylum

Ir'renhäusler ['ɪrənhɔɪzlər] m (–s;–) inmate of an insane asylum

ir'rereden intr rave; talk deliriously

Irrfahrt ['ɪrfart] f odyssey

Irrgang ['ɪrgaŋ] m winding path

Irrgarten ['ɪrgartən] m labyrinth

Irrglaube ['ɪrglaubə] m heresy

irrgläubig ['ɪrglɔɪbɪç] adj heretical

irrig ['ɪrɪç] adj mistaken

Irri·gator [ɪrɪ'gator] m (–s;-gatoren [ga·torən]) douche

irritieren [ɪrɪ'tirən] tr irritate; (coll) confuse

Irrlehre ['ɪrlerə] f false doctrine

Irrlicht ['ɪrlɪçt] n jack-o'-lantern

Irrsinn ['ɪrzɪn] m insanity

irr'sinnig adj insane

Irrtum ['ɪrtum] n (–s;-er) error

irrtümlich ['ɪrtymlɪç] adj erroneous

Irrweg ['ɪrvek] m wrong track

Irrwisch ['ɪrvɪʃ] m (–es;-e) jack-o'-lantern; (coll) fireball

Islam [ɪs'lam] m (–s;) Islam

Island ['islant] n (–s;) Iceland

Iso·lator [izo'lator] m (–s;-latoren [la'torən]) (elec) insulator

Isolier– [ɪzolir] comb.fm. isolation; insulating; insulated

Isolier'band n (–[e]s;-er) friction tape

isolieren [ɪzo'lirən] tr (Kranke) isolate; (abdichten) insulate

Isolier'haft f solitary confinement

Insolier'station f isolation ward

Isolie'rung f (–;-en) isolation; (elec) insulation

Isotop [izo'top] n (–[e]s;-e) isotope

Israel ['ɪsra·el] n (– & –s;) Israel

Israeli [ɪsra'eli] m (–s;–s) Israeli

israelisch [ɪsra'elɪʃ] adj Israeli

Israelit –in [ɪsra·e'lit(ɪn)] §7 mf Israelite

israelitisch [ɪsra·e'litɪʃ] adj Israelite

Ist– [ɪst] comb.fm. actual

Ist-'Bestand m actual stock; (fin) actual balance; (mil) actual stockpile

Ist-'Stand m, **Ist-'Stärke** f (mil) effective strength

Italien [ɪ'taljən] n (–s;) Italy

Italiener –in [ɪtal'jenər(ɪn)] §6 mf Italian

italienisch [ɪtal'jenɪʃ] adj Italian

J

J, j [jɔt] invar n J, j

ja [ja] adv yes; indeed, certainly; of course ‖ **Ja** n (–s;–s) yes

Jacht [jaxt] f (–;-en) yacht

Jacke ['jakə] f (–;-n) jacket, coat

Jackenkleid [Jak'kenkleid] n lady's two-piece suit

Jackett [ʒa'kɛt] n (–s;–s) jacket

Jagd [jakt] f (–;-en) hunt(ing); **auf die J. gehen** go hunting; **J. machen auf** (acc) hunt for

Jagd'abschirmung f (aer) fighter screen

Jagd'aufseher m gamewarden

jagdbar ['jaktbar] adj in season, fair (game)

Jagd'bomber m (aer) fighter-bomber

Jagd'flieger m fighter pilot

Jagd'flugzeug n (aer) fighter plane

Jagd'gehege n game preserve

Jagd'geleit n (aer) fighter escort

Jagd'hund m hunting dog, hound

Jagd'rennen n steeplechase

Jagd'revier n hunting ground

Jagd'schein m hunting license

Jagd'schutz m (aer) fighter protection

Jagd'verband m (aer) fighter unit

Jagd'wild n game; game bird

jagen ['jagən] tr hunt; pursue; chase; (fig) follow close on; **in die Luft j.** blow up ‖ intr go hunting; **j. nach** pursue ‖ intr (SEIN) rush

Jäger ['jegər] m (–s;–) hunter; (aer) fighter plane; (mil) rifleman

Jägerei [jega'rai] f (–;) hunting

Jä'gerlatein n (coll) fish story

Jaguar ['jagu·ar] m (–s;–s) jaguar

jäh [je] adj sudden; steep ‖ **Jähe** f (–;) suddenness; steepness

jählings ['jelɪŋs] adv suddenly; steeply

Jahr [jar] n (–[e]s;-e) year

jahraus' adv—**j. jahrein** year in year out, year after year

Jahr'buch n almanac; yearbook; annual

jahrelang ['jarəlaŋ] adj long-standing ‖ adv for years

jähren ['jerən] ref be a year ago

Jahres– [jarəs] comb.fm. annual, yearly, of the year

Jah′resfeier *f* anniversary
Jah′resfrist *f* period of a year
Jah′resrente *f* annuity
Jah′restag *m* anniversary
Jah′reszahl *f* date, year
Jah′reszeit *f* season
jah′reszeitlich *adj* seasonal
Jahr′gang *m* age group; class, year; crop; vintage; **er gehört zu meinem J.** he was born in the same year as I
Jahrhun′dert *n* century
–jährig [jɛrɪç] *comb.fm.* –year-old
jährlich [′jɛrlɪç] *adj* yearly, annual
Jahr′markt *m* fair
Jahr′marktplatz *m* fairground
Jahrtau′send *n* millennium
Jahrzehnt [jɑr′tsɛnt] *n* (–[e]s;–e) decade
Jäh′zorn *m* fit of anger; hot temper
jäh′zornig *adj* quick-tempered
Jalou·sie [ʒalu′zi] *f* (–;–sien [′zi·ən]) louvre; Venetian blind
Jammer [′jamər] *m* (–s;) misery; wailing; **es ist ein J.,** **daß** it's a pity that
Jam′merlappen *m* (pej) jellyfish
jämmerlich [′jɛmərlɪç] *adj* miserable, pitiful; (*Anblick*) sorry
jammern [′jamərn] *tr* move to pity ‖ *intr* (**über** *acc,* **um**) moan (about); **j. nach** (or **um**) whimper for
jam′merschade *adj* deplorable
Jänner [′jɛnər] *m* (–s & –;–) (Aust) January
Januar [′janu·ɑr] *m* (–s & –;–e) January
Japan [′japan] *n* (–s;) Japan
Japaner –in [ja′panər(ɪn)] §6 *mf* Japanese
japanisch [ja′panɪʃ] *adj* Japanese
jappen [′japən] *intr* pant, gasp
Jasager [′jazagər] *m* (–s;–) yes-man
jäten [′jɛtən] *tr* weed; **das Unkraut j.** pull out weeds ‖ *intr* weed
Jauche [′jauxə] *f* (–;–n) liquid manure; (sl) slop
jauchen [′jauxən] *tr* manure
Jau′chegrube *f* cesspool
jauchzen [′jauxtsən] *intr* rejoice; **vor Freude j.** shout for joy ‖ **Jauchzen** *n* (–s;) jubilation
Jauch′zer *m* (–s;–) shout of joy
jawohl [ja′vol] *interj* yes, indeed!
Ja′wort *n* (–[e]s;) consent
Jazz [dʒɛz], [jats] *m* (–;) jazz
je [je] *adv* ever; **denn je** than ever; **je länger, je** (or **desto**) **besser** the longer the better; **je nach** according to, depending on; **je nachdem, ob** according to whether; **je Pfund** per pound; **je zwei** two each; two by two, in twos; **seit je** always
Jeans [dʒinz] *pl* jeans
jedenfalls [′jedənfals] *adv* at any rate; **ich j.** I for one
jeder [′jedər] §3 *indef adj* each, every ‖ *indef pron* each one, everyone
jederlei [′jedər ′lai] *invar adj* every kind of
je′dermann *indef pron* everyone, everybody
je′derzeit *adv* at all times, at any time
je′desmal *adv* each time, every time
jedoch [je′dɔx] *adv* however

jeglicher [′jeklɪçər] §3 *indef adj* each, every ‖ *indef pron* each one, everyone
je′her *adv*—**von j.** since time immemorial
Jelän′gerjelie′ber *m & n* honeysuckle
jemals [′jemals] *adv* ever
jemand [′jemant] *indef pron* someone, somebody; anyone, anybody
jener [′jenər] §3 *dem adj* that ‖ *dem pron* that one
jenseitig [′jenzaitɪç] *adj* opposite, beyond, otherworldly
jenseits [′jenzaits] *prep* (*genit*) on the other side of; beyond ‖ **Jenseits** *n* (–;) beyond
jetzig [′jetsɪç] *adj* present, current
jetzt [jetst] *adv* now
jeweilig [′jevailiç] *adj* at that time
jeweils [′jevails] *adv* at that time
jiddisch [′jidɪʃ] *adj* Yiddish
Joch [jɔx] *n* (–[e]s;–e) yoke; yoke of oxen; (*e–r Brücke*) span; (*e–s Berges*) saddleback
Joch′bein *n* cheekbone
Joch′brücke *f* pile bridge
Jockei [′dʒɔki] *m* (–s;–s) jockey
Jod [jot] *n* (–s;) iodine
jodeln [′jodəln] *intr* yodel
Jodler –in [′jodlər(ɪn)] §6 *mf* yodeler ‖ *m* yodel
Jodtinktur [′jottɪŋktur] *f* (–;) (pharm) iodine
Johannisbeere [jo′hanısberə] *f* currant
johlen [′jolən] *intr* yell, boo
jonglieren [ʒɔŋ ′(g)lirən] *tr & intr* juggle
Journalist –in [ʒurna′lɪst(ɪn)] §7 *mf* journalist
jovial [jo′vjal] *adj* jovial
Jubel [′jubəl] *m* (–s;) jubilation
Ju′belfeier *f,* **Ju′belfest** *n* jubilee
Ju′beljahr *n* jubilee year
jubeln [′jubəln] *intr* rejoice; shout for joy
Jubilä·um [jubɪ′le·um] *n* (–s;–en [ən]) jubilee
juche [jux′he] *interj* hurray!
juchei [jux′hai] *interj* hurray!
juchzen [′juxtsən] *intr* shout for joy
jucken [′jukən] *tr* itch; scratch ‖ *ref* scratch ‖ *intr* itch ‖ *impers*—**es juckt mich** I feel itchy; **es juckt mir** (or **mich**) **in den Fingern zu** (*inf*) **I** am itching to (*inf*); **es juckt sie in den Beinen** she is itching to dance
Jude [′judə] *m* (–n;–n) Jew
Ju′denschaft *f* (–;) Jewry
Ju′denstern *m* star of David
Judentum [′judəntum] *n* (–s;) Judaism; **das J.** the Jews
Jüdin [′jydɪn] *f* (–;–nen) Jewish woman
jüdisch [′jydɪʃ] *adj* Jewish
Jugend [′jugənt] *f* (–;) youth
Ju′gendalter *n* youth; adolescence
Ju′gendgericht *n* juvenile court
Ju′gendherberge *f* youth hostel
Ju′gendkriminalität *f* juvenile delinquency
jugendlich [′jugəntlɪç] *adj* youthful ‖ **Jugendliche** §5 *mf* youth, teenager
Ju′gendliebe *f* puppy love
Ju′gendstrich *m* youthful prank

Jugoslawien [jugo'slavjən] *n* (-s;) Yugoslavia

jugoslawisch [jugo'slavɪʃ] *adj* Yugoslav

Juli ['juli] *m* (-[s];-s) July

jung [juŋ] *adj* (**jünger** ['jyŋər]; **jüngste** ['jyŋstə] §9) young; (*Erbsen*) green; (*Wein*) new || **Junge** §5 *m* boy || *n* newly born; young

jungen ['juŋən] *intr* produce young

jun'genhaft *adj* boyish

Jünger ['jyŋər] *m* (-s;-) disciple

Jungfer ['juŋfər] *f* (-;-n) maiden; virgin

jüngferlich ['jyŋfərlɪç] *adj* maidenly

Jung'fernfahrt *f* maiden voyage

Jung'fernhäutchen *n* hymen

Jung'fernkranz *m* bridal wreath

Jung'fernschaft *f* virginity

Jung'frau *f* virgin

jungfräulich ['juŋfrɔɪlɪç] *adj* maidenly; virgin

Jung'fräulichkeit *f* virginity

Jung'geselle *m* bachelor

Jung'gesellenstand *m* bachelorhood

Jung'gesellin *f* single girl

Jüngling ['jyŋlɪŋ] *m* (-s;-e) young man

jüngst [jyŋst] *adv* recently

jüng'ste *adj* see **jung**

Juni ['juni] *m* (-[s];-s) June

Junker ['juŋkər] *m* (-s;-) young nobleman; nobleman

Jura ['jura] *pl*—J. **studieren** study law

Jurist –in [ju'rɪst(ɪn)] §7 *mf* lawyer; (educ) law student

Juristerei [jurɪstə'raɪ] *f* (-;) jurisprudence

juristisch [ju'rɪstɪʃ] *adj* legal, law; **juristische Person** legal entity, corporation

just [just] *adv* just, precisely

justieren [jus'tirən] *tr* adjust

Justiz [jus'tits] *f* (-;) justice; administration of justice

Justiz'irrtum *m* miscarriage of justice

Justiz'minister *m* minister of justice; attorney general; Lord Chancellor (Brit)

Jutesack ['jutəzak] *m* gunnysack

Juwel [ju'vel] *n* (-s;-en) jewel, gem; **Juwelen** jewelry

Juwe'lenkästchen *n* jewel box

Juwelier –in [juve'lir(ɪn)] §6 *mf* jeweler

Juwelier'waren *pl* jewelry

Jux [juks] *m* (-es;-e) spoof, joke; **aus Jux** as a joke; **sich** [*dat*] **e–n Jux mit j–m machen** play a joke on s.o.

K

K, k [ka] *invar n* K, k

Kabale [ka'balə] *f* (-;-n) intrigue

Kabarett [kaba'ret] *n* (-[e]s;-e) cabaret; floor show; (*drehbare Platte*) lazy Suzan

Kabel ['kabəl] *n* (-s;-) cable

Ka'belgramm *n* (-es;-e) cablegram

Kabeljau ['kabəljau] *m* (-s;-e) codfish

kabeln ['kabəln] *tr* cable

Kabine [ka'binə] *f* (-;-n) cabin; booth; (aer) cockpit

Kabinett [kabɪ'net] *n* (-s;-e) closet; small room; (& pol) cabinet

Kabriolett [kabrɪ·o'let] *n* (-[e]s;-e) (aut) convertible

Kachel ['kaxəl] *f* (-;-n) glazed tile

kacken ['kakən] *intr* (sl) defecate

Kadaver [ka'davər] *m* (-s;-) cadaver

Kada'vergehorsam *m* blind obedience

Kadenz [ka'dents] *f* (-;-en) cadence

Kader ['kadər] *m* (-s;-) cadre

Kadett [ka'det] *m* (-en;-en) cadet

Käfer ['kefər] *m* (-s;-) beetle

Kaffee ['kafe] *m* (-s;-s) coffee

Kaf'feebohne *f* coffee bean

Kaf'feeklatsch *m* coffee klatsch

Kaf'feemaschine *f* coffee maker

Kaf'feepflanzung *f*, **Kaf'feeplantage** *f* coffee plantation

Kaf'feesatz *m* coffee grounds

Kaf'feetante *f* coffee fiend

Käfig ['kefɪç] *m* (-[e]s;-e) cage

kahl [kal] *adj* bald; (*Baum*) bare; (*Landschaft*) bleak, barren

kahl'köpfig *adj* bald-headed

Kahm [kam] *m* (-[e]s;-e) mold; scum

kahmig ['kamɪç] *adj* moldy; scummy

Kahn [kan] *m* (-[e]s;-e) boat; barge

Kai [kaɪ], [ke] *m* (-s;-s) quay, wharf

Kaiser ['kaɪzər] *m* (-s;-) emperor

Kaiserin ['kaɪzərɪn] *f* (-;-nen) empress

kai'serlich *adj* imperial

Kai'serreich *n*, **Kaisertum** ['kaɪzərtum] *n* (-[e]s;ꞏer) empire

Kai'serschnitt *m* Caesarian operation

Kai'serzeit *f* (hist) Empire

Kajüte [ka'jytə] *f* (-;-n) (naut) cabin

Kaju'tenjunge *m* cabin boy

Kaju'tentreppe *f* (naut) companionway

Kakao [ka'ka·o] *m* (-s;-) cocoa; **j–n durch den K. ziehen** pull s.o.'s leg

Kaktee [kak'te·ə] *f* (-;-n), **Kaktus** ['kaktus] *m* (-;-se) cactus

Kalauer ['kalau·ər] *m* (-s;-) pun

Kalb [kalp] *n* (-[e]s;ꞏer) calf

Kalbe ['kalbə] *f* (-;-n) heifer

kalbern ['kalbərn] *intr* be silly

Kalb'fell *n* calfskin

Kalb'fleisch *n* veal

Kalbs'braten *m* roast veal

Kalbs'kotelett *n* veal cutlet

Kalbs'schnitzel *n* veal cutlet

Kaleidoskop [kalaɪdo'skop] *n* (-s;-e) kaleidoscope

Kalender [ka'lendər] *m* (-s;-) calendar

Kali ['kali] *n* (-s;) potash

Kaliber [ka'libər] *m* (-s;-) caliber

kalibrieren [kalɪ'brirən] *tr* calibrate; gauge

Kaliko ['kaliko] *m* (-s;-s) calico

Kalium ['kaljum] *n* (-s;) potassium

Kalk [kalk] *m* (-[e]s;-e) lime; calcium
kalken ['kalkən] *tr* whitewash; lime
kalkig ['kalkɪç] *adj* limy
Kalk'ofen *m* limekiln
Kalk'stein *m* limestone
Kalk'steinbruch *m* limestone quarry
Kalkül [kal'kyl] *m & n* (-s;-e) calculation; (math) calculus
kalkulieren [kalku'lirən] *tr* calculate
Kal·mar ['kalmar] *m* (-s;-mare ['marə]) squid
Kalo·rie [kalo'ri] *f* (-;-rien ['ri·ən]) calorie
Kalotte [ka'lɔtə] *f* (-;-n) skullcap
kalt [kalt] *adj* (kälter ['keltər); kälteste ['keltəstə] §9) cold
kaltblütig ['kaltblytɪç] *adj* cold-blooded
Kälte ['keltə] *f* (-;) cold, coldness
käl'tebeständig *adj* cold-resistant
Käl'tegrad *m* degree below freezing
kälten ['keltən] *tr* chill
Käl'tewelle *f* (meteor) cold wave
Kalt'front *m* cold front
kalt'herzig *adj* cold-hearted
kalt'machen *tr* (sl) bump off
kaltschnäuzig ['kalt/nɔɪtsɪç] *adj* (coll) callous; (coll) cool, unflappable
kalt'stellen *tr* render harmless
kam [kam] *pret of* kommen
Kambodscha [kam'bɔtʒa] *n* (-s;) Cambodia
kambodschanisch [kambə'dʒanɪʃ] *adj* Cambodian
Kamel [ka'mel] *n* (-[e]s;-e) camel
Kamel'garn *n* mohair
Kamera ['kamera] *f* (-;-s) camera
Kamerad [kamə'rat] *m* (-en;-en), Kameradin [kamə'radɪn] *f* (-;-nen) comrade
Kamerad'schaft ((-;-en) comradeship
Kamin [ka'min] *m* (-s;-e) chimney; fireplace
Kamin'platte *f* hearthstone
Kamin'sims *m* mantelpiece
Kamm [kam] *m* (-[e]s;ːːe) comb; (e-s Gebirges) ridge; (e-r Welle) crest
kämmen ['kemən] *tr* comb; (Wolle) card
Kammer ['kamər] *f* (-;-n) chamber; (adm) board; (anat) ventricle
Kam'merdiener *m* valet
Kämmerer ['kemərər] *m* (-s;-) chamberlain; (Schatzmeister) treasurer
Kam'mermusik *f* chamber music
Kamm'garn *n* (tex) worsted
Kamm'rad *n* cogwheel
Kampagne [kam'panjə] *f* (-;-n) campaign
Kämpe ['kempə] *m* (-n;-n) warrior
Kampf [kampf] *m* (-[e]s;ːːe) fight
Kampf'bahn *f* (sport) stadium, arena
kämpfen ['kempfən] *tr & intr* fight
Kampfer ['kampfər] *m* (-s;) camphor
Kämpfer -in ['kempfər(ɪn)] §6 *mf* fighter
kämpferisch ['kempfərɪʃ] *adj* fighting
kampf'erprobt *adj* battle-tested
kampf'fähig *adj* fit to fight; (mil) fit for active service
Kampf'hahn *m* gamecock; (fig) scrapper
Kampf'handlung *f* (mil) action

Kampf'müdigkeit *f* combat fatigue
Kampf'parole *f* (pol) campaign slogan
Kampf'platz *m* battleground
Kampf'raum *m* battle zone
Kampf'richter *m* referee, umpire
Kampf'schwimmer *m* (nav) frogman
Kampf'spiel *n* (sport) competition
Kampf'staffel *f* tactical squadron
kampf'unfähig *adj* disabled; k. machen put out of action
Kampf'veranstalter *m* (sport) promotor
Kampf'verband *m* combat unit
Kampf'wert *m* fighting efficiency
Kampf'ziel *n* (mil) objective
kampieren [kam'pirən] *intr* camp
Kanada ['kanada] *n* (-s;) Canada
Kanadier -in [ka'nadjər(ɪn)] §6 *mf* Canadian ‖ *m* canoe
kanadisch [ka'nadɪʃ] *adj* Canadian
Kanaille [ka'naljə] *f* (-;-n) bum; (Pöbel) riffraff
Kanal [ka'nal] *m* (-s;ːːe) canal; (für Abwasser) drain, sewer; (agr) irrigation ditch; (anat, elec) duct; (geol, telv) channel
Kanalisation [kanalıza'tsjon] *f* (-;) drainage; sewerage system
Kanalräumer [ka'nalrɔɪmər] *m* (-s;-) sewer worker
Kanal'wähler *m* (telv) channel selector
Kanapee ['kanape] *n* (-s;-s) sofa
Kanarienvogel [ka'narjənfogəl] *m* canary
Kandare [kan'darə] *f* (-;-n) bit, curb; j-n an die K. nehmen take s.o. in hand
Kanda'renkette *f* curb chain
Kandelaber [kande'labər] *m* (-s;-) candelabrum
Kandidat -in [kandɪ'dat(ɪn)] §7 *mf* candidate
Kandidatur [kandıda'tur] *f* (-;-en) candidacy
kandideln [kan'didəln] *ref* get drunk
kandidieren [kandɪ'dirən] *intr* be a candidate, run for office
Kandis ['kandɪs] *m* (-s;) rock candy
Kaneel [ka'nel] *m* (-s;-e) cinnamon
Känguruh ['kɛŋguru] *n* (-s;-s) kangaroo
Kaninchen [ka'ninçən] *n* (-s;-) rabbit
Kanister [ka'nɪstər] *m* (-s;-) canister
Kanne ['kanə] *f* (-;-n) can; pot; jug
Kannelüre [kanə'lyrə] *f* (-;-n) (archit) flute
Kannibale [kanɪ'balə] *m* (-n;-n), Kannibalin [kanɪ'balɪn] *f* (-;-nen) cannibal
kannte ['kantə] *pret of* kennen
Ka·non ['kanɔn] *n* (-s;-s) (Maßstab; Gebet bei der Messe) canon; (mus) round ‖ *m* (-s;-nones ['nonəs] canon (of Canon Law)
Kanone [ka'nonə] *f* (-;-n) (arti) gun; (hist) canon; (coll) expert; unter aller K. indescribably bad
Kano'nenboot *n* gunboat
Kano'nenrohr *n* gun barrel; heiliges K.! holy smokes!
kanonisieren [kanɔnɪ'zirən] *tr* canonize
Kante ['kantə] *f* (-;-n) edge

kanten ['kantən] *tr* set on edge; *(beim Schifahren)* cant || **Kanten** *m* (-s;-) end of a loaf, crust

Kanthaken ['kanthɑkən] *m* grappling hook

kantig ['kantıç] *adj* angular; squared

Kantine [kan'tinə] *f* (-;-n) canteen; (mil) post exchange

Kanton [kan'ton] *m* (-s;-e) canton

Kan·tor ['kantər] *m* (-s;-toren ['torən]) choir master; organist

Kanu [ka'nu] *n* (-s;-s) canoe

Kanzel ['kantsəl] *f* (-;-n) pulpit; (aer) cockpit

Kanzlei [kants'lɑɪ] *f* (-;-en) office; chancellery

Kanzlei'papier *n* official foolscap

Kanzlei'sprache *f* legal jargon

Kanzler ['kantslər] *m* (-s;-) chancellor

Kap [kap] *n* (-s;-s) cape, headland

Kapaun [ka'paun] *m* (-s;-e) capon

Kapazität [kapatsı'tet] *f* (-;-en) capacity; *(Könner)* authority

Kapelle [ka'pelə] *f* (-;-n) chapel; (mus) band

Kapell'meister *m* band leader; orchestra conductor

kapern ['kɑpərn] *tr* capture; (coll) nab

kapieren [ka'pirən] *tr* get, understand || *intr* get it; **kapiert?** got it?

kapital [kapı'tal] *adj* excellent || **Kapital** *n* (-s;-e & -ien [jən]) (fin) capital; **K. schlagen aus** capitalize on; **K. und Zinsen** principal and interest

Kapital'anlage *f* investment

Kapital'ertragssteuer *f* tax on unearned income

kapitalisieren [kapıtalı'zirən] *tr* (fin) capitalize

Kapitalismus [kapıta'lısmʊs] *m* (-s;) capitalism

Kapitalist -in [kapıta'lıst(ın)] *m* §7 capitalist

Kapital'verbrechen *n* capital offense

Kapitän [kapı'ten] *m* (-s;-e) captain, skipper; **K. zur See** (nav) captain

Kapitän'leutnant *m* (nav) lieutenant

Kapitel [ka'pıtəl] *n* (-s;-) chapter

Kapitell [kapı'tel] *n* (-s;-e) (archit) capital

kapitulieren [kapıtu'lirən] *intr* capitulate, surrender; reenlist

Kaplan [ka'plan] *m* (-s;¨e) chaplain; (R.C.) assistant (pastor)

Kapo ['kapo] *m* (-s;-s) prisoner overseer; (mil) (coll) N.C.O.

Kappe ['kapə] *f* (-;-n) cap; hood, cover; **etw auf seine eigene K. nehmen** take the responsibility for s.th.

Käppi ['kepı] *n* (-s;-s) garrison cap

Kaprice [ka'prisə] *f* (-;-n) caprice

Kapriole [kaprı'olə] *f* (-;-n) caper

kaprizieren [kaprı'tsirən] *ref*—**sich k. auf** (acc) be dead set on

kapriziös [kaprı'tsjøs] *adj* capricious

Kapsel ['kapsəl] *f* (-;-n) capsule; *(e-r Flasche)* cap; *(e-s Sprengkörpers)* detonator

kaputt [ka'pʊt] *adj* (sl) broken; (sl) ruined; (sl) exhausted; (sl) dead

kaputt'gehen §82 *intr* (SEIN) get ruined

kaputt'machen *tr* ruin

Kapuze [ka'putsə] *f* (-;-n) hood; (eccl) cowl

Kapuziner [kapu'tsinər] *m* (-s;-) Capuchin

Kapuzi'nerkresse *f* Nasturtium

Karabiner [kara'binər] *m* (-s;-) carbine

Karabi'nerhaken *m* snap

Karaffe [ka'rafə] *f* (-;-n) carafe

Karambolage [karambo'laʒə] *f* (-;-n) (coll) collision

karambolieren [karambo'lirən] *intr* (coll) collide

Karamelle [kara'melə] *f* (-;-n) caramel

Karat [ka'rat] *n* (-[e]s;) carat

-karätig [karetıç] *comb.fm.* –carat

Karawane [kara'vanə] *f* (-;-n) caravan

Karbid [kar'bit] *n* (-[e]s;-e) carbide

Karbolsäure [kar'bolzɔırə] *f* (-;) carbolic acid

Karbon [kar'bon] *n* (-s;) (geol) carbon

Karbunkel [kar'bʊŋkəl] *n* (-s;-) carbuncle

Kardinal- [kardınal] *comb.fm.* cardinal, principal || **Kardinal** *m* (-s;¨e) (eccl, orn) cardinal

Karenzzeit [ka'rentstsaıt] *f* (ins) waiting period

Karfreitag [kɑr'fraıtak] *m* Good Friday

karg [kark] *adj* (karger & kärger ['kergər]; kärgste & kärgste ['kerstə] §9) *(ärmlich)* meager; *(Boden)* poor; *(Landschaft)* bleak

kargen ['kargən] *intr* be sparing

Karg'heit *f* (-;) bleakness; meagerness; frugality

kärglich ['kerlıç] *adj* meager, poor

kariert [ka'rirt] *adj* checked, squared

Karikatur [karıka'tur] *f* (-;-en) caricature; cartoon

karikieren [karı'kirən] *tr* caricature

Karl [karl] *m* (-s;) Charles; **Karl der Große** Charlemagne

Karmeliter [karme'litər] *m* (-s;-) Carmelite Friar

Karmelitin [karme'litın] *f* (-;-nen) Carmelite nun

karmesinrot [karme'zinrot], **karminrot** [kar'minrot] *adj* crimson

Karneval ['karneval] *m* (-s;-s & -e) carnival

Karnickel [kar'nıkəl] *n* (-s;-) (coll) rabbit; *(Sündenbock)* (coll) scapegoat; *(Einfaltspinsel)* simpleton

Karo ['karo] *n* (-s;-s) diamond; check, square; (cards) diamond(s)

Karosse [ka'rosə] *f* (-;-n) state carriage

Karosse·rie [karosə'ri] *f* (-;-rien ['ri-ən] (aut) body

Karotte [ka'rotə] *f* (-;-n) carrot

Karpfen ['karpfən] *m* (-s;-) carp

Karre ['karə] *f* (-;-n), **Karren** ['karən] *m* (-s;-) cart; wheelbarrow; **die alte K.** the old rattletrap

Karriere [kar'rjerə] *f* (-;-n) career; gallop; **K. machen** get ahead

Karte ['kartə] *f* (-;-n) card; ticket; *(Landkarte)* map; *(Speise-)* menu

Kartei [kar'taı] *f* (-;-en) card file

Kartei'karte *f* index card

Kartell [kar'tel] *n* (-s;-e) cartel
Kar'tenkunststück *n* card trick
Kartenlegerin ['kartənlegərın] *f* (-;
-nen) fortuneteller
Kar'tenstelle *f* ration board
Kartoffel [kar'tɔfəl] *f* (-;-n) potato
Kartof'felbrei *m* mashed potatoes
Kartoffelpuffer [kar'tɔfəlpufər] *m* (-s;
-) potato pancake
Karton [kar'tɔn] *m* (-s;-s) cardboard;
carton; (paint) cartoon
Kartonage [kartɔ'naʒə] *f* (-;-n) card-
board box
kartoniert [kartɔ'nirt] *adj* (bb) soft-
cover
Karton'papier *n* (thin) cardboard
Karthothek [kartɔ'tek] *f* (-;-en) card
index; card filing system
Karthothek'ausgabe *f* loose-leaf edition
Karussell [karu'sel] *n* (-s;-e) merry-
go-round
Karwoche ['karvɔxə] *f* Holy Week
Karzer ['kartsər] *m* (-s;-) (educ) detention room; **K. bekommen** get a
detention
Kaschmir ['kaʃmɪr] *m* (-s;-e) cashmere
Käse ['kezə] *m* (-s;-) cheese; (sl)
baloney
Kaserne [ka'zernə] *f* (-;-n) barracks
käsig ['kezɪç] *adj* cheesy; (Gesichtsfarbe) pasty
Kasino [ka'zino] *n* (-s;-s) casino;
(mil) officer's mess
Kas'pisches Meer' ['kaspɪʃəs] *n* Cas-
pian Sea
Kassa ['kasa] *f*—per **K.** in cash
Kassa— *comb.fm.* cash, spot
Kasse ['kasə] *f* (-;-n) money box; till;
cash register; cashiers desk; (Bar-
geld) cash; (adm) finance depart-
ment; (educ) bursars office; (sport)
ticket window; (theat) box office;
gegen (or **per**) **K.** cash, for cash;
gut bei K. sein (coll) be flush
Kas'senabschluß *m* balancing of ac-
counts
Kas'senbeamte *m* cashier; teller
Kas'senbeleg *m* sales slip
Kas'senbestand *m* cash on hand
Kas'senerfolg *m* (theat) hit
Kas'senführer **-in** §6 *mf* cashier
Kas'senschalter *m* teller's window
Kas'senschrank *m* safe
Kas'senzettel *m* sales slip
Kasserolle [kasə'rɔlə] *f* (-;-n) casse-
role
Kassette [ka'setə] *f* (-;-n) base, box;
(cin, phot) cassette
kassieren [ka'sirən] *tr* (Geld) take in;
get; (Urteil) annul; (coll) confiscate;
(coll) arrest; (mil) break
Kassie'rer **-in** §6 *mf* cashier; teller
Kastagnette [kastan'jetə] *f* (-;-n)
castanet
Kastanie [kas'tanjə] *f* (-;-n) chestnut
Kästchen ['kestçən] *n* (-s;-) case, box
Kaste ['kastə] *f* (-;-n) caste
kasteien [kas'taɪən] *tr & ref* mortify;
sein Leib k. mortify the flesh
Kastell [kas'tel] *n* (-s;-e) small fort
Kasten ['kastən] *m* (-s;·· & -) chest,
case, box; cupboard, cabinet; (Auto)

(coll) crate; (Boot) (coll) tub; (Gefängnis) (coll) jug
Ka'stengeist *m* snobbishness
Ka'stenwagen *m* (aut) panel truck; (rr)
boxcar
Ka'stenwesen *n* caste system
Kastrat [kas'trat] *m* (-en;-en) eunuch
kastrieren [kas'trirən] *tr* castrate
Katakomben [kata'kɔmbən] *pl* cata-
combs
Katalog [kata'lok] *m* (-[e]s;-e) catalogue
katalogisieren [katalɔgi'zirən] *tr* catalogue
Katapult [kata'pult] *m & n* (-[e]s;-e)
catapult
katapultieren [katapul'tirən] *tr* catapult
Katarakt [kata'rakt] *m* (-[e]s;-e) cataract, rapids; (pathol) cataract
Katasteramt [ka'tastəramt] *n* land-
registry office
katastrophal [katastro'fal] *adj* cata-
strophic, disastrous
Katastrophe [kata'strofə] *f* (-;-n)
catastrophe, disaster
Katastro'phengebiet *m* disaster area
Kategorie [katego'ri] *f* (-;-rien
['ri·ən] category
kategorisch [kate'goriʃ] *adj* categori-
cal
Kater ['katər] *m* (-s;-) tomcat; (coll)
hangover
Katheder [ka'tedər] *n & m* (-s;-)
teacher's desk
Kathe'derblüte *f* teacher's blunder
Kathedrale [kate'dralə] *f* (-;-n) cathe-
dral
Kathode [ka'todə] *f* (-;-n) cathode
Katholik **-in** [katɔ'lik(ɪn)] §7 *mf*
Catholic
katholisch [ka'toliʃ] *adj* Catholic
Kattun [ka'tun] *m* (-s;-e) calico
Kätzchen ['ketsçən] *n* (-s;-) kitten
Katze ['katsə] *f* (-;-n) cat; **für die K.**
(coll) for the birds
kat'zenartig *adj* cat-like, feline
Kat'zenauge *n* reflector
Kat'zenbuckel *m* cat's arched back;
vor j-m K. machen lick s.o.'s boots
kat'zenfreundlich *adj* overfriendly
Kat'zenjammer *m* hangover; blues
Kat'zenkopf *m* (coll) cobblestone;
(box) rabbit punch
Kat'zensprung *m* stone's throw
Kauderwelsch ['kaudərvelʃ] *n* (-es;)
gibberish
kauen ['kau·ən] *tr* chew
kauern ['kau·ərn] *ref & intr* cower
Kauf [kauf] *m* (-[e]s;·e) purchase;
in K. nehmen (fig) take, put up with;
leichten Kaufes davonkommen get
off cheaply; **zum K. stehen** be for
sale
Kauf'auftrag *m* (com) order
kaufen ['kaufən] *tr* purchase, buy
Käufer **-in** ['kɔɪfər(ɪn)] §6 *mf* buyer
Kauf'haus *n* department store
Kauf'kraft *f* purchasing power
käuflich ['kɔɪflɪç] *adj* for sale; (bestechlich) open to bribes
Kauf'mann *m* (-[e]s;-leute) businessman; salesman

kaufmännisch ['kaufmenɪʃ] *adj* commercial, business
Kauf/mannsdeutsch *n* business German
Kauf/zwang *m* obligation to buy
Kaugummi ['kaugumɪ] *m* chewing gum
kaukasisch [kau'kazɪ] *adj* Caucasian
Kaulquappe ['kaulkvapə] *f* (-;-n) tadpole, polliwog
kaum [kaum] *adv* hardly, scarcely
Kautabak ['kautabak] *m* chewing tobacco
Kaution [kau'tsjon] *f* (-;-en) (jur) bond; (*Bürgschaft*) (jur) bail; **gegen K.** on bail
Kautschuk ['kaut/uk] *m* (-s;-e) rubber
Kauz [kauts] *m* (-es;-e) owl; (sl) crackpot
Kavalier [kava'lir] *m* (-s;-e) cavalier; gentleman; beau
Kavalkade [kaval'kadə] *f* (-;-n) cavalcade
Kavalle-rie [kavalə'ri] *f* (-;-rien ['ri·ən]) cavalry
Kavallerist [kavalə'rɪst] *m* (-en;-en) cavalryman, trooper
Kaviar ['kavjar] *m* (-s;-e) caviar
keck [kek] *adj* bold; impudent; cheeky
Kegel ['kegəl] *m* (-s;-) tenpin; (geom) cone; **K. schieben** bowl
Ke/gelbahn *f* bowling alley
kegeln ['kegəln] *intr* bowl
Keg/ler *m* §6 *mf* bowler
Kehle ['kelə] *f* (-;-n) throat
kehlig ['kelɪç] *adj* throaty
Kehlkopf ['kelkopf] *m* larynx
Kehl/kopfentzündung *f* laryngitis
Kehre ['kerə] *f* (-;-n) turn, bend
kehren ['kerən] *tr* sweep; (*wenden*) turn; **alles zum besten k.** make the best of it; **j-m den Rücken k.** turn one's back on s.o. || *ref* turn; **ich bin gekehrt sein** be lost in thought; **sich an nichts k.** not care about anything; **sich k. an** (*acc*) heed || *intr* sweep
Kehricht ['kerɪçt] *m* & *n* (-[e]s;) sweepings; trash, rubbish
Keh/richteimer *m* trash can
Keh/richtschaufel *f* dustpan
Kehr/maschine *f* street cleaner
Kehr/reim *m* refrain, chorus
Kehr/seite *f* reverse; (fig) seamy side
kehrtmachen ['kertmaxən] *intr* turn around; (mil) about-face
Kehrt/wendung *f* about-face
keifen ['kaifən] *intr* nag
Keiferei [kaifə'rai] *f* (-;-en) nagging; squabble
Keil [kail] *m* (-[e]s;-e) wedge
keilen ['kailən] *tr* wedge; (coll) recruit || *recip* scrap
Keilerei [kailə'rai] *f* (-;-en) scrap
keil/förmig *adj* wedge-shaped; tapered
Keil/hammer *m* sledgehammer
Keil/hose *f* tapered trousers
Keil/schrift *f* cuneiform writing
Keim [kaim] *m* (-[e]s;-e) germ; embryo; (fig) seeds; (bot) bud, sprout; **im K. ersticken** nip in the bud; **im K. vorhanden** at an embryonic stage; **Keime treiben** germinate
keimen ['kaimən] *intr* germinate;

sprout || **Keimen** *n*—**zum K. bringen** cause to germinate
keim/frei *adj* germ-free, sterile
Keimling ['kaimlɪŋ] *m* (-s;-e) embryo; sprout; seedling
keimtötend ['kaimtøtənt] *adj* germicidal; antiseptic, sterilizing
Keim/zelle *f* germ cell, sex cell
kein [kain] §2,2 *adj* no, not any
keiner ['kainər] §2,4 *indef pron* none; no one, nobody, not one; **k. von beiden** neither of them
keinerlei ['kainər'lai] *invar adj* no... of any kind, no...whatsoever
keineswegs ['kainəs'veks] *adv* by no means, not at all
Keks [keks] *m* & *n* (-es;-e) biscuit, cracker; cookie
Kelch [kelç] *m* (-[e]s;-e) cup; (bot) calyx; (eccl) chalice
Kelch/blatt *n* (bot) sepal
Kelle ['kelə] *f* (-;-n) ladle; (hort, mas) trowel
Keller ['kelər] *m* (-s;-) cellar
Kel/lergeschoß *n* basement
Kel/lergewölbe *n* underground vault
Kellner ['kelnər] *m* (-s;-) waiter
Kellnerin ['kelnərɪn] *f* (-;-nen) waitress
Kelte ['keltə] *m* (-n;-n) Celt
Kelter ['keltər] *f* (-;-n) wine press
keltern ['keltərn] *tr* press
Keltin ['keltɪn] *f* (-;-nen) Celt
keltisch ['keltɪʃ] *adj* Celtic
kennbar ['kenbar] *adj* recognizable
kennen ['kenən] §97 *tr* be acquainted with, know
ken/nenlernen *tr* get to know, meet
Ken/ner **-in** §6 *mf* expert
Ken/nerblick *m* knowing glance
Ken/ner **-in** §6 *mf* expert
Kennkarte ['kenkartə] *f* identity card
kenntlich ['kentlɪç] *adj* identifiable, recognizable; conspicuous
Kenntnis ['kentnɪs] *f* (-;-se) knowledge; **gute Kenntnisse haben in** (*dat*) be well versed in; **j-n von etw in K. setzen** apprise s.o. of s.th.; **Kenntnisse** knowledge; skills; know-how; **oberflächliche Kenntnisse** a smattering; **von etw K. nehmen** take note of s.th.; **zur K. nehmen** take note of s.th.
Kennwort ['kenvort] *n* (-[e]s;-er) code word; (mil) password
Kennzeichen ['kentsaiçən] *n* distinguishing mark; hallmark; criterion; (aer) marking; (aut) license number
kennzeichnen ['kentsaiçnən] *tr* characterize; identify; brand
Kennziffer ['kentsifər] *f* code number
kentern ['kentərn] *intr* (SEIN) capsize
Keramik [ke'ramɪk] *f* (-;) ceramics; pottery
keramisch [ke'ramɪʃ] *adj* ceramic
Kerbe ['kerbə] *f* (-;-n) notch, groove
kerben ['kerbən] *tr* notch, nick; make a groove in; serrate
Kerbholz ['kerpholts] *n*—**etw auf dem K. haben** have a crime chalked up against one
Kerbtier ['kerptir] *n* insect
Kerker ['kerkər] *m* (-s;-) jail

Kerl [kɛrl] *m* (-s;-e) fellow, guy; (*Mädchen*) lass

Kern [kɛrn] *m* (-[e]s;-e) kernel; (*im Obst*) pit, stone, pip; hard core; (*e-s Problems*) crux; (phys) nucleus

Kern- *comb.fm.* core; central, basic; through and through; (phys) nuclear

Kern′aufbau *m* nuclear structure

kern′deutsch′ *adj* German through and through

Kern′energie *f* nuclear energy

Kern′fächer *pl* core curriculum

kern′gesund′ *adj* perfectly sound

Kern′holz *n* heartwood

kernig [′kɛrnɪç] *adj* full of seeds; robust, vigorous

kern′los *adj* seedless

Kern′physik *f* nuclear physics

Kern′punkt *m* gist, crux; focal point

Kern′schußweite *f*—**auf K.** at point-blank range

Kern′spaltung *f* nuclear fission

Kern′truppen *pl* crack troops

Kern′verschmelzung *f* nuclear fusion

Kern′waffe *f* nuclear weapon

Kerosin [kero′zin] *n* (-s;) kerosene

Kerze [′kɛrtsə] *f* (-;-n) candle; (aut) plug

ker′zengera′de *adj* straight as an arrow || *adv* bolt upright

Kessel [′kɛsəl] *m* (-s;-) kettle; cauldron; boiler; (geog) basin-shaped valley; (mil) pocket

Kes′selpauke *f* kettledrum

Kes′selraum *m* boiler room

Kes′selschmied *m* boilermaker

Kes′selwagen *m* (aut) tank truck; (rr) tank car

Kette [′kɛtə] *f* (-;-n) chain; (e-s Panzers) track

ketten [′kɛtən] *tr* (**an** *acc*) chain (to)

Ket′tengeschäft *n* chain store

Ket′tenglied *n* chain link

Ket′tenhund *m* watch dog

Ket′tenrad *n* sprocket

Ket′tenraucher **-in** §6 *mf* chain smoker

Ket′tenstich *m* chain stitch, lock stitch

Ketzer **-in** [′kɛtsər(ɪn)] §6 *mf* heretic

Ketzerei [kɛtsə′raɪ] *f* (-;-en) heresy

ketzerisch [′kɛtsərɪʃ] *adj* heretical

keuchen [′kɔɪçən] *intr* pant, gasp

Keuch′husten *m* (-s;) whooping cough

Keule [′kɔɪlə] *f* (-;-n) club; (culin) leg, drumstick

keusch [kɔɪʃ] *adj* chaste

Keusch′heit *f* (-;) chastity

KG *abbr* (**Kommanditgesellschaft**) Ltd.

Khaki [′kaki] *m* (-;) (tex) khaki

kichern [′kɪçərn] *intr* giggle

kicken [′kɪkən] *tr* (fb) kick

Kicker [′kɪkər] *m* (-s;-) soccer player

Kiebitz [′kibɪts] *m* (-[e]s;-e) (orn) lapwing; (*Zugucker*) kibitzer

kiebitzen [′kibɪtsən] *intr* kibitz

Kiefer [′kifər] *m* (-s;-) jaw(bone) || *f* (-;-n) pine; **gemeine K.** Scotch pine

Kiel [kil] *m* (-[e]s;-e) (*Feder*) quill; (naut) keel

Kiel′raum *m* hold

Kiel′wasser *n* wake

Kieme [′kimə] *f* (-;-n) gill

Kien [′kin] *m* (-[e]s;-e) pine cone

Kien′span *m* pine torch

Kiepe [′kipə] *f* (-;-n) basket (*carried on one's back*)

Kies [kis] *m* (-es;-e) gravel

Kiesel [′kizəl] *m* (-s;-) pebble

Kilo [′kilo] *n* (-s;-s & -) kilogram

Kilogramm [kilo′gram] *n* (-s;-e & -) kilogram

Kilometer [kilo′metər] *m* & *n* (-s;-) kilometer

Kilome′terfresser *m* (coll) speedster

Kilowatt [kilo′vat] *n* (-s;-) kilowatt

Kimm [kɪm] *m* (-es;-e) horizon || *f* (-;-e) (naut) bilge

Kimme [′kɪmə] *f* (-;-n) notch; groove; (e-s Gewehrs) sight

Kind [kɪnt] *n* (-[e]s;-er) child; baby

Kinder- [kɪndər] *comb.fm.* child's, children's

Kin′derarzt *m*, **Kin′derärztin** *f* pediatrician

Kinderei [kɪndə′raɪ] *f* (-;-en) childish behavior, childish prank

Kin′derfrau *f* nursemaid

Kin′derfräulein *n* governess

Kin′derfürsorge *f* child welfare

Kin′dergarten *m* nursery school, playschool

Kin′dergärtnerin *f* nursery school attendant

Kin′dergeld *n* see **Kinderzulage**

Kin′derheilkunde *f* pediatrics

Kin′derheim *n* children's home

Kin′derhort *m* day nursery

Kin′derlähmung *f* polio

kin′derleicht *adj* easy as pie

Kin′derlied *n* nursery rhyme

kin′derlos *adj* childless

Kin′dermädchen *n* nursemaid

Kin′derpuder *m* baby powder

Kin′derreim *m* nursery rhyme

Kin′derschreck *m* bogeyman

Kin′dersportwagen *m* stroller

Kin′derstube *f* nursery; (*Erziehung*) upbringing

Kin′derstuhl *m* highchair

Kin′derwagen *m* baby carriage

Kin′derzulage *f* family allowance (*paid by the employer*)

Kin′desalter *n* childhood; infancy

Kin′desannahme *f* adoption

Kin′desbeine *pl*—**von Kindesbeinen an** from childhood on

Kin′desentführer **-in** §6 *mf* kidnaper

Kin′desentführung *f*, **Kin′desraub** *m* kidnaping

Kind′heit *f* (-;) childhood

kindisch [′kɪndɪʃ] *adj* childish

kindlich [′kɪntlɪç] *adj* childlike

Kinetik [ki′netɪk] *f* (-;) kinetics

kinetisch [ki′netɪʃ] *adj* kinetic

Kinkerlitzchen [′kɪŋkərlɪtsçən] *pl* trifles; gimmicks

Kinn [kɪn] *n* (-[e]s;-e) chin

Kinn′backen *m* jawbone

Kinn′haken *m* (box) uppercut

Kinn′kette *f* curb chain

Kino [′kino] *n* (-s;-s) movie theater

Ki′nobesucher **-in** §6 *mf* moviegoer

Ki′nokamera *f* movie camera

Ki′nokasse *f* box office

Kiosk [ki′ɔsk] *m* (-[e]s;-e) stand

Kipfel [′kɪpfəl] *n* (-s;-) (Aust) (culin) crescent roll

Kippe ['kɪpə] *f* (-;-n) edge; *(Zigarettenstummel)* butt; **auf der K. stehen** stand on edge; (fig) be touch and go || *intr* (SEIN) tilt; overturn
kippen ['kɪpən] *tr* tilt, tip over; dump || *intr* (SEIN) tilt; overturn
Kipper ['kɪpər] *m* (-s;-) dump truck
Kirche ['kɪrçə] *f* (-;-n) church
Kirchen– [kɪrçən] *comb.fm.* church, ecclesiastical
Kir'chenbann *m* excommunication; **in den K. tun** excommunicate
Kir'chenbau *m* (-[e]s;) building of churches || *m* (-[e]s;-ten) church
Kir'chenbesuch *m* church attendance
Kir'chenbuch *n* parish register
Kir'chendiener *m* sacristan, sexton
Kir'chengut *n* church property
Kir'chenlied *n* hymn
Kir'chenschändung *f* desecration of a church
Kir'chenschiff *n* (archit) nave
Kir'chenspaltung *f* schism
Kir'chenstaat *m* Papal States
Kir'chenstuhl *m* pew
Kir'chentag *m* Church congress
Kirchgang ['kɪrçgaŋ] *m* going to church
Kirch'gänger –in §6 *mf* church-goer
Kirch'hof *m* churchyard
kirch'lich *adj* church, ecclesiastical
Kirch'spiel *n* parish
Kirch'turm *m* steeple
Kirch'turmpolitik *f* (pej) parochialism
Kirch'turmspitze *f* spire
Kirchweih ['kɪrçvaɪ] *f* (-;-en) church picnic
Kirch'weihe *f* dedication of a church
Kirch'weihfest *n* church picnic
Kirsch [kɪrʃ] *m* (-es;-) cherry brandy
Kirsche ['kɪrʃə] *f* (-;-n) cherry
Kirsch'wasser *n* cherry brandy
Kissen ['kɪsən] *n* (-s;-) cushion, pillow; *(Polster)* pad
Kis'senbezug *m* pillowcase
Kiste ['kɪstə] *f* (-;-n) box, crate, case; (aer) crate; (aut) rattletrap; (naut) tub
Kitsch [kɪtʃ] *m* (-es;) kitsch
kitschig ['kɪtʃɪç] *adj* trashy; mawkish
Kitt [kɪt] *m* (-[e]s;-e) putty; cement; **der ganze Kitt** the whole caboodle
Kittchen ['kɪtçən] *n* (-s;-) (coll) jail
Kittel ['kɪtəl] *m* (-s;-) smock, coat; (Aust) skirt
Kit'telkleid *n* house dress
kitten ['kɪtən] *tr* putty; cement, glue; (fig) patch up
Kitzel ['kɪtsəl] *m* (-s;) tickle; (fig) itch
kitzeln ['kɪtsəln] *tr* tickle
kitzlig ['kɪtslɪç] *adj* ticklish
Kladderadatsch [kladəra'datʃ] *m* (-es;) crash, bang; mess, muddle
klaffen ['klafən] *intr* gape, yawn
kläffen ['klɛfən] *intr* yelp
Klafter ['klaftər] *f* (-;- & -n), *m & n* (-s;-) fathom; *(Holz-)* cord
klagbar ['klakbar] *adj* (jur) actionable
Klage ['klaːgə] *f* (-;-n) complaint; (jur) (civil) suit
Kla'gelied *n* dirge, threnody
klagen ['klaːgən] *tr*—**j-m seinen Kummer k.** pour out one's troubles to s.o.

|| *intr* complain; **auf Scheidung k.** sue for divorce; **k. über** *(acc)* complain about; **k. um** lament
Kläger –in ['klɛgər(ɪn)] §6 *mf* (jur) plaintiff
Kla'geweib *n* hired mourner
kläglich ['klɛklɪç] *adj* plaintive, pitiful; *(Zustand)* sorry; *(Ergebnis, Ende)* miserable
klaglos ['klaːkloːs] *adv* uncomplainingly
klamm [klam] *adj* *(erstarrt)* numb; *(feuchtkalt)* clammy; **k. an Geld** (coll) short of dough || **Klamm** *f* (-;-en) gorge
Klammer ['klamər] *f* (-;-n) clamp; clip; paper clip; *(Schließe)* clasp; clothespin; hair clip, bobby pin; **eckige K.** bracket; **runde K.** parenthesis
klammern ['klamərn] *tr* clamp; clasp || *ref*—**sich k. an** *(acc)* cling to
Klamotte [kla'mɔtə] *f* (-;-n)—**alte K.** oldy; (aer, aut) old crate; **Klamotten** things, clothes
Klampfe ['klampfə] *f* (-;-n) guitar
klang [klaŋ] *pret* of **klingen** || **Klang** *m* (-[e]s;-e) tone, sound
Klang'farbe *f* timbre
klang'getreu *adj* high-fidelity
Klang'regler *m* (rad) tone-control knob
Klang'taste *f* tone-control push button
klang'voll *adj* sonorous
Klappe ['klapə] *f* (-;-n) flap; *(Mund)* (sl) trap; (anat, mach) valve; **in die K. gehen** (sl) hit the sack
klappen ['klapən] *tr* flip || *intr* flap, fold || *impers*—**es klappt** (coll) it clicks, it turns out well
Klapper ['klapər] *f* (-;-n) rattle
klap'perdürr *adj* skinny
Klap'pergestell *n* (coll) beanpole; *(Kiste)* (coll) rattletrap
klappern ['klapərn] *intr* rattle, clatter; *(Zähne)* chatter
Klap'perschlange *f* rattlesnake
Klap'perstorch *m* stork
Klappflügel ['klapflyːgəl] *m* (aer) folding wing *(of carrier plane)*
Klappmesser ['klapmɛsər] *n* jackknife
klapprig ['klaprɪç] *adj* rickety
Klappstuhl ['klapʃtuːl] *m* folding chair
Klapptisch ['klaptɪʃ] *m* drop-leaf table
Klapptür ['klaptyːr] *f* trap door
Klaps [klaps] *m* (-es;-e) smack, slap; **e-n K. kriegen** (sl) go nuts
klapsen ['klapsən] *tr* smack, slap
Klaps'mühle *f* (coll) booby hatch
klar [klaːr] *adj* clear; **klar zum Start** ready for take-off
Kläranlage ['klɛranlaːgə] *f* sewage-disposal plant
klären ['klɛrən] *tr* clear; *(Mißverständnis)* clear up || *ref* become clear
Klar'heit *f* (-;) clearness, clarity
Klarinette [klarɪ'nɛtə] *f* (-;-n) clarinet
klar'legen, klar'stellen *tr* clear up
Klärung ['klɛːruŋ] *f* (-;) clarification
Klasse ['klasə] *f* (-;-n) class; (educ) grade, class
Klas'senarbeit *f* test
Klas'senaufsatz *m* composition *(written in class)*
klas'senbewußt *adj* class-conscious

Klas′seneinteilung f classification
Klas′senkamerad –in §7 mf classmate
Klas′sentreffen n (–s;–) class reunion
klassifizieren [klasɪfɪ′tsirən] tr classify
Klassifizie′rung f (–;–en) classification
–klassig [klasɪç] comb.fm. –class, –grade
Klassik [′klasɪk] f (–;) classical antiquity, classical period
Klas′siker –in §6 mf classical author
klassisch [′klasɪ∫] adj classic(al)
Klatsch [klat∫] m (–es;) clap; gossip
Klatsch′base f gossipmonger; tattletale
Klatsch′blatt n scandal sheet
Klatsche [′klat∫ə] f (–;–n) fly swatter; tattletale; (educ) pony
klatschen [′klat∫ən] tr smack, slap; **dem Lehrer etw k.** tattletale to the teacher about s.th.; **in Beifall k.** applaud s.o. || intr clap; (Regen) patter; (fig) gossip; **in die Hände (or mit den Händen) k.** clap the hands
Klatscherei [klat∫ə′raɪ] f (–;–en) gossip
klatsch′naß/ adj soaking wet
Klatsch′spalte f glossip column
klauben [′klaʊbən] tr pick
Klaue [′klaʊ-ə] f (–;–n) claw, talon; (Spalthuf) hoof; (coll) scrawl
klauen [′klaʊ-ən] tr (coll) snitch
Klause [′klaʊzə] f (–;–n) hermitage; (Schlucht) defile; (coll) den, pad
Klausel [′klaʊzəl] f (–;–n) clause; (Abmachung) stipulation
Klausner [′klaʊznər] m (–s;–) hermit
Klausur [klaʊ′zur] f (–;–en) seclusion; (educ) final examination
Klausur′arbeit f final examination
Klaviatur [klavja′tur] f (–;–en) keyboard
Klavier [kla′vir] n (–[e]s;–e) piano
Klavier′auszug m piano score
Klebemittel [′klebəmɪtəl] n (–s;–) adhesive, glue
kleben [′klebən] tr & intr stick
Kleberolle [′klebərələ] f roll of gummed tape
Klebestreifen [′klebə/traɪfən] m adhesive tape; Scotch tape (trademark)
Klebezettel [′klebətsetəl] m label, sticker
klebrig [′klebrɪç] adj sticky
Klebstoff [′klep/tof] m adhesive
Klecks [klɛks] m (–es;–e) stain; dab
klecksen [′klɛksən] tr splash || intr make blotches
Kleckser –in [′klɛksər(ɪn)] §6 mf scribbler; dauber
Klee [kle] m (–s;) clover
Klee′blatt n cloverleaf; (fig) trio
Kleid [klaɪt] n (–[e]s;–er) garment; dress; robe; **Kleider** clothes
kleiden [′klaɪdən] tr dress; **j–n gut k.** look good on s.o.
Klei′derablage f cloakroom; (Kleiderständer) clothes rack
Klei′derbestand m wardrobe
Klei′derbügel m coat hanger
Klei′dersack m (mil) duffle bag
Klei′derschrank m clothes closet
Klei′derständer m clothes rack
kleidsam [′klaɪtzəm] adj well-fitting, becoming

Klei′dung f (–;) clothing
Kleie [′klaɪ-ə] f (–;–n) bran
klein [klaɪn] adj small, little; short; **ein k. wenig** a little bit || **Kleine** §5 m little boy || f little girl || n little one
Klein′anzeigen pl classified ads
Klein′arbeit f detailed work
Klein′asien n Asia Minor
Klein′bahn f narrow-gauge railroad
Klein′bauer m small farmer
Klein′betrieb m small business
Kleinbild– comb.fm. (phot) 35mm
klein′bürgerlich adj lower middle-class
Klein′geld n change
klein′gläubig adj of little faith
Klein′handel m retail business
Klein′händler –in §6 mf retailer
Klein′hirn n (anat) cerebellum
Klein′holz n kindling; **K. aus j–m machen** (coll) beat s.o. to a pulp
Klei′nigkeit f small object; trifle, minor detail; small matter
Klei′nigkeitskrämer m fusspot
kleinkalibrig [′klaɪnkalibrɪç] adj small-bore
Klein′kind n infant
Klein′kinderbewahranstalt f day care center
Klein′kram m odds and ends; details
klein′laut adj subdued
klein′lich adj stingy; (Betrag) paltry; (engstirnig) narrow-minded, pedantic
Klein′mut m despondency; faintheartedness
klein′mütig adj despondent; faint-hearted
Klei′nod [′klaɪnot] n (–[e]s;–node & –nodien [′nodjən] jewel, gem
klein′schneiden §106 tr chop up
Klein′schreibmaschine f portable typewriter
Kleister [′klaɪstər] m (–s;–) paste
Klemme [′klemə] f (–;–n) clamp, clip; (coll) tight spot, fix; (elec) terminal; (surg) clamp
klemmen [′klemən] tr tuck, put; (stehlen) pinch, swipe || **ref–sich** [dat] **den Finger k.** smash one's finger; **sich hinter die Arbeit k.** get down to business; **sich k. hinter** (acc) get after || intr be stuck
Klempner [′klempnər] m (–s;–) tinsmith; plumber
Klempnerei [klempnə′raɪ] f (–;) plumbing
Kleptomane [klepto′manə] §5 mf kleptomaniac
klerikal [klerɪ′kal] adj clerical
Kleriker [′klerɪkər] m (–s;–) clergyman, priest
Klerus [′klerus] m (–;) clergy
Klette [′kletə] f (–;–n) (bot) burr; (coll) pain in the neck
Klet′tergarten m training area (for mountain climbing)
klettern [′kletərn] intr (SEIN) climb
Klet′terpflanze f (bot) creeper
Klet′terrose f rambler
Klet′tertour f climbing expedition
Klient [klɪ′ent] m (–en;–en) client
Klientel [klɪ-en′tel] f (–;–en) clientele (of a lawyer)

Klientin [klɪˈɛntɪn] *f* (-;-nen) client

Klima [ˈklima] *n* (-s;-s) climate

Kli'maanlage *f* air conditioner

kli'magerecht *adj* air-conditioned

klimatisch [klɪˈmatɪʃ] *adj* climatic

klimatisieren [klɪmatɪˈzirən] *tr* air-condition

Klimatisie'rung *f* (-;) air conditioning

Klimbim [klɪmˈbɪm] *m* (-s;) (coll) junk; (coll) racket; (coll) fuss

klimmen [ˈklɪmən] §164 *intr* (SEIN) climb

klimpern [ˈklɪmpərn] *intr* jingle; *(auf der Gitarre)* strum; **mit den Wimpern k.** flutter one's eyelashes

Klinge [ˈklɪŋə] *f* (-;-n) blade; sword, saber; **über die K. springen lassen** put to the sword

Klingel [ˈklɪŋəl] *f* (-;-n) bell

Klin'gelbeutel *m* collection basket

Klin'gelknopf *m* doorbell button

klingeln [ˈklɪŋəln] *intr* ring, tinkle; *(Vers, Reim)* jingle || *impers*—es klingelt the doorbell is ringing; there goes the (school) bell; the phone is ringing

kling'klang *interj* ding-dong!

Klinik [ˈklinɪk] *f* (-;-en) teaching hospital *(of a university)*; private hospital; nursing home

klinisch [ˈklinɪʃ] *adj* clinical; hospital

Klinke [ˈklɪŋkə] *f* (-;-n) door handle; (telp) jack; **Klinken putzen** beg or peddle from door to door

Klippe [ˈklɪpə] *f* (-;-n) rock, reef

klirren [ˈklɪrən] *intr* rattle, clang; *(Gläser)* clink; *(Waffen)* clash

Klischee [klɪˈʃe] *n* (-s;-s) cliché

Klistier [klɪsˈtir] *n* (-s;-e) enema

klistieren [klɪsˈtirən] *tr* give an enema to

klitschig [ˈklɪtʃɪç] *adj* doughy

Klo [klo] *n* (-s;-s) (coll) john

Kloake [kloˈakə] *f* (-;-n) sewer

Kloben [ˈklobən] *m* (-s;-) pulley; *(Holz)* block; *(Schraubenstock)* vise

klobig [ˈklobɪç] *adj* clumsy; bulky

klomm [klɔm] *pret of* **klimmen**

klopfen [ˈklɔpfən] *tr (Nagel)* drive; *(Teppich)* beat; *(Fleisch)* pound || *intr* knock; *(Herz)* beat, pound; *(Motor)* ping; **j-m auf die Schulter k.** pat s.o. on the back || *impers*—es klopft s.o. is knocking

klopffest [ˈklɔpffɛst] *adj* antiknock

Klöppel [ˈklœpəl] *m* (-s;-) bobbin; *(e-r Glocke)* clapper; (mus) mallet

klöppeln [ˈklœpəln] *tr* make (lace) with bobbins

Klops [klɔps] *m* (-es;-e) meatball

Klosett [kloˈzet] *n* (-s;-e & -s) (flush) toilet

Klosett'becken *n* toilet bowl

Klosett'brille *f* toilet seat

Klosett'deckel *m* toilet-seat lid

Klosett'papier *n* toilet paper

Kloß [klos] *m* (-es;ⁿe) dumpling; **e-n K. im Hals haben** have a lump in one's throat

Kloster [ˈklostər] *n* (-s;ⁿ) monastery; convent

Kloster- *comb.fm.* monastic

Klo'sterbruder *m* lay brother, friar

Klo'sterfrau *f* nun

klösterlich [ˈkløstərlɪç] *adj* monastic

Klotz [klɔts] *m* (-es;ⁿe) block; toy building block; (coll) blockhead; **ein K. am Bein** (coll) a drag; **wie ein K. schlafen** sleep like a log

klotzig [ˈklɔtsɪç] *adj* clumsy; uncouth || *adv*—**k. reich** filthy rich

Klub [klup] *m* (-s;-s) club

Klub'jacke *f* blazer

Klub'sessel *m* easy chair

Kluft [kluft] *f* (-;ⁿe) gorge, ravine; (fig) gulf; (poet) chasm || *f* (-;-en) outfit, uniform

klug [kluk] *adj* (klüger [ˈklygər], klügste [ˈklygstə] §9) clever, bright; wise; **aus Schaden k. werden** learn the hard way; **nicht k. werden können aus** be unable to figure out

klügeln [ˈklygəln] *intr* quibble

Klug'heit *f* (-;) cleverness; intelligence; wisdom

klüglich [ˈklyklɪç] *adv* wisely

Klug'redner *m* wise guy, know-it-all

Klumpen [ˈklumpən] *m* (-s;-) lump, clod; *(Haufen)* heap; (min) nugget

Klumpfuß [ˈklumpfus] *m* clubfoot

klumpig [ˈklumpɪç] *adj* lumpy

Klüngel [ˈklyŋəl] *m* (-s;-) clique

knabbern [ˈknabərn] *intr* nibble

Knabe [ˈknabə] *m* (-n;-n) boy

Kna'benalter *n* boyhood

kna'benhaft *adj* boyish

knack [knak] *interj* crack!; snap!; click!

knacken [ˈknakən] *tr* crack || *intr* crack; *(Schloß)* click; *(Feuer)* crackle

Knacks [knaks] *m* (-es;-e) crack; snap; click; **e-n K. kriegen** get a crack; **e-n K. weg haben** be badly hit; **sich** [*dat*] **e-n K. holen** suffer a blow

Knack'wurst *f* pork sausage; smoked sausage

Knall [knal] *m* (-[e]s;-e) crack, bang; **K. und Fall** on the spot, at once

Knallblättchen [ˈknalbletçən] *n* (-s;-) cap *(for a toy pistol)*

Knall'bonbon *m & n* noise maker

Knall'büchse *f* popgun

Knall'dämpfer *m* silencer

Knall'effekt *m* big surprise

knall'rot *adj* fiery red

knapp [knap] *adj (eng)* close, tight; *(Mehrheit)* bare; *(Zeit)* short; *(Stil)* concise; **k. werden** run short, run low

Knappe [ˈknapə] *m* (-n;-n) (hist) squire; (min) miner

Knapp'heit *f* (-;) closeness, tightness; shortage; conciseness

Knapp'schaft *f* (-;-en) miner's union

Knapp'schaftskasse *f* miner's insurance

knarren [ˈknarən] *intr* creek

Knaster [ˈknastər] *m* (-s;-) tobacco

knattern [ˈknatərn] *intr* crackle; *(Maschinengewehr)* rattle || *intr* (SEIN) put-put along

Knäuel [ˈknɔɪəl] *m & n* (-s;-) *(Garn-)* ball; *(Menschen-)* throng

Knauf [knauf] *m* (-[e]s;ⁿe) knob

Knauser **-in** [ˈknauzər(ɪn)] §6 *mf* tightwad

Knauserei [knauzə'raɪ] *f* (-;) stinginess
knauserig ['knauzərɪç] *adj* stingy
knausern ['knauzərn] *intr* be stingy
knautschen ['knautʃən] *tr* crumple || *intr* crumple; (coll) wimper
Knebel ['knebəl] *m* (-s;-) gag
Kne'belbart *m* handlebar moustache
knebeln ['knebəln] *tr* gag; (fig) muzzle
Kne'belpresse *f* tourniquet
Kne'belung *f*—K. der Presse muzzling of the press
Knecht [knɛçt] *m* (-[e]s;-e) servant; farmhand; serf; slave
knechten ['knɛçtən] *tr* enslave; oppress
knechtisch ['knɛçtɪʃ] *adj* servile
Knecht'schaft *f* (-;) servitude
kneifen ['knaɪfən] §88 & §109 *tr* pinch || §88 *intr* (*Kleid*) be too tight; back out, back down; (fencing) retreat; **k. vor** (*dat*) shirk, dodge
Kneifzange ['knaɪftsaŋə] *f* (pair of) pincers
Kneipe ['knaɪpə] *f* (-;-n) saloon
kneipen ['knaɪpən] *intr* (coll) booze
Knei'penwirt *m* saloon keeper
Kneiperei [knaɪpə'raɪ] *f* (-;-en) drinking bout
kneten ['knetən] *tr* knead; massage
Knick [knɪk] *m* (-[e]s;-e) bend; (*Bruch*) break; (*Falte*) fold, crease
knicken ['knɪkən] *tr* bend; break; fold; (*Hoffnungen*) dash || *intr* (SEIN) snap
Knicker ['knɪkər] *m* (-s;-) tightwad
Knicks [knɪks] *m* (-es;-e) curtsy
knicksen ['knɪksən] *intr* curtsy
Knie [kni] *n* (-s;- ['kni·ə]) knee
Knie'beuge *f* knee bend
Knie'beugung *f* genuflection
knie'fällig *adj* on one's knees
knie'frei *adj* above-the-knee
Knie'freiheit *f* legroom
Knie'kehle *f* hollow of the knee
knien ['kni·ən] *intr* kneel
Knie'scheibe *f* kneecap
Knie'schützer *m* (sport) kneepad
kniff [knɪf] *pret* of **kneifen** || **Kniff** *m* (-[e]s;-e) crease, fold; (*Kunstgriff*) knack
kniff(e)lig ['knɪf(ə)lɪç] *adj* tricky
kniffen ['knɪfən] *tr* crease, fold
Knigge ['knɪgə] *m* (-;) (fig) Emily Post
knipsen ['knɪpsən] *tr* (*Karte*) punch; (phot) snap || *intr* snap a picture; **mit den Fingern k.** snap one's fingers
Knirps [knɪrps] *m* (-es;-e) (coll) shrimp
knirschen ['knɪrʃən] *intr* crunch; **mit den Zähnen k.** gnash one's teeth
knistern ['knɪstərn] *intr* crackle; (*Seide*) rustle
knitterfest ['knɪtərfest] *adj* wrinkle-proof
knittern ['knɪtərn] *tr* wrinkle; crumple
knobeln ['knobəln] *intr* play dice; **an e-m Problem k.** puzzle over a problem
Knoblauch ['knoblaux] *m* (-[e]s;) garlic
Knöchel ['knœçəl] *m* (-s;-) knuckle, joint; ankle
Knochen ['knɔxən] *m* (-s;-) bone

Kno'chenbruch *m* fracture
Kno'chengerüst *n* skeleton
Kno'chenmark *n* marrow
Kno'chenmühle *f* (coll) sweat shop
knöchern ['knœçərn] *adj* bone; bony
knochig ['knɔxɪç] *adj* bony
Knödel ['knødəl] *m* (-s;-) dumpling; **e-n K. im Hals haben** have a lump in one's throat
Knolle ['knɔlə] *f* (coll) bulbous nose; (bot) tuber
Knollen ['knɔlən] *m* (-s;-) lump; (coll) bulbous nose
knollig ['knɔlɪç] *adj* bulbous
Knopf [knɔpf] *m* (-[e]s;ː-e) button; knob; (*e-r Stechnadel*) head; **alter K.** old fogey
knöpfen ['knœpfən] *tr* button
Knopf'loch *n* buttonhole
knorke ['knɔrkə] *adj* (coll) super
Knorpel ['knɔrpəl] *m* (-s;-) cartilage
Knorren ['knɔrən] *m* (-s;-) knot, gnarl
knorrig ['knɔrɪç] *adj* gnarled, knotty
Knospe ['knɔspə] *f* (-;-n) bud
knospen ['knɔspən] *intr* bud
knoten ['knotən] *tr* & *intr* knot || **Knoten** *m* (-s;-) knot; (*Schwierigkeit*) snag; (*Haarfrisur*) chignon; (*Seemeile*) knot; (astr, med, phys) node; (theat) plot
Kno'tenpunkt *m* intersection, interchange; (rr) junction
knotig ['knotɪç] *adj* knotty
Knuff [knʊf] *m* (-[e]s;ː-e) (coll) poke
knuffen ['knʊfən] *tr* (coll) poke
knüllen ['knʏlən] *tr* crumple
Knüller ['knʏlər] *m* (-s;-) (coll) hit
knüpfen ['knʏpfən] *tr* tie, knot; (*Teppich*) weave; (*Bündnis*) form; (*befestigen*) fasten; **k. an** (*acc*) tie in with || *ref*—**sich k. an** (*acc*) be tied in with
Knüppel ['knʏpəl] *m* (-s;-) cudgel; (*e-s Polizisten*) blackjack; (aer) control stick
knurren ['knʊrən] *intr* growl, snarl; (*Magen*) rumble; (fig) grumble
knurrig ['knʊrɪç] *adj* grumpy
knusprig ['knʊsprɪç] *adj* crisp; (*Mädchen*) attractive
Knute ['knutə] *f* (-;-n) whip; (*Gewalt*) power; (*Gewaltherrschaft*) tyranny
knutschen ['knutʃən] *tr*, *recip* & *intr* (coll) neck, pet
Knüttel ['knʏtəl] *m* (-s;-) cudgel
Knüt'telvers *m* doggerel
k.o. ['ka'o] *adj* knocked out || *adv*—**k.o. schlagen** knock out || **K.O.** *m* (-[s];-s) knockout
Koalition [ko·alɪ'tsjon] *f* (-;-en) coalition
Kobalt ['kobalt] *n* (-es;) cobalt
Koben ['kobən] *m* (-s;-) pigsty
Kobold ['kobɔlt] *m* (-[e]s;-e) goblin
Kobolz [ko'bɔlts] *m*—**e-n K. schießen** do a somersault
Koch [kɔx] *m* (-[e]s;ː-e) cook
Koch'buch *n* cookbook
kochen ['kɔxən] *tr* & *intr* cook; boil
Kocher ['kɔxər] *m* (-s;-) cooker; boiler

Köcher ['kœçər] *m* (-s;-) quiver; golf bag
Koch'fett *n* shortening
Koch'geschirr *n* (mil) mess kit
Koch'herd *m* kitchen range
Köchin ['kœçɪn] *f* (-;-nen) cook
Koch'löffel *m* wooden spoon
Koch'salz *n* table salt
Köder ['kødər] *m* (-s;-) bait; lure
ködern ['kødərn] *tr* bait; lure
Kodex ['kodɛks] *m* (-es;-e) codex; (jur) code
kodifizieren [kodɪfɪ'tsirən] *tr* codify
Koffein [kɔfe'in] *n* (-s;) caffeine
Koffer ['kɔfər] *m* (-s;-) suitcase; trunk; case (*for portable items*)
Kof'ferfernseher *m* portable television
Kof'fergerät *n* (rad, telv) portable set
Kof'ferraum *m* (aut) trunk
Kof'ferschreibmaschine *f* portable typewriter
Kognak ['kɔnjak] *m* (-s;-s) cognac
Kohl [kol] *m* (-s;) cabbage; nonsense
Kohle ['kolə] *f* (-;-n) coal; (*Holzkohle*) charcoal
Kohlehydrat ['koləhydrat] *n* (-[e]s;-e) carbohydrate
kohlen ['kolən] *tr & intr* carbonize
Koh'lenbergbau *m* coal mining
Koh'lenbergwerk *n* coal mine
Koh'lendioxyd *n* carbon dioxide
Koh'lenoxyd *n* carbon monoxide
Koh'lenrevier *n* coal field
Koh'lensäure *f* carbonic acid
Koh'lenstoff *m* carbon
Koh'lenwagen *m* coal truck; (rr) coal car
Koh'lepapier *n* carbon paper
Koh'leskizze *f* charcoal sketch
kohl'ra'benschwarz' *adj* jet black
Koitus ['ko·ɪtus] *m* (-;) coitus
Koje ['kojə] *f* (-;-n) bunk, berth
Kojote [ko'jotə] *m* (-;-n) coyote
Kokain [koka'in] *n* (-s;) cocaine
Kokerei [kokə'raɪ] *f* (-;-en) coking plant
kokett [ko'kɛt] *adj* flirtatious ‖ **Kokette** *f* (-;-n) flirt
kokettieren [koke'tirən] *intr* flirt
Kokon [ko'kõ] *m* (-s;-s) cocoon
Kokosnuß ['kokosnus] *f* coconut
Kokospalme ['kokospalmə] *f* coconut palm, coconut tree
Koks [koks] *m* (-es;-e) coke; (coll) nonsense; (*Geld*) (coll) dough
Kolben ['kɔlbən] *m* (-s;-) butt; (*Keule*) mace; (*Löt-*) soldering iron; (aut) piston; (chem) flask; (culin) cob; (elec) bulb
Kol'benhub *m* piston stroke
Kol'benring *m* piston ring
Kol'benstange *f* piston rod
Kolchose [kɔl'çozə] *f* (-;-n) collective farm
Kolibri ['kolibri] *m* (-s;-s) humming bird
Kolik ['kolɪk] *f* (-;-en) colic
Kolkrabe ['kɔlkrabə] *m* (-n;-n) raven
Kollaborateur [kɔlabɔra'tør] *m* (-s;-) collaborator (*with the enemy*)
kollaborieren [kɔlabo'rirən] *intr* collaborate
Kollaps [kɔ'laps] *m* (-es;-e) collapse

kollationieren [kɔlatsjo'nirən] *tr* collate
Kol·leg [kɔ'lek] *n* (-s;-s & -legien ['legjən]) lecture; course of lectures; theological college
Kollege [kɔ'legə] *m* (-n;-n) colleague
Kolleg'heft *n* lecture notes
Kollegin [kɔ'legɪn] *f* (-;-nen) colleague
Kollekte [kɔ'lɛktə] *f* (-;-n) collection; (eccl) collect
Kollektion [kɔlɛk'tsjon] *f* (-;-en) collection
kollektiv [kɔlɛk'tif] *adj* collective ‖ **Kollektiv** *n* (-s;-e) collective
Koller ['kɔlər] *m* (-s;) rage, temper
kollern ['kɔlərn] *ref* roll about; (vor Lachen*) double over ‖ *intr* (*Puter*) gobble; (*Magen*) rumble ‖ *intr* (SEIN) roll
kollidieren [kɔlɪ'dirən] *intr* (SEIN) collide
Kollier [kɔ'lir] *n* (-s;-s) necklace
Kollision [kɔlɪ'zjon] *f* (-;-en) collision
Köln [kœln] *n* (-s;) Cologne
Kölnischwasser [kœlnɪʃ'vasər] *n* cologne
kolonial [kolo'njal] *adj* colonial
Kolonial'waren *pl* groceries
Kolonial'warengeschäft *n* grocery store
Kolo·nie [kolo'ni] *f* (-;-nien ['ni·ən]) colony
Kolonnade [kolo'nadə] *f* (-;-n) colonnade
Kolonne [ko'lɔnə] *f* (-;-n) column; (mil) convoy (*of vehicles*)
kolorieren [kolo'rirən] *tr* color
Kolorit [kolo'rit] *n* (-[e]s;-e) coloring
Ko·loß [ko'lɔs] *m* (-losses;-losse) colossus; giant
kolossal [kolo'sal] *adj* colossal
Kolportage [kɔlpɔr'taʒə] *f* (-;-n) trashy literature; spreading of rumors
kolportieren [kɔlpɔr'tirən] *tr* peddle; (*Gerüchte*) spread
Kolumnist -in [kolum'nɪst(ɪn)] §7 *mf* columnist
Kombi ['kɔmbi] *m* (-s;-s) (coll) station wagon
Kombination [kɔmbɪna'tsjon] *f* (-;-en) combination; (*Flieger-*) flying suit; (*e-s Monteurs*) coveralls; sport suit; reasoning, deduction; conjecture
kombinieren [kɔmbɪ'nirən] *tr* combine ‖ *intr* reason
Kom'biwagen *m* station wagon
Kombüse [kɔm'byzə] *f* (-;-n) (naut) galley, kitchen
Komik ['komɪk] *f* (-;) humor
Komiker ['komɪkər] *m* (-s;-) comedian
Komikerin ['komɪkərɪn] *f* (-;-nen) comedienne
komisch ['komɪʃ] *adj* funny
Komitee [komi'te] *n* (-s;-s) committee
Komma ['koma] *n* (-s;-s) comma; (*Dezimalzeichen*) decimal point
Kommandant [koman'dant] *m* (-en;-en) commanding officer; commandant

Kommandantur [kəmandan'tur] *f* (-;
-en) headquarters
Kommandeur [kɔman'dør] *m* (-s;-e)
commanding officer, commander
kommandieren [kɔman'dirən] *tr* command, order; be in command of;
(mil) detail; (mil) detach ‖ *intr* command, be in command
Kommanditgesellschaft [kɔman'ditga-
zel∫aft] *f* limited partnership; **K. auf
Aktien** partnership limited by shares
Kommando [kə'mando] *n* (-s;-s) command, order; (mil) command; (mil)
detachment, detail; **K. zurück!** as
you were!
Komman′dobrücke *f* (nav) bridge
Komman′doraum *m* control room
Komman′dostab *m* baton
Komman′dostand *m*, **Komman′dostelle**
f command post; (nav) bridge
Komman′dotruppe *f* commando unit
Komman′doturm *m* conning tower;
control tower (*of an aircraft carrier*)
kommen ['kɔmən] §99 *intr* (SEIN)
come; (*geschehen*) happen; **auf etw**
[*acc*] **k.** hit on s.th.; **auf jeden k. drei
Mark** each one gets three marks; **das
kommt bloß daher, daß** that's entirely due to; **dazu k.** get around to
it; get hold of it; **hinter etw** [*acc*] **k.**
find s.th. out; **j—m grob k.** be rude
to s.o.; **k. lassen** send for; **nichts k.
lassen auf** (*acc*) defend; **so weit k.,
daß** reach the point where; **ums
Leben k.** lose one's life; **wenn Sie
mir so k.** if you talk like that to me;
weit k. get far; **wieder zu sich k.**
come to, regain consciousness; **wie
kam er denn dazu?** how come he did
it? **wie komme ich zum Bahnhof?**
how do I get to the train station?
Kommentar [kɔmen'tar] *m* (-s;-e)
commentary; **kein K.!** no comment!
Kommen·tator [kɔmen'tator] *m* (-s;
-tatoren [ta'torən]) commentator
kommentieren [kɔmen'tirən] *tr* comment on
Kommers [kə'mers] *m* (-es;-e) drinking party
Kommers′buch *n* students' song book
kommerziell [komer'tsjel] *adj* commercial
Kommilitone [kɔmɪlɪ'tonə] *m* (-n;-n)
fellow student
Kom·mis [kə'mi] *m* (-mis ['mis];
-mis ['mis]) clerk
Kom·miß [kə'mis] *m* (-misses;) (coll)
army; (coll) army life
Kommissar [kɔmɪ'sar] *m* (-s;-e) commissioner; (pol) commissar
kommissarisch [kɔmɪ'sarɪ∫] *adj* provisional, temporary
Kommission [kɔmɪ'sjon] *f* (-;-en)
commission, board; **in K.** (com) on
consignment; on a commission basis
Kommissionär [kɔmɪsjo'nɛr] *m* (-s;-e)
agent; wholesale bookseller
Kommissions′gebühr *f* (com) commission
kommissions′weise *adv* on a commission basis
Kommiß′stiefel *m* army boot
kommod [kə'mot] *adj* comfortable

Kommode [kə'modə] *f* (-;-n) bureau,
chest of drawers
kommunal [kɔmu'nal] *adj* municipal,
local
Kommunal′politik *f* local politics
Kommune [kə'munə] *f* (-;-n) munici-
pality; **die K.** the Commies
Kommunikant -in [kɔmunɪ'kant(ɪn)]
§7 *mf* communicant
Kommunion [kɔmu'njon] *f* (-;-en)
Communion
Kommuniqué [kɔmynɪ'ke] *n* (-s;-s)
communiqué
Kommunismus [kɔmu'nɪsmus] *m* (-;)
communism
Kommunist -in [kɔmu'nɪst(ɪn)] §7 *mf*
communist
kommunistisch [kɔmu'nɪstɪ∫] *adj* com-
munist(ic)
Komödiant [kɔmø'djant] *m* (-en;-en)
comedian; (pej) ham
Komödie [kə'mødjə] *f* (-;-n) comedy;
K. spielen (coll) put on an act
Kompagnon [kɔmpan'jõ] *m* (-s;-s)
(business) partner; associate
kompakt [kɔm'pakt] *adj* compact
Kompa·nie [kɔmpa'ni] *f* (-;-nien
['ni·ən]) company
Kompanie′chef *m* company commander
komparativ [kɔmpara'tif] *adj* comparative ‖ **Komparativ** *m* (-s;-e)
comparative
Komparse [kɔm'parzə] *m* (-n;-n)
(theat) extra
Kom·paß ['kɔmpas] *m* (-passes;
-passe) compass
Kompen·dium [kɔm'pendjum] *n* (-s;
-dien [djən]) compendium
Kompensation [kɔmpenza'tsjon] *f* (-;
-en) compensation
Kompensations′geschäft *n* fair-value
exchange
kompensieren [kɔmpen'zirən] *tr* compensate for, offset
Kompetenz [kɔmpe'tents] *f* (-;-en)
(jur) jurisdiction
komplementär [kɔmplemen'ter] *adj*
complementary
Komplet [kõ'ple] *n* (-s;-s) dress with
matching coat
komplett [kɔm'plet] *adj* complete;
everything included
komplex [kɔm'pleks] *adj* complex ‖
Komplex *m* (-es;-e) complex
Komplice [kɔm'plitsə] *m* (-n;-n) accomplice
komplizieren [kɔmplɪ'tsirən] *tr* complicate
Komplott [kɔm'plɔt] *n* (-[e]s;-e) plot
Komponente [kɔmpə'nentə] *f* (-;-n)
component
komponieren [kɔmpə'nirən] *tr* compose
Komponist -in [kɔmpə'nɪst(ɪn)] §7 *mf*
composer
Komposition [kɔmpozɪ'tsjon] *f* (-;-en)
composition
Komposi·tum [kɔm'pozɪtum] *n* (-s;
-ta [ta] & -ten [tən]) compound
(word)
Kompott [kɔm'pɔt] *n* (-[e]s;-e) stewed fruit

Kompres·sor [kɔm'presɔr] *m* (**–s;**
–soren ['soːrən]) compressor; (aut)
supercharger

komprimieren [kɔmprɪ'miːrən] *tr* compress

Kompro·miß [kɔmprə'mɪs] *m* (**–mis-**
ses; –misse) compromise

kompromittieren [kɔmprəmɪ'tiːrən] *tr*
compromise

kondensieren [kɔndɛn'ziːrən] *tr, ref* &
intr (SEIN) condense

Kondensmilch [kɔn'dɛnsmɪlç] *f* evap-
orated milk

Kondens'streifen [kɔn'dɛns/traɪfən] *m*
contrail

Konditorei [kɔndɪtə'raɪ] *f* (**–;–en**)
pastry shop

Konfekt [kɔn'fɛkt] *n* (**–[e]s;**) candy,
chocolates; fancy cookies

Konfektion [kɔnfɛk'tsjoːn] *f* (**–;**) readymade clothes; manufacture of ready-
made clothes

Konfektionär [kɔnfɛktsjo'nɛːr] *m* (**–s;**
–e) clothing manufacturer; clothing
retailer

konfektionieren [kɔnfɛktsjo'niːrən] *tr*
manufacture (*clothes*)

Konferenz [kɔnfe'rɛnts] *f* (**–;–en**) conference

konferieren [kɔnfe'riːrən] *intr* confer,
hold a conference

Konfession [kɔnfe'sjoːn] *f* (**–;–en**) religious denomination; (eccl) confession; confession of faith, creed

konfessionell [kɔnfɛsjo'nɛl] *adj* denominational

konfessions'los *adj* nondenominational

Konfessions'schule *f* denominational
school, parochial school

konfirmieren [kɔnfɪr'miːrən] *tr* (eccl)
(Prot) confirm

konfiszieren [kɔnfɪs'tsiːrən] *tr* confiscate

Konfitüre [kɔnfɪ'tyːrə] *f* (**–;–n**) jam

Konflikt [kɔn'flɪkt] *m* (**–[e]s;–e**) conflict

konform [kɔn'fɔrm] *adj* concurring;
mit j–m k. gehen agree with s.o.

Konfrontation [kɔnfrɔnta'tsjoːn] *f* (**–;**
–en) confrontation

konfrontieren [kɔnfrɔn'tiːrən] *tr* confront

konfus [kɔn'fuːs] *adj* confused, puzzled

Kongruenz [kɔngru'ɛnts] *f* (**–;**) (geom)
congruence; (gram) agreement

König ['køːnɪç] *m* (**–[e]s;–e**) king

Königin ['køːnɪgɪn] *f* (**–;–nen**) queen

kö'niglich *adj* kingly, royal

Kö'nigreich *n* kingdom

Kö'nigsadler *m* golden eagle

Kö'nigsrose *f* (bot) peony

Kö'nigsschlange *f* boa constrictor

kö'nigstreu *adj* royalist

Kö'nigswürde *f* kingship

Königtum ['køːnɪçtum] *n* (**–s;**) royalty,
kinship; monarchy

konisch ['koːnɪʃ] *adj* conical

konjugieren [kɔnju'giːrən] *tr* conjugate

Konjunktion [kɔnjuŋk'tsjoːn] *f* (**–;–en**)
conjunction

Konjunktiv [kɔnjuŋk'tiːf] *m* (**–s;–e**)
subjunctive mood

Konjunktur [kɔnjuŋk'tuːr] *f* (**–;–en**)

economic situation; business trend;
(*Hochstand*) boom

konkav [kɔn'kaːf] *adj* concave

konkret [kɔn'kreːt] *adj* concrete

Konkurrent –in [kɔnku'rɛnt(ɪn)] §7
mf competitor

Konkurrenz [kɔnku'rɛnts] *f* (**–;–en**)
competition; **K. machen** (*dat*) compete with

konkurrenz'fähig *adj* competitive

konkurrieren [kɔnku'riːrən] *intr* compete

Konkurs [kɔn'kurs] *m* (**–es;–e**) bankruptcy; **in K. gehen** (or geraten) go
bankrupt; **K. anmelden** declare bankruptcy

Konkurs'masse *f* bankrupt company's
assets

können ['kœnən] §100 *tr* able to do;
know; **ich kann nichts dafür** I can't
help it || *intr*—**ich kann nicht hinein**
I can't get in || *mod aux* be able to;
know how to; be allowed; **das kann
sein** that may be; **ich kann nicht
sehen** I can't see || **Können** *n* (**–s;**)
ability

Könner ['kœnər] *m* (**–s;–**) expert

konnte ['kɔntə] *pret* of **können**

konsequent [kɔnze'kvɛnt] *adj* consistent

Konsequenz [kɔnze'kvɛnts] *f* (**–;–en**)
consistency; (*Folge*) consequence

konservativ [kɔnzɛrva'tiːf] *adj* conservative

Konservato·rium [kɔnzɛrva'toːrjum] *n*
(**–s;–rien** [rjən]) conservatory

Konserve [kɔn'zɛrvə] *f* (**–;–n**) canned
food

Konser'venbüchse *f*, **Konser'vendose** *f*
can

Konser'venfabrik *f* cannery

Konser'venöffner *m* can opener

konservieren [kɔnzɛr'viːrən] *tr* preserve

Konservie'rung *f* (**–;**) preservation

Konsisto·rium [kɔnzɪs'toːrjum] *n* (**–s;**
–rien [rjən]) (eccl) consistory

Konsole [kɔn'zoːlə] *f* (**–;–n**) bracket;
(archit) console

konsolidieren [kɔnzɔlɪ'diːrən] *tr* consolidate

Konsonant [kɔnzo'nant] *m* (**–en;–en**)
consonant

Konsorte [kɔn'zɔrtə] *m* (**–n;–n**) (pej)
accomplice; (fin) member of a syndicate

Konsor·tium [kɔn'zɔrtjum] *n* (**–s;–tien**
[tjən]) (fin) syndicate

konstant [kɔn'stant] *adj* constant ||
Konstante §5 *f* (math, phys) constant

konstatieren [kɔnsta'tiːrən] *tr* ascertain; state; (med) diagnose

konsterniert [kɔnstɛr'niːrt] *adj* stunned

konstituieren [kɔnstɪtu'iːrən] *tr* consti-
tute || *ref* be established; **sich als
Ausschuß k.** form a committee of the
whole

konstitutionell [kɔnstɪtutsjo'nɛl] *adj*
constitutional

konstruieren [kɔnstru'iːrən] *tr* construct; (*entwerfen*) design; (gram)
construe

Konsul ['kɔnzul] *m* (**–s;–n**) consul

konsularisch [kɔnzu'larɪʃ] *adj* consular

Konsulat [kɔnzu'lɑt] *n* (-[e]s;-e) consulate; (hist) consulship

Konsulent –in [kɔnzu'lent(ɪn)] §7 *mf* (jur) counsel

konsultieren [kɔnzul'tirən] *tr* consult

Konsum [kɔn'zum] *m* (-s;-s) cooperative store; (com) consumption

Konsument –in [kɔnzu'ment(ɪn)] §7 *mf* consumer

Konsum'güter *pl* consumer goods

konsumieren [kɔnzu'mirən] *tr* consume

Konsum'verein *m* cooperative society

Kontakt [kɔn'takt] *m* (-[e]s;-e) contact

Kontakt'glas *n*, **Kontakt'schale** *f* contact lens

Konteradmiral ['kɔntəratmirɑl] *m* rear admiral

Konterfei [kɔntər'faɪ] *n* (-s;-e) portrait, likeness

kontern ['kɔntərn] *tr* counter

Kontinent ['kɔntinənt] *m* (-[e]s;-e) continent

Kontingent [kɔntɪŋ'gent] *n* (-[e]s;-e) quota; (mil) contingent

Kon·to ['kɔnto] *n* (-s;-s & -ten [tən]) account

Kon'toauszug *m* bank statement

Kontor [kɔn'tor] *n* (-s;-e) (com) office

Kontorist –in [kɔntə'rɪst(ɪn)] §7 *mf* clerk (*in an office*)

Kontrahent [kɔntra'hent] *m* (-en;-en) contracting party; dueller

kontrahieren [kɔntra'hirən] *tr & intr* contract

Kontrakt [kɔn'trakt] *m* (-[e]s;-e) contract

Kontrapunkt ['kɔntrapuŋkt] *m* (mus) counterpoint

konträr [kɔn'trer] *adj* contrary

Kontrast [kɔn'trast] *m* (-[e]s;-e) contrast

konstrastieren [kɔntras'tirən] *intr* contrast

Kontrast'regelung *f* (telv) contrast button

Kontroll– [kɔntrɔl] *comb.fm.* checking; control

Kontroll'abschnitt *m* stub (*of ticket*)

Kontrolle [kɔn'trɔlə] *f* (-;-n) control, check, inspection

Kontrolleur [kɔntrɔ'lør] *m* (-s;-e) inspector, supervisor; (aer) air-traffic controller; (indust) timekeeper

kontrollieren [kɔntrɔ'lirən] *tr* control; check, inspect; (*Bücher*) audit

Kontroll'kasse *f* cash register

Kontroll'leuchte *f* (aut) warning light (*on dashboard*)

Kontroll'turm *m* (aer) control tower

Kontroverse [kɔntrə'verzə] *f* (-;-n) controversy

Kontur [kɔn'tur] *f* (-;-en) contour

Konvent [kɔn'vent] *m* (-[e]s;-e) convent; monastery; (*Versammlung*) convention

Konvention [kɔnven'tsjon] *f* (-;-en) convention

konventionell [kɔnventsjə'nel] *adj* conventional

Konversation [kɔnverza'tsjon] *f* (-;-en) conversation

Konversations'lexikon *n* encyclopedia; **wandelndes K.** (coll) walking encyclopedia

konvertieren [kɔnver'tirən] *tr* convert || *intr* be converted

Konvertit –in [kɔnver'tit(ɪn)] §7 *mf* convert

konvex [kɔn'veks] *adj* convex

Konvikt [kɔn'vɪkt] *n* (-s;-e) minor seminary

Konvoi ['kɔnvɔɪ] *m* (-s;-s) convoy

Konvolut [kɔnvə'lut] *n* (-[e]s;-e) bundle, roll

Konzentration [kɔntsentra'tsjon] *f* (-; -en) concentration

Konzentrations'lager *n* concentration camp

konzentrieren [kɔntsen'trirən] *tr & ref* (**auf** *acc*) concentrate (*on*)

konzentrisch [kɔn'tsentrɪʃ] *adj* concentric

Konzept [kɔn'tsept] *n* (-[e]s;-e) rough draft; **aus dem K. bringen** confuse, throw off; **aus dem K. kommen** lose one's train of thought

Konzept'papier *n* scribbling paper

Konzern [kɔn'tsern] *m* (-s;-e) (com) combine

Konzert [kɔn'tsert] *n* (-[e]s;-e) concert

Konzert'flügel *m* grand piano

Konzession [kɔntse'sjon] *f* (-;-en) concession; license

konzessionieren [kɔntsesjo'nirən] *tr* (com) license

Kon·zil [kɔn'tsil] *n* (-[e]s;-e & -zilien ['tsiljən]) (eccl) council

konziliant [kɔntsi'ljant] *adj* conciliatory; understanding

konzipieren [kɔntsi'pirən] *tr* conceive

koordiniren [kɔ·ɔrdi'nirən] *tr* coordinate

Kopf [kɔpf] *m* (-es;¨e) head; **aus dem Kopfe** by heart; **j-m über den K. wachsen** be taller than s.o.; (fig) be too much for s.o.; **mit dem K. voran** head first; **seinen eigenen K. haben** have a mind of one's own; **seinen K. lassen müssen** lose one's life

Kopf'bedeckung *f* headgear, head wear

Kopf'brett *n* headboard

köpfen ['kœpfən] *tr* behead; (*Baum*) top; (fb) head

Kopf'ende *n* head (*of bed, etc.*)

Kopf'geld *n* reward (*for capture of criminal*)

Kopf'haut *f* scalp

Kopf'hörer *m* headset, earphones

-köpfig [kœpfɪç] *comb.fm.* -headed; -man

Kopf'kissen *n* pillow

Kopf'kissenbezug *m* pillowcase

kopf'lastig *adj* top-heavy

Kopf'lehne *f* headrest

Kopf'rechnen *n* (-s) mental arithmetic

Kopf'salat *m* head lettuce

kopf'scheu *adj* (*Pferd*) nervous; (*Person*) shy; **k. werden** become alarmed

Kopf'schmerzen *pl* headache

Kopf'schuppen *pl* dandruff

Kopf'sprung *m* dive; **e-n K. machen** dive

Kopf'stand *m* handstand; **e-n K. machen** (aer) nose over

Kopf'stärke *f* (mil) strength

kopf'stehen §146 *intr* stand on one's head; (fig) be upside down

Kopf'steinpflaster *n* cobblestones

Kopf'steuer *f* poll tax

Kopf'stimme *f* falsetto

Kopf'stoß *m* butt; (fb) header

Kopf'tuch *n* kerchief, babushka

kopfü'ber *adv* head over heels

kopfun'ter *adv*—**kopfüber k.** head over heels

Kopf'weh *n* headache

Kopf'wellenknall *m* sonic boom

Ko·pie [ko'pi] *f* (–;–pien ['pi·ən]) copy, duplicate; (phot) print

kopieren [ko'pirən] *tr* copy; (phot) print

Kopier'maschine *f* copier, photocopying machine

Kopier'papier *n* tracing paper; carbon paper; (phot) printing paper

Kopier'stift *m* indelible pencil

Koppel ['kɔpəl] *f* (–;–n) leash; (*Gehege*) enclosure, paddock ‖ *n* (–s;–) (mil) belt

koppeln ['kɔpəln] *tr* tie together, yoke; (fig) tie in; (elec) connect; (rad, rr) couple; (rok) dock ‖ **Koppeln** (–s;) (aer, naut) dead reckoning; (rok) docking

Kopplungsgeschäft ['kɔpluŋsgəʃɛft] *n* package deal

Koralle [ko'ralə] *f* (–;–n) coral

Korb [kɔrp] *m* (–[e]s;ⁱ̈e) basket; **j–m den K. geben** (fig) give s.o. the brush-off

Korb'ball *m* basketball

Körbchen ['kœrpçən] *n* (–s;–) little basket; (*e-s Büstenhalters*) cup

Korb'flasche *f* demijohn

Korb'geflecht *n* wickerwork

Korb'möbel *pl* wicker furniture

Korb'weide *f* (bot) osier

Kordel ['kɔrdəl] *f* (–;–n) cord

Kordon [kɔr'dõ] *m* (–s;–s) cordon; (*Ordensband*) ribbon

Korea [ko're·a] *n* (–s;) Korea

koreanisch [ko're'aniʃ] *adj* Korean

Korinthe [ko'rɪntə] *f* (–;–n) currant

Kork [kɔrk] *m* (–[e]s;–e) cork

Korken ['kɔrkən] *m* (–s;–) cork, stopper

Korkenzieher ['kɔrkəntsi·ər] *m* (–s;–) corkscrew

Korn [kɔrn] *n* (–[e]s;ⁱ̈er) grain; seed; (*am Gewehr*) bead; (*Getreide*) rye; (*e-r Münze*) fineness; (phot) graininess; **j–n aufs K. nehmen** draw a bead on s.o.

Korn'ähre *f* ear of grain

Korn'branntwein *m* whiskey

Kornett [kɔr'nɛt] *n* (–[e]s;–e) (mus) cornet

körnig ['kœrnɪç] *adj* granular

Korn'kammer *f* granary; (fig) breadbasket

koronar [kɔrə'nɑr] *adj* coronary

Körper ['kœrpər] *m* (–s;–) body; (geom, phys) solid

Kör'perbau *m* (–[e]s;) build, physique

kör'perbehindert *adj* physically handicapped

Kör'perbeschaffenheit *f* constitution

Körperchen [kœrpərçən] *n* (–s;–) corpuscle

Kör'perfülle *f* plumpness, corpulence

Kör'pergeruch *m* body odor

Kör'perhaltung *f* posture, bearing

Kör'perkraft *f* physical strength

kör'perlich *adj* physical; (*stofflich*) corporeal

Kör'perpflege *f* personal hygiene

Kör'perpuder *m* talcum powder

Kör'perschaft *f* (–;–en) body (*of persons*); corporation

Kör'perverletzung *f* bodily injury

Korporation [kɔrpora'tsjon] *f* (–;–en) corporation

Korps [kor] *n* (– [kors];– [kors]) corps

Korps'geist *m* esprit de corps

Korps'student *m* member of a fraternity

korrekt [kɔ'rɛkt] *adj* correct, proper

Korrek·tor [kɔ'rɛktər] *m* (–s;–toren ['torən]) proofreader

Korrektur [kɔrɛk'tur] *f* (–;–en) correction; proofreading

Korrektur'bogen *m* page proof

Korrektur'fahne *f* galley proof

Korrelat [kɔre'lat] *n* (–[e]s;–e) correlative

Korrespondent –in [kɔrɛspon'dɛnt(ɪn)] §7 *mf* correspondent

Korrespondenz [kɔrɛspon'dɛnts] *f* (–;–en) correspondence

Korrespondenz'karte *f* (Aust) postcard

Korridor ['kɔridor] *m* (–s;–e) corridor

korrigieren [kɔri'girən] *tr* correct

korrodieren [kɔro'dirən] *tr & intr* corrode

Korse ['kɔrzə] *m* (–n;–n) Corsican

Korsett [kɔr'zɛt] *n* (–[e]s;–e & –s) corset

Korsika ['kɔrzika] *n* (–s;) Corsica

Korvette [kɔr'vetə] *f* (–;–n) corvette

Kosak [ko'zak] *m* (–en;–en) Cossack

K.-o.-Schlag [ka'o/lak] *m* knockout punch

kosen ['kozən] *tr* fondle, caress

Kosename ['kozənamə] *m* pet name

Kosmetik [kɔs'metik] *f* (–;) beauty treatment; **chirurgische K.** cosmetic surgery, plastic surgery

Kosme'tikartikel *m* cosmetic

Kosmeti·kum [kɔs'metikum] *n* (–s;–ka [ka]) cosmetic

kosmisch ['kɔzmiʃ] *adj* cosmic

kosmopolitisch [kɔzmopo'litiʃ] *adj* cosmopolitan

Kosmos ['kɔsmos] *m* (–;) cosmos

Kost [kɔst] *f* (–;) food, board

kostbar ['kɔstbar] *adj* costly; costly precious thing

Kost'barkeit *f* (–;–en) costliness; (fig) precious thing

kosten [kɔstən] *tr* cost; taste, sip ‖ **Kosten** *pl* costs; **auf K.** (*genit*) at the expense of; **auf seine K. kommen** get one's money's worth; **sich in K. stürzen** go to great expense

Ko'stenanschlag *m* estimate

Ko'stenaufwand *m* expenditure, outlay

Ko'stenberechnung *f* cost accounting

Ko'stenersatz *m*, **Ko'stenerstattung** *f* reimbursement of expenses

ko'stenlos *adj* free of charge

Ko'stenvoranschlag *m* estimate

Kost'gänger **-in** §6 *mf* boarder

köstlich [ˈkœstlɪç] *adj* delicious; delightful || *adv*—**sich k. amüsieren** have a grand time

Kost'probe *f* sample (*to taste*)

kostspielig [ˈkost/piliç] *adj* expensive

Kostüm [kos'tym] *n* (-s;-e) costume; woman's suit; fancy dress

kostümieren [kɔsty'mirən] *tr & ref* dress up

Kostüm'probe *f* dress rehearsal

Kot [kot] *m* (-[e]s;) mud, dirt; (*tierischer*) dirt, dung; excrement

Kotelett [kɔtə'let] *n* (-[e]s;-e & -s) pork chop; cutlet

Köter [ˈkøtər] *m* (-s;-) mut, mongrel

Kot'flügel *m* (aut) fender

kotig [ˈkotɪç] *adj* muddy, dirty

kotzen [ˈkotsən] *intr* (sl) puke || **Kotzen** *n*—**es ist zum K.** it's enough to make you throw up

Krabbe [ˈkrabə] *f* (-;-n) crab; shrimp; (*niedliches Kind*) little darling

krabbeln [ˈkrabəln] *tr & intr* tickle || *intr* (SEIN) crawl

Krach [krax] *m* (-[e]s;-s & -e) crash, bang; (*Lärm*) racket; (*Streit*) row; (fin) crash; **K. machen** kick up a row

krachen [ˈkraxən] *intr* crash, crack

krächzen [ˈkrɛçtsən] *intr* croak, caw

kraft [kraft] *prep* (*genit*) by virtue of || **Kraft** *f* (-;-̈e) strength, power, force; **außer K. setzen** repeal; **in K. sein** be in force; **in K. treten** come into force

Kraft'anlage *f* (elec) power plant

Kraft'anstrengung *f* strenuous effort

Kraft'aufwand *m* effort

Kraft'ausdruck *m* swear word; **Kraftausdrücke** strong language

Kraft'brühe *f* concentrated broth

Kraft'fahrer **-in** §6 *mf* motorist

Kraft'fahrzeug *n* motor vehicle

kräftig [ˈkreftɪç] *adj* strong, powerful; (*Speise*) nutritious || *adv* hard; heartily

kräftigen [ˈkreftɪgən] *tr* strengthen

Kraft'leistung *f* feat of strength

kraft'los *adj* powerless; weak

Kraft'meier *m* (coll) bully; (coll) muscle man

Kraft'probe *f* test of strength

Kraft'protz *m* (coll) powerhouse

Kraft'rad *n* motorcycle

Kraft'stoff *m* fuel

Kraft'stoffleitung *f* fuel line

kraftstrotzend [ˈkraft/trotsənt] *adj* strapping

Kraft'übertragung *f* (aut) transmission

Kraft'wagen *m* motor vehicle

Kraft'werk *n* generating plant

Kraft'wort *n* (-[e]s;-̈er) swear word

Kragen [ˈkragən] *m* (-s;-) collar

Krähe [ˈkre·ə] *f* (-;-n) crow

krähen [ˈkre·ən] *intr* crow

Krähenfüße [ˈkre·ənfysə] *pl* crow's feet (*wrinkles*)

Krakeel [kra'kel] *m* (-s;-e) (coll) rumpus; (*lauter Streit*) brawl

krakeelen [kra'kelən] *intr* (coll) kick up a storm

Kralle [ˈkralə] *f* (-;-n) claw

Kram [kram] *m* (-[e]s;) (coll) things, stuff; (coll) business, affairs

kramen [ˈkramən] *intr* rummage

Krämer **-in** [ˈkremər(ɪn)] §6 *mf* shopkeeper || *m* (pej) philistine

Krä'merseele *f* philistine

Kram'laden *m* general store

Krampe [ˈkrampə] *f* (-;-n) staple

Krampf [krampf] *m* (-[e]s;-̈e) cramp, spasm; convulsion; (*Unsinn*) nonsense

Krampf'ader *f* varicose vein

krampf'artig *adj* spasmodic

krampf'haft *adj* convulsive

Kran [kran] *m* (-[e]s;-̈e & -e) (mach) crane

Kranich [ˈkranɪç] *m* (-s;-e) (orn) crane

krank [kraŋk] *adj* sick, ill || **Kranke** §5 *mf* patient

-krank *comb.fm.* suffering from

kränkeln [ˈkrɛŋkəln] *intr* be sickly

kranken [ˈkraŋkən] *intr*—**k. an** (*dat*) suffer from

kränken [ˈkrɛŋkən] *tr* hurt, offend || *ref* (*über acc*) feel hurt (at)

Kran'kenanstalt *f* hospital

Kran'kenbahre *f* stretcher

Kran'kenbett *n* sickbed

Kran'kenfahrstuhl *m* wheel chair

Kran'kengeld *n* sick benefit

Kran'kenhaus *n* hospital; **ins K. einweisen** hospitalize

Kran'kenkasse *f* medical insurance plan

Kran'kenlager *n* sickbed

Kran'kenpflege *f* nursing

Kran'kenpfleger **-in** §6 *mf* nurse

Kran'kenrevier *n* (mil) sick quarters; (nav) sick bay

Kran'kensaal *m* hospital ward

Kran'kenschwester *f* nurse

Kran'kenstube *f* infirmary

Kran'kenstuhl *m* wheel chair

Kran'kenurlaub *m* sick leave

Kran'kenversicherung *f* health insurance

Kran'kenwagen *m* ambulance

krank'feiern *intr* (coll) play sick

krank'haft *adj* morbid, pathological

Krank'heit *f* (-;-en) sickness, disease

Krank'heitsbericht *m* medical bulletin

Krank'heitserscheinung *f* symptom

kränklich [ˈkrɛŋklɪç] *adj* sickly

Kränk'lichkeit *f* (-;) poor health

Kränkung [ˈkrɛŋkʊŋ] *f* (-;-en) offense

Kran'wagen *m* (aut) wrecker, tow truck

Kranz [krants] *m* (-[e]s;-̈e) wreath

Kränzchen [ˈkrentsçən] *n* (-s;-) small wreath; ladies' circle; informal dance

kränzen [ˈkrentsən] *tr* wreathe

Krapfen [ˈkrapfən] *m* (-s;-) doughnut

kraß [kras] *adj* crass, gross

Krater [ˈkratər] *m* (-s;-) crater

Kratzbürste [ˈkratsbYrstə] *f* wire brush; (fig) stand-offish woman

Krätze [ˈkretsə] *f* (-;) itch, scabies

kratzen [ˈkratsən] *tr & intr* scratch

Krat'zer *m* (-s;-) scratch; scraper

krauen ['krau·ən] *tr* scratch gently
kraus [kraus] *adj* (*Haar*) frizzy; (*Gedanken*) confused; **die Stirn k. ziehen** knit one's brows
Krause ['krauzə] *f* (-;-n) ruffle
kräuseln ['krɔɪzəln] *tr & ref* curl
Krau'seminze *f* (bot) spearmint
Kraus'haar *n* frizz
Kraut [kraut] *n* (-[e]s;̈-er) herb, plant; leafy top; (*Kohl*) cabbage; **ins K. schießen** run wild
Krawall [kra'val] *m* (-[e]s;-e) riot; (coll) rumpus
Krawatte [kra'vatə] *f* (-;-n) necktie
Krawat'tenhalter *m* tie clip
kraxeln [kra'ksəln] *intr* (SEIN) climb
Kreatur [krea'tur] *f* (-;-en) creature
Krebs [kreps] *m* (-es;-e) crawfish, crab; (pathol) cancer
krebs'artig *adj* (pathol) cancerous
Kredenz [kre'dents] *f* (-;-en) buffet, credenza, sideboard
kredenzen [kre'dentsən] *tr* (*Wein*) serve
Kredit [kre'dit] *m* (-[e]s;-e) credit
Kredit'bank *f* commercial bank
kreditieren [kredi'tirən] *tr* credit || *intr* give credit
Kredit'karte *f* credit card
Kredit'würdigkeit *f* trustworthiness; (com) credit rating
Kreide ['kraɪdə] *f* (-;-n) chalk, piece of chalk, crayon
kreieren [kre'irən] *tr* create
Kreis [kraɪs] *m* (-es;-e) circle; (*Bereich*) field; (*Bezirk*) district; (adm) county; (elec) circuit
Kreis'abschnitt *m* segment
Kreis'amt *n* district office
Kreis'ausschnitt *m* sector
Kreis'bahn *f* orbit
Kreis'bogen *m* (geom) arc
kreischen ['kraɪ/ən] *intr* shriek
Kreisel ['kraɪzəl] *m* (-s;-) gyroscope; top (*toy*)
Krei'selbewegung *f* gyration
Krei'selhorizont *m* artificial horizon
kreiseln ['kraɪzəln] *intr* spin, rotate, gyrate; spin the top
Krei'selpumpe *f* centrifugal pump
kreisen ['kraɪzən] *intr* circle; revolve; (*Blut*) circulate
kreis'förmig *adj* circular
Kreis'lauf *m* circulation; cycle
Kreis'laufsstörung *f* circulatory disorder
kreis'rund *adj* circular
Kreis'säge *f* circular saw, buzz saw
kreißen ['kraɪsən] *intr* be in labor
Kreißsaal ['kraɪssal] *m* delivery room
Kreis'stadt *f* (rural) county seat
Kreis'umfang *m* circumference
Kreis'verkehr *m* traffic circle
Krem [krem] *f* (-;-s) & *m* (-s;-s) cream
Kreml ['kreməl] *m* (-[e]s;) Kremlin
Krempe ['krempə] *f* (-;-n) brim, rim
Krempel ['krempəl] *m* (-s;) (coll) stuff, junk || *f* (-;-n) (tex) card
Kren [kren] *m* (-[e]s;) horseradish
krepieren [kre'pirən] *intr* (SEIN) (*Tiere*) die; (*Granate*) explode, burst; (sl) kick the bucket

Krepp [krep] *m* (-s;-s) crepe
Kreta ['kreta] *n* (-s;) Crete
Kretonne [kre'tonə] *f* (-;-n) cretonne
kreuz [krɔɪts] *adv*—**k. und quer** crisscross || **Kreuz** *n* (-es;-e) cross; small of the back; (cards) club(s) (anat)
Kreuz'abnahme *f* deposition
Kreuz'band *n* (-[e]s;̈-er) mailing wrapper (*for newspapers, etc.*)
kreuz'brav *adj* (coll) very honest; (coll) very well-behaved
kreuzen ['krɔɪtsən] *tr* cross || *recip* cross; interbreed || *intr* cruise
Kreuzer ['krɔɪtsər] *m* (-s;-) penny; (nav) cruiser
Kreuz'fahrer *m* crusader
Kreuz'fahrt *f* cruise; (hist) crusade
Kreuz'feuer *n* crossfire
kreuz'fidel *adj* very cheerful
Kreuz'gang *m* (archit) cloister(s)
kreuzigen ['krɔɪtsɪgən] *tr* crucify
Kreu'zigung *f* (-;-en) crucifixion
Kreuz'otter *f* adder
Kreuz'ritter *m* crusader; Knight of the Teutonic Order
Kreuz'schiff *m* transept (*of church*)
Kreuz'schlitzschraubenzieher *m* Phillips screwdriver
Kreu'zung *f* (-;-en) intersection; crossbreeding; hybrid; (rr) crossing
Kreuz'verhör *n* cross-examination; **j-n ins K. nehmen** cross-examine s.o.
Kreuz'verweis *m* cross reference
Kreuz'weg *m* crossroad; (eccl) stations of the cross
Kreuz'worträtsel *n* crossword puzzle
Kreuz'zeichen *n* (eccl) sign of the cross; (typ) dagger
Kreuz'zug *m* crusade
kribbelig ['krɪbəlɪç] *adj* irritable; (nervös) edgy, on edge
kribbeln ['krɪbəln] *intr* tickle
kriechen ['kriçən] §102 *intr* (SEIN) creep, crawl
kriecherisch ['kriçərɪ/] *adj* fawning
Kriechtier ['kriçtir] *n* reptile
Krieg [krik] *m* (-[e]s;-e) war
kriegen ['krigən] *tr* (coll) get, catch
Krie'ger *m* (-s;-) warrior
kriegerisch ['krigərɪ/] *adj* warlike; (*Person*) belligerent
krieg'führend *adj* warring
Kriegs'akademie *f* war college
Kriegs'bemalung *f* war paint
Kriegs'berichter *m*, **Kriegs'berichterstatter** *m* war correspondent
Kriegs'dienst *m* military service
Kriegs'dienstverweigerer *m* conscientious objector
Kriegs'einsatz *m* (mil) action
Kriegs'entschädigung *f* reparations
Kriegs'fall *m*—**im K.** in case of war
Kriegs'flotte *f* fleet; naval force
Kriegs'fuß *m*—**mit j-m auf K. stehen** be at loggerheads with s.o.
Kriegs'gebiet *n* war zone
Kriegs'gefangene §5 *mf* prisoner of war
Kriegs'gericht *n* court martial
Kriegs'gewinnler ['kriksgəvɪnlər] *m* (-s;-) war profiteer
Kriegs'hafen *m* naval base
Kriegs'hetzer *m* warmonger

Kriegs′kamerad m fellow soldier
Kriegs′lazarett n base hospital
Kriegs′list f stratagem
Kriegs′marine f navy
Kriegs′ministerium n war department
Kriegs′opfer n war victim
Kriegs′pfad m warpath
Kriegs′rat m council of war
Kriegs′recht n martial law
Kriegs′rüstung f arming for war; war production
Kriegs′schauplatz m theater of war
Kriegs′schuld f war debt; war guilt
Kriegs′teilnehmer m combatant; (*ehemaliger*) ex-serviceman, veteran
Kriegs′verbrechen n war crime
Kriegs′versehrte §5 m disabled veteran
kriegs′verwendungsfähig adj fit for active duty
Kriegs′wesen n warfare, war
Kriegs′zug m (mil) campaign
Kriegs′zustand n state of war
Krim [krɪm] f (-;) Crimea
Krimi [′krimi] m (-s;-s) & (-;-) (coll) murder mystery; (telv) thriller
kriminal [krɪmɪ′nɑl] adj criminal
Kriminal− comb.fm. criminal, crime
Kriminal′beamte m criminal investigator
Kriminal′roman m detective novel
Kriminal′stück n (telv) thriller
kriminell [krɪmɪ′nɛl] adj criminal ‖
Kriminelle §5 mf criminal
Krimskrams [′krɪmskrams] m (-es;) (coll) junk
Kripo [′kripo] abbr (**Kriminalpolizei**) crime squad
Krippe [′krɪpə] f (-;-n) crib, manger; day nursery (*for infants up to 3 years*)
Krise [′krizə] f (-;-n) crisis
kriseln [′krizəln] impers—es kriselt there's a crisis, trouble is brewing
Kristall [krɪs′tal] m (-s;-e) crystal
Kristalleuchter (**Kristall′leuchter**) m crystal chandelier
Kristall′glas n crystal
kristallisieren [krɪstalɪ′zirən] ref & intr crystallize
Kristall′zucker m granulated sugar
Krite·rium [krɪ′terjum] n (-s;-rien [rjən]) criterion
Kritik [krɪ′tik] f (-;-en) criticism; critique; **unter aller K.** abominable
Kritikaster [krɪtɪ′kaster] m (-s;-) (pej) faultfinder
Kritiker −in [′kritɪkər(ɪn)] §6 mf critic; reviewer
kritik′los adj uncritical
kritisch [′kritɪʃ] adj critical
kritisieren [krɪtɪ′zirən] tr criticize; (*werten*) review
Krittelei [krɪtə′laɪ] f (-;-en) faultfinding; petty criticism
kritteln [′krɪtəln] intr (an dat) find fault (with), grumble (about)
Kritzelei [krɪtsə′laɪ] f (-;-en) scribbling, scrawling; scribble, scrawl
kritzeln [′krɪtsəln] tr & intr scribble
kroch [krɔx] pret of **kriechen**
Krokodil [kroko′dil] n (-[e]s;-e) crocodile
Krokus [′krokus] m (-;- & -se) crocus

Krone [′kronə] f (-;-n) crown
krönen [′krønən] tr crown
Kronerbe [′kronerbə] m, **Kronerbin** [′kronerbɪn] f heir apparent
Kronleuchter [′kronlɔɪçtər] m chandelier
Kronprinz [′kronprɪnts] m crown prince
Kronprinzessin [′kronprɪntsesɪn] f crown princess
Krö′nung f (-;-en) coronation
Kropf [krɔpf] m (-[e]s;⸚e) crop (*of bird*); (pathol) goiter
Kröte [′krøtə] f (-;-n) toad; **Kröten** (coll) coins, coppers
Krücke [′krykə] f (-;-n) crutch
Krückstock [′kryk/tɔk] m walking stick
Krug [kruk] m (-[e]s;⸚e) jar, jug; mug; pitcher; (*Wirtshaus*) tavern
Krume [′krumə] f (-;-n) crumb; topsoil
Krümel [′kryməl] m (-s;-) crumb
krümeln [′kryməln] tr & intr crumble
krumm [krum] adj (krummer & krümmer [′krymər]; krummste & krümmste [′krymstə] §9) bent, stooping; crooked
krumm′beinig adj bowlegged
krümmen [′krymən] tr bend, curve ‖ ref (vor Schmerzen) writhe; (vor Lachen) double up; (Wurm) wriggle; (Holz) warp; (Fluß, Straße) wind
Krümmer [′krymər] m (-s;-) (tech) elbow
krumm′nehmen §116 tr (coll) take the wrong way, take amiss
Krumm′stab m (eccl) crozier
Krüm′mung f (-;-en) bend, curve; winding
krumpeln [′krumpəln] tr & intr (coll) crumple, crease
Krüppel [′krypəl] m (-s;-) cripple; **zum K. machen** cripple
krüp′pelhaft adj deformed
krüp′pelig adj crippled; stunted
Kruste [′krustə] f (-;-n) crust
Kru′stentier n crustacean
krustig [′krustɪç] adj crusty
Kruzifix [krutsɪ′fɪks] n (-es;-e) crucifix
Kryp·ta [′krypta] f (-;-ten [tən]) crypt
Kübel [′kybəl] m (-s;-) tub; bucket
Kü′belwagen m jeep
kubieren [ku′birən] tr (math) cube
Kubik− [kubik] comb.fm. cubic
Kubik′maß n cubic measure
kubisch [′kubɪʃ] adj cubic
Kubismus [ku′bɪsmus] m (-;) cubism
Küche [′kyçə] f (-;-n) kitchen; (culin) cuisine
Kuchen [′kuxən] m (-s;-) cake, pie
Ku′chenblech n cookie sheet
Küchenchef m chef
Kü′chendienst m (mil) K.P.
Ku′chenform f cake pan
Kü′chengerät n kitchen utensil
Kü′chengeschirr n kitchen utensils
Kü′chenherd m kitchen range, stove
Kü′chenmaschine f electric kitchen appliance
Kü′chenmeister m chef

Kü'chenzettel *m* menu

Küchlein ['kʏçlaɪn] *n* (-s;-) chick; (culin) small cake

Kuckuck ['kʊkʊk] *m* (-s;-e) cuckoo; **zum K. gehen** (coll) go to hell

Kufe ['kufə] *f* (-;-n) vat; (*Schlitten-*) runner

Küfer ['kyfər] *m* (-s;-) cooper

Kugel ['kugəl] *f* (-;-n) ball; sphere; (*Geschoß*) bullet; (sport) shot

ku'gelfest *adj* bulletproof

ku'gelförmig *adj* spherical

Ku'gelgelenk *n* (mach) ball-and-socket joint; (anat) socket joint

Ku'gellager *n* ball bearing

kugeln ['kugəln] *tr* roll ‖ *ref* roll around; **sich vor Lachen k.** double over with laughter ‖ *intr* (SEIN) roll

Ku'gelregen *m* hail of bullets

ku'gelrund' *adj* round; (coll) tubby

Ku'gelschreiber *m* ball-point pen

Ku'gelstoßen *n* (sport) shot put

Kuh [ku] *f* (-;-e) cow

Kuh'dorf *n* hick town

Kuh'fladen *m* cow dung

Kuh'handel *m* (pol) horse trading

Kuh'haut *f* cowhide; **das geht auf keine K.** but that's a long story

kühl [kyl] *adj* cool

Kühl'anlage *f* refrigerator; cooling system; cold storage (room)

Kühle ['kylə] *f* (-;) cool, coolness

kühlen ['kylən] *tr* cool; (*Wein*) chill

Küh'ler *m* (-s;-) cooler; (aut) radiator

Küh'lerverschluß *m* radiator cap

Kühl'mittel *n* coolant

Kühl'schrank *m* refrigerator

Kühl'truhe *f* freezer

Kühl'wagen *m* refrigerator truck; (rr) refrigerator car

Kuh'magd *f* milkmaid

Kuh'mist *m* cow dung

kühn [kyn] *adj* bold, daring

Kühn'heit *f* (-;) boldness, daring

Kuhpocken ['kupokən] *pl* cowpox

Kuh'stall *m* cowshed, cow barn

Kujon [ku'jon] *m* (-s;-e) (pej) louse

kujonieren [kujo'nirən] *tr* bully

Küken ['kykən] *n* (-s;-) chick

Kukuruz ['kukuruts] *m* (-es;) (Aust) corn

kulant [ku'lant] *adj* obliging; generous

Kuli ['kuli] *m* (-s;-s) coolie

kulinarisch [kuli'narɪʃ] *adj* culinary

Kulisse [ku'lisə] *f* (-;-n) (theat) wing; **hinter den Kulissen** behind the scenes; **Kulissen** scenery

Kulis'senfieber *n* stage fright

kullern ['kulərn] *intr* (SEIN) roll

kulminieren [kulmi'nirən] *intr* culminate

Kult [kult] *m* (-[e]s;-e) cult

kultivieren [kulti'virən] *tr* cultivate

Kultur [kul'tur] *f* (-;-en) culture, civilization; (agr) cultivation; (bact, chem) culture

Kultur'austausch *m* cultural exchange

kulturell [kultu'rel] *adj* cultural

Kultur'erbe *n* cultural heritage

Kultur'film *m* educational film

Kultur'geschichte *f* history of civilization; cultural history

Kultur'volk *n* civilized people

Kul·tus ['kultus] *m* (-;-te [tə]) cult

Kümmel ['kʏməl] *m* (-s;-) caraway seed; caraway brandy

Küm'melbrot *n* seeded rye bread

Kummer ['kumər] *m* (-s;) grief, sorrow; worry, concern, trouble; **j-m großen K. bereiten** cause s.o. a lot of worry; **sich** [*dat*] **K. machen über** (*acc*) worry about

kümmerlich ['kʏmərlɪç] *adj* wretched; (*dürftig*) needy

Kümmerling ['kʏmərlɪŋ] *m* (-s;-e) stunted animal; stunted plant

kümmern ['kʏmərn] *tr* trouble, worry; concern ‖ *ref*—**sich k. um** worry about; take care of; **sich nicht k. um** not bother about; neglect

Kümmernis ['kʏmərnɪs] *f* (-;-se) worry, trouble

kum'mervoll *adj* grief-stricken

Kumpan [kum'pan] *m* (-s;-e) companion; buddy

Kumpel ['kumpəl] *m* (-s;-) buddy, sidekick; (min) miner

kund [kunt] *adj* known

kündbar ['kʏntbar] *adj* (*Vertrag*) terminable; (fin) redeemable

Kunde ['kundə] *m* (-n;-n) customer; **übler K.** (fig) tough customer ‖ *f* (-;) news, information; lore

-kunde *f* comb.fm. –ology; –graphy; science of; guide to, study of

Kun'dendienst *m* customer service; warranty service

Kun'denkreis *m* clientele

kund'geben §80 *tr* make known, announce

Kundgebung ['kuntgebuŋ] *f* (-;-en) manifestation; (pol) rally

kundig ['kundɪç] *adj* well-informed; **k. sein** (*genit*) know

-kundig comb.fm. well versed in; able to

kündigen ['kʏndɪgən] *tr* (*Vertrag*) give notice to terminate; (*Wohnung*) give notice to vacate; (*Stellung*) give notice of quitting; (*Kapital*) call in; (*Hypothek*) foreclose on; **j-n fristlos k.** (coll) sack s.o. ‖ *intr* (*dat*) given notice to, release

Kün'digung *f* (-;-en) (*seitens des Arbeitnehmers*) resignation; (*seitens des Arbeitgebers*) notice (*of termination*); **mit monatlicher K.** subject to a month's notice

Kün'digungsfrist *f* period of notice

kund'machen *tr* make known, announce

Kund'machung *f* (-;-en) announcement

Kund'schaft *f* (-;) clientele, customer(s); (mil) reconnaissance

kundschaften ['kuntʃaftən] *intr* go on reconnaissance, scout

Kund'schafter *m* (-s;-) scout, spy

kund'tun §154 *tr* make known, announce

kund'werden §159 *intr* (SEIN) become known

künftig ['kʏnftɪç] *adj* future, to come, next ‖ *adv* in the future, from now on

künf'tighin' *adv* from now on, hereafter

Kunst [kunst] *f* (-;-e) art; skill; **das ist keine K.** it's easy

Kunstbanause ['kunstbanauzə] *m* (-n; -n) philistine

Kunst'dünger *m* chemical fertilizer

Künstelei [kynstə'laɪ] *f* (-;-en) affectation

Kunst'faser *f* synthetic fiber

Kunst'fehler *m*—**ärztlicher K.** malpractice

kunst'fertig *adj* skillful, skilled

Kunst'flieger *m* stunt pilot

Kunst'flug *m* stunt flying

Kunst'freund **–in** §8 *mf* art lover; patron of the arts

Kunst'gegenstand *m* objet d'art

kunst'gerecht *adj* skillful; expert

Kunst'gewerbe *n* arts and crafts

Kunst'glied *n* artificial limb

Kunst'griff *m* trick

Kunst'händler **–in** §6 *mf* art dealer

Kunst'kenner **–in** §6 *mf* art connoisseur

Kunst'laufen *n* figure skating

Künstler **–in** ['kynstlər(ɪn)] §6 *mf* artist; performer

künstlerisch ['kynstlərɪʃ] *adj* artistic

künstlich ['kynstlɪç] *adj* artificial; (chem) synthetic

Kunst'liebhaber **–in** §6 *mf* art lover

kunst'los *adj* unaffected

Kunst'maler **–in** §6 *mf* painter, artist

Kunst'pause *f* pause for effect

kunst'reich *adj* ingenious

Kunst'reiter *m* equestrian

Kunst'seide *f* rayon

Kunst'springen *n* (sport) diving

Kunst'stoff *m* plastic material; synthetic material; (tex) synthetic fiber

Kunststoff– *comb.fm.* plastic; plastics

Kunst'stopfen *n* invisible mending

Kunst'stück *n* trick, feat

Kunst'tischler *m* cabinet maker

Kunstverständige ['kunstfer/tendɪgə] §5 *mf* art expert

kunst'voll *adj* elaborate, ornate

Kunst'werk *n* work of art

kunterbunt ['kuntərbunt] *adj* chaotic

Kupfer ['kupfər] *n* (-s;) copper

kupfern ['kupfərn] *adj* copper

kupieren [ku'piːrən] *tr* (*Schwanz, Ohren*) cut off; (*Spielkarten*) cut; (*Fahrkarten*) punch

Kuppe ['kupə] *f* (-;-n) top, summit

Kuppel ['kupəl] *f* (-;-n) cupola

Kuppelei [kupə'laɪ] *f* (-;) procuring

kuppeln ['kupəln] *tr* couple, connect ‖ *intr* be a pimp; be a procuress; (aut) operate the clutch

Kuppler ['kuplər] *m* (-s;-) pimp

Kupplerin ['kuplərɪn] *f* (-;-nen) procuress

Kupplung ['kupluŋ] *f* (-;-en) (aut) clutch; (rr) coupling

Kur [kuːr] *f* (-;-en) cure (*at a spa*); **j–n in die Kur nehmen** give s.o. a talking to

Kuratel [kura'tel] *f* (-;) guardianship; **j–n unter K. stellen** appoint a guardian for s.o.

Ku·rator [ku'raːtər] *m* (-s;-ratoren [ra'toːrən]) (*e–s Museums*) curator; (educ) trustee; (jur) guardian

Kurato·rium [kura'torjum] *n* (-s;-rien [rjən]) (educ) board of trustees

Kurbel ['kurbəl] *f* (-;-n) crank, handle, winch

Kurbelei [kurbə'laɪ] *f* (-;-en) shooting a film; (aer) dogfight

Kur'belgehäuse *n* (aut) crankcase

kurbeln ['kurbəln] *tr* crank; (*Film*) shoot ‖ *intr* engage in a dogfight

Kur'belstange *f* (mach) connecting rod

Kur'belwelle *f* (mach) crankshaft

Kürbis ['kyrbɪs] *m* (-ses;-se) pumpkin; (*Kopf*) (sl) bean

küren ['kyːrən] §165 & §109 *tr* elect

Kurfürst ['kurfyrst] *m* (-en;-en) elector (*of the Holy Roman Empire*)

Kur'haus *n* spa; hotel

Kurie ['kurjə] *f* (-;-n) (eccl) curia

Kurier [ku'riːr] *m* (-s;-e) courier

kurieren [ku'riːrən] *tr* cure

kurios [ku'rjoːs] *adj* odd, curious

Kuriosität [kurjozi'tet] *f* (-;-en) quaintness; curio, curiosity

Kur'ort *m* health resort, spa

Kurpfuscher ['kurpfu/ər] *m* (-s;-) quack

Kurrentschrift [ku'rent/rɪft] *f* cursive script

Kurs [kurs] *m* (-es;-e) (educ) course; (fin) rate of exchange; (fin) circulation; (naut) course; (st. exch.) price; **außer K.** setzen take out of circulation; **hoch im K. stehen** be at a premium; (fig) rate high; **zum Kurse von** at the rate of

Kurs'bericht *m* (st. exch.) market report

Kurs'buch *n* (rr) timetable

Kürschner ['kyr/nər] *m* (-s;-) furrier

Kurs'entwicklung *f* price trend

Kurs'gewinn *m* (st. exch.) gain

kursieren [kur'ziːrən] *intr* circulate

Kursive [kur'ziːvə] *f* (-;), **Kursivschrift** [kur'zif/rɪft] *f* (-;) italics

Kurs'stand *m* (st. exch.) price level

Kur·sus ['kurzus] *m* (-;-se [zə]) (educ) course

Kurs'veränderung *f* (fin) change in exchange rates; (naut) change of course; (pol) change of policy; (st. exch.) price change

Kurs'wert *m* (st. exch.) market value

Kurve ['kurvə] *f* (-;-n) curve; **in die K. gehen** (aer) bank

kurz [kurts] *adj* (**kürzer** ['kyrtsər]; **kürzeste** ['kyrtsəstə] §9) short, brief; **auf das kürzeste** very briefly; **binnen kurzem** within a short time; **in kurzem** before long; **k. und gut** in a word; **seit kurzem** for the last few days or weeks; **über k. oder lang** sooner or later; **zu k. kommen** (coll) get the short end of it ‖ *adv* shortly; briefly; curtly

kurzatmig ['kurtsaːtmɪç] *adj* shortwinded; (*Pferd*) broken-winded

Kürze ['kyrtsə] *f* (-;) shortness; brevity; **in K.** shortly; briefly

kürzen ['kyrtsən] *tr* shorten; (*Gehalt*) cut; (math) reduce

kurzerhand' *adv* offhand

Kurz'fassung *f* abridged version

Kurz'film *m* (cin) short

kurzfristig [ˈkurtsfrɪstɪç] *adj* short-term
Kurz′geschichte *f* short story
kurzlebig [ˈkurtslebɪç] *adj* short-lived
kürzlich [ˈkʏrtslɪç] *adj* lately, recently
Kurz′meldung *f* news flash
Kurz′nachrichten *pl* news summary
kurz′schließen §76 *tr* short-circuit
Kurz′schluß *m* short circuit
Kurz′schlußbrücke *f* (elec) jumper
Kurz′schrift *f* shorthand
kurz′sichtig *adj* near-sighted; (fig) short-sighted
Kurz′streckenlauf *m* sprint
Kurz′streckenläufer –in §6 *mf* sprinter
kurzum′ *adv* in short, in a word
Kür′zung *f* (–;–en) reduction; curtailment; (*e–s Buches*) abridgment
Kurz′waren *pl* sewing supplies
kurz′weg *adv* bluntly, flatly
Kurzweil [ˈkurtsvaɪl] *f* (–;) pastime
kurzweilig [ˈkurtsvaɪlɪç] *adj* amusing
kusch [kuʃ] *interj* lie down! (*to a dog*)
kuschen [ˈkuʃən] *ref* lie down; crouch || *intr* lie down; crouch, cringe; (*Person*) knuckle under, submit
Kusine [kuˈzinə] *f* (–;–n) female cousin
Kuß [kus] *m* (**Kusses; Küsse**) kiss; **kalter K.** popsicle

küssen [ˈkʏsən] *tr & intr* kiss
Kuß′hand *f*—*j–m* e–e **K. zuwerfen** throw s.o. a kiss; **mit K.** with pleasure
Küste [ˈkʏstə] *f* (–;–n) coast, shore
Kü′stenfahrer *m* coasting vessel
Kü′stenfischerei *f* inshore fishing
Kü′stengewässer *n* coastal waters
Kü′stenlinie *f* coastline, shoreline
kü′stennah *adj* offshore; coastal
Kü′stenschiffahrt *f* coastal shipping
Kü′stenstreife *f* shore patrol
Küster [ˈkʏstər] *m* (–s;–) sexton
Kustos [ˈkustɔs] *m* (–; **Kustoden** [kusˈtodən]) custodian
Kutsche [ˈkutʃə] *f* (–;–n) coach
Kut′scher *m* (–s;–) coachman
kutschieren [kuˈtʃirən] *intr* drive a coach || *intr* (SEIN) ride in a coach
Kutte [ˈkutə] *f* (–;–n) (eccl) cowl
Kutteln [ˈkutəln] *pl* tripe
Kutter [ˈkutər] *m* (–s;–) (naut) cutter
Kuvert [kuˈvert] *n* (–s;–s) & (–[e]s;–e) envelope; table setting
kuvertieren [kuverˈtirən] *tr* put into an envelope
Kux [kuks] *m* (–es;–e) mining share
Kyklon [kyˈklon] *m* (–s;–e) cyclone
Kyniker [ˈkynɪkər] *m* (–s;–) (philos) cynic

L

L, l [el] *invar n* L, l
laben [ˈlabən] *tr* refresh
Labial [laˈbjal] *m* (–s;–e) labial
labil [laˈbil] *adj* unstable
Labor [laˈbor] *n* (–s;–s) (coll) lab
Laborant [laboˈrant] (ɪn) §7 *mf* laboratory technician
Laborato·rium [laboraˈtorjum] *n* (–s; **rien** [rjən]) laboratory
laborieren [laboˈrirən] *intr* experiment; **l. an** (*dat*) suffer from
Labsal [ˈlapzal] *n* (–[e]s;–e) refreshment
La′bung *f* (–;–en) refreshment
Labyrinth [labyˈrɪnt] *n* (–[e]s;–e) labyrinth
Lache [ˈlaxə] *f* (–;–n) puddle, pool; laugh; **e–e gellende L. anschlagen** break out in laughter
lächeln [ˈleçəln] *intr* (**über** *acc*) smile (at) || **Lächeln** *n* (–s;) smile; **höhnisches L.** sneer
lachen [ˈlaxən] *intr* laugh; **daß ich nicht lache!** don't make me laugh! || **Lachen** *n* (–s;) laugh, laughter; **du hast gut L.!** you can laugh!
lächerlich [ˈleçərlɪç] *adj* ridiculous; **l. machen** ridicule; **sich l. machen** make a fool of oneself
lachhaft [ˈlaxhaft] *adj* ridiculous
Lachkrampf [ˈlaxkrampf] *m* fit of laughter
Lachs [laks] *m* (–es;–e) salmon
Lachsalve [ˈlaxzalvə] *f* (–;–n) peal of laughter

Lachs′schinken *m* raw, lightly smoked ham
Lack [lak] *m* (–[e]s;–e) lacquer, varnish
Lackel [ˈlakəl] *m* (–s;–) (coll) dope
lackieren [laˈkirən] *tr* lacquer, varnish; (*Autos*) paint
Lack′leder *n* patent leather
Lackmuspapier [ˈlakmuspapir] *n* litmus paper
Lack′schuhe *pl* patent-leather shoes
Lade [ˈladə] *f* (–;–n) box, case; (*Schublade*) drawer
La′dearbeiter *m* loader
La′debaum *m* derrick
La′defähigkeit *f* loading capacity
La′dehemmung *f* jamming (*of a gun*); **L. haben** jam
La′deklappe *f* tailgate
laden [ˈladən] §103 *tr* load; (*Gast*) invite; (elec) charge; (jur) summon; **geladen sein** (coll) be burned up || **Laden** *m* (–s;-) store, shop; (*Fenster–*) shutter; **den L. schmeißen** pull it off, lick it
La′dendieb *m*, **La′dendiebin** *f* shoplifter
La′dendiebstahl *m* shoplifting
La′denhüter *m* drug on the market
La′deninhaber –in §6 *mf* shopkeeper
La′denkasse *f* till
Lä′denmädchen *n* salesgirl
La′denpreis *m* retail price
La′denschluß *m* closing time

La′denschwengel *m* (pej) stupid shop clerk

La′dentisch *m* counter

La′derampe *f* loading platform

La′deschein *m* bill of lading

La′destock *m* ramrod

La′destreifen *m* cartridge clip

La′dung *f* (–;–en) loading; load; (*Güter*) freight; (elec) charge; (jur) summons; (mil) charge; (naut) cargo

Lafette [la′fetə] *f* (–;–n) gun mount

Laffe [′lafə] *m* (–n;–n) jazzy dresser

lag [lak] *pret* of **liegen**

Lage [′lagə] *f* (–;–n) site, location; situation; (*Zustand*) condition, state; (*Haltung*) posture; (*Schicht*) layer, deposit; (*Salve*) volley; (*Bier*) round; (bb) quire; (mil) position; (mus) pitch; **mißliche L.** predicament; **versetzen Sie sich in meine L.** put yourself in my position

Lager [′lagər] *n* (–s;–) bed; (*e-s Wildes*) lair; (*Stapelplatz*) dump; (*Partei*) side, camp; (*von Waffen*) cache; (*Vorrat*) stock; (*Warenlager*) stockroom; (geol) stratum, vein; (mach) bearing; (mil) camp; **auf L.** in stock; (fig) up one′s sleeve; **ein L. halten von** keep stock of

La′geraufnahme *f* inventory

La′gerbier *n* lager beer

La′gerfähigkeit *f* shelf life

La′gerfeuer *n* campfire

La′gergebühr *f* storage charges

La′gerhalter *m* stock clerk

La′gerhaus *n* warehouse

Lagerist –in [lagə′rɪst(ɪn)] §7 *mf* warehouse clerk

La′gerleben *n* camp life

lagern [′lagərn] *tr* lay down; (*Waren*) stock, store; (*altern*) season; (mach) mount on bearings ‖ *ref* lie down, rest ‖ *intr* lie down, rest; (*Waren*) be stored; (*Wein*) season; (geol) be deposited; (mil) camp

La′gerort *m*, **La′gerplatz** *m* resting place; (*Stapelplatz*) dump; (mil) camp site

La′gerraum *m* storeroom, stockroom

La′gerstand *m* stock on hand, inventory

La′gerstätte *f*, **La′gerstelle** *f* resting place; (geol) deposit; (mil) camp site

La′gerung *f* (–;–en) storage; (*Alterung*) seasoning; (geol) stratification

La′gervorrat *m* stock, supply

Lagune [la′gunə] *f* (–;–n) lagoon

lahm [lam] *adj* lame; paralyzed ‖ **Lahme** §5 *mf* paralytic

lahmen [′lamən] *intr* be lame, limp

lähmen [′lɛmən] *tr* paralyze; (*Verkehr*) tie up; (fig) cripple

lahm′legen *tr* cripple, paralyze; (mil) neutralize

Läh′mung *f* (–;–en) paralysis

Laib [laɪp] *m* (–[e]s;–e) loaf

Laich [laɪç] *m* (–[e]s;–e) spawn

laichen [′laɪçən] *intr* spawn

Laie [′laɪə] *m* (–n;–n) layman; **Laien** laity

Lai′enbruder *m* lay brother

lai′enhaft *adj* layman′s

Lakai [la′kaɪ] *m* (–en;–en) lackey

Lake [′lakə] *f* (–;–n) brine, pickle

Laken [′lakən] *n* (–s;–) sheet

lakonisch [la′koniʃ] *adj* laconic

Lakritze [la′krɪtsə] *f* (–;–n) licorice

Lakune [la′kunə] *f* (–;–n) lacuna

lallen [′lalən] *tr & intr* stammer

lamellenförmig [la′mɛlənfœrmɪç] *adj* laminate

lamentieren [lamen′tirən] *intr* wail

Lametta [la′mɛta] *n* (–s;) tinsel

Lamm [lam] *n* (–[e]s;⸚er) lamb

Lamm′braten *m* roast lamb

Lämmerwolke [′lɛmərvɔlkə] *f* cirrus

Lamm′fleisch *n* (culin) lamb

lamm′fromm′ *adj* meek as a lamb

Lampe [′lampə] *f* (–;–n) lamp; light

Lam′penfieber *n* stage fright

Lam′penschirm *m* lamp shade

Lampion [lam′pjõ] *m* (–s;–s) Chinese lantern

lancieren [lɑ̃′sirən] *tr* launch, promote; (*Kandidaten*) (pol) groom

Land [lant] *n* (–[e]s;⸚er & –e) land; (*Ackerboden*) ground, soil; (*Staat*) country; (*Provinz*) state; (*Gegensatz: Stadt*) country; **ans L.** ashore; **auf dem Lande** in the country; **aufs L.** into the country; **aus aller Herren Ländern** from everywhere; **außer Landes gehen** go abroad; **zu Lande** by land

Land′arbeiter *m* farm hand

Land′armee *f* land forces

Land′bau *m* farming, agriculture

Land′besitz *m* landed property

Land′besitzer –in §6 *mf* landowner

Landebahn [′landəban] *f* runway

Landedeck [′landədɛk] *n* flight deck

Land′edel·mann *m* (–es;–leute) country gentleman

Landefeuer [′landəfɔɪ·ər] *n* runway lights

land′einwärts *adv* inland

Landekopf [′landəkɔpf] *m* beachhead

landen [′landən] *tr & intr* (SEIN) land

Land′enge *f* isthmus, neck of land

Landeplatz [′landəplats] *m* wharf; (aer) landing field

Länderei [lɛndə′raɪ] *f* (–;–en) or **Ländereien** *pl* lands, estates

Länderkunde [′lɛndərkundə] *f* geography

Landes– [landəs] *comb.fm.* national, native, of the land

Lan′desaufnahme *f* land survey

Lan′desbank *f* national bank

Lan′desbeschreibung *f* topography

lan′deseigen *adj* state-owned

Lan′deserzeugnis *n* domestic product

Lan′desfarben *pl* national colors

Lan′desfürst *m* sovereign

Lan′desgesetz *n* law of the land

Lan′desherr *m* sovereign

Lan′desherrschaft *f*, **Lan′deshoheit** *f* sovereignty

Lan′dessprache *f* vernacular

Lan′destracht *f* national costume

Lan′desträuer *f* public mourning

lan′desüblich *adj* customary

Lan′desvater *m* sovereign

Lan′desverrat *m* high treason

Lan′desverräter –in §6 *mf* traitor

Lan′desverteidigung *f* national defense

Land′flucht f rural exodus
land′flüchtig adj exiled, fugitive
Land′friedensbruch m disturbance of the peace
Land′gericht n district court, superior court
Land′gewinnung f land reclamation
Land′gut n country estate
Land′haus n country house
Land′jäger m rural policeman; (culin) sausage
Land′junker m country squire
Land′karte f map
Land′kreis m rural district
land′läufig adj customary
Ländler [′lɛntlər] m (-s;-) waltz
Land′leute pl country folk
ländlich [′lɛntlɪç] adj rural, rustic
Land′luft f country air
Land′macht f land forces
Land′mann m (-[e]s;-leute) farmer
Land′marke f landmark (for travelers and sailors)
Land′maschinen pl farm machinery
Land′messer m surveyor
Land′partie f outing, picnic
Land′plage f nation-wide plague; (coll) big nuisance
Land′rat m regional governor
Land′ratte f (fig) landlubber
Land′recht n common law
Land′regen m steady rain
Land′rücken m ridge
Land′schaft f (-;-en) landscape, scenery; (Bezirk) district, region
land′schaftlich adj scenic; regional
Landser [′lantsər] m (-s;-) G.I.
Lands′knecht m mercenary
Lands′mann m (-[e]s;-leute) fellow countryman
Land′spitze f promontory
Land′straße f highway
Land′streicher m (-s;-) tramp, hobo
Land′strich m tract of land
Land′sturm m home guard
Land′tag m state assembly
landumschlossen [′lantum/lɔsən] adj landlocked
Lan′dung f (-;-en) landing
Lan′dungsboot n landing craft
Lan′dungsbrücke f jetty, pier
Lan′dungsgestell n landing gear
Lan′dungssteg m gangplank
Land′vermessung f surveying
Land′volk n country folk
Land′weg m overland route
Land′wehr f militia, home guard
Land′wirt m farmer
Land′wirtschaft f agriculture; **L. be-treiben** farm
land′wirtschaftlich adj farm, agricultural
Land′zunge f spit of land
lang [laŋ] adj (länger [′lɛŋər]; längste [′lɛŋstə] §9) long; (Person) tall ‖ adv—**die ganze Woche l.** all week; **e-e Stunde l.** for an hour
langatmig [′laŋatmɪç] adj long-winded
lang′beinig adj long-legged
lange [′laŋə] adv long, a long time; **es ist noch l. nicht fertig** it is far from ready; **schon l. her** long ago; **schon l. her, daß** a long time since;

so l. bis until; **so l. wie** as long as; **wie l.?** how long?
Länge [′lɛŋə] f (-;-n) length; long syllable; (geog) longitude; (pros) quantity; **auf die L.** in the long run; **der L. nach** lengthwise; **in die L. ziehen** drag out
langen [′laŋən] tr reach, hand; **j-m eine l.** (coll) give s.o. a smack ‖ intr be enough; **l. nach** reach for ‖ impers—**es langt mir** I have enough; **jetzt langt′s mir aber! I′ve** had it!
Län′gengrad m degree of longitude
Län′genkreis m meridian
Län′genmaß n linear measure
Lan′geweile f boredom; **sich [dat] die L. vertreiben** (coll) kill time
Lang′finger m pickpocket
langfingerig [′laŋfɪŋərɪç] adj (fig) thievish
langfristig [′laŋfrɪstɪç] adj long-term
lang′jährig adj long-standing
Lang′lauf m crosscountry skiing
langlebig [′laŋlebɪç] adj long-lived
Lang′lebigkeit f (-;) longevity
lang′legen ref lie down, stretch out
länglich [′lɛŋlɪç] adj oblong
läng′lichrund adj oval, elliptical
Lang′mut f patience
lang′mütig adj patient
Lang′mütigkeit f patience
längs [lɛŋs] prep (genit or dat) along
langsam [′laŋzam] adj slow
Lang′spielplatte f long-playing record
längst [lɛŋst] adv long since, long ago
längstens [′lɛŋstəns] adv at the latest; (höchstens) at the most
Langstrecken– comb.fm. long-range; (sport) long-distance
langweilen [′laŋvailən] tr bore ‖ ref feel bored
Lang′weiler m (-s;-) slowpoke
langweilig [′laŋvailɪç] adj boring
langwierig [′laŋvirɪç] adj lengthy
Lanolin [lano′lin] n (-s;) lanolin
Lanze [′lantsə] f (-;-n) lance, spear
Lan′zenstechen n (-s;) jousting
Lappalie [la′paljə] f (-;-n) trifle
Lappen [′lapən] m (-s;-) rag; wash-rag; (Flicken) patch; (anat) lobe
läppisch [′lɛpɪ/] adj silly, trifling
Lappland [′laplant] n (-s;) Lapland
Lärche [′lɛrçə] f (-;-n) (bot) larch
Lärm [lɛrm] m (-[e]s;) noise; **L. schlagen** (fig) make a fuss
lärmen [′lɛrmən] intr make noise
lär′mend adj noisy
Larve [′larfə] f (-;-n) mask; larva
las [las] pret of lesen
lasch [la/] adj limp; (Speise) insipid
Lasche [′la/ə] f (-;-n) (Klappe) flap; (Schuh–) tongue; (rr) fishplate
lasieren [la′zirən] tr glaze
lassen [′lasən] §104 tr let; (erlauben) allow; (bewirken) have, make; leave (behind, undone, open, etc.); **den Film entwickeln l.** have the film developed; **etw fallen l.** drop s.th.; **ich kann es nicht l.** I can′t help it; **j-n warten l.** keep s.o. waiting; **kommen l.** send for; **laß den Lärm!** stop

the noise!; **laß es!** cut it out!; **laßt uns gehen** let us go; **sein Leben l.** lose one's life; **sein Leben l. für** sacrifice one's life for ‖ *ref*—**das läßt sich denken** I can imagine; **das läßt sich hören!** now you're talking!; **es läßt sich nicht beschreiben** it defies description; **es läßt sich nicht leugnen, daß** it cannot be denied that; **sich** [*dat*] **Zeit l.** take one's time

lässig [ˈlɛsɪç] *adj* (*faul*) lazy; sluggish; (*nachlässig*) remiss

Läs′sigkeit *f* (–;) laziness; negligence

läßlich [ˈlɛslɪç] *adj* venial

Last [last] *f* (–;-en) load, weight; (*Bürde*) burden; (*Hypotek*) encumbrance; (aer, naut) cargo, freight; **j–m etw zur L. legen** blame s.o. for s.th.; **L. der Beweise** weight of evidence; **ruhende L.** dead weight; **zur L. fallen** (*dat*) become a burden for

Last′auto *n* truck

lasten [ˈlastən] *intr* (**auf** *dat*) weigh (on)

la′stenfrei *adj* unencumbered

La′stensegler *m* transport glider

Laster [ˈlastər] *m* (-s;-) (coll) truck ‖ *n* (-s;-) vice

Lästerer –in [ˈlɛstərər(ɪn)] §6 *mf* slanderer; blasphemer

la′sterhaft *adj* vicious

La′sterleben *n* life of vice

lästerlich [ˈlɛstərlɪç] *adj* slanderous; blasphemous

Lästermaul [ˈlɛstərmaul] *n* scandalmonger

lästern [ˈlɛstərn] *tr* slander; blaspheme

Lä′sterung *f* (–;-en) slander; blasphemy

lästig [ˈlɛstɪç] *adj* troublesome; **j–m l. fallen** bother s.o.

Last′kahn *m* barge

Last′kraftwagen *m* truck

Last′schrift *f* (acct) debit

Last′tier *n* beast of burden

Last′träger *m* porter

Last′wagen *m* truck

Last′zug *m* tractor-trailer (*consisting of several trailers*)

Lasur [laˈzur] *f* (–;) glaze

Latein [laˈtaɪn] *n* (-s;) Latin

lateinisch [laˈtaɪnɪʃ] *adj* Latin

Laterne [laˈtɛrnə] *f* (–;-n) lantern; lamp

Latrine [laˈtrinə] *f* (–;-n) latrine

Latri′nenparole *f* scuttlebut

Latsche [ˈlatʃə] *f* (–;-n) (coll) slipper ‖ [ˈlatʃə] *f* (–;-n) (bot) dwarf pine

latschen [ˈlatʃən] *intr* (SEIN) shuffle along

Latte [ˈlatə] *f* (–;-n) lath

Lat′tenkiste *f* crate

Lat′tenzaun *m* picket fence

Lattich [ˈlatɪç] *m* (-[e]s;-e) lettuce

Latz [lats] *m* (-es;¨e) bib; (*Klappe*) flap; (*Schürzchen*) pinafore

Lätzchen [ˈlɛtsçən] *n* (-s;-) bib

lau [lau] *adj* lukewarm; (*Wetter*) mild; (fig) half-hearted

Laub [laup] *n* (-[e]s;) foliage

Laub′baum *m* deciduous tree

Laube [ˈlaubə] *f* (–;-n) arbor; (*Säulen-*

gang) portico; (*Bogengang*) arcade; (theat) box

Lau′bengang *m* arcade

Laub′säge *f* fret saw

Laub′sägearbeit *f* fretwork

Laub′werk *n* foliage

Lauer [ˈlau·ər] *f* (–;) ambush; **auf der L. liegen** lie in wait

lauern [ˈlau·ərn] *intr* lurk; **l. auf** (*acc*) lie in wait for, watch for

lau′ernd *adj* (*Blick*) wary; (*Gefahr*) lurking

Lauf [lauf] *m* (-[e]s;¨e) running; run; (*e–s Flusses*) course; (*Strömung*) current; (*Wettlauf*) race; (*e–s Gewehrs*) barrel; (astr) path, orbit; **den Dingen freien L. lassen** let things take their course; **im Laufe der Zeit** in the course of time; **im vollen Laufe** at full speed

Lauf′bahn *f* career; (astr) orbit; (sport) lane

Lauf′bursche *m* errand boy; office boy

laufen [ˈlaufən] §105 *intr* (SEIN) run; (*zu Fuß gehen*) walk; (*leck sein*) leak; (*Zeit*) pass; **die Dinge l. lassen** let things slide; **j–n l. lassen** let s.o. go; (*straflos*) let s.o. off

lau′fend *adj* (*ständig*) steady; (*Jahr, Preis*) current; (*Nummern*) consecutive; (*Wartung, Geschäft*) routine; (*Meter, usw.*) running; **auf dem laufenden** up to date; **laufendes Band** conveyor belt; assembly line

Läufer [ˈlɔɪfər] *m* (-s;-) runner; (*Teppich*) runner; (chess) bishop; (fb) halfback; (mach) rotor; (mus) run

Lauferei [laufəˈraɪ] *f* (–;-en) running around

Lauf′feuer *n* (-s;) wildfire

Lauf′fläche *f* tread (*on tire*)

Lauf′gewicht *n* sliding weight

Lauf′gitter *n* playpen

Lauf′graben *m* trench

läufig [ˈlɔɪfɪç] *adj* in heat

Läu′figkeit *f* (–;) heat

Lauf′junge *m* errand boy; office boy

Lauf′kran *m* (mach) traveling crane

Lauf′kunde *m* chance customer

Lauf′masche *f* run (in stocking)

lauf′maschenfrei *adj* runproof

Lauf′paß *m* (coll) walking papers; (coll) brush-off

Lauf′planke *f* gangplank

Lauf′rad *n* (*e–r Turbine*) rotor; (aer) landing wheel

Lauf′schritt *m* double-quick time

Lauf′steg *m* footbridge

Laufställchen [ˈlaufˌʃtɛlçən] *n* (-s;-) playpen

Lauf′zeit *f* rutting season; (*e–s Vertrags*) term; (cin) running time; (mach) (service) life

Lauge [ˈlaugə] *f* (–;-n) lye; (*Salzlauge*) brine; (*Seifenlauge*) suds

Lau′gensalz *n* alkali

lau′gensalzig *adj* alkaline

Laune [ˈlaunə] *f* (–;-n) mood, humor; (*Grille*) whim

lau′nenhaft *adj* capricious

launig [ˈlaunɪç] *adj* humorous, witty

lau′nisch *adj* moody

Laus [laus] *f* (–;¨e) louse

Laus'bub m rascal

lauschen ['lauʃən] intr listen; eavesdrop; **l. auf** (acc) listen to

Lau'scher –in §6 mf eavesdropper

lauschig ['lauʃɪç] adj cosy, peaceful

Lau'sebengel m, **Lau'sejunge** m, **Lau'sekerl** m (coll) rascal, brat

lausen ['lauzən] tr pick lice from; **ich denke, mich laust der Affe** (coll) I couldn't believe my eyes

lausig ['lauzɪç] adj lousy

laut [laut] adj loud; (lärmend) noisy; **l. werden** become public; **l. werden lassen** divulge || prep (genit & dat) according to; (com) as per; **l. Bericht** according to the report || **Laut** m (–[e]s;–e) sound

Laute ['lautə] f (–;–n) lute

lauten ['lautən] intr sound; (Worte) read, go, say; **das Urteil lautet auf Tod** the sentence is death

läuten ['lɔɪtən] tr & intr ring, toll || impers—**es läutet** the bell is ringing || **Läuten** n (–s;) toll

lauter ['lautər] adj pure; (aufrecht) sincere || invar adj (nichts als) nothing but

Lau'terkeit f (–;) purity; sincerity

läutern ['lɔɪtərn] tr purify; (Metall, Zucker) refine; (veredeln) ennoble

Laut'gesetz n phonetic law

Laut'lehre f phonetics, phonology

laut'lich adj phonetic

laut'los adj soundless

Laut'malerei f onomatopoeia

Laut'schrift f phonetic spelling

Laut'sprecher m loudspeaker

Laut'sprecheranlage f public address system

Laut'sprecherwagen m sound truck

Laut'stärke f volume

Laut'stärkeregler m volume control

Laut'system n phonetic system

Laut'zeichen n phonetic symbol

lau'warm adj lukewarm

Lava ['lava] f (–;) lava

Lavendel [la'vendəl] m (–s;) (bot) lavender

laven'delfarben adj lavender

lavieren [la'virən] intr (fig) maneuver; (naut) tack

Lawine [la'vinə] f (–;–n) avalanche

lax [laks] adj lax

Lax'heit f (–;) laxity

Laxiermittel [la'ksirmɪtəl] n laxative

Layout ['le·aut] n (–s;–s) layout

Lazarett [latsa'ret] n (–[e]s;–e) (mil) hospital

Lebedame ['lebədamə] f woman of leisure

Lebehoch [lebə'hox] n (–s;–s) cheer; toast; **ein dreimaliges L.** three cheers

Lebemann ['lebəman] m playboy

leben ['lebən] tr & intr live || **Leben** n (–s;–) life; existence; **am L. bleiben** survive; **am L. erhalten** keep alive; **ins L. rufen** bring into being; **sein L. lang** all his life; **ums L. kommen** lose one's life

lebendig [lɛ'bendɪç] adj living, alive; (lebhaft) lively; (Darstellung) vivid

Le'bensalter n age, period of life

Le'bensanschauung f outlook on life

Le'bensart f manners

Le'bensaufgabe f mission in life

Le'bensbaum m (bot) arbor vitae

Le'bensbedingungen pl living conditions

Le'bensbeschreibung f biography

Le'bensdauer f life span

Le'benserwartung f life expectancy

le'bensfähig adj viable

Le'bensfrage f vital question

le'bensgefährlich adj perilous

Le'bensgefährte m, **Le'bensgefährtin** f life companion, spouse

le'bensgroß adj life-size

Le'benshaltung f standard of living

Le'benshaltungskosten pl cost of living

Le'bensinteressen pl vital interests

Le'benskraft f vitality

Le'benskünstler m—**er ist ein L.** nothing can get him down

lebenslänglich ['lebənsleŋlɪç] adj life

Le'benslauf m curriculum vitae

Le'bensmittel pl groceries

Le'bensmittelgeschäft n grocery store

Le'bensmittelkarte f food ration card

Le'bensmittellieferant m caterer

lebensmüde adj weary of life

le'bensnotwendig adj vital, essential

Le'bensprozeß m vital function

Le'bensstandard m standard of living

Le'bensstellung f lifetime job; tenure

Le'bensstil m life style

Le'bensunterhalt m livelihood

le'bensuntüchtig adj impractical

Le'bensversicherung f life insurance

Le'benswandel m conduct; life

Le'bensweise f way of life

Le'bensweisheit f worldly wisdom

le'benswichtig adj vital, essential

Le'benszeichen n sign of life

Le'benszeit f lifetime; **auf L.** for life

Leber ['lebər] f (–;–n) liver; **frei von der L. weg reden** speak frankly

Le'berfleck m mole

Leberkäs ['lebərkɛs] m (–es;) meat loaf (made with liver)

Le'bertran m cod-liver oil

Lebewesen ['lebəvezən] n living being

Lebewohl [lebə'vol] n (–[e]s;–e) farewell

lebhaft ['lephaft] adj lively; full of life; (Farbe) bright; (Straße) busy; (Börse) brisk; (Interesse) keen

Lebkuchen ['lepkuxən] m gingerbread

leblos ['leplos] adj lifeless

Lebtag ['leptak] m—**mein L.** in all my life

Lebzeiten ['leptsaɪtən] pl—**zu meinen L.** in my lifetime

lechzen ['lɛçtsən] intr (nach) thirst (for)

leck [lek] adj leaky || **Leck** n (–[e]s;–e) leak; **ein L. bekommen** spring a leak

lecken ['lekən] tr lick || intr leak; (naut) have sprung a leak

lecker ['lekər] adj dainty; (köstlich) delicious

Leckerbissen (**Lek'kerbissen**) m delicacy, dainty

Leckerei [lɛkə'raɪ] f (–;–en) daintiness; sweets

leckerhaft (**lek'kerhaft**) adj dainty

Leckermaul (Lek'kermaul) *n*—**ein L. sein** have a sweet tooth
Leder ['ledər] *n* (–s;) leather
ledern ['ledərn] *adj* leather; (fig) dull, boring
ledig ['ledɪç] *adj* single; (*Kind*) illegitimate; **l.** (*genit*) free of; **lediger Stand** single state; celibacy
le'diglich *adv* merely, only
leer [ler] *adj* empty, void; (fig) vain ||
Leere *f* (–;) emptiness, void; vacuum || *n*—**der Schlag ging ins L.** the blow missed; **ins L. starren** stare into space
leeren ['lerən] *tr* empty
Leer'gut *n* empties (*bottles, cases*)
Leer'lauf *m* (aut) idling, idle; (*Gang*) (aut) neutral
leer'laufen §105 *intr* (SEIN) idle
leer'stehend *adj* unoccupied, vacant
Leer'taste *f* (typ) space bar
legal [le'gal] *adj* legal
legalisieren [legalɪ'zirən] *tr* legalize
Legat [le'gat] *m* (–en;–en) legate || *n* (–[e]s;–e) legacy, bequest
legen ['legən] *tr* lay, put; **auf die Kette l.** chain, tie up; **j–m ans Herz l.** recommend warmly to s.o.; **Nachdruck l. auf** (*acc*) emphasize; **Wert l. auf** (*acc*) attach importance to || *ref* lie down; go to bed; (*Wind*) die down; **die Krankheit hat sich ihm auf die Lungen gelegt** his sickness affected his lungs
legendär [legen'der] *adj* legendary
Legende [le'gendə] *f* (–;–n) legend
legieren [le'girən] *tr* alloy
Legie'rung *f* (–;–en) alloy
Legion [le'gjon] *f* (–;–en) legion
Legionär [legjo'ner] *m* (–s;–e) legionnaire, legionary
legislativ [legɪsla'tif] *adj* legislative ||
Legislative [legɪsla'tivə] *f* (–;–n) legislature
Legis·lator [legɪs'lator] *m* (–s;–latoren [la'torən]) legislator
Legislatur [legɪsla'tur] *f* (–;–en) legislature
legitim [legɪ'tim] *adj* legitimate
Legitimation [legɪtɪma'tsjon] *f* (–;–) proof of identity
legitimieren [legɪtɪ'mirən] *tr* legitimize; (*berechtigen*) authorize || *ref* prove one's identity
Lehen ['le·ən] *n* (–s;–) (hist) fief
Le'hensherr *m* liege lord
Le'hens·mann *m* (–[e]s;–leute) vassal
Lehm [lem] *m* (–[e]s;–e) clay, loam
lehmig ['lemɪç] *adj* clayey, loamy
Lehne ['lenə] *f* (–;–n) support; (*e–s Stuhls*) arm, back; (*Abhang*) slope
lehnen ['lenən] *tr, ref & intr* lean
Lehnsessel ['lenzesəl] *m*, **Lehnstuhl** ['len/tul] *m* armchair, easy chair
Lehn'wort ['lenvɔrt] *n* (–[e]s;–er) loan word
Lehramt ['leramt] *n* teaching profession; professorship
Lehranstalt ['leran/talt] *f* educational institution
Lehrbrief ['lerbrif] *m* apprentice's diploma
Lehrbube ['lerbubə] *m* apprentice

Lehrbuch ['lerbux] *n* textbook
Lehrbursche ['lerbur/ə] *m* apprentice
Lehre ['lerə] *f* (–;–n) doctrine, teaching; (*Wissenschaft*) science; (*Theorie*) theory; (*Unterweisung*) instruction; (*Warnung*) lesson; (*e–r Fabel*) moral; (*Richtschnur*) rule, precept; (*e–s Lehrlings*) apprenticeship; (tech) gauge; **in der L. sein** be serving one's apprenticeship
lehren ['lerən] *tr* teach, instruct
Lehrer –in ['lerər(ɪn)] §6 *mf* teacher
Leh'rerbildungsanstalt *f* teacher's college
Leh'rerkollegium *n* teaching staff
Lehrfach ['lerfax] *n* subject
Lehrfilm ['lerfɪlm] *m* educational film
Lehrgang ['lergaŋ] *m* (educ) course
Lehrgedicht ['lergədɪçt] *n* didactic poem
Lehrgegenstand ['lergegən/tant] *m* (educ) subject
Lehrgeld ['lergelt] *n*—**L. zahlen** (fig) learn the hard way
lehrhaft ['lerhaft] *adj* didactic
Lehrjunge ['lerjuŋə] *m* apprentice
Lehrkörper ['lerkœrpər] *m* teaching staff; faculty (*of a university*)
Lehrling ['lerlɪŋ] *m* (–s;–e) apprentice
Lehrmädchen ['lermetçən] *n* girl apprentice
Lehrmeister ['lermaɪstər] *m* master, teacher, instructor
Lehrmittel ['lermɪtəl] *n* teaching aid
Lehrplan ['lerplan] *m* curriculum
lehrreich ['lerraɪç] *adj* instructive
Lehrsaal ['lerzal] *m* lecture hall
Lehrsatz ['lerzats] *m* (eccl) dogma; (math) theorem
Lehrspruch ['ler/prux] *m* maxim
Lehrstelle ['ler/telə] *f* position as an apprentice
Lehrstoff ['ler/tɔf] *m* subject matter
Lehrstuhl ['ler/tul] *m* (educ) chair
Lehrstunde ['ler/tundə] *f* lesson
Lehrzeit ['lertsart] *f* apprenticeship
Leib [laɪp] *m* (–[e]s;–er) body; (*Bauch*) belly, abdomen; (*Taille*) waist; (*Mutterleib*) womb; **am ganzen L. zittern** tremble all over; **bleib mir nur damit vom Leibe!** (coll) don't bother me with that: **e–n harten L. haben** be constipated; **gesegneten Leibes** with child; **L. und Leben** life and limb; **mit L. und Seele** through and through; **sich** [*dat*] **j–n vom Leibe halten** keep s.o. at arm's length; **zu Leibe gehen** (*dat*) tackle (*s.th.*), attack (*s.o.*)
Leib'arzt *m* personal physician
Leib'binde *f* sash
Leibchen ['laɪpçən] *n* (–s;–) bodice; vest
leib'eigen *adj* in bondage || **Leibeigene** §5 *mf* serf
Leib'eigenschaft *f* (–;) serfdom, bondage
Lei'besbeschaffenheit *f* (–;–en) constitution
Lei'beserbe *m* (–n;–n) offspring
Lei'beserziehung *f* physical education
Lei'besfrucht *f* fetus
Lei'beskräfte *pl*—**aus Leibeskräften**

schreien scream at the top of one's lungs
Lei'besübungen *pl* physical education
Lei'besvisitation *f* body search
Leib'garde *f* bodyguard
Leibgardist ['laɪpgardɪst] *m* (-en;-en) bodyguard
Leib'gericht *n* favorite dish
leibhaft(ig) ['laɪphaft(ɪç)] *adj* incarnate, real
leib'lich *adj* bodily, corporal; **leiblicher Vetter** first cousin; **sein leiblicher Sohn** his own son
Leib'rente *f* annuity for life
Leib'schmerzen *pl*, **Leib'schneiden** *n* abdominal pains
Leibstandarte ['laɪp/tandartə] *f* (-;-n) (hist) SS bodyguard
Leib'wache *f* bodyguard
Leib'wäsche *f* underwear
Leiche ['laɪçə] *f* (-;-n) corpse, body; carcass; (dial) funeral
Leichenbegängnis ['laɪçənbəgɛŋnɪs] *n* (-ses;-se) funeral, interment
Leichenbeschauer ['laɪçənbə/au-ər] *m* (-s;-) coroner
Leichenbestatter ['laɪçənbə/tatər] *m* (-s;-) undertaker
Lei'chenbittermiene *f* woe-begone look
Leichenfledderer ['laɪçənfledərər] *m* (-s;-) body stripper
Lei'chengift *n* ptomaine poison
lei'chenhaft *adj* corpse-like
Lei'chenhalle *f* mortuary
Lei'chenöffnung *f* autopsy
Lei'chenräuber *m* body snatcher
Lei'chenrede *f* eulogy
Lei'chenschau *f* post mortem
Lei'chenschauhaus *m* morgue
Lei'chenstarre *f* rigor mortis
Lei'chenträger *m* pallbearer
Lei'chentuch *n* shroud
Lei'chenverbrennung *f* cremation
Lei'chenwagen *m* hearse
Lei'chenzug *m* funeral cortege
Leichnam ['laɪçnam] *m* (-[e]s;-e) corpse
leicht [laɪçt] *adj* light; (*nicht schwierig*) easy; (*gering*) slight; **leichten Herzens** light-heartedly
Leicht'atletik *f* track and field
Leicht'bauweise *f* lightweight construction
Leicht'benzin *n* cleaning fluid
leichtbeschwingt ['laɪçtbə/vɪŋt] *adj* gay
leicht'blütig *adj* light-hearted
leicht'entzündlich *adj* highly flammable
Leichter ['laɪçtər] *m* (-s;-) (naut) lighter
leicht'fertig *adj* frivolous, flippant; careless
leicht'flüchtig *adj* highly volatile
leicht'flüssig *adj* thin
Leicht'gewicht *n* lightweight division
Leichtgewichtler ['laɪçtgəvɪçtlər] *m* (-s;-) lightweight boxer
leicht'gläubig *adj* gullible
leicht'hin' *adv* lightly, casually
Leich'tigkeit *f* (-;) ease
leichtlebig ['laɪçtlebɪç] *adj* easygoing
Leicht'sinn *m* frivolity, irresponsibility;

(*Sorglosigkeit*) carelessness; (*Unbedachtsamkeit*) imprudence
leicht'sinnig *adj* frivolous, irresponsible
leicht'verdaulich *adj* easy to digest
leicht'verderblich *adj* perishable
leid [laɪt] *adj*—**er tut mir l.** I feel sorry for him; **es tut mir l., daß I** am sorry that; **es ist** (or **tut**) **mir l. um** I feel sorry for, I regret; **ich bin es l.** I'm fed up with it ‖ **Leid** *n* (-[e]s;) (*Betrübnis*) sorrow; (*Schaden*) harm; (*Unrecht*) wrong; **j-m ein L. antun** harm s.o.
Leideform ['laɪdəform] *f* (gram) passive voice
leiden ['laɪdən] §106 *tr* suffer; (*ertragen*) stand ‖ *intr* (**an** *dat*) suffer (*from*) ‖ **Leiden** *n* (-s;-) suffering; (*Krankheit*) ailment
Lei'denschaft *f* (-;-en) passion
lei'denschaftlich *adj* passionate
lei'denschaftslos *adj* dispassionate
Lei'densgefährte *m*, **Lei'densgefährtin** *f* fellow sufferer
Lei'densgeschichte *f* tale of woe; (relig) Passion
Lei'densweg *m* way of the cross
leider ['laɪdər] *adv* unfortunately
leiderfüllt ['laɪtərfʏlt] *adj* sorrowful
leidig ['laɪdɪç] *adj* tiresome
leidlich ['laɪtlɪç] *adv* tolerable; (*halbwegs gut*) passable ‖ *adv* so-so
leidtragend ['laɪttragənt] *adj* in mourning ‖ **Leidtragende** §5 *mf* mourner; **er ist der L. dabei** he is the one that suffers for it
Leid'wesen *n*—**zu meinem L.** to my regret
Leier ['laɪ-ər] *f* (-;-n) (mus) lyre
Lei'erkasten *m* hand organ, hurdygurdy
Lei'ermann *m* (-[e]s;̈-er) organ grinder
leiern ['laɪ-ərn] *tr* (*winden*) crank; (*Gebete, Verse*) drone ‖ *intr* drone
Leih- [laɪ] *comb.fm.* loan, rental
Leih'amt *n*, **Leih'anstalt** *f* loan office
Leih'bibliothek *f* rental library
leihen ['laɪ-ən] *tr* lend, loan out; (*entleihen*) (**von**) borrow (*from*)
Leih'gebühr *f* rental fee
Leih'haus *n* pawnshop
Leim [laɪm] *m* (-[e]s;-e) glue; birdlime; **aus dem L. gehen** fall apart; **j-m auf den L. gehen** be taken in by s.o.
leimen ['laɪmən] *tr* glue; (*betrügen*) take in, fool
Leim'farbe *f* distemper
leimig ['laɪmɪç] *adj* gluey
Lein [laɪn] *m* (-[e]s;-e) flax
Leine ['laɪnə] *f* (-;-n) line, cord; (*Hunde*—) leash
Leinen ['laɪnən] *n* (-s;-) linen
Lei'neneinband *m* (-[e]s;̈-e) (bb) cloth binding
Lei'nenschuh *m* sneaker, canvas shoe
Lei'nenzeug *n* linen fabric
Lein'öl *n* linseed oil
Lein'tuch *n* sheet
Lein'wand *f* linen cloth; canvas; (cin) screen
leise ['laɪzə] *adj* soft, low; (*sanft*) gentle; (*gering*) faint; (*Schlaf*) light

lei′sestellen *tr* (rad) turn down

Lei′setreter *m* (-s;-) pussyfoot

Leiste [′laɪstə] *f* (-;-n) (*Rand*) border; (anat) groin; (carp) molding

leisten [′laɪstən] *tr* do, perform, accomplish; (*Dienst*) render; (*Eid*) take; (*Abbitte, Hilfe, Widerstand*) offer; **Bürgschaft l. für** put up bail for; **Folge l.** (*dat*), **Gehorsam l.** (*dat*) obey; **Genüge l.** (*dat*) satisfy; **j–m Gesellschaft l.** keep s.o. company; **sich** [*dat*] **etw l. können** be able to afford s.th. ‖ **Leisten** *m* (-s;-) last; **alles über e–n L. schlagen** (fig) be undiscriminating

Lei′stenbruch *m* hernia, rupture

Lei′stung *f* (-;-en) performance; efficiency; ability; feat, achievement; (*Ergebnis*) result; (*Erzeugung*) production; (*Abgabe, Ausstoß*) output; (*Beitrag*) contribution; (*Dienstleistungen*) services rendered; (elec) power, wattage; (indust) output, production; (insur) benefits; (mach) capacity

Lei′stungsanreiz *m* incentive

lei′stungsfähig *adj* (*Person*) efficient; (*Motor*) powerful; (*Fabrik*) productive; (phys) efficient

Lei′stungsfähigkeit *f* efficiency; proficiency; (*e–s Autos*) performance; (*e–s Motors*) power; (mach) output

lei′stungsgerecht *adj* based on merit

Lei′stungsgrenze *f* peak of performance

Lei′stungslohn *m* pay based on performance

Lei′stungszulage *f* bonus

Leit– [laɪt] *comb.fm.* leading, dominant, guiding

Leit′artikel *m* editorial

Leit′bild *n* (good) example, ideal

leiten [′laɪtən] *tr* lead, guide; (*Verkehr*) route; (*Betrieb*) direct, run; (*Versammlung*) preside over; (arti) direct; (elec, mus, phys) conduct

Lei′ter *m* (-s;-) leader; director; (educ) principal; (elec, mus) conductor ‖ *f* (-;-n) ladder

Lei′terin *f* (-;-nen) leader; director

Leit′faden *m* manual, guide

Leit′fähigkeit *f* conductivity

Leit′gedanke *m* main idea, main theme

Leit′hammel *m* (fig) boss, leader

Leit′motiv *n* keynote; (mus) leitmotiv

Leit′satz *m* basic point

Leit′spruch *m* motto

Leit′stelle *f* head office

Leit′stern *m* polestar, lodestar

Lei′tung *f* (-;-en) direction, guidance; (*Beaufsichtigung*) management; (*Rohr*) pipeline; (*für Gas, Wasser*) main; (elec) lead; (phys) conduction; (telp) line; **e–e lange L. haben** be rather dense; **L. besetzt!** line is busy!

Lei′tungsdraht *m* (elec) lead

Lei′tungsmast *m* telephone pole

Lei′tungsnetz *n* (elec) power lines

Lei′tungsrohr *n* pipe, main

Lei′tungsvermögen *n* conductivity

Lei′tungswasser *n* tap water

Leit′werk *n* (aer) tail assembly

Leit′zahl *f* code number

Lektion [lɛk′tsjon] *f* (-;-en) lesson; (fig) lecture, rebuke

Lek·tor [′lɛktɔr] *m* (-s;-toren [′tɔrən]) lecturer; (*e–s Verlags*) reader

Lektüre [lɛk′tyrə] *f* (-;) reading matter, literature

Lende [′lɛndə] *f* (-;-n) loin; (*Hüfte*) hip

Len′denbraten *m* roast loin, sirloin

len′denlahm *adj* stiff; (*Ausrede*) lame

Len′denschurz *m* loincloth

Len′denstück *n* tenderloin, sirloin

lenkbar [′lɛŋkbar] *adj* manageable; steerable, maneuverable; **lenkbares Luftschiff** dirigible

lenken [′lɛŋkən] *tr* guide, control; (*Wagen*) drive; (*wenden*) turn; (*steuern*) steer; **Aufmerksamkeit l. auf** (*acc*) call attention to

Len′ker –in §6 *mf* ruler; (aut) driver

Lenkrad [′lɛŋkrat] *n* steering wheel

Lenksäule [′lɛŋkzɔɪlə] *f* steering column

Lenkstange [′lɛŋkʃtaŋə] *f* handlebar; (aut) connecting rod

Len′kung *f* (-;-en) guidance, control; (aut) steering mechanism

Lenz [lɛnts] *m* (-es;-e) (fig) prime of life; (poet) spring

Lenz′pumpe *f* bilge pump

Lepra [′lepra] *f* (-;) leprosy

Lerche [′lɛrçə] *f* (-;-n) (orn) lark

lernbegierig [′lɛrnbəgiriç] *adj* eager to learn, studious

lernen [′lɛrnən] *tr* & *intr* learn; study

Lesart [′lezart] *f* version

lesbar [′lezbar] *adj* legible; readable

Lesbierin [′lɛsbi·ərɪn] *f* (-;-nen) lesbian

lesbisch [′lɛsbɪʃ] *adj* lesbian; **lesbische Liebe** lesbianism

Lese [′lezə] *f* (-;-n) gathering, picking; (*Wein–*) vintage

Lese– [lezə] *comb.fm.* reading; lecture

Le′sebrille *f* reading glasses

Le′sebuch *n* reader

Le′sehalle *f* reading room

lesen [′lezən] §107 *tr* read; gather; (*Messe*) say ‖ *intr* read; lecture; **l. über** (*acc*) lecture on

le′senswert *adj* worth reading

Le′seprobe *f* specimen from a book; (theat) reading rehearsal

Le′ser –in §6 *mf* reader; picker

Le′seratte *f* (coll) bookworm

le′serlich *adj* legible

Le′serzuschrift *f* letter to the editor

Le′sestoff *m* reading matter

Le′sezeichen *n* bookmark

Le′sung *f* (-;-en) reading

Lette [′lɛtə] *m* (-n;-n), **Lettin** [′lɛtɪn] *f* (-;-nen) Latvian

lettisch [′lɛtɪʃ] *adj* Latvian

Lettland [′lɛtlant] *n* (-[e]s;) Latvia

letzte [′lɛtstə] §9 *adj* last; (*endgültig*) final, ultimate; (*neueste*) latest; (*Ausweg*) last; **bis ins l.** to the last detail; **in den letzten Jahren** in recent years; **in der letzten Zeit** lately; **letzten Endes** in the final analysis ‖ **Letzte** §5 *pron* last, last one; **am Letzten** on the last of the month; **sein Letztes hergeben** do one's utmost; **zu guter Letzt** finally, last but not least

letztens ['lɛtstəns] *adv* lately

letztere ['lɛtstərə] §5 *mfn* latter

letzthin [lɛtst'hɪn] *adv* lately

letztlich ['lɛtstlɪç] *adv* lately, recently; in the final analysis

letztwillig ['lɛtstvɪlɪç] *adj* testamentary

Leucht– [lɔɪçt] *comb.fm.* luminous; illuminating

Leucht/bombe *f* flare bomb

Leuchte ['lɔɪçtə] *f* (–;–n) light, lamp; lantern; (fig) luminary

leuchten ['lɔɪçtən] *intr* shine

leuch/tend *adj* shining, bright; luminous

Leuchter ['lɔɪçtər] *m* (–s;–) candlestick; chandelier

Leucht/farbe *f* luminous paint

Leucht/feuer *n* (aer) flare; (naut) beacon

Leucht/käfer *m* lightning bug

Leucht/körper *m* light bulb; light fixture

Leucht/kugel *f* tracer bullet; flare

Leucht/pistole *f* Very pistol

Leucht/rakete *f* (aer) flare

Leucht/reklame *f* neon sign

Leucht/röhre *f* fluorescent lamp

Leucht/spurgeschoß *n* tracer bullet

Leucht/turm *m* lighthouse

Leucht/zifferblatt *n* luminous dial

leugnen ['lɔɪgnən] *tr* deny; disclaim

Leukoplast [lɔɪko'plast] *n* (–[e]s;–) adhesive tape

Leumund ['lɔɪmʊnt] *m* (–[e]s;) reputation

Leu/mundszeugnis *n* character reference

Leute ['lɔɪtə] *pl* people, persons, men; (*Dienstleute*) servants

Leu/teschinder *m* oppressor; slave driver

Leutnant ['lɔɪtnant] *m* (–s;–s) lieutenant

Leut/priester *m* secular priest

leut/selig *adj* affable

Lexikograph [lɛksɪko'graf] *m* (–en;–en) lexicographer

Lexikon ['lɛksɪkɔn] *n* (–s;–s) encyclopedia

Libanon ['libanɔn] *n* (–s;) Lebanon

Libelle [lɪ'bɛlə] *f* (–;–n) dragonfly; (carp) level

liberal [libe'ral] *adj* liberal

Liberalismus [lɪbera'lɪsmʊs] *m* (–s;) liberalism

Libyen ['liby.ən] *n* (–s;) Libya

licht [lɪçt] *adj* light, bright; (*durchsichtig*) clear ‖ **Licht** *n* (–[e]s;–er) light; (*Kerze*) candle

licht/beständig *adj* non-fading

Licht/bild *n* photograph

Licht/bildervortrag *m* illustrated lecture

licht/blau *adj* light-blue

Licht/blick *m* (fig) bright spot

Licht/bogen *m* (elec) arc

Licht/bogenschweißung *f* arc welding

Licht/brechung *f* (–;–en) refraction of light

Licht/druck *m* phototype

licht/durchlässig *adj* translucent

licht/echt *adj* non-fading

licht/empfindlich *adj* sensitized; **l. machen** sensitize

Licht/empfindlichkeit *f* (phot) speed

lichten ['lɪçtən] *tr* clear; thin; (*Anker*) weigh

lichterloh ['lɪçtərlo] *adv* ablaze; **l. brennen** be ablaze

Licht/hof *m* (archit) light well, inner court; (phot) halo

Licht/kegel *m* beam of light

Licht/maschine *f* generator, dynamo

Licht/pause *f* blueprint

Licht/punkt *m* (fig) ray of hope

Licht/schacht *m* light well

Licht/schalter *m* light switch

licht/scheu *adj*—**lichtscheues Gesindel** shady characters

Licht/schirm *m* lamp shade

Licht/seite *f* (fig) bright side

Licht/spiele *pl*, **Licht/spielhaus** *n*, **Licht/spieltheater** *n* movie theater

licht/stark *adj* (*Objektiv*) high-powered; (phot) high-speed

Lich/tung *f* (–;–en) clearing

Lid [lit] *n* (–[e]s;–er) eyelid

Lid/schatten *m* eye shadow

lieb [lip] *adj* dear; (*nett*) nice; **der liebe Gott** the good Lord; **es ist mir l., daß I am glad that; seien Sie so l. und** please; **sich lieb Kind machen** bei ingratiate oneself with

lieb/äugeln *intr*—**l. mit** (& *fig*) flirt with

Liebchen ['lipçən] *n* (–s;–) darling

Liebe ['libə] *f* (–;) (zu) love (*for, of*)

liebedienerisch ['libədinərɪʃ] *adj* fawning

Liebelei [libə'laɪ] *f* (–;–en) flirtation

lieben ['libən] *tr* love, be fond of

lieb/bend *adj* loving ‖ *adv*—**l. gern** gladly ‖ **Liebende** §5 *mf* lover

lieb/benswert *adj* lovable

lieb/benswürdig *adj* lovable; charming; **das ist sehr l. von Ihnen** that's very kind of you

lieber ['libər] *adv* rather, sooner; **l. haben** prefer

Liebes– ['libəs] *comb.fm.* love, of love

Lie/besdienst *m* favor, good turn

Lie/beserlebnis *n* romance

Lie/besgabe *f* charitable gift

Lie/beshandel *m* love affair

Lie/besmahl *n* love feast

Lie/besmühe *f*—**verlorene L.** wasted effort

Lie/bespaar *n* couple (of lovers)

Lie/bespfand *n* token of love

Lie/bestrank *m* love potion

Lie/beswerben *n* advances

lieb/bevoll *adj* loving, affectionate

Lieb/frauenkirche *f* Church of Our Lady

lieb/gewinnen §121 *tr* grow fond of

lieb/haben §89 *tr* love, be fond of

Liebhaber ['liphabər] *m* (–s;–) lover, beau; amateur; fan, buff; **erster L.** leading man

lieb/kosen *tr* caress, fondle

lieb/lich *adj* lovely, sweet; charming

Liebling ['liplɪŋ] *m* (–s;–e) darling; (*Haustier*) pet; (*Günstling*) favorite

Lieblings– *comb.fm.* favorite

Lieb′lingsgedanke *m* pet idea
Lieb′lingswunsch *m* dearest wish
lieb′los *adj* unkind
lieb′reich *adj* kind, affectionate
Lieb′reiz *m* charm, attractiveness
lieb′reizend *adj* charming
Lieb′schaft *f* (-;-en) love affair
liebste ['lipstə] §9 *adj* favorite; **am liebsten trinke ich Wein** I like wine best of all
Lied [lit] *n* (-[e]s;-er) song; **er weiß ein L. davon zu singen** he can tell you all about it; **geistliches L.** hymn
liederlich ['lidərlɪç] *adj* dissolute; (*unordentlich*) disorderly
lief [lif] *pret* of **laufen**
Lieferant -in [lifə'rant(ɪn)] §7 *mf* supplier; (*Verteiler*) distributor; (*von Lebensmitteln*) caterer
Lieferauto ['lifərauto] *n* delivery truck
lieferbar ['lifərbar] *adj* available, deliverable
Liefergebühr ['lifərgə'byr] *f* delivery charge
liefern ['lifərn] *tr* deliver; (*beschaffen*) supply, furnish; (*Ertrag*) yield; **ich bin geliefert** (coll) I'm done for
Lieferschein ['lifər/aɪn] *m* delivery receipt
Lie′ferung *f* (-;-en) delivery, shipment; supply; (*e-s Werkes*) installment, number; **zahlbar bei L.** cash on delivery
Lieferwagen ['lifərvagən] *m* delivery truck
Liege ['ligə] *f* (-;-n) couch
Lie′gekur *f* rest cure
liegen ['ligən] §108 *intr* lie, be situated; **gut auf der Straße l.** hug the road; **l. an** (*dat*) lie near; (fig) be due to; **wie die Sache jetzt liegt** as matters now stand || *impers*—**es liegt an ihm zu** (*inf*) it's up to him to (*inf*); **es liegt auf der Hand** it is obvious; **es liegt mir nichts daran** it doesn't matter to me; **es liegt mir (sehr viel) daran** it matters (a great deal) to me
lie′genbleiben §62 *intr* (SEIN) stay in bed; (*Waren*) remain unsold; (*stekkenbleiben*) have a breakdown; (*Arbeit*) be left undone
lie′genlassen §104 *tr* let lie; leave alone; (*Arbeit*) leave undone
Lie′genschaft *f* (-;-en) real estate
Lie′gestuhl *m* deck chair
Lie′gestütz *n* (gym) pushup
lieh [li] *pret* of **leihen**
ließ [lis] *pret* of **lassen**
Li·ga ['ligə] *f* (-;-gen [gən]) league
Liguster [lɪ'gustər] *m* (-s;-) privet
liieren [lɪ'irən] *ref*—**sich l. mit** ally oneself with
Likör [lɪ'kør] *m* (-s;-e) liqueur
lila ['lila] *adj* lilac
Lilie ['liljə] *f* (-;-n) lily
Limonade [lɪmo'nadə] *f* (-;-n) soft drink, soda
lind [lɪnt] *adj* mild, gentle
Linde ['lɪndə] *f* (-;-n) (bot) linden
lindern ['lɪndərn] *tr* alleviate; (*Übel*) mitigate; (*mildern*) soften

Lindwurm ['lɪntvurm] *m* dragon
Lineal [lɪnɛ'al] *n* (-s;-e) ruler
Linguist -in [lɪŋgu'ɪst(ɪn)] §7 *mf* linguist
Linie ['linjə] *f* (-;-n) line; **auf gleicher L. mit** on a level with; **in erster L.** in the first place
Li′nienpapier *n* lined paper
Li′nienrichter *m* (sport) linesman
Li′nienschiff *n* ship of the line
li′nientreu *adj*—**l. sein** follow the party line
linieren [lɪ'nirən] *tr* line, rule
linke ['lɪŋkə] §9 *adj* left; (*Seite*) wrong, reverse || §5 **Linke** *m* (box) left || §5 *f* left side; left hand; **die L.** (pol) the left
linkisch ['lɪŋkɪʃ] *adj* clumsy, awkward
links [lɪŋks] *adv* left; to the left; on the left; (*verkehrt*) inside out; **l. liegenlassen** bypass, ignore; **links um!** left, face!
links′drehend *adj* counterclockwise
linksgängig ['lɪŋksgɛŋɪç] *adj* counterclockwise
Linkshänder ['lɪŋkshɛndər] *m* (-s;-) left-hander
links′läufig *adj* counterclockwise
links′stehend *adj* (pol) leftist
Linnen ['lɪnən] *n* (-s;-) linen
Linse ['lɪnzə] *f* (-;-n) (bot) lentil; (opt) lens
Lippe ['lɪpə] *f* (-;-n) lip; **e-e L. riskieren** (fig) speak out of turn
Lip′penbekenntnis *n* lip service
Lip′penlaut *m* labial
Lip′penstift *m* lipstick
liquid [lɪ'kvit] *adj* (*Geldmittel*) liquid; (*Gesellschaft*) solvent
Liquidation [lɪkvɪda'tsjon] *f* (-;-en) liquidation; (*Kostenrechnung*) bill
liquidieren [lɪkvɪ'dirən] *tr* liquidate; (*Geschäft*) wind up; (*Honorar*) charge
lispeln ['lɪspəln] *tr & intr* lisp; (*flüstern*) whisper
Lissabon ['lɪsa'bɔn] *n* (-s;) Lisbon
List [lɪst] *f* (-;-en) cunning; trick
Liste ['lɪstə] *f* (-;-n) list; **schwarze L.** blacklist
Li′stenwahl *f* block voting
listig ['lɪstɪç] *adj* cunning, sly
Litanei [lɪta'naɪ] *f* (-;-en) litany
Litauen ['litau·ən] *n* (-s;) Lithuania
litauisch ['litau·ɪʃ] *adj* Lithuanian
Liter ['litər] *m & n* (-s;-) liter
literarisch [lɪtə'rarɪʃ] *adj* literary
Literatur [lɪtera'tur] *f* (-;-en) literature
Litfaßsäule ['lɪtfaszɔɪlə] *f* advertising pillar
Litur·gie [lɪtur'gi] *f* (-;-gien ['gi·ən]) liturgy
Litze ['lɪtsə] *f* (-;-n) cord; (elec) strand
Li·vree [lɪ'vre] *f* (-;-vreen ['vre·ən]) uniform, livery
Lizenz [lɪ'tsɛnts] *f* (-;-en) license
Lob [lop] *n* (-[e]s;) praise
loben ['lobən] §109 *tr* praise
lo′benswert *adj* praiseworthy
Lobhudelei [lophudə'laɪ] *f* (-;-en) flattery

lob'hudeln tr heap praise on
löblich ['løplɪç] adj commendable
lob'preisen tr extol, praise
Lob'rede f panegyric
Loch [lɔx] n (-es;ːer) hole
Loch'bohrer m auger
lochen ['lɔxən] tr punch, perforate
Locher ['lɔxər] m (-s;-) punch
löcherig ['lœçərɪç] adj full of holes
Loch'karte f punch card
Lo'chung f (-;-en) perforation
Locke ['lɔkə] f (-;-n) lock, curl
locken ['lɔkən] tr allure, entice; de-coy; (Hund) whistle to
locker ['lɔkər] adj loose; (nicht straff) slack; spongy; (moralisch) loose
lockern ['lɔkərn] tr loosen
lockig ['lɔkɪç] adj curly, curled
Lock'mittel n, **Lock'speise** f (& fig) bait
Lockspitzel ['lɔkʃpɪtsəl] m stool-pigeon
Lo'ckung f (-;-en) allurement
Lock'vogel m (& fig) decoy
Loden ['lodən] m (-s;-) coarse woolen cloth
lodern ['lodərn] intr blaze; (fig) glow
Löffel ['lœfəl] m (-s;-) spoon; (culin) spoonful; (coll & hunt) ear; **über den L. balbieren** hoodwink
Löf'felbagger m power shovel
löffeln ['lœfəln] tr spoon out
log [lok] pret of **lügen**
Logbuch ['lɔkbux] n logbook
Loge ['loʒə] f (-;-n) (der Freimau-rer) lodge; (theat) box
Lo'genbruder m freemason
Logierbesuch [lo'ʒirbəzux] m house-guest(s)
logieren [lo'ʒirən] intr (bei) stay (with)
Logik ['loːɡɪk] f (-;) logic
Logis [lo'ʒi] invar f lodgings
logisch ['loːɡɪʃ] adj logical
Lohe ['loːə] f (-;-n) blaze, flame
Lohgerber ['loːɡɛrbər] m (-s;-) tanner
Lohn [lon] m (-[e]s;ːe) pay, wages; (fig) reward
Lohn'abbau m wage cut
lohnen ['lonən] tr compensate, reward; (Arbeiter) pay; **j-m etw l.** reward s.o. for s.th. || ref pay, be worth-while
löhnen ['lønən] tr pay, pay wages to
Lohn'erhöhung f raise, wage increase
Lohn'gefälle n wage differential
Lohn'herr m employer
lohn'intensiv adj with high labor costs
Lohn'liste f payroll
Lohn'satz m pay rate
Lohn'stopp m wage freeze
Lohn'tag m payday
Lohn'tüte f pay envelope
Löh'nung f (-;-en) payment
lokal [lo'kal] adj local || **Lokal** n (-[e]s;-e) locality, premises; (Wirts-haus) restaurant, pub, inn
lokalisieren [lokalɪ'zirən] tr localize
Lokalität [lokalɪ'tɛt] f (-;-en) locality
Lokomotive [lokomo'tivə] f (-;-n) lo-comotive
Lokomotiv'führer m (rr) engineer
Lokus ['lokus] m (-;-se) (coll) john
Lorbeer ['lɔrbər] m (-s;-en) laurel

los [los] adj loose; **es ist etw los** there is s.th. going on; **es ist nichts los** there is nothing going on; **etw los haben** have s.th. on the ball; **j-n** (or **etw**) **los sein** be rid of s.o. (or s.th.); **los!** go on!, scram!; (sprich!) fire away!; (mach schnell!) let's go!; (sport) play ball!; **mit ihm ist nicht viel los** he's no great shakes; **was ist los?** what's the matter? || **Los** n (-[e]s;-e) lot; (Lotterie-) ticket; (Anteil) lot, portion; (Schicksal) fate; **das Große Los** first prize; **das Los ziehen** draw lots; **die Lose sind gefallen** the die is cast
los- comb.fm. un-, e.g., **losmachen** undo
los'arbeiten tr extricate || ref get loose, extricate oneself || intr (auf acc) work away (at)
lösbar ['løsbar] adj solvable
los'binden §59 tr loosen, untie
los'brechen §64 tr break off || intr (SEIN) break loose
Löschblatt ['lœʃblat] n blotter
Löscheimer ['lœʃaɪmər] m fire bucket
löschen ['lœʃən] tr put out; (Durst) quench; (Schuld) cancel; (Schrift) blot; (Bandaufnahme) erase; (Firma) liquidate; (Hypotek) pay off; (naut) unload
Lö'scher m (-s;-) blotter; (Feuer-) fire extinguisher
Löschgerät ['lœʃɡəret] n fire extin-guisher
Löschmannschaft ['lœʃmanʃaft] f fire brigade
Löschpapier ['lœʃpapir] n blotting paper
Lö'schung f (-;-en) extinction; (Til-gung) cancellation; (naut) unloading
los'drehen tr unscrew, twist off
los'drücken tr fire || intr pull the trigger
lose ['loze] §9 adj loose
Lösegeld ['løzəɡɛlt] n ransom
loseisen ['losaɪzən] tr—**Geld l. von** wangle money out of; **j-n l. aus** get s.o. out of; **j-n l. von** get s.o. away from || ref (von) worm one's way from (out of)
losen ['lozən] intr draw lots
lösen ['løzən] tr loosen, untie; (ab-trennen) sever; (Bremse) release; (Fahrkarte) buy; (loskaufen) ransom; (lossprechen) absolve; (Rätsel) solve; (Schuß) fire; (Verlobung) break off || ref come loose, come undone; dis-solve; (sich befreien) free oneself
los'fahren §71 intr (SEIN) drive off; **l. auf** (acc) head for; rush at; attack (verbally)
los'gehen §82 intr (SEIN) (coll) begin; (Gewehr) go off; (sich lösen) come loose; **auf j-n l.** attack s.o.
los'haken tr unhook
los'kaufen tr ransom
los'ketten tr unchain
los'kommen §99 intr (SEIN) come loose, come off; **ich komme nicht davon los** I can't get over it; **l. von** get away from; get rid of
los'lachen intr burst out laughing

los'lassen §104 *tr* let go; release; den Hund l. auf (*acc*) sic the dog on

los'legen *intr* (coll) start up, let fly; (*reden*) (coll) open up; leg los! (coll) fire away!

löslich ['løslɪç] *adj* soluble

los'lösen *tr* detach

los'machen *tr* undo, untie; (*freimachen*) free || *ref* disengage onself

los'platzen *intr* (SEIN) burst out laughing; l. mit blurt out

los'reißen §53 *tr* & *ref* break loose

los'sagen *ref*—sich l. von renounce

los'schlagen §132 *tr* knock off; (*verkaufen*) dispose of, sell cheaply || *intr* open the attack; l. auf (*acc*) let fly at

los'schnallen *tr* unbuckle

los'schrauben *tr* unscrew

los'sprechen §64 *tr* absolve

los'steuern *intr*—l. auf (*acc*) head for

Lo'sung *f* (-;-en) (*Kot*) dung; (mil) password; (pol) slogan

Lö'sung *f* (-;-en) solution

Lö'sungsmittel *n* solvent; thinner

los'werden §159 *tr* (SEIN) get rid of

los'ziehen §163 *intr* (SEIN) set out, march away; l. auf (*acc*) talk about, run down

Lot [lot] *n* (-[e]s;-e) plummet; plumb line; (*Lötmetall*) solder; (geom) perpendicular; im Lot perpendicular; (fig) in order; ins Lot bringen (fig) set right

Löteisen ['løtaɪzən] *n* soldering iron

loten ['lotən] *tr* (naut) plumb || *intr* (naut) take soundings

löten ['løtən] *tr* solder

Lötkolben ['løtkɔlbən] *m* soldering iron

Lötlampe ['løtlampə] *f* blowtorch

Lötmetall ['løtmetal] *n* solder

lot'recht *adj* perpendicular

Lotse ['lotsə] *m* (-n;-n) (aer) air traffic controller; (naut) pilot

lotsen ['lotsən] *tr* (*Flugzeuge*) guide in; (naut) pilot

Lotte-rie [lɔtə'ri] *f* (-;-rien ['ri·ən]) lottery, sweepstakes

Lotterie'los *n* lottery ticket

lotterig ['lɔtərɪç] *adj* sloppy

Lotterleben ['lɔtərlebən] *n* dissolute life

Lotto ['lɔto] *n* (-s;-s) state-owned numbers game

Löwe ['løvə] *m* (-n;-n) lion

Lö'wenanteil *m* lion's share

Lö'wenbändiger -in §6 *mf* lion tamer

Lö'wengrube *f* lion's den

Lö'wenmaul *n* (bot) snapdragon

Lö'wenzahn *m* (bot) dandelion

Löwin ['løvɪn] *f* (-;-nen) lioness

loyal [lɔ·a'jal] *adj* loyal

Luchs [luks] *m* (-es;-e) lynx

Lücke ['lykə] *f* (-;-n) gap, hole; (*Mangel*) deficiency; (im *Gesetz*) loophole; (*Zwischenraum*) interval; auf L. stehend staggered

Lückenbüßer ['lykənbysər] *m* (-s;-) stop-gap

lückenhaft (lük'kenhaft) *adj* defective, fragmentary

Luder ['ludər] *n* (-s;-) carrion; (coll)

cad; (*Weibsbild*) slut; das arme L.! the poor thing!; dummes L.! fathead!

Lu'derleben *n* dissolute life

ludern ['ludərn] *intr* lead a dissolute life

Luft [luft] *f* (-;-e) air; (*Atem*) breath; (*Brise*) breeze; die L. ist rein the coast is clear; es ist dicke L. there is trouble brewing; es liegt etw in der L. (fig) there's s.th. in the air; frische L. schöpfen get a breath of fresh air; in die L. fliegen be blown up; in die L. gehen blow one's top; in die L. sprengen blow up; j-n an die L. setzen give s.o. the air; nach L. schnappen gasp for breath; seinem Zorn L. machen give vent to one's anger; tief L. holen take a deep breath

Luft'alarm *m* air-raid alarm

Luft'angriff *m* air raid

Luft'ansicht *f* aerial view

Luft'aufklärung *f* air reconnaissance

Luft'bild *n* aerial photograph

Luft'bremse *f* air brake

Luft'brücke *f* airlift

Lüftchen ['lyftçən] *n* (-s;-) gentle breeze

luft'dicht *adj* airtight

Luft'druck *m* atmospheric pressure; (*e-r Explosion*) blast; (aut) air pressure

Luft'druckbremse *f* air brake

Luft'druckmesser *m* barometer

Luft'druckprüfer *m* tire gauge

Luft'düse *f* air nozzle, air jet

lüften ['lyftən] *tr* air, ventilate; den Hut l. tip one's hat

Luft'fahrt *f* aviation

Luft'fahrzeug *n* aircraft

Luft'flotte *f* air force

luft'förmig *adj* gaseous

Luft'hafen *m* airport

Luft'heizung *f* hot-air heating

Luft'herrschaft *f* air supremacy

Luft'hülle *f* atmosphere

luftig ['luftɪç] *adj* airy; (*windig*) windy; (*Person*) flighty; (*Kleidung*) loosely woven, light

Luftikus ['luftɪkus] *m* (-;-se) lightheaded person

Luft'klappe *f* air valve

luft'krank *adj* airsick

Luft'kurort *m* mountain resort

Luft'landetruppen *pl* airborne troops

luft'leer *adj* vacuous; luftleerer Raum vacuum

Luft'linie *f* beeline; fünfzig Kilometer L. 50 kilometers as the crow flies

Luft'loch *n* vent; (aer) air pocket

Luft'parade *f* flyover

Luft'post *f* airmail

Luft'raum *m* atmosphere; air space

Luft'reifen *m* tire

Luft'reklame *f* sky writing

Luft'röhre *f* (anat) windpipe

Luft'schiff *n* airship

Luft'schiffahrt *f* aviation

Luft'schloß *n* castle in the air

Luft'schutz *m* air-raid protection

Luft'schutzkeller *m* air-raid shelter

Luft'schutzwart *m* air-raid warden

Luft'spiegelung *f* mirage

Luft′sprung m caper
Luft′streitkräfte pl air force
Luft′strom m air current
Luft′strudel m (aer) wash
Luft′stützpunkt m air base
luft′tüchtig adj air-worthy
Lüf′tung f (–;) airing, ventilation
Luft′veränderung f change of climate
Luft′verkehrsgesellschaft f, **Luft′verkehrslinie** f airline
Luft′vermessung f aerial survey
Luft′verpestung f (–;), **Luft′verschmutzung** f (–;), **Luft′verunreinigung** f (–;) air pollution
Luft′waffe f air force
Luft′warnung f air-raid warning
Luft′weg m air route; **auf dem Luftwege** by air
Luft′widerstand m (phys) air resistance
Luft′zug m draft
Lug [luk] m (–[e]s;) lie; **Lug und Trug** pack of lies
Lüge [′lygə] f (–;–n) lie; **fromme L.** white lie; **j–n Lügen strafen** prove s.o. a liar
lugen [′lugən] intr peep
lügen [′lygən] §111 tr—**das Blaue vom Himmel herunter l.** lie like mad ‖ intr lie, tell a lie
Lügendetek·tor [′lygəndetektɔr] m (–s; –toren [′torən]) lie detector
Lü′gengeschichte f cock-and-bull story
Lü′gengespinst n, **Lü′gengewebe** n tissue of lies
lü′genhaft adj (Person) dishonest, lying; (Nachricht) untrue
Lügner –in [′lygnər(in)] §6 mf liar
lügnerisch [′lygnərɪʃ] adj dishonest
Luke [′lukə] f (–;–n) (am Dach) dormer window; (naut) hatch
Lümmel [′lʏməl] m (–s;–) lout
Lump [lump] m (–en;–en) scoundrel
lumpen [′lumpən] intr lead a wild life; **sich nicht l. lassen** (coll) be generous ‖ **Lumpen** m (–s;–) rag
Lum′pengeld n measly sum; **für ein L.** dirtcheap
Lum′pengesindel n mob, rabble
Lum′penhändler m ragman
Lum′penkerl m (coll) bum
Lum′penpack n rabble, riffraff
Lumperei [′lumpə′raɪ] f (–;–en) shady deal; dirty trick; (Kleinigkeit) trifle
lumpig [′lumpɪç] adj ragged; shabby

Lunge [′luŋə] f (–;–n) lung
Lungen– comb.fm. pulmonary
Lun′genentzündung f pneumonia
Lun′genflügel m lung
lun′genkrank adj consumptive ‖ **Lungenkranke** §5 mf consumptive
Lun′genschwindsucht f tuberculosis
lungern [′luŋərn] intr (HABEN & SEIN) loiter about, lounge about
Lunte [′luntə] f (–;–n) fuse; **L. riechen** smell a rat
Lupe [′lupə] f (–;–n) magnifying glass; **unter die L. nehmen** examine closely
lüpfen [′lʏpfən] tr lift gently
Lust [lust] f (–;⸚e) pleasure; (Verlangen) desire; (Wollust) lust; **L. haben zu** (inf) feel like (ger); **mit L. und Liebe** with heart and soul
Lust′barkeit f (–;–en) amusement, entertainment
Lüster [′lʏstər] m (–s;–) luster
lüstern [′lʏstərn] adj (nach) desirous (of); lustful; (Bilder, Späße) lewd
Lü′sternheit f (–;) greediness; lustfulness; lewdness
Lust′fahrt f pleasure ride
lustig [′lustɪç] adv gay, jolly; (belustigend) amusing; **du bist vielleicht l.!** you must be joking!; **l. sein** have a gay time; **sich l. machen über** (acc) poke fun at
Lüstling [′lʏstlɪŋ] m (–s;–e) lecher
lust′los adj listless; (Börse) inactive
Lustmolch [′lustmɔlç] m (–[e]s;–e) sex fiend
Lust′mord m sex murder
Lust′reise f pleasure trip
Lust′seuche f venereal disease
Lust′spiel n comedy
lust′wandeln intr (SEIN) stroll
Lutheraner –in [lutə′ranər(in)] §6 mf Lutheran
lutherisch [′lutərɪʃ] adj Lutheran
lutschen [′lutʃən] tr & intr suck
Lut′scher m (–s;–) nipple, pacifier
Luxus [′luksus] m (–;) luxury
Lu′xusausgabe f deluxe edition
Luzerne [lu′tsernə] f (–;–n) alfalfa
Lymphe [′lʏmfə] f (–;–n) lymph
lynchen [′lʏnçən] tr lynch
Lyrik [′lʏrɪk] f (–;) lyric poetry
lyrisch [′lʏrɪʃ] adj lyric(al)
Lyze·um [lʏ′tse·um] n (–s;–en [ən]) girls' high school

M

M, m [εm] invar n M, m
M abbr (Mark) (fin) mark
Maar [mɑr] n (–[e]s;–e) crater lake
Maat [mɑt] m (–[e]s;–e) (naut) mate
Machart [′maxɑrt] f make, type
Mache [′maxə] f (–;) (coll) make-believe; **er hat es schon in der M.** he is working on it
machen [′maxən] tr make; (tun) do; (bewirken) produce; (verursachen) cause; (Prüfung, Reise, Spaziergang)

take; (Begriff) form; (Besuch) pay; (Freude) give; (Holz) chop; (Konkurrenz) offer; **das macht mir zu schaffen** that causes me trouble; **das macht nichts** it doesn't matter; never mind; **das macht Spaß** that's fun; **Dummheiten m.** behave foolishly; **Ernst m. be in earnest; gemacht!** right!; O.K.!; **Geschäfte m.** do business; **Geschichten m.** make a fuss; **Hochzeit m.** get married; **ich mache**

Spaß I'm joking; **mach dir nichts daraus!** don't worry about it; **mach's gut!** so long!; **wieviel macht es?** how much is it? || *ref* make progress, do all right; **sich auf den Weg m.** set out; **sich** [*dat*] **etw m. lassen** have s.th. made to order; **sich m. an** (*acc*) get down to; **sich** [*dat*] **nichts daraus m.** not care for (or about) || *intr*— **laß mich nur m.!** just leave it to me; **mach, daß . . . !** see to it that . . . !; **m. in** (*dat*) deal in; dabble in; **mach schon** (or **zu**)! get going!; **nichts zu m!** (coll) nothing doing! no dice!

Machenschaften ['maxən/aftən] *pl* intrigues

Macher ['maxər] *m* (-s;-) instigator; (coll) big shot

Macht [maxt] *f* (-;⸚e) might, power; (*Kraft*) force, strength; **aus eigener M.** on one's own responsibility; **an der Macht** in power; **an die M. kommen** come to power

Macht'ausgleich *m* balance of power

Macht'befugnis *f* authority

Machthaber ['maxthabər] *m* (-s;-) ruler; dictator

machthaberisch ['maxthabərɪ/] *adj* dictatorial

mächtig ['mɛçtɪç] *adj* mighty, powerful; (*riesig*) huge

macht'los *adj* powerless

Macht'losigkeit *f* (-;) impotence

Macht'politik *f* power politics

Macht'vollkommenheit *f* absolute power; **aus eigener M.** on one's own authority

Macht'wort *n* (-[e]s;⸚e)—**ein M. sprechen** put one's foot down

Machwerk ['maxverk] *n* bad job

Mädchen ['mɛtçən] *n* (-s;-) girl; maid

mäd'chenhaft *adj* girlish; maidenly

Mäd'chenhandel *m* white slavery

Mäd'chenname *m* maiden name; girl's name

Made ['madə] *f* (-;-n) maggot

Mädel ['medəl] *n* (-s;-) (coll) girl

madig ['madɪç] *adj* wormy

Magazin [maga'tsin] *n* (-s;-e) warehouse; (*Zeitschrift; Fernsehprogramm; am Gewehr*) magazine

Magd [makt] *f* (-;⸚e) maid; (poet) maiden

Magen ['magən] *m* (-s;⸚ & -) stomach; **auf nüchternen M.** on an empty stomach

Ma'genbeschwerden *pl* stomach trouble

Ma'gengrube *f* pit of the stomach

Ma'gensaft *m* gastric juice

Ma'genweh *n* stomach ache

mager ['magər] *adj* lean; (*Ernte*) poor

Magie [ma'gi] *f* (-;) magic

Magier -in ['magiər(ɪn)] §6 *mf* magician

magisch ['magɪ/] *adj* magic(al)

Magister [ma'gɪstər] *m* (-s;-) school teacher; **M. der freien Künste** Master of Arts

Magistrat [magɪs'trat] *m* (-[e]s;-e) city council; (hist) magistracy

Magnat [mag'nat] *m* (-en;-en) magnate

Magnet [mag'net] *m* (-[e]s;-e) or (-en;-en) magnet

magnetisch [mag'netɪ/] *adj* magnetic

magnetisieren [magnetɪ'zirən] *tr* magnetize

Magnetismus [magne'tɪsmus] *m* (-;) magnetism

Mahagoni [maha'goni] *n* (-s;) mahogony

Mahd [mat] *f* (-;-en) mowing

Mähdrescher ['medrə/ər] *m* (agr) combine

mähen ['me.ən] *tr* mow; (*Getreide*) reap

Mä'her *m* (-s;-) mower; reaper

Mahl [mal] *n* (-[e]s;⸚er) meal

mahlen ['malən] (*pp* **gemahlen**) *tr* grind || *intr* spin

Mahl'zahn *m* molar

Mahl'zeit *f* meal; **prost M.!** that's a nice mess!

Mähmaschine ['mema/inə] *f* reaper; (*Rasen-*) lawn mower

Mähne ['menə] *f* (-;-n) mane

mahnen ['manən] *tr* (**an** *acc*) remind (of); (**an** *acc*) warn (about or of)

Mahnmal ['manmal] *n* (-s;-e) monument

Mah'nung *f* (-;-en) admonition; (com) reminder, notice

Mähre ['merə] *f* (-;-n) old nag

Mähren ['merən] *n* (-s;) Moravia

Mai [maɪ] *m* (-[e]s;-e) May

Mai'baum *m* maypole

Mai'blume *f* lily of the valley

Maid [maɪt] *f* (-;-en) (poet) maiden

Mai'glöckchen *n* lily of the valley

Mai'käfer *m* June bug

Mailand ['maɪlant] *n* (-[e]s) Milan

Mais [maɪs] *m* (-es;) Indian corn

Maische ['maɪ/ə] *f* (-;) mash

Mais'hülse *f* corn husk

Mais'kolben *m* corncob

Majestät [majes'tet] *f* (-;-en) majesty

majestätisch [majes'tetɪ/] *adj* majestic

Major [ma'jor] *m* (-s;-e) major

Majoran [majo'ran] *m* (-s;-e) marjoram

majorenn [majo'ren] *adj* of age

Majorität [majorɪ'tet] *f* (-;-en) majority

Makel ['makəl] *m* (-s;-) spot, stain

Mäkelei [mekə'laɪ] *f* (-;-en) carping

mäkelig ['mekəlɪç] *adj* critical; (*im Essen*) picky

ma'kellos *adj* spotless; (fig) impeccable

mäkeln ['mekəln] *intr* (**an** *dat*) carp (at), find fault (with)

Makkaroni [maka'roni] *pl* macaroni

Makler -in ['maklər(ɪn)] §6 *mf* agent, broker

Mäkler -in ['meklər(ɪn)] §6 *mf* faultfinder

Mak'lergebühr *f* brokerage

Makrele [ma'krelə] *f* (-;-n) mackerel

Makrone [ma'kronə] *f* (-;-n) macaroon

Makulatur [makula'tur] *f* (-;) waste

mal [mal] *adv* (coll) once; (arith) times; **komm mal her!** come here once!; **zwei mal drei** two times three; **zwei mal Spinat** two (orders of) spinach || **Mal** n (-[e]s;-e) mark, sign; (*Mutter*-) birthmark, mole; (*Fleck*) stain; time; **dieses Mal** this time; **manches liebe Mal** many a time; **mit e-m Male** all at once

Malbuch ['malbux] n coloring book

malen ['malən] tr & intr paint

Ma'ler –in §6 mf painter

Malerei [malə'raı] f (-;-en) painting

malerisch ['malərıʃ] adj picturesque

Ma'lerleinwand f canvas

Malkunst ['malkunst] f art of painting

Malstrom ['mal/trom] m maelstrom

malträtieren [maltre'tirən] tr maltreat

Malve ['malvə] f (-;-n) mallow

Malz [malts] n (-es;) malt

Malz'bonbon m cough drop

Mal'zeichen n multiplication sign

Mama [ma'ma], ['mama] f (-;-s) mom, ma

Mamsell [mam'zel] f (-;-en) miss; (*Wirtschafterin*) housekeeper

man [man] indef pron one, they, people, you; **man hat mir gesagt** I have been told

manch [manç] invar adj—**manch ein** many a || **mancher** §3 adj many a; **manche** pl some, several || pron many a person; many a thing

mancherlei ['mançərlaı] invar adj all sorts of, various

Manchester [man'ʃestər] m (-s;) corduroy

manch'mal adv sometimes

Mandant –in [man'dant(ın)] §7 mf client

Mandarine [manda'rinə] f (-;-n) tangerine

Mandat [man'dat] n (-[e]s;-e) mandate

mandatieren [manda'tirən] tr mandate

Mandel ['mandəl] f (-;-n) almond; (*15 Stück*) fifteen; (anat) tonsil

Man'delentzündung f tonsilitis

Mandoline [mando'linə] f (-;-n) mandolin

Mandschurei [mantʃu'raı] f (-;) Manchuria

Mangan [maŋ'gan] n (-s;) manganese

Mangel ['maŋəl] m (-s;ᵘ) lack, deficiency; (*Knappheit*) shortage; (*Fehler*) shortcoming; **aus M. an** (dat) for lack of; **M. haben an** (dat) be deficient in; **M. leiden an** (dat) be short of || f (-;-n) mangle

Mangel– comb.fm. in short supply

Man'gelberuf m undermanned profession

man'gelhaft adj defective; faulty; unsatisfactory, deficient

Man'gelkrankheit f nutritional deficiency

mangeln ['maŋəln] tr (*Wäsche*) mangle || intr (an dat) be short of, lack || impers—**es mangelt mir an** (dat) I lack

Mängelrüge ['meŋəlrygə] f (-;-n) (com) complaint (*about a shipment*)

mangels ['maŋəls] prep (genit) for want of, for lack of

Ma·nie [ma'ni] f (-;-nien ['ni-ən]) mania

Manier [ma'nir] f (-;-en) manner

maniert [ma'nirt] adj affected

Manieriert'heit f (-;-en) mannerism

manier'lich adj mannerly, polite

Manifest [manı'fest] n (-es;-e) (aer, naut) manifest; (pol) manifesto

Maniküre [manı'kyrə] f (-;-n) manicure; manicurist

maniküren [manı'kyrən] tr manicure

manipulieren [manıpu'lirən] tr manipulate

manisch ['manıʃ] adj maniacal

Manko ['maŋko] n (-s;-s) deficit; (com) shortage

Mann [man] m (-[e]s;ᵘer) man; (*Gatte*) husband; **an den M. bringen** manage to get rid of; **der M. aus dem Volke** the man in the street; **seinen M. stehen** hold one's own

mannbar ['manbar] adj marriageable

Mann'barkeit f (-;) puberty; marriageable age (*of girls*)

Männchen ['mençən] n (-s;-) little man; (*Ehemann*) hubby; (zool) male; **M. machen** sit on its hind legs

Männerchor ['menərkor] m men's choir

Mannesalter ['manəsaltər] n manhood

Manneszucht ['manəstsuxt] f discipline

mann'haft adj manly, valiant

mannigfaltig ['manıçfaltıç] adj manifold

Man'nigfaltigkeit f (-;) diversity

männlich ['menlıç] adj male; (fig) manly; (gram) masculine

Männ'lichkeit f (-;) manhood; virility

Mannsbild ['mansbılt] n (pej) man

Mann'schaft f (-;-en) crew; (sport) team, squad; **Mannschaften** (mil) enlisted men

Mann'schaftsführer –in §6 mf (sport) captain

Mann'schaftswagen m (mil) personnel carrier

Mannsleute ['manslaıtə] pl menfolk

mannstoll ['manstol] adj man-crazy

Manns'tollheit f (-;) nymphomania

Mann'weib n mannish woman

Manometer [mano'metər] n pressure gauge

Manöver [ma'nøvər] n (-s;-) maneuver

manövrieren [manø'vrirən] intr maneuver

manövrier'fähig adj maneuverable

Mansarde [man'zardə] f (-;-n) attic

manschen ['manʃən] tr & intr splash

Manschette [man'ʃetə] f (-;-n) cuff

Manschet'tenknopf m cuff link

Mantel ['mantəl] m (-s;ᵘ) overcoat; (*Fahrrad*-) tire; (*e-s Kabels*) sheathing; (*Geschoß*-) jacket, case; (geol, orn) mantle

manuell [manu'el] adj manual

Manufaktur [manufak'tur] f (-;-en) manufacture

Manufaktur'waren pl manufactured goods

Manuskript [manu'skrıpt] n (-[e]s;-e) manuscript

Mappe ['mapə] f (-;-n) briefcase; (*Aktendeckel*) folder

Märchen ['merçən] n (-s;-) fairy tale

mär'chenhaft adj legendary; (*fig*) fabulous

Mär′chenland n fairyland
Marchese [mar′kezə] m (-;-n) marquis
Marder [′mardər] m (-s;-) marten; (fig) thief
Margarine [marga′rinə] f (-;) margarine
Marienbild [ma′ri·ənbɪlt] n image of the Virgin
Marienfäden [ma′ri·ənfedən] pl gossamer(s)
Marienglas [ma′ri·ənglas] n mica
Marienkäfer [ma′ri·ənkefər] m ladybug
Marine [ma′rinə] f (-;-n) (Kriegs-) navy; (Handels-) merchant marine
mari′neblau adj navy-blue
Mari′neflugzeug n seaplane
Mari′neinfanterie f marines
Mari′neminister m secretary of the navy
Mari′neoffizier –in §6 mf naval officer
Mari′nesoldat m marine
marinieren [marɪ′nirən] tr marinate
Marionette [marɪ·ə′netə] f (-;-n) puppet
Marionet′tentheater n puppet show
Mark [mark] f (-;-) (fin) mark; (hist) borderland, march ‖ n (-[e]s;) marrow; (im Holz) pith; **bis ins M. to the quick; er hat M.** (fig) he has guts; **j–m durch M. und Bein gehen** (fig) go right through s.o.
markant [mar′kant] adj (einprägsam) marked; (außergewöhnlich) striking; (Geländepunkt) prominent
Marke [′markə] f (-;-n) mark; (Brief-) stamp; (Handelszeichen) trademark; (Sorte) brand; (Fabrikat) make; (Spiel-) counter
mark′erschütternd adj piercing
Marketenderei [markətendə′raɪ] f (-; –en) post exchange, PX
Marketing [′markɪtɪŋ] n (-s;) (com) marketing
markieren [mar′kirən] tr mark; (spielen) pretend to be
Markise [mar′kizə] f (-;-n) awning
Mark′stein m landmark
Markt [markt] m (-[e]s;ᵘe) market; (Jahrmarkt) fair
Markt′bude f booth, stall
markten [′marktən] intr (um) bargain (for)
markt′fähig adj marketable
Markt′flecken m market town
marktgängig [′marktgɛŋɪç] adj marketable
Markt′platz m market place
Markt′schreier m quack
Marmelade [marmə′ladə] f (-;-n) jam
Marmor [′marmor] m (-s;-e) marble
Mar′morbruch m marble quarry
marmorn [′marmərn] adj marble
marode [ma′rodə] adj (coll) tired out
Marodeur [marə′dør] m (-s;-e) marauder
marodieren [marə′dirən] intr maraud
Marone [ma′ronə] f (-;-n) chestnut
Maroquin [marə′kē] m (-s;) morocco
Marotte [ma′rotə] f (-;-n) whim
marsch [marʃ] interj march!; be off!; **m., m.!** on the double ‖ **Marsch** m (-es; ᵘe) march; **in M. setzen** get

going; **j–m den M. blasen** (coll) chew s.o. out; **(sich) in M. setzen** set out
Marschall [′marʃal] m (-s;ᵘe) marshal
Mar′schallstab m marshal's baton
Marsch′gepäck n full field pack
marschieren [mar′ʃirən] intr (SEIN) march
Marsch′kompanie f replacement company
Marsch′lied n marching song
Marsch′verpflegung f field rations
Marter [′martər] f (-;-n) torture
martern [′martərn] tr torture, torment
Mar′terpfahl m stake
Märtyrer –in [′mertyrər(ɪn)] §6 mf martyr
Märtyrertum [′mertyrərtum] n (-s;) martyrdom
März [merts] m (-[es];-e) March
Masche [′maʃə] f (-;-n) mesh; stitch; (fig) trick
Ma′schendraht m chicken wire; screen; wire mesh
ma′schenfest adj runproof
Maschine [ma′ʃinə] f (-;-n) machine; (aer) airplane
maschinell [maʃɪ′nɛl] adj mechanical ‖ adv by machine
Maschi′nenantrieb m—**mit M.** machine-driven
Maschi′nenbau m (-[e]s;) mechanical engineering
Maschi′nengewehr n machine gun
Maschi′nengewehrschütze m machine gunner
maschi′nenmäßig adj mechanical
Maschi′nenpistole f tommy gun
Maschi′nenschaden m engine trouble
Maschi′nenschlosser m machinist
maschi′nenschreiben tr type ‖ **Maschinenschreiben** n (-s;-) typing; typewritten letter
Maschi′nenschrift f typescript
Maschi′nensprache f computer language
Maschinerie [maʃɪnə′ri] f (-;) (& fig) machinery
Maschinist –in [maʃɪ′nɪst(ɪn)] §7 mf machinist
Masern [′mazərn] pl measles
Maserung [′mazərʊŋ] f (-;) grain (in wood)
Maske [′maskə] f (-;-n) mask; (fig) disguise; (theat) make-up
Ma′skenball m masquerade
Maskerade [maskə′radə] f (-;-n) masquerade
maskieren [mas′kirən] tr mask
Maskotte [mas′kotə] f (-;-n) mascot
maskulin [maskʊ′lin] adj masculine
Maskuli·num [maskʊ′linʊm] n (-s;-na [na]) masculine noun
maß [mas] pret of **messen** ‖ **Maß** n (-es;-e) measure; (Messung) measurement; (Ausdehnung) extent, dimension; (Verhältnis) rate, proportion; (Grad) degree; (Mäßigung) moderation; **das Maß ist voll!** I've had it!; **das Maß überschreiten** go too far; **er hat sein gerütteltes Maß an Kummer gehabt** he had his full share of trouble; **in gewissem Maße** to a certain extent; **in hohem Maße**

highly; **j-m Maß nehmen zu** take s.o.'s measurements for; **Maß halten** observe moderation; **mit Maße** in moderation; **nach Maß angefertigt** custom-made; **ohne Maß und Ziel** without limit; **weder Maß noch Ziel kennen** know no bounds; **zweierlei Maß** double standard ‖ *f* (-;- & -e) quart (*of beer*), stein

massakrieren [masa'kri:rən] *tr* massacre

Maß'anzug *m* tailor-made suit

Maß'arbeit *f* work made to order

Masse ['masə] *f* (-;-n) mass; bulk; (*Menge*) volume; (*Volk*) crowd; (*Hinterlassenschaft*) estate; (elec) ground; **die breite M.** the masses; the rank and file; **e-e Masse...** (coll) lots of

Maß'einheit *f* unit of measure

Masseleisen ['masəlaɪzən] *n* pigiron

Massen- *comb.fm.* mass, bulk, wholesale

Mas'senabsatz *m* wholesale selling

Mas'senangriff *m* mass attack

Mas'senanziehung *f* gravitation

mas'senhaft *adj* in large quantities

Maß'gabe *f*—**mit der M., daß** with the understanding that; **nach M.** (genit) in proportion to; according to; (jur) as provided in

maß'gebend, maßgeblich ['masgeplɪç] *adj* standard; authoritative; (*Kreise*) leading, influential; **das ist nicht maßgebend für** that is no criterion for

maß'gerecht *adj* to scale

maß'halten §90 *intr* observe moderation

maß'haltig *adj* precise

massieren [ma'si:rən] *tr* massage; (*Truppen*) mass

massig ['masɪç] *adj* bulky; solid; (*Person*) stout ‖ *adv*—**m. viel** (coll) very much

mäßig ['mesɪç] *adj* moderate; frugal; (*Leistung*) mediocre

mäßigen ['mesɪgən] *tr* moderate; tone down ‖ *ref* control oneself

Mä'ßigkeit *f* moderation; frugality; temperance

Mä'ßigung *f* (-;) moderation

massiv [ma'si:f] *adj* massive; solid

Maß'krug *m* beer mug, stein

Maß'liebchen *n* daisy

maß'los *adj* immoderate ‖ *adv* extremely

Maß'nahme *f* (-;-n), **Maß'regel** *f* (-; -n) measure, step, move

maß'regeln *tr* reprimand

Maß'schneider *m* custom tailor

Maß'stab *m* ruler; (fig) yardstick, standard; (*auf Landkarten*) scale; **jeden M. verlieren** lose all sense of proportion

maß'voll *adj* moderate; (*Benehmen*) discreet

Mast [mast] *m* (-es;-en & -e) pole; (naut) mast ‖ *f* (-;) (*Schweinfutter*) mast

Mast'baum *m* (naut) mast

Mast'darm *m* rectum

mästen ['mestən] *tr* fatten

Mast'korb *m* masthead, crow's nest

Material [materɪ'al] *n* (-s;-ien [1·ən]) material

Materialismus [materɪa'lɪsmus] *m* (-;) materialism

materialistisch [materɪa'lɪstɪʃ] *adj* materialistic

Material'waren *pl* (Aust) medical supplies

Materie [ma'te:rɪə] *f* (-;-n) matter

materiell [materɪ'el] *adj* material; (*Schwierigkeiten*) financial; (*Recht*) substantive

Mathe ['matə] *f* (-;) (coll) math

Mathematik [matema'tik] *f* (-;) mathematics

Mathematiker -in [mate'matɪkər(ɪn)] §6 *mf* mathematician

mathematisch [mate'matɪʃ] *adj* mathematical

Matratze [ma'tratsə] *f* (-;-n) mattress

Mätresse [me'tresə] *f* (-;-n) mistress

Matrize [ma'tritsə] *f* (-;-n) stencil; (*Stempel*) die, matrix

Matrone [ma'tro:nə] *f* (-;-n) matron

matro'nenhaft *adj* matronly

Matrose [ma'tro:zə] *m* (-n;-n) sailor

Matro'senanzug *m* sailor's uniform

Matro'senjacke *f* (nav) peacoat

Matsch [matʃ] *m* (-es;) (*Brei*) mush; (*Schlamm*) mud; (*halbgetauter Schnee*) slush

matschig ['matʃɪç] *adj* mushy; muddy; slushy

matt [mat] *adj* dull; weak; limp; (*Glas, Birne*) frosted; (*Börse*) slack; (*erschöpft*) exhausted; (*Kugel*) spent; (*Licht*) dim; (*Metall*) tarnished; (phot) matt; **m. machen** dull; tarnish; **m. setzen** checkmate

Matte ['matə] *f* (-;-n) mat; (*Wiese*) Alpine meadow; (poet) mead

Matt'glas *n* frosted glass

Matt'gold *n* dull gold

Matt'heit *f* dullness; fatigue

matt'herzig *adj* faint-hearted

Mat'tigkeit *f* (-;) fatigue

Matura [ma'tu:ra] *f* (-;) (Aust) final examination (*before graduation*)

Mätzchen ['metsçən] *n* (-s;-) trick; **M. machen** play tricks; put on airs

Mauer ['mau·ər] *f* (-;-n) wall

Mau'erblümchen *n* (fig) wallflower

Mau'erkalk *m* mortar

mauern ['mau·ərn] *tr* build (*in stone or brick*)

Mau'erstein *m* brick

Mau'erwerk *n* brickwork; masonry

Mau'erziegel *m* brick

Maul [maul] *n* (-[e]s;¨er) mouth; maw; **halt's M.!** (sl) shut up!

Maul'affe *m* gaping fool

Maul'beerbaum *m* mulberry tree

Maul'beere *f* mulberry

maulen ['maulən] *intr* gripe

Maul'esel *m* mule

maul'faul *adj* too lazy to talk

Maul'held *m* braggart

Maul'korb *m* muzzle

Maul'schelle *f* slap in the face

Maul'sperre *f* lock jaw

Maul'tier *n* mule

Maul'trommel *f* Jew's-harp

Maul'– und Klau'enseuche f hoof and mouth disease

Maul'werk n—**ein großes M. haben** have the gift of gab

Maul'wurf m (zool) mole

Maul'wurfshaufen m, **Maul'wurfshügel** m molehill

Maure ['maurə] m (–n;–n) Moor

Maurer ['maurər] m (–s;–) mason; bricklayer

Mau'rerkelle f trowel

Mau'rerpolier m bricklayer foreman

Maus [maus] f (–;:̈e) mouse

Mäuschen ['mɔisçən] n (–s;–) little mouse; (fig) pet, darling; wench

Mau'sefalle f mousetrap

mausen ['mauzən] tr pilfer, swipe || intr catch mice

Mauser ['mauzər] f (–;) molting season; **in der M. sein** be molting

mausern ['mauzərn] ref molt

mau'setot' adj dead as a doornail

mausig ['mauziç] adj—**sich m. machen** put on airs, be stuck-up

Mauso·leum [mauzo'le·um] n (–s; –leen ['le·ən]) mausoleum

Maxime [ma'ksimə] f (–;–n) maxim

Mayonnaise [majo'nezə] f (–;) mayonnaise

Mechanik [me'çanık] f (–;–en) mechanics; (Triebwerk) mechanism

Mechaniker [me'çanıkər] m (–s;–) mechanic

mechanisch [me'çanıʃ] adj mechanical; power-

mechanisieren [meçanı'zirən] tr mechanize

Mechanis·mus [meça'nısmus] m (–; –men [mən]) mechanism; (Uhrwerk) works

Meckerer ['mekərər] m (–s;–) (coll) grumbler

meckern ['mekərn] intr bleat; (coll) grumble

Medaille [me'daljə] f (–;–n) medal

Medaillon [medal'jɔ̃] n (–s;–s) medallion; locket

Medikament [medika'ment] n (–s;–e) medication

Meditation [medıta'tsjon] f (–;–en) meditation

meditieren [medı'tirən] intr meditate

Medizin [medı'tsin] f (–;–en) medicine

Medizinalassistant [medıtsı'nalasıstant(ın)] §7 mf intern

Medizinalbeamte [medıtsı'nalbə·amtə] m health officer

Medizinalbehörde [medıtsı'nalbəhørdə] f board of health

Mediziner –in [medı'tsinər(ın)] §6 mf physician; medical student

medizinisch [medı'tsinıʃ] adj medical, medicinal; medicated; **medizinische Fakultät** medical school

Meer [mer] n (–[e]s;–e) sea; **am Meere** at the seashore; **übers M.** overseas

Meer'busen m bay, gulf

Meer'enge f straits

Meeres– [merəs] comb.fm. sea, marine

Mee'resarm m inlet

Mee'resboden m bottom of the sea

Mee'resbucht f bay

Mee'resgrund m bottom of the sea

Mee'reshöhe f sea level

Mee'resküste f seacoast

Mee'resleuchten n phosphorescence

Mee'resspiegel m sea level

meer'grün adj sea-green

Meer'rettich m horseradish

Meer'schaum m meerschaum

Meer'schwein n porpoise

Meer'schweinchen n guinea pig

Meer'ungeheuer n sea monster

Meer'weib n mermaid

Mehl [mel] n (–[e]s;) (grobes) meal; (feines) flour; (Staub) dust, powder

Mehl'kloß m dumpling

Mehl'speise f pastry; pudding

Mehl'suppe f gruel

Mehl'tau m mildew

mehr [mer] invar adj & adv more; **immer m.** more and more; **kein Wort m.!** not another word!; **m. oder weniger** more or less, give or take; **nicht m.** no more, no longer; **nie m.** never again || **Mehr** n (–s;) majority; (Zuwachs) increase; (Überschuß) surplus

Mehr'arbeit f extra work; (Überstunden) overtime

Mehr'aufwand m, **Mehr'ausgabe** f additional expenditure

Mehr'betrag m surplus; extra charge

mehr'deutig adj ambiguous

mehren ['merən] tr & ref increase

mehrere ['merərə] adj & pron several

mehr'fach adj manifold; repeated, multiple

mehr'farbig adj multicolored

Mehr'gebot n higher bid

Mehr'gepäck n excess luggage

Mehr'gewicht n excess weight

Mehr'heit f (–;–en) majority; (pol) plurality

Mehr'heitsbeschluß m, **Mehr'heitsentscheidung** f plurality vote

mehr'jährig adj (bot) perennial

Mehr'kosten pl extra charges

Mehr'ladegewehr n repeater

Mehr'leistung f increased performance; (ins) extended benefits

mehrmalig ['mermaliç] adj repeated

mehrmals ['mermals] adv several times, on several occasions; repeatedly

Mehr'porto n additional postage

Mehr'preis m extra charge

mehr'seitig adj multilateral; many-sided; (Brief) of many pages

mehrsilbig ['merzılbıç] adj polysyllabic

mehrsprachig ['merʃpraxıç] adj polyglot

mehrstöckig ['merʃtœkıç] adj multistory

mehrstufig ['merʃtufıç] adj multistage

Meh'rung f (–;) increase, multiplication

Mehr'verbrauch m increased consumption

Mehr'wertsteuer f added value tax

Mehr'zahl f majority; (gram) plural

meiden ['maidən] §112 tr avoid, shun

Meier ['maɪ·ər] m (–s;–) tenant farmer; dairy farmer

Meierei [maɪ·ə'raɪ] f (–;–en) dairy

Mei'ergut n, **Mei'erhof** m dairy farm

Meile ['maɪlə] f (-;-n) mile

mei'lenweit adj extending for miles, miles and miles of || adv far away; **m. auseinander** miles apart

Mei'lenzahl f mileage

mein [maɪn] §2,2 poss adj my || §2,4,5 pron mine; **das Meine** my share; my due; **die Meinen** my family

Meineid ['maɪnaɪt] m (-[e]s;) perjury; **e–n M. schwören** (or **leisten**) commit perjury

meineidig ['maɪnaɪdɪç] adj perjured; **m. werden** perjure oneself

meinen ['maɪnən] tr think; (im Sinne haben) mean, intend; **das will ich m.** I should think so; **die Sonne meint es heute gut** the sun is very warm today; **es ehrlich m.** have honorable intentions; **es gut m.** mean well; **ich meinte dich im Recht** I thought you were in the right; **m. Sie das ernst** (or **im Ernst**)? do you really mean it?; **was m. Sie damit?** what do you mean by that?; **was m. Sie dazu?** what do you think of that? || intr think; **m. Sie?** do you think so?; **m. Sie nicht auch?** don't you agree?; **wie m. Sie?** I beg your pardon?

meinerseits ['maɪnər'zaɪts] adv for my part

meinesgleichen ['maɪnəs'glaɪçən] pron people like me, the likes of me

meinethlben ['maɪnət'halbən], **meinet-wegen** ['maɪnət'veɡən] adv for my sake, on my account; for all I care

meinetwillen ['maɪnət'vɪlən] adv—**um m.** for my sake, on my behalf

meinige ['maɪnɪɡə] §2,5 pron mine

Mei'nung f (-;-en) opinion; **anderer M. mit j–m sein über** (acc) disagree with s.o. about; **der M. sein** be of the opinion; **geteilter M. sein** be of two minds; **j–m die** (or **seine**) **M. sagen** give s.o. a piece of one's mind; **meiner M. nach** in my opinion; **vorgefaßte M.** preconceived idea

Mei'nungsäußerung f expression of opinion

Mei'nungsaustausch m exchange of views

Mei'nungsbefragung f, **Mei'nungsfor-schung** f public opinion poll

Mei'nungsumfrage f public opinion poll

Mei'nungsverschiedenheit f difference of opinion, disagreement

Meise ['maɪzə] f (-;-n) titmouse

Meißel ['maɪsəl] m (-s;-) chisel

meißeln ['maɪsəln] tr & intr chisel

meist [maɪst] adj most; **am meisten** most; **das meiste** the most; **die meisten Menschen** most people; **die meiste Zeit** most of the time; **die meiste Zeit des Jahres** most of the year || adv usually, generally

Meist'begünstigungsklausel f most-favored nation clause

Meist'bietende §5 mf highest bidder

meistens ['maɪstəns] adv mostly

Meister ['maɪstər] m (-s;-) master; boss; (im Betrieb) foreman; (sport) champion

mei'sterhaft adj masterly

Meisterin ['maɪstərɪn] f (-;-nen) master's wife; (sport) champion

mei'sterlich adj masterly

meistern ['maɪstərn] tr master

Mei'sterschaft f (-;-en) mastery; (sport) championship

Mei'sterstück n, **Mei'sterwerk** n masterpiece

Mei'sterzug m master stroke

Melancholie [melaŋkɔ'li] f (-;) melancholy

melancholisch [melaŋ'kolɪʃ] adj melancholy

Melasse [me'lasə] f (-;-n) molasses

Meldeamt ['meldə·amt] n. **Meldebüro** ['meldəbyro] n registration office

Meldefahrer ['meldəfarər] m (mil) dispatch rider

Meldegänger ['meldəɡeŋər] m (mil) messenger, runner

melden ['meldən] tr report; (polizei-lich) turn (s.o.) in; **den Empfang m.** (genit) acknowledge the receipt of; **er hat nichts zu m.** he has nothing to say in the matter; **gemeldet wer-den zu** (sport) be entered in; **j–m m. lassen, daß** send s.o. word that || ref report; (Alter) begin to show; (Gläubiger) come forward; (Kind) cry; (Magen) growl; (polizeilich) register; (Winter) set in; (telp) answer; **sich auf e–e Anzeige m.** answer an ad; **sich krank m.** (mil) go on sick call; **sich m. zu** apply for; (freiwillig) volunteer for; (mil) enlist in; (sport) enter; **sich zum Dienst m.** (mil) report for duty; **sich zum Wort m.** ask to speak; (in der Schule) hold up the hand

Mel'der m (-s;-) (mil) runner

Meldezettel ['meldətsetəl] m registration form

Mel'dung f (-;-en) report; message, notification; (Bewerbung) application

Melkeimer ['melkaɪmər] m milk pail

melken ['melkən] §113 tr milk

Melo·die [melə'di] f (-;-dien ['di·ən]) melody

melodisch [me'lodɪʃ] adj melodious

Melone [me'lonə] f (-;-n) melon; (coll) derby

Meltau ['meltau] m (-[e]s;) honeydew

Membran [mem'bran] f (-;-en), **Mem-brane** [mem'branə] f (-;-n) membrane

Memme ['memə] f (-;-n) coward

Memoiren [memo'arən] pl memoirs

memorieren [memo'rirən] tr memorize

Menge ['meŋə] f (-;-n) quantity, amount; crowd; **e–e M.** a lot of

mengen ['meŋən] tr mix || ref (unter acc) mingle (with); (in acc) meddle (in)

Men'genlehre f (math) theory of sets

men'genmäßig adj quantitative

Mengsel ['meŋzəl] n (-s;-) hodgepodge

Mennige ['menɪɡə] f (-;) rust-preventive paint

Mensch [menʃ] m (-en;-en) human being, man; person, individual; **die Menschen** the people; **kein M.** no one || n (-es; -er) hussy, slut

Menschen– [menʃən] *comb.fm.* man, of men; human
Men'schenalter *n* generation, age
Men'schenfeind **–in** §8 *mf* misanthropist
Men'schenfresser *m* cannibal
Men'schenfreund **–in** §8 *mf* philanthropist
men'schenfreundlich *adj* philanthropic, humanitarian
Men'schengedenken *n*—**seit M.** since time immemorial
Men'schengeschlecht *n* mankind
Men'schengewühl *n* milling crowd
Men'schenglück *n* human happiness
Men'schenhandel *m* slave trade
Men'schenhaß *m* misanthropy
Men'schenjagd *f* manhunt
Men'schenkenner **–in** §6 *mf* judge of human nature
Men'schenkind *n* human being; **armes M.** poor soul
men'schenleer *adj* deserted
Men'schenliebe *f* philanthropy
Men'schenmaterial *n* manpower
men'schenmöglich *adj* humanly possible
Men'schenraub *m* kidnaping
Men'schenräuber **–in** §6 *mf* kidnaper
Men'schenrechte *pl* human rights
men'schenscheu *adj* shy, unsociable
Men'schenschinder *m* oppressor, slave driver
Men'schenschlag *m* race
Men'schenseele *f* human soul; **keine M.** not a living soul
Men'schenskind *interj* man alive!
Men'schensohn *m* (Bib) Son of man
men'schenunwürdig *adj* degrading
Men'schenverächter **–in** §6 *mf* cynic
Men'schenverstand *m*—**guter M.** common sense
Men'schenwürde *f* human dignity
men'schenwürdig *adj* decent
Mensch'heit *f* (–;) mankind, humanity
mensch'lich *adj* human; (*human*) humane
Mensch'lichkeit *f* (–;) humanity
Menschwerdung ['menʃverduŋ] *f* (–;) incarnation
Menstruation [mentrʊ·a'tsjon] *f* (–;-en) menstruation
Mensur [men'zur] *f* (–;-en) measure; (*Meßglas*) measuring glass; students' duel
Mentalität [mentali'tet] *f* (–;) mentality
Menuett [menu'et] *n* (–[e]s;-e) minuet
Meridian [meri'djan] *m* (–s;-e) (astr) meridian
merkbar ['merkbar] *adj* noticeable
Merkblatt ['merkblat] *n* instruction sheet
Merkbuch ['merkbux] *n* notebook
merken ['merkən] *tr* notice; realize; etw m. lassen show s.th., betray s.th.; **man merkte es sofort an ihrem Ausdruck, daß** one noticed immediately by her expression that || *ref*—m. **Sie sich** [*dat*], **was ich sage!** mark my word!; sich [*dat*] etw m. bear s.th. in mind; sich [*dat*] nichts m. lassen not give oneself away || *intr*—m. **auf** (*acc*) pay attention to, heed
merk'lich *adj* noticeable

Merkmal ['merkmal] *n* (–[e]s;-e) mark, feature, characteristic
Merkur [mer'kur] *m* & *n* (–s;) mercury
Merk'wort *n* (–[e]s;ˮer) catchword; (theat) cue
merk'würdig *adj* remarkable; (*seltsam*) curious, strange
merkwürdigerweise ['merkvʏrdɪgərvaɪzə] *adv* strange to say
Merk'würdigkeit *f* (–;-en) strange thing
Merk'zeichen *n* mark
meschugge [me'ʃugə] *adj* (coll) nuts
Mesner ['mesnər] *m* (–s;-) sexton
Meß– [mes] *comb.fm.* measuring; (eccl) mass
Meß'band *n* (–[e]s;ˮer) measuring tape
meßbar ['mesbar] *adj* measurable
Meß'buch *n* (relig) missal
Meß'diener *m* acolyte
Messe ['mesə] *f* (–;-n) fair; (eccl) mass; (nav) officers' mess
messen ['mesən] §70 *tr* measure; (*Zeit*) time, clock; (*mustern*) size up || *ref* —sich m. mit cope with; (*geistig*) match wits with; sich nicht m. können mit be no match for || *intr* measure
Messer ['mesər] *m* (–s;-) gauge; meter || *n* (–s;-) knife; (surg) scalpel; **bis aufs M.** to the death
Mes'serheld *m* (coll) cutthroat
mes'serscharf *adj* razor-sharp
Mes'serschmied *m* cutler
Messerschmiedewaren ['mesərʃmidəvarən] *pl* cutlery
Mes'serschneide *f* knife edge
Meß'gewand *n* (eccl) vestment; chasuble
Meß'hemd *n* (eccl) alb
Messias [me'si·as] *invar m* Messiah
Messing ['mesɪŋ] *n* (–s;) brass
messingen ['mesɪŋən] *adj* brass
Meß'opfer *n* sacrifice of the mass
Mes'sung *f* (–;-en) measurement
Metall [me'tal] *n* (–s;-e) metal
Metall'baukasten *m* erector set
metallen [me'talən], **metallisch** [me'talɪʃ] *adj* metallic
Mettall'säge *f* hacksaw
Metallurgie [metalʊr'gi] *f* (–;) metallurgy
metall'verarbeitend *adj* metal-processing
Metall'waren *pl* hardware
Metapher [me'tafər] *f* (–;-n) metaphor
Meteor [mete'or] *m* (–s;-e) meteor
Meteorologe [mete·oro'logə] *m* (–n;-) meteorologist
Meteorologie [mete·orolo'gi] *f* (–;) meteorolgy
Meteorologin [mete·oro'logɪn] *f* (–;-nen) meteorologist
meteorologisch [mete·oro'logɪʃ] *adj* meteorological
Meteor'stein *m* meteorite, aerolite
Meter ['metər] *m* & *n* (–s;-) meter
Me'termaß *n* tape measure
Methode [me'todə] *f* (–;-n) method
methodisch [me'todɪʃ] *adj* methodical
Metrik ['metrɪk] *f* (–;) metrics
metrisch ['metrɪʃ] *adj* metrical

Metropole [metro'polə] *f* (-;-n) metropolis

Mette ['mɛtə] *f* (-;-n) matins

Mettwurst ['mɛtvurst] *f* soft sausage

Metzelei [mɛtsə'laɪ] *f* (-;-en) massacre, slaughter

metzeln ['mɛtsəln] *tr* massacre

Metzger ['mɛtsgər] *m* (-s;-) butcher

Metzgerei [mɛtsgə'raɪ] *f* (-;-en) butcher shop

Meuchelmord ['mɔɪçəlmɔrt] *m* assassination

Meuchelmörder –in ['mɔɪçəlmœrdər (ɪn)] §6 *mf* assassin

meucheln ['mɔɪçəln] *tr* murder

meuchlerisch ['mɔɪçlərɪʃ] *adj* murderous

meuchlings ['mɔɪçlɪŋs] *adv* treacherously

Meute ['mɔɪtə] *f* (-;-n) pack (*of hounds*); (fig) horde, gang

Meuterei [mɔɪtə'raɪ] *f* (-;-en) mutiny

meuterisch ['mɔɪtərɪʃ] *adj* mutinous

meutern ['mɔɪtərn] *intr* mutiny

Mexikaner –in [mɛksɪ'kanər(ɪn)] §6 *mf* Mexican

mexikanisch [mɛksɪ'kanɪʃ] *adj* Mexican

Mexiko ['mɛksɪko] *n* (-s;) Mexico

miauen [mɪ'aʊ.ən] *intr* meow

mich [mɪç] §11 *pers pron* me ‖ §11 *reflex pron* myself

mied [mit] *pret of* meiden

Mieder ['midər] *n* (-s;-) bodice

Mie'derwaren *pl* foundation garments

Mief [mif] *m* (-;-n) foul air

Miene ['minə] *f* (-;-n) mien; facial expression; M. machen zu (*inf*) make a move to (*inf*); ohne die M. zu verziehen without flinching

mies [mis] *adj* (coll) miserable, lousy

Mies'macher *m* (-s;-) alarmist

Miet– [mit] *comb.fm.* rental, rented; rent

Miet'auto *n* rented car

Miete ['mitə] *f* (-;-n) rent; (Zins) rental; (Erd-) pit (*for storing vegetables*); in M. geben rent out; in M. nehmen rent; kalte M. rent not including heat; zur M. wohnen live in a rented apartment (or home)

mieten ['mitən] *tr* rent, hire; (Flugzeug) charter

Miet'entschädigung *f* allowance for house rent

Mie'ter –in §6 *mf* tenant

Miet'ertrag *m* rent, rental

Miet'kontrakt *m* lease

Mietling ['mitlɪŋ] *m* (-s;-e) hireling

Miets'haus *n* apartment building

Miets'kaserne *f* tenement house

Miet'vertrag *m* lease

Miet'wagen *m* rented car

Miet'wohung *f* apartment

Miet'zins *m* rent

Mieze ['mitsə] *f* (-;-n) pussy

Migräne [mɪ'grɛnə] *f* (-;-n) migraine

Mikrobe [mɪ'krobə] *f* (-;-n) microbe

Mikrofilm ['mikrofɪlm] *m* microfilm

Mikrophon [mɪkro'fon] *n* (-s;-e) microphone

Mikroskop [mɪkro'skop] *n* (-s;-e) microscope

mikroskopisch [mɪkro'skopɪʃ] *adj* microscopic

Milbe ['mɪlbə] *f* (-;-n) (ent) mite

Milch [mɪlç] *f* (-;) milk

Milch'bart *m* sissy

Milch'brot *n*, **Milch'brötchen** *n* French roll

Milch'bruder *m* foster brother

Milch'drüse *f* mammary gland

Milch'eimer *m* milk pail

Milch'geschäft *n* creamery, dairy

Milch'glas *n* milk glass

milchig ['mɪlçɪç] *adj* milky

Milch'mädchen *n* milkmaid

Milch'mädchenrechnung *f* oversimplification

Milch'mixgetränk *n* milkshake

Milch'pulver *n* powdered milk

Milch'reis *m* rice pudding

Milch'schwester *f* foster sister

Milch'straße *f* Milky Way

Milch'tüte *f* carton of milk

Milch'wirtschaft *f* dairy

Milchzähne ['mɪlçtsɛnə] *pl* baby teeth

mild [mɪlt] *adj* mild; (nicht streng) lenient; (Stiftung) charitable; (Wein) smooth; (Lächeln) faint ‖ **Milde** *f* (-;) mildness; leniency; kindness

mildern ['mɪldərn] *tr* soften, alleviate; **mildernde Umstände** extenuating circumstances

Mil'derung *f* (-;) softening, alleviation, mitigation

mild'herzig, mild'tätig *adj* charitable

Militär [mɪlɪ'tɛr] *n* (-s;) military, army; zum M. gehen join the army ‖ *m* (-s;-s) professional soldier

Militär'dienst *m* military service

Militär'geistliche §5 *m* chaplain

Militär'gericht *n* military court

militärisch [mɪlɪ'tɛrɪʃ] *adj* military

Militarismus [mɪlɪta'rɪsmus] *m* (-;) militarism

Miliz [mɪ'lɪts] *f* (-;) militia

Miliz'soldat *m* militiaman

Milliardär –in [mɪljar'der(ɪn)] §8 *mf* multimillionaire

Milliarde [mɪl'jardə] *f* (-;-n) billion

Milligramm [mɪlɪ'gram] *n* milligram

Millimeter [mɪlɪ'metər] *n & m* millimeter

Millime'terpapier *n* graph paper

Million [mɪl'jon] *f* (-;-en) million

Millionär –in [mɪljo'ner(ɪn)] §8 *mf* millionaire

millionste [mɪl'jonstə] §9 *adj & pron* millionth

Milz [mɪlts] *f* (-;) spleen

Mime ['mimə] *m* (-n;-n) mime

Mimiker –in ['mimɪkər(ɪn)] §6 *mf* mimic

Mimose [mɪ'mozə] *f* (-;-n) mimosa

minder ['mɪndər] *adj* lesser, smaller; (geringer) minor, inferior ‖ *adv* less; m. gut inferior; nicht m. likewise

min'derbedeutend *adj* less important

min'derbegabt *adj* less talented

min'derbemittelt *adj* of moderate means

Min'derbetrag *m* shortage, deficit

Min'derheit *f* (-;-en) minority

min'derjährig *adj* underage ‖ **Minderjährige** §5 *mf* minor

mindern ['mɪndərn] *tr* lessen, diminish

Min'derung *f* (-;-en) diminution

min'derwertig *adj* inferior

Min'derwertigkeit *f* inferiority

Min'derwertigkeitskomplex *m* inferiority complex

Min'derzahl *f* minority

Mindest- [mɪndəest] *comb.fm.* minimum

mindeste ['mɪndəstə] §9 *adj* least; (*kleinste*) smallest; **nicht die mindesten Aussichten** not the slightest chance; **nicht im mindesten** in the least; **zum mindesten** at the very least

mindestens ['mɪndəstəns] *adv* at least

Min'destgebot *n* lowest bid

Min'destlohn *m* minimum wage

Mine ['mɪnə] *f* (-;-n) (*im Bleistift*) lead; (mil, min) mine; **alle Minen springen lassen** (fig) pull out all the stops

Minenleger ['mɪnənlegər] *m* (-s;-) minelayer

Minenräumboot ['mɪnənrɔɪmbot] *n* minesweeper

Mineral [mɪnə'ral] *n* (-s;-e & -ien [jən]) mineral

mineralisch [mɪnə'ralɪʃ] *adj* mineral

Mineralogie [mɪnəralə'gi] *f* (-;) mineralogy

Miniatur [mɪnja'tur] *f* (-;-en) miniature

minieren [mɪ'nirən] *tr* (fig) undermine; (mil) mine

minimal [mɪnɪ'mal] *adj* minimal

Minirock ['mɪnɪrɔk] *m* miniskirt

Minister [mɪ'nɪstər] *m* (-s;-) minister, secretary

Ministe·rium [mɪnɪs'terjum] *n* (-s; -rien [rjən]) ministry, department

Mini'sterpräsident *m* prime minister

Mini'sterrat *m* (-[e]s;⁎e) cabinet

Ministrant [mɪnɪs'trant] *m* (-en;-en) altar boy, acolyte

Minne ['mɪnə] *f* (-;) (obs) love

Min'nesänger *m* minnesinger; troubadour

minorenn [mɪnə'ren] *adj* underage

minus ['mɪnus] *adv* minus || **Minus** *n* (-;-) minus; (com) deficit

Minute [mɪ'nutə] *f* (-;-n) minute

Minu'tenzeiger *m* minute hand

-minutig [mɪnutɪç] *comb.fm.* -minute

Minze ['mɪntsə] *f* (-;-n) (bot) mint

mir [mir] §11 *pers pron* me, to me, for me; **mir ist kalt** I am cold; **mir nichts, dir nichts** suddenly; **von mir aus** for all I care || §11 *reflex pron* myself, to myself, for myself

Mirabelle [mɪra'belə] *f* (-;-n) yellow plum

Mirakel [mɪ'rakəl] *n* (-s;-) miracle

Mira'kelspiel *n* miracle play

Mischehe ['mɪʃ·e·ə] *f* mixed marriage

mischen ['mɪʃən] *tr* mix, blend; (cards) shuffle

Mischling ['mɪʃlɪŋ] *m* (-es;-e) half-breed; mongrel

Mischmasch ['mɪʃmaʃ] *m* (-es;-e) hodgepodge

Mischpult ['mɪʃpult] *n* (rad, telv) master console

Mischrasse ['mɪʃrasə] *f* cross-breed

Mi'schung *f* (-;-en) mixture, blend

Misere [mɪ'zerə] *f* (-;-n) misery

Miß-, miß- [mɪs] *comb.fm.* mis-, dis-, amiss; bad, wrong, false

mißach'ten *tr* disregard; (*geringschätzen*) slight

mißartet [mɪs'artət] *adj* degenerate

miß'behagen *intr* (dat) displeasure || **Mißbehagen** *n* (-s;) displeasure

miß'bilden *tr* misshape, deform

Miß'bildung *f* (-;-en) deformity

miß'billigen *tr* disapprove

Miß'billigung *f* (-;-en) disapproval

Miß'brauch *m* abuse; (*falsche Anwendung*) misuse

mißbrau'chen *tr* abuse; misuse

mißbräuchlich ['mɪsbrɔɪçlɪç] *adj* improper

mißdeu'ten *tr* misinterpret

missen ['mɪsən] *tr* miss; do without

Miß'erfolg *m* failure, flop

Miß'ernte *f* bad harvest

Missetat ['mɪsətat] *f* misdeed; (*Verstoß*) offense; (*Verbrechen*) felony; (*Sünde*) sin

Missetäter -in ['mɪsətetər(ɪn)] §6 *mf* wrongdoer; offender; felon; sinner

mißfal'len §72 *intr* (dat) displease || **Mißfallen** *n* (-s;) displeasure

miß'fällig *adj* displeasing; (*anstößig*) shocking; (*verächtlich*) disparaging

miß'farben, miß'farbig *adj* discolored

Miß'geburt *f* freak

mißgelaunt ['mɪsgəlaunt] *adj* in bad humor, sour

Miß'geschick *n* (-s;-e) mishap; misfortune

Miß'gestalt *f* deformity; monster

miß'gestaltet *adj* deformed, misshapen

mißgestimmt ['mɪsgəʃtɪmt] *adj* grumpy

miß'glücken (mißglük'ken) *intr* (SEIN) fail, not succeed

mißgön'nen *tr* begrudge

Miß'griff *m* mistake

Miß'gunst *f* grudge, jealousy

mißgün'stig *adj* envious

mißhan'deln *tr* mistreat

Miß'heirat *f* mismarriage

Mißhelligkeit ['mɪshelɪçkaɪt] *f* (-;-en) friction, disagreement

Mission [mɪ'sjon] *f* (-;-en) mission

Missionar [mɪsjo'nar] *m*, **Missionär** [mɪsjo'ner] *m* (-s;-e) missionary

Miß'klang *m* dissonance; (fig) sour note

Miß'kredit *m* discredit, disrepute

mißlang [mɪs'laŋ] *pret* of **mißlingen**

miß'lich *adj* awkward; (*gefährlich*) dangerous; (*bedenklich*) critical

miß'liebig *adj* unpopular

mißlingen [mɪs'lɪŋən] §142 *intr* (SEIN) go wrong, misfire, prove a failure || **Mißlingen** *n* (-s;) failure

Miß'mut *m* bad humor; discontent

miß'mutig *adj* sullen; discontented

mißra'ten §63 *intr* (SEIN) go wrong, misfire; **mißratene Kinder** spoiled children

Miß'stand *m* bad state of affairs; **Mißstände abschaffen** remedy abuses

Miß'stimmung *f* dissension; (*Mißmut*) bad humor

Miß'ton *m* dissonance; (fig) sour note

mißtrau'en intr (dat) mistrust, distrust
|| **Miß'trauen** n (–s;) mistrust
mißtrauisch ['mɪstrav·ɪʃ] adj distrustful
Miß'vergnügen n displeasure
miß'vergnügt adj cross; discontented
Miß'verhältnis n disproportion
Miß'verständnis n misunderstanding
miß'verstehen §146 tr & intr misunderstand
Miß'wirtschaft f mismanagement
Mist [mɪst] m (–es;) dung, manure;
(Schmutz) dirt; (fig) mess, nonsense;
M. machen (coll) blow the job;
(Spaß machen) (coll) horse around;
viel M. verzapfen talk a lot of nonsense
Mist'beet n hotbed
Mistel ['mɪstəl] f (–;-n) mistletoe
misten ['mɪstən] tr (Stall) muck;
(Acker) fertilize
Mist'fink m (coll) dirty brat
Mist'haufen m manure pile
mistig ['mɪstɪç] adj dirty; (sehr unangenehm) very unpleasant
mit [mɪt] adv along; also, likewise;
simultaneously || prep (dat) with;
mit 18 Jahren at the age of eighteen
Mit'angeklagte §5 mf codefendant
Mit'arbeit f cooperation, collaboration
mit'arbeiten intr cooperate, collaborate; **m. an** (dat) contribute to
Mit'arbeiter –in §6 mf co-worker
Mit'arbeiterstab m staff
mit'bekommen §99 tr receive when leaving; (verstehen) get, catch
mit'benutzen tr use jointly
Mit'bestimmung f share in decision making
mit'bewerben ref (um) compete (for)
Mit'bewerber –in §6 mf competitor
mit'bringen §65 tr bring along
Mitbringsel ['mɪtbrɪŋzəl] n (–s;)
little present
Mit'bürger –in §6 mf fellow citizen
Mit'eigentümer –in §6 mf co-owner
miteinan'der adv together
mit'empfinden §59 tr sympathize with
Mit'erbe m, **Mit'erbin** f coheir
Mitesser ['mɪtɛsər] m (–s;-) pimple,
blackhead
mit'fahren §71 intr (SEIN) ride along;
j–n m. lassen give s.o. a lift
mit'fühlen tr share, sympathize with
mit'fühlend adj sympathetic
mit'gehen §82 intr (SEIN) (mit) go
along (with)
Mit'gift f dowry
Mit'giftjäger m fortune hunter
Mit'glied n member; **M. auf Lebenszeit** life member
Mit'gliederversammlung f general
meeting
Mit'gliederzahl f membership
Mit'gliedsbeitrag m dues
Mit'gliedschaft f (–;-en) membership
Mit'gliedskarte f membership card
Mit'gliedstaat m member nation
Mit'haftung f joint liability
mit'halten §90 intr be one of a party;
ich halte mit I'll join you
mit'helfen §96 intr help along, pitch
in

Mit'helfer –in §6 mf assistant
Mit'herausgeber –in §6 mf coeditor
Mit'hilfe f assistance
mithin' adv consequently
mit'hören tr listen in on; (zufällig)
overhear; (rad, telp) monitor
Mit'inhaber –in §6 mf copartner
Mit'kämpfer –in §6 mf fellow fighter
mit'klingen §142 intr resonate
mit'kommen §99 intr (SEIN) come
along; (fig) keep up
mit'kriegen tr (coll) see **mitbekommen**
Mit'läufer –in §6 mf (pol) fellow
traveler
Mit'laut m consonant
Mit'leid n compassion, pity
Mit'leidenschaft f—**j–n in M. ziehen**
affect s.o.
mit'leidig adj compassionate; pitiful
Mit'leidsbezeigung f condolences
mit'leidslos adj pitiless
mit'leidsvoll adj full of pity
mit'machen tr participate in, join in
on; (ertragen) suffer, endure
Mit'mensch m fellow man
mit'nehmen §116 tr take along; (erschöpfen) wear out, exhaust; (abholen) pick up; (Ort, Museum) visit,
take in; **j–n arg m.** treat s.o. roughly
mitnichten [mɪt'nɪçtən] adv by no
means, not at all
mit'rechnen tr include || intr count
mit'reden tr—**ein Wort mitzureden
haben bei** have a say in || intr join
in a conversation
Mit'reisende §5 mf travel companion
mit'reißen §53 tr (& fig) carry away
mit'reißend adj stirring
mitsamt [mɪt'zamt] prep (dat) together with
mit'schreiben §62 intr take notes
Mit'schuld f (an dat) complicity (in)
mit'schuldig adj (an dat) accessory
(to) || **Mitschuldige** §5 mf accomplice
Mit'schüler –in §6 mf schoolmate
mit'singen §142 intr sing along
mit'spielen intr play along; (fig) be
involved; **j–m arg (or übel) m.** play
s.o. dirty
Mit'spieler –in §6 mf partner
Mit'spracherecht n right to share in
decision making
mit'sprechen §64 tr say with (s.o.) ||
intr be involved; (an e–r Entscheidung beteiligt sein) share in decision making
Mit'tag m noon; (poet) South; **M.
machen** stop for lunch; **zu M. essen**
eat lunch
Mittag– comb.fm. midday, noon; lunch
Mit'tagbrot n, **Mit'tagessen** n lunch
mit'täglich adj midday, noontime
mittags ['mɪtaks] adv at noon
Mit'tagskreis m, **Mit'tagslinie** f meridian
Mit'tagsruhe f siesta
Mit'tagsstunde f noon; lunch hour
Mit'tagstisch m lunch table; lunch; **gut
bürglicher M.** good home cooking
Mit'tagszeit f noontime; lunch time
Mit'täter –in §6 mf accomplice
Mit'täterschaft f complicity

Mitte ['mɪtə] f (-;-n) middle, midst; (*Mittelpunkt*) center; **ab durch die M.!** (coll) scram!; **aus unserer M.** from among us; **die goldene M.** the golden mean; **die richtige M. treffen** hit a happy medium; **er ist M. Vierzig** he is in his mid-forties; **in die M. nehmen** take by both arms; (sport) sandwich in; **j—n um die M. fassen** put one's arms around s.o.'s waist

mit'teilbar adj communicable

mit'teilen tr tell; (*im Vertrauen*) intimate; **ich muß Ihnen leider m.,** **daß** I regret to inform you that

mitteilsam ['mɪttaɪlzam] adj communicative

Mit'teilung f (-;-en) communication; information; (*amtliche*) communiqué; (*an die Presse*) release

mittel ['mɪtəl] adj medium, average || **Mittel** n (-s;-) middle; means; (*Heil-*) remedy; (*Maßnahme*) measure; (*Ausweg*) expedient; (*Durchschnitt*) average; (math) mean; (phys) medium; **im M.** on the average; **ins M. treten** (or **sich ins M. legen**) intervene, intercede; **letztes M.** last resort; **mit allen Mitteln** by every means; **Mittel** pl resources, means; funds; **M. und Wege** ways and means; **M. zum Zweck** means to an end; **sicheres M.** reliable method

Mit'telalter n Middle Ages

mittelalterlich ['mɪtəlaltərlɪç] adj medieval

Mit'telamerika n Central America

mittelbar ['mɪtəlbar] adj indirect

Mit'telgang m center aisle

Mit'telgebirge n highlands

Mit'telgewicht n (box) middleweight class

Mittelgewichtler ['mɪtəlgəvɪçtlər] m (-s;-) middleweight boxer

Mit'telgröße f medium size

mit'telhochdeutsch adj Middle High German || **Mittelhochdeutsch** n (-es;) Middle High German

Mit'teilage f central position; (mus) middle range

mittelländisch ['mɪtəllendɪʃ] adj Mediterranean

Mit'telläufer m (fb) center halfback

mit'tellos adj penniless, destitute

Mit'telmaß n medium; balance; average

mitt'telmäßig adj medium, mediocre; (*leidlich*) indifferent, so–so

Mit'telmäßigkeit f mediocrity

Mit'telmeer n Mediterranean

Mit'telmast m mainmast

Mit'telohr n middle ear

Mit'telpreis m average price

Mit'telpunkt m center

mittels ['mɪtəls] prep (*genit*) by means of

Mit'telschiff n (archit) nave

Mit'telschule f secondary school

Mit'tels·mann m (-[e]s;̈er & -leute) go-between; (com) middleman

Mit'telsorte f medium quality

Mit'telsperson f see Mittelsmann

Mit'telstand m middle class

Mit'telstürmer m (fb) center forward

Mit'telweg m middle course; **der goldene M.** the golden mean; **e–n M.** **einschlagen** steer a middle course

Mit'telwort n (-[e]s;̈er) (gram) participle

mitten ['mɪtən] adv—m. am Tage in broad daylight; **m. auf dem Wege** well on the way; **m. auf der Straße;** right in the middle of the street; **m. aus** from the midst of, from among; **m. darin** right in the very center (of it, of them); **m. entzwei brechen** break right in two; **m. im Winter** in the dead of winter; **m. in der Luft** in midair; **m. ins zwanzigste Jahrhundert** well into the twentieth century

Mitternacht ['mɪtərnaxt] f midnight

mitternächtig ['mɪtərneçtɪç], **mitternächtlich** ['mɪtərneçtlɪç] adj midnight

Mittler –in ['mɪtlər(ɪn)] §6 mf mediator; (com) middleman

mittlere ['mɪtlərə] §9 adj middle, central; (*durchschnittlich*) average; (*mittelmäßig*) medium; (math) mean; **der Mittlere Osten** the Middle East; **in mittleren Jahren sein** be middleaged; **von mittlerer Größe** mediumsized

mitt'lerweile adv in the meantime

mittschiffs ['mɪtʃɪfs] adv amidships

Mittwoch ['mɪtvɔx] m (-[e]s;-e) Wednesday

mitun'ter adv now and then

mit'unterzeichnen tr & intr countersign

mit'verantwortlich adj jointly responsible

Mit'verantwortung f joint responsibility

Mit'verschworene §5 mf co-conspirator

Mit'welt f present generation; our (his, etc.) contemporaries

mit'wirken intr (an dat or bei) cooperate (in)

Mit'wirkung f cooperation

Mit'wissen n—ohne mein M. without my knowledge

Mitwisser –in ['mɪtvɪsər(ɪn)] §6 mf accessory; one in the know

mit'zählen tr include || intr count along

mixen ['mɪksən] tr mix

Mixgetränk ['mɪksgətrɛŋk] n mixed drink

Mixtur [mɪks'tur] f (-;-en) mixture

Möbel ['møbəl] n (-s;-) piece of furniture; **Möbel** pl furniture

Mö'belstück n piece of furniture

Möbeltransporteur ['møbəltransportør] m (-s;-e) mover

Mö'belwagen m moving van

mobil [mo'bil] adj movable; (*flink*) chipper; (mil) mobile

Mobiliar [mobɪl'jar] n (-[e]s;) furniture

Mobilien [mo'biljən] pl movables

mobilisieren [mobɪlɪ'zirən] tr mobilize

Mobilisierung [mobɪlɪ'ziruŋ] f (-;) mobilization

mobil'machen *tr* mobilize

Mobilmachung [mɔ'bilmaxʊŋ] *f* (-;) mobilization

möblieren [mø'bliːrən] *tr* furnish; **möbliert wohnen** (coll) live in a furnished room; **neu m.** refurnish

mochte ['mɔxtə] *pret* of **mögen**

Mode ['moːdə] *f* (-;-n) fashion, style

Mo'debild *n* fashion plate

Modell [mɔ'del] *n* (-[e]s;-e) model; (*Muster*) pattern; (fig) prototype; **M. stehen zu** (*dat*) model for

modellieren [mɔde'liːrən] *tr* fashion, shape

Modell'puppe *f* mannequin

modeln ['moːdəln] *tr* fashion, shape; (**nach**) model (on) ‖ *ref*—**zu alt sein, um sich m. zu lassen** be too old to change

Mo'dengeschäft *n* dress shop

Mo'denschau *f* fashion show

Mo'denzeitung *f* fashion magazine

Moder ['moːdər] *m* (-;) mold; mustiness; (*Schlamm*) mud

Mo'derduft *m*, **Mo'dergeruch** *m* musty smell

moderig ['moːdərɪç] *adj* moldy, musty

modern [mɔ'dern] *adj* modern ‖ ['moːdərn] *intr* rot, decay ‖ **Modern** *n* (-s;) decay

modernisieren [mɔdernɪ'ziːrən] *tr* modernize; bring up to date

Mo'deschmuck *m* costume jewelry

Mo'deschriftsteller **-in** §6 *mf* popular writer

Mo'dewaren *pl* (com) novelties

modifizieren [mɔdifɪ'tsiːrən] *tr* modify

modisch ['moːdɪʃ] *adj* fashionable

Modistin [mɔ'dɪstɪn] *f* (-;-nen) milliner

modrig ['moːdrɪç] *adj* moldy

modulieren [moːdu'liːrən] *tr* modulate; (*Stimme*) inflect

Mo·dus ['moːdʊs] *m* (-;-di [diː]) mode, manner; (gram) mood

mogeln ['moːgəln] *intr* cheat ‖ **Mogeln** *n* (-s;) cheating

mögen ['møːgən] §114 *tr* like, care for; **ich mag lieber** I prefer ‖ *mod aux* may; can; care to; **er mag nicht nach Hause gehen** he doesn't care to go home; **ich möchte lieber bleiben** I'd rather stay; **ich möchte wissen** I should like to know; **mag kommen was da will** come what may; **wer mag das nur sein?** who can that be?; **wie mag das geschehen sein?** how could this have happened?

möglich ['møːklɪç] *adj* possible; (*ausführbar*) feasible; **sein möglichstes tun** do one's utmost ‖ **Mögliche** §5 *n* possibility; **er muß alles Mögliche bedenken** he must consider every possibility; **im Rahmen des Möglichen** within the realm of possibility

möglichenfalls ['møːklɪçənfals], **möglicherweise** ['møːklɪçərvaɪzə] *adv* possibly, if possible

Mög'lichkeit *f* (-;-en) possibility; potentiality; **ist es die M.!** well, I never!; **finanzielle Möglichkeiten** financial means; **nach M.** as far as possible

möglichst ['møːklɪçst] *adv* as ... as possible

Mohn [moːn] *m* (-[e]s;-e) poppyseed; (bot) poppy

Mohn'samen *m* poppyseed

Mohr [moːr] *m* (-en;-en) Moor

Möhre ['møːrə] *f* (-;-n) carrot

Mohr'rübe *f* carrot

Mokka ['mɔka] *m* (-s;-s) mocha (*coffee*)

Molch [mɔlç] *m* (-[e]s;-e) salamander

Mole ['moːlə] *f* (-;-n) mole, breakwater

Molekül [mɔle'kyːl] *n* (-s;-e) molecule

molekular [mɔleku'laːr] *adj* molecular

Molke ['mɔlkə] *f* (-;) whey

Molkerei [mɔlkə'raɪ] *f* (-;-en) dairy

Moll [mɔl] *invar n* (mus) minor

mollig ['mɔlɪç] *adj* plump; (*Frau*) buxom; (*behaglich*) snug, cozy

Moll'tonart *f* (mus) minor key

Moment [mɔ'ment] *m* (-[e]s;-e) moment ‖ *n* (-[e]s;-e) momentum; (*Antrieb*) impulse, impetus; (*Faktor*) factor, point; (*Beweggrund*) motive

momentan [mɔmen'taːn] *adj* momentary

Moment'aufnahme *f* snapshot; (*Bewegungsaufnahme*) action shot

Monarch [mɔ'narç] *m* (-en;-en) monarch

Monar·chie [mɔnar'çiː] *f* (-;-chien ['çiː·ən]) monarchy

Monat ['moːnat] *m* (-[e]s;-e) month

monatelang ['moːnatəlaŋ] *adj* lasting for months ‖ *adv* for months

mo'natlich *adj* monthly

Mo'natsbinde *f* sanitary napkin

Mo'natsfluß *m* menstruation

mo'natsweise *adv* monthly

Mönch [mœnç] *m* (-[e]s;-e) monk, friar

Mönchs'kappe *f* monk's cowl

Mönchs'kloster *n* monastery

Mönchs'kutte *f* monk's habit

Mönchs'orden *m* monastic order

Mönchs'wesen *n* monasticism

Mond [moːnt] *m* (-[e]s;-e) moon; **abnehmender M.** waning moon; **zunehmender M.** waxing moon

mondän [mɔn'dɛːn] *adj* sophisticated

Mond'fähre *f* (rok) lunar lander

Mond'finsternis *f* lunar eclipse

mond'hell *adj* moonlit

Mond'jahr *n* lunar year

Mond'kalb *n* (fig) born fool

Mond'schein *m* moonlight

Mond'sichel *f* crescent moon

Mond'sucht *f* lunacy; somnambulism

mond'süchtig *adj* moonstruck

Moneten [mɔ'neːtən] *pl* (coll) dough

monieren [mɔ'niːrən] *tr* criticize; remind

Monogramm [mɔno'gram] *n* (-s;-e) monogram

Monolog [mɔno'loːk] *m* (-s;-e) monologue

Monopol [mɔno'poːl] *n* (-s;-e) monopoly

monopolisieren [mɔnopɔli'ziːrən] *tr* monopolize

monoton [mɔno'toːn] *adj* monotonous

Monotonie [mɔnɔto'niː] *f* (-;) monotony

Monsterfilm ['mɔnstərfɪlm] *m* (cin) spectacular

Monstranz [mɔn'strants] *f* (-;-en) monstrance

monströs [mɔn'strøs] *adj* monstrous

Monstrosität [mɔnstrozɪ'tet] *f* (-;-en) monstrosity

Mon·strum ['mɔnstrum] *n* (-;-stra [stra]) monster

Monsun [mɔ'zun] *m* (-s;-e) monsoon

Montag ['mɔntak] *m* (-[e]s;-e) Monday

Montage [mɔn'taʒə] *f* (-;-n) mounting, fitting; (mach) assembly

Monta'gebahn *f*, **Monta'geband** *n* assembly line

Monta'gehalle *f* assembly room

montags ['mɔntaks] *adv* Mondays

Montan– [mɔntan] *comb.fm.* mining

Monteur [mɔn'tør] *m* (-s;-e) assembly-man, mechanic

Monteur'anzug *m* coveralls

montieren [mɔn'tirən] *tr* mount, fit; (*zusammenbauen*) assemble; (*einrichten*) install; (*aufstellen*) set up

Montur [mɔn'tur] *f* (-;-en) uniform

Moor [mor] *n* (-[e]s;-e) swamp

Moor'bad *n* mud bath

moorig ['moriç] *adj* swampy

Moos [mos] *n* (-es;) moss; (*Geld*) (coll) dough

Mop [mɔp] *m* (-s;-s) mop

Moped ['moped] *n* (-s;-s) motor bike, moped

moppen ['mɔpən] *tr* mop

mopsen ['mɔpsən] *tr* (coll) swipe ‖ *ref* be bored stiff; be upset

Moral [mo'ral] *f* (-;) morality; (*Nutzwendung*) moral; (mil) morale

moralisch [mo'ralɪʃ] *adj* moral

moralisieren [mɔralɪ'zirən] *intr* moralize

Moralität [mɔralɪ'tet] *f* (-;) morality

Morast [mo'rast] *m* (-es;-e & ⁼e) mire; morass, quagmire

Mord [mɔrt] *m* (-[e]s;-e) murder

Mord'anschlag *m* murder attempt; (pol) assassination attempt

Mord'brennerei *f* arson and murder

Mord'bube *m* murderer, assassin

morden ['mɔrdən] *tr & intr* murder

Mörder –in ['mœrdər(ɪn)] §6 murderer

möderisch ['mœrdərɪʃ] *adj* murderous; (coll) awful, terrible

mord'gierig *adj* bloodthirsty

Mord'kommission *f* homicide squad

mord'lustig *adj* bloodthirsty

Mords– [mɔrts] *comb.fm.* huge; terrible, awful; fantastic, incredible

Mords'angst *f* mortal fear

Mords'geschichte *f* tall story

Mords'geschrei *n* loud shouting

Mords'kerl *m* (coll) great guy

mords'mäßig *adv* (coll) awfully

Mords'spektakel *n* awful din

Mord'tat *f* murder

Mord'waffe *f* murder weapon

Mores ['mores] *pl*—j—n M. lehren teach s.o. manners

morgen ['mɔrgən] *adv* tomorrow; m. abend tomorrow evening (or night); m. früh tomorrow morning; m. in

acht Tagen (or über acht Tage) a week from tomorrow; **m. mittag** tomorrow noon ‖ **Morgen** *m* (-s;-) morning; acre; **des Morgens** in the morning ‖ *n* (-;) tomorrow

Mor'genblatt *n* morning paper

Mor'gendämmerung *f* dawn, daybreak

mor'gendlich *adj* morning

Mor'gengabe *f* wedding present

Mor'gengrauen *n* dawn, daybreak

Mor'genland *n* Orient

Morgenländer –in ['mɔrgənlendər(ɪn)] §6 *mf* Oriental

Mor'genrock *m* house robe

Mor'genrot *n*, **Mor'genröte** *f* dawn, sunrise; (fig) dawn, beginning

morgens ['mɔrgəns] *adv* in the morning

Mor'genstern *m* morning star

Mor'genstunde *f* morning hour

Mor'genzeitung *f* morning paper

morgig ['mɔrgɪç] *adj* tomorrow's

Morphium ['mɔrfjum] *n* (-s;) morphine

morsch [mɔrʃ] *adj* rotten; (*baufällig*) dilapidated; (*brüchig*) brittle; (fig) decadent

Morsealphabet ['mɔrzə-alfabet] *n* Morse code

Mörser ['mœrzər] *m* (-s;-) (& mil) mortar

Mör'serkeule *f* pestle

Mörtel ['mœrtəl] *m* (-s;-) mortar; plaster; **mit M. bewerfen** roughcast

Mör'telkelle *f* trowel

Mör'teltrog *m* hod

Mosaik [moza'ik] *n* (-s;-en) mosaic

mosaisch [mo'za·ɪʃ] *adj* Mosaic

Moschee [mo'ʃe] *f* (-;-n) mosque

Moskau ['mɔskau] *n* (-s;) Moscow

Moslem ['mɔsləm] *m* (-s;-s) Moslem

moslemisch [mɔs'lemɪʃ] *adj* Moslem

Most [mɔst] *m* (-es;-e) must, grape juice; new wine

Mostrich ['mɔstrɪç] *m* (-[e]s;-e) mustard

Motel [mo'tel] *n* (-s;-s) motel

Motiv [mo'tif] *n* (-[e]s;-e) (*Beweggrund*) motive; (mus, paint) motif

motivieren [motɪ'virən] *tr* justify

Mo·tor ['motɔr], [mo'tor] *m* (-s;-toren** ['torən] & **-tore** ['torə]) motor

Mo'tordefekt *m* motor trouble

Mo'torhaube *f* (aer) cowl; (aut) hood

–motorig [motorɪç] *comb.fm.* –motor, –engine

Mo'torpanne *f* (aut) breakdown

Mo'torpflug *m* tractor plow

Mo'torrad *n* motorcycle

Mo'torradfahrer –in §6 *mf* motorcyclist

Mo'torrasenmäher *m* power mower

Mo'torroller *m* motor scooter

Mo'torsäge *f* power saw

Mo'torschaden *m* engine trouble

Motte ['mɔtə] *f* (-;-n) moth

mot'tenfest *adj* mothproof

Mot'tenkugel *f* mothball

Motto ['mɔto] *n* (-s;-s) motto

moussieren [mu'sirən] *intr* fizz; (*Wein*) sparkle

Möwe ['møvə] *f* (-s;-n) sea gull

Mucke ['mʊkə] *f* (-;-n) whim; (dial) gnat; **Mucken haben** have moods

Mücke ['mykə] *f* (-;-n) gnat; mosquito; (dial) fly

Mucker ['mʊkər] *m* (-s;-) hypocrite; bigot; grouch; (coll) awkward guy

Muckerei [mʊkə'raɪ] *f* (-;) hypocrisy

muckerhaft ['mʊkərhaft] *adj* hypocritical, bigoted

Mucks [mʊks] *m* (-es;-e) faint sound; **keinen M. mehr!** not another sound!

mucksen ['mʊksən] *ref & intr* stir, say a word; **nicht gemuckst!** stay pat!

müde ['mydə] *adj* tired; **zum Umfallen m.** ready to drop

Mü'digkeit *f* (-;) weariness

Muff [mʊf] *m* (-[e]s;-e) (Handwärmer) muff; (Schimmel) mold; musty smell

Muffe ['mʊfə] *f* (-;-n) (mach) sleeve

muffeln ['mʊfəln] *intr* sulk, be grouchy; (anhaltend kauen) munch; mumble

muffig ['mʊfɪç] *adj* musty; (Person) sulky; (Luft) stale, frowzy

Mühe ['myə] *f* (-;-n) trouble, pains; (Anstrengung) effort; **geben Sie sich keine M.!** don't bother; **j-m M. machen** cause s.o. trouble; **mit M.** with difficulty; **mit M. und Not** barely; **nicht der M. wert** not worthwhile; **sich** [dat] **große M. machen** go to great pains; **verlorene M.** wasted effort

mü'helos *adj* easy, effortless

muhen ['mu-ən] *intr* moo, low

mühen ['my-ən] *ref* take pains

mü'hevoll *adj* hard, troublesome

Mühewaltung ['my-əvaltʊŋ] *f* (-;) trouble, efforts; **für Ihre M. dankend, verbleiben wir ...** thanking you for your cooperation, we remain ...

Mühle ['mylə] *f* (-;-n) mill

Mühlrad ['mylrat] *n* water wheel

Mühlstein ['mylʃtaɪn] *m* millstone

Muhme ['mumə] *f* (-;-n) aunt; cousin

Mühsal ['myzal] *f* (-s;-e) trouble

mühsam ['myzam] *adj* wearisome; (Leben) hard; (Arbeit) painstaking || *adv* with effort, with difficulty

mühselig ['myzelɪç] *adj* (Arbeit) hard; (Leben) miserable, tough

Mulatte [mu'latə] *m* (-n;-n), **Mulattin** [mu'latɪn] *f* (-;-nen) mulatto

Mulde ['mʊldə] *f* (-;-n) trough; (geol) depression, basin

Mull [mʊl] *m* (-[e]s;) gauze

Müll [myl] *m* (-[e]s;) dust, ashes; (Abfälle) trash, garbage

Müll'abfuhr *f* garbage disposal

Müll'abfuhrwagen *m* garbage truck

Müll'eimer *m* trash can, garbage can

Müller ['mylər] *m* (-s;-) miller

Müllerin ['mylərɪn] *f* (-;-nen) miller's wife; miller's daughter

Müll'fahrer *m* garbage man

Müll'haufen *m* scrap heap

Müll'platz *m* garbage dump

Müll'schaufel *f* dustpan

Mulm [mʊlm] *m* (-[e]s;) rotten wood

mul'mig *adj* rotten; dusty; (Luft) sticky; (Lage) ticklish

Multiplikation [mʊltɪplɪka'tsjon] *f* (-;) multiplication

multiplizieren [mʊltɪplɪ'tsirən] *tr* multiply

Mumie ['mumjə] *f* (-;-n) mummy

Mumm [mʊm] *m* (-s;) (coll) drive, grit

Mummelgreis ['mʊməlgraɪs] *m* (coll) old fogey

mummeln ['mʊməln] *tr & intr* mumble

Mund [mʊnt] *m* (-[e]s;ːer) mouth; **den M. aufreißen** brag; **den M. halten** shut up; **den M. vollnehmen** talk big; **e-n losen M. haben** answer back; **sich** [dat] **den Mund verbrennen** put one's foot into it; **wie auf den M. geschlagen** dumbfounded

Mund'art *f* dialect

Mündel ['myndəl] *m & n* (-s;-) & *f* (-;-n) ward

Mündelgelder ['myndəlgeldər] *pl* trust-fund

mün'delsicher *adj* gilt-edged; absolutely safe

munden ['mʊndən] *intr* taste good

münden ['myndən] *intr*—**m. in** (acc) empty into, flow into

mund'faul *adj* too lazy to talk

mund'gerecht *adj* palatable

Mund'geruch *m* halitosis

Mund'harmonika *f* mouth organ

Mund'höhle *f* oral cavity

mündig ['myndɪç] *adj* of age

Mün'digkeit *f* (-;) majority, full age

mündlich ['myntlɪç] *adj* oral, verbal

Mund'pflege *f* oral hygiene

Mund'sperre *f* lockjaw

Mund'stück *n* mouthpiece; (Zigaretten-) tip; (Düse) nozzle

mund'tot *adj*—**j-n m. machen** (fig) silence s.o.

Mund'tuch *n* table napkin

Mün'dung *f* (e-s Flusses) mouth; (e-r Feuerwaffe) muzzle

Mün'dungsfeuer *n* muzzle flash

Mün'dungsweite *f* (arti) bore

Mund'vorrat *m* provisions

Mund'wasser *n* mouthwash

Mund'werk *n* (fig) mouth, tongue

Mund'winkel *m* corner of the mouth

Munition [mʊni'tsjon] *f* (-;) ammunition

Munitions'lager *n* ammunition dump

munkeln ['mʊŋkəln] *tr & intr* whisper

Münster ['mynstər] *n* (-s;-) cathedral

munter ['mʊntər] *adj* awake; (lebhaft) lively; (rüstig) vigorous; gay

Münz- [mynts] *comb.fm.* monetary; of the mint; coin; coinage; coin-operated

Münz'anstalt *f* mint

Münze ['myntsə] *f* (-;-n) coin; change; (Münzanstalt) mint; (Denkmünze) medal; **bare M.** hard cash; **für bare Münze nehmen** take at face value

Münz'einheit *f* monetary unit

Münz'einwurf *m* coin slot

münzen ['myntsən] *tr* coin, mint; **das ist auf ihn gemünzt** that is meant for him || **Münzen** *n* (-s;) mintage, coinage

Münz'fälscher *m* counterfeiter

Münz'fernsprecher *m* public telephone

Münz'kunde f numismatics
Münz'wesen n monetary system
Münz'wissenschaft f numismatics
mürb [mʏrp], **mürbe** ['mʏrbə] adj
(Fleisch) tender; (sehr reif) mellow;
(gut durchgekocht) well done; (Gebäck) crisp and flaky; (brüchig)
brittle; (erschöpft) worn out; (mil)
demoralized; j-n **mürbe machen** (fig)
break s.o. down; **mürbe werden**
soften, give in
Murks [murks] m (-es;) bungling job
murksen ['murksən] intr bungle
Murmel ['murməl] f (-;-n) marble
murmeln ['murməln] tr & intr murmur
Mur'meltier n ground hog, woodchuck
murren ['murən] intr grumble
mürrisch ['mʏrɪʃ] adj grouchy, crabby
Mus [mus] n (-es;-e) purée; sauce
Muschel ['muʃəl] f (-;-n) mussel;
(Schale) shell; (anat) concha
Muse ['muzə] f (-;-n) (myth) Muse
Muse·um [mu'ze·um] n (-s;-en) mu-
seum
Musik [mu'zik] f (-;) music
Musikalien [muzi'kaljən] pl music
book
musikalisch [muzi'kalɪʃ] adj musical
Musikant [muzi'kant] m (-en;-en)
musician
Musikan'tenknochen m funny bone
Musik'automat m, **Musikbox** ['mjuzɪk-
bɔks] f (-;-en) juke box
Musiker -in ['muzikər(ɪn)] §6 mf
musician
Musik'hochschule f conservatory
Musik'kapelle f band
Musik'korps n military band
Musik'pavillon m bandstand
Musik'schrank m, **Musik'truhe** f radio-
phonograph console
Musi·kus ['muzikus] m (-;-zi [tsi])
(hum) musician
Musik'wissenschaft f musicology
musisch ['muzɪʃ] adj artistic
musizieren [muzi'tsirən] intr play
music
Muskat [mus'kat] m (-[e]s;-e) nut-
meg
Muskateller [muska'telər] m (-s;)
muscatel
Muskat'nuß f nutmeg
Muskel ['muskəl] f (-s;-n) muscle
Mus'kelkater m (coll) charley horse
Mus'kelkraft f brawn
Mus'kelriß m torn muscle
Mus'kelschwund m muscular distrophy
Mus'kelzerrung f pulled muscle
Muskete [mus'ketə] f (-;-n) musket
Muskulatur [muskula'tur] f (-;-en)
muscles, muscular system
muskulös [musku'løs] adj muscular
Muß [mus] invar n must, necessity
Muße ['musə] f (-;) leisure; **mit M.**
at leisure
Muß'ehe f shotgun wedding
Musselin [musə'lin] m (-s;-e) muslin
müssen ['mʏsən] intr—**ich muß nach
Hause** I must go home || mod aux—
ich muß (inf) I must (inf), I have to
(inf); **ich muß nicht** I don't have to;
muß das wirklich sein? is it really
neecessary?; **sie hätten hier sein m.**

they ought to have been here; **sie
müssen bald kommen** they are bound
to come soon
müßig ['mʏsɪç] adj idle; (unnütz) unprofitable; (zwecklos) useless; (überflüssig) superfluous
Mu'ßiggang m idleness
Müßiggänger m loafer
mußte ['mustə] pret of **müssen**
Muster ['mustər] n (-s;-) pattern;
(Probestück) sample; (Vorbild) example, model; **das M. e-r Hausfrau**
a model housewife; **nach dem M.
von** along the lines of; **sich** [dat]
ein M. nehmen an (dat) model oneself on
Mu'sterbeispiel n typical example
Mu'sterbild n ideal, paragon
Mu'stergatte m model husband
Mu'stergattin f model wife
mu'stergültig adj model, ideal
Mu'stergut n model farm
mu'sterhaft adj model, ideal
Mu'sterknabe m (pej) sissy
Mu'sterkollektion f (kit of) samples
mustern ['mustərn] tr examine, eye,
size up; (mil) inspect, review
Mu'sterprozeß m test case
Mu'sterschüler -in §6 mf model pupil
Mu'sterstück n specimen, sample
Mu'sterstudent -in §7 mf model stu-
dent
Mu'sterung f (-;-en) inspection; ex-
amination; (mil) review
Mu'sterungsbescheid m induction no-
tice
Mu'sterungskommission f draft board
Mu'sterwerk n standard work
Mu'sterwort n (-[e]s;⸚er) (gram) paradigm
Mut [mut] m (-[e]s;) courage; **den
Mut sinken lassen** lose heart; **guten
Mutes sein** feel encouraged; **j-m
den Mut nehmen** discourage s.o.;
nur Mut! cheer up!
Mutation [muta'tsjon] f (-;-en) (biol)
mutation, sport
Mütchen ['mʏtçən] n—**sein M. kühlen
an** (dat) take it out on
mutieren [mu'tirən] intr (Stimme)
change
mutig ['mutɪç] adj courageous, brave
-mütig [mʏtɪç] comb.fm. -minded,
-feeling
mut'los adj discouraged
Mut'losigkeit f (-;) discouragement
mutmaßen ['mutmasən] tr suppose,
conjecture
mutmaßlich ['mutmaslɪç] adj supposed, alleged; **mutmaßlicher Erbe**
heir presumptive || adv presumably
Mut'maßung f (-;-en) conjecture,
guesswork; **Mutmaßungen anstellen**
conjecture
Mutter ['mutər] f (-;⸚) mother; **wer-
dende M.** expectant mother || f (-;
-n) nut
Mut'terboden m rich soil
Mütterchen ['mʏtərçən] n (-s;-)
mummy; little old lady
Mut'tererde f rich soil; native soil
Mut'terfürsorge f maternity welfare
Mut'terkuchen m (anat) placenta

Mut'terleib *m* womb

Mütterlich ['mʏtərlɪç] *adj* motherly, maternal; **m. verwandt** related on the mother's side

mut'terlos *adj* motherless

Mut'termal *n* birthmark

Mut'terpferd *n* mare

Mut'terschaf *n* ewe

Mut'terschaft *f* (-;) motherhood, maternity

Mut'terschlüssel *m* (mach) wrench

mut'terseelenallein' *adj* all alone

Muttersöhnchen ['mʊtərzøŋçən] *n* (-s;-) mamma's boy

Mut'tersprache *f* mother tongue

Mut'terstelle *f*—bei **j-m die M. vertreten** be a mother to s.o.

Mut'terstute *f* mare

Mut'tertier *n* (zool) dam

Mut'terwitz *m* common sense

Mutti ['mʊti] *f* (-;-s) (coll) mom

mut'voll *adj* courageous

Mut'wille *m* mischievousness

mut'willig *adj* mischievous, willful

Mütze ['mʏtsə] *f* (-;-n) cap

Myriade [mʏri'adə] *f* (-;-n) myriad

Myrrhe ['mʏrə] *f* (-;-n) myrrh

Myrte ['mʏrtə] *f* (-;-n) myrtle

Mysterienspiel [mʏs'terjən/pil] *n* (theat) mystery play

mysteriös [mʏste'rjøs] *adj* mysterious

Myste-rium [mʏs'terjʊm] *n* (-s;-rien [rjən]) mystery

mystifizieren [mʏstifi'tsirən] *tr* mystify; (*täuschen*) hoax

Mystik ['mʏstɪk] *f* (-;) mysticism

My'stiker **-in** §6 *mf* mystic

mystisch ['mʏstɪʃ] *adj* mystic(al)

Mythe ['mʏtə] *f* (-;-n) myth

mythisch ['mʏtɪʃ] *adj* mythical

Mytholo-gie [mʏtolo'gi] *f* (-;-gien ['gi-ən]) mythology

mythologisch [mʏto'logɪʃ] *adj* mythological

My-thus ['mʏtʊs] *m* (-;-then [tən]) myth

N

N, n [ɛn] *invar n* N, n

na [na] *interj* well!; **na also!** there you are!; **na, so was!** don't tell me!; **na, und ob!** I'll say!; **na, warte!** just you wait!

Nabe ['nabə] *f* (-;-n) hub

Nabel ['nabəl] *m* (-s;-) navel

Na'belschnur *f* umbilical cord

nach [nax] *adv* after; **n. und n.** little by little; **n. wie vor** now as ever || *prep* (*dat*) (*Zeit*) after; (*Reihenfolge*) after, behind; (*Ziel, Richtung*) to, towards, for; (*Art, Maß, Vorbild, Richtschnur*) according to, after

Nach-, nach- *comb.fm.* subsequent, additional, supplementary; post-; over, over again, re-; after

nach'äffen *tr* ape, imitate

nachahmen ['naxamən] *tr* imitate, copy

Nach'ahmer **-in** §6 *mf* imitator

Nach'ahmung *f* (-;-en) imitation, copy

nach'arbeiten *tr* copy; (*ausbessern*) touch up; (*Versäumtes*) make up for

nach'arten *intr* (SEIN) (*dat*) take after

Nachbar ['naxbar] *m* (-s & -n;-n), Nachbarin ['naxbarɪn] *f* (-;-nen) neighbor

nach'barlich *adj* neighborly; neighboring

Nach'barschaft *f* (-;-en) neighborhood; **gute N. halten** be on friendly terms with neighbors

Nach'bau *m* (-s;) imitation, duplication; licensed manufacture; **unerlaubter N.** illegal manufacture

Nach'behandlung *f* (med) follow-up treatment

nach'bestellen *tr* reorder, order more of

Nach'bestellung *f* (-;-en) repeat order

nach'beten *tr & intr* repeat mechanically

nach'bezahlen *tr* pay afterwards; pay the rest of || *intr* pay afterwards

Nach'bild *n* copy

nach'bilden *tr* copy

Nach'bildung *f* (-;-en) copying; (*Kopie*) copy, reproduction; (*Modell*) mock-up; (*Attrappe*) dummy

nach'bleiben §62 *intr* (SEIN) remain behind; (educ) stay in; **hinter j-m n.** lag behind s.o.

nach'blicken *intr* (*dat*) look after

nach'brennen §97 *intr* smolder || Nach'brennen *n* (-s;) (rok) afterburn

Nach'brenner *m* (aer) afterburner

nach'datieren *tr* postdate

nachdem [nax'dem] *adv* afterwards; **je n.** as the case may be, it all depends || *conj* after, when; **je n.** according to how, depending on how

nach'denken §66 *intr* think it over; **n. über** (*acc*) think over, reflect on || Nachdenken *n* (-s;) reflection; **bei weiterem N.** on second thought

nach'denklich *adj* reflective, thoughtful; (*Buch*) thought-provoking; (*abwesend*) lost in thought

Nach'dichtung *f* (-;-en) free poetical rendering

nach'drängen *intr* (SEIN) (*dat*) crowd after; pursue

nach'dringen §142 *intr* be in hot pursuit; (*dat*) pursue

Nach'druck *m* (*Betonung*) stress, emphasis; energy; (*Raubdruck*) pirated edition; (typ) reprint; **mit N.** emphatically; **N. verboten** all rights reserved

nach'drucken *tr* reprint

nach'drücklich *adj* emphatic; **n. betonen** emphasize

nach'dunkeln *intr* get darker

nach'eifern *intr* (*dat*) emulate

nach'eilen *intr* (SEIN) (*dat*) hasten after, rush after

nacheinan'der *adv* one after another

nach'empfinden §59 *tr* have a feeling for; **j-m etw n.** sympathize with s.o. about s.th.

Nachen ['naxən] *m* (-s;-) (poet) boat

nach'erzählen *tr* repeat, retell

Nachfahr ['naxfɑr] *m* (-s;-en) descendant

nach'fahren §71 *intr* (SEIN) (*dat*) drive after, follow

nach'fassen *tr* (mil) get a second helping of ‖ *intr* (econ) do a follow-up

Nach'folge *f* succession

nach'folgen *intr* (*dat*) succeed, follow; follow in the footsteps of

nach'folgend *adj* following, subsequent

Nach'folger –in §6 *mf* follower; successor

nach'fordern *tr* charge extra; claim subsequently

nach'forschen *intr* (*dat*) investigate

Nach'frage *f* inquiry; (com) demand

nach'fragen *intr* (nach) ask (about)

Nach'frist *f* time extension

nach'fühlen *tr*—**j-m etw n.** sympathize with s.o. about s.th.

nach'füllen *tr* refill, fill up

nach'geben §80 *tr* give later; (beim Essen) give another helping of; **j-m nichts an Eifer n.** not be outdone by s.o. in zeal ‖ *intr* give way, give; (schlaff werden) slacken, give; (dat) give in to, yield to

nach'geboren *adj* younger; posthumous

Nach'gebühr *f* postage due

nach'gehen §82 *intr* (SEIN) (*dat*) follow; (Geschäften) attend to; (untersuchen) investigate, check on

nachgemacht ['naxgəmaxt] *adj* false, imitation; (künstlich) artificial

nachgeordnet ['naxgə‧ɔrdnət] *adj* subordinate

nach'gerade *adv* by now; (allmählich) gradually; (wirklich) really

Nach'geschmack *m* aftertaste, bad taste

nachgewiesenermaßen ['naxgəvizənər‧masən] *adv* as has been shown (or proved)

nachgiebig ['naxgibɪç] *adj* elastic, yielding, compliant; (nachsichtig) indulgent; (st. exch.) declining

nach'gießen §76 *tr* fill up, refill ‖ *intr* add more

nach'glühen *tr* (tech) temper ‖ *intr* smolder

nach'grübeln *intr* (dat or über acc) mull (over), ponder (on)

Nach'hall *m* echo, reverberation

nach'hallen *intr* echo, reverberate

nachhaltig ['naxhaltɪç] *adj* lasting

nach'hängen §92 *intr* (dat) give free rein to ‖ *impers*—**es hängt mir nach** I still feel the effects of it

nach'helfen §96 *intr* (dat) help along

nach'her *adv* afterwards, later, then; **bis n.!** so long!

nachherig ['naxherɪç] *adj* later

Nach'hilfe *f* assistance, help

Nach'hilfelehrer –in §6 *mf* tutor

Nach'hilfestunde *f* tutoring lesson

Nach'hilfeunterricht *m* tutoring

nach'hinken *intr* (dat) lag behind

Nachholbedarf ['naxholbədarf] *m* backlog of unsatisfied demands

nach'holen *tr* make up for

Nach'hut *f* (mil) rear guard

nach'jagen *tr*—**j-m etw n.** send s.th. after s.o. ‖ *intr* (SEIN) (dat) pursue

Nach'klang *m* echo; (fig) reminiscence

nach'klingen §142 *intr* reecho, resound

Nachkomme ['naxkɔmə] *m* (-n;-n) offspring, descendant

nach'kommen §99 *intr* (SEIN) (dat) follow; join (s.o.) later; (Vorschriften, e-m Gesetz) obey; (e-m Versprechen) keep; (e-r Pflicht) live up to

Nach'kommenschaft *f* (-;) posterity

Nachkömmling ['naxkœmlɪŋ] *m* (-s; -e) offspring, descendant

Nach'laß ['naxlas] *m* (-lasses;-lässe) remission; (am Preis) reduction; (Erbschaft) estate; **literarischer N.** unpublished works

nach'lassen §104 *tr* leave behind; (lockern) slacken; **j-m 15% vom Preise n.** give s.o. a fifteen percent reduction in price ‖ *intr* (sich lockern) slacken; (sich vermindern) diminish; (milder werden) relent; (Regen) let up; (Kräfte) give out; (Wind, Sturm) die down; (schlechter werden) get worse

Nach'laßgericht *n* probate court

nach'lässig *adj* careless, negligent

Nach'lässigkeit *f* carelessness, negligence

nach'laufen §105 *intr* (SEIN) (dat) run after, pursue

nach'leben *intr* (dat) live up to ‖ **Nachleben** *n* afterlife

Nach'lese *f* gleanings

nach'lesen §107 *tr* glean; (Stelle im Buch) reread, look up

nach'liefern *tr* deliver subsequently

nach'machen *tr* imitate; (fälschen) counterfeit; **j-m alles n.** imitate s.o. in everything

nach'malen *tr* copy

nachmalig ['naxmalɪç] *adj* later

nachmals ['naxmals] *adv* afterwards

nach'messen §70 *tr* measure again

Nach'mittag *m* afternoon

nach'mittags *adv* in the afternoon

Nach'mittagsvorstellung *f* matinée

Nach'nahme *f* (-;) C.O.D.

Nach'name *m* last name, family name

nach'plappern *tr* repeat mechanically

Nach'porto *n* postage due

nachprüfbar ['naxpryfbɑr] *adj* verifiable

nach'prüfen *tr* verify, check out

nach'rechnen *tr* (acct) check

Nach'rede *f* epilogue; **j-n in üble N. bringen** bring s.o. into bad repute; **üble N.** slander; **üble N. verbreiten** spread nasty rumors

nach'reden *tr*—**j-m etw n.** say s.th. behind s.o.'s back

Nachricht ['naxrɪçt] *f* (-;-en) news; (Bericht) report; (kurzer Bericht) notice; (Auskunft) information; **e-e N. verbreiten** spread the news; **geben Sie mir von Zeit zu Zeit N.!** keep me advised; **Nachrichten** (rad, telv) news, news report; **Nachrichten einholen** make inquiries; **Nachrichten einziehen** gather information; **zur N.!** for your information

Nach′richtenabteilung f (mil) intelligence section

Nach′richtenagentur f news agency

Nach′richtenbüro n news room; news agency

Nach′richtendienst m news service; (mil) army intelligence

Nach′richtensatellit m communications satellite

Nach′richtensendung f newscast

Nach′richtenwesen n communications

nach′rücken intr (SEIN) (im Rang) move up; (mil) (dat) follow up; **j-m n.** move up into s.o.'s position

Nach′ruf m obituary

nach′rufen §122 tr (dat) call after

Nach′ruhm m posthumous fame

nach′rühmen tr—j-m etw n. say s.th. nice about s.o.

nach′sagen tr—j-m etw n. repeat s.th. after s.o.; say s.th behind s.o.'s back; **das lasse ich mir nicht n.** I won't let that be said of me

Nach′satz m concluding clause

nach′schaffen tr replace

nach′schauen intr (dat) gaze after

nach′schicken tr forward

Nachschlagebuch [′nɑx/lɑgəbux] n reference book

nach′schlagen §132 tr look up; (Buch) consult ‖ intr (box) counter

Nachschlagewerk [′nɑx/lɑgəverk] n reference work

Nach′schlüssel m skeleton key

nach′schreiben §62 tr copy; take down from dictation

Nach′schrift f postscript

Nach′schub m (mil) supply, fresh supplies; (mil) supply lines

Nach′schublinie f (mil) supply line

Nach′schubstützpunkt m (mil) supply base

Nach′schubweg m supply line

nach′sehen §138 tr (nachschlagen) look up; (nachprüfen) check; (acct) audit; (mach) overhaul; **j-m vieles n.** overlook much in s.o. ‖ intr (dat) gaze after ‖ **Nachsehen** n—**das N. haben** get the short end

nach′senden §140 tr send after, forward

nach′setzen intr (dat) run after

Nach′sicht f patience; **mit j-m N. üben** have patience with s.o.

nach′sichtig, nach′sichtsvoll adj lenient, considerate

Nach′silbe f suffix

nach′sinnen §121 intr (über acc) reflect (on), muse (over)

nach′sitzen intr be kept in after school

Nach′sommer m Indian summer

Nach′speise f dessert

Nach′spiel n (fig) sequel

nach′spüren intr (dat) track down

nächst [neçst] prep (dat) next to

nächst′beste §9 adj second-best

nächstdem′ adv thereupon

nächste [′neçstə] §9 adj (super of

nahe) next; (Weg) shortest; (Beziehungen) closest ‖ **Nächste** §5 mf neighbor, fellow man, fellow creature

nach′stehen §146 intr (dat) be inferior to

nach′stehend adj following ‖ adv (mentioned) below

nach′stellen tr (Schraube) reset, adjust; (Uhr) set back ‖ intr (dat) be after; (e-m Mädchen) run after

Nach′stellung f (-;-en) persecution; ambush; (gram) postposition

nächsten [′neçstən] adv one of these days, before long; next time

Näch′stenliebe f charity

nächst′liegend adj nearest

nach′stöbern intr rummage about

nach′stoßen §150 intr (SEIN) (dat) (mil) follow up

nach′streben intr (dat) strive after; (e-r Person) emulate

nach′strömen, nach′strümen, nach′stürzen intr (SEIN) (dat) crowd after

nach′suchen tr search for ‖ intr—n. um apply for

Nach′suchung f (-;-en) search, inquiry; petition

Nacht [nɑxt] f (-;⸗e) night; **bei N. und Nebel** under cover of night

Nacht′ausgabe f final (edition)

Nacht′teil m disadvantage

nacht′teilig adj disadvantageous

Nacht′essen n supper

Nacht′eule f night owl

Nacht′falter m (ent) moth

Nacht′geschirr n chamber pot

Nacht′gleiche f equinox

Nacht′hemd n nightgown

Nachtigall [′nɑxtɪgal] f (-;-n) nightingale

nächtigen [′neçtɪgən] intr pass the night

Nach′tisch m dessert

Nacht′klub m, **Nacht′lokal** n nightclub

Nacht′lager n accommodations for the night

nächtlich [′neçtlɪç] adj night, nightly

Nacht′mal n supper

Nacht′musik f serenade

nach′tönen intr resound; (Note) linger

Nacht′quartier n accommodations for the night

Nachtrag [′nɑxtrak] m (-[e]s;⸗e) supplement, addition

nach′tragen §132 tr add; **j-m etw n.** carry s.th. after s.o.; (fig) hold s.th. against s.o.

nachträgerisch [′nɑxtregərɪʃ] adj resentful, vindictive

nachträglich [′nɑxtreklɪç] adj supplementary; (später) subsequent

Nachtrags- comb.fm. supplementary

Nach′trupp m (-s) rear guard

nachts [nɑxts] adv at night

Nacht′schicht f night shift

nacht′schlafend adj—**bei** (or **zu**) **nacht′schlafender Zeit** late at night

Nacht′schwärmer -in §6 mf reveler

Nacht′tisch m night table

Nacht′topf m chamber pot

nach′tun §154 tr—j-m etw n. imitate s.o. in s.th.

Nacht′wache f night watch, vigil

Nacht′wächter m night watchman

Nachtwandler –in ['naxtvandlər(ɪn)] §6 *mf* sleepwalker, somnambulist

Nacht/zeug *n* overnight things

Nach/urlaub *m* extended leave

nach/wachsen §155 *intr* (SEIN) grow again

Nach/wahl *f* special election

Nachwehen ['naxve-ən] *pl* afterpains; (fig) painful consequences

nach/weinen *intr*—**keine Tränen n.** (*dat*) waste no tears over ‖ *intr* (*dat*) cry over

Nachweis ['naxvaɪs] *m* (–es;–e) proof; **den N. bringen** (or **führen**) furnish proof

nach/weisbar *adj* demonstrable

nach/weisen §118 *tr* point, show; (*beweisen*) prove; (*begründen*) substantiate; (*verweisen*) refer to

nach/weislich *adj* demonstrable

Nach/welt *f* posterity

nach/wiegen §57 *tr* verify the weight of

nach/wirken *intr* have an aftereffect

Nach/wirkung *f* (–;–en) aftereffect

Nach/wort *n* (–[e]s;–e) epilogue

Nach/wuchs *m* younger generation; younger set; children

nach/zahlen *tr & intr* pay extra

nach/zählen *tr* count over, check

nach/zeichnen *tr* draw a copy of ‖ *intr* copy

nach/ziehen §163 *tr* drag; tow; (*Linien*) trace; (*Schraube*) tighten ‖ *intr* (SEIN) (*dat*) follow after

nach/zotein *intr* (SEIN) (coll) trot after

Nachzügler –in ['naxtsyklər(ɪn)] §6 *mf* straggler; latecomer

Nackedei ['nakədaɪ] *m* (–[e]s;–e) naked child; nude

Nacken ['nakən] *m* (–s;–) nape of the neck

nackend ['nakənt] *adj* var of **nackt**

Nackenschlag (Nak'kenschlag) *m* rabbit punch; (fig) hard blow

-nackig [nakɪç] *comb.fm.* –necked

nackt [nakt] *adj* nude, bare; (*Tatsache*) hard; **sich n. ausziehen** strip bare

Nackt/heit *f* (–;) nudity, nakedness

Nadel ['nadəl] *f* (–;–n) needle; pin; **wie auf Nadeln sitzen** be on pins and needles

Na'delbaum *m* coniferous tree

Na'delkissen *n* pin cushion

Nadelöhr ['nadəlør] *n* (–s;–e) eye of a needle

Na'delstich *m* pinprick; (sew) stitch

Nagel ['nagəl] *m* (–s;:-) nail; **an den N. hängen** (fig) shelve; **an den Nägeln kauen** bite one's nails

Na'gelhaut *f* cuticle

nageln ['nagəln] *tr & intr* nail

na'gelneu/ *adj* brand-new

nagen ['nagən] *tr* gnaw; **das Fleisch vom Knochen n.** pick the meat off the bone ‖ *intr* (an *dat*) gnaw (at), nibble (at); (fig) (an *dat*) rankle

Nagetier ['nagetir] *n* rodent

Nah– [na] *comb.fm.* close-range, short-range

Näh– [ne] *comb.fm.* sewing, needlework

Näh/arbeit *f* sewing, needlework

Näh/aufnahme *f* (phot) close-up

nahe ['na·ə] *adj* (**näher** ['ne·ər]; **nächste** ['nɛçstə] §9) near, close; nearby; (*bevorstehend*) forthcoming; (*Gefahr*) imminent ‖ *adv*—**j–m zu n. treten** hurt s.o.'s feelings; **n. an.** (*dat* or *acc*), **n. bei** close to; **n. daran sein zu** (*inf*) be on the point of (*ger*)

Nähe ['ne·ə] *f* (–;–n) nearness; vicinity; **in der N.** close by

na'hebei *adv* nearby

na'hebringen §65 *tr* drive home

na'hegehen §82 *intr* (SEIN) (*dat*) affect, touch, grieve

na'hekommen §99 *intr* (SEIN) approach; (*dat*) come near to; **der Wahrheit n.** get at the truth

na'helegen *tr* suggest

na'heliegen §108 *intr* be close by; be obvious; be easy

na'heliegend *adj* obvious

nahen ['na·ən] *ref & intr* (SEIN) approach; (*dat*) draw near to

nähen ['ne·ən] *tr & intr* sew, stitch

näher ['ne·ər] *adj* (*comp* of **nahe**) nearer; **bei näherer Betrachtung** upon further consideration ‖ *adv* closer; **immer n. kommen** close in; **treten Sie n.!** this way, please! ‖ **Nähere** §5 *n* details, particulars; **das N. auseinandersetzen** explain fully; **Näheres erfahren** learn further particulars; **sich des Näheren entsinnen** remember all particulars; **wenn Sie Näheres wissen wollen** if you want details

Näherin ['ne·ərɪn] *f* (–;–nen) seamstress

nähern ['ne·ərn] *ref* approach; (*dat*) draw near to, approach

Nä'herungswert *m* approximate value

na'hestehen §146 *intr* (*dat*) share the view of

na'hetreten §152 *intr* (SEIN) (*dat*) come into close contact with

na'hezu *adv* almost, nearly

Näh/garn *n* thread

Näh/kampf *m* hand-to-hand fighting; (box) in-fighting

nahm [nam] *pret* of **nehmen**

Näh/maschine *f* sewing machine

-nahme [namə] *f* (–;–n) *comb.fm.* taking

Nähr– [ner] *comb.fm.* nutritive

Nähr/boden *m* rich soil; (fig) breeding ground; (biol) culture medium

nähren ['nerən] *tr* nourish, feed; (*Kind*) nurse ‖ *ref* make a living; **sich n. von** subsist on ‖ *intr* be nutritious

nahrhaft ['narhaft] *adj* nourishing, nutritious, nutritive

Nähr/mittel *pl* (*Teigwaren*) noodles; (*Hülsenfrüchte*) beans and peas

Nahrung ['narʊŋ] *f* (–;) nourishment; (*Kost*) diet; (*Unterhalt*) livelihood

Nah'rungsmittel *pl* food

Nah'rungsmittelvergiftung *f* food poisoning

Nah'rungssorgen *pl* difficulty in making ends meet

Nähr/wert *m* nutritive value

Näh/stube *f* sewing room

Naht [nat] *f* (–;:-e) seam

Nah'verkehr *m* local traffic

Näh'zeug *n* sewing kit

naiv [na'if] *adj* naive

Name ['namə] *m* (-ns;-n), **Namen** ['namən] *m* (-s;-) name

na'menlos *adj* nameless; *(unsäglich)* indescribable

namens ['naməns] *adv* named, called || *prep (genit)* in the name of, on behalf of

Na'mensschild *n* nameplate

Na'menstag *m* name day

Na'mensvetter *m* namesake

namentlich ['naməntlɪç] *adj*—**namentliche Abstimmung** roll-call vote || *adv* by name, individually; *(besonders)* especially

Na'menverzeichnis *n* index of names; nomenclature

namhaft ['namhaft] *adj* distinguished; *(beträchtlich)* considerable; **n. machen** name, specify

nämlich ['nemlɪç] *adv* namely, that is; (coll) you know, you see

nannte ['nantə] *pret* of **nennen**

nanu [na'nu] *interj* gee!

Napf [napf] *m* (-es;-e) bowl

Narbe ['narbə] *f* (-;-n) scar; *(des Leders)* grain; (agr) topsoil

narbig ['narbɪç] *adj* scarred

Narkose [nar'kozə] *f* (-;-n) anesthesia

Narkoti·kum [nar'kotɪkum] *n* (-s;-ka [ka]) narcotic, dope

narkotisch [nar'kotɪʃ] *adj* narcotic

Narr [nar] *m* (-en;-en) fool; (hist) jester; **j-n zum Narren halten** make a fool of s.o.

Närrchen ['nɛrçən] *n* (-s;-) silly little goose

narren ['narən] *tr* make a fool of

Narrenfest ['narənfest] *n* masquerade

Narrenhaus ['narənhaus] *n* madhouse

Narrenkappe ['narənkapə] *f* cap and bells

narrensicher ['narənzɪçər] *adj* (coll) foolproof

Narren(s)possen ['narən(s)pɔsən] *pl* horseplay; **laß die N.!** stop horsing around!

Narr'heit *f* (-;-en) folly

närrisch ['nerɪʃ] *adj* foolish; *(verrückt)* crazy; *(Kauz)* eccentric; **n. sein auf** *(acc)* be crazy about

Narzisse [nar'tsɪsə] *f* (-;-n) (bot) narcissus; **gelbe N.** daffodil

naschen ['naʃən] *tr* nibble at || *intr* (an *dat*, von) nibble (on); **gern n.** have a sweet tooth

Näscher -in ['neʃər(ɪn)] §6 *mf* nibbler

Näscherei [neʃə'raɪ] *f* (-;-en) snack

naschhaft ['naʃhaft] *adj* sweet-toothed

Naschkatze ['naʃkatsə] *f* nibbler

Naschmaul ['naʃmaul] *n* nibbler

Naschwerk ['naʃverk] *n* sweets, tidbits

Nase ['nazə] *f* (-;-n) nose; **auf der N. liegen** be laid up in bed; **aufgeworfene N.** turned-up nose; **das sticht ihm in die N.** it annoys him; he's itching to have it; **daß du die N. im Gesicht behältst!** keep your shirt on!; **dem Kind die N. putzen** wipe the child's nose; **die N. läuft ihm blau an** his nose is getting red; **die N. rüm-**

pfen über *(acc)* turn up one's nose at; **die N. voll haben von** be fed up with; **e-e tüchtige N. voll bekommen** (or **einstecken müssen**) get chewed out; **faß dich an deine eigene N.!** mind your own business!; **feine N. für** flair for; **immer der N. nach!** follow your nose!; **in der N. bohren** poke one's nose; **j-m e-e lange N. machen** thumb one's nose at s.o.; **j-m e-e N. drehen** outwit s.o.; **j-m die Würmer aus der N. ziehen** worm it out of s.o.; **j-m etw auf die N. binden** divulge s.th. to s.o.; **j-m in die N. fahren** (or **steigen**) annoy s.o.; **j-n an der N. herumführen** lead s.o. by the nose; **man kann es ihm an der N. ansehen** it's written all over his face; **mit langer N. abziehen** be the loser; **pro N.** per head; **sich** *[dat]* **die N. begießen** wet one's whistle

näseln ['nezəln] *intr* speak through the nose || **Näseln** *n* (-s;) nasal twang

nä'selnd *adj* nasal

Na'senbein *n* nasal bone

Na'senbluten *n* (-s;) nosebleed

na'senlang *adv*—**alle n.** constantly

Na'senlänge *f*—**um e-e N.** by a nose

Na'senlaut *m* (phonet) nasal

Na'senloch *n* nostril

Na'senrücken *m* bridge of the nose

Na'senschleim *m* mucus

Na'senschleimhaut *f* mucous membrane

Nasenspray ['nazənspre] *m* (-s;-s) nose spray

Na'sentropfen *m* nose drop

na'seweis *adj* fresh, wise || **Naseweis** *m* (-es;-e) wise guy

Na'seweisheit *f* freshness

nasführen ['nasfyrən] *tr* lead by the nose; *(foppen)* fool

Nashorn ['nashɔrn] *n* (-[e]s;-er) rhinoceros

naß [nas] *adj* (**nasser** ['nasər] or **nässer** ['nesər]; **nasseste** ['nasəstə] or **nässeste** ['nesəstə] §9) wet; *(feucht)* moist || **Naß** *n* (Nasses) (poet) liquid

Nassauer ['nasau·ər] *m* (-s;-) sponger, chiseler

nassauern ['nasau·ərn] *intr* (coll) sponge

Nässe ['nesə] *f* (-;) wetness; moisture

nässen ['nesən] *tr* wet; moisten || *intr* ooze

naß'forsch *adj* rash, bold

naß'kalt *adj* raw, cold and damp

Nation [na'tsjon] *f* (-;-en) nation

national [natsjo'nal] *adj* national

National'hymne *f* national anthem

nationalisieren [natsjonalɪ'zirən] *tr* nationalize

Nationalismus [natsjona'lɪsmus] *m* (-;) nationalism

Nationalität [natsjonalɪ'tet] *f* (-;-en) nationality; ethnic minority

National'sozialismus *m* national socialism, Nazism

National'sozialist -in §7 *mf* national socialist, Nazi

National'tracht *f* national costume

Nativität [natɪvɪ'tet] *f* (-;-en) horoscope

Natrium ['nɑtrɪ·um] n (-s;) sodium

Natter ['natər] f (-;-n) adder, viper

Natur [na'tur] f (-;-en) nature; (*Körperbeschaffenheit*) constitution; (*Gemütsart*) disposition; (*Art*) character; (*Person*) creature; **von N.** by nature

Natura [na'tura] f—**in N.** in kind

Naturalien [natu'raljən] pl produce

naturalisieren [naturalɪ'zirən] tr naturalize || ref—**sich n. lassen** become naturalized

Natur'anlage f disposition

Natur'arzt m naturopath

Naturell [natu'rel] n (-[e]s;-e) nature, temperament

Natur'erscheinung f phenomenon

Natur'forscher –in §6 mf naturalist

Natur'gabe f natural gift, talent

natur'gemäß adv naturally

Natur'geschichte f natural history

Natur'gesetz n natural law

natur'getreu adj life-like

Natur'kunde f, **Natur'lehre** f natural science

natürlich [na'tyrlɪç] adj natural; (*echt*) real; (*ungezwungen*) natural; **das geht aber nicht mit natürlichen Dingen zu** there is s.th. fishy about it; **das geht ganz n. zu** there is nothing strange about it || adv naturally, of course

Natur'mensch m primitive man; nature enthusiast

Natur'philosoph m natural philosopher

Natur'recht n natural right

Natur'schutz m preservation of natural beauty

Natur'schutzgebiet n wildlife preserve

Natur'schutzpark m national park

Natur'spiel n freak of nature

Natur'theater n outdoor theater

Natur'trieb m instinct

Natur'verehrung f natural religion

Natur'volk n primitive people

natur'widrig adj contrary to nature

Natur'wissenschaft f natural science

Natur'wissenschaftler –in §6 mf scientist

naturwüchsig [na'turvyksɪç] adj unspoiled by civilization

Natur'zustand m natural state

nautisch ['nautɪʃ] adj nautical

Navigation [naviga'tsjon] f (-;) navigation

navigieren [navi'girən] intr navigate

Nazi ['nɑtsi] m (-s;-s) Nazi

Nazismus [na'tsɪsmus] m (-;) Nazism

nazistisch [na'tsɪstɪç] adj Nazi

Nebel ['nebəl] m (-s;-) fog, mist; (*Dunst*) haze

Ne'belbank f (-;˙-e) fog bank

Ne'belfeld n patch of fog

Ne'belferne f hazy distance; (fig) dim future

Ne'belfleck m (astr) nebula

ne'belhaft adj foggy, hazy; (*Ferne*) dim

Ne'belhorn n foghorn

nebeln ['nebəln] intr be foggy

Ne'belscheinwerfer m (aut) fog light

Ne'belschicht f fog bank

Ne'belschirm m smoke screen

Ne'belvorhang m smoke screen

neben ['nebən] prep (dat & acc) by, beside; side by side with, alongside, close to, next to; (*verglichen mit*) compared with; (*außer*) besides, aside from; in addition to; extra

Neben– comb.fm. secondary, accessory, by–, side–, subordinate

Ne'benabsicht f ulterior motive

Ne'benaltar m side altar

Ne'benamt n additional duties

nebenan' adv close by; next-door

Ne'benanschluß m (telp) extension; (telp) party line

Ne'benarbeit f extra work

Ne'benarm m tributary, branch

Ne'benausgaben pl incidentals, extras

Ne'benausgang m side exit

Ne'benbahn f (rr) branch line

Ne'benbedeutung f (-;-en) secondary meaning

nebenbei' adv close by; (*außerdem*) besides, on the side; (*beiläufig*) incidentally

Ne'benberuf m sideline, side job

ne'benberuflich adj sideline, spare-time

Ne'benbeschäftigung f sideline

Nebenbuhler –in ['nebənbulər(ɪn)] §6 mf competitor, rival

ne'benbuhlerisch adj rival

Ne'bending n secondary matter

nebeneinan'der adv side by side; neck and neck; (*gleichzeitig*) simultaneously; **n. bestehen** coexist

Nebeneinan'derleben n coexistence

nebeneinan'derstellen tr juxtapose

Ne'beneingang m side entrance

Ne'beneinkünfte pl, **Ne'beneinnahmen** pl extra income

Ne'benerzeugnis n by-product

Ne'benfach n (educ) minor; **als N. studieren** minor in

Ne'benflügel m (archit) wing

Ne'benfluß m tributary

Ne'benfrage f side issue

Ne'benfrau f concubine

Ne'bengang m side aisle

Ne'bengasse f side street, alley

Ne'bengebäude n annex, wing

Ne'bengedanke m ulterior motive

Ne'bengericht n side dish

Ne'bengeschäft n (com) branch

Ne'bengleis n (rr) siding, sidetrack

Ne'benhandlung f (-;-en) subplot

nebenher' adv on the side; besides; along

nebenhin' adv incidentally, by the way

Ne'benkosten pl incidentals, extras

Ne'benlinie f (rr) branch line

Ne'benmann m (-[e]s;˙-er) neighbor

Ne'benprodukt n by-product

Ne'benpunkt m minor point

Ne'benrolle f supporting role

Ne'bensache f side issue

ne'bensächlich adj subordinate; incidental; (*unwesentlich*) unimportant

Ne'bensächlichkeit f unimportance; triviality

Ne'bensatz m subordinate clause

Ne'benschaltung f (-;-en) (elec) shunt

Ne'benschluß m (elec) shunt

Ne'benspesen pl additional charges

ne'benstehend adj marginal, in the margin || **Nebenstehende** §5 mf bystander

Ne′benstelle *f* branch; (telp) extension
Ne′benstraße *f* side street
Ne′bentisch *m* next table
Ne′bentür *f* side door
Ne′benverdienst *m* extra pay; side job
Ne′benvorstellung *f* side show
Ne′benweg *m* side road
Ne′benwirkung *f* (–en) side effect
Ne′benzimmer *n* adjoining room
Ne′benzweck *m* secondary aim
neblig [′neblɪç] *adj* foggy, misty
nebst [nepst] *prep* (dat) including
necken [′nekən] *tr & recip* tease, kid
Neckerei [nekə′raɪ] *f* (–;–en) teasing
neckisch [′nekɪʃ] *adj* fond of teasing; (coll) cute
nee [ne] *adv* (dial) no
Neffe [′nefə] *m* (–n;–n) nephew
Negation [nɛga′tsjon] *f* (–;–en) negation
negativ [nega′tif] *adj* negative ‖ **Negativ** *n* (–s;–e) negative
Neger –in [′negər(ɪn)] §6 *mf* black, Negro
Negligé [negli′ʒe] *n* (–s;–e) negligee
nehmen [′nemən] §116 *tr* take; (weg–) take away; (anstellen) take on, hire; (Anwalt) retain; (Hindernis) clear, take; (Kurve) negotiate; (Schaden) suffer; **Anfang n.** begin; **Anstand n.** hesitate; **an sich n.** pocket, misappropriate; collect; retrieve; **Anstoß n. an** (dat) take offense at; **auf sich n.** assume, take upon oneself; **das Wort n.** begin to speak; **den Mund voll n.** (coll) talk big; **die Folgen auf sich n.** bear the consequences; **ein Ende n.** come to an end; **ein gutes Ende n.** turn out all right; **er versteht es, die Kunden richtig zu n.** he knows how to handle customers; **etw genau n.** take s.th. literally; **ich lasse es mir nicht n. zu** (inf) I insist on (ger); **im Grunde genommen** basically; **in Angriff n.** begin; **in Arbeit n.** start making; **in die Hand n.** pick up; (fig) take in hand; **j–m etw n.** take s.th. away from s.o.; deprive s.o. of s.th.; **kein Ende n.** go on endlessly; **man nehme zwei Eier, usw.** (im Kochbuch) take two eggs, etc.; **n. Sie bitte Platz!** please sit down; **n. wir den Fall, daß** let's suppose that; **Rücksicht n. auf** (acc) show consideration for; **sich** [dat] **das Leben n.** take one's life; **sich** [dat] **nichts von seinen Rechten n.** lassen insist on one's rights; **streng genommen** strictly speaking; **Stunden n.** take lessons; **Urlaub n.** take a vacation; (mil) go on furlough; **wie man's nimmt** it all depends; **zu Hilfe n. use; zur Ehe n. marry; zu sich** [dat] **n.** put into one's pocket; (Speise) eat; (Kind) take charge of
Neid [naɪt] *m* (–es) envy; **blasser (or gelber) N.** pure envy; **vor N. vergehen** die of envy
neiden [′naɪdən] *tr—j–m etw n.** envy s.o. for s.th.
Neid′hammel *m* envious person
nei′dig *adj* (dial) var of neidisch
neidisch [′naɪdɪʃ] *adj* (auf acc) envious (of)

neid′los *adj* free of envy
Neid′nagel *m* hangnail
Neige [′naɪgə] *f* (–;–n) slope; (Abnahme) decline; (Überbleibsel) sediment, dregs; **zur N. gehen** (Geld, Vorräte) run low; (Sonne) go down; (Tag, Jahr) draw to a close
neigen [′naɪgən] *tr* incline, bend; **geneigt** sloping; (fig) friendly, favorable ‖ *ref* (vor *dat*) bow (to); (Abhang) slope; **sich zum Ende n.** draw to a close ‖ *intr—n. zu* be inclined to
Nei′gung *f* (–;–en) slope, incline; (des Hauptes) bowing; (e–s Schiffes) list; (in der Straße) dip; (Gefälle) gradient; (Hang) inclination; (Anlage) tendency; (Vorliebe) taste, liking; (Zuneigung) affection; **e–e N. nach rechts haben** lean towards the right; **N. fassen zu** take (a fancy) to
nein [naɪn] *adv* no ‖ **Nein** *n* (–s;) no
Nein′stimme *f* (parl) nay
Nekrolog [nekrə′lok] *m* (–[e]s;–e) obituary
Nektar [′nektar] *m* (–s;) nectar
Nelke [′nelkə] *f* (–;–n) carnation; (Gewürz) clove
Nel′kenöl *n* oil of cloves
Nel′kenpfeffer *m* allspice
Nemesis [′nemezɪs] *f* (–;) Nemesis
nennbar [′nenbar] *adj* mentionable
nennen [′nenən] §97 *tr* name, call; (erwähnen) mention; (benennen) term ‖ *ref* be called, be named
nen′nenswert *adj* worth mentioning
Nenner [′nenər] *m* (–s;–) (math) denominator; **auf e–n gemeinsamen N. bringen** reduce to a common denominator
Nennform [′nenform] *f* (gram) infinitive
Nenngeld [′nengelt] *n* entry fee
Nen′nung *f* (–;) naming; mentioning
Nennwert [′nenvert] *m* face value
Neologis·mus [ne·olo′gɪsmus] *m* (–;-men [mən]) neologism
Neon [′ne·on] *n* (–s;) neon
Ne′onlicht *n* neon light
Nepotismus [nepo′tɪsmus] *m* (–;) nepotism
neppen [′nepən] *tr* (coll) gyp, clip
Nepplokal [′neplokal] *n* (sl) clip joint
Neptun [nep′tun] *m* (–s;) Neptune
Nerv [nerf] *m* (–s;–en) nerve; **die Nerven behalten** keep cool; **die Nerven verlieren** lose one's head; **j–m auf die Nerven gehen** get on s.o.'s nerves; **mit den Nerven herunter sein** be a nervous wreck
Nerven–, nerven– [′nerfən] *comb.fm.* nervous, neuro–, of nerves
Ner′venarzt *m*, **Ner′venärztin** *f* neurologist
ner′venaufreibend *adj* nerve-racking
Ner′venberuhigungsmittel *n* sedative
Ner′venbündel *n* (fig) bundle of nerves
Ner′venentzündung *f* neuritis
Ner′venfaser *f* nerve fiber
Ner′venheilanstalt *f* mental institution
Ner′venheilkunde *f* neurology
Ner′venkitzel *m* thrill, suspense
Ner′venknoten *m* ganglion
ner′venkrank *adj* neurotic

Ner'venkrieg *m* war of nerves
Ner'venlehre *f* neurology
Ner'vensäge *f* (coll) pain in the neck
Ner'venschmerz *m* neuralgia
Ner'venschwäche *f* nervousness
Ner'venzentrum *n* (fig) nerve center
Ner'venzusammenbruch *m* nervous breakdown
nervig ['nɛrvɪç], ['nɛrfɪç] *adj* sinewy
nervös [nɛr'vøs] *adj* nervous
Nervosität [nɛrvozi'tɛt] *f* (–;) nervousness
Nerz [nɛrts] *m* (–es;-e) (zool) mink
Nerz'mantel *m* mink coat
Nessel ['nɛsəl] *f* (–;-n) nettle; **sich in die Nesseln setzen** (fig) get oneself into hot water
Nest [nɛst] *n.* (–es;-er) nest; (*Schlupfwinkel*) hideout; small town; dead town; (*Bett*) (coll) bed
nesteln ['nɛstəln] *tr* lace, tie || *intr* —n. an (*dat*) fiddle with, fuss with
Nesthäkchen ['nɛsthɛkçən] *n* (–s;–), Nestküken ['nɛstkykən] *n* (–s;–) baby (*of the family*)
nett [nɛt] *adj* nice; (*sauber*) neat; (*niedlich*) cute; **das kann ja n. werden!** (iron) that's going to be just dandy!
netto ['nɛto] *adv* net; clear
Net'togewicht *n* net weight
Net'togewinn *m* clear profit
Net'tolohn *m* take-home pay
Net'topreis *m* net price
Netz [nɛts] *n* (–es;-e) net; network; grid
netzen ['nɛtsən] *tr* wet, moisten
Netz'haut *f* retina
Netz'werk *n* netting, webbing
neu [nɔɪ] *adj* new; (*frisch*) fresh; (*unlängst geschehen*) recent; **aufs neue** anew; **neuere Geschichte** modern history; **neuere Sprachen** modern languages; **von neuem** all over again || *adv* newly; recently; anew; afresh || **Neue** §5 *mf* newcomer || §5 *n*— **was gibt es Neues?** what's new?
Neu–, neu– *comb.fm.* new–, newly; re–; neo–
Neu'anlage *f* new installation; (fin) reinvestment
Neu'anschaffung *f* recent acquisition
neu'artig *adj* novel; modern
Neu'aufführung *f* (–;-en) (theat) revival
Neu'ausgabe *f* new edition, republication; (*Neudruck*) reprint
Neu'bau *m* (–[e]s;-bauten) new building
neu'bearbeiten *tr* revise
Neubelebung ['nɔɪbəlebuŋ] *f* (–;-en) revival
Neu'bildung *f* (–;-en) new growth; (gram) neologism
Neu'druck *m* reprint
neuerdings ['nɔɪ·ərdɪŋs] *adv* recently; (*vom neuem*) anew
Neuerer –in ['nɔɪ·ərər(ɪn)] §6 *mf* innovator
Neuerung ['nɔɪ·əruŋ] *f* (–;-en) innovation
neuestens ['nɔɪ·əstəns] *adv* recently
Neu'fassung *f* revision

Neufundland [nɔɪ'fʊntlant] *n* (–s;) Newfoundland
neu'gebacken *adj* fresh-baked; brand-new
neu'geboren *adj* new-born
neu'gestalten *tr* reorganize
Neu'gier *f,* Neugierde ['nɔɪgɪrdə] *f* (–;) curiosity, inquisitiveness
neu'gierig *adj* curious, nosey
Neu'gründung *f* (–;-en) reestablishment
Neu'gruppierung *f* (–;-en) regrouping; reshuffling
Neu'heit *f* (–;-en) novelty
neu'hochdeutsch *adj* modern High German
Neu'igkeit *f* (–;-en) news, piece of news
Neu'jahr *n* New Year
Neu'land *n* virgin soil; (fig) new ground
neu'lich *adv* lately
Neuling ['nɔɪlɪŋ] *m* (–[e]s;-e) beginner
neu'modisch *adj* fashionable; newfangled
neun [nɔɪn] *invar adj & pron* nine || Neun *f* (–;-en) nine
Neunmalkluge ['nɔɪnmalklugə] §5 *mf* wiseacre
neunte ['nɔɪntə] §9 *adj & pron* ninth
Neuntel ['nɔɪntəl] *n* (–s;–) ninth
neun'zehn *invar adj & pron* nineteen || Neunzehn *f* (–;-en) nineteen
neun'zehnte §9 *adj & pron* nineteenth
neunzig ['nɔɪntsɪç] *invar adj & pron* ninety || Neunzig *f* (–;-en) ninety
neunziger ['nɔɪntsɪgər] *invar adj* of the nineties; **die n. Jahre** the nineties || Neunziger –in §6 *mf* nonagenarian
neunzigste ['nɔɪntsɪçstə] §9 *adj & pron* ninetieth
Neu'ordnung *f* (–;-en) reorganization
Neural·gie [nɔɪral'gi] *f* (–;-gien ['gi·ən]) neuralgia
Neu'regelung *f* (–;-en) rearrangement
Neu·ron ['nɔɪrɔn] *n* (–;-ronen ['rɔnən]) neuron
Neurose [nɔɪ'rozə] *f* (–;-n) neurosis
Neurotiker –in [nɔɪ'rotɪkər(ɪn)] §6 *mf* neurotic
neurotisch [nɔɪ'rotɪʃ] *adj* neurotic
Neusee'land *n* (–s;) New Zealand
Neu'silber *n* German silver
Neusprachler –in ['nɔɪʃpraxlər(ɪn)] §6 *mf* modern-language teacher
Neu'stadt *f* new section of town
Neu'steinzeit *f* neolithic age
neu'steinzeitlich *adj* neolithic
neutral [nɔɪ'tral] *adj* neutral
neutralisieren [nɔɪtralɪ'zirən] *tr* neutralize
Neutralität [nɔɪtralɪ'tɛt] *f* (–;) neutrality
Neu·tron ['nɔɪtrɔn] *n* (–;-tronen ['trɔnən]) neutron
Neu·trum ['nɔɪtrum] *n* (–s;-tra [tra] & -tren [trən]) (gram) neuter
neuvermählt ['nɔɪfermɛlt] *adj* newly married || Neuvermählte §5 *pl* newlyweds
Neu'zeit *f* recent times
Nibelung ['nibəluŋ] *m* (–s;) (myth)

(King) Nibelung ‖ *m* (-en;-en) Nibelung

nicht [nıçt] *adv* not; **auch...nicht** not ...either; **n. doch!** please don't; **n. einmal** not even, not so much as; **n. mehr** no longer, no more; **n. um die Welt** not for the world; **n. wahr?** isn't it so?, no?, right?

Nicht-, nicht- *comb.fm.* in-, im-, un-, non-

Nicht'achtung *f* disregard, disrespect; **N. des Gerichts** contempt of court

nicht'amtlich *adj* unofficial

Nicht'angriffspakt *m* nonaggression pact

Nicht'annahme *f* nonacceptance

Nichte ['nıçtə] *f* (-;-n) niece

Nicht'einmischung *f* noninterference

Nicht'eisenmetall *n* nonferrous metal

nichtig ['nıçtıç] *adj* invalid; void; (*eitel*) vain; (*vergänglich*) transitory; **für n. erklären** annul

Nich'tigkeit *f* (-;-en) invalidity; futility; (*Kleinigkeit*) trifle; **Nichtigkeiten** trivia

Nich'tigkeitserklärung *f* annulment

Nicht'kämpfer *m* noncombatant

nicht'öffentlich *adj* private; (*Sitzung*) closed

nicht'rostend *adj* rustproof; (*Stahl*) stainless

nichts [nıçts] *indef pron* nothing; **gar n.** nothing at all; **n. als** nothing but; **n. mehr davon!** not another word about it!; **n. und wieder n.** absolutely nothing; **soviel wie n.** next to nothing; **um n.** for nothing, to no avail; **weiter n.?** is that all?; **wenn es weiter n. ist!** if it's nothing worse than that ‖ **Nichts** *n* (-s;) nothingness; nonentity; (*Leere*) void; (*Kleinigkeit*) trifle; **vor dem N. stehen** be faced with utter ruin

nichtsdestowe'niger *adv* nevertheless

Nichts'könner *m* incompetent person; ignoramus

Nichts'nutz *m* good-for-nothing

nichts'nutzig *adj* good-for-nothing

nichts'sagend *adj* insignificant; (*Antwort*) vague; noncommittal; (*Gesicht*) vacuous; (*Redensart*) trite

Nichts'tuer -in §6 *mf* loafer

Nichts'wisser -in §6 *mf* ignoramus

nichts'würdig *adj* contemptible

Nicht'zutreffende §5 *n*—**Nichtzutreffendes streichen** delete if not applicable

Nickel ['nıkəl] *n* (-s;-) (metal) nickel

nicken ['nıkən] *intr* nod; (*schlummern*) nap

Nickerchen ['nıkərçən] *n* (-s;-) nap

nie [ni] *adv* never, at no time

nieder ['nidər] *adj* low; (*gemein*) base ‖ *adv* down

nie'derbrechen §64 *tr & intr* (SEIN) break down

nie'derbrennen §97 *tr & intr* (SEIN) burn down

nie'derdeutsch *adj* Low German ‖ **Niederdeutsch** *n* Low German ‖ **Niederdeutsche** §5 *mf* North German

nie'derdonnern *tr* (coll) shout down ‖ *intr* go (or come) crashing down

Nie'derdruck *m* low pressure

nie'derdrücken *tr* press down (fig) weigh down; (*unterdrücken*) oppress; (*entmutigen*) depress

nie'derfallen §72 *intr* (SEIN) fall down

Nie'derfrequenz *f* low frequency; audio frequency

Nie'dergang *m* descent; (*der Sonne*) setting; (fig) decline, fall

nie'dergehen §82 *intr* (SEIN) go down; (*Flugzeug*) land; (*Regen*) fall; (*Vorhang*) drop

nie'dergeschlagen *adj* dejected

nie'derhalten §90 *tr* hold down, keep down

nie'derholen *tr* lower, haul down

Nie'derholz *n* underbrush

nie'derkämpfen *tr* (& fig) overcome

nie'derkommen §99 *intr* (SEIN) (mit) give birth (to)

Niederkunft ['nidərkʊnft] *f* (-;) confinement, childbirth

Nie'derlage *f* defeat; (*Lager*) warehouse; (*Filiale*) branch

Niederlande, die ['nidərlandə] *pl* The Netherlands, Holland

Niederländer ['nidərlɛndər] *m* (-s;-) Dutchman

niederländisch ['nidərlɛndɪʃ] *adj* Dutch

nie'derlassen §104 *tr* let down ‖ *ref* sit down, recline; (*Wohnsitz nehmen*) settle; (*ein Geschäft eröffnen*) set oneself up in business; (*Vogel, Flugzeug*) land

Nie'derlassung *f* (-;-en) settlement, colony; establishment; (*e-r Bank*) branch; (com) plant

nie'derlegen *tr* lay down, put down; (*Amt*) resign; (*Geschäft*) give up; (*Krone*) abdicate; (*schriftlich*) set down in writing; **die Arbeit n.** go on strike ‖ *ref* lie down; go to bed

nie'dermachen *tr* butcher, massacre

nie'dermähen *tr* mow down

nie'dermetzeln *tr* butcher, massacre

Nie'derschlag *m* (*Bodensatz*) sediment; (box) knockdown; (chem) precipitate; (meteor) precipitation; **radioaktiver N.** fallout

nie'derschlagen §132 *tr* knock down; (*Augen*) cast down; (*Aufstand*) put down; (*vertuschen*) hush up; (*Verfahren*) quash; (*Forderung*) waive; (*Hoffnungen*) dash; (chem) precipitate

nie'derschmettern *tr* knock to the ground; (fig) crush

nie'derschreiben §62 *tr* write down

nie'dersetzen *tr* set down ‖ *ref* sit down

nie'dersinken §143 *intr* (SEIN) sink down

nie'derstimmen *tr* vote down

Nie'dertracht *f* nastiness, meanness

nie'derträchtig *adj* nasty; underhand

Nie'derung *f* (-;-en) low ground, depression

niederwärts ['nidərverts] *adv* downward

nie'derwerfen §160 *tr* knock down; (*Aufstand*) put down ‖ *ref* fall down

Nie'derwild *n* small game

niedlich ['nitlıç] *adj* nice, cute

Niednagel ['nitnagəl] *m* hangnail

niedrig ['niːdrɪç] *adj* low; (*Herkunft*) humble; (*gemein*) mean, base

niemals ['niːmals] *adv* never

niemand ['niːmant] *indef pron* no one, nobody

Nie′mandsland *n* no man's land

Niere ['niːrə] *f* (-;-n) kidney; **das geht mir an die Nieren** (fig) that cuts me deep

nieseln ['niːzəln] *impers*—**es nieselt it is drizzling**

Nie′selregen *m* drizzle

niesen ['niːzən] *intr* sneeze

Niet [niːt] *m* (-[e]s;-e) rivet

Niete ['niːtə] *f* (-;-n) rivet; (*in der Lotterie*) blank; (*Versager*) flop

nieten ['niːtən] *tr* rivet

niet-′ und na′gelfest *adj* nailed down

Nihilismus [nihiˈlɪsmɪs] *m* (-;) nihilism

Nikotin [nikoˈtiːn] *n* (-s;) nicotine

nikotin′arm *adj* low in nicotine

Nil [niːl] *m* (-s;) Nile

Nil′pferd *n* hippopotamus

Nimbus ['nɪmbus] *m* (-;-se) halo; aura; (*Ansehen*) prestige; (meteor) nimbus

nimmer ['nɪmər] *adv* never; (dial) no more

nim′mermehr *adv* never more; by no means

Nippel ['nɪpəl] *m* (-s;-) (mach) nipple

nippen ['nɪpən] *tr & intr* sip

Nippsachen ['nɪpzaxən] *pl* knicknacks

nirgends ['nɪrgənts] *adv* nowhere

nirgendwo ['nɪrgəntvo] *adv* nowhere

Nische ['niːʃə] *f* (-;-n) niche

nisten ['nɪstən] *intr* nest

Nitrat [niˈtraːt] *n* (-[e]s;-e) nitrate

Nitrid [niˈtriːt] *n* (-[e]s;-e) nitride

Nitroglyzerin [nɪtroˈɡlytsəˈriːn] *n* (-s;) nitroglycerin

Niveau [niˈvo] *n* (-s;-s) level; **N. haben** have class; **unter dem N. sein** be substandard

Niveau′übergang *m* (rr) grade crossing

nivellieren [nivəˈliːrən] *tr* level

nix [nɪks] *indef pron* (dial) nothing ‖ **Nix** *m* (-[e]s;-e) water sprite

Nixe ['nɪksə] *f* (-;-n) water nymph

nobel ['noːbəl] *adj* noble; elegant; (*freigebig*) generous

noch [nɔx] *adv* still, yet; even; else; **heute n.** this very day; **n. besser even bettter; n. dazu** over and above that; **n. einer** one more, still another; **n. einmal** once more; **n. einmal so viel** twice as much; **n. etwas** one more thing; **n. etwas?** anything else?; **n. heute** even today; **n. immer** still; **n. nicht** not yet; **n. nie** never before; **n. und n.** (coll) over and over; **sei es n. so klein** now matter how small it is; **was denn n. also?** what next? **wer kommt n.?** who else is coming?

noch′mal *adv* once more

nochmalig ['nɔxmaːlɪç] *adj* repeated

nochmals ['nɔxmals] *adv* once more

Nocke ['nɔkə] *f* (-;-n) (mach) cam

Nockenwelle (**Nok′kenwelle**) *f* camshaft

Nockerl ['nɔkərl] *n* (-s;- & -n) (Aust) dumpling

Nomade [noˈmaːdə] *m* (-n;-n) nomad

nominell [nomiˈnɛl] *adj* nominal

nominieren [nomiˈniːrən] *tr* nominate

Nonne ['nɔnə] *f* (-;-n) nun

Non′nenkloster *n* convent

Noppe ['nɔpə] *f* (-;-n) (tex) nap

Nord [nɔrt] *m* (-[e]s;) North; (poet) north wind

Norden ['nɔrdən] *m* (-s;) North; **im N. von** north of

nordisch ['nɔrdɪʃ] *adj* northern; (*Rasse*) Nordic; (*skandinavisch*) Norse

nördlich ['nœrtlɪç] *adj* northern

Nord′licht *n* northern lights

nordwärts ['nɔrtvɛrts] *adv* northward

Nörgelei [nœrɡəˈlaɪ] *f* (-;-en) griping

nörgelig ['nœrɡəlɪç] *adj* nagging

nörgeln ['nœrɡəln] *intr*—**n. an** (dat) gripe about, kick about

Norm [nɔrm] *f* (-;-en) norm, standard

normal [nɔrˈmaːl] *adj* normal, standard

normalisieren [nɔrmaliˈziːrən] *tr* normalize

Normal′zeit *f* standard time

Normanne [nɔrˈmanə] *m* (-n;-n) Norman

normen ['nɔrmən], **normieren** [nɔrˈmiːrən] *tr* normalize, standardize

Norwegen ['nɔrveːɡən] *n* (-s;) Norway

Norweger **-in** ['nɔrveːɡər(ɪn)] §6 *mf* Norwegian

norwegisch ['nɔrveːɡɪʃ] *adj* Norwegian

Not [noːt] *f* (-;ːe) need, want; (*Notlage*) necessity; (*Gefahr*) distress; (*Dringlichkeit*) emergency; **es hat keine Not** there's no hurry about it; **es tut not** it is necessary; **in der Not** in a pinch; **in Not geraten** fall upon hard times; **j—m große Not machen** give s.o. a lot of trouble; **j—m seine Not klagen** cry on s.o.'s shoulders; **mit knapper Not** narrowly; **mit Not** scarcely; **Not haben zu** (inf) be scarcely able to (inf); **Not leiden** suffer want; **ohne Not** needlessly; **seine liebe Not haben mit** have a lot of trouble with; **sie haben Not auszukommen** they have difficulty making ends meet; **zur Not** if need be, in a pinch

Nota ['noːta] *f* (-;-s) note; **etw in N. geben** place an order for s.th.; **etw in N. nehmen** make a note of s.th.

Notar **-in** [noˈtaːr(ɪn)] §8 *mf* notary public

Notariat [notaˈrjaːt] *n* (-[e]s;-e) notary office

notariell [notaˈrjɛl] *adv*—**n. beglaubigen** notarize

Not′ausgang *m* emergency exit

Not′ausstieg *m* escape hatch

Not′behelf *m* makeshift, stopgap

Not′bremse *f* (rr) emergency brake

Not′durft ['noːtdurft] *f* (-;) want; necessities of life; **seine N. verrichten** relieve oneself

not′dürftig *adj* scanty, poor; hard up; (*behelfsmäßig*) temporary

Note ['noːtə] *f* (-;-n) note; (*Banknote*) bill; (*Eigenart*) trait; (educ) mark; (mus) note; **in Noten setzen** set to music; **nach Noten** (fig) thoroughly; **persönliche Note** personal

touch; **wie nach Noten** like clock-work
No'tenblatt n sheet music
No'tenbuch n, **No'tenheft** n music book
No'tenlinie f (mus) line
No'tenschlüssel m (mus) clef
No'tenständer m music stand
No'tensystem n (mus) staff
Not'fall m emergency
notfalls ['nɔtfals] adv if necessary
notgedrungen ['nɔtgədrʊŋən] adj compulsory || adv of necessity
notieren [no'tirən] tr note down; jot down; (Preise) quote
Notie'rung f (-;-en) noting; (st. exch.) quotation
nötig ['nøtɪç] adj necessary; **das habe ich nicht n.!** I don't have to stand for that!; **n. haben** need
nötigen ['nøtɪgən] tr urge; (zwingen) force || ref—**lassen Sie sich nicht n.!** don't wait to be asked; **sich genötigt sehen zu** (inf) feel compelled to (inf)
nö'tigenfalls adv in case of need
Nö'tigung f (-;) compulsion; urgent request; (jur) duress
Notiz [no'tits] f (-;-en) notice; (Vermerk) note, memorandum; **keine N. nehmen von** take no notice of; **sich** [dat] **Notizen machen** jot down notes
Notiz'block m scratch pad
Not'lage f predicament; emergency
Not'landung f emergency landing
Not'lüge f white lie
Not'maßnahme f emergency measure
Not'nagel m (fig) stopgap
notorisch [nɔ'tɔrɪʃ] adj notorious
Not'pfennig m savings; **sich e-n N. aufsparen** save up for a rainy day
Not'ruf m (telp) emergency
Not'signal n distress signal
Not'stand m state of emergency
Not'standsgebiet n disaster area
Not'treppe f fire escape
Not'wehr f—**aus N.** in self-defense
notwendig ['nɔtvendɪç] adj necessary
Not'wendigkeit f (-;-en) necessity
Not'zeichen n distress signal
Not'zucht f rape
not'züchtigen tr rape, ravish
Nougat ['nugat] m & n (-s;-s) nougat
Novelle [nɔ'vɛlə] f (-;-n) short story; (parl) amendment, rider
November [nɔ'vɛmbər] m (-s;-) November
Novität [nɔvi'tɛt] f (-;-en) novelty
Novize [nɔ'vitsə] m (-n;-n), **Novizin** [nɔ'vitsɪn] f (-;-nen), novice
Noviziat [nɔvi'tsjat] n (-[e]s;-e) noviziate
Nu [nu] invar m—**im Nu** in a jiffy
Nuance [nY'ãsə] f (-;-n) nuance
nüchtern ['nyçtərn] adj fasting; not having had breakfast; (Magen) empty; (nicht betrunken) sober; (leidenschaftslos) cool; (geistlos) dull; (unsentimental) matter-of-fact
Nudel ['nudəl] f (-;-n) noodle; **e-e komische N.** (coll) a funny person
Nu'delholz n rolling pin

nudeln ['nudəln] tr force-feed
Nugat ['nugat] m (-s;-s) nougat
nuklear [nukle'ar] adj nuclear
Nukle·on ['nukle·ɔn] n (-s;-onen ['ɔnən]) nucleon
null [nʊl] adj null; **n. und nichtig** null and void; **n. und nichtig machen** annul || **Null** f (-;-en) naught; zero; (fig) nobody; **in N. Komma nichts** in less than no time, in no time
Null'punkt m zero; freezing point; **auf dem N. angekommen sein** hit bottom
Numera·le [nume'ralə] n (-s;-lien ljən] & -**lia** [lja]) numeral
numerieren [nume'rirən] tr number; **numerierten Platz** reserved seat
numerisch [nu'merɪʃ] adj numerical
Nummer ['nʊmər] f (-;-n) number; (Größe) size; (e-r Zeitung) issue; **auf N. Sicher sitzen** (sl) be in jail; **bei j-m e-e gute N. haben** (coll) be in good with s.o.; **e-e bloße N.** a mere figurehead; **er ist e-e N.!** he's quite a character; **laufende N.** serial number; **N. besetzt!** line is busy!
Num'mernfolge f numerical order
Num'mernscheibe f (telp) dial
Num'mernschild n (aut) license plate
nun [nʊn] adv now; now? well?; **nun aber** now; **nun also!** well now!; **nun gut!** all right then!; **nun und nimmer(mehr)** never more; **von nun ab** from now on; **wenn er nun käme?** what if he came?
nun'mehr' adv now; from now on
nur [nur] adv only, merely, but; (lauter) nothing but; **nicht nur ... sondern auch** not only ... but also; **nur daß** except that; **nur eben** scarcely; (zeitlich) a moment ago; **nur zu!** go to it!; **wenn nur** if only, provided that
Nürnberg ['nYrnberk] n (-s;) Nuremberg
nuscheln ['nuʃəln] intr (coll) mumble
Nuß [nʊs] f (-; Nüsse) nut
nuß'braun adj nut-brown; (Augen) hazel
Nuß'kern m kernel
Nußknacker ['nusknakər] m (-s;-) nutcracker
Nuß'schale f nutshell
Nüster ['nystər] f (-;-n) nostril
Nut [nut] f (-;-en), **Nute** ['nutə] f (-;-n) groove, rabbet
Nutte ['nutə] f (-;-n) whore
nutz [nuts] adj useful; **zu nichts n. sein** be good for nothing || **Nutz** m (-es;) use; benefit; profit; **zu j-s N. und Frommen** for s.o.'s benefit
Nutz'anwendung f utilization
nutzbar ['nutsbar] adj useful; **sich** [dat] **etw n. machen** utilize s.th.
nutz'bringend adj useful, profitable
nütze ['nYtsə] adj useful; **nichts n. of** no use; **zu nichts n. sein** be good for nothing
Nutz'effekt m efficiency
nutzen ['nutsən], **nützen** ['nYtsən] tr make use of; **das kann mir viel (wenig, nichts) n.** this can do me much (little, no) good; **was nützt das**

alles? what's the good of all this? ‖ *intr* do good ‖ *impers—es nützt nichts* it's no use ‖ **Nutzen** *m* (-s;-) use; benefit; (*Gewinn*) profit; (*Vorteil*) advantage; **von N. sein** be of use

Nutz'fahrzeug *n* commercial vehicle

Nutz'garten *m* vegetable garden

Nutz'holz *n* lumber

Nutz'leistung *f* (mech) output

nützlich ['nʏtslɪç] *adj* useful

nutz'los *adj* useless

Nutz'losigkeit *f* (-;) uselessness

Nutz'schwelle *f* break-even point

Nut'zung *f* (-;) use

Nylon ['naɪlɔn] *n* (-s;) nylon

Nymphe ['nʏmfə] *f* (-;-n) nymph

Nymphomanin [nʏmfo'manɪn] *f* (-; -nen) nymphomaniac

O

O, o [o] *invar n* O, o

Oase [ɔ'azə] *f* (-;-n) oasis

ob [ɔp] *prep* (*dat*) above; (*genit*) on account of ‖ *conj* whether; **als ob** as if; **na ob!** rather!; **und ob!** and how!

Obacht ['obaxt] *f* (-;)—**in O. nehmen** take care of; **O.!** watch out!; **O. geben auf** (*acc*) pay attention to; take care of

Obdach ['ɔpdax] *n* (-[e]s;) shelter

ob'dachlos *adj* homeless

Obduktion [ɔpduk'tsjon] *f* (-;-en) autopsy

obduzieren [ɔpdu'tsirən] *tr* perform an autopsy on

O—Beine ['obaɪnə] *pl* bow legs

O'-beinig *adj* bowlegged

Obelisk [obe'lɪsk] *m* (-en;-en) obelisk

oben ['obən] *adv* above; (*in der Höhe*) up; (*im Himmelsraum*) on high; (*im Hause*) upstairs; (*auf der Spitze*) at the top; (*auf der Oberfläche*) on the surface; (*Aufschrift auf Kisten*) this side up; **da o.** up there; **nach o. gehen** go up, go upstairs; **o. am Tische sitzen** sit at the head of the table; **o. auf** (*dat*) at the top of, on the top of; **von o.** from above; **von o. bis unten** from top to bottom; from head to foot; **von o. herab** (fig) condescendingly; **wie o. angegeben** as stated above

obenan' *adv* at the top, at the head

obenauf' *adv* on top; **immer o. sein** be always in top spirits

obendrein [obən'draɪn] *adv* on top of it, into the bargain

o'benerwähnt, o'bengenannt *adj* above-mentioned

o'bengesteuert *adj* (aut) overhead

obenhin' *adv* superficially; perfunctorily

obenhinaus' *adv*—**o. wollen** have big ideas

o'ben-oh'ne *adj* (coll) topless

o'benstehend *adj* given above

Ober ['obər] *m* (-s;-) (coll) waiter; **Herr O.!** waiter!

Ober- *comb.fm.* upper, higher; superior; chief, supreme, head; southern

O'berägypten *n* Upper Egypt

O'berarm *m* upper arm

O'beraufseher *m* inspector general; superintendent

O'beraufsicht *f* superintendence

O'berbau *m* (-[e]s;-ten) superstructure

O'berbefehl *m* supreme command; **O. führen** have supreme command

O'berbefehlshaber *m* commander in chief

O'berbegriff *m* wider concept

O'berdeck *n* upper deck

O'berdeckomnibus *m* double-decker bus

o'berdeutsch *adj* of southern Germany

obere ['obərə] §9 *adj* higher, upper; chief, superior; supreme ‖ **Obere** §5 *m* (eccl) father superior ‖ *n* top

O'berfaul *adj* (fig) fishy

O'berfeldwebel *m* sergeant first class

O'berfläche *f* surface

o'berflächlich *adj* superficial

O'bergefreite §5 *m* corporal

O'bergeschoß *n* upper floor

O'bergewalt *f* supreme authority

o'berhalb *prep* (*genit*) above

O'berhand *f* (fig) upper hand; **die O. gewinnen über** (*acc*) get the better of

O'berhaupt *n* head, chief

O'berhaus *n* upper house

O'berhaut *f* epidermis

O'berhemd *n* shirt, dress shirt

O'berherr *m* sovereign

O'berherrschaft *f* sovereignty; supremacy

O'berhirte *m* prelate

O'berhofmeister *m* Lord Chamberlain

O'berhoheit *f* supreme authority

Oberin ['obərɪn] *f* (-;-nen) mother superior; (med) head nurse

O'beringenieur *m* chief engineer

o'berirdisch *adj* above-ground; overhead

O'berkellner *m* head waiter

O'berkiefer *m* upper jaw

O'berkleidung *f* outer wear

O'berkommando *n* general headquarters

O'berkörper *m* upper part of the body

O'berland *n* highlands

Oberländer -in ['obərlɛndər(ɪn)] §6 *mf* highlander

o'berlastig *adj* top-heavy

O'berleder *n* uppers

O'berlehrer -in §6 *mf* secondary school teacher, high school teacher

O'berleitung *f* supervision; (elec) overhead line (*of trolley, etc.*)

O'berleutnant *m* first lieutenant

O'berlicht n skylight
O'berliga f (sport) upper division
O'berlippe f upper lip
O'berpostamt n general post office
O'berprima f senior class
Obers ['obərs] m (-;) (Aust) cream
O'berschenkel m thigh
O'berschicht f upper layer; (der Bevölkerung) upper classes; geistige O. intelligentsia
O'berschule f high school
O'berschwester f (med) head nurse
O'berseite f topside, right side
Oberst ['obərst] m (-en;-en) colonel
O'berstaatsanwalt m attorney general
oberste ['obərstə] §9 adj (super of obere) uppermost, highest, top ‖ Oberste §5 mf senior, chief
O'berstimme f treble, soprano
O'berstleutnant m lieutenant colonel
O'berstock m upper floor
O'berwasser n—O. haben (fig) have the upper hand
O'berwelt f upper world
O'berwerk n upper manual (of organ)
obgleich' conj though, although
Ob'hut f (-;) care, protection
obig ['obɪç] adj above, above-mentioned
Objekt [ɔp'jɛkt] n (-[e]s;-e) object
objektiv [ɔpjɛk'tif] adj objective; (unparteiisch) impartial ‖ Objektiv n (-s;-e) objective lens
Objektivität [ɔpjɛktivi'tɛt] f (-;) objectivity; impartiality
Objekt'träger m slide (of microscope)
Oblate [ɔ'blatə] f (-;-n) wafer; (eccl) host
obliegen [ɔp'ligən] §108 intr (dat) apply oneself to, devote oneself to; (dat) be incumbent upon ‖ impers—es obliegt mir zu (inf) it's up to me to (inf)
Ob'liegenheit f (-;-en) obligation
obligat [ɔblɪ'gat] adj obligatory; (unerläßlich) indispensable; (unvermeidlich) inevitable
Obligation [ɔblɪga'tsjon] f (-;-en) bond; obligation
obligatorisch [ɔblɪga'torɪʃ] adj obligatory
Ob·mann ['ɔpman] m (-[e]s;⁼er & -leute) chairman; (jur) foreman
Oboe [o'bo·ə] f (-;-n) oboe
Obrigkeit ['obrɪçkaɪt] f (-;-en) authority; (coll) authorities
o'brigkeitlich adj government(al)
obschon' conj though, although
Observato·rium [ɔpzɛrva'torjum] n (-s;-rien) [rjən] observatory
obsiegen ['ɔpzigən] intr be victorious; (dat) triumph over
obskur [ɔps'kur] adj obscure
Obst [ɔpst] n (-es;) (certain kinds of) fruit (mainly central-European, e.g., apples, plums; but not bananas, oranges); O. und Südfrüchte European and (sub)tropical fruit
Obst'garten m orchard
Obst'kern m stone; seed, pip
Obstruktion [ɔpstruk'tsjon] f (-;-en) obstruction; (pol) filibuster; O. treiben filibuster

obszön [ɔps'tsøn] adj obscene
Obszönität [ɔpstsønɪ'tɛt] f (-;-en) obscenity
ob'walten, obwal'ten intr exist; prevail; hold sway
obwohl' conj though, although
Ochse ['ɔksə] m (-n;-n) ox
ochsen ['ɔksən] intr (educ) cram
O'chsenfleisch n beef
O'chsenfrosch m bullfrog
öde ['ødə] adj bleak ‖ Öde f (-;-n) wasteland; (fig) bleakness
Ödem [ø'dem] n (-s;-e) edema
oder ['odər] conj or
Öd·land ['øtlant] n (-[e]s;-ländereien [lɛndə'raɪ·ən]) wasteland
Ofen ['ofən] m (-s;⁼) stove; (Back-) oven; (Hoch-) furnace; (Brenn-, Dürr-) kiln
O'fenklappe f damper
O'fenrohr n stovepipe
O'fenröhre f warming oven
offen ['ɔfən] adj open; (öffentlich) public; (fig) frank, open
offenbar ['ɔfənbar] adj obvious, manifest
offenbaren [ɔfən'barən] tr reveal
Offenba'rung f (-;-en) revelation
Of'fenheit f (-;) openness
of'fenherzig adj forthright; (Kleid) (hum) low-cut
of'fenkundig adj well-known; (offensichtlich) obvious; (Beweis) clear
of'fensichtlich adj obvious
offensiv [ɔfɛn'zif] adj offensive ‖ Offensive [ɔfɛn'zivə] f (-;-n) offensive
öffentlich ['œfəntlɪç] adj public; (Dienst) civil; öffentliches Haus brothel
Öf'fentlichkeit f (-;) public; publicity; an die Ö. treten appear in public; im Licht der Ö. in the limelight; in aller Ö. in public; sich in die Ö. flüchten rush into print
offerieren [ɔfə'rirən] tr offer
Offerte [ɔ'fɛrtə] f (-;-n) offer
Offerto·rium [ɔfɛr'torjum] n (-s;-rien [rjən]) offertory
Offiziant [ɔfɪ'tsjant] m (-en;-en) officiating priest
offiziell [ɔfɪ'tsjɛl] adj official
Offizier –in [ɔfɪ'tsir(ɪn)] §6 mf officer
Offiziers'anwärter –in §6 mf officer candidate
Offiziers'bursche m orderly
Offiziers'deck n quarter deck
Offiziers'kasino n officers' club
Offiziers'patent n officer's commission
Offizin [ɔfɪ'tsin] f (-;-en) drugstore; (Druckerei) print shop, press
offiziös [ɔfɪ'tsjøs] adj semiofficial
öffnen ['œfnən] tr & ref open
Öff'ner m (-s;-) opener
Öff'nung f (-;-en) opening
oft [ɔft], öfter(s) ['œftər(s)] adv often
oftmals ['ɔftmals] adv often(times)
oh [o] interj oh!, O!
Oheim ['ohaɪm] m (-s;-e) uncle
Ohm [om] m (-s;-e) (poet) uncle ‖ n (-s;-) (elec) ohm
ohne ['onə] prep (acc) without; o. daß (ind) without (ger); o. mich! count

me out!; **o. weiteres** right off; **o. zu**
(*inf*) without (*ger*)

ohnedies' *adv* anyhow, in any case

ohneglei'chen *adj* unequaled

ohnehin' *adv* anyhow, as it is

Ohnmacht ['onmaxt] *f* (-;) faint, un-
consciousness; helplessness; **in O.
fallen** (or **sinken**) faint, pass out

ohnmächtig ['onmeçtıç] *adj* unconscious; helpless; **o. werden** faint

Ohr [or] *n* (-[e]s;-en) ear; (*im Buch*)
dog-ear; **die Ohren spitzen** prick up
the ears; **es dick hinter den Ohren
haben be sly; ganz Ohr sein** be all
ears; **j—m in den Ohren liegen** keep
dinning it into s.o.'s ears; **j—n hinter
die Ohren hauen** box s.o.'s ears; **j—n
übers Ohr hauen** cheat s.o.; **sich aufs
Ohr legen** take a nap; **zum e—n Ohr
hinein, zum anderen wieder hinaus**
in one ear and out the other

Öhr [ør] *n* (-[e]s;-e) eye (*of needle*);
ax hole, hammer hole

ohrenbetäubend *adj* earsplitting

Oh'renklingen *n* ringing in the ears

Oh'rensausen *n* buzzing in the ear

Oh'renschmalz *n* earwax

Oh'renschmaus *m* treat for the ears

Ohrenschützer *m* earmuff

Ohr'feige *f* (-;-n) box on the ear

ohrfeigen ['orfaıgən] *tr* box on the ear

Ohrläppchen ['orlɛpçən] *n* (-s;-) ear-
lobe

Ohr'muschel *f* auricle

okkult [ɔ'kult] *adj* occult

Ökologie [økɔlo'gi] *f* (-;) ecology

ökologisch [økɔ'logıʃ] *adj* ecological

Ökonom [øko'nom] *m* (-en;-en) economist

Ökono•mie [økənɔ'mi] (-;-mien ['mi-
ən]) economy; economics

ökonomisch [øko'nomıʃ] *adj* economical

Oktav [ɔk'taf] *n* (-s;-e) octavo

Oktave [ɔk'tavə] *f* (-;-n) octave

Oktober [ɔk'tobər] *m* (-s;-) October

oktroyieren [ɔktrwa'jirən] *tr* impose

Okular [ɔku'lar] *n* (-s;-e) eyepiece

okulieren [ɔku'lirən] *tr* inoculate

Ökumene [øku'menə] *f* (-;) ecume-
nism

ökumenisch [øku'menıʃ] *adj* ecumeni-
cal

Okzident ['ɔktsıdɛnt] *m* (-s;) Occident

Öl [øl] *n* (-[e]s;-e) oil; **Öl ins Feuer
gießen** (fig) add fuel to the fire

Öl'baum *m* olive tree

Öl'berg *m* Mount of Olives

ölen ['ølən] *tr* oil; (mach) lubricate

Öl'heizung *f* oil heat

ölig ['ølıç] *adj* oily

Oligar•chie [ɔligar'çi] *f* (-;-chien
['çi-ən]) oligarchy

Olive [ɔ'livə] *f* (-;-n) olive

Oli'venöl *n* olive oil

Öl'leitung *f* pipeline

Öl'quelle *f* oil well

Öl'schlick *m* oil slick

Öl'stand *m* (aut) oil level

Öl'standanzeiger *m* oil gauge

Öl'standmesser *m* (aut) oil gauge; dip
stick

Öl'lung *f* (-;-en) oiling; anointing; **die
Letzte Ö.** extreme unction

Olymp [ɔ'lymp] *m* (-s;) Mt. Olympus

Olmypiade [ɔlym'pjadə] *f* (-;-n) olympiad

olympisch [ɔ'lympıʃ] *adj* Olympian;
Olympic; **die Olympischen Spiele** the
Olympics

Öl'zweig *m* olive branch

Oma ['oma] *f* (-;-s) (coll) grandma

Omelett [ɔm(ə)'lɛt] *n* (-[e]s;-e & -s)
omelette

O•men ['omen] *n* (-s;-mina [mına])
omen

ominös [ɔmı'nøs] *adj* ominous

Omnibus ['ɔmnıbus] *m* (ses;-se) bus

Onanie [ona'ni] *f* (-;) masturbation

ondulieren [ɔndu'lirən] *tr* (*Haar*) wave

Onkel ['ɔŋkəl] *m* (-s;- & -s) uncle;
der große O. (coll) the big toe

Opa ['opa] *m* (-s;-s) (coll) grandpa

Oper ['opər] *f* (-;-n) opera

Operateur [ɔpera'tør] *m* (-s;-s) operator; (cin) projectionist; (surg) operating surgeon

Operation [ɔpera'tsjon] *f* (-;-en) operation

Operations'gebiet *n* theater of operations

Operations'saal *m* operating room

operativ [ɔpera'tif] *adj* surgical; operational, strategic

operieren [ɔpe'rirən] *tr* operate on;
sich o. lassen undergo an operation

O'pernglas *n*, **O'perngucker** *m* opera
glasses

O'pernhaus *n* opera house, opera

Opfer ['ɔpfər] *n* (-s;-) sacrifice; victim; **zum O. fallen** (*dat*) fall victim
to

op'ferfreudig *adj* self-sacrificing

Op'fergabe *f* offering

Op'ferkasten *m* poor box

Op'ferlamm *n* sacrificial lamb; **Lamb
of God**; (fig) victim

opfern ['ɔpfərn] *tr* sacrifice, offer up

Op'ferstock *m* poor box

Op'fertier *n* victim

Op'fertod *m* sacrifice of one's life

Op'fertrank *m* libation

Op'ferung *f* (-;-en) offering, sacrifice

op'ferwillig *adj* willing to make sacri-
fices

opponieren [ɔpo'nirən] *intr* (*dat*) oppose

opportun [ɔpɔr'tun] *adj* opportune

optieren [ɔp'tirən] *intr*—**o. für** opt for

Optik ['ɔptık] *f* (-;) optics

Optiker **-in** ['ɔptıkər(ın)] §6 *mf* optician

optimistisch [ɔptı'mıstıʃ] *adj* optimistic

optisch ['ɔptıʃ] *adj* optic(al)

Orakel [ɔ'rakəl] *n* (-s;-) oracle

ora'kelhaft *adj* oracular

orange [ɔ'rã:ʒə] *adj* orange || **Orange**
f (-;-n) orange

oran'genfarben, oran'genfarbig *adj* or-
ange-colored

oratorisch [ora'torıʃ] *adj* oratorical

Orchester [ɔr'kɛstər] n (-s;-) orches-tra

orchestral [ɔrçɛs'tral] adj orchestral

orchestrieren [ɔrkɛs'triːrən] tr orches-trate

Orchidee [ɔrçɪ'deːə] f (-;-n) orchid

Orden ['ɔrdən] m (-s;-) medal, deco-ration; (eccl) order

Or'densband n (-[e]s;⸚er) ribbon

Or'densbruder m monk, friar

Or'denskleid n (eccl) habit

Or'densschwester f nun, sister

ordentlich ['ɔrdəntlɪç] adj orderly; (aufgeräumt) tidy; (anständig) de-cent, respectable; (regelrecht) regu-lar; (tüchtig) sound; (Frühstück) solid; (Mitglied) active; (Professor) full; **e-e ordentliche Leistung** a pretty good job; **in ordentlichem Zustand** in good condition || adv thoroughly, properly; (sehr) awfully, very; really

Order ['ɔrdər] f (-;-n) (com, mil) order

ordinär [ɔrdɪ'nɛr] adj ordinary; vul-gar; rude

Ordina·rius [ɔrdɪ'narjʊs] m (-;-rien [rjən]) professor; (eccl) ordinary

Ordinär'preis m retail price

ordinieren [ɔrdɪ'niːrən] tr ordain || intr (med) have office hours

ordnen ['ɔrdnən] tr arrange; (regeln) put in order; (säubern) tidy up

Ord'nung f (-;-en) order, arrangement; classification; system; class; rank; regulation; (mil) formation; **aus der O. bringen** disturb; **in bester O.** in tiptop shape; **in O. bringen** set in order; **in O. sein** be all right; **nicht in O. sein** be out of order; be wrong; be out of sorts

ord'nungsgemäß adv duly

Ord'nungsliebe f tidiness, orderliness

ord'nungsmäßig adj orderly, regular || adv duly

Ord'nungsruf m (parl) call to order

Ord'nungssinn m sense of order

Ord'nungsstrafe f fine

ord'nungswidrig adj irregular, illegal

Ord'nungszahl f ordinal number

Ordonnanz [ɔrdɔ'nants] f (-;-en) (mil) orderly

Organ [ɔr'gan] n (-s;-e) organ

Organisation [ɔrganiza'tsjon] f (-;-en) organization

organisch [ɔr'ganɪʃ] adj organic; (Ge-webe) structural || adv organically

organisieren [ɔrganɪ'ziːrən] tr organize; (mil) scrounge || ref unionize; **or-ganisierter Arbeiter** union worker

Organis·mus [ɔrga'nɪsmʊs] m (-;-men [mən]) organism

Organist **-in** [ɔrga'nɪst(ɪn)] §7 mf organist

Orgas·mus [ɔr'gasmʊs] m (-;-men [mən]) orgasm

Orgel ['ɔrgəl] f (-;-n) organ

Or'gelzug m organ stop

Orgie ['ɔrgjə] f (-;-n) orgy

Orient ['ɔrjɛnt] m (-s;) Orient

Orientale [ɔrjɛn'talə] m (-n;-n) Ori-entalin [ɔrjɛn'talɪn] f (-;-nen) Ori-ental

orientalisch [ɔrjɛn'talɪʃ] adj oriental

orientieren [ɔrjɛn'tirən] tr orient; (fig) inform, instruct; (mil) brief

Orientie'rung f (-;-en) orientation; in-formation, instruction; **die O. ver-lieren** lose one's bearings

Orientie'rungssinn m sense of direction

original [ɔrigi'nal] adj original || **Original** n (-s;-e) original; (typ) copy

Original'ausgabe f first edition

Originalität [ɔriginalɪ'tet] f (-;) orig-inality

Original'sendung f live broadcast

originell [ɔrigi'nɛl] adj original

Orkan [ɔr'kan] m (-[e]s;-e) hurricane

Ornament [ɔrna'mɛnt] n (-[e]s;-e) ornament

Ornat [ɔr'nat] m (-[e]s;-e) robes

Ort [ɔrt] m (-[e]s;-e) place, spot; (Örtlichkeit) locality; (Dorf) village; **am Ort sein** be appropriate; **an allen Orten** everywhere; **an Ort und Stelle** on the spot; **an Ort und Stelle gelangen** reach one's destination; **höheren Ortes** at higher levels; **Ort der Handlung** scene of action; **vor Ort** on location; **vor Ort arbeiten** (min) work at the face || m (-[e]s;⸚er) position, locus

Örtchen ['œrtçən] n (-s;-) toilet

orten ['ɔrtən] tr get the bearing on, locate || intr take a bearing

orthodox [ɔrto'dɔks] adj orthodox

Orthographie [ɔrtogra'fi] f (-;) orthog-raphy

Orthopäde [ɔrto'pɛdə] m (-n;-n), **Orthopädin** [ɔrto'pɛdɪn] f (-;-nen) orthopedist

orthopädisch [ɔrto'pɛdɪʃ] adj ortho-pedic

örtlich ['œrtlɪç] adj local, topical

Ört'lichkeit f (-;-en) locality

Orts-, orts- [ɔrts] comb.fm. local

Orts'amt n (telp) local exchange

Orts'angabe f address

orts'ansässig adj resident || **Ortsan-sässige §5** mf resident

Orts'behörde f local authorities

Orts'beschreibung f topography

Ort'schaft f (-;-en) place; (Dorf) vil-lage

orts'fremd adj nonlocal, out-of-town

Orts'gespräch n (telp) local call

Orts'kenntnis f familiarity with a place

orts'kundig adj familiar with the lo-cality

Orts'name m place name

Orts'sinn m sense of direction

Orts'veränderung f change of scenery

Orts'verkehr m local traffic

Orts'zeit f local time

Orts'zustellung f local delivery

Or'tung f (-;-en) (aer, naut) taking of bearings, navigation

Öse ['øzə] f (-;-n) loop, eye; (des Schuhes) eyelet

Ost [ɔst] m (-es;-e) East; (poet) east wind

Ost- comb.fm. eastern, East

Osten ['ɔstən] m (-s;) East; **der Ferne O.** the Far East; **der Nahe O.** the Near East; **nach O.** eastward

ostentativ [ɔstenta'tif] adj ostentatious

Oster– ['ostər] *comb.fm.* Easter
O'sterei *n* Easter egg
O'sterfest *n* Easter
O'sterhase *m* Easter bunny
O'sterlamm *m* paschal lamb
Ostern ['ostərn] *n* (–;–) & *pl* Easter
Österreich ['østəraıç] *n* (–;) Austria
Österreicher **–in** ['østəraıçər(ın)] §6 *mf* Austrian
österreichisch ['østəraıçıʃ] *adj* Austrian
O'sterzeit *f* Eastertide
Ost'front *f* eastern front
Ost'gote *m* Ostrogoth
östlich ['œstlıç] *adj* eastern, easterly; Oriental; **ö.** von east of
Ost'mark *f* East-German mark
Ost'see *f* Baltic Sea
ostwärts ['ostverts] *adv* eastward

Otter ['ɔtər] *m* (–s;–) otter ‖ *f* (–;–n) (*Schlange*) adder
Ouvertüre [uver'tyrə] *f* (–;–n) (mus) overture
oval [ɔ'val] *adj* oval ‖ **Oval** *n* (–s;–e) oval
Ovar [ɔ'var] *n* (–s;–e & –ien [jən]) ovary
Overall ['ovərol] *m* (–s;–s) overalls
Oxyd [ɔ'ksyt] *n* (–[e]s;–e) oxide
Oxydation [ɔksyda'tsjon] *f* (–;) oxidation
oxydieren [ɔksy'dirən] *tr* & *intr* (SEIN) oxidize
Ozean ['otse.an] *m* (–s;–e) ocean; **der Große** (or **Stille) O.** the Pacific
Ozeanographie [otse.anogra'fi] *f* (–;) oceanography
Ozon [ɔ'tson] *n* (–s;) ozone

P

P, p [pe] *invar n* P, p
paar [par] *adj* even ‖ *invar adj*—**ein p.** a couple of, a few ‖ **Paar** *n* (–[e]s;–e) pair, couple; **zu Paaren treiben** rout
paaren ['parən] *tr* match, mate ‖ *ref* mate
paarig ['parıç] *adj* in pairs
paar'laufen §105 *intr* (SEIN) skate as a couple
paar'mal *adv*—**ein p.** a couple of times
Paa'rung *f* (–;) pairing, matching; (*Begattung*) mating
Paa'rungszeit *f* mating season
paar'weise *adv* in pairs, two by two
Pacht [paxt] *f* (–;–en) lease; (*Geld*) rent; **in P. geben** lease out; **in P. nehmen** lease, rent
Pacht'brief *m* lease
pachten ['paxtən] *tr* take a lease on
Pächter **–in** ['pɛçtər(ın)] §6 *mf* tenant
Pacht'ertrag *m*, **Pacht'geld** *n* rent
Pacht'gut *n*, **Pacht'hof** *m* leased farm
Pacht'kontrakt *m* lease
Pach'tung *f* (–;–en) leasing; leasehold
Pacht'vertrag *m* lease
Pacht'zeit *f* term of lease
Pacht'zins *m* rent
Pack [pak] *m* (–[e]s;–e & ⸚e) pack; (*Paket*) parcel; (*Ballen*) bale; **ein P. Spielkarten** a pack of cards ‖ *n* (–[e]s;) rabble; **ein P. von Lügnern** a pack of liars
Päckchen ['pɛkçən] *n* (–s;–) small package; (*Zigaretten*–) pack
packen ['pakən] *tr* pack, pack up; (*fassen*) seize, grab; (fig) grip, thrill; **pack dich!** scram! ‖ **Packen** *m* (–s;–) pack; (*Ballen*) bale ‖ *n* (–s;) packing
Pack'esel *m* (fig) drudge
Pack'papier *n* wrapping paper
Pack'pferd *n* packhorse
Pack'tier *n* pack animal
Packung (Pak'kung) *f* (–;–en) packing; (*Paket*) packet; **P. Zigaretten** pack of cigarettes

Pack'wagen *m* (rr) baggage car
Pädadoge [peda'gogə] *m* (–n;–n) pedagogue
Pädagogik [peda'gogık] *f* (–;) pedagogy
pädagogisch [peda'gogıʃ] *adj* pedagogical, educational
Paddel ['padəl] *n* (–s;–) paddle
Pad'delboot *n* canoe
paddeln ['padəln] *intr* paddle, canoe
Pädiatrie [pedi·a'tri] *f* (–;) pediatrics
paff [paf] *interj* bang!
paffen ['pafən] *tr* & *intr* puff
Page ['paʒə] *m* (–n;–n) page
Pa'genfrisur *f*, **Pa'genkopf** *m* pageboy
Pagode [pa'godə] *f* (–;–n) pagoda
Pair [per] *m* (–s;–s) peer
Pak [pak] *f* (–; & –s) (Panzerabwehrkanone) antitank gun
Paket [pa'ket] *n* (–[e]s;–e) parcel; (*Bücher–, Post–*) bundle
Paket'adresse *f* gummed label
Paket'post *f* parcel post
Pakt [pakt] *m* (–[e]s;–e) pact
paktieren [pak'tirən] *intr* make a pact
Paläontologie [pale.ontolo'gi] *f* (–;) paleontology
Palast [pa'last] *m* (–es;⸚e) palace
palast'artig *adj* palatial
Palästina [pale'stina] *n* (–s;) Palestine
Palette [pa'letə] *f* (–;–n) palette
Palisade [palı'zadə] *f* (–;–n) palisade
Palme ['palmə] *f* (–;–n) palm tree; palm branch; **j–n auf die P. bringen** (coll) drive s.o. up the wall
Palm'wedel *m*, **Palm'zweig** *m* palm branch
Pampelmuse ['pampəlmuzə] *f* (–;–n) grapefruit
Pamphlet [pam'flet] *n* (–[e]s;–e) lampoon
Panama ['panama] *n* (–s;) Panama
Paneel [pa'nel] *n* (–s;–e) panel
paneelieren [pane'lirən] *tr* panel
Panier [pa'nir] *n* (–s;–e) slogan
panieren [pa'nirən] *tr* (culin) bread

Panik ['pɑnɪk] f (-;) panic
panisch ['pɑnɪʃ] adj panic-stricken
Panne ['panə] f (-;-n) breakdown;
(Reifenpanne) blowout; (fig) mishap
Panora·ma [panə'rɑma] n (-s;-men
[mən]) panorama
panschen ['panʃən] tr adulterate, water
down || intr splash about; mix
Panther ['pantər] m (-s;-) panther
Pantine [pan'tinə] f (-;-n) clog
Pantoffel [pan'tɔfəl] m (-s;-n) slipper;
unter dem P. stehen be henpecked
Pantof'felheld m henpecked husband
Panzer ['pantsər] m (-s;-) armor; ar-
mor plating; (mil) tank; (zool) shell
Pan'zerabwehrkanone f antitank gun
pan'zerbrechend adj armor-piercing
Pan'zerfalle f tank trap
Pan'zerfaust f bazooka
Pan'zergeschoß n, Pan'zergranate f
armor-piercing shell
Pan'zerhandschuh m gauntlet
Pan'zerhemd n coat of mail
Pan'zerkreuzer m battle cruiser
panzern ['pantsərn] tr armor || ref
arm oneself
Pan'zerschrank m safe
Panzerspähwagen ['pantsər/pevagən]
m (mil) armored car
Pan'zersperre f antitank obstacle
Pan'zerung f (-;-en) armor plating
Pan'zerwagen m armored car
Papagei [papa'gaɪ] m (-en;-en) &
(-[e]s;-e) parrot
Papier [pa'pir] n (-[e]s;-e) paper
Papier'bogen m sheet of paper
Papier'brei m paper pulp
papieren [pa'pirən] adj paper
Papier'fabrik f paper mill
Papier'format n size of paper
Papier'korb m wastebasket
Papier'krieg m (fig) red tape
Papier'mühle f paper mill
Papier'schlange f paper streamer
Papier'tüte f paper bag
Papier'waren pl stationery
Papp [pap] m (-[e]s;-e) (Brei) pap;
(Kleister) paste
Papp- [pap] comb.fm. sticky; card-
board
Papp'band m (-[e]s;-e) paperback
Papp'deckel m piece of cardboard
Pappe ['papə] f (-;) cardboard
Pappel ['papəl] f (-;-n) poplar
päppeln ['pepəln] tr feed lovingly
pappen ['papən] tr paste, glue || intr
stick
Pap'penstiel m (coll) trifle; das ist
keinen P. wert (coll) this isn't worth
a thing
papperlapapp [papərla'pap] interj non-
sense!
pap'pig adj sticky
Papp'karton m, Papp'schachtel f card-
board box, cardboard carton
Papp'schnee m sticky snow (for skiing)
Paprika ['paprɪka] m (-s;) paprika
Pap'rikaschote f (green) pepper
Papst [papst] m (-es;-̈e) pope
päpstlich ['pepstlɪç] adj papal
Papsttum ['papsttum] n (-s;) papacy
Papy·rus [pa'pyrus] m (-;-ri) [rɪ])
papyrus

Parabel [pa'rabəl] f (-;-n) parable;
(geom) parabola
Parade [pa'radə] f (-;-n) parade;
(fencing) parry; (mil) review; (fb)
save
Para'deanzug m (mil) dress uniform
Paradeiser [para'daɪzər] m (-s;-)
(Aust) tomato
Para'depferd n (fig) show-off
Para'deplatz m parade ground
Para'deschritt m goose step
paradieren [para'dirən] intr parade;
(fig) show off
Paradies [para'dis] n (-es;-e) paradise
Paradies'apfel m tomato
paradox [para'dɔks] adj paradoxical ||
Paradox n (-es;-e) paradox
Paraffin [para'fin] n (-s;-e) paraffin
Paragraph [para'grɑf] m (-en & -s;
-en) paragraph; (jur) section
parallel [para'lel] adj parallel || Paral-
lele f (-;-n) parallel
Paralyse [para'lyzə] f (-;-n) paralysis
paralysieren [paraly'zirən] tr paralyze
Paralytiker -in [para'lytɪkər(ɪn)] §6
mf paralytic
Paranuß ['paranus] f Brazil nut
Parasit [para'zit] m (-en;-en) parasite
parat [pa'rɑt] adj ready
Pardon [par'dɔ̃] m (-s;) pardon; kei-
nen P. geben (mil) given no quarter
Parenthese [paren'tezə] f (-;-n) parenthesis
Parfüm [par'fym] n (-[e]s;-e) perfume
Parfüme·rie [parfymə'ri] f (-;-rien
['ri·ən]) perfume shop
parfümieren [parfy'mirən] tr perfume
pari ['pari] adv at par || Pari m (-
[s];) par; auf P. at par
Paria ['parja] m (-s;-s) pariah
parieren [pa'rirən] tr (Pferd) rein in;
(Hieb) parry || intr (dat) obey
Pa'rikurs m (com) parity
Paris [pa'ris] n (-;) Paris
Pariser -in [pa'rizər(ɪn)] §6 mf Pari-
sian
Parität [parɪ'tet] f (-;) equality; (fin,
st. exch.) parity
paritätisch [parɪ'tetɪʃ] adj on a footing of equality
Park [park] m (-s;-s & -e) park
Park'anlage f park; Parkanlagen
grounds
parken ['parkən] tr & intr park
Parkett [par'ket] n (-[e]s;-e) (Fußboden) parquet; (theat) parquet
Parkett'fußboden m parquet flooring
Park'licht n parking light
Park'platz m parking lot
Park'platzwärter m parking lot attendant
Park'uhr f parking meter
Parlament [parla'ment] n (-[e]s;-e)
parliament
Parlamentär [parlamen'ter] m (-s;-e)
truce negotiator
parlamentarisch [parlamen'tɑrɪʃ] adj
parliamentary
parlamentieren [parlamen'tirən] intr
(coll) parley
Paro·die [parə'di] f (-;-dien ['di·ən])
parody
parodieren [parə'dirən] tr parody

Parole [pa'rolə] *f* (-;-n) (mil) password; (pol) slogan

Partei [par'taɪ] *f* (-;-en) party; (*Mieter*) tenant(s); (jur, pol) party; (sport) side; j-s P. ergreifen or P. nehmen für j-n side with s.o.

Partei'bonze *m* (pol) party boss

Partei'gänger –in §6 *mf* (pol) party sympathizer

Partei'genosse *m*, **Partei'genossin** *f* party member

Partei'grundsatz *m* party plank

parteiisch [par'taɪɪʃ] *adj* partial, biased; (pol) partisan

partei'lich *adj* partisan

Partei'lichkeit *f* (-;) partiality

partei'los *adj* (pol) independent ‖ **Parteilose** §5 *mf* independent

Partei'losigkeit *f* (-;) impartiality; political independence

Partei'nahme *f* (-;) taking sides

Partei'programm *n* party platform

Partei'tag *m* party rally

Partei'zugehörigkeit *f* party affiliation

Parterre [par'ter] *n* (-s;-s) ground floor; (theat) parterre

Par-tie [par'ti] *f* (-;-tien ['ti-ən]) part; (*Gesellschaft*) party; (*Spiel*) game; (*Ausflug*) outing; (com) lot; (theat) role; e-e gute P. machen (coll) marry rich; ich bin mit von der P.! count me in!

partiell [par'tsjel] *adj* partial ‖ *adv* partly, partially

Partikel [par'tikəl] *f* (-;-n) particle

Partisan –in [partɪ'zan(ɪn)] §7 *mf* partisan

Partitur [partɪ'tur] *f* (-;-en) (mus) score

Partizip [partɪ'tsip] *n* (-s;-ien [jən]) participle

Partner –in ['partnər(ɪn)] §6 *mf* partner

Part'nerschaft *f* (-;-en) partnership

Parzelle [par'tsele] *f* (-;-n) lot

parzellieren [partse'lirən] *tr* parcel out, allot

paschen ['paʃən] *tr* smuggle ‖ *intr* smuggle; (*würfeln*) play dice

Paß [pas] *m* (-sses; Pässe) pass; passport; (geog) mountain pass

passabel [pa'sabəl] *adj* tolerable

Passage [pa'saʒə] *f* (-;-n) passage; (mus) run

Passagier [pasa'ʒir] *m* (-s;-e) passenger; **blinder P.** stowaway

Passagier'dampfer *m* passenger liner

Passagier'gut *n* luggage

Passah ['pasa] *n* (-s;), **Pas'sahfest** *n* Passover

Paß'amt *n* passport office

Passant –in [pa'sant(ɪn)] §7 *mf* passerby

Paß'ball *m* (sport) pass

Paß'bild *n* passport photograph

passen ['pasən] *ref* be proper ‖ *intr* fit; (*dat*) suit; (cards, fb) pass; **p. auf** (*acc*) watch for, wait for; **p. zu** suit, fit; **sie p. zueinander** they are a good match

pas'send *adj* suitable; convenient; (*Kleidungsstück*) matching; **für p. halten** think it proper

Paß'form *f* —e–e **gute P. haben** be form-fitting

passierbar [pa'sirbar] *adj* passable

passieren [pa'sirən] *tr* pass, cross; (culin) sift, sieve ‖ *intr* (SEIN) happen

Passier'schein *m* pass, permit

Passion [pa'sjon] *f* (-s;-en) passion

passioniert [pasjo'nirt] *adj* ardent

Passions'spiel *n* passion play

passiv [pa'sif] *adj* passive; (*Handelsbilanz*) unfavorable; **passives Wahlrecht** eligibility ‖ **Passiv** *n* (-s;-e) (gram) passive

Passiva [pa'siva] *pl*, **Passiven** [pa'sivən] *pl* debts, liabilities

Paß'kontrolle *f* passport inspection

Paste ['pastə] *f* (-;-n) paste

Pastell [pa'stel] *n* (-s;-e) pastel; crayon

pastell'farben *adj* pastel

Pastell'stift *m* crayon

Pastete [pas'tetə] *f* (-;-n) meat pie, fish pie

pasteurisieren [pastœrɪ'zirən] *tr* pasteurize

Pastille [pa'stɪlə] *f* (-;-n) lozenge

Pa-stor ['pastor] *m* (-s;-storen ['torən]) pastor, minister, vicar

Pate ['patə] *m* (-n;-n) godfather ‖ *f* (-;-n) godmother

Pa'tenkind *n* godchild

patent [pa'tent] *adj* neat; smart; **ein patenter Kerl** quite a fellow ‖ **Patent** *n* (-[e]s;-e) patent; (mil) commission; **P. angemeldet** patent pending

Patent'amt *n* patent office

patentieren [paten'tirən] *tr* patent

Pater ['patər] *m* (-s; Patres ['patres]) (eccl) Father

pathetisch [pa'tetɪʃ] *adj* impassioned; solemn

Pathologe [pato'logə] *m* (-n;-n) pathologist

Pathologie [patolo'gi] *f* (-;) pathology

Pathologin [pato'login] *f* (-;-nen) pathologist

Patient –in [pa'tsjent(ɪn)] §7 *mf* patient

Patin ['patɪn] *f* (-;-nen) godmother

Patriarch [patrɪ'arç] *m* (-en;-en) patriarch

Patriot –in [patrɪ'ot(ɪn)] §7 *mf* patriot

patriotisch [patrɪ'otɪʃ] *adj* patriotic

Patrize [pa'tritsə] *f* (-;-n) die, stamp

Patrizier –in [pa'tritsjər(ɪn)] §6 *mf* patrician

Patron [pa'tron] *m* (-s;-e) patron; (pej) guy

Patronat [patro'nat] *n* (-[e]s;-e) patronage

Patrone [pa'tronə] *f* (-;-n) cartridge

Patro'nengurt *m* cartridge belt

Patro'nenhülse *f* cartridge case

Patronin [pa'tronɪn] *f* (-;-nen) patroness

Patrouille [pa'truljə] *f* (-;-n) patrol

patrouillieren [patru'ljirən] *tr & intr* patrol

Patsche ['patʃə] *f* (-;-en) (*Pfütze*) puddle; (coll) jam, scrape; **in der P. lassen** leave in a lurch; **in e-e P. geraten** get into a jam

patschen ['patʃ ən] *tr* slap || *intr* splash; **in die Hände p.** clap hands
patsch'naß *adj* soaking wet
patzig ['patsɪç] *adj* snappy, sassy
Pauke ['paukə] *f* (-;-n) kettledrum; **j-m e-e P. halten** give s.o. a lecture
pauken ['paukən] *tr* (educ) cram || *intr* beat the kettledrum; (educ) cram
Pau'ker *m* (-s;-) (coll) martinet
pausbackig ['pausbakɪç], **pausbäckig** ['pausbɛkɪç] *adj* chubby-faced
pauschal [pau'ʃɑl] *adj* (*Summe*) flat
Pauschal'betrag *m* flat rate
Pauscha·le [pau'ʃɑlə] *n* (-s;-lien [ljən]) lump sum
Pauschal'preis *m* package price
Pauschal'reise *f* all-inclusive tour
Pauschal'summe *f* flat sum
Pause ['pauzə] *f* (-;-n) pause; (*Pauszeichnung*) tracing; (educ) recess, break; (mus) rest; (theat) intermission; **e-e P. machen** take a break
pausen ['pauzən] *tr* trace
pau'senlos *adj* continuous
Pau'senzeichen *n* (rad) station identification
pausieren [pau'zirən] *intr* pause; rest
Pauspapier ['pauzpapir] *n* tracing paper
Pavian ['pɑvjɑn] *m* (-s;-e) baboon
Pavillon ['pɑviljɔ] *m* (-s;-s) pavilion
Pazifik [pa'tsifik] *m* (-s;) Pacific
pazifisch [pa'tsifɪʃ] *adj* Pacific
Pazifist –in [patsi'fɪst(ɪn)] §7 *mf* pacifist
Pech [pɛç] *n* (-[e]s;-e) pitch; **P. haben** (coll) have tough luck
Pech'fackel *f* torch
Pech'kohle *f* bituminous coal
pech'ra'benschwarz' *adj* pitch-black
pech'schwarz' *adj* pitch-dark
Pech'strähne *f* streak of bad luck
Pech'vogel *m* (coll) unlucky fellow
Pedal [pe'dɑl] *n* (-s;-e) pedal
Pedant [pe'dant] *m* (-en;-en) pedant
pedantisch [pe'dantɪʃ] *adj* pedantic
Pegel ['pegəl] *m* (-s;-) water gauge
Pe'gelstand *m* water level
Peil– [paɪl] *comb.fm.* direction-finding, sounding
peilen ['paɪlən] *tr* take the bearings of; (*Tiefe*) sound; **über den Daumen p.** (coll) estimate roughly || *intr* take bearings
Pei'lung *f* (-;-en) bearings; taking of bearings; sounding
Pein [paɪn] *f* (-;) pain, torment
peinigen ['paɪnɪgən] *tr* torment
pein'lich *adj* painful; embarrassing; (*genau*) painstaking; (*sorgfältig*) scrupulous || *adv* scrupulously; carefully
Peitsche ['paɪtʃə] *f* (-;-n) whip; **mit der P. knallen** crack the whip
peitschen ['paɪtʃən] *tr* whip
Peit'schenhieb *m* whiplash
Peit'schenknall *m* crack of the whip
Pelerine [pelə'rinə] *f* (-;-n) cape
Pelikan ['pelɪkɑn] *m* (-s;-e) pelican
Pelle ['pelə] *f* (-;-n) peel, skin
pellen ['pelən] *tr* peel, skin
Pellkartoffeln ['pelkartɔfəln] *pl* potatoes in their jackets

Pelz [pelts] *m* (-es;-e) fur; (*Fell*) pelt; fur coat
Pelz'besatz *m* fur trimming
Pelz'futter *n* fur lining
Pelz'händler –in §6 *mf* furrier
pel'zig *adj* furry; (*Gefühl im Mund*) cottony
Pelz'tier *n* fur-bearing animal
Pelz'tierjäger *m* trapper
Pelz'werk *n* furs
Pendel ['pendəl] *n* (-s;-) pendulum
pendeln ['pendəln] *intr* swing, oscillate; (*zwischen zwei Orten*) commute
Pen'deltür *f* swinging door
Pen'delverkehr *m* commuter traffic; shuttle service
Pen'delzug *m* shuttle train
Pendler ['pendlər] *m* (-s;-) commuter
Penizillin [penɪtsɪ'lin] *n* (-s;) penicillin
Pension [pen'zjon] *f* (-;-en) pension, retirement pay; (*Fremdenhaus*) boarding house; (*Unterkunft und Verpflegung*) room and board; (*Pensionat*) girls' boarding school; **in P. gehen** go on pension
Pensionär [penzjo'ner] *m* (-s;-e) pensioner; boarder
Pensionat [penzjo'nɑt] *n* (-[e]s;-e) girls boarding school
pensionieren [penzjo'nirən] *tr* put on pension; (mil) retire on half pay; **sich p. lassen** retire
Pensions'kasse *f* pension fund
Pensions'preis *m* price of room and board
Pen·sum ['penzum] *n* (-s;-sen [zən] & -sa [za]) task, assignment; quota
per [per] *prep* (*acc*) per, by, with; (*zeitlich*) by, until; **per Adresse** care of, c/o; **per sofort** at once
perfekt [per'fɛkt] *adj* perfect; concluded || **Perfekt** *n* (-[e]s;-e) perfect
Pergament [perga'ment] *n* (-[e]s;-e) parchment
Periode [per'jodə] *f* (-;-n) period
periodisch [per'jodɪʃ] *adj* periodic
Periphe·rie [perife'ri] *f* (-;-rien ['ri·ən]) periphery
Periskop [perɪ'skop] *n* (-s;-e) periscope
Perle ['perlə] *f* (-;-n) pearl; (*aus Glas*) bead; (*Tropfen*) drop, bead; (*Bläschen*) bubble; (fig) gem
perlen ['perlən] *intr* sparkle
Per'lenauster *f* pearl oyster
Per'lenkette *f*, **Per'lenschnur** *f* pearl necklace, string of pearls
Perlhuhn ['perlhun] *n* guinea fowl
perlig ['perlɪç] *adj* pearly
Perl'muschel *f* pearl oyster
Perlmutt ['perlmut] *n* (-s;), **Perl'mutter** *f* mother of pearl
perplex [per'pleks] *adj* perplexed
Persenning [per'zenɪŋ] *f* (-;-en) tarpaulin
Persien ['perzjən] *n* (-s;) Persia
persisch [perzɪʃ] *adj* Persian
Person [per'zon] *f* (-;-en) person; (theat) character; **ich für meine P.** I for one; **klein von P.** small of stature
Personal [perzo'nɑl] *n* (-s;) personnel
Personal'akte *f* personal file, dossier

Personal'angaben pl personal data

Personal'aufzug m passenger elevator

Personal'ausweis m identity card

Personal'chef m personnel manager

Personalien [pɛrzoˈnɑːljən] pl personal data, particulars

Personal'pronomen n personal pronoun

Perso'nengedächtnis n good memory for names

Perso'nenkraftwagen m passenger car

Perso'nenschaden m personal injury

Perso'nenverzeichnis n list of persons; (theat) dramatis personae, cast

Perso'nenwagen m passenger car

Perso'nenzug m passenger train; (rr) local

personifizieren [pɛrzonɪfiˈtsiːrən] tr personify

persönlich [pɛrˈzønlɪç] adj personal ‖ adv personally, in person

Persön'lichkeit f (-;-en) personality

Perspektiv [pɛrspɛkˈtiːf] n (-s;-e) telescope

Perücke [pɛˈrʏkə] f (-;-n) wig

pervers [pɛrˈvɛrs] adj perverse

pessimistisch [pɛsiˈmɪstɪʃ] adj pessimistic

Pest [pɛst] f (-;) plague

pest'artig adj pestilential

Pestilenz [pɛstiˈlɛnts] f (-;-en) pestilence

Petersilie [petərˈziːljə] f (-;) parsley

Petroleum [peˈtroːleːʊm] n (-s;) petroleum

Petschaft [ˈpɛtʃaft] n (-s;-e) seal

Petting [ˈpɛtɪŋ] n (-s;) petting

petto [ˈpɛto]—**in p.** haben have in reserve; (coll) have up one's sleeve

Petunie [peˈtuːnjə] f (-;-n) petunia

Petze [ˈpɛtsə] f (-;-n) tattletale

petzen [ˈpɛtsən] intr tattle, squeal

Pfad [pfat] m (-[e]s;-e) path, track

Pfadfinder [ˈpfatfɪndər] m (-s;-) boy scout

Pfadfinderin [ˈpfatfɪndərɪn] f (-;-nen) girl scout

Pfaffe [ˈpfafə] m (-n;-n) (pej) priest

Pfahl [pfaːl] m (-[e]s;ːe) stake; post

Pfahl'bau m (-[e]s;-bauten) lake dwelling

Pfahl'werk n palisade, stockade

Pfahl'wurzel f taproot

Pfahl'zaun m palisade, stockade

Pfälzer -in [ˈpfɛltsər(ɪn)] §6 mf inhabitant of the Palatinate

Pfand [pfant] n (-[e]s;ːer) pledge; deposit; (Bürgschaft) security, pawn (auf Immobilien) mortgage; **zum Pfande geben** (or **setzen**) pawn, mortgage

pfändbar [ˈpfɛntbar] adj (jur) attachable

Pfand'brief m mortgage papers

pfänden [ˈpfɛndən] tr attach, impound

Pfand'geber m mortgagor

Pfand'gläubiger m mortgagee

Pfand'haus n, **Pfand'leihe** f pawnshop

Pfand'leiher -in §6 mf pawnbroker

Pfand'recht n lien

Pfand'schein m pawn ticket

Pfand'schuldner m mortgagor

Pfän'dung f (-;-en) attachment, confiscation

Pfanne [ˈpfanə] f (-;-n) pan; (anat) socket; **etw auf der P. haben** (fig) have s.th. up one's sleeve; **in die P. hauen** (fig) make mincemeat of

Pfan'nenstiel m panhandle

Pfann'kuchen m pancake; **Berliner P.** doughnut

Pfarr- [pfar] comb.fm. parish, parochial

Pfarr'amt n rectory

Pfarr'bezirk m parish

Pfarr'dorf n parish seat

Pfarre [ˈpfarə] f (-;-n) parish; (Pfarrhaus) rectory

Pfarrei [pfaˈraɪ] f (-;-en) parish; (Pfarrhaus) rectory

Pfarrer [ˈpfarər] m (-s;-) pastor

Pfarr'gemeinde f parish

Pfarr'haus n rectory

Pfarr'kind n parishioner

Pfarr'kirche f parish church

Pfarr'schule f parochial school

Pfau [pfau] m (-[e]s;-en) peacock

Pfau'enhenne f peahen

Pfeffer [ˈpfɛfər] m (-s;) pepper

pfefferig [ˈpfɛfərɪç] adj peppery

Pfef'ferkorn n peppercorn

Pfef'ferkuchen m gingerbread

Pfef'ferminze f (bot) peppermint

Pfef'ferminzplätzchen n peppermint cookie

pfeffern [ˈpfɛfərn] tr pepper

Pfef'fernuß f ginger nut

Pfeife [ˈpfaɪfə] f (-;-n) whistle; (Orgel-) pipe; (zum Rauchen) (tobacco) pipe

pfeifen [ˈpfaɪfən] tr whistle; **ich pfeife ihm was** he can whistle for it ‖ intr whistle; (Schiedsrichter) blow the whistle; (Maus) squeak; (Vogel) sing; (dat) whistle for or to; **auf dem letzten Loche p.** be on one's last legs; **ich pfeife darauf!** I couldn't care less!

Pfei'fenkopf m pipe bowl

Pfei'fenrohr n pipestem

Pfei'fer -in §6 mf whistler; (mus) piper, fife player

Pfei'fkessel m, **Pfeif'topf** m whistling kettle

Pfeil [pfaɪl] m (-[e]s;-e) arrow, dart; **P. und Bogen** bow and arrow

Pfei'ler m (-s;-) (& fig) pillar; (e-r Brücke) pier

pfeil'gera'de adj straight as an arrow

pfeil'schnell' adj swift as an arrow ‖ adv like a shot

Pfeil'schütze m archer

Pfeil'spitze f arrowhead

Pfennig [ˈpfɛnɪç] m (-[e]s;-e & -) pfennig, penny (one hundredth of a mark)

Pfennigfuchser [ˈpfɛnɪçfʊksər] m (-s; -) penny pincher

Pferch [pfɛrç] m (-[e]s;-e) fold, pen

pferchen [ˈpfɛrçən] tr herd together, pen in

Pferd [pfɛrt] n (-[e]s;-e) horse; **zu Pferde** on horseback

Pferde- [pfɛrdə] comb.fm. horse

Pfer'deapfel m horse manure

Pfer'debremse f horsefly

Pfer'dedecke f horse blanket

Pfer'defuß m (*Kennzeichen des Teufels*) cloven hoof; (pathol) clubfoot

Pfer'degeschirr n harness

Pfer'degespann n team of horses

Pfer'deknecht m groom

Pfer'dekoppel f corral

Pfer'delänge f (*beim Rennen*) length

Pfer'derennbahn f race track

Pfer'derennen n horse racing

Pfer'destärke f horsepower

Pfer'dezucht f horse breeding

pfiff [pfɪf] pret of **pfeifen** || **Pfiff** m (-[e]s;-e) whistle; **den P. heraushaben** (fig) know the ropes

Pfifferling ['pfɪfərlɪŋ] m (-s;-e) (bot) chanterelle; **keinen P. wert** not worth a thing

pfiffig ['pfɪfɪç] adj shrewd, sharp

Pfiffikus ['pfɪfɪkʊs] m (-;-), (-ses;-se) (coll) sly fox

Pfingsten ['pfɪŋstən] n (-s;) Pentecost

Pfingst'son'ntag m Whitsunday

Pfingst'rose f (bot) peony

Pfirsich ['pfɪrzɪç] m (-[e]s;-e) peach

Pflanze ['pflantsə] f (-;-n) plant

pflanzen ['pflantsən] tr plant

Pflan'zenfaser f vegetable fiber

Pflan'zenfett n vegetable shortening

pflan'zenfressend adj herbivorous

Pflan'zenkost f vegetable diet

Pflan'zenkunde f botany

Pflan'zenleben n plant life, vegetation

Pflan'zenlehre f botany

Pflan'zenöl n vegetable oil

Pflan'zenreich n vegetable kingdom

Pflan'zensaft m sap, juice

Pflan'zenschutzmittel n pesticide

Pflan'zenwelt f flora

Pflan'zer -in §6 mf planter

pflanz'lich adj vegetable

Pflanz'schule f, **Pflanz'stätte** f nursery; (fig) hotbed

Pflan'zung f (-;-en) plantation

Pflaster ['pflastər] n (-s;-) pavement; (*Fleck*) patch; (med) Band-Aid; **als P.** (fig) in compensation; **ein teueres P.** (fig) an expensive place; **P. treten** (fig) pound the sidewalks

Pflasterer ['pflastərər] m (-s;-) paver

pfla'stermüde adj tired of walking the streets

pflastern ['pflastərn] tr pave

Pfla'sterstein m paving stone; (*Kopfstein*) cobblestone

Pfla'stertreter m (-s;-) loafer

Pfla'sterung f (-;) paving

Pflaume ['pflaumə] f (-;-n) plum; (*spitze Bemerkung*) dig

pflaumen ['pflaumən] intr (coll) tease

pflau'menweich adj (fig) spineless

Pflege ['pfleɡə] f (-;-n) care; (*e-s Kranken*) nursing; (*Wartung*) tending; (*e-s Gartens, der Künste*) cultivation; **gute P. haben** be well cared for; **in P. nehmen** take charge of

Pflegebefohlene ['pfleɡəbəfoːlənə] §5 mf charge; fosterchild

Pfle'geeltern pl foster parents

Pfle'geheim n nursing home

Pfle'gekind n foster child

pflegen ['pfleɡən] tr take care of, look after; (*Kranken*) nurse; (*Garten, Kunst*) cultivate; (*Freundschaft*) foster; **Geselligkeit p.** lead an active social life; **Umgang p. mit** associate with || intr—p. zu (inf) be wont to (inf), be in the habit of (ger); **sein Vater pflegte zu sagen** his father used to say; **sie pflegt morgens zeitig aufzustehen** she usually gets up early in the morning || intr (pp **gepflegt & gepflogen**) (genit) carry on; **der Liebe p.** enjoy the pleasures of love; **der Ruhe p.** take a rest; **Rats p. mit** consult with

Pfle'ger -in §6 mf nurse; (jur) guardian

Pfle'gesohn m foster son

Pfle'gestelle f foster home

Pfle'getocher f foster daughter

Pfle'gevater m foster father

pfleglich ['pfleːklɪç] adj careful

Pflegling ['pfleːklɪŋ] m (-s;-e) foster child; (*Pflegebefohlener*) charge

Pflegschaft ['pfleːkʃaft] f (-;-en) (jur) guardianship

Pflicht [pflɪçt] f (-;-en) duty; **sich seiner P. entziehen** evade one's duty

pflicht'bewußt adj conscientious

Pflicht'bewußtsein n conscientiousness

Pflicht'eifer m zeal

pflicht'eifrig adj zealous

Pflicht'erfüllung f performance of duty

Pflicht'fach n (educ) required course

Pflicht'gefühl n sense of duty

pflicht'gemäß adj dutiful

-pflichtig [pflɪçtɪç] comb.fm. obligated, e.g., **schulpflichtig** obligated to attend school

pflicht'schuldig adj duty-bound

pflicht'treu adj dutiful, loyal

pflicht'vergessen adj forgetful of one's duty; (*untreu*) disloyal

Pflicht'vergessenheit f dereliction of duty; disloyalty

Pflicht'verletzung f, **Pflicht'versäumnis** n neglect of duty

Pflock [pflɔk] m (-[e]s;⁻e) peg; **e-n P. zurückstecken** (fig) come down a peg

pflog [pfloːk] pret of **pflegen**

pflücken ['pflʏkən] tr pluck, pick

Pflug [pfluːk] m (-[e]s;⁻e) plow

pflügen ['pflyːɡən] tr & intr plow

Pflug'schar f plowshare

Pforte ['pfɔrtə] f (-;-n) gate

Pförtner -in ['pfœrtnər(ɪn)] §6 mf gatekeeper || m doorman; (anat) pylorus

Pfosten ['pfɔstən] m (-s;-) post; (carp) jamb

Pfote ['pfoːtə] f (-;-n) paw; **j-m eins auf die Pfoten geben** rap s.o.'s knuckles

Pfriem [pfriːm] m (-[e]s;-e) awl

Pfropf [pfrɔpf] m (-[e]s;-e) stopper, plug, cork

pfropfen ['pfrɔpfən] tr cork, plug; (*stopfen*) cram; (hort) graft || **Pfropfen** m (-s;-) stopper, plug, cork

Pfrop'fenzieher m corkscrew

Pfropf'reis n (hort) graft

Pfründe ['pfrʏndə] f (-;-n) benefice; (*ohne Seelsorge*) sinecure; **fette P.** (fig) cushy, well-paying job

Pfuhl [pfuːl] m (-[e]s;-e) pool, puddle; (fig) pit

Pfühl [pfyl] *m* (-[e]s;-e) (poet) cushion
pfui ['pfu·ɪ] *interj* phooey!; **p. über dich!** shame on you!
Pfund [pfunt] *n* (-[e]s;-e) pound
pfundig ['pfundɪç] *adj* (coll) great
-fündig [pfyndɪç] *comb.fm.* -pound
Pfundskerl ['pfuntskerl] *m* (coll) great guy
pfund'weise *adv* by the pound
Pfuscharbeit ['pfuʃarbaɪt] *f* bungling
pfuschen ['pfuʃən] *tr & intr* bungle; **j-m ins Handwerk p.** meddle in s.o.'s business
Pfuscherei [pfuʃə'raɪ] f (-;-en) bungling
Pfütze ['pfytsə] *f* (-;-n) puddle
Phänomen [fenɔ'men] *n* (-s;-e) phenomenon
phänomenal [fenɔme'nal] *adj* phenomenal
Phanta·sie [fanta'zi] *f* (-;-sien ['zi·ən]) imagination
Phantasie'gebilde *n* daydream
phantasieren [fanta'zirən] *intr* daydream; (mus) improvise; (pathol) be delirious
phantasie'voll *adj* imaginative
Phantast *-in* [fan'tast(ɪn)] §7 *mf* visionary
phantastisch [fan'tastɪʃ] *adj* fantastic
Phantom [fan'tom] *n* (-s;-e) phantom
Parisäer [farɪ'ze·ər] *m* (-s;-) Pharisee; (fig) pharisee
pharmazeutisch [farma'tsɔɪtɪʃ] *adj* pharmaceutical
Pharmazie [farma'tsi] *f* (-;) pharmacy
Phase ['fazə] *f* (-;-n) phase
Philantrop *-in* [fɪlan'trop(ɪn)] §7 *mf* philanthropist
philanthropisch [fɪlan'tropɪʃ] *adj* philanthropic
Philister [fɪ'lɪstər] *m* (-s;-) Philistine
Phiole [fɪ'olə] *f* (-;-n) vial, phial
Philologe [fɪlo'logə] *m* (-n;-n) philologist
Philologie [fɪlolo'gi] *f* (-;) philology
Philologin [fɪlo'logɪn] *f* (-;-nen) philologist
Philosoph [fɪlo'zof] *m* (-en;-en) philosopher
Philoso·phie [fɪlozo'fi] *f* (-;-fien ['fi·ən]) philosophy
philosophieren [fɪlozo'firən] *intr* philosophize
philosophisch [fɪlo'zofɪʃ] *adj* philosophic(al)
Phlegma ['flegma] *n* (-s;) indolence
Phonetik [fo'netɪk] *f* (-;) phonetics
phonetisch [fo'netɪʃ] *adj* phonetic
Phönix ['fønɪks] *m* (-[e]s;-e) phoenix
Phönizien [fø'nitsjən] *n* (-s;) Phoenicia
Phönizier *-in* [fø'nitsjər(ɪn)] §6 *mf* Phoenician
Phosphor ['fosfɔr] *m* (-s;) phosphorus
phos'phorig *adj* phosphorous
Photo ['foto] *n* (-s;-) photo
Pho'toapparat *m* camera
photogen [foto'gen] *adj* photogenic
Photograph [foto'graf] *m* (-en;-en) photographer
Photogra·phie [fotogra'fi] *f* (-;-fien ['fi·ən]) photography

photographieren [fotogra'firən] *tr & intr* photograph; **sich p. lassen** have one's photograph taken
Photographin [foto'grafɪn] *f* (-;-nen) photographer
photographisch [foto'grafɪʃ] *adj* photographic
Photokopie' *f* photocopy
photokopie'ren *tr* photocopy
Pho'tozelle *f* photoelectric cell
Phrase ['frazə] *f* (-;-n) phrase; (fig) platitude; **das sind nur Phrasen** that's just talk
phra'senhaft *adj* empty, trite; windy
Physik [fy'zik] *f* (-;) physics
physikalisch [fyzɪ'kalɪ/] *adj* physical
Physiker *-in* ['fysɪkər(ɪn)] §6 *mf* physicist
Physiogno·mie [fyzjɔgnɔ'mi] *f* (-;-mien ['mi·ən]) physiognomy
Physiologie [fyzjolo'gi] *f* (-;) physiology
physiologisch [fyzjo'logɪʃ] *adj* physiological
physisch ['fyzɪʃ] *adj* physical
Pianino [pɪ·a'nino] *n* (-s;-s) small upright piano
Pianist *-in* [pɪ·a'nɪst(ɪn)] §7 *mf* pianist
picheln ['pɪçəln] *tr & intr* tipple
pichen ['pɪçən] *tr* pitch, cover with pitch
Pichler *-in* ['pɪçlər(ɪn)] §6 *mf* tippler
Picke ['pɪkə] *f* (-;-n) pickax
Pickel ['pɪkəl] *m* (-s;-) pimple; (*Picke*) pickax; (*Eispicke*) ice ax
Pickelhaube (Pik'kelhaube) *f* spiked helmet
Pickelhering (Pik'kelhering) *m* pickled herring
pickelig (pik'kelig) *adj* pimply
picken ['pɪkən] *tr & intr* peck
picklig ['pɪklɪç] *adj* var of **pickelig**
Picknick ['pɪknɪk] *n* (-s;-s) picnic
pieken ['pikən] *tr* sting; (coll) prick
piekfein ['pik'faɪn] *adj* tiptop
pieksauber ['pik'zaubər] *adj* spick and span
piepen ['pipən] *intr* chirp; (*Maus*) squeal; **bei dir piept's wohl?** are you quite all there? ‖ **Piepen** *n*— **das ist zum P.!** that's ridiculous
Pier [pir] *m* (-s;-e) pier
piesacken ['pizakən] *tr* (coll) pester
Pietät [pɪ·e'tet] *f* (-;) piety
pietät'los *adj* irreverent
pietät'voll *adj* reverent(ial)
Pigment [pɪg'ment] *n* (-[e]s;-e) pigment
Pik [pik, pɪk] *m* (-s;-s & -e) (*Bergspitze*) peak ‖ *m* (-s;-e) (coll) grudge; **e-n Pik auf j-n haben** hold a grudge against s.o. ‖ *n* (-s;-e) (cards) spade(s)
pikant [pɪ'kant] *adj* piquant, pungent; (*Bemerkung*) suggestive
Pikante·rie [pɪkantə'ri] *f* (-;-rien ['ri·ən]) piquancy; spicy story, suggestive remark
Pike ['pikə] *f* (-;-n) pike, spear; **von der P. auf dienen** (fig) rise through the ranks
pikiert [pɪ'kirt] *adj* (**über** *acc*) piqued (at)

Pikkolo ['pɪkɔlo] *m* (-s;-s) apprentice waiter; (mus) piccolo
Pik′koloflöte *f* (mus) piccolo
Pilger ['pɪlgər] *m* (-s;-) pilgrim
Pil′gerfahrt *f* pilgrimage
Pilgerin ['pɪlgərɪn] *f* (-;-nen) pilgrim
pilgern ['pɪlgərn] *intr* (SEIN) go on a pilgrimage, make a pilgrimage
Pille ['pɪlə] *f* (-;-n) pill; **P. danach** morning-after pill
Pilot –in [pɪ'lot(ɪn)] §7 *mf* pilot
Pilz [pɪlts] *m* (-es;-e) fungus; mushroom
pimp(e)lig ['pɪmp(ə)lɪç] *adj* sickly, delicate; (*verweichlicht*) effeminate
Pinguin [pɪŋgu'in] *m* (-s;-e) penguin
Pinie ['pinjə] *f* (-;-n) umbrella pine
Pinke ['pɪŋkə] *f* (-) (coll) dough
Pinkel ['pɪŋkəl] *m* (-s;-) (coll) dude
pinkeln ['pɪŋkəln] *intr* (sl) pee
Pinne ['pɪnə] *f* (-;-n) pin; tack; (naut) tiller
Pinscher ['pɪnʃər] *m* (-s;-) terrier
Pinsel ['pɪnzəl] *m* (-s;-) brush; (fig) simpleton, dope
Pinselei [pɪnzə'laɪ] *f* (-;-en) daubing; (*schlechte Malerei*) daub
pinseln ['pɪnzəln] *tr & intr* paint
Pinzette [pɪn'tsɛta] *f* (-;-n) pair of tweezers, tweezers
Pionier [pɪ̯o'nir] *m* (-s;-e) (fig) pioneer; (mil) engineer
Pionier′arbeit *f* (fig) spadework
Pionier′truppe *f* (mil) engineers
Pirat [pɪ'rat] *m* (-en;-en) pirate
Piraterie [pɪratə'ri] *f* (-;) piracy
Pirol [pɪ'rol] *m* (-s;-e) oriole
Pirsch [pɪrʃ] *f* (-;) hunt
pirschen ['pɪrʃən] *intr* stalk game
Pirsch′jagd *f* hunt
Pistazie [pɪs'tatsjə] *f* (-;-n) pistachio
Piste ['pɪstə] *f* (-;-n) beaten track; ski run; toboggan run; (aer) runway
Pistole [pɪs'tolə] *f* (-;-n) pistol
Pisto′lentasche *f* holster
pitsch(e)naß ['pɪt∫(ə)'nas] *adj* soaked to the skin
pittoresk [pɪto'rɛsk] *adj* picturesque
Pkw., PKW *abbr* (**Personenkraftwagen**) passenger car
placieren [pla'sirən] *tr* place
placken ['plakən] *tr* pester, plague ‖ *ref* toil, drudge
Plackerei [plakə'raɪ] *f* (-;) drudgery
plädieren [plɛ'dirən] *intr* plead
Plädoyer [pledwa'je] *n* (-s;-s) plea
Plage ['plaɡə] *f* (-;-n) trouble, bother; torment; (*Seuche*) plague
Pla′gegeist *m* pest, pain in the neck
plagen ['plaɡən] *tr* trouble, bother; (*mit Fragen, usw.*) pester
Plagiat [pla'gjat] *n* (-[e]s;-e) plagiarism
Pla′giator [pla'gjatɔr] *m* (-s;-giatoren [gja'torən]) plagiarist
Plakat [pla'kat] *n* (-[e]s;-e) poster
Plakat′träger *m* sandwich man
Plakette [pla'kɛtə] *f* (-;-n) plaque
plan [plan] *adj* plain, clear; (*eben*) level ‖ **Plan** *m* (-[e]s;-e) plan; (*Stadt–*) map; (poet) battlefield; **auf den P. treten** appear on the scene
Plane ['planə] *f* (-;-n) tarpaulin

Plänemacher ['plɛnəmaxər] *m* (-s;-) schemer
planen ['planən] *tr* plan
Pläneschmied ['plɛnə/mit] *m* schemer
Planet [pla'net] *m* (-en;-en) planet
Planeta·rium [plane'tarjum] *n* (-s; -rien [rjən]) planetarium
Planeten– [planetən] *comb.fm.* planetary
Plane′tenbahn *f* planetary orbit
plan′gemäß *adv* according to plan
planieren [pla'nirən] *tr* level, grade
Planier′raupe *f* bulldozer
Planimetrie [planime'tri] *f* (-;) plane geometry
Planke ['plaŋkə] *f* (-;-n) plank
Plänkelei [plɛŋkə'laɪ] *f* (-;-en) skirmish, skirmishing
plänkeln ['plɛŋkəln] *intr* skirmish
plan′los *adj* aimless; indiscriminate
plan′mäßig *adj* systematic; fixed, regular; (*Verkehr*) scheduled ‖ *adv* according to plan
planschen ['plan∫ən] *intr* splash
Plantage [plan'taʒə] *f* (-;-n) plantation
Pla′nung *f* (-;) planning
plan′voll *adj* systematic, methodical
Plan′wagen *m* covered wagon
Plan′wirtschaft *f* planned economy
Plapperei [plapə'raɪ] *f* (-;) chatter
Plap′permaul ['plapərmaʊl] *n* chatterbox
plappern ['plapərn] *intr* chatter; prattle
plärren ['plɛrən] *intr* (coll) bawl
Plas·ma ['plasma] *n* (-s;-men [mən]) plasma
Plastik ['plastɪk] *f* (-;-en) (*Bildwerk*) sculpture; (surg) plastic surgery ‖ *n* (-s;) plastic
plastisch ['plastɪ∫] *adj* plastic; (*anschaulich*) graphic
Platane [pla'tanə] *f* (-;-n) sycamore
Plateau [pla'to] *n* (-s;-s) plateau
Plateau′schuhe *pl* platform shoes
Platin [pla'tin] *n* (-s;) platinum
platin′blond *adj* platinum-blonde
Platoniker [pla'tonɪkər] *m* (-s;-) Platonist
platonisch [pla'tonɪ∫] *adj* Platonic
plätschern ['plɛt∫ərn] *intr* splash; (*Bach*) babble
platt [plat] *adj* flat; (*nichtssagend*) trite; (coll) flabbergasted
Plättbrett ['plɛtbrɛt] *n* ironing board
platt′deutsch *adj* Low German
Platte ['platə] *f* (-;-n) plate; top, surface; slab; (*Präsentierteller*) tray; (*Speise*) dish; (fig) pate, bean; (mus) record; (phot) plate
Plätteisen ['plɛtaɪzən] *n* flatiron
plätten ['plɛtən] *tr & intr* iron
Plat′tenjockey *m* disc jockey
Plat′tenspieler *m* record player
Plat′tenteller *m* turntable
Plat′tenwechsler *m* record changer
Platt′form *f* platform
Platt′fuß *m* (aut) flat; **Plattfüße** flat feet
platt′füßig *adj* flat-footed
Platt′heit *f* (-;-en) flatness; (fig) banality

plattieren [pla'tirən] *tr* plate

Plättwäsche ['plɛtvɛ/ə] *f* ironing

Platz [plats] *m* (**-es;ᵘe**) place; spot; locality; square; (*Sitz*) seat; (*Raum*) room, space; (*Stellung*) position; (sport) ground, field; (tennis) court; **auf die Plätze, fertig, los!** on your marks, get set, go! **fester P.** (mil) fortified position; **freier P.** open space; **immer auf dem Platze sein** be always on the alert; **nicht am P. sein** be out of place; be irrelevant; **P. da!** make way; **P. greifen** (fig) take effect, gain ground; **P. machen** make room; **P. nehmen** sit down; **seinen P. behaupten** stand one's ground

Platz′anweiser –in §6 *mf* usher

Plätzchen ['plɛtsçən] *n* (**-s;-**) little place; little square; (*Süßware*) candy wafer; (*Gebäck*) cookie, cracker

platzen ['platsən] *intr* (SEIN) burst; split; crack; (*Granate*) explode; (*Luftreifen*) blow out; (fig) come to nothing; **da plᵘtzte ihm endlich der Kragen** he finally blew his top; **der Wechsel ist geplatzt** the check bounced

Platz′karte *f* reserved-seat ticket

Platz′kommandant *m* commandant

Platz′konzert *n* open-air concert

Platz′patrone *f* blank cartridge; **mit Platzpatronen schießen** fire blanks

Platz′regen *m* cloudburst

Platz′runde *f* (aer) circuit of a field

Platz′wechsel *m* change of place; (sport) change in lineup

Platz′wette *f* betting on a horse to finish in first, second, or third place, bet to place

Plauderei [plaudə'raɪ] *f* (**-;-en**) chat; small talk

Plau′derer –in §6 *mf* talker, chatterer

plaudern ['plaudərn] *intr* chat, chatter; **aus der Schule p.** tell tales out of school

Plaudertasche ['plaudərta/ə] *f* chatterbox

Plauderton ['plaudərton] *m* conversational tone

plausibel [plau'zibəl] *adj* plausible

plauz [plauts] *interj* crash!

pleite ['plaɪtə] *adj* (coll) broke || *adv* —**p. gehen** go broke || **Pleite** *f* (**-;-**) (coll) bankruptcy; **P. machen** (coll) go broke

Plenarsitzung [ple'narzɪtsuŋ] *f* (**-;-en**) plenary session

Plenum ['plenum] *n* (**-s;**) plenary session

Pleuelstange ['plɔɪ·əl/taŋə] *f* (mach) connecting rod

Plexiglas ['plɛksɪglas] *n* (**-es;**) plexiglass

Plinse ['plɪnzə] *f* (**-;-n**) pancake; fritter

Plissee [plɪ'se] *n* (**-s;-s**) pleat

Plissee′rock *m* pleated skirt

plissieren [plɪ'sirən] *tr* pleat

Plombe ['plɔmbə] *f* (**-;-n**) lead seal; (dent) filling

plombieren [plɔm'birən] *tr* seal with lead; (dent) fill

---

plötzlich ['plœtslɪç] *adj* sudden || *adv* suddenly, all of a sudden

plump [plump] *adj* (*unförmig*) shapeless; (*schwerfällig*) heavy, slow; (*derb*) coarse; (*unbeholfen*) ungainly; (*taktlos*) tactless, blunt

plumps [plumps] *interj* plop! thump!

plumpsen ['plumpsən] *intr* (HABEN & SEIN) plop, flop

Plunder ['plundər] *m* (**-s;**) junk

plündern ['plyndərn] *tr & intr* plunder

Plural ['plural] *m* (**-s;-e**) plural

plus [plus] *adv* plus || **Plus** *n* (**-;-**) plus; (*Überschuß*) surplus; (*Vorteil*) advantage, edge

Plus′pol *m* (elec) positive pole

Plutokrat [pluto'krat] *m* (**-en;-en**) plutocrat

Plutonium [plu'tonjum] *n* (**-s;**) plutonium

pneumatisch [pnɔɪ'matɪ/] *adj* pneumatic

Pöbel ['pøbəl] *m* (**-s;**) mob, rabble

pö′belhaft *adj* rude, rowdy

Pö′belherrschaft *f* mob rule

pochen ['pɔxən] *tr* (min) crush || *intr* knock; (*Herz*) pound; **p. an** (dat) knock on; **p. auf** (acc) pound on; (fig) insist on

Pochmühle ['pɔxmylə] *f*, **Pochwerk** ['pɔxvɛrk] *n* crushing mill

Pocke ['pɔkə] *f* (**-;-n**) pockmark; **Pocken** (pathol) smallpox

Pockennarbe [Pɔk′kɛnnarbe] *f* pockmark

pockennarbig (pok′kennarbig) *adj* pockmarked

Podest [pɔ'dɛst] *m & n* (**-es;-e**) pedestal; (*Treppenabsatz*) landing; podium

Po·dium ['pɔdjum] *n* (**-s;-dien** [djən]) podium, platform

Poesie [pɔ·ɛ'zi] *f* (**-;**) poetry

Poet [pɔ'et] *m* (**-en;-en**) poet

Poetik [pɔ'etɪk] *f* (**-;**) poetics

poetisch [pɔ'etɪ/] *adj* poetic

Pointe [pɔ'ɛ̃tə] *f* (**-;**) point (*of joke*)

Pokal [pɔ'kal] *m* (**-s;-e**) goblet; (sport) cup

Pökel ['pøkəl] *m* (**-s;**) brine

Pö′kelfleisch *n* salted meat

Pö′kelhering *m* pickled herring

pökeln ['pøkəln] *tr* pickle, salt

Poker ['pokər] *n* (**-s;**) poker

Pol [pol] *m* (**-s;-e**) pole

Polar– [polar] *comb.fm.* polar

polarisieren [polarɪ'zirən] *tr* polarize

Polarität [polarɪ'tet] *f* (**-;-en**) polarity

Polar′kreis *m* polar circle; **nördlicher P.** Arctic Circle; **südlicher P.** Antarctic Circle

Polar′licht *n* polar lights

Polar′stern *m* polestar

Polar′zone *f* frigid zone

Pole ['polə] *m* (**-n;-n**) Pole

Polemik [po'lemɪk] *f* (**-;**) polemics

polemisch [po'lemɪ/] *adj* polemical

Polen ['polən] *n* (**-s;**) Poland

Police [po'lisə] *f* (**-;-n**) (ins) policy

Polier [po'lir] *m* (**-s;-e**) foreman

polieren [po'lirən] *tr* polish

Polin ['polɪn] *f* (**-;-nen**) Pole

Politik [poli'tik] *f* (**-;-en**) policy; (*Staatsangelegenheiten*) politics

Politiker –in [po'litɪkər(ɪn)] §6 *mf* politician

Politi·kum [po'litɪkum] *n* (-s;-ka [ka]) political issue, political matter

politisch [po'litɪʃ] *adj* political

politisieren [polɪti'ziːrən] *intr* talk politics

Politur [polɪ'tuːr] *f* (-;-en) polish

Polizei [polɪ'tsaɪ] *f* (-;) police

Polizei'aufgebot *n* posse

Polizei'aufsicht *f*—**unter P. stehen** have to report periodically to the police

Polizei'beamte §5 *m* police officer

Polizei'büro *n*, **Polizei'dienststelle** *f* police station

Polizei'knüppel *m* billy club

Polizei'kommissar *m* police commissioner

polizei'lich *adj* police

Polizei'präsident *m* chief of police

Polizei'revier *n* police station

Polizei'spion *m*, **Polizei'spitzel** *m* stool-pigeon

Polizei'streife *f* raid; police patrol

Polizei'streifenwagen *m* squad car

Polizei'stunde *f* closing time; curfew

Polizei'wache *f* police station

polizei'widrig *adj* against police regulations

Polizist [polɪ'tsɪst] *m* (-en;-en) policeman

Polizistin [polɪ'tsɪstɪn] *f* (-;-nen) policewoman

Polizze [po'lɪtsə] *f* (-;-n) (Aust) insurance policy

Polka ['polka] *f* (-;-s) polka

polnisch ['polnɪʃ] *adj* Polish

Polo ['polo] *n* (-s;) (sport) polo

Polster ['polstər] *m* & *n* (-s;-) cushion

Pol'stergarnitur *f* living-room suite

Pol'stermöbel *pl* upholstered furniture

polstern ['polstərn] *tr* upholster

Pol'stersessel *m* upholstered chair

Pol'sterstuhl *m* padded chair

Pol'sterung *f* (-;) padding, stuffing

Polterabend ['poltərabant] *m* eve of the wedding day

Poltergeist ['poltərgaɪst] *m* poltergeist

poltern ['poltərn] *intr* make noise; (*rumpeln*) rumble; (*zanken*) bluster

Polyp [po'lyp] *m* (-en;-en) (pathol, zool) polyp; (*Polizist*) (sl) cop

Polytechni·kum [poly'tɛçnɪkum] *n* (-s; -ka [ka]) polytechnic institute

Pomade [po'mɑːdə] *f* (-;-n) pomade

Pomeranze [pomə'rantsə] *f* (-;-n) bitter orange

Pommern ['pomərn] *n* (-s;) Pomerania

Pommes frites [pom'fʀit] *pl* French fries

Pomp [pomp] *m* (-es;) pomp

Pompadour ['pompadur] *m* (-s;-e & -s) lady's string-drawn bag

pomp'haft, pompös [pom'pøs] *adj* pompous

pontifikal [pontɪfɪ'kɑl] *adj* pontifical

Pontifikat [pontɪfɪ'kɑt] *n* (-s;) pontificate

Pontius ['pontsjus] *m*—**von P. zu Pilatus geschickt werden** (coll) get the run-around

Pony ['poni] *m* (-s;-s) (*Damenfrisur*) pony ‖ *n* (-s;-s) (*Pferd*) pony

Popo [po'po] *m* (-s;-s) (coll) backside

populär [popu'lɛr] *adj* popular

Popularität [popularɪ'tɛt] *f* (-;) popularity

Pore ['poːrə] *f* (-;-n) pore

porig ['poːrɪç] *adj* porous

Pornofilm ['pornofɪlm] *m* (coll) smoker, pornographic movie

Pornoladen ['pornoladən] *m* (coll) porn shop

Pornographie [pornogra'fi] *f* (-;) pornography

poros [po'roːs] *adj* porous

Porphyr ['porfyr] *m* (-s;) porphyry

Porree ['pore] *m* (-s;-s) (bot) leek

Portal [por'tɑl] *n* (-s;-e) portal

Portemonnaie [portmo'ne] *n* (-s;-s) wallet

Portier [por'tje] *m* (-s;-s) doorman

Portion [por'tsjon] *f* (-;-en) portion; (culin) serving, helping; **halbe P.** (coll) half pint; **zwei Portionen Kaffee** two cups of coffee

Por·to ['porto] *n* (-s;-ti [ti]) postage

Por'togebühren *pl* postage

Por'tokasse *f* petty cash

Porträt [por'tret] *n* (-s;-s), (-[e]s;-e) portrait

porträtieren [portre'tirən] *tr* portray

Portugal ['portugal] *n* (-s;) Portugal

Portugiese [portu'gizə] *m* (-n;-n), **Portugiesin** [portu'gizɪn] *f* (-;-nen) Portuguese

portugiesisch [portu'gizɪʃ] *adj* Portuguese

Porzellan [portsə'lɑn] *n* (-s;-e) porcelain; china; **Meißener Porzellan** Dresden china

Porzellan'brennerei *f* porcelain factory

Posament [poza'mɛnt] *n* (-[e]s;-en) trimming, lace

Posaune [po'zaunə] *f* (-;-n) trombone

posaunen [po'zaunən] *intr* play the trombone

Pose ['poːzə] *f* (-;-n) pose

posieren [po'zirən] *intr* pose

Position [pozɪ'tsjon] *f* (-;-en) position

Positions'lampe *f* **Positions'licht** *n* (aer, naut) navigation light

positiv [pozɪ'tif] *adj* (*bejahend*) affirmative; (*Kritik*) favorable; (elec, math, med) positive ‖ *adv* in the affirmative; (coll) for certain ‖ **Positiv** *m* (-s;-e) (gram) positive degree ‖ *n* (-s;-e) (mus) small organ; (phot) positive

Positur [pozɪ'tur] *f* (-;-en) posture, attitude; **sich in P. setzen** (or **stellen** or **werfen**) strike a pose

Posse ['posə] *f* (-;-n) (theat) farce

Possen ['posən] *pl* (-s;) trick, practical joke; **j-m e-n P. spielen** play a practical joke on s.o.; **laß die P.!** cut out the nonsense; **P. treiben** (or **reißen**) crack jokes

pos'senhaft *adj* farcical, comical

Possenreißer ['posənraɪsər] *m* (-s;-) joker

Pos'senspiel *n* farce, burlesque

possierlich [po'sirlɪç] *adj* funny

Post [post] *f* (-;-en) mail; (*Postgebäude*) post office

postalisch [pos'tɑlɪʃ] *adj* postal

Postament [pɔsta'mɛnt] *n* (-[e]s;-e) pedestal
Post'amt *n* post office
Post'anweisung *f* money order
Post'auto *n* mail truck
Post'beamte *m* postal clerk
Post'beutel *m* mailbag
Post'bote *m* mailman
Post'direktor *m* postmaster
Posten ['pɔstən] *m* (-s;-) post; (*Stellung*) position; (acct) entry, item; (com) line, lot; (mil) guard, sentinel; **auf dem P. sein** (fig) be on guard; **auf verlorenem P. kämpfen** (coll) play a losing game; **nicht recht auf dem P. sein** be out of sorts; **P. aufstellen** post sentries; **P. stehen** stand guard; **ruhiger P.** (mil) soft job
Po'stenjäger -in §6 *mf* job hunter
Po'stenkette *f* line of outposts
Post'fach *n* post-office box
Post'gebühr *f* postage
posthum [pɔst'hum] *adj* posthumous
postieren [pɔs'tirən] *tr* post, place
Postille [pɔs'tilə] *f* (-;-n) devotional book
Post'karte *f* post card
Post'kasten *m* mail box
Post'kutsche *f* stagecoach
post'lagernd *adj* general-delivery || *adv* general delivery
Postleitzahl ['pɔstlarttsal] *f* zip code
Post'minister *m* postmaster general
Post'nachnahme *f* (-;-n) C.O.D.
Post'sack *m* mailbag
Post'schalter *m* post-office window
Post'scheck *m* postal check
Postschließfach ['pɔst/lisfax] *n* post-office box
Postskript [pɔst'skript] *n* (-[e]s;-e) postscript
Post'stempel *m* postmark
Post'überweisung *f* money order
post'wendend *adj* & *adv* by return mail
Post'wertzeichen *n* postage stamp
Post'wesen *n* postal system
potent [po'tɛnt] *adj* potent
Potential [poten'tsjal] *n* (-s;-e) potential
Potenz [po'tɛnts] *f* (-;-en) potency; (math) power; **dritte P.** (math) cube; **zweite P.** (math) square
potenzieren [poten'tsirən] *tr* raise to a higher power; (fig) intensify
Pottasche ['pɔta/ə] *f* (-;) potash
Pottwal ['pɔtval] *m* sperm whale
potz [pɔts] *interj*—**p. Blitz!** holy smoke!
potztau'send *interj* holy smoke!
poussieren [pu'sirən] *tr* (coll) flirt with; (coll) butter up || *intr* flirt
Pracht [praxt] *f* (-;) splendor, magnificence
Pracht'ausgabe *f* deluxe edition
Pracht'exemplar *n* beauty, beaut
prächtig ['prɛçtɪç] *adj* splendid
Pracht'kerl *m* (coll) great guy
Pracht'stück *n* (coll) beauty, beaut
pracht'voll *adj* gorgeous
Pracht'zimmer *n* stateroom (*in palace*)
Prädikat [predɪ'kat] *n* (-[e]s;-e) title; (educ) mark, grade; (gram) predicate

Prädikatsnomen [predɪ'katsnomən] *n* (-s;-s) (gram) complement
Präfix [pre'fɪks] *n* (-es;-e) prefix
Prag [prak] *n* (-s;) Prague
Prägeanstalt ['prega-anstalt] *f* mint
prägen ['pregən] *tr* stamp, coin || *ref* —**das hat sich mir tief in das Gedächtnis geprägt** that made a lasting impression on me
Prä'gestempel *m* (mach) die
pragmatisch [prag'matɪ/] *adj* pragmatic
prägnant [pre'gnant] *adj* pithy, terse
Prä'gung *f* (-;-en) coining, minting; (fig) coinage
prahlen ['pralən] *intr* (mit) brag (about); (mit) show off (with)
Prah'ler *m* (-s;-) braggart; show-off
Prahlerei [pralə'rar] *f* (-;-en) bragging, boasting; (*Prunken*) showing off
Prah'lerin *f* (-;-nen) braggart; show-off
prahlerisch ['pralərɪ/] *adj* bragging
Prahlhans ['pralhans] *m* (-es;-̈e) braggart
Prahm [pram] *m* (-[e]s;-e) flat-bottomed lighter
Praktik ['praktɪk] *f* (-;-en) practice; (*Kniff*) trick
Praktikant -in [praktɪ'kant(ɪn)] §7 *mf* student in on-the-job training
Praktiker ['praktɪkər] *m* (-s;-) practical person
Prakti·kum ['praktɪkʊm] *n* (-s;-ka [ka]) practical training
Praktikus ['praktɪkʊs] *m* (-;-se) old hand
praktisch ['praktɪ/] *adj* practical; **praktischer Arzt** general practitioner
praktizieren [praktɪ'tsirən] *tr* practice; **etw in die Tasche p.** manage to slip s.th. into the pocket
Prälat [pre'lat] *m* (-en;-en) prelate
Praline [pra'linə] *f* (-;-n) chocolate
prall [pral] *adj* (*straff*) tight; (*Brüste*) full; (*Backen*) chubby; (*Arme, Beine*) shapely; (*Sonne*) blazing || **Prall** *m* (-[e]s;-e) impact; collision
prallen ['pralən] *intr* (SEIN) bounce, rebound; (*Sonne*) beat down
Prämie ['premjə] *f* (-;-n) award, prize; premium; bonus
prämieren [premɪ'irən] *tr* award a prize to
prangen ['praŋən] *intr* shine; look beautiful
Pranger ['praŋər] *m* (-s;-) pillory
Pranke ['praŋkə] *f* (-;-n) claw
pränumerando [prenumə'rando] *adv* in advance, beforehand
Präparat [prepa'rat] *n* (-[e]s;-e) preparation
präparieren [prepa'rirən] *tr* prepare
Präposition [prepozɪ'tsjon] *f* (-;-en) preposition
Prä·rie [pre'ri] *f* (-;-rien ['ri-ən]) prairie
Präsens ['prezens] *n* (-; Präsentia [pre'zentsɪ-a]) (gram) present
präsent [pre'zent] *adj* present || **Präsent** *n* (-s;-e) present, gift
präsentieren [prezen'tirən] *tr* present
Präsentier'teller *m* tray

Präsenzstärke [prɛˈzɛnts/tɛrkə] *f* effective strength

Präservativ [prɛzɛrvaˈtif] *m* (-s;-e) prophylactic, condom

Präsident [prɛziˈdɛnt] *m* (-en;-en) president

Präsidenten– [prɛzidɛntən] *comb.fm.* presidential

Präsident'schaft *f* (-;-en) presidency

präsidieren [prɛziˈdiːrən] *intr* preside

Präsi·dium [prɛˈzidjum] *n* (-s;-dien [djən]) presidency; chairmanship

prasseln [ˈprasəln] *intr* crackle; (*Regen*) patter

prassen [ˈprasən] *intr* lead a dissipated life

Prasserei [prasəˈrai] *f* (-;) luxurious living, high life

Prätendent [pretɛnˈdɛnt] *m* (-en;-en) (auf *acc*) pretender (to)

Pra·xis [ˈpraksis] *f* (-;-xen [ksən]) practice; experience; doctor's office; law office; (jur) clientele; (med) patients

Präzedenzfall [pretseˈdɛntsfal] *m* precedent

präzis [preˈtsis] *adj* precise

Präzision [pretsiˈzjon] *f* (-;) precision

predigen [ˈprediɡən] *tr & intr* preach

Prediger [ˈprediɡər] *m* (-s;-) preacher

Predigt [ˈprediçt] *f* (-;-en) sermon

Preis [prais] *m* (-es;-e) price, rate, cost; (poet) praise, glory; **äußerst P.** (coll) rock-bottom price; **um jeden P.** (fig) at all costs; **um keinen P.** (fig) on no account; **zum P. von** at the rate of

Preis'aufgabe *f* project in a competition

Preis'aufschlag *m* extra charge

Preis'ausschreiben *n* competition

Preisdrückerei [ˈpraisdrykərai] *f* (-;-en) price cutting

Preiselbeere [ˈpraizəlberə] *f* cranberry

preisen [ˈpraizən] *tr* praise

Preis'ermäßigung *f* price reduction

Preis'frage *f* question in a competition; question of price (coll) sixty-four-dollar question

Preis'gabe *f* abandonment, surrender

preis'geben §80 *tr* abandon, surrender; (*Geheimnis*) betray; **j–n dem Spott p.** hold s.o. up to ridicule

preisgekrönt [ˈpraisɡəkrønt] *adj* prize-winning

Preis'gericht *n* jury

Preis'grenze *f* price limit; **obere P.** ceiling; **untere P.** minimum price

preis'günstig *adj* worth the money

Preis'lage *f* price range

Preis'niveau *n* price level

Preis'notierung *f* rate of exchange

Preis'richter *m* judge (*in competition*)

Preis'schießen *n* shooting competition

Preis'schild *n* price tag

Preis'schlager *m* bargain price

Preis'schrift *f* prize-winning essay

Preis'stopp *m* price freezing

Preis'sturz *m* drop in prices

Preis'träger –in §6 *mf* prize winner

Preistreiberei [praistraibəˈrai] *f* (-;) price rigging

Preis'überwachung *f* price control

Preis'verzeichnis *n* price list

preis'wert, preis'würdig *adj* worth the money, reasonable

Preis'zuschlag *m* markup

prekär [preˈkɛr] *adj* precarious

Prellbock [ˈprɛlbɔk] *m* (rr) buffer

prellen [ˈprɛlən] *tr* bump; bounce; toss up (*in a blanket*); (um) cheat (out of) || *ref*—**sich** [*dat*] **den Arm p.** bruise one's arm

Prel'ler *m* (-s;-) bump; ricochet; bilker, cheat

Prellerei [prɛləˈrai] *f* (-;-en) (act of) cheating

Prell'schuß *m* ricochet

Prell'stein *m* curbstone

Prel'lung *f* (-;-en) bruise

Premier [prəˈmje] *m* (-s;-s) premier

Premiere [prəˈmjerə] *f* (-;-n) (theat) premiere, first night, opening

Premier'minister *m* prime minister

Presbyterianer –in [presbytəˈrjanər (in)] §6 *mf* Presbyterian

presbyterianisch [presbytəˈrjaniʃ] *adj* Presbyterian

preschen [ˈpreʃən] *intr* charge

pressant [preˈsant] *adj* pressing

Presse [ˈpresə] *f* (-;-n) (& journ) press; (educ) cram class

Pres'seagentur *f* press agency

Pres'seamt *n* public-relations office

Pres'seausweis *m* press card

Pres'sebericht *m* press report

Pres'sechef *m* press secretary

Pres'sekonferenz *f* press conference

Pres'semeldung *f* news item

Pres'sestelle *f* public-relations office

Pres'severtreter *m* reporter; public-relations officer

Preßkohle [ˈpreskolə] *f* briquette

Preßluft [ˈpresluft] *f* compressed air

Preß'lufthammer *m* jackhammer

Preuße [ˈprɔisə] *m* (-n;-n) Prussian

Preußen [ˈprɔisən] *n* (-s;) Prussia

Preußin [ˈprɔisin] *f* (-;-nen) Prussian

preußisch [ˈprɔisiʃ] *adj* Prussian

prickeln [ˈprikəln] *intr* tingle

Priem [prim] *m* (-[e]s;-e) plug (*of tobacco*)

priemen [ˈprimən] *intr* chew tobacco

pries [pris] *pret* of **preisen**

Priester [ˈpristər] *m* (-s;-) priest

Prie'steramt *n* priesthood

Priesterin [ˈpristərin] *f* (-;-nen) priestess

prie'sterlich *adj* priestly

Prie'sterrock *m* cassock

Priestertum [ˈpristərtum] *n* (-s;) priesthood

Prie'sterweihe *f* (eccl) ordination

prima [ˈprima] *invar adj* first-class; terrific, swell

primär [priˈmer] *adj* primary || *adv* primarily

Primat [priˈmat] *m & n* (-[e]s;-e) primacy, priority || *m* (-en;-en) primate

Primel [ˈprimel] *f* (-;-n) primrose

primitiv [primiˈtif] *adj* primitive

Prinz [prints] *m* (-en;-en) prince

Prinzessin [prinˈtsesin] *f* (-;-nen) princess

Prinz'gemahl *m* prince consort

Prin·zip [prɪn'tsip] n (-s;-zipien ['tsipjən]) principle
prinzipiell [prɪntsɪ'pjɛl] adj in principle, fundamentally
Prinzi'pienreiter m (coll) pedant
prinz'lich adj princely
Pri·or ['pri·or] m (-s;-oren ['orən]) (eccl) prior
Priorität [prɪ·orɪ'tɛt] f (-;-en) priority
Prise ['prizə] f (-;-n) pinch (of salt, etc.); (nav) prize
Pris·ma ['prɪsma] n (-s;-men [men]) prism
privat [prɪ'vat] adj private; personal
Privat'adresse f, **Privat'anschrift** f home address
Privat'dozent –in §7 mf non-salaried university lecturer
Privat'druck m private printing
Privat'eigentum n private property
Privat'gespräch n (telp) personal call
privatim [prɪ'vatɪm] adv privately; confidentially
privatisieren [prɪvatɪ'zirən] intr be financially independent
Privat'lehrer –in §6 mf tutor
Privat'recht n civil law
privat'rechtlich adj (jur) civil
Privi·leg [prɪvɪ'lek] n (-[e]s;-legien ['legjən]) privilege
privilegiert [prɪvɪle'girt] adj privileged
probat [pro'bat] adj tried, tested
Probe ['probə] f (-;-n) (Versuch) trial, experiment; (Prüfung) test; (Muster) sample; (Beweis) proof; (theat) rehearsal; **auf die P. stellen** put to the test; **auf (or zur) P.** on approval
Pro'beabdruck m, **Pro'beabzug** m (typ) proof
Pro'bebild n (phot) proof
Pro'bebogen m proof sheet
Pro'bedruck m (typ) proof
Pro'befahrt f road test, trial run
Pro'beflug m test flight
Pro'belauf m trial run; dry run
Pro'besendung f sample sent on approval
Pro'bestück n sample, specimen
pro'beweise adv on trial; on approval
Pro'bezeit f probation period
probieren [pro'birən] tr try out, test; try, taste; (metal) assay
Probier'glas n test tube
Probier'stein m touch-stone
Problem [pro'blem] n (-s;-e) problem
Produkt [pro'dukt] n (-[e]s;-e) product; (des Bodens) produce
Produktion [produk'tsjon] f (-;-en) production; (indust) output
produktiv [produk'tif] adj productive
Produzent [produ'tsent] m (-en;-en) (& cin) producer
produzieren [produ'tsirən] tr produce ‖ ref perform; (pej) show off
profan [pro'fan] adj profane
profanieren [profa'nirən] tr profane
Profession [profe'sjon] f (-;-en) profession
Professional [profesjə'nal] m (-s;-e) (sport) professional
professionell [profesjə'nel] adj professional
Profes·sor [pro'fesor] m (-s;-soren

['sorən]), **Professorin** [profe'sorɪn] f (-;-nen) professor; **außerordentlicher P.** associate professor; **ordentlicher P.** full professor
Professur [profe'sur] f (-;-en) professorship
Profi ['profi] m (-s;-s) (coll) pro
Profil [pro'fil] n (-s;-e) profile; (aut) tread; **im P.** in profile
profiliert [profɪ'lirt] adj outstanding
Profit [pro'fit] m (-[e]s;-e) profit
profitabel [profɪ'tabəl] adj profitable
Profit'gier f profiteering
profitieren [profɪ'tirən] tr & intr profit
Prognose [pro'gnozə] f (-;-n) (med) prognosis; (meteor) forecast
Programm [pro'gram] n (-s;-e) program; (pol) platform
programmieren [progra'mirən] tr (data proc) program
Projekt [pro'jekt] n (-[e]s;-e) project
Projektil [projek'til] n (-s;-e) projectile
Projektion [projek'tsjon] f (-;-en) projection
Projektions'apparat m, **Projektions'gerät** n, **Projek·tor** [pro'jektor] m (-s;-toren ['torən]) projector
projizieren [proji'tsirən] tr project
proklamieren [prokla'mirən] tr proclaim
Prokura [pro'kura] f (-;) power of attorney; **per P.** by proxy
Prolet [pro'let] m (-en;-en) (pej) cad
Proletariat [proleta'rjat] n (-[e]s;-e) proletariat
Proletarier –in [prole'tarjər(ɪn)] §6 mf proletarian
proletarisch [prole'tarɪʃ] adj proletarian
Prolog [pro'lok] m (-[e]s;-e) prologue
prolongieren [prolɔŋ'girən] tr extend; (cin) hold over
Promenade [promə'nadə] f (-;-n) avenue; (Spaziergang) promenade
promenieren [promə'nirən] intr stroll
prominent [promɪ'nent] adj prominent
Promotion [promo'tsjon] f (-;-en) awarding of the doctor's degree
promovieren [promo'virən] intr attain a doctor's degree
prompt [prɔmpt] adj prompt, quick
Prono·men [pro'nomən] n (-s;-mina [mɪna]) pronoun
Propaganda [propa'ganda] f (-;) propaganda
propagieren [propa'girən] tr propagate
Propeller [pro'pelər] m (-s;-) propeller
Prophet [pro'fet] m (-en;-en) prophet
Prophetin [pro'fetɪn] f (-;-nen) prophetess
prophetisch [pro'fetɪʃ] adj prophetic
prophezeien [profe'tsar-ən] tr prophesy
Prophezei'ung f (-;-en) prophecy
Proportion [propor'tsjon] f (-;-en) proportion
proportional [proportsjo'nal] adj proportional
proportioniert [proportsjo'nirt] adj proportionate
Propst [propst] m (-es;ᴇe) provost

Prosa ['proza] *f* (-;) prose

prosaisch [pro'za·ɪʃ] *adj* prosaic

prosit ['prozɪt] *interj* to your health! || **Prosit** *n* (-s;-s) toast

Prospekt [pro'spekt] *m* (-[e]s;-e) prospect, view; brochure, folder

prostituieren [prostitu'irən] *tr* prostitute

Prostituierte [prostitu'irtə] §5 *f* prostitute

protegieren [protə'girən] *tr* patronize; (*schützen*) protect

Protektion [protek'tsjon] *f* (-;) pull, connections

Protest [pro'test] *m* (-es;-e) protest

Protestant –in [protes'tant(ɪn)] §7 *mf* Protestant

protestantisch [protes'tantɪʃ] *adj* Protestant

protestieren [protes'tirən] *tr & intr* protest

Protokoll [proto'kɔl] *n* (-s;-e) protocol; record, minutes; **P. führen** take the minutes; **zu P. nehmen** take down

Protokoll'führer –in §6 *mf* recording secretary; (jur) clerk

protokollieren [protokɔ'lirən] *tr* record

Pro·ton ['proton] *n* (-s;-tonen ['tonən]) (phys) proton

Protz [prɔts] *m* (-es;-en) show-off

protzen ['prɔtsən] *intr* show off

prot'zenhaft, protzig ['prɔtsɪç] *adj* show-offish

Prozedur [protsə'dur] *f* (-;-en) procedure; (jur) proceeding

Prozent [pro'tsent] *n* (-[e]s;-e) percent

Prozent'satz *m* percentage

Pro·zeß [pro'tses] *m* (-zesses;-zesse) process; (jur) case, suit; (jur) proceedings; **e–en P. anstrengen** (or **führen**) **gegen** sue; **kurzen P. machen mit** make short work of

Prozeß'akten *pl* (jur) record

Prozeß'führer –in §6 *mf* litigant

prozessieren [protsə'sirən] *intr* go to court; **p. gegen** sue

Prozession [protse'sjon] *f* (-;-en) procession

Prozeß'kosten *pl* (jur) court costs

Prozeß'vollmacht *f* power of attorney

prüde ['prydə] *adj* prudish

prüfen ['pryfən] *tr* test; (*nachprüfen*) check, verify; (*untersuchen*) examine; (*kosten*) taste; (acct) audit

Prüfer –in §6 *mf* examiner; (acct) auditor

Prüfling ['pryflɪŋ] *m* (-s;-e) examinee

Prüfstein ['pryfʃtaɪn] *m* touchstone

Prü'fung *f* (-;-en) test; examination; check, verification; (acct) audit; (jur) review

Prü'fungsarbeit *f* test paper

Prü'fungsausschuß *m*, **Prü'fungskommission** *f* examining board

Prügel ['prygəl] *m* (-s;-) stick, cudgel; **Prügel** *pl* whipping

Prügelei [prygə'laɪ] *f* (-;-en) brawl; free-for-all

Prü'gelknabe *m* whipping boy, scapegoat

prügeln ['prygəln] *tr* beat, whip || *ref* have a fight

Prü'gelstrafe *f* corporal punishment

Prunk [prʊŋk] *m* (-[e]s;) pomp, show

prunken ['prʊŋkən] *intr* show off

Prunk'gemach *n* stateroom

prunk'haft *adj* showy

Prunk'sucht *f* ostentatiousness

prunk'süchtig *adj* ostentatious

prunk'voll *adj* gorgeous

Prunk'zimmer *n* stateroom

prusten ['prustən] *intr* snort

Psalm [psalm] *m* (-s;-en) psalm

Psalter ['psaltər] *m* (-s;-) psalter

Pseudonym [psɔɪdo'nym] *n* (-s;-e) pseudonym

Psychiater (psyçɪ'atər] *m* (-s;-) psychiatrist

Psychiatrie [psyçɪ·a'tri] *f* (-;) psychiatry

psychiatrisch [psyçɪ'atrɪʃ] *adj* psychiatric

psychisch ['psyçɪʃ] *adj* psychic(al)

Psychoanalyse [psyço·ana'lyzə] *f* (-;) psychoanalysis

Psychoanalytiker –in [psyço·ana'lytɪkər(ɪn)] §6 *mf* psychoanalyst

Psychologe [psyço'logə] *m* (-;-n) psychologist

Psychologie [psyçolo'gi] *f* (-;) psychology

Psychologin [psyço'logɪn] *f* (-;-nen) psychologist

psychologisch [psyço'logɪʃ] *adj* psychological

Psychopath –in [psyço'pat(ɪn)] §7 *mf* psychopath

Psychose [psy'çozə] *f* (-;-n) psychosis

Psychotherapie [psyçotera'pi] *f* (-;) psychotherapy

Pubertät [puber'tet] *f* (-;) puberty

publik [pub'lik] *adj* public

Publi·kum ['publikʊm] *n* (-s;-ka [ka]) public; (theat) audience

publizieren [publɪ'tsirən] *tr* publish

Publizist –in [publɪ'tsɪst(ɪn)] §7 *mf* (journ) writer on public affairs; teacher or student of journalism

Publizität [publɪtsɪ'tet] *f* (-;) publicity

Pudel ['pudəl] *m* (-s;-) poodle; **des Pudels Kern** (fig) gist of the matter

Pu'delmütze *f* fur cap; woolen cap

pu'delnaß *adj* (coll) soaking wet

Puder ['pudər] *m* (-s;-) powder

Pu'derdose *f* powder box; compact

Pu'derquaste *f* powder puff

Pu'derzucker *m* powdered sugar

Puff [puf] *m* (-[e]s;ᵉe & -e) (*Stoß*) poke; (*Knall*) pop; (*Bausch*) puff; || *m* (-s;-s) (coll) brothel

Puff'ärmel *m* puffed sleeve

puffen ['pufən] *tr* poke; (coll) prod || *intr* puff; (*knallen*) pop, bang away

Puffer ['pufər] *m* (-s;-) buffer; popgun; (culin) potato pancake

Puf'ferbatterie *f* booster battery

Puf'ferstaat *m* buffer state

Puff'mais *m* popcorn

Puff'reis *m* (-es;) puffed rice

Pulli ['puli] *m* (-s;-s) (coll) sweater

Pullover [pu'lovar] *m* (-s;-) sweater

Puls [puls] *m* (-es;-e) pulse

Puls'ader *f* artery

pulsieren [pul'zirən] *intr* pulsate

Puls'schlag *m* pulse beat

Pult [pult] n (-[e]s;-e) desk
Pulver ['pulfər] n (-s;-) powder; (Schieß-) gunpowder; (coll) dough
pul'verig adj powdery
pulverisieren [pulfərı'zirən] tr pulverize
Pul'verschnee m powdery snow
Pummel ['puməl] m (-s;-) butterball (chubby child)
pummelig ['puməlıç] adj (coll) chubby
Pump [pump] m—auf P. (coll) on tick
Pumpe ['pumpə] f (-;-n) pump
pumpen ['pumpən] tr pump; (coll) give on tick; (coll) get on tick ‖ intr pump
Pum'penschwengel m pump handle
Pumpernickel ['pumpərnıkəl] m (-s; -) pumpernickel
Pump'hosen f pair of knickerbockers
Punkt [puŋkt] m (-[e]s;-e) point; (Tüpfelchen) dot; (Stelle) spot; (Einzelheit) item; (gram) period; **der tote P.** a deadlock; **dunkler P.** (fig) skeleton in the closet; **nach Punkten siegen** win on points; **P. sechs Uhr** at six o'clock sharp; **springender P.** crux; **strittiger P.** point at issue; **wunder P.** (fig) sore spot
Punkt'gleichheit f (sport) tie
punktieren [puŋk'tirən] tr dot, stipple; **punktierte Linie** dotted line
pünktlich ['pyŋktlıç] adj punctual
Punkt'sieg m (box) winning on points
punktum ['puŋktum] interj—**und damit p.!** and that's it!; period!
Punkt'zahl f (sport) score
Punsch [punʃ] m (-es;) punch (drink)
Punze ['puntsə] f (-;-n) punch, stamp
punzen ['puntsən] tr punch, stamp
Pupille [pu'pılə] f (-;-n) (anat) pupil
Puppe ['pupə] f (-;-n) doll; puppet; (Schneider-) dummy; (zool) pupa
Pup'penspiel n puppet show
Pup'penwagen m doll carriage
pur [pur] adj pure, sheer

Püree [py're] n (-s;-s) mashed potatoes; puree
purgieren [pur'girən] tr & intr purge
Purpur ['purpur] m (-s;) purple
pur'purfarben adj purple
purpurn [purpurn] adj purple
Purzelbaum ['purtsəlbaum] m somersault; **e-en P. schlagen** do a somersault
purzeln ['purtsəln] intr (SEIN) tumble
pusselig ['pusəlıç] adj fussy
Puste ['pustə] f (-;) (coll) breath
Pustel ['pustəl] f (-;-n) pustule
pusten ['pustən] tr—**ich puste dir was!** (coll) you may whistle for it! ‖ intr puff, pant
Pu'sterohr n peashooter
Pute ['putə] f (-;-n) turkey (hen)
Puter ['putər] m (-s;-) turkey (cock)
Putsch [putʃ] m (-es;-e) putsch, uprising
Putz [puts] m (-es;) finery; trimming; ornaments; plaster
putzen ['putsən] tr (reinigen) clean; (Schuhe) polish; (Zähne) brush; (Person) dress; (schmücken) adorn ‖ ref dress; **sich** [dat] **die Nase p.** blow one's nose
Put'zer m (-s;-) cleaner; (mil) orderly
Putzerei [putsə'raı] f (-;-en) (Aust) dry cleaner's; (Aust) laundry
Putz'frau f cleaning woman
putzig ['putsıç] adj funny
Putz'lappen m cleaning cloth
Putz'mittel n cleaning agent
Putz'wolle f cotton waste
Putz'zeug n cleaning things
Pygmäe [pyg'me·ə] m (-n;-n) pygmy
Pyjama [pı'dʒama] m (-s;-s) pajamas
Pyramide [pyra'midə] f (-;-n) pyramid; (mil) stack
Pyrenäen [pyre'ne·ən] pl Pyrenees
Pyrotechnik [pyro'tɛçnık] f (-;) pyrotechnics
Pythonschlange ['pytən/laŋə] f python

Q

Q, q [ku] invar n Q, q
quabbelig ['kvabəlıç] adj flabby; quivering, jelly-like
quabbeln ['kvabəln] intr quiver
Quackelei [kvakə'laı] f (-;-en) silly talk; (unnützes Zeug) rubbish
Quacksalber ['kvakzalbər] m (-s;-) quack
Quader ['kvadər] m (-s;-) ashlar
Quadrant [kva'drant] m (-en;-en) quadrant
Quadrat [kva'drat] n (-[e]s;-e) square; **e-e Zahl ins Q. erheben** square a number; **zwei Fuß im Q.** two feet square
quadratisch [kva'dratıʃ] adj square; quadratic
Quadrat'meter n square meter
Quadrat'wurzel f square root
quadrieren [kva'drirən] tr square

quaken ['kvakən] intr (Ente) quack; (Frosch) croak
quäken ['kvekən] intr bawl
Qual [kval] f (-;-en) torment, agony
quälen ['kvelən] tr torment; worry; (ständig bedrängen) pester ‖ ref—**sich mit e-r Arbeit q.** slave at a job; **sich umsonst q.** labor in vain; **sich zu Tode q.** worry oneself to death
Quälgeist ['kvelgaıst] m pest
Qualifikation [kvalıfıka'tsjon] f (-; -en) qualification
qualifizieren [kvalıfı'tsirən] tr & ref (zu) qualify (for)
Qualität [kvalı'tet] f (-;-en) quality
Qualitäts- comb.fm. high-quality, high-grade, quality
Qualle ['kvalə] f (-;-n) jellyfish
Qualm [kvalm] m (-[e]s;) smoke; vapor

qualmen ['kvalmən] *tr* smoke ‖ *intr* smoke; (coll) smoke like a chimney
qual′mig *adj* smoky
qual′voll *adj* agonizing
Quantentheorie ['kvantəntə‧ori] *f* quantum theory
Quantität [kvantı'tet] *f* (–;–en) quantity
Quan·tum ['kvantum] *n* (–s;–ten [tən]) quantum; quantity; (*Anteil*) portion
Quappe ['kvapə] *f* (–;–n) tadpole
Quarantäne [kvaran'tenə] *f* (–;–n) quarantine
Quark [kvark] *m* (–[e]s;) curds; cottage cheese; (fig) nonsense
Quark′käse *m* cottage cheese
quarren ['kvarən] *intr* (*Frosch*) croak; (fig) groan
Quart [kvart] *n* (–s;–e) quart; quarto ‖ *f* (–;–en) (mus) fourth
Quartal [kvar'tal] *n* (–s;–e) quarter (*of a year*)
Quartals′abrechnung *f* (fin) quarterly statement
Quartals′säufer *m* periodic drunkard
Quart′band *m* (–[e]s;–e) quarto volume
Quarte ['kvartə] *f* (–;–n) (mus) fourth
Quartett [kvar'tet] *n* (–[e]s;–e) quartet
Quart′format *n* quarto
Quartier [kvar'tir] *n* (–s;–e) (*Stadtviertel*) quarter; (*Unterkunft*) quarters; (mil) quarters, billet
Quartier′meister *m* (mil) quartermaster
Quarz [kvarts] *m* (–es;–e) quartz
quasseln ['kvasəln] *tr* (coll) talk ‖ *intr* talk nonsense
Quast [kvast] *m* (–[e]s;–e) brush
Quaste ['kvastə] *f* (–;–n) tassel
Quatsch [kvatʃ] *m* (–es;) (coll) baloney
quatschen ['kvatʃən] *intr* chatter; talk nonsense; (*durch Schlamm*) slog
Quecksilber ['kvekzılbər] *n* mercury
queck′silbrig *adj* fidgety
Quell [kvel] *m* (–[e]s;–e) (poet) var of Quelle
Quelle ['kvelə] *f* (–;–n) fountainhead; source; spring
quellen ['kvelən] §119 *tr* cause to swell; soak ‖ *intr* (SEIN) spring, gush; (*Tränen*) well up; (*anschwellen*) swell; **ihm quollen die Augen fast aus dem Kopf** his eyes almost popped out
Quel′lenangabe *f* citation; bibliography
quel′lenmäßig *adj* according to the best authorities, authentic
Quel′lenmaterial *n* source material
Quel′lenstudium *n* original research

Quell′fluß *m* source
Quell′gebiet *n* headwaters
Quell′wasser *n* spring water
Quengelei [kvenə'lai] *f* (–;–en) nagging
quengeln ['kvenəln] *intr* nag
quer [kver] *adj* cross, transverse ‖ *adv* crosswise; **q. über** (*acc*) across
Quer′balken *m* crossbeam
Quere ['kverə] *f* (–;) diagonal direction; **j–m in die Q. kommen** run across s.o.; (fig) disturb s.o.
queren ['kverən] *tr* traverse, cross
querfeldein′ *adv* cross-country
Quer′kopf *m* contrary person
quer′köpfig *adj* contrary
Quer′pfeife *f* (mus) fife
Quer′ruder *n* (aer) aileron
Quer′schiff *n* (archit) transept
Quer′schläger *m* ricochet
Quer′schnitt *m* cross section
Quer′treiber *m* schemer, plotter
querü′ber *adv* straight across
Querulant –in [kveru'lant(ın)] §7 *mf* grumbler, grouch
Quetsche ['kvetʃə] *f* (–;–n) squeezer; (pej) joint
quetschen ['kvetʃən] *tr* squeeze, pinch; bruise; (*zerquetschen*) crush, mash
Quetsch′kartoffeln *pl* mashed potatoes
Quet′schung *f* (–;–en) bruise, contusion
Quetsch′wunde *f* bruise
quick [kvık] *adj* brisk, lively
quick′lebendig *adj* (coll) very lively
quieken ['kvikən] *intr* squeal, squeak
quietschen ['kvitʃən] *intr* (*Tür*) creak; (*Ferkel*) squeal; (*Bremsen*) screetch
Quintessenz ['kvıntesents] *f* (–;) quintessence
Quintett [kvın'tet] *n* (–[e]s;–e) quintet
Quirl [kvırl] *m* (–[e]s;–e) (fig) fidgeter; (culin) whisk, mixer
quirlen ['kvırlən] *tr* beat, mix
quitt [kvıt] *adj* even, square
Quitte ['kvıtə] *f* (–;–n) quince
quittieren [kvı'tirən] *tr* give a receipt for; (*aufgeben*) quit
Quit′tung *f* (–;–en) receipt
Quiz [kvıs] *n* (–;–) quiz
quoll [kvol] *pret* of quellen
Quotation [kvota'tsjon] *f* (–;–en) (st. exch.) quotation
Quote ['kvotə] *f* (–;–en) quota
Quotient [kvo'tsjent] *m* (–en;–en) quotient
quotieren [kvo'tirən] *tr* quote

R

R, r [er] *invar n* R, r
Rabatt [ra'bat] *m* (–[e]s;–e) reduction, discount
Rabatt′marke *f* trading stamp
Rabatz [ra'bats] *m*—**R. machen** (coll) raise Cain
Rab·bi ['rabi] *m* (–[s];–s & –binen [binən]), **Rabbiner** [ra'binər] *m* (–s;–) rabbi
Rabe ['rabə] *m* (–n;–n) raven; **weißer R.** (fig) rare bird
Ra′benaas *n* (coll) beast
Ra′benmutter *f* hard-hearted mother
ra′benschwarz′ *adj* jet-black

rabiat [ra'bjat] *adj* rabid, raving

Rache ['raxə] *f* (–;) revenge

Rachen ['raxən] *m* (–s;–) throat; mouth; (fig) jaws

rächen ['rɛçən] *tr* avenge || *ref* (an *dat*) avenge oneself (on)

Ra'chenhöhle *f* pharynx

Ra'chenkatarrh *m* sore throat

Rä'cher –in §6 *mf* avenger

Rachgier ['raxgir] *f* revengefulness

rach'gierig, rach'süchtig *adj* vengeful

Rad [rat] *n* (–[e]s;ᵘer) wheel; bike; ein Rad schlagen turn a cartwheel; (*Pfau*) fan the tail

Radar ['radar], [ra'dar] *n* (–s;) radar

Ra'dargerät *n* radar

Ra'darschirm *m* radarscope

Radau [ra'dau] *m* (–s;–) (coll) row

Radau'macher *m* rowdy

Rädchen ['rɛtçən] *n* (–s;–) little wheel

Rad'dampfer *m* river boat

radebrechen ['radəbrɛçən] §64 *tr* murder (*a language*)

radeln ['radəln] *intr* (SEIN) (coll) ride a bike

Rädelsführer ['redəlsfyrər] *m* ringleader

rädern ['redərn] *tr* torture; **wie gerädert sein** (coll) be bushed

Räderwerk ['redərverk] *n* gears; (fig) clockwork

rad'fahren §71 *intr* (SEIN) ride a bicycle

radieren [ra'dirən] *tr* erase; etch

Radie'rer *m* (–s;–) eraser; etcher

Radier'gummi *m* eraser

Radier'kunst *f* art of etching

Radier'messer *n* scraper, eraser

Radie'rung *f* (–;–en) erasure; etching

Radieschen [ra'disçən] *n* (–s;–) radish

radikal [radɪ'kal] *adj* radical || **Radikale** §5 *mf* radical, extremist

Radio ['radjo] *n* (–s;–s) radio; **im R.** on the radio; **R. hören** listen to the radio

Ra'dioamateur *m* (rad) ham

Ra'dioapparat *m*, **Ra'diogerät** *n* radio set

Radiologe [radjo'logə] *m* (–n;–n) radiologist

Radiologie [radjolo'gi] *f* (–;) radiology

Ra'dioröhre *f* radio tube

Ra'diosender *m* radio transmitter

Radium ['radjum] *n* (–s;) radium

Ra·dius ['radjus] *m* (–;–dien [djən]) radius

Rad'kappe *f* hubcap

Rad'kranz *m* rim

Radler –in ['radlər(ɪn)] §6 *mf* cyclist

Rad'nabe *f* hub

Rad'rennen *n* bicycle race

–rädrig [redrɪç] *comb.fm.* –wheeled

rad'schlagen §132 *intr* turn a cartwheel

Rad'spur *f* rut, track

Rad'stand *m* wheelbase

Rad'zahn *m* cog

raffen ['rafən] *tr* snatch up, gather up; (sew) take up

Raffgier ['rafgir] *f* rapacity

raffgierig ['rafgirɪç] *adj* rapacious

Raffine·rie [rafɪnə'ri] *f* (–;–rien ['ri·ən]) refinery

raffinieren [rafɪ'nirən] *tr* refine

raffiniert [rafɪ'nirt] *adj* refined; (fig) shrewd, cunning

Raffzahn ['raftsan] *m* canine tooth

ragen ['ragən] *intr* tower, loom

Ragout [ra'gu] *n* (–s;–s) (culin) stew

Rahe ['ra·ə] *f* (–;–n) (naut) yard

Rahm [ram] *m* (–[e]s;) cream

Rahmen ['ramən] *m* (–s;–) frame; (*Gefüge*) framework; (*Bereich*) scope, limits; (fig) setting; (aut) chassis; **aus dem R. fallen** be out of place; **e–n R. abgeben für** form a setting for; **im R.** (*genit*) in the course of; **im R. von** (or *genit*) within the scope of; within the framework of

Rah'menerzählung *f* story within a story

rahmig ['ramɪç] *adj* creamy

Rakete [ra'ketə] *f* (–;–n) rocket

Rake'tenabschußrampe *f* launch pad

Rake'tenbunker *m* silo

Rake'tenstart *m* rocket launch

Rake'tenwerfer *m* rocket launcher

Rake'tenwesen *n* rocketry

Rakett [ra'ket] *n* (–[e]s;–e & –s) (tennis) racket

Rammbär ['ramber] *m*, **Rammbock** ['rambɔk] *m*, **Ramme** ['ramə] *f* (–;–n) rammer; pile driver

rammeln ['raməln] *tr* shove; (*zusammenpressen*) pack; (*belegen*) copulate with || *intr* copulate

rammen ['ramən] *tr* ram; (*Beton*) tamp

Rampe ['rampə] *f* (–;–n) ramp; (rok) launch pad; (rr) platform; (theat) apron

Ram'penlicht *n* footlights; (fig) limelight

Ramsch [ramʃ] *m* (–es;) odds and ends; junk; (com) rummage

Ramsch'verkauf *m* rummage sale

Ramsch'waren *pl* junk

Rand [rant] *m* (–[e]s;ᵘer) edge, border; (*e–s Druckseite*) margin; **am Rande bemerken** note in passing; **außer R. und Band** completely out of control; **bis zum Rande** to the brim; **e–n R. hinterlassen** leave a ring (*e.g., from a wet glass*); **Ränder unter den Augen** circles under the eyes

Rand'auslöser *m* (typ) margin release

Rand'bemerkung *f* marginal note; (fig) snide remark

rändeln ['rendəln], **rändern** ['rendərn] *tr* border, edge; (*Münzen*) mill

Rand'gebiet *n* borderland; (*e–r Stadt*) outskirts

rand'los *adj* rimless

Rand'staat *m* border state

Ranft [ranft] *m* (–[e]s;ᵘe) crust

rang [ran] *pret of* ringen || **Rang** *m* (–[e]s;ᵘe) rank; (theat) balcony; **j–m den R. ablaufen** (fig) run rings around s.o.

Rang'abzeichen *n* insignia of rank

Rang'älteste §5 *mf* ranking officer

Range ['ranə] *m* (–n;–n) & *f* (–;–n) brat

Rangier'bahnhof *m* (rr) marshaling yard

rangieren [rã'ʒirən] *tr* rank; (rr) shunt, switch || *intr* rank

Rang′ordnung f order of precedence
Rang′stufe f rank
rank [raŋk] adj slender
Ranke [′raŋkə] f (-;-n) tendril
Ränke [′reŋkə] pl schemes; **R. schmie-**
den scheme
ranken [′raŋkən] ref & intr creep,
climb; **sich r. um** wind around
rän′kevoll adj scheming
rann [ran] pret of **rinnen**
rannte [′rantə] pret of **rennen**
Ranzen [′rantsən] m (-s;-) knapsack;
school bag; (Bauch) belly; (mil) field
pack
ranzig [′rantsiç] adj rancid
rapid [ra′pit], **rapide** [ra′pidə] adj
rapid
Rappe [′rapə] m (-n;-n) black horse
rar [rar] adj rare, scarce
Rarität [rari′tɛt] f (-;-en) rarity
rasant [ra′zant] adj grazing, point-
blank (fire); (fig) impetuous
Rasanz [ra′zants] f (-;) flat trajectory;
(fig) impetuosity
rasch [raʃ] adj quick; (hastig) hasty
rascheln [′raʃəln] intr rustle
Rasch′heit f (-;) haste, speed
rasen [′razən] intr rage, rave || intr
(SEIN) rush; (aut) speed || **Rasen** m
(-s;-) lawn, grass
ra′send adj raging, raving; wild, mad;
(Hunger) ravenous; (Wut) towering;
(Tempo) break-neck; **r. werden** see
red
Ra′sendecke f turf
Ra′senmäher m lawn mower
Ra′senplatz m lawn
Ra′sensprenger m lawn sprinkler
Raserei [razə′rai] f (-;) rage, mad-
ness; (aut) reckless driving
Rasier- [razir] comb.fm. shaving,
razor
Rasier′apparat m safety razor
rasieren [ra′zirən] tr & ref shave
Rasier′klinge f razor blade
Rasier′messer n straight razor
Rasier′napf m shaving mug
Rasier′pinsel m shaving brush
Rasier′wasser n after-shave lotion
Rasier′zeug n shaving outfit
Raspel [′raspəl] f (-;-n) rasp; (culin)
grater
raspeln [′raspəln] tr rasp; grate
Rasse [′rasə] f (-;-n) race; (Zucht)
breed, blood, stock; (fig) good breed-
ing
Rassel [′rasəl] f (-;-n) rattle
rasseln [′rasəln] intr rattle; **durchs**
Examen r. (coll) flunk the exam
Rassen- [rasən] comb.fm. racial
Ras′senfrage f racial problem
Ras′senhaß m racism, race hatred
Ras′senkreuzung f miscegenation;
crossbreeding
Ras′senkunde f ethnology
ras′senmäßig adj racial
Ras′senmerkmal n racial characteristic
Ras′sentrennung f segregation
Ras′senunruhen pl racial disorders
ras′sepferd n thoroughbred (horse)
ras′serein adj racially pure; thorough-
bred
Ras′sevieh n purebred cattle

rassig [′rasiç] adj racy; thoroughbred
rassisch [′rasiʃ] adj racial
Rast [rast] f (-;-en) rest; station,
stage; (mach) notch, groove; (mil)
halt; **e-e R. machen** take a rest
rasten [′rastən] intr rest; (mil) halt
rast′los adj restless
Rast′losigkeit f (-;) restlessness
Rast′platz m, **Rast′stätte** f resting place
Rast′tag m day of rest
Rasur [ra′zur] f (-;-en) shave
Rat [rat] m (-[e]s; **Ratschläge** [′rat-
ʃlegə]) advice, piece of advice, counsel; (Beratung) deliberation; (Ausweg) means, solution; **auf e-n Rat**
hören listen to reason; **sich** [dat]
keinen Rat mehr wissen be at one's
wits' end; **zu Rate ziehen** consult (a
person, dictionary, etc.) || m (-[e]s;
⸚e) council, board; (Person) councilor, alderman; advisor; (jur) counsel
Rate [′ratə] f (-;-n) installment; **auf**
Raten on the installment plan
raten [′ratən] §63 tr guess; (Rätsel)
solve; **das will ich dir nicht geraten**
haben! you had better not!; **geraten!**
you guessed it!; **j-m etw r.** advise
s.o. about s.th.; **komm nicht wieder.**
das rate ich dir! take my advice and
don't come back! || intr guess; give
advice; (dat) advise; **gut r.** take a
good guess; **hin und her r.** make random guesses; **j-m gut r.** give s.o.
good advice; **j-m zu etw r.** recom-
mend s.th. to s.o. || **Raten** n (-s;)
guesswork; advice
ra′tenweise adv by installments
Ra′tenzahlung f payment in installments; **auf R.** on the installment plan
Räterepublik [′rɛtərepublik] f Soviet
Union, Soviet Republic
Rat′geber -in §6 mf adviser, counselor
Rat′haus n city hall
ratifizieren [ratifi′tsirən] tr ratify
Ratifizie′rung f (-;-en) ratification
Ration [ra′tsjon] f (-;-en) ration
rational [ratsjo′nal] adj rational
rationalisieren [ratsjonali′zirən] tr
streamline (operations in industry)
rationell [ratsjo′nel] adj rational
rationieren [ratsjo′nirən] tr ration
rätlich [′retliç] adj advisable
rat′los adj helpless, perplexed
ratsam [′ratzam] adj advisable
Ratsche [′ratʃə] f (-;-n) rattle; (coll)
chatterbox; (tech) ratchet
ratschen [′ratʃən] intr make noise with
a rattle; (coll) chat
Rat′schlag m advice, piece of advice
rat′schlagen §132 intr deliberate, consult
Rat′schluß m decision, decree, resolution
Rätsel [′retsəl] n (-s;-) puzzle; (fig)
riddle, enigma, mystery
rät′selhaft adj puzzling; mysterious
Ratte [′ratə] f (-;-n) rat
Rat′tenschwanz m rat tail; (fig) tangle;
(coll) whole string (of questions,
etc.); (Haarzopf) (coll) pigtail
rattern [′ratərn] intr rattle
ratzekahl [′ratsə′kal] adj (Person)

completely bald; (*Landschaft*) completely barren || *adv* completely

Raub [raup] *m* (-[e]s;) robbery; plunder; (*Beute*) prey, spoils; **zum Raube fallen** fall prey, fall victim

Raub– comb.fm. predatory, rapacious

Raub'bau *m* (-[e]s;) excessive exploitation (*of natural resources*)

rauben ['rauben] *tr*—j–m etw r. rob s.o. of s.th.; **e–m Mädchen die Unschuld r.** seduce a girl; **e–n Kuß r.** steal a kiss || *intr* rob

Räuber ['rɔɪbər] *m* (-s;–) robber; **R. und Gendarm spielen** play cops and robbers

Räu'berbande *f* gang of robbers

Räu'berhauptmann *m* gang leader

räuberisch ['rɔɪbərɪʃ] *adj* predatory

Raub'fisch *m* predatory fish

Raub'gesindel *n* gang of robbers

Raub'lust *f* rapacity

raub'gierig *adj* rapacious

Raub'lust *f* rapacity

Raub'mord *m* murder with robbery

Raub'mörder *m* robber and murderer

Raub'schiff *n* corsair, pirate ship

Raub'tier *n* beast of prey

Raub'überfall *m* holdup, robbery

Raub'vogel *m* bird of prey

Raub'zug *m* plundering raid

Rauch [raux] *m* (-[e]s;) smoke

rauchen ['rauxən] *tr & intr* smoke

Raucher ['rauxər] *m* (-s;–) smoker

Räucher– [rɔɪxər] *comb.fm.* smoked

Rau'cherabteil *n* smoking section

Räu'cherfaß *n* (eccl) censer

Räu'cherhering *m* smoked herring

Rau'cherhusten *m* cigarette cough

Räu'cherkammer *f* smokehouse

räuchern ['rɔɪxərn] *tr* smoke, cure; (*desinzieren*) fumigate

Räu'cherschinken *m* smoked ham

Räu'cherung *f* (-;) smoking; fumigation

Rau'cherwagen *m* (rr) smoker

Rauch'fahne *f* trail of smoke

Rauch'fang *m* (*über dem Herd*) hood; (*im Schornstein*) flue

Rauch'fleisch *n* smoked meat

rauchig ['rauxɪç] *adj* smoky

rauch'los *adj* smokeless

Rauch'schleier *m* (mil) smoke screen

Rauch'waren *pl* (*Pelze*) furs; (*Tabakwaren*) tobacco supplies

Räude ['rɔɪdə] *f* (-;) mange

räudig ['rɔɪdɪç] *adj* mangy; **räudiges Schaf** (fig) black sheep

Raufbold ['raufbɔlt] *m* (-[e]s;-e) roughneck, bully

Raufe ['raufə] *f* (-;-n) hayrack

raufen ['raufən] *tr* tear, pull out || *recip & intr* fight, brawl, scuffle

Rauferei [raufə'raɪ] *f* (-;-en) fight, scuffle

rauf'lustig *adj* scrappy, belligerent

rauh [rau] *adj* rough; (*Hals*) hoarse; (*Behandlung*) harsh; **rauhe Wirklichkeit** hard facts

Rauh'bein *n* (fig) roughneck, churl

rauh'beinig *adj* tough, churlish

Rau'heit *f* (-;) roughness; hoarseness

rauhen ['rau·ən] *tr* roughen

Rauh'futter *n* roughage

rauh'haarig *adj* shaggy, hirsute

Rauh'reif *m* hoarfrost

Raum [raum] *m* (-[e]s;-̈e) room, space; (*Zimmer*) room; (*Bereich*) area; (*e–s Schiffes*) hold; **am Rande R. lassen** (typ) leave a margin; **freier R.** open space; **gebt R.!** make way! **luftleerer R.** vacuum; **R. bieten für** accommodate; **R. einnehmen** take up space; **R. geben** (*dat*) give way to; comply with

Raum'anzug *m* space suit

Räumboot ['rɔɪmboːt] *n* minesweeper

Raum'dichte *f* (phys) density by volume

räumen ['rɔɪmən] *tr* clear; (*Wohnung*) vacate; (*Minen*) sweep; (mil) evacuate; **den Saal r.** clear the room; **das Lager r.** (com) clear out the stock; **j–n aus dem Wege r.** (fig) finish s.o. off

Raum'ersparnis *f* economy of space; **der R. wegen** to save space

Raum'fahrer *m* spaceman

Raum'fahrt *f* space travel

Raum'flug *m* space flight

Raum'gestaltung *f* interior decorating

Raum'inhalt *m* volume, capacity

Raum'kunst *f* interior decorating

Raum'lehre *f* geometry

räumlich ['rɔɪmlɪç] *adj* spatial

Räum'lichkeit *f* (-;-en) room

Raum'mangel *m* lack of space

Raum'medizin *f* space medicine

Raum'meter *n* cubic meter

Raum'schiff *n* space ship

Raum'schiffart *f* space travel

Raum'schiffkapsel *f* space capsule

Raum'sonde *f* unmanned space explorer

Raum'ton *m* stereophonic sound

Räu'mung *f* (-;-en) clearing, removal; (com) clearance; (mil) evacuation

Räu'mungsausverkauf *m* clearance sale

Räu'mungsbefehl *m* eviction notice; (mil) evacuation order

raunen ['raunən] *tr & intr* whisper

raunzen ['rauntsən] *intr* grumble

Raupe ['raupə] *f* (-;-n) (ent, mach) caterpillar

Rau'penfahrzeug *n* full-track vehicle

Rau'penkette *f* caterpillar track

Rau'penschlepper *m* caterpillar tractor

Rausch [rau∫] *m* (-es;-e) drunkenness; (fig) intoxication, ecstasy; **e–n R. haben** be drunk; **sich** [*dat*] **e–n R. antrinken** get drunk

rauschen ['rau∫ən] *intr* (*Blätter, Seide*) rustle; (*Bach*) murmur; (*Brandung, Sturm*) roar || *intr* (SEIN) strut; rush

rau'schend *adj* rustling; (*Fest*) uproarious; (*Beifall*) thunderous

Rausch'gift *n* drug, dope

Rausch'gifthandel *m* drug traffic

Rausch'giftschieber –in §6 *mf* pusher

Rausch'giftsucht *f* drug addiction

Rausch'giftsüchtige §5 *mf* dope addict

Rausch'gold *n* tinsel

räuspern ['rɔɪspərn] *ref* clear one's throat

Rausschmeißer ['raus/maɪsər] *m* (-s;–) (coll) bouncer

Raute ['rautə] *f* (-;-n) (cards) diamond; (geom) rhombus

Rayon [re'jõ] *m* (-s;-s) (*Bezirk*) district, region; (*im Warenhaus*) department

Raz-zia ['ratsja] *f* (-;-zien [tsjən]) police raid

Reagenzglas [re·a'gentsglɑs] *n* test tube

reagieren [re·a'girən] *intr* (auf *acc*) react (to)

Reaktion [re·ak'tsjon] *f* (-;-en) reaction

reaktionär [re·aktsjə'ner] *adj* reactionary ‖ **Reaktionär** *m* (-s;-e) reactionary

Reak·tor [re'aktɔr] *m* (-s;-toren ['torən]) (phys) reactor

real [re'al] *adj* real

Real/gymnasium *n* high school (*where modern languages, mathematics, or sciences are stressed*)

Realien [re'uljən] *pl* real facts, realities; exact sciences

realisieren [re·ali'zirən] *tr* realize

Realist -in [re·a'lɪst(ɪn)] §7 *mf* realist

realistisch [re·a'lɪstɪʃ] *adj* realistic

Realität [re·ali'tet] *f* (-;-en) reality; **Realitäten** real property

Real/lexikon *n* encyclopedia

Real/lohn *m* purchasing power of wages

Real/schule *f* non-classical secondary school

Rebe ['rebə] *f* (-;-n) vine; tendril

Rebell [re'bel] *m* (-en;-en) rebel

rebellieren [rebe'lirən] *intr* rebel

Rebellin [re'belɪn] *f* (-;-nen) rebel

Rebellion [rebel'jon] *f* (-;-en) rebellion

rebellisch [re'belɪʃ] *adj* rebellious

Re/bensaft *m* (poet) juice of the grape

Rebhuhn ['rephun] *n* partridge

Rebstock ['rep/tɔk] *m* vine

rechen ['reçən] *tr* rake ‖ **Rechen** *m* (-s;-) rake; grate

Re/chenaufgabe *f* arithmetic problem

Re/chenautomat *m* computer

Re/chenbrett *n* abacus

Re/chenbuch *n* arithmetic book

Re/chenexemplar *n* arithmetic problem

Re/chenkunst *f* arithmetic

Re/chenmaschine *f* calculator

Re/chenpfennig *m* counter

Re/chenschaft *f* (-;) account; j-n zur R. ziehen call s.o. to account

Re/chenschaftsbericht *m* report

Re/chenschieber *m* slide rule

rechnen ['reçnən] *tr* reckon, calculate, figure out ‖ *intr* reckon; calculate; **falsch r.** miscalculate; **r. auf** (*acc*) count on; **r. mit** be prepared for; expect; take into account; **r. zu** be counted among ‖ **Rechnen** *n* (-s;) arithmetic; calculation

Rech/ner *m* (-s;-) calculator, computer; **er ist ein guter R.** he is good at numbers

rechnerisch ['reçnərɪʃ] *adj* arithmetical

Rech/nung *f* (-;-en) calculation; account; bill; (*Warenrechnung*) invoice; (*im Restaurant*) check; **auf j-s R. setzen** (or **stellen**) charge to s.o.'s

account; **auf R. kaufen** buy on credit; **auf seine R. kaufen** get one's money's worth; **außer R. lassen** overlook; **das geht auf meine R.** this is on me; **die R. begleichen** settle an account (or bill); **j-m in R. stellen** charge to s.o.'s account; **in R. ziehen** take into account; **R. tragen** (*dat*) make allowance for

Rech/nungsabschluß *m* closing of accounts

Rech/nungsauszug *m* (com) statement

Rech/nungsführer -in §6 *mf* accountant

Rech/nungsführung *f* accounting

Rech/nungsjahr *n* fiscal year

Rech/nungsprüfer -in §6 *mf* auditor

Rech/nungswesen *n* accounting

recht [reçt] *adj* right; (*richtig*) correct; (*echt*) real; (*gerecht*) all right, right; (*geziemend*) suitable, proper; **es ist mir nicht r.** I don't like it; **es ist schon r.** that's all right; **mir soll's r. sein** I don't mind; **zur rechten Zeit** at the right moment ‖ *adv* right; quite; (*sehr*) very; **das kommt mir gerade r.** that comes in handy; **erst r.** all the more; **es j-m r. machen** please s.o.; **es geschieht ihm r.** it serves him right; **j-m r. geben** agree with s.o.; **nun erst r. nicht** now less than ever; **r. daran tun zu** (*inf*) do right to (*inf*); **r. haben** be right ‖ **Recht** *n* (-[e]s;-e) right; (*Vorrecht*) privilege; (jur) law; **alle Rechte vorbehalten** all rights reserved; **die Rechte studieren** study law; **mit R.** with good reason; **R. sprechen** dispense justice; **sich** [*dat*] **selbst R. verschaffen** take the law into one's hands; **von Rechts wegen** by rights; **wieder zu seinem Rechte kommen** come into one's own again; **zu R. bestehen** be justified ‖ **Rechte** §5 *mf* right person; **an den Rechten kommen** meet one's match; **du bist mir der R.!** you're a fine fellow! ‖ *f* right hand; (box) right; **die R.** (pol) the right ‖ *n* right; **er dünkt sich** [*dat*] **was Rechtes** he thinks he's somebody; **nach dem Rechten sehen** look after things

Recht/eck *n* rectangle, oblong

recht/eckig *adj* rectangular

recht/fertigen *tr* justify, vindicate

Recht/fertigung *f* (-;-en) justification

recht/gläubig *adj* orthodox

rechthaberisch ['reçthabərɪʃ] *adj* dogmatic

recht/lich *adj* legal, lawful; (*ehrlich*) honest, honorable

Recht/lichkeit *f* (-;) legality; (*Redlichkeit*) honesty

recht/los *adj* without rights

recht/mäßig *adj* legal; legitimate

Recht/mäßigkeit *f* (-;) legality; legitimacy

rechts [reçts] *adv* on the right; right, to the right

Rechts- *comb.fm.* legal

Rechts/angelegenheit *f* legal matter

Rechts/anspruch *m* legal claim

Rechts/anwalt *m* lawyer, attorney

Rechts′ausdruck m legal term
Rechts′auskunft f legal advice
Rechts′außen m (–;–) (fb) right wing
Rechts′beistand m legal adviser
recht′schaffen adj honest
Recht′schaffenheit f (–;) honesty
Recht′schreibung f orthography
Rechts′fall m case, legal case
Rechts′gang m legal procedure
Rechts′gefühl n sense of justice
Rechts′gelehrsamkeit f jurisprudence
Rechts′grund m legal grounds; (Anspruch) title, claim
rechts′gültig adj legal, valid
Rechts′gültigkeit f legality
Rechts′gutachten n legal opinion
Rechts′handel m lawsuit
rechtshändig [′reçtshendiç] adj right-handed
rechts′herum adv clockwise
Rechts′kraft f legal force
rechts′kräftig adj valid
Rechts′lage f legal status
Rechts′lehre f jurisprudence
Rechts′mittel n legal remedy
Rechts′pflege f administration of justice
Recht′sprechung f (–;) administration of justice; die R. (coll) the judiciary
Rechts′schutz m legal protection
Rechts′spruch m verdict
Rechts′streit m legal dispute; pending case: difference of opinion in the interpretation of the law
rechtsum′ interj (mil) right face!
rechts′ungültig adj illegal, invalid
rechts′verbindlich adj legally binding
Rechtsverdreher –in [′reçtsferdre.ər(ın)] §6 mf pettifogger
Rechts′verletzung f (–;–en) violation of the law; infringement of another's rights
Rechts′weg m recourse to the law; auf dem Rechtswege by the courts; den R. beschreiten take legal action
Rechts′wissenschaft f jurisprudence
Reck [rek] n (–[e]s;–e) horizontal bar
recken [′rekən] tr stretch; den Hals r. crane one's neck
Redakteur [redak′tør] m (–s;–e) editor
Redaktion [redak′tsjon] f (–;–en) editorship; (Arbeitskräfte) editorial staff; (Arbeitsraum) editorial office
redaktionell [redaktsjo′nel] adj editorial
Redaktions′schluß m press time, deadline
Rede [′redə] f (–;–n) speech; (Gespräch) conversation; (Gerücht) rumor; das ist nicht der R. wert that is not worth mentioning; davon kann keine R. sein that's out of the question; die in R. stehende Person the person in question; e–e R. halten give a speech; es geht die R., daß it is rumored that; gebundene R. verse; gehobene R. lofty language; j–m in die R. fallen interrupt s.o.; j–m R. und Antwort stehen explain oneself to s.o.; j–n zur R. stellen take s.o. to task; keine R.! absolutely not!; lose Reden führen engage in loose talk; ungebundene R. prose

Re′defigur f figure of speech
Re′defluß m flow of words
Re′defreiheit f freedom of speech
Re′degabe f eloquence, fluency
re′degewandt adj fluent; (iron) glib
Re′degewandtheit f fluency, eloquence
Re′dekunst f eloquence
reden [′redən] tr speak, talk ‖ ref— mit sich r. lassen listen to reason; sich heiser r. talk oneself hoarse; von sich r. machen cause a lot of talk ‖ intr speak, talk; converse; du hast gut r.! it's easy for you to talk; j–m ins Gewissen r. appeal to s.o.'s conscience; j–m nach dem Munde r. humor s.o.; mit j–m deutsch r. (fig) talk turkey to s.o.
Re′densart f phrase, expression; idiom
Rederei [redə′raɪ] f (–;–en) empty talk
Re′deschwall m verbosity
Re′deteil m part of speech
Re′deweise f style of speaking
Re′dewendung f phrase, expression
redigieren [redɪ′girən] tr edit
redlich [′retlıç] adj upright, honest ‖ adv—es r. meinen mean well; sich r. bemühen make an honest effort
Red′lichkeit f (–;) honesty, integrity
Redner –in [′rednər(ın)] §6 mf speaker
Red′nerbühne f podium, platform
Red′nergabe f (gift of) eloquence
rednerisch [′rednərıʃ] adj rhetorical
Redoute [re′dutə] f (–;–n) masquerade; (mil) redoubt
redselig [′retzelıç] adj talkative
Reduktion [reduk′tsjon] f (–;–en) reduction
reduplizieren [reduplı′tsirən] tr reduplicate
reduzieren [redu′tsirən] tr (auf acc) reduce (to)
Reede [′redə] f (–;–n) (naut) roadstead
Reeder [′redər] m (–s;–) shipowner
Reederei [redə′raɪ] f (–;–en) shipping company; shipping business
reell [re′el] adj honest; (Preis) fair; (Geschäft) sound ‖ adv—r. bedient werden get one's money's worth
Reep [rep] n (–[e]s;–e) (naut) rope
Referat [refə′rat] n (–[e]s;–e) report; (Vortrag) paper; ein R. halten give a paper
Referendar [referen′dar] m (–s;–e) junior lawyer; in-service teacher
Referent –in [refe′rent(ın)] §7 mf reader of a paper; (Berichterstatter) reporter; (Gutachter) official adviser
Referenz [refe′rents] f (–;–en) reference; j–n als R. angeben give s.o. as a reference; über gute Referenzen verfügen have good references
referieren [refe′rirən] intr (über acc) give a report (on); (über acc) read a paper (on)
reffen [′refən] tr (naut) reef
reflektieren [reflek′tirən] tr reflect ‖ intr reflect; r. auf (acc) reflect on; (com) think of buying
Reflek·tor [re′flektor] m (–s;–toren [′torən]) reflector
Reflex [re′fleks] m (–es;–e) reflex
Reflex′bewegung f reflex action

Reflexion [refle'ksjon] *f* (-;-en) reflection

reflexiv [refle'ksif] *adj* reflexive

Reform [re'form] *f* (-;-en) reform

Reformation [reforma'tsjon] *f* (-;-en) reformation

Refor·mator [refor'mator] *m* (-s; [ma'torən]) reformer

Reform'haus *n* health-food store

reformieren [refor'mirən] *tr* reform

Reform'kost *f* health food

Refrain [rə'frɛ̃] *m* (-s;-s) refrain; **den R. mitsingen** join in the refrain

Regal [re'gal] *n* (-s;-e) shelf

Regat·ta [re'gata] *f* (-;-ten [tən]) regatta

rege ['regə] *adj* brisk, lively

Regel ['regəl] *f* (-;-n) rule, regulation; (pathol) menstruation; **in der R. as a rule**

re'gellos *adj* irregular; disorderly

Re'gellosigkeit *f* (-;-en) irregularity

re'gelmäßig *adj* regular

Re'gelmäßigkeit *f* regularity

regeln ['regəln] *tr* regulate; arrange; control

re'gelrecht *adj* regular; downright

Re'gelung *f* (-;-en) regulation; control

re'gelwidrig *adj* against the rules; (sport) foul

regen ['regən] *tr* & *ref* move, stir ‖ **Regen** *m* (-s;-) rain; **vom R. unter die Traufe kommen** jump out of the frying pan into the fire

re'genarm *adj* rainless, dry

Re'genbogen *m* rainbow

Re'genbogenhaut *f* (anat) iris

re'gendicht *adj* rainproof

Re'genfall *m* rainfall

re'genfest *adj* rainproof

Re'genguß *m* downpour

Re'genhaut *f* oilskin coat

Re'genmantel *m* raincoat

Re'genmenge *f* amount of rainfall

Re'genmesser *m* rain gauge

Re'genpfeifer *m* (orn) plover

Re'genschauer *m* shower

Re'genschirm *m* umbrella

Regent –in [re'gent(ɪn)] §7 *mf* regent

Re'gentag *m* rainy day

Re'gentropfen *m* raindrop

Re'genumhang *m* cape

Re'genwetter *n* rainy weather

Re'genwurm *m* earthworm

Re'genzeit *f* rainy season

Re·gie [re'ʒi] *f* (-;-gien ['ʒi·ən]) management, administration; (com) state monopoly; (cin, theat) direction

Regie'assistent –in §7 *mf* (cin, theat) assistant director

Regie'pult *n* (rad) control console

Regie'raum *m* (rad) control room

regieren [re'girən] *tr* govern, rule; (gram) govern, take ‖ *intr* reign; (fig) predominate

Regie'rung *f* (-;-en) government, rule; administration; reign

Regie'rungsanleihe *f* government loan

Regie'rungsantritt *m* accession

Regie'rungsbeamte §5 *m* government official

Regie'rungssitz *m* seat of government

Regie'rungszeit *f* reign; administration

Regime [re'ʒim] *n* (-s;-s) regime

Regiment [regɪ'ment] *n* (-[e]s;-e) rule, government ‖ *n* (-[e]s;-er) (mil) regiment

Regiments– *comb.fm.* regimental

Regiments'kommandeur *m* regimental commander

Region [re'gjon] *f* (-;-en) region

regional [regjo'nal] *adj* regional

Regisseur [reʒɪ'sør] *m* (-s;-e) (cin, theat) director

Register [re'gɪstər] *n* (-s;-) file clerk; (*Inhaltsverzeichnis*) index; (*Orgel*–) stop

Regi·strator [regɪs'trator] *m* (-s; -stratoren [stra'torən]) registrar

Registratur [regɪstra'tur] *f* (-;-en) filing; filing cabinet

registrieren [regɪs'trirən] *tr* register; (*Betrag*) ring up

Registrier'kasse *f* cash register

Registrie'rung *f* (-;-en) registration

Reglement [reglə'mã] *n* (-s;-s) regulation(s), rule(s)

Regler ['reglər] *m* (-s;-) regulator; (mach) governor

reglos ['reklos] *adj* motionless

regnen ['regnən] *impers*—**es regnet** it is raining; **es regnet Bindfäden** it's raining cats and dogs; **es regnete Püffe** blows came thick and fast

regnerisch ['regnərɪʃ] *adj* rainy

Re·greß [re'gres] *m* (-gresses;-gresse) recourse, remedy; **R. nehmen zu** have recourse to

regsam ['rekzam] *adj* lively; quick

regulär [regu'ler] *adj* regular

regulierbar [regu'lirbar] *adj* adjustable

regulieren [regu'lirən] *tr* regulate; adjust

Regung ['regʊŋ] *f* (-;-en) motion, stirring; emotion; impulse

Reh [re] *n* (-[e]s;-e) deer

rehabilitieren [rehabɪlɪ'tirən] *tr* rehabilitate

Rehabilitie'rung *f* (-;-en) rehabilitation

Reh'bock *m* roebuck

Reh'braten *m* roast venison

Reh'kalb *n* fawn

Reh'keule *f* leg of venison

Rehkitz ['rekɪts] *n* (-es;-e) fawn

Reh'leder *n* doeskin

Reibahle ['raipalə] *f* (-;-n) reamer

Reibe ['raibə] *f* (-;-n) (coll) grater

Reibeisen ['raipaizən] *n* (culin) grater

reiben ['raibən] §62 *tr* rub; grate; grind ‖ *ref*—**sich r. an** (*dat*) take offense at ‖ *intr* rub

Reiberei [raibə'rai] *f* (-;-en) (coll) friction, squabble

Rei'bung *f* (-;-en) friction

rei'bungslos *adj* frictionless; (fig) smooth

reich [raiç] *adj* wealthy; (an *dat*) rich (in); (*Fang*) big; (*Phantasie*) fertile; (*Mahlzeit*) lavish ‖ **Reich** *n* (-[e]s; -e) empire, realm; kingdom

reichen ['raiçən] *tr* reach; hand, pass ‖ *intr* reach, extend; do, manage; **das reicht!** that will do!

reich'haltig *adj* rich; abundant

reich'lich adj plentiful, abundant || adv pretty, fairly
Reichs'kanzlei f chancellery
Reichs'kanzler m chancellor
Reichs'mark f reichsmark
Reichs'tag m (hist) diet; (hist) Reichstag (lower house)
Reichtum ['raiçtum] n (-s;-er) riches
Reich'weite f reach, range
reif [raif] adj ripe; (fig) mature || **Reif** m (-[e]s;) frost
Reife ['raifə] f (-;) ripeness; (fig) maturity
reifen ['raifən] intr (SEIN) ripen; mature || impers—es reift there is frost || **Reifen** m (-s;-) tire; hoop
Rei'fendruckmesser m tire gauge
Rei'fenpanne f, **Rei'fenschaden** m flat tire, blowout
Rei'feprüfung f final examination (as prerequisite for entering university)
Rei'fezeugnis n high school diploma
reif'lich adj careful
Reigen ['raigən] m (-s;-) square dance
Reihe ['rai·ə] f (-;-n) row, string; set, series; rank, file; turn; **an der R. sein** be next; **an die R. kommen** get one's turn; **aus der R. tanzen** (fig) go one's own way; **die R. ist an mir** it's my turn; **nach der R.** in succession
reihen ['rai·ən] tr range, rank; (Perlen) string
Rei'hendorf n one-street village
Rei'henfabrikation f assembly-line production
Rei'henfolge f succession, sequence
Rei'henhaus n row house
Rei'henschaltung f (elec) series connection
reih'enweise adv in rows
Reiher ['rai·ər] m (-s;-) heron
Reim [raim] m (-[e]s;-e) rhyme
reimen ['raimən] tr (auf acc) make rhyme (with) || ref rhyme; (fig) make sense; (auf acc) rhyme (with) || intr rhyme
reim'los adj unrhymed, blank
rein [rain] adj pure; (sauber) clean; (klar) clear; (Gewinn) net; (Wahrheit) simple; (Wahnsinn) sheer, absolute; **etw ins reine bringen** clear up s.th.; **etw ins reine schreiben** write (or type) a final copy of s.th.; **mit j—m ins reine kommen** come to an understanding with s.o. || adv quite, downright; **r. alles** almost everything || **Rein** f (-;-en) pan
Reindl ['raindəl] n (-s; & -n) pan
Rei'nemachen n (-s;) housecleaning
Rein'ertrag m clear profit
Rein'fall m flop, disappointment
Rein'gewicht n net weight
Rein'gewinn m net profit
Rein'heit f (-;) purity; cleanness
reinigen ['rainigən] tr clean, cleanse; (fig) purify, refine
Rei'nigung f (-;-en) cleaning; purification; dry cleaning
Rei'nigungsanstalt f dry cleaner's
Rei'nigungsmittel n cleaning agent
Reinmachefrau ['rainmaxəfrau] f cleaning woman
Rein'schrift f final copy

reinweg ['rainvɛk] adv (coll) flatly, absolutely
rein'wollen adj all-wool
Reis [rais] m (-es;) rice || n (-es;-er) twig; (fig) scion
Reis'brei m rice pudding
Reise ['raizə] f (-;-n) trip, tour; (aer) flight; (naut) voyage; **auf der R.** while traveling; **auf Reisen sein** be traveling
Rei'sebericht m travelogue
Rei'sebeschreibung f travel book
Rei'sebüro n travel agency
rei'sefertig adj ready to leave
Rei'seführer m guidebook
Rei'segefährte m, **Rei'segefährtin** f travel companion
Rei'segenehmigung f travel permit
Rei'segepäck n luggage; (rr) baggage
Rei'segesellschaft f tour operator(s); travel group
Rei'sehandbuch n guidebook
Rei'seleiter —in §6 mf courier, guide
rei'selustig adj fond of traveling
reisen ['raizən] intr (SEIN) travel
Reisende ['raizəndə] §5 mf traveler
Rei'sepaß m passport
Rei'seplan m itinerary
Rei'seprospekt m travel folder
Rei'seroute f itinerary
Rei'sescheck m traveler's check
Rei'seschreibmaschine f portable typewriter
Rei'sespesen pl travel expenses
Rei'setasche f overnight bag, flight bag
Rei'seziel n destination
Reisig ['raiziç] n (-s;) brushwood
Rei'sigbündel n faggot
Reisige ['raizigə] §5 m cavalryman
Reißaus [rais'aus] n—R. nehmen (coll) take to one's heels
Reißbrett ['raisbret] n drawing board
reißen ['raisən] §53 tr tear, rip; (ziehen) pull, yank; (wegschnappen) wrest, snatch || intr tear; pull, tug; break, snap; (sich spalten) split, burst; **das reißt ins Geld** this is running into money; **mir reißt die Geduld** I am losing all patience || ref—**an sich r.** seize; (com) monopolize; **die Führung an sich r.** take the lead; **sich an e—m Nagel r.** scratch oneself on a nail; **sich um etw r.** scramble for s.th. || **Reißen** n (-s;) tearing; bursting; sharp pains; rheumatism
rei'ßend adj rapid; (Schmerz) sharp; (Tier) rapacious; **reißenden Absatz finden** (coll) sell like hotcakes
Reißer ['raisər] m (-s;-) bestseller; (cin) box-office hit; (com) good seller
Reißfeder ['raisfedər] f drawing pen
Reißleine ['raislainə] f rip cord
Reißnagel ['raisnagəl] m thumbtack
Reißschiene ['rais/inə] f T-square
Reißverschluß ['raisfer/lus] m zipper
Reißzahn ['raistsan] m canine tooth
Reißzeug ['raistsoik] n mechanical-drawing tools
Reißzwecke ['raistsvekə] f thumbtack
Reit– [rait] comb.fm. riding
Reit'anzug m riding habit

Reit'bahn f riding ring
reiten ['raɪtən] §86 tr ride; **e-n Weg r.** ride along a road; **ihn reitet der Teufel** (coll) he is full of the devil; **krumme Touren r.** (coll) pull shady deals; **Prinzipien r.** (fig) stick rigidly to principles; **über den Haufen r.** knock down || intr (SEIN) go horseback riding; **geritten kommen** come on horseback; **vor Anker r.** ride at anchor
Rei'ter –in §86 mf rider
Rei'terstandbild n equestrian statue
Reit'gerte f riding crop
Reit'hose f riding breeches
Reit'knecht m groom
Reit'kunst f horsemanship
Reit'peitsche f riding crop
Reit'pferd n saddle horse
Reit'schule f riding academy
Reit'stiefel m riding boot
Reit'weg m bridle path
Reiz [raɪts] m (–es;–e) charm, appeal; (Erregung) irritation; (physiol, psychol) stimulus; **e-n R. ausüben auf** (acc) attract; **sie läßt ihre Reize spielen** she turns on the charm
reizbar ['raɪtsbar] adj irritable; (empfindlich) sensitive, touchy
reizen ['raɪtsən] tr (entzünden, ärgern) irritate; (locken) allure; (anziehen) attract; (anregen) excite, stimulate; (aufreizen) provoke; (Appetit) whet || intr (cards) bid || impers **es reizt mich zu** (inf) I'm itching to (inf)
rei'zend adj charming; cute, sweet; (pathol) irritating
Reiz'entzug m sensory deprivation
Reiz'husten m (–s;) constant cough
reiz'los adj unattractive; (Kost) bland
Reiz'mittel n stimulant; (fig) incentive
Reiz'stoff m irritant
Rei'zung f (–;–en) irritation; (Lokkung) allurement; (Anregung) stimulation; (Aufreizung) provocation
reiz'voll adj charming, attractive; fascinating; (verlockend) tempting
rekeln ['rekəln] ref (coll) lounge
Reklamation [reklama'tsjon] f (–;–en) complaint, protest
Reklame [re'klamə] f (–;–n) advertisement, ad; publicity; **R. machen für** advertise
Rekla'mebüro n advertising agency
Rekla'mefeldzug m advertising campaign
reklamieren [rekla'mirən] tr claim || intr (gegen) protest (against); (wegen) complain (about)
rekognoszieren [rekɔs'tsirən] tr & intr reconnoiter
Rekonvaleszent –in [rekɔnvales'tsent (ɪn)] §7 mf convalescent
Rekonvaleszenz [rekɔnvales'tsents] f (–;) convalescence
Rekord [re'kɔrt] m (–[e]s;–e) record
Rekord'ernte f bumper crop, record crop
Rekordler –in [re'kɔrtlər(ɪn)] §6 mf (coll) record holder
Rekord'versuch m attempt to break the record

Rekrut [re'krut] m (–en;–en) recruit
Rekru'tenausbildung f basic training
Rekru'tenaushebung f recruitment
rekrutieren [rekru'tirən] tr recruit || ref—**sich r. aus** be recruited from
Rek·tor ['rektɔr] m (–s;–toren ['torən]) principal; (e-r Universität) president
Relais [rə'le] n (–lais ['le(s)];–lais ['les]) relay
relativ [rela'tif] adj relative
Relegation [relega'tsjon] f (–;–en) expulsion
relegieren [rele'girən] tr expel
Relief [re'ljef] n (–s;–s & –e) relief
Religion [reli'gjon] f (–;–en) religion
Religions'ausübung f practice of religion
Religions'bekenntnis n religious denomination
religiös [reli'gjøs] adj religious
Reling ['relɪŋ] f (–s;–s) (naut) rail
Reliquie [re'likvjə] f (–;–n) relic
Reli'quienschrein m reliquary
remis [rə'mi] adj (cards) tied || **Remis** n (–;–) (chess) tie, draw
remittieren [remi'tirən] tr (Geld) remit; (Waren) return || intr (Fieber) go down
rempeln ['rempəln] tr bump, jostle || intr (fb) block
Remter ['remtər] m (–s;–) refectory; assembly hall
Ren [ren] (–s;–e) reindeer
Renaissance [rənɛ'sãs] f (–;–n) renaissance
Rendite [ren'ditə] f (–;–n) return
Renn– [ren] comb.fm. race, racing
Renn'bahn f race track; (aut) speedway
Renn'boot n racing boat
rennen ['renən] §97 tr run; **j-m den Degen durch den Leib r.** run s.o. through with a sword; **über den Haufen r.** run over; **zu Boden r.** knock down || intr (SEIN) run; race || **Rennen** n (–s;–) running; race; (Einzelrennen) heat; **das R. machen** win the race; **totes R.** dead heat, tie
Ren'ner m (–s;–) (good) race horse
Renn'fahrer m (aut) race driver
Renn'pferd n race horse
Renn'platz m race track; (aut) speedway
Renn'rad n racing bicycle, racer
Renn'sport m racing
Renn'strecke f race track; distance (to be raced); (aut) speedway
Renn'wagen m racing car, racer
Renommee [renɔ'me] n (–s;–s) reputation
renommieren [renɔ'mirən] intr (mit) brag (about), boast (about)
renommiert' adj (wegen) renowned (for)
Renommist [renɔ'mɪst] m (–en;–en) braggart
renovieren [renɔ'virən] tr renovate; redecorate
rentabel [ren'tabəl] adj profitable
Rentabilität [rentabɪlɪ'tet] f (–;–en) (e-r Investition) return; (fin) productiveness

Rente ['rɛntə] f (-;-n) income, revenue; pension; annuity
Ren'tenbrief m annuity bond
Ren'tenempfänger -in §6 mf pensioner
Rentier [rɛn'tje] m (-s;-s) person of independent means || ['rɛntir] n (-s; -s;) reindeer
rentieren [rɛn'tirən] ref pay
Rentner -in ['rɛntnər(ɪn)] §6 mf person on pension
Reparatur [repara'tur] f (-;-en) repair
Reparatur'werkstatt f repair shop; (aut) garage
reparieren [repa'rirən] tr repair, fix
Reportage [repor'taʒə] f (-;-n) report; coverage
Reporter -in [re'pɔrtər(ɪn)] §6 mf reporter
Repräsentant -in [reprezɛn'tant(ɪn)] §7 mf representative
repräsentieren [reprezɛn'tirən] tr represent || intr be a socialite
Repressalie [reprɛ'saljə] f (-;-n) reprisal
Reprise [re'prizə] f (-;-n) (cin) rerun; (mus) repeat; (theat) revival
reproduzieren [reprodu'tsirən] tr reproduce
Reptil [rɛp'til] n (-s;-ien [jən] & -e) reptile
Republik [repu'blik] f (-;-en) republic
Republikaner -in [republi'kanər(ɪn)] §6 mf republican
republikanisch [republi'kanɪʃ] adj republican
Requisit [rekvi'zit] n (-[e]s;-en) requisite; **Requisiten** (theat) props
Reservat [rezɛr'vat] n (-[e]s;-e) reservation
Reserve [re'zɛrvə] f (-;-n) reserve
Reser'vebank f (-;-e) (sport) bench
Reser'vereifen m spare tire
Reser'veteil m spare part
Reser'vetruppen pl (mil) reserves
reservieren [rezɛr'virən] tr reserve
Reservie'rung f (-;-en) reservation
Residenz [rezi'dɛnts] f (-;-en) residence
Residenz'stadt f capital
residieren [rezi'dirən] intr reside
resignieren [rezɪg'nirən] intr resign
Respekt [re'spɛkt] m (-[e]s;) respect
respektabel [rɛspɛk'tabəl] adj respectable
respektieren [rɛspɛk'tirən] tr respect
respekt'los adj disrespectful
respekt'voll adj respectful
Ressort [re'sor] n (-s;-s) department
Rest [rɛst] m (-es;-e & -er) rest; (Stoff-) remnant; (Zahlungs-) balance; (Bodensatz) residue; (math) remainder; **irdische** (or **sterbliche**) **Reste** earthly (or mortal) remains; **j-m den R. geben** (coll) finish s.o. off
Rest'auflage f remainders
Restaurant [rɛsto'rã] n (-s;-s) restaurant
Restauration [rɛstaura'tsjon] f (-;-en) restoration; (Aust) restaurant
Rest'bestand m remainder
Rest'betrag m balance, remainder
Re'steverkauf m remnant sale

rest'lich adj remaining
rest'los adj complete
Resultat [rezul'tat] n (-[e]s;-e) result; upshot; (sport) score
retten ['rɛtən] tr save, rescue
Ret'ter m (-s;-) rescuer; (Heiland) Savior
Rettich ['rɛtɪç] m (-s;-e) radish
Ret'tung f (-;-en) rescue; salvation
Ret'tungsaktion f rescue operation
Ret'tungsboot n lifeboat
Ret'tungsfloß n life raft
Ret'tungsgürtel m life preserver
Ret'tungsleine f life line
ret'tungslos adj irretrievable
Ret'tungsmannschaft f rescue party
Ret'tungsring m life preserver
Ret'tungsstation f first-aid station
retuschieren [retu'ʃirən] tr retouch
Reue ['rɔɪə] f (-;) remorse
reu'elos adj remorseless, impenitent
reuen ['rɔɪən] tr—**die Tat reut mich** I regret having done it; **die Zeit reut mich** I regret wasting the time || impers—es **reut mich, daß** I regret that, I am sorry that
reu'evoll adj repentant, contrite
Reugeld ['rɔɪgɛlt] n forfeit
reumütig ['rɔɪmytɪç] adj repentant
Revanche [re'vãʃə] f (-;) revenge
Revan'chekrieg m punitive war
revan'chelustig adj vengeful
Revan'chepartie f (sport) return game
revanchieren [revã'ʃirən] ref (an dat) take revenge (on); **sich für e-n Dienst r.** return a favor
Revers [re'vɛrs] m (-es;-e) (e-r Münze) reverse; (Erklärung) statement || (re'ver] m (Aust) & n (-;-) lapel; cuff
revidieren [revi'dirən] tr revise; (nachprüfen) check; (com) audit
Revier [re'vir] n (-s;-e) district; quarter; hunting ground; police station; (mil) sick quarters
Revier'stube f (mil) sickroom
Revision [revi'zjon] f (-;-en) revision; (com) audit; (jur) appeal
Re'visor [re'vizor] m (-s;-visoren [vi'zorən]) reviser; (com) auditor
Revolte [re'vɔltə] f (-;-n) revolt
revoltieren [revɔl'tirən] intr revolt
Revolution [revolu'tsjon] f (-;-en) revolution
revolutionär [revolutsjo'ner] adj revolutionary || **Revolutionär** -in §8 mf revolutionary
Revolver [re'vɔlvər] m (-s;-) revolver
Revol'verblatt n (coll) scandal sheet
Revol'verschnauze f (coll) lip, sass
Re·vue [re'vy] f (-;-vuen ['vy.ən]) review; (theat) revue
Rezensent -in [retsɛn'zɛnt(ɪn)] §7 mf reviewer, critic
rezensieren [retsɛn'zirən] tr review
Rezension [retsɛn'zjon] f (-;-en) review
Rezept [re'tsɛpt] n (-[e]s;-e) (culin) recipe; (med) prescription
rezitieren [retsɪ'tirən] tr recite
Rhabarber [ra'barbər] m (-s;) rhubarb
Rhapso·die [rapso'di] f (-;-dien ['di.ən]) rhapsody

Rhein [raɪn] *m* (-[e]s;) Rhine
Rhesusfaktor ['rezuzfaktər] *m* (-s;) Rh factor
Rhetorik [re'torɪk] *f* (-;) rhetoric
rhetorisch [re'torɪʃ] *adj* rhetorical
rheumatisch [rɔɪ'matɪʃ] *adj* rheumatic
Rheumatismus [rɔɪma'tɪsmus] *m* (-;) rheumatism
rhythmisch ['rʏtmɪʃ] *adj* rhythmical
Rhyth·mus ['rʏtmus] *m* (-;-men [mən]) rhythm
Richtbeil ['rɪçtbaɪl] *n* executioner's ax
Richtblei ['rɪçtblaɪ] *n* plummet
richten ['rɪçtən] *tr* arrange, adjust; put in order; (*lenken*) direct; (*Waffe, Fernrohr*) (**auf** *acc*) point (at), aim (at); (*Bitte, Brief, Frage, Rede*) (**an** *acc*) address (to); (*Augenmerk, Streben*) (**auf** *acc*) concentrate (on), focus (on); (*Bett*) make; (*Essen*) prepare; (*ausbessern*) fix; (*gerade biegen*) straighten; (*jur*) judge, sentence; (*mil*) dress; **zugrunde r.** ruin ‖ *ref* (**auf** *acc*, **gegen**) be directed (at); **das richtet sich ganz danach, ob** it all depends on whether; **sich** [*dat*] **die Haare r.** do one's hair; **sich r. nach** follow the example of; **sich selbst r.** commit suicide ‖ *intr* judge, sit in judgment
Rich'ter *m* (-s;-) judge
Rich'teramt *n* judgeship
Rich'terin *f* (-;-nen) judge
Rich'terkollegium *n* (jur) bench
rich'terlich *adj* judicial
Rich'terspruch *m* judgment; sentence
Rich'terstand *m* judiciary
Rich'terstuhl *m* tribunal, bench
richtig ['rɪçtɪç] *adj* right, correct; (*echt*) real, genuine; (*genau*) exact; (*Zeit*) proper ‖ *adv* right, really, downright; **die Uhr geht r.** the clock keeps good time; **und r., da kam sie!** and sure enough, there she was!
rich'tiggehend *adj* (*Uhr*) keeping good time; (fig) regular
Rich'tigkeit *f* (-;) correctness; accuracy
rich'tigstellen *tr* rectify
Richtlinien ['rɪçtlinjən] *pl* guidelines
Richtlot ['rɪçtlot] *n* plumbline
Richtmaß ['rɪçtmas] *n* standard, gauge
Richtplatz ['rɪçtplats] *m* place of execution
Richtpreis ['rɪçtpraɪs] *m* standard price
Richtschnur ['rɪçt/nur] *f* plumbline; (fig) guiding principle
Richtschwert ['rɪçt/vert] *n* executioner's sword
Richtstätte ['rɪçt/tetə] *f* place of execution
Rich'tung *f* (-;-en) direction; (*Weg*) course; (*Entwicklung*) trend; (*Einstellung*) slant, view
Rich'tungsanzeiger *m* (aut) direction signal
Richtwaage ['rɪçtvagə] *f* level
rieb [rip] *pret* of reiben
riechen ['riçən] §102 *tr* smell; (fig) stand; **kein Pulver r. können** have no guts ‖ *intr* smell; **r. an** (*dat*) sniff at; **r. nach** smell of
Riechsalz ['riçzalts] *n* smelling salts

rief [rif] *pret* of rufen
Riefe ['rifə] *f* (-;-n) groove; (archit) flute
Riege ['rigə] *f* (-;-n) (gym) squad
Riegel ['rigəl] *m* (-s;-) bolt; (*Seife*) cake; (*Schokolade*) bar
riegeln ['rigəln] *tr* bolt, bar
Riemen ['rimən] *m* (-s;-) strap; (*Leib-, Trieb-*) belt; (*Ruder*) oar; (*e-s Gewehrs*) sling
Rie'menscheibe *f* pulley
Ries [ris] *n* (-es;-e) ream (*of one thousand sheets*)
Riese ['rizə] *m* (-;-n) giant
rieseln ['rizəln] *intr* (HABEN & SEIN) trickle; (*Bach*) purl ‖ *impers*—**es rieselt** it is drizzling
Rie'selregen *m* drizzle
Rie'senbomber *m* superbomber
Rie'senerfolg *m* smash hit
rie'sengroß *adj* gigantic
rie'senhaft *adj* gigantic
Rie'senrad *n* Ferris wheel
Rie'senschlange *f* boa constrictor
Rie'sentanne *f* (bot) sequoia
riesig ['rizɪç] *adj* gigantic, huge ‖ *adv* (coll) awfully
Riesin ['rizɪn] *f* (-;-nen) giant
riet [rit] *pret* of raten
Riff [rɪf] *n* (-[e]s;-e) reef
Rille ['rɪlə] *f* (-;-n) groove; small furrow; (archit) flute
Rimesse [rɪ'mesə] *f* (-;-n) (com) remittance
Rind [rɪnt] *n* (-[e]s;-er) head of cattle; **Rinder** cattle
Rinde ['rɪndə] *f* (-;-n) rind; (*Baum-*) bark; (*Brot-*) crust; (anat) cortex
Rin'derbraten *m* roast beef
Rin'derbremse *f* horsefly
Rin'derherde *f* herd of cattle
Rin'derhirt *m* cowboy
Rind'fleisch *n* beef
Rinds'leder *n* cowhide
Rinds'lendenstück *n* rump steak, tenderloin
Rinds'rückenstück *n* sirloin of beef
Rind'vieh *n* cattle; (sl) idiot
Ring [rɪŋ] *m* (-[e]s;-e) ring; (*Kreis*) circle; (*Kettenglied*) link; (*Kartell*) combine; (astr) halo
Ringel ['rɪŋəl] *m* (-s;) small ring; (*Locke*) ringlet, curl
Rin'gelblume *f* marigold
ringeln ['rɪŋəln] *tr* & *ref* curl
Rin'gelreihen *m* ring-around-the-rosy
Rin'gelspiel *n* merry-go-round
ringen [rɪŋən] §142 *tr* wrestle; (*Wäsche, Hände*) wring; (*herauswinden*) wrest ‖ *intr* wrestle; (fig) struggle
Rin'ger –**in** §6 *mf* wrestler
Ring'kampf *m* wrestling match
Ring'mauer *f* town wall, city wall
Ring'richter *m* (box) referee
rings [rɪŋs] *adv* around; **r. um all** around
Ring'schlüssel *m* socket wrench
rings'herum', rings'um', rings'umher' *adv* all around
Rinne ['rɪnə] *f* (-;-n) groove; (*Strombett*) channel; (*Leitung*) duct; (*Gosse*) gutter; (*Erdfurche*) furrow

rinnen ['rınən] §121 *intr* (SEIN) run, flow; trickle || *intr* (HABEN) leak

Rinnsal ['rınzal] *n* (-[e]s;-e) little stream

Rinn'stein *m* gutter; (*Ausgußbecken*) sink; (*unterirdisch*) culvert

Rippchen ['rıpçən] *n* (-s;-) cutlet

Rippe ['rıpə] *f* (-;-n) rib; (*Schokolade*) bar; (*archit*) groin

rippen ['rıpən] *tr* rib, flute

Rip'penfellentzündung *f* pleurisy

Rip'penstoß *m* nudge (in the ribs)

Rip'penstück *n* loin end

Risi·ko ['rizıko] *n* (-s;-s & -ken [kən]) risk; **ein R. eingehen** take a risk

riskant [rıs'kant] *adj* risky

riskieren [rıs'kirən] *tr* risk

riß [rıs] *pret of* **reißen** || **Riß** *m* (Risses; Risse) tear, rip; (*Bruch*) fracture; (*Lücke*) gap; (*Kratzer*) scratch; (*Spalt*) split, cleft; (*Spaltung*) fissure; (*Sprung*) crack; (*Zeichnung*) sketch; (eccl) schism; (geol) crevasse

rissig ['rısıç] *adj* torn; cracked; split; (*Haut*) chapped

Rist [rıst] *m* (-es;-e) wrist; (*des Fußes*) instep

ritt [rıt] *pret of* **reiten** || **Ritt** *m* (-[e]s; -e) ride

Ritter ['rıtər] *m* (-s;-) knight; cavalier; **zum R. schlagen** knight

Rit'tergut *n* manor

Rit'terkreuz *n* (mil) Knight's Cross (*of the Iron Cross*)

rit'terlich *adj* knightly; (fig) chivalrous

Rit'terlichkeit *f* (-;) chivalry

Rit'terzeit *f* age of chivalry

rittlings ['rıtlıŋs] *adv*-r. **auf** (*dat or acc*) astride

Ritual [rıtu'al] *n* (-s;-e & -ien [jən]) ritual

rituell [rıtu'el] *adj* ritual

Ri·tus ['rıtus] *m* (-;-ten [tən]) rite

Ritz [rıts] *m* (-es;-e), **Ritze** ['rıtsə] *f* (-;-en) crack, crevice; (*Schlitz*) slit; (*Schramme*) scratch

ritzen ['rıtsən] *tr* scratch; (*Glas*) cut

Rivale [rı'valə] *m* (-n;-n), **Rivalin** [rı'valın] *f* (-;-nen) rival

rivalisieren [rıvalı'zirən] *intr* be in rivalry; **r. mit** rival

Rivalität [rıvalı'tet] *f* (-;-en) rivalry

Rizinusöl ['rıtsınusøl] *n* castor oil

Robbe ['robə] *f* (-;-n) seal

robben ['robən] *intr* (HABEN & SEIN) (mil) crawl (*using one's elbows*)

Rob'benfang *m* seal hunt

Robe ['robə] *f* (-;-n) robe, gown

Roboter ['robotər] *m* (-s;-) robot

robust [ro'bust] *adj* robust

roch [rox] *pret of* **riechen**

röcheln ['ræçəln] *tr* gasp out || *intr* rattle (*in one's throat*)

rochieren [ro'ʃirən] *intr* (chess) castle

Rock [rok] *m* (-[e]s;¨e) skirt; jacket

Rock'schoß *m* coattail

Rodel ['rodəl] *m* (-s;-) & *f* (-;-n) toboggan; (*mit Steuerung*) bobsled

Ro'delbahn *f* toboggan slide

rodeln ['rodəln] *intr* (HABEN & SEIN) toboggan

Ro'delschlitten *m* toboggan; bobsled

roden ['rodən] *tr* root out; (*Wald*) clear; (*Land*) make arable

Rogen ['rogən] *m* (-s; roe, spawn

Roggen ['rogən] *m* (-s;) rye

roh [ro] *adj* raw; crude; (*Steine*) unhewn; (*Dielen*) bare; (fig) uncouth, brutal

Roh'bau *m* (-[e]s;-ten) rough brickwork

Roh'diamant *m* uncut diamond

Roh'einnahme *f* gross receipts

Roh'eisen *n* pig iron

Roh'heit *f* (-;) rawness, raw state; crudeness; brutality

Roh'entwurf *m* rough sketch

Roh'gewicht *n* gross weight

Roh'gewinn *m* gross profit

Roh'gummi *m* crude rubber

Roh'haut *f* rawhide

Roh'kost *f* uncooked vegetarian food

Rohling ['rolıŋ] *m* (-s;-e) blank; slug; (fig) thug, hoodlum

Roh'material *n* raw material

Roh'öl *n* crude oil

Rohr [ror] *n* (-[e]s;-e) reed, cane; (*Röhre*) pipe, tube; (*Kanal*) duct, channel; (*Gewehrlauf*) barrel

Rohr'anschluß *m* pipe joint

Rohr'bogen *m* elbow

Röhre ['rørə] *f* (-;-n) tube, pipe; (electron) tube

Röh'renblitz *m* electronic flash

Röh'renblitzgerät *n* electronic flash unit

Rohr'leger *m* pipe fitter

Rohr'leitung *f* pipeline, main

Rohr'schäftung *f* sleeve joint

Rohr'schelle *f* pipe clamp

Rohr'zange *f* pipe wrench

Rohr'zucker *m* cane sugar

Roh'stoff *m* raw material

Rolladen (Roll'laden) *m* sliding shutter; sliding cover

Rollbahn ['rolban] *f* (aer) runway; (mil) road leading up to the front

Röllchen ['rælçən] *n* (-s;-) caster

Rolldach ['roldax] *n* (aut) sun roof

Rolle ['rolə] *f* (-;-n) roll; (*Walze*) roller; (*Flaschenzug*) pulley; (*Spule*) spool, reel; (*unter Möbeln*) caster; (*Mangel*) mangle; (*Liste*) list, register; (theat) role; **aus der R. fallen** (fig) misbehave; **spielt keine R.!** never mind!, forget it!

rollen ['rolən] *tr* roll; (*auf Rädern*) wheel; (*Wäsche*) mangle; || *ref* curl up || *intr* (HABEN & SEIN) roll; (*Flugzeug*) taxi; (*Geschütze*) roar || **Rollen** *n*-ins. **R. kommen** get going

Rol'lenbesetzung *f* (theat) cast

Rol'lenlager *n* roller bearing

Rol'lenzug *m* block and tackle

Rol'ler *m* (-s;-) scooter; motor scooter

Roll'feld *n* (aer) runway

Roll'kragen *m* turtleneck

Roll'mops *m* pickled herring

Rollo ['rolo] *n* (-s;-s) (coll) blind, shade

Roll'schuh *m* roller skate; **R. laufen** roller-skate

Roll'schuhbahn *f* roller-skating rink

Roll'stuhl *m* wheelchair

Roll'treppe *f* escalator

Roll'wagen *m* truck
Rom [rom] *n* (–s;) Rome
Roman [rɔ'man] *m* (–s;–e) novel
Roman'folge *f* serial
roman'haft *adj* fictional
romanisch [rɔ'manıʃ] *adj* (*Sprache*) Romance; (*archit*) Romanesque
Romanist –in [roma'nıst(ın)] §7 *mf* scholar of Romance languages
Roman'schriftsteller –in §6 *mf* novelist
Romantik [rɔ'mantık] *f* (–;) Romanticism
romantisch [rɔ'mantıʃ] *adj* romantic
Romanze [rɔ'mantsə] (–;–n) romance
Römer –in ['rømər(ın)] §6 *mf* Roman
römisch ['rømıʃ] *adj* Roman
rö'misch-katho'lisch *adj* Roman Catholic
röntgen ['rœntgən] *tr* x-ray
Rönt'genapparat *m* x-ray machine
Rönt'genarzt *m*, **Rönt'genärztin** *f* radiologist
Rönt'genaufnahme *f*, **Rönt'genbild** *n* x-ray
Rönt'genstrahlen *pl* x-rays
rosa ['roza] *adj* pink || **Rosa** *n* (–s;– & –s) pink
Rose ['rozə] *f* (–;–n) rose
Ro'senkohl *m* Brussels sprouts
Ro'senkranz *m* (*eccl*) rosary
ro'senrot *adj* rosy, rose-colored
Ro'senstock *m* rosebush
rosig ['rozıç] *adj* (& *fig*) rosy; (*Laune*) happy
Rosine [rɔ'zinə] *f* (–;–n) raisin
Roß [rɔs] *n* (Rosses; Rosse) horse; (sl) jerk; (poet) steed
Rost [rɔst] *m* (–es;) rust; mildew || *m* (–es;–e) grate; grill; **auf dem R. braten** grill
Rost'braten *m* roast beef
Röstbrot ['røstbrot] *n* toast
rosten ['rɔstən] *intr* rust
rösten ['røstən] *tr* (*auf dem Rost*) grill; (*in der Pfanne*) roast; (*Brot*) toast; (*Mais*) pop; (*Kaffee*) roast
Rö'ster *m* (–s;–) roaster; toaster
Rost'fleck *m* rust stain
rost'frei *adj* rust-proof; (*Stahl*) stainless
rostig ['rɔstıç] *adj* rusty, corroded
rot [rot] *adj* (röter ['røtər]; röteste ['røtəstə] §9) red || **Rot** *n* (–es;) red; (*Schminke*) rouge
Rotation [rota'tsjon] *f* (–;–en) rotation
Rotations'maschine *f* rotary press
rotbäckig ['rotbɛkıç] *adj* red-cheeked
Rot'dorn *m* (bot) pink hawthorn
Röte ['røtə] *f* (–;) red(ness); blush
Röteln ['røtəln] *pl* German measles
rotieren [rɔ'tirən] *intr* rotate
Rotkäppchen ['rotkɛpçən] *n* (–s;) Little Red Riding Hood
Rotkehlchen ['rotkelçən] *n* (–s;–) robin
rötlich ['røtlıç] *adj* reddish
Ro·tor ['rotɔr] *m* (–s;–toren ['torən]) (aer) rotor; (elec) armature
Rot'schimmel *m* roan (*horse*)
Rot'tanne *f* spruce
Rotte ['rɔtə] *f* (–;–n) gang, mob
Rotz [rɔts] *m* (–es;–e) (sl) snot
rot'zig *adj* (sl) snotty

Rouleau [ru'lo] *n* (–s;–s) window shade
Route ['rutə] *f* (–;–n) route
Routine [ru'tinə] *f* (–;) routine; practice, experience
routiniert [rutı'nirt] *adj* experienced
Rübe ['rybə] *f* (–;–n) beet; **gelbe R.** carrot; **weiße R.** turnip
Rubin [ru'bin] *m* (–s;–e) ruby
Rubrik [ru'brik] *f* (–;–en) rubric; heading; (*Spalte*) column
ruchbar ['ruxbar] *adj* known, public
ruchlos ['ruxlos] *adj* wicked
Ruck [ruk] *m* (–[e]s;–e) jerk; yank; jolt; **auf e-n R.** at once; **mit e-m R.** in one quick move
Rück-, rück- [ryk] *comb.fm.* re-, back, rear; return
Rück'ansicht *f* rear view
Rück'antwort *f* reply; **Postkarte mit R.** prepaid reply postcard
rück'bezüglich *adj* (gram) reflexive
Rück'bleibsel *n* remainder
rücken ['rykən] *tr* move, shove || *intr* (SEIN) move; (*Platz machen*) move over; (*marschieren*) march; **höher r.** be promoted; **näher r.** approach || **Rücken** *m* (–s;–) back; (*Rückseite*) rear; (*der Nase*) bridge
Rückendeckung (Rük'kendeckung) *f* (fig) backing, support
Rückenlehne (Rük'kenlehne) *f* back rest
Rückenmark (Rük'kenmark) *n* spinal cord
Rückenschwimmen (Rük'kenschwimmen) *n* backstroke
Rückenwind (Rük'kenwind) *m* tail wind
Rückenwirbel (Rük'kenwirbel) *m* (anat) vertebra
rück'erstatten *tr* reimburse, refund
Rück'fahrkarte *f*, **Rück'fahrschein** *m* round-trip ticket
Rück'fahrt *f* return trip
Rück'fall *m* relapse
rück'fällig *adj* habitual, relapsing
Rück'flug *m* return flight
Rück'frage *f* further question
Rück'führung *f* repatriation
Rück'gabe *f* return, restitution
Rück'gang *m* return; regression; (*der Preise*) drop; (econ) recession
rückgängig ['rykgɛnıç] *adj* retrogressive; dropping; **r. machen** cancel
rück'gewinnen §121 *tr* recover
Rück'grat *n* backbone, spine
Rück'griff *m* (auf acc) recourse (to)
Rück'halt *m* backing; (mil) reserves; **e-n R. an j–m haben** have s.o.'s backing; **ohne R.** without reservation
rück'haltlos *adj* frank, unreserved || *adv* without reserve
Rück'handschlag *m* (tennis) back-hand stroke
Rück'kauf *m* repurchase
Rück'kehr *f* return; (fig) comeback
Rück'kopplung *f* (electron) feedback
Rück'lage *f* reserves, savings
Rück'lauf *m* reverse; (mil) recoil
Rück'läufer *m* letter returned to sender
rückläufig ['ryklɔıfıç] *adj* retrograde

Rück′licht n (aut) taillight
rücklings [′rʏklɪŋs] adv backwards
Rück′nahme f withdrawal, taking back
Rück′porto n return postage
Rück′prall m bounce, rebound, recoil
Rück′reise f return trip
Rück′sack m knapsack
Rück′schau m—**R. halten auf** (acc) look back on
Rück′schlag m back stroke; (e-s Balles) bounce; (fig) setback
Rück′schluß m conclusion, inference
Rück′schritt m backward step; (fig) falling off, retrogression
Rück′seite f back; reverse; wrong side
Rück′sicht f regard, respect, consideration; **aus R. auf** (acc) out of consideration for; **in** (or **mit**) **R. auf** (acc) in regard to; **ohne R. auf** (acc) irrespective of; **R. nehmen auf** (acc) take into account, show consideration for
rück′sichtlich prep (genit) considering
rück′sichtslos adj inconsiderate; reckless; ruthless
rück′sichtsvoll adj considerate
Rück′sitz m (aut) rear seat
Rück′spiegel m (aut) rear-view mirror
Rück′spiel n return match
Rück′sprache f discussion; conference; **R. nehmen mit** consult with
Rück′stand m arrears; (Satz) sediment; (Rest) remainder; (von Aufträgen, usw.) backlog; (chem) residue
rück′ständig adj behind, in arrears; (Geld) outstanding; (Raten) delinquent; (altmodisch) backward
Rück′stau m back-up water
Rück′stelltaste f backspace key
Rück′stoß m repulsion; recoil, kick
Rückstrahler [′rʏkstraːlər] m (-s;-) reflector
Rück′strahlung f reflection
Rück′tritt m resignation
Rück′trittbremse f coaster brake
Rück′umschlag m return envelope
rückwärts [′rʏkvɛrts] adv backward(s)
Rück′wärtsgang m (aut) reverse
Rück′weg m way back, return
ruck′weise adv by fits and starts
rück′wirkend adj retroactive
Rück′wirkung f (-;-en) reaction; repercussion
rück′zahlen tr repay, refund
Rück′zug m withdrawal; retreat; **zum R. blasen** sound the retreat
Rück′zugsgefecht n running fight
rüde [′ryːdə] adj rude, coarse ‖ **Rüde** m (-n;-n) male (wolf, fox, etc.)
Rudel [′ruːdəl] n (-s;-) herd; flock; (von Wölfen, U-Booten) wolf pack
Ruder [′ruːdər] n (-s;-) (aer, naut) rudder; (naut) oar
Ru′derblatt n blade of an oar
Ru′derboot n rowboat
Ru′derer –**in** §6 mf rower
Ru′derklampe f oarlock
rudern [′ruːdərn] tr & intr row
Ru′derschlag m stroke of the oar
Ru′dersport m (sport) crew
Ruf [ruːf] m (-[e]s;-e) call; shout; yell; (Berufung) vocation; (Nach-

rede) reputation; appointment; (com) credit
rufen [′ruːfən] §122 tr call; shout; **r. lassen** send for ‖ intr call; shout
Ruf′mord m character assassination
Ruf′name m first name
Ruf′nummer f telephone number
Ruf′weite f—**in R.** within earshot
Ruf′zeichen n (rad) station identification; (telp) call sign
Rüge [′ryːgə] f (-;-n) reprimand
rügen [′ryːgən] tr reprimand
Ruhe [′ruːə] f (-;) rest; quiet; calm; (Frieden) peace; (Stille) silence; **immer mit der R.!** (coll) take it easy!
ru′hebedürftig adj in need of rest
Ru′hegehalt n pension
Ru′hekur f rest cure
ru′helos adj restless
ruhen [′ruːən] intr rest; sleep
Ru′hepause f pause, break
Ru′heplatz m resting place
Ru′hestand m retirement
Ru′hestätte f resting place
Ru′hestörer –**in** §6 mf disturber of the peace
Ru′hetag m day of rest, day off
Ru′hezeit f leisure
ruhig [′ruːɪç] adj still, quiet; calm
Ruhm [ruːm] m (-[e]s;) glory, fame
rühmen [′ryːmən] tr praise ‖ ref (genit) boast (about)
rühmlich [′ryːmlɪç] adj praiseworthy
ruhm′los adj inglorious
ruhmredig [′ruːmreːdɪç] adj vainglorious
ruhm′reich adj glorious
ruhm′voll adj famous, glorious
ruhm′würdig adj praiseworthy
Ruhr [ruːr] f (-;) dysentery; **Ruhr** (river)
Rührei [′ryːraɪ] n scrambled egg
rühren [′ryːrən] tr stir; touch, move; (Trommel) beat; **alle Kräfte r.** exert every effort ‖ ref stir, move; get a move on; **rührt euch!** (mil) at ease! ‖ intr stir, move; **r. an** (acc) touch; (fig) mention; **r. von** originate in
rührig [′ryːrɪç] adj active; agile
Rührlöffel [′ryːrlœfəl] m ladle
rührselig [′ryːrzeːlɪç] adj sentimental
Rührstück [′ryːr/tʏk] n soap opera
Rüh′rung f (-;-en) emotion
Ruin [ruˈiːn] m (-s;) ruin; decay
Ruine [ruˈiːnə] f (-;-n) ruins; (fig) wreck
rui′nenhaft adj ruinous
ruinieren [ruˈiˈniːrən] tr ruin
Rülps [rʏlps] m (-es;-e) belch
rülpsen [′rʏlpsən] intr belch
Rülp′ser m (-s;-) belch
Rum [rum] m (-s;-s) rum
Rumäne [ruˈmeːnə] m (-n;-n) Rumanian
Rumänien [ruˈmeːnjən] n (-s;) Rumania
Rumänin [ruˈmeːnɪn] f (-;-nen) Rumanian
rumänisch [ruˈmeːnɪʃ] adj Rumanian
Rummel [′ruməl] m (-s;) junk; racket; hustle and bustle; **auf den R. gehen** go to the fair; **den ganzen R. kaufen** (coll) buy the works
Rum′melplatz m amusement park, fair
Rumor [ruˈmoːr] m (-s;) noise, racket

Rumpel ['rʊmpəl] f (-;-n) scrub board
Rum'pelkammer f storage room, junk room
Rum'pelkasten m (aut) jalopy
rumpeln ['rʊmpəln] tr (Wäsche) scrub ‖ intr rumble, rattle
Rumpf [rʊmpf] m (-[e]s;ːe) trunk, body; torso; (aer) fuselage; (naut) hull
rümpfen ['rʏmpfən] tr—**die Nase r. über** (acc) turn up one's nose at
rund [rʊnt] adj round; (Absage) flat ‖ adv around; about, approximately; **r. um** around
Rund'blick m panorama
Rund'brief m circular letter
Runde ['rʊndə] f (-;-n) round; (box) round; (beim Rennsport) lap
runden ['rʊndən] tr make round; round off ‖ ref become round
Rund'erlaß m circular
rund'erneuern tr (aut) retread; **runderneuerter Reifen** m retread
Rund'fahrt f sightseeing tour
Rund'flug m (aer) circuit
Rund'frage f questionnaire, poll
Rund'funk m radio; **im R.** on the radio
Rund'funkansage f radio announcement
Rund'funkansager **-in** §6 mf radio announcer
Rund'funkgerät n radio set
Rund'funkgesellschaft f broadcasting company
Rund'funkhörer **-in** §6 mf listener
Rund'funknetz n radio network
Rund'funksender m broadcasting station
Rund'funksendung f radio broadcast
Rund'funksprecher **-in** §6 mf announcer
Rund'funkwerbung f (rad) commercial
Rund'gang m tour; stroll
rund'heraus adv plainly, flatly
rundherum adv all around
rund'lich adj round; (dick) plump
Rund'reise f sightseeing tour
Rund'schau f panorama; (journ) news in brief
Rund'schreiben n circular letter
rundweg ['rʊnt'vɛk] adv bluntly, flatly

Runzel ['rʊntsəl] f (-;-n) wrinkle
runzelig ['rʊntsəlɪç] adj wrinkled
runzeln ['rʊntsəln] tr wrinkle; **die Brauen r.** knit one's brows; **die Stirn r.** frown ‖ ref wrinkle
Rüpel ['rʏpəl] m (-s;-) boor
rü'pelhaft adj rude, boorish
rupfen ['rʊpfən] tr pluck; (fig) fleece
ruppig ['rʊpɪç] adj shabby; (fig) rude
Ruprecht ['ruːprɛçt] m (-s;)—**Knecht R.** Santa Claus
Ruß [ruːs] m (-es;) soot
Russe ['rʊsə] m (-n;-n) Russian
Rüssel ['rʏsəl] m (-s;-) snout; (Elephanten-) trunk; (coll) snoot; (ent) proboscis
rußig ['ruːsɪç] adj sooty
Russin ['rʊsɪn] f (-;-nen) Russian
russisch ['rʊsɪ] adj Russian
Rußland ['rʊslant] n (-s;) Russia
Rüst- [rʏst] comb.fm. scaffolding; armament, munition
rüsten ['rʏstən] tr arm, equip; prepare ‖ ref get ready ‖ intr (zu) get ready (for); **zum Krieg r.** mobilize
Rüster ['rʏstər] f (-;-n) elm
rüstig ['rʏstɪç] adj vigorous; alert
Rüst'kammer f armory, arsenal
Rü'stung f (-;-en) preparation; equipment; armament; mobilization; armor; implements; (archit) scaffolding
Rü'stungsbetrieb m munitions factory
Rü'stungsfertigung f war production
Rü'stungsindustrie f war industry
Rü'stungskontrolle f arms control
Rü'stungsmaterial n war materiel
Rü'stungsstand m state of preparedness
Rüst'zeug n kit; (fig) knowledge
Rute ['ruːtə] f (-;-n) rod; twig; tail; (anat) penis
Rutsch [rʊtʃ] m (-es;-e) slip, slide
Rutsch'bahn f slide; chute
Rutsche ['rʊtʃə] f (-;-n) slide; chute
rutschen ['rʊtʃən] intr (SEIN) slip, slide; (aut) skid
rutschig ['rʊtʃɪç] adj slippery
rütteln ['rʏtəln] tr shake; jolt; (Getreide) winnow; (aus dem Schlafe) rouse ‖ intr—**r. an** (acc) cause to rattle; (fig) try to undermine

S

S, s [ɛs] invar n S, s
SA abbr (mil) (Sturmabteilung) storm troopers
Saal [zaːl] m (-[e]s; Säle ['zɛːlə]) hall
Saat [zaːt] f (-;-en) seed; (Säen) sowing; (Getreide auf dem Halm) crop(s); **die S. bestellen** sow
Saat'bestellung f sowing
Saat'kartoffel f seed potato
Sabbat ['zabat] m (-s;-e) Sabbath
Sabberei [zabə'raɪ] f (-;-en) drooling; (Geschwätz) drivel
sabbern ['zabərn] intr drool, drivel

Säbel ['zɛːbəl] m (-s;) saber; **mit dem S. rasseln** (pol) rattle the saber
sä'belbeinig adj bowlegged
säbeln ['zɛːbəln] tr (coll) hack
Sä'belrasseln n (pol) saber rattling
Sabotage [zabo'taːʒə] f (-;-n) sabotage
Saboteur [zabo'tøːr] m (-s;-e) saboteur
sabotieren [zabo'tiːrən] tr sabotage
Saccharin [zaxa'riːn] n (-s;) saccharin
Sach- [zax] comb.fm. of facts, factual
Sach'anlagevermögen n tangible fixed assets
Sach'bearbeiter **-in** §6 mf specialist

Sach'beschädigung f property damage
Sach'bezüge pl compensation in kind
Sach'buch n nonfiction (work)
Sach'darstellung f statement of facts
sach'dienlich adj relevant, pertinent
Sache ['zaxə] f (-;-n) thing; matter; cause; (jur) case; **bei der S. sein** be on the ball; **beschlossene S.** foregone conclusion; **die S. der Freiheit** the cause of freedom; **große S.** big affair; **gute S.** good cause; **heikle S.** delicate point; **in eigner S.** on one's own behalf; **in Sachen X gegen Y** (jur) in the case of X versus Y; **meine sieben Sachen** all my belongings; **nicht bei der S. sein** not be with it; **nicht zur S. gehörig** irrelevant; **von der S. abkommen** get off the subject; **zur S.!** come to the point! (parl) question!
sach'gemäß adj proper, pertinent || adv in a suitable manner
Sach'kenner –in §6 mf expert
Sach'kenntnis f, **Sach'kunde** f expertise
sach'kundig adj expert || **Sach'kundige** §5 mf expert
Sach'lage f state of affairs, circumstances
Sach'leistung f payment in kind
sach'lich adj (treffend) to the point; (gegenständlich) objective; (tatsächlich) factual; (unparteiisch) impartial; (nüchtern) matter-of-fact || adv to the point
sächlich ['zɛçlɪç] adj (gram) neuter
Sach'lichkeit f (-;) objectivity; reality; impartiality; matter-of-factness
Sach'register n index
Sach'schaden m property damage
Sach'schadenersatz m indemnity (for property damage)
Sachse ['zaksə] m (-n;-n) Saxon
Sachsen ['zaksən] n (-s;) Saxony
sächsisch ['zɛksɪʃ] adj Saxon
sacht(e) ['zaxt(ə)] adj soft, gentle; (langsam) slow || adv gingerly; **immer sacht!** easy does it!
Sach'verhalt m facts of the case
Sach'vermögen n real property
sach'verständig adj experienced || **Sachverständige** §5 mf expert
Sach'wert m actual value; **Sachwerte** material assets
Sach'wörterbuch n encyclopedia
Sack [zak] m (-[e]s;=e) sack, bag; pocket; **j-n in den S. stecken** (coll) be way above s.o.; **mit S. und Pack** bag and baggage
Säckel ['zɛkəl] m (-s;-) little bag; pocket; purse
sacken ['zakən] tr bag || ref be baggy || intr (SEIN) sag; (archit) settle; (naut) founder
Sack'gasse f blind alley, dead end; (fig) stalemate, dead end
Sack'leinwand f burlap
Sack'pfeife f bagpipe
Sack'tuch n handkerchief
Sadist –in [za'dɪst(ɪn)] §7 mf sadist
sadistisch [za'dɪstɪ] adj sadistic
säen ['zɛ·ən] tr & intr sow
Saffian ['zafjan] m (-s;) morocco

Safran ['zafran] m (-s;-e) saffron
Saft [zaft] m (-[e]s;=e) juice; sap; (culin) gravy
saftig ['zaftɪç] adj juicy; (Witze) spicy
saft'los adj juiceless; (fig) wishy-washy
saft'reich adj juicy, succulent
Sage ['zagə] f (-;-n) legend, saga
Säge ['zɛgə] f (-;-n) saw
Sä'geblatt n saw blade
Sä'gebock m sawhorse, sawbuck
Sä'gefisch m sawfish
Sä'gemehl n sawdust
sagen ['zagən] tr say; (mitteilen) tell; **das hat nichts zu s.** that's neither here nor there; **das will nicht s.** that is not to say; **gesagt, getan** no sooner said than done; **j-m s. lassen** send s.o. word; **laß dir gesagt sein** let it be a warning to you; **sich [dat] nichts s. lassen** not listen to reason
sägen ['zɛgən] tr saw || intr saw; (coll) snore, cut wood
sa'genhaft adj legendary
Sägespäne ['zɛgəʃpɛnə] pl sawdust
Sä'gewerk n sawmill
sah [za] pret of **sehen**
Sahne ['zanə] f (-;) cream
Saison [se'zõ] f (-;-s) season
Saison– comb.fm. seasonal
saison'bedingt, saison'mäßig adj seasonal
Saite ['zaɪtə] f (-;-n) string, chord
Sai'teninstrument n string instrument
Sakko ['zako] m & n (-s;-s) suit coat
Sak'koanzug m sport suit
Sakrament [zakra'ment] n (-[e]s;-e) sacrament; **das S. des Altars** the Eucharist || interj (sl) dammit!
Sakrileg [zakri'lek] n (-s;-e) sacrilege
Sakristan [zakrɪs'tan] m (-s;-e) sacristan
Sakristei [zakrɪs'taɪ] f (-;-en) sacristy
Säkular– [zekular] comb.fm. secular; centennial
säkularisieren [zekularɪ'zirən] tr secularize
Salami [za'lami] f (-;-s) salami
Salat [za'lat] m (-[e]s;-e) salad; lettuce; **gemischter S.** tossed salad
Salat'soße f salad dressing
salbadern [zal'badərn] intr talk hypocritically, put on the dog
Salbe ['zalbə] f (-;-n) salve
salben ['zalbən] tr put salve on; anoint
Sal'bung f (-;-en) anointing
sal'bungsvoll adj unctuous
saldieren [zal'dirən] tr (com) balance
Sal·do ['zaldo] m (-s;-s & di [di]) (acct) balance; **e-n S. aufstellen** (or ziehen) strike a balance; **e-n S. ausweisen** show a balance
Saline [za'linə] f (-;-n) saltworks
Salmiak [zal'mjak] m (-s;) ammonium chloride, sal ammoniac
Salmiak'geist m ammonia
Salon [za'lõ] m (-s;-s) salon; parlor, living room
salon'fähig adj (Aussehen) presentable; (Ausdruck) fit for polite company
Salon'held m, **Salon'löwe** m ladies' man
salopp [za'lɔp] adj sloppy; (ungezwungen) casual
Salpeter [zal'petər] m (-s;) saltpeter

salpeterig [zal'petərɪç] *adj* nitrous
Salpe'tersäure *f* nitric acid
Salto ['zalto] *m* (-s;-s) somersault
Salut [za'lut] *m* (-[e]s;-e) salute; **S. schießen** fire a salute
salutieren [zalu'tirən] *tr & intr* salute
Salve ['zalvə] *f* (-;-n) volley, salvo
Salz [zalts] *n* (-es;-e) salt
Salz'bergwerk *n* salt mine
Salz'brühe *f* brine
salzen ['zaltsən] *tr* salt
Salz'faß *n* salt shaker
Salz'fleisch *n* salted meat
Salz'gurke *f* pickle
salz'haltig *adj* saline
Salz'hering *m* pickled herring
salzig ['zaltsɪç] *adj* salty; saline
Salz'kartoffeln *pl* boiled potatoes
Salz'lake *f* brine
Salz'säure *f* hydrochloric acid, muriatic acid
Salz'sole *f* brine
Salz'werk *n* salt works
Samariter –in [zama'ritər(ɪn)] §6 *mf* Samaritan
Same ['zamə] *m* (-ns;-n), **Samen** ['zamən] *m* (-s;-) seed; (biol) semen
Sa'menkorn *n* grain of seed
Sa'menstaub *m* pollen
Samentierchen ['zaməntirçən] *n* (-s;-) spermatozoon
sämig ['zemɪç] *adj* (culin) thick, creamy
Sämischleder ['zemɪʃledər] *n* chamois
Sämling ['zemlɪŋ] *m* (-s;-e) seedling
Sammel- [zaməl] *comb.fm.* collecting, collective
Sam'melbatterie *f* storage battery
Sam'melbecken *n* reservoir; storage tank
Sam'melbegriff *m* collective noun
Sam'melbüchse *f* poor box
Sam'mellinse *f* convex lens
sammeln ['zaməln] *tr* gather; collect; (*Aufmerksamkeit, Truppen*) concentrate || *ref* gather; compose oneself; **sich wieder s.** (mil) reassemble
Sam'melname *m* collective noun
Sam'melplatz *m* collecting point; meeting place; (mil) rendezvous
Sam'melverbindung *f* conference call
Sam'melwerk *n* compilation
Sammler ['zamlər] *m* (-s;-) collector; compiler; (elec) storage cell
Samm'lung *f* (-;-en) collection; (*Zusammenstellung*) compilation; (*Fassung*) composure; concentration
Samstag ['zamstak] *m* (-[e]s;-e) Saturday
samt [zamt] *adv*—**s. und sonders** each and everyone, without exception || *prep* (*dat*) together with || **Samt** *m* (-[e]s;-e) velvet
samt'artig *adj* velvety
sämtlich ['zemtlɪç] *adj* all, complete || *adv* all together
Sanato·rium [zana'torjum] *n* (-s;-rien [rjən]) sanatorium
Sand [zant] *m* (-[e]s;-e) sand; **im Sande verlaufen** (fig) peter out
Sandale [zan'dalə] *f* (-;-n) sandal
Sand'bahn *f* (sport) dirt track
Sand'bank *f* (-;⁀e) sandbank

Sand'boden *m* sandy soil
Sand'düne *f* sand dune
Sand'grube *f* sand pit
sandig ['zandɪç] *adj* sandy
Sand'kasten *m* sand box
Sand'korn *n* grain of sand
Sand'mann *m* (-[e]s;) (fig) sandman
Sand'papier *n* sandpaper; **mit S. abschleifen** sand, sandpaper
Sand'sack *m* sandbag
Sand'stein *m* sandstone
Sand'steingebäude *n* brownstone
sand'strahlen *tr* sandblast
Sand'sturmgebiet *n* dust bowl
sandte ['zantə] *pret* of **senden**
Sand'torte *f* sponge cake
Sand'uhr *f* hour glass
Sand'wüste *f* sandy desert
sanft [zanft] *adj* soft, gentle
Sänfte ['zenftə] *f* (-;-n) sedan chair
Sanft'mut *f* gentleness, meekness
sanft'mütig *adj* gentle, meek, mild
sang [zaŋ] *pret* of **singen** || **Sang** *m* (-[e]s;⁀e) song; **mit S. und Klang** (fig) with great fanfare
sang'und klang'los *adv* unceremoniously
Sänger ['zeŋər] *m* (-s;-) singer
Sän'gerchor *m* glee club
Sängerin ['zeŋərɪn] *f* (-;-nen) singer
Sanguiniker [zaŋ'gwinɪkər] *m* (-s;-) optimist
sanguinisch [zaŋ'gwiniʃ] *adj* sanguine
sanieren [za'nirən] *tr* cure; improve the sanitary conditions of; disinfect; (fin) put on a firm basis
Sanie'rung *f* (-;-en) restoration; reorganization
sanitär [zani'ter] *adj* sanitary
Sanitäter [zani'tetər] *m* (-s;-) first-aid-man; (mil) medic
Sanitäts- [zanitets] *comb.fm.* first-aid, medical
Sanitäts'korps *n* army medical corps
Sanitäts'soldat *m* medic
Sanitäts'wache *f* first-aid station
Sanitäts'wagen *m* ambulance
Sanitäts'zug *m* hospital train
sank [zaŋk] *pret* of **sinken**
Sanka ['zaŋka] *m* (-s;-s) (**Sanitätskraftwagen**) field ambulance
Sankt [zaŋkt] *invar mf* Saint
Sanktion [zaŋk'tsjon] *f* (-;-en) sanction
sanktionieren [zaŋktsjo'nirən] *tr* sanction
sann [zan] *pret* of **sinnen**
Saphir ['zafir] *m* (-s;-e) sapphire
sapperment [zapər'ment] *interj* the deuce!
Sardelle [zar'delə] *f* (-;-n) anchovy
Sardine [zar'dinə] *f* (-;-n) sardine
Sardinien [zar'dinjən] *n* (-s;) Sardinia
sardinisch [zar'diniʃ] *adj* Sardinian
Sarg [zark] *m* (-[e]s;⁀e) coffin
Sarg'tuch *n* pall
Sarkasmus [zar'kasmus] *m* (-;) sarcasm
sarkastisch [zar'kastiʃ] *adj* sarcastic
Sarkophag [zarkə'fak] *m* (-s;-e) sarcophagus
saß [zas] *pret* of **sitzen**
Satan ['zatan] *m* (-s;-e) Satan

satanisch [za'tɑnɪʃ] adj satanic(al)
Satellit [zate'lit] m (-en;-en) satellite
Satin [sa'tē] m (-s;-s) satin
Satire [za'tirə] f (-;-n) satire
Satiriker -in [za'tirɪkər(ɪn)] §6 mf satirist
satirisch [za'tirɪʃ] adj satirical
satt [zat] adj satisfied; satiated; (Farben) deep, rich; (chem) saturated; etw s. bekommen (or haben) be fed up with s.th.; ich bin s. I've had enough; sich s. essen eat one's fill
Sattel ['zatəl] m (-s;⁚) saddle
sat'telfest adj (fig) well-versed
Sat'telgurt m girth
satteln ['zatəln] tr saddle
Sat'telschlepper m semi-trailer
Sat'teltasche f saddlebag
Satt'heit f (-;) saturation; (der Farben) richness
sättigen ['zɛtɪgən] tr satisfy, satiate; saturate
Sät'tigung f (-;) satiation; saturation
Sattler ['zatlər] m (-s;-) harness maker
sattsam ['zatzam] adv sufficiently
saturieren [zatu'rirən] tr saturate
Satz [zats] m (-es;⁚e) sentence; clause; phrase; (Behauptung) proposition; (Bodensatz) grounds; sediment; (Betrag) amount; (Tarif) rate; (Gebühr) fee; (Garnitur) set; (Sprung) leap; (Wette) stake; (Menge) batch; (math) theorem; (mus) movement; (tennis) set; (typ) typesetting, composition; e-n S. machen jump; e-n S. aufstellen set down an article of faith; einfacher S. simple sentence; hauptwörtlicher S. substantive clause; in S. geben go to press; verkürzter S. phrase; zum S. von at the rate of; zusammengesetzter S. compound sentence
Satz'aussage f gram) predicate
Satz'bau m (-[e]s;) (gram) construction
Satz'gefüge n complex sentence
Satz'gegenstand m (gram) subject
Satz'lehre f syntax
Satz'teil m (gram) part of speech
Sat'zung f (-;-en) rule, regulation; (Vereins-) bylaw; statute
sat'zungsgemäß, sat'zungsmäßig adj statutory, according to the bylaws
Satz'zeichen n punctuation mark
Sau [zau] f (-;⁚e) sow; (pej) pig; wie e-e gesengte Sau fahren drive like a maniac
Sau'arbeit f (coll) sloppy work; (coll) tough job; (coll) dirty job
sauber ['zaubər] adj clean; exact
säuberlich ['zɔɪbərlɪç] adj clean, neat; (anständig) decent
sau'bermachen tr clean, clean up
säubern ['zɔɪbərn] tr clean; (freimachen) clear; (Buch) expurgate; (mil) mop up; (pol) purge
Säu'berungsaktion f (mil) mopping-up operation; (pol) purge
Sau'borste f hog bristle
Sauce ['zosə] f (-;-n) sauce; gravy; (Salat-) dressing
sau'dumm' adj (coll) awfully dumb
sauer ['zau-ər] adj sour

Sau'erbraten m braised beef soaked in vinegar
Sauerei [zau-ə'raɪ] f (-;-en) filth, filthy joke
Sau'erkohl, Sau'erkraut n sauerkraut
säuerlich ['zɔɪ-ərlɪç] adj sourish, acidulous; (Lächeln) forced
säuern ['zɔɪ-ərn] tr sour; (Teig) leaven || intr turn sour, acidify
Sau'erstoff m (-[e]s;) oxygen
Sau'erstoffflasche f oxygen tank
Sau'erteig m leaven
Sau'ertopf m (coll) sourpuss
Sau'erwasser n sparkling water
Saufaus ['zaufaus] m (-;), Saufbold ['zaufbolt] m (-[e]s;-e), Saufbruder ['zaufbrudər] m (coll) booze hound
saufen ['zaufən] §124 tr drink, guzzle || intr drink; (sl) booze
Säufer -in ['zɔɪfər(ɪn)] §6 mf drunkard
Saufgelage ['zaufgəlagə] n booze party
Sau'fraß m terrible food, slop
Säugamme ['zɔɪkamə] f wet nurse
saugen ['zaugən] §109 & §125 tr suck || ref—sich [dat] etw aus den Fingern s. invent s.th., make up s.th.
säugen ['zɔɪgən] tr suckle, nurse
Sauger ['zaugər] m (-s;-) sucker; nipple; pacifier
Säuger ['zɔɪgər] m (-s;-), Säugetier ['zɔɪgətir] n mammal
Saug'flasche f baby bottle
Säugling ['zɔɪklɪŋ] m (-s;-e) baby
Säug'lingsausstattung f layette
Säug'lingsheim n nursery
Sau'glück n (coll) dumb luck
Saug'napf m suction cup
Saug'pumpe f suction pump
Saug'watte f absorbent cotton
Saug'wirkung f suction
Sau'hund m (sl) louse, dirty dog
Sau'igel m (sl) dirty guy
sauigeln ['zau-igəln] intr (sl) tell dirty jokes
Sau'kerl m (sl) cad, skunk
Säule ['zɔɪlə] f (-;-n) column; (& fig) pillar; (elec) dry battery; (phys) pile
Säu'lenfuß m base of a column
Säu'lengang m colonnade, peristyle
Säu'lenhalle f portico, gallery
Säu'lenkapitell n, Säu'lenknauf m, Säu'lenknopf m (archit) capital
Säu'lenschaft m shaft of a column
Säu'lenvorbau m portico, (front) porch
Saum [zaum] m (-[e]s;⁚e) seam, hem; (Rand) border; (e-r Stadt) outskirts
säumen ['zɔɪmən] tr hem; border; (Straßen) line || intr tarry
Sau'mensch n (vulg) slut
säumig ['zɔɪmɪç] adj tardy
Säumnis ['zɔɪmnɪs] f (-;-nisse) dilatoriness; (Verzug) delay; (Nichterfüllung) default
Saum'pfad m mule track
Saum'tier n beast of burden
Sau'pech n (coll) rotten luck
Säure ['zɔɪrə] f (-;-n) sourness; acidity; tartness; (chem) acid
Sauregur'kenzeit f slack season
Säu'remesser m (aut) battery tester
Saures ['zaurəs] n—gib ihm S. (coll) give it to 'im!

Saus [zaus] *m*—in S. und Braus leben live high

säuseln ['zɔɪzəln] *intr* rustle; **mit säuselnder Stimme** in whispers

sausen ['zauzən] *intr* (*Wind, Kugel*) whistle; (*Wasser*) gush ‖ *intr* (SEIN) rush, whiz ‖ *impers*—**mir saust es in den Ohren** my ears are ringing ‖ **Sausen** *n* (-s;) rush and roar; humming, ringing (*in the ears*)

Sau'stall *m* pigsty; (fig) terrible mess

Sau'wetter *n* (coll) nasty weather

Sau'wirtschaft *f* (coll) helluva mess

sau'wohl' *adj* (coll) in great shape

Saxophon [zakso'fɔn] *n* (-s;-e) saxophone

Schabe ['ʃabə] *f* (-;-n) cockroach

Schabeisen ['ʃʹaparzən] *n* scraper

schaben ['ʃabən] *tr* scrape; grate, rasp

Scha'ber *m* (-s;-) scraper

Schabernack ['ʃabərnak] *m* (-[e]s;-e) practical joke

schäbig ['ʃebɪç] *adj* shabby; (fig) mean

Schablone [ʃa'blonə] *f* (-;-n) (*Muster*) pattern, model; (*Matrize*) stencil; (*mechanische Arbeit*) routine; **nach der S.** mechanically

schablo'nenhaft, schablo'nenmäßig *adj* mechanical; (*Arbeit*) routine

Schach [ʃax] *n* (-[e]s;) chess; **in S. halten** (fig) keep in check; **S. bieten** (or **geben**) check; (fig) defy; **S. dem König!** check!

Schach'brett *n* chessboard

Schacher ['ʃaxər] *m* (-s;) haggling; **S. treiben** haggle, huckster

Schach'feld *n* (chess) square

Schach'figur *f* chessman; (fig) pawn

schach'matt' *adj* checkmated; (fig) beat

Schach'partie *f*, **Schach'spiel** *n* game of chess

Schacht [ʃaxt] *m* (-[e]s;¨e) shaft; manhole

Schacht'deckel *m* manhole cover

Schachtel ['ʃaxtəl] *f* (-;-n) box; (*von Zigaretten*) pack; (fig) frump

Schach'zug *m* (chess & fig) move

schade ['ʃadə] *adj* too bad

Schädel ['ʃedəl] *m* (-s;-) skull; **mir brummt** (or **dröhnt**) **der S.** my head is throbbing

Schä'delbruch *m*, **Schä'delfraktur** *f* skull fracture

Schä'delhaut *f* scalp

Schä'delknochen *m* cranium

Schä'dellehre *f* phrenology

schaden ['ʃadən] *intr* do harm; (*dat*) harm, damage; **das wird ihr nichts s.** it serves her right; **ein Versuch kann nichts s.** there's no harm in trying ‖ *impers*—**es schadet nichts** it doesn't matter ‖ **Schaden** *m* (-s;¨) damage, injury; (*Verlust*) loss; (*Nachteil*) disadvantage; **er will deinen S. nicht** he means you no harm; **j-m S. zufügen** inflict loss on s.o.; (coll) give s.o. a black eye; **mit S. verkaufen** sell at a loss; **S. nehmen** come to grief; **zu meinem S.** to my detriment

Scha'denersatz *m* compensation, damages; (*Wiedergutmachung*) reparation; **S. leisten** pay damages; make amends

Scha'denersatzklage *f* damage suit

Scha'denfreude *f* gloating

scha'denfroh *adj* gloating, malicious

Scha'denversicherung *f* comprehensive insurance

schadhaft ['ʃathaft] *adj* damaged; (*Material*) faulty; (*Zähne*) decayed; (*baufällig*) dilapidated

schädigen ['ʃedɪgən] *tr* inflict financial damage on; (*benachteiligen*) wrong; (*Ruf*) damage; (*Rechte*) infringe on

Schä'digung *f* (-;) damage

schädlich ['ʃetlɪç] *adj* harmful; (*nachteilig*) detrimental; (*verderblich*) noxious; (*Speise*) unwholesome

Schädling ['ʃetlɪŋ] *m* (-s;-e) (*Person*) parasite; (ent) pest; **Schädlinge vermin**

Schäd'lingsbekämpfung *f* pest control

schadlos ['ʃatlos] *adj*—**sich an j-m s. halten** make s.o. pay (*for an injury done to oneself*); **sich für etw s. halten** compensate oneself for s.th., make up for s.th.

Schaf [ʃaf] *n* (-[e]s;-e) sheep; (fig) blockhead, dope

Schaf'bock *m* ram

Schäfchen ['ʃefçən] *n* (-s;-) lamb; (*Wolken*) fleecy clouds

Schäf'chenwolke *f* fleecy cloud

Schäfer ['ʃefər] *m* (-s;-) shepherd

Schä'ferhund *m* sheep dog; **deutscher S.** German shepherd

Schaf'fell *n* sheepskin

schaffen ['ʃafən] §109 *tr* do; get; put; manage, manage to do; (*erreichen*) accomplish; (*liefern*) supply; (*erschaffen*) bring, cause; (*wegbringen*) take; **auf die Seite s.** put aside; (*betrügerisch*) embezzle; **ich schaffe es noch, daß** I'll see to it that; **Rat s.** know what to do; **vom Halse s.** get off one's neck ‖ §126 *tr* create; produce; **wie geschaffen sein für** cut out for ‖ §109 *intr* do; (*arbeiten*) work; **j-m viel zu s. machen** cause s.o. a lot of trouble; **sich zu s. machen** be busy, putter around

schaf'fend *adj* working; (*schöpferisch*) creative; (*produktiv*) productive

Schaf'fensdrang *m* creative urge

Schaf'fenskraft *f* creative power

Schaffner ['ʃafnər] *m* (-s;-) (rr) conductor

Schaf'fung *f* (-;-en) creation

Schaf'hirt *m* shepherd

Schaf'pelz *m* sheepskin coat

Schaf'pferch *m* sheepfold

Schafs'kopf *m* (sl) mutton-head

Schaf'stall *m* sheepfold

Schaft [ʃaft] *m* (-[e]s;¨e) shaft; (*e-r Feder*) stem; (*e-s Gewehrs*) stock; (*e-s Ankers*) shank; (bot) stem, stalk

Schaft'stiefel *m* high boot

Schaf'zucht *f* sheep raising

Schakal [ʃa'kal] *m* (-s;-e) jackal

schäkern ['ʃekərn] *intr* joke around; flirt

schal [ʃal] *adj* stale, insipid; (fig) flat ‖ **Schal** *m* (-s;-e & -s) scarf; shawl

Schale ['ʃalə] *f* (-;-n) bowl; (*Tasse*) cup; (*von Obst*) peel, skin; (*Hülse*) shell; (*Schote*) pod; (*Rinde*) bark;

(*Waagschale*) scale; (zool) shell; **sich in S. werfen** (coll) doll up

schälen [ˈʃeːlən] *tr* peel; (*Mais*) husk; (*Baumrinde*) bark ‖ *ref* peel off

Scha'lentier *n* (zool) crustacean

Schalk [ʃalk] *m* (-[e]s;-e & ⸚e) rogue

schalk'haft *adj* roguish

Schall [ʃal] *m* (-[e]s;-e & ⸚e) sound; (*Klang*) ring; (*Lärm*) noise

Schall'boden *m* sounding board

Schall'dämpfer *m* (*an Schußwaffen*) silencer; (aut) muffler; (mus) soft pedal

schall'dicht *adj* soundproof

Schall'dose *f* (electron) pickup

Schall'druck *m* sonic boom

Schallehre (**Schall'lehre**) *f* acoustics

schallen [ˈʃalən] *intr* sound, resound

Schall'grenze *f* sound barrier

Schall'mauer *f* sound barrier

Schall'meßgerät *n* sonar

Schall'pegel *m* sound level

Schall'platte *f* phonograph record

Schall'plattenaufnahme *f* recording

Schall'wand *f* baffle

Schall'welle *f* sound wave

Schalotte [ʃaˈlɔtə] *f* (-;-n) (bot) scallion

schalt [ʃalt] *pret of* **schelten**

Schalt- *comb.fm.* switch; connecting; breaking; shifting

Schalt'bild *n* circuit diagram

Schalt'brett *n* switchboard; control panel; (aut) dashboard

Schalt'dose *f* switch box

schalten [ˈʃaltən] *tr* switch; (*anlassen*) start; (*Gang*) (aut) shift ‖ *intr* switch; (*regieren*) be in command; (aut) shift gears; **s. und walten mit** do as one pleases with

Schal'ter *m* (-s;-) switch; (*Ausschalter*) circuit breaker; (*für Kundenverkehr*) window, ticket window

Schal'terdeckel *m* switch plate

Schalt'hebel *m* (aut) gearshift; (elec) switch lever

Schalt'jahr *n* leap year

Schalt'kasten *m* switch box

Schalt'pult *n* (rad, telv) control desk

Schalt'tafel *f* switchboard, instrument panel; (aut) dashboard

Schalt'uhr *f* timer

Schal'tung *f* (-;-en) switching; (elec) connection; (elec) circuit

Schaluppe [ʃaˈlupə] *f* (-;-n) sloop

Scham [ʃɑm] *f* (-;) shame; (anat) genitals

Scham'bein *n* (anat) pubis

schämen [ˈʃeːmən] *ref* (**über** *acc*) feel ashamed (of)

Scham'gefühl *n* sense of shame

Scham'haar *n* pubic hair

scham'haft *adj* modest, bashful

scham'los *adj* shameless

Schampun [ʃamˈpuːn] *n* (-s;-s) shampoo

schampunieren [ʃampuˈniːrən] *tr* shampoo

scham'rot *adj* blushing; **s. werden** blush

Scham'teile *pl* genitals

Schand- [ʃant] *comb.fm.* of shame

schandbar [ˈʃantbɑːr] *adj* shameful; infamous

Schande [ˈʃandə] *f* (-;) shame, disgrace

schänden [ˈʃendən] *tr* disgrace; (*entweihen*) desecrate; (*Mädchen*) rape

Schän'der *m* (-s;-) violator; rapist

Schand'fleck *m* stain; (fig) blemish; (fig) good-for-nothing; **der S. der Familie** the disgrace of the family

schändlich [ˈʃentlɪç] *adj* shameful, disgraceful; scandalous ‖ *adv* (coll) awfully

Schand'mal *n* stigma

Schand'tat *f* shameful deed, crime

Schän'dung *f* (-;-en) desecration; disfigurement; rape

Schank [ʃaŋk] *m* (-[e]s;⸚e) bar, saloon

Schank'bier *n* draft beer

Schank'erlaubnis *f*, **Schank'gerechtigkeit** *f*, **Schank'konzession** *f* liquor license

Schank'stätte *f* bar, tavern

Schank'tisch *m* bar

Schank'wirt *m* bartender

Schank'wirtschaft *f* bar, saloon

Schanzarbeit [ˈʃantsarbaɪt] *f* earthwork; **Schanzarbeiten** entrenchments

Schanze [ˈʃantsə] *f* (-;-n) entrenchments, trenches; (naut) quarter-deck; (sport) take-off ramp (*of ski jump*)

Schanz'gerät *n* entrenching tool

Schar [ʃɑr] *f* (-;-en) group, bunch; crowd; (*von Vögeln*) flock, flight

Scharade [ʃaˈrɑːdə] *f* (-;-n) charade

scharen [ˈʃɑːrən] *ref* (**um**) gather (around)

scharf [ʃarf] *adj* (**schärfer** [ˈʃerfər]; **schärfste** [ˈʃerfstə] §9) sharp; (*Tempo*) fast; (*Bemerkung*) cutting; (*Blick*) hard; (*Brille*) strong; (*Fernrohr*) powerful; (*Geruch*) pungent; (*Munition*) live; (*Pfeffer, Senf*) hot; (*streng*) severe; (*genau*) exact; (*Ton*) shrill; (*wahrnehmend*) keen; **s. machen** sharpen; **s. sein auf** (acc) be keen on ‖ *adv* hard; fast; **j-n s. nehmen** be very strict with s.o.; **s. ansehen** look hard at; **s. geladen** loaded; **s. schießen** shoot with live ammunition; **s. umreißen** define clearly

Scharf'blick *m* (fig) sharp eye

Schärfe [ˈʃerfə] *f* (-;-n) sharpness; keenness; pungency; severity; accuracy

Scharf'einstellung *f* (phot) focusing

schärfen [ˈʃerfən] *tr* sharpen, whet; make pointy; (fig) intensify

scharf'kantig *adj* sharp-edged

scharf'machen *tr* stir up; (*Bomben*) arm; (*Zünder*) activate

Scharf'macher *m* demagogue, agitator

Scharf'richter *m* executioner

Scharf'schütze *m* (mil) sharpshooter

scharf'sichtig *adj* sharp-eyed; (fig) clear-sighted

Scharf'sinn *m* sagacity, acumen

scharf'sinnig *adj* sharp, sagacious

Scharlach [ˈʃarlax] *m* (-s;-e) scarlet; (pathol) scarlet fever

schar'lachfarben *adj* scarlet

schar'lachrot *adj* scarlet

Scharlatan [ˈʃarlatan] *m* (-s;-e) charlatan, quack

scharmant [ʃar'mant] *adj* charming

Scharmützel [ʃar'mytsəl] *n* (-s;-) skirmish

Scharnier [ʃar'nir] *n* (-s;-e) hinge; joint

Schärpe ['ʃerpə] *f* (-;-n) sash

Scharre ['ʃarə] *f* (-;-n) scraper

Scharreisen ['ʃaraɪzən] *n* scraper

scharren ['ʃarən] *tr* scrape, paw || *intr* scrape; (an *acc*) scratch (on); **auf den Boden s.** paw the ground; **mit den Füßen scrape the feet** (*in disapproval*)

Scharte ['ʃartə] *f* (-;-n) nick, dent; (*Kerbe*) notch; (*Kratzer*) scratch; (*Riß*) crack; (*Bergsattel*) gap; (fig) mistake; **e-e S. auswetzen** (fig) make amends

Scharteke [ʃar'tekə] *f* (-;-n) worthless old book; (fig) frump

schartig ['ʃartɪç] *adj* jagged; notched

Schatten ['ʃatən] *m* (-s;-) shade; shadow; **in den S. stellen** throw into the shade

Schat'tenbild *n* silhouette; (fig) phantom

Schat'tendasein *n* shadowy existence

Schat'tengestalt *f* shadowy figure

schat'tenhaft *adj* shadowy

Schat'tenriß *m* silhouette

Schat'tenseite *f* shady side; dark side; (fig) seamy side

schattieren [ʃa'tirən] *tr* shade; (*schraffieren*) hatch; (*abtönen*) tint

Schattie'rung *f* (-;-en) shading; (*Farbton*) shade, tint

schattig ['ʃatɪç] *adj* shadowy; shady

Schatulle [ʃa'tulə] *f* (-;-n) cash box; (*für Schmuck*) jewelry box; (hist) private funds (*of a prince*)

Schatz [ʃats] *m* (-es;̈e) treasure; (*Vorrat*) store; (fig) sweetheart

Schatz'amt *n* treasury department

Schatz'anweisung *f* treasury bond

schätzbar ['ʃetsbar] *adj* valuable

schätzen ['ʃetsən] *tr* (*Grundstücke, Häuser, Schaden*) estimate, appraise; (*urteilen, vermuten*) guess; (*achten*) esteem, value; (*würdigen*) appreciate; **er schätzte mich auf 20 Jahre** he took me for 20 years old; **zu hoch s.** overestimate, overrate; **zu s. wissen** appreciate || *ref*—**sich** [*dat*] **es zu Ehre s.** consider it an honor; **sich glücklich s.** consider oneself lucky || *recip*—**sie s. sich nicht** there's no love lost between

schät'zenswert *adj* valuable

Schät'zer -in §6 *mf* appraiser; (*zur Besteuerung*) assessor

Schatz'kammer *m* treasury; (fig) storehouse

Schatz'meister -in §6 *mf* treasurer

Schät'zung *f* (-;-en) estimate; (*Meinung*) estimation; (*Hochachtung*) esteem; (*Hochschätzung*) appreciation; (*zur Besteuerung*) assessment

schät'zungsweise *adv* approximately

Schät'zungswert *m* estimated value; assessed value; (*des Schadens*) appraisal

Schatz'wechsel *m* treasury bill

Schau [ʃau] *f* (-;-en) view; (*Ausstel-*

lung) exhibition, show; (mil) review; (telv) show; **zur S. stehen** be on display; **zur S. stellen** put on display; **zur S. tragen** feign

Schau'bild *n* diagram, chart

Schauder ['ʃaudar] *m* (-s;-) shudder, shiver; (*Schrecken*) horror, terror

schauderbar ['ʃaudərbar] *adj* terrible

schau'dererregend *adj* horrifying

schau'derhaft *adj* horrible, awful

schaudern ['ʃaudərn] *intr* (vor *dat*) shudder (at) || *impers*—**es schaudert mich** I shudder

schauen ['ʃau-ən] *tr* look at; (*beobachten*) observe || *intr* look

Schauer ['ʃau-ər] *m* (-s;-) shower, downpour; (*Schauder*) shudder, chill; thrill; (*Anfall*) fit, attack; **einzelne S.** scattered showers

Schau'erdrama *n* (theat) thriller

schau'erlich *adj* dreadful, horrible

schauern ['ʃau-ərn] *intr* shudder || *impers*—**es schauert** it is pouring; **es schauert mich** (or **mir**) **vor** (*dat*) I shudder at; I shiver with

Schau'erroman *m* thriller

Schaufel ['ʃaufəl] *f* (-;-n) shovel; scoop; (*Rad-*) paddle; (*Turbinen-*) blade, vane

schaufeln ['ʃaufəln] *tr* shovel; (*Grab*) dig || *intr* shovel

Schau'felrad *n* paddle wheel

Schau'fenster *n* display window; **die S. ansehen** go window-shopping

Schau'fensterauslage *f* window display

Schau'fensterbummel *m* window-shopping

Schau'fensterdekoration *f* window dressing

Schau'fliegen *n* stunt flying

Schau'flug *m* air show

Schau'gepränge *n* pageantry

Schau'gerüst *n* grandstand

Schau'kampf *m* (box) exhibition fight

Schau'kasten *m* showcase

Schaukel ['ʃaukəl] *f* (-;-n) swing

Schau'kelbrett *n* seesaw

schaukeln ['ʃaukəln] *tr* swing; rock || *intr* swing; rock; sway

Schau'kelpferd *n* rocking horse

Schau'kelreck *n* trapeze

Schau'kelstuhl *m* rocking chair

Schau'loch *n* peephole

Schaum [ʃaum] *m* (-[e]s;̈e) foam, froth; (*Abschaum*) scum; (*Geifer*) slaver; **zu S. schlagen** whip; **zu S. werden** (fig) come to nothing

Schaum'bad *n* bubble bath

schäumen ['ʃɔɪmən] *intr* foam; (*Wein*) sparkle; (aus *Wut*) fume, boil

Schaum'gummi *n & m* foam rubber

Schaum'haube *f* head (*on beer*)

schaumig ['ʃaumɪç] *adj* foamy

Schaum'krone *f* whitecap (*on wave*)

Schau'modell *n* mock-up

Schaum'wein *m* sparkling wine

Schau'platz *m* scene, theater

Schau'prozeß *m* mock trial

schaurig ['ʃaurɪç] *adj* horrible

Schau'spiel *n* play, drama; spectacle

Schau'spieler *m* actor

Schau'spielerin *f* actress

schau'spielerisch *adj* theatrical

schauspielern [ˈʃaʊʃpiːlərn] *intr* act; (*schwindeln*) act, make believe
Schau/spielhaus *n* theater
Schau/spielkunst *f* dramatic art
Schau/stück *n* show piece; (*Muster*) sample
Scheck [ʃɛk] *m* (-s;-s & -e) check; **e-n S. ausstellen an** (*acc*) **über** (*acc*) write out a check to (*s.o.*) in the amount of; **e-n S. einlösen** cash a check; **e-n S. sperren lassen** stop payment on a check; **offener S.** blank check
Scheck/abschnitt *m* check stub
Scheck/formular *n* blank check
Scheck/heft *n* check book
scheckig [ˈʃɛkɪç] *adj* dappled
Scheck/konto *n* checking account
scheel [ʃeːl] *adj* squinting; squint-eyed; (fig) envious, jealous
Scheffel [ˈʃɛfəl] *m* (-s;-) bushel
scheffeln [ˈʃɛfəln] *tr* amass
Scheibe [ˈʃaɪbə] *f* (-;-n) disk; sheet; plate; (*Glas-*) pane; (*Honig-*) honeycomb; (*Ziel*) target; (*Schnitte*) slice; (astr) orb, disk; (mach) washer; (telp) dial
Schei/benbremse *f* disk brake
Schei/benkönig *m* top marksman
Schei/benschießen *n* target practice
Schei/benwäscher *m* windshield washer
Schei/benwischer *m* windshield wiper
Scheide [ˈʃaɪdə] *f* (-;-n) sheath; border, boundary; (anat) vagina
Schei/debrief *m* farewell letter
Schei/degruß *m* goodbye
scheiden [ˈʃaɪdən] §112 *tr* separate, divide; (*zerlegen*) decompose; (*Ehe*) dissolve; (*Eheleute*) divorce; (chem) analyze; (chem) refine || *ref* part; **sich s. lassen** get a divorce || *intr* (SEIN) part; depart; (*aus dem Amt*) resign, retire
schei/dend *adj* (*Tag*) closing; (*Sonne*) setting
Schei/dewand *f* partition
Schei/deweg *m* fork, crossroad; (fig) moment of decision
Schei/dung *f* (-;-en) separation; (*Ehe-*) divorce
Schein [ʃaɪn] *m* (-[e]s;-e) shine; (*Licht*) light; (*Schimmer*) gleam, glitter; (*Strahl*) flash; (*Erscheinung*) appearance; (*Anschein*) pretense, show; (*Urkunde*) certificate, papers, license, ticket; (*Geldschein*) bill; (*Quittung*) receipt; **dem Scheine nach** apparently; **den äußeren S. wahren** save face; **sich** [*dat*] **den S. geben** make believe; **zum S.** pro forma
Schein- *comb.fm.* sham, mock, make-believe
scheinbar [ˈʃaɪnbar] *adj* seeming, apparent; likely; (*vorgeblich*) make-believe
Schein/bild *n* illusion; phantom
scheinen [ˈʃaɪnən] §128 *intr* shine; seem, appear || *impers*—**es scheint** it seems
Schein/grund *m* pretext
schein/heilig *adj* sanctimonious, hypocritical
Schein/tod *m* suspended animation

Schein/werfer *m* flashlight; (aer) beacon; (aut) headlight
Scheit [ʃaɪt] *n* (-[e]s;-e) piece of chopped wood; **Holz in Scheite hakken** chop wood
Scheitel [ˈʃaɪtəl] *m* (-s;-) apex, top; top of the head; (*des Haares*) part; **e-n S. ziehen** make a part
scheiteln [ˈʃaɪtəln] *tr & ref* part
Schei/telpunkt *m* (fig) summit; (astr) zenith; (math) vertex
Schei/telwinkel *m* opposite angle
Scheiterhaufen [ˈʃaɪtərhaʊfən] *m* funeral pile; **auf dem S. sterben** die at the stake
scheitern [ˈʃaɪtərn] *intr* (SEIN) run aground, be wrecked; (*Plan*) miscarry || **Scheitern** *n* (-s;) shipwreck; (fig) failure
Schelle [ˈʃɛlə] *f* (-;-n) bell; (*Fessel*) handcuff; (*Ohrfeige*) box on the ear
schellen [ˈʃɛlən] *tr & intr* ring
Schel/lenkappe *f* cap and bells
Schellfisch [ˈʃɛlfɪʃ] *m* haddock
Schelm [ʃɛlm] *m* (-[e]s;-e) rogue; (Lit) knave; **armer S.** poor devil
Schel/menstreich *m* prank
schelmisch [ˈʃɛlmɪʃ] *adj* roguish, impish
Schelte [ˈʃɛltə] *f* (-;-n) scolding
schelten [ˈʃɛltən] *tr & intr* scold
Scheltwort [ˈʃɛltvɔrt] *n* (-[e]s;-e & ≈er) abusive word; word of reproof
Sche•ma [ˈʃema] *n* (-s;-s & -mata [mata] & -men [mən]) scheme; diagram; (*Muster*) pattern, design
Schemel [ˈʃeməl] *m* (-s;-) stool
Schemen [ˈʃemən] *m* (-s;-) phantom, shadow
sche/menhaft *adj* shadowy
Schenk [ʃɛŋk] *m* (-[e]s;-en) bartender
Schenke [ˈʃɛŋkə] *f* (-;-n) bar, tavern
Schenkel [ˈʃɛŋkəl] *m* (-s;-) thigh; (*e-s Winkels*) side; (*e-r Schere*) blade; (*e-s Zirkels*) leg
schenken [ˈʃɛŋkən] *tr* give, offer; pour (out); (*Aufmerksamkeit*) pay; (*Schuld*) remit; **das ist geschenkt** that's dirt cheap; **das kann ich mir s.** I can pass that up; **das kannst du dir s.!** keep it to yourself! **j-m Beifall s.** applaud *s.o.*; **j-m das Leben s.** grant *s.o.* pardon
Schenk/stube *f* taproom, barroom
Schenk/tisch *m* bar
Schen/kung *f* (-;-en) donation
Schenk/wirt *m* bartender
scheppern [ˈʃɛpərn] *intr* (coll) rattle
Scherbe [ˈʃɛrbə] *f* (-;-n), **Scherben** [ˈʃɛrbən] *m* (-s;-) broken piece; potsherd; **in Scherben gehen** go to pieces
Scher/bengericht *n* ostracism
Scherbett [ʃɛrˈbɛt] *m* (-[e]s;-e) sherbe(r)t
Schere [ˈʃerə] *f* (-;-n) (pair of) scissors; shears; (*Draht-*) cutter; (zool) claw
scheren [ˈʃerən] *tr* bother; **was schert dich das?** what's that to you? §129 *tr* cut, clip, trim; (*Schafe*) shear; || §109 *ref*—**scher dich ins Bett!** off to bed with you!; **scher dich zum Teu-**

fel! the devil with you!; **sich um etw s.** trouble oneself about s.th.

Schererei [ʃerəˈraɪ] f (–s;-en) trouble

Scherflein [ˈʃɛrflaɪn] n (–s;-) bit; **sein S. beitragen** contribute one's bit

Scherz [ʃɛrts] m (–es;-e) joke; **im (or zum) S.** for fun; **S. treiben mit** make fun of

scherzen [ˈʃɛrtsən] intr joke, kid

scherz'haft adj joking, humorous

Scherz'name m nickname

scherz'weise adv in jest, as a joke

scheu [ʃɔɪ] adj shy; **s. machen** frighten; startle || **Scheu** f (–;) shyness

Scheuche [ˈʃɔɪçə] f (–;-n) scarecrow

scheuchen [ˈʃɔɪçən] tr scare (away)

scheuen [ˈʃɔɪ·ən] tr shun; shrink from; fear; (*Mühen, Kosten*) spare; **ohne die Kosten zu s.** regardless of expenses || ref (**vor** dat) be afraid (of); **ich s. mich zu** (inf) I am reluctant to (inf) || intr—s. **vor** (dat) shy at

Scheuer [ˈʃɔɪ·ər] f (–;-n) barn

Scheu'erbürste f scrub brush

Scheu'erfrau f scrubwoman

Scheu'erlappen m scrub rag

scheuern [ˈʃɔɪ·ərn] tr scrub, scour; (*reiben*) rub

Scheu'erpulver n scouring powder

Scheu'klappe f blinder (*for horses*)

Scheune [ˈʃɔɪnə] f (–;-n) barn

Scheu'nendrescher m—**er ißt wie ein S.** (coll) he eats like a horse

Scheusal [ˈʃɔɪzal] n (–s;-e) monster

scheußlich [ˈʃɔɪslɪç] adj dreadful, atrocious; (coll) awful, rotten

Scheuß'lichkeit f (–;-en) hideousness; (*Tat*) atrocity

Schi [ʃi] m (–s;- & -er) ski; **Schi fahren** (or laufen) ski

Schicht [ʃɪçt] f (–;-en) layer, film; (*Farb-*) coat; (*Arbeiter-*) shift; (*Gesellschafts-*) class; (geol) stratum; (phot) emulsion; **Leute aus allen Schichten** people from all walks of life; **S. machen** (coll) knock off from work

Schicht'arbeit f shift work

schichten [ˈʃɪçtən] tr arrange in layers; laminate; (*Holz*) stack (up); (*in Klassen einteilen*) classify; (geol) stratify; (*Ladung*) (naut) stow

–schichtig [ʃɪçtɪç] comb.fm. -layer, -ply

Schicht'linie f contour

Schicht'linienplan m contour map

Schicht'meister m shift foreman

schicht'weise adv in layers; in shifts

schick [ʃɪk] adj chic, swank || **Schick** m (–[e]s;) stylishness; (*Geschick*) skill; (*Geschmack*) tact, taste; **S. haben für** have a knack for

schicken [ˈʃɪkən] tr send || ref—**sich s. für** (or zu) be suitable for; **sich s. in** (acc) adapt oneself to; resign oneself to || intr—**nach j-m s.** send for s.o. || impers—**es schickt sich** it is proper; (*sich ereignen*) come to pass

schick'lich adj proper; decent

Schick'lichkeit f (–;) propriety

Schick'lichkeitsgefühl n sense of propriety

Schicksal [ˈʃɪkzal] n (–[e]s;-e) destiny, fate

Schick'salsgefährte m fellow sufferer

Schick'salsglaube m fatalism

Schick'salsgöttinnen pl (myth) Fates

Schick'salsschlag m stroke of fate

Schickung (Schik'kung) f (–;-en) (divine) dispensation

Schiebe– [ʃibə] comb.fm. sliding, push

Schie'beleiter f extension ladder

schieben [ˈʃibən] §130 tr push, shove; traffic in; **auf die lange Bank s.** put off; **e-e ruhige Kugel s.** have a cushy job; **Kegel s.** bowl; **Wache s.** (mil) pull guard duty || ref move, shuffle || intr shuffle along; profiteer

Schieber [ˈʃibər] m (–s;-) slide valve; (*Riegel*) bolt; (*am Schornstein*) damper; (fig) racketeer

Schie'bergeschäft f (com) racket

Schiebertum [ˈʃibərtum] n (–s;) (com) racketeering

Schie'betür f sliding door

schied [ʃit] pret of **scheiden**

Schieds– [ʃits] comb.fm. of arbitration

Schieds'gericht n board of arbitration; **an ein S. verweisen** refer to arbitration

Schieds'mann m (–[e]s;-er) arbitrator

Schieds'richter m arbitrator; (sport) referee, umpire

schieds'richterlich adj of an arbitration board || adv by arbitration

Schieds'spruch m decision; **e-n S. fällen** render a decision

schief [ʃif] adj (*abfallend*) slanting; (*krumm*) crooked; (*einseitig*) lopsided; (*geneigt*) inclined; (*Winkel*) oblique; (*falsch*) false, wrong; **auf die schiefe Ebene geraten** (fig) go downhill; **schiefe Lage** (fig) tight spot; **schiefes Licht** (fig) bad light || adv at an angle; awry; obliquely; wrong; **s. ansehen** look askance at; **s. halten** tip, tilt; **s. nehmen** take amiss

Schiefer [ˈʃifər] m (–s;-) slate; (*Splitter*) splinter

Schie'ferbruch m slate quarry

Schie'feröl n shale oil

Schie'fertafel f (educ) slate

schief'gehen §82 intr (SEIN) go wrong

schief'treten §152 tr—**die Abstätze s.** wear down the heels

schieläugig [ˈʃilɔɪgɪç] adj squint-eyed; cross-eyed

schielen [ˈʃilən] intr squint; **s. nach** squint at; leer at

schie'lend adj squinting; cross-eyed; furtive

schien [ʃin] pret of **scheinen**

Schienbein [ˈʃinbaɪn] n shinbone, tibia

Schien'beinschützer m shinguard

Schiene [ˈʃinə] f (–;-n) (rr) rail, track; (surg) splint; **aus den Schienen springen** jump the track

schienen [ˈʃinən] tr put in splints

Schie'nenbahn f track, rails; streetcar; railroad

Schie'nenfahrzeug n rail car

Schie'nengleis n track

schier [ʃir] *adj* sheer || *adv* almost
Schierling [ˈʃirlɪŋ] *m* (–s;–e) (bot) hemlock
Schieß– [ʃis] *comb.fm.* shooting
Schieß′baumwolle *f* guncotton
Schieß′bedarf *m* ammunition
Schieß′bude *f* shooting gallery
Schieß′eisen *n* (hum) shooting iron
schießen [ˈʃisən] §76 *tr* shoot, fire; **e–n Bock s.** (coll) pull a boner; **ein Tor s.** make a goal || *intr* (auf *acc*) shoot (at); **aus dem Hinterhalt s.** snipe; **gut s.** be a good shot; **scharf s.** shoot with live ammunition || *intr* (SEIN) shoot up; spurt; zig, fly; **das Blut schoß ihm ins Gesicht his face got red; in Samen s.** go to seed; **ins Kraut s.** sprout || **Schießen** *n* (–s;) shooting; **das ist ja zum s.!** (coll) that's a riot!
Schießerei [ʃisəˈraɪ] *f* (–;–en) gun fight; pointless firing
Schieß′gewehr *n* firearm
Schieß′hund *m* (hunt) pointer
Schieß′lehre *f* ballistics
Schieß′platz *m* firing range
Schieß′prügel *m* (hum) shooting iron
Schieß′pulver *n* gunpowder
Schieß′scharte *f* loophole
Schieß′scheibe *f* target
Schieß′stand *m* shooting gallery; (mil) firing range, rifle range
Schieß′übung *f* firing practice
Schi′fahrer –in §6 *mf* skier
Schiff [ʃɪf] *n* (–[e]s;–e) ship; (archit) nave; (typ) galley
Schiffahrt (Schiff′fahrt) *f* navigation
Schiffahrtslinie (Schiff′fahrtslinie) *f* steamship line
Schiffahrtsweg (Schiff′fahrtsweg) *m* shipping lane
schiffbar [ˈʃɪfbɑr] *adj* navigable
Schiff′bau *m* (–[e]s;) shipbuilding
Schiff′bruch *m* shipwreck
schiff′brüchig *adj* shipwrecked
Schiff′brücke *f* pontoon bridge; (naut) bridge
Schiffchen [ˈʃɪfçən] *n* (–s;–) little ship; (mil) overseas cap; (tex) shuttle
schiffen [ˈʃɪfən] *intr* (vulg) pee || *impers*—**es schifft** (vulg) it's pouring
Schiffer [ˈʃɪfər] *m* (–s;–) seaman; skipper; (*Schiffsführer*) navigator
Schif′ferklavier *n* (coll) concertina
Schiffs′journal *n* log, logbook
Schiffs′junge *m* cabin boy
Schiffs′küche *f* galley
Schiffs′ladung *f* cargo
Schiffs′luke *f* hatch
Schiffs′mannschaft *f* crew
Schiffs′ortung *f* dead reckoning
Schiffs′raum *m* hold; tonnage
Schiffs′rumpf *m* hull
Schiffs′schraube *f* propeller
Schiffs′tau *n* hawser
Schiffs′taufe *f* christening of a ship
Schiffs′werft *f* shipyard, dockyard
Schiffs′winde *f* winch, capstan
Schiffs′zimmermann *m* ship's carpenter; (*Schiffs*) shipwright
Schikane [ʃɪˈkɑnə] *f* (–;–n) chicanery; **mit allen Schikanen** with all the frills; (aut) fully loaded

schikanieren [ʃɪkaˈnirən] *tr* harass
schikanös [ʃɪkaˈnøs] *adj* annoying
Schi′langlauf *m* cross-country skiing
Schi′lauf *m* skiing
schi′laufen §105 *intr* (SEIN) ski || **Schilaufen** *n* (–s;) skiing
Schi′läufer –in §6 *mf* skier
Schild [ʃɪlt] *m* (–[e]s;–e) shield; (heral) coat of arms; **etw im Schilde führen** have s.th. up one's sleeve || *n* (–[e]s;–er) sign; road sign; name-plate; (*e–s Arztes, usw.*) shingle; (*Etikett*) label; (*Mützenschirm*) visor, shade
Schild′bürger *m* (fig) dunce
Schild′bürgerstreich *m* boner
Schild′drüse *f* thyroid gland
Schilderhaus [ˈʃɪldərhaʊs] *n* sentry box
Schil′dermaler *m* sign painter
schildern [ˈʃɪldərn] *tr* depict, describe
Schil′derung *f* (–;–en) description
Schild′kröte *f* tortoise, turtle
Schildpatt [ˈʃɪltpat] *n* (–[e]s;) tortoise shell, turtle shell
Schilf [ʃɪlf] *n* (–[e]s;–e) reed
Schilf′rohr *n* reed
Schi′lift *m* ski lift
Schiller [ˈʃɪlər] *m* (–s;) luster; iridescence
schillern [ˈʃɪlərn] *intr* be iridescent
Schil′lerwein *m* bright-red wine
Schilling [ˈʃɪlɪŋ] *m* (–s;– & –e) shilling; (Aust) schilling
Schimäre [ʃɪˈmɛrə] *f* (–;–n) chimera
Schimmel [ˈʃɪməl] *m* (–s;–) white horse; mildew, mold
schimmelig [ˈʃɪməlɪç] *adj* moldy
schimmeln [ˈʃɪməln] *intr* (HABEN & SEIN) get moldy
Schimmer [ˈʃɪmər] *m* (–s;) glimmer
schimmern [ˈʃɪmərn] *intr* glimmer
schimmlig [ˈʃɪmlɪç] *adj* moldy
Schimpanse [ʃɪmˈpanzə] *m* (–n;–n) chimpanzee
Schimpf [ʃɪmpf] *m* (–[e]s;–e) insult, abuse
schimpfen [ˈʃɪmpfən] *tr* scold, abuse || *intr* be abusive; (über *acc* or auf *acc*) curse (at), swear (at)
schimpf′lich *adj* disgraceful
Schimpf′name *m* nickname; **j–m Schimpfnamen geben** call s.o. names
Schimpf′wort *n* (–[e]s;–e & ⸚er) swear word
Schindaas [ˈʃɪntɑs] *n* carrion
Schindel [ˈʃɪndəl] *f* (–;–n) shingle
schindeln [ˈʃɪndəln] *tr* shingle
schinden [ˈʃɪndən] §167 *tr* skin; torment; oppress; exploit; **Eindruck s.** try to make an impression; **Eintrittsgeld s.** crash the gate; **Zeilen s.** pad the writing; **Zigaretten s.** bum cigarettes || *ref* break one's back
Schin′der *m* (–s;–) slave driver
Schinderei [ʃɪndəˈraɪ] *f* (–;–en) drudgery, grind
Schindluder [ˈʃɪntludər] *n* carrion; **mit j–m S. treiben** treat s.o. outrageously
Schindmähre [ˈʃɪntmɛrə] *f* old nag
Schinken [ˈʃɪŋkən] *m* (–s;–) ham; (hum) tome; (hum) huge painting
Schinnen [ˈʃɪnən] *pl* dandruff

Schippe [ˈʃɪpə] ƒ (-;-n) shovel, scoop; (cards) spade(s); e-e S. machen (or ziehen) pout; j-n auf die S. nehmen (coll) pull s.o.'s leg

schippen [ˈʃɪpən] tr & intr shovel

Schirm [ʃɪrm] m (-[e]s;-e) screen; umbrella; x-ray screen; lampshade; visor; (fig) protection, shelter; (hunt) blind

Schirm′bild n x-ray

Schirm′bildaufnahme ƒ x-ray

Schirm′dach n lean-to

schirmen [ˈʃɪrmən] tr protect

Schirm′futteral n umbrella case

Schirm′herr m protector, patron

Schirm′herrin ƒ protectress, patroness

Schirm′herrschaft ƒ protectorate; patronage

Schirm′ständer m umbrella stand

Schir′mung ƒ (-;-en) (elec) shielding

schirren [ˈʃɪrən] tr harness

Schis·ma [ˈʃɪsma] n (-;-mata [mata] & -men [mən] schism

Schi′sprung m ski jump

Schi′stock m ski pole

schizophren [sçɪtsoˈfren] adj schizophrenic

Schizophrenie [sçɪtsofreˈni] ƒ (-;) schizophrenia

schlabbern [ˈʃlabərn] tr lap up || intr (geifern) slobber; (fig) babble

Schlacht [ʃlaxt] ƒ (-;-en) battle; die S. bei the battle of

schlachten [ˈʃlaxtən] tr slaughter

Schlach′tenbummler m camp follower; (sport) fan

Schlächter [ˈʃlɛçtər] m (-s;-) butcher

Schlacht′feld n battlefield

Schlacht′flieger m combat pilot; close-support fighter

Schlacht′geschrei n battle cry

Schlacht′haus n slaughterhouse

Schlacht′kreuzer m heavy cruiser

Schlacht′opfer n sacrifice; (fig) victim

Schlacht′ordnung ƒ battle array

Schlacht′roß n (hist) charger

Schlacht′ruf m battle cry

Schlacht′schiff n battleship

Schlach′tung ƒ (-;-en) slaughter

Schlacke [ˈʃlakə] ƒ (-;-n) cinder; lava; (metal) slag, dross

schlackig [ˈʃlakɪç] adj sloppy (weather)

Schlaf [ʃlaf] m (-[e]s;) sleep

Schlaf′abteil n sleeping compartment

Schlaf′anzug m pajamas

Schläfchen [ˈʃlɛfçən] n (-s;-) nap; ein S. machen take a nap

Schläfe [ˈʃlɛfə] ƒ (-;-n) temple

schlafen [ˈʃlafən] §131 tr sleep || intr sleep; sich s. legen go to bed

Schla′fenszeit ƒ bedtime

Schläfer -in [ˈʃlɛfər(ɪn)] §6 mƒ sleeper

schläfern [ˈʃlɛfərn] impers—es schläfert mich I'm sleepy

schlaff [ʃlaf] adj slack; limp; flabby; (locker) loose

Schlaf′gelegenheit ƒ sleeping accommodations

Schlaf′kammer ƒ bedroom

Schlaf′krankheit ƒ sleeping sickness

schlaf′los adj sleepless

Schlaf′losigkeit ƒ (-;) sleeplessness

Schlaf′mittel n sleeping pill

Schlaf′mütze ƒ nightcap; (fig) sleepyhead

schläfrig [ˈʃlefrɪç] adj sleepy, drowsy

Schläf′rigkeit ƒ (-;) sleepiness, drowsiness

Schlaf′rock m housecoat

Schlaf′saal m dormitory

Schlaf′sack m sleeping bag

Schlaf′stätte ƒ, **Schlaf′stelle** ƒ place to sleep

Schlaf′stube ƒ bedroom

Schlaf′trunk m (hum) nightcap

schlaf′trunken adj still half-asleep

Schlaf′wagen m (rr) sleeping car

schlaf′wandeln intr (SEIN) walk in one's sleep

Schlafwandler -in [ˈʃlafvandlər(ɪn)] §6 mƒ sleepwalker

Schlaf′zimmer n bedroom

Schlag [ʃlak] m (-[e]s;-̈e) blow; stroke; (Puls-) beat; (Faust-) punch; (Hand-) slap; (Donner-) clap; (Tauben-) loft; (Art, Sorte) kind, sort, breed; (e-s Taues) coil; (der Vögel) song; (vom Pferd) kick; (e-r Kutsche) door; (Holz-) cut; (Pendel) swing; (agr) field; (elec) shock; (mil) scoop, ladleful; (pathol) stroke; ein S. ins Wasser a vain attempt; Leute seines Schlages the likes of him; S. zwölf Uhr at the stroke of twelve; von gutem S. of the right sort

Schlag′ader ƒ artery

Schlag′anfall m (pathol) stroke

schlag′artig adj sudden, surprise; (heftig) violent || adv all of a sudden; with a bang

Schlag′baum m barrier

Schlag′besen m eggbeater

Schlag′bolzen m firing pin

Schlägel [ˈʃlegəl] m (-s;-) sledge hammer

schlagen [ˈʃlagən] §132 tr hit; strike; beat; (besiegen) defeat; (strafen) spank; (Alarm) sound; (Brücke) build; (Eier) beat; (Geld) coin; (Holz) fell; (Saiten) strike; (Schlacht) fight; die Augen zu Boden s. cast down the eyes; durch ein Sieb s. strain, sift; e-e geschlagene Stunde (coll) a solid hour; in die Flucht s. put to flight; in Fesseln s. put in chains; in Papier s. wrap in paper; Wurzel s. take root; zu Boden s. knock down || ref come to blows; fight a duel; fence; sich gut s. stand one's ground; sich s. zu side with; um sich s. flail about || intr strike; beat; (Pferd) kick; (Vogel) sing; mit den Flügeln s. flap the wings; nach j-m s. take a swing at s.o.; (fig) be like s.o., take after s.o.

schla′gend adj striking, impressive; convincing; schlagende Verbindung dueling fraternity; schlagende Wetter firedamp

Schla′ger m (-s;-) (tolle Sache) hot item; (mus, theat) hit

Schläger [ˈʃlegər] m (-s;-) beater; hitter; batter; baseball bat; golf club; tennis racket; eggbeater; mallet; (Singvogel) warbler; (Raufbold) bully

Schlägerei [ʃlɛgəˈraɪ] f (-;-en) fight, fighting; brawl
Schla'gerpreis m rock-bottom price
Schla'gersänger –in §6 mf pop singer
schlag'fertig adj quick with an answer; (Antwort) ready
Schlag'holz n club, bat
Schlag'instrument n percussion instrument
Schlag'kraft f striking power
schlag'kräftig adj (Armee) powerful; (Beweis) conclusive
Schlag'licht n strong light; glare
Schlag'loch n pothole
Schlag'mal n (baseball) home plate
Schlag'ring m brass knuckles
Schlag'sahne f whipped cream
Schlag'schatten m deep shadow
Schlag'seite f (naut) list; **S. haben** have a list; (hum) be drunk
Schlag'uhr f striking clock
Schlag'weite f striking distance
Schlag'welle f breaker, comber
Schlag'wetter pl (min) firedamp
Schlag'wort n (-[e]s;̈er & -e) slogan; key word, subject (in cataloguing); (Phrasendrescherei) claptrap
Schlag'wörterkatalog m (libr) subject index
Schlag'zeile f headline
Schlag'zeug n percussion instruments f
Schlaks [ʃlaks] m (-es;-e) lanky person
schlaksig [ˈʃlaksɪç] adj lanky
Schlamassel [ʃlaˈmasəl] m & n (-s;-) (coll) jam, pickle, mess
Schlamm [ʃlam] m (-[e]s;-e) mud, slime; (im Motor) sludge; (fig) mire
Schlamm'bad n mud bath
schlämmen [ˈʃlɛmən] tr dredge; (metal) wash
schlammig [ˈʃlamɪç] adj muddy
Schlampe [ˈʃlampə] f (-;-n) frump; (sl) slut
Schlamperei [ʃlampəˈraɪ] f (-;-en) slovenliness; untidiness, mess
schlampig [ˈʃlampɪç] adj sloppy
schlang [ʃlaŋ] pret of schlingen
Schlange [ˈʃlaŋə] f (-;-n) snake; queue, waiting line; (Wasserschlauch) hose; **Schlange stehen** line up for
schlängeln [ˈʃlɛŋəln] ref wind; (Fluß) meander; (sich krümmen) squirm; wriggle; (fig) worm one's way
Schlan'genbeschwörer –in §6 mf snake charmer
Schlan'genlinie f wavy line
schlank [ʃlaŋk] adj slender, slim; im schlanken Trabe at a fast clip
Schlank'heit f (-;) slenderness
Schlank'heitskur f—e—e **S. machen** diet
schlankweg [ˈʃlaŋkvɛk] adv flatly; downright
schlapp [ʃlap] adj slack, limp; flabby; (milde) washed out || **Schlappe** f (-;-n) setback; (Verlust) loss
schlappen [ˈʃlapən] intr flap; shuffle along || **Schlappen** m (-s;-) slipper
schlappern [ˈʃlapərn] tr lap up
schlapp'machen intr (zusammenbrechen) collapse; (ohnmächtig werden) faint; (nicht durchhalten) call it quits

Schlapp'schwanz m (coll) weakling, sissy; (Feigling) coward
Schlaraffenland [ʃlaˈrafənlant] n paradise
Schlaraffenleben [ʃlaˈrafənlebən] n life of Riley
schlau [ʃlau] adj sly; clever
Schlauch [ʃlaux] m (-[e]s;̈e) hose; tube; (fig) souse; (aut) inner tube; (educ) pony
Schlauch'boot n rubber dinghy
schlauchen [ˈʃlauxən] tr drive hard; (mil) drill mercilessly
Schlauch'ventil n (aut) valve
Schläue [ˈʃlɔɪə] f (-;) slyness
schlau'erweise adv prudently
Schlaufe [ˈʃlaufə] f (-;-n) loop
Schlau'kopf m, Schlau'meier m sly fox
schlecht [ʃlɛçt] adj bad, poor; **mir wird s.** I'm getting sick; **schlechter werden** get worse; **s. werden** go bad || adv poorly; **die Uhr geht s.** the clock is off; **s. daran sein** be badly off; **s. und recht** somehow; **s. zu sprechen sein auf** (acc) have it in for
schlechterdings [ˈʃlɛçtərdɪŋs] adv utterly, absolutely
schlecht'gelaunt adj in a bad mood
schlecht'hin' adv simply, downright
schlecht'machen tr talk behind the back of
schlechtweg [ˈʃlɛçtvɛk] adv simply, downright
schlecken [ˈʃlɛkən] tr lick || intr eat sweets, nibble
Schleckerei [ʃlɛkəˈraɪ] f (-;-en) sweets
schleckern [ˈʃlɛkərn] intr have a sweet tooth || impers—mich schleckert es nach I have a yen for
Schlegel [ˈʃlegəl] m (-s;-) sledge hammer; (Holz) mallet; (culin) leg; (mus) drumstick
schleichen [ˈʃlaɪçən] §85 ref & intr (SEIN) sneak
schlei'chend adj creeping; furtive; (Krankheit) lingering; (Gift) slow
Schlei'cher m (-s;-) sneak, hypocrite
Schleicherei [ʃlaɪçəˈraɪ] f (-;-en) sneaking; underhand dealing
Schleich'gut n contraband
Schleich'handel m underhand dealing; smuggling; black-marketing
Schleich'weg m secret path; **auf Schleichwegen** in a roundabout way
Schleier [ˈʃlaɪər] m (-s;-) veil; haze; gauze
schlei'erhaft adj hazy; mysterious; (fig) veiled; **das ist mir s.** I don't know what to make of it
Schleif- [ʃlaɪf] comb.fm. sliding; grinding, abrasive
Schleif'bürste f (elec) brush
Schleife [ˈʃlaɪfə] f (-;-n) (am Kleid, im Haar) bow; (in Schnüren) slipknot; (e-r Straße) hairpin curve; (e-s Flusses) bend; (Wende-) loop; (mit langen Bändern) streamer; (Rutschbahn) slide, chute; (aer) loop
schleifen [ˈʃlaɪfən] tr drag; (Kleid) trail along; demolish; raze; (mus) slur || §88 tr grind; whet; polish; (Glas, Edelstein) cut; (mil) drill hard || §109 intr drag, trail

Schleif′mit′tel n abrasive
Schleif′papier n sandpaper
Schleif′rad n emery wheel
Schleif′stein m whetstone
Schleim [ʃlaɪm] m (-[e]s;-e) slime; mucus, phlegm
Schleim′haut f mucous membrane
schleimig [′ʃlaɪmɪç] adj slimy; mucous
schleißen [′ʃlaɪsən] §53 tr split; slit; (Federkiele) strip ‖ intr wear out
Schlemm [ʃlɛm] m (-s;-e) (cards) slam
schlemmen [′ʃlɛmən] intr carouse; gorge oneself; live high
Schlem′mer –in §6 mf glutton, guzzler; gourmet
schlem′merhaft adj gluttonous; (üppig) plentiful, luxurious
Schlem′merlokal n gourmet restaurant
Schlempe [′ʃlɛmpə] f (-;-n) slop
schlendern [′ʃlɛndərn] intr (SEIN) stroll
Schlendrian [′ʃlɛndri‧an] m (-s;) routine
schlenkern [′ʃlɛŋkərn] tr dangle, swing ‖ intr dangle; mit den Armen s. swing the arms
Schlepp– [ʃlɛp] comb.fm. towing, drag
Schlepp′dampfer m tugboat
Schlepp′dienst m towing service
Schleppe [′ʃlɛpə] f (-;-n) train
schleppen [′ʃlɛpən] tr drag; lug, tote; (aer, naut) tow ‖ ref drag along; sich mit etw s. be burdened with s.th.
Schlepp′penkleid n dress with a train
Schlep′per m (-s;-) hauler; tractor; tugboat; tender, lighter
Schlepp′fischerei f trawling
Schlepp′netz n dragnet, dredge; trawling net
Schlepp′netzboot n trawler
Schlepp′schiff n tugboat
Schlepp′tau n towline; ins S. nehmen take in tow
Schleuder [′ʃlɔɪdər] f (-;-n) sling, slingshot; (aer) catapult; (mach) centrifuge
schleudern [′ʃlɔɪdərn] tr fling; sling; (aer) catapult ‖ intr (aut) skid; (com) undersell
Schleu′derpreis m cutrate price
Schleu′dersitz m (aer) ejection seat
schleunig [′ʃlɔɪnɪç] adj speedy ‖ adv in all haste; (sofort) at once
schleunigst [′ʃlɔɪnɪçst] adv as soon as possible; right away
Schleuse [′ʃlɔɪzə] f (-;-n) lock, sluice, sluice way; drain, sewer
schleusen [′ʃlɔɪzən] tr (fig) maneuver
schlich [ʃlɪç] pret of schleichen ‖ **Schlich** [ʃlɪç] m (-[e]s;-e) trick; alle Schliche kennen know all the ropes; j–m auf die Schliche (or hinter j–s Schliche) kommen be on to s.o.
schlicht [ʃlɪçt] adj smooth; plain
schlichten [′ʃlɪçtən] tr smooth; (fig) settle, arbitrate
Schlich′ter –in §6 mf arbitrator
Schlich′tung f (-;-en) arbitration; settlement
schlief [ʃlif] pret of schlafen
Schließe [′ʃlisə] f (-;-n) clasp; pin
schließen [′ʃlisən] §76 tr shut, close; lock; end, conclude; (Betrieb) shut

down; (Bücher) balance; (Konto; Klammer) close; (Bündnis) form; (Frieden; Rede) conclude; (Kompromiß) reach; (Heirat) form; (Geschäft, Handel) strike; (Versammlung) adjourn; (Wette) make; (Reihen) (mil) close; ans Herz s. press to one's heart; aus etw. s., daß conclude from s.th. that; den Zug s. (mil) bring up the rear; e–n Vergleich s. come to an agreement; ins Herz s. take a liking to; kurz s. (elec) short ‖ ref shut, close; in sich s. comprise, include; (bedeuten) imply; (umfassen) involve; von sich auf andere s. judge others by oneself ‖ intr shut, close; end
Schließ′fach n post office box; safe-deposit box
schließlich [′ʃlislɪç] adj final, eventual ‖ adv finally
schliff [ʃlɪf] pp of schleifen ‖ **Schliff** m (-[e]s;-e) polish; (e–s Diamanten) cut; (fig) polish; (mil) rigorous training
schlimm [ʃlɪm] adj bad; (bedenklich) serious; (traurig) sad; (wund) sore; (eklig) nasty; am schlimmsten worst; immer schlimmer worse and worse; s. daran sein be badly off
schlimmstenfalls [′ʃlɪmstənfals] adv at worst
Schlinge [′ʃlɪŋə] f (-;-n) loop; coil; (fig) trap, difficulty; (bot) tendril; (hunt) snare; (surg) sling; in die S. gehen (fig) fall into a trap
Schlingel [′ʃlɪŋəl] m (-s;-) rascal; fauler S. lazybones
schlingen [′ʃlɪŋən] §142 tr tie; twist; wind; wrap; gulp ‖ ref wind, coil; climb, creep ‖ intr gulp down food
Schlingerbewegung [′ʃlɪŋərbəveguŋ] f (naut) roll
schlingern [′ʃlɪŋərn] intr (naut) roll
Schlinggewächs [′ʃlɪŋgəvɛks] n,
Schlingpflanze [′ʃlɪŋpflantsə] f climber
Schlips [ʃlɪps] m (-es;-e) necktie
Schlitten [′ʃlɪtən] m (-s;-) sled; (an der Schreibmaschine) carriage
schlit′tenfahren §71 intr go sleigh riding; mit j–m s. make life miserable for s.o.
schlittern [′ʃlɪtərn] intr (HABEN & SEIN) slide; (Wagen) skid
Schlittschuh [′ʃlɪtʃu] m ice skate; S. laufen skate, go ice-skating
Schlitt′schuhläufer –in §6 mf ice skater
Schlitz [ʃlɪts] m (-es;-e) slit, slot; (Hosen-) fly
schlitz′äugig adj slit-eyed, sloe-eyed
schlitzen [′ʃlɪtsən] tr slit; rip
Schloß [ʃlɔs] n (Schlosses; Schlösser) castle; country mansion; lock; snap, clasp; hinter S. und Riegel behind bars; unter S. und Riegel under lock and key
Schloße [′ʃlɔsə] f (-;-n) hailstone
Schlosser [′ʃlɔsər] m (-s;-) mechanic; locksmith
Schloß′graben m moat
Schlot [ʃlot] m (-[e]s;-e & ⁼e) chimney, smokestack; (fig) louse

Schlot'baron *m* (coll) tycoon

Schlot'feger *m* chimney sweep

schlotterig ['ʃlɔtərɪç] *adj* loose, dangling; wobbly; (*liederlich*) slovenly

schlottern ['ʃlɔtərn] *intr* fit loosely; (*baumeln*) dangle; (*zittern*) tremble; (*wackeln*) wobble

Schlucht [ʃluχt] *f* (-;-en) gorge; ravine

schluchzen ['ʃluxtsən] *intr* sob

Schluck [ʃlʊk] *m* (-[e]s;-e) gulp; sip

Schluck'auf *m* (-s;) hiccups

schlucken ['ʃlʊkən] *tr & intr* gulp

Schlucker ['ʃlʊkər] *m* (-s;-)—armer S. (coll) poor devil

schlucksen ['ʃlʊksən] *intr* have the hiccups

schluderig ['ʃludərɪç] *adj* slipshod

schludern ['ʃludərn] *intr* do slipshod work

Schlummer ['ʃlʊmər] *m* (-s;) slumber

Schlum'merlied *n* lullaby

schlummern ['ʃlʊmərn] *intr* slumber

schlum'mernd *adj* latent

Schlum'merrolle *f* cushion

Schlund [ʃlʊnt] *m* (-[e]s;-e) gullet; pharynx; (*e-s Vulcans*) crater; (fig) abyss

Schlund'röhre *f* esophagus

Schlupf [ʃlʊpf] *m* (-[e]s;⸚e) hole; (elec, mach) slip

schlüpfen ['ʃlʏpfən] *intr* (SEIN) slip; sneak

Schlüp'fer *m* (-s;-) (pair of) panties; (pair of) bloomers

Schlupf'jacke *f* sweater

Schlupf'loch *n* hiding place; loophole

schlüpfrig ['ʃlʏpfrɪç] *adj* slippery; (*obszön*) off-color

Schlupf'winkel *m* hiding place; haunt

schlurfen ['ʃlʊrfən] *intr* (SEIN) shuffle

schlürfen ['ʃlʏrfən] *tr* slurp; lap up

Schluß [ʃlʊs] *m* (Schlusses; Schlüsse) end, close; (*Ablauf*) expiration; (*Folgerung*) conclusion; S. damit! time!; cut it out!; S. folgt to be concluded; S. machen mit put an end to; knock off from (*work*); break up with (*s.o.*); zum S. in conclusion

Schluß'effekt *m* upshot

Schlüssel ['ʃlʏsəl] *m* (-s;-) key; wrench; quota; code key; (fig) key, clue

Schlüs'selbein *n* collarbone, clavicle

Schlüs'selblume *f* cowslip; helle S. primrose

Schlüs'selbrett *n* keyboard

Schlüs'selbund *m* bunch of keys

schlüs'selfertig *adj* ready for occupancy

Schlüs'selloch *n* keyhole

Schluß'ergebnis *n* final result

Schluß'folge *f*, Schluß'folgerung *f* conclusion, deduction

Schluß'formel *f* complimentary close

schlüssig ['ʃlʏsɪç] *adj* determined; logical; (*Beweis*) conclusive; sich [*dat*] noch nicht s. sein, ob be undecided whether

Schluß'licht *n* (aut) taillight

Schluß'linie *f* (typ) dash

Schluß'rennen *n* (sport) final heat

Schluß'runde *f* (sport) finals

Schluß'schein *m* sales agreement

Schluß'verkauf *m* clearance sale

Schmach [ʃmɑx] *f* (-;) disgrace, shame; insult; humiliation

schmachten ['ʃmaxtən] *intr* (vor *dat*) languish (with); s. nach long for

Schmachtfetzen ['ʃmaxtfetsən] *m* sentimental song or book; melodrama

schmächtig ['ʃmɛçtɪç] *adj* scrawny

Schmachtriemen ['ʃmaxtrimən] *m*—den S. enger schnallen (fig) tighten one's belt

schmach'voll *adj* disgraceful; humiliating

schmackhaft ['ʃmakhaft] *adj* tasty

schmähen ['ʃmɛ-ən] *tr* revile, abuse; speak ill of

schmählich ['ʃmɛlɪç] *adj* disgraceful, scandalous; humiliating

Schmährede ['ʃmɛredə] *f* abuse; diatribe

Schmähschrift ['ʃmɛʃrɪft] *f* libel

schmähsüchtig ['ʃmɛzʏçtɪç] *adj* abusive

Schmä'hung *f* (-;-en) abuse; slander

schmal [ʃmɑl] *adj* narrow; slim; meager

schmälern ['ʃmɛlərn] *tr* curtail; belittle

Schmal'spurbahn *f* narrow-gauge railroad

Schmalz [ʃmalts] *n* (-[e]s;) lard, grease; (fig) schmaltz

schmalzen ['ʃmaltsən] *tr* lard, grease

schmalzig ['ʃmaltsɪç] *adj* greasy; fatty; (fig) schmaltzy

schmarotzen [ʃma'rɔtsən] *intr* (bei) sponge (on)

Schmarot'zer *m* (-s;-) sponger; (zool) parasite

schmarotzerisch [ʃma'rɔtsərɪʃ] *adj* sponging; (zool) parasitic(al)

Schmarre ['ʃmarə] *f* (-;-n) scar; scratch

schmarrig ['ʃmarɪç] *adj* scary

Schmatz [ʃmats] *m* (-es;-e) hearty kiss

schmatzen ['ʃmatsən] *tr* (coll) kiss loudly ‖ *intr* smack one's lips

Schmaus [ʃmaʊs] *m* (-es;⸚e) feast; treat

schmausen ['ʃmaʊzən] *intr* (von) feast (on)

schmecken ['ʃmekən] *tr* taste, sample; (fig) stand ‖ *intr* taste good; s. nach taste like

Schmeichelei [ʃmaɪçə'laɪ] *f* (-;-en) flattery; coaxing

schmeichelhaft ['ʃmaɪçəlhaft] *adj* flattering

schmeicheln ['ʃmaɪçəln] *ref*—sich [*dat*] s. zu (*inf*) pride oneself on (*ger*) ‖ *intr* be flattering; (*dat*) flatter

Schmeich'ler -in §6 *mf* flatterer

schmeichlerisch ['ʃmaɪçlərɪʃ] *adj* flattering; complimentary; fawning

schmeißen ['ʃmaɪsən] §53 *tr* (coll) throw; (coll) manage; e-e Runde Bier s. set up a round of beer ‖ *ref*—mit Geld um sich s. throw money around

Schmelz [ʃmelts] *m* (-es;-e) enamel; glaze; melodious ring; (fig) bloom

schmelzen ['ʃmeltsən] §133 *tr* melt; smelt ‖ *intr* (SEIN) melt; (fig) soften

schmel′zend adj mellow; melodious
Schmelzerei [ʃmeltsə′raɪ] f (-;-en) foundry
schmelz′flüssig adj molten
Schmelz′hütte f foundry
Schmelz′käse m soft cheese
Schmelz′ofen m smelting furnace
Schmelz′punkt m melting point
Schmelz′tiegel m crucible, melting pot
Schmer [ʃmer] m & n (-s;) fat, grease
Schmer′bauch m (coll) potbelly
Schmerz [ʃmerts] m (-es;-en) pain, ache; **mit Schmerzen** (coll) anxiously, impatiently
schmerzen [′ʃmertsən] tr & intr hurt
schmer′zend adj aching, sore
Schmer′zensgeld n damages (for pain or anguish)
Schmer′zenskind n problem child
schmerz′haft adj painful, aching
schmerz′lich adj painful, severe
schmerz′lindernd adj soothing
schmerz′los adj painless
Schmerz′schwelle f threshold of pain
Schmetterling [′ʃmetərlɪŋ] m (-s;-e) butterfly
Schmet′terlingsstil m (sport) butterfly
schmettern [′ʃmetərn] tr smash; **zu Boden s.** knock down || intr (Trompete) blare; (Vogel) warble
Schmied [ʃmit] m (-[e]s;-e) smith
Schmiede [′ʃmidə] f (-;-n) forge; blacksmith shop
Schmie′deeisen n wrought iron
Schmie′dehammer m sledge hammer
schmieden [′ʃmidən] tr forge; hammer; (Pläne, usw.) devise, concoct
schmiegen [′ʃmigən] tr—**das Kinn** (or **die Wange**) **in die Hand s.** prop one's chin (or cheek) in one's hand || ref (an acc) snuggle up (to); **sich s. und biegen vor** (dat) bow and scrape before
schmiegsam [′ʃmikzam] adj flexible
Schmier- [ʃmir] comb.fm. grease, lubricating; smearing
Schmiere [′ʃmira] f (-;-n) grease; lubricant; salve; (Schmutz) muck; (fig) mess; (fig) spanking; (theat) barnstormers; **S. stehen** be the lookout man
schmieren [′ʃmirən] tr grease, lubricate; smear; (Butter) spread; (Brot) butter; (bestechen) bribe; **j-m e-e s.** (coll) paste s.o.; **wie geschmiert** like greased lightning || ref—**sich** (dat) **die Kehle s.** (coll) wet one's whistle || intr scribble
Schmie′renkomödiant -in §7 mf (theat) barnstormer, ham
Schmiererei [ʃmira′raɪ] f (-;-en) greasing; smearing; scribbling
Schmier′fink m scrawler; (Schmutzkerl) dirty fellow
Schmier′geld n (coll) bribe; (coll) hush money; (pol) slush fund
schmierig [′ʃmirɪç] adj smeary, greasy; oily; (Geschäfte) dirty
Schmier′käse m cheese spread
Schmier′mittel n lubricant
Schmier′pistole f, **Schmier′presse** f grease gun
Schmie′rung f (-;-en) lubrication

Schminke [′ʃmɪŋkə] f (-;-n) rouge; make-up
schminken [′ʃmɪŋkən] tr apply make-up to; rouge; **die Lippen s.** put on lipstick || ref put on make-up
Schminkunterlage [′ʃmɪŋkunterlagə] f base
Schmirgel [′ʃmɪrgəl] m (-s;) emery
Schmir′gelleinen n, **Schmir′gelleinwand** f emery cloth
Schmir′gelpapier n emery paper
Schmir′gelscheibe f emery wheel
Schmiß [ʃmɪs] m (Schmisses; Schmisse) (coll) stroke, blow; (coll) gash; (coll) dueling scar; (coll) zip
schmissig [′ʃmɪsɪç] adj (coll) snazzy
schmollen [′ʃmɔlən] intr pout, sulk
schmolz [ʃmɔlts] pret of **schmelzen**
Schmorbraten [′ʃmorbratən] m braised meat
schmoren [′ʃmorən] tr braise, stew || intr (fig) swelter; **laß ihn s.!** let him stew!
schmuck [ʃmʊk] adj nice, cute; smart, dapper; (sauber) neat || **Schmuck** m (-[e]s;) ornament; decoration; trimmings; trinket(s); jewelry
schmücken [′ʃmʏkən] tr adorn; decorate, trim; (Aufsatz) embellish || ref spruce up, dress up
Schmuck′kästchen n jewel box
schmuck′los adj unadorned, plain
Schmuck′waren pl jewelry
Schmuddel [′ʃmʊdəl] m (-s;-) slob
schmuddelig [′ʃmʊdəlɪç] adj dirty
Schmuggel [′ʃmʊgəl] m (-s;), **Schmuggelei** [ʃmʊgə′laɪ] f (-;-en) smuggling
schmuggeln [′ʃmʊgəln] tr & intr smuggle
Schmug′gelware f contraband
Schmuggler -in [′ʃmʊglər(ɪn)] §6 mf smuggler
schmunzeln [′ʃmʊntsəln] intr grin || **Schmunzeln** n (-s;) big grin
Schmutz [ʃmʊts] m (-es;) dirt, filth; (Zote) smut
schmutzen [′ʃmʊtsən] tr & intr soil
Schmutz′fink m (coll) slob
Schmutz′fleck m stain, smudge, blotch
schmut′zig adj dirty
Schnabel [′ʃnabəl] m (-s;ö) beak, bill; **halt den S.!** (sl) shut up!
Schna′belhieb m peck
schnäbeln [′ʃnebəln] tr & intr peck; (fig) kiss
Schnalle [′ʃnalə] f (-;-n) buckle; (vulg) whore
schnallen [′ʃnalən] tr buckle, fasten
schnalzen [′ʃnaltsən] intr—**mit den Fingern s.** snap one's fingers; **mit der Zunge s.** click one's tongue
schnapp [ʃnap] interj snap!
schnappen [′ʃnapən] tr grab; (Dieb) nab || intr snap; **ins Schloß s.** snap shut; **mit den Fingern s.** snap one's fingers; **nach Luft s.** gasp for air; **s. nach** snap at
Schnapp′messer n jackknife
Schnapp′schuß m (phot) snapshot
Schnaps [ʃnaps] m (-es;ö-e) hard liquor
Schnaps′brennerei f distillery
Schnaps′bruder m (coll) booze hound

Schnaps'idee f (coll) crazy idea
schnarchen ['ʃnarçən] tr snore
Schnarre ['ʃnarə] f (-;-n) rattle
schnarren ['ʃnarən] intr rattle; (Säge) buzz; (Insekten) drone, buzz
schnattern ['ʃnatərn] intr (Enten) cackle; (Zähne) chatter; (fig) gab
schnauben ['ʃnaubən] intr pant, puff; (Pferd) snort; **nach Rache s.** breathe revenge; **vor Wut s.** fume with rage || ref blow one's nose
schnaufen ['ʃnaufən] intr pant; wheeze
Schnau'fer m (-s;-) (coll) deep breath
Schnauzbart ['ʃnautsbart] m mustache
Schnauze ['ʃnautsə] f (-;-n) snout, muzzle; spout; (sl) snoot; (sl) big mouth
Schnauzer ['ʃnautsər] m (-s;-) schnauzer
schnauzig ['ʃnautsɪç] adj rude
Schnecke ['ʃnɛkə] f (-;-n) snail; (Nacht-) slug; (e-r Säule) volute; spiral; (anat) cochlea; (mach) worm; (e-r Violine) (mus) scroll
Schneckenhaus (Schnek'kenhaus) n snail shell
Schneckentempo (Schnek'kentempo) n (fig) snail's pace
Schnee ['ʃne] m (-s;) snow; whipped egg white
Schnee'besen m eggbeater
Schnee'brett n snow slide, avalanche
Schnee'brille f snow goggles
Schnee'decke f blanket of snow
Schnee'flocke f snowflake
Schnee'gestöber n snow flurry
schneeig ['ʃne·ɪç] adj snowy
Schnee'matsch m slush
Schnee'pflug m snowplow
Schnee'schaufel f, **Schnee'schippe** f snow shovel
Schnee'schläger m eggbeater
Schnee'schmelze f thaw
Schnee'treiben n blizzard
schneeverweht ['ʃnefervet] adj snowbound
Schnee'verwehung f snowdrift
Schnee'wehe f snowdrift
Schneewittchen ['ʃnevɪtçən] n (-s) Snow White
Schneid ['ʃnaɪt] m (-[e]s;) (coll) pluck; (Mut) (coll) guts
Schneid'brenner m cutting torch
Schneide ['ʃnaɪdə] f (-;-n) (cutting) edge; (e-s Hobels) blade; **auf des Messers S.** (fig) on the razor's edge
Schnei'debrett n cutting board
Schnei'demaschine f cutter, slicer
Schnei'demühle f sawmill
schneiden ['ʃnaɪdən] §106 tr cut; (Baum) prune; (Fingernägel) pare; (Hecke) trim; (nicht grüßen) snub; (surg) operate on; (tennis) slice; **Gesichter s.** make faces; **klein s.** cut up || ref (fig) be mistaken; (fig) be disappointed; (math) intersect; **sich in den Finger s.** cut one's finger || intr cut
Schnei'der m (-s;-) m cutter; tailor
Schneiderei [ʃnaɪdə'raɪ] f (-;-en) tailoring; (Werkstatt) tailorshop
Schnei'derin f (-;-nen) dressmaker

schneidern ['ʃnaɪdərn] tr make || intr do tailoring; be a dressmaker
Schnei'derpuppe f dummy
Schnei'dezahn m incisor
schneidig ['ʃnaɪdɪç] adj sharp-edged; energetic; smart, sharp
schneien ['ʃnaɪ·ən] impers—**es schneit** it is snowing
Schneise ['ʃnaɪzə] f (-;-n) lane (between rows of trees)
schnell [ʃnel] adj fast, quick
Schnell'lauf (Schnell'lauf) m race; sprint; speed skating
Schnell'bahn f high-speed railroad
Schnelle ['ʃnelə] f (-;-n) speed; (Strom-) rapids; **auf die S.** (coll) in a hurry, very briefly
schnellen ['ʃnelən] tr let fly || intr (SEIN) spring, jump up; (Preise) shoot up; **mit dem Finger s.** snap one's fingers
Schnell'gang m (aut) overdrive
Schnellhefter ['ʃnelheftər] m (-s;-) folder, file
Schnell'imbiß m snack
Schnell'kraft f elasticity
schnellstens ['ʃnelstəns] adv as fast as possible
Schnell'verfahren n quick process; (jur) summary proceeding
Schnell'zug m express train
Schneppe ['ʃnepə] f (-;-n) spout; (sl) prostitute
schneuzen ['ʃnɔɪtsən] ref blow one's nose
schniegeln ['ʃnigəln] ref dress up; **geschniegelt und gebügelt** dressed to kill
schnipfeln ['ʃnɪpfəln] tr & intr snip
Schnippchen ['ʃnɪpçən] n—**j-m ein S. schlagen** (coll) pull a fast one on s.o.; outwit s.o.
Schnippel ['ʃnɪpəl] m & n (-s;-) chip
schnippeln ['ʃnɪpəln] tr & intr snip
schnippen ['ʃnɪpən] intr—**mit den Fingern s.** (coll) snap one's fingers
schnippisch ['ʃnɪpɪʃ] adj fresh || adv pertly; **s. erwidern** snap back
schnitt [ʃnɪt] pret of **schneiden** || **Schnitt** m (-[e]s;-e) cut, incision; (Kerbe) notch; (Schnitte) slice; (Quer-) profile, cross section; (Durch-) average; (e-s Anzuges) cut, style; (Gewinn) cut; (agr) reaping; (bb) edge; (cin) editing; (geom) intersection; **weicher Schnitt** (cin) dissolve
Schnitt'ansicht f sectional view
Schnitt'ball m (tennis) slice
Schnitt'blumen pl cut flowers
Schnitt'bohnen pl string beans
Schnittchen ['ʃnɪtçən] n (-s;-) thin slice; sandwich
Schnitte ['ʃnɪtə] f (-;-n) slice
Schnit'ter –in §6 mf reaper, mower
Schnitt'fläche f (geom) plane
Schnitt'holz n lumber
schnittig ['ʃnɪtɪç] adj smart-looking; (aut) streamlined
Schnitt'lauch ['ʃnɪtlaux] m (-[e]s;) (bot) chive
Schnitt'linie f (geom) secant
Schnitt'meister m (cin) editor

Schnitt′muster n pattern (*of dress, etc.*)

Schnitt′punkt m intersection

Schnitt′waren pl dry goods

Schnitt′wunde f cut, gash

Schnitz [ʃnɪts] m (-es;-e) cut; slice; chop; chip

Schnitzel [′ʃnɪtsəl] n (-s;-) chip; slice; shred; (*Abfälle*) parings; (culin) cutlet

schnitzeln [′ʃnɪtsəln] tr cut up; shred; (*Holz*) whittle

schnitzen [′ʃnɪtsən] tr carve

Schnit′zer m (-s;-) carver; (*Fehler*) blunder; **grober S.** boner

Schnitzerei [ʃnɪtsə′raɪ] f (-;-en) wood carving, carved work

schnob [ʃnop] pret of schnauben

schnodderig [′ʃnodərɪç] adj brash

schnöde [′ʃnøːdə] adj vile; disdainful; (*Gewinn*) filthy

Schnorchel [′ʃnorçəl] m (-s;-) snorkel

Schnörkel [′ʃnœrkəl] m (-s;-) (*beim Schreiben*) flourish; (fig) frills; (archit) scroll

schnorren [′ʃnorən] tr (coll) chisel, bum ‖ intr (coll) sponge, chisel

Schnösel [′ʃnøːzəl] m (-s;-) wise guy

schnüffeln [′ʃnʏfəln] intr snoop around; (an *dat*) sniff (at)

Schnüff′ler -in §6 mf (coll) snoop

Schnuller [′ʃnʊlər] m (-s;-) pacifier

Schnultze [′ʃnʊltsə] f (-;-n) (coll) tear-jerker

schnultzig [′ʃnʊltsɪç] adj (coll) corny, mawkish

schnupfen [′ʃnʊpfən] tr snuff ‖ intr take snuff ‖ **Schnupfen** m (-s;-) cold; **den S. bekommen** catch a cold

Schnupftabak [′ʃnʊpftabak] m snuff

schnuppe [′ʃnʊpə] adj—**das ist mir s.** it's all the same to me ‖ **Schnuppe** f (-;-n) shooting star; (e-r *Kerze*) snuff

Schnur [ʃnur] f (-;̈e & -en) string; (*Band*) braid; (elec) flexible cord; **nach der S.** regularly

Schnürband [′ʃnʏrbant] n (-[e]s;̈er) shoestring; corset lace

Schnürchen [′ʃnʏrçən] n (-s;-) string; **etw am S. haben** have at one's fingertips; **wie am S.** like clockwork

schnüren [′ʃnʏrən] tr tie; lace; (*Perlen*) string ‖ ref put on a corset

schnur′gerade adj straight ‖ adv straight, as the crow flies

schnurr [ʃnur] interj purr!; buzz!

Schnurrbart [′ʃnʊrbart] m mustache

schnurren [′ʃnʊrən] intr (*Katze*) purr; (*Rad*) whir; (*Maschine*) hum; (*schnorren*) sponge, chisel

schnurrig [′ʃnʊrɪç] adj funny; queer

Schnürschuh [′ʃnʏrʃu] m oxford shoe

Schnürsenkel [′ʃnʏrzɛŋkəl] m shoestring

schnurstracks [′ʃnur′traks] adv right away; directly; **s. entgegengesetzt** diametrically opposite; **s. losgehen auf** (*acc*) make a beeline for

schob [ʃop] pret of schieben

Schober [′ʃobər] m (-s;-) stack

Schock [ʃok] m (-[e]s;-s) shock ‖ n (-[e]s;-e) threescore

schockant [ʃo′kant] adj shocking

schockieren [ʃo′kirən] tr shock

schofel [′ʃofəl] adj mean; miserable; (*schäbig*) shabby; (*geizig*) stingy

Schöffe [′ʃœfə] m (-n;-n) juror

Schokolade [ʃoko′ladə] f (-;-n) chocolate

schokoladen [ʃoko′ladən] adj chocolate

Schokola′dentafel f chocolate bar

scholl [ʃol] pret of schallen

Scholle [′ʃolə] f (-;-n) clod; sod; stratum; ice floe; (ichth) sole; **heimatliche S.** native soil

schon [ʃon] adv already; as early as; yet, as yet; (*sogar*) even; (*bloß*) the bare, the mere; **ich komme s.!** all right, I'm coming!; **s. am folgenden Tage** on the very next day; **s. der Gedanke** the mere thought; **s. früher** before now; **s. gut!** all right!; **s. immer** always; **s. lange** long since, for a long time; **s. wieder** again

schön [ʃøn] adj beautiful; nice; (*Künste*) fine; (*Mann*) handsome; (*Summe*) nice round; (*Geschlecht*) fair; **schönen Dank!** many thanks!; **schönen Gruß an** (*acc*) best regards to ‖ adv nicely; **der Hund macht s.** the dog sits up and begs; **s. warm** nice and warm

schonen [′ʃonən] tr spare; take it easy on; treat with consideration ‖ ref take care of oneself

scho′nend adj careful; considerate

schön′färben tr gloss over

Schon′frist f period of grace

Schon′gang m (aut) overdrive

Schön′heit f (-;-en) beauty

Schön′heitsfehler m flaw

Schön′heitskönigin f beauty queen

Schön′heitspflege f beauty treatment

schön′tun §154 intr (*dat*) flatter; (*dat*) flirt (with)

Scho′nung f (-;-en) care, careful treatment; mercy; consideration; tree nursery; wild-game preserve

scho′nungslos adj unsparing; merciless; relentless

scho′nungsvoll adj considerate

Schon′zeit f (hunt) closed season

Schopf [ʃopf] m (-[e]s;̈e) tuft of hair; (orn) crest

schöpfen [′ʃœpfən] tr draw; bail; scoop, ladle; (*frische Luft*) breathe; (*Mut*) take; **Verdacht s.** become suspicious; **wieder Atem** (or **Luft**) **s.** (fig) breathe freely again

Schöp′fer m (-s;-) creator; author; composer; painter; sculptor; dipper, ladle

schöpferisch [′ʃœpfərɪʃ] adj creative

Schöp′ferkraft f creative power

Schöpf′kelle f scoop

Schöpf′löffel m ladle

Schöp′fung f (-;-en) creation

Schoppen [′ʃopən] m (-s;-) pint; glass of beer, glass of wine

schor [ʃor] pret of scheren

Schorf [ʃorf] m (-[e]s;-e) scab

Schornstein [′ʃornʃtaɪn] m chimney; smokestack

Schorn′steinfeger m chimney sweeper

Schoß [ʃos] m (**Schosses; Schosse**)

sprout || *ʃ*os] *m* (-es;≃e) lap; womb; (fig) bosom; **die Hände in den S. legen** cross one's arms; (fig) be idle

Schößling [ʃœslɪŋ] *m* (-s;-e) shoot

Schote [ʃoːtə] *f* (-;-n) pod, shell

Schotte [ʃɔtə] *m* (-n;-n) Scotchman || *f* (-;-n) (naut) bulkhead

Schotter [ʃɔtər] *m* (-s;-) gravel; macadam, crushed stone; (rr) ballast

Schottin [ʃɔtɪn] *f* (-;-nen) Scotchwoman

schottisch [ʃɔtɪʃ] *adj* Scotch

schraffieren [ʃraˈfiːrən] *tr* hatch

schräg [ʃreːk] *adj* oblique; *(abfallend)* slanting, sloping; diagonal || *adv* obliquely; **s. gegenüber von** diagonally across from; **s. geneigt** sloping

Schräg′linie *f* diagonal

schrak [ʃrak] *pret* of **schrecken**

Schramme [ʃramə] *f* (-;-n) scratch, abrasion; scar

schrammen [ʃramən] *tr* scratch; skin

Schrank [ʃraŋk] *m* (-[e]s;≃e) closet

Schranke [ʃraŋkə] *f* (-;-n) barrier; (fig) bounds, limit; (jur) bar; (rr) gate; (sport) starting gate

schran′kenlos *adj* boundless; exaggerated

Schran′kenwärter *m* (rr) signalman

Schrank′fach *n* compartment

Schrank′koffer *m* wardrobe trunk

Schrapnell [ʃrapˈnɛl] *n* (-s;-e & -s) shrapnel, piece of shrapnel

Schraubdeckel [ʃraupdekəl] *m* screw-on cap

Schraube [ʃraubə] *f* (-;-n) screw; bolt; (aer, naut) propeller

schrauben [ʃraubən] *tr* screw; **in die Höhe s.** raise || *ref*—**sich in die Höhe s.** circle higher and higher

Schrau′benflügel *m* propeller blade

Schrau′bengang *m,* **Schrau′bengewinde** *n* thread (of a screw)

Schrau′benmutter *f* (-;-n) nut

Schrau′benschlüssel *m* wrench; **verstellbarer S.** monkey wrench

Schrau′benstrahl *m,* **Schrau′benstrom** *m* (aer) slipstream

Schraubenzieher [ʃraubəntsiːər] *m* (-s;-) screwdriver

Schraubstock [ʃraupʃtɔk] *m* vice

Schrebergarten [ʃreːbərɡartən] *m* garden plot *(at edge of town)*

Schreck [ʃrek] *m* (-[e]s;-e) var of **Schrecken**

Schreck′bild *n* frightful sight; boogeyman

schrecken [ʃrekən] *tr* frighten, scare || **Schrecken** *m* (-s;-) fright, fear

Schreckensbotschaft (**Schrek′kensbotschaft**) *f* alarming news

Schreckensherrschaft (**Schrek′kensherrschaft**) *f* reign of terror

Schreckenskammer (**Schrek′kenskammer**) *f* chamber of horrors

Schreckensregiment (**Schrek′kensregiment**) *n* reign of teror, terrorism

Schreckenstat (**Schrek′kenstat**) *f* atrocity

schreck′haft *adj* timid

schreck′lich *adj* frightful, terrible

Schrecknis [ʃreknɪs] *n* (-ses;-se) horror

Schreck′schuß *m* warning shot

Schreck′sekunde *f* reaction time

Schrei [ʃrai] *m* (-[e]s;-e) cry, shout; **letzter S.** latest fashion

Schreib- [ʃraip] *comb.fm.* writing

Schreib′art *f* style; spelling

Schreib′bedarf *m* stationery

Schreib′block *m* writing pad, note pad

schreiben [ʃraibən] §62 *tr* write; spell; type; **ins Konzept s.** make a rough draft of; **ins reine s.** make a clean copy; **Noten s.** copy music || *ref* spell one's name || *intr* write; spell; type || **Schreiben** *n* (-s;-) writing; (com) letter

Schrei′ber *m* (-s;-) writer; clerk; recording instrument, recorder

schreib′faul *adj* too lazy to write

Schreib′feder *f* pen

Schreib′fehler *m* slip of the pen

Schreib′heft *n* copybook, exercise book

Schreib′mappe *f* portfolio

Schreib′maschine *f* typewriter; **mit der S. geschrieben** typed; **S. schreiben** type

Schreib′maschinenfarbband *n* (-[e]s; ≃er) typewriter ribbon

Schreib′maschinenschreiber –in §6 *mf* typist

Schreib′maschinenschrift *f* typescript

Schreib′materialien *pl,* **Schreib′papier** *n* stationery

Schreib′schrift *f* (typ) script

Schreib′stube *f* (mil) orderly room

Schreib′tisch *m* desk

Schrei′bung *f* (-;-en) spelling

Schreib′unterlage *f* desk pad

Schreib′waren *pl* stationery

Schreib′warenhandlung *f* stationery store

Schreibweise *f* style; spelling

Schreib′zeug *n* writing materials

schreien [ʃraiən] §135 *tr* cry, shout, scream, howl || *ref*—**sich heiser s.** shout oneself hoarse; **sich tot s.** yell one's lungs out || *intr* cry, shout, scream, howl; *(Esel)* bray; *(Eule)* screech; *(Schwein)* squeal; **s. nach** clamor for; **s. über** *(acc)* cry out against; **s. vor** *(dat)* shout for *(joy)*; cry out in *(pain)*; roar with *(laughter)* || **Schreien** *n* (-s;) shouting; **das ist zum S.!** that's a scream!

schrei′end *adj* shrill; *(Farbe)* loud; *(Unrecht)* flagrant

Schrei′hals *m* (coll) crybaby

Schrei′krampf *m* crying fit

Schrein [ʃrain] *m* (-[e]s;-e) reliquary

Schreiner [ʃrainər] *m* (-s;-) carpenter; cabinetmaker

schreiten [ʃraitən] §86 *intr* (SEIN) step; stride; **zur Abstimmung s.** proceed to vote; **zur Tat s.** proceed to act

schrie [ʃriː] *pret* of **schreien**

schrieb [ʃriːp] *pret* of **schreiben**

Schrift [ʃrɪft] *f* (-;-en) writing; handwriting; letter, character; document; book; publication; periodical; *(auf Münzen)* legend; (typ) type, font; **die Heilige S.** Holy Scripture; **nach der S. sprechen** speak standard German

Schrift′art f type, font
Schrift′auslegung f exegesis
Schrift′bild n type face
Schrift′deutsch n literary German
Schrift′führer –in §6 mf secretary
Schrift′leiter –in §6 mf editor
schrift′lich adj written || adv in writing; **s. wiedergeben** transcribe
Schrift′satz m (jur) brief; (typ) composition
Schrift′setzer m typesetter
Schrift′sprache f literary language
Schriftsteller –in [′ʃrɪft/ʃtɛlər(ɪn)] §6 mf writer, author
Schrift′stück n piece of writing; document
Schrifttum [′ʃrɪfttum] n (–s;) literature
Schrift′verkehr m, **Schrift′wechsel** m correspondence
Schrift′zeichen n letter, character
schrill [ʃrɪl] adj shrill
schrillen [′ʃrɪlən] intr ring loudly
schritt [ʃrɪt] pret of **schreiten** || **Schritt** m (–[e]s;–e) step; pace; stride; (e–r Hose) crotch; (fig) step
Schritt′macher m pacemaker
schritt′weise adv gradually; step by step
schroff [ʃrɔf] adj steep; rugged; rude, uncouth; rough, harsh; (Ablehnung, Widerspruch) flat
schröpfen [′ʃrœpfən] tr (fig) milk, fleece; (med) bleed, cup
Schrot [ʃrot] m & n (–[e]s;–e) scrap; (Getreide) crushed grain, grits; (zum Schießen) buckshot
Schrot′brot n whole grain bread
Schrot′flinte f shotgun
Schrot′korn n, **Schrot′kugel** f pellet
Schrott [ʃrɔt] m (–[e]s;) scrap metal
Schrott′platz m junk yard
schrubben [′ʃrubən] tr scrub
Schrulle [′ʃrulə] f (–;–n) (coll) nutty idea
schrul′lenhaft, schrullig [′ʃrulɪç] adj whimsical
schrumpelig [′ʃrumpəlɪç] adj crumpled; wrinkled, shriveled
schrumpeln [′ʃrumpəln] intr shrivel
schrumpfen [′ʃrumpfən] intr (SEIN) shrink; shrivel; (pathol) atrophy
Schub [ʃup] m (–[e]s;"e) shove, push; batch; (phys) thrust
Schub′fach n drawer
Schub′karre f, **Schub′karren** m wheelbarrow
Schub′kasten m drawer
Schub′kraft f thrust
Schub′lade f drawer
Schub′kraft f thrust
Schubs [ʃups] m (–es;–e) (coll) shove
schubsen [′ʃupsən] tr & intr shove
Schub′stange f (aut) connecting rod
schüchtern [′ʃʏçtərn] adj shy, bashful
schuf [ʃuf] pret of **schaffen**
Schuft [ʃuft] m (–[e]s;–e) cad
schuften [′ʃuftən] intr drudge, slave
Schufterei [ʃuftə′raɪ] f (–;) drudgery; (Schuftigkeit) meanness
schuftig [′ʃuftɪç] adj (fig) rotten
Schuh [ʃu] m (–[e]s;–e) shoe; boot
Schuh′band n (–[e]s;"er) shoestring

Schuhflicker [′ʃuflɪkər] m (–s;–) shoe repairman, shoemaker
Schuh′krem m shoe polish
Schuh′laden m shoe store
Schuh′leisten m last
Schuh′löffel m shoehorn
Schuh′macher m shoemaker
Schuhplattler [′ʃuplatlər] m (–s;–) Bavarian folk dance
Schuh′putzer m shoeshine boy
Schuh′sohle f sole
Schuhspanner [′ʃu/ʃpanər] m (–s;–) shoetree
Schuh′werk n footwear
Schuh′wichse f shoe polish
Schuh′zeug n footwear
Schul– [ʃul] comb.fm. school
Schul′amt n school board
Schul′arbeit f homework; (Aust) classroom work
Schul′aufsicht f school board
Schul′bank f (–;"e) school desk
Schul′behörde f school board; board of education
Schul′beispiel n (fig) test case
Schul′besuch m attendance at school
Schul′bildung f schooling, education
schuld [ʃult] adj at fault, to blame || **Schuld** f (–;–en) debt; fault; guilt
schuld′bewußt adj conscious of one's guilt
schulden [′ʃuldən] tr owe
schuld′haft adj culpable || **Schuld′haft** f imprisonment for debt
Schul′diener m school janitor
schuldig [′ʃuldɪç] adj guilty; responsible; **j–m etw s. sein** owe s.o. s.th. || **Schuldige** §5 mf culprit; guilty party
Schul′digkeit f (–;–en) duty, obligation; **seine S. tun** do one's duty
Schul′direktor m §7 mf principal
schuld′los adj innocent
Schuld′losigkeit f (–;) innocence
Schuldner –in [′ʃuldnər(ɪn)] §6 mf debtor
Schuld′schein m promissory note, IOU
Schuld′spruch m verdict of guilty
Schuld′verschreibung f promissory note, IOU; (Obligation) bond
Schule [′ʃulə] f (–;–n) school; **auf der S.** in school; **S. machen** (fig) set a precedent; **von der S. abgehen** quit school
schulen [′ʃulən] tr train; (pol) indoctrinate
Schüler [′ʃylər] m (–s;–) pupil (in grammar school or high school); trainee; (Jünger) disciple
Schü′leraustausch m student exchange
Schülerin [′ʃylərɪn] f (–;–nen) pupil
Schul′film m educational film
Schul′flug m training flight
schul′frei adj;—**schulfreier Tag** holiday; **s. haben** have off
Schul′gelände n school grounds; campus
Schul′geld n tuition
Schul′gelehrsamkeit f book learning
Schul′hof m schoolyard, playground
Schul′kamerad m school chum
Schul′lehrer –in §6 mf schoolteacher
Schul′mappe f schoolbag
Schul′meister m schoolmaster; pedant
schul′meistern intr criticize

Schul'ordnung f school regulation
Schul'pflicht f compulsory school attendance
schul'pflichtig adj of school age; schulpflichtiges Alter school age
Schul'plan m curriculum
Schul'ranzen m schoolbag
Schul'rat m (-[e]s;-̈e) (educ) superintendent
Schul'reise f field trip
Schul'schiff n training ship
Schul'schluß m close of school
Schul'schwester f teaching nun
Schul'stunde f lesson, period
Schul'tasche f schoolbag
Schulter ['ʃultər] f (-;-n) shoulder
Schul'terblatt n shoulder blade
schul'terfrei adj off-the-shoulder; (trägerfrei) strapless
schultern ['ʃultərn] tr shoulder
Schul'terstück n epaulet
Schul'unterricht m instruction; schooling; im S. in school
Schul'wesen n school system
Schul'zeugnis n report card
Schul'zimmer n classroom
Schul'zwang m compulsory education
schummeln ['ʃuməln] intr (coll) cheat
schund [ʃunt] pret of schinden || Schund m (-[e]s) junk, trash
Schund'literatur f trashy literature
Schund'roman m dime novel
Schupo ['ʃupo] m (-s;-s) (Schutzpolizist) policeman, copy || f (-;) (Schutzpolizei) police
Schuppe [ʃupə] f (-;-n) scale; Schuppen pl dandruff
schuppen ['ʃupən] tr scale; scrape || Schuppen m (-s;-) shed; (aer) hangar; (aut) garage
schuppig ['ʃupɪç] adj scaly, flaky
Schups [ʃups] m (-es;-e) shove
schupsen ['ʃupsən] tr shove
Schüreisen ['ʃyraɪzən] n poker
schüren ['ʃyrən] tr poke, stir; (fig) stir up, foment
schürfen ['ʃyrfən] tr scratch, scrape; dig for || intr (nach) prospect (for)
schurigeln ['ʃurigəln] tr (coll) bully
Schurke ['ʃurkə] m (-n;-n) bum, punk
Schur'kenstreich m, Schur'kentat f, Schurkerei [ʃurkə'raɪ] f (-;-en) mean trick
schurkisch ['ʃurkɪʃ] adj mean, low-down
Schürze ['ʃyrtsə] f (-;-n) apron
schürzen ['ʃyrtsən] tr tuck up; tie
Schür'zenband n (-[e]s;-̈er) apron
Schür'zenjäger m skirt chaser, wolf
Schuß [ʃus] m (Schusses; Schüsse) shot; (Ladung) round; (rasche Bewunde) gunshot wound; (rasche Bewegung) rush; (Brot) batch; (bot) shoot; (culin) dash; (sport) shot; blinder S. blank; e-n S. abgeben fire a shot; ein S. ins Blaue a wild shot; ein S. ins Schwarze a bull's-eye; im S. haben have under control; im vollen S. in full swing; in S. bekommen get going; in S. bringen get (s.th.); j-m vor den S. kommen come within s.o.'s range; (fig) come across s.o.; scharfer S.

live round; weit vom S. out of harm's way
Schüssel ['ʃysəl] f (-;-n) bowl; (fig) dish
schuß'fest, schuß'sicher adj bulletproof
Schuß'waffe f firearm
Schuß'weite f range
Schuster ['ʃustər] m (-s;-) shoemaker; (fig) bungler
schustern ['ʃustərn] intr bungle
Schutt [ʃut] m (-es;) rubbish; rubble
Schutt'abladeplatz m dump
Schüttboden ['ʃytbodən] m granary
Schüttelfrost ['ʃytəlfrɔst] m shivers
schütteln ['ʃytəln] tr shake; j-m die Hand s. shake hands with s.o.
schütten ['ʃytən] tr pour, spill || impers —es schüttet it is pouring
Schutz [ʃuts] m (-es;) protection, defense; (Obdach) shelter; (Deckung) cover; (Schirm) screen; (Schutzgeleit) safeguard; zu S. und Trutz defensive and offensive
Schutz'brille f safety goggles
Schütze ['ʃytsə] m (-n;-n) marksman, shot; (astr) Sagittarius; (mil) rifleman || f (-;-n) sluice gate
schützen ['ʃytsən] tr (gegen) protect (against), defend (against); (vor dat) preserve (from) || Schützen m (-s;-) (tex) shuttle
schüt'zend adj protective; tutelary
Schutz'engel m guardian angle
Schüt'zengraben m (mil) foxhole
Schüt'zenkompanie f rifle company
Schüt'zenkönig m crack shot
Schüt'zenloch n (mil) foxhole
Schüt'zenmine f anti-personnel mine
Schutz'geleit n escort; safe conduct; (aer) air cover; (nav) convoy
Schutz'glocke f (aer) umbrella
Schutz'gott m, Schutz'göttin f tutelary deity
Schutz'haft f protective custody
Schutzheilige §5 mf patron saint
Schutz'herr m protector; patron
Schutz'herrin f protectress; patroness
Schutz'impfung f immunization
Schutz'insel f traffic island
Schützling ['ʃytslɪŋ] m (-s;-e) ward
schutz'los adj defenseless
Schutz'mann m (-[e]s;-̈er & -leute) policeman
Schutz'marke f trademark
Schutz'mittel n preservative; preventive
Schutz'patron -in §8 mf patron saint
Schutz'polizei f police
Schutz'polizist m policeman, cop
Schutz'scheibe f (aut) windshield
Schutz'staffel f SS troops
Schutz'umschlag m dust jacket
Schutz-'und-Trutz-'Bündnis f defensive and offensive alliance
Schutz'waffe f defensive weapon
Schutz'zoll m protective tariff
Schwabe ['ʃvabə] m (-n;-n) Swabian
Schwaben ['ʃvabən] n (-s;) Swabia
Schwäbin ['ʃvebɪn] f (-;-nen) Swabian
schwäbisch ['ʃvebɪʃ] adj Swabian; das Schwäbische Meer Lake Constance
schwach [ʃvax] adj (schwächer ['ʃveçər]; schwächste ['ʃveçstə] §9)

weak; (*Hoffnung, Ton, Licht*) faint; (*unzureichend*) scanty; sparse; (*armselig*) poor

Schwäche ['ʃvɛçə] *f* (-;-n) weakness

Schwach'kopf *m* dunce; sap, dope

schwächlich ['ʃvɛçlɪç] *adj* feeble, delicate

Schwächling ['ʃvɛçlɪŋ] *m* (-s;-e) weakling

schwach'sinnig *adj* feeble-minded ‖ **Schwachsinnige** §5 *mf* dimwit, moron

Schwach'strom *m* low-voltage current

Schwaden ['ʃvɑdən] *m* (-s;-) swath; cloud (*of smoke, etc.*)

Schwadron [ʃva'droːn] *f* (-;-en) squadron

schwadronieren [ʃvadroˈniːrən] *intr* (coll) brag

schwafeln ['ʃvɑfəln] *intr* talk nonsense

Schwager ['ʃvɑgər] *m* (-s;⁔) brother-in-law

Schwägerin ['ʃvɛgərɪn] *f* (-;-nen) sister-in-law

Schwalbe ['ʃvalbə] *f* (-;-n) swallow

Schwal'bennest *n* (aer) gun turret

Schwal'benschwanz *m* (*Frack*) tails; (carp) dovetail

Schwall [ʃval] *m* (-[e]s;-e) flood; (*von Worten*) torrent

schwamm [ʃvam] *pret* of **schwimmen** ‖ **Schwamm** *m* (-[e]s;⁔e) sponge; mushroom; fungus; dry rot; **S. darüber!** skip it!

schwammig ['ʃvamɪç] *adj* spongy

Schwan [ʃvan] *m* (-[e]s;⁔e) swan

schwand [ʃvant] *pret* of **schwinden**

schwang [ʃvaŋ] *pret* of **schwingen**

schwanger ['ʃvaŋər] *adj* pregnant

schwängern ['ʃvɛŋərn] *tr* make pregnant; (fig) impregnate

Schwan'gerschaft *f* (-;-en) pregnancy

Schwan'gerschaftsverhütung *f* contraception

schwank [ʃvaŋk] *adj* flexible; unsteady ‖ **Schwank** *m* (-[e]s;⁔e) prank; joke; funny story; (theat) farce

schwanken ['ʃvaŋkən] *intr* stagger; (*schaukeln*) rock; (*schlingern*) roll; (*stampfen*) pitch; (*Flamme*) flicker; (*pendeln*) oscillate; (*vibrieren*) vibrate; (*wellenartig*) undulate; (*zittern*) shake; (*Preise*) fluctuate; (*zögern*) vacillate, hesitate

Schwanz [ʃvants] *m* (-es;⁔e) tail; (*Gefolge*) train; (vulg) pecker; **kein S.** not a living soul; **mit dem S. wedeln** (or **wippen**) wag its tail

schwänzeln ['ʃvɛntsəln] *intr* wag its tail; **s. um** fawn on

schwänzen ['ʃvɛntsən] *tr*—**die Schule s.** play hooky from school; **e-e Stunde s.** cut a class ‖ *intr* play hooky

schwappen ['ʃvapən] *intr* slosh around; **s. über** (*acc*) spill over

schwapps [ʃvaps] *interj* slap!; splash!

Schwäre ['ʃvɛrə] *f* (-;-n) abscess

schwären ['ʃvɛrən] *intr* fester

Schwarm [ʃvarm] *m* (-[e]s;⁔e) swarm; flock, herd; (*von Fischen*) school; (fig) idol; (fig) craze; (aer) flight of five aircraft; **sie ist mein S.** (coll) I have a crush on her

schwärmen ['ʃvɛrmən] *intr* swarm; stray; daydream; go out on the town; **s. für** (or **über** *acc* or **von**) rave about

Schwär'mer *m* (-s;-) enthusiast; reveler; daydreamer; firecracker; (religious) fanatic; (ent) hawk moth

Schwärmerei [ʃvɛrmə'raɪ] *f* (-;-en) enthusiasm; daydreaming; revelry; fanaticism

schwärmerisch ['ʃvɛrmərɪʃ] *adj* enthusiastic; gushy; fanatic; fanciful

Schwarte ['ʃvartə] *f* (-;-n) rind, skin; (coll) old book

schwarz [ʃvarts] *adj* black; dark; (*ungesetzlich*) illegal; (*schmutzig*) dirty; (*düster*) gloomy; (*von der Sonne*) tanned; **schwarze Kunst** black magic; **schwarzes Brett** bulletin board ‖ *adv* illegally

Schwarz'arbeit *f* moonlighting; non-union work; illicit work

Schwarz'brenner *m* moonshiner

Schwärze ['ʃvɛrtsə] *f* (-;-n) blackness; darkness; printer's ink

schwärzen ['ʃvɛrtsən] *tr* darken; blacken

schwarz'fahren §71 *intr* (SEIN) drive without a license; ride without a ticket

Schwarz'fahrer -in §6 *mf* unlicensed driver; rider without a ticket

Schwarz'fahrt *f* joy ride; ride without a ticket

Schwarz'handel *m* black-marketing

Schwarz'händler -in §6 *mf* black marketeer; (*mit Eintrittskarten*) scalper

schwärzlich ['ʃvɛrtslɪç] *adj* blackish

Schwarz'markt *m* black market

Schwarz'seher -in §6 *mf* pessimist

Schwarz'sender *m* illegal transmitter

schwatzen ['ʃvatsən], **schwätzen** ['ʃvɛtsən] *tr* (coll) talk ‖ *intr* (coll) yap, talk nonsense; (coll) gossip

Schwät'zer -in §6 *mf* windbag; gossip

schwatz'haft *adj* talkative

Schwatz'maul *n* blabber mouth

Schwebe ['ʃveːbə] *f* (-;-) suspense; **in der S. sein** be undecided; be pending

Schwe'bebahn *f* cablecar

Schwe'beflug *m* hovering, soaring

schweben ['ʃveːbən] *intr* (HABEN & SEIN) be suspended, hang; float; (*Hubschrauber*) hover; (*Segelflugzeug*) soar; glide; (fig) waver, be undecided; **in Gefahr s.** be in danger; **in Ungewißheit s.** be in suspense

Schwede ['ʃveːdə] *m* (-n;-n) Swede

Schweden ['ʃveːdən] *n* (-s;) Sweden

Schwedin ['ʃveːdɪn] *f* (-;-nen) Swede

schwedisch ['ʃveːdɪʃ] *adj* Swedish

Schwefel ['ʃveːfəl] *m* (-s;) sulfur

Schwe'felsäure *f* sulfuric acid

Schweif [ʃvaɪf] *m* (-[e]s;-e) tail; (fig) train

schweifen ['ʃvaɪfən] *tr* curve; (*spülen*) rinse ‖ *intr* (SEIN) roam, wander

Schweigegeld ['ʃvaɪgəgɛlt] *n* hush money

schweigen ['ʃvaɪgən] §148 *intr* be silent, keep silent; (*aufhören*) stop; **ganz zu s. von** to say nothing of; **s. zu** make no reply to

schwei′gend *adj* silent || *adv* in silence
schweigsam [′ʃvaɪkzəm] *adj* taciturn
Schwein [ʃvaɪn] *n* (-[e]s;-e) pig, hog; **S. haben** be lucky, have luck
Schwei′nebraten *m* roast pork
Schwei′nefleisch *n* pork
Schwei′nehund *m* (pej) filthy swine
Schwei′nekoben *m* pigsty, pig pen
Schweinerei [ʃvaɪnə′raɪ] *f* (-;-en) mess; dirty business
Schwei′nerippchen *pl* pork chops
Schwei′newirtschaft *f* dirty mess
Schweins′kotelett *n* pork chop
Schweiß [ʃvaɪs] *m* (-es;) perspiration
schweißen [′ʃvaɪsən] *tr* weld || *intr* begin to melt, fuse; (hunt) bleed
Schwei′ßer *m* §6 *mf* welder
Schweißfüße [′ʃvaɪsfysə] *pl* sweaty feet
schweißig [′ʃvaɪsɪç] *adj* sweaty; (hunt) bloody
Schweiß′perle *f* bead of sweat
Schweiz [ʃvaɪts] *f* (-;)—**die S.** Switzerland
Schwei′zer *m* Swiss; dairyman
schweizerisch [′ʃvaɪtsərɪʃ] *adj* Swiss
schwelen [′ʃvelən] *intr* smolder
schwelgen [′ʃvelgən] *intr* feast; **s. in** (*dat*) (fig) revel in; wallow in
Schwelgerei [ʃvelgə′raɪ] *f* (-;-en) feasting, carousing
schwelgerisch [′ʃvelgərɪʃ] *adj* riotous; luxurious
Schwelle [′ʃvelə] *f* (-;-n) sill; doorstep; (fig) verge; (psychol) threshold; (rr) railroad tie
schwellen [′ʃvelən] §119 *tr* swell || *intr* (SEIN) swell; (*Wasser*) rise; (*anwachsen*) increase
Schwel′lung *f* (-;-en) swelling
Schwemme [′ʃvemə] *f* (-;-n) watering place; (coll) taproom; (com) glut
schwemmen [′ʃvemən] *tr* wash off, rinse; (*Vieh*) water; (*Holz*) float
Schwengel [′ʃvenəl] *m* (-s;-) pump handle; (*e-r Glocke*) hammer
schwenkbar [′ʃvenkbar] *adj* rotating
schwenken [′ʃvenkən] *tr* swing; shake; (*drohend*) brandish; (*Hut*) wave; (*spülen*) rinse || *intr* (SEIN) turn; swivel, pivot; (*Geschütz*) traverse; (mil) wheel; (pol) change sides
Schwen′kung *f* (-;-en) turn; wheeling, traversing; (fig) change of mind
schwer [ʃver] *adj* heavy; difficult, hard; serious; (*schwerfällig*) ponderous; (*Strafe*) severe; (*Wein*) strong; (*Speise*) rich; (*unbeholfen*) clumsy; (*Kompanie*) heavy-weapons; **drei Pfund s. sein** weigh three pounds; **schweres Geld bezahlen** pay a stiff price || *adv* hard; with difficulty; (coll) very
Schwere [′ʃverə] *f* (-;) weight; seriousness; (*des Weines*) body; difficulty; significance; (phys) gravity
schwe′relos *adj* weightless
schwer′fällig *adj* heavy; clumsy, slow
Schwer′gewicht *n* heavyweight class; (*Nachdruck*) emphasis
Schwergewichtler -in [′ʃvergəvɪçtlər (ɪn)] §6 *mf* (sport) heavyweight
schwer′hörig *adj* hard of hearing

Schwer′industrie *f* heavy industry
Schwer′kraft *f* gravity
schwer′lich *adv* hardly
Schwer′mut *f* melancholy, depression
schwer′mütig *adj* melancholy, depressed
schwer′nehmen §116 *tr* take hard
Schwer′punkt *m* center of gravity; crucial point, focal point
Schwert [ʃvert] *n* (-[e]s;-er) sword
Schwer′verbrecher -in §6 *mf* felon
schwer′verdient *adj* hard-earned
schwer′wiegend *adj* weighty
Schwester [′ʃvestər] *f* (-;-n) sister; nurse; nun
Schwe′sterhelferin *f* nurse's aide
schweig [ʃvik] *pret* of **schweigen**
Schwieger- [′ʃvigər] *comb.fm.* -in-law
Schwie′germutter *f* mother-in-law
Schwie′gersohn *m* son-in-law
Schwie′gertochter *f* daughter-in-law
Schwie′gervater *m* father-in-law
Schwiele [′ʃvilə] *f* (-;-n) callus
schwielig [′ʃvilɪç] *adj* callous
schwierig [′ʃvirɪç] *adj* hard, difficult
Schwie′rigkeit *f* (-;-en) difficulty
Schwimm- [′ʃvɪm] *comb.fm.* swimming
Schwimm′anstalt *f*, **Schwimm′bad** *n*, **Schwimm′bassin** *n*, **Schwimm′becken** *n* swimming pool
schwimmen [′ʃvɪmən] §136 *intr* (HABEN & SEIN) swim; float
Schwimm′gürtel *m* life belt
Schwimm′haut *f* web
Schwimm′hose *f* bathing trunks
Schwimm′kraft *f* buoyancy
Schwimm′panzer *m* amphibious tank
Schwimm′weste *f* life jacket
Schwindel [′ʃvɪndəl] *m* (-s;-) dizziness; swindle, gyp; (*Unsinn*) bunk; (pathol) vertigo; **der ganze S.** the whole caboodle
Schwin′delanfall *m* dizzy spell
Schwin′delfirma *f* fly-by-night
schwin′delhaft *adj* fraudulent, bogus
schwindelig [′ʃvɪndəlɪç] *adj* dizzy
schwindeln [′ʃvɪndəln] *tr* swindle || *intr* fib || *impers*—**mir schwindelt** I feel dizzy
Schwin′delunternehmen *n* fly-by-night
schwinden [′ʃvɪndən] §59 *intr* (SEIN) dwindle; decline; (*Farbe*) fade
Schwind′ler -in §6 *mf* swindler; fibber
schwindlig [′ʃvɪntlɪç] *adj* dizzy
Schwindsucht [′ʃvɪntzuçt] *f* tuberculosis
Schwinge [′ʃvɪnə] *f* (-;-n) wing; fan; winnow; (poet) pinion
schwingen [′ʃvɪnən] §142 *tr* swing; wave; brandish; (agr) winnow; (tex) swingle || *ref* vault; soar || *intr* swing; sway; oscillate; vibrate
Schwin′ger *m* (-s;-) oscillator; (box) haymaker
Schwin′gung *f* (-;-en) oscillation; vibration; swinging
Schwips [ʃvɪps] *m*—**e-n S. haben** (coll) be tight, be tipsy
schwirren [′ʃvɪrən] *intr* (HABEN & SEIN) whiz, whir; buzz; (*Gerüchte*) fly
Schwitzbad [′ʃvɪtsbat] *n* Turkish bath
schwitzen [′ʃvɪtsən] *tr & intr* sweat

schwoll [ʃvɔl] *pret of* **schwellen**

schwor [ʃvor] *pret of* **schwören**

schwören [ˈʃvøːrən] §137 *tr & intr* swear; **auf j—n** (or **etw**) **s.** swear by s.o. (or s.th.)

schwul [ʃvul] *adj* (vulg) homosexual

schwül [ʃvyl] *adj* sultry, muggy

Schwulität [ʃvuliˈtɛt] *f* (-;-en) trouble

Schwulst [ʃvulst] *m* (-es;ːe) bombast

schwülstig [ˈʃvylstıç] *adj* bombastic

schwummerig [ˈʃvumərıç] *adj* (coll) shaky

Schwund [ʃvunt] *m* (-[e]s;) dwindling; shrinkage; loss; leakage; (des Haares) falling out; (rad) fading; (pathol) atrophy

Schwung [ʃvuŋ] *m* (-[e]s;ːe) swing; vault; (Tatkraft) zip, go; (der Phantasie) flight; **in S. bringen** start; **S. bekommen** gather momentum

schwung′haft *adj* brisk, lively

Schwung′kraft *f* centrifugal force; (fig) zip, pep; (phys) momentum

Schwung′rad *n* (mach) flywheel

schwung′voll *adj* enthusiastic, lively

schwur [ʃvur] *pret of* **schwören** ‖ **Schwur** *m* (-[e]s;ːe) oath

Schwur′gericht *n* jury

sechs [zɛks] *invar adj & pron* six ‖ **Sechs** *f* (-;-en) six

Sechs′eck *n* hexagon

Sechser [ˈzɛksər] *m* (-s;-) six; (in der Lotterie) jackpot

Sechsta′gerennen *n* six-day bicycle race

sechste [ˈzɛkstə] §9 *adj & pron* sixth

Sechstel [ˈzɛkstəl] *n* (-s;-) sixth

sech′zehn *invar adj & pron* sixteen ‖ **Sech′zehn** *f* (-;-en) sixteen

sech′zehnte §9 *adj & pron* sixteenth

Sech′zehntel *n* (-s;-) sixteenth

sechzig [ˈzɛçtsıç] *invar adj & pron* sixty ‖ **Sechzig** *f* (-;-en) sixty

sechziger [ˈzɛçtsıgər] *invar adj* of the sixties; **die s. Jahre** the sixties ‖ **Sechziger** *m* (-s;-) sexagenarian

sechzigste [ˈzɛçtsıçstə] §9 *adj & pron* sixtieth

See [ze] *m* (Sees; Seen [ˈze·ən] lake ‖ *f* (See; Seen [ˈze·ən]) sea; ocean; **an der See** at the seashore; **an die See gehen** go to the seashore; **auf See** at sea; **in See gehen** (or **stechen**) put out to sea; **in See sein** be in open water; **Kapitän zur See** navy captain; **zur See gehen** go to sea

See′bad *n* seashore resort

See′bär *m* (fig) sea dog

see′fähig *adj* seaworthy

See′fahrer *m* seafarer

See′fahrt *f* seafaring; voyage

see′fest *adj* seaworthy; **s. werden** get one's sea legs

See′gang *m*—**hoher** (or **schwerer** or **starker**) **S.** heavy seas

See′hafen *m* seaport

See′handel *m* maritime trade

See′hund *m* (zool) seal

See′jungfer *f*, **See′jungfrau** *f* mermaid

See′kadett *m* naval cadet

See′karte *f* (naut) chart

see′krank *adj* seasick

See′krebs *m* lobster

Seele [ˈzelə] *f* (-;-n) soul; mind; (Ein-**

wohner) inhabitant, soul; (e-s Geschützes) bore; (e-s Kabels) core

See′lenangst *f* mortal fear

See′lenfriede *m* peace of mind

See′lenheil *n* salvation

See′lennot *f* mental distress

See′lenpein *f*, **See′lenqual** *f* mental anguish

See′lenruhe *f* peace of mind; composure

see′lensgut *adj* good-hearted

seelisch [ˈzelıʃ] *adj* mental, psychic

Seel′sorge *f* ministry

Seel′sorger *m* (-s;-) minister, pastor

See′macht *f* sea power

See′mann *m* (-[e]s;-leute) seaman

See′meile *f* nautical mile

See′möwe *f* sea gull

See′not *f* (naut) distress

See′ratte *f* (fig) old salt

See′raub *m* piracy

See′räuber *m* pirate; corsair

See′räuberei *f* piracy

See′recht *n* maritime law

See′reise *f* voyage; cruise

See′sperre *f* naval blockade

See′stadt *f* seaport town; coastal town

See′straße *f* shipping lane

See′streitkräfte *pl* naval forces

See′tang *m* seaweed

see′tüchtig *adj* seaworthy

See′warte *f* oceanographic institute

See′weg *m* sea route; **auf dem S. by sea**

See′wesen *n* naval affairs

Segel [ˈzegəl] *n* (-s;-) sail

Se′gelboot *n* sailboat; (sport) yacht

Se′gelfliegen *n* gliding

Se′gelflieger –in §6 *mf* glider pilot

Se′gelflug *m* glide, gliding

Se′gelflugzeug *n* glider

Se′gelleinwand *f* sailcloth, canvas

segeln [ˈzegəln] *intr* (HABEN & SEIN) sail; (aer) glide

Se′gelschiff *n* sailing vessel

Se′gelsport *m* sailing

Se′geltuch *n* sailcloth, canvas

Se′geltuchhülle *f*, **Se′geltuchplane** *f* tarpaulin

Segen [ˈzegən] *m* (-s;-) blessing

se′gensreich *adj* blessed, blissful

Segler [ˈzeglər] *m* (-s;-) yachtsman; (aer) glider; (naut) sailing vessel

segnen [ˈzegnən] *tr* bless

Seh- [ze] *comb.fm.* visual, of vision

sehen [ˈze·ən] §138 *tr* see ‖ *intr* see; look; **s. auf** (*acc*) look at; take care of; face (*a direction*); **s. nach** look for, look around for; **schlecht s.** have poor eyes ‖ **Sehen** *n* (-s;) sight; eyesight, vision; **vom S. by sight**

se′henswert *adj* worth seeing

Se′henswürdigkeit *f* object of interest; **Sehenswürdigkeiten** sights

Seher [ˈze·ər] *m* (-s;-) seer, prophet

Se′hergabe *f* gift of prophecy

Seh′feld *n* field of vision

Seh′kraft *f* eyesight

Sehne [ˈzenə] *f* (-;-n) tendon, sinew; (Bogen-) string; (geom) secant

sehnen [ˈzenən] *ref*—**sich s. nach** long for, crave ‖ **Sehnen** *n* (-s;) longing

Seh′nerv *m* optic nerve

sehnig [ˈzeniç] *adj* sinewy; *(Fleisch)* stringy
sehnlich [ˈzenliç] *adj* longing; ardent
Sehnsucht [ˈzenzuçt] *f* (-;) yearning
sehr [zer] *adv* very; very much
Seh'rohr *n* periscope
Seh'vermögen *n* sight, vision
Seh'weite *f* visual range; **in S. within sight**
seicht [zaiçt] *adj* (& fig) shallow
Seide [ˈzaidə] *f* (-;-n) silk
seiden [ˈzaidən] *adj* silk, silky
Sei'denatlas *m* satin
Sei'denpapier *n* tissue paper
Sei'denraupe *f* silkworm
Sei'denspinnerei *f* silk mill
Sei'denstoff *m* silk cloth
seidig [ˈzaidiç] *adj* silky
Seife [ˈzaifə] *f* (-;-n) soap
Sei'fenblase *f* soap bubble
Sei'fenbrühe *f* soapsuds
Sei'fenflocken *pl* soap flakes
Sei'fenlauge *f* soapsuds
Sei'fenpulver *n* soap powder
Sei'fenschale *f* soap dish
Sei'fenschaum *m* lather
seifig [ˈzaifiç] *adj* soapy
seihen [ˈzai-ən] *tr* strain, filter
Sei'her *m* (-s;-) strainer, filter
Seil [zail] *n* (-[e]s;-e) rope; cable
Sei'lbahn *f* cable railway; cable car
seil'springen *intr* jump rope
Seil'tänzer -in §6 *mf* ropewalker
sein [zain] §139 *intr* (SEIN) be; exist; **es ist mir, als wenn** I feel as if; **es sei denn, daß** unless; **lassen Sie das s.!** stop it!; **wenn dem so ist** if that is the case; **wie dem auch sein mag** however that may be ‖ *aux* (to form compound past tenses of intransitive verbs of motion, change of condition, etc.) have, e.g., **ich bin gegangen** I have gone, I went ‖ §2,2 *poss adj* his; its; one's; her ‖ §2,4,5 *poss pron* his; hers; **die Seinen** his family; **er hat das Seine getan** he did his share; **jedem das Seine** to each his own ‖ **Sein** *n* (-s;) being; existence; reality
seinerseits [ˈzainərˌzaits] *adv* for his part
seinerzeit [ˈzainərˌtsait] *adv* in its time; in those days; in due time
seinesgleichen [ˈzainəsˌglaiçən] *pron* people like him, the likes of him
seinethalben [ˈzainətˌhalbən], **seinetwegen** [ˈzainətˌvegən] *adv* for his sake; on his account; *(von ihm aus)* for all he cares
seinetwillen [ˈzainətˌvilən] *adv*—**um s.** for his sake, on his behalf
Seinige [ˈzainigə] §2,5 *pron* his; **das S.** his property, his own; his due; his share; **die Seinigen** his family
seit [zait] *prep* (dat) since, for; **seit einem Jahr** for one year; **seit einiger Zeit for some time past; s. kurzem** lately; **s. langem** for a long time; **s. wann** since when ‖ *conj* since
seitdem [zaitˈdem] *adv* since that time ‖ *conj* since
Seite [ˈzaitə] *f* (-;-n) side; page; direction; *(Quelle)* source; (mil) flank
Sei'tenansicht *f* side view, profile

Sei'tenbau *m* (-[e]s;-ten) annex
Sei'tenblick *m* side glance
Sei'tenflosse *f* (aer) horizontal stabilizer
Sei'tenflügel *m* (archit) wing
Sei'tengang *m* side aisle
Sei'tengeleise *n* sidetrack
Sei'tenhieb *m* snide remark, dig
sei'tenlang *adj* pages of
Sei'tenriß *m* profile
sei'tens *prep* (genit) on the part of
Sei'tenschiff *n* (archit) aisle
Sei'tenschwimmen *n* sidestroke
Sei'tensprung *m* (fig) escapade
Sei'tenstück *n* (fig) counterpart
Sei'tenwind *m* cross wind
seither [zaitˈher] *adv* since then
—**seitig** [zaitiç] *comb.fm.* -sided
seit'lich *adj* lateral
seitwärts [ˈzaitverts] *adv* sideways, sidewards; aside
Sekretär -in [zekreˈter(in)] §8 *mf* secretary
Sekt [zekt] *m* (-[e]s;-e) champagne
Sekte [ˈzektə] *f* (-;-n) sect
Sek·tor [ˈzektɔr] *m* (-s;-toren [ˈtorən]) sector; (fig) field
Sekundant [zekunˈdant] *m* (-en;-en) (box) second
sekundär [zekunˈder] *adj* secondary
Sekunde [zeˈkundə] *f* (-;-n) second
Sekun'denbruchteil *m* split second
Sekun'denzeiger *m* second hand
Sekurit [zekuˈrit] *n* (-s;) safety glass
selber [ˈzelbər] *invar pron* (coll) var of **selbst**
selbst [zelpst] *invar pron* self; in person, personally; *(sogar)* even; by oneself; **ich s.** I myself; **von s.** voluntarily; spontaneously; automatically ‖ *adv* even; **s. ich** even I; **s. wenn** even if, even when
Selbst'achtung *f* self-respect
selbständig [ˈzelpˌtendiç] *adj* independent
Selbst'bedienung *f* self-service
Selbst'beherrschung *f* self-control
Selbst'beobachtung *f* introspection
Selbst'bestimmung *f* self-determination
Selbst'betrug *m* self-deception
selbst'bewußt *adj* self-confident
Selbst'binder *m* necktie; (agr) combine
Selbst'erhaltung *f* self-preservation
selbst'gebacken *adj* homemade
selbst'gefällig *adj* complacent, smug
Selbst'gefühl *n* self-confidence
selbst'gemacht *adj* homemade
selbst'gerecht *adj* self-righteous
Selbst'gespräch *n* soliloquy
selbst'gezogen *adj* home-grown
selbst'herrlich *adj* high-handed
Selbst'herrschaft *f* autocracy
Selbst'herrscher *m* autocrat
Selbst'kosten *pl* production costs
Selbst'kostenpreis *m* factory price; **zum S. abgeben** sell at cost
Selbstlader [ˈzelpstladər] *m* (-s;-) automatic (weapon)
Selbst'laut *m* vowel
Selbst'mord *m* suicide
selbst'los *adj* unselfish
selbst'sicher *adj* self-confident
Selbst'steuer *n* automatic pilot

Selbst′sucht f egotism, selfishness
selbst′süchtig adj egotistical
selbst′tätig adj automatic
Selbst′täuschung f self-deception
Selbstüberhebung ['zɛlpstybərhebuŋ] f (–;) self-conceit, presumption
Selbst′verbrennung f spontaneous combustion; self-immolation
Selbst′verlag m—im S. printed privately
Selbst′verleugnung f self-denial
Selbst′versorger m (–s;–) self-supporter
selbst′verständlich adj obvious; natural ‖ adv of course
Selbst′verständlichkeit f foregone conclusion, matter of course
Selbst′verteidigung f self-defense
Selbst′vertrauen n self-confidence
Selbst′verwaltung f autonomy
Selbst′wähler m (–s;–) dial telephone
Selbst′zucht f self-discipline
selbst′zufrieden adj self-satisfied
Selbst′zufriedenheit f self-satisfaction
Selbst′zweck m end in itself
selig ['zelɪç] adj blessed; (verstorben) late; (fig) ecstatic; (fig) tipsy; **seligen Angedenkens** of blessed memory; **s. werden** attain salvation, be saved
Se′ligkeit f (–;) happiness; salvation
Se′ligpreisung f (Bib) beatitude
se′ligsprechen §64 tr beatify
Sellerie ['zɛləri] m (–s;) & f (–;) celery (bulb)
selten ['zɛltən] adj rare, scarce ‖ adv seldom, rarely
Selterswasser ['zɛltərsvasər] n seltzer, soda water
seltsam ['zɛltzam] adj odd, strange
Semester [ze′mɛstər] n (–s;–) semester
Semikolon ['zemikolɔn] n semicolon
Seminar [zemɪ′nɑr] n (–s;–e) seminary; (educ) seminar
Seminarist [zemɪna′rɪst] m (–en;–en) seminarian
semitisch [ze′mɪtɪʃ] adj Semitic
Semmel ['zɛməl] f (–;–n) roll
Senat [ze′nat] m (–[e]s;–e) senate
Se·nator [ze′natɔr] m (–s;–natoren [na′torən]) senator
Sende– [zɛndə] comb.fm. transmitting, transmitter, broadcasting
senden ['zɛndən] tr & intr transmit, broadcast; telecast ‖ §120 & §140 tr send ‖ intr—s. nach send for
Sen′der m (–s;–) (rad, telv) transmitter; (rad) broadcasting station
Sen′deraum m broadcasting studio
Sen′dezeichen n station identification
Sen′dezeit f air time
Sen′dung f (–;–en) sending; (fig) mission; (com) shipment; (rad) broadcast; (telv) telecast
Senf [zɛnf] m (–[e]s;–e) mustard
sengen ['zɛŋən] tr singe, scorch
seng(e)rig ['zɛŋ(ə)rɪç] adj burnt; (fig) suspicious, fishy
senil [ze′nil] adj senile
Senilität [zenili′tɛt] f (–;) senility
senior ['zɛnjɔr] adj senior
Senkblei ['zɛŋkblaɪ] n plummet; (naut) sounding lead
Senke ['zɛŋkə] f (–;–n) depression
senken ['zɛŋkən] tr lower; sink; (Kopf)

bow ‖ ref sink, settle; dip, slope; (Mauer) sag
Senkfüße ['zɛŋkfysə] pl flat feet, fallen arches
Senk′fußeinlage f arch support
Senkgrube ['zɛŋkgrubə] f cesspool
Senkkasten ['zɛŋkkastən] m caisson
senkrecht ['zɛŋkrɛçt] adj vertical; (geom) perpendicular
Sen′kung f (–;–en) sinking; depression; dip, slope; sag; (der Preise) lowering
Sensation [zenza′tsjon] f (–;–en) sensation
sensationell [zenzatsjə′nɛl] adj sensational
Sensations′blatt n (pej) scandal sheet
Sensations′lust f sensationalism
Sensations′meldung f, **Sensations′nachricht** f (journ) scoop
Sensations′presse f yellow journalism
Sense ['zɛnzə] f (–;–n) scythe
sensibel [zen′zibəl] adj sensitive; (Nerven) sensory
Sensibilität [zenzibɪli′tɛt] f (–;) sensitivity, sensitiveness
sentimental [zentɪmɛn′tal] adj sentimental
separat [zepa′rat] adj separate
September [zep′tɛmbər] m (–[s];) September
Serenade [zere′nadə] f (–;–n) serenade
Serie ['zerjə] f (–;–n) series; line
Se′rienanfertigung f, **Se′rienbau** m, **Se′rienfabrikation** f, **Se′rienherstellung** f mass production
se′rienmäßig adj—**serienmäßige Herstellung** mass production ‖ adv—**s. herstellen** mass-produce
Se′riennummer f serial number
Se′rienproduktion f mass production
seriös [ze′rjøs] adj serious; reliable
Se·rum ['zerum] n (–s;–ren [rən] & –ra [ra]) serum
Service ['zɔrvɪs] m (Services ['zɔr-vɪs(əs);) (Kundendienst) service ‖ [zer′vis] n (Services [zer′vis]; Service [zer′vis(ə)];) (Tafelgeschirr) service
Servierbrett [zer′virbret] n tray
servieren [zer′virən] tr serve; **es ist serviert!** dinner is ready! ‖ intr wait at table
Serviertisch [zer′virtɪʃ] m sideboard
Servierwagen [zer′virvagən] m serving cart
Serviette [zer′vjetə] f (–;–n) napkin
Servo– [zervə] comb.fm. booster, auxiliary, servo, power, automatic
Ser′vobremsen pl power brakes
Ser′vokupplung f automatic transmission
Ser′volenkung f power steering
Servus ['servus] interj (Aust) hello!; (coll) so long!
Sessel ['zesəl] m (–s;–) easy chair
Ses′sellift m chair lift
seßhaft ['zeshaft] adj settled; **sich s. machen** settle down
Setzei ['zetsaɪ] n fried egg
setzen ['zetsən] tr set, put, place; seat; (beim Spiel) bet; (Denkmal) erect; (Frist) fix; (Junge) breed; (Fische) stock; (Pflanzen) plant; (mus) com-

pose; (typ) set ‖ *ref* sit down; (*Kaffee*) settle ‖ *intr* set type; **s. auf** (*acc*) bet on ‖ *intr* (SEIN)—**s. über** (*acc*) jump over

Set'zer *m* (-s;-) typesetter, compositor

Setz'fehler *m* typographical error

Seuche ['zɔɪçə] *f* (-;-n) epidemic

seufzen ['zɔɪftsən] *intr* sigh

Seuf'zer *m* (-s;-) sigh

Sex [zɛks] *m* (-es;) sex

Sex-Appeal ['zɛks ə'pil] *m* (-s;) sex appeal

Sex'-Bombe *f* (coll) sex pot

Sexual– [zɛksuɑl] *comb.fm.* sex

sexuell [zɛksu'ɛl] *adj* sexual

Sexus ['zɛksʊs] *m* (-;-) sex

sezieren [ze'tsirən] *tr* dissect

Shampoo [ʃam'pu] *n* (-s;-s) shampoo

Sibirien [zɪ'birjən] *n* (-s;) Siberia

sich [zɪç] §11 *reflex pron* oneself; himself; herself; itself; themselves; an (**und für**) **s.** in itself; **außer s. sein** be beside oneself ‖ *recip pron* each other, one another

Sichel ['zɪçəl] *f* (-;-n) sickle

sicher ['zɪçər] *adj* sure; positive; reliable; (**vor** *dat*) safe (from), secure (from) ‖ *adv* surely, certainly

Si'cherheit *f* (-;-en) safety, security; (*Gewißheit*) certainty; (*Zuverlässigkeit*) reliability; (*im Auftreten*) assurance; (com) security; (jur) bail

Si'cherheitsgurt *m*, **Si'cherheitsgürtel** *m* (aer, aut) seat belt

Si'cherheitsnadel *f* safety pin

Si'cherheitspolizei *f* security police

Si'cherheitsspielraum *m* margin of safety, leeway

si'cherlich *adv* surely, certainly

sichern ['zɪçərn] *tr* secure; fasten; guarantee; (*Gewehr*) put on safety

Si'cherstellung *f* safekeeping; guarantee

Si'cherung *f* (-;-en) protection; guarantee; (*an Schußwaffe*) safety catch; (elec) fuse; **durchgebrannte S.** blown fuse

Si'cherungskasten *m* fuse box

Sicht [zɪçt] *f* (-;) sight; (*Aussicht*) view; (*Sichtigkeit*) visibility; **auf kurze S.** short-range; **auf S.** at sight

sichtbar ['zɪçtbar] *adj* visible

sichten ['zɪçtən] *tr* sight; (fig) sift

sichtig ['zɪçtɪç] *adj* clear

sicht'lich *adj* visible

Sicht'vermerk *m* visa

sickern ['zɪkərn] *intr* (HABEN & SEIN) trickle, seep, leak

sie [zi] §11 *pers pron* she, her; it; they, them ‖ §11 **Sie** *pers pron* you

Sieb [zip] *n* (-[e]s;-e) sieve, colander; screen; (rad) filter

sieben ['zibən] *invar adj & pron* seven ‖ *tr* sift, strain; (fig) screen; (rad) filter ‖ **Sieben** *f* (-;-en) seven

siebente ['zibəntə] §9 *adj & pron* seventh

Siebentel ['zibəntəl] *n* (-s;-) seventh

siebte ['ziptə] §9 *adj & pron* seventh

Siebtel ['ziptəl] *n* (-s;-) seventh

siebzehn ['ziptsən] *invar adj & pron* seventeen ‖ **Siebzehn** *f* (-;-en) seventeen

siebzehnte ['ziptsəntə] §9 *adj & pron* seventeenth

Siebzehntel ['ziptsəntəl] *n* (-s;-) seventeenth

siebzig ['ziptsɪç] *invar adj & pron* seventy ‖ **Siebzig** *f* (-;-en) seventy

siebziger ['ziptsɪgər] *invar adj* of the seventies; **die s. Jahre** the seventies ‖ **Siebziger** *m* (-s;-) septuagenarian

siebzigste ['ziptsɪçstə] §9 *adj & pron* seventieth

siech [ziç] *adj* sickly

siechen ['ziçən] *intr* be sickly

Siechtum ['ziçtum] *n* (-s;) lingering illness

siedeheiß ['zidə'haɪs] *adj* piping hot

siedeln ['zidəln] *intr* settle

sieden ['zidən] §141 *tr & intr* boil

Siedepunkt ['zidəpuŋkt] *m* boiling point

Siedler –**in** ['zidlər(ɪn)] §6 *mf* settler

Sied'lerstelle *f* homestead

Sied'lung *f* (-;-en) settlement; colony; housing development

Sieg [zik] *m* (-[e]s;-e) victory

Siegel ['zigəl] *n* (-s;-) seal

siegeln ['zigəln] *tr* seal

Sie'gelring *m* signet ring

siegen ['zigən] *intr* win, be victorious

Sie'ger –**in** §6 *mf* winner, victor; **zweiter Sieger** runner-up

Sieges– [zigəs] *comb.fm.* victory, of victory, triumphal

Sie'gesbogen *m* triumphal arch

sieg'reich *adj* victorious

Signal [zɪg'nɑl] *n* (-s;-e) signal

signalisieren [zɪgnɑlɪ'zirən] *tr* signal

Silbe ['zɪlbə] *f* (-;-n) syllable

Sil'bentrennung *f* syllabification

Silber ['zɪlbər] *n* (-s;) silver

silbern ['zɪlbərn] *adj* silver, silvery

Sil'berzeug *n* silver, silverware

Silhouette [zɪlu'ɛtə] *f* (-;-n) silhouette

Silo ['zilo] *m* (-s;-s) silo

Silvester [zɪl'vɛstər] *m* (-s;-), **Silve'sterabend** *m* New Year's Eve

simpel ['zɪmpəl] *adj* simple ‖ **Simpel** *m* (-s;-) simpleton

Sims [zɪms] *m & n* (-es;-e) ledge; (*Fenster–*) sill; (*Kamin–*) mantelpiece

Simulant –**in** [zɪmu'lant(ɪn)] §7 *mf* faker; (mil) goldbrick

simulieren [zɪmu'lirən] *tr* simulate, fake ‖ *intr* loaf

simultan [zɪmul'tɑn] *adj* simultaneous

Sinfo•nie [zɪnfo'ni] *f* (-;-nien ['ni-ən]) symphony

singen ['zɪŋən] §142 *tr & intr* sing

Singsang ['zɪŋzaŋ] *m* (-[e]s;) singsong

Sing'spiel *n* musical comedy, musical

Sing'stimme *f* vocal part

Singular ['zɪŋgular] *m* (-s;-e) singular

sinken ['zɪŋkən] §143 *intr* (SEIN) sink, slump, sag; (*Preise*) drop; **s. lassen** lower; (*Mut*) lose

Sinn [zɪn] *m* (-[e]s;-e) sense; mind; meaning; taste

Sinn'bild *n* emblem, symbol

sinn'bildlich *adj* symbolic(al) ‖ *adv* symbolically; **s. darstellen** symbolize

sinnen ['zɪnən] §121 *tr* plan; plot ‖ *intr* (**auf** *acc*) plan, plot; (**über** *acc*)

think (about) ‖ **Sinnen** n (-s;) reflection, meditation, reverie
sin'nend adj pensive, reflective
Sin'nenlust f sensuality
Sin'nenmensch m sensualist
Sin'nenwelt f material world
Sin'nesänderung f change of mind
Sin'nesart f character, disposition
Sin'nestäuschung f illusion, hallucination, mirage
sinn'lich adj sensual; material
sinn'los adj senseless
sinn'reich adj ingenious, bright
sinn'verwandt adj synonymous
sinn'voll adj meaningful; sensible
Sintflut [ˈzɪntflut] f deluge, flood
Sippe [ˈzɪpə] f (-;-n) kin; clan
Sipp'schaft f (-;-en) clique, set
Sirup [ˈziːrup] m (-s;-e) syrup
Sitte [ˈzɪtə] f (-;-n) custom; habit; usage; **die Sitten** the morals
Sit'tenbild n, **Sit'tengemälde** n description of the manners (*of an age*)
Sit'tengesetz n moral law
Sit'tenlehre f ethics
sit'tenlos adj immoral
Sit'tenpolizei f vice squad
sit'tenrein adj chaste
Sit'tenrichter m censor
sit'tenstreng adj puritanical, prudish
Sittich [ˈzɪtɪç] m (-s;-e) parakeet
sittlich [ˈzɪtlɪç] adj moral, ethical
Sittlichkeit f (-;) morality
Sitt'lichkeitsverbrechen n indecent assault
sittsam [ˈzɪtzam] adj modest, decent
Situation [zɪtu·aˈtsjon] f (-;-en) situation
situiert [zɪtuˈirt] adj;—**gut s.** well-to-do
Sitz [zɪts] m (-es;-e) seat; residence; (e–s Kleides) fit; (eccl) see
sitzen [ˈzɪtsən] §144 intr sit; dwell; (Vögel) perch; (Kleider) fit; (Hieb) hit home; (coll) be in jail
sit'zenbleiben §62 intr (SEIN) remain seated; (beim Tanzen) be a wallflower; (bei der Heirat) remain unmarried; (educ) stay behind, flunk
sit'zenlassen §104 tr leave, abandon; (Mädchen) jilt
Sitz'gelegenheit f seating accommodation
Sitz'ordnung f seating arrangement
Sitz'platz m seat
Sitz'streik m sit-down strike
Sitz'ung f (-;-en) session
Sit'zungsbericht m minutes
Sit'zungsperiode f session; (jur) term
Sizilien [zɪˈtsiljən] n (-s;) Sicily
Ska·la [ˈskala] f (-;-len [lən]) scale
Skandal [skanˈdal] m (-s;-e) scandal
skandalös [skandaˈløs] adj scandalous
Skandinavien [skandɪˈnavjən] n (-s;) Scandinavia
Skelett [skeˈlet] n (-[e]s;-e) skeleton
Skepsis [ˈskepsɪs] f (-;) skepticism
Skeptiker -**in** [ˈskeptɪkər(ɪn)] §6 mf skeptic
skeptisch [ˈskeptɪʃ] adj skeptical
Ski [ʃi] m (-s;) **Skier** [ˈʃi·ər]) ski
Skizze [ˈskɪtsə] f (-;-n) sketch
skizzieren [skɪˈtsirən] tr & intr sketch
Sklave [ˈsklavə] m (-n;-n) slave

Sklaverei [sklavəˈraɪ] f (-;) slavery
sklavisch [ˈsklavɪʃ] adj slavish
Skonto [ˈskonto] m & n (-s;-s) discount
Skrupel [ˈskrupəl] m (-s;-) scruple
skru'pellos adj unscrupulous
skrupulös [skrupuˈløs] adj scrupulous
Skulptur [skulpˈtur] f (-;-en) sculpture
Slalom [ˈslalom] m & n (-s;-s) slalom
Slawe [ˈslavə] m (-n;-n), **Slawin** [ˈslavɪn] f (-;-nen) Slav
slawisch [ˈslavɪʃ] adj Slavic
Smaragd [smaˈrakt] m (-[e]s;-e) emerald
Smoking [ˈsmokɪŋ] m (-s;-s) tuxedo
so [zo] adv so; this way, thus; **so ein** such a; **so oder so** by hook or by crook; **so...wie** as...as
sobald' conj as soon as
Socke [ˈzokə] f (-;-n) sock
Sockenhalter (Sok'kenhalter) m garter
Soda [ˈzoda] f (-;) & n (-s;) soda
sodann' adv then
Sodbrennen [ˈzotbrenən] n (-s;) heartburn
soeben [zoˈebən] adv just now, just
Sofa [ˈzofa] n (-s;-s) sofa
sofern' conj provided, if
soff [zof] pret of saufen
sofort' adv at once, right away
sofortig [zoˈfortɪç] adj immediate
sog [zok] pret of saugen ‖ **Sog** m (-[e]s;) suction; undertow; (aer) wash
sogar' adv even
so'genannt adj so-called; would-be
sogleich' adv at once, right away
Sohle [ˈzolə] f (-;-n) sole; bottom
Sohn [zon] m (-[e]s;ꞏe) son
solan'ge conj as long as
solch [zolç] adj such
Sold [zolt] m (-[e]s;-e) pay
Soldat [zolˈdat] m (-en;-en) soldier
Söldner [ˈzœldnər] m (-s;-) mercenary
Sole [ˈzolə] f (-;-n) brine
solid [zoˈlit] adj solid; sound; reliable; steady; respectable; (Preis) reasonable; (com) sound, solvent
solide [zoˈlidə] adj var of solid
Solist -**in** [zoˈlɪst(ɪn)] §7 mf soloist
Soll [zol] n (-s;) quota; (acct) debit side; **S. und Haben** debit and credit
Soll- comb.fm. estimated; debit
sollen [ˈzolən] §145 mod (inf) be obliged to (inf), have to (inf); (inf) be supposed to (inf); (inf) be said to (inf)
Soll'wert m face value
solo [ˈzolo] adv (mus) solo ‖ **So·lo** n (-s;-s & -li [li]) solo
somit' adv so, consequently
Sommer [ˈzomər] m (-s;-) summer
Som'merfrische f health resort; **in die S. fahren** go to the country
Sommerfrischler [ˈzomərfrɪʃlər] m (-s;-) vacationer
som'merlich adj summery
Som'mersprosse f freckle
sonach' adv consequently, so
Sonate [zoˈnatə] f (-;-n) sonata
Sonde [ˈzondə] f (-;-n) probe
Sonder- [ˈzondər] comb.fm. special, extra; separate

sonderbar ['zɔndərbɑr] *adj* strange, odd; peculiar
son'derlich *adj* special, particular
Sonderling ['zɔndərlɪŋ] *m* (-s;-e) odd person, strange character
sondern ['zɔndərn] *tr* separate; sever; part; sort out; classify || *conj* but
Son'derrecht *n* privilege
Son'derung *f* (-;-en) separation; sorting, sifting; classifying
Son'derverband *m* (mil) task force
Son'derzug *m* (rr) special
sondieren [zɔn'dirən] *tr* probe; (fig) sound out; (naut) sound
Sonnabend ['zɔnɑbənt] *m* (-s;-e) Saturday
Sonne ['zɔnə] *f* (-;-n) sun
sonnen ['zɔnən] *tr* sun || *ref* sun oneself
Son'nenaufgang *m* sunrise
Son'nenbad *n* sun bath
Son'nenblende *f* (aut) sun visor; (phot) lens shade
Sonnenbrand *m* sunburn
Son'nenbräune *f* suntan
Son'nenbrille *f* (pair of) sun glasses
Son'nendach *n* awning
Son'nenenergie *f* solar energy
Son'nenfinsternis *f* eclipse of the sun
Son'nenfleck *m* sunspot
Son'nenjahr *n* solar year
son'nenklar' *adj* sunny; (fig) clear as day
Son'nenlicht *n* sunlight
Son'nenschein *m* sunshine
Son'nenschirm *m* parasol
Son'nensegel *n* awning
Son'nenseite *f* sunny side
Son'nenstich *m* sunstroke
Son'nenstrahl *m* sunbeam
Son'nensystem *n* solar system
Son'nenuhr *f* sundial
Son'nenuntergang *m* sunset
son'nenverbrannt *adj* sunburnt, tanned
Son'nenwende *f* solstice
sonnig ['zɔnɪç] *adj* sunny
Sonntag ['zɔntɑk] *m* (-s;-e) Sunday
sonn'tags *adv* on Sundays
Sonn'tagsfahrer **-in** §6 *mf* Sunday driver
Sonn'tagskind *n* person born under a lucky star
Sonn'tagsstaat *m* Sunday clothes
sonor [zɔ'nor] *adj* sonorous
sonst [zɔnst] *adv* otherwise; else; (*ehemals*) formerly; **s. etw** something else; **s. keiner** no one else; **s. nichts** nothing else; **s. noch was?** anything else?; **wie s.** as usual; **wie s. was** (coll) like anything
sonstig ['zɔnstɪç] *adj* other
sonst'wer *pron* someone else
sonst'wie *adv* in some other way
sonst'wo *adv* somewhere else
Sopran [zo'prɑn] *m* (-s;-e) soprano; treble
Sopranist **-in** [zopra'nɪst(ɪn)] §7 *mf* soprano
Sorge ['zɔrgə] *f* (-;-n) care; worry; **außer S. sein** be at ease; **keine S.!** don't worry; **sich** [*dat*] **Sorgen machen über** (*acc*) or **um** be worried about

sorgen ['zɔrgən] *intr*—**dafür s., daß** take care that, see to it that; **s. für** take care of || *ref* be uneasy; **sich s. über** (*acc*) grieve over; **sich s. um** be worried about
sor'genfrei *adj* carefree; untroubled
Sor'genkind *n* problem child
sor'genlos *adj* carefree
sor'genvoll *adj* uneasy, anxious
Sor'gerecht *n* (für) custody (of)
Sorgfalt ['zɔrkfalt] *f* (-;) care, carefulness; accuracy
sorgfältig ['zɔrkfɛltɪç] *adj* careful
sorglich ['zɔrklɪç] *adj* careful
sorglos ['zɔrklos] *adj* careless; thoughtless; carefree
sorgsam ['zɔrkzɑm] *adj* careful; cautious
Sorte ['zɔrtə] *f* (-;-n) sort, kind
sortieren [zɔr'tirən] *tr* sort out
Sortiment [zɔrtɪ'mɛnt] *n* (-[e]s;-e) assortment
Soße ['zosə] *f* (-;-n) sauce; gravy
sott [zɔt] *pret of* **sieden**
Souffleur [zu'flør] *m* (-s;-s), **Souffleuse** [zu'fløzə] *f* (-;-n) prompter
soufflieren [zu'flirən] *intr* (*dat*) prompt
Soutane [zu'tɑnə] *f* (-;-n) cassock
Souvenir [zuvə'nir] *n* (-s;-s) souvenir
souverän [zuvə'ren] *adj* sovereign || **Souverän** *m* (-s;-e) sovereign ||
Souveränität [zuvərenɪ'tet] *f* (-;) sovereignty
soviel *adv* so much; **noch einmal s.** twice as much || *conj* as far as
soweit' *conj* as far as
sowie' *conj* as well as
sowieso' *adv* in any case, anyhow
Sowjet [zɔv'jet] *m* (-s;-s) Soviet
sowjetisch [zɔv'jetɪʃ] *adj* Soviet
sowohl *conj*—**sowohl...als auch as** well as, both...and
sozial [zo'tsjal] *adj* social
Sozial'fürsorge *f* social welfare
sozialisieren [zotsjalɪ'zirən] *tr* nationalize
Sozialismus [zotsja'lɪsmus] *m* (-;) socialism
Sozialist **-in** [zotsja'lɪst(ɪn)] §7 *mf* socialist
sozialistisch [zotsja'lɪstɪʃ] *adj* socialistic
Sozial'wissenschaft *f* social science
Soziologie [zotsjolo'gi] *f* (-;) sociology
Sozius ['zotsjus] *m* (-;-se) associate, partner; (*auf dem Motorrad*) rider
sozusa'gen *adv* so to speak, as it were
Spachtel ['ʃpaxtəl] *m* (-s;-) & *f* (-;-n) spatula; putty knife
Spach'telmesser *n* putty knife
Spagat [ʃpa'gɑt] *m* (-[e]s;-e) (gym) split; (dial) string
spähen ['ʃpe·ən] *intr* peer; spy
Spä'her *m* (-s;-) lookout; (mil) scout
Spä'herblick *m* searching glance
Spähtrupp ['ʃpetrup] *m* reconnaissance squad
Späh'wagen *m* reconnaissance car
Spalier [ʃpa'lir] *n* (-s;-e) trellis; double line (*of people*)
Spalt [ʃpalt] *m* (-[e]s;-e) split; crack; slit; (geol) cleft

Spalte [ˈʃpaltə] ƒ (-;-n) split; crack; slit; (typ) column

spalten [ˈʃpaltən] tr (pp **gespaltet** or **gespalten**) split; slit; crack; (Holz) chop

Spal′tung ƒ (-;-en) split; (der Meinungen) division; (chem) decomposition; (eccl) schism; (phys) fission

Span [ʃpan] m (-[e]s;ːe) chip; splinter; **Späne** shavings

Span′ferkel n suckling pig

Spange [ˈʃpaŋə] ƒ (-;-n) clasp; hair clip; (Schnalle) buckle

Spanien [ˈʃpanjən] n (-s;) Spain

Spanier –in [ˈʃpanjər(ɪn)] §6 mf Spaniard

spanisch [ˈʃpanɪʃ] adj Spanish; **das kommt mir s. vor** (coll) that's Greek to me; **spanischer Pfeffer** paprika; **spanische Wand** folding screen

spann [ʃpan] pret of spinnen ‖ **Spann** m (-s;-e) instep

Spanne [ˈʃpanə] ƒ (-;-n) span; (com) margin

spannen [ˈʃpanən] tr stretch; strain; make tense; (Bogen) bend; (Feder) tighten; (Flinte) cock; (Erwartungen) raise; (Pferde) hitch; **straff s.** tighten; ‖ intr be (too) tight; **s. auf** (acc) wait eagerly for; listen closely to

span′nend adj tight; exciting

Spann′kraft ƒ tension; elasticity; (fig) resiliency

spann′kräftig adj elastic

Span′nung ƒ (-;-en) stress; strain; pressure; close attention; suspense; excitement; strained relations; (elec) voltage

Spar– [ʃpar] comb.fm. savings

Spar′buch n bank book, pass book

Spar′büchse ƒ piggy bank

sparen [ˈʃparən] tr & intr save

Spar′flamme ƒ pilot light

Spargel [ˈʃpargəl] m (-s;-) asparagus

Spar′kasse ƒ savings bank

Spar′konto n savings account

spärlich [ˈʃpɛrlɪç] adj scanty; scarce; sparse; frugal; (Haar) thin ‖ adv poorly; scantily; sparsely

Sparren [ˈʃparən] m (-s;-) rafter

sparsam [ˈʃparzam] adj thrifty

Spaß [ʃpas] m (-es;ːe) joke; fun; **aus S. in** fun; **S. beiseite!** all joking aside; **S. haben an** (dat) enjoy; **S. machen** be joking; be fun; **viel S.!** have fun!; **zum S.** for fun

spaß′haft, spaßig [ˈʃpasɪç] adj funny, facetious

Spaß′macher m joker

Spaßverderber [ˈʃpasvɛrdɛrbər] m (-s;-) (coll) kill-joy

Spaß′vogel m joker

spät [ʃpet] adj late; **wie s. ist es?** what time is it? ‖ adv late

Spaten [ˈʃpatən] m (-s;-) spade

später [ˈʃpetər] adv later

späterhin [ˈʃpetərhɪn] adv later on

spätestens [ˈʃpetəstəns] adv at the latest

Spät′jahr n autumn, fall

Spatz [ʃpats] m (-es & -en;-en) sparrow

spazieren [ʃpaˈtsirən] intr (SEIN) stroll, take a walk

spazie′renfahren §71 intr (SEIN) go for a drive

spazie′renführen tr walk (e.g., a dog)

spazie′rengehen §82 intr (SEIN) go for a walk

Spazier′fahrt ƒ drive

Spazier′gang m stroll, walk; **e–n S. machen** take a walk

Spazier′gänger –in §6 mf stroller

Spazier′weg m walk

Specht [ʃpeçt] m (-[e]s;-e) woodpecker

Speck [ʃpɛk] m (-[e]s;-) fat; bacon; (beim Wal) blubber

Speck′bauch m (coll) potbelly

speckig [ˈʃpɛkɪç] adj greasy, dirty

spedieren [ʃpeˈdirən] tr dispatch, ship

Spediteur [ʃpediˈtør] m (-s;-e) shipper; furniture mover

Spedition [ʃpediˈtsjon] ƒ (-;-en) shipment; moving company, movers

Speer [ʃper] m (-[e]s;-e) spear; (sport) javelin

Speiche [ˈʃpaɪçə] ƒ (-;-n) spoke

Speichel [ˈʃpaɪçəl] m (-s;) saliva

Spei′chellecker m brown-noser

speicheln [ˈʃpaɪçəln] intr drool

Speicher [ˈʃpaɪçər] m (-s;-) warehouse; grain elevator; attic, loft

speichern [ˈʃpaɪçərn] tr store

speien [ˈʃpaɪ·ən] §135 tr vomit; spit; (Feuer) belch; (Wasser) spurt ‖ intr vomit, throw up; spit

Speise [ˈʃpaɪzə] ƒ (-;-n) food; meal; (Gericht) dish

Spei′seeis n ice cream

Spei′sekammer ƒ pantry

Spei′sekarte ƒ menu

speisen [ˈʃpaɪzən] tr feed; (fig) supply ‖ intr eat; **auswärts s.** dine out

Spei′senfolge ƒ menu

Spei′sereste pl leftovers

Spei′serohr n (mach) feed pipe

Spei′seröhre ƒ esophagus

Spei′sesaal m dining room

Spei′seschrank m cupboard

Spei′sewagen m (rr) diner

Spei′sezimmer n dining room

Spektakel [ʃpɛkˈtakəl] m (-s;-) noise, racket

Spekulant –in [ʃpekuˈlant(ɪn)] §7 mf speculator

Spekulation [ʃpekulaˈtsjon] ƒ (-;-en) speculation; venture

spekulieren [ʃpekuˈlirən] intr speculate, reflect; (fin) speculate

Spelunke [ʃpeˈluŋkə] ƒ (-;-n) (coll) drive, joint

Spende [ˈʃpɛndə] ƒ (-;-n) donation

spenden [ˈʃpɛndən] tr give; donate; (Sakramente) administer; (Lob) bestow; **j–m Trost s.** comfort s.o.

spendieren [ʃpɛnˈdirən] tr—**j–m etw s.** treat s.o. to s.th.

Sperling [ˈʃpɛrlɪŋ] m (-s;-e) sparrow

Sperr– [ʃpɛr] comb.fm. barrage; barred

Sperr′baum m barrier, bar

Sperre [ˈʃpɛrə] ƒ (-;-n) shutting; close; blockade; embargo; barricade; catch; lock; (rr) gate

sperren [ˈʃpɛrən] tr shut; (Gas, Licht) cut off; (Straße) block off; cordon off; (*blockieren*) blockade; (*mit Schloß*) lock; (*verriegeln*) bolt; (*Konto, Gelder*) freeze; (*Scheck*) stop payment on; (*verbieten*) stop; (sport) block; (sport) suspend; (typ) space || *intr* jam, be stuck

Sperr′feuer *n* barrage

Sperr′gebiet *n* restricted area

Sperr′holz *n* plywood

sperrig [′ʃpɛrɪç] *adj* bulky

Sperr′sitz *m* (*im Kino*) rear seat; (*im Zirkus*) front seat

Sperr′stunde *f* closing time; curfew

Sper′rung *f* (-;-en) stoppage; blocking; blockade; embargo; suspension (*of telephone service, etc.*)

Spesen [′ʃpezən] *pl* costs, expenses

Spezi [′ʃpetsi] *m* (-s;-s) (coll) buddy

spezial [ʃpe′tsjɑl] *adj* special

Spezial′arzt *m*, **Spezial′ärztin** *f* specialist

Spezial′fach *n* specialty

Spezial′geschäft *n* specialty shop

spezialisieren [ʃpetsjɑlɪ′zirən] *ref* (*auf acc*) specialize (in)

Spezialist -in [ʃpetsjɑ′lɪst(ɪn)] §7 *mf* specialist

Spezialität [ʃpetsjɑlɪ′tet] *f* (-;-en) specialty

speziell [ʃpe′tsjel] *adj* special

spezifisch [ʃpe′tsifɪʃ] *adj* specific

Sphäre [′sferə] *f* (-;-n) sphere

sphärisch [′sferɪʃ] *adj* spherical

Spickaal [′ʃpɪkɑl] *m* smoked eel

spicken [′ʃpɪkən] *tr* lard; (fig) bribe

spie [ʃpi] *pret* of **speien**

Spiegel [′ʃpigəl] *m* (-s;-) mirror

Spie′gelbild *n* reflection (*in mirror*)

spie′gelblank *adj* spick and span

Spie′gelei *n* fried egg

spie′gelglatt *adj* glassy

spiegeln [′ʃpigəln] *tr* reflect; mirror || *ref* be reflected || *intr* shine

Spiel [ʃpil] *n* (-[e]s;-e) game; play; set (*of chessmen or checkers*); (cards) deck; (mach) play; (mus) playing; (sport) match; (theat) acting, performance; **auf dem S. stehen** be at stake; **aufs S. setzen** risk; **bei etw im S. sein** be at the bottom of s.th.; **leichtes S. haben mit** have an easy time with; **S. der Natur** freak of nature

Spiel′art *f* (biol) variety

Spiel′automat *m* slot machine

Spiel′bank *f* (-;-en) gambling table; gambling casino

Spiel′dose *f* music box

spielen [′ʃpilən] *tr & intr* play

Spielerei [ʃpilə′raɪ] *f* (-;-en) fooling around; child's play

Spiel′ergebnis *n* (sport) score

spielerisch [′ʃpilərɪʃ] *adj* playful

Spiel′feld *n* (sport) playing field

Spiel′film *m* feature film

Spiel′folge *f* program

Spiel′gefährte *m*, **Spiel′gefährtin** *f* playmate

Spiel′karten *pl* (playing) cards

Spiel′leiter *m* (cin, theat) director

Spiel′marke *f* chip, counter

Spiel′plan *m* program

Spiel′platz *m* playground; playing field

Spiel′raum *m* (fig) elbowroom; (mach) play

Spiel′sachen *pl* toys

Spiel′tisch *m* gambling table

Spiel′verderber *m* kill-joy

Spiel′verlängerung *f* overtime

Spiel′waren *pl* toys

Spiel′zeug *n* toy(s)

Spieß [ʃpis] *m* (-es;-e) spear, pike; (sl) top kick; (culin) spit; **den S. umdrehen gegen** turn the tables on

Spieß′bürger *m* Philistine, lowbrow

spieß′bürgerlich *adj* narrow-minded

spießen [′ʃpisən] *tr* spear; spit

Spie′ßer *m* (-s;-) Philistine, lowbrow

Spieß′gesell *m* accomplice

Spießruten [′ʃpisrutən] *pl*—**S. laufen** run the gauntlet

spinal [ʃpi′nɑl] *adj* spinal; **spinale Kinderlähmung** infantile paralysis

Spinat [ʃpi′nɑt] *m* (-[e]s;-e) spinach

Spind [ʃpɪnt] *m & n* (-[e]s;-e) wardrobe; (mil) locker

Spindel [′ʃpɪndəl] *f* (-;-n) spindle; (*Spinnrocken*) distaff

spin′deldürr′ *adj* skinny, scrawny

Spinne [′ʃpɪnə] *f* (-;-n) spider

spinnen [′ʃpɪnən] *tr* spin; **Ränke s.** hatch plots || *intr* purr; (*im Gefängnis sitzen*) do time; (sl) be looney

Spin′nengewebe *n* spider web

Spin′ner *m* (-s;-) spinner; (sl) nut

Spinnerei [ʃpɪnə′raɪ] *f* (-;-en) spinning; spinning mill

Spinn′faden *m* spider thread; **Spinn-fäden** gossamer

Spinn′gewebe *n* (-s;-) cobweb

Spinn′rad *n* spinning wheel

Spinn′webe *f* (-;-n) (Aust) cobweb

Spion [ʃpi′on] *m* (-[e]s;-e) spy

Spionage [ʃpi·o′nɑʒə] *f* (-;) spying, espionage

Spiona′geabwehr *f* counterintelligence

spionieren [ʃpi·o′nirən] *intr* spy

Spirale [ʃpi′rɑlə] *f* (-;-n) spiral

Spirituosen [ʃpiritu′ozən] *pl* liquor

Spiritus [′ʃpiritus] *m* (-;-se) alcohol

Spital [ʃpi′tɑl] *n* (-s;¨er) hospital

spitz [ʃpɪts] *adj* pointed; sharp; (*Winkel*) acute

Spitz′bart *m* goatee

Spitz′bube *m* rascal; thief; swindler

Spitze [′ʃpɪtsə] *f* (-;-n) point; tip; top; summit; (tex) lace; **an der S. liegen** be in the lead; **auf die S. treiben** carry to extremes

Spitzel [′ʃpɪtsəl] *m* (-s;-) spy; stool pigeon; plain-clothes man

spitzen [′ʃpɪtsən] *tr* point; sharpen; (*Ohren*) prick up; **den Mund s.** purse the lips || *ref*—**sich s. auf** (*acc*) look forward to || *intr* be on one's toes

Spitzen- *comb.fm.* top; peak; leading; topnotch; maximum; (tex) lace

Spit′zenform *f* (sport) top form

Spit′zenleistung *f* top performance

Spit′zenmarke *f* (com) top brand

Spit′zer *m* (-s;-) pencil sharpener

spitz′findig *adj* subtle; sharp

Spitz′hacke *f*, **Spitz′haue** *f* pickax

spitzig [′ʃpɪtsɪç] *adj* pointed; (& fig) sharp

Spitz′marke f (typ) heading
Spitz′name m nickname; pet name
Spitz′nase f pointed nose
spleißen [′ʃplaɪsən] §53 tr splice
spliß [ʃplɪs] pret of spleißen
Splitter [′ʃplɪtər] m (–s;–) splinter;
chip; fragment
split′ternackt′ adj stark-naked
Split′terpartei f splinter party
split′tersicher adj shatterproof
spontan [ʃpɔn′tɑn] adj spontaneous
Spore [′ʃporə] f (–;–n) spore
Sporn [ʃpɔrn] m (–[e]s; Sporen
[′ʃporən] spur; (fig) stimulus; (aer)
tail skid; (naut) ram
spornen [′ʃpɔrnən] tr spur
Sport [ʃpɔrt] m (–[e]s;–) sport(s); S.
ausüben (or treiben) play sports
Sport′freund –in §8 mf sports fan
Sport′hose f shorts, trunks
Sport′jacke f sport jacket, blazer
Sport′kleidung f sportswear
Sportler –in [′ʃpɔrtlər(ɪn)] §6 mf
athlete
sport′lich adj sportsmanlike; (Figur)
athletic; (Kleidung) sport
Sport′wagen m sports car; (Kinder-
wagen) stroller
Sport′wart m trainer
Spott [ʃpɔt] m (–[e]s;) mockery; scorn
Spott′bild n caricature
spott′bil′lig adj dirt-cheap
Spott′drossel f mockingbird
Spöttelei [ʃpœtə′laɪ] f (–;–en) mockery
spotten [′ʃpɔtən] intr (über acc) scoff
(at), ridicule; das spottet jeder Be-
schreibung that defies description
Spötterei [ʃpœtə′raɪ] f (–;–en) mock-
ery
Spott′gebot n (com) ridiculous offer
spöttisch [′ʃpœtɪʃ] adj mocking, satir-
ical; sneering
Spott′name m nickname
Spott′schrift f satire
sprach [ʃprɑx] pret of sprechen
Sprach– comb.fm. speech; grammati-
cal; linguistic; philological
Sprache [′ʃprɑxə] f (–;–n) language,
tongue; speech; diction; style; idiom
Sprach′eigenheit f, Sprach′eigentüm-
lichkeit f idiom, idiomatic expression
Sprach′fehler m speech defect
Sprach′forschung f linguistics
Sprach′führer m phrase book
Sprach′gebrauch m usage
Sprach′gefühl n feeling for a language
sprach′gewandt adj fluent
sprach′kundig adj proficient in lan-
guages
Sprach′lehre f grammar
Sprach′lehrer –in §6 mf language
teacher
sprach′lich adj grammatical; linguistic
sprach′los adj speechless
Sprach′rohr n megaphone; (fig) mouth-
piece
Sprach′schatz m vocabulary
Sprach′störung f speech defect
Sprach′wissenschaft f philology; lin-
guistics
sprang [ʃpraŋ] pret of springen
Sprech– [ʃprɛç] comb.fm. speaking
Sprech′art f way of speaking

Sprech′bühne f legitimate theater
sprechen [′ʃprɛçən] §64 tr speak; talk;
(Gebet) say; (Urteil) pronounce;
speak to, see ‖ intr (über acc, von)
speak (about), talk (about); er ist
nicht zu s. he's not available
Spre′cher –in §6 mf speaker, talker
Sprech′fehler m slip of the tongue
Sprech′funkgerät n walkie-talkie
Sprech′probe f audition
Sprech′sprache f spoken language
Sprech′stunde f office hours
Sprech′stundenhilfe f receptionist
Sprech′zimmer n office (of doctor,
etc.)
Spreize [′ʃpraɪtsə] f (–;–n) prop, strut;
(gym) split
spreizen [′ʃpraɪtsən] tr spread, stretch
out ‖ ref sprawl out; (fig) (mit) boast
(of); sich s. gegen resist
Spreng– [ʃprɛŋ] comb.fm. high-explo-
sive
Sprengel [′ʃprɛŋəl] m (–s;–) diocese;
parish
sprengen [′ʃprɛŋən] tr break, burst;
(mit Sprengstoff) blow up; (Tür)
force; (Versammlung) break up;
(Mine) set off; (besprizten) sprinkle;
(Garten) water ‖ intr (SEIN) gallop
Spreng′kommando n bomb disposal
unit
Spreng′kopf m warhead
Spreng′körper m, Spreng′stoff m explosive
Spreng′wagen m sprinkling truck
Sprenkel [′ʃprɛŋkəl] m (–s;–) speck
sprenkeln [′ʃprɛŋkəln] tr speckle
Spreu [ʃprɔɪ] f (–;) chaff
Sprichwort [′ʃprɪçvɔrt] n (–[e]s;–er)
proverb, saying
sprichwörtlich [′ʃprɪçvœrtlɪç] adj proverbial
sprießen [′ʃprisən] §76 intr (SEIN)
sprout
Springbrunnen [′ʃprɪŋbrʊnən] m
(–s;–) fountain
springen [′ʃprɪŋən] §142 intr (SEIN)
jump; dive; burst; (Eis) crack; (coll)
rush, hurry
Sprin′ger m (–s;–) jumper; (chess)
knight; (sport) diver
Spring′insfeld m (–[e]s;–e) (coll) live
wire
Spring′kraft f (& fig) resiliency
Spring′seil n jumping rope
Sprint [ʃprɪnt] m (–s;–s) sprint
Sprit [ʃprit] m (–[e]s;–e) alcohol;
(coll) gasoline
Spritze [′ʃprɪtsə] f (–;–n) squirt; (Feuerwehr) fire engine; (med) injection,
shot; (med) syringe
spritzen [′ʃprɪtsən] tr squirt; splash;
(sprühen) spray; (sprengen) sprinkle;
(Wein) mix with soda water; (med)
inject ‖ intr spurt, spout ‖ impers—
es spritzt it is drizzling ‖ intr
(SEIN) dash, flit
Spritz′tour f (coll) side trip
spröde [′ʃprødə] adj brittle; (Haut)
chapped; (fig) prudish, coy
sproß [ʃprɔs] pret of sprießen ‖ Sproß
m (Sprosses; Sprosse) offspring, descendant; (bot) shoot

Sprosse ['ʃprɔsə] *f* (-;-n) rung; prong
sprossen ['ʃprɔsən] *intr* (HABEN & SEIN) sprout
Sprößling ['ʃprœslɪŋ] *m* (-s;-e) offspring, descendant; (bot) sprout
Spruch [ʃprux] *m* (-[e]s;-̈e) saying; motto; text, passage; (jur) sentence; (jur) verdict; **e-n S. fällen** give the verdict
Spruch'band *n* (-[e]s;-̈er) banderole
Sprudel ['ʃprudəl] *m* (-s;-) mineral water
sprudeln ['ʃprudəln] *intr* bubble
sprühen ['ʃpry-ən] *tr* emit || *intr* spray; sparkle; (fig) flash || *impers*—**es sprüht** it is drizzling
Sprüh'regen *m* drizzle
Sprüh'teufel *m* (coll) spitfire
Sprung [ʃpruŋ] *m* (-[e]s;-̈e) jump; crack; (sport) dive
Sprung'brett *n* diving board; (fig) stepping stone
Spucke ['ʃpukə] *f* (-;) (coll) spit
spucken ['ʃpukən] *tr* spit || *intr* spit; (*Motor*) sputter
Spuk [ʃpuk] *m* (-[e]s;-e) ghost, spook; (*Lärm*) racket; (*Alptraum*) nightmare
spuken ['ʃpukən] *intr* linger on || *impers*—**es spukt hier** this place is haunted
spuk'haft *adj* spooky
Spülabort ['ʃpylabɔrt] *m* flush toilet
Spül'becken *n* sink
Spule ['ʃpulə] *f* (-;-n) spool, reel; (elec) coil
Spüle ['ʃpylə] *f* (-;-n) wash basin
spulen ['ʃpulən] *tr* reel, wind
spülen ['ʃpylən] *tr* wash, rinse; (*Abort*) flush; **an Land s.** wash ashore || *intr* flush the toilet; undulate
Spü'ler *m* (-s;-) dishwasher
Spülicht ['ʃpylɪçt] *n* (-[e]s;-e) dishwater; swill, slop
Spül'maschine *f* dishwasher
Spül'mittel *n* detergent
Spülwasser *n* dishwater
Spund [ʃpunt] *m* (-[e]s;-̈e) bung, plug; (carp) feather, tongue
Spur [ʃpur] *f* (-;-en) trace; track, rut; (hunt) scent; **S. Salz** pinch of salt
spürbar ['ʃpyrbar] *adj* perceptible
spüren ['ʃpyrən] *tr* trace; track, trail; (*fühlen*) feel; (*wahrnehmen*) perceive
spur'los *adj* trackless || *adv* without a trace
Spür'nase *f* (coll) good nose
Spür'sinn *m* flair
Spur'weite *f* (aut) tread; (rr) gauge
sputen ['ʃputən] *ref* hurry up
SS ['ɛs'ɛs] *f* (-;) (Schutzstaffel) S.S.
Staat [ʃtat] *m* (-[e]s;-en) state; government; (*Aufwand*) show; (*Putz*) finery
Staats– *comb.fm.* state; government; national; public; political
Staatsangehörigkeit ['ʃtatsangəhøriçkaıt] *f* (-;) nationality
Staats'anwalt *m* district attorney
Staats'bauten *pl* public works
Staats'beamte *m* civil servant

Staats'bürger –in §6 *mf* citizen
Staats'bürgerkunde *f* civics
Staats'bürgerschaft *f* citizenship
Staats'dienst *m* civil service
staats'eigen *adj* state-owned
Staats'feind *m* public enemy
staats'feindlich *adj* subversive
Staats'form *f* form of government
Staats'gewalt *f* supreme power
Staats'hoheit *f* sovereignty
staats'klug *adj* politic, diplomatic
Staats'klugheit *f* statecraft
Staats'kunst *f* statesmanship
Staats'mann *m* (-[e]s;-̈er) statesman
staats'männisch *adj* statesmanlike
Staats'oberhaupt *n* head of state
Staats'papiere *pl* government bonds
Staats'recht *n* public law
Staats'streich *m* coup d'état
Staats'wirtschaft *f* political economy
Staats'wissenschaft *f* political science
Stab [ʃtap] *m* (-[e]s;-̈e) staff; rod; bar; (*e-r Jalousie*) slat; (eccl) crozier; (mil) staff; (mil) headquarters; (mus, sport) baton
stab'hochspringen §142 *intr* (SEIN) pole-vault
stabil [ʃta'bil] *adj* stable, steady
stabilisieren [ʃtabılı'zirən] *tr* stabilize
stach [ʃtax] *pret* of **stechen**
Stachel ['ʃtaxəl] *m* (-s;-n) prick; quill; (bot) thorn; (ent) sting
Sta'chelbeere *f* gooseberry
Sta'cheldraht *m* barbed wire
stachelig ['ʃtaxəlıç] *adj* prickly; (& fig) thorny
Sta'chelschwein *n* porcupine
Sta·dion ['ʃtadjən] *n* (-s;-dien [djən]) stadium
Sta·dium ['ʃtadjυm] *n* (-s;-dien [djən]) stage
Stadt [ʃtat] *f* (-;-̈e) city, town
Städtchen ['ʃtɛtçən] *n* (-s;-) town
Städtebau ['ʃtɛtəbau] *m* (-[e]s;) city planning
Stadt'gemeinde *f* township
Stadt'gespräch *n* talk of the town
städtisch ['ʃtɛtɪʃ] *adj* municipal
Stadt'plan *m* map of the city
Stadt'rand *m* outskirts
Stadt'rat *m* (-[e]s;-̈e) city council; (*Person*) city councilor
Stadt'teil *m* **Stadt'viertel** *n* quarter (of the city)
Stafette [ʃta'fɛtə] *f* (-;-n) courier; (sport) relay
Staffel ['ʃtafəl] *f* (-;-n) step, rung; (*Stufe*) degree; (aer) squadron (*of nine aircraft*); (sport) relay team
Staffelei [ʃtafə'laı] *f* (-;-en) easel
Staf'felkeil *m* (aer) V-formation
Staf'fellauf *m* relay race
staffeln ['ʃtafəln] *tr* graduate; (*Arbeitszeit, usw.*) stagger
stahl [ʃtal] *pret* of **stehlen** || **Stahl** *m* (-[e]s;-e) steel
Stahl'beton *m* reinforced concrete
stählen ['ʃtɛlən] *tr* temper; (fig) steel
Stahl'kammer *f* steel vault
Stahlspäne ['ʃtal/pɛnə] *pl* steel wool
stak [ʃtak] *pret* of **stecken**
Stalag ['ʃtalak] *n* (-s;-s) (Stammlager) main camp (*for P.O.W.'s*)

Stall [ʃtal] *m* (-[e]s;ᵁe) stable; shed
Stall′knecht *m* groom
Stamm [ʃtam] *m* (-[e]s;ᵁe) stem; stalk; trunk; stock; race; tribe; breed
Stamm′aktie *f* common stock
Stamm′baum *m* family tree; pedigree
stammeln [′ʃtaməln] *tr & intr* stammer
Stamm′eltern *pl* ancestors
stammen [′ʃtamən] *intr* (SEIN) (**aus, von**) come (from); (**von**) date (from); (**gram**) (**von**) be derived (from)
Stamm′gast *m* regular customer
stämmig [′ʃtemɪç] *adj* stocky; husky
Stamm′kneipe *f* favorite bar
Stamm′kunde *m*, **Stamm′kundin** *f* regular customer
Stamm′personal *n* skeleton staff
Stamm′tisch *m* reserved table
Stammutter (**Stamm′mutter**) *f* ancestress
Stamm′vater *m* ancestor
stampfen [′ʃtampfən] *tr* tamp, pound; (*Kartoffeln*) mash; (*Boden*) paw || *intr* stamp the ground; (*durch Schnee*) trudge; (*naut*) pitch
stand [ʃtant] *pret* of **stehen** || **Stand** *m* (-[e]s;ᵁe) stand; footing, foothold; level, height; condition; status, rank; class, caste; booth; profession; trade; (*sport*) score; **seinen S. behaupten** hold one's ground
Standard [′ʃtandart] *m* (-s;-s) standard
Standarte [ʃtan′dartə] *f* (-;-n) banner; standard
Stand′bild *n* statue
Ständchen [′ʃtentçən] *n* (-s;-) serenade; **j-m ein S. bringen** serenade s.o.
Ständer [′ʃtendər] *m* (-s;-) stand, rack; pillar; stud; (*mach*) column
Stan′desamt *n* bureau of vital statistics
stan′desamtlich *adj & adv* before a civil magistrate
stan′desgemäß *adj* according to rank
Stan′desperson *f* dignitary
stand′fest *adj* stable, steady, sturdy
stand′haft *adj* steadfast
stand′halten §90 *intr* hold out; (*dat*) withstand
ständig [′ʃtendɪç] *adj* permanent; steady, constant
Stand′licht *n* parking light
Stand′ort *m* position; station; (*mil*) base; (*mil*) garrison
Stand′pauke *f* (coll) lecture
Stand′punkt *m* standpoint
Stand′recht *n* martial law
Stand′uhr *f* grandfather's clock
Stange [′ʃtaŋə] *f* (-;-n) pole; rod, bar; perch, roost; **e-e S. Zigaretten** a carton of cigarettes; **von der S.** readymade (*clothes*)
stank [ʃtaŋk] *pret* of **stinken**
stänkern [′ʃteŋkərn] *intr* (coll) stink; (coll) make trouble
Stanniol [ʃta′njol] *n* (-s;-e), **Stanniol′papier** *n* tinfoil
Stanze [′ʃtantsə] *f* (-;-n) stanza; punch, die, stamp
stanzen [′ʃtantsən] *tr* (mach) punch
Stapel [′ʃtapəl] *m* (-s;-) stack; depot;

stock; (naut) slip; (tex) staple; **auf S. liegen** be in drydock; **vom S. laufen lassen** launch
Sta′pellauf *m* launching
stapeln [′ʃtapəln] *tr* stack, pile up
Sta′pelplatz *m* lumberyard; depot
stapfen [′ʃtapfən] *intr* (SEIN) slog
Star [ʃtar] *m* (-[e]s;-e) (orn) starling; (pathol) cataract; **grauer S.** cataract; **grüner S.** glaucoma || *m* (-s;-s) (cin, theat) star
starb [ʃtarp] *pret* of **sterben**
stark [ʃtark] *adj* (**stärker** [′ʃterkər]; **stärkste** [′ʃterkstə] §9) strong; stout; (*Erkältung*) bad; (*Familie*) big; (*Kälte*) severe; (*Frost, Verkehr*) heavy; (*Wind*) high; (*Stunde*) full || *adv* much; hard; very
Stärke [′ʃterkə] *f* (-;-n) strength; force; stoutness; thickness; might; violence; intensity; (*Anzahl*) number; (fig) forte; (chem) starch
stärken [′ʃterkən] *tr* strengthen; (*Wäsche*) starch || *ref* take some refreshment
Stark′strom *m* high-voltage current
Stär′kung *f* (-;-en) strengthening; refreshment; (*Imbiß*) snack
starr [ʃtar] *adj* stiff, rigid; fixed; inflexible; obstinate; dumbfounded; numb || *adv* **s. ansehen** stare at
starren [′ʃtarən] *intr* (**auf** *acc*) stare (at); **s. von** be covered with
Starr′kopf *m* stubborn fellow
starr′köpfig *adj* stubborn
Starr′krampf *m* (-es;) tetanus
Starr′sinn *m* (-[e]s;) stubbornness
Start [ʃtart] *m* (-[e]s;-s & -e) start; (aer) take-off; (rok) launching
Start′bahn *f* (aer) runway
starten [′ʃtartən] *tr* start; launch || *intr* (SEIN) start; (aer) take off; (rok) lift off, be launched
Start′rampe *f* (rok) launch pad
Station [ʃta′tsjon] *f* (-;-en) station; (med) ward; **freie S.** free room and board
statisch [′ʃtatɪʃ] *adj* static
Statist -**in** [ʃta′tɪst(ɪn)] §7 *mf* (cin) extra; (theat) supernumerary
Statistik [ʃta′tɪstɪk] *f* (-;-en) statistic; (*Wissenschaft*) statistics
statistisch [ʃta′tɪstɪʃ] *adj* statistical
Stativ [ʃta′tif] *n* (-s;-e) stand; (phot) tripod
statt [ʃtat] *prep* (*genit*) instead of; **s. zu** (*inf*) instead of (*ger*) || **Statt** *f* (-;) place, stead; **an Kindes S. annehmen** adopt
Stätte [′ʃtetə] *f* (-;-n) place, spot; (*Wohnung*) abode; room
statt′finden §59 *intr* take place
statt′haft *adj* admissible; legal
Statthalter [′ʃtathaltər] *m* (-s;-) governor
statt′lich *adj* stately; imposing
Statue [′ʃtatu·ə] *f* (-;-n) statue
statuieren [ʃtatu′irən] *tr* establish; **ein Exempel s. an** (*dat*) make an example of
Statur [ʃta′tur] *f* (-;-en) stature
Statut [ʃta′tut] *n* (-[e]s;-en) statute; **Statuten** bylaws

Stau [ʃtau] *m* (-[e]s;-e) dammed-up water; updraft; (aut) tie-up

Staub [ʃtaup] *m* (-[e]s;) dust

Stau′becken *n* reservoir

stauben [′ʃtaubən] *intr* make dust

stäuben [′ʃtɔɪbən] *tr* dust; sprinkle, powder; (*Flüssigkeit*) spray ‖ *intr* make dust; throw off spray

staubig [′ʃtaubɪç] *adj* dusty

staub′saugen *tr & intr* vacuum

Staub′sauger *m* vacuum cleaner

Staub′wedel *m* feather duster

Staub′zucker *m* powdered sugar

stauchen [′ʃtauçən] *tr* knock, jolt; compress; (sl) chew out

Stau′damm *m* dam

Staude [′ʃtaudə] *f* (-;-n) perennial

stauen [′ʃtau-ən] *tr* dam up; (*Waren*) stow away; (*Blut*) stanch ‖ *ref* be blocked, jam up

Stau′er *m* (-s;-) stevedore

staunen [′ʃtaunən] *intr* (*über acc*) be astonished (at) ‖ **Staunen** *n* (-s;) astonishment

stau′nenswert *adj* astonishing

Staupe [′ʃtaupə] *f* (-;) (vet) distemper

Stau′see *m* reservoir

Stau′ung *f* (-;-en) damming up; blockage; (*Engpaß*) bottleneck; (*Verkehrs-*) jam-up; (pathol) congestion

stechen [′ʃteçən] §64 *tr* prick; sting, bite; (*mit e-r Waffe*) stab; (*Torf*) cut; (*Star*) remove; (*Kontrolluhr*) punch; (*Wein*) draw; (*Näherei*) stitch; (*gravieren*) engrave; (cards) trump; (cards) take (*a trick*) ‖ *intr* sting, bite; (*Sonne*) be hot; (cards) be trump; **j-m in die Augen s.** catch s.o.'s eye ‖ *impers*—**es sticht mich in der Brust** I have a sharp pain in my chest

ste′chend *adj* (*Blick*) piercing; (*Geruch*) strong; (*Schmerz*) sharp, stabbing

Stech′karte *f* timecard

Stech′schritt *m* goosestep

Stech′uhr *f* time clock

Steckbrief [′ʃtekbrif] *m* warrant for arrest

steck′brieflich *adv*—**s. verfolgen** put out a "wanted" notice for

Steckdose [′ʃtekdozə] *f* (elec) outlet

stecken [′ʃtekən] *tr & intr* stick ‖ **Stecken** *m* (-s;-) stick

steckenbleiben (stek′kenbleiben) §62 *intr* (SEIN) get stuck

Steckenpferd (Stek′kenpferd) *n* hobbyhorse; (fig) hobby

Stecker (Stek′ker) *m* (-s;-) (elec) plug

Steck′kontakt *m* (elec) plug

Steck′nadel *f* pin

Steg [ʃtek] *m* (-[e]s;-e) footpath; footbridge; (*e-r Brille, Geige*) bridge; (*Landungs-*) jetty; (naut) gangplank

Steg′reif *m*—**aus dem S.** extempore

stehen [′ʃte-ən] §146 *tr*—**e-m Maler Modell s.** sit for a painter; **Schlange s.** stand in line; **Schmiere s.** (coll) be a lookout; **Wache s.** stand guard ‖ *intr* (HABEN & SEIN) stand; stop; be; (gram) occur, be used; (*Kleider*) fit; **das steht bei Ihnen** that depends

on you; **gut s.** (*dat*) fit, suit; **gut s. mit** be on good terms with; **wie steht's?** (coll) how is it going?

ste′henbleiben §62 *intr* (SEIN) stop

ste′henlassen §104 *tr* leave standing; (*nicht anrühren*) leave alone; (*Fehler*) leave uncorrected; (*vergessen*) forget; (culin) allow to stand or cool

Ste′her *m* (-s;-) long-distance cyclist

Stehlampe [′ʃtelampə] *f* floor lamp

Stehleiter [′ʃtelaɪtər] *f* stepladder

stehlen [′ʃtelən] §147 *tr & intr* steal

Stehplatz [′ʃteplats] *m* standing room

steif [ʃtaɪf] *adj* stiff; rigid; (*Lächeln*) forced; (*förmlich*) formal; (*starr*) numb

steifen [′ʃtaɪfən] *tr* stiffen; (*Wäsche*) starch

Steig [ʃtaɪk] *m* (-[e]s;-e) path

Steig′bügel *m* stirrup

steigen [′ʃtaɪgən] §148 *tr* (*Treppen*) climb ‖ *intr* (SEIN) climb; rise; go up; (*Nebel*) lift; (*Blut in den Kopf*) rush ‖ **Steigen** *n* (-s;) rise; increase

steigern [′ʃtaɪgərn] *tr* raise, increase; (*verstärken*) enhance; (gram) compare ‖ *ref* increase, go up

Stei′gerung *f* (-;-en) rising; increase; intensification; (gram) comparison

Stei′gerungsgrad *m* (gram) degree of comparison

Stei′gung *f* (-;-en) rise; (*Hang*) slope; (*e-s Propellers*) pitch

steil [ʃtaɪl] *adj* steep

Stein [ʃtaɪn] *m* (-[e]s;-e) stone; rock; (horol) jewel; (pathol) stone

stein′alt′ *adj* old as the hills

Stein′bruch *m* quarry

Stein′druck *m* lithography; (*Bild*) lithograph

steinern [′ʃtaɪnərn] *adj* stone

Stein′gut *n* earthenware

steinig [′ʃtaɪnɪç] *adj* stony, rocky

steinigen [′ʃtaɪnɪgən] *tr* stone

Stein′kohle *f* hard coal

Stein′metz *m* stonemason

stein′reich′ *adj* (coll) filthy rich

Stein′salz *n* rock salt

Stein′schlag *m* (public sign) falling rocks

Stein′wurf *m* stone's throw

Stein′zeit *f* stone age

Steiß [ʃtaɪs] *m* (-es;-e) buttocks

Stelldichein [′ʃteldɪçaɪn] *n* (-[s]; -[s]) (coll) date

Stelle [′ʃtelə] *f* (-;-n) place, spot; position; job; agency, department; quotation; (math) digit; **an S. von** in place of; **auf der S.** on the spot; **auf der S. treten** (fig & mil) mark time; **freie** (or **offene**) **S.** opening; **zur S. sein** be on hand

stellen [′ʃtelən] *tr* put; place; set; stand; (*ein-*) regulate, adjust; (*anordnen*) fix, arrange; (*Frage*) ask; (*Horoskop*) cast; (*Diagnose*) give; (*Falle, Wecker*) set; (*Kaution*) put up; (*Zeugen*) produce; **e-n Antrag s.** make a motion; **in Dienst s.** appoint; put into service ‖ *ref* place oneself, stand; give oneself up; **der Preis stellt sich auf...** the price is...; **sich s., als ob** act as if

Stel'lenangebot *n* help wanted
Stel'lenbewerber –in §6 *mf* applicant
Stel'lengesuch *n* situation wanted
Stel'lenjagd *f* job hunting
Stel'lennachweis *m*, **Stel'lenvermitt-lungsbüro** *n* employment agency
stel'lenweise *adv* here and there
–stellig [ʃtɛlɪç] *comb.fm.* –digit
Stell'schraube *f* set screw
Stel'lung *f* (–;–en) position; situation; job; standing; status; rank; posture; (mil) line, position; (mil) emplacement; **S. nehmen zu** express one's opinion on; (*erklären*) explain; (*beantworten*) answer
Stel'lungnahme *f* (–;–n) attitude, point of view; (*Erklärung*) comment; (*Gutachten*) opinion; (*Bericht*) report; (*Beantwortung*) answer; (*Entscheid*) decision; **sich** [*dat*] **e–e S. vorbehalten** not commit oneself
Stel'lungsgesuch *n* (job) application
stel'lungslos *adj* jobless
stell'vertretend *adj* acting
Stell'vertreter –in §6 *mf* representative; deputy; proxy; substitute
Stell'vertretung *f* (–;–en) representation; substitution; **in S.** by proxy
Stelzbein [ʃteltsbaɪn] *n* wooden leg
Stelze [ʃteltsə] *f* (–;–n) stilt
stelzen [ʃteltsən] *intr* (SEIN) stride
Stemmeisen [ʃtɛmaɪzən] *n* crowbar
stemmen [ʃtɛmən] *tr* support; (*Gewicht*) lift; (*Loch*) chisel ‖ *ref*—**sich s. gegen** oppose
Stempel [ʃtɛmpəl] *m* (–s;–) stamp; prop; (*Kolben*) piston; (bot) pistil
Stem'pelkissen *n* ink pad, stamp pad
stempeln [ʃtɛmpəln] *tr* stamp ‖ *intr*—**s. gehen** (coll) collect unemployment insurance
Stengel [ʃtɛŋəl] *m* (–s;–) stalk
Steno [ʃteno] *f* (–;) stenography
Stenograph [ʃtenoˈgraf] *m* (–en;–en) stenographer
Stenographie [ʃtenograˈfi] *f* (–;) stenography, shorthand
stenographieren [ʃtenogrˈfirən] *tr* take down in shorthand ‖ *intr* do shorthand
Stenographin [ʃtenoˈgrafɪn] *f* (–;–nen) stenographer
Stenotypistin [ʃtenoˈtypɪstɪn] *f* (–;–nen) stenographer
Step [ʃtɛp] *m* (–s;–) tap dance; **S. tanzen** tap-dance
Steppdecke [ʃtɛpdɛkə] *f* comforter
Steppe [ʃtɛpə] *f* (–;–n) steppe
steppen [ʃtɛpən] *tr* quilt ‖ *intr* tap-dance ‖ **Steppen** *n* (–s;) tap-dancing
Sterbe– [ʃtɛrbə] *comb.fm.* dying, death
Ster'befall *m* death
Ster'begeld *n* death benefit
Ster'behilfe *f* euthanasia
sterben [ʃtɛrbən] §149 *intr* (SEIN) (an *dat*) die (of)
sterb'lich *adj* mortal ‖ *adv*—**s. verliebt in** (*acc*) head over heals in love with
Sterb'lichkeit *f* (–;) mortality
Sterb'lichkeitsziffer *f* death rate
stereotyp [stereoˈtyp] *adj* stereotyped
steril [ʃteˈril] *adj* sterile
sterilisieren [ʃterɪlɪˈzirən] *tr* sterilize

Stern [ʃtern] *m* (–[e]s;–e) star; (typ) asterisk
Stern'bild *n* constellation
Stern'blume *f* aster
Sterndeuter [ʃterndɔɪtər] *m* (–s;–) astrologer
Sterndeuterei [ʃterndɔɪtəˈraɪ] *f* (–;) astrology
Ster'nenbanner *n* Stars and Stripes
stern'ha'gelvoll *adj* (sl) dead drunk
stern'hell *adj* starlit
Stern'himmel *m* starry sky
Stern'kunde *f* astronomy
Stern'schuppe *f* shooting star
Stern'warte *f* observatory
stet [ʃtet], **stetig** [ʃtetɪç] *adj* steady
stets [ʃtets] *adv* constantly, always
Steuer [ʃtɔɪ.ər] *f* (–;–en) tax; duty ‖ *n* (–s;–) rudder, helm; (aer) controls; (aut) steering wheel; **am S.** at the helm; (aut) behind the wheel
Steu'eramt *n* tax office
Steu'erbord *n* (naut) starboard
Steu'ererhebung *f* levy of taxes
Steu'ererklärung *f* tax return
Steu'erflosse *f* vertical stabilizer
Steu'erhinterziehung *f* tax evasion
Steu'erjahr *n* fiscal year
Steu'erknüppel *m* control stick
Steu'ermann *m* (–[e]s;–er & –leute) helmsman
steuern [ʃtɔɪ.ərn] *tr* steer; control; regulate; (aer, naut) pilot; (aut) drive ‖ *intr* (*dat*) curb, check
steu'erpflichtig *adj* taxable; dutiable
Steu'errad *n* steering wheel
Steu'erruder *n* rudder, helm
Steu'ersatz *m* tax rate
Steu'ersäule *f* (aer) control column; (aut) steering column
Steu'erstufe *f* tax bracket
Steu'erung *f* (–;–en) steering; (*Bekämpfung*) control; (*Verhinderung*) prevention; (aer) piloting; (aut) steering mechanism
Steu'erveranlagung *f* tax assessment
Steu'erwerk *n* (aer) controls
Steu'erzahler –in §6 *mf* tax payer
Steu'erzuschlag *m* surtax
Steven [ʃtevən] *m* (–s;–) (naut) stem
Stewar·deß [ˈstju.əˌrdes] *f* (–;–dessen [desən]) (aer) stewardess
stibitzen [ʃtɪˈbɪtsən] *tr* snitch
Stich [ʃtɪç] *m* (–[e]s;–e) prick; (*Messer–*) stab; (*Insekten–*) sting, bite; (*Stoß*) thrust; (*Seitenstechen*) sharp pain; (*Kupfer–*) engraving; (cards) trick; (naut) knot; (sew) stitch; **im S. lassen** abandon
Stichelei [ʃtɪçəˈlaɪ] *f* (–;–en) taunt
sticheln [ʃtɪçəln] *intr*—**gegen j–n s.** (fig) needle s.o.
Stich'flamme *f* flash
stich'haltig *adj* valid, sound
Stich'probe *f* spot check
Stich'tag *m* effective date; due date
Stich'wahl *f* run-off election
Stich'wort *n* (–[e]s;–er) key word; dictionary entry ‖ *n* (–[e]s;–e) (theat) cue
Stich'wunde *f* stab wound
sticken [ʃtɪkən] *tr* embroider ‖ *intr* embroider

Stickerei [ʃtɪkə'raɪ] *f* (-;-en) embroidery
Stick'husten *m* whooping cough
stickig ['ʃtɪkɪç] *adj* stuffy, close
Stick'stoff *m* nitrogen
stieben ['ʃtiːbən] §130 *intr* (HABEN & SEIN) fly; (*Menge*) disperse
Stief [ʃtiːf] *comb.fm.* step-
Stief'bruder *m* stepbrother
Stiefel ['ʃtiːfəl] *m* (-s;-) boot
Stie'felknecht *m* bootjack
Stief'mutter *f* stepmother
Stief'mütterchen *n* (bot) pansy
Stief'vater *m* stepfather
stieg [ʃtiːk] *pret* of **steigen**
Stiege ['ʃtiːgə] *f* (-;-n) staircase
Stiel [ʃtiːl] *m* (-[e]s;-e) handle; (bot) stalk
stier [ʃtiːr] *adj* staring, glassy || **Stier** *m* (-[e]s;-e) bull; (astr) Taurus
stieren ['ʃtiːrən] *intr* (**auf** *acc*) stare (at)
Stier'kampf *m* bullfight
stieß [ʃtiːs] *pret* of **stoßen**
Stift [ʃtɪft] *m* (-[e]s;-e) pin; peg; pencil; crayon; (*Zwecke*) tack; (coll) apprentice || *n* (-[e]s;-e & -er) charitable foundation or institution
stiften ['ʃtɪftən] *tr* (*gründen*) found; (*spenden*) donate; (*verursachen*) cause; (*Unruhe*) stir up; (*Frieden*) make; (*Brand*) start; (*e-e Runde Bier*) set up
Stif'ter -in §6 *mf* founder; donor; (fig) author, cause
Stif'tung *f* (-;-en) foundation; donation; grant; **fromme S.** religious establishment; **milde S.** charitable institution
Stif'tungsfest *n* founder's day
Stil [ʃtiːl] *m* (-[e]s;-e) style
stil'gerecht *adj* in good taste
stilisieren [ʃtiːli'ziːrən] *tr* word
stilistisch [ʃti'lɪstɪʃ] *adj* stylistic
still [ʃtɪl] *adj* calm; silent; (com) slack; **im stillen** in secret; **Stiller Ozean** Pacific Ocean || **Stille** *f* (-;) stillness; silence
still'bleiben §62 *intr* (SEIN) keep still
Stilleben (**Still'leben**) *n* still life
stillegen (**still'legen**) *tr* (*Betrieb*) shut down; (*Verkehr*) stop; (*Schiff*) put into mothballs
stillen ['ʃtɪlən] *tr* still; (*Hunger*) appease; (*Durst*) quench; (*Blut*) stanch; (*Begierde*) gratify
stilliegen (**still'liegen**) §108 *intr* lie still; (*Betrieb*) lie idle; (*Verkehr*) be at a standstill
still'schweigen §148 *intr* be silent; **s. zu** acquiesce in || **Stillschweigen** *n* (-s;) silence; secrecy
still'schweigend *adj* silent; (fig) tacit
Still'stand *m* standstill; (*Sackgasse*) stalemate, deadlock
still'stehen §146 *intr* stand still; (*Betrieb*) be idle; (mil) stand at attention; **stillgestanden!** (mil) attention!
Stil'möbel *pl* period furniture
stil'voll *adj* stylish
Stimm– [ʃtɪm] *comb.fm.* vocal; voting
Stimm'abgabe *f* vote, voting
Stimm'band *n* (-[e]s;-̈er) vocal cord

Stimm'block *m* (parl) bloc
Stimm'bruch *m* change of voice
Stimme ['ʃtɪmə] *f* (-;-n) voice; vote
stimmen ['ʃtɪmən] *tr* make feel (*happy, etc.*); (mus) tune || *intr* be right; vote; (mus) be in tune
Stim'menrutsch *m* (pol) landslide
Stimm'enthaltung *f* abstention
Stimm'gabel *f* tuning fork
Stimm'recht *n* right to vote, suffrage
Stim'mung *f* (-;-en) tone; (*Laune*) mood; (mil) morale; (mus) tuning; (st.exch.) trend
stim'mungsvoll *adj* cheerful
Stimm'zettel *m* ballot
stinken ['ʃtɪŋkən] §143 *intr* stink
Stink'tier *n* skunk
Stipen·dium ['ʃtiː'pɛndjum] *n* (-s;-dien [djən]) scholarship, grant
stippen ['ʃtɪpən] *tr* (coll) dunk
Stippvisite ['ʃtɪpvizitə] *f* (-;-n) short visit
Stirn [ʃtɪrn] *f* (-;-en), **Stirne** ['ʃtɪrnə] *f* (-;-n) forehead, brow; (fig) insolence, gall; **die S. runzeln** frown
Stirn'runzeln *n* (-s;) frown(ing)
stob [ʃtoːp] *pret* of **stieben**
stöbern ['ʃtøːbərn] *tr* (*Wild*) flush; (*aus dem Bett*) yank || *intr* poke around; browse; (*Schnee*) drift
stochern ['ʃtɔxərn] *intr* poke around; **im Essen s.** pick at one's food; **im Feuer s.** stoke the fire; **in den Zähnen s.** pick one's teeth
Stock [ʃtɔk] *m* (-[e]s;-̈e) stick; cane; wand; baton; stem; vine; tree stump; cleaning rod; beehive; massif; story, floor; **im ersten S.** on the second floor
Stock–, stock– *comb.fm.* thoroughly
stock'blind *adj* stone-blind
stock'dun'kel *adj* pitch-dark
Stöckel ['ʃtœkəl] *m* (-s;-) high heel
stocken ['ʃtɔkən] *intr* stop; (*Geschäft*) slack off; (*Blut*) coagulate; (*in der Rede*) get stuck; (*Milch*) curdle; (*Stimme*) falter; (*schimmeln*) get moldy; (*Unterhandlungen*) become deadlocked; (*Verkehr*) get tied up; (*zögern*) hesitate || **Stocken** *n* (-s;) stopping; hesitation; **ins S. bringen** tie up
stock'fin'ster *adj* pitch-black
Stock'fleck *m* mildew
stock'fleckig *adj* mildewy
stockig ['ʃtɔkɪç] *adj* moldy
–stöckig [ʃtœkɪç] *comb.fm.* –story
stock'nüch'tern *adj* dead-sober
stock'steif' *adj* stiff as a board
stock'taub' *adj* stone-deaf
Stockung (**Stok'kung**) *f* (-;-en) stoppage; (*des Verkehrs*) tie-up; (*des Blutes*) congestion; (*Unterbrechung*) interruption; (*Verlangsamung*) slow-down; (*Zeitverlust*) delay; (*Pause*) pause; (*Zögern*) hesitation; (*der Unterhandlungen*) deadlock
Stock'werk *n* story, floor
Stoff [ʃtɔf] *m* (-[e]s;-e) stuff, matter; fabric; material; cloth; subject, topic; (chem) substance
stoff'lich *adj* material
Stoff'rest *m* (tex) remnant

Stoff'wechsel m metabolism
stöhnen ['ʃtøːnən] intr groan, moan
Stolle ['ʃtɔlə] f (-;-n) fruit cake
Stollen ['ʃtɔlən] m (-s;-) fruit cake; tunnel; (Pfosten) post; (Stütze) prop
stolpern ['ʃtɔlpərn] intr (SEIN) stumble, trip
stolz [ʃtɔlts] adj (auf acc) proud (of) ‖ **Stolz** m (-es;) pride
stolzieren [ʃtɔl'tsiːrən] intr (SEIN) strut; (Pferd) prance
stopfen ['ʃtɔpfən] tr stuff, cram; (Pfeife) fill; (Strumpf) darn; (mus) mute; **j-m den Mund s.** shut s.o. up ‖ intr be filling; cause constipation
Stopf'garn n darning yarn
Stoppel ['ʃtɔpəl] f (-;-n) stubble
stoppelig ['ʃtɔpəlɪç] adj stubbly
stoppeln ['ʃtɔpəln] tr glean; (fig) patch
stoppen ['ʃtɔpən] tr stop; clock, time ‖ intr stop
Stopp'licht n tail light; stoplight
Stopp'uhr f stopwatch
Stöpsel ['ʃtœsəl] m (-s;-) stopper, cork; (coll) squirt; (elec) plug
stöpseln ['ʃtœpsəln] tr plug; cork
Storch [ʃtɔrç] m (-[e]s;̈-e) stork
stören ['ʃtøːrən] tr disturb, bother; (Pläne) cross; (Vergnügen) spoil; (mil) harass; (rad) jam
Störenfried ['ʃtøːrənfriːt] m (-[e]s;-e) pain in the neck
störrig ['ʃtœrɪç], **störrisch** ['ʃtœrɪʃ] adj stubborn
Stö'rung f (-;-en) disturbance, trouble; breakdown; interruption; annoyance; intrusion; (rad) static; (rad) jamming
Stoß [ʃtoːs] m (-es;̈-e) push, shove; hit, blow; nudge, poke; (Einschlag) impact; (Erschütterung) shock; (Fecht-) pass; (Feuer-) burst (of fire); (Fuß-) kick; (Haufen) pile, bundle; (Rück-) recoil; (Saum) seam, hem; (Schwimm-) stroke; (Trompeten-) blast; (Wind-) gust; (mil) thrust; (orn) tail
Stoß'dämpfer m shock absorber
Stößel ['ʃtøːsəl] m (-s;-) pestle
stoßen ['ʃtoːsən] §150 tr push, shove; hit, knock; kick; punch; jab, nudge, poke; ram; pound; pulverize; oust ‖ ref bump oneself; **sich s. an** (dat) take offense at; take exception to ‖ intr kick; (mit den Hörnen) butt; (Gewehr) recoil, kick; (Wagen) jolt (Schiff) toss; **in die Trompete s.** blow the trumpet; **s. auf** (acc) swoop down on ‖ intr (SEIN)—**s. an** (acc) bump against; adjoin; be next-door to; **s. auf** (acc) run into; come across; (naut) dash against; **s. durch** (mil) smash through; **vom Lande s.** shove off; **zu j-m s.** side with s.o.
Stoß'stange f (aut) bumper
Stoß'trupp m assault party; **Stoßtruppen** shock troops; commandos, rangers
Stoß'zahn m tusk
stottern ['ʃtɔtərn] tr stutter, stammer ‖ intr stutter, stammer; (aut) sputter
stracks [ʃtraks] adv immediately; (geradeaus) straight ahead
Straf- [ʃtraːf] comb.fm. penal; criminal

Straf'anstalt f penal institution
Straf'arbeit f (educ) extra work
Straf'aufschub m reprieve
strafbar ['ʃtraːfbar] adj punishable
Strafe ['ʃtraːfə] f (-;-n) punishment; penalty; (Geld-) fine; **bei S. von** under pain of; **zur S.** as punishment
strafen ['ʃtraːfən] tr punish
straff [ʃtraf] adj tight; (Seil) taut; (gespannt) tense; (aufrecht) erect; (fig) strict; **s. spannen** tighten
straf'fällig adj punishable; culpable
Straf'geld n fine
Straf'gesetzbuch n penal code
sträflich ['ʃtreːflɪç] adj culpable
Sträfling ['ʃtreːflɪŋ] m (-s;-e) convict
straf'los adj unpunished
Straf'porto n postage due
Straf'predigt f talking-to, lecture
Straf'raum m (sport) penalty box
Straf'recht n criminal law
Straf'stoß m (sport) penalty kick
Straf'umwandlung f (jur) commutation
Straf'verfahren n criminal proceedings
Strahl [ʃtraːl] m (-[e]s;-en) ray; beam; flash; jet; (geom) radius
Strahl'antrieb m jet propulsion
strahlen ['ʃtraːlən] intr beam, shine
Strahl'motor m, **Strahl'triebwerk** n jet engine
Strah'lung f (-;-en) radiation
Strähne ['ʃtreːnə] f (-;-n) strand; lock; hank, skein
strähnig ['ʃtreːnɪç] adj wispy
stramm [ʃtram] adj tight; (kräftig) strapping; (Zucht) strict; (Arbeit) hard; (Soldat) smart; (Mädel) buxom ‖ adv—**s. stehen** stand at attention
stramm'ziehen §163 tr draw tight
strampeln ['ʃtrampəln] intr kick
Strand [ʃtrant] m (-[e]s;̈-e) beach, seashore, shore
stranden ['ʃtrandən] intr (SEIN) be beached, run aground, be stranded
Strand'gut n flotsam, jetsam
Strand'gutjäger –in §6 mf beachcomber
Strand'korb m hooded beach chair
Strand'schirm m beach umbrella
Strang [ʃtraŋ] m (-[e]s;̈-e) rope; (Strähne) hank; (Zugseil) trace; (rr) track; **wenn alle Stränge reißen** (rr) if worse comes to worst
Strapaze [ʃtra'patsə] f (-;-n) fatigue; exertion, strain
strapazieren [ʃtrapa'tsiːrən] tr tire out; (Kleider) wear hard
strapazier'fähig adj heavy-duty
strapaziös [ʃtrapa'tsjøs] adj tiring
Straße ['ʃtraːsə] f (-;-n) street; road, highway; (Meerenge) strait
Stra'ßenanzug m business suit
Stra'ßenbahn f streetcar, trolley; trolley line
Stra'ßenbahnwagen m streetcar
Stra'ßendirne f streetwalker
Stra'ßengraben m ditch, gutter
Stra'ßenhändler –in §6 mf street vendor
Stra'ßenjunge m urchin
Stra'ßenkarte f street map
Stra'ßenkreuzung f intersection
Stra'ßenlage f (aut) roadability
Stra'ßenrennen n drag race

Stra'ßenrinne f gutter
Stra'ßenschild n street sign
Stra'ßensperrung f (public sign) road closed
Stra'ßenstreife f highway patrol
strategisch [ʃtra'tegɪʃ] adj strategic
sträuben ['ʃtrɔɪbən] tr ruffle || ref bristle, stand on end; sich s. gegen resist, struggle against
Strauch [ʃtraux] m (-[e]s;⁼er) shrub
straucheln ['ʃtrauxəln] intr (SEIN) stumble, trip; (fig) go wrong
Strauß [ʃtraus] m (-[e]s;⁼e) bouquet || m (-[e]s;-e) ostrich
Strebe ['ʃtrebə] f (-;-n) prop, strut
Stre'bebogen m flying buttress
streben ['ʃtrebən] intr (nach) strive (after); (nach) tend (toward) || Stre-ben n (-s;-) striving; pursuit; (Hang) tendency; (Anstrengung) endeavor
Stre'ber m (-s;-) go-getter, eager beaver; social climber; (in der Schule) grind
strebsam ['ʃtrepzam] adj zealous
Streb'samkeit f (-;) zeal; industry
Strecke ['ʃtrekə] f (-;-n) stretch; extent; distance; stage, leg; (geom) straight line; (hunt) bag; (rr) section; zur S. bringen catch up with; (box) defeat; (hunt) bag
strecken ['ʃtrekən] tr stretch; (Metalle) laminate; (Wein) dilute; (fig) make last; die Waffen s. lay down one's arms || ref stretch (oneself)
Streich [ʃtraɪç] m (-[e]s;-e) blow; (fig) trick, prank
streicheln ['ʃtraɪçəln] tr stroke; pat
streichen ['ʃtraɪçən] §85 tr stroke; (Butter, usw.) spread; (an-) paint; (Geige) play; (Messer) whet; (Rasiermesser) strop; (Streichholz) strike; (Flagge, Segel) lower; (Ärmel) roll down; (Ziegel) make; (mit Ruten) flog; delete; (sport) scratch || intr—mit der Hand s. über (acc) pass one's hand over || intr (SEIN) stretch, extend; wander; pass, move; rush
Streich'holz n match
Streich'holzbrief m matchbook
Streich'instrument n stringed instrument
Streich'orchester n string band
Streich'riemen m razor strop
Streif [ʃtraɪf] m (-[e]s;-e) streak, stripe; strip
Streif'band n (-[e]s;⁼er) wrapper
Streife ['ʃtraɪfə] f (-;-n) raid; (Runde) beat; (mil) patrol
streifen ['ʃtraɪfən] tr stripe; streak; graze; skim over; (abziehen) strip; (grenzen an) verge on; (Thema) touch on || intr (SEIN) roam; (mil) patrol; s. an (acc) brush against; (fig) verge on; s. über (acc) scan || Streifen m (-s;-) stripe; streak; strip; slip; (cin) movie
Strei'fendienst m patrol duty
Strei'fenwagen m patrol car, squad car
streifig ['ʃtraɪfɪç] adj striped
Streif'licht n flash, streak of light; S. werfen auf (acc) shed light on
Streif'wunde f scratch

Streif'zug m exploratory trip, look-see
Streik [ʃtraɪk] m (-[e]s;-s) strike, walkout; wilder S. wildcat strike
streiken ['ʃtraɪkən] intr go on strike
Strei'kende §5 mf striker
Streik'posten m picket; S. stehen picket
Streit [ʃtraɪt] m (-[e]s;-e) fight; argument, quarrel; (jur) litigation
Streit'axt f battle-ax; die S. begraben (fig) bury the hatchet
streitbar ['ʃtraɪtbar] adj belligerent
streiten ['ʃtraɪtən] §86 recip & intr quarrel
Streit'frage f point at issue
streitig ['ʃtraɪtɪç] adj controversial; at issue
Streit'kräfte pl (mil) forces, troops
streit'lustig adj belligerent, scrappy
Streit'objekt n bone of contention
Streit'punkt m issue, point at issue
streit'süchtig adj quarrelsome
streng [ʃtrɛŋ] adj severe, stern; austere; strict; (Geschmack) sharp ||
Strenge f (-;) severity, sternness; austerity; strictness; sharpness
streng'genommen adv strictly speaking
streng'gläubig adj orthodox
Streu [ʃtrɔɪ] f (-;-en) straw bed
Streu'büchse f shaker
streuen ['ʃtrɔɪ·ən] tr strew, sprinkle; (ausbreiten) spread; (verbreiten) scatter || intr spread, scatter
strich [ʃtrɪç] pret of streichen || Strich m (-[e]s;-e) stroke; line; (Streif) stripe; (Landstrich) tract; (carp) grain; (tex) nap; (typ) dash; auf den S. gehen walk the streets (as prostitute); gegen den S. gehen go against the grain; (fig) rub the wrong way
Strich'mädchen n streetwalker
Strich'punkt m semicolon
Strich'regen m local shower
strich'weise adv here and there
Strick [ʃtrɪk] m (-[e]s;-e) rope, cord; (fig) rogue, good-for-nothing
stricken ['ʃtrɪkən] tr & intr knit
Strick'garn n knitting yarn
Strick'jacke f cardigan
Strick'kleid n knitted dress
Strick'leiter f rope ladder
Strick'waren pl knitwear
Strick'zeug n knitting things
Striemen ['ʃtrimən] m (-s;-) stripe, streak; (in der Haut) weal
Strippe ['ʃtrɪpə] f (-;-n) string; strap; shoestring; (telp) line
stritt [ʃtrɪt] pret of streiten
strittig ['ʃtrɪtɪç] adj controversial
Stroh [ʃtro] n (-[e]s) straw
Stroh'dach n thatched roof
Stroh'halm m straw; drinking straw
Stroh'mann m (-[e]s;⁼er) scarecrow; (cards) dummy
Stroh'puppe f scarecrow
Stroh'sack m straw mattress; heiliger S.! holy smokes!
Strolch [ʃtrɔlç] m (-[e]s;-e) bum
strolchen ['ʃtrɔlçən] intr bum around
Strom [ʃtrom] m (-[e]s;⁼e) river; stream; (von Worten) torrent; (& elec) current

strom ab' wärts *adv* downstream
strom auf' wärts *adv* upstream
Strom' ausfall *m* (elec) power failure
strömen ['ʃtrømən] *intr* (HABEN & SEIN) stream; (*Regen*) pour (down)
Stro' mer *m* (–s;–) (coll) tramp
Strom' kreis *m* (elec) circuit
strom' linienförmig *adj* streamlined
Strom' richter *m* (elec) converter
Strom' schnelle *f* rapids
Strom' spannung *f* voltage
Strom' stärke *f* (elec) amperage
Strö' mung *f* (–;–en) current; trend
Strom' unterbrecher *m* (elec) circuit breaker
Strom' wandler *m* (elec) transformer
Strom' zähler *m* electric meter
Strophe ['ʃtrofə] *f* (–;–n) stanza
strotzen ['ʃtrɔtsən] *intr*—**s. von** or **vor** (*dat*) abound in, teem with
Strudel ['ʃtruːdəl] *m* (–s;–) eddy, whirlpool; (fig) maelstrom; (culin) strudel
strudeln ['ʃtruːdəln] *intr* eddy, whirl
Struktur [ʃtrʊk'tur] *f* (–;–en) structure; (tex) texture
Strumpf [ʃtrʊmpf] *m* (–[e]s;ˤe) stocking
Strumpf' band *n* (–[e]s;ˤer), **Strumpf' halter** *m* garter
Strumpf' waren *pl* hosiery
struppig ['ʃtrʊpɪç] *adj* shaggy, unkempt
Stube ['ʃtubə] *f* (–;–n) room
Stu' benmädchen *n* chambermaid
stu' benrein *adj* housebroken
Stubsnase ['ʃtupsnazə] *f* snub nose
Stuck [ʃtʊk] *m* (–[e]s;) stucco
Stück [ʃtʏk] *n* (–[e]s;–e) piece; lot; plot; stretch distance; (*Butter*) pat; (*Zucker*) lump; (*Seife*) cake; (*Vieh*) head; (mus) piece, number; (theat) play, show; **pro S.** apiece
stückeln ['ʃtʏkəln] *tr* cut or break into small pieces; piece together
stück' weise *adv* piecemeal
Stück' werk *n* patchwork
Student [ʃtu'dɛnt] *m* (–en;–en) college student
Studen' tenheim *n* dormitory
Studen' tenverbindung *f* fraternity
Studentin [ʃtu'dɛntɪn] *f* (–;–nen) college student, coed
Studie ['ʃtudjə] *f* (–;–n) (Lit) essay; (paint) study, sketch
Stu' diengang *m* (educ) course
Stu' dienplan *m* curriculum
Stu' dienrat *m* (–[e]s;ˤe) high school teacher
Stu' dienreferendar –in §8 *mf* practice teacher
Stu' dienreise *f* (educ) field trip
studieren [ʃtu'diːrən] *tr* & *intr* study (*at college*); examine
studiert [ʃtu'dirt] *adj* college-educated; (*gekünstelt*) affected
Studier' zimmer *n* study
Stu' dium ['ʃtudjʊm] *n* (–s;–dien [djən]) study (*at college*); studies
Stufe ['ʃtufə] *f* (–;–n) step, stair; (*e-r Leiter*) rung; (*Grad*) degree; (*Niveau*) level; stage; (mus) interval
Stu' fenfolge *f* graduation; succession
Stu' fenleiter *f* stepladder; (fig) gamut
stu' fenweise *adv* by degrees

Stuhl [ʃtul] *m* (–[e]s;ˤe) chair; (*Stuhlgang*) stool, feces; **der Heilige S.** the Holy See
Stuhl' bein *n* leg of a chair
Stuhl' drang *m* urgent call of nature
Stuhl' gang *m* stool, feces; **S. haben** have a bowel movement
Stuhl' lehne *f* back of a chair
Stulpe ['ʃtʊlpə] *f* (–;–n) cuff
Stülpnase ['ʃtʏlpnazə] *f* snub nose
stumm [ʃtʊm] *adj* dumb; mute; (*schweigend*) silent; (gram) mute
Stummel ['ʃtʊməl] *m* (–s;–) (*e-s Armes, Baumes, e–r Zigarette*) stump
Stümper ['ʃtʏmpər] *m* (–s;–) bungler
Stümperei [ʃtʏmpə'raɪ] *f* (–;–en) bungling
stüm' perhaft *adj* bungling
stümpern ['ʃtʏmpərn] *tr* & *intr* bungle
stumpf [ʃtʊmpf] *adj* blunt; (& fig) obtuse ‖ **Stumpf** *m* (–[e]s;ˤe) stump
Stumpf' sinn *m* apathy, dullness
stumpf' sinnig *adj* dull, stupid
Stunde ['ʃtʊndə] *f* (–;–n) hour; (educ) class, lesson, period
stunden ['ʃtʊndən] *tr* grant postponement of
Stun' dengeld *n* tutoring fee
Stun' dengeschwindigkeit *f* miles per hour
Stun' denkilometer *pl* kilometers per hour
stun' denlang *adv* for hours
Stun' denlohn *m* hourly wage(s)
Stun' denplan *m* roster, schedule
stun' denweise *adv* by the hour
Stun' denzeiger *m* hour hand
–stündig [ʃtʏndɪç] *comb.fm.* –hour
stündlich ['ʃtʏntlɪç] *adj* hourly
Stun' dung *f* (–;–en) period of grace
Stunk [ʃtʊŋk] *m* (–[e]s;) stink; **S. machen** (sl) raise a stink
Stups [ʃtʊps] *m* (–es;–e) nudge
stupsen ['ʃtʊpsən] *tr* nudge
Stups' nase *f* snub nose
stur [ʃtur] *adj* stubborn; (*Blick*) fixed
Sturm [ʃtʊrm] *m* (–[e]s;ˤe) storm; gale
Sturm' abteilung *f* storm troopers
stürmen ['ʃtʏrmən] *tr* storm ‖ *intr* rage, roar ‖ *intr* (SEIN) rush ‖ *impers*—**es stürmt** it is stormy
Stürmer ['ʃtʏrmər] *m* (–s;–) (fb) forward
stürmisch ['ʃtʏrmɪʃ] *adj* stormy; impetuous ‖ *adv*—**nicht so s.!** not so fast!
Sturm' schritt *m* (mil) double time
Sturm' trupp *m* assault party
Sturm' welle *f* (mil) assault wave
Sturm' wind *m* gale, hurricane
Sturz [ʃtʊrts] *m* (–es;ˤe) fall, sudden drop; overthrow; collapse; (archit) lintel; (aut) camber; (com) slump
Sturz' bach *m* torrent
Sturz' bomber *m* dive bomber
Stürze ['ʃtʏrtsə] *f* (–;–n) lid
stürzen ['ʃtʏrtsən] *tr* throw down; upset, overturn; overthrow; (*tauchen*) plunge; **nicht s.!** this side up! ‖ *ref* rush; plunge ‖ *intr* (SEIN) fall, tumble; rush; (*Tränen*) pour; (aer) dive
Sturz' flug *m* (aer) dive
Sturz' helm *m* crash helmet

Sturz'regen *m* downpour
Sturz'see *f* heavy seas
Stute ['ʃtutə] *f* (-;-n) mare
Stütze ['ʃtʏtsə] *f* (-;-n) support, prop; (fig) help, support
stutzen ['ʃtutsən] *tr* cut short; (*Flügel*) clip; (*Bäume*) prune; (*Ohren*) crop; (*Bart*) trim || *intr* stop short; be startled; (*Pferd*) shy
stützen ['ʃtʏtsən] *tr* support; prop; shore up; (fig) support || *ref—sich s. auf* (*acc*) lean on; (fig) depend on
Stutzer ['ʃtutsər] *m* (-s;-) car coat; (coll) snazzy dresser
Stutz'flügel *m* baby grand piano
stutzig ['ʃtutsɪç] *adj* suspicious
Stütz'pfeiler *m* abutment
Stütz'punkt *m* footing; (mil) base; (phys) fulcrum
Subjekt [zup'jekt] *n* (-[e]s;-e) (coll) guy, character; (gram) subject
subjektiv [zupjek'tif] *adj* subjective
Substantiv [zupstan'tif] *n* (-[e]s;-e) (gram) substantive, noun
Substanz [zup'stants] *f* (-;-en) substance
subtil [zup'til] *adj* subtle
subtrahieren [zuptra'hirən] *tr* subtract
Subtraktion [zuptrak'tsjon] *f* (-;-en) subtraction
Subvention [zupven'tsjon] *f* (-;-en) subsidy
Such- [zux] *comb.fm.* search
Such'anzeige *f* want ad
Such'büro *n*, Such'dienst *m* missing-persons bureau
Suche ['zuxə] *f* (-;-en) search; *auf der S. nach* in search of, in quest of
suchen ['zuxən] *tr* search for, look for; (*erstreben*) seek; want, desire; (*in der Zeitung*) advertise for; (*Gefahr*) court; *das Weite s.* run away || *intr* search; *nach etw s.* look for s.th.
Sucht [zuxt] *f* (-;̈e) passion, mania; (*nach*) addition (to)
süchtig ['zʏçtɪç] *adj* addicted || Süch'tige §5 *mf* addict
Sud [zut] *m* (-[e]s;-e) brewing; brew
Süd [zyt] *m* (-[e]s;) south
sudelhaft ['zudəlhaft], sudelig ['zu-dəlɪç] *adj* slovenly, sloppy
sudeln ['zudəln] *tr & intr* mess up
Süden ['zydən] *m* (-s;) south
Sudeten [zu'detən] *pl* Sudeten mountains (*along northern border of Czechoslovakia*)
Süd'früchte *pl* (tropical and subtropical) fruit (*e.g., bananas, oranges*)
süd'lich *adj* south, southern, southerly; *s. von* south of || *adv* south
Südost' *m*, Südo'sten *m* southeast
südöst'lich *adj* southeast(ern)
Süd'pol *m* (-s;) South Pole
südwärts ['zytverts] *adv* southward
Südwest' *m*, Südwe'sten *m* southwest
süffig ['zʏfɪç] *adj* tasty
suggerieren [zugə'rirən] *tr* suggest
suggestiv [zuges'tif] *adj* suggestive
Suggestiv'frage *f* leading question
suhlen ['zulən] *ref* wallow
Sühne ['zynə] *f* (-;) atonement
sühnen ['zynən] *tr* atone for, expiate
Sülze ['zʏltsə] *f* (-;-n) jellied meat

summarisch [zu'marɪʃ] *adj* summary
Summe ['zumə] *f* (-;-n) sum, total
summen ['zumən] *tr* hum || *intr* hum; buzz
Sum'mer *m* (-s;-) buzzer
summieren [zu'mirən] *tr* sum up, total || *ref* run up, pile up
Summton ['zumton] *m* (telp) dial tone
Sumpf [zumpf] *m* (-[e]s;̈e) swamp
sumpfig ['zumpfɪç] *adj* swampy, marshy
Sünde ['zyndə] *f* (-;-n) sin
Sün'denbock *m* scapegoat
Sün'denerlaß *m* absolution
Sün'denfall *m* original sin
Sün'der *m* (-s;-) sinner
Sünd'flut ['zyntflut] *f* Deluge
sünd'haft, sündig ['zyndɪç] *adj* sinful
sündigen ['zyndɪgən] *intr* sin
Superlativ ['zuperlatif] *m* (-s;-e) (gram) superlative
Su'permarkt *m* supermarket
Suppe ['zupə] *f* (-;-n) soup
Sup'penschüssel *f* tureen
surren ['zurən] *intr* buzz
Surrogat [zurə'gat] *n* (-[e]s;-e) substitute
suspendieren [zuspen'dirən] *tr* suspend
süß [zys] *adj* sweet || Süße *f* (-;) sweetness
süßen ['zysən] *tr* sweeten
Sü'ßigkeit *f* (-;-en) sweetness; Süßig-keiten sweets, candy
Süß'kartoffel *f* sweet potato
süß'lich *adj* sweetish; (fig) mawkish
Süß'stoff *m* artificial sweetener
Süß'waren *pl* sweets, candy
Süß'wasser *n* fresh water
Symbol [zym'bol] *n* (-s;-e) symbol
Symbolik [zym'bolɪk] *f* (-;) symbolism
symbolisch [zym'bolɪʃ] *adj* symbolic(al)
Symme·trie [zyme'tri] *f* (-;-trien) ['tri-ən] symmetry
symmetrisch [zy'metrɪʃ] *adj* symmetrical
Sympa·thie [zympa'ti] *f* (-;-thien) ['ti-ən] liking
sympathisch [zym'patɪʃ] *adj* likeable; *er ist mir s.* I like him
sympathisieren [zympatɪ'zirən] *intr—s. mit* sympathize with; like
Sympho·nie [zymfo'ni] *f* (-;-nien) ['ni-ən] symphony
Symptom [zymp'tom] *n* (-s;-e) symptom
symptomatisch [zympto'matɪʃ] *adj* (*für*) symptomatic (of)
Synagoge [zyna'gogə] *f* (-;-n) synagogue
synchronisieren [zynkronɪ'zirən] *tr* synchronize
Syndikat [zyndɪ'kat] *n* (-[e]s;-e) syndicate
Syndi·kus ['zyndɪkus] *m* (-;-kusse & -ki [ki]) corporation lawyer
synonym [zyno'nym] *adj* synonymous || Synonym *n* (-s;) synonym
Syntax ['zyntaks] *f* (-;) syntax
synthetisch [zyn'tetɪʃ] *adj* synthetic
Syrien ['zyrjən] *n* (-s;) Syria

System [zʏs'tem] *n* (–s;–e) system
systematisch [zʏste'matɪʃ] *adj* systematic
Szene ['stsenə] *f* (–;–n) scene; **in S.**

setzen stage; **sich in S. setzen** put on
an act
Sze'nenaufnahme *f* (cin) take
Szenerie [stenə'riː] *f* (–;) scenery

T

T, t [te] *invar n* T, t
Tabak [ta'bak], ['tabak] *m* (–[e]s;–e)
tobacco
Tabaks'beutel *m* tobacco pouch
Tabak'trafik *f* (Aust) cigar store
Tabak'waren *pl* tobacco products
tabellarisch [tabe'lariːʃ] *adj* tabular
tabellarisieren [tabelarɪ'zirən] *tr* tabu-
late
Tabelle [ta'belə] *f* (–;–n) table, chart;
graph
Tabernakel [taber'nakəl] *m & n* (–s;–)
tabernacle
Tablett [ta'blɛt] *n* (–[e]s;–e) tray
Tablette [ta'bletə] *f* (–;–n) tablet, pill
tabu [ta'bu] *adj* taboo || **Tabu** *n* (–s;
–s) taboo
Tachometer [taxo'metər] *n* speedometer
Tadel ['tadəl] *m* (–s;–) scolding;
(*Schuld*) blame; (educ) demerit
ta'dellos *adj* blameless; flawless
tadeln ['tadəln] *tr* scold, reprimand;
blame, find fault with
Tafel ['tafəl] *f* (–;–n) (*Tisch, Diagramm*) table; (*Anschlag–*) billboard;
(*Glas–*) pane; (*Holz–, Schalt–*) panel;
(*Mahlzeit*) meal, dinner; (*Metall–*)
sheet, plate; (*Platte*) slab; (*Schiefer–*)
slate; (*Schreib–*) tablet; (*Schokolade*)
bar; (*Wand–*) blackboard; **bei T.** at
dinner; **die T. decken** set the table;
offene T. halten have open house
Ta'felaufsatz *m* centerpiece
Ta'felbesteck *n* knife, fork, and spoon
ta'felförmig *adj* tabular
Ta'felgeschirr *n* table service
Ta'felland *n* tableland, plateau
Ta'felmusik *f* dinner music
tafeln ['tafəln] *intr* dine, feast
täfeln ['tɛfəln] *tr* (*Wand*) wainscot,
panel; (*Fußboden*) parquet
Ta'felöl *n* salad oil
Ta'felservice *n* tableware
Tä'felung *f* (–;–en) inlay; paneling
Taft [taft] *m* (–[e]s;–e) taffeta
Tag [tak] *m* (–[e]s;–e) day; daylight;
am Tage by day; **am Tage nach** the
day after; **an den Tag bringen** bring
to light; **bei Tage** by day, in the daytime; **den ganzen Tag** all day long;
e–n Tag um den andern every other
day; **e–s Tages** someday; **es wird Tag**
day is breaking; **guten Tag!** hello!;
how do you do?; (*bei Verabschiedung*) good day!; goodby!; **Tag der
offenen Tür** open house; **unter Tage**
(min) underground, below the surface
tagaus', tagein' *adv* day in and day out
Tage– [tagə] *comb.fm.* day–, daily

Ta'geblatt *n* daily, daily paper
Ta'gebuch *n* diary, journal
Ta'gegeld *n* per diem allowance
ta'gelang *adv* for days
Ta'gelohn *m* daily wage
Tagelöhner –in ['tagəløːnər(ɪn)] §6 *mf*
day laborer
tagen ['tagən] *intr* dawn; (*beraten*)
meet; (jur) be in session
Ta'gesanbruch *m* daybreak
Ta'gesangriff *m* (aer) daylight raid
Ta'gesbefehl *m* (mil) order of the day
Ta'gesbericht *m* daily report
Ta'geseinnahme *f* daily receipts
Ta'gesgespräch *n* topic of the day
ta'geshell *adj* as light as day
Ta'geskasse *f* (theat) box office
Ta'gesleistung *f* daily output
Ta'geslicht *n* daylight
Ta'geslichtaufnahme *f* (phot) daylight
shot
Ta'gesordnung *f* agenda; (coll) order
of the day
Ta'gespreis *m* market price
Ta'gespresse *f* daily press
Ta'gesschau *f* (telv) news
Ta'geszeit *f* time of day; daytime; **zu
jeder T.** at any hour
Ta'geszeitung *f* daily paper
ta'geweise *adv* by the day
Ta'gewerk *n* day's work
–tägig [tegɪç] *comb.fm.* –day
täglich ['tekliç] *adj* daily
tags [taks] *adv* —**t. darauf** the follow-
ing day; **t. zuvor** the day before
Tag'schicht *f* day shift
tags'über *adv* during the day, in the
daytime
Tagung ['tagʊŋ] *f* (–;–en) convention,
conference, meeting
Ta'gungsort *m* meeting place
Taifun [taɪ'fun] *m* (–s;–e) typhoon
Taille [['taljə] *f* (–;–n) waist; (*Mieder*) bodice
Takel ['takəl] *n* (–s;–) tackle
Takelage [takə'laʒə] *f* (–;–n) rigging
takeln ['takəln] *tr* rig
Ta'kelwerk *n* var of **Takelage**
Takt [takt] *m* (–[e]s;–e) tact; (mach)
stroke; (mus) time, beat; (mus) bar;
den T. schlagen mark time; **im T.** in
time; in step; **T. halten** mark time
takt'fest *adj* keeping good time; (fig)
reliable
Taktik ['taktɪk] *f* (–;–en) (& fig)
tactics
Tak'tiker *m* (–s;–) tactician
taktisch ['taktɪʃ] *adj* tactical
takt'los *adj* tactless
Takt'messer *m* metronome
Takt'stock *m* baton

Takt'strich *m* (mus) bar

takt'voll *adj* tactful

Tal [tɑl] *n* (-[e]s;⁼er) valley

Talar [ta'lɑr] *m* (-s;-e) robe, gown

Tal'boden *m* valley floor

Talent [ta'lɛnt] *n* (-[e]s;-e) talent

talentiert [talɛn'tirt] *adj* talented

Tal'fahrt *f* descent

Talg [talk] *m* (-[e]s;-e) suet; tallow

Talg'kerze *f*, Talg'licht *n* tallow candle

Talisman ['tɑlɪsman] *m* (-s;-e) talisman

Talk(um)puder ['talk(ʊm)pudər] *m* talcum powder

Talmi ['talmi] *n* (-s;) (fig) imitation

Tal'sperre *f* dam

Tamburin [tambʊ'rin] *n* (-s;-e) tambourine

Tampon [tã'põ] *m* (-s;-s) (med) tampon

Tamtam [tam'tam] *n* (-s;-s) gong; (fig) fanfare, drum beating

Tand [tant] *m* (-[e]s;) trifle; bauble

tändeln ['tɛndəln] *intr* trifle; flirt

Tang [taŋ] *m* (-[e]s;-e) seaweed

Tangente [taŋ'gɛntə] *f* (-;-n) (geom) tangent

tangieren [taŋ'girən] *tr* concern

Tango ['taŋgo] *m* (-s;-s) tango

Tank [taŋk] *m* (-[e]s;-e & -s) tank

tanken ['taŋkən] *intr* get gas; refuel

Tan'ker *m*, Tank'schiff *n* tanker

Tank'stelle *f* gas (or service) station

Tank'wagen *m* tank truck; (rr) tank car

Tankwart ['taŋkvart] *m* (-[e]s;-e) gas station attendant

Tanne ['tanə] *f* (-;-n) fir (tree)

Tan'nenbaum *m* fir tree

Tan'nenzapfen *m* fir cone

Tante ['tantə] *f* (-;-n) aunt; T. Meyer (coll) john

Tantieme [tã'tjemə] *f* (-;-n) dividend; (com) royalty

Tanz [tants] *m* (-es;⁼e) dance

Tanz'bein *n*—das T. schwingen (coll) cut a rug

Tanz'diele *f* dance hall

tänzeln ['tɛntsəln] *intr* (HABEN & SEIN) skip about; (*Pferd*) prance

tanzen ['tantsən] *tr & intr* dance

Tänzer -in ['tɛntsər(ɪn)] §6 *mf* dancer

Tanz'fläche *f* dance floor

Tanz'kapelle *f* dance band

Tanz'lokal *n* dance hall

Tanz'saal *m* ballroom

Tanz'schritt *m* dance step

Tanz'stunde *f* dancing lesson

Tapete [ta'petə] *f* (-;-n) wallpaper

Tape'tenpapier *n* wallpaper (*in rolls*)

Tape'tentür *f* wallpapered door

Tapezierarbeit [tape'tsirarbaɪt] *f* paperhanging

tapezieren [tape'tsirən] *tr* wallpaper

Tapezie'rer *m* (-s;-) paperhanger

tapfer ['tapfər] *adj* brave, valiant

Ta'pferkeit *f* (-;) bravery, valor

tappen ['tapən] *intr* (HABEN & SEIN) grope about; t. nach grope for

täppisch ['tɛpɪʃ] *adj* clumsy

tapsen ['tapsən] *intr* (SEIN) clump along

Tara ['tɑra] *f* (-;) (com) tare

Tarif [ta'rif] *m* (-s;-e) tariff; price list; wage scale; postal rates

Tarif'lohn *m* standard wages

Tarif'verhandlung *f* collective bargaining

Tarif'vertrag *m* wage agreement

Tarn- [tarn] *comb.fm.* camouflage

tarnen ['tarnən] *tr* camouflage

Tarn'kappe *f* (myth) magic cap (*rendering wearer invisible*)

Tar'nung *f* (-;) camouflage

Tasche ['taʃə] *f* (-;-n) pocket; handbag; pocketbook; schoolbag; flight bag; pouch; briefcase

Ta'schenausgabe *f* pocket edition

Ta'schenbuch *n* paperback

Ta'schendieb *m* pickpocket

Ta'schendiebstahl *m* pickpocketing

Ta'schengeld *n* pocket money

Ta'schenlampe *f* flashlight

Ta'schenmesser *n* pocketknife

Ta'schenrechner *m* pocket calculator

Ta'schenspieler -in §6 *mf* magician

Ta'schenspielerei *f* sleight of hand

Ta'schentuch *n* handkerchief

Ta'schenuhr *f* pocket watch

Ta'schenwörterbuch *n* pocket dictionary

Tasse ['tasə] *f* (-;-n) cup

Tastatur [tasta'tur] *f* (-;-en) keyboard

Taste ['tastə] *f* (-;-n) key

tasten ['tastən] *tr* feel, touch; (telg) send || *ref* feel one's way || *intr* (nach) grope (for)

Tastsinn ['tastzɪn] *m* sense of touch

tat [tat] *pret* of tun || Tat *f* (-;-en) deed, act; (*Verbrechen*) crime; auf frischer Tat ertappen catch red-handed; in der Tat in fact; in die Tat umsetzen implement

Tat'bestand *m* facts of the case

Tat'bestandsaufnahme *f* factual statement

tatenlos ['tɑtənlos] *adj* inactive

Ta'tenlosigkeit *f* (-;) inactivity

Täter -in ['tɛtər(ɪn)] §6 *mf* doer, perpetrator; culprit

Tat'form *f* (gram) active voice

tätig ['tɛtɪç] *adj* active; busy; t. sein bei be employed by

tätigen ['tɛtɪgən] *tr* conclude

Tä'tigkeit *f* (-;-en) activity; occupation, job, profession

Tä'tigkeitsbericht *m* progress report

Tä'tigkeitsfeld *n* field, line

Tä'tigung *f* (-;-en) transaction

Tat'kraft *f* energy, strength; vigor

tat'kräftig *adj* energetic; vigorous

tätlich ['tɛtlɪç] *adj* violent; tätliche Beleidigung (jur) assault and battery; t. werden gegen assault || *adv* —t. beleidigen (jur) assault

Tät'lichkeit *f* (-;-en) (act of) violence; es kam zu Tätlichkeiten it came to blows

Tat'ort *m* scene of the crime

tätowieren [tɛto'virən] *tr* tattoo

Tätowie'rung *f* (-;-en) tattoo

Tat'sache *f* fact

Tat'sachenbericht *m* factual report

tat'sächlich *adj* actual, real, factual

tätscheln ['tɛtʃəln] *tr* pet, stroke

Tatterich ['tatərɪç] *m* (-s;) shakes
Tatze ['tatsə] *f* (-;-n) paw
Tau [tau] *m* (-[e]s;) dew ‖ *n* (-[e]s; -e) rope; (naut) hawser
taub [taup] *adj* deaf; (*betäubt*) numb; (*unfruchtbar*) barren; (*Gestein*) not containing ore; (*Nuß*) hollow; (*Ei*) unfertile; (*Hafer*) wild; **t. gegen** deaf to; **t. vor Kälte** numb with cold
Taube ['taubə] *f* (-;-n) pigeon; (pol) dove
Tau/benhaus *n*, **Tau/benschlag** *m* dovecote
Taub/heit *f* (-;) deafness; numbness
taub/stumm *adj* deaf and dumb ‖ **Taub-stumme** §5 *mf* deaf-mute
Tauchboot ['tauxbot] *n* submarine
tauchen ['tauxən] *tr* dip, duck, immerse ‖ *intr* (HABEN & SEIN) dive, plunge; (naut) submerge, dive
Tau/cher -in §6 *mf* (& orn) diver
Tau/cheranzug *m* diving suit
Tau/chergerät *n* aqualung
Tau/cherglocke *f* diving bell
Tauch/krankheit *f* bends
Tauch/schwimmer *m* (nav) frogman
tauen ['tau-ən] *tr* thaw, melt; (*schleppen*) tow ‖ *intr* (HABEN & SEIN) thaw ‖ *impers*—**es taut** dew is falling ‖ *impers* (HABEN & SEIN)—**es taut** it is thawing ‖ **Tauen** *n* (-s;) thaw
Tauf- [tauf] *comb.fm.* baptismal
Tauf/becken *n* baptismal font
Tauf/buch *n* parish register
Taufe ['taufə] *f* (-;-n) baptism, christening
taufen ['taufən] *tr* baptize, christen
Täufer ['tɔɪfər] *m*—**Johannes der T.** John the Baptizer
Täufling ['tɔɪflɪŋ] *m* (-s;-e) child (or person) to be baptized
Tauf/name *m* Christian name
Tauf/pate *m* godfather
Tauf/patin *f* godmother
Tauf/schein *m* baptismal certificate
taugen ['taugən] *intr* be of use; **zu etw t.** be good for s.th.
Taugenichts ['taugənɪçts] *m* (-es;-e) good-for-nothing
tauglich ['tauklɪç] *adj* (**für, zu**) good (for), fit (for); suitable (for); (mil) able-bodied; **t. zu** (*inf*) able to (*inf*)
Taumel ['tauməl] *m* (-s;) giddiness; (*Überschwang*) ecstasy
taumelig ['tauməlɪç] *adj* giddy; reeling
taumeln ['tauməln] *intr* (SEIN) reel, stagger; be giddy; be ecstatic
Tausch [tauʃ] *m* (-es;-e) exchange
tauschen ['tauʃən] *tr* (**gegen**) exchange (for) ‖ *intr*—**mit j-m t.** exchange places with s.o.
täuschen ['tɔɪʃən] *tr* deceive, fool; (*betrügen*) cheat; (*Erwartungen*) disappoint ‖ *ref* be mistaken
täu/schend *adj* deceptive, illusory; (*Ähnlichkeit*) striking
Tausch/geschäft *n* exchange, swap
Tausch/handel *m* barter; **T. treiben** barter
Täu/schung *f* (-;-en) deception, deceit; fraud; **optische T.** optical illusion
Täu/schungsangriff *m* (mil) feint attack
Täu/schungsmanöver *n* feint

Tausch/wert *m* trade-in value
tausend ['tauzənt] *invar adj & pron* thousand ‖ **Tausend** *m*—**ei der T.!** (or **potz T.!**) holy smokes! ‖ *f* (-; -en) thousand ‖ *n* (-s;-e) thousand
Tau/sendfuß *m*, **Tausendfüß(l)er** ['tauzəntfys(l)ər] *m* (-s;-) centipede
tausendste ['tauzəntstə] §9 *adj & pron* thousandth
Tausendstel ['tauzəntstəl] *n* (-s;-) thousandth
Tau/tropfen *m* dewdrop
Tau/werk *n* (naut) rigging
Tau/wetter *n* thaw
Tau/ziehen *n* tug of war
Taxameter [taksa'metər] *m* taxi meter
Taxe ['taksə] *f* (-;-n) tax; (*Schätzung*) appraisal; (*Gebühr*) fee; (*Taxi*) taxi
Taxi ['taksi] *n* (-s;-s) taxi, cab
taxieren [ta'ksirən] *tr* appraise; rate
Taxifahrer -in §6 *mf* taxi driver
Ta/xistand *m* taxi stand
Taxus ['taksus] *m* (-;-) (bot) yew
Team [tim] *n* (-s;-s) team
Technik ['tɛçnɪk] *f* (-;-en) technique; workmanship; technology
Tech/niker -in §6 *mf* technician; engineer
Techni/kum ['tɛçnɪkum] *n* (-s;-ka [ka] & -ken [kən]) technical school; school of engineering
technisch ['tɛçnɪʃ] *adj* technical; **tech-nische Angelegenheit** technicality; **technische Hochschule** technical institute
Technologie [tɛçnələ'gi] *f* (-;) technology
technologisch [tɛçnə'logɪʃ] *adj* technological
Tee [te] *m* (-s;-s) tea
Tee/gebäck *n* tea biscuit, cookie
Tee/kanne *f* teapot
Tee/kessel *m* teakettle
Tee/löffel *m* teaspoon; teaspoonful
Teenager ['tinedʒər] *m* (-s;-) teenager
Teer [ter] *m* (-[e]s;-e) tar
Teer/decke *f* tar surface, blacktop
teeren ['terən] *tr* tar
Teer/pappe *f* tar paper
Tee/satz *m* tealeaves
Teich [taɪç] *m* (-[e]s;-e) pond, pool
Teig [taɪk] *m* (-[e]s;-e) dough
teigig ['taɪgɪç] *adj* doughy
Teig/mulde *f* kneading trough
Teig/waren *pl* noodles; pastries
Teil [taɪl] *m & n* (-[e]s;-e) part; piece; portion; (*Abschnitt*) section; (jur) party; **der dritte T. von** one third of; **edle Teile des Körpers** vital parts; **zu gleichen Teilen** fifty-fifty; **zum größten T.** for the most part; **zum T.** partly, in part
Teil- *comb.fm.* partial
teilbar ['taɪlbar] *adj* divisible
Teilchen ['taɪlçən] *n* (-s;-) particle
teilen ['taɪlən] *tr* divide; (**mit**) share (with) ‖ *ref* (*Weg*) divide; (*An-sichten*) differ; **sich t. in** (acc) share
teil/haben §89 *intr* (an dat) participate (in), share (in)
Teilhaber -in ['taɪlhabər(ɪn)] §6 *mf* participant; (com) partner
Teil/haberschaft *f* (-;-en) partnership

–teilig [taılıç] *comb.fm.* –piece
Teil'nahme *f* (–;) participation; sympathy; interest
teilnahmslos ['taılnamslos] *adj* indifferent; apathetic
Teil'nahmslosigkeit *f* (–;) indifference; apathy
teilnahmsvoll ['taılnamsfol] *adj* sympathetic; (*besorgt*) solicitous
teil'nehmen §116 *intr* (an *dat*) participate (in), take part (in); (an *dat*) attend; (fig) (an *dat*) sympathize (with)
Teil'nehmer –in §6 *mf* participant; (*Mitglied*) member; (sport) competitor; (telp) customer, party
teils [taıls] *adv* partly
Teil'strecke *f* section, stage
Tei'lung *f* (–;-en) division; partition; separation; (*Grade*) graduation, scale; (*Anteile*) sharing
teil'weise *adv* partly
Teil'zahlung *f* partial payment; **auf T. kaufen** buy on the installment plan
Teint [tɛ̃] *m* (–s;-s) complexion
Telefon [tele'fon] *n* (–s;-e) telephone
Telegramm [tele'gram] *n* (–s;-e) telegram
Telegraph [tele'graf] *m* (–en;-en) telegraph
Telegra'phenstange *f* telegraph pole
telegraphieren [telegra'firən] *tr & intr* telegraph; (*nach Übersee*) cable
Teleobjektiv ['tele-objektif] *n* telephoto lens
Telephon [tele'fon] *n* (–s;-e) telephone, phone; **ans T. gehen** answer the phone
Telephon'anruf *m* telephone call
Telephon'anschluß *m* telephone connection
Telephon'gespräch *n* telephone call
Telephon'hörer *m* receiver
telephonieren [telefo'nirən] *intr* telephone; **mit j–m t.** phone s.o.
telephonisch [tele'fonıʃ] *adj* telephone || *adv* by telephone
Telephonist –in [telefo'nıst(ın)] §7 *mf* telephone operator
Telephon'vermittlung *f* telephone exchange
Telephon'zelle *f* telephone booth
Telephon'zentrale *f* telephone exchange
Teleskop [tele'skop] *n* (–s;-e) telescope
Television [televı'zjon] *f* (–;) television
Teller ['tɛlər] *m* (–s;-) plate
Tel'lereisen *n* trap
Tel'lermine *f* antitank mine
Tel'lertuch *n* dishtowel
Tempel ['tɛmpəl] *m* (–s;-) temple
Temperament [tɛmpəra'mɛnt] *n* (–[e] s;-e) temperament; enthusiasm; **er hat kein T.** he has no life in him; **hitziges T.** hot temper
temperament'los *adj* lifeless, boring
temperament'voll *adj* lively, vivacious
Temperatur [tɛmpera'tur] *f* (–;-en) temperature
Temperenzler [tɛmpe'rɛntslər] *m* (–s; –) teetotaler
temperieren [tɛmpe'rirən] *tr* temper; cool; air-condition; (mus) temper

Tem·po ['tɛmpo] *n* (–s;-s & pi [pi]) tempo; speed; (mus) movement
Tem·pus ['tɛmpus] *n* (–; –pora [pɔra]) (gram) tense
Tendenz [tɛn'dɛnts] *f* (–;-en) tendency
Tender ['tɛndər] *m* (–s;-) (nav, rr) tender
Tenne ['tɛnə] *f* (–;-n) threshing floor
Tennis ['tɛnıs] *n* (–;) tennis
Ten'nisplatz *m* tennis court
Ten'nisschläger *m* tennis racket
Ten'nisturnier *n* tennis tournament
Tenor ['tenor] *m* (–s;) (*Wortlaut*) tenor, purport || [te'nor] *m* (–[e]s; ·e) tenor
Teppich ['tɛpıç] *m* (–s;-e) rug, carpet
Teppichkehrmaschine ['tɛpıçkerma-jinə] *f* carpet sweeper
Termin [tɛr'min] *m* (–s;-e) date, time, day; deadline; (com) due date; **er hat heute T.** he is to appear in court today; **äußerster T.** deadline
termin'gemäß *adv* on time, punctually
Termin'geschäft *n* futures
Termin'kalender *m* appointment book; (jur) court calendar
Terminolo·gie [tɛrmınolə'gi] *f* (–; –gien ['gi·ən]) terminology
termin'weise *adv* (com) on time
Terpentin [tɛrpɛn'tin] *m* (–s;) turpentine
Terrain [te'rɛ̃] *n* (–s;-s) ground; (*Grundstück*) lot; (mil) terrain; **T. gewinnen** (fig & mil) gain ground
Terrasse [te'rasə] *f* (–;-n) terrace
terras'senförmig *adj* terraced
Terrine [te'rinə] *f* (–;-n) tureen
Territo·rium [tɛrı'torjum] *n* (–s;-rien [rjən]) territory
Terror ['tɛror] *m* (–s;) terror
terrorisieren [tɛrɔri'zirən] *tr* terrorize
Terrorist –in [tɛrɔ'rıst(ın)] §7 *mf* terrorist
Terz [tɛrts] *f* (–;-en) (mus) third
Terzett [tɛr'tsɛt] *n* (–[e]s;-e) trio
Test [tɛst] *m* (–[e]s;-e & -s) test
Testament [tɛsta'mɛnt] *n* (–[e]s;-e) will; (eccl) Testament
testamentarisch [tɛstamɛn'tarıʃ] *adj* testamentary || *adv* by will; **t. bestimmen** will
Testaments'vollstrecker –in §6 *mf* executor
testen ['tɛstən] *tr* test
teuer ['tɔɪər] *adj* dear, expensive; (*Preis*) high
Teu'erung *f* (–;-en) rise in price
Teu'erungswelle *f* rise in prices
Teu'erungszulage *f* cost-of-living increase
Teufel ['tɔɪfəl] *m* (–s;-) devil; **des Teufels sein** be mad; **wer zum T.?** who the devil?
Teufelei [tɔɪfə'laɪ] *f* (–;-en) deviltry
Teufelsbanner ['tɔɪfəlsbanər] *m* (–s;-) exorcist
Teu'felskerl *m* helluva fellow
teuflisch ['tɔɪflıʃ] *adj* devilish
Teutone [tɔɪ'tonə] *m* (–n;-n) Teuton
teutonisch [tɔɪ'tonıʃ] *adj* Teutonic
Text [tɛkst] *m* (–[e]s;-e) text, words; (cin) script; (mus) libretto; (typ) double pica; **aus dem T. kommen**

lose the train of thought; **j-m den T. lesen** give s.o. a lecture

Text'buch n (mus) libretto

Texter **-in** ['tɛkstər(ɪn)] §6 mf ad writer, ad man; (mus) lyricist

Textil- ['tɛkstil] comb.fm. textile

Textilien [teks'tiljən] pl, **Textil'waren** pl textiles

text'lich adj textual

Theater [te'atər] n (-s;-) theater; **T. machen** (fig) make a fuss; **T. spielen** (fig) make believe, put on

Thea'terbesucher **-in** §6 mf theater-goer

Thea'terdichter **-in** §6 mf playwright

Thea'terkarte f theater ticket

Thea'terkasse f box office

Thea'terprobe f rehearsal

Thea'terstück n play

Thea'terzettel m program

theatralisch [te·a'tralɪʃ] adj theater; (fig) theatrical

Theke ['tekə] f (-;-n) counter; bar

The·ma ['tema] n (-s;-men [mən] & -mata [mata]) theme, subject

Theologe [te·ɔ'logə] m (-n;-n) theologian

Theologie [te·ɔ'logi] f (-;) theology

theologisch [te·ɔ'logɪʃ] adj theological

theoretisch [te·ɔ'retɪʃ] adj theoretic(al)

Theo·rie [te·ɔ'ri] f (-;-rien ['ri·ən]) theory

Thera·pie [tera'pi] f (-;-pien ['pi·ən]) therapy

Thermalbad [ter'malbat] n thermal bath

Thermometer [termɔ'metər] n thermometer

Thermome'terstand m thermometer reading

Thermosflasche ['termɔsflaʃə] f thermos bottle

Thermostat [termɔ'stat] m (-[e]s;-e & (-en;-en) thermostat

These ['tezə] f (-;-n) thesis

Thrombose [trɔm'bozə] f (-;-n) thrombosis

Thron [tron] m (-[e]s;-e) throne

Thron'besteigung f accession to the throne

Thron'bewerber m pretender to the throne

Thron'folge f succession to the throne

Thron'folger m successor to the throne

Thron'himmel m canopy, baldachin

Thron'räuber m usurper

Thunfisch ['tunfɪʃ] m tuna

Tick [tɪk] m (-[e]s;-s & -e) tic; (fig) eccentricity; **e-n T. auf j-n haben** have a grudge against s.o.; **e-n T. haben** (coll) be balmy

ticken ['tɪkən] intr tick

ticktack ['tɪk'tak] adv ticktock || **Ticktack** n (-s;) ticktock

tief [tif] adj deep; profound; (niedrig) low; (Schlaf) sound; (Farbe) dark; (äußerst) extreme; **aus tiefstem Herzen** from the bottom of one's heart; **im tiefsten Winter** in the dead of winter || adv deeply; **zu t. singen** be flat || **Tief** n (-[e]s;-e) (meteor) low

Tief'angriff m low-level attack

Tief'bau m (-[e]s;) underground engineering; underground work

tief'betrübt adj deeply grieved

Tief'druckgebiet n (meteor) low

Tiefe ['tifə] f (-;-n) depth; profundity

Tief'ebene f lowlands, plain

teif'empfunden adj heartfelt

Tie'fenanzeiger m (naut) depth gauge

Tie'fenschärfe f (phot) depth of field

Tief'flug m low-level flight

Tief'gang m (fig) depth; (naut) draft

tief'gekühlt adj deep-freeze

tief'greifend adj far-reaching; radical; deep-seated

Tief'kühlschrank m deep freeze

Tief'land n lowlands

tief'liegend adj low-lying; deep-seated; (Augen) sunken

Tief'punkt m (& fig) low point

Tief'schlag m (box) low blow

Tiefsee- [tifze] comb.fm. deep-sea

tief'sinnig adj pensive; melancholy

Tief'stand m low level

Tiegel ['tigəl] m (-s;-) saucepan; (zum Schmelzen) crucible; (typ) platen

Tier [tir] n (-[e]s;-e) animal; (& fig) beast; **großes** (or **hohes**) **T.** (coll) big shot, big wheel

Tier'art f species (of animal)

Tier'arzt m veterinarian

Tier'bändiger **-in** §6 mf wild-animal tamer

Tier'garten m zoo

Tier'heilkunde f veterinary medicine

tierisch ['tirɪʃ] adj animal (fig) brutish, bestial

Tier'kreis m zodiac

Tier'kreiszeichen n sign of the zodiac

Tier'quälerei f cruelty to animals

Tier'reich n animal kingdom

Tier'schutzverein m society for the prevention of cruelty to animals

Tier'wärter m keeper (at zoo)

Tier'welt f animal kingdom

Tiger ['tigar] m (-s;-) tiger

Tigerin ['tigərɪn] f (-;-nen) tigress

tilgen ['tɪlgən] tr wipe out; (ausrotten) eradicate; (Schuld) pay off; (Sünden) expiate; (streichen) delete

Til'gung f (-;-en) eradication, extinction; payment; deletion

Til'gungsfonds m sinking fund

Tingeltangel ['tɪŋəltaŋəl] m & n (-s;-) honky-tonk

Tinktur [tɪŋk'tur] f (-;-en) tincture

Tinte ['tɪntə] f (-;-n) ink; **in der T. sitzen** (coll) be in a pickle

Tin'tenfaß n inkwell

Tin'tenfisch m cuttlefish

Tin'tenfleck m, **Tin'tenklecks** m ink spot

Tin'tenstift m indelible pencil

Tip [tɪp] m (-s;-s) tip, hint

Tippelbruder ['tɪpəlbrudər] m tramp

tippeln ['tɪpəln] intr (SEIN) (coll) tramp; (coll) toddle

tippen ['tɪpən] tr type || intr type; tap; (wetten) bet; **an j-n nicht t. können** not be able to come near s.o. (in performance); **daran kannst du nicht t.** that's beyond your reach; **t. auf** (acc) predict || ref—**sich an die Stirn t.** tap one's forehead

Tippfehler ['tɪpfɛlər] m typographical error

Tippfräulein ['tɪpfrɔɪlaɪn] n (coll) typist

tipptopp ['tɪp'tɔp] adj tiptop

Tirol [tɪ'rol] n (-s;) Tyrol

Tiroler –in [tɪ'rolər(ɪn)] §6 mf Tyrolean

tirolerisch [tɪ'rolərɪʃ] adj Tyrolean

Tisch [tɪʃ] m (-es;-e) table; (Mahl-zeit) meal, dinner, supper; **bei T.** during the meal; **nach T.** after the meal; **reinen T. machen** make a clean sweep of it; **unter den T. fallen** be ignored; **vom grünen T.** arm-chair; bureaucratic; **vor T.** before the meal; **zu T., bitte!** dinner is ready

Tisch'aufsatz m centerpiece

Tisch'besen m crumb brush

Tisch'besteck n knife, fork, and spoon

Tisch'blatt n leaf of a table

Tisch'decke f tablecloth

Tisch'gast m dinner guest

Tisch'gebet n—T. sprechen say grace

Tisch'gesellschaft f dinner party

Tisch'glocke f dinner bell

Tisch'karte f name plate

Tisch'lampe f table lamp; desk lamp

Tischler ['tɪʃlər] m (-s;-) cabinet maker

Tisch'platte f table top

Tisch'rede f after-dinner speech

Tisch'tennis n Ping-Pong

Tisch'tuch n tablecloth

Tisch'zeit f mealtime, dinner time

Tisch'zeug n table linen and tableware

Titan [tɪ'tan] m (-en;-en) Titan || n (-s;) (chem) titanium

titanisch [tɪ'tanɪʃ] adj titanic

Titel ['tital] m (-s;-) title; (Anspruch) claim; **e-n T. innehaben** (sport) hold a title

Ti'telbild n frontispiece; (e-r Illu-strierten) cover picture

Ti'telblatt n title page

Ti'telkampf m (box) title bout

Ti'telrolle f title role

titulieren [tɪtu'lirən] tr title

Toast [tost] m (-es;-e & -s) toast

toasten ['tostən] tr (Brot) toast || intr propose a toast, drink a toast; **auf j–n t.** toast s.o.

toben ['tobən] intr rage; (Kinder) raise a racket || **Toben** n (-s;) rage, raging; racket; noise

Tob'sucht f frenzy, madness

tob'süchtig adj raving, mad; frantic

Tochter ['tɔxtər] f (-;-ͤ) daughter

Toch'terfirma f, **Toch'tergesellschaft** f (com) subsidiary, affiliate

Tod [tot] m (-es;-e) death; (jur) de-cease; **des Todes sein** be a dead man; **sich** [dat] **den Tod holen** catch a death of a cold

tod'ernst' adj dead serious

Todes— [todəs] comb.fm. of death; deadly

To'desanzeige f obituary

To'desfall m death

To'desgefahr f mortal danger

To'deskampf m death struggle

To'deskandidat m one at death's door

To'desstoß m coup de grâce

To'desstrafe f death penalty; **bei T.** on pain of death

To'destag m anniversary of death

To'desursache f cause of death

To'desurteil n death sentence

Tod'feind –in §8 mf mortal enemy

todgeweiht ['totgəvaɪt] adj doomed

tödlich ['tøtlɪç] adj deadly, fatal

tod'müde adj dead tired

tod'schick' adj (coll) very chic

tod'si'cher adj (coll) dead sure

Tod'sünde f mortal sin

Toilette [twa'letə] f (-;-n) toilet

Toilet'tentisch m dressing table

tolerant [tole'rant] adj (gegen) tolerant (toward)

Toleranz [tole'rants] f (-;-en) tolera-tion; (mach) tolerance

tolerieren [tole'rirən] tr tolerate

toll [tɔl] adj mad, crazy; fantastic, terrific; **das wird noch toller kom-men** the worst is yet to come; **er ist nicht so t.** (coll) he's not so hot; **es zu t. treiben** carry it a bit too far; **t. nach** crazy about

tollen ['tɔlən] intr (HABEN & SEIN) romp about

Toll'haus n (fig) bedlam

Toll'heit f (-;) madness

Toll'kopf m (coll) crackpot

toll'kühn adj foolhardy, rash

Toll'wut f rabies

Tolpatsch ['tɔlpatʃ] m (-es;-e), **Tölpel** ['tœlpəl] m (-s;-) (coll) clumsy ox

töl'pelhaft adj clumsy

Tomate [to'matə] f (-;-n) tomato

Ton [ton] m (-[e]s;-ͤe) tone; sound; tint, shade; (Betonung) accent, stress; (fig) fashion; **den Ton ange-ben** (fig) set the tone; (mus) give the keynote; **e-n anderen Ton anschla-gen** change one's tune; **große Töne reden** talk big; **guter Ton** (fig) good taste; **hast du Töne!** can you beat that! || m (-s;-e) clay

Ton'abnehmer m (electron) pickup

Ton'angebend adj leading

Ton'arm m pickup arm

Ton'art f type of clay; (mus) key

Ton'atelier n (cin) sound studio

Ton'band n (-[e]s;-ͤer) (cin) sound track; (electron) tape

Ton'bandgerät n tape recorder

tönen ['tønən] tr tint, shade || intr sound; (läuten) ring

tönern ['tønərn] adj clay, of clay

Ton'fall m intonation, accent

Ton'farbe f timbre

Ton'film m sound film

Ton'folge f melody

Ton'frequenz f audio frequency

Ton'geschirr n earthenware

Ton'höhe f, **Ton'lage** f pitch

Ton'leiter f (mus) scale

ton'los adj voiceless; unstressed

Ton'malerei f onomotopoeia

Ton'meister m sound engineer

Tonnage [tɔ'naʒə] f (-;-n) (naut) ton-nage

Tonne ['tɔnə] f (-;-n) barrel; ton

Ton'silbe f accented syllable

Ton'spur f groove (of record)

Ton'streifen m (cin) sound track

Tonsur [tɔn'zur] *f* (-;-en) tonsure
Ton'taube *f* clay pigeon
Ton'taubenschießen *n* trapshooting
Tö'nung *f* (-;-en) tint; (phot) tone
Ton'verstärker *m* amplifier
Ton'waren *pl* earthenware
Topas [to'pas] *m* (-es;-e) topaz
Topf [tɔpf] *m* (-[e]s;-̈e) pot
Topf'blume *f* potted flower
Töpfer ['tœpfər] *m* (-s;-) potter
Töpferei [tœpfə'raɪ] *f* (-;-en) potter's shop
Töp'ferscheibe *f* potter's wheel
Töp'ferwaren *pl* pottery
Topf'lappen *m* potholder
Topf'pflanze *f* potted plant
Topp [tɔp] *m* (-s;-e) (naut) masthead || **topp** *interj* it's a deal
Tor [tor] *m* (-en;-en) fool || *n* (-[e]s; -e) gate; gateway; (sport) goal
Torbogen *m* archway
Torf [tɔrf] *m* (-[e]s) peat
Tor'flügel *m* door (*of double door*)
Torf'moos *n* peat moss
Tor'heit *f* (-;-en) foolishness, folly
Tor'hüter *m* gatekeeper; (sport) goalie
töricht ['tørɪçt] *adj* foolish, silly
Törin ['tørɪn] *f* (-;-nen) fool
torkeln ['tɔrkəln] *intr* (HABEN & SEIN) (coll) stagger
Tor'latte *f* (sport) crossbar
Tor'lauf *m* slalom
Tor'linie *f* (sport) goal line
Tornister [tɔr'nɪstər] *m* (-s;-) knapsack; school bag; (mil) field pack
torpedieren [tɔrpe'dirən] *tr* torpedo
Torpedo [tɔr'pedo] *m* (-s;-s) torpedo
Tor'pfosten *m* doorpost; (fb) goal post
Tor'schluß *m*—**kurz vor T.** (fig) at the eleventh hour
Torte ['tɔrtə] *f* (-;-n) cake; pie
Tortur [tɔr'tur] *f* (-;-en) torture
Tor'wächter *m*, **Torwart** ['torvart] (-[e]s;-e) (sport) goalie
Tor'weg *m* gateway
tosen ['tozən] *intr* (HABEN & SEIN) rage, roar || **Tosen** *n* (-s) rage, roar
tot [tot] *adj* dead; (*Kapital*) idle; (*Wasser*) stagnant; **toter Punkt** dead center; (fig) snag; **totes Rennen** dead heat; **tote Zeit** dead season
total [to'tal] *adj* total; all-out
totalitär [totali'tɛr] *adj* totalitarian
tot'arbeiten *ref* work oneself to death
Tote ['totə] §5 *mf* dead person
töten ['tøtən] *tr* kill; (*Nerv*) deaden
To'tenacker *m* churchyard
To'tenbett *n* deathbed
to'tenblaß' *adj* deathly pale
To'tenblässe *f* deathly pallor
to'tenbleich' *adj* deathly pale
To'tengräber *m* gravedigger
To'tengruft *f* crypt
To'tenhemd *n* shroud, winding sheet
To'tenklage *f* lament
To'tenkopf *m* skull
To'tenkranz *m* funeral wreath
To'tenmaske *f* death mask
To'tenmesse *f* requiem
To'tenreich *n* (myth) underworld
To'tenschau *f* coroner's inquest
To'tenschein *m* death certificate
To'tenstadt *f* necropolis

To'tenstarre *f* rigor mortis
To'tenstille *f* dead silence
To'tenwache *f* wake
tot'geboren *adj* stillborn
Tot'geburt *f* stillbirth
tot'lachen *ref* die laughing
Toto ['toto] *m* (-s;-s) football pool
tot'schießen §76 *tr* shoot dead
Tot'schlag *m* manslaughter
tot'schlagen §132 *tr* strike dead; (*Zeit*) kill
tot'schweigen §148 *tr* hush up; keep under wraps || *intr* hush up
tot'stellen *ref* feign death, play dead
tot'treten §152 *tr* trample to death
Tö'tung *f* (-;-en) killing
Tour [tur] *f* (-;-en) tour; turn; (*Umdrehung*) revolution; **auf die krumme T.** by hook or by crook; **auf die langsame T.** very leisurely; **auf höchsten Touren** at full spead; (fig) full blast; **auf Touren bringen** (aut) rev up; **auf Touren kommen** pick up speed; (fig) get worked up; **auf Touren sein** (coll) be in good shape
Tou'renzahl *f* revolutions per minute
Tourismus [tu'rɪsmus] *m* (-s) tourism
Tourist [tu'rɪst] *m* (-en;-en) tourist
Touri'stenverkehr *m*, **Touristik** [tu'rɪstɪk] *f* (-;) tourism
Touristin [tu'rɪstɪn] *f* (-;-nen) tourist
Tour·nee [tur'ne] *f* (-;-neen ['ne-ən]) (mus, theat) tour
Trab [trap] *m* (-[e]s;) trot; **im T.** at a trot
Trabant [tra'bant] *m* (-en;-en) satellite
traben ['trabən] *intr* (HABEN & SEIN) trot
Tra'ber *m* (-s;-) trotter
Tra'berwagen *m* sulky
Trab'rennen *n* harness racing
Tracht [traxt] *f* (-;-en) costume; (*Last*) load; (*Ertrag*) yield
trachten ['traxtən] *intr*—**t. nach** strive for; **t. zu** (*inf*) endeavor to (*inf*)
trächtig ['trɛçtɪç] *adj* pregnant
Tradition [tradɪ'tsjon] *f* (-;-en) tradition
traditionell [tradɪtsjo'nel] *adj* traditional
traf [traf] *pret of* **treffen**
Trafik [tra'fɪk] *f* (-;-en) (Aust) cigar store
träg [trek] *adj var of* **träge**
Tragbahre ['trakbarə] *f* (-;-n) stretcher, litter
Trag'balken ['trakbalkən] *m* supporting beam; girder; joist
Tragband ['trakbant] *n* (-[e]s;-̈er) strap; shoulder strap
tragbar ['trakbar] *adj* portable; (*Kleid*) wearable; (fig) bearable
Trage ['tragə] *f* (-;-n) litter
träge ['tregə] *adj* lazy; slow; inert
tragen ['tragən] §132 *tr* carry; bear; endure; support; (*Kleider*) wear, have on; (*hervorbringen*) produce, yield; (*Bedenken*) have; (*Folgen*) take; (*Risiko*) run; (*Zinsen*) yield; **bei sich t.** have on one's person; **getragen sein von** be based on; **zur Schau t.** show off || *ref* dress; **sich**

gut t. wear well || *intr* (*Stimme*) carry; (*Schußwaffe*) have a range; (*Baum, Feld*) bear, yield; (*Eis*) be thick enough

Träger ['trɛgər] *m* (-s;-) carrier; porter; (*Inhaber*) bearer; shoulder strap; (archit) girder, beam

Trä′gerflugzeug *n* carrier plane

trä′gerlos *adj* strapless

tragfähig ['trakfɛ-ɪç] *adj* strong enough, capable of carrying; **tragfähige Grundlage** (fig) sound basis

Trag′fähigkeit *f* (-;-en) capacity, load limit; (naut) tonnage

Tragfläche ['trakflɛçə] *f*, **Tragflügel** ['trakflygəl] *m* airfoil

Träg′heit ['trɛkhaɪt] *f* (-;) laziness; (phys) inertia

Traghimmel ['trakhɪməl] *m* canopy

Tragik ['tragɪk] *f* (-;) tragedy

tragisch ['tragɪʃ] *adj* tragic

Tragödie [tra'gødjə] *f* (-;-n) tragedy

Tragriemen ['trakrimən] *m* strap

Tragsessel ['trakzɛsəl] *m* sedan chair

Tragtasche ['traktaʃə] *f* shopping bag

Tragtier ['traktir] *n* pack animal

Tragweite ['trakvaɪtə] *f* range; (*Bedeutung*) significance, moment

Tragwerk ['trakverk] *n* (aer) airfoil

Trainer ['trɛnər] *m* (-s;-) coach

trainieren [trɛ'nirən] *tr & intr* train; coach

Training ['trenɪŋ] *n* (-s;) training

Trai′ningsanzug *m* sweat suit

traktieren [trak'tirən] *tr* treat; treat rougly

Trak·tor ['traktɔr] *m* (-s;-toren ['torən]) tractor

trällern ['trɛlərn] *tr & intr* hum

trampeln ['trampəln] *tr* trample

Tram′pelpfad *m* beaten path

Tran [tran] *m* (-[e]s;-e) whale oil; **im T. sein** be drowsy; be under the influence of alcohol

tranchieren [trã'firən] *tr* carve

Träne ['trɛnə] *f* (-;-n) tear

tränen ['trɛnən] *intr* water

Trä′nengas *n* tear gas

trank [traŋk] *pret* of **trinken** || **Trank** *m* (-[e]s;⁼e) drink, draught; potion

Tränke ['trɛŋkə] *f* (-;-n) watering hole

tränken ['trɛŋkən] *tr* give (*s.o.*) a drink; (*Tiere*) water; soak

Transfor·mator [transfɔr'matɔr] *m* (-s; -matoren [ma'torən] transformer

transformieren [transfɔr'mirən] *tr* transform; step up; step down

Transfusion [transfu'zjon] *f* (-;-en) transfusion

Tran·sistor [tran'zɪstɔr] *m* (-s;-sistoren [zɪs'torən]) transistor

transitiv [tranzɪ'tif] *adj* transitive

Transmission [transmɪ'sjon] *f* (-;-en) transmission

transparent [transpa'rent] *adj* transparent || **Transparent** *n* (-[e]s;-e) transparency; (*Spruchband*) banderol

transpirieren [transpɪ'rirən] *intr* perspire

Transplantation [transplanta'tsjon] *f* (-;-en) (surg) transplant

Transport [trans'pɔrt] *m* (-[e]s;-e) transportation

transportabel [transpɔr'tabəl] *adj* transportable

Transporter [trans'pɔrtər] *m* (-s;-) troopship; transport plane

transport′fähig *adj* transportable

transportieren [transpɔr'tirən] *tr* transport, ship

Transport′unternehmen *n* carrier

Trapez [tra'pets] *n* (-es;-e) trapeze; (geom) trapezoid

trappeln ['trapəln] *intr* (SEIN) clatter; (*Kinder*) patter

Trassant [tra'sant] *m* (-en;-en) (fin) drawer

Trassat [tra'sat] *m* (-en;-en) drawee

trassieren [tra'sirən] *tr* trace, lay out; **e-n Wechsel t. auf** (*acc*) write out a check to

trat [trat] *pret* of **treten**

Tratsch [tratʃ] *m* (-es;) gossip

tratschen ['tratʃən] *intr* gossip

Tratte ['tratə] *f* (-;-n) (fin) draft

Trau- [trau] *comb.fm.* wedding, marriage

Traube ['traubə] *f* (-;-n) grape; bunch of grapes; (fig) bunch

Trau′bensaft *m* grape juice

Trau′benzucker *m* glucose

trauen ['trau-ən] *tr* (*Brautpaar*) marry; **sich t. lassen** get married || *ref* dare || *intr* (*dat*) trust (in), have confidence (in)

Trauer ['trau-ər] *f* (-;) grief, sorrow; mourning; (*Trauerkleidung*) mourning clothes; **T. anlegen** put on mourning clothes; **T. haben** be in mourning

Trau′eranzeige *f* obituary

Trau′erbotschaft *f* sad news

Trau′erfall *m* death

Trau′erfeier *f* funeral ceremony

Trau′erflor *m* mourning crepe

Trau′ergefolge *n*, **Trau′ergeleit** *n* funeral procession

Trau′ergottesdienst *m* funeral service

Trau′erkloß *m* (coll) sad sack

Trau′ermarsch *m* funeral march

trauern ['trau-ərn] *intr* (um) mourn (for); (um) wear mourning (for)

Trau′erspiel *n* tragedy

Trau′erweide *f* weeping willow

Trau′erzug *m* funeral cortege

Traufe ['traufə] *f* (-;-n) eaves

träufeln ['trɔfəln] *tr & intr* drip

Trauf′rinne *f* rain gutter

Trauf′röhre *f* rain pipe

traulich ['traulɪç] *adj* intimate; cozy

Traum [traum] *m* (-[e]s;⁼e) dream; (fig) daydream, reverie

Traum′bild *n* vision, phantom

Traum′deuter -in §6 *mf* interpreter of dreams

träumen ['trɔɪmən] *tr & intr* dream

Träu′mer *m* (-s;-) dreamer

Träumerei [trɔɪmə'raɪ] *f* (-;-en) dreaming; daydream

Träumerin ['trɔɪmərɪn] *f* (-;-nen) dreamer

träumerisch ['trɔɪmərɪʃ] *adj* dreamy; absent-minded

Traum′gesicht *n* vision, phantom

traum′haft *adj* dream-like

traurig ['traurɪç] *adj* sad

Trau′ring *m* wedding ring (or band)

Trau'schein *m* marriage certificate

traut [traut] *adj* dear; cozy; intimate

Trau'ung *f* (-;-en) marriage ceremony; **kirchliche T.** church wedding; **standesamtliche T.** civil ceremony

Trau'zeuge *m* best man

Trecker [trɛkər] *m* (-s;-) tractor

Treff [trɛf] *n* (-s;-s) (cards) club(s)

treffen [trɛfən] §151 *tr* hit; (*begegnen*) meet; (*betreffen*) concern || *ref* meet; assemble; **sich t. mit** meet with || *intr* hit home; (box) land, connect || **Treffen** *n* (-s;-) meeting; (mil) encounter; (sport) meet

tref'fend *adj* pertinent; to the point; (*Ähnlichkeit*) striking

Tref'fer *m* (-s;-) hit; winner; prize

treff'lich *adj* excellent

Treff'punkt *m* rendezvous, meeting place

Treib- [traip] *comb.fm.* moving; driving

treiben [traibən] §62 *tr* drive; propel; chase, expel; (*Beruf*) pursue; (*Blätter*, *Blüten*) put forth; (*Geschäft*) run, carry on; (*Metall*) work; (*Musik*, *Sport*) go in for; (*Sprachen*) study; (*Pflanzen*) force; **es zu weit t.** go too far; **was treibst du denn?** (coll) what are you doing? || *intr* blossom; sprout; (*Teig*) ferment || *intr* (SEIN) drift, float || **Treiben** *n* (-s;) doings, activity; drifting, floating

Treib'haus *n* hothouse

Treib'holz *n* driftwood

Treib'kraft *f* driving force

Treib'mine *f* floating mine

Treib'rakete *f* booster rocket

Treib'riemen *m* drive belt

Treib'sand *m* drifting sand; quicksand

Treib'stange *f* connecting rod

Treib'stoff *m* fuel; propellant

Treib'stoffbehälter *m* fuel tank

trennbar [trɛnbar] *adj* separable

trennen [trɛnən] *tr* separate; sever; (*Naht*) undo; (*Ehe*) dissolve; (elec, telp) cut off || *ref* part; separate; (*Weg*) branch off

Tren'nung *f* (-;-en) separation; parting; dissolution

Tren'nungsstrich *m* dividing line; hyphen

Trense [trɛnzə] *f* (-;-n) snaffle

Treppe [trɛpə] *f* (-;-n) stairs, stairway; flight of stairs; **die T. hinauffallen** (coll) be kicked upstairs; **zwei Treppen hoch wohnen** live two flights up

Trep'penabsatz *m* landing

Trep'penflucht *f* flight of stairs

Trep'pengeländer *n* banister

Trep'penhaus *n* staircase

Trep'penläufer *m* stair carpet

Trep'penstufe *f* step, stair

Tresor [trɛ'zor] *m* (-s;-e) safe; vault

Tresse [trɛsə] *f* (-;-n) (mil) stripe

treten [tretən] §152 *tr* tread; tread on; trample; (*Fußhebel*) work; (*Orgel*) pump; **mit Füßen t.** (fig) trample under foot || *intr* (SEIN) step, walk; tread; **an j-s Stelle t.** succeed s.o.; **auf der Stelle t.** (mil) mark time; **in**

Kraft t. go into effect; **j–m zu nahe t.** offend s.o.; **t. in** (*acc*) enter (into)

Tretmühle [tretmylə] *f* treadmill

treu [trɔɪ] *adj* loyal, faithful, true

Treu'bruch *m* breach of faith

Treue [trɔɪ·ə] *f* (–;) loyalty, fidelity; allegiance; **j–m die T. halten** remain loyal to s.o.

Treu'eid *m* oath of allegiance

Treu'hand *f* (jur) trust

Treuhänder –in [trɔɪhɛndər(m)] §6 *mf* trustee

Treu'handfonds *m* trust fund

treu'herzig *adj* trusting; sincere

treu'los *adj* unfaithful; (gegen) disloyal (to)

Tribüne [tri'bynə] *f* (–;-n) rostrum; (mil) reviewing stand; (sport) grandstand

Tribut [tri'but] *m* (-[e]s;-e) tribute

Trichter [trɪçtər] *m* (-s;-) funnel; (*Bomben–*) crater, pothole; (mus) bell (*of wind instrument*); **auf den T. kommen** (coll) catch on

Trick [trɪk] *m* (-s;-s & -e) trick

Trick'film *m* animated cartoon

trieb [trip] *pret of* **treiben** || **Trieb** *m* (-[e]s;-e) sprout, shoot; urge, drive; instinct

Trieb'feder *f* (horol) mainspring

Trieb'kraft *f* motive power

trieb'mäßig *adj* instinctive

Trieb'werk *n* motor, engine

triefäugig [trifɔɪgɪç] *adj* bleary-eyed

triefen [trifən] §153 *intr* drip; (*Augen*) water; (*Nase*) run

triezen [tritsən] *tr* (coll) tease

Trift [trɪft] *f* (–;-en) pasture land; cattle track; log-running

triftig [trɪftɪç] *adj* cogent; valid

Trigonometrie [trigonome'tri] *f* (–;) trigonometry

Trikot [tri'ko] *m* & *n* (-s;-s) knitted cloth; (sport) trunks, tights

Triller [trɪlər] *m* (-s;-) trill; (mus) quaver

trillern [trɪlərn] *intr* trill; (*Vogel*) warble

Tril'lerpfeife *f* whistle

Trink- [trɪŋk] *comb.fm.* drinking

trinkbar [trɪŋkbar] *adj* drinkable

Trink'becher *m* drinking cup

trinken [trɪŋkən] §143 *tr* & *intr* drink

Trin'ker –in §6 *mf* drinker

trink'fest *adj* able to hold one's liquor

Trink'gelage *n* drinking party

Trink'geld *n* tip, gratuity

Trink'glas *n* drinking glass

Trink'halm *m* straw

Trink'spruch *m* toast

Trink'wasser *n* drinking water

Trio [tri·o] *n* (-s;-s) trio

trippeln [trɪpəln] *intr* (SEIN) patter

Tripper [trɪpər] *m* (-s;) gonorrhea

trist [trɪst] *adj* dreary

tritt [trɪt] *pret of* **treten** || *m* (-[e]s; -e) step; kick; pace; footstep; footprint; small stepladder; pedal; **j–m e–n T. versetzen** give s.o. a kick

Tritt'brett *n* running board

Tritt'leiter *f* stepladder

Triumph [tri'umf] *m* (-[e]s;-e) triumph

Triumph′bogen m triumphal arch

triumphieren [trɪ·um′fi:rən] intr triumph

Triumph′zug m triumphal procession

trocken [′trɔkən] adj dry; arid; **trokkenes Brot** plain bread

Trockenbagger (**Trok′kenbagger**) m (mach) excavator

Trockendock (**Trok′kendock**) n drydock

Trockenei (**Trok′kenei**) n dehydrated eggs

Trockeneis (**Trok′keneis**) n dry ice

Trockenhaube (**Trok′kenhaube**) f hair drier

Trockenheit (**Trok′kenheit**) f (–;) dryness, aridity

trockenlegen (**trok′kenlegen**) tr (Sumpf) drain; (Säugling) change (the diapers of)

Trockenmaß (**Trok′kenmaß**) n dry measure

Trockenmilch (**Trok′kenmilch**) f powdered milk

Trockenschleuder (**Trok′kenschleuder**) f spin-drier, clothes drier

Trockenübung (**Trok′kenübung**) f dry run

trocknen [′trɔknən] tr dry || intr (SEIN) dry, dry up

Troddel [′trɔdəl] f (–;–n) tassel

Trödel [′trø:dəl] m (–s;) secondhand goods; old clothes; junk; (fig) nuisance, waste of time

Trö′delkram m junk

trödeln [′trø:dəln] intr waste time

Tröd′ler –in §6 mf secondhand dealer

troff [trɔf] pret of triefen

trog [tro:k] pret of trügen **Trog** m (–[e]s;ːe) trough

Trommel [′trɔməl] f (–;–n) drum

Trom′melfell n drumhead; (anat) eardrum

trommeln [′trɔməln] tr & intr drum

Trom′melschlag m drumbeat

Trom′melschlegel m, **Trom′melstock** m drumstick

Trom′melwirbel m drum roll

Trommler [′trɔmlər] m (–s;–) drummer

Trompete [trɔm′pe:tə] f (–;–n) trumpet

trompeten [trɔm′pe:tən] intr blow the trumpet; (Elefant) trumpet

Trompe′ter –in §6 mf trumpeter

Tropen [′tro:pən] pl tropics

Tropf [trɔpf] m (–[e]s;ːe) simpleton; **armer T.** poor devil

tröpfeln [′trœpfəln] tr & intr drip || intr (SEIN) trickle || impers—es **tröpfelt** it is sprinkling

tropfen [′trɔpfən] tr & intr drip || intr (SEIN) trickle || m **Tropfen** m (–s;–) drop; **ein T. auf den heißen Stein** a drop in the bucket

trop′fenweise adv drop by drop

Trophäe [tro′fɛ:ə] f (–;–n) trophy

tropisch [′tro:pɪʃ] adj tropical

Troß [trɔs] m (Trosses; Trosse) (coll) load, baggage; (coll) hangers-on

Trosse [′trɔsə] f (–;–n) cable; (naut) hawser

Trost [tro:st] m (–es;) consolation, comfort; **geringer T.** cold comfort;

wohl nicht bei T. sein not be all there

trösten [′trø:stən] tr console, comfort || ref cheer up; feel consoled

tröstlich [′trø:stlɪç] adj comforting

trost′los adj disconsolate; bleak

Trost′preis m consolation prize

trost′reich adj comforting

Trö′stung f (–;–en) consolation

Trott [trɔt] m (–[e]s;ːe) trot; (coll) routine

Trottel [′trɔtəl] m (–s;–) (coll) dope

trotten [′trɔtən] intr (SEIN) trot

Trottoir [trɔ′twar] n (–s;–e & –s) sidewalk

trotz [trɔts] prep (genit) in spite of; **t. alledem** for all that || **Trotz** m (–es;) defiance; **j–m T. bieten** defy s.o.

trotz′dem adv nevertheless || conj although

trotzen [′trɔtsən] intr be stubborn; (schmollen) sulk; (dat) defy

trotzig [′trɔtsɪç] adj defiant; sulky; obstinate

Trotz′kopf m defiant child (or adult)

trüb [try:p], **trübe** [′try:bə] adj turbid, muddy; (Wetter) dreary; (glanzlos) dull; (Erfahrung) sad

Trubel [′tru:bəl] m (–s;) bustle

trüben [′try:bən] tr make turbid, muddy; dim; dull; disturb, trouble (Freude, Stimmung) spoil || ref grow cloudy; become muddy; become strained

Trübsal [′try:pzal] f (–;–en) distress, misery; **T. blasen** be in the dumps

trüb′selig adj gloomy, sad

Trüb′sinn m (–[e]s;) gloom

trüb′sinnig adj gloomy

Trü′bung f (–;) muddiness; blurring

trudeln [′tru:dəln] intr go into a spin || **Trudeln** n (–s;) spin; **ins T. kommen** (aer) go into a spin

trug [tru:k] pret of tragen || **Trug** m (–[e]s;) deceit; fraud; delusion

Trug′bild n phantom; illusion

trügen [′try:gən] §111 tr & intr deceive

trügerisch [′try:gərɪʃ] adj deceptive, illusory; (verräterisch) treacherous

Trug′schluß m fallacy

Truhe [′tru:ə] f (–;–n) trunk, chest

Trulle [′trulə] f (–;–n) slut

Trümmer [′trymər] pl ruins; rubble

Trumpf [trumpf] m (–[e]s;ːe) trump

Trunk [truŋk] m (–[e]s;ːe) drinking; **im T.** when drunk

trunken [′truŋkən] adj drunk; **t. vor** (dat) elated with

Trunkenbold [′truŋkənbɔlt] m (–[e]s; –e) drunkard

Trun′kenheit f (–;) drunkenness; **T. am Steuer** (jur) drunken driving

trunk′süchtig adj alcoholic || **Trunksüchtige** §5 mf alcoholic

Trupp [trup] m (–s;–s) troop, gang; (mil) detail, detachment

Truppe [′trupə] f (–;–n) (mil) troop; (theat) troupe; **Truppen** (mil) troops

Trup′peneinheit f unit

Trup′penersatz m reserves

Trup′pengattung f branch of service

Trup′penschau f (mil) review, parade

Trup'pentransporter *m* (aer) troop carrier; (nav) troopship
Trüp'penübung *f* field exercise
Trup'penverband *m* unit; task force
Trup'penverbandplatz *m* (mil) first-aid station
Trust [trʊst] *m* (-[e]s;-e & -s) (com) trust
Truthahn ['truthan] *m* turkey (cock)
Truthenne ['truthenə] *f* turkey (hen)
trutzig ['trʊtsɪç] *adj* defiant
Tscheche ['t/eçə] *m* (-n;-n), **Tschechin** ['t/eçɪn] *f* (-;-nen) Czech
tschechisch ['t/eçɪʃ] *adj* Czech
Tschechoslowakei [t/eçɔslɔva'kaɪ] *f* (-;)—**die T.** Czechoslovakia
Tube ['tubə] *f* (-;-n) tube; **auf die T. drücken** (aut) step on it
Tuberkulose [tuberku'lozə] *f* (-;) tuberculosis
Tuch [tux] *n* (-[e]s;-e) cloth; fabric || *n* (-[e]s;-̈er) kerchief; shawl; scarf
tuchen ['tuxən] *adj* cloth, fabric
Tuch'fühlung *f*—**T. haben mit** (mil) stand shoulder to shoulder with; **T. halten mit** keep in close touch with
Tuch'seite *f* right side (*of cloth*)
tüchtig ['tʏçtɪç] *adj* able, capable, efficient; sound, thorough; excellent; good; (*Trinker*) hard; **t. in** (*dat*) good at; **t. zu** qualified for || *adv* very much; hard; soundly, throughly; (sl) awfully
Tüch'tigkeit *f* (-;) ability, efficiency; soundness, thoroughness; excellency
Tuch'waren *pl* dry goods
Tücke ['tʏkə] *f* (-;-n) malice; **mit List und T.** by cleverness
tückisch ['tʏkɪʃ] *adj* insidious
tüfteln ['tʏftəln] *intr*—**t. an** (*dat*) (coll) puzzle over
Tugend ['tugənt] *f* (-;-en) virtue
Tugendbold ['tugəntbɔlt] *m* (-[e]s;-e) (pej) paragon of virtue
tu'gendhaft *adj* virtuous
Tulpe ['tʊlpə] *f* (-;-n) tulip
tummeln ['tʊməln] *tr* (*Pferd*) exercise || *ref* hurry; (*Kinder*) romp about
Tum'melplatz *m* playground; (fig) arena
Tümmler ['tʏmlər] *m* (-s;-) dolphin; (*Taube*) tumbler
Tumor ['tumɔr] *m* (-s; **Tumoren** [tu'morən]) tumor
Tümpel ['tʏmpəl] *m* (-s;-) pond
Tumult [tu'mʊlt] *m* (-[e]s;-e) uproar; uprising
tun [tun] §154 *tr* do; make; take; **dazu tun** add to it; **e-n Zug tun** take a swig; **es zu tun bekommen mit** have trouble with; **j-n in ein Internat tun** send s.o. to a boarding school || *intr* do; be busy; **alle Hände voll zu tun haben** have one's hands full; **es ist mir darum zu tun I** am anxious about it; **groß tun** talk big; **mir ist sehr darum zu tun zu** (*inf*) it is very important for me to (*inf*); **nur so tun, als ob** pretend that; **spröde tun** be prudish; **stolz tun** be proud; **weh tun** hurt; **zu t. haben** be busy; have one's work cut out; **zu tun haben mit** have trouble with || *impers*—**es tut mir**

leid I am sorry; **es tut nichts** it doesn't matter || **Tun** *n* (-s;) doings; action; **Tun und Treiben** doings
Tünche ['tʏnçə] *f* (-;-n) whitewash
tünchen ['tʏnçən] *tr* whitewash
Tunichtgut ['tunɪçtgut] *m* (- & -[e]s; -e) good-for-nothing
Tunke ['tʊŋkə] *f* (-;-n) sauce; gravy
tunken ['tʊŋkən] *tr* dip, dunk
tunlichst ['tunlɪçst] *adv*—**das wirst du t. bleiben lassen** you had better leave it alone
Tunnel ['tʊnəl] *m* (-s;- & -s) tunnel
Tüpfchen ['tʏpfçən] *n* (-s;-) dot
Tüpfel ['tʏpfəl] *m & n* (-s;-) dot
tüpfen ['tʏpfən] *tr* dab; dot || **Tupfen** *m* (-s;-) dot, spot
Tür [tyr] *f* (-;-en) door
Tür'angel *f* door hinge
Tür'anschlag *m* doorstop
Turbine [tur'binə] *f* (-;-n) turbine
Turboprop ['turbɔprɔp] *m* (-s;-s) turboprop
Tür'drücker *m* latch
Tür'flügel *m* door (*of double door*)
Tür'griff *m* door handle; door knob
Türke ['tʏrkə] *m* (-n;-n) Turk
Türkei [tyr'kaɪ] *f* (-;)—**die T.** Turkey
Türkin ['tʏrkɪn] *f* (-;-nen) Turk
Türkis [tyr'kis] *m* (-es;-e) turquoise
türkisch ['tʏrkɪʃ] *adj* Turkish
türkisen [tyr'kizən] *adj* turquoise
Tür'klingel *f* doorbell
Tür'klinke *f* door handle
Turm [turm] *m* (-[e]s;-̈e) tower; steeple; turret; (chess) castle
Türmchen ['tʏrmçən] *n* (-s;-) turret
türmen ['tʏrmən] *tr & ref* pile up || *intr* (SEIN) run away, bolt
turm'hoch *adj* towering || *adv* (by) far
Turm'spitze *f* spire
Turm'springen *n* high diving
Turn- [turn] *comb.fm.* gymnastic, gym, athletic
turnen ['turnən] *intr* do exercises || **Turnen** *n* (-s;) gymnastics
Tur'ner –in §6 *mf* gymnast
turnerisch ['turnərɪʃ] *adj* gymnastic
Turn'gerät *n* gymnastic apparatus
Turn'halle *f* gymnasium, gym
Turn'hemd *n* gym shirt
Turn'hose *f* trunks
Turnier [tur'nir] *n* (-s;-e) tournament
Turn'schuhe *pl* sneakers
Tür'pfosten *m* doorpost
Tür'rahmen *m* doorframe
Tür'schild *n* doorplate
Tür'schwelle *f* threshold
Tusche ['tu/ə] *f* (-;-n) (paint) wash; **chinesische T.** India ink
tuscheln ['tu/əln] *intr* whisper
Tute ['tutə] *f* (-;-n) (aut) horn
Tüte ['tytə] *f* (-;-n) paper bag; paper cone; ice cream cone
tuten ['tutən] *intr* blow the horn; (coll) blare away
Twen [tven] *m* (-s;-s) young man (*in his twenties*)
Typ [typ] *m* (-s;-en) type; (*Bauart*) model
Type ['typə] *f* (-;-n) type; (coll) strange character
Ty'pennummer *f* model number

Typhus ['tyfʊs] *m* (–;) typhoid
typisch ['typɪ] *adj* (für) typical (of)
Tyrann [ty'ran] *m* (–en;–en) tyrant
Tyrannei [tyra'naɪ] *f* (–;–en) tyranny

tyrannisch [ty'ranɪʃ] *adj* tyrannical
tyrannisieren [tyranɪ'zirən] *tr* tyrannize, oppress
Tz ['tetset] *n*—**bis ins Tz** thoroughly

U

U, u [u] *invar n* U, u
u.A.w.g. *abbr* (**um Antwort wird gebeten**) R.S.V.P.
U-Bahn ['uban] *f* (**Untergrundbahn**) subway
übel ['ybəl] *adj* evil; (*schlecht*) bad; (*unwohl*) queasy, sick; (*Geruch, usw.*) nasty, foul; **er ist ein übler Geselle** he's a bad egg; **mir ist ü.** I feel sick; **ü. daran sein** have it rough || *adv* badly; **est steht ü. mit** things don't look good for; **ü. auslegen** misconstrue; **ü. deuten** misinterpret; **ü. ergehen** fare badly; **ü. gelaunt** in bad humor || **Übel** *n* (–s;–) evil; ailment
ü'belgelaunt *adj* ill-humored
ü'belgesinnt *adj* evil-minded
Ü'belkeit *f* (–;) nausea
ü'belnehmen §116 *tr* take amiss; take offense at, resent
ü'belnehmend *adj* resentful
ü'belriechend *adj* foul-smelling
Ü'belstand *m* evil; bad state of affairs
Ü'beltat *f* misdeed, crime, offense
Ü'beltäter **–in** §6 *mf* wrongdoer; criminal
ü'belwollen §162 *intr* (*dat*) be ill-disposed towards || **Übelwollen** *n* (–s;) ill will, malevolence
ü'belwollend *adj* malevolent
üben ['ybən] *tr* practice, exercise; (*e–e Kunst*) cultivate; (*Handwerk*) pursue; (*Gewalt*) use; (*Verrat*) commit; (mil) drill; (sport) train; **Barmherzigkeit ü. an** (*dat*) have mercy on; **Gerechtigkeit ü. gegen** be fair to; **Nachsicht ü. gegen** be lenient towards; **Rache ü. an** (*dat*) take revenge on || *ref*—**sich im Schifahren ü.** practice skiing
über ['ybər] *adv*—**j–m ü. sein in** (*dat*) be superior to s.o. in; **ü. und ü.** over and over || *prep* (*dat*) over; above, on top of || *prep* (*acc*) by way of, via; (*bei, während*) during; (*nach*) past; over; across; (*betreffend*) about, concerning; **Briefe ü. Briefe** letter after letter; **ein Scheck ü. 10 DM** a check for 10 marks; **es geht nichts ü.** there is nothing better than; **heute übers Jahr** a year from today; **ü. Gebühr** more than was due; **ü. kurz oder lang** sooner or later; **ü. Land** crosscountry
überall' *adv* everywhere, all over
überallher' *adv* from all sides
überallhin' *adv* in every direction
Ü'berangebot *n* over-supply
überan'strengen *tr* overexert, strain || *ref* overexert oneself, strain oneself

überar'beiten *tr* revise, touch up || *ref*—**sich ü.** overwork oneself
Überar'beitung *f* (–;–en) revision, touching up; revised text
ü'beraus *adv* extremely, very
überbacken (überbak'ken) §50 *tr* bake lightly
Ü'berbau *m* (–[e]s; –e & –ten [tən]) superstructure
ü'berbeanspruchen *tr* overwork
ü'berbelasten *tr* overload
ü'berbelegt *adj* overcrowded
ü'berbelichten *tr* (phot) overexpose
ü'berbetonen *tr* overemphasize
überbie'ten §58 *tr* outbid; (fig) outdo
Überbleibsel ['ybərblaɪpsəl] *n* (–s;–) remains; leftovers
Überblen'dung *f* (cin) dissolve
Ü'berblick *m* survey; (fig) synopsis
überblicken (überblik'ken) *tr* survey
überbrin'gen §65 *tr* deliver; convey
Überbrin'ger **–in** §6 *mf* bearer
überbrücken (überbrük'ken) *tr* (& fig) bridge
Überbrückung (Überbrük'kung) *f* (–; –en) bridging; (rr) overpass
Überbrückungs– *comb.fm.* emergency, stop-gap
überdachen [ybər'daxən] *tr* roof over
überdau'ern *tr* outlast
überdecken (überdek'ken) *tr* cover
überdies' *adv* moreover, besides
überden'ken §66 *tr* think over
überdre'hen *tr* (Uhr) overwind
Ü'berdruck *m* excess pressure
Ü'berdruckanzug *m* space suit
Ü'berdruckkabine *f* pressurized cabin
Über'druß ['ybərdrʊs] *m* (–drusses;) boredom; (*Übersättigung*) satiety; (*Ekel*) disgust; **bis zum Ü.** ad nauseam
überdrüssig ['ybərdrʏsɪç] *adj* (*genit*) sick of, disgusted with
ü'berdurchschnittlich *adj* above the average
Ü'bereifer *m* excessive zeal
ü'bereifrig *adj* overzealous
überei'len *tr* precipitate; rush || *ref* be in too big a hurry; act rashly
übereilt [ybər'aɪlt] *adj* hasty, rash
übereinan'der *adv* one on top of the other
übereinan'derschlagen §132 *tr* cross
überein'kommen §99 *intr* (SEIN) come to an agreement || **Übereinkommen** *n* (–s;–) agreement
Überein'kunft *f* agreement
überein'stimmen *intr* be in agreement; concur; (Farben, usw.) harmonize
Überein'stimmung *f* agreement; accord; (*Gleichförmigkeit*) conformity;

(*Einklang*) harmony; **in Ü. mit** in line with

ü'berempfindlich *adj* oversensitive

überfah'ren §71 *tr* run over, run down; (*Fluß, usw.*) cross; **ein Signal ü.** go through a traffic light; **ü. werden** (coll) be taken in || **ü'berfahren** §71 *tr* (*über e-n Fluß, usw.*) take across || *intr* (SEIN) drive over, cross

Ü'berfahrt *f* crossing

Ü'berfall *m* surprise attack, assault; (*Raubüberfall*) holdup; (*Einfall*) raid

überfal'len §72 *tr* (*räuberisch*) hold up; assault; (mil) surprise; (mil) invade, raid; **ü. werden** be overcome (*by sleep*); be seized (*with fear*)

ü'berfällig *adj* overdue

Ü'berfallkommando *n* riot squad

überflie'gen §57 *tr* fly over; (*Buch*) skim through

ü'berfließen §76 *intr* (SEIN) overflow

überflügeln [ybər'flygəln] *tr* outflank; (fig) outstrip

ü'berflüssig *adj* superfluous

überflu'ten *tr* overflow, flood, swamp || **ü'berfluten** *intr* (SEIN) overflow

überfor'dern *tr* demand too much of; overwork

Ü'berfracht *f* excess luggage

ü'berführen *tr* carry across; (*Leiche*) transport in state || **überfüh'ren** *tr* (genit) convince of; (genit) convict of

Überfüh'rung *f* (–;–en) overpass; (*e–s Verbrechers*) conviction

Ü'berfülle *f* superabundance

überfül'len *tr* stuff, jam, pack

Ü'bergabe *f* delivery; (& mil) surrender

Ü'bergang *m* passage; crossing; transition; (jur) transfer; (mil) desertion; (paint) blending; (rr) crossing

Ü'bergangsbeihilfe *f* severance pay

Ü'bergangsstadium *n* transition stage

Ü'bergangszeit *f* transitional period

überge'ben §80 *tr* hand over; give up; (*einreichen*) submit; (& mil) surrender; **dem Verkehr ü.** open to traffic || *ref* vomit, throw up

überge'hen §82 *tr* omit; overlook; **mit Stillschweigen ü.** pass over in silence || **ü'bergehen** §82 *intr* (SEIN) go over, cross; (*sich verändern*) (**in** *acc*) change (into); **auf j–n ü.** devolve upon s.o.; **in andere Hände ü.** change hands; **in Fäulnis ü.** become rotten

Ü'bergewicht *n* overweight; (fig) preponderance; **das Ü. bekommen** become top-heavy; (fig) get the upper hand

übergießen §76 *tr* spill || **übergie'ßen** §76 *tr* pour over, pour on; (*Braten*) baste; **mit Zuckerguß ü.** (culin) ice

übergreifen §88 *intr* (**auf** *acc*) spread (to); (**auf** *acc*) encroach (on)

Ü'bergriff *m* encroachment

ü'bergroß *adj* huge, colossal; oversize

ü'berhaben §89 *tr* have left; (*Kleider*) have on; (fig) be fed up with

überhand'nehmen §116 *intr* get the upper hand; run riot

ü'berhängen §92 *tr* (*Mantel*) put on;

(*Gewehr*) sling over the shoulders || *intr* overhang, project

überhäu'fen *tr* overwhelm, swamp

überhaupt' *adv* really; anyhow; (*besonders*) especially; (*überdies*) besides; at all; **ü. kein** no...whatever; **ü. nicht** not at all; **wenn ü. if...at** all; **if...really**

überheblich [ybər'heplıç] *adj* arrogant

überhei'zen, überzhit'zen *tr* overheat

überhöhen [ybər'hø·ən] *tr* (*Kurve*) bank; (*Preise*) raise too high

ü'berholen *tr* take across; **die Segel ü.** shift sails || *intr* (naut) heel || **überho'len** *tr* outdistance, outrun; (*ausbessern*) overhaul; (*Fahrzeug*) pass; (fig) outstrip

überholt [ybər'hɔlt] *adj* obsolete, out of date; (*repariert*) reconditioned

überhö'ren *tr* not hear, miss; ignore; misunderstand

ü'berirdisch *adj* supernatural

überkandidelt ['ybərkandidəlt] *adj* (coll) nutty, wacky

ü'berkippen *intr* (SEIN) tilt over

überkle'ben *tr* paper over; **ü. mit** cover with

Ü'berkleid *n* outer garment; overalls

ü'berklug *adj* (pej) wise, smart

ü'berkochen *intr* (SEIN) boil over

überkom'men *adj* traditional || §99 *tr* overcome || *intr* (SEIN) be handed down to

überla'den *adj* overdone || §103 *tr* overload

Ü'berlandbahn *f* interurban trolley line

Ü'berlandleitung *f* (elec) high-tension line; (telp) long-distance line

überlas'sen §104 *tr* yield, leave, relinquish; entrust; (com) sell; **das bleibt ihm ü.** he is free to do as he pleases || *ref* (*dat*) give way to

Ü'berlast *f* overload; overweight

ü'berla'sten *tr* overload

überlau'fen *adj* overcrowded; (fig) swamped || §105 *tr* overrun; (*belästigen*) pester; **Angst überlief ihn** fear came over him || **ü'berlaufen** §105 *intr* (SEIN) run over, overflow; boil over; (fig & mil) desert; **die Galle läuft mir über** (fig) my blood boils || *impers*—**mich überläuft es kalt** I shudder

Ü'berläufer –in §6 *mf* (mil) deserter; (pol) turncoat

ü'berlaut *adj* too noisy

überle'ben *tr* outlive, survive || *ref* go out of style

überle'bend *adj* surviving || **Überlebende** §5 *mf* survivor

ü'berlebensgroß *adj* bigger than life

überlebt [ybər'lept] *adj* antiquated

überle'gen *adj* (dat) superior (to); (an *dat*) superior (in) || *tr* consider, think over || *ref—sich* [*dat*] **anders ü.** change one's mind; **sich** [*dat*] **ü.** consider, think over || *intr* think it over || **ü'berlegen** *tr* lay across; (*Mantel*) put on

Überle'genheit *f* (–;) superiority

überlegt' *adj* well considered; (jur) willful

Überle′gung f (–;–en) consideration
überle′sen §107 tr read over, peruse
überlie′fern tr deliver; hand down, transmit; (mil) surrender
Überlie′ferung f (–;–en) delivery; (fig) tradition; (mil) surrender
überli′sten tr outwit, outsmart
überma′chen tr bequeath
U′bermacht f superiority; (fig) predominance
ü′bermächtig adj overwhelming; predominant
überma′len tr paint over
übermannen [ybər′manən] tr overpower
U′bermaß n excess; **bis zum U.** to excess
ü′bermäßig adj excessive ‖ adv excessively; overly
U′bermensch m superman
ü′bermenschlich adj superhuman
übermitteln [ybər′mɪtəln] tr transmit, convey, forward
Übermitt′lung f (–;–en) transmission, conveyance, forwarding
ü′bermorgen adv the day after tomorrow
übermüdet [ybər′mydət] adj overtired
U′bermut m exuberance, mischievousness
übermütig adj exuberant; haughty
ü′bernächste §9 adj next but one; **am übernächsten Tag** the day after tomorrow; **ü. Woche** week after next
übernach′ten intr spend the night
Übernach′tung f (–;–en) accommodations for the night; spending the night
U′bernahme f taking over, takeover
ü′bernatürlich adj supernatural
überneh′men §116 tr take over; assume; undertake; take upon oneself; accept, receive ‖ **ü′bernehmen** §116 tr (Mantel, Schal) put on; (Gewehr) shoulder ‖ **überneh′men** §116 ref overreach oneself; **sich beim Essen ü.** overeat
ü′berordnen tr place over, set over
ü′berparteilich adj nonpartisan
U′berproduktion f overproduction
überprü′fen tr examine again, check; verify; (Personen) screen
Überprü′fung f (–;–en) checking; checkup
ü′berquellen §119 intr (SEIN) (Teig) run over; **überquellende Freude** irrepressible joy
überqueren [ybər′kverən] tr cross
überra′gen tr tower over; (fig) surpass
überraschen [ybər′ra/ən] tr surprise
Überra′schung f (–;–en) surprise
überrech′nen tr count over
überre′den tr persuade; **j-n zu etw ü.** talk a person into s.th.
Überre′dung f (–;–en) persuasion
ü′berreich adj (an dat) abounding (in) ‖ adv–**ü. ausgestattet** well equipped
überrei′chen tr hand over, present
ü′berreichlich adj superabundant
ü′berreif adj overripe
überrei′zen tr overexcite; (Augen, Nerven) strain
überreizt′ adj overwrought

überren′nen §97 tr overrun; (fig) overwhelm
U′berrest m rest, remainder; **irdische Überreste** mortal remains
U′berrock m topcoat, overcoat
überrum′peln tr take by surprise
Überrum′pelung f (–;–en) surprise
überrun′den tr (sport) lap
übersät [ybər′zet] adj (fig) strewn, dotted
übersät′tigen tr stuff; cloy; (chem) saturate, supersaturate
Übersät′tigung f (chem) supersaturation
Überschall– comb.fm. supersonic
überschat′ten tr overshadow
überschät′zen tr overestimate
U′berschau f survey
überschau′en tr look over, survey; overlook (a scene)
überschla′fen §131 tr (fig) sleep on
U′berschlag m rough estimate; (aer) loop; (gym) somersault
überschla′gen adj lukewarm ‖ §132 tr skip, omit; estimate roughly; consider ‖ ref go head over heels; do a somersault; (Auto) overturn; (Boot) capsize; (Flugzeug) do a loop; (beim Landen) turn over; (Stimme) break; (fig) (vor dat) outdo oneself (in) ‖ **ü′berschlagen** §132 tr (Beine) cross; flip over; (es) **ü. in** (acc) (fig) change suddenly to
ü′berschnappen intr (SEIN) (Stimme) squeak; (coll) flip one's lid
überschnei′den §106 ref (Linien) intersect; (& fig) overlap
überschrei′ben §62 tr sign over
überschrei′en §135 tr shout down ‖ ref strain one's voice
überschrei′ten §86 tr cross, step over; (Kredit) overdraw; (Gesetz) violate, transgress; (fig) exceed, overstep
U′berschrift f heading, title
U′berschuh m overshoe
U′berschuß m surplus, excess; profit
ü′berschüssig adj surplus, excess
überschüt′ten tr shower; (& fig) overwhelm, flood
Überschwang′ m (–[e]s;) rapture
überschwem′men tr flood, inundate
Überschwem′mung f (–;–en) flood, inundation
überschwenglich [′ybər/venlɪç] adj effusive, gushing
Übersee′ f (–;) overseas
U′berseedampfer m ocean liner
U′berseehandel m overseas trade
übersehbar [ybər′zebar] adj visible at a glance
überse′hen §138 tr survey, look over; (nicht bemerken) overlook; (absichtlich) ignore; (erkennen) realize
übersen′den §140 tr send, forward; transmit; (Geld) remit
Übersen′dung f (–;–en) forwarding; transmission; consignment
ü′bersetzen tr ferry across ‖ **übersetz′zen** tr translate
Überset′zung f (–;–en) translation; (mach) gear, transmission
U′bersicht f survey, review; (Abriß) abstract; (Zusammenfassung) sum-

mary; (*Umriß*) outline; (*Ausblick*) perspective; **jede Ü. verlieren** lose all perspective

ü'bersichtlich *adj* clear; (*Gelände*) open

Ü'bersichtsplan *m* general plan

ü'bersiedeln *intr* (SEIN) move; emigrate

ü'bersinnlich *adj* transcendental

überspan'nen *tr* span; cover; overstrain; (fig) exaggerate

überspannt [ybər'/pant] *adj* eccentric; extravagant

Überspannt'heit *f* (-;-en) eccentricity

Überspan'nung *f* (-;-en) overstraining; (fig) exaggeration; (elec) excess voltage

überspie'len *tr* outplay; outwit; (*Tonbandaufnahme*) transcribe; (*Schüchternheit*) hide

überspitzt [ybər'/pItst] *adj* oversubtle

übersprin'gen §142 *tr* jump; (*auslassen*) omit, skip || **ü'berspringen** §142 *intr* (SEIN) jump

ü'bersprudeln *intr* (SEIN) bubble over

ü'berständig *adj* leftover; (*Bier*) flat; (*Obst*) overripe

überste'hen §146 *tr* stand, endure; (*Krankheit, usw.*) get over; (*Operation*) pull through; (*überleben*) survive || **ü'berstehen** §146 *intr* jut out

übersteig'gen §148 *tr* climb over; (*Hindernisse*) overcome; (*Erwartungen*) exceed || **ü'bersteigen** §148 *intr* (SEIN) step over

überstim'men *tr* vote down, defeat

überstrah'len *tr* shine upon; (*verdunkeln*) outshine, eclipse

überstrei'chen §85 *tr* paint over

ü'berstreifen *tr* slip on

überströ'men *tr* flood, inundate || **ü'berströmen** *intr* (SEIN) overflow

Ü'berstunde *f* hour of overtime; **Überstunden machen** work overtime

überstür'zen *tr* rush, hurry || *ref* be in too big a hurry; act rashly; (*Ereignisse*) follow one another rapidly

überstürzt [ybər'/tyrtst] *adj* hasty

überteuern [ybər'tɔɪ-ərn] *tr* overcharge

übertölpeln [ybər'tœpəln] *tr* dupe

übertö'nen *tr* drown out

Übertrag ['ybərtrak] *m* (-[e]s;-̈e) (acct) carryover, balance

übertragbar [ybər'trakbar] *adj* transferable; (pathol) contagious

übertra'gen *adj* figurative, metaphorical || §132 *tr* carry over, transfer; (*Amt, Titel*) confer; (*Aufgabe*) assign; (*Vollmacht*) delegate; (*Kurzschrift*) transcribe; (**in** acc) translate (into); (acct) transfer; (pathol) spread, communicate; (rad) broadcast, transmit; (*mit Relais*) relay; (telv) televise

Übertra'gung *f* (-;-en) carrying over; transfer; assignment; delegation; conferring; transcription; translation; copy; (pathol) spread; (rad) broadcast; relay; (telv) televising

übertref'fen §151 *tr* surpass, outdo

übertrei'ben §62 *tr* overdo; exaggerate; (theat) overact

Übertrei'bung *f* (-;-en) overdoing; exaggeration; (theat) overacting

übertre'ten §152 *tr* (*Gesetz*) transgress, break || *ref—sich* [*dat*] **den Fuß ü.** sprain one's ankle || **ü'bertreten** §152 *intr* (SEIN) (sport) go off sides; **ü. zu** (fig) go over to; (relig) be converted to

Übertre'tung *f* (-;-en) violation

Ü'bertritt *m* change, going over; (relig) conversion

übervölkern [ybər'fœlkərn] *tr* overpopulate

Übervöl'kerung *f* (-;) overpopulation

ü'bervoll *adj* brimful; crowded

übervorteilen [ybər'fortaɪlən] *tr* take advantage of, get the better of

überwa'chen *tr* watch over; supervise; (*kontrollieren*) inspect, check; (*polizeilich*) shadow; (rad, telv) monitor

Überwa'chung *f* (-;-en) supervision; inspection; control; surveillance

Überwa'chungsausschuß *m* watchdog committee

überwäl'tigen [ybər'vɛltɪgən] *tr* overpower (fig) overwhelm

überwei'sen §118 *tr* (*Geld*) send; (zu e-m Spezialisten) refer

Überwei'sung *f* (-;-en) sending, remittance; referral

ü'berweltlich *adj* otherworldly

ü'berwerfen §160 *tr* throw over || **überwer'fen** §160 *ref* (**mit**) have a run-in (with)

überwie'gen §57 *tr* outweigh || *intr* prevail, preponderate || **Überwiegen** *n* (-s;) prevalence, preponderance

überwie'gend *adj* prevailing; (*Mehrheit*) vast || *adv* predominantly

überwin'den §59 *tr* conquer, overcome || *ref—sich* **ü. zu** (*inf*) bring oneself to (*inf*)

überwintern [ybər'vIntərn] *intr* pass the winter; (bot) survive the winter

überwu'chern *tr* overrun; (fig) stifle

Ü'berwurf *m* wrap; shawl

Ü'berzahl *f* numerical superiority; majority

überzah'len *tr* & *intr* overpay

überzäh'len *tr* count over, recount

überzählig ['ybərtselɪç] *adj* surplus

überzeu'gen *tr* convince || *ref—sich* **ü. Sie sich selbst davon!** go and see for yourself!

Überzeu'gung *f* (-;-en) conviction

überzie'hen §163 *tr* cover; (*mit Farbe*) coat; (*Bett*) put fresh linen on; (*Konto*) overdraw; **ein Land mit Krieg ü.** invade a country || **ü'berziehen** §163 *tr* (*Mantel, usw.*) slip on; **j-m eins ü.** (coll) give s.o. a whack

Ü'berzieher *m* (-s;-) overcoat

überzuckern (überzuk'kern) *tr* (& fig) sugarcoat

Ü'berzug *m* coat, film; (*Decke*) cover; (*Hülle*) case; pillow case; (*Kruste*) crust; (*Schale, Rinde*) skin

üblich ['yplIç] *adj* usual, customary

U'-Boot *n* (Unterseeboot) submarine

U'-Bootbunker *m* submarine pen

U'-Bootjäger *m* (aer) antisubmarine aircraft; (nav) subchaser

U'-Bootortungsgerät *n* sonar

U'-Bootrudel *n* (nav) wolf pack

übrig ['ybrIç] *adj* left (over), remaining, rest (of); **die übrigen** the others, the rest; **ein übriges tun** do more than is necessary; **etw ü. haben für** have a soft spot for; **im übrigen** for the rest, otherwise

ü′brigbehalten §90 *tr* keep, spare

ü′brigbleiben §62 *intr* (SEIN) be left (over) ‖ *impers*—**es blieb mir nichts anderes ü. als zu** (*inf*) I had no choice but to (*inf*)

übrigens [′ybrigəns] *adv* moreover; after all; by the way

ü′briglassen §104 *tr* leave, spare

Übung [′ybuŋ] *f* (-;-en) exercise; practice; (*Gewohnheit*) use; (*Ausbildung*) training; (mil) drill

Ü′bungsbeispiel *n* practical example

Ü′bungsbuch *n* composition book; workbook

Ü′bungsgelände *n* training ground; (*für Bomben*) target area

Ü′bungshang *m* (sport) training slope

Ü′bungsheft *n* composition book; workbook

Ufer [′ufər] *n* (-s;-) (*e-s Flusses*) bank; (*e-s Meers*) shore

U′ferdamm *m* embankment, levee

u′ferlos *adj* fruitless

Uhr [ur] *f* (-;-en) clock; watch; o′clock; **um wieviel Uhr?** at what time; **um zwölf Uhr** at twelve o′clock; **wieviel Uhr ist es?** what time is it?

Uhr′armband *n* (-[e]s;:er) watchband

Uhr′feder *f* watch spring

Uhr′glas *n* watch crystal

Uhr′macher *m* watchmaker

Uhr′werk *n* works, clockwork

Uhr′zeiger *m* hand

Uhr′zeigerrichtung *f*—**entgegen der U.** counterclockwise; **in der U.** clockwise

Uhr′zeigersinn *m*—**in U.** clockwise

Uhu [′uhu] *m* (-s;-s) owl

Ukraine [u′krainə] *f* (-;)—**die U.** the Ukraine

ukrainisch [u′krainiʃ] *adj* Ukrainian

UK-Stellung [u′ka/teluŋ] *f* (-;-en) military deferment

Ulk [ulk] *m* (-[e]s;-e) joke, fun

ulken [′ulkən] *intr* (coll) make fun

ulkig [′ulkıç] *adj* funny

Ulme [′ulmə] *f* (-;-n) elm

Ultima•tum [ulti′matum] *n* (-s;-ten [tən] & -ta [ta]) ultimatum

Ultra-, ultra- [ultra] *comb.fm.* ultra-

Ul′trakurzfrequenz *f* ultrashort frequency

ultramontan [ultramon′tan] *adj* strict Catholic

ul′trarot *adj* infrared

Ultraschall- *comb.fm.* supersonic

ul′traviolett *adj* ultraviolet

um [um] *adv*—**deine Zeit ist um** your time is up; **je. . .um so the. . .the; um so besser** all the better; **um so weniger** all the less; **um und um** round and round ‖ *prep* (*acc*) around, about; for; at; **um die Hälfte mehr** half as much again; **um die Wette laufen** race; **um ein Jahr älter** one year older; **um etw eintauschen** exchange for s.th.; **um jeden Preis** at any price; **um. . .Uhr** at. . .o′clock; **um. . .zu** (*inf*) in order to (*inf*)

um′ackern *tr* plow up, turn over

um′adressieren *tr* readdress

um′ändern *tr* change (around)

Um′änderung *f* (-;-en) change, alteration

um′arbeiten *tr* rework; (*Metall*) recast; (*Buch*) revise; (*Haus*) remodel; (*berichtigen*) emend, correct; (*verbessern*) improve

umar′men *tr* embrace, hug

Umar′mung *f* (-;-en) embrace, hug

Um′bau *m* (-[e]s;-e & -ten) rebuilding; alterations, remodeling; reorganization

um′bauen *tr* remodel; reorganize ‖ umbau′en *tr* build around; **umbauter Raum** floor space

um′besetzen *tr* (*Stellungen*) switch around; (pol) reshuffle; (theat) recast

um′biegen §47 *tr* bend (over); bend up, bend down

um′bilden *tr* remodel; reconstruct; (adm) reorganize, (pol) reshuffle

Um′bildung *f* (-;-en) remodeling; reconstruction; reorganization; reshuffling

um′binden §59 *tr* (*Schürze, usw.*) put on ‖ umbin′den §59 *tr* (*verletztes Glied, usw.*) bandage

um′blättern *tr* turn ‖ *intr* turn the page(s)

um′brechen §64 *tr* (*Bäume, usw.*) knock down; (*Acker*) plow up ‖ umbre′chen *tr* make into page proof

um′bringen §65 *tr* kill

Um′bruch *m* upheaval; (typ) page proof

um′buchen *tr* transfer to another account; book for another date

um′denken §66 *tr* rethink

um′dirigieren *tr* redirect

um′disponieren *tr* rearrange

umdrän′gen *tr* crowd around

um′drehen *tr* turn around; (*Hals*) wring; (*j-s Worte*) twist ‖ *ref* turn around ‖ *intr* turn around

Umdre′hung *f* (-;-en) turn; revolution

Um′druck *m* reprint; (typ) transfer

umeinan′der *adv* around each other

um′erziehen §163 *tr* reeducate

um′fahren §71 *tr* run down ‖ umfah′ren §71 *tr* drive around; sail around

um′fallen §72 *intr* (SEIN) fall over, fall down; collapse; give in

Um′fang *m* circumference; perimeter; (*Bereich*) range; (*Ausdehnung*) extent; (*des Leibes*) girth; (fig) scope; (mus) range; **im großen U.** on a large scale

umfan′gen §73 *tr* surround; embrace

um′fangreich *adj* extensive; (*körperlich*) bulky; (*geräumig*) spacious

umfas′sen *tr* embrace, clasp; comprise, cover; include; contain; (mil) envelop

umfas′send *adj* comprehensive; extensive

Umfas′sung *f* (-;-en) embrace, clasp; enclosure, fence; (mil) envelopment

Umfas'sungsmauer *f* enclosure
umflat'tern *tr* flutter around
umflech'ten §74 *tr* braid
umflie'gen §57 *tr* fly around ‖ **um'flie-**
gen §57 *intr* (SEIN) (coll) fall down
umflie'ßen §76 *tr* flow around
um'formen *tr* reshape; (elec) convert
Um'former *m* (-s;-) (elec) converter
Um'frage *f* inquiry, poll; **öffentliche**
U. public opinion poll
umfrieden [ʊmˈfridən] *tr* enclose
Um'gang *m* round, circuit; revolution,
rotation; (*Zug*) procession; association, company; (archit) gallery; **ge-**
schlechtlicher U. sexual intercourse;
schlechter U. bad company; **U. mit**
j-m haben (or **pflegen**) associate
with s.o.
umgänglich [ˈʊmgɛŋlɪç] *adj* sociable
Um'gangsformen *pl* social manners
Um'gangssprache *f* colloquial speech
um'gangssprachlich *adj* colloquial
umgar'nen *tr* (fig) trap
umge'ben §80 *tr* surround
Umgebung [ʊmˈgebʊŋ] *f* (-;-en) surroundings, environs, neighborhood;
company, associates; background,
environment
Umgegend [ˈʊmgegənt] *f* (-;) (coll)
neighborhood
umgehen §82 *tr* go around; evade; bypass; (mil) outflank ‖ **um'gehen** §82
intr (SEIN) go around; (*Gerücht*) circulate; **an** (or **in**) **e-m Ort u. haben**
a place; **mit dem Gedanken** (or
Plan) **u. zu** (*inf*) be thinking of (*ger*);
u. mit deal with, handle; manage; be
occupied with; hang around with
um'gehend *adj* immediate; **mit umge-**
hender Post by return mail; **umge-**
hende Antwort erbeten! please answer at your earliest convenience ‖
adv immediately
Umge'hung *f* (-;-en) going around;
bypassing; (fig) evasion; (mil) flank-
ing movement
Umge'hungsstraße *f* bypass
umgekehrt [ˈʊmgəkert] *adj* reverse;
contrary ‖ *adv* on the contrary; vice
versa; upside down; inside out
um'gestalten *tr* alter; remodel
um'graben §87 *tr* dig up
umgren'zen *tr* fence in; (fig) limit
Umgren'zung *f* (-;-en) enclosure; (fig)
limit, boundary
um'gruppieren *tr* regroup; (pol) reshuffle
um'gucken *ref* look around
um'haben §89 *tr* have on, be wearing
Um'hang *m* wrap; cape; shawl
um'hängen *tr* put on; (*Gewehr*) sling;
(*Bild*) hang elsewhere
Um'hängetasche *f* shoulder bag
um'hauen §93 *tr* cut down; (coll) bowl
over
umher' *adv* around, about
umher'blicken *tr* look around
umher'fuchteln *intr* gesticulate
umher'schweifen, **umher'streifen** *intr*
(SEIN) rove, roam about
umhin' *adv*—**ich kann nicht u.** I can't
do otherwise; **ich kann nicht u. zu**
(*inf*) I can't help (*ger*)

umhül'len *tr* wrap up, cover; envelop
Umhül'lung *f* (-;-en) wrapping
Umkehr [ˈʊmker] *f* (-;) return;
change; conversion; (elec) reversal
um'kehren *tr* turn around; overturn;
(*Tasche*) turn out; (elec) reverse;
(gram, math, mus) invert ‖ *intr*
(SEIN) turn back, return
Um'kehrung *f* (-;-en) overturning; reversal; conversion; inversion
um'kippen *tr* upset ‖ *intr* (SEIN) tilt
over
umklam'mern *tr* clasp; cling to; (mil)
envelop; **einander u.** (box) clinch
Umklam'merung *f* (-;-en) embrace;
(box) clinch; (mil) envelopment
umklei'den *tr* clothe ‖ *ref* change
around ‖ **um'kleiden** *tr* change the
clothes of
Um'kleideraum *m* dressing room
um'kommen §99 *intr* (SEIN) perish;
(*Essen*) spoil
Um'kreis *m* circuit; vicinity; (geom)
circumference; **5 km im U.** within a
radius of 5 km
umkrei'sen *tr* circle, revolve around
um'krempeln *tr* (*Ärmel*) roll up; **völ-**
lig u. (coll) change completely
um'laden §103 *tr* reload; transship
Um'lauf *m* circulation; (*Umdrehung*)
revolution, rotation; (*Flugblatt*) circular; (*Rundschreiben*) circular letter; **in U. setzen** circulate
Um'laufbahn *f* orbit
um'laufen §105 *tr* run down ‖ *intr*
(SEIN) circulate ‖ **umlau'fen** §105 *tr*
walk around
Um'laut *m* (-es;-e) umlaut, vowel mutation; mutated vowel
umlegbar [ˈʊmlekbar] *adj* reversible
um'legen *tr* lay down; turn down; (*an-**
**ders legen*) shift; (*Kragen*) put on;
(*gleichmäßig verteilen*) apportion;
(coll) knock down; (vulg) lay
um'leiten *tr* detour, divert
Um'leitung *f* (-;-en) detour
um'lenken *tr* turn back
um'lernen *tr* relearn, learn anew
um'liegend *adj* surrounding
ummau'ern *tr* wall in
um'modeln *tr* remodel
umnachtet [ʊmˈnaxtət] *adj* deranged
Umnach'tung *f* (-;)—**geistige U.** mental derangement
um'nähen *tr* hem
umne'beln *tr* fog; (fig) dull; **umnebelter**
Blick glassy eyes
um'nehmen §116 *tr* put on
um'packen *tr* repack
um'pflanzen *tr* transplant ‖ **umpflan'-**
zen *tr*—**etw mit Blumen u.** plant
flowers around s.th.
um'pflügen *tr* plow up, turn over
umrah'men *tr* frame
umranden [ʊmˈrandən] *tr* edge, border
Umran'dung *f* (-;-en) edging, edge
umran'ken *tr* twine around; **mit Efeu**
umrankt ivy-clad
um'rechnen *tr* convert; **umgerechnet**
auf (*acc*) expressed in
Um'rechnungskurs *m* rate of exchange
Um'rechnungstabelle *f* conversion table
Um'rechnungswert *m* exchange value

um'reißen §53 *tr* pull down; knock down || **umrei'ßen** §53 *tr* outline
umrin'gen *tr* surround
Um'riß *m* outline
Um'rißzeichnung *f* sketch
um'rühren *tr* stir, stir up
um'satteln *tr* resaddle || *intr* change jobs; (*educ*) change one's course or major; (*pol*) switch parties
Um'satz *m* turnover, sales
Um'satzsteuer *f* sales tax
umsäu'men *tr* enclose, hem in
um'schalten *tr* switch; (*Strom*) convert || *intr* (*auf acc*) switch back (to)
Um'schalter *m* (*elec*) switch; (*typ*) shift key
Um'schaltung *f* (–;–en) switching; shifting
Um'schau *f* look around; **U. halten** have a look around
um'schauen *ref* look around
um'schichten *tr* regroup, reshuffle
umschichtig ['ʊmʃɪçtɪç] *adv* alternately
umschif'fen *tr* circumnavigate; (*ein Kap*) double
Um'schlag *m* (sudden) change, shift; envelope; (*e-s Buches*) cover, jacket; cuff; hem; transshipment; (*med*) compress
um'schlagen §132 *tr* knock down; (*Ärmel*) roll up; (*Bäume*) fell; (*Saum*) turn up; (*Seite*) turn; (*umladen*) transship || *intr* (SEIN) (*Laune*, *Wetter*) change; (*Wind*) shift; (*kentern*) capsize
Um'schlagpapier *n* wrapping paper
umschlie'ßen §76 *tr* surround, enclose
umschlin'gen §142 *tr* clasp; embrace; wind around
um'schmeißen §53 *tr* (coll) throw over
um'schnallen *tr* buckle on
um'schreiben §62 *tr* rewrite; (*abschreiben*) transcribe; (*Wechsel*) re-endorse; **u. auf** (*acc*) transfer to || **umschrei'ben** §62 *tr* circumscribe; paraphrase
Um'schreibung *f* (–;–en) transcription; transfer || **Umschrei'bung** *f* (–;–en) paraphrase
Um'schrift *f* transcription; (*e-r Münze*) legend
um'schulen *tr* retrain
um'schütteln *tr* shake (up)
um'schütten *tr* spill; pour into another container
umschwär'men *tr* swarm around; (fig) idolize
Um'schweif *m* digression; **ohne Um-schweife** point-blank; **Umschweife machen** beat around the bush
umschweifig [um'ʃvaɪfɪç] *adj* round-about
um'schwenken *intr* wheel around; (fig) change one's mind
Um'schwung *m* change; (*Drehung*) revolution; (*Umkehrung*) reversal; (*der Gesinnung*) revulsion
umse'geln *tr* sail around; (*Kap*) double
Umse'gelung *f* (–;–en) circumnavigation
um'sehen §138 *ref* (**nach**) look around (for); (fig) (**nach**) look out (for)

um'sein §139 *intr* (SEIN) (*Zeit*) be up; (*Ferien*) be over
um'setzen *tr* shift; transplant; (*Nährstoffe*) assimilate; (*Schüler*) switch around; (*Ware*) sell; (*verwandeln*) convert; (mus) transpose; **Geld u. in** (*acc*) spend money on; **in die Tat u.** translate into action || *ref*—**sich u. in** (*acc*) (biochem) be converted into
Um'sicht *f* (–;) circumspection
umsichtig ['ʊmzɪçtɪç] *adj* circumspect
um'siedeln *tr & intr* (SEIN) resettle
Um'siedlung *f* (–;–en) resettlement
umsonst' *adv* for nothing, gratis; (*vergebens*) in vain
um'spannen *tr* (*Wagenpferde*) change; (*elec*) transform || **umspan'nen** *tr* span; encompass; include
Um'spanner *m* (–s;–) (elec) transformer
um'springen §142 *intr* (SEIN) (*Wind*) shift; **mit j–m rücksichtslos u.** (coll) treat s.o. thoughtlessly
Um'stand *m* circumstance; factor; fact; (*Einzelheit*) detail; (*Aufheben*) fuss; **in anderen Umständen** (coll) pregnant; **sich** [*dat*] **Umstände machen** go to the trouble; **Umstände machen** be formal; **unter Umständen** under certain conditions
umständehalber ['ʊmʃtɛndəhalbər] *adv* owing to circumstances
umständlich ['ʊmʃtɛntlɪç] *adj* detailed; (*förmlich*) formal; (*zu genau*) fussy; (*verwickelt*) complicated; (*Erzählung*) long-winded, round-about
Um'standskleid *n* maternity dress
Um'standskrämer *m* fusspot
Um'standswort *n* (–[e]s;–er) adverb
um'stehend *adj* (*Seite*) next || **Umstehende** §5 *mf* bystander
Um'steige(fahr)karte *f* transfer
um'steigen §148 *intr* (SEIN) transfer
um'stellen *tr* put into a different place, shift; (*Möbel*) rearrange; (*auf acc*) convert (to) || *ref* (*auf acc*) adjust (to) || **umstel'len** *tr* surround
Um'stellung *f* (–;–en) change of position, shift; conversion; readjustment
um'stimmen *tr* tune to another pitch; make (*s.o.*) change his mind
um'stoßen §150 *tr* knock down; (*Pläne*) upset; (*Vertrag*) annul; (*Urteil*) reverse
umstricken (umstrik/ken) *tr* ensnare
umstritten [um'ʃtrɪtən] *adj* contested; controversial
Um'sturz *m* overthrow
um'stürzen *tr* overturn; overthrow; (*Mauer*) tear down; (*Plan*) change, throw out || *intr* (SEIN) fall down
Umstürzler –in ['ʊmʃtyrtslər(ɪn)] §6 *mf* revolutionary, subversive
umstürzlerisch ['ʊmʃtyrtslərɪʃ] *adj* revolutionary; subversive
Um'tausch *m* exchange
um'tauschen *tr* (**gegen**) exchange (for)
um'tun §154 *tr* (*Kleider*) put on || *ref*—**sich u. nach** look around for
um'wälzen *tr* roll around; (fig) revolutionize
umwäl'zend *adj* revolutionary
Umwäl'zung *f* (–;–en) revolution

umwandelbar ['ʊmvandəlbɑr] *adj* (com) convertible

um'wandeln *tr* change; (elec, fin) convert; (jur) commute

Um'wandlung *f* (–;–en) change; (elec, fin) conversion; (jur) commutation

um'wechseln *tr* exchange; (fin) convert

Um'weg *m* detour; **auf Umwegen** indirectly

um'wehen *tr* knock down || **umwe'hen** *tr* blow around

Um'welt *f* environment

Um'weltverschmutzung *f* ecological pollution

um'wenden §140 *tr* turn over || *ref & intr* turn around

umwer'ben §149 *tr* court, go with

um'werfen §160 *tr* throw down; upset; (*Plan*) ruin; (*Kleider*) throw about one's shoulders

umwickeln (umwik'keln) *tr* (*mit Band*) tape

umwin'den *tr* wreathe

umwölken [ʊm'vœlkən] *ref & intr* cloud over

umzäunen [ʊm'tsɔɪnən] *tr* fence in

um'ziehen §163 *ref* change one's clothes || *intr* (SEIN) move || **umzie'hen** §163 *ref*—**der Himmel hat sich umzogen** the sky has become overcast

umzingeln [ʊm'tsɪŋəln] *tr* encircle

Um'zug *m* procession, parade; (*Wohnungswechsel*) moving; (pol) march

un– [ʊn] *comb.fm.* un–, in–, ir–, non–

unabän'derlich *adj* unalterable

un'abhängig (**von**) *adj* independent (of) || **Unabhängige** §5 *mf* (pol) independent

Un'abhängigkeit *f* independence

unabkömm'lich *adj* unavailable; indispensable; (mil) essential (*on the homefront*); **ich bin augenblicklich u.** I can't get away at the moment

unablässig ['ʊnaplesɪç] *adj* incessant

unablösbar ['ʊn'løsbɑr], **unablöslich** [ʊnap'løslɪç] *adj* unpayable

unabsetz'bar *adj* irremovable

unabsicht'lich *adj* unintentional

unabwendbar [ʊnap'ventbɑr] *adj* inevitable

un'achtsam *adj* careless, inattentive

um'ähnlich *adj* dissimilar, unlike

unanfecht'bar *adj* indisputable

un'angebracht *adj* out of place

un'angefochten *adj* undisputed

un'angemessen *adj* improper; inadequate; unsuitable

un'angenehm *adj* unpleasant, disagreeable; awkward

un'annehmbar *adj* unacceptable

Un'annehmlichkeit *f* unpleasantness; annoyance, inconvenience; **Unannehmlichkeiten** trouble

un'ansehnlich *adj* unsightly; (*unscheinbar*) plain, inconspicuous

un'anständig *adj* indecent; obscene

un'antastbar *adj* unassailable

un'appetitlich *adj* unappetizing; (*ekelhaft*) unsavory

Un'art *f* bad habit; (*Ungezogenheit*)

naughtiness; (*schlechte Manieren*) bad manners

un'artig *adj* ill-behaved, naughty

un'aufdringlich *adj* unostentatious; unobtrusive

un'auffällig *adj* inconspicuous

unauffindbar ['ʊnauffɪntbɑr] *adj* not to be found

unaufgefordert ['ʊnaufgəfɔrdərt] *adj* unasked, uncalled for || *adv* spontaneously

unaufhaltbar ['ʊnaufhaltbɑr], **unaufhaltsam** ['ʊnaufhaltzam] *adj* irresistible; relentless

unaufhörlich ['ʊnaufhørlɪç] *adj* incessant

un'aufmerksam *adj* inattentive

un'aufrichtig *adj* insincere

unaufschiebbar ['ʊnauf'ipbɑr] *adj* not to be postponed, urgent

unausbleiblich ['ʊnausblaɪplɪç] *adj* inevitable

unausführbar ['ʊnausfyrbɑr] *adj* unfeasible, impracticable

unausgeglichen ['ʊnausgəglɪçən] *adj* uneven; (fig) unbalanced

unauslöschbar ['ʊnauslœ/bɑr], **unauslöschlich** ['ʊnauslœ/lɪç] *adj* inextinguishable; (*Tinte*) indelible

unaussprechlich ['ʊnaus/preçlɪç] *adj* unspeakable, ineffable

unausstehlich ['ʊnaus/telɪç] *adj* intolerable, insufferable

unbändig ['ʊnbendɪç] *adj* wild

un'barmherzig *adj* unmerciful

un'beabsichtigt *adj* unintentional

un'beachtet *adj* unobserved, unnoticed

unbeanstandet ['ʊnbə-an/tandət] *adj* unopposed, unhampered

unbearbeitet ['ʊnbə-arbaɪtət] *adj* unworked; (*roh*) raw; (*Land*) untilled; (mach) unfinished

unbebaut ['ʊnbəbaut] *adj* uncultivated; (*Gelände*) undeveloped

unbedacht ['ʊnbədaxt] *adj* thoughtless

un'bedenklich *adj* unhesitating; unswerving; unobjectionable, harmless || *adv* without hesitation

un'bedeutend *adj* unimportant; slight

un'bedingt *adj* unconditional, unqualified; implicit

un'befahrbar *adj* impassable

un'befangen *adj* unembarrassed; (*unparteiisch*) impartial; natural, unaffected

unbefleckt ['ʊnbəflɛkt] *adj* immaculate

un'befriedigend *adj* unsatisfactory

un'befriedigt *adj* unsatisfied

un'befugt *adj* unauthorized; (jur) incompetent || **Unbefugte** §5 *mf* unauthorized person

un'begabt *adj* untalented

unbegreif'lich *adj* incomprehensible

un'begrenzt *adj* unlimited

un'begründet *adj* unfounded

Un'behagen *n* discomfort, uneasiness

un'behaglich *adj* uncomfortable

unbehelligt ['ʊnbəhelɪçt] *adj* undisturbed, unmolested

unbehindert ['ʊnbəhɪndərt] *adj* unhindered; unrestrained

unbeholfen ['ʊnbəholfən] *adj* clumsy

unbeirrbar ['unbə·ırbar] *adj* unwavering

unbeirrt ['unbə·ırt] *adj* unswerving

un'bekannt *adj* unknown; unfamiliar; unacquainted; (*Ursache*) unexplained ‖ **Unbekannte** §5 *mf* stranger ‖ *f* (math) unknown quantity

unbekümmert ['unbəkʏmərt] *adj* (um) unconcerned (about)

un'beladen *adj* unloaded

unbelastet ['unbəlastət] *adj* unencumbered; (*Wagen*) unloaded; carefree

un'belebt *adj* inanimate; (*Straße*) quiet; (com) slack

unbelichtet ['unbəlıçtət] *adj* (Film) unexposed

un'beliebt *adj* unpopular, disliked

unbemannt ['unbəmant] *adj* unmanned

un'bemerkbar *adj* imperceptible

un'bemittelt *adj* poor

un'benommen *adj*—**es bleibt Ihnen u. zu** (*inf*) you are free to (*inf*); **es ist mir u., ob** it's up to me whether

unbenutzbar ['unbənutsbar] *adj* unusable

unbenutzt ['unbənutst] *adj* unused

un'bequem *adj* inconvenient; uncomfortable

unberechenbar ['unbəreçənbar] *adj* incalculable; unpredictable

un'berechtigt *adj* unauthorized; unjustified

unbeschadet ['unbəʃadət] *prep* (genit) without prejudice to

unbeschädigt ['unbəʃedıçt] *adj* unhurt; undamaged

un'bescheiden *adj* pushy

unbescholten ['unbəʃoltən] *adj* of good reputation

un'beschränkt *adj* unlimited; absolute

unbeschreiblich ['unbəʃraıplıç] *adj* indescribable

unbesehen ['unbəze·ən] *adv* sight unseen

un'besetzt *adj* unoccupied, vacant

unbesiegbar ['unbəzikbar] *adj* invincible

unbesoldet ['unbəzoldət] *adj* unsalaried

un'besonnen *adj* thoughtless; careless; rash

un'besorgt *adj* unconcerned; carefree

un'beständig *adj* unsteady, inconstant; (*Preise*) fluctuating; (*Wetter*) changeable; (*Person*) fickle, unstable

unbestätigt ['unbəʃtetıçt] *adj* unconfirmed

un'bestechlich *adj* incorruptible

un'bestimmt *adj* indeterminate; vague; (*unsicher*) uncertain; (*unentschieden*) undecided; (gram) indefinite

unbestraft ['unbəʃtraft] *adj* unpunished

unbestreit'bar *adj* indisputable

unbestritten ['unbəʃtrıtən] *adj* undisputed, uncontested

unbeteiligt ['unbətaılıçt] *adj* uninterested; indifferent; impartial

un'beträchtlich *adj* trifling, slight

unbeugsam ['unbɔʏkzam] *adj* inflexible

unbewacht ['unbəvaxt] *adj* unguarded

unbewaffnet ['unbəvafnət] *adj* unarmed; (*Auge*) naked

un'beweglich *adj* immovable; motionless

unbewiesen ['unbəvizən] *adj* unproved

unbewohnt ['unbəvont] *adj* uninhabited

un'bewußt *adj* unconscious; involuntary

unbezähmbar [unbə'tsembar] *adj* untamable; (fig) uncontrollable

Un'bilden *pl*—**U. der Witterung** inclement weather

Un'bildung *f* lack of education

un'billig *adj* unfair

unbotmäßig ['unbotmesıç] *adj* unruly; insubordinate

unbrauch'bar *adj* useless, of no use

un'bußfertig *adj* unrepentant

un'christlich *adj* unchristian

und [unt] *conj* and; **und?** so what? **und wenn** even if

Un'dank *m* ingratitude

un'dankbar *adj* ungrateful; thankless

Un'dankbarkeit *f* ingratitude

undatiert ['undatirt] *adj* undated

undenk'bar *adj* unthinkable

undenklich [un'denklıç] *adj*—**seit undenklichen Zeiten** from time immemorial

un'deutlich *adj* unclear, indistinct

un'deutsch *adj* un-German

un'dicht *adj* not tight; leaky

Un'ding *n* nonsense, absurdity

un'duldsam *adj* intolerant

undurchdring'lich *adj* (für) impervious (to); **undurchdringliche Miene** poker face

undurchführ'bar *adj* not feasible

un'durchlässig *adj* (für) impervious (to)

un'durchsichtig *adj* opaque; (*Beweggründe*) hidden; (*Machenschaften*) shady

un'eben *adj* uneven; bumpy; **nicht u.!** (coll) not bad!

un'echt *adj* false, spurious; artificial, imitation; (*Farbe*) fading

un'edel *adj* ignoble; (*Metall*) base

un'ehelich *adj* illegitimate

Un'ehre *f* dishonor

un'ehrenhaft *adj* dishonorable

un'ehrerbietig *adj* disrespectful

un'ehrlich *adj* dishonest; underhand

un'eigennützig *adj* unselfish

un'einig *adj* disunited; at odds

Un'einigkeit *f* disagreement

uneinnehm'bar *adj* impregnable

un'eins *adj* at odds, at variance

un'empfänglich *adj* (für) insusceptible (to)

un'empfindlich *adj* (gegen) insensitive (to); (gegen) insensible (to)

unend'lich *adj* endless; infinite; **auf u. einstellen** (phot) set at infinity ‖ *adv* endlessly; infinitely; **u. viele an** endless number of

unentbehr'lich *adj* indispensable

unentrinnbar [unent'rınbar] *adj* inescapable

un'entschieden *adj* undecided; (*schwankend*) indecisive; (sport) tie ‖ **Unentschieden** *n* (-s;-) (sport) tie

Un'entschiedenheit *f* indecision

un'entschlossen *adj* irresolute

Un′entschlossenheit *f* indecision
unentschuld′bar *adj* inexcusable
unentwegt [′unɛntvekt] *adj* staunch; unswerving ‖ *adv* continuously; untiringly ‖ **Unentwegte** §5 *mf* die-hard
unentwirrbar [′unɛntvɪrbar] *adj* inextricable
unerbittlich [unɛr′bɪtlɪç] *adj* inexorable; *(Tatsache)* hard
un′erfahren *adj* inexperienced
unerfindlich [unɛr′fɪntlɪç] *adj* incomprehensible, mysterious
unerforschlich [unɛr′fɔrʃlɪç] *adj* inscrutable
unerfreulich [′unɛrfrɔɪlɪç] *adj* unpleasant
unerfüllbar [unɛr′fʏlbar] *adj* unattainable
un′ergiebig *adj* unproductive
un′ergründlich *adj* unfathomable
un′erheblich *adj* insignificant; **(für)** irrelevant (to)
unerhört [unɛr′hørt] *adj* unheard-of, unprecedented; outrageous ‖ **un′erhört** *adj (Bitte)* unanswered
un′erkannt *adj* unrecognized ‖ *adv* incognito
unerklär′lich *adj* inexplicable
unerläßlich [unɛr′lɛslɪç] *adj* indispensable
un′erlaubt *adj* illicit, unauthorized
un′erledigt *adj* unsettled, unfinished
unermeßlich [unɛr′mɛslɪç] *adj* immense
unermüdlich [unɛr′mydlɪç] *adj* untiring; *(Person)* indefatigable
unerquicklich [unɛr′kvɪklɪç] *adj* unpleasant
unerreich′bar *adj* unattainable, out of reach
unerreicht [′unɛrraɪçt] *adj* unrivaled
unersättlich [unɛr′zɛtlɪç] *adj* insatiable
unerschlossen [′unɛr′lɔsən] *adj* undeveloped; *(Boden)* unexploited
unerschöpflich [unɛr′ʃøpflɪç] *adj* inhaustible
unerschrocken [′unɛr′ʃrɔkən] *adj* intrepid, fearless
unerschütterlich [unɛr′ʃʏtɛrlɪç] *adj* unshakable; imperturbable
unerschwing′lich *adj* unattainable; beyond one's means; exorbitant
unersetz′bar, unersetz′lich *adj* irreplaceable; *(Schaden)* irreparable
unerträg′lich *adj* intolerable
unerwähnt [′unɛrvent] *adj* unmentioned; **u. lassen** pass over in silence
unerwartet [′unɛrvartət] *adj* unexpected, sudden
unerweis′lich *adj* unprovable
un′erwünscht *adj* undesired; unwelcome
unerzogen [′unɛrtsogən] *adj* ill-bred
un′fähig *adj* incapable, unable; unqualified, inefficient
Un′fähigkeit *f* inability; inefficiency
Un′fall *m* accident, mishap
Un′fallflucht *f* hit-and-run offense
Un′fallstation *f* first-aid station
Un′falltod *m* accidental death
Un′fallversicherung *f* accident insurance
Un′fallziffer *m* accident rate

unfaß′bar, unfaß′lich *adj* incomprehensible; inconceivable
unfehl′bar *adj* infallible; unfailing
Unfehl′barkeit *f* infallibility
un′fein *adj* coarse; indelicate
un′fern *adj* near; **u. von** not far from ‖ *prep (genit)* not far from
un′fertig *adj* not ready; not finished; immature
Unflat [′unflat] *m* (-s;) dirt, filth
unflätig [′unfletɪç] *adj* dirty, filthy
un′folgsam *adj* disobedient
Un′folgsamkeit *f* disobedience
unförmig [′unfœrmɪç] *adj* shapeless
un′förmlich *adj* informal
unfrankiert [′unfraŋkirt] *adj* unfranked, unstamped
un′frei *adj* not free; unstamped ‖ *adv* **—u. schicken** send c.o.d.
un′freiwillig *adj* involuntary
un′freundlich *adj* unfriendly, unkind
Un′friede *m* dissension, discord
un′fruchtbar *adj* unfruitful, sterile; *(fig)* fruitless
Unfug [′unfuk] *m* (-[e]s;) nuisance, disturbance; mischief; misdemeanor; **U. treiben** cause mischief
ungang′bar *adj* impassable; unsalable
Ungar [′ungar] *m* (-;-n), **Ungarin** [′uŋgarɪn] *f* (-;-nen) Hungarian
ungarisch [′uŋgarɪʃ] *adj* Hungarian
Ungarn [′uŋgarn] *n* (-s;) Hungary
un′gastlich *adj* inhospitable
ungeachtet [′uŋgə-axtət] *adj* not esteemed ‖ *prep (genit)* regardless of
ungeahnt [′uŋgə-ant] *adj* unexpected
ungebärdig [′uŋgəberdɪç] *adj* unruly
ungebeten [′uŋgəbetən] *adj* unbidden
ungebeugt [′uŋgəbɔɪkt] *adj* unbowed; (gram) uninflected
un′gebildet *adj* uneducated
un′gebräuchlich *adj* unusual; *(veraltet)* obsolete
un′gebraucht *adj* unused
Un′gebühr *f* indecency, impropriety
un′gebührlich *adj* indecent, improper
ungebunden [′uŋgəbundən] *adj* unbound; *(ausschweifend)* loose, dissolute; *(frei)* unrestrained; **ungebundene Rede** prose
ungedeckt [′uŋgədekt] *adj* uncovered; *(Tisch)* unset; *(Haus)* roofless; *(Kosten)* unpaid; *(Scheck)* overdrawn
Un′geduld *f* impatience
un′geduldig *adj* impatient
un′geeignet *adj* unfit, unsuitable; unqualified
ungefähr [′uŋgəfer] *adj* approximate ‖ *adv* approximately, about; **nicht von u.** on purpose
un′gefährdet [′uŋgəferdət] *adj* safe, unendangered
un′gefährlich *adj* not dangerous
un′gefällig *adj* discourteous
un′gefüge *adj* monstrous; clumsy
un′gefügig *adj* unyielding, inflexible
ungefüttert [′uŋgəfʏtərt] *adj* unlined
un′gehalten *adj (Versprechen)* unkept, broken; **(über** *acc)* indignant (at)
ungeheißen [′uŋgəhaɪsən] *adv* of one's own accord
ungehemmt [′uŋgəhemt] *adj* unchecked

ungeheuer ['ʊngəhɔɪ-ər] *adj* huge; monstrous ‖ *adv* tremendously ‖ **Ungeheuer** *n* (-s;-) monster

un'geheuerlich *adj* monstrous ‖ *adv* (coll) tremendously

ungehobelt ['ʊngəhobəlt] *adj* unplaned; (fig) uncouth

un'gehörig *adj* improper; (*Stunde*) ungodly

Un'gehörigkeit *f* (-;-en) impropriety

un'gehorsam *adj* disobedient ‖ **Ungehorsam** *m* (-s;) disobedience

un'gekünstelt *adj* unaffected, natural

un'gekürzt *adj* unabridged

un'gelegen *adj* inconvenient

Un'gelegenheiten *pl* inconvenience

un'gelehrig *adj* unteachable

un'gelenk *adj* clumsy; stiff

un'gelernt *adj* (coll) unskilled

Un'gemach *n* discomfort; trouble

un'gemein *adj* uncommon

un'gemütlich *adj* uncomfortable; (*Zimmer*) dreary; (*Person*) disagreeable

un'genannt *adj* anonymous

un'genau *adj* inaccurate, inexact

ungeniert [ʊnʒenirt] *adj* informal ‖ *adv* freely

ungenieß'bar *adj* inedible; undrinkable; (& fig) unpalatable

un'genügend *adj* insufficient; **u. bekommen** get a failing grade

ungepflastert ['ʊngəpflastərt] *adj* unpaved, dirt

un'gerade *adj* uneven; crooked; (*Zahl*) odd

un'geraten *adj* spoiled

un'gerecht *adj* unjust, unfair

Un'gerechtigkeit *f* injustice

ungereimt ['ʊngəraimt] *adj* unrhymed; (*unvernünft*) absurd; **ungereimtes Zeug reden** talk nonsense

un'gern *adv* unwillingly, reluctantly

ungerührt ['ʊngəryrt] *adj* (fig) unmoved

un'geschehen *adj* undone; **u. machen** undo

ungescheut ['ʊngəʃɔɪt] *adv* without fear

Un'geschick *n*, **Un'geschicklichkkeit** *f* awkwardness

un'geschickt *adj* awkward, clumsy

un'geschlacht ['ʊngəʃlaxt] *adj* uncouth

ungeschliffen ['ʊngəʃlifən] *adj* unpolished; (*Messer*) blunt; (*Edelstein*) uncut; (fig) rude

ungeschminkt ['ʊngəʃmɪŋkt] *adj* without makeup; (*Wahrheit*) unvarnished

un'gesellig *adj* unsociable

un'gesetzlich *adj* illegal

ungesittet ['ʊngəzɪtət] *adj* unmannerly; uncivilized

ungestört ['ʊngəʃtørt] *adj* undisturbed

ungestraft ['ʊngəʃtraft] *adj* unpunished ‖ *adv* scot-free

ungestüm ['ʊngəʃtym] *adj* impetuous, violent ‖ **Ungestüm** *n* (-[e]s;) impetuosity, violence

un'gesund *adj* unhealthy; unwholesome

ungeteilt ['ʊngətailt] *adj* undivided

un'getreu *adj* disloyal, untrue

ungetrübt ['ʊngətrypt] *adj* cloudless, clear; (fig) untroubled

Ungetüm ['ʊngətym] *n* (-[e]s;-e) monster

ungeübt ['ʊngə-ypt] *adj* untrained; (*Arbeiter*) inexperienced

un'gewandt *adj* unskillful; clumsy

un'gewiß *adj* uncertain; **j-n im ungewissen lassen** keep s.o. in suspense

Un'gewißheit *f* uncertainty

Un'gewitter *n* storm

un'gewöhnlich *adj* unusual

un'gewohnt *adj* unusual; (*genit*) unaccustomed (to)

ungezählt ['ʊngətselt] *adj* countless

Ungeziefer ['ʊngətsifər] *n* (-s;) vermin, bugs

ungeziemend ['ʊngətsimənt] *adj* improper; (*frech*) impudent

un'gezogen *adj* rude; naughty

ungezügelt ['ʊngətsygəlt] *adj* unbridled

un'gezwungen *adj* unforced; natural, easy-going

Un'glaube *m* disbelief, unbelief

un'gläubig *adj* incredulous; (*heidnisch*) infidel ‖ **Ungläubige** §5 *mf* infidel

unglaub'lich *adj* incredible

un'glaubwürdig *adj* untrustworthy; incredible

un'gleich *adj* uneven, unequal; (*unähnlich*) unlike, dissimilar; (*Zahl*) odd ‖ *adv* much, far, by far

un'gleichartig *adj* heterogeneous

un'gleichförmig *adj* unequal; irregular

Un'gleichheit *f* inequality; difference, dissimilarity; unevenness

un'gleichmäßig *adj* disproportionate

Unglimpf ['ʊnglɪmpf] *m* (-[e]s;-e) harshness; wrong, insult

glimpf'lich *adj* harsh

Un'glück *n* (-s;) bad luck; (*Unfall*) accident; disaster, calamity

un'glücklich *adj* unlucky; unfortunate; unhappy

un'glücklicherweise *adv* unfortunately

Un'glücksbote *m* bearer of bad news

Un'glücksbringer *m* (-s;-) jinx

un'glückselig *adj* miserable; disastrous

Un'glücksfall *m* accident, misfortune

Un'glücksmensch *m* unlucky person

Un'glücksrabe *m*, **Un'glücksvogel** *m* unlucky fellow

Un'gnade *f* (-;) disfavor, displeasure

un'gnädig *adj* ungracious; **etw u. aufnehmen** take s.th. amiss

un'gültig *adj* null and void, invalid; **für u. erklären** nullify, void

Un'gültigkeit *f* invalidity

Un'gültigkeitserklärung *f* annulment

Un'gunst *f* disfavor; **zu meinen Ungunsten** to my disadvantage

un'günstig *adj* unfavorable, bad, adverse

un'gut *adj* unkind; **nichts für u.!** no offense!; **ungutes Gefühl** misgivings

un'haltbar *adj* not durable; untenable

un'handlich *adj* unwieldy, unhandy

Un'heil *n* disaster; mischief; **U. anrichten** cause mischief; **U. heraufbeschwören** ask for trouble

unheil'bar *adj* incurable; irreparable

un'heilvoll *adj* ominous; disastrous

un'heimlich *adj* uncanny; sinister

un'höflich *adj* impolite, uncivil

Un'höflichkeit f impoliteness
un'hold adj unkind || Unhold m (–[e]s; –e) fiend
un'hörbar adj inaudible
un'hygienisch adj unsanitary
Uni ['uni] f (–;–s) (Universität) (coll) university
uniform [uni'form] adj uniform || Uniform f (–;–en) uniform
Uni·kum ['uːnɪkum] n (–s;–s & –ka [ka]) unique example; (coll) queer duck
un'interessant adj uninteresting
un'interessiert adj (an dat) uninterested (in)
Union [un'join] f (–;–en) union
universal [univer'zal] adj universal
Universal'mittel n panacea, cure-all
Universal'schlüssel m monkey wrench
Universität [univerzi'tet] f (–;–en) university
Universitäts'auswahlmannschaft f varsity (team)
Universum [uni'verzum] n (–s;) universe
Unke ['uŋkə] f (–;–n) toad
unken ['uŋkən] intr (coll) be a prophet of doom
un'kenntlich adj unrecognizable; u. machen disguise
Un'kenntnis f (–;) ignorance
Un'kenruf m croak
un'keusch adj unchaste
un'kindlich adj precocious; (Verhalten) disrespectful
un'kirchlich adj secular, worldly
un'klar adj unclear; muddy; misty; im unklaren sein über (acc) be in the dark about
Un'klarheit f obscurity
un'kleidsam adj unbecoming
un'klug adj unwise, imprudent
Un'klugheit f imprudence; foolish act
un'kontrollierbar adj unverifiable
un'körperlich adj incorporeal
Un'kosten pl expenses, costs; overhead; sich in U. stürzen go to great expense
Un'kraut n weed, weeds; U. jäten pull weeds
Un'krautvertilgungsmittel n weed killer
un'kündbar adj binding; (Darlehen) irredeemable; (Stellung) permanent
un'kundig adj (genit) ignorant (of), unacquainted (with)
unlängst ['unleŋst] adv recently, the other day
un'lauter adj unfair
un'leidlich adj intolerable
un'lenksam adj unruly
unles'bar, unle'serlich adj illegible
unleugbar ['unlɔikbar] adj indisputable, undeniable
un'lieb adj disagreeable; es ist mir u. I am sorry
un'logisch adj illogical
unlös'bar adj (Problem) unsolvable; (untrennbar) inseparable; (chem) insoluble
unlös'lich adj (chem) insoluble
Un'lust f reluctance; listlessness
un'lustig adj reluctant; listless

un'manierlich adj impolite
un'männlich adj unmanly
Un'maß n excess; im U. to excess
Un'masse f (coll) vast amount, lots
un'maßgeblich adj unauthoritative; irrelevant; nach meiner unmaßgeblichen Meinung in my humble opinion
un'mäßig adj immoderate; excessive
Un'menge f (coll)—e–e U. von lots of
Un'mensch m brute, monster
un'menschlich adj inhuman, brutal
Un'menschlichkeit f brutality
un'marklich adj imperceptible
un'methodisch adj unmethodical
un'mißverständlich adj unmistakable
un'mittelbar adj direct, immediate
un'möbliert adj unfurnished
un'modern adj outmoded
un'möglich, unmög'lich adj impossible
Un'möglichkeit f impossibility
Un'moral f immorality
un'moralisch adj immoral
un'mündig adj underage
un'musikalisch adj unmusical
Un'mut m (über acc) displeasure (at)
un'mutig adj displeased, annoyed
unnachahmlich ['unnaxamlɪç] adj inimitable
un'nachgiebig adj unyielding
un'nachsichtig adj unrelenting, inexorable; strict
unnahbar [un'nabar] adj inaccessible
un'natürlich adj unnatural
unnenn'bar adj inexpressible
un'nötig adj unnecessary
unnütz ['unnyts] adj useless; vain
un'ordentlich adj disorderly; untidy
Un'ordnung f disorder; mess; in U. bringen throw into disorder
un'organisch adj inorganic
un'paar, un'paarig adj unpaired, odd
un'parteiisch, un'parteilich adj impartial, disinterested
Un'parteilichkeit f impartiality
un'passend adj unsuitable; (unschicklich) improper; (unzeitgemäß) untimely
un'passierbar adj impassable
unpäßlich ['unpeslɪç] adj indisposed, ill
un'patriotisch adj unpatriotic
un'persönlich adj impersonal
un'politisch adj nonpolitical
un'populär adj unpopular
un'praktisch adj impractical; (unerfahren) unskillful
Un'rast f restlessness
Un'rat m (–[e]s;) garbage; dirt; U. wittern (coll) smell a rat
un'rätlich, un'ratsam adj inadvisable
un'recht adj wrong || Unrecht n (–[e]s;) —im U. sein be in the wrong; j–m U. geben decide against s.o.; mit (or zu) U. wrongly; unjustly; illegally
un'redlich adj dishonest
Un'redlichkeit f dishonesty
un'reell adj unfair
un'regelmäßig adj irregular
Un'regelmäßigkeit f irregularity
un'reif adj unripe, green; (fig) immature
Un'reife f unripeness; immaturity
un'rein adj unclean; (& fig) impure;

ins u. schreiben make a rough copy
of
Un'reinheit f uncleanness; (& fig) impurity
un'reinlich adj dirty
un'rentabel adj unprofitable
un'rettbar adj irrecoverable
un'richtig adj incorrect, wrong
un'ritterlich adj unchivalrous
Un'ruh f (-;-en) (horol) balance wheel
Un'ruhe f restlessness; uneasiness;
(Aufruhr) commotion, riot; (Störung) disturbance; (Besorgnis) anxiety
un'ruhig adj restless; uneasy; (laut)
noisy; (Pferd) restive; (Meer)
choppy; (nervös) jumpy
un'rühmlich adj inglorious
Un'ruhstifter –in §6 mf agitator,
troublemaker; (Wirrkopf) screwball
uns [ʊns] pers pron us; to us || reflex
pron ourselves; wir sind doch unter
uns we are by ourselves || recip pron
each other, one another; wir sehen
uns später we'll meet later
un'sachgemäß adj inexpert
un'sachlich adj subjective; personal
unsagbar [ʊnˈzakbar], **unsäglich** [ʊn-
ˈzeklɪç] adj unspeakable; (fig) immense
un'sauber adj unclean; (unlauter) unfair, dirty
un'schädlich adj harmless
un'scharf adj (Apparat) out of focus;
(Bild) blurred; (Begriff) poorly de-
fined
un'schätzbar adj inestimable, invaluable
un'scheinbar adj inconspicuous, insignificant
un'schicklich adj unbecoming; indecent
Un'schicklichkeit f impropriety
un'schlüssig adj indecisive
Un'schlüssigkeit f indecision, hesitation
un'schmackhaft adj insipid, unpalatable
un'schön adj unlovely; plain, homely;
(Angelegenheit) unpleasant
Un'schuld f innocence; ich wasche
meine Hände in U. I wash my hands
of it
un'schuldig adj innocent; (keusch)
chaste; harmless; sich für u. erklären (jur) plead not guilty
un'schwer adj not difficult
Un'segen m adversity; (Fluch) curse
un'selbständig adj dependent, helpless
un'selig adj unfortunate; (Ereignis)
fatal
unser [ˈʊnzər] §2,3 poss adj our ||
§2,4 poss pron ours || pers pron us;
of us; erinnerst du dich unser noch?
do you still remember us?; es waren
unser vier there were four of us
unseresgleichen [ˈʊnzarəsˈglaɪçən] pron
people like us; the likes of us
unserige [ˈʊnzərɪgə] §2,5 pron ours
unserthalben [ˈʊnzərtˈhalbən], **unsertwegen** [ˈʊnzərtˈvegən] adv for our
sake, on our behalf, on our account
un'sicher adj unsafe; shaky; precarious

Un'sicherheit f unsafeness; shakiness;
insecurity; precariousness
un'sichtbar adj invisible
Un'sinn m (-[e]s;) nonsense, rubbish;
U. machen fool around
un'sinnig adj nonsensical
Un'sitte f bad habit
un'sittlich adj immoral, indecent
Un'sittlichkeit f immorality
un'solid(e) adj unsolid; (Person)
loose; (Firma) unreliable, shaky
unsortiert [ˈʊnzɔrtirt] adj unsorted
un'sozial adj antisocial
un'sportlich adj unsportsmanlike
unsrerseits [ˈʊnzər'zaɪts] adv as for
us, for our part
unsrige [ˈʊnzrɪgə] §2,5 poss pron ours
un'ständig adj impermanent, temporary
un'statthaft adj inadmissible; forbidden
unsterb'lich adj immortal
Unsterb'lichkeit f immortality
Un'stern m unlucky star; (fig) disaster
un'stet adj unsteady; restless; changeable
un'stillbar adj unappeasable; (Durst)
unquenchable; (Hunger) unsatiable
unstimmig [ˈʊnʃtɪmɪç] adj discrepant;
inconsistent
Un'stimmigkeit f (-;-en) discrepancy;
inconsistency; (Widerspruch) disagreement
un'sträflich adj blameless; guileless
un'streitig adj indisputable
Un'summe f enormous sum
un'symmetrisch adj asymmetrical
un'sympathisch adj unpleasant; er ist
mir u. I don't like him
un'tadelhaft adj blameless; flawless
Un'tat f crime
un'tätig adj inactive
un'tauglich adj unfit, unsuitable; useless; (Person) incompetent; u. machen disqualify
un'teilbar adj indivisible
unten [ˈʊntən] adv below; beneath;
downstairs; da u. down there; er ist
bei ihnen u. durch they are through
with him; nach u. downstairs; downwards; tief u. far below; u. am Berge
at the foot of the mountain; u. an
der Seite at the bottom of the page;
von u. her from underneath
unter [ˈʊntər] prep (dat) under, below;
beneath, underneath; (zwischen)
among; (während) during; ganz u.
uns gesagt just between you and me;
u. aller Kritik beneath contempt; u.
anderem among other things; u. diesem Gesichtspunkt from this point
of view; u. Null below zero; was
versteht man unter...? what is meant
by...? || prep (acc) under, below;
beneath, underneath; among || Unter
m (-[s]:) (cards) jack
Unter-, unter- comb.fm. under-, sub-;
lower
Un'terabteilung f subdivision
Un'terarm m forearm
Un'terart f subspecies
Un'terausschuß m subcommittee
Un'terbau m (-[e]s;–ten) foundation

un'terbelichten tr underexpose

un'terbewußt adj subconscious

Un'terbewußtsein n subconscious

unterbie'ten §58 tr undercut, undersell; underbid

un'terbinden §59 tr tie underneath || **unterbin'den** §59 tr (Verkehr) tie up; (Blutgefäß) tie off; (verhindern) prevent; (Angriff) neutralize

Unterbin'dung f stoppage; (surg) ligature

unterblei'ben §62 intr (SEIN) remain undone; not take place; be discontinued; **das muß u.** that must be stopped

unterbre'chen §64 tr interrupt; (einstellen) suspend; (Schweigen, Stille, Kontakt) break; (Verkehr) hold up; (telp) disconnect; **die Reise in München u.** have a stopover in Munich || ref stop short

Unterbre'cher m (elec) circuit breaker

Unterbre'chung f interruption; disconnection; (e-r Fahrt) stopover

unterbrei'ten tr submit

un'terbringen §65 tr provide a place for; find room for; (Gäste) accommodate, put up; (Stapeln) store; (Anleihe) place; (Geld) invest; (Pferde) stable; (Wagen) park; (Truppe) billet; **e-n Artikel bei e-r Zeitung u.** have an article published in a newspaper; **j-n auf e-m Posten** (or **in e-r Stellung**) **u.** find s.o. a job, place s.o.

Un'terbringung f (-;-en) accommodations, housing; billet; storage; investment; placement

Un'terbringungsmöglichkeiten pl accommodations

unterdes [untǝr'des], **unterdessen** [untǝr'desǝn] adv meanwhile

Un'terdruck m low pressure

unterdrücken (unterdrük'ken) tr suppress; (Aufstand) quell; (bedrücken) oppress; (ersticken) stifle; (Seufzer) repress

Un'terdruckgebiet n low-pressure area

Unterdrückung (Unterdrük'kung) f (-;) oppression; suppression

untere ['untǝrǝ] §9 adj lower, inferior

untereinan'der adv among one another; mutually; reciprocally

unterentwickelt ['untǝrentvɪkǝlt] adj underdeveloped

unterernährt ['untǝrernert] adj undernourished

Un'terernährung f (-;) undernourishment

Un'terfamilie f subfamily

unterfer'tigen tr sign

Unterführ'rung f (-;-en) underpass

unterfüt'tern tr line

Un'tergang m setting; (fig) decline, fall; (naut) sinking

unterge'ben adj (dat) subject (to), inferior (to) || **Untergebene** §5 mf subordinate

un'tergehen §82 intr (SEIN) go down, sink; (fig) perish; (astr) set

untergeordnet ['untǝrgǝ-ɔrdnǝt] adj subordinate || **Untergeordnete** §5 mf subordinate

Un'tergeschoß n ground floor; (Kellergeschoß) basement

Un'tergestell n undercarriage

Un'tergewand n underwear

un'tergliedern tr subdivide

untergra'ben §87 tr undermine

Un'tergrund m subsoil

Un'tergrundbahn f subway

Un'tergrundbewegung f underground movement

un'terhalb prep (genit) below

Un'terhalt m (-[e]s;) support; maintenance, upkeep; livelihood

un'terhalten §90 tr hold under || **unterhal'ten** §90 tr maintain; support; (Briefwechsel) keep up; (Feuer) feed; entertain, amuse || ref enjoy oneself, have a good time; amuse oneself; **sich u. mit** talk with

unterhaltsam [untǝr'haltzam] adj entertaining, amusing, enjoyable

Un'terhaltsbeitrag m alimony; (für Kinder) support

Unterhaltsberechtigte ['untǝrhaltsbǝreçtIgtǝ] §5 mf dependent

Un'terhaltskosten pl living expenses

Unterhal'tung f (-;-en) entertainment, amusement; (Gespräch) conversation; (Aufrechterhaltung) upkeep; (Unterstützung) support

Unterhal'tungskosten pl maintenance cost, maintenance

Unterhal'tungslektüre f light reading

unterhan'deln intr negotiate

Un'terhändler -in §6 mf negotiator; (Vermittler) mediator

Unterhand'lung f (-;-en) negotiation

Un'terhaus n (parl) lower house

Un'terhemd n undershirt

unterhöh'len tr undermine

Un'terholz n undergrowth, underbrush

Un'terhose f shorts; panties; **in Unterhosen zeigen** (coll) debunk

un'terirdisch adj underground, subterranean; (myth) of the underworld

Un'terjacke f vest

unterjo'chen tr subjugate

Unterjo'chung f (-;) subjugation

Un'terkiefer m lower jaw

Un'terkinn n double chin

Un'terkleid n slip

Un'terkleidung f (-;) underwear

Un'terkommen §99 intr (SEIN) find accommodations; find employment || **Unterkommen** n (-s;) accommodations; (Stellung) job

Un'terkörper m lower part of the body

un'terkriegen tr (coll) get the better of; **er läßt sich nicht u.** he won't knuckle under

Unterkunft ['untǝrkunft] f (-;¨e) accommodations; apartment; (Obdach) shelter, place to stay; (mil) quarters; **U. und Verpflegung** room and board

Un'terlage f foundation; base; pad; desk pad; rubber pad (for a bed); (Teppich-) underpad; (Beleg) voucher; (Urkunde) document; (archit) support; (geol) substratum; **keine Unterlagen haben** have nothing to go on; **Unterlagen** documentation; data

Un'terland n lowland

Unterlaß ['ʊntərlas] *m*—**ohne U.** without letup

unterlas'sen §104 *tr* omit; neglect; skip; stop, cut out

Unterlas'sung *f* (–;–en) omission; neglect; failure

Unterlas'sungssünde *f* sin of omission

unterlau'fen *adj*—**blau u.** black-and-blue; **mit Blut u.** bloodshot || **un'terlaufen** §105 *intr* (SEIN) (*Fehler*) slip in

un'terlegen *tr* lay under, put under; (*Bedeutung, Sinn*) attach; **der Musik Worte u.** set words to music || **unterle'gen** *adj* defeated; (*dat*) inferior (to) || **Unterlegene** §5 *mf* loser

Unterle'genheit *f* (–;) inferiority

Unterlegring ['ʊntərlekrɪŋ], **Unterlegscheibe** ['ʊntərlekʃaibə] *f* washer

Un'terleib *m* abdomen

Unterleibs- *comb.fm.* abdominal

unterlie'gen §108 *intr* (SEIN) (*dat*) be beaten (by), lose (to); **e-m Rabatt u.** be subject to discount || *impers* (SEIN)—**es unterliegt keinem Zweifel, daß** there is no doubt that

Un'terlippe *f* lower lip

unterma'len *tr* put the primer on; **mit Musik u.** accompany with music

untermau'ern *tr* support

Un'termiete *f* (–;) subletting; **in U. abgeben** sublet; **in U. wohnen bei** sublet from

Un'termieter –in §6 *mf* subtenant

unterminie'ren *tr* (fig) undermine

unterneh'men §116 *tr* undertake; (*versuchen*) attempt; **Schritte u.** (fig) take steps || **Unternehmen** *n* (–s;–) undertaking; venture; enterprise; (mil) operation

unterneh'mend *adj* enterprising

Unterneh'mensberater *m* management consultant

Unterneh'mer –in §6 *mf* entrepreneur; (*Arbeitgeber*) employer; (*Bau–*) contractor

Unterneh'mung *f* (–;–en) undertaking; enterprise, business; (mil) operation

Unterneh'mungsgeist *m* initiative

unterneh'mungslustig *adj* enterprising

Un'teroffizier *m* noncommissioned officer, N.C.O.

un'terordnen *tr* (*dat*) subordinate (to) || *ref* (*dat*) submit (to)

unterre'den *ref* (mit) confer (with)

Unterre'dung *f* (–;–en) conference

Unterricht ['ʊntərrɪçt] *m* (–[e]s;–e) instruction, lessons

unterrich'ten *tr* instruct; **u. von** (or **über** *acc*) inform (of, about)

Un'terrichtsfach *n* subject, course

Un'terrichtsfilm *m* educational film; (mil) training film

Un'terrichtsministerium *n* department of public instruction

Un'terrichtsstunde *f* (educ) period

Un'terrichtswesen *n* education; teaching

Un'terrock *m* slip

untersa'gen *tr* forbid, prohibit

Un'tersatz *m* saucer; support; (*Gestell*) stand; (archit) socle; (log) minor premise

unterschät'zen *tr* underrate, underestimate; undervalue

unterschei'den §112 *tr* distinguish || *ref* (von) differ (from)

Unterschei'dung *f* (–;–en) difference, distinction

Un'terschenkel *m* shank

un'terschieben §130 *tr* shove under; (statt *genit*) substitute (for); (*dat*) impute (to), foist (on)

Unterschied ['ʊntərʃit] *m* (–[e]s;–e) difference, distinction; **zum U. von** as distinct from, unlike

un'terschiedlich *adj* different; varying

un'terschiedslos *adj* indiscriminate

unterschla'gen §132 *tr* embezzle; (*Nachricht*) suppress; (*Brief*) intercept

Unterschla'gung *f* (–;–en) embezzlement; suppression; interception

Unterschlupf ['ʊntərʃlupf] *m* (–[e]s;) shelter; hide-out

unterschrei'ben §62 *tr* sign; (fig) subscribe to, agree to

Un'terschrift *f* signature

Un'terseeboot *n* submarine

unterseeisch ['ʊntərze·ɪʃ] *adj* submarine

Un'terseekabel *n* transoceanic cable

Un'terseite *f* underside

untersetzt [ʊntər'zetst] *adj* stocky

Un'tersetzung *f* (–;–en) (mech) reduction

un'tersinken §143 *intr* (SEIN) go down

Un'terstand *m* (mil) dugout

unterste ['ʊntərstə] §9 *adj* lowest, bottom

unterste'hen §146 *ref* dare; **untersteh dich!** don't you dare! || *intr* (*dat*) be under (*s.o.*) || **un'terstehen** §146 *intr* take shelter

un'terstellen *tr* place under; (*Auto*) put into the garage || *ref* take cover || **unterstel'len** *tr* assume, suppose; (*dat*) impute (to); (mil) (*dat*) put under the command (of)

Unterstel'lung *f* (–;–en) assumption; imputation

unterstrei'chen §85 *tr* underline

unterstüt'zen *tr* support, back; help

Unterstüt'zung *f* (–;–en) support, backing; assistance; (*Beihilfe durch Geld*) relief; (ins) benefit

untersu'chen *tr* examine, inspect; investigate; study, do research on; (chem) analyze

Untersu'chung *f* (–;–en) examination; inspection; investigation; study, research; (chem) analysis

Untersu'chungsausschuß *m* fact-finding committee

Untersu'chungsgericht *n* court of inquiry

Untersu'chungshaft *f* (jur) detention

Untersu'chungsrichter *m* examining judge

Untertagebau [ʊntər'tagəbau] *m* (–[e]s;) mine

Untertan ['ʊntərtan] *m* (–s & –en;–en) subject

untertänig [ʊntər'teniç] *adj* submissive

Un'tertasse *f* saucer; **fliegende U.** flying saucer

un'tertauchen *tr* submerge; duck || *intr* (SEIN) dive; (fig) disappear || **Unter-tauchen** *n* (-s;) dive; disappearance
Un'terteil *m* & *n* lower part, bottom
untertei'len *tr* subdivide
Untertei'lung *f* (-;-en) subdivision
Un'tertitel *m* subtitle; caption
Un'terton *m* undertone
un'tertreten §152 *intr* (SEIN) take cover
un'tervermieten *tr* sublet
Un'tervertrag *m* subcontract
unterwan'dern *tr* infiltrate
Un'terwäsche *f* underwear
Unterwasser— *comb.fm.* underwater, submarine
Un'terwasserbombe *f* depth charge
Un'terwasserhorchgerät *n* hydrophone
Un'terwasserortungsgerät *n* sonar
unterwegs [untər'veks] *adv* on the way; (com) in transit
unterwei'sen §118 *tr* instruct
Unterwei'sung *f* (-;-en) instruction
Un'terwelt *f* underworld; (myth) lower world
unterwer'fen §160 *tr* subjugate; (*dat*) subject (to) || *ref* (*dat*) submit to, subject oneself to; **sich** [*dat*] **ein Volk u.** subjugate a people
Unterwer'fung *f* (-;) subjugation; submission
unterworfen [untər'vorfən] *adj* subject
unterwürfig ['untərvʏrfɪç] *adj* submissive, subservient
unterzeich'nen *tr* sign
Unterzeich'ner –in §6 *mf* signer; signatory
Unterzeichnete [untər'tsaɪçnətə] §5 *mf* undersigned
Unterzeich'nung *f* (-;-en) signing; signature
un'terziehen §163 *tr* put on underneath || **unterzie'hen** §163 *tr* (*dat*) subject (to) || *ref*—**sich der Mühe u. zu** (*inf*) take the trouble to (*inf*); **sich e-r Operation u.** have an operation; **sich e-r Prüfung u.** take an examination
un'tief *adj* shallow || **Untiefe** *f* (-;-n) shoal
Un'tier *n* (& fig) monster
untilg'bar *adj* inextinguishable; (*Tinte*) indelible; (*Anleihe*) irredeemable
untrag'bar *adj* unbearable; (*Kleidung*) unwearable; (*Kosten*) prohibitive
untrenn'bar *adj* inseparable
un'treu *adj* unfaithful || **Untreue** *f* unfaithfulness; infidelity
untröst'lich *adj* inconsolable
untrüg'lich *adj* unerring, infallible
un'tüchtig *adj* incapable; inefficient
Un'tugend *f* bad habit, vice
un'überlegt *adj* thoughtless; rash
unüberseh'bar *adj* vast, huge; incalculable || *adv* very
unübersetz'bar *adj* untranslatable
un'übersichtlich *adj* unclear; (*Kurve*) blind
unübersteig'bar, unübersteig'lich *adj* insurmountable
unübertreff'lich *adj* unsurpassable
unübertroffen [unʏbər'trofən] *adj* unsurpassed
unüberwind'lich *adj* invincible; (*Schwierigkeiten*) insurmountable

unumgäng'lich *adj* indispensable
unumschränkt ['unum/reŋkt] *adj* unlimited; (pol) absolute
unumstößlich ['unum/tøslɪç] *adj* irrefutable; (*unwiderruflich*) irrevocable
unumwunden ['unumvundən] *adj* blunt
un'unterbrochen *adj* continuous
unverän'derlich *adj* unchangeable, invariable
unverant'wortlich *adj* irresponsible
unveräu'ßerlich *adj* inalienable
unverbesserlich [unfer'besərlɪç] *adj* incorrigible
unverbind'lich *adj* without obligation; (*Verhalten*) proper, formal; (*Antwort*) noncommittal
un'verblümt *adj* blunt, plain
unverbürgt [unfer'bʏrkt] *adj* unwarranted; (*Nachricht*) unconfirmed
un'verdächtig *adj* unsuspected
un'verdaulich *adj* indigestible
unverderbt ['unferderpt], **unverdorben** ['unferdorbən] *adj* unspoiled
unverdient ['unferdint] *adj* undeserved
un'verdrossen *adj* indefatigable
unverdünnt ['unferdʏnt] *adj* undiluted
unverehelicht ['unfere-əlɪçt] *adj* unmarried, single
un'vereinbar *adj* incompatible; contradictory
unverfälscht ['unferfelʃt] *adj* genuine; (*Wein*) undiluted
un'verfänglich *adj* innocent
un'verfroren *adj* brash
un'vergänglich *adj* imperishable
un'vergeßlich *adj* unforgettable
unvergleich'bar *adj* incomparable
unvergleichlich ['unferglaɪçlɪç] *adj* incomparable
un'verhältnismäßig *adj* disproportionate
un'verheiratet *adj* unmarried
unvergolten ['unfergoltən] *adj* unrewarded
unverhofft ['unferhoft] *adj* unhoped-for
unverhohlen ['unferholən] *adj* unconcealed; (fig) open
un'verkäuflich *adj* unsalable
unverkennbar ['unferkenbar] *adj* unmistakable
unverkürzt ['unferkʏrtst] *adj* unabridged
unverlangt ['unferlaŋt] *adj* unsolicited
un'verletzbar, un'verletzlich *adj* undamageable; (fig) inviolable
unverletzt ['unferletst] *adj* safe and sound, unharmed; (*Sache*) undamaged
unvermeid'lich *adj* inevitable
unvermindert ['unfermɪndərt] *adj* undiminished
unvermittelt ['unfermɪtəlt] *adj* sudden
Un'vermögen *n* inability; impotence
un'vermögend *adj* poor; impotent
unvermutet ['unfermutət] *adj* unexpected
un'vernehmlich *adj* imperceptible
Un'vernunft *f* unreasonableness; folly
un'vernünftig *adj* unreasonable; foolish
un'verschämt *adj* brazen, shameless

unverschuldet [ˈunferʃuldət] *adj* un-encumbered; (*unverdient*) unde-served
un'versehens *adv* unawares, suddenly
unversehrt [ˈunferzert] *adj* undamaged (*Person*) unharmed
unversichert [ˈunferziçərt] *adj* unin-sured
unversiegbar [unferˈziːkbɑr] **unversieg-lich** [unferˈziːkliç] *adj* inexhaustible
unversiegelt [ˈunferziːgəlt] *adj* unsealed
un'versöhnlich *adj* irreconcilable
unversorgt [ˈunferzɔrkt] *adj* unpro-vided for
Un'verstand *m* lack of judgment
un'verständig *adj* foolish
un'verständlich *adj* incomprehensible
unversucht [ˈunferzuxt] *adj* untried
un'verträglich *adj* unsociable; quarrel-some; incompatible, contradictory
un'verwandt *adj* steady, unflinching
unverwelklich [unferˈvelkliç] *adj* un-fading
un'verwendbar *adj* unusable
unverweslich [ˈunferveːzliç] *adj* incor-ruptible
unverwindbar [unferˈvɪntbɑr] *adj* ir-reparable; (*Enttäuschung*) lasting
un'verwundbar *adj* invulnerable
unverwüstlich [ˈunfervyːstliç] *adj* in-destructible; (*Stoff*) durable; (fig) irrepressible
unverzagt [ˈunfertsɑkt] *adj* undaunted
un'verzeihlich *adj* unpardonable
unverzerrt [ˈunfertsert] *adj* undistorted
unverzinslich [ˈunfertsɪnsliç] *adj* (fin) without interest
unverzüglich [ˈunfertsyːkliç] *adj* prompt, immediate ‖ *adv* without delay
unvollendet [ˈunfɔləndət] *adj* unfin-ished
un'vollkommen *adj* imperfect
Un'vollkommenheit *f* imperfection
un'vollständig *adj* incomplete; (gram) defective
un'vorbereitet *adj* unprepared; (*Rede*) extemporaneous ‖ *adv* extempore
un'voreingenommen *adj* unbiased
un'vorhergesehen *adj* unforeseen
un'vorsätzlich *adj* unintentional
un'vorsichtig *adj* incautious; careless
un'vorteilhaft *adj* disadvantageous; unprofitable; (*Kleid*) unflattering
un'wahr *adj* untrue
un'wahrhaftig *adj* untruthful
Un'wahrheit *f* untruth, falsehood
un'wahrnehmbar *adj* imperceptible
un'wahrscheinlich *adj* unlikely, improb-able
unwan'delbar *adj* unchangeable
unwegsam [ˈunveːkzɑm] *adj* impass-able
unweigerlich [unˈvaɪɡərliç] *adj* un-hesitating; (*Folge*) necessary ‖ *adv* without fail
un'weit *adj*—**u. von** not far from ‖ *prep* (*genit*) not far from
Un'wesen *n* mischief; **sein U. treiben** be up to one's old tricks
un'wesentlich *adj* unessential; unim-portant; (für) immaterial (to)
Un'wetter *n* storm

un'wichtig *adj* unimportant
unwiederbringlich [unviːdərˈbrɪŋliç] *adj* irretrievable, irreparable
unwiderleg'bar *adj* irrefutable
unwiderruf'lich *adj* irrevocable
unwidersteh'lich *adj* irresistible
Un'wille *m*, **Un'willen** *m* indignation, displeasure; reluctance
un'willig *adj* (über *acc*) indignant (at), displeased (at); **u. zu** (*inf*) reluctant to (*inf*)
un'willkommen *adj* unwelcome
un'willkürlich *adj* involuntary
un'wirklich *adj* unreal
un'wirksam *adj* ineffective; inefficient; (chem) inactive; (jur) null and void
Un'wirksamkeit *f* ineffectiveness; inef-ficiency; (chem) inactivity
unwirsch [ˈunvɪrʃ] *adj* surly
un'wirtlich *adj* inhospitable
un'wirtschaftlich *adj* uneconomical
unwissend [ˈunvɪsənt] *adj* ignorant
Unwissenheit [ˈunvɪsənhaɪt] *f* (-;) ig-norance
un'wissenschaftlich *adj* unscientific
un'wissentlich *adv* unwittingly
un'wohl *adj* sickish; **ich fühle mich u.** I don't feel well
un'wohnlich *adj* uninhabitable; (*un-behaglich*) uncomfortable
un'würdig *adj* unworthy
Un'zahl *f* (von) huge number (of)
unzähl'bar, **unzählig** [unˈtseːliç] *adj* countless, innumerable
un'zart *adj* indelicate
Unze [ˈuntsə] *f* (-;-n) ounce
Un'zeit *f* wrong time
un'zeitgemäß *adj* out-of-date
un'zeitig *adj* untimely; (*Obst*) unripe
unzerbrech'lich *adj* unbreakable
unzerstör'bar *adj* indestructible
unzertrennlich [untserˈtrenliç] *adj* in-separable
unziemend [ˈuntsimənt], **un'ziemlich** *adj* unbecoming, unseemly
Un'zucht *f* unchastity; lewdness
un'züchtig *adj* unchaste; lewd
un'zufrieden *adj* dissatisfied
un'zugänglich *adj* inaccessible; aloof
un'zulänglich *adj* inadequate
un'zulässig *adj* inadmissible; (*Beein-flussung, Einmischung*) undue
un'zurechnungsfähig *adj* unaccountable
un'zureichend *adj* inadequate
un'zusammenhängend *adj* incoherent
un'zuträglich *adj* (dat) bad (for)
un'zutreffend *adj* not applicable
un'zuverlässig *adj* unreliable
un'zweckmäßig *adj* inappropriate; un-suitable; impractical
un'zweideutig *adj* unambiguous
un'zweifelhaft *adj* undoubted
üppig [ˈʏpɪç] *adj* luxurious, plush; (*Mahl*) sumptuous; (*Pflanzenwuchs*) luxuriant; (*sinnlich*) voluptuous
Ur-, **ur-** [uːr] *comb.fm.* original; very
ur'alt *adj* very old, ancient
Uran [uˈrɑn] *n* (-s;) uranium
Ur'aufführung *f* world première
urbar [ˈurbɑr] *adj* arable; **u. machen** reclaim
Urbarmachung [ˈurbɑrmaxʊŋ] *f* (-;) reclamation

Ur'bewohner pl aborigines
Ur'bild n prototype; original
ur'deutsch adj hundred-percent German
ur'eigen adj one's very own; original
Ur'einwohner pl aborigines
Ur'eltern pl ancestors
Ur'enkel m great-grandson
Ur'geschichte f prehistory
Ur'großmutter f great-grandmother
Ur'großvater m great-grandfather
Urheber **-in** ['urhebər(ɪn)] §6 mf originator, author
Ur'heberrecht n copyright
Ur'heberschaft f (-;-e) authorship
Urin [u'rin] m (-s;) urine
urinieren [urɪ'nirən] intr urinate
ur'ko'misch adj very funny
Urkunde ['urkundə] f (-;-n) document; deed; (Vertrag) instrument
Ur'kundenmaterial n documentation
urkundlich ['urkuntlɪç] adj documentary; (verbürgt) authentic
Urlaub ['urlaup] m (-[e]s;-e) vacation; (mil) furlough
Ur'lauber **-in** §6 mf vacationer
Ur'laubsschein m (mil) pass
Ur'laubstag m day off
Urne ['urnə] f (-;-n) urn; ballot box; **zur U. gehen** go to the polls
Ur'nengang m balloting

ur'plötz'lich adj sudden || adv all of a sudden
Ur'sache f cause, reason; **keine U.!** don't mention it!
ur'sächlich adj causal
Ur'schleim m (-es;) protoplasm
Ur'schrift f original text, original
Ur'sprung m origin, source; beginning; (Ursache) cause
ursprünglich ['ur/pryŋlɪç] adj original
Ur'stoff m primary matter; (chem) element
Ur'teil n judgment; (Ansicht) view, opinion; (jur) verdict; (Strafmaß) (jur) sentence
urteilen ['urtailən] intr judge; **u. nach** judge by
Ur'teilskraft f discernment
Ur'teilsspruch m verdict; sentence
Ur'text m original text
Ur'tier n protozoon
Ur'volk n aborigines
Ur'wald m virgin forest; jungle
ur'weltlich adj primeval
urwüchsig ['urvyksɪç] adj original; (fig) rough
Ur'zeit f remote antiquity
Utensilien [uten'ziljən] pl utensils
Uto·pie [uto'pi] f (-;-pien ['pi·ən]) utopia; pipe dream
uzen ['utsən] tr tease, kid

V

V, v [fau] invar n V, v
vag [vak] adj vague
Vagabund [vaga'bunt] m (-en;-en) vagabond, tramp, bum
vagabundieren [vagabun'dirən] intr (HABEN & SEIN) bum around
vage ['vagə] adj vague
vakant [va'kant] adj vacant
Vakanz [va'kants] f (-;-en) vacancy
Vaku·um ['vaku·um] n (-s;-ua [u·a]) vacuum
Vakzine [vak'tsinə] f (-;-n) vaccine
vakzinieren [vaktsi'nirən] tr vaccinate
Valet [va'let] n (-s;-s) farewell
Valu·ta [va'luta] f (-;-ten [tən]) value; (foreign) currency
Vampir ['vampir] m (-s;-e) vampire
Vandale [van'dalə] m (-n;-n) Vandal; (fig) vandal
Vanille [va'nɪljə] f (-;) vanilla
Variante [varɪ'antə] f (-;-n) variant
Varietät [varɪ·e'tet] f (-;-en) variety
Varieté [varɪ·e'te] n (-s;-s) vaudeville; vaudeville stage
variieren [varɪ'irən] tr & intr vary
Vase ['vazə] f (-;-n) vase
Vaselin [vaze'lin] n (-s;-e), **Vaseline** [vaze'linə] f (-;-n) vaseline
Vater ['fatər] m (-s;⁻) father
Va'terland n (native) country
vaterländisch ['fatərlendɪʃ] adj national || adv—v. gesinnt patriotic
Va'terlandsliebe f patriotism
väterlich ['fetərlɪç] adj fatherly

väterlicherseits ['fetərlɪçər'zaɪts] adv on the father's side
Va'terliebe f paternal love
Va'terschaft f (-;) fatherhood
Va'terschaftsklage f paternity suit
Va'tersname m family name, last name
Va'terstadt f home town
Va'terstelle f—**bei j-m V. vertreten** be a father to s.o.
Vaterun'ser n (-s;⁻) Lord's Prayer
Vati ['fati] m (-s;-s) dad, daddy
Vatikan [vatɪ'kan] m (-s;) Vatican
v. Chr. abbr (vor Christus) B.C.
Vegetarier **-in** [vege'tarjər(ɪn)] §6 mf vegetarian
Vegetation [vegeta'tsjon] f (-;) vegetation
vegetieren [vege'tirən] intr vegetate
Veilchen ['failçən] n (-s;⁻) (bot) violet
Vene ['venə] f (-;-n) (anat) vein
Venedig [ve'nedɪç] n (-s;) Venice
venerisch [ve'neriʃ] adj venereal; **venerisches Leiden** venereal disease
Ventil [ven'til] n (-s;-e) valve; (bei der Orgel) stop; (fig) outlet
Ventilation [ventɪla'tsjon] f (-;) ventilation
Venti·lator [ventɪ'lator] m (-s;-latoren [la'torən]) ventilator; fan
ver- pref up, e.g., **verbrauchen** use up; away, e.g., **verjagen** chase away; mis-, wrongly, e.g., **verstellen** misplace, **verdrehen** turn the wrong

way; (to form verbs from other parts of speech) **verwirklichen** realize, (to express a sense **vergöttern** deify; opposite that of the simple verb) **verlernen** forget, **verkaufen** sell; (to indicate consumption or waste through the action of the verb) **verschreiben** use up in writing; (to indicate intensification or completion) **verhungern** die of hunger; (to indicate cessation of action) **vergären** cease to ferment; (to indicate conversion to another state) **verflüssigen** liquify

verabfolgen [fɛr'ʔpfɔlgən] *tr* hand over; deliver; (*Arznei*) give, administer

verabreden [fɛr'apredən] *tr* agree upon; **schon anderweitig verabredet sein** have a prior engagement || *ref* make an appointment

Verab'redung *f* (-;-en) agreement; appointment

verabreichen [fɛr'apraiçən] *tr* give

verabsäumen [fɛr'apzɔimən] *tr* var of **versäumen**

verabscheuen [fɛr'apʃɔiən] *tr* detest, loath, abhor

verab'scheuenswert, verab'scheunswürdig detestable

verabschieden [fɛr'apʃidən] *tr* dismiss; (*Beamte*) put on pension; (*Gesetz*) pass; (mil) disband || *ref* (**von**) take leave (of), say goodbye (to)

Verab'schiedung *f* (-;-en) dismissal; pensioning; (mil) disbanding; (parl) passing, enactment

verach'ten *tr* despise; **nicht zu v.** not to be sneezed at

verächtlich [fɛr'ɛçtlɪç] *adj* contemptuous; (*verachtungswert*) contemptible

Verach'tung *f* (-;) contempt

veralbern [fɛr'albərn] *tr* tease

verallgemeinern [fɛralgə'mainərn] *tr & intr* generalize

Verallgemei'nerung *f* (-;-en) generalization

veralten [fɛr'altən] *intr* become obsolete; (*Kleider*) go out of style

veraltet [fɛr'altət] *adj* obsolete; out of date, old-fashioned

Veran-da [ve'randa] *f* (-;-den [dən]) veranda, porch

veränderlich [fɛr'ɛndərlɪç] *adj* changeable; (math) variable

Verän'derlichkeit *f* (-;-en) changeableness; fluctuation; instability

verän'dern [fɛr'ɛndərn] *tr* change; vary || *ref* change; look for a new job

Verän'derung *f* (-;-en) change

verängstigt [fɛr'ɛŋstɪçt] *adj* intimidated

verankern [fɛr'aŋkərn] *tr* anchor, moor

Veran'kerung *f* (-;-en) anchorage, mooring

veranlagen [fɛr'anlagən] *tr* (*zu* or *Steuer*) assess; **gut veranlagt** highly talented; **künstlerisch veranlagt** artificially inclined; **schlecht veranlagt** poorly endowed

Veran'lagung *f* (-;-en) talents; disposition; (fin) assessment

veran'lassen *tr* cause, occasion, make; (*bereden*) induce

Veran'lassung *f* (-;-en) cause, occasion; **auf V. von** at the suggestion of; **ohne jede V.** without provocation; **V. geben zu** give rise to

veranschaulichen [fɛr'anʃaulɪçən] *tr* make clear, illustrate

veran'schlagen §132 *tr* rate, value; (*im voraus berechnen*) estimate; **zu hoch v.** overrate

Veran'schlagung *f* (-;) estimate

veranstalten [fɛr'anʃtaltən] *tr* organize, arrange; (*Empfang*) give; (*Sammlung*) take up; (*Versammlung*) hold

Veran'stalter **-in** §6 *mf* organizer

Veran'staltung *f* (-;-en) organization, arrangement; affair; performance, show; meeting; (sport) event, meet

veran'tworten *tr* answer for, account for; (*verteidigen*) defend || *ref* defend oneself, justify oneself

verantwortlich [fɛr'antvɔrtlɪç] *adj* responsible, answerable; **für etw v. zeichnen** sign for s.th.

Verant'wortlichkeit *f* (-;) responsibility; (jur) liability

Verant'wortung *f* (-;-en) responsibility; (*Rechtfertigung*) justification; **auf eigene V.** at one's own risk; **die V. abwälzen auf** (acc) pass the buck to; **zur V. ziehen** call to account

Verant'wortungsbewußtsein *n* sense of responsibility

verant'wortungsfreudig *adj* willing to assume responsibility

verant'wortungsvoll *adj* responsible

veräppeln [fɛr'ɛpəln] *tr* (coll) tease

verar'beiten *tr* manufacture, process; (*zu*) make (into); (*verdauen*) digest; (fig) assimilate

verar'beitend *adj* manufacturing

Verar'beitung *f* (-;-en) manufacturing; digestion; (fig) assimilation

verargen [fɛr'argən] *tr*—**j-m etw v.** blame s.o. for s.th.

verär'gern *tr* annoy

verarmen [fɛr'armən] *intr* (SEIN) grow poor

verästeln [fɛr'ɛstəln] *ref* branch out

verausgaben [fɛr'ausgabən] *tr* pay out || *ref* run short of money

veräußern [fɛr'ɔisərn] *tr* sell

Verb [vɛrp] *n* (-s;-en) verb

verbal [vɛr'bal] *adj* verbal

Verband [fɛr'bant] *m* (-[e]s;⸚e) association, union, federation; (aer, nav) formation; (mil) unit; (surg) bandage, dressing; **sich aus dem V. lösen** (aer) peel off

Verband'kasten *m* first-aid kit

Verband'päckchen *n* first-aid pack

Verband'platz *m* first-aid station

Verband'stoff *m* bandage, dressing

verbannen [fɛr'banən] *tr* banish, exile

Verbannte [fɛr'bantə] §5 *mf* exile

Verban'nung *f* (-;-en) banishment; place of exile

verbarrikadie'ren *tr* barricade

verbau'en *tr* (*Gelände*) build up; use up (*in building*); (*Geld*) spend (*in building*); build poorly; **j-m den Weg v. zu** bar s.o.'s way to

verbei′ßen §53 *tr* swallow, suppress ‖
ref (**in** *acc*) stick (to)
verber′gen §54 *tr* & *ref* hide
verbes′sern *tr* improve; correct; (*Aufsatz*) grade; (*Gesetz*) amend; (*Tatsache*) rectify ‖ *ref* improve; better
oneself
Verbes′serung *f* (–;–en) improvement;
correction; amendment
verbeu′gen *ref* bow
Verbeu′gung *f* (–;–en) bow; curtsy
verbeulen [fɛr′bɔɪlən] *tr* dent; batter
verbie′gen §57 *tr* bend ‖ *ref* warp
verbie′ten §58 *tr* forbid
verbil′den *tr* spoil; educate badly
verbil′ligen *tr* reduce the price of
Verbil′ligung *f* (–;–en) reduction
verbin′den §59 *tr* tie, tie up; join,
unite; (*verketten*) link; (*zu Dank verpflichten*) obligate; (*chem*) combine;
(*med*) bandage; (*telp*) (**mit**) connect
(with), put through (to); **j–m die
Augen v.** blindfold s.o. ‖ *ref* unite
verbindlich [fɛr′bɪntlɪç] *adj* obliging;
binding; **verbindlichsten Dank!** thank
you ever so much!
Verbind′lichkeit *f* (–;–en) obligation;
commitment; polite way; (*e–s Vertrags*) binding force
Verbin′dung *f* (–;–en) union; association; alliance; combination; contact;
touch; (*Fuge, Gelenk*) joint; (*chem*)
compound; (*educ*) fraternity; (*mach,
rr, telp*) connection; (*mil*) liaison;
die V. verlieren mit lose touch with;
e–e V. eingehen (*chem*) form a compound; **er hat gute Verbindungen** he
has good connections; **in V. mit** in
conjunction with; **sich in V. setzen
mit** get in touch with; **unmittelbare
V.** (*telp*) direct call
Verbin′dungsbahn *f* connecting train
Verbin′dungsleitung *f* (*telp*) trunk line
Verbin′dungslinie *f* line of communication
Verbin′dungsoffizier *m* liaison officer
Verbin′dungspunkt *m*, **Verbin′dungs-
stelle** *f* joint, juncture
Verbin′dungsstück *n* joint, coupling
verbissen [fɛr′bɪsən] *adj* dogged, grim;
(*Zorn*) suppressed; **v. sein in** (*dat*)
stick doggedly to
Verbis′senheit *f* (–;) doggedness, grimness
verbitten [fɛr′bɪtən] §60 *ref*—**sich**
[*dat*] **etw v.** not stand for s.th.
verbittern [fɛr′bɪtərn] *tr* embitter
Verbit′terung *f* (–;) bitterness
verblassen [fɛr′blasən] *intr* (SEIN)
grow pale; (fig) fade
verblättern [fɛr′blɛtərn] *tr*—**die Seite
v.** lose the page
Verbleib [fɛr′blaɪp] *m* (–[e]s;) whereabouts
verblei′ben §62 *intr* (SEIN) remain, be
left; (**bei**) persist (in); **wir sind so
verblieben, daß** we finally agreed
that
verblei′chen §85 *intr* (SEIN) fade
verblen′den *tr* blind; dazzle; (*Mauer*)
face; (*Fenster*) wall up
Verblen′dung *f* (–;–en) blindness, infatuation; (archit) facing

verblichen [fɛr′blɪçən] *adj* faded
verblödet [fɛr′blødət] *adj* idiotic
verblüffen [fɛr′blʏfən] *tr* dumbfound,
flabbergast; bewilder, perplex
Verblüf′fung *f* (–;) bewilderment
verblü′hen *intr* (SEIN) wither; fade
verblümt [fɛr′blymt] *adj* euphemistic
verblu′ten *ref* & *intr* (SEIN) bleed to
death
verbocken [fɛr′bɔkən] *tr* bungle
verboh′ren *ref*—**sich v. in** (*acc*) stick
stubbornly to
verbohrt [fɛr′bort] *adj* stubborn; odd
verbolzen [fɛr′bɔltsən] *tr* bolt
verbor′gen *adj* secret; latent; hidden ‖
tr lend out ‖ **Verborgene** §5 *n*—**im
Verborgenen** in secret, on the sly
Verbor′genheit *f* (–;) secrecy; concealment; seclusion
Verbot [fɛr′bot] *n* (–[e]s;–e) prohibition; (jur) injunction
verboten [fɛr′botən] *adj* forbidden;
Eintritt v.! no admittance; **Plakat-
kleben v.!** post no bills!; **Stehenbleiben v.!** no loitering
verbrämen [fɛr′brɛmən] *tr* trim, edge;
(fig) sugar-coat
verbrannt [fɛr′brant] *adj* burnt; torrid; **Politik der verbrannten Erde**
scorched-earth policy
Verbrauch′ *m* (–[e]s;) use, consumption
verbrau′chen *tr* use up, consume;
waste; (*abnutzen*) wear out
Verbrau′cher *m* (–s;–) consumer; (*Be-
nützer*) user; (*Kunde*) customer
Verbrau′chergenossenschaft *f* co-op
Verbrauchs′güter *pl* consumer goods
verbraucht′ *adj* used up, consumed;
worn out; (*Geld*) spent; (*Luft*) stale
verbre′chen §64 *tr* commit, do ‖ **Verbrechen** *n* (–s;–) crime
Verbre′cher *m* (–s;–) criminal
Verbre′cheralbum *n* rogues′ gallery
Verbre′cherin *f* (–;–nen) criminal
verbrecherisch [fɛr′breçərɪʃ] *adj* criminal
Verbre′cherkolonie *f* penal colony
verbreiten [fɛr′braɪtən] *tr* spread;
(*Frieden, Licht*) shed ‖ *ref* spread;
sich v. über (*acc*) expatiate on
verbreitern [fɛr′braɪtərn] *tr* & *ref*
widen, broaden
Verbrei′terung *f* (–;) widening, broad-
ening
Verbrei′tung *f* (–;) spreading; dissemi-
nation; diffusion
verbren′nen §97 *tr* burn; scorch; (*bräunen*) tan; (*Leichen*) cremate ‖ *ref*
burn oneself; **sich** [*dat*] **die Finger
v.** (& fig) burn one′s fingers
Verbren′nung *f* (–;–en) burning, combustion; cremation; (*Brandwunde*)
burn
Verbren′nungskraftmaschine *f*, **Ver-
bren′nungsmotor** *m* internal combustion engine
Verbren′nungsraum *m* combustion
chamber
verbrin′gen §65 *tr* spend, pass; (*wegbringen*) take away
verbrüdern [fɛr′brydərn] *ref* (**mit**) fraternize (with)

Verbrü'derung *f* (-;) fraternizing

verbrü'hen *tr* scald

verbu'chen *tr* book; **etw als Erfolg v.** chalk s.th. up as a success

Ver·bum ['vɛrbʊm] *n* (-s;-ba [ba]) verb

verbunden [fɛr'bʊndən] *adj* connected; **falsch v.!** sorry, wrong number!; **untereinander v.** interconnected; **zu Dank v.** obligated

verbün'den *ref*—**sich mit j-m v.** ally oneself with s.o.

Verbun'denheit *f* (-;) connection, ties; solidarity, union

Verbündete [fɛr'bʏndətə] §5 *mf* ally

verbür'gen *tr* guarantee, vouch for ‖ *ref*—**sich v. für** vouch for

verbürgt [fɛr'bʏrkt] *adj* authenticated

verbüßen [fɛr'bysən] *tr* atone for, pay for; **seine Strafe v.** serve one's time

verchromen [fɛr'kromən] *tr* chromeplate

Verchro'mung *f* (-;-en) chromeplating

Verdacht [fɛr'daxt] *m* (-[e]s;) suspicion; **in V. kommen** come under suspicion; **V. hegen gegen** have suspicions about; **V. schöpfen** get suspicious

verdächtig [fɛr'dɛçtɪç] *adj* suspicious; (*genit*) suspected (of)

verdächtigen [fɛr'dɛçtɪgən] *tr* cast suspicion on; (*genit*) suspect (of)

Verdäch'tigung *f* (-;-en) insinuation

verdammen [fɛr'damən] *tr* condemn; damn

Verdammnis [fɛr'damnɪs] *f* (-;) damnation, perdition

verdammt' *adj* (sl) damn ‖ *interj* (sl) damn it!

verdampf'en *tr* & *intr* (SEIN) evaporate

Verdampf'ung *f* (-;) evaporation

verdan'ken *tr*—**j-m etw v.** be indebted to s.o. for s.th.

verdarb [fɛr'darp] *pret of* verderben

verdattert [fɛr'datərt] *adj* (coll) shook up

verdauen [fɛr'dau·ən] *tr* digest

verdaulich [fɛr'daʊlɪç] *adj* digestible

Verdau'ung *f* (-;) digestion

Verdau'ungsbeschwerden *pl* Verdau'ungsstörung *f* indigestion

Verdau'ungswerkzeug *n* digestive track

Verdeck [fɛr'dɛk] *n* (-[e]s;-e) hood (*of baby carriage*); (aut) convertible top; (naut) deck

verdecken (verdek'ken) *tr* cover; hide

verden'ken §66 *tr*—**j-m etw v.** blame s.o. for s.th.

Verderb [fɛr'dɛrp] *m* (-[e]s;) ruin; decay

verderben [fɛr'dɛrbən] §149 *tr* spoil; ruin; (*Magen*) upset; (*verführen*) corrupt ‖ *intr* (SEIN) spoil, go bad; (fig) go to pot ‖ **Verderben** (-s;) ruin; **j-n ins V. stürzen** ruin s.o.

verderblich [fɛr'dɛrplɪç] *adj* ruinous; (*Lebensmittel*) perishable

Verderbnis [fɛr'dɛrpnɪs] *f* (-;) depravity

verderbt [fɛr'dɛrpt] *adj* depraved

Verderbt'heit *f* (-;) depravity

verdeutlichen [fɛr'dɔɪtlɪçən] *tr* make plain, explain

verdeutschen [fɛr'dɔɪt/ən] *tr* translate into (or express in) German

verdich'ten *tr* condense, thicken ‖ *ref* condense; solidify; thicken; (*Nebel, Rauch*) grow thicker; (*Verdacht*) become stronger, grow

verdicken [fɛr'dɪkən] *tr* & *ref* thicken

verdie'nen *tr* deserve; (*Geld*) earn

Verdienst [fɛr'dinst] *m* (-es;-e) earnings; gain, profit ‖ *n* (-es;-e) merit; deserts; **es ist dein V., daß it is owing to you that; nach V.** deservedly; **nach V. behandelt werden** get one's due; **sich** [*dat*] **als** (or **zum**) **V. anrechnen** take credit for it; **V. um** services to

Verdienst'ausfall *m* loss of wages

verdienst'lich *adj* meritorious

Verdienst'spanne *f* margin of profit

verdienst'voll *adj* meritorious

verdient [fɛr'dint] *adj*—**sich um j-n v. machen** serve s.o. well

verdol'metschen *tr* translate orally; interpret

Verdol'metschung *f* (-;) oral translation; interpretation

verdonnern [fɛr'dɔnərn] *tr* (coll) condemn

verdop'peln *tr* & *ref* double

verdorben [fɛr'dɔrbən] *adj* spoiled; (*Luft*) foul; (*Magen*) upset; (*moralisch*) depraved

verdorren [fɛr'dɔrən] *intr* (SEIN) dry up, wither

verdrän'gen *tr* push aside, crowd out; dislodge; (phys) displace; (psychol) repress, inhibit

Verdrän'gung *f* (-;-en) (phys) displacement; (psychol) repression, inhibition

verdre'hen *tr* twist; (*Augen*) roll; (*Glied*) sprain; (fig) distort; **j-m den Kopf v.** make s.o. fall in love with one

verdreht' *adj* twisted; (fig) distorted; (fig) (*verrückt*) cracked

verdreifachen [fɛr'draɪfaxən] *tr* triple

verdre'schen §67 *tr* (coll) spank

verdrießen [fɛr'drisən] §76 *tr* bother, annoy, get down; **laß es dich nicht v.!** don't let it get you down; **sich keine Mühe v. lassen** spare no pains ‖ *impers*—**es verdrießt mich, daß it** bothers me that

verdrießlich [fɛr'drislɪç] *adj* glum; tiresome, depressing; annoyed

verdroß [fɛr'drɔs] *pret of* verdrießen

verdro'ßen *adj* cross; (*mürrisch*) surly; (*lustlos*) listless

verdrucken (verdruk'ken) *tr* misprint

verdrücken (verdrük'ken) *tr* wrinkle; (coll) eat up, polish off ‖ *ref* (coll) sneak away

Ver·druß [fɛr'drʊs] *m* (-drusses; -drusse) annoyance, vexation; **j-m etw zum V. tun** do s.th. to spite s.o.

verduften [fɛr'dʊftən] *intr* (SEIN) lose its aroma; (coll) take off, scram

verdummen [fɛr'dʊmən] *tr* make stupid ‖ *intr* (SEIN) become stupid

verdunkeln [fɛr'dʊŋkəln] *tr* darken; obscure; (*Glanz*) dull; (fig) cloud; (astr) eclipse; (mil) black out ‖ *ref* darken; (*Himmel*) cloud over

Verdun'kelung f (-;-en) darkening; (astr) eclipse; (mil) blackout
verdünnen [fɛr'dʏnən] tr thin; dilute; (Gase) rarefy
verdun'sten intr (SEIN) evaporate
Verdun'stung f (-;) evaporation
verdur'sten intr (SEIN) die of thirst
verdutzen [fɛr'dʊtsən] tr bewilder
veredeln [fɛr'edəln] tr ennoble; (verfeinen) refine; (Rohstoff) process; (Boden) enrich; (Pflanze, Tier) improve
Vere'delung f (-;) refinement; processing; enrichment; improvement
verehelichen [fɛr'e·əliçən] ref get married
verehren [fɛr'erən] tr revere; worship; (fig) adore; **j-m etw v.** present s.o. with s.th.
Vereh'rer -in §6 mf worshiper; (Liebhaber) admirer
verehrt [fɛr'ert] adj—**Sehr verehrte gnädige Frau!** Dear Madam; **Sehr verehrter Herr!** Dear Sir; **Verehrte Anwesende** (or **Gäste**)**!** Ladies and Gentlemen!
Vereh'rung f (-;) reverence, veneration; worship, adoration
vereiden [fɛr'aɪdən], **vereidigen** [fɛr'aɪdɪgən] tr swear in
Verein [fɛr'aɪn] m (-[e]s;-e) society
vereinbar [fɛr'aɪnbar] adj compatible
vereinbaren [fɛr'aɪnbarən] tr agree to, agree upon ‖ ref—**das läßt sich mit meinen Grundsätzen nicht v.** that is inconsistent with my principles
Verein'barkeit f (-;) compatibility
Verein'barung f (-;) agreement, arrangement; terms; **nur nach V.** by appointment only
vereinen [fɛr'aɪnən] tr unite, join
vereinfachen [fɛr'aɪnfaxən] tr simplify
Verein'fachung f (-;-en) simplification
vereinheitlichen [fɛr'aɪnhaɪtlɪçən] tr standardize
vereinigen [fɛr'aɪnɪgən] tr unite, join; (verbinden) combine; (verschmelzen) merge; (versammeln) assemble ‖ ref unite, join; (Flüsse) meet; **sich v. mit** team up with; **sich v. lassen mit** be compatible with, square with
Verei'nigten Staa-ten -pl United States
Verein'igung f (-;-en) union; combination; society, association
vereinnahmen [fɛr'aɪnnamən] tr take in
vereinsamen [fɛr'aɪnzamən] intr (SEIN) become lonely; become isolated
Verein'samung f (-;) loneliness; isolation
Vereins'meier -in §6 mf (coll) joiner
vereinzeln [fɛr'aɪntsəln] tr isolate
verein'zelt adj isolated; sporadic
vereisen [fɛr'aɪzən] tr (surg) freeze ‖ intr (SEIN) become covered with ice; (aer) ice up
vereiteln [fɛr'aɪtəln] tr frustrate; baffle
verekeln [fɛr'ɛkəln] tr—**j-m etw v.** spoil s.th. for s.o.
veren'den intr (SEIN) die
verengen [fɛr'ɛŋən] tr & ref narrow
verer'ben tr bequeath, leave; (über-

mitteln) hand down; (Krankheit) transmit ‖ ref run in the family
Verer'bung f (-;-en) inheritance; transmission; heredity
Verer'bungslehre f genetics
verewigen [fɛr'evɪgən] tr perpetuate
verewigt [fɛr'evɪçt] adj late, deceased
verfah'ren adj bungled, messed up ‖ §71 tr bungle; (Geld, Zeit) spend (on travel) ‖ ref lose one's way, take a track ‖ intr (SEIN) proceed; act ‖ wrong turn; (fig) be on the wrong **Verfahren** n (-s;-) procedure, method; system; (chem) process; (jur) proceedings, case
Verfall m (-[e]s;) deterioration, decay; decline, downfall; (Fristablauf) expiration; (von Wechseln) maturity; **in V. geraten** become delapidated
verfal'len adj delapidated; **e-m Rauschgift v. sein** be addicted to a drug ‖ §72 intr (SEIN) decay, go to ruin, decline; (ablaufen) expire; (Kranker) waste away; (Recht) lapse; (Pfand) be forfeited; (Wechsel) mature
Verfall'tag m due date; date of maturity
verfäl'schen tr falsify; (Geld) counterfeit; (Wein) adulterate; (Urkunde) forge
Verfäl'schung f (-;-en) falsification; forging; adulteration
verfan'gen §73 ref become entangled ‖ intr (bei) have an effect (on)
verfänglich [fɛr'fɛŋlɪç] adj (Frage) loaded; (Situation) awkward
verfär'ben ref change color
verfas'sen tr compose, write
Verfas'ser -in §6 mf author
Verfas'sung f (-;-en) constitution; (Zustand) condition; frame of mind, mood
verfas'sungsgemäß, verfas'sungsmäßig adj constitutional
verfas'sungswidrig adj unconstitutional
verfau'len intr (SEIN) rot
verfech'ten §74 tr defend, stand up for
Verfech'ter m (-s;-) champion
verfeh'len tr (Abzweigung, Ziel, Zug) miss; (Wirkung) fail to achieve, not have; **ich werde nicht v. zu** (inf) I will not fail to (inf) ‖ recip—**wir haben uns verfehlt** we missed each other
verfehlt [fɛr'felt] adj wrong
Verfeh'lung f (-;-en) offense; mistake
verfeinden [fɛr'faɪndən] recip become enemies
verfeinern [fɛr'faɪnərn] tr refine, improve ‖ ref become refined, improve
verfertigen [fɛr'fertɪgən] tr manufacture, make
Verfer'tigung f (-;) manufacture
verfilmen [fɛr'fɪlmən] tr adapt to the screen, make into a movie
Verfil'mung f (-;-en) film version
verfilzen [fɛr'fɪltsən] ref get tangled
verfinstern [fɛr'fɪnstərn] ref get dark
verflachen [fɛr'flaxən] tr flatten ‖ ref & intr (SEIN) flatten out
verflech'ten §74 tr interweave; (fig) implicate, involve
verflie'gen §57 ref (aer) lose one's

bearings ‖ *intr* (SEIN) fly away; (*Zeit*) fly; evaporate; (fig) vanish

verflie/ßen §76 *intr* (SEIN) flow off; (*Frist*) run out, expire; (*Farben*) blend; (*Begriffe, Grenzen*) overlap

verflixt [fer'flıkst] *adj* (sl) darn

verflossen [fer'flɔsən] *adj* past; former

verflu/chen *tr* curse, damn

verflucht/ *adj* (sl) damn ‖ *interj* (sl) damn it!

verflüchtigen [fer'flʏçtıgən] *tr* volatilize ‖ *ref* evaporate; (fig) disappear

verflüssigen [fer'flʏsıgən] *tr* & *ref* liquefy

Verfolg [fer'fɔlk] *m* (-s;) course; **im V.** (*genit*) in pursuance of

verfol/gen *tr* pursue; follow up; persecute; haunt; (hunt) track; (jur) prosecute; **j-n steckbrieflich v.** send out a warrant for the arrest of s.o.

Verfol/ger –in §6 *mf* pursuer; persecutor

Verfol/gung *f* (-;-en) pursuit; persecution; (jur) prosecution

Verfol/gungswahn *m*, **Verfol/gungswahnsinn** *m* persecution complex

verfrachten [fer'fraxtən] *tr* ship; (coll) bundle off

Verfrach/ter –in §6 *mf* shipper

verfrühen [fer'fry·ən] *ref* be too early

verfügbar [fer'fykbar] *adj* available, at one's disposal

verfü/gen *tr* decree, order ‖ *ref*—**sich v. nach** betake oneself to ‖ *intr*—**v. über** (*acc*) have at one's disposal, have control over

Verfü/gung *f* (-;-en) decree, order; disposal; **einstweilige V.** (jur) injunction; **j-m zur V. stehen** be at s.o.'s disposal; **j-m zur V. stellen** put at s.o.'s disposal; **letztwillige V.** last will and testament

verfüh/ren *tr* mislead; (*zum Irrtum*) lead; (*verlocken*) seduce

Verfüh/rer –in §6 *mf* seducer

verführerisch [fer'fyrərıʃ] *adj* seductive, tempting

Verfüh/rung *f* (-;-en) seduction

vergaffen [fer'gafən] *ref* (coll) (**in** *acc*) fall in love (with)

vergammeln [fer'gaməln] *intr* (SEIN) (coll) go to the dogs

vergangen [fer'gaŋən] *adj* past; (*Schönheit*) faded

Vergan/genheit *f* (-;) past; background; (gram) past tense

vergänglich [fer'geŋlıç] *adj* transitory

vergasen [fer'gazən] *tr* gas

Verga/ser *m* (-s;-) carburetor

vergaß [fer'gas] *pret* of **vergessen**

verge/ben §80 *tr* forgive (s.th.); give away; (*Chance*) miss, pass up; (*Amt, freie Stelle*) fill; (*Auftrag*) place; (*Karten*) misdeal; (*verleihen*) confer; **v. sein** have a previous engagement; be engaged (*to a man*) ‖ *ref*—**sich** [*dat*] **etw. v.** compromise on s.th. ‖ *intr* (dat) forgive (*s.o.*)

verge/bens [fer'gebəns] *adv* in vain

vergeb/lich [fer'geplıç] *adj* vain, futile

Verge/bung *f* (-;) forgiveness; bestowal

vergegenwärtigen [fer'gegənvertıgən] *ref*—**sich** [*dat*] **etw. v.** visualize s.th.

verge/hen §82 *ref*—**sich an j–m v.** offend s.o.; (*sexuell*) violate s.o. ‖ *intr* (SEIN) pass, go away; fade ‖ **Verge/hen** *n* (-s;-) offense, misdemeanor

vergel/ten §83 *tr* requite; **vergelt's Gott!** (coll) thank you!

Vergel/tung *f* (-;) repayment; retaliation, reprisal

Vergel/tungswaffe *f* V-1 or V-2

vergesellschaften [fergə'zelʃaftən] *tr* socialize; nationalize

vergessen [fer'gesən] §70 *tr* forget

Verges/senheit *f* (-;)—**in V. geraten** fall (or sink) into oblivion

vergeßlich [fer'geslıç] *adj* forceful

Vergeß/lichkeit *f* (-;) forgetfulness

vergeuden [fer'gɔidən] *tr* waste

Vergeu/dung *f* (-;) waste, squandering

vergewaltigen [fergə'valtıgən] *tr* do violence to; (*Mädchen*) rape

Vergewal/tigung *f* (-;-en) rape

vergewerkschaften [fergə'verkʃaftən] *tr* unionize

vergewissern [fergə'visərn] *ref* (*genit*) make sure of, ascertain

vergie/ßen §76 *tr* spill; (*Tränen*) shed

vergiften [fer'gıftən] *tr* (& fig) poison; (*verseuchen*) contaminate ‖ *ref* take poison

Vergif/tung *f* (-;-en) poisoning; contamination

vergipsen [fer'gıpsən] *tr* plaster

Vergißmeinnicht [fer'gısmaınnıçt] *n* (-[e]s;-e) forget-me-not

vergittern [fer'gıtərn] *tr* bar up

Vergleich [fer'glaıç] *m* (-[e]s;-e) comparison; (*Verständigung*) agreement; (*Ausgleich*) settlement; **e–n V. anstellen zwischen** make a comparison between; **e–n V. treffen** reach a settlement, come to an agreement

vergleichbar [fer'glaıçbar] *adj* comparable

verglei/chen [fer'glaıçən] §85 *tr* (**mit**) compare (with, to) ‖ *ref* (**mit**) come to an agreement (with)

Vergleichs/grundlage *f* basis for comparison

vergleichs/weise *adv* by way of comparison

Verglei/chung *f* (-;-en) comparison; matching; contrasting

verglü/hen *intr* (SEIN) cease to glow

vergnügen [fer'gnygən] *tr* amuse, delight ‖ *ref* enjoy oneself, amuse oneself ‖ **Vergnügen** *n* (-s;-) delight, pleasure; **mit V. with** pleasure; **V. finden an** (*dat*) take delight in; **viel V.!** (coll) have fun!; **zum V. for** fun

vergnügt [fer'gnykt] *adj* cheerful, gay; (**über** *acc*) delighted (with)

Vergnü/gung *f* (-;-en) pleasure, amusement

Vergnü/gungspark *m* amusement park

Vergnü/gungsreise *f* pleasure trip

Vergnü/gungssteuer *f* entertainment tax

vergnü/gungssüchtig *adj* pleasure-loving

vergolden [fer'gɔldən] *tr* gild

Vergol/dung *f* (-;-en) gilding

vergönnen [fer'gœnən] *tr* not begrudge

vergöttern [fer'gœtərn] *tr* deify; (fig) idolize

vergra/ben §87 *tr* (& fig) bury

vergrämen [fer'grɛmən] *tr* annoy, anger

vergrämt [fer'grɛmt] *adj* haggard

vergrei′fen §88 *ref* (mus) hit the wrong note; **sich v. an** (*dat*) lay violent hands on; (*fremdem Gut*) encroach on; (*Geld*) misappropriate; (*Mädchen*) assault; **sich im Ausdruck v.** express oneself poorly

vergreisen [fer'graɪzən] *intr* (SEIN) age; become senile

vergriffen [fer'grɪfən] *adj* sold out; (*Buch*) out of print

vergröbern [fer'grøbərn] *tr* roughen || *ref* become coarser

vergrößern [fer'grøsərn] *tr* enlarge; increase; (*ausdehnen*) expand; (opt) magnify || *ref* become larger

Vergrö′ßerung *f* (-;-en) enlargement; increase; expansion; (opt) magnification

Vergrö′ßerungsapparat *m* (phot) enlarger

Vergrö′ßerungsglas *m* magnifying glass

Vergünstigung [fer'gʏnstɪguŋ] *f* (-;-en) privilege; (*bevorzugte Behandlung*) preferential treatment

vergüten [fer'gytən] *tr* make good; (*Stahl*) temper; **j–m etw v.** reimburse (or compensate) s.o. for s.th.

Vergü′tung *f* (-;-en) reimbursement, compensation; tempering

verhaften [fer'haftən] *tr* apprehend

Verhaf′tung *f* (-;-en) apprehension

verhal′ten *adj* (*Atem*) bated; (*Stimme*) low || §90 *tr* hold back; (*Atem*) hold; (*Lachen*) suppress; (*Stimme*) keep down; **den Schritt v.** slow down; (*stehenbleiben*) stop || *ref* behave, act; be; **A verhält sich zu B wie X zu Y** A is to B as X is to Y; **sich anders v.** be different; **sich ruhig v.** keep quiet || *impers ref*—**wenn es sich so verhält** if that's the case || **Verhalten** *n* (-s;) conduct, behavior; attitude

Verhältnis [fer'hɛltnɪs] *n* (-ses;-se) proportion, ratio; (*Beziehung*) relation; (*Liebes*–) love affair; **aus kleinen Verhältnissen** of humble birth; **bei sonst gleichen Verhältnissen** other things being equal; **das steht in keinem V. zu** that is all out of proportion to; **Verhältnisse** circumstances, conditions; matters; means

verhält′nismäßig *adj* proportionate || *adv* relatively, comparatively

Verhält′nismaßregeln *pl* instructions

Verhält′niswahl *f* proportional representation

verhält′niswidrig *adj* disproportionate

Verhält′niswort *n* (-[e]s;–er) preposition

verhan′deln *tr* discuss; (*Waren*) sell || *intr* negotiate; argue; (*beraten*) confer; (jur) plead a case; **gegen j–n wegen etw v.** (jur) try s.o. for s.th.

Verhand′lung *f* (-;-en) negotiation; discussion; proceedings, trial

verhangen [fer'haŋən] *adj* overcast

verhän′gen *tr* (*Fenster*) put curtains on; (*Strafe*) impose; (*Untersuchung*) order; (*Belagerungszustand*) pro- | claim; **mit verhängtem Zügel at full speed**

Verhängnis [fer'hɛŋnɪs] *n* (-ses;-se) destiny, fate; (*Unglück*) disaster

verhäng′nisvoll *adj* fateful; disastrous

verhärmt [fer'hɛrmt] *adj* haggard

verharren [fer'harən] *intr* (HABEN & SEIN) remain; (**auf** *dat*, **in** *dat*, **bei**) stick (to)

verhärten [fer'hɛrtən] *tr & ref* harden

verhaßt [fer'hast] *adj* hated, hateful

verhätscheln [fer'hɛtʃəln] *tr* pamper

Verhau [fer'hau] *m* (-[e]s;-e) barbwire entanglement

verhau′en §93 *tr* lick, beat up; (*Kind*) spank; (*Auftrag, Ball, usw.*) muff || *ref* make a blunder

verheddern [fer'hedərn] *ref* get tangled up

verheeren [fer'herən] *tr* devastate

verhee′rend *adj* terrible; (coll) awful

Verhee′rung *f* (-;) devastation

verhehlen [fer'helən] *tr* conceal

verhei′len *intr* (SEIN) heal up

verheimlichen [fer'haɪmlɪçən] *tr* keep secret, conceal

Verheim′lichung *f* (-;) concealment

verhei′raten *tr* marry; (*Tochter*) give away || *ref* (**mit**) get married (to)

Verhei′ratung *f* (-;) marriage

verhei′ßen §95 *tr* promise

Verhei′ßung *f* (-;-en) promise

verhei′ßungsvoll *adj* promising

verhel′fen §96 *intr*—**j–m zu etw v.** help s.o. to acquire s.th.

verherrlichen [fer'herlɪçən] *tr* glorify

Verherr′lichung *f* (-;) glorification

verhet′zen *tr* instigate

verhexen [fer'heksən] *tr* bewitch, hex

verhimmeln [fer'hɪməln] *tr* praise to the skies; (*Schauspieler*) idolize

verhin′dern *tr* prevent

Verhin′derung *f* (-;) prevention; **im Falle seiner V.** in case he's unavailable

verhohlen [fer'holən] *adj* hidden

verhöh′nen *tr* jeer at; make fun of

Verhöh′nung *f* (-;) jeering; ridicule

Verhör [fer'hør] *n* (-s;-e) interrogation, questioning, hearing

verhö′ren *tr* interrogate, question || *ref* hear wrong

verhudeln [fer'hudəln] *tr* (coll) bungle

verhüllen [fer'hylən] *tr* cover, veil; wrap up; disguise

Verhül′lung *f* (-;-en) cover; disguise

verhun′gern *intr* (SEIN) starve to death

verhunzen [fer'huntsən] *tr* (coll) botch

verhü′ten *tr* prevent, avert

verinnerlicht [fer'ɪnərlɪçt] *adj* introspective

verir′ren *ref* lose one's way; (*Augen, Blick*) wander; (*fig*) make a mistake

verirrt [fer'ɪrt] *adj* stray

verja′gen *tr* chase away

verjähren [fer'jerən] *intr* (SEIN) fall under the statute of limitations

verjubeln [fer'jubəln] *tr* squander

verjüngen [fer'jʏŋən] *tr* rejuvenate; reduce in scale; taper || *ref* be rejuvenated; taper, narrow

Verjün′gung *f* (-;) rejuvenation; tapering; scaling down

verkatert [fɛr'kɑtərt] *adj* suffering from a hangover

Verkauf' *m* (-[e]s;⸗e) sale

verkau'fen *tr* sell

Verkäu'fer –in §6 *mf* seller; salesclerk; vendor ‖ *m* salesman ‖ *f* salesgirl, saleswoman

verkäuf'lich *adj* salable

Verkaufs'anzeige *f* for-sale ad

Verkaufs'automat *m* vending machine

Verkaufs'leiter –in §6 *mf* sales manager

Verkaufs'schlager *m* good seller

Verkaufs'steigerung *f* sales promotion

Verkaufs'vertrag *m* agreement of sale

Verkehr [fɛr'ker] *m* (-s;) traffic; commerce; company, association; (*sexuell*) intercourse; (aer, rr) service; (fin) circulation

verkeh'ren *tr* reverse, invert; turn upside down; convert, change; (*Sinn, Worte*) twist ‖ *intr* (*Fahrzeug*) run, run regularly; **mit j-m geschlechtlich v.** have intercourse with s.o.; **mit j-m v.** associate with s.o.

Verkehrs'ader *f* main artery

Verkehrs'ampel *f* traffic light

Verkehrs'andrang *m* heavy traffic

Verkehrs'betrieb *m* public transportation company

Verkehrs'delikt *n* traffic violation

Verkehrs'flugzeug *n* airliner

Verkehrs'insel *f* traffic island

Verkehrs'mittel *n* means of transportation

Verkehrs'ordnungen *pl* traffic regulations

Verkehrs'polizist –in §7 *mf* traffic cop

verkehrs'reich *adj* crowded, congested

verkehrs'stark *adj* busy

Verkehrs'stockung *f*, **Verkehrs'störung** *f* traffic jam

Verkehrs'unfall *m* traffic accident

Verkehrs'unternehmen *n* transportation company

Verkehrs'vorschrift *f* traffic regulation

Verkehrs'wesen *n* traffic, transportation

Verkehrs'zeichen *n* traffic sign

verkehrt [fɛr'kert] *adj* reversed, upside down; inside out; wrong

verken'nen §97 *tr* misunderstand; (*Person*) misjudge, mistake

verketten [fɛr'ketən] *tr* chain together; (fig) link

Verket'tung *f* (-;) chaining; (fig) concatenation; (fig) coincidence

verkit'ten *tr* cement; putty; seal, bond

verkla'gen *tr* accuse; (jur) sue

Verklagte [fɛr'klɑktə] §5 *mf* defendant

verklat'schen *tr* (coll) slander; (educ) squeal on

verkle'ben *tr* glue, cement; **v. mit** cover with

verklei'den *tr* disguise, dress up; (*täfeln*) panel; line, face; (mil) camouflage

Verklei'dung *f* (-;-en) disguise; paneling; lining, facing; (mil) camouflage

verkleinern [fɛr'klɑɪnərn] *tr* lessen, diminish; (fig) disparage; (math) reduce; **maßstäblich v.** scale down

Verklei'nerung *f* (-;-en) diminution, reduction; (fig) detraction

Verklei'nerungsform *f* diminutive

verklin'gen §142 *intr* (SEIN) die away

verkloppen [fɛr'klɔpən] *tr* (coll) beat up

verknacken [fɛr'knakən] *tr* (coll) sentence

verknallt [fɛr'knalt] *adj*—**in j-n v. sein** (coll) have a crush on s.o.

verknappen [fɛr'knapən] *intr* (SEIN) run short, run low

Verknap'pung *f* (-;) shortage

verknei'fen §88 *ref*—**sich** [*dat*] **etw v.** deny oneself s.th.

verkniffen [fɛr'knɪfən] *adj* wry

verknip'sen *tr* (*Film*) waste

verknöchern [fɛr'knœçərn] *intr* (SEIN) ossify; (*Glieder*) become stiff

verknöchert [fɛr'knœçərt] *adj* pedantic; (*Junggeselle*) inveterate

verknoten [fɛr'knotən] *tr* snarl, tie up

verknüp'fen *tr* tie together; (fig) connect, combine, relate

verknusen [fɛr'knuzən] *tr* (coll) stand

verkohlen [fɛr'kolən] *tr* carbonize; char; **j-n v.** (coll) pull s.o.'s leg

verkom'men *adj* decayed; degenerate; (*Gebäude*) squalid ‖ §99 *intr* (SEIN) decay, spoil; (fig) go to the dogs; **v. zu** degenerate into

Verkom'menheit *f* (-;) depravity

verkop'peln *tr* couple; (*Interessen*) (com) consolidate

verkorken [fɛr'kɔrkən] *tr* cork up

verkorksen [fɛr'kɔrksən] *tr* (coll) bungle ‖ *ref*—**sich** [*dat*] **den Magen v.** (coll) upset one's stomach

verkörpern [fɛr'kœrpərn] *tr* embody, personify; (*Rolle*) play

Verkör'perung *f* (-;-en) embodiment, incarnation

verkra'chen *ref*—**sich mit j-m v.** have an argument with s.o. ‖ *intr* (SEIN) (coll) go bankrupt

verkrampft [fɛr'krampft] *adj* cramped

verkrie'chen §102 *ref* hide; (& fig) crawl into a hole; **neben ihm kannst du dich v.!** you're no match for him!

verkrümeln [fɛr'krymaln] *tr* crumble ‖ *ref* (fig) disappear

verkrüm'men *tr* & *ref* bend

Verkrüm'mung *f* (-;) bend, crookedness; curvature

verkrüppeln [fɛr'krypəln] *tr* cripple ‖ *intr* (SEIN) become crippled; (*verkümmern*) become stunted

verkrustet [fɛr'krustət] *adj* caked

verküh'len *ref* catch a cold

verküm'mern *intr* (SEIN) become stunted; (pathol) atrophy

Verküm'merung *f* (-;) atrophy

verkünden [fɛr'kyndən], **verkündigen** [fɛr'kyndɪgən] *tr* announce, proclaim; (*Urteil*) pronounce

Verkün'digung *f* (-;-en), **Verkün'dung** *f* (-;-en) announcement, proclamation; pronouncement; **Mariä Verkündigung** (feast of the) Annunciation

verkup'peln *tr* couple; (*Mädchen, Mann*) procure; (*Tochter*) sell into prostitution

verkür′zen *tr* shorten; abridge; (*beschränken*) curtail; (*Zeit*) pass

Verkür′zung *f* (-;-en) shortening; abridgement; curtailment

verla′chen *tr* laugh at

verla′den §103 *tr* load, ship

Verlag [fer′lak] *m* (-[e]s;-e) publisher; **im V. von** published by

verla′gern *tr* shift; (*aus Sicherheitsgründen*) evacuate || *ref* shift

Verla′gerung *f* (-;-en) shift, shifting; evacuation

Verlags′anstalt *f* publisher

Verlags′buchhandlung *f* publisher and dealer

Verlags′recht *n* copyright

verlangen [fer′laŋən] *tr* demand, require; want, ask || *intr—v.* **nach** ask for; long for || **Verlangen** *n* (-s;) demand; request; wish; claim; (*Sehnsucht*) longing, yearning; **auf V.** upon demand, upon request

verlängern [fer′leŋərn] *tr* lengthen; prolong, extend; **seinen Paß v. lassen** have one's passport renewed

Verlän′gerung *f* (-;-en) lengthening; prolongation, extension; (*sport*) overtime

Verlän′gerungsschnur *f* extension cord

verlangsamen [fer′laŋzamən] *tr* slow down

verläppern [fer′lepərn] *tr* (coll) fritter away

Ver-laß [fer′las] *m* (-lasses;) reliance; **es ist kein V. auf ihn** you can't rely on him

verlas′sen *adj* abandoned, deserted; lonesome || §104 *tr* leave; forsake, desert || *ref—sich v. auf* (*acc*) rely on

Verlas′senheit *f* (-;) loneliness

verläßlich [fer′leslıç] *adj* reliable

verlästern [fer′lestərn] *tr* slander

Verlä′sterung *f* (-;-en) slander

Verlaub [fer′laup] *m—mit* **V. mit** your permission; **mit V. zu sagen** if I may say so

Verlauf′ *m* (-[e]s;) course; **e-n guten V. haben** turn out well; **nach V. von** after a lapse of

verlau′fen §105 *intr* (SEIN) (*Zeit*) pass, lapse; (*ablaufen*) turn out, come off; (*vorgehen*) proceed, run || *ref* lose one's way; (*Wasser*) run off; (*Menschenmenge*) disperse

verlau′ten *intr* (SEIN) become known, be reported; **kein Wort davon v. lassen** not breathe a word about it; **wie verlautet** as reported || *impers—es verlautet* it is reported

verle′ben *tr* spend, pass

verlebt [fer′lept] *adj* haggard

verle′gen *adj* embarrassed; confused; **v. um** (*e-e Antwort*) at a loss for; (*Geld*) short of || *tr* move, shift; transfer; misplace; (*Buch*) publish; (*Geleise, Kabel, Rohre*) lay; (*sperren*) block; (*verpassen*) postpone || *ref—sich v. auf* (*acc*) apply onself to; devote oneself to; resort to

Verle′genheit *f* (-;) embarrassment; difficulties; predicament; **in V. bringen** embarrass

Verle′ger *m* (-s;-) publisher

Verle′gung *f* (-;-en) move, shift; transfer; postponement; (*von Kabeln, usw.*) laying

verlei′den *tr* spoil, take the joy out of

Verleih [fer′laı] *m* (-s;-e) rental service

verlei′hen §81 *tr* lend out, loan; rent out; (*Gunst*) grant; (*Titel*) confer; (*Auszeichnung*) award

Verlei′her -in §6 *mf* lender; grantor; (*von Filmen*) distributor

Verlei′hung *f* (-;-en) lending out; rental; grant; bestowal

verlei′ten *tr* mislead; (*zur Sünde, zum Trunk*) lead; (*jur*) suborn

verler′nen *tr* unlearn, forget

verle′sen §107 *tr* read out; (*Namen*) read off; (*Salat*) clean; (*Gemüse*) sort out || *ref* misread

verletzen [fer′letsən] *tr* (& fig) injure, hurt; (*kränken*) offend; (*Gesetz*) break; (*Recht*) violate

verlet′zend *adj* offensive

Verletzte [fer′letstə] §5 *mf* injured party

Verlet′zung *f* (-;-en) injury; offense; (*e-s Gesetzes*) breaking; (*e-s Rechtes*) violation

verleug′nen *tr* deny; (*Kind*) disown; (*Glauben*) renounce || *ref—sich selbst v.* act contrary to one's nature; **sich vor Besuchern v. lassen** refuse to see visitors

Verleug′nung *f* (-;-en) denial; renunciation; disavowal

verleumden [fer′lɔımdən] *tr* slander

verleumderisch [fer′lɔımdərıʃ] *adj* slanderous, libelous

Verleum′dung *f* (-;-en) slander

verlie′ben *ref—sich in j-n v.* fall in love with s.o.

verliebt [fer′lipt] *adj* in love

verlieren [fer′lirən] §77 *tr* lose || *ref* lose one's way; disappear; disperse

Verlies [fer′lis] *n* (-es;-e) dungeon

verlo′ben *ref* (mit) become engaged (to)

Verlöbnis [fer′løpnıs] *n* (-ses;-se) engagement

Verlobte [fer′loptə] §5 *m* fiancé; **die Verlobten** the engaged couple || *f* fiancée

Verlo′bung *f* (-;-en) engagement

verlocken [fer′lokən] *tr* lure, tempt; (*verführen*) seduce

verlockend [fer′lokənt] *adj* tempting

Verlockung (Verlok′kung) *f* (-;-en) allurement, temptation

verlogen [fer′logən] *adj* dishonest

verlohn′nen *impers ref—es verlohnt sich nicht** it doesn't pay || *impers—es* **verlohnt der Mühe nicht** it is not worth the trouble

verlor [fer′lor] *pret* of **verlieren**

verloren [fer′lorən] *pp* of **verlieren** || *adj* lost; (*hilflos*) forlorn; (*Ei*) poached; **der verlorene Sohn** the prodigal son

verlo′rengehen §80 *tr* give up for lost

verlo′rengehen §82 *intr* (SEIN) be lost

verlö′schen §110 *tr* extinguish; (*Schrift*) erase || *intr* (SEIN) (*Licht, Kerze*) go out; (*Zorn*) cease

verlo′sen *tr* raffle off, draw lots for

verlö′ten *tr* solder; **e–n v.** (coll) belt one down

verlottern [fɛr′lɔtərn] *intr* (coll) go to the dogs

verlumpen [fɛr′lʊmpən] *tr* (coll) blow, squander ‖ *intr* (coll) go to the dogs

Verlust [fɛr′lʊst] *m* (–[e]s;–e) loss; **in V. geraten** get lost; **Verluste** (mil) casualties

Verlust′liste *f* (mil) casualty list

verma′chen *tr* bequeath, leave

Vermächtnis [fɛr′mɛçtnɪs] *n* (–ses;–se) bequest, legacy

vermählen [fɛr′mɛlən] *tr* marry ‖ *ref* (mit) get married (to)

Vermäh′lung *f* (–;–en) marriage, wedding

vermah′nen *tr* admonish, warn

Vermah′nung *f* (–;–en) admonition

vermaledeien [fɛrmalə′daɪ·ən] *tr* curse

vermanschen [fɛr′manʃən] *tr* (coll) make a mess of

vermasseln [fɛr′masəln] *tr* (coll) bungle, muff

vermassen [fɛr′masən] *intr* (SEIN) lose one's individuality

vermauern [fɛr′maʊ·ərn] *tr* wall up

vermehren [fɛr′merən] *tr* & *ref* increase; **(an Zahl)** multiply; **vermehrte Auflage** enlarged edition

vermei′den *tr* avoid

vermeidlich [fɛr′maɪtlɪç] *adj* avoidable

Vermei′dung *f* (–;) avoidance

vermei′nen *tr* suppose; presume, allege

vermeintlich [fɛr′maɪntlɪç] *adj* supposed, alleged; **(erdacht)** imaginary

vermel′den *tr* (poet) announce

vermen′gen *tr* mix, mingle; confound ‖ *ref* (mit) meddle (with)

Vermerk [fɛr′mɛrk] *m* (–[e]s;–e) note

vermer′ken *tr* note, record

vermes′sen *adj* daring, bold ‖ §70 *tr* measure; **(Land)** survey ‖ *ref* measure wrong; **sich v. zu** (*inf*) have the nerve to (*inf*)

Vermes′sung *f* (–;–en) surveying

vermie′ten *tr* rent out; lease out

Vermie′ter **–in** §6 *mf* (jur) lessor ‖ *m* landlord ‖ *f* landlady

vermindern [fɛr′mɪndərn] *tr* diminish, lessen; **(beschränken)** reduce, cut ‖ *ref* diminish, decrease

Vermin′derung *f* (–;–en) diminution, decrease; reduction, cut

verminen [fɛr′minən] *tr* (mil) mine

vermi′schen *tr* & *ref* mix

Vermi′schung *f* (–;–en) mixture

vermissen [fɛr′mɪsən] *tr* miss

vermißt [fɛr′mɪst] *adj* (mil) missing in action ‖ **Vermißte** §5 *mf* missing person

vermitteln [fɛr′mɪtəln] *tr* negotiate; arrange, bring about; **(beschaffen)** get, procure ‖ *intr* mediate; intercede

vermittels [fɛr′mɪtəls] *prep* (genit) by means of, through

Vermitt′ler **–in** §6 *mf* mediator, go-between; (com) agent

Vermitt′lung *f* (–;–en) negotiation; mediation; procuring; providing; intercession; **(Mittel)** means; agency;

brokerage; (telp) exchange; **durch gütige V.** (genit) through the good offices of

Vermitt′lungsamt *n* (telp) exchange

Vermitt′lungsgebühr *f,* **Vermitt′lungsprovision** *f* commission; brokerage

vermo′dern *intr* (SEIN) rot, decay

vermöge [fɛr′møgə] *prep* (genit) by virtue of

vermö′gen §114 *tr* be able to do; **j–n v. zu** (*inf*) induce s.o. to (*inf*); **sie vermag bei ihm viel** (or **wenig**) she has great (or little) influence with him; **v. zu** (*inf*) be able to (*inf*), have the power to (*inf*) ‖ **Vermögen** *n* (–s;–) ability; capacity; power; fortune, means; property; (fin) capital, assets; **nach bestem V.** to the best of one's ability

vermö′gend *adj* well-to-do, well-off

Vermö′genslage *f* financial situation

Vermö′genssteuer *f* property tax

vermorscht [fɛr′mɔrʃt] *adj* rotten

vermottet [fɛr′mɔtət] *adj* moth-eaten

vermummen [fɛr′mʊmən] *tr* disguise ‖ *ref* disguise oneself

vermuten [fɛr′mutən] *tr* suppose, presume

vermutlich [fɛr′mutlɪç] *adj* presumable ‖ *adv* presumably, I suppose

Vermu′tung *f* (–;–en) guess, conjecture

vernachlässigen [fɛr′naxlɛsɪgən] *tr* neglect

Vernach′lässigung *f* (–;) neglect

verna′geln *tr* nail up; board up

vernä′hen *tr* sew up

vernarben [fɛr′narbən] *intr* (SEIN) heal up

vernarren [fɛr′narən] *ref*—**sich v. in** (acc) be crazy about, be stuck on

verna′schen *tr* spend on sweets; **(Mädchen)** make love to

vernebeln [fɛr′nebəln] *tr* (mil) screen with smoke; (fig) hide, cover over

vernehmbar [fɛr′nembar] *adj* perceptible

verneh′men §116 *tr* perceive; **(erfahren)** hear, learn; (jur) question; **sich v. lassen** be heard, express an opinion ‖ **Vernehmen** *n* (–s;–)—**dem V. nach** reportedly, according to the report

vernehmlich [fɛr′nemlɪç] *adj* perceptible, audible; distinct

Verneh′mung *f* (–;–en) interrogation

vernei′gen *ref* bow; curtsy

Vernei′gung *f* (–;–en) bow; curtsy

verneinen [fɛr′naɪnən] *tr* say no to; reject, refuse; disavow

vernei′nend *adj* negative

Vernei′nung *f* (–;–en) negation; denial

vernichten [fɛr′nɪçtən] *tr* destroy, annihilate; **(Hoffnung)** dash

vernich′tend *adj* (Kritik) scathing; (Niederlage) crushing

Vernich′tung *f* (–;–en) destruction

vernickeln [fɛr′nɪkəln] *tr* nickel-plate

vernie′ten *tr* rivet

Vernunft [fɛr′nʊnft] *f* (–;) reason; good sense; senses; **die gesunde V.** common sense; **V. annehmen** listen to reason; **zur V. bringen** bring to one's senses

Vernunft'ehe *f* marriage of convenience

vernunft'gemäß *adj* reasonable

vernünftig [fɛr'nʏnftɪç] *adj* rational; reasonable; sensible; level-headed

vernunft'los *adj* senseless

vernunft'mäßig *adj* rational; reasonable

veröden [fɛr'ødən] *intr* (SEIN) become desolate

veröffentlichen [fɛr'œfəntlɪçən] *tr* publish; announce

Veröf'fentlichung *f* (-;-en) publication; announcement

verord'nen *tr* decree; (med) prescribe

Verord'nung *f* (-;-en) decree, order; (med) prescription

verpach'ten *tr* farm out; lease, rent out

Verpäch'ter –in §6 *mf* lessor

verpacken (verpak'ken) *tr* pack up

Verpackung (Verpak'kung) *f* (-;-en) packing (material); wrapping

verpas'sen *tr* (Gelegenheit, Anschluß, usw.) miss; **j–m e–n Anzug v.** fit s.o. with a suit; **j–m e–e v.** (coll) give s.o. a smack

verpatzen [fɛr'patsən] *tr* (coll) make a mess of

verpesten [fɛr'pɛstən] *tr* infect, contaminate

verpet'zen *tr* (coll) squeal on

verpfän'den *tr* pawn; mortgage; **sein Wort v.** give one's word of honor

verpflan'zen *tr* (bot, surg) transplant

Verpflan'zung *f* (-;-en) (bot, surg) transplant

verpfle'gen *tr* feed; (mil) supply

Verpfle'gung *f* (-;) feeding; board; (mil) rations, supplies

verpflichten [fɛr'pflɪçtən] *tr* obligate, bind; **zu Dank v.** put under obligation

Verpflich'tung *f* (-;-en) obligation; commitment; (jur) liability

verpfuschen [fɛr'pfuʃən] *tr* (coll) botch, bungle, muff

verplap'pern *ref* blab out a secret

verplau'dern *tr* waste in chatting

verpönt [fɛr'pønt] *adj* taboo

verprü'geln *tr* (coll) wallop, thrash

verpuf'fen *intr* (SEIN) fizzle; (fig) fizzle out

verpulvern [fɛr'pulfərn] *tr* (coll) waste, fritter away

verpum'pen *tr* (coll) loan

verpusten [fɛr'pustən] *ref* (coll) catch one's breath

Verputz [fɛr'puts] *m* (-es;-e) finishing coat (of plaster)

verput'zen *tr* plaster; (aufessen) polish off; (coll) stand

verquicken [fɛr'kvɪkən] *tr* interrelate

verquollen [fɛr'kvɔlən] *adj* (Augen) swollen; (Gesicht) puffy; (Holz) warped

verrammeln [fɛr'raməln] *tr* barricade

verramschen [fɛr'ramʃən] *tr* (coll) sell dirt-cheap

verrannt [fɛr'rant] *adj*—**v. sein in** (acc) be stuck on

Verrat' *m* (-[e]s;) betrayal; treason

verra'ten §63 *tr* betray

Verräter –in [fɛr'retər(ɪn)] §6 *mf* traitor; betrayer

verräterisch [fɛr'retərɪʃ] *adj* treacherous; (Spur, usw.) telltale

verrau'chen *tr* spend on smokes

verräu'chern *tr* fill with smoke

verrech'nen *tr* (ausgleichen) balance; (Scheck) deposit; (fin) clear || *ref* miscalculate; (fig) be mistaken

Verrech'nung *f* (-;-en) miscalculation; (fin) clearing; **nur zur V.** for deposit only

Verrech'nungsbank *f*, **Verrech'nungskasse** *f* clearing house

verrecken [fɛr'rɛkən] *intr* (SEIN) die; (sl) croak; **verrecke!** drop dead!

verreg'nen *tr* spoil with too much rain

verrei'sen *intr* (SEIN) go on a trip; **v. nach** depart for

verreist [fɛr'raist] *adj* out of town

verren'ken *tr* wrench, dislocate || *ref*—**sich** [*dat*] **den Arm v.** wrench one's arm; **sich** [*dat*] **den Hals v.** (coll) crane one's neck

Verren'kung *f* (-;-en) dislocation

verrich'ten *tr* do; (Gebet) say; **seine Notdurft v.** ease oneself

Verrich'tung *f* (-;-en) performance; task, duty

verrie'geln *tr* bolt, bar

verringern [fɛr'rɪŋərn] *tr* diminish, reduce || *ref* diminish; be reduced

Verrin'gerung *f* (-;-en) diminution; reduction

verrin'nen §121 *intr* (SEIN) run off; (Zeit) pass

verro'sten *intr* (SEIN) rust

verrotten [fɛr'rɔtən] *intr* (SEIN) rot

verrucht [fɛr'ruxt] *adj* wicked

verrücken (verrük'ken) *tr* move, shift

verrückt [fɛr'rʏkt] *adj* crazy; **v. auf** *etw* crazy about s.th.; **v. nach** j–m crazy about s.o. || **Verrückte** §5 *mf* lunatic

Verrückt'heit *f* (-;-en) craziness, madness; crazy action or act

Verruf' *m* (-[e]s;) discredit, disrepute

verru'fen *adj* disreputable

verrüh'ren *tr* stir thoroughly

verrut'schen *intr* (SEIN) slip

Vers [fɛrs] *m* (-es;-e) verse

versa'gen *tr* refuse; **versagt sein** have a previous engagement || *ref*—**sich** [*dat*] **etw v.** deny oneself s.th.; **ich kann es mir nicht v. zu** (*inf*) I can't refrain from (*ger*) || *intr* fail; (Beine, Stimme, usw.) give out; (Gewehr) misfire; (Motor) fail to start; **bei e–r Prüfung v.** flunk a test || **Versagen** *n* (-s;-) failure, flop; misfire

Versa'ger *m* (-s;-) failure, flop; (Patrone) dud

versal'zen *tr* oversalt; (fig) spoil

versam'meln *tr* gather together, assemble; convoke || *ref* gather, assemble

Versamm'lung *f* (-;-en) assembly, meeting

Versand [fɛr'zant] *m* (-[e]s;) shipment; mailing

Versand'abteilung *f* shipping department

versanden [fɛr'zandən] *intr* (SEIN) silt up; (fig) bog down

Versand'geschäft n, **Versand'haus** n mail-order house

versäu'men tr (Gelegenheit, Schule, Zug) miss; (Geschäft, Pflicht) neglect; **v. zu** (inf) fail to (inf)

Versäumnis [fer'zɔɪmnɪs] ƒ (-;-se), n (-ses;-se) omission, neglect; (educ) absence; (jur) default

verschaf'fen tr get, obtain || ref—**sich** [dat] **etw v.** get; **sich** [dat] **Geld v.** raise money; **sich** [dat] **Respekt v.** gain respect

verschämt [fer'ʃɛmt] adj bashful, coy

Verschämt'heit ƒ (-;) bashfulness

verschandeln [fer'ʃandəln] tr deface

verschan'zen tr fortify || ref entrench oneself; **sich v. hinter** (dat) (fig) hide behind

Verschan'zung ƒ (-;-en) entrenchment

verschär'fen tr intensify; aggravate; **verschärfter Arrest** detention on a bread-and-water diet || ref get worse

verschei'den §112 intr (SEIN) pass away

verschen'ken tr give away

verscher'zen ref—**sich** [dat] **etw v.** throw away, lose (frivolously)

verscheu'chen tr scare away

verschicken (**verschik'ken**) tr send away; (deportieren) deport

Verschie'behahnhof m marshaling yard

verschie'ben §130 tr postpone; shift; displace; black-market; (rr) shunt, switch || ref shift

Verschie'bung ƒ (-;-en) postponement; shift, shifting

verschieden [fer'ʃidən] adj different, various; distinct

verschie'denartig adj of a different kind

verschiedenerlei [fer'ʃidənərlaɪ] invar adj different kinds of

Verschie'denheit ƒ (-;-en) difference; variety, diversity

verschiedentlich [fer'ʃidəntlɪç] adv repeatedly; at times, occasionally

verschie'ßen §76 tr (Schießvorrat) use up, expend || intr (SEIN) (Farbe) fade

verschif'fen tr ship

Verschif'fung ƒ (-;) shipment

verschim'meln intr (SEIN) get moldy

verschla'fen adj sleepy, drowsy || §131 tr miss by sleeping; (Zeit) sleep away || intr oversleep

Verschla'fenheit ƒ (-;) sleepiness

Verschlag' m partition; crate

verschla'gen adj sly; (lau) lukewarm || §132 tr partition off; board up; (Kisten) nail shut; (Seite im Buch) lose; (naut) drive off course; (tennis) misserve; **j-m den Atem v.** take s.o.'s breath away; **j-m die Sprache (or Rede, Stimme) v.** make s.o. speechless; **v. werden auf** (acc) (or **in** acc) be driven to || **impers—es verschlägt nichts** it doesn't matter

verschlammen [fer'ʃlamən] intr (SEIN) silt up

verschlampen [fer'ʃlampən] tr ruin (through neglect); (verlegen) misplace || intr get slovenly

verschlechtern [fer'ʃlɛçtərn] tr make worse || ref get worse, deteriorate

Verschlech'terung ƒ (-;) deterioration

verschleiern [fer'ʃlaɪ·ərn] tr veil; (Tatsachen) cover up; (Stimme) disguise; (mil) screen; **die Bilanz v.** juggle the books || ref cloud up

verschleiert [fer'ʃlaɪ·ərt] adj hazy; (Stimme) husky; (Augen) misty

Verschlei'erung ƒ (-;) coverup; camouflaging; (jur) suppression of evidence

verschlei'fen §88 tr slur, slur over

Verschleiß [fer'ʃlaɪs] m (-es;) wear and tear; (Aust) retail trade

verschlei'ßen §53 tr wear out; (Aust) retail || ref wear out

verschleiß'fest adj durable

verschlep'pen tr drag off; abduct; (im Krieg) displace; (Verhandlungen) drag out; (Seuche) spread; (verzögern) delay

verschleu'dern tr waste, squander; (Waren) sell dirt-cheap

verschlie'ßen §76 tr shut; lock; put under lock and key || ref (dat) close one's mind to

verschlimmern [fer'ʃlɪmərn] tr make worse; (fig) aggravate || ref get worse

verschlin'gen §142 tr devour, wolf down; (verflechten) intertwine

verschlissen [fer'ʃlɪsən] adj frayed

verschlossen [fer'ʃlosən] adj shut; (fig) reserved, tight-lipped

verschlucken (**verschluk'ken**) tr swallow || ref swallow the wrong way

verschlungen [fer'ʃluŋən] adj (Weg) winding; (fig) intricate

Ver·schluß' m (-schlusses;-schlüsse) fastener; (Schnapp-) catch; (Schloß) lock; (e-r Flasche) stopper; (Stöpsel) plug; (Plombe) seal; (e-s Gewehrs) breechlock; (phot) shutter; **unter V.** under lock and key

verschlüsseln [fer'ʃlʏsəln] tr code

Verschluß'laut m (ling) stop, plosive

verschmach'ten intr (SEIN) pine away; **vor Durst v.** be dying of thirst

verschmä'hen tr disdain

verschmel'zen §133 tr & intr (SEIN) fuse, merge; blend

Verschmel'zung ƒ (-;-en) fusion; (com) merger

verschmer'zen tr get over

verschmie'ren tr smear; soil, dirty; (verwischen) blur

verschmitzt [fer'ʃmɪtst] adj crafty

verschmut'zen tr dirty || intr (SEIN) get dirty

verschnap'pen ref give oneself away

verschnau'fen ref & intr stop for breath

verschnei'den §106 tr clip, trim; cut wrong; castrate; (Branntwein, Wein) blend

verschneit [fer'ʃnaɪt] adj snow-covered

Verschnitt' m (-[e]s;) blend

verschnup'fen tr annoy; **verschnupft sein** have a cold; (coll) be annoyed

verschnü'ren tr tie up

verschollen [fer'ʃolən] adj missing, never heard of again; (jur) presumed dead

verscho'nen tr spare; **j-n mit etw v.** spare s.o. s.th.

verschönern [fer'ʃønərn] tr beautify

verschossen [fer'ʃɔsən] *adj* faded, discolored; (**in** *acc*) (coll) be madly in love (with)
verschränken [fer'ʃreŋkən] *tr* fold (one's arms)
verschrau'ben *tr* screw tight
verschrei'ben §62 *tr* use up (*in writing*); (jur) make over; (med) prescribe || *ref* make a mistake (*in writing*)
Verschrei'bung *f* (–;-en) prescription
verschrei'en §135 *tr* decry
verschrien [fer'ʃriːən] *adj*—**v. sein als** have the reputation of being
verschroben [fer'ʃroːbən] *adj* eccentric
Verschro'benheit *f* (–;-en) eccentricity
verschrotten [fer'ʃrɔtən] *tr* scrap
verschüch'tern *tr* intimidate
verschul'den *tr* encumber with debts; **etw v.** be guilty of s.th.; be the cause of s.th. || **Verschulden** *n* (–s;) fault
verschuldet [fer'ʃuldət] *adj* in debt
Verschul'dung *f* (–;-en) indebtedness; encumbrance
verschüt'ten *tr* spill; (*ausfüllen*) fill up; (*Person*) bury alive
verschwägert [fer'ʃvɛːgərt] *adj* related by marriage
verschwei'gen §148 *tr* keep secret; **j-m etw v.** keep s.th. from s.o.
Verschwei'gung *f* (–;) concealment
verschwei'ßen *tr* weld (together)
verschwenden [fer'ʃvɛndən] *tr* (**an** *acc*) waste (on), squander (on)
Verschwen'der –**in** §6 *mf* spendthrift
verschwenderisch [fer'ʃvɛndərɪʃ] *adj* wasteful; lavish, extravagant
Verschwen'dung *f* (–;) waste; extravagance
verschwiegen [fer'ʃviːgən] *adj* discreet, reserved, reticent
Verschwie'genheit *f* (–;) discretion; reticence; secrecy
verschwim'men §136 *intr* (SEIN) become blurred; (fig) fade
verschwin'den §59 *intr* (SEIN) disappear; **ich muß mal v.** (coll) I have to go (to the toilet); **v. lassen** put out of the way; spirit off || **Verschwinden** *n* (–s;) disappearance
verschwistert [fer'ʃvɪstərt] *adj* closely related
verschwit'zen *tr* sweat up; (coll) forget
verschwollen [fer'ʃvɔlən] *adj* swollen
verschwommen [fer'ʃvɔmən] *adj* hazy, indistinct; (*Bild*) blurred
Verschwom'menheit *f* (–;) haziness
verschwö'ren §137 *tr* forswear || *ref* (**gegen**) plot (against); **sich zu etw v.** plot s.th.
Verschwö'rer –**in** §6 *mf* conspirator
Verschwö'rung *f* (–;-en) conspiracy
verse'hen §138 *tr* (*Amt, Stellung*) hold; (*Dienst, Pflicht*) perform; (*Haushalt, usw.*) look after; (**mit**) provide (with); (eccl) administer the last rites to; **j-s Dienst v.** fill in for s.o.; **mit e-m Saum v.** hem; **mit Giro v.** endorse; **mit Unterschrift v.** sign || *ref* make a mistake; **ehe man es sich versieht** before you know it; **sich v.** (*genit*) expect || **Versehen** *n* (–s;–) mistake, slip; oversight; **aus V.** by mistake

versehentlich [fer'zeː.əntlɪç] *adv* by mistake, erroneously, inadvertently
versehren [fer'zeːrən] *tr* injure
Versehrte [fer'zeːrtə] §5 *mf* disabled person
versen'den §140 *tr* send, ship; **ins Ausland v.** export
versen'gen *tr* scorch; (*Haar*) singe
versen'ken *tr* sink; submerge; lower; (*Kabel*) lay; (*Schraube*) countersink; (naut) scuttle || *ref*—**sich v. in** (*acc*) become engrossed in
Versen'kung *f* (–;) sinking; (theat) trapdoor; **in der V. verschwinden** (fig) vanish into thin air
versessen [fer'zɛsən] *adj*—**v. auf** (*acc*) crazy about, obsessed with
verset'zen *tr* move, shift; (*Pflanze*) transplant; (*Schulkind*) promote; (*Beamte*) transfer; (*Schlag*) deal, give; (*verpfänden*) pawn; (*vermischen*) mix; (*Metall*) alloy; (*erwidern*) reply; (*vergeblich warten lassen*) (coll) stand up; (mus) transpose; **in Angst v.** terrify; **in Erstaunen v.** amaze; **in den Ruhestand v.** retire; **in Zorn v.** anger || *ref*—**v. Sie sich in meine Lage** put yourself in my place
Verset'zung *f* (–;-en) moving, shifting; transplanting; transfer; mixing; alloying; (educ) promotion
Verset'zungszeichen *n* (mus) accidental
verseuchen [fer'zɔɪçən] *tr* infect, contaminate
Verseu'chung *f* (–;) infection; contamination
Vers'fuß *m* (pros) foot
versicherbar [fer'zɪçərbar] *adj* insurable
versichern [fer'zɪçərn] *tr* assure; assert, affirm; insure || *ref* (*genit*) assure oneself of
Versicherte [fer'zɪçərtə] §5 *mf* insured
Versi'cherung *f* (–;-en) assurance; affirmation; insurance
Versi'cherungsanstalt *f* insurance company
Versi'cherungsbeitrag *m* premium
versi'cherungsfähig *adj* insurable
Versi'cherungsgesellschaft *f* insurance company
Versi'cherungsleistung *f* insurance benefit
Versi'cherungsmathematiker –**in** §6 *mf* actuary
Versi'cherungsnehmer –**in** §6 *mf* insured
versi'cherungspflichtig *adj* subject to mandatory insurance
Versi'cherungspolice *f*, **Versi'cherungsschein** *m* insurance policy
Versi'cherungsträger *m* underwriter
Versi'cherungszwang *m* compulsory insurance
versickern (versik'kern) *intr* (SEIN) seep out, trickle away
versie'geln *tr* seal (up); (jur) seal off
Versie'gelung *f* (–;) sealing (off)
versie'gen *intr* (SEIN) dry up
versil'bern *tr* silver-plate; (coll) sell
Versil'berung *f* (–;) silver-plating

versin'ken §143 *intr* (SEIN) (in *acc*) sink (into); (fig) (in *acc*) lapse (into)

versinnbildlichen [fɛr'zɪnbɪltlɪçən] *tr* symbolize

Version [ver'zjon] *f* (-;-en) version

versippt [fɛr'zɪpt] *adj* (mit) related (to)

versklaven [fɛr'sklavən] *tr* enslave

Vers'kunst *f* versification

Vers'macher –in §6 *mf* versifier

Vers'maß *n* meter

versoffen [fɛr'zɔfən] *adj* (coll) drunk

versohlen [fɛr'zolən] *tr* (coll) give (s.o.) a good licking

versöhnen [fɛr'zønən] *tr* (mit) reconcile (with) || *ref* become reconciled

versöhnlich [fɛr'zønlɪç] *adj* conciliatory

Versöh'nung *f* (-;) reconciliation

Versöh'nungstag *m* Day of Atonement

versonnen [fɛr'zɔnən] *adj* wistful

versor'gen *tr* look after; provide for; (mit) supply (with), provide (with)

Versor'ger –in §6 *mf* provider, breadwinner

Versor'gung *f* (-;) providing, supplying; (*Unterhalt*) maintenance; (*Alters- und Validen-*) social security

Versor'gungsbetrieb *m* public utility

Versor'gungstruppen *pl* service troops

Versor'gungswege *pl* supply lines

verspan'nen *tr* guy, brace

verspäten [fɛr'pɛtən] *ref* come late; (rr) be behind schedule

verspätet [fɛr'pɛtət] *adj* belated, late

Verspä'tung *f* (-;-en) lateness, delay; **mit e–r Stunde V.** one hour behind schedule; **V. haben** be late

verspei'sen *tr* eat up

verspekulie'ren *tr* lose on a gamble || *ref* lose all through speculation

versper'ren *tr* bar, block, obstruct; (*Tür*) lock

verspie'len *tr* lose, gamble away || *intr* **—bei j–m v.** lose favor with s.o.

verspielt [fɛr'pilt] *adj* playful; frivolous

versponnen [fɛr'pɔnən] *adj*—**in Gedanken versponnen** lost in thought

verspot'ten *tr* mock, deride

Verspot'tung *f* (-;) mockery, derision

verspre'chen §64 *tr* promise || *ref* make a mistake in speaking; **ich verspreche mir viel davon** I expect a lot from that || **Versprechen** *n* (-;-) promise; slip of the tongue

Verspre'chung *f* (-;-en) promise

verspren'gen *tr* scatter, disperse

Versprengte [fɛr'prɛŋtə] §5 *mf* (mil) straggler

versprit'zen *tr* squirt, spatter

versprü'hen *tr* spray

verspü'ren *tr* feel, sense

verstaatlichen [fɛr'tatlɪçən] *tr* nationalize

Verstaat'lichung *f* (-;) nationalization

verstädtern [fɛr'tɛtərn] *tr* urbanize

Verstäd'terung *f* (-;) urbanization

Verstand' *m* (-[e]s;) understanding; intellect; intelligence, brains; (*Vernunft*) reason; (*Geist*) mind; senses; sense; **den V. verlieren** lose one's

mind; **gesunder V.** common sense; **klarer V.** clear head; **nicht bei V. sein** be out of one's mind

Verstan'deskraft *f* intellectual power

verstan'desmäßig *adj* rational

Verstan'desmensch *m* matter-of-fact person

verstän'dig *adj* intelligent; sensible, reasonable; wise

verständigen [fɛr'tɛndɪgən] *tr* (von) inform (about), notify (of) || *ref*— **sich v. mit** make oneself understood to; come to an understanding with

Verstän'digung *f* (-;) understanding; information; communication; (telp) quality of reception

verständlich [fɛr'tɛntlɪç] *adj* understandable, intelligible; **sich v. machen** make oneself understood

Verständnis [fɛr'tɛntnɪs] *n* (-ses;-se) (für) understanding (of), appreciation (for)

verständ'nislos *adj* uncomprehending

verständ'nisinnig *adj* with deep mutual understanding; (*Blick*) knowing

verständ'nisvoll *adj* understanding; appreciative; (*Blick*) knowing

verstär'ken *tr* stiffen up

verstär'ken *tr* strengthen; (*steigern*) intensify; (elec) boost; (mil) reinforce; (rad) amplify

Verstär'ker *m* (-s;-) (rad) amplifier

Verstär'kung *f* (-;-en) strengthening; intensification; (mil) reinforcement; (rad) amplification

verstatten [fɛr'tatən] *tr* permit

verstau'ben *intr* (SEIN) get dusty

verstäu'ben *intr* atomize

verstaubt [fɛr'taupt] *adj* dusty; (fig) antiquated

verstau'chen *tr* sprain

Verstau'chung *f* (-;-en) sprain

verstau'en *tr* stow away

Versteck [fɛr'tɛk] *m* (-[e]s;-e) hiding place; hideout; **V. spielen** play hide-and-seek

verstecken (verstek'ken) *tr & ref* hide

versteckt [fɛr'tɛkt] *adj* hidden, veiled; (*Absicht*) ulterior

verste'hen §146 *tr* understand, see; make out; realize; (*Sprache*) know; **e–n Spaß v.** take a joke; **ich verstehe es zu** (*inf*) I know how to (*inf*); **falsch v.** misunderstand; **verstanden?** get it?; **v. Sie mich recht!** don't get me wrong!; **was v. Sie unter** (*dat*)? what do you mean by? || *ref*—(**das**) **versteht sich!** that's understood!; **das versteht sich von selbst!** that goes without saying; **sich gut v. mit** get along well with; **sich v. auf** (*acc*) be skilled in; **sich zu etw v.** (*sich zu etw entschließen*) bring oneself to do s.th.; (*in etw einwilligen*) agree to s.th. || *recip* understand each other

verstei'fen *tr* stiffen; strut, brace, reinforce || *ref* stiffen; **sich v. auf** (*acc*) insist on

verstei'gen §148 *ref* lose one's way in the mountain; **sich dazu v., daß** go so far as to (*inf*)

Verstei'gerer *m* (-s;-) auctioneer

verstei'gern *tr* auction off

Verstei′gerung f (-; -en) auction
verstei′nern intr (SEIN) become petrified; (fig) be petrified
verstell′bar adj adjustable
verstell′en tr (regulieren) adjust; (versperren) block; (Stimme, usw.) disguise; (Weiche) throw; (Verkehrsampel) switch; (Zeiger e-r Uhr) move; misplace; **j-m den Weg v.** block s.o.'s way ‖ ref put on an act
Verstel′lung f (-; -en) adjusting; disguise
versteu′ern tr pay taxes on
Versteu′erung f (-;) paying of taxes
verstiegen [fer′ʃtigən] adj (Idee, Plan) extravagant, fantastic
verstim′men tr put out of tune; (fig) put out of humor
verstimmt [fer′ʃtɪmt] adj out of tune; (Magen) upset; **v. über** (acc) upset over
Verstim′mung f (-;) bad humor; (zwischen zweien) bad feeling, bad blood
verstockt [fer′ʃtɔkt] adj stubborn; (Verbrecher) hardened; (eccl) impenitent
Verstockt′heit f (-;) stubbornness; (eccl) impenitence
verstohlen [fer′ʃtolən] adj furtive
verstop′fen tr stop up, clog; (Straße) block, jam; (Leib) constipate
Verstop′fung f (-;) stopping up, clogging; congestion; (pathol) constipation
verstorben [fer′ʃtɔrbən] adj late, deceased ‖ **Verstorbene** §5 mf deceased
verstört [fer′ʃtørt] adj shaken, bewildered, distracted
Verstört′heit f (-;) bewilderment
Verstoß′ m (gegen) violation (of), offense (against)
versto′ßen §150 tr disown ‖ intr—**v. gegen** violate, break
verstre′ben tr prop, brace
verstrei′chen §85 tr (Butter) spread; (Risse) plaster up ‖ intr (SEIN) pass, elapse; (Gelegenheit) slip by; (Frist) expire
verstreu′en tr scatter, disperse, strew
verstricken (verstrik′ken) tr use up in knitting; (fig) involve, entangle ‖ ref get entangled
verstümmeln [fer′ʃtyməln] tr mutilate; (Funkspruch) garble
Verstüm′melung f (-; -en) mutilation; (rad) garbling
verstummen [fer′ʃtumən] intr (SEIN) become silent; (vor Erstaunen) be dumbstruck; (Geräusch) cease
Versuch [fer′zux] m (-[e]s; -e) try, attempt; (Probe) test, trial; (wissenschaftlich) experiment; **e-n V. machen mit** have a try at
versu′chen tr try; tempt; (kosten) taste
Versuchs′anstalt f research institute
Versuchs′ballon m (& fig) trial balloon
Versuchs′flieger m test pilot
Versuchs′flug m test flight
Versuchs′kaninchen n (fig) guinea pig
Versuchs′reihe f series of tests
versuchs′weise adv by way of a test; on approval
Versu′chung f (-; -en) temptation

versumpfen [fer′zumpfən] intr (SEIN) become marshy; (coll) go to the dogs
versün′digen ref (an dat) sin (against)
versunken [fer′zuŋkən] adj sunk; **v. in** (acc) (fig) lost in
versü′ßen tr sweeten
verta′gen tr & ref (auf acc) adjourn (till), recess (till)
Verta′gung f (-; -en) adjournment
vertändeln [fer′tendəln] tr trifle away
vertäuen [fer′tɔɪ.ən] tr (naut) moor
vertau′schen tr (gegen) exchange (for)
Vertau′schung f (-;) exchange
verteidigen [fer′taɪdɪgən] tr defend
Vertei′diger **-in** §6 mf defender; (Befürworter) advocate; (jur) counsel for the defense ‖ m (fb) back
Vertei′digung f (-; -en) defense
Vertei′digungsbündnis n defensive alliance
Vertei′digungsminister m secretary of defense
Vertei′digungsministerium n department of defense
Vertei′digungsschrift f written defense
Vertei′digungsstellung f defensive position
vertei′len tr distribute; (zuteilen) allot; (über e-e große Fläche) scatter; (steuerlich) spread out; (Rollen) (theat) cast ‖ ref spread out
Vertei′ler m (-s; -) distributer; (Anschriftenliste) mailing list; (von Durchschlägen) distribution; (aut) distributor
Vertei′lung f (-; -en) distribution; allotment; (theat) casting
verteuern [fer′tɔɪ.ərn] tr raise the price of
verteufelt [fer′tɔɪfəlt] adj devilish; **a devil of a**
vertiefen [fer′tifən] tr make deeper; (fig) deepen ‖ ref—**sich v. in** (acc) become absorbed in
Vertie′fung f (-; -en) deepening; (Höhlung) hollow, depression; (Nische) niche; (Loch) hole; (fig) absorption
vertiert [fer′tirt] adj bestial
vertikal [vertɪ′kal] adj vertical ‖ **Vertikale** f (-; -n) vertical
vertil′gen tr exterminate, eradicate; (aufessen) (coll) eat, polish off
Vertil′gung f (-;) extermination
vertip′pen tr type incorrectly ‖ ref make a typing error
verto′nen tr set to music
Verto′nung f (-; -en) musical arrangement
vertrackt [fer′trakt] adj (coll) odd, strange; (coll) blooming
Vertrag [fer′trak] m (-[e]s; ‑e) contract, agreement; (dipl) treaty
vertra′gen §132 tr stand, take; tolerate ‖ recip agree, be compatible; (Farben) harmonize; (Personen) get along
vertrag′lich adj contractual ‖ adv by contract, as stipulated; **sich v. verpflichten zu** (inf) contract to (inf)
verträglich [fer′treklɪç] adj sociable, personable; (Speise) digestible
Vertrags′bruch m breach of contract
vertragsbrüchig [fer′traksbryçɪç] adj —**v. werden** break a contract

vertrags'gemäß *adj* contractual

vertrags'widrig *adj* contrary to the terms of a contract or treaty

vertrau'en *intr* (*dat*) trust; **v. auf** (*acc*) trust in, have confidence in ‖ **Vertrauen** *n* (*-s*;) trust, confidence; **ganz im V.** just between you and me; **im V.** confidentially

vertrau'enerweckend *adj* inspiring confidence

Vertrau'ensbruch *m* breach of trust

Vertrau'ens·mann *m* (*-[e]s;-er* & *-leute*) confidential agent; (*Vertrauter*) confidant; (*Sprecher*) spokesman; (*Gewährsmann*) informant

Vertrau'ensposten *m*, **Vertrau'ensstellung** *f* position of trust

vertrau'ensvoll *adj* confident; trusting

Vertrau'ensvotum *n* vote of confidence

vertrau'enswürdig *adj* trustworthy

vertrauern [fer'trau·ərn] *tr* spend in mourning

vertraulich [fer'traulɪç] *adj* confidential; intimate

Vertrau'lichkeit *f* (*-;-en*) intimacy, familiarity; **sich** [*dat*] **Vertraulichkeiten herausnehmen** take liberties

verträu'men *tr* dream away

verträumt [fer'trɔɪmt] *adj* dreamy

vertraut [fer'traut] *adj* familiar; friendly, intimate ‖ **Vertraute §5** *mf* intimate friend ‖ *m* confidant ‖ *f* confidante

Vertraut'heit *f* (*-;*) familiarity

vertrei'ben §62 *tr* drive away, expel; (*aus dem Hause*) chase out; (*aus dem Lande*) banish; (*Ware*) sell, market; (*Zeit*) pass, kill

Vertrei'bung *f* (*-;*) expulsion

vertre'ten §152 *tr* represent; substitute for; (*Ansicht, usw.*) advocate ‖ *ref* —**sich** [*dat*] **den Fuß v.** sprain one's ankle; **sich** [*dat*] **die Beine v.** (coll) stretch one's legs

Vertre'ter –**in §6** *mf* representative; substitute; (*Bevollmächtigte*) proxy; (*im Amt*) deputy; (*Fürsprecher*) advocate; (*com*) agent

Vertre'tung *f* (*-;-en*) representation; substitution; (*com*) agency; (*pol*) mission; **in V.** by proxy; **in V.** (*genit*) signed for

Vertrieb' *m* (*-[e]s;-e*) sale, turnover; retail trade; sales department

Vertriebs'abkommen *n* franchise agreement

Vertriebs'abteilung *f* sales department

Vertriebs'kosten *pl* distribution costs

Vertriebs'leiter –**in §6** *mf* sales manager

Vertriebs'recht *n* franchise

vertrin'ken §143 *tr* drink up

vertrock'nen *intr* (SEIN) dry up

vertrödeln [fer'trøːdəln] *tr* fritter away

vertrö'sten *tr* string along; **auf später v.** put off till later

vertun' **§154** *tr* waste ‖ *ref* (coll) make a mistake

vertu'schen *tr* hush up

verübeln [fer'yːbəln] *tr* take (s.th.) the wrong way; **j-m etw v.** blame s.o. for s.th.

verü'ben *tr* commit, perpetrate

verul'ken *tr* (coll) kid

verunehren [fer'unˀeːrən] *tr* dishonor

veruneinigen [fer'unˀaɪnɪgən] *tr* disunite ‖ *recip* fall out, quarrel

verunglimpfen [fer'unglɪmpfən] *tr* slander, defame

verunglücken [fer'unglykən] *intr* (SEIN) have an accident; (coll) fail

Verunglückte [fer'unglyktə] **§5** *mf* victim, casualty

verunreinigen [fer'unˀraɪnɪgən] *tr* soil, dirty; (*Luft, Wasser*) pollute

Verun'reinigung *f* (*-;*) pollution

verunstalten [fer'unˀʃtaltən] *tr* disfigure, deface

veruntreuen [fer'untrɔɪ·ən] *tr* embezzle

Verun'treuung *f* (*-;*) embezzlement

verunzieren [fer'untsiːrən] *tr* mar

verursachen [fer'urˀzaxən] *tr* cause

verur'teilen *tr* condemn; sentence

Verur'teilung *f* (*-;-en*) condemnation; sentence

vervielfachen [fer'fiːlfaxən] *tr* multiply ‖ *ref* increase considerably

vervielfältigen [fer'fiːlfɛltɪgən] *tr* multiply; duplicate; mimeograph; (*nachbilden*) reproduce

Verviel'fältigung *f* (*-;-en*) duplication; mimeographing; reproduction; (phot) printing

Verviel'fältigungsapparat *m* duplicator

vervollkommnen [fer'fɔlkɔmnən] *tr* improve on, perfect

Vervoll'kommnung *f* (*-;*) improvement, perfection

vervollständigen [fer'fɔlʃtɛndɪgən] *tr* complete

Vervoll'ständigung *f* (*-;*) completion

verwach'sen *adj* overgrown; deformed; hunchbacked; **mit etw v. sein** (fig) be attached to s.th. ‖ *intr* (SEIN) grow together; become deformed; (*Wunde*) heal up; **zu e-r Einheit v.** form a whole

Verwach'sung *f* (*-;-en*) deformity

verwackelt [fer'vakəlt] *adj* (phot) blurred

verwah'ren *tr* keep; **v. vor** (*dat*) protect against ‖ *ref*—**sich v. gegen** protest against

verwahrlosen [fer'vɑrloːzən] *tr* neglect ‖ *intr* (SEIN) (*Gebäude*) deteriorate; (*Kinder*) run wild; (*Personen*) go to the dogs

verwahrlost [fer'vɑrloːst] *adj* uncared-for; (*Person*) unkempt; (*sittlich*) degenerate; (*Garten*) overgrown with weeds

Verwahr'losung *f* (*-;*) neglect

Verwah'rung *f* (*-;*) care, safekeeping, custody; (fig) protest; **etw in V. nehmen** take care of s.th.; **j-m in V. geben** entrust to s.o.'s care

verwaisen [fer'vaizən] *intr* (SEIN) become an orphan, be orphaned

verwaist [fer'vaist] *adj* orphaned; (fig) deserted

verwalten [fer'valtən] *tr* administer, manage

Verwal'ter –**in §6** *mf* administrator, manager

Verwal'tung *f* (*-;-en*) administration, management

Verwal'tungsapparat *m* administrative machinery

Verwal'tungsbeamte *m* civil service worker; administrative official

Verwal'tungsdienst *m* civil service

Verwal'tungsrat *m* advisory board; (*e-r Aktiengesellschaft*) board of directors; (*e-s Instituts*) board of trustees

verwan'deln *tr* change, turn, convert; (*Strafe*) commute || *ref* change, turn

Verwand'lung *f* (-;-en) change, transformation; (jur) commutation

verwandt [fɛr'vant] *adj* (mit) related (to); (*Wissenschaften*) allied; (*Wörter*) cognate; (*Seelen*) kindred || Verwandte §5 *mf* relative, relation

Verwandt'schaft *f* (-;-en) relationship; relatives; (chem) affinity

verwandt'schaftlich *adj* kindred

Verwandt'schaftsgrad *m* degree of relationship

verwanzt [fɛr'vantst] *adj* (coll) full of bugs, lousy

verwar'nen *tr* warn, caution

Verwar'nung *f* (-;-en) warning, caution

verwa'schen *adj* washed-out, faded; (*verschwommen*) vague, fuzzy

verwäs'sern *tr* dilute; (fig) water down

verwe'ben §94 *tr* interweave

verwe'chseln *tr* confuse, get (*various items*) mixed up; (*Hüte, Mäntel*) take by mistake || Verwechseln *n* (-s;)—sie sehen sich zum V. ähnlich they are as alike as two peas

Verwechs'lung *f* (-;-en) mix-up

verwegen [fɛr'vegən] *adj* bold, daring

verwe'hen *tr* (*Blätter*) blow away; (*Spur*) cover up (with snow) || *intr* (SEIN) be blown in all directions; (*Spur*) be covered up; (*Worte*) drift away

verweh'ren *tr*—j—m etw *v*. refuse s.o. s.th.; prevent s.o. from getting s.th.

Verwe'hung *f* (-;-en) (snow)drift

verweichlichen [fɛr'vaɪçlɪçən] *tr* make effeminate; (*Kind*) coddle || *ref* & *intr* become effeminate; grow soft

verweichlicht [fɛr'vaɪçlɪçt] *adj* effeminate; soft, flabby

Verweich'lichung *f* (-;) effeminacy

verwei'gern *tr* refuse, deny, turn down

Verwei'gerung *f* (-;-en) refusal

verweilen [fɛr'vaɪlən] *intr* linger, tarry; (fig) dwell

verweint [fɛr'vaɪnt] *adj* red with tears

Verweis [fɛr'vaɪs] *m* (-es;-e) reprimand, rebuke; (*Hinweis*) reference

verwei'sen §118 *tr* banish; (*Schüler*) expel; j—m etw *v*. reprimand s.o. for s.th.; j—n an j—n *v*. refer s.o. to s.o.; j—n auf etw *v*. refer s.o. to s.th.

Verwei'sung *f* (-;-en) banishment; expulsion; (an *acc*) referral (to); (auf *acc*) reference (to)

verwel'ken *intr* (SEIN) wither, wilt

verweltlichen [fɛr'vɛltlɪçən] *tr* secularize

verwendbar [fɛr'vɛntbar] *adj* applicable; available; usable

Verwend'barkeit *f* (-;) availability; usefulness

verwen'den §140 *tr* use, employ; (auf *acc*, für) apply (to); Zeit und Mühe *v*. auf (*acc*) spend time and effort on || *ref*—sich bei j—m *v*. für intercede with s.o. for

Verwen'dung *f* (-;-en) use, employment; application; keine V. haben für have no use for; vielseitige V. versatility

verwen'dungsfähig *adj* usable

verwer'fen §160 *tr* reject; (*Plan*) discard; (*Berufung*) turn down; (*Klage*) dismiss; (*Urteil*) overrule || *ref* (*Holz*) warp; (geol) fault

verwerf'lich *adj* objectionable

Verwer'fung *f* (-;-en) rejection; warping; (geol) fault

verwer'ten *tr* utilize

Verwer'tung *f* (-;-en) utilization

verwesen [fɛr'vezən] *intr* (SEIN) rot

verweslich [fɛr'vezlɪç] *adj* perishable

Verwe'sung *f* (-;) decay

verwet'ten *tr* lose (*in betting*)

verwich'sen *tr* (coll) clobber

verwickeln (verwik'keln) *tr* snarl, entangle; complicate; (fig) involve || *ref*—sich *v*. in (*acc*) get entangled in; (fig) get involved in

Verwick'lung *f* (-;-en) snarl, tangle; involvement; complexity; complication

verwil'dern *intr* become overgrown; (*Person*) become depraved; (*Kind*) run wild, go wild

verwildert [fɛr'vɪldərt] *adj* wild, savage; weed-grown

verwin'den §59 *tr* get over; (*Verlust*) recover from

verwir'ken *tr* forfeit; (*Strafe*) incur || *ref*—sich [*dat*] j—s Gunst *v*. lose favor with s.o.

verwirklichen [fɛr'vɪrklɪçən] *tr* realize, make come true || *ref* come true

Verwirk'lichung *f* (-;) realization

Verwir'kung *f* (-;) forfeiture

verwirren [fɛr'vɪrən] *tr* throw into disorder; (*Haar*) muss up; confuse

verwirrt [fɛr'vɪrt] *adj* confused

Verwir'rung *f* (-;-en) confusion; in V. geraten become confused

verwirt'schaften *tr* squander

verwi'schen *tr* wipe out; (*teilweise*) blur; (*verschmieren*) smear; (*Spuren*) cover || *ref* become blurred

verwit'tern *intr* (SEIN) become weather-beaten; (*zerfallen*) crumble away

verwittert [fɛr'vɪtərt] *adj* weather-beaten

verwitwet [fɛr'vɪtvət] *adj* widowed

verwöhnen [fɛr'vønən] *tr* pamper, spoil

verworfen [fɛr'vorfən] *adj* depraved

Verwor'fenheit *f* (-;) depravity

verworren [fɛr'vorən] *adj* confused

verwundbar [fɛr'vuntbar] *adj* vulnerable

verwun'den *tr* wound

verwunderlich [fɛr'vundərlɪç] *adj* remarkable, astonishing

verwun'dern *tr* astonish || *ref* (über *acc*) be astonished (at), wonder (at)

Verwun'derung *f* (-;) astonishment; j—n in V. setzen astonish s.o.

verwundet [fɛr'vundət] *adj* wounded

|| **Verwundete** §5 *mf* wounded person

verwunschen [fɛr'vunʃən] *adj* enchanted

verwün'schen *tr* damn, curse; (*in Märchen*) bewitch, put a curse on

verwünscht [fɛr'vynʃt] *adj* confounded, darn || *interj* darn it!

Verwün'schung *f* (-;-en) curse

verwurzelt [fɛr'vurtsəlt] *adj* deeply rooted

verwüsten [fɛr'vystən] *tr* devastate

Verwü'stung *f* (-;-en) devastation

verzagen [fɛr'tsagən] *intr* (SEIN) lose heart, despair; **v. an** (*dat*) give up on

verzagt [fɛr'tsakt] *adj* despondent

Verzagt'heit *f* (-;) despondency

verzäh'len *ref* miscount

verzärteln [fɛr'tsertəln] *tr* pamper

verzau'bern *tr* bewitch, charm; **v. in** (*acc*) change into

Verzehr [fɛr'tser] *m* (-[e]s;) consumption

verzeh'ren *tr* consume; (*Geld*) spend; (*Mahlzeit*) eat || *ref* (*in dat*, *vor dat*) pine away (with); (*nach*) yearn (for)

verzeh'rend *adj* (*Blick*) longing; (*Fieber*) wasting; (*Leidenschaft*) burning

Verzeh'rung *f* (-;) consumption

verzeich'nen *tr* draw wrong; make a list of; register; catalogue; (opt) distort

Verzeichnis [fɛr'tsaɪçnɪs] *n* (-ses;-se) list; catalogue; (*im Buch*) index; (*Inventar*) inventory; (*Tabelle*) table; (telp) directory

verzeihen [fɛr'tsaɪ·ən] §81 *tr* forgive, pardon (*s.th.*); condone || *intr* (*dat*) forgive, pardon (*s.o.*)

verzeihlich [fɛr'tsaɪlɪç] *adj* pardonable

Verzei'hung *f* (-;) pardon

verzer'ren *tr* distort; contort

Verzer'rung *f* (-;-en) distortion; contortion; grimace

verzetteln [fɛr'tsetəln] *tr* fritter away; catalogue || *ref* spread oneself too thin

Verzicht [fɛr'tsɪçt] *m* (-[e]s;) renunciation; **V. leisten auf** (*acc*) waive

verzichten [fɛr'tsɪçtən] *intr*—**v. auf** (*acc*) do without; (*verabsäumen*) pass up; (*aufgeben*) give up, renounce; (*Rechte*) waive

verzieh [fɛr'tsi] *pret* of **verzeihen**

verzie'hen §163 *tr* distort; (*Kind*) spoil; **den Mund v.** make a face; **ohne e–e Miene zu v.** without batting an eye || *ref* disappear; (*Schmerz*) go away; (*Menge, Wolken*) disperse; (*Holz*) warp; (*durch Druck*) buckle; (coll) sneak off

verzie'ren *tr* decorate

Verzie'rung *f* (-;-en) decoration; (*Schmuck*) ornament

verzinsen [fɛr'tsɪnzən] *tr* pay interest on; **e–e Summe zu 6% v.** pay 6% interest on a sum || *ref* yield interest; **sich mit 6% v.** yield 6% interest

verzinslich [fɛr'tsɪnslɪç] *adj* bearing interest || *adv*—**v. anlegen** put out at interest

Verzin'sung *f* (-;) interest

verzog [fɛr'tsok] *pret* of **verziehen**

verzogen [fɛr'tsogən] *adj* distorted; (*Kind*) spoiled; (*Holz*) warped

verzö'gern *tr* delay; put off, postpone || *ref* be late

Verzö'gerung *f* (-;-en) delay; postponement

verzollen [fɛr'tsɔlən] *tr* pay duty on; (naut) clear; **haben Sie etw zu v.?** do you have anything to declare?

verzückt [fɛr'tsʏkt] *adj* ecstatic

Verzückung [fɛr'tsʏkuŋ] *f* (-;) ecstasy

Verzug' *m* (-[e]s;) delay; (*in der Leistung*) default; **in V. geraten mit** fall behind in; **ohne V.** without delay

verzwei'feln *intr* (HABEN & SEIN) (**an** *dat*) despair (of) || **Verzweifeln n—es ist zum V.** it's enough to drive one to despair

verzweifelt [fɛr'tsvaɪfəlt] *adj* desperate

Verzweif'lung *f* (-;) despair

verzweigen [fɛr'tsvargən] *ref* branch out

verzweigt [fɛr'tsvaɪkt] *adj* having many branches; (fig) complex

verzwickt [fɛr'tsvɪkt] *adj* (coll) tricky, ticklish

Vestibül [vɛstɪ'byl] *n* (-s;-e) vestibule; (theat) lobby

Veteran [vete'ran] *m* (-en;-en) veteran, ex-serviceman

Veterinär –**in** [veterɪ'ner(ɪn)] §8 *mf* veterinarian

Veto ['veto] *n* (-s;-s) veto

Vetter ['fɛtər] *m* (-s;-) cousin

Vet'ternwirtschaft *f* nepotism

Vexierbild [vɛ'ksirbɪlt] *n* picture puzzle

vexieren [vɛ'ksirən] *tr* tease; pester

V-förmig ['faufœrmɪç] *adj* V-shaped

vibrieren [vɪ'briːrən] *intr* vibrate

Vieh [fi] *n* (-[e]s;) livestock; cattle; animal, beast

Vieh'bestand *m* livestock

Vieh'bremse *f* horsefly

viehisch ['fi·ɪʃ] *adj* brutal

Vieh'tränke *f* water hole

Vieh'wagen *m* (rr) cattle car

Vieh'weide *f* cow pasture

Vieh'zucht *f* cattle breeding

Vieh'züchter –**in** §6 *mf* rancher

viel [fil] *adj* much; many; a lot of || *adv* much; a lot || *pron* much; many

viel'beschäftigt *adj* very busy

viel'deutig *adj* ambiguous

Viel'eck *n* polygon

vielerlei ['filər'laɪ] *invar adj* many kinds of

viel'fach *adj* multiple; manifold || *adv* (coll) often

Vielfach– *comb.fm.* multiple

viel'fältig *adj* manifold, various

Viel'fältigkeit *f* (-;) multiplicity; variety

vielleicht' *adv* maybe, perhaps

vielmalig ['filmalɪç] *adj* oft repeated

vielmals ['filmals] *adv* frequently; **danke v.!** many thanks!

vielmehr' *adv* rather, on the contrary

viel'sagend *adj* suggestive

viel'seitig *adj* many-sided, versatile

vielstufig ['fil'tufɪç] *adj* multistage

viel'teilig *adj* of many parts

viel'versprechend *adj* very promising

vier [fir] *adj* four; **unter vier Augen** confidentially || *pron* four; **auf allen vieren** on all fours || **Vier** *f* (-;-en) four

vier′beinig *adj* four-legged

Vier′eck *n* quadrangle

vier′eckig *adj* quadrangular

viererlei [′firər′lai] *invar adj* four different kinds of

vier′fach, vier′fältig *adv* fourfold, quadruple

Vierfüßer [′firfysər] *m* (-s;-) quadruped

vierhändig [′firhendıç] *adv*—**v. spielen** (mus) play a duet

Vierlinge [′firlıŋə] *pl* quadruplets

vier′mal *adv* four times

vierschrötig [′fir′ʃrøtıç] *adj* stocky

vierstrahlig [′fir′ʃtralıç] *adj* four-engine (jet)

viert [firt] *pron*—**zu v.** in fours; **wir gehen zu v.** the four of us are going

Viertakter [′firtaktər] *m* (-s;-), **Viertaktmotor** [′firtaktmotər] *m* four-cycle engine

Vierte [′firtə] §9 *adj & pron* fourth

vier′teilen *tr* quarter

Viertel [′firtəl] *n* (-s;-) quarter; fourth (*part*); (*Stadtteil*) quarter, section

Vierteljahr′ *n* quarter (*of a year*)

vierteljäh′rig, vierteljähr′lich *adj* quarterly

vierteln [′firtəln] *tr* quarter

Vier′telnote *f* (mus) quarter note

Viertelpfund′ *n* quarter of a pound

Viertelstun′de *f* quarter of an hour

viertens [′firtəns] *adv* fourthly

vier′zehn *invar adj & pron* fourteen || **Vierzehn** *f* (-;-en) fourteen

vier′zehnte §9 *adj & pron* fourteenth

Vier′zehntel *n* (-s;-) fourteenth (*part*)

vierzig [′firtsıç] *invar adj & pron* forty || **Vierzig** *f* (-;-en) forty

vierziger [′firtsıgər] *invar adj* of the forties; **die v. Jahre** the forties

vierzigste [′firtsıçstə] §9 *adj & pron* fortieth

Vikar [vı′kar] *m* (-s;-e) vicar

Vil·la [′vıla] *f* (-;-len [lən]) villa

violett [vı·o′let] *adj* violet

Violine [vı·o′linə] *f* (-;-n) violin

Violin′schlüssel *m* treble clef

Viper [′vipər] *f* (-;-n) viper

viril [vı′ril] *adj* virile

virtuos [vırtu′os] *adj* masterly || **Virtuose** [vırtu′ozə] *m* (-n;-n), **Virtuosin** [vırtu′ozın] *f* (-;-nen) virtuoso

Vi·rus [′virus] *n* (-;-ren [rən]) virus

Visage [vı′zaʒə] *f* (-;-n) (coll) mug

Visier [vı′zir] *n* (-s;-e) visor; (am Gewehr) sight

visieren [vı′zirən] *tr* (eichen) gauge; (Paß) visa

Vision [vı′zjon] *f* (-;-en) vision

visionär [vızjo′ner] *adj* visionary || **Visionär** *m* (-s;-e) visionary

Visitation [vızıta′tsjon] *f* (-;-en) inspection; search

Visite [vı′zitə] *f* (-;-n) formal call; **Visiten machen** (med) make the rounds

Visi′tenkarte *f* calling card

visuell [vızu′el] *adj* visual

Vi·sum [′vizum] *n* (-s;-sa [za]) visa

vital [vı′tal] *adj* energetic

Vitalität [vıtalı′tet] *f* (-;) vitality

Vitamin [vıta′min] *n* (-s;-e) vitamin

Vitamin′mangel *m* vitamin deficiency

Vitrine [vı′trinə] *f* (-;-n) showcase

Vize- [fitsə], [vitsə] *comb.fm.* vice-

Vi′zekönig *m* viceroy

Vlies [flis] *n* (-es;-e) fleece

Vogel [′fogəl] *m* (-s;˝) bird; (coll) chap, bird; **den V. abschießen** (coll) bring down the house; **du hast e-n V.!** (coll) you're cuckoo!

Vo′gelbauer *n* birdcage

Vogelbeerbaum [′fogəlberbaum] *m* mountain ash

vo′gelfrei *adj* outlawed

Vo′gelfutter *n* birdseed

Vo′gelkunde *f* ornithology

Vo′gelmist *m* bird droppings

vögeln [′føgəln] *tr & intr* (vulg) screw

Vo′gelperspektive *f*, **Vo′gelschau** *f* bird's-eye view

Vo′gelpfeife *f* bird call

Vo′gelscheuche *f* scarecrow

Vo′gelstange *f* perch

Vogel-Strauß′-Politik *f* burying one's head in the sand; **V. betreiben** bury one's head in the sand

Vo′gelstrich *m*, **Vo′gelzug** *m* migration of birds

Vöglein [′føglain] *n* (-s;-) little bird

Vogt [fokt] *m* (-[e]s;˝e) (obs) steward; (obs) governor, prefect, magistrate

Vokabel [vo′kabəl] *f* (-;-n) vocabulary word

Vokal [vo′kal] *m* (-s;-e) vowel

Volk [folk] *n* (-[e]s;˝er) people, nation; lower classes; (von Bienen) swarm; (von Rebhühnern) covey

Völker- [fœlkər] *comb.fm.* international

Völ′kerbund *m* League of Nations

Völ′kerfriede *m* international peace

Völ′kerkunde *f* ethnology

Völ′kermord *m* genocide

Völ′kerrecht *n* international law

Völ′kerschaft *f* (-;-en) tribe

Völ′kerwanderung *f* barbarian invasions

volk′reich *adj* populous

Volks′abstimmung *f* plebiscite

Volks′aufwiegler *m* rabble rouser

Volks′ausdruck *m* household expression

Volks′befragung *f* public opinion poll

Volks′begehren *n* national referendum

Volks′bibliotek *f* free library

Volks′charakter *m* national character

Volks′deutsche §5 *mf* German national

Volks′dichter *m* popular poet

volks′eigen *adj* state-owned

Volks′entscheid *m* referendum

Volks′feind *m* public enemy

Volks′gunst *f* popularity

Volks′haufen *m* crowd, mob

Volks′herrschaft *f* democracy

Volks′hochschule *f* adult evening school

Volks′justiz *f* lynch law

Volks'küche f soup kitchen
Volks'kunde f folklore
Volks'lied n folksong
volks'mäßig adj popular
Volks'meinung f popular opinion
Volks'menge f populace, crowd of people
Volks'musik f popular music
Volks'partei f people's party
Volks'republik f people's republic
Volks'schule f grade school
Volks'sitte f national custom
Volks'sprache f vernacular
Volks'stamm m tribe; race
Volks'stimme f popular opinion
Volks'stimmung f mood of the people
Volks'tracht f national costume
Volkstum ['fɔlkstum] n (-s;) nationality
volkstümlich ['fɔlkstymlɪç] adj national; popular
Volks'verführer –in §6 mf demagogue
Volks'versammlung f public meeting
Volks'vertreter –in §6 mf representative
Volks'wirt m political economist
Volks'wirtschaft f national economy
Volks'wirtschaftslehre f (educ) political economy
Volks'wohl n public good
Volks'wohlfahrt f public welfare
Volks'zählung f census
voll [fɔl] adj full, filled; whole, entire; (Tageslicht) broad; (coll) drunk; **aus dem vollen schöpfen** have unlimited resources; **j–n für v. ansehen** (or **nehmen**) take s.o. seriously || adv fully, in full; **v. und ganz** fully
vollauf' adv—**das genügt v.** that's quite enough; **v. beschäftigt** plenty busy; **v. zu tun haben** have plenty to do
Voll'beschäftigung f full employment
Voll'besitz m full possession
Voll'blut n, **Voll'blutpferd** n thoroughbred
vollblütig ['fɔlblytɪç] adj full-blooded
vollbrin'gen §65 tr achieve
vollbusig ['vɔlbuzɪç] adj big-breasted
Voll'dampf m full steam; **mit V.** (fig) at full blast, full speed
vollenden [fɔl'ɛndən] tr bring to a close, finish, complete; (vervollkommnen) perfect; **er hat sein Leben vollendet** (poet) he died
vollendet [fɔl'ɛndət] adj perfect
vollends ['fɔlɛnts] adv completely
Vollen'dung f (–;) finishing, completing; (Vollkommenheit) perfection
Völlerei ['fœlə'raɪ] f (–;) gluttony
voll'führen tr carry out, execute
voll'füllen tr fill up
Voll'gas n full throttle
Voll'gefühl n—**im V.** (genit) fully conscious of
Voll'genuß m full enjoyment
vollgepfropft ['fɔlgəprɔpft] adj jammed, packed
voll'gießen §76 tr fill up
völlig ['fœlɪç] adj full, complete
voll'jährig adj of age
Voll'jährigkeit f legal age, majority
vollkom'men, voll'kommen adj perfect || adv (coll) absolutely

Vollkom'menheit f (–;) perfection
Voll'kornbrot n whole-grain bread
Voll'kraft f full vigor, prime
voll'machen tr fill up; (coll) dirty
Voll'macht f full authority; (jur) power of attorney; **in V. for**...(prefixed to the signature of another at end of letter)
Voll'matrose m able-bodied seaman
Voll'milch f whole milk
Voll'mond m full moon
Voll'pension f full board and lodging
voll'saftig adj juicy, succulent
voll'schenken tr fill up
voll'schlagen §132 ref—**sich** [dat] **den Bauch v.** (coll) stuff oneself
voll'schlank adj well filled out
Voll'sitzung f plenary session
Voll'spur f (rr) standard-gauge track
voll'ständig adj full; complete, entire || adv completely, quite
Voll'ständigkeit f (–;) completeness
voll'stopfen tr stuff, cram
vollstrecken (vollstrek'ken) tr (Urteil) carry out; (Testament) execute; **ein Todesurteil an j–m v.** execute s.o.
Vollstreckung (Vollstrek'kung) f. (–;) execution
voll'tanken tr (aut) fill up || intr (aut) fill it up
volltönend ['fɔltønənt] adj (Stimme) rich; (Satz) well-rounded
Voll'treffer m direct hit
Voll'versammlung f plenary session
Voll'waise f (full) orphan
voll'wertig adj of full value; complete, perfect
vollzählig ['fɔltsɛlɪç] adj complete; **sind wir v.?** are we all here? || adv in full force
vollzie'hen §163 tr execute, carry out, effect; (Vertrag) ratify; (Ehe) consummate || ref take place
vollzie'hend adj executive
Vollzie'hung f, **Vollzug'** m execution, carrying out
Vollzugs'ausschuß m executive committee
Volontär –in [vɔlɔn'ter(ɪn)] §8 mf volunteer; trainee
volontieren [vɔlɔn'tirən] intr work as a trainee
Volt [vɔlt] n (–[e]s;–) (elec) volt
Volu•men [vo'lumən] n (–s;– & –mina [mɪna]) (Band; Rauminhalt) volume
vom [fɔm] abbr **von dem**
von [fɔn] prep (dat) (beim Passiv) by; **für den Genitiv**) of; (räumlich, zeitlich) from; (über) about, of; **von**...**an** from...on; **von Holz** (made) of wood; **von Kindheit auf** from earliest childhood; **von mir aus** as far as I am concerned; **von selbst** automatically
voneinan'der adv from each other; of each other; apart
vonnöten [fɔn'nøtən] invar adj—**v. sein** be necessary
vonstatten [fɔn'statən] adv—**gut v. gehen** go well; **v. gehen** take place
vor [for] prep (dat) (örtlich) in front of, before; (zeitlich) before, prior to; (Abwehr) against, from; (wegen) of,

with, for; **etw vor sich haben** face s.th.; **heute vor acht Tagen** today a week ago; **vor sich gehen** take place, occur; **vor sich hin** to oneself ‖ *prep (acc)* in front of

vorab′ *adv* in advance

Vor′abend *m*—**am V.** (*genit*) on the eve of

Vor′ahnung *f* (coll) hunch, idea

voran′ *adv* in front, out ahead ‖ *interj* go ahead!, go on!

voran′gehen §82 *intr* (SEIN) go on ahead, take the lead; (fig) set an example; **die Arbeit geht gut voran** the work is coming along well

voran′kommen §99 *intr* (SEIN) make progress; **gut v.** come along well

Vor′anschlag *m* rough estimate

Vor′anzeige *f* preliminary announcement; (cin) preview of coming attractions

Vor′arbeit *f* preliminary work

vor′arbeiten *intr* do the work in advance; do the preliminary work

vorauf′ *adv* ahead, in front

voraus′ *adv* in front; (*dat*) ahead (of) ‖ **vor′aus** *adv*—**im v.** in advance

Voraus′abteilung *f* (mil) vanguard

voraus′bedingen §142 *tr* stipulate beforehand

voraus′bestellen *tr* reserve

voraus′bestimmen *tr* predetermine

voraus′bezahlen *tr* pay in advance

voraus′eilen *intr* (SEIN) rush ahead

vorausgesetzt [fo′rausgazetst] *adj*—**v., daß** provided that

Voraus′sage *f* prediction; prophecy; (*des Wetters*) forecast; (*Wink*) tip

voraus′sagen *tr* predict; prophesy; (*Wetter*) forecast

Voraus′sagung *f* var of **Voraussage**

voraus′schauen *intr* look ahead

voraus′schicken *tr* send ahead; (fig) mention beforehand

voraus′sehen §138 *tr* foresee

voraus′setzen *tr* presume, presuppose

Voraus′setzung *f* assumption; prerequisite; premise

Voraus′sicht *f* foresight

voraus′sichtlich *adj* probable, presumable ‖ *adv* probably, presumably, the way it looks

Voraus′zahlung *f* advance payment

Vor′bau *m* (-[e]s;-ten) projection; balcony, porch

vor′bauen *tr* build out ‖ *intr* (*dat*) take precautions against

vor′bedacht *adj* premeditated ‖ **Vorbedacht** *m* (-[e]s;)—**mit V.** on purpose; **ohne V.** unintentionally

vor′bedeuten *tr* forebode

Vor′bedeutung *f* (-;-en) foreboding; omen, portent

Vor′bedingung *f* (-;-en) precondition

Vorbehalt [′forbahalt] *m* (-[e]s;-e) reservation; proviso; **mit allem V. hinnehmen!** take it for what it's worth!; **mit** (*or* **unter**) **dem V., daß** with the proviso that; **stiller** (*or* **innerer**) **V.** mental reservation; **unter V. aller Rechte** all rights reserved

vor′behalten §90 *tr* reserve; **Änderungen v.!** subject to change without

notice ‖ *ref*—**sich** [*dat*] **etw v.** reserve s.th. for oneself

vor′behaltlich *prep* (*genit*) subject to

vor′behaltlos *adj* unreserved, unconditional

vorbei′ *adv* over, past, gone; **es ist drei Uhr v.** it's past three o'clock; **v. an** (*dat*) past, by; **v. ist v.** done is done; **v. können** be able to pass

vorbei′eilen *intr* (SEIN)—**an j-m v.** rush past s.o.

vorbei′fahren §71 *intr* (SEIN) drive by

vorbei′fliegen §57 *intr* (SEIN) fly past

vorbei′fließen §76 *intr* (SEIN) flow by

vorbei′gehen §82 *intr* (SEIN) pass; **an j-m v.** pass by s.o. ‖ **Vorbeigehen** *n* —**im V.** in passing

vorbei′gelingen §142 *intr* (SEIN) fail

vorbei′kommen §99 *intr* (SEIN) pass by; (coll) stop in

vorbei′lassen §104 *tr* let pass

Vorbei′marsch *m* parade

vorbei′marschieren *intr* (SEIN) march by

Vor′bemerkung *f* (-;-en) preliminary remark; (parl) preamble

vorbenannt [′forbənant] *adj* aforementioned

vor′bereiten *tr* prepare ‖ *ref* (**auf** *acc*, **für**) get ready (for)

vor′bereitend *adj* preparatory

Vor′bereitung *f* (-;-en) preparation

Vor′bericht *m* preliminary report

Vor′besprechung *f* (-;-en) preliminary discussion

vor′bestellen *tr* order in advance; (*Zimmer, usw.*) reserve

Vor′bestellung *f* (-;-en) advance order; reservation

vor′bestraft *adj* previously convicted

vor′beten *tr* keep repeating ‖ *intr* lead in prayer

vor′beugen *ref* bend forward ‖ *intr* (*dat*) prevent

vor′beugend *adj* preventive

Vor′beugung *f* (-;-en) prevention

Vor′beugungsmittel *n* preventive

Vor′bild *n* model; (*Beispiel*) example

vor′bildlich *adj* exemplary, model

Vor′bildung *f* (-;-en) educational background

Vor′bote *m* forerunner; (fig) harbinger

vor′bringen §65 *tr* bring forward, produce; (*Gründe*) give; (*Plan*) propose; (*Klagen*) prefer; (*Wunsch*) express

vor′buchstabieren *tr* spell out

Vor′bühne *f* apron, proscenium

vor′datieren *tr* antedate

vordem [for′dem] *adv* formerly

Vorder– [′fordər] *comb.fm.* front, fore-

Vor′derachse *f* front axle

Vor′derarm *m* forearm

Vor′derbein *n* foreleg

vordere [′fordərə] §9 *adj* front

Vor′derfront *f* front; (fig) forefront

Vor′derfuß *m* front foot

Vor′dergrund *m* foreground

vor′derhand *adv* for the time being

vor′derlastig *adj* (aer) nose-heavy

Vor′derlauf *m* (hunt) foreleg

Vor′dermann *m* (-[e]s;⸚er) man in front; **j-n auf V. bringen** (coll) put s.o. straight; **V. halten** keep in line

Vor′derpfote f front paw
Vor′derrad n front wheel
Vor′derradantrieb m front-wheel drive
Vor′derreihe f front row; front rank
Vor′dersicht f front view
Vor′derseite f front side, front; (e-r Münze) obverse, heads
Vor′dersitz m front seat
vorderste [′fɔrdərstə] §9 adj farthest front
Vor′dersteven m (naut) stem
Vor′derteil m & n front section; (naut) prow
Vor′dertür f front door
Vor′derzahn m front tooth
Vor′derzimmer n front room
vor′drängen tr & ref press forward
vor′dringen §142 intr (SEIN) forge ahead, advance
vor′dringlich adj urgent
vor′druck m printed form, blank
vor′ehelich adj premarital
vor′eilig adj hasty, rash
Vor′eiligkeit f (-;) haste, rashness
vor′eingenommen adj biased, prejudiced
Vor′eingenommenheit f (-;-en) bias, prejudice
Vor′eltern pl ancestors, forefathers
vor′enthalten §90 tr—j-m etw v. withhold s.th. from s.o.
Vor′entscheidung f (-;-en) preliminary decision
vor′erst adv first of all; for the time being, for the present
vorerwähnt [′fɔrervent] adj aforesaid
Vorfahr [′fɔrfar] m (-en;-en) forebear
vor′fahren §71 intr (SEIN) (bei) drive up (to)
Vor′fahrt f, **Vor′fahrt(s)recht** n right of way
Vor′fall m incident; event
vor′fallen §72 intr (SEIN) happen
Vor′feld n (aer) apron (of airport); (mil) approaches
vor′finden §59 tr find there
Vor′freude f anticipation
Vor′frühling m early spring
vor′fühlen intr—bei j-m v. feel s.o. out, put out feelers to s.o.
Vorführdame [′fɔrfyrdamə] f mannequin
vor′führen tr bring forward, produce; display, demonstrate; (Kleider) model; (Film) show; (Stück) (theat) present
Vor′führer -in §6 mf projectionist
Vor′führung f (-;-en) production; demonstration; showing; show, performance
Vor′gabe f points, handicap
Vor′gaberennen n handicap (race)
Vor′gabespiel n handicap
Vor′gang m event, incident, phenomenon; (Verfahren) process, procedure; (Präzedenzfall) precedent; (in den Akten) previous correspondence
Vor′gänger -in §6 mf predecessor
Vor′garten m front yard
vor′geben §80 tr pretend; give as an excuse; j-m zehn Punkte v. give s.o. ten points odds || intr—j-m v. give

s.o. odds || **Vorgeben** n (-s;-) pretext
Vor′gebirge n foothills; (Kap) cape
vorgeblich [′fɔrgepliç] adj ostensible
vorgefaßt [′fɔrgəfast] adj preconceived
Vor′gefühl n inkling; banges V. misgivings; im V. von or genit in anticipation of
vor′gehen §82 intr (SEIN) advance; go first; act; take action, proceed; (sich ereignen) go on, happen; (Uhr) be fast; (dat) take precedence (over); die Arbeit geht vor work comes first; was geht hier vor? what's going on here? || **Vorgehen** n (-s;) advance; action, proceeding; gemeinschaftliches V. concerted action
vorgelagert [′fɔrgəlagərt] adj offshore
Vor′gelände n foreground
vorgenannt [′fɔrgənant] adj aforementioned
Vor′gericht n appetizer
Vor′geschichte f previous history; (Urgeschichte) prehistory
vor′geschichtlich adj prehistoric
Vor′geschmack m foretaste
Vorgesetzte [′fɔrgəzetstə] §5 mf superior; boss; (mil) senior officer
vor′gestern adv day before yesterday
vor′gestrig adj of the day before yesterday
vorgetäuscht [′fɔrgətɔɪʃt] adj make-believe
vor′greifen §88 intr (dat) anticipate
Vor′griff m anticipation
vor′gucken intr (Unterkleid) show
vor′haben §89 tr have in mind, plan; intend to do; (ausfragen) question; (schelten) scold; (Schürze) (coll) have on || **Vorhaben** n (-s;-) intention, plan; project
Vor′halle f entrance hall; lobby
vor′halten §90 tr—j-m etw v. hold s.th. in front of s.o.; (fig) reproach s.o. with s.th. || intr last
Vor′haltung f (-;-en) reproach; j-m Vorhaltungen machen über (acc) reproach s.o. for
Vor′hand f (cards) forehand; (tennis) forehand stroke; die V. haben (cards) lead off
vorhanden [for′handən] adj present, at hand, available; (com) in stock; v. sein exist
Vorhan′densein n existence; presence
Vor′hang m (-[e]s;̈e) curtain; (theat) (coll) curtain call; Eiserner V. iron curtain
Vorhängeschloß [′fɔrheŋəʃlɔs] n padlock
Vor′hangstange f curtain rod
Vor′hangstoff m drapery material
Vor′haut f foreskin
Vor′hemd n dicky, shirt front
vor′her adv before, previously; (im voraus) in advance
vorher′bestellen tr reserve
vorher′bestimmen tr predetermine; (eccl) predestine
Vorher′bestimmung f predestination
vorher′gehend, vorherig [for′heriç] adj preceding, previous; prior
Vor′herrschaft f predominance

vor'herrschen *intr* predominate, prevail

vor'herrschend *adj* predominant, prevailing

Vorher'sage *f* prediction; forecast

vorher'sagen *tr* predict, foretell; (*Wetter*) forecast

vorhin' *adv* a little while ago

vor'historisch *adj* prehistoric

Vor'hof *m* front yard; (anat) auricle

Vor'hut *f* (mil) vanguard

vorige ['forigə] §9 *adj* previous, former; **voriges Jahr** last year

Vor'jahr *n* preceding year

vor'jährig *adj* last year's

Vor'kammer *f* (anat) auricle; (aut) precombustion chamber

Vor'kampf *m* (box) preliminary bout; (sport) heat

Vor'kämpfer –in §6 *mf* pioneer

Vorkehrung ['forkeruŋ] *f* (–;–en) precaution; **Vorkehrungen treffen** take precautions

Vor'kenntnis *f* (von) basic knowledge (of); **Vorkenntnisse** rudiments, basics; **Vorkenntnisse nicht erforderlich** no previous experience necessary

vor'knöpfen *ref*—**sich** [dat] **j–n** v. (coll) chew s.o. out

Vor'kommando *n* (mil) advance party

vor'kommen §99 *intr* (SEIN) happen; (*Fall*) come up; (als Besucher) be admitted; (scheinen) seem, look; (sich finden) be found; (zu Besuch) call on || *ref*—**er kam sich** [dat] **dumm vor** he felt silly || *impers*—**es kommt dir nur so vor** you are just imagining it; **es kommt mir vor** it seems to me || **Vorkommen** *n* (–s;–) occurrence; (min) deposit

Vorkommnis ['forkomnis] *n* (–ses;–se) event, occurrence

Vorkriegs— *comb.fm.* prewar

vor'laden §103 *tr* (jur) summon; (unter Strafandrohung) (jur) subpoena

Vor'ladung *f* (–;–en) (jur) summons; (unter Strafandrohung) (jur) subpoena

Vor'lage *f* submission, presentation; proposal; (Muster) pattern; bedside carpet; (fb) forward pass; (parl) bill

vor'lassen §104 *tr* let go ahead; (Auto) let pass; (zulassen) admit

Vor'lauf *m* (sport) qualifying heat

Vor'läufer –in §6 *mf* forerunner

vor'läufig *adj* preliminary; temporary || *adv* provisionally; temporarily, for the time being

vor'laut *adj* forward, fresh

Vor'leben *n* past life, former life

Vorlegebesteck ['forlegəbə/stek] *n* carving set

Vorlegegabel ['forlegəgabəl] *f* carving fork

Vorlegelöffel ['forlegəlœfəl] *m* serving spoon

Vorlegemesser ['forlegəmesər] *n* carving knife

vor'legen *tr* put forward; propose; (Ausweis, Paß) show; (Essen) serve; (zur Prüfung, usw.) submit, present; **den Ball v.** (fb) pass the ball; **ein scharfes Tempo v.** (coll) speed it up;

j–m e–e Frage v. ask s.o. a question || *ref* lean forward

Ver'leger *m* (–s;–) throw rug

Vorlegeschloß ['forlegə/los] *n* padlock

vor'lesen §107 *tr*—**j–m etw v.** read s.th. to s.o.

Vor'lesung *f* (–;–en) reading; lecture; **e–e V. halten über** (acc) give a lecture on

Vor'lesungsverzeichnis *n* university catalogue

vor'letzte §9 *adj* second last; (gram) penultimate

Vor'liebe *f* preference

vorliebnehmen [for'lipnemən] §116 *intr* take pot luck; **v. mit** put up with

vor'liegen §108 *intr* be present; exist; be under consideration; **dem Richter v.** be up before the judge; **heute liegt nichts vor** there's nothing doing today; **mir liegt e–e Beschwerde vor** I have a complaint here; **was liegt gegen ihn vor?** what is the charge against him?

vor'liegend *adj* present, at hand

vor'lügen §111 *tr*—**j–m etw v. über** (acc) tell s.o. lies about

vor'machen *tr*—**du kannst mir doch nichts v.** you can't put anything over on me; **j–m etw v.** show s.o. how to do s.th. || *ref*—**er läßt sich** [dat] **nichts v.** he's nobody's fool; **sich** [dat] **selbst etw v.** fool oneself

Vor'macht *f* leading power; supremacy

Vor'machtstellung *f* (position of) supremacy

vormalig ['formaliç] *adj* former

vormals ['formals] *adv* formerly

Vor'marsch *m* advance

vor'merken *tr* note down; reserve; **sich v. lassen für** put in for

Vor'mittag *m* forenoon, morning

vor'mittags *adv* in the forenoon

Vor'mund *m* guardian

Vor'mundschaft *f* (–;–en) guardianship

vor'mundschaftlich *adj* guardian's

Vor'mundschaftsgericht *n* orphans' court

vorn [forn] *adv* in front; ahead; **ganz v.** all the way up front; **nach v.** forward; **nach v. heraus wohnen** live in the front part of the house; **nach v. liegen** face the front; **von v.** from the front; **von v. anfangen** begin at the beginning

Vor'nahme *f* undertaking

Vor'name *m* first name

vorne ['fornə] *adv* (coll) var of **vorn**

vornehm ['fornem] *adj* distinguished, high-class; **vornehme Welt** high society; **vornehmste Aufgabe** principal task || *adv*—**v. tun** put on airs

vor'nehmen §116 *tr* (umbinden) put on; undertake, take up; (Änderungen) make; **wieder v.** resume || *ref*—**sich** [dat] **ein Buch v.** take up a book; **sich** [dat] **etw v.** decide upon s.th.; **sich** [dat] **j–n v.** take s.o. to task; **sich** [dat] **v. zu** (inf) make up one's mind to (inf); **sich** [dat] **zuviel v.** bite off more than one can chew

Vor'nehmheit *f* (–;) distinction, high rank; distinguished bearing

vor'nehmlich *adv* especially

vor'neigen *ref* bend forward

vorn'herein *adv*—**von v.** from the first

vornweg ['fornvɛk], **[forn'vɛk]** *adv*—**er ist weit v.** he is way out in front; **mit dem Kopf v.** head first; **mit dem Mund v. sein** be fresh

Vor'ort *m* suburb

Vorort– *comb.fm.* suburban

Vor'ortbahn *f* (tr) suburban line

Vor'ortzug *m* commuter train

Vor'platz *m* front yard; *(Diele)* entrance hall; *(Vorfeld)* (aer) apron

Vor'posten *m* (mil) outpost

Vor'rang *m* precedence; priority; preeminence; **den V. vor j-m haben** have precedence over s.o.

Vor'rat *m* (-[e]s;⸚e) (an *dat*) stock (of), supply (of); **auf V. kaufen** buy in quantity; **e-n V. anlegen an** (*dat*) stock

vorrätig ['forrɛtɪç] *adj* in stock

Vor'ratskammer *f* pantry, storeroom

Vor'ratsraum *m* storeroom

Vor'ratsschrank *m* pantry

Vor'raum *m* anteroom

vor'rechnen *tr*—**j-m etw v.** figure out s.th. for s.o.; **j-m seine Fehler v.** enumerate s.o.'s mistakes to s.o.

Vor'recht *n* privilege, prerogative

Vor'rede *f* preface, introduction

vor'reden *tr*—**j-m etw v.** try to make s.o. believe s.th.

Vor'redner –in §6 *mf* previous speaker

Vor'richtung *f* (-;-en) preparation; *(Gerät)* device, appliance, mechanism; (mach) fixture

vor'rücken *tr* move forward ‖ *intr* (SEIN) *(Truppen)* advance; *(Polizei)* move in; *(im Dienst)* be promoted

Vor'runde *f* (sport) play-offs

vors [fors] *abbr* vor das

vor'sagen *tr*—**j-m etw v.** recite s.th. to s.o. ‖ *intr* (*dat*) prompt

Vor'sager –in §6 *mf* prompter

Vor'satz *m* purpose, intention; (jur) premeditation; **den V. fassen zu** (*inf*) make up one's mind to (*inf*); **mit V.** on purpose; **seinen V. ausführen** gain one's ends

Vor'satzblatt *n* (bb) end paper

Vor'satzgerät *n* adapter

vorsätzlich ['forzetslɪç] *adj* deliberate; *(Mord)* premeditated

Vor'schau *f* (cin) preview

vor'schieben §130 *tr* push forward; offer as an excuse; (fig) plead; **den Riegel v.** (*dat*) (fig) prevent; **Truppen v.** move troops forward

vor'schießen §76 *tr* *(Geld)* (coll) advance ‖ *intr* (SEIN) dart ahead

Vor'schiff *n* (naut) forecastle

Vor'schlag *m* proposal; *(Angebot)* offer; *(Anregung)* suggestion; *(Empfehlung)* recommendation; (mus) grace note; (parl) motion; **in V. bringen** propose; (parl) move

vor'schlagen §132 *tr* propose; suggest; recommend; **zur Wahl v.** nominate

Vor'schlagsliste *f* slate of candidates

Vor'schlußrunde *f* (sport) semifinal

vor'schnell *adj* rash, hasty

vor'schreiben §62 *tr* prescribe, order;

specify; write out; **ich lasse mir nichts v.** I take orders from no one

vor'schreiten §86 *intr* (SEIN) step forward; advance

Vor'schrift *f* order, direction; regulation; (med) prescription

vor'schriftsmäßig *adj* & *adv* according to regulations

vor'schriftswidrig *adj* & *adv* against regulations

Vor'schub *m* assistance; (mach) feed; **V. leisten** (*dat*) encourage; (jur) aid and abet

Vor'schule *f* prep school; *(Elementarschule)* elementary school

Vor'schuß *m* *(Geld*–) advance; (jur) retainer

vor'schützen *tr* pretend, plead

Vor'schützung *f* (-;) pretense

vor'schweben *intr*—**mir schwebte etw anderes vor** I had s.th. else in mind; **das schwebt mir dunkel vor** I have a dim recollection of it

vor'schwindeln *tr*—**j-m etw v.** fool s.o. about s.th.

vor'sehen §138 *tr* schedule, plan; provide; (fin) earmark; **das Gesetz sieht vor, daß** the law provides that ‖ *ref* be careful, take care; **sich mit etw v.** provide oneself with s.th.; **sich v. vor** (*dat*) be on one's guard against

Vor'sehung *f* (-;) Providence

vor'setzen *tr* put forward; *(Silbe)* prefix; **j-m etw v.** set s.th. before s.o. *(to eat)*; **j-m j-n v.** set s.o. over s.o.

Vor'sicht *f* caution, care; *(Umsicht)* prudence; **V.!** watch out! *(auf Kisten)* handle with care!; **V., Stufe!** watch your step!

vor'sichtig *adj* cautious, careful

Vor'sichtigkeit *f* (-;) caution

vorsichtshalber ['forzɪçtshalbər] *adv* to be on the safe side, as a precaution

Vor'sichtsmaßnahme *f*, **Vor'sichtsmaßregel** *f* precaution

Vor'silbe *f* prefix

vor'singen §142 *tr*—**j-m etw v.** sing s.th. to s.o. ‖ *intr* lead the choir

Vor'sitz *m* chairmanship, chair; presidency; **den V. haben** (or **führen**) **bei** preside over; **unter V. von** presided over by

Vorsitzende ['forzɪtsəndə] §5 *mf* chairperson; president

Vor'sorge *f* provision; **V. tragen** (or **treffen**) **für** make provision for, provide for

vor'sorgen *intr* (**für**) provide (for)

vorsorglich ['forzorklɪç] *adv* as a precaution, just in case

Vor'spann *m* (cin) credits; *(Kurzfilm)* (cin) short

Vor'speise *f* appetizer

vor'spiegeln *tr*—**j-m etw v.** delude s.o. with s.th.; **j-m falsche Tatsachen v.** misrepresent facts to s.o.

Vor'spiegelung *f* (-;) sham; pretense; **V. falscher Tatsachen** misrepresentation of facts

Vor'spiel *n* prelude; *(beim Geschlechtsverkehr)* foreplay; (mus) overture; (theat) curtain raiser; **das**

war nur das V.! (fig) that was only the beginning!

vor'spielen tr—j—m etw v. play s.th. for s.o.

vor'sprechen §64 tr—j—m etw v. pronounce s.th. for s.o.; teach s.o. how to pronounce s.th. || intr—bei j—m v. drop in on s.o.; j—m v. audition before s.o.

vor'springen §142 intr (SEIN) leap forward; (aus dem Versteck) jump out; (vorstehen) stick out, protrude

Vor'sprung m projection; (Sims) ledge; (Vorteil) advantage; (sport) head start; (sport) lead

Vor'stadt f suburb

vor'städtisch adj suburban

Vor'stand m board of directors; executive committee, executive board; (Person) chairman of the board

vor'stehen §146 intr protrude; (dat) be at the head of, direct, manage

Vor'steher m (-s;-) head, director, manager; (educ) principal

Vor'steherdrüse f prostate gland

Vor'steherin f (-;-nen) head, director, manager; (educ) principal

vor'stellen tr place in front, put ahead; (Uhr) set ahead; (einführen) introduce, present; (darstellen) represent; (bedeuten) mean; (hinweisen auf) point out || ref—sich [dat] etw v. imagine s.th., picture s.th.

Vor'stellung f (-;-en) introduction, presentation; (Begriff) idea; (Einspruch) remonstrance, protest; (cin) show; (theat) performance

Vor'stellungsvermögen n imagination

Vor'stoß m (fig & mil) thrust, drive

vor'stoßen §150 tr push forward || intr (SEIN) push forward, advance

Vor'strafe f previous conviction

Vor'strafenregister n previous record

vor'strecken tr stretch out; (Geld) advance

Vor'stufe f preliminary stage

Vor'tag m previous day

vor'täuschen tr pretend, put on

Vor'teil m advantage; profit; (tennis) advantage

vor'teilhaft adj advantageous; profitable

Vortrag ['fortrak] m (-[e]s;-e) performance; (Bericht) report; (e-s Gedichtes) recitation; (e-r Rede) delivery; (Vorlesung) lecture; (acct) balance (carried over); (mus) recital; e-n V. halten über (acc) give a lecture on

vor'tragen §132 tr perform; present

Vortragende ['fortragəndə] §5 mf performer; speaker; lecturer

Vor'tragsfolge f program

vortrefflich ['fortreflɪç] adj excellent

vor'treten §152 intr (SEIN) step forward; (fig) stick out, protrude

Vor'tritt m (-[e]s) precedence

vorü'ber adv past, by, along; (zeitlich) over, gone by

vorü'bergehen §82 intr (SEIN) pass; (an dat) pass by; (fig) disregard

vorü'bergehend adj passing, transitory || **Vorübergehende** §5 mf passer-by

vorü'berziehen §163 intr (SEIN) march by; (Gewitter) blow over

Vor'übung f warmup

Vor'untersuchung f preliminary investigation

Vor'urteil n prejudice

vor'urteilsfrei, vor'urteilslos adj unprejudiced

Vor'vergangenheit f (gram) past perfect

Vor'verkauf m advance sale; (theat) advance reservation

vor'verlegen tr advance, move up

Vor'wahl f (pol) primary

vor'wählen intr dial the area code

Vor'wählnummer f (telp) area code

Vor'wand m (-[e]s;-e) pretext; excuse

vorwärts ['forverts] adv forward, on, ahead || interj go on!

vor'wärtsbringen §65 tr bring forward; (fig) advance

vor'wärtsgehen §82 intr (SEIN) progress

vor'wärtskommen §99 intr (SEIN) go ahead; progress, make headway

vorweg [for'vek] adv beforehand; out in front

Vorweg'nahme f anticipation

vorweg'nehmen §116 tr anticipate; presuppose, assume

vor'weisen §118 tr produce, show

Vor'welt f prehistoric world

vor'weltlich adj primeval

vor'werfen §160 tr—j—m etw v. throw s.th. to s.o.; (fig) throw s.th. up to s.o.

vorwiegend ['forvigənt] adj predominant || adv predominantly, chiefly

Vor'wissen n foreknowledge

vor'witzig adj inquisitive; brash

Vor'wort n (-[e]s;-e) foreword

Vor'wurf m reproach, blame; (e-s Dramas) subject; j—m Vorwürfe machen blame s.o.

vor'wurfslos adj irreproachable

vor'wurfsvoll adj reproachful

vor'zählen tr enumerate

Vor'zeichen n omen; (math) sign; (mus) accidental; negatives V. minus sign

vor'zeichnen tr—j—m etw v. draw or sketch s.th. for s.o.

Vor'zeichnung f (-;-en) drawing; (mus) signature

vor'zeigen tr produce, show; (Wechsel) present

Vor'zeiger -in §6 mf bearer

Vor'zeigung f (-;-en) producing, showing; presentation

Vor'zeit f remote antiquity

vor'zeiten adv in days of old

vor'zeitig adj premature

vor'ziehen §163 tr draw forth; pull out; prefer; (mil) move up

Vor'zimmer n anteroom; entrance hall

Vor'zug m preference; (Vorteil) advantage; (Überlegenheit) superiority; (Vorrang) priority; (Vorrecht) privilege; (Vorzüglichkeit) excellence; e-r Sache den V. geben prefer s.th.

vorzüglich ['fortsyklɪç] adj excellent, first-rate || adv especially

Vor'züglichkeit f (-;) excellence

Vor'zugsaktie f preferred stock

Vor'zugsbehandlung *f* preferential treatment
Vor'zugspreis *m* special price
Vor'zugsrecht *n* priority; privilege
vor'zugsweise *adv* preferably
votieren [vo'tirən] *intr* vote
Votiv- [votif] *comb.fm.* votive
Vo·tum ['votum] *n* (-s;-ten [tən] & -ta [ta]) vote

vulgär [vul'ger] *adj* vulgar
Vulkan [vul'kan] *m* (-s;-e) volcano
Vulkan'ausbruch *m* eruption
vulkanisch [vul'kaniʃ] *adj* volcanic
vulkanisieren [vulkanı'zirən] *tr* vulcanize
Vulkan'schlot *m* volcanic vent
VW *abbr* (Volkswagen) VW
V-Waffe *f* (Vergeltungswaffe) V-1, V-2

W

W, w [ve] *invar n* W, w
Waage ['vagə] *f* (-;-n) (pair of) scales; (astr) Libra; (gym) horizontal position; **die beiden Dinge halten sich** [dat] **die W.** the two things balance each other; **die W. halten** (*dat*) counterbalance; **j—m die W. halten** be a match for s.o.
waa'gerecht, waagrecht ['vakrɛçt] *adj* horizontal, level
Waagschale ['vakʃalə] *f* scale(s); **in die W. fallen** carry weight; **in die W. werfen** bring to bear
wabbelig ['vabəlıç] *adj* (coll) flabby
Wabe ['vabə] *f* (-;-n) honeycomb
wach [vax] *adj* awake; (*lebhaft*) lively; (*Geist*) alert; **ganz w.** wide awake
Wach'ablösung *f* changing of the guard
Wach'dienst *m* guard duty
Wache ['vaxə] *f* (-;-n) guard, watch; (*Wachstube*) guardroom; (*Wachlokal*) guardhouse; (*Polizei-*) police station; (*Wachdienst*) guard duty; (*Posten*) guard, sentinel; **auf W. on guard; auf W. ziehen** mount guard; **W. schieben** (coll) pull guard duty
wachen ['vaxən] *intr* be awake; **bei j—m w.** sit up with s.o.; **w. über** (*acc*) watch over, guard
wach'habend *adj* on guard duty
wach'halten §90 *tr* keep awake; (fig) keep alive
Wach'hund *m* watchdog
Wach'lokal *n* guardroom; police station
Wach'mann *m* (-[e]s;-leute) (Aust) policeman
Wach'mannschaft *f* (mil) guard detail
Wacholder [va'xoldər] *m* (-s;-) juniper
Wachol'derbranntwein *m* gin
Wach'posten *m* sentry
wach'rufen §122 *tr* wake up; (*Erinnerung*) bring back
Wachs [vaks] *n* (-es;-e) wax
wachsam ['vaxzam] *adj* vigilant
Wach'samkeit *f* (-) vigilance
Wachs'bohne *f* wax bean
wachsen ['vaksən] *tr* wax || §155 *intr* (SEIN) grow; (an *dat*) increase (in)
wächsern ['vɛksərn] *adj* wax; (fig) waxy
Wachs'figurenkabinett *n* wax museum
Wachs'kerze *f*, **Wachs'licht** *n* wax candle
Wachs'leinwand *f* oilcloth

Wach'stube *f* guardroom
Wachs'tuch *n* oilcloth
Wachstum ['vaxstum] *n* (-s;) growth; increase
Wacht [vaxt] *f* (-;-en) guard, watch
Wächte ['vɛçtə] *f* (-;-n) snow cornice
Wachtel ['vaxtəl] *f* (-;-n) quail
Wach'telhund *m* spaniel
Wächter ['vɛçtər] *m* (-s;-) guard
Wacht'meister *m* police sergeant
Wach'traum *m* daydream
Wacht'turm *m* watchtower
wackelig ['vakəlıç] *adj* wobbly; (*Zahn*) loose; (fig) shaky
Wackelkontakt ['vakəlkɔntakt] *m* (elec) loose connection, poor contact
wackeln ['vakəln] *intr* wobble; shake; (*locker sein*) be loose
wacker ['vakər] *adj* decent, honest; (*tapfer*) brave || *adv* heartily
wacklig ['vakliç] *adj* var of **wackelig**
Wade ['vadə] *f* (-;-n) (anat) calf
Wa'denbein *n* (anat) fibula
Wa'denkrampf *m* leg cramp
Wa'denstrumpf *m* calf-length stocking
Waffe ['vafə] *f* (-;-n) weapon; branch of service; **die Waffen strecken** surrender; (fig) give up; **zu den Waffen greifen** take up arms
Waffel ['vafəl] *f* (-;-n) waffle
Waf'fenbruder *m* comrade in arms
waf'fenfähig *adj* capable of bearing arms
Waf'fengang *m* armed conflict
Waf'fengattung *f* branch of service
Waf'fengewalt *f* force of arms
Waf'fenkammer *f* armory
Waf'fenlager *n* ordnance depot; **heimliches W.** cache of arms
waf'fenlos *adj* unarmed
Waf'fenruhe *f* truce
Waf'fenschein *m* gun permit
Waf'fenschmied *m* gunsmith
Waf'fenschmuggel *m* gunrunning
Waf'fen-SS *f* (-;) SS combat unit
Waf'fenstillstand *m* armistice
Wagehals ['vagəhals] *m* daredevil
Wagemut ['vagəmut] *m* daring
wagen ['vagən] *tr* dare; risk || *ref* venture, dare || **Wagen** *m* (-s;-) wagon; (*Fahrzeug; Teil e—r Schreibmaschine*) carriage; (aut, rr) car; **der Große Wagen** the Big Dipper; **j—m an den W. fahren** (fig) step on s.o.'s toes
wägen ['vegən] *tr* (& fig) weigh
Wa'genabteil *n* (rr) compartment

Wa'genburg *f* barricade of wagons
Wa'genheber *m* (aut) jack
Wa'genpark *m* fleet of cars
Wa'genpflege *f* (aut) maintenance
Wa'genschlag *m* car door, carriage door
Wa'genschmiere *f* (aut) grease
Wa'genspur *f* wheel track, rut
Wa'genwäsche *f* car wash
Wagestück ['vɑgə/tyk] *n* hazardous venture, daring deed
Waggon [va'gõ] *m* (-s;-s) railroad car
waghalsig ['vɑkhalzɪç] *adj* foolhardy
Wagnis ['vɑknɪs] *n* (-ses;-se) risk
Wahl [vɑl] *f* (-;-en) choice, option; (*Auswahl*) selection; (*Alternative*) alternative; (pol) election; **e-e W. treffen** make a choice; **vor der W. stehen** have the choice
wählbar ['vɛlbɑr] *adj* eligible
Wähl'barkeit *f* (-;) eligibility
Wahl'beeinflussung *f* interference with the election process
wahl'berechtigt *adj* eligible to vote
Wahl'beteiligung *f* election turnout
Wahl'bezirk *m* ward
wählen ['vɛlən] *tr* choose; select; (pol) elect; (telp) dial || *intr* vote
Wäh'ler *m* (-s;-) voter
Wahl'ergebnis *n* election returns
Wäh'lerin *f* (-;-nen) voter
wählerisch ['vɛlərɪʃ] *adj* choosy, particular
Wäh'lerschaft *f* (-;-en) constituency
Wäh'lerscheibe *f* (telp) dial
Wahl'fach *n* (educ) elective
wahl'fähig *adj* eligible for election; having a vote
wahl'frei *adj* (educ) elective
Wahl'gang *m* ballot
Wahl'kampf *m* election campaign
Wahl'kreis *m* constituency; district
Wahl'leiter *m* campaign manager
Wahl'list *f* (pol) slate, ticket
Wahl'lokal *n* polling place
Wahl'lokomotive *f* (coll) vote getter
wahl'los *adj* indiscriminate
Wahl'parole *f* campaign slogan
Wahl'programm *n* (pol) platform
Wahl'recht *n* right to vote, suffrage
Wahl'rede *f* campaign speech
Wahl'spruch *m* motto; (com, pol) slogan
Wahl'urne *f* ballot box
Wahl'versammlung *f* campaign rally
wahl'verwandt *adj* congenial
Wahl'zelle *f* voting booth
Wahl'zettel *m* ballot
Wahn [vɑn] *m* (-[e]s;) delusion; error; folly; madness
Wahn'bild *n* phantom, delusion
wähnen ['vɛnən] *tr* fancy, imagine
Wahn'idee *f* delusion; (coll) crazy idea
Wahn'sinn *m* (& fig) madness
wahn'sinnig *adj* (vor *dat*) mad (with); (coll) terrible || *adv* madly; (coll) awfully || **Wahnsinnige** §5 *mf* lunatic
Wahn'vorstellung *f* hallucination
Wahn'witz *m* (& fig) madness
wahn'witzig *adj* mad; (*unverantwortlich*) irresponsible
wahr [vɑr] *adj* true; (*wirklich*) real; (*echt*) genuine; **nicht w.?** right?

wahren ['vɑrən] *tr* keep; (*Anschein*) keep up; (**vor** *dat*) protect (against)
währen ['vɛrən] *intr* last
während ['vɛrənt] *prep* (*genit*) during; (jur) pending || *conj* while; whereas
wahr'haben §89 *tr* admit
wahr'haft, wahr'haftig *adj* true, truthful; (*wirklich*) real || *adv* actually
Wahr'haftigkeit *f* (-;) truthfulness
Wahr'heit *f* (-;-en) truth; **j-m die W. sagen** give s.o. a piece of one's mind
wahr'heitsgemäß, wahr'heitsgetreu *adj* true, faithful; truthful
Wahr'heitsliebe *f* truthfulness
wahr'heitsliebend *adj* truthful
wahr'lich *adv* truly; (Bib) verily
wahrnehmbar ['vɑrnembɑr] *adj* noticeable
wahr'nehmen §116 *tr* notice; (*benutzen*) make use of; (*Interesse*) protect; (*Recht*) assert
Wahr'nehmung *f* (-;-en) observation, perception; (*der Interessen*) safeguarding
wahr'sagen *ref*—**sich** [*dat*] **w. lassen** have one's fortune told || *intr* prophesy; tell fortunes
Wahr'sagerin *f* (-;-nen) fortuneteller
wahrscheinlich ['vɑr'ʃɑɪnlɪç] *adj* probable, likely || *adv* probably
Wahrschein'lichkeit *f* (-;) probability
Wahr'spruch *m* verdict
Wah'rung *f* (-;) safeguarding
Wäh'rung *f* (-;-en) currency; standard
Wäh'rungsabwertung *f* devaluation
Wäh'rungseinheit *f* monetary unit
Wahr'zeichen *n* landmark
Waise ['vaɪzə] *f* (-;-n) orphan
Wai'senhaus *n* orphanage
Wal [vɑl] *m* (-[e]s;-e) whale
Wald [valt] *m* (-[e]s;̈er) forest, woods
Wald- *comb.fm.* forest; sylvan; wild
Wald'aufseher *m* forest ranger
Wald'brand *m* forest fire
waldig ['valdɪç] *adj* wooded
Waldung ['valduŋ] *f* (-;-en) forest
Wald'wirtschaft *f* forestry
Wal'fang *m* whaling
Wal'fänger *m* (-s;-) whaler
walken ['valkən] *tr* full
Wal'ker *m* (-s;-) fuller
Wall [val] *m* (-[e]s;̈e) mound; embankment; (mil) rampart
Wallach ['valax] *m* (-[e]s;-e) gelding
wallen ['valən] *intr* (*sieden*) boil; (*sprudeln*) bubble; (*Gewand, Haar*) flow, fall in waves || *intr* (SEIN) go on a pilgrimage; travel, wander
wall'fahren *insep intr* (SEIN) go on a pilgrimage
Wall'fahrer -in §6 *mf* pilgrim
Wall'fahrt *f* pilgrimage
Wall'graben *m* moat
Wal'lung *f* (-;) simmering, boiling; bubbling; flow; flutter; (*Blutandrang*) congestion; **in W. bringen** enrage; **in W. geraten** fly into a rage; **Wallungen** hot flashes
Walnuß ['valnus] *f* walnut
Walroß ['valrɔs] *n* walrus
Wal'speck *m* blubber
walten ['valtən] *intr* rule; hold sway;

Gnade w. lassen show mercy; seines Amtes w. attend to one's duties

Wal'tran *m* whale oil

Walze ['valtsə] *f* (-;-n) cylinder, drum; roll, roller; (*der Schreibmaschine*) platen

walzen ['valtsən] *tr* roll

wälzen ['veltsən] *tr* roll; (*Bücher*) pore over; (*Gedanken*) turn over in one's mind; **die Schuld auf j-n w.** shift the blame to s.o. else || *ref* roll, toss; (*im Kot*) wallow; (*im Blut*) welter

Wal'zer *m* (-s;-) waltz

Wäl'zer *m* (-s;-) (coll) thick tome

Walz'werk *n* rolling mill

Wamme ['vamə] *f* (-;-n) dewlap; (coll) potbelly

Wampe ['vampə] *f* (-;-n) (coll) potbelly

wand [vant] *pret* of **winden** || **Wand** *f* (-;̈e) wall; partition; (*Fels-*) cliff; **spanische W.** folding screen

Wand'apparat *m* (telp) wall phone

Wand'bekleidung *f* wainscot

Wandel ['vandəl] *m* (-s;) change

wandelbar ['vandəlbar] *adj* changeable

Wan'delgang *m*, **Wan'delhalle** *f* lobby

wandeln ['vandəln] *tr* change || *ref* (in *acc*) change (into) || *intr* (SEIN) (poet) wander; (poet) walk

Wan'derer **-in** §6 *mf* wanderer; hiker

Wan'derlust *f* wanderlust, itch to travel

wandern ['vandərn] *intr* (SEIN) wander; hike; (*Vögel*) migrate

Wan'derniere *f* floating kidney

Wan'derpreis *m* challenge trophy

Wan'derschaft *f* (-;) travels, wanderings

Wan'derstab *m* walking stick

Wan'derung *f* (-;-en) hike; migration

Wan'dervogel *m* migratory bird; (coll) rover

Wand'gemälde *n* mural

Wand'karte *f* wall map

Wand'leuchter *m* sconce

Wand'lung *f* (-;-en) change, transformation; (eccl) consecration

Wand'malerei *f* wall painting

Wand'pfeiler *m* pilaster

Wand'schirm *m* folding screen

Wand'schrank *m* wall shelves

Wand'spiegel *m* wall mirror

Wand'steckdose *f*, **Wand'stecker** *m* (elec) wall outlet

Wand'tafel *f* blackboard

wandte ['vantə] *pret* of **wenden**

Wand'teppich *m* tapestry

Wange ['vaŋə] *f* (-;-n) cheek

-wangig [vaŋɪç] *comb.fm.* -cheeked

Wan'kelmut *m* fickleness

wan'kelmütig *adj* fickle

wanken ['vaŋkən] *intr* stagger; sway, rock; (fig) waver

wann [van] *adv & conj* when; **w. immer** anytime, whenever

Wanne ['vanə] *f* (-;-n) tub

Wanst [vanst] *m* (-es;̈e) belly, paunch

-wanstig [vanstɪç] *comb.fm.* -bellied

Wanze ['vantsə] *f* (-;-n) bedbug

Wappen ['vapən] *n* (-s;-) coat of arms

Wap'penkunde *f* heraldry

Wap'penschild *m* escutcheon

wappnen ['vapnən] *ref* arm oneself; **sich mit Geduld w.** have patience

war [var] *pret* of **sein**

warb [varp] *pret* of **werben**

ward [vart] *pret* of **werden**

Ware ['varə] *f* (-;-n) ware; article; commodity; **Waren** goods, merchandise

-waren [varən] *pl comb.fm.* -ware

Wa'renaufzug *m* freight elevator

Wa'renausgabe *f* wrapping department

Wa'renbestand *m* stock

Wa'renbörse *f* commodity market

Wa'renhaus *n* department store

Wa'renlager *n* warehouse; stockroom

Wa'renmarkt *m* commodity market

Wa'renmuster *n*, **Wa'renprobe** *f* sample

Wa'renrechnung *f* invoice

Wa'renzeichen *n* trademark

warf [varf] *pret* of **werfen**

warm [varm] *adj* (**wärmer** ['vermər]; **wärmste** ['vermstə] §9) warm

Warmblüter ['varmblytər] *m* (-s;-) warm-blooded animal

warmblütig ['varmblytɪç] *adj* warm-blooded

Wärme ['vermə] *f* (-;) warmth, heat

wär'mebeständig *adj* heatproof

Wär'meeinheit *f* thermal unit; calory

Wär'megrad *m* degree of heat, temperature

wärmen ['vermən] *tr* warm, heat

Wär'meplatte *f*—**elektrische W.** hotplate

Wärm'flasche *f* hot-water bottle

warm'halten §90 *tr* keep warm

warm'herzig *adj* warm-hearted

warm'laufen §105 *intr*—**den Motor w. lassen** let the motor warm up

Warmluft'heizung *f* hot-air heating

Warmwas'serbehälter *m* hot-water tank

Warmwas'serheizung *f* hot-water heating

Warmwas'serspeicher *m* hot-water tank

Warn- [varn] *comb.fm.* warning

Warn'anlage *f* warning system

warnen ['varnən] *tr* (**vor** *dat*) warn (of), caution (against)

Warn'gebiet *n* danger zone

Warn'schuß *m* warning shot

Warn'signal *n* warning signal

War'nung *f* (-;-en) warning, caution; **zur W.** as a warning

War'nungsschild *n*, **Warn'zeichen** *n* danger sign

Warschau ['varʃau] *n* (-s;) Warsaw

Warte ['vartə] *f* (-;-n) watchtower, lookout

War'tefrau *f* attendant; nurse

War'tefrist *f* waiting period

warten ['vartən] *tr* tend, attend to; (*pflegen*) nurse || *intr* (**auf** *acc*) wait (for)

Wärter ['vertər] *m* (-s;-) attendant; (*Pfleger*) male nurse; (*Aufseher*) caretaker; (*Gefängnis-*) guard; (rr) signalman

War'teraum *m* waiting room

Wärterin ['vertərɪn] *f* (-;-nen) attendant; nurse

War'tesaal *m*, War'tezimmer *n* waiting room
War'tung *f* (–;) maintenance
warum [va'rum] *adv* why
Warze ['vartsə] *f* (–;–n) wart; (Brust–) nipple
was [vas] *indef pron* something; na, so was! well, I never! ‖ *interr pron* what; ach was! go on! was für ein what kind of, what sort of; was haben wir gelacht! how we laughed! ‖ *rel pron* what; which, that; was auch immer no matter what; was immer whatever
Wasch– [vaʃ] *comb.fm.* wash, washing
waschbar ['vaʃbar] *adj* washable
Wasch'bär *m* racoon
Wasch'becken *n* sink
Wasch'benzin *n* cleaning fluid
Wasch'blau *n* bluing
Wasch'bütte *f* washtub
Wäsche ['vɛʃə] *f* (–;–n) wash, laundry; linen; underwear
Wä'schebeutel *m* laundry bag
wasch'echt *adj* washable; (fig) genuine
Wä'scheklammer *f* clothespin
Wä'schekorb *m* clothesbasket
Wä'scheleine *f* clothesline
waschen ['vaʃən] §158 *tr* wash; launder; (Gold) pan; (Haar) shampoo; (reinigen) purify ‖ *ref* wash; sich [dat] die Hände w. wash one's hands ‖ *intr* wash
Wä'scher ['vɛʃər] *m* (–s;–) washer; laundryman
Wäscherei [vɛʃə'raɪ] *f* (–;–en) laundry
Wäscherin ['vɛʃərɪn] *f* (–;–nen) washerwoman, laundress
Wä'scherolle *f* mangle
Wä'scheschleuder *f* spin-drier
Wä'scheschrank *m* linen closet
Wä'schezeichen *n* laundry mark
Wasch'frau *f* laundress
Wasch'haus *n* laundry
Wasch'korb *m* clothesbasket
Wasch'küche *f* laundry
Wasch'lappen *m* washcloth; (fig) wishy-washy person
Wasch'maschine *f* washmachine, washer
Wasch'mittel *n* detergent
Wasch'raum *m* washroom, lavatory
Wasch'schüssel *f* wash basin
Wasch'tisch *m* washstand
Wasch'trog *m* washtub
Wa'schung *f* (–;–en) washing; ablution
Wasch'weib *n* (coll) gossip (woman)
Wasch'zettel *m* laundry list; (am Schutzumschlag) blurb
Wasser ['vasər] *n* (–s;–) water; das W. läuft mir im Mund zusammen my mouth is watering; j–m das W. abgraben pull the rug out from under s.o.; mit allen Wassern gewaschen sharp as a needle
was'serabstoßend *adj* water-repellent
was'serarm *adj* arid
Was'serball *m* water polo
Was'serbau *m* (–[e]s;) harbor and canal construction
Was'serbehälter *m* water tank; reservoir; cistern

Was'serblase *f* bubble; (auf der Haut) blister
Was'serbombe *f* depth charge
Was'serbüffel *m* water buffalo
Was'serdampf *m* steam
was'serdicht *adj* watertight, waterproof
Was'sereimer *m* bucket
Was'serfall *m* waterfall, cascade
Was'serfarbe *f* watercolor
Was'serflasche *f* water bottle
Was'serflugzeug *n* seaplane
Was'sergeflügel *n* waterfowl
Was'sergraben *m* drain; moat
Was'serhahn *m* faucet, spigot
Was'serhose *f* waterspout
wässerig ['vesərɪç] *adj* watery
Was'serjungfer *f* dragonfly
Was'serkessel *m* cauldron
Was'serklosett *n* toilet
Was'serkraftwerk *n* hydroelectric plant
Was'serkrug *m* water jug, water pitcher
Was'serkur *f* spa
Was'serland'flugzeug *n* amphibian plane
Was'serland'panzerwagen *m* amphibian tank
Was'serlauf *m* watercourse
Was'serleitung *f* water main; aqueduct
Was'sermangel *m* water shortage
Was'sermann *m* (–[e]s;) (astr) Aquarius
Was'sermelone *f* watermelon
wassern ['vasərn] *intr* land on water; (rok) splash down
wässern ['vesərn] *tr* water; irrigate; (phot) wash ‖ *intr* (Augen, Mund) water
Was'serratte *f* water rat; (fig) old salt
Was'serrinne *f* gutter
Was'serrohr *n* water pipe
Was'serscheide *f* watershed, divide
was'serscheu *adj* afraid of water
Was'serschi *m* water ski
Was'serschlauch *m* hose
Wasserspeier ['vasər/paɪ·ər] *m* (–s;–) gargoyle
Was'serspiegel *m* surface; water level
Was'sersport *m* aquatics
Was'serstand *m* water level
Was'serstiefel *m* rubber boots
Was'serstoff *m* hydrogen
was'serstoffblond *adj* peroxide-blond
Was'serstoffbombe *f* hydrogen bomb
Was'serstrahl *m* jet of water
Was'serstraße *f* waterway
Was'sersucht *f* dropsy
Was'serung *f* (–;–en) (aer) landing on water; (rok) splashdown
Wäs'serung *f* (–;) watering; irrigation
Was'serverdrängung *f* displacement
Was'serversorgung *f* water supply
Was'servogel *m* waterfowl
Was'serwaage *f* (carp) level
Was'serweg *m* waterway; auf dem W. by water
Was'serwerk *n* waterworks
Was'serzähler *m* water meter
Was'serzeichen *n* watermark
wässrig ['vesrɪç] *adj* watery
waten ['vatən] *intr* (SEIN) wade
Watsche ['vatʃə] *f* (–;–n) slap
watscheln ['vatʃəln] *intr* (SEIN) waddle
watschen ['vatʃən] *tr* slap

Watt [vat] *n* (-s;-) (elec) watt

Watte ['vatə] *f* (-;-en) absorbent cotton; wadding

Wat'tebausch *m* swab

Wat'tekugel *f* cotton ball

Wat'tenmeer *n* shallow coastal waters

Wat'testäbchen *n* Q-tip, cotton swab

wattieren [va'tirən] *tr* pad, wad

Wattie'rung *f* (-;-en) padding, wadding

wauwau ['vau˙vau] *interj* bow-wow! || Wauwau *m* (-s;-s) bow-wow, doggy

weben ['vebən] §109 & §94 *tr* & *intr* weave

We'ber *m* (-s;-) weaver

Weberei [vebə'raɪ] *f* (-;-en) weaving

We'berin *f* (-;-nen) weaver

We'berknecht *m* daddy-long-legs

Webstuhl ['vep/tul] *m* loom

Webwaren ['vepvʊrən] *pl* textiles

Wechsel ['veksəl] *m* (-s;-) change, shift; (*für Studenten*) allowance; (agr) rotation (*of crops*); (fin) bill of exchange; (hunt) run, beaten track; gezogener W. draft; offener W. letter of credit; trockener (or eigener) W. promissory note

Wech'selbeziehung *f* correlation

Wechselfälle ['veksəlfelə] *pl* ups and downs, vicissitudes

Wech'selfieber *n* intermittent fever; malaria

Wech'selfrist *f* period of grace (*before bill of exchange falls due*)

Wech'selgeld *n* change, small change

Wech'selgesang *m* antiphony

Wech'selgespräch *n* dialogue

wech'selhaft *adj* changeable

Wech'selkurs *m* rate of exchange

Wech'selmakler -in §6 *mf* bill-broker

wechseln ['veksəln] *tr* change; vary; (*austauschen*) exchange; den Besitzer w. change hands; die Zähne w. get one's second set of teeth; seinen Wohnsitz w. move || *intr* change; vary

Wech'selnehmer *m* (fin) payee

Wech'selnotierung *f* foreign exchange rate

Wech'selrichter *m* (elec) vibrator (*producing a.c.*)

wech'selseitig *adj* mutual, reciprocal

Wech'selseitigkeit *f* (-;) reciprocity

Wech'selspiel *n* interplay

Wech'selsprechanlage *f* intercom

Wech'selstrom *m* alternating current

Wech'selstube *f* money-exchange office

Wech'seltierchen *n* amoeba

wech'selvoll *adj* (*Landschaft*) changing; (*Leben*) checkered; (*Wetter*) changeable

wech'selweise *adv* mutually; alternately

Wech'selwirkung *f* interaction

Wech'selwirtschaft *f* crop rotation

wecken ['vekən] *tr* wake, awaken, rouse

Wecker (Wek'ker) *m* (-s;-) alarm clock

Weck'ruf *m* (mil) reveille

Wedel ['vedəl] *m* (-s;-) brush, whisk; (*Schwanz*) tail; (eccl) sprinkler

wedeln ['vedəln] *tr* brush away || *intr*

—mit dem Fächer w. fan oneself; mit dem Schwanz w. wag its tail

weder ['vedər] *conj*—weder...noch neither...nor

weg [vek] *adv* away, off; gone; lost || Weg [vek] *m* (-[e]s;-e) way, path; road; route, course; (*Art und Weise*) way; (*Mittel*) means; am Wege by the roadside; auf dem besten Wege sein be well on the way; auf gütlichem Wege amicably; auf halbem Wege halfway; aus dem Weg räumen remove; (fig) bump off; etw in die Wege leiten prepare the way for s.th.; introduce s.th.; j—m aus dem Wege gehen make way for s.o.; steer clear of s.o.; Weg und Steg kennen know every turn in the road

weg'bekommen §99 *tr* (*Fleck*) get out; (*Krankheit*) catch; (*verstehen*) get the hang of; e—e w. (coll) get a crack

weg'bleiben §62 *intr* (SEIN) stay away; be omitted

weg'blicken *intr* glance away

weg'bringen §65 *tr* take away; (*Fleck*) get out

Wegebau ['vegəbau] *m* (-[e]s;) road building

Wegegeld ['vegəgelt] *n* mileage allowance; turnpike toll

wegen ['vegən] *prep* (*genit*) because of, on account of; for the sake of; (*mit Rücksicht auf*) in consideration of; (*infolge*) in consequence of; (jur) on (the charge of); von Amts w. officially; von Rechts w. by right

Wegerecht ['vegəreçt] *n* right of way

weg'essen §70 *tr* eat up

weg'fahren §71 *tr* remove || *intr* (SEIN) drive away, leave

weg'fallen §72 *intr* (SEIN) fall away, fall off; (*ausgelassen werden*) be omitted; (*aufhören*) cease; (*abgeschafft werden*) be abolished

weg'fangen §73 *tr* snap away, snatch

weg'fliegen §57 *intr* (SEIN) fly away

weg'fressen §70 *tr* devour

weg'führen *tr* lead away

Weggang ['vekgaŋ] *m* departure

weg'geben §80 *tr* give away

weg'gehen §82 *intr* (SEIN) go away; w. über (*acc*) pass over; wie warme Semmeln w. go like hotcakes

weg'haben §89 *tr* get rid of; (*Schläge, usw.*) have gotten one's share of; (*verstehen*) catch on to; der hat eins weg (sl) he has a screw loose; (sl) he's loaded

weg'jagen *tr* chase away

weg'kehren *tr* sweep away; (*Gesicht*) avert || *ref* turn away

weg'kommen §99 *intr* (SEIN) come away; get away (*verlorengehen*) get lost; nicht w. über (*acc*) not get over

weg'können §100 *intr*—nicht w. not be able to get away

Wegkreuzung ['vekkrɔɪtsuŋ] *f* (-;-en) crossing, intersection

weg'kriegen *tr* (*Fleck*) get out

weg'lassen §104 *tr* leave out; let go; cross out; (gram) elide; (math) cancel

weg'legen *tr* put aside

weg'machen *tr* take away; *(Fleck)* take out

wegmüde ['vekmydə] *adj* travel-weary

weg'müssen §115 *intr* have to go

Wegnahme ['veknɑːmə] *f* (-;-n) taking away; confiscation; (mil) capture

weg'nehmen §116 *tr* take away; *(Raum, Zeit)* take up; *(beschlagnahmen)* confiscate; (mil) capture

weg'packen *tr* pack away || *ref* pack off

weg'raffen *tr* snatch away

Wegrand ['vekrant] *m* wayside

weg'räumen *tr* clear away

weg'reißen §53 *tr* tear off, tear away

weg'rücken *tr* move away

weg'schaffen *tr* remove; get rid of

weg'scheren §129 *tr* clip || *ref* scram

weg'scheuchen *tr* scare away

weg'schicken *tr* send away

weg'schleichen §85 *ref* & *intr* (SEIN) sneak away, steal away

weg'schmeißen §53 *tr* (coll) throw away

weg'schneiden §106 *tr* cut away

weg'sehen §138 *intr* look away; **w. über** *(acc)* shut one's eyes to

weg'setzen *tr* put away || *ref—sich* **w. über** *(acc)* not mind; feel superior to || *intr* (SEIN)—**w. über** *(acc)* jump over

weg'spülen *tr* wash away; (geol) erode

weg'stehlen §147 *ref* slip away

weg'stellen *tr* put aside

weg'stoßen §150 *tr* shove aside

weg'streichen §85 *tr* cross out

weg'treten §152 *intr* (SEIN) step aside; (mil) break ranks; **weggetreten!** (mil) dismissed!; **w. lassen** (mil) dismiss

weg'tun §154 *tr* put away

Wegweiser ['vekvaɪzər] *m* (-s;-) roadsign; *(Buch, Reiseführer)* guide

weg'wenden §120 & §140 *tr* & *ref* turn away

weg'werfen §160 *tr* throw away || *ref* degrade oneself

weg'werfend *adj* disparaging

weg'wischen *tr* wipe away

weg'zaubern *tr* spirit away

weg'ziehen §163 *tr* pull away || *intr* (SEIN) move; (mil) pull out

weh [veː] *adj* painful, sore; **mir ist weh ums Herz** I am sick at heart || *adv—* **sich** *[dat]* **weh tun** hurt oneself; **weh tun ache** || *interj* woe! **weh mir!** woe is me! || **Weh** *n* (-[e]s;-e) pain, ache

wehe ['veː·ə] *adj, adv,* & *interj* var of **weh** || **Wehe** *f* (-;-n) drift

wehen ['veː·ən] *tr* blow; *(Schnee)* drift || *intr* *(Wind)* blow; *(Fahne, Kerzenflamme)* flutter || **Wehen** *pl* labor, labor pains; (fig) travail

Weh'geschrei *n* wails, wailing

Weh'klage *f* wail

weh'klagen *intr* *(über acc)* wail (over); **w. um** lament for

weh'leidig *adj* complaining, whining; **W. tun** whine

Weh'mut *f* (-;) melancholy; nostalgia

weh'mütig *adj* melancholy; nostalgic

Wehr [veːr] *f* (-;-en) weapon; *(Abwehr)* defense, resistance; *(Brüstung)*

parapet; **sich zur W. setzen** offer resistance || **Wehr** *n* (-[e]s;-e) dam

Wehr'dienst *m* military service

wehr'dienstpflichtig *adj* subject to military service

Wehr'dienstverweigerer *m* (-s;-) conscientious objector

wehren ['veːrən] *tr—j—m etw* **w.** keep s.o. (away) from s.th. || *ref* defend oneself; resist, put up a fight; **sich seiner Haut w.** save one's skin || *intr* *(dat)* resist; *(dat)* check

wehr'fähig *adj* fit for military service

wehr'haft *adj* *(Person)* full of fight; *(Burg)* strong

wehr'los *adj* defenseless

Wehr'macht *f* (hist) German armed forces

Wehr'meldeamt *n* draft board

Wehr'paß *m* service record

Wehr'pflicht *f* compulsory military service; **allgemeine W.** universal military training

wehr'pflichtig *adj* subject to military service

Weib [vaɪp] *n* (-[e]s;-er) woman; wife; **ein tolles W.** a luscious doll

Weibchen ['vaɪpçən] *n* (-s;-) *(Tier)* female; *(Ehefrau)* little woman

Weiberfeind ['vaɪbərfaɪnt] *m* womanhater

Weiberheld ['vaɪbərhelt] *m* ladies' man

Weibervolk ['vaɪbərfɔlk] *n* womenfolk

weibisch ['vaɪbɪʃ] *adj* womanish, effeminate

weib'lich *adj* female; womanly; (& gram) feminine

Weib'lichkeit *f* (-;) womanhood; feminine nature; **die holde W.** (hum) the fair sex

Weibs'bild *n* female; (pej) wench

Weibs'stück *n* (sl) woman

weich [vaɪç] *adj* soft; *(Ei)* soft-boiled; *(zart)* tender; *(schwach)* weak; **w. machen** soften up; **w. werden** (& fig) soften; relent

Weich'bild *n* urban area, outskirts

Weiche ['vaɪçə] *f* (-;-n) (anat) side, flank; (rr) switch; **Weichen stellen** throw the switch

weichen ['vaɪçən] *tr* & *intr* soften; soak || §85 *intr* (SEIN) yield; give ground; *(Boden)* give way; *(dat)* give in to; **j—m nicht von der Seite w.** not leave s.o.'s side; **nicht von der Stelle w.** not budge from the spot; **von j—m w.** leave s.o.

Weichensteller ['vaɪçənstelər] *m* (-s; -) (rr) switchman

Weich'heit *f* (-;) softness; tenderness

weich'herzig *adj* soft-hearted

Weich'käse *m* soft cheese

weich'lich *adj* soft; tender; flabby; insipid; *(weibisch)* effeminate; *(lässig)* indolent

Weichling ['vaɪçlɪŋ] *m* (-s;-e) weakling

Weich'tier *n* mollusk

Weide ['vaɪdə] *f* (-;-n) pasture; (bot) willow

Wei'deland *n* pasture land

weiden ['vaɪdən] *tr* graze; *(Augen)*

feast || *ref—sich w. an* (*dat*) feast
one's eyes on || *intr* graze
Wei′denkorb *m* wicker basket
weidlich [′vaıtlıç] *adv* heartily
weidmännisch [′vaıtmenıʃ] *adj* (hunt)
sportsmanlike
weigern [′vaıgərn] *ref—sich w. zu* (*inf*)
refuse to (*inf*)
Wei′gerung *f* (-;-en) refusal
Weihe [′vaı·ə] *f* (-;-n) consecration;
(*e-s Priesters*) ordination
weihen [′vaı·ən] *tr* consecrate; (*zum
Priester*) ordain; (*widmen*) dedicate;
dem Tode geweiht doomed to death
|| *ref* devote oneself
Wei′her *m* (-s;-) pond
wei′hevoll *adj* solemn
Weihnachten [′vaınaxtən] *n* (-s;) & *pl*
Christmas; **zu W.** for or at Christmas
Weih′nachtsabend *m* Christmas Eve
Weih′nachtsbaum *m* Christmas tree;
(coll) bombing markers
Weih′nachtsbescherung *f* exchange of
Christmas presents
Weih′nachtsfeier *f* Christmas celebra-
tion; (*in Betrieben*) Christmas party
Weih′nachtsfest *n* feast of Christmas
Weih′nachtsgeschenk *n* Christmas pres-
ent
Weih′nachtsgratifikation *f* Christmas
bonus
Weih′nachtslied *n* Christmas carol
Weih′nachtsmann *m* (-[e]s;) Santa
Claus
Weih′nachtsmarkt *m* Christmas fair
(*at which Christmas decorations are
sold*)
Weih′nachstag *m* Christmas day
Weih′rauch *m* incense
Weih′rauchfaß *n* censer
Weih′wasser *n* holy water
Weih′wedel *m* (eccl) sprinkler
weil [vaıl] *conj* because, since
weiland [′vaılant] *adv* formerly
Weilchen [′vaılçən] *n* (-s;) little while
Weile [′vaılə] *f* (-;) while
weilen [′vaılən] *intr* stay, linger
Wein [vaın] *m* (-[e]s;-e) wine;
(*Pflanze*) vine
Wein′bau *m* (-[e]s;) winegrowing
Wein′bauer -in §6 *mf* winegrower
Wein′beere *f* grape
Wein′berg *m* vineyard
Wein′blatt *n* vine leaf
Wein′brand *m* brandy
weinen [′vaınən] *tr* (*Tränen*) shed ||
intr cry, weep; **vor Freude w.** weep
for joy; **w. um** cry over
weinerlich [′vaınərlıç] *adj* tearful;
(*Stimme*)) whining
Wein′ernte *f* vintage
Wein′essig *m* wine vinegar
Wein′faß *n* wine barrel
Wein′händler *m* wine merchant
Wein′jahr *n* vintage year
Wein′karte *f* wine list
Wein′keller *m* wine cellar
Wein′kelter *f* wine press
Wein′kenner *m* connoisseur of wine
Wein′krampf *m* crying fit
Wein′laub *n* vine leaves
Wein′lese *f* grape picking
Wein′presse *f* wine press

Wein′ranke *f* vine tendril
Wein′rebe *f* grapevine
wein′selig *adj* tipsy, tight
Wein′stock *m* vine
Wein′traube *f* grape; bunch of grapes
weise [′vaızə] *adj* wise || **Weise** §5 *m*
wise man, sage || *f* (-;-n) way;
(*Melodie*) tune; **auf diese W.** in this
way
-weise *comb.fm.* -wise; by, e.g., **dut-
zendweise** by the dozen; -ly, e.g.,
glücklicherweise luckily
weisen [′vaızən] §118 *tr* point out,
show; (*aus dem Lande*) banish; (*aus
der Schule*) expel; **j-n w. an** (*acc*)
refer s.o. to; **j-n w. nach** direct s.o.
to; **j-n w. von** order s.o. off (*premises, etc.*); **von der Hand w.** refuse;
weit von der Hand w. have nothing
to do with || *ref—von sich w.* refuse
|| *intr—w. auf* (*acc*) point to
Weis′heit *f* (-;-en) wisdom; wise saying; **Weisheiten** words of wisdom
Weis′heitszahn *m* wisdom tooth
weis′lich *adv* wisely, prudently
weismachen [′vaısmaxən] *tr—j—m etw
w.* put s.th. over on s.o.; **mach das
anderen weis!** tell it to the marines!
weiß [vaıs] *adj* white
weissagen [′vaızzagən] *tr* foretell
Weiß′blech *n* tin plate, tin
Weiß′blechdose *f* tincan
weiß′bluten *tr* bleed white
Weiß′brot *n* white bread
Weiß′dorn *m* (bot) hawthorn
Weiße [′vaısə] *f* (-;-n) whiteness;
(Berlin) ale || §5 *m* white man || *f*
white woman || *n* (*im Auge, im Ei*)
white
weißen [′vaısən] *tr* whiten; (*tünchen*)
whitewash
weiß′glühend *adj* white-hot
Weiß′glut *f* white heat, incandescence
Weiß′kohl *m*, **Weiß′kraut** *n* cabbage
weiß′lich *adj* whitish
Weiß′metall *n* pewter; Babbitt metal
Weiß′waren *pl* linens
Weiß′wein *m* white wine
Wei′sung *f* (-;-en) directions, instructions; directive
weit [vaıt] *adj* far, distant; (*ausgedehnt*) extensive; (*breit*) wide, broad;
(*geräumig*) large; (*Gewissen*) elastic;
(*Herz*) big; (*Kleid*) full, big; (*Meer*)
broad; (*Reise, Weg*) long; (*Welt*)
wide; **bei weitem besser** better by
far; **von weitem** from afar || *adv* far,
way; widely; greatly; **w. besser** far
better
weit′ab′ *adv* (**von**) far away (from)
weit′aus′ *adv* by far
Weit′blick *m* farsightedness
weit′blickend *adj* farsighted
Weite [′vaıtə] *f* (-;-n) width, breadth;
(*Ferne*) distance; (*Umfang*) size;
(*Ausdehnung*) extent; (*Durchmesser*)
diameter; (fig) range; **in die W.
ziehen** go out into the world
weiten [′vaıtən] *tr* widen; (*Loch*) en-
large; (*Schuh*) stretch || *ref* widen
weiter [′vaıtər] *adj* farther; further;
wider; **bis auf weiteres** until further
notice; **des weiteren** furthermore;

ohne weiteres without further ado ‖ *adv* farther; further; furthermore; (*voran*) on; **er kann nicht w.** he can't go on; **nur s. w.!** keep it up!; **und so w.** and so forth, and so on

weiter– *comb.fm.* on; keep on, continue to

wei′terbefördern *tr* forward

Wei′terbestand *m* continued existence

wei′terbestehen §146 *intr* survive

wei′terbilden *tr* develop ‖ *ref* continue one's studies

wei′tererzählen *tr* spread (*rumors*)

wei′terfahren §71 *intr* (SEIN) drive on

wei′tergeben §80 *tr* pass on, relay

wei′tergehen §82 *intr* (SEIN) go on

wei′terhin′ *adv* furthermore; again

wei′terkommen §99 *intr* (SEIN) get ahead, make progress

wei′terkönnen §100 *intr* be able to go on; **ich kann nicht weiter** I'm stuck

wei′terleben *intr* live on, survive

wei′termachen *tr* & *intr* continue ‖ *interj* (mil) as you were!, carry on!

weit′gehend *adj* far-reaching

weit′gereist *adj* widely traveled

weit′greifend *adj* far-reaching

weit′her′ *adv*—**von w.** from afar

weit′her′geholt *adj* far-fetched

weit′herzig *adj* broad-minded

weit′hin′ *adv* far off

weitläufig [′vaɪtlɔɪfɪç] *adj* lengthy, detailed; complicated; (*Verwandte*) distant; (*geräumig*) roomy ‖ *adv* at length, in detail

weit′reichend *adj* far-reaching

weitschweifig [′vaɪt/vaɪfɪç] *adj* detailed, lengthy; long-winded

weit′sichtig *adj* (& fig) far-sighted

Weit′sprung *m* (sport) long jump

Weit′streckenflug *m* long-distance flight

weit′tragend *adj* long-range; (fig) far-reaching

Weit′winkelobjektiv *n* wide-angle lens

Welzen [′vaɪtsən] *m* (–s;–) wheat

Wei′zenmehl *n* wheat flour

welch [vɛlç] *interr adj* which ‖ *interr pron* which one; (*in Ausrufen*) what ...!; **mit welcher** (or **mit welch einer**) **Begeisterung arbeitet er!** with what enthusiasm he works! ‖ *indef pron* any; some ‖ *rel pron* who, which, that

welcherlei [′vɛlçər′laɪ] *invar adj* what kind of; whatever

welk [vɛlk] *adj* withered; (*Haut, Lippen*) wrinkled; (fig) faded

welken [′vɛlkən] *intr* (SEIN) wither; (fig) fade

Wellblech [′vɛlblɛç] *n* corrugated iron

Well′blechhütte *f* Quonset hut

Welle [′vɛlə] *f* (–;–n) wave; (*Wellbaum*) shaft; (gym) circle (*around horizontal bar*); (mach) shaft

wellen [′vɛlən] *tr* & *ref* wave

Wel′lenbereich *m* wave band

Wel′lenberg *m* crest (*of wave*)

Wel′lenbewegung *f* undulation

Wel′lenbrecher *m* breakwater

wel′lenförmig *adj* wavy

Wel′lenlänge *f* wavelength

Wel′lenlinie *f* wavy line

wel′lenreiten §86 *intr* surf; waterski ‖ **Wellenreiten** *n* (–s;) surfing, surfboard riding; waterskiing

Wel′lenreiter **–in** §6 *mf* surfer; water-skier

Wel′lenreiterbrett *n* surfboard; water ski

Wel′lental *n* trough (*of wave*)

wellig [′vɛlɪç] *adj* wavy

Well′pappe *f* corrugated cardboard

Welt [vɛlt] *f* (–;–en) world

Weit′all *n* universe; outer space

Welt′anschauung *f* outlook on life; ideology

Welt′ausmaß *m*—**im W.** on a global scale

Welt′ausstellung *f* world's fair

welt′bekannt, welt′berühmt *adj* world-renowned

Welt′enbummler *m* globetrotter

welt′erfahren *adj* sophisticated

Weltergewicht [′vɛltərgəvɪçt] *n* welterweight class

Weltergewichtler [′vɛltərgəvɪçtlər] *m* (–s;–) welterweight boxer

welt′erschütternd *adj* earth-shaking

welt′fremd *adj* secluded; innocent

Welt′friede *m* world peace

Welt′geistlicher *m* secular priest

welt′gewandt *adj* worldly-wise

Welt′karte *f* map of the world

welt′klug *adj* worldly-wise

Welt′körper *m* heavenly body

Welt′krieg *m* world war

Welt′kugel *f* globe

Welt′lage *f* international situation

welt′lich *adj* worldly; secular

Welt′macht *f* world power

Welt′mann *m* (–[e]s;–er) man of the world

welt′männisch *adj* sophisticated

Welt′meer *n* ocean

Welt′meinung *f* world opinion

Welt′meister **–in** §6 *mf* world champion

Welt′meisterschaft *f* world championship

Welt′ordnung *f* cosmic order

Welt′postverein *m* postal union

Welt′priester *m* secular priest

Welt′raum *m* (–[e]s;) outer space

Welt′raumfahrer *m* spaceman

Welt′raumfahrt *f* space travel

Welt′raumfahrzeug *n* spacecraft

Welt′raumforschung *f* exploration of outer space

Welt′raumgeschoß *n* space shot

Welt′raumkapsel *f* space capsule

Welt′raumstation *f* space station

Welt′raumstrahlen *pl* cosmic rays

Welt′reich *n* world empire

Welt′reise *f* trip around the world

Welt′rekord *m* world record

Welt′ruf *m* world-wide renown

Welt′ruhm *m* world-wide fame

Welt′schmerz *m* world-weariness

Welt′sicherheitsrat *m* U.N. Security Council

Welt′stadt *f* metropolis (*city with more than one million inhabitants*)

Welt′teil *m* continent

welt′umfassend *adj* world-wide

Welt′weisheit *f* philosophy

wem [vem] *interr & rel pron* to whom
Wem′fall *m* dative case
wen [ven] *interr & rel pron* whom
Wende [′vendə] *f* (−;-n) turn; turning point; (gym) face vault, front vault
Wen′dekreis *m* (geog) tropic
Wendeltreppe [′vendəltrepə] *f* spiral staircase
Wen′demarke *f* (aer) pylon; (sport) turn post
wenden [′vendən] §140 *tr* turn; turn around; turn over; (Geld, Mühe) spend || *ref* turn; (Wind, Wetter) change || *intr* turn, turn around
Wen′depunkt *m* turning point
wendig [′vendɪç] *adj* maneuverable; (Person) versatile, resourceful
Wen′dung *f* (−;-en) turn; change; (Redensart) idiomatic expression
Wen′fall *m* accusative case
wenig [′venɪç] *adj* little; **ein w.** a little, a bit of; **wenige** few, a few, some || *adv* little; not very; seldom || *indef pron* little; **wenige** few, a few
weniger [′venɪgər] *adj* fewer; less; (arith) minus
We′nigkeit *f* (−;) fewness; smallness; pittance; trifle; **meine W.** (coll) poor little me
wenigste [′venɪçstə] §9 *adj* least; very few, fewest; **am wenigsten** least of all
wenigstens [′venɪçstəns] *adv* at least
wenn [ven] *conj* if, in case; (zeitlich) when, whenever; **auch w.** even if; **außer w.** except when, except if, unless; **w. anders** provided that; **w. auch** although, even if; **w. schon, denn schon** go all the way || **Wenn** *n* (−;-) if
wenngleich′, wennschon′ *conj* although
Wenzel [′ventsəl] *m* (−;-) (cards) jack
wer [ver] *interr pron* who, which one; **wer auch immer** whoever; **wer da?** who goes there? || *rel pron* he who, whoever || *indef pron* somebody, anybody
Werbe- [verbə] *comb.fm.* advertising; publicity; commercial
Wer′befernsehen *n* commercial television
Wer′befilm *m* commercial
Wer′befläche *f* advertising space
Wer′begraphik *f* commercial art
Wer′begraphiker −in §6 *mf* commercial artist
werben [′verbən] §149 *tr* (neue Kunden) try to get; (mil) recruit || *intr* advertise; **für e−n neuen Handelsartikel w.** advertise a new product; **um ein Mädchen w.** court a girl
Wer′beschrift *f* folder
Wer′bestelle *f* advertising agency
Wer′bung *f* (−;-en) advertising; publicity; courting; recruiting
Werdegang [′verdəgaŋ] *m* career, background; (Entwicklung) development; (Wachstum) growth; (Ablauf der Herstellung) process of production
werden [′verdən] §159 *intr* (SEIN) become, grow, get, turn; **w. zu** change into; **zu nichts w.** come to nought ||

aux (SEIN) (to form the future) **er wird gehen** he will go; (to form the passive) **er wird geehrt** he is being honored || **Werden** *n* (−;) becoming, growing; (Entstehung) evolution; (Wachstum) growth; **im W. sein** be in the process of development; be in the making
wer′dend *adj* nascent; (Mutter) expectant; (Arzt) future
Werder [′verdər] *m* (−;-) islet
Wer′fall *m* subjective case
werfen [′verfən] §160 *tr* throw, cast; (Junge) produce; (Blasen) form, blow; **Falten w.** wrinkle || *ref* (Holz) warp; **sich hin und her w.** toss; **sich in die Brust w.** throw out one's chest || *intr* throw; (Tieren) produce young
Werft [verft] *f* (−;-e) shipyard
Werft′halle *f* (aer) repair hangar
Werg [verk] *n* (−[e]s;) oakum, tow
Werk [verk] *n* (−[e]s;-e) work; (Tat) deed; (Erzeugnis) production; (Leistung) performance; (Unternehmen) undertaking; (Fabrik) works, plant, mill; (horol) clockwork; **das ist dein W.** that's your doing; **gutes W.** good deed; **im Werke sein** be in the works; **zu Werke gehen** go to it
Werk′anlage *f* plant, works
Werk′bank *f* (−;-e) workbench
werk′fremd *adj* (Personen) unauthorized
Werk′meister *m* foreman
Werk′nummer *f* factory serial number
Werks′angehörige §5 *mf* employee
Werk′schutz *m* security force
Werks′kantine *f* factory cafeteria
Werk′statt *f*, **Werk′stätte** *f* workshop
Werk′stattwagen *m* maintenance truck
Werk′stoff *m* manufacturing material
Werk′stück *n* (indust) piece
Werk′tag *m* weekday; working day
werk′tägig *adj* workaday, ordinary
werk′tags *adv* (on) weekdays
werk′tätig *adj* working; practical
Werk′zeug *n* tool
Werk′zeugmaschine *f* machine tool
Wermut [′vermut] *m* (−[e]s;) vermouth; (bot) wormwood
wert [vert] *adj* worth; worthy; esteemed; **etw** [genit or acc] **w. sein** be worth s.th.; **nicht der Rede w. sein** not worth mentioning; **nichts w.** good for nothing; **Werter Herr X** Dear Mr. X || **Wert** *m* (−[e]s;-e) worth, value; price, rate; (Wichtigkeit) importance; (chem) valence; **äußerer W.** face value; **im W. von** valued at; **innerer W.** intrinsic value; **Werte** (com) assets; (phys) data
Wert′angabe *f* valuation
wert′beständig *adj* of lasting value; (Währung) stable
Wert′bestimmung *f* appraisal
Wert′brief *m* insured letter
werten [′vertən] *tr* (bewerten) value; (nach Leistung) rate; (auswerten) evaluate
Wert′gegenstand *m* valuable article; **Wertgegenstände** valuables
−wertig [vertɪç] *comb.fm.* −value, −quality, e.g., **geringwertig** low-qual-

ity; (chem) –valent, e.g., **zweiwertig** bivalent

Wer′tigkeit *f* (–;–en) (chem) valence

wert′los *adj* worthless

Wert′papiere *pl* securities

Wert′sachen *pl* valuables

wert′voll *adj* valuable

Wert′zeichen *n* stamp; *(Briefmarke)* postage stamp; *(Banknote)* bill

Wesen [′vezən] *n* (–s;–) being, creature; entity; *(inneres Sein, Kern)* essence; *(Betragen)* conduct, way; *(Getue)* fuss; *(Natur)* nature, character; **einnehmendes W.** pleasing personality; **höchtes W.** Supreme Being –**wesen** *n comb.fm.* system

we′senhaft *adj* real; characteristic

we′senlos *adj* unreal; incorporeal

wesentlich [′vezəntlɪç] *adj* essential; *(beträchtlich)* substantial

Weser [′vezər] *f* (–;) Weser (River)

Wes′fall *m* genitive case

weshalb [ves′halp] *adv* why; wherefore

Wespe [′vespə] *f* (–;–n) wasp

wessen [′vesən] *interr pron* whose

West [vest] *m* (–s;) west; (poet) west wind

Weste [′vestə] *f* (–;–n) vest; **e-e reine W.** a clean slate

Westen [′vestən] *m* (–s;) west; **im W. von** west of; **nach W.** westward

Westfalen [vest′fɑlən] *n* (–s;) Westphalia

westfälisch [vest′felɪʃ] *adj* Westphalian

West′gote *m* (–n;–n) Visigoth

Westindien [vest′ɪndjən] *n* (–s;) the West Indies

west′lich *adj* west, western; westerly

Westmächte [′vestmɛçtə] *pl* Western Powers

westwärts [′vestverts] *adv* westward

weswegen [ves′vegən] *adv* why; wherefore

wett [vet] *adj* even, quits

Wett– *comb.fm.* competitive

Wett′bewerb *m* (–s;–e) competition, contest; *(Treffen)* meet

Wett′bewerber –in §6 *mf* competitor

Wette [′vetə] *f* (–;–n) bet, wager; **e–e W. abschließen (or eingehen)** make a bet; **mit j–m um die W. laufen race s.o.; was gilt die W.?** what do you bet?

Wett′eifer *m* competitiveness, rivalry

wetteifern [′vetarfərn] *insep intr* compete; **w. um** compete for

Wetter [′vetər] *n* (–s;) weather; (min) ventilation; **alle W.!** holy smokes!

wet′terbeständig, wet′terfest *adj* weatherproof

Wet′terglas *n* barometer

wet′terhart *adj* hardy

Wet′terkunde *f* meteorology

Wet′terlage *f* weather conditions

wet′terleuchten *insep impers*—**es wetterleuchtet** there is summer lightning ‖ **Wetterleuchten** *n* (–s;) summer lightning, heat lightning

Wet′terverhältnisse *pl* weather conditions

Wet′tervorhersage *f* weather forecast

Wet′terwarte *f* meteorological station

Wet′terwechsel *m* change in the weather

wetterwendisch [′vetərvendɪʃ] *adj* moody

Wett′fahrer –in §6 *mf* racer

Wett′fahrt *f* race

Wett′kampf *m* competition, contest

Wett′kämpfer –in §6 *mf* competitor, contestant

Wett′lauf *m* race, foot race

Wett′läufer –in §6 *mf* runner

wett′machen *tr* make up for

Wett′rennen *n* race

Wett′rudern *n* boat race

Wett′rüsten *n* armaments race

Wett′schwimmen *n* swimming meet

Wett′segeln *n* regatta

Wett′spiel *n* game, match

Wett′streit *m* contest, match, game

Wett′zettel *m* betting ticket

wetzen [′vetsən] *tr* whet, sharpen

Wetzstein [′vetsˌtaɪn] *m* whetstone

Whisky [′vɪski] *m* (–s;–s) whiskey

wich [vɪç] *pret of* **weichen**

Wichs [vɪks] *m* (es–;–e) gala; **in vollem W.** in full dress; **sich in W. werfen** dress up

Wichse [′vɪksə] *f* (–;–n) shoepolish ‖ *f* (–;) (coll) spanking

wichsen [′vɪksən] *tr* polish; (coll) spank, beat up

Wicht [vɪçt] *m* (–[e]s;–e) elf; dwarf

Wichtel [′vɪçtəl] *m* (–s;–) dwarf

wichtig [′vɪçtɪç] *adj* important ‖ *adv* —**w. tun** act important

Wich′tigkeit *f* (–;) importance

Wichtigtuer [′vɪçtɪçtuˌər] *m* (–s;–) busybody

wichtigtuerisch [′vɪçtɪçtuˌərɪʃ] *adj* officious

Wicke [′vɪkə] *f* (–;–n) (bot) vetch

Wickel [′vɪkəl] *m* (–s;–) wrapper; curler, roller; *(von Garn)* ball; (med) compress

wickeln [′vɪkəln] *tr* wrap; wind *(Haar)* curl; *(Kind)* diaper; *(Zigaretten)* roll

Widder [′vɪdər] *m* (–s;–) ram; (astr) Ram

wider [′vidər] *prep (acc)* against, contrary to

wider– *comb.fm.* re–, con–, un–, counter–, contra–, anti–, with–

wi′derborstig *adj* stubborn, contrary

widerfah′ren §71 *intr* (SEIN) *(dat)* befall, happen to

Wi′derhaken *m* barb

Wi′derhall *m* echo, reverberation; (fig) response, reaction

wi′derhallen *intr* echo, resound

Wi′derlager *n* abutment

widerle′gen *tr* refute

wi′derlich *adj* repulsive

wi′dernatürlich *adj* unnatural

widerra′ten §63 *tr*—**j–m etw w.** dissuade s.o. from s.th.

wi′derrechtlich *adj* illegal

Wi′derrede *f* contradiction

Wi′derruf *m* recall; cancellation; retraction; denial; **bis auf W.** until further notice

widerru′fen §122 *tr* revoke; *(Auftrag)*

cancel; (*Befehl*) countermand; (*Behauptung*) retract

Widersacher –in [ˈvidərzaxər(ɪn)] §6 *mf* adversary

Wi'derschein *m* reflection

widerset'zen *ref* (*dat*) oppose, resist

widersetz'lich *adj* insubordinate

wi'dersinnig *adj* absurd, nonsensical

widerspenstig [ˈvidərʃpɛnstɪç] *adj* refractory, contrary; (*Haar*) stubborn

wi'derspiegeln *tr* reflect ‖ *ref* (in *dat*) be reflected (in)

Wi'derspiel *n* contrary, reverse

widerspre'chen §64 *intr* (*dat*) contradict; (*dat*) oppose

widerspre'chend *adj* contradictory

Wi'derspruch *m* contradiction; opposition; **auf heftigen W. stoßen bei** meet with strong opposition from

widersprüchlich [ˈvidərʃprʏçlɪç] *adj* contradictory

wi'derspruchsvoll *adj* full of contradictions

Wi'derstand *m* resistance; opposition; (elec) resistance; (elec) resistor

Wi'derstandsnest *n* pocket of resistance

widerste'hen §146 *intr* (*dat*) withstand, resist; (*dat*) be repugnant to

widerstre'ben *intr* (*dat*) oppose, resist; (*dat*) be repugnant to ‖ *impers*—**es widerstrebt mir zu** (*inf*) I hate to (*inf*)

widerstre'bend *adj* reluctant

Wi'derstreit *m* opposition, antagonism; (fig) conflict, clash

widerstrei'ten §86 *intr* (*dat*) clash with

widerwärtig [ˈvidərvɛrtɪç] *adj* nasty

Wi'derwille *m* (gegen) dislike (of, for), aversion (to); (*Widerstreben*) reluctance; **mit W.** reluctantly

wi'derwillig *adj* reluctant, unwilling

widmen [ˈvɪtmən] *tr* dedicate, devote ‖ *ref* (*dat*) devote oneself to

Wid'mung *f* (–;–en) dedication

widrig [ˈvidrɪç] *adj* contrary; (*ungünstig*) unfavorable, adverse

wid'rigenfalls *adv* otherwise, or else

wie [vi] *adv* how; (*vergleichend*) as, such as, like; **so . . . wie as . . . as**; **und wie!** and how!; **wie, bitte?** what did you say?; **wie dem auch sei** be that as it may; **wie wäre es mit . . . ?** how about . . . ?

wieder [ˈvidər] *adv* again; anew; (*zurück*) back; (*als Vergeltung*) in return

wieder– *comb.fm.* re–

Wie'derabdruck *m* reprint

wiederan'knüpfen *tr* resume

Wiederauf'bau *m* (–[e]s;) rebuilding

wiederauf'bauen *tr* rebuild, reconstruct

wiederauf'erstehen §146 *intr* (SEIN) rise from the dead

Wiederauf'erstehung *f* resurrection

Wiederauf'führung *f* (theat) revival

wiederauf'kommen §99 *intr* (SEIN) (*Kranker*) recover; (*Mode*) come in again

Wiederauf'nahme *f* resumption; (jur) reopening

Wiederauf'nahmeverfahren *n* retrial

Wiederauf'rüstung *f* rearmament

Wie'derbeginn *m* reopening

wie'derbekommen §99 *tr* recover

wie'derbeleben *tr* revive, resuscitate

wie'derbeschaffen *tr* replace

wie'derbringen §65 *tr* bring back; restore, give back

wiederein'bringen §65 *tr* make up for

wiederein'setzen *tr* (in *acc*) reinstate (in); **in Rechte w.** restore to former rights

wiederein'stellen *tr* rehire; (mil) reenlist

Wie'dereintritt *m* (rok) reentry

wie'derergreifen §88 *tr* recapture

wie'dererhalten §90 *tr* get back

wie'dererkennen §97 *tr* recognize

wie'dererlangen *tr* recover, retrieve

wie'dererstatten *tr* restore; (*Geld*) refund

Wie'dergabe *f* return; reproduction; rendering

wie'dergeben §80 *tr* give back; (*Ton*) reproduce; (spielen, übersetzen) render; (*Ehre, Gesundheit*) restore

Wie'dergeburt *f* rebirth

wie'dergenesen §84 *intr* (SEIN) recover

wie'dergewinnen §52 *tr* regain

Wiedergut'machen *tr* make good

Wiedergut'machung *f* (–;–en) reparation

wiederher'stellen *tr* restore

wie'derholen *tr* bring back; take back ‖ **wiederho'len** *tr* repeat

wiederholt [vidərˈholt] *adv* repeatedly

Wiederho'lung *f* (–;–en) repetition

Wiederho'lungszeichen *n* dittomarks; (mus) repeat

Wie'derhören *n*—**auf W.!** (telp) goodbye!

wie'derimpfen *tr* give (*s.o.*) a booster shot

wiederinstand'setzen *tr* repair

wiederkäuen [ˈvidərkɔɪ-ən] *tr* ruminate; (fig) repeat over and over ‖ *intr* chew the cud

Wiederkehr [ˈvidərker] *f* (–;) return; recurrence; anniversary

wie'derkehren *intr* (SEIN) return; recur

wie'derkommen §99 *intr* (SEIN) come back

Wiederkunft [ˈvidərkunft] *f* (–;) return

wie'dersehen §138 *tr* see again ‖ *recip* meet again ‖ **Wiedersehen** *n* (–s;–) meeting again; **auf W.!** see you!

Wie'dertäufer *m* Baptist

wie'dertun §154 *tr* do again, repeat

wie'derum *adv* again; on the other hand

wie'dervereinigen *tr* reunite; reunify

Wie'dervereinigung *f* reunion; (pol) reunification

wie'derverheiraten *tr* & *recip* remarry

Wie'derverkäufer –in §6 *mf* retailer

Wie'derwahl *f* reelection

wie'derwählen *tr* reelect

wiederzu'lassen §104 *tr* readmit

Wiege [ˈvigə] *f* (–;–n) cradle

wiegen [ˈvigən] *tr* (schaukeln) rock ‖ *ref*—**sich in den Hüften w.** sway one's hips; **sich w. in** (*acc*) lull oneself into ‖ §57 *tr* & *intr* weigh

Wie'gendruck *m* incunabulum

Wie'genlied *n* lullaby

wiehern ['vi·ərn] *intr* neigh; **wiehern-des Gelächter** horselaugh

Wien [vin] *n* (-s;) Vienna

Wiener -in ['vinər(ın)] §6 *mf* Viennese

wienerisch ['vinərıʃ] *adj* Viennese

wies [vis] *pret* of **weisen**

Wiese ['vizə] *f* (-;-n) meadow

Wiesel ['vizəl] *n* (-s;-) weasel

Wie'senland *n* meadowland

wieso' *adv* why, how come

wieviel' *adj* how much; **w. Uhr ist es?** what time is it? || *adv & pron* how much || **vieviele** *adj & pron* how many

wievielte [vi'filtə] §9 *adj* which, what; **den wievielten haben wir?** (or **der w. ist heute?**) what day of the month is it?

wiewohl' *conj* although

wild [vılt] *adj* wild; savage; (*grausam*) ferocious; (*Flucht*) headlong; (*auf acc*) wild (about); **wilde Ehe** concubinage; **wilder Streik** wildcat strike || **Wild** *n* (-es;) game

Wild'bach *m* torrent

Wild'braten *m* roast venison

Wildbret ['vıltbret] *n* (-s;) game; venison

Wild'dieb *m* poacher

Wilde ['vıldə] §5 *mf* savage; **wie ein Wilder** like a madman

Wild'ente *f* wild duck

Wilderer ['vıldərər] *m* (-s;-) poacher

wildern ['vıldərn] *intr* poach

Wild'fleisch *n* game; venison

wild'fremd' *adj* completely strange

Wild'hüter *m* game warden

Wild'leder *n* doeskin, buckskin; chamois; suede

Wildnis ['vıltnıs] *f* (-;) wilderness

Wild'schwein *n* wild boar

Wild'wasser *n* rapids

Wildwest'film *m* western

wildwüchsig ['vıltvyksıç] *adj* wild

Wille ['vılə] *m* (-ns;-n), **Willen** ['vılən] *m* (-s;-) will; (*Absicht*) intention; **mit W.** on purpose; **um j-s willen** for s.o.'s sake; **wider Willen** unwillingly; unintentionally; **willens sein zu** (*inf*) be willing to (*inf*)

wil'lenlos *adj* irresolute; unstable

Wil'lensfreiheit *f* free will

Wil'lenskraft *f* will power

wil'lensschwach *adj* weak-willed

wil'lensstark *adj* strong-willed

willfah'ren *intr* (*dat*) comply with

willig ['vılıç] *adj* willing, ready

Wil'ligkeit *f* (-;) willingness

willkom'men *adj* welcome; **j-n w. heißen** welcome s.o. || **Willkommen** *m & n* (-s;) welcome

Willkür ['vılkyr] *f* (-;) arbitrariness

will'kürlich *adj* arbitrary

wimmeln ['vıməln] *intr* (**von**) team (with)

wimmern ['vımərn] *intr* whimper

Wimpel ['vımpəl] *m* (-s;-) streamer; pennant

Wimper ['vımpər] *f* (-;-n) eyelash; **ohne mit der W. zu zucken** without batting an eye

Wim'perntusche *f* mascara

Wind [vınt] *m* (-[e]s;-e) wind; flatulence; (hunt) scent

Wind'beutel *m* (fig) windbag; (aer) windsock; (culin) cream puff

Winde ['vındə] *f* (-;-n) winch, windlass; reel; (naut) capstan

Windel ['vındəl] *f* (-;-n) diaper

win'delweich *adj*—**w. schlagen** (coll) beat to a pulp

winden ['vındən] §59 *tr* wind; twist; coil; (*Kranz*) weave, make || *ref* wriggle; (*Fluß*) wind; (*vor Schmerzen*) writhe

Wind'fang *m* storm porch

Wind'hose *f* tornado

Wind'hund *m* greyhound; (coll) windbag

windig ['vındıç] *adj* windy; (fig) flighty

Wind'kanal *m* wind tunnel

Wind'licht *n* hurricane lamp

Wind'mühle *f* windmill

Wind'pocken *pl* chicken pox

Wind'sack *m* windsock

Wind'schatten *m* lee

Wind'schutzscheibe *f* windshield

Wind'stärke *f* wind velocity

wind'still *adj* calm || **Windstille** *f* calm

Wind'stoß *m* gust

Wind'strömung *f* air current

Win'dung *f* (-;-en) winding, twisting; (*Kurve*) bend; (*e-r Schlange*) coil; (*e-r Schraube*) thread, worm; (*e-r Muschel*) whorl

Wind'zug *m* air current, draft

Wink [vıŋk] *m* (-[e]s;-e) sign; (*Zwinkern*) wink; (*mit der Hand*) wave; (*mit dem Kopfe*) nod; (*Hinweis*) hint, tip; **W. mit dem Zaunpfahl** broad hint

Winkel ['vıŋkəl] *m* (-s;-) corner; (carp) square; (geom) angle; (mil) chevron

winkelig ['vıŋkəlıç] *adj* angular; (*Straße*) crooked

Win'kellinie *f* diagonal

Win'kelmaß *n* (carp) square

Win'kelzug *m* subterfuge; evasion

winken ['vıŋkən] *intr* signal; **mit der Hand** wave; (*mit dem Kopfe*) nod; (*mit dem Auge*) wink; **mit dem Taschentuch w.** wave the handkerchief

Win'ker *m* (-s;-) signalman; (aut) direction signal

winseln ['vınzəln] *intr* whimper, whine

Winter ['vıntər] *m* (-s;-) winter

win'terfest *adj* winterized; (*Pflanzen*) hardy

win'terlich *adj* wintry

Win'terschlaf *m* hibernation; **W. halten** hibernate

Win'tersonnenwende *f* winter solstice

Winzer ['vıntsər] *m* (-s;-) vinedresser; (*Traubenleser*) grape picker

winzig ['vıntsıç] *adj* tiny

Wipfel ['vıpfəl] *m* (-s;-) treetop

Wippe ['vıpə] *f* (-;-n) seesaw

wippen ['vıpən] *intr* seesaw; rock; balance oneself

wir [vir] §11 *pers pron* we

Wirbel ['vırbəl] *m* (-s;-) whirl; eddy; whirlpool; (*Trommel-*) roll; (*Violin-*)

peg; (anat) vertebra; **e–n W. machen**
(coll) raise Cain
wirbelig ['vɪrbəlɪç] *adj* whirling; giddy
Wir'belknochen *m* (anat) vertebra
wir'bellos *adj* spineless, invertebrate
wirbeln ['vɪrbəln] *tr* warble ‖ *intr*
whirl; (*Wasser*) eddy; (*Trommel*)
roll; (*Lerche*) warble; **mir wirbelt
der Kopf** my head is spinning
Wir'belsäule *f* spinal column, spine
Wir'belsturm *m* hurricane, typhoon
Wir'beltier *n* vertebrate
Wir'belwind *m* whirlwind
wirken ['vɪrkən] *tr* work, bring about,
effect; (*Teig*) knead; (*Teppich*)
weave; (*Pullover*) knit; **Gutes w.** do
good; **Wunder w.** work wonders ‖
intr work; be active; function; look,
appear; (*Worte*) tell, hit home; **als
Arzt w.** be a doctor; **an e–r Schule
(als Lehrer) w.** teach school; **anregend w.** act as a stimulant; **berauschend w. auf** (*acc*) intoxicate; **beruhigend w. auf** (*acc*) have a soothing
effect on; **gut w.** work well; **lächerlich w.** look ridiculous; **stark w. auf**
(*acc*) touch deeply; **w. auf** (*acc*)
affect, have an effect on; **w. bei** have
an effect on; **w. für** work for; **w. gegen** work against, counteract ‖
Wirken *n* (–s;) action, performance;
operation
wirk'lich *adj* real, actual; true ‖ *adv*
really, actually; truly
Wirk'lichkeit *f* (–;–en) reality; actual
fact
Wirk'lichkeitsform *f* indicative mood
wirksam ['vɪrkzam] *adj* active; effective; (*Hieb*) telling; **w. für** good for
Wirk'samkeit *f* (–;) effectiveness
Wirk'stoff *m* metabolic substance
(*vitamin, hormone, or enzyme*)
Wir'kung *f* (–;–en) effect; result; operation, action; influence, impression
Wir'kungsbereich *m* scope; effective
range; (mil) zone of fire
wir'kungsfähig *adj* active; effective;
efficient
Wir'kungskreis *m* domain, province
wir'kungslos *adj* ineffective; inefficient
wir'kungsvoll *adj* effective; efficacious
Wirk'waren *pl* knitwear
wirr [vɪr] *adj* confused; (*verworren*)
chaotic; (*Haar*) disheveled
Wirren ['vɪrən] *pl* disorders, troubles
Wirr'kopf *m* scatterbrain
Wirrwarr ['vɪrvar] *m* (–s;) mix-up,
mess
Wirt [vɪrt] *m* (–[e]s;–e) host; innkeeper; landlord; (biol) host
Wirtin ['vɪrtɪn] *f* (–;–nen) hostess;
innkeeper, innkeeper's wife; landlady
wirt'lich *adj* hospitable
Wirt'schaft *f* (–;–en) economy; business; industry and trade; (*Haushal-
tung*) housekeeping; (*Hauswesen*)
household; (*Gasthaus*) inn; (*Treiben*)
goings-on; (*Durcheinander*) mess;
(*Umstände*) fuss, trouble; **die W. besorgen** (or **führen**) keep house; **ge-
lenkte W.** planned economy
wirtschaften ['vɪrtʃaftən] *intr* keep

house; economize; (*herumhantieren*)
bustle about; **gut w.** manage well
Wirt'schafter –in §6 *mf* manager ‖ *f*
housekeeper
Wirt'schaftler –in §6 *mf* economist;
economics teacher
wirt'schaftlich *adj* economical, thrifty;
economic; industrial; (*vorteilhaft*)
profitable
Wirt'schaftsgeld *n* housekeeping
money
Wirt'schaftshilfe *f* economic aid
Wirt'schaftsjahr *n* fiscal year
Wirt'schaftslehre *f* economics
Wirt'schaftspolitik *f* economic policy
Wirt'schaftsprüfer –in §6 *mf* certified
public accountant, CPA
Wirts'haus *n* inn, restaurant; bar
wischen ['vɪʃən] *tr* wipe
Wisch'lappen *m* dustcloth
Wisch'tuch *n* dishtowel
wispern ['vɪspərn] *tr* & *intr* whisper
Wißbegierde ['vɪsbəgirdə] *f* (–;) crav-
ing for knowledge; curiosity
wissen ['vɪsən] §161 *tr* & *intr* know ‖
Wissen *n* (–s;) knowledge; learning;
know-how; **meines Wissens** as far as
I know
Wis'senschaft *f* (–;–en) knowledge;
science
Wis'senschaftler –in §6 *mf* scientist
wis'senschaftlich *adj* scientific; scholarly; learned
Wis'sensdrang *m*, **Wis'sensdurst** *m*
thirst for knowledge
Wis'sensgebiet *n* field of knowledge
wis'senswert *adj* worth knowing
wis'sentlich *adj* conscious; willful ‖
adv knowingly; on purpose
wittern ['vɪtərn] *tr* scent, smell
Wit'terung *f* (–;–en) weather; (hunt)
scent; **bei günstiger W.** weather per-
mitting; **e–e feine W. haben** have a
good nose
Wit'terungsverhältnisse *pl* weather
conditions
Witwe ['vɪtvə] *f* (–;–n) widow
Witwer ['vɪtvər] *m* (–s;–) widower
Witz [vɪts] *m* (–es;–e) joke; wisecrack;
wit; wittiness; **das ist der ganze W.**
that's all; **Witze machen** (or **reißen**)
crack jokes
Witz'blatt *n* comics
Witzbold ['vɪtsbɔlt] *m* (–[e]s;–e) joker
witzig ['vɪtsɪç] *adj* witty; funny
wo [vo] *adv* where; **wo auch** (or **wo
immer**) wherever; **wo nicht** if not;
wo nur wherever
woan'ders *adv* somewhere else
wob [vop] *pret of* **weben**
wobei' *adv* whereby; whereat; whereto;
at which; in the course of which
Woche ['vɔxə] *f* (–;–n) week; **heute in
e–r W.** a week from today; **in den
Wochen** sein be in labor; **in die
Wochen kommen** go into labor;
unter der W. (coll) during the week
Wo'chenbeihilfe *f* maternity benefits
Wo'chenbett *n* post-natal period
Wo'chenblatt *n* weekly (newspaper)
Wo'chenende *n* weekend
Wo'chengeld *n* weekly allowance; (*für
Mütter*) maternity benefits

wo'chenlang *adj* lasting many weeks ‖ *adv* for weeks

Wo'chenlohn *m* weekly wages

Wo'chenschau *f* (cin) newsreel

wöchentlich ['vœçəntliç] *adj* weekly ‖ *adv* every week; **einmal w.** once a week

–wöchig [vœçiç] *comb.fm.* –week

Wöchnerin ['vœçnərin] *f* (–;–nen) recent mother

Wodka ['vɔtka] *m* (–s;) vodka

wodurch' *adv* whereby, by which; how

wofern' *conj* provided that; **w. nicht** unless

wofür' *adv* wherefore, for which; what for; **w. halten Sie mich?** what do you take me for?

wog [vok] *pret* of **wägen** & **wiegen**

Woge ['vogə] *f* (–;–n) billow; **Wogen der Erregung** waves of excitement

woge'gen *adv* against what; against which; in exchange for what

wogen ['vogən] *intr* billow, surge, heave; (*Getreide*) wave; **hin und her w.** fluctuate

woher' *adv* from where; **w. wissen Sie das?** how do you know this?

wohin' *adv* whereto, where

wohinge'gen *conj* whereas

wohl [vol] *adj* well ‖ *adv* well; (*freilich*) to be sure, all right; I guess; possibly, probably; perhaps; **es sich** [*dat*] **w. sein lassen** have a good time; **nun w.!** well! **w. daran tun zu** (*inf*) do well to (*inf*); **w. dem, der** happy he who; **w. kaum** hardly; **w. oder übel** willy-nilly ‖ **Wohl** *n* (–[e]s;) good health, well-being; (*Wohlfahrt*) welfare; (*Gedeihen*) prosperity; **auf Ihr W.!** to your health! **gemeines W.** common good

wohlan' *interj* all right then!

wohlauf' *adj* in good health, well ‖ *interj* all right then!

wohlbedacht ['volbədaxt] *adj* well-thought-out

Wohl'befinden *n* (–;) well-being

Wohl'behagen *n* comfort, contentment

wohl'behalten *adj* safe and sound

wohl'bekannt *adj* well-known

wohl'beschaffen *adj* in good condition

Wohl'ergehen *n* well-being

wohl'erzogen *adj* well-bred

Wohl'fahrt *f* (–;) welfare

Wohl'fahrtsarbeit *f* social work

wohl'feil *adj* cheap

Wohl'gefallen *n* (–s;) pleasure, satisfaction

wohl'gefällig *adj* pleasant, agreeable

wohl'gemeint *adj* well-meant

wohlgemut ['volgəmut] *adj* cheerful

wohl'genährt *adj* well-fed

wohl'geneigt *adj* affectionate

Wohl'geruch *m* fragrance, perfume

wohl'gesinnt *adj* well-disposed

wohl'habend *adj* well-to-do

wohlig ['voliç] *adj* comfortable

Wohl'klang *m* melodious sound

wohl'klingend *adj* melodious

Wohl'leben *n* good living, luxury

wohl'riechend *adj* fragrant

wohl'schmeckend *adj* tasty

Wohl'sein *n* good health, well-being

Wohl'stand *m* prosperity, wealth

Wohl'tat *f* benefit; (*Gunst*) kindness, good deed; **e–e W. sein** hit the spot

Wohl'täter –in §6 *mf* benefactor

wohl'tätig *adj* charitable; beneficent

Wohl'tätigkeit *f* charity

wohltuend ['voltu-ənt] *adj* pleasant

wohl'tun §154 *intr* do good; (*dat*) be pleasant (to)

wohl'unterrichtet *adj* well-informed

wohl'verdient *adj* well-deserved

wohl'verstanden *interj* mark my words!

wohl'weislich *adv* very wisely

wohl'wollen §162 *intr* (*dat*) be well-disposed towards ‖ **Wollwollen** *n* (–s;) good will; (*Gunst*) favor

Wohn– [von] *comb.fm.* residential; dwelling, living

Wohn'anhänger *m* house trailer

Wohn'block *m* block of apartments

wohnen ['vonən] *intr* live, reside; (*als Mieter*) room

wohn'haft *adj* residing, living

Wohn'haus *n* dwelling; apartment house

Wohn'küche *f* efficiency apartment

Wohn'laube *f* garden house

wohn'lich *adj* livable; cozy

Wohn'möglichkeit *f* living accommodations

Wohn'ort *m* place of residence; (jur) domicile; **ständiger W.** permanent address

Wohn'raum *m* living space; room (*of a house*)

Wohn'sitz *m* place of residence

Woh'nung *f* (–;–en) dwelling, home; apartment; room; accommodations

Woh'nungsamt *n* housing authority

Woh'nungsbau *m* (–[e]s;) housing construction

Woh'nungsfrage *f* housing problem

Woh'nungsinhaber –in §6 *mf* occupant

Woh'nungsmangel *m*, **Woh'nungsnot** *f* housing shortage

Wohn'viertel *n* residential district

Wohn'wagen *m* mobile home

Wohn'wagenparkplatz *m* trailer camp

Wohn'zimmer *n* living room

wölben ['vœlbən] *tr* vault, arch ‖ *ref* (über *dat* or *acc*) arch (over)

Wöl'bung *f* (–;–en) curvature; vault

Wolf [vɔlf] *m* (–[e]s;–e) wolf; (*Fleisch–*) meat grinder; (astr) Lupus; (pathol) lupus

Wolfram ['vɔlfram] *n* (–s;) tungsten

Wolke ['vɔlkə] *f* (–;–n) cloud

Wol'kenbildung *f* cloud formation

Wol'kenbruch *m* cloudburst

Wol'kendecke *f* cloudcover

Wol'kenfetzen *m* wispy cloud

Wol'kenhöhe *f* (meteor) ceiling

Wol'kenkratzer *m* (–s;–) skyscraper

Wol'kenwand *f* cloud bank

wolkig ['vɔlkiç] *adj* cloudy, clouded

Wolldecke ['vɔldɛkə] *f* woolen blanket

Wolle ['vɔlə] *f* (–;–n) wool

wollen ['vɔlən] *adj* woolen, wool ‖ §162 *tr* want, wish; mean, intend; (*gern haben*) like ‖ *intr* wish, like; **dem sei, wie ihm wolle** be that as it may; **wie Sie w.** as you please ‖ *mod aux* want (to), wish (to), intend (to);

be going (to) ‖ **Wollen** n (–s;) will; volition

Wollfett ['vɔlfet] n lanolin

Wollgarn ['vɔlgarn] n worsted

wollig ['vɔlɪç] adj woolly

Wolljacke ['vɔljakə] f cardigan

Wollsachen ['vɔlzaxən] pl woolens

Wollstoff ['vɔl/tɔf] m woolen fabric

Wollust ['vɔllʊst] f (–;⁺e) lust

wollüstig ['vɔllYstɪç] adj voluptuous; (geil) lewd, lecherous

Wollüstling ['vɔllYstlɪŋ] m (–s;–e) voluptuary

Wollwaren ['vɔlvarən] pl woolens

womit' adv with which; with what; wherewith; **w. kann ich dienen?** (com) can I help you?

womög'lich adv possibly, if possible

wonach' adv after which, whereupon; according to which

Wonne ['vɔnə] f (–;–n) delight; bliss

Won'negefühl n blissful feeling

Won'neschauer m thrill of delight

won'netrunken adj enraptured

won'nevoll, wonnig ['vɔnɪç] adj blissful

woran' adv at which; at what; **ich weiß nicht, w. ich bin** I don't know where I stand

worauf' adv on which; on what; whereupon; **w. warten Sie?** what are you waiting for?

woraus' adv out of what, from what; out of which, from which; **w. ist das gemacht?** what is this made of?

worden ['vɔrdən] pp of **werden**

worin' adv in what; in which

Wort [vɔrt] n (–[e]s;⁺er) word (individual; literal) ‖ n (–[e]s;–e) word (expression; figurative); (Ausspruch) saying; (Ehrenwort) word (of honor); **auf ein W.!** may I have a word with you!; **auf mein W.!** word of honor!; **aufs W.** implicitly, to the letter; **das W. ergreifen** begin to speak; (parl) take the floor; **das W. erhalten** (or **haben**) be allowed to speak; (parl) have the floor; **das W. führen** be the spokesman; **hast du Worte!** (coll) can you beat that!; **in Worten** in writing; **j–m das W. erteilen** allow s.o. to speak; **j–m ins W. fallen** cut s.o. short

Wort'art f (gram) part of speech

Wort'bedeutungslehre f semantics

Wort'beugung f declension

Wort'bildung f word formation

wort'brüchig adj—**w. werden** break one's word

Wörterbuch ['vœrtərbux] n dictionary

Wörterverzeichnis ['vœtərfertsaɪçnɪs] n word index; vocabulary; glossary

Wort'folge f word order

Wort'führer –in §6 mf spokesman

Wort'gefecht n dispute

wort'getreu adj literal; verbatim

wort'karg adj taciturn

Wortklauber –in ['vɔrtklaubər(ɪn)] §6 mf quibbler, hairsplitter

Wort'laut m wording; (fig) letter

wörtlich ['vœrtlɪç] adj word-for-word; literal; (Rede) direct

wort'los adv without saying a word

Wort'register n word index

Wort'schatz m vocabulary

Wort'schwall m flood of words, verbiage

Wort'spiel n pun

Wort'stamm m stem

Wort'stellung f word order

Wort'streit m, **Wort'wechsel** m argument

worüber [vo'rybər] adv over what, over which

worum [vo'rum] adv about what, about which

worunter [vo'runtər] adv under what, under which; among which

wovon' adv from what, of what, from which, of which; **w. ist die Rede?** what are they talking about?

wovor' adv of what; before which

wozu' adv for what; why; to which

Wrack [vrak] n (–[e]s;–e & –s) (& fig) wreck

Wrack'gut n wreckage

wrang [vraŋ] pret of **wringen**

wringen ['vrɪŋən] §142 tr wring

Wringmaschine ['vrɪŋma/inə] f wringer

Wucher ['vuxər] m (–s) profiteering; **das ist ja W.!** (coll) that's highway robbery!; **W. treiben** profiteer

Wu'cherer –in §6 mf profiteer; loan shark

Wu'chergewinn m excess profit

wu'cherhaft, wucherisch ['vuxərɪ/] adj profiteering, exorbitant

Wu'chermiete f excessive rent

wuchern ['vuxərn] intr grow luxuriantly; (Wucher treiben) profiteer

Wu'cherung f (–;–en) (bot) rank growth; (pathol) growth

Wu'cherzinsen pl excessive interest

wuchs [vuks] pret of **wachsen** ‖ **Wuchs** m (–es) growth; groß von W. tall

–wüchsig ['vYksɪç] comb.fm. –growing, –grown

Wucht [vuxt] f (–;–en) weight, force

wuchten ['vuxtən] tr lift with effort

wuchtig ['vuxtɪç] adj heavy; massive

Wühlarbeit ['vylarbaɪt] f subversive activity

wühlen ['vylən] intr dig, burrow; (Schwein) root about; (suchend) rummage about; (pol) engage in subversive activities; **im Geld w.** be rolling in money; **in Schmutz w.** wallow in filth

Wüh'ler –in §6 mf subversive, agitator

Wulst [vulst] m (–es;⁺e) & f (–;⁺e) bulge; (aut) rim (of tire)

wulstig ['vulstɪç] adj bulging; (Lippen) thick

wund [vunt] adj sore; (poet) wounded

Wunde ['vundə] f (–;–n) wound; sore

Wunder ['vundər] n (–s;–) wonder; miracle; **W. wirken** work wonders

wunderbar ['vundərbar] adj wonderful; (& fig) miraculous

Wun'derding n wonder

Wun'derdoktor m faith healer

Wun'derkind n child prodigy

Wun'derkraft f miraculous power

wun'derlich adj queer, odd

wundern ['vundərn] tr amaze ‖ ref

(über *acc*) be amazed (at) ‖ *impers* —es sollte mich w., wenn I'd be surprised if; **es wundert mich, daß** I am surprised that

wun'derschön' *adv* lovely, gorgeous

Wun'dertat *f* miracle

Wun'dertäter –in §6 *mf* wonder worker

wundertätig *adj* miraculous

wun'dervoll *adj* wonderful, marvelous

Wun'derwerk *n* (& fig) miracle

Wun'derzeichen *n* omen, prodigy

Wund'klammer *f* (surg) clamp

wund'liegen §108 *ref* get bedsores

Wund'mal *n* scar, sore; (relig) wound

wund'reiten §86 *ref* become saddlesore

Wunsch [vʊnʃ] *m* (-es;⁓e) wish; (nach) desire (for); **auf W.** upon request; **ein frommer W.** wishful thinking; **nach W.** as desired

Wünschelrute ['vynʃəlruːtə] *f* divining rod

Wün'schelrutengänger *m* dowser

wünschen ['vynʃən] *tr* wish; wish for, desire; **was w. Sie?** (com) may I help you? ‖ *intr* wish, please

wün'schenswert *adj* desirable

Wunsch'form *f* (gram) optative

Wunsch'konzert *n* (rad) request program

wunsch'los *adj* contented ‖ *adv*—w. glücklich perfectly happy

wuppdich ['vʊpdɪç] *interj* zip!, in a flash!; all of a sudden!

wurde ['vʊrdə] *pret* of **werden**

Würde ['vyrdə] *f* (-;-n) honor; title; dignity; post, office; **akademische W.** academic degree; **unter aller W.** beneath contempt

wür'delos *adj* undignified

Wür'denträger –in §6 *mf* dignitary

wür'devoll *adj* dignified

würdig ['vyrdɪç] *adj* dignified; (*genit*) worthy (of), deserving (of)

würdigen ['vyrdɪgən] *tr* appreciate, value; (*genit*) deem worthy (of)

Wurf [vʊrf] *m* (-[e]s;⁓e) throw, cast, pitch; (fig) hit, success; (zool) litter, brood

Wurf'anker *m* grapnel

Würfel ['vyrfəl] *m* (-s;-) die; cube,

square; (geom) cube; **W. spielen** play dice

Wür'felbecher *m* dice box

würfelig ['vyrfəlɪç] *adj* cube-shaped; (*Muster*) checkered

würfeln ['vyrfəln] *intr* play dice

Wür'felzucker *m* cube sugar

Wurf'geschoß *n* projectile, missile

Wurf'pfeil *m* dart

würgen ['vyrgən] *tr* choke; strangle ‖ *intr* choke; **am Essen w.** gag on food

Wurm [vʊrm] *m* (-s;⁓er) (& mach) worm

wurmen ['vʊrmən] *tr* (coll) bug

wurmig ['vʊrmɪç] *adj* wormy; worm-eaten

wurmstichig ['vʊrmʃtɪçɪç] *adj* worm-eaten

Wurst [vʊrst] *f* (-;⁓e) sausage; **es geht um die W.** now or never; **es ist mir W.** I couldn't care less

Würstchen ['vyrstçən] *n* (-s;-), **Würstel** ['vyrstəl] *n* (-s;-n) hotdog

wursteln ['vʊrstəln] *intr* muddle along

Würze ['vyrtsə] *f* (-;-n) spice, seasoning; (fig) zest

Wurzel ['vʊrtsəl] *f* (-;-n) root; **W. fassen** (or **schlagen**) take root

wurzeln ['vʊrtsəln] *intr* (HABEN & SEIN) take root; **w. in** (*dat*) be rooted in

würzen ['vyrtsən] *tr* spice, season

würzig ['vyrtsɪç] *adj* spicy; aromatic

Würz'stoff *m* seasoning

wusch [vʊʃ] *pret* of **waschen**

wußte ['vʊstə] *pret* of **wissen**

Wust [vʊst] *m* (-es) jumble, mess

wüst [vyst] *adj* desert, waste; (*roh*) coarse; (*wirr*) confused

Wüste ['vyːstə] *f* (-;-en) desert

Wüstling ['vystlɪŋ] *m* (-s;-e) debauchee

Wut [vuːt] *f* (-;) rage, fury; madness

Wut'anfall *m* fit of rage

wüten ['vyːtən] *intr* rage

wü'tend *adj* (auf *acc*) furious (at)

Wüterich ['vyːtərɪç] *m* (-s;-e) madman; bloodthirsty villain

wut'schäumend *adj* foaming with rage

wut'schnaubend *adj* in a towering rage

Wut'schrei *m* shout of anger

X

X, x [ɪks] *invar n* X, x

X'-Beine *pl* knock-knees

x'-beinig *adj* knock-kneed

x'-beliebig *adj* any, whatever ‖ **X-beliebige** §5 *m*—**jeder X.** every Tom, Dick, and Harry

x'-fach *adj* (coll) hundredfold

x'-mal *adv* umpteen times

X'-Strahlen *pl* x-rays

X'-Tag *m* D-day

x-te ['ɪkstə] §9 *adj* umpteenth; **die x-te Potenz** (math) the nth power

Xylophon [ksylə'foːn] *n* (-s;-e) xylophone

Y

Y, y [ypsilɔn] *invar n* Y, y

Yacht [jaxt] *f* (-;-en) yacht

Yamswurzel ['jamsvʊrtsəl] *f* (-;-n) (bot) yam

Yankee ['jɛŋki] *m* (-s;-s) Yankee

Yoghurt ['joɡurt] *m & n* (-s;) yogurt

Yo-Yo ['joːjoː] *n* (-s;-s) yo-yo

Ypsilon ['ypsilɔn] *n* (-[s];-s) y

Z

Z, z [tset] *invar n* Z, z
Zacke ['tsakə] *f* (–;–n) sharp point; (*Zinke*) prong; (*Fels–*) crag; (*e-s Kamms, e–r Säge*) tooth; (*am Kleid*) scallop
zacken ['tsakən] *tr* notch; scallop || **Zacken** *m* (–s;–) *var of* Zacke
zackig ['tsakıç] *adj* toothed; notched; (*Felsen*) jagged; (*spitz*) pointed; (*Kleid*) scalloped; (fig) sharp
zagen ['tsagən] *intr* be faint-hearted
zaghaft ['tsakhaft] *adj* timid
zäh [tse] *adj* tough; (*klebig*) viscous; (*beharrlich*) persistent; (*Gedächtnis*) tenacious; (*halsstarrig*) dogged
zäh'flüssig *adj* viscous
Zäh'flüssigkeit *f* (–;) viscosity
Zä'higkeit *f* (–;) toughness; tenacity; viscosity; doggedness
Zahl [tsal] *f* (–;–en) number; (*Betrag, Ziffer*) figure; **an Z. übertreffen** outnumber; **arabische Z.** Arabic numeral; **der Z. nach** in number; **ganze Z.** integer; **gebrochene Z.** fraction; **gerade Z.** even number; **in roten Zahlen stecken** be in the red; **ungerade Z.** odd number; **wenig an der Z.** few in number
zahlbar ['tsalbar] *adj* payable; **z. bei Lieferung** cash on delivery
zählebig ['tselebıç] *adj* hardy
zahlen ['tsalən] *tr* pay; (*Schuld*) pay off || *intr* pay
zählen ['tselən] *tr* count; number, amount to || *intr* count; be of importance, count; **nach Tausenden z.** number in the thousands; **z. auf** (*dat*) count on; **z. zu** be numbered among, belong to
Zah'lenangaben *pl* figures
Zah'lenfolge *f* numerical order
zah'lenmäßig *adj* numerical
Zah'ler –in §6 *mf* payer
Zäh'ler (–s;–) counter; recorder; (*für Gas, Elektrizität*) meter; (math) numerator; (parl) teller; (sport) scorekeeper
Zählerableser ['tseləraplezər] *m* (–s;–) meter man
Zahl'karte *f* money-order form
zahl'los *adj* countless, innumerable
Zahl'meister *m* paymaster; (mil) pay officer; (nav) purser
zahl'reich *adj* numerous
Zähl'rohr *n* Geiger counter
Zahl'stelle *f* cashier's window; (*e-r Bank*) branch office
Zahl'tag *m* payday
Zah'lung *f* (–;–en) payment; (*e-r Schuld*) settlement
Zäh'lung *f* (–;–en) counting; computation
Zah'lungsanweisung *f* draft; check; postal money order
Zah'lungsausgleich *m* balance of payments
Zah'lungsbedingungen *pl* (fin) terms
Zah'lungsbestätigung *f* receipt

Zah'lungsbilanz *f* balance of payments; **aktive (or passive) Z.** favorable (or unfavorable) balance of payments
zah'lungsfähig *adj* solvent
Zah'lungsfähigkeit *f* (–;) solvency
Zah'lungsfrist *f* due date
Zah'lungsmittel *n* medium of exchange; **gesetzliches Z.** legal tender; **bargeldloses Z.** instrument of credit
Zah'lungsschwierigkeiten *pl* financial embarrassment
Zah'lungssperre *f* stoppage of payments
Zah'lungstermin *m* date of payment; (fin) date of maturity
Zah'lungsverzug *m* (fin) default
Zähl'werk *n* meter
Zahl'wort *n* (–[e]s;–er) numeral
Zahl'zeichen *n* figure, cipher
zahm [tsam] *adj* tame; domesticated
zähmen ['tsemən] *tr* tame; domesticate; (fig) control || *ref* control oneself
Zäh'mung *f* (–;) taming; domestication
Zahn [tsan] *m* (–[e]s;–e) tooth; (mach) tooth, cog; **j-m auf den Z. fühlen** sound s.o. out; **mit den Zähnen knirschen** grind one's teeth
Zahn'arzt *m*, **Zahn'ärztin** *f* dentist
Zahn'bürste *f* toothbrush
Zahn'creme *f* toothpaste
zahnen ['tsanən] *intr* cut one's teeth
Zahn'ersatz *m* denture
Zahn'fäule *f* tooth decay, caries
Zahn'fleisch *n* gum
Zahn'füllung *f* (dent) filling
Zahn'heilkunde *f* dentistry
Zahn'klammer *f* (–;–n) (dent) brace
Zahn'krem *f* toothpaste
Zahn'krone *f* (dent) crown
Zahn'laut *m* (phonet) dental
Zahn'lücke *f* gap between the teeth
Zahn'paste *f* toothpaste
Zahn'pflege *f* dental hygiene
Zahn'pulver *n* tooth powder
Zahn'rad *n* cog wheel; (*Kettenrad*) sprocket
Zahn'radbahn *f* cog railway
Zahn'schmerz *m* toothache
Zahn'spange *f* (–;–n) (dent) brace
Zahn'stein *m* (dent) tartar
Zahnstocher ['tsan/toxər] *m* (–s;–) toothpick
Zahn'techniker –in §6 *mf* dental technician
Zahn'weh *n* toothache
Zange ['tsaŋə] *f* (–;–en) (pair of) pliers; (pair of) tongs; (*Pinzette*) (pair of) tweezers; (dent, surg, zool) forceps; **j-n in die Z. nehmen** corner s.o. (*with tough questioning*)
Zank [tsaŋk] *m* (–[e]s;) quarrel, fight
Zank'apfel *m* apple of discord
zanken ['tsaŋkən] *tr* scold || *recip & intr* quarrel, fight
zank'haft, zänkisch ['tseŋkıʃ], **zank'süchtig** *adj* quarrelsome

Zäpfchen ['tsɛpfçən] n (-s;-) little peg; (anat) uvula; (med) suppository

zapfen ['tsapfən] tr (Bier, Wein) tap ‖ **Zapfen** m (-s;-) plug, bung; (Stift) stud; (Drehpunkt) pivot; (Eis-) icicle; (Tannen-) cone; (carp) tenon; (mach) pin; (mach) journal

Zap'fenstreich m (mil) taps

Zapfhahn ['tsapfhɑn] m tap, spigot

Zapfsäule ['tsapfzɔɪlə] f (-;-n) (aut) gasoline pump

Zapfstelle ['tsapf/tɛlə] f (-;-n) (aut) service station, gas station

Zapfwart ['tsapfvart] m (-[e]s;-e) (aut) service station attendant

zappelig ['tsapəlɪç] adj fidgety

zappeln ['tsapəln] intr fidget; squirm; (im Wasser) founder

Zar [tsɑr] m (-en;-en) czar

Zarge ['tsargə] f (-;-n) border; frame

zart [tsɑrt] adj tender; (Farbe, Haut) soft; (Gesundheit) delicate

zart'fühlend adj tender; sensitive

Zart'gefühl n sensitivity; tact

Zart'heit f (-;) tenderness

zärtlich ['tsɛrtlɪç] adj tender, affectionate

Zärt'lichkeit f (-;-en) tenderness; (Liebkosung) caress

Zaster ['tsastər] m (-s;) (coll) dough

Zauber ['tsaubər] m (-s;-) spell; magic; (fig) charm, glamor

Zauber- comb.fm. magic

Zauberei [tsaubə'raɪ] f (-;-en) magic; witchcraft, sorcery

Zau'berer m (-s;-) magician; sorcerer

Zau'berformel f incantation, spell

zau'berhaft adj magic; enchanting

Zau'berin f (-;-nen) sorceress, witch; enchantress

zauberisch ['tsaubərɪ/] adj magic

Zau'berkraft f magic power

Zau'berkunst f magic

Zau'berkünstler -in §6 mf magician

Zau'berkunststück n magic trick

Zau'berland n fairyland

zaubern ['tsaubərn] tr produce by magic ‖ intr practice magic; do magic tricks

Zau'berspruch m incantation, spell

Zau'berstab m magic wand

Zau'bertrank m magic potion

Zau'berwerk n witchcraft

Zau'berwort n (-[e]s;-e) magic word

zaudern ['tsaudərn] intr procrastinate; hesitate; linger

Zaum [tsaum] m (-[e]s;ⁱe) bridle; im Z. halten keep in check

zäumen ['tsɔɪmən] tr bridle

Zaun [tsaun] m (-[e]s;ⁱe) fence; e-n Streit vom Z. brechen pick a quarrel

Zaun'gast m non-paying spectator

Zaun'könig m (orn) wren

Zaun'pfahl m fence post

zausen ['tsauzən] tr tug at; tousle, ruffle ‖ recip tug at each other

Zebra ['tsebra] n (-s;-s) zebra

Ze'brastreifen m zebra stripe; (auf der Fahrbahn) passenger crossing

Zech- [tsɛç] comb.fm. drinking

Zech'bruder m boozehound

Zeche ['tsɛçə] f (-;-n) (Wirtshausrechnung) check; (min) mine die Z.

prellen (coll) sneak out without paying the bill

zechen ['tsɛçən] intr booze

Ze'cher -in §6 mf heavy drinker

Zech'gelage n drinking party

Zechpreller ['tsɛçprɛlər] m (-s;-) cheat, bilker

Zech'tour f binge; e-e Z. machen go on a binge

Zecke ['tsɛkə] f (-;-n) (ent) tick

Zeder ['tsedər] f (-;-n) cedar

Zehe ['tse.ə] f (-;-n) toe; (Knoblauch-) clove

Ze'hennagel m toenail

Ze'henspitze f tip of the toe; auf den Zehenspitzen (on) tiptoe

zehn [tsen] invar adj & pron ten ‖ Zehn f (-;-en) ten

Zehner ['tsenər] m (-s;-) ten; ten-mark bill

zehn'fach, zehn'fältig adj tenfold

Zehnfin'gersystem n touch-type system

Zehn'kampf m decathlon

zehn'mal adv ten times

zehnte ['tsentə] §9 adj & pron tenth ‖ Zehnte §5 mfn tenth

Zehntel ['tsentəl] n (-s;-) tenth (part)

zehren ['tserən] intr be debilitating; an den Kräften z. drain one's strength; an der Gesundheit z. undermine one's health; z. an (dat) (fig) gnaw at; z. von live on, live off

Zeh'rung f (-;) provisions; expenses

Zeichen ['tsaɪçən] n (-s;-) sign; signal; token; (Merkmal) distinguishing mark; (Beweis) proof; symbol; (astr) sign; (com) brand; (med) symptom; (rad) call sign; er ist seines Zeichens Anwalt he is a lawyer by profession; zum Z., daß as proof that

Zei'chenbrett n drawing board

Zei'chenbuch n sketchbook

Zei'chengerät n drafting equipment

Zei'chenheft n sketchbook

Zei'chenlehrer -in §6 mf art teacher

Zei'chenpapier n drawing paper

Zei'chensetzung f punctuation

Zei'chensprache f sign language

Zei'chentisch m drawing board

Zei'chentrickfilm m animated cartoon

Zei'chenunterricht m drawing lesson

zeichnen ['tsaɪçnən] tr draw; sketch; (entwerfen) design; (brandmarken) brand; (Anleihe) take out; (Aktien) buy; (Geld) pledge; (Wäsche) mark; (Brief) sign ‖ intr draw; sketch; (hunt) leave a trail of blood; z. für sign for

Zeich'ner -in §6 mf draftsman; (Mode-) designer; (e-r Anleihe) subscriber

zeichnerisch ['tsaɪçnərɪ/] adj (Begabung) for drawing; (Darstellung) graphic

Zeich'nung f (-;-en) drawing; sketch; design; picture, illustration; diagram; signature; (e-r Anleihe) subscription; (des Holzes) grain

zeich'nungsberechtigt adj authorized to sign

Zeigefinger ['tsaɪgəfɪŋər] m index finger

zeigen ['tsaɪgən] tr show, indicate;

(in e-r Rede) point out; (zur Schau stellen) display; (beweisen) prove; (dartun) demonstrate || ref appear, show up; prove to be || intr point; z. auf (acc) point to; z. nach point toward || impers ref—es zeigt sich, daß it turns out that; es wird sich ja z., ob we shall see whether

Zei′ger m (-s;-) pointer; indicator; (e-r Uhr) hand

Zeigestock [ˈtsaɪɡəʃtɔk] m pointer

Zeile [ˈtsaɪlə] f (-;-n) line; (Reihe) row

Zeit [tsaɪt] f (-;-en) time; auf Z. (com) on credit, on time; in der letzten Z. lately; in jüngster Z. quite recently; mit der Z. in time, in the course of time; vor Zeiten in former times; zu meiner Z. in my time; zu rechter Z. in the nick of time; on time; zur Z. at present; zur Z. (genit) at the time of

Zeit′abschnitt m period, epoch
Zeit′abstand m interval of time
Zeit′alter n age
Zeit′angabe f time; date; exact date and hour; ohne Z. undated
Zeit′ansage f (rad) (giving of) time
Zeit′aufnahme f (phot) time exposure
Zeit′aufwand m loss of time; (für) time spent (on)
Zeit′dauer f term, period of time
Zeit′einteilung f timetable; timing
Zei′tenfolge f sequence of tenses
Zei′tenwende f beginning of the Christian era
Zeit′folge f chronological order
Zeit′form f tense
Zeit′geist m spirit of the times
zeit′gemäß adj timely; up-to-date
Zeit′genosse m, **Zeit′genossin** f contemporary
zeitgenössisch [ˈtsaɪtɡənœsɪʃ] adj contemporary
Zeit′geschichte f contemporary history
zeitig [ˈtsaɪtɪç] adj early; (reif) mature, ripe
zeitigen [ˈtsaɪtɪɡən] tr ripen
Zeit′karte f commuter ticket
Zeit′lage f state of affairs
Zeit′lang f—e-e Z. for some time
Zeit′lauf m course of time
zeit′lebens adv during my (his, your, etc.) life
zeit′lich adj temporal; chronological || adv in time || Zeitliche §5 n—das Z. segnen depart this world
zeit′los adj timeless
Zeit′lupe f (cin) slow motion
Zeit′mangel m lack of time
Zeit′maß n (mus) tempo; (pros) quantity
Zeit′nehmer –in §6 mf timekeeper
Zeit′ordnung f chronological order
Zeit′punkt m point of time, moment
Zeitraffer [ˈtsaɪtrafər] m (-s;-) time-lapse photography
zeit′raubend adj time-consuming
Zeit′raum m space of time, period
Zeit′rechnung f era
Zeit′schaltgerät n timer
Zeit′schrift f periodical, magazine
Zeit′spanne f span (of time)

Zeit′tafel f chronological table
Zei′tung f (-;-en) newspaper; journal
Zei′tungsarchiv n (journ) morgue
Zei′tungsartikel m newspaper article
Zei′tungsausschnitt m newspaper clipping
Zei′tungsbeilage f supplement
Zei′tungsdeutsch n journalese
Zei′tungsente f (journ) hoax, spoof
Zei′tungskiosk m newsstand
Zei′tungsmeldung f, **Zei′tungsnotiz** f newspaper item
Zei′tungspapier n newsprint
Zei′tungsverkäufer –in §6 mf newsvendor
Zei′tungswesen n—das Z. the press
Zeit′vergeudung f waste of time
zeit′verkürzend adj entertaining
Zeit′verlust m loss of time
Zeit′vermerk m date
Zeit′verschwendung f waste of time
Zeit′vertreib m pastime
zeitweilig [ˈtsaɪtvaɪlɪç] adj temporary; periodic || adv temporarily; at times, from time to time
Zeit′wende f beginning of a new era
Zeit′wert m current value
Zeit′wort n (-[e]s;ːer) verb
Zeit′zeichen n time signal
Zeit′zünder m time fuse
Zelle [ˈtselə] f (-;-n) cell; (aer) fuselage; (telp) booth
Zel′lenlehre f cytology
Zellophan [tselɔˈfan] n (-s;) cellophane
Zellstoff [ˈtselʃtɔf] m cellulose
Zelluloid [tseluˈlɔɪt] n (-s;) celluloid
Zellulose [tseluˈlozə] f (-;) cellulose
Zelt [ˈtselt] n (-[e]s;-e) tent
zelten [ˈtseltən] intr camp out
Zelt′leinwand f canvas
Zelt′pfahl m tent pole
Zelt′pflock m tent peg, tent stake
Zelt′stange f, **Zelt′stock** m tent pole
Zement [tseˈment] m (-[e]s;) cement
zementieren [tsemenˈtirən] tr cement
Zenit [tseˈnit] m (-[e]s;) zenith
zensieren [tsenˈzirən] tr censor; (educ) mark, grade
Zen·sor [ˈtsenzɔr] m (-s;-soren [ˈzorən]) censor
Zensur [tsenˈzur] f (-;-en) censorship; (educ) grade, mark
Zentimeter [tsentiˈmetər] m & n centimeter
Zentner [ˈtsentnər] m (-s;-) hundredweight
Zent′nerlast f (fig) heavy load
zentral [tsenˈtral] adj central
Zentral′behörde f central authority
Zentrale [tsenˈtralə] f (-;-n) central office; telephone exchange, switchboard; (elec) power station
Zentral′heizung f central heating
Zen·trum [ˈtsentrum] m (-s;-tren [trən]) center
Zephir [ˈtsefir] m (-s;-e) zephyr
Zepter [ˈtseptər] n (-s;-) scepter
zer- [tser] pref up, to pieces, apart
zerbei′ßen §53 tr bite to pieces
zerber′sten §55 intr (SEIN) split apart
zerbre′chen §64 tr break to pieces, shatter, smash || ref—sich [dat] den

Kopf z. über (acc) rack one's brains over ‖ intr (SEIN) shatter
zerbrech'lich adj fragile, brittle
zerbröckeln (zerbrök'keln) tr & intr (SEIN) crumble
zerdrücken (zerdrük'ken) tr crush; (Kleid) wrinkle; (Kartoffeln) mash
Zeremonie [tseremɔ'ni] f (–;-nien ['ni-ən]) ceremony
zeremoniell [tseremɔ'njel] adj ceremonial ‖ **Zeremoniell** n (–s;-e) ceremonial
Zeremo'nienmeister m master of ceremonies
zerfah'ren adj (Weg) rutted; (zerstreut) absent-minded; (konfus) scatterbrained
Zerfall' m (–s;) decay, ruin; disintegration; (geistig) decadence
zerfal'len adj—z. sein mit be at variance with ‖ §72 intr (SEIN) fall into ruin; decay; disintegrate; z. in (acc) divide into; z. mit fall out with
zerfa'sern tr unravel ‖ intr fray
zerfet'zen tr tear to shreds
zerflei'schen tr mangle; lacerate
zerflie'ßen §76 intr (SEIN) melt; (Farben) run
zerfres'sen §70 tr eat away, chew up; erode, eat a hole in; corrode
zerge'hen §82 intr (SEIN) melt
zerglie'dern tr dissect; analyze
zerhacken (zerhak'ken) tr chop up
zerkau'en tr chew well
zerkleinern [tser'klaɪnərn] tr cut into small pieces; chop up
zerklop'fen tr pound
zerklüftet [tser'klyftət] adj jagged
zerknirscht [tser'knɪrʃt] adj contrite
Zerknir'schung f (–;) contrition
zerknit'tern tr (Papier) crumple; (Kleider) rumple
zerknül'len tr crumple up
zerko'chen tr overcook
zerkrat'zen tr scratch up
zerkrü'meln tr & intr (SEIN) crumble
zerlas'sen §104 tr melt, dissolve
zerlegbar [tser'lekbar] adj collapsible; (chem) decomposable; (math) divisible
zerle'gen tr take apart; (zerstückeln) cut up; (Braten) carve; (Licht) disperse; (anat) dissect; (chem) break down; (geom, mus) resolve; (gram & fig) analyze; (mach) tear down
zerle'sen adj well-thumbed
zerlö'chern tr riddle with holes
zerlumpt [tser'lʊmpt] adj tattered
zermah'len tr grind
zermal'men tr crush
zermür'ben tr wear down
Zermür'bung f (–;) attrition, wear
zerna'gen tr gnaw, chew up; (chem) corrode
zerplat'zen intr (SEIN) burst; explode
zerquet'schen tr crush; (culin) mash
Zerrbild ['tserbɪlt] n distorted picture; caricature
zerrei'ben §62 tr grind, pulverize
zerrei'ßen §95 tr tear; tear up; (zerfleischen) mangle; (fig) split; (pathol) rupture; j—m das Herz z. break s.o.'s heart ‖ ref—sich z. für

(fig) knock oneself out for ‖ intr (SEIN) tear
zerren ['tserən] tr drag; (Sehne) pull ‖ intr (an dat) tug (at)
zerrin'nen §121 intr (SEIN) melt away
zerrissen [tser'rɪsən] adj torn
Zer'rung f (–;-en) strain, muscle pull
zerrütten [tser'rytən] tr disorganize; (Geist) unhinge; (Gesundheit) undermine; (Nerven) shatter; (Ehe) wreck
zersä'gen tr saw up
zerschel'len intr (SEIN) be wrecked; (Schiff) break up
zerschie'ßen §76 tr shoot up
zerschla'gen adj battered, broken; exhausted, beat ‖ §132 tr beat up; break to pieces; smash; batter
zerschmel'zen tr & intr (SEIN) melt
zerschmet'tern tr smash, crush
zerschnei'den §106 tr cut up; mince
zerset'zen tr decompose; electrolyze; (fig) undermine ‖ ref decompose, disintegrate
zerspal'ten tr split
zersplit'tern tr split up; splinter; (Menge) disperse; (Kraft, Zeit) fritter away ‖ ref spread oneself thin
zerspren'gen tr blow up; (Kette) break; (mil) rout
zersprin'gen §142 intr (SEIN) break, burst; (Glas) crack; (Saite) snap; (Kopf) split; (vor Wut) explode; (vor Freude) burst
zerstamp'fen tr crush, pound; trample
zerstäu'ben tr pulverize, spray
Zerstäu'ber m (–s;–) sprayer; (für Parfüm) atomizer
zerste'chen §64 tr sting; bite
zerstie'ben intr §130 tr (SEIN) scatter
zerstö'ren tr destroy; (Fernsprechleitung) disrupt; (Leben, Ehe, usw.) ruin; (Illusionen) shatter
Zerstö'rer m (–s;–) (& nav) destroyer
Zerstö'rung f (–;-en) destruction; ruin; disruption
Zerstö'rungswerk n work of destruction
Zerstö'rungswut f vandalism
zersto'ßen §150 tr pound, crush
zerstreu'en tr scatter, disperse; (Bedenken, Zweifel) dispel; (ablenken) distract; (Licht) diffuse ‖ ref scatter; amuse oneself
zerstreut' adj dispersed; (Licht) diffused; (fig) absent-minded
Zerstreut'heit f (–;) absent-mindedness
Zerstreu'ung f (–;) scattering; diffusion; diversion; absent-mindedness
zerstückeln [tser'ʃtykəln] tr chop up; (Körper) dismember; (Land) parcel out
zertei'len tr divide; (zerstreuen) disperse; (Braten, usw.) cut up ‖ ref divide, separate
Zertifikat [tsertɪfɪ'kɑt] n (–[e]s;-e) certificate
zertren'nen tr sever
zertre'ten §152 tr trample, squash; (Feuer) stamp out
zertrümmern [tser'trymərn] tr smash, demolish; (Atome) split
zerwüh'len tr root up; (Haar) dishevel; (Bett, Kissen) rumple

Zerwürfnis [tsɛr'vʏrfnɪs] n (-ses;-se) disagreement, quarrel

zerzau'sen tr (Haar) muss; (Federn) ruffle

Zeter ['tsetər] n (-s;) —Z. und Mordio schreien (coll) cry bloody murder

zetern ['tsetərn] intr cry out, raise an outcry

Zettel ['tsetəl] m (-s;-) slip of paper; note; (Anschlag) poster; (zum Ankleben) sticker; (zum Anhängen) tag

Zet'telkartei f, **Zet'telkasten** m, **Zet'telkatalog** m card file

Zeug [tsɔɪk] n (-[e]s;-e) stuff, material; (Stoff) cloth, fabric; (Sachen) things; (Waren) goods; (Geräte) tools; (Plunder) junk; **dummes Z.** silly nonsense; **er hat das Z.** he has what it takes

-zeug n comb.fm. stuff; tools; equipment; tackle; instrument; things; -wear

Zeuge ['tsɔɪgə] m (-n;-n) witness; **als Z. aussagen** testify

zeugen ['tsɔɪgən] tr beget; (fig) produce, generate || intr produce offspring; testify; **z. für** testify in favor of; **z. von** bear witness to

Zeu'genaussage f deposition

Zeu'genbank f witness stand

Zeu'genbeeinflussung f suborning of witnesses

Zeu'genstand m witness stand

Zeugin ['tsɔɪgɪn] f (-;-nen) witness

Zeugnis ['tsɔɪknɪs] n (-ses;-se) evidence, testimony; proof; (Schein) certificate; (educ) report card; **j-m ein Z. ausstellen** (or **schreiben**) write s.o. a letter of recommendation; **Z. ablegen** testify; **zum Z. dessen** in witness whereof

Zeu'gung f (-;) procreation; breeding

Zeu'gungstrieb m sexual drive

zeu'gungsunfähig adj impotent

Zicke ['tsɪkə] f (-;-n) (pej) old nanny goat; **Zicken machen** (coll) play tricks

Zicklein ['tsɪklaɪn] n (-s;-) kid

Zickzack ['tsɪktsak] m (-[e]s;-e) zigzag; **im Z. laufen** run zigzag

Zick'zackkurs m—**im Z. fahren** zigzag

Ziege ['tsigə] f (-;-n) she-goat

Ziegel ['tsigəl] m (-s;-) brick; (Dach-) tile

Zie'gelbrenner m brickmaker; tilemaker

Zie'gelbrennerei f brickyard; tileworks

Zie'geldach n tiled roof

Zie'gelstein m brick

Zie'genbart m goatee

Zie'genbock m billy goat

Zie'genhirt m goatherd

Zie'genpeter m (pathol) mumps

Zieh- [tsi] comb.fm. draw; tow-; foster

ziehen ['tsi·ən] §163 tr pull; (Folgerung, Kreis, Linie, Los, Schwert, Seitengewehr, Vorhang, Wechsel) draw; (Glocke) ring; aus der Tasche) pull out; (Zahn) extract, pull; (züchten) grow, breed; (Kinder) raise; (beim Schach) move; (den Hut) tip; (Graben) dig; (Mauer) build; (Schiff) tow; (Blasen) raise; (Vergleich) make; (Gewehrlauf) rifle; (math) extract; **auf Fäden z.** string (pearls); **auf Flaschen z.** bottle; **auf seine Seite z.** win over to one's side; **den kürzeren z.** get the short end of it; **die Bilanz z.** balance accounts; **die Stirn kraus z.** knit the brows; **Grimassen z.** make faces; **ins Vertrauen z.** take into confidence; **j-n auf die Seite z.** take s.o. aside; **Nutzen z.** derive benefit; **Wasser z.** leak || ref (Holz) warp; (Stoff) stretch; (geog) extend, run; **an sich** (or **auf sich**) **z.** attract; **sich in die Länge z.** drag on || intr ache; (an dat) pull (on); (theat) (coll) pull them in; **an e-r Zigarette z.** puff on a cigarette || intr (SEIN) go; march; (Vögel) migrate; (Wohnung wechseln) move || impers—**es zieht** there is a draft; **es zieht mich nach I** feel drawn to || **Ziehen** n (-s;) drawing; cultivation; growing; raising; breeding; migration

Zieh'harmonika f accordion

Zieh'kind n foster child

Zie'hung f (-;-en) drawing (of lots)

Ziel [tsil] n (-[e]s;-e) aim; mark; goal; (beim Rennsport) finish line; (e-r Reise) destination; (beim Schießen) target; (Grenze) limit, boundary; (Zweck) end, object; (des Spottes) butt; (Frist) term; (mil) objective; **auf Z.** (com) on credit; **durchs Z. gehen** pass the finish line; **gegen zwei Jahre Z.** (or **mit zwei Jahren Z.**) with two years to pay; **j-m zwei Jahre Z. gewähren** give s.o. two years to pay; **seinem Ehrgeiz ein Z. setzen** set a limit to one's ambition

Ziel'anflug m (aer) bomb run

Ziel'band n (-[e]s;ˈer) (sport) tape

ziel'bewußt adj purposeful; single-minded

zielen ['tsilən] intr take aim; **z. auf** (acc) or **nach** aim at

Ziel'fernrohr n telescopic sight

Ziel'gerade f homestretch

Ziel'gerät n gunsight; (aer) bombsight

Ziel'landung f pinpoint landing

Ziel'linie f (sport) finish line

ziel'los adj aimless

Ziel'photographie f photo finish

Ziel'punkt m objective; bull's-eye

Ziel'scheibe f target; (fig) butt

Ziel'setzung f objective, target

ziel'sicher adj steady, unerring

Ziel'sprache f target language

zielstrebig ['tsil/trebɪç] adj single-minded, determined

Ziel'sucher m (rok) homing device

Ziel'vorrichtung f gunsight; bombsight

ziemen ['tsimən] ref be proper; **sich für j-n z.** become s.o. || intr (dat) be becoming to

ziemlich ['tsimlɪç] adj fit, suitable; (leidlich) middling; (mäßig) fair; (beträchtlich) considerable || adv pretty, rather, fairly; (fast) almost, practically

Zier [tsir] *f* (-;), **Zierat** ['tsirɑt] *m* (-s;) ornament, decoration
Zierde ['tsirdə] *f* (-;-n) ornament decoration; (fig) credit, honor
zieren ['tsirən] *tr* decorate, adorn ‖ *ref* be affected, be coy; (*beim Essen*) need to be coaxed; **zier dich doch nicht so!** don't be coy!
Zier'leiste *f* trim(ming)
zier'lich *adj* delicate; (*nett*) nice
Zier'pflanze *f* ornamental plant
Zier'puppe *f* glamour girl
Ziffer ['tsɪfər] *f* (-;-n) digit, figure
Zi'ferblatt *n* face (*of a clock*)
zig [tsɪç] *invar adj* (coll) umpteen
Zigarette [tsigaˈretə] *f* (-;-n) cigarette
Zigaret'tenautomat *m* cigarette machine
Zigaret'tenetui *n* cigarette case
Zigaret'tenspitze *f* cigarette holder
Zigaret'tenstummel *m* cigarette butt
Zigarre [tsɪˈɡarə] *f* (-;-n) cigar
Zigeuner **-in** [tsɪˈɡɔinər(ɪn)] §6 *mf* gipsy
Zimbel ['tsɪmbəl] *f* (-;-n) cymbal
Zimmer ['tsɪmər] *n* (-s;-) room
Zim'merantenne *f* indoor antenna
Zim'merarbeit *f* carpentry
Zim'merdienst *m* room service
Zim'mereinrichtung *f* furniture
Zim'merer *m* (-s;-) carpenter
Zim'merflucht *f* suite
Zim'mermädchen *n* chambermaid
Zim'mer·mann *m* (-[e]s;-leute) carpenter
zimmern ['tsɪmərn] *tr* carpenter, build ‖ *intr* carpenter
Zim'mervermieter *m* landlord
-zimmrig [tsɪmrɪç] *comb.fm.* -room
zimperlich ['tsɪmpərlɪç] *adj* prudish; fastidious; (*gegen Kälte*) oversensitive
Zimt [tsɪmt] *m* (-[e]s;) cinnamon
Zink [tsɪŋk] *m & n* (-[e]s;) zinc
Zinke ['tsɪŋkə] *f* (-;-n) prong; (*e-s Kammes*) tooth; (carp) dovetail
zinken ['tsɪŋkən] *tr* dovetail; (*Karten*) mark ‖ **Zinken** *m* (-s;-) (sl) schnozzle
-zinkig [tsɪŋkɪç] *comb.fm.* -pronged
Zinn [tsɪn] *n* (-[e]s;) tin
Zinne ['tsɪnə] *f* (-;-n) pinnacle; battlement
zinnoberrot [tsɪˈnobərrot] *adj* vermilion
Zins [tsɪns] *m* (-es;-en) interest; (*Miete*) rent; **auf Zinsen anlegen** put out at interest; **j-m mit Zinsen (und Zinseszinsen) heimzahlen** (coll) pay s.o. back in full; **Zinsen berechnen** charge interest
zins'bringend *adj* interest-bearing
Zin'senbelastung *f* interest charge
Zinseszinsen ['tsɪnzəstsɪnzən] *pl* compound interest
zins'frei *adj* rent-free; interest-free
Zins'fuß *m*, **Zins'satz** *m* rate of interest
Zins'schein *m* (interest) coupon; dividend warrant
Zionismus [tsɪˈc·nɪsmus] *m* (-;) Zionism
Zipfel ['tsɪpfəl] *m* (-s;-) tip, point;

edge; (*Ecke*) corner; (*e-r Wurst*) end piece
Zip'felmütze *f* nightcap, tasseled cap
zirka ['tsɪrka] *adv* approximately
Zirkel ['tsɪrkəl] *m* (-s;-) circle; (*Reißzeug*) compass; (fig) circle
Zir'kelschluß *m* vicious circle
zirkulieren [tsɪrkuˈlirən] *intr* (SEIN) circulate; **z. lassen** circulate
Zirkus ['tsɪrkʊs] *m* (-;-se) circus
zirpen ['tsɪrpən] *intr* chirp
zischeln ['tsɪʃəln] *tr & intr* whisper
zischen ['tsɪʃən] *intr* hiss; sizzle; (*schwirren*) whiz ‖ **Zischen** *n* (-s;) hissing; sizzle; whiz
Zisch'laut *m* hissing sound; (phonet) sibilant
ziselieren [tsizeˈlirən] *tr* chase
Zisterne [tsɪsˈtɛrnə] *f* (-;-n) cistern
Zitadelle [tsɪtaˈdɛlə] *f* (-;-n) citadel
Zitat [tsɪˈtɑt] *n* (-[e]s;-e) quotation
Zither ['tsɪtər] *f* (-;-n) zither
zitieren [tsɪˈtirən] *tr* quote; **j-n vor Gericht z.** issue s.o. a summons
Zitronat [tsɪtroˈnɑt] *n* (-[e]s;-e) candied lemon peel
Zitrone [tsɪˈtronə] *f* (-;-n) lemon
Zitro'nenlimonade *f* lemonade; (*mit Sodawasser*) lemon soda
Zitro'nenpresse *f* lemon squeezer
Zitro'nensaft *m* lemon juice
Zitro'nensäure *f* citric acid
zitterig ['tsɪtərɪç] *adj* shaky
zittern ['tsɪtərn] *intr* quake, tremble; quiver; (*flimmern*) dance; (*vor dat*) shake (with), shiver (with); **beim dem Gedanken an etw** [*acc*] **z.** shudder at the thought of s.th.
Zit'terpappel ['tsɪtərpapəl] *f* aspen
Zitze ['tsɪtsə] *f* (-;-n) teat
zivil [tsɪˈvil] *adj* civil; civilian; (*Preise*) reasonable ‖ **Zivil** *n* (-s;) civilians; **in Z.** in plain clothes
Zivil'courage *f* courage of one's convictions, moral courage
Zivil'ehe *f* civil marriage
Zivilisation [tsɪvɪlɪzaˈtsjon] *f* (-;-en) civilization
zivilisieren [tsɪvɪlɪˈzirən] *tr* civilize
Zivilist **-in** [tsɪvɪˈlɪst(ɪn)] §7 *mf* civilian
Zivil'klage *f* (jur) civil suit
Zivil'kleidung *f* civilian clothes
Zivil'person *f* civilian
Zobel ['tsobəl] *m* (-s;-) (zool) sable
Zofe ['tsofə] *f* (-;-n) lady-in-waiting
zog [tsok] *pret of* ziehen
zögern ['tsøːɡərn] *intr* hesitate; delay ‖ **Zögern** *n* (-s;) hesitation; delay
Zögling ['tsøːklɪŋ] *m* (-s;-e) pupil
Zölibat [tsøliˈbɑt] *m & n* (-[e]s;) celibacy
Zoll [tsɔl] *m* (-[e]s;-ᵉe) duty, customs; (*Brückenzoll*) toll; (*Maß*) inch
Zoll'abfertigung *f* customs clearance
Zoll'amt *n* customs office
Zoll'beamte §5 *m* customs official
zollen ['tsɔlən] *tr* give, pay; **j-m Achtung z.** show s.o. respect; **j-m Beifall z.** applaud s.o.; **j-m Dank z.** thank s.o.; **j-m Lob z.** praise s.o.
Zoll'erklärung *f* customs declaration

zoll'frei *adj* duty-free
Zoll'grenze *f* customs frontier
–zöllig [tsœlɪç] *comb.fm.* –inch
Zoll'kontrolle *f* customs inspection
zoll'pflichtig *adj* dutiable
Zoll'schein *m* customs clearance
Zoll'schranke *f* customs barrier
Zoll'stab *m*, **Zoll'stock** *m* foot rule
Zoll'tarif *m* tariff
Zone ['tsona] *f* (–;–n) zone; **blaue Z.** limited-parking area; **Z. der Windstille** doldrums
Zoo [tso] *m* (– & –s;–s) zoo
Zoologe [tsoˑoˈloga] *m* (–n;–n) zoologist
Zoologie [tsoˑoloˈgi] *f* (–;) zoology
Zoologin [tsoˑoˈlogin] *f* (–;–nen) zoologist
zoologisch [tsoˑoˈlogɪʃ] *adj* zoological
Zopf [tsɔpf] *m* (–[e]s;–̈e) plait of hair; pigtail; twisted (bread) roll; **alter Z.** outdated custom
zopfig ['tsɔpfɪç] *adj* pedantic; old-fashioned
Zorn [tsɔrn] *m* (–[e]s;) anger, rage
Zorn'anfall *m* fit of anger
Zorn'ausbruch *m* outburst of anger
zornig ['tsɔrnɪç] *adj* (**auf** *acc*) angry (at)
zorn'mütig *adj* hotheaded
Zote ['tsota] *f* (–;–n) obscenity; dirty joke; **Zoten reißen** crack dirty jokes; talk dirty
zo'tenhaft, zotig ['tsotɪç] *adj* obscene, dirty
Zotte ['tsota] *f* (–;–n) tuft of hair; strand of hair
Zottel ['tsotal] *f* (–;–n) strand of hair
Zot'telhaar *n* stringy hair
zottelig ['tsotalɪç] *adj* stringy (hair)
zotteln ['tsotaln] *intr* (SEIN) (coll) saunter
zottig ['tsotɪç] *adj* shaggy; matted
zu [tsu] *adj* closed, shut ‖ *adv* too; **immer zu!** (or **nur zu!**) go on! ‖ *prep* (*dat*) at, in, on; to; along with; in addition to; beside, near; **zu Anfang** at the beginning; **zu dritt** in threes; **zu Wasser und zu Lande** by land and by sea
zuallererst [tsu·alərˈerst] *adv* first of all
zuallerletzt [tsu·alərˈletst] *adv* last of all
zuballern ['tsubalərn] *tr* (coll) slam
zu'bauen *tr* wall up, wall in
Zubehör ['tsubahør] *m & n* (–s;) accessories; fittings; trimmings; **Wohnung mit allem Z.** apartment with all utilities
zu'behörteil *m* accessory, attachment, component
zu'beißen §53 *intr* bite; snap at people
zu'bekommen §99 *tr* get in addition; (*Tür, usw.*) manage to close
zu'bereiten *tr* prepare; (*Speise*) cook; (*Getränk*) mix
Zu'bereitung *f* (–;–en) preparation
zu'billigen *tr* grant, allow, concede
zu'binden §59 *tr* tie up; **j–m die Augen z.** blindfold s.o.
zu'bleiben §62 *intr* (SEIN) remain closed

zu'blinzeln *intr* (*dat*) wink at
zu'bringen §65 *tr* (*Zeit*) spend; (coll) manage to shut; (tech) feed
Zu'bringer *m* (–s;–) (tech) feeder
Zu'bringerdienst *m* shuttle service
Zu'bringerstraße *f* access road
Zucht [tsuxt] *f* (–;) breeding; rearing; (*Rasse*) race, stock; (*Pflanzen-*) cultivation; (*Schul-*) education; discipline; training, drill; **Z. halten** maintain discipline
züchten ['tsyçtən] *tr* breed; rear, raise; (bot) grow, cultivate
Züch'ter **–in** §6 *mf* breeder; grower
Zucht'haus *n* penitentiary, hard labor; **lebenslängliches Z.** life imprisonment
Zuchthäusler **–in** ['tsuxthɔɪzlər(ɪn)] §6 *mf* convict, prisoner at hard labor
Zucht'hengst *m* studhorse
züchtig ['tsyçtɪç] *adj* modest, chaste
züchtigen ['tsyçtɪgən] *tr* chastise
zucht'los *adj* undisciplined
Zucht'losigkeit *f* (–;) lack of discipline
Zucht'meister *m* disciplinarian
Zucht'perle *f* cultured pearl
Züch'tung *f* (–;) breeding; rearing; growing, cultivation
zucken ['tsukən] *tr* (*Achseln*) shrug ‖ *intr* twitch, jerk; (*Blitz*) flash; (*vor Schmerzen*) wince; **mit keiner Wimper z.** not bat an eye; **ohne zu z.** without wincing ‖ *impers*—**es zuckte mir in den Fingern zu** (*inf*) my fingers were itching to (*inf*) ‖ **Zucken** *n* (–s;) twitch
zücken ['tsykən] *tr* (*Schwert*) draw
Zucker ['tsukər] *m* (–s;) sugar
Zuckerdose (**Zuk'kerdose**) *f* sugar bowl
Zuckererbse (**Zuk'kererbse**) *f* sweet pea
Zuckerguß (**Zuk'kerguß**) *m* frosting
Zuckerharnruhr (**Zuk'kerharnruhr**) *f* diabetes
Zuckerhut (**Zuk'kerhut**) *m* sugar loaf
zuckerig ['tsukərɪç] *adj* sugary
zuckerkrank (**zuk'kerkrank**) *adj* diabetic ‖ **Zuckerkranke** §5 *mf* diabetic
Zuckerkrankheit (**Zuk'kerkrankheit**) *f* diabetes
Zuckerlecken (**Zuk'kerlecken**) *n* (–s;) (fig) pushover, picnic
Zuckerrohr (**Zuk'kerrohr**) *n* sugar cane
Zuckerrübe (**Zuk'kerrübe**) *f* sugar beet
zuckersüß (**zuk'kersüß**) *adj* sweet as sugar
Zuckerwerk (**Zuk'kerwerk**) *n*, **Zuckerzeug** (**Zuk'kerzeug**) *n* candy
Zuckung (**Zuk'kung**) *f* (–;–en) twitch, spasm, convulsion
Zu'decke *f* (coll) bed covering
zu'decken *tr* cover up
zudem [tsuˈdem] *adv* moreover, besides
zu'denken §66 *tr*—**j–m etw z.** intend s.th. as a present for s.o.
Zu'drang *m* crowding, rush
zu'drehen *tr* turn off; **j–m den Rücken z.** turn one's back on s.o.
zu'dringlich *adj* obtrusive; **z. werden** make a pass
zu'drücken *tr* close, shut
zu'eignen *tr* dedicate
Zu'eignung *f* (–;–en) dedication

zu'erkennen §97 *tr* confer, award; (jur) adjudge, award
zuerst' *adv* first; at first
zu'erteilen *tr* award; confer, bestow
zu'fahren §71 *intr* (SEIN) drive on; z. **auf** (acc) drive in the direction of (s.th.); rush at (s.o.)
Zu'fahrt *f* access
Zu'fahrtsrampe *f* on-ramp
Zu'fahrtsstraße *f* access road
Zu'fall *m* chance; coincidence; accident; **durch Z.** by chance
zu'fallen §72 *intr* (SEIN) close, shut; **j-m z.** fall to s.o.'s share
zufällig ['tsufɛlɪç] *adj* chance, fortuitous; accidental; casual ‖ *adv* by chance; accidentally
zu'fälligerweise *adv* by chance
Zufalls— *comb.fm.* chance
zu'fassen *intr* set to work; lend a hand; (e-e Gelegenheit wahrnehmen) seize the opportunity
Zu'flucht *f* refuge; (fig) recourse; **seine Z. nehmen zu** take refuge in; have recourse to
Zu'fluß *m* influx; (Nebenfluß) tributary; (mach) feed
zu'flüstern *intr* (dat) whisper to
zufolge [tsu'fɔlgə] *prep* (genit & dat) in consequence of; according to
zufrieden [tsu'fridən] *adj* satisfied; **j-n z. lassen** leave s.o. alone
zufrie'dengeben §80 *ref* (mit) be satisfied (with), acquiesce (in)
Zufrie'denheit *f* (—;) satisfaction
zufrie'denstellen *tr* satisfy
zufrie'denstellend *adj* satisfactory
Zufrie'denstellung *f* satisfaction
zu'frieren §77 *intr* (SEIN) freeze up
zu'fügen *tr* add; (Niederlage) inflict; (Kummer, Schaden, Schmerz) cause
Zufuhr ['tsufur] *f* (—;) supply; importation; supplies; (mach) feed
zu'führen *tr* convey, bring; (Waren) supply; (mach) feed
Zu'führung *f* (—;-en) conveyance; supply; importation; (elec) lead; (mach) feed
Zug [tsuk] *m* (-[e]s;ⁿe) train; pull, tug; drawing, pulling; (Spannung) tension; strain; (beim Rauchen) puff; (beim Atmen) breath, gasp; (Schluck) drink, gulp, swig; (Luft-) draft; (Reihe) row, line; (Um—) procession; parade; (Kriegs—) campaign; (Geleit) escort; (von Vögeln) flock; flight, migration; (von Fischen) school; (Rudel) pack; (Trupp) platoon; (Gespann) team, yoke; (Gesichts-) feature; (Charakter-) trait; characteristic; (Neigung) trend, tendency; (im Gewehrlauf) groove, rifling; (Strich) stroke; (Schnörkel) flourish; (Umriß) outline; (beim Brettspiel) move; **auf dem Zuge** on the march; **auf e-n Zug** in one gulp; at one stroke; at a stretch; **du bist am Zug** (& fig) it's your move; **e-n guten Zug haben** drink like a fish; **e-n Zug tun** take a puff; make a move; take a drink; **gut im Zuge sein** (or **im besten Zuge sein**) be going strong; **in e-m Zuge** in one gulp; in one breath; at one stroke; at a stretch; **in großen Zügen** in broad outlines; **in vollen Zügen** thoroughly; **in Zug bringen** start; **nicht zum Zug kommen** not get a chance; **ohne rechten Zug** half-heartedly; **Zug um Zug** in rapid succession
Zu'gabe *f* addition; (theat) encore
Zu'gang *m* access; approach; entrance; (Zunahme) increase; (libr) accession
zugänglich ['tsugɛnlɪç] *adj* accessible; (Person) affable; (benutzbar) available; (dat, für) open (to); **nicht z. für** proof against
Zug'artikel *m* (com) popular article
Zug'brücke *f* drawbridge
zu'geben §80 *tr* add; (erlauben) allow; (anerkennen) admit, concede; (eingestehen) confess; (com) throw into the bargain
zugegen [tsu'gegən] *adj* (bei) present (at)
zu'gehen §82 *intr* (SEIN) go on; walk faster; (sich schließen) shut; **auf j-n z.** go up to s.o.; **j-m etw z. lassen** send s.th. to s.o.
zu'gehören *intr* (dat) belong to
zu'gehörig *adj* (dat) belonging to
Zu'gehörigkeit *f* (—;) (zu) membership (in)
Zügel ['tsygəl] *m* (-s;-) rein; bridle; (fig) curb
zü'gellos *adj* (& fig) unbridled; (ausschweifig) dissolute
Zü'gellosigkeit *f* (—;) licentiousness
zügeln ['tsygəln] *tr* bridle; (fig) curb
Zu'geständnis *n* admission, concession
zu'gestehen §146 *tr* admit, concede
zu'getan *adj* (dat) fond of
Zug'feder *f* tension spring
Zug'führer *m* (mil) platoon leader; (rr) chief conductor
zu'gießen §76 *tr* add
zugig ['tsugɪç] *adj* drafty
zügig ['tsygɪç] *adj* speedy, fast
Zug'klappe *f* damper
Zug'kraft *f* tensile force; (fig) drawing power
zug'kräftig *adj* attractive, popular
zugleich' *adv* at the same time; **z. mit** together with
Zug'luft *f* draft
Zug'maschine *f* tractor
Zug'mittel *n* (fig) attraction, draw
zu'graben §87 *tr* cover up
zu'greifen §88 *intr* grab hold; lend a hand; (fig) go into action; **greifen Sie zu!** (bei Tisch) help yourself!; (bei Reklamen) don't miss this opportunity!
Zu'griff *m* grip; (fig) clutches
zugrunde [tsu'grundə] *adv*—**z. gehen** go to ruin; **z. legen** (dat) take as a basis (for); **z. liegen** (dat) underlie
Zug'tier *n* draft animal
zu'gucken *intr* (coll) look on
zugunsten [tsu'gunstən] *prep* (genit) in favor of; for the benefit of
zugute [tsu'gutə] *adv*—**j-m etw z. halten** make allowance for s.o. for s.th.; **j-m z. kommen** stand s.o. in good stead
Zug'verkehr *m* train service

Zug'vogel *m* migratory bird
zu'haben §89 *tr* (*Augen*) have closed; (*Mantel*) have buttoned up ‖ *intr* (*Geschäft*) be closed
zu'halten §90 *tr* keep closed; (*Ohren*) shut ‖ *intr*—z. auf (*acc*) head for
Zuhälter ['tsuhɛltər] *m* (–s;–) pimp
Zuhälterei [tsuhɛlte'raɪ] *f* (–;) pimping
zuhanden [tsu'handən] *prep* (*genit*) (*auf Briefumschlägen*) Attn:
Zuhause [tsu'hauzə] *n* (–s;) home
zu'heilen *intr* (SEIN) heal up
zu'hören *intr* (*dat*) listen (to)
Zu'hörer –in §6 *mf* hearer, listener; die Z. the audience
Zu'hörerschaft *f* (–;) audience
zu'jauchzen, zu'jubeln *intr* cheer
zu'klappen *tr* shut, slam shut
zu'kleben *tr* glue up, paste up
zu'knallen *tr* bang, slam shut
zu'kneifen §88 *tr*—die Augen z. blink; ein Auge z. wink
zu'knöpfen *tr* button up
zu'kommen §99 *intr* (SEIN) (*dat*) reach; (*dat*) be due to; auf j–n z. come up to s.o.; **das kommt dir nicht zu** you're not entitled to it; j–m etw z. lassen let s.o. have s.th.; send s.th. to s.o. ‖ *impers*—mir kommt es nicht zu zu (*inf*) it's not up to me to (*inf*)
zu'korken *tr* put the cork on
Zu'kost *f* vegetables; trimmings
Zukunft ['tsukʊnft] *f* (–;) future; (*gram*) future (tense)
zukünftig ['tsukʏnftɪç] *adj* future ‖ *adv* in the future ‖ **Zukünftige** §5 *m* (coll) fiancé ‖ *f* (coll) fiancée
Zu'kunftsmusik *f* wishful thinking
Zu'kunftsroman *m* science fiction
zu'lächeln *intr* (*dat*) smile at; (*dat*) smile on
Zu'lage *f* extra pay; pay raise
zulande [tsu'landə] *adv*—bei uns z. in my (or our) country
zu'langen *intr* suffice, do; (*bei Tisch*) help oneself
zu'länglich *adj* adequate, sufficient
zu'lassen §104 *tr* admit; (*erlauben*) allow; (*Tür*) leave shut; (*Fahrzeug*) license; (*Zweifel*) admit of
zulässig ['tsulɛsɪç] *adj* permissible; **zulässige Abweichung** allowance, tolerance
Zu'lassung *f* (–;–en) admission; permission; approval; license
Zu'lassungsprüfung *f* college entrance examination
Zu'lassungsschein *m* registration card
Zu'lauf *m* crowd, rush; Z. haben be popular; (theat) have a long run
zu'laufen §105 *intr* (SEIN) run on; run faster; (*dat*) flock to; auf j–n z. run up to s.o.; spitz z. end in a point
zu'legen *tr* add; etw z. up one's offer ‖ *ref*—sich [*dat*] etw. z. (coll) get oneself s.th.
zuleide [tsu'laɪdə] *adv*—j–m etw z. tun hurt s.o., do s.o. wrong
zu'leiten *tr* (*Wasser*) (*dat*) let in (to); (*dat*) direct (s.o.) (to); (*Schreiben*) (*dat*) pass on (to); auf dem Amtsweg) channel (to); (tech) feed

Zu'leitung *f* (–;–en) feed pipe; (elec) lead-in wire; (elec) conductor
zuletzt [tsu'lɛtst] *adv* last; at last; finally; after all
zuliebe [tsu'libə] *prep* (*dat*) for (s.o.'s) sake
zum [tsum] *abbr* **zu dem; es ist zum ...it's** enough to make one...
zu'machen *tr* shut; (*Loch*) close up; (*zuknöpfen*) button up
zumal [tsu'mal] *adv* especially; **z. da** all the more because
zu'mauern *tr* wall up
zumindest [tsu'mɪndəst] *adv* at least
zumute [tsu'mutə] *adv*—mir ist gut (or wohl) z. I feel good; **mir ist nicht zum Lachen z.** I don't feel like laughing
zumuten ['tsumutən] *tr*—j–m etw z. expect s.th. of s.o. ‖ *ref*—sich [*dat*] **zuviel z.** attempt too much
Zu'mutung *f* (–;–en) imposition
zunächst [tsu'nɛçst] *adv* first, at first, first of all; (*erstens*) to begin with; (*vorläufig*) for the time being ‖ *prep* (*dat*) next to
zu'nageln *tr* nail up, nail shut
zu'nähen *tr* sew up
Zu'nahme *f* (–;–n) increase; growth; rise
Zu'name *m* last name, family name
Zünd– (tsynt) *comb.fm.* ignition
zünden ['tsyndən] *tr* ignite; kindle; (*Sprengstoff*) detonate ‖ *intr* ignite, catch fire; (fig) catch on
Zün'der *m* (–s;–) fuse; detonator
Zünd'flamme *f* pilot light
Zünd'holz *n* match
Zünd'kerze *f* (aut) spark plug
Zünd'nadel *f* firing pin
Zünd'satz *m* primer
Zünd'schlüssel *m* ignition key
Zünd'schnur *f* fuse
Zünd'stein *m* flint
Zünd'stoff *m* fuel
Zün'dung *f* (–;–en) (aut) ignition
zu'nehmen §116 *intr* (*dat*) increase (in); (*steigen*) rise; grow longer
zu'neigen *tr* (*dat*) tilt toward ‖ *ref &* *intr* incline toward(s); sich dem Ende z. draw to a close
Zu'neigung *f* (–;) (für, zu) liking (for)
Zunft [tsunft] *f* (–;–en) guild
Zunge ['tsuŋə] *f* (–;–n) tongue
züngeln ['tsyŋəln] *intr* dart out the tongue; (*Flamme*) dart, leap up
Zun'genbrecher *m* tongue twister
zun'genfertig *adj* glib
Zun'genspitze *f* tip of the tongue
zunichte [tsu'nɪçtə] *adv*—z. machen destroy; (*Plan*) spoil; (*Theorie*) explode; **z. werden** come to nothing
zu'nicken *intr* (*dat*) nod to
zunutze [tsu'nutsə] *adv*—sich etw z. machen utilize s.th.
zuoberst [tsu'obərst] *adv* at the top
zupfen ['tsupfən] *tr* pull; pluck ‖ *intr* (an *dat*) tug (at)
zu'prosten *intr* (*dat*) toast
zur [tsur] *abbr* **zu der**
zu'rechnen *tr* add; (*dat*) number among, classify with; (*dat*) attribute to

zu'rechnungsfähig *adj* accountable; responsible; of sound mind
Zu'rechnungsfähigkeit *f* responsibility; sound mind
zurecht– [tsu'reçt] *comb.fm.* right, in order; at the right time
zurecht'biegen §57 *tr* straighten out
zurecht'bringen §65 *tr* set right
zurecht'finden §59 *ref* find one's way; (fig) see one's way
zurecht'kommen §99 *intr* (SEIN) come on time; get on, manage; turn out all right; mit etw nicht z. make a mess of s.th.; mit j–m z. get along with s.o.
zurecht'legen *tr* lay out in order || *ref–sich* [*dat*] z. figure out
zurecht'machen *tr & ref* get ready
zurecht'schneiden §106 *tr* cut to size
zurecht'setzen *tr* set right, fix, adjust
zurecht'weisen §118 *tr* reprimand
zu'reden *intr* (*dat*) try to persuade; (*dat*) encourage
zu'reichen *tr* reach, pass || *intr* do
zu'reichend *adj* sufficient
zu'reiten §86 *tr* break in
zu'richten *tr* prepare; cook
zu'riegeln *tr* bolt
zürnen ['tsʏrnən] *intr* (*dat*) be angry (with)
zurren ['tsurən] *tr* (naut) lash down
Zurschau'stellung *f* display
zurück [tsu'rʏk] *adv* back; backward; behind; ein paar Jahre z. a few years ago || *interj* back up!
zurück– *comb.fm.* back; behind; re–
zurück'behalten §90 *tr* keep back
zurück'bekommen §99 *tr* get back
zurück'bleiben §62 *intr* (SEIN) stay behind; fall behind; (Uhr) lose time; (hinter *dat*) fall short (of)
Zurück'blenden *n* (cin) flashback
zurück'blicken *intr* look back
zurück'bringen §65 *tr* bring back; z. auf (*acc*) (math) reduce to
zurück'datieren *tr* antedate
zurück'drängen *tr* force back; repress
zurück'dürfen §69 *intr* be allowed to return
zurück'erobern *tr* reconquer, win back
zurück'erstatten *tr* return; (Ausgaben) refund; (Kosten) reimburse
zurück'fahren §71 *tr* drive back || *intr* (SEIN) drive back, ride back; (vor Schreck) recoil, start
zurück'finden §59 *ref* find one's way back
zurück'fordern *tr* reclaim, demand back
zurück'führen *tr* lead back; trace back; z. auf (*acc*) refer to; attribute to
zurück'geben §80 *tr* give back, return
zurück'gehen §82 *intr* (SEIN) go back; (Fieber, Preise) drop; (Geschwulst) go down; (mil) fall back
zurück'gezogen *adj* secluded
zurück'greifen §88 *intr–z. auf** (*acc*) (fig) fall back on
zurück'halten §90 *tr* hold back; j–n davon z. zu (*inf*) keep s.o. from (ger) || *intr* mit etw z. conceal s.th.
zurück'haltend *adj* reserved; shy
Zurück'haltung *f* (–;–en) reserve

zurück'kehren *intr* (SEIN) return
zurück'kommen §99 *intr* (SEIN) return; z. auf (*acc*) come back to, revert to; (hinweisen) refer to
zurück'können §100 *intr* be able to return
zurück'lassen §104 *tr* leave behind; outstrip, outrun
zurück'legen *tr* (Kopf) lean back; (Geld) put aside; (Strecke) complete; (Ware) lay away || *ref* lean back
zurück'lehnen *ref* lean back
zurück'liegen §108 *intr* belong to the past || *impers–es liegt jetzt zehn Jahre zurück, daß* it's ten years now that
zurück'müssen §115 *intr* have to return
zurück'nehmen §116 *tr* take back; (widerrufen) revoke; (Auftrag) cancel; (Vorwurf) retract; (Klage) withdraw; (Versprechen) go back on; (Truppen) pull back; das Gas z. slow down
zurück'prallen *intr* (SEIN) rebound; (vor Schreck) start, be startled
zurück'rufen §122 *tr* call back, recall
zurück'schauen *intr* look back
zurück'schicken *tr* send back
zurück'schlagen §132 *tr* beat back, throw back || *intr* strike back
zurück'schrecken *tr* frighten away; (von) deter (from) || §109 & §134 *intr* (SEIN) (von, vor *dat*) shrink back (from)
zurück'sehnen *ref* yearn to return
zurück'sein §139 *intr* (SEIN) be back; (in *dat*) be behind (in)
zurück'setzen *tr* put back; (im Preis) reduce; (fig) snub || *ref* sit back
zurück'stecken *tr* put back
zurück'stellen *tr* (Uhr) set back; (Plan) shelve; (mil) defer
zurück'stoßen §150 *tr* push back; repel
zurück'strahlen *tr* reflect
zurück'streifen *tr* (Ärmel) roll up
zurück'treten §152 *intr* (SEIN) step back; (vom Amt) resign; (Wasser, Berge) recede
zurück'tun §154 *tr* put back
zurück'verfolgen *tr* (Schritte) retrace; (fig) trace back
zurück'verweisen §118 *tr* (an *acc*) refer back (to); (parl) remand (to)
zurück'weichen §85 *intr* (SEIN) fall back, make way; (Hochwasser) recede; (vor dem Feind) give ground; z. vor (*dat*) shrink from
zurück'weisen §118 *tr* turn back; (ablehnen) turn down; (Angriff) repel || *intr–z. auf* (*acc*) refer to
Zurück'weisung *f* (–;–en) rejection
zurück'wenden §140 *tr & ref* turn back
zurück'werfen §160 *tr* throw back; (e–n Patienten) set back; (Strahlen) reflect; (Feind) hurl back
zurück'wirken *intr* (auf *acc*) react (on); (Gesetz) be retroactive
zurück'zahlen *tr* pay back; (fin) refund
zurück'ziehen §163 *tr* draw back; (Antrag) withdraw; (Geld) call in; (Truppen) pull back; (sport) scratch || *ref* withdraw; (schlafengehen) re-

tire; (mil) pull back || intr (SEIN) move back; (mil) fall back, retreat

Zu′ruf m call; cheer; (parl) acclamation

zu′rufen §122 tr—j—m etw z. shout s.th. to s.o.

Zu′sage f (-;-n) assent; promise

zu′sagen tr promise || intr accept an invitation; (dat) please; (dat) agree (with)

zusammen [tsu'zamən] adv together; in common; at the same time

Zusam′menarbeit f cooperation

zusam′menarbeiten intr cooperate

zusam′menballen tr (Faust) clench

zusam′menbeißen §53 tr—die Zähne z. grit one's teeth

zusam′menbinden §59 tr tie together

zusam′menbrauen tr concoct || ref (Sturm) brew

zusam′menbrechen §64 intr (SEIN) break down; collapse

Zusam′menbruch m collapse; breakdown

zusam′mendrängen tr crowd together

zusam′mendrücken tr compress

zusam′menfahren §71 intr (SEIN) be startled; (mit) collide (with)

zusam′menfallen §72 intr (SEIN) fall in, collapse; (Teig) fall; (Person) lose weight; (mit) coincide (with)

Zusam′menfall m coincidence

zusam′menfalten tr fold

zusam′menfassen tr (in sich fassen) comprise; (verbinden) combine; (Macht, Funktionen) concentrate; (Bericht) summarize

zusam′menfassend adj comprehensive; summary

Zusam′menfassung f (-;-en) summary, résumé

zusam′menfinden §59 ref meet

zusam′menfügen tr join together; (Scherben, Teile) piece together

zusam′mengehen §82 intr (SEIN) go together; match; close; shrink

zusam′mengehören intr belong together

zusam′mengeraten §63 intr (SEIN) collide

zusammengewürfelt [tsu'zamɛngevyr-fəlt] adj mixed, motely

Zusam′menhalt m cohesion; consistency

zusam′menhalten §90 tr hold together; compare || intr stick together

Zusam′menhang m connection, relation; context; coherence

zusam′menhängend adj coherent; allied

zusam′menklappen tr fold up; die Hacken z. click one's heels || intr (SEIN) collapse

zusam′menkommen §99 intr (SEIN) come together

Zusammenkunft [tsu'zamənkunft] f (-;⸚e) meeting

zusam′menlaufen §105 intr (SEIN) run together; come together; flock; (Milch) curdle; (Farben) run; (einschrumpfen) shrink up; (geom) converge

zusammenlegbar [tsu'zamənlekbɑr] adj collapsible

zusam′menlegen tr put together; (fal-

ten) fold; (Geld) pool; (vereinigen) combine, consolidate || intr pool money

zusam′mennehmen §116 tr gather up; (Gedanken) collect; (Kräfte, Mut) muster; alles zusammengenommen considering everything || ref pull oneself together

zusam′menpacken tr pack up

zusam′menpassen tr & intr match

zusam′menpferchen tr crowd together

Zusam′menprall m collision; (fig) (mit) impact (on)

zusam′menprallen intr collide

zusam′menraffen tr collect in haste; (ein Vermögen) amass; (Kräfte) summon up, marshal || ref pull oneself together

zusam′menreißen §53 ref (coll) pull oneself together

zusam′menrollen tr roll up

zusam′menrotten ref band together, form a gang; (Aufrührer) riot

zusam′menrücken tr push together || intr (SEIN) move closer together

zusam′menschießen tr (Stadt) shoot up; (Menschen) shoot down; (Geld) pool

zusam′menschlagen §132 tr smash up; (Absätze) click; (Beine, Zeitung) fold; (Hände) clap; (zerschlagen) beat up; die Hände über den Kopf z. (fig) throw up one's hands || intr (SEIN)—aneinander z. clash

zusam′menschließen §76 tr join; link together || ref join together, unite

Zusam′menschluß m union; alliance

zusam′menschmelzen intr (SEIN) fuse; melt away; (fig) dwindle

zusam′menschnüren tr tie up

zusam′menschrumpfen intr (SEIN) shrivel; (fig) (coll) dwindle away

zusam′mensetzen tr put together; (mach) assemble || ref sit down together; sich z. aus consist of

Zusam′mensetzung f (-;-en) composition; (Bestandteile) ingredients; (Struktur) structure; (chem, gram) compound

Zusam′menspiel n teamwork

zusam′menstauchen tr browbeat, chew out

zusam′menstellen tr put together; (Liste) compile; (Farben) match; organize

Zusam′menstoß m collision; (der Meinungen) clash; (Treffen) encounter; (mil) engagement

zusam′menstoßen §150 tr knock together; (Gläser) touch || intr adjoin; mit den Gläsern z. clink glasses || intr (SEIN) collide; (Gegner) clash

zusam′menstückeln tr piece together

zusam′menstürzen intr (SEIN) collapse

zusam′mentragen §132 tr collect

zusam′mentreffen §151 intr (SEIN) meet; coincide || Zusammentreffen n (-s;) encounter, meeting; coincidence

zusam′mentreiben §62 tr round up; (Geld) scrape up

zusam′mentreten §152 intr (SEIN) meet

zusam′menwirken intr cooperate; collaborate; interact || **Zusammen-wirken** n (-s;) cooperation; interaction

zusam'menzählen tr count up, add up

zusam'menziehen §163 tr draw together, contract; (Lippen) pucker; (Brauen) knit; (Summe) add up; (kürzen) shorten; (Truppen) concentrate || ref contract; (Gewitter) brew || intr (SEIN)—mit j-m z. move in with s.o.

Zu'satz m addition; (Ergänzung) supplement; (Anhang) appendix; (Nachschrift) postscript; (Beimischung) admixture; (zu e-m Testament) codicil; (parl) rider; unter Z. von with the addition of

Zu'satzgerät n attachment

zusätzlich ['tsuzetslɪç] adj additional, extra || adv in addition

zuschanden [tsuˈʃandən] adv—z. machen ruin; z. werden go to ruin

zu'schauen intr look on; (dat) watch

Zu'schauer –in §6 mf spectator

Zu'schauerraum m auditorium

zu'schicken tr (dat) send (to)

zu'schieben §130 tr close, shut; (Riegel) push forward; j-m die Schuld z. push the blame on s.o.

Zu'schlag m extra charge; den Z. erhalten get the contract (on a bid)

zu'schlagen §132 tr (Tür) slam; (Buch) shut; (auf Auktionen) knock down; (hinzurechnen) add || intr hit hard

zu'schließen §76 tr shut, lock

zu'schnallen tr buckle (up)

zu'schnappen intr snap shut; z. lassen snap shut

zu'schneiden §106 tr cut out; (Anzug) cut to size

Zu'schnitt m cut; (fig) style

zu'schnüren tr lace up

zu'schrauben tr screw tight

zu'schreiben §62 tr ascribe; (Bedeutung) attach; (Grundstück, usw.) transfer, sign over || ref—er hat es sich [dat] selbst zuzuschreiben he has himself to thank for it

Zu'schrift f letter, communication

zuschulden [tsuˈʃuldən] adv—sich [dat] etw. z. kommen lassen take the blame for s.th.

Zu'schuß m subsidy; grant; allowance

zu'schütten tr add; (Graben) fill up

zu'sehen §138 intr look on; (dat) watch; z., daß see to it that

zusehends ['tsuze-ənts] adv visibly

zu'senden §120 & §140 tr (dat) send to

zu'setzen tr add; (Geld) lose || intr (dat) pester; (dat) be hard on; (mil) (dat) put pressure on

zu'sichern tr—j-m etw z. assure s.o. of s.th.

Zu'sicherung f (-;-en) assurance

zu'siegeln tr seal up

Zu'speise f side dish

zu'sperren tr lock

zu'spielen tr—j-m den Ball z. pass the ball to s.o.; j-m etw z. slip s.th. to s.o.

zu'spitzen tr sharpen, make pointy || ref (Lage) come to a head

zu'sprechen §64 tr (& jur) award

Zu'spruch m consolation, encouragement; (com) customers, clientele

zu'springen §142 intr (SEIN) snap shut

Zu'stand m state, condition; gegenwärtiger Z. status quo; in gutem Z. in good condition; Zustände state of affairs

zustande [tsuˈʃtandə] adv—z. bringen bring about; put across; get away with; z. kommen come about, come off; happen; be realized; (Gesetz) pass; (Vertrag) be reached

zu'ständig adj competent; (Behörde) proper; (verantwortlich) responsible

Zu'ständigkeit f (-;) jurisdiction

zustatten [tsuˈʃtatən] adv—z. kommen come in handy

zu'stehen §146 intr (dat) be due to

zu'stellen tr deliver; (jur) serve

Zu'stellung f (-;-en) delivery; (jur) serving

zu'steuern tr (Geld) contribute, kick in || intr (dat, auf acc) head for

zu'stimmen intr (dat) agree to, approve of (s.th.); (dat) agree with (s.o.)

Zu'stimmung f (-;) consent, approval

zu'stopfen tr plug up

zu'stoßen §150 tr slam || intr (SEIN) lunge; (dat) happen to

zu'streben intr (dat) strive for

zutage [tsuˈtagə] adv to light; z. liegen be evident

Zutaten ['tsutatən] pl ingredients

zuteil [tsuˈtaɪl] adv—j-m z. werden fall to s.o.'s share

zu'teilen tr allot; ration; award; (gewähren) grant; confer; (mil) assign

Zu'teilung f (-;-en) allotment, allocation; rationing; (mil) assignment

zu'tragen §132 tr carry; (Neuigkeiten) report || ref happen

zuträglich ['tsutreklɪç] adj advantageous; (Klima) healthful; (Nahrung) wholesome; j-m z. sein agree with s.o.

zu'trauen tr—j-m etw z. give s.o. credit for s.th.; imagine s.o. capable of s.th. || Zutrauen n (-s;) (zu) confidence (in)

zu'traulich adj trustful; (zahm) tame

zu'treffen §151 intr (SEIN) prove right; come true; hold true, be conclusive; z. auf (acc) apply to

zu'treffend adj correct; to the point; (anwendbar) applicable

zu'trinken §143 intr (dat) drink to

Zu'tritt m access; admission; entrance; kein Z.! no admittance!

zu'tun §154 tr close; (hinzufügen) add

zu'verlässig adj reliable; von zuverlässiger Seite on good authority

Zu'verlässigkeit f (-;) reliability

Zuversicht ['tsuferzɪçt] f (-;) confidence

zu'versichtlich adj confident

zuviel [tsuˈfil] adv & indef pron too much; einer z. one too many

zuvor [tsuˈfor] adv before, previously; first (of all); kurz z. shortly before

zuvor– comb.fm. beforehand

zuvor'kommen §99 intr (SEIN) (dat) anticipate; j-m z. get the jump on s.o.

zuvor'kommend *adj* obliging; polite

zuvor'tun §154 *tr*—es j-m z. outdo s.o.

Zu'wachs *m* increase; growth; **auf Z.** (big enough) to allow for growth

zu'wachsen §155 *intr* (SEIN) grow together; (*Wunde*) heal up; (*dat*) accrue (to)

Zu'wachsrate *f* rate of increase

zuwege [tsu'vega] *adv*—z. bringen bring about; achieve; finish; **gut z. sein** be fit as a fiddle

zuweilen [tsu'vaɪlən] *adv* sometimes

zu'weisen §118 *tr* assign, allot

zu'wenden §120 & §140 *tr* (*dat*) turn (*s.th.*) towards; (*dat*) give (*s.th.*) to, devote (*s.th.*) to || *ref* (*dat*) devote oneself to, concentrate on

Zu'wendung *f* (—;-en) gift, donation

zuwenig [tsu'venɪç] *adv & pron* too little

zu'werfen §160 *tr* (*Tür*) slam; (*Blick*) cast; (*Grube*) fill up; **j-m etw z.** throw s.o. s.th.

zuwider [tsu'vidər] *adj* (*dat*) distasteful (to) || *prep* (*dat*) contrary to

zuwi'derhandeln *intr* (*dat*) go against

Zuwi'derhandlung *f* (—;-en) violation

zu'winken *intr* (*dat*) wave to; beckon to

zu'zahlen *tr* pay extra

zu'zählen *tr* add

zuzeiten [tsu'tsaɪtən] *adv* at times

zu'ziehen §163 *tr* (*Vorhang*) draw; (*Knoten*) tighten; (*Arzt, Experten*) call in || *ref*—**sich** [*dat*] **etw z.** incur s.th.; contract s.th. || *intr* (SEIN) move in; move (*to a city*)

Zu'ziehung *f*—**unter Z.** (*genit* or **von**) in consultation with

zuzüglich ['tsutsyklɪç] *prep* (*genit*) plus; including

zwang [tsvaŋ] *pret* of **zwingen** || **Zwang** *m* (—[e]s;) coercion, force; restraint; obligation; (*Druck*) pressure; (jur) duress; **auf j-n Z.** ausüben put pressure on s.o. || *ref*—**sich** [*dat*] **keinen Z. antun** (or **auferlegen**) relax

zwängen ['tsveŋən] *tr* force, squeeze || *ref* (**durch**) squeeze (through)

zwang'los *adj* free and easy; informal

Zwang'losigkeit *f* (—;) ease; informality

Zwangs— [tsvaŋs] *comb.fm.* force, compulsory

Zwangs'arbeit *f* hard labor

Zwangs'arbeitslager *n* labor camp

Zwangs'jacke *f* strait jacket

Zwangs'lage *f* tight spot

zwangs'läufig *adj* inevitable

zwangs'mäßig *adj* forced; coercive

Zwangs'maßnahme *f*—**zu Zwangsmaßnahmen greifen** resort to force

Zwangs'verschleppte §5 *mf* displaced person

Zwangs'verwaltung *f* receivership

Zwangs'vorstellung *f* hallucination

zwangs'weise *adv* by force

Zwangs'wirtschaft *f* (econ) government control, controlled economy

zwanzig ['tsvantsɪç] *invar adj & pron* twenty || **Zwanzig** *f* (—;-en) twenty

zwanziger ['tsvansɪgər] *invar adj* of the twenties; **die z. Jahre** the twenties

zwanzigste ['tsvantsɪçstə] §9 *adj & pron* twentieth

Zwanzigstel ['tsvantsɪçstəl] *n* (—s;—) twentieth (*part*)

zwar [tsvar] *adv* indeed, no doubt, it is true; **und z.** namely, that is

Zweck [tsvɛk] *m* (—[e]s;-e) purpose, aim, object, point; **es hat keinen Z.** there's no point to it

zweck'dienlich *adj* serviceable, useful

Zwecke ['tsvɛkə] *f* (—;-n) tack; thumbtack

zweck'entfremden *tr* misuse

zweck'entsprechend *adj* appropriate

zweck'los *adj* pointless

zweck'mäßig *adj* serving its purpose; (*Möbel*) functional

zwecks [tsvɛks] *prep* (*genit*) for the purpose of

zwei [tsvaɪ] *adj & pron* two; **alle z.** (coll) both; **zu zweien in** twos, two by two, in pairs; **zu zweien hintereinander** in double file || **Zwei** *f* (—;-en) two

zwei'beinig *adj* two-legged

Zwei'bettzimmer *n* double room

Zweidecker ['tsvaɪdɛkər] *m* (—s;—) biplane

zweideutig ['tsvaɪdɔɪtɪç] *adj* ambiguous; (*Witz*) off-color; (*schlüpfrig*) suggestive

zweierlei ['tsvaɪ-ər'laɪ] *invar adj* two kinds of; **das ist z.** (coll) that's different

zwei'fach, zwei'fältig *adj* twofold, double; **in zweifacher Ausfertigung in** duplicate

Zweifami'lienhaus *n* duplex

zwei'farbig *adj* two-tone

Zweifel ['tsvaɪfəl] *m* (—s;—) doubt; **in Z. stellen** (or **ziehen**) call into question; **über allen Zweifeln erhaben** beyond reproach

zwei'felhaft *adj* doubtful; questionable; (*Persönlichkeit*) suspicious

zwei'fellos *adj* doubtless

zweifeln ['tsvaɪfəln] *intr* be in doubt; waver, hesitate; **z. an** (*dat*) doubt

Zwei'felsfall *m*—**im Z.** in case of doubt

Zweif'ler **-in** §6 *mf* skeptic

Zweig [tsvaɪk] *m* (—[e]s;-e) branch

Zweig'anstalt *f*, **Zweig'geschäft** *n* (com) branch

Zweig'gesellschaft *f* (com) affiliate

Zweig'niederlassung *f*, **Zweig'stelle** *f* (com) branch

Zwei'kampf *m* duel, single combat

zwei'mal *adv* twice

zweimalig ['tsvaɪmalɪç] *adj* repeated

zweimotorig ['tsvaɪmɔtorɪç] *adj* two-engine, twin-engine

zweireihig ['tsvaɪraɪ-ɪç] *adj* (*Sakko*) double-breasted

zwei'schneidig *adj* double-edged

zwei'seitig *adj* bilateral; reversible

zweisprachig ['tsvaɪʃpraxɪç] *adj* bilingual

Zweistür'kenglas *n* bifocal lens; (*Brille*) bifocals

zwei'stimmig *adj* for two voices

zweistufig ['tsvaɪtufɪç] *adj* (rok) two-stage

zwei'stündig *adj* two-hour

zwei'stündlich *adj & adv* every two hours

zweit [tsvart] *adv*—**zu z.** by twos; **wir sind zu z.** there are two of us

Zwei'taktmotor *m* two-cycle engine

Zweit'ausfertigung *f* duplicate

zweit'beste §9 *adj* second-best

zweite ['tsvartə] §9 *adj & pron* second; another; **aus zweiter Hand** second-hand; at second hand; **zum zweiten** secondly ‖ **Zweite** §5 *mf* (sport) runner-up

zwei'teilig *adj* two-piece; two-part

zweitens ['tsvartəns] *adv* secondly

zweit'klassig *adj* second-class

Zwerchfell ['tsverçfel] *n* diaphragm

Zwerg [tsverk] *m* (-[e]s;-e) dwarf

zwer'genhaft *adj* dwarfish

Zwetsche ['tsvetʃə] *f* (-;-n), **Zwetsche** ['tsvetʃgə] *f* (-;-n) plum

Zwetsch'genwasser *n* plum brandy

zwicken ['tsvikən] *tr* pinch

Zwicker (Zwik'ker) *m* (-s;-) pince-nez

Zwickmühle ['tsvikmylə] *f* (fig) fix

zwie- [tsvi] *comb.fm.* dis-, two-, double

Zwieback ['tsvibak] *m* (-s;⁻e & -e) zwieback

Zwiebel ['tsvibəl] *f* (-;-n) onion; (*Blumen-*) bulb

Zwie'gespräch *n* dialogue

Zwie'licht *n* twilight

Zwiesel ['tsvizəl] *f* (-;-n) fork (*of tree*)

Zwie'spalt *m* dissension; schism; discrepancy; **im Z. sein mit** be at variance with

zwiespältig ['tsvi/pɛltiç] *adj* disunited, divided; divergent

Zwie'tracht *f* (-;) discord

Zwilling ['tsvilɪŋ] *m* (-s;-e) twin; **eineiige Zwillinge** identical twins

Zwil'lingsbruder *m* twin brother

Zwil'lingsschwester *f* twin sister

Zwinge ['tsviŋə] *f* (-;-n) ferrule; clamp; (*Schraubstock*) vise

zwingen ['tsviŋən] §142 *tr* force, compel; (*schaffen*) accomplish, swing

zwin'gend *adj* forceful, cogent

Zwin'ger *m* (-s;-) dungeon; cage; dog kennel; bear pit; lists

zwinkern ['tsviŋkərn] *intr* blink

Zwirn [tsvirn] *m* (-[e]s;-e) thread

Zwirns'faden *m* thread

zwischen ['tsvi/ən] *prep* (*dat & acc*) between, among

Zwi'schenbemerkung *f* interruption

Zwi'schendeck *n* steerage

Zwi'schending *n* cross, mixture

zwischendurch' *adv* in between; at times

Zwi'schenergebnis *n* incomplete result

Zwi'schenfall *m* (unexpected) incident

Zwi'schenhändler **-in** §6 *mf* middleman

Zwi'schenlandung *f* stopover

Zwi'schenlauf *m* (sport) quarterfinal; (sport) semifinal

Zwi'schenpause *f* break, intermission

Zwi'schenraum *m* space, interval

Zwi'schenruf *m* boo; interruption

Zwi'schenrunde *f* (sport) quarterfinal; (sport) semifinal

Zwi'schenspiel *n* interlude

zwi'schenstaatlich *adj* international; interstate

Zwi'schenstation *f* (rr) way station

Zwi'schenstecker *m* (elec) adapter

Zwi'schenstellung *f* (-;-en) intermediate position

Zwi'schenstück *n* insert; (*Verbindung*) connection; (elec) adapter

Zwi'schenstufe *f* intermediate stage

Zwi'schenträger **-in** §6 *mf* gossip

Zwi'schenwand *f* partition wall

Zwi'schenzeit *f* interval, meanwhile

Zwist [tsvist] *m* (-es;-e) discord; quarrel; (*Feindschaft*) enmity

Zwi'stigkeit *f* (-;-en) hostility

zwitschern ['tsvit/ərn] *tr*—**e-n z.** (coll) have a shot of liquor ‖ *intr* chirp

Zwitter ['tsvitər] *m* (-s;-) hermaphrodite

Zwit'terfahrzeug *n* (mil) half-track

zwo [tsvo] *adj & pron* (coll) two

zwölf ['tsvœlf] *invar adj & pron* twelve ‖ **Zwölf** *f* (-;-en) twelve

Zwölffin'gerdarm *m* duodenum

zwölfte ['tsvœlftə] §9 *adj & pron* twelfth

Zwölftel ['tsvœftəl] *n* (-s;-) twelfth (*part*)

Zyklon [tsy'klon] *m* (-s;-e), **Zyklone** [tsy'klonə] *f* (-;-n) cyclone

Zyk·lus ['tsyklus] *m* (-;-len [lən]) cycle; (*Reihe*) series, course

Zylinder [tsy'lindər] *m* (-s;-) cylinder (*e-r Lampe*) chimney; (*Hut*) top hat

zylindrisch [tsy'lindri/] *adj* cylindrical

Zyniker ['tsynikər] *m* (-s;-) cynic; (philos) Cynic

zynisch ['tsyni/] *adj* cynical

Zypern ['tsypərn] *n* (-s;) Cyprus

Zypresse [tsy'presə] *f* (-;-n) cypress

Zyste ['tsystə] *f* (-;-n) cyst

GRAMMATICAL EXPLANATIONS

All [...]ers [...]
(In [...] their [...]
of the [...] column [...]
trans[...] [...]p 4

German Pronunciation

All the German letters and their variant spellings are listed below (in column 1) with their IPA symbols (in column 2), a description of their sounds (in column 3), and German examples with phonetic transcription (in column 4).

		VOWELS	
SPELLING	SYMBOL	APPROXIMATE SOUND	EXAMPLES
a	[a]	Like *a* in English *swat*	Apfel ['apfəl], lassen ['lasən], Stadt [ʃtat]
a	[ɑ]	Like *a* in English *father*	Vater ['fɑtər], laden ['lɑdən]
aa	[ɑ]	" "	Paar [pɑr], Staat [ʃtɑt]
ah	[ɑ]	" "	Hahn [hɑn], Zahl [tsɑl]
ä	[ɛ]	Like *e* in English *met*	Äpfel ['epfəl], lässig ['lesɪç], Städte ['ʃtetə]
ä	[e]	Like *e* in English *they* (without the following sound of *y*)	mäßig ['mesɪç], Väter ['fetər]
äh	[e]	" "	ähnlich ['enlɪç], Zähne ['tsenə]
e	[ə]	Like *e* in English *system*	Bitte ['bɪtə], rufen ['rufən]
e	[ɛ]	Like *e* in English *met*	Kette ['ketə], messen ['mesən]
e	[e]	Like *e* in English *they* (without the following sound of *y*)	Feder ['fedər], regnen ['regnən]
ee	[e]	" "	Meer [mer], Seele ['zelə]
eh	[e]	" "	Ehre ['erə], zehn [tsen]
i	[ɪ]	Like *i* in English *sin*	bin [bɪn], Fisch [fɪʃ]
i	[i]	Like *i* in English *machine*	Maschine [ma'ʃinə], Lid [lit]
ih	[i]	" "	ihm [im], ihr [ir]
ie	[i]	" "	dieser ['dizər], tief [tif]
o	[ɔ]	Like *o* in English *often*	Gott [gɔt], offen ['ɔfən]
o	[o]	Like *o* in English *note*, but without the diphthongal glide	holen ['holən], Rose ['rozə]
oo	[o]	" "	Boot [bot], Moos [mos]
oh	[o]	" "	Bohne ['bonə], Kohle ['kolə]
ö	[œ]	The lips are rounded for [ɔ] and held without moving while the sound [ɛ] is pronounced.	Götter ['gœtər], öffnen ['œfnən]

3a

SPELLING	SYMBOL	APPROXIMATE SOUND	EXAMPLES
ö	[ø]	The lips are rounded for [o] and held without moving while the sound [e] is pronounced.	böse ['bøzə], Löwe ['løvə]
öh	[ø]	" "	Röhre ['rørə], Söhne ['zønə]
u	[ʊ]	Like *u* in English *bush*	Busch [bʊʃ], muß [mʊs], Hund [hʊnt]
u	[u]	Like *u* in English *rule*	Schule ['ʃulə], Gruß [grus]
uh	[u]	" "	Uhr [ur], Ruhm [rum]
ü	[ʏ]	The lips are rounded for [u] and held without moving while the sound [ɪ] is pronounced.	Hütte ['hʏtə], müssen ['mʏsən]
ü	[y]	The lips are rounded for [u] and held without moving while the sound [i] is pronounced.	Schüler ['ʃylər], Grüße ['grysə]
üh	[y]	" "	Mühle ['mylə], kühn [kyn]
y	[ʏ]	Like *ü* [ʏ] above	Mystik ['mʏstɪk]
y	[y]	Like *ü* [y] above	Mythe ['mytə]

DIPHTHONGS

SPELLING	SYMBOL	APPROXIMATE SOUND	EXAMPLES
ai	[aɪ]	Like *i* in English *night*	Saite ['zaɪtə], Mais [maɪs]
au	[aʊ]	Like *ou* in English *ouch*	kaufen ['kaufən], Haus [haus]
äu	[ɔɪ]	Like *oy* in English *toy*	träumen ['trɔɪmən], Gebäude [gə'bɔɪdə]
ei	[aɪ]	Like *i* in English *night*	Zeit [tsaɪt], nein [naɪn]
eu	[ɔɪ]	Like *oy* in English *toy*	heute ['hɔɪtə], Eule ['ɔɪlə]

CONSONANTS

SPELLING	SYMBOL	APPROXIMATE SOUND	EXAMPLES
b	[b]	Like *b* in English *boy*	Buch [bux], haben ['habən]
b	[p]	Like *p* in English *lap*	gelb [gelp], lieblich ['liplɪç]
c	[k]	Like *c* in English *car*	Clown [klaun], Café [ka'fe]
c	[ts]	Like *ts* in English *its*	Cäsar ['tsezar], Centrale [tsen'tralə]
ch	[x]	This sound is made by breathing through a space between the back of the tongue and the soft palate.	auch [aux], Buche ['buxə]
ch	[ç]	This sound is made by breathing through a space left when the front of the tongue is pressed close to the hard palate with the tip of the tongue behind the lower teeth.	ich [ɪç], Bücher ['byçər], Chemie [çɛ'mi], durch [durç]

4a

SPELLING	SYMBOL	APPROXIMATE SOUND	EXAMPLES
ch	[k]	Like *k* in English *key*	Charakter [ka'raktər], Chor [kor]
ch	[ʃ]	Like *sh* in English *shall*	Chef [ʃef], Chassis [ʃa'si]
chs	[ks]	Like *x* in English *box*	sechs [zɛks], Wachs [vaks]
ck	[k]	Like *k* in English *key* When *ck* in a vocabulary entry in this Dictionary has to be divided by an accent mark, the word is first spelled with *ck* and is then repeated in parentheses with the *ck* changed to *kk* in accordance with the principle which requires this change when the division comes at the end of the line, e.g., Deckenlicht (Dek'kenlicht).	wecken ['vɛkən], Ruck [rʊk]
đ	[d]	Like *d* in English *door*	laden ['lɑdən], deutsch [dɔɪtʃ]
đ	[t]	Like *t* in English *time*	Freund [frɔɪnt], Hund [hʊnt]
đt	[t]	" "	verwandt [fer'vant], Stadt [ʃtat]
f	[f]	Like *f* in English *five*	Fall [fal], auf [aʊf]
g	[g]	Like *g* in English *go*	geben ['gebən], Regen ['regən]
g	[k]	Like *k* in English *key*	Krieg [krik], Weg [vek]
g	[ç]	See ch [ç] above	wenig ['veniç], häufig ['hɔɪfɪç]
h	[h]	Like *h* in English *hat*	Haus [haʊs], Freiheit ['fraɪhaɪt]
j	[j]	Like *y* in English *yet*	Jahr [jɑr], jener ['jenər]
k	[k]	Like *k* in English *key*	Kaffee [ka'fe], kein [kaɪn]
l	[l]	This sound is made with the tip of the tongue against the back of the upper teeth and the side edges of the tongue against the side teeth.	laden ['lɑdən], fahl [fɑl]
m	[m]	Like *m* in English *man*	mehr [mer], Amt [amt]
n	[n]	Like *n* in English *neck*	Nase ['nɑzə], kaufen ['kaʊfən]
n	[ŋ]	Like *n* in English *sink*	sinken ['zɪŋkən], Funke ['fʊŋkə]
ng	[ŋ]	" "	Finger ['fɪŋər], Rang [raŋ]
p	[p]	Like *p* in English *pond*	Perle ['pɛrlə], Opfer ['ɔpfər]
ph	[f]	Like *f* in English *five*	Phase ['fɑzə], Graphik ['grɑfɪk]
qu	[kv]	Does not occur in English.	Quelle ['kvɛlə], bequem [bə'kvem]
r	[r]	This sound is a trilled sound made by vibrating the tip of the tongue against the upper gums or by vibrating the uvula.	rufen ['rufən], Rede ['redə]

5a

SPELLING	SYMBOL	APPROXIMATE SOUND	EXAMPLES
s	[s]	Like s in English sock	Glas [glɑs], erst [erst]
s	[z]	Like z in English zest	sind [zɪnt], Eisen ['aɪzən]
sch	[ʃ]	Like sh in English shall	Schuh [ʃu], Schnee [ʃne]
sp	[ʃp]	Does not occur in English in the initial position.	sparen ['ʃpɑrən], Spott [ʃpɔt]
ss	[s]	This spelling is used only in the intervocalic position and when the preceding vowel sound is one of the following: [a], [e], [ɪ], [ə], [œ], [ʊ], [ʏ]	Klasse ['klasə], essen ['esən], wissen ['vɪsən], Gosse ['gɔsə], Rössel ['rœsəl], Russe ['rusə], müssen ['mʏsən]
ß	[s]	This spelling is used instead of ss (a) when in the final position in a word or component, (b) when followed by a consonant, or (c) when intervocalic and preceded by a diphthong or one of the following vowel sounds: [ɑ], [e], [i], [o], [ø], [u], [y]	(a) Fluß [flʊs], Flußufer ['flʊsufər], (b) läßt [lest], (c) dreißig ['draɪsɪç], Straße ['ʃtrɑsə], mäßig ['mesɪç], schießen ['ʃisən], stoßen ['ʃtosən], Stößel ['ʃtøsəl], Muße ['musə], müßig ['mysɪç]
st	[ʃt]	Does not occur in English in the initial position.	Staub [ʃtaʊp], stehen ['ʃte·ən]
t	[t]	Like t in English time	Teller ['tɛlər], Tau [taʊ]
th	[t]	" "	Theater [te'ɑtər], Thema ['tema]
ti+ vowel	[tsj]	Does not occur in English.	Station [sta'tsjon], Patient [pa'tsjent]
tz	[ts]	Like ts in English its	schätzen ['ʃɛtsən], jetzt [jetst]
v	[f]	Like f in English five	Vater ['fɑtər], brav [brɑf]
v	[v]	Like v in English vat	November [nɔ'vembər], Verb [verp]
w	[v]	" "	Wasser ['vasər], wissen ['vɪsən]
x	[ks]	Like x in English box	Export [ɛks'pɔrt], Taxe ['taksə]
z	[ts]	Like ts in English its	Zahn [tsɑn], reizen ['raɪtsən]

German Grammar References

§1. Declension of the Definite Article

	SINGULAR			PLURAL
	MASC	FEM	NEUT	MASC, FEM, NEUT
NOM	der	die	das	die
ACC	den	die	das	die
DAT	dem	der	dem	den
GENIT	des	der	des	der

§2. Declension of the Indefinite Article and the Numeral Adjective

	SINGULAR			PLURAL
1.	MASC	FEM	NEUT	MASC, FEM, NEUT
NOM	ein	eine	ein	
ACC	einen	eine	ein	
DAT	einem	einer	einem	
GENIT	eines	einer	eines	

2. Other words that are declined like **ein** are: **kein** *no, not any* and the possessive adjectives **mein** *my;* **dein** *thy, your;* **sein** *his; her; its;* **ihr** *her; their;* **Ihr** *your;* **unser** *our;* **euer** *your.* Unlike **ein**, they have plural forms, as shown in the following paradigm.

	SINGULAR			PLURAL
	MASC	FEM	NEUT	MASC, FEM, NEUT
NOM	kein	keine	kein	keine
ACC	keinen	keine	kein	keine
DAT	keinem	keiner	keinem	keinen
GENIT	keines	keiner	keines	keiner

3. The **e** of **er** of **unser** and **euer** is generally dropped when followed by an ending, as shown in the following paradigm. And instead of the **e** of **er** dropping, the **e** of final **em** and **en** in these words may drop.

	SINGULAR			PLURAL
	MASC	FEM	NEUT	MASC, FEM, NEUT
NOM	unser	uns(e)re	unser	uns(e)re
ACC	uns(e)ren or unsern	uns(e)re	unser	uns(e)re
DAT	uns(e)rem or unserm	uns(e)rer	uns(e)rem or unserm	uns(e)ren or unsern
GENIT	uns(e)res	uns(e)rer	uns(e)res	uns(e)rer

All adjectives that follow these words are declined in the mixed declension.

4. The pronouns **einer** and **keiner**, as well as all the possessive pronouns, are declined according to the strong declension of adjectives. The neuter forms **eines** and **keines** have the variants **eins** and **keins**.

5. When the possessive adjectives are used as possessive pronouns, they are declined according to the strong declension of adjectives. When preceded by the definite article, they are declined according to the weak declension of adjectives. There are also possessive pronouns with the infix **ig** which are always preceded by the definite article and capitalized and are declined according to the declension of adjectives, e.g., **der, die, das Meinige** *mine*.

§3. Declension of the Demonstrative Pronoun

	SINGULAR			PLURAL
	MASC	FEM	NEUT	MASC, FEM, NEUT
NOM	dieser	diese	dieses or dies	diese
ACC	diesen	diese	dieses or dies	diese
DAT	diesem	dieser	diesem	diesen
GENIT	dieses	dieser	dieses	dieser

Other words that are declined like **dieser** are **jeder** *each;* **jener** *that;* **mancher** *many a;* **welcher** *which.* All adjectives that come after these words are declined in the weak declension.

§4. Declension of Adjectives.

Adjectives have three declensions: 1) the strong declension, 2) the weak declension, and 3) the mixed declension. On both sides of this Dictionary, adjectives occurring in the expressions consisting solely of an adjective and a noun are entered in their weak forms.

1. The strong declension of adjectives, whose endings are shown in the following table, is used when the adjective is not preceded by **der** or by **dieser** or any of the other words listed in §3 or by **ein** or any of the other words listed in §2.

	SINGULAR			PLURAL
	MASC	FEM	NEUT	MASC, FEM, NEUT
NOM	–er	–e	–es	–e
ACC	–en	–e	–es	–e
DAT	–em	–er	–em	–en
GENIT	–en	–er	–en	–er

2. The weak declension of adjectives, whose endings are shown in the following table, is used when the adjective is preceded by **der** or **dieser** or any of the other words listed in §3.

	SINGULAR			PLURAL
	MASC	FEM	NEUT	MASC, FEM, NEUT
NOM	–e	–e	–e	–en
ACC	–en	–e	–e	–en
DAT	–en	–en	–en	–en
GENIT	–en	–en	–en	–en

3. The **der** component of **derselbe** and **derjenige** is the article **der** and is declined like it, while the **–selbe** and **–jenige** components are declined according to the weak declension of adjectives.

4. The mixed declension of adjectives, whose endings are shown in the following table, is used when the adjective is preceded by **ein** or **kein** or any of the other words listed in §2.

8a

	SINGULAR			PLURAL
	MASC	FEM	NEUT	MASC, FEM, NEUT
NOM	−er	−e	−es	−en
ACC	−en	−e	−es	−en
DAT	−en	−en	−en	−en
GENIT	−en	−en	−en	−en

§5. Adjectives Used as Nouns. When an adjective is used as a masculine, feminine, or neuter noun, it is spelled with an initial capital letter and is declined as an adjective in accordance with the principles set forth in §4. We have, for example, der or die **Fremde** the foreigner; der or die **Angestellte** *the employee;* ein **Angestellter** *a (male) employee,* eine **Angestellte** *a (female) employee;* das **Deutsche** German (i.e., *language*). These nouns are entered on both sides of this Dictionary in the weak form of the adjective and their genitives and plurals are not shown.

§6. Many masculine nouns ending in −er and −ier have feminine forms made by adding −in. The masculine forms have genitives made by adding s and remain unchanged in the plural, while the feminine forms remain unchanged in the singular and have plurals made by adding −nen. For example:

	MASC	FEM
NOM SG	**Verkäufer** *salesperson (salesman)*	**Verkäuferin** *salesperson (saleslady)*
GENIT SG	**Verkäufers**	**Verkäuferin**
NOM PL	**Verkäufer**	**Verkäuferinnen**

§7. Many masculine nouns ending in −at (e.g., Advokat), or in −ant (e.g., Musikant), or in −ist (*e.g.,* Artist), or in −ent (e.g., Student), or in −graph (e.g., Choreograph), or in −ot (e.g., Pilot), or in −et (e.g.,Analphabet), or in −it (e.g., Israelit), or in −ast (e.g., Phantast), etc., have feminine forms made by adding −in. The masculine forms have genitives and plurals made by adding −en, while the femine forms remain unchanged in the singular and have plurals made by adding −nen. For example:

	MASC	FEM
NOM SG	**Advokat** *attorney*	**Advokatin** *attorney*
GENIT SG	**Advokaten**	**Advokatin**
NOM PL	**Advokaten**	**Advokatinnen**

§8. Many masculine nouns ending in −ar (e.g., Antiquar) or in −är (e.g., Milliardär) have feminine forms made by adding −in. The masculine forms have genitives made by adding −(e)s and plurals made by adding −e, while the feminine forms remain unchanged in the singular and have plurals made by adding −nen. For example:

	MASC	FEM
NOM SG	**Antiquar** *antique dealer*	**Antiquarin** *antique dealer*
GENIT SG	**Antiquar(e)s**	**Antiquarin**
NOM PL	**Antiquare**	**Antiquarinnen**

§9. Adjectives are generally given in their uninflected form, the form in which they appear in the predicate, e.g., **billig, reich, alt.** However, those adjectives which do not occur in an uninflected form are given with the weak ending −e, which in the nominative is the same for all genders, e.g., **andere, besondere, beste, hohe.**

§10. Adjectives which denote languages may be used as adverbs. When so used with **sprechen, schreiben, können,** and a few others, they are translated in English by the corresponding noun, and actual and immediate action is implied, e.g., **deutsch sprechen** *to speak German* (i.e., to be speaking German right now). Adjectives which denote languages may be capitalized and used as invariable nouns, and when so used with **sprechen, schreiben, können,** and a few other verbs, general action is implied, e.g., **Deutsch sprechen** *to speak German* (i.e., to know how to speak German, to be a speaker of German).

With other verbs, these adjectives used as adverbs are translated by the corresponding noun preceded by "auf" or "in", e.g., **sich auf (or in) deutsch unterhalten** *to converse in German.*

§11. Personal and Reflexive Pronouns

PERSONS	SUBJECT	PERSONAL DIRECT OBJECT	PERSONAL INDIRECT OBJECT	REFLEXIVE DIRECT OBJECT	REFLEXIVE INDIRECT OBJECT
SG					
1	ich *I*	mich *me*	mir *(to) me*	mich *myself*	mir *(to) myself*
2	du *you*	dich *you*	dir *(to) you*	dich *yourself*	dir *(to) yourself*
3 MASC	er *he; it*	ihn *him; it*	ihm *(to) him; (to) it*	sich *himself; itself*	sich *(to) himself; (to) itself*
3 FEM	sie *she; it*	sie *her; it*	ihr *(to) her; (to) it*	sich *herself; itself*	sich *(to) herself; (to) itself*
3 NEUT	es *it; she; he*	es *it; her; him*	ihm *(to) it; (to) her; (to) him*	sich *itself; herself; himself*	sich *(to) itself; (to) herself; (to) himself*
PL					
1	wir *we*	uns *us*	uns *(to) us*	uns *ourselves*	uns *(to) ourselves*
2	ihr *you*	euch *you*	euch *(to) you*	euch *yourselves*	euch *(to) yourselves*
3	sie *they*	sie *them*	ihnen *(to) them*	sich *themselves*	sich *(to) themselves*
2 FORMAL SG & PL	Sie *you*	Sie *you*	Ihnen *(to) you*	sich *yourself; yourselves*	sich *(to) yourself; (to) yourselves*

er means *it* when it stands for a masculine noun that is the name of an animal or a thing, as **Hund, Tisch**. **sie** means *it* when it stands for a feminine noun that is the name of an animal or a thing, as **Hündin, Feder**. **es** means *she* when it stands for a neuter noun that is the name of a female person, as **Fräulein, Mädchen, Weib**; it means *he* when it stands for a neuter noun that is the name of a male person, as **Söhnchen, Söhnlein**. The dative means also *from me, from you*, etc., with certain verbs expressing separation such as **entnehmen**.

11a

§12. Separable and Inseparable Prefixes. Many verbs can be compounded either with a prefix, which is always inseparable and unstressed, or with a combining form (conventionally called also a prefix), which can be separable and stressed or inseparable and unstressed. Exceptions are indicated by the abbreviations *sep* and *insep*.

1. The inseparable prefixes are be–, emp–, ent–, er–, ge–, ver–, and zer–, e.g., beglei′ten, erler′nen, verste′hen. They are never stressed.

2. The separable prefixes (i.e., combining forms) are prepositions, e.g., auf– as in auf′tragen, adverbs, e.g., vorwärts– as in vor′wärtsbringen, adjectives, e.g., tot– as in tot′schlagen, nouns, e.g., maschine– as in maschi′neschreiben, or other verbs, e.g., stehen– as in ste′henbleiben. They are always stressed except as provided for those listed in the following section.

3. The prefixes (combining forms) durch, hinter, über, um, unter, wider, and wieder, when their meaning is literal, are separable and stressed, e.g. durch′schneiden *cut through, cut in two,* and, when their meaning is figurative or derived, are inseparable and unstressed, e.g., durchschnei′den *cut across, traverse.*

4. A compound prefix is (a) inseparable if it consists of an inseparable prefix plus a separable prefix, e.g., beauf′tragen, (b) separable if it consists of a separable prefix plus an inseparable prefix, e.g.,vor′bereiten—er bereitet etwas vor, and (c) separable if it consists of two separable prefixes, e.g., vorbei′laufen—sie lief vorbei. Although verbs falling under (b) are separable, they do not take –ge– in the past participle, e.g., vor′bereitet (past participle of vorbereiten). But they do take the infix –zu– in the infinitive, e.g., vor′zubereiten. Note that compound prefixes falling under (c) are stressed on the second of the two separable components.

§13. German verbs are regarded as reflexive regardless of whether the reflexive pronoun is the direct or indirect object of the verb.

§14. The declension of German nouns is shown by giving the genitive singular followed by the nominative plural, in parentheses after the abbreviation indicating gender. This is done by presenting the whole noun by a hyphen with which the ending and/or the umlaut may or may not be shown according to the inflection; e.g., Stadt [/tat] *f* (–/tat) means der Stadt and die Städte. If the noun has no plural, the closing parenthesis comes immediately after the semicolon following the genitive singular, e.g., Kleidung [′klaidʊŋ] *f* (–;). In loan words in which the ending changes in the plural, the centered period is used to mark off the portion of the word that has to be detached before the portion showing the plural form is added, e.g., Da·tum [′dɑtʊm] *n* (–s;-ten [tən]).

When a vowel is added to a word ending in ß, the ß remains if it is preceded by a diphthong or one of the following vowel sounds: [ɑ], [e], [i], [o], [ø], [y], e.g., Stoß [/tos], plural: Stöße; Strauß, plural: Sträuße, but changes to ss if it is preceded by one of the following vowel sounds: [a], [ɛ], [ɪ], [ɔ], [œ], [ʊ], [ʏ], e.g., Roß [rɔs], plural Rosses. In this Dictionary the inflection of words in which ß does not change is shown in the usual way, e.g., Stoß [/tos] *m* (–es;̈e); Strauß [/traus] *m* (–es;̈e), while the inflection of words in which ß changes to ss is shown in monosyllables by repeating the full word in its inflected forms, e.g., Roß [rɔs] *n* (Rosses; Rosse) and in polysyllables by marking off with a centered dot the final syllable and then repeating it in its inflected forms, e.g., Ver·laß [fer′las] *m* (–lasses;).

§15. When a word ending in a double consonant is combined with a following word beginning with the same single consonant followed by a vowel, the resultant group of three identical consonants is shortened to two, e.g., Schiff combined with Fahrt makes Schiffahrt and Schall combined with Lehre makes

12a

Schallehre.[1] However, when such a compound as a vocabulary entry has to be divided by an accent mark, the word is first spelled with two identical consonants and is then repeated in parentheses with three identical consonants, e.g., **Schiffahrt (Schiff/fahrt).** Furthermore, when such a compound has to be divided because the first component comes at the end of a line and is followed by a hyphen and the second component begins the following line, the three consonants are used, e.g., **Schiff–fahrt** and **Schall–lehre.**

When the medial group **ck** in a vocabulary entry has to be divided by an accent mark, the word is first spelled with **ck** and is then repeated in parentheses with the **ck** changed to **kk** in accordance with the orthographic principle which requires this change when the division comes at the end of the line, e.g., **Deckenlicht (Dek/kenlicht).**

---

[1] If the intial consonant of the following word is followed by a consonant instead of a vowel, the group of three identical consonants remains, e.g., **Fetttropfen, Rohstofffrage.**

German Model Verbs

These verbs are models for all the verbs that appear as vocabulary entries in the German-English part of this Dictionary. If a section number referring to this table is not given with an entry, it is understood that the verb is a weak verb conjugated like **loben, reden, handeln,** or **warten.** If a section number is given, it is understood that the verb is a strong, mixed, or irregular verb and that it is identical in all forms with the model referred to in its radical vowel or diphthong and the consonants that follow the radical. Thus **schneiden** is numbered §106 to refer to the model **leiden.** Such words include the model itself, e.g., **denken,** numbered §66 to refer to the model **denken,** compounds of the model, e.g., **bekommen,** numbered §99 to refer to the model **kommen,** and verbs that have the same radical component, e.g., **empfehlen,** numbered §51 to refer to the model **befehlen.**

If a strong or mixed verb in a given function (transitive or intransitive) and/or meaning may be conjugated also as a weak verb, this is indicated by the insertion of the section number of the appropriate weak verb (**loben, handeln, reden,** or **warten**) after the section number of the model strong verb, e.g., **dingen** §142 & §109.

If a strong or mixed verb in a different function is conjugated as a weak verb, this is indicated by dividing the two functions by parallels and showing the conjugation of each by the insertion of the appropriate section numbers, e.g., **hängen** §92 *tr* . . . || §109 *intr.*

If a strong or mixed verb in a different meaning is conjugated as a weak verb, this is indicated by dividing the two meanings by parallels and showing the conjugation of each by the insertion of the appropriate section numbers, e.g., **bewegen** *tr* move, set in motion . . . || §56 *tr* move, induce.

It is understood that verbs with inseparable prefixes, verbs with compound separable prefixes of which the first component is separable and the second inseparable, and verbs ending in –ieren do not take ge in the past participle.

No account is taken here of the auxiliary used in forming compound tenses. The use of SEIN is indicated in the body of the Dictionary.

Alternate forms are listed in parentheses immediately below the corresponding principal part of the model verb.

14a

§	INFINITIVE	3D SG PRESENT INDICATIVE	IMPERFECT INDICATIVE	IMPERFECT SUBJUNCTIVE	PAST PARTICIPLE
§50	backen	bäckt	buk	büke	gebacken
§51	befehlen	befiehlt	befahl	beföhle	befohlen
§52	beginnen	beginnt	begann	begönne (begänne)	begonnen
§53	beißen	beißt	biß	bisse	gebissen
§54	bergen	birgt	barg	bärge (bürge)	geborgen
§55	bersten	birst (berstet)	barst	bärste (börste)	geborsten
§56	bewegen	bewegt	bewog	bewöge	bewogen
§57	biegen	biegt	bog	böge	gebogen
§58	bieten	bietet	bot	böte	geboten
§59	binden	bindet	band	bände	gebunden
§60	bitten	bittet	bat	bäte	gebeten
§61	blasen	bläst	blies	bliese	geblasen
§62	bleiben	bleibt	blieb	bliebe	geblieben
§63	braten	brät	briet	briete	gebraten
§64	brechen	bricht	brach	bräche	gebrochen
§65	bringen	bringt	brachte	brächte	gebracht
§66	denken	denkt	dachte	dächte	gedacht
§67	dreschen	drischt	drosch (drasch)	drösche (dräsche)	gedroschen
§68	dünken	dünkt (deucht)	dünkte (deuchte)	dünkte (deuchte)	gedünkt (gedeucht)

	INFINITIVE	3D SG PRESENT INDICATIVE	IMPERFECT INDICATIVE	IMPERFECT SUBJUNCTIVE	PAST PARTICIPLE
§69	dürfen	darf	durfte	dürfte	gedurft (dürfen)
§70	essen	ißt	aß	äße	gegessen
§71	fahren	fährt	fuhr	führe	gefahren
§72	fallen	fällt	fiel	fiele	gefallen
§73	fangen	fängt	fing	finge	gefangen
§74	fechten	ficht	focht	föchte	gefochten
§75	fliehen	flieht	floh	flöhe	geflohen
§76	fließen	fließt	floß	flösse	geflossen
§77	frieren	friert	fror	fröre	gefroren
§78	gären	gärt	gor	göre	gegoren
§79	gebären	gebiert	gebar	gebäre	geboren
§80	geben	gibt	gab	gäbe	gegeben
§81	gedeihen	gedeiht	gedieh	gediehe	gediehen
§82	gehen	geht	ging	ginge	gegangen
§83	gelten	gilt	galt	gälte (gölte)	gegolten
§84	genesen	genest	genas	genäse	genesen
§85	gleichen	gleicht	glich	gliche	geglichen
§86	gleiten	gleitet	glitt	glitte	geglitten
§87	graben	gräbt	grub	grübe	gegraben
§88	greifen	greift	griff	griffe	gegriffen
§89	haben	hat	hatte	hätte	gehabt
§90	halten	hält	hielt	hielte	gehalten

16a

	INFINITIVE	3D SG PRESENT INDICATIVE	IMPERFECT INDICATIVE	IMPERFECT SUBJUNCTIVE	PAST PARTICIPLE
§91	handeln	handelt	handelte	handelte	gehandelt
§92	hängen	hängt	hing	hinge	gehangen
§93	hauen	haut	hieb	hiebe	gehauen
§94	heben	hebt	hob	höbe	gehoben
§95	heißen	heißt	hieß	hieße	geheißen
§96	helfen	hilft	half	hälfe	geholfen
				(hülfe)	
§97	kennen	kennt	kannte	kennte	gekannt
§98	kiesen	kiest	kor	köre	gekoren
§99	kommen	kommt	kam	käme	gekommen
§100	können	kann	konnte	könnte	gekonnt (können)
§101	kreischen	kreischt	kreischte (krisch)	kreischte (krische)	gekreischt (gekrischen)
§102	kriechen	kriecht	kroch	kröche	gekrochen
§103	laden	lädt	lud	lüde	geladen
§104	lassen	läßt	ließ	ließe	gelassen
§105	laufen	läuft	lief	liefe	gelaufen
§106	leiden	leidet	litt	litte	gelitten
§107	lesen	liest	las	läse	gelesen
§108	liegen	liegt	lag	läge	gelegen
§109	loben	lobt	lobte	lobte	gelobt
§110	löschen	lischt	losch	lösche	geloschen
§111	lügen	lügt	log	löge	gelogen

	INFINITIVE	3D SG PRESENT INDICATIVE	IMPERFECT INDICATIVE	IMPERFECT SUBJUNCTIVE	PAST PARTICIPLE
§112	meiden	meidet	mied	miede	gemieden
§113	melken	melkt	molk	mölke	gemolken
§114	mögen	mag	mochte	möchte	gemocht (mögen)
§115	müssen	muß	mußte	müßte	gemußt (müssen)
§116	nehmen	nimmt	nahm	nähme	genommen
§117	pflegen	pflegt	pflog	pflöge	gepflogen
§118	preisen	preist	pries	priese	gepriesen
§119	quellen	quillt	quoll	quölle	gequollen
§120	reden	redet	redete	redete	geredet
§121	rinnen	rinnt	rann	ränne (rönne)	geronnen
§122	rufen	ruft	rief	riefe	gerufen
§123	salzen	salzt	salzte	salzte	gesalzen
§124	saufen	säuft	soff	söffe	gesoffen
§125	saugen	saugt	sog	söge	gesogen
§126	schaffen	schafft	schuf	schüfe	geschaffen
§127	schallen	schallt	scholl	schölle	geschollen
§128	scheinen	scheint	schien	schiene	geschienen
§129	scheren	schert (schiert)	schor	schöre	geschoren
§130	schieben	schiebt	schob	schöbe	geschoben
§131	schlafen	schläft	schlief	schliefe	geschlafen

18a

	INFINITIVE	3D SG PRESENT INDICATIVE	IMPERFECT INDICATIVE	IMPERFECT SUBJUNCTIVE	PAST PARTICIPLE
§132	schlagen	schlägt	schlug	schlüge	geschlagen
§133	schmelzen	schmilzt	schmolz	schmölze	geschmolzen
§134	schrecken	schrickt	schrak	schräke	geschrocken
§135	schreien	schreit	schrie	schriee	geschrie(e)n
§136	schwimmen	schwimmt	schwamm	schwämme (schwömme)	geschwommen
§137	schwören	schwört	schwur (schwor)	schwüre	geschworen
§138	sehen	sieht	sah	sähe	gesehen
§139	sein	ist	war	wäre	gewesen
§140	senden	sendet	sandte	sendete	gesandt
§141	sieden	siedet	sott	sötte	gesotten
§142	singen	singt	sang	sänge	gesungen
§143	sinken	sinkt	sank	sänke	gesunken
§144	sitzen	sitzt	saß	säße	gesessen
§145	sollen	soll	sollte	sollte	gesollt (sollen)
§146	stehen	steht	stand	stände (stünde)	gestanden
§147	stehlen	stiehlt	stahl	stähle (stöhle)	gestohlen
§148	steigen	steigt	stieg	stiege	gestiegen
§149	sterben	stirbt	starb	stürbe	gestorben
§150	stoßen	stößt	stieß	stieße	gestoßen

	INFINITIVE	3D SG PRESENT INDICATIVE	IMPERFECT INDICATIVE	IMPERFECT SUBJUNCTIVE	PAST PARTICIPLE
§151	treffen	trifft	traf	träfe	getroffen
§152	treten	tritt	trat	träte	getreten
§153	triefen	trieft	troff	tröffe	getroffen
§154	tun	tut	tat	täte	getan
§155	wachsen	wächst	wuchs	wüchse	gewachsen
§156	wägen	wiegt	wog	wöge	gewogen
§157	warten	wartet	wartete	wartete	gewartet
§158	waschen	wäscht	wusch	wüsche	gewaschen
§159	werden	wird	wurde (ward)	würde	geworden (worden)
§160	werfen	wirft	warf	würfe	geworfen
§161	wissen	weiß	wußte	wüßte	gewußt
§162	wollen	will	wollte	wollte	gewollt (wollen)
§163	ziehen	zieht	zog	zöge	gezogen
§164	klimmen	klimmt	klomm	klömme	geklommen
§165	küren	kürt	kor	köre	gekoren
§166	schinden	schindet	schund	schünde	geschunden

Die Aussprache des Englischen

Die nachstehenden Lautzeichen bezeichnen fast alle Laute der englischen Sprache:

VOKALE		
LAUTZEICHEN	**UNGEFÄHRER LAUT**	**BEISPIEL**
[æ]	Offener als *ä* in *hätte*	hat [hæt]
[ɑ]	Wie *a* in *Vater*	father [ˈfɑðər]
	Wie *a* in *Mann*	proper [ˈprɑpər]
[ɛ]	Wie *e* in *Fett*	met [mɛt]
[e]	Offener als *eej* in *Seejungfrau*	fate [fet]
		they [ðe]
[ə]	Wie *e* in *finden*	haven [ˈhɛvən]
		pardon [ˈpɑrdən]
[i]	Wie *ie* in *sie*	she [ʃi]
		machine [məˈʃin]
[ɪ]	Offener als *i* in *bitte*	fit [fɪt]
		beer [bɪr]
[o]	Offenes *o* mit anschließendem kurzem (halbvokalischem) *u*	nose [noz]
		road [rod]
		row [ro]
[ɔ]	Wie *o* in *oft*	bought [bɔt]
		law [lɔ]
[ʌ]	Wie *er* in *jeder* (umgangssprachlich)	cup [kʌp]
		come [kʌm]
		mother [ˈmʌðər]
[ʊ]	Wie *u* in *Fluß*	pull [pʊl]
		book [bʊk]
		wolf [wʊlf]
[u]	Wie *u* in *Fluß*	move [muv]
		tomb [tum]

DIPHTHONGE		
LAUTZEICHEN	**UNGEFÄHRER LAUT**	**BEISPIEL**
[aɪ]	Wie *ei* in *nein*	night [naɪt]
		eye [aɪ]
[aʊ]	Wie *au* in *Haus*	found [faʊnd]
		cow [kaʊ]
[ɔɪ]	Wie *eu* in *heute*	voice [vɔɪs]
		oil [ɔɪl]

KONSONANTEN		
LAUTZEICHEN	**UNGEFÄHRER LAUT**	**BEISPIEL**
[b]	Wie *b* in *bin*	bed [bɛd]
		robber [ˈrɑbər]

21a

LAUTZEICHEN	UNGEFÄHRER LAUT	BEISPIEL
[d]	Wie d in du	dead [dɛd] add [æd]
[dʒ]	Wie dsch in Dschungel	gem [dʒɛm] jail [dʒel]
[ð]	d als Reibelaut ausgesprochen	this [ðɪs] Father ['faðər]
[f]	Wie f in fett	face [fes] phone [fon]
[g]	Wie g in gehen	go [go] get [gɛt]
[h]	Wie h in Haus	hot [hɑt] alcohol ['ælkə ˌhɔl]
[j]	Wie j in ja	yes [jɛs] unit ['junɪt]
[k]	Wie k in kann	cat [kæt] chord [kɔrd] kill [kɪl]
[l]	Wie l in lang, aber mit angehobenem Zungenrücken	late [let] allow [ə'lau]
[m]	Wie m in mehr	more [mor] command [kə'mænd]
[n]	Wie n in Nest	nest [nɛst] manner ['mænər]
[ŋ]	Wie ng in singen	king [kɪŋ] conquer ['kɑŋkər]
[p]	Wie p in Pech	pen [pɛn] cap [kæp]
[r]	Im Gegensatz zum deutschen gerollten Zungenspitzen- oder Zäpfchen-r, ist das englische r mit retroflexer Zungenstellung und gerundeten Lippen zu artikulieren.	run [rʌn] far [fɑr] art [ɑrt] carry ['kæri]
[s]	Wie s in es	send [sɛnd] cellar ['sɛlər]
[ʃ]	Wie sch in Schule	shall [ʃæl] machine [mə'ʃin] nation ['neʃən]
[t]	Wie t in Tee	ten [tɛn] dropped [drɑpt]
[tʃ]	Wie tsch in deutsch	child [tʃaɪld] much [mʌtʃ] nature ['netʃər]
[θ]	Ist als stimmloser linguadentaler Lispellaut zu artikulieren	think [θɪŋk] truth [truθ]
[v]	Wie w in was	vest [vɛst] over ['ovər] of [ɑv]
[w]	Ist als Halbvokal zu artikulieren	work [wʌrk] tweed [twid] queen [kwin]
[z]	Ist stimmhaft zu artikulieren wie s in so	zeal [zil] busy ['bɪzi] his [hɪz] winds [wɪndz]
[ʒ]	Wie j in Jalousie	azure ['eʒər] measure ['mɛʒər]

Aussprache der zusammengesetzten Wörter

Im englisch-deutschen Teil dieses Wörterbuches ist die Aussprache aller einfachen englischen Wörter in einer Neufassung der Lautzeichen des Internationalen Phonetischen Alphabets in eckigen Klammern angegeben.

22a

Außer den mit Präfixen, Suffixen und Wortbildungselementen gebildeten Zusammensetzungen gibt es im Englischen drei Arten von zusammengesetzten Wörtern: (1) zusammengeschriebene, z.B. **bookcase** Bücherregal, (2) mit Bindestrich geschriebene, z.B. **short-circuit** kurzschließen, und (3) getrennt geschriebene, z.B. **post card** Postkarte. Die Aussprache der englischen zusammengesetzten Wörter ist nicht angegeben, sofern die Aussprache der Bestandteile an der Stelle angegeben ist, wo sie als selbständige Stichwörter erscheinen; angegeben ist jedoch die Betonung durch Haupt- und Nebentonakzent und zwar jeweils am Ende der betonten Silben, z.B. **book′case′**, **short′-cir′cuit**, **post′ card′**.

In Hauptwörtern, in denen der Nebenton auf den Bestandteilen –man und –men liegt, wird der Vokal dieser Bestandteile wie in den Wörtern **man** und **men** ausgesprochen, z.B. **mailman** ['mel‚mæn] und **mailmen** ['mel‚mɛn]. In Hauptwörtern, in denen diese Bestandteile unbetont bleiben, wird der Vokal beider Bestandteile als schwa ausgesprochen, z.B. **policeman** [pə'lismən] und **policemen** [pə'lismən]. Es gibt Hauptwörter, in denen diese Bestandteile entweder mit dem Nebenton oder unbetont ausgesprochen werden, z.B. **doorman** ['dor‚mæn] oder ['dormən] und **doormen** ['dor‚men] oder ['dormən]. In diesem Wörterbuch ist die Lautschrift für diese Wörter nicht angegeben, sofern sie für den ersten Bestandteil dort angeführt ist, wo er als Stichwort erscheint; angegeben sind jedoch Haupt- und Nebenton:

> mail′man s (–men′)
> police′man s (–men)
> door′man′ & door′man s (–men′ & –men)

Aussprache des Partizip Perfekt

Bei Wörtern, die auf –ed (oder –d nach stummem e) enden und nach den nachstehenden Regeln ausgesprochen werden, ist die Aussprache in diesem Wörterbuch nicht angegeben, sofern sie für die endungslose Form dort angegeben ist, wo diese als Stichwort erscheint. Die Doppelschreibung des Schlußkonsonanten nach einfachem betontem Vokal hat keinen Einfluß auf die Aussprache der Endung –ed.

Die Endung –ed (oder –d nach stummem e) der Vergangenheit, des Partizip Perfekt und gewisser Adjektive hat drei verschiedene Aussprachen je nach dem Klang des Konsonanten am Stammende.

1) Wenn der Stamm auf einen stimmhaften Konsonanten mit Ausnahme von [d] ausgeht, nämlich [b], [g], [l], [m], [n], [ŋ], [r], [v], [z], [ʒ], oder auf einen Vokal, wird –ed als [d] ausgesprochen.

KLANG DES STAMMENDES	INFINITIV	VERGANGENHEIT UND PARTIZIP PERFEKT
[b]	ebb [ɛb]	ebbed [ɛbd]
	rob [rɑb]	robbed [rɑbd]
	robe [rob]	robed [robd]
[g]	egg [ɛg]	egged [ɛgd]
	sag [sæg]	sagged [sægd]
[l]	mail [mel]	mailed [meld]
	scale [skel]	scaled [skeld]
[m]	storm [stɔrm]	stormed [stɔrmd]
	bomb [bɑm]	bombed [bɑmd]
	name [nem]	named [nemd]
[n]	tan [tæn]	tanned [tænd]
	sign [saɪn]	signed [saɪnd]
	mine [maɪn]	mined [maɪnd]
[ŋ]	hang [hæŋ]	hanged [hæŋd]
[r]	fear [fɪr]	feared [fɪrd]
	care [ker]	cared [kerd]
[v]	rev [rev]	revved [revd]
	save [sev]	saved [sevd]
[z]	buzz [bʌz]	buzzed [bʌzd]
[ð]	smooth [smuð]	smoothed [smuðd]
	bathe [beð]	bathed [beðd]
[ʒ]	massage [mə'sɑʒ]	massaged [mə'sɑʒd]
[dʒ]	page [pedʒ]	paged [pedʒd]
Klang des Vokals	key [ki]	keyed [kid]
	sigh [saɪ]	sighed [saɪd]
	paw [pɔ]	pawed [pɔd]

2) Wenn der Stamm auf einen stimmlosen Konsonanten mit Ausnahme von [t]
ausgeht, nämlich: [f], [k], [p], [s], [θ], [ʃ] oder [tʃ], wird –ed als [t] ausgesprochen.

KLANG DES STAMMENDES	INFINITIV	VERGANGENHEIT UND PARTIZIP PERFEKT
[f]	loaf [lof] knife [naɪf]	loafed [loft] knifed [naɪft]
[k]	back [bæk] bake [bek]	backed [bækt] baked [bekt]
[p]	cap [kæp] wipe [waɪp]	capped [kæpt] wiped [waɪpt]
[s]	hiss [hɪs] mix [mɪks]	hissed [hɪst] mixed [mɪkst]
[θ]	lath [læθ]	lathed [læθt]
[ʃ]	mash [mæʃ]	mashed [mæʃt]
[tʃ]	match [mætʃ]	matched [mætʃt]

3) Wenn der Stamm auf einen Dentallaut ausgeht, nämlich: [t] oder [d], wird
–ed als [ɪd] oder [əd] ausgesprochen.

KLANG DES STAMMENDES	INFINITIV	VERGANGENHEIT UND PARTIZIP PERFEKT
[t]	wait [wet] mate [met]	waited ['wetɪd] mated ['metɪd]
[d]	mend [mɛnd] wade [wed]	mended ['mɛndɪd] waded ['wedɪd]

Es ist zu beachten, daß die Doppelschreibung des Schlußkonsonanten nach
einem einfachen betonten Vokal die Aussprache der Endung –ed nicht beein-
flußt: **batted** ['bætɪd], **dropped** [drɑpt], **robbed** [rɑbd].

Diese Regeln gelten auch für zusammengesetzte Adjektive, die auf –ed enden.
Für diese Adjektive ist nur die Betonung angegeben, sofern die Aussprache der
beiden Bestandteile ohne die Endung –ed dort angegeben ist, wo sie als Stichwörter erscheinen, z.B. o'pen-mind'ed.

Es ist jedoch zu beachten, daß bei manchen Adjektiven, deren Stamm auf
einen anderen Konsonanten als [d] oder [t] ausgeht, das –ed als [ɪd] ausgesprochen wird; in diesem Fall ist die volle Aussprache in phonetischer Umschrift angegeben, z.B. **blessed** ['blɛsɪd], **crabbed** ['kræbɪd].

PART TWO

English-German

ENGLISH—GERMAN

A

A, a [e] *s* erster Buchstabe des englischen Alphabets; (mus) A *n*; **A flat** As *n*; **A sharp** Ais *n*

a [e], [ə] *indef art* ein ‖ *prep* pro; **once a year** einmal im Jahr

abandon [ə'bændən] *s*—**with a.** rückhaltlos ‖ *tr* (*forsake*) verlassen; (*give up*) aufgeben; (*a child*) aussetzen; (*a position*) (mil) überlassen; **a. oneself to** sich ergeben (*dat*)

abase [ə'bes] *tr* demütigen

abasement [ə'besmənt] *s* Demütigung *f*

abashed [ə'bæʃt] *adj* fassungslos

abate [ə'bet] *tr* mäßigen ‖ *intr* nachlassen

abbess ['æbrs] *s* Äbtissin *f*

abbey ['æbi] *s* Abtei *f*

abbot ['æbət] *s* Abt *m*

abbreviate [ə'brivɪ‚et] *tr* abkürzen

abbreviation [ə‚brivɪ'eʃən] *s* Abkürzung *f*

ABC's [‚e‚bi'siz] *spl* Abc *n*

abdicate ['æbdɪ‚ket] *tr* niederlegen; (*a right, claim*) verzichten auf (*acc*) ‖ *intr* abdanken

abdomen ['æbdəmən] *s* Unterleib *m*

abdominal [æb'dɑmɪnəl] *adj* Unterleibs-

abduct [æb'dʌkt] *tr* entführen

abet [ə'bet] *v* (*pret & pp* **abetted**; *ger* **abetting**) *tr* (*a person*) aufhetzen; (*a crime*) Vorschub leisten (*dat*)

abeyance [ə'be‚əns] *s*—**in a.** in der Schwebe

ab·hor [æb'hɔr] *v* (*pret & pp* **-horred**; *ger* **-horring**) *tr* verabscheuen

abhorrent [æb'hɔrənt] *adj* verhaßt

abide [ə'baɪd] *v* (*pret & pp* **abode** [ə'bod] **& abided**) *intr*—**a. by** (*an agreement*) sich halten an (*acc*); (*a promise*) halten

ability [ə'bɪlɪti] *s* Fähigkeit *f*; **to the best of one's a.** nach bestem Vermögen

abject [æb'dʒekt] *adj* (*servile*) unterwürfig; (*poverty*) äußerst

ablative ['æblətɪv] *s* Ablativ *m*

ablaze [ə'blez] *adj* in Flammen; (**with**) glänzend (vor *dat*); (*excited*) (**with**) erregt (vor *dat*)

able ['ebəl] *adj* fähig, tüchtig; **be a. to** (*inf*) können (*inf*)

able-bodied ['ebəl'badid] *adj* kräftig; (mil) wehrfähig; **a. seaman** Vollmatrose *m*

ably ['ebli] *adv* mit Geschick

abnormal [æb'nɔrməl] *adj* abnorm

abnormality [‚æbnɔr'mælɪti] *s* Ungewöhnlichkeit *f*; (pathol) Mißbildung *f*

abnor'mal psychol'ogy *s* Psychopathologie *f*

aboard [ə'bord] *adv* an Bord; **all a.!** (*a ship*) alles an Bord! (*a bus, plane, train*) alles einsteigen! ‖ *prep* (*a ship*) an Bord (*genit*); (*a bus, train*) in (*dat*)

abode [ə'bod] *s* Wohnsitz *m*

abolish [ə'balɪʃ] *tr* aufheben, abschaffen

abominable [ə'bɑmɪnəbəl] / *adj* abscheulich

aborigines [‚æbə'rɪdʒɪ‚niz] *spl* Ureinwohner *pl*, Urvolk *n*

abort [ə'bɔrt] *tr* (rok) vorzeitig zur Explosion bringen ‖ *intr* fehlgebären; (fig) fehlschlagen

abortion [ə'bɔrʃən] *s* Abtreibung *f*

abortive [ə'bɔrtɪv] *adj* (fig) mißlungen; **prove a.** fehlschlagen

abound [ə'baʊnd] *intr* reichlich vorhanden sein; **a. in** reich sein an (*dat*)

about [ə'baʊt] *adv* umher, herum; (*approximately*) ungefähr, etwa; **be a. to** (*inf*) im Begriff sein zu (*inf*) ‖ *prep* (*around*) um (*acc*); (*concerning*) über (*acc*); (*approximately at*) gegen (*acc*)

about' face' *interj* kehrt!

about'-face' *s*—**do an a.** (fig) umschwenken; **complete a.** (fig) völliger Umschwung *m*

above [ə'bʌv] *adj* obig ‖ *adv* oben, droben ‖ *prep* (*position*) über (*dat*); (*direction*) über (*acc*); (*physically*) oberhalb (*genit*); **a. all** vor allem

above'board' *adj & adv* ehrlich, redlich

above'-men'tioned *adj* obenerwähnt, obig

abrasion [ə'breʒən] *s* Abschleifen *n*; (*of the skin*) Abschürfung *f*

abrasive [ə'bresɪv] *adj* abschleifend; (*character*) auf die Nerven gehend ‖ *s* Schleifmittel *n*

abreast [ə'brest] *adj & adv* nebeneinander; **keep a. of** Schritt halten mit

abridge [ə'brɪdʒ] *tr* verkürzen

abridgement [ə'brɪdʒmənt] *s* Verkürzung *f*

abroad [ə'brɔd] *adv* im Ausland; (*direction*) ins Ausland; (*out of doors*) draußen

abrogate ['æbrə‚get] *tr* abschaffen

abrupt [ə'brʌpt] *adj* (*sudden*) jäh; (*curt*) schroff; (*change*) unvermittelt; (*style*) abgerissen

abscess ['æbses] *s* Geschwür *n*, Abszeß *m*

abscond [æb'skand] *intr* (**with**) durchgehen (mit)

absence ['æbsəns] *s* Abwesenheit *f*; (*lack*) Mangel *m*; **in the a. of** in Ermangelung von (or *genit*)

ab'sence without' leave' s unerlaubte Entfernung f von der Truppe

absent ['æbsənt] adj abwesend; **be a.** fehlen || [æb'sent] tr—a. **oneself** (stay away) fernbleiben; (go away) sich entfernen

absentee [ˌæbsən'ti] s Abwesende mf

ab'sent-mind'ed adj geistesabwesend

absolute ['æbsəˌlut] adj absolut

absolutely ['æbsəˌlutli] adv absolut, völlig || [ˌæbsə'lutli] adv (coll) ganz bestimmt, jawohl; **a. not!** keine Rede!

absolve [æb'salv] tr (from sin, an obligation) lossprechen; (sins) vergeben

absorb [æb'sɔrb] tr aufsaugen; (a shock) dämpfen; (engross) ganz in Anspruch nehmen; **be absorbed in** vertieft sein in (acc)

absorbent [æb'sɔrbənt] adj aufsaugend **absor'bent cot'ton** s Verbandswatte f

absorb'ing adj (fig) packend

abstain [æb'sten] intr (from) sich enthalten (genit); (parl) sich der Stimme enthalten

abstention [æb'stenʃən] s (from) Enthaltung f (von); (parl) Stimmenthaltung f

abstinence ['æbstɪnəns] s Enthaltsamkeit f; (from) Enthaltung f (von)

abstinent ['æbstɪnənt] adj enthaltsam

abstract ['æbstrækt] adj abstrakt || s (summary) Abriß m; **in the a.** im und für sich (betrachtet) || [æb-'strækt] tr (the general from the specific) abstrahieren; (summarize) kurz zusammenfassen; (purloin) entwenden

abstruse [æb'strus] adj dunkel

absurd [æb'sʌrd] adj unsinnig

absurdity [æb'sʌrdɪti] s Unsinn m

abundance [ə'bʌndəns] s (of) Fülle f (von), Überfluß m (an dat, von)

abundant [ə'bʌndənt] adj reichlich; **a. in** reich an (dat)

abuse [ə'bjus] s (misuse) Mißbrauch m; (insult) Beschimpfung f; (physical ill-treatment) Mißhandlung f || [ə'bjuz] tr mißhandeln; (insult) beschimpfen; (ill-treat) mißhandeln; (a girl) schänden

abusive [ə'bjusɪv] adj mißbräuchlich; (treatment) beleidigend; **a. language** Schimpfworte pl; **become a.** ausfällig werden

abut [ə'bʌt] v (pret & pp abutted; ger abutting) intr—**a. on** grenzen an (acc)

abutment [ə'bʌtmənt] s (of arch) Strebepfeiler m; (of bridge) Widerlager n

abyss [ə'bɪs] s Abgrund m

academic [ˌækə'demɪk] adj akademisch

academ'ic gown' s Talar m

academy [ə'kædəmi] s Akademie f

accede [æk'sid] intr beistimmen; **a. to** (s.o.'s wishes) gewähren; (an agreement) beitreten (dat); **a. to the throne** den Thron besteigen

accelerate [æk'seləˌret] tr & intr beschleunigen

accelerator [æk'seləˌretər] s Gashebel m

accent ['æksent] s (stress) Betonung f; (peculiar pronunciation) Akzent m || [æk'sent] tr betonen

ac'cent mark' s Tonzeichen n, Akzent m

accentuate [æk'sentʃʊˌet] tr betonen

accept [æk'sept] tr annehmen; (one's fate, blame) auf sich [acc] nehmen; (put up with) hinnehmen; (recognize) anerkennen

acceptable [æk'septəbəl] adj annehmbar; (pleasing) angenehm; (welcome) willkommen

acceptance [æk'septəns] s Annahme f; (recognition) Anerkennung f

access ['ækses] s Zugang m; (to a person) Zutritt m; (data proc) Zugriff m

accessible [æk'sesɪbəl] adj (to) zugänglich (für)

accession [æk'seʃən] s (to an office) Antritt m; **a. to the throne** Thronbesteigung f

accessory [æk'sesəri] adj (subordinate) untergeordnet; (additional) zusätzlich || s Zubehörteil n; (to a crime) Teilnehmer –in mf; (after the fact) Begünstiger –in mf; (before the fact) Anstifter –in mf

ac'cess road' s Zufahrtsstraße f; (on a turnpike) Zubringerstraße f

accident ['æksɪdənt] s (mishap) Unfall m; (chance) Zufall m; **by a.** zufälligerweise; **have an a.** verunglücken

accidental [ˌæksɪ'dentəl] adj zufällig; **a. death** Unfalltod m || s (mus) Versetzungszeichen n

acclaim [ə'klem] s Beifall m || tr (e.g., as king) begrüßen, akklamieren

acclamation [ˌæklə'meʃən] s Beifall m

acclimate ['æklɪˌmet] tr akklimatisieren || intr (to) sich gewöhnen (an acc)

accommodate [ə'kaməˌdet] tr (oblige) aushelfen (dat); (have room for) Platz haben für

accom'modating adj gefällig

accommodation [əˌkamə'deʃən] s (convenience) Annehmlichkeit f; (adaptation, adjustment) Anpassung f; (willingness to please) Gefälligkeit f; (compromise) Übereinkommen n; **accommodations** (lodgings) Unterkunft f

accompaniment [ə'kʌmpənɪmənt] s Begleitung f

accompanist [ə'kʌmpənɪst] s Begleiter –in mf

accompa·ny [ə'kʌmpəni] v (pret & pp –nied) tr begleiten

accomplice [ə'kʌmplɪs] m Mitschuldige mf

accomplish [ə'kʌmplɪʃ] tr (a task) vollenden; (a goal) erreichen

accom'plished adj (skilled) ausgezeichnet

accomplishment [ə'kʌmplɪʃmənt] s (completion) Vollendung f; (achievement) Leistung f

accord [ə'kɔrd] s Übereinstimmung f; **in a. with** übereinstimmend mit; **of**

one's own a. aus eigenem Antriebe
|| *tr* gewähren || *intr* übereinstimmen
accordingly [ə'kɔrdɪŋli] *adv* demgemäß
accord'ing to' *prep* gemäß (*dat*), laut
(*genit* or *dat*), nach (*dat*)
accordion [ə'kɔrdɪ-ən] *s* Akkordeon *n*
accost [ə'kɔst] *tr* ansprechen
account [ə'kaʊnt] *s* Rechnung *f*; (*narrative*) Erzählung *f*; (*report*) Bericht
m; (*importance*) Bedeutung *f*; (com)
Konto *n*; **by all accounts** nach allem,
was man hört; **call to a.** zur Rechenschaft ziehen; **on a. of** wegen; **on no
a.** auf keinen Fall; **render an a. of
s.th. to s.o.** j-m Rechenschaft von
etw ablegen; **settle accounts with**
(coll) abrechnen mit; **take into a.** in
Betracht ziehen
accountable [ə'kaʊntəbəl] *adj* (*explicable*) erklärlich; (*responsible*) (**for**)
verantwortlich (für)
accountant [ə'kaʊntənt] *s* Rechnungsführer –in *mf*, Buchhalter –in *mf*
account'ing *s* Rechnungswesen *n*
accouterments [ə'kutərmənts] *spl* Ausrüstung *f*
accredit [ə'krɛdɪt] *tr* (*e.g., an ambassador*) beglaubigen; (*a school*) bestätigen; (*a story*) als wahr anerkennen; (*give credit for*) gutschreiben
accrue [ə'kru] *intr* anwachsen; (*said
of interest*) auflaufen || *intr* sich
anhäufen
accumulation [ə‚kjumjə'leʃən] *s* Anhäufung *f*
accuracy ['ækjərəsi] *s* Genauigkeit *f*
accurate ['ækjərɪt] *adj* genau
accursed [ə'kʌrsɪd], [ə'kʌrst] *adj* verwünscht
accusation [‚ækjə'zeʃən] *s* Anschuldigung *f*; (jur) Anklage *f*
accusative [ə'kjuzətɪv] *s* Akkusativ *m*
accuse [ə'kjuz] *tr* (**of**) beschuldigen
(*genit*); (jur) (**of**) anklagen (wegen)
accustom [ə'kʌstəm] *tr* (**to**) gewöhnen
(an *acc*); **become accustomed to** sich
gewöhnen an (*an acc*)
ace [es] *s* (aer, cards) As *n*
acetate ['æsɪ‚tet] *s* Azetat *n*; (tex)
Azetatseide *f*
ace'tic ac'id [ə'sitɪk] *s* Essigsäure *f*
acetone ['æsɪ‚ton] *s* Azeton *n*
acet'ylene torch' [ə'sɛtɪ‚lin] *s* Schweißbrenner *m*
ache [ek] *s* Schmerz *m* || *intr* schmerzen; **a. for** (coll) sich sehnen nach
achieve [ə'tʃiv] *tr* erlangen; (*success*)
erzielen; (*a goal*) erreichen
achievement [ə'tʃivmənt] *s* (*something
accomplished*) Leistung *f*; (*great
deed*) Großtat *f*; (*heroic deed*)
Heldentat *f*; (*of one's object*) Erreichung *f*
achieve'ment test' *s* Leistungsprüfung *f*
Achil'les' ten'don [ə'kɪlis] *s* Achillessehne *f*
acid ['æsɪd] *adj* sauer || *s* Säure *f*
acidity [ə'sɪdɪti] *s* Säure *f*, Schärfe *f*;
(*of the stomach*) Magensäure *f*
ac'id test' *s* (fig) Feuerprobe *f*
acidy ['æsɪdi] *adj* säuerlich, säurig
acknowledge [æk'nɑlɪdʒ] *tr* anerkennen; (*admit*) zugeben; (*receipt*) bestätigen
acknowledgment [æk'nɑlɪdʒmənt] *s*
Anerkennung *f*; (*e.g., of a letter*)
Bestätigung *f*
acme ['ækmi] *s* Höhepunkt *m*
acne ['ækni] *s* (pathol) Akne *f*
acolyte ['ækə‚laɪt] *s* Ministrant *m*
acorn ['ekɔrn] *s* Eichel *f*
acoustic(al) [ə'kustɪk(əl)] *adj* akustisch, Gehör–, Hör–
acous'tical tile' *s* Dämmplatte *f*
acoustics [ə'kustɪks] *s* & *spl* Akustik *f*
acquaint [ə'kwent] *tr*—**a. s.o. with
s.th.** j-n mit etw bekanntmachen,
j-m etw mitteilen; **be acquainted
with** kennen; **get acquainted with**
kennenlernen
acquaintance [ə'kwentəns] *s* Bekanntschaft *f*; (*person*) Bekannte *mf*
acquiesce [‚ækwɪ'es] *intr* (**in**) einwilligen (in *acc*)
acquiescence [‚ækwɪ'esəns] *s* (**in**) Einwilligung *f* (in *acc*)
acquire [ə'kwaɪr] *tr* erwerben, sich
[*dat*] anschaffen; **a. a taste for** Geschmack gewinnen an (*dat*)
acquisition [‚ækwɪ'zɪʃən] *s* Anschaffung *f*
acquisitive [ə'kwɪzɪtɪv] *adj* gewinnsüchtig
acquit [ə'kwɪt] *v* (*pret* & *pp* acquitted;
ger acquitting) *tr* freisprechen
acquittal [ə'kwɪtəl] *s* Freispruch *m*
acre ['ekər] *s* Acre *m*
acreage ['ekərɪdʒ] *s* Fläche *f*
acrid ['ækrɪd] *adj* beißend, scharf
acrobat ['ækrə‚bæt] *s* Akrobat –in *mf*
acrobatic [‚ækrə'bætɪk] *adj* akrobatisch || **acrobatics** *spl* Akrobatik *f*;
(aer) Kunstflug *m*
acronym ['ækrənɪm] *s* Akronym *n*
across [ə'krɔs] *adv* herüber, hinüber;
a. from gegenüber (*dat*); **ten feet a.**
zehn Fuß im Durchmesser || *prep*
(quer) über (*acc*); (*on the other side
of*) jenseits (*genit*); **come a.** (*a person*) treffen; (*a thing*) stoßen auf
(*acc*); **come a. with it!** (*say it!*) heraus damit!; (*give it!*) her damit!
across'-the-board' *adj* allgemein
acrostic [ə'krɔstɪk] *s* Akrostichon *n*
act [ækt] *s* Tat *f*, Handlung *f*; (coll)
Theater *n*; (jur) Gesetz *n*; (telv)
Nummer *f*; (theat) Akt *m*, Aufzug
m; **catch in the act** auf frischer Tat
ertappen || *tr* spielen; || *intr* (*take
action*) handeln; (*function*) wirken;
(*behave*) (**like**) sich benehmen (wie);
(theat & fig) Theater spielen; **act as**
dienen als; **act as if** so tun, als ob;
act on (*follow*) befolgen; (*affect*)
(ein)wirken auf (*acc*)
act'ing *adj* stellvertretend; (theat)
Bühnen– || *s* (*as an art*) Schauspielkunst *f*
action ['ækʃən] *s* Tätigkeit *f*, Tat *f*;
(*effect*) Wirkung *f*; (jur) Klage *f*;
(mil) Gefecht *n*; (tech) Wirkungsweise *f*; **go into a.** eingreifen; **put
out of a.** (mil) außer Gefecht setzen;
(tech) außer Betrieb setzen; **see a.**
(mil) an der Front kämpfen

activate ['æktɪ‚vet] *tr* aktivieren; (mil) aufstellen

active ['æktɪv] *adj* tätig; *(member)* ordentlich; *(gram, mil)* aktiv

ac'tive voice' *s* Tätigkeitsform *f*

activist ['æktɪvɪst] *s* Aktivist –in *mf*

activity [æk'tɪvɪti] *s* Tätigkeit *f*

act' of God' *s* höhere Gewalt *f*

act' of war' *s* Angriffshandlung *f*

actor ['æktər] *s* Schauspieler *m*

actress ['æktrɪs] *s* Schauspielerin *f*

actual ['æktʃʋ-əl] *adj* wirklich

actually ['æktʃʋ-əli] *adv* *(really)* wirklich; *(as a matter of fact)* eigentlich

actuary ['æktʃʋ‚eri] *s* Aktuar –in *mf*

actuate ['æktʃʋ‚et] *tr* in Bewegung setzen; *(incite)* antreiben

acumen [ə'kjumən] *s* Scharfsinn *m*

acupuncture ['ækjə‚pʌŋkt∫ər] *s* Akupunktur *f*

acute [ə'kjut] *adj* *(stage, appendicitis)* akut; *(pain)* scharf; *(need)* vordringlich; *(vision)* scharf; *(hearing)* fein; *(problem)* brennend; *(shortage)* bedenklich; *(angle)* spitz

A.D. *abbr* n. Chr. *(nach Christus)*

ad [æd] *s* (coll) Anzeige *f*; **put an ad in the papers** inserieren

adage ['ædɪdʒ] *s* Sprichwort *n*

adamant ['ædəmənt] *adj* unnachgiebig

Ad'am's ap'ple ['ædəmz] *s* Adamsapfel *m*

adapt [ə'dæpt] *tr* *(to)* anpassen *(dat* or an *acc)*; **a. to the stage** für die Bühne bearbeiten; **a. to the screen** verfilmen || *intr* sich anpassen

adaptation [‚ædæp'teʃən] *s* *(adjustment)* *(to)* Anpassung *f* *(an acc)*; *(reworking, rewriting)* *(for)* Bearbeitung *f* (für)

adapter [ə'dæptər] *s* Zwischenstück *n*; (elec) Zwischenstecker *m*

add [æd] *tr* hinzufügen; (math) addieren; **add** *(e.g., 10%)* **to the price** auf den Preis aufschlagen; **add up** zusammenrechnen || *intr* (math) addieren; **add to** *(in number)* vermehren; *(in size)* vergrößern; **add up** (coll) stimmen; **add up to** betragen

adder ['ædər] *s* Natter *f*, Otter *f*

addict ['ædɪkt] *s* Süchtige *mf* || [ə'dɪkt] *tr*—**a. oneself to** sich ergeben *(dat)*

addict'ed *adj* ergeben; **a. to drugs** rauschgiftsüchtig

addiction [ə'dɪk/ən] *s* *(to)* Sucht *f* *(nach)*

add'ing machine' *s* Addiermaschine *f*

addition [ə'dɪʃən] *s* Hinzufügung *f*, Zusatz *m*; *(to a family, possessions)* Zuwachs *m*; *(to a building)* Anbau *m*; (math) Addition *f*; **in a.** außerdem; **in a. to** außer

additional [ə'dɪʃənəl] *adj* zusätzlich

additive ['ædɪtɪv] *s* Zusatz *m*

address [ə'drɛs], ['ædrɛs] *s* Adresse *f*, Anschrift *f* || [ə'drɛs] *s* Rede *f*; **deliver an a.** e–e Rede halten || *tr* *(a letter)* *(to)* adressieren *(an acc)*; *(words, a question)* *(to)* richten *(an acc)*; *(an audience)* e–e Ansprache halten an *(acc)*

adduce [ə'd(j)us] *tr* anführen

adenoids ['ædə‚nɔɪdz] *spl* Polypen *pl*

adept [ə'dɛpt] *adj* *(in)* geschickt (in *dat)*

adequate ['ædɪkwɪt] *adj* angemessen; *(to)* ausreichend (für)

adhere [æd'hɪr] *intr* *(to)* haften (an *dat)*; (fig) *(to)* festhalten (an *dat)*

adherence [æd'hɪrəns] *s* *(to)* Festhalten *n* (an *dat)*; (fig) *(to)* Festhalten *n* *(an dat)*, Beharren *n* (bei)

adherent [æd'hɪrənt] *s* Anhänger –in *mf*

adhesion [æd'hiʒən] *s* *(sticking)* Ankleben *n*; *(loyalty)* Anhänglichkeit *f*; *(pathol, phys)* Adhäsion *f*

adhesive [æd'hisɪv] *adj* anklebend || Klebemittel *n*, Klebstoff *m*

adhe'sive tape' *s* Heftpflaster *m*

adieu [ə'd(j)u] *s* *(adieus & adieux)* Lebewohl *n* || *interj* lebe wohl!

adjacent [ə'dʒesənt] *adj* *(to)* angrenzend (an *acc)*; *(angles)* Nebenzend

adjective ['ædʒɪktɪv] *s* Eigenschaftswort *n*, Adjektiv *n*

adjoin [ə'dʒɔɪn] *tr* angrenzen an *(acc)* || *intr* angrenzen, naheliegen

adjoin'ing *adj* angrenzend; **a. rooms** Nebenzimmer *pl*

adjourn [ə'dʒʌrn] *tr* vertagen || *intr* sich vertagen

adjournment [ə'dʒʌrnmənt] *s* Vertagung *f*

adjudge [ə'dʒʌdʒ] *tr* *(a prize)* zusprechen; **a. s.o. guilty** j–n für schuldig erklären

adjudicate [ə'dʒudɪ‚ket] *tr* gerichtlich entscheiden

adjunct ['ædʒʌŋkt] *s* *(to)* Zusatz *m* (zu)

adjust [ə'dʒʌst] *tr* *(to the right position)* einstellen; *(to an alternate position)* verstellen; *(fit)* (to an) anpassen *(dat* or an *acc)*; *(differences)* ausgleichen; *(an account)* bereinigen; (ins) berechnen || *intr* *(to)* sich anpassen *(dat* or an *acc)*

adjustable [ə'dʒʌstəbəl] *adj* verstellbar

adjuster [ə'dʒʌstər] *s* (ins) Schadenssachverständiger –in *mf*

adjustment [ə'dʒʌstmənt] *s* *(to)* Anpassung *f* *(dat* or an *acc)*; *(of an account)* Bereinigung *f*; (ins) Berechnung *f*; *(mach)* Einstellung *f*

adjutant ['ædʒətənt] *s* Adjutant *m*

ad-lib ['æd'lɪb] *v (pret & pp)* **–libbed**; *ger* **–libbing** *s & intr* improvisieren

ad-man ['ædmæn] *s* (–men) Werbefachmann *m*; *(writer)* Werbetexter *m*

administer [æd'mɪnɪstər] *tr* verwalten; *(help)* leisten; *(medicine)* eingeben; *(an oath)* abnehmen; *(punishment)* verhängen; *(a sacrament)* spenden; **a. justice** Recht sprechen || *intr*—**a. to** dienen *(dat)*

administration [æd‚mɪnɪs'treʃən] *s* *(of an institution)* Verwaltung *f*; *(of an official)* Amtsführung *f*; *(government)* Regierung *f*; *(period of government)* Regierungszeit *f*; *(of a president)* Amtszeit *f*; *(of tests)* Durchführung *f*; *(of an oath)* Abnahme *f*; *(of a sacrament)* Spendung *f*; **a. of justice** Rechtspflege *f*

administrator [æd'mɪnɪs‚tretər] *s* Verwalter –in *mf*

admiral ['ædmɪrəl] *s* Admiral *m*

admiration [‚ædmɪ'reʃən] *s* Bewunderung *f*

admire [æd'maɪr] *tr* (**for**) bewundern (wegen)

admirer [æd'maɪrər] *s* Bewunderer –in *mf*; (*of a woman*) Verehrer *m*

admissible [æd'mɪsɪbəl] *adj* (& jur) zulässig

admission [æd'mɪʃən] *s* (*entry*) Eintritt *m*; (*permission to enter*) Eintrittserlaubnis *f*; (*entry fee*) Eintrittsgebühr *f*; (*of facts*) Anerkennung *f*; (*of guilt*) Eingeständis *n*; (*enrollment*) (**to, into**) Aufnahme *f* (in *acc*); (**to**) (*a profession*) Zulassung *f* (zu)

ad·mit [æd'mɪt] *v* (*pret & pp* **–mitted;** *ger* **–mitting**) *tr* (hin)einlassen; (**to**) (*a hospital, a society*) aufnehmen (in *acc*); (**to**) (*a profession*) zulassen (zu); (*accept*) anerkennen; (*concede*) zugeben; (*a crime, guilt*) eingestehen ‖ *intr*—**a. of** zulassen

admittance [æd'mɪtəns] *s* Eintritt *m*; **no a.** Eintritt verboten

admittedly [æd'mɪtɪdli] *adv* anerkanntermaßen

admixture [æd'mɪkstʃər] *s* Beimischung *f*

admonish [æd'manɪʃ] *tr* ermahnen

admonition [‚ædmə'nɪʃən] *s* Ermahnung *f*

ado [ə'du] *s* Getue *n*; **much ado about nothing** viel Lärm um nichts; **without further ado** ohne weiteres

adobe [ə'dobi] *s* Lehmstein *m*

adolescence [‚ædə'lesəns] *s* Jugendalter *n*

adolescent [‚ædə'lesənt] *adj* jugendlich ‖ *s* Jugendliche *mf*

adopt [ə'dapt] *tr* (*a child*) adoptieren; (*an idea*) annehmen

adopt'ed child' *s* Adoptivkind *n*

adoption [ə'dapʃən] *s* (*of a child*) Adoption *f*; (*of an idea*) Annahme *f*

adorable [ə'dorəbəl] *adj* anbetungswürdig; (coll) entzückend

adore [ə'dor] *tr* anbeten; (coll) entzückend finden

adorn [ə'dɔrn] *tr* schmücken

adornment [ə'dɔrnmənt] *s* Schmuck *m*

adrenaline [ə'drenəlɪn] *s* Adrenalin *n*

adrift [ə'drɪft] *adj*—**be a.** treiben; (fig) weder aus noch ein wissen

adroit [ə'drɔɪt] *adj* geschickt, gewandt

adulation [‚ædjə'leʃən] *s* Schmeichelei *f*

adult [ə'dʌlt], ['ædʌlt] *adj* erwachsen ‖ *s* Erwachsene *mf*

adult' educa'tion *s* Erwachsenenbildung *f*

adulterate [ə'dʌltə‚ret] *tr* verfälschen; (*e.g., wine*) panschen

adulterer [ə'dʌltərər] *s* Ehebrecher *m*

adulteress [ə'dʌltərɪs] *s* Ehebrecherin *f*

adulterous [ə'dʌltərəs] *adj* ehebrecherisch

adultery [ə'dʌltəri] *s* Ehebruch *m*

advance [æd'væns] *s* Fortschritt *m*; (*money*) Vorschuß *m*; **in a.** im vor-

aus; **make advances to** (*e.g., a girl*) Annäherungsversuche machen bei ‖ *tr* vorrücken; (*a clock*) vorstellen; (*money*) vorschießen; (*a date*) aufschieben; (*an opinion*) vorbringen; (*s.o.'s interests*) fördern; (*in rank*) befördern ‖ *intr* vorrücken

advancement [æd'vænsmənt] *s* Fortschritt *m*; (*promotion*) Beförderung *f*; (*of a cause*) Förderung *f*

advance' pay'ment *s* Voraus(be)zahlung *f*

advantage [æd'væntɪdʒ] *s* Vorteil *m*; **be of a.** nützlich sein; **take a. of** ausnutzen; **to a.** vorteilhaft

advantageous [‚ædvən'tedʒəs] *adj* vorteilhaft

advent ['ædvent] *s* Ankunft *f*; **Advent** Advent *m*, Adventszeit *f*

adventure [æd'ventʃər] *s* Abenteuer *n*

adventurer [æd'ventʃərər] *s* Abenteurer *m*

adventuress [æd'ventʃərɪs] *s* Abenteurerin *f*

adventurous [æd'ventʃərəs] *adj* (*person*) abenteuerlustig; (*undertaking*) abenteuerlich

adverb ['ædvərb] *s* Umstandswort *n*

adverbial [æd'vʌrbɪ·əl] *adj* adverbial

adversary ['ædvər‚seri] *s* Gegner –in *mf*

adverse [æd'vʌrs], ['ædvʌrs] *adj* ungünstig, nachteilig

adversity [æd'versɪti] *s* Unglück *n*, Not *f*

advertise ['ædvər‚taɪz] *tr* Reklame machen für ‖ *intr* Reklame machen; **a. for** durch Inserat suchen

advertisement [‚ædvər'taɪzmənt], [əd-'vertɪsmənt] *s* Anzeige *f*, Reklame *f*

ad'vertising a'gency *s* Reklamebüro *n*

ad'vertising campaign' *s* Werbefeldzug *m*

ad'vertising man' *s* (*solicitor*) Anzeigenvermittler *m*; (*writer*) Werbetexter *m*

advice [æd'vaɪs] *s* Rat *m*, Ratschlag *m*; **a piece of a.** ein Rat *m*; **get a. from** sich [*dat*] Rat holen bei; **give a. to** raten (*dat*)

advisable [æd'vaɪzəbəl] *adj* ratsam

advise [æd'vaɪz] *tr* raten (*dat*); (**of**) benachrichtigen (von); (**on**) beraten (über *acc*); **a. s.o. against s.th.** j–m von etw abraten

advisement [æd'vaɪzmənt] *s*—**take under a.** in Betracht ziehen

adviser [æd'vaɪzər] *s* Berater –in *mf*

advisory [æd'vaɪzəri] *adj* Beratungs-

advi'sory board' *s* Beirat *m*

advocate ['ædvə‚ket] *s* Fürsprecher –in *mf*; (jur) Advokat –in *mf* ‖ *tr* befürworten

aeon ['i·ən], ['i·an] *s* Äon *m*

aerial ['ɛrɪ·əl] *adj* Luft– ‖ *s* Antenne *f*

aerodynamic [‚ɛroda'næmɪk] *adj* aerodynamisch ‖ **aerodynamics** *s* Aerodynamik *f*

aeronautic(al) [‚ɛrə'nɔtɪk(əl)] *adj* aeronautisch ‖ **aeronautics** *s* Aeronautik *f*, Luftfahrt *f*

aerosol ['ɛrə‚sol] *s* Sprühdose *f*

aerospace ['ɛrəspes] *adj* Raum—
aesthetic [ɛs'θɛtɪk] *adj* ästhetisch ‖
   aesthetics *s* Ästhetik *f*
afar [ə'far] *adv*—a. off weit weg; from
   a. von weit her
affable ['æfəbəl] *adj* leutselig
affair [ə'fer] *s* Angelegenheit *f*; (event,
   performance) Veranstaltung *f*; (romantic involvement) Verhältnis *n*
affect [ə'fɛkt] *tr* (influence) berühren;
   (injuriously) angreifen; (pretend)
   vortäuschen
affectation [ˌæfɛk'teʃən] *s* Geziertheit
   f
affect′ed *adj* affektiert
affection [ə'fɛkʃən] *s* (for) Zuneigung
   f (zu); (pathol) Erkrankung *f*
affectionate [ə'fɛkʃənɪt] *adj* liebevoll
affidavit [ˌæfɪ'devɪt] *s* (schriftliche)
   eidesstattliche Erklärung *f*
affiliate [ə'fɪlɪˌet] *s* Zweiggesellschaft
   f ‖ *tr* angliedern ‖ *intr* sich angliedern
affinity [ə'fɪnɪti] *s* Verwandschaft *f*
affirm [ə'fʌrm] *tr & intr* behaupten
affirmation [ˌæfər'meʃən] *s* Behauptung *f*
affirmative [ə'fʌrmətɪv] *adj* bejahend
   ‖ *s* Bejahung *f*; in the a. bejahend,
   positiv
affix [ə'fɪks] *tr* (a seal) aufdrücken;
   (to) befestigen (an dat), anheften (an
   acc)
afflict [ə'flɪkt] *tr* plagen; **afflicted with**
   erkrankt an (dat)
affliction [ə'flɪkʃən] *s* Elend *n*, Leiden
   n; (grief) Betrübnis *f*
affluence ['æflu.əns] *s* Wohlstand *m*
affluent ['æflu.ənt] *adj* wohlhabend
af′fluent socie′ty *s* Wohlstandsgesell-
   schaft *f*
afford [ə'ford] *tr* (confer) gewähren;
   (time) erübrigen; (be able to meet
   the expense of) sich [dat] leisten
affront [ə'frʌnt] *s* Beleidigung *f* ‖ *tr*
   beleidigen
afire [ə'faɪr] *adj & adv* in Flammen
aflame [ə'flem] *adj & adv* in Flammen
afloat [ə'flot] *adj* flott, schwimmend;
   (awash) überschwemmt; (at sea) auf
   dem Meer; (in circulation) im Umlauf; **keep a.** (& fig) über Wasser
   halten; **stay a.** (& fig) sich über
   Wasser halten
afoot [ə'fut] *adj & adv* (on foot) zu
   Fuß; (in progress) im Gange
aforesaid [ə'forˌsed] *adj* vorerwähnt
afoul [ə'faul] *adj* (entangled) verwickelt ‖ *adv*—**run a. of the law** mit
   dem Gesetz in Konflikt geraten
afraid [ə'fred] *adj* ängstlich; **be a.** (of)
   (inf) sich scheuen zu (inf)
afresh [ə'frɛʃ] *adv* aufs neue
Africa ['æfrɪkə] *s* Afrika *n*
African ['æfrɪkən] *adj* afrikanisch ‖
   s Afrikaner –in *mf*
aft [æft] *adv* (nach) achtern
after ['æftər] *adj* später; (naut) achter
   ‖ *adv* nachher, darauf ‖ *prep* nach
   (dat); **a. all** immerhin; **a. that** darauf; **be a. s.o.** hinter j–m her sein ‖
   conj nachdem
af′ter-din′ner speech′ *s* Tischrede *f*

af′tereffect′ *s* Nachwirkung *f*; **have an**
   a. nachwirken
af′terlife′ *s* (later life) zukünftiges
   Leben *n*; (life after death) Leben *n*
   nach dem Tode
aftermath ['æftərˌmæθ] *s* Nach-
   wirkungen *pl*; (agr) Grummet *n*
af′ternoon′ *s* Nachmittag *m*; in the a.
   am Nachmittag, nachmittags; **this a.**
   heute nachmittag
af′ter-shave′ lo′tion *s* Rasierwasser *n*
af′tertaste′ *s* Nachgeschmack *m*
af′terthought′ *s* nachträglicher Einfall
   m
afterward(s) ['æftərwəd(z)] *adv* später
af′terworld′ *s* Jenseits *n*
again [ə'gɛn] *adv* wieder, noch einmal;
   half as much a. anderthalbmal so
   viel; **what′s his name a.?** wie heißt
   er doch schnell?
against [ə'gɛnst] *prep* gegen (acc); **a.**
   it dagegen; **a. the rules** regelwidrig;
   be up a. it (coll) in der Klemme sein
age [edʒ] *s* Alter *n*, Lebensalter *n*;
   (period of history) Zeitalter *n*; **at the**
   age of mit, im Alter von; **come of**
   age mündig werden; **for ages** e—e
   Ewigkeit; **of age** volljährig; **of the**
   same age gleichaltrig; **twenty years**
   of age zwanzig Jahre alt ‖ *tr* alt
   machen; (wine) ablagern ‖ *intr*
   altern; (said of wine) lagern
aged [edʒd] *adj* alt, e.g., **a. three** drei
   Jahre alt ‖ ['edʒɪd] *adj* bejahrt
age′ lim′it *s* Altersgrenze *f*
agency ['edʒənsi] *s* (instrumentality)
   Vermittlung *f*; (activity) Tätigkeit
   f; (adm) Behörde *f*; (com) Agentur *f*
agenda [ə'dʒɛndə] *s* Tagesordnung *f*
agent ['edʒənt] *s* Handelnde *mf*; (biol,
   chem) Agens *n*; (com) Agent –in *mf*
agglomeration [əˌglɑmə're∫ən] *s* Anhäufung *f*
aggravate ['ægrəˌvet] *tr* erschweren,
   verschärfen; (coll) ärgern
aggravation [ˌægrə've∫ən] *s* Erschwe-
   rung *f*, Verschärfung *f*; (coll) Ärger
   m
aggregate ['ægrɪˌget] *adj* gesamt ‖ *s*
   Aggregat *n*; **in the a.** im ganzen ‖ *tr*
   anhäufen
aggression [ə'grɛʃən] *s* Aggression *f*
aggressive [ə'grɛsɪv] *adj* aggressiv
aggressor [ə'grɛsər] *s* Aggressor *m*
aggrieved [ə'grivd] *adj* (saddened) betrübt; (jur) geschädigt
aghast [ə'gæst] *adj* entsetzt
agile ['ædʒɪl] *adj* flink; (mind) rege
agility [ə'dʒɪlɪti] *s* Flinkheit *f*; (of the
   mind) Regsamkeit *f*
agitate ['ædʒɪˌtet] *tr* hin und her bewegen; (fig) beunruhigen ‖ *intr* agitieren
agitator ['ædʒɪˌtetər] *s* Unruhestifter
   –in *mf*; (in a washer) Rührapparat *m*
aglow [ə'glo] *adj & adv* (er)glühend
agnostic [æg'nɑstɪk] *adj* agnostisch ‖
   s Agnostiker –in *mf*
ago [ə'go] *adv* vor (dat), e.g., **a year**
   ago vor e–m Jahr; **long ago** vor langer Zeit
agog [ə'gɑg] *adv* gespannt, erpicht
agonize ['ægəˌnaɪz] *intr* sich quälen

ag′onizing adj qualvoll

agony ['ægəni] s Qual f; (death struggle) Todeskampf m

agrarian [ə'grɛrɪ·ən] adj landwirtschaftlich, agrarisch

agree [ə'gri] intr übereinstimmen; **a.
on** (or **upon**) sich einigen über (acc);
a. to zustimmen (dat); **a. to** (inf)
übereinkommen zu (inf); **a. with** (&
gram) übereinstimmen mit; (affect
one's health) bekommen (dat)

agreeable [ə'gri·əbəl] adj angenehm

agreed′ interj abgemacht!, einverstanden!

agreement [ə'grimənt] s Abkommen
n, Vereinbarung f; (contract) Vertrag m; (& gram) Übereinstimmung f

agriculture ['ægrɪ‚kʌltʃər] s Landwirtschaft f, Ackerbau m

aground [ə'graund] adv gestrandet;
run a. stranden, auf Grund laufen

ahead [ə'hɛd] adj & adv (in the front)
vorn; (to the front) nach vorn; (in
advance) voraus; (forward) vorwärts;
a. of vor (dat); **get a.** vorwärtskommen; **go a.** vorangehen; **go a.!** los!;
go a. with fortfahren mit; **look a. an**
die Zukunft denken

ahoy [ə'hɔɪ] interj ahoi!

aid [ed] s Hilfe f, Beihilfe f ‖ tr helfen
(dat); **aid and abet** Vorschub leisten
(dat)

aide [ed] s Gehilfe m

aide-de-camp ['eddə'kæmp] s (aides-
de-camp) Adjutant m

ail [el] tr schmerzen; **what ails you?**
was fehlt Ihnen? ‖ intr (have pain)
Schmerzen haben; (be ill) erkrankt
sein

ail′ing adj leidend, kränklich

ailment ['elmənt] s Leiden n

aim [em] s Ziel n; (fig) Ziel n, Zweck
m; **is your aim good?** zielen Sie gut?;
take aim zielen ‖ tr (a gun, words)
(at) richten auf (acc); **aim to** (inf)
beabsichtigen zu (inf) ‖ intr zielen;
aim at (& fig) zielen auf (acc); **aim
for** streben nach

aimless ['emlɪs] adj ziellos, planlos

air [er] s Luft f; (mus) Melodie f; **be on
the air** (an announcer) senden; (a
program) gesendet werden; **be up in
the air** (fig) in der Luft hängen; **by
air** per Flugzeug; **go off the air** die
Sendung beenden; **go on the air** die
Sendung beginnen; **in the open air**
im Freien; **put on airs** groß tun;
walk on air sich wie im Himmel
fühlen ‖ tr lüften

air′base′ s Flugstützpunkt m

airborne ['ɛr‚bɔrn] adj aufgestiegen;
a. troops Luftlandetruppen pl

air′brake′ s Druckluftbremse f

air′-condi′tion tr klimatisieren

air′ condi′tioner s Klimaanlage f

air′ cov′er s Luftsicherung f

air′craft′ s (pl aircraft) Flugzeug n

air′craft car′rier s Flugzeugträger m

air′ cur′rent s Luftströmung f

air′ fare′ s Flugpreis m

air′field′ s Flugplatz m

air′force′ s Luftstreitkräfte pl

air′ing s Lüftung f

air′ lane′ s Flugschneise f

air′lift′ s Luftbrücke f ‖ tr auf dem
Luftwege transportieren

air′line(s)′ s Luftverkehrsgesellschaft f

air′line pi′lot s Flugkapitän m

air′lin′er s Verkehrsflugzeug n

air′mail′ s Luftpost f

air′-mail let′ter s Luftpostbrief m

air′-mail stamp′ s Luftpostbriefmarke
f

air′plane′ s Flugzeug n

air′ pock′et s Luftloch n

air′ pollu′tion s Luftverunreinigung f

air′port′ s Flughafen m, Flugplatz m

air′ raid′ s Fliegerangriff m

air′-raid drill′ s Luftschutzübung f

air′-raid shel′ter s Luftschutzraum m

air′-raid war′den s Luftschutzwart m

air′-raid warn′ing s Fliegeralarm m

air′ recon′naissance s Luftaufklärung f

air′show′ s Flugvorführung f

air′sick′ adj luftkrank

air′sleeve′, air′sock′ s Windsack m

air′strip′ s Start- und Landestreifen m

air′ suprem′acy s Lufherrschaft f

air′tight′ adj luftdicht

air′ time′ s (rad, telv) Sendezeit f

air′-traffic control′ s Flugsicherung f

air′waves′ spl Rundfunk m; **on the a.**
im Rundfunk

air′way′ s Luft(verkehrs)linie f

air′wor′thy adj lufttüchtig

airy ['eri] adj (room) luftig; (lively)
lebhaft; (flippant) leichtsinnig

aisle [aɪl] s Gang m; (archit) Seitenschiff n

ajar [ə'dʒɑr] adj angelehnt

akimbo [ə'kɪmbo] adj—**with arms a.**
die Arme in die Hüften gestemmt

akin [ə'kɪn] adj verwandt; **a. to** ähnlich (dat)

alabaster ['ælə‚bæstər] s Alabaster m

alacrity [ə'lækrɪti] s Bereitwilligkeit f

alarm [ə'lɑrm] s Alarm m; (sudden
fear) Bestürzung f; (apprehension)
Unruhe f ‖ tr alarmieren

alarm′ clock′ s Wecker m

alas [ə'læs] interj o weh!

Albania [æl'beni·ə] s Albanien n

Albanian [æl'beni·ən] adj albanisch ‖
s Alban(i)er –in mf

albatross ['ælbə‚trɔs] s Albatros m

album ['ælbəm] s Album n

albumen [æl'bjumən] s Eiweiß n

alchemy ['ælkɪmi] s Alchimie f

alcohol ['ælkə‚hɔl] s Alkohol m

alcoholic [‚ælkə'hɔlɪk] adj alkoholisch
‖ s Alkoholiker –in mf

alcove ['ælkov] s Alkoven m

alder ['ɔldər] s (bot) Erle f

al′der·man s (–men) Stadtrat m

ale [el] s Ale n, englisches Bier n

alert [ə'lʌrt] adj wachsam ‖ s (state
of readiness) Alarmbereitschaft f; **on
the a.** alarmbereit; (fig) auf der Hut
‖ tr alarmieren

alfalfa [æl'fælfə] s Luzerne f

algae ['ældʒi] spl Algen pl

algebra ['ældʒɪbrə] s Algebra f

Algeria [æl'dʒɪrɪ·ə] s Algerien n

Algerian [æl'dʒɪrɪ·ən] adj algerisch ‖
s Algerier –in mf

Algiers [æl'dʒɪrz] s Algier n

alias ['eɪlɪəs] *adv* alias, sonst...genannt ‖ *s* Deckname *m*
ali·bi ['ælɪ ˌbaɪ] *s* (–bis) Alibi *n*; (*excuse*) Ausrede *f*
alien ['eɪljən], ['eɪlɪ·ən] *adj* fremd ‖ *s* Fremde *mf*, Ausländer –in *mf*
alienate ['eɪljə ˌnet], ['eɪlɪ·ə ˌnet] *tr* entfremden; (*jur*) übertragen
alight [ə'laɪt] *v* (*pret & pp* **alighted &** **alit** ['ɪt]) *intr* aussteigen; (*said of a bird*) (**on**) sich niederlassen (auf *dat* or *acc*); (aer) landen
align [ə'laɪn] *tr* (**with**) ausrichten (nach); (aut) einstellen; **a. oneself** **with** sich anschließen an (*acc*) ‖ *intr* **—a. with** sich ausrichten nach
alignment [ə'laɪnmənt] *s* Ausrichten *n*; (pol) Ausrichtung *f*; **bring into a.** gleichschalten; **out of a.** schlecht ausgerichtet
alike [ə'laɪk] *adj* gleich, ähnlich; **look** **a.** sich [*dat*] ähnlich sehen; (*resemble completely*) gleich aussehen
alimony ['ælɪ ˌmoni] *s* Unterhaltskosten *pl*
alive [ə'laɪv] *adj* lebendig; (*vivacious*) lebhaft; **keep a.** am Leben bleiben; **keep s.o. a.** j–n am Leben erhalten
alka·li ['ælkə ˌlaɪ] *s* (–lis & –lies) Laugensalz *n*, Alkali *n*
alkaline ['ælkə ˌlaɪn] *adj* alkalisch
all [ɔl] *adj* all, ganz; **all day long den** ganzen Tag; **all kinds of** allerlei; **all** **the time** fortwährend; **for all that** trotzdem ‖ *adv* ganz, völlig; **all along** schon immer; **all at once** auf einmal; **all gone alle; all in** (coll) völlig erschöpft; (aut) übertragen **all over** (*everywhere*) überall; (*ended*) ganz vorbei; **all right** gut, schön; **all the better** um so besser; **all the same** dennoch; **not be all** **there** (coll) nicht ganz richtig im Kopf sein ‖ *s*—**after all** schließlich; **all in all** im großen und ganzen; **and** **all** gesamt, e.g., **he went, family and** **all** er ging mit gesamter Familie; **in** **all** insgesamt; **not at all** überhaupt nicht, gar nicht ‖ *indef pron* alle; (*everything*) alles
all'-around' *adj* vielseitig
allay [ə'le] *tr* beschwichtigen; (*hunger,* *thirst*) stillen
all'-clear' *s* Entwarnung *f*
allege [ə'ledʒ] *tr* behaupten; (*advance* *as an excuse*) vorgeben
alleged' *adj* angeblich, mutmaßlich
allegiance [ə'lidʒəns] *s* Treue *f*
allegoric(al) [ˌælɪ'gɔrɪk(əl)] *adj* allegorisch
allegory ['ælɪ ˌgori] *s* Allegorie *f*
allergic [ə'lʌrdʒɪk] *adj* allergisch
allergy ['ælərdʒi] *s* Allergie *f*
alleviate [ə'livɪ ˌet] *tr* lindern
alley ['æli] *s* Gasse *f*; (*for bowling*) Kegelbahn *f*
alliance [ə'laɪəns] *s* Bündnis *n*
allied' *adj* (*field*) benachbart; (*science*) verwandt; (mil, pol) alliiert
alligator ['ælɪ ˌgetər] *s* Alligator *m*
all'-inclu'sive *adj* Pauschal–
alliteration [ə ˌlɪtə'reʃən] *s* Stabreim *m*, Alliteration *f*
all'-know'ing *adj* allwissend

allocate ['ælə ˌket] *tr* zuteilen
al·lot [ə'lɑt] (*pret & pp* **–lotted; ger** **–lotting**) *tr* zuteilen, austeilen
all'-out' *adj* vollkommen, total
allow [ə'laʊ] *tr* erlauben, gestatten; (*admit*) zugeben; (*e.g., a discount*) gewähren; **be allowed to** (*inf*) dürfen (*inf*) ‖ *intr*—**a. for** bedenken
allowable [ə'laʊ·əbəl] *adj* zulässig
allowance [ə'laʊ·əns] *s* (*tolerance*) Duldung *f*; (*permission*) Erlaubnis *f*; (*ration*) Zuteilung *f*, Ration *f*; (*pocket money*) Taschengeld *n*; (*discount*) Abzug *m*; (*salary for a particular expense*) Zuschuß *m*, Zulage *f*; (*for groceries*) Wirtschaftsgeld *n*; (mach) Toleranz *f*; **make a. for** berücksichtigen
alloy ['ælɔɪ] *s* Legierung *f* ‖ [ə'lɔɪ] *tr* legieren
all'-pow'erful *adj* allmächtig
all' right' *adj*—**be a. in** Ordnung sein ‖ *interj* schon gut!
All' Saints' Day' *s* Allerheiligen *n*
All' Souls' Day' *s* Allerseelen *n*
all'spice' *s* Nelkenpfeffer *m*
all'-star' *adj* (*sport*) aus den besten Spielern bestehend
allude [ə'lud] *intr*—**a. to** anspielen auf (*acc*)
allure [ə'lʊr] *s* Charme *m* ‖ *tr* anlocken
allurement [ə'lʊrmənt] *s* Verlockung *f*
allur'ing *adj* verlockend
allusion [ə'luʒən] *s* (**to**) Anspielung *f* (auf *acc*)
al·ly ['ælar], [ə'laɪ] *s* Alliierte *mf*, Verbündete *mf* ‖ [ə'laɪ] *v* (*pret &* *pp* **–lied**) *tr*—**a. oneself with** sich verbünden mit
almanac ['ɔlmə ˌnæk] *s* Almanach *m*
almighty [ɔl'maɪti] *adj* allmächtig
almond ['amənd] *s* Mandel *f*
almost ['ɔlmost], [ɔl'most] *adv* fast
alms [amz] *s & spl* Almosen *n*
aloft [ə'lɔft] *adv* (*position*) oben; (*direction*) nach oben; **raise a.** emporheben
alone [ə'lon] *adj* allein; **let a.** (*not to* *mention*) geschweige denn; (*not* *bother*) in Ruhe lassen ‖ *adv* allein
along [ə'lɔŋ] *adv* vorwärts, weiter; **all** **a.** schon immer; **a. with** zusammen mit; **get a. with** sich gut vertragen mit; **go a. with** mitgehen mit; (*agree* *with*) sich einverstanden erklären mit ‖ *prep* (*direction*) entlang (*acc*); (*position*) an (*dat*), längs (*genit*)
along'side' *adv* (naut) längsseits; **a. of** im Vergleich zu ‖ *prep* neben (*dat*); (naut) längsseits (*genit*)
aloof [ə'luf] *adj* zurückhaltend ‖ *adv*— **keep a.** (**from**) sich fernhalten (von); **stand a.** für sich bleiben
aloud [ə'laʊd] *adv* laut
alphabet ['ælfə ˌbet] *s* Alphabet *n*
alphabetic(al) [ˌælfə'betɪk(əl)] *adj* alphabetisch
alpine ['ælpaɪn] *adj* alpin, Alpen–
Alps [ælps] *spl* Alpen *pl*
already [ɔl'redi] *adv* schon, bereits
Alsace [æl'ses], ['ælsæs] *s* Elsaß *n*
Alsatian [æl'seʃən] *adj* elsässisch ‖ *s*

Elsässer –in *mf;* *(dog)* deutscher Schäferhund *m*

also ['ɔlso] *adv* auch

altar ['ɔltər] *s* Altar *m*

al'tar boy' *s* Ministrant *m*

alter ['ɔltər] *tr* ändern; *(castrate)* kastrieren ‖ *intr* sich ändern

alteration [ˌɔltə'reʃən] *s* Änderung *f;* **alterations** *(in construction)* Umbau *m*

alternate ['ɔltərnɪt] *adj* abwechselnd ‖ *s* Ersatzmann *m* ‖ ['ɔltər͵net] *tr* (ab)wechseln; *(e.g., hot and cold compresses)* zwischen *(dat)* und *(dat)* abwechseln ‖ *intr* miteinander abwechseln

al'ternating cur'rent *s* Wechselstrom *m*

alternative [ɔl'tʌrnətɪv] *adj* Ausweich-, Alternativ- ‖ *s* Alternative *f*

although [ɔl'ðo] *conj* obgleich, obwohl

altimeter [æl'tɪmɪtər] *s* Höhenmesser *m*

altitude ['æltɪˌt(j)ud] *s* Höhe *f*

al·to ['ælto] *s* (–tos) Alt *m,* Altstimme *f;* *(singer)* Altist *m*

altogether [ˌɔltə'ɡeðər] *adv* durchaus; *(in all)* insgesamt

altruist ['æltru-ɪst] *s* Altruist –in *mf*

alum ['æləm] *s* Alaun *m*

aluminum [ə'luminəm] *s* Aluminium *n*

alu'minum foil' *s* Aluminiumfolie *f*

alum·na [ə'lʌmnə] *s* (–nae [ni]) ehemalige Studentin *f*

alum·nus [ə'lʌmnəs] *s* (–ni [naɪ]) ehemaliger Student *m*

always ['ɔlwɪz], ['ɔlwez] *adv* immer

A.M. *abbr* (ante meridiem) vormittags; **(amplitude modulation)** Amplitudenmodulation *f*

amalgam [ə'mælɡəm] *s* Amalgam *n;* (fig) Mischung *f,* Gemenge *n*

amalgamate [ə'mælɡə͵met] *tr* amalgamieren ‖ *intr* sich amalgamieren

amass [ə'mæs] *tr* aufhäufen, ansammeln

amateur ['æmətʃər] *adj* Amateur- ‖ *s* Amateur *m,* Liebhaber *m*

amaze [ə'mez] *tr* erstaunen

amaz'ing *adj* erstaunlich

Amazon ['æmə͵zan] *s* *(river)* Amazonas *m;* (fig) Mannweib *n;* *(myth)* Amazone *f*

ambassador [æm'bæsədər] *s* Botschafter –in §6 *mf;* (fig) Bote *m*

ambassadorial [æm͵bæsə'dɔri-əl] *adj* Botschafts-

amber ['æmbər] *adj* Bernstein-; (in color) bernsteinfarben ‖ *s* Bernstein *m*

ambiguity [ˌæmbɪ'ɡju-ɪti] *s* Doppelsinn *m,* Zweideutigkeit *f*

ambiguous [æm'bɪɡjʊ-əs] *adj* doppelsinnig, zweideutig

ambit ['æmbɪt] *s* Bereich *m*

ambition [æm'bɪʃən] *s* Ehrgeiz *m;* *(aim, object)* Ambition *f*

ambitious [æm'bɪʃəs] *adj* ehrgeizig

ambivalent [æm'bɪvələnt] *adj* (chem) ambivalent; (psychol) zwiespältig

amble ['æmbəl] *s* *(of a person)* gemächlicher Gang *m;* *(of a horse)* Paßgang *m* ‖ *intr* schlendern; *(said of a horse)* im Paßgang gehen

ambulance ['æmbjələns] *s* Krankenwagen *m*

ambulatory ['æmbjələˌtori] *adj* gehfähig

ambuscade [ˌæmbəs'ked] *s* Hinterhalt *m*

ambush ['æmbʊʃ] *s* Hinterhalt *m* ‖ *tr* aus dem Hinterhalt überfallen

ameliorate [ə'miljə͵ret] *tr* verbessern ‖ *intr* besser werden

amen ['e'men], ['ɑ'men] *s* Amen *n* ‖ *interj* amen!

amenable [ə'menəbəl] *adj* (docile) fügsam; **a. to** *(e.g., flattery)* zugänglich *(dat);* *(e.g., laws)* unterworfen *(dat)*

amend [ə'mend] *tr* *(a law)* (ver)bessern; *(one's ways)* (ab)ändern ‖ *intr* sich bessern

amendment [ə'mendmənt] *s* Änderungsantrag *m;* (by addition) Zusatzantrag *m;* *(to the constitution)* Zusatzartikel *m*

amends [ə'mendz] *s & spl* Genugtuung *f;* **make a.** für wiedergutmachen

amenity [ə'menɪti] *s* *(pleasantness)* Annehmlichkeit *f;* **amenities** *(of life)* Annehmlichkeiten *pl*

America [ə'merɪkə] *s* Amerika *n*

American [ə'merɪkən] *adj* amerikanisch ‖ *s* Amerikaner –in *mf*

Americanize [ə'merɪkə͵naɪz] *tr* amerikanisieren

amethyst ['æmɪθɪst] *s* Amethyst *m*

amiable ['emɪ-əbəl] *adj* liebenswürdig

amicable ['æmɪkəbəl] *adj* freundschaftlich, gütlich

amid [ə'mɪd] *prep* inmitten (genit)

amidships [ə'mɪd/ɪps] *adv* mittschiffs

amiss [ə'mɪs] *adj* *(improper)* unpassend; *(wrong)* verkehrt; **there is s.th. a.** etwas stimmt nicht ‖ *adv* verkehrt; **go a.** danebengehen; **take a.** übelnehmen

amity ['æmɪti] *s* Freundschaft *f*

ammo ['æmo] *s* (sl) Muni *m*

ammonia [ə'monɪ-ə] *s* *(gas)* Ammoniak *n;* *(solution)* Salmiakgeist *m*

ammunition [ˌæmjə'nɪ/ən] *s* Munition *f*

amnesia [æm'niʒɪ-ə] *s* Amnesie *f*

amnes·ty ['æmnɪsti] *s* Amnestie *f* ‖ *v* *(pret & pp. –tied) tr* begnadigen

amoeba [ə'mibə] *s* Amöbe *f*

among [ə'mʌŋ] *prep (position)* unter *(dat);* *(direction)* unter *(acc);* **a. other things** unter anderem

amorous ['æmərəs] *adj* amourös

amortize ['æmər͵taɪz] *tr* tilgen

amount [ə'maʊnt] *s* *(sum)* Betrag *m;* *(quantity)* Menge *f* ‖ *intr*—**a. to** betragen

ampere ['æmpɪr] *s* Ampere *n*

amphibian [æm'fɪbɪ-ən] *s* Amphibie *f*

amphibious [æm'fɪbɪ-əs] *adj* amphibisch

amphitheater ['æmfɪˌθi-ətər] *s* Amphitheater *n*

ample ['æmpəl] *adj* *(sufficient)* genügend; *(spacious)* geräumig

amplifier ['æmplɪˌfaɪ-ər] *s* Verstärker *m*

ampli·fy ['æmplɪˌfaɪ] *v* *(pret & pp –fied) tr* *(a statement)* erweitern; (electron, rad, phys) verstärken

amplitude ['æmplɪ‚t(j)ud] s Weite f; (electron, rad, phys) Amplitude f

am'plitude modula'tion s Amplitudenmodulation f

amputate ['æmpjə‚tet] tr amputieren

amputee [‚æmpje'ti] s Amputierte mf

amuck [ə'mʌk] adv—**run a.** Amok laufen

amulet ['æmjəlɪt] s Amulett n

amuse [ə'mjuz] tr amüsieren, belustigen

amusement [ə'mjuzmənt] s Vergnügen n

amuse'ment park' s Vergnügungspark m

amus'ing adj amüsant

an [æn], [ən] indef art ein

anachronism [ə'nækrə‚nɪzəm] s Anachronismus m

analogous [ə'næləgəs] adj (to) analog (dat), ähnlich (dat)

analogy [ə'nælədʒi] s Analogie f

analy·sis [ə'nælɪsɪs] s (-ses [‚siz]) Analyse f; (of a literary work) Zergliederung f

analyst ['ænəlɪst] s Analytiker –in m

analytic(al) [‚ænə'lɪtɪk(əl)] adj analytisch

analyze ['ænə‚laɪz] tr analysieren

anarchist ['ænərkɪst] s Anarchist –in mf

anarchy ['ænərki] s Anarchie f

anatomic(al) [‚ænə'tɑmɪk(əl)] adj anatomisch

anatomy [ə'nætəmi] s Anatomie f

ancestor ['ænsestər] s Vorfahr m, Ahne m

ancestral [æn'sestrəl] adj angestammt, Ahnen–; (inherited) Erb–, ererbt

ancestry ['ænsestri] s Abstammung f

anchor ['æŋkər] s Anker m; **cast a.** vor Anker gehen; **weigh a.** den Anker lichten || tr verankern || intr ankern

anchorage ['æŋkərɪdʒ] s Ankerplatz m

anchovy ['æntʃovi] s Anschovis f

ancient ['entʃənt] adj (very old) uralt; (civilization) antik || **the ancients** spl die alten Griechen und Römer

an'cient his'tory s alte Geschichte f

and [ænd], [ənd] conj und; **and how!** und ob! **and so forth** und so weiter

andiron ['ænd‚aɪ‚ərn] s Kaminbock m

anecdote ['ænɪk‚dot] s Anekdote f

anemia [ə'nimɪ‚ə] s Anämie f

anemic [ə'nimɪk] adj anämisch, blutarm

anesthesia [‚ænɪs'θiʒə] s Anästhesie f; **general a.** Vollnarkose f; **local a.** Lokalanästhesie f

anesthetic [‚ænɪs'θetɪk] adj betäubend || s Betäubungsmittel n; **local a.** örtliches Betäubungsmittel n

anesthetize [æ'nesθɪ‚taɪz] tr betäuben

anew [ə'n(j)u] adv von neuem, aufs neue

angel ['endʒəl] s Engel m; (financial backer) Hintermann m

angelic(al) [æn'dʒelɪk(əl)] adj engelgleich, engelhaft

anger ['æŋgər] s Zorn m || tr erzürnen

angina pectoris [æn'dʒaɪnə'pektərɪs] s Brustbeklemmung f, Herzbräune f

angle ['æŋgəl] s Winkel m; (point of view) Gesichtswinkel m; (ulterior motive) Hintergedanken m; (side) Seite f

angler ['æŋglər] s Angler –in mf

angry ['æŋgri] adj zornig, böse; (wound) entzündet; **a. at** (s.th.) zornig über (acc); **a. with** (s.o.) zornig auf (acc)

anguish ['æŋgwɪʃ] s Qual f, Pein f

angular ['æŋgjələr] adj kantig

animal ['ænɪməl] adj tierisch, Tier— || s Tier n

animate ['ænɪmɪt] adj belebt; (lively) lebhaft || ['ænɪ‚met] tr beleben, beseelen; (make lively) aufmuntern

an'imated cartoon' s Zeichentrickfilm m

animation [‚ænɪ'meʃən] s Lebhaftigkeit f; (cin) Herstellung f von Zeichentrickfilm

animosity [‚ænɪ'mɑsɪti] s Feindseligkeit f

anion ['æn‚aɪ‚ən] s Anion n

anise ['ænɪs] s Anis m

anisette [‚ænɪ'set] s Anisett m

ankle ['æŋkəl] s Fußknöchel m

an'kle support' s Knöchelstütze f

anklet ['æŋklɪt] s (ornament) Fußring m; (sock) Söckchen n

annals ['ænəlz] spl Annalen pl

anneal [ə'nil] tr ausglühen; (the mind) stählen

annex ['æneks] s (building) Anbau m, Nebengebäude n; (supplement) Zusatz m || [ə'neks] tr annektieren

annexation [‚æneks'eʃən] s Einverleibung f; (pol) Annexion f

annihilate [ə'naɪ‚ɪ‚let] tr vernichten; (fig) zunichte machen

annihilation [ə‚naɪ‚ɪ'leʃən] s Vernichtung f

anniversary [‚ænɪ'vʌrsəri] s Jahrestag m

annotate ['ænə‚tet] tr mit Anmerkungen versehen

annotation [‚ænə'teʃən] s Anmerkung f

announce [ə'naʊns] tr ankündigen, anmelden; (rad) ansagen, melden

announcement [ə'naʊnsmənt] s Ankündigung f; (rad) Durchsage f

announcer [ə'naʊnsər] s Ansager –in mf

annoy [ə'nɔɪ] tr ärgern; **be annoyed at** sich ärgern über (acc)

annoyance [ə'nɔɪ‚əns] s Ärger m

annoy'ing adj ärgerlich

annual ['ænju‚əl] adj jährlich, Jahres–; (plant) einjährig || s (book) Jahrbuch n; (bot) einjährige Pflanze f

annuity [ə'n(j)u‚ɪti] s Jahresrente f

an·nul [ə'nʌl] v (pret & pp –nulled; ger –nulling) tr annullieren

annulment [ə'nʌlmənt] s Annullierung f; (of marriage) Nichtigkeitserklärung f

anode ['ænod] s Anode f

anoint [ə'nɔɪnt] tr salben

anomaly [ə'nɑməli] s Anomalie f

anonymous [ə'nɑnɪməs] adj anonym

another [ə'nʌðər] adj (a different) ein anderer; (an additional) noch ein; **a. Caesar** ein zweiter Cäsar || pron (*a different one*) ein anderer; (*an additional one*) noch einer

answer ['ænsər] *s* Antwort *f*; (*to a problem*) Lösung *f* || *tr* (*a person*) antworten (*dat*); (*a question, letter*) beantworten; (*need, description*) entsprechen (*dat*); (*enemy fire*) antworten auf (*acc*); **a. an ad** sich auf e-e Anzeige melden; **a. the door** die Tür öffnen; **a. the telephone** ans Telefon gehen || *intr* antworten; (*telp*) sich melden; **a. back** e-n losen Mund haben; **a. for** verantworten; **a. to** (*a description*) entsprechen (*dat*)

an'swering serv'ice *s* Fernsprechauftragsdienst *m*

ant [ænt] *s* Ameise *f*

antagonism [æn'tægə,nɪzəm] *s* Feindseligkeit *f*

antagonize [æn'tægə,naɪz] *tr* sich [*dat*] zum Gegner machen

antarctic [ænt'ɑrktɪk] *adj* antarktisch || **the Antarctic** *s* die Antarktis

Antarc'tic Cir'cle *s* südlicher Polarkreis *m*

Antarc'tic O'cean *s* südliches Eismeer *n*

ante ['ænti] *s* (*cards*) Einsatz *m*; (*com*) Scherflein *n* || *tr* (*cards*) einsetzen || *intr* (*in a joint venture*) sein Scherflein beitragen; (*pay up*) (*coll*) blechen; (*cards*) einsetzen

antecedent [,æntɪ'sidənt] *adj* vorhergehend || *s* (*gram*) Beziehungswort *n*; **antecedents** Antezedenzien *pl*

antechamber ['æntɪ,tʃembər] *s* Vorzimmer *n*

antelope ['æntɪ,lop] *s* Antilope *f*

anten·na ['æntɪna] *s* (*-nae* [ni]) (*ent*) Fühler *m* || *s* (*-nas*) (*rad*) Antenne *f*

antepenult [,æntɪ'pinʌlt] *s* drittletzte Silbe *f*

anthem ['ænθəm] *s* Hymne *f*

ant'hill' *s* Ameisenhaufen *m*

anthology [æn'θɑlədʒi] *s* Anthologie *f*

anthropology [,ænθrə'pɑlədʒi] *s* Anthropologie *f*, Lehre *f* vom Menschen

antiaircraft [,ænti'er,kræft] *adj* Flak-, Flugabwehr- || *s* Flak *f*

antiair'craft gun' *s* Flak *f*

antibiotic [,æntibaɪ'ɑtɪk] *s* Antibiotikum *n*

antibody ['ænti,bɑdi] *s* Antikörper *m*

anticipate [æn'tɪsɪ,pet] *tr* (*expect*) erwarten; (*remarks, criticism, etc.*) vorwegnehmen; (*trouble*) voraussehnen; (*pleasure*) vorausempfinden; (*s.o.'s wish or desire*) zuvorkommen (*dat*)

anticipation [æn,tɪsɪ'peʃən] *s* Erwartung *f*, Vorfreude *f*

antics ['æntɪks] *spl* Possen *pl*

antidote ['æntɪ,dot] *s* Gegengift *n*

antifreeze ['ænti,friz] *s* Gefrierschutzmittel *n*

antiknock [,ænti'nɑk] *adj* klopffest || *s* Antiklopfmittel *n*

antipathy [æn'tɪpəθi] *s* Abneigung *f*, Antipathie *f*

antiquarian [,ænti'kweri·ən] *adj* altertümlich || *s* Altertumsforscher –in *mf*

antiquated ['ænti,kwetɪd] *adj* veraltet

antique [æn'tik] *adj* (*ur*)alt, antik || *s* Antiquität *f*

antique' deal'er *s* Antiquitätenhändler –in *mf*

antique' shop' *s* Antiquitätenladen *m*

antiquity [æn'tɪkwɪti] *s* Altertum *n*, Vorzeit *f*; **antiquities** Antiquitäten *pl*, Altertümer *pl*

antirust [,ænti'rʌst] *adj* Rostschutz–

anti-Semitic [,æntɪsɪ'mɪtɪk] *adj* antisemitisch, judenfeindlich

antiseptic [,ænti'septɪk] *adj* antiseptisch || *s* Antiseptikum *n*

antitank [,ænti'tæŋk] *adj* Panzer–: (*unit*) Panzerjäger–

antitank' mine' *s* Tellermine *f*

antithe·sis [æn'tɪθɪsɪs] *s* (*-ses* [,siz]) Gegensatz *m*, Antithese *f*

antitoxin [,ænti'tɑksɪn] *s* Gegengift *n*

antitrust [,ænti'trʌst] *adj* Antitrust–

antiwar [,ænti'wɔr] *adj* antimilitaristisch

antler ['æntlər] *s* Geweihsprosse *f*; (*pair of*) antlers Geweih *n*

antonym ['æntənɪm] *s* Antonym *n*

anus ['enəs] *s* After *m*

anvil ['ænvɪl] *s* Amboß *m*

anxiety [æŋ'zaɪ·əti] *s* (*over*) Besorgnis *f* (um); (*psychol*) Beklemmung *f*

anxious ['æŋk/əs] *adj* (*about*) besorgt (um or wegen); (*for*) gespannt (auf *acc*), begierig (auf *acc*); **I am a. to** (*inf*) es liegt mir daran zu (*inf*)

any ['ɛni] *indef adj* irgendein, irgendwelch; (*a little*) etwas; **any** (*possible*) etwaig; **any** (*you wish*) jeder beliebige; **do you have any money on you?** haben Sie Geld bei sich?; **I do not have any money** ich habe kein Geld || *adv*—any more (*e.g., coffee*) noch etwas; (*e.g., apples*) noch ein paar; **not any better** keinwegs besser; **not ... any longer** nicht mehr; **not ... any more** nicht mehr

an'ybod'y *indef pron* var of **anyone**

an'yhow' *adv* sowieso, trotzdem; (*in any event*) jedenfalls

an'yone' *indef pron* (*irgend*)jemand, irgendeiner; **a. but** you jeder andere als du; **a. else** sonstnochwer; **ask a.** frag wen du willst; **I don't see a.** ich sehe niemand

an'yplace' *adv* (*coll*) var of **anywhere**

an'ything' *indef pron* (*irgend*)etwas, (*irgend*)was; **a. but** alles andere als; **a. else?** noch etwas?, sonst etwas?; **a. you want** was du willst; **not ... a.** nichts; **not for a. in the world** um keinen Preis

an'ytime' *adv* zu jeder (*beliebig*) Zeit; (*at some unspecified time*) irgendwann

an'yway' *adv* sowieso, trotzdem

an'ywhere' *adv* (*position*) irgendwo; (*everywhere*) an jedem beliebigen Ort; (*direction*) irgendwohin; (*everywhere*) an jeden beliebigen Ort; (*to any extent*) einigermaßen, e.g., **a. near correct** einigermaßen richtig; **get a.** (*achieve success*) es zu etwas bringen

apace [ə'pes] *adv* schnell, rasch

apart [ə'pɑrt] *adv* (*to pieces*) auseinander; (*separately*) einzeln, für sich; a. **from** abgesehen von

apartment [ə'pɑrtmənt] *s* Wohnung *f*

apart'ment house' *s* Apartmenthaus *n*

apathetic [,æpə'θetɪk] *adj* apathisch, teilnahmslos

apathy ['æpəθi] *s* Apathie *f*

ape [ep] *s* Affe *m* || *tr* nachäffen

aperture ['æpərt/ər] *s* Öffnung *f*; (phot) Blende *f*

apex ['epeks] *s* (**apexes & apices** ['æpɪ,siz]) Spitze *f*; (fig) Gipfel *m*

aphid ['æfɪd] *s* Blattlaus *f*

aphorism ['æfə,rɪzəm] *s* Aphorismus *m*

apiary ['epɪ,eri] *s* Bienenhaus *n*

apiece [ə'pis] *adv* pro Stück; (*per person*) pro Person

aplomb [ə'plom] *s* sicheres Auftreten *n*

apogee ['æpə,dʒi] *s* Erdferne *f*

apologetic [ə,pɑlə'dʒetɪk] *adj* (*remark*) entschuldigend; (*letter, speech*) Entschuldigungs–; be a. (about) Entschuldigungen vorbringen (für)

apologize [ə'pɑlə,dʒaɪz] *intr* sich entschuldigen; a. **to s.o. for s.th.** sich bei j–m wegen etw entschuldigen

apology [ə'pɑlədʒi] *s* (*excuse*) Entschuldigung *f*; (*apologia*) Verteidigung *f*

apoplec'tic stroke' [,æpə'plektɪk] *s* Schlaganfall *m*

apoplexy ['æpə,pleksi] *s* Schlaganfall *m*

apostle [ə'pɑsəl] *s* Apostel *m*

apostolic [,æpəs'tɑlɪk] *adj* apostolisch

apostrophe [ə'pɑstrəfi] *s* (gram) Apostroph *m*; (rhet) Anrede *f*

apothecary [ə'pɑθə,keri] *s* (*druggist*) Apotheker *m*; (*drugstore*) Apotheke *f*

appall [ə'pɔl] *tr* entsetzen

appall'ing *adj* entsetzlich

appara·tus [,æpə'retəs], [,æpə'rætəs] *s* (**-tus & -tuses**) Apparat *m*

apparel [ə'pærəl] *s* Kleidung *f*, Tracht *f*

apparent [ə'pærənt] *adj* (*visible*) sichtbar; (*obvious*) offenbar; (*seeming*) scheinbar

apparition [,æpə'rɪ/ən] *s* Erscheinung *f*; (*ghost*) Gespenst *n*

appeal [ə'pil] *s* (*request*) Appell *m*, dringende Bitte *f*; (*to reason, etc.*) Appell *m*; (*charm*) Anziehungskraft *f*; (jur) (**to**) Berufung *f* (an *acc*) || *tr*—a case Berufung einlegen in e–r Rechtssache || *intr*—a. **to** (*entreat*) dringend bitten; (*be attractive to*) reizen; (jur) appellieren an (*acc*)

appear [ə'pɪr] *intr* erscheinen; (*seem*) scheinen; (*come before the public*) sich zeigen; (jur) sich stellen; (theat) auftreten; a. **as a guest** (telv) gastieren

appearance [ə'pɪrəns] *s* Erscheinen *n*; (*outward look*) Aussehen *n*; (*semblance*) Anschein *m*; (*on the stage*) Auftreten *n*; (jur) Erscheinen *n*; **for the sake of appearances** anstandshalber; **to all appearances** allem Anschein nach

appease [ə'piz] *tr* beruhigen; (*hunger*)

stillen; (*pain*) mildern; (dipl) beschwichtigen

appeasement [ə'pizmənt] *s* Beruhigung *f*; (*of hunger*) Stillung *f*; (dipl) Beschwichtigung *f*

appel'late court' [ə'pelɪt] *s* Berufungsgericht *n*

append [ə'pend] *tr* anhängen; (*a signature*) hinzufügen

appendage [ə'pendɪdʒ] *s* Anhang *m*

appendectomy [,æpən'dektəmi] *s* Blinddarmoperation *f*

appendicitis [ə,pendɪ'saɪtɪs] *s* Blinddarmentzündung *f*, Appendizitis *f*

appen·dix [ə'pendɪks] *s* (**-dixes & -dices** [dɪ,siz]) Anhang *m*; (anat) Appendix *m*

appertain [,æpər'ten] *intr* (**to**) gehören (zu), gebühren (*dat*)

appetite ['æpɪ,taɪt] *s* (**for**) Appetit *m* (auf *acc*)

appetizer ['æpɪ,taɪzər] *s* Vorspeise *f*

ap'petizing *adj* appetitlich

applaud [ə'plɔd] *tr* Beifall klatschen (*dat*); (*praise*) billigen || *intr* Beifall klatschen

applause [ə'plɔz] *s* Beifall *m*, Applaus *m*

apple ['æpəl] *s* Apfel *m*

ap'plecart' *s*—**upset the a.** die Pläne über den Haufen werfen

ap'ple of one's eye' *s* Augapfel *m*

ap'ple pie' *s* gedeckte Apfeltorte *f*

ap'ple-pol'isher *s* (coll) Speichellecker *m*

ap'plesauce' *s* Apfelmus *n*

ap'ple tree' *s* Apfelbaum *m*

appliance [ə'plaɪ·əns] *s* Gerät *n*, Vorrichtung *f*

applicable ['æplɪkəbəl] *adj* (**to**) anwendbar (auf *acc*); **not a.** nicht zutreffend

applicant ['æplɪkənt] *s* Bewerber –in *mf*

application [,æplɪ'ke/ən] *s* (*use*) Anwendung *f*; (*for a job*) Bewerbung *f*; (*for a grant*) Antrag *m*; (*zeal*) Fleiß *m*; (med) Anlegen *n*

applica'tion blank' *s* (*for a job*) Bewerbungsformular *n*; (*for a grant*) Antragsformular *n*

applied' *adj* angewandt

apply [ə'plaɪ] *v* (*pret & pp* –**plied**) *tr* anwenden; (med) anlegen; a. **oneself to** sich befleißigen (*genit*); a. **the brakes** bremsen || *intr* gelten; a. **for** (*a job*) sich bewerben um; (*a grant*) beantragen

appoint [ə'pɔɪnt] *tr* (*a person*) ernennen; (*a time, etc.*) festsetzen

appointment [ə'pɔɪntmənt] *s* Ernennung *f*; (*post*) Stelle *f*; (*engagement*) Verabredung *f*; **by a. only** nur nach Vereinbarung; **have an a. with** (*e.g., a dentist*) bestellt sein zu

appoint'ment book' *s* Terminkalender *m*

apportion [ə'pɔr/ən] *tr* zumessen

appraisal [ə'prezəl] *s* Abschätzung *f*

appraise [ə'prez] *tr* (ab)schätzen

appraiser [ə'prezər] *s* Schätzer –in *mf*

appreciable [ə'pri/ɪ·əbəl] *adj* (*notice-*

able) merklich; (*considerable*) erheblich

appreciate [ə'pri/ɪ,et] *tr* dankbar sein für; (*danger*) erkennen; (*regard highly*) hochschätzen || *intr* (im Werte) steigen

appreciation [ə,pri/ɪ'eʃən] *s* (*gratitude*) Dank *m*. Anerkennung *f*; (*for art*) Verständnis *n*; (*high regard*) Schätzung *f*; (*increase in value*) Wertzuwachs *m*

appreciative [ə'pri/ɪ·ətɪv] *adj* (*of*) dankbar (für)

apprehend [,æprɪ'hɛnd] *tr* verhaften, ergreifen; (*understand*) begreifen

apprehension [,æprɪ'hɛnʃən] *s* (*arrest*) Verhaftung *f*; (*fear*) Befürchtung *f*; (*comprehending*) Begreifen *n*

apprehensive [,æprɪ'hɛnsɪv] *adj* (*of*) besorgt (um)

apprentice [ə'prɛntɪs] *s* Lehrling *m*

appren'ticeship *s* Lehre *f*; **serve an a.** in der Lehre sein

apprise, apprize [ə'praɪz] *tr* (*of*) benachrichtigen (von)

approach [ə'protʃ] *s* Annäherung *f*; (*e.g., a road*) Zugang *m*, Zufahrt *f*; (*e.g., a problem*) Behandlung *f*; (*tentative sexual approach*) Annäherungsversuch *m*; (*aer*) Anflug *m* || *tr* sich nähern (*dat*); (*e.g., a problem*) behandeln; (*perfection*) nahekommen (*dat*); (*aer*) anfliegen || *intr* sich nähern

approachable [ə'protʃəbəl] *adj* zugänglich

approbation [,æprə'beʃən] *s* (*approval*) Beifall *m*; (*sanction*) Billigung *f*

appropriate [ə'propri·ɪt] *adj* (*to*) angemessen (*dat*) || [ə'propri,et] *tr* (*take possession of*) sich [*dat*] aneignen; (*authorize*) bewilligen

approval [ə'pruvəl] *s* (*approbation*) Beifall *m*; (*sanction*) Billigung *f*; **meet with s.o.'s a.** j–s Beifall finden; **on a.** auf Probe

approve [ə'pruv] *tr* (*sanction*) genehmigen; (*judge favorably*) billigen; (*a bill*) (parl) annehmen || *intr*—**a. of** billigen

approvingly [ə'pruvɪŋli] *adv* beifällig

approximate [ə'praksɪmɪt] *adj* annähernd || [ə'praksɪ,met] *tr* (*come close to*) nahekommen (*dat*); (*estimate*) schätzen; (*simulate closely*) täuschend nachahmen

approximately [ə'praksɪmɪtli] *adv* ungefähr, etwa

apricot ['eprɪ,kat] *s* Aprikose *f*

ap'ricot tree' *s* Aprikosenbaum *m*

April ['eprɪl] *s* April *m*

A'pril fool' *interj* April, April!

A'pril Fools' Day' *s* der erste April *m*

apron ['eprən] *s* Schürze *f*; (aer) Vorfeld *n*; (theat) Vorbühne *f*

apropos [,æprə'po] *adj* passend || *adv* —**a. of** in Bezug auf (*acc*)

apse [æps] *s* Apsis *f*

apt [æpt] *adj* (*suited to the occasion*) passend; (*suited to the purpose*) geeignet; (*metaphor*) zutreffend; **be apt to** (*inf*) (*be prone to*) dazu neigen zu

(*inf*); **he is apt to believe it** er wird es wahrscheinlich glauben

aptitude ['æptɪ,t(j)ud] *s* Eignung *f*

ap'titude test' *s* Eignungsprüfung *f*

aqualung ['ækwə,lʌŋ] *s* Tauchergerät *n*

aquamarine [,ækwəmə'rin] *adj* blaugrün || *s* Aquamarin *m*

aquari·um [ə'kwɛrɪ·əm] *s* (**–ums & –a** [ə]) Aquarium *n*

aquatic [ə'kwætɪk] *adj* Wasser– || **aquatics** *spl* Wassersport *m*

aqueduct ['ækwə,dʌkt] *s* Aquädukt *n*

aq'uiline nose' ['ækwɪ,laɪn] *s* Adlernase *f*

Arab ['ærəb] *adj* arabisch || *s* Araber –in *mf*

Arabia [ə'rebɪ·ə] *s* Arabien *n*

Arabic ['ærəbɪk] *adj* arabisch || *s* Arabisch *n*

arable ['ærəbəl] *adj* urbar, Ackerland *n*

arbiter ['arbɪtər] *s* Schiedsrichter *m*

arbitrary ['arbɪ,trɛri] *adj* (*act*) willkürlich; (*number*) beliebig; (*person, government*) tyrannisch

arbitrate ['arbɪ,tret] *tr* schlichten || *intr* als Schiedsrichter fungieren

arbitration [,arbɪ'treʃən] *s* Schlichtung *f*

arbitrator ['arbɪ,tretər] *s* Schiedsrichter *m*

arbor ['arbər] *s* Laube *f*; (mach) Achse *f*

arbore·tum [,arbə'ritəm] *s* (**–tums & –ta** [tə]) Baumgarten *m*

arc [ark] *s* (astr, geom, mach) Bogen *m*; (elec) Lichtbogen *m*

arcade [ar'ked] *s* Bogengang *m*, Arkade *f*

arcane [ar'ken] *adj* geheimnisvoll

arch [artʃ] *adj* (*liar, etc.*) abgefeimt || *s* Bogen *m* || *tr* wölben; (*span*) überwölben || *intr* sich wölben

archaeologist [,arkɪ'alədʒɪst] *s* Archäolog(e) *m*, Archäologin *f*

archaeology [,arkɪ'alədʒi] *s* Archäologie *f*

archaic [ar'ke·ɪk] *adj* (*word*) veraltet; (*manner, notion*) antiquiert

archangel ['ark,endʒəl] *s* Erzengel *m*

archbishop ['artʃ'bɪʃəp] *s* Erzbischof *m*

archduke ['artʃ'd(j)uk] *s* Erzherzog *m*

archenemy ['artʃ,ɛnɪmi] *s* Erzfeind *m*

archer ['artʃər] *s* Bogenschütze *m*

archery ['artʃəri] *s* Bogenschießen *n*

archipela·go [,arkɪ'pelago] *s* (**–gos & –goes**) Inselmeer *n*; (*group of islands*) Inselgruppe *f*, Archipel *m*

architect ['arkɪ,tɛkt] *s* Architekt –in *mf*

architecture ['arkɪ,tɛktʃər] *s* Architektur *f*, Baukunst *f*

archives ['arkaɪvz] *spl* Archiv *n*

arch'way' *s* Bogengang *m*, Torbogen *m*

arctic ['arktɪk] *adj* arktisch, nördlich || **the Arctic** *s* die Arktis

Arc'tic Cir'cle *s* nördlicher Polarkreis *m*

arc' weld'ing *s* Lichtbogenschweißung *f*

ardent ['ardənt] *adj* feurig, eifrig

ardor ['ardər] *s* Eifer *m*, Inbrust *f*

arduous ['ɑrdʒu·əs] *adj* mühsam

area ['eri·ə] *s (surface)* Fläche *f*; *(district)* Gegend *f*; *(field of enterprise)* Bereich *m*, Gebiet *n*; *(of danger)* Zone *f*

arena [ə'rinə] *s* Arena *f*, Kampfbahn *f*

Argentina [,ɑrdʒən'tinə] *s* Argentinien *n*

argue ['ɑrgju] *tr* erörtern; *(maintain)* behaupten; **a. into** *(ger)* dazu überreden zu *(inf)* ‖ *intr (with)* streiten (mit); **a. for** (or **against**) s.th. für (or gegen) etw eintreten; **don't a.!** keine Widerrede

argument ['ɑrgjəmənt] *s (discussion)* Erörterung *f*; *(point)* Beweisgrund *m*; *(disagreement)* Auseinandersetzung *f*; *(theme)* Thema *n*

argumentative [,ɑrgjə'mentətɪv] *adj* streitsüchtig

aria ['ɑri·ə], ['eri·ə] *s* Arie *f*

arid ['ærɪd] *adj* trocken, dürr

aridity [ə'rɪdɪti] *s* Trockenheit *f*

arise [ə'raɪz] *v (pret* arose [ə'roz]; *pp* arisen [ə'rɪzən]) *intr (come into being) (from)* entstehen (aus); *(get out of bed)* aufstehen; *(from a seat)* sich erheben; *(occur)* aufkommen, auftauchen; *(said of an opportunity)* sich bieten; *(stem) (from)* stammen (von)

aristocracy [,ærɪs'tɑkrəsi] *s* Aristokratie *f*

aristocrat [ə'rɪstə,kræt] *s* Aristokrat –in *mf*

aristocratic [ə,rɪstə'krætɪk] *adj* aristokratisch

arithmetic [ə'rɪθmətɪk] *s* Arithmetik *f*

arithmetical [,ærɪθ'metɪkəl] *adj* arithmetisch, rechnerisch

ark [ɑrk] *s* Arche *f*

ark' of the cov'enant *s* Bundeslade *f*

arm [ɑrm] *s* Arm *m*; *(of a chair)* Seitenlehne *f*; *(weapon)* Waffe *f*; **keep s.o. at arm's length** sich j–m vom Leibe halten; **take up arms** zu den Waffen greifen; **up in arms** in Aufruhr ‖ *tr* bewaffnen; ‖ *intr* sich bewaffnen

armament ['ɑrməmənt] *s* Kriegsausrüstung *f*, Bewaffnung *f*

ar'maments race' *s* Rüstungswettlauf *m*

armature ['ɑrmə,tʃər] *s (of doorbell or magnet)* Anker *m*; *(of a motor or dynamo)* Läufer *m*; *(biol)* Panzer *m*

arm'chair' *s* Lehnsessel *m*; *(unpadded)* Lehnstuhl *m*

armed' for'ces *spl* Streitkräfte *pl*

armed' rob'bery *s* bewaffneter Raubüberfall *m*

Armenia [ɑr'mini·ə] *s* Armenien *n*

armful ['ɑrm,fʊl] *s* Armvoll *m*

armistice ['ɑrmɪstɪs] *s* Waffenstillstand *m*

armor ['ɑrmər] *s* Panzer *m* ‖ *tr* panzern

ar'mored car' *s* Panzerwagen *m*

armor-piercing ['ɑrmər,pɪrsɪŋ] *adj* panzerbrechend

ar'mor plat'ing ['pletɪŋ] *s* Panzerung *f*

armory ['ɑrməri] *s (large arms storage)* Arsenal *n*; *(arms repair and storage room of a unit)* Waffenkam-

-mer *f*; *(arms factory)* Waffenfabrik *f*; *(drill hall)* Exerzierhalle *f*

arm'pit' *s* Achselhöhle *f*

arm'rest' *s* Armlehne *f*

army ['ɑrmi] *adj* Armes–, Heeres– ‖ *s* Armee *f*, Heer *n*; **join the a.** zum Militär gehen

aroma [ə'romə] *s* Aroma *n*, Duft *m*

aromatic [,ærə'mætɪk] *adj* aromatisch

around [ə'raʊnd] *adv* ringsherum; **be a. in der Nähe sein; get a.** viel herumkommen; **get a. to** *(inf)* dazukommen zu *(inf)* ‖ *prep* um *(acc)* herum; *(approximately)* etwa; *(near)* bei *(dat)*; **a. town** in der Stadt

arouse [ə'raʊz] *tr* aufwecken; *(fig)* erwecken

arraign [ə'ren] *tr (accuse)* anklagen; *(jur)* vor Gericht stellen

arrange [ə'rendʒ] *tr* arrangieren; *(in a certain order)* (an)ordnen; *(a time)* festsetzen; *(mus)* bearbeiten ‖ *intr—* **a. for** Vorkehrungen treffen für

arrangement [ə'rendʒmənt] *s* Anordnung *f*; *(agreement)* Vereinbarung *f*; *(mus)* Bearbeitung *f*; **make arrangements to** *(inf)* Vorbereitungen treffen, um zu *(inf)*

array [ə're] *s (of troops, facts)* Ordnung *f*; *(large number or quantity)* Menge *f*; *(apparel)* Staat *m* ‖ *tr* ordnen; *(dress up)* putzen

arrears [ə'rɪrz] *spl* Rückstand *m*; **in a.** rückständig

arrest [ə'rest] *s* Verhaftung *f*; **make an a. e–e** Verhaftung vornehmen; **place under a. in** Haft nehmen; **under a.** verhaftet ‖ *tr* verhaften; *(attention)* fesseln; *(a disease, progress)* hemmen

arrival [ə'raɪvəl] *s* Ankunft *f*; *(of merchandise)* Eingang *m*; *(a person)* Ankömmling *m*

arrive [ə'raɪv] *intr* ankommen; *(said of time, an event)* kommen; **a. at** *(a conclusion, decision)* erlangen

arrogance ['ærəgəns] *s* Anmaßung *f*

arrogant ['ærəgənt] *adj* anmaßend

arrogate ['ærə,get] *tr* sich [*dat*] anmaßen

arrow ['æro] *s* Pfeil *m*

ar'rowhead' *s* Pfeilspitze *f*

arsenal ['ɑrsənəl] *s* Arsenal *n*

arsenic ['ɑrsɪnɪk] *s* Arsen *n*

arson ['ɑrsən] *s* Brandstiftung *f*

arsonist ['ɑrsənɪst] *s* Brandstifter –in *mf*

art [ɑrt] *s* Kunst *f*

artery ['ɑrtəri] *s* Pulsader *f*; *(highway)* Verkehrsader *f*

artful ['ɑrtfəl] *adj (cunning)* schlau, listig; *(skillful)* kunstvoll

arthritic [ɑr'θrɪtɪk] *adj* arthritisch, gichtisch ‖ *s* Arthritiker –in *mf*

arthritis [ɑr'θraɪtɪs] *s* Arthritis *f*

artichoke ['ɑrtɪ,tʃok] *s* Artischocke *f*

article ['ɑrtɪkəl] *s (object)* Gegenstand *m*; *(com, gram, journ, jur)* Artikel *m*

articulate [ɑr'tɪkjəlɪt] *adj* deutlich ‖ [ɑr'tɪkjə,let] *tr & intr* deutlich aussprechen

artifact ['ɑrtɪ,fækt] *s* Artefakt *n*

artifice ['ɑrtɪfɪs] *s* Kunstgriff *m*

artificial [,ɑrtɪ'fɪʃəl] *adj* Kunst–,

künstlich; (*emotion, smile*) gekünstelt

artillery [ɑr'tɪləri] *s* Artillerie *f*

artil/lery·man *s* (**-men**) Artillerist *m*

artisan ['ɑrtɪzən] *s* Handwerker –in *mf*

artist ['ɑrtɪst] *s* Künstler –in *mf*

artistic [ɑr'tɪstɪk] *adj* künstlerisch

artistry ['ɑrtɪstri] *s* Kunstfertigkeit *f*

artless ['ɑrtlɪs] *adj* (*lacking art*) unkünstlerisch; (*made without skill*) stümperhaft; (*ingenuous*) unbefangen

arts/ and crafts/ *spl* Kunstgewerbe *n*

arts/ and sci/ences *spl* Geistes- und Naturwissenschaften *pl*

arty ['ɑrti] *adj* (coll) gekünstelt

Aryan ['ɛrɪ·ən], ['ɑrjən] *adj* arisch || *s* Arier –in *mf*; (*language*) Arisch *n*

as [æz], [əz] *adv* wie; as... as (eben)so ...wie; **as far as Berlin** bis nach Berlin; **as far as I know** soviel ich weiß; **as far back as 1900** schon im Jahre 1900; **as for me** was mich betrifft; **as if** als ob; **as long as** solange; (*with the proviso that*) vorausgesetzt, daß; **as soon as** sobald wie; **as though** als ob; **as well** ebensogut, auch; **as yet** bis jetzt || *rel pron* wie, was || *prep* als; **as a rule** in der Regel || *conj* wie; (*while*) als, während; (*because*) da, weil, indem; **as it were** sozusagen

asbestos [æs'bɛstəs] *adj* Asbest– || *s* Asbest *m*

ascend [ə'sɛnd] *tr* (*stairs*) hinaufsteigen; (*a throne, mountain*) besteigen || *intr* emporsteigen; (*said of a balloon, plane*) aufsteigen

ascendancy [ə'sɛndənsi] *s* Überlegenheit *f*

ascension [ə'sɛnʃən] *s* Aufsteigen *n*

Ascen/sion Day/ *s* Himmelfahrtstag *m*

ascent [ə'sɛnt] *s* (*on foot*) Besteigung *f*; (*by vehicle*) Auffahrt *f*; (*upward slope*) Steigung *f*; (& fig) Aufstieg *m*

ascertain [ˌæsər'ten] *tr* feststellen

ascetic [ə'sɛtɪk] *adj* asketisch || *s* Asket –in *mf*

ascribe [ə'skraɪb] *tr*—**a. to** zuschreiben (*dat*)

aseptic [ə'sɛptɪk] *adj* aseptisch

ash [æʃ] *s* Asche *f*; (*tree*) Esche *f*; **ashes** Asche *f*; (*mortal remains*) sterbliche Überreste *pl*

ashamed [ə'ʃemd] *adj*—**be** (or **feel**) **a.** (of) sich schämen (*genit*)

ash/can/ *s* Ascheneimer *m*

ashen ['æʃən] *adj* aschgrau

ashore [ə'ʃor] *adv* (*position*) am Land; (*direction*) ans Land

ash/tray/ *s* Aschenbecher *m*

Ash/ Wednes/day *s* Aschermittwoch *m*

Asia ['eʒə], ['eʃə] *s* Asien *n*

A/sia Mi/nor *s* Kleinasien *n*

aside [ə'saɪd] *adv* zur Seite; **a. from** außer || *s* (theat) Seitenbemerkung *f*

asinine ['æsɪˌnaɪn] *adj* eselhaft

ask [æsk] *tr* (*request*) bitten; (*demand*) auffordern; (*a high price*) fordern; (*inquire of*) fragen; **ask a question** (of s.o.) (j–m) e-e Frage stellen; **ask in** hereinbitten; **that is asking too much** das ist zuviel verlangt || *intr*

fragen; **ask for** bitten um; **ask for trouble** sich [*dat*] selbst Schwierigkeiten machen

askance [ə'kæns] *adv*—**look a. at** schief ansehen

askew [ə'skju] *adv* schräg

ask/ing *s*—**for the a.** umsonst

asleep [ə'slip] *adj* schlafend; (*numb*) eingeschlafen; **be a.** schlafen; **fall a.** einschlafen

asp [æsp] *s* Natter *f*

asparagus [ə'spærəgəs] *s* Spargel *m*

aspect ['æspɛkt] *s* Gesichtspunkt *m*

aspen ['æspən] *s* Espe *f*

aspersion [ə'spʌrʒən] *s* (eccl) Besprengung *f*; **cast aspersions on** verleumden

asphalt ['æsfɔlt], ['æsfælt] *s* Asphalt *m* || *tr* asphaltieren

asphyxiate [æs'fɪksɪˌet] *tr* & *intr* ersticken

aspirant [ə'spaɪrənt] *s* Bewerber –in *mf*

aspirate ['æspɪrɪt] *s* Hauchlaut *m* || ['æspɪˌret] *tr* behauchen

aspire [ə'spaɪr] *intr* (*after, to*) streben (*nach*); **a. to** (*inf*) danach streben zu (*inf*)

aspirin ['æspɪrɪn] *s* Aspirin *n*

ass [æs] *s* Esel *m*; (*vulg*) Arsch *m*; **make an ass of oneself** (sl) sich lächerlich machen

assail [ə'sel] *tr* angreifen, anfallen; (*with questions*) bestürmen

assassin [ə'sæsɪn] *s* Meuchelmörder –in *mf*

assassinate [ə'sæsɪˌnet] *tr* ermorden

assassination [əˌsæsɪ'neʃən] *s* Meuchelmord *m*, Ermordung *f*

assault [ə'sɔlt] *s* Überfall *m*; (*rape*) Vergewaltigung *f*; (*physical violence*) (jur) tätlicher Angriff *m*; (*threat of violence*) (jur) unmittelbare Bedrohung *f*; (mil) Sturm *m* || *tr* (er)stürmen, anfallen; (jur) tätlich beleidigen

assault/ and bat/tery *s* schwere tätliche Beleidigung *f*

assay [ə'se], ['æse] *s* Prüfung *f* || [ə'se] *tr* prüfen

assemble [ə'sɛmbəl] *tr* versammeln; (mach) montieren || *intr* sich versammeln

assembly [ə'sɛmbli] *s* Versammlung *f*; (mach) Montage *f*; (pol) Unterhaus *n*

assem/bly line/ *s* Fließband *n*

assent [ə'sɛnt] *s* Zustimmung *f* || *intr* (**to**) zustimmen (*dat*)

assert [ə'sʌrt] *tr* behaupten; **a. oneself** sich behaupten

assertion [ə'sʌrʃən] *s* Behauptung *f*; (*of rights*) Geltendmachung *f*

assess [ə'sɛs] *tr* (*damage*) festsetzen; (*property*) (at) (ab)schätzen (auf *acc*); **assessed value** Schätzungswert *m*

assessment [ə'sɛsmənt] *s* (*of damage*) Festsetzung *f*; (*valuation*) Einschätzung *f*; (*of real estate*) Veranlagung *f*

assessor [ə'sɛsər] *s* Steuereinschätzer *m*

asset ['æset] *s* Vorzug *m;* (com) Aktivposten *m;* **assets** Vermögenswerte *pl;* **assets and liabilities** Aktiva und Passiva *pl*

assiduous [ə'sɪdʒʊ-əs] *adj* emsig

assign [ə'saɪn] *tr* zuweisen; (*homework*) aufgeben; (*transfer*) (jur) abtreten; (mil) zuteilen

assignment [ə'saɪnmənt] *s* Zuweisung *f;* (*homework*) Aufgabe *f;* (*task*) Auftrag *m,* Aufgabe *f;* (*transference*) (jur) Abtretung *f;* (*to a unit*) (mil) Zuteilung *f*

assimilate [ə'sɪmɪ‚let] *tr* angleichen || *intr* sich angleichen

assimilation [ə‚sɪmɪ'leʃən] *s* Assimilierung *f,* Angleichung *f*

assist [ə'sɪst] *s* (sport) Zuspiel *n* || *tr* beistehen (*dat*) || *intr*—**a. in** beistehen bei, behilflich sein bei

assistance [ə'sɪstəns] *s* Hilfe *f*

assistant [ə'sɪstənt] *adj* Hilfs-, Unter- || *s* (*helper*) Gehilfe *m,* Gehilfin *f*

associate [ə'soʃɪ‚ɪt] *adj* Mit-, beigeordnet; (*member*) außerordentlich || *s* (*companion*) Gefährte *m,* Gefährtin *f;* (*colleague*) Kollege *m,* Kollegin *f;* (com) Partner –in *mf* || [ə'soʃɪ‚et] *tr* verbinden || *intr* (with) verkehren (mit)

asso'ciate profes'sor *s* außerordentlicher Professor *m*

association [ə‚soʃɪ'eʃən] *s* (*connection*) Verbindung *f;* (*social intercourse*) Verkehr *m;* (*society*) Verband *m;* (*suggested ideas, feelings*) Assoziation *f*

assonance ['æsənəns] *s* Assonanz *f*

assorted [ə'sɔrtɪd] *adj* verschieden

assortment [ə'sɔrtmənt] *s* Sortiment *n*

assuage [ə'swedʒ] *tr* (*pain*) lindern; (*hunger*) befriedigen; (*thirst*) stillen

assume [ə's(j)um] *tr* (*a fact as true; a certain shape, property, habit*) annehmen; (*a duty*) auf sich nehmen; (*office*) antreten; (*power*) ergreifen; **assuming that** vorausgesetzt, daß

assumed' *adj* (*feigned*) erheuchelt; **a. name** Deckname *m*

assumption [ə'sʌmpʃən] *s* (*supposition*) Annahme *f;* (*e.g., of power*) Übernahme *f*

assurance [ə'ʃʊrəns] *s* Versicherung *f*

assure [ə'ʃʊr] *tr* versichern

aster ['æstər] *s* Aster *f*

asterisk ['æstə‚rɪsk] *s* Sternchen *n*

astern [ə'stɜrn] *adv* achtern, achteraus

asthma ['æzmə] *s* Asthma *n*

astonish [ə'stɑnɪʃ] *tr* in Erstaunen setzen; **be astonished at** staunen über (*acc*), sich wundern über (*acc*)

aston'ishing *adj* erstaunlich

astonishment [ə'stɑnɪʃmənt] *s* Erstaunen *n,* Verwunderung *f*

astound [ə'staʊnd] *tr* überraschen

astound'ing *adj* erstaunlich

astray [ə'stre] *adv*—**go a.** irregehen; **lead a.** irreführen

astride [ə'straɪd] *adv* rittlings || *prep* (*a road*) an beiden Seiten (*genit*); (*a horse*) rittlings auf (*dat*)

astringent [ə'strɪndʒənt] *adj* stopfend || *s* Stopfmittel *n*

astrology [ə'strɑlədʒɪ] *s* Astrologie *f*

astronaut ['æstrə‚nɔt] *s* Astronaut *m*

astronautics [‚æstrə'nɔtɪks] *s* Raumfahrtwissenschaft *f,* Astronautik *f*

astronomer [ə'strɑnəmər] *s* Astronom –in *mf*

astronomic(al) [‚æstrə'nɑmɪk(əl)] *adj* astronomisch

astronomy [ə'strɑnəmɪ] *s* Astronomie *f*

astute [ə'st(j)ut] *adj* scharfsinnig; (*cunning*) schlau

asunder [ə'sʌndər] *adv* auseinander

asylum [ə'saɪləm] *s* (*refuge*) Asyl *n;* (*for the insane*) Irrenhaus *n*

at [æt], [ət] *prep* (*position*) an (*dat*), auf (*dat*), bei (*dat*), zu (*dat*); (*direction*) auf (*acc*), gegen (*acc*), nach (*dat*), zu (*dat*); (*manner, circumstance*) auf (*acc*), in (*dat*), unter (*dat*), bei (*dat*), zu (*dat*); (*time*) um (*acc*), bei (*dat*), auf (*dat*) zu (*dat*); **at all** (*in questions*) überhaupt; **at high prices** zu hohen Preisen; **even at that** sogar so

atheism ['eθɪ‚ɪzəm] *s* Atheismus *m*

atheist ['eθɪ‚ɪst] *s* Atheist –in *mf*

Athens ['æθɪns] *s* Athen *n*

athlete ['æθlit] *s* Sportler –in *mf*

ath'lete's foot' *s* Fußflechte *f*

athletic [æθ'letɪk] *adj* athletisch, Sport-, Turn- || **athletics** *s* Athletik *f*

Atlantic [æt'læntɪk] *adj* atlantisch || *s* Atlantik *m*

atlas ['ætləs] *s* Atlas *m*

atmosphere ['ætməs‚fɪr] *s* (& fig) Atmosphäre *f*

atmospheric [‚ætməs'ferɪk] *adj* atmosphärisch

atom ['ætəm] *s* Atom *n*

atomic [ə'tɑmɪk] *adj* atomisch, atomar, Atom-

atom'ic age' *s* Atomzeitalter *n*

atom'ic bomb' *s* Atombombe *f*

atom'ic pow'er *s* Atomkraft *f;* **atomic powers** (pol) Atommächte *pl*

atomizer ['ætə‚maɪzər] *s* Zerstäuber *m*

atone [ə'ton] *intr*—**a. for** büßen

atonement [ə'tonmənt] *s* Buße *f*

atrocious [ə'troʃəs] *adj* gräßlich

atrocity [ə'trɑsɪtɪ] *s* Greueltat *f*

atro•phy ['ætrəfɪ] *s* Verkümmerung *f,* Atrophie *f* || *v* (*pret & pp* **-phied**) *tr* auszehren || *intr* verkümmern

attach [ə'tætʃ] *tr* (*with glue, stitches, tacks*) (to) anheften (an *acc*); (*connect*) (to) befestigen (an *acc*); (*importance*) (to) beimessen (*dat*); (*a person*) (jur) verhaften; (*a thing*) (jur) beschlagnahmen; (mil) (to) zuteilen (*dat*); **a. oneself to** sich anschließen an (*acc*); **be attached to** festhalten an (*dat*); (fig) verwachsen sein mit

attaché [‚ætə'ʃe] *s* Attaché *m*

attaché' case' *s* Aktenköfferchen *n*

attachment [ə'tætʃmənt] *s* Befestigung *f;* (*regard*) (to) Zuneigung *f* (zu); (*device*) Zusatzgerät *n;* (*of a person*) (jur) Verhaftung *f;* (*of a thing*) (jur) Beschlagnahme *f*

attack [ə'tæk] *s* Angriff *m;* (pathol)

Anfall *m* ‖ *tr & intr* angreifen; (pathol) überfallen

attain [ə'ten] *tr* erreichen, erzielen ‖ *intr*—**a. to** erreichen

attainment [ə'tenmənt] *s* Erreichen *n*; **attainments** Fertigkeiten *pl*

attempt [ə'tempt] *s* Versuch *m*; (*assault*) Attentat *n* ‖ *tr* versuchen

attend [ə'tend] *tr* beiwohnen (*dat*); (*school, church*) besuchen; (*accompany*) begleiten; (*a patient*) behandeln ‖ *intr*—**a. to** nachgehen (*dat*), erledigen

attendance [ə'tendəns] *s* Besuch *m*; (*number in attendance*) Besucherzahl *f*; (med) Behandlung *f*

attendant [ə'tendənt] *s* (*servant, waiter*) Diener –in *mf*; (*keeper*) Wärter –in *mf*; (*at a gas station*) Tankwart *m*; (*escort*) Begleiter –in *mf*

attention [ə'tenʃən] *s* Aufmerksamkeit *f*; Acht *f*; **a. Mr. X.** zu Händen von Herrn X; **call a. to** hinweisen auf (*acc*); **call s.o.'s a. to** j–n aufmerksam machen auf (*acc*); **pay a.** achtgeben; **pay a. to** achten auf (*acc*); **stand at a.** stillstehen ‖ *interj* (mil) Achtung!

attentive [ə'tentɪv] *adj* aufmerksam

attenuate [ə'tenjʊ͵et] *tr* (*dilute, thin*) verdünnen; (*weaken*) abschwächen

attest [ə'test] *tr* bezeugen ‖ *intr*—**a. to** bezeugen

attic ['ætɪk] *s* Dachboden *m*; (*as living quarters*) Mansarde *f*

attire [ə'taɪr] *s* Putz *m* ‖ *tr* kleiden

attitude ['ætɪ͵t(j)ud] *s* Haltung *f*; (aer, rok) Lage *f*

attorney [ə'tarni] *s* Rechtsanwalt *m*

attor'ney gen'eral *s* (attorneys general) Justizminister *m*

attract [ə'trækt] *tr* anziehen, reizen; (*attention*) erregen

attraction [ə'trækʃən] *s* Anziehungskraft *f*; (*that which attracts*) Anziehungspunkt *m*; (*in a circus, variety show*) Attraktion *f*; (theat) Zugstück *n*

attractive [ə'træktɪv] *adj* reizvoll; (*price, offer*) günstig

attribute ['ætrɪ͵bjut] *s* Attribut *n* ‖ [ə'trɪbjut] *tr* (**to**) zuschreiben (*dat*)

attrition [ə'trɪʃən] *s* Abnutzung *f*, Verschleiß *m*

attune [ə't(j)un] *tr* (**to**) abstimmen (auf *acc*)

auburn ['ɔbərn] *adj* kastanienbraun

auction ['ɔkʃən] *s* Auktion *f* ‖ *tr*—**a. off** versteigern; **be auctioned off** unter den Hammer kommen

auctioneer [͵ɔkʃən'ɪr] *s* Versteigerer –in *mf*

audacious [ɔ'deʃəs] *adj* (*daring*) kühn; (*brazen*) keck

audacity [ɔ'dæsɪti] *s* (*daring*) Kühnheit *f*; (*insolence*) Unverschämtheit *f*

audience ['ɔdɪ͵əns] *s* (*spectators*) Publikum *n*; (*formal hearing*) Audienz *f*; (rad) Zuhörerschaft *f*; (telv) Fernsehpublikum *n*

au'dio fre'quency ['ɔdɪ͵o] *s* Tonfrequenz *f*, Hörfrequenz *f*

au'dio-vis'ual *adj* audiovisuell; **a. aids** Lehrmittel *pl*

audit ['ɔdɪt] *s* Rechnungsprüfung *f* ‖ *tr* prüfen, revidieren; (*a lecture*) als Gasthörer belegen

audition [ɔ'dɪʃən] *s* Hörprobe *f* ‖ *tr* vorspielen (or vorsingen) lassen ‖ *intr* vorspielen, vorsingen

auditor ['ɔdɪtər] *s* (com) Rechnungsprüfer –in *mf*; (educ) Gasthörer –in *mf*

auditorium [͵ɔdɪ'torɪ͵əm] *s* Hörsaal *m*

auger ['ɔgər] *s* Bohrer *m*

augment [ɔg'ment] *tr* (*in size*) vergrößern; (*in number*) vermehren ‖ *intr* sich vergrößern; sich vermehren

augur ['ɔgər] *s* Augur *m* ‖ *intr* weissagen; **a. well for** Gutes versprechen für

augury ['ɔgəri] *s* Weissagung *f*

august [ɔ'gʌst] *adj* erhaben ‖ **August** ['ɔgəst] *s* August *m*

aunt [ænt], [ɑnt] *s* Tante *f*

auricle ['ɔrɪkəl] *s* äußeres Ohr *n*; (*of the heart*) Herzohr *n*

auspices ['ɔspɪsɪz] *spl* Auspizien *pl*

auspicious [ɔs'pɪʃəs] *adj* glückverheißend

austere [ɔs'tɪr] *adj* (*stern*) streng; (*simple*) einfach; (*frugal*) genügsam; (*style*) schmucklos

Australia [ɔ'streljə] *s* Australien *n*

Australian [ɔ'streljən] *adj* australisch ‖ *s* Australier –in *mf*

Austria ['ɔstrɪ͵ə] *s* Österreich *n*

Austrian ['ɔstrɪ͵ən] *adj* österreichisch ‖ *s* Österreicher –in *mf*; (*dialect*) Österreichisch *n*

authentic [ɔ'θentɪk] *adj* authentisch

authenticate [ɔ'θentɪ͵ket] *tr* (*establish as genuine*) als echt erweisen; (*a document*) beglaubigen

author ['ɔθər] *s* (*of a book*) Autor –in *mf*; (*creator*) Urheber –in *mf*

authoritative [ɔ'θɔrɪ͵tetɪv] *adj* maßgebend

authority [ə'θɔrɪti] *s* (*power; expert*) Autorität *f*; (*right*) Recht *n*; (*approval*) Genehmigung *f*; (*source*) Quelle *f*; (*commanding influence*) Ansehen *n*; (*authoritative body*) Behörde *f*; **on one's own a.** auf eigene Verantwortung; **the authorities** die Behörden

authorize ['ɔθə͵raɪz] *tr* autorisieren

au'thorship' *s* Autorschaft *f*

au-to ['ɔto] *s* (–tos) Auto *n*

autobiography [͵ɔtobaɪ'ɑgrəfi] *s* Selbstbiographie *f*

autocratic [͵ɔtə'krætɪk] *adj* autokratisch

autograph ['ɔtə͵græf] *s* Autogramm *n* ‖ *tr* autographieren

automat ['ɔtə͵mæt] *s* Automatenrestaurant *n*

automatic [͵ɔtə'mætɪk] *adj* automatisch ‖ *s* Selbstladepistole *f*

automat'ic transmis'sion *s* Automatik *f*

automation [͵ɔtə'meʃən] *s* Automation *f*

automa·ton [ɔ'tɑmə͵tɑn] *s* (–tons & –ta [tə]) Automat *m*

automobile [ˌɔtəmoˈbil] s Automobil n

automotive [ˌɔtəˈmotɪv] adj Auto-

autonomous [ɔˈtʌnəməs] adj autonom

autonomy [ɔˈtɑnəmi] s Autonomie f

autopsy [ˈɔtɑpsi] s Obduktion f

autumn [ˈɔtəm] adj Herbst– ‖ s Herbst m

autumnal [ɔˈtʌmnəl] adj herbstlich

auxiliary [ogˈzɪljəri] adj Hilfs– ‖ s (helper) Helfer –in mf; (gram) Hilfszeitwort n; **auxiliaries** (mil) Hilfstruppen pl

avail [əˈvel] s—to no a. nutzlos; **without a.** vergeblich ‖ tr nützen (dat); **a. oneself of** sich bedienen (genit) ‖ intr nützen

available [əˈveləbəl] adj vorhanden; (articles, products) erhältlich; (e.g., documents) zugänglich; **be a.** (for consultation, etc.) zu sprechen sein; **make a. (to)** zur Verfügung stellen (dat)

avalanche [ˈævəˌlænt∫] s Lawine f

avarice [ˈævərɪs] s Habsucht f, Geiz m

avaricious [ˌævəˈrɪ∫əs] adj geizig

avenge [əˈvendʒ] tr (a person) rächen; (a crime) ahnden; **a. oneself on** sich rächen an (dat)

avenger [əˈvendʒər] s Rächer –in mf

avenue [ˈævəˌn(j)u] s (wide street) Straße f; (fig) Weg m

average [ˈævərɪdʒ] adj Durchschnitts– ‖ s Durchschnitt m; (naut) Havarie f; **on the a.** im Durchschnitt ‖ tr (amount to, as a mean quantity) durchschnittlich betragen; (find the average of) den Durchschnitt berechnen von; (earn on the average) durchschnittlich verdienen; (travel on the average) durchschnittlich zurücklegen

averse [əˈvʌrs] adj (to) abgeneigt (dat)

aversion [əˈvʌrʒən] s (to) Abneigung f (gegen)

avert [əˈvʌrt] tr abwenden

aviary [ˈevɪˌeri] s Vogelhaus n

aviation [ˌevɪˈe∫ən] s Flugwesen n

aviator [ˈevɪˌetər] s Flieger –in mf

avid [ˈævɪd] adj gierig

avocation [ˌævəˈke∫ən] s Nebenbeschäftigung f

avoid [əˈvɔɪd] tr (a person) meiden; (a thing) vermeiden

avoidable [əˈvɔɪdəbəl] adj vermeidbar

avoidance [əˈvɔɪdəns] s (of a person) Meidung f; (of a thing) Vermeidung f

avow [əˈvau] tr bekennen, gestehen

avowal [əˈvau·əl] s Bekenntnis n

avowed' adj (declared) erklärt; (acknowledged) offen anerkannt

await [əˈwet] tr erwarten

awake [əˈwek] adj wach, munter ‖ v (pret & pp **awoke** [əˈwok] & **awaked**) tr wecken; (fig) erwecken ‖ intr erwachen

awaken [əˈweken] tr wecken; (fig) erwecken ‖ intr erwachen

awak′ening s Erwachen n; **a rude a.** ein unsanftes Erwachen

award [əˈword] s Preis m, Prämie f ‖ tr (to) zuerkennen (dat)

aware [əˈwer] adj—**be a. of** sich [dat] bewußt sein (genit)

awareness [əˈwernɪs] s Bewußtsein n

awash [əˈwɑ∫] adj überschwemmt

away [əˈwe] adj abwesend; (on a trip) verreist; (sport) Auswärts– ‖ adv fort, (hin)weg; **do a. with** abschaffen; **make a. with** (kill) umbringen

awe [ɔ] s (of) Ehrfurcht f (vor dat); **stand in awe of s.o.** vor j–m Ehrfurcht haben

awesome [ˈɔsəm] adj ehrfurchtgebietend

awful [ˈɔfəl] adj ehrfurchtgebietend; (coll) furchtbar

awfully [ˈɔfəli] adv (coll) furchtbar

awhile [əˈhwaɪl] adv eine Zeitlang

awkward [ˈɔkwərd] adj ungeschickt; (situation) peinlich

awl [ɔl] s Ahle f, Pfriem m

awning [ˈɔnɪŋ] s Markise f

awry [əˈraɪ] adv—**go a.** schiefgehen

ax [æks] s Axt f, Beil n

axiom [ˈæksɪ·əm] s Axiom n

axiomatic [ˌæksɪ·əˈmætɪk] adj axiomatisch

axis [ˈæksɪs] s (**axes** [ˈæksiz]) Achse f

axle [ˈæksəl] s Achse f

ay(e) [aɪ] adv (yes) ja; aye, aye, sir! zu Befehl, Herr (Leutnant, etc.) ‖ s Ja n, Jastimme f; **the ayes have it** die Mehrheit ist dafür

azalea [əˈzeljə] s Azalee f

azure [ˈəʒər] adj azurblau ‖ s Azur m

B

B, b [bi] zweiter Buchstabe des englischen Alphabets; (mus) H n; **B flat** B n; **B sharp** His n

babble [ˈbæbəl] s Geschwätz n; (of brook) Geplätscher n ‖ tr schwätzen ‖ intr schwätzen; (said of a brook) plätschern

babe [beb] s Kind n; (naive person) Kindskopf m; (pretty girl) Puppe f

baboon [bæˈbun] s (zool) Pavian m

ba·by [ˈbebi] s Baby n; (youngest child) Nesthäkchen n ‖ v (pret & pp **–bied**) tr verzärteln

ba′by bot′tle s Saugflasche f

ba′by car′riage s Kinderwagen m

ba′by grand′ s Stutzflügel m

ba′by pow′der s Kinderpuder m

ba′by-sit′ v (pret & pp **–sat**; ger **–sitting**) intr Kinder hüten

ba′by-sit′ter s Babysitter m

ba′by talk′ s Babysprache f
ba′by teeth′ spl Milchzähne pl
baccalaureate [ˌbækəˈlɔːrɪ·ɪt] s (bachelor's degree) Bakkalaureat n; (service) Gottesdienst m bei der akademischen Promotion
bacchanal [ˈbækənəl] s (devotee) Bacchantin f; (orgy) Bacchanal n
bachelor [ˈbætʃələr] s Junggeselle m
bach′elorhood′ s Junggesellenstand m
Bach′elor of Arts′ s Bakkalaureus m der Geisteswissenschaften
Bach′elor of Sci′ence s Bakkalaureus m der Naturwissenschaften
bacil·lus [bəˈsɪləs] s (-li [laɪ]) Bazillus m, Stäbchenbakterie f
back [bæk] adj Hinter–, Rück– ‖ s (of a man, animal) Rücken m, Kreuz n; (of a hand, book, knife, mountain) Rücken m; (of a head, house, door, picture, sheet) Rückseite f; (of a fabric) linke Seite f; (of a seat) Rückenlehne f; (of a coin) Kehrseite f; (of clothing) Rückenteil m; (sport) Verteidiger m; at the b. of (e.g., a room) hinten in (dat); b. to b. (coll) nacheinander; behind s.o.'s b. hinter j-s Rücken; have one's b. to the wall an die Wand gedrückt sein; turn one's b. on s.o. (& fig) j–m den Rücken kehren ‖ adv zurück; b. and forth hin und her; b. home bei uns (zulande); ‖ tr (a person) den Rücken decken (dat); (a candidate, product) befürworten; (a horse) setzen auf (acc); b. up (a car) rückwärts laufen lassen; b. water rückwärts rudern; das Schiff rückwärts fahren lassen; (fig) sich zurückziehen ‖ intr —b. down klein beigeben; b. down from abstehen von; b. out of zurücktreten von; b. up zurückfahren, zurückgehen; (said of a sewer) zurückfließen
back′ache′ s Rückenschmerzen pl
back′bit′ing s Anschwärzerei f
back′bone′ s Rückgrat n; (fig) Willenskraft f
back′break′ing adj mühsam
back′ door′ s Hintertür f
back′drop′ s (fig & theat) Hintergrund m
backer [ˈbækər] s Förderer m, Unterstützer m; (com) Hintermann m
back′fire′ s Fehlzündung f ‖ intr fehlzünden; (fig) nach hinten losgehen
back′ground′ adj Hintergrund– ‖ s (& fig) Hintergrund m; (e.g., of an applicant) Vorbildung f, Erfahrung f
back′hand′ s (tennis) Rückhandschlag m
back′hand′ed adj Rückhand–; (compliment) zweideutig
back′ing s Unterstützung f; (material) versteifende Ausfütterung f
back′lash′ s (& fig) Rückschlag m; (mach) toter Gang m
back′log′ s Rückstand m
back′ or′der s rückständiger Auftrag m
back′ pay′ s rückständiger Lohn m
back′ seat′ s Rücksitz m
back′side′ s Rückseite f; (coll) Gesäß n

back′space′ intr den Wagen zurückschieben
back′space key′ s Rücktaste f
back′spin′ s Rückeffet n
back′stage′ adv hinten auf der Bühne
back′ stairs′ spl Hintertreppe f
back′stop′ s (baseball) Ballfang m
back′ stretch′ s Gegengerade f
back′stroke′ s Rückenschwimmen n
back′swept′ adj pfeilförmig
back′ talk′ s freche Antworten pl
back′track′ intr denselben Weg zurückgehen; (fig) e–n Rückzieher machen
back′up′ s (stand-by) Beistand m; (in traffic) Verkehrsstauung f
back′up light′ s (aut) Rückfahrscheinwerfer m
backward [ˈbækwərd] adj rückwärts gerichtet, Rück–; (country) rückständig; (in development) zurückgeblieben; (shy) zurückhaltend ‖ adv rückwärts, zurück; (fig) verkehrt; b. and forward vor und zurück
backwardness [ˈbækwərdnɪs] s Rückständigkeit f; (shyness) Zurückhaltung f
back′wash′ s zurücklaufende Strömung f
back′wa′ter s Rückstau m; (fig) Öde f
back′woods′ spl Hinterwälder pl
back′yard′ s Hinterhof m
bacon [ˈbekən] s Speck m; bring home the b. (sl) es schaffen
bacteria [bækˈtɪrɪ·ə] spl Bakterien pl
bacteriological [bækˌtɪrɪ·əˈlɑdʒɪkəl] adj bakteriologisch
bacteriology [bækˌtɪrɪˈɑlədʒɪ] s Bakteriologie f, Bakterienkunde f
bacteri·um [bækˈtɪrɪ·əm] s (-a [ə]) Bakterie f
bad [bæd] adj schlecht, schlimm; (unfavorable) ungünstig; (risk) zweifelhaft; (debt) uneinbringlich; (check) ungedeckt; (blood) böse; (breath) übelriechend; (language) anstößig; (pain) stark; bad for schädlich (dat); from bad to worse immer schlimmer; I feel bad about it es tut mir leid; too bad! schade!
bad′ egg′ s (sl) übler Kunde m
badge [bædʒ] s Abzeichen n
badger [ˈbædʒər] s Dachs m ‖ tr quälen
bad′ luck′ s Unglück n, Pech n
badly [ˈbædli] adv schlecht, übel; (coll) dringend; b. wounded schwerverwundet; be b. off übel dran sein
badminton [ˈbædmɪntən] s Federballspiel n
bad′-tem′pered adj schlecht gelaunt
baffle [ˈbæfəl] s Sperre f; (on loudspeaker) Schallwand f ‖ tr verwirren; (gas) drosseln
baf′fling adj verwirrend
bag [bæg] s Sack m; (for small items) Tüte f; (for travel) Reisetasche f; (sl) Frauenzimmer n; (hunt) Strecke f; bag and baggage mit Sack und Pack; it's in the bag das haben wir in der Tasche ‖ v (pret & pp bagged; ger bagging) tr einsacken; (hunt) zur Strecke bringen ‖ intr sich bauschen
baggage [ˈbægɪdʒ] s Gepäck n

bag′gage car′ s Gepäckwagen m

bag′gage check′ s Gepäckschein m

bag′gage count′er s Gepäckabfertigung f

bag′gage room′ s Gepäckaufbewahrung f

baggy ['bægi] adj bauschig

bag′pipe′ s Dudelsack m; play the b. dudeln

bail [bel] s Kaution f; be out on b. gegen Kaution auf freiem Fuß sein; put up b. for bürgen für || tr—b. out (water) aussschöpfen; (fig) retten; (jur) durch Kaution aus der Haft befreien || intr Wasser schöpfen; b. out (aer) abspringen

bailiff ['belif] s (agr) Gutsverwalter m; (jur) Gerichtsvollzieher m

bailiwick ['belıwık] s (fig) Spezialgebiet n; (jur) Amtsbezirk m

bait [bet] s (& fig) Köder m || tr (traps) mit Köder versehen; (lure) ködern; (harass) quälen

bake [bek] tr (bread) backen; (meat) braten; (in a kiln) brennen || intr backen; (meat) braten

baked′ goods′ spl Gebäck n, Backwaren pl

baked′ pota′to s gebackene Pellkartoffel f

baker ['bekər] s Bäcker –in mf

bak′er′s doz′en s dreizehn Stück pl

bakery ['bekəri] s Bäckerei f

bak′ing pow′der s Backpulver n

bak′ing so′da s Backpulver n

balance ['bæləns] s (equilibrium) Gleichgewicht n; (remainder) Rest m; (scales) Waage f; (in a bank account) Bankguthaben n; (fig) Fassung f; (com) Bilanz f; || tr balancieren; (offset) abgleichen; (make come out even) ausgleichen || intr balancieren

bal′ance of pay′ments s Devisenbilanz f

bal′ance of pow′er s Gleichgewicht n der Kräfte

bal′ance sheet′ s Bilanz f

bal′ance wheel′ s (horol) Unruh f

balcony ['bælkəni] s Balkon m; (theat) Rang m

bald [bɔld] adj kahl; (eagle) weißköpfig; (fig) unverblümt

bald′head′ed adj kahlköpfig

baldness ['bɔldnıs] s Kahlheit f

bald′ spot′ s Kahlstelle f

bale [bel] s Ballen m || tr in Ballen verpacken

baleful ['belfəl] adj unheilvoll

balk [bɔk] intr (at) scheuen (vor dat)

Balkan ['bɔlkən] adj Balkan– || s— the Balkans die Balkans m

balky ['bɔki] adj störrisch

ball [bɔl] s Ball m; (dance) Ball m; (of yarn) Knäuel m & n; (of the foot) Ballen m; be on the b. (coll) bei der Sache sein; have a lot on the b. (coll) viel auf dem Kasten haben

ballad ['bæləd] s Ballade f

ball′-and-sock′et joint′ s Kugelgelenk n

ballast ['bæləst] s (aer, naut) Ballast m; (rr) Schotter m || tr (aer, naut) mit Ballast beladen; (rr) beschottern

ball′ bear′ing s Kugellager n

ballerina [,bælə'rinə] s Ballerina f

ballet [bæ'le] s Ballett n

ball′ han′dling s (sport) Balltechnik f

ballistic [bə'lıstık] adj ballistisch || ballistics s Ballistik f

balloon [bə'lun] s Ballon m

ballot ['bælət] s Stimmzettel m || intr abstimmen

bal′lot box′ s Wahlurne f

ball′-point pen′ s Kugelschreiber m

ball′room′ s Ballsaal m, Tanzsaal m

ballyhoo ['bælı,hu] s Tamtam n || tr Tamtam machen um

balm [bam] s (& fig) Balsam m

balmy ['bami] adj mild, lind; be b. (coll) e–n Tick haben

baloney [bə'loni] s (sausage) (coll) Bolognawurst f; (sl) Quatsch m

balsam ['bɔlsəm] s Balsam m

Baltic ['bɔltık] adj baltisch || s Ostsee f

baluster ['bæləstər] s Geländersäule f

balustrade ['bæləs,tred] s Brüstung f

bamboo [bæm'bu] s Bambus m, Bambusrohr n

bamboozle [bæm'buzəl] tr (cheat) anschmieren; (mislead) irreführen; (perplex) verwirren

ban [bæn] s Verbot n; (eccl) Bann m; || v (pret & pp banned; ger banning) tr verbieten

banal ['benəl] adj banal

banana [bə'nænə] s Banane f; (tree) Bananenbaum m

band [bænd] s (e.g., of a hat) Band n; (stripe) Streifen m; (gang) Bande f; (mus) Musikkapelle f; (rad) Band n || intr—b. together sich zusammenrotten

bandage ['bændıdʒ] s Verband m || tr verbinden

Band′-Aid′ s (trademark) Schnellverband m

bandit ['bændıt] s Bandit m

band′lead′er s Kapellmeister m

band′ saw′ s Bandsäge f

band′stand′ s Musikpavillon m

band′wag′on s—climb the b. mitlaufen

bane [ben] s Ruin m

baneful ['benfəl] adj verderblich

bang [bæŋ] s Knall m; bangs Ponyfrisur f; with a b. mit Krach || tr knallen lassen; (a door) zuschlagen; || intr knallen; (said of a door) zuschlagen; || interj bums! paff!

bang′-up′ adj (sl) tipptopp, prima

banish ['bænıʃ] tr verbannen

banishment ['bænıʃmənt] s Verbannung f

banister ['bænıstər] s Geländer n

bank [bæŋk] s Bank f; (of a river) Ufer n; (in a road) Überhöhung f; (aer) Schräglage f; (rr) Böschung f; || tr (money) in e–r Bank deponieren; (a road) überhöhen; (aer) in Schräglage bringen || intr (at) ein Bankkonto haben (bei); (aer) in die Kurve gehen; b. on bauen auf (acc)

bank′ account′ s Bankkonto n

bank′ bal′ance s Bankguthaben n

bank′book′ s Sparbuch n, Bankbuch n

banker ['bæŋkər] s Bankier –in mf

bank′ing *s* Bankwesen *n*

bank′ note′ *s* Geldschein *m*

bank′roll′ *s* Rolle *f* von Geldscheinen ‖ *tr* (sl) finanzieren

bankrupt [′bæŋkrʌpt] *adj* bankrott; **go b.** Pleite machen ‖ *tr* bankrott machen

bankruptcy [′bæŋkrʌptsi] *s* Bankrott *m*

bank′ state′ment *s* Bankausweis *m*

bank′ tell′er *s* Kassierer –in *mf*

banner [′bænər] *s* Fahne *f*, Banner *n*

banquet [′bæŋkwɪt] *s* Bankett *n* ‖ *intr* tafeln

banter [′bæntər] *s* Neckerei *f* ‖ *intr* necken

baptism [′bæptɪzəm] *s* Taufe *f*

baptismal [bæp′tɪzməl] *adj* Tauf-

baptis′mal certi′ficate *s* Taufschein *m*

bap′tism of fire′ *s* Feuertaufe *f*

Baptist [′bæptɪst] *s* Baptist –in *mf*, Wiedertäufer *m*

baptistery [′bæptɪstəri] *s* Taufkapelle *f*

baptize [bæp′taɪz] *tr* taufen

bar [bar] *s* Stange *f*; (*of a door, window*) Riegel *m*; (*of gold, etc.*) Barren *m*; (*of chocolate, soap*) Riegel *m*; (*barroom*) Bar *f*; (*counter*) Schanktisch *m*; (*obstacle*) (**to**) Schranke *f* (*gegen*); (*jur*) Gerichtshof *m*, Anwaltschaft *f*; (*bar line*) (*mus*) Taktstrich *m*; (*measure*) Takt *m*; (*naut*) Barre *f*; **be admitted to the bar** zur Advokatur zugelassen werden; **behind bars** hinter Gittern; ‖ *prep*— **bar none** ohne Ausnahme ‖ *v* (*pret & pp* **barred;** *ger* **barring**) *tr* (*a door*) verriegeln; (*a window*) vergittern; (*the way*) versperren; **bar s.o. from** j-n hindern an (*dat*)

barb [barb] *s* Widerhaken *m*; (fig) Stachelrede *f*; (bot) Bart *m*

barbarian [bar′berɪən] *s* Barbar *m*

barbaric [bar′bærɪk] *adj* barbarisch

barbarism [′barbə,rɪzəm] *s* Barbarei *f*; (gram) Barbarismus *m*

barbarity [bar′berɪti] *s* Barbarei *f*

barbarous [′barbərəs] *adj* barbarisch

barbecue [′barbɪ,kju] *s* am Spieß (*or* am Rost) gebratenes Fleisch *n*; (*grill*) Bratrost *m*; (*outdoor meal*) Gartengrillfest *n* ‖ *tr* am Spieß (*or* am Rost) braten

barbed′ wire′ *s* Stacheldraht *m*

barbed′-wire entan′glement *s* Drahtverhau *m*

barber [′barbər] *s* Friseur *m*

bar′ber chair′ *s* Friseursessel *m*

bar′bershop′ *s* Friseurladen *m*

bard [bard] *s* Barde *m*

bare [ber] *adj* nackt, bloß; (*tree, wall*) kahl; (*facts*) nackt; (*majority*) knapp ‖ *tr* entblößen; (*heart, thoughts*) offenbaren; (*teeth*) fletschen

bare′back′ *adj* & *adv* sattellos

bare′faced′ *adj* unverschämt

bare′foot′ *adj* & *adv* barfuß

bare′head′ed *adj* & *adv* barhäuptig

barely [′berli] *adv* kaum, bloß

bar′fly′ *s* Kneipenhocker *m*

bargain [′bargɪn] *s* (*deal*) Geschäft *n*; (*cheap purchase*) Sonderangebot *n*; **into the b.** obendrein; **it′s a b.!** abge-

macht! ‖ *tr*—**b. away** mit Verlust verkaufen ‖ *intr* handeln; **b. for** verhandeln über (*acc*)

bar′gain price′ *s* Preisschlager *m*

bar′gain sale′ *s* Sonderverkauf *m*

barge [bardʒ] *s* Lastkahn *m*; ‖ *intr*— **b. in** hereinstürzen; **b. into** stürzen in (*acc*)

baritone [′bærɪ,ton] *s* Bariton *m*

barium [′berɪ-əm] *s* Barium *n*

bark [bark] *s* (*of a tree*) Rinde *f*; (*of a dog*) Bellen *n*, Gebell *n*; (*boat*) Barke *f*; ‖ *tr*—**b. out** bellend hervorstoßen ‖ *intr* bellen; **b. at** anbellen

barker [′barkər] *s* Anreißer *m*

barley [′barli] *s* Gerste *f*; **grain of b.** Graupe *f*

bar′maid′ *s* Schankmädchen *n*, Bardame *f*

barn [barn] *s* Scheune *f*; (*for animals*) Stall *m*

barnacle [′barnəkəl] *s* Entenmuschel *f*

barn′storm′ *intr* auf dem Lande Theateraufführungen veranstalten; (pol) auf dem Lande Wahlreden halten

barn′yard′ *s* Scheunenhof *m*

barometer [bə′ramɪtər] *s* Barometer *n*

barometric [,bærə′metrɪk] *adj* barometrisch

baron [′bærən] *s* Baron *m*

baroness [′bærənɪs] *s* Baronin *f*

baroque [bə′rok] *adj* barock ‖ *s* (*style, period*) Barock *m* & *n*

barracks [′bærəks] *s* (*temporary wooden structure*) Baracke *f*; (mil) Kaserne *f*

barrage [bə′raʒ] *s* Sperrfeuer *n*; **moving b.** Sperrfeuerwalze *f*

barrel [′bærəl] *s* Faß *n*, Tonne *f*; (*of a gun*) Lauf *m*; (*of money, fun*) große Menge *f*; **have over the b.** (sl) in der Gewalt haben ‖ *intr* (coll) rasen, sausen

barren [′bærən] *adj* dürr, unfruchtbar; (*landscape*) kahl

barricade [′bærɪ,ked] *s* Barrikade *f* ‖ *tr* verbarrikadieren

barrier [′bærɪ-ər] *s* Schranke *f*, Schlagbaum *m*; (*e.g., on a street*) Sperre *f*

bar′room′ *s* Schenkstube *f*, Bar *f*

bartend [′bar,tend] *intr* Getränke ausschenken

bar′tend′er *s* Schankwirt *m*, Barmixer *m*

barter [′bartər] *s* Tauschhandel *m* ‖ *tr* tauschen ‖ *intr* Tauschhandel treiben

basalt [bə′sɔlt], [′bæsɔlt] *s* Basalt *m*

base [bes] *adj* gemein, niedrig; (*metal*) unedel ‖ *s* (*cosmetic*) Schminkunterlage *f*; (fig) Grundlage *f*; (archit) Basis *f*, Fundament *n*; (baseball) Mal *n*; (chem) Base *f*; (geom) Grundlinie *f*, Grundfläche *f*; (math) Basis *f*; (mil) Stützpunkt *m* ‖ *tr* (mil) stationieren; **b. on** stützen auf (*acc*), gründen auf (*acc*)

base′ball′ *s* Baseball *m*

base′board′ *s* Wandleiste *f*

basement [′besmənt] *s* Kellergeschoß *n*

bash [bæʃ] *s* heftiger Schlag *m*

bashful [′bæʃfəl] *adj* schüchtern

basic ['besɪk] *adj* grundsätzlich; (*e.g.*, *salary*) Grund-; (chem) basisch

basically ['besɪkəli] *adv* grundsätzlich

ba'sic train'ing *s* Grundausbildung *f*

basilica [bə'sɪlɪkə] *s* Basilika *f*

basin ['besɪn] *s* Becken *n*; (geol) Mulde *f*; (naut) Bassin *n*

ba·sis ['besɪs] *s* (-ses [siz]) Basis *f*, Grundlage *f*; **b. of comparison** Vergleichsgrundlage *f*; **put on a firm b.** (fin) sanieren

bask [bæsk] *intr* (& fig) sich sonnen

basket ['bæskɪt] *s* (& sport) Korb *m*

bas'ketball *s* Basketball *m*, Korbball *m*

bas-relief [,barɪ'lif] *s* Flachrelief *n*

bass [bes] *adj* Baß- ‖ *s* (mus) Baß *m* ‖ [bæs] *s* (ichth) Flußbarsch *m*, Seebarsch *m*

bass' clef' *s* Baßschlüssel *m*

bass' drum' *s* große Trommel *f*

bass' fid'dle *s* Baßgeige *f*

bassoon [bə'sun] *s* Fagott *n*

bass viol ['bes'vaɪ-əl] *s* Gambe *f*

bastard ['bæstərd] *adj* Bastard-; (*illegitimate in birth*) unehelich ‖ *s* Bastard *m*; (vulg) Schweinehund *m*

baste [best] *tr* (*thrash*) verprügeln; (*scold*) schelten; (culin) begießen; (*sew*) lose (an)heften

bastion ['bæst/ən] *s* Bastion *f*

bat [bæt] *s* (sport) Schläger *m*; (zool) Fledermaus *f*; **go to bat for s.o.** (fig) für j-n eintreten ‖ *v* (*pret & pp* **batted**; *ger* **batting**) *tr* schlagen; **without batting an eye** ohne mit der Wimper zu zucken

batch [bæt/] *s* Satz *m*, Haufen *m*; (*of bread*) Schub *m*; (*of letters*) Stoß *m*

bated ['betɪd] *adj*—**with b. breath** mit verhaltenem Atem

bath [bæθ] *s* Bad *n*; **take a b.** ein Bad nehmen

bathe [beð] *tr & intr* baden

bather ['beðər] *s* Badende *mf*

bath'house' *s* Umkleideräume *pl*

bath'ing *s* Baden *n*, Bad *n*

bath'ing cap' *s* Badehaube *f*

bath'ing suit' *s* Badeanzug *m*

bath'ing trunks' *spl* Badehose *f*

bath'robe' *s* Bademantel *m*

bath'room' *s* Badezimmer *n*

bath'room fix'tures *spl* Armaturen *pl*

bath'room scales *spl* Personenwaage *f*

bath' tow'el *s* Badetuch *n*

bath'tub' *s* Badewanne *f*

baton [bæ'tɑn] *s* (mil) Kommandostab *m*; (mus) Taktstock *m*

battalion [bə'tæljən] *s* Bataillon *n*

batter ['bætər] *s* Teig *m*; (baseball) Schläger -in *mf* ‖ *tr* zerschlagen; (aer) bombardieren; **b. down** niederschlagen; **b. in** einschlagen

bat'tering ram' *s* Sturmbock *m*

battery ['bætəri] *s* Batterie *f*; (*secondary cell*) Akkumulator *m*; (arti) Batterie *f*; (nav) Geschützgruppe *f*

battle ['bætəl] *s* Schlacht *f*; (& fig) Kampf *m*; **do b.** kämpfen; **in b.** im Felde ‖ *tr* bekämpfen ‖ *intr* kämpfen

bat'tle array' *s* Schlachtordnung *f*

bat'tleax' *s* Streitaxt *f*; (fig) Drachen *m*

bat'tle cruis'er *s* Schlachtkreuzer *m*

bat'tle cry' *s* Schlachtruf *m*; (fig) Schlagwort *n*

bat'tle fatigue' *s* Kriegsneurose *f*

bat'tlefield' *s* Schlachtfeld *n*

bat'tlefront' *s* Front *f*, Hauptkampflinie *f*

bat'tleground' *s* Kampfplatz *m*

battlement ['bætəlmənt] *s* Zinne *f*

bat'tle scar' *s* Kampfmal *n*

bat'tleship' *s* Schlachtschiff *n*

bat'tle wag'on *s* (coll) Schlachtschiff *n*

batty ['bæti] *adj* (sl) doof

bauble ['bɔbəl] *s* Tand *m*; (*jester's staff*) Narrenstab *m*

Bavaria [bə'verɪ-ə] *s* Bayern *n*

Bavarian [bə'verɪ-ən] *adj* bayerisch ‖ *s* Bayer -in *mf*

bawd [bɔd] *s* Dirne *f*

bawdy ['bɔdi] *adj* unzüchtig

bawl [bɔl] *s* Geplärr *n* ‖ *tr*—**b. out** (*names, etc.*) ausschreien; (*scold*) anschnauzen ‖ *intr* (coll) plärren

bay [be] *adj* kastanienbraun ‖ *s* Bucht *f*; (*horse*) Rotfuchs *m*; (bot) Lorbeer *m*; **keep at bay** in Schach halten ‖ *intr* laut bellen; **bay at** anbellen

bayo·net ['be-ənɪt] *s* Bajonett *n*, Seitengewehr *n*; **with fixed bayonets** mit aufgepflanztem Bajonett ‖ *v* (*pret & pp* **-net(t)ed**; *ger* **-net(t)ing**) *tr* mit dem Bajonett erstechen

bay' win'dow *s* Erkerfenster *n*

bazaar [bə'zɑr] *s* Basar *m*, Markt *m*

bazooka [bə'zukə] *s* Panzerfaust *f*

be [bi] *v* (*pres am* [æm], *is* [ɪz]) ‖ [ɑr]; *pret was* [wɑz], [wʌz], *were* [wʌr]; *pp been* [bɪn]) *intr* sein; **be about to** (*inf*) im Begriff sein zu (*inf*); **be after s.o.** hinter j-m her sein; **be along** hier sein; **be behind in** im Rückstand sein mit; **be behind s.o.** j-m den Rücken decken; **be from** (*a country*) stammen aus, sein aus; **be in** zu Hause sein; **be in for u** erwarten haben; **be in for it** in der Patsche sitzen; **be in on** dabei sein bei; **be off** weggehen; **be on to s.o.** j-m auf die Schliche kommen; **be out** nicht zu Hause sein, aus sein; **be out for s.th.** auf der Suche nach etw sein; **be up** auf sein; **be up to s.th.** etw im Sinn haben; **how are you?** wie geht es Ihnen?, wie befinden Sie sich?; **how much is that?** wieviel kostet das?; **there are, there is es gibt** (*acc*) ‖ *aux*—**he is studying** er studiert; **he is to go** er soll gehen; **he was hit** er ist getroffen worden ‖ *impers*—**how is it that...?** wie kommt es, daß...?; **it is cold** es ist kalt; **it is to be seen that** es ist darauf zu sehen, daß

beach [bit/] *s* Strand *m*; **on the b.** am Strand, an der See ‖ *tr* auf den Strand ziehen; **be beached** stranden

beach'comb'er *s* Strandgutjäger *m*; (*wave*) Strandwelle *f*

beach'head' *s* Landekopf *m*

beach' tow'el *s* Badetuch *n*

beach' umbrel'la *s* Strandschirm *m*

beacon ['bikən] *s* Leuchtfeuer *n*, Bake *f*; (*lighthouse*) Leuchtturm *m*; (aer)

Scheinwerfer *m* ‖ *tr* lenken ‖ *intr* leuchten

bead [bid] (*of glass, wood, sweat*) Perle *f*; (*of a gun*) Korn *n*; **beads** (eccl) Rosenkranz *m*; **draw a b.** on zielen auf (*acc*)

beagle ['bigel] *s* Spürhund *m*

beak [bik] *s* Schnabel *m*; (*nose*) (sl) Rübe *f*

beam [bim] *s* (*of wood*) Balken *m*; (*of light, heat, etc.*) Strahl *m*; (fig) Glanz *m*; (aer) Leitstrahl *m*; (*width of a vessel*) (naut) größte Schiffsbreite *f*; (*horizontal structural member*) (naut) Deckbalken *m*; **b. of light** Lichtkegel *m*; **off the b.** (sl) auf dem Holzweg; **on the b.** (sl) auf Draht ‖ *intr* strahlen; **b. at** anstrahlen

bean [bin] *s* Bohne *f*; (*head*) (sl) Birne *f*; **spill the beans** (sl) alles ausquatschen

bean'pole' *s* (& coll) Bohnenstange *f*

bear [ber] *adj* (market) flau, Baisse– ‖ *s* Bär *m*; (st. exch.) Baissier *m* ‖ *v* (*pret* **bore** [bor]; *pp* **borne** [born]) *tr* (*carry*) tragen; (*endure*) dulden, ertragen; (*children*) gebären; (*date*) tragen; (*a name, sword*) führen; (*a grudge, love*) hegen; (*a message*) überbringen; (*the consequences*) auf sich [*acc*] nehmen; **bear in mind** bedenken, beachten; **bear fruit** Früchte tragen; (fig) Frucht tragen; **bear out** bestätigen ‖ *intr*—**bear down on** losgehen auf (*acc*); (naut) zufahren auf (*acc*); **bear left** sich links halten; **bear on** sich beziehen auf (*acc*); **bear up (well) against** gut ertragen; **bear up with** Geduld haben mit

bearable ['berəbəl] *adj* erträglich

beard [bɪrd] *s* Bart *m*

beard'ed *adj* bärtig

beardless ['bɪrdlɪs] *adj* bartlos

bearer ['berər] *s* Träger –in *m*f; (*of a message*) Überbringer –in *m*f; (com) Inhaber –in *m*f

bear' hug' *s* (coll) Knutsch *m*

bear'ing *s* Körperhaltung *f*; (mach) Lager *n*; (on) Beziehung *f* (auf *acc*); **bearings** (aer, naut) Lage *f*, Richtung *f*, Peilung *f*; **lose one's bearings** die Richtung verlieren

bear'skin' *s* Bärenfell *n*

beast [bist] *s* Tier *n*; (fig) Bestie *f*

beastly ['bistlɪ] *adj* bestialisch; **b. weather** Hundewetter *n*

beast' of bur'den *s* Lasttier *n*

beat [bit] *adj* (sl) erschöpft ‖ *s* (*of the heart*) Schlag *m*; (*of a policeman*) Runde *f*, Revier *n*; (mus) Takt *m* ‖ *v* (*pret* **beat**; *pp* **beat & beaten**) *tr* (*eggs, a child, record, team, etc.*) schlagen; (*a carpet*) ausklopfen; (*metal*) hämmern; (*a path*) treten; **b. it!** hau ab!; **b. one's brains out** sich [*dat*] den Kopf zerbrechen; **b. s.o. to it** j–m zuvorkommen; **b. up** verprügeln ‖ *intr* schlagen, klopfen; **b. against** peitschen gegen; **b. down** niederprallen

beati•fy [bɪ'ætɪ͵faɪ] *v* (*pret & pp* **–fied**) *tr* seligsprechen

beat'ing *s* Prügel *pl*

beatitude [bɪ'ætɪ͵t(j)ud] *s* Seligpreisung *f*

beau [bo] *s* (**beaus & beaux** [boz]) Liebhaber *m*

beautician [bju'tɪʃən] *s* Kosmetiker –in *m*f; (*hairdresser*) Friseuse *f*

beautiful ['bjutɪfəl] *adj* schön

beauti•fy ['bjutɪ͵faɪ] *v* (*pret & pp* **–fied**) *tr* verschönern

beauty ['bjutɪ] *s* (*quality; woman*) Schönheit *f*; (coll) Prachtexemplar *n*

beau'ty queen' *s* Schönheitskönigin *f*

beau'ty shop' *s* Frisiersalon *m*

beau'ty sleep' *s* Schönheitsschlaf *m*

beau'ty spot' *s* Schönheitsmal *n*

beaver ['bivər] *s* Biber *m*

because [bɪ'kɔz] *conj* weil, da ‖ *interj* darum!

because' of' *prep* wegen (*genit*)

beck [bek] *s* Wink *m*; **be at s.o.'s b. and call** j–m ganz zu Diensten sein

beckon ['bekən] *tr* zuwinken (*dat*); (*summon*) heranwinken ‖ *intr* winken; **b. to s.o.** j–m zuwinken

become [bɪ'kʌm] *v* (*pret* **–came**; *pp* **–come**) *tr* (*said of clothes*) gut anstehen (*dat*); (*said of conduct*) sich schicken für ‖ *intr* werden; **what has b. of him?** was ist aus ihm geworden?

becom'ing *adj* (*said of clothes*) kleidsam; (*said of conduct*) schicklich

bed [bed] *s* (*for sleeping; of a river*) Bett *n*; (*of flowers*) Beet *n*; (*of straw*) Lager *n*; (geol) Lager *n*; (rr) Unterbau *m*; **put to bed** zu Bett bringen

bed'bug' *s* Wanze *f*

bed'clothes' *spl* Bettwäsche *f*

bed'ding *s* Bettzeug *n*; (*for animals*) Streu *f*

bed'fel'low *s*—**strange bedfellows** ein seltsames Paar *n*

bedlam ['bedləm] *s* (fig) Tollhaus *n*; **there was b.** es ging zu wie im Tollhaus

bed' lin'en *s* Bettwäsche *f*

bed'pan' *s* Bettschüssel *f*

bed'post' *s* Bettpfosten *m*

bedraggled [bɪ'dræɡəld] *adj* beschmutzt

bedridden ['bed͵rɪdən] *adj* bettlägerig

bed'rock' *s* Grundgestein *n*; (fig) Grundlage *f*

bed'room' *s* Schlafzimmer *n*

bed'side' *s*—**at s.o.'s b.** an j–s Bett

bed'sore' *s* wundgelegene Stelle *f*; **get bedsores** sich wundliegen

bed'spread' *s* Bettdecke *f*, Tagesdecke *f*

bed'spring' *s* (*one coil*) Sprungfeder *f*; (*framework of springs*) Sprungfedermatratze *f*

bed'stead' *s* Bettgestell *n*

bed'time' *s* Schlafenszeit *f*; **it's past b.** es ist höchste Zeit, zu Bett zu gehen

bee [bi] *s* Biene *f*

beech [bitʃ] *s* Buche *f*

beech'nut' *s* Buchecker *f*

beef [bif] *s* Rindfleisch *n*; (*brawn*) (coll) Muskelkraft *f*; (*human flesh*) (coll) Fleisch *n*; (*complaint*) (sl) Gemecker *n* ‖ *tr*—**b. up** ver-

stärken ‖ *intr* (*complain*) (sl)
meckern
beef′ broth′ *s* Kraftbrühe *f*
beef′steak′ *s* Beefsteak *n*
beefy [′bifi] *adj* muskulös
bee′hive′ *s* Bienenstock *m*, Bienenkorb
m
bee′line′ *s*—**make a b. for** schnurstracks losgehen auf (*acc*)
beer [bɪr] *s* Bier *n*
bee′ sting′ *s* Bienenstich *m*
beeswax [′biz‚wæks] *s* Bienenwachs *n*
beet [bit] *s* Rübe *f*
beetle [′bitəl] *s* Käfer *m*
be•fall [bɪ′fɔl] *v* (*pret* **–fell** [′fel]; *pp*
–fallen [′fɔlən] *tr* betreffen, zustoßen
‖ *intr* sich ereignen
befit′ting *adj* passend
before [bɪ′fɔr] *adv* vorher, früher ‖
prep (*position or time*) vor (*dat*); (*direction*) vor (*acc*); **b. now** schon früher ‖
kurzem; **b. now** schon früher ‖ *conj*
bevor, ehe
before′hand′ *adv* zuvor, vorher
befriend [bɪ′frend] *tr* sich [*dat*] (*j–n*)
zum Freund machen, sich anfreun-
den mit
befuddle [bɪ′fʌdəl] *tr* verwirren
beg [beg] *v* (*pret & pp* begged; *ger*
begging) *tr* bitten um; (*a meal*)
betteln um; **beg s.o.** to (*inf*) *j–n*
bitten zu (*inf*); **I beg your pardon**
(*ich bitte um*) Verzeihung! ‖ *intr*
betteln; (*said of a dog*) Männchen
machen; **beg for** bitten um, flehen
um; **beg off** absagen
be•get [bɪ′get] *v* (*pret* **–got** [′gɑt];
pp **–gotten** –got; *ger* –getting) *tr*
erzeugen
beggar [′begər] *s* Bettler –in *mf*
be•gin [bɪ′gɪn] *v* (*pret* **–gan** [′gæn]; *pp*
–gun [′gʌn]; *ger* **–ginning** [′gɪnɪŋ])
tr beginnen, anfangen ‖ *intr* beginnen, anfangen; **to b. with** zunächst
beginner [bɪ′gɪnər] *s* Anfänger –in *mf*
begin′ning *s* Beginn *m*, Anfang *m*
begrudge [bɪ′grʌdʒ] *tr*—**b. s.o. s.th.**
j–m etw mißgönnen
beguile [bɪ′gaɪl] *tr* (*mislead*) verleiten;
(*charm*) betören
behalf [bɪ′hæf] *s*—**on b. of** zugunsten
(*genit*), für; (*as a representative of*)
im Namen (*genit*), im Auftrag von
behave [bɪ′hev] *intr* sich benehmen
behavior [bɪ′hevjər] *s* Benehmen *n*
behead [bɪ′hed] *tr* enthaupten
behind [bɪ′haɪnd] *adj* (*in arrears*) (*in*)
im Rückstand (*mit*); **the clock is ten
minutes b.** die Uhr geht zehn Mi-
nuten nach ‖ *adv* (*in the rear*) hinten, hinterher; (*to the rear*) nach
hinten, zurück; **from b.** von hinten
‖ *s* (sl) Hintern *m*, Popo *m* ‖ *prep*
(*position*) hinter (*dat*); (*direction*)
hinter (*acc*); **be b. schedule** sich verspäten; **b. time** zu spät; **b. the times**
hinter dem Mond
be•hold [bɪ′hold] *v* (*pret & pp* **–held**
[′held] *tr* betrachten ‖ *interj* schau!
behoove [bɪ′huv] *impers*—**it behooves
me** es geziemt mir
beige [beʒ] *adj* beige ‖ *s* Beige *n*
be′ing *adj*—**for the time b.** einstweilen

‖ *s* Dasein *n*; (*creature*) Wesen *n*;
come into b. entstehen
belabor [bɪ′lebər] *tr* herumreiten auf
(*dat*)
belated [bɪ′letɪd] *adj* verspätet
belch [beltʃ] *s* Rülpser *m* ‖ *tr* (*fire*)
ausspeien ‖ *intr* rülpsen
beleaguer [bɪ′ligər] *tr* belagern
belfry [′belfri] *s* Glockenturm *m*
Belgian [′beldʒən] *adj* belgisch ‖ *s* Belgier –in *mf*
Belgium [′beldʒəm] *s* Belgien *n*
belief [bɪ′lif] *s* (in) Glaube(n) *m* (an
acc)
believable [bɪ′livəbəl] *adj* glaublich
believe [bɪ′liv] *tr* (*a thing*) glauben;
(*a person*) glauben (*dat*) ‖ *intr* glauben; **b. in** glauben an (*acc*); **I don't
b. in war** ich halte nicht viel vom
Kriege
believer [bɪ′livər] *s* Gläubige *mf*
belittle [bɪ′lɪtəl] *tr* herabsetzen
bell [bel] *s* Glocke *f*; (*small bell*) Klingel *f*; (*of a wind instrument*) Schall-
trichter *m*; (*box*) Gong *m*
bell′boy′ *s* Hotelboy *m*
bell′hop′ *s* (sl) Hotelpage *m*
belligerent [bə′lɪdʒərənt] *adj* streit-
lustig ‖ *s* kriegführender Staat *m*
bell′ jar′ *s* Glasglocke *f*
bellow [′belo] *s* Gebrüll *n*; **bellows**
Blasebalg *m*; (phot) Balgen *m* ‖ *tr*
& *intr* brüllen
bell′ tow′er *s* Glockenturm *m*
bel•ly [′beli] *s* Bauch *m*; (*of a sail*)
Bausch *m* ‖ *v* (*pret & pp* **–lied**) *intr*
bauschen
bel′lyache′ *s* (coll) Bauchweh *n* ‖ *intr*
(sl) jammern
bel′ly but′ton *s* Nabel *m*
bel′ly danc′er *s* Bauchtänzerin *f*
bel′ly flop′ *s* Bauchklatscher *m*
bellyful [′belɪ‚fʊl] *s*—**have a b. of** die
Nase voll haben von
bel′ly-land′ing *s* Bauchlandung *f*
belong [bɪ′lɔŋ] *intr* **b.** to (*designating
ownership*) gehören (*dat*); (*designating membership*) gehören zu; **where
does this table b.?** wohin gehört
dieser Tisch?
belongings [bɪ′lɔŋɪŋz] *spl* Sachen *pl*
beloved [bɪ′lʌvɪd], [bɪ′lʌvd] *adj* ge-
liebt ‖ *s* Geliebte *mf*
below [bɪ′lo] *adv* (*position*) unten;
(*direction*) nach unten, hinunter ‖
prep (*position*) unter (*dat*), unterhalb (*genit*); (*direction*) unter (*acc*)
belt [belt] *s* Riemen *m*, Gurt *m*, Gürtel
m; (geol) Gebiet *n*; (mach) Treibriemen *m*; **tighten one's b.** den Riemen
enger schnallen ‖ *tr* (sl) e–n heftigen
Schlag versetzen (*dat*)
belt′ buck′le *s* Gürtelschnalle *f*
belt′way′ *s* Verkehrsgürtel *m*
bemoan [bɪ′mon] *tr* betrauern, beklagen
bench [bentʃ] *s* Bank *f*; (jur) Gerichtshof *m*; (sport) Reservebank *f*, Bank
f
bend [bend] *s* Biegung *f*; (*in a road*)
Kurve *f*; **bends** (pathol) Tauchkrank-
heit *f* ‖ *v* (*pret & pp* bent [bent])
biegen, beugen; (*a bow*) spannen ‖

intr sich biegen, sich beugen; **b. down** sich bücken; **b. over backwards** (fig) sich [*dat*] übergroße Mühe geben

beneath [bɪ'niθ] *adv* unten ‖ *prep* (*position*) unter (*dat*), unterhalb (*genit*); (*direction*) unter (*acc*); **b. me** unter meiner Würde

benediction [,benɪ'dɪkʃən] *s* Segen *m*

benefactor ['benɪ,fæktər] *s* Wohltäter –in *m*

beneficence [bɪ'nefɪsəns] *s* Wohltätigkeit *f*

beneficent [bɪ'nefɪsənt] *adj* wohltätig

beneficial [,benɪ'fɪʃəl] *adj* heilbringend, gesund; (to) nützlich (*dat*)

beneficiary [,benɪ'fɪʃɪ,erɪ] *s* Begünstigte *mf*; (ins) Bezugsberechtigte *mf*

benefit ['benɪfɪt] *s* Nutzen *m*; (*fundraising performance*) Benefiz *n*; (ins) Versicherungsleistung *f*

benevolence [bɪ'nevələns] *s* Wohlwollen *n*

benevolent [bɪ'nevələnt] *adj* wohlwollend

benign [bɪ'naɪn] *adj* gütig; (pathol) gutartig

bent [bent] *adj* krumm, verbogen; **b. on** versessen auf (*acc*) ‖ *s* Hang *m*

benzene [ben'zin] *s* Benzol *n*

bequeath [bɪ'kwið] *tr* vermachen

bequest [bɪ'kwest] *s* Vermächtnis *n*

berate [bɪ'ret] *tr* ausschelten, rügen

be·reave [bɪ'riv] *v* (*pret & pp* –reaved & –reft* ['reft]) *tr* (of) berauben (*genit*)

bereavement [bɪ'rivmənt] *s* Trauerfall *m*

beret [bə're] *s* Baskenmütze *f*

Berlin [bər'lɪn] *adj* Berliner, berlinerisch ‖ *s* Berlin *n*

Berliner [bər'lɪnər] *s* Berliner –in *mf*

berry ['berɪ] *s* Beere *f*

berserk [bər'sʌrk] *adj* wütend ‖ *adv*—**go b.** wütend werden

berth [bʌrθ] *s* Schlafkoje *f*; (naut) Liegeplatz *m*; (rr) Bett *n*; **give s.o. wide b.** um j–n e–n weiten Bogen machen ‖ *tr* am Kai festmachen

be·seech [bɪ'sit/] *v* (*pret & pp* –sought ['sɔt] & –seeched) *tr* anflehen

be·set [bɪ'set] *v* (*pret & pp* –set; *ger* –setting) *tr* bedrängen, umringen

beside [bɪ'saɪd] *prep* (*position*) neben (*dat*), bei (*dat*); (*direction*) neben (*acc*); **be b. oneself with** außer sich [*dat*] sein vor (*dat*)

besides [bɪ'saɪdz] *adv* überdies, außerdem ‖ *prep* außer (*dat*)

besiege [bɪ'sidʒ] *tr* belagern

besmirch [bɪ'smʌrtʃ] *tr* beschmutzen

be·speak [bɪ'spik] *v* (*pret* –spoke ['spok]; *pp* –spoken ['spokən]) *tr* bezeigen

best [best] *adj* beste; **b. of all, very b. allerbeste** ‖ *adv* am besten; **had b. es wäre am besten, wenn** ‖ *s*—at b. bestenfalls; **be at one's b.** in bester Form sein; **for the b.** zum Besten; **make the b. of** sich abfinden mit; **to the b. of one's ability** nach bestem Vermögen

bestial ['bestʃəl] *adj* bestialisch

best' man' *s* Brautführer *m*

bestow [bɪ'sto] *tr* verleihen

bestowal [bɪ'sto·əl] *s* Verleihung *f*

best' sel'ler *s* (*book*) Bestseller *m*

bet [bet] *s* Wette *f*; **make a bet** e–e Wette abschließen (or eingehen) ‖ *v* (*pret & pp* **bet** & **betted**; *ger* betting) *tr* (on) wetten (auf *acc*) ‖ *intr* wetten; **you bet! aber sicher!**

betray [bɪ'tre] *tr* verraten; (*a secret*) preisgeben; (*ignorance*) offenbaren; (*a trust*) mißbrauchen

betrayal [bɪ'tre·əl] *s* Verrat *m*

betrayer [bɪ'tre·ər] *s* Verräter –in *mf*

better ['betər] *adj* besser; **the b. part of** der größere Teil (*genit*) ‖ *s*—**change for the b.** sich zum Besseren wenden; **get the b. of** übervorteilen; **one's betters** die Höherstehenden *pl*; ‖ *adv* besser; **all the b.** um so besser; **b. off** besser daran; (*financially*) wohlhabender; **so much the b.** desto besser; **you had b. do it at once** am besten tust du es sofort; **you had b. not** das will ich dir nicht geraten haben ‖ *tr* verbessern; **b. oneself** sich verbessern

bet'ter half' *s* (coll) bessere Hälfte *f*

betterment ['betərmənt] *s* Besserung *f*

bettor ['betər] *s* Wettende *mf*

between [bɪ'twin] *adv*—**in b.** dazwischen ‖ *prep* (*position*) zwischen (*dat*); (*direction*) zwischen (*acc*); **just b. you and me** ganz unter uns gesagt

bev·el ['bevəl] *adj* schräg ‖ *s* schräge Kante *f* ‖ *v* (*pret & pp* –el(l)ed; *ger* –el(l)ing) *tr* abschrägen

beverage ['bevərɪdʒ] *s* Getränk *n*

bevy ['bevɪ] *s* Schar *f*

bewail [bɪ'wel] *tr* beklagen

beware [bɪ'wer] *intr* sich hüten; **b.! gib acht!; b. of** sich hüten vor (*dat*); **b. of imitations** vor Nachahmungen wird gewarnt

bewilder [bɪ'wɪldər] *tr* verblüffen

bewilderment [bɪ'wɪldərmənt] *s* Verblüffung *f*

bewitch [bɪ'wɪtʃ] *tr* (fig) bezaubern

beyond [bɪ'jɑnd] *adv* jenseits ‖ *s*—**the b.** das Jenseits ‖ *prep* jenseits (*genit*), über (*acc*) hinaus; (fig) über (*acc*), außer (*dat*); **he is b. help** ihm ist nicht mehr zu helfen; **that's b. me** das geht über meinen Verstand

B'-girl' *s* (coll) Animiermädchen *n*

bias ['baɪ·əs] *s* Voreingenommenheit *f* ‖ *tr* (against) einnehmen (gegen)

bi'ased *adj* voreingenommen

bib [bɪb] *s* Latz *m*, Lätzchen *n*

Bible ['baɪbəl] *s* Bibel *f*

Biblical ['bɪblɪkəl] *adj* biblisch

bibliographer [,bɪblɪ'ɑgrəfər] *s* Bibliograph –in *mf*

bibliography [,bɪblɪ'ɑgrəfɪ] *s* Bücherverzeichnis *n*; (*science*) Bücherkunde *f*

bi·ceps ['baɪseps] *s* (–cepses [sepsɪz] & –ceps) Bizeps *m*

bicker ['bɪkər] *intr* sich zanken

bick'ering *s* Gezänk *n*

bicuspid [baɪ'kʌspɪd] *s* kleiner Backenzahn *m*

bicycle ['baɪsɪkəl] s Fahrrad n
bid [bɪd] s Angebot n; (cards) Meldung f; (com) Kostenvoranschlag m ‖ v (pret **bade** [bæd] & **bid**; pp **bidden** ['bɪdən]) tr (ask) heißen; (at auction) bieten; (cards) melden, reizen ‖ intr (cards) reizen; (com) ein Preisangebot machen; **bid for** sich bewerben um
bidder ['bɪdər] s (at an auction) Bieter -in mf; **highest b.** Meistbietende m
bid′ding s (at an auction) Bieten n; (request) Geheiß n; (cards) Reizen n
bide [baɪd] tr—**b. one's time** seine Gelegenheit abwarten
biennial [baɪ'enɪəl] adj zweijährig
bier [bɪr] s Totenbahre f
bifocals [baɪ'fokəlz] spl Zweistärkenbrille f
big [bɪg] adj (bigger; biggest) groß
bigamist ['bɪgəmɪst] s Bigamist m
bigamous ['bɪgəməs] adj bigamisch
bigamy ['bɪgəmi] s Bigamie f
big′-boned′ adj starkknochig
big′ busi′ness s das große Geschäft; (collectively) Großunternehmertum n
Big′ Dip′per s Großer Bär m
big′ game′ s Hochwild n
big′-heart′ed adj großherzig
big′mouth′ s (sl) Großmaul n
bigot ['bɪgət] s Fanatiker -in mf
bigoted ['bɪgətɪd] adj bigott, fanatisch
bigotry ['bɪgətri] s Bigotterie f
big′ shot′ s (coll) hohes Tier n, Bonze m
big′-time′ adj groß, erstklassig; **b. operator** Großschieber -in mf
big′ toe′ s große Zehe f
big′ top′ s (coll) großes Zirkuszelt n
big′ wheel′ s (coll) hohes Tier n
big′wig′ s (coll) Bonze m
bike [baɪk] s (coll) Rad n
bikini [bɪ'kini] s Bikini m
bilateral [baɪ'lætərəl] adj beiderseitig verbindlich
bile [baɪl] s Galle f
bilge [bɪldʒ] s Bilge f, Kielraum m
bilge′ wat′er s Bilgenwasser n
bilingual [baɪ'lɪŋgwəl] adj zweisprachig
bilk [bɪlk] tr (out of) prellen (um)
bill [bɪl] s Rechnung f; (paper money) Geldschein m, Schein m; (of a bird) Schnabel m; (parl) Gesetzesvorlage f; **pass a b.** ein Gesetz verabschieden ‖ tr in Rechnung stellen
bill′board′ s Anschlagtafel f
bill′ collec′tor s Einkassierer -in mf
billet ['bɪlɪt] s (mil) Quartier n ‖ tr (mil) einquartieren, unterbringen
bill′fold′ s Brieftasche f
bil′liard ball′ s Billardkugel f
billiards ['bɪljərdz] s Billard n
bil′liard ta′ble s Billardtisch m
billion ['bɪljən] s Milliarde f; (Brit) Billion f (million million)
bill′ of exchange′ s Tratte f, Wechsel m
bill′ of fare′ s Speisekarte f
bill′ of health′ s Gesundheitszeugnis n; **he gave me a clean b.** (fig) er hat mich für einwandfrei befunden
bill′ of lad′ing ['ledɪŋ] s Frachtbrief m

bill′ of rights′ s erste zehn Zusatzartikel pl zur Verfassung (der U.S.A.)
bill′ of sale′ s Kaufurkunde f
billow ['bɪlo] s Woge f ‖ intr wogen
bil′ly club′ ['brli] s Polizeiknüppel m
bil′ly goat′ s (coll) Ziegenbock m
bind [baɪnd] s—**in a b.** in der Klemme ‖ v (pret & pp **bound** [baʊnd]) tr binden; (obligate) verpflichten; (bb) einbinden
binder ['baɪndər] s Binder -in mf; (e.g., cement) Bindemittel n; (for loose papers) Aktendeckel m; (mach) Garbenbinder m
bindery ['baɪndəri] s Buchbinderei f
bind′ing (on) adj verbindlich (für) ‖ s Binden n; (for skis) Bindung f; (bb) Einband f
binge [bɪndʒ] s (sl) Zechtour f; **go on a b.** (sl) e-e Zechtour machen
binoculars [baɪ'nakjələrz] spl Fernglas n
biochemistry [ˌbaɪ-ə'kemɪstri] s Biochemie f
biographer [baɪ'agrəfər] s Biograph -in mf
biographic(al) [ˌbaɪ-ə'græfɪk(əl)] adj biographisch
biography [baɪ'agrəfi] s Biographie f
biologic(al) [ˌbaɪ-ə'ladʒɪk(əl)] adj biologisch
biologist [baɪ'alədʒɪst] s Biologe m, Biologin f
biology [baɪ'alədʒi] s Biologie f
biophysics [ˌbaɪ-ə'fɪzɪks] s Biophysik f
biopsy ['baɪ-apsi] s Biopsie f
bipartisan [baɪ'partɪzən] adj Zweiparteien-
biped ['baɪped] s Zweifüßer m
bird [bɪrd] s Vogel m; **for the birds** für die Katz; **kill two birds with one stone** zwei Fliegen mit e-r Klappe schlagen
bird′cage′ s Bauer n, Vogelkäfig m
bird′ call′ s Vogelruf m, Lockpfeife f
bird′ dog′ s Hühnerhund m
bird′ of prey′ s Raubvogel m
bird′seed′ s Vogelfutter n
bird′s′-eye view′ s Vogelperspektive f
birth [bʌrθ] s Geburt f; (origin) Herkunft f; **give b. to** gebären
birth′ certi′ficate s Geburtsurkunde f
birth′ control′ s Geburtenbeschränkung f
birth′day′ s Geburtstag m
birth′day cake′ s Geburtstagskuchen m
birth′day par′ty s Geburtstagsfeier f
birth′day pres′ent s Geburtstagsgeschenk n
birth′day suit′ s (hum) Adamskostüm n
birth′mark′ s Muttermal n
birth′place′ s Geburtsort m
birth′ rate′ s Geburtenziffer f
birth′right′ s Geburtsrecht n
biscuit ['brskɪt] s Keks m
bisect [baɪ'sekt] tr halbieren ‖ intr sich teilen
bishop ['bɪʃəp] s Bischof m; (chess) Läufer m
bison ['baɪsən] s Bison m
bit [bɪt] s Bißchen n; (of food) Stück-

chen n; (of time) Augenblick m; (part of a bridle) Gebiß n; (drill) Bohrer m; **a bit** (somewhat) ein wenig; **a little bit** ein klein wenig; **bit by bit** brockenweise; **bits and pieces** Brocken pl; **every bit as** ganz genauso

bitch [bɪtʃ] s Hündin f; (vulg) Weibsbild n

bite [baɪt] s Biß m; (wound) Bißwunde f; (of an insect) Stich m; (of a snake) Biß m; (snack) Imbiß m; (fig) Bissigkeit f; **I have a b.** (in fishing) es beißt e–r an || v (pret bit [bɪt]; pp bit & bitten [ˈbɪtən]) tr beißen; (said of insects) stechen; (said of snakes) beißen; **b. one's nails** an den Nägeln kauen || intr beißen; (said of fish) anbeißen; (said of the wind) schneiden; **b. into** anbeißen

bit'ing adj (remark) bissig; (cold, wind) schneidend

bit' part' s kleine Rolle f

bitter [ˈbɪtər] adj (& fig) bitter; (Person, Blick) bitterböse

bitterly [ˈbɪtərli] adv bitterlich

bitterness [ˈbɪtərnɪs] s Bitterkeit f

bitters [ˈbɪtərz] spl Magenbitter m

bitu'minous coal' [bɪˈt(j)umɪnəs] s Fettkohle f

bivouac [ˈbɪvwæk] s Biwak n || intr biwakieren

bizarre [bɪˈzɑr] adj bizarr

blab [blæb] v (pret & pp blabbed; ger blabbing) tr ausplaudern || intr plaudern

blabber [ˈblæbər] intr schwatzen

blab'bermouth' s Schwatzmaul n

black [blæk] adj schwarz || s Schwarz n; (black person) Neger –in mf, Schwarze mf || tr schwärzen; **b. out** (mil) verdunkeln || intr—**b. out** die Besinnung verlieren

black'-and-blue' adj blau unterlaufen; **beat s.o. b.** j–n grün und blau schlagen

black' and white' s—**in b.** schwarz auf weiß, schriftlich

black'-and-white' adj schwarzweiß

black'ball' tr (ostracize) ausschließen; (vote against) stimmen gegen

black'ber'ry s Brombeere f

black'berry bush' s Brombeerstrauch m

black'bird' s Amsel f

black'board' s Tafel f, Wandtafel f

blacken [ˈblækən] tr schwärzen; (a name) anschwärzen

black' eye' s blaues Auge n; **give s.o. a b.** (fig) j–m Schaden zufügen

black'head' s Mitesser m

blackish [ˈblækɪʃ] adj schwärzlich

black'jack' s (club) Totschläger m; (cards) Siebzehnundvier n || tr niederknüppeln

black'list' s schwarze Liste f || tr auf die schwarze Liste setzen

black' mag'ic s schwarze Kunst f

black'mail' s Erpressung f || tr erpressen

blackmailer [ˈblæk͵melər] s Erpresser –in mf

black' mar'ket s Schwarzmarkt m

black' marketeer' s Schwarzhändler –in mf

black'out' s (fainting) Bewußtlosigkeit f; (of memory) kurze Gedächtnisstörung f; (of news) Nachrichtensperre f; (mil) Verdunkelung f; (telv) Sperre f; (theat) Auslöschen n aller Rampenlichter

black' sheep' s (fig) schwarzes Schaf n

black'smith' s Grobschmied m; (person who shoes horses) Hufschmied m

bladder [ˈblædər] s Blase f

blade [bled] s (of a sword, knife) Klinge f; (of grass) Halm m; (of a saw, ax, shovel, oar) Blatt n; (of a propeller) Flügel m

blame [blem] s Schuld f || tr die Schuld geben (dat); **b. s.o. for** j–m Vorwürfe machen wegen; **I don't b. you for laughing** ich nehme es Ihnen nicht übel, daß Sie lachen

blameless [ˈblemlɪs] adj schuldlos

blame'wor'thy adj tadelnswert, schuldig

blanch [blæntʃ] tr erbleichen lassen; (celery) bleichen; (almonds) blanchieren || intr erbleichen

bland [blænd] adj sanft, mild

blandish [ˈblændɪʃ] tr schmeicheln (dat)

blank [blæŋk] adj (cartridge) blind; (piece of paper, space, expression) leer; (form) unausgefüllt; (tape) unbespielt; (nonplussed) verblüfft; **my mind went b.** ich konnte mich an nichts erinnern || s (cartridge) Platzpatrone f; (unwritten space) leere Stelle f; (form) Formular n; (unfinished piece of metal) Rohling m || tr (sport) auf Null halten

blank' check' s Blankoscheck m

blanket [ˈblæŋkɪt] adj generell, umfassend || s Decke f

blank' verse' s Blankvers m

blare [bler] s Lärm m; (of trumpets) Geschmetter n || intr schmettern; (aut) laut hupen

blasé [blɑˈze] adj blasiert; **b. attitude** Blasiertheit f

blaspheme [blæsˈfim] tr & intr lästern

blasphemous [ˈblæsfɪməs] adj lästerlich

blasphemy [ˈblæsfɪmi] s Lästerung f

blast [blæst] s (of an explosion) Luftdruck m; (of a horn, trumpet, air) Stoß m; (of air) Luftzug m; **at full b.** (fig) auf höchsten Touren || tr (e.g., a tunnel) sprengen; (ruin) (fig) verderben; (criticize) wettern gegen; (blight) versengen; **b. it!** verdammt! || intr—**b. off** (rok) starten

blast' fur'nace s Hochofen m

blast'-off' s (rok) Start m

blatant [ˈbletənt] adj (lie, infraction) eklatant; (nonsense) schreiend

blaze [blez] s Brand m; **b. of color** Farbenpracht f; **b. of glory** Ruhmesglanz m; **b. of light** Lichterglanz m; **go to blazes!** (sl) geh zum Teufel!; **like blazes** wie verrückt || tr—**b. a trail** e–n Weg markieren; (fig) e–n Weg bahnen || intr lodern; **b. away at** drauflosschießen auf (acc)

blazer ['blezər] s Sportjacke f

blaz'ing adj (sun) prall

bleach [blitʃ] s Bleichmittel n || tr bleichen; (hair) blondieren || intr bleichen

bleachers ['blitʃərs] spl Zuschauersitze pl im Freien

bleak [blik] adj öde, trostlos

bleary-eyed ['blɪrɪ,aɪd] adj triefäugig

bleat [blit] s Blöken n || intr blöken; (said of a goat) meckern

bleed [blid] v (pret & pp **bled** [bled]) tr (brakes) entlüften; (med) zur Ader lassen; **b. white** (fig) zum Weißbluten bringen || intr bluten; **b. to death** verbluten

blemish ['blemɪʃ] s Fleck m, Makel m; (fig) Schandfleck m

blend [blend] s Mischung f; (liquor) Verschnitt m || v (pret & pp **blended** & **blent** [blent]) tr mischen; (wine, liquor) verschneiden || intr sich vermischen; (said of colors) zueinander passen, zusammenpassen

bless [bles] tr segnen; **God b. you!** (after a sneeze) Gesundheit!

blessed ['blesɪd] adj selig

bless'ing s Segen m, Gnade f; **b. in disguise** Glück n im Unglück

blight [blaɪt] s (fig) Gifthauch m; (agr) Brand m, Mehltau m || tr (fig) verderben; (agr) schädigen

blight'ed adj brandig

blimp [blɪmp] s unstarres Luftschiff n

blind [blaɪnd] adj blind; (curve) unübersichtlich; **go b.** erblinden || s Jalousie f; (hunt) Attrappe f || tr blenden; (fig) verblenden

blind' al'ley s (& fig) Sackgasse f

blind' date' s Verabredung f mit e-r (or e-m) Unbekannten

blinder ['blaɪndər] s Scheuklappe f

blind' fly'ing s Blindflug m

blind'fold' adj mit verbundenen Augen || adv blindlings || tr die Augen verbinden (dat)

blind' man' s Blinder m

blind'man's' bluff' s Blindekuhspiel n

blindness ['blaɪndnɪs] s Blindheit f

blink [blɪŋk] s Blinken n; **on the b.** (sl) kaputt || tr—**b. one's eyes** mit den Augen zwinkern || intr (said of a light) blinken; (said of the eyes) blinzeln

blinker ['blɪŋkər] s (for horses) Scheuklappe f; (aut) Blinker m

blip [blɪp] s (radar) Leuchtfleck m

bliss [blɪs] s Wonne f

blissful ['blɪsfəl] adj glückselig

blister ['blɪstər] s Blase f; (from a burn) Brandblase f || intr (said of the skin) Blasen ziehen; (said of paint) Blasen werfen

blithe [blaɪð] adj fröhlich

blitzkrieg ['blɪts,krig] s Blitzkrieg m

blizzard ['blɪzərd] s Blizzard m

bloat [blot] tr aufblähen || intr anschwellen

bloc [blɑk] s (parl) Stimmblock m; (pol) Block m

block [blɑk] s (of wood) Klotz m; (toy) Bauklotz m; (for chopping) Hackklotz m; (of houses) Häuser-

block m; (of seats) Reihe f; (mach) Rolle f; (sport) Block m; **five blocks from here** fünf Straßen weiter || tr versperren; (traffic, a street, a player) blockieren; (a ball) abfangen; (a hat) aufdämpfen; **be blocked** sich stauen; **b. off** (a street) absperren; **b. up** verstopfen, versperren

blockade [blɑ'ked] s Blockade f, Sperre f || tr blockieren, sperren

blockade' run'ner s Blockadebrecher m

blockage ['blɑkɪdʒ] s Stockung f

block' and tac'kle s Flaschenzug m

block'head' s Klotz m, Dummkopf m

blond [blɑnd] adj blond || s Blonde m

blonde [blɑnd] s Blondine f

blood [blʌd] s Blut n; (lineage) Geblüt n; **in cold b.** kaltblütig

blood' circula'tion s Blutkreislauf m

blood' clot' s Blutgerinnsel n

bloodcurdling ['blʌd,kʌrdlɪŋ] adj haarsträubend

blood' do'nor s Blutspender –in m f

blood'hound' s (& fig) Bluthund m

bloodless ['blʌdlɪs] adj blutlos; (revolution) unblutig

blood' poi'soning s Blutvergiftung f

blood' pres'sure s Blutdruck m

blood' rela'tion s Blutsverwandte m f

blood'shed' s Blutvergießen n

blood'shot' adj blutunterlaufen

blood'stain' s Blutfleck m, Blutspur f

blood'stained' adj blutbefleckt

blood'stream' s Blutstrom m

blood'suck'er s (& fig) Blutsauger m

blood' test' s Blutprobe f

blood'thirst'y adj blutdürstig

blood' transfu'sion s Blutübertragung f

blood' type' s Blutgruppe f

blood' ves'sel s Blutgefäß n

blood-y ['blʌdɪ] adj blutig; (blood-stained) blutbefleckt || v (pret & pp –ied) tr mit Blut beflecken

bloom [blum] s Blüte f || intr blühen

blossom ['blɑsəm] s Blüte f || intr blühen

blot [blɑt] s Fleck m; (fig) Schandfleck m || v (pret & pp **blotted**; ger **blotting**) tr (smear) beschmieren; (with a blotter) (ab)löschen; **b. out** ausstreichen; (fig) auslöschen || intr (said of ink) klecksen

blotch [blɑtʃ] s Klecks m; (on the skin) Ausschlag m

blotter ['blɑtər] s Löscher m

blot'ting pa'per s Löschpapier n

blouse [blaus] s Bluse f

blow [blo] s Schlag m, Hieb m; (fig) Schlag m; **come to blows** handgemein werden || v (pret **blew** [blu]; pp **blown**) tr blasen; (money) (sl) verschwenden; (a fuse) durchbrennen; **b. a whistle** pfeifen; **b. off** steam sich austoben; **b. one's top** (coll) hochgehen; **b. out** (a candle) ausblasen; **b. up** (inflate) aufblasen; (with explosives) sprengen; (phot) vergrößern || intr blasen; **b. out** (said of a candle) auslöschen; (said of a tire) platzen; **blow over** vorübergehen; **b. up** (& fig) in die Luft gehen

blower ['blo-ər] s Gebläse n, Bläser m

blow'out' s (sl) Gelage n; (aut) Reifen-panne f

blow'pipe' s Blasrohr n

blow'torch' s Lötlampe f

blubber ['blʌbər] s Tran m || intr (cry noisily) jaulen

bludgeon ['blʌdʒən] s Knüppel m || tr mit dem Knüppel bearbeiten

blue [blu] adj blau; (fig) bedrückt || s Blau n; **blues** (mus) Blues m; **have the blues** trüb gestimmt sein; **out of the b.** aus heiterem Himmel

blue'ber'ry s Heidelbeere f

blue'bird' s Blaukehlchen n

blue' chip' s (cards) blaue Spielmarke f; (fin) sicheres Wertpapier n

blue'-col'lar work'er s Arbeiter m

blue' jeans' spl Jeans pl

blue' moon' s—once in a b. alle Jubel-jahre einmal

blue'print' s Blaupause f

blue' streak' s—talk a b. (coll) in e-r Tour reden

bluff [blʌf] adj schroff; (person) derb || s (coll) Bluff m; (geol) Steilküste f; **call s.o.'s b.** j—m beim Wort neh-men || tr & intr bluffen

bluffer ['blʌfər] s Bluffer m

blu'ing s Waschblau n

bluish ['blu·ɪʃ] adj bläulich

blunder ['blʌndər] s Schnitzer m; || intr e-n Schnitzer machen; **b.** into stolpern in (acc); **b. upon** zufällig geraten auf (acc)

blunt [blʌnt] adj stumpf; (fig) plump, unverblümt || tr abstumpfen

bluntly ['blʌntlɪ] adv unverblümt

blur [blʌr] s Verschwommenheit f || v (pret & pp **blurred**; ger **blurring**) tr verwischen || intr verschwommen werden

blurb [blʌrb] s Reklametext m

blurred adj verschwommen; (vision) unscharf

blurt [blʌrt] tr—**b. out** herausplatzen

blush [blʌʃ] s Röte f, Schamröte f || intr (at) erröten (über acc)

bluster ['blʌstər] s Prahlerei f || intr (said of a person) prahlen, poltern; (said of wind) toben

blustery ['blʌstərɪ] adj stürmisch

boa constrictor ['bo·ə kən'strɪktər] s Abgottschlange f, Königsschlange f

boar [bor] s Eber m; (wild boar) Wild-schwein n

board [bord] s Brett n; (of administra-tors) Ausschuß m, Behörde f, Rat m; (meals) Kost f; (educ) Schultafel f; **above b.** offen; **on b.** an Bord || tr (a ship) besteigen; (a plane, train) einsteigen in (acc); (paying guests) beköstigen; **b. up** mit Brettern ver-nageln || intr (with) in Kost sein (bei)

boarder ['bordər] s Kostgänger –in mf

board'inghouse' s Pension f

board'ing pass' s Bordkarte f

board'ing school' s Internat n

board'ing stu'dent s Interne mf

board' of direc'tors s Verwaltungsrat m, Aufsichtsrat m

board' of educa'tion s Unterrichtsmi-nisterium n

board' of health' s Gesundheitsbehörde f

board' of trade' s Handelskammer f

board' of trustees' s Verwaltungsrat m

board'walk' s Strandpromenade f

boast [bost] s Prahlerei f; (cause of pride) Stolz m || tr sich rühmen (genit) || intr (about) prahlen (mit)

boastful ['bostfəl] adj prahlerisch

boat [bot] s Boot n; **in the same b.** (fig) in der gleichen Lage

boat'house' s Bootshaus n

boat'ing s Bootsfahrt f; **go b.** e-e Boot-fahrt machen

boat'race' s Bootrennen n

boat' ride' s Bootsfahrt f

boatswain ['bosən] s Hochbootsmann m

bob [bab] s (jerky motion) Ruck m; (hairdo) Bubikopf m; (of a fishing line) Schwimmer m; (of a plumb line) Senkblei n || v (pret & pp **bobbed**; ger **bobbing**) tr (hair) kurz schneiden || intr sich hin und her be-wegen; **bob up and down** sich auf und ab bewegen

bobbin ['babɪn] s Klöppel m

bobble ['babəl] tr (coll) ungeschickt handhaben

bob'by pin' ['babɪ] s Haarklammer f

bob'sled' s Bob m, Rennschlitten m

bode [bod] tr bedeuten

bodily ['badɪlɪ] adj leiblich; **b. injury** Körperverletzung f || adv leibhaftig

body ['badɪ] s Körper m; (of a person or animal) Körper m; (corpse) Leiche f; (collective group) Körperschaft f; (of a plane, ship) Rumpf m; (of a vehicle) Karosserie f; (of beer, wine) Schwere f; (of a letter) Text m; **b. of water** Gewässer n; **in a b.** geschlos-sen

bod'yguard' s Leibgarde f

bod'y o'dor s Körpergeruch m

bog [bag] s Sumpf m || v (pret & pp **bogged**; ger **bogging**) intr—**bog down** steckenbleiben

bogey-man ['bogɪ,mæn] s (–men) Kin-derschreck m

bogus ['bogəs] adj schwindelhaft

Bohemia [bo'himɪ·ə] s Böhmen n

Bohemian [bo'himɪ·ən] adj böhmisch || s (person) Böhme m, Böhmin f; (fig) Bohemien m; (language) Böh-misch n

boil [bɔɪl] s (pathol) Geschwür n; **bring to a b.** zum Sieden bringen || tr kochen, sieden || intr kochen, sie-den; **b. away** verkochen; **b. over** überkochen

boiled' ham' s gekochter Schinken m

boiled' pota'toes spl Salzkartoffeln pl

boiler ['bɔɪlər] s (electrical water tank) Boiler m; (kettle) Kessel m

boil'ermak'er s Kesselschmied m

boil'er room' s Heizraum m

boil'ing adj siedend || adv—**be b. mad** vor Zorn kochen; **b. hot** siedeheiß

boil'ing point' s Siedepunkt m

boisterous ['bɔɪstərəs] adj ausgelassen

bold [bold] adj kühn, gewagt; (out-lines) deutlich

bold'face' s Fettdruck m

boldness ['bouldnɪs] s Kühnheit f
Bolshevik ['bɔl/əvɪk] adj bolschewistisch ‖ s Bolschewik –in mf
bolster ['boulstər] s Nackenrolle f ‖ tr unterstützen
bolt [boult] s Bolzen m; (door lock) Riegel m; (of cloth) Stoffballen m; (of lightning) Blitzstrahl m; b. out of the blue Blitz m aus heiterem Himmel ‖ tr (a door) verriegeln; (a political party) im Stich lassen; (food) hinunterschlingen ‖ intr davonstürzen; (said of a horse) durchgehen
bomb [bɑm] s (dropped from the air) Bombe f; (planted) Sprengladung f; (fiasco) (sl) Versager m ‖ tr (from the air) bombardieren; (blow up) sprengen ‖ intr (sl) versagen
bombard [bɑm'bɑrd] tr bombardieren, beschießen; (fig) bombardieren
bombardier [ˌbɑmbər'dɪr] s Bombenschütze m
bombardment [bɑm'bɑrdmənt] s Bombardement n, Beschießung f
bombast ['bɑmbæst] s Schwulst m
bombastic [bɑm'bæstɪk] adj schwülstig
bomb′ bay′ s Bombenschacht m
bomb′ cra′ter s Bombentrichter m
bomber ['bɑmər] s Bomber m
bomb′ing s Bombenabwurf m
bomb′ing run′ s Bomben(ziel)anflug m
bomb′proof′ adj bombenfest, bombensicher
bomb′shell′ s (& fig) Bombe f
bomb′ shel′ter s Bombenkeller m
bomb′sight′ s Bombenzielgerät n
bomb′ squad′ s Entschärfungskommando n
bona fide ['bonə ˌfaɪd] adj ehrlich, echt; (offer) solide
bonanza [bo'nænzə] s Goldgrube f
bond [bɑnd] s Fessel f; (fin) Obligation f
bondage ['bɑndɪdʒ] s Knechtschaft f
bond′hold′er s Inhaber –in mf e–r Obligation
bonds·man ['bɑndzmən] s (–men) Bürge m
bone [bon] s Knochen m, Bein n; (of fish) Gräte f; bones Gebein n; (mortal remains) Gebeine pl; have a b. to pick with ein Hühnchen zu rupfen haben mit; make no bones about it nicht viel Federlesens machen mit; to the b. bis ins Mark ‖ tr (meat) ausbeinen; (fish) ausgräten ‖ intr— b. up for (sl) büffeln für
bone′-dry′ adj knochentrocken
bone′head′ s Dummkopf m
boneless ['bonlɪs] adj ohne Knochen; (fish) ohne Gräten
boner ['bonər] s (coll) Schnitzer m; pull a b. (coll) e–n Schnitzer machen
bonfire ['bɑn ˌfaɪr] s Freudenfeuer n
bonnet ['bɑnɪt] s Haube f
bonus ['bonəs] s Gratifikation f
bony ['boni] adj knochig; (fish) grätig
boo [bu] s Pfuiruf m ‖ tr niederbrüllen ‖ intr pfui rufen ‖ interj (to jeer) pfui; (to scare someone) huh!
boob [bub] s (sl) Blödkopf m
booby ['bubi] s (sl) Blödkopf m
boo′by hatch′ s (sl) Affenkasten m

boo′by prize′ s Trostpreis m
boo′by trap′ s Minenfalle f
boogey·man ['bugi ˌmæn], ['bogiˌmæn] s (–men′) Schreckgespenst n
book [buk] s Buch n; (of stamps, tickets, matches) Heftchen n; keep books Bücher führen ‖ tr buchen; (e.g., seats) vorbestellen
book′bind′er s Buchbinder –in mf
book′bind′ery s Buchbinderei f
book′bind′ing s Buchbinderei f
book′case′ s Bücherschrank m
book′ end′ s Bücherstütze f
bookie ['buki] s (coll) Buchmacher –in mf
book′ing s Buchung f
bookish ['bukɪʃ] adj lesefreudig
book′keep′er s Buchhalter –in mf
book′keep′ing s Buchhaltung f
book′ learn′ing s Schulweisheit f
booklet ['buklɪt] s Büchlein n
book′mak′er s Buchmacher –in mf
book′mark′ s Lesezeichen n
book′rack′ s Büchergestell n
book′ review′ s Buchbesprechung f
book′sel′ler s Buchhändler –in mf
book′shelf′ s (–shelves) Bücherregal n
book′stand′ s Bücher(verkaufs)stand m
book′store′ s Buchhandlung f
book′worm′ s (& fig) Bücherwurm m
boom [bum] s (noise) dumpfes Dröhnen n; (of a crane) Ausleger m; (cin, telv) Galgen m; (econ) Boom m, Hochkonjunktur f; (naut) Baum m, Spiere f; (st.exch.) Hausse f ‖ intr dröhnen; (said of an organ) brummen
boomerang ['bumə ˌræŋ] s Bumerang m
boon [bun] s Wohltat f, Segen m
boon′ compan′ion s Zechkumpan m
boor [bur] s Rüpel m, Flegel m
boorish ['burɪʃ] adj flegelhaft
boost [bust] s (push) Auftrieb m; (in pay) Gehaltserhöhung f ‖ tr fördern; (prices) in die Höhe treiben; (elec) verstärken; b. business die Wirtschaft ankurbeln
booster ['bustər] s (backer) Förderer m, Förderin f
boost′er rock′et s Hilfsrakete f
boost′er shot′ s (med) Nachimpfung f
boot [but] s Stiefel m; (kick) Fußtritt m; to b. noch dazu; you can bet your boots on that (sl) darauf kannst du Gift nehmen ‖ tr (sl) stoßen; (fb) kicken; b. out (sl) 'rausschmeißen
booth [buθ] s (at a fair) Marktbude f; (for telephone, voting) Zelle f
boot′leg′ adj geschmuggelt ‖ v (pret & pp –legged; ger –legging) tr (make illegally) illegal brennen; (smuggle) schmuggeln
bootlegger ['but ˌlegər] s Alkoholschmuggler m, Bootlegger m
bootlicker ['but ˌlɪkər] s (sl) Kriecher m
booty ['buti] s Beute f
booze [buz] s (coll) Schnaps m ‖ intr (coll) saufen
booze′ hound′ s Saufbold m, Saufaus m
border ['bɔrdər] s Rand m; (of a country) Grenze f; (of a dress, etc.) Saum

m, Borte *f* ‖ *tr* umranden, begrenzen; **be bordered by** grenzen an (*acc*) ‖ *intr*—**b. on** (& fig) grenzen an (*acc*)

bor'derline' *s* Grenzlinie *f*

bor'derline case' *s* Grenzfall *m*

bore [bor] *s* (*drill hole*) Bohrloch *n*; (*of a gun*) Bohrung *f*; (*of a cylinder*) innerer Zylinderdurchmesser *m*; (fig) langweiliger Mensch *m* ‖ *tr* bohren; (fig) langweilen

boredom ['bordəm] *s* Langeweile *f*

bor'ing *adj* langweilig ‖ *s* Bohren *n*

born [bɔrn] *adj* geboren; **he was b.** (*said of a living person*) er ist geboren; (*said of a deceased person*) er war geboren

borough ['bʌro] *s* Städtchen *n*

borrow ['bɔro] *tr* leihen

borrower ['bɔro·ər] *s* Entleiher –in *mf*; (fin) Kreditnehmer –in *mf*

bor'rowing *s* Borgen *n*; (fin) Kreditaufnahme *f*; (ling) Lehnwort *n*

bosom ['buzəm] *s* Busen *m*; (fig) Schoß *m*

bos'om friend' *s* Busenfreund *m*

boss [bɔs] *s* (coll) Chef *m*, Boß *m*; (*of a shield*) Buckel *m*; (pol) Bonze *m* ‖ *tr* (**around**) herumkommandieren

bossy ['bɔsɪ] *adj* herrschsüchtig

botanical [bə'tænɪkəl] *adj* botanisch

botanist ['batənɪst] *s* Botaniker –in *mf*

botany ['batənɪ] *s* Botanik *f*

botch [batʃ] *tr* (coll) verpfuschen

both [boθ] *adj* & *pron* beide ‖ *conj*—**both...and** sowohl... als auch

bother ['baðər] *s* Belästigung *f*, Mühe *f* ‖ *tr* (**annoy**) belästigen, stören; (**worry**) bedrücken; (*said of a conscience*) quälen ‖ *intr* sich bemühen; **b. about** sich bekümmern um; **b. with** (*a thing*) sich befassen mit; (*a person*) verkehren mit

bothersome ['baðərsəm] *adj* lästig

bottle ['batəl] *s* Flasche *f* ‖ *tr* in Flaschen abfüllen; **bottled up** aufgestaut

bot'tleneck' *s* Flaschenhals *m*; (fig) Engpaß *m*, Stauung *f*

bot'tle o'pener *s* Flaschenöffner *m*

bottom ['batəm] *adj* niedrigste, unterste ‖ *s* Boden *m*; (*of a well, shaft, river, valley*) Sohle *f*; (*of a mountain*) Fuß *m*; (*of an affair*) Grund *m*; (**buttocks**) Hintern *m*; **at the b. of the page** unten auf der Seite; **bottoms up!** prosit, ex!; **get to the b. of a problem** e-r Frage auf den Grund gehen; **reach b.** (fig) den Nullpunkt erreichen

bottomless ['batəmlɪs] *adj* bodenlos

bough [bau] *s* Ast *m*

bouillon ['buljan] *s* Kraftbrühe *f*

bouil'lon cube' *s* Bouillonwürfel *m*

boulder ['boldər] *s* Felsblock *m*

bounce [bauns] *s* Aufprall *m*; (fig) Schwung *m* ‖ *tr* (*a ball*) aufprallen lassen; (*throw out*) (sl) 'rausschmeißen ‖ *intr* aufprallen, aufspringen; (*said of a check*) (coll) platzen

bouncer ['baunsər] *s* (sl) Rausschmeißer *m*

bounc'ing *adj* (**baby**) stramm

bound [baund] *adj* gebunden, gefesselt; (**book**) gebunden; (*in duty*) verpflichtet; **be b. for** unterwegs sein nach; **be b. up with** eng verbunden sein mit; **I am b. to** (*inf*) ich muß (*inf*) ‖ *s* Sprung *m*, Satz *m*; **bounds** Grenzen *pl*, Schranken *pl*; **in bounds** (sport) in: **keep within bounds in** Schranken halten; **know no bounds** weder Maß noch Ziel kennen; **out of bounds** (sport) aus; **within the bounds of** im Bereich (**genit**) ‖ *tr* begrenzen ‖ *intr* aufprallen, aufspringen

boundary ['baundəri] *s* Grenze *f*; (fig) Umgrenzung *f*

boun'dary line' *s* Grenzlinie *f*

boun'dary stone' *s* Grenzstein *m*

boundless ['baundlɪs] *adj* grenzenlos

bountiful ['bauntɪfəl] *adj* (**generous**) freigebig; (**ample**) reichlich

bounty ['bauntɪ] *s* (**generosity**) Freigebigkeit *f*; (**gift**) Geschenk *n*; (**reward**) Prämie *f*

bouquet [bu'ke] *s* Strauß *m*; (**aroma**) Blume *f*

bout [baut] *s* (**box**) Kampf *m*; (**fencing**) Gang *m*; (pathol) Anfall *m*

bow [bau] *s* Verbeugung *f*; (naut) Bug *m* ‖ *intr* sich verbeugen; **bow and scrape before** sich schmiegen und biegen vor (*dat*); **bow down** sich bücken; **bow out** sich geschickt zurückziehen; **bow to** sich (ver)neigen vor (*dat*) ‖ [bo] *s* (**weapon**) Bogen *m*; (*of a violin*) Geigenbogen *m*; (**bowknot**) Schleife *f*; **bow and arrow** Pfeil *m* und Bogen *m* ‖ *intr* (mus) geigen

bowel ['bau·əl] *s* Darm *m*; **bowels** Eingeweide *pl*; **bowels of the earth** Erdinnere *n*

bow'el move'ment *s* Stuhlgang *m*

bowl [bol] *s* Napf *m*, Schüssel *f*; (*of a pipe*) Kopf *m*; (**washbowl, toilet bowl**) Becken *n*; (*of a spoon*) Höhlung *f*; (sport) Stadion *n* ‖ *tr* umhauen; (fig) umwerfen ‖ *intr* kegeln

bowlegged ['bo,leg(ɪ)d] *adj* O-beinig

bowler ['bolər] *s* Kegler –in *mf*

bowl'ing *s* Kegeln *n*

bowl'ing al'ley *s* Kegelbahn *f*

bowl'ing ball' *s* Kegelkugel *f*

bowl'ing pin' *s* Kegel *m*

bowstring ['bo,strɪŋ] *s* Bogensehne *f*

bow' tie' [bo] *s* Schleife *f*, Fliege *f*

bow' win'dow [bo] *s* Bogenfenster *n*

bowwow ['bau'wau] *interj* wauwau!

box [baks] *s* (*small and generally of cardboard*) Schachtel *f*; (*larger and generally of cardboard*) Karton *m*; (*generally of wood*) Kasten *m*; (*larger and generally of wood*) Kiste *f*; (*of strips of wood*) Spanschachtel *f*; (theat) Loge *f*; (pop) Kasten *m*; **box of candy** Bonbonniere *f*; **box on the ear** Ohrfeige *f* ‖ *tr* (sport) boxen; **box in** einschließen; **box s.o.'s ears** j–n ohrfeigen ‖ *intr* (sport) boxen

box'car' *s* geschlossener Güterwagen *m*

boxer ['baksər] *s* (sport, zool) Boxer *m*

box'ing *s* Boxen *n*, Boxsport *m*

box'ing glove' *s* Boxhandschuh *m*

box′ing match′ s Boxkampf m
box′ kite′ s Kastendrachen m
box′ of′fice s (cin, theat) Kasse f
box′ seat′ s Logenplatz m
box′wood′ s Buchsbaum m
boy [bɔɪ] s Junge m; (servant) Boy m
boycott [′bɔɪkat] s Boykott m ‖ tr boykottieren
boy′friend′ s Freund m
boy′hood′ s Knabenalter n
boyish [′bɔɪ·ɪʃ] adj jungenhaft
boy′ scout′ s Pfadfinder m
bra [bra] s (coll) BH m
brace [bres] s (carp) Strebe f, Stütze f; (dent) Zahnklammer f, Zahnspange f; (hunt) Paar n; (med) Schiene f; (typ) geschweifte Klammer f ‖ tr verstreben; (fig) stärken; **b. oneself** sich zusammenreißen; **b. oneself against** sich stemmen gegen; **b. oneself for** seinen Mut zusammennehmen für; **b. up** (fig) aufpulvern
brace′ and bit′ s Bohrwinde f
bracelet [′breslɪt] s Armband n
brac′ing adj (invigorating) erfrischend
bracket [′brækɪt] s Winkelstütze f, Konsole f; (wall bracket) Wandarm m; (mounting clip) Befestigungsschelle f; (typ) eckige Klammer f ‖ tr einklammern; (arti) eingabeln
brackish [′brækɪʃ] adj brackig
brag [bræg] v (pret & pp bragged; ger bragging) intr (about) prahlen
braggart [′brægərt] s Prahler –in mf
brag′ging adj prahlerisch ‖ s Prahlerei f
braid [bred] s (of hair) Flechte f; (flat trimming) Tresse f, Litze f; (round trimming) Kordel f ‖ tr (hair, rope) flechten; (trim with braid) mit Tresse (or Borten) besetzen
braille [brel] s Blindenschrift f
brain [bren] s Hirn n; **brains** Hirn n; (fig) Grütze f ‖ tr (coll) den Schädel einschlagen (dat)
brain′child′ s Geistesfrucht f
brainless [′brenlɪs] adj hirnlos
brain′storm′ s (coll) Geistesblitz m
brain′wash′ s Gehirnwäsche vornehmen bei
brain′wash′ing s Gehirnwäsche f
brain′ wave′ s Hirnwelle f; (fig) Geistesblitz m
brain′work′ s Gehirnarbeit f
brainy [′breni] adj geistreich
braise [brez] tr schmoren, dünsten
brake [brek] s Bremse f; **put on the brakes** bremsen ‖ intr bremsen
brake′ drum′ s Bremstrommel f
brake′ light′ s Bremslicht n
brake′ lin′ing s Bremsbelag m
brake′man s (–men) Bremser m
brake′ped′al s Bremspedal n
brake′ shoe′ s (aut) Bremsbacke f
bramble [′bræmbəl] s Dornbusch m
bran [bræn] s Kleie f
branch [bræntʃ] s (of a tree) Ast m; (smaller branch; of lineage) Zweig m; (of river) Arm m; (of a road, railroad) Abzweigung f; (of science, work, a shop) Branche f, Unterabteilung f; (com) Filiale f, Nebenstelle

f ‖ intr—**b. off** abzweigen; **b. out** sich verzweigen
branch′ line′ s Seitenlinie f
branch′ of′fice s Zweigstelle f
branch′ of serv′ice s Truppengattung f
brand [brænd] s (kind) Marke f; (trademark) Handelsmarke f; (on cattle) Brandmal n; (branding iron) Brandeisen n; (dishonor) Schandfleck m ‖ tr (& fig) brandmarken
brand′ing i′ron s Brandeisen n
brandish [′brændɪʃ] tr schwingen; (threateningly) schwenken
brand′-new′ adj nagelneu
brandy [′brændi] s Branntwein m
brash [bræʃ] adj schnodd(e)rig, frech
brass [bræs] adj Messing– ‖ s Messing n; (mil) hohe Offiziere pl; (mus) Blechinstrumente pl
brass′ band′ s Blechblaskapelle f
brassiere [brə′zɪr] s Büstenhalter m
brass′ knuck′les spl Schlagring m
brass′ tacks′ spl—**get down to b.** (coll) zur Sache kommen
brat [bræt] s (coll) Balg m
bravado [brə′vado] s Bravour f, Angabe f
brave [brev] adj tapfer, mutig ‖ s indianischer Krieger m ‖ tr trotzen (dat)
bravery [′brevəri] s Tapferkeit f
bra·vo [′bravo] s (–vos) Bravo n ‖ interj bravo!
brawl [brɔl] s Rauferei f ‖ intr raufen
brawler [′brɔlər] s Raufbold m
brawn [brɔn] s Muskelkraft f
brawny [′brɔni] adj muskulös, kräftig
bray [bre] s Eselsschrei m ‖ intr schreien, iahen
braze [brez] tr (brassplate) mit Messing überziehen; (solder) hartlöten
brazen [′brezən] adj Messing–, ehern; (fig) unverschämt ‖ tr—**b. it out** unverschämt durchsetzen
Brazil [brə′zɪl] s Brasilien n
Brazilian [brə′zɪljən] adj brasilianisch, brasilisch ‖ s Brasilier –in mf
Brazil′ nut′ s Paranuß f
breach [britʃ] s Bruch m; (mil) Bresche f ‖ tr (mil) durchbrechen
breach′ of con′tract s Vertragsbruch m
breach′ of prom′ise s Verlöbnisbruch m
breach′ of the peace′ s Friedensbruch m
breach′ of trust′ s Vertrauensbruch m
bread [bred] s Brot n; (money) (sl) Pinke f ‖ tr (culin) panieren
bread′ and but′ter s Butterbrot n; (livelihood) Lebensunterhalt m
bread′ box′ s Brotkasten m
bread′ crumb′ s Brotkrume f
bread′ed adj paniert
bread′ed veal′ cut′let s Wiener Schnitzel n
bread′ knife′ s Brotmesser n
breadth [bredθ] s Breite f
bread′win′ner s Brotverdiener –in mf
break [brek] s Bruch m; (split, tear) Riß m; (crack) Sprung m; (in relations) Bruch m; (in a forest) Lichtung f; (in the clouds) Lücke f; (recess) Pause f; (rest from work)

Arbeitspause *f;* (*luck*) Glück *n;* (*chance*) Chance *f;* (*box*) Lösen *n;* **bad b. in the weather** Wetterumschlag *m;* **give s.o. a b.** j–m e–e Chance geben; **make a b. for** losstürzen auf (*acc*); **take a b.** e–e Pause machen; **tough b.** Pech *n;* **without a b.** ohne Unterbrechung ‖ *v* (*pret* **broke** [brok]; *pp* **broken** ['brokən]) *tr* (& *fig*) brechen; (*snap*) zerreißen; (*a string*) durchreißen; (*a dish*) zerbrechen; (*an appointment*) nicht einhalten; (*contact*) unterbrechen; (*an engagement*) auflösen; (*a law, limb*) verletzen; (*monotony*) auflockern; (*a record*) brechen; (*a seal*) erbrechen; (*a window*) einschlagen; (*one's word, promise*) nicht halten; **b. down** (*into constituents*) zerlegen; (*s.o.'s resistance*) überwinden; (*mach*) abmontieren; **b. in** (*a horse*) zureiten; (*a car*) einfahren; (*a person*) anlernen; **b. loose** losreißen; **b. off** abbrechen, losbrechen; (*an engagement*) lösen; **b. open** aufbrechen; **b. s.o. from s.th.** j–m etw abgewöhnen; **b. the news (to)** die Nachricht eröffnen (*dat*), die Nachricht beibringen (*dat*); **b. to pieces** zerbrechen; (*a meeting*) auflösen; (*forcibly*) sprengen; **break wind** e–n Darmwind abgehen lassen ‖ *intr* brechen; (*snap*) reißen; (*said of the voice*) mutieren; (*said of waves*) sich brechen; (*said of large waves*) sich überschlagen; (*said of the weather*) umschlagen; **b. down** zusammenbrechen; (*mach*) versagen; **b. even** gerade die Unkosten decken; **b. loose** losbrechen, sich losreißen; **b. out** (*said of fire, an epidemic, prisoner*) ausbrechen; **b. up** (*said of a meeting*) sich auflösen

breakable ['brekəbəl] *adj* zerbrechlich
breakage ['brekɪdʒ] *s* Bruch *m;* (*cost of broken articles*) Bruchschaden *m*
break'down' *s* (*of health, discipline, morals*) Zusammenbruch *m;* (*disintegration*) Zersetzung *f;* (*of costs, etc.*) Aufgliederung *f;* (*aut*) Panne *f;* (*chem*) Analyse *f;* (*elec*) Durchschlag *m;* (*of a piece of equipment*) (*mach*) Versagen *n;* (*e.g., of power supply, factory equipment*) Betriebsstörung *f*
breaker ['brekər] *s* Sturzwelle *f;* **breakers** Brandung *f*
breakfast ['brekfəst] *s* Frühstück *n* ‖ *intr* frühstücken
break'neck' *adj* halsbrecherisch
break' of day' *s* Tagesanbruch *m*
break'through' *s* Durchbruch *m*
break'up' *s* Aufbrechen *n;* (*of a meeting*) Auflösung *f*
break'wa'ter *s* Wellenbrecher *m*
breast [brest] *s* Brust *f;* (*of a woman*) Brust *f,* Busen *m;* **beat one's b.** sich an die Brust schlagen; **make a clean b. of** sich [*dat*] vom Herzen reden
breast'bone' *s* Brustbein *n*
breast' feed'ing *s* Stillen *n*
breast'plate' *s* Brustharnisch *m*
breast'stroke' *s* Brustschwimmen *n*

breath [brɛθ] *s* Atem *m;* (*single inhalation*) Atemzug *m;* (*fig*) Hauch *m;* **b. of air** Lüftchen *n;* **gasp for b.** nach Luft schnappen; **have bad b.** aus dem Mund riechen; **in the same b.** im gleichen Atemzug; **save one's b.** sich [*dat*] seine Worte ersparen; **take a deep b.** tief Luft holen; **take one's b. away** j–m den Atem verschlagen; **waste one's b.** in den Wind reden
breathe [brið] *tr* atmen, schöpfen; **b. a sigh of relief** aufatmen; **b. life into** beseelen; **b. one's last** die Seele aushauchen; **b. out** ausatmen; **not b. a word about it** kein Wort davon verlauten lassen ‖ *intr* atmen, hauchen; **b. again** aufatmen; **b. on** anhauchen
breath'ing space' *s* Atempause *f*
breathless ['brɛθlɪs] *adj* atemlos
breath'-tak'ing *adj* atemberaubend
breech [britʃ] *s* Verschlußstück *n*
breed [brid] *s* Zucht *f,* Stamm *m;* (*sort, group*) Schlag *m;* (*of animals*) Rasse *f* ‖ *v* (*pret & pp* **bred** [brɛd]) *tr* (*beget*) erzeugen; (*raise*) züchten; (*fig*) hervorrufen ‖ *intr* sich vermehren
breeder ['bridər] *s* Züchter –in *mf*
breed'ing *s* (*of animals*) Züchtung *f,* Aufzucht *f;* (*fig*) Erziehung *f*
breeze [briz] *s* Lüftchen *n,* Brise *f* ‖ *intr***—b. by** vorbeiflitzen; **b. in** frisch und vergnügt hereinkommen
breezy ['brizi] *adj* luftig; (*fig*) keß
brevity ['brɛvɪti] *s* Kürze *f*
brew [bru] *s* Brühe *f;* (*of beer*) Bräu *m* ‖ *tr* (*tea, coffee*) aufbrühen; (*beer*) brauen ‖ *intr* ziehen; (*said of a storm*) sich zusammenbrauen; **something is brewing** etwas ist im Anzuge
brewer ['bru·ər] *s* Brauer –in *mf*
brewery ['bru·əri] *s* Brauerei *f*
bribe [braɪb] *s* Bestechungsgeld *n* ‖ *tr* bestechen
bribery ['braɪbəri] *s* Bestechung *f*
brick [brɪk] *s* Ziegelstein *m*
bricklayer ['brɪk‚le·ər] *s* Maurer *m*
brick'work' *s* Mauerwerk *n*
brick'yard' *s* Ziegelei *f*
bridal ['braɪdəl] *adj* Braut–, Hochzeits–
brid'al gown' *s* Brautkleid *n*
brid'al veil' *s* Brautschleier *m*
bride [braɪd] *s* Braut *f*
bride'groom' *s* Bräutigam *m*
brides'maid' *s* Brautjungfer *f*
bridge [brɪdʒ] *s* (*over a river*) Brücke *f;* (*of eyeglasses*) Steg *m;* (*of a nose*) Nasenrücken *m;* (*cards*) Bridge *n;* (*dent*) Zahnbrücke *f;* (*naut*) Kommandobrücke *f* ‖ *tr* (& *fig*) überbrücken
bridge'head' *s* Brückenkopf *m*
bridge'work' *s* (*dent*) Brückenarbeit *f*
bridle ['braɪdəl] *s* Zaum *m,* Zügel *m* ‖ *tr* aufzäumen, zügeln
bri'dle path' *s* Reitweg *m*
brief [brif] *adj* kurz; **be b.** sich kurz fassen ‖ *s* (*jur*) Schriftsatz *m* ‖ *tr* einweisen, orientieren
brief' case' *s* Aktentasche *f*

brief′ing s Einsatzbesprechung f
brier ['braɪ.ər] s Dornbusch m
brig [brɪg] s (naut) Brigg f; (nav) Knast m
brigade [brɪ'ged] s Brigade f
brigadier′ gen′eral [ˌbrɪgə'dɪr] s Brigadegeneral m
brigand ['brɪgənd] s Brigant m
bright [braɪt] adj hell; (color) lebhaft; (face) strahlend; (weather) heiter; (smart) gescheit, aufgeweckt || adv —b. and early in aller Frühe
brighten ['braɪtən] tr aufhellen || intr sich aufhellen
bright′-eyed adj helläugig
brightness ['braɪtnɪs] s Helle f
bright′ side s (fig) Lichtseite f
bright′ spot′ s (fig) Lichtblick m
brilliance ['brɪljəns], **brilliancy** ['brɪljənsi] s Glanz m
brilliant ['brɪljənt] adj (& fig) glänzend
brim [brɪm] s Rand m; (of a hat) Krempe f; to the b. bis zum Rande || v (pret & pp brimmed; ger brimming) intr—b. over (with) (fig) überschwämmen (vor dat)
brimful ['brɪm‚ful] adj übervoll
brim′stone′ s Schwefel m
brine [braɪn] s Salzwasser n, Sole f; (for pickling) Salzlake f
bring [brɪŋ] v (pret & pp brought [brɔt]) tr bringen; **b. about** zustande bringen; **b. back** zurückbringen; (memories) zurückrufen; **b. down** herunterbringen; (shoot down) abschießen; **b. down the house** (fig) Lachstürme entfesseln; **b. forth** (e.g., complaints) hervorbringen; **b. forward** vorbringen; **b. it about** that es durchsetzen, daß; **b. on** herbeiführen; **b. oneself** to (inf) sich überwinden zu (inf); **b. to** wieder zu sich bringen; **b. together** zusammenbringen; **b. up** (children) erziehen; (a topic) zur Sprache bringen
bring′ing-up′ s Erziehung f
brink [brɪŋk] s (& fig) Rand m
brisk [brɪsk] adj (pace, business) flott; (air) frisch, scharf
bristle ['brɪsəl] s Borste f || intr sich sträuben
bristly ['brɪsli] adj borstig
Britain ['brɪtən] s Britannien n
British ['brɪtɪʃ] adj britisch || **the B.** spl die Briten pl
Britisher ['brɪtɪʃər] s Brite m, Britin f
Briton ['brɪtən] s Brite m, Britin f
Brittany ['brɪtəni] s die Bretagne f
brittle ['brɪtəl] adj brüchig, spröde
broach [brotʃ] tr zur Sprache bringen
broad [brɔd] adj breit; (daylight) hellicht; (outline) grob; (sense) weit; (view) allgemein, umfassend
broad′cast′ s Sendung f, Übertragung f || v (pret & pp —cast) (rumors, etc.) ausposaunen || (pret & pp —cast & —casted) tr & intr senden, übertragen
broadcaster ['brɔd‚kæstər] s Rundfunksprecher –in mf
broad′casting sta′tion s Sender m
broad′casting stu′dio s Senderaum m

broad′cloth′ s feiner Wäschestoff m
broaden ['brɔdən] tr verbreitern || intr sich verbreitern
broad′-gauge′ adj (rr) breitspurig
broad′-mind′ed adj großzügig
broad′-shoul′dered adj breitschultrig
broad′side′ s (guns on one side of ship) Breitseite f; (fig) Schimpfkanonade f
brocade [bro'ked] s Brokat m
broccoli ['brakəli] s Spargelkohl m
brochure [bro'ʃur] s Broschüre f
broil [brɔɪl] tr am Rost braten, grillen
broiler ['brɔɪlər] s Bratrost m
broke [brok] adj (coll) abgebrannt, pleite; go b. (coll) pleite gehen
broken ['brokən] adj zerbrochen; (limb, spirit, English) gebrochen; (home) zerrüttet; (line) gestrichelt
bro′ken-down′ adj erschöpft; (horse) abgearbeitet
bro′ken-heart′ed adj mit gebrochenem Herzen
broker ['brokər] s Makler –in mf
brokerage ['brokərɪdʒ] s Maklergeschäft n; (fee) Maklergebühr f
bromide ['bromaɪd] s Bromid n; (coll) Binsenweisheit f
bromine ['bromin] s Brom n
bronchial ['braŋkɪ.əl] adj bronchial
bron′chial tube′ s Luftröhre f, Bronchie f
bronchitis [braŋ'kaɪtɪs] s Bronchitis f
bron-co ['braŋko] s (–cos) kleines halbwildes Pferd n
bronze [branz] adj Bronze– || s Bronze f || tr bronzieren || intr sich bräunen
brooch [brotʃ], [brutʃ] s Brosche f
brood [brud] s Brut f, Junge pl || tr ausbrüten || intr brüten; (coll) sinnieren; **b. over** grübeln über (acc)
brook [bruk] s Bach m || tr dulden
broom [brum] s Besen m
broom′stick′ s Besenstiel m
broth [brɔθ] s Brühe f
brothel ['braθəl] s Bordell n
brother ['brʌðər] s Bruder m; **brother(s) and sister(s)** Geschwister pl
broth′erhood′ s (& relig) Brüderschaft f
broth′er-in-law′ s (brothers-in-law) Schwager m
brotherly ['brʌðərli] adj brüderlich
brow [brau] s Stirn f
brow′beat′ v (pret –beat; pp –beaten) tr einschüchtern
brown [braun] adj braun || s Bräune f || tr & intr bräunen
brownish ['braunɪʃ] adj bräunlich
brown′-nose′ tr (sl) kriechen (dat)
brown′ sug′ar s brauner Zucker m
browse [brauz] intr grasen, weiden; (through books) schmökern, stöbern; (through a store) herumsuchen
bruise [bruz] s Quetschung f || tr quetschen
brunette [bru'nɛt] adj brünett || s Brünette f
brunt [brʌnt] s Anprall m; bear the b. die Hauptlast tragen
brush [brʌʃ] s Bürste f; (of an artist; for shaving) Pinsel m; (brief encoun-

ter) kurzer Zusammenstoß *m*; *(light touch)* leichte Berührung *f*; *(bot)* Gebüsch *n*; *(elec)* Bürste *f*; || *tr* bürsten; **b. aside** beiseite schieben; **b. off** abbürsten; *(devour)* verschlingen; *(make light of)* abwimmeln || *intr*—**b. against** streifen; **b. up on** auffrischen

brush'-off' *s* (coll) Laufpaß *m*

brush'wood' *s* Unterholz *n*, Niederwald *m*

brusque [brʌsk] *adj* brüsk

Brussels ['brʌsəlz] *s* Brüssel *n*

Brus'sels sprouts' *spl* Rosenkohl *m*

brutal ['brutəl] *adj* brutal

brutality [bru'tælɪtɪ] *s* Brutalität *f*

brute [brut] *adj* viehisch; *(strength)* roh || *s* Tier *n*; *(fig)* Unmensch *m*

brutish ['brutɪʃ] *adj* tierisch, roh

bubble ['bʌbəl] *s* Blase *f*, Bläschen *n* || *intr* sprudeln; **b. over (with)** übersprudeln (vor *dat*)

bub'ble bath' *s* Schaumbad *n*

bub'ble gum' *s* Knallkaugummi *m*

bubbly ['bʌblɪ] *adj* sprudelnd; *(Person)* lebhaft

buck [bʌk] *s* Bock *m*; *(sl)* Dollar *m*; **pass the b.** (coll) die Verantwortung abschieben || *tr* (fig) kämpfen gegen; **b. off** abwerfen || *intr* bocken; **b. for** *(a promotion)* sich bemühen um

bucket ['bʌkɪt] *s* Eimer *m*

buck'et seat' *s* Schalensitz *m*

buckle ['bʌkəl] *s* Schnalle *f*; *(bend)* Ausbuchtung *f* || *tr* zuschnallen || *intr (from heat, etc.)* zusammensacken; **b. down** sich auf die Hosen setzen

buck' pri'vate *s* gemeiner Soldat *m*

buckram ['bʌkrəm] *s* Buckram *n*

buck'shot' *s* Rehposten *m*

buck'tooth' *s* (**-teeth**) vorstehender Zahn *m*

buck'wheat' *s* Buchweizen *m*

bud [bʌd] *s* Knospe *f*, Keim *m*; **nip in the bud** (fig) im Keime ersticken || *v (pret & pp* **budded;** *ger* **budding)** *intr* knospen, keimen, ausschlagen

buddy ['bʌdɪ] *s* (coll) Kumpel *m*

budge [bʌdʒ] *tr* (von der Stelle) bewegen || *intr* sich (von der Stelle) bewegen

budget ['bʌdʒɪt] *s* Budget *n*, Haushaltsplan *m*; *(of a state)* Staatshaushalt *m* || *tr* einteilen, vorausplanen

budgetary ['bʌdʒɪ,terɪ] *adj* Budget-

buff [bʌf] *adj* lederfarben || *s* Lederfarbe *f*; (coll) Schwärmer –in *mf* || *tr* polieren

buffa·lo ['bʌfə,lo] *s* (**-loes & -los**) Büffel *m*

buffer ['bʌfər] *s* Puffer *m*; *(polisher)* Polierer *m*; *(rr)* Prellbock *m*

buff'er state' *s* Pufferstaat *m*

buffet [bu'fe] *s (meal)* Büfett *n*; *(furniture)* Kredenz *f* || ['bʌfɪt] *tr* herumstoßen

buffoon [bə'fun] *s* Hanswurst *m*

bug [bʌg] *s* Insekt *n*, Käfer *m*; *(defect)* (coll) Defekt *m*; *(electron)* Abhörgerät *n*, Wanze *f*; **bugs** Ungeziefer *n* || *v (pret & pp* **bugged;** *ger* **bugging)** *tr (annoy)* (sl) ärgern;

(electron) **(sl)** Abhörgeräte einbauen in *(dat)*

bug'-eyed' *adj* (sl) mit großen Augen

buggy ['bʌgɪ] *adj* verwanzt; *(crazy)* (sl) verrückt || *s* Wagen *m*

bugle ['bjugəl] *s* Signalhorn *n*

bu'gle call' *s* Signal *n*

bugler ['bjuglər] *s* Hornist –in *mf*

build [bɪld] *s* Bauart *f*, Gestalt *f*; *(of a person)* Körperbau *m* || *v (pret & pp* **built** [bɪlt]) *tr* bauen; *(a bridge)* schlagen; *(with stone or brick)* mauern; *(a fire)* anmachen; **b. up** aufbauen; *(an area)* ausbauen; *(hopes)* erwecken

builder ['bɪldər] *s* Baumeister *m*

build'ing *s* Gebäude *n*

build'ing and loan' associa'tion *s* Bausparkasse *f*

build'ing block' *s* Zementblock *m*; *(for children)* Bauklötzchen *n*

build'ing con'tractor *s* Bauunternehmer *m*

build'ing in'dustry *s* Bauindustrie *f*

build'ing lot' *s* Bauplatz *m*, Grundstück *n*

build'ing mate'rial *s* Baustoff *m*

build'-up' *s* (coll) Propaganda *f*

built'-in' *adj* Einbau-

built'-up' *adj* bebaut

bulb [bʌlb] *s (bot)* Knolle *f*, Zwiebel *f*; *(elec)* Glühbirne *f*; *(phot)* Blitzlampe *f*

Bulgaria [bʌl'gɑrɪ·ə] *s* Bulgarien *n*

Bulgarian [bʌl'gɑrɪ·ən] *adj* bulgarisch || *s* Bulgare *m*, Bulgarin *f*; *(language)* Bulgarisch *n*

bulge [bʌldʒ] *s* Ausbauchung *f*, Beule *f*; *(of a sail)* Bausch *m*; *(mil)* Frontvorsprung *m* || *intr* sich bauschen; *(said of eyes)* hervortreten

bulg'ing *adj (belly, muscles)* hervorspringend; *(eyes)* hervorquellend; *(sails)* gebläht; **b. with** bis zum Platzen gefüllt mit

bulk [bʌlk] *adj* Massen–, unverpackt || *s* Masse *f*; *(main part)* Hauptteil *m*; **in b.** unverpackt || *intr*—**b. large** e–e große Rolle spielen

bulk'head' *s (aer)* Spant *m*; *(naut)* Schott *n*

bulky ['bʌlkɪ] *adj* sperrig

bull [bul] *s* Bulle *m*, Stier *m*; (sl) Quatsch *m*; *(eccl)* Bulle *f*; *(st. exch.)* Haussier *m*; **like a b. in a china shop** wie ein Elefant im Porzellanladen; **shoot the b.** (sl) quatschen; **take the b. by the horns** den Stier an den Hörnern packen; **throw the b.** (sl) aufschneiden

bull'dog' *s* Bulldogge *f*

bull'doze' *tr* planieren; (fig) überfahren

bulldozer ['bʌl,dozər] *s* Planierraupe *f*

bullet ['bulɪt] *s* Kugel *f*

bul'let hole' *s* Schußöffnung *f*

bulletin ['bulətɪn] *s (report)* Bulletin *n*; *(flyer)* Flugschrift *f*

bul'letin board' *s* Anschlagbrett *n*

bul'letproof' *adj* kugelsicher

bull'fight' *s* Stierkampf *m*

bull'fight'er *s* Stierkämpfer –in *mf*

bull'frog' *s* Ochsenfrosch *m*

bull'-head'ed adj dickköpfig

bull' horn' s Richtungslautsprecher m

bullion ['buljən] s Barren m; (mil, nav) Kordel f

bull' mar'ket s Spekulationsmarkt m

bullock ['bulək] s Ochse m

bull'pen' s Stierpferch m; (baseball) Übungsplatz m für Reservewerfer

bull'ring's Stierkampfarena f

bull' ses'sion s (sl) zwanglose Diskussion f

bull's'-eye' s (of a target) Schwarze n; (round window) Bullauge n; hit the b. ins Schwarze treffen

bul-ly ['buli] adj—b. for you! großartig! || s Raufbold m || v (pret & pp –lied) tr tyrannisieren

bulrush ['bul‚rʌ∫] s Binse f

bulwark ['bulwərk] s Bollwerk n

bum [bʌm] s (sl) Strolch m; give s.o. the bum's rush j-n auf den Schub bringen || v (pret & pp bummed; ger bumming) tr (sl) schinden, schnorren || intr—bum around bummeln

bumblebee ['bʌmbəl‚bi] s Hummel f

bump [bʌmp] s Stoß m, Bums m; (swelling) Beule f; (in the road) holp(e)rige Stelle f || tr (an)stoßen; b. off (sl) abknallen; b. one's head against s.th. mit dem Kopf gegen etw stoßen || intr zusammenstoßen; b. against stoßen an (acc); b. into stoßen gegen; (meet unexpectedly) in die Arme laufen (dat)

bumper ['bʌmpər] s Stoßstange f

bumpkin ['bʌmpkɪn] s Tölpel m

bumpy ['bʌmpi] adj holperig; (aer) böig

bum' steer' s—give s.o. a b. (coll) nasführen

bun [bʌn] s Kuchenbrötchen n; (of hair) Haarknoten m

bunch [bʌnt∫] s Bündel n; (of grapes) Traube f; (group) Schar f, Bande f; b. of flowers Blumenstrauß m; b. of grapes Weintraube f || tr—b. together zusammenfassen || intr—b. together sich zusammendrängen

bundle ['bʌndəl] s Bündel n; (heap) Stoß m; (of straw) Schütte f; b. of nerves Nervenbündel n || tr bündeln; b. off (coll) verfrachten; b. up sich warm anziehen

bung [bʌŋ] s Spund m || tr verspunden

bungalow ['bʌŋɡə‚lo] s Bungalow m

bung'hole' s Spundloch n

bungle ['bʌŋɡəl] s Pfuscherei f || tr verpfuschen || intr pfuschen

bungler ['bʌŋɡlər] s Pfuscher –in mf

bun'gling adj stümperhaft || s Stümperei f

bunk [bʌŋk] s Schlafkoje f; (sl) Unsinn m || intr (with) schlafen (mit)

bunk' bed' s Etagenbett n

bunker ['bʌŋkər] s Bunker m

bunny ['bʌni] s Kaninchen n

bunt'ing s (cloth) Fahnentuch n; (decoration) Fahnenschmuck m; (orn) Ammer f

buoy [bɔɪ], ['bu·i] s Boje f || tr—b. up flott erhalten; (fig) Auftrieb geben (dat)

buoyancy ['bɔɪ·ənsi] s Auftrieb m; (fig) Spannkraft f

buoyant ['bɔɪ·ənt] adj schwimmend; (fig) lebhaft

burden ['bʌrdən] s Bürde f, Last f; (fig) Belastung f || tr belasten

bur'den of proof' s Beweislast f

burdensome ['bʌrdənsəm] adj lästig

bureau ['bjuro] s Kommode f; (office) Büro n; (department) Amt n

bureaucracy [bju'rɑkrəsi] s Bürokratie f, Beamtenschaft f

bureaucrat ['bjurə‚kræt] s Bürokrat –in mf

bureaucratic [‚bjurə'krætɪk] adj bürokratisch

burglar ['bʌrɡlər] s Einbrecher –in mf

bur'glar alarm' s Einbruchssicherung f

burglarize ['bʌrɡlə‚raɪz] tr einbrechen in (acc)

bur'glarproof' adj einbruchssicher

burglary ['bʌrɡləri] s Einbruchdiebstahl m

Burgundy ['bʌrɡəndi] s Burgund n; (wine) Burgunder m

burial ['beri·əl] s Beerdigung f

bur'ial ground' s Begräbnisplatz m

burlap ['bʌrlæp] s Sackleinwand f

burlesque [bʌr'lesk] adj burlesk || s Burleske f || tr burlesk behandeln

burlesque' show' s Variété n

burly ['bʌrli] adj stämmig, beleibt

Burma ['bʌrmə] s Birma n

Bur-mese [bʌr'miz] adj birmanisch || s (-mese) (person) Birmane m, Birmanin f; (language) Birmanisch n

burn [bʌrn] s Brandwunde f || v (pret & pp burned & burnt [bʌrnt]) tr (ver)brennen; be burned up (coll) fauchen; b. down niederbrennen; b. up (coll) wütend machen || intr (ver)brennen; (said of food) anbrennen; b. out ausbrennen; (elec) durchbrennen; b. up ganz verbrennen; (during reentry) verglühen

burner ['bʌrnər] s Brenner m

burn'ing adj (& fig) brennend

burnish ['bʌrnɪ∫] tr polieren

burn'out' s (rok) Brennschluß m

burnt adj verbrannt; (smell) brenzlig

burp [bʌrp] s Rülpser m || tr rülpsen lassen || intr rülpsen

burr [bʌr] s (growth on a tree) Auswuchs m; (in metal) Grat m; (bot) Klette f

burrow ['bʌro] s Bau m || tr graben || intr sich eingraben, wühlen

bursar ['bʌrsər] s Schatzmeister m

burst [bʌrst] s Bersten n; (split) Riß m; Bruch m; b. of gunfire Feuerstoß m || v (pret & pp burst) tr (auf)sprengen, zum Platzen bringen || intr bersten, platzen; (split) reißen; (said of a boil) aufgehen; b. into (e.g., a room) hereinstürzen in (acc); b. into tears in Tränen ausbrechen; b. open aufplatzen; b. out laughing loslachen

bur-y ['beri] v (pret & pp –ied) tr beerdigen, begraben; be buried in thought in Gedanken versunken sein; b. alive verschütten

bus [bʌs] s (busses & buses) Autobus m, Bus m || v (pret & pp) bussed &

bused; (*ger* **bussing & busing**) *tr &*
intr mit dem Bus fahren
bus′ boy′ *s* Pikkolo *m*
bus′ driv′er *s* Autobusfahrer –in *mf*
bush [buʃ] *s* Busch *m;* **beat around
the b.** um die Sache herumreden
bushed *adj* (coll) abgeklappert
bushel [′buʃəl] *s* Scheffel *m;* **by the b.**
scheffelweise
bush′ing *s* Buchse *f*
bushy [′buʃi] *adj* strauchbewachsen;
(*brows*) buschig
business [′bɪznɪs] *adj* Geschäfts– || *s*
Geschäft *n;* (*company*) Firma *f,* Betrieb *m;* (*employment*) Beruf *m,* Gewerbe *n;* (*duty*) Pflicht *f;* (*right*)
Recht *n;* (coll) Sache *f;* **be in b.** ge-
schäftlich tätig sein; **do b. with** Geschäfte machen mit; **get down to b.**
(coll) zur Sache kommen; **go about
one's b.** seiner Arbeit nachgehen; **he
means b.** (coll) er meint es ernst;
know one's b. seine Sache verstehen;
make s.th. one's b. sich [*dat*] etw
angelegen sein lassen; **mind your
own b.** kümmere dich um deine
eigenen Sachen; **that's none of your
b.** das geht dich gar nichts an; **the
whole b.** die ganze Geschichte; **you
have no b. here** du hast hier nichts
zu suchen
busi′ness call′ *s* Dienstgespräch *n*
busi′ness card′ *s* Geschäftskarte *f*
busi′ness cen′ter *s* Geschäftszentrum *n*
busi′ness col′lege *s* Handelsschule *f*
busi′ness dis′trict *s* Geschäftsviertel *n*
busi′ness expens′es *spl* Geschäftsspesen
pl
busi′ness hours′ *s* Geschäftszeit *f*
busi′ness let′ter *s* Geschäftsbrief *m*
busi′nesslike′ *adj* sachlich; (pej) ge-
schäftsmäßig
busi′ness·man′ *s* (–men′) Geschäfts-
mann *m*
busi′ness reply′ card′ *s* Rückantwort-
karte *f*
busi′ness suit′ *s* Straßenanzug *m*
busi′ness·wom′an *s* (–wom′en) Ge-
schäftsfrau *f*
bus′ line′ *s* Autobuslinie *f*
bus′ stop′ *s* Autobushaltestelle *f*
bust [bʌst] *s* (*chest*) Busen *m;* (*measurement*) Oberweite *f;* (*statue*) Brustbild *n;* (*blow*) (sl) Faustschlag *m;*
(*failure*) (sl) Platzen *n;* (*binge*) (sl)
Sauftour *f* || *tr* (sl) kaputtmachen;
(mil) degradieren || *intr* (*break*) (sl)
kaputtgehen
bustle [′bʌsəl] *s* (*activity*) Hochbe-
trieb *m,* Trubel *m* || *intr* umher-
hasten; **b. about** herumsausen
bus′tling *adj* geschäftig
bus·y [′bɪzi] *adj* tätig, beschäftigt;
(*day, life*) arbeitsreich; (*street*) lebhaft, verkehrsreich; (telp) belegt, besetzt; **be b.** (*be occupied*) zu tun
haben; (*be unavailable*) nicht zu
sprechen sein || *v* (*pret & pp* –**ied**)
tr beschäftigen
bus′ybod′y *s* Wichtigtuer –in *mf*
bus′y sig′nal *s* (telp) Besetztzeichen *n*
but [bʌt] *adv* nur, lediglich, bloß;
(*just, only*) erst; **all but** beinahe ||

prep außer (*dat*); (*after negatives*)
als; **all but one** alle bis auf einen ||
conj aber; (*after negatives*) sondern
butcher [′butʃər] *s* Fleischer –in *mf,*
Metzger –in *mf;* (fig) Schlächter –in
mf || *tr* schlachten; (fig) abschlachten
butch′er knife′ *s* Fleischermesser *n*
butch′er shop′ *s* Metzgerei *f*
butchery [′butʃəri] *s* (*slaughterhouse*)
Schlachthaus *n;* (fig) Gemetzel *n*
butler [′bʌtlər] *s* Haushofmeister *m*
butt [bʌt] *s* (*of a gun*) Kolben *m;* (*of
a cigarette*) Stummel *m;* (*with the
horns, head*) Stoß *m;* (*of ridicule*)
Zielscheibe *f* || *tr* stoßen || *intr*
stoßen; **b. in** (sl) sich einmischen,
dazwischenfahren
butter [′bʌtər] *s* Butter *f* || *tr* mit But-
ter bestreichen; (*bread*) schmieren;
b. s.o. up (coll) j–m Honig um den
Mund schmieren
but′terball′ *s* Butterkugel *f;* (*chubby
child*) Pummelchen *n*
but′tercup′ *s* Butterblume *f,* Hahnenfuß *m*
but′ter dish′ *s* Butterdose *f*
but′terfly′ *s* Schmetterling *m;* (sport)
Schmetterlingsstil *m*
but′ter knife′ *s* Buttermesser *n*
but′termilk′ *s* Buttermilch *f*
buttocks [′bʌtəks] *spl* Hinterbacken *pl*
button [′bʌtən] *s* Knopf *m* || *tr* knöp-
fen; **button up** zuknöpfen
but′tonhole′ *s* Knopfloch *n* || *tr* im
Gespräch festhalten
buttress [′bʌtrɪs] *s* Strebepfeiler *m;*
(fig) Stütze *f* || *tr* (durch Strebepfei-
ler) stützen; (fig) (unter)stützen
butt′-weld′ *tr* stumpfschweißen
buxom [′bʌksəm] *adj* beleibt
buy [baɪ] *s* Kauf *m* || *v* (*pret & pp*
bought [bɔt]) *tr* kaufen; (*bus ticket,
train ticket*) lösen; (*accept, believe*)
glauben; **buy off** (*bribe*) bestechen;
buy out auskaufen; **buy up** aufkaufen
buyer [′baɪər] *s* Käufer –in *mf*
buzz [bʌz] *s* Summen *n,* Surren *n;*
(telp) (coll) Anruf *m* || *tr* (coll) (aer)
dicht vorbeisausen an (*dat*); (telp)
(coll) anrufen || *intr* summen, sur-
ren; **b. around** herumsausen
buzzard [′bʌzərd] *s* Bussard *m*
buzz′ bomb′ *s* Roboterbombe *f,* V-
Waffe *f*
buzzer [′bʌzər] *s* Summer *m;* **did the
b. sound?** ist der Summer ertönt
buzz′ saw′ *s* Kreissäge *f,* Rundsäge *f*
by [baɪ] *adv* vorüber, vorbei; **by and
by** nach und nach; **by and large** im
großen und ganzen || *prep* (*agency*)
von (*dat*), durch (*acc*); (*position*)
bei (*dat*), an (*dat*), neben (*dat*); (*no
later than*) bis spätestens; (*in division*) durch (*acc*); (*indicating mode
of transportation*) mit (*dat*); (*indicating authorship*) von (*dat*); (*according to*) nach (*dat*); (*past*) an
(*dat*) vorbei; (*by means of*) mit
(*dat*); **by** (*ger*) indem (*ind*); **by an
inch** um e–n Zoll; **by day** bei Tag;
by far bei weitem; **by heart** auswendig; **by itself** (*automatically*) von
selbst; **by land** zu Lande; **by mail**

per Post; **by myself** ganz allein; **by nature** von Natur aus; **by now** schon; **by the pound** per Pfund; **two by four** zwei mal vier

bye [baɪ] *s* (sport) Freilos *n*

bye'bye' *interj* Wiedersehen!

bygone ['baɪ,gɒn] *adj* vergangen ‖ *s*—**let bygones be bygones** laß(t) das Vergangene ruhen

by'law' *s* Satzung *f*; **bylaws** (*of an organization*) Statuten *pl*, Satzungen *pl*

by'-line' *s* (journ) Verfasserangabe *f*

by'pass' *s* Umgehungsstraße *f*, Umleitung *f*; (elec) Nebenschluß *m* ‖ *tr* umgehen

by'prod'uct *s* Nebenprodukt *n*

bystander ['baɪ,stændər] *s* Umstehende *mf*

by'way' *s* Seitenweg *m*

by'word' *s* Sprichwort *n*

Byzantine ['bɪzən,tin], [bɪ'zæntin] *adj* byzantinisch ‖ *s* Byzantiner –in *mf*

Byzantium [bɪ'zænʃɪ·əm], [bɪ'zæntɪ·əm] *s* Byzanz *n*

C

C, c [si] *s* dritter Buchstabe des englischen Alphabets; (mus) C *n*; **C flat** Ces *n*; **C sharp** Cis *n*

cab [kæb] *s* Taxi *n*; (*of a truck*) Fahrerkabine *f*

cabaret [,kæbə're] *s* Kabarett *n*

cabbage ['kæbɪdʒ] *s* Kohl *m*, Kraut *n*

cab'driv'er *s* Taxifahrer –in *mf*

cabin ['kæbɪn] *s* Hütte *f*; (aer) Kabine *f*; (naut) Kajüte *f*, Kabine *f*

cab'in boy' *s* Schiffsjunge *m*

cabinet ['kæbɪnɪt] *adj* Kabinetts– ‖ *s* (*in a kitchen*) Küchenschrank *m*; (*for a radio*) Gehäuse *n*; (pol) Kabinett *n*, Ministerrat *m*

cab'inetmak'er *s* Tischler *m*

cable ['kebəl] *s* Kabel *n*, Seil *n*; (naut) Tau *n*; (telg) Kabelnachricht *f* ‖ *tr & intr* kabeln

ca'ble car' *s* Seilbahn *f*, Schwebebahn *f*

ca'blegram' *s* Kabelnachricht *f*

caboose [kə'bus] *s* (rr) Dienstwagen *m*

cab'stand' *s* Taxistand *m*

cache [kæʃ] *s* Geheimlager *n*, Versteck *n*; **c. of arms** Waffenlager *n*

cachet [kæ'ʃe] *s* Siegel *n*; (fig) Stempel *m*; (pharm) Kapsel *f*

cackle ['kækəl] *s* (*of chickens*) Gegacker *n*; (*of geese*) Geschnatter *n* ‖ *intr* gackern, gackeln; schnattern

cac·tus ['kæktəs] *s* (–tuses & –ti [taɪ]) Kaktus *m*

cad [kæd] *s* (sl) Saukerl *m*, Schuft *m*

cadaver [kə'dævər] *s* Kadaver *m*, Leiche *f*

caddie ['kædi] *s* Golfjunge *m* ‖ *intr* die Schläger tragen

cadence ['kedəns] *s* (*rhythm*) Rhythmus *m*; (*flow of language*) Sprechrhythmus *m*; (mus) Kadenz *f*

cadet [kə'det] *s* Offizier(s)anwärter –in *mf*

cadre ['kædri] *s* Kader *m*

Caesar'ean opera'tion [sɪ'zɛrɪ·ən] *s* Kaiserschnitt *m*

café [kæ'fe] *s* Cafe *n*

cafeteria [,kæfə'tɪrɪ·ə] *s* Selbstbedienungsrestaurant *n*

caffeine ['kæfin] *s* Koffein *n*

cage [kedʒ] *s* Käfig *m* ‖ *tr* in e–n Käfig sperren

cagey ['kedʒi] *adj* (coll) schlau

cahoots [kə'huts] *s*—**be in c.** (sl) unter e–r Decke stecken

Cain [ken] *s*—**raise C.** Krach schlagen

caisson ['kesən] *s* Senkkasten *m*

cajole [kə'dʒol] *tr* beschwatzen

cake [kek] *s* Kuchen *m*; (*round cake*) Torte *f*; (*of soap*) Riegel *m*; **he takes the c.** (coll) er schießt den Vogel ab; **that takes the c.** (coll) das ist die Höhe ‖ *intr* zusammenbacken; **c. on** anbacken

calamitous [kə'læmɪtəs] *adj* unheilvoll

calamity [kə'læmɪti] *s* Unheil *n*

calci·fy ['kælsɪ,faɪ] *v* (*pret & pp* –fied) *tr & intr* verkalken

calcium ['kælsɪ·əm] *s* Kalzium *n*

calculate ['kælkjə,let] *tr* berechnen ‖ *intr* rechnen

cal'culated risk' *s*—**take a c.** ein bewußtes Risiko eingehen

cal'culating *adj* berechnend

calculation [,kælkjə'leʃən] *s* Berechnung *f*; **rough c.** Überschlagsrechnung *f*

calculator ['kælkjə,letər] *s* Rechenmaschine *f*; (data proc) Rechner *m*

calcu·lus ['kælkjələs] *s* (–luses & –li [,laɪ]) (math) Differenzial– und Integralrechnung *f*; (pathol) Stein *m*

caldron ['kɔldrən] *s* Kessel *m*

calendar ['kæləndər] *s* Kalender *m*

calf [kæf] *s* (calves [kævz]) (*of a cow*) Kalb *n*; (*of certain other mammals*) Junge *n*; (anat) Wade *f*

calf'skin' *s* Kalbleder *n*

caliber ['kælɪbər] *s* (& fig) Kaliber *n*

calibrate ['kælɪ,bret] *tr* kalibrieren

cali·co ['kælɪ,ko] *s* (–coes & –cos) Kaliko *m*

calisthenics [,kælɪs'θɛnɪks] *spl* Leibesübungen *pl*

calk [kɔk] *tr* abdichten, kalfatern

calk'ing *s* Kalfaterung *f*

call [kɔl] *s* Ruf *m*; (*visit*) Besuch *m*; (*reason*) Grund *m*; (com) (for) Nachfrage *f* (nach); (naut) Anlaufen *n*; (telp) Anruf *m*; **on c.** auf Abruf ‖ *tr* rufen; (*name*) nennen; (*wake*) wecken; (*a meeting*) einberufen; (*a strike*) ausrufen; (*by phone*) anrufen; (*a witness*) vorladen; (*a doctor; taxi*) kommen las-

sen; **be called** heißen; **c. down** (coll)
herunterputzen; **c. in** (a doctor, specialist) hinzuziehen; (for advice) zu
Rate ziehen; (currency) einziehen;
(capital) kündigen; **c. it a day** (coll)
Schluß machen; **c. off** absagen; **c.
out** ausrufen; (the police) einsetzen;
c. s.o. names j-n beschimpfen; **c. up**
(mil) einberufen; (telp) anrufen ||
intr rufen; (cards) ansagen; **c. for**
(require) erfordern; (fetch) abholen;
(help) rufen um; (a person) rufen
nach; **c. on** (a pupil) aufrufen; (visit)
e-n Besuch machen bei; **c. to s.o.**
j-m zurufen; **c. upon** auffordern

call′ bell′ s Rufglocke f
call′ boy′ s Hotelpage m; (theat) In-
spezierengehilfe m
caller [′kɔlər] s Besucher –in mf
call′ girl′ s Callgirl n
call′ing s Beruf m; (relig) Berufung f
call′ing card′ s Visitenkarte f
call′ing-down′ s (coll) Standpauke f
call′ num′ber s (libr) Standortnummer
f
callous [′kæləs] adj schwielig; (fig)
gefühllos, abgestumpft
call′up′ s (mil) Einberufung f
callus [′kæləs] s Schwiele f
calm [kam] adj ruhig || s Ruhe f;
(naut) Flaute f || tr beruhigen; **c.
down** beruhigen || intr—**c. down** sich
beruhigen
calorie [′kæləri] s Kalorie f
calumny [′kæləmni] s Verleumdung f
Calvary [′kælvəri] s Golgatha n
calve [kæv] intr kalben
cam [kæm] s Nocken m
camel [′kæməl] s Kamel n
camellia [kə′miljə] s Kamelie f
cameo [′kæmɪ‚o] s (-os) Kamee f
camera [′kæmərə] s Kamera f
cam′era-man′ s (-men′) Kameramann
m
camouflage [′kæmə‚flɑʒ] s Tarnung f
|| tr tarnen
camp [kæmp] s (& fig) Lager n || intr
kampieren, lagern, campen
campaign [kæm′pen] s (& fig) Feldzug
m; (pol) Wahlfeldzug m || intr an
e-m Feldzug teilnehmen; **c. for** (pol)
Wahlpropaganda machen für
campaigner [kæm′penər] s (for a specific cause) Befürworter –in mf;
(pol) Wahlredner –in mf
campaign′ slo′gan s Wahlparole f
campaign′ speech′ s Wahlrede f
camper [′kæmpər] s Camper m
camp′fire′ s Lagerfeuer n
camp′ground′ s Campingplatz m
camphor [′kæmfər] s Kampfer m
camp′ing s Camping n
campus [′kæmpəs] s Universitätsge-
lände n
cam′shaft′ s Nockenwelle f
can [kæn] s Dose f, Büchse f; (for
gasoline, water) Kanister m || v
(pret & pp **canned**; ger **canning**) tr
einmachen; (sl) ′rausschmeißen || v
(pret & cond) (**could**) aux—**I can
come** ich kann kommen; **I cannot
come** ich kann nicht kommen
Canada [′kænədə] s Kanada n

Canadian [kə′nedɪ‚ən] adj kanadisch
|| s Kanadier –in mf
canal [kə′næl] s Kanal m; (anat)
Gang m
canary [kə′neri] s Kanarienvogel m ||
the Canaries spl die Kanarischen
Inseln pl
can·cel [′kænsəl] v (pret & pp –el(l)ed;
ger –el(l)ing) tr (an event) absagen;
(an order) rückgängig machen;
(something written) (aus)streichen,
annulieren; (stamps) entwerten; (a
debt) tilgen; (a newspaper) abbestellen; (math) streichen; **c. out** ausgleichen
cancellation [‚kænsə′leʃən] s (of an
event) Absage f; (of an order) Annullierung f; (of something written)
Streichung f; (of a debt) Tilgung f;
(of a stamp) Entwertung f; (of a
newspaper) Abbestellung f
cancer [′kænsər] s Krebs m
cancerous [′kænsərəs] adj krebsartig
candela·brum [‚kændə′labrəm] s
(-bra [brə] & –brums) Armleuchter
m
candid [′kændɪd] adj offen
candidacy [′kændɪdəsi] s Kandidatur
f
candidate [′kændɪ‚det] s (for) Kandidat –in mf (für)
candied [′kændɪd] adj kandiert
candle [′kændəl] s Kerze f
can′dlelight′ s Kerzenlicht n
can′dlepow′er s Kerzenstärke f
can′dlestick′ s Kerzenhalter m
candor [′kændər] s Offenheit f
can·dy [′kændi] s Süßwaren pl; **piece
of c.** Bonbon m & n || v (pret & pp
–died) tr glacieren, kandieren
can′dy store′ s Süßwarengeschäft n
cane [ken] s (plant; stem) Rohr n;
(walking stick) Stock m || tr mit e-m
Stock züchtigen
cane′ sug′ar s Rohrzucker m
canine [′kenaɪn] adj Hunde– || s
(tooth) Eckzahn m, Reißzahn m
canister [′kænɪstər] s Dose f
canker [′kæŋkər] s (bot) Brand m;
(pathol) Mundgeschwür n
canned′ goods′ spl Dosenkonserven pl
canned′ mu′sic s Konservenmusik f
canned′ veg′etables spl Gemüsekon-
serven pl
cannery [′kænəri] s Konservenfabrik f
cannibal [′kænɪbəl] s Kannibale m
can′ning adj Konserven– || s Konser-
venfabrikation f
cannon [′kænən] s Kanone f
cannonade [‚kænə′ned] s Kanonade f,
Beschießung f || tr beschießen
can′nonball′ s Kanonenkugel f
can′non fod′der s Kanonenfutter n
canny [′kæni] adj (shrewd) schlau;
(sagacious) klug
canoe [kə′nu] s Kanu n
canoe′ing s Kanufahren n
canoeist [kə′nu·ɪst] s Kanufahrer m
canon [′kænən] s Kanon m; (of a
cathedral) Domherr m
canonical [kə′nɑnɪkəl] adj kanonisch
|| **canonicals** spl kirchliche Amts-
tracht f

canonize ['kænə ,naız] *tr* heiligsprechen

can'on law' *s* kanonisches Recht *n*

can' o'pener *s* Dosenöffner *m*

canopy ['kænəpi] *s* Baldachin *m*; (*above a king or pope*) Thronhimmel *m*; (*of a bed*) Betthimmel *m*

cant [kænt] *s* (*insincere statements*) unaufrichtiges Gerede *n*; (*jargon of thieves*) Gaunersprache *f*; (*technical phraseology*) Jargon *m*

cantaloupe ['kæntə ,lop] *s* Kantalupe *f*

cantankerous [kæn'tæŋkərəs] *adj* mürrisch, zänkisch

cantata [kən'tatə] *s* Kantate *f*

canteen [kæn'tin] *s* (*service club, service store*) Kantine *f*; (*flask*) Feldflasche *f*

canter ['kæntər] *s* kurzer Galopp *m* || *intr* im kurzen Galopp reiten

canticle ['kæntıkəl] *s* Lobgesang *m*

canton ['kæntən] *s* Kanton *m*

canvas ['kænvəs] *s* Leinwand *f*; (naut) Segeltuch *n*; (*a painting*) Gemälde *n*

canvass ['kænvəs] *s* (econ) Werbefeldzug *m*; (pol) Wahlfeldzug *m* || *tr* (*a district*) (pol) bearbeiten; (*votes*) (pol) werben

canyon ['kænjən] *s* Schlucht *f*

cap [kæp] *s* Kappe *f*, Mütze *f*; (*of a jar*) Deckel *m*; (*twist-off type*) Kapsel *f*; (*for a toy pistol*) Knallblättchen *n*; (typ) großer Buchstabe *m*; **use caps** (typ) großschreiben || *v* (*pret & pp* **capped**; *ger* **capping**) *tr* (*a bottle*) mit e–r Kapsel versehen; (*e.g., with snow*) bedecken; (*outdo*) übertreffen; (*success*) krönen

capability [,kepə'bılıti] *s* Fähigkeit *f*

capable ['kepəbəl] *adj* tüchtig; **c. of** fähig (*genit*); (*ger*) fähig zu (*inf*)

capacious [kə'pe/əs] *adj* geräumig

capacity [kə'pæsıti] *adj* maximal, Kapazitäts– || *s* (*ability*) Fähigkeit *f*; (*content*) Fassungsvermögen *n*; (*of a truck, bridge*) Tragfähigkeit *f*; (tech) Kapazität *f*; **in my c.** as in meiner Eigenschaft als

cap' and gown' *s* Barett *n* und Talar *m*

cape [kep] *s* Umhang *m*; (geog) Kap *n*

Cape' of Good' Hope' *s* Kap *n* der Guten Hoffnung

caper ['kepər] *s* Luftsprung *m*; (*prank*) Schabernack *m*; (culin) Kaper *f* || *intr* hüpfen

capita ['kæpıtə] *spl*—**per c.** pro Kopf, pro Person

capital ['kæpıtəl] *adj* (*importance*) äußerste, höchste; (*city*) Haupt–; (*crime*) Kapital– || *s* (*city*) Hauptstadt *f*; (archit) Kapitell *n*; (fin) Kapital *n*; (typ) Großbuchstabe *m*

cap'ital gains' *spl* Kapitalzuwachs *m*

capitalism ['kæpıtə ,lızəm] *s* Kapitalismus *m*

capitalist ['kæpıtəlıst] *s* Kapitalist *–in m*f

capitalistic [,kæpıtə'lıstık] *adj* kapitalistisch

capitalize ['kæpıtə ,laız] *tr* (fin) kapitalisieren; (typ) groß schreiben (or

drucken) || *intr*—**c. on** Nutzen ziehen aus

cap'ital let'ter *s* Großbuchstabe *m*

cap'ital pun'ishment *s* Todesstrafe *f*

capitol ['kæpıtəl] *s* Kapitol *n*

capitulate [kə'pıt/ə ,let] *intr* kapitulieren

capon ['kepən] *s* Kapaun *m*

caprice [kə'pris] *s* Grille *f*, Kaprice *f*

capricious [kə'prı/əs] *adj* kapriziös

capsize ['kæpsaız] *tr* zum Kentern bringen || *intr* kentern

capsule ['kæpsəl] *s* Kapsel *f*

captain ['kæptən] *s* (*of police, of firemen, in the army*) Hauptmann *m*; (naut, sport) Kapitän *m*; (nav) Kapitän *m* zur See; (sport) Mannschaftsführer *m*

caption ['kæp/ən] *s* (*heading of an article*) Überschrift *f*; (*wording under a picture*) Bildunterschrift *f*; (cin) Untertitel *m*

captivate ['kæptı ,vet] *tr* fesseln

captive ['kæptıv] *adj* gefangen || *s* Gefangene *m*f

cap'tive au'dience *s* unfreiwillige Zuhörerschaft *f*

captivity [kæp'tıvıti] *s* Gefangenschaft *f*

captor ['kæptər] *s* Fänger *–in m*f

capture ['kæpt/ər] *s* Fangen *n*, Gefangennahme *f*; (naut) Kaperung *f* || *tr* (*animals*) fangen; (*soldiers*) gefangennehmen; (*a ship*) kapern; (*a town*) erobern; (*a prize*) gewinnen

car [kar] *s* (aut, rr) Wagen *m*

carafe [kə'ræf] *s* Karaffe *f*

caramel ['kærəməl] *s* Karamelle *f*

carat ['kærət] *s* Karat *n*

caravan ['kærə ,væn] *s* Karawane *f*

car'away seed' ['kærə ,we] *s* Kümmelkorn *n*

carbide ['karbaıd] *s* Karbid *n*

carbine ['karbaın] *s* Karabiner *m*

carbohydrate [,karbo'haıdret] *s* Kohlenhydrat *n*

carbol'ic ac'id [kar'balık] *s* Karbolsäure *f*

carbon ['karbən] *s* (chem) Kohlenstoff *m*; (elec) Kohlenstift *m*

carbonated ['karbə ,netıd] *adj* kohlensäurehaltig, Brause–

car'bon cop'y *s* Durchschlag *m*; **make a c. of** durchschlagen

car'bon diox'ide *s* Kohlendioxyd *n*

car'bon monox'ide *s* Kohlenoxyd *n*

car'bon pa'per *s* Kohlepapier *n*

carbuncle ['karbʌŋkəl] *s* (*stone*) Karfunkel *m*; (*pathol*) Karbunkel *m*

carburetor ['karb(j)ə ,retər] *s* Vergaser *m*

carcass ['karkəs] *s* Kadaver *m*, Aas *n*; (*without offal*) Rumpf *m*

car' coat' *s* Stutzer *m*

card [kard] *s* Karte *f*; (*person*) (coll) Kerl *m*; (*text*) Krempel *f* || *tr* (text) kardätschen

card'board' *s* Kartonpapier *n*; (*thick pasteboard*) Pappe *f*; **piece of c.** Papp(en)deckel *m*

card'board box' *s* Pappkarton *m*, Pappschachtel *f*

card' cat'alogue *s* Kartothek *f*

card′ file′ *s* Kartei *f*
cardiac ['kɑrdɪˌæk] *adj* Herz– ‖ *s*
(*remedy*) Herzmittel *n*; (*patient*)
Herzkranke *mf*
cardinal ['kɑrdɪnəl] *adj* Kardinal– ‖ *s*
(eccl, orn) Kardinal *m*
card′ in′dex *s* Karthotek *f*, Kartei *f*
card′sharp′ *s* Falschspieler –in *mf*
card′ trick′ *s* Kartenkunststück *n*
care [ker] *s* (*accuracy*) Sorgfalt *f*;
(*worry*) Sorge *f*, Kummer *m*; (*pru-dence*) Vorsicht *f*; (*upkeep*) Pflege
f; **be under a doctor's c.** unter der
Aufsicht e–s Arztes stehen; **c. of** (*on
letters*) bei; **take c.** aufpassen; **take
c. not to** (*inf*) sich hüten zu (*inf*);
take c. of s.o. (*provide for s.o.*) für
j–n sorgen; (*attend to*) sich um j–n
kümmern; **take c. of s.th.** etw be-sorgen; (*e.g.*, *one's clothes*) schonen
‖ *intr*—**c. about** sich kümmern um;
c. for (*like*) mögen, gern haben;
(*have concern for*) sorgen für; (*at-tend to*) pflegen; **c. to** (*inf*) Lust
haben zu (*inf*); **for all I c.** von mir
aus
careen [kəˈrin] *tr* auf die Seite legen
‖ *intr* (aut) sich in die Kurve neigen
career [kəˈrɪr] *adj* Berufs– ‖ *s* Kar-riere *f*
career′ wo′man *s* berufstätige Frau *f*
care′free′ *adj* unbelastet, sorgenfrei
careful ['kerfəl] *adj* (*cautious*) vor-sichtig; (*accurate*) sorgfältig; **b. c.!**
gib acht!
careless ['kerlɪs] *adj* (*incautious*) un-vorsichtig; (*remark*) unbedacht; (*in-accurate*) nachlässig
carelessness ['kerlɪsnɪs] *s* Unvorsich-tigkeit *f*; Nachlässigkeit *f*
caress [kəˈres] *s* Liebkosung *f* ‖ *tr*
liebkosen
caret ['kærət] *s* Auslassungszeichen *n*
caretaker ['kerˌtekər] *s* Verwalter *m*
care′worn′ *adj* abgehärmt, vergrämt
car′fare′ *s* Fahrgeld *n*
car·go ['kɑrgo] *s* (–goes & –gos)
Fracht *f*
car′go compart′ment *s* Frachtraum *m*
car′go plane′ *s* Frachtflugzeug *n*
Caribbean [ˌkærɪˈbiˌən], [kəˈrɪbɪˌən]
adj karibisch ‖ *s* Karibisches Meer *n*
caricature ['kærɪkətˌʃər] *s* Karikatur *f*
‖ *tr* karikieren
caries ['kɛriz] *s* (dent) Karies *f*
carillon ['kærɪˌlɑn] *s* Glockenspiel *n*
car′ lift′ *s* (aut) Hebebühne *f*
car′load′ *s* Wagenladung *f*
carnage ['kɑrnɪdʒ] *s* Blutbad *n*
carnal ['kɑrnəl] *adj* fleischlich
car′nal know′ledge *s* Geschlechtsver-kehr *m*
carnation [kɑrˈneʃən] *s* Nelke *f*
carnival ['kɑrnɪvəl] *s* Karneval *m*
carnivorous [kɑrˈnɪvərəs] *adj* fleisch-fressend
car·ol ['kærəl] *s* Weihnachtslied *n* ‖
v (*pret* & *pp* –ol(l)ed; *ger* –l(l)ing)
intr Weihnachtslieder singen
carom ['kærəm] *s* (*billiards*) Karam-bolage *f* ‖ *intr* (*fig*) zusammen-stoßen; (*billiards*) karambolieren
carouse [kəˈrauz] *intr* zechen

carp [kɑrp] *s* Karpfen *m* ‖ *intr* nör-geln
carpenter ['kɑrpəntər] *s* Zimmermann
m
carpentry ['kɑrpəntri] *s* Zimmerei *f*
carpet ['kɑrpɪt] *s* Teppich *m* ‖ *tr* mit
Teppichen belegen
car′pet sweep′er *s* Teppichkehr-maschine *f*
car′port′ *s* Autoschuppen *m*
car′-ren′tal serv′ice *s* Autovermietung
f
carriage ['kærɪdʒ] *s* Kutsche *f*; (*of a
typewriter*) Wagen *m*; (*bearing*)
Körperhaltung *f*; (econ) Transport-kosten *pl*
car′ ride′ *s* Autofahrt *f*
carrier ['kærɪˌər] *s* Träger *m*; (*com-pany*) Transportunternehmen *n*
car′rier pig′eon *s* Brieftaube *f*
carrion ['kærɪˌən] *s* Aas *n*
carrot ['kærət] *s* Karotte *f*, Mohrrübe
f
carrousel [ˌkærəˈzel] *s* Karussell *n*
car·ry ['kæri] *v* (*pret* & *pp* –ried) *tr*
tragen; (*wares*) führen; (*a message*)
überbringen; (*a tune*) halten; (*said
of transportation*) befördern; (*insur-ance*) haben; (math) übertragen;
(parl) durchbringen; **be carried**
(*said of a motion, bill*) angenommen
werden; **be carried away by** (& fig)
mitgerissen werden von; **c. away** (*an
audience*) mitreißen; **c. off** (*a prize*)
davontragen; **c. on** weiterführen; (*a
business*) betreiben, führen; **c. out**
hinaustragen; (*a duty*) erfüllen;
(*measures*) durchführen; (*a sen-tence*) vollstrecken; (*an order*) aus-führen; **c. over** (acct) übertragen;
c. s.th. too far etw übertreiben; **c.
through** durchsetzen; ‖ *intr* (*said of
sounds*) tragen; (parl) durchgehen;
c. on (*continue*) weitermachen; (*act
up*) (coll) toben; **c. on with** ein Ver-hältnis haben mit
car′rying char′ges *spl* Kreditgebühren
pl
car′ry-o′ver *s* Überbleibsel *n*; (acct)
Übertrag *m*
cart [kɑrt] *s* Karren *m* ‖ *tr* mit dem
Handwagen befördern; **c. away** (or
c. off) abfahren
cartel [kɑrˈtel] *s* Kartell *n*
cartilage ['kɑrtɪlɪdʒ] *s* Knorpel *m*
carton [kɑrˈtun] *s* Karton *m*; **a c. of
cigarettes** e–e Stange Zigaretten
cartoon [kɑrˈtun] *s* Karikatur *f*;
(*comic strip*) Karikaturenreihe *f*;
(cin) Zeichentrickfilm *m*; (paint)
Entwurf *m* natürlicher Größe ‖ *tr*
karikieren
cartoonist [kɑrˈtunɪst] *s* Karikaturen-zeichner –in *mf*
cartridge ['kɑrtrɪdʒ] *s* Patrone *f*;
(phot) Filmpatrone *f*
car′tridge belt′ *s* Patronengurt *m*
cart′wheel′ *s* Wagenrad *n*; **turn a c.**
ein Rad schlagen
carve [kɑrv] *tr* (*wood*) schnitzen;
(*meat*) tranchieren, vorschneiden;
(*stone*) meißeln; **c. out** (*e.g.*, *a ca-reer*) aufbauen

carver ['kɑrvər] s (at table) Vor-
schneider –in mf

carv'ing knife' s Tranchiermesser n

car' wash' s Wagenwäsche f

cascade [kæs'ked] s Kaskade f ‖ intr
kaskadenartig herabstürzen

case [kes] s (instance) Fall m; (situation) Sache f; (box) Kiste f; (for
a knife, etc.) Hülle f; (for cigarettes)
Etui n; (for eyeglasses) Futteral n;
(for shipping) Schutzkarton m; (of
a watch) Gehäuse n; (of sickness)
Krankheitsfall m; (sick person) Patient –in mf; (gram) Fall m; (jur)
Fall m, Sache f, Prozeß m; (typ)
Setzkasten m; as the c. may be je
nachdem; have a strong c. schlüssige
Beweise haben; if that's the c. wenn
es sich so verhält; in any c. auf jeden
Fall, jedenfalls; in c. falls; in c. of
im Falle (genit); in c. of emergency
im Notfall; in no c. keinesfalls ‖ tr
(sl) genau ansehen; the c. at issue
der vorliegende Fall

case' his'tory s Vorgeschichte f; (med)
Krankengeschichte f

casement ['kesmənt] s Fensterflügel m

case'ment win'dow s Flügelfenster n

cash [kæʃ] adj Bar– ‖ s Bargeld n;
(cash payment) Barzahlung f; c. and
carry nur gegen Barzahlung und
eigenen Transport; in c. per Kasse;
out of c. nicht bei Kasse; pay c. for
bar bezahlen ‖ tr einlösen ‖ intr —
c. in on (coll) Nutzen ziehen aus

cash'box' s Schatulle f, Kasse f

cash' dis'count s Kassaskonto n

cashew' nut' [kə'ʃu], ['kæʃu] s Ka-
schunuß f

cashier [kæ'ʃɪr] s Kassierer –in mf

cashmere ['kæʃmɪr] s Kaschmir m

cash' on deliv'ery adv per Nachnahme

cash' reg'ister m Registrierkasse f

cas'ing s (wrapping) Verpackung f;
(housing) Gehäuse n; (of a window
or door) Futter n; (of a tire) Mantel
m; (of a sausage) Wurstdarm m

casi·no [kə'sino] s (–nos) Kasino n

cask [kæsk] s Faß n, Tonne f

casket ['kæskɪt] s Sarg m

casserole ['kæsə͵rol] s Kasserolle f

cassette [kæ'set] s Kassette f

cassock ['kæsək] s (eccl) Soutane f

cast [kæst] s (throw) Wurf m; (act of
molding) Guß m; (mold) Gußform
f; (object molded) Abguß m; (hue)
Abtönung f; (surg) Gipsverband m;
(theat) Rollenbesetzung f ‖ v (pret
& pp cast) tr werfen; (a net, anchor)
auswerfen; (a ballot) abgeben; (lots)
ziehen; (skin, horns) abwerfen; (a
shadow, glance) werfen; (metal)
gießen; (a play or motion picture)
die Rollen besetzen in (dat); be c.
down niedergeschlagen sein; c. aside
(reject) verwerfen; ‖ intr (angl) die
Angel auswerfen; c. off (naut) los-
werfen

castanet [͵kæstə'net] s Kastagnette f

cast'away' adj verworfen; (naut)
schiffbrüchig ‖ s (naut) Schiff-
brüchige mf

caste [kæst] s Kaste f

caster ['kæstər] s (under furniture)
Rolle f; (shaker) Streuer m

castigate ['kæstɪ͵get] tr züchtigen;
(fig) geißeln

cast'ing s Wurf m; (act of casting)
(metal) Guß m; (the object cast)
(metal) Gußstück n; (theat) Rollen-
verteilung f

cast'ing rod' s Wurfangel f

cast' i'ron s Gußeisen n

cast'-i'ron adj gußeisern; (fig) eisern

castle ['kæsəl] s Schloß n, Burg, f;
(chess) Turm m ‖ intr (chess) rochieren

cast'off' adj abgelegt ‖ s (e.g., dress)
abgelegtes Kleidungsstück n; (person) Verstoßene mf

cas'tor oil' ['kæstər] s Rizinusöl n

castrate ['kæstret] tr kastrieren

casual ['kæʒʊ·əl] adj (cursory) beiläufig; (occasional) gelegentlich; (incidental) zufällig; (informal) zwanglos; (unconcerned) gleichgültig

casualty ['kæʒʊ·əltɪ] s (victim) Opfer
n; (accident) Unfall m; (person injured) Verunglückte mf; (person
killed) (mil) Gefallene mf; (person
wounded) (mil) Verwundete mf;
casualties (in an accident) Verunglückte pl; (in war) Verluste pl

cas'ualty list' s Verlustliste f

cat [kæt] s Katze f; (guy) (sl) Typ m;
(malicious woman) (sl) falsche Katze
f

catacomb ['kætə͵kom] s Katakombe f

catalog(ue) ['kætə͵ləg] s Katalog m;
(list) Verzeichnis n; (of a university)
Vorlesungsverzeichnis n ‖ tr katalogisieren

catalyst ['kætəlɪst] s Katalysator m

catapult ['kætə͵pʌlt] s Katapult m &
n ‖ tr katapultieren, abschleudern

cataract ['kætə͵rækt] s Katarakt m;
(pathol) grauer Star m; remove
s.o.'s c. j-m den Star stechen

catastrophe [kə'tæstrəfɪ] s Katastrophe f

cat'call' s Auspfeifen n ‖ tr auspfeifen

catch [kætʃ] s Fang m; (of fish) Fisch-
fang m; (device) Haken m, Klinke
f; (desirable partner) Partie f; (fig)
Haken m; ‖ v (pret & pp caught
[kɔt]) tr fangen; (s.o. or s.th. falling) auffangen; (by pursuing) abfangen; (s.o. or s.th. that has es-
caped) einfangen; (by surprise)
ertappen, erwischen; (in midair)
aufschnappen; (take hold of) fassen;
(said of a storm) überraschen; (e.g.,
a train) erreichen; c. a cold sich erkälten; c. fire in Brand geraten; c.
hold of ergreifen; c. it (coll) sein
Fett kriegen; c. one's breath wieder
Atem schöpfen; c. one's eye j-m ins
Auge fallen; get caught on hängenbleiben an (dat) ‖ intr (said of a
bolt, etc.) einschnappen; c. on (said
of an idea) Anklang finden; c. on to
(fig) kapieren; catch up aufholen;
c. up on nachholen; c. up with einholen

catch'ing adj (disease) ansteckend;
(attractive) anziehend

catch′word′ s (slogan) Schlagwort n; (actor's cue) Stichwort n; (pol) Parteiparole f

catchy [ˈkætʃi] adj einschmeichelnd

catechism [ˈkætɪˌkɪzəm] s Katechismus m

category [ˈkætɪˌgori] s Kategorie f

cater [ˈketər] tr Lebensmittel liefern für ‖ intr—c. to schmeicheln (dat); (deliver food to) Lebensmittel liefern für

cater-corner [ˈkætərˌkɔrnər] adj & adv diagonal

caterer [ˈketərər] s Lebensmittellieferant –in mf

caterpillar [ˈkætərˌpɪlər] s (ent, mach) Raupe f

cat′fish′ s Katzenwels m, Katzenfisch m

cat′gut′ s (mus) Darmseite f; (surg) Katgut m

cathedral [kəˈθidrəl] s Dom m

catheter [ˈkæθɪtər] s Katheter m

cathode [ˈkæθod] s Kathode f

catholic [ˈkæθəlɪk] adj universal; Catholic katholisch ‖ Catholic s Katholik –in mf

cat′nap′ s Nickerchen n

catnip [ˈkætnɪp] s Baldrian m

catsup [ˈkætsəp], [ˈketʃəp] s Ketschup m

cattle [ˈkætəl] spl Vieh n

cat′tle car′ s (rr) Viehwagen m

cat′tle·man s (–men) Viehzüchter m

cat′tle ranch′ s Viehfarm f

catty [ˈkæti] adj boshaft

cat′walk′ s Steg m, Laufplanke f

Caucasian [kɔˈkeʒən] adj kaukasisch ‖ s Kaukasier –in mf

caucus [ˈkɔkəs] s Parteiführerversammlung f

cauliflower [ˈkɔliˌflau·ər] s Blumenkohl m

cause [kɔz] s (origin) Ursache f; (reason) Grund m; (person) Urheber –in mf; (occasion) Anlaß m; for a good c. für e–e gute Sache ‖ tr verursachen; c. s.o. to (inf) j–n veranlassen zu (inf)

cause′way′ s Dammweg m

caustic [ˈkɔstɪk] adj (& fig) ätzend

cauterize [ˈkɔtəˌraɪz] tr verätzen

caution [ˈkɔʃən] s (carefulness) Vorsicht f; (warning) Warnung f ‖ tr (against) warnen (vor dat)

cautious [ˈkɔʃəs] adj vorsichtig

cavalcade [ˈkævəlˌked] s Kavalkade f

cavalier [ˌkævəˈlɪr] adj hochmütig ‖ s Kavalier m

cavalry [ˈkævəlri] s Kavallerie f

cav′alry·man s (–men) Kavallerist m

cave [kev] s Höhle f ‖ intr—c. in (collapse) einstürzen

cave′-in′ s Einsturz m

cave′ man′ s Höhlenmensch m

cavern [ˈkævərn] s (große) Höhle f

caviar [ˈkæviˌɑr] s Kaviar m

cav·il [ˈkævɪl] v (pret & pp –l(l)ed; ger –l(l)ing) intr (at, about) herumnörgeln (an dat)

cavity [ˈkævɪti] s Hohlraum m; (anat) Höhle f; (dent) Loch n

cavort [kəˈvɔrt] intr (coll) herumtollen

caw. [kɔ] s Krächzen n ‖ intr krächzen

cease [sis] s—without c. unaufhörlich ‖ tr einstellen; (ger) aufhören (zu inf); c. fire das Feuer einstellen ‖ intr aufhören

cease′fire′ s Feuereinstellung f

ceaseless [ˈsislɪs] adj unaufhörlich

cedar [ˈsidər] s Zeder f

cede [sid] tr abtreten, überlassen

cedilla [sɪˈdɪlə] s Cedille f

ceiling [ˈsilɪŋ] s Decke f; (fin) oberste Grenze f; hit the c. (coll) platzen

ceil′ing light′ s Deckenlicht n

ceil′ing price′ s Höchstpreis m

celebrant [ˈsɛlɪbrənt] s Zelebrant m

celebrate [ˈsɛlɪˌbret] tr (a feast) feiern; (mass) zelebrieren ‖ intr feiern; (eccl) zelebrieren

cel′ebrat′ed adj (for) berühmt (wegen)

celebration [ˌsɛlɪˈbreʃən] s Feier f; (eccl) Zelebrieren n; in c. of zur Feier (genit)

celebrity [sɪˈlɛbrɪti] s Berühmtheit f; (person) Prominente mf

celery [ˈsɛləri] s Selleriestengel m

celestial [sɪˈlɛstʃəl] adj himmlisch; (astr) Himmels-

celibacy [ˈsɛlɪbəsi] s Zölibat m & n

celibate [ˈsɛlɪbɪt] adj ehelos

cell [sɛl] s Zelle f

cellar [ˈsɛlər] s Keller m

cellist [ˈtʃɛlɪst] s Cellist –in mf

cel·lo [ˈtʃɛlo] s (–los) Cello n

cellophane [ˈsɛləˌfɛn] s Zellophan n

celluloid [ˈsɛljəˌlɔɪd] s Zelluloid f

Celt [sɛlt], [kɛlt] s Kelte m, Keltin f

Celtic [ˈsɛltɪk], [ˈkɛltɪk] adj keltisch

cement [sɪˈmɛnt] s (glue) Bindemittel n; (used in building) Zement m ‖ tr zementieren; (glue) kitten; (fig) (be)festigen

cement′ mix′er s Betonmischmaschine f

cemetery [ˈsɛmɪˌtɛri] s Friedhof m

censer [ˈsɛnsər] s Räucherfaß n

censor [ˈsɛnsər] s (of printed matter, films) Zensor m; (of morals) Sittenrichter m ‖ tr zensieren

cen′sorship′ s Zensur f

censure [ˈsɛnʃər] s Tadel m ‖ tr tadeln

census [ˈsɛnsəs] s Volkszählung f

cent [sɛnt] s Cent m

centaur [ˈsɛntɔr] s Zentaur m

centennial [sɛnˈtɛni·əl] adj hundertjährig ‖ s Hundertjahrfeier f

center [ˈsɛntər] s Zentrum n, Mittelpunkt m; (pol) Mitte f ‖ tr in den Mittelpunkt stellen; (tech) zentrieren ‖ intr—c. on sich konzentrieren auf (acc)

cen′ter aisle′ s Mittelgang m

cen′ter cit′y s Stadtmitte f

cen′terpiece′ s Tischaufsatz m

centigrade [ˈsɛntɪˌgred] s Celsius, e.g., one degree c. ein Grad Celsius

centimeter [ˈsɛntɪˌmitər] s Zentimeter m

centipede [ˈsɛntɪˌpid] s Hundertfüßler m

central [ˈsɛntrəl] adj zentral

Cen′tral Amer′ica s Mittelamerika n

centralize [ˈsɛntrəˌlaɪz] tr zentralisieren

centri′fugal force′ [sen′trɪfjəgəl] *s* Fliehkraft *f*

centrifuge [′sentrɪ‚fjudʒ] *s* Zentrifuge *f*

century [′sentʃəri] *s* Jahrhundert *n*

ceramic [sɪ′ræmɪk] *adj* keramisch ‖ **ceramics** *s* (art) Keramik *f*; *spl* Töpferwaren *pl*

cereal [′sɪrɪ‚əl] *adj* Getreide- ‖ *s* (*grain*) Getreide *n*; (*dish*) Getreideflockengericht *n*

cerebral [′serɪbrəl] *adj* Gehirn-

ceremonial [‚serɪ′monɪ‚əl] *adj* zeremoniell, feierlich

ceremonious [‚serɪ′monɪ‚əs] *adj* zeremoniös, umständlich

ceremony [′serɪ‚moni] *s* Zeremonie *f*

certain [′sʌrtən] *adj* (*sure*) sicher, bestimmt; (*particular but unnamed*) gewiß; **be c.** feststehen; **for c.** gewiß; **make c. of** sich vergewissern (*genit*); **make c. that** sich vergewissern, daß

certainly [′sʌrtənli] *adv* sicher(lich); (*as a strong affirmative*) allerdings

certainty [′sʌrtənti] *s* Sicherheit *f*

certificate [sər′tɪfɪkɪt] *s* Schein *m*; (*educ*) Abgangszeugnis *n*

certification [‚sʌrtɪfɪ′keʃən] *s* Bescheinigung *f*, Beglaubigung *f*

cer′tified *adj* beglaubigt

cer′tified check′ *s* durch Bank bestätigter Scheck *m*

cer′tified pub′lic account′ant *s* amtlich zugelassener Wirtschaftsprüfer *m*

certi-fy [′sʌrtɪ‚faɪ] *v* (*pret & pp* –**fied**) bescheinigen, beglaubigen

cervix [′sʌrvɪks] *s* (**cervices** [sər′vaɪsiz]) Genick *n*

cessation [se′seʃən] *s* (*of territory*) Abtretung *f*; (*of activities*) Einstellung *f*

cesspool [′ses‚pul] *s* Senkgrube *f*

chafe [tʃef] *tr* (*the skin*) wundscheuern ‖ *intr* (*rub*) sich wundreiben; (*become sore*) sich wundreiben; (*be irritated*) (*at*) sich ärgern über (*acc*)

chaff [tʃæf] *s* Spreu *f*

chaf′ing dish′ *s* Speisenwärmer *m*

chagrin [ʃə′grɪn] *s* Verdruß *m* ‖ *tr* verdrießen

chain [tʃen] *s* Kette *f* ‖ *tr* (**to**) anketten (an *acc*)

chain′ gang′ *s* Kettensträflinge *pl*

chain′ reac′tion *s* Kettenreaktion *f*

chain′ smok′er *s* Kettenraucher –in *mf*

chain′ store′ *s* Kettenladen *m*

chair [tʃer] *s* Stuhl *m*; (*upholstered*) Sessel *m*; (*of the presiding officer*) Vorsitz *m*; (*presiding officer*) Vorsitzende *mf*; (*educ*) Lehrstuhl *m* ‖ *tr* den Vorsitz führen von

chair′la′dy *s* Vorsitzende *f*

chair′ lift′ *s* Sessellift *m*

chair′man *s* (–**men**) Vorsitzende *m*

chair′manship′ *s* Vorsitz *m*

chalice [′tʃælɪs] *s* Kelch *m*

chalk [tʃɔk] *s* Kreide *f* ‖ *tr*—**c. up** ankreiden; (*coll*) verbuchen

challenge [′tʃælɪndʒ] *s* Aufforderung *f*; (*to a duel*) Herausforderung *f*; (*jur*) Ablehnung *f*; (*mil*) Anruf *m* ‖ *tr* auffordern; (*to a duel*) herausfor-

dern; (*a statement, right*) bestreiten; (*jur*) ablehnen; (*mil*) anrufen

chamber [′tʃembər] *s* Kammer *f*; (*parl*) Sitzungssaal *m*

chamberlain [′tʃembərlɪn] *s* Kammerherr *m*

cham′bermaid′ *s* Stubenmädchen *n*

cham′ber of com′merce *s* Handelskammer *f*

chameleon [kə′milɪ‚ən] *s* Chamäleon *n*

chamfer [′tʃæmfər] *s* Schrägkante *f* ‖ *tr* abschrägen; (*furrow*) auskehlen

cham-ois [′ʃæmi] *s* (–**ois**) Sämischleder *n*; (*zool*) Gemse *f*

champ [tʃæmp] *s* (*coll*) Meister *m* ‖ *tr* kauen; **champ the bit am** Gebiß kauen

champagne [ʃæm′pen] *s* Champagner *m*, Sekt *m*

champion [′tʃæmpɪ‚ən] *s* (*of a cause*) Verfechter –in *mf*; (*sport*) Meister –in *mf* ‖ *tr* eintreten für

cham′pionship′ *s* Meisterschaft *f*

chance [tʃæns] *adj* zufällig ‖ *s* (*accident*) Zufall *m*; (*opportunity*) Chance *f*, Gelegenheit *f*; (*risk*) Risiko *n*; (*possibility*) Möglichkeit *f*; (*lottery ticket*) Los *n*; **by c.** zufällig; **c. of a lifetime** einmalige Gelegenheit *f*; **chances are (that)** aller Wahrscheinlichkeit nach; **on the c. that** für den Fall, daß; **take a c.** ein Risiko eingehen; **take no chances** nichts riskieren; ‖ *tr* riskieren ‖ *intr* geschehen; **c. upon** stoßen auf (*acc*)

chancel [′tʃænsəl] *s* Altarraum *m*

chancellery [′tʃænsələri] *s* Kanzlei *f*

chancellor [′tʃænsələr] *s* Kanzler *m*; (*hist*) Reichskanzler *m*

chandelier [‚ʃændə′lir] *s* Kronleuchter *m*

change [tʃendʒ] *s* Veränderung *f*; (*in times, styles, etc.*) Wechsel *m*; (*in attitude, relations, etc.*) Wandel *m*; (*small coins*) Kleingeld *n*; (*of weather*) Umschlag *m*; **c. for the better** Verbesserung *f*; **c. for the worse** Verschlechterung *f*; **for a c.** zur Abwechslung; **give c. for a dollar** auf e–n Dollar herausgeben; **need a c.** Luftveränderung brauchen ‖ *tr* ändern; (*plans*) ändern; (*money, subject, oil*) wechseln; (*a baby*) trockenlegen; (*stations, channels*) umschalten; **c. around** umändern; **c. hands** den Besitzer wechseln; **c. one's mind** sich anders besinnen; **c. trains (or buses, streetcars)** umsteigen ‖ *intr* sich verändern; (*said of a mood, wind, weather*) umschlagen; (*said of a voice*) mutieren; (*change clothes*) sich umziehen **change into** sich wandeln in (*acc*)

changeable [′tʃendʒəbəl] *adj* veränderlich

changeless [′tʃendʒlɪs] *adj* unveränderlich

change′ of heart′ *s* Sinnesänderung *f*

change′ of life′ *s* Wechseljahre *pl*

change′ of scen′ery *s* Ortsveränderung *f*

change′-o′ver *s* Umstellung *f*

chan·nel ['tʃænəl] *s* (*strait*) Kanal *m*; (*of a river*) Fahrrinne *f*; (*groove*) Rinne *f*; (*furrow*) Furche *f*; (fig) Weg *m*; (telv) Kanal *m*; **through official channels** auf dem Amtswege || *v* (*pret & pp* **–nel(l)ed**; *ger* **–nel(l)ing**) *tr* lenken; (*furrow*) kanalisieren

chant [tʃænt] *s* Gesang *m*; (*singsong*) Singsang *m*; (eccl) Kirchengesang *m* || *tr* singen

chanter ['tʃæntər] *s* Kantor *m*

chaos ['ke·as] *s* Chaos *n*

chaotic [ke'atɪk] *adj* chaotisch

chap [tʃæp] *s* (*in the skin*) Riß *m*; (coll) Kerl *m* || *v* (*pret & pp* **chapped**; *ger* **chapping**) *tr* (*the skin*) rissig machen || *intr* rissig werden, aufspringen

chapel ['tʃæpəl] *s* Kapelle *f*

chaperon ['ʃæpə‚ron] *s* Begleiter –in *mf*; (*of a young couple*) Anstandsdame *f* || *tr* als Anstandsdame begleiten

chaplain ['tʃæplɪn] *s* Kaplan *m*

chapter ['tʃæptər] *s* Kapitel *n*; (*of an organization*) Ortsgruppe *f*

char [tʃar] *v* (*pret & pp* **charred**; *ger* **charring**) *tr* verkohlen

character ['kærɪktər] *s* Charakter *m*; (*letter*) Schriftzeichen *n*; (*typewriter space*) Anschlag *m*; (coll) Kauz *m*; (theat) handelnde Person *f*; **be out of c.** nicht passen

characteristic [‚kærɪktə'rɪstɪk] *adj* (*of*) charakteristisch (für) || *s* Charakterzug *m*, Kennzeichen *n*

characterize ['kærɪktə‚raɪz] *tr* charakterisieren, kennzeichnen

charade [ʃə'red] *s* Scharade *f*

charcoal ['tʃar‚kol] *s* Holzkohle *f*; (*for sketching*) Zeichenkohle *f*

charge [tʃardʒ] *s* (*accusation*) Anklage *f*; (*fee*) Gebühr *f*; (*custody*) Obhut *f*; (*responsibility*) Pflicht *f*; (*ward*) Pflegebefohlene *mf*; (*of an explosive or electricity*) Ladung *f*; (*assault*) Ansturm *m*; (*of a judge to the jury*) Rechtsbelehrung *f*; **be in c. of** verantwortlich sein für; **charges** Spesen *pl*; **take c. of** die Verantwortung übernehmen für; **there is no c.** es kostet nichts; **under s.o.'s c.** unter j-s Aufsicht || *tr* (*a battery*) (auf)laden; (*with*) anklagen (wegen); (*a jury*) belehren; (mil) stürmen; **c. s.o. ten marks for** j-m zehn Mark berechnen für; **c. s.o.'s account** auf j-s Rechnung setzen || *intr* (mil) anrechnen für; **c. to s.o.'s account** auf j-s Rechnung setzen || *intr* (mil) anstürmen

charge′ account′ *s* laufendes Konto *n*

charger ['tʃardʒər] *s* (elec) Ladevorrichtung *f*; (hist) Schlachtroß *n*

chariot ['tʃærɪ·ət] *s* Kampfwagen *m*

charitable ['tʃærɪtəbəl] *adj* (*generous*) freigebig; (*lenient*) nachsichtig; **c. institution** wohltätige Stiftung *f*

charity ['tʃærɪti] *s* (*giving of alms*) Wohltätigkeit *f*; (*alms*) Almosen *n*; (*institution*) Wohlfahrtsinstitut *n*; (*love of neighbor*) Nächstenliebe *f*

charlatan ['ʃarlətən] *s* Scharlatan *m*

Charles [tʃarlz] *s* Karl *m*

char′ley horse′ ['tʃarli] *s* (coll) Muskelkater *m*

charm [tʃarm] *s* Charme *m*; (*trinket*) Amulett *n* || *tr* verzaubern; (fig) entzücken

charm′ing *adj* scharmant, reizend

chart [tʃart] *s* Karte *f*; (*table*) Tabelle *f*; (naut) Seekarte *f* || *tr* entwerfen, auf e-r Karte graphisch darstellen

charter ['tʃartər] *adj* (*plane, etc.*) Charter– || *s* Freibrief *m*, Charter *m*; (*of an organization*) Gründungsurkunde *f* und Satzungen *pl* || *tr* chartern

char′ter mem′ber *s* gründendes Mitglied *n*

char–woman ['tʃar‚wumən] *s* (**–women** [‚wɪmɪn]) Putzfrau *f*

chase [tʃes] *s* (*pursuit*) Verfolgung *f*; (*hunt*) Jagd *f* || *tr* jagen; (*girls*) nachsteigen (*dat*); **c. away** verjagen; **c. out** vertreiben || *intr*—**c. after** nachlaufen (*dat*)

chasm ['kæzəm] *s* (& fig) Abgrund *m*

chas·sis ['tʃæsi] *s* (**–sis** [siz]) Chassis *n*; (aut) Fahrgestell *n*

chaste [tʃest] *adj* keusch

chasten ['tʃesən] *tr* züchtigen

chastise [tʃæs'taɪz] *tr* züchtigen

chastity ['tʃæstɪti] *s* Keuschheit *f*

chat [tʃæt] *s* Plauderei *f* || *v* (*pret & pp* **chatted**; *ger* **chatting**) *intr* plaudern

chattel ['tʃætəl] *s* Sklave *m*; **chattels** Hab und Gut *n*

chatter ['tʃætər] *s* (*talk*) Geplapper *n*; (*of teeth*) Klappern *n* || *intr* (*talk*) plappern; (*said of teeth*) klappern

chat′terbox′ *s* (coll) Plappermaul *n*

chauffeur ['ʃofər], [ʃo'fʌr] *s* Chauffeur *m* || *tr* fahren

cheap [tʃip] *adj* (*inexpensive*) billig; (*shoddy*) minderwertig; (*base*) gemein; (*stingy*) geizig; **feel c.** sich verlegen fühlen || *adv* billig; **get off c.** mit e-m blauen Auge davonkommen

cheapen ['tʃipən] *tr* herabsetzen

cheat [tʃit] *s* Betrüger –in *mf* || *tr* (**out of**) betrügen (um) || *intr* schwindeln; (*at cards*) mogeln; **c. on** (*e.g., a wife*) betrügen

cheat′ing *s* Betrügerei *f*; (*at cards*) Mogelei *f*

check [tʃek] *s* (*of a bank*) Scheck *m*; (*for luggage*) Schein *m*; (*in a restaurant*) Rechnung *f*; (*inspection*) Kontrolle *f*; (*test*) Nachprüfung *f*; (*repulse*) Rückschlag *m*; (*restraint*) (**on**) Hemmnis *n* (für); (*square*) Karo *n*; (chess) Schach *f*; **hold in c.** in Schach halten || *tr* (*restrain*) hindern; (*inspect*) kontrollieren; (*test*) nachprüfen, überprüfen; (*a hat, coat*) abgeben, (*luggage*) aufgeben; (*figures*) nachrechnen; (chess) Schach bieten (*dat*); **c. off** abhaken || *intr* (*agree*) übereinstimmen; **c. out** (*of a hotel*) sich abmelden; **c. up on** (*a person*) sich erkun-

digen über (acc); **c. with** (correspond to) übereinstimmen mit; (con-
sult) sich besprechen mit || interj
Schach!
check'book' s Scheckbuch n, Scheck-
heft n
checker ['tʃɛkər] s Kontrolleur m; (in
checkers) Damestein m; **checkers**
Damespiel n
check'erboard' s Damebrett n
check'ered adj kariert; (life, career)
wechselvoll
check'ing account' s Scheckkonto n
check'list' s Kontrolliste f
check'mate' s Schachmatt n; (fig)
Niederlage f || tr (& fig) matt setzen
|| interj schachmatt!
check'-out count'er s Kasse f
check'point' s Kontrollstelle f
check'room' s Garderobe f
check'up' s Überprüfung f; (med) ärzt-
liche Untersuchung f
cheek [tʃik] s Backe f, Wange f; (coll)
Frechheit f
cheek'bone' s Backenknochen m
cheek'by jowl' adv Seite an Seite
cheeky ['tʃiki] adj (coll) frech
cheer [tʃɪr] s (applause) Beifallsruf
m; (encouragement) Ermunterung f;
(sport) Ermunterungsruf m; **three
cheers** for ein dreifaches Hoch auf
(acc) || tr zujubeln (dat); **c. on** an-
feuern; **c. up** aufmuntern; **c. up!** nur
Mut!
cheerful ['tʃɪrfəl] adj heiter; (room,
surroundings) freundlich
cheer'lead'er s Anführer –in mf beim
Beifallsrufen
cheerless ['tʃɪrlɪs] adj freudlos
cheese [tʃiz] s Käse m
cheeseburger ['tʃiz‚bʌrgər] s belegtes
Brot n mit Frikadelle und über-
backenem Käse
cheese'cake' s Käsekuchen m
cheese'cloth' s grobe Baumwollgaze f
cheesy ['tʃizi] adj (sl) minderwertig
chef [ʃɛf] s Küchenchef m
chemical ['kɛmɪkəl] adj chemisch;
(fertilizer) Kunst– || s Chemikalie f
chemist ['kɛmɪst] s Chemiker –in mf
chemistry ['kɛmɪstri] s Chemie f
cherish ['tʃɛrɪʃ] tr (hold dear) schätzen; (hopes, thoughts) hegen
cherry ['tʃɛri] s Kirsche f
cher'ry tree' s Kirschbaum m
cher·ub ['tʃɛrəb] s (–ubim [əbɪm])
Cherub m || s (–ubs) Engelskopf m
chess [tʃɛs] s Schach n
chess'board' s Schachbrett n
chess'man' s (–men') Schachfigur f
chest [tʃɛst] s Truhe f; (anat) Brust f
chestnut ['tʃɛsnət] adj kastanienbraun
|| s Kastanie f; (tree) Kastanien-
baum m; (horse) Rotfuchs m
chest' of drawers' s Kommode f
chevron ['ʃɛvrən] s (mil) Winkel m
chew [tʃu] s Kauen n; (stick of to-
bacco) Priem m || tr kauen; **c. the
cud** wiederkäuen; **c. the rag** (sl)
schwatzen
chew'ing gum' s Kaugummi m
chew'ing tobac'co s Kautabak m
chic [ʃik] adj schick || s Schick m

chicanery [ʃɪ'kenəri] s Schikane f
chick [tʃɪk] s Küken n; (girl) (sl) kesse
Biene f
chicken ['tʃɪkən] adj Hühner–; (sl)
feig(e) || s Huhn n, Hühnchen n
chick'en coop' s Hühnerstall m
chick'en-heart'ed adj feig(e)
chick'en pox' s Windpocken pl
chick'en wire' s Maschendraht m
chick'pea' s Kichererbse f
chicory ['tʃɪkəri] s Zichorie f
chide [tʃaɪd] v (pret & pp chided &
chid [tʃɪd]; pp chided) tr tadeln
chief [tʃif] adj Haupt–, Ober–, oberste;
(leading) leitend || s Chef m, Ober-
haupt n; (of an Indian tribe) Häuptling m
chief' exec'utive s Regierungsober-
haupt n
chief' jus'tice s Vorsitzender m des
obersten Gerichtshofes
chiefly ['tʃifli] adv vorwiegend
chief' of police' s Polizeipräsident m
chief' of staff' s Generalstabschef m
chief' of state' s Staatschef m
chieftain ['tʃiftən] s Häuptling m
chiffon ['ʃɪfɑn] s Chiffon m
child [tʃaɪld] s (children ['tʃɪldrən])
Kind n; **with c.** schwanger
child' abuse' s Kindermißhandlung f
child'birth' s Niederkunft f
child'hood' s Kindheit f
childish ['tʃaɪldɪʃ] adj kindisch
childless ['tʃaɪldlɪs] adj kinderlos
child'like' adj kindlich
child' prod'igy s Wunderkind n
child's' play' s (fig) Kinderspiel n
child' support' s Alimente pl
child' wel'fare s Jugendfürsorge f
Chile ['tʃɪli] s Chile n
chili ['tʃɪli] s Cayennepfeffer m
chil'i sauce' s Chillisoße f
chill [tʃɪl] s (coldness) Kälte f; (sensation of cold or fear) Schau(d)er
m; **chills** Fieberschau(d)er m || tr
kühlen; (hopes, etc.) dämpfen; (metals) abschrecken; **be chilled to the
bone** durchfrieren || intr abkühlen
chilly ['tʃɪli] adj (& fig) frostig; **feel
chilly** frösteln
chime [tʃaɪm] s Geläut n; **chimes**
Glockenspiel n || intr (said of bells)
läuten; (said of a doorbell) ertönen;
(said of a clock) schlagen; **c. in**
(coll) beipflichten
chimera [kaɪ'mɪrə] s Hirngespinst n
chimney ['tʃɪmni] s Schornstein m;
(of a lamp) Zylinder m
chimpanzee [tʃɪm'pænzi] s Schimpanse m
chin [tʃɪn] s Kinn n; **keep one's c. up**
die Ohren steifhalten; **up to the c.**
bis über die Ohren
china ['tʃaɪnə] s Porzellan n || **China**
s China n
chi'na clos'et s Porzellanschrank m
chi'na-man s (–men) (pej) Chinese m
chin'aware' s Porzellanwaren pl
Chi·nese [tʃaɪ'niz] adj chinesisch || s
(–nese) Chinese m, Chinesin f; (language) Chinesisch n
Chi·nese' lan'tern s Lampion m
chink [tʃɪŋk] s Ritze f; (of coins or

glasses) Klang *m* || *tr* (*glasses*) anstoßen

chin'-up' *s* Klimmzug *m*

chip [tʃɪp] *s* Span *m*, Splitter *m*; (*in china*) angestoßene Stelle *f*; (*in poker*) Spielmarke *f*; **a c. off the old block** (coll) ganz der Vater; **have a c. on one's shoulder** (coll) vor Zorn geladen sein || *v* (*pret & pp* **chipped**; *ger* **chipping**) *tr* (*e.g., a cup*) anschlagen; **c. in** (coll) beitragen; **c. off** abbrechen || *intr* (leicht) abbrechen; **c. in** (with) einspringen (mit); **c. off** (*said of paint*) abblättern

chipmunk ['tʃɪp ˌmʌŋk] *s* Streifenhörnchen *n*

chipper ['tʃɪpər] *adj* (coll) munter

chiropodist [kaɪ'rapədɪst], [kɪ'rapədɪst] *s* Fußpfleger –in *mf*

chiropractor ['kaɪrə ˌpræktər] *s* Chiropraktiker –in *mf*

chirp [tʃʌrp] *s* Gezwitscher *n* || *intr* zwitschern

chis·el ['tʃɪzəl] *s* Meißel *m* || *v* (*pret & pp* **-el[l]ed**; *ger* **-il[l]ing**) *tr* meißeln; (sl) bemogeln || *intr* meißeln; (sl) mogeln

chiseler ['tʃɪzələr] *s* (sl) Mogler *m*

chitchat ['tʃɪt ˌtʃæt] *s* Schnickschnack *m*

chivalrous ['ʃɪvəlrəs] *adj* ritterlich

chivalry ['ʃɪvəlri] *s* Rittertum *n*; (*politeness*) Ritterlichkeit *f*

chive [tʃaɪv] *s* Schnittlauch *m*

chloride ['kloraɪd] *s* Chlorid *n*

chlorine ['klorin] *s* Chlor *n*

chloroform ['klorə ˌfɔrm] *s* Chloroform *n* || *tr* chloroformieren

chlorophyll ['klorəfɪl] *s* Chlorophyll *n*

chock-full ['tsak'fʊl] *adj* zum Bersten voll

chocolate ['tʃɔkəlɪt] *adj* Schokoladen–; (*in color*) schokoladenfarben || *s* Schokolade *f*; (*chocolate-covered candy*) Praline *f*

choc'olate bar' *s* Schokoladentafel *f*

choice [tʃɔɪs] *adj* (aus)erlesen || *s* Wahl *f*; (*selection*) Auswahl *f*

choir [kwaɪr] *s* Chor *m*; (archit) Chor *m*

choir'boy' *s* Chorknabe *m*

choir' loft' *s* Chorgalerie *f*

choir'mas'ter *s* Chordirigent *m*

choke [tʃok] *s* (aut) Starterklappe *f* || *tr* erwürgen, ersticken; **c. back** (*tears*) herunterschlucken; **c. down** herunterwürgen; **c. up** verstopfen || *intr* ersticken; **c. on** ersticken an (*dat*)

choker ['tʃokər] *s* enges Halsband *n*

cholera ['kalərə] *s* Cholera *f*

cholesterol [kə'lestə ˌrol] *s* Blutfett *n*

choose [tʃuz] *v* (*pret* **chose** [tʃoz]; *pp* **chosen** ['tʃozən]) *tr & intr* wählen

choosy ['tʃuzi] *adj* (coll) wählerisch

chop [tʃap] *s* Hieb *m*; (culin) Kotelett *n*, Schnitzel *n*; **chops** (sl) Maul *n* || *v* (*pret & pp* **chopped**; *ger* **chopping**) *tr* hacken; **c. down** niederhauen; **c. off** abhacken; **c. up** zerhacken

chopper ['tʃapər] *s* (ax) Hackbeil *n*; (coll) Hubschrauber *m*

chop'ping block' *s* Hackklotz *m*

choppy ['tʃapi] *adj* (sea) bewegt

chop'stick' *s* Eßstäbchen *n*

choral ['korəl] *adj* Chor–, Sänger–

chorale [ko'ral] *s* Choral *m*

chord [kɔrd] *s* (anat) Band *n*; (geom) Sehne *f*; (*combination of notes*) (mus) Akkord *m*; (mus & fig) Saite *f*

chore [tʃor] *s* Hausarbeit *f*

choreography [ˌkɔrɪ'agrəfi] *s* Choreographie *f*

chorus ['korəs] *s* Chor *m*; (*refrain*) Kehrreim *m*

cho'rus girl' *s* Revuetänzerin *f*

chowder ['tʃaudər] *s* Fischsuppe *f*

Christ [kraɪst] *s* Christus *m*

Christ' child' *s* Christkind *n*

christen ['krɪsən] *tr* taufen

Christendom ['krɪsəndəm] *s* Christenheit *f*

chris'tening *s* Taufe *f*; **c. of a ship** Schiffstaufe *f*

Christian ['krɪstʃən] *adj* christlich || Christ –in *mf*

Chris'tian E'ra *s* christliche Zeitrechnung *f*

Christianity [ˌkrɪstɪ'æniti] *s* (*faith*) Christentum *n*; (*all Christians*) Christenheit *f*

Chris'tian name' *s* Taufname *m*

Christmas ['krɪsməs] *s* Weihnachts– || *s* Weihnachten *pl*, Weihnachtsfest *n*

Christ'mas card' *s* Weihnachtskarte *f*

Christ'mas car'ol *s* Weihnachtslied *n*

Christ'mas Eve' *s* Heiliger Abend *m*

Christ'mas gift' *s* Weihnachtsgeschenk *n*

Christ'mas tree' *s* Christbaum *m*

Christ'mas tree' lights' *spl* Weihnachtskerzen *pl*

Christopher ['krɪstəfər] *s* Christoph *m*

chromatic [kro'mætɪk] *adj* chromatisch

chrome [krom] *adj* Chrom– || *s* Chrom *n* || *tr* verchromen

chrome'plate' *tr* verchromen

chromium ['kromɪ·əm] *s* Chrom *n*

chromosome ['kromə ˌsom] *s* Chromosom *n*

chronic ['kranɪk] *adj* chronisch

chronicle ['kranɪkəl] *s* Chronik *f* || *tr* aufzeichnen

chronicler ['kranɪklər] *s* Chronist –in *mf*

chronological [ˌkranə'ladʒɪkəl] *adj* chronologisch

chronology [krə'nalədʒi] *s* Chronologie *f*

chronometer [krə'namɪtər] *s* Chronometer *n*

chrysanthemum [krɪ'sænθɪməm] *s* Chrysantheme *f*

chubby ['tʃʌbi] *adj* pummelig

chuck [tʃʌk] *s* (culin) Schulterstück *n*; (mach) Klemmfutter *n* || *tr* schmeißen

chuckle ['tʃʌkəl] *s* Glucksen *n* || *intr* glucksen

chug [tʃʌg] *s* Tuckern *n* || *v* (*pret & pp* **chugged**; *ger* **chugging**) *intr* tuckern; **c. along** tuckernd fahren

chum [tʃʌm] s (coll) Kumpel m || v (pret & pp chummed; ger chumming) intr—c. around with sich eng anschließen an (acc)
chummy ['tʃʌmi] adj eng befreundet
chump [tʃʌmp] s (coll) Trottel m
chunk [tʃʌŋk] s Klotz m, Stück m
church [tʃʌrtʃ] adj Kirchen-, kirchlich || s Kirche f
churchgoer ['tʃʌrtʃ,goə·ər] s Kirchgänger –in mf
church' pic'nic s Kirchweih f
church'yard' s Kirchhof m
churl [tʃʌrl] s Flegel m
churlish ['tʃʌrlɪʃ] adj flegelhaft
churn [tʃʌrn] s Butterfaß n || tr (cream) buttern; c. up aufwühlen || intr sich heftig bewegen
chute [ʃut] s (for coal, etc.) Rutsche f; (for laundry, etc.) Abwurfschacht m; (sliding board) Rutschbahn f; (in a river) Stromschnelle f; (aer) Fallschirm m
cider ['saɪdər] s Apfelwein m
cigar [sɪ'gɑr] s Zigarre f
cigarette [,sɪgə'ret] s Zigarette f
cigarette' cough' s Raucherhusten m
cigarette' light'er s Feuerzeug n
cigar' store' s Rauchwarenladen m
cinch [sɪntʃ] s Sattelgurt m; (sure thing) totsichere Sache f; (snap) (sl) Kinderspiel n; (likely candidate) totsicherer Kandidat m || tr (sl) sich [dat] sichern
cinder ['sɪndər] s (ember) glühende Kohle f; (slag) Schlacke f; cinders Asche f
Cinderella [,sɪndə'relə] s Aschenbrödel n
cin'der track' s (sport) Aschenbahn f
cinema ['sɪnəmə] s Kino n
cinematography [,sɪnəmə'tɑgrəfi] s Kinematographie f
cinnamon ['sɪnəmən] s Zimt m
cipher ['saɪfər] s Ziffer f; (zero) Null f; (code) Chiffre f || tr chiffrieren
circle ['sʌrkəl] s Kreis m; circles under the eyes Ränder pl unter den Augen || tr einkreisen; (go around) umkreisen || intr kreisen
circuit ['sʌrkɪt] s (course) Kreislauf m; (elec) Stromkreis m; (jur) Bezirk m
cir'cuit break'er s Ausschalter m
cir'cuit court' s Bezirksgericht n
circuitous [sər'kju·ɪtəs] adj weitschweifig
circular ['sʌrkjələr] adj kreisförmig; (saw) Kreis– || s Rundschreiben n
circulate ['sʌrkjə,let] tr in Umlauf setzen; (a rumor) verbreiten; (fin) girieren || intr umlaufen; (said of blood) kreisen; (said of a rumor) umgehen
circulation [,sʌrkjə'leʃən] s (blood) Kreislauf m; (of a newspaper) Auflage f; (of money) Umlauf m
circumcize ['sʌrkəm,saɪz] tr beschneiden
circumference [sər'kʌmfərəns] s Umfang m
circumflex ['sʌrkəm,fleks] s Zirkumflex m

circumlocution [,sʌrkəmlo'kju/ən] s Umschreibung f
circumscribe ['sʌrkəm,skraɪb] tr (geom) umschreiben; (fig) umgrenzen
circumspect ['sʌrkəm,spekt] adj umsichtig
circumstance ['sʌrkəm,stæns] s Umstand m; circumstances (financial situation) Verhältnisse pl
cir'cumstan'tial ev'idence [,sʌrkəm-'stæn/əl] s Indizienbeweis m
circumvent [,sʌrkəm'vent] tr umgehen
circus ['sʌrkəs] s Zirkus m
cistern ['sɪstərn] s Zisterne f
citadel ['sɪtədəl] s Burg f
citation [sar'teʃən] s Zitat n; (jur) Vorladung f; (mil) Belobung f
cite [saɪt] tr (quote) anführen; (jur) vorladen; (mil) belobigen
citizen ['sɪtɪzən] s Bürger –in mf
cit'izenship' s Staatsangehörigkeit f
cit'rus fruit' ['sɪtrəs] s Zitrusfrucht f
city ['sɪti] s Stadt f
cit'y coun'cil s Stadtrat m
cit'y fa'ther s Stadtrat m
cit'y hall' s Rathaus m
cit'y plan'ning s Stadtplanung f
civic ['sɪvɪk] adj bürgerlich, Bürger– || civics s Staatsbürgerkunde f
civil ['sɪvɪl] adj (life, duty) bürgerlich; (service) öffentlich; (polite) höflich; (jur) privatrechtlich
civ'il cer'emony s standesamtliche Trauung f
civ'il defense' s zivile Verteidigung f
civ'il engineer'ing s Hoch– und Tiefbau m
civilian [sɪ'vɪljən] adj bürgerlich, Zivil– || s Zivilist –in mf
civilization [,sɪvɪlɪ'zeʃən] s Zivilisation f, Kultur f
civilize ['sɪvɪ,laɪz] tr zivilisieren
civ'il rights' spl Bürgerrechte pl
civ'il serv'ant s Staatsbeamte m, Staatsbeamtin f
civ'il serv'ice s Staatsdienst m
civ'il war' s Bürgerkrieg m
claim [klem] s Anspruch m; (assertion) Behauptung f; (for public land) beanspruchtes Land n || tr beanspruchen; (assert) behaupten; (attention) erfordern; c. to be sich ausgeben für
claim' check' s Aufgabeschein m
clairvoyance [kler'vɔɪ·əns] s Hellsehen n
clairvoyant [kler'vɔɪ·ənt] adj hellseherisch; be c. hellsehen || s Hellseher –in mf
clam [klæm] s eßbare Meermuschel f
clamber ['klæmər] intr klettern
clammy ['klæmi] adj feuchtkalt
clamor ['klæmər] s Geschrei n || intr (for) schreien (nach)
clamorous ['klæmərəs] adj schreiend
clamp [klæmp] s Klammer f; (surg) Klemme f || tr (ver)klammern || intr —c. down on einschreiten gegen
clan [klæn] s Stamm m; (pej) Sippschaft f
clandestine [klæn'destɪn] adj heimlich
clang [klæŋ] s Geklirr n || intr klirren

clank [klæŋk] *s* Geklirr *n*, Gerassel *n* || *intr* klirren, rasseln

clannish ['klænɪʃ] *adj* stammesbewußt

clap [klæp] *s* (*of the hands*) Klatschen *n*; (*of thunder*) Schlag *m* || *v* (*pret & pp* **clapped**; *ger* **clapping**) *tr* (*a tax, fine, duty*) (**on**) auferlegen (*dat*); **clap hands** in die Hände klatschen || *intr* Beifall klatschen

clapper ['klæpər] *s* Klöppel *m*

clap'trap' *s* Phrasendrescherei *f*

claque [klæk] *s* Claque *f*

clari•fy ['klærɪ‚faɪ] *v* (*pret & pp* **-fied**) *tr* erklären

clarinet [‚klærɪ'nɛt] *s* Klarinette *f*

clarity ['klærɪti] *s* Klarheit *f*

clash [klæʃ] *s* (*sound*) Geklirr *n*; (*of interests, etc.*) Widerstreit *m* || *intr* (*conflict*) kollidieren; (*said of persons*) aufeinanderstoßen; (*said of ideas*) im Widerspruch stehen; (*said of colors*) nicht zusammenpassen

clasp [klæsp] *s* (*fastener*) Schließe *f*, Spange *f*; (*on a necktie*) Klammer *f*; (*embrace*) Umarmung *f*; (*of hands*) Händedruck *m* || *tr* umklammern; **c. s.o.'s hand** j–m die Hand drücken

class [klæs] *s* (*group*) Klasse *f*; (*period of instruction*) Stunde *f*; (*year*) Jahrgang *m*; **have c.** (sl) Niveau haben || *tr* einstufen

classic ['klæsɪk] *adj* klassisch || *s* Klassiker *m*

classical ['klæsɪkəl] *adj* klassisch; **c. antiquity** Klassik *f*; **c. author** Klassiker *m*

classicist ['klæsɪsɪst] *s* Kenner –in *mf* der Klassik

classification [‚klæsɪfɪ'keʃən] *s* Klassifikation *f*, Anordnung *f*

clas'sified *adj* geheimhaltend

clas'sified ad' *s* kleine Anzeige *f*

classi•fy ['klæsɪ‚faɪ] *v* (*pret & pp* **-fied**) *tr* klassifizieren

class'mate' *s* Klassenkamerad *m*

class' reun'ion *s* Klassentreffen *n*

class'room' *s* Klassenzimmer *n*

classy ['klæsi] *adj* (sl) pfundig

clatter ['klætər] *s* Geklapper *n* || *intr* klappern

clause [klɔz] *s* Satzteil *m*; (jur) Klausel *f*

clavicle ['klævɪkəl] *s* Schlüsselbein *n*

claw [klɔ] *s* Klaue *f*, Kralle *f*; (*of a crab*) Schere *f* || *tr* zerkratzen; (*a hole*) scharren || *intr* kratzen

clay [kle] *adj* tönern || *s* Ton *m*, Lehm *m*

clay' pig'eon *s* Tontaube *f*

clean [klin] *adj* sauber, rein; (*cut*) glatt; (*features*) klar || *adv* (coll) völlig || *tr* reinigen, putzen; **c. out** (*clear out by force*) räumen; (*empty*) ausleeren; (sl) ausbeuten; **c. up** (*a room*) aufräumen || *intr* putzen; **c. up** sich zurechtmachen; (*in gambling*) (sl) schwer einheimsen

clean'-cut' *adj* (*person*) ordentlich; (*clearly outlined*) klar umrissen

cleaner ['klinər] *s* (*person, device*) Reiniger *m*; **cleaners** (*establishment*) Reinigungsanstalt *f*

clean'ing flu'id *s* flüssiges Reinigungsmittel *n*

clean'ing wo'man *s* Reinemachefrau *f*

cleanliness ['klɛnlɪnɪs] *s* Sauberkeit *f*

cleanse [klɛnz] *tr* reinigen

cleanser ['klɛnzər] *s* Reinigungsmittel *n*

clean'-shav'en *adj* glattrasiert

clean'up' *s* Reinemachen *n*; (*e.g., of vice, graft*) Säuberungsaktion *f*

clear [klɪr] *adj* klar; (*sky, weather*) heiter; (*light*) hell; (*profit*) netto; (*conscience*) rein; (*proof*) offenkundig || *adv* (coll) völlig; (fin) netto || *tr* klären; (*streets*) freimachen; (*the table*) abräumen; (*a room*) räumen; (*a forest*) roden; (*the air*) reinigen; (*an obstacle without touching it*) setzen über (*acc*); (*a path*) bahnen; (*as profit*) rein gewinnen; (*at customs*) zollamtlich abfertigen; (*one's name*) reinwaschen; **c. away** wegräumen; (*doubts*) beseitigen; **c. up** klarlegen || *intr* sich klären; **c. out** (coll) sich davonmachen; **c. up** sich aufklären

clearance ['klɪrəns] *s* (*approval*) Genehmigung *f*; (*at customs*) Zollabfertigung *f*; (*of a bridge*) lichte Höhe *f*; (aer) Starterlaubnis *f*; (mach) Spielraum *m*

clear'ance sale' *s* Räumungsverkauf *m*

clear'-cut' *adj* klar, eindeutig

clear'-head'ed *adj* verständig

clear'ing *s* (*in a woods*) Lichtung *f*

clear'ing house' *s* Abstimmungszentrale *f*; (fin) Verrechnungsstelle *f*

clear'-sight'ed *adj* scharfsichtig

cleat [klit] *s* Stollen *m*

cleavage ['klivɪdʒ] *s* Spaltung *f*

cleave [kliv] *v* (*pret & pp* **cleft** [klɛft] & **cleaved**) *tr* zerspalten || *intr* (*split*) sich spalten; (to) kleben (an *dat*)

cleaver ['klivər] *s* Hackbeil *n*

clef [klɛf] *s* Notenschlüssel *m*

cleft [klɛft] *s* Riß *m*, Spalt *m*

clemency ['klɛmənsi] *s* Milde *f*; (jur) Begnadigung *f*

clement ['klɛmənt] *adj* mild

clench [klɛntʃ] *tr* (*a fist*) ballen; (*the teeth*) zusammenbeißen

clerestory ['klɪr‚stori] *s* Lichtgaden *m*

clergy ['klɜrdʒi] *s* Geistlichkeit *f*

cler'gy•man *s* (**-men**) Geistliche *m*

cleric ['klɛrɪk] *s* Kleriker *m*

clerical ['klɛrɪkəl] *adj* Schreib-, Büro-; (eccl) geistlich

cler'ical er'ror *s* Schreibfehler *m*

cler'ical staff' *s* Schreibkräfte *pl*

cler'ical work' *s* Büroarbeit *f*

clerk [klɑrk] *s* (*in a store*) Verkäufer –in *mf*; (*in an office*) Büroangestellte *mf*; (*in a post office*) Schalterbeamte *m*; (jur) Gerichtsschreiber –in *mf*

clever ['klɛvər] *adj* (*intelligent*) klug; (*adroit*) geschickt; (*witty*) geistreich; (*ingenious*) findig

cleverness ['klɛvərnɪs] *s* (*intelligence*) Klugheit *f*; (*adroitness*) Geschicklichkeit *f*; (*ingeniousness*) Findigkeit *f*

cliché [kli'ʃe] *s* Klischee *n*

click [klɪk] s Klicken n; (of the tongue) Schnalzen n; (of a lock) Einschnappen n || intr klicken lassen; **c. one's heels** die Hacken zusammenschlagen || intr klicken; (said of heels) knallen; (said of a lock) einschnappen || impers—**it clicks** (coll) es klappt

client ['klaɪ·ənt] s (customer) Kunde m, Kundin f; (of a company) Auftraggeber –in mf; (jur) Klient –in mf

clientele [,klar·ən'tel] s Kundschaft f; (com, jur) Klientel f

cliff [klɪf] s Klippe f, Felsen m

climate ['klaɪmɪt] s Klima n

climax ['klaɪmæks] s Höhepunkt m

climb [klaɪm] s Aufstieg m, Besteigung f; (aer) Steigungsflug m || tr ersteigen, besteigen; (stairs) hinaufsteigen; **climb a tree** auf e–n Baum klettern; || intr steigen, klettern; (said of a street) ansteigen

climber ['klaɪmər] s Kletterer –in mf; (of a mountain) Bergsteiger –in mf; (bot) Kletterpflanze f

clinch [klɪntʃ] s (box) Clinch m || tr (settle) entscheiden || intr clinchen

clincher ['klɪntʃər] s (coll) Trumpf m

cling [klɪŋ] v (pret & pp **clung** [klʌŋ]) intr haften; **c. to** sich anklammern an (acc); (said of a dress) sich anschmiegen an (acc); (fig) festhalten an (dat)

clinic ['klɪnɪk] s Klinik f

clinical ['klɪnɪkəl] adj klinisch

clink [klɪŋk] s Klirren n; (prison) (sl) Kittchen n || tr—**c. glasses** mit den Gläsern anstoßen || intr klirren

clip [klɪp] s Klammer f; **go at a good c.** ein scharfes Tempo gehen || v (pret & pp **clipped**; ger **clipping**) tr (a hedge) beschneiden; (hair) schneiden; (wings) stutzen; (sheep) scheren; (from newspapers, etc.) ausschneiden; (syllables) verschlucken; (sl) schröpfen; **c. together** zusammenklammern

clip'board' s Manuskripthalter m

clip' joint' s (sl) Nepplokal n

clipper ['klɪpər] s (aer) Klipperflugzeug n; (naut) Klipper m; **clippers** Haarschneidemaschine f

clip'ping s (act) Stutzen n; (from newspapers) Ausschnitt m; **clippings** (of paper) Schnitzel pl; (scraps) Abfälle pl

clique [klik] s Sippschaft f

cliquish ['klikɪʃ] adj cliquenhaft

cloak [klok] s Umhang m; (fig) Deckmantel m; **under the c. of darkness** im Schutz der Dunkelheit || tr (fig) bemänteln

cloak'-and-dag'ger adj Spionage-

cloak'room' s Garderobe f

clobber ['klabər] tr (coll) verwichsen

clock [klak] s Uhr f || tr (a runner) abstoppen

clock'mak'er s Uhrmacher –in mf

clock' tow'er s Uhrturm m

clock'wise' adv im Uhrzeigersinn

clock'work' s Uhrwerk n; **like c.** wie am Schnürchen

clod [klad] s Klumpen m, Scholle f

clodhopper ['klad,hapər] s Bauerntölpel m

clog [klag] s Verstopfung f; (shoe) Holzschuh m || v (pret & pp **clogged**; ger **clogging**) tr verstopfen || intr sich verstopfen

cloister ['klɔɪstər] s Kloster n; (covered walk) Kreuzgang m

close [klos] adj (near) nahe; (tight) knapp; (air) schwül; (ties) friend) eng; (attention) gespannt; (game) beinahe gleich; (observer) scharf; (surveillance) streng; (supervision) genau; (inspection) eingehend; (resemblance) (competition) stark; (shave) glatt; (translation) wortgetreu; (stingy) geizig; (order) (mil) geschlossen; **c. to** (position) nahe an (dat), neben (dat); (direction) nahe an (acc), neben (acc) || adv dicht, eng; **from c. up** in der Nähe || [kloz] s Schluß m, Ende n; **bring to a c.** zu Ende bringen; **draw to a c.** zu Ende gehen || tr schließen; (an account, deal) abschließen; **c. down** stillegen; **c. off** abschließen; (a road) sperren; **c. out** (com) ausverkaufen; **c. up** zumachen || intr sich schließen; **c. in** immer näher kommen; **c. in on** umschließen

close-by ['klos'bar] adj nebenan

close-cropped ['klos'krapt] adj kurz geschoren

closed [klozd] adj geschlossen; **c. today** (public sign) heute Betriebsruhe

closed' shop' s Unternehmen n mit Gewerkschaftszwang

closefisted ['klos'fɪstəd] adj geizig

close-fitting ['klos'fɪtɪŋ] adj eng anliegend

close-mouthed ['klos'mavðd] adj verschwiegen

close' or'der drill' [klos] s (mil) geschlosssenes Exerzieren n

closeout ['kloz,aut] s Räumungsausverkauf m

close' shave' [klos] s glatte Rasure f; (fig) knappes Entkommen n; **have a c.** mit knapper Not davonkommen

closet ['klazɪt] s Schrank m

close-up ['klos,ʌp] s Nahaufnahme f

clos'ing adj Schluß-; (day) scheidend || s Schließung f; (of an account) Abschluß m; (of a factory) Stillegung f; (of a road) Sperrung f

clos'ing price' s Schlußkurs m

clos'ing time' s (of a shop) Geschäftsschluß m; (of bars) Polizeistunde f

clot [klat] s Klumpen m; (of blood) Gerinnsel n || v (pret & pp **clotted**; ger **clotting**) intr gerinnen

cloth [klɔθ] s Stoff m, Tuch n; (for cleaning, etc.) Lappen m; **the c.** die Geistlichkeit

clothe [kloð] v (pret & pp **clothed** & **clad** [klæd]) tr ankleiden, (be)kleiden; (fig) (in) einhüllen (in acc)

clothes [kloz], [kloθz] spl Kleider pl; **change one's clothes** sich umziehen; **put on one's clothes** sich anziehen

clothes'bas'ket s Wäschekorb m

clothes'brush' s Kleiderbürste f

clothes' clos'et s Kleiderschrank m

clothes′ dri′er s Wäschetrockner m
clothes′ hang′er s Kleiderbügel m
clothes′line′ s Wäscheleine f
clothes′pin′ s Wäscheklammer f
clothier [′kloðjər] s Kleiderhändler m; (cloth maker) Tuchmacher m; (cloth dealer) Tuchhändler m
clothing [′kloðɪŋ] s Kleidung f
cloud [klaud] s Wolke f; **be up in the clouds** (fig) in höheren Regionen schweben || tr bewölken; (a liquid) trüben; (fig) verdunkeln || intr—c. over (or up) sich bewölken
cloud′burst′ s Wolkenbruch m
cloud′-capped′ adj von Wolken bedeckt
cloudiness [′klaudɪnɪs] s Bewölktheit f
cloudless [′klaudlɪs] adj unbewölkt
cloudy [′klaudɪ] adj bewölkt; (liquid) trüb(e)
clout [klaut] s (blow) (coll) Hieb m; (influence) (coll) Einfluß m || tr—c. s.o. (coll) j—m eins herunterhauen
clove [klov] s Gewürznelke f; c. of garlic Knoblauchzehe f
clo′ven hoof′ [′klovən] s (as a sign of the devil) Pferdefuß m
clover [′klovər] s Klee m
clo′ver-leaf′ s (–leaves) Kleeblatt n
clown [klaun] s Clown m, Hanswurst m
clownish [′klaunɪʃ] adj närrisch
cloy [klɔɪ] tr übersättigen
club [klʌb] s (weapon) Keule f; (organization) Klub m; (cards) Kreuz n; (golf) Schläger m || (pret & pp clubbed; ger clubbing) tr verprügeln
club′ car′ s (rr) Salonwagen m
club′house′ s Klubhaus n
cluck [klʌk] s Glucken n || intr glucken
clue [klu] s Schlüssel m, Anhaltspunkt m
clump [klʌmp] s (of earth) Klumpen m; (of hair, grass) Büschel n; (of trees) Gruppe f; (heavy tramping sound) schwerer Tritt m; c. of bushes Gebüsch n || intr—c. along trapsen
clumsy [′klʌmzɪ] adj ungeschickt, plump; c. ox Tölpel m
cluster [′klʌstər] s (bunch growing together) Büschel n; (of grapes) Traube f; (group) Gruppe f || intr—c. around sich zusammendrängen um
clutch [klʌtʃ] s Griff m; (aut) Kupplung f; fall into s.o.'s clutches j—m in die Klauen geraten; let out the c. einkuppeln; step on the c. auskuppeln || tr packen
clutter [′klʌtər] s Durcheinander n || tr—c. up vollstopfen
Co. abbr (Company) Gesellschaft f
c/o abbr (care of) per Adresse, bei
coach [kotʃ] s Kutsche f; (rr) Personenwagen m; (sport) Trainer m || tr Nachhilfeunterricht geben (dat); (sport) trainieren || intr (sport) trainieren
coach′ing s Nachhilfeunterricht m; (sport) Training n
coach′man s (–men) Kutscher m

coagulate [ko′ægjə‚let] tr gerinnen lassen || intr gerinnen
coal [kol] s Kohle f
coal′bin′ s Kohlenkasten m
coal′-black′ adj kohlrabenschwarz
coal′ car′ s (rr) Kohlenwagen m
coal′deal′er s Kohlenhändler m
coalesce [‚ko·ə′les] intr zusammenwachsen, sich vereinigen
coalition [‚ko·ə′lɪʃən] s Koalition f
coal′ mine′ s Kohlenbergwerk n
coal′ min′ing s Kohlenbergbau m
coal′ oil′ s Petroleum n
coal′yard′ s Kohlenlager n
coarse [kors] adj (& fig) grob
coast [kost] s Küste f; the c. is clear (coll) die Luft ist rein || intr im Leerlauf fahren; c. along (fig) sich mühelos fortbewegen
coastal [′kostəl] adj küstennah, Küsten-
coaster [′kostər] s (for a glass) Untersatz m; (naut) Küstenfahrer m
coast′guard′ s Küstenwachdienst m
coast′line′ s Küstenlinie f
coat [kot] s (of a suit) Jacke f, Rock m; (topcoat) Mantel m; (of fur) Fell n; (of enamel, etc.) Belag m; (of paint) Anstrich m || tr (e.g., with teflon) beschichten; (e.g., with chocolate) überziehen; (e.g., with oil) beschmieren
coat′ed adj überzogen; (tongue) belegt
coat′ hang′er s Kleiderbügel m
coat′ing s Belag m, Überzug m
coat′ of arms′ s Wappen n
coat′rack′ s Kleiderständer m
coat′room′ s Garderobe f
coat′tail′ s Rockschoß m; (of formal wear) Frackschoß m
coauthor [′ko‚ɔθər] s Mitautor m
coax [koks] tr schmeicheln (dat); c. s.o. to (inf) j—n überreden zu (inf)
cob [kab] s Kolben m
cobalt [′kobɔlt] s Kobalt m
cobbler [′kablər] s Flickschuster m
cobblestone [′kabəl‚ston] s Pflasterstein m, Kopfstein m
cobra [′kobrə] s Kobra f
cob′web′ s Spinn(en)gewebe n
cocaine [ko′ken] s Kokain n
cock [kak] s Hahn m; (faucet) Wasserhahn m; (of a gun) Gewehrhahn m || tr (one's ears) spitzen; (one's hat) schief aufsetzen; (the firing mechanism) spannen
cock-a-doodle-doo [′kakə‚dudəl′du] s Kikeriki n
cock′-and-bull′ sto′ry s Lügengeschichte f
cockeyed [′kak‚aɪd] adj (cross-eyed) nach innen schielend; (slanted to one side) (sl) schief; (drunk) (sl) blau; (absurd) (sl) verrückt
cock′fight′ s Hahnenkampf m
cock′pit′ s Hahnenkampfplatz m; (aer) Kabine f, Kanzel f
cock′roach′ s Schabe f
cock′sure′ adj todsicher
cock′tail′ s Cocktail m
cock′tail dress′ s Cocktailkleid n
cock′tail par′ty s Cocktailparty f

cock′tail shak′er s Cocktailmischgefäß n

cocky [ˈkaki] adj (coll) frech

cocoa [ˈkoko] s Kakao m

coconut [ˈkokə‚nʌt] s Kokosnuß f

co′conut palm′, co′conut tree′ s Kokospalme f

cacoon [kəˈkun] s Kokon m

C.O.D., c.o.d. abbr (**cash on delivery**) per Nachnahme

cod [kad] s Kabeljau m

coddle [ˈkadəl] tr hätscheln

code [kod] s Geheimschrift f; (jur) Kodex m || tr verschlüsseln, chiffrieren

codefendant [‚kodɪˈfɛndənt] s Mitangeklagte mf

code′ name′ s Deckname m

code′ of hon′or s Ehrenkodex m

code′ of laws′ s Gesetzsammlung f

code′ word′ s Kennwort n

codex [ˈkodɛks] s (**codices** [ˈkodɪ‚siz]) Kodex m

cod′fish′ s Kabeljau m

codicil [ˈkadɪsɪl] s Kodizill n

codi·fy [ˈkodɪ‚faɪ] v (pret & pp **–fied**) tr kodifizieren

cod′-liver oil′ s Lebertran m

coed, co-ed [ˈko‚ɛd] s Studentin f

coeducation [‚ko‚ɛdʒəˈkeʃən] s Koedukation f

coeducational [‚ko‚ɛdʒəˈkeʃənəl] adj Koedukations–

coefficient [‚ko·ɪˈfɪʃənt] s Koeffizient m

coerce [koˈʌrs] tr zwingen

coercion [koˈʌrʃən] s Zwang m

coexist [‚ko·ɪgˈzɪst] intr koexistieren

coexistence [‚ko·ɪgˈzɪstəns] s Koexistenz f

coffee [ˈkɔfi] s Kaffee m

cof′fee bean′ s Kaffeebohne f

cof′fee break′ s Kaffeepause f

cof′fee fiend′ s Kaffeetante f

cof′fee grounds′ spl Kaffeesatz m

cof′fee pot′ s Kaffeekanne f

cof′fee shop′ s Kaffeestube f

coffer [ˈkɔfər] s Truhe f; (archit) Deckenfeld n; **coffers** Schatzkammer

cof′ferdam′ s (caisson) Kastendamm m; (naut) Kofferdamm m

coffin [ˈkɔfɪn] s Sarg m

cog [kag] s Zahn m; (cogwheel) Zahnrad n

cogency [ˈkodʒənsi] s Beweiskraft f

cogent [ˈkodʒənt] adj triftig

cognac [ˈkonjæk], [ˈkɑnjæk] s Kognak m

cognizance [ˈkɑgnɪzəns] s Kenntnis f; **take c. of s.th.** etw zur Kenntnis nehmen

cognizant [ˈkɑgnɪzənt] adj—**be c. of** Kenntnis haben von

cog′wheel′ s Zahnrad m

cohabit [koˈhæbɪt] intr in wilder Ehe leben

coheir [koˈɛr] s Miterbe m, Miterbin f

cohere [koˈhɪr] intr zusammenhängen

cohesion [koˈhiʒən] s Kohäsion f

coiffeur [kwaˈfʌr] s Friseur m

coiffure [kwaˈfjur] s Frisur f

coil [kɔɪl] s (something wound in a

spiral) Spirale f, Rolle f; (of tubing) Schlange f; (single wind) Windung f; (elec) Spule f || tr aufrollen; (naut) aufschießen || intr—**c. up** sich zusammenrollen

coil′ spring′ s Spiralfeder f

coin [kɔɪn] s Münze f, Geldstück n || tr münzen, (& fig) prägen

coinage [ˈkɔɪnɪdʒ] s (minting) Prägen n; (coins collectively) Münzen pl; (fig) Prägung f

coincide [‚ko·ɪnˈsaɪd] intr (with) zusammentreffen (mit); (in time) (with) gleichzeitig geschehen (mit)

coincidence [koˈɪnsɪdəns] s Zufall m; **by mere c.** rein zufällig

coin′ machine′ s Münzautomat m

coin′ slot′ s Münzeinwurf m

coition [koˈɪ/ən], **coitus** [ˈko·ɪtəs] s Koitus m, Beischlaf m

coke [kok] s Koks m; (coll) Coca-Cola n

colander [ˈkʌləndər] s Sieb n

cold [kold] adj kalt || s Kälte f; (indisposition) Erkältung f

cold′ blood′ s—**in c.** kaltblütig

cold′-blood′ed adj kaltblütig

cold′ cream′ s Cold Cream n

cold′ cuts′ spl kalter Aufschnitt m

cold′ feet′ spl—**have c.** (fig) Angst haben

cold′ front′ s Kaltfront f

cold′-heart′ed adj kaltherzig

coldness [ˈkoldnɪs] s Kälte f

cold′ should′er s—**give s.o. the c.** j–m die kalte Schulter zeigen

cold′ snap′ s plötzlicher Kälteeinbruch m

cold′ stor′age s Lagerung f im Kühlraum

cold′ war′ s kalter Krieg m

cold′ wave′ s (meteor) Kältewelle f

coleslaw [ˈkol‚slɔ] s Krautsalat m

colic [ˈkalɪk] s Kolik f

coliseum [‚kalɪˈsi·əm] s Kolosseum n

collaborate [kəˈlæbə‚ret] intr mitarbeiten; (pol) kollaborieren

collaboration [kə‚læbəˈreʃən] s Mitarbeit f; (pol) Kollaboration f

collaborator [kəˈlæbə‚retər] s Mitarbeiter –in mf; (pol) Kollaborateur m

collapse [kəˈlæps] s (of a bridge, etc.) Einsturz m; (com) Krach m; (pathol) Zusammenbruch m, Kollaps m || intr einstürzen; (fig) zusammenbrechen

collapsible [kəˈlæpsɪbəl] adj zusammenklappbar

collaps′ible boat′ s Faltboot n

collar [ˈkalər] s Kragen m; (of a dog) Halsband n; (of a horse) Kummet n; (mach) Ring m, Kragen m

col′larbone′ s Schlüsselbein n

collate [kəˈlet] tr kollationieren

collateral [kəˈlætərəl] adj kollateral, Seiten– || s (fin) Deckung f

collation [kəˈleʃən] s Kollation f

colleague [ˈkalig] s Kollege m, Kollegin f

collect [ˈkalɛkt] s (eccl) Kollekte f || [kəˈlɛkt] adj—**make a c. call** ein R-

Gespräch führen || adv—call c. ein R-Gespräch führen; send c. gegen Nachnahme schicken || tr (money) (ein)kassieren; (stamps, coins) sammeln; (e.g., examination papers) einsammeln; (taxes) abheben; (one's thoughts) zusammennehmen; c. oneself sich fassen || intr sich (ver)sammeln; (pile up) sich anhäufen

collect'ed adj (works) gesammelt; (self-possessed) gefaßt

collection [kə'lɛkʃən] s (of stamps, etc.) Sammlung f; (accumulation) Ansammlung f; (of money) Einziehung f; (in a church) Kollekte f; (of mail) Leerung f des Briefkastens; (com) Kollektion f

collec'tion a'gency s Inkassobüro n

collec'tion bas'ket s Klingelbeutel m

collective [kə'lɛktɪv] adj kollektiv, Sammel-, Gesamt- || s (pol) Kollektiv n

collec'tive bar'gaining s Tarifverhandlungen pl

collec'tive farm' s Kolchose f

collector [kə'lɛktər] s (e.g., of stamps) Sammler –in mf; (bill collector) Einkassierer –in mf; (of taxes) Einnehmer –in mf; (of tickets) Fahrkartenabnehmer –in mf

college ['kɑlɪdʒ] s College n; (e.g., of cardinals) Kollegium n

collide [kə'laɪd] intr zusammenstoßen

collie ['kɑli] s Collie m

collision [kə'lɪʒən] s Zusammenstoß m

colloquial [kə'lokwɪ·əl] adj umgangssprachlich, Umgangs-

colloquialism [kə'lokwɪ·ə‚lɪzəm] s Ausdruck m der Umgangssprache

colloquy ['kɑləkwi] s Gespräch n

collusion [kə'luʒən] s Kollusion f; be in c. kolludieren

colon ['kolən] s (anat) Dickdarm m; (gram) Doppelpunkt m

colonel ['kʌrnəl] s Oberst m

colonial [kə'lonɪ·əl] adj Kolonial- || s Einwohner –in mf e-r Kolonie

colonialism [kə'lonɪ·ə‚lɪzəm] s Kolonialismus m

colonize ['kɑlə‚naɪz] tr besiedeln

colonnade [‚kɑlə'ned] s Säulengang m

colony ['kɑləni] s Kolonie f

color ['kʌlər] adj (film, photo, photography, slide, television) Farb- || s Farbe f; lend c. to beleben; show one's colors sein wahres Gesicht zeigen; the colors die Flagge; with flying colors glänzend || tr färben; (fig) (schön)färben || intr sich verfärben; (become red) erröten

col'or-blind' adj farbenblind

col'ored adj farbig

col'or-fast' adj farbecht

colorful ['kʌlərfəl] adj bunt, farbenreich; (fig) farbig

col'oring s Kolorit n, Färbung f

col'oring book' s Malbuch n

colorless ['kʌlərlɪs] adj farblos

col'or ser'geant s Fahnenträger m

colossal [kə'lɑsəl] adj kolossal

colossus [kə'lɑsəs] s Koloß m

colt [kolt] s Füllen n

Columbus [kə'lʌmbəs] s Kolumbus m

column ['kɑləm] s Säule f; (syndicated article) Kolumne f; (mil) Kolonne f; (typ) Spalte f, Rubrik f; c. of smoke Rauchsäule f

columnist ['kɑləmɪst] s Kolumnist –in mf

coma ['komə] s Koma n

comb [kom] s Kamm m; (honeycomb) Wabe f; (of a rooster) Kamm m || tr kämmen; (an area) absuchen

com·bat ['kɑmbæt] (e.g., pilot, strength, unit, zone) Kampf- || s Kampf m, Streit m || ['kɑmbæt], [kəm'bæt] v (pret & pp –bat[t]ed; ger –bat[t]ing) tr bekämpfen || intr kämpfen

combatant ['kɑmbətənt] s Kämpfer –in mf

com'bat fatigue' s Kriegsneurose f

combative ['kɑmbətɪv] adj streitsüchtig

comber ['komər] s Sturzwelle f

combination [‚kɑmbɪ'neʃən] s Verbindung f; (com) Konzern m

combine ['kɑmbaɪn] s (agr) Mähdrescher m; (com) Interessengemeinschaft f || [kəm'baɪn] tr kombinieren, verbinden

combustible [kəm'bʌstɪbəl] adj (ver)brennbar || s Brennstoff m

combustion [kəm'bʌstʃən] s Verbrennung f

combus'tion cham'ber s Brennkammer f

combus'tion en'gine s Verbrennungsmaschine f

come [kʌm] v (pret came [kem]; pp come) intr kommen; c. about geschehen, sich ereignen; c. across (discover) stoßen auf (acc); (said of a speech, etc.) ankommen; c. across with (coll) blechen; c. after folgen (dat); (fetch) holen kommen; c. along mitkommen; (coll) vorwärtskommen; c. apart auseinanderfallen; c. around herumkommen; (said of a special day) wiederkehren; (improve) wieder zu sich kommen; (change one's view) von e-r Ansicht abgehen; c. back zurückkehren; (recur to the mind) wieder einfallen; c. between treten zwischen (acc); c. by vorbeikommen; (acquire) geraten an (acc); c. clean (sl) mit der Wahrheit herausrücken; c. down (said of prices) sinken; (& fig) herunterkommen; c. down with erkranken an (dat); c. first (have priority) zuerst an die Reihe kommen; c. for abholen; c. forward vortreten; c. from herkommen; (e.g., a rich family) stammen aus; (e.g., school) kommen aus; c. in hereinkommen; c. in for (coll) erhalten; c. in second den zweiten Platz belegen; c. off (said of a button) abgehen; (come loose) losgehen; (said of an event) verlaufen; c. on! los!; c. out herauskommen; (said of a spot) herausgehen; (said of a publication) erscheinen; c. out against (or for) sich erklären gegen (or für); c. over (said of fear, etc.) überlaufen; c. to (amount to) betragen; (*after fainting*) wieder zu sich kommen; **c. together** zusammenkommen; **c. up** (*occur*) vorkommen; (*said of a number*) herauskommen; (*said of plants*) aufgehen; (*in conversation*) zur Sprache kommen; (*said of a storm*) heranziehen; **c. upon** kommen auf (*acc*); **c. up to** entsprechen (*dat*); **for years to c.** auf Jahre hinaus; **how c.?** (coll) wieso?; **it comes easy to he** es fällt mir leicht

come′back′ *s* Comeback *n*

comedian [kə′midɪ·ən] *s* Komiker *m*; (pej) Komödiant –in *mf*

comedienne [kə‚midɪ′en] *s* Komikerin *f*

come′down′ *s* (coll) Abstieg *m*

comedy [′kamədɪ] *s* Komödie *f*

comely [′kʌmlɪ] *adj* anmutig

come′-on′ *s* (sl) Lockmittel *n*

comet [′kamɪt] *s* Komet *m*

comfort [′kʌmfərt] *s* (*solace*) Trost *m*; (*of a room, etc.*) Behaglichkeit *f*; (*person or thing that comforts*) Tröster *m*; (*bed cover*) Steppdecke *f* ‖ *tr* trösten

comfortable [′kʌmfərtəbəl] *adj* behaglich, bequem; (*income*) ausreichend; **be (or feel) c.** sich wohl fühlen

comforter [′kʌmfərtər] *s* Tröster *m*; (*bed cover*) Steppdecke *f*

com′forting *adj* tröstlich

com′fort sta′tion *s* Bedürfnisanstalt *f*

comic [′kamɪk] *adj* komisch ‖ *s* Komiker *m*; **comics** Comics *pl*, Witzblatt *n*

comical [′kamɪkəl] *adj* komisch

com′ic op′era *s* Operette *f*

com′ic strip′ *s* Bildstreifen *m*

com′ing *adj* künftig, kommend; **c. soon** (*notice at theater*) demnächst ‖ *s* Kommen *n*, Ankunft *f*; **c. of age** Mündigwerden *n*

comma [′kamə] *s* Komma *n*, Beistrich *m*

command [kə′mænd] *s* (*order*) Befehl *m*; (*of language*) Beherrschung *f*; (mil) Kommando *n*; (*jurisdiction*) (mil) Kommandobereich *m*; **at s.o.'s c.** auf j-s Befehl; **be in c. of** (mil) das Kommando führen über (*acc*); **have a good c. of** gut beherrschen; **take c. of** (mil) das Kommando übernehmen über (*acc*) ‖ *tr* (*a person*) befehlen (*dat*); (*respect, silence*) gebieten; (*troops*) führen; (*a high price*) erzielen ‖ *intr* (mil) kommandieren

commandant [‚kamən′dænt] *s* Kommandant *m*

commandeer [‚kamən′dɪr] *tr* (coll) organisieren; (mil) requirieren

commander [kə′mændər] *s* Truppenführer *m*; (*of a company*) Chef *m*; (*of a military unit from battalion to corps*) Kommandeur *m*; (*of an army*) Befehlshaber *m*; (nav) Fregattenkapitän *m*

comman′der in chief′ *s* Oberbefehlshaber *m*

command′ing *adj* (*appearance*) eindrucksvoll; (*view*) weit; (*position*) beherrschend; (*general*) kommandierend

command′ing of′ficer *s* Einheitsführer *m*

commandment [kə′mændmənt] *s* Gebot *n*

command′ post′ *s* Befehlsstand *m*

commemorate [kə′memə‚ret] *tr* gedenken (*genit*), feiern

commemoration [kə‚memə′reʃən] *s* Gedenkfeier *f*; **in c. of** zum Gedächtnis von

commence [kə′mens] *tr & intr* anfangen

commencement [kə′mensmənt] *s* Anfang *m*; (educ) Schulentlassungsfeier *f*

commend [kə′mend] *tr* (*praise*) (& mil) belob(ig)en; (*entrust*) empfehlen

commendable [kə′mendəbəl] *adj* lobenswert

commendation [‚kamən′deʃən] *s* Belobigung *f*

comment [′kamənt] *s* Bemerkung *f*, Stellungnahme *f*; **no c.!** kein Kommentar! ‖ *intr* Bemerkungen machen; **c. on** kommentieren

commentary [′kamən‚terɪ] *s* Kommentar *m*

commentator [′kamən‚tetər] *s* Kommentator –in *mf*; (*of a text*) Erklärer –in *mf*

commerce [′kamərs] *s* Handel *m*

commercial [kə′marʃəl] *adj* Handels-, Geschäfts-, kommerziell ‖ *s* (rad, telv) Werbesendung *f*

commer′cial art′ *s* Gebrauchsgraphik *f*

commercialism [kə′marʃə‚lɪzəm] *s* Handelsgeist *m*

commercialize [kə′marʃə‚laɪz] *tr* kommerzialisieren

commiserate [kə′mɪzə‚ret] *intr*—**c. with** bemitleiden

commissar [′kamɪ‚sar] *s* (pol) Kommissar *m*

commissary [′kamɪ‚serɪ] *s* (*deputy*) Kommissar *m*; (*store*) Militärversorgungsstelle *f*

commission [kə′mɪʃən] *s* (*order*) Auftrag *m*; (*of a crime*) Begehung *f*; (*committee*) Kommission *f*; (*percentage*) Provision *f*; (mil) Offizierspatent *n*; **out of c.** außer Betrieb; ‖ *tr* beauftragen; (*a work*) bestellen; (*a ship*) in Dienst stellen; (mil) ein Offizierspatent verleihen (*dat*)

commis′sioned of′ficer *s* Offizier –in *mf*

commissioner [kə′mɪʃənər] *s* Kommissar –in *mf*

com·mit [kə′mɪt] *v* (*pret & pp* –mitted; *ger* –mitting) *tr* (*a crime*) begehen; (*entrust*) anvertrauen; (*give over*) übergeben; (*to an institution*) einweisen; **c. oneself to** sich festlegen auf (*acc*); **c. to memory** auswendig lernen; **c. to writing** zu Papier bringen

commitment [kə′mɪtmənt] *s* (**to**) Festlegung *f* (*auf acc*); (*to an asylum*) Anstaltsüberweisung *f*

committee [kə′mɪtɪ] *s* Ausschuß *m*

commode [kə′mod] *s* Kommode *f*

commodious [kə'modɪ·əs] *adj* geräumig

commodity [kə'madɪtɪ] *s* Ware *f*

common ['kamən] *adj* (*language, property, interest*) gemeinsam; (*general*) allgemein; (*people*) einfach; (*soldier*) gemein; (*coarse, vulgar*) gemein; (*frequent*) häufig || *s*—**in c.** gemeinsam

com'mon denom'inator *s* gemeinsamer Nenner *m*; **reduce to a** c. auf e-n gemeinsamen Nenner bringen

commoner ['kamənər] *s* Bürger –in *mf*

com'mon-law mar'riage *s* wilde Ehe *f*

Com'mon Mar'ket *s* Gemeinsamer Markt *m*

com'mon noun' *s* Gattungsname *m*

com'monplace' *adj* alltäglich || *s* Gemeinplatz *m*

com'mon sense' *s* gesunder Menschenverstand *m*

com'mon stock' *s* Stammaktien *pl*

commonweal ['kamən,wil] *s* Gemeinwohl *n*

com'monwealth' *s* (*republic*) Republik *f*; (*state in U.S.A.*) Bundesstaat *m*

commotion [kə'moʃən] *s* Aufruhr *m*

commune ['kamjun] *s* Kommune *f* || [kə'mjun] *intr* sich vertraulich besprechen

communicable [kə'mjunɪkəbəl] *adj* übertragbar

communicant [kə'mjunɪkənt] *s* Kommunikant –in *mf*

communicate [kə'mjunɪ,ket] *tr* mitteilen; (*a disease*) (**to**) übertragen (auf *acc*) || *intr* sich besprechen

communication [kə,mjunɪ'keʃən] *s* Mitteilung *f*; (*message*) Nachricht *f*; **communications** Nachrichtenwesen *n*; (mil) Fernmeldewesen *n*

communicative [kə'mjunɪ,ketɪv] *adj* mitteilsam

communion [kə'mjunjən] *s* Gemeinschaft *f*; (Prot) Abendmahl *n*; (R. C.) Kommunion *f*

commun'ion rail' *s* Altargitter *n*

communiqué [kə,mjunɪ'ke] *s* Kommuniqué *n*

communism ['kamjə,nɪzəm] *s* Kommunismus *m*

communist ['kamjənɪst] *s* kommunistisch *s* Kommunist –in *mf*

community [kə'mjunɪtɪ] *s* Gemeinschaft *f*; (*people living together*) Gemeinde *f*

communize ['kamjə,naɪz] *tr* kommunistisch machen

commutation [,kamjə'teʃən] *s* (jur) Umwandlung *f*

commuta'tion tick'et *s* Zeitkarte *f*

commutator ['kamjə,tetər] *s* (elec) Kommutator *m*, Kollektor *m*

commute ['kamjut] *tr* (jur) umwandeln || *intr* pendeln

commuter [kə'mjutər] *s* Pendler –in *mf*

commut'er train' *s* Pendelzug *m*

compact [kəm'pækt] *adj* kompakt, dicht || ['kampækt] *s* (*for cosmetics*) Kompaktdose *f*; (*agreement*) Vertrag *m*; (aut) Kompaktwagen *m*

companion [kəm'pænjən] *s* Kumpan –in *mf*; (*one who accompanies*) Begleiter –in *mf*

companionable [kə'pænjənəbəl] *adj* gesellig

compan'ionship' *s* Gesellschaft *f*

compan'ionway' *s* Kajütstreppe *f*

company ['kʌmpənɪ] *s* (*companions*) Umgang *m*; (& com) Gesellschaft *f*; (mil) Kompanie *f*; (theat) Truppe *f*; **keep c. with** verkehren mit; **keep s.o. c.** j–m Gesellschaft leisten

com'pany command'er *s* Kompaniechef *m*

comparable ['kampərəbəl] *adj* vergleichbar

comparative [kəm'pærətɪv] *adv* vergleichend; (gram) komparativ || *s* (gram) Komparativ *m*

comparatively [kəm'pærətɪvlɪ] *adv* verhältnismäßig

compare [kəm'per] *s*—**beyond c.** unvergleichlich || *tr* (**with, to**) vergleichen (mit); (gram) steigern; **as compared with** im Vergleich zu

comparison [kəm'pærɪsən] *s* Vergleich *m*; (gram) Steigerung *f*

compartment [kəm'partmənt] *s* Fach *n*; (rr) Abteil *n*

compass ['kʌmpəs] *s* Kompaß *m*; (geom) Zirkel *m*; **within the c. of** innerhalb (*genit*)

com'pass card' *s* Kompaßrose *f*

compassion [kəm'pæʃən] *s* Mitleid *n*

compassionate [kəm'pæʃənɪt] *adj* mitleidig

compatible [kəm'pætɪbəl] *adj* vereinbar

com·pel [kəm'pel] *v* (*pret & pp* **–pelled;** *ger* **–pelling**) *tr* zwingen, nötigen

compendious [kəm'pendɪ·əs] *adj* gedrängt

compendi·um [kəm'pendɪ·əm] *s* (**–ums** & **–a** [ə]) Abriß *m*, Kompendium *n*

compensate ['kampən,set] *tr* entschädigen || *intr*—**c. for** Ersatz leisten (or bieten) für

compensation [,kampən'seʃən] *s* (*for damages*) Entschädigung *f*; (*remuneration*) Entgeld *n*

compete [kəm'pit] *intr* (**with**) konkurrieren (mit); (**for**) sich mitbewerben (um); (sport) am Wettkampf teilnehmen

competence ['kampɪtəns] *s* (*mental state*) Zurechnungsfähigkeit *f*; (*ability*) (**in**) Fähigkeit *f* (zu)

competent ['kampɪtənt] *adj* (*able*) fähig, tüchtig; (*witness*) zulässig

competition [,kampɪ'tɪʃən] *s* Wettbewerb *m*; (com) Konkurrenz *f*; (sport) Wettkampf *m*

competitive [kəm'petɪtɪv] *adj* (*bidding*) Konkurrenz–; (*prices*) konkurrenzfähig; (*person*) ehrgeizig; (*exam*) Auslese–

competitor [kəm'petɪtər] *s* Mitbewerber –in *mf*; (com) Konkurrent –in *mf*; (sport) Wettkämpfer –in *mf*

compilation [,kampɪ'leʃən] *s* Zusammenstellung *f*; (*book*) Sammelwerk *n*

compile [kəm'paɪl] *tr* zusammenstellen, kompilieren; (*Material*) zusammentragen

complacence [kəm'pleɪsəns], **complacency** [kəm'pleɪsənsi] *s* Selbstgefälligkeit *f*

complacent [kəm'pleɪsənt] *adj* selbstgefällig

complain [kəm'pleɪn] *intr* klagen; **c. to s.o. about** sich bei j-m beklagen über (*acc*)

complaint [kəm'pleɪnt] *s* Klage *f*; (*ailment*) Beschwerde *f*

complement ['kamplɪmənt] *s* (& *gram*) Ergänzung *f*; (*geom*) Komplement *n*; (*nav*) Bemannung *f* || ['kamplɪ,ment] *tr* ergänzen

complete [kəm'plit] *adj* ganz, vollkommen, vollständig; (*works*) sämtlich || *tr* (*make whole*) vervollständigen; (*make perfect*) vollenden; (*finish*) beenden; (*a job*) erledigen

completely [kəm'plitli] *adv* völlig

completion [kəm'pliʃən] *s* Vollendung *f*

complex [kəm'pleks], ['kampleks] *adj* verwickelt || ['kampleks] *s* Komplex *m*

complexion [kəm'plekʃən] *s* Gesichtsfarbe *f*; (*appearance*) Aussehen *n*

complexity [kəm'pleksɪti] *s* Kompliziertheit *f*

compliance [kəm'plaɪəns] *s* Einwilligung *f*; **in c. with your wishes** Ihren Wünschen gemäß

complicate ['kamplɪ,ket] *tr* komplizieren

com'plicat'ed *adj* kompliziert

complication [,kamplɪ'keʃən] *s* Verwicklung *f*; (& *pathol*) Komplikation *f*

complicity [kəm'plɪsɪti] *s* (**in**) Mitschuld *f* (**an** *dat*)

compliment ['kamplɪmənt] *s* Kompliment *n*; (*praise*) Lob *n*; **compliments** Empfehlungen *pl*; **pay s.o. a (high) c.** j-m ein (großes) Lob spenden || *tr* (**on**) beglückwünschen (zu)

complimentary [,kamplɪ'mentəri] *adj* (*remark*) schmeichelhaft; (*free*) Frei-

com·ply [kəm'plaɪ] *v* (*pret & pp* **-plied**) *intr* sich fügen; **c. with** einwilligen in (*acc*); **c. with the rules** sich an die Vorschriften halten

component [kəm'ponənt] *adj* Teil- || *s* Bestandteil *m*; (*math, phys*) Komponente *f*

compose [kəm'poz] *tr* (*writings*) verfassen; (*a sentence*) bilden; (*mus*) komponieren; (*typ*) setzen; **be composed of** bestehen aus; **c. oneself** sich fassen

composed' *adj* ruhig, gefaßt

composer [kəm'pozər] *s* Verfasser –in *mf*; (*mus*) Komponist –in *mf*

composite [kəm'pazɪt] *adj* zusammengesetzt || *s* Zusammensetzung *f*

composition [,kampə'zɪʃən] *s* (*chem*) Zusammensetzung *f*; (*educ*) Aufsatz *m*; (*mus, paint*) Komposition *f*; (*typ*) Schriftsatz *m*

composi'tion book' *s* Übungsheft *n*

compositor [kəm'pazɪtər] *s* Setzer –in *mf*

composure [kəm'poʒər] *s* Fassung *f*

compote ['kampot] *s* (*stewed fruit*) Kompott *n*; (*dish*) Kompottschale *f*

compound ['kampaund] *adj* zusammengesetzt; (*fracture*) kompliziert || *s* Zusammensetzung *f*; (*enclosure*) umzäuntes Gelände *n*; (*chem*) Verbindung *f*; (*gram*) Kompositum *n*; (*mil*) Truppenlager *n* || [kam'paund] *tr* zusammensetzen

com'pound in'terest *s* Zinseszinsen *pl*

comprehend [,kamprɪ'hend] *tr* auffassen

comprehensible [,kamprɪ'hensɪbəl] *adj* faßlich, begreiflich

comprehension [,kamprɪ'henʃən] *s* Auffassung *f*; (*ability to understand*) Fassungskraft *f*

comprehensive [,kamprɪ'hensɪv] *adj* umfassend

compress ['kampres] *s* (*med*) Kompresse *f* || [kəm'pres] *tr* komprimieren

compressed' *adj* komprimiert; (*air*) Druck-; (*fig*) gedrängt

compression [kəm'preʃən] *s* Kompression *f*, Druck *m*

comprise [kəm'praɪz] *tr* umfassen; **be comprised of** bestehen aus

compromise ['kamprə,maɪz] *s* Kompromiß *m* || *tr* kompromittieren; (*principles*) preisgeben || *intr* (**on**) e-n Kompromiß schließen (über *acc*)

comptroller [kəm'trolər] *s* Rechnungsprüfer *m*

compulsion [kəm'pʌlʃən] *s* Zwang *m*

compulsive [kəm'pʌlsɪv] *adj* triebhaft

compulsory [kəm'pʌlsəri] *adj* obligatorisch, Zwangs-; **c. military service** allgemeine Wehrpflicht *f*

compute [kəm'pjut] *tr* berechnen || *intr* rechnen

computer [kəm'pjutər] *s* Computer *m*

comput'er lan'guage *s* Maschinensprache *f*

comrade ['kamræd] *s* Kamerad *m*

con [kan] *v* (*pret & pp* **conned**; *ger* **conning**) *tr* beschwindeln

concave [kan'kev] *adj* konkav

conceal [kən'sil] *tr* verheimlichen

concealment [kən'silmənt] *s* Verheimlichung *f*; (*place*) Versteck *n*

concede [kən'sid] *tr* zugestehen, zubilligen; **c. victory** (pol) den Wahlsieg überlassen || *intr* nachgeben

conceit [kən'sit] *s* (*vanity*) Einbildung *f*, Dünkel *m*; (*witty expression*) Witz *m*

conceit'ed *adj* eingebildet

conceivable [kən'sivəbəl] *adj* denkbar

conceive [kən'siv] *tr* begreifen; (*a desire*) hegen; (*a child*) empfangen

concentrate ['kansən,tret] *tr* konzentrieren; (*troops*) zusammenziehen || *intr* (**on**) sich konzentrieren (auf *acc*); (*gather*) sich sammeln

concentration [,kansən'treʃən] *s* Konzentration *f*

concentric [kən'sentrɪk] *adj* konzentrisch

concept ['kansept] *s* Begriff *m*

conception [kən'sepʃən] s (idea) Vorstellung f; (design) Entwurf m; (biol) Empfängnis f

concern [kən'sʌrn] s (worry) Besorgnis f; (matter) Angelegenheit f; (com) Firma f; that is no c. of mine das geht mich nichts an || tr betreffen, angehen; as far as I am concerned von mir aus; c. oneself about sich bekümmern um; c. oneself with sich befassen mit; to whom it may c. Bescheinigung

concern'ing prep betreffend (acc), betreffs (genit), über (acc)

concert ['kansərt] s (mus) Konzert n; in c. (with) im Einvernehmen (mit) || [kən'sʌrt] tr zusammenfassen

concession [kən'seʃən] s Konzession f

conciliate [kən'sɪlɪ,et] tr versöhnen

conciliatory [kən'sɪlɪ-ə,tori] adj versöhnlich

concise [kən'sais] adj kurz, bündig

conclude [kən'klud] tr schließen; c. from s.th. that aus etw schließen, daß; to be concluded Schluß folgt || intr (with) schließen (mit)

conclusion [kən'kluʒən] s Schluß m; draw conclusions from Schlüsse ziehen aus; in c. zum Schluß; jump at conclusions voreilige Schlüsse ziehen

conclusive [kən'klusɪv] adj (decisive) entscheidend; (proof) schlagkräftig

concoct [kən'kakt] tr (brew) zusammenbrauen; (plans) schmieden

concoction [kən'kakʃən] s Gebräu n

concomitant [kən'kamitənt] adj begleitend || s Begleitumstand m

concord ['kaŋkərd] s Eintracht f

concordance [kən'kərdəns] s Übereinstimmung f; (book) Konkordanz f

concourse ['kankors] s (of people) Zusammenlaufen n, Anlauf m; (of rivers) Zusammenfluß m; (rr) Bahnhofshalle f

concrete ['kankrit], [kan'krit] adj (not abstract) konkret; (solid) fest; (evidence) schlüssig; (of concrete) Beton–; (math) benannt || s Beton m || tr betonieren

con'crete block' s Betonblock m

con'crete noun' s Konkretum n

concubine ['kaŋkjə,bain] s Nebenfrau f; (mistress) Konkubine f

con-cur [kən'kʌr] v (pret & pp –curred; ger –curring) intr (agree) übereinstimmen; (coincide) (with) zusammenfallen (mit); c. in (an opinion) beistimmen (dat)

concurrence [kən'kʌrəns] s (agreement) Einverständnis n; (coincidence) Zusammentreffen n; (geom) Schnittpunkt m

condemn [kən'dem] tr verdammen; (& jur) verurteilen; (a building) für unbewohnlich erklären

condemnation [,kandem'neʃən] s Verurteilung f; (of a building, ship, plane) Untauglichkeitserklärung f

condense [kən'dens] tr (make thicker) verdichten; (writing) zusammendrängen; || intr kondensieren

condenser [kən'densər] s Kondensator m

condescend [,kandi'send] intr sich herablassen

condescend'ing adj herablassend

condescension [,kandi'senʃən] s Herablassung f

condiment ['kandimənt] s Würze f

condition [kən'dɪʃən] s (state) Zustand m; (state of health) Verfassung f; (stipulation) Bedingung f; conditions (e.g. for working; of the weather) Verhältnisse pl; on c. that unter der Bedingung, daß || tr (impose stipulations on) bedingen; (accustom) (to) gewöhnen (an acc); (sport) in Form bringen

conditional [kən'dɪʃənəl] adj bedingt

condi'tional clause' s Bedingungssatz m

conditionally [kən'dɪʃənəli] adv bedingungsweise

condole [kən'dol] intr (with) kondolieren (dat)

condolence [kən'doləns] s Beileid n

condom ['kandəm] s Präservativ n

condominium [,kandə'mɪni-əm] s Eigentumswohnung f

condone [kən'don] tr verzeihen

conducive [kən'd(j)usɪv] adj—c. to förderlich (dat)

conduct ['kandʌkt] s (behavior) Betragen n; (guidance) Führung f || [kən'dʌkt] tr (business, a campaign, a tour) führen; (elec, phys) leiten; (mus) dirigieren; c. oneself sich betragen || intr (mus) dirigieren

conductor [kən'dʌktər] s (elec, phys) Leiter m; (mus) Dirigent m; (rr) Schaffner m

conduit ['kand(ʊ)ɪt] s Röhre f; (elec) Isolierrohr n

cone [kon] s (ice cream cone; paper cone) Tüte f; (bot) Zapfen m; (geom) Kegel m, Konus m

confection [kən'fekʃən] s Konfekt n

confectioner [kən'fekʃənər] s Zuckerbäcker –in mf

confec'tioner's sug'ar s Puderzucker m

confectionery [kən'fekʃə,neri] s (shop) Konditorei f; (sweets) Zuckerwerk n

confederacy [kən'fedərəsi] s Bündnis n; (conspiracy) Verschwörung f

confederate [kən'fedərit] adj verbündet || s Bundesgenosse m, Bundesgenossin f; (accomplice) Helfershelfer –in mf || [kən'fedə,ret] tr verbünden || intr sich verbünden

confederation [kən,fedə'reʃən] s Bund m

con-fer [kən'fʌr] v (pret & pp –ferred; ger –ferring) tr (on, upon) verleihen (dat) || intr sich besprechen, konferieren

conference ['kanfərəns] s Konferenz f; (sport) Verband m

con'ference call' s Sammelverbindung f

confess [kən'fes] tr (ein)gestehen, bekennen; (sins) beichten || intr gestehen

confession [kən'feʃən] s Geständnis n, Bekenntnis n; (of sins) Beichte f; go to c. beichten

confessional [kən'feʃənəl] s Beicht-stuhl m

confes'sion of faith' s Glaubensbe-kenntnis n

confessor [kən'fesər] s Beichtvater m

confidant [,kʌnfɪ'dænt] s Vertraute mf

confide [kən'faɪd] tr (to) anvertrauen (dat) ‖ intr—c. in vertrauen (dat)

confidence ['kʌnfɪdəns] s (trust) (in) Vertrauen n (auf acc, zu); (assurance) Zuversicht f; **in c.** im Vertrauen

con'fidence man' s Bauernfänger m

confident ['kʌnfɪdənt] adj zuversichtlich; **be c. of** sich [dat] sicher sein (genit)

confidential [,kʌnfɪ'denʃəl] adj vertraulich

confine ['kʌnfaɪn] s—**the confines** die Grenzen pl ‖ tr [kən'faɪn] tr (limit) (to) beschränken (auf acc); (shut in) einsperren; **be confined** (in pregnancy) niederkommen; **be confined to bed** bettlägerig sein

confinement [kən'faɪnmənt] s Beschränkung f; (arrest) Haft f; (childbirth) Niederkunft f

confirm [kən'fʌrm] tr bestätigen; (Prot) konfirmieren; (R.C.) firmen; **confirm in writing** verbriefen

confirmation [,kʌnfər'meʃən] s Bestätigung f; (Prot) Konfirmation f; (R.C.) Firmung f

confirmed' adj (e.g., report) bestätigt; (inveterate) unverbesserlich; **c. bachelor** Hagestolz m

confiscate ['kʌnfɪs,ket] tr beschlagnahmen, konfiszieren

confiscation [,kʌnfɪs'keʃən] s Beschlagnahme f

conflagration [,kʌnflə'greʃən] s Brand m, Feuerbrunst f

conflict ['kʌnflɪkt] s (of interests, of evidence) Konflikt m; (fight) Zusammenstoß m ‖ [kən'flɪkt] intr (with) im Widerspruch stehen (zu)

conflict'ing adj einander widersprechend

con'flict of in'terest s Interessenkonflikt m, Interessenkollision f

confluence ['kʌnfluəns] s Zusammenfluß m

conform [kən'fɔrm] tr anpassen ‖ intr übereinstimmen; (to) sich anpassen (dat)

conformity [kən'fɔrmɪti] s (adaptation) (to) Anpassung f (an acc); (agreement) (with) Übereinstimmung f (mit)

confound [kən'faʊnd] tr (perplex) verblüffen; (throw into confusion) verwirren; (erroneously identify) (with) verwechseln (mit) ‖ ['kʌn'faʊnd] tr—**c. it!** zum Donnerwetter!

confound'ed adj (coll) verwünscht

confrere ['kʌnfrer] s Kollege m

confront [kən'frʌnt] tr (face) gegenüberstehen (dat); (a problem, an enemy) entgegentreten (dat); **be confronted with** gegenüberstehen (dat); **c. s.o. with** j-n konfrontieren mit

confrontation [,kʌnfrən'teʃən] s Konfrontation f; (of witnesses) Gegenüberstellung f

confuse [kən'fjuz] tr (e.g., names) verwechseln; (persons) verwirren

confused' adj konfus, verwirrt, wirr

confusion [kən'fjuʒən] s Verwechslung f; (disorder, chaos) Verwirrung f

confute [kən'fjut] tr widerlegen

congeal [kən'dʒil] tr erstarren lassen ‖ intr erstarren

congenial [kən'dʒinjəl] adj (person) sympathisch; (surroundings) angenehm

congenital [kən'dʒenɪtəl] adj angeboren

congen'ital de'fect s Geburtsfehler m

congest [kən'dʒest] tr überfüllen

congest'ed adj überfüllt; (area) übervölkert; (with traffic) verkehrsreich

congestion [kən'dʒestʃən] s Überfüllung f; (of traffic) Verkehrsstockung f; (of population) Übervölkerung f; (pathol) Blutandrang m

congratulate [kən'grætʃə,let] tr gratulieren (dat); **c. s.o. on** j-m gratulieren zu

congratulations [kən,grætʃə'leʃənz] spl Glückwunsch m; **c.!** ich gratuliere!

congregate ['kʌŋgrɪ,get] intr sich (ver)sammeln, zusammenkommen

congregation [,kʌŋgrɪ'geʃən] s Versammlung f; (eccl) Gemeinde f

congress ['kʌŋgres] s Kongreß m

congressional [kən'greʃənəl] adj Kongreß–

congress·man ['kʌŋgrɪsmən] s (-men) Abgeordnete m

con'gress·wom'an s (-wom'en) Abgeordnete f

congruent ['kʌŋgru·ənt] adj kongruent

conical ['kʌnɪkəl] adj kegelförmig

conjecture [kən'dʒekʃər] s Vermutung f, Mutmaßung f ‖ tr & intr vermuten

conjugal ['kʌndʒəgəl] adj ehelich

conjugate ['kʌndʒə,get] tr abwandeln

conjugation [,kʌndʒə'geʃən] s Abwandlung f

conjunction [kən'dʒʌŋkʃən] s Bindewort n; **in c. with** in Verbindung mit

conjure [kən'dʒur] tr (appeal solemnly to) beschwören ‖ ['kʌndʒər] tr—**c. away** wegzaubern; **c. up** heraufbeschwören

conk [kʌŋk] tr (sl) hauen ‖ intr—**c. out** (sl) versagen

connect [kə'nekt] tr verbinden; (& fig) verknüpfen; (elec) (to) anschließen (an acc); (telp) (with) verbinden (mit) ‖ intr verbunden sein; (said of trains, etc.) (with) Anschluß haben (an acc); (box) treffen

connect'ing adj Verbindungs–, Binde–; (trains, buses) Anschluß–; (rooms) mit Zwischentür

connect'ing rod' s Schubstange f

connection [kə'nekʃən] s (e.g., of a pipe) Verbindung f; (of ideas) Verknüpfung f; (context) Zusammenhang m; (part that connects) Verbindungsteil m; (elec) Schaltung f;

(mach, rr, telp) Verbindung *f*; connections Beziehungen *pl*; in c. with
in Zusammenhang mit

con'ning tow'er ['kɑnɪŋ] *s* Kommandoturm *m*

connive [kə'naɪv] *intr*—c. at ein Auge
zudrücken bei; c. with im geheimen
Einverständnis stehen mit

connotation [,kɑno'teʃən] *s* Nebenbedeutung *f*

connote [kə'not] *tr* mitbezeichnen

conquer ['kɑŋkər] *tr* (win in war) erobern; (overcome) überwinden

conquerer ['kɑŋkərər] *s* Eroberer *m*

conquest ['kɑŋkwest] *s* Eroberung *f*

conscience ['kɑnʃəns] *s* Gewissen *n*

conscientious [,kɑnʃɪ'enʃəs] *adj* ge-
wissenhaft, pflichtbewußt

conscien'tious objec'tor [əb'dʒektər]
s Wehrdienstverweigerer *m*

conscious ['kɑnʃəs] *adj* bei Bewußtsein; c. of bewußt (genit)

consciousness ['kɑnʃəsnɪs] *s* Bewußtsein *n*; (awareness) (of) Kenntnis *f*
(genit or von); regain c. wieder zu
sich kommen

conscript ['kɑnskrɪpt] *s* Dienstpflichtige *m*; (mil) Wehrdienstpflichtige
m || [kən'skrɪpt] *tr* ausheben

conscription [kən'skrɪpʃən] *s* Dienst-
pflicht *f*; (draft) Aushebung *f*

consecrate ['kɑnsɪ,kret] *tr* weihen

consecration [,kɑnsɪ'kreʃən] *s* Einweihung *f*; (at Mass) Wandlung *f*

consecutive [kən'sekjətɪv] *adj* aufeinanderfolgend

consensus [kən'sensəs] *s* allgemeine
Übereinstimmung *f*; the c. of opinion
die übereinstimmende Meinung

consent [kən'sent] *s* Zustimmung *f*; by
common c. mit allgemeiner Zustim-
mung || *intr* zustimmen; c. to (inf)
sich bereit erklären zu (inf)

consequence ['kɑnsɪ,kwens] *s* Folge
f; (influence) Einfluß *m*; in c. of
infolge (genit); it is of no c. es hat
nichts auf sich; suffer the consequences die Folgen tragen

consequently ['kɑnsɪ,kwentli] *adv*
folglich, infolgedessen, mithin

conservation [,kɑnsər'veʃən] *s* Bewahrung *f*; (of energy, etc.) Erhal-
tung *f*; (supervision of natural resources) Naturschutz *m*; (ecology)
Umweltschutz *m*

conservatism [kən'sʌrvə,tɪzəm] *s*
Konservatismus *m*

conservative [kən'sʌrvətɪv] *adj* kon-
servativ; (estimate) vorsichtig || *s*
Konservative *mf*

conservatory [kən'sʌrvə,tori] *s* Treibhaus *n*; (mus) Konservatorium *n*

conserve [kən'sʌrv] *tr* sparsam umgehen mit

consider [kən'sɪdər] *tr* (take into account) berücksichtigen; (show consideration for) Rücksicht nehmen
auf (acc); (reflect on) sich [dat]
überlegen; (regard as) halten für,
betrachten als; all things considered
in allem

considerable [kən'sɪdərəbəl] *adj* beträchtlich, erheblich

considerate [kən'sɪdərɪt] *adj* (towards) rücksichtsvoll (gegen)

consideration [kən,sɪdə'reʃən] *s* (taking into account) Berücksichtigung
f; (regard) (for) Rücksicht *f* (auf
acc); be an important c. e-e wich-
tige Rolle spielen; be under c. in
Betracht gezogen werden; for a c.
entgeltlich; in c. of in Anbetracht
(genit); take into c. in Betracht ziehen; with c. rücksichtsvoll

consid'ering *adv* (coll) den Umständen
nach || *prep* in Anbetracht (genit)

consign [kən'saɪn] *tr* (ship) versenden;
(address) adressieren

consignee [,kɑnsaɪ'ni] *s* Adressat –in
mf

consignment [kən'saɪnmənt] *s* (act of
sending) Versand *m*; (merchandise
sent) Sendung *f*; on c. in Kommission

consist [kən'sɪst] *intr*—c. in bestehen
in (dat); c. of bestehen aus

consistency [kən'sɪstənsi] *s* Konsequenz *f*; (firmness) Festigkeit *f*; (viscosity) Dickflüssigkeit *f*; (agreement) Übereinstimmung *f*; (stead-
fastness) (in) Beständigkeit *f* (in
dat)

consistent [kən'sɪstənt] *adj* (performer) stetig; (performance) gleichmäßig; (free from contradiction)
konsequent; c. with in Übereinstimmung mit

consistory [kən'sɪstəri] *s* Konsisto-
rium *n*

consolation [,kɑnsə'leʃən] *s* Trost *m*

console ['kɑnsol] *s* (for radio or record player) Musiktruhe *f*; (of an
organ) Spieltisch *m*; (television)
Fernsehtruhe *f* || [kən'sol] *tr* trösten

consolidate [kən'sɑlɪ,det] *tr* (a position) festigen; (debts) konsolidieren;
(combine) zusammenlegen

consonant ['kɑnsənənt] *adj* (with) im
Einklang *m* || *s* Mitlaut *m*

consort ['kɑnsɔrt] *s* (male) Gemahl *m*;
(female) Gemahlin *f* || [kən'sɔrt]
intr (with) Umgang haben (mit)

consorti·um [kən'sɔrtɪ·əm] *s* (-a [ə])
Konsortium *n*

conspicuous [kən'spɪkju·əs] *adj* auffallend, auffällig; c. for bemerkenswert wegen

conspiracy [kən'spɪrəsi] *s* Verschwörung *f*

conspirator [kən'spɪrətər] *s* Ver-
schwörer –in *mf*

conspire [kən'spaɪr] *intr* sich verschwören

constable ['kɑnstəbəl] *s* Gendarm *m*

constancy ['kɑnstənsi] *s* Beständigkeit
f

constant ['kɑnstənt] *adj* (continuous)
dauernd, ständig; (faithful) treu;
(resolute) standhaft; (element, time
element) fest; (fig & tech) konstant
|| *s* (math, phys) Konstante *f*

constantly ['kɑnstəntli] *adv* immerfort

constellation [,kɑnstə'leʃən] *s* Sternbild *n*

consternation [,kɑnstər'neʃən] *s* Bestürzung *f*

constipate ['kʌnstɪ‚pet] *tr* verstopfen
constipation [‚kʌnstɪ'peʃən] *s* Verstopfung *f*
constituency [kən'stɪt/ʊ‧ənsi] *s* Wählerschaft *f*
constituent [kən'stɪt/ʊ‧ənt] *adj* wesentlich; **c. part** Bestandteil *m* ‖ *s* Komponente *f*; (pol) Wähler –in *mf*
constitute ['kʌnstɪ‚t(j)ut] *tr* (*make up*) ausmachen, bilden; (*found*) gründen
constitution [‚kʌnstɪ't(j)uʃən] *s* (*of a country or organization*) Verfassung *f*; (*bodily condition*) Konstitution *f*; (*composition*) Zusammensetzung *f*
constitutional [‚kʌnstɪ't(j)uʃənəl] *adj* (*according to a constitution*) konstitutionell; (*crisis, amendment, etc.*) Verfassungs–
constrain [kən'stren] *tr* zwingen
constraint [kən'strent] *s* Zwang *m*; (jur) Nötigung *f*
constrict [kən'strɪkt] *tr* zusammenziehen
construct [kən'strʌkt] *tr* errichten; (eng, geom, gram) konstruieren
construction [kən'strʌkʃən] *s* (*act of building*) Errichtung *f*; (*manner of building*) Bauweise *f*; (*interpretation*) Auslegung *f*; (eng, geom, gram) Konstruktion *f*; **under c.** im Bau
constructive [kən'strʌktɪv] *adj* konstruktiv
construe [kən'stru] *tr* (*interpret*) auslegen; (gram) konstruieren
consul ['kʌnsəl] *s* Konsul *m*
consular ['kʌns(j)ələr] *adj* konsularisch
consulate ['kʌns(j)əlɪt] *s* Konsulat *n*
con′sul gen′eral *s* Generalkonsul *m*
consult [kən'sʌlt] *tr* konsultieren, um Rat fragen; (*a book*) nachschlagen ‖ *intr*–**c. with** sich beraten mit
consultant [kən'sʌltənt] *s* Berater –in *mf*
consultation [‚kʌnsəl'teʃən] *s* Beratung *f*; (& med) Konsultation *f*
consume [kən's(j)um] *tr* verzehren; (*use up*) verbrauchen; (*time*) beanspruchen
consumer [kən's(j)umər] *s* Konsument –in *mf*, Verbraucher –in *mf*
consum′er goods′ *spl* Konsumgüter *pl*
consummate [kən'sʌmɪt] *adj* vollendet; (pej) abgefeimt ‖ ['kʌnsə‚met] *tr* vollziehen
consumption [kən'sʌmpʃən] *s* (*of food*) Verzehr *m*; (econ) (**of**) Verbrauch *m* (an *dat*); (pathol) Schwindsucht *f*
consumptive [kə'sʌmptɪv] *adj* schwindsüchtig ‖ *s* Schwindsüchtige *mf*
contact ['kʌntækt] *s* Kontakt *m*, Berührung *f*; (fig) (**with**) Verbindung *f* (mit); (elec) Kontakt *m* ‖ *tr* (coll) sich in Verbindung setzen mit
con′tact lens′ *s* Haftschale *f*
contagion [kən'tedʒən] *s* Ansteckung *f*
contagious [kən'tedʒəs] *adj* ansteckend
contain [kən'ten] *tr* enthalten; (*an*

enemy) aufhalten; (*one′s feelings*) verhalten; **c. oneself** sich beherrschen
container [kən'tenər] *s* Behälter *m*
containment [kən'tenmənt] *s* (mil, pol) Eindämmung *f*
contaminate [kən'tæmɪ‚net] *tr* verunreinigen; (fig) vergiften
contamination [kən‚tæmɪ'neʃən] *s* Verunreinigung *f*; (fig) Vergiftung *f*
contemplate ['kʌntəm‚plet] *tr* betrachten; (*intend*) beabsichtigen ‖ *intr* nachdenken
contemplation [‚kʌntəm'pleʃən] *s* Betrachtung *f*; (*consideration*) Erwägung *f*
contemporaneous [kən‚tempə'renɪ‧əs] *adj* (**with**) gleichzeitig (mit)
contemporary [kən'tempə‚reri] *adj* zeitgenössisch; (*modern*) modern ‖ *s* Zeitgenosse *m*, Zeitgenossin *f*
contempt [kən'tempt] *s* Verachtung *f*; **beneath c.** unter aller Kritik
contemptible [kən'temptɪbəl] *adj* verachtungswürdig
contempt′ of court′ *s* Mißachtung *f* des Gerichtes
contemptuous [kən'temptʃʊ‧əs] *adj* verachtungsvoll, verächtlich
contend [kən'tend] *tr* behaupten ‖ *intr* (**for**) sich bewerben (um); (**with**) kämpfen (mit)
contender [kən'tendər] *s* (**for**) Bewerber –in *mf* (um)
content [kən'tent] *adj* (**with**) zufrieden (mit); **c. to** (*inf*) bereit zu (*inf*) ‖ *s* Zufriedenheit *f*; **to one′s heart′s c.** nach Herzenslust ‖ ['kʌntənt] *s* Inhalt *m*; (chem) Gehalt *m*; **contents** Inhalt *m* ‖ [kən'tent] *tr* zufriedenstellen; **c. oneself with** sich begnügen mit
content′ed *adj* zufrieden
contention [kən'tenʃən] *s* (*strife*) Streit *m*; (*assertion*) Behauptung *f*
contest ['kʌntest] *s* (**for**) Wettkampf *m* (um); (*written competition*) Preisausschreiben *n* ‖ [kən'test] *tr* (*argue against*) bestreiten; (*a will*) anfechten; (mil) kämpfen um; **contested** umstritten
contestant [kən'testənt] *s* Bewerber –in *mf*; (sport) Wettkämpfer –in *mf*
context ['kʌntekst] *s* Zusammenhang *m*
contiguous [kən'tɪgjʊ‧əs] *adj* einander berührend; (**to**) angrenzend (an *acc*)
continence ['kʌntɪnəns] *s* Enthaltsamkeit *f*
continent ['kʌntɪnənt] *adj* enthaltsam ‖ *s* Kontinent *m*
continental [‚kʌntɪ'nentəl] *adj* kontinental, Kontinental–
contingency [kən'tɪndʒənsi] *s* Zufall *m*
contingent [kən'tɪndʒənt] *adj* (**upon**) abhängig (von) ‖ *s* (mil) Kontingent *m*
continual [kən'tɪnjʊ‧əl] *adj* immer wiederkehrend
continuation [kən‚tɪnjʊ'eʃən] *s* Fortsetzung *f*; (*continued existence*) Fortdauer *f*
continue [kən'tɪnju] *tr* fortsetzen; **c.**

to (*inf*) fortfahren zu (*inf*); weiter–, e.g., **c. to read** weiterlesen; **to be continued** Fortsetzung folgt ‖ *intr* fortfahren; (*said of things*) anhalten

continuity [ˌkɑntɪ'n(j)u·ɪti] *s* Stetigkeit *f*

continuous [kən'tɪnju·əs] *adj* ununterbrochen, anhaltend

contortion [kən'tɔrʃən] *s* Verzerrung *f*

contour ['kɑntʊr] *s* Kontur *f*

con'tour line' *s* Schichtlinie *f*

con'tour map' *s* Landkarte *f* mit Schichtlinien

contraband ['kɑntrəˌbænd] *adj* Schmuggel– ‖ *s* Konterbande *f*, Schmuggelware *f*

contraceptive [ˌkɑntrə'sɛptɪv] *adj* empfängnisverhütend ‖ *s* Empfängnisverhütungsmittel *n*

contract ['kɑntrækt] *s* Vertrag *m*, Kontrakt *m*; (*order*) Auftrag *m* ‖ [kən'trækt] *tr* (*marriage*) abschließen; (*a disease*) sich [*dat*] zuziehen; (*e.g., a muscle*) zusammenziehen; (*debts*) geraten in (*acc*); (*ling*) kontrahieren ‖ *intr* (*shrink*) sich zusammenziehen; **c. to** (*inf*) sich vertraglich verpflichten zu (*inf*)

contract'ing *adj* vertragsschließend

contraction [kən'trækʃən] *s* (& ling) Zusammenziehung *f*, Kontraktion *f*; (*contracted word*) Verkürzung *f*

contractor ['kɑntræktər] *s* (*supplier*) Lieferant *m*; (*builder*) Bauunternehmer *m*

contradict [ˌkɑntrə'dɪkt] *tr* widersprechen (*dat*)

contradiction [ˌkɑntrə'dɪkʃən] *s* Widerspruch *m*

contradictory [ˌkɑntrə'dɪktəri] *adj* widerspruchsvoll

contrail ['kɑnˌtrel] *s* Kondensstreifen *m*

contral·to [kən'trælto] *s* (–tos) (*person*) Altistin *f*; (*voice*) Alt *m*

contraption [kən'træpʃən] *s* (coll) Vorrichtung *f*; (*car*) (coll) Kiste *f*

contrary ['kɑntreri] *adj* konträr, gegensätzlich; (*person*) querköpfig; **c. to** entgegen (*dat*); **c. to nature** naturwidrig ‖ *s* Gegenteil *n*; **on the c.** im Gegenteil

contrast ['kɑntræst] *s* Gegensatz *m* ‖ [kən'træst] *tr* (**with**) gegenüberstellen (*dat*) ‖ *intr* (**with**) im Gegensatz stehen (**zu**)

contravene [ˌkɑntrə'vin] *tr* zuwiderhandeln (*dat*)

contribute [kən'trɪbjut] *tr* beitragen, spenden ‖ *intr*—**c. to** beitragen zu; (*with help*) mitwirken an (*dat*)

contribution [ˌkɑntrɪ'bjuʃən] *s* Beitrag *m*; (*of money*) Spende *f*

contributor [kən'trɪbjutər] *s* Spender –in *mf*; (*to a periodical*) Mitarbeiter –in *mf*

contrite [kən'traɪt] *adj* reuig

contrition [kən'trɪʃən] *s* Reue *f*

contrivance [kən'traɪvəns] *s* (*device*) Vorrichtung *f*; (*expedient*) Kunstgriff *m*; (*act of contriving*) Aushecken *n*

contrive [kən'traɪv] *tr* (*invent*) erfin-

den; (*devise*) ersinnen; **c. to** (*inf*) es fertig bringen zu (*inf*) ‖ *intr* Anschläge aushecken

con·trol [kən'trol] *s* Kontrolle *f*, Gewalt *f*; (mach) Steuerung *f*; (mach) (*devise*) Regler *m*; **be out of c.** nicht zu halten sein; **be under c.** in bester Ordnung sein; **controls** (aer) Steuerwerk *n*; **gain c. over** die Herrschaft gewinnen über (*acc*); **have c. over** s.o. über j–n Gewalt haben; **keep under c.** im Zaume halten ‖ *v* (*pret* & *pp* –**trolled**; *ger* –**trolling**) *tr* (*dominate*) beherrschen; (*verify*) kontrollieren; (*contain*) eindämmen; (*steer*) steuern; (*regulate*) regeln; **c. oneself** sich beherrschen

control' pan'el *s* Schaltbrett *n*

control' room' *s* Kommandoraum *m*; (rad) Regieraum *m*

control' stick' *s* (aer) Steuerknüppel *m*

control' tow'er *s* (*at an airport*) Kontrollturm *m*; (*on an aircraft carrier*) Kommandoturm *m*

controversial [ˌkɑntrə'vɑrʃəl] *adj* umstritten, strittig; **c. subject** Streitfrage *f*

controversy ['kɑntrəˌvɑrsi] *s* Kontroverse *f*, Auseinandersetzung *f*

controvert [ˌkɑntrə'vɑrt] *tr* (*argue against*) bestreiten; (*argue about*) streiten über (*acc*)

contusion [kən't(j)uʒən] *s* Quetschung *f*

convalesce [ˌkɑnvə'lɛs] *intr* genesen

convalescence [ˌkɑnvə'lɛsəns] *s* Genesung *f*

convalescent [ˌkɑnvə'lɛsənt] *s* Genesende *mf*

convales'cent home' *s* Genesungsheim *n*

convene [kən'vin] *tr* versammeln ‖ *intr* sich versammeln

convenience [kən'vinjəns] *s* Bequemlichkeit *f*; **at one's c.** nach Belieben; **at your earliest c.** möglichst bald; **modern conveniences** moderner Komfort *m*

convenient [kən'vinjənt] *adj* gelegen

convent ['kɑnvent] *s* Nonnenkloster *n*

convention [kən'venʃən] *s* (*professional meeting*) Tagung *f*; (*political meeting*) Konvent *m*; (*accepted usage*) Konvention *f*

conventional [kən'venʃənəl] *adj* konventionell, herkömmlich

converge [kən'vɑrdʒ] *intr* zusammenlaufen; **c. on** sich stürzen auf (*acc*)

conversation [ˌkɑnvər'seʃən] *s* Gespräch *n*

conversational [ˌkɑnvər'seʃənəl] *adj* Gesprächs–

converse ['kɑnvɑrs] *adj* gegenteilig ‖ *s* (**of**) Gegenteil *n* (**von**) ‖ [kən'vɑrs] *intr* sich unterhalten

conversion [kən'vɑrʒən] *s* (**into**) Umwandlung *f* (in *acc*); (*of a factory*) (**to**) Umstellung *f* (auf *acc*); (*of a building*) (**into**) Umbau *m* (**zu**); (*of currency*) (**into**) Umwechslung *f* (in *acc*); (elec) (**to**) Umformung *f* (in *acc*); (math) Umrechnung *f*; (phys) Umsetzung *f*; (relig) Bekehrung *f*

convert ['kɒnvɑrt] *s* (**to**) Bekehrte *mf* (zu) ‖ [kən'vɑrt] *tr* (**into**) umwandeln (in *acc*); (*a factory*) (**to**) umstellen (auf *acc*); (*a building*) (**into**) umbauen (zu); (*currency*) (**into**) umwechseln (in *acc*); (*biochem*) (**into**) umsetzen (in *acc*); (*chem*) (**into**) umwandeln (in *acc*), verwandeln (in *acc*); (*elec*) (**to**) umformen (in *acc*); (*math*) (**to**) umrechnen (in *acc*); (*phys*) (**to**) umsetzen (in *acc*); (*relig*) (**to**) bekehren (zu) ‖ *intr* (**to**) sich bekehren (zu)

converter [kən'vɑrtər] *s* (*elec*) Umformer *m*, Stromrichter *m*

convertible [kən'vɑrtɪbəl] *adj* umwandelbar; (*fin*) konvertierbar ‖ *s* (*aut*) Kabriolett *n*

convex ['kɒnveks], [kən'veks] *adj* konvex

convey [kən've] *tr* (*transport*) befördern; (*greetings, message*) übermitteln; (*sound*) fortpflanzen; (*meaning*) ausdrücken; (*a property*) abtreten

conveyance [kən've-əns] *s* (*act*) Beförderung *f*; (*means*) Transportmittel *n*; (*jur*) Abtretung *f*

conveyor [kən've-ər] *s* Beförderer –in *mf*

convey'or belt' *s* Förderband *n*

convict ['kɒnvɪkt] *s* Sträfling *m* ‖ [kən'vɪkt] *tr* (**of**) überführen (*genit*)

conviction [kən'vɪkʃən] *s* (*of a crime*) Verurteilung *f*; (*certainty*) Überzeugung *f*; **convictions** Gesinnung *f*

convince [kən'vɪns] *tr* (**of**) überzeugen (von)

convivial [kən'vɪvɪ-əl] *adj* gesellig

convocation [ˌkɒnvə'keʃən] *s* Zusammenberufung *f*; (*educ*) Eröffnungsfeier *f*

convoke [kən'vok] *tr* zusammenberufen

convoy ['kɒnvɔɪ] *s* (*of vehicles*) Kolonne *f*, Konvoi *m*; (*nav*) Geleitzug *m*

convulse [kən'vʌls] *tr* erschüttern

convulsion [kən'vʌlʃən] *s* Krampf *m*; **go into convulsions** Krämpfe bekommen

coo [ku] *intr* girren

cook [kʊk] *s* Koch *m*, Köchin *f* ‖ *tr* braten, backen; (*boil*) kochen; **c. up** (fig) zusammenbrauen ‖ *intr* braten, backen; (*boil*) kochen

cook'book' *s* Kochbuch *n*

cookie ['kʊki] *s* Plätzchen *n*, Keks *m* & *n*; **cookies** *pl* Gebäck *n*

cook'ing *s* Kochen *n*; **do one's own c.** sich selbst beköstigen

cool [kul] *adj* (& fig) kühl; **keep c.!** ruhig Blut!; **keep one's c.** (coll) ruhig Blut bewahren ‖ *s* Kühle *f* ‖ *tr* kühlen; **c. down** (fig) beruhigen; **c. off** abkühlen ‖ *intr* (& fig) sich abkühlen

cooler ['kulər] *s* Kühler *m*; (sl) Kittchen *n*

cool'-head'ed *adj* besonnen

coolie ['kuli] *s* Kuli *m*

coolness ['kulnɪs] *s* (& fig) Kühle *f*

coon [kun] *s* (zool) Waschbär *m*

coop [kup] *s* (*building*) Hühnerstall *m*; (*enclosure*) Hühnerhof *m*; (*jail*) (sl) Kittchen *n*; **fly the c.** (sl) auskneifen ‖ *tr*—**c. up** einsperren

co-op ['ko-ɑp] *s* Konsumverein *m*

cooper ['kupər] *s* Küfer *m*, Böttcher *m*

cooperate [ko'ɑpə,ret] *intr* (**in**) mitwirken (an *dat*, bei); (**with**) mitarbeiten (mit)

cooperation [ko,ɑpə're(ʃən] *s* Mitwirkung *f*, Mitarbeit *f*

cooperative [ko'ɑpə,retɪv] *adj* hilfsbereit

coordinate [ko'ɔrdɪnɪt] *adj* gleichrangig; (*gram*) beigeordnet ‖ *s* (*math*) Koordinate *f* ‖ [ko'ɔrdɪ,net] *tr* koordinieren

coordination [ko,ɔrdɪ'neʃən] *s* Koordination *f*; (*gram*) Beiordnung *f*

cootie ['kuti] *s* (sl) Laus *f*

co-owner ['ko,onər] *s* Miteigentümer –in *mf*

cop [kɑp] *s* (sl) Bulle *m* ‖ *v* (*pret & pp* **copped**; *ger* **copped**) *tr* (*catch*) (sl) erwischen; (*steal*) (sl) klauen ‖ *intr*—**cop out** (coll) auskneifen

copartner [ko'pɑrtnər] *s* Mitinhaber –in *mf*

cope [kop] *intr*—**c. with** sich messen mit, aufkommen gegen

cope'stone' *s* Schlußstein *m*

copier ['kɑpɪ-ər] *s* Kopiermaschine *f*

copilot ['ko,paɪlət] *s* Kopilot *m*

coping ['kopɪŋ] *s* Mauerkappe *f*

copious ['kopɪ-əs] *adj* reichlich

cop'-out' *s* (*act*) Kneifen *n*; (*person*) Drückeberger *m*

copper ['kɑpər] *adj* kupfern, Kupfer–; (*color*) kupferrot ‖ *s* Kupfer *n*; (*coin*) Kupfermünze *f*; (sl) Schupo *m*

cop'persmith' *s* Kupferschmied *m*

copter ['kɑptər] *s* (coll) Hubschrauber *m*

copulate ['kɑpjə,let] *intr* sich paaren

cop·y ['kɑpi] *s* Kopie *f*; (*of a book*) Exemplar *n*; (*typ*) druckfertiges Manuskript *n* ‖ *v* (*pret & pp* **-ied**) *tr* kopieren; (*in school*) abschreiben

cop'ybook' *s* Schreibheft *n*, Heft *n*

cop'ycat' *s* (*imitator*) Nachäffer –in *mf*

cop'yright' *s* Urheberrecht *n*, Verlagsrecht *n* ‖ *tr* urheberrechtlich schützen, verlagsrechtlich schützen

cop'ywrit'er *s* Texter –in *mf*

coquette [ko'ket] *s* Kokette *f*

coquettish [ko'ketɪʃ] *adj* kokett

coral ['kɒrəl] *adj* Korallen– ‖ *s* Koralle *f*

cor'al reef' *s* Korallenriff *n*

cord [kɔrd] *s* Schnur *f*, Strick *m*; (*of wood*) Klafter *n*; (*elec*) Leitungsschnur *f*

cordial ['kɔrdʒəl] *adj* herzlich ‖ *s* Likör *m*; (*med*) Herzstärkung *f*

cordiality [kɔr'dʒælɪti] *s* Herzlichkeit *f*

cordon ['kɔrdən] *s* Kordon *m*, Absperrkette *f* ‖ *tr*—**c. off** absperren

corduroy ['kɔrdə,rɔɪ] *s* Kordsamt *m*; **corduroys** Kordsamthose *f*

core [kor] *s* (*of fruit*) Kern *m*; (*of a*

cable) Seele *f*; (fig) Kern *m*, Mark *n*; (elec) Spulenkern *m*

cork [kɔrk] *s* Kork *m*; (*stopper*) Pfropfen *m*, Korken *m* || *tr* verkorken

corker ['kɔrkər] *s* (sl) Schlager *m*

cork'ing *adj* (sl) fabelhaft

cork'oak', cork' tree' *s* Korkeiche *f*

cork'screw' *s* Korkenzieher *m*

corn [kɔrn] *s* (*Indian corn*) Mais *m*; (*on a foot*) Hühnerauge *n*; (*joke*) (sl) Kalauer *m*

corn'bread' *s* Maisbrot *m*

corn'cob' *s* Maiskolben *m*

corn'cob pipe' *s* Maiskolbenpfeife *f*

corn'crib' *s* Maisspeicher *m*

cornea ['kɔrnɪ·ə] *s* Hornhaut *f*

corned' beef' ['kɔrnd] *s* Pökelfleisch *n*

corner ['kɔrnər] *adj* Eck– || *s* Ecke *f*; (*secluded spot*) Winkel *m*; (*curve*) Kurve *f*; **c. of the eye** Augenwinkel *m*; **from all corners of the world** von allen Ecken und Enden; **turn the c.** um die Ecke biegen || *tr* (*a person*) in die Zange nehmen; (*the market*) aufkaufen

cor'nerstone' *s* Eckstein *m*; (*of a new building*) Grundstein *m*

cornet [kɔr'nɛt] *s* (mus) Kornett *n*

corn' exchange' *s* Getreidebörse *f*

corn'field' *s* Maisfeld *n*; (*grain field*) (Brit) Kornfeld *n*

corn'flakes' *spl* Maisflocken *pl*

corn' flour' *s* Maismehl *n*

corn'flow'er *s* Kornblume *f*

corn' frit'ter *s* Maispfannkuchen *m*

corn'husk' *s* Maishülse *f*

cornice ['kɔrnɪs] *s* Gesims *n*

corn' liq'uor *s* Maisschnaps *m*

corn' meal' *s* Maismehl *n*

corn' on the cob' *s* Mais *m* am Kolben

corn' silk' *s* Maisfasern *pl*

corn'stalk' *s* Maisstengel *m*

corn'starch' *s* Maisstärke *f*

cornucopia [,kɔrnə'kopɪ·ə] *s* Füllhorn *n*

corny ['kɔrni] *adj* (*sentimental*) rührselig; (*joke*) blöd

corollary ['kɔrə,lɛri] *s* (**to**) Folge *f* (von)

coron·a [kə'ronə] *s* (**–nas** & **–nae** [ni]) (astr) Hof *m*, Korona *f*; (archit) Kranzleiste *f*

coronary ['kɔrə,nɛri] *adj* koronar

coronation [,kɔrə'neʃən] *s* Krönung *f*

coroner ['kɔrənər] *s* Gerichtsmediziner *m*

cor'oner's in'quest *s* Totenschau *f*

coronet ['kɔrə,nɛt] *s* Krönchen *n*; (*worn by the nobility*) Adelskrone *f*; (*worn by women*) Diadem *n*

corporal ['kɔrpərəl] *adj* körperlich || *s* (mil) Obergefreite *m*

corporate ['kɔrpərɪt] *adj* korporativ

corporation [,kɔrpə'reʃən] *s* (fin) Aktiengesellschaft *f*; (jur) Körperschaft *f*

corpora'tion law'yer *s* Syndikus *m*

corporeal [kɔr'porɪ·əl] *adj* körperlich

corps [kɔr] *s* (**corps** [kɔrz]) Korps *n*

corpse [kɔrps] *s* Leiche *f*, Leichnam *m*

corps'man *s* (**–men**) Sanitäter *m*

corpulent ['kɔrpjələnt] *adj* beleibt

corpuscle ['kɔrpəsəl] *s* Blutkörperchen *n*

cor·ral [ke'ræl] *s* Pferch *m* || *v* (*pret* & *pp* **–ralled;** *ger* **–ralling**) *tr* zusammenpferchen

correct [kə'rɛkt] *adj* richtig; (*manners*) korrekt; (*time*) genau; **be c.** (*said of a thing*) stimmen; (*said of a person*) recht haben || *tr* korrigieren; (*examination papers*) verbessern; (*beat*) züchtigen; (*scold*) zurechtweisen; (*an unjust situation*) ausgleichen

correction [kə'rɛkʃən] *s* Berichtigung *f*; (*of examination papers*) Verbesserung *f*, Korrektur *f*; (*punishment*) Bestrafung *f*

corrective [kə'rɛktɪv] *adj* (*measures*) Gegen–; (*lenses, shoes*) Ausgleichs–

correctness [kə'rɛktnɪs] *s* Richtigkeit *f*; (*in manners*) Korrektheit *f*

correlate ['kɔrə,let] *tr* in Wechselbeziehung bringen || *intr* in Wechselbeziehung stehen

correlation [,kɔrə'leʃən] *s* Wechselbeziehung *f*, Korrelation *f*

correlative [kə'rɛlətɪv] *adj* korrelativ || *s* Korrelat *n*

correspond [,kɔrɪ'spand] *intr* einander übereinstimmen; (**to, with**) entsprechen (*dat*); (*exchange letters*) (**with**) im Briefwechsel stehen (**mit**)

correspondence [,kɔrɪ'spandəns] *s* (*act of corresponding*) Übereinstimmung *f*; (*instance of correspondence*) Entsprechung *f*; (*exchange of letters; letters*) Korrespondenz *f*

correspon'dence course' *s* Fernkursus *m*

correspondent [,kɔrɪ'spandənt] *s* Briefpartner *–in mf*; (journ) Korrespondent *–in mf*

correspond'ing *adj* entsprechend

corridor ['kɔrɪdər] *s* Korridor *m*

corroborate [kə'rabə,ret] *tr* bestätigen

corrode [kə'rod] *tr* & *intr* korrodieren

corrosion [kə'roʒən] *s* Korrosion *f*

corrosive [kə'rosɪv] *adj* ätzend; (*influence*) schädigend || *s* Ätzmittel *n*

cor'rugated card'board ['kɔrə,getɪd] *s* Wellpappe *f*

cor'rugated i'ron *s* Wellblech *n*

corrupt [kə'rʌpt] *adj* (*text*) verderbt; (*morally*) verdorben; (*open to bribes*) bestechlich || *tr* verderben; (*bribe*) bestechen

corruption [kə'rʌpʃən] *s* Verderbtheit *f*; (*bribery*) Korruption *f*

corsage [kɔr'saʒ] *s* Blumensträußchen *n* zum Anstecken

corsair ['kɔrsɛr] *s* Korsar *m*

corset ['kɔrsɪt] *s* Korsett *n*

Corsica ['kɔrsɪkə] *s* Korsika *f*

Corsican ['kɔrsɪkən] *adj* korsisch

cortege [kɔr'tɛʒ] *s* Gefolge *n*; (*at a funeral*) Leichenzug *m*

cor·tex ['kɔr,tɛks] *s* (**–tices** [tɪ,siz]) Rinde *f*, Kortex *m*

cortisone ['kɔrtɪ,son] *s* Cortison *n*

corvette [kɔr'vɛt] *s* (naut) Korvette *f*

cosmetic [kaz'mɛtɪk] *adj* kosmetisch || *s* Kosmetikum *n*; **cosmetics** Kosmetikartikel *pl* cosmic ['kɑzmɪk] adj kosmisch

cosmonaut ['kɑzmə‚nɔt] s Kosmonaut –in mf

cosmopolitan [‚kɑzə'pɑlɪtən] adj kosmopolitisch || s Kosmopolit –in mf

cosmos ['kɑzməs] s Kosmos m

cost [kɔst] s Preis m; at all costs (fig) um jeden Preis; at c. zum Selbstkostenpreis; at the c. of auf Kosten (genit); costs Kosten pl; (jur) Gerichtskosten pl || v (pret & pp cost) intr kosten

cost' account'ing s Kostenrechnung f

costly ['kɔstlɪ] adj kostspielig; (of great value) kostbar

cost' of liv'ing s Lebenshaltungskosten pl

costume ['kɑst(j)um] s Kostüm n; (national dress) Tracht f

cos'tume ball' s Kostümball m

cos'tume jew'elry s Modeschmuck m

cot [kɑt] s Feldbett n

coterie ['kotərɪ] s Klüngel m, Koterie f

cottage ['kɑtɪdʒ] s Hütte f; (country house) Landhaus n

cot'tage cheese' s Quark m, Quarkkäse m

cot'ter pin' ['kɑtər] s Schließbolzen m

cotton ['kɑtən] s (fiber, yarn) Baumwolle f; (unspun cotton) Watte f; (sterilized cotton) Verbandswatte f

cot'ton field' s Baumwollfeld n

cot'ton gin' s Entkörnungsmaschine f

cot'ton mill' s Baumwollspinnerei f

cot'ton pick'er ['pɪkər] s Baumwollpflücker –in m; (machine) Baumwollpflückmaschine f

cot'tonseed oil' s Baumwollsamenöl n

cot'ton waste' s Putzwolle f

couch [kaʊt͡ʃ] s Couch f, Liege f || tr (words) fassen; (thoughts) ausdrücken

cougar ['kugər] s Puma m

cough [kɔf] s Husten m || tr—c. up aushusten; (money) (sl) blechen || intr husten; (in order to attract attention) sich räuspern

cough' drop' s Hustenbonbon m & n

cough' syr'up s Hustentropfen pl

could [kʊd] aux—he c. (was able) er konnte; if he c. (were able) wenn er könnte

council ['kaʊnsəl] s Rat m; (eccl) Konzil n

coun'cil-man s (-men) Stadtratsmitglied n

councilor ['kaʊnsələr] s Rat m

coun·sel ['kaʊnsəl] s Rat m; (for the defense) Verteidiger –in mf; (for the prosecution) Anklagevertreter –in mf || v (pret & pp -sel[l]ed; ger -sel[l]ing) tr raten (dat) || intr Rat geben

counselor ['kaʊnsələr] s Berater –in mf

count [kaʊnt] s Zahl f; (nobleman) Graf m; (jur) Anklagepunkt m; lose c. sich verzählen || tr zählen; (the costs) berechnen; c. in einschließen; c. off abzählen; c. out (money, a boxer) auszählen || intr zählen; c. for little (or much) wenig (or viel)

gelten; c. off (mil) abzählen; c. on zählen auf (acc)

count'down' s Countdown m & n

countenance ['kaʊntɪnəns] s Antlitz n || tr (tolerate) zulassen; (approve) billigen

counter ['kaʊntər] adj Gegen– || adv —c. to wider; run c. to zuwiderlaufen (dat) || s Zähler m; (in games) Spielmarke f; (in a store) Ladentisch m, Theke f; (in a restaurant) Büffet n; (in a bank) Schalter m; under the c. (fig) heimlich || tr widerstreben (dat); (in speech) widersprechen (dat) || intr Gegenmaßnahmen treffen; (box) kontern, nachschlagen

coun'teract' tr entgegenwirken (dat)

coun'terattack' s Gegenangriff m || coun'terattack' tr e–n Gegenangriff machen auf (acc) || intr e–n Gegenangriff machen

coun'terbal'ance s Gegengewicht n || coun'terbal'ance tr das Gegengewicht halten (dat)

coun'terclock'wise adj linksläufig || adv entgegen der Uhrzeigerrichtung

coun'teres'pionage s Gegenspionage f

counterfeit ['kaʊntərfɪt] adj gefälscht || s Fälschung f; (money) Falschgeld n || tr fälschen

counterfeiter ['kaʊntər‚fɪtər] s Falschmünzer –in mf

coun'terfeit mon'ey s Falschgeld n

coun'terintel'ligence s Spionageabwehr f

countermand ['kaʊntər‚mænd] s Gegenbefehl m || tr widerrufen

coun'termeas'ure s Gegenmaßnahme f

coun'teroffen'sive s Gegenoffensive f

coun'terpart' s Gegenstück n; (person) Ebenbild n

coun'terpoint' s (mus) Kontrapunkt m

coun'terrevolu'tion s Konterrevolution f

coun'tersign' s Gegenzeichen n || tr & intr mitunterzeichnen

coun'tersink' v (pret & pp –sunk) tr (a screw) versenken; (a hole) ausfräsen

coun'terspy' s Gegenspion –in mf

coun'terstroke' s Gegenstoß m

coun'terweight' s Gegengewicht n

countess ['kaʊntɪs] s Gräfin f

countless ['kaʊntlɪs] adj zahllos

countrified ['kʌntrɪ‚faɪd] adj ländlich; (boorish) bäu(e)risch

country ['kʌntrɪ] adj (air, house, life, road) Land– || s (state; rural area) Land n; (land of birth) Heimatland n; in the c. auf dem Lande; to the c. aufs Land

coun'try club' s exklusiver Klub m auf dem Lande

coun'tryfolk' spl Landvolk n

coun'try gen'tleman s Landedelmann m

coun'try-man s (–men) Landsmann m

coun'tryside' s Landschaft f, Land n

coun'try-wide' adj über das ganze Land verbreitet (or ausgedehnt)

county ['kaʊntɪ] s Kreis m

coun'ty seat' s Kreisstadt f

coup [ku] *s* Coup *m*

coup d'état [ku de 'ta] *s* Staatsstreich *m*

coupe [ku'pe], [kup] *s* Coupé *n*

couple [ˈkʌpəl] *s* Paar *n*; (*of lovers*) Liebespaar *n*; (*man and wife*) Ehepaar *n*; (phys) Kräftepaar *n*; **a c. of** ein paar, eine, **a c. of days ago** vor ein paar Tagen ‖ *tr* koppeln ‖ *intr* sich paaren

couplet [ˈkʌplɪt] *s* Verspaar *n*

coupling [ˈkʌplɪŋ] *s* Verbindungsstück *n*; (rad) Kopplung *f*; (rr) Kupplung *f*

coupon [ˈk(j)upɑn] *s* Gutschein *m*

courage [ˈkʌrɪdʒ] *s* Mut *m*, Courage *f*; **get up the c. to** (*inf*) sich [*dat*] ein Herz fassen zu (*inf*)

courageous [kəˈredʒəs] *adj* mutig

courier [ˈkʌrɪ·ər] *s* Eilbote *m*; (*tour guide*) Reiseleiter –in *mf*

course [kors] *s* (*direction*) Richtung *f*, Kurs *m*; (*of a river, of time*) Lauf *m*; (*method of procedure*) Weg *m*, Weise *f*, Kurs *m*; (*in racing*) Bahn *f*; (archit) Schicht *f*; (culin) Gang *m*; (educ) Kurs *m*; **c. of action** Handlungsweise *f*; **go off c.** (aer) sich verfliegen; **in due c.** zur rechten Zeit; **in the c. of** im Verlaufe von (or *genit*); (*with expressions of time*) im Laufe (*genit*); **of c.** natürlich; **run its c.** seinen Verlauf nehmen

court [kort] *s* (*of a king*) Hof *m*; (*of justice*) Gericht *n*; (*yard*) Hof *m*; (tennis) Platz *m*; (**in c.** (or **into c.** or **to c.**) vor Gericht; **out of c.** außergerichtlich ‖ *tr* (*a girl*) werben um; (*danger*) suchen; (*disaster*) heraufbeschwören

courteous [ˈkʌrtɪ·əs] *adj* höflich

courtesan [ˈkortɪʒən] *s* Kurtisane *f*

courtesy [ˈkʌrtɪsɪ] *s* Höflichkeit *f*; **by c. of** freundlicherweise zur Verfügung gestellt von

court'house' *s* Gerichtsgebäude *n*

courtier [ˈkortɪ·ər] *s* Höfling *m*

court' jest'er *s* Hofnarr *m*

court'-mar'tial *s* (**courts-martial**) Kriegsgericht *n* ‖ *v* (*pret & pp* **-tial[l]ed**; *ger* **-tial[l]ing**) *tr* vor ein Kriegsgericht stellen

court'room' *s* Gerichtssaal *m*

court'ship' *s* Werbung *f*

court'yard' *s* Hof *m*

cousin [ˈkʌzɪn] *s* Vetter *m*; (*female*) Kusine *f*

cove [kov] *s* Bucht *f*

covenant [ˈkʌvənənt] *s* Vertrag *m*; (Bib) Bund *m*

cover [ˈkʌvər] *s* Decke *f*; (*lid*) Deckel *m*; (*wrapping*) Hülle *f*; (*e.g., of a bed*) Bezug *m*; (*of a book*) Einband *m*; (*protection*) Schutz *m*; (*of*) Deckung *f*; **from c. to c.** von vorn bis hinten; **take c.** sich unterstellen; **under c.** im Geheimen; **under c. of night** im Schutz der Dunkelheit ‖ *tr* bedecken, decken; (*conceal*) verdecken; (*distances*) zurücklegen; (*a sales territory*) bearbeiten; (*a bet*) die gleiche Summe setzen gegen; (*expenses, losses*) decken; (*upholstered furniture*) beziehen; (*deal with*) behandeln; (*include*) umfassen; (*material in class*) durchnehmen; (*said of a reporter*) berichten über (*acc*); (*said of plants*) bewachsen; (*with insurance*) versichern, decken; (*protect with a gun*) sichern; (*threaten with a gun*) in Schach halten; (*have within range*) beherrschen; **c. up** zudecken; (*conceal*) verheimlichen ‖ *intr*—**c. for** einspringen für

coverage [ˈkʌvərɪdʒ] *s* (*area covered*) Verbreitungsgebiet *n*; (*of news*) Berichterstattung *f*; (ins) Versicherungsschutz *m*; (rad, telv) Sendebereich *m*

coveralls [ˈkʌvər͵ɔlz] *spl* Monteuranzug *m*

cov'ered wag'on *s* Planwagen *m*

cov'er girl' *s* Covergirl *n*

cov'ering *s* Decke *f*, Bedeckung *f*

covert [ˈkovərt] *adj* verborgen

cov'erup' *s* Beschönigung *f*, Bemäntelung *f*

covet [ˈkʌvɪt] *tr* begehren

covetous [ˈkʌvɪtəs] *adj* begehrlich

covetousness [ˈkʌvɪtəsnɪs] *s* Begehrlichkeit *f*

covey [ˈkʌvi] *s* (*brood*) Brut *f*; (*small flock*) Schwarm *m*; (*bevy*) Schar *f*

cow [kau] *s* Kuh *f* ‖ *tr* einschüchtern

coward [ˈkau·ərd] *s* Feigling *m*, Memme *f*

cowardice [ˈkau·ərdɪs] *s* Feigheit *f*

cowardly [ˈkau·ərdli] *adj* feig(e)

cow'bell' *s* Kuhglocke *f*

cow'boy' *s* Cowboy *m*

cower [ˈkau·ər] *intr* kauern

cow'herd' *s* Kuhhirt *m*

cow'hide' *s* Rindsleder *n*

cowl [kaul] *s* (*on a chimney*) Schornsteinkappe *f*; (*aer*) Motorhaube *f*; (eccl) Kapuze *f*

cowling [ˈkaulɪŋ] *s* (aer) Motorhaube *f*

co-worker [ˈko ͵wʌrkər] *s* Mitarbeiter –in *mf*

cowpox [ˈkau ͵pɑks] *s* Kuhpocken *pl*

coxswain [ˈkɑksən] *s* Steuermann *m*

coy [kɔɪ] *adj* spröde

coyote [kaɪˈoti], [ˈkaɪ·ot] *s* Kojote *m*, Präriewolf *m*, Steppenwolf *m*

cozy [ˈkozi] *adj* gemütlich

C.P.A. [ˈsi·pi'e] *s* (**certified public accountant**) amtlich zugelassener Wirtschaftsprüfer *m*

crab [kræb] *s* Krabbe *f*; (*grouch*) Sauertopf *m*

crab' ap'ple *s* Holzapfel *m*

crabbed [ˈkræbɪd] *adj* mürrisch; (*handwriting*) unleserlich; (*style*) schwer verständlich, verworren

crabby [ˈkræbi] *adj* mürrisch, grämlich

crack [kræk] *adj* erstklassig; (*troops*) Elite– ‖ *s* Riß *m*, Sprung *m*; (*of a whip or rifle*) Knall *m*; (*blow*) (sl) Klaps *m*; (*opportunity*) (sl) Gelegenheit *f*; (*try*) (sl) Versuch *m*; (*cutting remark*) (sl) Seitenhieb *m*; **at the c. of dawn** bei Tagesanbruch; **take a c. at** (sl) versuchen ‖ *tr* spalten; (*a nut, safe*) knacken; (*an egg*) aufschlagen;

(a code) entziffern; *(hit)* (sl) e-n Klaps geben *(dat)*; (chem) spalten; **c. a joke** e-n Witz reißen; **c. a smile** lächeln ‖ *intr (make a cracking sound)* knacken, krachen; *(develop a crack)* rissig werden; *(said of a whip or rifle)* knallen; *(said of a voice)* umschlagen; *(said of ice)* (zer) springen; **c. down on** scharf vorgehen gegen; **c. up** (coll) überschnappen; (aut) aufknallen

cracked *adj (split)* rissig; *(crazy)* (sl) übergeschnappt

cracker ['krækər] *s* Keks *m* & *n*

crack'erjack' *adj* (coll) erstklassig ‖ *s* (coll) Kanone *f*

crackle ['krækəl] *s* Krakelierung *f* ‖ *tr* krakelieren ‖ *intr* prasseln

crack'pot' *adj* (sl) verrückt ‖ *s* (sl) Verrückte *mf*

crack' shot' *s* Meisterschütze *m*

crack'-up' *s* (aut) Zusammenstoß *m*

cradle ['kredəl] *s* Wiege *f*; (telp) Gabel *f* ‖ *tr* in den Armen wiegen

craft [kræft] *s* Handwerk *n*, Gewerbe *n*; (naut) Fahrzeug *n*; **by c.** durch List ‖ *spl* Fahrzeuge *pl*, Schiffe *pl*; **small c.** kleine Schiffe *pl*

craftiness ['kræftɪnɪs] *s* List *f*

crafts·man ['kræftsmən] *s* (–men) Handwerker *m*

crafts'manship' *s* Kunstfertigkeit *f*

crafty ['kræftɪ] *adj* arglistig

crag [kræg] *s* Felszacke *f*

cram [kræm] *v* *(pret & pp* crammed; *ger* cramming) *tr* vollstopfen; **c. into** hineinstopfen in *(acc)* ‖ *intr* (educ) büffeln, ochsen; **c. into** sich hineinzwängen in *(acc)*

cram' course' *s* Presse *f*

cramp [kræmp] *s* Krampf *m*; *(clamp)* Klammer *f* ‖ *tr* einschränken, beengen

cramped *adj* eng

cranberry ['kræn,beri] *s* Preiselbeere *f*

crane [kren] *s* (mach) Kran *m*; (orn) Kranich *m* ‖ **c. one's neck** den Hals recken

crani·um ['krenɪ·əm] *s* (–a [ə]) *s* Hirnschale *f*, Schädel *m*

crank [kræŋk] *s* Kurbel *f*; *(grouch)* (coll) Griesgram *m*; *(eccentric)* (coll) Sonderling *m* ‖ *tr* kurbeln; **c. up** ankurbeln

crank'case' *s* Kurbelgehäuse *n*

crank'shaft' *s* Kurbelwelle *f*

cranky ['kræŋkɪ] *adj* launisch

cranny ['krænɪ] *s* Ritze *f*

crap [kræp] *s* *(nonsense)* (sl) Unsinn *m*; **craps** Würfel *pl*; **shoot craps** Würfel spielen

crash [kræʃ] *s* Krach *m*; (aer) Absturz *m*; (aut) Zusammenstoß *m*; (econ) Zusammenbruch *m* ‖ *tr* zerschmettern; *(a party)* hineinplatzen in *(acc)*; (aer) zum Absturz bringen ‖ *intr (produce a crashing sound)* krachen; *(shatter)* zerbrechen; *(collapse)* zusammenstürzen; (aer) abstürzen; (aut) zusammenstoßen; **c. into** fahren gegen

crash' dive' *s* Schnelltauchen *n*

crash'-dive' *intr* schnelltauchen

crash' hel'met *s* Sturzhelm *m*

crash' land'ing *s* Bruchlandung *f*

crash' pro'gram *s* Gewaltkur *f*

crass [kræs] *adj* kraß

crate [kret] *s* Lattenkiste *f*; *(old car, old plane)* (coll) Kiste *f* ‖ *tr* in e-r Lattenkiste verpacken

crater ['kretər] *s* Krater *m*; *(of a bomb)* Trichter *m*

crave [krev] *tr* ersehnen ‖ *intr*—**c. for** verlangen nach

craven ['krevən] *adj* feige ‖ *s* Feigling *m*

crav'ing *s* *(for)* Verlangen *n* (nach)

craw [krɔ] *s* Kropf *m*

crawl [krɔl] *s* Kriechen *n* ‖ *intr* kriechen; *(said of the skin)* kribbeln; *(said of a swimmer)* kraulen; *(said of cars)* schleichen; **c. along** im Schneckentempo gehen (or fahren); **c. into a hole** (& fig) sich verkriechen; **c. with** wimmeln von

crayon ['kre·ən] *s* *(wax crayon)* Wachsmalkreide *f*; *(colored pencil)* Farbstift *m*; *(artist's crayon)* Zeichenkreide *f*

craze [krez] *s* Mode *f*, Verrücktheit *f* ‖ *tr* verrückt machen

crazy ['krezi] *adj* verrückt; *(senseless)* sinnlos; **c. about** verrückt nach; **c. idea** Wahnidee *f*; **drive c.** verrückt machen

cra'zy bone' *s* Musikantenknochen *m*

creak [krik] *s* *(high-pitched sound)* Quietschen *n*; *(low-pitched sound)* Knarren *n* ‖ *intr* quietschen; knarren

creaky ['kriki] *adj* quietschend; knarrend

cream [krim] *adj* Sahne–, Rahm–; *(color)* creme, cremefarben ‖ *s* Sahne *f*, Rahm *m*; *(cosmetic)* Creme *f*; *(color)* Cremefarbe *f*; (fig) Creme *f* ‖ *tr (milk)* abrahmen; *(trounce)* (sl) schlagen

cream' cheese' *s* Rahmkäse *m*, Sahnekäse *m*

creamery ['kriməri] *s* Molkerei *f*

cream' pit'cher *s* Sahnekännchen *n*

cream' puff' *s* Windbeutel *m*

cream' sep'arator ['sepə,retər] *s* Milchschleuder *f*, Milchzentrifuge *f*

creamy ['krimi] *adj* sahnig

crease [kris] *s* Falte *f*; *(in trousers)* Bügelfalte *f* ‖ *tr* falten; *(trousers)* bügeln ‖ *intr* knittern

create [kri'et] *tr* (er)schaffen; *(excitement, an impression)* hervorrufen; *(noise)* verursachen; *(appoint)* ernennen, machen zu; *(a role, fashion)* kreieren

creation [kri'eʃən] *s* Schaffung *f*; *(of the world)* Schöpfung *f*; *(in fashions)* Modeschöpfung *f*

creative [kri'etɪv] *adj* schöpferisch

creator [kri'etər] *s* Schöpfer *m*

creature ['kritʃər] *s* Kreatur *f*, Geschöpf *n*; **every living c.** jedes Lebewesen *n*

credence ['kridəns] *s* Glaube *m*

credentials [krɪ'denʃəlz] *spl* Beglaubigungsschreiben *n*, Akkreditiv *n*

credenza [krɪ'denzə] *s* Kredenz *f*

credibility [ˌkredɪ'bɪlɪti] s Glaubwürdigkeit f

credibil'ity gap' s Vertrauenslücke f

credible ['kredɪbəl] adj glaubwürdig

credit ['kredɪt] s (credence) Glaube m; (honor) Ehre f; (recognition) Anerkennung f; (educ) Anrechnungspunkt m; (fin) Kredit m; (credit balance) (fin) Guthaben n; **be a c. to** Ehre machen (dat); **credits** (cin) Vorspann m; **give** s.o. c. **for** s.th. j-m etw hoch anrechnen; **on c.** auf Kredit; **on thirty days' c.** auf dreißig Tage Ziel; **als Verdienst anrechnen; to s.o.'s c.** zu j-s Ehre || tr (believe) glauben (dat); (an account) gutschreiben (dat); **c.** s.o. **with** s.th. j-m etw hoch anrechnen

creditable ['kredɪtəbəl] adj ehrenwert

cre'dit card' s Kreditkarte f

cre'dit hour' s (educ) Anrechnungspunkt m

creditor ['kredɪtər] s Gläubiger –in mf

cre'dit rat'ing s Bonität f

credulous ['kredʒələs] adj leichtgläubig

creed [krid] s (& fig) Glaubensbekenntnis n

creek [krik] s Bach m

creep [krip] s Kriechen n; (sl) Spinner m; **it gives me the creeps** mir gruselt || v (pret & pp **crept** [krept]) intr kriechen, schleichen; (said of plants) kriechen; **c. along** dahinschleichen; **c. up on** heranschleichen an (acc); **it makes my flesh c.** es macht mich schaudern

creeper ['kripər] s Kletterpflanze f

creepy ['kripi] adj schaudererregend; (sensation) gruselig; **have a c. feeling** gruseln

cremate ['krimet] tr einäschern

cremation [krɪ'meʃən] s Einäscherung f

crematory ['krimə‚tori] s Krematorium n

crepe [krep] s Krepp m; (mourning band) Trauerflor m

crepe' pa'per s Kreppapier n

crescent ['kresənt] s Mondsichel f

cres'cent roll' s Hörnchen n

cress [kres] s (bot) Kresse f

crest [krest] s (of a hill, wave, or rooster) Kamm m; (of a helmet) Helmbusch m; (of a bird) Federbüschel n

crestfallen ['krest‚fɔlən] adj niedergeschlagen

Crete [krit] s Kreta n

crevice ['krevɪs] s Riß m

crew [kru] s Gruppe f; (aer, nav) Besatzung f; (of a boat) (sport) Mannschaft f; (rowing) (sport) Rudersport m

crew' cut' s Bürstenschnitt m

crib [krɪb] s (manger) Krippe f; (for children) Kinderbettstelle f; (bin) Speicher m; (student's pony) Eselsbrücke f || v (pret & pp **cribbed**; ger **cribbing**) tr & intr abbohren

cricket ['krɪkɪt] s (ent) Grille f;

(sport) Kricketspiel n; **not c.** (coll) nicht fair

crime [kraɪm] s Verbrechen n

criminal ['krɪmɪnəl] adj verbrecherisch; (act, case, code, court, law) Straf–; (investigation, trial, police) Kriminal– || s Verbrecher –in mf

crim'inal charge' s Strafanzeige f

crim'inal neg'ligence s grobe Fahrlässigkeit f

crim'inal offense' s strafbare Handlung f

crim'inal rec'ord s Strafregister n

crimp [krɪmp] s Welle f; **put a c. in** (coll) e–n Dämpfer aufsetzen (dat) || tr wellen, riffeln

crimson ['krɪmzən] adj karmesinrot || s Karmesin n

cringe [krɪndʒ] intr sich krümmen; (fawn) kriechen

crinkle ['krɪŋkəl] s Runzel f || tr runzeln; (one's nose) rümpfen

cripple ['krɪpəl] s Krüppel m || tr verkrüppeln; (fig) lähmen, lahmlegen

cri·sis ['kraɪsɪs] s (–ses [siz]) Krise f

crisp [krɪsp] adj (brittle) knusprig; (firm and fresh) mürb; (air, clothes) frisch; (manner) forsch

crisscross ['krɪs‚krɔs] adj & adv kreuz und quer || tr kreuz und quer markieren || intr sich kreuzen

criteri·on [kraɪ'tɪrɪ·ən] s (–a [ə] & –ons) Kennzeichen n, Kriterium n

critic ['krɪtɪk] s Kritiker –in mf

critical ['krɪtɪkəl] adj kritisch

criticism ['krɪtɪ‚sɪzəm] s Kritik f

criticize ['krɪtɪ‚saɪz] tr kritisieren

critique [krɪ'tik] s (review) Rezension f; (critical discussion) Kritik f

croak [krok] s (of a frog) Quaken n; (of a raven) Krächzen n || intr quaken; krächzen; (die) (sl) verrecken

cro·chet [kro'ʃə] s Häkelarbeit f || v (pret & pp **–cheted** ['ʃed]); ger **–cheting** ['ʃe‚ɪŋ] tr & intr häkeln

crochet' nee'dle s Häkelnadel f

crock [krak] s irdener Topf m, Krug m

crockery ['krakəri] s irdenes Geschirr n

crocodile ['krakə‚daɪl] s Krokodil n

croc'odile tears' spl Krokodilstränen pl

crocus ['krokəs] s (bot) Krokus m

crone [kron] s altes Weib n

crony ['kroni] s alter Kamerad m

crook [kruk] s (of a shepherd) Hirtenstab m; (sl) Gauner m || tr krümmen

crooked ['krʊkɪd] adj krumm; (dishonest) unehrlich

croon [krun] tr & intr schmalzig singen

crooner ['krunər] s Schnulzensänger m

crop [krap] s Ernte f; (whip) Peitsche f; (of a bird) Kropf m; (large number) Menge f; **the crops** die ganze Ernte || v (pret & pp **cropped**; ger **cropping**) tr stutzen; (said of an animal) abfressen || intr—**c. up** auftauchen

crop' fail'ure s Mißerte f

croquet [kro'ke] s Krocket n

croquette [kro'ket] s (culin) Krokette f

crosier ['kroʒər] s Bischofsstab m

cross [krɔs] adj Quer-, Kreuz-; (biol) Kreuzungs-; (angry) (with) ärgerlich (auf acc, über acc) || s (& fig) Kreuz n; (biol) Kreuzung f || tr (arms, legs, streets, plans, breeds) kreuzen; (a mountain) übersteigen; (oppose) in die Quere kommen (dat); c. my heart! Hand aufs Herz!; c. oneself sich bekreuzigen; c. s.o.'s mind j-m durch den Kopf gehen; c. out ausstreichen || intr sich kreuzen; c. over to hinübergehen zu

cross'bones' spl gekreuzte Skelettknochen pl

cross'bow' s (hist) Armbrust f

cross'breed' v (pret & pp –bred) tr kreuzen

cross'-coun'try adj (vehicle) geländegängig || cross'-coun'try s (sport) Langlauf m

cross'cur'rent s Gegenströmung f

cross'-exam'ine tr ins Kreuzverhör nehmen

cross'-examina'tion s Kreuzverhör n

cross'-eyed' adj schieläugig

cross'fire' s Kreuzfeuer n

cross'ing s (of streets) Kreuzung f; (of the ocean) Überfahrt f, Überquerung f; (rr) Übergang m

cross'piece' s Querstück n

cross'-pur'pose s—be at cross-purposes einander entgegenarbeiten

cross' ref'erence s Querverweis m

cross'road' s Querweg m; crossroads Straßenkreuzung f; (fig) Scheideweg m

cross' sec'tion s Querschnitt m

cross'wind' s Seitenwind m

cross'wise' adj & adv quer, in die Quere

cross'word puz'zle s Kreuzworträtsel n

crotch [krɑt∫] s (of a tree) Gabelung f; (of a body or trousers) Schritt m

crotchety ['krɑt∫ɪti] adj verschroben

crouch [kraut∫] s Hocke f || intr hocken

croup [krup] s (of a horse) Kruppe f; (pathol) Halsbräune f

croupier ['krupɪ-ər] s Croupier –in mf

crouton ['krutɑn] s gerösteter Brotwürfel m

crow [kro] s (cry) Krähen n; (bird) Krähe f; as the c. flies schnurgrade; eat c. klein beigeben || intr krähen

crow'bar' s Stemmeisen n

crowd [kraud] s Menge f; (mob) Masse f; (set) Gesellschaft f || tr vollstopfen; (push) stoßen; c. out verdrängen || intr (around) sich drängen (um); c. into sich hineindrängen in (acc)

crowd'ed adj überfüllt; (street) belebt

crown [kraun] s Krone f; (dent) Zahnkrone f || tr krönen; bekränzen; (checkers) zur Dame machen; (sl) eins aufs Dach geben (dat); (dent) überkronen

crown' jew'els spl Kronjuwelen pl

crown' prince' s Kronprinz m

crown' prin'cess s Kronprinzessin f

crow's'-feet' spl (wrinkles) Krähenfüße pl

crow's'-nest' s (naut) Krähennest n

crucial ['kru∫əl] adj entscheidend; (point) springend; c. question Gretchenfrage f; c. test Feuerprobe f

crucible ['krusɪbəl] s Schmelztiegel m

crucifix ['krusɪfɪks] s Kruzifix n

crucifixion [,krusɪ'fɪk∫ən] s Kreuzigung f

cruci-fy ['krusɪ,faɪ] v (pret & pp –fied) tr kreuzigen

crude [krud] adj (raw, unrefined) roh; (person) grob, ungeschliffen; c. joke plumper Scherz m

crudity ['krudɪti] s Roheit f

cruel ['kru-əl] adj (to) grausam (gegen)

cruelty ['kru-əlti] s Grausamkeit f; c. to animals Tierquälerei f

cruet ['kru-ɪt] s Fläschchen n; (relig) Meßkännchen n

cruise [kruz] s Kreuzfahrt f || intr (aer) mit Reisegeschwindigkeit fliegen; (aut) herumfahren; (naut) kreuzen

cruiser ['kruzər] s (nav) Kreuzer m

cruise' ship' s Vergnügungsdampfer m

cruller ['krʌlər] s Krapfen m

crumb [krʌm] s Krümel m; (& fig) Bröckchen n; (sl) Schweinehund m

crumble ['krʌmbəl] tr & intr zerbröckeln

crumbly ['krʌmbli] adj bröcklig

crummy ['krʌmi] adj (sl) schäbig

crumple ['krʌmpəl] tr zerknittern || intr (said of clothes) faltig werden; (collapse) zusammenbrechen

crunch [krʌnt∫] s Knacken n; (of snow) Knirschen n; (tight situation) Druck m || intr knirschend kauen || intr (said of snow) knirschen; c. on knirschend kauen

crusade [kru'sed] s Kreuzzug m

crusader [kru'sedər] s Kreuzfahrer m

crush [krʌ∫] s Gedränge n; have a c. on s.o. (coll) in j–n vernarrt sein || tr (zer)quetschen, zerdrücken; (grain) schroten; (stone) zerkleinern; (suppress) unterdrücken; (oppress) bedrücken; (hopes) knicken; (overwhelm) zerschmettern; (min) pochen; c. out (a cigarette) ausdrücken || intr zerdrückt werden

crush'ing adj (victory) entscheidend; (defeat) vernichtend; (experience) überwältigend

crust [krʌst] s Kruste f; (sl) Frechheit f

crustacean [krʌs'te∫ən] s Krebstier n

crustaceous [krʌs'te∫əs] adj Krebs-

crusty ['krʌsti] adj krustig, rösch; (surly) mürrisch

crutch [krʌt∫] s (& fig) Krücke f

crux [krʌks] s Kern m, Kernpunkt m

cry [kraɪ] s (cries) (shout) Schrei m, Ruf m; (weeping) Weinen n; a far cry from etw ganz anderes als; cry for help Hilferuf m; have a good cry sich ordentlich ausweinen || v (pret & pp cried) tr schreien, rufen; cry one's eyes out sich [dat] die Augen aus dem Kopf weinen || intr (weep)

weinen; (*shout*) schreien; **cry for
help** um Hilfe rufen; **cry on s.o.'s
shoulder** j-m seine Not klagen; **cry
out against** scharf verurteilen; **cry
out in** (*pain*) schreien vor (*dat*); **cry
over** nachweinen (*dat*)

cry′ba′by s (**-bies**) Schreihals m

cry′ing adj—**c.** jag Schreikrampf m;
c. shame schreiende Ungerechtigkeit
f || s Weinen n; **for c. out loud!** um
Himmels willen!

crypt [krɪpt] s Totengruft f, Krypta f

cryptic(al) [′krɪptɪk(əl)] adj (*secret*)
geheim; (*puzzling*) rätselhaft; (*coded*)
verschlüsselt

crystal [′krɪstəl] adj Kristall- || s
Kristall m; (*cut glass*) Kristallglas
n; (*of a watch*) Uhrglas n

crys′tal ball′ s Kristall m

crystalline [′krɪstəlɪn], [′krɪstə‚laɪn]
adj kristallinisch, kristallen

crystallize [′krɪstə‚laɪz] tr kristal-
lisieren || intr kristallisieren; (fig)
feste Form annehmen

cub [kʌb] s Junge n

Cuba [′kjubə] s Kuba n

Cuban [′kjubən] adj kubanisch || s
Kubaner –in mf

cubbyhole [′kʌbɪ‚hol] s gemütliches
Zimmerchen n

cube [kjub] s Würfel m; (math) dritte
Potenz f || tr in Würfel schneiden;
(math) kubieren

cubic [′kjubɪk] adj Raum–; (math)
kubisch; **c. foot** Kubikfuß m

cub′ report′er s unerfahrener Reporter
m

cub′ scout′ s Wölfling m

cuckold [′kʌkəld] s Hahnrei m || tr
zum Hahnrei machen

cuckoo [′kuku] adj (sl) verrückt || s
Kuckuck m

cuck′oo clock′ s Kuckucksuhr f

cucumber [′kjukʌmbər] s Gurke f

cud [kʌd] s—**chew the cud** wiederkäuen

cuddle [′kʌdəl] tr herzen || intr sich
kuscheln; **c. up** sich behaglich zu-
sammenkuscheln

cudg·el [′kʌdʒəl] s Prügel m || v (*pret
& pp* **-el[l]ed**; *ger* **-el[l]ing**) tr verprügeln

cue [kju] s Hinweis m; (billiards) Bil-
lardstock m; (theat) Stichwort n;
take the cue from s.o. sich nach
j-m richten || tr das Stichwort geben
(*dat*)

cuff [kʌf] s (*of a shirt*) Manschette f;
(*of trousers*) Aufschlag m; (*blow*)
Ohrfeige f; **off the c.** aus dem Handgelenk

cuff′ link′ s Manschettenknopf m

cuisine [kwi′zin] s Küche f

culinary [′kjulɪ‚nerɪ] adj kulinarisch,
Koch–; **c. art** Kochkunst f

cull [kʌl] tr (*choose*) auslesen; (*pluck*)
pflücken

culminate [′kʌlmɪ‚net] intr (**in**) kulminieren (in *dat*), gipfeln (in *dat*)

culmination [‚kʌlmɪ′neʃən] s Gipfel m

culpable [′kʌlpəbəl] adj schuldhaft

culprit [′kʌlprɪt] s Schuldige mf

cult [kʌlt] s Kult m, Kultus m

cultivate [′kʌltɪ‚vet] tr (*soil*) bearbeiten; (*plants*) ziehen; (*activities*)
betreiben; (*an art*) pflegen; (*friendship*) hegen

cul′tivat′ed adj kultiviert

cultivation [‚kʌltɪ′veʃən] s (*of the
soil*) Bearbeitung f; (*of the arts*)
Pflege f; (*of friendship*) Hegen n;
under c. bebaut

cultivator [′kʌltɪ‚vetər] s (mach) Kul-
tivator m

cultural [′kʌltʃərəl] adj kulturell,
Kultur–

culture [′kʌltʃər] s Kultur f

cul′tured adj kultiviert

cul′ture me′dium s Nährboden m

culvert [′kʌlvərt] s Rinnstein m

cumbersome [′kʌmbərsəm] adj (*unwieldy*) unhandlich; (*slow-moving*)
schwerfällig; (*burdensome*) lästig

cunning [′kʌnɪŋ] adj (arg)listig || s
List f, Arglist f, Schlauheit f

cup [kʌp] s Tasse f; (*of a bra*) Körbchen n; (fig, bot, relig) Kelch m;
(sport) Pokal m || v (*pret & pp*
cupped; *ger* **cupping**) tr (*the hands*)
wölben; (med) schröpfen

cupboard [′kʌbərd] s Schrank m

cupidity [kju′pɪdɪti] s Habgier f

cupola [′kjupələ] s Kuppel f

cur [kʌr] s Köter m; (pej) Halunke m

curable [′kjurəbəl] adj heilbar

curate [′kjurɪt] s Kaplan m

curative [′kjurətɪv] adj heilend, Heil–

curator [kju′retər] s Kustos m

curb [kʌrb] s (*of a street*) Randstein
m; (*of a horse*) Kandare f || tr (&
fig) zügeln; (*a person*) an die Kandare nehmen

curb′stone′ s Bordstein m

curd [kʌrd] s Quark m; **curds** Quark
m

curdle [′kʌrdəl] tr gerinnen lassen;
(fig) erstarren lassen || intr gerinnen,
stocken; (fig) erstarren

cure [kjur] s (*restoration to health*)
Heilung f; (*remedy*) Heilmittel n;
(*treatment*) Kur f || tr (*a disease,
evil*) heilen; (*by smoking*) räuchern;
(*by drying*) trocknen; (*by salting*)
einsalzen || intr heilen

cure′-all′ s Allheilmittel n

curfew [′kʌrfju] s Ausgehverbot n;
(*enforced closing time*) Polizeistunde
f

curi·o [′kjurɪ‚o] s (**-os**) Kuriosität f

curiosity [‚kjurɪ′asɪti] s Neugier f;
(*strange article*) Kuriosität f

curious [′kjurɪ‚əs] adj neugierig; (*odd*)
kurios, merkwürdig

curl [kʌrl] s (*of hair*) Locke f; (*of
smoke*) Rauchkringel m || tr locken;
(*lips*) verächtlich schürzen || intr
sich kräuseln; **c. up** sich zusammenrollen; (*said of an edge*) sich um-
biegen

curler [′kʌrlər] s Haarwickler m

curlicue [′kʌrlɪ‚kju] s Schnörkel m

curly [′kʌrli] adj lockig; (*leaves, etc.*)
gekräuselt

currant [′kʌrənt] s (*raisin*) Korinthe
f; (genus *Ribes*) Johannisbeere f

currency ['kʌrənsi] s (money) Währung f; (circulation) Umlauf m; foreign c. Devisen pl; gain c. in Gebrauch kommen

current ['kʌrənt] adj (year, prices, account) laufend; (events) aktuell, Tages-; be c. Gültigkeit haben; (said of money) gelten ‖ s (& elec) Strom m

currently ['kʌrəntli] adv gegenwärtig

curricu·lum [kə'rɪkjələm] s (-lums & -la [lə]) Lehrplan m

cur·ry ['kʌri] s Curry m ‖ v (pret & pp -ried) tr (a horse) striegeln; c. favor with s.o. sich bei j-m einzuschmeicheln suchen

cur'rycomb' s Striegel m

cur'ry pow'der s Currypulver n

curse [kʌrs] s Fluch m; put a c. on verwünschen ‖ tr verfluchen ‖ intr (at) fluchen (auf acc)

cursed ['kʌrsɪd], [kʌrst] adj verflucht

curse' word' s Fluchwort n, Schimpfwort n

cursive ['kʌrsɪv] adj Kurrent—

cursory ['kʌrsəri] adj flüchtig

curt [kʌrt] adj barsch, schroff

curtail [kər'tel] tr einschränken

curtain ['kʌrtɪn] s Gardine f; (drape) Vorhang m; (theat) Vorhang m ‖ tr—c. off mit Vorhängen abteilen

cur'tain call' s Vorhang m, Hervorruf m

cur'tain rod' s Gardinenstange f

curt·sy ['kʌrtsi] s Knicks m ‖ v (pret & pp -sied) intr (to) knicksen (vor dat)

curvaceous [kʌr've/əs] adj kurvenreich

curvature ['kʌrvət/ər] s (of the spine) Verkrümmung f; (of the earth) Krümmung f

curved adj krumm

cushion ['ku/ən] s Kissen n, Polster m & n; (billiards) Bande f ‖ tr polstern; (a shock) abfedern

cuss [kʌs] s (sl) Kerl m; (curse) (sl) Fluch m ‖ tr (sl) verfluchen ‖ intr (sl) fluchen

cussed ['kʌsɪd] adj (sl) verflucht

cussedness ['kʌsɪdnɪs] s (sl) Bosheit f

custard ['kʌstərd] s Eierkrem f

custodian [kəs'todɪ·ən] s (e.g., of records) Verwalter m; (of inmates) Wärter m; (caretaker) Hausmeister m

custody ['kʌstədi] s Verwahrung f, Obhut f; (jur) Gewahrsam m; c. of (children) Sorgerecht für; in the c. of in der Obhut (genit); take into c. in Gewahrsam nehmen

custom ['kʌstəm] s Brauch m, Sitte f; (habit) Gewohnheit f; customs Zollkontrolle f; pay customs on s.th. für etw Zoll bezahlen

customary ['kʌstə,meri] adj gebräuchlich

cus'tom-built' adj nach Wunsch gebaut

customer ['kʌstəmər] s Kunde m, Kundin f; (in a restaurant) Gast m; (telp) Teilnehmer -in mf

cus'tom-made' adj nach Maß angefertigt

cus'toms clear'ance s Zollabertigung f

cus'toms declara'tion s Zollerklärung f; (form) Abfertigungsschein m

cus'toms inspec'tion s Zollkontrolle f

cus'toms of'fice s Zollamt n

customs of'ficer s Zollbeamte m, Zollbeamtin f

cus'tom tai'lor s Maßschneider m

cut [kʌt] adj (glass) geschliffen; cut flowers Schnittblumen pl; cut out for wie geschaffen für (or zu) ‖ s Schnitt m; (piece cut off) Abschnitt m; (slice) Schnitte f; (wound) Schnittwunde f; (of a garment) Schnitt m, Fasson f; (of the profits) Anteil m; (in prices, pay) Kürzung f, Senkung f; (absence from school) Schwänzen n; (of meat) Stück n; (cards) Abheben n; (tennis) Drehschlag m; a cut above e-e Stufe besser als ‖ v (pret & pp cut; ger cutting) tr schneiden; (glass, precious stones) schleifen; (grass) mähen; (hedges) stutzen; (hay) machen; (a tunnel) bohren; (a motor) abstellen; (production) drosseln; (pay) kürzen, vermindern; (class) (coll) schwänzen; (prices) herabsetzen, kürzen; (whiskey) (coll) panschen; (cards) abheben; (tennis) schneiden; cut back (plants) stutzen; (fig) abbauen; cut down fällen; cut it out! Schluß damit!; cut off abschneiden; (a tail) kupieren; (gas, telephone, electricity) absperren; (troops) absprengen; cut one's finger sich in den Finger schneiden; cut out the nonsense! laß den Quatsch!; cut short (e.g., a vacation) abkürzen; (a person) das Wort abschneiden (dat); cut up zerstückeln ‖ intr schneiden; cut down on einschränken, verringern; cut in sich einmischen; (at a dance) ablösen; cut in ahead of s.o. vor j-m einbiegen; cut up (sl) wild darauf losschießen

cut-and-dried ['kʌtən'draɪd] adj fix und fertig

cut'away' s Cut m

cut'back' s Einschränkung f

cute [kjut] adj (pretty) niedlich; (shrewd) (coll) klug

cut' glass' s geschliffenes Glas n

cuticle ['kjutɪkəl] s Nagelhaut f

cutie ['kjuti] s (sl) flotte Biene f

cutlass ['kʌtləs] s Entermesser n

cutlery ['kʌtləri] s Schneidwerkzeuge pl

cutlet ['kʌtlɪt] s Schnitzel n

cut'-off' s (turn-off) Abzweigung f; (cut-off point) (acct) gemeinsamer Endpunkt m; (elec) Ausschaltvorrichtung f; (mach) Absperrvorrichtung f

cut'-off date' s Abschlußtag m

cut'-out' s Ausschnitt m; (design to be cut out) Ausschneidemuster n; (aut) Auspuffklappe f

cut'-rate' adj (price) Schleuder—

cutter ['kʌtər] s (naut) Kutter m

cut'throat' adj halsabschneiderisch ‖ s Halsabschneider -in mf

cut'ting adj schneidend; (tools)

Schneide–; (*remark*) scharf ‖ *s* Abschnitt *m*; (*of prices*) Herabsetzung *f*; (hort) Steckling *m*; **cuttings** Abfälle *pl*

cut'ting board' *s* Schneidebrett *n*

cut'ting edge' *s* Schnittkante *f*

cut'ting room' *s* (cin) Schneideraum *m*

cuttlefish ['kʌtəl‚fɪʃ] *s* Tintenfisch *m*

cyanamide [saɪ'ænə‚maɪd] *s* (chem) Zyanamid *n*; (com) Kalkstickstoff *m*

cycle ['saɪkəl] *s* Kreis *m*; (*of an internal combustion engine*) Takt *m*; (phys) Periode *f* ‖ *intr* radeln

cyclic(al) ['sɪklɪk(əl)] *adj* zyklisch, kreisförmig

cyclist ['saɪklɪst] *s* Radfahrer –in *mf*

cyclone ['saɪklon] *s* Zyklon *m*

cyclotron ['saɪklə‚tran] *s* Zyklotron *n*, Beschleuniger *m*

cylinder ['sɪlɪndər] *s* Zylinder *m*

cyl'inder block' *s* Zylinderblock *m*

cyl'inder bore' *s* Zylinderbohrung *f*

cyl'inder head' *s* Zylinderkopf *m*

cylindric(al) [sɪ'lɪndrɪk(əl)] *adj* zylindrisch

cymbal ['sɪmbəl] *s* Becken *n*

cynic ['sɪnɪk] *adj* (philos) zynisch ‖ *s* Menschenverächter –in *mf*; (philos) Zyniker *m*

cynical ['sɪnɪkəl] *adj* zynisch

cynicism ['sɪnɪ‚sɪzəm] *s* Zynismus *m*; (*cynical remark*) zynische Bemerkung *f*

cypress ['saɪprəs] *s* Zypresse *f*

Cyprus ['saɪprəs] *s* Zypern *n*

Cyrillic [sɪ'rɪlɪk] *adj* kyrillisch

cyst [sɪst] *s* Zyste *f*

czar [zar] *s* Zar *m*

czarina [za'rinə] *s* Zarin *f*

Czech [tʃɛk] *adj* tschechisch ‖ *s* Tscheche *m*, Tschechin *f*; (*language*) Tschechisch *n*

Czechoslovakia [‚tʃɛkəslo'vækɪ‚ə] *s* die Tschechoslowakei *f*

D

D, d [di] *s* vierter Buchstabe des englischen Alphabets; (mus) D; **D flat** Des *n*; **D sharp** Dis *n*

D.A. *abb* (**District Attorney**) Staatsanwalt *m*

dab [dæb] *s* (*of color*) Klecks *m*; (*e.g., of butter*) Stückchen *n* ‖ *v* (*pret & pp* **dabbed**; *ger* **dabbing**) *tr* betupfen ‖ *intr*—**dab at** betupfen

dabble ['dæbəl] *tr* bespritzen ‖ *intr* (*splash about*) plantschen; **d. in** herumstümpern in (*dat*)

dachshund ['daks‚hund] *s* Dachshund *m*

dad [dæd] *s* (coll) Vati *m*

daddy ['dædi] *s* (coll) Vati *m*

dad'dy-long'legs' *s* (**–legs**) Weberknecht *m*

daffodil ['dæfədɪl] *s* gelbe Narzisse *f*

daffy ['dæfi] *adj* (coll) doof

dagger ['dægər] *s* Dolch *m*; (typ) Kreuzzeichen *n*; **look daggers at s.o.** j–n mit Blicken durchbohren

dahlia ['dæljə] *s* Georgine *f*, Dahlie *f*

daily ['deli] *adj* täglich, Tages– ‖ *adv* täglich ‖ *s* Tageszeitung *f*

dainty ['denti] *adj* zart; (*food*) lecker; (*finiky*) wählerisch

dairy ['deri] *s* Molkerei *f*

dair'y farm' *s* Meierei *f*

dair'y farm'er *s* Meier –in *mf*

dais ['de·ɪs] *s* Tribüne *f*

daisy ['dezi] *s* Gänseblümchen *n*

dal·ly ['dæli] *v* (*pret & pp* **–lied**) *intr* (*delay*) herumtrödeln; (*play amorously*) liebäugeln

dam [dæm] *s* Damm *m*; (*female quadruped*) Muttertier *n* ‖ *v* (*pret & pp* **dammed**; *ger* **damming**) *tr* eindämmen; **dam up** anstauen

damage ['dæmɪdʒ] *s* Schaden *m*; **damages** (jur) Schadenersatz *m*; **do d.** Schaden anrichten; **sue for damages**

auf Schadenersatz klagen ‖ *tr* beschädigen; (*a reputation*) beeinträchtigen

dam'aging *adj* (*influence*) schädlich; (*evidence*) belastend

dame [dem] *s* Dame *f*; (sl) Weibsbild *n*

damn [dæm] *adj* (sl) verflucht ‖ *s*— **I don't give a d. about it** (sl) ich mache mir e–n Dreck daraus; **not be worth a d.** (sl) keinen Pfifferling wert sein ‖ *tr* verdammen; (*curse*) verfluchen; **d. it!** (sl) verflucht!

damnation [dæm'neʃən] *s* Verdammnis *f*

damned *adj* verdammt; (sl) verflucht ‖ *adv* (sl) verdammt ‖ **the d.** *spl* die Verdammten *pl*

damp [dæmp] *adj* feucht ‖ *s* Feuchtigkeit *f* ‖ *tr* (be)feuchten; (*a fire; enthusiasm*) dämpfen; (elec, mus, phys) dämpfen

dampen ['dæmpən] *tr* befeuchten; (fig) dämpfen

damper ['dæmpər] *s* (*of a fireplace*) Schieber *m*; (*of a stove*) Ofenklappe *f*; (mus) Dämpfer *m*; **put a d. on** e–n Dämpfer aufsetzen (*dat*)

dampness ['dæmpnɪs] *s* Feuchtigkeit *f*

damsel ['dæmzəl] *s* Jungfrau *f*

dance [dæns] *s* Tanz *m* ‖ *tr & intr* tanzen

dance' band' *s* Tanzkapelle *f*

dance' floor' *s* Tanzfläche *f*

dance' hall' *s* Tanzsaal *m*, Tanzlokal *n*

dancer ['dænsər] *s* Tänzer –in *mf*

dance' step' *s* Tanzschritt *m*

danc'ing part'ner *s* Tanzpartner –in *mf*

dandelion ['dændɪ‚laɪ·ən] *s* Löwenzahn *m*

dandruff ['dændrəf] *s* Schuppen *pl*

dandy ['dændɪ] adj (coll) pfundig, nett || s Stutzer m

Dane [den] s Däne m, Dänin f

danger ['dendʒər] s (to) Gefahr f (für)

dan'ger list' s—be on the d. in Lebensgefahr sein

dangerous ['dendʒərəs] adj gefährlich

dangle ['dæŋgəl] tr schlenkern, baumeln lassen || intr baumeln

Danish ['denɪʃ] adj dänisch || s (language) Dänisch n

Dan'ish pas'try s feines Hefegebäck n

dank [dæŋk] adj feucht

Danube ['dænjub] s Donau f

dapper ['dæpər] adj schmuck

dappled ['dæpəld] adj scheckig, bunt

dare [der] s Herausforderung f || tr wagen; (a person) herausfordern; d. to (inf) es wagen zu (inf); don't you d. go unterstehen Sie sich, wegzugehen!; I d. say ich darf wohl behaupten || intr—don't you d.! unterstehen Sie sich!

dare'dev'il s Waghals m, Draufgänger m

dar'ing adj (deed) verwegen; (person) wagemutig || s Wagemut m

dark [dɑrk] adj finster; (color, beer, complexion) dunkel; (fig) düster || s Finsternis n, Dunkel n; be in the d. about im unklaren sein über (acc)

Dark' A'ges spl frühes Mittelalter n

dark-complexioned ['dɑrkkəm'plekʃənd] adj dunkelhäutig

darken ['dɑrkən] tr (a room) verfinstern || intr sich verfinstern; (fig) sich verdüstern

dark'-eyed' adj schwarzäugig

dark' horse' s Außenseiter m

darkly ['dɑrkli] adv geheimnisvoll

darkness ['dɑrknɪs] s Finsternis f

dark'room' s (phot) Dunkelkammer f

darling ['dɑrlɪŋ] adj lieb || s Liebchen n

darn [dɑrn] adj (coll) verwünscht || adv (coll) verdammt || s—I don't give a d. about it ich pfeif drauf! || tr (stockings) stopfen; d. it! (coll) verflixt!; I'll be darned if der Kukkuck soll mich holen, wenn

darn'ing nee'dle s Stopfnadel f

dart [dɑrt] s Wurfspieß m, Pfeil m; (sew) Abnäher m; darts (game) Pfeilwerfen n; play darts Pfeile werfen || intr huschen; d. ahead vorschießen; d. off davonstürzen

dash [dæʃ] s (rush) Ansturm m; (smartness) Schneidigkeit f; (spirit) Schwung m; (of solids) Prise f; (of liquids) Schuß m; (sport) Kurzstreckenlauf m; (typ) Gedankenstrich m; make a d. for losstürzen auf (acc) || tr (throw) schleudern; (hopes) niederschlagen, knicken; d. off (a letter) hinwerfen || intr stürmen, stürzen

dash'board' s (aut) Armaturenbrett n

dash'ing adj schneidig, forsch

dastardly ['dæstərdli] adj feige

data ['detə] s or spl Daten pl, Angaben pl

da'ta proc'essing s Datenverarbeitung f

date [det] s Datum n; (fixed time) Termin m; (period) Zeitraum m; (appointment) (coll) Verabredung f; (person on a date) Freund –in mf; (bot) Dattel f; (jur) Termin m; have a d. with verabredet sein mit; make a d. with sich verabreden mit; out of d. veraltet; to d. bis heute; what is the d. today? der wievielte ist heute? || tr datieren; (coll) ausgehen mit || intr—d. back to zurückgehen auf (acc); d. from stammen aus

dat'ed adj (provided with a date) datiert; (out-of-date) zeitgebunden

date' line' s Datumsgrenze f

date'line' s (journ) Datumszeile f

date' palm' s Dattelpalme f

dative ['detɪv] adj Dativ m, Wemfall m

daub [dɔb] s Bewurf m || tr (a canvas) beschmieren; (a wall) bewerfen; (e.g. mud, plaster) (on) schmieren (auf acc) || intr (paint) klecksen

daughter ['dɔtər] s Tochter f

daugh'ter-in-law' s (daughters-in-law) Schwiegertochter f

daunt [dɔnt] tr einschüchtern

dauntless ['dɔntlɪs] adj furchtlos

davenport ['dævən‚pɔrt] s Diwan m

davit ['devɪt] s (naut) Bootskran m

daw [dɔ] s (orn) Dohle f

dawdle ['dɔdəl] intr trödeln, bummeln

dawn [dɔn] s Morgendämmerung f; (fig) Anbeginn m || intr dämmern; d. on s.o. j–m zum Bewußtsein kommen

day [de] s Tage-, Tages- || s Tag m; (specific date) Termin m; all day long den ganzen Tag; by day am Tage, bei Tage; by the day tageweise; call it a day (coll) Feierabend machen; day after day Tag für Tag; day by day Tag für Tag; day in, day out tagaus, tagein; day off Urlaubstag m, Ruhetag m; every other day jeden zweiten Tag; in days of old in alten Zeiten; in his day zu seiner Zeit; in those days damals; one day e–s Tages; one of these days demnächst; the day after am folgenden Tag; the day after tomorrow übermorgen; the day before am Vortag; the day before yesterday vorgestern; the other day neulich, unlängst; these days heutzutage; to this very day bis auf den heutigen Tag; what day of the week is it? welchen Wochentag haben wir?

day' bed' s Ruhebett n, Liege f

day'break' s Tagesanbruch m

day'-by-day' adj tagtäglich, Tag für Tag

day'-care cen'ter s Kindertagesstätte f, Kindergarten m

day' coach' s (rr) Personenwagen m

day'dream' s Träumerei f, Wachtraum m; (wild ideas) Phantasterei f || intr mit offenen Augen träumen

day'dream'er s Träumer –in mf

day' la'borer s Tagelöhner –in mf

day'light' adj Tageslicht- || s Tageslicht n; in broad d. am hellichten Tag; knock the daylights out of (sl) zur Sau machen

day′light-sav′ing time′ s Sommerzeit f

day′ nurs′ery s Kleinkinderbewahranstalt f

day′ of reck′oning s Jüngster Tag m

day′ shift′ s Tagschicht f

day′time′ s Tageszeit f; **in the d.** bei Tage, am Tage

daze [dez] s Benommenheit f; **be in a d.** benommen sein ‖ tr betäuben

dazzle [′dæzəl] s Blenden n ‖ tr (& fig) blenden

dazz′ling adj blendend

D-day [′di‚de] s X-Tag m; (hist) Invasionstag m

deacon [′dikən] s Diakon m

deaconess [′dikənɪs] s Diakonisse f

dead [ded] adj tot; (plant) abgestorben, dürr; (faint, sleep) tief; (numb) gefühllos; (volcano, fire) erloschen; (elec) stromlos; (sport) tot, nicht im Spiel; **d. as a doornail** mausetot; **d. shot** unfehlbarer Schütze m; **d. silence** Totenstille f ‖ adv völlig, tod– ‖ s— **in the d. of night** mitten in der Nacht; **in the d. of winter** im tiefsten Winter

dead′ beat′ s (sl) Nichtstuer –in mf

dead′ bolt′ s Absteller m

dead′ calm′ s Windstille f

dead′ cen′ter s genaue Mitte f; (dead point) (mach) toter Punkt m

deaden [′dedən] tr (pain) betäuben; (a nerve) abtöten; (sound) dämpfen

dead′ end′ s (& fig) Sackgasse f

dead′head′ s Dummkopf m

dead′ heat′ s totes Rennen n

dead′-let′ter of′fice s Abteilung f für unbestellbare Briefe

dead′line′ s (letzter) Termin m; (journ) Redaktionsschluß m; **meet the d.** den Termin einhalten; **set a d. for** terminieren

dead′lock′ s Stillstand m; **break the d.** den toten Punkt überwinden; **reach a d.** steckenbleiben ‖ tr zum völligen Stillstand bringen; **become deadlocked** stocken

deadly [′dedli] adj (fatal) tödlich; **d. enemy** Todfeind –in mf; **d. fear** Todesangst f ‖ adv—**d. dull** sterbenlangweilig; **d. pale** leichenblaß

dead′ly sins′ spl Todsünden pl

dead′pan′ adj (look) ausdruckslos; (person) schafsgesichtig

dead′ pan′ s (coll) Schafsgesicht n

dead′ reck′oning s (naut) Koppelkurs m

dead′ ring′er [′rɪŋər] s (coll) Doppelgänger m

dead′wood′ s (& fig) totes Holz n

deaf [def] adj taub; **d. and dumb** taubstumm; **d. to** (fig) taub gegen; **turn a d. ear to** taube Ohren haben für

deafen [′defən] tr betäuben

deaf′ening adj ohrenbetäubend

deaf′-mute′ adj taubstumm ‖ s Taubstumme mf

deafness [′defnɪs] s Taubheit f

deal [dil] s (business transaction) Geschäft n; (underhanded agreement) Schiebung f; (cards) Austeilen n, Geben n; **a good d. of** (coll) ziemlich

viel; **a good d. worse** (coll) viel (or weit) schlechter; **a great d. of** (coll) sehr viel; **give s.o. a good d.** (be fair to s.o.) j–n fair behandeln; (make s.o. a good offer) j–m ein gutes Angebot machen; **give s.o. a raw d.** j–m übel mitspielen; **it is my d.** (cards) ich muß geben; **it's a d.!** abgemacht!; **make a d.** (coll) ein Abkommen treffen ‖ v (pret & pp **dealt** [delt]) tr (a blow) versetzen; (cards) austeilen, geben ‖ intr (cards) geben; **d. at** (a store) kaufen bei; **d. in** handeln mit; **d. with** (settle) erledigen; (occupy oneself or itself with) sich befassen mit; (treat, e.g., fairly) behandeln; (patronize) kaufen bei; (do business with) in Geschäftsbeziehungen stehen mit; **I'll d. with you later** mit Ihnen werde ich später abrechnen!

dealer [′dilər] s Geber –in mf; (com) Händler –in mf

deal′ings spl (business dealings) Handel m; (relations) Umgang m; **I'll have no d. with** ich will nichts zu tun haben mit

dean [din] s (eccl, educ) Dekan m

dean′ship′ s (eccl, educ) Dekanat n

dear [dɪr] adj lieb, traut; (expensive) teuer; **Dear Madam** Sehr verehrte gnädige Frau!; **Dear Mrs. X** Sehr geehrte Frau X; **Dear Mr. X** Sehr geehrter Herr X!; **Dear Sir** Sehr geehrter Herr! ‖ s Liebling m, Schatz m ‖ interj—**oh d.!** ach herrje!

dearie [′dɪri] s (coll) Liebchen n

dearth [dʌrθ] s (of) Mangel m (an dat)

death [deθ] s Tod m; (in the family) Todesfall m; **at death's door** sterbenskrank; **catch a d. of a cold** sich [dat] den Tod holen; **he'll be the d. of me yet** er bringt mich noch ins Grab; **put to d.** hinrichten; **to the d.** bis aufs Messer; **work to d.** totarbeiten

death′bed′ s Totenbett n, Sterbebett n

death′blow′ s Gnadenstoß m; (fig) Todesstoß m

death′ certif′icate s Totenschein m

death′ house′ s Todeshaus n

death′ knell′ s Grabgeläute n

deathless [′deθlɪs] adj unsterblich

deathly [′deθli] adj tödlich, Todes-, Toten– ‖ adv toten–

death′ mask′ s Totenmaske f

death′ pen′alty s Todesstrafe f

death′ rate′ s Sterblichkeitsziffer f

death′ rat′tle s Todesröcheln n

death′ sen′tence s Todesurteil n

death′ strug′gle s Todeskampf m

death′ trap′ s (fig) Mausefalle f

death′ war′rant s Hinrichtungsbefehl m

debacle [de′bakəl] s Zusammenbruch m

de·bar [dɪ′bɑr] v (pret & pp **–barred**; ger **–barring**) tr (from) ausschließen (aus)

debark [dɪ′bɑrk] tr ausschiffen ‖ intr sich ausschiffen, an Land gehen

debarkation [‚dibɑr′keʃən] s Ausschiffung f

debase [dɪ'bes] *tr* entwürdigen; (*currency*) entwerten

debatable [dɪ'betəbəl] *adj* strittig

debate [dɪ'bet] *s* Debatte *f* || *tr & intr* debattieren

debauch [dɪ'bɔtʃ] *s* Schwelgerei *f* || *tr* verderben; (*seduce*) verführen; **d. oneself** verkommen

debauched' *adj* ausschweifend

debauchee [,debə'tʃi] *s* Wüstling *m*

debauchery [dɪ'bɔtʃəri] *s* Schwelgerei *f*

debenture [dɪ'bentʃər] *s* (*bond*) Obligation *f*; (*voucher*) Schuldschein *m*

debilitate [dɪ'bɪlɪ,tet] *tr* entkräften

debility [dɪ'bɪlɪti] *s* Schwäche *f*

debit ['dɛbɪt] *s* Debet *n*, Soll *n*; (*as entry*) Belastung *f*

de'bit bal'ance *s* Sollsaldo *n*

de'bit side' *s* Soll *n*, Sollseite *f*

debonair [,debə'ner] *adj* (*courteous*) höflich; (*carefree*) heiter und sorglos

debris [de'bri] *s* Trümmer *pl*

debt [dɛt] *s* Schuld *f*; **be in s.o.'s d.** j-m verpflichtet sein; **run into d.** in Schulden geraten

debtor ['dɛtər] *s* Schuldner –in *mf*

de·bug [di'bʌg] *v pret & pp* –bugged; *ger* –bugging) *tr* (*remove defects from*) bereinigen; (*electron*) Abhörgeräte entfernen aus

debut [de'bju] *s* Debüt *n*; **make one's d.** debütieren

debutante ['debju,tɑnt] *s* Debütantin *f*

decade ['dɛked] *s* Jahrzehnt *n*, Dekade *f*

decadence ['dɛkədəns] *s* Dekadenz *f*

decadent ['dɛkədənt] *adj* dekadent; (*art*) entartet

decal ['dɪkæl] *s* Abziehbild *n*

decanter [dɪ'kæntər] *s* Karaffe *f*

decapitate [dɪ'kæpɪ,tet] *tr* enthaupten

decathlon [dɪ'kæθlɑn] *s* Zehnkampf *m*

decay [dɪ'ke] *s* (*rotting*) Verwesung *f*; (*fig*) Verfall *m*; (*dent*) Karies *f*; **fall into d.** (& *fig*) in Verfall geraten || *intr* verfaulen; (fig) verfallen

decease [dɪ'sis] *s* Ableben *n*

deceased' *adj* verstorben || *s* Verstorbene *mf*

deceit [dɪ'sit] *s* Betrügerei *f*

deceitful [dɪ'sitfəl] *adj* betrügerisch

deceive [dɪ'siv] *tr* betrügen || *intr* trügen

decelerate [di'selə,ret] *tr* verlangsamen || *intr* seine Geschwindigkeit verringern

December [dɪ'sembər] *s* Dezember *m*

decency ['disənsi] *s* Anstand *m*; **decencies** Anstandsformen *pl*

decent ['disənt] *adj* anständig

decentralize [di'sentrə,laɪz] *tr* dezentralisieren

deception [dɪ'sepʃən] *s* (*act of deceiving*) Betrug *m*; (*state of being deceived*) Täuschung *f*

deceptive [dɪ'septɪv] *adj* trügerisch; (*misleading*) irreführend; (*similarity*) täuschend

decide [dɪ'saɪd] *tr* entscheiden || *intr* (on) sich entscheiden, sich entschließen (über *acc*, für)

deciduous [dɪ'sɪdʒu·əs] *adj* blattabwerfend; **d. tree** Laubbaum *m*

decimal ['dɛsɪməl] *adj* dezimal || *s* Dezimalzahl *f*

dec'imal place' *s* Dezimalstelle *f*

dec'imal point' *s* (*in German the comma is used to separate the decimal fraction from the integer*) Komma *n*

decimate ['dɛsɪ,met] *tr* dezimieren

decipher [dɪ'saɪfər] *tr* entziffern

decision [dɪ'sɪʒən] *s* Entscheidung *f*, Entschluß *m*; (jur) Urteil *n*

decisive [dɪ'saɪsɪv] *adj* entscheidend

deck [dɛk] *s* (of cards) Spiel *n*; (data proc) Kartensatz *m*; (naut) Deck *n*, Verdeck *n* || *tr* (coll) zu Boden schlagen; **d. out** ausschmücken

deck' chair' *s* Liegestuhl *m*

deck' hand' *s* gemeiner Matrose *m*

deck' land'ing *s* (aer) Trägerlandung *f*

declaim [dɪ'klem] *tr & intr* deklamieren

declaration [,dɛklə're ʃən] *s* Erklärung *f*; (at customs) Zollerklärung *f*

declarative [dɪ'klærətɪv] *adj*–**d. sentence** Aussagesatz *m*

declare [dɪ'kler] *tr* erklären; (*tourist's belongings*) verzollen; (*commercial products*) deklarieren; **d. oneself against** sich aussprechen gegen

declension [dɪ'klenʃən] *s* Deklination *f*

declinable [dɪ'klaɪnəbəl] *adj* deklinierbar

decline [dɪ'klaɪn] *s* (decrease) Abnahme *f*; (in prices) Rückgang *m*; (deterioration) Verschlechterung *f*; (slope) Abhang *m*; (fig) Niedergang *m*; **be on the d.** in Abnahme begriffen sein || *tr* (refuse) ablehnen; (gram) deklinieren || *intr* (refuse) ablehnen; (descend) sich senken; (sink) sinken; (draw to a close) zu Ende gehen

declivity [dɪ'klɪvɪti] *s* Abhang *m*

decode [di'kod] *tr* entschlüsseln

decompose [,dikəm'poz] *tr* zerlegen || *intr* sich zersetzen, verwesen

decomposition [,dikɑmpə'zɪʃən] *s* Zersetzung *f*, Verwesung *f*

decompression [,dikəm'preʃən] *s* Dekompression *f*

decontaminaiton [,dikən,tæmɪ'neʃən] *s* Entseuchung *f*

décor [de'kɔr] *s* Dekor *m*

decorate ['dɛkə,ret] *tr* dekorieren, (aus)schmücken; (a new room) einrichten; (e.g., with a badge) auszeichnen

decoration [,dɛkə're ʃən] *s* Schmuck *m*; (medal) Orden *m*, Ehrenzeichen *n*, Dekoration *f*

decorative ['dɛkərətɪv] *adj* dekorativ

decorator ['dɛkə,retər] *s* Dekorateur –in *mf*

decorous ['dɛkərəs] *adj* schicklich

decorum [dɪ'korəm] *s* Schicklichkeit *f*

decoy ['dikɔɪ] *s* (bird or person) Lockvogel *m*; (anything used as a lure) Lockmittel *n* || [dɪ'kɔɪ] *tr* locken

decrease ['dikris] *s* Abnahme *f* ||

[dɪˈkris] *tr* verringern ‖ *intr* abnehmen
decree [dɪˈkri] *s* Dekret *n*, Verordnung *f* ‖ *tr* dekretieren, verordnen
decrepit [dɪˈkrɛpɪt] *adj* (*age-worn*)
altersschwach; (*frail*) gebrechlich
de·cry [dɪˈkraɪ] *v* (*pret & pp* **–cried**)
tr (*disparage*) herabsetzen; (*censure
openly*) kritisieren
dedicate [ˈdɛdɪ͵ket] *tr* (*a book, one's
life*) (**to**) widmen (*dat*); (*a building*)
einweihen
dedication [͵dɛdɪˈkeʃən] *s* Widmung
f; (*of a building, etc.*) Einweihung *f*;
(**to**) Hingabe *f* (an *acc*)
deduce [dɪˈd(j)us] *tr* (**from**) schließen
(aus)
deduct [dɪˈdʌkt] *tr* abziehen, abrechnen
deduction [dɪˈdʌkʃən] *s* Abzug *m*;
(*conclusion*) Schluß *m*, Folgerung *f*
deed [did] *s* (*act*) Tat *f*; (*jur*) Besitz-
urkunde *f*
deem [dim] *tr* halten für; **d. s.o.
worthy of my confidence** j-n meines
Vertrauens für würdig halten
deep [dip] *adj* tief; (*recondite*) dunkel; (*impression*) tiefgehend; (*color,
sound*) tief, dunkel; **be d. in debt**
tief in Schulden stecken; **four** (**ranks**)
d. in Viererreihen; **in d. water** (fig)
in Schwierigkeiten; **that's too d. for
me** das ist mir zu hoch ‖ *adv* tief;
d. down in tief innen in (*dat*) ‖ *s*
Tiefe *f*, Meer *n*
deepen [ˈdipən] *tr* (& fig) vertiefen ‖
intr sich vertiefen
deep'-freeze' *v* (*pret* **–freezed & –froze**;
pp **–freezed & –frozen**) *tr* tiefkühlen
deep'-fry' *v* (*pret & pp* **–fried**) *tr* fri-
tieren
deep'-laid' *adj* schlau angelegt
deep' mourn'ing *s* tiefe Trauer *f*
deep'-root'ed *adj* tiefsitzend
deep'-set' *adj* (*eyes*) tiefliegend
deer [dɪr] *s* Hirsch *m*, Reh *n*, Rotwild
n
deer'skin' *s* Hirschleder *n*, Wildleder *n*
deface [dɪˈfes] *tr* (*disfigure*) verunstalten; (*make illegible*) unleserlich
machen
defacement [dɪˈfesmənt] *s* Verunstal-
tung *f*
de facto [diˈfækto] *adj & adv* tatsächlich, de facto
defamation [͵dɛfəˈmeʃən] *s* Verleumdung *f*
defame [dɪˈfem] *tr* verleumden
default [dɪˈfɔlt] *s* (*in duties*) Unterlassung *f*; (fin) Verzug *m*; **by d.** (jur)
durch Nichterscheinen; (sport) durch
Nichtantreten; **in d. of** in Ermangelung (*genit*) ‖ *tr* nicht erfüllen; (fin)
nicht zahlen ‖ *intr* seinen Verpflich-
tungen nicht nachkommen; (fin) in
Verzug sein
defeat [dɪˈfit] *s* Niederlage *f*; (parl)
Niederstimmen *n*; **admit d.** sich geschlagen geben ‖ *tr* besiegen, schlagen; (*frustrate*) hilflos machen;
(*plans*) zunichte machen; (*a bill*)
niederstimmen; **d. the purpose** den
Zweck verfehlen

defeatism [dɪˈfitɪzəm] *s* Defätismus *m*
defeatist [dɪˈfitɪst] *s* Defätist –in *mf*
defecate [ˈdɛfɪ͵ket] *intr* Stuhl haben
defect [ˈdifɛkt] *s* Defekt *m*; (*physical
or mental defect*) Gebrechen *n*; (*imperfection*) Mangel *m*; (*in manufacture*) Fabrikationsfehler *m* ‖ [dɪ-
ˈfɛkt] *intr* (**from**) (*a religion*) abfallen
(von); (*a party*) abtrünnig werden
(von); (**to**) überlaufen (zu)
defection [dɪˈfɛkʃən] *s* Abfall *m*; (**to**)
Übertritt *m* (zu)
defective [dɪˈfɛktɪv] *adj* fehlerhaft;
(gram) unvollständig; (tech) defekt
defector [dɪˈfɛktər] *s* (pol) Abtrünnige
mf, Überläufer –in *mf*
defend [dɪˈfɛnd] *tr* verteidigen
defendant [dɪˈfɛndənt] *s* (*in civil suit*)
Beklagte *mf*; (*in criminal suit*) Angeklagte *mf*
defender [dɪˈfɛndər] *s* Verteidiger –in
mf; (sport) Titelverteidiger –in *mf*
defense [dɪˈfɛns] *s* (& jur, sport) Verteidigung *f*; (*tactical*) (mil) Abwehr
f; **d. against** (*e.g., disease*) Schutz *m*
vor (*dat*)
defenseless [dɪˈfɛnslɪs] *adj* schutzlos
defensible [dɪˈfɛnsɪbəl] *adj* verteidi-
gungsfähig; (*argument, claim*) ver-
fechtbar
defensive [dɪˈfɛnsɪv] *adj* defensiv;
(mil) Verteidigungs-, Abwehr– ‖ *s*
Defensive *f*; (*tactical*) Abwehr *f*; **be
on the d.**—sich in der Defensive befinden
de·fer [dɪˈfʌr] *v* (*pret & pp* **ferred**;
ger **–ferring**) *tr* verschieben; (mil)
zurückschieben ‖ *intr*—**d. to** nachgeben (*dat*)
deference [ˈdɛfərəns] *s* (*courteous regard*) Ehrerbietung *f*; (*yielding*)
Nachgiebigkeit *f*; **in d. to** aus Rücksicht gegen; **with all due d. to** bei
aller Achtung vor (*dat*)
deferential [͵dɛfəˈrɛnʃəl] *adj* ehrerbietig, rücksichtsvoll
deferment [dɪˈfʌrmənt] *s* Aufschub *m*;
(mil) Zurückstellung *f*
defiance [dɪˈfaɪəns] *s* Trotz *m*; **in d.
of s.o.** j–m zum Trotz
defiant [dɪˈfaɪənt] *adj* trotzig
deficiency [dɪˈfɪʃənsi] *s* (**of**) Mangel
m (an *dat*); (*shortcoming*) Defekt
m; (*deficit*) Defizit *n*
deficient [dɪˈfɪʃənt] *adj* mangelhaft;
be d. in Mangel haben an (*dat*);
mentally d. schwachsinnig
deficit [ˈdɛfɪsɪt] *s* Defizit *n*
defilade [͵dɛfiˈled] *s* Deckung *f* ‖ *tr*
gegen Feuer sichern
defile [dɪˈfaɪl], [ˈdɪfaɪl] *s* Hohlweg *m*
‖ [dɪˈfaɪl] *tr* beflecken
defilement [dɪˈfaɪlmənt] *s* Befleckung
f
define [dɪˈfaɪn] *tr* definieren, bestimmen; (*e.g., boundaries*) festlegen
definite [ˈdɛfɪnɪt] *adj* bestimmt
definition [͵dɛfɪˈnɪʃən] *s* Definition *f*,
Bestimmung *f*; (opt) Bildschärfe *f*
definitive [dɪˈfɪnɪtɪv] *adj* endgültig
deflate [dɪˈflet] *tr* Luft ablassen aus;
(*prices*) herabsetzen; (*s.o.'s ego,
hopes*) e–n Stoß versetzen (*dat*)

deflation [dɪ'fleʃən] s (fin) Deflation f

deflect [dɪ'flɛkt] tr ablenken ‖ intr (from) abweichen (von)

deflection [dɪ'flɛkʃən] s Ablenkung f; Abweichung f; (of an indicator) Ausschlag m; (of light rays) Beugung f; (radar, telv) Ablenkung f

deflower [dɪ'flau-ər] tr entjungfern

defoliate [dɪ'folɪ,et] tr entblättern

deforest [dɪ'fɔrest] tr abholzen

deform [dɪ'fɔrm] tr entstellen

deformed' adj verwachsen, mißförmig

deformity [dɪ'fɔrmɪtɪ] s (state of being deformed) Mißgestalt f; (deformed part) Verwachsung f; (ugliness) Häßlichkeit f

defraud [dɪ'frɔd] tr (of) betrügen (um)

defray [dɪ'fre] tr tragen, bestreiten

defrock [dɪ'frɑk] tr das Priesteramt entziehen (dat)

defrost [dɪ'frɔst] tr entfrosten

defroster [dɪ'frɔstər] s Entfroster m

deft [dɛft] adj flink, fingerfertig

defunct [dɪ'fʌŋkt] adj (person) verstorben; (no longer in operation) stillgelegt; (no longer in effect) außer Kraft (befindlich); (newspaper) eingegangen

de•fy [dɪ'faɪ] v (pret & pp –fied) tr trotzen (dat); (challenge) herausfordern; **d. description** sich nicht beschreiben lassen

degeneracy [dɪ'dʒenərəsi] s Entartung f

degenerate [dɪ'dʒenərɪt] adj entartet, verkommen ‖ [dɪ'dʒenə,ret] intr entarten; (into) ausarten (in acc)

degrade [dɪ'gred] tr degradieren; (bring into low esteem) entwürdigen

degrad'ing adj entwürdigend

degree [dɪ'gri] s Grad m; (gram) Steigerungsstufe f; **by degrees** gradweise; **d. of latitude** Breitengrad m; **d. of longitude** Längengrad m; **take one's d.** promovieren; **to a d.** einigermaßen; **to a high d.** in hohem Maße

dehumanize [dɪ'hjumə,naɪz] tr entmenschlichen

dehumidifier [,dɪhju'mɪdɪ,faɪ-ər] s Luftentfeuchter m

dehumidi•fy [,dɪhju'mɪdɪ,faɪ] v (pret & pp –fied) entfeuchten

dehydrate [dɪ'haɪdret] tr (vegetables) dörren, das Wasser entziehen (dat); (chem) dehydrieren ‖ intr das Wasser verlieren

dehy'drated adj (vegetables) Trocken–; (body) dehydriert

deice [dɪ'aɪs] tr enteisen

dei•fy ['di·ɪ,faɪ] v (pret & pp –fied) tr (a man) zum Gott erheben; (a woman) zur Göttin erheben

deject'ed adj niedergeschlagen

dejection [dɪ'dʒɛkʃən] s Niedergeschlagenheit f, Mutlosigkeit f

delay [dɪ'le] s Aufschub m, Verzögerung f; **without d.** unverzüglich ‖ tr (postpone) aufschieben; (detain) aufhalten ‖ intr zögern

delectable [dɪ'lɛktəbəl] adj ergötzlich

delegate ['dɛlɪ,get], ['dɛlɪgɪt] s Delegierte mf ‖ ['dɛlɪ,get] tr delegieren; (authority) übertragen

delegation [,dɛlɪ'geʃən] s (persons delegated) Delegation f; (e.g., of authority) Übertragung f

delete [dɪ'lit] tr tilgen

deletion [dɪ'liʃən] s Tilgung f

deliberate [dɪ'lɪbərɪt] adj (intentional) vorsätzlich, bewußt; (slow) gemessen, bedächtig ‖ [dɪ'lɪbə,ret] intr überlegen; (said of several persons) beratschlagen; **d. on** sich beraten über (acc)

deliberately [dɪ'lɪbərɪtlɪ] adv mit Absicht

deliberation [dɪ,lɪbə'reʃən] s Überlegung f; (by several persons) Beratung f; (slowness) Bedächtigkeit f

delicacy ['dɛlɪkəsɪ] s Zartheit f; (fine food) Delikatesse f

delicate ['dɛlɪkɪt] adj fein, delikat; (situation) heikel; (health) zart

delicatessen [,dɛlɪkə'tesən] s (food) Delikatessen pl; (store) Delikatessengeschäft n

delicious [dɪ'lɪʃəs] adj köstlich

delight [dɪ'laɪt] s Freude f; (high degree of pleasure) Entzücken n; **take d. in** Freude finden an (dat) ‖ tr entzücken, erfreuen; **be delighted by** sich freuen an (dat); **I'll be delighted to come** ich komme mit dem größten Vergnügen ‖ intr—**d. in** sich ergötzen an (dat)

delightful [dɪ'laɪtfəl] adj entzückend

delimit [dɪ'lɪmɪt] tr abgrenzen

delineate [dɪ'lɪnɪ,et] tr zeichnen

delinquency [dɪ'lɪŋkwənsi] s Pflichtvergessenheit f; (misdeed) Vergehen n

delinquent [dɪ'lɪŋkwənt] adj pflichtvergessen; (guilty) straffällig; (overdue) rückständig; (in default) säumig ‖ s Straffällige mf

delirious [dɪ'lɪrɪ·əs] adj irre; (with) rasend (vor dat)

delirium [dɪ'lɪrɪ·əm] s Fieberwahn m

deliver [dɪ'lɪvər] tr liefern; (a message) überreichen; (free) befreien; (mail) zustellen; (a speech) halten; (a blow) versetzen; (a verdict) aussprechen; (a child) zur Welt bringen; (votes) bringen; (a ball) werfen; (relig) erlösen

deliverance [dɪ'lɪvərəns] s Erlösung f

delivery [dɪ'lɪvərɪ] s Lieferung f; (freeing) Befreiung f; (of mail) Zustellung f; (of a speaker, actor, singer) Vortragsweise f; (of a pitcher) Wurf m; (childbirth) Entbindung f

deliv'ery·man [–'men] s Austräger m

deliv'ery room' s Kreißsaal m

deliv'ery truck' s Lieferwagen m

dell [dɛl] s enges Tal m

delouse [dɪ'laʊs] tr entlausen

delta ['dɛltə] s Delta n

delude [dɪ'lud] tr täuschen

deluge ['dɛljudʒ] s Überschwemmung f; (fig) Hochflut f; **Deluge** (Bib) Sintflut f ‖ tr überschwemmen; (with letters, etc.) überschütten

delusion [dɪ'luʒən] s (state of being deluded) Täuschung f; (misconcep-

tion) Wahnvorstellung *f;* (*psychiatry*) Wahn *m;* **delusions of grandeur** Größenwahn *m*

deluxe [dɪˈlʊks], [dɪˈlʌks] *adj* Luxus-

delve [dɛlv] *intr*—d. into sich vertiefen in (*acc*)

demagogue [ˈdɛməˌgag] *s* Volksverführer –in *mf*

demand [dɪˈmænd] *s* Verlangen *n;* (*com*) (**for**) Nachfrage *f* (nach); **in** (**great**) **d.** (sehr) gefragt; **make demands on** Ansprüche erheben auf (*acc*); **on d.** auf Verlangen ‖ *tr* (**from** or **of**) verlangen (von), fordern (von)

demand'ing *adj* anspruchsvoll; (*strict*) streng

demarca'tion line' [ˌdimarˈkeʃən] *s* Demarkationslinie *f*

demean [dɪˈmin] *tr* erniedrigen

demeanor [dɪˈminər] *s* Benehmen *n*

demented [dɪˈmɛntɪd] *adj* wahnsinnig

demerit [diˈmɛrɪt] *s* (*fault*) Fehler *m;* (*deficiency mark*) Minuspunkt *m*

demigod [ˈdɛmɪˌgad] *s* Halbgott *m*

demijohn [ˈdɛmɪˌdʒan] *s* Korbflasche *f*

demilitarize [diˈmɪlɪtəˌraɪz] *tr* entmilitarisieren

demise [dɪˈmaɪz] *s* Ableben *n*

demitasse [ˈdɛmɪˌtæs], [ˈdɛmɪˌtas] *s* Mokkatasse *f*

demobilize [diˈmobɪˌlaɪz] *tr & intr* demobilisieren

democracy [dɪˈmakrəsi] *s* Demokratie *f*

democrat [ˈdɛməˌkræt] *s* Demokrat –in *mf*

democratic [ˌdɛməˈkrætɪk] *adj* demokratisch

demolish [dɪˈmalɪʃ] *tr* (*raze*) niederreißen; (*destroy*) zertrümmern; (*an argument*) vernichten; (*devour*) (*coll*) verschlingen

demolition [ˌdɛməˈlɪʃən], [ˌdiməˈlɪʃən] *s* (*act of razing*) Abbruch *m;* (*by explosives*) Sprengung *f;* **demolitions** Sprengstoff *m*

demoli'tion squad' *s* Sprengkommando *n*

demoli'tion work' *s* Sprengarbeiten *pl*

demon [ˈdimən] *s* Dämon *m,* böser Geist *m*

demonstrable [dɪˈmanstrəbəl] *adj* beweisbar

demonstrate [ˈdɛmənˌstret] *tr* (*prove*) beweisen; (*explain*) erklären; (*display*) zeigen; (*a product, process*) vorführen ‖ *intr* (pol) demonstrieren

demonstration [ˌdɛmənˈstreʃən] *s* (*com*) Vorführung *f;* (pol) Demonstration *f*

demonstrative [dɪˈmanstrətɪv] *adj* (*showing emotions*) gefühlvoll; (*illustrative*) anschaulich; (*gram*) hinweisend

demonstrator [ˈdɛmənˌstretər] *s* (*of products*) Vorführer –in *mf;* (*model used in demonstration*) Vorführmodell *n;* (pol) Demonstrant –in *mf*

demoralize [dɪˈmɔrəˌlaɪz] *tr* demoralisieren

demote [dɪˈmot] *tr* (*an employee*) her-

abstufen; (*a student*) zurückversetzen; (mil) degradieren

demotion [dɪˈmoʃən] *s* (*of an employee*) Herabstufung *f;* (*of a student*) Zurückversetzung *f;* (mil) Degradierung *f*

de-mur [dɪˈmʌr] *v* (*pret & pp* **-murred;** *ger* **-murring**) *intr* Einwände erheben

demure [dɪˈmjur] *adj* zimperlich

den [dɛn] *s* (*of animals; of thieves*) Höhle *f;* (*comfortable room*) Freizeitraum *m*

denaturalize [diˈnætʃərəˌlaɪz] *tr* ausbürgern

denial [dɪˈnaɪəl] *s* (*of an assertion*) Leugnung *f;* (*of guilt*) Leugnen *n;* (*of a request*) Ablehnung *f;* (*of faith*) Ableugnung *f;* (*of rights*) Verweigerung *f;* (*of a report*) Dementi *n*

denigrate [ˈdɛnɪˌgret] *tr* anschwärzen

denim [ˈdɛnɪm] *s* Drillich *m*

denizen [ˈdɛnɪzən] *s* Bewohner –in *mf*

Denmark [ˈdɛnmark] *s* Dänemark *n*

denomination [dɪˌnamɪˈneʃən] *s* Bezeichnung *f;* (*class, kind*) Klasse *f;* (*of money*) Nennwert *m;* (*of shares*) Stückelung *f;* (relig) Konfession *f,* Bekenntnis *n;* **in denominations of five and ten dollars** in Fünf- und Zehndollarnoten

denotation [ˌdinoˈteʃən] *s* Bedeutung *f*

denote [dɪˈnot] *tr* (*mean*) bedeuten; (*indicate*) anzeigen

dénouement [deˈnumã] *s* Auflösung *f*

denounce [dɪˈnauns] *tr* (*inform against*) denunzieren; (*condemn openly*) brandmarken, anprangern; (*a treaty*) kündigen

dense [dɛns] *adj* dicht; (coll) beschränkt

density [ˈdɛnsɪti] *s* Dichte *f*

dent [dɛnt] *s* Beule *f* ‖ *tr* einbeulen

dental [ˈdɛntəl] *adj* Zahn–; (ling) dental ‖ *s* (ling) Zahnlaut *m*

den'tal hygiene' *s* Zahnpflege *f*

den'tal sur'geon *s* Zahnarzt *m,* Zahnärztin *f*

dentifrice [ˈdɛntɪfrɪs] *s* Zahnputzmittel *n*

dentist [ˈdɛntɪst] *s* Zahnarzt *m,* Zahnärztin *f*

dentistry [ˈdɛntɪstri] *s* Zahnheilkunde *f*

denture [ˈdɛntʃər] *s* künstliches Gebiß *n*

denunciation [dɪˌnʌnsɪˈeʃən] *s* (*informing against*) Denunzierung *f;* (*public condemnation*) Brandmarkung *f*

de-ny [dɪˈnaɪ] *v* (*pret & pp* **-nied**) *tr* (*a statement*) leugnen; (*officially*) dementieren; (*a request*) ablehnen; (*one's faith*) ableugnen; (*rights*) verweigern; **d. oneself s.th.** sich [dat] etw versagen; **d. s.o. s.th.** j-m etw aberkennen

deodorant [diˈodərənt] *s* Deodorant *n*

deodorize [diˈodəˌraɪz] *tr* desodorieren

deoxidize [diˈaksɪˌdaɪz] *tr* desoxydieren

depart [dɪ'pɑrt] *intr* (*on foot*) fortgehen; (*in a vehicle or boat*) abfahren; (*by plane*) abfliegen; (*on horseback*) abreiten; (*on a trip*) abreisen; (*deviate*) abweichen

department [dɪ'pɑrtmənt] *s* (*subdivision*) Abteilung *f*; (*field*) Fach *n*; (*principal branch of government*) Ministerium *n*; (*government office*) Amt *n*; (*educ*) Abteilung *f*

depart'ment head' *s* Abteilungsleiter –in *mf*

depart'ment store' *s* Kaufhaus *n*, Warenhaus *n*

departure [dɪ'pɑrtʃər] *s* (*on foot*) Weggehen *n*; (*by car, boat, train*) Abfahrt *f*, Abreise *f*; (*by plane*) Abflug *m*; (*deviation*) Abweichung *f*

depend [dɪ'pɛnd] *intr* (**on**) abhängen (von); (*rely on*) sich verlassen (auf *acc*); **depending on** je nach; **depending on how** je nachdem; **it all depends** (coll) es kommt darauf an

dependable [dɪ'pɛndəbəl] *adj* zuverlässig

dependence [dɪ'pɛndəns] *s* Abhängigkeit *f*

dependency [dɪ'pɛndənsi] *s* Schutzgebiet *n*

dependent [dɪ'pɛndənt] *adj* (**on**) abhängig (von) || *s* Abhängige *mf*; (*for tax purposes*) Unterhaltsberechtigte *mf*

depict [dɪ'pɪkt] *tr* schildern

deplete [dɪ'plit] *tr* entleeren; (*fig*) erschöpfen

deplorable [dɪ'plɔrəbəl] *adj* (*situation*) beklagenswert; (*regrettable*) bedauerlich; (*bad*) schlecht

deplore [dɪ'plɔr] *tr* bedauern

deploy [dɪ'plɔɪ] *tr* entfalten || *intr* sich entfalten

deployment [dɪ'plɔɪmənt] *s* Entfaltung *f*

depolarize [di'polə,raɪz] *tr* depolarisieren

deponent [dɪ'ponənt] *s* (*gram*) Deponens *n*; (*jur*) Deponent –in *mf*

depopulate [di'pɑpjə,let] *tr* entvölkern

deport [dɪ'pɔrt] *tr* deportieren; **d. oneself** sich benehmen

deportation [,dipɔr'teʃən] *s* Deportation *f*

deportment [dɪ'pɔrtmənt] *s* Benehmen *n*

depose [dɪ'poz] *tr* (*from office*) absetzen; (*jur*) bezeugen || *intr* (*jur*) unter Eid aussagen; (*in writing*) (*jur*) eidesstattlich versichern

deposit [dɪ'pɑzɪt] *s* (*partial payment*) Anzahlung *f*; (*at a bank*) Einlage *f*; (*for safekeeping*) Hinterlegung *f*; (*geol*) Ablagerung *f*; (*min*) Vorkommen *n*; **for d. only** nur zur Verrechnung || *tr* (*set down*) niederlegen; (*money at a bank*) einlegen; (*a check*) verrechnen; (*as part payment*) anzahlen; (*for safekeeping*) deponieren; (*geol*) ablagern; (*a coin*) (telp) einwerfen

depositor [dɪ'pɑzɪtər] *s* Einzahler –in *mf*; (*of valuables*) Hinterleger –in *mf*

depos'it slip' *s* Einzahlungsbeleg *m*

depot ['dipo], ['depo] *s* (*bus station; storage place*) Depot *n*; (*train station*) Bahnhof *m*

depraved [dɪ'prevd] *adj* verworfen

depravity [dɪ'prævɪti] *s* Verworfenheit *f*

deprecate ['deprɪ,ket] *tr* mißbilligen

depreciate [dɪ'priʃɪ,et] *tr* (*money, stocks*) abwerten; (*for tax purposes*) abschreiben; (*value or price*) herabsetzen; (*disparage*) geringschätzen || *intr* im Wert sinken

depreciation [dɪ,priʃɪ'eʃən] *s* (*decrease in value*) Wertminderung *f*; (*of currency or stocks*) Abwertung *f*; (*for tax purposes*) Abschreibung *f*

depress [dɪ'pres] *tr* niederdrücken; (*sadden*) deprimieren; (*cause to sink*) herunterdrücken

depressed' *adj* (*saddened*) niedergeschlagen; (*market*) flau

depressed' ar'ea *s* Notstandsgebiet *n*

depress'ing *adj* deprimierend

depression [dɪ'preʃən] *s* (*mental state; economic crisis*) Depression *f*; (*geol*) Vertiefung *f*

deprive [dɪ'praɪv] *tr*—**d. s.o. of s.th.** j-m etw entziehen; (*withhold*) j-m etw vorenthalten

depth [depθ] *s* Tiefe *f*; **go beyond one's d.** den Boden unter den Füßen verlieren; **in d.** gründlich

depth' charge' *s* Wasserbombe *f*

depth' of field' *s* (phot) Tiefenschärfe *f*

deputation [,depjə'teʃən] *s* Abordnung *f*

deputize ['depjə,taɪz] *tr* abordnen

deputy ['depjəti] *s* Vertreter –in *mf*; (pol) Abgeordnete *mf*

derail [dɪ'rel] *tr* zum Entgleisen bringen || *intr* entgleisen

derailment [dɪ'relmənt] *s* Entgleisung *f*

deranged [dɪ'rendʒd] *adj* geistesgestört

derangement [dɪ'rendʒmənt] *s* Geistesgestörtheit *f*

derby ['dʌrbi] *s* (*hat*) Melone *f*; (*race*) Derbyrennen *n*

derelict ['derɪlɪkt] *adj* (*negligent*) (**in**) nachlässig (in *dat*); (*abandoned*) herrenlos || *s* (*ship; bum*) Wrack *n*

dereliction [,derɪ'lɪkʃən] *s* (*neglect*) Vernachlässigung *f*

deride [dɪ'raɪd] *tr* verspotten

derision [dɪ'rɪʒən] *s* Spott *m*

derivation [,derɪ'veʃən] *s* (gram, math) Ableitung *f*

derivative [dɪ'rɪvətɪv] *adj* abgeleitet || *s* (chem) Derivat *n*; (gram, math) Ableitung *f*

derive [dɪ'raɪv] *tr* (*obtain*) gewinnen; (gram, math) ableiten; **d. pleasure from s.th.** Freude an etw finden || *intr* (*from*) herstammen (von)

dermatologist [[,dʌrmə'tɑlədʒɪst] *s* Hautarzt *m*, Hautärztin *f*

derogatory [dɪ'rɑgə,tori] *adj* abfällig

derrick ['derɪk] *s* (*over an oil well*) Bohrturm *m*; (naut) Ladebaum *m*

dervish ['dʌrvɪʃ] *s* Derwisch *m*

desalinization [di,sælɪnɪ'zeʃən] *s* Entsalzung *f*

desalt [di'sɔlt] *tr* entsalzen

descend [dɪ'send] *tr* hinuntergehen || *intr* (*dismount, alight*) absteigen; (*said of a plane*) niedergehen; (*from a tree, from heaven*) herabsteigen; (*said of a road*) sich senken; (*pass by inheritance*) (**to**) übergehen (auf *acc*); **be descended from** abstammen von; **d. upon** hereinbrechen über (*acc*)

descendant [dɪ'sendənt] *s* Abkömmling *m*, Nachkomme *m*; **descendants** Nachkommenschaft *f*

descendent [dɪ'sendənt] *adj* absteigend

descent [dɪ'sent] *s* Abstieg *m*; (*lineage*) Herkunft *f*; (*of a plane or parachute*) Niedergehen *n*; (*slope*) Abhang *m*; (*hostile raid*) (**on**) Überfall *m* (auf *acc*)

describe [dɪ'skraɪb] *tr* beschreiben

description [dɪ'skrɪpʃən] *s* Beschreibung *f*; (*type*) Art *f*; **beyond d.** unbeschreiblich

descriptive [dɪ'skrɪptɪv] *adj* beschreibend

de∙scry [dɪ'skraɪ] *v* (*pret & pp* **-scried**) *tr* erspähen, erblicken

desecrate ['desɪ‚kret] *tr* entweihen

desecration [‚desɪ'kreʃən] *s* Entweihung *f*

desegregate [di'segrɪ‚get] *tr* die Rassentrennung aufheben in (*dat*)

desegregation [di‚segrɪ'geʃən] *s* Aufhebung *f* der Rassentrennung

desert ['dezərt] *adj* öde, wüst; (*sand, warfare, etc.*) Wüsten- || *s* Wüste *f*; (*fig*) Öde *f* || [dɪ'zʌrt] *s* Verdienst *m*; **get one's just deserts** seinen wohlverdienten Lohn empfangen || *tr* verlassen || *intr* (mil) desertieren; (**to**) überlaufen (zu)

deserter [dɪ'zʌrtər] *s* Deserteur *m*

desertion [dɪ'zʌrʃən] *s* Verlassen *n*; (*of a party*) Abfall *m*; (mil) Fahnenflucht *f*

deserve [dɪ'zʌrv] *tr* verdienen

deservedly [dɪ'zʌrvɪdli] *adv* mit Recht

deserv∙ing *adj* (**of**) würdig (*genit*)

design [dɪ'zaɪn] *s* (*outline*) Entwurf *m*; (*pattern*) Muster *n*; (*plan*) Plan *m*; (*plot*) Anschlag *m*; (*of a building, etc.*) Bauart *f*; (*aim*) Absicht *f*; **designs on** böse Absichten auf (*acc*) || *tr* (*make a preliminary sketch of*) entwerfen; (*draw up detailed plans for*) konstruieren; **designed for** gedacht für

designate ['dezɪg‚net] *tr* (**as**) bezeichnen (als); (**to**) ernennen (zu)

designation [‚dezɪg'neʃən] *s* (*act of designating*) Kennzeichnung *f*; (*title*) Bezeichnung *f*; (*appointment*) Ernennung *f*

designer [dɪ'zaɪnər] *s* (*of patterns*) Musterzeichner -in *mf*; (*of fashions*) Modeschöpfer -in *mf*; (theat) Dekorateur -in *mf*

design∙ing *adj* intrigant; (*calculating*) berechnend

desirable [dɪ'zaɪrəbəl] *adj* wünschenswert, begehrenswert

desire [dɪ'zaɪr] *s* (*wish*) Wunsch *m*; (*interest*) Lust *f*; (*craving*) Begierde *f*; (*thing desired*) Gewünschte *n* || *tr* wünschen

desirous [dɪ'zaɪrəs] *adj* (**of**) begierig (nach)

desist [dɪ'zɪst] *intr* (**from**) ablassen (von)

desk [desk] *s* Schreibtisch *m*; (*of a teacher*) Pult *n*; (*of a pupil*) Schulbank *f*; (*in a hotel*) Kasse *f*

desk′ cop′y *s* Freiexemplar *n*

desk′ lamp′ *s* Tischlampe *f*

desk′ pad′ *s* Schreibunterlage *f*

desolate ['desəlɪt] *adj* (*barren*) öde; (*joyless*) trostlos; (*deserted*) verlassen; (*delapidated*) verfallen || ['desə‚let] *tr* verwüsten

desolation [‚desə'leʃən] *s* (*devastation*) Verwüstung *f*; (*dreariness*) Trostlosigkeit *f*

despair [dɪs'per] *s* Verzweiflung *f* || *intr* (**of**) verzweifeln (an *dat*)

despair′ing *adj* verzweifelt

despera∙do [‚despə'rado], [‚despə'redo] *s* (**-does & -dos**) Desperado *m*

desperate ['despərɪt] *adj* verzweifelt

desperation [‚despə'reʃən] *s* Verzweiflung *f*

despicable ['despɪkəbəl] *adj* verächtlich, verachtungswürdig

despise [dɪs'paɪz] *tr* verachten

despite [dɪs'paɪt] *prep* trotz (*genit*)

despondency [dɪs'pandənsi] *s* Kleinmut *m*

despondent [dɪs'pandənt] *adj* kleinmütig

despot ['despat] *s* Despot -in *mf*

despotic [des'patɪk] *adj* despotisch

despotism ['despə‚tɪzəm] *s* Despotie *f*; (*as a system*) Despotismus *m*

dessert [dɪ'zʌrt] *s* Nachtisch *m*

destination [‚destɪ'neʃən] *s* (*of a trip*) Bestimmungsort *m*, Reiseziel *n*; (*purpose*) Bestimmung *f*

destine ['destɪn] *tr* (**for**) bestimmen (zu or für)

destiny ['destɪni] *s* Schicksal *n*; (*doom*) Verhängnis *n*

destitute ['destɪ‚t(j)ut] *adj* mittellos; **d. of** ohne

destitution [‚destɪ't(j)uʃən] *s* äußerste Armut *f*

destroy [dɪ'strɔɪ] *tr* vernichten, zerstören; (*animals, bacteria*) töten

destroyer [dɪ'strɔɪ‚ər] *s* (nav) Zerstörer *m*

destroy′er es′cort *s* Zerstörergeleitschutz *m*

destruction [dɪ'strʌkʃən] *s* Zerstörung *f*; (*of species*) Ausrottung *f*

destructive [dɪ'strʌktɪv] *adj* zerstörend; (*criticism*) vernichtend; (*tendency*) destruktiv

desultory ['desəl‚tori] *adj* (*without plan*) planlos; (*fitful*) sprunghaft; (*remark*) deplaciert

detach [dɪ'tætʃ] *tr* ablösen; (*along a perforation*) abtrennen; (mil) abkommandieren

detachable [dɪ'tætʃəbəl] *tr* abnehmbar, ablösbar

detached′ *adj* (*building*) alleinstehend; (*objective*) objektiv; (*aloof*) distanziert

detachment [dɪˈtætʃmənt] *s* Objektivität *f*; (*aloofness*) Abstand *m*; (*mil*) Trupp *m*, Kommando *n*

detail [dɪˈtel], [ˈditel] *s* Enzelheit *f*, Detail *n*; (*mil*) Kommando *n*, Trupp *m*; **details** (*pej*) Kleinkram *m*; **in d.** ausführlich ‖ [dɪˈtel] (*relate in detail*) ausführlich berichten; (*list*) einzeln aufzählen; (*mil*) abkommandieren

de'tail draw'ing *s* Detailzeichnung *f*

detailed *adj* ausführlich; **d. work** Kleinarbeit *f*

detain [dɪˈten] *tr* zurückhalten; (*jur*) in Haft behalten

detect [dɪˈtekt] *tr* (*discover*) entdecken; (*catch*) ertappen

detection [dɪˈtekʃən] *s* Entdeckung *f*

detective [dɪˈtektɪv] *s* Detektiv *m*

detec'tive sto'ry *s* Kriminalroman *m*

detector [dɪˈtektər] *s* (*e.g., of smoke*) Spürgerät *n*; (*of objects*) Suchgerät *n*; (*rad*) Detektor *m*

détente [deˈtɑnt] *s* Entspannung *f*, Détente *f*

detention [dɪˈtenʃən] *s* (*jur*) Haft *f*

deten'tion camp' *s* Internierungslager *n*

deten'tion home' *s* Haftanstalt *f*

de·ter [dɪˈtʌr] *v* (*pret & pp* **-terred**; *ger-terring*) *tr* (*from*) abschrecken (*von*), abhalten (*von*)

detergent [dɪˈtʌrdʒənt] *s* Reinigungsmittel *n*; (*in a washer*) Waschmittel *n*

deteriorate [dɪˈtɪrɪ·əˌret] *tr* verschlechtern ‖ *intr* sich verschlechtern

deterioration [dɪˌtɪrɪ·əˈreʃən] *s* Verschlechterung *f*, Verfall *m*

determination [dɪˌtʌrmɪˈneʃən] *s* Bestimmung *f*; (*resoluteness*) Entschlossenheit *f*; (*of boundaries*) Festlegung *f*

determine [dɪˈtʌrmɪn] *tr* (*fix conclusively*) bestimmen; (*boundaries*) festlegen; (*decide*) entscheiden

deter'mined *adj* entschlossen

deterrent [dɪˈtʌrənt] *adj* abschreckend ‖ *s* Abschreckungsmittel *n*

detest [dɪˈtest] *tr* verabscheuen

detestable [dɪˈtestəbəl] *adj* abscheulich

dethrone [dɪˈθron] *tr* entthronen

detonate [ˈdetəˌnet] *tr* explodieren lassen ‖ *intr* explodieren

detour [ˈditur] *s* (*for cars*) Umleitung *f*; (*for pedestrians*) Umweg *m* ‖ *tr* umleiten ‖ *intr* e-n Umweg machen

detract [dɪˈtrækt] *tr* ablenken ‖ *intr*—**d. from** beeinträchtigen

detraction [dɪˈtrækʃən] *s* Beeinträchtigung *f*

detractor [dɪˈtræktər] *s* Verleumder –in *mf*

detrain [dɪˈtren] *tr* ausladen ‖ *intr* aussteigen

detriment [ˈdetrɪmənt] *s* Nachteil *m*

detrimental [ˌdetrɪˈmentəl] *adj* (**to**) nachteilig (für), schädlich (für)

deuce [d(j)us] *s* (*in cards or dice*) Zwei *f*; (*in tennis*) Einstand *m*; **what the d.?** was zum Teufel?

devaluate [diˈvæljuˌet] *tr* abwerten

devaluation [diˌvæljuˈeʃən] *s* Abwertung *f*

devastate [ˈdevəsˌtet] *tr* verheeren

develop [dɪˈveləp] *tr* entwickeln; (*one's mind*) (aus)bilden; (*a habit*) annehmen; (*a disease*) sich [*dat*] zuziehen; (*cracks*) bekommen; (*land*) nutzbar machen; (*a mine*) ausbauen; (*phot*) entwickeln ‖ *intr* sich entwickeln; (*said of habits*) sich herausbilden; **d. into** sich entwickeln zu

developer [dɪˈveləpər] *s* (*of land*) Spekulant –in *mf*; (*phot*) Entwickler *m*

development [dɪˈveləpmənt] *s* Entwicklung *f*; (*of relations, of a mine*) Ausbau *m*; (*of land*) Nutzbarmachung *f*; (*of housing*) Siedlung *f*; (*an event*) Ereignis *n*; (*educ*) Ausbildung *f*; (*phot*) Entwicklung *f*

deviate [ˈdivɪˌet] *intr* abweichen

deviation [ˌdivɪˈeʃən] *s* Abweichung *f*

device [dɪˈvaɪs] *s* Vorrichtung *f*, Gerät *n*; (*means*) Mittel *n*; (*crafty scheme*) Kniff *m*; (*literary device*) Kunstgriff *m*; (*heral*) Sinnbild *n*; **leave s.o. to his own devices** j–n sich [*dat*] selbst überlassen

dev·il [ˈdevəl] *s* Teufel *m*; **a d. of a** (*coll*) verteufelt; **between the d. and the deep blue sea** zwischen zwei Feuern; **poor d.** armer Teufel; **the d. with you!** (*coll*) scher dich zum Teufel!; **what (who, etc.) the d.?** was (wer, *etc.*) zum Teufel? ‖ *v* (*pret & pp* **-il[l]ed**; *ger* **-il[l]ing**) *tr* (*culin*) mit viel Gewürz zubereiten

devilish [ˈdev(ə)lɪʃ] *adj* teuflisch

dev'il-may-care' *adj* (*informal*) wurstig; (*reckless*) verwegen

devilment [ˈdevɪlmənt] *s* Unfug *m*

deviltry [ˈdevɪltrɪ] *s* Unfug *m*

devious [ˈdivɪ·əs] *adj* abweichend; (*tricky*) unredlich; (*reasoning*) abwegig

devise [dɪˈvaɪz] *tr* ersinnen; (*jur*) vermachen

devoid [dɪˈvɔɪd] *adj*—**d. of** ohne

devolve [dɪˈvɑlv] *intr*—**d. on** zufallen (*dat*)

devote [dɪˈvot] *tr* widmen

devot'ed *adj* (*dedicated*) ergeben; (*affectionate*) liebevoll

devotee [ˌdevəˈti] *s* Anhänger –in *mf*

devotion [dɪˈvoʃən] *s* Ergebenheit *f*; (*devoutness*) Frömmigkeit *f*; (*special prayer*) (**to**) Gebet *n* (zu); **devotions** Andacht *f*

devour [dɪˈvaur] *tr* verschlingen; (*said of fire*) verzehren

devout [dɪˈvaut] *adj* fromm; (*e.g., hope*) innig

dew [d(j)u] *s* Tau *m*; **dew is falling** es taut

dew'drop' *s* Tautropfen *m*

dew'lap' *s* Wamme *f*

dewy [ˈd(j)u·i] *adj* tauig

dexterity [deksˈterɪtɪ] *s* Geschicklichkeit *f*, Handfertigkeit *f*

dexterous [ˈdekstərəs] *adj* handfertig

dextrose [ˈdekstroz] *s* Traubenzucker *m*

diabetes [ˌdaɪ·əˈbitɪs] *s* Zuckerkrankheit *f*

diabetic [ˌdaɪ·ə'bɛtɪk] *adj* zucker-krank *mf*

diabolic(al) [ˌdaɪ·ə'bɑlɪk(ə)l] *adj* teuflisch

diacritical [ˌdaɪ·ə'krɪtɪkəl] *adj* dia-kritisch

diadem ['daɪ·ə‚dɛm] *s* Diadem *n*

diaere·sis [daɪ'ɛrɪsɪs] *s* (**-ses** [‚sɪz]) Diäresis *f*; (*mark*) Trema *n*

diagnose [ˌdaɪ·əg'nos], [ˌdaɪ·əg'noz] *tr* diagnostizieren

diagno·sis [ˌdaɪ·əg'nosɪs] *s* (**-ses** [sɪz]) Diagnose *f*

diagonal [daɪ'ægənəl] *adj* diagonal || *s* Diagonale *f*

diagonally [daɪ'ægənəli] *adv*—**d. across from** schräg gegenüber von

diagram ['daɪ·ə‚græm] *s* Diagramm *n*

di·al ['daɪ·əl] *s* Zifferblatt *n*; (*tech*) Skalenscheibe *f*; (telp) Wählscheibe *f* || *v* (*pret & pp* **-aled;** *ger* **-al[l]ing**) *tr & intr* (telp) wählen

di'aling *s* (telp) Wählen *n* der Nummer

dialogue ['daɪ·ə‚lɔg] *s* Dialog *m*

di'al tel'ephone *s* Selbstanschlußtelefon *n*

di'al tone' *s* Summton *m*, Amtszeichen *n*

diameter [daɪ'æmɪtər] *s* Durchmesser *m*

diamond ['daɪmənd] *adj* diamanten; (*in shape*) rautenförmig || *s* Diamant *m*; (*cut diamond*) Brillant *m*; (*rhombus*) Raute *f*; (baseball) Spielfeld *n*; (cards) Karo *f*

dia'mond ring' *s* Brillantring *m*

diaper ['daɪpər] *s* Windel *f*; **change the diapers of** trockenlegen, wickeln

diaphanous [daɪ'æfənəs] *adj* durch-sichtig, durchscheinend

diaphragm ['daɪ·ə‚fræm] *s* (*for birth control*) Gebärmutterkappe *f*; (anat) Zwerchfell *n*; (phot) Blende *f*; (tech, telp) Membran *f*

diarrhea [ˌdaɪ·ə'ri·ə] *s* Durchfall *m*

diary ['daɪ·əri] *s* Tagebuch *n*

diastole [daɪ'æstəli] *s* Diastole *f*

diatribe ['daɪ·ə‚traɪb] *s* Schmährede *f*

dice [daɪs] *spl* Würfel *pl* || *tr* in Würfel schneiden

dice'box' *s* Würfelbecher *m*

dichotomy [daɪ'katəmi] *s* Zweiteilung *f*; (bot) Gabelung *f*

dicker ['dɪkər] *intr* (**about**) feilschen (**um**)

dickey ['dɪki] *s* Hemdbrust *f*

dictaphone ['dɪktə‚fon] *s* Diktaphon *n*

dictate ['dɪktet] *s* Diktat *n*; **the dictates of conscience** das Gebot des Gewissens || *tr & intr* diktieren

dictation [dɪk'te/ən] *s* Diktat *n*

dictator ['dɪktetər] *s* Diktator *m*

dictatorial [ˌdɪktə'tori·əl] *adj* dikta-torisch; (*power*) unumschränkt

dic'tatorship' *s* Diktatur *f*

diction ['dɪk/ən] *s* Ausdrucksweise *f*

dictionary ['dɪk/ə‚neri] *s* Wörterbuch *n*

dic·tum ['dɪktəm] *s* (**-ta** [tə]) (*saying*) Spruch *m*; (*pronouncement*) Aus-spruch *m*

didactic [daɪ'dæktɪk] *adj* lehrhaft

die [daɪ] *s* (**dice** [daɪs]) Würfel *m*; **the die is cast** die Würfel sind gefallen || *s* (**dies**) (*coining die*) Präge-stempel *m*; (*casting die*) Form *f*; (*forging die*) Gesenk *n*; (*threader*) Schneidkopf *m* || *v* (*pret & pp* **died;** *ger* **dying**) *tr*—**die a natural death** e-s natürlichen Todes sterben || *intr* sterben; (*said of plants and animals*) eingehen; **be dying for** (coll) sich sehnen nach; **die down** (*said of the wind*) sich legen; (*said of noise*) er-sterben; **die from** sterben an (*dat*); **die laughing** sich totlachen; **die of hunger** verhungern; **die of thirst** ver-dursten; **die out** aussterben; (*said of fire*) erlöschen; **I am dying to** (*inf*) (coll) ich würde schrecklich gern (*inf*)

die'-hard' *s* Unentwegte *mf*

die'sel en'gine ['dizəl] *s* Dieselmotor *m*

die'sel oil' *s* Dieselöl *n*

die'stock' *s* Gewindeschneidkluppe *f*

diet ['daɪ·ət] *s* Kost *f*; (*special menu*) Diät *f*; (parl) Reichstag *m*; **be on a d.** diät leben; **put on a d.** auf Diät setzen || *intr* diät leben

dietary ['daɪ·ə‚teri] *adj* Diät–; **d. laws** rituelle Diätvorschriften *pl*

dietetic [ˌdaɪ·ə'tɛtɪk] *adj* diätetisch || **dietetics** *spl* Diätetik *f*

dietitian [ˌdaɪ·ə'tɪ/ən] *s* Diätspezialist *-in mf*

differ ['dɪfər] *intr* sich unterscheiden; (*said of opinions*) auseinandergehen; **d. from** abweichen von; **d. in** ver-schieden sein in (*dat*); **d. with** an-derer Meinung sein als

difference ['dɪfərəns] *s* Unterschied *m*; (*argument*) Streit *m*; (math) Dif-ferenz *f*; **d. of opinion** Meinungsver-schiedenheit *f*; **it makes no d. to me** es ist mir gleich; **split the d.** den Rest teilen

different ['dɪfərənt] *adj* verschieden; **a d. kind of** e-e andere Art von; **d. from** anders als, verschieden von; **d. kinds of** verschiedene

differential [ˌdɪfə'rɛn/əl] *adj* (econ, elec, mach, math, phys) Differential– || *s* (*difference*) Unterschied *m*; (mach) Differentialgetriebe *n*; (math) Differential *n*

differen'tial cal'culus *s* Differential-rechnung *f*

differentiate [ˌdɪfə'rɛn/ɪ‚et] *tr* unter-scheiden; (math) differenzieren || *intr* —**d. between** unterscheiden zwischen (*dat*)

difficult ['dɪfɪ‚kʌlt] *adj* schwierig, schwer

difficulty ['dɪfɪ‚kʌlti] *s* Schwierigkeit *f*; **I have d. in** (*inf*) es fällt mir schwer zu (*inf*); **with d.** mit Mühe

diffuse [dɪ'fjus] *adj* (weit) zerstreut; (*style*) diffus || [dɪ'fjuz] *tr* (*spread*) verbreiten; (*pour out*) ausgießen; (phys) diffundieren || *intr* sich zer-streuen

diffusion [dɪ'fju/ən] *s* (*spread*) Ver-breitung *f*; (phys) Diffusion *f*

dig [dɪg] *s* (*jab*) Stoß *m*; (*sarcasm*)

Seitenhieb *m;* (archeol) Ausgrabung *f* ‖ *v (pret & pp* dug [dʌg] & digged; *ger* digging) *tr* graben; *(a ditch)* auswerfen; *(potatoes)* ausgraben; *(understand)* (sl) kapieren; *(look at)* (sl) anschauen; *(appreciate)* (sl) schwärmen für; dig up ausgraben; *(find)* auftreiben; *(information)* ausfindig machen; *(money)* aufbringen; ‖ *intr* graben, wühlen; dig in *(with the hands)* hineinfassen; *(work hard)* (coll) schuften; (mil) sich eingraben; dig for *(e.g., gold)* schürfen nach

digest ['daɪdʒɛst] *s* Zusammenfassung *f;* (jur) Gesetzessammlung *f* ‖ [daɪ-'dʒɛst] *tr* verdauen; *(in the mind)* verarbeiten ‖ *intr* verdauen

digestible [daɪ'dʒɛstɪbəl] *adj* verdaulich, verträglich

digestion [daɪ'dʒɛstʃən] *s* Verdauung *f*

digestive [daɪ'dʒɛstɪv] *adj* Verdauungs–; d. tract Verdauungsapparat *m*

digit ['dɪdʒɪt] *s* (math) Ziffer *f* (unter zehn); (math) Stelle *f*

digital ['dɪdʒɪtəl] *adj* digital, Digital–

dig'ital comput'er *s* digitale Rechenanlage *f*

digitalis [dɪdʒɪ'tælɪs] *s* Digitalis *n*

dignified ['dɪgnɪˌfaɪd] *adj* würdig

dig·ni·fy ['dɪgnɪˌfaɪ] *v (pret & pp* –fied) *tr* ehren

dignitary ['dɪgnɪˌteri] *s* Würdenträger –in *mf*

dignity ['dɪgnɪti] *s* Würde *f;* d. of man Menschenwürde *f;* stand on one's d. sich *[dat]* nichts vergeben

digress [daɪ'grɛs] *intr* (from) abschweifen (von)

digression [daɪ'grɛʃən] *s* Abschweifung *f*

dike [daɪk] *s* Deich *m*

dilapidated [dɪ'læpɪˌdetɪd] *adj* baufällig

dilate [daɪ'let] *tr* ausdehnen ‖ *intr* sich ausdehnen

dilation [daɪ'leʃən] *s* Ausdehnung *f*

dilatory ['dɪlaˌtori] *adj* saumselig; *(tending to cause delay)* hinhaltend

dilemma [dɪ'lɛmə] *s* Dilemma *n*

dilettan·te [ˌdɪlə'tænti], ['dɪləˌtɑnt] *s* (–tes & –ti [ti]) Dilettant –in *mf*

diligence ['dɪlɪdʒəns] *s* Fleiß *m*

diligent ['dɪlɪdʒənt] *adj* fleißig

dill [dɪl] *s* Dill *m*

dillydal·ly ['dɪlɪˌdæli] *v (pret & pp* –lied) *intr* herumtrödeln

dilute [dɪ'lut], [daɪ'lut] *adj* verdünnt ‖ [dɪ'lut] *tr* verdünnen; *(with water)* verwässern ‖ *intr* sich verdünnen

dilution [dɪ'luʃən] *s* Verdünnung *f;* *(with water)* Verwässerung *f*

dim [dɪm] *adj (dimmer; dimmest) adj (light, eyesight)* schwach; *(poorly lighted)* schwach beleuchtet; *(dull)* matt; *(chances, outlook)* schlecht; *(indistinct)* undeutlich; take a dim view of *(disapprove of)* mißbilligen; *(be pessimistic about)* sich *[dat]* etw schwarz ausmalen ‖ *v (pret & pp* dimmed; *ger* dimming) *tr* trüben; *(lights)* abblenden ‖ *intr* sich ver-

dunkeln; *(said of lights, hopes)* verblassen

dime [daɪm] *s* Zehncentstück *n*

dime' nov'el *s* Groschenroman *m*

dimension [dɪ'mɛnʃən] *s* Maß *n,* Ausdehnung *f;* dimensions Ausmaß *n*

diminish [dɪ'mɪnɪʃ] *tr* (ver)mindern, verringern ‖ *intr* sich vermindern

diminutive [dɪ'mɪnjətɪv] *adj* winzig; (gram) Verkleinerungs– ‖ *s* Verkleinerungsform *f*

dimmer ['dɪmər] *s* (aut) Abblendvorrichtung *f*

dimple ['dɪmpəl] *s* Grübchen *n*

dim'wit' *s* Schwachsinnige *mf*

din [dɪn] *s* Getöse *n* ‖ *v (pret & pp* dinned; *ger* dinning) *tr* betäuben; din s.th. into s.o. j–m etw einhämmern

dine [daɪn] *intr* speisen; d. out auswärts speisen

diner ['daɪnər] *s* Tischgast *m;* *(small restaurant)* speisewagenähnliches Speiselokal *n;* (rr) Speisewagen *m*

dinette [daɪ'nɛt] *s* Speisenische *f*

dingbat ['dɪŋˌbæt] *s* (sl) *(person)* Dingsda *m;* *(thing)* Dingsda *n*

ding-dong ['dɪŋˌdɒŋ] *interj* bimbam!, klingklang!

dinghy ['dɪŋgi] *s* Beiboot *n;* rubber d. Schlauchboot *n*

dingy ['dɪndʒi] *adj (gloomy)* düster; *(shabby)* schäbig

din'ing car' *s* (rr) Speisewagen *m*

din'ing hall' *s* Speisesaal *m*

din'ing room' *s* Eßzimmer *n*

dinner ['dɪnər] *s (supper)* Abendessen *n;* *(main meal)* Hauptmahlzeit *f;* *(formal meal)* Diner *n;* after d. nach Tisch; at d. bei Tisch; before d. vor Tisch

din'ner guest' *s* Tischgast *m*

din'ner jac'ket *s* Smoking *m*

din'ner mu'sic *s* Tafelmusik *f*

din'ner par'ty *s* Tischgesellschaft *f*

din'ner time' *s* Tischzeit *f*

dinosaur ['daɪnəˌsɔr] *s* Dinosaurier *m*

dint [dɪnt] *s*—by d. of kraft *(genit)*

diocesan [daɪ'ɑsɪsən] *adj* Diözesan–

diocese ['daɪ-əˌsis] *s* Diözese *f*

diode ['daɪ-od] *s* (electron) Diode *f*

dioxide [daɪ'ɑksaɪd] *s* Dioxyd *n*

dip [dɪp] *s (in the road)* Neigung *f;* *(short swim)* kurzes Bad *n;* *(dunk)* Eintauchen *n;* *(sauce)* Tunke *f;* *(of ice cream)* Portion *f* ‖ *v (pret & pp* dipped; *ger* dipping) *tr* eintauchen; *(e.g., doughnuts)* eintunken; *(a flag)* senken ‖ *intr* sich senken; dip into *(e.g., reserves)* angreifen; dip into one's pockets (fig) in die Tasche greifen

diphtheria [dɪf'θɪrɪ-ə] *s* Diphtherie *f*

diphthong ['dɪfθɒŋ] *s* Doppelvokal *m*

diploma [dɪ'plomə] *s* Diplom *n*

diplomacy [dɪ'ploməsi] *s* Diplomatie *f*

diplomat ['dɪpləˌmæt] *s* Diplomat –in *mf*

diplomatic [ˌdɪplə'mætɪk] *adj (& fig)* diplomatisch

dipper ['dɪpər] *s* Schöpflöffel *m*

dipsomania [ˌdɪpsə'menɪ-ə] *s* Trunksucht *f*

dip′ stick′ *s* (aut) Ölstandmesser *m*

dire [daɪr] *adj* (*terrible*) gräßlich; (*need*) äußerste

direct [dɪ'rɛkt] *adj* direkt, unmittelbar; (*frank*) unverblümt; (*quotation*) wörtlich ‖ *tr* (*order*) beauftragen; (*a company*) leiten; (*traffic*) regeln; (*a movie*, *play*) Regie führen bei; (*an orchestra*) dirigieren; (*attention*, *glance*) (**to**) richten (auf *acc*); (*a person*) (**to**) verweisen (an *acc*); (*words*, *letter*) (**to**) richten (an *acc*)

direct′ call′ *s* Selbstwählverbindung *f*

direct′ cur′rent *s* Gleichstrom *m*

direct′ dis′course *s* direkte Rede *f*

direct′ hit′ *s* Volltreffer *m*

direction [dɪ'rɛk/ən] *s* Richtung *f*; (*order*) Anweisung *f*; (*leadership*) Leitung *f*, Führung *f*; (cin, theat) Regie *f*; (mus) Stabführung *f*; **directions** Weisungen *pl*; (*for use*) Gebrauchsanweisung *f*; **in all directions** nach allen Richtungen

directional [dɪ'rɛk/ənəl] *adj* Richt–

direc′tion find′er *s* Peilgerät *n*

direc′tion sig′nal *s* (aut) Richtungsanzeiger *m*

directive [dɪ'rɛktɪv] *s* Anweisung *f*

direct′ ob′ject *s* direktes Objekt *n*

direct′ op′posite *s* genaues Gegenteil *n*

director [dɪ'rɛktər] *s* Leiter –in *mf*, Direktor –in *mf*; (cin, theat) Regisseur –in *mf*; (mus) Dirigent –in *mf*; (rad, telv) Sendeleiter –in *mf*

direc′torship *s* Direktorat *n*

directory [dɪ'rɛktəri] *s* Verzeichnis *n*

dirge [dʌrdʒ] *s* Trauergesang *m*

dirigible [′dɪrɪdʒɪbəl] *s* lenkbares Luftschiff *n*

dirt [dʌrt] *s* Schmutz *m*, Dreck *m*; (*moral filth*) Schmutz *m*; (*soil*) Erde *f*

dirt′-cheap′ *adj* spottbillig

dirt′ farm′er *s* kleiner Farmer *m*

dirt′ road′ *s* unbefestigte Straße *f*

dirt•y [′dʌrti] *adj* schmutzig, dreckig; (*morally*) schmutzig; **d. business** Schweinerei *f*; **d. dog** Sauhund *m*; **d. joke** Zote *f*; **d. lie** gemeine Lüge *f*; **d. linen** schmutzige Wäsche *f*; **d. look** böser Blick *m*; **d. trick** übler Streich *m*; **that's a d. shame** das ist e–e Gemeinheit! ‖ *v* (*pret & pp –ied*) *tr* beschmutzen

disability [,dɪsə'bɪlɪti] *s* Invalidität *f*

disable [dɪs'ebəl] *tr* (e.g., *a worker*) arbeitsunfähig machen; (*make unsuited for combat*) kampfunfähig machen; (jur) rechtsunfähig machen

disa′bled *adj* invalide; (mil) kampfunfähig; **d. veteran** Kriegsversehrte *mf*; **d. person** Invalide *mf*

disabuse [,dɪsə'bjuz] *tr*—**d. of** befreien von

disadvantage [,dɪsəd'væntɪdʒ] *s* Nachteil *m*; **place at a d.** benachteiligen

disadvantageous [dɪs,ædvən'tedʒəs] *adj* nachteilig

disagree [,dɪsə'gri] *intr* nicht übereinstimmen; (*be contradictory*) einander widersprechen; (*quarrel*) (sich) streiten; **d. with** (*said of food*) nicht bekommen (*dat*); **d. with s.o. on**
anderer Meinung über (*acc*) als j–d sein

disagreeable [,dɪsə'gri·əbəl] *adj* unangenehm

disagreement [,dɪsə'grimənt] *s* (*unlikeness*) Verschiedenheit *f*; (*dissention*) Uneinigkeit *f*; (*quarrel*) Meinungsverschiedenheit *f*

disappear [,dɪsə'pɪr] *intr* verschwinden

disappearance [,dɪsə'pɪrəns] *s* Verschwinden *n*

disappoint [,dɪsə'pɔɪnt] *tr* enttäuschen; **be disappointed at** (or **with**) enttäuscht sein über (*acc*)

disappointment [,dɪsə'pɔɪntmənt] *s* Enttäuschung *f*

disapproval [,dɪsə'pruvəl] *s* Mißbilligung *f*

disapprove [,dɪsə'pruv] *tr* mißbilligen; (e.g., *an application*) nicht genehmigen ‖ *intr*—**d. of** mißbilligen

disarm [dɪs'ɑrm] *tr* (& fig) entwaffen; (*a bomb*) entschärfen ‖ *intr* abrüsten

disarmament [dɪs'ɑrməmənt] *s* Abrüstung *f*

disarm′ing *adj* (fig) entwaffend

disarray [,dɪsə're] *s* Unordnung *f* ‖ *tr* in Unordnung bringen, verwirren

disassemble [,dɪsə'sɛmbəl] *tr* zerlegen

disaster [dɪ'zæstər] *s* Unheil *n*

disas′ter ar′ea *s* Katastrophengebiet *n*

disastrous [dɪ'zæstrəs] *adj* unheilvoll

disavow [,dɪsə'vau] *tr* ableugnen

disavowal [,dɪsə'vau·əl] *s* Ableugnung *f*

disband [dɪs'bænd] *tr* auflösen ‖ *intr* sich auflösen

dis•bar [dɪs'bɑr] *v* (*pret & pp –barred; ger –barring*) *tr* aus dem Anwaltsstand ausschließen

disbelief [,dɪsbɪ'lif] *s* Unglaube *m*

disbelieve [,dɪsbɪ'liv] *tr & intr* nicht glauben

disburse [dɪs'bʌrs] *tr* auszahlen

disbursement [dɪs'bʌrsmənt] *s* Auszahlung *f*

disc [dɪsk] *s* var of **disk**

discard [dɪs'kɑrd] *s* Ablegen *n* ‖ *tr* (*clothes*, *cards*, *habits*) ablegen; (*a plan*) verwerfen

discern [dɪ'sʌrn] *tr* (*perceive*) wahrnehmen; **be able to d. right from wrong** zwischen Gut und Böse unterscheiden können

discern′ing *adj* scharfsinnig

discernment [dɪ'sʌrnmənt] *s* Scharfsinn *m*

discharge [dɪs'tʃɑrdʒ] *s* (*of a gun*) Abfeuern *n*; (*of a battery*) Entladung *f*; (*of water*) Abfluß *m*; (*of smoke*) Ausströmen *n*; (*of duties*) Erfüllung *f*; (*of debts*) Tilgung *f*; (*of employees*, *patients*, *soldiers*) Entlassung *f*; (*of a prisoner*) Freilassung *f*; (pathol) Ausfluß *m* ‖ *tr* (*a gun*) abfeuern; (*a battery*) ergießen; (*smoke*) ausstoßen; (*debts*) tilgen; (*duties*) erfüllen; (*an office*) verwalten; (*an employee*, *patient*, *soldier*) entlassen ‖ *intr* (*said of a gun*) losgehen; (*said of a battery*) sich entladen; (*pour out*) abfließen; (pathol) eitern

disciple [dɪ'saɪpəl] *s* Jünger *m*

disciplinarian [ˌdɪsɪplɪ'nerɪ·ən] *s* Zuchtmeister *m*

disciplinary ['dɪsɪplɪ ˌneri] *adj* Disziplinar–

discipline ['dɪsɪplɪn] *s* Disziplin *f*; (*punishment*) Züchtigung *f* ‖ *tr* disziplinieren; (*punish*) züchtigen

disclaim [dɪs'klem] *tr* leugnen; (jur) verzichten auf (*acc*)

disclose [dɪs'kloz] *tr* enthüllen

disclosure [dɪs'kloʒər] *s* Enthüllung *f*

discolor [dɪs'kʌlər] *tr* verfärben ‖ *intr* sich verfärben

discoloration [dɪsˌkʌlə'reʃən] *s* Verfärbung *f*

discomfiture [dɪs'kʌmfɪtʃər] *s* (*defeat*) Niederlage *f*; (*frustration*) Enttäuschung *f*; (*confusion*) Verwirrung *f*

discomfort [dɪs'kʌmfərt] *s* Unbehagen *n* ‖ *tr* Unbehagen verursachen (*dat*)

disconcert [ˌdɪskən'sʌrt] *tr* aus der Fassung bringen

dis'concert'ed *adj* fassungslos

disconnect [ˌdɪskə'nekt] *tr* trennen; (elec) ausschalten; (mach) auskuppeln; (telp) unterbrechen

disconsolate [dɪs'kɑnsəlɪt] *adj* trostlos

discontent [ˌdɪskən'tent] *s* Unzufriedenheit *f* ‖ *tr* unzufrieden machen

dis'content'ed *adj* (with) mißvergnügt (über *acc*)

discontinue [ˌdɪskən'tɪnju] *tr* (*permanently*) einstellen; (*temporarily*) aussetzen; (*a newspaper*) abbestellen; **d.** (ger) aufhören zu (*inf*)

discord ['dɪskɔrd] *s* Mißklang *m*; (*dissention*) Zwietracht *f*

discordance [dɪs'kɔrdəns] *s* Uneinigkeit *f*

discotheque [ˌdɪsko'tek] *s* Diskothek *f*

discount ['dɪskaunt] *s* (*in price*) Rabatt *m*; (*cash discount*) Kassaskonto *n*; (*deduction from nominal value*) Diskont *m*; **at a d.** mit Rabatt; (st. exch.) unter pari ‖ *tr* (*disregard*) außer acht lassen; (*minimize*) geringen Wert beimessen (*dat*); (*for cash payment*) e–n Abzug gewähren auf (*acc*); (e.g., *a promissory note*) diskontieren

dis'count store' *s* Rabattladen *m*

discourage [dɪs'kʌrɪdʒ] *tr* (*dishearten*) entmutigen; **d. s.o. from** (ger) (*deter*) j–n davon abschrecken zu (*inf*); (*dissuade*) j–m davon abraten zu (*inf*)

discour'aged *adj* mutlos

discouragement [dɪs'kʌrɪdʒmənt] *s* (*act*) Entmutigung *f*; (*state*) Mutlosigkeit *f*; (*deterrent*) Abschreckung *f*

discourse ['dɪskɔrs] *s* (*conversation*) Gespräch *n*; (*formal treatment*) Abhandlung *f*; (*lecture*) Vortrag *m* ‖ [dɪs'kɔrs] *intr* (on) sich unterhalten (über *acc*)

discourteous [dɪs'kʌrtɪ·əs] *adj* unhöflich

discourtesy [dɪs'kʌrtəsi] *s* Unhöflichkeit *f*

discover [dɪs'kʌvər] *tr* entdecken

discovery [dɪs'kʌvəri] *s* Entdeckung *f*

discredit [dɪs'kredɪt] *s* (*disrepute*) Mißkredit *m*; (*disbelief*) Zweifel *m* ‖ *tr* (*destroy confidence in*) in Mißkredit bringen; (*disbelieve*) anzweifeln; (*disgrace*) in Verruf bringen

discreditable [dɪs'kredɪtəbəl] *adj* schändlich

discreet [dɪs'krit] *adj* diskret

discrepancy [dɪs'krepənsi] *s* Unstimmigkeit *f*

discretion [dɪs'kreʃən] *s* Diskretion *f*, Besonnenheit *f*; **at one's d.** nach Belieben; **leave to s.o.'s d.** in j–s Belieben stellen

discriminate [dɪs'krɪmɪˌnet] *tr* voneinander unterscheiden ‖ *intr*—**d. against** diskriminieren

discrimination [dɪsˌkrɪmɪ'neʃən] *s* (*distinction*) Unterscheidung *f*; (*prejudicial treatment*) Diskriminierung *f*

discriminatory [dɪs'krɪmɪnəˌtori] *adj* diskriminierend

discus ['dɪskəs] *s* Diskus *m*

discuss [dɪs'kʌs] *tr* besprechen, diskutieren; (*formally*) erörtern

discussion [dɪs'kʌʃən] *s* Diskussion *f*; (*formal consideration*) Erörterung *f*

disdain [dɪs'den] *s* Geringschätzung *f* ‖ *tr* geringschätzen

disdainful [dɪs'denfəl] *adj* geringschätzig; **be d. of** geringschätzen

disease [dɪ'ziz] *s* Krankheit *f*

diseased' *adj* krank, erkrankt

disembark [ˌdɪsem'bɑrk] *tr* ausschiffen, landen ‖ *intr* an Land gehen, landen

disembarkation [dɪsˌembɑr'keʃən] *s* Ausschiffung *f*

disembow·el [ˌdɪsem'bau·əl] *v* (*pret & pp* -el[l]ed; *ger* -el[l]ing) *tr* ausweiden

disenchant [ˌdɪsen't'fænt] *tr* ernüchtern

disenchantment [ˌdɪsen't'fæntmənt] *s* Ernüchterung *f*

disengage [ˌdɪsen'gedʒ] *tr* (*a clutch*) ausrücken; (*the enemy*) sich absetzen von; (*troops*) entflechten; **d. the clutch** auskuppeln ‖ *intr* loskommen; (mil) sich absetzen

disengagement [ˌdɪsen'gedʒmənt] *s* Lösung *f*; (mil) Truppenentflechtung *f*

disentangle [ˌdɪsen'tæŋgəl] *tr* entwirren

disentanglement [ˌdɪsen'tæŋgəlmənt] *s* Entwirrung *f*

disfavor [dɪs'fevər] *s* Ungunst *f*

disfigure [dɪs'fɪgjər] *tr* entstellen

disfigurement [dɪs'fɪgjərmənt] *s* Entstellung *f*

disfranchise [dɪs'fræntʃaɪz] *tr* die Bürgerrechte entziehen (*dat*)

disgorge [dɪs'gɔrdʒ] *tr* ausspeien ‖ *intr* sich ergießen

disgrace [dɪs'gres] *s* Schande *f*; (*of a family*) Schandfleck *m* ‖ *tr* in Schande bringen; (*a girl*) schänden; **be disgraced** in Schande kommen

disgraceful [dɪsˈgresfəl] *adj* schänd-lich, schimpflich

disgruntled [dɪsˈgrʌntəld] *adj* mürrisch

disguise [dɪsˈgaɪz] *s* (*clothing*) Ver-kleidung *f*; (*insincere manner*) Ver-stellung *f* ‖ *tr* (*by dress*) verkleiden; (*e.g., the voice*) verstellen

disgust [dɪsˈgʌst] *s* (at) Ekel *m* (vor *dat*) ‖ *tr* anekeln

disgust'ing *adj* ekelhaft

dish [dɪ/] *s* Schüssel *f*, Platte *f*; (*food*) Gericht *n*; **do the dishes** das Ge-schirr spülen ‖ *tr*—**d. out** (coll) aus-teilen

dish'cloth' *s* Geschirrlappen *m*

dishearten [dɪsˈhɑrtən] *tr* entmutigen

disheveled [dɪˈ/ɛvəld] *adj* unordentlich

dishonest [dɪsˈɑnɪst] *adj* unehrlich

dishonesty [dɪsˈɑnɪsti] *s* Unehrlichkeit *f*

dishonor [dɪsˈɑnər] *s* Unehre *f* ‖ *tr* verunehren

dishonorable [dɪsˈɑnərəbəl] *adj* (*per-son*) ehrlos; (*action*) unehrenhaft

dishon'orable dis'charge *s* Entlassung *f* wegen Wehrunwürdigkeit

dish'pan' *s* Aufwaschschüssel *f*

dish'rack' *s* Abtropfkörbchen *n*

dish'rag' *s* Spüllappen *m*

dish'tow'el *s* Geschirrtuch *n*

dish'wash'er *s* (*person*) Aufwäscher –in *mf*; (*appliance*) Geschirrspül-maschine *f*

dish'wa'ter *s* Spülwasser *n*

disillusion [ˌdɪsɪˈluʒən] *s* Ernüchte-rung *f* ‖ *tr* ernüchtern

disillusionment [ˌdɪsɪˈluʒənmənt] *s* Er-nüchterung *f*

disinclination [ˌdɪsˌɪnklɪˈne/ən] *s* Ab-neigung *f*, Abgeneigtheit *f*

disinclined [ˌdɪsɪnˈklaɪnd] *adj* abge-neight

disinfect [ˌdɪsɪnˈfɛkt] *tr* desinfizieren

disinfectant [ˌdɪsɪnˈfɛktənt] *adj* des-infizierend ‖ *s* Desinfektionsmittel *n*

disinherit [ˌdɪsɪnˈhɛrɪt] *tr* enterben

disintegrate [dɪsˈɪntɪˌgret] *tr* (& fig) zersetzen ‖ *intr* zerfallen

disintegration [dɪsˌɪntɪˈgre/ən] *s* (& fig) Zerfall *m*

disin·ter [ˌdɪsɪnˈtʌr] *v* (*pret & pp* –terred; *ger* –terring) *tr* ausgraben

disinterested [dɪsˈɪntəˌrɛstɪd] *adj* (*un-biased*) unparteiisch; (*uninterested*) desinteressiert

disjunctive [dɪsˈdʒʌŋktɪv] *adj* disjunk-tiv

disk [dɪsk] *s* Scheibe *f*

disk' brake' *s* Scheibenbremse *f*

disk' jock'ey *s* Schallplattenjockei *m*

dislike [dɪsˈlaɪk] *s* (of) Abneigung *f* (gegen) ‖ *tr* nicht mögen

dislocate [ˈdɪslo͜ˌket] *tr* verschieben; (*a shoulder*) verrenken; (fig) stören

dislocation [ˌdɪsloˈke/ən] *s* Verschie-bung *f*; (*of a shoulder*) Verrenkung *f*; (fig) Störung *f*

dislodge [dɪsˈlɑdʒ] *tr* losreißen; (mil) aus der Stellung werfen

disloyal [dɪsˈlɔɪ-əl] *adj* untreu

disloyalty [dɪsˈlɔɪ-əlti] *s* Untreue *f*

dismal [ˈdɪzməl] *adj* trübselig, düster

dismantle [dɪsˈmæntəl] *tr* demontieren

dismay [dɪsˈme] *s* Bestürzung *f* ‖ *tr* bestürzen

dismember [dɪsˈmɛmbər] *tr* zerstük-keln

dismiss [dɪsˈmɪs] *tr* verabschieden; (*an employee*) (**from**) entlassen (aus); (*a case*) (jur) abweisen; (mil) weg-treten lassen; **d. as** abtun als; **dis-missed!** (mil) wegtreten!

dismissal [dɪsˈmɪsəl] *s* Entlassung *f*; (jur) Abweisung *f*

dismount [dɪsˈmaʊnt] *tr* (*throw down*) abwerfen; (*mach*) abmontieren ‖ *intr* (*from a carriage*) herabsteigen; (*from a horse*) absitzen

disobedience [ˌdɪsəˈbidɪ-əns] *s* Unge-horsam *m*, Unfolgsamkeit *f*

disobedient [ˌdɪsəˈbidɪ-ənt] *adj* unge-horsam, unfolgsam

disobey [ˌdɪsəˈbe] *tr* nicht gehorchen (*dat*) ‖ *intr* nicht gehorchen

disorder [dɪsˈɔrdər] *s* Unordnung *f*; (*public disturbance*) Unruhe *f*; (pathol) Erkrankung *f*; **throw into d.** in Unordnung bringen

disorderly [dɪsˈɔrdərli] *adj* unordent-lich, liederlich

disor'derly con'duct *s* ungebührliches Benehmen *n*

disor'derly house' *s* Bordell *n*; (*gam-bling house*) Spielhölle *f*

disorganize [dɪsˈɔrgəˌnaɪz] *tr* zerrüt-ten, desorganisieren

disown [dɪsˈon] *tr* verleugnen

disparage [dɪˈspærɪdʒ] *tr* herabsetzen, geringschätzen

disparate [ˈdɪspərɪt] *adj* ungleichartig

disparity [dɪˈspærɪti] *s* (*inequality*) Ungleichheit *f*; (*difference*) Unter-schied *m*

dispassionate [dɪsˈpæ/ənɪt] *adj* leiden-schaftslos

dispatch [dɪˈspæt/] *s* Abfertigung *f*; (*message*) Depesche *f*; **with d.** in Eile ‖ *tr* (*send off*) absenden; (*e.g., a truck*) abfertigen; (*e.g., a task*) schnell erledigen; (*kill*) töten; (*eat fast*) (coll) verputzen

dispatcher [dɪˈspæt/ər] *s* (*of vehicles*) Fahrbereitschaftsleiter –in *mf*

dis·pel [dɪˈspɛl] *v* (*pret & pp* –pelled; *ger* –pelling) *tr* vertreiben; (*thoughts, doubts*) zerstreuen

dispensary [dɪˈspɛnsəri] *s* Arzneiaus-gabestelle *f*; (mil) Krankenrevier *n*

dispensation [ˌdɪspɛnˈse/ən] *s* (eccl) (**from**) Dispens *m* (von); **by divine d.** durch göttliche Fügung

dispense [dɪˈspɛns] *tr* (*exempt*) (**from**) entbinden (von); (pharm) zubereiten und ausgeben; **d. justice** Recht sprechen ‖ *intr*—**d. with** verzichten auf (*acc*)

dispersal [dɪˈspʌrsəl] *s* Auflockerung *f*

disperse [dɪˈspʌrs] *tr* zerstreuen; (*a crowd*) zersprengen; (*one's troops*) auflockern; (*the enemy*) auseinander-sprengen ‖ *intr* (*said of clouds, etc.*) sich verziehen; (*said of crowds*) aus-einandergehen

dispirited [dɪˈspɪrɪtɪd] *adj* niederge-schlagen

displace 88 **distant**

displace [dɪs'pleɪs] *tr (people in war)* verschleppen; *(phys)* verdrängen
displacement [dɪs'pleɪsmənt] *s* Vertreibung *f; (phys)* Verdrängung *f*
display [dɪ'spleɪ] *s (of energy, wealth)* Entfaltung *f; (of goods)* Ausstellung *f; (pomp)* Aufwand *m;* **on d.** zur Schau ‖ *tr (wares)* ausstellen; *(reveal)* entfalten; *(flaunt)* protzen mit
display' case' *s* Vitrine *f*
display' room' *s* Ausstellungsraum *m*
display' win'dow *s* Schaufenster *n*
displease [dɪs'pliːz] *tr* mißfallen *(dat);* **be displeased with** mißfallen finden an *(dat)* ‖ *intr* mißfallen
displeas'ing *adj* mißfällig
displeasure [dɪs'pleʒər] *s* Mißfallen *n*
disposable [dɪ'spozəbəl] *adj* Einweg-
disposal [dɪ'spozəl] *s (riddance)* Beseitigung *f; (of a matter)* Erledigung *f; (distribution)* Anordnung *f;* **be at s.o.'s d.** j-m zur Verfügung stehen; **have at one's d.** verfügen über *(acc);* **put at s.o.'s d.** j-m zur Verfügung stellen
dispose [dɪ'spoz] *tr (incline)* **(to)** geneigt machen (zu); *(arrange)* anordnen ‖ *intr*—**d. of** *(a matter)* erledigen; *(get rid of)* loswerden
disposed' *adj* gesinnt; **d. to** *(ger)* geneigt zu *(inf)*
disposition [ˌdɪspə'zɪʃən] *s (settlement)* Erledigung *f; (nature)* Gemütsart *f; (inclination)* Neigung *f*
dispossess [ˌdɪspə'zes] *tr*—**d. s.o. of s.th.** j-m etw enteignen
disproof [dɪs'pruːf] *s* Widerlegung *f*
disproportionate [ˌdɪsprə'pɔrʃənɪt] *adj* unverhältnismäßig **be d. to** im Mißverhältnis stehen zu
disprove [dɪs'pruːv] *tr* widerlegen
dispute [dɪs'pjuːt] *s (quarrel)* Streit *m; (debate)* Wortgefecht *n;* **beyond d.** unstreitig; **in d.** umstritten ‖ *tr* bestreiten ‖ *intr* disputieren
disqualification [dɪsˌkwɑlɪfɪ'keʃən] *s* Disqualifizierung *f*
disqual•i•fy [dɪs'kwɑlɪˌfaɪ] *v (pret & pp –fied) tr (make unfit)* **(for)** untauglich machen (für); *(declare ineligible)* disqualifizieren
disquiet [dɪs'kwaɪət] *tr* beunruhigen
disqui'eting *adj* beunruhigend
disregard [ˌdɪsrɪ'gɑrd] *s (lack of attention)* Nichtbeachtung *f* ‖ *tr (not pay attention to)* nicht beachten; *(treat without due respect)* mißachten
disrepair [ˌdɪsrɪ'per] *s* Verfall *m;* **fall into d.** verfallen
disreputable [dɪs'repjətəbəl] *adj* verrufen
disrepute [ˌdɪsrɪ'pjuːt] *s* Verruf *m*
disrespect [ˌdɪsrɪ'spekt] *s* Nichtachtung *f,* Mißachtung *f* ‖ *tr* nicht achten
disrespectful [ˌdɪsrɪ'spektfəl] *adj* respektlos, unehrerbietig
disrobe [dɪs'rob] *tr* entkleiden ‖ *intr* sich entkleiden
disrupt [dɪs'rʌpt] *tr (throw into confusion)* in Verwirrung bringen; *(interrupt)* unterbrechen; *(cause to break down)* zum Zusammenbruch bringen
dissatisfaction [ˌdɪssætɪs'fækʃən] *s* Unzufriedenheit *f*
dissat'isfied' *adj* unzufrieden
dissatis•fy [dɪs'sætɪsˌfaɪ] *v (pret & pp –fied) tr* nicht befriedigen
dissect [dɪ'sekt] *tr (fig)* zergliedern; *(anat)* sezieren
dissection [dɪ'sekʃən] *s (fig)* Zergliederung *f; (anat)* Sektion *f*
dissemble [dɪ'sembəl] *tr* verbergen ‖ *intr* heucheln
disseminate [dɪ'semɪˌnet] *tr* verbreiten
dissension [dɪ'senʃən] *s* Uneinigkeit *f*
dissent [dɪ'sent] *s* abweichende Meinung *f* ‖ *intr* **(from)** anderer Meinung sein (als)
dissenter [dɪ'sentər] *s* Andersdenkende *mf; (relig)* Dissident –in *mf*
dissertation [ˌdɪsər'teʃən] *s* Dissertation *f*
disservice [dɪ'sʌrvɪs] *s* schlechter Dienst *m;* **do s.o. a d.** j-m e-n schlechten Dienst erweisen
dissidence ['dɪsɪdəns] *s* Meinungsverschiedenheit *f*
dissident ['dɪsɪdəns] *adj* andersdenkend ‖ *s* Dissident –in *mf*
dissimilar [dɪ'sɪmɪlər] *adj* unähnlich
dissimilate [dɪ'sɪmɪˌlet] *tr (phonet)* dissimilieren
dissimulate [dɪ'sɪmjəˌlet] *tr* verheimlichen ‖ *intr* heucheln
dissipate ['dɪsɪˌpet] *tr (squander)* vergeuden; *(scatter)* zerstreuen; *(dissolve)* auflösen ‖ *intr (scatter)* sich zerstreuen; *(dissolve)* sich auflösen
dis'sipat'ed *adj* ausschweifend
dissipation [ˌdɪsɪ'peʃən] *s (squandering)* Vergeudung *f; (dissolute mode of life)* Ausschweifung *f; (phys)* Dissipation *f*
dissociate [dɪ'soʃɪˌet] *tr* trennen; **d. oneself from** abrücken von
dissolute ['dɪsəˌluːt] *adj* ausschweifend
dissolution [ˌdɪsə'luːʃən] *s* Auflösung *f*
dissolve [dɪ'zɑlv] *s (cin)* Überblendung *f* ‖ *tr* auflösen; *(cin)* überblenden ‖ *intr* sich auflösen; *(cin)* überblenden
dissonance ['dɪsənəns] *s* Mißklang *m*
dissuade [dɪ'swed] *tr* **(from)** abbringen (von); **d. s.o. from** *(ger)* j-n davon abbringen zu *(inf)*
dissyllabic [ˌdɪsɪ'læbɪk] *adj* zweisilbig
distaff ['dɪstæf] *s* Spinnrocken *m; (fig)* Frauen *pl*
dis'taff side' *s* weibliche Linie *f*
distance ['dɪstəns] *s* Entfernung *f; (between two points)* Abstand *m; (stretch)* Strecke *f; (of a race)* Rennstrecke *f;* **from a d.** aus einiger Entfernung; **go the d.** bis zum Ende aushalten; **in the d.** in der Ferne; **keep one's d.** zurückhaltend sein; **keep your d.** bleib mir vom Leib!; **within easy d. of** nicht weit weg von; **within walking d. of** zu Fuß erreichbar von
distant ['dɪstənt] *adj* entfernt; *(reserved)* zurückhaltend

distaste [dɪsˈtest] s (for) Abneigung f (gegen), Ekel m (vor dat)

distasteful [dɪsˈtestfəl] adj (unpleasant) (to) unangenehm (dat); (offensive) (to) ekelhaft (dat)

distemper [dɪsˈtempər] s (of dogs) Staupe f; (paint) Temperafarbe f

distend [dɪsˈtend] tr (swell) aufblähen; (extend) ausdehnen || intr (swell) anschwellen; (extend) (aus)dehnen

distension [dɪsˈtenʃən] s Aufblähung f; Ausdehnung f

distill [dɪˈstɪl] tr destillieren; (e.g., whiskey) brennen

distillation [ˌdɪstɪˈleʃən] s Destillation f; (of whiskey) Brennen n

distiller [dɪsˈtɪlər] s Brenner m

distillery [dɪsˈtɪləri] s Brennerei f

distinct [dɪˈstɪŋkt] adj (clear) deutlich; (different) verschieden; **as d. from** zum Unterschied von; **keep d.** auseinanderhalten

distinction [dɪsˈtɪŋkʃən] s (difference) Unterschied m; (differentiation) Unterscheidung f; (honor) Auszeichnung f; (eminence) Vornehmheit f; **have the d. of** (ger) den Vorzug haben zu (inf)

distinctive [dɪsˈtɪŋktɪv] adj (distinguishing) unterscheidend; (characteristic) kennzeichnend

distinguish [dɪsˈtɪŋgwɪʃ] tr (differentiate) unterscheiden; (classify) einteilen; (honor) auszeichnen; (characterize) kennzeichnen; (discern) erkennen || intr (between) unterscheiden (zwischen dat)

distin′guished adj (eminent) prominent; (for) berühmt (wegen)

distort [dɪsˈtɔrt] tr verzerren; (the truth) entstellen; **distorted picture** Zerrbild n

distortion [dɪsˈtɔrʃən] s Verzerrung f; (of the truth) Entstellung f

distract [dɪˈstrækt] tr ablenken

distraction [dɪˈstrækʃən] s (diversion of attention) Ablenkung f; (entertainment) Zerstreuung f; **drive s.o. to d.** j-n zum Wahnsinn treiben

distraught [dɪˈstrɔt] adj (bewildered) verwirrt; (deeply agitated) (with) aufgewühlt (von); (crazed) (with) rasend (vor dat)

distress [dɪsˈtres] s (anxiety) Kummer m; (mental pain) Betrübnis f; (danger) Notstand m, Bedrängnis f; (naut) Seenot f || tr betrüben

distress′ing adj betrüblich

distress′ sig′nal s Notzeichen n

distribute [dɪsˈtrɪbjut] tr verteilen; (divide) einteilen; (apportion) (jur) aufteilen

distribution [ˌdɪstrɪˈbjuʃən] s Verteilung f; (geographic range) Verbreitung f; (of films) Verleih m; (marketing) Vertrieb m; (of dividends) Ausschüttung f; (jur) Aufteilung f

distributor [dɪsˈtrɪbjətər] s Verteiler –in mf; (of films) Verleiher –in mf; (dealer) Lieferant –in mf; (aut) Verteiler m

distri′butorship′ s Vertrieb m

district [ˈdɪstrɪkt] s Bezirk m

dis′trict attor′ney s Staatsanwalt m

distrust [dɪsˈtrʌst] s Mißtrauen n || tr mißtrauen (dat)

distrustful [dɪsˈtrʌstfəl] adj (of) mißtrauisch (gegen)

disturb [dɪsˈtʌrb] tr stören; (disquiet) beunruhigen; **d. the peace** die öffentliche Ruhe stören

disturbance [dɪsˈtʌrbəns] s (interruption) Störung f; (breach of peace) Unruhe f

disunited [ˌdɪsjuˈnaɪtɪd] adj uneinig

disunity [dɪsˈjunɪti] s Uneinigkeit f

disuse [dɪsˈjus] s Nichtverwendung f; **fall into d.** außer Gebrauch kommen

ditch [dɪtʃ] s Graben m || tr (discard) (sl) wegschmeißen; (aer) (coll) auf dem Wasser notlanden mit || intr (aer) (coll) notwassern

dither [ˈdɪðər] s—**be in a d.** verdattert sein

dit•to [ˈdɪto] adj (coll) dito || s (–tos) Kopie f || tr vervielfältigen

dit′to mark′ s Wiederholungszeichen n

ditty [ˈdɪti] s Liedchen n

diva [ˈdivɑ] s (mus) Diva f

divan [ˈdarvæn], [dɪˈvæn] s Diwan m

dive [daɪv] s Kopfsprung m; (coll) Spelunke f; (aer) Sturzflug m; (nav) Tauchen n; (sport) Kunstsprung m; **make a d. for** (fig) sich stürzen auf (acc) || v (pret & pp dived & dove [dov]) intr (submerge) tauchen; (plunge head first) e-n Kopfsprung machen; (aer) e-n Sturzflug machen; (nav) (unter)tauchen; (sport) e-n Kunstsprung machen

dive′-bomb′ tr & intr im Sturzflug mit Bomben angreifen

dive′ bomb′er s Sturzkampfbomber m

diver [ˈdaɪvər] s Taucher –in mf; (orn) Taucher m; (sport) Kunstspringer –in mf

diverge [daɪˈvʌrdʒ] intr (said of roads, views) sich teilen; (from the norm) abweichen; (geom, phys) divergieren

diverse [daɪˈvʌrs] adj (different) verschieden; (of various kinds) vielförmig

diversi•fy [daɪˈvʌrsɪˌfaɪ] v (pret & pp –fied) tr abwechslungsreich gestalten

diversion [daɪˈvʌrʒən] s Ablenkung f; (recreation) Zeitvertreib m; (mil) Ablenkungsmanöver n

diversity [daɪˈvʌrsɪti] s Mannigfaltigkeit f

divert [daɪˈvʌrt] tr (attention) ablenken; (traffic) umleiten; (a river) ableiten; (money) abzweigen; (entertain) zerstreuen

divest [daɪˈvest] tr—**d. oneself of** sich entäußern (genit); **d. s.o. of** (e.g., office, power) j-n entkleiden (genit); (e.g., rights, property) j-m (seine Rechte, etc.) entziehen

divide [dɪˈvaɪd] s (geol) Wasserscheide f || tr teilen; (cause to disagree) entzweien; (math) (by) teilen (durch); **d. into** einteilen in (acc); **d. off** (a room) abteilen; **d. up** (among) aufteilen (unter acc) || intr (*said of a road*) sich teilen; **d. into** sich teilen in (*acc*)

dividend ['dɪvɪ‚dend] *s* Dividende *f*; (math) Dividend *m*; **pay dividends** Dividenden ausschütten; (fig) sich lohnen

divid′ing line′ *s* Trennungsstrich *m*

divination [‚dɪvɪ′neʃən] *s* Weissagung *f*

divine [dɪ′vaɪn] *adj* göttlich ‖ *s* Geistlicher *m* ‖ *tr* (er)ahnen

divine′ prov′idence *s* göttliche Vorsehung *f*

divine′ right′ of kings′ *s* Königtum *n* von Gottes Gnaden

div′ing *s* Tauchen *n* (sport) Kunstspringen *n*

div′ing bell′ *s* Taucherglocke *f*

div′ing board′ *s* Sprungbrett *n*

div′ing suit′ *s* Taucheranzug *m*

divin′ing rod′ *s* Wünschelrute *f*

divinity [dɪ′vɪnɪti] *s* (*divine nature*) Göttlichkeit *f;* (*deity*) Gottheit *f*

divisible [dɪ′vɪzɪbəl] *adj* teilbar

division [dɪ′vɪʒən] *s* Teilung *f;* (*dissention*) Uneinigkeit *f;* (adm) Abteilung *f;* (math, mil) Division *f;* (sport) Sportklasse *f*

divisor [dɪ′vaɪzər] *s* (math) Teiler *m;* Divisor *m*

divorce [dɪ′vors] *s* Scheidung *f;* **apply for a d.** die Scheidungsklage einreichen; **get a d.** sich scheiden lassen ‖ *tr* (*said of a spouse*) sich scheiden lassen von; (*said of a judge*) scheiden; (*separate*) trennen

divorcee [dɪvor′si] *s* Geschiedene *f*

divulge [dɪ′vʌldʒ] *tr* ausplaudern

dizziness [′dɪzɪnɪs] *s* Schwindel *m*

dizzy [′dɪzi] *adj* schwindlig; (*causing dizziness*) schwindelerregend; (*mentally confused*) benommen; (*foolish*) damisch; (*feeling, spell*) Schwindel-

do [du] *v* (*3d pers* **does** [dʌz]; *pret* **did** [dɪd]; *pp* **done** [dʌn]; *ger* **doing** [′du‚ɪŋ]) *tr* tun, machen; (*damage*) anrichten; (*one's hair*) frisieren; (*an injustice*) antun; (*a favor, disservice*) erweisen; (*time in jail*) absitzen; (*miles per hour*) fahren; (*tour*) (coll) besichtigen; (*Shakespeare, etc., in class*) durchnehmen; **do duty as** dienen als; **do in** (sl) umbringen; **do over** (*with paint*) neu anstreichen; (*with covering*) neu überziehen; **what can I do for you?** womit kann ich dienen? ‖ *intr* tun, machen; (*suffice*) genügen; **do away with** abschaffen; (*persons*) aus dem Wege räumen; **do away with oneself** sich [*dat*] das Leben nehmen; **do without** auskommen ohne; **I am doing well** es geht mir gut; (*financially*) ich verdiene gut; (*e.g., in history*) ich komme gut voran; **I'll make it** do ich werde schon damit auskommen; **nothing doing!** ausgeschlossen! **that will do!** genug davon!; **that won't do!** das geht nicht! ‖ *aux* used in English but not specifically expressed in German: 1) in questions, e.g., **do you speak German?** sprechen Sie deutsch?; 2) in negative sentences,

e.g., **I do not live here** ich wohne hier nicht; 3) for emphasis, e.g., **I do feel better** ich fühle mich wirklich besser; 4) in imperative entreaties, e.g., **do come again** besuchen Sie mich doch wieder!; 5) in elliptical sentences, e.g., **I like Berlin. So do I** Mir gefällt Berlin. Mir auch.; **he drinks, doesn't he?** er trinkt, nicht wahr?; 6) in inversions after adverbs such as hardly, rarely, scarcely, little, e.g., **little did she realize that...sie** hatte keine Ahnung, daß... ‖ *impers*—**it doesn't do to** (*inf*) es ist unklug zu (*inf*); **it won't do you any good to stay here** es wird Ihnen nicht viel nützen, hier zu bleiben

docile [′dɑsɪl] *adj* gelehrig; (*easy to handle*) fügsam, lenksam

dock [dɑk] *s* Anlegeplatz *m;* (jur) Anklagebank *f;* **docks** Hafenanlagen *pl;* **in the d.** (jur) auf der Anklagebank ‖ *tr* (*a ship, space vehicle*) docken; (*a tail*) stutzen; (*pay*) kürzen; **d. an employee (for)** e-m Arbeitnehmer den Lohn kürzen (um) ‖ *intr* (naut) (am Kai) anlegen; (rok) docken, koppeln

docket [′dɑkɪt] *s* (*agenda*) Tagesordnung *f;* (jur) Prozeßliste *f*

dock′ hand′ *s* Hafenarbeiter *m*

dock′ing *s* (naut) Anlegen *n;* (rok) Andocken *n*

dock′ work′er *s* Dockarbeiter *m*

dock′yard′ *s* Werft *f*

doctor [′dɑktər] *s* Doktor *m;* (*physician*) Arzt *m,* Ärztin *f* ‖ *tr* (*records*) frisieren; (*adapt, edit, a play*) zurechtmachen ‖ *intr* (coll) in ärztlicher Behandlung stehen

doctorate [′dɑktərɪt] *s* Doktorwürde *f*

doctrine [′dɑktrɪn] *s* Doktrin *f,* Lehre *f*

document [′dɑkjəmənt] *s* Urkunde *f* ‖ [′dɑkjə‚ment] *tr* dokumentieren

documentary [‚dɑkjə′mentəri] *adj* dokumentarisch ‖ *s* Dokumentarfilm *m*

documentation [‚dɑkjəmən′teʃən] *s* Dokumentation *f*

doddering [′dɑdərɪŋ] *adj* zittrig

dodge [dɑdʒ] *s* Winkelzug *m* ‖ *tr* (*e.g., a blow*) ausweichen (*dat*); (*e.g., a responsibility*) sich drücken vor (*dat*) ‖ *intr* ausweichen

do-do [′dodo] *s* (–**does** & –**dos**) (coll) Depp *m*

doe [do] *s* Rehgeiß *f,* Damhirschkuh *f*

doer [′du‚ər] *s* Täter –in *mf*

doe′skin′ *s* Rehleder *n*

doff [dɑf] *tr* (*a hat*) abnehmen; (*clothes*) ausziehen; (*habits*) ablegen

dog [dɔg] *s* Hund *m;* **dog eats dog** jeder für sich; **go to the dogs** (coll) vor die Hunde gehen; **lucky dog!** (coll) Glückspilz!; **put on the dog** (coll) großtun ‖ *v* (*pret* & *pp* **dogged**; *ger* **dogging**) *tr* nachspüren (*dat*)

dog′ bis′cuit *s* Hundekuchen *m*

dog′ days′ *spl* Hundstage *pl*

dog′-eared′ *adj* mit Eselsohren

dog′face′ *s* (mil) Landser *m*

dog'fight' s (aer) Kurbelei f
dogged ['dɔgɪd] adj verbissen
doggerel ['dɔgərəl] s Knittelvers m
doggone ['dɔg'gɔn] adj (sl) verflixt
dog'house' s Hundehütte f; **in the d.** (fig) in Ungnade
dog' ken'nel s Hundezwinger m
dogma ['dɔgmə] s Dogma n
dogmatic [dɔg'mætɪk] adj dogmatisch
do-gooder ['du'gudər] s Humanitäts-apostel m
dog' show' s Hundeschau f
dog's' life' s Hundeleben n
Dog' Star' s Hundestern m
dog' tag' s Hundemarke f; (mil) Erkennungsmarke f
dog'-tired' adj hundemüde
dog'wood' s Hartriegel m
doily ['dɔɪlɪ] s Zierdeckchen n
do'ing s Werk n; **doings** Tun und Treiben n; (events) Ereignisse pl
doldrums ['dɔldrəmz] spl Kalmengürtel m; **in the d.** (fig) deprimiert
dole [dol] s Spende f; **be on the d.** stempeln gehen ‖ tr—**d. out** verteilen
doleful ['dolfəl] adj trübselig
doll [dɑl] s Puppe f ‖ tr—**d. up** (coll) aufdonnern ‖ intr (coll) sich aufdonnern
dollar ['dɑlər] s Dollar m
doll' car'riage s Puppenwagen m
dolly ['dɑlɪ] s Püppchen n; (cart) Schiebkarren m
dolphin ['dɑlfɪn] s Delphin m
dolt [dolt] s Tölpel m
domain [do'men] s (& fig) Domäne f
dome [dom] s Kuppel f
dome' light' s (aut) Deckenlicht n
domestic [də'mestɪk] adj (of the home) Haus-, häuslich, Haushalts-; (produced at home) einheimisch, inländisch, Landes-; (tame) Haus-; (e.g., policy) Innen-, innere ‖ s Hausangestellte mf
domesticate [də'mestɪ ,ket] tr zähmen
domicile ['dɑmɪ ,saɪl] s Wohnsitz m
dominance ['dɑmɪnəns] s Vorherrschaft f
dominant ['dɑmɪnənt] adj vorherrschend; (factor) entscheidend
dominate ['dɑmɪ ,net] tr beherrschen ‖ intr (over) herrschen (über acc)
domination [,dɑmɪ'neʃən] s Beherrschung f, Herrschaft f
domineer [,dɑmɪ'nɪr] tr & intr tyrannisieren
domineer'ing adj tyrannisch
dominion [də'mɪnjən] s (sovereignty) (over) Gewalt f (über acc); (domain) Domäne f; (of British Empire) Dominion n
domi·no ['dɑmɪ ,no] s (–noes & nos) Dominostein m; **dominoes** ssg Dominospiel n
don [dɑn] s Universitätsprofessor m ‖ v (pret & pp donned; ger donning) tr anlegen; (a hat) sich [dat] aufsetzen
donate ['donet] tr schenken, spenden
donation [do'neʃən] s Schenkung f; (small contribution) Spende f
done [dʌn] adj erledigt; (culin) gar, fertig; **d. for** kaputt; **d. with** (com-

pleted) fertig; **get** (s.th.) **d.** fertigbekommen; **well d.** (culin) durchgebraten
donkey ['dʌŋkɪ] s Esel m
donor ['donər] s Spender –in mf
doodad ['dudæd] s (gadget) Dings n; (decoration) Tand m
doodle ['dudəl] s Gekritzel n ‖ tr bekritzeln ‖ intr kritzeln
doom [dum] s Verhängnis n ‖ tr verdammen, verurteilen
doomed adj todgeweiht
doomsday ['dumz ,de] s der Jüngste Tag
door [dor] s Tür f; **from d. to d.** von Haus zu Haus; **out of doors** draußen, im Freien; **show s.o. the d.** j–m die Tür weisen; **two doors away** zwei Häuser weiter
door'bell' s Türklingel f; **the d. is ringing** es klingelt
door'but'ton s Klingelknopf m
door'frame' s Türrahmen m
door'han'dle s Türgriff m, Türklinke f
door'jamb' s Türpfosten m
door'knob' s Türknopf m
door'man' s (–men') Portier m
door'mat' s Abtreter m, Türmatte f
door'nail' s—**dead as a d.** mausetot
door'post' s Türpfosten m
door'sill' s Türschwelle f
door'step' s Türstufe f
door'stop' s Türanschlag m
door'-to-door' sales'man s Hausierer m
door'-to-door sel'ling s Hausieren n
door'way' s Türöffnung f; (fig) Weg m
dope [dop] s (drug) (sl) Rauschgift n; (information) (sl) vertraulicher Tip m; (fool) (sl) Trottel m; (aer) Lack m ‖ tr (a racehorse) (sl) dopen; (a person) (sl) betäuben, verdrogen; (aer) lackieren; **d. out** (sl) herausfinden, ausarbeiten; **d. up** (sl) verdrogen
dope' ad'dict s (sl) Rauschgiftsüchtige mf
dope' push'er s (sl) Rauschgiftschieber –in mf
dope'sheet' s (sl) vertraulicher Bericht m
dope' traf'fic s (sl) Rauschgifthandel m
dopey ['dopi] adj (dopier; dopiest) (sl) dämlich; (from sleep) (coll) schlaftrunken
dormant ['dɔrmənt] adj ruhend, untätig; (bot) in der Winterruhe
dormer ['dɔrmər] s Bodenfenster n; (the whole structure) Mansarde f
dor'mer win'dow s Bodenfenster n
dormitory ['dɔrmɪ ,tori] s (building) Studentenheim n; (room) Schlafsaal m
dormouse ['dɔr ,maʊs] s (mice [,maɪs]) Haselmaus f
dor'sal fin' ['dɔrsəl] s Rückenflosse f
dosage ['dosɪdʒ] s Dosierung f
dose [dos] s (& fig) Dosis f
dossier ['dɑsɪ ,e] s Dossier m
dot [dɑt] s Punkt m, Tupfen m; **on the dot** auf die Sekunde; **three o'clock on the dot** Punkt drei Uhr ‖ v (pret

& *pp* dotted; *ger* dotting) *tr* punktieren; tüpfeln; **dot one's i's** den Punkt aufs i setzen; (fig) übergenau sein

dotage ['dotɪdʒ] *s*—**be in one's d.** senil sein

dotard ['dotərd] *s* kindischer Greis *m*

dote [dot] *intr*—**d. on** vernarrt sein in (*acc*)

dot'ing *adj* (on) vernarrt (in *acc*)

dots' and dash'es *spl* (telg) Punkte und Striche *pl*

dot'ted *adj* (*pattern*) getüpfelt; (*with flowers, etc.*) übersät; (*line*) punktiert

double ['dʌbəl] *adj* doppelt || *s* Doppelte *n*; (*person*) Doppelgänger *m* (cin, theat) Double *n*; **doubles** (tennis) Doppel *n*; **on the d.** im Geschwindschritt || *tr* (ver)doppeln; (*the fist*) ballen; (cards) doppeln; (naut) umsegeln || *intr* sich verdoppeln; (cards) doppeln; **d. back** umkehren; **d. up with** sich biegen vor (*dat*)

dou'ble-bar'reled *adj* (*gun*) doppelläufig; (fig) mit zweifacher Wirkung

dou'ble bass' [bes] *s* Kontrabaß *m*

dou'ble bed' *s* Doppelbett *n*

dou'ble-breast'ed *adj* doppelreihig

dou'ble' chin' *s* Doppelkinn *n*

dou'ble cross' *s* Schwindel *m*

dou'ble-cross' *tr* beschwindeln

dou'ble-cross'er *s* Schwindler –in *mf*

dou'ble date' *s* Doppelrendezvous *n*

dou'ble-deal'er *s* Betrüger –in *mf*

dou'ble-deal'ing *s* Doppelzüngigkeit *f*

dou'ble-deck'er *s* (*ship, bus*) Doppeldecker *m*; (*sandwich*) Doppelsandwich *n*; (*bed*) Etagenbett *n*

dou'ble-edged' *adj* (& fig) zweischneidig

double entendre ['dʌbələn'tandrə] *s* (*ambiguity*) Doppelsinn *m*; (*ambiguous term*) doppelsinniger Ausdruck *m*

dou'ble en'try *s* (com) doppelte Buchführung *f*

dou'ble expo'sure *s* Doppelbelichtung *f*

dou'ble fea'ture *s* Doppelprogramm *n*

dou'blehead'er *s* Doppelspiel *n*

dou'ble-joint'ed *adj* mit Gummigelenken

dou'blepark' *tr* & *intr* falsch parken

dou'ble-spaced' *adj* mit doppeltem Zeilenabstand

dou'ble stand'ard *s* zweierlei Maß *n*

doublet ['dʌblɪt] *s* (*duplicate; counterfeit stone*) Dublette *f*; (hist) Wams *m*; (ling) Doppelform *f*

dou'ble take' *s* (fig) Spätzündung *f*

dou'ble-talk' *s* zweideutige Rede *f*

dou'ble time' *s* (*wage rate*) doppelter Lohn *m*; (mil) Eilschritt *m*

dou'ble track' *s* (rr) doppelgleisige Bahnlinie *f*

doubly ['dʌbli] *adv* doppelt

doubt [daut] *s* Zweifel *m*; **be still in d.** (*said of things*) noch zweifelhaft sein; **beyond d.** ohne (jeden) Zweifel; **in case of d.** im Zweifelsfalle; **no d.** zweifellos; **raise doubts** Bedenken

erregen; **there is no d. that** es unterliegt keinem Zweifel, daß || *tr* bezweifeln || *intr* zweifeln

doubter ['dautər] *s* Zweifler –in *mf*

doubtful ['dautfəl] *adj* zweifelhaft

doubtless ['dautlɪs] *adj* & *adv* zweifellos

douche [duʃ] *s* (*device*) Irrigator *m*; (*act of cleansing*) Spülung *f* || *tr* & *intr* spülen

dough [do] *s* Teig *m*; (sl) Pinke *f*

dough'boy' *s* (sl) Landser *m*

dough'nut' *s* Krapfen *m*

doughty ['dauti] *adj* wacker

doughy ['do·i] *adj* teigig

dour [daur], [dur] *adj* mürrisch

douse [daus] *tr* eintauchen; (**with**) übergießen (mit); (*a fire*) auslöschen

dove [dʌv] *s* (& pol) Taube *f*

dovecote ['dʌv‚kot] *s* Taubenschlag *m*

dove'tail' *s* (carp) Schwalbenschwanz *m* || *tr* verzinken; (fig) ineinanderfügen || *intr* ineinanderpassen

dowager ['dau·ədʒər] *s* Witwe *f* (von Stand); (coll) Matrone *f*

dowdy ['daudi] *adj* schlampig

dow·el ['dau·əl] *s* Dübel *m* || *v* (*pret* & *pp* **-el[l]ed;** *ger* **-el[l]ing**) *tr* (ein)dübeln

down [daun] *adj* (*prices*) gesunken; (*sun*) untergegangen; **be d. for** vorgemerkt sein für; **be d. on s.o.** auf j–m herumtrampeln; **be d. three points** (sport) drei Punkte zurück sein; **be d. with a cold** mit e–r Erkältung im Bett liegen; **d. and out** völlig erledigt; **d. in the mouth** niedergedrückt || *adv* herunter, hinunter; **d. from** von...herab; **d. there** da unten; **d. to** bis hinunter zu; **d. to the last man** bis zum letzten Mann; **d. with...!** nieder mit...! || *s* (*of fowl*) Daune *f*; (*fine hair*) Flaum *m*; **downs** grasbedecktes Hügelland *n* || *prep* (postpositive) (*acc*) herunter, hinunter; **a little way d. the road** etwas weiter auf der Straße; **d. the river** flußabwärts || *tr* niederschlagen; (*a glass of beer*) (coll) hinunterstürzen; (aer) abschießen

down'cast' *adj* niedergeschlagen

down'draft' *s* Abwind *m*, Fallwind *m*

down'fall' *s* Untergang *m*

down'grade' *s* Gefälle *n*; **on the d.** (fig) im Niedergang || *tr* herabsetzen; niedrig einstufen

down'heart'ed *adj* niedergeschlagen

down'hill' *adj* bergabgehend; (*in skiing*) Abfahrts– || *adv* bergab; **he's going d.** (coll) mit ihm geht es abwärts

down' pay'ment *s* Anzahlung *f*

down'pour' *s* Regenguß *m*, Sturzregen *m*

down'right' *adj* ausgesprochen; (*lie*) glatt; (*contradiction*) schroff || *adv* ausgesprochen

down'spout' *s* Fallrohr *n*

down'stairs' *adj* unten befindlich || *adv* (*position*) unten; (*direction*) nach unten

down'stream' *adv* stromabwärts

down'stroke' s (in writing) Grund-
strich m; (of a piston) Abwärtshub
m

down'-the-line' adj vorbehaltlos

down-to-earth' adj nüchtern

down'town' adj im Geschäftsviertel
gelegen || adv (position) im Ge-
schäftsviertel; (direction) ins Ge-
schäftsviertel, in die Stadt || s
Geschäftsviertel n

down'trend' s Baissestimmung f

downtrodden ['daun,trɑdən] adj un-
terdrückt

downward ['daunwərd] adj Abwärts–
|| adv abwärts

downwards ['daunwərdz] adv abwärts

downy ['dauni] adj flaumig; (soft)
weich wie Flaum

dowry ['dauri] s Mitgift f

dowser ['dauzər] s (rod) Wünschelrute f; (person) Wünschelrutengän-
ger m

doze [doz] s Schläfchen n || intr dösen

dozen ['dʌzən] s Dutzend n; a d. times
dutzendmal

Dr. abbr (**Doctor**) Dr.; (in addresses:
Drive) Str.

drab [dræb] adj (**drabber; drabbest**)
graubraun; (fig) trüb

drach·ma ['drækmə] s (**-mas & –mae**
[mi]) Drachme f

draft [dræft] s (of air, drink) Zug m;
(sketch) Entwurf m; (fin) Tratte f;
(mil) Einberufung f; on d. vom Faß
|| tr (sketch) entwerfen, abfassen;
(mil) einberufen

draft' age' s wehrpflichtiges Alter n

draft' beer' s Schankbier n

draft' board' s Wehrmeldeamt n

draft' dodg'er ['dadʒər] s Drückeberger m

draftee [,dræf'ti] s Dienstpflichtige
f

draft'ing s (of a document) Abfassung
f; (mechanical drawing) Zeichnen n;
(mil) Aushebung f

draft'ing board' s Zeichenbrett n

draft'ing room' s Zeichenbüro n

drafts·man ['dræftsmən] s (**-men**)
Zeichner m

drafty ['dræfti] adj zugig

drag [dræg] s (sledge) Lastschlitten
m; (in smoking) (coll) Zug m; (boring person) langweiliger Mensch m;
(s.th. tedious) etwas langweiliges;
(encumbrance) (on) Hemmschuh m
(für); (aer) Luftwiderstand m; (for
recovering objects) (naut) Schleppnetz n; (for retarding motion) (naut)
Schleppanker m || v (pret & pp
dragged; ger **dragging**) tr schleppen,
schleifen; **d. one's feet** schlurfen;
(fig) sich [dat] Zeit lassen; **d. out**
dahinschleppen; (protract) verschleppen; **d. through the mud** (fig) in den
Schmutz zerren; **d. up** (fig) aufwär-
men || intr (said of a long dress,
etc.) schleifen; (said of time) dahin-
schleichen; **d. on** (be prolonged) sich
hinziehen

drag'net' s Schleppnetz n

dragon ['drægən] s Drache m

drag'onfly' s Libelle f

dragoon [drə'gun] s Dragoner m || tr
(coerce) zwingen

drag' race' s Straßenrennen n; (sport)
Kurzstreckenrennen n

drain [dren] s (sewer) Kanal m; (under a sink) Abfluß m; (fig) (on)
Belastung f (genit); (surg) Drain m;
down the d. (fig) zum Fenster hin-
aus || tr (land) entwässern; (water)
ableiten; (a cup, glass) austrinken;
(fig) verzehren || intr ablaufen;
(culin) abtropfen

drainage ['drenidʒ] s Ableitung f;
(e.g., of land) Entwässerung f; (surg)
Drainage f

drain'age ditch' s Abflußgraben m

drain' cock' s Entleerungshahn m

drain'pipe' s Abflußrohr n

drain' plug' s Abflußstöpsel m

drake [drek] s Enterich m

dram [dræm] s Dram f

drama ['drɑmə] s Drama n; (art and
genre) Dramatik f

dra'ma crit'ic s Theaterkritiker –in mf

dramatic [drə'mætɪk] adj dramatisch
|| **dramatics** s Dramatik f; spl (pej)
Schauspielerei f

dramatist ['dræmətɪst] s Dramatiker
–in mf

dramatize ['dræmə,taɪz] tr dramati-
sieren

drape [drep] s Vorhang m; (hang of a
drape or skirt) Faltenwurf m || tr
drapieren

drapery ['drepəri] s Vorhänge pl

dra'pery mate'rial s Vorhangstoff m

drastic ['dræstɪk] adj drastisch

draught [dræft] s & tr var of **draft**

draw [drɔ] s (in a lottery) Ziehen n;
(that which attracts) Schlager m;
(power of attraction) Anziehungskraft f; end in a d. unentschieden
ausgehen || v (pret **drew** [dru]; pp
drawn [drɔn]) tr (pictures) zeichnen;
(a line, comparison, parallel, conclusion, lots, winner, sword, wagon)
ziehen; (a crowd) anlocken; (a distinction) machen; (blood) vergießen; (curtains) zuziehen; (a check)
ausstellen; (water) schöpfen; (cards)
nehmen; (rations) (mil) in Empfang
nehmen; **d. a blank** (coll) e-e Niete
ziehen; **d. aside** beiseiteziehen; **d. attention to** die Aufmerksamkeit lenken auf (acc); **d. into** (e.g., an argument) hineinziehen in (acc); **d. lots
for** losen um; **d. out** (protract) in
die Länge ziehen; (money from a
bank) abheben; **d. s.o. out** j–n aus-
holen; **d. the line** (fig) e–e Grenze
ziehen; **d. up** (a document) verfas-
sen; (plans) entwerfen || intr zeich-
nen; **d. away** sich entfernen; **d. back**
sich zurückziehen; **d. near** heran-
nahen; **d. on** zurückgreifen auf (acc);
d. to a close sich dem Ende zuneigen

draw'back' s Nachteil m

draw'bridge' s Zugbrücke f

drawee [,drɔ'i] s Trassat –in mf

drawer ['drɔər] s Zeichner –in mf;
(com) Trassant –in mf & ['drɔr] s
Schublade f; **drawers** Unterhose f

draw'ing s (of pictures) Zeichnen n;

(picture) Zeichnung *f; (in a lottery)* Ziehung *f,* Verlosung *f*
draw′ing board′ *s* Reißbrett *n*
draw′ing card′ *s* Zugnummer *f*
draw′ing room′ *s* Empfangszimmer *n*
drawl [drɔl] *s* gedehntes Sprechen *n* || *intr* gedehnt sprechen
drawn [drɔn] *adj (face)* **(with)** verzerrt (vor *dat*); *(sword)* blank
dray [dre] *s* niedriger Rollwagen *m; (sledge)* Schleife *f*
dread [dred] *adj* furchtbar || *s* Furcht *f* || *tr* fürchten
dreadful [′dredfəl] *adj* furchtbar
dream [drim] *s* Traum *m; (aspiration, ambition)* Wunschtraum *m; (ideal)* **(coll)** Gedicht *n* || *v (pret & pp* **dreamed & dreamt** [dremt] *tr* träumen; **d. away** verträumen; **d. up** zusammenträumen || *intr* träumen; **d. of** *(long for)* sich [*dat*] enträumen; **I dreamt of her** mir träumte von ihr
dreamer [′drimər] *s* Träumer –in *mf*
dream′land′ *s* Traumland *n*
dream′-like′ *adj* traumhaft
dream′world′ *s* Traumwelt *f*
dreamy [′drimi] *adj (place)* verträumt; *(eyes)* träumerisch
dreary [′driri] *adj* trüb, trist
dredge [dredʒ] *s* Bagger *m* || *tr* (aus)-baggern || *intr* baggern
dredger [′dredʒər] *s* Bagger *m*
dredg′ing *s* Baggern *n*
dregs [dregz] *spl* Bodensatz *m; (of society)* Abschaum *m,* Auswurf *m*
drench [drentʃ] *tr* durchnässen
Dres′den chi′na [′drezdən] *s* Meißner Porzellan *n*
dress [dres] *s* Kleidung *f; (woman's dress)* Kleid *n* || *tr* anziehen; *(a store window)* dekorieren; *(skins)* gerben; *(a salad, goose, chicken)* zubereiten; *(vines)* beschneiden; *(stones)* behauen; *(ore)* aufbereiten; *(wounds)* verbinden; *(hair)* frisieren; *(tex)* appretieren; **d. down** **(coll)** ausschimpfen; **d. ranks** die Glieder ausrichten; **get dressed** sich anziehen || *intr* sich anziehen; **d. up** sich fein machen
dress′ affair′ *s* Galaveranstaltung *f*
dresser [′dresər] *s* Frisierkommode *f;* **be a good d.** sich gut kleiden
dress′ing *s (stuffing for fowl)* Füllung *f; (for salad)* Soße *f; (surg)* Verband *m*
dress′ing down′ *s* Gardinenpredigt *f*
dress′ing room′ *s* Umkleideraum *m; (theat)* Garderobe *f*
dress′ing sta′tion *s* Verbandsplatz *m*
dress′ing ta′ble *s* Frisierkommode *f*
dress′mak′er *s* Schneiderin *f*
dress′mak′ing *s* Modenschneiderei *f*
dress′ rehear′sal *s* Kostümprobe *f*
dress′ shirt′ *s* Frackhemd *n*
dress′ shop′ *s* Modenhaus *n,* Modengeschäft *n*
dress′ suit′ *s* Frackanzug *m,* Frack *m*
dress′ un′iform *s* Paradeuniform *f*
dressy [′dresi] *adj (showy)* geschniegelt; *(stylish)* modisch; *(for formal affairs)* elegant
dribble [′drıbəl] *s (trickle)* Getröpfel

n; **(sport)** Dribbeln *n* || *tr & intr* tröpfeln; **(sport)** dribbeln
driblet [′drıblıt] *s* Bißchen *n*
dried [draıd] *adj* Trocken–, Dörr–
dried′ beef′ *s* Dörrfleisch *n*
dried′ fruit′ *s* Dörrobst *n*
dried′-up′ *adj* ausgetrocknet, verdorrt
drier [′draıər] *s* Trockner *m; (for the hair)* Haartrockenhaube *f; (hand model)* Fön *m*
drift [drıft] *s (of sand, snow)* Wehe *f; (tendency)* Richtung *f,* Neigung *f; (intent)* Absicht *f; (meaning)* Sinn *m; (aer, naut, rad)* Abtrift *f; (flow of the ocean current)* (naut) Drift *f* || *intr (said of sand, snow)* sich anhäufen; *(said of a boat)* treiben; **d. away** *(said of sounds)* verwehen; *(said of a crowd)* sich verlaufen; **d. shut** verweht werden
drifter [′drıftər] *s* zielloser Mensch *m*
drift′ ice′ *s* Treibeis *n*
drift′wood′ *s* Treibholz *n*
drill [drıl] *s (tool)* Bohrer *m; (exercise)* Drill *m; (tex)* Drillich *m* || *tr* bohren; *(exercise)* drillen; **d. s.th. into s.o.** j–m etw einpauken || *intr* bohren; *(exercise)* drillen
drill′mas′ter *s* (mil) Ausbilder *m*
drill′ press′ *s* Bohrpresse *f*
drink [drıŋk] *s* Trunk *m* || *v (pret* **drank** [dræŋk]; *pp* **drunk** [drʌŋk] *tr* trinken; *(said of animals)* saufen; *(pej)* saufen; **d. away** *(money)* versaufen; **d. down** hinunterkippen; **d. in** *(air)* einschlürfen; *(s.o.'s words)* verschlingen || *intr* trinken; *(excessively)* saufen; **d. to** trinken auf *(acc);* **d. up** austrinken
drinkable [′drıŋkəbəl] *adj* trinkbar
drinker [′drıŋkər] *s* Trinker –in *mf;* **heavy drinker** Zecher –in *mf*
drink′ing foun′tain *s* Trinkbrunnen *m*
drink′ing par′ty *s* Zechgelage *n*
drink′ing song′ *s* Trinklied *n*
drink′ing straw′ *s* Strohhalm *m*
drink′ing trough′ *s* Viehtränke *f*
drink′ing wa′ter *s* Trinkwasser *n*
drip [drıp] *s* Tröpfeln *n* || *v (pret & pp* **dripped**; *ger* **dripping**) *tr & intr* tröpfeln
drip′ cof′fee *s* Filterkaffee *m*
drip′-dry′ *adj* bügelfrei
drip′ pan′ *s* Bratpfanne *f*
drip′pings *spl* Bratenfett *n*
drive [draıv] *s (in a car)* Fahrt *f; (road)* Fahrweg *m; (energy)* Schwungkraft *f; (inner urge)* Antrieb *m; (campaign)* Aktion *f; (for raising money)* Spendeaktion *f; (golf)* Treibschlag *m; (mach)* Antrieb *m; (mil)* Vorstoß *m; (tennis)* Treibschlag *m;* **go for a d.** spazierenfahren || *v (pret* **drove** [drov]; *pp* **driven** [′drıvən]) *tr (a car, etc.)* fahren; *(e.g., cattle)* treiben; *(a tunnel)* vortreiben; **d. a hard bargain** zäh um den Preis feilschen; **d. away** abtreiben; **d. *(oneself, a horse)* hard** abjagen; **d. home** nahebringen; **d. in** *(a nail)* einschlagen; **d. off course** (naut) verschlagen; **d. on** antreiben; **d. out** austreiben; **d. s.o. to** *(inf)* j–n

dazu bringen zu (inf); **d. to despair** zur Verzweiflung treiben ‖ intr fahren; **d. along** mitfahren; **d. at** abzielen auf (acc); **d. away** wegfahren; **d. by** vorbeifahren an (dat); **d. in** einfahren; **d. on** weiterfahren; **d. out** herausfahren; **d. up** anfahren

drive′ belt′ s Treibriemen m

drive′-in′ s Autorestaurant n; (cin) Autokino n

driv·el [′drɪvəl] s (slobber) Geifer m; (nonsense) Faselei f ‖ v (pret & pp -el[l]ed; ger -el[l]ing) intr sabbern; (fig) faseln

driver [′draɪvər] s (of a car) Fahrer -in mf; (of a locomotive, streetcar) Führer m; (golf) Treibschläger m; (mach) Treibhammer m

driv′er's li′cense s Führerschein m

drive′ shaft′ s Antriebswelle f

drive′ way′ s Einfahrt f

drive′-yourself′ serv′ice s Autovermietung f an Selbstfahrer

driv·ing adj (rain) stürmisch ‖ s (aut) Steuerung f

driv′ing instruc′tor s Fahrlehrer -in mf

driv′ing les′son s Fahrstunde f

driv′ing school′ s Autofahrschule f

drizzle [′drɪzəl] s Nieselregen m ‖ impers—**it is drizzling** es nieselt

droll [drol] adj drollig

dromedary [′drɑmə͵derɪ] s Dromedar n

drone [dron] s (bee; loafer) Drohne f; (buzz) Gesumme n; (monotonous speech) Geleier n ‖ tr (e.g., prayers) leiern ‖ intr summen; (fig) leiern

drool [drul] intr sabbern

droop [drup] s Herabhängen n; (stoop) gebeugte Haltung f ‖ intr herabhängen; (said of flowers) zu welken beginnen; (fig) den Kopf hängen lassen

droopy [′drupɪ] adj (saggy) schlaff herabhängend; (dejected) mutlos; (shoulders) abfallend; (flowers) welkend

drop [drɑp] s (of liquid) Tropfen m; (candy) Fruchtbonbon m & n; (fall) Fall m; (height differential) Gefälle n; (reduction) Abnahme f; (in prices) Rückgang m; (in temperature) Sturz m; (of bombs or supplies) Abwurf m; (of paratroopers) Absprung m; **a fifty-meter d.** ein Fall m aus e-r Höhe von fünfzig Metern; **d. by d.** tropfenweise; **d. in the bucket** Tropfen m auf e-n heißen Stein ‖ v (pret & pp **dropped;** ger **dropping**) tr (let fall) fallenlassen; (bombs, supplies) abwerfen; (a subject, remarks, hints) fallenlassen; (the eyes, voice) senken; (anchor; young of animals) werfen; (money in gambling) (sl) verlieren; (terminate) einstellen; (from membership roll) ausschließen; (paratroopers) absetzen; **d. it!** laß das!; **d. s.o. a line** j-m ein paar Zeilen schreiben ‖ intr fallen; (drip) tropfen; (said of prices, temperature) sinken, fallen; (keel over) umfallen; (said of a curtain) niedergehen; **d. behind** zurück-

fallen; **d. dead!** (sl) laß dich begraben!; **d. in on s.o.** auf e-n Sprung bei j-m vorbeikommen; **d. off to sleep** einschlafen; **d. out** sich zurückziehen; (sport) ausscheiden; **d. out of school** von der Schule abgehen

drop′ ar′ea s (aer) Abwurfraum m

drop′ cur′tain s (bemalter) Vorhang m

drop′ ham′mer s Fallhammer m

drop′-leaf ta′ble s Tisch m mit herunterklappbaren Flügeln

drop′light′ s Hängelampe f

drop′out′ s Gescheiterte mf; (educ) Abgänger -in mf

dropper [′drɑpər] s (med) Tropfer m

drop′ping adj (prices) rückgängig ‖ s (of bombs, supplies) Abwurf m; **droppings** tierischer Kot m

dropsy [′drɑpsɪ] s Wassersucht f

drop′ ta′ble s Klapptisch m

dross [drɔs] s (slag) Schlacke f; (waste) Abfall m

drought [draʊt] s Dürre f

drove [drov] s Herde f

drown [draʊn] tr (& fig) ertränken; **d. out** übertönen ‖ intr ertrinken

drowse [draʊz] intr dösen

drowsiness [′draʊzɪnɪs] s Schläfrigkeit f

drowsy [′draʊzɪ] adj schläfrig, dösig

drub [drʌb] v (pret & pp **drubbed;** ger **drubbing**) tr (flog) verprügeln; (sport) entscheidend schlagen

drudge [drʌdʒ] s Packesel m ‖ intr sich placken, schuften

drudgery [′drʌdʒərɪ] s Plackerei f

drug [drʌg] s Droge f, Arznei f; (narcotic) Betäubungsmittel n; (addictive narcotic) Rauschgift n ‖ v (pret & pp **drugged;** ger **drugging**) tr betäuben

drug′ ad′dict s Rauschgiftsüchtige mf

drug′ addic′tion s Rauschgiftsucht f

druggist [′drʌgɪst] s Apotheker -in mf

drug′store′ s Apotheke f, Drogerie f

drug′ traf′fic s Rauschgifthandel m

druid [′druːɪd] s Druide m

drum [drʌm] s (musical instrument; container) Trommel f ‖ v (pret & pp **drummed;** ger **drumming**) tr trommeln; **d. s.th. into s.o.** j-m etw einpauken; **d. the table** auf den Tisch trommeln; **d. up** zusammentrommeln ‖ intr trommeln

drum′ and bu′gle corps′ s Musikzug m

drum′beat′ s Trommelschlag m

drum′fire′ s (mil) Trommelfeuer n

drum′head′ s Trommelfell n

drum′ ma′jor s Tambourmajor m

drum′ majorette′ s Tambourmajorin f

drummer [′drʌmər] s Trommler -in mf

drum′stick′ s Trommelschlegel m; (culin) Unterschenkel m

drunk [drʌŋk] adj betrunken ‖ s Säufer -in mf

drunkard [′drʌŋkərd] s Trunkenbold m

drunken [′drʌŋkən] adj betrunken

dry [draɪ] adj trocken; (boring) trocken; (wine) herb; (thirsty) durstig; (rainless) regenarm; (wood) dürr ‖ v (pret & pp **-dried**) tr (ab)trocknen;

(*e.g., fruit*) dörren; **dry off** abtrocknen; **dry out** austrocknen; **dry up** austrocknen; (*fig*) erschöpfen ‖ *intr* trocknen; **dry out** austrocknen; **dry up** vertrocknen; (*said of grass, flowers*) verdorren; (*fig*) versiegen; (*keep quiet*) (*sl*) die Klappe halten

dry′ bat′tery *s* Trockenbatterie *f*
dry′ cell′ *s* Tockenelement *n*
dry′-clean′ *tr* (*chemically*) reinigen
dry′ clean′er′s *s* Reinigungsanstalt *f*
dry′ clean′ing *s* chemische Reinigung *f*
dry′ dock′ *s* Trockendock *n*
dry′-eyed′ *adj* ungerührt
dry′ goods′ *spl* Schnittwaren *pl*
dry′ ice′ *s* Trockeneis *n*
dry′ land′ *s* fester Boden *m*
dry′ meas′ure *s* Trockenmaß *n*
dryness [′draɪnɪs] *s* Trockenheit *f*, Dürre *f*; (*fig*) Nüchternheit *f*
dry′ nurse′ *s* Säuglingsschwester *f*
dry′ rot′ *s* Trockenfäule *f*
dry′ run′ *s* Vorübung *f*; (*test run*) Probelauf *m*; (*with blank ammunition*) Zielübung *f*
dry′ sea′son *s* Trockenzeit *f*
dual [′d(j)u-əl] *adj* Zwei-, doppelt; (*tech*) Doppel-
dualism [′d(j)u-ə‚lɪzəm] *s* Dualismus *m*
du′al-pur′pose *adj* e-m doppelten Zweck dienend
dub [dʌb] *v* (*pret & pp* **dubbed;** *ger* **dubbing**) *tr* (*nickname*) betiteln; (*cin*) synchronisieren; (*golf*) schlecht treffen; (*hist*) zum Ritter schlagen
dub′bing *s* (*cin*) Synchronisierung *f*
dubious [′d(j)ubɪ-əs] *adj* zweifelhaft
ducal [′d(j)ukəl] *adj* herzoglich
duchess [′dʌt∫ɪs] *s* Herzogin *f*
duchy [′dʌt∫i] *s* Herzogtum *n*
duck [dʌk] *s* Ente *f* ‖ *tr* (*the head*) ducken; (*in water*) (unter)tauchen; (*evade*) sich drücken vor (*dat*) ‖ *intr* ducken; (*go under the surface*) untertauchen
duck′ing *s*—**give s.o. a d.** j-n untertauchen
duck′ pond′ *s* Ententeich *m*
duck′ soup′ *s* (*sl*) Kinderspiel *n*
ducky [′dʌki] *adj* (*coll*) nett, lieb
duct [dʌkt] *s* Rohr *n*, Kanal *m*, Leitung *f*; (*anat, elec*) Kanal *m*
duct′less gland′ [′dʌktlɪs] *s* endokrine Drüse *f*
duct′work′ *s* Rohrleitungen *pl*
dud [dʌd] *s* (*sl & mil*) Versager *m*, Blindgänger *m*; **duds** (*coll*) Klamotten *pl*
dude [d(j)ud] *s* (*dandy*) Geck *m*
dude′ ranch′ *s* Vergnügungsfarm *f*
due [d(j)u] *adj* (*payment; bus, train*) fällig; (*proper*) gehörig; (*consideration*) reiflich; **be due to** (*as a cause*) beruhen auf (*dat*); (*said of an honor*) gebühren (*dat*); (*said of money*) zustehen (*dat*); **be due to** (*inf*) sollen, müssen; **in due course** im gegebenen Moment; **in due time** zur rechten Zeit ‖ *adv* (*naut*) genau ‖ *s*—**dues** Beitrag *m*; **get one′s due** nach Verdienst behandelt werden; **give every-**

one his **due** jedem geben, was ihm gebührt
due′ date′ *s* (*of a payment*) Termin *m*
duel [′d(j)u-əl] *s* Duell *n*; **fight a d.** sich duellieren ‖ *v* (*pret & pp* **duel[l]ed;** *ger* **duel[l]ing**) *intr* sich duellieren
dues-paying [′d(j)uz‚pe-ɪŋ] *adj* beitragzahlend
duet [d(j)u′et] *s* Duett *n*
due′ to′ *prep* wegen (*genit*)
duf′fle bag′ [′dʌfəl] *s* (*mil*) Kleidersack *m*
dug′out′ *s* (*boat*) Einbaum *m*; (*baseball, mil*) Unterstand *m*
duke [d(j)uk] *s* Herzog *m*
dukedom [′d(j)ukdəm] *s* Herzogtum *n*
dull [dʌl] *adj* (*not sharp*) stumpf; (*pain*) dumpf; (*not shining*) glanzlos, matt; (*uninteresting*) nüchtern, geistlos; (*stupid*) stumpfsinnig; (*com*) flau ‖ *tr* stumpf machen; (*fig*) abstumpfen ‖ *intr* stumpf werden; (*fig*) abstumpfen
dullard [′dʌlərd] *s* Dummkopf *m*
dullness [′dʌlnɪs] *s* (*of a blade*) Stumpfheit *f*; (*of color*) Mattheit *f*; (*of a speech, etc.*) Stumpfsinn *m*
duly [′d(j)uli] *adv* ordnungsgemäß
dumb [dʌm] *adj* stumm; (*stupid*) dumm ‖ *adv*—**play d.** sich unwissend stellen
dumb′bell′ *s* Hantel *f*; (*sl*) Dummkopf *m*
dumbstruck [′dʌm‚strʌk] *adj* wie auf den Mund geschlagen
dumb′ wait′er *s* (*elevator*) Speiseaufzug *m*; (*serving table*) Serviertisch *m*
dumdum [′dʌm‚dʌm] *s* Dumdumgeschoß *n*
dumfound [′dʌm‚faund] *tr* verblüffen
dummy [′dʌmi] *adj* (*not real*) Schein-; (*mil*) blind, Übungs- ‖ *s* (*representation for display*) Attrappe *f*; (*clothes form*) Schneiderpuppe *f*; (*dolt*) Ölgötze *m*; (*cards*) Strohmann *m*; (*mil*) Übungspatrone *f*; (*typ*) Blindband *m*
dump [dʌmp] *s* (*trash heap*) Schuttabladeplatz *m*; (*sl*) Bude *f*; (*mil*) Lager *n*; **be down in the dumps** (*coll*) Trübsal blasen ‖ *tr* (aus)kippen; (*fling down*) hinplumpsen; (*garbage*) abladen; (*com*) verschleudern; **be dumped** (*be fired*) entlassen werden; **no dumping** (*public sign*) Schuttabladen verboten
dumpling [′dʌmplɪŋ] *s* Kloß *m*, Knödel *m*
dump′ truck′ *s* Kipper *m*
dumpy [′dʌmpi] *adj* rundlich
dun [dʌn] *adj* schwarzbraun ‖ *v* (*pret & pp* **dunned;** *ger* **dunning**) *tr* drängen
dunce [dʌns] *s* Schwachkopf *m*
dunce′ cap′ *s* Narrenkappe *f*
dune [d(j)un] *s* Düne *f*
dung [dʌŋ] *s* Dung *m*, Mist *m* ‖ *tr* düngen
dungarees [‚dʌŋgə′riz] *spl* Drillichhose *f*, Drillichanzug *m*
dungeon [′dʌndʒən] *s* Verlies *n*; (*hist*) Bergfried *m*

dung′hill′ s Düngerhaufen m
dunk [dʌŋk] tr eintunken
duo [′d(j)u‧o] s (duet) Duett n; (a pair) Duo n
duode‧num [‚d(j)u‧ə′dinəm] s (-na [nə]) Zwölffingerdarm m
dupe [d(j)up] s Düpierte mf ‖ tr düpieren, übertölpeln
duplex [′d(j)upleks] s Doppelhaus n
duplicate [′d(j)uplɪkɪt] adj Duplikat–; (parts) Ersatz–; **d. key** Nachschlüssel m ‖ s Duplikat n, Abschrift f; **in d.** abschriftlich ‖ [′d(j)uplɪ‚ket] tr (make a copy of) kopieren; (make many copies of) vervielfältigen; (reproduce by writing) abschreiben; (repeat) wiederholen; (perform again) nachmachen
duplication [‚d(j)uplɪ′keʃən] s Vervielfältigung f
duplicator [′d(j)uplɪ‚ketər] s Vervielfältigungsapparat m
duplicity [d(j)u′plɪsɪtɪ] s Duplizität f
durable [′d(j)urəbəl] adj dauerhaft
duration [d(j)u′reʃən] s Dauer f
duress [′d(j)ures] s (jur) Nötigung f
during [′d(j)urɪŋ] prep während (genit), bei (dat); **d. the meal** bei Tisch; **the day** tagsüber
dusk [dʌsk] s Abenddämmerung f
dust [dʌst] s Staub m; **cover with d.** bestauben; **make d.** stauben ‖ tr (free of dust) abstauben; (sprinkle, spray with insecticides) bestäuben
dust′ bowl′ s Staubsturmgebiet n
dust′ cloth′ s Staubtuch n
dust′ collec′tor s Staubfänger m
duster [′dʌstər] s (feather duster) Staubwedel m; (for insecticides) Zerstäuber m
dust′ing pow′der s Streupulver n
dust′ jac′ket s Schutzumschlag m
dust′ mop′ s Mop m
dust′pan′ s Kehrichtschaufel f
dust′proof′ adj staubdicht
dust′ rag′ s Staublappen m
dusty [′dʌsti] adj staubig
Dutch [dʌtʃ] adj niederländisch; **go D.** (coll) getrennt bezahlen ‖ s (language) Niederländisch n; **in D.** (coll)

in der Patsche; **the D.** die Niederländer
Dutch′man s (-men) Niederländer m
Dutch′ treat′ s (coll) Beisammensein n bei getrennter Kasse
dutiable [′d(j)utɪ‧əbəl] adj steuerpflichtig
dutiful [′d(j)utɪfəl] adj pflichtgetreu
duty [′d(j)uti] s (to) Pflicht f (gegenüber dat); (service) Dienst m; (task) Aufgabe f; (tax) Zoll m, Abgabe f; **be in d.** bound to (inf) pflichtgemäß müssen (inf); **do d. as** (said of a thing) dienen als; (said of a person) Dienst tun als; **off d.** außer Dienst, dienstfrei; **on d.** im Dienst; **pay d. on** verzollen
du′ty-free′ adj zollfrei
du′ty ros′ter s (mil) Diensteinteilung f
dwarf [dwɔrf] adj zwergenhaft, Zwerg– ‖ s Zwerg m ‖ tr (stunt) in der Entwicklung behindern; (fig) in den Schatten stellen
dwell [dwel] v (pret & pp dwelled & dwelt [dwelt]) intr wohnen; **d. on** verweilen bei
dwell′ing s Wohnung f
dwell′ing house′ s Wohnhaus n
dwindle [′dwɪndəl] intr schwinden, abnehmen; **d. away** dahinschwinden
dye [daɪ] s Farbe f ‖ v (pret & pp dyed) ger dyeing) tr färben
dyed′-in-the-wool′ adj (fig) in der Wolle gefärbt
dye′ing s Färben n
dyer [′daɪ‧ər] s Färber –in mf
dy′ing adj (person) sterbend; (words) letzte ‖ s Sterben n
dynamic [daɪ′næmɪk] adj dynamisch ‖ **dynamics** s Dynamik f; **dynamics** spl (fig) Triebkraft f
dynamite [′daɪnə‚maɪt] s Dynamit n ‖ tr sprengen
dyna‧mo [′daɪnə‚mo] s (-mos) Dynamo m
dynastic [daɪ′næstɪk] adj dynastisch
dynasty [′daɪnəstɪ] s Dynastie f
dysentery [′dɪsən‚terɪ] s Ruhr f
dyspepsia [dɪs′pɛpsɪ‧ə] s Verdauungsstörung f

E

E, e [i] s fünfter Buchstabe des englischen Alphabets; (mus) E n; **E flat** Es n; **E sharp** Eis n
each [itʃ] indef adj jeder; **e. and every** jeder einzelne ‖ adv je, pro Person, pro Stück ‖ indef pron jeder; **e. other** einander, sich
eager [′igər] adj eifrig; **e. for** begierig nach; **e. to** (inf) begierig zu (inf)
ea′ger bea′ver s (coll) Streber –in mf
eagerness [′igərnɪs] s Eifer m
eagle [′igəl] s Adler m
ea′gle-eyed′ adj adleräugig
ear [ɪr] s Ohr n; (of corn, wheat) Ähre f; (fig) Gehör n; **be all ears**

ganz Ohr sein; **bend s.o.'s ears** (sl) j–m die Ohren vollreden; **be up to one's ears** in bis über die Ohren stecken in (dat); **by ear** nach Gehör; **ear for music** musikalisches Gehör n; **fall on deaf ears** kein Gehör finden; **in one ear and out the other** zu e–m Ohr hinein und zum anderen hinaus; **turn a deaf ear to** taub sein gegen
ear′ache′ s Ohrenschmerzen pl
ear′drops′ spl (med) Ohrentropfen pl
ear′drum′ s Trommelfell n
earl [ʌrl] s Graf m
ear′lobe′ s Ohrläppchen n

early ['ʌrli] *adj* früh; *(reply)* baldig; *(far back in time)* Früh–; **at the earliest possible moment** baldigst; **at your earliest convenience** bei erster Gelegenheit; **be too e.** sich verfrühen || *adv* früh, frühzeitig; *(too soon)* zu früh; **as e. as** schon

ear'ly bird' *s* Frühaufsteher –in *mf*

ear'ly ris'er *s* Frühaufsteher –in *mf*

ear'ly warn'ing sys'tem *s* Vorwarnungssystem *n*

ear'mark' *s* (fig) Kennzeichen *n* || *tr (mark out)* kennzeichnen; *(e.g., funds)* **(for)** bestimmen (für)

ear'muffs' *spl* Ohrenschützer *m*

earn [ʌrn] *tr (money)* verdienen; *(a reputation)* sich [*dat*] erwerben; *(interest)* einbringen

earnest ['ʌrnɪst] *adj* ernst, ernsthaft || *s*—**are you in e.?** ist das Ihr Ernst?; **be in e. about** es ernst meinen mit; **in e.** im Ernst

ear'phone' *s* Kopfhörer *m*

ear'piece' *s (earphone)* Hörer *m*; *(of eyeglasses)* Bügel *m*

ear'ring' *s* Ohrring *m*

ear'shot' *s*—**within e.** in Hörweite

ear'split'ting *adj* ohrenbetäubend

earth [ʌrθ] *s* Erde *f*; **come down to e.** auf den Boden der Wirklichkeit zurückkehren; **on e.** (coll) in aller Welt

earthen ['ʌrθən] *adj* irden

earth'enware' *s* Tonwaren *pl*

earthly ['ʌrθli] *adj* irdisch; **be of no e. use** völlig unnütz sein; **e. possessions** Glücksgüter *pl*

earth'quake' *s* Erdbeben *n*

earth'shak'ing *adj* welterschütternd

earth'work' *s* Schanze *f*

earth'worm' *s* Regenwurm *m*

earthy ['ʌrθi] *adj* erdig; (fig) deftig

ear'wax' *s* Ohrenschmalz *m*

ease [iz] *s (facility)* Leichtigkeit *f*; *(comfort)* Bequemlichkeit *f*; *(informality)* Zwanglosigkeit *f*; **at e.!** (mil) rührt euch!; **feel at e. with s.o.** sich in j-s Gegenwart wohl fühlen; **put at e.** beruhigen; **with e.** mühelos || *tr (work)* erleichtern; *(pain)* lindern; *(move carefully)* lavieren; **e. out** *(of a job)* hinausmanövrieren || *intr*—**e. up** nachlassen; **e. up on** *(work)* es sich [*dat*] leichter machen mit

easel ['izəl] *s* Staffelei *f*

easement ['izmənt] *s* (jur) Dienstbarkeit *f*

easily ['izəli] *adv* leicht, mühelos; **e. satisfied** genügsam

easiness ['izɪnɪs] *s* Leichtigkeit *f*

east [ist] *adj* Ost–, östlich || *adv* ostwärts, nach Osten; **e. of** östlich von || *s* Osten *m*; **the East** der Osten

east'bound' *adj* nach Osten fahrend

Easter ['istər] *adj* Oster– || *s* Ostern *n & pl*

easterly ['istərli] *adj* österlich

eastern ['istərn] *adj* Ost–

East'ertide' *s* Osterzeit *f*

East'-Ger'man mark' *s* Ostmark *f*

eastward ['istwəd] *adv* ostwärts

easy ['izi] *adj* leicht; *(terms)* günstig; *(virtue)* locker; *(pace)* gemächlich; **e. on the eye** knusprig; **e. to digest**

leichtverdaulich; **have an e. time of it** leichtes Spiel haben; **it's e. for you to talk** du hast gut reden!; **make e.** erleichtern || *adv*—**e. come, e. go** wie gewonnen, so zerronnen; **get off e.** gnädig davonkommen; **take it e.** *(relax)* es sich [*dat*] leicht machen; *take one'e time)* sich [*dat*] Zeit lassen; *(in parting)* mach's gut! *(remain calm)* reg dich nicht auf!; **take it e. on** *(a person)* schonend umgehen mit; *(a thing)* sparsam umgehen mit

eas'y chair' *s* Lehnsessel *m*

eas'ygo'ing *adj* ungeniert, ungezwungen

eas'y mark' *s* (coll) leichte Beute *f*

eat [it] *s*—**eats** *pl* (coll) Essen *n* || *v (pret* ate [et]; *pp* eaten ['itən]) *tr* essen; *(said of animals)* fressen; **eat away** zerfressen; **eat one's fill** sich satt essen; **eat one's heart out** sich in Kummer verzehren; **eat one's words** das Gesagte zurücknehmen; **eat up** aufessen; **what's eating him?** was hat er denn? || *intr* essen; **eat out** auswärts essen

eatable ['itəbəl] *adj* eßbar

eaves [ivz] *spl* Dachrinne *f*, Traufe *f*

eaves'drop' *v (pret & pp* –dropped; *ger* –dropping) *intr* horchen; **e. on** belauschen

eaves'drop'per *s* Horcher –in *mf*

ebb [eb] *s* Ebbe *f*; **at a low ebb** sehr heruntergekommen || *intr* ebben; (fig) nachlassen

ebb' and flow' *s* Ebbe und Flut *f*

ebb' tide' *s* Ebbe *f*

ebony ['ebəni] *s* Ebenholz *n*

ebullient [ɪ'bʌljənt] *adj* überschwenglich, hochbegeistert

eccentric [ek'sentrɪk] *adj* (& fig) exzentrisch || *s* Sonderling *m*, Kauz *m*; (mach) Exzenter *m*

eccentricity [ˌeksen'trɪsɪti] *s* Verschrobenheit *f*, Tick *m*

ecclesiastic [ɪˌklizi'æstɪk] *adj* kirchlich; *(law)* Kirchen– || *s* Geistlicher *m*

echelon ['eʃəˌlɑn] *s (level)* Befehlsebene *f*; *(group occupying a particular level)* Stabsführung *f*; *(flight formation)* Staffel *f*; **in echelons** staffelförmig || *tr* staffeln

ech·o ['eko] *s* (–oes) Echo *n* || *tr (sounds)* zurückwerfen; (fig) nachsprechen || *intr* widerhallen, echoen

éclair [e'kler] *s* Eclair *n*

eclectic [ek'lektɪk] *adj* eklektisch || *s* Eklektiker –in *mf*

eclipse [ɪ'klɪps] *s* Verfinsterung *f*; **go into e.** sich verfinstern; **in e.** im Schwinden || *tr* verfinstern; (fig) in den Schatten stellen

eclogue ['eklɔg] *s* Ekloge *f*

ecological [ˌekə'lɑdʒɪkəl] *adj* ökologisch

ecology [ɪ'kalədʒi] *s* Ökologie *f*

economic [ˌikə'namɪk], [ˌekə'namɪk] *adj* wirtschaftlich, Wirtschafts–

economical [ˌikə'namɪkəl], [ˌekə'namɪkəl] *adj* sparsam

economics [ˌikə'namɪks], [ˌekə'namɪks] *s* Wirtschaftswissenschaften *pl*

economist [ɪˈkɑnəmɪst] s Volkswirt-schaftler –in mf

economize [ɪˈkɑnəˌmaɪz] intr sparen

economy [ɪˈkɑnəmi] s Wirtschaft f; (thriftiness) Sparsamkeit f; (a saving) Ersparnis f

ecstasy [ˈɛkstəsi] s Verzückung f; go into e. in Verzückung geraten

ecstatic [ɛkˈstætɪk] adj verzückt

ecumenic(al) [ˌɛkjəˈmɛnɪk(əl)] adj ökumenisch

eczema [ˈɛgˈzimə] s Ausschlag m

ed·dy [ˈɛdi] s Strudel m || v (pret & pp –died) intr strudeln

edelweiss [ˈɛdəlˌvaɪs] s Edelweiß n

edge [ɛdʒ] s (of a knife) Schneide f; (of a forest, town, water, road) Rand m; (e.g., of a table) Kante f; (keenness) Schärfe f; (bb) Schnitt m; have an e. on s.o. den Vorteil gegenüber j-m haben; on e. (said of a person or teeth) kribbelig; (said of nerves) aufs äußerste gespannt; take the e. off abstumpfen; (fig) die Schärfe nehmen (dat) || tr (a lawn) beschneiden; (put a border on) einfassen; e. out (sport) knapp schlagen || intr —e. forward langsam vorrücken

edge'wise' adv—not get a word in e. nicht zu Worte kommen können

edg'ing s Umrandung f, Besatz m

edgy [ˈɛdʒi] adj kribbelig

edible [ˈɛdɪbəl] adj eßbar, genießbar

edict [ˈidɪkt] s Edikt n, Erlaß m

edification [ˌɛdɪfɪˈkeʃən] s Erbauung f

edifice [ˈɛdɪfɪs] s Bauwerk n, Gebäude n

edi·fy [ˈɛdɪˌfaɪ] v (pret & pp –fied) tr erbauen; be edified by sich erbauen an (dat)

**ed'ifying adj erbaulich

edit [ˈɛdɪt] tr (a book) herausgeben; (a newspaper) redigieren; (cin) schneiden

edition [ɛˈdɪʃən] s Ausgabe f

editor [ˈɛdɪtər] s (of a newspaper or magazine) Redakteur –in mf; (of a book) Herausgeber –in mf; (of editorials) Leitartikler –in mf; (cin) Schnittmeister –in mf

editorial [ˌɛdɪˈtorɪəl] adj redaktionell, Redaktions– || s Leitartikel m

editorialize [ˌɛdɪˈtorɪəˌlaɪz] intr (on) seine Meinung zum Ausdruck bringen (über acc); (report with a slant) tendenziös berichten

edito'rial of'fice s Redaktion f

edito'rial staff s Redaktion f

ed'itor in chief' s Chefredakteur –in mf

educate [ˈɛdʒuˌket] tr bilden, erziehen

education [ˌɛdʒuˈkeʃən] s Bildung f, Erziehung f; (educ) Pädagogik f

educational [ˌɛdʒuˈkeʃənəl] adj Bildungs–; e. background Vorbildung f; e. film Lehrfilm m; e. institution Lehranstalt f

educator [ˈɛdʒuˌketər] s Erzieher –in mf

educe [ɪˈd(j)us] tr hervorholen

eel [il] s Aal m

eerie, eery [ˈɪri] adj unheimlich

efface [ɪˈfes] tr austilgen; e. oneself sich zurückhalten

effect [ɪˈfɛkt] s (on) Wirkung f (auf acc); (consequence) (on) Auswirkung f (auf acc); (impression) Eindruck m; effects (movable property) Habe f; for e. zum Effekt; go into e. in Kraft treten; have an e. on wirken auf (acc); in e. praktisch; put into e. in Kraft setzen; take e. zur Geltung kommen; to the e. that des Inhalts, daß || tr bewirken

effective [ɪˈfɛktɪv] adj wirkungsvoll; (actual) effektiv; e. against wirksam gegen; e. date Tag m des Inkrafttretens; e. from mit Wirkung von; e. immediately mit sofortiger Wirkung; e. strength (mil) Iststärke f

effectual [ɪˈfɛktʃu·əl] adj wirksam

effectuate [ɪˈfɛktʃu·ˌet] tr bewirken

effeminacy [ɪˈfɛmɪnəsi] s Verweichlichung f

effeminate [ɪˈfɛmɪnɪt] adj verweichlicht

effervesce [ˌɛfərˈvɛs] intr aufbrausen

effervescence [ˌɛfərˈvɛsəns] s Aufbrausen n, Moussieren n

effervescent [ˌɛfərˈvɛsənt] adj (liquid; personality) aufbrausend

effete [ɪˈfit] adj entkräftet

efficacious [ˌɛfɪˈkeʃəs] adj wirksam

efficacy [ˈɛfɪkəsi] s Wirksamkeit f, Wirkungskraft f

efficiency [ɪˈfɪʃənsi] s Tüchtigkeit f; (phys) Nutzeffekt m; (tech) Leistungsfähigkeit f

efficient [ɪˈfɪʃənt] adj tüchtig; (tech) leistungsfähig

effigy [ˈɛfɪdʒi] s Abbild n; hang in e. symbolisch hängen

effort [ˈɛfort] s (exertion) Mühe f; (attempt) Bestreben n; efforts Bemühungen pl; make an honest e. to (inf) sich redlich bemühen zu (inf)

effortless [ˈɛfortlɪs] adj mühelos

effrontery [ɪˈfrʌntəri] s Frechheit f, Unverschämtheit f

effusion [ɪˈfjuʒən] s Erguß m

effusive [ɪˈfjusɪv] adj überschwenglich

egg [ɛg] s Ei n; bad egg (sl) übler Geselle m; good egg (sl) feiner Kerl m; lay an egg ein Ei legen; (fig) e–e völlige Niete sein || tr—egg on anstacheln

egg'beat'er s Schneeschläger m

egg'cup' s Eierbecher m

egg'head' s (coll) Intelligenzler –in mf

eggnog [ˈɛgˌnɑg] s Eierlikör m, Egg-Nog m

egg'plant' s Eierfrucht f

egg'shell' s Eierschale f

egg' white' s Eiweiß n

egg' yolk' s Eigelb n, Eidotter m

ego [ˈigo] s Ego n, Ich n; (coll) Ichsucht f

egocentric [ˌigoˈsɛntrɪk] adj egozentrisch

egoism [ˈigoˌɪzəm] s Selbstsucht f

egoist [ˈigo·ɪst] s Egoist m

egotism [ˈigoˌtɪzəm] s Ichsucht f

egotistic(al) [ˌigoˈtɪstɪk(əl)] adj egotistisch, geltungsbedürtig egregious [ɪˈgridʒəs] adj unerhört

egress [ˈigres] s Ausgang m

Egypt [ˈidʒɪpt] s Ägypten n

Egyptian [ɪˈdʒɪpʃən] adj ägyptisch ‖ s Ägypter –in mf; (language) Ägyptisch n

eiderdown [ˈaɪdərˌdaun] s Eiderdaunen pl; (cover) Daunenbett n

eight [et] adj & pron acht ‖ s Acht f

eight'ball' s—be behind the e. (sl) in der Klemme sitzen

eighteen [ˈetˈtin] adj & pron achtzehn ‖ s Achtzehn f

eighteenth [ˈetˈtinθ] adj achtzehnte ‖ s (fraction) Achtzehntel n; the e. (in dates or in a series) der Achtzehnte

eighth [etθ] adj achte ‖ s (fraction) Achtel n; the e. (in dates or in a series) der Achte

eighth' note' s (mus) Achtelnote f

eightieth [ˈetiˌiθ] adj achtzigste ‖ s (fraction) Achtzigstel n; the e. der Achtzigste

eighty [ˈeti] adj & pron achtzig ‖ s Achtzig f; the eighties die achtziger Jahre pl

eigh'ty-one' adj & pron einundachtzig

either [ˈiðər], [ˈaɪðər] adj—e. one is correct beides ist richtig; e. way auf die e–e oder andere Art; in e. case in jedem der beiden Fälle; on e. side auf beiden Seiten ‖ adv—not...e. auch nicht ‖ pron einer von beiden; e. of you einer von euch beiden; I didn't see e. ich habe beide nicht gesehen ‖ conj—e....or entweder... oder

ejaculate [ɪˈdʒækjəˌlet] tr ausstoßen; (physiol) ejakulieren

eject [ɪˈdʒɛkt] tr ausstoßen; (from a property) (from) hinauswerfen (aus)

ejection [ɪˈdʒɛkʃən] s Ausstoßung f

ejec'tion seat' s Schleudersitz m

eke [ik] tr—eke out a living das Leben fristen

el [ɛl] s (coll) Hochbahn f

elaborate [ɪˈlæbərɪt] adj (detailed) weitläufig; (ornate) kunstvoll; (idea) kompliziert ‖ [ɪˈlæbəˌret] tr ausarbeiten ‖ intr—e. on sich verbreiten über (acc)

elaboration [ɪˌlæbəˈreʃən] s Ausarbeitung f

elapse [ɪˈlæps] intr verrinnen

elastic [ɪˈlæstɪk] adj elastisch; (conscience) weit ‖ s Gummiband n

elasticity [ˌɪlæsˈtɪsɪti] s Elastizität f

elated [ɪˈletɪd] adj freudig erregt

elation [ɪˈleʃən] s Hochgefühl n

elbow [ˈelbo] s Ellbogen m; (of a pipe) Rohrknie n; at one's e. bei der Hand; rub elbows with s.o. mit j–m in nähere Berührung kommen ‖ tr—e. one's way sich [dat] seinen Weg bahnen

el'bow grease' s (coll) Knochenschmalz n

el'bowroom' s Spielraum m

elder [ˈeldər] adj älter ‖ s Ältere mf; (bot) Holunder m; (eccl) Kirchenälteste mf

el'derber'ry s Holunderbeere f

elderly [ˈeldərli] adj ältlich

el'der states'man s profilierter Staatsmann m

eldest [ˈeldɪst] adj älteste

elect [ɪˈlekt] adj erlesen; (elected but not yet installed) zukünftig; (relig) auserwählt ‖ the e. spl die Auserwählten pl ‖ tr wählen; e. s.o. president j–n zum Präsidenten wählen

election [ɪˈlekʃən] adj Wahl– ‖ s Wahl f

elec'tion campaign' s Wahlkampf m

elec'tion day' s Wahltag m

electioneer [ɪˌlekʃəˈnɪr] intr Stimmen werben

elective [ɪˈlektɪv] adj (educ) wahlfrei; (pol) Wahl– ‖ s (educ) Wahlfach n

electoral [ɪˈlektərəl] adj Wahl–

elec'toral col'lege s Wahlmänner pl

electorate [ɪˈlektərɪt] s Wählerschaft f

electric(al) [ɪˈlektrɪk(əl)] adj elektrisch, Elektro–

elec'trical appli'ance s Elektrogerät n

elec'trical engineer' s Elektroingenieur m

elec'trical engineer'ing s Elektrotechnik f

elec'tric blan'ket s Heizdecke f

elec'tric bulb' s Glühbirne f

elec'tric chair' s elektrischer Stuhl m; (penalty) Hinrichtung f auf dem elektrischen Stuhl

elec'tric cir'cuit s Stromkreis m

elec'tric eel' s Zitteraal m

elec'tric eye' s Photozelle f

elec'tric fan' s Ventilator m

elec'tric fence' s elektrisch geladener Drahtzaun m

electrician [ɪˌlekˈtrɪʃən] s Elektriker –in mf

electricity [ˌɪlekˈtrɪsɪti] s Elektrizität f; (current) Strom m

elec'tric light' s elektrisches Licht n

elec'tric me'ter s Stromzähler m

elec'tric saw' s Motorsäge f

elec'tric shav'er s elektrischer Rasierapparat m

elec'tric storm' s Gewittersturm m

elec'tric stove' s Elektroherd m

electri·fy [ɪˈlektrɪˌfaɪ] v (pret & pp –fied) tr (& fig) elektrisieren; (a streetcar, railroad) elektrifizieren

electrocute [ɪˈlektrəˌkjut] tr durch elektrischen Strom töten; (jur) auf dem elektrischen Stuhl hinrichten

electrode [ɪˈlektrod] s Elektrode f

electrolysis [ɪˌlekˈtralɪsɪs] s Elektrolyse f

electrolyte [ɪˈlektrəˌlaɪt] s Elektrolyt m

electromagnet [ɪˌlektrəˈmægnət] s Elektromagnet m

electromagnetic [ɪˌlektrəmægˈnetɪk] adj elektromagnetisch

electron [ɪˈlektran] s Elektron n

electronic [ɪˌlekˈtranɪk] adj elektronisch, Elektronen– ‖ electronics s Elektronik f

electron'ic flash' s Röhrenblitz m; (device) Blitzgerät n

electronic [ɪˌlekˈtranɪk] adj elektroplattieren, galvanisieren

electrostatic [ɪ ˌlektrə'stætɪk] *adj* elektrostatisch

electrotype [ɪ'lektrə ˌtaɪp] *s* Galvano *n* ‖ *tr* galvanoplastisch vervielfältigen

elegance ['elɪgəns] *s* Eleganz *f*

elegant ['elə ˌgənt] *adj* elegant

elegiac [ˌelɪ'dʒaɪ-æk] *adj* elegisch

elegy ['elɪdʒɪ] *s* Elegie *f*

element ['elɪmənt] *s* (& *fig*) Element *n*; (*e.g.*, *of truth*) Körnchen *n*

elementary [ˌelɪ'mentərɪ] *adj* elementar, grundlegend

elemen'tary school' *s* Grundschule *f*

elephant ['elɪfənt] *s* Elefant *m*

elevate ['elɪ ˌvet] *tr* erheben, erhöhen

el'evated *adj* (*eyes*) erhoben; (*style*) erhaben ‖ *s* (coll) Hochbahn *f*

elevation [ˌelɪ'veʃən] *s* (*height*) Höhe *f*; (*hill*) Anhöhe *f*; (*above sealevel*) Seehöhe *f*; (*to the throne*) Erhebung *f*; (*archit*) Aufriß *m*; (*arti*) Richthöhe *f*; (*astr*, *relig*) Elevation *f*

elevator ['elɪ ˌvetər] *s* Aufzug *m*, Fahrstuhl *m*; (aer) Höhenruder *n*; (agr) Getreidespeicher *m*

el'evator op'erator *s* Fahrstuhlführer –in *mf*

el'evator shaft' *s* Fahrstuhlschacht *m*

eleven [ɪ'levən] *adj* & *pron* elf ‖ *s* Elf *f*

eleventh [ɪ'levənθ] *adj* elfte ‖ *s* (*fraction*) Elftel *n*; **the e.** (*in dates and in a series*) der Elfte

elev'enth hour' *s*—**at the e.** (fig) kurz vor Torschluß

elf [elf] *s* (**elves** [elvz]) Elf *m*, Elfe *f*

elicit [ɪ'lɪsɪt] *tr* hervorlocken; (*an answer*) entlocken

elide [ɪ'laɪd] *tr* elidieren

eligible ['elɪdʒɪbəl] *adj* qualifiziert; (*entitled*) berechtigt; (*for office*) wählbar; (*for marriage*) heiratsfähig

el'igible bach'elor *s* Heiratskandidat *m*

eliminate [ɪ'lɪmɪ ˌnet] *tr* ausscheiden; (alg) eliminieren

elimination [ɪ ˌlɪmɪ'neʃən] *s* Ausscheidung *f*

elimina'tion bout' *s* Ausscheidungskampf *m*

elision [ɪ'lɪʒən] *s* Auslassung *f*

elite [e'lit] *adj* Elite– ‖ *s* Elite *f*

elixir [ɪ'lɪksər] *s* Elixier *n*

elk [elk] *s* Elch *m*

ellipse [ɪ'lɪps] *s* (geom) Ellipse *f*

ellip·sis [ɪ'lɪpsɪs] *s* (**-ses** [siz]) (gram) Ellipse *f*

elliptic(al) [ɪ'lɪptɪk(əl)] *adj* elliptisch

elm [elm] *s* Ulme *f*

elocution [ˌelə'kju:ʃən] *s* (*art*) Vortragskunst *f*; (*style*) Vortragsweise *f*

elope [ɪ'lop] *intr* ausreißen

elopement [ɪ'lopmənt] *s* Ausreißen *n*

eloquence ['eləkwəns] *s* Beredsamkeit *f*

eloquent ['eləkwənt] *adj* beredt

else [els] *adj* sonst; someone **else's house** das Haus e–s anderen; **what e.?** was sonst?; (*in addition*) was noch? ‖ *adv* sonst, anders; **nowhere e.** sonst nirgends; **or e.** sonst, andernfalls; **where e.?** wo sonst?

else'where' *adv* (*position*) woanders;

(*direction*) sonstwohin; **from e.** anderswoher

elucidate [ɪ'lusɪ ˌdet] *tr* erläutern

elucidation [ɪ ˌlusɪ'deʃən] *s* Erläuterung *f*

elude [ɪ'lud] *tr* entgehen (dat)

elusive [ɪ'lusɪv] *adj* schwer zu fassen; (*memory*) unzuverlässig

emaciated [ɪ'meʃɪ ˌetɪd] *adj* abgezehrt

emanate ['emə ˌnet] *intr*—**e. from** (*said of gases*) ausströmen aus; (*said of rays*) ausstrahlen aus; (fig) ausgehen von

emancipate [ɪ'mænsɪ ˌpet] *tr* emanzipieren

emasculate [ɪ'mæskjə ˌlet] *tr* (& *fig*) entmannen

embalm [em'bam] *tr* einbalsamieren

embankment [em'bæŋkmənt] *s* Damm *m*

embar·go [em'bargo] *s* (**-goes**) Sperre *f*, Embargo *n* ‖ *tr* sperren

embark [em'bark] *intr* (**for**) sich einschiffen (nach); **e. upon** sich einlassen auf (acc)

embarkation [ˌembar'keʃən] *s* Einschiffung *f*

embarrass [em'bærəs] *tr* in Verlegenheit bringen

embar'rassed *adj* verlegen; **feel e.** sich genieren

embar'rassing *adj* peinlich

embarrassment [em'bærəsmənt] *s* Verlegenheit *f*

embassy ['embəsɪ] *s* Botschaft *f*

em·bed [em'bed] *v* (*pret* & *pp* **-bedded**; *ger* **-bedding**) *tr* einbetten; **e. in concrete** einbetonieren

embellish [em'belɪʃ] *tr* verschönern

embellishment [em'belɪʃmənt] *s* Verschönerung *f*

ember ['embər] *s* glühende Kohle *f*; **embers** Glut *f*

Em'ber day' *s* Quatember *m*

embezzle [em'bezəl] *tr* unterschlagen

embezzlement [em'bezəlmənt] *s* Unterschlagung *f*, Veruntreuung *f*

embezzler [em'bezlər] *s* Veruntreuer –in *mf*

embitter [em'bɪtər] *tr* verbittern

emblazon [em'blezən] *tr* (*decorate*) verzieren; (*extol*) verherrlichen; (heral) heraldisch darstellen

emblem ['embləm] *s* Sinnbild *n*

emblematic(al) [ˌemblə'mætɪk(əl)] *adj* sinnbildlich

embodiment [em'badɪmənt] *s* Verkörperung *f*

embod·y [em'badɪ] *v* (*pret* & *pp* **-ied**) *tr* verkörpern

embolden [em'boldən] *tr* ermutigen

embolism ['embə ˌlɪzəm] *s* Embolie *f*

emboss [em'bas] *tr* bossieren

embossed' *adj* getrieben

embrace [em'bres] *s* Umarmung *f* ‖ *tr* umarmen; (*include*) umfassen; (*a religion*, *idea*) annehmen ‖ *intr* sich umarmen

embrasure [em'breʒər] *s* Schießscharte *f*

embroider [em'brɔɪdər] *tr* sticken

embroidery [em'brɔɪdərɪ] *s* Stickerei *f*

embroi'dery nee'dle *s* Sticknadel *f*

embroil [em'brɔil] *tr* verwickeln

embroilment [em'brɔilmənt] *s* Verwicklung *f*

embry•o ['embrɪ,o] *s* (**-os**) Embryo *m*

embryology [,embrɪ'alədʒi] *s* Embryologie *f*

embryonic [,embrɪ'anɪk] *adj* embryonal

emend [ɪ'mend] *tr* berichtigen

emendation [,imen'deʃən] *s* Berichtigung *f*

emerald ['emərəld] *adj* smaragdgrün || *s* Smaragd *m*

emerge [ɪ'mʌrdʒ] *intr* (*come forth*) hervortreten; (*surface*) auftauchen; (*result*) (*from*) herauskommen (bei)

emergence [ɪ'mʌrdʒəns] *s* Hervortreten *n*; (*surfacing*) Auftauchen *n*

emergency [ɪ'mʌrdʒənsi] *adj* Not– || *s* Notlage *f*; **in case of e.** im Notfall

emeritus [ɪ'merɪtəs] *adj* emeritiert

emersion [ɪ'mʌrʒən] *s* Auftauchen *n*

emery ['eməri] *s* Schmirgel *m*

em'ery cloth' *s* Schmirgelleinwand *f*

em'ery wheel' *s* Schmirgelrad *n*

emetic [ɪ'metɪk] *adj* Brech– || *s* Brechmittel *n*

emigrant ['emɪgrənt] *s* Auswanderer –in *mf*

emigrate ['emɪ,gret] *intr* auswandern

emigration [,emɪ'greʃən] *s* Auswanderung *f*

eminence ['emɪnəns] *s* (*height*) Anhöhe *f*; (*fame*) Berühmtheit *f*; **Eminence** (*title of a cardinal*) Eminenz *f*; **rise to e.** zu Ruhm und Würde gelangen

eminent ['emɪnənt] *adj* hervorragend

emissary ['emɪ,seri] *s* Abgesandte *mf*

emission [ɪ'mɪʃən] *s* (biol) Erguß *m*; (phys) Austrahlung *f*, Ausströmung *f*

emis'sion control' *s* Abgasentgiftung *f*

emit [ɪ'mɪt] *v* (*pret & pp* **emitted**; *ger* **emitting**) *tr* von sich geben; (*rays*) ausstrahlen; (*gases*) ausströmen; (*sparks*) sprühen

emolument [ɪ'maljəmənt] *s* Vergütung *f*

emotion [ɪ'moʃən] *s* Gemütsbewegung *f*

emotional [ɪ'moʃənəl] *adj* (*e.g., disorder*) Gemüts–; (*person*) gefühlvoll; (*e.g., sermon*) ergreifend; (*mawkish*) rührselig

emperor ['empərər] *s* Kaiser *m*

empha•sis ['emfəsɪs] *s* (**-ses** [,siz]) Betonung *f*

emphasize ['emfə,saɪz] *tr* betonen

emphatic [em'fætɪk] *adj* nachdrücklich

emphysema [,emfɪ'simə] *s* Emphysem *n*

empire ['empaɪr] *s* Reich *n*; (*Roman period*) Kaiserzeit *f*

Em'pire fur'niture *s* Empiremöbel *n*

empiric(al) [em'pɪrɪk(əl)] *adj* erfahrungsmäßig, empirisch

empiricist [em'pɪrɪsɪst] *s* Empiriker –in *mf*

emplacement [em'plesmənt] *s* Stellung *f*

employ [em'plɔɪ] *s* Dienst *m* || *tr* (*hire*) anstellen; (*keep in employ-*ment) beschäftigen; (*use*) verwenden; (*troops, police*) einsetzen

employee [em'plɔɪ·i], [,emplɔɪ'i] *s* Arbeitnehmer –in *mf*

employer [em'plɔɪ·ər] *s* Arbeitgeber –in *mf*

employment [em'plɔɪmənt] *s* (*work*) Beschäftigung *f*, Arbeit *f*; (*use*) Verwendung *f*; (*e.g., of troops*) Einsatz *m*; **out of e.** arbeitslos

employ'ment a'gency *s* Arbeitsvermittlung *f*

empower [em'pau·ər] *tr* ermächtigen

empress ['empris] *s* Kaiserin *f*

emptiness ['emptɪnɪs] *s* Leere *f*; (fig) Nichtigkeit *f*

emp•ty ['empti] *adj* leer; **e. talk** leere Worte *pl*; **on an e. stomach** auf nüchternem Magen || **empties** *spl* Leergut *n* || *v* (*pret & pp* **-tied**) *tr* (aus)leeren || *intr*—**e. into** münden in (*acc*)

emp'ty-hand'ed *adj* mit leeren Händen

emp'ty-head'ed *adj* hohlköpfig

emulate ['emjə,let] *tr* nacheifern (*dat*)

emulation [,emjə'leʃən] *s* Nacheiferung *f*

emulator [,emjə'letər] *s* Nacheiferer –in *mf*

emulsi•fy [ɪ'mʌlsɪ,faɪ] *v* (*pret & pp* **-fied**) *tr* emulgieren

emulsion [ɪ'mʌlʃən] *s* Emulsion *f*; (phot) Schicht *f*

enable [en'ebəl] *tr* befähigen

enact [en'ækt] *tr* erlassen

enactment [en'æktmənt] *s* Erlassen *n*

enam•el [ɪ'næməl] *s* Email *n*; (dent) Zahnschmelz *m* || *v* (*pret & pp* **-el[l]ed**; *ger* **-el[l]ing**) *tr* emaillieren

enam'el paint' *s* Emaillack *m*

enam'elware' *s* Emailwaren *pl*

enamored [e'næmərd] *adj*—**be e. of** verliebt sein in (*acc*)

encamp [en'kæmp] *tr* in e–m Lager unterbringen || *intr* lagern, sich lagern

encampment [en'kæmpmənt] *s* (*camping*) Lagern *n*; (*campsite*) Lager *n*

encase [en'kes] *tr* einschließen

enchant [en'tʃænt] *tr* verzaubern; (fig) bezaubern

enchanter [en'tʃæntər] *s* Zauberer –in *mf*

enchant'ing *adj* bezaubernd

enchantment [en'tʃæntmənt] *s* (*state*) Verzauberung *f*; (*cause of enchantment*) Zauber *m*

enchantress [en'tʃæntrɪs] *s* Zauberin *f*

encircle [en'sʌrkəl] *tr* umgeben; (mil) einschließen

encirclement [en'sʌrkəlmənt] *s* (mil) Einschließung *f*

enclave ['enklev] *s* Enklave *f*

enclitic [en'klɪtɪk] *adj* enklitisch || *s* Enklitikon *n*

enclose [en'kloz] *tr* einschließen; (*land*) umzäunen; (*in a letter*) beilegen; **e. in parentheses** einklammern; **please find enclosed** in der Anlage erhalten Sie

enclosure [en'kloʒər] *s* Umzäunung *f*; (*in a letter*) Anlage *f*

encomi·um [en'komɪ·əm] *s* (**–ums &** **–a** [ə]) Lobpreisung *f*, Enkomion *n*

encompass [en'kʌmpəs] *tr* umfassen

encore ['ɑnkor] *s* (*performance*) Zugabe *f*; (*recall*) Dakaporuf *m* ‖ *interj* da capo!; noch einmal!

encounter [en'kaʊntər] *s* Begegnung *f*; (*hostile meeting*) Zusammenstoß *m*; (mil) Gefecht *n* ‖ *tr* begegnen (*dat*)

encourage [en'kʌrɪdʒ] *tr* ermutigen

encouragement [en'kʌrɪdʒmənt] *s* Ermutigung *f*

encroach [en'krotʃ] *intr*—**e. on** übergreifen auf (*acc*); (*rights*) beeinträchtigen

encroachment [en'krotʃmənt] *s* Übergriff *m*

encrust [en'krʌst] *tr* überkrusten

encumber [en'kʌmbər] *tr* belasten; (*with debts*) verschulden

encumbrance [en'krʌmbrəns] *s* Belastung *f*

encyclical [en'sɪklɪkəl] *s* Enzyklika *f*

encyclopedia [en‚saɪklə'pidɪ·ə] *s* Enzyklopädie *f*

encyclopedic [en‚saɪklə'pidɪk] *adj* enzyklopädisch

end [end] *s* Ende *n*; (*purpose*) Zweck *m*; (*goal*) Ziel *n*; (*closing*) Schluß *m*; (*outcome*) Ausgang *m*, Ergebnis *n*; **at the end of one's strength** am Rande seiner Kraft; **come to a bad end** ein schlimmes Ende finden; **come to an end** zu Ende gehen; **end in itself** Selbstzweck *m*; **gain one's ends** seinen Vorsatz ausführen; **go off the deep end** sich unnötig aufregen; **in the end** schließlich; **make both ends meet** gerade auskommen; **no end of** unendlich viel(e); **on end** hochkant; (*without letup*) ununterbrochen; **put an end to** ein Ende machen (*dat*); **that will be the end of me** das überlebe ich nicht; **to no end** vergebens ‖ *tr* beenden ‖ *intr* enden; (gram) auslauten; **end in a point** spitz zulaufen; **end up** (in) (coll) landen (in *dat*); **end up with** beenden mit

end′-all′ *s* Schluß *m* vom Ganzen

endanger [en'dendʒər] *tr* gefährden

endear [en'dɪr] *tr*—**e. s.o. to** j-n einschmeicheln bei

endear′ing *adj* gewinnend

endearment [en'dɪrmənt] *s* Beliebtheit *f*

endeavor [en'devər] *s* Bestreben *n* ‖ *intr*—**e. to** (*inf*) sich bestreben zu (*inf*), versuchen zu (*inf*)

endemic [en'demɪk] *adj* endemisch ‖ *s* Endemie *f*, endemische Krankheit *f*

end′ing *s* Beendigung *f*, Abschluß *m*; (gram) Endung *f*

endive ['endaɪv] *s* Endivie *f*

endless ['endlɪs] *adj* endlos; **an e. number of** unendlich viele

end′most′ *adj* entfernteste

endocrine ['endo‚kraɪn] *adj* endokrin

endorse [en'dors] *tr* (*confirm*) bestätigen; (*a check*) indossieren

endorsee [‚endor'si] *s* Indossat –in *mf*

endorsement [en'dorsmənt] *s* Indossament *n*; (*approval*) Bestätigung *f*

endorser [en'dorsər] *s* Indossant –in *mf*; (*backer*) Hintermann *m*

endow [en'daʊ] *tr* (*provide with income*) dotieren; (*with talent*) begaben

endowment [en'daʊmənt] *s* Dotierung *f*; (*talent*) Begabung *f*

endow′ment fund′ *s* Stiftungsvermögen *n*

endurance [en'd(j)ʊrəns] *s* Dauer *f*; (*ability to hold out*) Ausdauer *f*

endur′ance test′ *s* Dauerprobe *f*

endure [en'd(j)ʊr] *tr* aushalten ‖ *intr* fortdauern

endur′ing *adj* dauerhaft

enema ['enəmə] *s* Einlauf *m*

enemy ['enəmi] *adj* feindlich, Feind– ‖ *s* Feind *m*; **become enemies** sich verfeinden

energetic [‚enər'dʒetɪk] *adj* energisch

energy ['enərdʒi] *s* Energie *f*

enervate ['enər‚vet] *tr* entkräften

enfeeble [en'fibəl] *tr* entkräften

enfilade ['enfɪ‚led] *s* (mil) Flankenfeuer *n* ‖ *tr* mit Flankenfeuer bestreichen

enfold [en'fold] *tr* einhüllen

enforce [en'fors] *tr* durchsetzen; (*obedience*) erzwingen

enforcement [en'forsmənt] *s* Durchsetzung *f*

enfranchise [en'fræntʃaɪz] *tr* (*admit to citizenship*) einbürgern; (*give the right to vote to*) das Wahlrecht verleihen (*dat*)

engage [en'gedʒ] *tr* (*hire*) anstellen; (*reserve*) vorbestellen; (*attention*) fesseln; (*gears*) einrücken; (*one's own troops*) einsetzen; (*the enemy*) angreifen; **be engaged in** beschäftigt sein mit; **e. in** verwickelt in (*acc*) ‖ *intr* (mach) (ein)greifen; **e. in** sich einlassen in (*acc*)

engaged′ *adj* verlobt; **get e. (to)** sich verloben (mit)

engaged′ cou′ple *s* Brautleute *pl*

engagement [en'gedʒmənt] *s* (*betrothal*) Verlobung *f*; (*appointment*) Verabredung *f*; (*obligation*) Verpflichtung *f*; (mil) Gefecht *n*; **have a previous e.** verabredet sein

engage′ment ring′ *s* Verlobungsring *m*

engag′ing *adj* gewinnend

engender [en'dʒendər] *tr* hervorbringen

engine ['endʒɪn] *s* Maschine *f*; (aer, aut) Motor *m*; (rr) Lokomotive *f*

engineer [‚endʒə'nɪr] *s* Ingenieur *m*, Techniker *m*; (mil) Pionier *m*; (rr) Lokomotivführer *m*; **engineers** (mil) Pioniertruppe *f* ‖ *tr* errichten; (fig) bewerkstelligen

engineer′ing *s* Ingenieurwesen *n*

engineer′ing school′ *s* Technikum *n*

en′gine house′ *s* Spritzenhaus *n*

en′gine room′ *s* Maschinenraum *m*

England ['ɪŋglənd] *s* England *n*

English ['ɪŋglɪʃ] *adj* englisch ‖ *s* (*spin*) Effet *n*; (*language*) Englisch *n*; **in plain E.** unverblümt; **the E.** die Engländer

Eng′lish Chan′nel s Ärmelkanal m
Eng′lish horn′ s Englischhorn n
Eng′lish-man s (–men) Engländer m
Eng′lish-speak′ing adj englischsprechend
Eng′lish-wom′an s (–wom′en) Engländerin f
engraft [ɛn'græft] tr aufpropfen; (fig) einprägen
engrave [ɛn'grev] tr gravieren
engraver [ɛn'grevər] s Graveur m
engrav′ing s Kupferstich m
engross [ɛn'gros] tr in Anspruch nehmen; (a document) mit großen Buchstaben schreiben; **become engrossed in** sich versenken in (acc)
engross′ing adj fesselnd
engulf [ɛn'gʌlf] tr (fig) verschlingen
enhance [ɛn'hæns] tr erhöhen; **be enhanced** sich erhöhen
enhancement [ɛn'hænsmənt] s Erhöhung f
enigma [ɪ'nɪgmə] s Rätsel n
enigmatic(al) [ˌɪnɪg'mætɪk(əl)] adj rätselhaft
enjoin [ɛn'dʒɔɪn] tr (forbid) (from ger) verbieten (dat) (zu inf); **e. s.o. to** (inf) j-m auferlegen zu (inf)
enjoy [ɛn'dʒɔɪ] tr (take pleasure in) Gefallen finden an (dat); (have the advantage of) genießen, sich erfreuen (genit); **e. doing s.th.** gern etw tun; **e. oneself** sich gut unterhalten; **e. to the full** auskosten; **I e. the wine** mir schmeckt der Wein
enjoyable [ɛn'dʒɔɪ-əbəl] adj erfreulich; **thoroughly e.** genußreich
enjoyment [ɛn'dʒɔɪmənt] s Genuß m
enkindle [ɛn'kɪndəl] tr entzünden
enlarge [ɛn'lɑrdʒ] tr vergrößern ‖ intr sich vergrößern; **e. upon** näher eingehen auf (acc)
enlargement [ɛn'lɑrdʒmənt] s Vergrößerung f
enlarger [ɛn'lɑrdʒər] s (phot) Vergrößerungsapparat m
enlighten [ɛn'laɪtən] tr aufklären
enlightenment [ɛn'laɪtənmənt] s (act) Aufklärung f; (state) Aufgeklärtheit f
enlist [ɛn'lɪst] tr (services) in Anspruch nehmen; (mil) anwerben; **e. s.o. in a cause** j-n für e-e Sache gewinnen ‖ intr (in) sich freiwillig melden (zu)
enlist′ed man′ s Soldat m; **enlisted men** Mannschaften pl
enlistment [ɛn'lɪstmənt] s Anwerbung f; (period of service) Militärdienstzeit f
enliven [ɛn'laɪvən] tr beleben
enmesh [ɛn'mɛʃ] tr verstricken
enmity ['ɛnmɪti] s Feindschaft f
ennoble [ɛn'nobəl] tr veredeln, adeln
ennui ['ɑnwi] s Langeweile f
enormity [ɪ'nɔrmɪti] s Ungeheuerlichkeit f
enormous [ɪ'nɔrməs] adj enorm, ungeheuer
enough [ɪ'nʌf] adj & adv genug, genügend; **be e.** genügen; **I have e. of it** ich bin es satt; **it's e. to drive one crazy** es ist zum Verrücktwerden

enounce [ɪ'naʊns] tr (declare) verkünden; (pronounce) aussprechen
enrage [ɛn'redʒ] tr wütend machen
enraged′ adj (at) wütend (über acc)
enrapture [ɛn'ræptʃər] tr hinreißen
enrich [ɛn'rɪtʃ] tr (a person with money; the mind, a program) bereichern; (soil) fruchtbarer machen; (food, metals, gases) anreichern
enrichment [ɛn'rɪtʃmənt] s Bereicherung f; (of food, metals, gases) Anreicherung f
enroll [ɛn'rol] tr als Mitglied aufnehmen ‖ intr (educ) sich immatrikulieren lassen
enrollment [ɛn'rolmənt] s (in a course or school) Schülerzahl f; (of a society) Mitgliederzahl f
en route [ɑn'rut] adv unterwegs
ensconce [ɛn'skɑns] tr verbergen
ensemble [ɑn'sɑmbəl] s Ensemble n
ensign ['ɛnsɪn] s (flag) (mil) Fahne f; (flag) (nav) Flagge f; (emblem) Abzeichen n; (nav) Leutnant m zur See
enslave [ɛn'slev] tr versklaven
enslavement [ɛn'slevmənt] s Versklavung f
ensnare [ɛn'sner] tr (fig) umgarnen
ensue [ɛn's(j)u] intr (from) (er)folgen (aus)
ensu′ing adj darauffolgend
ensure [ɛn'ʃʊr] tr gewährleisten
entail [ɛn'tel] tr mit sich bringen
entangle [ɛn'tæŋgəl] tr verwickeln; **get entangled** sich verwickeln
entanglement [ɛn'tæŋgəlmənt] s Verwicklung f; (mil) Drahtverhau m
enter ['ɛntər] tr (a room) betreten, treten in (acc); (political office) antreten; (a university) beziehen; (a protest) erheben; (a career) einschlagen; (in the records) eintragen; **e. the army** Soldat werden ‖ intr eintreten, hereinkommen; (by car) einfahren; (sport) melden; (theat) auftreten; **e. into** (an agreement) treffen; (a contract) abschließen; **e. upon** anfangen; (a career) einschlagen; (an office, inheritance) antreten; (year of life) eintreten in (acc)
enterprise ['ɛntər ˌpraɪz] s Unternehmen n; (spirit) Unternehmungsgeist m
en′terprising adj unternehmungslustig
entertain [ˌɛntər'ten] tr unterhalten; (guests) bewirten; (doubts, hopes, suspicions) hegen ‖ intr Gäste haben
entertainer [ˌɛntər'tenər] s Unterhaltungskünstler –in mf
entertain′ing adj unterhaltsam ‖ s—**do a lot of e.** ein großes Haus führen
entertainment [ˌɛntər'tenmənt] s Unterhaltung f
entertain′ment tax′ s Vergnügungssteuer f
enthrall [ɛn'θrɔl] tr bezaubern, fesseln
enthrone [ɛn'θron] tr auf den Thron setzen; **be enthroned** thronen
enthuse [ɛn'θ(j)uz] tr (coll) begeistern
enthusiasm [ɛn'θ(j)uzɪ ˌæzəm] s Begeisterung f, Schwärmerei f

enthusiast [ɛn'θ(j)uzɪ‚æst] *s* Schwärmer –in *mf*
enthusiastic [ɛn‚θ(j)uzɪ'æstɪk] *adj* **(about)** begeistert (über *acc* or von)
entice [ɛn'taɪs] *tr* (ver)locken
enticement [ɛn'taɪsmənt] *s* Verlockung *f*
entic'ing *adj* verlockend
entire [ɛn'taɪr] *adj* ganz, gesamt; **(trust)** voll
entirely [ɛn'taɪrlɪ] *adv* ganz, gänzlich
entirety [ɛn'taɪrtɪ] *s*—**in its e.** in seiner Gesamtheit
entitle [ɛn'taɪtəl] *tr* **(call)** betiteln; **(to)** berechtigen (zu); **be entitled to** Anspruch haben auf **(acc)**; **be entitled to (inf)** berechtigt sein zu **(inf)**
entity ['ɛntɪtɪ] *s* Wesen *n*
entomb [ɛn'tum] *tr* bestatten
entombment [ɛn'tummənt] *s* Bestattung *f*
entomology [‚ɛntə'malədʒɪ] *s* Entomologie *f*
entourage [‚antu'raʒ] *s* Begleitung *f*
entrails ['ɛntrelz] *spl* Eingeweide *pl*
entrain [ɛn'tren] *tr* verladen ‖ *intr* einsteigen
entrance ['ɛntrəns] *s* Eingang *m*; **(drive)** Einfahrt *f*; **(of a home)** Flur *m*; **(upon office)** Antritt *m*; **(theat)** Auftritt *m*; **make one's e.** eintreten ‖ [ɛn'træns] *tr* mitreißen
en'trance examina'tion *s* Aufnahmeprüfung *f*
en'trance fee' *s* Eintrittspreis *m*
entrant ['ɛntrənt] *s* **(in)** Teilnehmer –in *mf* **(an** *dat***)**
en·trap [ɛn'træp] *v* **(***pret* & *pp* **-trapped;** *ger* **-trapping)** *tr* verleiten
entreat [ɛn'trit] *tr* anflehen
entreaty [ɛn'tritɪ] *s* dringende Bitte *f*; **at his e.** auf seine Bitte
entrée ['antre] *s* **(access)** Zutritt *m*; **(before main course)** Vorspeise *f*; **(between courses)** Zwischengericht *n*; **(main course)** Hauptgericht *n*
entrench [ɛn'trentʃ] *tr* verschanzen; **be entrenched in** *(fig)* eingewurzelt sein in **(***dat***)**
entrenchment [ɛn'trentʃmənt] *s* **(activity)** Schanzbau *m*; **(the result)** Verschanzung *f*
entrepreneur [antrəprə'nʌr] *s* Unternehmer –in *mf*
entrust [ɛn'trʌst] *tr* **(to)** anvertrauen **(***dat***)**
entry ['ɛntrɪ] *s* Eintritt *m*; **(by car)** Einfahrt *f*; **(door)** Eingang *m*, Eingangstür *f*; **(into a country)** Einreise *f*; **(into office)** Antritt *m*; **(in a dictionary)** Stichwort *n*; **(into a race)** Nennung *f*; **(contestant)** Bewerber –in *mf*; **(com)** Buchung *f*; **(theat)** Auftritt *m*; **unlawful e.** Hausfriedensbruch *m*
entwine [ɛn'twaɪn] *tr* umwinden
enumerate [ɪ'n(j)umə‚ret] *tr* aufzählen
enunciate [ɪ'nʌnsɪ‚et] *tr* aussprechen ‖ *intr* deutlich aussprechen
envelop [ɛn'vɛləp] *tr* **(said of crowds, waves)** verschlingen; **(said of mist, clouds, darkness)** umhüllen; **(mil)** umfassen

envelope ['ɛnvə‚lop] *s* Umschlag *m*
envelopment [ɛn'vɛləpmənt] *s* Umhüllung *f*; **(mil)** Umfassung *f*
envenom [ɛn'vɛnəm] *tr* vergiften
enviable ['ɛnvɪ·əbəl] *adj* beneidenswert
envious ['ɛnvɪ·əs] *adj.* **(of)** neidisch **(auf** *acc***)**
environment [ɛn'vaɪrənmənt] *s* **(ecological condition)** Umwelt *f*; **(surroundings)** Umgebung *f*
environmental [ɛn‚vaɪrən'mɛntəl] *adj* Umwelt–; umgebend, Umgebungs-
environmentalist [ɛn‚vaɪrən'mɛntəlɪst] *s* Umweltschützer –in *mf*
environs [ɛn'vaɪrənz] *spl* Umgebung *f*
envisage [ɛn'vɪzɪdʒ] *tr* ins Auge fassen
envoy ['ɛnvɔɪ] *s* Gesandte *mf*
en·vy ['ɛnvɪ] *s* Neid *m* ‖ *v* **(***pret* & *pp* **-vied)** *tr* **(for)** beneiden (um)
enzyme ['ɛnzaɪm] *s* Enzym *n*
epaulet, epaulette ['ɛpə‚lɛt] *s* Epaulette *f*, Schulterstück *n*
ephemeral [ɪ'fɛmərəl] *adj* flüchtig
epic ['ɛpɪk] *adj* episch; **e. poetry** Epik *f* ‖ *s* Epos *n*, Heldengedicht *n*
epicure ['ɛpɪ‚kjur] *s* Feinschmecker –in *mf*
epicurean [‚ɛpɪkju'ri·ən] *adj* genußsüchtig; **(philos)** epikureisch ‖ *s* Genußmensch *m*; **(philos)** Epikureer *m*
epidemic [‚ɛpɪ'dɛmɪk] *adj* epidemisch ‖ *s* Epidemie *f*, Seuche *f*
epidermis [‚ɛpɪ'dʌrmɪs] *s* Oberhaut *f*
epigram ['ɛpɪ‚græm] *s* Epigramm *n*
epigraph ['ɛpɪ‚græf] *s* Inschrift *f*
epigraphy [ɛ'pɪgrəfɪ] *s* Inschriftenkunde *f*
epilepsy ['ɛpɪ‚lɛpsɪ] *s* Epilepsie *f*
epileptic [‚ɛpɪ'lɛptɪk] *adj* epileptisch ‖ *s* Epileptiker –in *mf*
epilogue ['ɛpɪ‚lɔg] *s* Nachwort *n*
Epiphany [ɪ'pɪfənɪ] *s* Dreikönigsfest *n*
episcopal [ɪ'pɪskəpəl] *adj* bischöflich
Episcopalian [ɪ‚pɪskə'pɛlɪ·ən] *adj* Episkopal– ‖ *s* Episkopale *m*, Episkopalin *f*
epis'copal see' *s* Bischofssitz *m*
episcopate [ɪ'pɪskə‚pɛt] *s* Bischofsamt *n*
episode ['ɛpɪ‚sod] *s* Episode *f*
epistemology [ɪ‚pɪstə'malədʒɪ] *s* Epistemologie *f*, Erkenntnistheorie *f*
epistle [ɪ'pɪsəl] *s* Epistel *f*
epitaph ['ɛpɪtæf] *s* Grabinschrift *f*
epithet ['ɛpɪ‚θɛt] *s* Beiwort *n*
epitome [ɪ'pɪtəmɪ] *s* Auszug *m*; *(fig)* Verkörperung *f*
epitomize [ɪ'pɪtə‚maɪz] *tr*—e–n Auszug machen von or aus; *(fig)* verkörpern
epoch ['ɛpək] *s* Epoche *f*
epochal ['ɛpəkəl] *adj* epochal
e'poch-mak'ing *adj* bahnbrechend
Ep'som salts' ['ɛpsəm] *spl* Bittersalz *n*
equable ['ɛkwəbəl] *adj* gleichmäßig; **(disposition)** gleichmütig
equal ['ikwəl] *adj* gleich; **(in birth or status)** ebenbürtig; **(in worth)** gleichwertig; **(in kind)** gleichartig; **be e. to** **(***e.g.***, a** *task***)** gewachsen sein **(***dat***)**; **be on e. terms** **(be on the same level)** auf gleichem Fuß stehen; **other**

things being e. bei sonst gleichen Verhältnissen ‖ s Gleiche *mfn;* her or their e.(s) ihresgleichen; my (your, *etc.*) e.(s) meines– (deines–, *etc.*) gleichen ‖ *v (pret & pp* equal[l]ed; *ger* equal[l]ing *tr* gleichkommen (*dat); (a record*) erreichen; (*math*) ergeben

equality [ɪˈkwɑlɪti] *s* Gleichheit *f;* (*in standing*) Gleichberechtigung *f*

equalize [ˈɛkwɪˌlaɪz] *tr* gleichmachen

equally [ˈikwəli] *adv* gleich, ebenso

equanimity [ˌikwəˈnɪmɪti] *s* Gleichmut *m*

equate [iˈkwet] *tr* (to or with) gleichsetzen (*dat* or mit)

equation [iˈkweʒən] *s* Gleichung *f*

equator [iˈkwetər] *s* Äquator *m*

equatorial [ˌikwəˈtɔrɪ·əl] *adj* äquatorial

equestrian [ɪˈkwestrɪ·ən] *adj* Reiter–; e. statue Reiterstandbild *n* ‖ *s* Kunstreiter –in *mf*

equilateral [ˌikwɪˈlætərəl] *adj* gleichseitig

equilibrium [ˌikwɪˈlɪbrɪ·əm] *s* Gleichgewicht *n;* (*fig*) Gleichmaß *n*

equinox [ˈikwɪˌnɑks] *s* Tagundnachtgleiche *f*

equip [ɪˈkwɪp] *v (pret & pp* equipped; *ger* equipping) *tr* ausrüsten, ausstatten

equipment [ɪˈkwɪpmənt] *s* Ausrüstung *f*, Ausstattung *f*

equipoise [ˈikwɪˌpɔɪz] *s* Gleichgewicht *n*

equitable [ˈɛkwɪtəbəl] *adj* gerecht

equity [ˈɛkwɪti] *s* (*fairness*) Unparteilichkeit *f;* (*fin*) Nettowert *m*

equivalent [ɪˈkwɪvələnt] *adj* gleichwertig; (to) gleichbedeutend (mit) ‖ *s* Gegenwert *m;* (of) Äquivalent *n* (für)

equivocal [ɪˈkwɪvəkəl] *adj* zweideutig

equivocate [ɪˈkwɪvəˌket] *intr* zweideutig reden

equivocation [ɪˌkwɪvəˌkeʃən] *s* Zweideutigkeit *f*

era [ˈɪrə], [ˈirə] *s* Zeitalter *n*

eradicate [ɪˈrædɪˌket] *tr* ausrotten

erase [ɪˈres] *tr* ausradieren; (*a tape recording*) löschen; (*a blackboard*) abwischen; (*fig*) auslöschen

eraser [ɪˈresər] *s* Radiergummi *m;* (*for a blackboard*) Tafelwischer *m*

erasure [ɪˈreʒər], [ɪˈreʒər] *s* (*action*) Ausradieren *n;* (*erased spot*) Rasur *f*

ere [ɛr] *prep* (poet) vor (*dat*) ‖ *conj* (poet) ehe, bevor

erect [ɪˈrɛkt] *adj* aufrecht, straff; (*hair*) gesträubt; with head e. erhobenen Hauptes ‖ *tr* errichten

erection [ɪˈrɛkʃən] *s* Errichtung *f;* (*of sexual organs*) Erektion *f*

erg [ʌrg] *s* Erg *n*

ermine [ˈʌrmɪn] *s* Hermelinpelz *m*

erode [ɪˈrod] *tr* (*corrode*) zerfressen; (*fig*) aushöhlen; (*geol*) erodieren ‖ *intr* zerfressen werden

erosion [ɪˈroʒən] *s* (*corrosion*) Zerfressen *n;* (*fig*) Unterhöhlung *f;* (*geol*) Erosion *f*

erotic [ɪˈrɑtɪk] *adj* erotisch

err [ʌr] *intr* irren, sich irren

errand [ˈɛrənd] *s* Besorgung *f;* run an e. e–e Besorgung machen

er'rand boy' *s* Laufbursche *m*

erratic [ɪˈrætɪk] *adj* regellos, ziellos; (*geol*) erratisch

erroneous [ɪˈroni·əs] *adj* irrtümlich

erroneously [ɪˈroni·əsli] *adv* irrtümlicherweise, versehentlich

error [ˈɛrər] *s* Fehler *m*, Irrtum *m*

erudite [ˈɛr(j)uˌdaɪt] *adj* gelehrt

erudition [ˌɛr(j)uˈdɪʃən] *s* Gelehrsamkeit *f*

erupt [ɪˈrʌpt] *intr* ausbrechen

eruption [ɪˈrʌpʃən] *s* Ausbruch *m;* (pathol) Ausschlag *m*

escalate [ˈɛskəˌlet] *tr & intr* eskalieren

escalation [ˌɛskəˈleʃən] *s* Eskalierung *f*

escalator [ˈɛskəˌletər] *s* Rolltreppe *f*

es'calator clause' *s* Indexklausel *f*

escapade [ˈɛskəˌped] *s* Eskapade *f*

escape [ɛsˈkep] *s* Flucht *f;* (*of gas or liquid*) Ausströmen *n;* have a narrow e. mit knapper Not davonkommen ‖ *intr* (*said of gas or liquid*) ausströmen; (*from*) flüchten (aus)

escape' clause' *s* Ausweichklausel *f*

escapee [ˌɛskəˈpi] *s* Flüchtling *m*

escape' hatch' *s* Notausstieg *m*

escapement [ɛsˈkepmənt] *s* (horol) Hemmung *f*

escape' wheel' *s* (horol) Hemmungsrad *n*

escapism [ɛsˈkepɪzəm] *s* Wirklichkeitsflucht *f*

escarpment [ɛsˈkɑrpmənt] *s* (geol) Steilabhang *m;* (mil) Abdachung *f*

eschew [ɛsˈt/u] *tr* (ver)meiden

escort [ˈɛskɔrt] *s* Geleit *n*, Schutzgeleit *n;* (*person*) Begleiter *m;* (mil) Begleitmannschaft *f*, Bedeckung *f;* (nav) Geleitschutz *m* ‖ [ɛsˈkɔrt] *tr* begleiten; (mil, nav) geleiten

es'cort ves'sel *s* Geleitschiff *n*

escutcheon [ɛsˈkʌtʃən] *s* Wappenschild *m;* (*doorplate*) Schlüssellochschild *n*

Eskimo [ˈɛskɪˌmo] *adj* Eskimo– ‖ *s* (–mos & –mo) Eskimo *m*

esophagus [iˈsɑfəgəs] *s* (–gi [ˌdʒaɪ]) Speiseröhre *f*

esoteric [ˌɛsoˈtɛrɪk] *adj* esoterisch

especial [ɛsˈpeʃəl] *adj* besondere

especially [ɛsˈpeʃəli] *adv* besonders

espionage [ˌɛspɪ·əˈnɑʒ] *s* Spionage *f*

espousal [ɛsˈpauzəl] *s* (of) Annahme *f* (von)

espouse [ɛsˈpauz] *tr* annehmen

esprit de corps [ɛsˈpri də ˈkɔr] *s* Korpsgeist *m*, Gemeinschaftsgeist *m*

espy [ɛsˈpaɪ] *v (pret & pp* espied) *tr* erspähen

essay [ˈɛse] *s* Aufsatz *m*, Essay *n* ‖ [ɛˈse] *tr* probieren

essayist [ˈɛse·ɪst] *s* Essayist –in *mf*

essence [ˈɛsəns] *s* Wesenheit *f;* (*scent*) Duft *m;* (*extract*) Essenz *f;* (philos) inneres Wesen *n;* in e. im wesentlichen

essential [ɛˈsenʃəl] *adj* (to) wesentlich (für) ‖ *s* Hauptsache *f;* the essentials die Grundzüge *pl*

establish [esˈtæblɪʃ] *tr (found)* gründen; *(a business, an account)* eröffnen; *(relations, connections)* herstellen; *(order)* schaffen; *(a record)* aufstellen; *(a fact)* feststellen

establishment [esˈtæblɪʃmənt] *s (act)* Gründung *f*; *(institution)* Anstalt *f*; *(business)* Unternehmen *n*; **the Establishment** das Establishment

estate [esˈtet] *s (landed property)* Landgut *n*; *(possessions)* Vermögen *n*; *(property of deceased person)* Nachlaß *m*; *(social station)* Stand *m*

esteem [esˈtim] *s* Hochachtung *f*; **hold in e.** achten ‖ *tr* achten

esthete [ˈesθit] *s* Ästhetiker –in *mf*

esthetic [esˈθetɪk] *adj* ästhetisch ‖ **esthetics** *s* Ästhetik *f*

estimable [ˈestɪməbəl] *adj* schätzenswert

estimate [ˈestɪˌmet], [ˈestɪmɪt] *s* Kostenanschlag *m*; *(judgment of value)* Schätzung *f*; **rough e.** Überschlag *m* ‖ [ˈestɪˌmet] *tr (costs)* veranschlagen; *(the value)* abschätzen; *(homes, damages)* schätzen; **(at)** beziffern (auf *acc*); **e. roughly** überschlagen

estimation [ˌestɪˈmeʃən] *s* Schätzung *f*; **in my e.** nach meiner Schätzung

Estonia [esˈtonɪ·ə] *s* Estland *n*

estrangement [esˈtrendʒmənt] *s* Entfremdung *f*

estuary [ˈestʃʊˌɛri] *s (of a river)* Mündung *f*; *(inlet)* Meeresarm *m*

etch [etʃ] *tr* radieren, ätzen

etcher [ˈetʃər] *s* Radierer –in *mf*

etch'ing *s* Radierung *f*; *(as an art)* Radierkunst *f*

eternal [ɪˈtʌrnəl] *adj* ewig

eternity [ɪˈtʌrnɪti] *s* Ewigkeit *f*

ether [ˈiθər] *s* Äther *m*

ethereal [ɪˈθɪrɪ·əl] *adj* ätherisch

ethical [ˈeθɪkəl] *adj* ethisch, sittlich

ethics [ˈeθɪks] *s* Ethik *f*, Sittenlehre *f*

Ethiopia [ˌiθɪˈopɪ·ə] *s* Äthiopien *n*

Ethiopian [ˌiθɪˈopɪ·ən] *adj* äthiopisch ‖ *s* Äthiopier –in *mf*; *(language)* Äthiopisch *n*

ethnic(al) [ˈeθnɪk(əl)] *adj* völkisch; **e. group** Volksgruppe *f*

ethnography [eθˈnɑgrəfi] *s* Ethnographie *f*

ethnology [eθˈnɑlədʒi] *s* Völkerkunde *f*

ethyl [ˈeθɪl] *s* Äthyl *m*

ethylene [ˈeθɪˌlin] *s* Äthylen *n*

etiquette [ˈetɪˌket] *s* Etikette *f*

etymology [ˌetɪˈmɑlədʒi] *s* Etymologie *f*

ety·mon [ˈetɪˌmɑn] *s (–mons & –ma [mə])* Etymon *n*

eucalyp·tus [ˌjukəˈlɪptəs] *s (–tuses & –ti [taɪ])* Eukalyptus *m*

Eucharist [ˈjukərɪst] *s*—**the E.** das heilige Abendmal, die Eucharistie *f*

eugenics [juˈdʒɛnɪks] *s* Rassenhygiene *f*

eulogize [ˈjuləˌdʒaɪz] *tr* lobpreisen

eulogy [ˈjulədʒi] *s* Lobrede *f*

eunuch [ˈjunək] *s* Eunuch *m*

euphemism [ˈjufɪˌmɪzəm] *s* Euphemismus *m*

euphemistic [ˌjufəˈmɪstɪk] *adj* euphemistisch, verblümt

euphonic [juˈfɑnɪk] *adj* wohlklingend

euphony [ˈjufəni] *s* Wohlklang *m*

euphoria [juˈforɪ·ə] *s* Euphorie *f*

euphoric [juˈforɪk] *adj* euphorisch

euphuism [ˈjufjuˌɪzəm] *s* gezierte Ausdrucksweise *f*

Europe [ˈjurəp] *s* Europa *n*

European [ˌjurəˈpi·ən] *adj* europäisch ‖ *s* Europäer –in *mf*

Europe'an plan' *s* Hotelpreis *m* ohne Mahlzeiten

euthanasia [ˌjuθəˈneʒə] *s* Euthanasie *f*

evacuate [ɪˈvækjuˌet] *tr* evakuieren; *(med)* entleeren; *(an area)* räumen ‖ *intr* sich zurückziehen

evacuation [ɪˌvækjuˈeʃən] *s* Evakuierung *f*; *(med)* Entleerung *f*

evade [ɪˈved] *tr* ausweichen *(dat)*; *(duties)* vernachlässigen; *(laws)* umgehen; *(prosecution, responsibility)* sich entziehen *(dat)*; *(taxes)* hinterziehen

evaluate [ɪˈvæljuˌet] *tr (e.g., jewels)* (ab)schätzen; *(e.g., a performance)* beurteilen

evaluation [ɪˌvæljuˈeʃən] *s* Abschätzung *f*; *(judgment)* Beurteilung *f*

evangelic(al) [ˌivænˈdʒelɪk(əl)], [ˌevənˈdʒelɪk(əl)] *adj* evangelisch

Evangelist [ɪˈvændʒəlɪst] *s* Evangelist *m*

evaporate [ɪˈvæpəˌret] *tr* eindampfen ‖ *intr (above boiling point)* verdampfen; *(below boiling point)* verdunsten; *(fig)* sich verflüchtigen

eva'porated milk' *s* Kondensmilch *f*

evasion [ɪˈveʒən] *s (dodge)* Ausweichen *n*; *(of the law)* Umgehung *f*; *(of responsibility)* Vernachlässigung *f*; *(in speech)* Ausflucht *f*

evasive [ɪˈvesɪv] *adj* ausweichend

eve [iv] *s* Vorabend *m*

even [ˈivən] *adj (smooth)* eben, gerade; *(number)* gerade; *(uniform)* gleichmäßig; *(chance)* gleich; *(temperament)* ruhig, ausgeglichen; **an e. dozen** genau ein Dutzend; **be e.** (coll) quitt sein; **e. with** auf gleicher Höhe mit; **get e. with** j–m abrechnen ‖ *adv* selbst, sogar; *(before comparatives)* noch; *(as intensifier before nouns and pronouns)* selbst; **break e.** gerade auf seine Kosten kommen; **e. if** selbst wenn, wenn auch; **e. so** trotzdem; **e. though** obgleich; **e. today** noch heute; **e. when** selbst wenn ‖ *tr* ebnen; **e. up** ausgleichen

e'ven-hand'ed *adj* unparteiisch

evening [ˈivnɪŋ] *adj* Abend– ‖ *s* Abend *m*; **in the e.** am Abend; **this e.** heute abend

eve'ning gown' *s* Abendkleid *n*

eve'ning pa'per *s* Abendblatt *n*

eve'ning school' *s* Abendschule *f*

evenly [ˈivənli] *adv* gleichmäßig; **e. matched** (sport) gleichwertig

ev'en-mind'ed *adj* gleichmütig

evenness [ˈivənnɪs] *s (smoothness)*

Ebenheit *f*; (*uniformity*) Gleich-mäßigkeit *f*

event [ɪ'vent] *s* Ereignis *n*; (sport) Veranstaltung *f*; **at all events, in any e.** auf jeden Fall; **in the e. of** im Falle (*genit*)

eventful [ɪ'ventfəl] *adj* ereignisvoll

eventual [ɪ'vent/ʊ·əl] *adj* schließlich

eventuality [ɪˌvent/ʊ'ælɪtɪ] *s* Möglich-keit *f*

eventually [ɪ'vent/ʊˌəlɪ] *adj* schließ-lich

ever ['evər] *adv* je, jemals; (*before comparatives*) immer; **did you e.!** hat man schon sowas gehört!; **e. after** die ganze Zeit danach; **e. so** noch so; **e. so much** (coll) sehr; **hardly e.** fast nie

ev'ergreen' *adj* immergrün || *s* Immer-grün *n*

ev'erlast'ing *adj* ewig; (*continual*) fortwährend; (iron) ewig

ev'ermore' *adv* immer; **for e.** in Ewig-keit

every ['evrɪ] *adj* jeder; (*confidence*) voll; **e. bit** (coll) völlig; **e. now and then** ab und zu; **e. once in a while** dann und wann; **e. other day** alle zwei Tage; **e. time (that)** jedesmal (wenn)

ev'erybod'y *indef pron* jeder, jeder-mann

ev'eryday' *adj* alltäglich, Alltags—

ev'eryone', ev'ery one' *indef pron* (of) jeder (von); **e. else** alle anderen

ev'erything' *indef pron* alles

ev'erywhere' *adv* (*position*) überall; (*direction*) überallhin

evict [ɪ'vɪkt] *tr* delogieren

eviction [ɪ'vɪk/ən] *s* Delogierung *f*

evidence ['evɪdəns] *s* Beweismaterial *n*, Beweise *pl*; (*piece of evidence*) Beweis *m*; **as e. of** zum Beweis (*genit*); **for lack of e.** wegen Mangels an Beweisen; **give e.** aussagen; **in e.** sichtbar

evident ['evɪdənt] *adj* (*obvious*) offen-sichtlich; (*visible*) ersichtlich; **be e.** zutage liegen

evidently ['evɪdəntlɪ] *adv* offenbar

evil ['evəl] *adj* übel, böse || *s* Übel *n*

e'vildo'er *s* Übeltäter –in *mf*

e'vildo'ing *s* Missetat *f*

e'vil eye' *s* böser Blick *m*

e'vil-mind'ed *adj* übelgesinnt

E'vil One' *s* Böse *m*

evince [ɪ'vɪns] *tr* bekunden

evoke [ɪ'vok] *tr* hervorrufen

evolution [ˌevə'luʃən] *s* Evolution *f*

evolve [ɪ'vɑlv] *tr* entwickeln, entfalten || *intr* sich entwickeln, sich entfalten

ewe [ju] *s* Mutterschaf *n*

ewer ['juˌər] *s* Wasserkanne *f*

exact [eg'zækt] *adj* genau || *tr* (*e.g., money*) beitreiben; (*obedience*) er-zwingen

exact'ing *adj* (*strict*) streng; (*task*) aufreibend; (*picky*) anspruchsvoll

exactly [eg'zæktlɪ] *adv* genau

exactness [eg'zæktnɪs] *s* Genauigkeit *f*

exact' sci'ences *spl* Realien *pl*

exaggerate [eg'zædʒəˌret] *tr* übertrei-ben

exaggeration [egˌzædʒə're/ən] *s* Über-treibung *f*

exalt [eg'zɔlt] *tr* erheben

exam [eg'zæm] *s* (coll) Prüfung *f*

examination [egˌzæmɪ'ne/ən] *s* Prü-fung *f*, Examen *n*; (jur) Verhör *n*, Vernehmung *f*; (med) Untersuchung *f*; **direct e.** (jur) direkte Befragung *f*; **fail an e.** bei e-r Prüfung durch-fallen; **on closer e.** bei näherer Prü-fung; **pass an e.** e-e Prüfung be-stehen; **take an e.** e-e Prüfung ab-legen

examine [eg'zæmɪn] *tr* prüfen; (jur) verhören, vernehmen; (med) unter-suchen

examinee [egˌzæmɪ'ni] *s* Prüfling *m*

examiner [eg'zæmɪnər] *s* (educ) Prü-fer –in *mf*; (med) Untersucher –in *mf*

example [eg'zæmpəl] *s* Beispiel *n*; **for e.** zum Beispiel; **make an e. of** ein Exempel statuieren an (*dat*); **set a good e.** mit gutem Beispiel voran-gehen

exasperate [eg'zæspəˌret] *tr* reizen

excavate ['ekskəˌvet] *tr* ausgraben

excavation [ˌekskə'veʃən] *s* Ausgra-bung *f*

excavator ['ekskəˌvetər] *s* (archeol) Ausgräber –in *mf*; (mach) Trocken-bagger *m*

exceed [ek'sid] *tr* überschreiten

exceedingly [ek'sidɪŋlɪ] *adv* außeror-dentlich

ex-cel [ek'sel] *v* (*pret & pp* **-celled;** *ger* **-celling**) *tr* übertreffen || *intr* (**in**) sich auszeichnen (in *dat*)

excellence ['eksəlens] *s* Vorzüglichkeit *f*

excellency ['ekséləns] *s* Vorzüglich-keit *f*; **Your Excellency** Eure Ex-zellenz

excellent ['ekséllənt] *adj* ausgezeichnet

excelsior [ek'selsɪˌər] *s* Holzwolle *f*

except [ek'sept] *adv*—**e. for** abgesehen von; **e. if** außer wenn; **e. that** außer daß; **e. when** außer wenn || *prep* außer (*dat*), ausgenommen (*acc*) || *tr* ausnehmen, ausschließen

exception [ek'sep/ən] *s* Ausnahme *f*; **by way of e.** ausnahmsweise; **take e. to** Anstoß nehmen an (*dat*); **without e.** ausnahmslos; **with the e. of** mit Ausnahme von

exceptional [ek'sep/ənəl] *adj* außerge-wöhnlich, Sonder—

excerpt ['eksˌʌrpt] *s* Auszug *m* || [ek-'sʌrpt] *tr* exzerpieren

excess ['ekses], [ek'ses] *adj* über-schüssig || [ek'ses] *s* (*surplus*) Überschuß *m*; (*immoderate amount*) (of) Übermaß *n* (von or an *dat*); **carry to e.** übertreiben; **excesses** Ausschreitungen *pl*; **in e. of** mehr als; **to e.** übermäßig

ex'cess bag'gage *s* Überfracht *f*

excessive [ek'sesɪv] *adj* übermäßig

ex'cess-prof'its tax' *s* Mehrgewinnsteu-er *f*

exchange [eks't/endʒ] *s* Austausch *m*; (*e.g., of purchases*) Umtausch *m*; (*of words*) Wechselgespräch *n*; (*of* *money)* Geldwechsel *m;* (fin) Börse *f;* (mil) Kantine *f;* (telp) Vermittlung *f;* e. of letters Briefwechsel *m;* in e. dafür; in e. for für ‖ *tr (trade)* tauschen; *(replace)* auswechseln; **e. for** umtauschen gegen; **e. places with** s.o. mit j—m tauschen

exchequer [eks't∫ekər] *s* Staatskasse *f; (department)* Schatzamt *n*

ex'cise tax' ['eksaiz] *s* Verbrauchssteuer *f*

excitable [ek'saitəbəl] *adj* erregbar

excite [ek'sait] *tr* erregen, aufregen

excitement [ek'saitmənt] *s* Erregung *f,* Aufregung *f*

excit'ing *adj* erregend, aufregend

exclaim [eks'klem] *tr & intr* ausrufen

exclamation [,ekskla'me∫ən] *s* Ausruf *m*

exclama'tion point' *s* Ausrufungszeichen *n*

exclude [eks'klud] *tr* ausschließen

exclusion [eks'kluʒən] *s* Ausschließung *f,* Ausschluß *m;* **to the e. of** unter Ausschluß *(genit)*

exclusive [eks'klusiv] *adj (rights, etc.)* alleinig, ausschließlich; *(club)* exklusiv; *(shop)* teuer; **e. of** ausschließlich *(genit)*

excommunicate [,ekskə'mjunɪ,ket] *tr* exkommunizieren

excommunication [,ekskə,mjunɪ'ke∫ən] *s* Exkommunikation *f,* Kirchenbann *m*

excoriate [eks'korɪ,et] *tr* (fig) heruntermachen

excrement ['ekskrəmənt] *s* Exkremente *pl*

excrescence [eks'kresəns] *s* Auswuchs *m*

excruciating [eks'kru∫ɪ,etɪŋ] *adj* qualvoll

exculpate ['ekskʌl,pet] *tr* entschuldigen

excursion [eks'kʌrʒən] *s (side trip)* Abstecher *m; (short trip)* Ausflug *m*

excusable [eks'kjuzəbəl] *adj* entschuldbar, verzeihlich

excuse [eks'kjus] *s* Ausrede *f;* **give as an e.** vorgeben; **make excuses** sich ausreden ‖ [eks'kjuz] *tr* entschuldigen; **e. me!** entschuldigen Sie!; **you may be excused now** Sie können jetzt gehen

execute ['eksɪ,kjut] *tr (a condemned man)* hinrichten; *(by firing squad)* erschießen; *(perform)* durchführen, vollziehen; *(a will, a sentence)* vollstrecken; (mus) vortragen

execution [,eksɪ'kju∫ən] *s* Hinrichtung *f; (by firing squad)* Erschießung *f; (performance)* Durchführung *f,* Vollziehung *f;* (mus) Vortrag *m*

executioner [,eksɪ'kju∫ənər] *s* Scharfrichter *m*

executive [eg'zekjətɪv] *adj* vollziehend, exekutiv ‖ *s* (com) Manager *m,* leitender Angestellte *mf;* **the Executive** *(pol)* die Exekutive *f*

exec'utive commit'tee *s* Vollzugsausschuß *m,* Vorstand *m*

exec'utive or'der *s* Durchführungsverordnung *f*

executor [eg'zekjətər] *s* Vollstrecker *m*

executrix [eg'zekjətrɪks] *s* Vollstreckerin *f*

exemplary [eg'zemplərɪ] *adj* vorbildlich, mustergültig

exempli·fy [eg'zemplɪ,faɪ] *v (pret & pp –fied) tr (demonstrate)* an Beispielen erläutern; *(embody)* als Beispiel dienen für

exempt [eg'zempt] *adj (from)* befreit (von) ‖ *tr* befreien; (mil) freistellen

exemption [eg'zemp∫ən] *s* Befreiung *f;* (mil) Freistellung *f*

exercise ['eksər,saɪz] *s (of the body)* Bewegung *f; (of power)* Ausübung *f;* (mil) Exerzieren *n;* **take e. sich** *[dat]* Bewegung machen ‖ *tr* üben; *(the body, a horse)* bewegen; *(power, influence)* ausüben; (mil) exerzieren ‖ *intr* üben; (mil) exerzieren

exert [eg'zʌrt] *tr* ausüben; **e. every effort** alle Kräfte rühren; **e. oneself** sich anstrengen

exertion [eg'zʌr∫ən] *s* Anstrengung *f; (e.g., of power)* Ausübung *f*

exhalation [,eks·hə'le∫ən] *s* Ausatmung *f; (of gases)* Gasabgabe *f*

exhale [eks'hel] *tr & intr* ausatmen

exhaust [eg'zɔst] *s* (aut) Auspuff *m* ‖ *tr* erschöpfen

exhaust'ed *adj* erschöpft

exhaust' fan' *s* Absaugventilator *m*

exhaust' gas' *s* Abgas *n*

exhaust'ing *adj* anstrengend, mühselig

exhaustion [eg'zɔst∫ən] *s* Erschöpfung *f*

exhaustive [eg'zɔstɪv] *adj* erschöpfend

exhaust' pipe' *s* Auspuffrohr *n*

exhaust' valve' *s* Auspuffventil *n*

exhibit [eg'zɪbɪt] *s (exhibition)* Ausstellung *f; (object exhibited)* Ausstellungsstück *n;* (jur) Beleg *m* ‖ *tr* zur Schau stellen; *(wares)* ausstellen; *(e.g., courage)* zeigen

exhibition [,eksɪ'bɪ∫ən] *s* Ausstellung *f*

exhilarating [eg'zɪlə,retɪŋ] *adj* erheiternd

exhort [eg'zɔrt] *tr* ermahnen

exhume [eks'hjum] *tr* exhumieren

exigency ['eksɪdʒənsɪ] *s (demand, need)* Erfordnis *n; (state of urgency)* Dringlichkeit *f*

exigent ['eksɪdʒənt] *adj* dringlich

exile ['egzaɪl] *s* Exil *n; (person)* Verbannte *mf* ‖ *tr* verbannen

exist [eg'zɪst] *intr* existieren; *(continue to be)* bestehen; **e. from day to day** dahinleben

existence [eg'zɪstəns] *s* Existenz *f,* Dasein *n;* **be in e.** bestehen; **come into e.** entstehen

existential [,egzɪs'ten∫əl] *adj* existentiell

existentialism [,egzɪs'ten∫ə,lɪzəm] *s* Existentialismus *m*

exit ['egzɪt] *s* Ausgang *m; (by car)* Ausfahrt *f;* (theat) Abgang *m* ‖ *intr* (theat) abtreten

exodus ['eksədəs] *s* Abwanderung *f*

exonerate [eg'zɑnə,ret] *tr* entlasten

exorbitant [eg'zɔrbɪtənt] *adj* schwindelhaft; **e. price** Wucherpreis *m*

exorcise ['eksɔr‚saɪz] *tr* exorzieren

exotic [eg'zɑtɪk] *adj* exotisch

expand [eks'pænd] *tr* (aus)dehnen; *(enlarge)* erweitern; *(math)* entwickeln ‖ *intr* sich ausdehnen

expanse [eks'pæns] *s* Weite *f*, Fläche *f*

expansion [eks'pænʃən] *s* Ausdehnung *f*; *(expanded part)* Erweiterung *f*

expansive [eks'pænsɪv] *adj* expansiv; (fig) mitteilsam

expatiate [eks'peʃɪ‚et] *intr* (on) sich verbreiten (über *acc*)

expatriate [eks'petrɪ‚ɪt] *adj* ausgebürgert ‖ *s* Ausgebürgerte *mf* ‖ [eks'petrɪ‚et] *tr* ausbürgern

expect [eks'pekt] *tr* erwarten ‖ *intr—***she's expecting** (coll) sie ist in anderen Umständen

expectancy [eks'pektənsɪ] *s* Ewartung *f*

expectant [eks'pektənt] *adj* erwartungsvoll; *(mother)* werdende

expectation [‚ekspek'teʃən] *s* Erwartung *f*

expectorate [eks'pektə‚ret] *tr* & *intr* spucken

expediency [eks'pidɪ‚ənsɪ] *s* Zweckmäßigkeit *f*

expedient [eks'pidɪ‚ənt] *adj* zweckmäßig ‖ *s* Mittel *n*, Hilfsmittel *f*

expedite ['ekspɪ‚daɪt] *tr* beschleunigen; *(a document)* ausstellen

expedition [‚ekspɪ'dɪʃən] *s* Expedition *f*

expedi'tionary force' [‚ekspɪ'dɪʃə‚-nerɪ] *s* (mil) Expeditionsstreitkräfte *pl*

expeditious [‚ekspɪ'dɪʃəs] *adj* schleunig

ex·pel [eks'pel] *v* *(pret* & *pp* **–pelled;** *ger* **–pelling)** *tr* (aus)treiben; *(a student)* **(from)** verweisen (von)

expend [eks'pend] *tr* *(time, effort, etc.)* aufwenden; *(money)* ausgeben

expendable [eks'pendəbəl] *adj* entbehrlich

expenditure [eks'pendɪt/ər] *s* Aufwand *m*; *(of money)* Ausgabe *f*

expense [eks'pens] *s* Ausgabe *f*; **at s.o.'s e.** (& fig) auf j-s Kosten; **expenses** Unkosten *pl*; **go to great e.** sich in Unkosten stürzen

expense' account' *s* Spesenkonto *n*

expensive [eks'pensɪv] *adj* kostspielig

experience [eks'pɪrɪ‚əns] *s* Erfahrung *f*; *(an event)* Erlebnis *n*; **no previous e. necessary** Vorkenntnisse nicht erforderlich ‖ *tr* erfahren; *(pain)* erdulden; *(loss)* erleiden

expe'rienced *adj* erfahren

experiment [eks'perɪmənt] *s* Experiment *n*, Versuch *m* ‖ [eks'perɪ‚ment] *intr* experimentieren, Versuche anstellen

experimental [eks‚perɪ'mentəl] *adj* experimentell, Versuchs-

expert ['ekspərt] *adj* fachmännisch, erfahren; **e. advice** Gutachten *n* ‖ *s* Fachmann *m*; (jur) Sachverständige *mf*

expertise [‚eksper'tiz] *s* *(opinion)* Gutachten *n*; *(skill)* Sachkenntnis *f*

expiate ['ekspɪ‚et] *tr* sühnen, büßen

expiation [‚ekspɪ'eʃən] *s* Sühnung *f*

expiration [‚ekspɪ'reʃən] *s* Verfall *m*

expira'tion date' *s* Verfalltag *m*

expire [eks'paɪr] *tr* ausatmen ‖ *intr* verfallen; *(die)* verscheiden

explain [eks'plen] *tr* erklären, erläutern; *(justify)* rechtfertigen

explanation [‚eksplə'neʃən] *s* Erklärung *f*, Erläuterung *f*

explanatory [eks'plænə‚torɪ] *adj* erklärend, erläuternd

expletive ['eksplɪtɪv] *s* Füllwort *n*

explicit [eks'plɪsɪt] *adj* ausdrücklich

explode [eks'plod] *tr* explodieren lassen; *(a theory)* verwerfen ‖ *intr* explodieren; *(said of a grenade)* krepieren; **(with)** platzen (vor *dat*)

exploit ['eksplɔɪt] *s* Heldentat *f*, Großtat *f* ‖ [eks'plɔɪt] *tr* ausnutzen; (pej) ausbeuten; (min) abbauen

exploitation [‚eksplɔɪ'teʃən] *s* Ausnutzung *f*; (pej) Ausbeutung *f*; (min) Abbau *m*

exploration [‚eksplə're/ən] *s* Erforschung *f*

explore [eks'plor] *tr* erforschen

explorer [eks'plorər] *s* Forscher –in *mf*

explosion [eks'ploʒən] *s* Explosion *f*

explosive [eks'plosɪv] *adj* explosiv, Spreng– ‖ *s* *(explosive substance)* Sprengstoff *m*; *(device)* Sprengkörper *m*

explo'sive charge' *s* Sprengladung *f*

exponent [eks'ponənt] *s* Exponent *m*

export ['eksport] *adj* Ausfuhr– ‖ *s* Ausfuhr *m*, Export *m*; **exports** Ausfuhrgüter *pl* ‖ [eks'port] *tr* ausführen

exportation [‚ekspor'teʃən] *s* Ausfuhr *m*

exporter ['eksportər], [eks'portər] *s* Ausfuhrhändler –in *mf*, Exporteur –in *mf*

expose [eks'poz] *tr* *(to danger, ridicule, sun)* aussetzen; *(bare)* entblößen; *(a person)* (as) bloßstellen (als), entlarven (als); (phot) belichten

exposé [‚ekspo'ze] *s* Enthüllung *f*

exposition [‚ekspə'zɪ/ən] *s* Ausstellung *f*; (rhet) Exposition *f*

expostulate [eks'pɑst/ə‚let] *intr* protestieren; **e. with s.o. about** j–m ernste Vorhaltungen machen über *(acc)*

exposure [eks'poʒər] *s* *(of a child)* Aussetzung *f*; *(laying bare)* Entblößung *f*; *(unmasking)* Entlarvung *f*; *(of a building)* Lage *f*; (phot) Belichtung *f*

expo'sure me'ter *s* Belichtungsmesser *m*

expound [eks'paund] *tr* erklären

express [eks'pres] *adj* ausdrücklich ‖ *s* (rr) Expreß *m*; **by e.** als Eilgut ‖ *tr* ausdrücken; *(feelings)* zeigen; **e. oneself** sich äußern

express' com'pany *s* Paketpostgesellschaft *f*

expression [eks'preʃən] *s* Ausdruck *m*

expressive [ɛks'prɛsɪv] *adj* ausdrucksvoll

express' train' *s* Expreßzug *m*

express'way' *s* Schnellverkehrsstraße *f*

expropriate [ɛks'propri ,et] *tr* enteignen

expulsion [ɛks'pʌl/ən] *s* Austreibung *f*; (*from school or a game*) Verweisung *f*

expunge [ɛks'pʌndʒ] *tr* ausstreichen

expurgate ['ɛkspər ,get] *tr* säubern

exquisite ['ɛkskwɪzɪt], [ɛks'kwɪzɪt] *adj* exquisit, vorzüglich

ex-service·man [,ɛks'sʌrvɪs ,mæn] *s* (**-men'**) ehemaliger Soldat *m*

extant ['ɛkstənt] *adj* noch bestehend

extemporaneous [ɛks ,tɛmpə'renɪ·əs] *adj* aus dem Stegreif, unvorbereitet

extempore [ɛks'tɛmpəri] *adj* unvorbereitet || *adv* aus dem Stegreif

extemporize [ɛks'tɛmpə ,raɪz] *tr & intr* extemporieren

extend [ɛks'tɛnd] *tr* (*expand*) ausdehnen; (*a line*) fortführen; (*time*) verlängern; (*congratulations, invitation*) aussprechen; (*one's hand*) ausstrecken; (*a building*) ausbauen || *intr* (**to**) sich erstrecken (bis); **e. beyond** hinausgehen über (*acc*)

extension [ɛks'tɛn/ən] *s* Ausdehnung *f*; (*of time, credit*) Verlängerung *f*; (*archit*) Anbau *m*; (*telp*) Nebenanschluß *m*

exten'sion cord' *s* Verlängerungsschnur *f*

exten'sion lad'der *s* Ausziehleiter *f*

exten'sion ta'ble *s* Ausziehtisch *m*

extensive [ɛks'tɛnsɪv] *adj* umfassend

extent [ɛks'tɛnt] *s* Umfang *m*, Ausmaß *n*; **to some e.** eingermaßen; **to the full e.** in vollem Umfang; **to what e.** inwiefern

extenuating [ɛks'tɛnju ,etɪŋ] *adj* mildernd

exterior [ɛks'tɪrɪ·ər] *adj* Außen-, äußere || *s* Äußere *n*

exterminate [ɛks'tʌrmɪ ,net] *tr* vertilgen, ausrotten

extermination [ɛks ,tʌrmɪ'ne/ən] *s* Vertilgung *f*; (*of vermin*) Rautentwesung *f*

exterminator [ɛks'tʌrmɪ ,netər] *s* Rautentweser *m*

external [ɛks'tʌrnəl] *adj* Außen-, äußerlich || **externals** *spl* Äußerlichkeiten *pl*

extinct [ɛks'tɪŋkt] *adj* (*volcano*) erloschen; (*animal*) ausgestorben; **become e.** aussterben

extinguish [ɛks'tɪŋgwɪ/] *tr* auslöschen; **be extinguished** erlöschen

extinguisher [ɛks'tɪŋgwɪ/ər] *s* Löschgerät *n*

extirpate ['ɛkstər ,pet] *tr* ausrotten

ex·tol [ɛks'tol] *v* (*pret & pp* **-tolled**, *ger* **-tolling**) *tr* erheben, lobpreisen

extort [ɛks'tort] *tr* erpressen

extortion [ɛks'tor/ən] *s* Erpressung *f*

extortionate [ɛks'tor/ənɪt] *adj* überhöht

extra ['ɛkstrə] *adj* übrig; (*special*) Sonder-, Extra-; **meals are e.** Mahlzeiten werden zusätzlich berechnet || *adv* extra, besonders || *s* (cin) Statist –in *mf*; (journ) Sonderausgabe *f*; (theat) Komparse *m*; **extras** (*expenses*) Nebenausgaben *pl*; (*accessories*) Zubehör *n*

extract ['ɛkstrækt] *s* Extrakt *m*, Auszug *m*; (*excerpt*) Ausschnitt *m* || [ɛks'trækt] *tr* extrahieren, ausziehen; (dent, math) ziehen

extraction [ɛks'træk/ən] *s* (*lineage*) Abstammung *f*; (dent) Zahnziehen *n*; (min) Gewinnung *f*

extracurricular [,ɛkstrəkə'rɪkjələr] *adj* außerplanmäßig

extradite ['ɛkstrə ,daɪt] *tr* ausliefern

extradition [,ɛkstrə'dɪ/ən] *s* Auslieferung *f*

ex'tra in'come *s* Nebeneinkünfte *pl*

ex'tramar'ital *adj* außerehelich

extramural [,ɛkstrə'mjurəl] *adj* außerhalb der Schule stattfindend

extraneous [ɛks'trenɪ·əs] *adj* unwesentlich

extraordinary [,ɛks'trɔrdɪ ,nerɪ] *adj* außerordentlich

ex'tra pay' *s* Zulage *f*

extrapolate [ɛks'træpə ,let] *tr & intr* extrapolieren

extrasensory [,ɛkstrə'sɛnsəri] *adj* übersinnlich

extravagance [ɛks'trævəgəns] *s* Verschwendung *f*

extravagant [ɛks'trævəgənt] *adj* verschwenderisch, extravagant; (*idea, plan*) überspannt

extreme [ɛks'trim] *adj* äußerst; (*radical*) extrem; (*old age*) höchst; (*necessity*) dringend || *s* Äußerste *n*; **at the other e.** am entgegengesetzten Ende; **carry to extremes** auf die Spitze treiben; **in the e.** äußerst

extremely [ɛks'trimli] *adv* äußerst

extreme' unc'tion *s* die Letzte Ölung

extremist [ɛks'trimɪst] *s* Extremist –in *mf*

extremity [ɛks'trɛmɪti] *s* Äußerste *n*, äußerstes Ende *n*; **be reduced to extremities** aus dem letzten Loch pfeifen; **extremities** (*hands and feet*) Extremitäten *pl*

extricate ['ɛkstrɪ ,ket] *tr* befreien

extrinsic [ɛks'trɪnsɪk] *adj* äußerlich

extrovert ['ɛkstrə ,vʌrt] *s* Extravertierte *mf*

extrude [ɛks'trud] *tr* ausstoßen

exuberant [ɛg'z(j)ubərənt] *adj* (*luxuriant*) üppig; (*lavish*) überschwenglich

exude [ɛg'zud] *tr* ausschwitzen; (fig) ausstrahlen

exult [ɛg'zʌlt] *intr* jauchzen

exultant [ɛg'zʌltənt] *adj* jauchzend

eye [aɪ] *s* Auge *n*; (*of a needle*) Öhr *n*; **an eye for an eye** ein Auge um Auge; **be all eyes** große Augen machen; **by eye** nach dem Augenmaß; **close one's eyes to** die Augen schließen vor (*dat*); **have an eye for** Sinn haben für; **have good eyes** gut sehen; **in my eyes** nach meiner Ansicht; **in the eyes of the law** vom Standpunkt des Gesetzes aus; **keep a close eye on s.o.** j–m auf die Finger sehen; **keep an eye on s.th.** ein wachsames Auge auf etw [*acc*] haben; **keep one's eyes peeled** scharf aufpassen; **lay eyes on** zu Gesicht bekommen; **makes eyes at** verliebte Blicke zuwerfen (*dat*); **see eye to eye with** völlig übereinstimmen mit; **with an eye to** mit Rücksicht auf (*acc*) || *v* (*pret* & *pp* **eyed**; *ger* **eying** & **eyeing**) *tr* mustern, schielen nach

eye′ball′ *s* Augapfel *m*

eye′brow′ *s* Augenbraue *f*

eye′brow pen′cil *s* Augenbrauenstift *m*

eye′ cat′cher *s* Blickfang *m*

eye′cup′ *s* Augenspülglas *n*

eye′ drops′ *spl* Augentropfen *pl*

eyeful [ˈaɪful] *s*—**get an e.** etw Hübsches sehen

eye′glass′ *s* Augenglas *n*; **eyeglasses** Brille *f*

eye′lash′ *s* Wimper *f*

eyelet [ˈaɪlɪt] *s* Öse *f*

eye′lid′ *s* Lid *n*, Augenlid *n*

eye′o′pener *s* (*surprise*) Überraschung *f*; (*liquor*) Schnäpschen *n*

eye′piece′ *s* Okular *n*

eye′shade′ *s* Augenschirm *m*

eye′shad′ow *s* Lidschatten *m*

eye′shot′ *s*—**within e.** in Sehweite

eye′sight′ *s* Augenlicht *n*, Sehkraft *f*; (*range*) Sehweite *f*; **have bad (or good) e.** schlechte (or gute) Augen haben

eye′ sock′et *s* Augenhöhle *f*

eye′sore′ *s* (fig) Dorn *m* im Auge

eye′strain′ *s* Überanstrengung *f* der Augen

eye′tooth′ *s* (**–teeth**) Augenzahn *m*; **cut one's eyeteeth** (fig) erfahrener werden

eye′wash′ *s* Augenwasser *n*; (sl) Schwindel *m*

eye′wit′ness *s* Augenzeuge *m*, Augenzeugin *f*

F

F, f [ef] *s* sechster Buchstabe des englischen Alphabets; (mus) F *n*; **F flat** Fes *n*; **F sharp** Fis *n*

fable [ˈfebəl] *s* Fabel *f*, Märchen *n*

fabric [ˈfæbrɪk] *s* Gewebe *n*; (*cloth*) Stoff *m*; (fig) Gefüge *n*

fabricate [ˈfæbrɪˌket] *tr* herstellen; (*lies*) erfinden

fabrication [ˌfæbrɪˈkeʃən] *s* Herstellung *f*; (fig) Erfindung *f*

fabulous [ˈfæbjələs] *adj* fabelhaft

façade [fəˈsad] *s* Fassade *f*

face [fes] *s* Gesicht *n*; (*dial*) Zifferblatt *n*; (tex) rechte Seite *f*; (typ) Satzspiegel *m*; **f. to f. with** Auge in Auge mit; **in the f. of** angesichts (*genit*); **lose f.** sich blamieren; **make faces at s.o.** j–m Gesichter schneiden; **on the f. of it** augenscheinlich; **save f.** das Gesicht wahren; **show one's f.** sich blicken lassen || *tr* (& fig) ins Auge sehen (*dat*); (*said of a building*) liegen nach; (*e.g., with brick*) verkleiden; **be faced with** stehen vor (*dat*); **facing** gegenüber (*dat*); **have to f. the music** die Suppe löffeln müssen || *intr* (*in some direction*) liegen; **about f.!** (mil) kehrt!; **he faced up to it like a man** er stellte seinen Mann

face′ card′ *s* Bildkarte *f*, Figur *f*

face′ cream′ *s* Gesichtskrem *f*

face′ lift′ing *s* Gesichtsstraffung *f*; (*of a building*) Schönheitsreparatur *f*

face′ pow′der *s* Gesichtspuder *m*

facet [ˈfæsɪt] *s* Facette *f*; (fig) Aspekt *m*

facetious [fəˈsiʃəs] *adj* scherzhaft

face′ val′ue *s* Nennwert *m*; **take at f.** (fig) für bare Münze nehmen

facial [ˈfeʃəl] *adj* Gesichts–; **f. expression** Miene *f* || *s* Gesichtspflege *f*

facilitate [fəˈsɪlɪˌtet] *tr* erleichtern

facility [fəˈsɪlɪti] *s* (*ease*) Leichtigkeit

f; (*skill*) Geschicklichkeit *f*; **facilities** Einrichtungen *pl*

fac′ing *s* (archit) Verkleidung *f*; (sew) Besatz *m*

facsimile [fækˈsɪmɪli] *s* Faksimile *n*

fact [fækt] *s* Tatsache *f*; **apart from the f. that** abgesehen davon, daß; **facts of the case** Tatbestand *m*; **in f.** tatsächlich; **it is a f. that es** steht fest, daß

fact′-find′ing *adj* Untersuchungs–

faction [ˈfækʃən] *s* Clique *f*

factional [ˈfækʃənəl] *adj* klüngelhaft

factor [ˈfæktər] *s* (& math) Faktor *m*

factory [ˈfæktəri] *s* Fabrik *f*

factual [ˈfæktʃʊ–əl] *adj* sachlich

faculty [ˈfækəlti] *s* Vermögen *n*; (educ) Lehrkörper *m*

fad [fæd] *s* Mode *f*; **latest fad** letzter Schrei *m*

fade [fed] *tr* verblassen lassen; **f. in** einblenden; **f. out** ausblenden || *intr* (*said of colors, memories*) verblassen; (*said of cloth, wallpaper, etc.*) verschießen; (*said of flowers*) verwelken; **f. away** (*said of sounds*) abklingen; **f. in** (cin, rad, telv) einblenden; **f. out** (cin, rad, telv) ausblenden

fade′-in′ *s* (cin, rad, telv) Einblenden *n*

fade′-out′ *s* (cin, rad, telv) Ausblenden *n*

fag [fæg] *s* (*cigarette*) (sl) Glimmstengel *m*; (*homosexual*) (sl) Schwuler *m* || *v* (*pret* & *pp* **fagged**; *ger* **fagging**) *tr*—**fag out** (sl) auspumpen

fagged *adj* (sl) erschöpft

fagot [ˈfægət] *s* Reisigbündel *n*

fail [fel] *s*—**without f.** ganz bestimmt || *tr* (*an examination*) durchfallen bei; (*a student*) durchfallen lassen; (*friends*) im Stich lassen; (*a father*) enttäuschen; **failing this** widrigenfalls; **I f. to see** ich kann nicht einsehen; **words f. me** mir fehlen die

Worte ‖ *intr* (*said of a person or device*) versagen; (*said of a project, attempt*) fehlschlagen; (*said of crops*) schlecht ausfallen; (*said of strength*) abnehmen; (*said of health*) sich verschlechtern; (com) in Konkurs geraten

failure [ˈfeljər] *s* Versagen *n;* (*person*) Versager –*m;* (*lack of success, unsuccessful venture*) Mißerfolg *m;* (*omission*) Versäumnis *n;* (*deterioration*) Schwäche *f;* (educ) ungenügende Zensur *f;* (com) Konkurs *m*

faint [fent] *adj* schwach; (*slight*) leise; **feel f.** sich schwach fühlen ‖ *s* Ohnmacht *f* ‖ *intr* ohnmächtig werden

faint'-heart'ed *adj* kleinmütig

faint'ing spell' *s* Ohnmachtsanfall *m*

fair [fer] *adj* (*just*) gerecht, fair; (*blond*) blond; (*complexion*) hell; (*weather*) heiter; (*chance, knowledge*) mittelmäßig; (*warning*) rechtzeitig; **f. to middling** gut bis mäßig ‖ *s* Jahrmarkt *m*, Messe *f*

fair' game' *s* (& fig) Freiwild *n*

fair'ground' *s* Jahrmarktplatz *m*

fairly [ˈferli] *adv* ziemlich

fair'-mind'ed *adj* unparteiisch

fairness [ˈfernɪs] *s* Gerechtigkeit *f;* **in f. to s.o.** um j–m Gerechtigkeit widerfahren zu lassen

fair' play' *s* fair Play *n*

fair' sex', the *s* das schöne Geschlecht

fair'way' *s* (golf) Spielbahn *f;* (naut) Fahrwasser *n*

fair'-weath'er *adj* (*friend*) unzuverlässig

fairy [ˈferi] *adj* Feen– ‖ *s* Fee *f;* (sl) Schwule *mf*

fair'y god'mother *s* gute Fee *f*

fair'yland' *s* Märchenland *n*

fair'ytale' *s* (& fig) Märchen *n*

faith [feθ] *s* Glaube(n) *m;* (in) Vertrauen *n* (auf *acc* or zu); **on the f.** of im Vertrauen auf (*acc*); **put one's f. in** Glauben schenken (*dat*)

faithful [ˈfeθfəl] *adj* (**to**) (ge)treu (*dat*); (*exact*) genau, wahrheitsgemäß ‖ **the f.** *spl* die Gläubigen

faith' heal'er *s* Gesundbeter –in *mf*

faithless [ˈfeθlɪs] *adj* treulos

fake [fek] *adj* verfälscht ‖ *s* Fälschung *f;* (*person*) Simulant –in *mf* ‖ *tr* vortäuschen, simulieren; (*forge*) fälschen

faker [ˈfekər] *s* Simulant –in *mf*

falcon [ˈfɔ(l)kən] *s* Falke *m*

falconer [ˈfɔ(l)kənər] *s* Falkner *m*

fall [fɔl] *adj* Herbst– ‖ *s* Fall *m;* (*of prices, of a government*) Sturz *m;* (*moral*) Verfall *m;* (*of water*) Fall *m;* (*autumn*) Herbst *m;* (Bib) Sündenfall *m;* ‖ *v* (*pret* **fell** [fel]; *pp* **fallen** [ˈfɔlən] *intr* (*said of a person, object, rain, snow, holiday, prices, temperature*) fallen; (*said of a town*) gestürzt werden; **f. apart** auseinanderfallen; **f. away** wegfallen; **f. back** zurückfallen; (mil) sich zurückziehen; **f. back on** zurückgreifen auf (*acc*); **f. behind** (**in**) zurückbleiben (mit); **f. below** unterschreiten; **f. down** umfallen; (*said only of per-*

sons) hinfallen; **f. down on the job** versagen; **f. due** fällig werden; **f. flat** (coll) flachfallen; **f. for** reinfallen auf (*acc*); **f. from** abfallen von; **f.. from grace** in Ungnade fallen; **f. in** (*said of a roof*) einstürzen; (mil) antreten; **f. in love with** sich verlieben in (*acc*); **f. in step** Tritt fassen; **f. into** (*e.g., a hole*) hereinfallen in (*acc*); (*e.g., trouble*) geraten in (*acc*); **f. into ruin** zerfallen; **f. in with s.o.** j–n zufällig treffen; **f. off** abfallen; (com) zurückgehen; **f. out** (*said of hair*) ausfallen; **f. out with** sich verfeinden mit; **f. over** umfallen; **f. short** knapp werden; (arti) kurz gehen; **f. short of** zurückbleiben hinter (*dat*); **f. through** durchfallen; **f. to s.o.'s share** j–m zufallen; **f. under s.o.'s influence** unter j–s Einfluß geraten; **f. upon** herfallen über (*acc*)

fallacious [fəˈleʃəs] *adj* trügerisch

fallacy [ˈfæləsi] *s* Trugschluß *m*, Fehlschluß *m*

fall' guy' *s* (sl) Sündenbock *m*

fallible [ˈfælɪbəl] *adj* fehlbar

fall'ing off' *s* Rückschritt *m*

fall'ing rocks' *spl* (public sign) Steinschlag *m*

fall'ing star' *s* Sternschnuppe *f*

fall'out' *s* radioaktiver Niederschlag *m*

fallow [ˈfælo] *adj* (agr) brach; **lie f.** (& fig) brachliegen

false [fɔls] *adj* falsch, Miß–; (*start, step*) Fehl–; (*bottom*) doppelt; (*ceiling*) Zwischen–

false' alarm' *s* blinder Alarm *m;* (fig) Schreckschuß *m*

false' face' *s* Maske *f*

false' front' *s* (fig) (coll) Mache *f*

false'-heart'ed *adj* treulos

false'hood' *s* Unwahrheit *f*

false' pretens'es *spl* Hochstapelei *f*

false' teeth' *spl* (künstliches) Gebiß *n*

falset·to [fɔlˈseto] *s* (–tos) Falset *n*

falsi·fy [ˈfɔlsɪˌfaɪ] *v* (*pret* & *pp* –**fied**) *tr* (ver)fälschen

falsity [ˈfɔlsɪti] *s* Falschheit *f*

falter [ˈfɔltər] *intr* schwanken; (*in speech*) stocken

fame [fem] *s* Ruf, *m*, Ruhm *m*

famed *adj* (**for**) berühmt (wegen, durch)

familiar [fəˈmɪljər] *adj* bekannt; (*expression*) geläufig; (*e.g., sight*) gewohnt; (*close*) vertraut; **become f. with** sich bekannt machen mit

familiarity [fəˌmɪliˈærɪti] *s* Vertrautheit *f;* (*closeness*) Vertraulichkeit *f*

familiarize [fəˈmɪljəˌraɪz] *tr* bekannt machen

family [ˈfæm(ɪ)li] *adj* Familien–; **in a f. way** in anderen Umständen ‖ *s* Familie *f*

fam'ily doc'tor *s* Hausarzt *m*

fam'ily man' *s* häuslicher Mann *m*

fam'ily name' *s* Familienname *m*

fam'ily tree' *s* Stammbaum *m*

famine [ˈfæmɪn] *s* Hungersnot *f*

famish [ˈfæmɪʃ] *tr* (ver)hungern lassen ‖ *intr* verhungern

fam'ished *adj* ausgehungert

famous [ˈfeməs] *adj* **(for)** berühmt (wegen, durch)

fan [fæn] *s* Fächer *m*, Wedel *m*; *(electric)* Ventilator *m*; (sl) Fan *m* ‖ *v* (*pret & pp* **fanned**; *ger* **fanning**) *tr* fächeln; *(a fire)* anfachen; *(passions)* entfachen ‖ *intr*—**fan out** *(said of roads)* fächerförmig auseinandergehen; (mil) ausschwärmen

fanatic [fəˈnætɪk] *adj* fanatisch ‖ *s* Fanatiker –in *mf*

fanatical [fəˈnætɪkəl] *adj* fanatisch

fanaticism [fəˈnætɪˌsɪzəm] *s* Fanatismus *m*

fan' belt' *s* (aut) Keilriemen *m*

fan'cied *adj* eingebildet

fancier [ˈfænsɪ-ər] *s* Liebhaber –in *mf*

fanciful [ˈfænsɪfəl] *adj* phantastisch

fan-cy [ˈfænsɪ] *adj* (extra)fein; (*e.g., dress*) Luxus–; (sport) Kunst–; **f. price** Phantasiepreis *m* ‖ *s* Phantasie *f*; passing **f.** vorübergehender Spleen *m*; **take a f.** to Gefallen finden an (*dat*) ‖ *v* (*pret & pp* **–cied**) *tr* sich [*dat*] vorstellen

fan'cy foods' *spl* Feinkost *f*

fan'cy-free' *adj* ungebunden

fan'fare' *s* Fanfare *f*; *(fuss)* Tamtam *n*

fang [fæŋ] *s* Fangzahn *m*; *(of a snake)* Giftzahn *m*

fan' mail' *s* Verehrerbriefe *pl*

fantastic(al) [fænˈtæstɪk(əl)] *adj* phantastisch, toll

fantasy [ˈfæntəsɪ] *s* Phantasie *f*

far [fɑr] *adj* (& fig) weit; **at the far end** am anderen Ende; **far cry from** etw ganz anderes als; **far side** andere Seite *f*; **in the far future** in der fernen Zukunft ‖ *adv* weit; **as far as** soweit; (*up to*) bis zu, bis an (*acc*); **as far as I am concerned** was mich anbelangt; **as far as I know** soviel ich weiß; **as far as that goes** was das betrifft; **by far** weitaus, bei weitem; **far and away** weitaus; **far away** weit entfernt; **far below** tief unten; **far better** weit besser; **far from it!** weit gefehlt!; **far from ready** noch lange nicht fertig; **far into the night** tief in die Nacht hinein; **far out** (sl) ausgefallen; **from far** von weitem; (*from a distant place*) von weit her; **go far** es weit bringen; **go far towards** (*ger*) viel beitragen zu (*inf*); **go too far** das Maß überschreiten; **not far from** unweit von; **so far** soweit, bisher

far'away' *adj* weit entfernt; (fig) träumerisch

farce [fɑrs] *s* Possenspiel *n*, Farce *f*; (fig) Posse *f*, Schwank *m*

farcical [ˈfɑrsɪkəl] *adj* possenhaft

fare [fer] *s* (*travel price*) Fahrpreis *m*; (*money for travel*) Fahrgeld *n*; (*passenger*) Fahrgast *m*; (*food*) Kost *f* ‖ *intr* (er)gehen; **how did you f., well or ill?** wie ist es Ihnen ergangen, gut oder schlecht?

Far' East', **the** *s* der Ferne Osten

Far' East'ern *adj* fernöstlich

fare'well' *s* Valet *n*, Lebewohl *n*; **bid s.o. f.** j–m Lebewohl sagen ‖ *interj* lebe wohl!; lebt wohl!

farewell' din'ner *s* Abschiedsschmaus *m*

farewell' par'ty *s* Abschiedsfeier *f*

far-fetched [ˈfɑrˈfetʃt] *adj* gesucht

far-flung [ˈfɑrˈflʌŋ] *adj* weit ausgedehnt

farina [fəˈrinə] *s* Grießmehl *n*

farm [fɑrm] *adj* landwirtschaftlich ‖ *s* Farm *f*, Bauernhof *m* ‖ *tr* bebauen, bewirtschaften ‖ *intr* Landwirtschaft betreiben, Bauer sein

farm' hand' *s* Landarbeiter *m*

farm'house' *s* Bauernhaus *n*

farm'ing *adj* landwirtschaftlich ‖ *s* Landwirtschaft *f*

farm'land' *s* Ackerland *n*

farm' machin'ery *s* Landmaschinen *pl*

farm'yard' *s* Bauernhof *m*

far'-off' *adj* fernliegend

far'-reach'ing *adj* weitreichend; (*decision*) folgenschwer

far'sight'ed *adj* weitsichtig; (fig) weitblickend

farther [ˈfɑrðər] *adj & adv* weiter

farthest [ˈfɑrðɪst] *adj* weiteste ‖ *adv* am weitesten

farthing [ˈfɑrðɪŋ] *s*—**not worth a f.** keinen Pfifferling wert

fascinate [ˈfæsɪˌnet] *tr* faszinieren

fas'cinating *adj* faszinierend

fascination [ˌfæsɪˈneʃən] *s* Faszination *f*

fascism [ˈfæʃɪzəm] *s* Faschismus *m*

fascist [ˈfæʃɪst] *s* Faschist –in *mf*

fashion [ˈfæʃən] *s* Mode *f*; (*manner*) Art *f*, Weise *f*; **after a f.** in gewisser Weise; **in f.** in Mode; **out of f.** aus der Mode ‖ *tr* gestalten, bilden

fashionable [ˈfæʃənəbəl] *adj* (*modern*) modisch; (*elegant*) elegant

fash'ion magazine' *s* Modenzeitschrift *f*

fash'ion plate' *s* Modedame *f*

fash'ion show' *s* Mode(n)schau *f*

fast [fæst] *adj* schnell; (*dye*) dauerhaft; (*company*) flott; (*life*) locker; (phot) lichtstark; **be f.** (*said of a clock*) vorgehen; **f. train** Schnellzug *m*; **pull a f. one on s.o.** (coll) j–m ein Schnippchen schlagen ‖ *adv* schnell; (*firmly*) fest; **as f. as possible** schnellstens; **be f. asleep** im tiefen Schlaf liegen; **hold f.** festhalten; **not so f.!** nicht so stürmisch! ‖ *s* Fasten *n* ‖ *intr* fasten

fast' day' *s* Fasttag *m*

fasten [ˈfæsən] *tr* festmachen, sichern; (*a buckle*) schnallen; (*to*) befestigen (an *dat*); **f. one's seat belt** sich anschnallen; **f. the blame on** die Schuld zuschieben (*dat*) ‖ *intr*—**f. upon** sich heften an (*acc*)

fastener [ˈfæsənər] *s* Verschluß *m*

fastidious [fæsˈtɪdɪ-əs] *adj* wählerisch

fast'ing *s* Fasten *n*

fat [fæt] *adj* (**fatter**; **fattest**) fett; (*plump*) dick, fett; (*profits*) reich ‖ *s* Fett *n*; **chew the fat** (sl) schwatzen

fatal [ˈfetəl] *adj* tödlich; (*mistake*) verhängnisvoll; **f. to** verhängnisvoll für

fatalism [ˈfetəˌlɪzəm] *s* Fatalismus *m*

fatalist [ˈfetəlɪst] *s* Fatalist –in *mf*

fatality [fə'tælɪti] s Todesfall m; (accident victim) Todesopfer n; (disaster) Unglück n

fat' cat' s (sl) Geldgeber –in mf

fate [fet] s Schicksal n, Verhängnis n; **the Fates** die Parzen pl

fated ['fetɪd] adj vom Schicksal bestimmt

fateful ['fetfəl] adj verhängnisvoll

fat'head' s (coll) dummes Luder n

father ['faðər] s Vater m; (eccl) Pater m ‖ tr (beget) erzeugen; (originate) hervorbringen

fa'therhood' s Vaterschaft f

fa'ther-in-law' s (fathers-in-law) Schwiegervater m

fa'therland' s Vaterland n

fatherless ['faðərlɪs] adj vaterlos

fatherly ['faðərli] adj väterlich

Fa'ther's Day' s Vatertag m

fathom ['fæðəm] s Klafter f ‖ tr sondieren; (fig) ergründen

fathomless ['fæðəmlɪs] adj unergründlich

fatigue [fə'tig] s Ermattung f; (mil) Arbeitsdienst m; **fatigues** (mil) Arbeitsanzug m ‖ tr abmatten

fat·so ['fætso] s (-sos & -soes) (coll) Fettkloß m

fatten ['fætən] tr mästen ‖ intr—f. up (coll) sich mästen

fatty ['fæti] adj fettig, fett; **f. tissue** Fettgewebe n ‖ s (coll) Dicke mf

fatuous ['fætʃu·əs] adj albern

faucet ['fɔsɪt] s Wasserhahn m

fault [fɔlt] s (blame) Schuld f; (misdeed) Vergehen n, Fehler m; (defect) Defekt m; (geol) Verwerfung f; (tennis) Fehlball m; **at f.** schuld; **find f. with** etw zu tadeln finden an (dat); **to a f.** allzusehr ‖ intr (geol) sich verwerfen

fault'find'er s Krittler –in mf

fault'find'ing adj tadelsüchtig ‖ s Krittelei f

faultless ['fɔltlɪs] adj fehlerfrei

faulty ['fɔlti] adj fehlerhaft

faun [fɔn] s (myth) Faun m

fauna ['fɔnə] s Fauna f

favor ['fevər] s (kind act) Gefallen m; (good will) Gunst f; **in f. of** zugunsten (genit), für; **in s.o.'s f.** zu j–s Gunsten; **lose f. with s.o.** sich [dat] j–s Gunst verwirken; **speak in f. of s.th.** für etw aussprechen ‖ tr begünstigen; (prefer) bevorzugen; (a sore limb) schonen

favorable ['fevərəbəl] adj günstig; (criticism) positiv; (report) beifällig

favorite ['fevərɪt] adj Lieblings– ‖ s Liebling m; (sport) Favorit –in mf

favoritism ['fevərɪ‚tɪzəm] s Günstlingswirtschaft f

fawn [fɔn] s Rehkalb n ‖ intr—f. on schmeicheln (dat)

fawn'ing adj schmeichlerisch

faze [fez] tr (coll) auf die Palme bringen

FBI [‚ɛf‚bi'aɪ] s (**Federal Bureau of Investigation**) Bundessicherheitspolizei f

fear [fɪr] s (of) Furcht f (vor dat), Angst f (vor dat); **for f. of** aus Angst vor (dat); **for f. of** (ger) um nicht zu (inf); **stand in f. of** sich fürchten vor (dat) ‖ tr fürchten, sich fürchten vor (dat); **f. the worst** das Schlimmste befürchten ‖ intr sich fürchten; **f. for** besorgt sein um

fearful ['fɪrfəl] adj (afraid) furchtsam; (terrible) furchtbar

fearless ['fɪrlɪs] adj furchtlos

feasible ['fizɪbəl] adj durchführbar

feast [fist] s Fest n; (sumptuous meal) Schmaus m ‖ tr—f. one's eyes on seine Augen weiden an (dat) ‖ intr schwelgen; **f. on** sich gütlich tun an (dat)

feast'day' s Festtag m

feast'ing s Schmauserei f

feat [fit] s Kunststück n; **f. of arms** Waffentat f

feather ['fɛðər] s Feder f; **a f. in his cap** ein Triumph für ihn ‖ tr mit Federn versehen; (aer) auf Segelstellung fahren; (crew) flach drehen; **f. one's nest** sich warm betten

feath'er bed' s Federbett n

feath'erbed'ding s Anstellung f unnötiger Arbeitskräfte

feath'erbrain' s Schwachkopf m

feath'er dust'er s Staubwedel m

feath'eredge' s feine Kante f

feath'erweight' adj Federgewichts– ‖ s (boxer) Federgewichtler m

feathery ['fɛðəri] adj federartig; (light as feathers) federleicht

feature ['fitʃər] s (of the face) Gesichtszug m; (characteristic) Merkmal n; **f. film** Spielfilm m; **main f.** Grundzug m; (cin) Hauptfilm m ‖ tr als Hauptschlager herausbringen; (cin) in der Hauptrolle zeigen

fea'ture writ'er s Sonderberichterstatter –in mf

February ['febru‚eri] s Februar m

feces ['fisiz] spl Kot m, Stuhl m

feckless ['fɛklɪs] adj (incompetent) unfähig; (ineffective) unwirksam; (without spirit) geistlos

fecund ['fikənd] adj fruchtbar

federal ['fedərəl] adj Bundes–, bundesstaatlich; **f. government** Bundesregierung f

federate ['fedə‚ret] adj verbündet ‖ tr zu e–m Bund vereinigen ‖ intr sich verbünden

federation [‚fedə'reʃən] s Staatenbund m

fed' up' [fed] adj—**be f.** die Nase voll haben; **be f. with s.th.** etw satt haben

fee [fi] s Gebühr f; (of a doctor) Honorar n

feeble ['fibəl] adj schwächlich

fee'ble-mind'ed adj schwachsinnig

feed [fid] s Futter n; (mach) Zuführung f ‖ v (pret & pp fed [fed]) tr (animals) füttern; (persons) zu Essen geben; (in a restaurant) verpflegen; (e.g., a nation) nähren; (a fire) unterhalten; (mach) zuführen ‖ intr fressen; **f. on** sich ernähren von

feed'back' s Rückwirkung f; (electron) Rückkoppelung f

feed' bag' s Futtersack m; **put on the f.** (sl) futtern

feeder ['fidər] *s* (elec) Speiseleitung *f*; (mach) Zubringer *m*

feed'er line' *s* (aer, rr) Zubringerlinie *f*

feed'ing *s* (*of animals*) Fütterung *f*; (& mach) Speisung *f*

feed' trough' *s* Futtertrog *m*

feed' wire' *s* (elec) Zuleitungsdraht *m*

feel [fil] *s* Gefühl *n*; get the f. of sich gewöhnen an (*acc*) || *v* (*pret & pp* **felt** [felt]) *tr* fühlen; (*a pain*) spüren; **f. one's way** sich vortasten; (fig) sondieren; **f. s.o. out** bei j–m vorfühlen || *intr* (*sick, tired, well*) sich fühlen; **f. about for** herumtasten nach; **f. for s.o.** mit j–m fühlen; **f. like** (*ger*) Lust haben zu (*inf*); **f. up to** sich gewachsen fühlen (*dat*); **his head feels hot** sein Kopf fühlt sich heiß an; **how do you f. about it?** was halten Sie davon?; **I don't quite f. myself** ich fühle mich nicht ganz wohl; **I f. as if** es ist mir, als wenn; **make itself felt** sich fühlbar machen

feeler ['filər] *s* (ent) Fühler *m*; **put out feelers to** vorfühlen bei

feel'ing [fen] *s* (ent) Gefühl *n*; bad f. Verstimmung *f*; **good f.** Wohlwollen *n*; **have a f. for** Sinn haben für; **have a f. that** das Gefühl haben, daß; **with f.** gefühlsvoll

feign [fen] *tr* vortäuschen; **f. death** sich totstellen

feint [fent] *s* (ent) Finte *f*, Scheinangriff *m*

feldspar ['feld ,spar] *s* Feldspat *m*

feline ['filaɪn] *adj* katzenartig

fell [fel] *adj* grausam || *tr* fällen

fellow ['felo] *s* (coll) Kerl *m*; (*of a society*) Mitglied *n*

fel'low be'ing *s* Mitmensch *m*

fel'low cit'izen *s* Mitbürger –in *mf*

fel'low coun'tryman *s* Landsmann *m*

fel'low crea'ture *s* Mitgeschöpf *n*

fel'lowman' *s* (–men') Mitmensch *m*

fel'low mem'ber *s* Mitglied *n*

fel'lowship' *s* Kameradschaft *f*; (educ) Stipendium *n*

fel'low stu'dent *s* Kommilitone *m*

fel'low trav'eler *s* Mitreisende *mf*; (pol) Mitläufer –in *mf*

felon ['felən] *s* Schwerverbrecher –in *mf*

felony ['feləni] *s* Schwerverbrechen *n*

felt [felt] *adj* Filz– || *s*

felt' pen' *s* Filzschreiber *m*, Faserstift *m*

female ['fimel] *adj* weiblich || *s* (*of animals*) Weibchen *n*; (pej) Weibsbild *n*

feminine ['femɪnɪn] *adj* weiblich

feminism ['femɪ ,nɪzəm] *s* Feminismus *m*

fen [fen] *s* Bruch *m* & *n*

fence [fens] *s* Zaun *m*; (*of stolen goods*) Hehler *m*; **on the f.** (fig) unentschlossen || *tr*—f. in einzäunen; **f. off** abzäunen || *intr* (sport) fechten

fence' post' *s* Zaunpfahl *m*

fenc'ing *s* Fechten *n*

fend [fend] *tr*—f. off abwehren || *intr* —f. for oneself für sich selbst sorgen

fender ['fendər] *s* (aut) Kotflügel *m*

fennel ['fenəl] *s* Fenchel *m*

ferment ['fʌrmɛnt] *s* Gärmittel *n*; (fig) Unruhe *f* || [fər'mɛnt] *tr* in Gärung bringen || *intr* gären

fermentation [,fʌrmən'teʃən] *s* Gärung *f*

fern [fʌrn] *s* Farn *m*

ferocious [fə'roʃəs] *adj* wild

ferocity [fə'rasɪti] *s* Wildheit *f*

ferret ['ferɪt] *s* Frettchen *n* || *tr*—f. out aufspüren

Fer'ris wheel' ['ferɪs] *s* Riesenrad *n*

ferrule ['ferul], ['ferəl] *s* Stockzwinge *f*, Zwinge *f*

fer·ry ['feri] *s* Fähre *f* || *v* (*pret & pp* **–ried**) *tr* übersetzen

fer'ryboat' *s* Fährboot *n*

fer'ry·man' *s* (–men') Fährmann *m*

fertile ['fʌrtɪl] *adj* fruchtbar

fertility [fər'tɪlɪti] *s* Fruchtbarkeit *f*

fertilization [,fʌrtɪlɪ'zeʃən] *s* Befruchtung *f*; (*of soil*) Düngung *f*

fertilize ['fʌrtɪ ,laɪz] *tr* (*a field*) düngen; (*an egg*) befruchten

fertilizer ['fʌrtɪ ,laɪzər] *s* Kunstdünger *m*

fervent ['fʌrvənt] *adj* inbrünstig

fervid ['fʌrvɪd] *adj* brennend

fervor ['fʌrvər] *s* Inbrunst *f*

fester ['festər] *intr* schwären, eitern; (fig) nagen

festival ['festɪvəl] *adj* festlich, Fest– || *s* Fest *n*; (mus, theat) Festspiele *pl*

festive ['festɪv] *adj* festlich

festivity [fes'tɪvɪti] *s* Feierlichkeit *f*

festoon [fes'tun] *s* Girlande *f* || *tr* mit Girlanden schmücken

fetch [fetʃ] *tr* holen, abholen

fetch'ing *adj* entzückend

fete [fet] *s* Fest *n*

fetid ['fetɪd], [fitɪd] *adj* stinkend

fetish ['fetɪʃ], ['fitɪʃ] *s* Fetisch *m*

fetlock ['fetlak] *s* Köte *f*; (*tuft of hair*) Kötenzopf *m*

fetter ['fetər] *s* Fessel *f* || *tr* fesseln

fettle ['fetəl] *s*—in fine f. in Form

fetus ['fitəs] *s* Leibesfrucht *f*

feud [fjud] *s* Fehde *f*

feudal ['fjudəl] *adj* feudal

feudalism ['fjudə ,lɪzəm] *s* Feudalismus *m*

fever ['fivər] *s* Fieber *n*

feverish ['fivərɪʃ] *adj* fieberig; **be f.** fiebern

few [fju] *adj* & *pron* wenige; **a few** ein paar

fiancé [,fi·an'se] *s* Verlobte *m*

fiancée [,fi·an'se] *s* Verlobte *f*

fias·co [fɪ'æsko] *s* (–cos & –coes) Fiasko *n*

fib [frb] *s* Flunkerei *f* || *v* (*pret & pp* **fibbed**; *ger* **fibbing**) *intr* flunkern

fibber ['fɪbər] *s* Flunkerer –in *mf*

fiber ['faɪbər] *s* Faser *f*

fibrous ['faɪbrəs] *adj* faserig

fickle ['fɪkəl] *adj* wankelmütig

fickleness ['fɪkəlnɪs] *s* Wankelmut *m*

fiction ['fɪkʃən] *s* Dichtung *f*, Romanliteratur *f*

fictional ['fɪkʃənəl] *adj* romanhaft

fic'tion writ'er *s* Romanschriftsteller –in *mf*

fictitious [fɪk'tɪʃəs] *adj* fingiert

fiddle ['fɪdəl] *s* Fiedel *f*, Geige *f* || *tr* fiedeln; **f. away** (*time*) vergeuden ||

intr fiedeln; **f. with** herumfingern an (*dat*)

fiddler ['fɪdlər] *s* Fiedler –in *mf*

fid'dlestick' *s* Fiedelbogen *m* ‖ **fiddlesticks** *interj* Quatsch!

fidelity [fɪ'delɪti] *s* Treue *f*

fidget ['fɪdʒɪt] *intr* zappeln; **f. with** nervös spielen mit

fidgety ['fɪdʒɪti] *adj* zappelig

fiduciary [fɪ'd(j)uʃɪ,erɪ] *adj* treuhänderisch; (*note*) ungedeckt ‖ *s* Treuhänder –in *mf*

fief [fif] *s* (hist) Lehen *n*

field [fild] *adj* (artillery, jacket, hospital, kitchen) Feld– ‖ *s* Feld *n*; (*under cultivation*) Acker *m*; (*contestants collectively*) Wettbewerbsteilnehmer *pl*; (*specialty*) Gebiet *n*; (aer) Flugplatz *m*; (elec) Feld *n*; (*of a motor*) (elec) Magnetfeld *n*; (sport) Spielfeld *n*

field' am'bulance *s* Sanitätskraftwagen *m*

field' day' *s* (fig) großer Tag *m*

fielder ['fildər] *s* Feldspieler *m*

field' ex'ercise *s* Truppenübung *f*

field' glass'es *spl* Feldstecher *m*

field' hock'ey *s* Rasenhockey *n*

field'mar'shal *s* Feldmarschall *m*

field' mouse' *s* Feldmaus *f*

field' of vi'sion *s* Blickfeld *n*

field' pack' *s* (mil) Tornister *m*

field' piece' *s* Feldgeschütz *n*

field' trip' *s* Studienfahrt *f*

field' work' *s* praktische Arbeit *f*

fiend [find] *s* (devil) Teufel *m*; (wicked person) Unhold *m*; (addict) Süchtige *mf*

fiendish ['findɪʃ] *adj* teuflisch

fierce [frrs] *adj* wild, wütend; (vehement) heftig; (menacing) drohend; (heat) glühend

fiery ['farrɪ], ['faɪ·ərɪ] *adj* feurig

fife [faɪf] *s* Querpfeife *f*

fifteen ['frf'tin] *adj* & *pron* fünfzehn ‖ *s* Fünfzehn *f*

fifteenth ['frf'tinθ] *adj* & *pron* fünfzehnte ‖ *s* (fraction) Fünfzehntel *n*; **the f.** (in dates or a series) der Fünfzehnte

fifth [fɪfθ] *adj* & *pron* fünfte ‖ *s* (fraction) Fünftel *n*; **the f.** (in dates or a series) der Fünfte

fifth' col'umn *s* (pol) Fünfte Kolonne *f*

fiftieth ['fɪftɪ·tθ] *adj* & *pron* fünfzigste ‖ *s* (fraction) Fünfzigstel *n*

fifty ['fɪftɪ] *adj* & *pron* fünfzig ‖ *s* Fünfzig *f*; **the fifties** die fünfziger Jahre

fif'ty-fif'ty *adv* halbpart; **go f. with s.o.** mit j–m halbpart machen

fig [fɪg] *s* Feige *f*; (fig) Pfifferling *m*

fight [faɪt] *s* Kampf *m*, Gefecht *n*; (quarrel) Streit *m*; (brawl) Rauferei *f*; (box) Boxkampf *m*; **pick a f.** Zank suchen ‖ *tr* bekämpfen; (a case) durchkämpfen; **f. back** (tears) niederkämpfen; **f. it out** ausfechten; **f. one's way out** sich durchkämpfen ‖ *intr* kämpfen; (quarrel) streiten; (brawl) raufen

fighter ['faɪtər] *adj* (aer) Jagd– ‖ *s* Kämpfer –in *mf*; (aer) Jäger *m*; (box) Boxkämpfer *m*

fight'er pi'lot *s* Jagdflieger *m*

fight'ing *s* Schlägerei *f*; (quarreling) Streiten *n*; (mil) Kampfhandlungen *pl*

fig' leaf' *s* Feigenblatt *n*

figment ['fɪgmənt] *s*—**f. of the imagination** Hirngespinst *n*

fig' tree' *s* Feigenbaum *m*

figurative ['fɪgjərətɪv] *adj* bildlich; (meaning) übertragen

figure ['fɪgjər] *s* Figur *f*; (personage) Persönlichkeit *f*; (number) Zahl *f*; **be good at figures** ein guter Rechner sein; **cut a fine** (or **poor**) **f.** e–e gute (or **schlechte**) Figur abgeben; **run into three figures** in die Hunderte gehen ‖ *tr* (coll) glauben, meinen; **f. out** ausknobeln ‖ *intr*—**f. large** e–e große Rolle spielen; **f. on** rechnen mit

fig'urehead' *s* Strohmann *m*; (naut) Bugfigur *f*; **a mere f.** e–e bloße Nummer

fig'ure of speech' *s* Redewendung *f*

fig'ure skat'ing *s* Kunstlauf *m*

figurine [,fɪgjə'rin] *s* Figurine *f*

filament ['fɪləmənt] *s* Faser *f*, Faden *m*; (elec) Glühfaden *m*

filbert ['fɪlbərt] *s* Haselnuß *f*

filch [fɪltʃ] *tr* mausen

file [faɪl] *s* (tool) Feile *f*; (record) Akte *f*; (cards) Kartei *f*; (row) Reihe *f*; **put on f.** zu den Akten legen ‖ *tr* (with a tool) feilen; (letters, etc.) ablegen, abheften; (a complaint) erheben; (a report) erstatten; (a claim) anmelden; (a petition) einreichen; **f. suit** e–n Prozeß anstrengen ‖ *intr*—**f. for** sich bewerben um; **f. out** im Gänsemarsch herausmarschieren; **f. past** vorbeidefilieren (an *dat*)

file' cab'inet *s* Aktenschrank *m*

file' card' *s* Karteikarte *f*

filial ['fɪlɪ·əl] *adj* kindlich

filibuster ['fɪlɪ,bʌstər] *s* Obstruktion *f* ‖ *intr* Obstruktion treiben

filigree ['fɪlɪ,gri] *s* Filigran *n*

fil'ing *s* Feilen *n*; (of records) Ablegen *n* von Akten; (of a claim) Anmeldung *f*; (of a complaint) Erhebung *f*; (of a petition) Einreichung *f*; **filings** Feilspäne *pl*

Filipi·no [,fɪlɪ'pino] *adj* filipinisch ‖ *s* (–nos) Filipino *m*

fill [fɪl] *s* (fullness) Fülle *f*; (land fill) Aufschüttung *f*; **eat one's f.** sich satt essen; **I have had my f. of it** ich habe es satt ‖ *tr* füllen; (an order) ausführen; (a pipe) stopfen; (a position) besetzen; (dent) plombieren, füllen; **f. full** vollfüllen; **f. in** (empty space) ausfüllen; (one's name) einsetzen; (a hole, grave) zuwerfen; **f. it up** (aut) volltanken; **f. up** auffüllen; (a tank) nachfüllen; (a bag) anfüllen; (a glass) vollschenken; **f. with smoke** verräuchern ‖ *intr* sich füllen; (said of sails) sich blähen; **f. in for** einspringen für; **f. out** rund werden; **f. up** sich füllen

filler ['fɪlər] *s* Füller *m*; (of a cigar)

Einlage *f;* (journ) Lückenbüßer *m;* (paint) Grundierfirnis *m*

fillet ['fɪlət] *s (headband)* Kopfbinde *f;* (archit) Leiste *f* || [fɪ'le] *s* (culin) Filet *n* || *tr* filetieren

fillet' of beef' *s* Rinderfilet *n*

fillet' of sole' *s* Seezungenfilet *n*

fill'ing *s* (culin, dent) Füllung *f*

fill'ing sta'tion *s* Tankstelle *f*

fillip ['fɪlɪp] *s* Schnippchen *n;* (*on the nose*) Nasenstüber *m*

filly ['fɪli] *s* Stutenfüllen *n*

film [fɪlm] *s (thin layer)* Schicht *f;* (cin, phot) Film *m;* **f. of grease** Fettschicht *f*

film' fes'tival *s* Filmfestspiele *pl*

film' li'brary *s* Filmarchiv *n*

film' speed' *s* Filmempfindlichkeit *f*

film' star' *s* Filmstar *m*

film'strip' *s* Bildstreifen *m*

filmy ['fɪlmi] *adj* trüb

filter ['fɪltər] *s* Filter *m;* (rad) Sieb *n* || *tr* filtern; (rad) sieben

fil'tering *s* Filtrierung *f*

fil'ter pa'per *s* Filterpapier *n*

fil'ter tip' *s* Filtermundstück *n;* (coll) Filterzigarette *f*

filth [fɪlθ] *s* Schmutz *m;* (fig) Unflätigkeit *f,* Zote *f*

filthy ['fɪlθi] *adj* schmutzig *(talk)* unflätig; *(lucre)* schnöd(e) || *adv*—**f. rich** (sl) klotzig reich

filtrate ['fɪltret] *s* Filtrat *n* || *tr & intr* filtrieren

filtration [fɪl'treʃən] *s* Filtrierung *f*

fin [fɪn] *s* Flosse *f;* (*of a shark or whale*) Finne *f;* (*of a bomb*) Steuerschwanz *m;* (aer) Flosse *f*

final ['faɪnəl] *adj* End-, Schluß-; *(definitive)* endgültig || *s* (educ) Abschlußprüfung *f;* **finals** (sport) Endrunde *f,* Endspiel *n*

finale [fɪ'nɑli] *s* Finale *n*

finalist ['faɪnəlɪst] *s* Finalist –in *mf*

finality [faɪ'nælɪti] *s* Endgültigkeit *f*

finally ['faɪnəli] *adv* schließlich

finance ['faɪnæns], [fɪ'næns] *s* Finanz *f;* **finances** Finanzwesen *n* || *tr* finanzieren

financial [fɪ'nænʃəl], [faɪ'nænʃəl] *adj* (*e.g., policy, situation, crisis, aid*) Finanz–; (*e.g., affairs, resources, embarrassment*) Geld–

financier [,fɪnən'sɪr], [,faɪnən'sɪr] *s* Finanzmann *m*

financ'ing, fi'nancing *s* Finanzierung *f*

finch [fɪntʃ] *s* Fink *s*

find [faɪnd] *s* Fund *m;* (archeol) Bodenfund *m* || *v (pret & pp* **found** [faʊnd]) *tr* finden; (math) bestimmen; **f. one's way** sich zurechtfinden; **f. one's way back** zurückfinden; **f. out** herausfinden; **f. s.o. guilty** j-n für schuldig erklären || *intr*—**f. out about s.th.** hinter etw [*acc*] kommen

finder ['faɪndər] *s* Finder –in *mf*

find'ing *s* Finden *n;* **findings** Tatbestand *m*

fine [faɪn] *adj* fein; *(excellent)* hervorragend; *(weather)* schön; **f.! gut!** || *s* Geldstrafe *f* || *tr* mit e-r Geldstrafe belegen

fine' arts' *spl* schöne Künste *pl*

fineness ['faɪnɪs] *s* Feinheit *f;* (*of a coin or metal*) Feingehalt *m*

fine' point' *s* Feinheit *f*

fine' print' *s* Kleindruck *m*

finery ['faɪnəri] *s* Putz *m,* Staat *m*

fine-spun ['faɪn,spʌn] *adj* feingesponnen

finesse [fɪ'nɛs] *s* Finesse *f;* (cards) Impaß *m* || *tr & intr* impassieren

fine-toothed ['faɪn,tuθt] *adj* feingezahnt; **go over with a f. comb** unter die Lupe nehmen

fine' touch' *s* Feinheit *f*

fine' tun'ing *s* Feineinstellung *f*

finger ['fɪŋgər] *s* Finger *m;* **have a f. in the pie** die Hand im Spiel haben; **keep your fingers crossed** halten Sie mir den Daumen; **not lift a f.** keinen Finger rühren; **put the f. on s.o.** (sl) j-n verpetzen; **snap one's fingers** mit den Fingern schnellen; **twist around one's little f.** um den kleinen Finger wickeln || *tr* befingern

fin'ger bowl' *s* Fingerschale *f*

fin'gering *s* (mus) Fingersatz *m*

fin'gernail' *s* Fingernagel *m*

fin'gernail pol'ish *s* Nagellack *m*

fin'gerprint' *s* Fingerabdruck *m* || *tr*—**f. s.o.** j-m die Fingerabdrücke abnehmen

fin'gertip' *s* Fingerspitze *f;* **have at one's fingertips** parat haben

finicky ['fɪnɪki] *adj* wählerisch

finish ['fɪnɪʃ] *s* Ende *n,* Abschluß *m;* *(polish)* Lack *m,* Politur *f;* **put a f. on** fertig bearbeiten || *tr* beenden; *(complete)* vollenden; *(put a finish on)* fertig bearbeiten; *(smooth)* glätten; *(polish)* polieren; *(ruin)* kaputt machen; **f. drinking** austrinken; **f. eating** aufessen; **f. off** *(supplies)* aufbrauchen; *(food)* aufessen; *(a drink)* austrinken; *(kill)* erledigen; **f. reading** *(a book)* auslesen

fin'ished *adj* beendet, fertig; **be all f.** fix und fertig sein

fin'ished pro'duct *s* Fertigprodukt *n*

fin'ishing coat' *s* Deckanstrich *m*

fin'ishing mill' *s* Nachwalzwerk *n*

fin'ishing school' *s* Mädchenpensionat *n*

fin'ishing touch'es *spl*—**put the f. to** die letzte Hand legen an *(acc)*

fin'ish line' *s* Ziel *n,* Ziellinie *f*

finite ['faɪnaɪt] *adj* endlich

fi'nite verb' *s* Verbum *n* finitum

fink [fɪŋk] *s (informer)* (sl) Verräter –in *mf;* *(strikebreaker)* (sl) Streikbrecher –in *mf*

Finland ['fɪnlənd] *s* Finnland *n*

Finn [fɪn] *s* Finne *m,* Finnin *f*

Finnish ['fɪnɪʃ] *adj* finnisch || *s (language)* Finnisch *n*

fir [fʌr] *s* Tanne *f*

fir' cone' *s* Tannenzapfen *m*

fire [faɪr] *s* Feuer *n;* *(conflagration)* Brand *m;* (mil) Feuer *n;* **come under f.** unter Beschuß geraten; **on f. in** Brand; **open f.** Feuer eröffnen; **set on f.** in Brand stecken || *tr* (*a gun, pistol, shot*) abfeuern; *(bricks, ceramics)* brennen; *(an oven)* befeuern; *(an employee)* entlassen; *(throw* *hard*) feuern; **f. questions at s.o.** j–n mit Fragen bombardieren; **f. up** (& fig) anfeuern ‖ *intr* feuern, schießen; **f. away!** schieß los!; **f. on** (mil) beschießen

fire′ alarm′ *s* Feuermeldung *f*; (*box*) Feuermelder *m*

fire′arm′ *s* Schußwaffe *f*

fire′ball′ *s* Feuerball *m*; (*hustler*) Draufgänger *m*

fire′bomb′ *s* Brandbombe *f* ‖ *tr* mit Brandbomben belegen

fire′brand′ *s* (fig) Aufwiegler –in *mf*

fire′break′ *s* Feuerschneise *f*

fire′ brigade′ *s* Feuerwehr *f*

fire′bug′ *m* (coll) Brandstifter –in *mf*

fire′ chief′ *s* Branddirektor *m*

fire′ com′pany *s* Feuerwehr *f*

fire′crack′er *s* Knallfrosch *m*

fire′damp′ *s* Schlagwetter *pl*

fire′ depart′ment *s* Feuerwehr *f*

fire′ drill′ *s* Feueralarmübung *f*; (*by a fire company*) Feuerwehrübung *f*

fire′ en′gine *s* Spritze *f*

fire′ escape′ *s* Feuerleiter *f*

fire′ extin′guisher *s* Feuerlöscher *m*

fire′fly′ *s* Glühwurm *m*

fire′ hose′ *s* Spritzenschlauch *m*

fire′house′ *s* Feuerwache *f*

fire′ hy′drant *s* Hydrant *m*

fire′ insur′ance *s* Brandversicherung *f*

fire′ i′rons *spl* Kamingeräte *pl*

fire′lane′ *s* Feuer(schutz)schneise *f*

fire′man *s* (**–men**) Feuerwehrmann *m*; (*stoker*) Heizer *m*

fire′place′ *s* Kamin *m*, Herd *m*

fire′plug′ *s* Hydrant *m*

fire′ pow′er *s* (mil) Feuerkraft *f*

fire′proof′ *adj* feuerfest ‖ *tr* feuerfest machen

fire′ sale′ *s* Ausverkauf *m* von feuerbeschädigten Waren

fire′ screen′ *s* Feuervorhang *m*

fire′side′ *s* Kamin *m*, Herd *m*

fire′trap′ *s* feuergefährdetes Gebäude *n*

fire′ wall′ *s* Brandmauer *f*

fire′wa′ter *s* (coll) Feuerwasser *n*

fire′wood′ *s* Brennholz *n*

fire′works′ *spl* Feuerwerk *n*

fir′ing *s* (*of a weapon*) Abfeuern *n*; (*of an employee*) Entlassung *f*

fir′ing line′ *s* Feuerlinie *f*

fir′ing range′ *s* Schießstand *m*

fir′ing squad′ *s* Erschießungskommando *n*; (*for ceremonies*) Ehrensalutkommando *n*; **put to the f.** an die Wand stellen

firm [fʌrm] *adj* fest ‖ *s* (com) Firma *f*

firmament ['fʌrməmənt] *s* Firmament *n*

firmness ['fʌrmnɪs] *s* Festigkeit *f*

first [fʌrst] *adj* erste; erste; **very f.** allererste ‖ *adv* erst, erstens; **f. of all** zunächst ‖ *s* (aut) erster Gang *m*; **at f.** zuerst; **f. come, f. served** wer zuerst kommt, mahlt zuerst; **f.** von vornherein; **the f.** (*in dates or in a series*) der Erste

first′ aid′ *s* Erste Hilfe *f*

first′-aid′ kit′ *s* Verbandpäckchen *n*

first′-aid′ sta′tion *s* Unfallstation *f*; (mil) Verbandsplatz *m*

first′-born′ *adj* erstgeboren

first′-class′ *adj* erstklassig ‖ *adv* erster Klasse

first′-class′ mail′ *s* Briefpost *f*

first′-class′ tic′ket *s* Fahrkarte *f* (or Flugkarte *f*) erster Klasse

first′ cous′in *s* leiblicher Vetter *m*, leibliche Cousine *f*

first′-degree′ *adj* ersten Grades

first′ draft′ *s* Konzept *n*

first′ fin′ger *s* Zeigefinger *m*

first′ floor′ *s* Parterre *n*, Erdgeschoß *n*

first′ fruits′ *spl* Erstlinge *pl*

first′ lieuten′ant *s* Oberleutnant *m*

firstly ['fʌrstli] *adv* erstens

first′ mate′ *s* Obersteuermann *m*

first′ name′ *s* Vorname *m*

first′ night′ *s* (theat) Erstaufführung *f*

first-nighter ['fʌrst'naɪtər] *s* (theat) Premierenbesucher –in *mf*

first′ offend′er *s* noch nicht Vorbestrafte *mf*

first′ of′ficer *s* erster Offizier *m*

first′ prize′ *s* Hauptgewinn *m*, Haupttreffer *m*

first′-rate′ *adj* erstklassig

first′ ser′geant *s* Hauptfeldwebel *m*

fir′ tree′ *s* Tannenbaum *m*

fiscal ['fɪskəl] *adj* (*period, year*) Rechnungs–; (*policy*) Finanz–

fish [fɪʃ] *s* Fisch *m*; **drink like a f.** wie ein Bürstenbinder saufen; **like a f. out of water** nicht in seinem Element ‖ *tr* fischen ‖ *intr* fischen; **f. for** angeln nach

fish′bone′ *s* Gräte *f*, Fischgräte *f*

fish′ bowl′ *s* Fischglas *n*

fisher ['fɪʃər] *s* Fischer –in *mf*

fish′er·man *s* (**–men**) Angler *m*

fishery ['fɪʃəri] *s* Fischerei *f*

fish′hook′ *s* Angelhaken *m*

fish′ing *adj* Fisch–, Angel– ‖ *s* Fischen *n*

fish′ing line′ *s* Angelschnur *f*

fish′ing reel′ *s* Angelschnurrolle *f*

fish′ing rod′ *s* Angelrute *f*

fish′ing tack′le *s* Fischgerät *n*

fish′ mar′ket *s* Fischmarkt *m*

fishmonger ['fɪʃ͵mʌŋgər] *s* Fischhändler –in *mf*

fish′pond′ *s* Fischteich *m*

fish′ sto′ry *s* Jägerlatein *n*

fish′tail′ *s* (aer) Abbremsen *n* ‖ *intr* (aer) abbremsen

fishy ['fɪʃi] *adj* fischig; (*eyes, look*) ausdruckslos; (*suspicious*) anrüchig; **there's s.th. f. about it** das geht nicht mit rechten Dingen zu

fission ['fɪʃən] *s* (phys) Spaltung *f*

fissionable ['fɪʃənəbəl] *adj* spaltbar

fissure ['fɪʃər] *s* Riß *m*, Spalt *m*

fist [fɪst] *s* Faust *f*; **make a f.** die Faust ballen; **shake one's f. at s.o.** j–m mit der Faust drohen

fist′ fight′ *s* Handgemenge *n*

fisticuffs ['fɪstɪ͵kʌfs] *spl* Faustschläge *pl*

fit [fɪt] *adj* (**fitter; fittest**) gesund; (**for**) tauglich (für, zu); (sport) gut in Form; **be fit as a fiddle** kerngesund sein; **be fit to be tied** Gift und Galle spucken; **feel fit** auf der Höhe sein; **fit for military service**

diensttauglich; **fit to eat** genießbar; **fit to drink** trinkbar; **keep fit in Form** bleiben; **see fit to** (inf) es für richtig halten zu (inf) || s (of clothes) Sitz m; **by fits and starts** ruckweise; **fit of anger** Wutanfall m; **fit of laughter** Lachkrampf m; **give s.o. fits** j-n auf die Palme bringen; **it is a good** (or **a bad**) **fit** es sitzt gut (or schlecht); **throw a fit** e-n Wutanfall kriegen || v (pret & pp **fitted**; ger **fitting**) tr passen (dat); **fit in** (for an appointment) einschieben; **fit out** ausrüsten, ausstatten || intr passen; **fit into** sich einfügen in (acc); **fit in with** passen zu; **fit together** zusammenpassen

fitful ['fɪtfəl] adj unregelmäßig

fitness ['fɪtnɪs] s Tauglichkeit f; **physical f.** gute körperliche Verfassung f

fit'ting adj passend, angemessen || s (of a garment) Anprobe f; (mach) Montage f; **fittings** Armaturen pl

five [faɪv] adj & pron fünf || s Fünf f

five'-year plan' s Fünfjahresplan m

fix [fɪks] s (determination of a position) Standortbestimmung f; (position) Standort m; (injection of heroin) (sl) Schuß m; **be in a fix** (coll) in der Klemme sein || tr befestigen; (a price, time) festsetzen; (repair) reparieren, wieder in Ordnung bringen; (get even with) (sl) erledigen, das Handwerk legen (dat); (one's glance) (on) heften (auf acc); (the blame) (on) zuschreiben (dat); (a game) (sl) auf unehrliche Weise beeinflussen; (bayonets) aufpflanzen; (phot) fixieren

fixed adj (unmovable) unbeweglich; (stare) starr; (income) fest; (idea, cost) fix; **f. date** Termin m

fixer ['fɪksər] s (phot) Fixiermittel n

fix'ing s (making fast) Befestigung f; (of a date, etc.) Festsetzung f; **fixings** (culin) Zutaten pl

fix'ing bath' s (phot) Fixierbad n

fixture ['fɪkstʃər] s Installationsteil m; **he is a permanent f.** er gehört zum Inventar

fizz [fɪz] s Zischen n || intr zischen

fizzle ['fɪzəl] s (coll) Pleite f || intr aufzischen; **f. out** verpuffen

flabbergast ['flæbər‚gæst] tr verblüffen

flabby ['flæbi] adj schlaff, schlapp

flag [flæg] s Fahne f, Flagge f || v (pret & pp **flagged**; ger **flagging**) tr signalisieren || intr nachlassen

flag'pole' s Fahnenmast m

flagrant ['flegrənt] adj schreiend

flag'ship' s Flaggschiff n

flag'staff' s Flaggenmast m

flag'stone' s Steinfliese f

flag' stop' s (rr) Bedarfshaltestelle f

flail [flel] s Dreschflegel m || tr dreschen || intr—**f. about** um sich schlagen

flair [fler] s Spürsinn m; feine Nase f

flak [flæk] s Flak f, Flakfeuer n

flake [flek] s (thin piece) Schuppe f; (of snow, soap) Flocke f || intr Schuppen bilden; **f. off** abblättern

flaky ['fleki] adj (skin) schuppig; (pastry) blätterig; (sl) überspannt

flamboyant [flæm'bɔɪ‚ənt] adj (person) angeberisch; (style) überladen

flame [flem] s Flamme f; **be in flames** in Flammen stehen; **burst into flames** in Flammen aufgehen || intr flammen

flamethrower ['flem‚θro‚ər] s Flammenwerfer m

flam'ing adj flammend

flamin•go [flə'mɪŋgo] s (-gos & -goes) (orn) Flamingo m

flammable ['flæməbəl] adj brennbar

Flanders ['flændərz] s Flandern n

flange [flændʒ] s (of a pipe) Flansch m; (of a wheel) (rr) Spurkranz m

flank [flæŋk] s (anat, mil, zool) Flanke f || tr flankieren

flank'ing move'ment s (mil) Umgehung f

flannel ['flænəl] adj flanellen || s Flanell m

flap [flæp] s Klappe f; **f. of the wing** Flügelschlag m || v (pret & pp **flapped**; ger **flapping**) tr—**f. the wings** mit den Flügeln schlagen || intr flattern

flare [fler] s Leuchtsignal n; (of anger, excitement) Aufbrausen n; (of a skirt) Glocke f; (mil) Leuchtrakete f, Leuchtbombe f || intr flackern; (said of a skirt) glockenförmig abstehen; **f. up** auflodern; (fig) aufbrausen

flare'-up' s Auflodern n; (of anger) Aufbrausen n

flash [flæʃ] s Blitz m; (of a gun) Mündungsfeuer n; (phot) Blitzlicht n; **f. of genious** Geistesblitz m; **f. of light** Lichtstrahl m; **f. of lightning** Blitzstrahl m; **in a f.** im Nu || tr (a glance) zuwerfen; (a message) funkeln; **f. a light in s.o.'s face** j-m ins Gesicht leuchten || intr blitzen; (said of eyes) funkeln; **f. by** vorbeisausen; **f. on** aufleuchten; **f. through one's mind** j-m durch den Kopf schießen

flash'back' s (cin) Rückblende f

flash' bulb' s Blitzlichtbirne f

flash' cube' s Blitzlichtwürfel m

flash' flood' s plötzliche Überschwemmung f

flash' gun' s Blitzlichtgerät n

flash'light' s Taschenlampe f

flash' pic'ture, flash' shot' s Blitzlichtaufnahme f

flashy ['flæʃi] adj auffällig; (clothes) protzig; (colors) grell

flask [flæsk] s Taschenflasche f; (for laboratory use) Glaskolben m

flat [flæt] adj (flatter; flattest) platt, flach; (food) fad(e); (rate) Pauschal–; (tire) platt; (color) matt; (beer, soda) schal; (lie) glatt; (denial) entschieden; (mus) erniedrigt; **be f.** (mus) zu tief singen || adv (e.g., in exactly ten minutes) genau; **fall f.** (fig) flachfallen; **go f.** schal werden; **lie f.** flach liegen || s (apartment) Wohnung f; (tire) Reifenpanne f

flat'boat' s Flachboot n

flat-broke ['flæt'brok] *adj* (coll) völlig pleite
flat'car' *s* Plattformwagen *m*
flat' feet' *spl* Plattfüße *pl*
flat'-foot'ed *adj* plattfüßig; **catch f.** auf frischer Tat ertappen
flat'i'ron *s* Bügeleisen *n*
flatly ['flætli] *adv* rundweg, reinweg
flatten ['flætən] *tr* (*paper, cloth*) glattstreichen; (*raze*) einebnen; **f. out** abplatten; (aer) abfangen || *intr* sich verflachen; (aer) ausschweben
flatter ['flætər] *tr* schmeicheln (*dat*); **be flattered** sich geschmeichelt fühlen; **f. oneself** sich [dat] einbilden
flatterer ['flætərər] *s* Schmeichler –in *mf*
flat'tering *adj* schmeichelhaft
flattery ['flætəri] *s* Schmeichelei *f*
flat' tire' *s* Reifenpanne *f*
flat'top' *s* (coll) Flugzeugträger *m*
flat' truc'tory *s* Rasanz *f*
flatulence ['flætʃələns] *s* Blähung *f*
flat'ware' *s* (silverware) Eßbestecke *pl*
flaunt [flɔnt] *tr* prunken mit
flavor ['flevər] *s* Aroma *n* || *tr* würzen
fla'voring *s* Würze *f*
flavorless ['flevərlɪs] *adj* fad(e)
flaw [flɔ] *s* Fehler *m*; (crack) Riß *m*; (in glass, precious stone) Blase *f*
flawless ['flɔlɪs] *adj* tadellos
flax [flæks] *s* Flachs *m*, Lein *m*
flaxen ['flæksən] *adj* flachsen
flax'seed' *s* Leinsamen *m*
flay [fle] *tr* ausbalgen
flea [fli] *s* Floh *m*
flea' bag' *s* (sleeping bag) (coll) Flohkiste *f*; (hotel) (coll) Penne *f*
flea'bite' *s* Flohbiß *m*
flea'mar'ket *s* Flohmarkt *m*
fleck [flɛk] *s* Fleck *m*
fledgling ['flɛdʒlɪŋ] *s* eben flügge gewordener Vogel *m*; (fig) Grünschnabel *m*
flee [fli] *v* (*pret & pp* **fled** [flɛd]) *intr* fliehen
fleece [flis] *s* Vlies *n* || *tr* (coll) rupfen
fleecy ['flisi] *adj* wollig; **f. clouds** Schäfchenwolken *pl*
fleet [flit] *adj* flink || *s* Flotte *f*; (aer) Geschwader *n*; (nav) Kriegsflotte *f*; **f. of cars** Wagenpark *m*
fleet'ing *adj* flüchtig
Flemish ['flɛmɪʃ] *adj* flämisch || *s* Flämisch *n*
flesh [flɛʃ] *s* Fleisch *n*; **in the f.** leibhaftig
flesh'-col'ored *adj* fleischfarben
fleshiness ['flɛʃɪnɪs] *s* Fleischigkeit *f*
flesh' wound' *s* Fleischwunde *f*
fleshy ['flɛʃi] *adj* fleischig
flex [flɛks] *tr* biegen; (muscles) anspannen
flexible ['flɛksɪbəl] *adj* biegsam
flex(i)time ['flɛks(ɪ) ,taɪm] *s* Gleitzeit *f*
flick [flɪk] *s* Schnippen *n* || *tr* (away) wegschnippen
flicker ['flɪkər] *s* (of a flame) Flakkern *n*; (of eyelids) Zucken *n* || *intr* flackern
flier ['flaɪ·ər] *s* Flieger –in *mf*; (handbill) Flugblatt *n*

flight [flaɪt] *s* Flug *m*; (fleeing) Flucht *f*; (of birds, geese) Schar *f*; (of stairs) Treppe *f*; **f. of stairs** Treppenflucht *f*; **f. of the imagination** Geistesschwung *m*; **live two flights up** zwei Treppen hoch wohnen; **put to f.** in die Flucht schlagen; **take to f.** sich davonmachen
flight' bag' *s* (aer) Reisetasche *f*
flight' deck' *s* (nav) Landedeck *n*
flight' engineer' *s* Bordmechaniker *m*
flight' instruc'tor *s* Fluglehrer –in *mf*
flight' path' *s* Flugstrecke *f*
flighty ['flaɪti] *adj* leichtsinnig
flim-flam ['flɪm ,flæm] *s* (nonsense) Unsinn *m*; (deception) Betrügerei *f* || *v* (pret & pp –flammed; ger –flamming) *tr* (coll) betrügen
flimsy ['flɪmzi] *adj* (material) hauchdünn; (excuse, construction) schwach
flinch [flɪntʃ] *intr* (at) zurückweichen (vor dat), zusammenfahren (vor dat)
flinch'ing *s*—**without f.** ohne mit der Wimper zu zucken
fling [flɪŋ] *s* Wurf *m*; **go on** (or **have**) **a f.** sich austoben; **have a f. at** versuchen || *v* (pret & pp **flung** [flʌŋ]) *tr* schleudern; **f. off** abschleudern; **f. open** aufreißen
flint [flɪnt] *s* Feuerstein *m*
flinty ['flɪnti] *adj* steinhart; (fig) hart
flip [flɪp] *adj* leichtfertig || *s* (of a coin) Hochwerfen *n*; (somersault) Purzelbaum *m* || *v* (pret & pp flipped; ger flipping) *tr* schnellen; (a coin) hochwerfen; **f. one's lid** (sl) rasend werden; **f. over** umdrehen
flippancy ['flɪpənsi] *s* Leichtfertigkeit *f*
flippant ['flɪpənt] *adj* leichtfertig
flipper ['flɪpər] *s* Flosse *f*
flirt [flʌrt] *s* Flirt *m* || *intr* kokettieren, flirten; (with an idea) liebäugeln
flirtation [flʌr'teʃən] *s* Liebelei *f*
flit [flɪt] *v* (pret & pp flitted; ger flitting) *intr* flitzen; **f. by** vorbeiflitzen; (said of time) verfliegen
float [flot] *s* Schwimmkörper *m*; (of a fishing line) Schwimmer *m*; (raft) Floß *n*; (in parades) Festwagen *m* || *tr* (logs) flößen; (a loan) auflegen || *intr* schwimmen; (in the air) schweben; **f. about** herumtreiben
float'ing kid'ney *s* Wanderniere *f*
float'ing mine' *s* Treibmine *f*
flock [flɑk] *s* (of sheep) Herde *f*; (of birds) Schar *f*, Schwarm *m*; (of people) Menge *f* || *intr* herbeiströmen; **come flocking** herbeigeströmt kommen; **f. around** sich scharen um; **f. into** strömen in (acc); **f. to** zulaufen (dat); **f. together** sich zusammenscharen
floe [flo] *s* Eisscholle *f*
flog [flɑg] *v* (pret & pp flogged; ger flogging) *tr* prügeln
flood [flʌd] *s* Flut *f*; (caused by heavy rains) Überschwemmung *f*; (sudden rise of a river) Hochwasser *n*; (fig) Schwall *m*; (Bib) Sintflut *f* || *tr* (& fig) überschwemmen; (e.g., with mail) überschütten

flood'gate' s (& fig) Schleusentor n

flood'light' s Flutlicht n || tr anstrahlen

flood' tide' s Flut f; **at f.** zur Zeit der Flut

flood' wa'ters spl Flutwasser n

floor [flor] s Fußboden m; (story) Stock m; (parl) Sitzungssaal m; **have the f.** das Wort haben; **may I have the f.?** ich bitte ums Wort; **on the third f.** im zweiten Stock || tr zu Boden strecken; (coll) verblüffen

floor'board' s Diele f

floor'ing s Fußbodenbelag m

floor' lamp' s Stehlampe f

floor' plan' s Grundriß m

floor' pol'ish s Bohnermasse f

floor' sam'ple s Vorführungsmuster n

floor' show' s Kabarett n

floor' tile' s Bodenfliese f

floor'walk'er s Abteilungsaufseher –in mf

floor' wax' s Bohnerwachs n

flop [flap] s (coll) Mißerfolg m; (person) Niete f; (fall) (coll) Plumps m; **take a f.** (coll) plumpsen || v (pret & pp **flopped;** ger **flopping**) intr (fall) (coll) plumpsen; (fail) (coll) versagen; (theat) (coll) durchfallen; **f. down in** (coll) sich plumpsen lassen in (acc)

flora ['florə] s Pflanzenwelt f

floral ['florəl] adj Blumen-

Florence ['florəns] s Florenz n

florescence [flo'resəns] s Blüte f

florid ['florɪd] adj (ornate) überladen; (complexion) blühend

florist ['florɪst] s Blumenhändler –in mf

floss [fləs] s Rohseide f; (of corn) Narbenfäden pl

floss' silk' s Florettseide f

flossy ['fləsi] adj seidenweich

flotilla [flo'tɪlə] s Flotille f

flotsam ['flɑtsəm] s Wrackgut n

flot'sam and jet'sam s Treibgut n; (trifles) Kleinigkeiten pl

flounce [flauns] s Volant m || tr mit Volants besetzen || intr erregt stürmen

flounder ['flaundər] s Flunder f || intr taumeln; (fig) ins Schwimmen kommen

flour [flaur] s Mehl n

flourish ['flʌrɪʃ] s (in writing) Schnörkel m; (in a speech) Floskel f; (gesture) große Geste f; (mus) Tusch m; **f. of trumpets** Trompetengeschmetter n || tr (banners) schwenken; (swords) schwingen || intr blühen, gedeihen

flour'ishing adj blühend; (business) schwunghaft

flour' mill' s Mühle f

floury ['flauri] adj mehlig

flout [flaut] tr verspotten || intr—**f. at** spotten über (acc)

flow [flo] s Fluß m || intr fließen, rinnen; (said of hair, clothes) wallen; **f. by** vorbeifließen; **f. into** zuströmen (dat)

flower ['flau·ər] s Blume f; **cut flowers** Schnittblumen pl || intr blühen

flow'er bed' s Blumenbeet n

flow'er gar'den s Blumengarten m

flow'er girl' s Blumenmädchen n

flow'erpot' s Blumentopf m

flow'er shop' s Blumenladen m

flow'er show' s Blumenausstellung f

flow'er stand' s Blumenstand m

flowery ['flau·əri] adj blumig; (fig) geziert; **f. phrase** Floskel f

flu [flu] s (coll) Grippe f

flub [flʌb] v (pret & pp **flubbed;** ger **flubbing**) tr (coll) verkorksen

fluctuate ['flʌkt/u ‚et] intr schwanken

fluctuation [‚flʌkt/u'e/ən] s Schwankung f

flue [flu] s Rauchrohr n

fluency ['flu·ənsi] s Geläufigkeit f

fluent ['flu·ənt] adj (speaker) redegewandt; (speech) fließend

fluently ['flu·əntli] adv fließend

fluff [flʌf] s Staubflocke f; (blunder) Schnitzer m || tr verpfuschen; **f. up** (a pillow) schütteln; (a rug) aufrauhen

fluffy ['flʌfi] adj flaumig

fluid ['flu·ɪd] adj flüssig || s Flüssigkeit f

fluke [fluk] s Ankerflügel m; (coll) Dusel m

flunk [flʌŋk] s Durchfallen n || tr (a test) (coll) durchfallen in (dat); (a student) (coll) durchfallen lassen || intr (coll) durchfallen

flunky ['flʌŋki] s Schranze mf

fluorescent [flo'resənt] adj fluoreszierend

fluores'cent light' s Leuchtstofflampe f

fluores'cent tube' s Leuchtröhre f

fluoridate ['florɪ ‚det] tr mit e–m Fluorid versetzen

fluoride ['florɑɪd] s Fluorid n

fluorine ['florin] s Fluor n

fluorite ['florɑɪt] s Fluorkalzium n

fluoroscope ['florə ‚skop] s Fluoroskop n

flurry ['flʌri] s (of snow) Schneegestöber m; (st. exch.) kurzes Aufflakkern n; **f. of activity** fieberhafte Tätigkeit f

flush [flʌʃ] adj (even) eben, glatt; (well-supplied) gut bei Kasse; (full to overflowing) übervoll || adv direkt || s (on the cheeks) Erröten n; (of youth) Blüte f; (of a toilet) Spülung f; (cards) Flöte f; **f. of victory** Siegesrausch m || tr (a toilet) spülen; (hunt) auftreiben; **f. down** hinunterspülen; **f. out** (animals) auftreiben || intr erröten

flush' switch' s Unterputzschalter m

flush' tank' s Spülkasten m

flush' toi'let s Spülklosett n

fluster ['flʌstər] s Verwirrung f || tr verwirren

flute [flut] s (archit) Kannelüre f; (mus) Flöte f || tr riffeln

flut'ing s (archit) Kannelierung f

flutist ['flutɪst] s Flötist –in mf

flutter ['flʌtər] s Flattern n; (excitement) Aufregung f || tr—**f. one's eyelashes** mit den Wimpern klimpern || intr flattern

flux [flʌks] s (*flow*) Fließen n, Fluß m; (*for fusing metals*) Schmelzmittel n; **in f.** im Fluß

fly [flai] s Fliege f; (*of trousers*) Schlitz m; (*angl*) künstliche Fliege f; **flies** (theat) Soffitten pl; **fly in the ointment** Haar n in der Suppe || v (*pret* **flew** [flu]; *pp* **flown** [flon]) tr fliegen || intr fliegen; (*rush*) stürzen; (*said of rumors*) schwirren; (*said of time*) verfliegen; **fly around** umherfliegen; (*e.g., the globe*) umfliegen; **fly at s.o.** auf j-n losgehen; **fly away** abfliegen; **fly in all directions** nach allen Seiten zerstieben; **fly low** tief fliegen; **fly off the handle** (fig) aus der Haut fahren; **fly open** aufspringen; **fly over** überfliegen; **fly past** vorbeifliegen (an *dat*); **let fly** (*e.g., an arrow*) schnellen

fly' ball' s (baseball) Flugball m
fly'-by-night' adj unverläßlich || s (coll) Schwindelunternehmen n
fly' cast'ing s Fischen n mit der Wurfangel
flyer ['flaɪ·ər] s var of **flier**
fly'-fish' intr mit künstlichen Fliegen angeln
fly'ing adj fliegend; (*boat, field, time*) Flug-; (*suit, club, school*) Flieger- || s Fliegen n
fly'ing but'tress s Strebebogen m
fly'ing col'ors spl—**come through with f. e-n** glänzenden Sieg erringen
fly'ing sau'cer s fliegende Untertasse f
fly'leaf' s (**-leaves'**) Vorsatzblatt n
fly'pa'per s Fliegenfänger m
fly' rod' s Angelrute f
fly'speck' s Fliegendreck m
fly' swat'ter [ˌswatər] s Fliegenklappe f
fly'trap' s Fliegenfalle f
fly'wheel' s Schwungrad n
foal [fol] s Fohlen n || intr fohlen
foam [fom] s Schaum m; (*of waves*) Gischt m; (*from the mouth*) Geifer m || intr schäumen; (*said of waves*) branden
foam' rub'ber s Schaumgummi m
foamy ['fomi] adj (*full of foam*) schaumig; (*beer*) schäumend; (*foam-like*) schaumartig
F.O.B., f.o.b. [ˌɛfˌoˈbi] adv (**free on board**) frei an Bord
focal ['fokəl] adj fokal; **be the f. point** im Brennpunkt stehen; **f. point** (fig & opt) Brennpunkt m
fo·cus ['fokəs] s (**-cuses & -ci** [saɪ]) (math, opt) Brennpunkt m; (pathol) Herd m; **bring into f.** richtig (or scharf) einstellen; **in f.** scharf eingestellt; **out of f.** unscharf || v (*pret* & *pp* **-cus[s]ed**; *ger* **-cus[s]ing**) tr (*a camera*) einstellen; (*attention, etc.*) (**on**) richten (auf *acc*) || intr sich scharf einstellen
fo'cusing s Scharfeinstellung f
fodder ['fadər] s Futter n
foe [fo] s Feind –in mf
fog [fɔg] s Nebel m; (fig) Verwirrung f; (phot) Grauschleier m || v (*pret* & *pp* **fogged**; *ger* **fogging**) tr ver-

nebeln; (fig) umnebeln || intr (phot) verschleiern; **fog up** beschlagen
fog' bank' s Nebelbank f
fog' bell' s Nebelglocke f
fog'-bound' adj durch Nebel festgehalten
fogey ['fogi] s Kauz m
foggy ['fɔgi] adj neblig, nebelhaft; (phot) verschleiert; **he hasn't the foggiest idea** er hat nicht die leiseste Ahnung
fog'horn' s Nebelhorn n
fog' light' s (aut) Nebelscheinwerfer m
foible ['fɔɪbəl] s Schwäche f
foil [fɔɪl] s (*of metal*) Folie f; (*of a mirror*) Spiegelbelag m; (fig) (**to**) Hintergrund m (für); (fencing) Florett n || tr (*a plan*) durchkreuzen; (*an attempt*) vereiteln
foist [fɔɪst] tr—**f. s.th. on s.o.** j-m etw anhängen
fold [fold] s Falte f; (*in stiff material*) Falz m; (*for sheep*) Pferch m; (*flock of sheep*) Schafherde f; (relig) Herde f || tr falten; (*stiff material*) falzen; (*e.g., a chair*) zusammenklappen; (*the arms*) kreuzen; (*the wash*) zusammenlegen || intr sich (zusammen) falten; (com) zusammenbrechen
folder ['foldər] s (*loose-leaf binder*) Schnellhefter m; (*manila folder*) Mappe f; (*brochure*) Prospekt m
fold'ing adj (*bed, chair, camera, wing*) Klapp-
fold'ing door' s Falttür f
fold'ing screen' s spanische Wand f
foliage ['folɪ·ɪdʒ] s Laubwerk n, Laub n
foli·o ['folɪˌo] adj Folio-, in Folio || s (**-os**) (*page*) Folioblatt n; (*book*) Foliant m || tr paginieren
folk [fok] adj Volks- || **folks** spl (*people*) Leute pl; (*family*) Angehörige pl
folk' dance' s Volkstanz m
folk'lore' s Volkskunde f
folk' mu'sic s Volksmusik f
folk' song' s Volkslied n
folksy ['foksi] adj (*person*) leutselig; (*speech, expression*) volkstümlich
folk' tale' s Volkssage f
folk'ways' spl volkstümliche Lebensweise f
follicle ['falɪkəl] s Follikel n
follow ['falo] tr folgen (*dat*); (*instructions*) befolgen; (*a goal, events, news*) verfolgen; (*in office*) folgen auf (*acc*); (*a profession*) ausüben; (*understand*) folgen können (*dat*); **f. one another** aufeinanderfolgen; (*said of events*) sich überstürzen; **f. up** nachgehen (*dat*); **f. your nose!** immer der Nase nach! || intr (nach)folgen; **as follows** folgendermaßen; **f. after** nachfolgen (*dat*); **f. through** (sport) ganz durchziehen; **f. upon** folgen auf (*acc*); **it follows that** daraus folgt, daß
follower ['falo·ər] s Anhänger –in mf
fol'lowing adj nachstehend, folgend || s Gefolgschaft f
fol'low-up' adj Nach– || s weitere Verfolgung f

folly ['fɑli] s Torheit *f;* **follies** (theat) Revue *f*

foment [fo'mɛnt] *tr* schüren, anstiften

fond [fɑnd] *adj* (*hope, wish*) sehnlich; **become f. of** lieb gewinnen; **be f. of** gern haben; **be f. of reading** gern lesen

fondle ['fɑndəl] *tr* liebkosen

fondness ['fɑndnɪs] *s* Verliebtheit *f;* (**for**) Hang *m* (zu), Vorliebe *f* (für)

font [fɑnt] *s* (*for holy water*) Weihwasserbecken *n;* (*for baptism*) Taufbecken *n;* (typ) Schriftart *f*

food [fud] *adj* Nähr-, Speise– ‖ *s* (*on the table*) Essen *n;* (*in a store*) Lebensmittel *pl;* (*requirement for life*) Nahrung *f;* (*for animals*) Futter *n;* (*for plants*) Nährstoff *m;* **f. and drink** Speis' und Trank; **f. for thought** Stoff *m* zum Nachdenken

food′ poi′soning *s* Nahrungsmittelvergiftung *f*

food′stuffs′ *spl* Nahrungsmittel *pl*

food′ val′ue *s* Nährwert *m*

fool [ful] *s* Narr *m;* **born f.** Mondkalb *n;* **make a f. of oneself** sich blamieren ‖ *tr* täuschen, anführen ‖ *intr*— **f. around** herumtrödeln; **f. around with** herumspielen mit; (*romantically*) sich herumtreiben mit

fool′har′dy *adj* tollkühn

fool′ing *s* Späße *pl;* **f. around** Firlefanz *m;* **no f.!** na, so was!

foolish ['fulɪʃ] *adj* töricht, albern

foolishness ['fulɪʃnɪs] *s* Torheit *f*

fool′-proof *adj* narrensicher

fools′cap′ *s* Narrenkappe *f;* (*paper size*) Kanzleipapier *n*

foot [fut] *s* (**feet** [fit]) Fuß *m;* **be (back) on one's feet** (wieder) auf den Beinen sein; **f. of the bed** Fußende *n* des Bettes; **on f.** zu Fuß; **put one's best f. forward** sich ins rechte Licht setzen; **put one's f. down** (fig) ein Machtwort sprechen; **put one's f. in it** (coll) ins Fettnäpfchen treten; **stand on one's own two feet** auf eigenen Füßen stehen ‖ *tr*—**f. the bill** blechen

footage ['futɪdʒ] *s* Ausmaß *n* in Fuß

foot′-and-mouth′ disease′ *s* Maul- und-Klauenseuche *f*

foot′ball′ *s* Fußball *m*

foot′board′ *s* (*in a car*) Trittbrett *n;* (*of a bed*) Fußbrett *n*

foot′bridge′ *s* Steg *m*

foot′fall′ *s* Schritt *m*

foot′hills′ *spl* Vorgebirge *n*

foot′hold′ *s* (& fig) Halt *m;* **gain a f.** festen Fuß fassen

foot′ing *s* Halt *m;* **lose one's f.** ausgleiten; **on an equal f. with** auf gleichem Fuße mit

foot′lights′ *spl* Rampenlicht *n*

foot′man *s* (**-men**) Lakai *m*

foot′note′ *s* Fußnote *f*

foot′path′ *s* Fußpfad *m,* Fußsteig *m*

foot′print′ *s* Fußstapfe *f*

foot′ race′ *s* Wettlauf *m*

foot′rest′ *s* Fußraste *f*

foot′ rule′ *s* Zollstock *m*

foot′ sol′dier *s* Infanterist *m*

foot′sore′ *adj* fußkrank

foot′step′ *s* Tritt *m;* **follow in s.o.'s footsteps** in j–s Fußstapfen treten

foot′stool′ *s* Schemel *m*

foot′wear′ *s* Schuhwerk *n*

foot′work′ *s* (sl) Lauferei *f;* (sport) Beinarbeit *f*

foot′worn′ *adj* abgetreten

fop [fɑp] *s* Geck *m*

for [fɔr] *prep* für; (*a destination*) nach (*dat*); (*with an English present perfect tense*) schon (*acc*), e.g., **I have been living here for a month** ich wohne hier schone e–n Monat (or seit e–m Monat; (*with an English future tense*) für or auf (*acc*); **for good** für immer; **for joy** vor Freude; **for years** jahrelang ‖ *conj* denn

forage ['fɔrɪdʒ] *s* Furage *f* ‖ *intr* furagieren

foray ['fɔre] *s* (*raid*) Raubzug *m;* (*e.g., into politics*) Streifzug *m* ‖ *intr* plündern

for·bear [fɔr'bɛr] *v* (*pret* **–bore** ['bor]; *pp* **–borne** ['born]) *tr* unterlassen ‖ *intr* ablassen

forbearance [fɔr'bɛrəns] *s* (*patience*) Geduld *f;* (*leniency*) Nachsicht *f*

for·bid [fɔr'bɪd] *v* (*pret* **–bade** ['bæd] & **–bad** ['bæd]; *pp* **–bidden** ['bɪdən]) *tr* verbieten

forbid′ding *adj* abschreckend; (*dangerous*) gefährlich

force [fɔrs] *s* (*strength*) Kraft *f;* (*compulsion*) Gewalt *f;* (phys) Kraft *f;* **be in f.** in Kraft sein; **by f.** gewaltsam; **come into f.** in Kraft treten; **forces** (mil) Streitkräfte *pl;* **have the f. of** gelten als; **resort to f.** zu Zwangsmaßnahmen greifen; **with full f.** mit voller Wucht ‖ *tr* zwingen; (*plants*) treiben; (*a door*) aufsprengen; (*e.g., an issue*) forcieren; (**into**) zwängen (in *acc*); **f. down** hinunterdrücken; (aer) zur Landung zwingen; **f. one's way** sich drängen; **f. s.th. on s.o.** j–m etw aufdrängen

forced′ land′ing *s* Notlandung *f*

forced′ march′ *s* Gewaltsmarsch *m*

forceful ['fɔrsfəl] *adj* eindrucksvoll

for·ceps ['fɔrseps] *s* (**–ceps** & **–cipes** [sɪ‚piz]) (dent, surg, zool) Zange *f*

forcible ['fɔrsɪbəl] *adj* (*strong*) kräftig; (*violent*) gewaltsam

ford [fɔrd] *s* Furt *f* ‖ *tr* durchwaten

fore [fɔr] *adj* Vorder– ‖ *adv* (naut) vorn ‖ *s*—**come to the f.** hervortreten ‖ *interj* (golf) Achtung!

fore′ and aft′ *adv* längsschiffs

fore′arm′ *s* Vorderarm *m,* Unterarm *m*

fore′bears′ *spl* Vorfahren *pl*

forebode [fɔr'bod] *tr* vorbedeuten

forebod′ing *s* (*omen*) Vorzeichen *n;* (*presentiment*) Vorahnung *f*

fore′cast′ *s* Voraussage *f* ‖ *v* (*pret* & *pp* **–cast** & **–casted**) *tr* voraussagen

forecastle ['foksəl] *s* Back *f*

foreclose *tr* (*a mortgage*) für verfallen erklären; (*shut out*) ausschließen

foredoom′ *tr* im voraus verurteilen

fore′fa′thers *spl* Vorfahren *pl*

fore′fin′ger *s* Zeigefinger *m*

fore′front′ *s* Spitze *f*

fore′go′ing *adj* vorhergehend

fore'gone' conclu'sion s ausgemachte Sache f

fore'ground' s Vordergrund m

forehead ['fɔrɪd] s Stirn(e) f

foreign ['fɔrɪn] adj (e.g., aid, product) Auslands-; (e.g., body, language, word, worker) Fremd-; (e.g., minister, office, policy, trade) Außen-; (e.g., affairs, service) auswärtig

foreigner ['fɔrɪnər] s Ausländer –in mf

for'eign exchange' s Devisen pl

fore'leg' s Vorderbein n

fore'lock' s Stirnlocke f

fore'man s (-men) Vorarbeiter m; (jur) Obmann m; (min) Steiger m

foremast ['fɔr,mæst] s Fockmast m

fore'most' adj vorderste || adv zuerst

fore'noon' s Vormittag m

fore'part' s vorderster Teil m

fore'paw' s Vorderpfote f

fore'quar'ter s Vorderviertel n

fore'run'ner s Vorbote m

fore'sail' s Focksegel n

fore-see' v (pret –saw'; pp –seen') tr voraussehen

foreseeable [fɔr'si·əbəl] adj absehbar

foreshad'ow tr ahnen lassen

foreshort'en tr verkürzen

fore'sight' s Voraussicht f

fore'sight'ed adj umsichtig

fore'skin' s Vorhaut f

forest ['fɔrɪst] s Wald m, Forst m

forestall' tr zuvorkommen (dat)

for'est fire' s Waldbrand m

for'est rang'er s Forstbeamte m

forestry ['fɔrɪstri] s Forstwirtschaft f

fore'taste' s Vorgeschmack m

fore-tell' v (pret & pp –told') tr vorhersagen, weissagen

fore'thought' s Vorsorge f, Vorbedacht m

forev'er adv ewig, für immer; f. and ever auf immer und ewig

forewarn' tr (of) vorher warnen (vor dat)

fore'word' s Vorwort n

forfeit ['fɔrfɪt] s Einbuße f || tr einbüßen, verwirken

forfeiture ['fɔrfɪt/ər] s Verwirkung f

forgather [fɔr'gæðər] intr sich treffen

forge [fɔrdʒ] s Schmiede f || tr schmieden; (documents) fälschen || intr— forge ahead vordringen

forger ['fɔrdʒər] s Fälscher –in mf

forgery ['fɔrdʒəri] s Fälschung f; (coin) Falschgeld n

for·get [fɔr'gɛt] v (pret –got; pp –got & –gotten; ger –getting) tr vergessen; f. it! spielt keine Rolle!; f. oneself sich vergessen

forgetful [fɔr'gɛtfəl] adj vergeßlich

forgetfulness [fɔr'gɛtfəlnɪs] s Vergeßlichkeit f

forget'-me-not' s Vergißmeinnicht n

forgivable [fɔr'gɪvəbəl] adj verzeihlich

for·give [fɔr'gɪv] v (pret –gave; pp –given) tr (a person) vergeben (dat); (a thing) vergeben

forgiveness [fɔr'gɪvnɪs] s Vergebung f

forgiv'ing adj versöhnlich

for·go [fɔr'go] v (pret –went; pp –gone) tr verzichten auf (acc)

fork [fɔrk] s Gabel f; (in the road) Gabelung f; (of a tree) Astgabelung f || tr gabeln; f. over (coll) übergeben

forked adj gabelförmig; (tongue) gespalten

fork'lift truck' s Gabelstapler m

forlorn [fɔr'lɔrn] adj (forsaken) verlassen; (wretched) elend; (attempt) verzweifelt

forlorn' hope' s aussichtsloses Unternehmen n

form [fɔrm] s Form f, Gestalt f; (paper to be filled out) Formular n || tr formen, bilden; (a plan) fassen; (a circle, alliance) schließen; (suspicions) schöpfen; (a habit) annehmen; (blisters) werfen || intr sich bilden

formal ['fɔrməl] adj formell, förmlich

for'mal call' s Höflichkeitsbesuch m

for'mal educa'tion s Schulbildung f

formality [fɔr'mælɪti] s Formalität f; without f. ohne Umstände

format ['fɔrmæt] s Format n

formation [fɔr'meʃən] s Bildung f; (aer) Verband m; (geol, mil) Formation f

former ['fɔrmər] adj ehemalig, früher; the f. jener

formerly ['fɔrmərli] adv ehemals, früher

form'-fit'ting adj—be f. e-e gute Paßform haben

formidable ['fɔrmɪdəbəl] adj (huge) gewaltig; (dreadful) schrecklich

formless ['fɔrmlɪs] adj formlos

form' let'ter s Rundbrief m

formu·la ['fɔrmjələ] s (-las & -lae [,li]) Formel f; (baby food) Kindermilch f

formulate ['fɔrmjə,let] tr formulieren

formulation [,fɔrmjə'leʃən] s Formulierung f

fornicate ['fɔrnɪ,ket] intr Unzucht treiben

fornication [,fɔrnɪ'keʃən] s Unzucht f

for·sake [fɔr'sek] v (pret –sook ['sʊk]; pp –saken ['sekən]) tr verlassen

fort [fɔrt] s Burg f; (mil) Fort n

forte [fɔrt] s Stärke f

forth [fɔrθ] adv hervor; and so f. und so fort; from that day f. von dem Tag an

forth'com'ing adj bevorstehend

forth'right' adj ehrlich, offen

forth'with' adv sofort

fortieth ['fɔrti·ɪθ] adj & pron vierzigste || s (fraction) Vierzigstel n; (in a series) Vierzigste mfn

fortification [,fɔrtɪfɪ'keʃən] s Befestigung f

forti·fy ['fɔrtɪ,faɪ] v (pret & pp –fied) tr (a place) befestigen; (e.g., with liquor) kräftigen; (encourage) ermutigen

fortitude ['fɔrtɪ,t(j)ud] s Seelenstärke f

fortnight ['fɔrtnaɪt] s vierzehn Tage pl

fortress ['fɔrtrɪs] s Festung f

fortuitous [fɔr't(j)u·ɪtəs] adj zufällig

fortunate ['fɔrt/ənɪt] adj glücklich

fortunately ['fɔrt/ənɪtli] adv glücklicherweise

fortune 126 **frantic**

fortune ['fɔrtʃən] s Glück n; (money) Vermögen n; **make a f.** sich [dat] ein Vermögen erwerben; **have one's f. told** sich [dat] wahrsagen lassen; **tell fortunes** wahrsagen
for'tune hunt'er s Mitgiftjäger –in mf
for'tunetell'er s Wahrsagerin f
forty ['fɔrti] adj & pron vierzig || s Vierzig f; **the forties** die vierziger Jahre
fo·rum ['fɔrəm] s (-rums & -ra [rə]) (& fig) Forum n
forward ['fɔrwərd] adj vordere, Vorwärts–; (person) keck; (mil) vorgeschoben || adv vorwärts, nach vorn; **bring f.** (an idea) vorschlagen; (a proposal) vorbringen; **come f.** sich melden; **look f. to** sich freuen auf (acc); **put f.** vorlegen || s (fb) Stürmer m || tr befördern; **please f.** bitte nachsenden || interj—f., march! im Gleichschritt, marsch!
fossil ['fɑsɪl] adj versteinert || s Fossil n
foster ['fɔstər] adj (child, father, mother, home) Pflege–; (brother, sister) Milch– || tr pflegen
foul [faʊl] adj übel; (in smell) übelriechend; (air, weather) schlecht; (language) unflätig; (means) unfair || s (sport) Foul n || tr (make dirty) besudeln; (the lines) verwickeln; (sport) foulen; **f. up** durcheinanderbringen || intr (sport) foulen
foul' line' s (baseball) Grenzlinie f; (basketball) Freiwurflinie f
foul-mouthed ['faʊl‚maʊðd], ['faʊl‚maʊθt] adj zotige Reden führend
foul' play' s unfaires Spiel n; (crime) Verbrechen n, Mord m
found [faʊnd] tr gründen; (cast) gießen
foundation [faʊn'deʃən] s (act) Gründung f; (of a structure) Fundament n; (fund) Stiftung f; (fig) Grundlage f; **lay the foundation of** (& fig) den Grund legen zu
founda'tion gar'ments spl Miederwaren pl
founda'tion wall' s Grundmauer f
founder ['faʊndər] s Gründer –in mf; (metal) Gießer –in mf || intr (said of a ship) sinken; (fail) scheitern
foundling ['faʊndlɪŋ] s Findling m
foundry ['faʊndri] s Gießerei f
found'ry·man s (-men) Gießer m
fount [faʊnt] s Quelle f
fountain ['faʊntən] s Springbrunnen m
foun'tainhead' s Urquell m
foun'tain pen' s Füller m
four [fɔr] adj & pron vier || s Vier f; **on all fours** auf allen vieren
four'-cy'cle adj (mach) Viertakt–
four'-en'gine adj viermotorig
fourflusher ['fɔr‚flʌʃər] s Angeber m
four'foot'ed adj vierfüßig
four' hun'dred adj & pron vierhundert || spl—**the Four Hundred** die oberen Zehntausend
four'lane' adj Vierbahn–
four'-leaf' adj vierblätterig
four'-leg'ged adj vierbeinig
four'-letter word' s unanständiges Wort n

foursome ['fɔrsəm] s Viererspiel n; (group of four) Quartet n
fourteenth [fɔr'tinθ] adj & pron vierzehnte || s (fraction) Vierzehntel n; **the f.** (in dates and in a series) der Vierzehnte
fourth [fɔrθ] adj & pron vierte || s (fraction) Viertel n; **the f.** (in dates and in a series) der Vierte
fourth' estate' s Presse f
fowl [faʊl] s Huhn n, Geflügel n
fox [fɑks] s (& fig) Fuchs m
fox'glove' s (bot) Fingerhut m
fox'hole' s (mil) Schützenloch n
fox' hound' s Hetzhund m
fox' hunt' s Fuchsjagd f
fox' ter'rier s Foxterrier m
fox' trot' s Foxtrott m
foyer ['fɔɪ·ər] s (of a theater) Foyer n; (of a house) Diele f
fracas ['frekəs] s Aufruhr m
fraction ['frækʃən] s Bruchteil m; (math) Bruch m
fractions Bruchrechnung f
fractional ['frækʃənəl] adj Bruch–
fracture ['fræktʃər] s Bruch m || tr sich [dat] brechen
fragile ['frædʒɪl] adj zerbrechlich
fragment ['frægmənt] s Bruchstück n; (of writing) Fragment n
fragmentary ['frægmən‚teri] adj bruchstückhaft; (writing) fragmentarisch
fragmenta'tion bomb' ['frægmən'teʃən] s Splitterbombe f
fragrance ['fregrəns] s Duft m
fragrant ['fregrənt] adj duftend; **be f.** duften
frail [frel] adj schwach, hinfällig; (fragile) zerbrechlich
frailty ['frelti] s Schwachheit f
frame [frem] s (e.g., of a picture, door) Rahmen m; (of glasses) Fassung f; (of a house) Balkenwerk n; (structure) Gestell n; (anat) Körperbau m; (cin, telv) Bild n; (naut) Spant n || tr (a picture) einrahmen; (a plan) ersinnen; (sl) reinhängen
frame' house' s Holzhaus n
frame' of mind' s Gemütsverfassung f
frame' of ref'erence s Bezugspunkte pl
frame'-up' s abgekartete Sache f
frame'work' s Gebälk n, Fachwerk n; (fig) Rahmen m; (aer) Aufbau m
franc [fræŋk] s Franc m; (Swiss) Franken m
France [fræns] s Frankreich n
Frances ['frænsɪs] s Franziska f
franchise ['fræntʃaɪz] s Konzession f; (right to vote) Wahlrecht n
Francis ['frænsɪs] s Franz m
Franciscan [fræn'sɪskən] adj Franziskaner– || s Franziskaner m
frank [fræŋk] adj offen || s Freivermerk m; **Frank** (masculine name) Franz m; (medieval German person) Franke m, Frankin f || tr franieren
frankfurter ['fræŋkfərtər] s Würstel m
frankincense ['fræŋkɪn‚sens] s Weihrauch m
Frankish ['fræŋkɪʃ] adj fränkisch
frankness ['fræŋknɪs] s Offenheit f; (bluntness) Freimut m
frantic ['fræntɪk] adj (with) außer sich (vor dat); (efforts) krampfhaft

fraternal [frəˈtʌrnəl] *adj* brüderlich; *(twins)* zweieiig

fraternity [frəˈtʌrnɪti] *s* Bruderschaft *f*; *(educ)* Studentenverbindung *f*

fraternize [ˈfrætərˌnaɪz] *intr* **(with)** sich anfreunden (mit)

fraud [frɔd] *s* Betrug *m*; *(person)* (coll) Betrüger –in *mf*

fraudulent [ˈfrɔdjələnt] *adj* betrügerisch

fraught [frɔt] *adj*—**f. with** voll mit; **f. with danger** gefahrvoll

fray [fre] *s* Schlägerei *f*; *(battle)* Kampf *m* || *tr* ausfranzen; *(the nerves)* aufreiben || *intr* (said of edges) sich ausfranzen; *(become threadbare)* sich durchscheuern

freak [frik] *s* Mißbildung *f*; *(whimsy)* Laune *f*; *(enthusiast)* Enthusiast –in *mf*; *(abnormal person)* verrückter Kerl *m*; **f. of nature** Monstrum *n*

freakish [ˈfrikɪʃ] *adj* grotesk; *(capricious)* launisch

freckle [ˈfrekəl] *s* Sommersprosse *f*

freckled [ˈfrekəld], **freckly** [ˈfrekli] *adj* sommersprossig

Frederick [ˈfredərɪk] *s* Friedrich *m*

free [fri] *adj* (freer [ˈfri‧ər]; freest [ˈfri‧ɪst]) frei; *(off duty)* dienstfrei; **for f.** (coll) gratis; **f. with** (e.g., money, praise) freigebig mit; **go f.** frei ausgehen; **he is f. to** (*inf*) es steht ihm frei zu (*inf*); **set f.** freilassen || *adv* umsonst, kostenlos || *v* (*pret & pp* freed [frid]; *ger* freeing [ˈfri‧ɪŋ] *tr* (liberate) befreien; *(untie)* losmachen

free′ and ea′sy *adj* zwanglos

freebooter [ˈfriˌbutər] *s* Freibeuter *m*

free′born′ *adj* freigeboren

freedom [ˈfridəm] *s* Freiheit *f*

free′dom of assem′bly *s* Versammlungsfreiheit *f*

free′dom of speech′ *s* Redefreiheit *f*

free′dom of the press′ *s* Pressefreiheit *f*

free′dom of wor′ship *s* Glaubensfreiheit *f*

free′ en′terprise *s* freie Wirtschaft *f*

free′-for-all′ *s* allgemeine Prügelei *f*

free′ hand′ *s* freie Hand *f*

free′hand′ draw′ing *s* *(activity)* Freihandzeichnen *n*; *(product)* Freihandzeichnung *f*

free′hand′ed *adj* freigebig

free′hold′ *s* (jur) Freigut *n*

free′ kick′ *s* (fb) Freistoß *m*

free′-lance′ *adj* freiberuflich || *intr* freiberuflich tätig sein

free-lancer [ˈfriˌlænsər] *s* Freiberufliche *mf*

free′ li′brary *s* Volksbibliothek *f*

free′man *s* (–men) Ehrenbürger *m*

Free′ma′son *s* Freimaurer *m*

Free′ma′sonry *s* Freimaurerei *f*

free′ of charge′ *adj & adv* kostenlos

free′ on board′ *adv* frei an Bord

free′ play′ *s* (fig & mach) Spielraum *m*

free′ port′ *s* Freihafen *m*

free′ sam′ple *s* *(of food)* Gratiskostprobe *f*; *(of products)* Gratismuster *n*

free′ speech′ *s* Redefreiheit *f*

free′-spo′ken *adj* freimütig

free′stone′ *adj* mit leicht auslösbarem Kern

free′think′er *s* Freigeist *m*

free′ thought′ *s* Freigeisterei *f*

free′ trade′ *s* Freihandel *m*

free′way′ *s* Autobahn *f*

free′ will′ *s* Willensfreiheit *f*; **of one′s own f.** aus freien Stücken

freeze [friz] *s* Frieren *n* || *v* (*pret* froze [froz]; *pp* frozen [ˈfrozən]) *tr* frieren; *(assets)* einfrieren; *(prices)* stoppen; *(food)* tiefkühlen; (surg) vereisen || *intr* (ge)frieren; (e.g., with fear) erstarren; **f. over** zufrieren; **f. to death** erfrieren; **f. up** vereisen

freeze′-dry′ *v* (*pret & pp* –dried) *tr* gefriertrocknen

freezer [ˈfrizər] *s* (chest) Tiefkühltruhe *f*; *(cabinet)* Tiefkühlschrank *m*

freez′er compart′ment *s* Gefrierfach *n*

freez′ing *s* Einfrieren *n*; **below f.** unter dem Gefrierpunkt

freight [fret] *s* (load) Fracht *f*; *(cargo)* Frachtgut *n*; *(fee)* Frachtgebühr *f*; **by f.** als Frachtgut || *tr* beladen

freight′ car′ *s* Güterwagen *m*

freight′ el′evator *s* Warenaufzug *m*

freighter [ˈfretər] *s* Frachter *m*

freight′ of′fice *s* Güterabfertigung *f*

freight′ train′ *s* Güterzug *m*

freight′ yard′ *s* Güterbahnhof *m*

French [frentʃ] *adj* französisch || *s* (language) Französisch *n*; **the F.** die Franzosen

French′ doors′ *spl* Glastüre *pl*

French′ fries′ *spl* Pommes frites *pl*

French′ horn′ *s* (mus) Waldhorn *n*

French′ leave′ *s*—**take F.** sich französisch empfehlen

French′man *s* (–men) Franzose *m*

French′ roll′ *s* Schrippe *f*

French′ toast′ *s* arme Ritter *pl*

French′ win′dow *s* Flügelfenster *n*

French′ wom′an *s* (–wom′en) Französin *f*

frenzied [ˈfrenzid] *adj* rasend

frenzy [ˈfrenzi] *s* Raserei *f*

frequency [ˈfrikwənsi] *s* Häufigkeit *f*; (phys) Frequenz *f*

fre′quency modula′tion *s* Frequenzmodulation *f*

frequent [ˈfrikwənt] *adj* häufig || [friˈkwənt] *tr* besuchen, frequentieren

frequently [ˈfrikwəntli] *adv* häufig

fres·co [ˈfresko] *s* (–coes & –cos) Fresko *n*, Freskogemälde *n*

fresh [freʃ] *adj* frisch; (coll) frech || *adv* neu, kürzlich

fresh′-baked′ *adj* neugebacken

freshen [ˈfreʃən] *tr* erfrischen; **f. up** auffrischen || *intr*—**f. up** sich auffrischen

freshet [ˈfreʃɪt] *s* Hochwasser *n*; *(fresh-water stream)* Fluß *m*

fresh′man *s* (–men) Fuchs *m*

freshness [ˈfreʃnɪs] *s* Frische *f*; (coll) Naseweisheit *f*

fresh′ wa′ter *s* Süßwasser *n*

fresh′-wa′ter *adj* Süßwasser-

fret [fret] *s* Verdruß *m*; (carp) Laubsägewerk *n*; (mus) Bund *n* || *v* (*pret*

& *pp* **fretted;** *ger* **fretting)** *tr* gitter-
förmig verzieren || *intr* sich ärgern
fretful ['frɛtfəl] *adj* verdrießlich
fret′work′ *s* Laubsägewerk *n*
Freudian ['frɔɪdɪ-ən] *adj* Freudsch ||
s Freudianer –in *mf*
friar ['fraɪ-ər] *s* Klosterbruder *m*
fricassee [ˌfrɪkə'si] *s* Frikassee *n*
friction ['frɪk/ən] *s* Reibung *f;* (fig)
Reiberei *f,* Mißhelligkeit *f*
fric′tion tape′ *s* Isolierband *n*
Friday ['fraɪdɪ] *s* Freitag *m*
fried [fraɪd] *adj* gebraten, Brat–,
Back–
fried′ chick′en *s* Backhuhn *n*
fried′ egg′ *s* Spiegelei *n*
fried′ pota′toes *spl* Bratkartoffeln *pl*
friend [frɛnd] *s* Freund –in *mf;* **be
(close) friends** (eng) befreundet sein; **
make friends (with)** sich anfreunden
(mit)
friendliness ['frɛndlɪnɪs] *s* Freundlichkeit *f*
friendly ['frɛndli] *adj* freundlich; **on f.
terms with** in freundschaftlichem
Verhältnis mit
friend′ship′ *s* Freundschaft *f*
frieze [friz] *s* Fries *m*
frigate ['frɪgɪt] *s* Fregatte *f*
fright [fraɪt] *s* Schrecken *m*
frighten ['fraɪtən] *tr* schrecken; **be
frightened** erschrecken; **f. away** ver-
scheuchen, vertreiben
frightful ['fraɪtfəl] *adj* schrecklich
frigid ['frɪdʒɪd] *adj* eiskalt; (pathol)
Frigid
frigidity [frɪ'dʒɪdɪti] *s* Kälte *f;* (pathol)
Frigidität *f*
Frig′id Zone′ *s* kalte Zone *f*
frill [frɪl] *s* (*ruffle*) Volant *m,* Krause
f; (*frippery*) Schnörkel *m;* **put on
frills** sich aufgeblasen benehmen; **
with all the frills** mit allen Schikanen
fringe [frɪndʒ] *s* Franse *f* || *tr* mit
Fransen besetzen; (fig) einsäumen
fringe′ ar′ea *s* Randgebiet *n*
fringe′ ben′efit *s* zusätzliche Sozial-
leistung *f*
frippery ['frɪpəri] *s* (*cheap finery, trifles*) Flitterkram *m*
frisk [frɪsk] *tr* (sl) durchsuchen || *intr*
—**f. about** herumtollen
frisky ['frɪski] *adj* ausgelassen
fritter ['frɪtər] *s* Beignet *m* || *tr*—**f.
away** vertrödeln, verzetteln
fritz [frɪts] *s*—**on the f.** kaputt
frivolous ['frɪvələs] *adj* leichtfertig;
(*object*) geringfügig
friz [frɪz] *s* (**frizzes**) Kraushaar *n* ||
v (*pret & pp* **frizzed;** *ger* **frizzing**) *tr*
kräuseln || *intr* sich kräuseln
frizzle ['frɪzəl] *s* Kraushaar *n* || *tr*
(*hair*) kräuseln; (*food*) knusprig bra-
ten || *intr* sich kräuseln; (*sizzle*)
zischen
frizzy ['frɪzi] *adj* kraus
fro [fro] *adv*—**to and fro** hin und her
frock [frɑk] *s* Kleid *n;* (eccl) Mönchs-
kutte *f*
frog [frɔg] *s* (*animal; slight hoarseness*) Frosch *m*
frog′man′ *s* (**-men′**) Froschmann *m*
frol·ic ['frɑlɪk] *s* Spaß *m* || *v* (*pret &*

pp **–icked;** *ger* **–icking**) *intr* Spaß
machen; (*frisk about*) herumtollen
frolicsome ['frɑlɪksəm] *adj* ausgelassen
from [frʌm] *prep* von (dat), aus (*dat*),
von (*dat*) aus; **f. afar** von weitem;
f. now on künftig; **f. ... on** von ... **
an**
front [frʌnt] *adj* Vorder–, vordere ||
s (*façade*) Vorderseite *f;* (*of a shirt,
dress*) Einsatz *m;* (*cover-up*) Aushängeschild *n;* (meteor, mil) Front
f; **from the f.** von vorn; **in f.** vorn;
in f. of vor (*dat or acc*); **in the f.
of the book** vorn im Buch; **put on
a bold f.** Mut zeigen; **they put on a
big f.** alles Fassade! || *tr* gegenüber-
liegen (*dat*) || *intr*—**f. for s.o.** j-m
als Strohmann dienen; **f. on** mit der
Front liegen nach
frontage ['frʌntɪdʒ] *s* Straßenfront *f*
frontal ['frʌntəl] *adj* Frontal–; (anat)
Stirn–
fron′tal view′ *s* Vorderansicht *f*
front′ door′ *s* Haustür *f*
front′ foot′ *s* Vorderfuß *m*
frontier [frʌn'tɪr] *s* (*border*) Grenze
f; (*area*) Grenzland *n;* (fig) Grenz-
bereich *m*
frontiers′man *s* (**-men**) Pionier *m*
frontispiece ['frʌntɪsˌpis] *s* Titelbild
n
front′ line′ *s* Front *f,* Frontlinie *f*
front′-line′ *adj* Front–, Gefechts–
front′ page′ *s* Titelseite *f*
front′ porch′ *s* Veranda *f*
front′ rank′ *s* (mil) vorderes Glied *n;*
be in the f. (fig) im Vordergrund
stehen
front′ row′ *s* erste Reihe *f*
front′ run′ner *s* (pol) Spitzenkandidat
–in *mf*
front′ seat′ *s* Vordersitz *m*
front′ steps′ *spl* Vordertreppe *f*
front′ yard′ *s* Vorgarten *m,* Vorplatz *m*
frost [frɔst] *s* (*freezing*) Frost *m;*
(*frozen dew*) Reif *m* || *tr* mit Reif
überziehen; (culin) glasieren
frost′bite′ *s* Erfrierung *f*
frost′bit′ten *adj* erfroren
frost′ed glass′ *s* Mattglas *n*
frost′ing *s* Glasur *f*
frost′ line′ *s* Frostgrenze *f*
frosty ['frɔsti] *adj* (& fig) frostig
froth [frɔθ] *s* (*foam*) Schaum *m;*
(*slaver*) Geifer *m* || *intr* schäumen
frothy ['frɔθi] *adj* schäumend
froward ['froward] *adj* eigensinnig
frown [fraun] *s* Stirnrunzeln *n* || *intr*
die Stirn runzeln; **f. at** böse anschauen; **f. on** mißbilligen
frowsy, frowzy ['frauzi] *adj* (*slovenly*)
schlampig; (*ill-smelling*) muffig
froz′en as′sets ['frozən] *spl* eingefro-
rene Guthaben *pl*
froz′en foods′ *spl* tiefgekühlte Lebensmittel *pl*
frugal ['frugəl] *adj* frugal
fruit [frut] *adj* (*tree*) Obst–, Süd-
frucht– || *s* Frucht *f,* Obst *n,* Süd-
früchte *pl;* (fig) Frucht *f*
fruit′ cake′ *s* Stolle *f,* Stollen *m*

fruit′ cup′ s gemischte Früchte pl

fruit′ fly′ s Obstfliege f

fruitful ['frutfəl] adj fruchtbar

fruition [fru'ɪʃən] s Reife f; **come to f.** zur Reife gelangen

fruit′ jar′ s Konservenglas n

fruit′ juice′ s Fruchtsaft m, Obstsaft m

fruitless ['frutlɪs] adj (& fig) fruchtlos

fruit′ sal′ad s Obstsalat m

fruit′ stand′ s Obststand m

frump [frʌmp] s Scharteke f

frumpish ['frʌmpɪʃ] adj schlampig

frustrate ['frʌstret] tr (discourage) frustrieren; (an endeavor) vereiteln

frustration [frʌs'treʃən] s Frustration f; (of an endeavor) Vereitelung f

fry [fraɪ] s Gebratenes n ‖ v (pret & pp fried) tr & intr braten

fry′ing pan′ s Bratpfanne f; **jump out of the f. into the fire** vom Regen unter die Traufe kommen

fuchsia ['fjuʃə] s (bot) Fuchsie f

fudge [fʌdʒ] s weiches, milchhaltiges, mit Kakao versetztes Zuckerwerk n

fuel ['fjuəl] s Brennstoff m; (for engines) Treibstoff m; (fig) Nahrung f; **add f. to the flames** Öl ins Feuer gießen ‖ v (pret & pp fuel[l]ed) ger fuel[l]ing) tr mit Brennstoff versorgen ‖ intr tanken

fu′el dump′ s Treibstofflager n

fu′el gauge′ s Benzinuhr f

fu′el tank′ s Treibstoffbehälter m

fugitive ['fjudʒɪtɪv] adj flüchtig ‖ s Flüchtling m

fugue [fjug] s (mus) Fuge f

ful·crum ['fʌlkrəm] s (-crums & -cra [krə]) Stützpunkt m, Drehpunkt m

fulfill [fʊl'fɪl] tr erfüllen

fulfillment [fʊl'fɪlmənt] s Erfüllung f

full [fʊl] adj voll; (with food) satt; (clothes) weit; (hour) ganz; (life) inhaltsreich; (voice) wohlklingend; (professor) ordentlich; **f. of** voller, voll von; **too f.** übervoll; **work f. time** ganztägig arbeiten ‖ adv—**f. well** sehr gut ‖ s—**in f.** voll, ganz ‖ tr (tex) walken

full′back′ s (fb) Außenverteidiger m

full′-blood′ed adj vollblütig

full-blown ['fʊl'blon] adj (flower) voll aufgeblüht; (fig) voll erblüht

full′-bod′ied adj (wine) stark, schwer

full′ dress′ s Gesellschaftsanzug m; (mil) Paradeanzug m

full′-dress′ adj Gala–, formell

full′-faced′ adj pausbackig; (portrait) mit voll zugewandtem Gesicht

full-fledged ['fʊl'fledʒd] adj richtiggehend

full-grown ['fʊl'gron] adj voll ausgewachsen

full′ house′ s (cards) Full house n; (theat) volles Haus n

full′-length′ adj (dress) in voller Größe; (portrait) lebensgroß; (movie) abendfüllend

full′ moon′ s Vollmond m

full′-page′ adj ganzseitig

full′ pay′ s volles Gehalt n

full′ profes′sor s Ordinarius m

full′-scale′ adj in voller Größe

full′-sized′ adj in natürlicher Größe

full′ speed′ adv auf höchsten Touren

full′ stop′ s (gram) Punkt m; **come to a f.** völlig stillstehen

full′ swing′—**in f.** in vollem Gange

full′ throt′tle s Vollgas m

full′ tilt′ adv auf höchsten Touren

full′-time′ adj ganztägig

full′ view′ s—**in f.** direkt vor den Augen

fully ['fʊl]i] adv völlig; **be f. booked** ausverkauft sein

fulsome ['fʊlsəm] adj (excessive) übermäßig; (offensive) widerlich

fumble ['fʌmbəl] tr (a ball) fallen lassen ‖ intr fummeln; **f. for** umherfühlen nach

fume [fjum] s Gas n, Dampf m ‖ intr dampfen; (smoke) rauchen; **f. with rage** vor Wut schnauben

fumigate ['fjumɪ‚get] tr ausräuchern

fun [fʌn] s Spaß m; **be (great) fun** (viel) Spaß machen; **for fun** zum Spaß; **for the fun of it** spaßeshalber; **have fun!** viel Spaß!; **make fun of** sich lustig machen über (acc); **poke fun at** witzeln über (acc)

function ['fʌŋkʃən] s Funktion f; (office) Amt n; (formal occasion) Feier f ‖ intr funktionieren; (officiate) fungieren

functional ['fʌŋkʃənəl] adj (practical) Zweck–, zweckmäßig; (disorder) funktionell, Funktions–

functionary ['fʌŋkʃə‚nerɪ] s Funktionär –in mf

fund [fʌnd] s Fonds m; (fig) Vorrat m **funds** Geldmittel pl ‖ tr fundieren

fundamental [‚fʌndə'mentəl] adj grundlegend, Grund– ‖ s Grundbegriff m

fundamentalist [‚fʌndə'mentəlɪst] s Fundamentalist –in mf

fundamentally [‚fʌndə'mentəli] adv im Grunde, prinzipiell

funeral ['fjunərəl] adj Leichen–, Trauer–, Begräbnis– ‖ s Begräbnis n

fu′neral direc′tor s Bestattungsunternehmer –in mf

fu′neral home′ s Aufbahrungshalle f

fu′neral proces′sion s Trauergefolge n

fu′neral serv′ice s Trauergottesdienst m

fu′neral wreath′ s Totenkranz m

funereal [fju'nɪrɪ·əl] adj düster

fungus ['fʌŋgəs] s (funguses & fungi ['fʌndʒaɪ]) Pilz m, Schwamm m

funicular [fju'nɪkjələr] s Drahtseilbahn f

funk [fʌŋk] s (fear) Mordsangst f; **be in a f.** niedergeschlagen sein

fun·nel ['fʌnəl] s Trichter m; (naut) Schornstein m ‖ v (pret & pp -nel[l]ed) ger -nel[l]ing) tr durch e–n Trichter gießen; (fig) (into) konzentrieren (auf acc)

funnies ['fʌnɪz] spl Witzseite f

funny ['fʌni] adj komisch; (strange, suspicious) sonderbar; **don't try anything f.** mach mir keine Dummheiten!

fun′ny bone′ s Musikantenknochen m

fun′ny bus′iness s dunkle Geschäfte pl

fun′ny ide′as spl Flausen pl

fun'ny pa'per s Witzblatt n
fur [fʌr] adj (coat, collar) Pelz– ‖ s
Pelz m; (on the tongue) Belag m
furbish ['fɜrbɪʃ] tr aufputzen
furious ['fjʊrɪ-əs] adj (at) wütend
(auf acc); **be f.** wüten
furl [fʌrl] tr zusammenrollen
fur'-lined' adj pelzgefüttert
furlong ['fʌrlɔŋ] s Achtelmeile f
furlough ['fʌrlo] s (mil) Urlaub m; **go
on f.** auf Urlaub kommen ‖ tr beurlauben
furnace ['fʌrnɪs] s Ofen m
furnish ['fʌrnɪʃ] tr (a room) möblieren; (e.g., an office) ausstatten;
(proof) liefern; (supply) (with) versehen (mit)
fur'nished room' s möbliertes Zimmer
n
furnishings ['fʌrnɪʃɪŋz] spl Ausstattung f
furniture ['fʌrnɪtʃər] s Möbel pl; **piece
of f.** Möbelstück n
fur'niture store' s Möbelhandlung f
furor ['fjʊrɔr] s (rage) Wut f; (uproar) Furore f; (vogue) Mode f;
cause a f. Furore machen
furrier ['fʌrɪ-ər] s Pelzhändler –in mf
furrow ['fʌro] s Furche f ‖ tr furchen
furry ['fʌri] adj pelzig
further ['fʌrðər] adj weiter; (particulars) näher ‖ adv weiter ‖ tr fördern
furtherance ['fʌrðərəns] s Förderung f
fur'thermore' adv überdies, außerdem
furthest ['fʌrðɪst] adj weiteste ‖ adv
am weitesten
furtive ['fʌrtɪv] adj verstohlen

fury ['fjʊri] s Wut f; **Fury** (myth)
Furie f
fuse [fjuz] s (of an explosive) Zünder
m; (elec) Sicherung f; **blown f.**
durchgebrannte Sicherung f ‖ tr verschmelzen ‖ intr verschmelzen; (fig)
sich vereinigen
fuse' box' s Sicherungskasten m
fuselage ['fjuzəlɪdʒ] s (aer) Rumpf m
fusible ['fjuzɪbəl] adj schmelzbar
fusillade ['fjusə,led] s Feuersalve f;
(fig) Hagel m
fusion ['fjuʒən] s Verschmelzung f;
(pol, phys) Fusion f
fuss [fʌs] s Getue n; **make a f. over**
viel Aufhebens machen von ‖ intr
sich aufregen; **f. around** herumwirt-
schaften; **f. over** viel Aufhebens machen von; **f. with** herumspielen mit
fuss' bud'get, fuss'pot' s Umstandskrä-
mer m
fussy ['fʌsi] adj (given to detail) umständlich; (fastidious) heikel; (irritable) reizbar; **be f.** Umstände machen
fustian ['fʌstʃən] s (bombast) Schwulst
m; (tex) Barchent m
fusty ['fʌsti] adj (musty) muffig; (old-
fashioned) veraltet
futile ['fjutəl] adj vergeblich, nutzlos
futility [fju'tɪlɪti] s Nutzlosigkeit f
future ['fjutʃər] adj (zu)künftig ‖ s
Zukunft f; **futures** (econ) Terminge-
schäfte pl; **in the f.** künftig
fuzz [fʌz] s (from cloth) Fussel f; (on
peaches) Flaum m
fuzzy ['fʌzi] adj flaumig; (unclear) unklar; (hair) kraus

G

G, g [dʒi] s siebenter Buchstabe des
englischen Alphabets
gab [gæb] s (coll) Geschwätz n ‖ v
(pret & pp gabbed; ger gabbing)
intr schwatzen
gabardine ['gæbər,din] s Gabardine m
gabble ['gæbəl] s Geschnatter n ‖ intr
schnattern
gable ['gebəl] s Giebel m
ga'ble end' s Giebelwand f
ga'ble roof' s Giebeldach n
gad [gæd] v (pret & pp gadded; ger
gadding) intr—**gad about** umher-
streifen
gad'about' s Bummler –in mf
gad'fly' s Viehbremse f; (fig) Störenfried m
gadget ['gædʒɪt] s (coll) Gerät n
Gaelic ['gelɪk] adj gälisch ‖ s (language) Gälisch n
gaff [gæf] s Fischhaken m
gag [gæg] s (something put into the
mouth) Knebel m; (joke) Witz m;
(hoax, trick) amüsanter Trick m ‖
v (pret & pp gagged; ger gagging) tr
knebeln; (said of a tight collar) würgen; (fig) mundtot machen ‖ intr
(on food) würgen

gage [gedʒ] s (challenge) Fehdehandschuh m; (pawn) Pfand m
gaiety ['ge-ɪti] s Fröhlichkeit f
gaily ['geli] adv fröhlich
gain [gen] s Gewinn m; (advantage)
Vorteil m; **g. in weight** Gewichtszunahme f ‖ tr gewinnen; (pounds)
zunehmen; (a living) verdienen; (a
victory) erringen; **g. a footing** festen
Fuß fassen; **g. ground** (mil & fig)
Terrain gewinnen; **g. speed** schneller
werden; **g. weight** an Gewicht zunehmen ‖ intr (said of a car) aufholen;
(said of a clock) vorgehen; **g. from**
Gewinn haben von; **g. in** gewinnen
an (dat); **g. on s.o.** j–m den Vorteil
abgewinnen
gainful ['genfəl] adj einträglich
gainfully ['genfəli] adv—**g. employed**
erwerbstätig
gain'say' v (pret & pp –said [,sed],
[,sed]) tr (a thing) verneinen; (a
person) widersprechen (dat)
gait [get] s Gang m, Gangart f
gala ['gælə], ['gelə] adj festlich ‖ s
(celebration) Feier f; (dress) Gala f
galaxy ['gæləksi] s Galaxis f; (fig)
glänzende Versammlung f

gale [gel] *s* Sturm *m*, Sturmwind *m*;
gales of laughter Lachensalven *pl*
gale' warn'ing *s* Sturmwarnung *f*
gall [gɔl] *s* Galle *f*; *(audacity)* Unverschämtheit *f* ‖ *tr (rub)* wundreiben;
(vex) ärgern, belästigen
gallant ['gælənt] *adj (tapfer)*; *(stately)*
stattlich ‖ [gə'lænt] *adj* galant ‖ *s*
Galan *m*
gallantry ['gæləntri] *s (bravery)* Tapferkeit *f*; *(courteous behavior)* Ritterlichkeit *f*
gall' blad'der *s* Gallenblase *f*
galleon ['gæli·ən] *s* Galeone *f*
gallery ['gæləri] *s (arcade)* Säulen-
halle *f*; *(art, theat)* Galerie *f*; *(min)*
Stollen *m*; **play to the g.** (coll) Effekthascherei treiben
galley ['gæli] *s (a ship)* Galeere *f*; *(a
kitchen)* Kombüse *f*; *(typ)* Setzschiff
n
gal'ley proof' *s (typ)* Fahne *f*
gal'ley slave' *s* Galeerensklave *m*
Gallic ['gælɪk] *adj* gallisch
gall'ing *adj* verdrießlich
gallivant ['gæli‚vænt] *intr* bummeln
gallon ['gælən] *s* Gallone *f*
galloon [gə'lun] *s* Tresse *f*
gallop ['gæləp] *s* Galopp *m*; **at full g.**
in gestrecktem Galopp ‖ *tr* in Ga-
lopp setzen ‖ *intr* galoppieren
gal·lows ['gæloz] *s (-lows & -lowses)*
Galgen *m*
gal'lows bird' *s* (coll) Galgenvogel *m*
gall'stone' *s* Gallenstein *m*
galore [gə'lor] *adv* im Überfluß
galosh [gə'lɑʃ] *s* Galosche *f*
galvanize ['gælvə‚naɪz] *tr* galvanisieren
gambit ['gæmbɪt] *s (fig)* Schachzug
m; *(chess)* Gambit *n*
gamble ['gæmbəl] *s* Hasardspiel *n*;
(risk) Risiko *n*; *(com)* Spekulations-
geschäft *n* ‖ *tr*—**g. away** verspielen
‖ *intr* spielen, hasardieren
gambler ['gæmblər] *s* Spieler –in *mf*;
(fig) Hasardeur *m*, Hasardeuse *f*
gam'bling *s* Spielen *n*, Spiel *n*
gam'bling house' *s* Spielhölle *f*
gam'bling ta'ble *s* Spieltisch *m*
gam·bol ['gæmbəl] *s* Luftsprung *m* ‖ *v
(pret & pp* **–bol[l]ed;** *ger* **–bol[l]ing)**
intr umhertollen
gambrel ['gæmbrəl] *s (hock)* Hachse
f; *(in a butcher shop)* Spriegel *m*
gam'brel roof' *s* Mansardendach *n*
game [gem] *adj* bereit; *(fight)* tapfer;
(leg) lahm; *(hunt)* Wild–, Jagd– ‖ *s*
Spiel *n*; *(e.g., of chess)* Partie *f*; *(fig)*
Absicht *f*; *(culin)* Wildbret *n*; *(hunt)*
Wild *n*, Jagdwild *n*; **have the g. in
the bag** den Sieg in der Tasche haben; **play a losing g.** auf verlorenem
Posten kämpfen; **the g. is up** das
Spiel ist aus
game' bird' *s* Jagdvogel *m*
game' board' *s* Spielbrett *n*
game'cock' *s* Kampfhahn *m*
gameness ['gemnɪs] *f* Tapferkeit *f*
game' of chance' *s* Glücksspiel *n*
game' preserve' *s* Wildpark *m*
game' war'den *s* Jagdaufseher *m*
gamut ['gæmət] *s* Skala *f*

gamy ['gemi] *adj* nach Wild riechend;
g. flavor Wildgeschmack *m*
gander ['gændər] *s* Gänserich *m*; **take
a g. at** (coll) e-n Blick werfen auf
(acc)
gang [gæŋ] *s (group of friends)* Gesellschaft *f*; *(antisocial group)* Bande
f; *(of workers)* Kolonne *f* ‖ *intr*—
g. up (on) sich zusammenrotten
(gegen)
gangling ['gæŋglɪŋ] *adj* schlaksig
gangli·on ['gæŋglɪ·ən] *s (-ons & -a
[ə])* *(cystic tumor)* Überbein *n*; *(of
nerves)* Nervenknoten *m*
gangly ['gæŋgli] *adj* schlaksig
gang'plank' *s* Laufplanke *f*, Steg *m*
gangrene ['gæŋgrin] *s* Gangrän *n*,
Brand *m* ‖ *intr* brandig werden
gangrenous ['gæŋgrɪnəs] *adj* brandig
gangster ['gæŋstər] *s* Gangster *m*
gang'way' *s (passageway)* Durchgang
m; *(naut)* Laufplanke *f* ‖ *interj* aus
dem Weg!
gantlet ['gɔntlət] *s (rr)* Gleisverschlin-
gung *f*
gantry ['gæntri] *s (rok)* Portalkran *m*;
(rr) Signalbrücke *f*
gan'try crane' *s* Portalkran *m*
gap [gæp] *s (fig)* Lücke *f*; *(in the mountains)* Schlucht *f*; *(mil)* Bresche *f*
gape [gep] *s* Riß *m*, Sprung *m*; *(gaping)* Gaffen *n* ‖ *intr* gaffen; *(said of
wounds, etc.)* klaffen; **g. at** angaffen
garage [gə'rɑʒ] *s* Garage *f*; *(repair
shop)* Reparaturwerkstatt *f*; **put into
the g.** unterstellen
garb [gɑrb] *s* Tracht *f*
garbage ['gɑrbɪdʒ] *s* Müll *m*; *(nonsense)* Unsinn *m*
gar'bage can' *s* Mülltonne *f*
gar'bage dispos'al *s* Müllabfuhr *f*
gar'bage dump' *s* Müllplatz *m*
gar'bage man' *s* Müllfahrer *m*
gar'bage truck' *s* Müllabfuhrwagen *m*
garble ['gɑrbəl] *tr* verstümmeln
garden ['gɑrdən] *s* Garten *m*; **gardens**
Gartenanlage *f*
gardener ['gɑrdənər] *s* Gärtner –in *mf*
gar'den hose' *s* Gartenschlauch *m*
gardenia [gɑr'dini·ə] *s* Gardenie *f*
gar'dening *s* Gartenarbeit *f*
gar'den par'ty *s* Gartengesellschaft *f*
gargle ['gɑrgəl] *s* Mundwasser *n* ‖ *tr
& intr* gurgeln
gargoyle ['gɑrgɔɪl] *s* Wasserspeier *m*
garish ['gerɪʃ], ['gærɪʃ] *adj* grell
garland ['gɑrlənd] *s* Girlande *f*
garlic ['gɑrlɪk] *s* Knoblauch *m*
garment ['gɑrmənt] *s* Kleidungsstück *n*
garner ['gɑrnər] *tr (grain)* aufspei-
chern; *(gather)* ansammeln
garnet ['gɑrnɪt] *s* Granat *m*
garnish ['gɑrnɪʃ] *s* Verzierung *f*;
(culin) Garnierung *f* ‖ *tr* verzieren;
(culin) garnieren
garret ['gærɪt] *s* Dachstube *f*
garrison ['gærɪsən] *s (troops)* Garnison *f*, Besatzung *f*; *(fort)* Festung *f*
‖ *tr* mit e-r Garnison versehen;
(troops) in Garnison stationieren
gar'rison cap' *s* Schiffchen *n*
garrote [gə'rɑt], [gə'rot] *s* Garrotte *f*
‖ *tr* garrottieren

garrulous ['gær(j)ələs] *adj* schwatzhaft
garter ['gɑrtər] *s* Strumpfband *n*
gar'ter belt' *s* Strumpfhaltergürtel *m*
gas [gæs] *adj* (e.g., *generator, light, main, meter*) Gas- ‖ *s* Gas *n*; (coll) Benzin *n*, Sprit *m*; (*empty talk*) (sl) leeres Geschwätz *n*; **get gas** (coll) tanken; **step on the gas** (coll) Gas geben ‖ *v* (*pret & pp* **gassed**; *ger* **gassing**) *tr* vergasen ‖ *intr* (sl) schwatzen; **gas up** (coll) volltanken
gas' attack' *s* Gasangriff *m*
gas' burn'er *s* Gasbrenner *m*
gas' en'gine *s* Gasmotor *m*
gaseous ['gæsɪ-əs], ['gæʃəs] *adj* gasförmig
gas' fit'ter *s* Gasinstallateur *m*
gash [gæʃ] *s* tiefe Schnittwunde *f* ‖ *tr* e-e tiefe Schnittwunde beibringen (*dat*)
gas' heat' *s* Gasheizung *f*
gas'hold'er *s* Gasbehälter *m*
gasi-fy ['gæsɪ‚faɪ] *v* (*pret & pp* **-fied**) *tr* in Gas verwandeln ‖ *intr* zu Gas werden
gas' jet' *s* Gasflamme *f*
gasket ['gæskɪt] *s* Dichtung *f*
gas' mask' *s* Gasmaske *f*
gasoline [‚gæsə'lin] *s* Benzin *n*
gasoline' pump' *s* Benzinzapfsäule *f*
gasp [gæsp] *s* Keuchen *n* ‖ *tr* (out) hervorstoßen ‖ *intr* keuchen; **g. for air** nach Luft schnappen; **g. for breath** nach Atem ringen
gas' range' *s* Gasherd *m*
gas' sta'tion *s* Tankstelle *f*
gas' sta'tion attend'ant *s* Tankwart *m*
gas' stove' *s* Gasherd *m*
gas' tank' *s* Benzinbehälter *m*
gastric ['gæstrɪk] *adj* gastrisch
gas'tric juice' *s* Magensaft *m*
gastronomy [gæs'trɑnəmi] *s* Gastronomie *f*
gas'works' *spl* Gasanstalt *f*
gate [get] *s* Tor *n*, Pforte *f*; (rr) Sperre *f*; (sport) eingenommenes Eintrittsgeld *n*; **crash the g.** ohne Eintrittskarte durchschlupfen
gate' crash'er [‚kræʃər] *s* unberechtigter Zuschauer *m*
gate'keep'er *s* Pförtner –in *mf*
gate'post' *s* Torpfosten *m*
gate'way' *s* Tor *n*, Torweg *m*
gather ['gæðər] *tr* (*things*) sammeln; (*people*) versammeln; (*flowers, fruit, peas*) pflücken; (*courage*) aufbringen; (*the impression*) gewinnen; (*information*) einziehen; (*strength, speed*) zunehmen an (*dat*); (*conclude*) (**from**) schließen (aus); **g. together** versammeln; **g. up** aufheben; (*curtains, dress*) raffen ‖ *intr* sich (an)sammeln; (*said of clouds*) sich zusammenziehen; **g. around** sich scharen um
gath'ered *adj* (*skirt*) gerafft
gath'ering *s* Versammlung *f*; (sew) Kräuselfalten *pl*
gaudy ['gɔdi] *adj* (*overdone*) überladen; (*color*) grell
gauge [gedʒ] *s* (*instrument*) Messer *m*, Anzeiger *m*; (*measurement*) Eichmaß *n*; (*of wire*) Stärke *f*; (*of a shot-*

gun) Kaliber *n*; (fig) Maß *n*; (mach) Lehre *f*; (rr) Spurweite *f* ‖ *tr* messen; (*check for accuracy*) eichen; (fig) abschätzen
Gaul [gɔl] *s* Gallien *n*; (*native*) Gallier –in *mf*
Gaulish ['gɔlɪʃ] *adj* gallisch
gaunt [gɔnt] *adj* hager
gauntlet ['gɔntlɪt] *s* Panzerhandschuh *m*; (fig) Fehdehandschuh *m*; **run the g.** Spießruten laufen
gauze [gɔz] *s* Gaze *f*
gavel ['gævəl] *s* Hammer *m*
gawk [gɔk] *s* (coll) Depp *m* ‖ *intr*—**g. at** (coll) blöde anstarren
gawky ['gɔki] *adj* schlaksig
gay [ge] *adj* lustig; (*homosexual*) schwul
gay' blade' *s* lebenslustiger Kerl *m*
gaze [gez] *intr* starren; **g. at** anstarren; (*in astonishment*) anstaunen
gazelle [gə'zɛl] *s* Gazelle *f*
gazetteer [‚gæzə'tɪr] *s* Ortslexikon *n*
gear [gɪr] *s* (*equipment*) Ausrüstung *f*; (aut) Schaltgetriebe *n*, Gang *m*; (mach) Zahnrad *n*; **gears** Räderwerk *n*; **in g.** eingeschaltet; **in high g.** im höchsten Gang; (fig) auf Touren; **shift gears** umschalten; **throw into g.** einschalten; **throw out of g.** (fig) aus dem Gleichgewicht bringen ‖ *tr*—**g. to** anpassen (*dat*)
gear'box' *s* Schaltgetriebe *n*
gear'shift' *s* Gangschaltung *f*; (*lever*) Schalthebel *m*
gear'wheel' *s* Zahnrad *n*
gee [dʒi] *interj* nanu!
Geiger counter ['gaɪgər ‚kaʊntər] *s* Geigerzähler *m*
gel [dʒɛl] *s* Gel *n* ‖ *v* (*pret & pp* **gelled**; *ger* **gelling**) *intr* gelieren; (coll) klappen
gelatin ['dʒɛlətɪn] *s* Gelatine *f*
geld [gɛld] *v* (*pret & pp* **gelded & gelt** [gɛlt]) *tr* kastrieren
geld'ing *s* Wallach *m*
gem [dʒɛm] *s* Edelstein *m*; (fig) Perle *f*
Gemini ['dʒɛmɪ‚naɪ] *s* (astr) Zwillinge *pl*
gender ['dʒɛndər] *s* Geschlecht *n*
gene [dʒin] *s* Gen *n*, Erbanlage *f*
genealogical [‚dʒinɪ-ə'lɑdʒɪkəl] *adj* genealogisch, Stamm-
genealog'ical ta'ble *s* Stammtafel *f*
genealog'ical tree' *s* Stammbaum *m*
genealogy [‚dʒini'ælədʒi] *s* Genealogie *f*
general ['dʒɛnərəl] *adj* allgemein, Gesamt- ‖ *s* General *m*; **in g.** im allgemeinen
Gen'eral Assem'bly *s* Vollversammlung *f*
gen'eral deliv'ery *adv* postlagernd
gen'eral head'quarters *spl* Oberkommando *n*
generalissi-mo [‚dʒɛnərə'lɪsɪmo] *s* (**-mos**) Generalissimus *m*
generality [‚dʒɛnə'rælɪti] *s* Allgemeingültigkeit *f*; **generalities** Gemeinplätze *pl*
generalization [‚dʒɛnərəlɪ'zeʃən] *s* Verallgemeinerung *f*

generalize ['dʒenərə‚laɪz] *tr & intr* verallgemeinern

generally ['dʒenərəli] *adv* im allgemeinen; (*usually*) gewöhnlich; (*mostly*) meistens

gen'eral man'ager *s* Generaldirektor –in *mf*

gen'eral plan' *s* Übersichtsplan *m*

gen'eral post' of'fice *s* Oberpostamt *n*

gen'eral practi'tioner *s* praktischer Arzt *m*

gen'eralship' *s* Führereigenschaften *pl*

gen'eral staff' *s* Generalstab *m*

gen'eral store' *s* Gemischtwarenhandlung *f*

gen'eral strike' *s* Generalstreik *m*

generate ['dʒenə‚ret] *tr* (*procreate*) zeugen; (fig) verursachen; (elec) erzeugen; (geom) bilden

gen'erating sta'tion *s* Kraftwerk *n*

generation [‚dʒenə'reʃən] *s* Generation *f*; **present g.** Mitwelt *f*; **younger g.** junge Generation *f*

genera'tion gap' *s* Generationsproblem *n*

generator ['dʒenə‚retər] *s* Erzeuger *m*; (chem, elec) Generator *m*; (elec) Stromerzeuger *m*

generic [dʒɪ'nerɪk] *adj* generisch, Gattungs-; **g. name** Gattungsname *m*

generosity [‚dʒenə'rɑsɪti] *s* Freigebigkeit *f*

generous ['dʒenərəs] *adj* freigebig

gene·sis ['dʒenɪsɪs] *s* (–ses [‚siz]) Genese *f*, Entstehung *f*; **Genesis** (Bib) Genesis *f*

genetic [dʒɪ'netɪk] *adj* genetisch

genet'ic engineer' *s* Gen-Ingineur *m*

genet'ic engineer'ing *s* Gen-Manipulation *f*

genetics [dʒɪ'netɪks] *s* Genetik *f*, Vererbungslehre *f*

Geneva [dʒɪ'nivə] *adj* Genfer ‖ *s* Genf *n*

Genevieve ['dʒenə‚viv] *s* Genoveva *f*

genial ['dʒinɪ·əl] *adj* freundlich

genie ['dʒini] *s* Kobold *m*

genital ['dʒenɪtəl] *adj* Genital– ‖ **genitals** *spl* Genitalien *pl*

genitive ['dʒenɪtɪv] *s* Genitiv *m*, Wesfall *m*

geni·us ['dʒinɪ·əs] *s* (geniuses) Genie *n* ‖ *s* (genii ['dʒinɪ‚aɪ]) Genius *m*

Genoa ['dʒeno·ə] *s* Genua *n*

genocidal [‚dʒenə'saɪdəl] *adj* rassenmörderisch

genocide ['dʒenə‚saɪd] *s* Rassenmord *m*

genre ['ʒɑnrə] *s* Genre *n*

genteel [dʒen'til] *adj* vornehm

gentile ['dʒentaɪl] *adj* nichtjüdisch; (*pagan*) heidnisch ‖ *s* Nichtjude *m*, Nichtjüdin *f*; (*pagan*) Heide *m*, Heidin *f*

gentility [dʒen'tɪlɪti] *s* Vornehmheit *f*

gentle ['dʒentəl] *adj* sanft, mild; (*tame*) zahm

gen'tle·man *s* (–men) Herr *m*, Gentleman *m*

gentlemanly ['dʒentəlmənli] *adj* weltmännisch

gen'tleman's agree'ment *s* Kavaliersab-

kommen *n*, Gentleman's Agreement *n*

gentleness ['dʒentəlnɪs] *s* Sanftmut *f*

gen'tle sex' *s* zartes Geschlecht *n*

gentry ['dʒentri] *s* feine Leute *pl*

genuflection [‚dʒenju'flekʃən] *s* Kniebeugung *f*

genuine ['dʒenju·ɪn] *adj* echt

genus ['dʒinəs] *s* (genera ['dʒenərə] & genuses) (biol, log) Gattung *f*

geographer [dʒɪ'ɑgrəfər] *s* Geograph –in *mf*

geographic(al) [‚dʒɪ·ə'græfɪk(əl)] *adj* geographisch

geography [dʒɪ'ɑgrəfi] *s* Geographie *f*

geologic(al) [‚dʒɪ·ə'lɑdʒɪk(əl)] *adj* geologisch

geolog'ical e'ra *s* Erdalter *n*

geologist [dʒɪ'ɑlədʒɪst] *s* Geologe *m*, Geologin *f*

geology [dʒɪ'ɑlədʒi] *s* Geologie *f*

geometric(al) [‚dʒɪ·ə'metrɪk(əl)] *adj* geometrisch

geometrician [dʒɪ‚ɑmɪ'trɪʃən] *s* Geometer –in *mf*

geometry [dʒɪ'ɑmɪtri] *s* Geometrie *f*

geophysics [‚dʒɪ·ə'fɪzɪks] *s* Geophysik *f*

geopolitics [‚dʒɪ·ə'pɑlɪtɪks] *s* Geopolitik *f*

George [dʒɔrdʒ] *s* Georg *m*

geranium [dʒɪ'renɪ·əm] *s* Geranie *f*

geriatrics [‚dʒerɪ'ætrɪks] *s* Geriatrie *f*

germ [dʒʌrm] *s* Keim *m*

German ['dʒʌrmən] *adj & adv* deutsch ‖ *s* Deutsche *mf*; (*language*) Deutsch *n*; **in G.** auf deutsch

germane [dʒer'men] *adj* (**to**) passend (zu)

Germanize ['dʒʌrmə‚naɪz] *tr* eindeutschen

Ger'man mea'sles *s & spl* Röteln *pl*

Ger'man shep'herd *s* deutscher Schäferhund *m*

Ger'man sil'ver *s* Alpaka *n*, Neusilber *n*

Germany ['dʒʌrməni] *s* Deutschland *n*

germ' cell' *s* Keimzelle *f*

germicidal [‚dʒʌrmɪ'saɪdəl] *adj* keimtötend

germicide ['dʒʌrmɪ‚saɪd] *s* Keimtöter *m*

germinate ['dʒʌrmɪ‚net] *intr* keimen

germ' war'fare *s* bakteriologische Kriegsführung *f*

gerontology [‚dʒerən'tɑlədʒi] *s* Gerontologie *f*

gerund ['dʒerənd] *s* Gerundium *n*

gerundive [dʒɪ'rʌndɪv] *s* Gerundiv *n*

gestation [dʒes'teʃən] *s* Schwangerschaft *f*; (*in animals*) Trächtigkeit *f*

gesticulate [dʒes'tɪkjə‚let] *intr* gestikulieren, sich gebärden

gesticulation [dʒes‚tɪkjə'leʃən] *s* Gebärdenspiel *n*, Gestikulation *f*

gesture ['dʒestʃər] *s* Geste *f* ‖ *intr* Gesten machen

get [get] *v* (*pret* got [gɑt]; *pp* got & gotten ['gɑtən]; *ger* getting) *tr* (*acquire*) bekommen; (*receive*) erhalten; (*procure*) beschaffen, besorgen; (*fetch*) holen; (*understand*) (coll) kapieren; (s.o. to do s.th.) dazu

bringing; (*reach by telephone*) erreichen; (*make, e.g., dirty*) machen;
(*convey, e.g., a message*) übermitteln; get across klarmachen; get back
zurückbekommen; get down (*depress*) verdrießen; (*swallow*) hin-
unterwürgen; get going in Gang setzen; get hold of (*a person*) erwischen; (*a thing*) erlangen; (*grip*)
ergreifen; get off (*e.g., a lid*) ab-
bekommen; get one's way sich durchsetzen; get out (*e.g., a spot*) heraus-
bekommen; get s.o. used to s.th. gewöhnen an (*acc*); get s.th. into one's
head sich [*dat*] etw in den Kopf setzen; get the hang of (coll) wegbe-
kommen; get the jump on s.o. j-m
zuvorkommen; get the worst of it
am schlechtesten dabei wegkommen;
get (*s.th.*) wrong falsch verstehen;
you're going to get it! (coll) du wirst
es kriegen! || *intr* (*become*) werden;
get about sich fortbewegen; get
ahead in the world in der Welt fort-
kommen; get along auskommen; get
along with zurechtkommen mit; get
around herumkommen; get around
to it dazu kommen; get at herankom-
men an (*acc*); (*e.g., the real reason*)
herausfinden; get away (*run away*)
entlaufen; (*escape*) entkommen; get
away from me! geh weg von mir!;
get away with davonkommen mit;
get back at s.o. es j-m heimzahlen;
get by (*e.g., the guards*) vorbeikommen an (*dat*); (*on little money*)
durchkommen; get down (*step
down*) absteigen; get down to brass
tacks (*or business*) zur Sache kommen; get going sich auf den Weg
machen; get going! mach, daß du
weiter kommst!; get into (*a vehicle*)
einsteigen in (*acc*); (*trouble, etc.*)
geraten in (*acc*); get loose sich losmachen; get lost verloren gehen, abhanden kommen; (*lose one's way*)
sich verirren; get lost! (sl) hau ab!;
get off aussteigen; get off with (*a
light sentence*) davonkommen mit;
get on (*e.g., a train*) einsteigen (in
acc); get on one's feet again sich
hochrappeln; get on with (*s.o.*) zurechtkommen; get out aussteigen;
get out of a tight spot sich aus der
Schlinge ziehen; get over (*a hurdle*)
nehmen; (*a misfortune*) überwinden;
(*a sickness*) überstehen; get ready
sich fertig machen; get through
durchkommen; get through to s.o.
sich verständlich machen (*dat*); (telp)
erreichen; get to be werden; get together (*meet*) sich treffen; (*agree*)
(on) sich einig werden (über *acc*);
get to the bottom of ergründen; get
up aufstehen; get used to sich gewöhnen an (*acc*); get well gesund
werden; get with it! (coll) zur
Sache!
get'away' s Entkommen n; (sport)
Start m; make one's g. entkommen
get'away car' s Fluchtwagen m
get'-togeth'er s zwangloses Treffen n
get'up' s (coll) Aufzug m

get' up' and go' s Unternehmungsgeist
m
gewgaw ['g(j)ugo] s Plunder m
geyser ['gaɪzər] s Geiser m
ghastly ['gæstlɪ] adj (*ghostly*) gespenstisch; (*e.g., crime*) grausig; (*in-
tensely unpleasant*) schrecklich
gherkin ['gɑrkɪn] s Essiggurke f
ghet-to ['geto] s (-tos) Getto n
ghost [gost] s Gespenst n, Geist m;
(telv) Doppelbild n; give up the g.
den Geist aufgeben; not a g. of a
chance nicht die geringsten Aussichten
ghostly ['gostlɪ] adj gespenstisch
ghost' sto'ry s Spukgeschichte f
ghost' town' s Geisterstadt f
ghost' writ'er s Ghostwriter m
ghoul [gul] s (& fig) Unhold m
ghoulish ['gulɪʃ] adj teuflisch
GHQ ['dʒi'et'kju] s (General Headquarters) Oberkommando n
GI ['dʒi'aɪ] s (GI's) (coll) Landser m
giant ['dʒaɪ-ənt] adj riesig, Riesen– ||
s Riese m, Riesin f
giantess ['dʒaɪ-əntɪs] s Riesin f
gibberish ['dʒɪbərɪʃ], ['gɪbərɪʃ] s
Klauderwelsch n
gibbet ['dʒɪbɪt] s Galgen m || tr hän-
gen
gibe [dʒaɪb] s Spott m || intr spotten;
g. at verspotten
giblets ['dʒɪblɪts] spl Gänseklein n
giddiness ['gɪdnɪs] s Schwindelgefühl
n; (*frivolity*) Leichtsinn m
giddy ['gɪdɪ] adj (*dizzy*) schwindlig;
(*height*) schwindelerregend; (*frivolous*) leichtsinnig
gift [gɪft] s Geschenk n; (*natural ability*) Begabung f
gift'ed adj begabt
gift'horse' s—never look a g. in the
mouth e-m geschenkten Gaul schaut
man nicht ins Maul
gift' of gab' s (coll) gutes Mundwerk n
gift' shop' s Geschenkartikelladen m
gift'-wrap' v (*pret & pp* -wrapped; *ger*
-wrapping) tr als Geschenk verpacken
gift'wrap'ping s Geschenkverpackung
f
gigantic [dʒaɪ'gæntɪk] adj riesig
giggle ['gɪgəl] s Gekicher n || intr
kichern
gigly ['gɪglɪ] adj allezeit kichernd
gigo·lo ['dʒɪgə,lo] s (-los) Gigolo m
gild [gɪld] v (*pret & pp* gilded & gilt
[gɪlt]) tr vergolden
gild'ing s Vergoldung f
gill [gɪl] s (*of a fish*) Kieme f; (*of a
cock*) Kehllappen m
gilt [gɪlt] adj vergoldet || s Vergol-
dung f
gilt' edge' s Goldschnitt m
gilt'-edged' adj mit Goldschnitt versehen; (*first-class*) (coll) erstklassig
gimlet ['gɪmlɪt] s Handbohrer m
gimmick ['gɪmɪk] s (sl) Trick m
gin [dʒɪn] s Wacholderbranntwein m,
Gin m; (*snare*) Schlinge f || v (*pret
& pp* ginned; *ger* ginning) tr ent-
körnen
ginger ['dʒɪndʒər] s Ingwer m

gin'ger ale' s Ingwerlimonade f
gin'gerbread' s Pfefferkuchen m
gingerly ['dʒɪndʒərli] adv sacht(e)
gin'gersnap' s Ingwerplätzchen n
gingham ['gɪŋəm] s Gingham m
giraffe [dʒɪ'ræf] s Giraffe f
gird [gʌrd] v (pret & pp girt [gʌrt] & girded) tr gürten; **g. oneself with a sword** sich [dat] ein Schwert umgürten
girder ['gʌrdər] s Tragbalken m
girdle ['gʌrdəl] s Gürtel m
girl [gʌrl] s Mädchen n, Mädel n
girl' friend' s Freundin f, Geliebte f
girl'hood' s Mädchenzeit f
girlish ['gʌrlɪʃ] adj mädchenhaft
girl' scout' s Pfadfinderin f
girth [gʌrθ] s Umfang m; (for a horse) Sattelgurt m
gist [dʒɪst] s Kernpunkt m; **g. of the matter** des Pudels Kern
give [gɪv] s Elastizität f; (yielding) Nachgeben n ‖ v (pret gave [gev]; pp given ['gɪvən]) tr geben; (a gift, credence) schenken; (free of charge) verschenken; (contribute) spenden; (hand over) übergeben; (a report) erstatten; (a reason, the time) angeben; (attention, recognition) zollen; (a lecture) halten; (an award) zusprechen; (homework) aufgeben; (a headache, etc.) verursachen; (joy) machen; (a reception) veranstalten; (a blow) versetzen; **g. away** weggeben; (divulge) verraten; **g. away the bride** Brautvater sein; **g. back** zurückgeben; **g. ground** zurückweichen; **g. it to 'em!** (coll) hau zu!; **g. off** von sich geben; (steam) ausströmen lassen; **g. oneself up** sich verplappern; **g. oneself away** sich verplappern; **g. oneself up** sich stellen; **g. or take** mehr oder weniger; **g. out** ausgeben; **g. rise to** Anlaß geben zu; **g. up** aufgeben; (a business) schließen; **g. up for lost** verlorengeben; **g. way** weichen; **g. way to** sich überlassen (dat) ‖ intr (yield) nachgeben; (collapse) einstürzen; **g. in to** nachgeben (dat), weichen (dat); **g. out** (said of the voice, legs) versagen; (said of strength) nachlassen; **g. up** aufgeben; (mil) die Waffen strecken; **g. up on** verzagen an (dat)
give'-and-take' s Kompromiß m & n; (exchange of opinion) Meinungsaustausch m
give'away' s (betrayal of a secret) unbeabsichtigte Preisgabe f; (promotional article) Gratisprobe f
give'away show' s Preisrätselsendung f
given ['gɪvən] adj gegeben; (time) festgesetzt; (math, philos) gegeben; **g. to drinking** dem Trunk ergeben
giv'en name' s Vorname m
giver ['gɪvər] s Geber –in mf; (of a contribution) Spender –in mf
gizzard ['gɪzərd] s Geflügelmagen m
gla'cial per'iod ['gleʃəl] s Eiszeit f
glacier ['gleʃər] s Gletscher m
glad [glæd] adj (gladder; gladdest) froh; **be g.** (about) sich freuen (über acc); **g. to** (inf) erfreut zu (inf); **g. to meet you** sehr erfreut!, sehr ange-

nehm!; **I'll be g. to do it for you** ich werde das gern für Sie tun
gladden ['glædən] tr erfreuen
glade [gled] s Waldwiese f, Waldlichtung f
gladiator ['glædɪ‚etər] s Gladiator m
gladiola [‚glædɪ'olə] s Gladiole f
gladly ['glædli] adv gern(e)
gladness ['glædnɪs] s Freude f
glad' rags' spl (sl) Sonntagsstaat m
glad' tid'ings spl Freundenbotschaft f
glamorous ['glæmərəs] adj bezaubernd
glamour ['glæmər] s (of a girl) Zauber m; (of an event) Glanz m
glam'our girl' s gefeierte Schönheit f; (pej) Zierpuppe f
glance [glæns] s Blick m; **at a g.**, **at first g.** auf den ersten Blick; ‖ intr (at) blicken (auf acc or nach); **g. around** umherblicken; **g. off** abgleiten an (dat); **g. through** (or over) flüchtig durchsehen; **g. up** aufblicken
gland [glænd] s Drüse f
glanders ['glændərz] spl Rotzkrankheit f
glare [gler] s grelles Licht n; (look) böser Blick m ‖ intr blenden; (look) böse starren; **g. at** böse anstarren
glar'ing adj (light) grell; (fig) schreiend, aufdringlich
glass [glæs] adj gläsern, Glas– ‖ s Glas n; **glasses** Brille f
glass' bead' s Glasperle f
glass' blow'er ['blo‚ər] s Glasbläser –in mf
glass' blow'ing s Glasbläserei f
glass' case' s Schaukasten m
glass' cut'ter s Glasschleifer –in mf; (tool) Glasschneider m
glassful ['glæsful] s Glas n
glass'ware' s Glaswaren pl
glass' wool' s Glaswolle f
glass'works' s Glasfabrik f, Glashütte f
glassy ['glæsi] adj (surface) spiegelglatt; (eyes) glasig
glaucoma [glau'komə] s Glaukom n, grüner Star m
glaze [glez] s (on ceramics) Glasur f; (on paintings) Lasur f; (of ice) Glatteis n ‖ tr (ceramics, baked goods) glasieren; (a window) verglasen; (a painting) lasieren
glazed adj (ceramics, baked goods) glasiert; (eyes) glasig; **g. tile** Kachel f
glazier ['gleʒər] s Glaser –in mf
gleam [glim] s Lichtstrahl m; **g. of hope** Hoffnungsschimmer m ‖ intr strahlen
glean [glin] tr & intr auflesen; (fig) zusammentragen
gleanings ['glinɪŋz] spl Nachlese f
glee [gli] s Frohsinn m
glee' club' s Gesangverein m
glen [glen] s Bergschlucht f
glib [glɪb] adj (glibber; glibbest) (tongue) beweglich; (person) zungenfertig
glide [glaɪd] s Gleiten n; (aer) Gleitflug m; (with a glider) (aer) Segelflug m; (ling) Gleitlaut m; (mus) Glissando n ‖ intr gleiten

glider ['glaɪdər] *s* (*porch swing*) Schaukelbett *n*; (aer) Segelflugzeug *n*

glid'er pi'lot *s* Segelflieger –in *mf*

glid'ing *s* Segelfliegen *n*

glimmer ['glɪmər] *s* Schimmer *m*; g. of hope Hoffnungsschimmer *m* || *intr* schimmern

glim'mering *adj* flimmernd || *s* Flimmern *n*

glimpse [glɪmps] *s* flüchtiger Blick *m*; catch a g. of flüchtig zu sehen bekommen || *tr* flüchtig erblicken || *intr*—g. at e-n flüchtigen Blick werfen auf (*acc*)

glint [glɪnt] *s* Lichtschimmer *m* || *intr* schimmern

glisten ['glɪsən] *s* Glanz *m* || *intr* glänzen

glitter ['glɪtər] *s* Glitzern *n*, Glanz *m* || *intr* glitzern, glänzen

gloat [glot] *intr* schadenfroh sein; g. over sich weiden an (*dat*)

gloat'ing *s* Schadenfreude *f*

global ['global] *adj* global, Welt-

globe [glob] *s* Erdkugel *f*, Globus *m*

globe'-trot'ter *s* Weltenbummler –in *mf*

globule ['glabjul] *s* Kügelchen *n*

glockenspiel ['glakən,spil] *s* Glockenspiel *n*

gloom [glum] *s* Düsternis *f*; (fig) Trübsinn *m*

gloominess ['gluminis] *s* Düsterkeit *f*; (fig) Trübsinn *m*

gloomy ['glumi] *adj* düster; (*depressing*) bedrückend; (*depressed*) trübsinnig

glorification ['glorifi,keʃən] *s* Verherrlichung *f*

glori-fy ['glori,faɪ] *v* (*pret & pp* –fied) *tr* verherrlichen

glorious ['glori-əs] *adj* (*full of glory*) glorreich; (*magnificent*) herrlich

glo-ry ['glori] *s* Ruhm *m*; (*magnificence*) Herrlichkeit *f*; be in one's g. im siebenten Himmel sein || *v* (*pret & pp* –ried) *intr*—g. in frohlocken über (*acc*)

gloss [glos] *s* (*shine*) Glanz *m*; (*notation*) Glosse *f* || *tr* glossieren; g. over verschleiern

glossary ['glosəri] *s* Glossar *n*

glossy ['glosi] *adj* glänzend

glottis ['glatis] *s* Stimmritze *f*

glove [glʌv] *s* Handschuh *m*; fit like a g. wie angegossen passen

glove' compart'ment *s* Handschuhfach *n*

glow [glo] *s* Glühen *n* || *intr* glühen; g. with (fig) erglühen vor (*dat*)

glower ['glaʊ-ər] *s* finsterer Blick *m* || *intr* finster blicken; g. at finster anblicken

glow'ing *adj* glühend; (*account*) begeistert

glow'worm' *s* Glühwurm *m*

glucose ['glukos] *s* Glukose *f*

glue [glu] *s* Leim *m*, Klebemittel *n* || *tr* (*wood*) leimen; (*paper*) kleben

gluey ['glu-i] *adj* leimig

glum [glʌm] *adj* (glummer; glummest) verdrießlich

glut [glʌt] *s* Übersättigung *f*; a g. on the market e-e Überschwemmung des Marktes || *v* (*pret & pp* glutted; *ger* glutting) *tr* übersättigen; (com) überschwemmen

glutton ['glʌtən] *s* Vielfraß *m*

gluttonous ['glʌtənəs] *adj* gefräßig

gluttony ['glʌtəni] *s* Gefräßigkeit *f*

glycerine ['glɪsərɪn] *s* Glyzerin *n*

gnarled [narld] *adj* knorrig

gnash [næʃ] *tr*—g. one's teeth mit den Zähnen knirschen

gnat [næt] *s* Mücke *f*

gnaw [no] *tr* zernagen; g. off abnagen || *intr* (on) nagen (an *dat*)

gnome [nom] *s* Gnom *m*, Berggeist *m*

go [go] *s*—be on the go auf den Beinen sein; have a lot of go viel Mumm in den Knochen haben; it's no go es geht nicht; let's have a go at it probieren wir's mal; make a go of it es zu e-m Erfolg machen || *v* (*pret* went [went]; *pp* gone [gon]) *tr*—go it alone es ganz allein(e) machen || *intr* gehen; (*depart*) weggehen; (*travel*) fahren, reisen; (*operate*) arbeiten; (*belong*) gehören; (*turn out*) verlaufen; (*collapse*) zusammenbrechen; (*fail, go out of order*) kaputtgehen; (*said of words*) lauten; (*said of bells*) läuten; (*said of a buzzer*) ertönen; (*said of awards*) zugeteilt werden; (*said of a road*) führen; be going to, e.g., I am going to study ich werde studieren; go about umhergehen; (*a task*) in Angriff nehmen; go about it darangehen; go after (*run after*) nachlaufen; (*strive for*) streben nach; go against the grain gegen den Strich gehen; go ahead vorausgehen; go ahead! voran!; go along with (*accompany*) mitgehen mit; (*agree with*) zustimmen mit; go and see for yourself überzeugen Sie sich selbst davon!; go around herumgehen; (*suffice*) (aus)reichen; (*an obstacle*) umgehen; go at (*a person*) losgehen auf (*acc*); (*a thing*) herangehen an (*acc*); go away weggehen; go back zurückkehren; (*ride back*) zurückfahren; go back on (*one's word*) brechen; go beyond überschreiten; go by (*pass by*) vorbeigehen (an *dat*); (*said of time*) vergehen; (*act according to*) sich richten nach; go down niedergehen; (*said of the sun or a ship*) untergehen; (*said of a swelling*) zurückgehen; (*said of a fever or a price*) sinken; go down in history in die Geschichte eingehen; go for (*fetch*) holen; (*apply to*) gelten für; (*be enthusiastic about*) schwärmen für; (*have a crush on*) verknallt sein in (*acc*); (*be sold for*) verkauft werden für; (*attack*) losgehen auf (*acc*); go in hineingehen; (*said of the sun*) verschwinden; go in for schwärmen für; (sport) treiben; go into eintreten in (*acc*); (arith) enthalten sein in (*dat*); go

into detail ins Detail gehen; **go in with s.o.** on sich beteiligen mit j-m an (*dat*); **go off** (*depart*) weggehen; (*said of a gun*) losgehen; (*said of a bomb*) explodieren; **go on** (*happen*) vorgehen; (*continue*) weitergehen; (*with*) fortfahren (mit); (*theat*) auftreten; **go on!** (*expressing encouragement*) nur zu!; (*expressing disbelief*) ach was!; **go on reading** weiterlesen; **go on to** (*another theme*) übergehen auf (*acc*); **go over** (*check*) überprüfen; (*review*) noch einmal durchgehen; (*figures*) nachrechnen; (*be a success*) einschlagen; **go over to** hinübergehen zu; (*the enemy*) übergehen zu; **go out** (*e.g., of the house*) hinausgehen; (*on an errand or socially; said of a light*) ausgehen; **go out of one's way** sich besonders anstrengen; **go out to dinner** auswärts essen; **go through** (*penetrate*) durchdringen; (*a traffic signal*) überfahren; (*endure*) durchmachen; **go through with** zu Ende führen; **go to** (*said of a prize*) zugeteilt werden (*dat*); **go together** zueinanderpassen; **go to it!** los!; **go to show** ein Beweis sein für; **go with** (*fit, match*) passen zu; (*associate with*) verkehren mit; **go without** entbehren; **go under an assumed name** e-n angenommenen Namen führen; **go up to s.o.** auf j-n zugehen

goad [god] *s* Stachel *m* || *tr* antreiben; **g. on** (fig) anstacheln

go′-ahead sig′nal *n* freie Bahn *f*

goal [gol] *s* Ziel *n;* (sport) Tor *n;* **make a goal** (sport) ein Tor schießen

goalie [′goli] *s* Torwart *m*

goal′keep′er *s* Torwart *m*

goal′ line′ *s* Torlinie *f*

goal′ post′ *s* Torpfosten *m*

goat [got] *s* Ziege *f*, Geiß *f;* (*male goat*) Ziegenbock *m;* **get s.o.'s g.** (sl) j-n auf die Palme bringen

goatee [go′ti] *s* Ziegenbart *m*, Spitzbart *m*

goat′ herd′ *s* Ziegenhirt *m*

goat′skin′ *s* Ziegenfell *n*

gob [gab] *s* (coll) Klumpen *m;* (*sailor*) (coll) Blaujacke *f;* **gobs of money** (coll) ein Haufen *m* Geld

gobble [′gabəl] *s* Kollern *n* || *tr* verschlingen; **g. up** (*food*) herunterschlingen; (*e.g., land*) zusammenraffen || *intr* (*said of a turkey*) kollern

gobbledegook [′gabəldɪ‚guk] *s* (coll) Amtssprache *f*

gobbler [′gablər] *s* (coll) Fresser –in *mf;* (orn) (coll) Puter *m*, Truthahn *m*

go′-between′ *s* Vermittler –in *mf*, Unterhändler *m*

goblet [′gablɪt] *s* Kelchglas *n*

goblin [′gablɪn] *s* Kobold *m*

go′cart′ *s* (*walker*) Laufstuhl *m;* (*stroller*) Sportwagen *m;* (*small racer*) Go-Kart *m;* (*handcart*) Handwagen *m*

god [gad] *s* Gott *m;* **God forbid!** Gott bewahre!; **God knows** weiß Gott; **my God!** du lieber Gott!; **so help me God!** so wahr mir Gott helfe!; **ye gods!** heiliger Strohsack!

god′child′ *s* (–chil′dren) Patenkind *n*

goddess [′gadɪs] *s* Göttin *f*

god′fa′ther *s* Pate *m;* **be a g.** Pate stehen

God′-fear′ing *adj* gottesfürchtig

god′forsak′en *adj* gottverlassen

god′head′ *s* Göttlichkeit *f;* **Godhead** Gott *m*

godless [′gadlɪs] *adj* gottlos

god′like′ *adj* göttlich

godly [′gadli] *adj* gottselig

god′moth′er *s* Patin *f;* **be a g.** Patin stehen

god′send′ *s* Segen *m*

God′speed′ *s*—**wish s.o. G.** j-m Lebewohl sagen

go-getter [′go‚getər] *s* Draufgänger *m*

goggle [′gagəl] *intr* glotzen

gog′gle-eyed′ *adj* glotzäugig

goggles [′gagəlz] *spl* Schutzbrille *f*

go′ing *adj* (*rate*) gültig, üblich; **g. on** (*e.g., six o'clock*) gegen; **I'm g. to do it** ich werde es tun

go′ing concern′ *s* schwunghaftes Geschäft *n*

go′ing-o′ver *s* Überprüfung *f;* (*beating*) Prügel *pl*

go′ings on′ *spl* Treiben *n*, Wirtschaft *f*

goiter [′gɔɪtər] *s* Kropf *m*

gold [gold] *adj* Gold– || *s* Gold *n*

gold′ bar′ *s* Goldbarren *m*

gold′brick′ *s* (mil) Drückeberger *m*

gold′-brick′ *intr* faulenzen

gold′-brick′ing *s* (mil) Drückebergerei *f*

gold′crest′ *s* Goldhähnchen *n*

gold′ dig′ger [′dɪgər] *s* Goldgräber *m;* (sl) Vamp *m*

golden [′goldən] *adj* golden; (*opportunity*) günstig

gold′en age′ *s* Glanzzeit *f*, Goldenes Zeitalter *n*

gold′en calf′, **the** *s* das Goldene Kalb

gold′en ea′gle *s* Goldadler *m*

Gold′en Fleece′, the (myth) das Goldene Vlies

gold′en mean′ *s* goldene Mitte *f*

gold′en rule′ *s* goldene Regel *f*

gold′en wed′ding *s* goldene Hochzeit *f*

gold′-filled′ *adj* vergoldet

gold′ fill′ing *s* (dent) Goldplombe *f*

gold′finch′ *s* Goldfink *m*, Stieglitz *m*

gold′fish′ *s* Goldfisch *m*

goldilocks [′goldɪ‚laks] *s* (bot) Hahnenfuß *m*

gold′ leaf′ *s* Blattgold *n*

gold′mine′ *s* Goldbergwerk *n*

gold′ nug′get *s* Goldklumpen *m*

gold′ plate′ *s* Goldgeschirr *n*

gold′-plate′ *tr* vergolden

gold′smith′ *s* Goldschmied –in *mf*

gold′ stand′ard *s* Goldwährung *f*

golf [galf] *s* Golf *n* || *intr* Golf spielen

golf′ bag′ *s* Köcher *m*

golf′ club′ *s* Golfschläger *m;* (*organization*) Golfklub *m*

golf′ course′ *s* Golfplatz *m*

golfer [′galfər] *s* Golfspieler –in *mf*

golf′ links′ *spl* Golfplatz *m*

gondola [′gandələ] *s* Gondel *f*

gon′dola car′ s offener Güterwagen m
gondolier [ˌɡɑndə′lɪr] s Gondelführer m
gone [ɡɔn] adj hin, weg; (ruined) futsch; **all g.** ganz weg; (sold out) ausverkauft; **he is g.** er ist fort
goner [′ɡɔnər] s (coll) verlorener Mensch m
gong [ɡɔŋ] s Gong m, Tamtam n
gonorrhea [ˌɡɑnə′riːə] s Tripper m
goo [ɡu] s (sl) klebrige Masse f
good [ɡud] adj (better; best) gut; (well behaved) brav, artig; (in health) gesund; (valid) gültig; **as g. as** so gut wie; **be g. enough to** (inf) so gut sein und; **g. and** recht, e.g., **g. and cheap** recht billig; **g. at** gut in (dat); **g. for** (suited to) geeignet zu; (effective against) wirksam für; (valid for) gültig für; **g. for you!** (serves you right!) das geschieht dir recht!; (expressing congratulations) ich gratuliere!, bravo!; **make g.** wiedergutmachen; (losses) vergüten; (a promise) erfüllen; **g.!** s Gut n; (welfare) Wohl n; (advantage) Nutzen m; (philos) Gut n, das Gute; **be up to no g.** nichts Gutes im Schilde führen; **catch with the goods** auf frischer Tat ertappen; **do g.** wohltun; **for g.** für immer; **goods** Waren pl; **to the g. als** Nettogewinn; **what g. is it?, what's the g. of it?** was nutzt es?
good′-by′, good′-bye′ s Lebewohl n; **say g.** (to) sich verabschieden (von) ‖ interj auf Wiedersehen!; (on the telephone) auf Wiederhören!
good′ day′ interj guten Tag!
good′ deed′ s Wohltat f
good′ egg′ s (sl) feiner Kerl m
good′ eve′ning interj guten Abend!
good′ fel′low s netter Kerl m
good′-fel′lowship s gute Kameradschaft f
good′-for-noth′ing adj nichtsnutzig ‖ s Taugenichts m, Nichtsnutz m
Good′ Fri′day s Karfreitag m
good′ grac′es spl—**be in s.o.'s g.** in j-s Gunst stehen
good′-heart′ed adj gutherzig
good′-hu′mored adj gutgelaunt, gutmütig
good′-look′ing adj gutaussehend, hübsch
goodly [′ɡudli] adj beträchtlich; **a g. number of** viele
good′ morn′ing interj guten Morgen!
good′-na′tured adj gutmütig
goodness [′ɡudnɪs] s Güte f; **for g. sake!** um Himmels willen!; **g. knows** weiß Gott; **thank g.** Gott sei Dank!
good′ night′ interj gute Nacht!
good′ sense′ s Sinn m; (common sense) gesunder Menschenverstand m; **make g. Sinn haben**
good′-sized′ adj ziemlich groß
good′-tem′pered adj ausgeglichen
good′ time′—**have a g.** sich gut unterhalten; **keep g.** taktfest sein
good′ turn′ s Gefallen m; **one g. deserves another** e-e Hand wäscht die andere

good′ will′ s Wohlwollen n; (com) Geschäftswert m
goody [′ɡudi] s Näscherei f ‖ interj pfundig!
gooey [′ɡu·i] adj klebrig
goof [ɡuf] s (person) (sl) Depp m; (mistake) (sl) Schnitzer m ‖ tr verpfuschen ‖ intr (sl) e-n Schnitzer machen; **g. off** (sl) faulenzen
goof′ball′ s (pill) (sl) Beruhigungspille f; (eccentric person) (sl) Sonderling m
goofy [′ɡufi] adj (sl) dämlich; **g. about** (sl) vernarrt in (acc)
goon [ɡun] s (sl) Dummkopf m; (in strikes) bestellter Schläger m
goose [ɡus] s (geese [ɡis]) Gans f; (culin) Gänsebraten m; **cook s.o.'s g.** j-n erledigen
goose′ber′ry s Stachelbeere f
goose′ egg′ s (sl) Gänseei s; (sl) Null f
goose′ flesh′ s Gänsehaut f
goose′ neck′ s Schwanenhals m
goose′ pim′ples spl Gänsehaut f
goose′ step′ s Stechschritt m
goose′-step′ v (pret & pp -stepped; ger -stepping) intr im Stechschritt marschieren
gopher [′ɡofər] s Taschenratte f
gore [ɡor] s geronnenes Blut n ‖ tr aufspießen
gorge [ɡɔrdʒ] s Schlucht f ‖ tr vollstopfen ‖ intr schlingen
gorgeous [′ɡɔrdʒəs] adj prachtvoll
gorilla [ɡə′rɪlə] s Gorilla m
gorse [ɡɔrs] s Stechginster m
gory [′ɡori] adj blutig
gosh [ɡɑʃ] interj herrjeh!
Gospel [′ɡɑspəl] s Evangelium n
gos′pel truth′ s reine Wahrheit f
gossamer [′ɡɑsəmər] s Sommerfäden pl
gossip [′ɡɑsɪp] s Klatsch m; (woman) Klatschweib n; (man) Schwätzer m ‖ intr klatschen, tratschen
gos′sip col′umn s Klatschspalte f
gossipmonger [′ɡɑsɪp ˌmʌŋɡər] s Klatschbase f
gossipy [′ɡɑsɪpi] adj tratschsüchtig
Goth [ɡɑθ] s Gote m, Gotin f
Gothic [′ɡɑθɪk] adj gotisch ‖ s (language) Gotisch n
Goth′ic arch′ s Spitzbogen m
gouge [ɡaudʒ] s (tool) Hohlmeißel m; (hole made by a gouge) ausgemeißelte Vertiefung f ‖ tr aushöhlen; (overcharge) überverteilen; **g. out** (eyes) herausdrücken
gouger [′ɡaudʒər] s Wucherer –in mf
goulash [′ɡulaʃ] s Gulasch n
gourd [ɡord], [ɡurd] s Kürbis m
gourmand [′ɡurmənd] s (glutton) Schlemmer –in mf; (gourmet) Feinschmecker m
gourmet [′ɡurme] s Feinschmecker m
gout [ɡaut] s Gicht f
govern [′ɡʌvərn] tr regieren; (fig) beherrschen; (gram) regieren ‖ intr regieren
governess [′ɡʌvərnɪs] s Gouvernante f
government [′ɡʌvərnmənt] adj Regierungs-, Staats- ‖ s Regierung f

gov′ernment con′tract s Staatsauftrag m

gov′ernment control′ s Zwangsbewirtschaftung f

gov′ernment employ′ee s Staatsbeamte m, Staatsbeamtin f

gov′ernment grant′ s Staatszuschuß m

gov′ernment-in-ex′ile s Exilregierung f

governor ['gʌvərnər] s Statthalter m, Gouverneur m; (mach) Regler m

gov′ernorship′ s Statthalterschaft f

gown [gaun] s Damenkleid n; (of a judge, professor) Robe f, Talar m

grab [græb] s—make a g. for grapschen nach ‖ v (pret & pp grabbed; ger grabbing) tr schnappen; g. hold of anpacken ‖ intr—g. for greifen nach

grab′ bag′ s Glückstopf m

grace [gres] s (mercy, divine favor) Gnade f; (charm) Grazie f; (table prayer) Tischgebet n; (charm) Grazie f; **Graces** (myth) Grazien pl

graceful ['gresfəl] adj graziös, anmutig

gracious ['grefəs] adj gnädig; (living) angenehm ‖ interj lieber Himmel!

gradation [gre'defən] s Stufenfolge f

grade [gred] s (level) Stufe f, Grad m; (quality) Qualität f; (class year) Schulklasse f; (mark in a course, test) Zensur f; (slope) Steigung f; (mil) Dienstgrad m ‖ tr (sort) einstufen; (evaluate) bewerten; (make level) planieren; (educ) zensieren

grade′ cross′ing s (rr) Schienenübergang m

grade′ school′ s Grundschule f

gradient ['gredɪ·ənt] s Neigung f

gradual ['grædʒʊ·əl] adj allmählich

graduate ['grædʒʊ·ɪt] adj (student) graduiert; (course) Graduierten– ‖ s Promovierte mf; (from a junior college) Abiturien –in mf; (from a university) Absolvent –in mf ‖ ['grædʒʊ‚et] tr & intr graduieren, promovieren; **g. from** absolvieren

grad′uated adj (tax) abgestuft; (marked by divisions of measurement) graduiert; **g. scale** Gradmesser m

graduation [‚grædʒʊ'efən] s Graduierung f, Promotion f; (marking on a vessel or instrument) Gradeinteilung f

gradua′tion ex′ercises spl Schlußfeier f

graft [græft] s (illegal gain) Schiebung f; (money involved in graft) Schmiergeld n; (twig) (hort) Pfropfreis n; (place where scion is inserted) (hort) Propfstelle f; (organ transplanted) (surg) verpflanztes Gewebe n; (transplanting) (surg) Gewebeverpflanzung f ‖ tr (hort) pfropfen; (surg) verpflanzen

gra′ham bread′ ['gre·əm] s Grahambrot n

gra′ham crack′er s Grahamplätzchen n

gra′ham flour′ s Grahammehl n

grain [gren] s Korn n; (of leather) Narbe f; (in wood, marble) Maserung f; (unit of weight) Gran n;

(cereals) Getreide n; (phot) Korn n; against the g. (& fig) gegen den Strich; **g. of truth** Körnchen n Wahrheit

grain′ el′evator s Getreidesilo m

grain′field′ s Saatfeld n, Kornfeld n

gram [græm] s Gramm n

grammar ['græmər] s Grammatik f

gram′mar school′ s Grundschule f

grammatical [grə'mætɪkəl] adj grammatisch, grammatikalisch

gramophone ['græmə‚fon] s Grammophon n

granary ['grenəri] s Getreidespeicher m

grand [grænd] adj großartig; (large and striking) grandios; (lofty) erhaben; (wonderful) (coll) herrlich

grand′aunt′ s Großtante f

grand′child′ s (–chil′dren) Enkelkind n

grand′daugh′ter s Enkelin f

grand′ duch′ess s Großfürstin f, Großherzogin f

grand′ duch′y s Großfürstentum n, Großherzogtum n

grand′ duke′ s Großfürst m, Großherzog m

grandee [græn'di] s Grande m

grandeur ['grændʒər], ['grændʒʊr] s Großartigkeit f, Erhabenheit f

grand′fath′er s Großvater m

grand′father's clock′ s Standuhr f

grandiose ['grændɪ‚os] adj grandios

grand′ ju′ry s Anklagekammer f

grand′ lar′ceny s schwerer Diebstahl m

grand′ lodge′ s Großloge f

grandma ['grænd(d)‚mɑ], ['græm‚mɑ] s (coll) Oma f

grand′moth′er s Großmutter f

grand′neph′ew s Großneffe m

grand′niece′ s Großnichte f

grandpa ['grænd(d)‚pɑ], ['græm‚pɑ] s (coll) Opa m

grand′par′ents spl Großeltern pl

grand′ pian′o s Konzertflügel m

grand′ slam′ s Schlemm m

grand′son′ s Enkel m

grand′stand′ s Tribüne f

grand′ to′tal s Gesamtsumme f

grand′un′cle s Großonkel m

grand′ vizier′ s Großwesir m

grange [grendʒ] s Farm f; (organization) Farmervereinigung f

granite ['grænɪt] adj Granit– ‖ s Granit m

granny ['græni] s (coll) Oma f

grant [grænt] s (of money) Beihilfe f; (of a pardon) Gewährung f; (of an award) Verleihung f ‖ tr (permission) geben; (credit) bewilligen; (a favor) gewähren; (a request) erfüllen; (a privilege, award) verleihen; (admit) zugeben; **granted that** angenommen, daß; **take for granted** als selbstverständlich hinnehmen

grantee [græn'ti] s Empfänger –in mf

grant′-in-aid′ s (grants-in-aid) (by the government) Subvention f; (educ) Stipendium n

grantor ['græntər] s Verleiher –in mf

granular ['grænjələr] adj körnig

granulate ['grænjə‚let] tr körnen

gran′ulated sug′ar s Streuzucker m
granule [′grænjul] s Körnchen n
grape [grep] s Weintraube f
grape′ ar′bor s Weinlaube f
grape′fruit′ s Pampelmuse f
grape′ juice′ s Most m, Traubensaft m
grape′ pick′er s Weinleser –in mf
grape′vine′ s Weinstock m; **through the g.** gerüchtweise
graph [græf] s Diagramm n
graphic(al) [′græfɪk(əl)] adj graphisch; (description) anschaulich, bildhaft
graph′ic arts′ spl Graphik f
graphite [′græfaɪt] s Graphit m
graph′ pa′per s Millimeterpapier n
grapnel [′græpnəl] s Wurfanker m
grapple [′græpəl] s Enterhaken m; (fight) Handgemenge n || tr packen || intr (use a grapple) (naut) e-n Enterhaken gebrauchen; **g. with** (& fig) ringen mit
grap′pling hook′, grap′pling i′ron s Wurfanker m; (naut) Enterhaken m
grasp [græsp] s Griff m; (control) Gewalt f; (comprehension) Verständnis n; (reach) Reichweite f; **have a good g. of** gut beherrschen || tr (& fig) fassen || intr—**g. at** schnappen nach
grasp′ing adj habgierig, geldgierig
grass [græs] s Gras n; (lawn) Rasen m; (pasture land) Weide f
grass′ court′ s Rasenspielplatz m
grass′hop′per s Grashüpfer m
grass′ land′ s Weideland n, Grasland n
grass′-roots′ adj (coll) volkstümlich
grass′ seed′ s Grassamen m
grass′ wid′ow s Strohwitwe f
grassy [′græsi] adj grasig
grate [gret] s (on a window) Gitter n; (of a furnace) Rost m || tr (e.g., cheese) reiben; **g. the teeth** mit den Zähnen knirschen || intr knirschen; **g. on one's nerves** an den Nerven reißen
grateful [′gretfəl] adj dankbar
grater [′gretər] s (culin) Reibeisen n
grati·fy [′grætɪ‚faɪ] v (pret & pp –fied) tr befriedigen; **be gratified by** sich freuen über (acc)
grat′ifying adj erfreulich
grat′ing adj knirschend || s Gitter n
gratis [′grætɪs], [′gretɪs] adj & adv unentgeltlich
gratitude [′grætɪ‚t(j)ud] s Dankbarkeit f
gratuitous [grə′t(j)u·ɪtəs] adj unentgeltlich; (undeserving) unverdient
gratuity [grə′t(j)u·ɪti] s Trinkgeld n
grave [grev] adj (face) ernst; (condition) besorgniserregend; (mistake) folgenschwer; (sound) tief || s Grab n; (accent) Gravis m
gravedigger [′grev‚dɪgər] s Totengräber m
gravel [′grævəl] s (rounded stones) Kies m; (crushed stones) Schotter m; (pathol) Harngrieß m || tr mit Kies (or Schotter) bestreuen
gravelly [′grævəli] adj heiser
grav′el pit′ s Kiesgrube f
grav′el road′ s Schotterstraße f

grave′stone′ s Grabstein m
grave′yard′ s Friedhof m
gravitate [′grævɪ‚tet] intr gravitieren; **g. towards** (fig) neigen zu
gravitation [‚grævɪ′teʃən] s Gravitation f, Massenanziehung f
gravitational [‚grævɪ′teʃənəl] adj Gravitations–, Schwer–
gravita′tional force′ s Schwerkraft f
gravita′tional pull′ s Anziehungskraft f
gravity [′grævɪti] s (seriousness) Ernst m; (of a situation) Schwere f; (phys) Schwerkraft f
gravy [′grevi] s Soße f; (coll) leichter Gewinn m
gra′vy boat′ s Soßenschüssel f
gra′vy train′ s (sl) Futterkrippe f
gray [gre] adj grau || s Grau n || intr ergrauen
gray′beard′ s Graubart m
gray′-haired′ adj grauhaarig
grayish [′gre·ɪʃ] adj gräulich
gray′ mat′ter s graue Substanz f
graze [grez] tr (said of a bullet) streifen; (cattle) weiden lassen || intr weiden
graz′ing land′ s Weide f
grease [gris] s Fett n, Schmiere f || [gris], [griz] tr (aut) schmieren
grease′ gun′ [gris] s Schmierpresse f
grease′ paint′ s Schminke f
grease′ pit′ s (aut) Schmiergrube f
grease′ spot′ s Fettfleck m
greasy [′grisi], [′grizi] adj fett(ig)
great [gret] adj groß; (wonderful) (coll) großartig; **a g. many (of)** e-e große Anzahl von; **g. fun** Heidenspaß m; **g. guy** Prachtkerl m
great′-aunt′ s Großtante f
Great′ Bear′ s Großer Bär m
Great′ Brit′ain s Großbritannien n
Great′ Dane′ s deutsche Dogge f
great′-grand′child′ s (–chil′dren) Urenkel m
great′-grand′daugh′ter s Urenkelin f
great′-grand′fa′ther s Urgroßvater m
great′-grand′moth′er s Urgroßmutter f
great′-grand′par′ents spl Urgroßeltern pl
great′-grand′son′ s Urenkel m
greatly [′gretli] adv sehr, stark
great′-neph′ew s Großneffe m
greatness [′gretnɪs] s Größe f
great′-niece′ s Großnichte f
great′-un′cle s Großonkel m
Grecian [′griʃən] adj griechisch
Greece [gris] s Griechenland n
greed [grid] s Habgier f, Gier f
greediness [′gridɪnɪs] s Gierigkeit f
greedy [′gridi] adj (for) gierig (nach)
Greek [grik] adj griechisch || s (person) Grieche m, Griechin f; (language) Griechisch n; **that's G. to me** das kommt mir spanisch vor
green [grin] adj grün; (unripe) unreif; (inexperienced) unerfahren, neu; **become g.** grünen; **turn g. with envy** grün vor Neid werden || s (& golf) Grün n; **greens** Blattgemüse n
green′back′ s (coll) Geldschein m
greenery [′grinəri] s Grün n

green'-eyed' *adj* grünäugig; *(fig)* neidisch

green'gro'cer *s* Obst- und Gemüsehändler –in *mf*

green'horn' *s* Ausländer –in *mf*

green'house' *s* Gewächshaus *n*

greenish ['grinɪʃ] *adj* grünlich

Green'land *s* Grönland *n*

green' light' *s* *(fig)* freie Fahrt *f*

greenness ['grinnɪs] *s* Grün *n*; *(inexperience)* Unerfahrenheit *f*

green' pep'per *s* Paprikaschote *f*

green'room' *s* *(theat)* Aufenthaltsraum *m*

greensward ['grin ˌswɔrd] *s* Rasen *m*

green' thumb' *s*—**have a g.** gärtnerisches Geschick besitzen

greet [grit] *tr* grüßen; *(welcome)* begrüßen

greet'ing *s* Gruß *m*; *(welcoming)* Begrüßung *f*; **greetings** Grüße *pl*

greet'ing card' *s* Glückwunschkarte *f*

gregarious [grɪ'gɛrɪ·əs] *adj* gesellig

Gregor'ian cal'endar [grɪ'gorɪ·ən] *s* Gregorianischer Kalender *m*

Gregor'ian chant' *s* Gregorianischer Gesang *m*

grenade [grɪ'ned] *s* Granate *f*

grenade' launch'er *s* Gewehrgranatgerät *n*

grey [gre] *adj*, *s*, & *intr* var of **gray**

grey'hound' *s* Windhund *m*

grid [grɪd] *s* *(on a map)* Gitternetz *n*; *(culin)* Bratrost *m*; *(electron)* Gitter *n*

griddle ['grɪdəl] *s* Bratpfanne *f*; *(cookie sheet)* Backblech *n*

grid'lecake' *s* Pfannkuchen *m*

grid'i'ron *s* Bratrost *m*; *(sport)* Spielfeld *n*; *(theat)* Schnürboden *m*

grid' leak' *s* *(electron)* Gitterwiderstand *m*

grief [grif] *s* Kummer *m*; **come to g.** zu Fall (*or* Schaden) kommen, scheitern

grief'-strick'en *adj* gramgebeugt

grievance ['grivəns] *s* Beschwerde *f*

grieve [griv] *tr* bekümmern ‖ *intr* *(over)* sich grämen (über *acc*)

grievous ['grivəs] *adj* *(causing grief)* schmerzlich; *(serious)* schwerwiegend

griffin ['grɪfɪn] *s* Greif *m*

grill [grɪl] *s* Grill *m* ‖ *tr* grillen; *(an accused person)* scharf verhören

grille [grɪl] *s* Gitter *n*

grim [grɪm] *adj* *(grimmer; grimmest)* grimmig; **g. humor** Galgenhumor *m*

grimace ['grɪməs], [grɪ'mes] *s* Grimasse *f* ‖ *intr* Grimassen schneiden

grime [graɪm] *s* Schmutz *m*, Ruß *m*

grimness ['grɪmnɪs] *s* Grimmigkeit *f*

grimy ['graɪmi] *adj* schmutzig, rußig

grin [grɪn] *s* Grinsen *n*, Schmunzeln *n* ‖ *v* *(pret & pp* grinned; *ger* grinning) *intr* grinsen, schmunzeln; **I had to g. and bear it** ich mußte gute Miene zum bösen Spiel machen

grind [graɪnd] *s* *(of coffee, grain)* Mahlen *n*; *(hard work)* Schinderei *f*; *(a student)* (coll) Streber –in *mf*; **the daily g.** der graue Alltag ‖ *v* *(pret & pp* ground [graund]) *tr* *(coffee,*

grain) mahlen; *(glass, tools)* schleifen; *(meat)* zermahlen; *(in a mortar)* stampfen; **g. down** zerreiben; **g. one's teeth** mit den Zähnen knirschen; **g. out** *(e.g., articles)* ausstoßen; *(tunes)* leiern

grinder ['graɪndər] *s* *(molar)* (dent) Backenzahn *m*; *(mach)* Schleifmaschine *f*

grind'stone' *s* Schleifstein *m*

grip [grɪp] *s* Griff *m*; *(handle)* Handgriff *m*; *(handbag)* Reisetasche *f*; *(power)* Gewalt *f*; **come to grips with** in Angriff nehmen; **have a good g. on** *(fig)* sicher beherrschen; **lose one's g.** *(fig)* den Halt verlieren ‖ *v* *(pret & pp* gripped; *ger* gripping) *tr* *(& fig)* packen

gripe [graɪp] *s* Meckerei *f* ‖ *intr* *(about)* meckern (über *acc*)

grippe [grɪp] *s* *(pathol)* Grippe *f*

grip'ping *adj* fesselnd, packend

grisly ['grɪzli] *adj* gräßlich

grist [grɪst] *s* Mahlkorn *n*; **that's g. for his mill** das ist Wasser auf seine Mühle

gristle ['grɪsəl] *s* Knorpel *m*

gristly ['grɪsli] *adj* knorpelig

grist'mill' *s* Getreidemühle *f*

grit [grɪt] *s* *(abrasive particles)* Grieß *m*; *(pluck)* (coll) Mumm *m*; **grits** Schrotmehl *n* ‖ *v* *(pret & pp* gritted; *ger* gritting) *tr* *(one's teeth)* zusammenbeißen

gritty ['grɪti] *adj* grießig

grizzly ['grɪzli] *adj* gräulich

griz'zly bear' *s* Graubär *m*

groan [gron] *s* Stöhnen *n*; **groans** Geächze *n* ‖ *intr* stöhnen; *(grumble)* (coll) brumen

grocer ['grosər] *s* Lebensmittelhändler –in *mf*

grocery ['grosəri] *s* *(store)* Lebensmittelgeschäft *n*; **groceries** Lebensmittel *pl*

gro'cery store' *s* Lebensmittelgeschäft *n*

grog [grɑg] *s* Grog *m*

groggy ['grɑgi] *adj* benommen

groin [grɔɪn] *s* *(anat)* Leiste *f*, Leistengegend *f*; *(archit)* Rippe *f*

groom [grum] *s* Bräutigam *m*; *(stableboy)* Reitknecht *m* ‖ *tr* *(a person, animal)* pflegen; *(for a position)* heranziehen

groove [gruv] *s* Kerbe *f*; *(for letting off water)* Rinne *f*; *(of a record)* Rille *f*; *(in a barrel)* Zug *m*; **in the g.** *(fig)* im richtigen Fahrwasser

grope [grop] *tr*—**g. one's way** sich vorwärtstasten ‖ *intr* tappen; **g. about** herumtappen; **g. for** tappen nach, tasten nach

gropingly ['gropɪŋli] *adv* tastend

gross [gros] *adj* *(coarse, vulgar)* roh, derb; *(mistake)* grob; *(crass, extreme)* kraß; *(after deductions)* Brutto– ‖ *s* Gros *n* ‖ *tr* e–n Bruttogewinn haben von

grossly ['grosli] *adv* sehr, stark

gross' na'tional prod'uct *s* Bruttosozialprodukt *n*

gross′ receipts′ *spl* Bruttoeinnahmen *pl*

grotesque [gro′tɛsk] *adj* grotesk

grot·to [′grɑto] *s* (−toes & −tos) Grotte *f*, Höhle *f*

grouch [graʊtʃ] *s* (coll) Brummbär *m*, Griesgram *m* ‖ *intr* brummen

grouchy [′graʊtʃi] *adj* (coll) brummig

ground [graʊnd] *s* Grund *m*, Boden *m*; (reason) Grund *m*; (elec) Erde *f*; **every inch of g.** jeder Fußbreit Boden; **grounds** (e.g., of an estate) Anlagen *pl*; (reasons) Gründe *pl*; (of coffee) Satz *m*; **break g.** mit dem Bau beginnen; **gain g.** (an) Boden gewinnen; **hold one′s g.** seinen Standpunkt behaupten; **level to the g.** dem Erdboden gleichmachen; **lose g.** (an) Boden verlieren; **low g.** Niederung *f*; **new g.** (fig) Neuland *n*; **on the grounds that** mit der Begründung, daß; **run into the g.** (fig) bis zum Überdruß wiederholen; **stand one′s g.** standhalten; **yield g.** (fig) nachgeben ‖ *tr* (a pilot) Startverbot erteilen (dat); (a ship) auflaufen lassen; (elec) erden; **be grounded by bad weather** wegen schlechten Wetters am Starten gehindert werden

ground′ connec′tion *s* (elec) Erdung *f*

ground′ crew′ *s* (aer) Bodenmannschaft *f*

ground′ floor′ *s* Parterre *n*, Erdgeschoß *n*

ground′ glass′ *s* Mattglas *n*

ground′ hog′ *s* Murmeltier *n*

groundless [′graʊndlɪs] *adj* grundlos

ground′ meat′ *s* Hackfleisch *n*

ground′ plan′ *s* Grundriß *m*; (fig) Entwurf *m*

ground′ speed′ *s* Geschwindigkeit *f* über Grund

ground′ swell′ *s* Dünung *f*; (fig) wogende Erregung *f*

ground′-to-air′ *adj* Boden-Bord-

ground′ wa′ter *s* Grundwasser *n*

ground′ wire′ *s* (elec) Erdleitung *f*

ground′work′ *s* Grundlage *f*

group [grup] *adj* Gruppen- ‖ *s* Gruppe *f*; (consisting of 18 aircraft) Geschwader *n* ‖ *tr* gruppieren ‖ *intr* sich gruppieren

group′ing *s* Gruppierung *f*

group′ insur′ance *s* Gruppenversicherung *f*

group′ ther′apy *s* Gruppentherapie *f*

grouse [graʊs] *s* Waldhuhn *n* ‖ *intr* (sl) meckern

grout [graʊt] *s* dünner Mörtel *m* ‖ *tr* verstreuen

grove [grov] *s* Gehölz *n*, Hain *m*

grov·el [′grʌvəl], [′grɑvəl] *v* (pret & pp −el[l]ed; ger −el[l]ing) *intr* (& fig) kriechen; **g. in filth** in Schmutz wühlen

grow [gro] *v* (pret grew [gru]; pp grown [gron]) *tr* (plants) planzen, züchten; (grain) anbauen; (a beard) sich [dat] wachsen lassen; **the ram grows horns** dem Widder wachsen Hörner ‖ *intr* wachsen; (become) werden; (become bigger) größer werden; **g. fond of** liebgewinnen; **g. luxuriantly** wuchern; **g. older** an Jahren zunehmen; **g. on s.o.** j-m ans Herz wachsen; **g. out of** (clothes) herauswachsen aus; (fig) entstehen aus; **g. pale** erblassen; **g. together** zusammenwachsen; (close) zuwachsen; **g. up** aufwachsen; **g. wild** (luxuriantly) wuchern; (in the wild) wild wachsen

grower [′gro‑ər] *s* Züchter −in *mf*

growl [graʊl] *s* (of a dog, stomach) Knurren *n*; (of a bear) Brummen *n* ‖ *tr* (words) brummen ‖ *intr* knurren; (said of a bear) brummen; **g. at** anknurren

grown [gron] *adj* erwachsen

grown′-up′ *adj* erwachsen ‖ *s* (grownups) Erwachsene *mf*

growth [groθ] *s* Wachstum *n*; (increase) Zuwachs *m*; (pathol) Gewächs *n*; **full g.** volle Größe *f*

grub [grʌb] *s* Larve *f*, Made *f*; (sl) Fraß *m* ‖ *v* (pret & pp grubbed; ger grubbing) *tr* ausjäten ‖ *intr* wühlen; **g. for** graben nach

grubby [′grʌbi] *adj* (dirty) schmutzig

grudge [grʌdʒ] *s* Mißgunst *f*, Groll *m*; **bear** (or **have**) **a g. against s.o.** j-m grollen ‖ *tr* mißgönnen

grudg′ing *adj* mißgünstig

grudg′ingly *adv* (nur) ungern

gruel [′gru‑əl] *s* Haferschleim *m*

gruel′ing *adj* strapaziös

gruesome [′grusəm] *adj* grausig

gruff [grʌf] *adj* barsch

grumble [′grʌmbəl] *s* Murren *n* ‖ *intr* (over) murren (über acc)

grumbler [′grʌmblər] *s* Brummbär *m*

grumpy [′grʌmpi] *adj* übellaunig

grunt [grʌnt] *s* Grunzen *n* ‖ *tr* & *intr* grunzen

G′-string′ *s* (of a dancer) letzte Hülle *f*; (of a native) Lendenschurz *m*

guarantee [ˌgærən′ti] *s* Garantie *f* ‖ *tr* garantieren für

guarantor [′gærən‚tɔr] *s* Garant *n* *mf*

guaranty [′gærənti] *s* Garantie *f* ‖ *v* (pret & pp −tied) *tr* garantieren

guard [gard] *s* (watch; watchman) Wache *f*; (person) Wächter −in *mf*; (fb) Verteidiger *m*; (mach) Schutzvorrichtung *f*; (soldier) (mil) Posten *m*; (soldiers) (mil) Wachmannschaft *f*, Wache *f*; **be on g. against** sich hüten vor (dat); **be on one′s g.** auf der Hut sein; **keep under close g.** scharf bewachen; **mount g.** Wache beziehen; **relieve the g.** die Wache ablösen; **stand g.** Posten (or Wache) stehen; (during a robbery) Schmiere stehen ‖ *tr* bewachen; (fig) hüten; **g. one′s tongue** seine Zunge im Zaum halten ‖ *intr*—**g. against** sich versehen gegen; **g. over** wachen über (acc)

guard′ de′tail *s* Wachmannschaft *f*

guard′ du′ty *s* Wachdienst *m*; **pull g.** Wache schieben

guard′house′ *s* (building used by guards) Wache *f*; (military jail) Arrestlokal *n* guardian ['gɑrdɪ-ən] s (custodian) Wächter –in mf; (jur) Vormund m

guard'ian an'gel s Schutzengel m

guard'ianship' s Obhut f; (jur) Vormundschaft f

guard'rail' s Geländer n

guard'room' s Wachstube f, Wachlokal n

guerrilla [gə'rɪlə] s Guerillakämpfer –in mf

gueril'la war'fare s Guerillakrieg m

guess [ges] s Vermutung f; anybody's g. reine Vermutung f; take a good g. gut raten || tr vermuten; you guessed it! geraten! || intr raten; g. at schätzen

guesser ['gesər] s Rater –in mf

guess'work' s Raten n, Mutmaßung f

guest [gest] adj Gast-, Gäste- || s Gast m; be a g. of zu Gaste sein bei

guest' book' s Gästebuch n

guest' perform'ance s Gastspiel n; give a g. (theat) gastieren

guest' perform'er s Gast m

guest' room' s Gästezimmer n

guest' speak'er s Gastredner –in mf

guffaw [gə'fɔ] s Gewieher n || intr wiehern

guidance ['gaɪdəns] s Leitung f, Führung f; (educ) Studienberatung f; for your g. zu Ihrer Orientierung

guid'ance coun'selor s Studienberater –in mf

guide [gaɪd] s Führer –in mf; (book) Reiseführer m; (tourist escort) Reiseführer –in mf; (for gardening, etc.) Leitfaden m || tr führen; (rok) lenken

guide'book' s Reiseführer m, Führer m

guid'ed mis'sile s Fernlenkkörper m

guid'ed tour' s Führung f

guide'line' s Richtlinie f

guide'post' s Wegweiser m

guide' word' s Stichwort n

guild [gɪld] s Zunft f, Gilde f

guile [gaɪl] s Arglist f

guileful ['gaɪlfəl] adj arglistig

guileless ['gaɪllɪs] adj arglos

guillotine ['gɪlə,tin] s Fallbeil n, Guillotine f || tr mit dem Fallbeil (or mit der Guillotine) hinrichten

guilt [gɪlt] s Schuld f

guilt'-rid'den adj schuldbeladen

guilty ['gɪlti] adj (of) schuldig (genit); (conscience) schlecht; plead g. sich schuldig bekennen; plead not g. sich für nicht schuldig erklären

guil'ty par'ty s Schuldige mf

guil'ty ver'dict s Schuldspruch m

guin'ea fowl' ['gɪni], guin'ea hen' s Perlhuhn n

guin'ea pig' s Meerschweinchen n; (fig) Versuchskaninchen n

guise [gaɪz] s Verkleidung f; under the g. of unter dem Schein (genit)

guitar [gɪ'tɑr] s Gitarre f

guitarist [gɪ'tɑrɪst] s Gitarrenspieler –in mf

gulch [gʌltʃ] s Bergschlucht f

gulf [gʌlf] s Golf m; (fig) Kluft f

Gulf' Stream' s Golfstrom m

gull [gʌl] s Möwe f; (coll) Tölpel m || tr übertölpeln

gullet ['gʌlɪt] s Gurgel f, Schlund m

gullible ['gʌlɪbəl] adj leichtgläubig

gully ['gʌli] s Wasserrinne f

gulp [gʌlp] s Schluck m, Zug m; at one g. in e-m Zuge || tr schlucken; g. down schlingen || intr schlucken

gum [gʌm] s Gummi m & n; (chewing gum) Kaugummi m & n; (anat) Zahnfleisch n || v (pret & pp gummed; ger gumming) tr (e.g., labels) gummieren; gum up the works (coll) die Arbeit (or das Spiel) vermasseln

gum' ar'abic s Gummiarabikum n

gum'boil' s (pathol) Zahngeschwür n

gum'drop' s Gummibonbon m & n

gummy ['gʌmi] adj klebrig

gumption ['gʌmpʃən] s Unternehmungsgeist m, Mumm m

gun [gʌn] s Gewehr n; (handgun) Handfeuerwaffe f; (arti) Geschütz n; stick to one's guns bei der Stange bleiben || v (pret & pp gunned; ger gunning) tr—gun down niederschießen; gun the engine Gas geben || intr auf die Jagd gehen; be out gunning for auf dem Korn haben; gun for game auf die Jagd gehen

gun' bar'rel s Gewehrlauf m; (arti) Geschützrohr n

gun' bat'tle s Feuerkampf m

gun' belt' s Wehrgehänge n

gun'boat' s Kanonenboot n

gun' car'riage s Lafette f

gun'cot'ton s Schießbaumwolle f

gun' crew' s Bedienungsmannschaft f

gun' emplace'ment s Geschützstand m

gun' fight' s Schießerei f

gun'fire' s Geschützfeuer n

gun'man s (–men) bewaffneter Bandit m

gun' met'al s Geschützlegierung f

gun' mount' s Lafette f; (of swivel type) Schwenklafette f

gunner ['gʌnər] s Kanonier m; (aer) Bordschütze m

gunnery ['gʌnəri] s Geschützwesen n

gun'nery prac'tice s Übungsschießen n

gunnysack ['gʌni,sæk] s Jutesack m

gun' per'mit s Waffenschein n

gun'point' s—at g. mit vorgehaltenem Gewehr

gun'pow'der s Schießpulver n

gun'run'ning s Waffenschmuggel m

gun'shot' s Schuß m; (range) Schußweite f

gun'shot wound' s Schußwunde f

gun'-shy' adj schußscheu

gun'sight' s Visier n

gun'smith' s Büchsenmacher m

gun'stock' s Gewehrschaft m

gun' tur'ret s Geschützturm m; (aer) Schwalbennest n

gunwale ['gʌnəl] s Schandeckel m

guppy ['gʌpi] s Millionenfisch m

gurgle ['gʌrgəl] s Glucksen n, Gurgeln n || intr glucksen, gurgeln

gush [gʌʃ] s Guß m; (fig) Erguß m || intr sich ergießen; g. out hervorströmen; g. over (fig) viel Aufhebens machen von

gusher ['gʌʃər] s Schwärmer –in mf; (oil well) sprudelnde Ölquelle f

gush'ing *adj* (fig) überschwenglich

gushy [ˈgʌʃi] *adj* schwärmerisch

gusset [ˈgʌsɪt] *s* Zwickel *m*

gust [gʌst] *s* Stoß *m*; (*of wind*) Windstoß *m*, Bö *f*

gusto [ˈgʌsto] *s* Gusto *m*

gusty [ˈgʌsti] *adj* böig

gut [gʌt] *s* Darm *m*; **guts** Eingeweide *pl*; (coll) Schneid *m* ‖ *v* (*pret & pp* **gutted**; *ger* **gutting**) *tr* ausbrennen; **be gutted** ausbrennen

gutter [ˈgʌtər] *s* Gosse *f*; (*of a roof*) Dachrinne *f*

gut'tersnipe' *s* (coll) Straßenjunge *m*

guttural [ˈgʌtərəl] *adj* kehlig; (ling) Kehl– ‖ *s* (ling) Kehllaut *m*

guy [gaɪ] *s* Halteseil *n*; (*of a tent*) Spannschnur *f*; (coll) Kerl *m*; **dirty guy** (coll) Saugeil *m*; **great guy** Prachtkerl *m* ‖ *tr* verspannen

guy' wire' *s* Spanndraht *m*

guzzle [ˈgʌzəl] *tr & intr* saufen

guzzler [ˈgʌzlər] *s* Säufer –in *mf*

gym [dʒɪm] *adj* (coll) Turn– ‖ *s* (coll) Turnhalle *f*

gym' class' *s* (coll) Turnstunde *f*

gymnasi·um [dʒɪmˈnɛzɪ·əm] *s* (–ums & –a [ə]) Turnhalle *f*

gymnast [ˈdʒɪmnæst] *s* Turner –in *mf*

gymnastic [dʒɪmˈnæstɪk] *adj* Turn–, gymnastisch; **g. exercise** Turnübung *f* ‖ **gymnastics** *spl* Gymnastik *f*, Turnen *n*

gynecologist [ˌgaɪnəˈkɑlədʒɪst] *s* Gynäkologe *m*, Gynäkologin *f*

gynecology [ˌgaɪnəˈkɑlədʒi] *s* Gynäkologie *f*

gyp [dʒɪp] *s* (sl) Nepp *m*; (*person*) Nepper *m*; **that's a gyp** das ist Nepp! ‖ *v* (*pret & pp* **gypped**; *ger* **gypping**) *tr* neppen

gyp' joint' *s* Nepplokal *n*

gypper [ˈdʒɪpər] *s* Nepper *m*

gypsy [ˈdʒɪpsi] *adj* Zigeuner– ‖ *s* Zigeuner –in *mf*

gyp'sy moth' *s* Großer Schwammspinner *m*

gyrate [ˈdʒaɪret] *intr* sich drehen; kreiseln

gyration [dʒaɪˈreʃən] *s* Kreiselbewegung *f*

gyroscope [ˈdʒaɪrəˌskop] *s* Kreisel *m*

H

H, h [etʃ] *s* achter Buchstabe des englischen Alphabets

haberdasher [ˈhæbərˌdæʃər] *s* Inhaber –in *mf* e–s Herrenmodengeschäfts

haberdashery [ˈhæbərˌdæʃəri] *s* Herrenmodengeschäft *n*

habit [ˈhæbɪt] *s* Gewohnheit *f*; (eccl) Ordenskleid *n*; **be in the h. of** (*ger*) pflegen zu (*inf*); **break s.o. of that h. of smoking** j–m das Rauchen abgewöhnen; **from h.** aus Gewohnheit; **get into the h. of smoking** sich [*dat*] das Rauchen angewöhnen; **make a h. of it** es zur Gewohnheit werden lassen

habitat [ˈhæbɪˌtæt] *s* Wohngebiet *n*

habitation [ˌhæbɪˈteʃən] *s* Wohnort *m*

habitual [həˈbɪtʃʊ·əl] *adj* gewohnheitsmäßig, Gewohnheits–

hack [hæk] *s* (*blow*) Hieb *m*; (*notch*) Kerbe *f*; (*rasping cough*) trockener Husten *m*; (*worn-out horse*) Schindmähre *f*; (*hackney*) Droschke *f*; (*taxi*) (coll) Taxi *n*; (*writer*) (coll) Schreiberling *m* ‖ *tr* hacken, hauen; (basketball) auf den Arm schlagen ‖ *intr* Taxi fahren

hackney [ˈhækni] *s* (*carriage*) Droschke *f*; (*horse*) gewöhnliches Gebrauchspferd *n*

hackneyed [ˈhæknid] *adj* abgedroschen

hack'saw' *s* Metallsäge *f*, Bügelsäge *f*

haddock [ˈhædək] *s* Schellfisch *m*

haft [hæft] *s* Griff *m*

hag [hæg] *s* Vettel *f*; (*witch*) Hexe *f*

haggard [ˈhægərd] *adj* hager

haggle [ˈhægəl] *intr* (**over**) feilschen (um)

hag'gling *s* Feilschen *n*

Hague, the [heg] *s* den Haag *n*

hail [hel] *s* Hagel *m*; **h. of bullets** Kugelhagel *m* ‖ *tr* (*a taxi, ship*) anrufen; (*acclaim*) preisen; (as) begrüßen (als) ‖ *intr* hageln; **h. from** stammen aus (or von) ‖ *interj* Heil!

Hail' Mar'y *s* Ave Maria *n*

hail'stone' *s* Hagelkorn *n*, Schloße *f*

hail'storm' *s* Hagelschauer *m*

hair [her] *s* (*single hair*) Haar *n*; (*collectively*) Haare *pl*; **by a h.** um ein Haar; **do s.o.'s h.** j–n frisieren; **get in s.o.'s h.** j–m auf die Nerven gehen lassen; **split hairs** Haarspalterei treiben

hair'breadth' *s*—**by a h.** um Haaresbreite

hair'brush' *s* Haarbürste *f*

hair' clip' *s* Spange *f*, Klammer *f*

hair'cloth' *s* Haartuch *n*

hair'curl'er *s* Lockenwickler *m*

hair'cut' *s* Haarschnitt *m*; **get a h.** sich [*dat*] die Haare schneiden lassen

hair'do' *s* (–**dos**) Frisur *f*

hair'dress'er *s* Friseur *m*, Friseuse *f*

hair'dri'er *s* Haartrockner *m*

hair' dye' *s* Haarfärbemittel *n*

hairiness [ˈherɪnɪs] *s* Behaartheit *f*

hairless [ˈherlɪs] *adj* haarlos

hair'line' *s* Haaransatz *m*

hair' net' *s* Haarnetz *n*

hair' oil' *s* Haaröl *n*

hair'piece' *s* Haarteil *m*

hair'pin' *s* Haarnadel *f*

hair'-pin curve' *s* Haarnadelkurve *f*

hair'-rais'ing *adj* haarsträubend

hair' rinse' *s* Spülmittel *n*

hair′roll′er s Haarwickler m
hair′ set′ s Wasserwelle f
hair′ shirt′ s Büßerhemd n
hair′split′ting s Haarspalterei f
hair′ spray′ s Haarspray m
hair′spring′ s Haarfeder f, Spirale f
hair′style′ s Frisur f
hair′ ton′ic s Haarwasser n
hairy ['heri] adj haarig, behaart
Haiti ['heti] s Haiti n
halberd ['hælbərd] s Hellebarde f
hal′cyon days′ ['hælsɪ·ən] spl (fig) glückliche Zeit f
hale [hel] adj gesund; **h. and hearty** gesund und munter
half [hæf] adj halb; **at h. price** zum halben Preis; **have h. a mind to** (inf) halb und halb entschlossen sein zu (inf); **one and a h.** eineinhalb || adv halb; **h. as much as** nur halb so wie; **h. as much again** um die Hälfte mehr; **h. past three** halb vier; **not h.** durchaus nicht || s (halves [hævz]) Hälfte f; **cut in h.** in die Hälfte schneiden; **go halves with** halbpart machen mit
half′-and-half′ adj & adv halb und halb || s Halb-und-halb-Mischung f
half′back′ s (fb) Läufer m
half′-baked′ adj halb gebacken; (plans, etc.) halbfertig; (person) unerfahren
half′-blood′ s Halbblut n
half′-breed′ s Halbblut n, Mischling m
half′ broth′er s Halbbruder m
half′-cocked′ adv (coll) nicht ganz vorbereitet
half′-day′ adv halbtags
half′-full′ adj halbvoll
half′-heart′ed adj zaghaft
half′-hour′ adj halbstündig || s halbe Stunde f; **every h.** halbstündlich
half′ leath′er s (bb) Halbleder n
half′-length′ adj halblang; (portrait) in Halbfigur
half′-length por′trait s Brustbild n
half′-light′ s Halbdunkel n
half-mast′ s—**at h.** auf halbmast
half′-meas′ure s Halbheit f
half′-moon′ s Halbmond m
half′ note′ s (mus) halbe Note f
half′ pay′ s Wartegeld n; **be on h.** Wartegeld beziehen
half′ pint′ s (sl) Zwerg m
half′ sis′ter s Halbschwester f
half′ sleeves′ spl halblange Ärmel pl
half′ sole′ s Halbsohle f
half′-staff′ s—**at h.** auf halbmast
half′-tim′bered adj Fachwerk-
half′ time′ s (sport) Halbzeit f
half′-time′ adj Halbzeit-
half′ ti′tle s Schmutztitel m
half′tone′ s (mus, paint, typ) Halbton m
half′-track′ s Halbkettenfahrzeug n
half′-truth′ s halbe Wahrheit f
half′way′ adj auf halbem Wege liegend || adv halbwegs, auf halbem Wege; **meet s.o. h.** j-m auf dem halbem Wege entgegenkommen
half′way meas′ure s Halbheit f
half′-wit′ s Schwachkopf m
half′-wit′ted adj blöd
halibut ['hælɪbət] s Heilbutt m

halitosis [,hælɪ'tosɪs] s Mundgeruch m
hall [həl] s (entranceway) Diele f, Flur m; (passageway) Gang m; (large meeting room) Saal m; (building) Gebäude n
hall′mark′ s Kennzeichen n
hal·lo [hə'lo] s (–los) Hallo n || interj hallo!
hall′ of fame′ s Ruhmeshalle f
hallow ['hælo] tr heiligen
hallucination [hə,lusɪ'neʃən] s Sinnestäuschung f, Halluzination f
hall′way′ s Flur m, Diele f; (passageway) Gang m
ha·lo ['helo] s (–los) Glorienschein m; (astr) Ring m, Hof m
halogen ['hælədʒən] s Halogen n
halt [həlt] s Halt m, Stillstand m; (rest) Rast f; **bring to a h.** zum Stillstand bringen; **call a h. to** halten lassen; **come to a h.** stehenbleiben || tr anhalten || intr halten; (rest) rasten || interj halt!
halter ['həltər] s (for a horse) Halfter m; (noose) Strick m
halt′ing adj (gait) hinkend; (voice) stockend
halve [hæv] tr halbieren
halyard ['hæljərd] s Fall n
ham [hæm] s (pork) Schinken m; (back of the knee) Kniekehle f; (actor) (sl) Schmierenschauspieler –in mf; (rad) (sl) Funkamateur m
hamburger ['hæm,bʌrgər] s Hackfleisch n, deutsches Beefsteak n
hamlet ['hæmlɪt] s Dörfchen n
hammer ['hæmər] s Hammer m; (of a bell) Klöppel m; (sport) Wurfhammer m || tr hämmern; **h. in** (a nail) einschlagen; (e.g., rules) einhämmern; **h. out** aushämmern || intr hämmern; **h. away at** (fig) herumarbeiten an (dat)
hammock ['hæmək] s Hängematte f
hamper ['hæmpər] s Wäschebehälter m || tr behindern
hamster ['hæmstər] s Hamster m
ham′string′ s Kniesehne f || v (pret & pp –strung) tr (fig) lähmen
hand [hænd] s Hand f; (applause) Beifall m; (handwriting) Handschrift f; (of a clock) Zeiger m; (help) Hilfe f; **all hands on deck!** (naut) alle Mann an Deck!; **at first h.** aus erster Hand; **at h.** vorhanden, zur Hand; **at the hands of** von seiten (genit); **be on h.** zur Stelle sein; **by h.** mit der Hand; **change hands** in andere Hände übergehen; **fall into s.o.'s hands** in j-s Hände fallen; **from h. to mouth** von der Hand in den Mund; **get one's hands on** in die Hände bekommen; **get the upper h.** die Oberhand gewinnen; **give s.o. a free h.** j-m freies Spiel lassen; **give s.o. a h.** (help s.o.) j-m helfen; (applaud s.o.) j-m Beifall spenden; **go h. in h. with** (fig) Hand in Hand gehen mit; **h. and foot** eifrig; **h. in h.** Hand in Hand; **hands off!** Hände weg!; **hands up!** Hände hoch!; **have a good h.** (cards) gute Karten haben; **have a**

in die Hand im Spiel haben bei; **have one's hands full** alle Hände voll zu tun haben; **have well in h.** gut in der Hand haben; **hold hands** sich bei den Händen halten; **in one's own h.** eigenhändig; **I wash my hands of it** ich wasche meine Hände in Unschuld; **join hands** (fig) sich zusammenschließen; **new h.** Neuling m; **on all hands** auf allen Seiten; **on h.** (com) vorrätig; **on one h. ... on the other** einerseits ... andererseits; **out of h.** außer Rand und Band; **play into s.o.'s hands** j-m in die Hände spielen; **put one's h. on** (fig) finden; **show one's h.** (fig) seine Karten aufdecken; **take a h. in** mitarbeiten an (dat); **throw up one's hands** verzweifelt die Hände hochwerfen; **try one's h. at** versuchen; **win hands down** spielend gewinnen; **with a heavy h.** streng || tr (zu)reichen; **h. down** (to s.o. below) herunterreichen; (e.g., traditions) überliefern; **h. in** (e.g., homework) abgeben; (an application) einreichen; **h. out** austeilen; **h. over** übergeben; (relinquish) aushändigen, hergeben; **I have to h. it to you** (coll) ich muß dir wohl lassen

hand′bag′ s Handtasche f, Tasche f
hand′ball′ s Handball m
hand′bill′ s Handzettel m
hand′book′ s Handbuch n
hand′ brake′ s (aut) Handbremse f
hand′breadth′ s Handbreit f
hand′ cart′ s Handkarren m
hand′clasp′ s Händedruck m
hand′cuff′ s Handschelle f || tr Handschellen anlegen (dat)
–handed [ˌhændɪd] suf –händig
hand′ful [ˈhændˌfʊl] s Handvoll f; (a few) ein paar; (fig) Nervensäge f
hand′glass′ s Leselupe f
hand′ grenade′ s Handgranate f
handi·cap [ˈhændɪˌkæp] s Handikap n, Benachteiligung f || v (pret & pp –capped; ger –capping) tr handikapen, benachteiligen
hand′icap race′ s Vorgaberennen n
handicraft [ˈhændɪˌkræft] s Handwerk n
handily [ˈhændɪli] adv (dexterously) geschickt; (easily) mit Leichtigkeit
handiwork [ˈhændɪˌwʌrk] s Handarbeit f; (fig) Werk n, Schöpfung f
handkerchief [ˈhæŋkərtʃɪf] s Taschentuch n
handle [ˈhændəl] s Griff m; (of a pot) Henkel m; (of a frying pan, broom, etc.) Stiel m; (of a crank) Handkurbel f; (of a pump) Schwengel m; (of a door) Drücker m; (name) (coll) Name m; (title) (coll) Titelkram m; **fly off the h.** vor Wut platzen || tr (touch) berühren; (tools, etc.) handhaben; (operate) bedienen; (fig) erledigen; (com) handeln mit; **h. with care!** Vorsicht!; **know how to h. customers** es verstehen, mit Kunden umzugehen || intr–**h. well** sich leicht lenken lassen

han′dlebars′ spl Lenkstange f, (mustache) (coll) Schnauzbart m
handler [ˈhændlər] s (sport) Trainer m
han′dling s (e.g., of a car) Lenkbarkeit f; (of merchandise, theme, ball) Behandlung f; (of a tool) Handhabung f
han′dling charg′es spl Umschlagspesen pl
hand′ lug′gage s Handgepäck n
hand′made′ adj handgemacht
hand′-me-downs′ spl getragene Kleider pl
hand′ mir′ror s Handspiegel m
hand′-op′erated adj mit Handbetrieb
hand′ or′gan s Drehorgel f
hand′out′ s milde Gabe f; (sheet) Handzettel m
hand′-picked′ adj handgepflückt; (fig) ausgesucht
hand′rail′ s Geländer n
hand′saw′ s Handsäge f
hand′shake′ s Handschlag m, Händedruck m
handsome [ˈhænsəm] adj schön
hand′-to-hand′ fight′ing s Nahkampf m
hand′-to-mouth′ adj von der Hand in den Mund
hand′work′ s Handarbeit f
hand′writ′ing s Handschrift f
handwritten [ˈhændˌrɪtən] adj handschriftlich; **h. letter** Handschreiben n
handy [ˈhændi] adj handlich; (practical) praktisch; (person) geschickt; **come in h.** gelegen kommen; **have h.** zur Hand haben
hand′y·man′ s (–men′) Handlanger m
hang [hæŋ] s (of curtains, clothes) Fall m; **get the h. of** (coll) sich einarbeiten in (acc); **I don't give a h. about it** (coll) es ist mir Wurst || v (pret & pp hung [hʌŋ]) tr hängen; (a door) einhängen; (wallpaper) ankleben; **h. one's head** den Kopf hängen lassen; **h. out** heraushängen; **h. up** aufhängen; (the receiver) (telp) auflegen; **I'll be hanged if I will** mich hängen lassen, wenn || intr hängen; (float) schweben; **h. around** herumlungern; **h. around the bar** sich in der Bar herumtreiben; **h. around with** umgehen mit; **h. back** sich zurückhalten; **h. by** (a thread, rope) hängen an (dat); **h. down** niederhängen; **h. in the balance** in der Schwebe sein; **h. on** durchhalten; **h. on s.o.'s words** an j-s Worten hängen; **h. on to** festhalten; (retain) behalten; **h. together** zusammenhalten; **h. up** (telp) einhängen || v (pret & pp hanged & hung) tr hängen
hangar [ˈhæŋər] s Hangar m
hang′-dog look′ s Armesündergesicht n
hanger [ˈhæŋər] s Kleiderbügel m
hang′er-on′ s (hangers-on) Mitläufer –in mf
hang′ing adj (herab)hängend || s Hängen n
hang′man s (–men) Henker m
hang′nail′ s Niednagel m

hang′out′ s Treffpunkt m

hang′o′ver s (coll) Kater m

hank [hæŋk] s Strähne f

hanker [′hæŋkər] intr (for) sich sehnen (nach)

hanky-panky [′hæŋki′pæŋki] s (coll) Schwindel m

haphazard [‚hæp′hæzərd] adj wahllos

haphazardly [‚hæp′hæzərdli] adv aufs Geratewohl

hapless [′hæplɪs] adj unglücklich

happen [′hæpən] intr geschehen; **h. to see** zufällig sehen; **h. upon** zufällig stoßen auf (acc); **what happens now?** was soll nun werden?

hap′pening s Ereignis n

happily [′hæpɪli] adv glücklich

happiness [′hæpɪnɪs] s Glück n

happy [′hæpi] adj glücklich; **be h. about s.th.** über etw erfreut sein; **be h. to** (inf) sich freuen zu (inf); **h. as a lark** quietschvergnügt

Hap′py Birth′day interj Herzlichen Glückwunsch zum Geburtstag!

hap′py-go-luck′y adj unbekümmert

hap′py me′dium s—**strike a h.** e-n glücklichen Ausgleich treffen

Hap′py New′ Year′ interj Glückliches Neujahr!

harangue [hə′ræŋ] s leidenschaftliche Rede f ‖ tr e-e leidenschaftliche Rede halten an (acc)

harass [hə′ræs], [′hærəs] tr schikanieren; (mil) stören

harass′ing fire′ s (mil) Störungsfeuer n

harassment [hə′ræsmənt], [′hærəsmənt] s Schikane f; (mil) Störung f

harbinger [′harbɪndʒər] s Vorbote m ‖ tr anmelden

harbor [′harbər] adj Hafen– ‖ s Hafen m ‖ tr (give refuge to) beherbergen; (hide) verbergen; (thoughts) hegen

har′bor mas′ter s Hafenmeister m

hard [hard] adj (substance, water, words) hart; (problem) schwierig; (worker) fleißig; (blow, times, work) schwer; (life) mühsam; (fact) nackt; (rain) heftig; (winter) streng; (drinks) alkoholisch; **be h. on s.o.** j-m schwer zusetzen; **have a h. time** Schwierigkeiten haben; **h. to believe** kaum zu glauben; **h. to please** anspruchsvoll; **h. to understand** schwer zu verstehen ‖ adv hart; (energetically) fleißig; **he was h. put to** (inf) es fiel ihm schwer zu (inf); **rain h.** stark regnen; **take h.** schwer nehmen; **try h.** mit aller Kraft versuchen

hard′-and-fast′ adj fest

hard-bitten [′hard‚bɪtən] adj verbissen

hard′-boiled′ adj (egg) hartgekocht; (coll) hartgesotten

hard′ can′dy s Bonbons pl

hard′ cash′ s bare Münze f

hard′ ci′der s Apfelwein m

hard′ coal′ s Steinkohle f

hard′-earned′ adj schwer verdient

harden [′hardən] tr & intr (er)härten

hard′ened adj (criminal) hartgesotten

hard′ening s Verhärtung f

hard′-head′ed adj nüchtern

hard′-heart′ed adj hartherzig

hardihood [′hardɪ‚hʊd] s Kühnheit f; (insolence) Frechheit f

hardiness [′hardɪnɪs] s Ausdauer f, Widerstandsfähigkeit f

hard′ la′bor s Zwangsarbeit f

hard′ luck′ s Pech n

hardly [′hardli] adv kaum, schwerlich; **h. ever** fast gar nicht

hardness [′hardnɪs] s Härte f

hard′-of-hear′ing adj schwerhörig

hard′-pressed′ adj schwer bedrängt

hard′-shell′ adj hartschalig; (coll) unnachgiebig

hard′ship′ s Mühsal f

hard′top′ s (aut) Hardtop n

hard′ up′ adj (for money) schlecht bei Kasse; **h. for** in Verlegenheit um

hard′ware′ s Eisenwaren pl; (e.g., on doors, windows) Beschläge pl; **military h.** militärische Ausrüstung f

hard′ware store′ s Eisenwarenhandlung f

hard′wood′ s Hartholz n

hard′wood floor′ s Hartholzboden m

hard′-work′ing adj fleißig

hardy [′hardi] adj (plants) winterfest; (person) widerstandsfähig

hare [her] s Hase m

hare′brained′ adj unbesonnen

hare′lip′ s Hasenscharte f

harem [′herəm] s Harem m

hark [hark] intr horchen; **h. back to** zurückgehen auf (acc)

harlequin [′harləkwɪn] s Harlekin m

harlot [′harlət] s Hure f

harm [harm] s Schaden m; **do h.** Schaden anrichten; **I meant no h. by it** ich meinte es nicht böse; **out of harm's way** in Sicherheit; **there's no h. in trying** ein Versuch kann nicht schaden ‖ tr beschädigen; (e.g., a reputation, chances) schaden (dat); **h. s.o.** (physically) j-m etw zuleide tun; (fig) schaden (dat)

harmful [′harmfəl] adj schädlich

harmless [′harmlɪs] adj unschädlich

harmonic [har′manɪk] adj harmonisch ‖ s (mus) Oberton m

harmonica [har′manɪkə] s Harmonika f

harmonious [har′monɪ‐əs] adj harmonisch

harmonize [′harmə‚naɪz] intr harmonieren

harmony [′harməni] s Harmonie f; **be in h. with** im Einklang stehen mit

harness [′harnɪs] s Geschirr n; **die in the h.** in den Sielen sterben ‖ tr anschirren; (e.g., a river, power) nutzbar machen

har′ness mak′er s Sattler m

har′ness rac′ing s Trabrennen n

harp [harp] s Harfe f ‖ intr—**h. on** herumreiten auf (dat)

harpist [′harpɪst] s Harfner –in mf

harpoon [har′pun] s Harpune f ‖ tr harpunieren

harpsichord [′harpsɪ‚kɔrd] s Cembalo n

harpy [′harpi] s (myth) Harpyie f

harrow [′hæro] s Egge f ‖ tr eggen

har′rowing adj schrecklich

har·ry ['hæri] v (pret & pp –ried) tr martern

Harry ['hæri] s Heinz m

harsh [hɑrʃ] adj (conditions) hart; (tone) schroff; (light) grell; (treatment) rauh

harshness ['hɑrʃnɪs] s Härte f; Schroffheit f; Grelle f; Rauheit f

hart [hɑrt] s Hirsch m

harum-scarum ['herəm'skerəm] adj wild || adv wie ein Wilder

harvest ['hɑrvɪst] s Ernte f; bad h. Mißernte f || tr & intr ernten

harvester ['hɑrvɪstər] s Schnitter –in mf; (mach) Mähmaschine f

har′vest moon′ s Erntemond m

has-been ['hæz‚bɪn] s (coll) Gestrige mf

hash [hæʃ] s Gehacktes n; make h. of (coll) verwursteln || tr zerhacken

hashish ['hæʃiʃ] s Haschisch n

hasp [hæsp] s Haspe f

hassle ['hæsəl] s (coll) Streit m

hassock ['hæsək] s Hocker m

haste [hest] s Hast f, Eile f; in (all) h. in (aller) Eile; make h. sich beeilen

hasten ['hesən] tr beschleunigen || intr hasten, eilen

hasty ['hesti] adj eilig; (rash) hastig

hat [hæt] s Hut m; keep under one's h. für sich behalten

hat′band′ s Hutband n

hat′block′ s Hutform f

hat′box′ s Hutschachtel f

hatch [hæt͡ʃ] s (opening) (aer, naut) Luke f; (cover) (naut) Lukendeckel m || tr (eggs) ausbrüten; (a scheme) aushecken; (mark with strokes) schraffieren || intr Junge ausbrüten; (said of chicks) aus dem Ei kriechen

hat′check girl′ s Garderobe(n)fräulein n

hatchet ['hæt͡ʃɪt] s Beil n; bury the h. die Streitaxt begraben

hatch′ing s Schraffierung f

hatch′way′ s (naut) Luke f

hate [het] s Haß m || tr hassen; I h. to (inf) es widerstrebt mir zu (inf)

hateful ['hetfəl] adj verhaßt

hatless ['hætlɪs] adj hutlos

hat′pin′ s Hutnadel f

hat′rack′ s Hutständer m

hatred ['hetrɪd] s Haß m

haughtiness ['hɔtɪnɪs] s Hochmut m

haughty ['hɔti] adj hochmütig

haul [hɔl] s Schleppen n; (hauling distance) Transportstrecke f; (amount caught) Fang m; make a big h. (fig) reiche Beute machen; over the long h. auf die Dauer || tr (tug) schleppen; (transport) transportieren; h. ashore ans Land ziehen; h. down (a flag) einholen; h. into court vor Gericht schleppen; h. out of bed aus dem Bett herausholen || intr—h. off (naut) abdrehen; h. off and hit ausholen um zu schlagen

haulage ['hɔlɪd͡ʒ] s Transport m; (costs) Transportkosten pl

haunch [hɔnt͡ʃ] s (hip) Hüfte f; (hind quarter of an animal) Keule f

haunt [hɔnt] s Aufenthaltsort m || tr verfolgen; h. a place an e–m Ort umgehen; this place is haunted es spukt hier

haunt′ed house′ s Haus n in dem es spukt

have [hæv] s—the haves and the have-nots die Besitzenden und die Besitzlosen || v (pret & pp had [hæd]) tr haben; (a baby) bekommen; (a drink) trinken; (food) essen; h. back (coll) zurückhaben; h. in mind vorhaben; h. it in for s.o. j–n auf dem Strich haben; h. it out with s.o. sich mit j–m aussprechen; h. it your way meinetwegen machen Sie es, wie Sie wollen; h. left übrig haben; h. on (clothes) anhaben; (a hat) aufhaben; (e.g., a program) vorhaben; h. on one's person bei sich tragen; h. to do with s.o. mit j–m zu tun haben; h. what it takes das Zeug dazu haben; I've had it! jetzt langt's mir aber!; I will not h. it! ich werde es nicht dulden!; you had better es wäre besser, wenn Sie; what would you h. me do? was soll ich machen? || intr—h. done with it fertig sein damit; h. off frei haben || aux (to form compound past tenses) haben, e.g., h. has paid the bill er hat die Rechnung bezahlt; (to form compound past tenses of certain intransitive verbs of motion and change of condition, of the verb bleiben, and of the transitive verb eingehen) sein, e.g., she has gone to the theater sie ist ins Theater gegangen; they h. become rich sie sind reich geworden; you h. stayed too long Sie sind zu lange geblieben; I h. assumed an obligation ich bin e–e Verpflichtung eingegangen; (to express causation) lassen, e.g., I am having a new suit made ich lasse mir e–n neuen Anzug machen; (to express necessity) müssen, e.g., I h. to study now jetzt muß ich studieren; that will h. to do das wird genügen müssen

haven ['hevən] s Hafen m

haversack ['hævər‚sæk] s Brotbeutel m

havoc ['hævək] s Verwüstung f; wreak h. on verwüsten

haw [hɔ] s (bot) Mehlbeere f; (in speech) Äh n || tr nach links lenken || intr nach links gehen || interj (to a horse) hü!

Hawaii [hə'wai‚i] s Hawaii n

Hawaiian [hə'waijən] adj hawaiisch

Hawai′ian Is′lands spl Hawaii-Inseln pl

hawk [hɔk] s Habicht m || tr (wares) verhökern; h. up aushusten || intr sich räuspern

hawker ['hɔkər] s Straßenhändler –in mf

hawse [hɔz] s (hole) (naut) Klüse f; (prow) (naut) Klüsenwand f

hawse′hole′ s (naut) Klüse f

hawser ['hɔzər] s (naut) Trosse f, Tau n

hawthorn ['hɔθɔrn] s Weißdorn m

hay [he] s Heu n; hit the hay (sl) sich

in die Falle hauen; **make hay** Heu machen
hay′ fe′ver s Heufieber n
hay′field′ s Kleefeld n
hay′fork′ s Heugabel f
hay′loft′ s Heuboden m
hay′mak′er s (box) Schwinger m
hay′rack′ s Heuraufe f
hayrick [′he͵rɪk] s Heuschober m
hay′ride′ s Ausflug m in e-m teilweise mit Heu gefüllten Wagen
hay′seed′ s (coll) Bauerntölpel m
hay′stack′ s Heuschober m
hay′wire′ adj (sl) übergeschnappt; **go h.** (go wrong) schiefgehen; (go insane) überschnappen
hazard [′hæzərd] s (danger) Gefahr f; (risk) Risiko n || tr riskieren
hazardous [′hæzərdəs] adj gefährlich
haze [hez] s Dunst m; (fig) Unklarheit f || tr (students) piesacken
hazel [′hezəl] adj (eyes) nußbraun || s (bush) Hasel f
ha′zelnut′ s Haselnuß f
haziness [′hezɪnɪs] s Dunstigkeit f; (fig) Verschwommenheit f
haz′ing s (of students) Piesacken n
hazy [′hezi] adj dunstig; (recollection) verschwommen
H-bomb [′etʃ͵bam] s Wasserstoffbombe f
he [hi] pers pron er || s Männchen n
head [hed] adj Kopf-; (chief) Haupt-, Ober-, Chef- || s (of a body, cabbage, nail, lettuce, pin) Kopf m; (of a gang, family) Haupt m; (of a firm) Chef m; (of a school) Direktor –in mf; (of a department) Leiter –in mf; (of a bed) Kopfende n; (of a coin) Bildseite f; (of a glass of beer) Blume f; (of cattle) Stück n; (of stairs) oberer Absatz m; (of a river) Quelle f; (of a parade, army) Spitze f; (toilet) Klo n; **a h.** pro Person, pro Kopf; **at the h. of** an der Spitze (genit); **be at the h. of** vorstehen (dat); **be h. and shoulders above** s.o. haushoch über j-m stehen; (be far superior to s.o.) j-m haushoch überlegen sein; **be over one's h.** über j-s Verstand gehen; **bring to a h.** zur Entscheidung bringen; **by a h.** um e-e Kopflänge; **from h. to foot** von Kopf bis Fuß; **go over** s.o.'s **h.** über j-s Verstand gehen; (adm) über j-s Kopf hinweg handeln; **go to** s.o.'s **h.** j-m zu Kopfe steigen; **have a good h. for** begabt sein für; **h. over heels** kopfüber; (in love) bis über die Ohren; (in debt) bis über den Hals; **heads or tails?** Kopf oder Wappen?; **heads up!** aufpassen!; **keep one's h.** kaltes Blut behalten; **keep one's h. above water** sich über Wasser halten; **lose one's h.** den Kopf verlieren; **my h. is spinning** es schwindelt mir; **not be able to make h. or tail of** nicht klug werden aus; **out of one's h.** nicht ganz richtig im Kopf; **per h.** pro Kopf; **put heads together** die Köpfe zusammenstecken; **talk over**

s.o.'s **h.** über j-s Kopf hinwegreden; **talk** s.o.'s **h. off** j-n dumm und dämlich reden; **take it into one's h.** es sich [dat] in den Kopf setzen || tr (be in charge of) leiten; (a parade, army, expedition) anführen; (steer, guide) lenken; **h. a list** als erster auf e-r Liste stehen; **h. off** abwehren; **h. up** (a committee) vorsitzen (dat) || intr—**h. back** zurückkehren; **h. for** auf dem Wege sein nach; (aer) anfliegen; (naut) ansteuern; **h. home** sich heimbegeben; **where are you heading?** wo wollen Sie hin?
head′ache′ s Kopfweh n, Kopfschmerzen pl
head′band′ s Kopfband n
head′board′ s Kopfbrett n
head′cold′ s Schnupfen m
head′ doc′tor s Chefarzt m, Chefärztin f
head′dress′ s Kopfputz m –**headed** [͵hedɪd] suf –köpfig
head first adv kopfüber; (fig) Hals über Kopf
head′gear′ s Kopfbedeckung f
head′hunt′er s Kopfjäger m
head′ing s Überschrift f; (aer) Steuerkurs m
headland [′hedlənd] s Landspitze f
headless [′hedlɪs] adj kopflos; (without a leader) führerlos
head′light′ s (aut) Scheinwerfer m
head′line′ s (in a newspaper) Schlagzeile f; (at the top of a page) Überschrift f; **hit the headlines** (coll) Schlagzeilen liefern
head′lin′er s Hauptdarsteller –in mf
head′long′ adj stürmisch || adv kopfüber
head′man s (–men) Häuptling m, Chef m
head′mas′ter s Direktor m
head′mis′tress s Direktorin f
head′ nurse′ s Oberschwester f
head′ of′fice s Hauptgeschäftsstelle f
head′ of gov′ernment s Regierungschef m
head′ of hair′ s—beautiful **h.** schönes volles Haar n
head′ of the fam′ily s Familienoberhaupt n
head′-on′ adj Frontal– || adv frontal
head′phones′ spl Kopfhörer pl
head′piece′ s Kopfbedeckung f; (brains) (coll) Kopf m; (typ) Zierleiste f
head′quar′ters s Hauptquartier n; (of police) Polizeidirektion f; (mil) Hauptquartier n, Stabsquartier n
head′quarters com′pany s Stabskompanie f
head′rest′ s Kopflehne f; (aut) Kopfstütze f
head′ restrain′er s (aut) Kopfstütze f
head′set′ s Kopfhörer m
head′ shrink′er s (coll) Psychiater –in mf
head′stand′ s Kopfstand m
head′ start′ s Vorsprung m
head′stone′ s Grabstein m
head′strong′ adj starrköpfig

head′ wait′er *s* Oberkellner *m*

head′ wa′ters *spl* Quellflüsse *pl*

head′way′ *s* Vorwärtsbewegung *f*; (fig) Fortschritte *pl*

head′wear′ *s* Kopfbedeckung *f*

head′wind′ *s* Gegenwind *m*

head′work′ *s* Kopfarbeit *f*

heady [′hɛdi] *adj* (wine) berauschend; (news) spannend; (impetuous) unbesonnen

heal [hil] *tr & intr* heilen; **h. up** zuheilen

healer [′hilər] *s* Heilkundige *mf*

heal′ing *s* Heilung *f*

health [hɛlθ] *s* Gesundheit *f*; **drink to s.o.'s h.** auf j-s Wohl trinken; **in good h.** gesund; **in poor h.** kränklich; **to your h.!** auf Ihr Wohl!

health′ certi′ficate *s* Gesundheitspaß *m*

healthful [′hɛlθfəl] *adj* heilsam; (climate) bekömmlich

health′ insur′ance *s* Krankenversicherung *f*

health′ resort′ *s* Kurort *m*

healthy [′hɛlθi] *adj* gesund; (respect) gehörig; **keep h.** sich gesund halten

heap [hip] *s* Haufen *m*; **in heaps** haufenweise ‖ *tr* beladen; **h.** (e.g., praise) **on s.o.** j-n überhäufen mit; **h. up** anhäufen

hear [hɪr] *v* (pret & pp heard [hʌrd]) *tr* hören; (find out) erfahren; (get word) Bescheid bekommen; **h. s.o.'s lessons** j-n überhören; **h. s.o. out** j-n ganz ausreden lassen ‖ *intr* hören; **h. about** hören über (acc) or von; **h. from** Nachricht bekommen von; **h. of** hören von; **h. wrong** sich verhören; **he wouldn't h. of it** er wollte nichts davon hören

hearer [′hɪrər] *s* Hörer –in *mf*; **hearers** Zuhörer *pl*

hear′ing *s* Hören *n*, Gehör *n*; (jur) Verhör *n*; **within h.** in Hörweite

hear′ing aid′ *s* Hörgerät *n*, Hörapparat *m*

hear′say′ *s* Hörensagen *n*; **know s.th. by h.** etw nur vom Hörensagen kennen; **that's mere h.** das ist bloßes Gerede

hearse [hʌrs] *s* Leichenwagen *m*

heart [hɑrt] *s* Herz *n*; **after my own h.** nach meinem Herzen; **at h.** im Grunde genommen; **be the h. and soul of** die Seele sein (genit); **by h.** auswendig; **cross my h.!** Hand aufs Herz!; **cry one's h. out** sich ausweinen; **eat one's h. out** sich vor Kummer verzehren; **get to the h. of** auf den Grund kommen (dat); **have a h.** (coll) ein Herz haben; **have one's h. in s.th.** mit dem Herzen bei etw sein; **have the h. to** (inf) es übers Herz bringen zu (inf); **h. and soul** mit Leib und Seele; **hearts** (cards) Herz *n*; **lose h.** den Mut verlieren; **lose one's h. to** sein Herz verlieren an (acc); **set one's h. on** sein Herz hängen an (acc); **take h.** Mut fassen; **take to h.** beherzigen; **to one's heart's content** nach Herzenslust; **wear one's h. on one's sleeve** das Herz auf der Zunge tragen; **with all one's h.** mit ganzem Herzen

heart′ache′ *s* Herzweh *n*

heart′ attack′ *s* Herzanfall *m*

heart′beat′ *s* Herzschlag *m*

heart′break′ *s* Herzeleid *n*

heart′break′er *s* Herzensbrecher –in *mf*

heartbroken [′hɑrt‚brokən] *adj* trostlos

heart′burn′ *s* Sodbrennen *n*

heart′ disease′ *s* Herzleiden *n*

–heart′ed [‚hɑrtɪd] *suf* –herzig

hearten [′hɑrtən] *tr* ermutigen

heart′ fail′ure *s* Herzschlag *m*

heartfelt [′hɑrt‚fɛlt] *adj* herzinnig, tiefempfunden; (wishes) herzlich

hearth [hɑrθ] *s* Herd *m*

hearth′stone′ *s* Kaminplatte *f*

heartily [′hɑrtɪli] *adv* (with zest) herzhaft; (sincerely) von Herzen

heartless [′hɑrtlɪs] *adj* herzlos

heart′ mur′mur *s* Herzgeräusch *n*

heart′-rend′ing *adj* herzzerreißend

heart′sick′ *adj* tief betrübt

heart′ strings′ *spl*—**pull at s.o.'s h.** j-m ans Herz greifen

heart′ throb′ *s* Schwarm *m*

heart′ trans′plant *s* Herzverpflanzung *f*

heart′ trou′ble *s* Herzbeschwerden *pl*

heart′wood′ *s* Kernholz *n*

hearty [′hɑrti] *adj* herzhaft; (meal) reichlich; (eater) stark; (appetite) gut

heat [hit] *s* Hitze *f*, Wärme *f*; (heating) Heizung *f*; (sexual) Brunst *f*; (in the case of dogs) Läufigkeit *f*; (of battle) Eifer *m*; (sport) Rennen *n*, Einzelrennen *n*; **be in h.** brunsten; (said of dogs) läufig sein; **final h.** Schlußrennen *n*; **put the h. on** (sl) unter Druck setzen; **qualifying h.** Vorlauf *m* ‖ *tr* (e.g., food) wärmen; (fluids) erhitzen; (a house) heizen; **h. up** aufwärmen ‖ *intr*—**h.** (up) warm (or heiß) werden

heat′ed *adj* erhitzt; (fig) erregt

heater [′hitər] *s* Heizkörper *m*; (oven) Heizofen *m*

heath [hiθ] *s* Heide *f*

hea·then [′hiðən] *adj* heidnisch ‖ *s* (–then & –thens) Heide *m*, Heidin *f*

heathendom [′hiðəndəm] *s* Heidentum *n*

heather [′hɛðər] *s* Heiderkraut *n*

heat′ing *s* Heizung *f*

heat′ing pad′ *s* Heizkissen *n*

heat′ing sys′tem *s* Heizanlage *f*

heat′ light′ning *s* Wetterleuchten *n*

heat′ prostra′tion *s* Hitzekollaps *m*

heat′-resis′tant *adj* hitzebeständig

heat′ shield′ *s* (rok) Hitzeschild *m*

heat′stroke′ *s* Hitzschlag *m*

heat′ treat′ment *s* Wärmebehandlung *f*

heat′ wave′ *s* Hitzewelle *f*

heave [hiv] *s* Hub *m*; (throw) Wurf *m*; **heaves** (vet) schweres Atmen *n* ‖ *v* (pret & pp heaved & hove [hov]) *tr* heben; (throw) werfen; (a sigh) ausstoßen; (the anchor) lichten ‖ *intr* (said of the breast or sea) wogen; (retch) sich übergeben; **h. in sight** auftauchen; **h. to** (naut) stoppen

heaven ['hevən] s Himmel m; **for heaven's sake** um Himmels willen; **good heavens!** ach du lieber Himmel!; **the heavens** der Himmel

heavenly ['hevənli] adj himmlisch

hea′venly bod′y s Himmelskörper m

heavenwards ['hevənwərdz] adv himmelwärts

heavily ['hevɪli] adv schwer; **h. in debt** überschuldet

heavy ['hevi] adj schwer; (food) schwer verdaulich; (fine, price) hoch; (walk) schwerfällig; (heart) bedrückt, schwer; (traffic, frost, rain) stark; (fog) dicht; (role) (theat) ernst, düster; **h. drinker** Gewohnheitstrinker –in mf; **h. seas** Sturzsee f; **h. with sleep** schlaftrunken

heavy′-armed′ adj schwerbewaffnet

heav′y-du′ty adj Hochleistungs–, Schwerlast–

heav′y-du′ty truck′ s Schwerlastwagen m

heav′y-heart′ed adj bedrückt

heav′y in′dustry s Schwerindustrie f

heav′yset′ adj untersetzt

heav′y weight′ adj Schwergewicht– ‖ s Schwergewichtler m

Hebrew ['hibru] adj hebräisch ‖ s Hebräer –in mf; (language) Hebräisch n

hecatomb ['hekə‚tom] s Hekatombe f

heck [hek] s—**give s.o. h.** (sl) j–m tüchtig einheizen; **what the h. are you doing?** (sl) was zum Teufel tust du? ‖ interj (sl) verflixt!

heckle ['hekəl] tr durch Zwischenrufe belästigen

heckler ['heklər] s Zwischenrufer –in mf

hectic ['hektɪk] adj hektisch

hectograph ['hektə‚græf] s Hektograph m ‖ tr hektographieren

hedge [hedʒ] s Hecke f ‖ tr—**h. in** (or **h. off**) einhegen ‖ intr sich den Rücken decken

hedge′hog′ s Igel m

hedge′hop′ v (pret & pp –hopped) ger hopping) intr (aer) heckenspringen

hedge′hop′ping s (aer) Heckenhüpfen n

hedge′row′ s Hecke f

hedonism ['hidə‚nɪzəm] s Hedonismus m

hedonist ['hidənɪst] s Hedonist –in mf

heed [hid] tr Acht f; **pay h. to** achtgeben auf ‹acc›; **take h.** achtgeben ‖ tr beachten ‖ intr achtgeben

heedful ['hidfəl] adj (of) achtsam (auf acc)

heedless ['hidlɪs] adj achtlos; **h. of** ungeachtet (genit)

heehaw ['hi‚hɔ] s Iah n ‖ interj iah!

heel [hil] s (of the foot) Ferse f; (of a shoe) Absatz m; (of bread) Brotende n; (sl) Schurke m; **down at the h.** abgerissen; **cool one's heels** sich [dat] die Beine in den Bauch stehen; **take to one's heels** Fersengeld geben ‖ intr (said of a dog) auf den Fersen folgen

hefty ['hefti] adj (heavy) schwer; (muscular) stämmig; (blow) zünftig

heifer ['hefər] s Färse f

height [haɪt] s Höhe f; (e.g., of power) Gipfel m; **h. of the season** Hochsaison f

heighten ['haɪtən] tr erhöhen; (fig) verschärfen

heinous ['henəs] adj abscheulich

heir [er] s Erbe; m; **become h. to** erben; **become s.o.'s h.** j–n beerben

heir′ appar′ent s (heirs apparent) Thronerbe m

heiress ['erɪs] s Erbin f

heir′loom′ s Erbstück n

heir′ presump′tive s (heirs presumptive) mutmaßlicher Erbe m

Helen ['helən] s Helene f

helicopter ['helɪ‚kaptər] s Hubschrauber m

heliport ['helɪ‚pɔrt] s Hubschrauberlandeplatz m

helium ['hilɪ‚əm] s Helium n

helix ['hilɪks] s (helixes & helices ['helɪ‚siz]) Spirale f; (archit) Schnecke f

hell [hel] s Hölle f

hell′bent′ adj—**h. on** (sl) erpicht auf ‹acc›

hell′cat′ s (shrew) Hexe f

Hellene ['helin] s Hellene m, Hellenin f

Hellenic [he'lenɪk] adj hellenisch

hell′fire′ s Höllenfeuer n

hellish ['helɪʃ] adj höllisch

hel·lo [he'lo] s (–los) Hallo n ‖ interj guten Tag!; (in southern Germany and Austria) Grüß Gott!; (to get s.o.'s attention and in answering the telephone) hallo!

helm [helm] s (& fig) Steuerruder n

helmet ['helmɪt] s Helm m

helms′man s (–men) Steuermann m

help [help] s Hilfe f; (domestic) Hilfe f, Hilfskraft f; (temporary) Aushilfe f; **h. wanted** (in newspapers) Stellenangebot n; **there's no h. for it** da ist nicht zu helfen; **with the h. of** mit Hilfe (genit) ‖ tr helfen (dat); **can I h. you?** womit kann ich (Ihnen) dienen?; **h. along** nachhelfen (dat); **h. down from** herunterhelfen (dat) von (dat); **h. oneself** sich helfen (at table) zugreifen; **h. oneself to** sich [dat] nehmen; **h. out** aushelfen (dat); **h. s.o. on** (or **off**) **with the coat** j–m in den (or aus dem) Mantel helfen; **I cannot h.** (ger), **I cannot h. but** (inf) ich kann nicht umhin zu (inf); **sorry, that can't be helped** es tut mir leid, aber es geht nicht anders ‖ intr helfen ‖ interj Hilfe!

helper ['helpər] s Gehilfe m, Gehilfin f

helpful ['helpfəl] adj (person) hilfsbereit; (e.g., suggestion) nützlich

help′ing s Portion f

help′ing hand′ s hilfreiche Hand f

helpless ['helplɪs] adj hilflos, ratlos

helter-skelter ['heltər 'skeltər] adj wirr ‖ adv holterdipolter

hem [hem] s Saum m ‖ v (pret & pp hemmed) ger hemming) tr säumen; **hem in** umringen ‖ intr stocken; **hem**

and **haw** nicht mit der Sprache herausvollen ‖ *interj* hml

hemisphere [ˈhemɪˌsfɪr] *s* Halbkugel *f*

hemistich [ˈhemɪˌstɪk] *s* Halbvers *m*

hem′line′ *s* Rocklänge *f*

hem′lock′ *s* (*conium*) Schierling *m*; (*poison*) Schierlingsgift *n*; (*Tsuga canadensis*) Kanadische Hemmlocktanne *f*

hemoglobin [ˌhiməˈglobɪn] *s* Blutfarbstoff *m*, Hämoglobin *n*

hemophilia [ˌhiməˈfɪlɪə] *s* Bluterkrankheit *f*, Hämophilie *f*

hemorrhage [ˈhemərɪdʒ] *s* Blutung *f*

hemorrhoids [ˈheməˌrɔɪdz] *spl* Hämorrhoiden *pl*

hemostat [ˈhiməˌstæt] *s* Unterbindungssklemme *f*

hemp [hemp] *s* Hanf *m*

hem′stitch′ *s* Hohlsaum *m* ‖ *tr* mit e–m Hohlsaum versehen

hen [hen] *s* Henne *f*, Huhn *n*

hence [hens] *adv* von hier; (*therefore*) daher, daraus; a year h. in e–m Jahr

hence′forth′ *adv* hinfort, von nun an

hench-man [ˈhentʃmən] *s* (–men) Anhänger *m*; (*gang member*) Helfershelfer *m*

hen′house′ *s* Hühnerstall *m*

henna [ˈhenə] *s* Henna *f*

hen′ par′ty *s* (coll) Damengesellschaft *f*

hen′peck′ *tr* unter dem Pantoffel haben; be henpecked unter dem Pantoffel stehen; henpecked husband Pantoffelheld *m*

Henry [ˈhenri] *s* Heinrich *m*

hep [hep] *adj* (to) eingeweiht (in *acc*)

her [hʌr] *poss adj* ihr; (*if the antecedent is neuter, e.g.*, Fräulein) sein ‖ *pers pron* sie; (*if the antecedent is neuter*) es; (*indirect object*) ihr; (*if the antecedent is neuter*) ihm

herald [ˈherəld] *s* Herold *m*; (fig) Vorbote *m* ‖ *tr* ankündigen; h. in einführen

heraldic [heˈrældɪk] *adj* heraldisch; h. figure Wappenbild *n*; h. motto Wappenspruch *m*

heraldry [ˈherəldri] *s* Wappenkunde *f*

herb [(h)ʌrb] *s* Kraut *n*, Gewürz *n*; (pharm) Arzneikraut *n*

herculean [hʌrkjuˈliən] *adj* herkulisch

herd [hʌrd] *s* Herde *f*; (*of game*) Rudel *n*; the common h. der Pöbel *m* ‖ *tr* hüten; h. together zusammenpferchen ‖ *intr* in e–r Herde gehen (or leben)

herds′man *s* (–men) Hirt *m*

here [hɪr] *adv* (*position*) hier; (*direction*) hierher, her; h. and there hie(r) und da; h. below in diesem Leben; h. goes! jetzt gilt's!; here's to you! auf Ihr Wohl!; neither h. nor there belanglos ‖ *interj* hier!

hereabouts [ˈhɪrəˌbauts] *adv* hier in der Nähe

hereaf′ter *adv* hiernach ‖ *s* Jenseits *n*

hereby′ *adv* hierdurch

hereditary [hɪˈrediˌteri] *adj* erblich, Erb–; be h. sich vererben

heredity [hɪˈrediti] *s* Vererbung *f*

herein′ *adv* hierin

hereof′ *adv* hiervon

hereon′ *adv* hierauf

heresy [ˈherəsi] *s* Ketzerei *f*

heretic [ˈherətɪk] *s* Ketzer –in *mf*

heretical [hɪˈretɪkəl] *adj* ketzerisch

heretofore′ [ˌhɪrtuˈfor] *adv* zuvor

here′upon′ *adv* daraufhin

herewith′ *adv* hiermit; (*in a letter*) anbei, in der Anlage

heritage [ˈherɪtɪdʒ] *s* Erbe *n*

hermet′ically sealed′ [hʌrˈmetɪkəli] *adj* hermetisch verschlossen

hermit [ˈhʌrmɪt] *s* Einsiedler –in *mf*; (eccl) Eremit *m*

hermitage [ˈhʌrmɪtɪdʒ] *s* Eremitage *f*

herni-a [ˈhʌrnɪə] *s* (–as & –ae [ˌi]) Bruch *m*

he-ro [ˈhɪro] *s* (–roes) Held *n*

heroic [hɪˈro·ɪk] *adj* heldenhaft, Helden–; (pros) heroisch ‖ **heroics** *spl* Heldentaten *pl*

hero′ic age′ *s* Helden(zeit)alter *n*

hero′ic coup′let *s* heroisches Reimpaar *n*

hero′ic verse′ *s* heroisches Versmaß *n*

heroin [ˈhero·ɪn] *s* Heroin *f*

heroine [ˈhero·ɪn] *s* Heldin *f*

heroism [ˈhero·ɪzəm] *s* Heldenmut *m*

heron [ˈherən] *s* (orn) Fischreiher *m*

he′ro wor′ship *s* Heldenverehrung *f*

herring [ˈherɪŋ] *s* Hering *m*

her′ringbone′ *s* (*pattern*) Grätenmuster *n*; (*parquetry*) Riemenparkett *n*

hers [hʌrz] *poss pron* der ihre (or ihrige), ihrer

herself *reflex pron* sich; she's not h. today sie ist heute gar nicht wie sonst ‖ *intens pron* selbst, selber

hesitancy [ˈherzɪtənsi] *s* Zaudern *n*

hesitant [ˈhezɪtənt] *adj* zögernd

hesitate [ˈhezɪˌtet] *intr* zögern

hesitation [ˌhezɪˈteʃən] *s* Zögern *n*

heterodox [ˈhetərəˌdaks] *adj* andersgläubig, heterodox

heterodyne [ˈhetərəˌdaɪn] *adj* Überlagerungs– ‖ *tr & intr* überlagern

heterogeneous [ˌhetərəˈdʒɪnɪ·əs] *adj* heterogen

hew [hju] *v* (*pret* hewed; *pp* hewed & hewn) *tr* (*stone*) hauen; (*trees*) fällen; hew down umhauen

hex [heks] *s* (*spell*) Zauber *m*; (*witch*) Hexe *f*; put a hex on (coll) behexen ‖ *tr* (coll) behexen

hexagon [ˈheksəgən] *s* Hexagon *n*

hey [he] *interj* heil; hey there! hedal

hey′day′ *s* Hochblüte *f*, Glanzzeit *f*

H′-hour′ *s* (mil) X-Zeit *f*

hi [haɪ] *interj* heil; hi there! hedal

hia-tus [haɪˈetəs] *s* (–tuses & –tus) Lücke *f*; (ling) Hiatus *m*

hibernate [ˈhaɪbərˌnet] *intr* (& fig) Winterschlaf halten

hibernation [ˌhaɪbərˈneʃən] *s* Winterschlaf *m*

hibiscus [haɪˈbɪskəs] *s* Hibiskus *m*

hiccough, hiccup [ˈhɪkəp] *s* Schluckauf *m*

hick [hɪk] *s* Tölpel *m*

hickory [ˈhɪkəri] *s* Hickorybaum *m*

hick′ town′ *s* Kuhdorf *n*

hidden ['hɪdən] *adj* verborgen, versteckt; *(secret)* geheim

hide [haɪd] *s* Haut *f*, Fell *n* ‖ *v (pret* **hid** [hɪd]; *pp* **hid** & **hidden** ['hɪdən] *tr* verstecken; *(a view)* verdecken; *(fig)* verbergen; **h. from** verheimlichen vor *(dat)* ‖ *intr* **(out)** sich verstecken

hide'-and-seek' *s* Versteckspiel *n;* **play h.** Versteck spielen

hide'away' *s* Schlupfwinkel *m*

hide'bound *adj* engherzig

hideous ['hɪdɪ·əs] *adj* gräßlich

hide'out' *s* (coll) Versteck *n*

hid'ing *s* Verstecken *n;* **be in h.** sich versteckt halten; **get a h.** (coll) Prügel bekommen

hid'ing place' *s* Versteck *n*

hierarchy ['haɪ·ə,rɑrkɪ] *s* Hierarchie *f*

hieroglyphic [,haɪ·ərə'glɪfɪk] *adj* Hieroglphen– ‖ *s* Hieroglyphe *f*

hi-fi ['haɪ'faɪ] *adj* Hifi– ‖ *s* Hi-Fi *n*

high [haɪ] *adj* hoch; *(wind)* stark; *(hopes)* hochgespannt; *(fever)* heftig *(spirits)* gehoben; **h. and dry** auf dem Trockenen; **h. and mighty** hochfahrend; **it is h. time** es ist höchste Zeit ‖ *adv* hoch; **h. and low** weit und breit ‖ *s (e.g., in prices)* Hochstand *m;* (aut) höchster Gang *m;* (meteor) Hoch *n;* **on h.** oben; **shift into h.** den höchsten Gang einschalten

high' al'tar *s* Hochaltar *m*

high'ball' *s* Highball *m*

high'born' *adj* hochgeboren

high'boy' *s* hochbeinige Kommode *f*

high'brow' *adj* intellektuell ‖ *s* Intellektuelle *mf*

high' chair' *s* Kinderstuhl *m*

High' Church' *s* Hochkirche *f*

high'-class' *adj* vornehm, herrschaftlich

high' command' *s* Oberkommando *n*

high' cost' of liv'ing *s* hohe Lebenshaltungskosten *pl*

high' div'ing *s* Turmspringen *n*

high'er educa'tion *s* Hochschulbildung *f*

high'er-up' *s* (coll) hohes Tier *n*

high'est bid' ['haɪ·ɪst] *s* Meistgebot *n*

high'est bid'der *s* Meistbietende *mf*

high' explo'sive *s* hochexplosiver Sprengstoff *m*

highfalutin [,haɪfə'lutən] *adj* hochtönend

high' fidel'ity *s* äußerst getreue Tonwiedergabe *f*, High Fidelity *f*

high'-fidel'ity *adj* klanggetreu

high' fre'quency *s* Hochfrequenz *f*

high'-fre'quency *adj* hochfrequent

high' gear' *s* höchster Gang *m;* **shift into h.** den höchsten Gang einschalten; (fig) auf Hochtouren gehen

High' Ger'man *s* Hochdeutsch *n*

high'-grade' *adj* hochfein, Qualitäts–

high'-grade steel' *s* Edelstahl *m*

high'-hand'ed *adj* anmaßend

high' heel' *s* Stöckel *m*

high'-heeled shoe' *s* Stöckelschuh *m*

high' horse' *s*—**come off one's h.** klein beigeben; **get up on one's h.** sich aufs hohe Roß setzen

high' jinks' [,dʒɪŋks] *spl* Ausgelassenheit *f*

high' jump' *s* (sport) Hochsprung *m*

highland ['haɪlənd] *s* Hochland *n;* **highlands** Hochland *n*

highlander ['haɪləndər] *s* Hochländer –in *mf*

high' life' *s* Prasserei *f*, Highlife *n*

high'light' *s* (big moment) Höhepunkt *m;* (in a picture) Glanzlicht *n* ‖ *tr* hervorheben; (in a picture) Glanzlichter aufsetzen (dat)

highly ['haɪlɪ] *adv* hoch, hoch–, höchst; **h. sensitive** hochempfindlich; **speak h. of** in den höchsten Tönen sprechen von; **think h. of** große Stücke halten auf (acc)

High' Mass' *s* Hochamt *n*

high'-mind'ed *adj* hochgesinnt

high'-necked' *adj* hochgeschlossen

highness ['haɪnɪs] *s* Höhe *f;* **Highness** (title) Hoheit *f*

high' noon' *s*—**at h.** am hellen Mittag

high'-oc'tane *adj* mit hoher Oktanzahl

high'-pitched' *adj* (voice) hoch; (roof) steil

high'-pow'ered *adj* starkmotorig; **h. engine** Hochleistungsmotor *m*

high' pres'sure *s* Hochdruck *m*

high'-pres'sure *adj* Hochdruck–; **h. area** Hochdruckgebiet *n* ‖ *tr* (com) bearbeiten

high'-priced' *adj* kostspielig

high' priest' *s* Hohe(r)priester *m*

high'-qual'ity *adj* Qualitäts–, hochwertig

high'-rank'ing *adj* hochgestellt

high' rise' *s* Hochbau *m*, Hochhaus *n*

high'road' *s* (fig) sicherer Weg *m*

high' school' *s* Oberschule *f*

high' sea' *s*—**on the high seas** auf offenem Meer

high' soci'ety *s* vornehme Welt *f*, High Society *f*

high'-sound'ing *adj* hochtönend

high'-speed' *adj* Schnell–; (phot) lichtstark

high'-speed steel' *s* Schnelldrehstahl *m*

high'-spir'ited *adj* hochgemut; (horse) feurig

high' spir'its *spl* gehobene Stimmung *f*

high-strung ['haɪ'strʌŋ] *adj* überempfindlich

high' ten'sion *s* Hochspannung *f*

high'-ten'sion *adj* Hochspannungs–

high'-test' gas'oline *s* Superbenzin *n*

high' tide' *s* Flut *f*

high' time' *s* höchste Zeit *f;* (sl) Heidenspaß *m*

high' trea'son *s* Hochverrat *m*

high' volt'age *s* Hochspannung *f*

high'-volt'age *adj* Hochspannungs–

high'-wa'ter mark' *s* Hochwassermarke *f;* (fig) Höhepunkt *m*

high'way' *s* Landstraße *f*, Chaussee *f*

high'way'man *s* (–men) Straßenräuber *m*

high'way patrol' *s* Straßenstreife *f*

high'way rob'bery *s* Straßenraub *m*

hijack ['haɪ,dʒæk] *tr* (a truck) überfallen und rauben; (a plane) entführen

hijacker ['haɪ ,dʒækər] s (of a truck) Straßenräuber –in mf; (of a plane) Entführer –in mf
hi'jack'ing s Entführung f
hike [haɪk] s Wanderung f; (in prices) Erhöhung f || tr (prices) erhöhen || intr wandern
hiker ['haɪkər] s Wanderer –in mf
hik'ing s Wandern n
hilarious [hɪ'lerɪ·əs] adj heiter
hill [hɪl] s Hügel m; go over the h. (mil) ausbüxen; over the h. (coll) auf dem absteigenden Ast || tr häufeln
hill'bil'ly adj hinterwäldlerisch || s Hinterwäldler –in mf
hill' coun'try s Hügelland n
hillock ['hɪlək] s Hügelchen n
hill'side' s Hang m
hilly ['hɪli] adj hügelig
hilt [hɪlt] s Griff m; armed to the h. bis an die Zähne bewaffnet; to the h. (fig) gründlich
him [hɪm] pers pron (dative) ihm; (accusative) ihn
himself' reflex pron sich; he is not h. today er ist heute gar nicht wie sonst || intens pron selbst, selber
hind [haɪnd] adj Hinter– || s Hirschkuh f
hinder ['hɪndər] tr (ver)hindern
hind'most' adj hinterste
hind'quar'ter s Hinterviertel n; (of a horse) Hinterhand f; (of venison) Ziemer m
hindrance ['hɪndrəns] s (to) Hindernis n (für)
hind'sight' s späte Einsicht f
Hindu ['hɪndu] adj Hindu– || s Hindu m
hinge [hɪndʒ] s Scharnier n; (of a door) Angel f || intr—h. on abhängen von
hint [hɪnt] s Wink m, Andeutung f; give a broad h. e-n Wink mit dem Zaunpfahl geben; take the h. den Wink verstehen || intr—h. at andeuten
hinterland ['hɪntər ,lænd] s Hinterland n
hip [hɪp] adj (sl) im Bild || s Hüfte f; (of a roof) Walm m
hip'bone' s Hüftbein n
hip'joint' s Hüftgelenk n
hipped adj—h. on (coll) erpicht auf (acc)
hippopota·mus [,hɪpə'patəməs] s (–muses & –mi [,maɪ]) Nilpferd n
hip' roof' s Walmdach n
hire [haɪr] s Miete f; (salary) Lohn m; for h. zu vermieten || tr (workers) anstellen; (rent) mieten; h. oneself out to sich verdingen bei; h. out vermieten
hired' hand' s Lohnarbeiter –in mf
hireling ['haɪrlɪŋ] s Mietling m
his [hɪz] poss adj sein || poss pron seiner, der seine (or seinige)
Hispanic [hɪs'pænɪk] adj hispanisch
hiss [hɪs] s Zischen n || tr auszischen || intr zischen
hiss'ing s Zischen n, Gezisch n

hiss'ing sound' s Zischlaut m
hist [hɪst] interj st!
historian [hɪs'torɪ·ən] s Historiker –in mf
historic [hɪs'tɔrɪk] adj historisch bedeutsam
historical [hɪs'tɔrɪkəl] adj historisch, geschichtlich
history ['hɪstəri] s Geschichte f
historionic [,hɪstrɪ'anɪk] adj schauspielerisch; (fig) übertrieben || histrionics spl theatralisches Benehmen n
hit [hɪt] s Schlag m, Stoß m; (a success) Schlager m; (sport) Treffer m; (theat) Zugstück n || v (pret & pp hit; ger hitting) tr (e.g., with the fist) schlagen; (a note, target) treffen; hit bottom (fig) auf den Nullpunkt angekommen sein; hit it off gut miteinander auskommen; hit one's head against mit dem Kopf stoßen gegen; hit s.o. hard (said of misfortunes, etc.) schwer treffen; hit the road sich auf den Weg machen; hit the sack sich hinhauen || intr schlagen; hit on (or upon) kommen auf (acc)
hit'-and-run' adj (driver) flüchtig; h. accident Unfall m mit Fahrerflucht; h. attack Zerstörangriff m
hitch [hɪtʃ] s (difficulty) Haken m; (knot) Stich m; (term of service) Dienstzeit f; that's the h. das ist ja gerade der Haken; without a h. reibungslos || tr spannen; h. a ride (to) per Anhalter fahren (nach); h. to the wagon vor (or an) den Wagen spannen; h. up (horses) anspannen; (trousers) hochziehen
hitch/hike' intr per Anhalter fahren
hitch'ing post' s Pfosten m (zum Anbinden von Pferden)
hither ['hɪðər] adv her, hierher; h. and thither hierhin und dorthin
hitherto adv bisher
hit' or miss' adv aufs Geratewohl
hit'-or-miss' adj planlos
hitter ['hɪtər] s Schläger m
hive [haɪv] s Bienenstock m; hives (pathol) Nesselausschlag m
hoard [hord] s Hort m || tr & intr horten; (food) hamstern
hoarder ['hordər] s Hamsterer –in mf
hoard'ing s Horten n; (of food) Hamstern n
hoarfrost ['hor ,frɔst] s Rauhreif m
hoarse [hors] adj heiser
hoarseness ['horsnɪs] s Heiserkeit f
hoary ['hori] adj ergraut; (fig) altersgrau
hoax [hoks] s Schnabernack m || tr anführen
hob [hab] s Kamineinsatz m
hobble ['habəl] s Humpeln n || intr humpeln
hobby ['habi] s Hobby n
hob'byhorse' s (stick with horse's head) Steckenpferd n; (rocking horse) Schaukelpferd n
hob'gob'lin s Kobold m; (bogy) Schreckgespenst n
hob'nail' s grober Schuhnagel m

hob·nob ['hab͵nɑb] *v* (*pret & pp* **-nobbed;** *ger* **-nobbing**) *intr*—h. **with** freundschaftlich verkehren mit

ho·bo ['hobo] *s* (**-bos** & **-boes**) Landstreicher *m*

hock [hak] *s* (*of a horse*) Sprunggelenk *n;* **in h.** verpfändet ‖ *tr* (*hamstring*) lähmen; (*pawn*) (coll) verpfänden

hockey ['hɑki] *s* Hockey *n*

hoc'key stick' *s* Hockeystock *m*

hock'shop' *s* (coll) Leihhaus *n*

hocus-pocus ['hokəs'pokəs] *s* Hokuspokus *m*

hod [had] *s* Mörteltrog *m*

hodgepodge ['hadʒ͵padʒ] *s* Mischmasch *m*

hoe [ho] *s* Hacke *f,* Haue *f* ‖ *tr* hacken

hog [hag] *s* Schwein *n* ‖ *v* (*pret & pp* **hogged;** *ger* **hogging**) *tr* (sl) gierig an sich reißen; **hog the road** rücksichtslos fahren

hog'back' *s* scharfer Gebirgskamm *m*

hog' bris'tle *s* Schweinsborste *f*

hoggish ['hagɪʃ] *adj* schweinisch, gefräßig

hog'wash' *s* (*nonsense*) Quatsch *m*

hoist [hɔɪst] *s* (*apparatus for lifting*) Hebezeug *n;* (*act of lifting*) Hochwinden *n* ‖ *tr* hochwinden; (*a flag, sail*) hissen

hokum ['hokəm] *s* (*nonsense*) (coll) Quatsch *m;* (*flimflam*) (coll) Effekthascherei *f*

hold [hold] *s* Halt *m,* Griff *m;* (naut) Raum *m;* (sport) Griff *m;* **get h. of** (*catch*) erwischen; (*acquire*) erwerben; **get h. of oneself** sich fassen; **take h. of anfassen** ‖ *v* (*pret & pp* **held** [hɛld] *tr* halten; (*contain*) enthalten; (*regard as*) halten für; (*one's breath*) anhalten; (*an audience*) fesseln; (*a meeting, election, court*) abhalten; (*an office, position*) bekleiden, innehaben; (*talks*) führen; (*a viewpoint*) vertreten; (*a meet*) (sport) veranstalten; **able to h. one's liquor** trinkfest; **h. back** zurückhalten; (*news*) geheimhalten; **h. dear** werthalten; **h. down** niederhalten; **h. in contempt** verachten; **h. it!** halt!; **h. off** abhalten; **h. office** amtieren; **h. one's ground** die Stellung halten; **h. one's own** seinen Mann stehen; **h. one's own against** sich behaupten gegen; **h. one's tongue** den Mund halten; **h. open** (*a door*) aufhalten; **h. out** (*a hand*) hinhalten; (*proffer*) vorhalten; **h. over** (*e.g., a play*) verlängern; **h. s.th. against s.o.** j-m etw nachtragen; **h. sway** walten; **h. under** niederhalten; **h. up** (*raise*) hochhalten; (*detain*) aufhalten; (*traffic*) behindern; (*rob*) (räuberisch) überfallen; **h. up to ridicule** dem Spott preisgeben; **h. the line** (telp) am Apparat bleiben; **h. the road well** e-e gute Straßenlage haben; **h. together** zusammenhalten; **h. water** (fig) stichhaltig sein ‖ *intr* (*said of a knot*) halten; **h. back** sich zurückhalten; **h. forth** (coll) dozieren; **h. on** warten; **h. on to** festhalten, sich

festhalten an (*dat*); **h. out** aushalten; **h. out for** abwarten; **h. true** gelten; **h. true for** zutreffen auf (*acc*); **h. up** (*wear well*) halten

holder ['holdər] *s* (*device*) Halter *m;* (*e.g., of a title*) Inhaber –*in m*

hold'ing *s* (*of a meeting*) Abhaltung *f;* (*of an office*) Bekleidung *f;* **holdings** Besitz *m,* Bestand *m*

hold'ing com'pany *s* Holdinggesellschaft *f*

hold'ing pat'tern *s* (aer) Platzrunde *f*

hold'-o'ver *s* Überbleibsel *n*

hold'up' *s* (*delay*) Aufenthalt *m;* (*robbery*) Raubüberfall *m;* (*in traffic*) Verkehrsstauung *f*

hold'up man' *s* Räuber *m*

hole [hol] *s* Loch *n;* (*of animals*) Bau *m;* **h. in the wall** Loch *n;* **in a h. in der Patsche;** **in the h.** hängengeblieben, e.g., **I am ten dollars in the h.** ich bin mit zehn Dollar hängengeblieben; **pick holes in** (fig) herumkritisieren an (*dat*); **wear holes in** völlig abtragen ‖ *intr*—h. **out** (golf) ins Loch spielen; **h. up** sich vergraben; (fig) sich verstecken

holiday ['hɑlɪ͵de] *s* Feiertag *m;* (*vacation*) Ferien *pl;* **take a h.** e-n freien Tag machen, Urlaub nehmen

hol'iday mood' *s* Ferienstimmung *f*

holiness ['holɪnɪs] *s* Heiligkeit *f;* **His Holiness** Seine Heiligkeit

Holland ['halənd] *s* Holland *n*

Hollander ['haləndər] *s* Holländer –*in mf*

hollow ['halo] *adj* hohl ‖ *s* Höhle *f,* Höhlung *f;* (geol) Talmulde *f* ‖ *tr*—h. **out** aushöhlen

hol'low-cheeked' *adj* hohlwangig

hol'low-eyed' *adj* hohläugig

holly ['hali] *s* Stechpalme *f*

holm' oak' [hom] *s* Steineiche *f*

holocaust ['hɑlə͵kɔst] *s* Brandopfer *n;* (*disaster*) Brandkatastrophe *f*

holster ['holstər] *s* Pistolentasche *f*

holy ['holi] *adj* heilig; **h. smokes!** (coll) heiliger Strohsack!

Ho'ly Commun'ion *s* Kommunion *f,* das Heilige Abendmahl

ho'ly day' *s* Feiertag *m*

Ho'ly Ghost' *s* Heiliger Geist *m*

Ho'ly of Ho'lies *s* Allerheiligste *n*

ho'ly or'ders *spl* Priesterweihe *f*

Ho'ly Scrip'ture *s* die Heilige Schrift

Ho'ly See' *s* Heiliger Stuhl *m*

Ho'ly Sep'ulcher *s* Heiliges Grab *n*

Ho'ly Spir'it *s* Heiliger Geist *m*

ho'ly wa'ter *s* Weihwasser *n*

Ho'ly Week' *s* Karwoche *f*

Ho'ly Writ' *s* die Heilige Schrift

homage ['(h)amɪdʒ] *s* Huldigung *f;* **pay h. to** huldigen (*dat*)

home [hom] *adj* inländisch, Innen- ‖ *adv* nach Hause, heim; **bring h. to s.o.** j-m beibringen ‖ *s* Heim *n;* (*house*) Haus *n,* Wohnung *f;* (*place of residence*) Wohnort *m;* (*institution*) Heim *n;* **at h.** zu Hause, daheim; **at h. and abroad** im In- und Ausland; **feel at h.** sich zu Hause fühlen; **for the h.** für den Hausbe-

darf; **from h.** von zu Hause; **h. for the aged** Altersheim *n;* **h. for the blind** Blindenheim *n;* **h. of one's own** Zuhause *n*
home′ address′ *s* Privatadresse *f*
home′-baked′ *adj* hausbacken
home′ base′ *s* (aer) Heimatflughafen *m*
home′bod′y *s* Stubenhocker –in *mf*
homebred [ˈhɒm‚bred] *adj* einheimisch
home′-brew′ *s* selbstgebrautes Getränk *n*
home′-brewed′ *adj* selbstgebraut
home′com′ing *s* Heimkehr *f*
home′ comput′er *s* Heimcomputer *m*
home′ coun′try *s* Heimatstaat *m*
home′ econom′ics *s* Hauswirtschaftslehre *f*
home′-fried pota′toes *spl,* **home′ fries′** [‚fraɪz] *spl* Bratkartoffeln *pl*
home′ front′ *s* Heimatfront *f*
home′-grown′ *adj* selbstgezogen
home′ guard′ *s* Landsturm *m*
home′land *s* Heimatland *n*
homeless [ˈhɒmlɪs] *adj* obdachlos ‖ *s* Obdachlose *mf*
home′like′ *adj* anheimelnd
homely [ˈhɒmli] *adj* unschön
home′made′ *adj* selbstgemacht; (culin) selbstgebacken
home′mak′er *s* Hausfrau *f*
home′ of′fice *s* Hauptbüro *n*
home′ own′er *s* Hausbesitzer –in *mf*
home′ plate′ *s* Schlagmal *n*
home′ rem′edy *s* Hausmittel *n*
home′ rule′ *s* Selbstverwaltung *f*
home′ run′ *s* (baseball) Vier-Mal-Lauf *m*
home′sick′ *adj*—**be h.** Heimweh haben
home′sick′ness *s* Heimweh *n*
homespun [ˈhɒm‚spʌn] *adj* selbstgemacht; (fig) einfach
home′stead′ *s* Siedlerstelle *f*
home′stretch′ *s* Zielgerade *f*
home′ team′ *s* Ortsmannschaft *f*
home′town′ *adj* Heimat– ‖ *s* Heimatstadt *f*
homeward [ˈhomwərd] *adv* heimwärts
home′ward jour′ney *s* Heimreise *f*
home′work′ *s* Hausaufgabe *f*
homey [ˈhomi] *adj* anheimelnd
homicidal [‚hɑmɪˈsaɪdəl] *adj* mörderisch
homicide [ˈhɑmɪ‚saɪd] *s* (act) Totschlag *m;* (person) Totschläger –in *mf*
hom′icide squad′ *s* Mordkommission *f*
homily [ˈhɑmɪli] *s* Homilie *f*
hom′ing device′ [ˈhomɪŋ] *s* Zielsucher *m*
hom′ing pi′geon *s* Brieftaube *f*
homogeneous [‚homəˈdʒɪnɪ·əs] *adj* homogen
homogenize [haˈmɑdʒə‚naɪz] *tr* homogenisieren
homonym [ˈhɑmənɪm] *s* Homonym *n*
homosexual [‚homəˈsɛkʃʊ·əl] *adj* homosexuell ‖ *s* Homosexuelle *mf*
hone [hon] *s* Wetzstein *m* ‖ *tr* honen
honest [ˈɑnɪst] *adj* ehrlich, aufrecht
honestly [ˈɑnɪstli] *adv* ehrlich; **to tell you h.** offengestanden ‖ *interj* auf mein Wort!

honesty [ˈɑnɪsti] *s* Ehrlichkeit *f*
hon•ey [ˈhʌni] *s* Honig *m;* (as a term of endearment) Schatz *m,* Liebling *m* ‖ *v* (pret & pp **–eyed** & **–ied**) *tr* versüßen; (speak sweetly to) schmeicheln (dat)
hon′eybee′ *s* Honigbiene *f*
hon′eycomb′ *s* Honigwabe *f* ‖ *tr* (e.g., a hill) wabenartig durchlöchern
hon′eyed *adj* mit Honig gesüßt; (fig) honigsüß
hon′ey lo′cust *s* Honigdorn *m*
hon′eymoon′ *s* Flitterwochen *pl* ‖ *intr* die Flitterwochen verbringen
hon′eysuck′le *s* Geißblatt *n*
honk [hɒŋk] *s* (aut) Hupensignal *n* ‖ *tr*—**h. the horn** hupen ‖ *intr* hupen
honkytonk [ˈhɒŋkɪ‚tɒŋk] *s* (sl) Tingeltangel *m & n*
honor [ˈɑnər] *s* Ehre *f;* (award) Auszeichnung *f;* (chastity) Ehre *f;* **be held in h.** in Ehren gehalten werden; **consider it an h.** es sich [dat] zur Ehre anrechnen; **do the honors** die Honneurs machen; **have the h. of** (ger) sich beehren zu (inf); **in s.o.'s h.** j-m zu Ehren; **your Honor** Euer Gnaden ‖ *tr* ehren; (favor) beehren; (a check) honorieren; **feel honored** sich geehrt fühlen
honorable [ˈɑnərəbəl] *adj* (person) ehrbar; (intentions) ehrlich; (peace treaty) ehrenvoll
honorari•um [‚ɑnəˈrɛrɪ·əm] *s* (**–ums** & **–a** [ə]) Honorar *n;* **give an h. to** honorieren
hon′orary degree′ *s* Ehrendoktorat *n*
honorific [‚ɑnəˈrɪfɪk] *adj* ehrend, Ehren– ‖ *s* Ehrentitel *m*
hooch [hutʃ] *s* (sl) Fusel *m,* Schnaps *m*
hood [hʊd] *s* Haube *f;* (of a monk) Kapuze *f;* (of a baby carriage) Verdeck *n;* (sl) Gangster *m;* (aut) Motorhaube *f;* (culin) Rauchabzug *m;* (educ) Talarüberwurf *m* ‖ *tr* mit e–r Haube versehen; (fig) verhüllen
hoodlum [ˈhʊdləm] *s* Ganove *m*
hoodoo [ˈhudu] *s* Unglücksbringer *m* ‖ *tr* Unglück bringen (dat)
hood′wink′ *tr* täuschen
hooey [ˈhu·i] *s* (sl) Quatsch *m*
hoof [huf], [hʊf] *s* Huf *m* ‖ *tr*—**h. it** auf Schusters Rappen reiten
hoof′beat′ *s* Hufschlag *m*
hook [hʊk] *s* Haken *m;* (angl) Angelhaken *m;* (baseball) Kurvball *m;* (box) Haken *m;* (golf) Hook *m;* **by h. or by crook** so oder so; **h., line, and sinker** mit allem Drum und Dran; **off the h.** (coll) aus der Schlinge; **on one's own h.** (coll) auf eigene Faust ‖ *tr* festhaken, einhaken; (e.g., a boyfriend) angeln; (steal) schnappen; (box) e–n Haken versetzen (dat); (golf) nach links verziehen; **h. up** zuhaken; (elec) anschließen ‖ *intr* sich krümmen; **h. up with s.o.** sich j–m anschließen
hook′ and eye′ *s* Haken *m* und Öse *f*
hook′-and-lad′der truck′ *s* Feuerwehrfahrzeug *n* mit Drehleiter

hooked *adj* hakenförmig; **h. on drugs** rauschgiftsüchtig

hooker ['hukər] *s* (sl) Nutte *f*

hook'nose' *s* Hakennase *f*

hook'up' *s* (elec, electron) Schaltung *f*; (electron) Schaltbild *n*; (rad, telv) Gemeinschaftsschaltung *f*

hook'worm' *s* Hakenwurm *m*

hooky ['huki] *s*—**play h.** schwänzen

hooligan ['hulɪgən] *s* Straßenlümmel *m*

hoop [hup] *s* Reifen *m* || *tr* binden

hoop' skirt' *s* Reifrock *m*

hoot [hut] *s* Geschrei *n*; **not give a h. about** keinen Pfifferling geben für || *intr* schreien; **h. at** anschreien

hoot' owl' *s* Waldkauz *m*

hop [hap] *s* Hopser *m*; (dance) Tanz *m*; **hops** (bot) Hopfen *m* || *v* (pret & pp **hopped**; ger **hopping**) *tr* (e.g., a train) aufspringen auf (acc); **hop a ride** (coll) mitfahren || *intr* hüpfen; **hop around** herumhüpfen

hope [hop] *s* (of) Hoffnung *f* (auf acc); **beyond h.** hoffnungslos; **not get up one's hopes** sich [dat] keine Hoffnungen machen || *tr* hoffen || *intr* hoffen; **h. for** hoffen auf (acc); **h. for the best** das Beste hoffen; **I h.** (parenthetical) hoffentlich

hope' chest' *s* Aussteuertruhe *f*

hopeful ['hopfəl] *adj* hoffnungsvoll || *s* (pol) Kandidat -in *mf*

hopefully ['hopfəli] *adv* hoffentlich

hopeless ['hoplɪs] *adj* hoffnungslos

hopper ['hapər] *s* Fülltrichter *m*; (in a toilet) Spülkasten *m*; (storage container) Vorratsbehälter *m*; (data proc) Kartenmagazin *n*

hop'per car' *s* (rr) Selbstentladewagen *m*

hop'ping mad' *adj* fuchsteufelswild

hop'scotch' *s* Himmel und Hölle

horde [hord] *s* Horde *f*

horehound ['hor,haund] *s* (lozenge) Hustenbonbon *m*; (bot) Andorn *m*

horizon [hə'raɪzən] *s* Horizont *m*

horizontal [,harɪ'zantəl] *adj* horizontal, waagrecht || *s* Horizontale *f*

horizon'tal bar' *s* (gym) Reck *n*

horizon'tal controls' *spl* (aer) Seitenleitwerk *n*

horizon'tal sta'bilizer *s* (aer) Höhenflosse *f*

hormone ['hormon] *s* Hormon *n*

horn [hɔrn] *s* (of an animal; wind instrument) Horn *n*; (aut) Hupe *f*; **blow one's own h.** (coll) ins eigene Horn stoßen; **blow the h.** (aut) hupen; **horns** (of an animal) Geweih *n* || *intr*—**h. in** (on) (coll) sich eindrängen (in acc)

hornet ['hɔrnɪt] *s* Hornisse *f*

hor'net's nest' *s*—**stir up a h.** in ein Wespennest stechen

horn' of plen'ty *s* Füllhorn *n*

horn'-rimmed glass'es *spl* Hornbrille *f*

horny ['hɔrni] *adj* (callous) schwielig; (having horn-like projections) verhornt; (sl) geil

horoscope ['hɔrə,skop] *s* Horoskop *n*; **cast s.o.'s h.** j-m das Horoskop stellen

horrible ['hɔrɪbəl] *adj* (& coll) schrecklich

horrid ['hɔrɪd] *adj* abscheulich

horri-fy ['hɔrɪ,faɪ] *v* (pret & pp **-fied**) *tr* erschrecken, entsetzen

horror ['hɔrər] *s* Schrecken *m*, Entsetzen *n*

hor'ror sto'ry *s* Schauergeschichte *f*

hors d'oeuvre [ɔr'dʌrv] *s* (**hors d'oeuvres** [ɔr'dʌrvz]) Vorspeise *f*

horse [hɔrs] *s* Pferd *n*; (carp) Sägebock *m*; **back the wrong h.** (fig) auf's falsche Pferd setzen; **bet on a h.** auf ein Pferd setzen; **hold your horses** immer mit der Ruhe!; **h. of another color** e-e andere Sache; **mount a h.** zu Pferd steigen; **straight from the horse's mouth** direkt von der Quelle || *intr*—**h. around** (sl) herumalbern; **stop horsing around** laß den Unsinn!

horse'back' *s*—**on h.** zu Pferd || *adv*—**ride h.** reiten

horse'back rid'ing *s* Reiten *n*

horse' blan'ket *s* Pferdedecke *f*

horse' chest'nut *s* Roßkastanie *f*

horse' col'lar *s* Kummet *n*

horse' doc'tor *s* (coll) Roßarzt *m*

horse'fly' *s* Pferdebremse *f*

horse'hair' *s* Roßhaar *n*, Pferdehaar *n*

horse'laugh' *s* wieherndes Gelächter *n*

horse'man *s* (**-men**) Reiter *m*

horse'manship' *s* Reitkunst *f*

horse' meat' *s* Pferdefleisch *n*

horse' op'era *s* (coll) Wildwestfilm *m*

horse'play' *s* grober Unfug *m*

horse'pow'er *s* Pferdestärke *f*

horse' race' *s* Pferderennen *n*

horse'rad'ish *s* Meerrettich *m*, Kren *m*

horse' sense' *s* gesunder Menschenverstand *m*

horse' shoe' *s* Hufeisen *n* || *tr* beschlagen

horse'shoe mag'net *s* Hufeisenmagnet *m*

horse' show' *s* Pferdeschau *f*

horse' tail' *s* Pferdeschwanz *m*

horse' trad'er *s* Pferdehändler *m*; (fig) Kuhhändler *m*

horse' trad'ing *s* Pferdehandel *m*; (fig) Kuhhandel *m*

horse'whip' *s* Reitpeitsche *f* || *v* (pret & pp **-whipped**; ger **-whipping**) *tr* mit der Reitpeitsche schlagen

horse'wom'an *s* (**-wom'en**) Reiterin *f*

horsy ['hɔrsi] *adj* pferdeartig; (horse-loving) pferdeliebend

horticultural [,hɔrtɪ'kʌlt/ərəl] *adj* Gartenbau-

horticulture ['hɔrtɪ,kʌlt/ər] *s* Gartenbau *m*, Gärtnerei *f*

hose [hoz] *s* Schlauch *m* || *s* (hose) Strumpf *m*; (collectively) Strümpfe *pl*

hosiery ['hoʒəri] *s* Strumpfwaren *pl*; (mill) Strumpffabrik *f*

hospice ['haspɪs] *s* Hospiz *n*

hospitable ['haspɪtəbəl], [has'pɪtəbəl] *adj* gastlich, gastfreundlich

hospital ['haspɪtəl] *s* Hospital *n*, Krankenhaus *n*; (mil) Lazarett *n*

hospitality [,haspɪ'tælɪti] *s* Gast-

freundschaft f; **show s.o. h.** j—m Gastfreundschaft gewähren
hospitalize ['hɑspitə,laiz] *tr* ins Krankenhaus einweisen
hos'pital ship' s Lazarettschiff f
hos'pital train' s Sanitätszug m
hos'pital ward' s Kranken(haus)station f
host [host] s Gastgeber m; *(at an inn)* Wirt m; *(in a television show)* Leiter m; *(multitude)* Heerschar f; *(army)* Heer m; **Host** (relig) Hostie f
hostage ['hɑstidʒ] s Geisel mf
hostel ['hɑstəl] s Herberge f
hostelry ['hɑstəlri] s Gasthaus n
hostess ['hostis] s Gastgeberin f; *(at an inn)* Wirtin f; *(on an airplane)* Stewardeß f; *(in a restaurant)* Empfangsdame f; *(on a television show)* Leiterin f
hostile ['hɑstil] *adj* feindlich; **(to)** feindselig (gegen)
hostility [hɑs'tiliti] s Feindseligkeit f; **hostilities** Feindseligkeiten pl
hot [hɑt] *adj* heiß; *(spicy)* scharf; *(meal)* warm; *(stolen, sought by the police, radioactive; jazz, tip)* heiß; *(trail, scent)* frisch; *(in heat)* geil; **be hot** *(said of the sun)* stechen; **get into hot water** in die Patsche geraten; **hot and bothered** aufgeregt; **hot from the press** frisch von der Presse; **hot on s.o.'s trail** j—m dicht auf der Spur; **hot stuff** (sl) toller Kerl m; **I am hot** mir ist heiß; **I don't feel so hot** (coll) ich fühle mich nicht besonders; **she's not so hot** (coll) sie is nicht so toll
hot' air' s Heißluft f; (sl) blauer Dunst m
hot'-air heat' s Heißluftheizung f
hot'bed' s Frühbeet n; *(fig)* Brutstätte f
hot'-blood'ed *adj* heißblütig
hot' cake' s Pfannkuchen m; **sell like hot cakes** wie warme Semmeln weggehen
hotchpotch ['hɑtʃ,pɑtʃ] s (coll) Mischmasch m
hot' dog' s warmes Würstel n
hotel [ho'tɛl] *adj* Hotel— ‖ s Hotel n; *(small hotel)* Gasthof m
hotel' busi'ness s Hotelgewerbe n
hotel'man s (—men) Hotelbesitzer m
hot'foot' *adv* in aller Eile ‖ tr—**h. it** schleunigst eilen; **h. it after s.o.** j—m nacheilen
hot'head' s Hitzkopf m
hot'-head'ed *adj* hitzköpfig
hot'house' s Treibhaus n, Gewächshaus n
hot' line' s (telp) heißer Draht m
hot' mon'ey s (sl) Fluchtkapital n
hot' pep'per s scharfe Paprikaschote f
hot' plate' s Heizplatte f
hot' pota'to s (coll) schwieriges Problem n
hot' rod' s (sl) frisiertes altes Auto n
hot' rod'der [,rɑdər] s (sl) Fahrer m e—s frisierten Autos
hot' seat' s (sl) elektrischer Stuhl m
hot' springs' spl Thermalquellen pl
hot' tem'per s hitziges Temperament n

hot'-tem'pered *adj* hitzig, hitzköpfig
hot' war' s Schießkrieg m
hot' wa'ter s Heißwasser n; **be in h.** (fig) in der Tinte sitzen; **get into h.** (fig) in die Patsche geraten
hot'-wa'ter bot'tle s Gummiwärmflasche f
hot'-wa'ter heat'er s Heißwasserbereiter m
hot'-wa'ter heat'ing s Heißwasserheizung f
hot'-wa'ter tank' s Heißwasserspeicher m
hound [haund] s Jagdhund m ‖ tr hetzen
hour [aur] s Stunde f; **after hours** nach Arbeitsschluß; **at any h.** zu jeder Tageszeit; **by the h.** stundenweise; **every h.** stündlich; **for an h.** e—e Stunde lang; **for a solid h.** e—e geschlagene Stunde lang; **for hours** stundenlang; **h. of death** Todesstunde f; **h. overtime** Überstunde f; **in the small hours** in den frühen Morgenstunden; **keep late hours** spät zu Bett gehen; **keep regular hours** zur Zeit aufstehen und schlafengehen; **on the h.** zur vollen Stunde
–hour *suf* —stündig
hour'glass' s Stundenglas n
hour' hand' s Stundenzeiger m
hourly ['aurli] *adj* stündlich; **h. rate** Stundensatz m; **h. wages** Stundenlohn m ‖ adv stündlich
house [haus] *adj* *(boat, dress)* Haus— ‖ s (**houses** ['hauziz]) Haus n; **h. and home** Haus und Hof; **h. for rent** Haus n zu vermieten; **keep h. (for s.o.)** (j—m) den Haushalt führen; **on the h.** auf Kosten des Wirts; **put one's h. in order** (fig) seine Angelegenheiten in Ordnung bringen ‖ [hauz] tr unterbringen
house' arrest' s Hausarrest m
house'boat' s Hausboot n
house'break'ing s Einbruchsdiebstahl m
housebroken ['haus,brokən] *adj* stubenrein
house' clean'ing s Hausputz m; *(fig)* Säuberungsaktion f
house'fly' s Stubenfliege f
houseful ['haus,ful] s Hausvoll m
house'guest' s Logierbesuch m
house'hold' *adj* Haushalts— ‖ s Haushalt m
house'hold'er s Haushaltsvorstand m
house'hold fur'nishings spl Hausrat m
house'hold needs' spl Hausbedarf m
house'hold word' s Alltagswort n
house' hunt'ing s Wohnungssuche f
house'keep'er s Haushälterin f
house'keep'ing s Hauswirtschaft f
house'maid' s Dienstmädchen n
house'moth'er s Hausmutter f
house' of cards' s Kartenhaus n
House' of Com'mons s Unterhaus n
house' of corec'tion s Zuchthaus n, Besserungsanstalt f
house' of ill' repute' s öffentliches Haus n
House' of Lords' s Oberhaus n

house/ physi/cian s Krankenhausarzt m; (in a hotel) Hausarzt m
house/-to-house/ adv von Haus zu Haus; sell h. hausieren
house/warm/ing s Einzugsfest n
house/wife/ s (wives') Hausfrau f
house/work/ s Hausarbeit f
hous/ing s Unterbringung f, Wohnung f; (mach) Gehäuse n
hous/ing devel/opment s Siedlung f
hous/ing proj/ect s Sozialsiedlung f
hous/ing short/age s Wohnungsnot f
hous/ing un/it s Wohneinheit f
hovel ['hʌvəl], ['hʊvəl] s Hütte f
hover ['hʌvər] intr schweben; (fig) pendeln; h. about sich herumtreiben in der Nähe von
Hov/ercraft/ s (trademark) Schwebefahrzeug n
how [haʊ] adv wie; and how! und wie!; how about ...? (would you care for ...?) wie wäre es mit ...?; (what's the progress of ...?) wie steht es mit ...?; (what do you think of ...?) was halten Sie von ...?; how are you? wie befinden Sie sich?; how beautiful! wie schön!; how come? wieso?, wie kommt es?; how do you do? (as a greeting) guten Tag!; (at an introduction) freut mich sehr!; how many wie viele; how much wieviel; how on earth wie in aller Welt; how the devil wie zum Teufel || s Wie n
how-do-you-do ['haʊdəjə'du] s—that's a fine h.! (coll) das ist e-e schöne Geschichte!
however adv jedoch, aber; (with adjectives and adverbs) wie ... auch immer; h. it may be wie es auch sein mag
howitzer ['haʊ·ɪtsər] s Haubitze f
howl [haʊl] s Geheul n, Gebrüll n || tr heulen, brüllen; h. down (a speaker) niederschreien; h. out hinausbrüllen || intr (said of a dog, wolf, wind, etc.) heulen; (in pain, anger) brüllen; h. with laughter vor Lachen brüllen
howler ['haʊlər] s (coll) Schnitzer m
hub [hʌb] s Nabe, f, Radnabe f
hubbub ['hʌbʌb] s Rummel m
hubby ['hʌbi] s (coll) Mann m
hub/cap/ s Radkappe f
huckleberry ['hʌkəl‚beri] s Heidelbeere f
huckster ['hʌkstər] s (hawker) Straßenhändler m; (peddler) Hausierer m; (adman) Reklamefachmann m || tr verhökern
huddle ['hʌdəl] s (fb) Zusammendrängen n; go into a h. die Köpfe zusammenstecken || intr sich zusammendrängen; (fb) sich um den Mannschaftsführer drängen
hue [hju] s Farbton m
hue/ and cry/ s Zetergeschrei n
huff [hʌf] s Aufbrausen n; in a h. beleidigt
huffy ['hʌfi] adj übelnehmerisch
hug [hʌg] s Umarmung f; give s.o. a hug j-n an sich drücken || v (pret & pp hugged; ger hugging) tr umar-

men; hug the road gut auf der Straße liegen; hug the shore sich dicht an der Küste halten || intr einander herzen
huge [hjudʒ] adj riesig, ungeheuer; h. success (theat) Bombenerfolg m
hulk [hʌlk] s (body of an old ship) Schiffsrumpf m; (old ship used as a warehouse, etc.) Hulk m & f; h. of a man Koloß m
hulk/ing adj ungeschlacht
hull [hʌl] s (of seed) Schale f; (naut) Schiffsrumpf m || tr schälen
hullabaloo [‚hʌləbə'lu] s Heidenlärm m
hum [hʌm] s Summen n || v (pret & pp hummed; ger humming) tr summen; hum (e.g., a tune) to oneself vor sich hin summen || intr summen; (fig) in lebhafter Bewegung sein
human ['hjumən] adj menschlich, Menschen-
hu/man be/ing s Mensch m, menschliches Wesen n
humane [hju'men] adj human
humaneness [hju'mennɪs] s Humanität f
humanistic [hjumə'nɪstɪk] adj humanistisch
humanitarian [hju‚mænɪ'terɪ·ən] adj menschenfreundlich || s Menschenfreund –in m
humanity [hju'mænɪti] s (mankind) Menschheit f; (humaneness) Humanität f, Menschlichkeit f; humanities Geisteswissenschaften pl; (Greek and Latin studies) klassische Philologie f
humanize ['hjumə‚naɪz] tr zivilisieren
hu/mankind/ s Menschengeschlecht n
humanly ['hjumənli] adv menschlich; h. possible menschenmöglich; h. speaking nach menschlichen Begriffen
hu/man na/ture s menschliche Natur f
hu/man race/ s Menschengeschlecht n
humble ['(h)ʌmbəl] adv demütig; (origens) niedrig; in my h. opinion nach meiner unmaßeblichen Meinung || tr demütigen
hum/ble pie/ s—eat h. sich demütigen
hum/drum/ adj eintönig
humer·us ['hjumərəs] s (–i [‚aɪ]) Oberarmknochen m
humid ['hjumɪd] adj feucht
humidifier [hju'mɪdɪ‚faɪ·ər] s Verdunster m
humidity [hju'mɪdɪti s Feuchtigkeit f
humiliate [hju'mɪlɪ‚et] tr erniedrigen
humil/iating adj schmachvoll
humiliation [hju‚mɪlɪ'eʃən] s Erniedrigung f
hum/mingbird/ s Kolibri m
humor ['(h)jumər] s (comic quality) Komik f; (frame of mind) Laune f; in bad (or good) h. bei schlechter (or guter) Laune || tr bei guter Laune halten
humorist ['(h)jumərɪst] s Humorist –in mf
humorous ['(h)jumərəs] adj humorvoll
hump [hʌmp] s Buckel m; (of a camel)

Höcker m; (slight elevation) kleiner Hügel m; over the h. (fig) über den Berg ‖ tr—h. its back (said of an animal) e-n Buckel machen
hump/back/ s Buckel m; (person) Bucklige mf

Hun [hʌn] s (hist) Hunne m, Hunnin f
hunch [hʌntʃ] s (hump) Buckel m; (coll) Ahnung f ‖ intr—h. over sich bücken über (acc)
hunch/back/ s Bucklige mf
hunch/backed/ adj bucklig
hunched adj—h. up zusammengekauert
hundred [ˈhʌndrəd] adj & pron hundert ‖ s Hundert n; by the h.(s) hundertweise; hundreds (and hundreds) of Hunderte (und aber Hunderte) von
hun/dredfold/ adj & adv hundertfach
hundredth [ˈhʌndrədθ] adj & pron hundertste; for the h. time (fig) zum X-ten Male; h. anniversary Hundertjahrfeier f ‖ s (fraction) Hundertstel n
hun/dredweight/ s Zentner n
Hungarian [hʌŋˈgɛri·ən] adj ungarisch ‖ s (person) Ungar -in mf; (language) Ungarisch n
Hungary [ˈhʌŋgəri] s Ungarn n
hunger [ˈhʌŋgər] s Hunger m ‖ intr hungern; h. for hungern nach
hun/ger strike/ s Hungerstreik m
hungry [ˈhʌŋgri] adj hungrig; be h. Hunger haben; be h. for (fig) begierig sein nach; go h. am Hungertuch nagen; I feel h. es hungert mich
hunk [hʌŋk] s großes Stück n
hunt [hʌnt] s Jagd f; (search) (for) Suche f (nach); on the h. for auf der Suche nach ‖ tr jagen; (a horse) jagen mit; (look for) suchen; h. down erjagen ‖ intr jagen; h. for suchen; (game) jagen; (a criminal) fahnden nach; go hunting auf die Jagd gehen
hunter [ˈhʌntər] s Jäger -in mf; (horse) Jagdpferd n
hunt/ing adj (e.g., dog, knife, season) Jagd- ‖ s Jägerei f; (on horseback) Parforcejagd f
hunt/ing ground/ s Jagdrevier n
hunt/ing li/cense s Jagdschein m
hunt/ing lodge/ s Jagdhütte f
huntress [ˈhʌntrɪs] s Jägerin f
hunts/man s (-men) Weidmann m
hurdle [ˈhʌrdəl] s Hürde f; (fig) Hindernis n; hurdles (sport) Hürdenlauf m ‖ tr überspringen; (fig) überwinden
hurdygurdy [ˈhʌrdiˈgɑrdi] s Drehorgel f
hurl [hʌrl] s Wurf m ‖ tr schleudern; h. abuse at s.o. j-m Beleidigungen ins Gesicht schleudern; h. down zu Boden werfen
hurrah [həˈrɑ], **hurray** [həˈre] s Hurra n ‖ interj hurra!
hurricane [ˈhʌrɪˌken] s Orkan m
hur/ricane lamp/ s Sturmlaterne f
hurried [ˈhʌrid] adj eilig, flüchtig
hurriedly [ˈhʌridli] adv eilig, eilends
hur-ry [ˈhʌri] s Eile f; be in too much of a h. sich übereilen; in a h. in Eile; there's no h. es hat keine Eile ‖ v

(pret & pp –ried) tr (prod) antreiben; (expedite) beschleunigen; (an activity) zu schnell tun; (to overhasty action) drängen ‖ intr eilen; h. away wegeilen; h. over s.th. etw flüchtig erledigen; h. up sich beeilen
hurt [hʌrt] adj (injured, offended) verletzt; feel h. (about) sich verletzt (or gekränkt) fühlen (durch) ‖ s Verletzung f ‖ v (pret & pp hurt) tr (a person, animal, feelings) verletzen; (e.g., a business) schaden (dat); it hurts him to think of it es schmerzt ihn, daran zu denken ‖ intr (& fig) weh tun, schmerzen; my arm hurts mir tut der Arm weh; that won't h. das schadet nichts; will it h. if I'm late? macht es etw aus, wenn ich zu spät komme?
hurtle [ˈhʌrtəl] tr schleudern ‖ intr stürzen
husband [ˈhʌzbənd] s Ehemann m; my h. mein Mann m ‖ tr haushalten mit
hus/bandman s (-men) Landwirt m
husbandry [ˈhʌzbəndri] s Landwirtschaft f
hush [hʌʃ] s Stille f ‖ tr zur Ruhe bringen; h. up (suppress) vertuschen ‖ intr schweigen ‖ interj still!
hush/-hush/ adj streng vertraulich und geheim
hush/ mon/ey s Schweigegeld n
husk [hʌsk] s Hülse f; (of corn) Maishülse f ‖ tr enthülsen
husky [ˈhʌski] adj stämmig; (voice) belegt ‖ s Eskimohund m
hussy [ˈhʌsi] s (prostitute) Dirne f; (saucy girl) Fratz m
hustle [ˈhʌsəl] s (coll) Betriebsamkeit f; h. and bustle Getriebe n ‖ tr (jostle, rush) drängen; (wares, girls) an den Mann bringen; (customers) bearbeiten; (money) betteln ‖ intr rührig sein; (shove) sich drängen; (hasten) hasten; (make money by fraud) Betrügereien verüben; (engage in prostitution) Prostitution betreiben
hustler [ˈhʌslər] s rühriger Mensch m
hut [hʌt] s Hütte f; (mil) Baracke f
hutch [hʌtʃ] s Stall m
hyacinth [ˈhaɪˌəsɪnθ] s Hyazinthe f
hybrid [ˈhaɪbrɪd] adj hybrid ‖ s Kreuzung f
hydrant [ˈhaɪdrənt] s Hydrant m
hydrate [ˈhaɪdret] s Hydrat n ‖ tr hydratisieren, hydrieren
hydraulic [haɪˈdrɔlɪk] adj hydraulisch ‖ hydraulics s Hydraulik f
hydrau/lic brakes/ spl Öldruckbremsen pl
hydrocarbon [ˌhaɪdrəˈkɑrbən] s Kohlenwasserstoff m
hydrochlor/ic ac/id [ˌhaɪdrəˈklorɪk] s Salzsäure f
hydroelectric [ˌhaɪdro·ɪˈlektrɪk] adj hydroelektrisch
hydroelec/tric plant/ s Wasserkraftwerk n
hydrofluo/ric ac/id [ˌhaɪdrəfluˈorɪk] s Flußsäure f
hydrofoil [ˈhaɪdrəˌfɔɪl] s Tragflügelboot n

hydrogen ['haɪdrədʒən] s Wasserstoff m

hy'drogen bomb' s Wasserstoffbombe f

hy'drogen perox'ide s Wasserstoffsuperoxyd n

hydrometer [haɪ'drɑmɪtər] s Hydrometer m

hydrophobia [ˌhaɪdrə'fobɪ·ə] s Wasserscheu f; (rabies) Tollwut f

hydrophone ['haɪdrəˌfon] s Unterwasserhorchgerät n, Hydrophon n

hydroplane ['haɪdrəˌplen] s (aer) Wasserflugzeug n; (aer) Gleitfläche f; (naut) Gleitboot n; (in a submarine) (nav) Tiefenruder n

hydroxide [haɪ'drɑksaɪd] s Hydroxyd n

hyena [haɪ'inə] s Hyäne f

hygiene ['haɪdʒin] s Hygiene f; (educ) Gesundheitslehre f

hygienic [haɪ'dʒinɪk] adj hygienisch

hymn [hɪm] s Hymne f; (eccl) Kirchenlied n

hymnal ['hɪmnəl] s Gesangbuch n

hymn'book' s Gesangbuch n

hyperacidity [ˌhaɪpərə'sɪdɪti] s Übersäuerung f

hyperbola [haɪ'pʌrbələ] s Hyperbel f

hyperbole [haɪ'pʌrbəli] s Hyperbel f

hypersensitive [ˌhaɪpər'sɛnsɪtɪv] adj (to) überempfindlich (gegen)

hypertension [ˌhaɪpər'tɛnʃən] s Hypertonie f

hyphen ['haɪfən] s Bindestrich m

hyphenate ['haɪfəˌnet] tr mit Bindestrich schreiben

hypnosis [hɪp'nosɪs] s Hypnose f

hypnotic [hɪp'nɑtɪk] adj hypnotisch

hypnotism ['hɪpnəˌtɪzəm] s Hypnotismus m

hypnotist ['hɪpnətɪst] s Hypnotiseur m

hypnotize ['hɪpnəˌtaɪz] tr hypnotisieren

hypochondriac [ˌhaɪpə'kɑndrɪˌæk] s Hypochonder m

hypocrisy [hɪ'pɑkrəsi] s Heuchelei f

hypocrite ['hɪpəkrɪt] s Heuchler –in mf; be a h. heucheln

hypocritical [ˌhɪpə'krɪtɪkəl] adj heuchlerisch

hypodermic [ˌhaɪpə'dʌrmɪk] adj subkutan || s (injection) subkutane Spritze f

hypoderm'ic nee'dle s Injektionsnadel f

hypotenuse [haɪ'pɑtɪˌn(j)us] s Hypotenuse f

hypothesis [haɪ'pɑθɪsɪs] s (–ses [ˌsiz]) Hypothese f

hypothetic(al) [ˌhaɪpə'θɛtɪk(əl)] adj hypothetisch

hysterectomy [ˌhɪstə'rɛktəmi] s Hysterektomie f

hysteria [hɪs'tɪrɪ·ə] s Hysterie f

hysteric [hɪs'tɛrɪk] adj hysterisch || **hysterics** spl Hysterie f; go into hysterics e–n hysterischen Anfall bekommen

hysterical [hɪs'tɛrɪkəl] adj hysterisch

I

I, i [aɪ] s elfter Buchstabe des englischen Alphabets

I pers pron ich

iambic [aɪ'æmbɪk] adj jambisch

Iberian [aɪ'bɪrɪ·ən] adj iberisch

ibex ['aɪbɛks] s (ibexes & ibices ['ɪbɪˌsiz]) Steinbock m

ice [aɪs] s Eis n; break the ice (coll) das Eis brechen; cut no ice (coll) nicht ziehen || tr (a cake) glasieren || intr—ice up vereisen

ice' age' s Eiszeit f

iceberg ['aɪsˌbʌrg] s Eisberg m

ice'boat' s (sport) Segelschlitten m

ice'bound' adj (boat) eingefroren; (port, river) zugefroren

ice'box' s Eisschrank m; (refrigerator) Kühlschrank m

ice'break'er s Eisbrecher m

ice' buck'et s Sektkübel m

ice'cap' s Eiskappe f

ice' cream' s Eis n, Eiskrem f

ice'-cream cone' s Tüte f Eis

ice' cube' s Eiswürfel m

ice'-cube tray' s Eiswürfelschale f

iced' tea' s Eistee m

ice' floe' s Eisscholle f

ice' hock'ey s Eishockey n

Iceland ['aɪslənd] s Island n

Icelander ['aɪsˌlændər] s Isländer –in mf

Icelandic [aɪs'lændɪk] adj isländisch || s (language) Isländisch n

ice'man' s (–men') Eismann m

ice' pack' s (geol) Packeis n; (med) Eisbeutel m

ice' pick' s Eispfriem m; (mount) Eispickel m

ice' skate' s Schlittschuh m

ice'-skate' intr eislaufen

ichthyology [ˌɪkθɪ'ɑlədʒi] s Ichthyologie f, Fischkunde f

icicle ['aɪsɪkəl] s Eiszapfen m

icing ['aɪsɪŋ] s Glasur f, Zuckerguß m; (aer) Vereisung f

icon ['aɪkɑn] s Ikone f

iconoclast [aɪ'kɑnəˌklæst] s Bilderstürmer –in mf

icy ['aɪsi] adj (& fig) eisig

id [ɪd] s (psychol) Es n

I.D. card ['aɪ'di'kɑrd] s Ausweis m

idea [aɪ'di·ə] s Idee f, Vorstellung f; (intimation) Ahnung f; crazy i. Schnapsidee f; have big ideas große Rosinen im Kopf haben; that's the i.! so ist's richtig!; the i.! na so was!; what's the i.? wie kommen Sie darauf?

ideal [aɪˈdɪəl] *adj* ideal ‖ *s* Ideal *n*

idealism [aɪˈdɪ·ə‚lɪzəm] *s* Idealismus *m*

idealist [aɪˈdɪ·əlɪst] *s* Idealist –in *mf*

idealistic [aɪ‚dɪ·əlˈɪstɪk] *adj* idealistisch

idealize [aɪˈdɪ·ə‚laɪz] *tr* idealisieren

identical [aɪˈdentɪkəl] *adj* identisch

identification [aɪˈdentɪfɪˈkeʃən] *s* Identifizierung *f*

identifica'tion tag' *s* Erkennungsmarke *f*

identi·fy [aɪˈdentɪ‚faɪ] *v* (*pret & pp* –**fied**) *tr* identifizieren; **i. oneself** sich ausweisen ‖ *intr*—**i. with** sich einfühlen in (*acc*)

identity [aɪˈdentɪti] *s* Identität *f*; **prove one's i.** sich ausweisen

iden'tity card' *s* Ausweis *m*

ideological [‚aɪdɪ·əˈlɑdʒɪkəl] *adj* ideologisch

ideology [‚aɪdɪˈɑlədʒi] *s* Ideologie *f*

idiocy [ˈɪdɪ·əsi] *s* Idiotie *f*

idiom [ˈɪdɪ·əm] *s* (*phrase*) Redewendung *f*; (*language, style*) Idiom *n*

idiomatic [‚ɪdɪ·əˈmætɪk] *adj* idiomatisch; **i. expression** (idiomatische) Redewendung *f*

idiosyncrasy [‚ɪdɪ·əˈsɪnkrəsi] *s* Idiosynkrasie *f*

idiot [ˈɪdɪ·ət] *s* Idiot *m*, Trottel *m*

idiotic [‚ɪdɪˈɑtɪk] *adj* idiotisch

idle [ˈaɪdəl] *adj* (*person, question, hours*) müßig; (*machine, factory*) stillstehend; (*capital*) tot; (*fears*) grundlos; (*talk, threats*) leer; **lie i.** stilliegen; **stand i.** stillstehen ‖ *s* (aut) Leerlauf *m* ‖ *tr* arbeitslos machen; **i. away** vertrödeln ‖ *intr* (aut) leerlaufen

idleness [ˈaɪdəlnɪs] *s* Müßiggang *m*

idler [ˈaɪdlər] *s* Müßiggänger *m*

i'dling *s* (aut) Leerlauf *m*

idol [ˈaɪdəl] *s* Abgott *m*; (fig) Idol *n*

idolatry [aɪˈdɑlətri] *s* Abgötterei *f*

idolize [ˈaɪdə‚laɪz] *tr* verhimmeln

idyll [ˈaɪdəl] *s* Idyll *n*, Idylle *f*

idyllic [aɪˈdɪlɪk] *adj* idyllisch

if [ɪf] *s* Wenn *n* ‖ *conj* wenn; (*whether*) ob

igloo [ˈɪglu] *s* Schneehütte *f*, Iglu *m* & *n*

ignite [ɪgˈnaɪt] *tr & intr* zünden

ignition [ɪgˈnɪʃən] *adj* Zünd– ‖ *s* Entzünden *n*; (aut) Zündung *f*

igni'tion key' *s* Zündschlüssel *m*

igni'tion switch' *s* Zündschloß *n*

ignoble [ɪgˈnobəl] *adj* unedel

ignominious [‚ɪgnəˈmɪnɪ·əs] *adj* schmachvoll, schändlich

ignoramus [‚ɪgnəˈreməs] *s* Ignorant –in *mf*

ignorance [ˈɪgnərəns] *s* Unwissenheit *f*; (of) Unkenntnis *f* (*genit*)

ignorant [ˈɪgnərənt] *adj* unwissend; **be i.** of nicht wissen

ignore [ɪgˈnor] *tr* ignorieren; (*words*) überhören; (*rules*) nicht beachten

ilk [ɪlk] *s*—**of that ilk** derselben Art

ill [ɪl] *adj* (*worse* [wʌrs]; *worst* [wʌrst]) krank; (*repute*) schlecht; (*feelings*) feindselig; **fall** (*or* **take**)

ill krank werden ‖ *adv* schlecht; **he can ill afford to** (*inf*) er kann es sich [*dat*] kaum leisten zu (*inf*); **take s.th. ill** etw übelnehmen

ill'-advised' *adj* (*person*) schlecht beraten; (*action*) unbesonnen

ill'-at-ease' *adj* unbehaglich

ill'-bred' *adj* ungezogen

ill'-consid'ered *adj* unbesonnen

ill'-disposed' *adj*—**be i. towards** übelgesinnt sein (*dat*)

illegal [ɪˈligəl] *adj* illegal

illegible [ɪˈledʒɪbəl] *adj* unlesbar

illegitimate [‚ɪlɪˈdʒɪtɪmɪt] *adj* unrechtmäßig; (*child*) illegitim

ill'-fat'ed *adj* unglücklich

ill-gotten [ˈɪl‚gatən] *adj* unrechtmäßig erworben

ill' health' *s* Kränklichkeit *f*

ill'-hu'mored *adj* übelgelaunt

illicit [ɪˈlɪsɪt] *adj* unerlaubt

illiteracy [ɪˈlɪtərəsi] *s* Analphabetentum *n*

illiterate [ɪˈlɪtərɪt] *adj* analphabetisch ‖ *s* Analphabet –in *mf*

ill'-man'nered *adj* ungehobelt

ill'-na'tured *adj* bösartig

illness [ˈɪlnɪs] *s* (& fig) Krankheit *f*

illogical [ɪˈlɑdʒɪkəl] *adj* unlogisch

ill'-spent' *adj* verschwendet

ill'-starred' *adj* unglücklich

ill'-suit'ed *adj* (**to**) unpassend (*dat*)

ill'-tem'pered *adj* schlechtgelaunt

ill'-timed' *adj* unpassend

ill'-treat' *tr* mißhandeln

illuminate [ɪˈlumɪ‚net] *tr* beleuchten; (*public buildings, manuscripts*) illuminieren; (*enlighten*) erleuchten; (*explain*) erklären

illumination [ɪ‚lumɪˈneʃən] *s* Beleuchten *n*; Erleuchtung *f*; Illuminierung *f*

illusion [ɪˈluʒən] *s* Illusion *f*

illusive [ɪˈlusɪv] *adj* trügerisch

illusory [ɪˈlusəri] *adj* illusorisch

illustrate [ˈɪləs‚tret] *tr* (*exemplify*) erläutern; (*a book*) illustrieren; **illustrated lecture** Lichtbildervortrag *m*; **richly illustrated** bilderreich

illustration [‚ɪləsˈtreʃən] *s* Erläuterung *f*; (*in a book*) Abbildung *f*

illustrative [ɪˈlʌstrətɪv] *adj* erläuternd; **i. material** Anschauungsmaterial *n*

illustrator [ˈɪləs‚tretər] *s* Illustrator *m*

illustrious [ɪˈlʌstrɪ·əs] *adj* berühmt

ill' will' *s* Feindschaft *f*

image [ˈɪmɪdʒ] *s* Bild *n*; (*reflection*) Spiegelbild *n*; (*statue*) Standbild *n*; (*before the public*) Image *n*; (opt, phot, telv) Bild *n*; **the spitting i. of his father** ganz der Vater

imagery [ˈɪmɪdʒ(ə)ri] *s* Bildersprache *f*

imaginable [ɪˈmædʒɪnəbəl] *adj* erdenklich

imaginary [ɪˈmædʒɪ‚neri] *adj* imaginär

imagination [ɪ‚mædʒɪˈneʃən] *s* Phantasie *f*, Einbildungskraft *f*; **that's pure i.** das ist pure Einbildung

imaginative [ɪˈmædʒɪnətɪv] *adj* phantasievoll

imagine [ɪˈmædʒɪn] *tr* sich [*dat*] vorstellen, sich [*dat*] denken; **i. oneself**

in sich hineindenken in (acc); **you're only imagining things** das bilden Sie sich [*dat*] nur ein || *intr*—**I can i.** das läßt sich denken; **I i. so ich glaube schon**; **just i.** denken Sie nur mal!

imbecile ['ɪmbɪsɪl] *adj* geistesschwach || *s* Geistesschwäche *mf*

imbecility [ˌɪmbɪ'sɪlɪti] *s* Geistesschwäche *f*, Blödheit *f*

imbibe [ɪm'baɪb] *tr* aufsaugen; (coll) trinken; (fig) (geistig) aufnehmen

imbue [ɪm'bju] *tr* durchfeuchten; (fig) (**with**) durchdringen (mit)

imitate ['ɪmɪ͵tet] *tr* nachahmen, nachmachen; **i. s.o. in everything** j-m alles nachmachen

imitation [ˌɪmɪ'teʃən] *adj* unecht, nachgemacht || *s* Nachahmung *f*; **in i. of** nach dem Muster (genit)

imitation leather *s* Kunstleder *n*

imitator ['ɪmɪ͵tetər] *s* Nachahmer –in *mf*

immaculate [ɪ'mækjəlɪt] *adj* makellos; (sinless) unbefleckt

immaterial [ˌɪmə'tɪrɪ-əl] *adj* immateriell, unkörperlich; (unimportant) unwesentlich; **it's i. to me** es is mir gleichgültig

immature [ˌɪmə'tjʊr] *adj* unreif

immaturity [ˌɪmə'tjʊrɪti] *s* Unreife *f*

immeasurable [ɪ'meʒərəbəl] *adj* unermeßlich

immediacy [ɪ'midɪ-əsi] *s* Unmittelbarkeit *f*

immediate [ɪ'midɪ-ɪt] *adj* sofortig; (direct) unmittelbar

immediately [ɪ'midɪ-ɪtli] *adv* sofort; **i. afterwards** gleich darauf

immemorial [ˌɪmɪ'morɪ-əl] *adj* uralt; **since time i.** seit Menschengedenken

immense [ɪ'mens] *adj* unermeßlich

immensity [ɪ'mensɪti] *s* Unermeßlichkeit *f*

immerse [ɪ'mʌrs] *tr* (unter)tauchen; **immersed in** (books, thought, work) vertieft in (acc); **i. oneself in** sich vertiefen in (acc)

immersion [ɪ'mʌrʒən] *s* Untertauchen *n*; (fig) Versunkenheit *f*

immigrant ['ɪmɪgrənt] *adj* einwandernd || *s* Einwanderer –in *mf*

immigrate ['ɪmɪ͵gret] *intr* einwandern

immigration [ˌɪmɪ'greʃən] *s* Einwanderung *f*

imminent ['ɪmɪnənt] *adj* drohend

immobile [ɪ'mobɪl] *adj* unbeweglich

immobilize [ɪ'mobɪ͵laɪz] *tr* unbeweglich machen; (tanks) bewegungsunfähig machen; (troops) fesseln; (med) ruhigstellen

immoderate [ɪ'mɑdərɪt] *adj* unmäßig

immodest [ɪ'mɑdɪst] *adj* unbescheiden

immolate ['ɪmə͵let] *tr* opfern

immoral [ɪ'mɔrəl] *adj* unsittlich

immorality [ˌɪmə'rælɪti] *s* Unsittlichkeit *f*

immortal [ɪ'mɔrtəl] *adj* unsterblich

immortality [ˌɪmɔr'tælɪti] *s* Unsterblichkeit *f*

immortalize [ɪ'mɔrtə͵laɪz] *tr* unsterblich machen

immovable [ɪ'muvəbəl] *adj* unbeweglich

immune [ɪ'mjun] *adj* (free, exempt) (**from**) immun (gegen); (not responsive) (**to**) gefeit (gegen); (med) (**to**) immun (gegen)

immunity [ɪ'mjunɪti] *s* Immunität *f*

immunization [ˌɪmjunɪ'zeʃən] *s* Schutzimpfung *f*, Immunisierung *f*

immunize ['ɪmjə͵naɪz] *tr* (**against**) immunisieren (gegen)

immutable [ɪ'mjutəbəl] *adj* unwandelbar

imp [ɪmp] *s* Schlingel *m*

impact ['ɪmpækt] *s* Anprall *m*; (of a shell) Aufschlag *m*; (fig) Einwirkung *f*

impair [ɪm'per] *tr* beeinträchtigen

impale [ɪm'pel] *tr* pfählen

impan·el [ɪm'pænəl] *v* (pret & pp **-el[l]ed**; ger **-el[l]ing**) *tr* in die Geschworenenliste eintragen

impart [ɪm'pɑrt] *tr* mitteilen

impartial [ɪm'pɑrʃəl] *adj* unparteiisch

impassable [ɪm'pæsɪbəl] *adj* (on foot) ungangbar; (by car) unbefahrbar

impasse ['ɪmpæs] *s* Sackgasse *f*; **reach an i.** in e-e Sackgasse geraten

impassible [ɪm'pæsɪbəl] *adj* (**to**) unempfindlich (für)

impassioned [ɪm'pæʃənd] *adj* leidenschaftlich

impassive [ɪm'pæsɪv] *adj* (person) teilnahmslos; (expression) ausdruckslos

impatience [ɪm'peʃəns] *s* Ungeduld *f*

impatient [ɪm'peʃənt] *adj* ungeduldig

impeach [ɪm'pitʃ] *tr* (an official) wegen Amtsmißbrauchs unter Anklage stellen; (a witness, motives) in Zweifel ziehen

impeachment [ɪm'pitʃmənt] *s* (of an official) öffentliche Anklage *f*; (of a witness, motives) Anzweiflung *f*

impeccable [ɪm'pekəbəl] *adj* makellos

impecunious [ˌɪmpɪ'kjunɪ-əs] *adj* mittellos

impede [ɪm'pid] *tr* behindern, erschweren

impediment [ɪm'pedɪmənt] *s* Behinderung *f*; (of speech) Sprachfehler *m*

im·pel [ɪm'pel] *v* (pret & pp **-pelled**; ger **-pelling**) *tr* antreiben

impending [ɪm'pendɪŋ] *adj* nahe bevorstehen; (threatening) drohend

impenetrable [ɪm'penɪtrəbəl] *adj* undurchdringlich; (fig) unergründlich

impenitent [ɪm'penɪtənt] *adj* unbußfertig

imperative [ɪm'perətɪv] *adj* dringend nötig || *s* Imperativ *m*

imper′ative mood′ *s* Befehlsform *f*

imperceptible [ˌɪmpər'septɪbəl] *adj* nicht wahrnehmbar, unmerklich

imperfect [ɪm'pɑrfɪkt] *adj* unvollkommen || *s* (gram) Imperfekt(um) *n*

imperfection [ˌɪmpər'fekʃən] *s* Unvollkommenheit *f*; (flaw) Fehler *m*

imperial [ɪm'pɪrɪ-əl] *adj* kaiserlich

imperialism [ɪm'pɪrɪ-ə͵lɪzəm] *s* Imperialismus *m*

imperialist [ɪm'pɪrɪ-əlɪst] *adj* imperialistisch || *s* Imperialist –in *mf* imper·il [ɪmˈperɪl] v (pret & pp -il[l]ed; ger -il[l]ing) tr gefährden

imperious [ɪmˈperɪ·əs] adj herrisch, anmaßend

imperishable [ɪmˈperɪʃəbəl] adj unvergänglich

impersonal [ɪmˈpʌrsənəl] adj unpersönlich

impersonate [ɪmˈpʌrsəˌnet] tr (imitate) nachahmen; (e.g., an officer) sich ausgeben als; (theat) darstellen

impersonator [ɪmˈpʌrsəˌnetər] s Imitator –in mf

impertinence [ɪmˈpʌrtɪnəns] s Ungezogenheit f

impertinent [ɪmˈpʌrtɪnənt] adj ungezogen

imperturbable [ˌɪmpʌrˈtʌrbəbəl] adj unerschütterlich

impetuous [ɪmˈpetʃʊ·əs] adj ungestüm

impetus [ˈɪmpɪtəs] s (& fig) Antrieb m

impiety [ɪmˈpaɪ·əti] s Gottlosigkeit f

impinge [ɪmˈpɪndʒ] intr—i. on (an) stoßen an (acc); (said of rays) fallen auf (acc); (fig) eingreifen in (acc)

impious [ˈɪmpɪ·əs] adj gottlos

impish [ˈɪmpɪʃ] adj spitzbübisch

implant [ɪmˈplænt] tr einpflanzen

implement [ˈɪmplɪmənt] s Werkzeug n, Gerät n ‖ [ˈɪmplɪˌment] tr durchführen

implicate [ˈɪmplɪˌket] tr (in) verwickeln (in acc)

implication [ˌɪmplɪˈkeʃən] s (involvement) Verwicklung f; (implying) Andeutung f; implications Folgerungen pl

implicit [ɪmˈplɪsɪt] adj (approval) stillschweigend; (trust) unbedingt

implied [ɪmˈplaɪd] adj stillschweigend

implore [ɪmˈplor] tr anflehen

im·ply [ɪmˈplaɪ] v (pret & pp –plied) tr (express indirectly) andeuten; (involve) in sich schließen; (said of words) besagen

impolite [ˌɪmpəˈlaɪt] adj unhöflich

import [ˈɪmport] s Import m, Einfuhr f; (meaning) Bedeutung f; imports Einfuhrwaren pl ‖ [ɪmˈport], [ˈɪmport] tr importieren, einführen

importance [ɪmˈportəns] s Wichtigkeit f; a man of i. ein Mann m von Bedeutung; of no i. unwichtig

important [ɪmˈportənt] adj wichtig

im′port du′ty s Einfuhrzoll m

importer [ɪmˈportər] s Importeur m

importune [ˌɪmporˈt(j)un] adj aufdringlich ‖ tr bestürmen

impose [ɪmˈpoz] tr (on, upon) auferlegen (dat) ‖ intr—i. on über Gebühr beanspruchen

impos′ing adj imposant

imposition [ˌɪmpəˈzɪʃən] s (of hands, of an obligation) Auferlegung f; (taking unfair advantage) Zumutung f

impossible [ɪmˈpɑsɪbəl] adj unmöglich

impostor [ɪmˈpɑstər] s Hochstapler m

imposture [ɪmˈpɑstʃər] s Hochstapelei f

impotence [ˈɪmpətəns] s Machtlosigkeit f; (pathol) Impotenz f

impotent [ˈɪmpətənt] adj machtlos; (pathol) impotent

impound [ɪmˈpaund] tr beschlagnahmen

impoverish [ɪmˈpɑvərɪʃ] tr arm machen; become impoverished verarmen

impracticable [ɪmˈpræktɪkəbəl] adj unausführbar

impractical [ɪmˈpræktɪkəl] adj unpraktisch

impregnable [ɪmˈpregnəbəl] adj uneinnehmbar

impregnate [ɪmˈpregnet] tr (saturate) imprägnieren; (& fig) schwängern

impresari·o [ˌɪmprɪˈsɑrɪˌo] s (–os) Impresario m

impress [ɪmˈpres] tr (affect) imponieren (dat), beeindrucken; (imprint, emphasize) einprägen; i. s.th. on s.o. j–m etw einprägen

impression [ɪmˈpreʃən] s Eindruck m; (stamp) Gepräge n; try to make an i. Eindruck schinden

impressive [ɪmˈpresɪv] adj eindrucksvoll

imprint [ˈɪmprɪnt] s Aufdruck m; (fig) Eindruck m ‖ [ɪmˈprɪnt] tr (on) aufdrucken (auf acc); i. on s.o.'s memory j–m ins Gedächtnis einprägen

imprison [ɪmˈprɪzən] tr einsperren

imprisonment [ɪmˈprɪzənmənt] s Haft f; (penalty) Freiheitsstrafe f; (captivity) Gefangenschaft f

improbable [ɪmˈprɑbəbəl] adj unwahrscheinlich

impromptu [ɪmˈprɑmpt(j)u] adj & adv aus dem Stegreif ‖ s Stegreifstück n

improper [ɪmˈprɑpər] adj ungehörig, unschicklich; (use) unzulässig

improve [ɪmˈpruv] tr verbessern; (relations) ausbauen; (land) kultivieren; (a salary) aufbessern; i. oneself sich bessern; (financially) sich verbessern ‖ intr bessern; (com) sich erholen; i. on Verbesserungen vornehmen an (dat)

improvement [ɪmˈpruvmənt] s Verbesserung f; (reworking) Umarbeitung f; (of money value) Erholung f; (of a salary) Aufbesserung f; (in health) Besserung f; be an i. on ein Fortschritt sein gegenüber

improvident [ɪmˈprɑvɪdənt] adj unbedacht

improvise [ˈɪmprəˌvaɪz] tr improvisieren ‖ intr improvisieren; (mus) phantasieren

imprudence [ɪmˈprudəns] s Unklugheit f

imprudent [ɪmˈprudənt] adj unklug

impudence [ˈɪmpjədəns] s Unverschämtheit f

impudent [ˈɪmpjədənt] adj unverschämt

impugn [ɪmˈpjun] tr bestreiten

impulse [ˈɪmpʌls] s Impuls m; act on i. impulsiv handeln

impulsive [ɪmˈpʌlsɪv] adj impulsiv

impunity [ɪmˈpjunɪti] s Straffreiheit f; with i. ungestraft

impure [ɪmˈpjur] adj (& fig) unrein

impurity [ɪmˈpjʊrɪti] s (& fig) Unreinheit f

impute [ɪmˈpjut] tr (to) unterstellen (dat)

in [ɪn] adv (position) drin, drinnen; (direction away from the speaker) hinein; (direction toward the speaker) herein; **be all in** ganz erschöpft sein; **be in** da sein; (said of a political party) an der Macht sein; (be in style) in Mode sein; **be in for** zu erwarten haben; **have it in** for auf dem Strich haben || s—**the ins and outs of** die Einzelheiten (genit) || prep (position) in (dat); (direction) in (acc); (e.g., the morning, afternoon, evening) an; (a field, the country; one eye) auf (dat); (one's opinion; all probability) nach (dat); (circumstances; a reign) unter (dat); (ink; one stroke) mit (dat); (because of pain, joy, etc.) vor (dat); **he doesn't have it in him to** (inf) er hat nicht das Zeug dazu zu (inf); **in German** auf deutsch

inability [ˌɪnəˈbɪlɪti] s Unfähigkeit f; **i. to pay** Zahlungsunfähigkeit f

inaccessible [ˌɪnækˈsesɪbəl] adj unzugänglich

inaccuracy [ɪnˈækjərəsi] s Ungenauigkeit f

inaccurate [ɪnˈækjərət] adj ungenau

inaction [ɪnˈækʃən] s Untätigkeit f

inactive [ɪnˈæktɪv] adj untätig; (chem) unwirksam; (st. exch.) lustlos

inactivity [ˌɪnækˈtɪvɪti] s Untätigkeit f

inadequate [ɪnˈædɪkwɪt] adj unangemessen

inadmissible [ˌɪnədˈmɪsɪbəl] adj unstatthaft, unzulässig

inadvertent [ˌɪnədˈvʌrtənt] adj versehentlich

inadvisable [ɪnədˈvaɪzəbəl] adj nicht ratsam

inalienable [ɪnˈeljənəbəl] adj unveräußerlich

inane [ɪnˈen] adj leer, unsinnig

inanimate [ɪnˈænɪmɪt] adj unbeseelt

inappropriate [ˌɪnəˈproprɪɪt] adj unangemessen

inarticulate [ˌɪnɑrˈtɪkjəlɪt] adj unartikuliert, undeutlich

inartistic [ˌɪnɑrˈtɪstɪk] adj unkünstlerisch, kunstlos

inasmuch as [ˌɪnəzˈmʌtʃˌæz] conj da

inattentive [ˌɪnəˈtentɪv] adv (to) unaufmerksam (or unachtsam) (gegenüber)

inaudible [ɪnˈɔdɪbəl] adj unhörbar

inaugural [ɪnˈɔg(j)ərəl] adj Antritts—

inaugurate [ɪnˈɔg(j)əˌret] tr feierlich eröffnen; (a new policy) einleiten

inauguration [ɪnˌɔg(j)əˈreʃən] s Eröffnung f; (of an official) Amtsantritt m

inauspicious [ˌɪnɔˈspɪʃəs] adj ungünstig

inborn [ˈɪnˌbɔrn] adj angeboren

inbred [ˈɪnˌbred] adj angeboren, ererbt

in'breed'ing s Inzucht f

incalculable [ɪnˈkælkjələbəl] adj unberechenbar

incandescent [ˌɪnkənˈdesənt] adj Glüh—

incantation [ˌɪnkænˈteʃən] s Beschwörung f

incapable [ɪnˈkepəbəl] adj untüchtig; **i. of** (ger) nicht fähig zu (inf)

incapacitate [ˌɪnkəˈpæsɪˌtet] tr unfähig machen; (jur) für geschäftsunfähig erklären

incarcerate [ɪnˈkɑrsəˌret] tr einkerkern

incarnate [ɪnˈkɑrnet] adj—**God i.** Gottmensch m; **the devil i.** der Teufel in Menschengestalt

incarnation [ˌɪnkɑrˈneʃən] s (fig) Verkörperung f; (eccl) Fleischwerdung f

incendiary [ɪnˈsendɪˌeri] adj Brand—; (fig) aufhetzend || s Brandstifter —in mf

incense [ˈɪnsəns] s Weihrauch m || tr (eccl) beräuchern || [ɪnˈsens] tr erzürnen

in'cense burn'er s Räuchergefäß n

incentive [ɪnˈsentɪv] s Anreiz m

inception [ɪnˈsepʃən] s Anfang m

incessant [ɪnˈsesənt] adj unaufhörlich

incest [ˈɪnsest] s Blutschande f

incestuous [ɪnˈsestʃʊəs] adj blutschänderisch

inch [ɪntʃ] s Zoll m; **beat within an i. of one's life** fast zu Tode prügeln; **by inches** nach und nach; **not yield an i.** keinen Fußbreit nachgeben || intr—**i. along** dahinschleichen; **i. forward** langsam vorrücken

incidence [ˈɪnsɪdəns] s Vorkommen n

incident [ˈɪnsɪdənt] s Vorfall m; (adverse event) Zwischenfall m

incidental [ˌɪnsɪˈdentəl] adj zufällig; **i. to** gehörig zu || **incidentals** spl Nebenausgaben pl

incidentally [ˌɪnsɪˈdentəli] adv übrigens

incinerate [ɪnˈsɪnəˌret] tr einäschern

incinerator [ɪnˈsɪnəˌretər] s Verbrennungsofen m

incipient [ɪnˈsɪpɪənt] adv beginnend

incision [ɪnˈsɪʒən] s Schnitt m

incisive [ɪnˈsaɪsɪv] adj (biting) beißend; (penetrating) durchdringend; (sharp) scharf

incisor [ɪnˈsaɪzər] s Schneidezahn m

incite [ɪnˈsaɪt] tr aufreizen, aufhetzen

inclement [ɪnˈklemənt] adj ungünstig

inclination [ˌɪnklɪˈneʃən] s (& fig) Neigung f

incline [ˈɪnklaɪn] s Abhang m || [ɪnˈklaɪn] tr neigen || intr (towards) sich neigen (nach or zu); (fig) (towards) neigen (zu); **the roof inclines sharply** das Dach fällt steil ab

include [ɪnˈklud] tr einschließen; **i. among** rechnen unter (acc); **i. in** einrechnen in (acc)

includ'ed adj (mit) inbegriffen

includ'ing prep einschließlich (genit)

inclusive [ɪnˈklusɪv] adj umfassend, gesamt; **all i.** alles inbegriffen; **from ... to ... i.** von ... zu ... einschließlich (or inklusive); **i. of** einschließlich (genit)

incognito [ɪn'kɑgnɪ ,to] *adv* inkognito
incoherent [,ɪnko'hɪrənt] *adj* unzusammenhängend; **be i.** (*said of a person*) nicht ganz bei sich sein
incombustible [,ɪnkəm'bʌstɪbəl] *adj* unverbrennbar
income ['ɪnkʌm] *s* (**from**) Einkommen *n* (aus)
in'come tax' *s* Einkommensteuer *f*
in'come-tax return' *s* Einkommensteuererklärung *f*
in'com'ing *adj* (*e.g., tide*) hereinkommend; (*bus, train*) ankommend; (*official*) neu eintretend; **i. goods, i. mail** Eingänge *pl*
incomparable [ɪn'kɑmpərəbəl] *adj* unvergleichlich
incompatible [,ɪnkəm'pætɪbəl] *adj* (**with**) unvereinbar (mit); (*persons*) unverträglich
incompetent [ɪn'kɑmpɪtənt] *adj* untauglich; (*not legally qualified*) nicht zuständig; (*not legally capable*) geschäftsunfähig; (*inadmissible*) unzulässig ‖ *s* Nichtkönner –in *mf*
incomplete [,ɪnkəm'plit] *adj* unvollständig
incomprehensible [,ɪnkɑmprɪ'hensɪbəl] *adj* unbegreiflich
inconceivable [,ɪnkən'sivəbəl] *adj* undenkbar
inconclusive [,ɪnkən'klusɪv] *adj* (*not convincing*) nicht überzeugend; (*leading to no result*) ergebnislos
incongruous [ɪn'kɑŋgru·əs] *adj* nicht übereinstimmend
inconsequential [ɪn ,kɑnsɪ'kwenʃəl] *adj* belanglos
inconsiderate [,ɪnkən'sɪdərɪt] *adj* unüberlegt; (**towards**) rücksichtslos (gegen)
inconsistency [,ɪnkən'sɪstənsɪ] *s* (*lack of logical connection*) Inkonsequenz *f*; (*contradiction*) Unstimmigkeit *f*; (*instability*) Unbeständigkeit *f*
inconsistent [,ɪnkən'sɪstənt] *adj* inkonsequent; (*uneven*) unbeständig
inconspicuous [,ɪnkən'spɪkju·əs] *adj* unauffällig
inconstant [ɪn'kɑnstənt] *adj* unbeständig
incontinent [ɪn'kɑntɪnənt] *adj* zügellos
incontrovertible [,ɪnkɑntrə'vʌrtɪbəl] *adj* unwiderlegbar
inconvenience [,ɪnkən'vini·əns] *s* Ungelegenheit *f* ‖ *tr* bemühen, belästigen
inconvenient [,ɪnkən'vini·ənt] *adj* ungelegen
incorporate [ɪn'kɔrpə ,ret] *tr* einverleiben; (*an organization*) zu e–r Körperschaft machen ‖ *intr* e–e Körperschaft werden
incorporation [ɪn ,kɔrpə'reʃən] *s* Einverleibung *f*; (*jur*) Körperschaftsbildung *f*
incorrect [,ɪnkə'rɛkt] *adj* unrichtig, falsch; (*conduct*) unschicklich
incorrigible [ɪn'kɔrɪdʒɪbəl] *adj* unverbesserlich
increase ['ɪnkris] *s* Zunahme *f*; **be on the i.** steigen; **i. in costs** Kostensteigerung *f*; **i. in pay** Gehaltser-

höhung *f*; (mil) Solderhöhung *f*; **i. in population** Bevölkerungszunahme *f*; **i. in prices** Preiserhöhung *f*; **i. in rent** Mieterhöhung *f*; **i. in taxes** Steuererhöhung *f*; **i. in value** Wertsteigerung *f*; **i. in weight** Gewichtszunahme *f* ‖ [ɪn'kris] *tr* (*in size*) vergrößern; (*in height*) erhöhen; (*in quantity*) vermehren; (*in intensity*) verstärken; (*prices*) heraufsetzen ‖ *intr* zunehmen, sich vergrößern; (*rise*) sich erhöhen; (*in quantity*) sich vermehren; (*in intensity*) sich verstärken; **i. in** zunehmen an (*dat*)
increasingly [ɪn'krisɪŋlɪ] *adv* immer mehr; **i. more difficult** immer schwieriger
incredible [ɪn'kredɪbəl] *adj* unglaublich
incredulous [ɪn'kredʒələs] *adj* ungläubig
increment ['ɪnkrɪmənt] *s* Zunahme *f*, Zuwachs *m*; (*in pay*) Gehaltszulage *f*
incriminate [ɪn'krɪmɪ ,net] *tr* belasten
incrust [ɪn'krʌst] *tr* überkrusten
incubate ['ɪnkjə ,bet] *tr & intr* brüten
incubator ['ɪnkjə ,betər] *s* Brutapparat *m*
inculcate [ɪn'kʌlket], ['ɪnkʌl ,ket] *tr* (**in**) einprägen (*dat*)
incumbency [ɪn'kʌmbənsɪ] *s* (*obligation*) Obliegenheit *f*; (*term of office*) Amtszeit *f*
incumbent [ɪn'kʌmbənt] *adj*—**be i. on** obliegen (*dat*) ‖ *s* Amtsinhaber –in *mf*
incunabula [,ɪnkju'næbjələ] *spl* (typ) Wiegendrucke *pl*
in·cur [ɪn'kʌr] *v* (*pret & pp* –**curred**; *ger* –**curring**) *tr* sich [*dat*] zuziehen; (*debts*) machen; (*a loss*) erleiden; (*a risk*) eingehen
incurable [ɪn'kjurəbəl] *adj* unheilbar ‖ *s* unheilbarer Kranke *m*
incursion [ɪn'kʌrʒən] *s* Einfall *m*
indebted [ɪn'detɪd] *adj* (**to**) verschuldet (bei); **be i. to s.o. for s.th.** j–m etw zu verdanken haben
indecency [ɪn'disənsɪ] *s* Unsittlichkeit *f*
indecent [ɪn'disənt] *adj* unsittlich; **i. assault** Sittlichkeitsvergehen *n*
indecision [,ɪndɪ'sɪʒən] *s* Unentschlossenheit *f*
indecisive [,ɪndɪ'saɪsɪv] *adj* (*person*) unentschlossen; (*battle*) nicht entscheidend
indeclinable [,ɪndɪ'klaɪnəbəl] *adj* undeklinierbar
indeed [ɪn'did] *adv* ja, zwar ‖ *interj* jawohl!
indefatigable [,ɪndɪ'fætɪgəbəl] *adj* unermüdlich
indefensible [,ɪndɪ'fensɪbəl] *adj* nicht zu verteidigen(d); (*argument*) unhaltbar; (*behavior*) unentschuldbar
indefinable [,ɪndɪ'faɪnəbəl] *adj* undefinierbar
indefinite [ɪn'defɪnɪt] *adj* (*unlimited*) unbegrenzt; (*not exact*) unbestimmt; (*answer*) ausweichend; (*vague*) undeutlich; (gram) unbestimmt

indelible [ɪnˈdelɪbəl] *adj* (*ink, pencil*) wasserfest; (*fig*) unauslöschlich

indelicate [ɪnˈdelɪkɪt] *adj* unzart

indemnification [ɪnˌdemnɪfɪˈkeʃən] *s* Schadenersatzleistung *f*

indemni‧fy [ɪnˈdemnɪˌfaɪ] *v* (*pret & pp* **-fied**) *tr* entschädigen

indemnity [ɪnˈdemnɪti] *s* Schadenersatz *m*

indent [ɪnˈdent] *tr* (*notch*) einkerben; (*the coast*) tiefe Einschnitte bilden in (*dat*); (*typ*) einrücken ‖ *intr* (*typ*) einrücken

indentation [ˌɪndenˈteʃən] *s* Kerbe *f*; (*typ*) Absatz *m*

indenture [ɪnˈdentʃər] *s* (*service contract*) Arbeitsvertrag *m*; (*apprentice contract*) Lehrvertrag *m* ‖ *tr* vertraglich binden

independence [ˌɪndɪˈpendəns] *s* Unabhängigkeit *f*

independent [ˌɪndɪˈpendənt] *adj* (*of*) unabhängig (von) ‖ *s* Unabhängige *mf*

indescribable [ˌɪndɪˈskraɪbəbəl] *adj* unbeschreiblich

indestructible [ˌɪndɪˈstrʌktɪbəl] *adj* unzerstörbar

index [ˈɪndeks] *s* (**indexes & indices** [ˈɪndɪˌsiz]) (*in a book*) Register *n*; (*fig*) (**to**) Hisweis *m* (auf *acc*); Index *m* ‖ *tr* registrieren; (*a book*) mit e-m Register versehen

in′dex card′ *s* Karteikarte *f*

in′dex fin′ger *s* Zeigefinger *m*

India [ˈɪndɪ‧ə] *s* Indien *n*

In′dia ink′ *s* chinesische Tusche *f*

Indian [ˈɪndɪ‧ən] *adj* indisch; (*e.g., chief, tribe*) Indianer– ‖ *s* (*of India*) Inder –in *mf*; (*of North America*) Indianer –in *mf*; (*of Central or South America*) Indio *m*

In′dian corn′ *s* Mais *m*

In′dian file′ *adv* in Gänsemarsch

In′dian O′cean *s* Indischer Ozean *m*

In′dian sum′mer *s* Altweibersommer *m*

indicate [ˈɪndɪˌket] *tr* angeben, anzeigen

indication [ˌɪndɪˈkeʃən] *s* Angabe *f*; (*of s.th. imminent*) (**of**) Anzeichen *n* (für); **give i. of** anzeigen

indicative [ɪnˈdɪkətɪv] *adj* (gram) indikativ; **be i. of** hindeuten auf (*acc*) ‖ *s* (gram) Wirklichkeitsform *f*, Indikativ *m*

indicator [ˈɪndɪˌketər] *s* Zeiger *m*

indict [ɪnˈdaɪt] *tr* (**for**) anklagen (wegen)

indictment [ɪnˈdaɪtmənt] *s* Anklage *f*

indifference [ɪnˈdɪfərəns] *s* (**to**) Gleichgültigkeit *f* (gegen or gegenüber)

indifferent [ɪnˈdɪfərənt] *adj* (*mediocre*) mittelmäßig; (**to**) gleichgültig (gegen)

indigenous [ɪnˈdɪdʒɪnəs] *adj* (**to**) einheimisch (in *dat*)

indigent [ˈɪndɪdʒənt] *adj* bedürftig

indigestible [ˌɪndɪˈdʒestɪbəl] *adj* unverdaulich

indigestion [ˌɪndɪˈdʒestʃən] *s* Verdauungsstörung *f*, Magenverstimmung *f*

indignant [ɪnˈdɪgnənt] *adj* (**at**) empört (über *acc*)

indignation [ˌɪndɪgˈneʃən] *s* (**at**) Empörung *f* (über *acc*)

indignity [ɪnˈdɪgnɪti] *s* Beleidigung *f*

indigo [ˈɪndɪˌgo] *adj* Indigo– ‖ *s* Indigo *m & n*

indirect [ˌɪndɪˈrekt] *adj* indirekt

in′direct dis′course *s* indirekte Rede *f*

in′direct ques′tion *s* indirekter Fragesatz *m*

indiscreet [ˌɪndɪsˈkrit] *adj* indiskret

indiscretion [ˌɪndɪsˈkreʃən] *s* Indiskretion *f*

indiscriminate [ˌɪndɪsˈkrɪmɪnɪt] *adj* unterschiedslos

indispensable [ˌɪndɪsˈpensəbəl] *adj* unentbehrlich

indisposed *adj* (*ill*) unpäßlich; **i. to** abgeneigt (*dat*)

indissoluble [ˌɪndɪˈsɑljəbəl] *adj* unauflösbar

indistinct [ˌɪndɪˈstɪŋkt] *adj* undeutlich

individual [ˌɪndɪˈvɪdʒʊ‧əl] *adj* individuell, Einzel–, einzeln ‖ *s* Individuum *n*

individ′ual case′ *s* Einzelfall *m*

individuality [ˌɪndɪˌvɪdʒʊˈælɪti] *s* Individualität *f*

individually [ˌɪndɪˈvɪdʒʊ‧əli] *adv* einzeln

indivisible [ˌɪndɪˈvɪzɪbəl] *adj* unteilbar

Indochina [ˈɪndoˈtʃaɪnə] *s* Indochina *n*

indoctrinate [ɪnˈdɑktrɪˌnet] *tr* (**in**) schulen (in *dat*), unterweisen (in *dat*)

indoctrination [ˌɪndɑktrɪˈneʃən] *s* Schulung *f*, Unterweisung *f*

Indo-European [ˈɪndoˌjʊrəˈpi‧ən] *adj* indogermanisch ‖ *s* (*language*) Indogermanisch *n*

indolence [ˈɪndələns] *s* Trägheit *f*

indolent [ˈɪndələnt] *adj* träge

Indonesia [ˌɪndoˈniʒə] *s* Indonesien *n*

Indonesian [ˌɪndoˈniʒən] *adj* indonesisch ‖ *s* Indonesier –in *mf*

indoor [ˈɪnˌdor] *adj* Haus–, Zimmer–, Innen–; (sport) Hallen–

indoors [ɪnˈdorz] *adv* innen, drin(nen)

in′door shot′ *s* (phot) Innenaufnahme *f*

induce [ɪnˈd(j)us] *tr* veranlassen, bewegen; (*bring about*) verursachen; (elec, phys) induzieren

inducement [ɪnˈd(j)usmənt] *s* Anreiz *m*

induct [ɪnˈdʌkt] *tr* (**into**) einführen (in *acc*); (mil) (**into**) einberufen (zu)

inductee [ˌɪnˈdʌkti] *s* Einberufene *mf*

induction [ɪnˈdʌkʃən] *s* Einführung *f*; (elec, log) Induktion *f*; (mil) Einberufung *f*

induc′tion coil′ *s* Induktionsspule *f*

indulge [ɪnˈdʌldʒ] *tr* (*a desire*) frönen (*dat*); (*a person*) befriedigen; (*children*) verwöhnen; **i. oneself in** schwelgen in (*dat*) ‖ *intr* (coll) trinken; **i. in s.th.** sich [*dat*] etw gestatten

indulgence [ɪnˈdʌldʒəns] *s* (*of a desire*) Frönen *n*; (*tolerance*) Duldung *f*; (relig) Ablaß *m*; **ask s.o.'s i.** j-n um Nachsicht bitten

indulgent [ɪnˈdʌldʒənt] *adj* schonend; (**toward**) nachsichtig (gegen)

industrial [ɪnˈdʌstrɪ‧əl] *adj* (*e.g., bank,*

center, alcohol, product, worker)
Industrie–; (e.g., accident, medicine)
Betriebs–; (e.g., revolution) industri-
ell; (e.g., school, engineering) Gewerbe–

industrialist [ɪn'dʌstrɪ·əlɪst] s In-
dustrielle mf

industrialize [ɪn'dʌstrɪ·ə‚laɪz] tr industrialisieren

indus'trial man'agement s Betriebs-
wirtschaft f

industrious [ɪn'dʌstrɪ·əs] adj fleißig

industry ['ɪndəstri] s Industrie f; (energy) Fleiß m

inebriated [ɪn'ibrɪ‚etɪd] adj betrunken

inedible [ɪn'edɪbəl] adj ungenießbar

ineffable [ɪn'efəbəl] adj unaussprechlich

ineffective [‚ɪnɪ'fɛktɪv] adj unwirksam; (person) untüchtig

ineffectual [‚ɪnɪ'fɛkt/ʊ·əl] adj unwirksam

inefficient [‚ɪnɪ'fɪ/ənt] adj untüchig;
(process, procedure) unrationell;
(mach) nicht leistungsfähig

ineligible [ɪn'elɪdʒɪbəl] adj nicht wählbar; (not suitable) ungeeignet

inept [ɪn'ept] adj ungeschickt

inequality [‚ɪnɪ'kwɑlɪti] s Ungleichheit f

inequity [ɪn'ekwɪti] s Ungerechtigkeit
f

inertia [ɪn'ʌr/ə] s Trägheit f

inescapable [‚ɪnes'kepəbəl] adj unentrinnbar, unabwendbar

inevitable [ɪn'evɪtəbəl] adj unvermeidlich, unausweichlich

inexact [‚ɪneg'zækt] adj ungenau

inexcusable [‚ɪneks'kjuzəbəl] adj unentschuldbar

inexhaustible [‚ɪneg'zɔstɪbəl] adj unerschöpflich

inexorable [ɪn'eksərəbəl] adj unerbittlich

inexpensive [‚ɪnek'spensɪv] adj billig

inexperience [‚ɪnek'spɪrɪ·əns] s Unerfahrenheit f

inexpe'rienced adj unerfahren

inexplicable [ɪn'eksplɪkəbəl] adj uner-
klärlich

inexpressible [‚ɪnek'spresɪbəl] adj unaussprechlich

infallibility [‚ɪnfælɪ'bɪlɪti] s Unfehl-
barkeit f

infallible [ɪn'fælɪbəl] adj unfehlbar

infamous ['ɪnfəməs] adj schändlich

infamy ['ɪnfəmi] s Schändlichkeit f

infancy ['ɪnfənsi] s Kindheit f; be still
in its i. (fig) noch in den Kinder-
schuhen stecken

infant ['ɪnfənt] adj Säuglings– || s
Kleinkind n, Säugling m

infantile ['ɪnfən‚taɪl] adj infantil

in'fantile paral'ysis s Kinderlähmung f

infantry ['ɪnfəntri] s Infanterie f

in'fantry‑man s (–men) Infanterist m

infatuated [ɪn'fæt/ʊ‚etɪd] adj betört

infatuation [ɪn‚fæt/ʊ'e/ən] s Betörung
f

infect [ɪn'fɛkt] tr anstecken, infizieren; **become infected** sich anstecken

infection [ɪn'fɛk/ən] s Ansteckung f

infectious [ɪn'fɛk/əs] adj (& fig) ansteckend

in‑fer [ɪn'fʌr] v (pret & pp –ferred;
ger –ferring) tr folgern

inference ['ɪnfərəns] s Folgerung f

inferior [ɪn'fɪrɪ·ər] adj (in rank) niedriger; (in worth) minderwertig; (to)
unterlegen (dat)

inferiority [ɪn‚fɪrɪ'ɑrɪti] s Unterlegen-
heit f; (in worth) Minderwertigkeit f

inferior'ity com'plex s Minderwertig-
keitskomplex m

infernal [ɪn'fʌrnəl] adj höllisch

infest [ɪn'fest] tr in Schwärmen überfallen; **be infested with** wimmeln von

infidel ['ɪnfɪdəl] adj ungläubig || s
Ungläubige mf

infidelity [‚ɪnfɪ'delɪti] s Untreue f

in'field' s (baseball) Innenfeld n

infiltrate [ɪn'fɪltret], ['ɪnfɪl‚tret] tr
(filter through) infiltrieren; (mil)
durchsickern durch; (pol) unterwan-
dern || intr infiltrieren

infinite ['ɪnfɪnɪt] adj unendlich

infinitive [ɪn'fɪnɪtɪv] s (gram) Nennform f, Infinitiv m

infinity [ɪn'fɪnɪti] s Unendlichkeit f;
to i. endlos

infirm [ɪn'fʌrm] adj schwach; (from
age) altersschwach

infirmary [ɪn'fʌrməri] s Krankenstube
f; (mil) Revier n

infirmity [ɪn'fʌrmɪti] s Schwachheit f

inflame [ɪn'flem] tr (fig & pathol) entzünden; **become inflamed** sich entzünden

inflammable [ɪn'flæməbəl] adj entzündbar, feuergefährlich

inflammation [‚ɪnflə'me/ən] s Entzündung f

inflammatory [ɪn'flæmə‚tori] adj aufrührerisch; (pathol) Entzündungs–

inflate [ɪn'flet] tr aufblasen; (tires)
aufpumpen

inflation [ɪn'fle/ən] s (econ) Inflation
f

inflationary [ɪn'fle/ə‚neri] adj infla-
tionistisch

inflect [ɪn'flɛkt] tr (the voice) modulieren; (gram) flektieren

inflection [ɪn'flɛk/ən] s (of the voice)
Tonfall m; (gram) Flexion f

inflexible [ɪn'flɛksɪbəl] adj unbiegsam;
(person) unbeugsam; (law) unabän-
derlich

inflict [ɪn'flɪkt] tr (punishment) (on)
auferlegen (dat); (a defeat) (on) zufügen (dat); (a wound) (on) beibringen (dat)

influence ['ɪnflu·əns] s (on) Einfluß m
(auf acc) || tr beeinflussen

influential [ɪnflu'en/əl] adj einfluß-
reich, maßgebend

influenza [‚ɪnflu'enzə] s Grippe f

influx ['ɪnflʌks] s Zufluß m

inform [ɪn'fɔrm] tr (of) benachrichti-
gen (von) || intr—i. against anzeigen

informal [ɪn'fɔrməl] adj zwanglos

informant [ɪn'fɔrmənt] s Gewährsmann m

information [‚ɪnfər'me/ən] s Nachricht
f, Auskunft f; (items of information)

Informationen *pl;* **a piece of i.** e–e Auskunft *f;* **for your i.** zu Ihrer Information

informa′tion desk′ *s* Auskunftstelle *f*

informative [ɪnˈfɔrmətɪv] *adj* belehrend

informed′ *adj* unterrichtet

informer [ɪnˈfɔrmər] *s* Denunziant –in *mf*

infraction [ɪnˈfrækʃən] *s* **(of)** Verstoß *m* **(gegen)**

infrared [ˌɪnfrəˈred] *adj* infrarot

infrequent [ɪnˈfrikwənt] *adj* selten

infringe [ɪnˈfrɪndʒ] *tr* verletzen ‖ *intr* **—i. on** eingreifen in *(acc)*

infringement [ɪnˈfrɪndʒmənt] *s* **(of a law)** Verletzung *f;* **(of a right)** Eingriff *m* **(in** *acc***)**

infuriate [ɪnˈfjurɪˌet] *tr* wütend machen

infuse [ɪnˈfjuz] *tr* **(& fig) (into)** einflößen *(dat)*

infusion [ɪnˈfjuʒən] *s* **(& fig)** Einflößung *f;* **(med)** Infusion *f*

ingenious [ɪnˈdʒinɪˌəs] *adj* erfinderisch

ingenuity [ˌɪndʒɪˈn(j)uˌɪti] *s* Erfindungsgabe *f,* Scharfsinn *m*

ingenuous [ɪnˈdʒɛnjuˌəs] *adj* aufrichtig; *(naive)* naiv

ingest [ɪnˈdʒɛst] *tr* zu sich nehmen

inglorious [ɪnˈglɔrɪˌəs] *adj* **(shameful)** unrühmlich; **(without honor)** ruhmlos

ingot [ˈɪŋgət] *s* Block *m;* **(of gold or silver)** Barren *m*

ingrained′, in′grained *adj* eingewurzelt

ingrate [ˈɪngret] *s* Undankbare *mf*

ingratiate [ɪnˈgreʃɪˌet] *tr*—**i. oneself with** sich einschmeicheln bei

ingra′tiating *adj* einschmeichelnd

ingratitude [ɪnˈgrætɪˌt(j)ud] *s* Undankbarkeit *f,* Undank *m*

ingredient [ɪnˈgridɪˌənt] *s* Bestandteil *m;* **(culin)** Zutat *f*

in′grown′ *adj* eingewachsen

inhabit [ɪnˈhæbɪt] *tr* bewohnen

inhabitant [ɪnˈhæbɪtənt] *s* Bewohner –in *mf,* Einwohner –in *mf*

inhale [ɪnˈhel] *tr & intr* einatmen; inhalieren

inherent [ɪnˈhɪrənt] *adj* innewohnend; *(right)* angeboren

inherit [ɪnˈhɛrɪt] *tr* **(biol, jur)** erben

inheritance [ɪnˈhɛrɪtəns] *s* Erbschaft *f*

inher′itance tax′ *s* Erbschaftssteuer *f*

inheritor [ɪnˈhɛrɪtər] *s* Erbe *m,* Erbin *f*

inhibit [ɪnˈhɪbɪt] *tr* hemmen, inhibieren

inhibition [ˌɪnɪˈbɪʃən] *s* Hemmung *f*

inhospitable [ɪnˈhɑspɪtəbəl] *adj* ungastlich; *(place)* unwirtlich

inhuman [ɪnˈhjumən] *adj* unmenschlich

inhumane [ˌɪnjuˈmen] *adj* inhuman

inhumanity [ˌɪnhjuˈmæniti] *s* Unmenschlichkeit *f*

inimical [ɪˈnɪmɪkəl] *adj* **(to)** abträglich *(dat)*

iniquity [ɪˈnɪkwɪti] *s* Niederträchtigkeit *f,* Ungerechtigkeit *f*

ini·tial [ɪnˈɪʃəl] *adj* anfänglich ‖ *s* Anfangsbuchstabe *m,* Initiale *f* ‖ *v*

(pret & pp **–tial[l]ed;** *ger* **–tial[l]ing)** *tr* mit den Initialen unterzeichnen

initially [ɪˈnɪʃəli] *adv* anfangs

initiate [ɪˈnɪʃɪˌet] *tr* einführen; *(reforms)* einleiten; **(into)** aufnehmen in *(acc)*

initiation [ɪˌnɪʃɪˈeʃən] *s* Einführung *f;* **(into)** Aufnahme *f* **(in** *acc***)**

initiative [ɪˈnɪʃ(ɪ)ətɪv] *s* Unternehmungsgeist *m;* **take the i.** die Initiative ergreifen

inject [ɪnˈdʒɛkt] *tr* **(a needle)** einführen; **(a word)** dazwischenwerfen; *(e.g., bigotry into a campaign)* einfließen lassen; **(a liquid) (med)** injizieren

injection [ɪnˈdʒɛkʃən] *s* **(mach)** Einspritzung *f;* **(med)** Injektion *f*

injudicious [ˌɪndʒuˈdɪʃəs] *adj* unverständig

injunction [ɪnˈdʒʌŋkʃən] *s* Gebot *n;* **(jur)** gerichtliche Verfügung *f*

injure [ˈɪndʒər] *tr* verletzen; *(fig)* schädigen

injurious [ɪnˈdʒurɪˌəs] *adj* schädlich

injury [ˈɪndʒəri] *s* Verletzung *f;* **(to)** Schädigung *f (genit)*

injustice [ɪnˈdʒʌstɪs] *s* Ungerechtigkeit *f*

ink [ɪŋk] *s* Tinte *f* ‖ *tr* schwärzen

inkling [ˈɪŋklɪŋ] *s* leise Ahnung *f*

ink′ pad′ *s* Stempelkissen *n*

ink′ spot′ *s* Tintenklecks *m*

inky [ˈɪŋki] *adj* tiefschwarz

inlaid [ˈɪnˌled] *adj* eingelegt

in′laid floor′ *s* Parkettfußboden *m*

inland [ˈɪnlənd] *adj* Binnen– ‖ *adv* landeinwärts ‖ *s* Binnenland *n*

in′-laws′ *spl* angeheiratete Verwandte *pl*

inlay [ˈɪnˌle] *s* Einlegearbeit *f;* **(dent)** gegossene Plombe *f*

inlet *s* Meeresarm *m;* **(opening)** Öffnung *f*

in′mate *s* Insasse *m,* Insassin *f*

inn [ɪn] *s* Gasthaus *n,* Wirtshaus *n*

innards [ˈɪnərdʒ] *spl* **(coll)** Innere *n*

innate [ɪˈnet] *adj* angeboren

inner [ˈɪnər] *adj* innere, inwendig, Innen–

in′nermost′ *adj* innerste

in′nerspring mat′tress *s* Federkernmatratze *f*

in′ner tube′ *s* Schlauch *m*

inning [ˈɪnɪŋ] *s* Runde *f*

inn′keep′er *s* Wirt *m,* Wirtin *f*

innocence [ˈɪnəsəns] *s* Unschuld *f;* **(of a crime)** Schuldlosigkeit *f*

innocent [ˈɪnəsənt] *adj* **(of)** unschuldig **(an** *dat***);** *(harmless)* harmlos; *(guileless)* arglos ‖ *s* Unschuldige *mf*

innocuous [ɪˈnɑkjuˌəs] *adj* harmlos

innovation [ˌɪnəˈveʃən] *s* Neuerung *f*

innovative [ˈɪnəˌvetɪv] *adj* *(person)* neuerungssüchtig; *(thing)* Neuerungs–

innuen·do [ˌɪnjuˈendo] *s* **(–does)** Unterstellung *f*

innumerable [ɪˈn(j)umərəbəl] *adj* unzählbar, unzählig

inoculate [ɪnˈɑkjəˌlet] *tr* impfen

inoculation [ɪnˌɑkjəˈleʃən] *s* Impfung *f*

inoffensive [ˌɪnəˈfensɪv] *adj* unschädlich

inopportune [ɪnˌɒpərˈt(j)un] *adj* ungelegen

inordinate [ɪnˈɔrdɪnɪt] *adj* übermäßig

inorganic [ˌɪnɔrˈgænɪk] *adj* unorganisch; (chem) anorganisch

in'put' *put'* (data proc) Eingabe– ‖ *s* (in production) Aufwand *m*; (data proc) Eingabe *f*, Eingangsinformation *f*; (elec) Stromzufuhr *f*

inquest [ˈɪnkwest] *s* Untersuchung *f*

inquire [ɪnˈkwaɪr] *intr* anfragen; **i. about** sich erkundigen nach; **i. into** untersuchen; **i. of** sich erkundigen bei

inquiry [ɪnˈkwaɪri], [ˈɪnkwɪri] *s* Anfrage *f*; (investigation) Untersuchung *f*; **make inquiries (about)** Erkundigungen einziehen (über *acc*)

inquisition [ˌɪnkwɪˈzɪʃən] *s* Inquisition *f*

inquisitive [ɪnˈkwɪzɪtɪv] *adj* wißbegierig

in'road *s* (raid) Einfall *m*; (fig) Eingriff *m*

ins' and outs' *spl* alle Kniffe *pl*

insane [ɪnˈsen] *adj* wahnsinnig; (absurd) unsinnig

insane' asy'lum *s* Irrenanstalt *f*

insanity [ɪnˈsænɪti] *s* Wahnsinn *m*

insatiable [ɪnˈseʃəbəl] *adj* unersättlich

inscribe [ɪnˈskraɪb] *tr* (a name) einschreiben; (a book) widmen; (a monument) mit e–r Inschrift versehen

inscription [ɪnˈskrɪpʃən] *s* Inschrift *f*; (of a book) Widmung *f*

inscrutable [ɪnˈskrutəbəl] *adj* unerforschlich

insect [ˈɪnsekt] *s* Insekt *n*, Kerbtier *n*

insecticide [ɪnˈsektɪˌsaɪd] *s* Insektenvertilgungsmittel *n*, Insektizid *n*

insecure [ˌɪnsɪˈkjur] *adj* unsicher

insecurity [ˌɪnsɪˈkjurɪti] *s* Unsicherheit *f*

insensitive [ɪnˈsensɪtɪv] *adj* (to) unempfindlich (gegen)

inseparable [ɪnˈsepərəbəl] *adj* untrennbar; (friends) unzertrennlich

insert [ˈɪnsʌrt] *s* Einsatzstück *n* ‖ [ɪnˈsʌrt] *tr* einfügen; (a coin) einwerfen

insertion [ɪnˈsʌrʃən] *s* Einfügung *f*; (of a coin) Einwurf *m*

in'set' (of a map) Nebenkarte *f*; (inserted piece) Einsatz *m*

in'shore' *adj* Küsten– ‖ *adv* auf die Küste zu

in'side' *adj* innere, Innen–; (information) vertraulich ‖ *adv* innen, drinnen; **come i.** hereinkommen; **i. of** innerhalb von; **i. out** verkehrt; **know i. out** in– und auswendig kennen; **turn i. out** umdrehen ‖ *s* Innenseite *f*, Innere *n*; **on the i.** innen ‖ *prep* innerhalb (genit)

insider [ɪnˈsaɪdər] *s* Eingeweihte *mf*

in'side track' *s* (sport) Innenbahn *f*; **have the i.** (fig) im Vorteil sein

insidious [ɪnˈsɪdɪ·əs] *adj* hinterlistig

in'sight' *s* Einsicht *f*

insigni·a [ɪnˈsɪgnɪ·ə] *s* (–a & –as) Abzeichen *n*; **i. of office** Amtsabzeichen *pl*; **i. of rank** Rangabzeichen *pl*

insignificant [ˌɪnsɪgˈnɪfɪkənt] *adj* bedeutungslos, geringfügig

insincere [ˌɪnsɪnˈsɪr] *adj* unaufrichtig

insincerity [ˌɪnsɪnˈserɪti] *s* Unaufrichtigkeit *f*

insinuate [ɪnˈsɪnju·ˌet] *tr* andeuten

insipid [ɪnˈsɪpɪd] *adj* (& fig) fad(e)

insist [ɪnˈsɪst] *intr*—**i. on** bestehen auf (dat); **i. on** (ger) darauf bestehen zu (inf)

insistent [ɪnˈsɪstənt] *adj* beharrlich

insofar as [ˌɪnsoˈfar ˌæz] *conj* insoweit als

insolence [ˈɪnsələns] *s* Unverschämtheit *f*

insolent [ˈɪnsələnt] *adj* unverschämt

insoluble [ɪnˈsaljəbəl] *adj* unlösbar

insolvency [ɪnˈsalvənsi] *s* Zahlungsunfähigkeit *f*, Insolvenz *f*

insolvent [ɪnˈsalvənt] *adj* zahlungsunfähig

insomnia [ɪnˈsamnɪ·ə] *s* Schlaflosigkeit *f*

insomuch as [ˌɪnsoˈmʌtʃəz] *conj* insofern als

inspect [ɪnˈspekt] *tr* (view closely) besichtigen; (check) kontrollieren; (aut) untersuchen; (mil) besichtigen

inspection [ɪnˈspekʃən] *s* Besichtigung *f*; Kontrolle *f*; (aut) Untersuchung *f*; (mil) Truppenbesichtigung *f*

inspector [ɪnˈspektər] *s* Kontrolleur *m*; (of police) Inspektor *m*

inspiration [ˌɪnspɪˈreʃən] *s* Begeisterung *f*

inspire [ɪnˈspaɪr] *tr* begeistern; (feelings) erwecken

inspir'ing *adj* begeisternd

instability [ˌɪnstəˈbɪlɪti] *s* Unbeständigkeit *f*

install [ɪnˈstɔl] *tr* (appliances) installieren; (in office) einführen

installation [ˌɪnstəˈleʃən] *s* (of appliances) Installation *f*; (mil) Anlage *f*

installment [ɪnˈstɔlmənt] *s* Installation *f*; (in a serialized story) Fortsetzung *f*; (partial payment) Rate *f*; **in installments** ratenweise

install'ment plan' *s* Teilzahlungsplan *m*

instance [ˈɪnstəns] *s* (case) Fall *m*; (example) Beispiel *n*; (jur) Instanz *f*; **for i.** zum Beispiel

instant [ˈɪnstənt] *adj* augenblicklich; (foods) gebrauchsfertig ‖ *s* Augenblick *m*; **this i.** sofort

instantaneous [ˌɪnstənˈtenɪ·əs] *adj* augenblicklich, sofortig

instead [ɪnˈsted] *adv* statt dessen

instead' of *prep* (an)statt (genit); (ger) anstatt zu (inf)

in'step' *s* Rist *m*

instigate [ˈɪnstɪˌget] *tr* anstiften

instigation [ˌɪnstɪˈgeʃən] *s* Anstiftung *f*

instigator [ˈɪnstɪˌgetər] *s* Anstifter –in *mf*

instill [ɪnˈstɪl] *tr* einflößen

instinct [ˈɪnstɪŋkt] *s* Trieb *m*, Instinkt *m*; **by i.** instinktiv

instinctive [ɪnˈstɪŋktɪv] *adj* instinktiv

institute ['instɪ‚t(j)ut] s Institut n ‖ tr einleiten

institution [‚ɪnstɪ't(j)uʃən] s Anstalt f

instruct [ɪn'strʌkt] tr anweisen, beauftragen; (teach) unterrichten

instruction [ɪn'strʌkʃən] s (teaching) Unterricht m; **instructions** Anweisungen pl; **instructions for use** Gebrauchsanweisung f

instructive [ɪn'strʌktɪv] adj lehrreich

instructor [ɪn'strʌktər] s Lehrer –in mf; (at a university) Dozent –in mf

instrument ['ɪnstrəmənt] s Instrument n; (tool) Werkzeug n; (jur) Dokument n

instrumental [‚ɪnstrə'mentəl] adj (mus) instrumental; he was i. in my getting an award er war mir behilflich, e-n Preis zu erhalten

instrumentality [‚ɪnstrəmən'tælɪti] s Vermittlung f

in'strument land'ing s Instrumentenlandung f

in'strument pan'el s Armaturenbrett n

insubordinate [‚ɪnsə'bɔrdɪnɪt] adj widersetzlich

insubordination [‚ɪnsəbɔrdɪ'neʃən] s Widersetzlichkeit f

insufferable [ɪn'sʌfərəbəl] adj unausstehlich

insufficient [‚ɪnsə'fɪʃənt] adj ungenügend, unzureichend

insular ['ɪns(j)ələr] adj insular

insulate ['ɪnsə‚let] tr isolieren

insulation [‚ɪnsə'leʃən] s Isolierung f; (insulating material) Isolierstoff m

insulator ['ɪnsə‚letər] s Isolator m

insulin ['ɪnsəlɪn] s Insulin n

insult ['ɪnsʌlt] s Beleidigung f ‖ [ɪn-'sʌlt] tr beleidigen, beschimpfen

insurance [ɪn'ʃurəns] adj Versicherungs- ‖ s Versicherung f

insure [ɪn'ʃur] tr versichern

insured' adj (letter, package) Wert- ‖ s Versicherungsnehmer –in mf

insurer [ɪn'ʃurər] s Versicherer –in mf

insurgent [ɪn'sʌrdʒənt] adj aufständisch ‖ s Aufständische mf

insurmountable [‚ɪnsər'mauntəbəl] adj unübersteigbar; (fig) unüberwindlich

insurrection [‚ɪnsə'rekʃən] s Aufstand m

intact [ɪn'tækt] adj unversehrt

in'take s (aut) Einlaß m; i. of food Nahrungsaufnahme f

in'take valve' s Einlaßventil n

intangible [ɪn'tændʒɪbəl] adj immateriell

integer ['ɪntɪdʒər] s ganze Zahl f

integral ['ɪntɪgrəl] adj wesentlich; (math) Integral- ‖ s Integral n

integrate ['ɪntɪ‚gret] tr eingliedern; (a school) die Rassentrennung aufheben in (dat); (& math) integrieren

integration [‚ɪntɪ'greʃən] s Integration f; (of schools) Aufhebung f der Rassentrennung

integrity [ɪn'tegrɪti] s Redlichkeit f

intellect ['ɪntə‚lekt] s Intellekt m

intellectual [‚ɪntə'lektʃʊ-əl] adj intellektuell; (freedom, history) Geistes- ‖ s Intellektuelle mf

intelligence [ɪn'telɪdʒəns] s Intelligenz f, Klugheit f; (information) Nachricht f; (department) Nachrichtendienst m; gather i. Nachrichten einziehen

intel'ligence quo'tient s Intelligenz-Quotient m

intel'ligence test' s Begabungsprüfung f

intelligent [ɪn'telɪdʒənt] adj intelligent, klug

intelligentsia [ɪn‚telɪ'dʒentsɪ-ə] s Intelligenz f, geistige Oberschicht f

intelligible [ɪn'telɪdʒɪbəl] adj (to) verständlich (dat)

intemperate [ɪn'tempərɪt] adj unmäßig; (in drink) trunksüchtig

intend [ɪn'tend] tr beabsichtigen; be intended for bestimmt sein für, gemünzt sein auf (acc) i. by bezwecken mit; i. for s.o. j-m zudenken

intend'ed s (coll) Verlobte mf

intense [ɪn'tens] adj intensiv, stark

intensify [ɪn'tensɪ‚faɪ] v (pret & pp –fied) tr steigern, verstärken ‖ intr sich steigern, stärker werden

intensity [ɪn'tensɪti] s Stärke f

intensive [ɪn'tensɪv] adj intensiv; (gram) verstärkend

inten'sive care' s Intensivstation f

intent [ɪn'tent] adj (on) erpicht (auf acc) ‖ s Absicht f; to all intents and purposes praktisch genommen

intention [ɪn'tenʃən] s Absicht f; good i. guter Wille m; have honorable intentions es ehrlich meinen; with the i. of (ger) in der Absicht zu (inf)

intentional [ɪn'tenʃənəl] adj absichtlich

intently [ɪn'tentli] adv gespannt

inter [ɪn'tar] v (pret & pp –terred; ger –terring) tr beerdigen

interact [‚ɪntər'ækt] intr zusammenwirken, aufeinander wirken

interaction [‚ɪntər'ækʃən] s Wechselwirkung f

inter·breed [‚ɪntər'brid] v (pret & pp –bred) tr kreuzen ‖ intr sich kreuzen

intercede [‚ɪntər'sid] intr Fürsprache einlegen; i. for s.o. with Fürsprache einlegen für j-n bei

intercept [‚ɪntər'sept] tr (a letter, aircraft) abfangen; (a radio message) abhören; (cut off, check) den Weg abschneiden (dat)

interceptor [‚ɪntər'septər] s (aer) Abfangjäger m

intercession [‚ɪntər'seʃən] s Fürsprache f; (relig) Fürbitte f

interchange [‚ɪntər‚tʃendʒ] s Wechsel m; (on a highway) Anschlußstelle f ‖ [‚ɪntər'tʃendʒ] tr auswechseln ‖ intr (with) abwechseln (mit)

interchangeable [‚ɪntər'tʃendʒəbəl] adj auswechselbar, austauschbar

intercom ['ɪntər‚kam] s Wechselsprachanlage f

intercourse ['ɪntər‚kors] s Verkehr m; (sexual) Geschlechtsverkehr m

interdependent [‚ɪntərdɪ'pendənt] adj voneinander abhängig

interdict ['ɪntər‚dɪkt] s Verbot n; (eccl) Interdikt n ‖ [‚ɪntər'dɪkt] tr

verbieten; **i. s.o. from** (*ger*) j—m verbieten zu (*inf*)
interest ['int(ə)rɪst] *s* (**in**) Interesse *n* (**an** *dat*, für); (fin) Zinsen *pl;* **at i.** gegen Zinsen; **be in s.o.'s i.** in j-s Interesse liegen; **have an i. in** beteiligt sein an (*dat*) or bei; **interests** Belange *pl;* **pay i.** (*bring in interest*) Zinsen abwerfen; (*pay out interest*) Zinsen zahlen; **i. in** sich interessieren für; **with i.** (& fig) mit Zinsen ‖ *tr* (**in**) interessieren (für)
in'terested *adj*—**i.** in interessiert an (*dat*); **the i. parties** die Beteiligten *pl*
in'teresting *adj* interessant
in'terest rate' *s* Zinsfuß *m,* Zinssatz *m*
interfere [,ɪntər'fɪr] *intr* (*said of a thing*) dazwischenkommen; (*said of a person*) eingreifen; (**in** or **with**) sich (ein)mengen (**in** *acc*); **i. with** (rad, telv) stören; **i. with s.o.'s work** j—n bei seiner Arbeit stören
interference [,ɪntər'fɪrəns] *s* Einmischung *f;* (phys) Interferenz *f;* (rad, telv) Störung *f*
interim ['ɪntərɪm] *adj* Zwischen– ‖ *s* Zwischenzeit *f*
interior [ɪn'tɪrɪ·ər] *adj* innere, Innen– ‖ *s* Innere *n;* (*of a building*) Innenraum *m;* (*of a country*) Inland *n*
inte'rior dec'orator *s* Innenarchitekt –in *mf*
interject [,ɪntər'dʒɛkt] *tr* dazwischenwerfen
interjection [,ɪntər'dʒɛkʃən] *s* Zwischenwurf *m;* (gram) Interjektion *f*
interlard [,ɪntər'lard] *tr* (& fig) spicken
interlinear [,ɪntər'lɪnɪ·ər] *adj* interlinear
interlock [,ɪntər'lɑk] *tr* miteinander verbinden ‖ *intr* sich ineinanderschließen
interloper [,ɪntər'lopər] *s* Eindringling *m*
interlude ['ɪntər,lud] *s* (*interval*) Pause *f;* (fig, mus, theat) Zwischenspiel *n*
intermediary [,ɪntər'midɪ,ɛri] *adj* vermittelnd ‖ *s* Vermittler –in *mf*
intermediate [,ɪntər'midɪ·ɪt] *adj* zwischenliegend, Zwischen–
interment [ɪn'tʌrmənt] *s* Beerdigung *f*
intermez·zo [,ɪntər'metso] *s* (**–zos** & **zi** [tsi]) Intermezzo *n*
intermingle [,ɪntər'mɪŋgəl] *tr* vermischen ‖ *intr* sich vermischen
intermission [,ɪntər'mɪʃən] *s* Unterbrechung *f;* (theat) Pause *f*
intermittent [,ɪntər'mɪtənt] *adj* intermittierend
intermix [,ɪntər'mɪks] *tr* vermischen ‖ *intr* sich vermischen
intern ['ɪntʌrn] *s* Assistenzarzt *m,* Assistenzärztin *f*
internal [ɪn'tʌrnəl] *adj* innere, intern; (*domestic*) einheimisch, (*trade, rhyme*) Binnen–
inter'nal-combus'tion en'gine *s* Verbrennungsmotor *m*
inter'nal med'icine *s* innere Medizin *f*
inter'nal rev'enue *s* Steueraufkommen *n*

international [,ɪntər'næʃənəl] *adj* international
interna'tional date' line' *s* internationale Datumsgrenze *f*
interna'tional law' *s* Völkerrecht *n*
interne'cine war' [,ɪntər'nisɪn] *s* gegenseitiger Vernichtungskrieg *m*
internee [,ɪntər'ni] *s* Internierte *mf*
internment [ɪn'tʌrnmənt] *s* Internierung *f*
in'ternship' *s* Pflichtzeit *f* als Assistenzarzt (or Assistenzärztin)
interoffice [,ɪntər'ɑfɪs] *adj* Haus–
interplanetary [,ɪntər'plænɪ,teri] *adj* interplanetarisch
interplay ['ɪntər,ple] *s* Wechselspiel *n*
interpolate [ɪn'tʌrpə,let] *tr* interpolieren
interpose [,ɪntər'poz] *tr* (*an obstacle*) dazwischensetzen; (*a remark*) einwerfen
interpret [ɪn'tʌrprɪt] *tr* (& mus) interpretieren; (*translate*) verdolmetschen ‖ *intr* dolmetschen
interpretation [ɪn,tʌrprɪ'teʃən] *s* (& mus) Interpretation *f*
interpreter [ɪn'tʌrprɪtər] *s* Dolmetscher –in *mf;* **act as i.** dolmetschen
interrogate [ɪn'terə,get] *tr* ausfragen; (jur) verhören, vernehmen
interrogation [ɪn,terə'geʃən] *s* Verhör *n*
interrogative [,ɪntər'rɑgətɪv] *adj* Frage–
interrupt [,ɪntə'rʌpt] *tr* unterbrechen
interruption [,ɪntə'rʌpʃən] *s* Unterbrechung *f;* (*in industry*) Betriebsstörung *f*
intersect [,ɪntər'sekt] *tr* durchschneiden ‖ *ref* sich kreuzen
intersection [,ɪntər'sekʃən] *s* Straßenkreuzung *f;* (math) Schnittpunkt *m*
intersperse [,ɪntər'spʌrs] *tr* durchsetzen
interstate ['ɪntər,stet] *adj* zwischenstaatlich
interstellar [,ɪntər'stelər] *adj* interstellar
interstice [ɪn'tʌrstɪs] *s* Zwischenraum *m*
intertwine [,ɪntər'twaɪn] *tr* verflechten ‖ *intr* sich verflechten
interval ['ɪntərvəl] *s* Abstand *m;* (mus) Stufe *f,* Intervall *n*
intervene [,ɪntər'vin] *intr* dazwischenkommen; (*interfere*) eingreifen; (*intercede*) intervenieren
intervention [,ɪntər'venʃən] *s* Dazwischenkommen *n;* Eingreifen *n;* Intervention *f*
interview ['ɪntər,vju] *s* Interview *n* ‖ *tr* interviewen
inter·weave [,ɪntər'wiv] *v* (*pret* **–wove** & **–weaved;** *pp* **–wove, –woven** & **–weaved**) *tr* durchweben, durchflechten
intestate [ɪn'testet] *adj* ohne Testament
intestine [ɪn'testɪn] *s* Darm *m;* **intestines** Gedärme *pl*
intimacy ['ɪntɪməsɪ] *s* Vertraulichkeit *f;* **intimacies** Intimitäten *pl*
intimate ['ɪntɪmɪt] *adj* intim, vertraut

|| *s* Vertraute *mf* || ['ɪntɪ ˌmet] *tr* andeuten

intimation [ˌɪntɪ'meʃən] *s* Andeutung *f*

intimidate [ɪn'tɪmɪ ˌdet] *tr* einschüchtern

intimidation [ˌɪntɪmɪ'deʃən] *s* Einschüchterung *f*

into ['ɪntu], ['ɪntu] *prep* in (*acc*)

intolerable [ɪn'tɑlərəbəl] *adj* unerträglich

intolerance [ɪn'tɑlərəns] *s* (of) Intoleranz *f* (gegen)

intolerant [ɪn'tɑlərənt] *adj* (of) intolerant (gegen)

intonation [ˌɪnto'neʃən] *s* Tonfall *m*

intone [ɪn'ton] *tr* intonieren

intoxicate [ɪn'tɑksɪ ˌket] *tr* berauschen; (*poison*) vergiften

intoxication [ɪn ˌtɑksɪ'keʃən] *s* (& fig) Rausch *m*; (*poisoning*) Vergiftung *f*

intractable [ɪn'træktəbəl] *adj* (*person*) störrisch; (*thing*) schwer zu bearbeiten(d)

intransigent [ɪn'trænsɪdʒənt] *adj* unversöhnlich

intransitive [ɪn'trænsɪtɪv] *adj* intransitiv

intravenous [ˌɪntrə'vinəs] *adj* intravenös

intrepid [ɪn'trɛpɪd] *adj* unerschrocken

intricate [ˈɪntrɪkɪt] *adj* verwickelt

intrigue [ɪn'trig], ['ɪntrig] *s* Intrige *f* || [ɪn'trig] *tr* fesseln || *intr* intrigieren

intrigu'ing *adj* fesselnd

intrinsic(al) [ɪn'trɪnsɪk(əl)] *adj* innere, innerlich; (*value*) wirklich

introduce [ˌɪntrə'd(j)us] *tr* einführen; (*strangers*) vorstellen

introduction [ˌɪntrə'dʌkʃən] *s* Einführung *f*; (*of strangers*) Vorstellung *f*; (*in a book*) Einleitung *f*

introductory [ˌɪntrə'dʌktəri] *adj* (*offer, price*) Einführungs-; (*remarks*) einleitend

introspection [ˌɪntrə'spɛkʃən] *s* Selbstbeobachtung *f*

introspective [ˌɪntrə'spɛktɪv] *adj* introspektiv

introvert ['ɪntrə ˌvʌrt] *s* Introvertierte *mf*

intrude [ɪn'trud] *intr* (on) sich aufdrängen (dat); **am I intruding?** störe ich?

intruder [ɪn'trudər] *s* Eindringling *m*

intrusion [ɪn'truʒən] *s* Eindringen *n*, Stören *n*

intrusive [ɪn'trusɪv] *adj* störend, lästig

intuition [ˌɪnt(j)u'ɪʃən] *s* Intuition *f*

inundate ['ɪnən ˌdet] *tr* überschwemmen

inundation [ˌɪnən'deʃən] *s* Überschwemmung *f*

inure [ɪn'jur] *tr* (to) abhärten (gegen)

invade [ɪn'ved] *tr* (*a country*) eindringen in (*acc*); (*rights*) verletzen; (*privacy*) stören

invader [ɪn'vedər] *s* Eindringling *m*; (mil) Angreifer *m*

invalid [ɪn'vælɪd] *adj* ungültig || ['ɪnvəlɪd] *adj* kränklich || *s* Invalide *m*

invalidate [ɪn'vælɪ ˌdet] *tr* ungültig machen; (*a law*) außer Kraft setzen

invalidity [ˌɪnvə'lɪdɪti] *s* Ungültigkeit *f*

invaluable [ɪn'vælju·əbəl] *adj* unschätzbar

invariable [ɪn'vɛrɪ·əbəl] *adj* unveränderlich

invasion [ɪn've/ən] *s* Invasion *f*

invective [ɪn'vɛktɪv] *s* Schmähung *f*

inveigh [ɪn've] *intr*—**i. against** schimpfen über (*acc*) or auf (*acc*)

inveigle [ɪn'vigel] *tr* verleiten; **i. s.o. into** (*ger*) j-n verleiten zu (*inf*)

invent [ɪn'vɛnt] *tr* erfinden; (*a story*) sich [*dat*] ausdenken

invention [ɪn'vɛnʃən] *s* Erfindung *f*

inventive [ɪn'vɛntɪv] *adj* erfinderisch

inventiveness [ɪn'vɛntɪvnɪs] *s* Erfindungsgabe *f*

inventor [ɪn'vɛntər] *s* Erfinder –in *mf*

invento·ry ['ɪnvən ˌtori] *s* (*stock*) Inventar *n*; (*act*) Inventur *f*; (*list*) Bestandsverzeichnis *n*; **take i.** Inventur machen || *v* (*pret & pp* –**ried**) *tr* inventarisieren

inverse [ɪn'vʌrs] *adj* umgekehrt

inversion [ɪn'vʌrʒən] *s* Umkehrung *f*; (gram) Umstellung *f*

invert [ɪn'vʌrt] *tr* umkehren; (gram) umstellen

invertebrate [ɪn'vʌrtɪ ˌbret] *adj* wirbellos || *s* wirbelloses Tier *n*

invest [ɪn'vɛst] *tr* (in) investieren (in *acc*); (mil) belagern; **i. with** ausstatten mit

investigate [ɪn'vɛstɪ ˌget] *tr* untersuchen

investigation [ɪn ˌvɛstɪ'geʃən] *s* Untersuchung *f*

investigator [ɪn'vɛstɪ ˌgetər] *s* Untersucher –in *mf*

investment [ɪn'vɛstmənt] *s* Anlage *f*, Investition *f*; (*with an office*) Amtseinführung *f*; (mil) Belagerung *f*

investor [ɪn'vɛstər] *s* Investor –in *mf*

inveterate [ɪn'vɛtərɪt] *adj* (*habitual*) eingefleischt; (*firmly established*) eingewurzelt

invidious [ɪn'vɪdɪ·əs] *adj* haßerregend

invigorate [ɪn'vɪgə ˌret] *tr* beleben

invig'orating *adj* belebend

invincible [ɪn'vɪnsɪbəl] *adj* unbesiegbar

invisible [ɪn'vɪzɪbəl] *adj* unsichtbar

invis'ible ink' *s* Geheimtinte *f*

invitation [ˌɪnvɪ'teʃən] *s* Einladung *f*

invite [ɪn'vaɪt] *tr* einladen; **i. in** hereinbitten

invit'ing *adj* lockend

invocation [ˌɪnvə'keʃən] *s* Anrufung *f*; (relig) Bittgebet *n*

invoice ['ɪnvɔɪs] *s* Faktura *f*, Warenrechnung *f*; **as per i.** laut Rechnung || *tr* fakturieren

invoke [ɪn'vok] *tr* anrufen; (*cite*) zitieren

involuntary [ɪn'vɑlən ˌteri] *adj* (*against one's will*) unfreiwillig; (*without one's will*) unwillkürlich

invol'untary man'slaughter *s* unbeabsichtigte Tötung *f*

involve [ɪn'vɑlv] *tr* verwickeln; (*include*) einschließen; (*affect*) betreffen; (*entail*) zur Folge haben

involved' *adj* verwickelt, kompliziert; **be i. in** (*e.g., construction*) beschäftigt sein bei; (*e.g., a crime*) verwickelt sein in (*acc*); **be i. with** (*e.g., a married person*) e–e Affäre haben mit

involvement [ɪn'vɑlʌmənt] *s* Verwicklung *f*

invulnerable [ɪn'vʌlnərəbəl] *adj* unverwundbar

inward ['ɪnwərd] *adj* inner(lich) || *adv* nach innen

inwardly ['ɪnwərdli] *adv* innerlich

iodine ['aɪ·ə,din] *s* (chem) Jod *n* || ['aɪ·ə,daɪn] *s* (pharm) Jodtinktur *f*

ion ['aɪ·ɑn], ['aɪ·ən] *s* Ion *n*

ionize ['aɪ·ə,naɪz] *tr* ionisieren

IOU ['aɪ,o'ju] *s* (**I owe you**) Schuldschein *m*

I.Q. ['aɪ'kju] *s* (**intelligence quotient**) Intelligenz-Quotient *m*

Iran [ɪ'rɑn], [aɪ'ræn] *s* Iran *m*

Iranian [aɪ'reni·ən] *adj* iranisch || *s* Iran(i)er –in *mf*

Iraq [ɪ'rɑk] *s* Irak *m*

Ira-qi [ɪ'rɑki] *adj* irakisch || *s* (–qis) Iraker –in *mf*

irascible [ɪ'ræsɪbəl] *adj* jähzornig

irate ['aɪret], [aɪ'ret] *adj* zornig

ire [aɪr] *s* Zorn *m*

Ireland ['aɪrlənd] *s* Irland *n*

iris ['aɪrɪs] *s* (anat, bot) Iris *f*

Irish ['aɪrɪʃ] *adj* irisch || *s* (*language*) Irisch *n*; **the I.** die Iren *pl*

I'rish·man *s* (–men) Ire *m*

I'rishwom'an *s* (–wom'en) Irin *f*

irk [ʌrk] *tr* ärgern

irksome ['ʌrksəm] *adj* ärgerlich

iron ['aɪ·ərn] *adj* (& fig) eisern || *s* Eisen *n*; (*for pressing clothes*) Bügeleisen *n* || *tr* bügeln; **i. out** ausbügeln; (fig) ins Reine bringen

ironclad ['aɪ·ərn,klæd] *adj* (fig) unumstößlich

i'ron cur'tain *s* eiserner Vorhang *m*

ironic(al) [aɪ'rɑnɪk(əl)] *adj* ironisch

i'roning *s* (*act*) Bügeln *n*; (*clothes*) Bügelwäsche *f*

i'roning board' *s* Bügelbrett *n*

i'ron lung' *s* eiserne Lunge *f*

i'ron ore' *s* Eisenerz *n*

irony ['aɪrəni] *s* Ironie *f*

irradiate [ɪ'redɪ,et] *tr* bestrahlen; (*light*) ausstrahlen; (*a face*) aufheitern

irrational [ɪ'ræʃənəl] *adj* irrational

irreconcilable [,ɪrekən'saɪləbəl] *adj* unversöhnlich

irredeemable [,ɪrɪ'diməbəl] *adj* (*loan, bond*) nicht einlösbar; (*hopeless*) hoffnunglos

irrefutable [,ɪrɪ'fjutəbəl] *adj* unwiderlegbar

irregular [ɪ'regjələr] *adj* unregelmäßig

irregularity [ɪ,regjə'lærɪti] *s* Unregelmäßigkeit *f*

irrelevant [ɪ'reləvənt] *adj* (**to**) nicht anwendbar (auf *acc*)

irreligious [,ɪrɪ'lɪdʒəs] *adj* irreligiös

irreparable [ɪ'repərəbəl] *adj* unersetzlich

irreplaceable [,ɪrɪ'plesɪbəl] *adj* unersetzlich

irrepressible [,ɪrɪ'presɪbəl] *adj* unbezähmbar

irreproachable [,ɪrɪ'protʃəbəl] *adj* untadelig

irresistible [,ɪrɪ'zɪstɪbəl] *adj* unwiderstehlich

irresolute [ɪ'rezəlut] *adj* unentschlossen, unschlüßig

irrespective [,ɪrɪ'spektɪv] *adj*—**i. of** ohne Rücksicht auf (*acc*)

irresponsible [,ɪrɪ'spɑnsɪbəl] *adj* unverantwortlich

irretrievable [,ɪrɪ'trivəbəl] *adj* unwiederbringlich, unrettbar

irreverent [ɪ'revərənt] *adj* unehrerbietig

irrevocable [ɪ'revəkəbəl] *adj* unwiderruflich

irrigate ['ɪrɪ,get] *tr* verwässern; (med) irrigieren

irrigation [,ɪrɪ'geʃən] *s* Bewässerung *f*

irritable ['ɪrɪtəbəl] *adj* reizbar

irritant ['ɪrɪtənt] *s* Reizstoff *m*

irritate ['ɪrɪ,tet] *tr* reizen, irritieren

irritation [,ɪrɪ'teʃən] *s* Reizung *f*

irruption [ɪ'rʌpʃən] *s* Einbruch *m*

isinglass ['aɪzɪŋ,glæs] *s* Fischleim *m*; (*mica*) Glimmer *m*

Islam ['ɪsləm] *s* Islam *m*

island ['aɪlənd] *s* Insel *f*

islander ['aɪləndər] *s* Insulaner –in *mf*

isle [aɪl] *s* kleine Insel *f*

isolate ['aɪsə,let] *tr* isolieren

isolation [,aɪsə'leʃən] *s* Isolierung *f*

isolationist [,aɪsə'leʃənɪst] *s* Isolationist –in *mf*

isola'tion ward' *s* Isolierstation *f*

isometric [,aɪsə'metrɪk] *adj* isometrisch

isosceles [aɪ'sɑsə,liz] *adj* gleichschenklig

isotope ['aɪsə,top] *s* Isotop *n*

Israel ['ɪzrɪ·əl] *s* Israel *n*

Israe-li [ɪz'reli] *adj* israelisch || *s* (–li) Israeli *m*

Israelite ['ɪzrɪ·ə,laɪt] *adj* israelitisch || *s* Israelit –in *mf*

issuance ['ɪʃu·əns] *s* Ausgabe *f*

issue ['ɪʃu] *s* (*of a magazine*) Nummer *f*; (*result*) Ausgang *m*; (*e.g., of securities*) Ausgabe *f*, Emission *f*; (*under discussion*) Streitpunkt *m*; (*offspring*) Nachkommenschaft *f*; **avoid the i.** der Frage ausweichen; **be at i.** zur Debatte stehen; **make an i. of it** e–e Streitfrage daraus machen; **take i.** with anderer Meinung sein als || *tr* (*orders, supplies, stamps, stocks*) ausgeben; (*a pass*) ausstellen || *intr* (**from**) herauskommen (aus)

isthmus ['ɪsməs] *s* Landenge *f*

it [ɪt] *pron* es; **about it** darüber, davon; **it is I** ich bin es

Italian [ɪ'tæljən] *adj* italienisch || *s* (*person*) Italiener –in *mf*; (*language*) Italienisch *n*

italicize [ɪ'tælɪ,saɪz] *tr* kursiv drucken

italics [ɪ'tælɪks] *spl* Kursivschrift *f*

Italy ['ɪtəli] *s* Italien *n*

itch [ɪtʃ] *s* Jucken *n*; (pathol) Krätze *f* ‖ *intr* jucken; **I am itching to** (*inf*) es reizt mich zu (*inf*); **my nose itches** me es juckt mich in der Nase

itchy ['ɪtʃi] *adj* juckend; (pathol) krätzig

item ['aɪtəm] *s* Artikel *m*; (*in a list*) Punkt *m*; (com) Posten *m*; (journ) Nachricht *f*; **hot i.** (coll) Schlager *m*

itemize ['aɪtə,maɪz] *tr* einzeln aufführen

itinerant [aɪ'tɪnərənt], [ɪ'tɪnərənt] *adj* Wander-, reisend ‖ *s* Reisende *mf*

itinerary [aɪ'tɪnə,reri] *s* Reiseplan *m*

its [ɪts] *poss adj* sein

itself *reflex pron* sich; **in i.** an und für sich ‖ *intens pron* selbst, selber

ivied ['aɪvid] *adj* efeubewachsen

ivory ['aɪvəri] *adj* elfenbeinern, Elfenbein–; (*color*) kremfarben ‖ *s* Elfenbein *n*; **tickle the ivories** in die Tasten greifen

i'vory tow'er *s* (fig) Elfenbeinturm *m*

ivy ['aɪvi] *s* Efeu *m*

J

J, j [dʒe] *s* zehnter Buchstabe des englischen Alphabets

jab [dʒæb] *s* Stoß *m*; (box) Gerade *f* ‖ *v* (*pret & pp* jabbed; *ger* jabbing) *tr* stoßen; (box) mit der Gerade stoßen

jabber ['dʒæbər] *tr & intr* plappern

jack [dʒæk] *s* (*money*) (sl) Pinke *f*; (aut) Wagenheber *m*; (cards) Bube *m*; (telp) Klinke *f*; **Jack Hans** *m* ‖ *tr*—**j. up** (aut) heben; (*prices*) hinaufschrauben

jackal ['dʒækəl] *s* Schakal *m*

jack'ass' *s* Esel *m*

jacket ['dʒækɪt] *s* Jacke *f*; (*of a book*) Umschlag *m*; (*of a potato*) Schale *f*

Jack' Frost' *s* Herr Winter *m*

jack'ham'mer *s* Preßlufthammer *m*

jack'-in-the-box' *s* Kastenteufel *m*

jack'knife' *s* (–knives) Klappmesser *n*; (*dive*) Hechtbeuge *f* ‖ *intr* zusammenklappen

jack'-of-all'-trades' *s* Hansdampf *m* in allen Gassen

jack'pot' *s* Jackpot *m*; **hit the j.** das Große Los gewinnen

jack' rab'bit *s* Hase *m*

Jacob ['dʒekəb] *s* Jakob *m*

jade [dʒed] *adj* jadegrün ‖ *s* (*stone*) Jade *m*; (*color*) Jadegrün *n*; (*horse*) Schindmähre *f*

jad'ed *adj* ermattet

jag [dʒæg] *s* Zacke *f*; **have a jag on** (sl) e–n Schwips haben

jagged ['dʒægɪd] *adj* zackig, schartig

jaguar ['dʒægwar] *s* Jaguar *m*

jail [dʒel] *s* Gefängnis *n*, Untersuchungsgefängnis *n*; **be in j.** sitzen ‖ *tr* einsperren

jail'bird' *s* Knastbruder *m*

jailer ['dʒelər] *s* Gefängniswärter *m*

jalopy [dʒə'lɑpi] *s* Rumpelkasten *m*

jal'ousie win'dow ['dʒæləsi] *s* Glasjalousie *f*

jam [dʒæm] *s* Marmelade *f*; **be in a jam** (coll) in der Patsche sitzen ‖ *v* (*pret & pp* jammed; *ger* jamming) *tr* (*a room*) überfüllen; (*a street*) verstopfen; (*a finger*) quetschen; (rad) stören; **be jammed** in eingezwängt sein; **jam on the brakes** auf die Bremsen drücken; **jam s.th. into**

etw stopfen in (*acc*) ‖ *intr* (*said of a window*) klemmen; (*said of gears*) sich verklemmen; (*said of a gun*) Ladehemmung haben; **jam into** sich hineinquetschen in (*acc*)

jamb [dʒæm] *s* Pfosten *m*

jamboree [,dʒæmbə'ri] *s* Trubel *m*; (*of scouts*) Pfadfindertreffen *n*

James [dʒemz] *s* Jakob *m*

jam'ming *s* (rad) Störung *f*

Jane [dʒen] *s* Johanna *f*

Janet ['dʒænɪt] *s* Hanna *f*

jangle ['dʒæŋgəl] *s* Rasseln *n* ‖ *tr* rasseln lassen; **j. s.o.'s nerves** j–m auf die Nerven gehen ‖ *intr* rasseln

janitor ['dʒænɪtər] *s* Hausmeister *m*

January ['dʒænju,eri] *s* Januar *m*

Japan [dʒə'pæn] *s* Japan *n*

Japanese [,dʒæpə'niz] *adj* japanisch ‖ *s* Japaner –in *mf*; (*language*) Japanisch *n*

Jap'anese bee'tle *s* Japankäfer *m*

jar [dʒɑr] *s* Krug *m*; (*e.g., of jam*) Glas *n*; (*jolt*) Stoß *m* ‖ *v* (*pret & pp* jarred; *ger* jarring) *tr* (*jolt*) anstoßen; (fig) erschüttern ‖ *intr* nicht harmonieren; **jar on the nerves** auf die Nerven gehen

jargon ['dʒɑrgən] *s* Jargon *m*

jasmine ['dʒæzmɪn] *s* Jasmin *m*

jaundice ['dʒɔndɪs] *s* Gelbsucht *f*

jaun'diced *adj* gelbsüchtig

jaunt [dʒɔnt] *s* Ausflug *m*

jaunty ['dʒɔnti] *adj* (*sprightly*) lebhaft; (*clothes*) fesch

javelin ['dʒævə(ə)lɪn] *s* Speer *m*

jaw [dʒɔ] *s* Kiefer *m*; **the jaws of death** die Klauen des Todes

jaw'bone' *s* Kiefer *m* ‖ *intr* (sl) sich stark machen

jay [dʒe] *s* (orn) Häher *m*

jay'walk' *intr* verkehrswidrig die Straße überqueren

jazz [dʒæz] *s* Jazz *m* ‖ *tr*—**j. up** (coll) aufmöbeln

jazz' band' *s* Jazzband *f*

jazzy ['dʒæzi] *adj* bunt, grell

jealous ['dʒeləs] *adj* (*of*) eifersüchtig (auf *acc*)

jealousy ['dʒeləsi] *s* Eifersucht *f*

jeans [dʒinz] *spl* Jeans *pl*

jeep [dʒip] s Jeep m

jeer [dʒɪr] s Hohn m ‖ tr verhöhnen ‖ intr höhnen; j. at verhöhnen

Jeffrey ['dʒefri] s Gottfried m

Jehovah [dʒɪ'hovə] s Jehova m

jell [dʒel] s Gelee n ‖ intr gelieren; (fig) zum Klappen kommen

jellied ['dʒelid] adj geliert

jelly ['dʒeli] s Gallerte f

jel'lyfish' s Qualle f; (pej) Waschlappen m

jeopardize ['dʒepər‚daɪz] tr gefährden

jeopardy ['dʒepərdi] s Gefahr f

jerk [dʒʌrk] s Ruck m; (sl) Knülch m ‖ tr ruckweise ziehen ‖ intr zucken

jerky ['dʒʌrki] adj ruckartig

jersey ['dʒʌrzi] s (material) Jersey m; (shirt) Jersey n; (sport) Trikot n

jest [dʒest] s Scherz m; in j. scherzweise ‖ intr scherzen

jester ['dʒestər] s Hofnarr m; (joker) Spaßvogel m

Jesuit ['dʒezʊ‚ɪt] adj Jesuiten- ‖ s Jesuit m

Jesus ['dʒizəs] s Jesus m

jet [dʒet] adj Düsen- ‖ s (stream) Strahl m; (nozzle) Düse f; (plane) Jet m, Düsenflugzeug n ‖ v (pret & pp jetted; ger jetting) herausströmen; (aer) jetten

jet'-black' adj rabenschwarz

jet' propul'sion s Düsenantrieb m

jetsam ['dʒetsəm] s Seewurfgut n

jet' stream' s Strahlströmung f

jettison ['dʒetɪsən] s Seewurf m ‖ tr (aer) abwerfen; (naut) über Bord werfen

jetty ['dʒeti] s (warf) Landungsbrücke f; (breakwater) Hafendamm m

Jew [dʒu] s Jude m, Jüdin f

jewel ['dʒu·əl] s (& fig) Juwel n; (in a watch) Stein m

jew'el box' s Schmuckkästchen n

jewel(l)er ['dʒu·ələr] s Juwelier -in mf

jewelry ['dʒu·əlri] s Jewelen pl; piece of j. Schmuckstück n

jew'elry store' s Juweliergeschäft n

Jewish ['dʒu·ɪʃ] adj jüdisch

Jew's' harp' s Maultrommel f

jib [dʒɪb] s Ausleger m; (naut) Klüver m

jibe [dʒaɪb] intr (coll) übereinstimmen

jiffy ['dʒɪfi] s—in a j. im Nu

jig [dʒɪg] s (dance) Gigue f; (tool) Spannvorrichtung f; the jig is up (sl) das Spiel ist aus

jigger ['dʒɪgər] s Schnapsglas n; (gadget) Dingsbums n; (naut) Besan m

jiggle ['dʒɪgəl] tr & intr rütteln

jig'saw' s Laubsäge f

jig'saw puz'zle s Puzzelspiel n

jilt [dʒɪlt] tr (a girl) sitzenlassen; (a boy) den Laufpaß geben (dat)

jim·my ['dʒɪmi] s Brecheisen n ‖ v (pret & pp -mied) tr mit dem Brecheisen aufbrechen

jingle ['dʒɪŋgəl] s (of coins) Klimpern n; (bell) Schelle f; (verse) Verseklingel n ‖ tr klimpern mit ‖ intr klimpern; (said of verses) klingeln

jin·go ['dʒɪŋgo] s (-goes) Chauvinist -in mf; by j.! alle Wetter!

jinx [dʒɪŋks] s Unglücksrabe m ‖ tr Pech bringen (dat); be jinxed vom Pech verfolgt sein

jitters ['dʒɪtərz] spl—have the j. wahnsinnig nervös sein; give s.o. the j. j-n wahnsinnig nervös machen

jittery ['dʒɪtəri] adj durchgedreht

Joan [dʒon] s Johanna f

job [dʒab] s (employment) Job m; (task, responsibility) Aufgabe f; bad job Machwerk n; do a good job gute Arbeit leisten; fall down on the job seine Pflicht nicht erfüllen; know one's job seine Sache verstehen; on the job bei der Arbeit; (fig) auf Draht; out of a job arbeitslos

jobber ['dʒabər] s (middleman) Zwischenhändler -in mf; (pieceworker) Akkordarbeiter -in mf

job'hold'er s Stelleninhaber -in mf

jobless ['dʒablɪs] adj stellungslos

jockey ['dʒaki] s Jockei m ‖ tr manövrieren

jog [dʒag] s Dauerlauf m; (of a horse) Trott m ‖ v (pret & pp jogged; ger jogging) tr (shake) rütteln; (the memory) auffrischen ‖ intr trotten; (for exercise) langsam rennen, Dauerlauf machen

John [dʒan] s Johann m; john (sl) Klo n

Johnny ['dʒani] s Hans m

John'ny-come'-late'ly s Neuling m, Nachzügler m

join [dʒɔɪn] tr verbinden; (a club) beitreten (dat); (a person) sich anschließen (dat); (two parts) zusammenfügen; j. the army zum Militär gehen ‖ intr sich verbinden; j. in sich beteiligen an (dat); j. up (mil) einrücken

joiner ['dʒɔɪnər] s (coll) Vereinsmeier m; (carp) Tischler m

joint [dʒɔɪnt] adj (account, venture) gemeinschaftlich; (return) gemeinsam; (committee) gemischt; (heir, owner) Mit- ‖ s Verbindungspunkt m; (in plumbing) Naht f; (sl) Bumslokal n; (anat, bot, mach) Gelenk n; (carp) Fuge f; (culin) Bratenstück n; throw out of j. auskugeln

jointly ['dʒɔɪntli] adv gemeinsam

joint'-stock' com'pany s Aktiengesellschaft f

joist [dʒɔɪst] s Tragbalken m

joke [dʒok] s Witz m; he can't take a j. er versteht keinen Spaß; make a j. of ins Lächerliche ziehen; play a j. on e-n Streich spielen (dat) ‖ intr Spaß machen; j. about witzeln über (acc); j. around schäkern; joking aside Spaß beiseite

joker ['dʒokər] s Spaßvogel m; (pej) Knülch m; (cards) Joker m

jolly ['dʒali] adj lustig

jolt [dʒolt] s Stoß m ‖ tr stoßen ‖ intr holpern; j. along dahinholpern

Jordan ['dʒɔrdən] s (country) Jordanien n; (river) Jordan m

josh [dʒaʃ] tr & intr hänseln

jostle ['dʒasəl] tr & intr drängeln

jot [dʒat] s—not a jot kein Jota ‖ v

(pret & pp **jotted;** ger **jotting**) tr—
jot down notieren

journal ['dʒɜːnəl] s (daily record) Tagebuch n; (magazine) Zeitschrift f

journalism ['dʒɜːnəˌlɪzəm] s Journalismus m, Zeitungswesen n

journalist ['dʒɜːnəlɪst] s Journalist –in mf

journey ['dʒɜːni] s Reise f; go on a j. verreisen || intr reisen

jour'ney-man adj tüchtig || s (-men) Geselle m

joust [dʒaʊst] s Tjost f || intr turnieren

jovial ['dʒoʊvɪəl] adj jovial

jowls [dʒaʊlz] spl Hängebacken pl

joy [dʒɔɪ] s Freude f

joyful ['dʒɔɪfəl] adj froh, freudig

joyless ['dʒɔɪlɪs] adj freudlos

joy' ride' s (coll) Schwarzfahrt f

joy' stick' s (aer) Steuerknüppel m

Jr. abbr (Junior) jr., jun.

jubilant ['dʒubɪlənt] adj frohlockend

jubilation [ˌdʒubɪ'leʃən] s Jubel m

jubilee ['dʒubɪˌli] s Jubiläum n

Judaea [dʒu'diə] s Judäa n

Judaic [dʒu'deɪk] adj jüdisch

Judaism ['dʒudəˌɪzəm] s Judaismus m

judge [dʒʌdʒ] s (in a competition) Preisrichter –in mf; (box) Punktrichter m; (jur) Richter –in mf || tr (by) beurteilen (nach); (distances) abschätzen; (jur) richten || intr urteilen; (jur) richten; **judging by his words** seinen Worten nach zu urteilen

judge' ad'vocate s Kriegsgerichtsrat m

judgment ['dʒʌdʒmənt] s (& jur) Urteil n; in my j. meines Erachtens; show good j. ein gutes Urteilsvermögen haben; sit in j. over zu Gericht sitzen über (acc)

Judg'ment Day' s Tag m des Gerichts

judicial [dʒu'drʃəl] adj Rechts-

judiciary [dʒu'drʃɪˌerɪ] adj richterlich || s (branch) richterliche Gewalt f; (judges) Richterstand m

judicious [dʒu'drʃəs] adj klug

judo ['dʒudo] s Judo n

jug [dʒʌg] s Krug m; (jail) Kittchen n

juggle ['dʒʌgəl] tr jonglieren; (accounts) frisieren || intr jonglieren

juggler ['dʒʌglər] s Gaukler –in mf

Jugoslav ['jugo,slav] adj jugoslawisch || s Jugoslawe m, Jugoslawin f

Jugoslavia [ˌjugo'slavɪə] s Jugoslawien n

jug'ular vein' ['dʒʌgjələr] s Halsader f

juice [dʒus] s Saft m

juicy ['dʒusi] adj saftig

jukebox ['dʒuk‚baks] s Musikautomat m

July [dʒu'laɪ] s Juli m

jumble ['dʒʌmbəl] s Wust m || tr durcheinanderwerfen

jumbo ['dʒʌmbo] adj Riesen-

jump [dʒʌmp] s Sprung m; (aer) Absprung m; get the j. on zuvorkommen (dat) || tr überspringen; (attack) überfallen; (a hurdle) nehmen; (in

checkers) schlagen; **j. bail** die Kaution verfallen lassen; **j. channels** den amtlichen Weg nicht einhalten; **j. rope** seilspringen; **j. ship** vom Schiff weglaufen; **j. the gun** übereilt handeln; (sport) zu früh starten; **j. the track** entgleisen || intr springen; (be startled) auffahren; **j. at** (a chance) stürzen auf (acc); **j. down s.o.'s throat** j–n anfahren

jump' ball' s (basketball) Sprungball m

jumper ['dʒʌmpər] s (dress) Jumper m; (elec) Kurzschlußbrücke f

jump'-off' s Beginn m; (sport) Start m

jump' rope' s Springseil n

jumpy ['dʒʌmpi] adj unruhig, nervös

junction ['dʒʌŋkʃən] s Verbindung f; (of roads, rail lines) Knotenpunkt m

juncture ['dʒʌŋktʃər] s Verbindungsstelle f; at this j. in diesem Augenblick

June [dʒun] s Juni m

June' bug' s Maikäfer m

jungle ['dʒʌŋgəl] s Dschungel m, n & f

junior ['dʒunjər] adj jünger || s Student –in mf im dritten Studienjahr

juniper ['dʒunɪpər] s Wacholder m

junk [dʒʌŋk] s Altwaren pl; (scrap iron) Schrott m; (useless stuff) Plunder m; (naut) Dschunke f

junket ['dʒʌŋkɪt] s Vergnügungsreise f auf öffentliche Kosten

junk' mail' s Wurfsendung f

junk'yard' s Schrottplatz m

junta ['hʌntə], ['dʒʌntə] s Junta f

jurisdiction [ˌdʒʊrɪs'dɪkʃən] s Zuständigkeit f; have j. over zuständig sein für

jurisprudence [ˌdʒʊrɪs'prudəns] s Rechtswissenschaft f

jurist ['dʒʊrɪst] s Jurist –in mf

juror ['dʒʊrər] s Geschworene mf

jury ['dʒʊri] s Geschworene pl

ju'ry box' s Geschworenenbank f

ju'ry tri'al s Schwurgerichtsverfahren n

just [dʒʌst] adj gerecht || adv gerade; (only) nur; (simply) einfach

justice ['dʒʌstɪs] s Gerechtigkeit f; (of a claim) Berechtigung f; (judge) Richter m; **bring to j.** vor Gericht bringen; **do j. to** (a meal) wacker zusprechen (dat); (said of a picture) gerecht werden (dat)

jus'tice of the peace' s Friedensrichter m

justification [ˌdʒʌstɪfɪ'keʃən] s Rechtfertigung f

justi·fy ['dʒʌstɪˌfaɪ] v (pret & pp –fied) tr rechtfertigen

justly ['dʒʌstli] adv mit Recht

jut [dʒʌt] v (pret & pp **jutted;** ger **jutting**) intr—**jut out** hervorragen

juvenile ['dʒuvə‚naɪl] adj (books, court) Jugend–; (childish) unreif

ju'venile delin'quency s Jugendkriminalität f

ju'venile delin'quent s jugendlicher Verbrecher m

juxtapose [ˌdʒʌkstə'poz] tr nebeneinanderstellen

K

K, k [ke] *s* elfter Buchstabe des englischen Alphabets

kale [kel] *s* Grünkohl *m*

kaleidoscopic [kə‚laɪdə'skɑpɪk] *adj* (& *fig*) kaleidoskopisch

kangaroo [‚kæŋgə'ru] *s* Känguruh *n*

kangaroo court' *s* Scheingericht *n*

kashmir ['kae/mɪr] *s* (tex) Kaschmir *m*

kayo ['ke'o] *s* K.o. *m* ‖ *tr* k.o. schlagen

keel [kil] *s* Kiel *m*; **on an even k.** (fig) gleichmäßig ‖ *intr*—**k. over** umkippen; (naut) kentern

keen [kin] *adj* (sharp) scharf; (interest) lebhaft; **k. on** scharf auf (acc)

keenness ['kinnɪs] *s* Schärfe *f*

keep [kip] *s* Unterhalt *m*; (of a castle) Bergfried *m*; **for keeps** (forever) für immer; (seriously) im Ernst ‖ *v* (pret & pp **kept** [kɛpt]) *tr* (retain) behalten; (detain) aufhalten; (save for s.o.) aufbewahren; (a secret) bewahren; (a promise) (ein)halten; (animals) halten; (books) (acct) führen; **be kept in school** nachsitzen müssen; **k. at arm's length** vom Leibe halten; **k. at bay** sich erwehren (genit); **k. away** fernhalten; **k. back** zurückhalten; (retain) zurückbehalten; **k.** (s.o.) **company** Gesellschaft leisten (dat); **k. down** (one's head) niederhalten; (one's voice) verhalten; (prices) niedrig halten; **k. from** abhalten von; **k. from** (ger) daran hindern zu (inf); **k. going** im Gange halten; **k. good time** gut gehen; **k. guard** Wache halten; **k. house** den Haushalt führen; **k. in good condition** instand halten; **k. in mind** sich [dat] merken; **k. it up!** nur so weiter; **k. on** (a garment) anbehalten; (a hat) aufbehalten; **k. oneself from** (ger) sich fertigbringen nicht zu (inf); **k. one's temper** sich beherrschen; **k. out** ausschließen; (light) nicht durchlassen; (rain) abhalten; **k. posted** auf dem laufenden halten; **k. score** die Punktliste führen; **k. secret** geheimhalten; **k. step** Tritt halten; **k. s.th. from s.o.** j-m etw verschweigen; **k. track of** sich [dat] merken; **k. under wraps** (coll) totschweigen; **k. up** instand halten; (appearances) wahren; (correspondence) unterhalten; **k. up the good work!** arbeiten Sie weiter so gut!; **k. waiting** warten lassen; **k. warm** warm halten; **k. your shirt on!** (coll) daß du die Nase im Gesicht behältst! ‖ *intr* (said of food) sich halten; **k. at** beharren bei; **k. at it!** bleib dabei!; **k. away** sich fernhalten; **k. cool** (fig) die Nerven behalten; **k. cool!** ruhig Blut!; **k. from** sich enthalten (genit); **k. from** (ger) es unterlassen zu (inf); **k. from laughing** sich das Lachen verkneifen;

k. going weitermachen; **k. moving** weitergehen; **k. on** (ger) weiter (inf), e.g., **k. on driving** weiterfahren; **k. out!** Eintritt verboten! **k. out of** sich fernhalten von; **k. quiet** sich ruhig verhalten; **k. quiet!** sei still!; **k. to the right** sich rechts halten; **k. up with** (work) nachkommen mit; **k. up with the Joneses** mit den Nachbarn Schritt halten; **k. within** bleiben innerhalb (genit)

keeper ['kipər] *s* (of animals) Halter –in *mf*; (at a zoo) Tierwärter –in *mf*; (watchman) Wächter *m*

keep'ing *s* Verwahrung *f*; **in k. with** in Einklang mit

keep'sake' *s* Andenken *n*

keg [kɛg] *s* Faß *n*

ken [kɛn] *s* Gesichtskreis *m*

kennel ['kɛnəl] *s* Hundezwinger *m*

kep‧i ['kepi], ['kepi] *s* (–is) Kappi *n*

kerchief ['kɑrt/ɪf] *s* (for the head) Kopftuch *n*; (for the neck) Halstuch *n*

kernel ['kʌrnəl] *s* (of fruit) Kern *m*; (of grain) Korn *n*; (fig) Kern *m*

kerosene [‚kerə'sin] *s* Petroleum *n*

kerplunk [kər'plʌŋk] *interj* bums!

ketchup ['ket/əp] *s* Ketchup *m* & *n*

kettle ['ketəl] *s* Kessel *m*

ket'tledrum' *s* Kesselpauke *f*

key [ki] *adj* (ring, hole, industry, position) Schlüssel– ‖ *s* (& *fig*) Schlüssel *m*; (of a map) Zeichenerklärung *f*; (of a typewriter, piano, organ) Taste *f*; (of windinstrument) Klappe *f*; (reef) Riff *n*; (low island) Insel *f*; (mus) Tonart *f*; **key of C major** C-dur; **off key** falsch ‖ *tr* (mach) festkeilen

key'board' *s* Tastatur *f*

keyed *adj*—**k. to** gestimmt auf (acc); **k. up** in Hochspannung

key' man' *s* Schlüsselfigur *f*

key'note *s* Grundgedanke *m*; (mus) Tonika *f*

key'note address' *s* programmatische Rede *f*

keynoter ['kɪ ‚notər] *s* Programmatiker –in *mf*

keypuncher ['ki ‚pʌnt/ər] *s* Locher –in *mf*

key'stone' *s* Schlußstein *m*; (fig) Grundlage *f*

key' word' *s* Stichwort *n*

kha‧ki ['kæki] *adj* Khaki– ‖ *s* (–kis) Khaki *m*; **khakis** Khakiuniform *f*

kibitz ['kɪbɪts] *intr* (coll) kiebitzen

kibitzer ['kɪbɪtsər] *s* (coll) Kiebitz *m*

kick [kɪk] *s* Fußtritt *m*; (of a rifle) Rückstoß *m*; (of a horse) Schlag *m*; (final spurt) (sport) Endspurt *m*; **give s.o. a k.** j-m e-n Fußtritt versetzen; **I get a (great) k. out of him** er macht mir (riesigen) Spaß ‖ *tr* treten, stoßen; (fb) kicken; **be kicked upstairs** (coll) die Treppe hinauffallen;

I could k. myself ich könnte mich ohrfeigen; k. a goal (fb) ein Tor schießen; k. (s.o.) around schlecht behandeln; (e.g., an idea) beschwatzen; k. in (money) beisteuern; k. open (a door) aufstoßen; k. out (coll) rausschmeißen; k. s.o. in the shins j-n gegen das Schienbein treten; k. the bucket (sl) krepieren; k. up a storm Krach schlagen || intr (said of a gun) stoßen; (said of a horse) ausschlagen; (complain) (about) meckern (über acc); k. around Europe in Europa herumbummeln; k. off (fb) anspielen

kick'back' s Schmiergeld n

kick'off' s (commencement) Beginn m; (fb) Anstoß m

kid [kɪd] s Zicklein n; (coll) Kind n || v (pret & pp kidded; ger kidding) tr necken || intr scherzen; no kidding! mach keine Witze!

kid' gloves' spl Glacéhandschuhe pl; handle with k. (fig) mit Glacéhandschuhen anfassen

kid'nap(p)er v (pret & pp -nap(p)ed; ger -nap(p)ing) tr kidnappen, entführen

kidnap(p)er ['kɪd,næpər] s Kidnapper m

kid'nap(p)ing s Kidnapping s

kidney ['kɪdni] s Niere f

kid'ney bean' s rote Bohne f

kid'ney-shaped' adj nierenförmig

kid'ney stone' s Nierenstein m

kid'ney trans'plant s Nierenverpflanzung f; (transplanted kidney) verpflanzte Niere f

kid'ney trou'ble s Nierenleiden n

kid' stuff' s (coll) Kinderei f

kill [kɪl] s (aer) Abschuß m; (hunt) Jagdbeute f; (nav) Versenkung f || tr töten; (murder) ermorden, killen; (plants) zum Absterben bringen; (time) totschlagen; (a proposal, plans, competition) zu Fall bringen; (the motor) abwürgen; (the ball) stark schlagen; (a bottle) austrinken; be killed in action (im Felde) fallen; it won't k. you (coll) es wird dich nicht umbringen; k. off abschlachten; k. oneself sich umbringen; k. two birds with one stone zwei Fliegen mit e-r Klappe schlagen; she is dressed to k. sie ist totschick angezogen

killer ['kɪlər] s Totschläger -in mf, Killer m

kill'er whale' s Schwertwal m

kill'ing s Tötung f; make a k. e-n unerhofften Gewinn erzielen

kill'joy' s Spaßverderber m

kiln ['kɪl(n)] s Brennofen m

kil·o ['kɪlo], ['kilo] s (-os) Kilo n

kilocycle ['kɪlə,saɪkəl] s Kilohertz n

kilogram ['kɪlə,græm] s Kilogramm n

kilohertz ['kɪlə,hʌrts] s Kilohertz n

kilometer [kɪ'lɑmɪtər] s Kilometer m; kilometers per hour Stundenkilometer pl

kilowatt ['kɪlə,wɑt] s Kilowatt n

kil'owatt'-hour' s Kilowattstunde f

kilt [kɪlt] s Kilt m

kilter ['kɪltər] s—out of k. nicht in Ordnung

kimo·no [kɪ'mono] s (-nos) Kimono m

kin [kɪn] s Sippe f; the next of kin die nächsten Angehörigen

kind [kaɪnd] adj liebenswürdig; (to) gütig (zu), freundlich (zu); would you be so k. as to (inf)? würden Sie so gefällig sein zu (inf)?; with k. regards mit freundlichen Grüßen || s Art f, Sorte f; all kinds of allerlei; another k. of ein anderer; any k. of irgendwelcher; every k. of jede Art von; in. k. (fig) auf gleiche Weise; k. of (coll) etwas; nothing of the k. nichts dergleichen; that k. of derartig; two (three) kinds of zweierlei (dreierlei); what k. of was für ein

kindergarten ['kɪndər,gɑrtən] s Vorschule f, Vorschuljahr n

kind'-heart'ed adj gutmütig

kindle ['kɪndəl] tr anzünden; (fig) erwecken || intr sich entzünden

kindling ['kɪndlɪŋ] s Entzündung f; (wood) Kleinholz n

kindly ['kaɪndli] adj gütig, freundlich || adv freundlich; (please) bitte

kindness ['kaɪndnɪs] s Freundlichkeit f; (deed) Gefälligkeit f

kindred ['kɪndrəd] adj verwandtschaftlich; (fig) verwandt || s Verwandtschaft f

kinescope ['kɪnɪ,skop] s (trademark) Fernsehempfangsröhre f

kinetic [kɪ'nɛtɪk] adj kinetisch || kinetics s Kinetik f

king [kɪŋ] s König m; (cards, chess) König m; (checkers) Dame f

kingdom ['kɪŋdəm] s Königreich n; (of animals, etc.) Reich n; k. of heaven Himmelreich n

king'fish'er s Königsfischer m

kingly ['kɪŋli] adj königlich

king'pin' s (coll) Boß m; (bowling) König m

king'ship' s Königtum n

king'-size' adj übergroß

kink [kɪŋk] s (in a wire) Knick m; (in the hair) Kräuselung f; (in a muscle) Muskelkrampf m; (flaw) Fehler m

kinky ['kɪŋki] adj gekräuselt

kin'ship' s Verwandtschaft f

kins'man s (-men) Blutsverwandte m

kins'wom'an s (-wom'en) Blutsverwandte f

kipper ['kɪpər] s Räucherhering m || tr einsalzen und räuchern

kiss [kɪs] s Kuß m || tr & intr küssen

kisser ['kɪsər] s (sl) Fresse f

kit [kɪt] s (equipment) Ausrüstung f; (tool kit) Werkzeugkasten m; (for models) Modellsatz m; (e.g., for a convention) Mappe f; the whole kit and caboodle (things) der ganze Kram; (persons) die ganze Sippschaft

kitchen ['kɪtʃən] s Küche f

kitchenette [,kɪtʃə'nɛt] s Kochnische f

kit'chen knife' s Küchenmesser n

kit'chen police' s (mil) Küchendienst m

kit'chen range' s Herd m, Kochherd m

kit′chen sink′ s Ausguß m

kit′chenware′ s Küchengeschirr n

kite [kaɪt] s Drachen m; (orn) Weih m; **fly a k.** e-n Drachen steigen lassen; **go fly a k.!** (coll) scher dich zum Kuckuck!

kith′ and kin′ [kɪθ] spl Freunde and Verwandte pl

kitten [′kɪtən] s Kätzchen n

kitty [′kɪtɪ] s Kätzchen n; (cards) gemeinsame Kasse f; **Kitty** Käthchen n

kleptomaniac [ˌkleptə′menɪˌæk] s Kleptomane m, Kleptomanin f

knack [næk] s—**have a k. for** Talent haben für; **have the k. of it** den Griff heraus haben

knapsack [′næpˌsæk] s Rucksack m

knave [nev] s Schelm m; (cards) Bube m

knavery [′nevərɪ] s Schelmenstreich m

knead [nid] tr kneten

knead′ing trough′ s Teigmulde f

knee [ni] s Knie n; **bring s.o. to his knees** j–n auf die Knie zwingen; **go down on one's knees** niederknien; **on bended knees** kniefällig

knee′ bend′ s Kniebeuge f

knee′ breech′es spl Kniehose f

knee′cap′ s Kniescheibe f

knee′-deep′ adj knietief

knee′-high′ adj kniehoch

knee′ jerk′ s Patellarreflex m

kneel [nil] v (pret & pp **knelt** [nelt] & **kneeled**) intr knien

knee′-length′ adj kniefreit

knee′ pad′ s (sport) Knieschützer m

knee′pan′ s Kniescheibe f

knee′ swell′ s (of organ) Knieschweller m

knell [nel] s Totengeläute n

knickers [′nɪkərz] spl Knickerbockerhosen pl

knickknack [′nɪkˌnæk] s Nippsache f

knife [naɪf] s (**knives** [naɪvz]) Messer n || tr erstechen

knife′ sharp′ener s Messerschleifer m

knife′ switch′ s (elec) Messerschalter m

knight [naɪt] s Ritter m; (chess) Springer m || tr zum Ritter schlagen

knight′hood′ s Ritterschaft f

knightly [′naɪtlɪ] adj ritterlich

knit [nɪt] v (pret & pp **knitted** & **knit**; ger **knitting**) tr stricken; **k. one's brows** die Brauen runzeln || intr stricken; (said of bones) zusammenheilen

knit′ goods′ spl Trikotwaren pl

knit′ted dress′ s Strickkleid n

knit′ting s (act) Strickerei f; (materials) Strickzeug n

knit′ting machine′ s Strickmaschine f

knit′ting nee′dle s Stricknadel f

knit′ting yarn′ s Strickgarn m

knit′wear′ s Strickwaren pl

knob [nab] s (of a door) Drücker m; (lump) Auswuchs m; (in wood) Knorren m; (of a radio) Knopf m

knock [nak] s (& aut) Klopfen n || tr (criticize) tadeln; **k. a hole through** durchbrechen; **k. around** herumstoßen; (mistreat) unsanft behandeln;

k. down niederschlagen; (with a car) umfahren; (trees) umbrechen; (at auctions) zuschlagen; **k. it off!** (sl) hör mal auf!; **k. oneself out** over sich [dat] die Zähne ausbeißen an (dat); **k. one's head against the wall** mit dem Kopf gegen die Wand rennen; **k. out** ausschlagen; (exhaust) (coll) strapazieren; (a tank) abschießen; (box) k.o. schlagen; **k. over** umwerfen; **k. together** (build hurriedly) schnell zusammenhauen; **k. to the ground** zu Boden schlagen; **k. up a girl** (sl) e–m Mädchen ein Kind anhängen || intr (an)klopfen; (aut) klopfen; **k. about** herumbummeln; **k. against** stoßen an (acc); **k. off** (from) (coll) aufhören (mit)

knock′down′ s (box) Niederschlag m

knocker [′nakər] s Türklopfer m; **knockers** (sl) Brüste pl

knock-kneed [′nakˌnid] adj x-beinig

knock′-knees′ spl X-beine pl

knock′out′ s (woman) (coll) Blitzmädel n; (box) Knockout m

knock′out drops′ spl Betäubungsmittel n

knock′-out punch′ s K.o.-Schlag m

knoll [nol] s Hügel m

knot [nat] s Knoten m; (in wood) Knorren m; (of people) Gruppe f; (naut) Knoten m; **tie a k.** e–n Knoten machen; **tie the k.** (coll) sich verheiraten || tr e–n Knoten machen in (acc); (two ends) zusammenknoten

knot′hole′ s Astloch n

knotty [′natɪ] adj knorrig; (problem) knifflig

know [no] s—**be in the k.** Bescheid wissen || v (pret **knew** [n(j)u]; pp **known**) tr (facts) wissen; (be familiar with) kennen; (a language) können; **come to k.** erfahren; **get to k.** kennenlernen; **known** bekannt; **k. one's way around** sich auskennen; **k. the ropes** (coll) Bescheid wissen; **k. what's what** (coll) den Rummel kennen || intr wissen; **he ought to k.** better er sollte mehr Verstand haben; **k. about** wissen über (acc); **k. of** wissen von; **not that I k. of** (coll) nicht, daß ich wüßte; **you k.** (coll) wissen Sie

knowable [′no-əbəl] adj kenntlich

know′-how′ s Sachkenntnis f

know′ing adj (glance) vielsagend

knowingly [′no-ɪŋlɪ] adv wissentlich; (intentionally) absichtlich

know′-it-all′ s Naseweis m

knowledge [′nalɪdʒ] s Wissen n, Kenntnisse pl; (information) (of) Kenntnis f (von); **basic k.** of Grundkenntnisse pl in (dat); **come to s.o.'s k.** j–m zur Kenntnis kommen; **to my k.** soweit (or soviel) ich weiß; **to the best of my k.** nach bestem Wissen; **without my k.** ohne mein Mitwissen; **working k.** of praktisch verwertbare Kenntnisse pl (genit)

knowledgeable [′nalɪdʒəbəl] adj kenntnisreich

known [non] adj bekannt; **become k.**

kundwerden; k. all over town stadtbekannt; make k. bekanntgeben

know'-noth'ing s Nichtswisser m

knuckle ['nʌkəl] s Knöchel m, Fingerknöchel m; (mach) Gelenkstück n; k. of ham Eisbein n || intr—k. down to work sich ernsthaft an die Arbeit machen; k. under klein beigeben

k.o. ['ke'o] s K.o. m || tr k.o.-schlagen

Koran [ko'ræn] s Koran m

Korea [ko'ri·ə] s Korea n

Korean [ko'ri·ən] adj koreanisch || s Koreaner –in mf; (language) Koreanisch n

kosher ['koʃər] adj (& coll) koscher

kowtow ['kau'tau] intr e–n Kotau machen; k. to kriechen vor (dat)

K.P. ['ke'pi] s (kitchen police) (mil) Küchendienst m

Kremlin ['kremlɪn] s Kreml m

kudos ['k(i)udɑs] s (coll) Ruhm m, Renommee n

L

L, l [ɛl] s zwölfter Buchstabe des englischen Alphabets

lab [læb] s (coll) Labor n

la·bel ['lebəl] s Etikett n; (brand) Marke f; (fig) Bezeichnung f || v (pret & pp –bel[l]ed; ger –bel[l]ing) tr etikettieren; (fig) bezeichnen

labial ['lebɪ·əl] adj Lippen– || s Lippenlaut m, Labial m

labor ['lebər] adj Arbeits–, Arbeiter– || s Arbeit f; (toil) Mühe f; be in l. in den Wehen liegen || tr (a point) ausführlich eingehen auf (acc) || intr sich abmühen; (at) arbeiten (an dat); (exert oneself) sich anstrengen; (staff of a ship) stampfen; l. under zu leiden haben unter (dat)

la'bor and man'agement spl Arbeitnehmer und Arbeitgeber pl

laboratory ['læbərə,tori] s Laboratorium n

lab'oratory techni'cian s Laborant –in mf

la'bor camp' s Zwangsarbeitslager n

la'bor con'tract s Tarifvertrag m

la'bor dis'pute s Arbeitsstreitigkeit f

la'bored adj (e.g., breathing) mühsam; (style) gezwungen

laborer ['lebərər] s Arbeiter –in mf; (unskilled) Hilfsarbeiter –in mf

la'bor force' s Arbeitskräfte pl

laborious [lə'borɪ·əs] adj mühsam, schwierig

la'bor law' s Arbeitsrecht n

la'bor lead'er s Arbeitsführer –in mf

la'bor mar'ket s Arbeitsmarkt m

la'bor move'ment s Arbeiterbewegung f

la'bor pains' spl Geburtswehen pl

la'bor-sav'ing adj arbeitssparend; l. device Hilfsgerät n

la'bor short'age s Mangel m an Arbeitskräften

la'bor supply' s Arbeitsangebot n

la'bor un'ion s Gewerkschaft f

laburnum [lə'bʌrnəm] s Goldregen m

labyrinth ['læbɪrɪnθ] s Labyrinth n

lace [les] adj (collar, dress) Spitzen– || s Spitze f; (shoestring) Schnürsenkel m || tr (e.g., shoes) schnüren; (braid) flechten; (drinks) (coll) mit e–m Schuß Branntwein versetzen; (beat) (coll) prügeln; l. up zuschnüren

lacerate ['læsə,ret] tr zerfleischen

laceration [,læsə'reʃən] s Fleischwunde f

lace' trim'ming s Spitzenbesatz m

lace'work' s Spitzenarbeit f

lachrymose ['lækrɪ,mos] adj tränenreich

lac'ing s Schnürung f; (coll) Prügel pl

lack [læk] s (of) Mangel m (an dat); for l. of aus Mangel an (dat); l. of space Raummangel m; l. of time Zeitmangel m || tr—I l. es mangelt mir an (dat) || intr—be lacking fehlen; he is lacking in courage ihm fehlt der Mut

lackadaisical [,lækə'dezɪkəl] adj teilnahmslos, gleichgültig

lackey ['læki] s Lakai m

lack'ing prep mangels (genit)

lack'lus'ter adj glanzlos

laconic [lə'kɑnɪk] adj lakonisch

lacquer ['lækər] s Lack m || tr lackieren

lac'quer ware' s Lackwaren pl

lacrosse [lə'krɔs] s Lacrosse n

lacu·na [lə'kjunə] s (–nas & –nae [ni]) Lücke f, Lakune f

lacy ['lesi] adj spitzenartig

lad [læd] s Bube m

la'dies' man' s Weiberheld m, Salonlöwe m

la'dies' room' s Damentoilette f

ladle ['ledəl] s Schöpflöffel m || tr ausschöpfen

lady ['ledi] s Dame f; ladies and gentlemen meine Damen und Herren!

la'dybird', la'dybug' s Marienkäfer m

la'dy compan'ion s Gesellschaftsdame f

la'dyfin'ger s Löffelbiskuit m & n

la'dy-in-wait'ing s (ladies-in-waiting) Hofdame f

la'dy-kil'ler s Schwerenöter m

la'dylike' adj damenhaft

la'dylove' s Geliebte f

la'dy of the house' s Hausherrin f

la'dy's maid' s Zofe f

la'dy's man' s var of ladies' man

lag [læg] s Zurückbleiben n; (aer) Rücktrift f; (phys) Verzögerung f || v (pret & pp lagged; ger lagging) intr (behind) zurückbleiben (hinter dat)

la'ger beer' ['lɑgər] s Lagerbier n

laggard ['lægərd] s Nachzügler m

lagoon [lə'gun] s Lagune f
laid' up' adj (with) bettlägerig (infolge von); **be l. in bed** auf der Nase liegen
lair [ler] s Höhle f, Lager n
laity ['le·ɪtɪ] s Laien pl
lake [lek] s See m
Lake' Con'stance ['kɑnstəns] s der Bodensee
lamb [læm] s Lamm n; (culin) Lammfleisch n
lambaste [læm'best] tr (berate) (coll) herunterputzen; (beat) (coll) verdreschen
lamb' chop' s Hammelrippchen n
lambkin ['læmkɪn] s Lammfell n
lame [lem] adj (person, leg; excuse) lahm; **be l. in one leg** auf e-m Bein lahm sein || tr lähmen
lament [lə'ment] s Jammer m; (dirge) Klagelied n || tr beklagen || intr wehklagen
lamentable ['læməntəbəl] adj beklagenswert; (pej) jämmerlich
lamentation [ˌlæmə'teʃən] s Wehklage f
laminate ['læmɪˌnet] tr schichten
lamp [læmp] s Lampe f
lamp' chim'ney s Lampenzylinder m
lamp'light' s Lampenlicht n
lamp'light'er s Laternenanzünder m
lampoon [læm'pun] s Schmähschrift f || tr mit e-r Schmähschrift verspotten
lamp'post' s Laternenpfahl m
lamp'shade' s Lampenschirm m
lance [læns] s Lanze f; (surg) Lanzette f || tr (surg) aufstechen
lance' cor'poral s (Brit) Hauptgefreite m
lancet ['lænsɪt] s Lanzette f
land [lænd] s (dry land; country) Land n; (ground) Boden m; **by l.** zu Lande || tr (a plane, troops, punch) landen; (a ship, fish) an Land bringen; (a job) (coll) kriegen; **l. s.o. in trouble** j-n in Schwierigkeiten bringen || intr (aer, naut, & fig) landen; (said of a blow) treffen; **l. on s.o.'s head** j-m auf den Kopf fallen; **l. on water** auf dem Wasser aufsetzen
land' breeze' s Landwind m
land'ed prop'erty s Landbesitz m
land'fall' s (sighting of land) Sichten n von Land; **make l.** landen
land' forc'es spl Landstreitkräfte pl
land'ing s Landung f; (of a staircase) Absatz m; **l. on the moon** Mondlandung f
land'ing craft' s Landungsboot n
land'ing field' s Landeplatz m
land'ing force' s Landekorps n
land'ing gear' s Fahrgestell n
land'ing par'ty s Landeabteilung f
land'ing stage' s Landungssteg m
land'ing strip' s Start- und Landestreifen m
land'la'dy s (of an apartment) Hauswirtin f; (of an inn) Gastwirtin f
land'locked' adj landumschlossen
land'lord' s (of an apartment) Hauswirt m; (of an inn) Gastwirt m
landlubber ['lænd ˌlʌbər] s Landratte f

land'mark' s Landmarke f; (cardinal event) Markstein m
land' of'fice s Grundbuchamt n
land'-office bus'iness s (fig) Bombengeschäft n
land'own'er s Grundbesitzer –in mf
landscape ['lænd ˌskep] s Landschaft f; (paint) Landschaftsbild n || tr landschaftlich gestalten
land'scape ar'chitect s Landschaftsarchitekt –in mf
land'scape paint'er s Landschaftsmaler –in mf
land'slide' s Bergrutsch m; (pol) Stimmenrutsch m
landward ['lændwərd] adv landwärts
land' wind' [wɪnd] s Landwind m
lane [len] s Bahn f; (country road) Feldweg m; (aer) Flugschneise f; (aut) Fahrbahn f; (naut) Fahrtroute f; (sport) Laufbahn f; (sport) Schwimmbahn f
language ['læŋgwɪdʒ] s Sprache f
lan'guage instruc'tion s Sprachunterricht m
lan'guage teach'er s Sprachlehrer –in mf
languid ['læŋgwɪd] adj schlaff
languish ['læŋgwɪʃ] intr schmachten
languor ['læŋgər] s Mattigkeit f
languorous ['læŋgərəs] adj matt
lank [læŋk] adj schlank; (hair) glatt
lanky ['læŋkɪ] adj schlaksig
lanolin ['lænəlɪn] s Lanolin n
lantern ['læntərn] s Laterne f
lan'tern slide' s Diapositiv n
lanyard ['lænjərd] s (around the neck) Halsschnur f; (naut) Taljereep n
Laos ['le·ɑs] s Laos n
Laotian [le'oʃən] adj laotisch || s Laote m, Laotin f; (language) Laotisch n
lap [læp] s (of the body or clothing) Schoß m; (of the waves) Plätschern n; (sport) Runde f || v (pret & pp lapped; ger lapping) tr schlappen; (sport) überrunden; **lap up auf(sch)-lecken** || intr—**lap against** (e.g., a boat, shore) plätschern gegen; **lap over** hinausragen über (acc)
lap' dog' s Schoßhund m
lapel [lə'pel] s Aufschlag m
Lap'land' s Lappland n
Laplander ['læp ˌlændər] s Lappländer –in mf
Lapp [læp] s Lappe m, Lappin f; (language) Lappisch n
lapse [læps] s (error) Versehen n; (of time) Ablauf m; **after a l. of** nach Ablauf von; **l. of duty** Pflichtversäumnis f; **l. of memory** Gedächtnislücke f || intr (said of a right, an insurance policy) verfallen; (said of time) ablaufen; **l. into** verfallen in (acc); **l. into unconsciousness** das Bewußtsein verlieren
lap'wing' s Kiebitz m
larceny ['lɑrsənɪ] s Diebstahl m
larch [lɑrtʃ] s (bot) Lärche f
lard [lɑrd] s Schmalz n || tr spicken
larder ['lɑrdər] s Speisekammer f
large [lɑrdʒ] adj groß; **at l.** (as a whole) gesamt; (at liberty) auf freiem

Fuß; (*said of an official*) zur besonderen Verfügung; **become larger** sich vergrößern; **on a l. scale** in großem Umfang

large′ intes′tine *s* Dickdarm *m*

largely [′lɑrdʒli] *adv* größtenteils

largeness [′lɑrdʒnɪs] *s* Größe *f*

large′-scale′ *adj* Groß–; (*map*) in großem Maßstab; (*production*) Serien–

largesse [′lɑrdʒes] *s* (*generosity*) Freigebigkeit *f*; (*handout*) Geldverteilung *f*

lariat [′læri·ət] *s* Lasso *m* & *n*; (*for grazing animals*) Halteseil *n*

lark [lɑrk] *s* (orn) Lerche *f*; **for a l.** zum Spaß

lark′spur′ *s* (bot) Rittersporn *m*

lar·va [′lɑrvə] *s* (–vae [vi]) Larve *f*

laryngitis [ˌlærɪn′dʒaɪtɪs] *s* Kehlkopfentzündung *f*, Laryngitis *f*

larynx [′lærɪŋks] *s* (**larynxes & larynges** [ləˈrɪndʒiz]) Kehlkopf *m*

lascivious [ləˈsɪvɪ·əs] *adj* wollüstig

lasciviousness [ləˈsɪvɪ·əsnɪs] *s* Wollüstigkeit *f*

laser [′lezər] *s* Laser *m*

lash [læʃ] *s* Peitsche *f*; (*as a punishment*) Peitschenhieb *m*; (*of the eye*) Wimper *f* ‖ *tr* (*whip*) peitschen; (*bind*) (**to**) anbinden (an *acc*); (*said of rain, storms*) peitschen ‖ *intr*—**l. out** (**at**) ausschlagen (nach)

lass [læs] *s* Mädel *n*

lassitude [′læsɪˌt(j)ud] *s* Mattigkeit *f*

last [læst] *adj* letzte; **very l.** allerletzte ‖ *adv* zuletzt; **l. of all** zuallerletzt ‖ *s* Letzte *mfn*; (*of a cobbler*) Schuhleisten *m*; **at l.** schließlich; **at long l.** zu guter Letzt; **look one′s l. on** zum letzten Mal blicken auf (*acc*); **see the l. of s.o.** j–n nicht mehr wiedersehen; **to the l.** bis zum Letzten ‖ *intr* (*remain unchanged*) anhalten; (*for a specific time*) dauern; (*said of money, supplies*) reichen; (*said of a person*) aushalten

last′ing *adj* dauerhaft, andauernd; **l. effect** Dauerwirkung *f*; **l. for months** monatelang

Last′ Judg′ment *s* Jüngstes Gericht *n*

lastly [′læstli] *adv* zuletzt

last′-min′ute *adj* in letzter Minute

last′-minute news′ *s* neueste Nachrichten *pl*

last′ night′ *adv* gestern abend

last′ quar′ter *s* (astr) abnehmendes Mondviertel *n*; (com) letztes Quartal *n*

last′ resort′ *s* letztes Mittel *n*

last′ sleep′ *s* Todesschlaf *m*

last′ straw′ *s*—that′s the **l.** das schlägt dem Faß den Boden aus

Last′ Sup′per *s* das Letzte Abendmahl

last′ week′ *adv* vorige Woche

last′ will′ and test′ament *s* letztwillige Verfügung *f*

last′ word′ *s* letztes Wort *n*; **the l.** (fig) der letzte Schrei

latch [lætʃ] *s* Klinke *f* ‖ *tr* zuklinken ‖ *intr* einschnappen; **l. on to** (coll) spitzkriegen

latch′key′ *s* Hausschlüssel *m*

late [let] *adj* (*after the usual time*) spät; (*at a late hour*) zu später Stunde; (*deceased*) verstorben; **be l.** sich verspäten; (*said of a train*) Verspätung haben; **keep l. hours** spät aufbleiben ‖ *adv* spät; **come l.** zu spät kommen; **of l.** kürzlich; **see you later** (coll) bis später!

latecomer [′let ˌkʌmər] *s* Nachzügler *m*

lateen′ sail′ [lætin] *s* Lateinsegel *n*

lateen′ yard′ *s* Lateinrah *f*

lately [′letli] *adv* neulich, unlängst

lateness [′letnɪs] *s* Verspätung *f*

latent [′letənt] *adj* latent, verborgen

later [′letər] *adj* später ‖ *adv* später, nachher; **l. on** späterhin

lateral [′lætərəl] *adj* seitlich, Seiten–

lath [læθ] *s* Latte *f* ‖ *tr* belatten

lathe [leð] *s* Drehbank *f*; **turn on a l.** drechseln

lather [′læðər] *s* Seifenschaum *m*; (*of a horse*) schäumender Schweiß *m* ‖ *tr* einseifen ‖ *intr* schäumen

lathing [′læθɪŋ] *s* Lattenwerk *n*

Latin [′lætɪn] *adj* lateinisch ‖ *s* (*Romance-speaking person*) Romane *m*, Romanin *f*; (*language*) Lateinisch *n*

La′tin Amer′ica *s* Lateinamerika *n*

La′tin-Amer′ican *adj* lateinamerikanisch ‖ *s* Lateinamerikaner –in *mf*

latitude [′lætɪˌt(j)ud] *s* Breite *f*; (fig) Spielraum *m*

latrine [ləˈtrin] *s* Latrine *f*

latter [′lætər] *adj* (*later*) später; (*final*) End–; (*recent*) letzte; **in the l. part of** (*e.g., the year*) in der zweiten Hälfte (*genit*); **the l.** dieser

lat′ter-day′ *adj* (*later*) später; (*recent*) letzte

Lat′ter-day Saint′ *s* Heilige *mf* der Jüngsten Tage

lattice [′lætɪs] *s* Gitter *n* ‖ *tr* vergittern

lat′ticework′ *s* Gitterwerk *n*

Latvia [′lætvɪ·ə] *s* Lettland *n*

Latvian [′lætvɪ·ən] *adj* lettisch ‖ *s* Lette *m*, Lettin *f*; (*language*) Lettisch *n*

laud [lɔd] *tr* loben, preisen

laudable [′lɔdəbəl] *adj* löblich

laudanum [′lɔd(ə)nəm] *s* Opiumtinktur *f*

laudatory [′lɔdəˌtɔri] *adj* Lob–

laugh [læf] *s* Lachen *n*, Gelächter *n*; **for laughs** zum Spaß; **have a good l.** sich auslachen ‖ *tr*—**l. off** sich lachend hinwegsetzen über (*acc*) ‖ *intr* lachen; **it′s easy for you to l.** Sie haben leicht lachen!; **l. about** lachen über (*acc*); **l. at** (*deride*) auslachen; (*find amusement in*) lachen über (*acc*)

laughable [′læfəbəl] *adj* lächerlich

laugh′ing *adj* lachend; **it′s no l. matter** es ist nichts zum Lachen

laugh′ing gas′ *s* Lachgas *n*

laugh′ingstock′ *s* Gespött *n*

laughter [′læftər] *s* Gelächter *n*, Lachen *n*; **roar with l.** vor Lachen brüllen

launch [lɔntʃ] *s* (*open boat*) Barkasse

f || *tr (a boat)* aussetzen; *(a ship)* vom Stapel laufen lassen; *(a plane)* katapultieren; *(a rocket)* starten; *(a torpedo)* abschießen; *(an offensive)* beginnen; **be launched** (naut) vom Stapel laufen; (rok) starten || *intr—* **l. into** sich stürzen in *(acc)*

launch′ing *s (of a ship)* Stapellauf *m; (of a torpedo)* Ausstoß *m; (of a rocket)* Abschuß *m,* Start *m*

launch′ pad′ *s* (rok) Startrampe *f*

launder [′lɔndər] *tr* waschen

laundress [′lɔndrɪs] *s* Wäscherin *f*

laundry [′lɔndrɪ] *s (clothes)* Wäsche *f; (room)* Waschküche *f; (business)* Wäscherei *f*

laun′drybag′ *s* Wäschebeutel *m*

laun′drybas′ket *s* Wäschekorb *m*

laun′dry list′ *s* Waschzettel *m*

laun′dry·man′ *s (-men′)* Wäscher *m*

laun′dry·wom′an *s (-wom′en)* Wäscherin *f*

laurel [′lɔrəl] *s* Lorbeer *m*

lau′rel tree′ *s* Lorbeerbaum *m*

lava [′lɑvə] *s* Lava *f*

lavatory [′lævə‚tori] *s* Waschraum *m; (toilet)* Toilette *f*

lavender [′lævəndər] *adj* lavendelfarben || *s* (bot) Lavendel *m*

lavish [′lævɪʃ] *adj (person)* verschwenderisch; *(dinner)* üppig || *tr—***l. care on** hegen und pflegen; **l. s.th. on s.o.** j-n mit etw überhäufen

lavishness [′lævɪʃnɪs] *s* Üppigkeit *f*

law [lɔ] *s* Gesetz *n; (system)* Recht *n; (as a science)* Rechtswissenschaft *f; (relig)* Gebot *n;* **according to law** dem Recht entsprechend; **act within the law** sich ans Gesetz halten; **against the law** gesetzwidrig; **become law** Gesetzkraft erlangen; **by law** gesetzlich; **go against the law** gegen das Gesetz handeln; **lay down the law** gebieterisch auftreten; **practice law** den Anwaltsberuf ausüben; **study law** Jura studieren; **take the law into one's own hands** sich *[dat]* selbst sein Recht verschaffen; **under the law** nach dem Gesetz

law′-abid′ing *adj* friedlich

law′ and or′der *s* Ruhe und Ordnung *pl*

law′-and-or′der *adj* für Ruhe und Ordnung

law′break′er *s* Rechtsbrecher *–in mf*

law′break′ing *s* Rechtsbruch *m*

law′court′ *s* Gerichtshof *m,* Gericht *n*

lawful [′lɔfəl] *adj* gesetzmäßig

lawless [′lɔlɪs] *adj* gesetzlos

lawlessness [′lɔlɪsnɪs] *s* Gesetzlosigkeit *f*

law′mak′er *s* Gesetzgeber *s*

lawn [lɔn] *s* Rasen *m;* (tex) Batist *m*

lawn′ mow′er *s* Rasenmäher *m*

lawn′ par′ty *s* Gartenfest *n*

lawn′ sprin′kler *s* Rasensprenger *m*

law′ of dimin′ishing returns′ *s* Gesetz *n* der abnehmenden Erträge

law′ of′fice *s* Anwaltsbüro *n*

law′ of na′tions *s* Völkerrecht *n*

law′ of na′ture *s* Naturgesetz *n*

law′ of probabil′ity *s* Wahrscheinlichkeitsgesetz *n*

law′ of supply′ and demand′ *s* Gesetz *n* von Angebot und Nachfrage

law′ of the land′ *s* Landesgesetz *n*

law′ school′ *s* juristische Fakultät *f*

law′ stu′dent *s* Student *–in mf* der Rechtswissenschaft

law′suit′ *s* Klage *f,* Prozeß *m*

lawyer [′lɔjər] *s* Advokat *–in m,* Anwalt *–in mf*

lax [læks] *adj* lax, nachlässig

laxative [′læksətɪv] *s* Abführmittel *n*

laxity [′læksɪti] *s* Laxheit *f*

lay [le] *adj (not of the clergy)* Laien–, weltlich; *(non-expert)* laienhaft || *s (poem)* Lied *n* || *v (pret & pp* **laid** [led]) *tr* legen; *(eggs; foundation, bricks, lineoleum)* legen; *(cables, pipes, tracks)* verlegen; *(vulg)* umlegen; **be laid up with** das Bett hüten müssen wegen *(genit);* **I'll lay you two to one** ich wette mit dir zwei zu eins; **lay aside** beiseite legen; *(save)* sparen; **lay bare** bloßlegen; **lay down** niederlegen; *(principles)* aufstellen; **lay claim to** Anspruch erheben auf *(acc);* **lay it on thick** dick auftragen; **lay low** *(said of an illness)* bettlägerig machen; **lay off** *(workers)* vorübergehend entlassen; **lay open** freilegen; **lay out** auslegen; *(a garden)* anlegen; *(money)* aufwenden; *(a corpse)* aufbahren; (surv) abstecken; **lay siege to** belagern; **lay waste** verwüsten || *intr (said of hens)* legen; **lay for** auflauern *(dat);* **lay into** *(beat)* (coll) verdreschen; *(scold)* (coll) heruntermachen; **lay off** *(abstain from)* sich enthalten *(genit); (let alone)* in Ruhe lassen; **lay over** *(on a trip)* sich aufhalten; **lay to** (naut) stilliegen

lay′ broth′er *s* Laienbruder *m*

layer [′le·ər] *s* Schicht *f;* (bot) Ableger *m;* **in layers** schichtenweise; **l. of fat** Fettschicht *f;* **thin l.** Hauch *m*

lay′er cake′ *s* Schichttorte *f*

layette [le′ɛt] *s* Babyausstattung *f*

lay′ fig′ure *s* Gliederpuppe *f*

lay′man *s (-men)* Laie *m;* **layman's** laienhaft

lay′off′ *s* vorübergehende Entlassung *f*

lay′ of the land′ *s* Gestaltung *f* des Terrains; (fig) Gesichtspunkt *m* der Angelegenheit

lay′out′ *s* Anlage *f,* Anordnung *f;* (typ) Layout *n;* **l. of rooms** Raumverteilung *f*

laziness [′lezɪnɪs] *s* Faulheit *f*

lazy [′lezi] *adj* faul

la′zybones′ *s* (coll) Faulpelz *m*

la′zy Su′san *s* drehbares Tablett *n*

lea [li] *s* (poet) Aue *f*

lead [led] *adj* Blei– || *s* Blei *n; (in a pencil)* Mine *f; (plumb line)* Bleilot *n* || *v (pret & pp* **leaded;** *ger* **leading)** *tr* verbleien; (typ) durchschießen || [lid] *s* Führung *f; (cards)* Vorhand *f;* (elec) Zuführung *f;* (sport) Vorsprung *m;* (theat) Hauptrolle *f;* **be in the l.** an der Spitze stehen; **have the l.** die Führung haben; **take the l.** Führung übernehmen || *v (pret & pp*

led [lɛd]) *tr* führen, leiten; *(to error, drinking, etc.)* verleiten; *(a parade)* anführen; *(a life)* führen; **l. astray** verführen; **l. away** wegführen; *(e.g., a criminal)* abführen; **l. back** zurückführen; **l. by the nose** an der Nase herumführen; **l. on** weiterführen; *(deceive)* täuschen; **l. the way** vorangehen ‖ *intr* führen; *(cards)* anspielen; **l. nowhere** zu nichts führen; **l. off** den Anfang machen; **l. to** hinausgehen auf *(acc)*; **l. up to** hinauswollen auf *(acc)* **where will all this l. to?** wo soll das alles hinführen?

leaden ['lɛdən] *adj* bleiern; *(in color)* bleifarbig; *(sluggish)* schwerfällig; **l. sky** bleierner Himmel *m*

leader ['lidər] *s* Führer –in *mf*; *(of a band)* Dirigent –in *mf*; *(of a film)* Vorspann *m*; *(lead article)* Leitartikel *m*

lead′ership′ *s* Führung *f*

leading ['lidɪŋ] *adj (person, position, power)* führend

lead′ing ide′a *s* Leitgedanke *m*

lead′ing la′dy *s* Hauptdarstellerin *f*

lead′ing man′ *s* Hauptdarsteller *m*

lead′ing ques′tion *s* Suggestivfrage *f*

lead′ing role′ *s* Hauptrolle *f*

lead′-in wire′ *s* Zuleitungsdraht *m*

lead′ pen′cil [lɛd] *s* Bleistift *m*

lead′ pipe′ [lɛd] *s* Bleirohr *n*

lead′ poi′soning [lɛd] *s* Bleivergiftung *f*

leaf [lif] *s* (**leaves** [livz]) Blatt *n*; *(of a folding door)* Flügel *m*; *(of a folding table)* Tischklappe *f*; *(insertable table board)* Einlegebrett *n*; **turn over a new l.** ein neues Leben anfangen ‖ *intr*—**l. through** durchblättern

leafage ['lifɪdʒ] *s* Laubwerk *n*

leafless ['liflɪs] *adj* blattlos

leaflet ['liflɪt] *s* Werbeprospekt *m*, Flugblatt *n*; *(bot)* Blättchen *n*

leafy ['lifi] *adj (abounding in leaves)* belaubt; *(e.g., vegetables)* Blatt–

league [lig] *s* Bund *m*; *(unit of distance)* Meile *f*; *(sport)* Liga *f*; **in l. with** verbündet mit ‖ *tr* verbünden ‖ *intr* sich verbünden

League′ of Na′tions *s* Völkerbund *m*

leak [lik] *s* Leck *n*; **spring a l.** ein Leck bekommen; **take a l.** *(vulg)* schiffen ‖ *tr (e.g., a story to the press)* durchsickern lassen ‖ *intr (said of a container)* leck sein; *(said of a boat)* lecken; *(said of a fluid)* auslaufen; *(said of a spigot)* tropfen; **l. out** (& fig) durchsickern

leakage ['likɪdʒ] *s* Lecken *n*; *(& fig)* Durchsickern *n*; *(com)* Schwund *m*; *(elec)* Streuung *f*

leaky ['liki] *adj* leck

lean [lin] *adj* mager ‖ *v (pret & pp leaned & leant* [lɛnt] *) tr (against)* lehnen (an *acc* or gegen) ‖ *intr* lehnen; **l. against** sich anlehnen an *(acc)*; **l. back** sich zurücklehnen; **l. forward** sich vorbeugen; **l. on** sich stützen auf *(acc)*; **l. over** *(e.g., a railing)* sich neigen über *(acc)*; **l. toward** (fig) neigen zu

lean′ing *adj* sich neigend; *(tower)* schief ‖ *s (toward)* Neigung *f* (zu)

leanness ['linnɪs] *s* Magerkeit *f*

lean′-to′ *s* (–**tos**) Anbau *m* mit Pultdach

lean′ years′ *spl* magere Jahre *pl*

leap [lip] *s* Sprung *m*, Satz *m*; **by leaps and bounds** sprungweise; **l. in the dark** (fig) Sprung *m* ins Ungewisse ‖ *v (pret & pp leaped & leapt* [lɛpt]*) tr* überspringen ‖ *intr* springen; **l. at** anspringen; **l. at an opportunity** e–e Gelegenheit beim Schopf ergreifen; **l. forward** vorspringen; **l. up** emporschnellen

leap′frog′ *s* Bocksprung *m*; **play l.** Bocksprünge machen

leap′ year′ *s* Schaltjahr *n*

learn [lʌrn] *v (pret & pp learned & learnt* [lʌrnt]*) tr* lernen; *(find out)* erfahren; **l. s.th. from s.o.**

learned ['lʌrnɪd] *adj (person, word)* gelehrt; *(for or of scholars)* Gelehrten–

learn′ed jour′nal *s* Gelehrtenzeitschrift *f*

learn′ed soci′ety *s* Gelehrtenvereinigung *f*

learn′ed world′ *s* Gelehrtenwelt *f*

learn′ing *s (act)* Lernen *n*; *(erudition)* Gelehrsamkeit *f*

lease [lis] *s* Mietvertrag *m*; *(of land)* Pachtvertrag *m* ‖ *tr (in the role of landlord)* vermieten; *(land)* verpachten; *(in the role of tenant)* mieten; *(land)* pachten

lease′hold′ *adj* Pacht– ‖ *s* Pachtbesitz *m*

leash [liʃ] *s* Leine *f*, Hundeleine *f*; **keep on the l.** an der Leine führen; **strain at the l.** (fig) an der Leine zerren ‖ *tr* an die Leine nehmen

leas′ing *s* Miete *f*; *(of land)* Pachtung *f*; **l. out** Vermietung *f*; *(of land)* Verpachtung *f*

least [list] *adj* mindeste, wenigste ‖ *adv* am wenigsten; **l. of all** am wenigsten von allen ‖ *s* Geringste *mfn*; **at l.** mindestens, wenigstens; **at the very l.** zum mindesten; **not in the l.** nicht im mindesten

leather ['lɛðər] *adj* ledern ‖ *s* Leder *n*

leath′er bind′ing *s* Ledereinband *m*

leath′erbound′ *adj* ledergebunden

leath′erneck′ *s* (sl) Marineinfanterist *m*

leathery ['lɛðəri] *adj (e.g., steak)* (coll) lederartig

leave [liv] *s (permission)* Erlaubnis *f*; *(mil)* Urlaub *m*; **on l.** auf Urlaub; **take l. (from)** Abschied nehmen (von); **take l. of one's senses** (coll) den Verstand verlieren ‖ *v (pret & pp left* [lɛft]*) tr (go away from)* verlassen; *(undone, open, etc.)* lassen; *(a message, bequest)* hinterlassen; *(a job)* aufgeben; *(a scar)* zurücklassen; *(forget)* liegenlassen, stehenlassen; *(e.g., some food for s.o.)* übriglassen; **be left** übrig sein; **l. alone** *(a thing)* bleibenlassen; *(a person)* in Frieden lassen; **l. behind** *(said of a deceased person)* hinterlassen; *(forget)* liegenlassen; **l. home von zu Hause** fortgehen; **l. it at that!** überlaß es mir!; **l. lying about herumliegen** lassen; **l. nothing to chance** nichts dem Zufall überlassen; **l. nothing undone** nichts unversucht lassen; **l. open** offen lassen; **l. out** auslassen; **l. standing** stehenlassen; **l.** *(e.g., work)* **undone** liegenlassen || *intr* fortgehen; *(on travels)* abreisen; *(said of vehicles)* abfahren; (aer) abfliegen; **l. off** *(e.g., from reading)* aufhören

leaven ['levən] *s* Treibmittel *n* || *tr* säuern

leav′ening *s* Treibstoff *m*

leave′ of ab′sence *s* Urlaub *m*

leave′-tak′ing *s* Abschiednehmen *n*

leavings ['livɪŋz] *spl* Überbleibsel *pl*

Leba•nese [ˌlebə′niz] *adj* libanesisch || *s (-nese)* Libanese *m*, Libanesin *f*

Lebanon ['lebənən] *s* Libanon *n*

lecher ['letʃər] *s* Lüstling *m*

lecherous ['letʃərəs] *adj* wollüstig

lechery ['letʃəri] *s* Wollust *f*

lectern ['lektərn] *s* Lesepult *n*

lector ['lektər] *s* (eccl) Lektor *m*

lecture ['lektʃər] *s* Vorlesung *f*, Vortrag *m*; (coll) Standpauke *f*; **give a l. on** e-n Vortrag halten über *(acc)*; **give s.o. a l.** j-m den Text lesen || *tr* (coll) abkanzeln || *intr* lesen

lecturer ['lektʃərər] *s* Vortragende *mf*; *(at a university)* Dozent –in *mf*

lec′ture room′ *s* Hörsaal *m*

ledge [ledʒ] *s* Sims *m & n*; *(of a cliff)* Felsenriff *n*

ledger ['ledʒər] *s* (acct) Hauptbuch *n*

lee [li] *s* Lee *f*

leech [litʃ] *s* Blutegel *m*; (fig) Blutsauger –in *mf*

leek [lik] *s* (bot) Porree *m*, Lauch *m*

leer [lɪr] *s* lüsterner Seitenblick *m* || *intr* (at) lüstern schielen (nach)

leery ['lɪri] *adj* mißtrauisch; **be l. of** mißtrauen *(dat)*

lees [liz] *spl* Hefe *f*

lee′ side′ *s* Leeseite *f*

leeward ['liwərd] *adv* leewärts || *s* Leeseite *f*

Lee′ward Is′lands *spl* Inseln *pl* unter dem Winde

lee′way′ *s* (coll) Spielraum *m*; (aer, naut) Abtrift *f*

left [left] *adj* linke; *(left over)* übrig || *adv* links; **l. face!** (mil) links um! || *s (left hand)* Linke *f*; **on our l.** zu unserer Linken; **the l.** (pol) die Linke; **the third street to the l.** die dritte Querstraße links; **to the l.** nach links; **to the l. of** links von

left′ field′er *s* (baseball) linkes Außenfeld *n*

left′ field′er ['fildər] *s* Spieler *m* im linken Außenfeld

left′-hand driver *s* Linkssteuerung *f*

left′-hand′ed *adj* linkshändig; *(compliment)* fragwürdig; *(counterclockwise)* linksgängig; *(clumsy)* linkisch

left-hander ['left′hændər] *s* Linkshänder –in *mf*

leftish ['leftɪʃ] *adj* linksgerichtet

leftist ['leftɪst] *s* Linksradikaler *m*; (pol) Linkspolitiker –in *mf*

left′o′ver *adj* übriggeblieben || **leftovers** *spl* Überbleibsel *pl*

left′-wing′ *adj* Links-

left′ wing′ *s* (pol) linker Flügel *m*; (sport) Linksaußen *m*

left-winger ['left′wɪŋər] *s* (coll) Linkspolitiker –in *mf*

lefty ['lefti] *adj* (coll) linkshändig || *s* (coll) Linkshänder –in *mf*

leg [leg] *s* *(of a body, of furniture, of trousers)* Bein *n*; *(stretch)* Etappe *f*; *(of a compass)* Schenkel *m*; *(of a boot)* Schaft *m*; **be on one's last legs** auf dem letzten Loche pfeifen; **pull s.o.'s leg** (coll) j-n auf die Schippe nehmen; **run one's legs off** sich abrennen; **you don't have a leg to stand on** Sie haben keinerlei Beweise

legacy ['legəsi] *s* Vermächtnis *n*

legal ['ligəl] *adj* *(according to the law)* gesetzlich, legal; *(pertaining to or approved by law)* Rechts–, juristisch; **take l. action** den Rechtsweg beschreiten; **take l. steps against s.o.** gerichtlich gegen j-n vorgehen

le′gal advice′ *s* Rechtsberatung *f*

le′gal advis′er *s* Rechtsberater –in *mf*

le′gal age′ *s* Volljährigkeit *f*; **of l.** großjährig

le′gal aid′ *s* Rechtshilfe *f*

le′gal ba′sis *s* Rechtsgrundlage *f*

le′gal case′ *s* Rechtsfall *m*

le′gal claim′ *s* Rechtsanspruch *m*

le′gal en′tity *s* juristische Person *f*

le′gal force′ *s* Rechtskraft *f*

le′gal grounds′ *spl* Rechtsgrund *m*

le′gal hol′iday *s* gesetzlicher Feiertag *m*

legality [lɪ′gælti] *s* Gesetzlichkeit *f*, Rechtlichkeit *f*

legalize ['ligəˌlaɪz] *tr* legalisieren

le′gal jar′gon *s* Kanzleisprache *f*

le′gal profes′sion *s* Rechtsanwaltsberuf *m*

le′gal rem′edy *s* Rechtsmittel *n*

le′gal ten′der *s* gesetzliches Zahlungsmittel *n*; **be l.** gelten

le′gal ti′tle *s* Rechtsanspruch *m*

legate ['legɪt] *s* Legat –in *mf*

legatee [ˌlegə′ti] *s* Legatar –in *mf*

legation [lɪ′geʃən] *s* Gesandtschaft *f*

legend ['ledʒənd] *s* Legende *f*

legendary ['ledʒənˌderi] *adj* legendär

legerdemain [ˌledʒərdɪ′men] *s* Taschenspielerei *f*

leggings ['legɪŋz] *spl* hohe Gamaschen *pl*

leggy ['legi] *adj* langbeinig

Leg′horn′ *s* (chicken) Leghorn *n*; *(town in Italy)* Livorno *m*

legibility [ˌledʒɪ′brɪlti] *s* Lesbarkeit *f*

legible ['ledʒɪbəl] *adj* lesbar

legion ['lidʒən] *s* Legion *f*; (fig) Heerschar *f*

legionnaire [ˌlidʒə′ner] *s* Legionär *m*

legislate ['ledʒɪsˌlet] *tr* durch Gesetzgebung bewirken || *intr* Gesetze geben

legislation [ˌledʒɪs′leʃən] *s* Gesetzgebung *f*

legislative ['lɛdʒɪs‚lɛtɪv] *adj* gesetzgebend

legislator ['lɛdʒɪs‚lɛtər] *s* Gesetzgeber –in *mf*

legislature ['lɛdʒɪs‚lɛtʃər] *s* Legislatur *f*

legitimacy [lɪ'dʒɪtɪməsi] *s* Rechtmäßigkeit *f*

legitimate [lɪ'dʒɪtɪmɪt] *adj* gesetzmäßig, legitim; (*child*) ehelich ‖ [lɪ'dʒɪtɪ‚met] *tr* legitimieren

legit′imate the′ater *s* literarisch wertvolles Theater *n*

legitimize [lɪ'dʒɪtɪ‚maɪz] *tr* legitimieren

leg′ of lamb′ *s* Lammkeule *f*

leg′ of mut′ton *s* Hammelkeule *f*

leg′ room′ *s* Beinfreiheit *f*

leg′work′ *s* Vorarbeiten *pl*

leisure ['liʒər] *s* Muße *f*; at l. mit Muße; at s.o.'s l. wenn es j–m paßt

lei′sure class′ *s* wohlhabende Klasse *f*

lei′sure hours′ *spl* Mußestunden *pl*

leisurely ['liʒərli] *adj & adv* gemächlich

lei′sure time′ *s* Freizeit *f*

lemon ['lɛmən] *adj* Zitronen– ‖ *s* Zitrone *f*; (sl) Niete *f*

lemonade [‚lɛmɪ'ned] *s* Zitronenlimonade *f*

lem′on squeez′er *s* Zitronenpresse *f*

lend [lɛnd] *v* (*pret & pp* lent [lɛnt]) *tr* leihen, borgen; l. at five percent interest zu fünf Prozent Zinsen anlegen; l. itself to sich eignen zu or für; l. oneself to sich hergeben zu; l. out ausleihen, verborgen; l. s.o. a hand j–m zur Hand gehen

lender ['lɛndər] *s* Verleiher –in *mf*

lend′ing li′brary *s* Leihbücherei *f*

length [lɛŋθ] *s* Länge *f*; (*of time*) Dauer *f*; (*in horse racing*) Pferdelänge *f*; at great l. sehr ausführlich; at l. ausführlich; (*finally*) schließlich; at some l. ziemlich ausführlich; go to any l. alles Erdenkliche tun; go to great lengths sich sehr bemühen; keep s.o. at arm's l. zu j–m Abstand wahren; stretch out full l. sich der Länge nach ausstrecken

lengthen ['lɛŋθən] *tr* verlängern; (*a vowel*) dehnen

length′ening *s* Verlängerung *f*; (ling) Dehnung *f*

length′wise′ *adj & adv* der Länge nach

lengthy ['lɛŋθi] *adj* langwierig

leniency ['linɪ‚ənsi] *s* Milde *f*

lens [lɛnz] *s* Linse *f*; (*combination of lenses*) Objektiv *n*

Lent [lɛnt] *s* Fastenzeit *f*

Lenten ['lɛntən] *adj* Fasten–

lentil ['lɛntɪl] *s* (bot) Linse *f*

leopard ['lɛpərd] *s* Leopard *m*

leper ['lɛpər] *s* Aussätzige *mf*

leprosy ['lɛprəsi] *s* Aussatz *m*, Lepra *f*

lesbian ['lɛzbɪ‚ən] *adj* lesbisch ‖ *s* Lesbierin *f*

lesbianism ['lɛzbɪ‚ə‚nɪzəm] *s* lesbische Liebe *f*

lesion ['liʒən] *s* Wunde *f*

less [lɛs] *comp adj* weniger, geringer; l. and l. immer weniger ‖ *adv* weniger, minder; l. than weniger als ‖ *s*—do with l. mit weniger auskommen; for l. billiger; in l. than no time in Null Komma nichts ‖ *prep* abzüglich (*genit* or *acc*); (arith) weniger (*acc*), minus (*acc*)

lessee [lɛ'si] *s* Mieter –in *mf*; (*of land*) Pächter –in *mf*

lessen ['lɛsən] *tr* vermindern ‖ *intr* sich vermindern, abnehmen

lesser ['lɛsər] *comp adj* minder, geringer

lesson ['lɛsən] *s* Unterrichtsstunde *f*, Stunde *f*; (*in a textbook*) Lektion *f*; (*warning*) Lehre *f*; learn a l. from e–e Lehre ziehen aus; let that be l. to you! lassen Sie sich das e–e Lehre sein

lessor ['lɛsər] *s* Vermieter –in *mf*; (*of land*) Verpächter –in *mf*

lest [lɛst] *conj* damit nicht; (after expressions of fear) daß

let [lɛt] *v* (*pret & pp* let; *ger* letting) *tr* lassen; I really let him have it! (coll) ich hab's ihm ordentlich gegeben!; let alone in Ruhe lassen; (*not to mention*) geschweige denn; let down herunterlassen; (*disappoint*) enttäuschen; let drop fallen lassen; let fly fliegen lassen; (coll) loslassen; let go fortlassen, loslassen; let go ahead vorlassen; let in hereinlassen; (*water*) zuleiten; let in on (e.g., a secret) einweihen in (*acc*); let it go, e.g., I'll let it go this time diesmal werde ich es noch hingehen lassen; let lie liegenlassen; let know wissen lassen, Bescheid geben (*dat*); let off (e.g., at the next corner) absetzen; let off easy noch so davonkommen lassen; let off scot-free straflos laufen lassen; let one's hair down (fig) sich gehenlassen; let out (*seams, air, water*) auslassen; (e.g., a yell) von sich geben; let pass durchlassen; let s.o. have s.th. j–m etw zukommen lassen; let stand (fig) gelten lassen; let through durchlassen; let things slide die Dinge laufen lassen; let things take their course den Dingen ihren Lauf lassen; let's go! los!; let us (or let's) (*inf*), e.g., let us (or let's) sing singen wir ‖ *intr* (*be rented out*) (*for*) vermietet werden (für); let fly with (coll) loslegen mit; let go of loslassen; let on that sich [*dat*] anmerken lassen, daß; let up nachlassen; let up on (coll) ablassen von

let′down′ *s* Hereinfall *m*

lethal ['liθəl] *adj* tödlich

lethargic [lɪ'θɑrdʒɪk] *adj* lethargisch

lethargy ['lɛθərdʒi] *s* Lethargie *f*

letter ['lɛtər] *s* Brief *m*, Schreiben *n*; (*of the alphabet*) Buchstabe *m*; by l. brieflich, schriftlich; to the l. aufs Wort ‖ *tr* beschriften

let′ter box′ *s* Briefkasten *m*

let′ter car′rier *s* Briefträger –in *mf*

let′ter drop′ *s* Briefeinwurf *m*

let′tered *adj* gelehrt

let′ter file′ *s* Briefordner *m*

let′terhead′ s Briefkopf m
let′tering s (act) Beschriften n; (inscription) Beschriftung f
let′ter of condol′ence s Beileidsbrief m
let′ter of cred′it s Kreditbrief m
let′ter of recommenda′tion s Empfehlungsbrief m
letter o′pener s Brieföffner m
let′terper′fect adj buchstabengetreu
let′terpress′ s (typ) Hochdruck m
let′ter scales′ spl Briefwaage f
let′ter to the ed′itor s Leserbrief m
lettuce [′letɪs] s Salat m
let′up′ s Nachlassen n; **without l.** ohne Unterlaß
leukemia [luˈkimɪ·ə] s Leukämie f
Levant [lɪˈvænt] s Levante f
Levantine [lɪˈvæntɪn] adj levantinisch ‖ s Levantiner –in mf
levee [′levɪ] s Uferdamm m
lev·el [′levəl] adj eben, gerade; (flat) flach; (spoonful) gestrichen; **be l. with** so hoch sein wie; **do one′s l. best** sein Möglichstes tun; **have a l. head** ausgeglichen sein; **keep a l. head** e–n klaren Kopf behalten ‖ s (& fig) Niveau n; (tool) Wasserwaage f; **at higher levels** höheren Ortes; **be up to the usual l.** (fig) auf der gewöhnlichen Höhe sein; **on a l. with** (& fig) auf gleicher Höhe mit; **on the l.** (fig) ehrlich ‖ v (pret & pp –el[l]ed; ger –el[l]ing or –el[l]ing) tr (a street, ground) planieren; **l.** (e.g., a rifle) **at** richten auf (acc); (e.g., complaints) richten gegen; **l. off** nivellieren; (aer) abfangen; **l. to the ground** dem Erdboden gleichmachen ‖ intr—**l. off** sich verflachen; (said of prices) sich stabilisieren; (aer) in Horizontalflug übergehen; **l. with s.o.** mit j–m offen sein
lev′elhead′ed adj besonnen, vernünftig
lever [′livər] s Hebel m, Brechstange f ‖ tr mit e–r Brechstange fortbewegen
leverage [′livərɪdʒ] s Hebelkraft f; (fig) Einfluß m
leviathan [lɪˈvaɪ·əθən] s Leviathan m
levitate [′levɪ‚tet] tr schweben lassen ‖ intr frei schweben
levitation [‚levɪˈteʃən] s Schweben n
levity [′levɪti] s Leichtsinn m
lev·y [′levɪ] s Truppenaushebung f; (of taxes) Erhebung f; (tax) Steuer f ‖ v (pret & pp –vied) tr (troops) ausheben; (taxes) erheben; **l. war on** Krieg führen gegen
lewd [lud] adj unzüchtig
lewdness [′ludnɪs] s Unzucht f
lexical [′leksɪkəl] adj lexikalisch
lexicographer [‚leksɪˈkɑgrəfər] s Lexikograph –in mf
lexicographic(al) [‚leksɪkəˈgræfɪk(əl)] adj lexikographisch
lexicography [‚leksɪˈkɑgrəfi] s Lexikographie f
lexicology [‚leksɪˈkɑlədʒi] s Wortforschung f, Lexikologie f
lexicon [′leksɪkən] s Wörterbuch n
liability [‚laɪ·əˈbɪlɪti] s (ins) Haftpflicht f; (jur) Haftung f; **liabilities** Schulden pl; (acct) Passiva pl

liabil′ity insur′ance s Haftpflichtversicherung f
liable [′laɪ·əbəl] adj (jur) haftbar (für); **be l. to** (inf) (coll) leicht können (inf); **l. for damages** schadenersatzpflichtig
liaison [liˈezɑn] s Verbindung f; (illicit affair) Liaison f; (ling) Bindung f
liai′son of′ficer s Verbindungsoffizier m
liar [′laɪ·ər] s Lügner –in mf
libation [laɪˈbeʃən] s Opfertrank m
li·bel [′laɪbəl] s Verleumdung f; (in writing) Schmähschrift f ‖ v (pret & pp –bel[l]ed; ger –bel[l]ing) tr verleumden
libelous [′laɪbələs] adj verleumderisch
li′bel suit′ s Verleumdungsklage f
liberal [′lɪbərəl] adj (views) liberal, freisinnig; (with money) freigebig; (gift) großzügig; (interpretation) weitherzig; (education) allgemeinbildend; (pol) liberal ‖ s Liberale mf
lib′eral arts′ spl Geisteswissenschaften pl
liberalism [′lɪbərə‚lɪzəm] s Liberalismus m
liberality [‚lɪbəˈrælti] s Freigebigkeit f, Großzügigkeit f
liberate [′lɪbə‚ret] tr befreien; (chem) freimachen
liberation [‚lɪbəˈreʃən] s Befreiung f; (chem) Freimachen n
liberator [′lɪbə‚retər] s Befreier –in mf
libertine [′lɪbər‚tin] s Wüstling m
liberty [′lɪbərti] s Freiheit f; **take liberties** sich [dat] Freiheiten herausnehmen; **you are at l. to** (inf) es steht Ihnen frei zu (inf)
libidinous [lɪˈbɪdɪnəs] adj wollüstig
libido [lɪˈbido] s Libido f
librarian [laɪˈbrerɪ·ən] s Bibliothekar –in mf
library [′laɪ‚brerɪ] s Bibliothek f
li′brary card′ s Benutzerkarte f
libret·to [lɪˈbreto] s (–tos) Operntext m, Libretto n
Libya [′lɪbɪ·ə] s Libyen n
Libyan [′lɪbɪ·ən] adj libysch ‖ s Libyer –in mf
license [′laɪsəns] s Lizenz f, Genehmigung f; (document) Zulassungsschein m; (for a business, restaurant) Konzession f; (to drive) Führerschein m; (excessive liberty) Zügellosigkeit f ‖ tr konzessionieren; (aut) zulassen
li′cense num′ber s (aut) Kennzeichen n
li′cense plate′ or **tag′** s Nummernschild n
licentious [laɪˈsenʃəs] adj unzüchtig
lichen [′laɪkən] s (bot) Flechte f
lick [lɪk] s Lecken n ‖ tr lecken; (thrash) (coll) wichsen; (defeat) (coll) schlagen; (said of a flame) züngeln an (dat); **l. clean** auslecken; **l. into shape** auf Hochglanz bringen; **l. off** ablecken; **l. one′s chops** sich [dat] die Lippen lecken; **l. s.o.′s boots** vor j–m kriechen; **l. up** auflecken
lick′ing s Prügel pl; **give s.o. a good l.** j–n versohlen

licorice [ˈlɪkərɪs] s Lakritze f
lid [lɪd] s Deckel m
lie [laɪ] s Lüge f; give the lie to s.o.
(or **s.th.**) j-n (or etw) Lügen strafen;
tell a lie lügen || v (pret & pp lied;
ger lying) tr—lie one's way out of
sich herauslügen aus || intr lügen;
lie like mad das Blaue vom Himmel
herunter lügen; lie to belügen || v
(pret lay [le]; pp lain [len]; ger
lying) intr liegen; lie down sich hin-
legen; lie down! (to a dog) leg dich!;
lie in wait auf der Lauer liegen; lie
in wait for auflauern (dat); lie low
sich versteckt halten; (bide one's
time) abwarten; take s.th. lying down
etw widerspruchslos hinnehmen
lie′ detec′tor s Lügendetektor m
lien [lin] s Pfandrecht n
lieu [lu] s—in l. of statt (genit)
lieutenant [luˈtenənt] s Leutnant m;
(nav) Kapitänleutnant m
lieuten′ant colo′nel s Oberstleutnant m
lieuten′ant comman′der s Korvetten-
kapitän m
lieuten′ant gen′eral s Generalleutnant
m
lieuten′ant gov′ernor s Vizegouverneur
m
lieuten′ant jun′ior grade′ s (nav) Oberleutnant m zur See
lieuten′ant sen′ior grade′ s (nav) Kapitänleutnant m
life [laɪf] adj (imprisonment) lebens-
länglich || s (lives [laɪvz]) Leben n;
(e.g., of a car) Lebensdauer f; all
my l. mein ganzes Leben lang; as big
as l. in voller Lebensgröße; bring
back to l. wieder zum Bewußtsein
bringen; bring to l. ins Leben bringen; for dear l. ums liebe Leben;
for l. auf Lebenszeit; full of l. voller
Leben; I can't for the l. of me ich
kann beim besten Willen nicht; lives
lost Menschenleben pl; not on your
l. auf keinen Fall; put l. into beleben; such is l.! so ist nun mal das
Leben; take one's l. sich [dat] das
Leben nehmen; upon my l.! so wahr
ich lebel; you can bet your l. on
that! darauf kannst du Gift nehmen!
life′-and-death′ adj auf Leben und Tod
life′ annu′ity s Lebensrente f
life′ belt′ s Schwimmgürtel m
life′blood′ s Lebensblut n
life′boat′ s Rettungsboot n
life′ buoy′ s Rettungsboje f
life′ expect′ancy s Lebenserwartung f
life′ guard′ s (at a pool) Bademeister
–in m/f; (at the shore) Strandwärter
–in m/f
life′ impris′onment s lebenslängliche
Haft f
life′ insur′ance s Lebensversicherung f
life′ jack′et s Schwimmweste f
lifeless [ˈlaɪflɪs] adj leblos m; (fig)
schwunglos
life′-like′ adj naturgetreu, lebensecht
life′ line′ s Rettungsleine f; (for a
diver) Signalleine f; (supply line)
Lebensader f
life′long′ adj lebenslänglich

life′ mem′ber s Mitglied n auf Lebenszeit
life′ of lei′sure s Wohlleben n
life′ of plea′sure s Wohlleben n
life′ of Ri′ley [ˈraɪli] s Herrenleben n
life′ of the par′ty s—be the l. die ganze
Gesellschaft unterhalten
life′ preserv′er [prɪ ˌzɑrvər] s Rettungs-
ring m
lifer [ˈlaɪfər] s (sl) Lebenslängliche m/f
life′ raft′ s Rettungsfloß n
lifesaver [ˈlaɪf ˌsevər] s Rettungs-
schwimmer –in m/f; (fig) rettender
Engel m
life′ sen′tence s Verurteilung f zu le-
benslänglicher Haft
life′-size(d)′ adj lebensgroß
life′ span′ s Lebensdauer f
life′ style′ s Lebensweise f
life′time′ adj lebenslänglich || s Leben
n; for a l. auf Lebenszeit; once in a
l. einmal im Leben
life′ vest′ s Schwimmweste f
life′work′ s Lebenswerk n
lift [lɪft] s (elevator) Aufzug m; (aer
& fig) Auftrieb m; give s.o. a l. j-n
im Wagen mitnehmen || tr heben;
(gently) lüpfen; (with effort) wuchten; (weights) stemmen; (the receiver) abnehmen; (an embargo) aufheben; (steal) (sl) klauen; l. up aufheben; (the eyes) erheben; not l. a
finger keinen Finger rühren || intr
(said of a mist) steigen; l. off (rok)
starten
lift′-off′ s (rok) Start m
lift′ truck′ s Lastkraftwagen m mit
Hebevorrichtung
ligament [ˈlɪgəmənt] s Band n
ligature [ˈlɪgətʃər] s (mus) Bindung f;
(act) (surg) Abbinden n; (filament)
(surg) Abbindungsschnur f; (typ)
Ligatur f
light [laɪt] adj (clothing, meal, music,
heart, wine, sleep, punishment,
weight) leicht; (day, beer, color,
complexion, hair) hell; as l. as day
tageshell; l. as a feather federleicht;
make l. of auf die leichte Schulter
nehmen; (belittle) als bedeutungslos
hinstellen || s Licht n; according to
his lights nach dem Maß seiner Einsicht; bring to l. ans Licht bringen;
come to l. ans Licht kommen; do
you have a l.? haben Sie Feuer?;
in the l. of im Lichte (genit), angesichts (genit); put in a false l. in ein
falsches Licht stellen; see the l. of
day (be born) das Licht der Welt
erblicken; shed l. on Licht werfen
auf (acc); throw quite a different l.
on ein ganz anderes Licht werfen
auf (acc) || v (pret & pp lighted &
lit [lɪt]) tr (a fire, cigarette) anzünden; (an oven) anheizen; (a
street) beleuchten; (a hall) erleuch-
ten; (a face) aufleuchten lassen ||
intr sich entzünden; l. up (said of a
face) aufleuchten; (light a cigarette)
sich [dat] e-e Zigarette anstecken
light′-blue′ adj lichtblau, hellblau
light′ bulb′ s Glühbirne f

light-complexioned [ˈlaɪtkəmˈplekʃənd] *adj* von heller Hautfarbe

lighten [ˈlaɪtən] *tr* (*in weight*) leichter machen; (*brighten*) erhellen; (*fig*) erleichtern || *intr* (*become brighter*) sich aufhellen; (*during a storm*) blitzen

lighter [ˈlaɪtər] *s* Feuerzeug *n*; (naut) Leichter *m*

ligh′ter flu′id *s* Feuerzeugbenzin *n*

light′-fin′gered *adj* geschickt; (*thievish*) langfingerig

light′-foot′ed *adj* leichtfüßig

light′-head′ed *adj* leichtsinnig; (*dizzy*) schwindlig

light′-heart′ed *adj* leichtherzig

light′-heavy′weight′ *adj* (box) Halbschwergewichts– || *s* Halbschwergewichtler *m*

light′house′ *s* Leuchtturm *m*

light′ing *s* Beleuchtung *f*

light′ing effects′ *spl* Lichteffekte *pl*

light′ing fix′ture *s* Beleuchtungskörper *m*

lightly [ˈlaɪtli] *adv* leicht; (*without due consideration*) leichthin; (*disparagingly*) geringschätzig

light′ me′ter *s* Lichtmesser *m*

lightness [ˈlaɪtnɪs] *s* (*in weight*) Leichtigkeit *f*; (*in shade*) Helligkeit *f*

lightning [ˈlaɪtnɪŋ] *s* Blitz *m* || *impers* —it is l. es blitzt

light′ning arrest′er [əˌrestər] *s* Blitzableiter *m*

light′ning bug′ *s* Leuchtkäfer *m*

light′ning rod′ *s* Blitzableiter *m*

light′ning speed′ *s* Windeseile *f*

light′ op′era *s* Operette *f*

light′ read′ing *s* Unterhaltungslektüre *f*

light′ship′ *s* Leuchtschiff *n*

light′ sleep′ *s* Dämmerschlaf *m*

light′ switch′ *s* Lichtschalter *m*

light′ wave′ *s* Lichtwelle *f*

light′weight′ *adj* (box) Leichtgewichts– || *s* (coll) geistig Minderbemittelter *m*; (box) Leichtgewichtler *m*

light′-year′ *s* Lichtjahr *n*

likable [ˈlaɪkəbəl] *adj* sympathisch, lieb

like [laɪk] *adj* gleich, ähnlich; **be l.** gleichen (*dat*) || *adv*—**l. crazy** (coll) wie verrückt || *s*—**and the l.** und dergleichen; **likes and dislikes** Neigungen und Abneigungen *pl* || *tr* gern haben, mögen; **I l. him** er ist mir sympathisch; **I l. the picture** das Bild gefällt mir; **I l. the food** das Essen schmeckt mir; **l. to** (*inf*), e.g., **I l. to read** ich lese gern || *intr*—**as you l.** wie Sie wollen; **if you l.** wenn Sie wollen || *prep* wie; **feel l.** (ger) Lust haben zu (*inf*); **feel l. hell** (sl) sich elend fühlen; **it looks l.** es sieht nach ... aus; **l. greased lightning** wie geschmiert; **that's just l. him** das sieht ihm ähnlich; **there's nothing l. traveling** es geht nichts übers Reisen

likelihood [ˈlaɪklɪˌhud] *s* Wahrscheinlichkeit *f*

likely [ˈlaɪkli] *adj* wahrscheinlich; **a l. story!** (iron) e-e glaubhafte Geschichte!; **it's l. to rain** es wird wahrscheinlich regen

like′-mind′ed *adj* gleichgesinnt

liken [ˈlaɪkən] *tr* (*to*) vergleichen (mit)

likeness [ˈlaɪknɪs] *s* Ähnlichkeit *f*; **a good l. of** ein gutes Portrait (*genit*)

like′wise′ *adv* gleichfalls, ebenso

lik′ing *s* (*for*) Zuneigung *f* (*zu*); **not to my l.** nicht nach meinem Geschmack; **take a l. to** Zuneigung fassen zu

lilac [ˈlaɪlək] *adj* lila || *s* Flieder *m*

lilt [lɪlt] *s* rhythmischer Schwung *m*; (*lilting song*) lustiges Lied *n*

lily [ˈlɪli] *s* Lilie *f*

lil′y of the val′ley *s* Maiglöckchen *n*

lil′y pad′ *s* schwimmendes Seerosenblatt *n*

lil′y-white′ *adj* lilienweiß

li′ma bean′ [ˈlaɪmə] *s* Limabohne *f*

limb [lɪm] *s* Glied *n*; (*of a tree*) Ast *m*; **go out on a l.** (fig) sich exponieren; **limbs** Gliedmaßen *pl*

limber [ˈlɪmbər] *adj* geschmeidig || *tr* —l. up geschmeidig machen || *intr*— sich geschmeidig machen

lim-bo [ˈlɪmbo] *s* (**-bos**) Vorhölle *f*; (fig) Vergessenheit *f*

lime [laɪm] *s* Kalk *m*; (bot) Limonelle *f*

lime′kiln′ *s* Kalkofen *m*

lime′light′ *s* (& fig) Rampenlicht *n*

limerick [ˈlɪmərɪk] *s* Limerick *m*

lime′stone′ *adj* Kalkstein– || *s* Kalkstein *m*

limit [ˈlɪmɪt] *s* Grenze *f*; **go the l.** zum Äußersten gehen; **off limits** Zutritt verboten; **set a l. to** e-e Grenze ziehen (*dat*); **that's the l.!** das ist denn doch die Höhe!; **there's a l. to everything** alles hat seine Grenzen; **within limits** in Grenzen; **without l.** schrankenlos || *tr* begrenzen; (**to**) beschränken (auf acc)

limitation [ˌlɪmɪˈteʃən] *s* Begrenzung *f*, Beschränkung *f*

lim′ited *adj* (**to**) beschränkt (auf acc) *f*

lim′ited-ac′cess high′way *s* Autobahn *f*

lim′ited mon′archy *s* konstitutionelle Monarchie *f*

limitless [ˈlɪmɪtlɪs] *adj* grenzenlos

limousine [ˈlɪməˌzin], [ˌlɪməˈzin] *s* Limousine *f*

limp [lɪmp] *adj* (& fig) schlaff || *s* Hinken *n*; **walk with a l.** hinken || *intr* (& fig) hinken

limpid [ˈlɪmpɪd] *adj* durchsichtig

linchpin [ˈlɪntʃˌpɪn] *s* Achsnagel *m*

linden [ˈlɪndən] *s* Linde *f*, Lindenbaum *m*

line [laɪn] *s* Linie *f*, Strich *m*; (*boundary*) Grenze *f*; (*of a page*) Zeile *f*; (*of verse*) Verszeile *f*; (*of a family*) Zweig *m*; (*sphere of activity*) Fach *n*; (*e.g., of a streetcar*) Linie *f*, Strecke *f*; (*wrinkle*) Furche *f*; (*of articles for sale*) Sortiment *n*; (*for wash*) Leine *f*; (*queue*) Schlange *f*; (sl) zungenfertiges Gerede *n*; (angl) Schnur *f*; (mil) Linie *f*, Front *f*; (telp) Leitung *f*; **all along the l.** (fig) auf der ganzen Linie; **along the lines**

of nach dem Muster von; **draw the l.** **(at)** (fig) e-e Grenze ziehen (bei); **fall into l.** sich einfügen; **forget one's lines** (theat) steckenbleiben; **form a l.** sich in e-r Reihe aufstellen; **get a l. on** (coll) herausklamüsern; **give s.o. a l.** (sl) j-m schöne Worte machen; **hold the l.** die Stellung halten; (telp) am Apparat bleiben; **in l. of duty** im Dienst; **in l. with** in Übereinstimmung mit; **keep in l.** in der Reihe bleiben; **keep s.o. in l.** j-n im Zaum halten; **stand in l.** Schlange stehen; **the l. is busy** (telp) Leitung besetzt! || *tr* linieren; (*e.g., a coat*) füttern; (*a face*) furchen; (*a drawer*) ausschlagen; (*a wall*) verkleiden; **l. one's purse** sich [*dat*] den Beutel spicken; **l. the streets** in den Straßen Spalier bilden; **l. up** ausrichten; (mil) aufstellen || *intr*—**l. up** Schlange stehen; (mil) antreten; **l. up for** sich anstellen nach

lineage ['lɪnɪ·ɪdʒ] *s* Abkunft *f*, Abstammung *f*

lineal ['lɪnɪ·əl] *adj* (*descent*) direkt; (*linear*) geradlinig

lineaments ['lɪnɪ·əmənts] *spl* Gesichtszüge *pl*

linear ['lɪnɪ·ər] *adj* (*arranged in a line*) geradlinig; (*involving a single dimension*) Längen-; (*using lines*) Linien-; (math) linear

lined′ pa′per *s* Linienpapier *n*

line′man *s* (**–men**) (rr) Streckenwärter *m*; (telp) Telephonarbeiter *m*

linen ['lɪnən] *adj* Leinen- || *s* Leinen *n*; (*in the household*) Wäsche *f*; (*of the bed*) Bettwäsche *f*; **linens** Weißzeug *n*; **put fresh l. on the bed** das Bett überziehen

lin′en clos′et *s* Wäscheschrank *m*

lin′en cloth′ *s* Leinwand *f*

lin′en goods′ *spl* Weißwaren *pl*

line′ of approach′ *s* (aer) Anflugschneise *f*

line′ of bus′iness *s* Geschäftszweig *m*

line′ of communica′tion *s* Verbindungslinie *f*

line′ of fire′ *s* Schußlinie *f*

line′ of sight′ *s* (*of a gun*) Visierlinie *f*; (astr) Sichtlinie *f*

liner ['laɪnər] *s* Einsatz *m*; (naut) Linienschiff *n*

lines′man *s* (**–men**) (sport) Linienrichter *m*

line′up′ *s* (*at a police station*) Gegenüberstellung *f*; (sport) Aufstellung *f*

linger ['lɪŋgər] *intr* (*tarry*) verweilen; (*said of memories*) nachwirken; (*said of a melody*) nachtönen; **l. over** verweilen bei

lingerie [ˌlænʒə'ri] *s* Damenunterwäsche *f*

lin′gering *adj* (*disease*) schleichend; (*tune*) nachklingend; (*memory, taste, feeling*) nachwirkend

lingo ['lɪŋgo] *s* Kauderwelsch *n*

linguist ['lɪŋgwɪst] *s* Sprachwissenschaftler –in *mf*

linguistic [lɪŋ'gwɪstɪk] *adj* (*e.g., skill*) sprachlich; (*of linguistics*) sprach-

wissenschaftlich || **linguistics** *s* Sprachwissenschaft *f*

liniment ['lɪnɪmənt] *s* Einreibemittel *n*

lin′ing *s* (*of a coat*) Futter *n*; (*of a brake*) Bremsbelag *m*; (*e.g., of a wall*) Verkleidung *f*

link [lɪŋk] *s* Glied *n*; (fig) Bindeglied *n* || *tr* verbinden; (fig) verketten; **l. to** verbinden mit; (fig) in Verbindung bringen mit || *intr*—**l. up** (rok) docken; **l. up with** sich anschließen an (acc)

linnet ['lɪnɪt] *s* (orn) Hänfling *m*

linoleum [lɪ'nolɪ·əm] *s* Linoleum *n*

linotype ['laɪnə,taɪp] *s* (trademark) Linotype *f*

lin′seed oil′ ['lɪn,sid] *s* Leinöl *n*

lint [lɪnt] *s* Fussel *f*

lintel ['lɪntəl] *s* Sturz *m*

lion ['laɪ·ən] *s* Löwe *m*

li′on cage′ *s* Löwenzwinger *m*

lioness ['laɪ·ənɪs] *s* Löwin *f*

lionize ['laɪ·ə,naɪz] *tr* zum Helden des Tages machen

li′ons′ den′ *s* Löwengrube *f*

li′on's share′ *s* Löwenanteil *m*

li′on tam′er *s* Löwenbändiger –in *mf*

lip [lɪp] *s* Lippe *f*; (*edge*) Rand *m*; **bite one's lips** sich auf die Lippen beißen; **smack one's lips** sich [*dat*] die Lippen lecken

lip′ read′ing *s* Lippenlesen *n*

lip′ serv′ice *s* Lippenbekenntnis *n*; **pay l. to** ein Lippenbekenntnis ablegen zu

lip′stick′ *s* Lippenstift *m*

lique·fy ['lɪkwɪ,faɪ] *v* (*pret & pp* **–fied**) *tr* verflüssigen || *intr* sich verflüssigen

liqueur [lɪ'kʌr] *s* Likör *m*

liquid ['lɪkwɪd] *adj* flüssig; (*clear*) klar || *s* Flüssigkeit *f*

liq′uid as′sets *spl* flüssige Mittel *pl*

liquidate ['lɪkwɪ,det] *tr* (*a debt*) tilgen; (*an account*) abrechnen; (*a company*) liquidieren

liquidation [ˌlɪkwɪ'deʃən] *s* (*of a debt*) Tilgung *f*; (*of an account*) Abrechnung *f*; (*of a company*) Liquidation *f*

liquidity [lɪ'kwɪdɪti] *s* flüssiger Zustand *m*; (fin) Liquidität *f*

liq′uid meas′ure *s* Hohlmaß *n*

liquor ['lɪkər] *s* Spirituosen *pl*, Schnaps *m*; **have a shot of l.** einen zwitschern

liquorice ['lɪkərɪs] *s* Lakritze *f*

li′quor li′cense *s* Schankerlaubnis *f*

Lisbon ['lɪzbən] *s* Lissabon *n*

lisp [lɪsp] *s* Lispeln *n* || *tr & intr* lispeln

lissome ['lɪsəm] *adj* biegsam, gelenkig

list [lɪst] *s* Liste *f*, Verzeichnis *n*; (naut) Schlagseite *f*; **enter the lists** (& fig) in die Schranken treten; **make a l. of** verzeichnen || *tr* verzeichnen || *intr* (naut) Schlagseite haben

listen ['lɪsən] *intr* horchen, zuhören; **l. closely** die Ohren aufsperren; **l. for** achten auf (acc); **l. in** mithören; **l. to** zuhören (dat); (*a thing*) horchen auf (acc); (*obey*) gehorchen (dat); (*take advice from*) hören auf (acc); **l. to reason** auf e-n Rat hören; **l. to the radio** Radio hören

listener ['lɪsənər] s Zuhörer –in mf; (rad) Rundfunkhörer –in mf

lis'tening adj Abhör–, Horch–

lis'tening post' s Horchposten m

listless ['lɪstlɪs] adj lustlos

list' price' s Listenpreis m

litany ['lɪtəni] s (& fig) Litanei f

liter ['lɪtər] s Liter m & n

literacy ['lɪtərəsi] s Kenntnis f des Lesens und Schreibens

literal ['lɪtərəl] adj buchstäblich; (person) pedantisch; **l. sense** wörtlicher Sinn m

literally ['lɪtərəli] adv buchstäblich

literary ['lɪtə‚reri] adj literarisch; **l. language** Literatursprache f; **l. reference** Schrifttumsangabe f

literate ['lɪtərɪt] adj des Lesens und des Schreibens kundig; (educated) gebildet || s Gebildete mf

literati [‚lɪtə'rati] spl Literaten pl

literature ['lɪtərətʃər] s Literatur f; (com) Drucksachen pl

lithe [laɪð] adj gelenkig

lithia ['lɪθɪ‚ə] s (chem) Lithiumoxyd n

lithium ['lɪθɪ‚əm] s Lithium n

lithograph ['lɪθə‚græf] s Steindruck m || tr lithographieren

lithographer [lɪ'θαgrəfər] s Lithograph –in mf

lithography [lɪ'θαgrəfi] s Steindruck m, Lithographie f

Lithuania [‚lɪθʊ'enɪ‚ə] s Litauen n

Lithuanian [‚lɪθʊ'enɪ‚ən] adj litauisch || s Litauer –in mf; (language) Litauisch n

litigant ['lɪtɪgənt] adj prozessierend; **the l. parties** die streitenden Parteien || s Prozeßführer m

litigate ['lɪtɪ‚get] tr prozessieren gegen || intr prozessieren

litigation [‚lɪtɪ'geʃən] s Rechsstreit m

lit'mus pa'per ['lɪtməs] s Lackmuspapier f

litter ['lɪtər] s (stretcher) Tragbahre f; (bedding for animals) Streu f; (of pigs, dogs) Wurf m; (trash) herumliegender Abfall m; (hist) Sänfte f || tr verunreinigen || intr (bear young) werfen; (strew litter) Abfälle wegwerfen; **no littering!** das Wegwerfen von Abfällen ist verboten!

lit'terbug' s—**don't be a l.** wirf keine Abfälle weg

little ['lɪtəl] adj (in size) klein; (in amount) wenig || adv wenig; **l. by l.** nach und nach || s—**after a l.** nach kurzer Zeit; **a l.** ein wenig, ein bißchen; **make l. of** wenig halten von

Lit'tle Bear' s Kleiner Bär m

Lit'tle Dip'per s Kleiner Wagen m, Kleiner Bär m

lit'tle fin'ger s kleiner Finger m

lit'tle peo'ple s kleine Leute pl; (myth) Heinzelmännchen pl

Lit'tle Red Rid'inghood' s Rotkäppchen n

lit'tle slam' s (cards) Klein-Schlemm m

liturgic(al) [lɪ'tʌrdʒɪk(əl)] adj liturgisch

liturgy ['lɪtərdʒi] s Liturgie f

livable ['lɪvəbəl] adj (place) wohnlich; (life) erträglich

live [laɪv] adj lebendig; (coals) glühend; (ammunition) scharf; (elec) stromführend; (rad, telv) live; **l. program** Originalsendung f || adv (rad, telv) live || [lɪv] tr leben; (a life) führen; **l. down** durch einwandfreien Lebenswandel vergessen machen; **l. it up** (coll) das Leben genießen; **l. out** (survive) überleben || intr leben; (reside) wohnen; (reside temporarily) sich aufhalten; **l. and learn!** man lernt nie aus!; **l. for the moment** in den Tag hineinleben; **l. high off the hog** in Saus und Braus leben; **l. off s.o.** j–m auf der Tasche liegen; **l. on** (subsist on) sich nähren von; (continue to live) fortleben; **l. through** durchmachen; **l. to see** erleben; **l. up to** gerecht werden (dat)

livelihood ['laɪvlɪ‚hud] s Lebensunterhalt m

liveliness ['laɪvlɪnɪs] s Lebhaftigkeit f

livelong ['lɪv‚lɔŋ] adj—**all the l. day** den lieben langen Tag

lively ['laɪvli] adj lebhaft; (street) belebt

liven ['laɪvən] tr aufmuntern || intr munter werden

liver ['lɪvər] s (anat) Leber f

liverwurst ['lɪvər‚wurst] s Leberwurst f

livery ['lɪvəri] s Livree f

liv'ery sta'ble s Mietstallung f

live' show' [laɪv] s Originalsendung f, Livesendung f

livestock ['laɪv‚stak] s Viehstand m

live' wire' [laɪv] s geladener Draht m; (coll) energiegeladener Mensch m

livid ['lɪvɪd] adj bleifarben; (enraged) wütend

living ['lɪvɪŋ] adj (alive) lebend, lebendig; (for living) Wohn–; **not a l. soul** keine Mutterseele f || s Unterhalt n; **good l.** Wohlleben n; **make a l.** (as) sein Auskommen haben (als); **what do you do for a l.?** wie verdienen Sie Ihren Lebensunterhalt?

liv'ing accommoda'tions spl Unterkunft f

liv'ing be'ing s Lebewesen n

liv'ing condi'tions spl Lebensbedingungen pl

liv'ing expens'es spl Unterhaltskosten pl

liv'ing quar'ters spl Unterkunft f

liv'ing room' s Wohnzimmer n

liv'ing-room set' (or suite') s Polstergarnitur f

liv'ing space' s Lebensraum m

liv'ing wage' s Existenzminimum n

lizard ['lɪzərd] s Eidechse f

load [lod] s Last f, Belastung f; (in a truck) Fuhre f; **get a l. of that!** schau dir das mal an!; **have a l. on** (sl) einen sitzen haben; **loads of** (coll) Mengen von; **that's a l. off my mind** mir ist dabei ein Stein vom Herzen gefallen || tr (a truck, gun) laden; (cargo on a ship) einladen; (with work) überladen; (with worries) belasten; **l. down** belasten; **l. the cam-**

era den Film einlegen; **l. up** aufladen || *intr* das Gewehr laden

load′ed *adj* (*rifle*) scharf geladen; (*dice*) falsch; (*question*) verfänglich; (*very rich*) (sl) steinreich; (*drunk*) (sl) sternhagelvoll; **fully l.** (aut) mit allen Schikanen

loader [′lodər] *s* (*worker*) Ladearbeiter –in *mf*; (*device*) Verladevorrichtung *f*

load′ing *s* Ladung *f*, Verladung *f*

load′ing plat′form *s* Ladebühne *f*

load′ing ramp′ *s* Laderampe *f*

load′ lim′it *s* Tragfähigkeit *f*; (elec) Belastungsgrenze *f*

load′stone′ *s* Magneteisenstein *m*

loaf [lof] *s* (**loaves** [lovz]) Laib *m* || *intr* faulenzen; **l. around** herumlungern

loafer [′lofər] *s* Faulenzer *m*

loaf′ing *s* Faulenzen *n*

loam [lom] *s* Lehm *m*

loamy [′lomi] *adj* lehmig

loan [lon] *s* Anleihe *f*, Darlehe(n) *n* || *tr* (ver)leihen, borgen; **l. out** leihen

loan′ com′pany *s* Leihanstalt *f*

loan′ shark′ *s* (coll) Wucherer *m*

loan′ word′ *s* Lehnwort *n*

loath [loθ] *adj*—**be l. to** (*inf*) abgeneigt sein zu (*inf*)

loathe [loð] *tr* verabscheuen

loathing [′loðɪŋ] *s* (for) Abscheu *m* (vor *dat*)

loathsome [′loðsəm] *adj* abscheulich

lob [lɑb] *s* (tennis) Lobball *m* || *v* (*pret & pp* **lobbed**; *ger* **lobbing**) *tr* lobben, hochschlagen

lob·by [′lɑbi] *s* (*of a hotel or theater*) Vorhalle *f*, Foyer *n*; (pol) Interessengruppe *f* || *v* (*pret & pp* **–bied**) *intr* antichambrieren

lob′bying *s* Beeinflussung *f* von Abgeordneten, Lobbying *n*

lobbyist [′lɑbɪ·ɪst] *s* Lobbyist –in *mf*

lobe [lob] *s* (anat) Lappen *m*

lobster [′lɑbstər] *s* Hummer *m*; **red as a l.** (fig) krebsrot

local [′lokəl] *adj* örtlich, Orts–; (*produce*) heimisch || *s* (*group*) Ortsgruppe *f*; (rr) Personenzug *m*

lo′cal anesthe′sia *s* Lokalanästhese *f*

lo′cal call′ *s* (telp) Ortsgespräch *n*

lo′cal col′or *s* Lokalkolorit *n*

lo′cal deliv′ery *s* Ortszustellung *f*

locale [lo′kæl] *s* Ort *m*

lo′cal gov′ernment *s* Gemeindeverwaltung *f*

locality [lo′kælɪti] *s* Örtlichkeit *f*

localize [′lokə‚laɪz] *tr* lokalisieren

lo′cal news′ *s* Lokalnachrichten *pl*

lo′cal pol′itics *s* Kommunalpolitik *f*

lo′cal show′er *s* Strichregen *m*

lo′cal tax′ *s* Gemeindesteuer *f*

lo′cal time′ *s* Ortszeit *f*

lo′cal traf′fic *s* Nahverkehr *m*, Ortsverkehr *m*

locate [lo′ket], [′loket] *tr* (*find*) ausfindig machen; (*a ship, aircraft*) orten; (*the trouble*) finden, feststellen; (*set up, e.g., an office*) errichten; **be located** liegen, gelegen sein || *intr* sich niederlassen

location [lo′keʃən] *s* Lage *f*; **on l.** (cin) auf Außenaufnahme

lock [lɑk] *s* Schloß *n*; (*of hair*) Locke *f*; (*of a canal*) Schleuse *f*; **l., stock, and barrel** mit allem Drum und Dran; **under l. and key** unter Verschluß || *tr* zusperren; (*arms*) verschränken; **l. in** einsperren; **l. out** aussperren; **l. up** (*a house*) zusperren; (*imprison*) einsperren || *intr* (*said of a lock*) zuschnappen; (*said of brakes*) sperren; **l. together** (*said of bumpers*) sich ineinander verhaken

locker [′lɑkər] *s* (*as in a gym or barracks*) Spind *m & n*; (*for luggage*) Schließfach *n*

lock′er room′ *s* Umkleideraum *m*

locket [′lɑkɪt] *s* Medaillon *n*

lock′jaw′ *s* Maulsperre *f*

lock′ nut′ *s* Gegenmutter *f*

lock′out′ *s* Aussperrung *f*

lock′smith′ *s* Schlosser –in *mf*

lock′smith shop′ *s* Schlosserei *f*

lock′ step′ *s* Marschieren *n* in dicht geschlossenen Gliedern

lock′ stitch′ *s* Kettenstich *m*

lock′up′ *s* (coll) Gefängnis *n*

lock′ wash′er *s* Sicherungsring *m*

locomotion [‚lokə′moʃən] *s* (act) Fortbewegung *f*; (power) Fortbewegungsfähigkeit *f*

locomotive [‚lokə′motɪv] *s* Lokomotive *f*

lo·cus [′lokəs] *s* (**–ci** [saɪ]) Ort *m*; (geom) geometrischer Ort *m*

locust [′lokəst] *s* (black locust) (bot) Robinie *f*; (carob) (bot) Johannisbrotbaum *m*; (Cicada) (ent) Zikade *f*

lode [lod] *s* (min) Gang *m*

lode′star′ *s* Leitstern *m*

lodge [lɑdʒ] *s* (of Masons) Loge *f*; (for hunting) Jagdhütte *f*; (for weekending) Wochenendhäuschen *n*; (summer house) Sommerhäuschen *n* || *tr* unterbringen; **l. a complaint** e-e Beschwerde einreichen || *intr* wohnen; (said of an arrow, etc.) steckenbleiben

lodger [′lɑdʒər] *s* Untermieter –in *mf*

lodg′ing *s* Unterkunft *f*; **lodgings** Logis *n*

loft [lɔft] *s* Speicher *m*; (for hay) Heuboden *m*; (of a church) Chor *m*; (of a golf club) Hochschlaghaltung *f* || *tr* (a golf club) in Hochschlaghaltung bringen; (a golf ball) hochschlagen

loftiness [′lɔftɪnɪs] *s* Erhabenheit *f*

lofty [′lɔfti] *adj* (style) erhaben; (high) hochragend; (elevated in rank) gehoben; (haughty) anmaßend

log [lɔg] *s* (trunk) Baumstamm *m*; (for the fireplace) Holzklotz *m*; (record book) Tagebuch *n*; (aer, naut) Log *n*; **sleep like a log** wie ein Klotz schlafen || *v* (*pret & pp* **logged**; *ger* **logging**) *tr* (trees) fällen und abästen; (cut into logs) in Klötze schneiden; (an area) abholzen; (enter into a logbook) in das Logbuch eintragen; (traverse) zurücklegen

logarithm [′lɔgə‚rɪðəm] *s* Logarithmus *m*

log′book′ s (aer, naut) Logbuch n

log′ cab′in s Blockhaus n, Blockhütte f

logger [ˈlɔɡər] s Holzfäller m

log′gerhead′ s—at loggerheads auf Kriegsfuß

log′ging s Holzarbeit f

logic [ˈlɑdʒɪk] s Logik f

logical [ˈlɑdʒɪkəl] adj logisch

logician [loˈdʒɪʃən] s Logiker –in mf

logistic(al) [loˈdʒɪstɪk(əl)] adj logistisch

logistics [loˈdʒɪstɪks] s Logistik f

log′jam′ s aufgestaute Baumstämme pl; (fig) völlige Stockung f

log′wood′ s Kampescheholz n

loin [lɔɪn] s (of beef) Lendenstück n; (anat) Lende f; gird up one's loins (fig) sich rüsten

loin′cloth′ s Lendentuch n

loin′ end′ s (of pork) Rippenstück n

loiter [ˈlɔɪtər] tr—l. away vertrödeln || intr trödeln; (hang around) herumlungern

loiterer [ˈlɔɪtərər] s Bummler –in mf

loi′tering s Trödelei f; no l. Herumlungern verboten!

loll [lɑl] intr sich bequem ausstrecken

lollipop [ˈlɑlɪˌpɑp] s Lutschbonbon n & n

Lombardy [ˈlɑmbərdi] s die Lombardei

London [ˈlʌndən] adj Londoner || s London n

Londoner [ˈlʌndənər] s Londoner –in mf

lone [lon] adj (sole) alleinig; (solitary) einzelstehend

loneliness [ˈlonlɪnɪs] s Einsamkeit f

lonely [ˈlonli] adj einsam; become l. vereinsamen

loner [ˈlonər] s Einzelgänger m

lonesome [ˈlonsəm] adj einsam; be l. for sich sehnen nach

lone′ wolf′ s (fig) Einzelgänger m

long [lɔŋ] adj (longer [ˈlɔŋɡər]; longest [ˈlɔŋɡɪst]) lang; (way, trip) weit; (detour) groß; a l. time lange; a l. time since schon lange her, daß; in the l. run auf die Dauer || adv lange; as l. as so lange wie; but not for l. aber nicht lange; l. after lange nach; l. ago vor langer Zeit; l. live ...! es lebe ...!; l. since längst; so l.! bis dann! || intr—l. for sich sehnen nach; l. to (inf) sich danach sehnen zu (inf)

long′boat′ s Pinasse f

long′ dis′tance s (telp) Ferngespräch n; call l. ein Ferngespräch anmelden

long′-dis′tance adj (sport) Langstrecken-

long′-dis′tance call′ s Ferngespräch n

long′-dis′tance flight′ s Langstreckenflug m

long′-drawn′-out′ adj ausgedehnt; (story) langatmig

longevity [lɑnˈdʒɛvɪti] s Langlebigkeit f

long′ face′ s langes Gesicht n

long′hair′ adj (fig) intellektuell || s (fig) Intellektueller m; (mus) (coll) konservativer Musiker m

long′hand′ s Langschrift f; in l. mit der Hand geschrieben

long′ing adj sehnsüchtig || s (for) Sehnsucht f (nach)

longitude [ˈlɑndʒɪˌt(j)ud] s Länge f

longitudinal [ˌlɑndʒɪˈt(j)udɪnəl] adj Longitudinal-

long′ jump′ s Weitsprung m

long-lived [ˈlɔŋˈlaɪvd] adj langlebig

long′-play′ing rec′ord s Langspielplatte f

long′-range′ adj (plan) auf lange Sicht; (aer) Langstrecken-

long′shore′man s (–men) Hafenarbeiter m

long′ shot′ s (coll) riskante Wette f; by a l. bei weitem

long′stand′ing adj althergebracht, alt

long′-suf′fering adj langmütig

long′ suit′ s (fig) Stärke f; (cards) lange Farbe f

long′-term′ adj langfristig

long-winded [ˈlɔŋˈwɪndɪd] adj langatmig

look [luk] s (glance) Blick m; (appearance) Aussehen n; (expression) Ausdruck m; from the looks of things wie die Sache aussieht; give a second l. sich (dat) genauer ansehen; have a l. around Umschau halten; have a l. at s.th. sich (dat) etw ansehen; I don't like the looks of it die Sache gefällt mir nicht; looks Ansehen n; new l. verändertes Aussehen n; (latest style) neueste Mode f; take a l. at s.th. sich (dat) etw ansehen || tr—he looks his age man sieht ihm sein Alter an; l. one's best sich in bester Verfassung zeigen; l. one's last at zum letzten Mal ansehen; l. s.o. in the eye j–m in die Augen sehen; l. s.o. over j–n mustern; l. s.th. over etw (über)prüfen (or durchsehen); l. up (e.g., a word) nachschlagen; (e.g., a friend) aufsuchen; l. up and down von oben bis unten mustern; l. intr schauen; (appear, seem) aussehen; l. after (e.g., children) betreuen; (a household, business) besorgen; (a departing person) nachblicken (dat); l. ahead vorausschauen; l. around (for) sich (dat) umsehen (nach); l. at anschauen; l. back (on) zurücksehen (auf acc); l. down herabsehen; (cast the eyes down) die Augen niederschlagen; l. down on herabsehen auf (acc); (in contempt) über die Achseln ansehen; l. for suchen; (e.g., a criminal) fahnden nach; l. forward to sich freuen auf (acc); l. hard at scharf ansehen; l. into (a mirror, the future) blicken in (acc); (a matter) nachgehen (dat); l. like gleichen (dat); (e.g., rain) aussehen nach; l. on zuschauen; l. on s.o. as j–n betrachten als; l. out aufpassen; l. out for aussehen nach; l. out on (a view) hinausgehen auf (acc); l. over hinwegsehen über (acc); l. sharp! jetzt aber hoppla!; l. through (e.g., a window) blicken durch; (s.o. or s.o.'s motives) durchschauen; l. up (raise one's gaze) aufschauen; l. up to s.o. zu j–m hinaufsehen; things are beginning to l. up es wird langsam besser; **things don't l. so good for** est steht übel mit; **what does he l. like?** wie sieht er aus?

look'ing glass' s Spiegel m

look'out' s (*watchman*) Wachposten m; (*observation point*) Ausguck m; (*matter of concern*) Sache f; **be a l.** Schmiere stehen; **be on the l.** (for) Auschau halten (nach)

look'out man' s—**be the l.** Schmiere stehen

look'out tow'er s Aussichtsturm m

loom [lum] s Webstuhl m || intr undeutlich und groß auftauchen; **l. large** von großer Bedeutung scheinen

loon [lun] s (orn) Taucher m

loony ['luni] adj verrückt; **be l.** spinnen

loop [lup] s Schleife f, Schlinge f; (*e.g., on a dress for a hook*) Öse f; (aer) Looping m; **do a l.** (aer) e-n Looping drehen || tr schlingen || intr Schlingen (or Schleifen) bilden

loop'hole' s Guckloch n; (*in a fortification*) Schießscharte f; (*in a law*) Lücke f

loose [lus] adj locker, los; (*wobbly*) wackelig; (*morally*) locker, unsolid; (*unpacked*) unverpackt; (*translation*) frei; (*interpretation*) dehnbar; (*dress, tongue*) lose; (*skin*) schlaff; **l. connection** (elec) Wackelkontakt m || adv—**break l.** (*from an enclosure*) ausbrechen; (*e.g., from a hitching*) sich losmachen; (*said of a storm, hell*) losbrechen; **come l.** losgehen; **cut l.** (act up) (coll) außer Rand und Band geraten; **turn l.** befreien; **work l.** sich lockern; (*said of a button*) abgehen; (*said of a brick, stone, shoestring*) sich lösen || s—**on the l.** ungehemmt, frei || tr (*a boat*) losmachen; (*a knot*) lösen

loose' change' s Kleingeld n

loose' end' s (fig) unerledigte Kleinigkeit f; **at loose ends** im ungewissen

loose'-leaf note'book s Loseblattbuch n

loosen ['lusən] tr lockern, locker machen || intr locker werden

looseness ['lusnɪs] s Lockerheit f

loot [lut] s Beute f || tr erbeuten; (*plunder*) plündern; (*e.g., art treasures*) verschleppen

lop [lap] v (pret & pp **lopped**; ger **lopping**) tr—**lop off** abhacken

lope [lop] s Trab m || intr—**l. along** in großen Schritten laufen

lop'sid'ed adj schief; (*score*) einseitig

loquacious [lo'kweʃəs] adj geschwätzig

lord [lɔrd] s Herr m; (Brit) Lord m; **Lord Herrgott** m || tr—**l. it over** sich als Herr aufspielen über (acc)

lordly ['lɔrdli] adj würdig; (*haughty*) hochmütig

Lord's' Day' s Tag m des Herrn

lord'ship' s Herrschaft f

Lord's' Prayer' s Vaterunser n

Lord's' Sup'per s heiliges Abendmahl n

lore [lor] s Kunde f; (*traditional wisdom*) überlieferte Kunde f

lorry ['lɔri] s (Brit) Lastkraftwagen m

lose [luz] v (pret & pp **lost** [lɔst]) tr verlieren; (*several minutes, as a clock does*) zurückbleiben; (*in betting*) verwetten; (*in gambling*) verspielen; (*the page in a book*) verblättern; **l. one's way** sich verirren; (*on foot*) sich verlaufen; (*by car*) sich verfahren || intr verlieren; (*sport*) geschlagen werden; **l. to** (sport) unterliegen (dat)

loser ['luzər] s Unterlegene mf; **be the l.** mit langer Nase abziehen

los'ing adj verlierend; (com) verlustbringend || **losings** spl Verluste pl

los'ing game' s aussichtsloses Spiel n

loss [lɔs] s (in) Verlust m (an dat); **at a l.** in Verlegenheit; (com) mit Verlust; **be at a l. for words** nach Worten suchen; **inflict l. on s.o.** j-m Schaden zufügen; **l. of appetite** Appetitlosigkeit f; **l. of blood** Blutverlust m; **l. of face** Blamage f; **l. of life** Verluste pl an Menschenleben; **l. of memory** Gedächtnisverlust m; **l. of sight** Erblindung f; **l. of time** Zeitverlust m; **straight l.** Barverlust m

lost [lɔst] adj verloren; **be l.** (*said of a thing*) verlorengehen; (*not know one's way*) sich verirrt haben; **be l. on s.o.** auf j-n keinen Eindruck machen; **get l.** in Verlust geraten; **get l.!** hau ab!; **l. in thought** in Gedanken versunken

lost'-and-found' depart'ment s Fundbüro n

lost' cause' s aussichtslose Sache f

lot [lat] s (fate) Los n, Schicksal n; (*in a drawing*) Los n; (*portion of land*) Grundstück n; (com) Posten m, Partie f; **a lot of** viel, sehr; **a lot of (or lots of)** viel(e); **the lot** das Ganze

lotion ['loʃən] s Wasser n

lottery ['latəri] s Lotterie f

lot'tery tick'et s Lotterielos n

lotto ['lato] s Lotto n

lotus ['lotəs] s Lotos m

loud [laud] adj laut; (*colors*) schreiend

loud-mouthed ['laud,mauðd] adj laut

loud'speak'er s Lautsprecher m

lounge [laundʒ] s Aufenthaltsraum m || intr sich recken; **l. around** herumlungern

lounge' chair' s Klubsessel m

lounge' liz'ard s (sl) Salonlöwe m

louse [laus] s (lice [laɪs]) Laus f; (sl) Sauhund m || tr—**l. up** (sl) versauen

lousy ['lauzi] adj verlaust; (sl) lausig; **l. with** (*people*) wimmelnd von; **l. with money** stinkreich

lout [laut] s Lümmel m

louver ['luvər] s Jalousie f

lovable ['lʌvəbəl] adj liebenswürdig

love [lʌv] adj Liebes– || s (for, of) Liebe f (zu); **be in l. with** verliebt sein in (acc); **for the l. of God** um Gottes willen; **fall (madly) in l. with** sich (heftig) verlieben in (acc); **Love** (at the end of a letter) herzliche Grüße; **l. at first sight** Liebe f auf den ersten Blick; **make l. to** herzen;

(sl) geschlechtlich verkehren mit;
not for l. or money nicht für Gold
und gute Worte; **there's no l. lost
between them** sie schätzen sich nicht
|| *tr* lieben; (*like*) gern haben; **l. to
dance** sehr gern tanzen

love′ affair′ *s* Liebeshandel *m*, Liebes-
verhältnis *n*

love′birds′ *spl* (coll) Unzertrennlichen
pl

love′ child′ *s* Kind *n* der Liebe

love′ feast′ *s* (eccl) Liebesmahl *n*

love′ game′ *s* (tennis) Nullpartie *f*

love′ knot′ *s* Liebesschleife *f*

loveless [′lʌvlɪs] *adj* lieblos

love′ let′ter *s* Liebesbrief *m*

lovelorn [′lʌv‚lɔrn] *adj* vor Liebe ver-
gehend

lovely [′lʌvli] *adj* lieblich

love′-mak′ing *s* Geschlechtsverkehr *m*

love′ match′ *s* Liebesheirat *f*

love′ po′em *s* Liebesgedicht *n*

love′ po′tion *s* Liebestrank *m*

lover [′lʌvər] *s* Liebhaber *m;* **lovers**
Liebespaar *n*

love′ scene′ *s* Liebesszene *f*

love′ seat′ *s* Sofasessel *m*

love′sick′ *adj* liebeskrank

love′ song′ *s* Liebeslied *n*

love′ to′ken *s* Liebespfand *n*

lov′ing *adj* liebevoll; **Your l. ...** Dich
liebender ...

lov′ing-kind′ness *s* Herzensgüte *f*

low [lo] *adj* (*building, mountain, forehead, birth, wages, estimate, prices,
rent*) niedrig; (*number*) nieder; (*altitude, speed*) gering; (*not loud*) leise;
(*vulgar*) gemein; (*grades, company*)
schlecht; (*fever*) leicht; (*pulse, pressure*) schwach; (*ground*) tiefgelegen;
(*bow, voice*) tief; (*almost empty*) fast
leer; (*supplies, funds*) knapp; **be low**
(*said of the sun, water*) niedrigste-
hen; **be low in funds** knapp bei
Kasse sein; **feel low** niedergeschlagen
sein; **have a low opinion of** e-e
geringe Meinung haben von || *adv*
niedrig; **lay low** über den Haufen
werfen; **lie low** sich versteckt halten;
(*bide one's time*) abwarten; **run low**
knapp werden; **sing low** tief singen;
sink low tief sinken || *s* (*low point*)
(fig) Tiefstand *m;* (meteor) Tief *n* ||
intr muhen, brüllen

low′ blow′ *s* (box) Tiefschlag *m*

low′born′ *adj* von niederer Herkunft

low′brow′ *s* Spießbürger *m*

low′-cost hous′ing *s* sozial geförderter
Wohnungsbau *m*

Low′ Coun′tries, the *spl* die Niederlande

low′-cut′ *adj* tiefausgeschnitten

low′-down′ *adj* schurkisch || *s* (*un-
adorned facts*) unverblümte Wahrheit *f;* (*inside information*) Geheim-
nachrichten *pl*

oneself sich herablassen || [′laʊ‚ər]
intr finster blicken; **l. at** finster an-
blicken

low′er ab′domen [′loər] *s* Unterbauch
m

low′er berth′ [′loər] *s* untere Koje *f*

low′er case′ [′loər] *s* Kleinbuchstaben
pl

lower-case [′loər′kes] *adj* klein

low′er course′ [′loər] *s* (*of a river*)
Unterlauf *m*

low′er mid′dle class′ [′loər] *s* Klein-
bürgertum *n*

lowermost [′loər‚most] *adj* niedrigste

low′er world′ [′loər] *s* Unterwelt *f*

low′-fly′ing *adj* tieffliegend

low′ fre′quency *s* Niederfrequenz *f*

low′-fre′quency *adj* Niederfrequenz-

low′ gear′ *s* erster Gang *m*

low′-grade′ *adj* minderwertig

low′ing *s* Gebrüll *n*

lowland [′loland] *s* Flachland *n;* **Lowlands** (*in Scotland*) Unterland *n*

low′ lev′el *s* Tiefstand *m*

low′-lev′el attack′ *s* Tiefangriff *m*

low′-lev′el flight′ *s* Tiefflug *m*

lowly [′loli] *adj* bescheiden; (*humble
in spirit*) niederträchtig

low′-ly′ing *adj* tiefliegend

Low′ Mass′ *s* stille Messe *f*

low′-mind′ed *adj* niedrig gesinnt

low′ neck′ *s* (*of a dress*) Ausschnitt *m*

low′-necked′ *adj* tief ausgeschnitten

low′-pitched′ *adj* (sound) tief; (roof)
mit geringer Neigung

low′-pres′sure *adj* Tiefdruck-, Unter-
druck-

low′-priced′ *adj* billig

low′ shoe′ *s* Halbschuh *m*

low′-speed′ *adj* mit geringer Geschwindigkeit; (*film*) unempfindlich

low′-spir′ited *adj* niedergeschlagen

low′ spir′its *spl* Niedergeschlagenheit
f; **be in l.** niedergeschlagen sein

low′ tide′ *s* Ebbe *f;* (fig) Tiefstand *m*

low′ wa′ter *s* Niedrigwasser *n*

low′-wa′ter mark′ *s* (fig) Tiefpunkt *m*

loyal [′lɔɪəl] *adj* treu, loyal

loyalist [′lɔɪ‚əlɪst] *s* Regierungstreue
mf

loyalty [′lɔɪ‚əlti] *s* Treue *f*

lozenge [′lazɪndʒ] *s* Pastille *f*

LP [′ɛl′pi] *s* (trademark) (**long-playing record**) Langspielplatte *f*

Ltd. *abbr* (Brit) (**Limited**) Gesellschaft
f mit beschränkter Haftung

lubricant [′lubrɪkənt] *s* Schmiermittel
n

lubricate [′lubrɪ‚ket] *tr* (ab)schmieren

lubrication [‚lubrɪ′keʃən] *s* Schmie-
rung *f*

lucerne [lu′sʌrn] *s* (bot) Luzerne *f;*
Lucerne Luzern *n*

lucid [′lusɪd] *adj* (*clear*) klar, deutlich;
(*bright*) hell

luck [lʌk] *s* Glück *n;* (*chance*) Zufall
m; **as l. would have it** wie es der
Zufall wollte; **be down on one's l.**
an seinem Glück verzagen; **be in l.**
Glück haben; **be out of l.** Unglück
haben; **dumb l.** (coll) Sauglück *n*
haben; **have tough l.** (coll) Pech haben;

lower [′loər] *comp adj* untere; (*e.g.,
deck, house, jaw, lip*) Unter– || *tr*
herunterlassen; (*the eyes, voice,
water level, temperature*) senken;
(*prices*) herabsetzen; (*a flag, sail*)
streichen; (*lifeboats*) aussetzen; **l.**

rotten l. (coll) Saupech *n;* **try one's l.** sein Glück versuchen; **with l. you should win** wenn Sie Glück haben, werden Sie gewinnen

luckily ['lʌkɪlɪ] *adv* zum Glück

luckless ['lʌklɪs] *adj* glücklos

lucky ['lʌki] *adj* glücklich; **be l.** Glück haben; **l. dog** (coll) Glückspilz *m;* **l. penny** Glückspfennig *m*

luck'y shot' *s* Glückstreffer *m*

lucrative ['lukrətɪv] *adj* gewinnbringend

ludicrous ['ludɪkrəs] *adj* lächerlich

lug [lʌg] *s* (pull, tug) Ruck *m;* (lout) (sl) Lümmel *m;* (elec) Öse *f* ‖ *v* (pret & pp lugged; ger lugging) *tr* schleppen

luggage ['lʌgɪdʒ] *s* Gepäck *n;* **excess l.** Mehrgepäck *n;* **piece of l.** Gepäckstück *n*

lug'gage car'rier *s* Gepäckträger *m*

lug'gage compart'ment *s* (aer) Frachtraum *m*

lug'gage rack' *s* Gepäckablage *f;* (on the roof of a car) Dachgepäckträger *m*

lug'gage receipt' *s* Aufgabeschein *m*

lugubrious [lu'g(j)ubrɪ-əs] *adj* tieftraurig

lukewarm ['luk,wɔrm] *adj* lau, lauwarm

lull [lʌl] *s* Windstille *f;* (com) Flaute *f* ‖ *tr* einlullen; (e.g., fears) beschwichtigen; **l. to sleep** einschläfern ‖ *intr* nachlassen

lullaby ['lʌlə,baɪ] *s* Wiegenlied *n*

lumbago [lʌm'bego] *s* Hexenschluß *m*

lumber ['lʌmbər] *s* Bauholz *n* ‖ *intr* sich schwerfällig fortbewegen

lum'berjack' *s* Holzfäller *m*

lum'ber-man' *s* (-men') (dealer) Holzhändler *m;* (lumberjack) Holzfäller *m*

lum'beryard' *s* Holzplatz *m*

luminary ['lumɪ,neri] *s* Leuchtkörper *m;* (fig) Leuchte *f*

luminescent [,lumɪ'nesənt] *adj* lumineszierend

luminous ['lumɪnəs] *adj* leuchtend, Leucht–

lu'minous di'al *s* Leuchtzifferblatt *n*

lu'minous paint' *s* Leuchtfarbe *f*

lummox ['lʌməks] *s* Lümmel *m*

lump [lʌmp] *s* (e.g., of clay) Klumpen *m;* (on the body) Beule *f;* **have a l. in one's throat** e–n Kloß (or Knödel) im Hals haben; **l. of sugar** Würfel *m* Zucker *f* ‖ *tr*—**l. together** (fig) zusammenwerfen

lumpish ['lʌmpɪʃ] *adj* klumpig

lump' sug'ar *s* Würfelzucker *m*

lump' sum' *s* Pauschalbetrag *m*

lumpy ['lʌmpi] *adj* klumpig; (sea) bewegt

lunacy ['lunəsɪ] *s* Irrsinn *m*

lu'nar eclipse' ['lunər] *s* Mondfinsternis *f*

lu'nar land'ing *s* Mondlandung *f*

lu'nar mod'ule *s* (rok) Mondfähre *f*

lu'nar year' *s* Mondjahr *n*

lunatic ['lunətɪk] *s* Irre *mf*

lu'natic asy'lum *s* Irrenhaus *n*

lu'natic fringe' *s* Extremisten *pl*

lunch [lʌntʃ] *s* (at noon) Mittagessen *n,* Lunch *m;* (light meal) Zwischenmahlzeit *f;* **eat l.** zu Mittag essen; **have** (s.th.) **for l.** zum Mittagessen haben ‖ *intr* zu Mittag essen, lunchen

lunch' coun'ter *s* Theke *f*

luncheon ['lʌntʃən] *s* gemeinsames Mittagessen *n*

luncheonette [,lʌntʃə'net] *s* Imbißstube *f*

lunch' hour' *s* Mittagsstunde *f*

lunch'room' *s* Imbißhalle *f*

lunch'time' *s* Mittagszeit *f*

lung [lʌŋ] *s* Lunge *f;* **at the top of one's lungs** aus voller Kehle

lunge ['lʌndʒ] *s* Sprung *m* vorwärts; (fencing) Ausfall *m* ‖ *tr* (a horse) an der Longe laufen lassen ‖ *intr*—e–n Sprung vorwärts machen; (with a sword) (at) e–n Ausfall machen (gegen); **l.** at losstürzen auf (acc)

lurch [lʌrtʃ] *s* Torkeln *n,* Taumeln *n;* **leave in a l.** im Stich lassen ‖ *intr* torkeln; (said of a ship) zur Seite rollen

lure [lur] *s* Köder *m* ‖ *tr* ködern; (fig) verlocken; **l. away** weglocken

lurid ['lurɪd] *adj* (light) gespenstisch; (sunset) düsterrot; (gruesome) grausig; (pallid) fahl

lurk [lʌrk] *intr* lauern

luscious ['lʌʃəs] *adj* köstlich; **a l. doll** (coll) ein tolles Weib

lush [lʌʃ] *adj* üppig

lust [lʌst] *s* Wollust *f;* (for) Begierde *f* (nach) ‖ *intr* (after, for) gieren (nach)

luster ['lʌstər] *s* Glanz *m;* (e.g., chandelier) Lüster *m*

lusterless ['lʌstərlɪs] *adj* matt

lus'terware' *s* Tongeschirr *n* mit Lüster

lustful ['lʌstfəl] *adj* lüstern, geil

lustrous ['lʌstrəs] *adj* glänzend

lusty ['lʌsti] *adj* kräftig

lute [lut] *s* Laute *f*

Lutheran ['luθərən] *adj* lutherisch ‖ *s* Lutheraner –in *mf*

luxuriance [lʌg'ʒurɪ-əns] *s* Üppigkeit *f*

luxuriant [lʌg'ʒurɪ-ənt] *adj* üppig

luxuriate [lʌg'ʒurɪ,et] *intr* (thrive) gedeihen; (delight) (in) schwelgen (in dat)

luxurious [lʌg'ʒurɪ-əs] *adj* luxuriös; **l. living** Prasserei *f*

luxury ['lʌgʒəri] *s* Extravaganz *f,* Luxus *m;* (object of luxury) Luxusartikel *m;* **live a life of l.** im vollen leben

lye [laɪ] *s* Lauge *f*

ly'ing *adj* lügenhaft ‖ *s* Lügen *n*

ly'ing-in' hos'pital *s* Entbindungsanstalt *f*

lymph [lɪmf] *s* Lymphe *f*

lymphatic [lɪm'fætɪk] *adj* lymphatisch

lynch [lɪntʃ] *tr* lynchen

lynch'ing *s* Lynchen *n*

lynch' law' *s* Lynchjustiz *f*

lynx [lɪŋks] *s* Luchs *m*

lynx'-eyed' *adj* luchsäugig

lyre [laır] s (mus) Leier f
lyric ['lırık] adj lyrisch; **l. poetry** Lyrik f ‖ s lyrisches Gedicht n; (of a song) Text m

lyrical ['lırıkəl] adj lyrisch
lyricism ['lırı‚sızəm] s Lyrik f
lyricist ['lırısıst] s (of a song) Texter –in mf; (poet) lyrischer Dichter m

M

M, m [ɛm] s dreizehnter Buchstabe des englischen Alphabets
ma [mɑ] s (coll) Mama f
ma'am [mæm] s (coll) gnädige Frau f
macadam [mə'kædəm] s Makadamdecke f
macadamize [mə'kædə‚maız] tr makadamisieren
maca'dam road' s Straße f mit Makadamdecke
macaroni [‚mækə'roni] spl Makkaroni pl
macaroon [‚mækə'run] s Makrone f
macaw [mə'kɔ] s (orn) Ara m
mace [mes] s Stab m, Amtsstab m
mace'bear'er s Träger m des Amtstabes
machination [‚mækı'neʃən] s Intrige f; **machinations** Machenschaften pl
machine [mə'ʃin] s Maschine f; (pol) Apparat m; **by m.** maschinell ‖ tr spannabhebend formen
machine'-driv'en adj mit Maschinenantrieb
machine' gun' s Maschinengewehr n
machine'-gun' v (pret & pp -gunned; ger -gunning) tr unter Maschinengewehrfeuer nehmen
machine' gun'ner s Maschinengewehrschütze m
machine'-made' adj maschinell hergestellt
machinery [mə'ʃinəri] s (& fig) Maschinerie f
machine' screw' s Maschinenschraube f
machine' shop' s Maschinenhalle f
machine' tool' s Werkzeugmaschine f
machinist [mə'ʃinıst] s (maker and repairer of machines) Maschinenbauer m; (machine operator) Maschinenschlosser –in mf
mackerel ['mækərəl] s Makrele f
mad [mæd] adj (madder; maddest) verrückt; (angry) böse; **be mad about** vernarrt sein in (acc); **be mad at** böse sein auf (acc); **drive mad** verrückt machen; **go mad** verrückt werden
madam ['mædəm] s gnädige Frau f; (of a brothel) (sl) Bordellmutter f
mad'cap' adj ausgelassen ‖ s Wildfang m
madden ['mædən] tr verrückt machen; (make angry) zornig machen
made'-to-or'der adj nach Maß angefertigt
made'-up' adj (story) erfunden; (artificial) künstlich; (with cosmetics) geschminkt

mad'house' s Irrenhaus n, Narrenhaus n
madly ['mædli] adv (coll) wahnsinnig
mad'man' s (-men') Verrückter m
madness ['mædnıs] s Wahnsinn m
Madonna [mə'dɑnə] s Madonna f
maelstrom ['melstrəm] s (& fig) Strudel m
magazine [‚mægə'zin] s (periodical) Zeitschrift f; (illustrated) Illustrierte f; (warehouse for munitions; cartridge container) Magazin n; (for a camera) Kassette f
magazine' rack' s Zeitschriftenständer m
Maggie ['mægi] s Gretchen n
maggot ['mægət] s Made f
Magi ['medʒaı] spl—**the three M.** (Bib) die drei Weisen pl aus dem Morgenland
magic ['mædʒık] adj (enchanting) zauberhaft; (trick, word, wand) Zauber– ‖ s Zauberkunst f
magician [mə'dʒıʃən] s Zauberer –in mf
ma'gic lan'tern s Laterna magica f
magisterial [‚mædʒıs'tırı‚əl] adj (of a magistrate) obrigkeitlich; (authoritative) autoritativ; (pompous) anmaßend
magistrate ['mædʒıs‚tret] s Polizeirichter m
magnanimous [mæg'nænıməs] adj großmütig
magnate ['mægnet] s Magnat m
magnesium [mæg'nizı‚əm] s Magnesium n
magnet ['mægnıt] s Magnet m
magnetic [mæg'netık] adj magnetisch; (personality) fesselnd
magnetism ['mægnı‚tızəm] s Magnetismus m; (fig) Anziehungskraft f
magnetize ['mægnı‚taız] tr magnetisieren
magnificence [mæg'nıfısəns] s Pracht f
magnificent [mæg'nıfısənt] adj prächtig
magnifier ['mægnı‚faı-ər] s (electron) Verstärker m
magni-fy ['mægnı‚faı] v (pret & pp -fied) tr vergrößern; (fig) übertreiben
mag'nifying glass' s Lupe f
magnitude ['mægnı‚t(j)ud] s (& astr) Größe f
magno'lia tree' [mæg'nolı‚ə] s Magnolia f
magpie ['mæg‚paı] s (& fig) Elster f
mahlstick ['mɑl‚stık] s Malerstock m

mahogany [məˈhɑgəni] s Mahagoni n
mahout [məˈhaut] s Elefantentreiber m
maid [med] s Dienstmädchen n
maiden [ˈmedən] s Jungfer f; (poet) Maid f
maid'enhair' s (bot) Jungfernhaar n
maid'enhead' s Jungfernhäutchen n
maid'enhood' s Jungfräulichkeit f
maidenly [ˈmedənli] adj jungfräulich
maid'en name' s Mädchenname m
maid'en voy'age s Jungfernfahrt f
maid'-in-wait'ing s (maids-in-waiting) Hofdame f
maid' of hon'or s erste Brautjungfer f
maid'serv'ant s Dienstmädchen n
mail [mel] adj Post– || s Post f; (armor) Kettenpanzer m; **by m.** brieflich; **by return m.** postwendend || tr (put into the mail) aufgeben; (send) abschicken; **m. to** zuschicken (dat)
mail'bag' s Postsack m
mail'boat' s Postschiff n
mail'box' s Briefkasten m
mail' car'rier s Briefträger –in mf
mail' deliv'ery s Postzustellung f
mail' drop' s Briefeinwurf m
mailer [ˈmelər] s (phot) Versandbeutel m
mail'ing s Absendung f
mail'ing list' s Postversandliste f
mail'ing per'mit s Zulassung f zum portofreien Versand
mail'man' s (-men') Briefträger m
mail' or'der s Bestellung f durch die Post
mail'-order house' s Versandhaus n
mail' plane' s Postflugzeug n
mail' train' s Postzug m
mail' truck' s Postauto n
maim [mem] tr verstümmeln
main [men] adj Haupt– || s Hauptleitung f; **in the main** hauptsächlich
main' clause' s (gram) Hauptsatz m
main' course' s Hauptgericht n
main' deck' s Hauptdeck n
main' floor' s Erdgeschoß n
mainland [ˈmen‚lænd] s Festland n
main' line' s (rr) Hauptstrecke f
mainly [ˈmenli] adv größtenteils
mainmast [ˈmen‚mæst] s Großmast m
main' of'fice s Hauptbüro n, Zentrale f
main' point' s springender Punkt m
mainsail [ˈmen‚sel] s Großsegel m
main'spring' s (horol & fig) Triebfeder f
main'stay' s (fig) Hauptstütze f; (naut) Großstag n
main' street' s Hauptstraße f
maintain [menˈten] tr aufrechterhalten; (e.g., a family) unterhalten; (assert) behaupten; (s.o.'s reputation) wahren; (e.g., in good condition) bewahren; (order, silence) halten; (a road) instand halten
maintenance [ˈmentɪnəns] s (upkeep) Instandhaltung f; (support) Unterhalt m; (e.g., of an automobile) Wardirektor m
maître d'hôtel [‚metərdoˈtel] s (head waiter) Oberkellner m; (owner) Hotelbesitzer m; (manager) Hotelführung f

majestic [məˈdʒestɪk] adj majestätisch
majesty [ˈmædʒɪsti] s Majestät f
major [ˈmedʒər] adj Haupt–; (mus) –Dur || s (educ) Hauptfach n; (mil) Major m || intr—**m. in** als Hauptfach studieren
majordomo [ˈmedʒərˈdomo] s Haushofmeister m
ma'jor gen'eral s Generalmajor m
majority [məˈdʒɔrɪti] adj Mehrheits– || s Mehrheit f; (full age) Mündigkeit f; (mil) Majorsrang m; (parl) Stimmenmehrheit f; **be in the m.** in der Mehrheit sein; **in the m. of cases** in der Mehrzahl der Fälle; **the m. of people** die meisten Menschen
major'ity vote' s Mehrheitsbeschluß m
ma'jor league' s Oberliga f
make [mek] s Fabrikat n, Marke f || tr machen; (in a factory) herstellen; (cause) lassen; (force) zwingen; (clothes) anfertigen; (money) verdienen; (a reputation, name) erwerben; (a choice) treffen; (a confession) ablegen; (a report) erstatten; (plans) schmieden; (changes) vornehmen; (a movie) drehen; (contact) herstellen; (a meal) (zu)bereiten; (conditions) stellen; (rules, assertions) aufstellen; (a bet, compromise, peace) schließen; (excuses, objections) vorbringen; (a protest) erheben; (a goal) schießen (or erzielen); (a comparison) ziehen; (a speech) halten; (e.g., a good father) abgeben; (be able to fit through, a window) gehen durch; (e.g., a train, bus, destination) erreichen; (e.g., ten miles) zurücklegen; (a girl) (sl) verführen; (arith) machen; **m.** (s.o.) **believe** weismachen (dat); **m. into** verarbeiten zu; **m.** of halten von; **m. out** (e.g., writing) entziffern; (e.g., a person at a distance) erkennen; (understand) kapieren; (a blank or form) ausfüllen; (a check, receipt) ausstellen; **m. over to** (jur) überschreiben auf (acc); **m. s.o. out to be a liar** j–n als Lügner hinstellen; **m. s.th. of oneself** es weit bringen; **m. the most of** ausnutzen; **m. time** Zeit gewinnen; **m. time with** (a woman) (coll) flirten mit; **m. up** (e.g., a list) zusammenstellen; (a bill) ausstellen; (a sentence) bilden; (a story) sich [dat] ausdenken; **m. up one's mind** (about) sich [dat] schlüssig werden (über acc); **m. way!** Platz da!; **m. way for** ausweichen vor (dat) || intr—**m. believe** schauspielern; **m. believe that** nur so tun, als ob; **m. do with** sich behelfen mit; **m. for** lossteuern auf (acc); **m. off with** durchbrennen mit; **m. out well** gut auskommen; **m. sure** of sich vergewissern (genit); **m. sure that** sich vergewissern, daß; **m. up** (after a quarrel) sich versöhnen; **m. up for** (past mistakes) wieder gutmachen; (lost time) wieder einbringen

make′-believe′ *adj* Schein-, vorgetäuscht ‖ *s* Schein *m*, Mache *f*
maker [′mekər] *s* Hersteller –in *mf*;
Maker Schöpfer *m*
make′shift′ *adj* behelfsmäßig, Behelfs-
‖ *s* Notbehelf *m*
make′-up′ *s* Aufmachung *f*; (*cosmetic*)
Make-up *n*, Schminke *f*; (*of a team*)
Aufstellung *f*; (*theat*) Maske *f*; (*typ*)
Umbruch *m*; **apply m.** sich schminken
make′weight′ *s* Gewichtszugabe *f*
mak′ing *s* Herstellung *f*; **be in the m.**
im Werden sein; **have the makings
of** das Zeug haben zu; **this is of his
own m.** dies ist sein eigenes Werk
maladjusted [‚mælə′dʒʌstɪd] *adj* unausgeglichen
maladroit [‚mælə′drɔɪt] *adj* ungeschickt
malady [′mælədi] *s* (& fig) Krankheit
f
malaise [mæ′lez] *s* (*physical*) Unwohl-
sein *n*; (*mental*) Unbehagen *n*
malaria [mə′lerɪ·ə] *s* Malaria *f*
Malaya [mə′le·ə] *s* Malaya *n*
Malaysia [mə′leʒɪ·ə] *s* Malaysia *n*
malcontent [′mælkən‚tent] *adj* unzufrieden ‖ *s* Unzufriedene *mf*
male [mel] *adj* männlich ‖ *s* Mann *m*;
(*bot*) männliche Pflanze *f*; (*zool*)
Männchen *n*
malediction [‚mælɪ′dɪkʃən] *s* Ver-
wünschung *f*
malefactor [′mælɪ‚fæktər] *s* Übeltäter
–in *mf*
male′ nurse′ *s* Pfleger *m*
malevolence [mæ′levələns] *s* Böswillig-
keit *f*
malevolent [mə′levələnt] *adj* böswillig
malfeasance [‚mæl′fizəns] *s* strafbare
Handlung *f*; **m. in office** Amtsver-
gehen *n*
malfunction [mæl′fʌŋkʃən] *s* technische Störung *f*
malice [′mælɪs] *s* Bosheit *f*
malicious [mə′lɪʃəs] *adj* boshaft
malign [mə′laɪn] *adj* böswillig ‖ *tr*
verleumden
malignancy [mə′lɪgnənsi] *s* (pathol)
Bösartigkeit *f*
malignant [mə′lɪgnənt] *adj* böswillig;
(pathol) bösartig
malinger [mə′lɪŋgər] *intr* simulieren
malingerer [mə′lɪŋgərər] *s* Simulant
–in *mf*
mall [mɔl] *s* (*promenade*) Lauben-
promenade *f*; (*shopping center*) über-
dachtes Einkaufszentrum *n*, Mall *f*
mallard [′mælərd] *s* Stockente *f*
malleable [′mælɪ·əbəl] *adj* schmiedbar
mallet [′mælɪt] *s* Schlegel *m*
mallow [′mælo] *s* Malve *f*
malnutrition [‚mæln(j)u′trɪʃən] *s* Unterernährung *f*
malodorous [mæl′odərəs] *adj* übelriechend
malpractice [mæl′præktɪs] *s* ärztlicher
Kunstfehler *m*
malt [mɔlt] *s* Malz *n*
maltreat [mæl′trit] *tr* mißhandeln
mamma [′mɑmə] *s* Mama *f*, Mutti *f*

mammal [′mæməl] *s* Säugetier *n*
mammalian [mæ′melɪ·ən] *adj* Säu-
getier- ‖ *s* Säugetier *n*
mam′mary gland′ [′mæməri] *s* Milch-
drüse *f*
mam′ma’s boy′ *s* Muttersöhnchen *n*
mammoth [′mæməθ] *adj* ungeheuer
(groß) ‖ *s* (zool) Mammut *n*
man [mæn] *s* (men [men]) (*adult male*)
Mann *m*; (*human being*) Mensch *m*;
(*servant*) Diener *m*; (*worker*) Arbeiter *m*; (*mankind*) die Menschheit
f; (*checkers*) Stein *m*; **man alive!**
Menschenskind! ‖ *v* (*pret & pp*
manned; *ger* **manning**) *tr* besetzen;
(nav, rok) bemannen
man′ about town′ *s* weltgewandter
Mann *m*
manacle [′mænəkəl] *s* Handschelle *f* ‖
tr fesseln
manage [′mænɪdʒ] *tr* (*a business,
household*) leiten; (*an estate*) verwalten; (*tools, weapons*) handhaben;
(*e.g., a boat, car*) völlig in der Gewalt haben; (*children*) fertig werden
mit; **I’ll m. it** ich werde es schon
schaffen; **m. the situation** die Sache
deichseln ‖ *intr* zurechtkommen;
(**with, on**) auskommen (mit); **m. to**
(*inf*) es fertigbringen zu (*inf*)
manageable [′mænɪdʒəbəl] *adj* handlich; (*hair*) fügsam
management [′mænɪdʒmənt] *s* Unter-
nehmensführung *f*; (*group which
manages*) Direktion *f*; (*as opposed
to labor*) Management *n*
man′agement consult′ant *s* Unterneh-
mungsberater –in *mf*
manager [′mænədʒər] *s* Manager *m*,
Geschäftsführer –in *mf*; (*of a bank
or hotel*) Direktor –in *mf*; (*of an
estate*) Verwalter –in *mf*; (*of a department*) Abteilungsleiter –in *mf*;
(*of a star, theater, athlete*) Manager
m
managerial [‚mænə′dʒɪrɪ·əl] *adj* Lei-
tungs-, Führungs-
man′aging *adj* geschäftsführend
man′aging direc′tor *s* Geschäftsführer
–in *mf*
Manchuria [mæn′tʃurɪ·ə] *s* Mandschurei *f*
man′darin or′ange [′mændərɪn] *s*
Mandarine *f*
mandate [′mændet] *s* Mandat *n* ‖ *tr*
(to) zuweisen (*dat*)
mandatory [′mændə‚tori] *adj* verbindlich
mandolin [′mændəlɪn] *s* Mandoline *f*
mandrake [′mændrek] *s* (bot) Alraune
f
mane [men] *s* Mähne *f*
maneuver [mə′nuvər] *s* Manöver *n*; **go
on maneuvers** (mil) ins Manöver ziehen ‖ *tr* manövrieren; **m. s.o. into**
(*ger*) j-n dazubringen zu (*inf*)
maneuverability [mə‚nuvərə′bɪlɪti] *s*
Manövrierbarkeit *f*
maneuverable [mə′nuvərəbəl] *adj* ma-
növrierfähig
manful [′mænfəl] *adj* mannhaft
manganese [′mæŋgə‚niz] *s* Mangan *n*

mange [mendʒ] *s* Räude *f*

manger ['mendʒər] *s* Krippe *f*

mangle ['mæŋgəl] *s* Mangel *f* ‖ *tr* (*tear apart*) zerfleischen; (*wash*) mangeln

mangy ['mendʒi] *adj* räudig; (fig) schäbig

man'han'dle *tr* grob behandeln

man'hole' *s* Kanalschacht *m*, Mannloch *n*

man'hole cov'er *s* Schachtdeckel *m*

man'hood' *s* (*virility*) Männlichkeit *f*; (*age*) Mannesalter *n*

man'-hour' *s* Arbeitsstunde *f* pro Mann

man'hunt' *s* Fahndung *f*

mania ['menɪ-ə] *s* Manie *f*

maniac ['menɪ‚æk] *s* Geisteskranke *mf*

maniacal [mə'naɪ-əkəl] *adj* manisch

manicure ['mænɪ‚kjʊr] *s* Maniküre *f*, Handpflege *f* ‖ *tr* maniküren

manicurist ['mænɪ‚kjʊrɪst] *s* Maniküre *f*

manifest ['mænɪ‚fest] *adj* offenkundig, offenbar ‖ *s* (aer, naut) Manifest *n* ‖ *tr* bekunden, bezeigen

manifestation [‚mænɪfes'teʃən] *s* (*manifesting*) Offenbarung *f*; (*indication*) Anzeichen *n*

manifes·to [‚mænɪ'festo] *s* (–toes) Manifest *n*

manifold ['mænɪ‚fold] *adj* mannigfaltig ‖ *s* (aut) Rohrverzweigung *f*

manikin ['mænɪkɪn] *s* Männchen *n*; (*for teaching anatomy*) anatomisches Modell *n*; (*mannequin*) Mannequin *n*

man' in the moon' *s* Mann *m* im Mond

man' in the streets' *s* Durchschnittsmensch *m*

manipulate [mə'nɪpjə‚let] *tr* manipulieren

man'kind' *s* Menschheit *f*

manliness ['mænlɪnɪs] *s* Männlichkeit *f*

manly ['mænli] *adj* mannhaft, männlich

man'-made' *adj* künstlich

manna ['mænə] *s* Manna *n*, Himmelsbrot *n*

manned' space'craft *s* bemanntes Raumfahrzeug *n*

mannequin ['mænɪkɪn] *s* (*clothes model*) Mannequin *n*; (*in a display window*) Schaufensterpuppe *f*

manner ['mænər] *s* Art *f*, Weise *f*; (*custom*) Sitte *f*; **after the m.** of nach der Art von; **by all m. of means** auf jeden Fall; **by no m. of means** auf keinen Fall; **in a m.** gewissermaßen; **in a m. of speaking** sozusagen; **in like m.** gleicherweise; **in the following m.** folgendermaßen; **in this m.** auf diese Weise; **it's bad manners to** (*inf*) es schickt sich nicht zu (*inf*); **m. of death** Todesart *f*; **manners** Manieren *pl*

mannerism ['mænə‚rɪzəm] *s* Manieriertheit *f*

mannerly ['mænərli] *adj* manierlich

mannish ['mænɪʃ] *adj* männisch; (*woman*) unweiblich

man' of let'ters *s* Literat *m*

man' of the world' *s* Weltmann *m*

man' of war' *s* Kriegsschiff *n*

manor ['mænər] *s* Herrengut *n*

man'or house' *s* Herrenhaus *n*

man'pow'er *s* Arbeitskräfte *pl*; (mil) Kriegsstärke *f*

man'serv'ant *s* (**menservants**) Diener *m*

mansion ['mænʃən] *s* Herrenhaus *n*

man'slaugh'ter *s* Totschlag *m*

mantel ['mæntəl] *s* Kaminsims *m & n*

man'telpiece' *s* Kaminsims *m & n*

mantilla [mæn'tɪlə] *s* Mantille *f*

mantle ['mæntəl] *s* (& fig) Mantel *m*; (*of a gaslight*) Glühstrumpf *m*; (geol) Mantel *m* ‖ *tr* verhüllen

manual ['mænjʊ-əl] *adj* manuell, Hand– ‖ *s* (*book*) Handbuch *n*, Leitfaden *m*; (mus) Manual *n*

man'ual control' *s* Handbedienung *f*

man'ual dexter'ity *s* Handfertigkeit *f*

man'ual la'bor *s* Handarbeit *f*

man'ual of arms' *s* (mil) Dienstvorschrift *f*

man'ual train'ing *s* Werkunterricht *m*

manufacture [‚mænjə'fækt/ər] *s* Herstellung *f*; (*production*) Erzeugnis *n* ‖ *tr* herstellen; (*clothes*) konfektionieren

manufac'tured goods' *spl* Fertigwaren *pl*

manufacturer [‚mænjə'fækt/ərər] *s* Hersteller –in *mf*

manure [mə'n(j)ʊr] *s* Mist *m* ‖ *tr* misten

manuscript ['mænjə‚skrɪpt] *adj* handschriftlich ‖ *s* Manuskript *n*

many ['meni] *adj* viele; **a good (or great) m.** sehr viele; **how m.** wieviele; **in so m. words** ausdrücklich; **m. a** mancher, manch ein; **m. a person** manch einer; **m. a time** manchmal; **twice as m.** noch einmal so viele ‖ *pron* viele; **as m. as ten** nicht weniger als zehn; **how m.** wieviele

man'y-sid'ed *adj* vielseitig

map [mæp] *s* Karte *f*, Landkarte *f*; (*of a city*) Plan *m*; (*of a local area*) Spezialkarte *f*; **map of the world** Weltkarte *f*; **put on the map** (coll) ausposaunen ‖ *v* (*pret & pp* **mapped**; *ger* **mapping**) *tr* kartographisch aufnehmen; **map out** planen

maple ['mepəl] *s* Ahorn *m*

ma'ple sug'ar *s* Ahornzucker *m*

ma'ple syr'up *s* Ahornsirup *m*

mar [mɑr] *v* (*pret & pp* **marred**; *ger* **marring**) *tr* (*detract from the beauty of*) verunzieren; (*e.g., a reputation*) beeinträchtigen

marathon ['mærə‚θɑn] *s* Dauerwettbewerb *m*

mar'athon race' *s* Marathonlauf *m*

maraud [mə'rɔd] *tr & intr* plündern

marauder [mə'rɔdər] *s* Plünderer *m*

marble ['mɑrbəl] *adj* marmorn ‖ *s* Marmor *m*; (*little glass ball*) Murmel *f*; **marbles** (*game*) Murmelspiel *n* ‖ *tr* marmorieren

mar'ble quar'ry *s* Marmorbruch *m*

march [mɑrt/] *s* Marsch *m*; (*festive parade*) Umzug *m*; **March** März *m*; **on the m.** auf dem Marsch; **steal a**

m. on s.o. j—m den Rang ablaufen; the m. of time der Lauf der Zeit ‖ *tr* marschieren ‖ *intr* marschieren; **m. by** vorbeimarschieren (an *dat*); **m. off** abmarschieren ‖ *interj* marsch!

marchioness ['mɑrʃənɪs] *s* Marquise *f*

mare [mer] *s* Stute *f*

Margaret ['mɑrgərɪt] *s* Margarete *f*

margarine ['mɑrdʒərɪn] *s* Margarine *f*

margin ['mɑrdʒɪn] *s* (*of a page*) Rand *m;* (*leeway*) Spielraum *m;* (*fin*) Spanne *f;* **by a narrow m.** mit knappem Abstand; **leave a m.** am Rande Raum lassen; **m. of profit** Gewinnspanne *f;* **m. of safety** Sicherheitsfaktor *m;* **win by a ten-second m.** mit zehn Sekunden Abstand gewinnen; **write in the m.** an dem Rand schreiben

marginal ['mɑrdʒɪnəl] *adj* (*costs, profits, case*) Grenz—; (*in the margin*) Rand—

mar′ginal note′ *s* Randbemerkung *f*

mar′gin release′ *s* Randauslöser *m*

mar′gin set′ter *s* Randsteller *m*

marigold ['mærɪˌgold] *s* Ringelblume *f*

marijuana [ˌmɑrɪ'hwɑnə] *s* Marihuana *n*

marinate ['mærɪˌnet] *tr* marinieren

marine [mə'rin] *adj* See—, Meer(es)— ‖ *s* (*fleet*) Marine *f;* (*fighter*) Marineinfanterist *m;* **marines** Marinetruppen *pl*

Marine′ Corps′ *s* Marineinfanteriekorps *n*

mariner ['mærɪnər] *s* Seemann *m*

marionette [ˌmærɪə'nɛt] *s* Marionette *f*

marital ['mærɪtəl] *adj* ehelich, Gatten—

mar′ital sta′tus *s* Familienstand *m*

maritime ['mærɪˌtaɪm] *adj* See—

marjoram ['mɑrdʒərəm] *s* Majoran *m*

mark [mɑrk] *s* (& fig) Zeichen *n;* (*stain, bruise*) Fleck *m*, Mal *n;* (*German unit of currency*) Mark *f;* (*educ*) Zensur *f;* **be an easy m.** (coll) leicht reinzulegen sein; **hit the m.** ins Schwarze treffen; **make one's m.** sich durchsetzen; **m. of confidence** Vertrauensbeweis *m;* **m. of favor** Gunstbezeichnung *f;* **m. of respect** Zeichen *n* der Hochachtung; **on your marks!** auf die Plätze!; **wide of the m.** am Ziel vorbei ‖ *tr* (aus)zeichnen, bezeichnen; (*student papers*) zensieren; (*cards*) zinken; (*labels*) beschriften; (*laundry*) zeichnen; (*the score*) anschreiben; **m. down** aufschreiben, niederschreiben; (com) im Preis herabsetzen; **m. my words!** merken Sie sich, was ich sage!; **m. off** abgrenzen; (surv) abstecken; **m. time** (mil & fig) auf der Stelle treten; (mus) den Takt schlagen; **m. up** (e.g., a wall) beschmieren; (com) im Preis heraufsetzen

mark′down′ *s* Preisnachlaß *m*

marked *adj* (*difference*) merklich; **a m. man** ein Gezeichneter *m*

marker ['mɑrkər] *s* (*of scores*) Anschreiber —in *mf;* (*commemorative marker*) Gedenktafel *f;* (*on a firing range*) Anzeiger *m;* (*bombing marker*) Leuchtbombe *f;* (*felt pen*) Filzschreiber *m*

market ['mɑrkɪt] *s* Markt *m;* (*grocery store*) Lebensmittelgeschäft *n;* (*stock exchange*) Börse *f;* (*ready sale*) Absatz *m;* **be in the m. for** Bedarf haben an (*dat*); **be on the m.** zum Verkauf stehen; **put on the m.** auf den Markt bringen ‖ *tr* verkaufen

marketable ['mɑrkɪtəbəl] *adj* marktfähig

mar′ket anal′ysis *s* Marktanalyse *f*

mar′keting *s* (econ) Marketing *n;* **do the m.** Einkäufe machen

mar′keting research′ *s* Absatzforschung *f*

mar′ketplace′ *s* Marktplatz *m*

mar′ket price′ *s* Marktpreis *m*

mar′ket town′ *s* Marktflecken *m*

mar′ket val′ue *s* Marktwert *m;* (st. exch.) Kurswert *m*

mark′ing *s* Kennzeichen *n*

marks·man ['mɑrksmən] *s* (—men) Schütze *m*

marks′manship′ *s* Schießkunst *f*

mark′up′ *s* (com) Gewinnaufschlag *m*

marl [mɑrl] *s* Mergel *m* ‖ *tr* mergeln

marmalade ['mɑrməˌled] *s* Marmelade *f*

maroon [mə'run] *adj* rotbraun, kastanienbraun ‖ *s* Kastanienbraun *n* ‖ *tr* aussetzen; **be marooned** von der Außenwelt abgeschnitten sein

marquee [mɑr'ki] *s* Schutzdach *n*

marquess ['mɑrkwɪs] *s* Marquis *m*

marquis ['mɑrkwɪs] *s* Marquis *m*

marquise [mɑr'kiz] *s* Marquise *f*

marriage ['mærɪdʒ] *s* Heirat *f;* (*state*) Ehe *f*, Ehestand *m;* **by m.** angeheiratet, schwägerlich; **give in m.** verheiraten

marriageable ['mærɪdʒəbəl] *adj* heiratsfähig; **m. age** (*of a girl*) Mannbarkeit *f*

mar′riage brok′er *s* Heiratsvermittler —in *mf*

mar′riage cer′emony *s* Trauung *f*

mar′riage li′cense *s* Heiratsurkunde *f*

mar′riage of conven′ience *s* Vernunftehe *f*

mar′riage por′tion *s* Mitgift *f*

mar′riage propos′al *s* Heiratsantrag *m*

mar′riage vow′ *s* Ehegelöbnis *n*

mar′ried cou′ple *s* Ehepaar *n*

mar′ried state′ *s* Ehestand *m*

marrow ['mæro] *s* Knochenmark *n;* (fig) Mark *n*

mar·ry ['mæri] *v* (*pret & pp* —ried) *tr* heiraten; (*said of a priest or minister*) trauen; **m. off (to)** verheiraten (mit) ‖ *intr* heiraten; **m. rich** e—e gute Partie machen

Mars [mɑrz] *s* Mars *m*

marsh [mɑrʃ] *s* Sumpf *m*

mar·shal ['mɑrʃəl] *s* Zeremonienmeister *m;* (*police officer*) Bezirkspolizeichef *m;* (mil) Marschall *m* ‖ *v* (*pret & pp* —shal[l]ed; *ger* —shal[l]ing) *tr* (*troops*) ordnungsgemäß aufstellen; (*strength*) zusammenraffen

marsh'land' s Sumpfland n
marsh'mal'low s (bot) Eibisch m
marsh'mal'low s (candy) Konfekt n aus Stärkesirup, Zucker, Stärke, Gelatine, und geschlagenem Eiweiß
marshy ['marʃi] adj sumpfig
mart [mart] s Markt m
marten ['martən] s (zool) Marder m
Martha ['marθə] s Martha f
martial ['marʃəl] adj Kriegs–
mar'tial law' s Standrecht n; **declare m.** das Standrecht verhängen; **under m.** standrechtlich
martin ['martin] s Mauerschwalbe f; **Martin** Martin m
martinet [,marti'net] s Pauker –in mf; (mil) Schleifer m
martyr ['martər] s Märtyrer –in mf || tr martern
martyrdom ['martərdəm] s Märtyrertum n
mar·vel ['marvəl] s Wunder n || v (pret & pp –vel[l]ed; ger –vel[l]ing) intr (at) sich wundern (über acc)
marvelous ['marvələs] adj wundervoll; (coll) pfundig
Marxist ['marksist] adj marxistisch || Marxist –in mf
marzipan ['marzi,pæn] s Marzipan n
mascara [mæs'kærə] s Lidtusche f
mascot ['mæskət] s Maskotte f
masculine ['mæskjəlin] adj männlich
mash [mæʃ] s Brei m; (in brewing) Maische f || tr zerquetschen; (potatoes) zerdrücken
mashed' pota'toes spl Kartoffelbrei m
mask [mæsk] s Maske f || tr maskieren
masked' ball' s Maskenball m
mason ['mesən] s Maurer m; **Mason** Freimaurer m
Masonic [mə'sanik] adj Freimaurer–
masonite ['mesə,nait] s Holzfaserplatte f
masonry ['mesənri] s Mauerwerk n; **Masonry** Freimaurerei f
masquerade [,mæskə'red] s (& fig) Maskerade f || intr (& fig) sich maskieren; **m. as** sich ausgeben als
mass [mæs] adj Massen– || s Masse f; (eccl) Messe; **the masses** die breite Masse f || tr massieren || intr sich ansammeln
massacre ['mæsəkər] s Massaker n || tr massakrieren, niedermetzeln
massage [mə'saʒ] s Massage f || tr massieren
masseur [mə'sʌr] s Masseur m
masseuse [mə'suz] s Masseuse f
massif ['mæsif] s Gebirgsstock m
massive ['mæsiv] adj massiv
mass' me'dia ['midi·ə] spl Massenmedien pl
mass' meet'ing s Massenversammlung f
mass' mur'der s Massenmord m
mass'-produce' tr serienmäßig herstellen
mass' produc'tion s Serienherstellung f
mast [mæst] s Mast m; (food for swine) Mast f
master ['mæstər] adj (bedroom, key, switch, cylinder) Haupt– || s Herr m;

Meister m; (male head of a household) Hausherr m; (of a ship) Kapitän m || tr beherrschen
mas'ter build'er s Baumeister m
mas'ter car'penter s Zimmermeister m
mas'ter cop'y s Originalkopie f
masterful ['mæstərfəl] adj herrisch; (masterly) meisterhaft
masterly ['mæstərli] adj meisterhaft
mas'ter mechan'ic s Schlossermeister m
mas'termind' s führender Geist m || tr planen und überwachen
Mas'ter of Arts' s Magister m der freien Künste
mas'ter of cer'emonies s Zeremonienmeister m
mas'ter of the house' s Hausherr m
mas'terpiece' s Meisterstück n
mas'ter ser'geant s Oberfeldwebel m
mas'ter stroke' s Meisterstreich m
mas'terwork' s Meisterwerk n
mastery ['mæstəri] s (of) Beherrschung f (genit); **gain m. over** die Oberhand gewinnen über (acc)
mast'head' s (naut) Topp m; (typ) Impressum n
masticate ['mæsti,ket] tr zerkauen || intr kauen
mastiff ['mæstif] s Mastiff m
masturbate ['mæstər,bet] intr onanieren
masturbation [,mæstər'beʃən] s Onanie f
mat [mæt] s (for a floor) Matte f; (before the door) Türvorleger m; (under cups, vases, etc.) Zierdeckchen n || v (pret & pp matted; ger matting) tr (cover with matting) mit Matten belegen; (the hair) verfilzen || intr sich verfilzen
match [mætʃ] s Streichholz n; (for marriage) Partie f; (sport) Match n; **be a good m.** zueinanderpassen; **be a m. for** gewachsen sein (dat); **be no m. for** sich nicht messen können mit; **meet one's m.** seinen Mann finden || tr (fit together) zusammenstellen; (harmonize with) passen zu; (equal) (in) gleichkommen (in dat); (funds) in gleicher Höhe aufbringen; (adapt) in Übereinstimmung bringen mit; **be well matched** auf gleicher Höhe sein; **m. up** zusammenpassen; **m. wits** with sich geistig messen mit || intr zueinanderpassen
match'book' s Streichholzbrief m
match' box' s Streichholzschachtel f
match'ing adj (clothes) passend; (funds) in gleicher Höhe || s Paarung f
match'mak'er s Heiratsvermittler –in mf; (sport) Veranstalter m
mate [met] s Genosse m, Kamerad m; (in marriage) Ehepartner m; (one of a pair, e.g., of gloves) Gegenstück n; (especially of birds) Männchen n, Weibchen n; (naut) Maat m || tr paaren || intr sich paaren
material [mə'tiri·əl] adj materiell; (important) wesentlich || s Material n, Stoff m; (tex) Stoff m

materialist [mə'tɪrɪ-əlɪst] s Materialist –in mf

materialistic [mə,tɪrɪ-ə'lɪstɪk] adj materialistisch

materialize [mə'tɪrɪ-ə,laɪz] intr sich verwirklichen

materiel [mə,tɪrɪ'el] s Material n; (mil) Kriegsmaterial n

maternal [mə'tʌrnəl] adj mütterlich; (relatives) mütterlicherseits

maternity [mə'tʌrnɪti] s Mutterschaft f

mater′nity dress′ s Umstandskleid n

mater′nity hos′pital s Wöchnerinnenheim n

mater′nity ward′ s Wöchnerinnenstation f

math [mæθ] s (coll) Mathe f

mathematical [,mæθɪ'mætɪkəl] adj mathematisch

mathematician [,mæθɪmə'tɪʃən] s Mathematiker –in mf

mathematics [,mæθɪ'mætɪks] s Mathematik f

matinée [,mætɪ'ne] s Nachmittagsvorstellung f

mat′ing sea′son s Paarungszeit f

matins ['mætɪnz] spl Frühmette f

matriarch ['metrɪ,ɑrk] s Stammesmutter f

matriarchal [,metrɪ'ɑrkəl] adj matriarchalisch

matriarchy ['metrɪ,ɑrki] s Matriarchat n

matricide ['mætrɪ,saɪd] s (act) Muttermord m; (person) Muttermörder –in mf

matriculate [mə'trɪkjə,let] tr immatrikulieren ‖ intr sich immatrikulieren

matriculation [mə,trɪkjə'leʃən] s Immatrikulation f

matrimonial [,mætrɪ'monɪ-əl] adj Ehe–

matrimony ['mætrɪ,moni] s Ehestand m

ma·trix ['metrɪks] s (–trices [trɪ,siz] & –trixes) (mold) Gießform f; (math) Matrix f; (typ) Matrize f

matron ['metrən] s Matrone f

matronly ['metrənli] adj matronenhaft, gesetzt

matt [mæt] adj (phot) matt

matter ['mætər] s Stoff m; (affair) Sache f, Angelegenheit f; (pus) Eiter m; (phys) Materie f; **as a m. of course** routinemäßig; **as matters now stand** wie die Sache jetzt liegt; **for that m.** was das betrifft; **it's a m. of** es handelt sich um; **it's a m. of life and death** es geht um Leben und Tod; **m. of opinion** Ansichtssache f; **m. of taste** Geschmackssache f; **something is the m. with his heart** er hat was am Herz; **no laughing m.** nichts zum Lachen; **no m.** ganz gleich; **what's the m. (with)?** was ist los (mit)? ‖ intr von Bedeutung sein; **it doesn't m.** es macht nichts (aus); **it doesn't m. to me** es liegt mir nichts daran; **it matters a great deal to me** es liegt mir sehr viel daran

mat′ter of fact′ s Tatsache f; **as a m.** tatsächlich

mat′ter-of-fact′ adj sachlich, nüchtern

Matthew ['mæθju] s Matthäus m

mattock ['mætək] s Breithacke f

mattress ['mætrɪs] s Matratze f

mature [mə't∫ʊr] adj (& fig) reif ‖ tr reifen lassen ‖ intr reifen; (fin) fällig werden

maturity [mə't∫ʊrɪti] s Reife f; (fin) Verfall m

maudlin ['mɔdlɪn] adj rührselig

maul [mɔl] tr schlimm zurichten

maulstick ['mɔl,stɪk] s Mahlstock m

mausole·um [,mɔsə'li-əm] s (–ums & –a [ə]) Mausoleum n

maw [mɔ] s (mouth of an animal) Rachen m; (stomach of an animal) Tiermagen m; (of birds) Kropf m

mawkish ['mɔkɪʃ] adj rührselig

maxim ['mæksɪm] s Maxime f, Lehrspruch m

maximum ['mæksɪməm] adj Höchst–; **m. load** Höchstbelastung f ‖ s Maximum n

May [me] s Mai m ‖ **may** v (pret **might** [maɪt]) aux (expressing possibility) mögen, können; (expressing permission) dürfen; (expressing a wish) mögen; **be that as it may** wie dem auch sei; **come what may** komme, was da wolle; **it may be too late** es ist vielleicht zu spät; **that may be** das kann (or mag) sein

maybe ['mebi] adv vielleicht

May′ Day′ s der erste Mai

mayhem ['mehəm] s Körperverletzung f

mayonnaise [,me·ə'nez] s Mayonnaise f

mayor [mer] s Bürgermeister m; (of a large city) Oberbürgermeister m

May′pole′ s Maibaum m

May′ queen′ s Maikönigin f

maze [mez] s Irrgarten m; (fig) Gewirr n

me [mi] pers pron (direct object) mich; (indirect object) mir; **this one is on me** das geht auf meine Rechnung

mead [mid] s (hist) Met m; (poet) Aue f

meadow ['medo] s Wiese f

mead′owland′ s Wiesenland n

meager ['migər] adj karg, kärglich

meal [mil] s Mahl n, Mahlzeit f; (grain) grobes Mehl n

meal′ tick′et s Gutschein m für e–e Mahlzeit

meal′time′ s Essenszeit f

mealy ['mili] adj mehlig

mealy-mouthed ['mili,mauðd] adj zurückhaltend

mean [min] adj (nasty) bösartig; (lowly) gemein, niedrig; (shabby) schäbig; (in statistics) mittlere; **no m.** kein schlechter ‖ s (log) Mittelbegriff m; (math) Mittel n; **by all means** unbedingt; **by every means** mit allen Mitteln; **by fair means or foul** ganz gleich wie; **by lawful means** auf dem Rechtswege; **by means of**

mittels (*genit*); **by no means** keineswegs; **live beyond one's means** über seine Verhältnisse leben; **live within one's means** seinen Verhältnissen entsprechend leben; **means** (*way*) Mittel *n*; (*resources*) Mittel *pl*, Vermögen *n*; **means of transportation** Verkehrsmittel *n*; **means to an end** Mittel *pl* zum Zweck; **of means** bemittelt ‖ *v* (*pret & pp* **meant** [ment]) *tr* (*intend, intend to say*) meinen; (*signify*) bedeuten; **be meant for** (*said, e.g., of a remark*) gelten (*dat*); (*said, e.g., of a gift*) bestimmt sein für; **it means a lot to me to** (*inf*) mir liegt viel daran zu (*inf*); **m. business** es ernst meinen; **m. little** (or **much**) wenig (or viel) gelten; **m. no harm** es nicht böse meinen; **m. s.o. no harm** j–n nicht verletzen wollen; **m. the world to s.o.** j–m alles bedeuten; **what is meant by ...?** was versteht man unter ...? ‖ *intr*—**m. well** es gut meinen

meander [mɪˈændər] *intr* sich winden

mean'ing *s* Bedeutung *f*; **take on m.** e–n Sinn bekommen; **what's the m. of this?** was soll das heißen?

meaningful [ˈminɪŋfəl] *adj* sinnvoll

meaningless [ˈminɪŋlɪs] *adj* sinnlos

mean'-look'ing *adj* bösartig aussehend

meanness [ˈminnɪs] *s* Gemeinheit *f*; (*nastiness*) Bösartigkeit *f*

mean'time', mean'while' *adv* mittlerweile ‖ *s*—**in the m.** mittlerweile, in der Zwischenzeit

measles [ˈmizəlz] *s* Masern *pl*; (*German measles*) Röteln *pl*

measly [ˈmizli] *adj* kümmerlich, lumpig

measurable [ˈmeʒərəbəl] *adj* meßbar

measure [ˈmeʒər] *s* Maß *n*; (*step*) Maßnahme *f*; (*law*) Gesetz *n*; (*mus*) Takt *m*; **beyond m.** übermäßig; **for good m.** obendrein; **in a great m.** in großem Maß; **to some m.** gewissermaßen; **take drastic measures** durchgreifen; **take measures to** (*inf*) Maßnahmen ergreifen um zu (*inf*); **take s.o.'s m.** (fig) j–n einschätzen ‖ *tr* messen; **m. off** abmessen; **m. out** ausmessen ‖ *intr* messen; **m. up to** gewachsen sein (*dat*)

measurement [ˈmeʒərmənt] *s* (*measured dimension*) Maß *n*; (*measuring*) Messung *f*; **measurements** Maße *pl*; **take s.o.'s measurements for** j–m Maß nehmen zu

meas'uring cup' *s* Meßbecher *m*

meas'uring tape' *s* Meßband *n*

meat [mit] *s* Fleisch *n*; (*of a nut, of the matter*) Kern *m*

meat'ball' *m* Fleischklößchen *n*

meat'grind'er *s* Fleischwolf *m*

meat'hook' *s* Fleischhaken *m*

meat'mar'ket *s* Fleischmarkt *m*

meat'pie' *s* Fleischpastete *f*

meaty [ˈmiti] *adj* fleischig; (fig) kernig

Mecca [ˈmekə] *s* Mekka *n*

mechanic [məˈkænɪk] *s* Mechaniker *m*, Schlosser *m*; (aut) Autoschlosser *m*; **mechanics** Mechanik *f*

mechanical [məˈkænɪkəl] *adj* mechanisch

mechan'ical engineer' *s* Maschinenbauingenieur *m*

mechan'ical engineer'ing *s* Maschinenbau *m*

mechanism [ˈmekə͵nɪzəm] *s* Mechanismus *m*

mechanize [ˈmekə͵naɪz] *tr* mechanisieren

medal [ˈmedəl] *s* Medaille *f*, Orden *m*

medallion [mɪˈdæljən] *s* Medaillon *n*

meddle [ˈmedəl] *intr* sich einmischen; **m. with** sich abgeben mit

meddler [ˈmedlər] *s* zudringliche Person *f*

meddlesome [ˈmedəlsəm] *adj* zudringlich

media [ˈmidɪ-ə] *spl* Medien *pl*

median [ˈmidɪ-ən] *adj* mittlere, Mittel- ‖ *s* (arith) Mittelwert *m*; (geom) Mittellinie *f*

me'dian strip' *s* Mittelstreifen *m*

mediate [ˈmidɪ͵et] *tr & intr* vermitteln

mediation [͵midɪˈeʃən] *s* Vermittlung *f*

mediator [ˈmidɪ͵etər] *s* Vermittler –in *mf*

medic [ˈmedɪk] *s* (mil) Sanitäter *m*

medical [ˈmedɪkəl] *adj* (*of a doctor*) ärztlich; (*of medicine*) medizinisch; (*of the sick*) Kranken-

med'ical bul'letin *s* Krankheitsbericht *m*

med'ical corps' *s* Sanitätstruppe *f*

med'ical profes'sion *s* Arztberuf *m*

med'ical school' *s* medizinische Fakultät *f*

med'ical sci'ence *s* Heilkunde *f*

med'ical stu'dent *s* Medizinstudent –in *mf*

medication [͵medɪˈkeʃən] *s* Medikament *n*

medicinal [məˈdɪsɪnəl] *adj* medizinisch

medicine [ˈmedɪsən] *s* Medizin *f*, Arznei *f*; (*profession*) Medizin *f*; **practice m.** den Arztberuf ausüben

med'icine cab'inet *s* Hausapotheke *f*

med'icine kit' *s* Reiseapotheke *f*

med'icine man' *s* Medizinmann *m*

medic·o [ˈmedɪ͵ko] *s* (–cos) (coll) Mediziner –in *mf*

medieval [͵midɪˈivəl], [͵medɪˈivəl] *adj* mittelalterlich

mediocre [͵midɪˈokər] *adj* mittelmäßig

mediocrity [͵midɪˈɑkrɪti] *s* Mittelmäßigkeit *f*

meditate [ˈmedɪ͵tet] *tr* vorhaben ‖ *intr* (on) meditieren (über *acc*)

meditation [͵medɪˈteʃən] *s* Meditation *f*

Mediterranean [͵medɪtəˈreni-ən] *adj* Mittelmeer- ‖ *s* Mittelmeer *n*

medi·um [ˈmidɪ-əm] *adj* Mittel-, mittlere ‖ *s* (–ums & –a [ə]) Mittel *n*; (*culture*) Nährboden *m*; (*in spiritualism, communications*) Medium *n*; **through the m.** of vermittels (*genit*)

me'dium of exchange' *s* Tauschmittel *n*

me'dium-rare' *adj* halb durchgebraten

me'dium size' *s* Mittelgröße *f*

med'ium-sized' *adj* mittelgroß

medley ['medli] *s* Mischmasch *m;* (mus) Potpourri *n*

medul·la [mɪ'dʌlə] *s* (**–las & –lae** [li]) Knochenmark *n*, Mark *n*

meek [mik] *adj* sanftmütig; **m. as a lamb** lammfromm

meekness ['miknɪs] *s* Sanftmut *m*

meerschaum ['mɪrʃəm] *s* Meerschaum *m*

meet [mit] *adj* passend ‖ *s* (sport) Treffen *n*, Veranstaltung *f* ‖ *v* (*pret & pp* **met** [met]) *tr* begegnen (*dat*), treffen; (*make the acquaintance of*) kennenlernen; (*demands*) befriedigen; (*obligations*) nachkommen (*dat*); (*wishes*) erfüllen; (*a deadline*) einhalten; **m. s.o. at the train** j–n von der Bahn abholen; **m. s.o. halfway** j–m auf halbem Wege entgegenkommen; **m. the train** zum Zug gehen; **pleased to m.** you freut mich sehr, sehr angenehm ‖ *intr* (*said of persons, of two ends*) zusammenkommen; (*said of persons*) sich treffen; (*in conference*) tagen; (*said of roads, rivers*) sich vereinigen; **make both ends m.** gerade mit dem Geld auskommen; **m. again** sich wiedersehen; **m. up with s.o.** j–n einholen; **m. with** zusammentreffen mit; **m. with an accident** verunglücken; **m. with a refusal** e–e Fehlbitte tun; **m. with approval** Beifall finden; **m. with success** Erfolg haben

meet'ing *s* (*of an organization*) Versammlung *f;* (*e.g., of a committee*) Sitzung *f;* (*of individuals*) Zusammenkunft *f*

meet'ing place' *s* Treffpunkt *m*

megacycle ['mega,saɪkəl], **megahertz** ['mega,hʌrts] *s* (elec) Megahertz *n*

megalomania [,megəlo'menɪə] *s* Größenwahn *m*

megaphone ['mega,fon] *s* Sprachrohr *n*

megohm ['meg,om] *s* Megohm *n*

melancholy ['melən,kɑli] *adj* schwermütig ‖ *s* Schwermut *f*

melee ['mele], ['mele] *s* Gemenge *n*

mellow ['melo] *adj* (*very ripe*) mürb(e); (*wine*) abgelagert; (*voice*) schmelzend; (*person*) gereift ‖ *tr zur* Reife bringen; (fig) mildern ‖ *intr* mürb(e) werden; (fig) mild werden

melodic [mɪ'lɑdɪk] *adj* melodisch

melodious [mɪ'lodɪ·əs] *adj* melodisch

melodrama ['melo,drɑmə] *s* (& fig) Melodrama *f*

melody ['melədi] *s* Melodie *f*

melon ['melən] *s* Melone *f*

melt [melt] *tr & intr* schmelzen

melt'ing point' *s* Schmelzpunkt *m*

melt'ing pot' *s* (& fig) Schmelztiegel *m*

member ['membər] *s* Glied *n;* (person) Mitglied *n*, Angehörige *mf;* **m. of the family** Familienangehörige *mf*

mem'bership *s* Mitgliedschaft *f;* (*collectively*) Mitglieder *pl;* (*number of members*) Mitgliederzahl *f*

mem'bership card' *s* Mitgliedskarte *f*

membrane ['membren] *s* Häutchen *n*, Membran(e) *f*

memen·to [mɪ'mento] *s* (**–tos & –toes**) Erinnerung *f*, Memento *n*

mem·o ['memo] *s* (**–os**) (coll) Notiz *f*

mem'o book' *s* Notizbuch *n*, Agenda *f*

memoirs ['memwɑrz] *spl* Memoiren *pl*

mem'o pad' *s* Notizblock *m*, Agenda *f*

memorable ['memərəbəl] *adj* denkwürdig

memoran·dum [,memə'rændəm] *s* (**–dums & –da** [də]) Notiz *f*, Vermerk *m;* (dipl) Memorandum *n*

memorial [mɪ'morɪ·əl] *adj* Gedächtnis–, Erinnerungs– ‖ *s* Denkmal *n*

Memor'ial Day' *s* Gefallenengedenktag *m*

memorialize [mɪ'morɪ·ə,laɪz] *tr* gedenken (*genit*)

memorize ['memə,raɪz] *tr* auswendig lernen

memory ['meməri] *s* (*faculty*) Gedächtnis *n;* (*of*) Gedenken *n* (an *acc*), Erinnerung *f* (an *acc*); **commit to m.** auswendig lernen; **escape one's m.** seinem Gedächtnis entfallen; **from m.** aus dem Gedächtnis; **in m. of** zur Erinnerung an (*acc*); **of blessed m.** seligen Angedenkens; **within the m. of men** seit Menschengedenken

menace ['menɪs] *s* (**to**) Drohung *f* (*genit*) ‖ *tr* bedrohen

menagerie [mə'nædʒəri] *s* Menagerie *f*

mend [mend] *s* Besserung *f;* **on the m.** auf dem Wege der Besserung ‖ *tr* (*clothes*) ausbessern; (*socks*) stopfen; (*repair*) reparieren

mendacious [men'deʃəs] *adj* lügnerisch

mendicant ['mendɪkənt] *adj* Bettel– ‖ *s* Bettelmönch *m*

menfolk ['men,fok] *spl* Mannsleute *pl*

menial ['minɪ·əl] *adj* niedrig ‖ *s* Diener –in *mf*

menopause ['menə,pɔz] *s* Wechseljahre *pl*

menses ['mensiz] *spl* Monatsfluß *m*

men's' room' *s* Herrentoilette *f*

men's' size' *s* Herrengröße *f*

men's' store' *s* Herrenbekleidungsgeschäft *n*

menstruate ['menstru,et] *intr* menstruieren

menstruation [,menstru'eʃən] *s* Menstruation *f*

men's' wear' *s* Herrenbekleidung *f*

mental ['mentəl] *adj* geistig, Geistes–

men'tal an'guish *s* Seelenpein *f*

men'tal arith'metic *s* Kopfrechnen *n*

men'tal capac'ity *s* Fassungskraft *f*

men'tal disor'der *s* Geistesstörung *f*

men'tal institu'tion *s* Nervenheilanstalt *f*

mentality [men'tælɪti] *s* Mentalität *f*

mentally ['mentəli] *adv* geistig, Geistes–; **m. alert** geistesgegenwärtig; **m. disturbed** geistesgestört; **m. lazy** denkfaul

men'tal reserva'tion *s* geistiger Vorbehalt *m*

men'tal teleg'athy *s* Gedankenübertragung *f*

mention ['menʃən] *s* Erwähnung *f;*

make m. of erwähnen ‖ *tr* erwähnen; nennen; **be mentioned** zur Sprache kommen; **don't m. it!** keine Ursache!; **not worth mentioning** nicht der Rede wert

menu ['menju] *s* Speisekarte *f*

meow [mi'au] *s* Miauen *n* ‖ *intr* miauen

mercantile ['mʌrkən‚til], ['mʌrkən‚tail] *adj* Handels-, kaufmännisch

mercenary ['mʌrsə‚neri] *adj* gewinnsüchtig ‖ *s* Söldner *m*

merchandise ['mʌrtʃən‚daiz] *s* Ware *f* ‖ *tr* handeln

mer'chandising *s* Verkaufspolitik *f*

merchant ['mʌrtʃənt] *s* Händler, Kaufmann *m*

mer'chant-man *s* (-men) Handelsschiff *n*

mer'chant marine' *s* Handelsmarine *f*

mer'chant ves'sel *s* Handelsschiff *n*

merciful ['mʌrsifəl] *adj* barmherzig

merciless ['mʌrsilis] *adj* erbarmungslos

mercurial [mer'kjuri·əl] *adj* quecksilbrig

mercury ['mʌrkjəri] *s* Quecksilber *n*

mercy ['mʌrsi] *s* Barmherzigkeit *f*; **be at s.o.'s m.** in j–s Gewalt sein; **be at the m. of** (*e.g., the wind, waves*) preisgegeben sein (*dat*); **beg for m.** um Gnade flehen; **show no m.** keine Gnade walten lassen; **show s.o. m.** sich j–s erbarmen; **throw oneself on the m. of** sich auf Gnade und Ungnade ergeben (*dat*); **without m.** ohne Gnade

mere [mir] *adj* bloß, rein

merely ['mirli] *adv* nur, lediglich

meretricious [‚meri'triʃəs] *adj* (*tawdry*) flitterhaft; (*characteristic of a prostitute*) dirnenhaft

merge [mʌrdʒ] *tr* verschmelzen ‖ *intr* sich verschmelzen

merger ['mʌrdʒər] *s* (com) Fusion *f*; (jur) Verschmelzung *f*

meridian [mə'ridi·ən] *s* (astr) Meridian *m*; (geog) Meridian *m*, Längenkreis *m*

meringue [mə'ræŋ] *s* (*topping*) Eierschnee *m*; (*pastry*) Schaumgebäck *n*

merit ['merit] *s* Verdienst *n*; **of great m.** hochverdient ‖ *tr* verdienen

meritorious [‚meri'tori·əs] *adj* verdienstvoll

merlin ['mʌrlin] *s* (orn) Merlinfalke *m*

mermaid ['mʌr‚med] *s* Seejungfer *f*

merriment ['merimənt] *s* Fröhlichkeit *f*

merry ['meri] *adj* fröhlich, heiter

Mer'ry Christ'mas *s* fröhliche Weihnachten *pl*

mer'ry-go-round' *s* Karussell *n*

mer'rymak'er *s* Zecher –in *mf*

mesh [meʃ] *s* Masche *f*; (*network*) Netzwerk *n*; (mach) Ineinandergreifen *n*; **meshes** (fig) Schlingen *pl* ‖ *intr* ineinandergreifen

mesmerize ['mesmə‚raiz] *tr* hypnotisieren

mess [mes] *s* (*disorder*) Durcheinander

n; (*dirty condition*) Schweinerei *f*; (*for officers*) Messe *f*; **a nice m.!** e–e schöne Wirtschaft!; **get into a m.** in die Klemme geraten; **make a m.** Schmutz machen; **make a m. of** verpfuschen; **what a m.!** nette Zustände! ‖ *tr*—**m. up** (*dirty*) beschmutzen; (*put into disarray*) in Unordnung bringen ‖ *intr*—**m. around** herumtrödeln; **m. around with** herummurksen an (*dat*)

message ['mesidʒ] *s* Botschaft *f*

messenger ['mesəndʒər] *s* Bote *m*, Botin *f*

mess' hall' *s* Messe *f*

Messiah [mə'sai·ə] *s* Messias *m*

mess' kit' *s* Eßgeschirr *n*

messy ['mesi] *adj* (*disorderly*) unordentlich; (*dirty*) dreckig

metabolism [mə'tæbə‚lizəm] *s* Stoffwechsel *m*

metal ['metəl] *s* Metall *n*

metallic [mi'tælik] *adj* metallisch

metallurgy ['metə‚lʌrdʒi] *s* Hüttenwesen *n*, Metallurgie *f*

met'alwork' *s* Metallarbeit *f*

metamorpho·sis [‚metə'mɔrfəsis] *s* (-ses [‚siz]) Verwandlung *f*

metaphor ['metə‚fɔr] *s* Metapher *f*

metaphorical [‚metə'fɔrikəl] *adj* bildlich

metaphysical [‚metə'fizikəl] *adj* metaphysisch

metaphysics [‚metə'fiziks] *s* Metaphysik *f*

metathe·sis [mi'tæθisis] *s* (-ses [‚siz]) Metathese *f*, Lautversetzung *f*

mete [mit] *tr*—**m. out** austeilen

meteor ['miti·ər] *s* Meteor *m*

meteoric [‚miti'ɔrik] *adj* meteorisch; (fig) kometenhaft

meteorite ['miti·ə‚rait] *s* Meteorit *m*

meteorologist [‚miti·ə'ralədʒist] *s* Meteorologe *m*, Meteorologin *f*

meteorology [‚miti·ə'ralədʒi] *s* Meteorologie *f*, Wetterkunde *f*

meter ['mitər] *s* Meter *m* & *n*; (*instrument*) Messer *m*, Zähler *m*; (pros) Versmaß *n*

me'ter read'er *s* Zählerableser –in *mf*

methane ['meθen] *s* Methan *n*, Sumpfgas *n*

method ['meθəd] *s* Methode *f*

methodic(al) [mi'θadik(əl)] *adj* methodisch

Methodist ['meθədist] *s* Methodist –in *mf*

methodology [‚meθə'dalədʒi] *s* Methodenlehre *f*

Methuselah [mi'θuzələ] *s* Methusalem *m*

meticulous [mi'tikjələs] *adj* übergenau

metric(al) ['metrik(əl)] *adj* metrisch

metrics ['metriks] *s* Metrik *f*

metronome ['metrə‚nom] *s* Metronom *n*

metropolis [mi'trapəlis] *s* Metropole *f*

metropolitan [‚metrə'palitən] *adj* großstädtisch ‖ *s* (eccl) Metropolit *m*

mettle ['metəl] *s* (*temperament*) Veranlagung *f*; (*courage*) Mut *m*

mettlesome ['metəlsəm] *adj* mutig

mew [mju] s Miau n ‖ intr miauen

Mexican ['meksɪkən] adj mexikanisch ‖ s Mexikaner –in mf

Mexico ['meksɪ‚ko] s Mexiko n

mezzanine ['mezə‚nin] s Zwischengeschoß n

mica ['maɪkə] s Glimmer m, Marienglas n

Michael ['maɪkəl] s Michel m

microbe ['maɪkrob] s Mikrobe f

microbiology [‚maɪkrəbaɪ'alədʒi] s Mikrobiologie f

microcosm ['maɪkrə‚kazəm] s Mikrokosmos m

microfilm ['maɪkrə‚fɪlm] s Mikrofilm m ‖ tr mikrofilmen

microgroove ['maɪkrə‚gruv] s Mikrorille f

mic'rogroove rec'ord s Schallplatte f mit Mikrorillen

microphone ['maɪkrə‚fon] s Mikrophon n

microscope ['maɪkrə‚skop] s Mikroskop n

microscopic [‚maɪkrə'skapɪk] adj mikroskopisch

microwave ['maɪkrə‚wev] s Mikrowelle f

mid [mɪd] adj mittlere

midair' s—in m. mitten in der Luft

mid'day' adj mittäglich, Mittags– ‖ s Mittag m

middle ['mɪdəl] adj mittlere ‖ s Mitte f, Mittel n; in the m. of inmitten (genit), mitten in (dat)

mid'dle age' s mittleres Lebensalter n; Middle Ages Mittelalter n

middle-aged ['mɪdəl‚edʒd] adj mittleren Alters

mid'dle class' s Mittelstand m

mid'dle-class' adj bürgerlich

mid'dle dis'tance s Mittelgrund m

mid'dle ear' s Mittelohr n

Mid'dle East', the s der Mittlere Osten

mid'dle fin'ger s Mittelfinger m

Mid'dle High' Ger'man s Mittelhochdeutsch n

Mid'dle Low' Ger'man s Mittelniederdeutsch n

mid'dle·man' s (–men') Mittelsmann m, Zwischenhändler m

mid'dleweight box'er s Mittelgewichtler m

mid'dleweight divi'sion s Mittelgewicht n

middling ['mɪdlɪŋ] adj mittelmäßig ‖ adv leidlich, ziemlich

middy ['mɪdi] s (nav) Fähnrich m zur See

midget ['mɪdʒɪt] s Zwerg m

mid'get rail'road s Liliputbahn f

mid'get submarine' s Kleinst-U-Boot n

midland ['mɪdlənd] adj binnenländisch

mid'night' adj mitternächtlich; burn the m. oil bis in die tiefe Nacht arbeiten ‖ s Mitternacht f; at m. um Mitternacht

midriff ['mɪdrɪf] s (of a dress) Mittelteil m; (diaphragm) Zwerchfell n; (middle part of the body) Magengrube f; have a bare m. die Taille frei lassen

mid'shipman' s (–men') Fähnrich m zur See

midst [mɪdst] s Mitte f; from our m. aus unserer Mitte; in the m. of mitten in (dat)

mid'stream' s—in m. in der Mitte des Stromes

mid'sum'mer s Mittsommer m

mid'-term' adj mitten im Semester ‖ midterms spl Prüfungen pl mitten im Semester

mid'way' adj in der Mitte befindlich ‖ adv auf halbem Weg ‖ s Mitte f des Weges; (at a fair) Mittelstraße f

mid'week' s Wochenmitte f

mid'wife' s (–wives') Hebamme f

mid'win'ter s Mittwinter m

mid'year' adj in der Mitte des Studienjahres ‖ midyears spl Prüfungen pl in der Mitte des Studienjahres

mien [min] s Miene f

miff [mɪf] s kleine Auseinandersetzung f ‖ tr ärgern

might [maɪt] s Macht f, Kraft f; with m. and main mit aller Kraft ‖ aux used to form the potential mood, e.g., she m. lose her way sie könnte sich verirren; we m. as well go es ist wohl besser, wenn wir gehen

mightily ['maɪtəli] adv gewaltig; (coll) enorm

mighty ['maɪti] adj mächtig ‖ adv (coll) furchtbar

migraine ['maɪgren] s Migräne f

mi'grant work'er ['maɪgrənt] s Wanderarbeiter –in mf

migrate ['maɪgret] intr wandern, ziehen

migration [maɪ'greʃən] s Wanderung f; (e.g., of birds) Zug m

migratory ['maɪgrə‚tori] adj Wander-

mi'gratory bird' s Zugvogel m

Milan [mɪ'læn] s Mailand m

mild [maɪld] adj mild, lind

mildew ['mɪl‚d(j)u] s Mehltau m

mildly ['maɪldli] adv leicht, schwach; to put it m. gelinde gesagt

mildness ['maɪldnɪs] s Milde f

mile [maɪl] s Meile f; for miles meilenweit; miles apart meilenweit auseinander; miles per hour Stundengeschwindigkeit

mileage ['maɪlɪdʒ] s Meilenzahl f; (charge) Meilengeld n

mile'post' s Wegweiser m mit Entfernungsangabe

mile'stone' s (& fig) Meilenstein m

militancy ['mɪlɪtənsi] s Kampfgeist m

militant ['mɪlɪtənt] adj militant ‖ s Kämpfer –in mf

militarism ['mɪlɪtə‚rɪzəm] s Militarismus m

militarize ['mɪlɪtə‚raɪz] tr auf den Krieg vorbereiten

military ['mɪlə‚teri] adj militärisch; (academy, band, government) Militär– ‖ s Militär n

mil'itary campaign' s Feldzug m

mil'itary cem'etery s Soldatenfriedhof m

mil'itary obliga'tions spl Wehrpflicht f

mil'itary police' s Militärpolizei f

mil'itary police'man s (–men) Militärpolizist m

mil'itary sci'ence s Kriegswissenschaft f

militate ['mılı ,tet] intr (against) entgegenwirken (dat)

militia [mı'lıʃə] s Miliz f

mili'tia-man s (–men) Milizsoldat m

milk [mılk] s Milch f ‖ tr (& fig) melken

milk' bar' s Milchbar f

milk' car'ton s Milchtüte f

milk'maid' s Milchmädchen n

milk'man' s (–men') Milchmann m

milk' pail' s Melkeimer m

milk'shake' s Milchmischgetränk n

milk'sop' s Milchbart m

milk' tooth' s Milchzahn m

milk'weed' s Wolfsmilch f, Seidenpflanze f

milky ['mılki] adj milchig

Milk'y Way' s Milchstraße f

mill [mıl] s Mühle f; (factory) Fabrik f, Werk n; (factory) durch e-e harte Schule schicken ‖ tr (grain) mahlen; (coins) rändeln; (with a milling machine) fräsern; (chocolate) quirlen ‖ intr—m. around durcheinanderlaufen

millenial [mı'lenı-əl] adj tausendjährig

millenni-um [mı'lenı-əm] s (–ums & –a [ə]) Jahrtausend n

miller ['mılər] s Müller m

millet ['mılıt] s Hirse f

milligram ['mılı ,græm] s Milligramm n

millimeter ['mılı ,mitər] s Millimeter m

milliner ['mılınər] s Putzmacher –in mf

mil'linery shop' ['mılı ,nerı] s Damenhutgeschäft n

mill'ing s (of grain) Mahlen n; (of wood or metal) Fräsen n

mill'ing machine' s Fräsmaschine f

million ['mıljən] adj—one m. people e-e Million Menschen; two m. people zwei Millionen Menschen ‖ s Million f

millionaire [,mıljən'er] s Millionär –in mf

millionth ['mıljənθ] adj & pron millionste ‖ s (fraction) Millionstel n

mill'pond' s Mühlteich m

mill'stone' s Mühlstein m

mill'wheel' s Mühlrad n

mime [maım] s Mime m, Mimin f ‖ tr mimen

mimeograph ['mımı-ə ,græf] s Vervielfältigungsapparat m ‖ tr vervielfältigen

mim·ic ['mımık] s Mimiker –in mf ‖ v (pret & pp –icked; ger –icking) tr nachäffen

mimicry ['mımıkrı] s Nachäffen n; (zool) Mimikry f

mimosa [mı'mosə] s Mimose f

minaret [,mınə'ret] s Minarett n

mince [mıns] tr (meat) zerhacken; not m. words kein Blatt vor den Mund nehmen

mince'meat' s Pastetenfüllung f;

(chopped meat) Hackfleisch n; **make m. of** (fig) in die Pfanne hauen

mind [maınd] s Geist m; **bear in m.** denken an (acc); **be of one m.** ein Herz und e-e Seele sein; **be of two minds** geteilter Meinung sein; **be out of one's m.** nicht bei Trost sein; **call to m.** erinnern; (remember) sich erinnern; **change one's m.** sich anders besinnen; **give s.o. a piece of one's m.** j-m gründlich die Meinung sagen; **have a good m. to** (inf) große Lust haben zu (inf); **have in m.** im Sinn haben zu (inf); **have one's m. on s.th.** ständig an etw denken müssen; **I can't get her out of my m.** sie will mir nicht aus dem Sinn; **know one's own m.** wissen, was man will; **of sound m.** zurechnungsfähig; **put s.th. out of one's m.** sich [dat] etw aus dem Sinn schlagen; **set one's m. on** sein Sinnen und Trachten richten auf (acc); **slip s.o.'s m.** j-m entfallen; **to my m.** meines Erachtens ‖ tr (watch over) aufpassen auf (acc); (obey) gehorchen (dat); (be troubled by; take care of) sich kümmern um; **do you m. if I smoke?** macht es Ihnen etw aus, wenn ich rauche?; **do you m. the smoke?** macht Ihnen der Rauch etw aus?; **I don't m. your smoking** ich habe nichts dagegen, daß (or wenn) Sie rauchen; **m. your own business** kümmere dich um deine Angelegenheit!; **m. you!** wohlgemerkt! ‖ intr—**I don't m.** es macht mir nichts aus; **I don't m. if I do** (coll) ja, recht gern; **never m.!** schon gut!

-minded [,maındıd] suf –mütig. –gesinnt, –sinnig

mindful ['maındfəl] adj (of) eingedenk (genit); **be m.** of achten auf (acc)

mind' read'er s Gedankenleser –in mf

mind'read'ing s Gedankenlesen n

mine [maın] s Bergwerk n, Mine f; (fig) Fundgrube f; (mil) Mine f ‖ poss pron meiner ‖ tr (e.g., coal) abbauen; (mil) verminen ‖ intr—**m. for** graben nach

mine' detec'tor s Minensuchgerät n

mine'field' s Minenfeld n

minelayer ['maın ,le-ər] s Minenleger m

miner ['maınər] s Bergarbeiter m

mineral ['mınərəl] adj mineralisch, Mineral– ‖ s Mineral n

mineralogy [,mınə'ralədʒı] s Mineralogie f

min'eral resourc'es spl Bodenschätze pl

min'eral wa'ter s Mineralwasser n

mine'sweep'er s Minenräumboot n

mingle ['mıŋgəl] tr vermengen ‖ intr (with) sich mischen (unter acc)

miniature ['mını-ət/ər], ['mınıt/ər] adj Miniatur–, Klein– ‖ s Miniatur f

minimal ['mınıməl] adj minimal, Mindest–

minimize ['mınə ,maız] tr auf das Minimum herabsetzen; (fig) bagatellisieren

minimum ['mınımǝm] *adj* minimal, Mindest- || *s* Minimum *n*; *(lowest price)* untere Preisgrenze *f*

min'imum wage' *s* Mindestlohn *m*

min'ing *adj* Bergbau- || *s* Bergbau *m*, Bergwesen *n*; *(mil)* Minenlegen *n*

minion ['mınjǝn] *s* Günstling *m*

miniskirt ['mını ˌskʌrt] *s* Minirock *m*

minister ['mınıstǝr] *s* (eccl) Geistlicher *m*; *(pol)* Minister *m* || *intr*—m. to dienen *(dat)*; *(aid)* Hilfe leisten *(dat)*

ministerial [ˌmınıs'tırı·ǝl] *adj* (eccl) geistlich; *(pol)* ministeriell

ministry ['mınıstri] *s* *(office)* (eccl) geistliches Amt *n*; *(the clergy)* (eccl) geistlicher Stand *m*; *(pol)* Ministerium *n*

mink [mıŋk] *s* (zool) Nerz *m*; *(fur)* Nerzfell *n*

mink' coat' *s* Nerzmantel *m*

minnow ['mıno] *s* Pfrille *f*, Elritze *f*

minor ['maınǝr] *adj* minder, geringer, Neben- || *s* *(person)* Minderjährige *mf*; *(educ)* Nebenfach *n*; *(log)* Untersatz *m*; *(mus)* Moll *n* || *intr*—m. in als Nebenfach studieren

minority [mı'nɔrıti] *adj* Minderheits- || *s* Minderheit *f*; *(of votes)* Stimmenminderheit *f*; *(ethnic group)* Minorität *f*

mi'nor key' *s* Molltonart *f*; **in a m.** in Moll

minstrel ['mınstrǝl] *s* (hist) Spielmann *m*

mint [mınt] *s* Münzanstalt *f*; *(bot)* Minze *f* || *tr* münzen

mintage ['mıntıdʒ] *s* Prägung *f*

minuet [ˌmınju'et] *s* Menuett *n*

minus ['maınǝs] *adj* negativ || *prep* minus, weniger; *(without)* (coll) ohne *(acc)*

mi'nus sign' *s* Minuszeichen *n*

minute [maı'n(j)ut] *adj* winzig || ['mınıt] *s* Minute *f*; **minutes** Protokoll *n*; **take the minutes** das Protokoll führen

-minute [mınıt] *suf* -minutig

min'ute hand' *s* Minutenzeiger *m*

minutiae [mı'n(j)u/ı·ı] *spl* Einzelheiten *pl*

minx [mıŋks] *s* Range *f*

miracle ['mırǝkǝl] *s* Wunder *n*

mir'acle play' *s* Mirakelspiel *n*

miraculous [mı'rækjǝlǝs] *adj* wunderbar; *(e.g., power)* Wunder-

mirage [mı'rɑʒ] *s* Luftspiegelung *f*; *(fig)* Luftbild *n*, Täuschung *f*

mire [maır] *s* Morast *m*, Schlamm *m*

mirror ['mırǝr] *s* Spiegel *m* || *tr* spiegeln

mirth [mʌrθ] *s* Fröhlichkeit *f*

miry ['maırı] *adj* sumpfig, schlammig

misadventure [ˌmısǝd'ventǝr] *s* Mißgeschick *n*

misanthrope ['mısǝn ˌθrop] *s* Menschenfeind *m*

misapprehension [ˌmısæprı'henʃǝn] *s* Mißverständnis *n*

misappropriate [ˌmısǝ'proprı ˌet] *tr* sich *(dat)* widerrechtlich aneignen

misbehave [ˌmısbı'hev] *intr* sich schlecht benehmen

misbehavior [ˌmısbı'hevı·ǝr] *s* schlechtes Benehmen *n*

miscalculate [mıs'kælkjǝ ˌlet] *tr* falsch berechnen || *intr* sich verrechnen

miscalculation [ˌmıskælkjǝ'leʃǝn] *s* Rechenfehler *m*

miscarriage [mıs'kærıdʒ] *s* Fehlgeburt *f*; *(fig)* Fehlschlag *m*

miscar'riage of jus'tice *s* Justizirrtum *m*

miscar·ry [mıs'kærı] *v* *(pret & pp -ried)* *intr* e–e Fehlgeburt haben; *(said of a plan)* scheitern, fehlschlagen

miscellaneous [ˌmısǝ'lenı·ǝs] *adj* vermischt

miscellany ['mısǝ ˌleni] *s* Gemisch *n*; *(of literary works)* Sammelband *m*

mischief ['mıstʃıf] *s* Unfug *m*; **be up to m.** e–n Unfug im Kopf haben; **cause m.** Unfug treiben; **get into m.** etw anstellen

mis'chief-mak'er *s* Störenfried *m*

mischievous ['mıstʃıvǝs] *adj* mutwillig

misconception [ˌmıskǝn'sepʃǝn] *s* falsche Auffassung *f*

misconduct [mıs'kɑndʌkt] *s* schlechtes Benehmen *n*; **m. in office** Amtsvergehen *n* || [ˌmıskǝn'dʌkt] *tr* schlecht verwalten; **m. oneself** sich schlecht benehmen

misconstrue [ˌmıskǝn'stru] *tr* falsch auffassen

miscount [mıs'kaunt] *s* Rechenfehler *m* || *tr* falsch zählen || *intr* sich verzählen

miscreant ['mıskrı·ǝnt] *s* Schurke *m*

miscue [mıs'kju] *s* (fig) Fehler *m*; *(billiards)* Kicks *m* || *intr* (billiards) kicksen; *(theat)* den Auftritt verpassen

mis·deal ['mıs ˌdil] *s* falsches Geben *n* || [mıs'dil] *v* *(pret & pp -delt* [delt]*)* *tr* falsch geben || *intr* sich vergeben

misdeed [mıs'did] *s* Missetat *f*

misdemeanor [ˌmısdı'minǝr] *s* Vergehen *n*

misdirect [ˌmısdı'rekt], [ˌmısdaı'rekt] *tr* *(& fig)* fehlleiten

misdoing [mıs'du·ıŋ] *s* Missetat *f*

miser ['maızǝr] *s* Geizhals *m*

miserable ['mızǝrǝbǝl] *adj* elend; **feel m.** sich elend fühlen; **make life m. for s.o.** j–m das Leben sauer machen

miserly ['maızǝrlı] *adj* geizig

misery ['mızǝrı] *s* Elend *n*

misfeasance [mıs'fizǝns] *s* (jur) Amtsmißbrauch *m*

misfire [mıs'faır] *s* Versagen *n* || *intr* versagen

misfit ['mısfıt] *s* *(clothing)* schlecht sitzendes Kleidungsstück *n*; *(person)* Gammler *m*

misfortune [mıs'fɔrtʃǝn] *s* Unglück *n*

misgiving [mıs'gıvıŋ] *s* böse Ahnung *f*; **full of misgivings** ahnungsvoll

misgovern [mıs'gʌvǝrn] *tr* schlecht verwalten

misguidance [mıs'gaıdǝns] *s* Irreführung *f*

misguide [mıs'gaıd] *tr* irreleiten

misguid'ed *adj* irregeleitet

mishap ['mɪshæp] s Unfall m

mishmash ['mɪʃ,mæʃ] s Mischmasch m

misinform [,mɪsɪn'fɔrm] tr falsch informieren, falsch unterrichten

misinterpret [,mɪsɪn'tʌrprɪt] tr mißdeuten, falsch auffassen

misjudge [mɪs'dʒʌdʒ] tr (e.g., a person, situation) falsch beurteilen; (distance) falsch schätzen

mis·lay [mɪs'le] v (pret & pp –laid) tr verlegen, verkramen

mis·lead [mɪs'lid] v (pret & pp –led) tr irreführen

mislead'ing adj irreführend

mismanage [mɪs'mænɪdʒ] tr schlecht verwalten; (funds) verwirtschaften

mismanagement [mɪs'mænɪdʒmənt] s Mißwirtschaft f, schlechte Verwaltung f

mismarriage [mɪs'mærɪdʒ] s Mißheirat f

misnomer [mɪs'nomər] s Felhbezeichnung f

misplace [mɪs'ples] tr verlegen

misprint ['mɪs,prɪnt] s Druckfehler m || [mɪs'prɪnt] tr verdrucken

mispronounce [,mɪsprə'naʊns] tr falsch aussprechen

mispronunciation [,mɪsprənʌnsɪ'eʃən] s falsche Aussprache f

misquote [mɪs'kwot] tr falsch zitieren

mis·read [mɪs'rid] v (pret & pp –read ['red]) tr falsch lesen || intr sich verlesen

misrepresent [,mɪsreprɪ'zent] tr falsch darstellen; m. the facts to s.o. j–m falsche Tatsachen vorspiegeln

miss [mɪs] s Fehlschlag m, Versager m; **Miss** Fräulein n; **Miss America** die Schönheitskönigin von Amerika || tr (a target; one's calling; a person, e.g., at the station; a town along the road; one's way) verfehlen; (feel the lack of) verpassen; (school, a train, an opportunity) versäumen; m. one's step fehltreten; m. the mark vorbeischießen; (fig) sein Ziel verfehlen; m. the point die Pointe nicht verstanden haben || intr fehlen; (in shooting) vorbeischießen

missal ['mɪsəl] s Meßbuch n

misshapen [mɪs'ʃepən] adj mißgestaltet

missile ['mɪsɪl] s Geschoß n; (rok) Rakete f

missing ['mɪsɪŋ] adj—be m. fehlen; (said, e.g., of a child) vermißt werden; m. in action vermißt

miss'ing per'son s Vermißte mf

miss'ing-per'sons bu'reau s Suchdienst m

mission ['mɪʃən] s Mission f; m. in life Lebensaufgabe f

missionary ['mɪʃən,ɛri] adj Missions– || s Missionar –in mf

missis ['mɪsɪz] s—the m. (the wife) die Frau; (of the house) (coll) die Frau des Hauses

missive ['mɪsɪv] s Sendschreiben n

mis·spell [mɪs'spel] v (pret & pp –spelled & –spelt) tr & intr falsch schreiben

misspell'ing s Schreibfehler m

misspent [mɪs'spent] adj vergeudet

misstate [mɪs'stet] tr falsch angeben

misstatement [mɪs'stetmənt] s falsche Angabe f

misstep [mɪs'step] s (& fig)Fehltritt m

mist [mɪst] s feiner Nebel m || tr umnebeln || intr (said of the eyes) sich trüben; **mist over** nebeln

mis·take [mɪs'tek] s Fehler m; **by m.** aus Versehen || (pret –took ['tuk]; pp –taken) tr verkennen; **m. s.o. for s.o. else** j–n mit e–m anderen verwechseln

mistaken [mɪs'tekən] adj falsch, irrig; **be m.** (about) sich irren (in dat); **unless I'm m.** wenn ich mich nicht irre

mistak'en iden'tity s Personenverwechslung f

mistakenly [mɪs'tekənli] adv versehentlich

mister ['mɪstər] s Herr m || interj (pej) Herr!

mistletoe ['mɪsəl,to] s Mistel f

mistreat [mɪs'trit] tr mißhandeln

mistreatment [mɪs'tritmənt] s Mißhandlung f

mistress ['mɪstrɪs] s Herrin f; (lover) Mätresse f, Geliebte f

mistrial [mɪs'traɪ·əl] s fehlerhaft geführter Prozeß m

mistrust [mɪs'trʌst] s Mißtrauen n || tr mißtrauen (dat)

misty ['mɪsti] adj neblig; (eyes) umflort; (fig) unklar

misunder·stand [,mɪsʌndər'stænd] v (pret & pp –stood) tr & intr mißverstehen

misunderstanding [,mɪsʌndər'stændɪŋ] s Mißverständnis n

misuse [mɪs'jus] s Mißbrauch m || [mɪs'juz] tr mißbrauchen; (mistreat) mißhandeln

misword [mɪs'wʌrd] tr in falsche Worte fassen

mite [maɪt] s (ent) Milbe f

miter ['maɪtər] s Bischofsmütze f || tr auf Gehrung verbinden

mi'ter box' s Gehrlade f

mitigate ['mɪtɪ,get] tr lindern

mitigation [,mɪtɪ'geʃən] s Linderung f

mitt [mɪt] s Fausthandschuh m; (sl) Flosse f; (baseball) Fängerhandschuh m

mitten ['mɪtən] s Fausthandschuh m

mix [mɪks] s Mischung f, Gemisch n || tr (ver)mischen; (a drink) mixen; (a cake) anrühren; **mix in** beimischen; **mix up** vermischen; (confuse) verwirren || intr sich (ver)mischen; **mix with** vekehren mit

mixed adj vermischt; (feelings, company, doubles) gemischt

mixed' drink' s Mixgetränk n

mixed' mar'riage s Mischehe f

mixer ['mɪksər] s Mischer –in mf; (of cocktails) Mixer –in mf; (mach) Mischmaschine f; **a good m.** ein guter Gesellschafter

mixture ['mɪkstʃər] s (e.g., of gases)

Gemisch n; (e.g., of tobacco, coffee) f, Maß n; **in m. mit** Maß; **observe m.**
Mischung f; (pharm) Mixtur f   Maß halten

mix'-up' s Wirrwar m, Verwechslung f **moderator** ['madə,retər] s Moderator
mizzen ['mɪzən] s Besan m   m
mnemonic [nə'manɪk] s Gedächtnis- **modern** ['madərn] adj modern, zeit-
hilfe f   gemäß
moan [mon] s Stöhnen n ‖ intr stöh- **mod'ern Eng'lish** s Neuenglisch n
nen; **m. about** jammern über (acc) **mod'ern his'tory** s Neuere Geschichte
or um   f
moat [mot] s Schloßgraben m **modernize** ['madər,naɪz] tr moderni-
mob [mab] s (populace) Pöbel m;   sieren
(crush of people) Andrang m; (gang **mod'ern lan'guages** spl neuere Spra-
of criminals) Verbrecherbande f ‖ v   chen pl
(pret & pp mobbed; ger mobbing) tr **mod'ern times'** spl die Neuzeit f
(crowd into) lärmend eindringen in **modest** ['madɪst] adj bescheiden
(acc); (e.g., a consulate) angreifen; **modesty** ['madɪsti] s Bescheidenheit f
(a celebrity) umringen **modicum** ['madɪkəm] s bißchen; **a m.**
mobile ['mobɪl] adj fahrbar; (mil) mo-   **of truth** ein Körnchen Wahrheit
torisiert **modification** [,madɪfɪ'keʃən] s Abän-
mo'bile home' s Wohnwagen m   derung f
mobility [mo'bɪlɪti] s (& mil) Beweg- **modifier** ['madɪ,faɪ·ər] s (gram)
lichkeit f   nähere Bestimmung f
mobilization [,mobɪlɪ'zeʃən] s Mobili- **modi-fy** ['madɪ,faɪ] v (pret & pp
sierung f   **-fied**) tr abändern; (gram) näher be-
mobilize ['mobɪ,laɪz] tr mobilisieren;   stimmen
(strength) aufbieten **modish** ['modɪʃ] adj modisch
mob' rule' s Pöbelherrschaft f **modulate** ['madjə,let] tr & intr modu-
mobster ['mabstər] s Gangster m   lieren
moccasin ['makəsɪn] s Mokassin m; **modulation** [,madjə'leʃən] s Modula-
(snake) Mokassinschlange f   tion f
Mo'cha cof'fee ['mokə] s Mokka m **mohair** ['mo,hɛr] s Mohair m
mock [mak] adj Schein- ‖ tr verspot- **Mohammedan** [mo'hæmɪdən] adj mo-
ten; (imitate) nachäffen ‖ intr spot-   hammedanisch ‖ s Mohammedaner
ten; **m. at** sich lustig machen über   –in mf
(acc); **m. up** improvisieren **Mohammedanism** [mo'hæmɪdə,nɪzəm]
mocker ['makər] s Spötter –in mf   s Mohammedanismus m
mockery ['makəri] s Spott m, Spöttelei **moist** [mɔɪst] adj feucht; (eyes) tränen-
f; **make a m.** of hohnsprechen (dat)   feucht
mock'ing adj spöttisch **moisten** ['mɔɪsən] tr anfeuchten; (lips)
mock'ingbird' s Spottdrossel f   befeuchten ‖ intr feucht werden
mock' tri'al s Schauprozeß m **moisture** ['mɔɪstʃər] s Feuchtigkeit f
mock' tur'tle soup' s falsche Schild- **molar** ['molər] s Backenzahn m
krötensuppe f **molasses** [mə'læsɪz] s Melasse f
mock'-up' s Schaumodell n **mold** [mold] s Form f; (mildew)
modal ['modəl] adj modal, Modal-   Schimmel m; (typ) Matrize f ‖ tr
mode [mod] s Modus m; (mus) Ton-   formen ‖ intr (ver)schimmeln
art f **molder** ['moldər] s Former –in mf;
mod·el ['madəl] adj vorbildlich; (stu-   (fig) Bildner –in mf ‖ intr modern
dent, husband) Muster- ‖ s (e.g., of **mold'ing** s Formen n; (carp) Gesims n
a building) Modell n; (at a fashion **moldy** ['moldɪ] adj modrig, schimm-
show) Vorführdame f; (for art or   lig
photography) Modell n; (example for **mole** [mol] s (breakwater) Hafendamm
imitation) Vorbild n, Muster n;   m; (blemish) Muttermal n; (zool)
(make) Typ m, Bauart f ‖ v (pret &   Maulwurf m
pp **-el[l]ed**; ger **-el[l]ing**) tr (clothes) **molecular** [mə'lekjələr] adj molekular
vorführen; **m. oneself on** sich [dat] **molecule** ['malɪ,kjul] s Molekül n
ein Muster nehmen an (dat); **m. s.th.** **mole'skin'** s (fur) Maulwurfsfell n;
on etw formen nach; (fig) etw ge-   (tex) Englischleder n
stalten nach ‖ intr (for) Modell ste- **molest** [mə'lɛst] tr belästigen
hen (zu dat) **molli-fy** ['malɪ,faɪ] v (pret & pp
mod'el air'plane s Flugzeugmodell n   **-fied**) tr besänftigen
mod'el num'ber s (aut) Typennummer **mollusk** ['maləsk] s Weichtier n
f **mollycoddle** ['malɪ,kadəl] s Weichling
moderate ['madərɪt] adj (climate) ge-   m ‖ tr verweichlichen
mäßigt; (demand) maßvoll; (price) **Mol'otov cock'tail** ['malətəf] s Fla-
angemessen; (e.g., in drinking)   schengranate f
mäßig; **of m. means** minderbemittelt **molt** [molt] s intr sich mausern
‖ ['madə,ret] tr mäßigen; (a meet- **molten** ['moltən] adj schmelzflüssig
ing) den Vorsitz führen über (acc) **molybdenum** [mə'lɪbdɪnəm] s Molyb-
or bei; (a television show) moderie-   dän n
ren ‖ intr sich mäßigen **mom** [mam] s (coll) Mama f, Mutti f
moderation [,madə'reʃən] s Mäßigung **moment** ['momənt] s Moment m, Au-

genblick *m;* a m. ago nur eben; at a
moment's notice jeden Augenblick;
at any m. jederzeit; at the m. im
Augenblick, zur Zeit; of great m.
von großer Tragweite; the very m.
I spotted her sobald ich sie erblickte
momentarily ['momən ‚terɪlɪ] *adv* momentan; (*in a moment*) gleich
momentary ['momən ‚terɪ] *adj* vorübergehend
momentous [mo'mentəs] *adj* folgenschwer
momen•tum [mo'mentəm] *s* (–tums &
–ta [tə]) (phys) Moment *n;* (fig)
Schwung *m;* gather m. Schwung bekommen
monarch ['monərk] *s* Monarch *m*
monarchical [mə'nɑrkɪkəl] *adj* mo-
narchisch
monarchy ['monərki] *s* Monarchie *f*
monastery ['monəs ‚terɪ] *s* Kloster *n*
monastic [mə'næstɪk] *adj* Kloster–,
Mönchs–
monasticism [mə'næstɪ ‚sɪzəm] *s*
Mönchswesen *n*
Monday ['mʌndi], ['mʌnde] *s* Montag
m; on M. am Montag
monetary ['monɪ ‚terɪ] *adj* (*e.g., crisis,
unit*) Währungs–; (*e.g., system,
value*) Geld–
mon'etary stand'ard *s* Münzfuß *m*
money ['mʌni] *adj* Geld– || *s* Geld *n;*
big m. schweres Geld; get one's
money's worth reell bedient werden;
make m. (on) Geld verdienen (an
dat); put m. on Geld setzen auf (*acc*)
mon'eybag' *s* Geldbeutel *m;* money-
bags (coll) Geldsack *m*
mon'ey belt' *s* Geldgürtel *m*
moneychanger ['monɪ ‚tʃendʒər] *s*
Wechsler –in *mf*
moneyed ['mʌnid] *adj* vermögend
mon'ey exchange' *s* Geldwechsel *m*
mon'eylend'er *s* Geldverleiher –in *mf*
mon'eymak'er *s* (fig) Goldgrube *f*
mon'ey or'der *s* Postanweisung *f*
Mongol ['mongəl] *adj* mongolid || *s*
Mongole *m,* Mongolin *f*
Mongolian [mɑŋ'golɪ·ən] *adj* mongo-
lisch || *s* (*language*) Mongolisch *n*
mon•goose ['mongus] *s* (–gooses)
Mungo *m*
mongrel ['mʌŋgrəl] *s* Bastard *m*
monitor ['monɪtər] *s* (*at school*) Klas-
senordner *m;* (rad, telv) Über-
wachungsgerät *n,* Monitor *m* || *tr*
überwachen
monk [mʌŋk] *s* Mönch *m*
monkey ['mʌŋki] *s* Affe *m;* (*female*)
Äffin *f;* make a m. of zum Narren
halten || *intr*—m. around (*trifle idly*)
herumalbern; m. around with s.o. es
mit j–m treiben; m. around with s.th.
an etw [*dat*] herummurksen
mon'keybusi'ness *s* (*underhanded conduct*) Gaunerei *f;* (*frivolous behavior*) (sl) Unfug *m*
mon'keyshine' *s* (sl) Possen *m*
mon'key wrench' *s* Engländer *m*
monocle ['monəkəl] *s* Monokel *n*
monogamous [mə'nɑgəməs] *adj* monog-
gam

monogamy [mə'nɑgəmi] *s* Einehe *f*
monogram ['monə ‚græm] *s* Monogramm *n*
monograph ['monə ‚græf] *s* Monogra-
phie *f*
monolithic [‚monə'lɪθɪk] *adj* (& fig)
monolithisch
monologue ['monə ‚lɔg] *s* Monolog *m*
monomania [‚monə'menɪ·ə] *s* Mono-
manie *f*
monoplane ['monə ‚plen] *s* Eindecker
m
monopolize [mə'nɑpə ‚laɪz] *tr* monopolisieren
monorail ['monə ‚rel] *s* Einschienen-
bahn *f*
monosyllable ['monə ‚sɪləbəl] *s* einsil-
biges Wort *n*
monotheism [‚monə'θi·ɪzəm] *s* Mono-
theismus *m*
monotonous [mə'nɑtənəs] *adj* eintönig
monotony [mə'nɑtəni] *s* Eintönigkeit *f*
monotype ['monə ‚taɪp] *s* Monotype *f*
monoxide [mɑ'nɑksaɪd] *s* Monoxyd *n*
monsignor [mɑn'sinjər] *s* (monsignors
& monsignori [‚monsi'njori]) (eccl)
Monsignore *m*
monsoon [mɑn'sun] *s* Monsun *m*
monster ['monstər] *s* (& fig) Ungeheuer *n*
monstrance ['monstrəns] *s* Monstranz
f
monstrosity [mɑns'trɑsɪti] *s* Monstrosität *f,* Ungeheuerlichkeit *f*
monstrous ['monstrəs] *adj* ungeheuer-
(lich)
month [mʌnθ] *s* Monat *m*
monthly ['mʌnθli] *adj* & *adv* monat-
lich || *s* Monatszeitschrift *f*
monument ['monjəmənt] *s* Denkmal *n*
monumental [‚monjə'mentəl] *adj*
monumental
moo [mu] *s* Muhen *n* || *intr* muhen
mood [mud] *s* Laune *f,* Stimmung *f;*
(gram) Aussageweise *f,* Modus *m;*
be in a bad m. schlechtgelaunt sein;
be in the m. for s.th. zu etw gelaunt
sein
moody ['mudi] *adj* launisch
moon [mun] *s* Mond *m* || *intr*—m.
about herumlungern
moon'beam' *s* Mondstrahl *m*
moon'light' *s* Mondschein *m* || *intr*
schwarzarbeiten
moon'light'er *s* Doppelverdiener –in *mf*
moon'light'ing *s* Schwarzarbeit *f*
moon'lit' *adj* mondhell
moon'shine' *s* Mondschein *m;* (sl)
schwarz gebrannter Whisky *m*
moonshiner ['mun ‚ʃaɪnər] *s* Schwarz-
brenner –in *mf*
moon'shot' *s* Mondgeschoß *n*
moor [mur] *s* Moor *n,* Heidemoor *n;*
Moor Mohr *m* || *tr* (naut) vertäuen
|| *intr* (naut) festmachen
moor'ing *s* (act) Festmachen *n;* moor-
ings (*cables*) Vertäuung *f;* (*place*)
Liegeplatz *m*
Moorish ['murɪʃ] *adj* maurisch
moose [mus] *s* (moose) amerikanischer
Elch *m*
moot [mut] *adj* umstritten

mop [map] *s* Mop *m*; (*of hair*) Wust *m* || *v* (*pret & pp* **mopped**; *ger* **mopping**) *tr* mit dem Mop wischen; **mop up** mit dem Mop aufwischen; (mil) säubern

mope [mop] *intr* Trübsal blasen

moped ['mopəd] *s* Moped *n*

mop'ping-up' opera'tion *s* (mil) Säuberungsaktion *f*

moral ['marəl] *adj* moralisch || *s* Moral *f*; **morals** Sitten *pl*

morale [mə'ræl] *s* Moral *f*

morality [mə'ræliti] *s* Sittlichkeit *f*

moralize ['marə‚laɪz] *intr* moralisieren

morass [mə'ræs] *s* Morast *m*

moratori·um [‚marə'torɪ-əm] *s* (**-ums** & **a-** [ə]) Moratorium *n*

Moravia [mə'revɪ·ə] *s* Mähren *n*

morbid ['marbɪd] *adj* krankhaft, morbid

mordacious [mar'deʃəs] *adj* bissig

mordant ['mardənt] *adj* beißend

more [mor] *comp adj* mehr; **one m. minute** noch e-e Minute || *comp adv* mehr; **all the m.** erst recht; **all the m. because** zumal; **m. and m.** immer mehr; **m. and m. expensive** immer teurer; **m. or less** gewissermaßen; **m. than anything** über alles; **no m.** nicht mehr; **not any m.** nicht mehr; **once m.** noch einmal; **the more ... the** (*expressing quantity*) je mehr ... desto; (*expressing frequency*) je öfter ... desto || *s* mehr; **see m. of s.o.** j-n noch öfter sehen; **what's m.** außerdem || *pron* mehr

more'o'ver *adv* außerdem, übrigens

morgue [marg] *s* Leichenschauhaus *n*; (journ) Archiv *n*, Zeitungsarchiv *n*

morning ['marnɪŋ] *adj* Morgen– || *s* Morgen *m*; **from m. till night** von früh bis spät; **in the early m.** in früher Morgenstunde; **in the m.** am Morgen; **this m.** heute morgen; **to-morrow m.** morgen früh

morn'ing-af'ter pill' *s* Pille *f* danach

morn'ing-glo'ry *s* Trichterwinde *f*

morn'ing sick'ness *s* morgendliches Erbrechen *n*

morn'ing star' *s* Morgenstern *m*

Moroccan [mə'rakən] *adj* marokkanisch || *s* Marokkaner *–in mf*

morocco [mə'rako] *s* (*leather*) Saffian *m*; **Morocco** Marokko *n*

moron ['maran] *s* Schwachsinnige *mf*

morose [mə'ros] *adj* mürrisch

morphine ['marfin] *s* Morphium *n*

morphology [mar'faləd͡ʒɪ] *s* Morphologie *f*

morrow ['maro] *s*—**on the m.** am folgenden Tag

Morse' code' [mars] *s* Morsealphabet *n*

morsel ['marsəl] *s* Bröckchen *n*

mortal ['martəl] *adj* sterblich || *s* Sterbliche *mf*

mor'tal dan'ger *s* Lebensgefahr *f*

mor'tal en'emy *s* Todfeind *m*

mor'tal fear' *s* Heidenangst *f*

mortality [mar'tæliti] *s* Sterblichkeit *f*

mortally ['martəli] *adv* tödlich

mor'tal remains' *spl* irdische Überreste *pl*

mor'tal sin' *s* Todsünde *f*

mor'tal wound' *s* Todeswunde *f*

mortar ['martər] *s* (*vessel*) Mörser *m*; (archit) Mörtel *m*; (mil) Granatwerfer *m*

mor'tarboard' *s* Mörtelbrett *n*

mor'tar fire' *s* Granatwerferfeuer *n*

mor'tar shell' *s* Granate *f*

mortgage ['margɪd͡ʒ] *s* Hypothek *f* || *tr* mit e-r Hypothek belasten

mortgagee [‚margɪ'd͡ʒi] *s* Hypothekengläubiger *–in mf*

mortgagor ['margɪd͡ʒər] *s* Hypothekenschuldner *–in mf*

mortician [mar'tɪʃən] *s* Leichenbestatter *–in mf*

morti·fy ['martɪ‚faɪ] *v* (*pret & pp* **-fied**) *tr* (*the flesh*) abtöten; (*humiliate*) demütigen; **m. oneself** sich kasteien

mortise ['martɪs] *s* (carp) Zapfenloch *n* || *tr* (carp) verzapfen

mortuary ['martʃʊ‚eri] *s* Leichenhalle *f*

mosaic [mo'ze·ɪk] *adj* mosaisch || *s* Mosaik *n*

Moscow ['masko], ['maskaʊ] *s* Moskau *n*

Moses ['mozɪz], ['mozɪs] *s* Moses *m*

mosey ['mozɪ] *intr* (coll) dahinschlürfen

Mos·lem ['mazləm] *adj* muselmanisch || *s* (**-lems** & **-lem**) Moslem *–in mf*

mosque [mask] *s* Moschee *f*

mosqui·to [məs'kito] *s* (**-toes** & **-tos**) Moskito *m*, Mücke *f*

mosqui'to net' *s* Moskitonetz *n*

moss [mas] *s* Moos *n*

mossy ['masi] *adj* bemoost

most [most] *super adj* meist || *super adv* am meisten; (*very*) höchst; **m. of all** am allermeisten || *s*—**at (the) m.** höchstens; **make the m. of** möglichst gut ausnützen; **m. of die meisten;** **m. of the day** der größte Teil des Tages; **the m.** das meiste, das Höchste || *pron* die meisten

mostly ['mostli] *adv* meistens

motel [mo'tel] *s* Motel *n*

moth [maθ] *s* Nachtfalter *m*; (*clothes moth*) Motte *f*

moth'ball' *s* Mottenkugel *f*; **put into mothballs** (nav) stillegen, einmotten || *tr* (& fig) einmotten

moth-eaten ['maθ‚itən] *adj* mottenzerfressen

mother ['mʌðər] *s* Mutter *f* || *tr* (*produce*) gebären; (*take care of as a mother*) bemuttern

moth'er coun'try *s* Mutterland *n*

moth'erhood' *s* Mutterschaft *f*

moth'er-in-law' *s* (**mothers-in-law**) Schwiegermutter *f*

motherless ['mʌðərlɪs] *adj* mutterlos

motherly ['mʌðərli] *adj* mütterlich

mother-of-pearl ['mʌðərəv'pʌrl] *adj* perlmuttern || *s* Perlmutter *f*

Moth'er's Day' *s* Muttertag *m*

moth'er's help'er *s* Stütze *f* der Hausfrau

moth′er supe′rior s (Schwester) Oberin f

moth′er tongue′ s Muttersprache f

moth′ hole′ s Mottenfraß m

mothy ['mɔθɪ] adj mottenzerfressen

motif [mo'tif] s (mus, paint) Motiv n

motion ['moʃən] s Bewegung f; (parl) Antrag m; **make a m.** e-n Antrag stellen; **set in m.** in Bewegung setzen ‖ tr zuwinken (dat); **m. s.o. to** (inf) j-n durch e-n Wink auffordern zu (inf)

motionless ['moʃənlɪs] adj bewegungslos

mo′tion pic′ture s Film m; **be in motion pictures** beim Film sein

mo′tion-pic′ture adj Film-

mo′tion-pic′ture the′ater s Kino n

motivate ['motɪ,vet] tr begründen, motivieren

motive ['motɪv] s Anlaß m, Beweggrund m

mo′tive pow′er s Triebkraft f

motley ['motlɪ] adj bunt zusammengewürfelt

motor ['motər] adj Motor- ‖ s Motor m

motorcade ['motər,ked] s Wagenkolonne f

mo′torcy′cle s Motorrad n

mo′torcy′clist s Motorradfahrer -in mf

mo′toring s Autofahren n

motorist ['motərɪst] s Autofahrer -in mf

motorize ['motə,raɪz] tr motorisieren

mo′tor launch′ s Motorbarkasse f

mo′tor-man s (-men) Straßenbahnführer m

mo′tor pool′ s Fahrbereitschaft f

mo′tor scoot′er s Motorroller m

mo′tor ve′hicle s Kraftfahrzeug n

mottle ['motəl] tr sprenkeln

mot-to ['moto] s (-toes & -tos) Motto n

mound [maund] s Wall m, Erdhügel m

mount [maunt] s (mountain) Berg m; (riding horse) Reittier n ‖ tr (a horse, mountain) besteigen; (stairs) hinaufgehen; (e.g., a machinegun) in Position bringen; (a precious stone) fassen; (photographs in an album) einkleben; (photographs on a backing) aufkleben; **m.** (e.g., a gun) **on** montieren auf (acc)

mountain ['mauntən] s Berg m; **down the m.** bergab; **up the m.** bergauf

moun′tain climb′er s Bergsteiger -in mf

moun′tain climb′ing s Bergsteigen n

mountaineer [,mauntə'nɪr] s Bergbewohner -in mf

mountainous ['mauntənəs] adj gebirgig

moun′tain pass′ s Gebirgspaß m, Paß m

moun′tain rail′road s Bergbahn f

moun′tain range′ s Gebirge s

moun′tain scen′ery s Berglandschaft f

mountebank ['mauntə,bæŋk] s Quacksalber m; (charlatan) Scharlatan m

mount′ing s Montage f; (of a precious stone) Fassung f

mourn [morn] tr betrauern ‖ intr trauern; **mourn for** betrauern, trauern um

mourner ['mornər] s Leidtragende mf

mournful ['mornfəl] adj traurig

mourn′ing s Trauer f; **be in m.** Trauer tragen

mourn′ing band′ s Trauerflor m

mourn′ing clothes′ spl Trauerkleidung f; **wear m.** Trauer tragen

mouse [maus] s (mice [maɪs]) Maus f

mouse′hole′ s Mauseloch n

mouse′trap′ s Mausefalle f

moustache [məs'tæʃ] s Schnurbart m

mouth [mauθ] s (mouths [mauðz]) Mund m; (of an animal) Maul n; (of a gun, bottle, river) Mündung f; (sl) Maul n; **keep one's m. shut** den Mund halten; **make s.o.'s m. water** j-m das Wasser im Munde zusammenlaufen lassen

mouthful ['mauθ,ful] s Mundvoll m; (sl) großes Wort n

mouth′ or′gan s Mundharmonika f

mouth′piece′ s (of an instrument) Ansatz m; (box) Mundstück n; (fig) Sprachrohr n

mouth′wash′ s Mundwasser n

movable ['muvəbəl] adj beweglich, mobil ‖ **movables** spl Mobilien pl

move [muv] s (movement) Bewegung f; (step, measure) Maßnahme f; (resettlement) Umzug m; (checkers) Zug m; (parl) Vorschlag m; **be on the m.** unterwegs sein; **don't make a m.!** keinen Schritt!; **get a m. on** (coll) sich rühren; **it's your m.** (& fig) du bist am Zug; **she won't make a m.** without him sie macht keinen Schritt ohne ihn ‖ tr bewegen; (emotionally) rühren; (shove) rücken; (checkers) e-n Zug machen mit; (parl) beantragen; **m. the bowels** abführen; **m. up** (mil) vorschieben ‖ intr (stir) sich bewegen; (change residence) umziehen; (in society) verkehren; (checkers) ziehen; (com) Absatz haben; **m. away** wegziehen; **m. back** zurückziehen; **m. for** (e.g., a new trial) beantragen; **m. in** zuziehen; **m. into** (a home) beziehen; **m. on** fortziehen; **m. out** (of) ausziehen (aus); **m. over** (make room) zur Seite rücken; **m. up** (to a higher position) vorrücken; (into a vacated position) nachrücken; (said of a team) aufsteigen

movement ['muvmənt] s (& fig) Bewegung f; (mus) Satz m

mover ['muvər] s Möbeltransporteur m; (parl) Antragsteller -in mf

movie ['muvi] adj (actor, actress, camera, projector) Film- ‖ s (coll) Film m; **movies** Kino n; **go to the movies** ins Kino gehen

mov′ie cam′era s Filmkamera f

moviegoer ['muvi,go·ər] s Kinobesucher -in mf

mov′ie house′ s Kino n

mov′ie screen′ s Filmleinwand f

mov′ie set′ s Filmkulisse f

mov′ie the′ater s Kino n

mov′ing adj beweglich; (force) trei-

bend; (fig) herzergreifend || s (change of residence) Umzug m
mov'ing pic'ture s Lichtspiel n, Film m
mov'ing spir'it s führender Kopf m
mow [mo] v (pret mowed; pp mowed & mown) tr mähen; **mow down** (enemies) niedermähen
mower ['mo·ər] s Mäher m
m.p.h. ['em'pi'et∫] spl (miles per hour) Stundenmeilen; **drive sixty m.p.h.** mit sechzig Stundenmeilen fahren
Mr. [mɪstər] s Herr m
Mrs. ['mɪsɪz] s Frau f
Ms. [mɪz] s Fräulein n
much [mʌt∫] adj, adv & pron viel; **as m. again** noch einmal soviel; **how m. wieviel; m. less** (not to mention) geschweige denn; **not so m.** as nicht einmal; **so m. so** so sehr; **so m. the better** um so besser; **very m.** sehr
mucilage ['mjusɪlɪdʒ] s Klebstoff m
muck [mʌk] s (& fig) Schmutz m
muck'rake' intr (coll) Korruptionsfälle enthüllen
muckraker ['mʌk,rekər] s (coll) Korruptionsschnüffler –in mf
mucky ['mʌki] adj schmutzig
mucous ['mjukəs] adj schleimig
muc'ous mem'brane s Schleimhaut f
mucus ['mjukəs] s Schleim m
mud [mʌd] s Schlamm m; **drag through the mud** (fig) in den Schmutz ziehen
mud' bath' s Schlammbad n, Moorbad n
muddle ['mʌdəl] s Durcheinander n || tr durcheinanderbringen || intr—**m. through** sich durchwursteln
mud'dlehead' s Wirrkopf m
mud-dy ['mʌdi] adj schlammig; (fig) trüb || v (pret & pp –died) trüben
mud'hole' s Schlammloch n
mudslinging ['mʌd,slɪŋɪŋ] s (fig) Verleumdung f
muff [mʌf] s Muff m || tr (coll) verpfuschen
muffin ['mʌfɪn] s Teekuchen m aus Backpulverteig
muffle ['mʌfəl] tr (sounds) dämpfen; **m. up** (wrap up) einhüllen
muf'fled adj dumpf
muffler ['mʌflər] s (scarf) Halstuch n; (aut) Auspufftopf m
mufti ['mʌfti] s Zivil n
mug [mʌg] s Krug m; (for beer) Seidel n; (thug) (sl) Rocker m; (face) (sl) Fratze f || v (pret & pp mugged; ger mugging) tr (sl) photographieren; (assault) (sl) überfallen || intr (sl) Gesichter schneiden
muggy ['mʌgi] adj schwül
mug' shot' s (sl) Polizeiphoto n
mulat·to [mə'læto] s (–toes) Mulatte m, Mulattin f
mulberry ['mʌl,beri] s Maulbeere f
mul'berry tree' s Maulbeerbaum m
mulch [mʌlt∫] s Streu n
mulct [mʌlkt] tr (of) betrügen (um)
mule [mjul] s Maulesel m, Maultier n
mulish ['mjulɪ∫] adj störrisch
mull [mʌl] intr—**m. over** nachgrübeln über (acc)
mullion ['mʌljən] s Mittelpfosten m

multicolored ['mʌltɪ,kələrd] adj bunt
multigraph ['mʌltɪ,græf] s (trademark) Vervielfältigungsmaschine f || tr vervielfältigen
multilateral [,mʌlti'lætərəl] adj mehrseitig
multimillionaire ['mʌltɪ,mɪljə'nɛr] s vielfacher Millionär m
multiple ['mʌltɪpəl] adj mehrfach, Vielfach– || s (math) Vielfaches n
multiplication [,mʌltɪplɪ'ke∫ən] s Vermehrung f; (arith) Multiplikation f
multiplica'tion ta'ble s Einmaleins n
multiplicity [,mʌltɪ'plɪsɪti] s Vielfältigkeit f
multi·ply ['mʌltɪ,plaɪ] v (pret & pp –plied) tr vervielfältigen; (biol) vermehren; (math) multiplizieren || intr sich vervielfachen; (biol) sich vermehren
multistage ['mʌltɪ,stedʒ] adj mehrstufig
multistory ['mʌltɪ,stori] adj mehrstöckig
multitude ['mʌltɪ,t(j)ud] s (large number) Vielheit f; (of people) Masse f
mum [mʌm] adj still; **keep mum about** Stillschweigen beobachten über (acc); **mum's the word!** Mund halten!
mumble ['mʌmbəl] tr & intr murmeln
mummery ['mʌməri] s Hokuspokus m
mummy ['mʌmi] s Mumie f
mumps [mʌmps] s Ziegenpeter m, Mumps m
munch [mʌnt∫] tr & intr geräuschvoll kauen
mundane [mʌn'den] adj irdisch
municipal [mju'nɪsɪpəl] adj städtisch
muni'cipal bond' s Kommunalobligation f
municipality [mju,nɪsɪ'pælɪti] s Stadt f, Gemeinde f; (governing body) Stadtverwaltung f
munificent [mju'nɪfɪsənt] adj freigebig
munificence [mju'nɪfɪsəns] s Freigebigkeit f
munitions [mju'nɪ∫əns] s Kriegsmaterial n, Munition f
muni'tions dump' s Munitionsdepot n
muni'tions fac'tory s Rüstungsfabrik f
mural ['mjurəl] s Wandgemälde n
murder ['mʌrdər] s Mord m || tr (er)morden; (a language) radebrechen
murderer ['mʌrdərər] s Mörder m
murderess ['mʌrdərɪs] s Mörderin f
mur'der mys'tery s Krimi m
murderous ['mʌrdərəs] adj mörderisch
mur'der plot' s Mordanschlag m
murky ['mʌrki] adj düster
murmur ['mʌrmər] s Gemurmel n || tr & intr murmeln
muscle ['mʌsəl] s Muskel m; **muscles** Muskulatur f
muscular ['mʌskjələr] adj muskulös
Muse [mjuz] s Muse f || **muse** intr (over) nachsinnen (über acc)
museum [mju'zi·əm] s Museum n
mush [mʌ∫] s (corn meal) Maismehlbrei m; (soft mass) Matsch m; (sentimental talk) Süßholzraspeln n
mush'room' s Pilz m, Champignon m

|| *intr* wie Pilze aus dem Boden schießen

mushy [ˈmʌʃi] *adj* matschig; *(sentimental)* rührselig

music [ˈmjuːzɪk] *s* Musik *f;* *(score)* Noten *pl;* **face the m.** die Sache ausbaden; **set to m.** vertonen

musical [ˈmjuːzɪkəl] *adj* musikalisch || *s* (cin) Singspielfilm *m;* (theat) Musical *n,* Singspiel *n*

mu'sical in'strument *s* Musikinstrument *n*

musicale [ˌmjuːzɪˈkæl] *s* Musikabend *m*

mu'sic box' *s* Spieldose *f*

musician [mjuˈzɪʃən] *s* Musikant –in *mf;* *(accomplished artist)* Musiker –in *mf*

musicology [ˌmjuːzɪˈkɑlədʒi] *s* Musikwissenschaft *f*

mu'sic stand' *s* Notenständer *m*

mus'ing *s* Grübelei *f*

musk [mʌsk] *s* Moschus *m*

musket [ˈmʌskɪt] *s* Muskete *f*

musk'rat' *s* Bisamratte *f*

muslin [ˈmʌzlɪn] *s* Musselin *m*

muss [mʌs] *tr* (hair) zerzausen; *(dirty)* schmutzig machen; *(rumple)* zerknittern

mussel [ˈmʌsəl] *s* Muschel *f*

mussy [ˈmʌsi] *adj* (hair) zerzaust; *(clothes)* zerknittert

must [mʌst] *s* *(a necessity)* Muß *n;* *(new wine)* Most *m;* *(mold)* Moder *m* || *mod*—**I m.** (inf) ich muß (inf)

mustache [məsˈtæʃ] *s* Schnurrbart *m*

mustard [ˈmʌstərd] *s* Senf *m*

mus'tard plas'ter *s* Senfpflaster *n*

muster [ˈmʌstər] *s* Appell *m;* **pass m.** die Prüfung bestehen || *tr* (troops) antreten lassen; *(courage, strength)* aufbringen; **m. out** ausmustern

musty [ˈmʌsti] *adj* mod(e)rig

mutation [mjuˈteʃən] *s* (biol) Mutation *f*

mute [mjut] *adj* (& ling) stumm || *s* (ling) stummer Buchstabe *m;* (mus) Dämpfer || *tr* (mus) dämpfen

mutilate [ˈmjutɪˌlet] *tr* verstümmeln

mutineer [ˌmjutɪˈnɪr] *s* Meuterer *m*

mutinous [ˈmjutɪnəs] *adj* meuterisch

muti·ny [ˈmjutɪni] *s* Meuterei *f* || *v* *(pret & pp* –**nied**) *intr* meutern

mutt [mʌt] *s* (coll) Köter *m*

mutter [ˈmʌtər] *s* Gemurmel *n* || *tr* & *intr* murmeln

mutton [ˈmʌtən] *s* (culin) Hammel *m*

mut'ton-head' *s* (sl) Hammel *m*

mutual [ˈmjutʃuəl] *adj* gegenseitig; *(friends)* gemeinsam

mu'tual fund' *s* Investmentfond *m*

mu'tual insur'ance com'pany *s* Versicherungsgesellschaft *f* auf Gegenseitigkeit

mutually [ˈmjutʃuəli] *adv* gegenseitig

muzzle [ˈmʌzəl] *s* Maulkorb *m;* *(of a gun)* Rohrmündung *f;* *(snout)* Schnauze *f* || *tr* (an animal) e-n Maulkorb anlegen (dat); *(e.g., the press)* mundtot machen

muz'zle flash' *s* Mündungsfeuer *n*

my [maɪ] *poss adj* mein

myopic [maɪˈɑpɪk] *adj* kurzsichtig

myriad [ˈmɪrɪəd] *adj* Myriade *f*

myrrh [mʌr] *s* Myrrhe *f*

myrtle [ˈmʌrtəl] *s* Myrte *f*

myself [maɪˈself] *reflex pron* mich; *(indirect object)* mir || *intens pron* selbst, selber

mysterious [mɪsˈtɪrɪəs] *adj* mysteriös

mystery [ˈmɪstəri] *s* Geheimnis *n;* (fi) Rätsel *n;* (relig) Mysterium *n*

mys'tery nov'el *s* Kriminalroman *m*

mys'tery play' *s* Mysterienspiel *n*

mystic [ˈmɪstɪk] *adj* mystisch || *s* Mystiker –in *mf*

mystical [ˈmɪstɪkəl] *adj* mystisch

mysticism [ˈmɪstɪˌsɪzəm] *s* Mystik *f*

mystification [ˌmɪstɪfɪˈkeʃən] *s* Verwirrung *f*

mysti·fy [ˈmɪstɪˌfaɪ] *v* *(pret & pp* –**fied**) *tr* verwirren

myth [mɪθ] *s* Mythe *f,* Mythos *m;* *(ill-founded belief)* Märchen *n*

mythical [ˈmɪθɪkəl] *adj* mythisch

mythological [ˌmɪθəˈlɑdʒɪkəl] *adj* mythologisch

mythology [mɪˈθɑlədʒi] *s* Mythologie *f*

N

N, n [en] *s* vierzehnter Buchstabe des englischen Alphabets

nab [næb] *v* *(pret & pp* **nabbed;** *ger* –**nabbing**) *tr* (coll) schnappen

nadir [ˈnedɪr] *s* (fig) Tiefpunkt *m;* (astr) Nadir *m*

nag [næg] *s* Gaul *m;* **old nag** Schindmähre *f* || *v* *(pret & pp* **nagged;** *ger* **nagging**) *tr* zusetzen (dat) || *intr* nörgeln; **nag at** herumnörgeln an (dat)

nag'ging *adj* nörgelnd || *s* Nörgelei *f*

naiad [ˈnaɪˌæd] *s* Najade *f*

nail [nel] *s* Nagel *m;* **hit the n. on the head** den Nagel auf den Kopf treffen || *tr* (to) annageln (an *acc*); *(catch)*

(coll) erwischen; (box) (coll) treffen; **n. down** (fig) festnageln; **n. shut** zunageln

nail' clip'pers *spl* Nagelzange *f*

nail' file' *s* Nagelfeile *f*

nail' pol'ish *s* Nagellack *m*

nail' scis'sors *s & spl* Nagelschere *f*

naïve [nɑˈiv] *adj* naiv

naked [ˈnekɪd] *adj* nackt; *(eye)* bloß

nakedness [ˈnekɪdnɪs] *s* Nacktheit *f*

name [nem] *s* Name *m;* *(reputation)* Name *m,* Ruf *m;* **by n.** dem Namen nach; **by the n. of** namens; **in n. only** nur dem Namen nach; **of the same n.** gleichnamig; **spell one's n.** sich schreiben; **what is your n.?** wie heißen Sie? || *tr* nennen; (*nominate*) ernennen; **be named after** heißen nach; **n. after** nennen nach; **named** namens

name'-call'ng *s* Beschimpfung *f*
name' day' *s* Namenstag *m*
nameless ['nemlɪs] *adj* namenlos
namely ['nemlɪ] *adv* nämlich, und zwar
name'plate' *s* Namensschild *n*
name'sake' *s* Namensvetter *m*
nanny ['næni] *s* Kindermädchen *n*
nan'ny goat' *s* (coll) Ziege *f*
nap [næp] *s* Schläfchen *n*; (tex) Noppe *f*; **take a nap** ein Schläfchen machen || *v* (*pret & pp* **napped;** *ger* **napping**) *intr* schlummern; **catch s.o. napping** (fig) j–n überrumpeln
napalm ['nepam] *s* Napalm *n*
nape [nep] *s*—**n. of the neck** Nacken *m*
naphtha ['næfθə] *s* Naphtha *f & n*
napkin ['næpkɪn] *s* Serviette *f*
nap'kin ring' *s* Serviettenring *m*
narcissism ['nɑrsɪ,sɪzəm] *s* Narzißmus *m*
narcissus [nɑr'sɪsəs] *s* (bot) Narzisse *f*
narcotic [nɑr'kɑtɪk] *adj* narkotisch || *s* (med) Betäubungsmittel *n*, Narkotikum *n*; (*addictive drug*) Rauschgift *n*; (*addict*) Rauschgiftsüchtige *mf*
narrate [næ'ret] *tr* erzählen
narration [næ're∫ən] *s* Erzählung *f*
narrative ['nærətɪv] *adj* erzählend || *s* Erzählung *f*
narrator [næ'retər] *s* Erzähler *m*; (telv) Moderator *m*
narrow ['næro] *adj* eng, schmal; (*e.g., margin*) knapp || **narrows** *spl* Meerenge *f* || *tr* verengen || *intr* sich verengen
nar'row escape' *s*—**have a n.** mit knapper Not entkommen
nar'row-gauge rail'road *s* Schmalspurbahn *f*
narrowly ['næroli] *adv* mit knapper Not
nar'row-mind'ed *adj* engstirnig
nasal ['nezəl] *adj* (*of the nose*) Nasen–; (*sound*) näselnd || *s* (phonet) Nasenlaut *m*
nasalize ['nezə,laɪz] *tr* nasalieren || *intr* näseln
na'sal twang' *s* Näseln *n*
nascent ['nesənt] *adj* werdend
nastiness ['næstɪnɪs] *s* Ekligkeit *f*
nasturtium [nə'stʌr/əm] *s* Kapuzinerkresse *f*
nasty ['næstɪ] *adj* (*person, smell, taste*) ekelhaft; (*weather*) scheußlich; (*dog, accident, tongue*) böse; **n. to** garstig zu or gegen
nation ['ne∫ən] *s* Nation *f*, Volk *n*
national ['næ∫ənəl] *adj* national, Landes– || *s* Staatsangehörige *mf*
na'tional an'them *s* Nationalhymne *f*
na'tional defense' *s* Landesverteidigung *f*
nationalism ['næ∫ənə,lɪzəm] *s* Nationalismus *m*
nationality [,næ∫ə'nælɪti] *s* (*citizen-*

ship) Staatsangehörigkeit *f*; (*ethnic identity*) Nationalität *f*
nationalization [,næ∫ənəlɪ'ze∫ən] *s* Verstaatlichung *f*
nationalize ['næ∫ənə,laɪz] *tr* verstaatlichen
na'tional park' *s* Naturschutzpark *m*
na'tional so'cialism *s* Nationalsozialismus *m*
na'tionwide' *adj* im ganzen Land
native ['netɪv] *adj* eingeboren; (*products*) heimisch, Landes– || *s* Eingeborene *mf*; **be a n. of** beheimatet sein in (*dat*)
na'tive coun'try *s* Vaterland *n*
na'tive land' *s* Heimatland *n*
na'tive tongue' *s* Muttersprache *f*
nativity [nə'tɪvɪti] *s* Geburt *f*; (astrol) Nativität *f*; **the Nativity** die Geburt Christi
NATO ['neto] *s* (**North Atlantic Treaty Organization**) NATO *f*
natty ['næti] *adj* elegant
natural ['næt∫ərəl] *adj* natürlich; (*behavior*) ungezwungen || *s* (mus) weiße Taste *f*; (*symbol*) (mus) Auflösungszeichen *n*; **a n.** (*person*) (coll) ein Naturtalent *n*; (*thing*) (coll) e–e totsichere Sache *f*
na'tural his'tory *s* Naturgeschichte *f*
naturalism ['næt∫ərə,lɪzəm] *s* Naturalismus *m*
naturalist ['næt∫ərəlɪst] *s* (*student of natural history*) Naturforscher –in *mf*; (paint, philos) Naturalist –in *mf*
naturalization [,næt∫ərəlɪ'ze∫ən] *s* Einbürgerung *f*
naturalize ['næt∫ərə,laɪz] *tr* einbürgern
na'tural law' *s* Naturgesetz *n*
na'tural phenom'enon *s* (*occurring in nature*) Naturereignis *n*; (*not supernatural*) natürliche Erscheinung *f*
na'tural re'sources *spl* Bodenschätze *pl*
na'tural sci'ence *s* Naturwissenschaft *f*
na'tural state' *s* Naturzustand *m*
nature ['net∫ər] *s* die Natur; (*qualities*) Natur *f*, Beschaffenheit *f*; **by n.** von Natur aus
naught [nɔt] *s* Null *f*; **all for n.** ganz umsonst; **bring to n.** zuschanden machen; **come to n.** zunichte werden
naughty ['nɔti] *adj* unartig, ungezogen
nausea ['nɔ∫ɪ·ə], ['nɔsɪ·ə] *s* Übelkeit *f*
nauseate ['nɔ∫ɪ,et], ['nɔsɪ,et] *tr* Übelkeit erregen (*dat*)
naus'eating *adj* Übelkeit erregend
nauseous ['nɔ∫ɪ·əs], ['nɔsɪ·əs] *adj* (*causing nausea*) Übelkeit erregend; **I feel n.** mir ist übel
nautical ['nɔtɪkəl] *adj* See–, nautisch
nau'tical mile' ['nɔtɪkəl] *s* Seemeile *f*
nau'tical term' *s* Ausdruck *m* der Seemannssprache *f*
naval ['nevəl] *adj* (*e.g., battle, blockade, cadet, victory*) See–; (*unit*) Flotten–; (*academy, officer*) Marine–
na'val base' *s* Flottenstützpunkt *m*
na'val cap'tain *s* Kapitän *m* zur See
na'val engage'ment *s* Seegefecht *n*
na'val forc'es *s* Seestreitkräfte *pl*
na'val suprem'acy *s* Seeherrschaft *f*

nave [nev] *s* (*of a church*) Schiff *n;* (*of a wheel*) Nabe *f*

navel ['nevəl] *s* Nabel *m*

na'vel or'ange *s* Navelorange *f*

navigable ['nævɪgəbəl] *adj* schiffbar

navigate ['nævɪ͵get] *tr* (*traverse*) befahren; (*steer*) steuern ‖ *intr* (aer, naut) navigieren

navigation [͵nævɪ'geʃən] *s* (*plotting courses*) Navigation *f;* (*sailing*) Schiffahrt *f*

naviga'tion chart' *s* Navigationskarte *f*

naviga'tion light' *s* (aer, naut) Positionslicht *n*

navigator ['nævɪ͵getər] *s* Seefahrer *m;* (aer) Navigator *m*

navy ['nevi] *adj* Marine– ‖ *s* Kriegsmarine *f*

na'vy bean' *s* Weiße Bohne *f*

na'vy blue' *adj* marineblau ‖ *s* Marineblau *n*

na'vy yard' *s* Marinewerft *f*

nay [ne] *adv* nein ‖ *s* Nein *n;* (parl) Neinstimme *f;* **the nays have it** die Mehrheit stimmt dagegen

Nazarene [͵næzə'rin] *adj* aus Nazareth ‖ *s* Nazarener *m*

Nazi ['natsi] *adj* Nazi– ‖ *s* Nazi *m*

Nazism ['natsizəm] *s* Nazismus *m*

N.C.O. ['en'si'o] *s* (noncommissioned officer) Unteroffizier *m*

neap' tide' [nip] *s* Nippflut *f*

near [nɪr] *adj* nahe(liegend); (*escape*) knapp; **n. at hand** zur Hand ‖ *adv* nahe; **draw n. (to)** sich nähern (*dat*); **live n.** (e.g., *a church*) in der Nähe wohnen (*genit*) ‖ *prep* nahe (*dat*), nahe an (*dat*), bei (*dat*); **n. here** hier in der Nähe

near'by' *adj* nahe(gelegen) ‖ *adv* in der Nähe

Near' East', **the** *s* der Nahe Osten

nearly ['nɪrli] *adv* beinahe, fast

nearness ['nɪrnɪs] *s* Nähe *f*

near'-sight'ed *adj* kurzsichtig

near'-sight'edness *s* Kurzsichtigkeit *f*

neat [nit] *adj* sauber, ordentlich; (*simple but tasteful*) nett; (*cute*) niedlich; (*tremendous*) (coll) prima

neatness ['nitnɪs] *s* Sauberkeit *f*

nebu·la ['nebjələ] *s* (–lae [͵li] & –las) (astr) Nebelfleck *m*

nebulous ['nebjələs] *adj* nebelhaft; (astr) Nebel–

necessarily [͵nesɪ'serɪli] *adv* notwendigerweise, unbedingt

necessary ['nesɪ͵seri] *adj* notwendig, nötig; (*consequence*) zwangsläufig; **if n.** notfalls

necessitate [nɪ'sesɪ͵tet] *tr* notwendig machen, erfordern

necessity [nɪ'sesɪti] *s* (state *of being necessary*) Notwendigkeit *f;* (*something necessary*) Bedürfnis *n;* (*poverty*) Not *f;* **in case of n.** im Notfall; **necessities of life** Lebensbedürfnisse *pl;* **of n.** notwendigerweise

neck [nek] *s* Hals *m;* (*of a dress*) Halsausschnitt *m;* **break one's n.** (& fig) sich [*dat*] den Hals brechen; **get it in the n.** (sl) eins aufs Dach kriegen; **get s.o. off one's n.** sich [*dat*] j-n

vom Halse schaffen; **n. and n.** Seite an Seite ‖ *intr* (coll) sich knutschen

–necked [͵nekt] *suf* –halsig, –nackig

neckerchief ['nekərtʃɪf] *s* Halstuch *n*

neck'ing *s* Abknutscherei *f*

necklace ['neklɪs] *s* Halsband *n;* (*metal chain*) Halskette *f*

neck'line' *s* Halsausschnitt *m;* **with a low n.** tief ausgeschnitten

neck'tie' *s* Krawatte *f*, Schlips *m*

necrology [ne'krɑlədʒi] *s* (*list of the dead*) Totenliste *f;* (*obituary*) Nekrolog *m*

necromancer ['nekrə͵mænsər] *s* Geistesbeschwörer –*in m f*

necromancy ['nekrə͵mænsi] *s* Geistesbeschwörung *f*

necropolis [ne'krɑpəlɪs] *s* Nekropolis *f*

nectar ['nektər] *s* (bot, myth) Nektar *m*

nectarine [͵nektə'rin] *s* Nektarine *f*

nee [ne] *adj* geborene, e.g., **Mrs. Mary Schmidt, nee Müller** Frau Maria Schmidt, geborene Müller

need [nid] *s* Bedarf *m*, Bedürfnis *n;* **be in n.** in Not sein; **be in n. of repair** reparaturbedürftig sein; **be in n. of s.th.** etw nötig haben; **if n. be** erforderlichenfalls; **meet s.o.'s needs** j-s Bedarf decken; **needs Bedarfsartikel** *pl* ‖ *tr* benötigen, brauchen; **as needed** nach Bedarf

needful ['nidfəl] *adj* nötig

needle ['nidəl] *s* Nadel *f* ‖ *tr* (*prod*) anstacheln; **n. s.o. about** gegen j–n stichein wegen

nee'dlepoint', **nee'dlepoint lace'** *s* Nadelspitze *f*

needless ['nidlɪs] *adj* unnötig; **n. to say** es erübrigt sich zu sagen

nee'dlework' *s* Näharbeit *f*

needy ['nidi] *adj* bedürftig

ne'er [ner] *adv* nie

ne'er'-do-well' *s* Tunichtgut *m*

nefarious [nɪ'feri·əs] *adj* ruchlos

negate [nɪ'get] *tr* verneinen

negation [nɪ'geʃən] *s* Verneinung *f*

negative ['negətɪv] *adj* negativ ‖ *s* Verneinung *f;* (elec) negativer Pol *m;* (gram) Verneinungswort *n;* (phot) Negativ *n*

neglect [nɪ'glekt] *s* Vernachlässigung *f* ‖ *tr* vernachlässigen; **n. to** (*inf*) unterlassen zu (*inf*)

négligée, **negligee** [͵neglɪ'ʒe] *s* Negligé *n*

negligence ['neglɪdʒəns] *s* Fahrlässigkeit *f*

negligent ['neglɪdʒənt] *adj* fahrlässig

negligible ['neglɪdʒɪbəl] *adj* geringfügig

negotiable [nɪ'goʃɪ·əbəl] *adj* diskutierbar; (fin) übertragbar, bankfähig

negotiate [nɪ'goʃɪ͵et] *tr* (*a contract*) abschließen; (*a curve*) nehmen ‖ *intr* verhandeln

negotiation [nɪ͵goʃɪ'eʃən] *s* Verhandlung *f;* **carry on negotiations with** in Verhandlungen stehen mit; **enter negotiations with** in Verhandlungen treten mit

negotiator [nɪˈgoʃɪˌetər] s Unterhändler -in mf

Ne·gro [ˈnigro] s (-groes) Neger -in mf

neigh [ne] s Wiehern n || intr wiehern

neighbor [ˈnebər] s Nachbar -in mf; (fellow man) Nächste m || tr angrenzen an (acc) || intr—**n. on** angrenzen an (acc)

neigh'borhood' s Nachbarschaft f; (vicinity) Umgebung f; **in the n. of** (coll) etwa

neigh'boring adj benachbart, Nachbar-, angrenzend

neighborliness [ˈnebərlɪnɪs] s gutnachbarliche Beziehungen pl

neighborly [ˈnebərli] adj (gut)nachbarlich

neither [ˈniðər] indef adj keiner || indef pron (of) keiner (von); **n. of them** keiner von beiden || conj noch, ebensowenig; auch nicht, e.g., **n. do I** ich auch nicht; **neither ... nor** weder ... noch; **that's n. here nor there** das hat nichts zu sagen

neme·sis [ˈneməsɪs] s (-ses [ˌsiz]) Nemesis f

Neolith'ic Age' [ˌni·əˈlɪθɪk] s Neusteinzeit f

neologism [niˈɑləˌdʒɪzəm] s Neubildung f, Neologismus m

neon [ˈni·ɑn] s Neon n

ne'on light' s Neonröhre f

ne'on sign' s Neonreklame f

neophyte [ˈni·əˌfaɪt] s Neuling m; (relig) Neubekehrte mf

nephew [ˈnefju] s Neffe m

nepotism [ˈnepəˌtɪzəm] s Nepotismus m

Neptune [ˈnept(j)un] s Neptun m

neptunium [nepˈt(j)uni·əm] s Neptunium n

nerve [nʌrv] adj Nerven- || s Nerv m; (courage) Wagemut m; (gall) (coll) Unverfrorenheit f; **get on s.o.'s nerves** j-m auf die Nerven gehen; **lose one's n.** die Nerven verlieren; **nerves of steel** Nerven pl wie Drahtseile

nerve' cen'ter s Nervenzentrum n

nerve'-rack'ing adj nervenaufreibend

nervous [ˈnʌrvəs] adj nervös; (system) Nerven-; (horse) kopfscheu; **be a n. wreck** mit den Nerven herunter sein

ner'vous break'down s Nervenzusammenbruch m

nervousness [ˈnʌrvəsnɪs] s Nervosität f

nervy [ˈnʌrvi] adj (brash) unverschämt; (courageous) mutig

nest [nest] s Nest n || intr nisten

nest' egg' s (fig) Sparpfennig m

nestle [ˈnesəl] intr (up to) sich anschmiegen (an acc)

net [net] adj Rein- || adv netto, rein || s Netz n; (for fire victims) Sprungtuch n || v (pret & pp netted; ger netting) tr (e.g., fish, butterflies) mit dem Netz fangen; (said of an enterprise) netto einbringen; (said of a person) rein verdienen

net'ball' s (tennis) Netzball m

Netherlander [ˈneðərˌlændər] s Niederländer -in mf

Netherlands, the [ˈneðərləndz] s & spl die Niederlande

net'ting s Netzwerk n

nettle [ˈnetəl] s Nessel f || tr reizen

net'work' s Netzwerk n; (rad, telv) Sendergruppe f

neuralgia [n(j)uˈrældʒə] s Neurologie f

neuritis [n(j)uˈraɪtɪs] s Nervenentzündung f

neurologist [n(j)uˈrɑlədʒɪst] s Nervenarzt m, Nervenärztin f

neurology [n(j)uˈrɑlədʒi] s Nervenheilkunde f, Neurologie f

neuron [ˈn(j)urɑn] s Neuron n

neuro·sis [n(j)uˈrosɪs] s (-ses [siz]) Neurose f

neurotic [n(j)uˈrɑtɪk] adj neurotisch || s Neurotiker -in mf

neuter [ˈn(j)utər] adj (gram) sächlich || s (gram) Neutrum n

neutral [ˈn(j)utrəl] adj neutral || s Neutrale mf; (aut) Leerlauf m

neutrality [n(j)uˈtrælɪti] s Neutralität f

neutralize [ˈn(j)utrəˌlaɪz] tr (a bomb) entschärfen; (& chem) neutralisieren; (troops) lahmlegen; (an attack) unterbinden

neutron [ˈn(j)utrɑn] s Neutron n

never [ˈnevər] adv nie(mals); **n. again** nie wieder; **n. before** noch nie; **n. mind!** spielt keine Rolle!

nevermore [ˈnevərˈmor] adv nimmermehr

nevertheless [ˌnevərðəˈlɛs] adv nichtsdestoweniger

new [n(j)u] adj neu; (wine) jung; (inexperienced) unerfahren; **what's new?** was gibt's Neues?

new' arriv'al s Neuankömmling m

new'born' adj neugeboren

New'cas'tle s—**carry coals to N.** Eulen nach Athen tragen

newcomer [ˈn(j)uˌkʌmər] s Neuankömmling m

newel [ˈn(j)u·əl] s Treppenspindel f

new'el post' s Geländerpfosten m

newfangled [ˈn(j)uˌfæŋgəld] adj neumodisch

Newfoundland [ˈn(j)ufənd,lænd] s Neufundland n || [n(j)uˈfaundlənd] s (dog) Neufundländer m

newly [ˈn(j)uli] adv neu, Neu-

new'lyweds' spl Neuvermählten pl

new' moon' s Neumond m

new-mown [ˈn(j)uˌmon] adj frischgemäht

newness [ˈn(j)unɪs] s Neuheit f

news [n(j)uz] s Nachricht f; (rad, telv) Nachrichten pl; **that's not n. to me** das ist mir nicht neu; **piece of n.** Neuigkeit f

news' a'gency s Nachrichtenagentur f

news'boy' s Zeitungsjunge m

news' bul'letin s Kurznachricht f

news'cast' s Nachrichtensendung f

news'cast'er s Nachrichtensprecher -in mf

news'deal'er s Zeitungshändler -in mf

news' ed'itor s Nachrichtenredakteur -in mf

news'let'ter s Rundschreiben n

news'man' s (–men') Journalist m; (dealer) Zeitungshändler m

news'pa'per adj Zeitungs– || s Zeitung f

news'paper clip'ping s Zeitungsausschnitt m

news'paper-man' s (–men') Journalist m; (dealer) Zeitungshändler m

news'paper se'rial s Zeitungsroman m

news'print' s Zeitungspapier n

news'reel' s Wochenschau f

news' report' s Nachrichtensendung f

news' report'er s Zeitungsreporter –in mf

news' room' s Nachrichtenbüro n

news'stand' s Zeitungskiosk m

news'wor'thy adj berichtenswert

New' Tes'tament s Neues Testament n

New' World' s Neue Welt f

New' Year' s Neujahr n; happy N.! glückliches Neues Jahr!

New' Year's' Eve' s Silvesterabend m

New' Zea'land s Neuseeland n

next [nekst] adj nächste; be n. an der Reihe sein; come n. folgen; in the n. place darauf; n. best nächstbeste; n. time das nächste Mal; n. to (locally) gleich neben (dat); (almost) sogut wie; the n. day am nächsten Tag || adv dann, danach; what should I do n.? was soll ich als Nächstes tun?

next'-door' adj—n. neighbor unmittelbarer Nachbar m || adv next'-door' adv nebenan; n. to direkt neben (dat)

next' of kin' s (pl: next of kin) nächster Angehöriger m

niacin ['naɪ-əsɪn] s Niacin n

Niag'ara Falls' [naɪ'ægrə] s Niagarafall m

nib [nɪb] s Spitze f; (of a pen) Federspitze f

nibble ['nɪbəl] tr knabbern || intr (on) knabbern (an dat)

Nibelung ['nibəluŋ] s (myth) Nibelung m

nice [naɪs] adj nett; (pretty) hübsch; (food) lecker; (well-behaved) artig; (distinction) fein; have a n. time sich gut unterhalten; n. and warm schön warm

nicely ['naɪsli] adv nett; he's doing n. es geht ihm recht gut; that will do n. das paßt gut

nicety ['naɪsəti] s Feinheit f; niceties of life Annehmlichkeiten pl des Lebens

niche [nɪtʃ] s Nische f; (fig) rechter Platz m

nick [nɪk] s Kerbe f, Scharte f; in the n. of time gerade im rechten Augenblick || tr kerben

nickel ['nɪkəl] s Nickel n; (coin) Fünfcentstück n || tr vernickeln

nick'el-plate' tr vernickeln

nick'name' s Spitzname m || tr e-n Spitznamen geben (dat)

nicotine ['nɪkə‚tin] s Nikotin n; low in n. nikotinarm

niece [nis] s Nichte f

nifty ['nɪfti] adj (coll) fesch, prima

niggard ['nɪgərd] s Knauser –in mf

niggardly ['nɪgərdli] adj knauserig

night [naɪt] adj (light, shift, train, watch) Nacht– || s Nacht f; all n. (long) die ganze Nacht (über); at n. nachts; last n. gestern abend; n. after n. Nacht für Nacht; n. before last vorgestern abend

night' cap' s Nachtmütze f; (drink) Schlummertrunk m

night' club' s Nachtklub m

night'fall' s Anbruch m der Nacht; at n. bei Anbruch der Nacht

night'gown' s Damennachthemd n

nightingale ['naɪtən‚gel] s Nachtigall f

night'light' s Nachtlicht n

night'long' adj & adv die ganze Nacht dauernd

nightly ['naɪtli] adj & adv allnächtlich

night'mare' s Alptraum m

nightmarish ['naɪt‚merɪʃ] adj alpartig

night' owl' s (coll) Nachteule f

night' school' s Abendschule f

night'time' s Nachtzeit f; at n. zur Nachtzeit

night' watch'man s Nachtwächter m

nihilism ['naɪ-ɪ‚lɪzəm] s Nihilismus m

nil [nɪl] s Nichts n, Null f

Nile [naɪl] s Nil m

nimble ['nɪmbəl] adj flink

nincompoop ['nɪnkəm‚pup] s Trottel m

nine [naɪn] adj & pron neun || s Neun f

nineteen ['naɪn'tin] adj & pron neunzehn || s Neunzehn f

nineteenth ['naɪn'tinθ] adj & pron neunzehnte || s (fraction) Neunzehntel n; the nineteenth (in dates or in a series) der neunzehnte

ninetieth ['naɪntɪ-ɪθ] adj & pron neunzigste || s (fraction) Neunzigstel n

ninety ['naɪnti] adj & pron neunzig || s Neunzig f; the nineties die neunziger Jahre

nine'ty-first' adj & pron einundneunzigste

nine'ty-one' adj & pron einundneunzig

ninny ['nɪni] s (coll) Trottel m

ninth [naɪnθ] adj & pron neunte || s (fraction) Neuntel n; the n. (in dates or in a series) der Neunte

nip [nɪp] s (pinch) Kneifen n; (of cold weather) Schneiden n; (of liquor) Schluck m || v (pret & pp nipped; ger nipping) tr (pinch) kneifen; (alcohol) nippen; nip in the bud im Keime ersticken

nippers ['nɪpərz] spl Zwickzange f

nipple ['nɪpəl] s (of a nursing bottle) Lutscher m; (anat) Brustwarze f; (mach) Schmiernippel m

nippy ['nɪpi] adj schneidend

nirvana [nɪr'vɑnə] s Nirwana n

nit [nɪt] s (ent) Nisse f

niter ['naɪtər] s Salpeter m

nit'pick'er s (coll) Pedant –in mf

nitrate ['naɪtret] s Nitrat n || tr nitrieren

ni'tric ac'id ['naɪtrɪk] s Salpetersäure f

nitride [ˈnaɪtraɪd] s Nitrid n
nitrogen [ˈnaɪtrədʒən] s Stickstoff m
nitroglycerin [ˌnaɪtrəˈglɪsərɪn] s Nitroglyzerin n
ni′trous ac′id [ˈnaɪtrəs] s salpetrige Säure f
ni′trous ox′ide s Stickstoffoxydul n
nit′wit′ s Trottel m
no [no] adj kein; **no admittance** Zutritt verboten; **no ... of any kind** keinerlei; **no offense!** nichts für ungut!; **no parking** Parkverbot; **no smoking** Rauchen verboten; **no thoroughfare** Durchgang verboten; **no ... whatever** überhaupt kein || adv nein; **no?** nicht wahr?; **no longer** (or **no more**) nicht mehr || s Nein n; **give no for an answer** mit (e-m) Nein antworten
No′ah′s Ark′ [ˈno-əz] s Arche f Noah(s)
nobility [noˈbɪlɪti] s (nobleness; aristocracy) Adel m; (noble rank) Adelsstand m; **n. of mind** Seelenadel m
noble [ˈnobəl] adj (rank) ad(e)lig; (character, person) edel || s Adliger m; **nobles** Edelleute pl
no′ble-man s (-men) Edelmann m
no′blemind′ed adj edelgesinnt
nobleness [ˈnobəlnɪs] s Vornehmheit f
no′ble-wom′an s (-wom′en) Edelfrau f
nobody [ˈno ˌbadi] s indef pron niemand, keiner; **n. else** sonst keiner || s (coll) Null f
nocturnal [nakˈtʌrnəl] adj nächtlich
nod [nad] s Kopfnicken n || v (pret & pp **nodded**; ger **nodding**) tr—**nod one′s head** mit dem Kopf nicken || intr nicken; **nod to** zunicken (dat)
node [nod] s (anat, astr, math, phys) Knoten m
nodule [ˈnadʒul] s Knötchen n; (bot) Knollen m
noise [nɔɪz] s Geräusch n; (disturbingly loud) Lärm m || tr—**n. abroad** ausposaunen
noiseless [ˈnɔɪzlɪs] adj geräuschlos
noisy [ˈnɔɪzi] adj lärmend, geräuschvoll
nomad [ˈnomæd] s Nomade m, Nomadin f
no′ man′s′ land′ s Niemandsland n
nomenclature [ˈnomən ˌkletʃər] s Nomenklatur f
nominal [ˈnamɪnəl] adj nominell
nominate [ˈnamɪ ˌnet] tr ernennen; **n. as candidate** als Kandidaten aufstellen
nomination [ˌnamɪˈneʃən] s Ernennung f; (of a candidate) Aufstellung f
nominative [ˈnamɪnətɪv] s Nominativ m
nominee [ˌnamɪˈni] s Designierte mf
non- [nan] pref Nicht-, nicht-
non′accept′ance s Nichtannahme f
non′belli′gerent adj nicht am Krieg teilnehmend
non′break′able adj unzerbrechlich
non′-Cath′olic nichtkatholisch || s Nichtkatholik m
nonchalant [ˌnanʃəˈlant] adj zwanglos

noncom [ˈnan ˌkam] s (coll) Kapo m
non′com′batant s Nichtkämpfer m
non′commis′sioned of′ficer s Unteroffizier m
noncommittal [ˌnankəˈmɪtəl] adj nichtssagend; (person) zurückhaltend
nondescript [ˈnandɪ ˌskrɪpt] adj unbestimmbar
none [nʌn] adv—**n. too** keineswegs zu || indef pron keiner; **that′s n. of your business** das geht dich nichts an
nonen′tity s Nichts n; (fig) Null f
non′exis′tent adj nichtexistent
nonfic′tion s Sachbücher pl
nonfulfill′ment s Nichterfüllung f
non′interven′tion s Nichteinmischung f
non′met′al s Nichtmetall n, Metalloid n
non′nego′tiable adj unübertragbar; (demands) unabdingbar
nonpar′tisan adj überparteilich
nonpay′ment s Nichtbezahlung f
non′polit′ical adj unpolitisch
non-plus [nanˈplʌs] s Verlegenheit f || v (pret & pp **-plus[s]ed**; ger **-plus[s]ing**) tr verblüffen
nonprof′it adj gemeinnützig
nonres′ident adj nicht ansässig || s Nichtansässige mf
non′return′able adj (bottles, etc.) Einweg-; (merchandise) nicht rücknehmbar
non′scienti′fic adj nichtwissenschaftlich
non′sectar′ian adj keiner Sekte angehörend
nonsense [ˈnansəns] s Unsinn m
nonsen′sical adj unsinnig, widersinnig
non′skid′ adj rutschsicher
nonsmok′er s Nichtraucher –in mf
non′stop′ adj & adv ohne Zwischenlandung
nonvi′olence s Gewaltlosigkeit f
nonvi′olent adj gewaltlos
noodle [ˈnudəl] s Nudel f; (head) (coll) Birne f
noo′dle soup′ s Nudelsuppe f
nook [nuk] s Ecke f; (fig) Winkel m
noon [nun] s Mittag m; **at n.** zu Mittag
no′ one′, no′-one′ indef pron niemand, keiner; **n. else** kein anderer
noon′ hour′ s Mittagsstunde f
noon′time′ adj mittäglich || s Mittagszeit f
noose [nus] s Schlinge f
nor [nɔr] conj (after **neither**) noch; auch nicht, e.g., **nor do I** ich auch nicht
Nordic [ˈnɔrdɪk] adj nordisch
norm [nɔrm] s Norm f
normal [ˈnɔrməl] adj normal
normalcy [ˈnɔrməlsi] s Normalzustand m
normalize [ˈnɔrmə ˌlaɪz] tr normalisieren
Norman [ˈnɔrmən] adj normannisch || s Normanne m, Normannin f
Normandy [ˈnɔrməndi] s die Normandie
Norse [nɔrs] adj altnordisch || s (language) Altnordisch n; **the N.** die Skandinavier pl
Norse′man s (-men) Nordländer m

north [norθ] *adj* nördlich, Nord– ‖ *adv* nach Norden ‖ *s* Norden *m*; **to the n. of** im Norden von

North′ Amer′ica *s* Nordamerika *n*

North′ Amer′ican *adj* nordamerikanisch ‖ *s* Nordamerikaner –in *mf*

north′east′ *adj & adv* nordöstlich ‖ *s* Nordosten *m*

north′east′er *s* Nordostwind *m*

northerly [′norðərli] *adj* nördlich

northern [′norðərn] *adj* (*direction*) nördlich; (*race*) nordisch

north′ern expo′sure *s* Nordseite *f*

North′ern Hem′isphere *s* nördliche Halbkugel *f*

north′ern lights′ *spl* Nordlicht *n*

nor′thernmost′ *adj* nördlichst

North′ Pole′ *s* Nordpol *m*

North′ Sea′ *s* Nordsee *f*

northward [′norθwərd] *adv* nach Norden

north′west′ *adj & adv* nordwestlich ‖ *s* Nordwesten *m*

north′ wind′ *s* Nordwind *m*

Norway [′norwe] *s* Norwegen *n*

Norwegian [nor′widʒən] *adj* norwegisch ‖ *s* Norweger –in *mf*; (*language*) Norwegisch *n*

nose [noz] *s* Nase *f*; (aer) Nase *f*, Bug *m*; **by a n.** (sport) um e–e Nasenlänge; **blow one's n.** sich schneuzen; **lead around by the n.** an der Nase herumführen; **pay through the n.** e–n zu hohen Preis bezahlen; **turn one's n. up at** die Nase rümpfen über (*acc*) ‖ *tr*—**n. out** (fig) mit knappem Vorsprung besiegen; (sport) um e–e Nasenlänge schlagen ‖ *intr*—**n. about** herumschnüffeln; **n. over** (aer) sich überschlagen

nose′bleed′ *s* Nasenbluten *n*

nose′ cone′ *s* (rok) Raketenspitze *f*

nose′ dive′ *s* (aer) Sturzflug *m*

nose′-dive′ *intr* e–n Sturzflug machen

nose′ drops′ *spl* Nasentropfen *pl*

nose′gay′ *s* Blumenstrauß *m*

nose′-heav′y *adj* (aer) vorderlastig

nostalgia [na′stældʒə] *s* Heimweh *n*

nostalgic [na′stældʒɪk] *adj* wehmütig

nostril [′nastrɪl] *s* (anat) Nasenloch *n*; (zool) Nüster *f*

nostrum [′nastrəm] *s* Allheilmittel *n*

nosy [′nozi] *adj* neugierig

not [nat] *adv* nicht; **not at all** überhaupt nicht; **not even** nicht einmal; **not one** keiner; **not only ... but also** nicht nur ... sondern auch

notable [′notəbəl] *adj* bemerkenswert ‖ *s* Standesperson *f*

notarial [no′teri·əl] *adj* notariell

notarize [′notə‚raɪz] *tr* notariell beglaubigen

no′tary pub′lic [′notəri] *s* (notaries public) Notar *m*, Notarin *f*

notation [no′teʃən] *s* (note) Aufzeichnung *f*; (system of symbols) Bezeichnung *f*; (method of noting) Schreibweise *f*

notch [natʃ] *s* Kerbe *f*; (in a belt) Loch *n*; (degree, step) Grad *m*; (of a wheel) Zahn *m* ‖ *tr* einkerben

note [not] *s* Notiz *f*; (to a text) Anmerkung *f*; (slip) Zettel *m*; (e.g., of doubt) Ton *m*; (mus) Note *f*; **jot down notes** sich [dat] Notizen machen; **make a n. of** sich [dat] notieren; **take n. of** zur Kenntnis nehmen; **take notes** sich [dat] Notizen machen ‖ *tr* beachten; **n. down** notieren; **n. in passing** am Rande bemerken

note′book′ *s* Heft *n*, Notizbuch *n*

note′ pad′ *s* Schreibblock *m*

note′wor′thy *adj* beachtenswert

nothing [′nʌθɪŋ] *indef pron* nichts; **be for n.** vergebens sein; **come to n.** platzen; **for n.** (gratis) umsonst; **have n. to go on** keine Unterlagen haben; **next to n.** soviel wie nichts; **n. at all** gar nichts; **n. but** lauter; **n. doing!** kommt nicht in Frage!; **n. else** sonst nichts; **n. new** nichts Neues; **there is n. like** es geht nichts über (*acc*)

nothingness [′nʌθɪŋnɪs] *s* (nonexistence) Nichts *n*; (utter insignificance) Nichtigkeit *f*

notice [′notɪs] *s* (placard) Anschlag *m*; (in the newspaper) Anzeige *f*; (attention) Beachtung *f*; (announcement) Ankündigung; (notice of termination) Kündigung *f*; **at a moment's n.** jeden Moment; **escape s.o.'s n.** j–m entgehen; **give s.o. a week's n.** j–m acht Tage vorher kündigen; **take n. of** Notiz nehmen von; **until further n.** bis auf weiteres ‖ *tr* (be)merken, wahrnehmen; **be noticed by s.o.** j–m auffallen; **n. s.th. about s.o.** j–m etw anmerken

noticeable [′notɪsəbəl] *adj* wahrnehmbar

notification [‚notɪfɪ′keʃən] *s* Benachrichtigung *f*

noti·fy [′notɪ‚faɪ] *v* (pret & pp –fied) *tr* (about) benachrichtigen (von)

notion [′noʃən] *s* (idea) Vorstellung *f*; **I have a good n. to** (inf) ich habe gute Lust zu (inf); **notions** Kurzwaren *pl*

notoriety [‚notə′raɪ·ɪti] *s* Verruf *m*

notorious [no′tori·əs] *adj* (for) notorisch (wegen)

no′-trump′ *adj* ohne Trumpf ‖ *s* Ohne Trumpf-Ansage *f*

notwithstanding [‚natwɪθ′stændɪŋ] *adv* trotzdem ‖ *prep* trotz (genit)

noun [naʊn] *s* Hauptwort *n*

nourish [′nʌrɪʃ] *tr* (er)nähren

nour′ishing *adj* nahrhaft, Nähr–

nourishment [′nʌrɪʃmənt] *s* (feeding) Ernährung *f*; (food) Nahrung *f*

Nova Scotia [′novə′skoʃə] *s* Neuschottland *n*

novel [′navəl] *adj* neuartig ‖ *s* Roman *m*

novelist [′navəlɪst] *s* Romanschriftsteller –in *mf*

novelty [′navəlti] *s* Neuheit *f*

November [no′vembər] *s* November *m*

novena [no′vinə] *s* Novene *f*

novice [′navɪs] *s* Neuling *m*; (eccl) Novize *m*, Novizin *f*

novitiate [no′vɪʃɪ·ɪt] *s* Noviziat *n*

novocaine [′novo‚ken] *s* Novokain *n*

now [naʊ] *adv* jetzt; (without tem-

poral force) nun; **before now** schon früher; **by now** nachgerade; **from now on** von nun ab, fortan; **now and then** dann und wann; **now ... now** bald ... bald; **now or never** jetzt oder nie

nowadays ['nau·ə‚dez] *adv* heutzutage

no'way', no'ways' *adv* keineswegs

no'where' *adv* nirgends

noxious ['nak/əs] *adj* schädlich

nozzle ['nazəl] *s* Düse *f*; *(on a can)* Schnabel *m*

nth [enθ] *adj*—**nth times** zig mal; **to the nth degree** (fig) im höchsten Maße

nuance ['n(j)u·ɑns] *s* Nuance *f*

nub [nʌb] *s* Knoten *m*; *(gist)* Kernpunkt *m*

nuclear ['n(j)uklɪ·ər] *adj* nuklear; *(energy, fission, fusion, physics, reactor, weapon)* Kern-

nu'clear pow'er *s* Atomkraft *f*

nu'clear pow'er plant' *s* Atomkraftwerk *n*

nucleolus [n(j)u'kli·ələs] *s* Nukleolus *m*

nucleon ['n(j)ukli·ɑn] *s* Nukleon *m*

nucle·us ['n(j)ukli·əs] *s* (**-uses** & **-i-** [‚aɪ]) Kern *m*

nude [n(j)ud] *adj* nackt ‖ *s* (*nude figure*) Akt *m*; **in the n.** nackt

nudge [nʌdʒ] *s* Stups *m* ‖ *tr* stupsen

nudist ['n(j)udɪst] *s* Nudist –in *mf*

nudity ['n(j)udɪti] *s* Nacktheit *f*

nugget ['nʌgɪt] *s* Klumpen *m*

nuisance ['n(j)usəns] *s* Ärgernis *n*; **be a n.** lästig sein

nui'sance raid' *s* Störungsangriff *m*

null' and void' [nʌl] *adj* null und nichtig

nulli·fy ['nʌlɪ‚faɪ] *v* (*pret* & *pp* **-fied**) *tr* (*e.g., a law*) für ungültig erklären; (*e.g., the effects*) aufheben

numb [nʌm] *adj* taub; (**with**) starr (vor *dat*); (fig) betäubt; **grow n.** erstarren ‖ *tr* (& fig) betäuben; (*said of cold*) starr machen

number ['nʌmbər] *s* Nummer *f*; (*count*) Zahl *f*, Anzahl *f*; (*article*) (com) Artikel *m*; (gram) Zahl *f*; (mus) Stück *n*; **in n.** der Zahl nach; **get s.o.'s n.** (coll) j-m auf die Schliche kommen ‖ *tr* (*e.g., pages*) numerieren; (*amount to*) zählen; **be numbered among** zählen zu; **n. among** zählen zu

numberless ['nʌmbərlɪs] *adj* zahllos

num'bers game' *s* Zahlenlotto *n*

numbness ['nʌmnɪs] *s* Taubheit *f*; (*from cold*) Starrheit *f*

numeral ['n(j)umərəl] *adj* Zahl- ‖ *s* Zahl *f*, Ziffer *f*; (gram) Zahlwort *n*

numerator ['n(j)umə‚retər] *s* Zähler *m*

numerical [n(j)u'merɪkəl] *adj* numerisch; **n. order** Zahlenfolge *f*; **n. superiority** Überzahl *f*; **n. value** Zahlenwert *m*

numerous ['n(j)umərəs] *adj* zahlreich

numismatic [‚n(j)umɪz'mætɪk] *adj* numismatisch ‖ **numismatics** *s* Münzkunde *f*

numskull ['nʌm‚skʌl] *s* Dummkopf *m*

nun [nʌn] *s* Nonne *f*

nunci·o ['nʌn/i·o] *s* (**-os**) Nuntius *m*

nuptial ['nʌp/əl] *adj* Braut-, Hochzeits- ‖ **nuptials** *spl* Trauung *f*

Nuremberg ['n(j)urəm‚bʌrg] *s* Nürnberg *n*

nurse [nʌrs] *s* Krankenschwester *f*; (*male*) Krankenpfleger *m*; (*wet nurse*) Amme *f* ‖ *tr* (*the sick*) pflegen; (*a child*) stillen; (*hopes*) hegen; **n. a cold** e-e Erkältung kurieren

nurse'maid' *s* Kindermädschen *n*

nursery ['nʌrsəri] *s* Kinderstube *f*; (*for day care*) Kindertagesstätte *f*; (hort) Baumschule *f*, Pflanzschule *f*

nurs'ery rhyme' *s* Kinderlied *n*

nurs'ery school' *s* Kindergarten *m*

nurse'ry's aide' *s* Schwesterhelferin *f*

nurs'ing *s* (*as a profession*) Krankenpflege *f*; (*of a person*) Pflege *f*; (*of a baby*) Stillen *n*

nurs'ing home' *s* Pflegeheim *n*

nurture ['nʌrt/ər] *s* Nahrung *f* ‖ *tr* (er)nähren

nut [nʌt] *s* Nuß *f*; (sl) verrückter Kerl *m*; (mach) Mutter *f*, Schraubenmutter *f*; **be nuts** (sl) verrückt sein; **be nuts about** (sl) vernarrt sein in (*acc*); **go nuts** (sl) e-n Klaps kriegen

nut'crack'er *s* Nußknacker *m*

nutmeg ['nʌt‚meg] *s* (*spice*) Muskatnuß *f*; (*tree*) Muskat *m*

nutrient ['nutri·ənt] *s* Nährstoff *m*

nutriment ['n(j)utrimənt] *s* Nährstoff *m*

nutrition [n(j)u'trɪ/ən] *s* Ernährung *f*

nutritious [n(j)u'trɪ/əs] *adj* nahrhaft

nutritive ['n(j)utrɪtɪv] *adj* nahrhaft, Nähr-

nut'shell' *s* Nußschale *f*; **in a n.** mit wenigen Worten

nutty ['nʌti] *adj* nußartig; (sl) spleenig, verrückt

nuzzle ['nʌzəl] *tr* sich mit der Schnauze (or Nase) reiben an (*dat*) ‖ *intr* (*burrow*) mit der Schnauze wühlen; **n. up to** sich anschmiegen an (*acc*)

nylon ['naɪlɑn] *s* Nylon *n*

nymph [nɪmf] *s* Nymphe *f*

nymphomaniac [‚nɪmfə'meni·æk] *s* Nymphomanin *f*

O

O, o [o] fünfzehnter Buchstabe des englischen Alphabets

oaf [of] *s* Tölpel *m*

oak [ok] *adj* eichen ‖ *s* Eiche *f*

oak' leaf' clus'ter *s* Eichenlaub *n*

oak' tree' *s* Eichbaum *m*

oakum ['okəm] *s* Werg *n*

oar [or], [ər] *s* Ruder *n*, Riemen *m*

oar'lock' s Ruderdolle f

oars'man' s (**-men'**) Ruderer m

oa·sis [o'esis] s (**-ses** [siz]) Oase f

oath [oθ] s (**oaths** [oðz]) Eid m; o. of allegiance Treueid m; o. of office Amtseid m; under o. eidlich

oat'meal' s Hafergrütze f, Hafermehl n

oats [ots] spl Hafer m; he's feeling his o. (coll) ihn sticht der Hafer; sow one's wild o. (coll) sich [dat] die Hörner ablaufen

obbligato [,ɑblɪ'gato] adj hauptstimmig || s Obligato m

obdurate ['ɑbdjərɪt] adj verstockt

obedience [o'bidɪ·əns] s (to) Gehorsam m (gegenüber dat, gegen); blind o. Kadavergehorsam m

obedient [o'bidɪ·ənt] adj (to) gehorsam (dat)

obeisance [o'bisəns] s Ehrerbietung f

obelisk ['ɑbəlɪsk] s Obelisk m

obese [o'bis] adj fettleibig

obesity [o'bisɪti] s Fettleibigkeit f

obey [o'be] tr gehorchen (dat); (a law, order) befolgen || intr gehorchen

obfuscate [ɑb'fʌsket] tr verdunkeln

obituary [o'bɪtʃu,ɛri] adj Todes- || s Todesanzeige f, Nachruf m

object ['ɑbdʒɪkt] s Gegenstand m; (aim) Ziel n, Zweck m; (gram) Ergänzung f, Objekt n; money is no o. Geld spielt keine Rolle || [ɑb'dʒɛkt] intr (to) Einwände erheben (gegen)

objection [ɑb'dʒɛkʃən] s Einwand m; I have no o. to his staying ich habe nichts dagegen (einzuwenden), daß er bleibe

objectionable [ɑb'dʒɛkʃənəbəl] adj nicht einwandfrei

objective [ɑb'dʒɛktɪv] adj sachlich, objektiv || s Ziel n

objec'tive case' s Objektsfall m

ob'ject les'son s Lehre f

obligate ['ɑblɪ,get] tr verpflichten; be obligated to s.o. j-m zu Dank verbunden sein

obligation [,ɑblɪ'geʃən] s Verpflichtung f

obligatory ['ɑblɪgə,tori], [ə'blɪgə,tori] adj verpflichtend, obligatorisch

oblige [ə'blaɪdʒ] tr (bind) verpflichten; (do a favor to) gefällig sein (dat); be obliged to (inf) müssen (inf); feel obliged to (inf) sich bemüßigt fühlen zu (inf); I'm much obliged to you ich bin Ihnen sehr verbunden

oblig'ing adj gefällig

oblique [ə'blik] adj schief

obliterate [ə'blɪtə,ret] tr auslöschen; (traces) verwischen; (writing) unleserlich machen

oblivion [ə'blɪvɪ·ən] s Vergessenheit f

oblivious [ə'blɪvɪ·əs] adj—be o. of sich [dat] nicht bewußt sein (genit)

oblong ['ɑblɔŋ] adj länglich || s Rechteck n

obnoxious [əb'nɑkʃəs] adj widerlich

oboe ['obo] s Oboe f

oboist ['obo·ɪst] s Oboist –in mf

obscene [ɑb'sin] adj obszön

obscenity [ɑb'sɛnɪti] s Obszönität f

obscure [əb'skjur] adj dunkel, obskur || tr verdunkeln

obscurity [əb'skjurɪti] s Dunkelheit f

obsequies ['ɑbsɪkwiz] spl Totenfeier f

obsequious [əb'sikwɪ·əs] adj unterwürfig

observance [əb'zʌrvəns] s Beachtung f, Befolgung f; (celebration) Feier f

observant [əb'zʌrvənt] adj beobachtend

observation [,ɑbzər've/ən] s Beobachtung f; keep under o. beobachten

observa'tion tow'er s Aussichtsturm m

observatory [əb'zʌrvə,tori] s Sternwarte f, Observatorium n

observe [əb'zʌrv] tr (a person, rules) beobachten; (a holiday) feiern; o. silence Stillschweigen bewahren

obsess [əb'sɛs] tr verfolgen; obsessed (by) besessen (von)

obsession [əb'sɛ/ən] s Besessenheit f

obsolescent [,ɑbsə'lɛsənt] adj veraltend

obsolete ['ɑbsə,lit] adj veraltet; become o. veralten

obstacle ['ɑbstəkəl] s Hindernis n

ob'stacle course' s Hindernisbahn f

obstetrical [ɑb'stɛtrɪkəl] adj Geburtshilfe-, Entbindungs-

obstetrician [,ɑbstə'trɪ/ən] s Geburtshelfer –in mf

obstetrics [ɑb'stɛtrɪks] s Geburtshilfe f

obstinacy ['ɑbstɪnəsi] s Starrheit f

obstinate ['ɑbstɪnɪt] adj starr

obstreperous [əb'strɛpərəs] adj (clamorous) lärmend; (unruly) widerspenstig

obstruct [əb'strʌkt] tr (e.g., a pipe) verstopfen; (a view, way) versperren; (traffic) behindern; o. justice die Rechtspflege behindern

obstruction [əb'strʌk/ən] s (of a view, way) Versperrung f; (of traffic) Behinderung f; (obstacle) Hindernis n; (parl, pathol) Obstruktion f

obtain [əb'ten] tr erhalten, erlangen || intr bestehen

obtrusive [əb'trusɪv] adj aufdringlich

obtuse [əb't(j)us] adj (fig & fig) stumpf

obviate ['ɑbvɪ,et] tr erübrigen

obvious ['ɑbvɪ·əs] adj naheliegend; it is o. es liegt auf der Hand

occasion [ə'keʒən] s Gelegenheit f; (reason) Anlaß m; on o. gelegentlich; on the o. of anläßlich (genit) || tr veranlassen

occasional [ə'keʒənəl] adj gelegentlich

occasionally [ə'keʒənəli] adv gelegentlich, zuweilen

occident ['ɑksɪdənt] s Abendland n

occidental [,ɑksɪ'dɛntəl] adj abendländisch || s Abendländer –in mf

occlusion [ə'kluʒən] s Okklusion f

occult [ə'kʌlt] adj geheim, okkult

occupancy ['ɑkjəpənsi] s Besitz m, Besitzergreifung f; (of a home) Einzug m

occupant ['ɑkjəpənt] s Besitzer –in mf; (of a home) Inhaber –in mf; (of a car) Insasse m, Insassin f

occupation [,ɑkjə'pe/ən] s (employ-

ment) Beruf *m*, Beschäftigung *f*;
(mil) Besetzung *f*, Besatzung *f*
occup'ational disease' [ˌɒkjəˈpeʃənəl]
s Berufskrankheit *f*
occupa'tional ther'apy *s* Beschäftigungstherapie *f*
occupa'tion troops' *spl* Besatzungstruppen *pl*
occu·py [ˈɒkjəˌpaɪ] *v* (*pret & pp* –**pied**)
tr in Besitz nehmen; (*a house*) bewohnen; (*time*) in Anspruch nehmen; (*keep busy*) beschäftigen; (mil) besetzen; **occupied** (*said of a seat or toilet*) besetzt; (*said of a person*) beschäftigt; **o. oneself with** sich befassen mit
oc·cur [əˈkʌr] *v* (*pret & pp* –**curred**; *ger* –**curring**) *intr* sich ereignen; (*come to mind*) (**to**) einfallen (*dat*)
occurrence [əˈkʌrəns] *s* Ereignis *n*; (*e.g., of a word*) Vorkommen *n*
ocean [ˈoʃən] *s* Ozean *m*
oceanic [ˌoʃɪˈænɪk] *adj* Ozean-, ozeanisch
o'cean lin'er *s* Ozeandampfer *m*
oceanography [ˌoʃənˈɒgrəfɪ] *s* Ozeanographie *f*
ocher [ˈokər] *s* Ocker *m & n*
o'clock [əˈklɑk] *adv* Uhr; **at ... o'clock** um ... Uhr
octane [ˈɑkten] *s* Oktan *m*
oc'tane num'ber *s* Oktanzahl *f*
octave [ˈɑktɪv], [ˈɑktev] *s* Oktave *f*
October [ɑkˈtobər] *s* Oktober *m*
octogenarian [ˌɑktədʒɪˈnɛrɪ·ən] *s* Achtzige *mf*
octo·pus [ˈɑktəpəs] *s* (–**puses** & –**pi** [ˌpaɪ]) Seepolyp *m*
ocular [ˈɑkjələr] *adj* Augen-
oculist [ˈɑkjəlɪst] *s* Augenarzt *m*, Augenärztin *f*
odd [ɑd] *adj* (*strange*) seltsam, eigenartig; (*number*) ungerade; (*e.g., glove*) einzeln; **two hundred odd pages** etwas über zweihundert Seiten || **odds** *spl* (*probability*) Wahrscheinlichkeit *f*; (*advantage*) Vorteil *m*; (*in gambling*) Vorgabe *f*; **at odds** uneinig; **lay** (*or* **give**) **odds** vorgeben; **the odds are two to one** die Chancen stehen zwei zu eins
odd' ball' *s* (sl) Sonderling *m*
oddity [ˈɑdɪtɪ] *s* Seltsamkeit *f*
odd' jobs' *spl* Gelegenheitsarbeit *f*; (*chores*) kleine Aufgaben *pl*
odds' and ends' *spl* Kleinkram *m*
ode [od] *s* Ode *f*
odious [ˈodɪ·əs] *adj* verhaßt
odor [ˈodər] *s* Duft *m*, Geruch *m*; **be in bad o.** in schlechtem Ruf stehen
odorless [ˈodərlɪs] *adj* geruchlos
odyssey [ˈɑdɪsɪ] *s* Irrfahrt *f*; **Odyssey** Odyssee *f*
of [ɑv], [əv] *prep* von (*dat*); genit, *e.g.,* **the name of the dog** der Name des Hundes
off [ɒf] *adj* (*free from work*) dienstfrei; (*poor, bad*) schlecht; (*electric current*) ausgeschaltet, abgeschaltet; **be badly off** in schlechten Verhältnissen sein; **be off** (*said of a clock*) nachgehen; (*said of a measurement*)

falsch sein; (*said of a person*) im Irrtum sein; (*be crazy*) nicht ganz richtig im Kopf sein; **be well off** in guten Verhältnissen sein; **the deal** (*or* **party**) **is off** es ist aus mit dem Geschäft (*or* mit der Party) || *adv* (*distant*) weg; **he was off in a flash** er war im Nu weg; **I must be off** ich muß fort || *prep* von (*dat*); **off duty** außer Dienst; **off limits** Zutritt verboten
offal [ˈɒfəl] *s* (*refuse*) Abfall *m*; (*of butchered meat*) Innereien *pl*
off' and on' *adv* ab und zu
off'beat' *adj* (sl) ungewöhnlich
off' chance' *s* geringe Chance *f*
off'-col'or *adj* schlüpfrig
off'-du'ty *adj* außerdienstlich
offend [əˈfɛnd] *tr* beleidigen || *intr*—**o. against** verstoßen gegen
offender [əˈfɛndər] *s* Missetäter –in *mf*; **first o.** nicht Vorbestrafte *mf*; **second o.** Vorbestrafte *mf*
offense [əˈfɛns] *s* (**against**) Vergehen *n* (gegen); **give o.** Anstoß geben; **no o.!** nichts für ungut!; **take o.** (**at**) Anstoß nehmen (an *dat*)
offensive [əˈfɛnsɪv] *adj* anstößig; (*odor*) ekelhaft; (*action*) offensiv || *s* Offensive *f*; **take the o.** die Offensive ergreifen
offer [ˈɒfər] *s* Angebot *n* || *tr* anbieten; (*a price*) bieten; (*help, resistance*) leisten; (*friendship*) schenken; **o. an excuse** e-e Entschuldigung vorbringen; **o. as an excuse** als Entschuldigung vorbringen; **o. for sale** feilbieten; **o. one's services** sich anbieten; **o. up** aufopfern || *intr*—**o. to** (*inf*) sich erbieten zu (*inf*)
of'fering [ˈɒfərɪŋ] *s* (*act*) Opferung *f*; (*gift*) Opfergabe *f*
offertory [ˈɒfərˌtorɪ] *s* Offertorium *n*
off'hand' *adj* (*excuse*) unvorbereitet; (*manner*) lässig || *adv* kurzerhand
office [ˈɒfɪs] *s* (*room*) Büro *n*, Amt *n*; (*position*) Amt *n*; (*of a doctor*) Sprechzimmer *n*; **be in o.** amtieren; **through the good offices of** durch die freundliche Vermittlung (*genit*); **run for o.** für ein Amt kandidieren
of'fice boy' *s* Bürojunge *m*
of'fice build'ing *s* Bürogebäude *n*
of'ficehold'er *s* Amtsträger –in *mf*
of'fice hours' *spl* Dienststunden *pl*; (*of a doctor, lawyer*) Sprechstunde *f*
officer [ˈɒfɪsər] *s* (adm) Beamte *m*, Beamtin *f*; (com) Direktor –in *mf*; (mil) Offizier –in *mf*
of'ficer can'didate *s* Offiziersanwärter –in *mf*
of'ficers' mess' *s* Offizierskasino *n*; (nav) Offiziersmesse *f*
of'fice seek'er *s* Amtsbewerber –in *mf*
of'fice supplies' *spl* Bürobedarf *m*
of'fice work' *s* Büroarbeit *f*
official [əˈfɪʃəl] *adj* amtlich; (*in line of duty*) Dienst-; (*visit*) offiziell; (*document*) öffentlich; **on o. business** dienstlich || *s* Beamte *m*, Beamtin *f*; **top officials** Spitzenkräfte *pl*
offi'cial busi'ness *s* Dienstsache *f*

offi′cial call′ s (telp) Dienstgespräch n

officialdom [ə′fɪʃəldəm] s Beamtentum n

officialese [ə‚fɪʃə′liz] s Amtssprache f

officially [ə′fɪʃəli] adv offiziell

offi′cial use′ s Dienstgebrauch m

officiate [ə′fɪʃɪ‚et] intr amtieren; o. at a marriage e-n Traugottesdienst halten

officious [ə′fɪʃəs] adj dienstbeflissen

offing [′ɔfɪŋ] s—in the o. in Aussicht

off′-lim′its adj gesperrt

off′print′ s Abdruck m, Sonderdruck m

off′-seas′on adj—o. prices Preise pl während der Vor- und Nachsaison ‖ s Vor- und Nachsaison f

off′set′ s (compensation) Ausgleich m; (typ) Offsetdruck m ‖ off′set′ v (pret –set; ger –setting) tr ausgleichen

off′set press′ s Offsetdruck m

off′shoot′ s Ableger m

off′shore′ adj küstennah

off′side′ adv (sport) abseits

off′spring′ s Sprößling m

off′stage′ adj hinter der Bühne befindlich ‖ adv hinter der Bühne

off′-the-cuff′ adj aus dem Stegreif

off′-the-rec′ord adj im Vertrauen

often [′ɔfən] adv oft, häufig; every so o. von Zeit zu Zeit; quite o. öfters

of′tentimes′ adv oftmals

ogive [′odʒaɪv] s (diagonal vaulting rib) Gratrippe f; (pointed arch) Spitzbogen m

ogle [′ogəl] tr liebäugeln mit ‖ intr liebäugeln

ogre [′ogər] s Scheusal n; (myth) Menschenfresser m

oh [o] interj oh!; oh, dear! o weh!

ohm [om] s Ohm n

oil [ɔɪl] s Öl n; strike oil auf Öl stoßen ‖ tr ölen

oil′ burn′er s Ölbrenner m

oil′can′ s Ölkanne f

oil′cloth′ s Wachsleinwand f

oil′ col′or s Ölfarbe f

oil′ drum′ s Ölfaß n

oil′ field′ s Ölfeld n

oil′ gauge′ s Ölstandsanzeiger m

oil′ heat′ s Ölheizung f

oil′ lev′el s Ölstand m

oil′man′ s (–men′) Ölhändler m

oil′ paint′ing s Ölgemälde n

oil′ pres′sure s Öldruck m

oil′ rig′ s Ölbohrinsel f

oil′ shale′ s Ölschiefer m

oil′ slick′ s Öllache f

oil′ tank′ s Ölbehälter m

oil′ tank′er s Öltanker m

oil′ well′ s Ölquelle f

oily [′ɔɪli] adj ölig; (unctious) salbungsvoll

ointment [′ɔɪntmənt] s Salbe f

O.K. [′o′ke] adj in Ordnung, okay ‖ s Billigung f ‖ v (pret & pp O.K.′d; ger O.K.′ing) tr billigen ‖ intr okay!

old [old] adj alt; as old as the hills uralt; (said of a person) steinalt

old′ age′ s Alter n, Greisenalter n

old′-age′ home′ s Altersheim n

old′ coun′try s Heimatland n

olden [′oldən] adj alt

old′-fash′ioned adj altmodisch

old′ fog′(e)y [′fogi] s alter Kauz m

Old′ Glo′ry s Sternenbanner n

old′ hand′ s alter Hase m

old′ hat′ adj bärtig

old′ la′dy s Greisin f; (wife) (pej) Alte f

old′ maid′ s alte Jungfer f

old′ man′ s Greis m; (mil) Alter m

old′ mas′ter s (paint) alter Meister m

old′ moon′ s letztes Viertel n

old′ salt′ s alter Seebär m

oldster [′oldstər] s alter Knabe m

Old′ Tes′tament s Altes Testament n

old′-time′ adj altväterisch

old′-tim′er s (coll) alter Hase m

old′ wives′/ tale′ s Altweibergeschichte f

Old′ World′ s alte Welt f

oleander [‚oli′ændər] s Oleander m

olfactory [al′fæktəri] adj Geruchs–

oligarchy [′alɪ‚garki] s Oligarchie f

olive [′alɪv] s Olive f

ol′ive branch′ s Ölzweig m

ol′ive grove′ s Olivenhain m

ol′ive oil′ s Olivenöl n

ol′ive tree′ s Olivenbaum m, Olivenbaum m

olympiad [o′lɪmpi‚æd] s Olympiade f

Olympian [o′lɪmpi·ən] adj olympisch

Olympic [o′lɪmpɪk] adj olympisch ‖ the Olympics spl die Olympischen Spiele

omelet, omelette [′amə‚let] s Eierkuchen m, Omelett n

omen [′omən] s Omen n, Vorzeichen n

ominous [′amɪnəs] adj ominös, unheilvoll

omission [o′mɪʃən] s Auslassung f; (of a deed) Unterlassung f

omit [o′mɪt] v (pret & pp omitted; ger omitting) tr (a word) auslassen; (a deed) unterlassen; be omitted ausfallen; o. (ger) es unterlassen zu (inf)

omnibus [′amnɪ‚bʌs] adj Sammel–, Mantel– ‖ s Omnibus m, Autobus m

omnipotent [am′nɪpətənt] adj allmächtig

omnipresent [‚amnɪ′prezənt] adj allgegenwärtig

omniscient [am′nɪʃənt] adj allwissend

on [on] adj (in progress) im Gange; (light, gas, water) an; (radio, television) angestellt; (switch) eingeschaltet; (brakes) angezogen; be on to s.o. j-n durchsehen; be on to s.th. über etw [acc] im Bilde sein ‖ adv weiter; on and off dann und wann; on and on in e-m fort ‖ prep auf (dat or acc), an (dat or acc); (concerning) über (acc)

once [wʌns] adv einmal; (formerly) einst; at o. auf einmal; (immediately) sofort; o. not ein einziges Mal; o. and for all ein für allemal; o. before früher einmal; o. in a while ab und zu; o. more noch einmal; o. upon a time there was es war einmal ‖ s—this o. dieses (eine) Mal ‖ conj sobald

once′-o′ver—give (s.o. or s.th.) the o. rasch mustern

one [wʌn] adj ein; (one certain, e.g.,

Mr. Smith) ein gewisser; **for one thing** zunächst; **her one care** ihre einzige Sorge; **it's all one to me** es ist mir ganz gleich; **one and a half hours** anderthalb Stunden; **one day** e–s Tages; **one more** noch ein; **one more thing** noch etwas; **one o'clock** ein Uhr, eins; **on the one hand ... on the other** einerseits ... andererseits ‖ *s* Eins *f* ‖ *pron* einer; **I for one** was mich betrifft, ich jedenfalls; **one after another** einer nach dem anderen; **one after the other** nacheinander; **one another** einander, sich; **one at a time, please!** einer nach dem anderen, bitte!; **one behind the other** hintereinander; **one by one** einer nach dem anderen; **one of these days** früher oder später; **one on top of the other** übereinander, aufeinander; **one to nothing** eins zu Null; **this one** dieser da, der da; **with one another** miteinander ‖ *indef pron* man; **one's** sein

one'-armed' *adj* einarmig

one'-eyed' *adj* einäugig

one'-horse town' *s* Kuhdorf *n*

one'-leg'ged *adj* einbeinig

onerous ['ɒnərəs] *adj* lästig

oneself' *reflex pron* sich; **be o.** sein, wie man immer ist; **by o.** allein; **to o.** vor sich [*acc*] hin

one'-sid'ed *adj* (& *fig*) einseitig

one'-track' *adj* eingleisig; (*fig*) einseitig

one'-way street' *s* Einbahnstraße *f*

one'-way tick'et *s* einfache Fahrkarte *f*

one'-week' *adj* achttägig

onion ['ʌnjən] *s* Zwiebel *f*; **know one's onions** (coll) Bescheid wissen

on'ionskin' *s* Durchschlagpapier *n*

on'look'er *s* Zuschauer –in *mf*

only ['onlɪ] *adj* (son, hope) einzig ‖ *adv* nur; **not only ... but also** nicht nur ... sondern auch; **o. too** nur (all)zu; **o. too well** zur Genüge; **o. yesterday** erst gestern ‖ *conj* aber; **o. that** nur daß

on'ly-begot'ten *adj* eingeboren

onomatopoeia [,ɑnə,mætə'pi·ə] *s* Lautmalerei *f*

on'-ramp' *s* Zufahrtsrampe *f*

on'rush' *s* Ansturm *m*

on'set' *s* Anfang *m*; (attack) Angriff *m*

onslaught ['ɒn,slɔt] *s* Angriff *m*

on'to *prep* auf (acc) hinauf; **be o. s.o.** hinter j–s Schliche kommen; **be o. s.th.** über etw [*acc*] im Bilde sein

onus ['onəs] *s* Last *f*; **o. of proof** Beweislast *f*

onward(s) ['ɒnwərd(z)] *adv* vorwärts

onyx ['ɒnɪks] *s* Onyx *m*

oodles ['udəlz] *spl* (coll) (of) Unmengen *pl* (von)

ooze [uz] *s* Sickern *n*; (mud) Schlamm *m* ‖ *tr* ausschwitzen ‖ *intr* sickern; **o. out** durchsickern

opal ['opəl] *s* Opal *m*

opaque [o'pek] *adj* undurchsichtig; (stupid) stumpf

open ['opən] *adj* (window, position, sea, question, vowel) offen; (air, field, seat) frei; (business, office)

geöffnet; (seam) geplatzt; (account) laufend; (meeting) öffentlich; **be o.** offenstehen; **get o.** aufbekommen; **have an o. mind** about s.th. sich noch nicht auf etw [*acc*] festgelegt haben; **keep o.** offenhalten; **lay oneself o. to** sich aussetzen (dat); **o. to** (the public) zugänglich (dat); (criticism) ausgesetzt (dat); (doubt) unterworfen (dat); **o. to bribery** bestechlich; **to question** strittig ‖ *s*—**come out into the o.** (fig) mit seinen Gedanken herauskommen; **in the o.** im Freien ‖ *tr* öffnen, aufmachen; (a business, account, meeting, hostilities, fire) eröffnen; (a book) aufschlagen; (eyes in surprise) aufreißen; (a box, bottle) anbrechen; (an umbrella) aufspannen; **o. the attack** losschlagen; **o. to traffic** dem Verkehr übergeben; **o. wide** weit aufreißen ‖ *intr* sich öffnen, aufgehen; (said of a school, speech, play) beginnen; **o. into** ausgehen auf (acc); **o. onto** hinausgehen auf (acc); **o. up** sich auftun; **o. with hearts** (cards) Herz ausspielen

o'pen-air' *adj* Freiluft–; (theat) Freilicht–; **o. concert** Konzert *n* im Freien

opener ['opənər] *s* Öffner *m*, **for openers** (coll) für den Anfang

o'pen-eyed' *adj* mit offenen Augen

o'pen-hand'ed *adj* freigebig

o'pen-heart'ed *adj* offenherzig

o'pen house' *s* allgemeiner Besuchstag *m*

o'pening *adj* (scene) erste; (remarks) Eröffnungs– ‖ *s* Öffnung *f*; (of a speech, play) Anfang *m*; (of a store, etc.) Eröffnung *f*; (vacant job) freie (or offene) Stelle *f*; (in the woods) Lichtung *f*; (good opportunity) günstige Gelegenheit *f*; (theat) Erstaufführung *f*

o'pening night' *s* Eröffnungsvorstellung *f*, Premiere *f*

o'pening num'ber *s* erstes Stück *n*

o'pen-mind'ed *adj* aufgeschlossen

openness ['opənnɪs] *s* Offenheit *f*

o'pen sea'son *s* Jagdzeit *f*

o'pen se'cret *s* offenes Geheimnis *n*

o'pen shop' *s* offener Betrieb *m* (für den kein Gewerkschaftszwang besteht)

opera ['ɑpərə] *s* Oper *f*

op'era glass'es *spl* Opernglas *n*

op'era house' *s* Opernhaus *n*

operate ['ɑpə,ret] *tr* (a machine, gun) bedienen; (a tool) handhaben; (a business) betreiben; **be operated by electricity** elektrisch betrieben werden ‖ *intr* (said of a device, machine) funktionieren, laufen; (surg) operieren, o. on (surg) operieren

operatic [,ɑpə'rætɪk] *adj* opernhaft

op'erating cost' *spl* Betriebskosten *pl*

op'erating instruc'tions *spl* Bedienungsanweisung *f*

op'erating room' *s* Operationssaal *m*

op'erating ta'ble *s* Operationstisch *m*

operation [,ɑpə're/ən] *s* (process) Verfahren *n*; (of a machine) Bedienung *f;* (*of a business*) Leitung *f;* (mil) Operation *f,* Aktion *f;* (surg) Operation *f;* **be in o.** (*said of a machine*) in Betrieb sein; (*said of a law*) in Kraft sein; **have** (or **undergo**) **an o.** sich e–r Operation unterziehen; **in a single o.** in e–m einzigen Arbeitsgang; **put into o.** in Betrieb setzen

operational [,ɑpəˈreʃənəl] *adj* (*ready to be used*) betriebsbereit; (*pertaining to operations*) Betriebs– Arbeits–; (mil) Einsatz–, Operations–

opera'tions room' *s* (aer) Bereitschaftsraum *m*

operative [ˈɑpərətɪv] *adj* funktionsfähig, wirkend; **become o.** in Kraft treten ‖ *s* Agent –in *mf*

operator [ˈɑpəˌretər] *s* (*of a machine*) Bedienende *mf;* (*of an automobile*) Fahrer –in *mf;* (sl) Schieber –in *mf;* (telp) Telephonist –in *mf;* **o.!** (telp) Zentrale!

op'erator's li'cense *s* Führerschein *m*

operetta [,ɑpəˈretə] *s* Operette *f*

ophthalmologist [,ɑfθəlˈmɑlədʒɪst] *s* Augenarzt *m,* Augenärztin *f*

ophthalmology [,ɑfθəlˈmɑlədʒi] *s* Augenheilkunde *f,* Ophthalmologie *f*

opiate [ˈopɪˌet] *s* Opiat *n;* (fig) Betäubungsmittel *n*

opinion [əˈpɪnjən] *s* Meinung *f;* **be of the o.** der Meinung sein; **give an o. on** begutachten; **have a high o. of** große Stücke halten auf (*acc*); **in my o.** meiner Meinung nach, meines Erachtens

opinionated [əˈpɪnjəˌnetɪd] *adj* von sich eingenommen

opin'ion poll' *s* Meinungsumfrage *f*

opium [ˈopɪəm] *s* Opium *n*

o'pium den' *s* Opiumhöhle *f*

o'pium pop'py *s* Schlafmohn *m*

opossum [əˈpɑsəm] *s* Opossum *n*

opponent [əˈponənt] *s* Gegner –in *mf*

opportune [,ɑpərˈt(j)un] *adj* gelegen

opportunist [,ɑpərˈt(j)unɪst] *s* Opportunist –in *mf*

opportunity [,ɑpərˈt(j)unɪti] *s* Gelegenheit *f*

oppose [əˈpoz] *tr* sich widersetzen (*dat*); (*for comparison*) gegenüberstellen; **be opposed to s.th.** gegen etw sein

oppos'ing *adj* (*team, forces*) gegnerisch; (*views*) entgegengesetzt

opposite [ˈɑpəsɪt] *adj* (*side, corner*) gegenüberliegend; (*meaning*) entgegengesetzt; (*view*) gegenteilig; **o. angle** (geom) Gegenwinkel *m;* **o. to** gegenüber (*dat*) ‖ *s* Gegensatz *m,* Gegenteil *n* ‖ *prep* gegenüber (*dat*)

op'posite num'ber *s* Gegenstück *n,* Gegenspieler –in *mf*

opposition [,ɑpəˈzɪʃən] *s* Widerstand *m;* (pol) Opposition *f;* **meet with stiff o.** auf heftigen Widerstand stoßen; **offer o.** Widerstand leisten

oppress [əˈpres] *tr* unterdrücken

oppression [əˈpreʃən] *s* Unterdrückung *f*

oppressive [əˈpresɪv] *adj* bedrückend

oppressor [əˈpresər] *s* Unterdrücker –in *mf*

opprobrious [əˈprobrɪ·əs] *adj* schändlich

opprobrium [əˈprobrɪ·əm] *s* Schande *f*

opt [ɑpt] *intr*—**opt for** optieren für

optic [ˈɑptɪk] *adj* Augen– ‖ **optics** *s* Optik *f*

optical [ˈɑptɪkəl] *adj* optisch

op'tical illus'ion *s* optische Täuschung *f*

optician [ɑpˈtɪʃən] *s* Optiker –in *mf*

op'tic nerve' *s* Augennerv *m*

optimism [ˈɑptɪˌmɪzəm] *s* Optimismus *m*

optimist [ˈɑptɪmɪst] *s* Optimist –in *mf*

optimistic [,ɑptɪˈmɪstɪk] *adj* optimistisch

option [ˈɑpʃən] *s* (*choice*) Wahl *f;* (*alternative*) Alternative *f;* (ins) Option *f*

optional [ˈɑpʃənəl] *adj* wahlfrei; **be o.** freistehen

optometrist [ɑpˈtɑmɪtrɪst] *s* Augenoptiker –in *mf*

optometry [ɑpˈtɑmɪtri] *s* Optometrie *f*

opulent [ˈɑpjələnt] *adj* (*wealthy*) reich; (*luxurious*) üppig

or [ɔr] *conj* oder

oracle [ˈɔrəkəl] *s* Orakel *n*

oracular [oˈrækjələr] *adj* orakelhaft

oral [ˈɔrəl] *adj* mündlich

o'ral hygiene' *s* Mundpflege *f*

orange [ˈɔrɪndʒ] *adj* orange ‖ *s* Orange *f,* Apfelsine *f*

orangeade [,ɔrɪndʒˈed] *s* Orangeade *f*

or'ange blos'som *s* Orangenblüte *f*

or'ange grove' *s* Orangenhain *m*

or'ange tree' *s* Orangenbaum *m*

orang-outang [oˈræŋuˌtæŋ] *s* Orang-Utan *m*

oration [oˈreʃən] *s* Rede *f*

orator [ˈɔrətər] *s* Redner –in *mf*

oratorical [,ɔrəˈtɔrɪkəl] *adj* rednerisch

oratori·o [ɔrəˈtɔrɪˌo] *s* (**–os**) Oratorium *n*

oratory [ˈɔrəˌtɔri] *s* Redekunst *f*

orb [ɔrb] *s* Kugel *f;* (*of the moon or sun*) Scheibe *f*

orbit [ˈɔrbɪt] *s* Umlaufbahn *f;* **send into o.** in die Umlaufbahn schicken ‖ *tr* umkreisen

orbital [ˈɔrbɪtəl] *adj* Kreisbahn–

orchard [ˈɔrtʃərd] *s* Obstgarten *m*

orchestra [ˈɔrkɪstrə] *s* Orchester *n*

or'chestra pit' *s* Orchesterraum *m*

orchestrate [ˈɔrkɪˌstret] *tr* orchestrieren

orchid [ˈɔrkɪd] *s* Orchidee *f*

ordain [ɔrˈden] *tr* verordnen; (eccl) ordinieren, zum Priester weihen

ordeal [ɔrˈdil] *s* Qual *f;* (hist) Gottesurteil *n,* **o. by fire** Feuerprobe *f*

order [ˈɔrdər] *s* (*command*) Befehl *m;* (*decree*) Verordnung *f;* (*order, arrangement*) Ordnung *f;* (*medal*) Orden *m;* (*sequence*) Reihenfolge *f;* (archit, bot, zool) Ordnung *f;* (com) (**for**) Auftrag *m* (auf *acc*), Bestellung *f* (auf *acc*); (eccl) Orden *m;* (jur) Beschluß *m;* **according to orders** befehlsgemäß; **be in good o.** in gutem

Zustand sein; **be the o. of the day** (coll) an der Tagesordnung sein; **be under orders to** (inf) Befehl haben zu (inf); **by o. of** auf Befehl von (or genit); **call to o.** (a meeting) für eröffnet erklären; (reestablish order) zur Ordnung rufen; **in o.** (functioning) in Ordnung; (proper, in place) angebracht; **in o.** of geordnet nach; **in o. that** damit; **in o. to** (inf) um ... zu (inf); **make to o.** nach Maß machen; **of a high o.** von ausgezeichneter Art; **on o.** (com) in Auftrag; **o.!, o.!** zur Ordnung! **out of o.** (defective) außer Betrieb; (not functioning at all) nicht in Ordnung; (disarranged) in Unordnung; (parl) im Widerspruch zur Geschäftsordnung, unzulässig; **put in o.** in Ordnung bringen; **restore to o.** die Ordnung wiederherstellen; **you are out of o.** Sie haben nicht das Wort || tr (command) befehlen, anordnen; (decree) verordnen; (com) bestellen; **as ordered** auftragsgemäß; **o. around** herumkommandieren; **o. in advance** vor(her)bestellen; **o. more** nachbestellen; **o. s.o. off** (e.g., the premises) j-n weisen von

or'der blank' s Auftragsformular n

orderliness ['ɔrdərlɪnɪs] s (of a person) Ordnungsliebe f; (of a room, etc.) Ordnung f

orderly ['ɔrdərli] adj ordentlich || s (med) Krankenwärter m; (mil) Bursche m

or'derly room' s (mil) Schreibstube f

or'der slip' s Bestellzettel m

ordinal ['ɔrdɪnəl] adj Ordnungs– || s Ordnungszahl f

ordinance ['ɔrdɪnəns] s Verfügung f; (of a city) Verordnung f

ordinary ['ɔrdɪ,nɛri] adj gewöhnlich; (member) ordentlich; **o. person** Alltagsmensch m || s Gewöhnliche n; (eccl) Ordinarius m; **nothing out of the o.** nichts Ungewöhnliches; **out of the o.** außerordentlich

ordination [,ɔrdɪ'neʃən] s Priesterweihe f

ordnance ['ɔrdnəns] s Waffen und Munition pl; (arti) Geschützwesen n

ore [or] s Erz n

organ ['ɔrgən] s (means) Werkzeug n; (publication) Organ n; (adm, biol) Organ n; (mus) Orgel f

organdy ['ɔrgəndi] s Organdy m

or'gan grind'er s Drehorgelspieler m

organic [ɔr'gænɪk] adj organisch

organism ['ɔrgə,nɪzəm] s Organismus m

organist ['ɔrgənɪst] s Organist –in mf

organization [,ɔrgənɪ'zeʃən] s Organisation f

organizational [,ɔrgənɪ'zeʃənəl] adj organisatorisch

organize ['ɔrgə,naɪz] tr organisieren

organizer ['ɔrgə,naɪzər] s Organisator –in mf

or'gan loft' s Orgelbühne f

orgasm ['ɔrgæzəm] s Orgasmus m

orgy ['ɔrdʒi] s Orgie f

Orient ['ori‿ənt] s Orient m || **orient** ['ori‿ent] tr orientieren

oriental [,ori'ɛntəl] adj orientalisch || **Oriental** s Orientale m, Orientalin f

orientation [,ori‿ən'teʃən] s Orientierung f; (of new staff members) Einführung f

orifice ['ɔrɪfɪs] s Öffnung f

origin ['ɔrɪdʒɪn] s Ursprung m; (of a person or word) Herkunft f

original [ə'rɪdʒɪnəl] adj ursprünglich; (first) Ur–; (novel, play) originell; (person) erfinderisch || s Original n

originality [ə,rɪdʒɪ'nælɪti] s Originalität f

ori'ginal research' s Quellenstudium n

ori'ginal sin' s Erbsünde f, Sündenfall m

originate [ə'rɪdʒɪ,net] tr hervorbringen; intr (from) entstehen (aus); **o. in** seinen Ursprung haben in (dat)

originator [ə'rɪdʒɪ,netər] s Urheber –in mf

oriole ['ori‿ol] s Goldamsel f, Pirol m

ormolu ['ɔrmə,lu] s Malergold n

ornament ['ɔrnəmənt] s Verzierung f, Schmuck m || ['ɔrnə,mɛnt] tr verzieren

ornamental [,ɔrnə'mɛntəl] adj Zier–

ornamentation [,ɔrnəmən'teʃən] s Verzierung f

ornate [ɔr'net] adj überladen; (speech) bilderreich

ornery ['ɔrnəri] adj (cantankerous) mürrisch; (vile) gemein

ornithology [,ɔrnɪ'θɑlədʒi] s Vogelkunde f, Ornithologie f

orphan ['ɔrfən] s Waise f; **become an o.** verwaisen

orphanage ['ɔrfənɪdʒ] s Waisenhaus n

or'phaned adj verwaist; **be o.** verwaisen

or'phans' court' s Vormundschaftsgericht n

orthodox ['ɔrθə,dɑks] adj orthodox

orthography [ɔr'θɑgrəfi] s Orthographie f, Rechtschreibung f

orthopedist [,ɔrθə'pidɪst] s Orthopäde m, Orthopädin f

oscillate ['ɑsɪ,let] intr schwingen

oscillation [,ɑsɪ'leʃən] s Schwingung f

oscillator ['ɑsɪ,letər] s Oszillator m

osier ['oʒər] s Korbweide f

osmosis [ɑs'mosɪs] s Osmose f

osprey ['ɑspri] s Fischadler m

ossi•fy ['ɑsɪ,faɪ] v (pret & pp **–fied**) tr verknöchern lassen || intr verknöchern

ostensible [ɑs'tɛnsɪbəl] adj vorgeblich

ostentation [,ɑstən'teʃən] s Zurschaustellung f, Prahlerei f

ostentatious [,ɑstən'teʃəs] adj prahlerisch, prunksüchtig

osteopath ['ɑstɪ‿ə,pæθ] s Osteopath –in mf

osteopathy [,ɑstɪ'ɑpəθi] s Osteopathie f

ostracism ['ɑstrə,sɪzəm] s Ächtung f; (hist) Scherbengericht n

ostracize ['ɑstrə,saɪz] tr verfemen

ostrich ['ɑstrɪtʃ] s Strauß m

Ostrogoth ['ɑstrə,gɑθ] s Ostgote m

other [ˈʌðər] *adj* andere, sonstig; among o. things unter anderem; every o. day jeden zweiten Tag; none o. than he kein anderer als er; on the o. hand andererseits; o. things being equal unter gleichen Voraussetzungen; someone or o. irgend jemand; some ... or o. irgendein; the o. day unlängst || *adv*—o. than anders als || *indef pron* andere; the others die anderen

otherwise [ˈʌðər‚waɪz] *adj* sonstig || *adv* sonst; I can't do o. ich kann nicht umhin; o. engaged anderweitig beschäftigt; think o. anders denken

otter [ˈɑtər] *s* Otter *m*; (*snake*) Otter *f*

Ottoman [ˈɑtəmən] *adj* osmanisch ||
ottoman *s* (*couch*) Ottomane *m*; (*cushioned stool*) Polsterschemel *m*; **O.** Osmane *m*

ouch [aʊtʃ] *interj* au!

ought [ɔt] *aux* used to express obligation, e.g., you o. to tell her Sie sollten es ihr sagen; they o. to have been here sie hätten hier sein sollen

ounce [aʊns] *s* Unze *f*

our [aʊr] *poss adj* unser

ours [aʊrz] *poss pron* der uns(e)rige, der uns(e)re, uns(e)rer; a friend of o. ein Freund von uns; this is o. das gehört uns

ourselves [aʊrˈselvz] *reflex pron* uns; we are by o. wir sind doch unter uns || *intens pron* selbst, selber

oust [aʊst] *tr* (**from**) verdrängen (aus); o. from office seines Amtes entheben

ouster [ˈaʊstər] *s* Amtsenthebung *f*

out [aʊt] *adj*—an evening out ein Ausgehabend *m*; be out (*of the house*) ausgegangen sein; (*said of a light, fire*) aus sein; (*said of a new book*) erschienen sein; (*said of a secret*) enthüllt sein; (*said of flowers*) aufgeblüht sein; (*said of a dislocated limb*) verrenkt sein; (*be out of style*) aus der Mode sein; (*be at an end*) aus sein; (*be absent from work*) der Arbeit fernbleiben; (*be on strike*) streiken; be out after s.o. hinter j-m her sein; be out for a good time dem Vergnügen nachgehen; be out on one's feet (*coll*) erledigt sein; be out ten marks zehn Mark eingebüßt haben; be out to (*inf*) darauf ausgehen (or aus sein) zu (*inf*); that's out das kommt nicht in Frage; the best thing out das Beste, was es gibt || *adv* (*gone forth; ended, terminated*) aus; out of (*curiosity, pity, etc.*) aus (*dat*); (*fear*) vor (*dat*); (*a certain number*) von (*dat*); (*deprived of*) beraubt (*genit*); out of breath außer Atem; out of money ohne Geld; out of place verlegt; (*not appropriate or proper*) unpassend; out of the window zum Fenster hinaus || *s* (*pretext*) Ausweg *m*; be on the outs with s.o. mit j-m auf gespanntem Fuße sein || *prep* aus (*dat*) || *interj* (*sport*) aus!; out with it! heraus damit!

out′ and away′ *adv* bei weitem

out′-and-out′ *adj* abgefeimt

out′-ar′gue *tr* in Grund und Boden argumentieren

out′bid′ *v* (*pret* –bid; *pp* –bid & –bidden; *ger* –bidding) *tr* überbieten

out′board mo′tor *s* Außenbordmotor *m*

out′bound′ *adj* nach auswärts bestimmt; (*traffic*) aus der Stadt fließend

out′break′ *s* Ausbruch *m*

out′build′ing *s* Nebengebäude *n*

out′burst′ *s* Ausbruch *m*; o. of anger Zornausbruch *m*

out′cast′ *adj* ausgestoßen || *s* Ausgestoßene *mf*

out′come′ *s* Ergebnis *n*

out′cry′ *s* Ausruf *m*; raise an o. ein Zetergeschrei erheben

out′dat′ed *adj* zeitlich überholt

out′dis′tance *tr* hinter sich [*dat*] lassen

out′do′ *v* (*pret* –did; *pp* –done) *tr* überbieten, übertreffen; not to be outdone by s.o. in zeal j-m nichts an Eifer nachgeben; o. oneself in sich überbieten in (*dat*)

out′door′ *adj* Außen—

out′doors′ *adv* draußen, im Freien || *s*—in the outdoors im Freien

out′door shot′ *s* (*phot*) Außenaufnahme *f*

out′door swim′ming pool′ *s* Freibad *n*

out′door the′ater *s* Naturtheater *n*

out′door toi′let *s* Abtritt *m*

outer [ˈaʊtər] *adj* äußere, Außen—

out′er ear′ *s* Ohrmuschel *f*

out′er gar′ment *s* Überkleid *n*

out′ermost′ *adj* äußerste

out′er space′ *s* Weltall *n*, Weltraum *m*

out′field′ *s* (*baseball*) Außenfeld *n*

out′fit′ *s* (*equipment*) Ausrüstung *f*; (*set of clothes*) Ausstattung *f*; (*uniform*) Kluft *f*; (*business firm*) Gesellschaft *f*; (*mil*) Einheit *f* || *v* (*pret* –fitted; *ger* –fitting) *tr* (*with equipment*) ausrüsten; (*with clothes*) neu ausstaffieren

out′flank′ *tr* überflügeln, umfassen

out′flow′ *s* Ausfluß *m*

out′go′ing *adj* (*sociable*) gesellig; (*officer*) bisherig; (*tide*) zurückgehend; (*train, plane*) abgehend

out′grow′ *v* (*pret* –grew; *pp* –grown) *tr* herauswachsen aus; (fig) entwachsen (*dat*)

out′growth′ *s* Auswuchs *m*; (fig) Folge *f*

out′ing *s* Ausflug *m*

outlandish [aʊtˈlændɪʃ] *adj* fremdartig; (*prices*) überhöht

out′last′ *tr* überdauern

out′law′ *s* Geächtete *mf* || *tr* ächten

out′lay′ *s* Auslage *f*, Kostenaufwand *m* || **out′lay′** *v* (*pret* & *pp* –laid) *tr* auslegen

out′let′ *s* (*for water*) Abfluß *m*, Ausfluß *m*; (fig) (*for*) Ventil *n* (für); (com) Absatzmarkt *m*; (elec) Steckdose *f*; find an o. for (fig) Luft machen (*dat*); no o. Sackgasse *f*

out′line′ *s* (*profile*) Umriß *m*; (*sketch*) Umrißzeichnung *f*; (*summary*) Grundriß *m*; rough o. knapper Umriß *m* || *tr* umreißen

out'live' *tr* überleben
out'look' *s* (*place giving a view*) Ausguck *m*; (*view from a place*) Ausblick *m*; (*point of view*) Anschauung *f*; (*prospects*) Aussichten *pl*
out'ly'ing *adj* Außen-
out'maneu'ver *tr* ausmanövrieren; (*fig*) überlisten
outmoded [ˌautˈmodɪd] *adj* unmodern
out'num'ber *tr* an Zahl übertreffen
out'-of-bounds' *adj* (*fig*) nicht in den Schranken; (*sport*) im Aus
out'-of-court' set'tlement *s* außergerichtlicher Vergleich *m*
out'-of-date' *adj* veraltet
out'-of-door' *adj* Außen-
out'-of-doors' *adj* Außen- ‖ *adv* im Freien, draußen ‖ *s*—in the o. im Freien
out'-of-pock'et *adj*—o. expenses Barauslagen *pl*
out' of print' vergriffen
out'-of-the-way' *adj* abgelegen
out' of tune' *adj* verstimmt
out' of work' *adj* arbeitslos, erwerbslos
out'pace' *tr* überholen
out'pa'tient *s* ambulant Behandelte *mf*
out'patient clin'ic *s* Ambulanz *f*
out'play' *tr* überspielen
out'point' *tr* (*sport*) nach Punkten schlagen
out'post' *s* (*mil*) Vorposten *m*
out'pour'ing *s* (& *fig*) Erguß *m*
out'put' *s* (*of a machine or factory*) Arbeitsleistung *f*; (*of a factory*) Produktion *f*; (*mech*) Nutzleistung *f*; (*min*) Förderung *f*
out'rage' *s* Unverschämtheit *f*; (*against*) Verletzung *f* (*genit*) ‖ *tr* gröblich beleidigen
outrageous [autˈredʒəs] *adj* unverschämt
out'rank' *tr* im Rang übertreffen
out'rid'er *s* Vorreiter *m*
outrigger [ˈautˌrɪgər] *s* Ausleger *m*; (*of a racing boat*) Outrigger *m*
out'right' *adj* (*lie, refusal*) glatt; (*loss*) total; (*frank*) offen ‖ *adv* (*completely*) völlig; (*without reserve*) ohne Vorbehalt; (*at once*) auf der Stelle; buy o. per Kasse kaufen; refuse o. glatt ablehnen
out'run' *v* (*pret* –ran; *pp* –run; *ger* –running) *tr* hinter sich [*dat*] lassen
out'sell' *v* (*pret* & *pp* –sold) *tr* e-n größeren Umsatz haben als
out'set' *s* Anfang *m*
out'shine' *v* (*pret* & *pp* –shone) *tr* überstrahlen
out'side' *adj* (*help, interference*) von außen; (*world, influence, impressions*) äußere; (*lane, work*) Außen- ‖ *adv* draußen ‖ *s* Außenseite *f*, Äußere *n*; at the (very) o. (aller-) höchstens; from the o. von außen ‖ *prep* außerhalb (*genit*)
outsider [ˌautˈsaɪdər] *s* Außenstehende *mf*; (*sport*) Außenseiter *m*
out'size' *adj* übergroß ‖ *s* Übergröße *f*
out'skirts' *spl* Randgebiet *n*, Stadtrand *m*

out'smart' *tr* überlisten
out'spo'ken *adj* freimütig
out'spread' *adj* (*legs*) gespreizt; (*arms, wings*) ausgebreitet
out'stand'ing *adj* hervorragend, profiliert; (*money, debts*) ausstehend
out'strip' *v* (*pret* & *pp* –stripped; *ger* –stripping) *tr* (& *fig*) hinter sich [*dat*] lassen
out'vote' *tr* überstimmen
outward [ˈautwərd] *adj* äußerlich, äußere ‖ *adv* auswärts, nach außen
outwardly [ˈautwərdlɪ] *adv* äußerlich
outwards [ˈautwərdz] *adv* auswärts
out'weigh' *tr* an Gewicht übertreffen; (*fig*) überwiegen
out'wit' *v* (*pret* & *pp* –witted; *ger* –witting) *tr* überlisten
oval [ˈovəl] *adj* oval ‖ *s* Oval *n*
ovary [ˈovərɪ] *s* Eierstock *m*
ovation [oˈveʃən] *s* Huldigung *f*, Ovation *f*
oven [ˈʌvən] *s* Ofen *m*; (*for baking*) Backofen *m*
over [ˈovər] *adj* (*ended*) vorbei, aus; it's all o. with him es ist vorbei mit ihm; o. and done with total erledigt ‖ *adv*—all o. (*everywhere*) überall; (*on the body*) über und über; children of twelve and o. Kinder von zwölf Jahren und darüber; come o.! komm herüber!; o.! (*turn the page*) bitte wenden!; o. again noch einmal; o. against gegenüber (*dat*); o. and above obendrein; o. and out! (*rad*) Ende!; o. and o. again immer wieder; o. in Europe drüben in Europa; o. there dort, da drüben ‖ *prep* (*position*) über (*dat*); (*motion*) über (*acc*); (*because of*) wegen (*genit*); (*in the course of, e.g., a cup of tea*) bei (*dat*); (*during; more than*) über (*acc*); all o. town (*position*) in der ganzen Stadt; (*direction*) durch die ganze Stadt; be o. s.o. über j-m stehen; b. o. s.o.'s head j-m zu hoch sein; from all o. Germany aus ganz Deutschland; o. and above außer (*genit*); o. the radio im Radio
o'veract' *tr* & *intr* (*theat*) übertreiben
o'verac'tive *adj* übermäßig tätig
overage [ˈovərˌedʒ] *adj* über das vorgeschriebene Alter hinaus
o'verall' *adj* Gesamt- ‖ o'veralls' *spl* Monteuranzug *m*; (*trousers*) Überziehhose *f*
o'verambi'tious *adj* allzu ehrgeizig
o'veranx'ious *adj* überängstlich; (*overeager*) übereifrig
o'verawe' *tr* einschüchtern
o'verbear'ing *adj* überheblich
o'verboard' *adv* über Bord; go o. about sich übermäßig begeistern für
o'vercast' *adj* bewölkt, bedeckt; become o. sich bewölken ‖ *s* Bewölkung *f*
o'vercharge' *s* Überteuerung *f*; (*elec*) Überladung *f* ‖ o'vercharge' *tr* e-n Überpreis abverlangen (*dat*); (*elec*) überladen
o'vercoat' *s* Mantel *m*, Überrock *m*
o'ver·come' *v* (*pret* –came; *pp* –come)

tr überwältigen; **be o. with joy** vor Freude hingerissen sein

o'vercon'fidence *s* zu großes Selbstvertrauen *n*

o'vercon'fident *adj* zu vertrauensvoll

o'vercook' *tr* (*overboil*) zerkochen; (*overbake*) zu lange backen, zu lange braten

o'vercrowd' *tr* überfüllen; (*a room, hotel, hospital*) überbelegen

o'ver-do' *v* (*pret* –**did**; *pp* –**done**) *tr* übertreiben; **o. it** sich überanstrengen

o'verdone' *adj* (culin) übergar

o'verdose' *s* Überdosis *f*

o'verdraft' *s* Überziehung *f*

o'ver-draw' *v* (*pret* –**drew**; *pp* –**drawn**) *tr* überziehen

o'verdress' *intr* sich übertrieben kleiden

o'verdrive' *s* (aut) Schongang *m*

o'verdue' *adj* überfällig

o'ver-eat' *v* (*pret* –**ate**; *pp* –**eaten**) *intr* sich überessen

o'verem'phasis *s* Überbetonung *f*

o'verem'phasize *tr* überbetonen

o'veres'timate *tr* überschätzen

o'verexcite' *tr* überreizen

o'verexert' *tr* überanstrengen

o'verexer'tion *s* Überanstrengung *f*

o'verexpose' *tr* (phot) überbelichten

o'verexpo'sure *s* Überbelichtung *f*

o'verextend' *tr* übermäßig ausweiten

o'verflow' *s* (*inundation*) Überschwemmung *f*; (*surplus*) Überschuß *m*; (*outlet for surplus liquid*) Überlauf *m*; **filled to o.** bis zum Überließen gefüllt ‖ o'verflow' *tr* überfluten; **o. the banks** über die Ufer treten ‖ *intr* überfließen

o'ver-fly' *v* (*pret* –**flew**; *pp* –**flown**) *tr* überfliegen

o'verfriend'ly *adj* katzenfreundlich

o'vergrown' *adj* überwachsen; (*child*) lang aufgeschossen; **become o.** (said *of a garden*) verwildern; **become o. with** überwuchert werden von

o'verhang' *s* Überhang *m* ‖ o'ver-hang' *v* (*pret & pp* –**hung**) *tr* hervorragen über (*acc*); (*threaten*) bedrohen ‖ *intr* überhängen

o'verhaul' *s* Überholung *f* ‖ o'verhaul' *tr* (*repair*; *overtake*) überholen

o'verhead' *adj* (*line*) oberirdisch; (*valve*) obengesteuert ‖ *adv* droben ‖ *s* (econ) Gemeinkosten *pl*, laufende Unkosten *pl*

o'verhead door' *s* Federhubtor *n*

o'verhead line' *s* (*of a trolley*) Oberleitung *f*

o'ver-hear' *v* (*pret & pp* –**heard**) *tr* mithören; **be o.** belauscht werden

o'verheat' *tr* überhitzen; (*a room*) überheizen ‖ *intr* heißlaufen

o'verindulge' *tr* verwöhnen ‖ *intr* (in) sich allzusehr ergehen (in *dat*)

o'verkill' *s* Overkill *m*

overjoyed [,ovər'dʒɔɪd] *adj* überglücklich

overland ['ovər‚lænd] *adj* Überland–; **o. route** Landweg *m* ‖ *adv* über Land

o'verlap' *s* Überschneiden *n* ‖ o'verlap' *v* (*pret & pp* –**lapped**; *ger* –**lapping**)

tr sich überschneiden mit ‖ *intr* (& fig) sich überschneiden

o'verlap'ping *s* (& fig) Überschneidung *f*

o'verlay' *s* Auflage *f*; (*for a map*) Planpause *f*; **o. of gold** Goldauflage *f*

o'verload' *s* Überbelastung *f*; (elec) Überlast *f* ‖ o'verload' *tr* überlasten; (*a truck*) überladen; (in radio communications) übersteuern; (elec) überlasten

o'verlook' *tr* (*by mistake*) übersehen; (*a mistake*) hinwegsehen über (*acc*); (*a view*) überblicken

overly ['ovərli] *adv* übermäßig

o'vernight' *adj*—**o. stop** Aufenthalt *m* von e–r Nacht; **o. things** Nachtzeug *n* ‖ *adv* über Nacht; **stay o.** übernachten

o'vernight' bag' *s* Nachtzeugtasche *f*

o'verpass' *s* Überführung *f*

o'ver-pay' *v* (*pret & pp* –**paid**) *tr & intr* überbezahlen

o'verpay'ment *s* Überbezahlung *f*

o'verpop'ulat'ed *adj* übervölkert

o'verpop'ula'tion *s* Übervölkerung *f*

o'verpow'er *tr* (& fig) überwältigen

o'verproduc'tion *s* Überproduktion *f*

o'verrate' *tr* zu hoch schätzen

o'verreach' *tr* (*extend beyond*) hinausragen über (*acc*); (*an arm*) zu weit ausstrecken; **o. oneself** sich übernehmen

o'verrefined' *adj* überspitzt

o'verripe' *adj* überreif

o'verrule' *tr* (*an objection*) zurückweisen; (*a proposal*) verwerfen; (*a person*) überstimmen

o'verrun' *s* Überproduktion *f* ‖ o'ver-run' *v* (*pret* –**ran**; *pp* –**run**; *ger* –**running**) *tr* überrennen; (*said of a flood*) überschwemmen; **o. with** (*weeds*) überwuchert von; (*tourists*) überlaufen von; (*vermin*) wimmeln von

o'versalt' *tr* versalzen

o'versea(s)' *adj* Übersee– ‖ *adv* nach Übersee

o'ver-see' *v* (*pret & pp* –**saw**; *pp* –**seen**) *tr* beaufsichtigen

o'verse'er *s* Aufseher –in *mf*

o'versen'sitive *adj* überempfindlich

o'vershad'ow *tr* überschatten; (fig) in den Schatten stellen

o'vershoe' *s* Überschuh *m*

o'ver-shoot' *v* (*pret & pp* –**shot**) *tr* (& fig) hinausschießen über (*acc*)

o'versight' *s* Versehen *n*; **through an o.** aus Versehen

o'versimplifica'tion *s* allzu große Vereinfachung *f*

o'versize' *adj* übergroß ‖ *s* Übergröße *f*

o'ver-sleep' *v* (*pret & pp* –**slept**) *tr & intr* verschlafen

o'verspe'cialized *adj* überspezialisiert

o'verstaffed' *adj* (mit Personal) übersetzt

o'verstay' *tr* überschreiten

o'ver-step' *v* (*pret & pp* –**stepped**; *ger* –**stepping**) *tr* überschreiten

o'verstock' *tr* überbevorraten

o'verstrain' *tr* überanstrengen

o'verstuffed' *adj* überfüllt; (*furniture*) überpolstert

o'versupply' *s* zu großer Vorrat *m*; (com) Überangebot *n* || o'versup-ply' *v* (*pret & pp* –plied) *tr* überreichlich versehen; (com) überreichlich anbieten

overt ['ovərt], [o'vʌrt] *adj* offenkundig

o'ver-take' *v* (*pret* –took; *pp* –taken) *tr* (*catch up to*) einholen; (*pass*) überholen; (*suddenly befall*) überfallen

o'vertax' *tr* überbesteuern; (fig) überfordern, übermäßig in Anspruch nehmen

o'ver-the-coun'ter *adj* (pharm) rezeptfrei; (st. exch.) freihändig

o'verthrow' *s* Sturz *m* || o'ver-throw' (*pret* –threw; *pp* –thrown) *tr* stürzen

o'vertime' *adj* Überstunden– || *adv*–work o. Überstunden arbeiten; work five hours o. fünf Überstunden machen || *s* Überstunden *pl*; (sport) Spielverlängerung *f*

o'vertired' *adj* übermüdet

o'vertone' *s* (fig) Nebenbedeutung *f*; (mus) Oberton *m*

o'vertrump' *tr* überstechen

overture ['ovərtʃər] *s* Antrag *m*; (mus) Ouvertüre *f*

o'verturn' *tr* umstürzen || *intr* umkippen; (aut) sich überschlagen

overweening [,ovər'winiŋ] *adj* hochmütig

o'verweight' *adj* zu schwer || *s* Übergewicht *n*; (of freight) Überfracht *f*

overwhelm [,ovər'whelm] *tr* (*with some feeling*) überwältigen; (*e.g.*, *with questions, gifts*) überschütten; (*with work*) überbürden

o'verwhelm'ing *adj* überwältigend

overwind [,ovər'waind] *v* (*pret & pp* –wound) *tr* überdrehen

o'verwork' *s* Überarbeitung *f*, Überanstrengung *f* || o'verwork' *tr* überfordern || *intr* sich überarbeiten

o'verwrought' *adj* überreizt

o'verzeal'ous *adj* übereifrig

ow [au] *interj* au!

owe [o] *tr* schulden (*dat*), schuldig sein (*dat*); he owes her everything er verdankt ihr alles

ow'ing *adj*—it is o. to you that es ist dein Verdienst, daß; o. to infolge (*genit*)

owl [aul] *s* Eule *f*; (barn owl, screech owl) Schleiereule *f*

own [on] *adj* eigen || *s*—be left on one's own sich [*dat*] selbst überlassen sein; be on one's own auf eigenen Füßen stehen; come into one's own zu seinem Recht kommen; hold one's own sich behaupten; of one's own für sich allein; on one's own (*initiative*) aus eigener Initiative; (*responsibility*) auf eigene Faust || *tr* besitzen; (*acknowledge*) anerkennen; who owns this house? wem gehört dieses Haus? || *intr*—own to sich bekennen zu; own up to zugeben (*dat*)

owner ['onər] *s* Eigentümer –in *mf*

own'ership' *s* Eigentum *n*; (legal right of possession) Eigentumsrecht *n*; under new o. unter neuer Leitung

ox [aks] *s* (oxen ['aksən]) Ochse *m*

ox'cart' *s* Ochsenkarren *m*

oxfords ['aksfərdz] *spl* Halbschuhe *pl*

oxide ['aksaid] *s* Oxyd *n*

oxidize ['aksı,daız] *tr & intr* oxydieren

oxydation [,aksı'deʃən] *s* Oxydation *f*

oxygen ['aksıdʒən] *s* Sauerstoff *m*

oxygenate ['aksıdʒə,net] *tr* mit Sauerstoff anreichern

ox'ygen mask' *s* Sauerstoffmaske *f*

ox'ygen tank' *s* Sauerstoffflasche *f*

ox'ygen tent' *s* Sauerstoffzelt *n*

oxytone ['aksı,ton] *adj* oxytoniert || *s* Oxytonon *n*

oyster ['ɔistər] *s* Auster *f*

oys'ter bed' *s* Austernbank *f*

oys'ter farm' *s* Austernpark *m*

oys'ter-man *s* (–men) Austernfischer *m*

oys'tershell' *s* Austernschale *f*

oys'ter stew' *s* Austernragout *n*

ozone ['ozon] *s* Ozon *n*

O'zone layer' *s* Ozonschicht *f*

P

P, p [pi] *s* sechzehnter Buchstabe des englischen Alphabets

pace [pes] *s* Schritt *m*; (speed) Tempo *n*; at a fast p. in schnellem Tempo; keep p. with Schritt halten mit; put s.o. through his paces j-n auf Herz und Nieren prüfen; set the p. das Tempo angeben; (sport) Schrittmacher sein || *tr* (the room, floor) abschreiten; p. off abschreiten || *intr*—p. up and down (in) auf und ab schreiten (in *dat*)

pace'mak'er *s* Schrittmacher *m*

pacific [pə'sıfık] *adj* pazifisch; the

Pacific Ocean der Pazifische (or Stille) Ozean || *s*—the Pacific der Pazifik

pacifier ['pæsı,faı·ər] *s* Friedensvermittler –in *mf*; (for a baby) Schnuller *m*

pacifism ['pæsı,fızəm] *s* Pazifismus *m*

pacifist ['pæsıfıst] *s* Pazifist –in *mf*

paci·fy ['pæsı,faı] *v* (*pret & pp* –fied) *tr* (a country) befrieden; (a person) beruhigen

pack [pæk] *s* Pack *m*, Packen *m*; (of a soldier) Gepäck *n*; (of wolves, submarines) Rudel *n*; (of hounds) Meute *f;* *(of cigarettes)* Päckchen *n,* Schachtel *f;* *(on pack animals)* Last *f;* *(med)* Packung *f;* **p. of cards** Spiel *n* Karten; **p. of lies** Lug und Trug || *tr* (a *trunk)* packen; *(clothes)* einpacken; *(seal)* abdichten; **p. in** *(above normal capacity)* einpferchen; **p. up** zusammenpacken || *intr* packen; **send s.o. packing** j-m Beine machen

package ['pækɪdʒ] *adj* *(price, tour, agreement)* Pauschal– || *s* Paket *n* || *tr* (ver)packen

pack′age deal′ *s* Koppelgeschäft *n*

pack′ an′imal *s* Packtier *n*

packet ['pækɪt] *s* Paket *n,* Päckchen *n;* *(naut)* Postschiff *n*

pack′ing *s* *(act)* Packen *n;* *(seal)* Dichtung *f;* *(wrapper)* Verpackung *f*

pack′ing case′ *s* Packkiste *f*

pack′ing house′ *s* Konservenfabrik *f*

pack′sad′dle *s* Packsattel *m*

pact [pækt] *s* Pakt *m;* **make a p. pak-tieren**

pad [pæd] *s* *(of writing paper)* Block *m;* *(ink pad)* Stempelkissen *n;* *(cushion)* Kissen *n;* *(of butter)* Stück *n;* *(under a rug)* Unterlage *f;* *(living quarters)* Bude *f;* *(rok)* Abschußrampe *f;* *(sport)* Schützer *m;* *(surg)* Bausch *m* || *v* *(pret & pp* padded; *ger* padding) *tr* *(e.g., the shoulders)* wattieren; *(writing)* ausbauschen

pad′ded cell′ *s* Gummizelle *f*

pad′ding *s* Wattierung *f;* *(coll)* Ballast *m*

paddle ['pædəl] *s* *(of a canoe)* Paddel *n;* *(for table tennis)* Schläger *m* || *tr* paddeln; *(spank)* prügeln || *intr* paddeln

pad′dle wheel′ *s* Schaufelrad *n*

paddock ['pædɒk] *s* Pferdekoppel *f;* *(at the races)* Sattelplatz *m*

pad′dy wag′on ['pædi] *s* (sl) Grüne Minna *f*

pad′lock′ *s* Vorhängeschloß *n* || *tr* mit e-m Vorhängeschloß verschließen

paean ['pi-ən] *s* Siegeslied *n*

pagan ['pegən] *adj* heidnisch || *s* Heide *m,* Heidin *f*

paganism ['pegə‚nɪzəm] *s* Heidentum *n*

page [pedʒ] *s* Seite *f;* *(in a hotel or club; at court)* Page *m* || *tr* *(summon)* über den Lautsprecher (or durch Pagen) holen lassen || *intr*— **p. through** durchblättern

pageant ['pædʒənt] *s* Festspiel *n;* *(procession)* Festzug *m*

pageantry ['pædʒəntri] *s* Schaugepränge *n*

page′boy′ *s* Pagenfrisur *f*

page′ proof′ *s* Umbruchabzug *m*

pagoda [pə'godə] *s* Pagode *f*

paid′ in full′ [ped] *adj* voll bezahlt

paid′-up′ *adj*(*debts*) abgezahlt; *(policy, capital)* voll eingezahlt

pail [pel] *s* Eimer *m*

pain [pen] *s* Schmerz *m;* **on p. of death** bei Todesstrafe; **take pains** sich bemühen || *tr & intr* schmerzen || *impers*—**it pains me to** *(inf)* es fällt mir schwer zu *(inf)*

painful ['penfəl] *adj* schmerzhaft; *(fig)* peinlich

pain′ in the neck′ *s* (coll) Nervensäge *f*

pain′kill′er *s* schmerzstillendes Mittel *n*

painless ['penlɪs] *adj* schmerzlos

pains′tak′ing *adj* *(work)* mühsam; *(person)* sorgfältig

paint [pent] *s* Farbe *f;* *(for a car)* Lack *m* || *tr* (be)malen; *(e.g., a house)* (an)streichen; *(a car)* lackieren; *(with watercolors)* aquarellieren; *(fig)* schildern; **p. the town red** tüchtig auf die Pauke hauen || *intr* malen; *(with house paint)* überstreichen

paint′box′ *s* Malkasten *m*

paint′brush′ *s* Pinsel *m*

paint′ can′ *s* Farbendose *f*

painter ['pentər] *s* Maler –in *mf;* *(of houses, etc.)* Anstreicher –in *mf*

paint′ing *s* Malerei *f;* *(picture)* Gemälde *n*

paint′ remov′er *s* Farbenabbeizmittel *n*

paint′ spray′er *s* Farbspritzpistole *f*

pair [pɛr] *s* Paar *n;* **a p. of glasses** e-e Brille *f;* **a p. of gloves** ein Paar *n* Handschuhe; **a p. of pants** e-e Hose *f;* **a p. of scissors** e-e Schere *f;* **a p. of twins** ein Zwillingspaar *n;* **in pairs** paarweise || *tr* paaren; **p. off** paarweise ordnen; *(coll)* verheiraten || *intr*—**p. off** sich paarweise absondern

pajamas [pə'dʒɑməz] *s* Pyjama *m*

Pakistan ['pækɪ‚stæn] *s* Pakistan *n*

Pakista·ni [‚pækɪ'stæni] *adj* pakistanisch || *s* (*-nis*) Pakistaner –in *mf*

pal [pæl] *s* Kamerad *m* || *v* *(pret & pp* palled; *ger* palling) *intr*—**pal around with** dick befreundet sein mit

palace ['pælɪs] *s* Palast *m*

palatable ['pælətəbəl] *adj* (& *fig*) mundgerecht

palatal ['pælətəl] *adj* Gaumen– || *s* (phonet) Gaumenlaut *m*

palate ['pælɪt] *s* Gaumen *m*

palatial [pə'leʃəl] *adj* palastartig

Palatinate [pə'lætɪ‚net] *s* Rheinpfalz *f*

pale [pel] *adj* *(face, colors, recollection)* blaß; **turn pale** erblassen, erbleichen || *s* Pfahl *m* || *intr* erblassen; **pale beside** (fig) verblassen neben *(dat)*

pale′face′ *s* Bleichgesicht *n*

Palestine ['pælɪs‚taɪn] *s* Palästina *n*

palette ['pælɪt] *s* Palette *f*

palisade [‚pælɪ'sed] *s* Palisade *f;* *(line of cliffs)* Flußklippen *pl*

pall [pɔl] *s* Bahrtuch *n;* *(of smoke, gloom)* Hülle *f* || *intr* (on) zuviel werden *(dat)*

pall′bear′er *s* Sargträger *m*

pallet ['pælɪt] *s* Lager *n*

palliate ['pælɪ‚et] *tr* lindern; *(fig)* bemänteln

pallid ['pælɪd] *adj* blaß, bleich

pallor ['pælər] *s* Blässe *f*

palm [pɑm] *s* *(of the hand)* Handfläche *f;* *(tree)* Palme *f;* **grease s.o.'s palm** j-n schmieren; **palm of victory** Siegespalme *f* || *tr* (a *card)* in der Hand verbergen; **palm s.th. off on s.o.** j-m etw andrehen

palmette [pæl'met] s Palmette f
palmet·to [pæl'meto] s (-tos & -toes)
Fächerpalme f
palmist ['pɑmɪst] s Wahrsager -in mf
palmistry ['pɑmɪstri] s Handlesekunst f
palm' leaf' s Palmblatt n
Palm' Sun'day s Palmsonntag m
palm' tree' s Palme f
palpable ['pælpəbəl] adj greifbar
palpitate ['pælpɪ‚tet] intr klopfen
palsied ['pɔlzid] adj lahm, gelähmt
palsy ['pɔlzi] s Lähmung f
paltry ['pɔltri] adj armselig
pamper ['pæmpər] tr verwöhnen
pamphlet ['pæmflɪt] s Flugschrift f
pan [pæn] s Pfanne f; (sl) Visage f || tr (gold) waschen; (a camera) schwenken; (criticize sharply) (coll) verreißen || intr (cin) panoramieren; pan out glücken, klappen
panacea [‚pænə'si·ə] s Allheilmittel n
Panama ['pænəmɑ] s Panama n
Pan'ama Canal' s Panamakanal m
Pan-American [‚pænə'merɪkən] adj panamerikanisch
pan'cake' s (flacher) Pfannkuchen m || intr (aer) absacken, bumslanden
pan'cake land'ing s Bumslandung f
panchromatic [‚pænkro'mætɪk] adj panchromatisch
pancreas ['pænkrɪ‚əs] s Bauchspeicheldrüse f
pandemic [pæn'demɪk] adj pandemisch
pandemonium [‚pændə'moni‚əm] s Höllenlärm m
pander ['pændər] s Kuppler m || intr kuppeln; p. to Vorschub leisten (dat)
pane [pen] s Scheibe f
panegyric [‚pænɪ'dʒɪrɪk] s Lobrede f
pan·el ['pænəl] s Tafel f, Feld n; (in a door) Füllung f; (for instruments) Schlattafel f; (of experts) Diskussionsgruppe f; (archit) Paneel n; (jur) Geschworenenliste f || v (pret & pp -el[l]ed; ger -el[l]ing) tr täfeln
pan'el discus'sion s Podiumsdiskussion f
pan'eling s Täfelung f
panelist ['pænəlɪst] s Diskussionsteilnehmer -in mf
pang [pæŋ] s stechender Schmerz m; (fig) Angst f; pangs of conscience Gewissensbisse pl; pangs of hunger nagender Hunger m
pan'han'dle s Pfannenstiel m; (geog) Landzunge f || intr (sl) betteln
pan'han'dler s (sl) Bettler -in mf
pan·ic ['pænɪk] s Panik f || v (pret & pp -icked; ger -icking) tr in Panik versetzen || intr von panischer Angst erfüllt werden
pan'ic-strick'en adj von panischem Schrecken erfaßt
panicky ['pænɪki] adj übernervös
panoply ['pænəpli] s Pracht f; (full suit of armor) vollständige Rüstung f
panorama [‚pænə'ræmə] s Panorama n
pansy ['pænzi] s Stiefmütterchen n
pant [pænt] s Keuchen n; pants Hose

f, Hosen pl || intr keuchen; p. for or after gieren nach
pantheism ['pænθɪ‚ɪzəm] s Pantheismus m
pantheon ['pænθɪ‚ɑn] s Pantheon n
panther ['pænθər] s Panther m
panties ['pæntiz] spl Schlüpfer m
pantomime ['pæntə‚maɪm] s Pantomime f
pantry ['pæntri] s Speisekammer f
pap [pæp] s Brei m, Kleister m
papa ['pɑpə] s Papa m, Vati m
papacy ['pepəsi] s Papsttum n
papal ['pepəl] adj päpstlich
Pa'pal State' s Kirchenstaat m
paper ['pepər] adj (money, plate, towel) Papier- || s Papier n; (before a learned society) Referat n; (newspaper) Zeitung f; papers (documents) Papiere pl || tr tapezieren
pa'perback' s Taschenbuch n, Pappband m
pa'per bag' s Papiertüte f, Tüte f
pa'perboy' s Zeitungsjunge m
pa'per clip' s Büroklammer f
pa'per cone' s Tüte f
pa'per cup' s Papierbecher m
pa'per cut'ter s Papierschneidemaschine f
pa'perhang'er s Tapezierer -in mf
pa'perhang'ing s Tapezierarbeit f
pa'pering s Tapezieren n
pa'per mill' s Papierfabrik f
pa'per nap'kin s Papierserviette f
pa'perweight' s Briefbeschwerer m
pa'perwork' s Schreibarbeit f
papier-mâché [‚pepərmə'ʃe] s Papier-mâché n, Pappmaché n
paprika [pæ'prikə] s Paprika m
papy·rus [pə'paɪrəs] s (-ri [raɪ]) Papyrus m
par [pɑr] s (fin) Pari n; (golf) festgesetzte Schlagzahl f; at par pari, auf Pari; on a par with auf gleicher Stufe mit; up to par (coll) auf der Höhe
parable ['pærəbəl] s Gleichnis n
parabola [pə'ræbələ] s Parabel f
parachute ['pærə‚ʃut] s Fallschirm m || tr mit dem Fallschirm abwerfen || intr abspringen
par'achute jump' s Fallschirmabsprung m
parachutist ['pærə‚ʃutɪst] s Fallschirmspringer -in mf
parade [pə'red] s Parade f || tr zur Schau stellen || intr paradieren; (mil) aufmarschieren
paradigm ['pærədɪm], ['pærə‚daɪm] s Musterbeispiel n, Paradigma n
paradise ['pærə‚daɪs] s Paradies n
paradox ['pærə‚dɑks] s Paradox n
paradoxical [‚pærə'dɑksɪkəl] adj paradox
paraffin ['pærəfɪn] s Paraffin n
paragon ['pærə‚gɑn] s Musterbild n
paragraph ['pærə‚græf] s Absatz m, Paragraph m
parakeet ['pærə‚kit] s Sittich m
paral·lel ['pærə‚lel] adj parallel; be (or run) p. to parallel verlaufen zu || s Parallele f; (of latitude) Breiten-

kreis *m;* (fig) Gegenstück *n;* without p. ohnegleichen ‖ *v* (*pret & pp* -lel[l]ed; *ger* -lel[l]ing) *tr* parallel verlaufen zu; (*match*) gleichkommen (*dat*); (*correspond to*) entsprechen (*dat*)

par′allel bars′ *spl* Barren *m*

paraly•sis [pə′rælɪsɪs] *s* (-ses [ˌsiz]) Lähmung *f*, Paralyse *f*

paralytic [ˌpærə′lɪtɪk] *adj* paralytisch ‖ *s* Paralytiker –in *mf*

paralyze [′pærəˌlaɪz] *tr* lähmen, paralysieren; (*traffic*) lahmlegen

parameter [pə′ræmɪtər] *s* Parameter *m*

paramilitary [ˌpærə′mɪlɪˌteri] *adj* halbmilitärisch

paramount [′pærəˌmaunt] *adj* oberste; be p. an erster Stelle stehen; of p. importance von äußerster Wichtigkeit

paranoia [ˌpærə′nɔɪ•ə] *s* Paranoia *f*

paranoiac [ˌpærə′nɔɪ•æk] *adj* paranoisch ‖ *s* Paranoiker –in *mf*

paranoid [′pærəˌnɔɪd] *adj* paranoid

parapet [′pærəˌpet] *s* (*of a wall*) Brustwehr *f;* (*of a balcony*) Geländer *n*

paraphernalia [ˌpærəfər′neli•ə] *s* Zubehör *n*, Ausrüstung *f*

paraphrase [′pærəˌfrez] *s* Umschreibung *f* ‖ *tr* umschreiben

parasite [′pærəˌsaɪt] *s* (& fig) Parasit *m*

parasitic(al) [ˌpærə′sɪtɪk(əl)] *adj* parasitisch

parasol [′pærəˌsɔl] *s* Sonnenschirm *m*

paratrooper [′pærəˌtrupər] *s* Fallschirmjäger *m*

par•cel [′pɑrsəl] *s* Paket *m;* (com) Posten *m* ‖ *v* (*pret & pp* -cel[l]ed; *ger* -cel[l]ing) *tr*—p. out aufteilen

par′cel post′ *s* Paketpost *f*

parch [pɑrtʃ] *tr* ausdörren; my throat is parched mir klebt die Zunge am Gaumen

parchment [′pɑrtʃmənt] *s* Pergament *n*

pardon [′pɑrdən] *s* Verzeihung *f;* (jur) Begnadigung *f;* I beg your p. ich bitte um Entschuldigung; p.? wie, bitte? ‖ *tr* (*a person*) verzeihen (*dat*); (*an act*) verzeihen; (*officially*) begnadigen

pardonable [′pɑrdənəbəl] *adj* verzeihlich

pare [per] *tr* (*nails*) schneiden; (*e.g., potatoes*) (ab)schälen; (*costs*) beschneiden

parent [′perənt] *s* Elternteil *m;* parents Eltern *pl*

parentage [′perəntɪdʒ] *s* Abstammung *f*

parental [pə′rentəl] *adj* elterlich

parenthe•sis [pə′renθɪsɪs] *s* (-ses [ˌsiz]) Klammer *f;* (*expression in parentheses*) Parenthese *f*

parenthetic(al) [ˌperən′θetɪk(əl)] *adj* parenthetisch

parenthood [′perəntˌhud] *s* Elternschaft *f*

pariah [pə′raɪ•ə] *s* Paria *m*

par′ing knife′ *s* Schälmesser *n*

Paris [′pærɪs] *s* Paris *n*

parish [′pærɪʃ] *adv* Pfarr– ‖ *s* Pfarrgemeinde *f*

parishioner [pə′rɪʃənər] *s* Gemeindemitglied *n*, Pfarrkind *n*

Parisian [pə′rɪʒən] *adj* Pariser ‖ *s* Pariser –in *mf*

parity [′pærɪti] *s* Parität *f*

park [pɑrk] *s* Park *m* ‖ *tr* abstellen, parken ‖ *intr* parken

park′ing *s* Parken *n;* no p. (public sign) Parken verboten

park′ing light′ *s* Parklicht *n*

park′ing lot′ *s* Parkplatz *m*

park′ing lot′ atten′dant′ *s* Parkplatzwärter –in *mf*

park′ing me′ter *s* Parkuhr *f*

park′ing place′, park′ing space′ *s* Parkplatz *m*, Parkstelle *f*

park′ing tick′et *s* gebührenpflichtige Verwarnung *f* (wegen falschen Parkens)

park′way′ *s* Aussichtsautobahn *f*

parley [′pɑrli] *s* Unterhandlung *f* ‖ *intr* unterhandeln

parliament [′pɑrləmənt] *s* Parlament *n*

parliamentary [ˌpɑrlə′mentəri] *adj* parlamentarisch

parlor [′pɑrlər] *s* Salon *m;* (*living room*) Wohnzimmer *n*

par′lor game′ *s* Gesellschaftsspiel *n*

parochial [pə′roki•əl] *adj* Pfarr–; (fig) beschränkt

paro′chial school′ *s* Pfarrschule *f*

paro•dy [′pærədi] *s* Parodie *f* ‖ *v* (*pret & pp* -died) *tr* parodieren

parole [pə′rol] *s* bedingte Strafaussetzung *f;* be out on p. bedingt entlassen sein ‖ *tr* bedingt entlassen

par•quet [pɑr′ke], [pɑr′ket] *v* (*pret & pp* -queted [′ked]; *ger* -queting [′ke•ɪŋ]) *tr* parkettieren

parquetry [′pɑrkɪtri] *s* Parkettfußboden *m*

parrot [′pærət] *s* Papagei *m* ‖ *tr* nachplappern

par•ry [′pæri] *s* Parade *f* ‖ *v* (*pret & pp* -ried) *tr* parieren

parse [pɑrs] *tr* zergliedern

parsimonious [ˌpɑrsɪ′moni•əs] *adj* sparsam

parsley [′pɑrsli] *s* Petersilie *f*

parsnip [′pɑrsnɪp] *s* Pastinak *m*

parson [′pɑrsən] *s* Pfarrer *m*

parsonage [′pɑrsənɪdʒ] *s* Pfarrhaus *n*

part [pɑrt] *adv*—p. ... p. zum Teil ... zum Teil ‖ *s* Teil *m & n;* (*section*) Abschnitt *m;* (spare part) Ersatzteil *m;* (*of a machine, etc.*) Bestandteil *m;* (*share*) Anteil *m;* (*of the hair*) Scheitel *m;* (mus) Partie *f;* (theat) Rolle *f;* do one′s p. das Seinige tun; for his p. seinerseits; for the most p. größtenteils; have a p. in Anteil haben an (*dat*); in p. zum Teil, teilweise; make a p. (*in the hair*) e–n Scheitel ziehen; on his p. seinerseits; p. and parcel ein wesentlicher Bestandteil *m;* take p. (in) teilnehmen (an *dat*); take s.o.′s p. j–s Partei ergreifen ‖ *tr* (ab)scheiden; (*the hair*) scheiteln; p. company von

einander scheiden || *intr* sich tren-
nen; **p. with** hergeben
par·take ['par'tek] *v* (*pret* –took; *pp*
taken) *intr*—**p.** in teilnehmen an
(*dat*); **p. of** zu sich nehmen
partial ['parʃəl] *adj* Teil-, partiell;
(*prejudiced*) parteiisch; **be p. to** bevorzugen
partiality [ˌparʃɪ'ælɪti] *s* Parteilichkeit *f*, Befangenheit *f*
partially ['parʃəli] *adv* teilweise
participant [par'tɪsɪpənt] *s* Teilnehmer –in *mf*
participate [par'tɪsɪˌpet] *intr* (in) teilnehmen (an *dat*)
participation [parˌtɪsɪ'peʃən] *s* (in)
Teilnahme *f* (an *dat*)
participle ['partɪˌsɪpəl] *s* Mittelwort
n, Partizip *n*
particle ['partɪkəl] *s* Teilchen *n*; (gram,
phys) Partikel *f*
particular [par'tɪkjələr] *adj* (specific)
bestimmt; (*individual*) einzeln; (*meticulous*) peinlich genau; (*especial*)
peinlich genau; (*choosy*) heikel || *s*
Einzelheit *f*; **in p.** insbesondere
partisan ['partɪzən] *adj* parteiisch || *s*
(mil) Partisan –in *mf*; (pol) Partei-
gänger –in *mf*
partition [par'tɪʃən] *s* Teilung *f*; (*wall*)
Scheidewand *f* || *tr* (auf)teilen; **p. off**
abteilen
partly ['partli] *adv* teils, teilweise
partner ['partnər] *s* Partner –in *mf*
part'nership' *s* Partnerschaft *f*
part' of speech' *s* Wortart *f*
partridge ['partrɪdʒ] *s* Rebhuhn *n*
part'-time' *adj & adv* nicht vollzeitlich
part'-time work' *s* Teilzeitarbeit *f*
party ['parti] *s* Gesellschaft *f*, Party *f*;
(jur) Partei *f*; (mil) Kommando *n*;
(pol) Partei *f*; (telp) Teilnehmer –in
mf; **be a p. to** sich hergeben zu
par'ty affilia'tion *s* Parteizugehörigkeit
f
par'ty line' *s* (pol) Parteilinie *f*; (telp)
Gemeinschaftsanschluß *m*
par'ty mem'ber *s* Parteigenosse *m*, Par-
teigenossin *f*
par'ty pol'itics *s* Parteipolitik *f*
paschal ['pæskəl] *adj* Oster-
pass [pæs] *s* (over a mountain; permit) Paß *m*; (erotic advance) An-
näherungsversuch *m*; (fencing) Stoß
m; (fb) Paßball *m*; (mil) Urlaubs-
schein *m*; (theat) Freikarte *f*; **make
a p. at** (flirt with) e–n Annäherungs-
versuch machen bei; (aer) vorbeiflie-
gen an (*dat*) || *tr* (*go by*) vorbeigehen
an (*dat*), passieren; (a test) bestehen;
(a student in a test) durchlassen; (a
bill) verabschieden; (hand over)
reichen; (judgment) abgeben; (sentence) sprechen; (time) verbringen;
(counterfeit money) in Umlauf bringen; (a car) überholen; (e.g., a kidney stone) ausscheiden; (a ball)
weitergeben; (to) zuspielen (*dat*); **p.
around** herumgehen lassen; **p. away**
(time) vertreiben; **p. in** einhändigen;
p. off as ausgeben als; **p. on** weiter-
leiten; (e.g., news) weitersagen; **p.**

out ausgeben; **p. over** in silence unerwähnt lassen; **p. up** verzichten auf
(*acc*) || *intr* (by) vorbeikommen (an
dat), vorbeigehen (an *dat*); (in a car)
(by) vorbeifahren (an *dat*); (in a
test) durchkommen; (e.g., from father
to son) übergehen; (cards) passen;
(parl) zustandekommen; **bring to p.**
herbeiführen; **come to p.** geschehen;
p.! (cards) passe!; **p. away** verscheiden; **p. for** gelten als; **p. on** ab-
scheiden; **p. out** ohnmächtig werden;
p. over (disregard) hinweggehen über
(*acc*); **p. through** durchgehen (durch);
(said of an army) durchziehen
(durch); (said of a train) berühren
passable ['pæsəbəl] *adj* (road) gangbar; (by car) befahrbar; (halfway
good) leidlich, passabel
passage ['pæsɪdʒ] *s* Korridor *m*, Gang
m; (crossing) Überfahrt *f*; (in a
book) Stelle *f*; (of a law) Annahme
f; (of time) Ablauf *m*; **book p. for**
e–e Schiffskarte bestellen nach
pas'sageway' *s* Durchgang *m*, Passage *f*
pass'book' *s* Sparbuch *n*
passenger ['pæsəndʒər] *s* Passagier –in
mf; (in public transportation) Fahrgast *m*; (in a car) Insasse *m*, Insassin *f*
pas'senger car' *s* Personenkraftwagen
m
pas'senger plane' *s* Passagierflugzeug *n*
pas'senger train' *s* Personenzug *m*
passer-by ['pæsər'baɪ] *s* (passers-by)
Passant –in *mf*
pass'ing *adj* vorübergehend; **a p. grade**
die Note „befriedigend" || *s* (act of
passing) Vorbeigehen *n*; (of a law)
Verabschiedung *f*; (of time) Ver-
streichen *n*; (dying) Hinscheiden *n*;
in p. im Vorbeigehen; (as under-
statement) beiläufig; **no p.** (public
sign) Überholen verboten
passion ['pæʃən] *s* Leidenschaft *f*; (of
Christ) Passion *f*; **fly into a p.** in
Zorn geraten; **have a p. for** e–e
Vorliebe haben für
passionate ['pæʃənɪt] *adj* leidenschaftlich
pas'sion play' *s* Passionsspiel *n*
passive ['pæsɪv] *adj* (& gram) passiv
|| *s* Passiv(um) *n*
pass'key' *s* (master key) Hauptschlüssel
m; (skeleton key) Nachschlüssel *m*
Pass'o'ver *s* Passah *n*
pass'port' *s* Paß *m*, Reisepaß *m*
pass'port of'fice *s* Paßamt *n*
pass'word' *s* (mil) Kennwort *n*
past [pæst] *adj* (e.g., week) vergangen;
(e.g., president) ehemalig, früher;
(gone) vorbei; **for some time p.** seit
einiger Zeit || *s* Vergangenheit *f* ||
prep (e.g., one o'clock) nach; (beyond) über (*acc*) hinaus; **get p.** (an
opponent) (sport) umspielen; **go p.**
vorbeigehen an (*dat*); **it's way p.**
bedtime es ist schon längst Zeit zum
Schlafengehen
paste [pest] *s* (glue) Kleister *m*,
Brei *m*, Paste *f* || *tr* (e.g., a wall)
(with) bekleben (mit); **p. on** aufkle-

ben auf (acc); **p. together** zusammen-kleben

paste'board' s Pappe f

astel [pæs'tel] adj pastellfarben || s Pastell n

astel' col'or s Pastellfarbe f

asteurize ['pæstə‚raɪz] tr pasteurisieren

astime ['pæs‚taɪm] s Zeitvertreib m

ast' mas'ter s Experte m

astor ['pæstər] s Pastor m

astoral ['pæstərəl] adj Schäfer-, Hirten-; (eccl) Hirten-, pastoral || s Schäfergedicht n

pas'toral let'ter s Hirtenbrief m

astorate ['pæstərɪt] s Pastorat n

astry ['pestri] s Gebäck n; **pastries** Backwaren pl

pas'try shop' s Konditorei f

past' tense' s Vergangenheit f

pasture ['pæstʃər] s Weide f || tr & intr weiden

pas'ture land' s Weideland n

pasty ['pesti] adj (sticky) klebrig; (complexion) bläßlich

pat [pæt] adj (answer) treffend; **have s.th. down pat** etw in- und auswendig wissen || adv—**stand pat** bei der Stange bleiben || s Klaps m; (of butter) Klümpchen n || tr tätscheln; **pat s.o. on the back** j-n auf die Schulter klopfen; (fig) j-n beglückwünschen

patch [pætʃ] s (of clothing, land, color) Fleck m; (garden bed) Beet n; (for clothing, inner tube) Flicken m; (over the eye) Binde f; (for a wound) Pflaster n || tr flicken; **p. together** (& fig) zusammenflicken; **p. up** (a friendship) kitten; (differences) beilegen

patch'work' s Flickwerk n; (fig) Stückwerk n

patch'work quilt' s Flickendecke f

pate [pet] s (coll) Schädel m

patent ['petənt] adj öffentlich || ['pætənt] adj Patent-, e.g., **p. lawyer** Patentanwalt m || s Patent n; **p. pending** Patent angemeldet || tr patentieren

pa'tent leath'er ['pætənt] s Lackleder n

pa'tent-leath'er shoe' s Lackschuh m

pat'ent med'icine ['pætənt] s rezeptfreies Medikament n

pat'ent rights' ['pætənt] spl Schutzrechte pl

paternal [pə'tʌrnəl] adj väterlich

paternity [pə'tʌrnɪti] s Vaterschaft f

path [pæθ] s Pfad m; (astr) Lauf m; **clear a p.** e-n Weg bahnen; **cross s.o.'s p.** j-s Weg kreuzen

pathetic [pə'θetɪk] adj (moving) rührend; (evoking contemptuous pity) kläglich

path'find'er s Pfadfinder m; (aer) Beleuchter m

pathologist [pə'θalədʒɪst] s Pathologe m, Pathologin f

pathology [pə'θalədʒi] s Pathologie f

pathos ['peθas] s Pathos n

path'way' s Weg m, Pfad m

patience ['peʃəns] s Geduld f

patient ['peʃənt] adj geduldig || s Patient –in mf

pati·o ['pæti·o] s (–os) Terasse f

patriarch ['petri‚ark] s Patriarch m

patrician [pə'trɪʃən] adj patrizisch || s Patrizier –in mf

patricide ['pætri‚saɪd] s (act) Vatermord m; (person) Vatermörder –in mf

patrimony ['pætri‚moni] s väterliches Erbe n

patriot ['petri·ət] s Patriot –in mf

patriotic [‚petri'atɪk] adj patriotisch

patriotism ['petri·ə‚tɪzəm] s Patriotismus m

pa·trol [pə'trol] s Patrouille f, Streife f || v (pret & pp –trolled; ger –trolling) tr & intr patrouillieren

patrol' car' s Streifenwagen m

patrol'man s (–men) Polizeistreife f

patrol' wag'on s Gefangenenwagen m

patron ['petrən] s Schutzherr m; (com) Kunde m, Kundin f; (eccl) Schutzpatron m

patronage ['petrənɪdʒ] s Patronat n

patroness ['petrənɪs] s Schutzherrin f; (eccl) Schutzpatronin f

patronize ['petrə‚naɪz] tr beschützen, protegieren; (com) als Kunde besuchen; (theat) regelmäßig besuchen

pa'tronizing adj gönnerhaft

pa'tron saint' s Schutzheilige mf

patter ['pætər] s (of rain) Prasseln n; (of feet) Getrappel n || intr (said of rain) prasseln; (said of feet) trappeln

pattern ['pætərn] s Muster m; (sew) Schnittmuster n

patty ['pæti] s Pastetchen n

paucity ['pasiti] s Knappheit f

paunch [pontʃ] s Wanst m

paunchy ['pontʃi] adj dickbäuchig

pauper ['papər] s Arme mf; (person on welfare) Unterstützte mf

pause [paz] s Pause f; (mus) Fermate f || intr pausieren

pave [pev] tr pflastern; **p. the way for** (fig) anbahnen

pavement ['pevmənt] s Pflaster n; (sidewalk) Bürgersteig m, Trottoir n

pavilion [pə'vɪljən] s Pavillon m

pav'ing s Pflasterung f

pav'ing stone' s Pflasterstein m

paw [po] s Pfote f || tr (scratch) kratzen; (coll) befummeln; **paw the ground** auf dem Boden scharren || intr (said of a horse) mit dem Huf scharren

pawl [pol] s Sperrklinke f

pawn [pon] s Pfand n; (fig) Schachfigur f; (chess) Bauer m || tr verpfänden

pawn'brok'er s Pfandleiher –in mf

pawn'shop' s Pfandhaus n

pawn' tick'et s Pfandschein m

pay [pe] s Lohn m; (mil) Sold m || v (pret & pp paid [ped]) tr bezahlen; (a visit) abstatten; (a dividend) ausschütten; (a compliment) machen; **pay back** zurückzahlen; **pay damages** Schadenersatz leisten; **pay down** anzahlen; **pay extra** nachzahlen; **pay in advance** vorauszahlen; **pay in full**

begleichen; **pay interest on** verzinsen; **pay off** (*a debt*) abbezahlen; (*a person*) entlohnen; **pay one's way** ohne Verlust arbeiten; **pay out** auszahlen; **pay s.o. back for s.th.** j-m etw heimzahlen; **pay taxes on** versteuern; **pay up** (*a debt*) abbezahlen; (ins) voll einzahlen ‖ *intr* zahlen; (*be worthwhile*) sich lohnen; **pay extra** zuzahlen; **pay for** (*a purchase*) (be)zahlen für; (*suffer for*) büßen

payable ['pe·əbəl] *adj* fällig, zahlbar
pay' check' *s* Lohnscheck *m*
pay'day' *s* Zahltag *m*
pay' dirt' —**hit p.** sein Glück machen
payee [pe'i] *s* (*of a draft*) Zahlungsempfänger –in *mf;* (*of a check*) Wechselnehmer –in *mf*
pay' en'velope *s* Lohntüte *f*
payer ['pe·ər] *s* Zahler –in *mf*
pay'load' *s* Nutzlast *f;* (*explosive energy*) Sprengladung *f*
pay'mas'ter *s* Zahlmeister *m*
payment ['pemənt] *s* Zahlung *f;* **in p. of** zur Bezahlung (*genit*)
pay' phone' *s* Münzfernsprecher *m*
pay' raise' *s* Gehaltserhöhung *f*
pay' rate' *s* Lohnsatz *m*
pay'roll' *s* Lohnliste *f;* (*money paid*) gesamte Lohnsumme *f*
pay' sta'tion *s* Telephonautomat *m*
pea [pi] *s* Erbse *f*
peace [pis] *s* Friede(n) *m;* (*quiet*) Ruhe *f;* **be at p. with** in Frieden leben mit; **keep the p.** die öffentliche Ruhe bewahren
peaceable ['pisəbəl] *adj* friedfertig
Peace' Corps' *s* Friedenskorps *n*
peace'-lov'ing *adj* friedliebend
peace'mak'er *s* Friedenstifter –in *mf*
peace' negotia'tions *spl* Friedensverhandlungen *pl*
peace' of mind' *s* Seelenruhe *f*
peace'pipe' *s* Friedenspfeife *f*
peace'time' *adj* Friedens– ‖ *s*—**in p.** in Friedenszeiten
peace' trea'ty *s* Friedensvertrag *m*
peach [pitʃ] *s* Pfirsich *m*
peach' tree' *s* Pfirsichbaum *m*
peachy ['pitʃi] *adj* (coll) pfundig
pea'cock' *s* Pfau *m*
pea'hen' *s* Pfauenhenne *f*
pea' jack'et *s* (nav) Matrosenjacke *f*
peak [pik] *adj* Spitzen– ‖ *s* (& fig) Gipfel *m;* (*of a cap*) Mützenschirm *m;* (elec) Leistungsspitze *f;* (phys) Scheitelwert *m*
peak' hours' *spl* (*of traffic*) Hauptverkehrszeit *f;* (elec) Stoßzeit *f*
peak' load' *s* (elec) Spitzenlast *f*
peak' vol'tage *s* Spitzenspannung *f*
peal [pil] *s* Geläute *n* ‖ *intr* erschallen
peal' of laugh'ter *s* Lachsalve *f*
peal' of thun'der *s* Donnergetöse *n*
pea'nut' *s* Erdnuß *f;* **peanuts** (coll) kleine Fische *pl*
pea'nut but'ter *s* Erdnußbutter *f*
pear [per] *s* Birne *f*
pearl [pʌrl] *adj* Perlen– ‖ *s* Perle *f*
pearl' neck'lace *s* Perlenkette *f*
pearl' oys'ter *s* Perlenauster *f*
pear' tree' *s* Birnbaum *m*

peasant ['pezənt] *adj* Bauern–, bäuerlich ‖ *s* Bauer *m,* Bäuerin *f*
peasantry ['pezəntri] *s* Bauernstand *m*
pea'shoot'er *s* Blasrohr *n*
pea' soup' *s* Erbsensuppe *f;* (fig) Waschküche *f*
peat [pit] *s* Torf *m*
peat' moss' *s* Torfmull *m*
pebble ['pebəl] *s* Kiesel *m;* **pebbles** Geröll *n*
peck [pɛk] *s* (*measure*) Viertelscheffel *m;* (*e.g., of a bird*) Schnabelhieb *n;* (*kiss*) (coll) flüchtiger Kuß *m;* (*of trouble*) (coll) Menge *f* ‖ *tr* hacken; (*food*) aufpicken ‖ *intr* hacken, picken; (*eat food*) picken; **p. at** hacken nach; (*food*) (coll) herumstochern in (*dat*)
peculation [ˌpɛkjə'leʃən] *s* Geldunterschlagung *f*
peculiar [pɪ'kjuljər] *adj* eigenartig, absonderlich; **p. to** eigen (*dat*)
peculiarity [ˌpɪkjulɪ'ærɪti] *s* Eigenheit *f,* Absonderlichkeit *f*
pedagogic(al) [ˌpɛdə'gadʒɪk(əl)] *adj* pädagogisch, erzieherisch
pedagogue ['pɛdəˌgag] *s* Pädagoge *m,* Erzieher *m*
pedagogy ['pɛdəˌgadʒi] *s* Pädagogik *f,* Erziehungskunde *f*
ped·al ['pɛdəl] *s* Pedal *n* ‖ *v* (*pret & pp* -al[l]ed; *ger* -al[l]ing) *tr* fahren ‖ *intr* die Pedale treten
pedant ['pɛdənt] *s* Pedant –in *mf*
pedantic [pɪ'dæntɪk] *adj* pedantisch
pedantry ['pɛdəntri] *s* Pedanterie *f*
peddle ['pɛdəl] *tr* hausieren mit ‖ *intr* hausieren
peddler ['pɛdlər] *s* Hausierer –in *mf*
pedestal ['pɛdɪstəl] *s* Sockel *m,* Postament *n;* **put s.o. on a p.** (fig) j-n aufs Podest erheben
pedestrian [pɪ'dɛstrɪ·ən] *adj* Fußgänger– *m;* (fig) schwunglos ‖ *s* Fußgänger –in *mf*
pediatrician [ˌpidɪ·ə'trɪʃən] *s* Kinderarzt *m,* Kinderärztin *f*
pediatrics [ˌpidɪ'ætrɪks] *s* Kinderheilkunde *f*
pediment ['pɛdɪmənt] *s* Giebelfeld *n*
peek [pik] *s* schneller Blick *m* ‖ *intr* gucken; **p. at** angucken
peekaboo ['pikəˌbu] *adj* durchsichtig ‖ *interj* guck, guck!
peel [pil] *s* Schale *f* ‖ *tr* schälen; **p. off** abschälen ‖ *intr* sich schälen; (*said of paint*) abbröckeln; **p. off** (aer) sich aus dem Verband lösen
peep [pip] *s* schneller Blick *m;* heimlicher Blick *m;* **not another p. out of you!** kein Laut mehr aus dir! ‖ *intr* gucken; (*look carefully*) lugen; **p. out** hervorlugen
peep'hole' *s* Guckloch *n*
peep' show' *s* Fleischbeschau *f*
peer [pɪr] *s* Gleichgestellte *mf* ‖ *intr* blicken; **p. at** mustern
peerless ['pɪrlɪs] *adj* unvergleichlich
peeve [piv] *s* (coll) Beschwerde *f* ‖ *tr* (coll) ärgern
peeved *adj* verärgert
peevish ['pivɪʃ] *adj* sauertöpfisch

peg [peg] s Pflock m; (for clothes) Haken m; (e.g., of a violin) Wirbel m; **take down a p. or two** ducken || v (pret & pp **pegged**; ger **pegging**) tr festpflocken; (prices) festlegen; (throw) (sl) schmeißen; (identify) (sl) erkennen

peg'board' s Klammerplatte f

Peggy ['pegɪ] s Gretchen n, Gretl f & n

peg' leg' s Stelzbein n

Pekin·ese [,pikɪ'niz] s (-ese) Pekinese m

pelf [pelf] s (pej) Mammon m

pelican ['pelɪkən] s Pelikan m

pellet ['pelɪt] s Kügelchen n; (bullet) Schrotkugel f, Schrotkorn n

pell-mell ['pel'mel] adj verworren || adv durcheinander

pelt [pelt] s Fell n, Pelz m; (whack) Schlag m || tr (with) bewerfen (mit); (with questions) bombardieren

pelvis ['pelvɪs] s Becken n

pen [pen] s Feder f; (fountain pen) Füllfederhalter m; (enclosure) Pferch m; (prison) (sl) Kittchen n || v (pret & pp **penned**; ger **penning**) tr (a letter) verfassen || (pret & pp **pent**; ger **penning**) tr—**pen in** pferchen

penal ['pinəl] adj strafrechtlich, Straf-

pe'nal code' s Strafgesetzbuch n

penalize ['pinə,laɪz] tr bestrafen; (box) mit Strafpunkten belegen

penalty ['penəltɪ] s Strafe f; (point deducted) (sport) Strafpunkt m; **under p. of death** bei Todesstrafe

pen'alty ar'ea s (sport) Strafraum m

pen'alty box' s Strafbank f

pen'alty kick' s Strafstoß m

penance ['penəns] s Buße f

penchant ['penʃənt] s (for) Hang m (zu)

pen·cil ['pensəl] s Bleistift m || v (pret & pp **-cil[l]ed**; ger **-cil[l]ing**) tr mit Bleistift anzeichnen

pen'cil push'er s (coll) Schreiberling m

pen'cil sharp'ener s Bleistiftspitzer m

pendant ['pendənt] s Anhänger m; (electrical fixture) Hängeleuchter m

pendent ['pendənt] adj (herab)hängend

pend'ing adj schwebend; **be p. in** (der) Schwebe sein || prep (during) während (genit); (until) bis zu (dat)

pendulum ['pendʒələm] s Pendel m

pen'dulum bob' s Pendelgewicht n

penetrate ['penɪ,tret] tr eindringen in (acc) || intr eindringen

penetration [,penɪ'treʃən] s Durchdringen n; (of, e.g., a country) Eindringen n (in acc); (in ballistics) Durchschlagskraft f

penguin ['peŋgwɪn] s Pinguin m

penicillin [,penɪ'sɪlɪn] s Penizillin n

peninsula [pə'nɪnsələ] s Halbinsel f

pe·nis ['pinɪs] s (-nes [niz] & -nises) Penis m

penitence ['penɪtəns] s Bußfertigkeit f

penitent ['penɪtənt] adj bußfertig || s Büßer –in mf; (eccl) Beichtkind n

penitentiary [,penɪ'tenʃərɪ] s Zuchthaus n

pen'knife' s (-knives') Federmesser n

penmanship ['penmən,ʃɪp] s Schreibkunst f

pen' name' s Schriftstellername m

pennant ['penənt] s Wimpel m; (nav) Stander m

penniless ['penɪlɪs] adj mittellos

penny ['penɪ] s Pfennig m; (U.S.A.) Cent m

pen'ny pinch'er [,pɪntʃər] s Pfennigfuchser m

pen' pal' s Schreibfreund –in mf

pension ['penʃən] s Pension f, Rente f; **put on p.** pensionieren || tr pensionieren

pensioner ['penʃənər] s Pensionär –in mf; (ins) Rentenempfänger –in mf

pen'sion fund' s Pensionskasse f

pensive ['pensɪv] adj sinnend

pentagon ['pentə,gan] s Fünfeck n; **the Pentagon** das Pentagon

Pentecost ['pentɪ,kɔst] s Pfingsten n

penthouse ['pent,haʊs] s Wetterdach n; (exclusive apartment) Penthouse n

pent-up ['pent'ʌp] adj verhalten

penult ['pinʌlt] s vorletzte Silbe f

penurious [pɪ'nʊrɪ·əs] adj karg

penury ['penjərɪ] s Kargheit f

peony ['pi·ənɪ] s Pfingstrose f

people ['pipəl] spl Leute pl, Menschen pl; **his p.** die Seinen; **p. like him** seinesgleichen; **p. say** man sagt, die Leute sagen || s (peoples) Volk n || tr bevölkern

pep [pep] s (coll) Schwungkraft f || v (pret & pp **pepped**; ger **pepping**) tr—**pep up** aufpulvern

pepper ['pepər] s (spice) Pfeffer m; (plant) Paprika f; (vegetable) Paprikaschote f || tr pfeffern

pep'per mill' s Pfeffermühle f

pep'permint' adj Pfefferminz– || s Pfefferminze f

pep'per shak'er s Pfefferstreuer m

peppery ['pepərɪ] adj pfefferig

per [pʌr] prep pro (acc); **as per** laut (genit & dat)

perambulator [pər'æmbjə,letər] s Kinderwagen m

per capita [pər'kæpɪtə] pro Kopf

perceivable [pər'sivəbəl] adj wahrnehmbar

perceive [pər'siv] tr wahrnehmen

percent [pər'sent] s Prozent n

percentage [pər'sentɪdʒ] s Prozentsatz m; **p. of** (e.g., the profit) Anteil m an (dat); (e.g., of a group) Teil m (genit)

perceptible [pər'septəbəl] adj wahrnehmbar

perception [pər'sepʃən] s Wahrnehmung f

perch [pʌrtʃ] s Stange f; (ichth) Barsch m || tr setzen || intr sitzen

percolate ['pʌrkə,let] tr durchseihen; (coffee) perkolieren || intr durchsickern

percolator ['pʌrkə,letər] s Perkolator m

percussion [pər'kʌʃən] s Schlag m; (med) Perkussion f

percus'sion in'strument s Schlaginstrument n

per di'em allow'ance [pər'daɪ·əm] s Tagegeld n

perdition [pər'dɪʃən] s Verdammnis f

perennial [pə'renɪ·əl] adj immerwährend; (bot) ausdauernd ‖ s ausdauernde Pflanze f

perfect ['pʌrfɪkt] adj perfekt, vollkommen; **he is a p. stranger to me** er ist mir völlig fremd ‖ s (gram) Perfekt(um) n ‖ [pər'fekt] tr vervollkommen

perfection [pər'fekʃən] s Vollkommenheit f; **to p.** vollkommen

perfectionist [pər'fekʃənɪst] s Perfektionist –in mf

perfectly ['pʌrfɪktlɪ] adv völlig, durchaus; **p. well** ganz genau

perfidious [pər'fɪdɪ·əs] adj treulos

perfidy ['pʌrfɪdɪ] s Treubruch m

perforate ['pʌrfə‚ret] tr durchlöchern

per'forated line' s durchlochte Linie f

perforation [‚pʌrfə'reʃən] s gelochte Linie f

perforce [pər'fors] adv notgedrungen

perform [pər'form] tr ausführen; (an operation) vornehmen; (theat) aufführen ‖ intr (öffentlich) auftreten; (mach) funktionieren

performance [pər'formans] s Ausführung f; (mach) Leistung f; (theat) Aufführung f

performer [pər'formər] s Künstler –in mf

perform'ing arts' spl darstellende Künste pl

perfume [pər'fjum] s Parfüm n ‖ tr parfümieren

perfunctorily [pər'fʌŋktərɪlɪ] adv oberflächlich

perfunctory [pər'fʌŋktərɪ] adj oberflächlich

perhaps [pər'hæps] adv vielleicht

per hour' pro Stunde, in der Stunde

peril ['perɪl] s Gefahr f; **at one's own p.** auf eigene Gefahr

perilous ['perɪləs] adj gefährlich

perimeter [pə'rɪmɪtər] s (math) Umfang m; (mil) Rand m

period ['pɪrɪ·əd] s Periode f, Zeitabschnitt m; (menstrual period) Periode f; (educ) Stunde f; (gram) Punkt m; (sport) Viertel n; **extra p.** (sport) Verlängerung f; **for a p. of** für die Dauer von; **p.!** und damit punktum!; **p. of grace** Frist f; **p. of life** Lebensalter n; **p. of time** Zeitdauer pl

pe'riod fur'niture s Stilmöbel pl

periodic [‚pɪrɪ'ɑdɪk] adj zeitweilig

periodical [‚pɪrɪ'ɑdɪkəl] s Zeitschrift f

peripheral [pə'rɪfərəl] adj peripher

periphery [pə'rɪfərɪ] s Peripherie f

periscope ['perɪ‚skop] s Periskop n

perish ['perɪʃ] intr umkommen; (said of wares) verderben

perishable ['perɪʃəbəl] adj vergänglich; (food) leicht verderblich

perjure ['pʌrdʒər] tr—**p. oneself** Meineid begehen

perjury ['pʌrdʒərɪ] s Meineid m; **commit p.** e–n Meineid leisten

perk [pʌrk] tr—**p. up** (the head) aufwerfen; (the ears) spitzen ‖ intr

(percolate) (coll) perkolieren; **p. up** lebhaft werden

permanence ['pʌrmənəns] s Dauer f

permanent ['pʌrmənənt] adj (fort)dauernd, bleibend ‖ s Dauerwelle f

per'manent address' s ständiger Wohnort m

per'manent job' s Dauerstellung f

per'manent wave' s Dauerwelle f

permeable ['pʌrmɪ·əbəl] adj durchlässig

permeate ['pʌrmɪ‚et] tr durchdringen ‖ intr durchsickern

permissible [pər'mɪsɪbəl] adj zulässig

permission [pər'mɪʃən] s Erlaubnis f; **with your p.** mit Verlaub

permissive [pər'mɪsɪv] adj nachsichtig

per-mit ['pʌrmɪt] s Erlaubnis f; (document) Erlaubnisschein m ‖ [pər'mɪt] v (pret & pp –mitted; ger –mitting) tr erlauben, gestatten; **be permitted to** (inf) dürfen (inf)

permute [pər'mjut] tr umsetzen; (math) permutieren

pernicious [pər'nɪʃəs] adj (to) schädlich (für)

perox'ide blonde' [pə'rɑksaɪd] s Wasserstoffblondine f

perpendicular [‚pʌrpən'dɪkjələr] adj senkrecht ‖ s Senkrechte f

perpetrate ['pʌrpɪ‚tret] tr verüben

perpetual [pər'petʃʊ·əl] adj (everlasting) ewig; (continual) unaufhörlich

perpetuate [pər'petʃʊ‚et] tr verewigen

perplex [pər'pleks] tr verblüffen

perplexed' adj verblüfft

perplexity [pər'pleksɪtɪ] s Verblüffung f

persecute ['pʌrsɪ‚kjut] tr verfolgen

persecution [‚pʌrsɪ'kjuʃən] s Verfolgung f

persecutor ['pʌrsɪ‚kjutər] s Verfolger –in mf

perseverance [‚pʌrsɪ'vɪrəns] s Ausdauer f, Beharrlichkeit f

persevere [‚pʌrsɪ'vɪr] intr ausdauern; **p. in** (cling to) beharren auf (acc); (e.g., efforts, studies) fortfahren mit

Persia ['pʌrʒə] s Persien n

Persian ['pʌrʒən] adj persisch ‖ s Perser –in mf; (language) Persisch n

Per'sian rug' s Perserteppich m

persimmon [pər'sɪmən] s Persimone f

persist [pər'sɪst] intr andauern; **p. in** verbleiben bei

persistent [pər'sɪstənt] adj andauernd

person ['pʌrsən] s Person f; **in p.** persönlich; **per p.** pro Person

personable ['pʌrsənəbəl] adj (attractive) ansehnlich; (good-natured) verträglich

personage ['pʌrsənɪdʒ] s Persönlichkeit f

personal ['pʌrsənəl] adj persönlich; (private) Privat–; **become p.** anzüglich werden

per'sonal da'ta spl Personalien pl

per'sonal hygiene' s Körperpflege f

per'sonal in'jury s Personenschaden m

personality [‚pʌrsə'nælɪtɪ] s Persönlichkeit f

personally ['pʌrsənəlɪ] adv persönlich

per'sonal pro'noun s Personalpronomen n

personi·fy ['pɜr'sɑnɪ,faɪ] v (pret & pp -fied) tr personifizieren, verkörpern

personnel [,pʌrsə'nel] s Personal n

per'son-to-per'son call' s Gespräch n mit Voranmeldung

perspective [pər'spɛktɪv] s Perspektive f

perspicacious [,pʌrspɪ'keʃəs] adj scharfsinnig

perspiration [,pʌrspɪ'reʃən] s Schweiß m; (perspiring) Schwitzen n

perspire [pər'spaɪr] intr schwitzen

persuade [pər'swed] tr überreden

persuasion [pər'sweʒən] s Überredung f

persuasive [pər'swesɪv] adj redegewandt

pert [pʌrt] adj keck; (sprightly) lebhaft

pertain [pər'ten] intr—p. to betreffen, sich beziehen auf (acc)

pertinacious [,pʌrtɪ'neʃəs] adj beharrlich

pertinent ['pʌrtɪnənt] adj einschlägig; be p. to sich beziehen auf (acc)

perturb [pər'tʌrb] tr beunruhigen

peruse [pə'ruz] tr sorgfältig durchlesen

pervade [pər'ved] tr durchdringen

perverse [pər'vʌrs] adj (abnormal) pervers; (obstinate) verstockt

perversion [pər'vʌrʒən] s Perversion f; (of truth) Verdrehung f

perversity [pər'vʌrsɪti] s Perversität f

pervert ['pʌrvərt] s perverser Mensch m ‖ [pər'vʌrt] tr (corrupt) verderben; (twist) verdrehen; (misapply) mißbrauchen

pesky ['peski] adj (coll) lästig

pessimism ['pɛsɪ,mɪzəm] s Pessimismus m

pessimist ['pɛsɪmɪst] s Pessimist –in mf

pessimistic [,pɛsɪ'mɪstɪk] adj pessimistisch

pest [pɛst] s (insect) Schädling m; (annoying person) Plagegeist m; (pestilence) Pest f

pest' control' s Schädlingsbekämpfung f

pester ['pɛstər] tr piesacken; (with questions) belästigen

pesticide ['pɛstɪ,saɪd] s Pestizid n

pestilence ['pɛstɪləns] s Pestilenz f

pestle ['pɛsəl] s Stößel m

pet [pɛt] adj Lieblings- ‖ s (animal) Haustier n; (person) Liebling m; (favorite child) Schoßkind n ‖ v (pret & pp petted; ger petting) tr streicheln ‖ intr sich abknutschen

petal ['pɛtəl] s Blumenblatt n

Peter ['pitər] s Peter m ‖ intr—peter out im Sande verlaufen

pet' ide'a s Lieblingsgedanke m

petition [pɪ'tɪʃən] s Eingabe f; (jur) Gesuch n ‖ tr (s.o.) ersuchen

pet' name' s Kosename m

petri·fy ['pɛtrɪ,faɪ] v (pret & pp -fied) tr (& fig) versteinern; be petrified versteinern; (fig) zu Stein werden

petroleum [pə'trolɪ·əm] s Petroleum n

pet' shop' s Tierhandlung f

petticoat ['pɛtɪ,kot] s Unterrock m

pet'ting s Petting n

petty ['pɛti] adj klein, geringfügig; (narrow) engstirnig

pet'ty cash' s Handkasse f

pet'ty lar'ceny s geringer Diebstahl m

pet'ty of'ficer s (nav) Bootsmann m

petulant ['pɛtʃələnt] adj verdrießlich

petunia [pə't(j)unɪ·ə] s Petunie f

pew [pju] s Bank f, Kirchenstuhl m

pewter ['pjutər] s Weißmetall n

Pfc. ['pi'ɛf'si] s (private first class) Gefreiter m

phalanx ['fælæŋks] s Phalanx f

phantasm ['fæntæzəm] s Trugbild n

phantom ['fæntəm] s Phantom n

Pharaoh ['fero] s Pharao m

Pharisee ['færɪ,si] s Pharisäer m

pharmaceutical [,farmə'sutɪkəl] adj pharmazeutisch

pharmacist ['farməsɪst] s Apotheker –in mf

pharmacy ['farməsi] s Apotheke f; (science) Pharmazie f

pharynx ['færɪŋks] s Rachenhöhle f

phase [fez] s Phase f ‖ tr in Phasen einteilen; p. out abwickeln

pheasant ['fɛzənt] s Fasan m

phenobarbital [,fino'barbɪ,tæl] s Phenobarbital n

phenomenal [fɪ'nɑmɪnəl] adj phänomenal

phenome·non [fɪ'nɑmɪ,nɑn] s (-na [nə]) (& fig) Phänomen n, Erscheinung f

phial ['faɪ·əl] s Phiole f

philanderer [fɪ'lændərər] s Schürzenjäger m

philanthropist [fɪ'lænθrəpɪst] s Menschenfreund –in mf, Philanthrop –in mf

philanthropy [fɪ'lænθrəpi] s Menschenliebe f, Philanthropie f

philately [fɪ'lætəli] s Briefmarkenkunde f

Philippine ['fɪlɪ,pin] adj philippinisch ‖ the Philippines spl die Philippinen

Philistine ['fɪlɪstɪn] adj (& fig) philisterhaft ‖ s (& fig) Philister m

philologist [fɪ'lɑlədʒɪst] s Philologe m, Philologin f

philology [fɪ'lɑlədʒi] s Philologie f

philosopher [fɪ'lɑsəfər] s Philosoph m

philosophic(al) [,fɪlə'sɑfɪk(əl)] adj philosophisch

philosophy [fɪ'lɑsəfi] s Philosophie f

phlebitis [flɪ'baɪtɪs] s Venenentzündung f

phlegm [flɛm] s Schleim m

phlegmatic(al) [flɛg'mætɪk(əl)] adj phlegmatisch

phobia ['fobɪ·ə] s Phobie f

Phoenicia [fɪ'nɪʃə] s Phönizien n

Phoenician [fɪ'nɪʃən] adj phönizisch ‖ s Phönizier m

phoenix ['finɪks] s Phönix m

phone [fon] s (coll) Telephon n; on the p. am Apparat ‖ tr (coll) anrufen ‖ intr telephonieren

phone' call' s (coll) Anruf m

phonetic [fo'nɛtɪk] *adj* phonetisch, Laut– || **phonetics** *s* Lautlehre *f*, Phonetik *f*
phonograph ['fonə‚græf] *s* Grammophon *n*
pho′nograph rec′ord *s* Schallplatte *f*
phonology [fə'nɑlədʒi] *s* Lautlehre *f*
phony ['foni] *adj* falsch, Schein– || *s* Schwindler –in *mf*
phosphate ['fɑsfet] *s* Phosphat *n*
phosphorescent [‚fɑsfə'rɛsənt] *adj* phosphoreszierend
phospho·rus ['fɑsfərəs] *s* (–ri [‚raɪ]) Phosphor *m*
pho·to ['foto] *s* (–tos) (coll) Photo *n*
pho′tocop′y *s* Photokopie *f* || *v* (*pret* & *pp* –ied) *tr* photokopieren
pho′toengrav′ing *s* Lichtdruckverfahren *n*
pho′to fin′ish *s* Zielphotographie *f*
photogenic [‚foto'dʒɛnɪk] *adj* photogen
photograph ['fotə‚græf] *s* Photographie *f* || *tr* & *intr* photographieren
photographer [fə'tɑgrəfər] *s* Photograph –in *mf*
photography [fə'tɑgrəfi] *s* Photographie *f*
photostat ['fotə‚stæt] *s* (trademark) Photokopie *f* || *tr* photokopieren
phrase [frez] *s* Sinngruppe *f* || *tr* formulieren; (mus) phrasieren
phrenology [frə'nɑlədʒi] *s* Schädellehre *f*
physic ['fɪzɪk] *s* Abführmittel *n*; **physics** *s* Physik *f*
physical ['fɪzɪkəl] *adj* körperlich, physisch || *s* (*examination*) ärztliche Untersuchung *f*
phys′ical condi′tion *s* Gesundheitszustand *m*
phys′ical de′fect *s* körperliches Gebrechen *n*
phys′ical educa′tion *s* Leibeserziehung *f*
phys′ical ex′ercise *s* Leibesübungen *pl*; (*calisthenics*) Bewegung *f*
phys′ical hand′icap *s* Körperbehinderung *f*
physician [fɪ'zɪʃən] *s* Arzt *m*, Ärztin *f*
physicist ['fɪzɪsɪst] *s* Physiker –in *mf*
physics ['fɪzɪks] *s* Physik *f*
physiognomy [‚fɪzi'ɑgnəmi] *s* Gesichtsbildung *f*, Physiognomie *f*
physiological [‚fɪzi·ə'lɑdʒɪkəl] *adj* physiologisch
physiology [‚fɪzi'ɑlədʒi] *s* Physiologie *f*
physique [fɪ'zik] *s* Körperbau *m*
pi [paɪ] *s* (math) Pi *n* || *tr* (typ) zusammenwerfen
pianist ['pi·ənɪst] *s* Pianist –in *mf*
pian·o [pɪ'æno] *s* (–os) Klavier *n*
pian′o stool′ *s* Klavierschemel *m*
picayune [‚pɪkə'jun] *adj* (*paltry*) geringfügig; (*person*) kleinlich
picco·lo ['pɪkəlo] *s* (–los) Pikkoloflöte *f*
pick [pɪk] *s* (*tool*) Spitzhacke *f*; (*choice*) Auslese *f*; **the p. of the crop** das Beste von allem || *tr* (*choose*) sich [*dat*] aussuchen; (*e.g., fruit*)

pflücken; (*one's teeth*) stochern in (*dat*); (*one's nose*) bohren in (*dat*); (*a lock*) mit e–m Dietrich öffnen; (*a quarrel*) suchen; (*a bone*) abnagen; **p. off** abpflücken; (*shoot*) (coll) abknallen; **p. out** auswählen; **p. s.o.'s brains** j–s Ideen klauen; **p. s.o.'s pocket** j–m die Tasche ausräumen; **p. up** (*lift up*) aufheben; (*a girl*) (coll) aufgabeln; (*a suspect*) aufgreifen; (*with a car*) abholen; (*passengers; the scent*) aufnehmen; (*a language; news*) aufschnappen; (*a habit*) annehmen; (*a visual object*) erkennen; (*strength*) wieder erlangen; (*weight*) zunehmen an (*dat*); **p. up speed** in Fahrt kommen || *intr*—**p. and choose** wählerisch suchen; **p. at** herumstochern in (*dat*); **p. on** herumreiten auf (*dat*); **p. up** (*improve in health or business*) sich (wieder) erholen
pick′ax′ *s* Picke *f*, Pickel *m*
picket ['pɪkɪt] *s* Holzpfahl *m*; (*of strikers*) Streikposten *m* || *tr* durch Streikposten absperren, Streikposten stehen vor (*dat*) || *intr* Streikposten stehen
pick′et fence′ *s* Lattenzaun *m*
pick′et line′ *s* Streikkette *f*
pickle ['pɪkəl] *s* Essiggurke *f*; **be in a p.** (coll) im Schlamassel sitzen || *tr* (ein)pökeln
pick′led *adj* (sl) blau
pick′led her′ring *s* Rollmops *m*
pick′pock′et *s* Taschendieb *m*
pick′up′ *s* (*of a car*) Beschleunigungsvermögen *n*; (*girl*) Straßenbekanntschaft *f*; (*restorative*) Stärkungsmittel *n*, Erfrischung *f*; (*a stop to pick up*) Abholung *f*; (*of a phonograph*) Schalldose *f*
pick′up truck′ *s* offener Lieferwagen *m*
picky ['pɪki] *adj* wählerisch
pic·nic ['pɪknɪk] *s* Picknick *n* || *v* (*pret* & *pp* –nicked; *ger* –nicking) *intr* picknicken
pictorial [pɪk'tori·əl] *adj* illustriert || *s* Illustrierte *f*
picture ['pɪktʃər] *s* Bild *n*; (fig) Vorstellung *f*; **look the p. of health** kerngesund aussehen || *tr* sich [*dat*] vorstellen
pic′ture gal′lery *s* Gemäldegalerie *f*
pic′ture post′card *s* Ansichtspostkarte *f*
picturesque [‚pɪktʃə'rɛsk] *adj* malerisch, pittoresk; (*language*) bilderreich
pic′ture tube′ *s* Bildröhre *f*
pic′ture win′dow *s* Panoramafenster *n*
piddling ['pɪdlɪŋ] *adj* lumpig
pie [paɪ] *s* Torte *f*; (*meat-filled*) Pastete *f*; **pie in the sky** Luftschloß *n*
piece [pis] *s* Stück *n*; (checkers) Stein *m*; (chess) Figur *f*; (mil) Geschütz *n*; (mus, theat) Stück *n*; **a p. of advice** ein Rat *m*; **a p. of bad luck** ein unglücklicher Zufall *m*; **a p. of furniture** ein Möbelstück *n*; **a p. of luggage** ein Gepäckstück *n*; **a p. of**

news e-e Neuigkeit *f*; a p. of paper ein Blatt Papier; a p. of toast e-e geröstete Brotscheibe *f*; say one's p. seine Meinung sagen

piece'meal' *adv* stückweise

piece'work' *s* Akkordarbeit *f*; do p. in Akkord arbeiten

piece'work'er *s* Akkordarbeiter –in *mf*

pier [pɪr] *s* Landungsbrücke *f*, Pier *m* & *f*; (*of a bridge*) Pfeiler *m*

pierce [pɪrs] *tr* durchstechen, durchbohren

pierc'ing *adj* (*look, pain*) scharf, stechend; (*cry*) gellend; (*cold*) schneidend

piety ['paɪ·əti] *s* Frömmigkeit *f*

pig [pɪg] *s* Schwein *n*

pigeon ['pɪdʒən] *s* Taube *f*

pi'geonhole' *s* Fach *n* || *tr* auf die lange Bank schieben

pi'geon loft' *s* Taubenschlag *m*

pi'geon-toed' *adj* & *adv* mit einwärts gerichteten Zehen

piggish ['pɪgɪʃ] *adj* säuisch

piggyback ['pɪgɪ‚bæk] *adv* huckepack

pig'gy bank' *s* Sparschweinchen *n*

pig'head'ed *adj* dickköpfig

pig' i'ron *s* Roheisen *n*

pigment ['pɪgmənt] *s* Pigment *n*

pig'pen' *s* Schweinekoben *m*

pig'skin' *s* Schweinsleder *n*; (sport) (coll) Fußball *m*

pig'sty' *s* Schweinestall *m*

pig'tail' *s* (*hair style*) Rattenschwanz *m*

pike [paɪk] *s* Pike *f*, Spieß *m*; (*highway*) Landstraße *f*; (ichth) Hecht *m*

piker ['paɪkər] *s* (coll) Knicker *m*

pilaster [pɪ'læstər] *s* Wandpfeiler *m*

pile [paɪl] *s* (*heap*) Haufen *m*; (*e.g., of papers*) Stoß *m*; (*stake*) Pfahl *m*; (*fortune*) (coll) Menge *f*; (atom. phys) Meiler *m*, Reaktor *m*; (elec, phys) Säule *f*; (tex) Flor *m*; **piles** (pathol) Hämorrhoiden *pl*; **piles of money** (coll) Heidengeld *n* || *tr* anhäufen, aufhäufen; **p. it on** (coll) dick auftragen || *intr—p.* **into** sich drängen in (acc); **p. on** sich übereinander stürzen; **p. out of** sich hinausdrängen aus; **p. up** sich (an)häufen

pile' driv'er *s* Pfahlramme *f*, Rammbär *m*

pilfer ['pɪlfər] *tr* mausen, stibitzen

pilgrim ['pɪlgrɪm] *s* Pilger –in *mf*

pilgrimage ['pɪlgrɪmɪdʒ] *s* Pilgerfahrt *f*; **go on a p.** pilgern

pill [pɪl] *s* (& fig) Pille *f*

pillar ['pɪlər] *s* Pfeiler *m*, Säule *f*

pill'box' *s* Pillenschachtel *f*; (mil) Bunker *m*

pillo·ry ['pɪləri] *s* Pranger *m* || *v* (*pret* & *pp* **–ried**) *tr* an den Pranger stellen; (fig) anprangern

pillow ['pɪlo] *s* Kopfkissen *n*

pil'lowcase' *s* Kopfkissenbezug *m*

pilot ['paɪlət] *adj* (*experimental*) Versuchs– || *s* (aer) Pilot *m*, Flugzeugführer –in *mf*; (naut) Lotse *m* || *tr* (aer) steuern, führen; (naut) steuern, lotsen

pi'lothouse' *s* (naut) Ruderhaus *n*

pi'lot light' *s* Sparflamme *f*

pi'lot's li'cense *s* Flugzeugführerschein *m*

pimp [pɪmp] *s* Zuhälter *m* || *intr* kuppeln

pimp'ing *s* Zuhälterei *f*

pimple ['pɪmpəl] *s* Pickel *m*

pimply ['pɪmpli] *adj* pickelig

pin [pɪn] *s* Stecknadel *f*; (*ornament*) Anstecknadel *f*; (bowling) Kegel *m*; (mach) Pinne *f*, Zapfen *m*; **be on pins and needles** wie auf Nadeln sitzen || *v* (*pret* & *pp* **pinned**); *ger* **pinning**) *tr* (*fasten with a pin*) mit e-r Nadel befestigen; (*e.g., a dress*) abstecken; (*e.g., under a car*) einklemmen; (*e.g., against the wall*) drücken; (*in wrestling*) auf die Schultern legen; **pin down** (*a person*) festlegen; (*troops*) niederhalten; **pin one's hopes on** seine Hofnungen setzen auf (*acc*); **pin s.th. on s.o.** (fig) j-m etw anhängen; **pin up** (*a sign*) anschlagen; (*the hair, a dress*) aufstecken

pinafore ['pɪnə‚for] *s* Latz *m*

pin'ball machine' *s* Spielautomat *m*

pin' boy' *s* Kegeljunge *m*

pincers ['pɪnsərz] *s* & *spl* Kneifzange *f*

pinch [pɪntʃ] *s* Kneifen *n*; (*of salt*) Prise *f*; **give s.o. a p.** j-n kneifen; **in a p.** zur Not, in der Not || *tr* kneifen, zwicken; (*steal*) (coll) klauen; (*arrest*) (coll) schnappen; **I got my finger pinched in the door** ich habe mir den Finger in der Tür geklemmt; **p. and scrape every penny** sich [*dat*] jeden Groschen vom Munde absparen; **p. off** abzwicken || *intr* (*said of shoe*) (& fig) drücken

pinchers ['pɪntʃərz] *s* & *spl* Kneifzange *f*

pinch'-hit' *v* (*pret* & *pp* **–hit**; *ger* **–hitting**) *intr* einspringen

pinch' hit'ter *s* Ersatzmann *m*

pin'cush'ion *s* Nadelkissen *n*

pine [paɪn] *adj* Kiefern– || *s* Kiefer *f* || *intr—p.* **away** sich abzehren; **p. for** sich sehnen nach

pine'ap'ple *s* Ananas *f*

pine' cone' *s* Kiefernzapfen *m*

pine' nee'dle *s* Kiefernnadel *f*

ping [pɪŋ] *s* Päng *n*; (*of a motor*) Klopfen *n* || *intr* (aut) klopfen

ping-pong ['pɪŋ‚pɑŋ] *s* Ping-pong *n*

pin'head' *s* (& fig) Stechnadelkopf *m*

pink [pɪŋk] *adj* rosa || *s* Rosa *n*

pin' mon'ey *s* Nadelgeld *n*

pinnacle ['pɪnəkəl] *s* Zinne *f*

pin'point' *adj* haarscharf; **p. landing** Ziellandung *f* || *tr* markieren

pin'prick' *s* Nadelstich *m*

pint [paɪnt] *s* Schoppen *m*, Pinte *f*

pin'up girl' *s* Pin-up-Girl *n*

pin'wheel' *s* (toy) Windmühle *f*; (*fireworks*) Feuerrad *n*

pioneer [‚paɪ·ə'nɪr] *s* Bahnbrecher –in *mf*; (fig & mil) Pionier *m* || *tr* (fig) den Weg freimachen für || *intr* (fig) Pionierarbeit leisten

pious ['paɪ·əs] *adj* fromm

pip [pɪp] *s* (*in fruit*) Kern *m*; (*on dice*) Punkt *m*; (*on a radarscope*) Leuchtpunkt *m*; (*of chickens*) Pips *m*

pipe [paɪp] s Rohr n; (for smoking; of an organ) Pfeife f ‖ tr durch ein Rohr (weiter)leiten ‖ intr pfeifen; **p. down** (sl) das Maul halten; **p. up** (coll) anfangen zu sprechen, loslegen

pipe′ clean′er s Pfeifenreiniger m

pipe′ dream′ s Wunschtraum m

pipe′ joint′ s Rohranschluß m

pipe′ line′ s Rohrleitung f, Pipeline f; (of information) Informationsquelle f

pipe′ or′gan s Orgel f

piper [′paɪpər] s Pfeifer –in mf

pipe′ wrench′ s Rohrzange f

piping [′paɪpɪŋ] adv—**p. hot** siedend heiß ‖ s Rohrleitung f; (on uniforms) Biese f; (sew) Paspel f

piquancy [′piːkənsi] s Pikanterie f

piquant [′piːkənt] adj pikant

pique [piːk] s Pik m ‖ tr verärgern; **be piqued at** pikiert sein über (acc)

piracy [′paɪrəsi] s Seeräuberei f

pirate [′paɪrɪt] s Seeräuber m ‖ tr (a book) (ungesetzlich) nachdrucken

pirouette [ˌpɪruˈet] s Pirouette f

pista′chio nut′ [pɪsˈtæʃ1ˈo] s Pistazien-nuß f

pistol [′pɪstəl] s Pistole f

pis′tol point′ s—**at p.** mit vorgehaltener Pistole

piston [′pɪstən] s Kolben m

pis′ton ring′ s Kolbenring m

pis′ton rod′ s Kolbenstange f

pis′ton stroke′ s Kolbenhub m

pit [pɪt] s Grube f; (in fruit) Kern m; (trap) Fallgrube f; (in the skin) Narbe f; (from corrosion) Rostgrüb-chen n; (in auto racing) Box f; (for cockfights) Kampfplatz m; (min) Schacht m; (theat) Parkett n; (mus) Orchester n; **pit of the stomach** Magengrube f ‖ v (pret & pp pitted; ger pitting) tr (a face) mit Narben be-decken; (fruit) entkernen; (through corrosion) anfressen; **pit A against B** A gegen B ausspielen; **pit one's strength against s.th.** seine Kraft mit etw messen

pitch [pɪtʃ] s Pech n; (of a roof) Dach-schräge f; (downward slope) Gefälle n; (of a ship) Stampfen n; (of a screw, thread) Teilung f; (of a pro-peller) Steigung f; (throw) Wurf m; (sales talk) Verkaufsgespräch n; (mus) Tonhöhe f ‖ tr (seal with pitch) verpichen; (a tent) aufschla-gen; (a ball) dem Schläger zuwerfen; (hay) mit der Heugabel werfen ‖ intr (naut) stampfen; **p. and toss** schlingern; **p. in** mithelfen

pitch′ ac′cent s musikalischer Tonak-zent m

pitch′-black′ adj pechrabenschwarz

pitcher [′pɪtʃər] s (jug) Krug m

pitch′fork′ s Heugabel f

pitch′ing s (naut) Stampfen n

pit′fall′ s Fallgrube f; (fig) Falle f

pith [pɪθ] s (& fig) Mark n

pithy [′pɪθi] adj (& fig) markig

pitiable [′pɪti·əbəl] adj erbarmenswert

pitiful [′pɪtifəl] adj erbärmlich

pitiless [′pɪtilɪs] adj erbarmungslos

pit′ted adj (by corrosion) angefressen; (fruit) entkernt

pit·y [′pɪti] s Erbarmen n, Mitleid n; **have p. on** Mitleid haben mit; **it's a p. that** (es ist) schade, daß; **move to p.** jammern; **what a p.!** wie schade! ‖ v (pret & pp –ied) tr sich erbar-men (genit), bemitleiden

pivot [′pɪvət] s Drehpunkt m ‖ intr (on) sich drehen (um); (mil) schwen-ken

placard [′plækɑrd] s Plakat n

placate [′pleket] tr begütigen

place [ples] s (seat; room) Platz m; (area, town, etc.) Ort m, Ortschaft f; (in a book; in a room) Stelle f; (situation) Lage f; (spot to eat in, dance in, etc.) Lokal n; **all over the p.** überall; **at your p.** (coll) bei Ihnen; **in my p.** an meiner Stelle; **in p. of** anstelle von (or genit); **in the first p.** erstens; **know one's p.** wissen, wohin man gehört; **out of p.** (& fig) nicht am Platz; **p. to stay** Unterkunft f; **put s.o. in his p.** j–n in seine Schran-ken verweisen; **take one's p.** antre-ten; **take p.** stattfinden; **take s.o.'s p.** an j–s Stelle treten ‖ tr setzen, stel-len; (an advertisement) aufgeben; (an order) erteilen; (find a job for) unterbringen; **I can't p. him** ich weiß nicht, wo ich ihn hintun soll; **p. a call** (telp) ein Gespräch anmelden ‖ intr (in horseracing) sich als Zweiter plazieren; (sport) sich plazieren

place·bo [pləˈsibo] s (–bos & –boes) Placebo n

place′ card′ s Tischkarte f

place′ mat′ s Tischmatte f

placement [′plesmənt] s Unterbringung f

place′-name′ s Ortsname m

place′ of birth′ s Geburtsort m

place′ of employ′ment s Arbeitsstätte f

place′ of res′idence s Wohnsitz m

placid [′plæsɪd] adj ruhig, sanftmütig

plagiarism [′pledʒəˌrɪzəm] s Plagiat n

plagiarist [′pledʒərɪst] s Plagiator –in mf

plagiarize [′pledʒəˌraɪz] intr ein Pla-giat begehen

plague [pleg] s Seuche f ‖ tr heim-suchen

plaid [plæd] adj buntkariert ‖ s Schot-tenkaro n

plain [plen] adj (simple) einfach; (clear) klar; (fabric) einfarbig; (homely) unschön; (truth) rein; (food) bürgerlich; (paper) unlin(i)-iert; (speech) unverblümt; (alcohol) unverdünnt ‖ s Ebene f

plain′ clothes′ spl—**in p.** in Zivil

plain′-clothes′ man′ s Geheimpolizist m

plaintiff [′plentif] s Kläger –in mf

plaintive [′plentɪv] adj Klage-, kla-gend

plait [plet], [plæt] s Flechte f; **p. of hair** Zopf m ‖ tr flechten

plan [plæn] s Plan m; (intention) Vor-haben n; **according to p.** planmäßig;

what are your plans for this evening? was haben Sie für heute abend vor? || v (pret & pp **planned;** ger **planning**) tr planen; (one's time) einteilen; **p. to** (inf) vorhaben zu (inf) || intr—**p. for** Pläne machen für; **p. on** rechnen mit

plane [plen] s (airplane) Flugzeug n, Maschine f; (airfoil) Tragfläche f; (carp) Hobel m; (geom) Ebene f; **on a high p.** (fig) auf e-m hohen Niveau || tr hobeln; **p. down** abhobeln

plane′ connec′tion s Fluganschluß m

plane′ geom′etry s Planimetrie f

planet [ˈplænɪt] s Planet m

planetari·um [ˌplænɪˈterɪ·əm] s (**-a** [ə] & **-ums**) Planetarium n

planetary [ˈplænəˌteri] adj Planeten-

plane′ tick′et s Flugkarte f

plane′ tree′ s Platane f

plank [plæŋk] s Brett n, Planke f; (pol) Programmpunkt m

planned′ par′enthood s Familienplanung f

plant [plænt] s (factory) Anlage f; (spy) Spion -in mf; (bot) Pflanze f || tr anpflanzen; (a field) bepflanzen; (a colony) gründen; (as a spy) als Falle aufstellen; (a bomb) verstecken; **p. oneself** sich hinstellen

plantation [plænˈteʃən] s Plantage f

planter [ˈplæntər] s (person who plants; plantation owner) Pflanzer -in mf; (decorative container) Blumentrog m; (mach) Pflanzmaschine f

plasma [ˈplæzmə] s Plasma n

plaster [ˈplæstər] s Verputz m; (med) Pflaster n || tr verputzen; (e.g., with posters) bepflastern; **be plastered** (sl) besoffen sein

plas′terboard′ s Gipsdiele f

plas′ter cast′ s (med) Gipsverband m; (sculp) Gipsabguß m

plasterer [ˈplæstərər] s Stukkateur m

plas′tering s Verputz m

plas′ter of Par′is s Gips m

plastic [ˈplæstɪk] adj Plastik- || s Plastik n

plas′tic sur′gery s Plastik f

plas′tic wood′ s Holzpaste f

plate [plet] s (dish) Teller m; (of metal) Platte f; (in a book) Tafel f; (elec, phot, typ) Platte f; (electron) Plattenelektrode f || tr plattieren

plateau [plæˈto] s Plateau n

plate′ glass′ s Tafelglas n

platen [ˈplætən] s Schreibmaschinenwalze f

platform [ˈplætˌfɔrm] s Plattform f; (for a speaker) Bühne f; (for loading) Rampe f; (pol) Programm n; (rr) Bahnsteig m

plat′form shoes′ spl Plateauschuhe pl

plat′ing s (e.g., of gold) Plattierung f; (armor) Panzerung f

platinum [ˈplætɪnəm] s Platin n

plat′inum blonde′ s Platinblondine f

platitude [ˈplætɪˌt(j)ud] s Gemeinplatz m

Plato [ˈpleto] s Plato m

Platonic [pləˈtɑnɪk] adj platonisch

platoon [pləˈtun] s Zug m

platter [ˈplætər] s Platte f

plausible [ˈplɔzɪbəl] adj plausibel

play [ple] s Spiel n; (mach) Spielraum m; (sport) Spielzug m; (theat) Stück n; **in p.** im Spiel; **out of p.** aus dem Spiel || tr spielen; (a card) ausspielen; (an opponent) spielen gegen; **p. back** (a tape, record) abspielen; **p. down** bagatellisieren; **p. the horses** bei Pferderennen wetten || intr spielen; (records, tapes) abspielen; **p. about** (the lips) umspielen; **p. along** mitspielen; **p. around with** herumspielen mit; **p. for** (stakes) spielen um; (a team) spielen für; **p. into s.o.'s hands** j-m in die Hände spielen; **p. safe** auf Nummer Sicher gehen; **p. up to** schmeicheln (dat)

play′back′ s (reproduction) Wiedergabe f; (device) Abspielgerät n

play′boy′ s Playboy m

player [ˈple·ər] s Spieler -in mf; (sport) Sportler -in mf; (theat) Schauspieler -in mf

playful [ˈplefəl] adj spielerisch

play′ground′ s Spielplatz m

play′house′ s Theater n; (for children) Spielhaus n

play′ing card′ s Spielkarte f

play′ing field′ s Spielfeld n

play′mate′ s Spielkamerad -in mf

play′-offs′ spl Vorrunde f

play′ on words′ s Wortspiel n

play′pen′ s Laufgitter n

play′room′ s Spielzimmer n

play′-school′ s Kindergarten m

play′thing′ s (& fig) Spielzeug n

playwright [ˈpleˌraɪt] s Schauspieldichter -in mf

plea [pli] s Bitte f; (jur) Plädoyer n

plead [plid] v (pret & pp **pleaded** & **pled** [pled]) tr (ignorance) vorschützen || intr plädieren; **p. guilty** sich schuldig bekennen; **p. not guilty** sich als nichtschuldig erklären; **p. with s.o.** j-n anflehen

pleasant [ˈplezənt] adj angenehm

pleasantry [ˈplezəntri] s Heiterkeit f; (remark) Witz m

please [pliz] tr gefallen (dat); **be pleased to** (inf) sich freuen zu (inf); **be pleased with** sich freuen über (acc); **pleased to meet you!** sehr angenehm || intr gefallen; **as one pleases** nach Gefallen; **do as you p.** tun Sie, wie Sie wollen; **if you p.** wenn ich bitten darf; (iron) gefälligst; **p.!** bitte!

pleas′ing adj angenehm, gefällig

pleasure [ˈpleʒər] s Vergnügen n

pleas′ure trip′ s Vergnügungsreise f

pleat [plit] s Plissee n || tr plissieren

pleat′ed skirt′ s Plisseerock m

plebeian [plɪˈbi·ən] adj plebejisch || s Plebejer -in mf

plectrum [ˈplektrəm] s (**-rums** & **-ra** [rə]) Plektron n; (for zither) Schlagring m

pledge [pledʒ] s (solemn promise) Gelübde n; (security for a payment)

Pfand *n*; (fig) Unterpfand *n* ‖ *tr* geloben; (*money*) zeichnen

plenary ['pli:nəri] *adj* Plenar-, Voll-

ple'nary indul'gence *s* vollkommener Ablaß *m*

ple'nary ses'sion *s* Plenum *n*

plenipotentiary [ˌplɛnɪpə'tɛnʃɪˌɛri] *adj* bevollmächtigt ‖ *s* Bevollmächtigte *mf*

plentiful ['plɛntɪfəl] *adj* reichlich

plenty ['plɛnti] *s* Fülle *f*; **have p. of** Überfluß haben an (*dat*); **have p. to do** vollauf zu tun haben ‖ *adv* (coll) reichlich

pleurisy ['plurɪsi] *s* Brustfellentzündung *f*

plexiglass ['plɛksɪˌglæs] *s* Plexiglas *n*

pliant ['plaɪənt] *adj* biegsam; (fig) gefügig

pliers ['plaɪərz] *s & spl* Zange *f*

plight [plaɪt] *s* Notlage *f*

plod [plad] *v* (*pret & pp* **plodded;** *ger* **plodding**) *intr* stapfen; **p. along** mühsam weitermachen

plop [plap] *v* (*pret & pp* **plopped;** *ger* **plopping**) *tr* plumpsen lassen ‖ *intr* plumpsen ‖ *interj* plumps!

plot [plat] *s* (*conspiracy*) Komplott *n*; (*of a story*) Handlung *f*; (*of ground*) Grundstück *n* ‖ *v* (*pret & pp* **plotted;** *ger* **plotting**) *tr* (*a course*) abstecken; (*intrigues*) schmieden; (*e.g., murder*) planen ‖ *intr* sich verschwören

plough [plaʊ] *s, tr & intr var of* plow

plow [plaʊ] *s* Pflug *m* ‖ *tr* pflügen; **p. up** umpflügen; **p. under** unterpflügen ‖ *intr* pflügen; **p. through the waves** durch die Wellen streichen

plow'man *s* (**-men**) Pflüger *m*

plow'share *s* Pflugschar *f*

pluck [plʌk] *s* (*tug*) Ruck *m*; (fig) Schneid *m* ‖ *tr* (*e.g., a chicken*) rupfen; (*flowers, fruit*) pflücken; (*eyebrows*) auszupfen; (mus) zupfen ‖ *intr*—**p. up** Mut fassen

plug [plʌg] *s* (*for a sink*) Pfropfen *m*; (*of tobacco*) Priem *m*; (*old horse*) alter Klepper *m*; (*advertising*) Befürwortung *f*; (aut) Zündkerze *f*; (elec) Stecker *m* ‖ *v* (*pret & pp* **plugged;** *ger* **plugging**) *tr* (*a hole*) zustopfen; **p. in** an die Steckdose anschließen ‖ *intr*—**p. away** (*work hard*) schuften; (*study hard*) pauken

plum [plʌm] *s* Pflaume *f*

plumage ['plumɪdʒ] *s* Gefieder *n*

plumb [plʌm] *adj* lotrecht ‖ *adv* (coll) völlig ‖ *s* Lot *n*; **out of p.** aus dem Lot ‖ *tr* loten, sondieren

plumb' bob' *s* Lot *n*

plumber ['plʌmər] *s* Installateur *m*

plumb'ing *s* (*plumbing work*) Installateurarbeit *f*; (*pipes*) Rohrleitung *f*

plumb' line' *s* Lotschnur *f*

plume [plum] *s* Feder *f*; (*on a helmet*) Helmbusch *m*; **p. of smoke** Rauchfahne *f* ‖ *tr* (*adorn with plumes*) mit Federn schmücken; **p. itself** sich putzen

plummet ['plʌmɪt] *s* Lot *n* ‖ *intr* stürzen

plump [plʌmp] *adj* rundlich ‖ *tr* plumpsen; **p. oneself down** sich schwerfällig hinwerfen

plum' tree' *s* Pflaumenbaum *m*

plunder ['plʌndər] *s* (*act*) Plünderung *f*; (*booty*) Beute *f* ‖ *tr & intr* plündern

plunderer ['plʌndərər] *s* Plünderer *m*

plunge [plʌndʒ] *s* Sturz *m* ‖ *tr* stürzen ‖ *intr* (*fall*) stürzen; (*throw oneself*) sich stürzen

plunger ['plʌndʒər] *s* Saugglocke *f*

plunk [plʌŋk] *adv* (*squarely*) (coll) genau ‖ *tr* (*e.g., a guitar*) zupfen; **p. down** klirrend auf den Tisch legen

pluperfect [ˌplu'pʌrfɛkt] *s* Vorvergangenheit *f*, Plusquamperfekt(um) *n*

plural ['plurəl] *adj* Plural- ‖ *s* Mehrzahl *f*, Plural *m*

plurality [plu'rælɪti] *s* Mehrheit *f*; (pol) Stimmenmehrheit *f*

plus [plʌs] *adj* Plus-; (elec) positiv ‖ *s* Plus *n* ‖ *prep* plus (*acc*)

plush [plʌʃ] *adj* (coll) luxuriös

plus' sign' *s* Pluszeichen *n*

plutonium [plu'toniəm] *s* Plutonium *n*

ply [plaɪ] *s* (*of wood, etc.*) Schicht *f*; (*of yarn*) Strähne *f* ‖ *v* (*pret & pp* **plied**) *tr* (*e.g., a needle*) (eifrig) handhaben; (*a trade*) betreiben; (*with questions*) bestürmen; (*a waterway*) regelmäßig befahren ‖ *intr* (*between*) verkehren (zwischen *dat*)

ply'wood' *s* Sperrholz *n*

pneumatic [n(j)u'mætɪk] *adj* pneumatisch

pneumat'ic drill' *s* Preßluftbohrer *m*

pneumonia [n(j)u'monɪ·ə] *s* Lungenentzündung *f*

poach [potʃ] *tr* (*eggs*) pochieren ‖ *intr* wildern

poached' egg' *s* verlorenes Ei *n*

poacher ['potʃər] *s* Wilderer *m*

pock [pak] *s* Pocke *f*, Pustel *f*

pocket ['pakɪt] *adj* (*comb, flap, knife, money, watch*) Taschen- ‖ *s* Tasche *f*; (billiards) Loch *n*; (mil) Kessel *m* ‖ *tr* in die Tasche stecken; (billiards) ins Loch spielen

pock'etbook' *s* Handtasche *f*; (*book*) Taschenbuch *n*

pock'et cal'culator *s* Taschenrechner *m*

pock'mark' *s* Pockennarbe *f*

pock'marked' *adj* pockennarbig

pod [pad] *s* Hülse *f*

podi·um ['podɪ·əm] *s* (**-ums & -a** [ə]) Podium *n*

poem ['po·ɪm] *s* Gedicht *n*

poet ['po·ɪt] *s* Dichter *m*, Poet *m*

poetaster ['po·ɪtˌæstər] *s* Dichterling *m*

poetess ['po·ɪtɪs] *s* Dichterin *f*

poetic [po'ɛtɪk] *adj* dichterisch, poetisch ‖ **poetics** *s* Poetik *f*

poetry ['po·ɪtri] *s* Dichtung *f*; **write p.** dichten, Gedichte schreiben

poignant ['poɪn(j)ənt] *adj* (*touching*) ergreifend; (*pungent*) scharf; (*cutting*) beißend

point [poɪnt] *s* (*dot, score*) Punkt *m*;

(tip) Spitze *f;* *(of a joke)* Pointe *f;* *(of a statement)* Hauptpunkt *m;* *(side of a character)* Seite *f;* *(purpose)* Sinn *m;* *(matter, subject)* Sache *f;* *(of a compass)* Kompaßstrich *m;* *(to show decimals)* Komma *n;* *(aut)* Zündkontakt *m;* *(geog)* Landspitze *f;* *(typ)* Punkt *m;* **at this p.** in diesem Augenblick; **be on the p. of** *(ger)* gerade im Begriff sein zu *(inf);* **come to the p.!** zur Sache!; **get the p.** verstehen; **in p. of fact** tatsächlich; **make a p. of** bestehen auf *(dat);* **make it a p. to** *(inf)* es sich *[dat]* zur Pflicht machen zu *(inf);* **not to the p.** nicht zur Sache gehörig; **off the p.** unzutreffend; **on points** *(sport)* nach Punkten; **p. at issue** strittiger Punkt *m;* **p. of order!** zur Tagesordnung!; **p. of time** Zeitpunkt *m;* **score a p.** *(fig)* e-n Punkt für sich buchen; **that's beside the p.** darum handelt es sich nicht; **there's no p. to it** es hat keinen Zweck; **to the p.** zutreffend; **up to a certain p.** bis zu e-m gewissen Grade || *tr* *(e.g., a gun)* *(at)* richten (auf *acc*); **p. out** (auf)zeigen; **p. s.th. out to s.o.** j-n auf etw *[acc]* hinweisen; **p. the finger at** mit dem Finger zeigen auf *(acc)* || *intr* mit dem Finger zeigen; **p. to** deuten auf *(acc);* *(fig)* hinweisen auf *(acc)*

point'-blank' *adj* *(refusal)* glatt; *(shot)* rasant, Kernschuß–; **at p. range** auf Kernschußweite || *adv* *(at close range)* aus nächster Nähe; *(fig)* glatt; *(arti)* auf Kernschußweite

point'ed *adj* spitzig; *(remark)* anzüglich; *(gun)* gerichtet; *(arch, nose)* Spitz–

pointer ['pɔɪntər] *s* *(of a meter)* Zeiger *m;* *(stick)* Zeigestock *m;* *(advice)* Tip *m;* *(hunting dog)* Vorstehhund *m*

pointless ['pɔɪntlɪs] *adj* zwecklos

point' of hon'or *s* Ehrensache *f*

point' of law' *s* Rechtsfrage *f*

point' of view' *s* Gesichtspunkt *m*

poise [pɔɪz] *s* sicheres Auftreten *n* || *tr* im Gleichgewicht halten || *intr* schweben

poison ['pɔɪzən] *s* Gift *n* || *tr* (& *fig*) vergiften

poi'son gas' *s* Giftgas *n*

poi'son i'vy *s* Giftṣumach *m*

poisonous ['pɔɪzənəs] *adj* giftig

poke [pok] *s* Stoß *m,* Knuff *m* || *tr* anstoßen, knuffen; *(the fire)* schüren; *(head, nose)* stecken; **p. fun at** sich lustig machen über *(acc);* **p. out** *(an eye)* ausstechen; **p. s.o. in the ribs** j-m e-n Rippenstoß geben || *intr* bummeln; **p. around** herumstochern; *(be slow)* herumbummeln; *(in another's business)* herumṣtöbern

poker ['pokər] *s* Schürhaken *m;* *(cards)* Poker *m*

pok'er face' *s* Pokergesicht *n*

poky ['poki] *adj* bummelig

Poland ['polənd] *s* Polen *n*

polar ['polər] *adj* Polar–

po'lar bear' *s* Eisbär *m*

polarity [po'lærɪti] *s* Polarität *f*

polarize ['polə ˌraɪz] *tr* polarisieren

pole [pol] *s* *(rod)* Stange *f;* *(for telephone lines, flags, etc.)* Mast *m;* *(astr, geog, phys)* Pol *m;* **Pole** Pole *m,* Polin *f* || *tr* *(a raft, boat)* staken

pole'cat' *s* Iltis *m*

polemic(al) [pə'lemɪk(əl)] *adj* polemisch

polemics [pə'lemɪks] *s* Polemik *f*

pole'star' *s* Polarstern *m*

pole'-vault' *intr* stabhochspringen

pole' vault'ing *s* Stabhochsprung *m*

police [pə'lis] *adj* polizeilich || *s* Polizei *f* || *tr* polizeilich überwachen; *(clean up)* *(mil)* säubern

police' es'cort *s* Polozeibedeckung *f*

police'man *s* (–men) Polizist *m*

police' of'ficer *s* Polizeibeamte *m,* Polizeibeamtin *f*

police' pre'cinct *s* Polizeirevier *n*

police' state' *s* Polizeistaat *m*

police' sta'tion *s* Polizeiwache *f*

police'wom'an *s* (–wom'en) Polizistin *f*

policy ['palɪsi] *s* Politik *f;* *(ins)* Police *f*

polio ['polɪ ˌo] *s* Polio *f*

polish ['palɪʃ] *s* *(material; shine)* Politur *f;* *(for shoes)* Schuhcreme *f;* *(fig)* Schliff *m* || *tr* polieren; *(fingernails)* lackieren; *(shoes, silver, etc.)* putzen; *(floors)* bohnern; *(fig)* abschleifen; **p. off** *(eat)* (sl) verdrücken; *(an opponent)* (sl) erledigen; *(work)* (sl) hinhauen || *intr*—**p. up on** auffpolieren || **Polish** ['polɪʃ] *adj* polnisch || *s* Polnisch *n*

polite [pə'laɪt] *adj* höflich

politeness [pə'laɪtnɪs] *s* Höflichkeit *f*

politic ['palɪtɪk] *adj* diplomatisch

political [pə'lɪtɪkəl] *adj* politisch

poli'tical econ'omy *s* Volkswirtschaft *f*

poli'tical sci'ence *s* Staatswissenschaften *pl*

politician [ˌpalɪ'tɪʃən] *s* Politiker –in *mf*

politics ['palɪtɪks] *s* Politik *f;* **be in p.** sich politisch betätigen; **talk p.** politisieren

polka ['po(l)kə] *s* Polka *f*

pol'ka-dot' *adj* getupft

poll [pol] *s* *(voting)* Abstimmung *f;* *(of public opinion)* Umfrage *f;* **be defeated at the polls** e-e Wahlniederlage erleiden; **go to the polls** zur Wahl gehen; **polls** *(voting place)* Wahllokal *n;* **take a p.** e-e Umfrage halten || *tr* befragen

pollen ['palən] *s* Pollen *m*

poll'ing booth' *s* Wahlzelle *f*

pollster ['polstər] *s* Meinungsforscher –in *mf*

poll' tax' *s* Kopfsteuer *f*

pollute [pə'lut] *tr* verunreinigen

pollution [pə'luʃən] *s* Verunreinigung *f*

polo ['polo] *s* *(sport)* Polo *n*

po'lo shirt' *s* Polohemd *n*

polygamist [pə'lɪgəmɪst] *s* Polygamist *m*

polygamy [pə'lɪgəmi] *s* Polygamie *f*

polyglot ['palɪ ˌglat] *s* Polyglott *m*

polygon ['pɑlɪ ‚gɑn] s Vieleck n
polyp ['pɑlɪp] s Polyp m
polytheism [‚pɑlɪ'θi ‚ɪzəm] s Vielgötterei f, Polytheismus m
polytheistic [‚pɑlɪθi'ɪstɪk] adj polytheistisch
pomade [pə'med] s Pomade f
pomegranate ['pɑm ‚grænɪt] s Granatapfel m; (tree) Granatapfelbaum m
Pomerania [‚pɑmə'renɪ-ə] s Pommern n
pom·mel ['pʌməl] s (of a sword) Degenkopf m; (of a saddle) Sattelknopf m ‖ v (pret & pp –mel[l]ed; ger –el[l]ing) tr mit der Faust schlagen
pomp [pɑmp] s Pomp m, Prunk m
pompous ['pɑmpəs] adj hochtrabend
pon·cho ['pɑnt/o] s (–chos) Poncho m
pond [pɑnd] s Teich m
ponder ['pɑndər] tr erwägen; (words) abwägen ‖ intr (over) nachsinnen (über acc)
ponderous ['pɑndərəs] adj schwerfällig
pontiff ['pɑntɪf] s (eccl) Papst m; (hist) Pontifex m
pontifical [pɑn'tɪfɪkəl] adj pontifikal
pontoon [pɑn'tun] s Ponton m; (aer) Schwimmer m
pony ['poni] s (small horse; hair style) Pony n; (crib) Eselsbrücke f
poodle ['pudəl] s Pudel m
pool [pul] s (small pond) Tümpel m; (of blood) Lache f; (swimming pool) Schwimmbecken n; (in betting) Pool m; (game) Billiard n; (fin) Pool m ‖ tr zusammenlegen
pool'room' s Billardsalon m
pool' ta'ble s Billardtisch m
poop [pup] s Heck n ‖ tr (sl) erschöpfen; **be pooped** (out) erschöpft sein
poor [pʊr] adj arm; (e.g., in spelling) schwach; (soil, harvest) schlecht; (miserable) armselig; **p. in** arm an (dat)
poor' box' s Opferstock m
poor'house' s Armenhaus n
poorly ['pʊrli] adv schlecht
pop [pɑp] adj (concert, singer, music) Pop– ‖ s Puff m, Knall m; (dad) Vati m; (soda) Brauselimonade f; (mus) Popmusik f ‖ v (pret & pp popped; ger popping) tr (corn) rösten; (cause to pop) knallen lassen; **pop the question** (coll) e-n Heiratsantrag machen ‖ intr (make a popping noise) knallen; (said of popcorn) aufplatzen; **pop in** (visit unexpectedly) (coll) hereinplatzen; **pop off** (sl) das Maul aufreißen; **pop up** (appear) (coll) auftauchen; (jump up) hochfahren
pop'corn' s Puffmais m
pope [pop] s Papst m
pop'eyed' adj glotzäugig
pop'gun' s Knallbüchse f
poplar ['pɑplər] s Pappel f
poppy ['pɑpi] s Mohnblume f, Mohn m
pop'pycock' s (coll) Quatsch m
pop'pyseed' s Mohn m
popsicle ['pɑp ‚sɪkəl] s Eis n am Stiel
populace ['pɑpjələs] s Pöbel m

popular ['pɑpjələr] adj populär; (e.g., music, expression). volkstümlich; **p. with** beliebt bei
popularity [‚pɑpjə'lærɪti] s Popularität f, Beliebtheit f
popularize ['pɑpjələ ‚raɪz] tr popularisieren
populate ['pɑpjə ‚let] tr bevölkern
population [‚pɑpjə'le/ən] s Bevölkerung f
popula'tion explo'sion s Bevölkerungsexplosion f
populous ['pɑpjələs] adj volkreich
porcelain ['pɔrs(ə)lɪn] s Porzellan n
porch [pɔrt/] s Vorbau m, Veranda f
porcupine ['pɔrkjə ‚paɪn] s Stachelschwein n
pore [por] s Pore f ‖ intr—**p. over** eifrig studieren
pork [pork] adj Schweine– ‖ s Schweinefleisch n
pork'chop' s Schweinekotelett n
pornography [pɔr'nɑgrəfi] s Pornographie f
porous ['porəs] adj porös
porphyry ['pɔrfɪri] s Porphyr m
porpoise ['pɔrpəs] s Tümmler m
porridge ['pɔrɪdʒ] s Brei m
port [port] s Hafen m; (wine) Portwein m; (slit for shooting) Schießscharte f; (naut) Backbord m & n; **to p.** (naut) backbord
portable ['portəbəl] adj tragbar; (radio, television, typewriter) Koffer–
portal ['portəl] s Portal n
portend [pɔr'tend] tr vorbedeuten
portent ['portənt] s schlimmes Vorzeichen n, böses Omen n
portentous [pɔr'tɛntəs] adj unheildrohend
porter ['portər] s (in a hotel) Hausdiener m; (at a station) Gepäckträger m; (doorman) Portier m
portfoli·o [port'foli ‚o] s (–os) Aktenmappe f; (fin) Portefeuille n; **without p.** ohne Geschäftsbereich
port'hole' s (for shooting) Schießscharte f; (naut) Bullauge n
porti·co ['portɪ ‚ko] s (–coes & –cos) Säulenvorbau m, Portikus m
portion ['pɔr/ən] s Anteil m; (serving) Portion f; (dowry) Heiratsgut n ‖ tr —**p. out** austeilen, einteilen
portly ['portli] adj wohlbeleibt
port' of call' s Anlaufhafen m
port' of en'try s Einfuhrhafen m
portrait ['portret] s Porträt n
portray [por'tre] tr porträtieren; (fig) beschreiben; (theat) darstellen
portrayal [por'tre-əl] s Porträtieren n; (fig) Beschreibung f; (theat) Darstellung f
port'side' s Backbord m & n
Portugal ['port/əgəl] s Portugal n
Portuguese ['port/ə ‚giz] adj portugiesisch ‖ s Portugiese m, Portugiesin f; (language) Portugiesisch n
port' wine' s Portwein m
pose [poz] s Haltung f, Pose f ‖ tr (a question, problem) stellen ‖ intr posieren; **p. as** sich ausgeben als; **p. for an artist** e-m Künstler Modell ste-

hen; **p.** for a picture sich e-m Photographen stellen

posh [pɑʃ] *adj* (sl) großartig

position [pə'ziʃən] *s* Stellung *f*; (*situation, condition*) Lage *f*; (*job; place of defense*) Stellung *f*; (*point of view*) Standpunkt *m*; (aer, naut) Standort *m*; (astr, mil, naut) Position *f*; **be in a p.** to (*inf*) in der Lage sein zu (*inf*); **in p.** am rechten Platz; **p.** wanted (*as in an ad*) Stelle gesucht; **take a p.** on Stellung nehmen zu; **take one's p.** sich aufstellen

positive ['pɑzitiv] *adj* (*reply, result, attitude*) positiv; (*answer*) zustimmend; (*sure*) sicher; (*offer*) fest; (elec, math, med, phot, phys) positiv ‖ *s* (gram) Positiv *m*; (phot) Positiv *n*

posse ['pɑsi] *s* Polizeiaufgebot *n*

possess [pə'zɛs] *tr* besitzen; **be possessed by the devil** von dem Teufel besessen sein

possession [pə'zɛʃən] *s* Besitz *m*; (*property*) Eigentum *n*; **be in p. of s.th.** etw besitzen; **take p. of s.th.** etw in Besitz nehmen

possessive [pə'zɛsiv] *adj* eifersüchtig; (gram) besitzanzeigend, Besitz-

possibility [,pɑsi'biliti] *s* Möglichkeit *f*

possible ['pɑsibəl] *adj* möglich; **make p.** ermöglichen

possibly ['pɑsibli] *adv* möglicherweise

possum ['pɑsəm] *s* Opossum *n*; **play p.** sich verstellen; (*play dead*) sich tot stellen

post [post] *s* (pole) Pfahl *m*; (*job; of a sentry*) Posten *m*; (*military camp*) Standort *m* ‖ *tr* (*a notice*) anschlagen; (*a guard*) aufstellen; (*a notice*) Kaution stellen; **p. no bills** Plakatankleben verboten

postage ['postidʒ] *s* Porto *n*

post'age due' *s* Nachporto *n*

post'age stamp' *s* Briefmarke *f*

postal ['postəl] *adj* Post-

post'al mon'ey or'der *s* Postanweisung *f*

post'card' *s* Ansichtskarte *f*

post'date' *tr* nachdatieren

post'ed *adj*—**keep s.o. p.** j-n auf dem laufenden halten

poster ['postər] *s* Plakat *n*

posterity [pɑs'tɛriti] *s* Nachkommenschaft *f*, Nachwelt *f*

postern ['postərn] *s* Hintertür *f*

post' exchange' *s* Marketenderei *f*

post'haste' *adv* schnellstens

posthumous ['pɑstʃuməs] *adj* posthum

post'man *s* (-men) Briefträger *m*

post'mark' *s* Poststempel *m* ‖ *tr* abstempeln

post'mas'ter *s* Postmeister *m*

post'master gen'eral *s* Postminister *m*

post-mortem [,post'mortəm] *s* Obduktion *f*

post' of'fice *s* Post *f*, Postamt *n*

post'-office box' *s* Postschließfach *n*

post'paid' *adv* frankiert

postpone [post'pon] *tr* (till, to) aufschieben (auf *acc*)

postponement [post'ponmənt] *s* Aufschub *m*

post'script' *s* Nachschrift *f*

posture ['pɑstʃər] *s* Haltung *f*

post'war' *adj* Nachkriegs-

posy ['pozi] *s* Sträußchen *n*

pot [pɑt] *s* Topf *m*; (*for coffee, tea*) Kanne *f*; (*in gambling*) Einsatz *m*; **go to pot** (sl) hops gehen; **pots and pans** Kochgeschirr *n*

potash ['pɑt,æʃ] *s* Pottasche *f*, Kali *n*

potassium [pə'tæsiəm] *s* Kalium *n*

pota•to [pə'teto] *s* (-toes) Kartoffel *f*

pota'to chips' *spl* Kartoffelchips *pl*

potbellied ['pɑt,belid] *adj* dickbäuchig

pot'bel'ly *s* Spitzbauch *m*

potency ['potənsi] *s* Stärke *f*; (physiol) Potenz *f*

potent ['potənt] *adj* (*powerful*) mächtig; (*persuasive*) überzeugend; (*e.g., drugs*) wirksam; (physiol) potent

potentate ['potən,tet] *s* Potentat *m*

potential [pə'tenʃəl] *adj* möglich; (phys) potentiell ‖ *s* (& elec, math, phys) Potential *n*

pot'hold'er *s* Topflappen *m*

pot'hole' *s* Schlagloch *n*

potion ['poʃən] *s* Trank *m*

pot'luck'—**take p.** mit dem vorliebnehmen, was es gerade gibt

pot' roast' *s* Schmorbraten *m*

pot'sherd' *s* Topfscherbe *f*

pot' shot' *s* müheloser Schuß *m*; **take a p. at** unfair bekritteln

pot'ted *adj* Topf-

potter ['pɑtər] *s* Töpfer *m*

pot'ter's clay' *s* Töpferton *m*

pot'ter's wheel' *s* Töpferscheibe *f*

pottery ['pɑtəri] *s* Tonwaren *pl*

potty ['pɑti] *s* (coll) Töpfchen *n*

pouch [pautʃ] *s* Beutel *m*

poultice ['poltis] *s* Breiumschlag *m*

poultry ['poltri] *s* Geflügel *n*

poul'try•man *s* (-men) Geflügelzüchter *m*; (*dealer*) Geflügelhändler *m*

pounce [pauns] *intr*—**p. on** sich stürzen auf (*acc*)

pound [paund] *s* Pfund *n*; (*for animals*) Pferch *m* ‖ *tr* (zer)stampfen; (*meat*) klopfen; **p. the sidewalks** Pflaster treten ‖ *intr* (*said of the heart*) klopfen; **p. on** (*e.g., a door*) hämmern an (*acc*)

-pound *suf*—pfündig

pound' ster'ling *s* Pfund *n* Sterling

pour [por] *tr* gießen; (*e.g., coffee*) einschenken; **p. away** wegschütten ‖ *intr* (meteor) gießen; **p. out of** (*e.g., a house*) strömen aus ‖ *impers*—**it's pouring** es gießt

pout [paut] *s* Schmollen *n* ‖ *intr* schmollen

pout'ing *adj* (lips) aufgeworfen ‖ *s* Schmollen *n*

poverty ['pɑvərti] *s* Armut *f*

pov'erty-strick'en *adj* verarmt

POW ['pi'o'dʌb,lju] *s* (prisoner of war) Kriegsgefangener *m*

powder ['paudər] *s* Pulver *n*; (*cosmetic*) Puder *m* ‖ *tr* (e.g., the face) pudern; (*plants*) stäuben; (*a cake*) bestreuen ‖ *intr* zu Pulver werden

pow'der box' s Puderdose f
pow'dered milk' s Milchpulver n
pow'dered sug'ar s Staubzucker m
pow'der keg' s Pulverfaß n
pow'der puff' s Puderquaste f
pow'der room' s Damentoilette f
powdery ['paudəri] adj pulverig
power ['pau·ər] s Macht f; (personal control) Gewalt f; (electricity) Strom m; (math) Potenz f; (opt) Vergrößerungskraft f; (phys) Leistung f; (pol) Macht f; **be in p.** an der Macht sein; **be in s.o.'s p.** in j–s Gewalt sein; **be within s.o.'s p.** in j–s Macht liegen; **come to p.** an die Macht gelangen; **have the p. to** (inf) vermögen zu (inf); **more p. to you!** viel Erfolg!; **the powers that be** die Obrigkeit f || tr antreiben
pow'er brake' s (aut) Servobremse f
pow'er dive' s (aer) Vollgassturzflug m
pow'er drill' s Elektrobohrer m
pow'er-driv'en adj mit Motorantrieb
pow'er fail'ure s Stromausfall m
powerful ['pau·ərfəl] adj mächtig; (opt) stark
pow'erhouse' s Kraftwerk n; (coll) Kraftprotz m
pow'erhun'gry adj herrschsüchtig
powerless ['pau·ərlɪs] adj machtlos
pow'er line' s Starkstromleitung f
pow'er mow'er s Motorrasenmäher m
pow'er of attorn'ey s Vollmacht f
pow'er plant' s (powerhouse) Kraftwerk n; (aer, aut) Triebwerk n
pow'er shov'el s Löffelbagger m
pow'er sta'tion s Kraftwerk n
pow'er steer'ing s Servolenkung f
pow'er supply' s Stromversorgung f
practicable ['præktɪkəbəl] adj praktikabel, durchführbar
practical ['præktɪkəl] adj praktisch
prac'tical joke' s Streich m
practically ['præktɪkəli] adv praktisch; (almost) fast, so gut wie
prac'tical nurse' s praktisch ausgebildete Krankenschwester f
practice ['præktɪs] s (exercise) Übung f; (habit) Gewohnheit f; (of medicine, law) Praxis f; **in p.** (in training) in der Übung; (in reality) in der Praxis; **make it a p. to** (inf) es sich [dat] zur Gewohnheit machen zu (inf); **out of p.** aus der Übung || tr (a profession) tätig sein als; (patience, reading, dancing, etc.) sich üben in (dat); (music, gymnastics) treiben; (piano, etc.) üben || intr üben; (said of a doctor) praktizieren; **p. on** (e.g., the violin, piano, parallel bars) üben auf (dat)
prac'tice game' s Übungsspiel n
prac'tice teach'er s Studienreferendar –in mf
practitioner [præk'tɪ/ənər] s Praktiker –in mf
pragmatic [præg'mætɪk] adj pragmatisch
pragmatism ['prægmə,tɪzəm] s Sachlichkeit f; (philos) Pragmatismus m
Prague [prɑg] s Prag n
prairie ['preri] s Steppe f, Prärie f

praise [prez] s Lob n || tr (for) loben (wegen); **p. to the skies** verhimmeln
praise'wor'thy adj lobenswert
prance [præns] intr tänzeln
prank [præŋk] s Schelmenstreich m
prate [pret] intr schwätzen
prattle ['prætəl] s Geplapper n || intr plappern, schwätzen
prawn [prɔn] s Garnele f
pray [pre] tr & intr beten
prayer [prer] s Gebet n; **say a p.** ein Gebet sprechen
prayer' book' s Gebetbuch n
preach [prit/] tr & intr predigen
preacher ['prit/ər] s Prediger m
preamble ['pri,æmbəl] s Präambel f
precarious [prɪ'kɛrɪ·əs] adj prekär
precaution [prɪ'kɔ/ən] s Vorsichtsmaßnahme f; **as a p.** vorsichtshalber; **take precautions** Vorkehrungen treffen
precede [prɪ'sid] tr vorausgehen (dat) || intr vorangehen
precedence ['prɛsɪdəns] s Vorrang m; **take p. over** den Vorrang haben vor (dat)
precedent ['prɛsɪdənt] s Präzedenzfall m; **set a p.** e–n Präzedenzfall schaffen
preced'ing adj vorhergehend
precept ['prisɛpt] s Vorschrift f
precinct ['prisɪŋkt] s Bezirk m
precious ['prɛ/əs] adj (expensive) kostbar; (valuable) wertvoll; (excessively refined) geziert; (child) lieb || adv **p. few** (coll) herzlich wenige
pre'cious stone' s Edelstein m
precipice ['prɛsɪpɪs] s Abgrund m
precipitate [prɪ'sɪpɪ,tet] adj steil abfallend || s (chem) Niederschlag m || tr (hurl) (into) stürzen (in acc); (bring about) heraufbeschwören; (vapor) (chem) niederschlagen; (from a solution) (chem) ausfällen || intr (chem, meteor) sich niederschlagen
precipitation [prɪ,sɪpɪ'te/ən] s (meteor) Niederschlag m
precipitous [prɪ'sɪpɪtəs] adj jäh
precise [prɪ'saɪs] adj präzis, genau
precision [prɪ'sɪʒən] s Präzision f
preclude [prɪ'klud] tr ausschließen
precocious [prɪ'ko/əs] adj frühreif
preconceived [,prikən'sivd] adj vorgefaßt
predatory ['prɛdə,tori] adj Raub–
predecessor ['prɛdɪ,sɛsər] s Vorgänger –in mf
predestination [,pridɛstɪ'ne/ən] s Prädestination f
predicament [prɪ'dɪkəmənt] s Mißliche Lage f
predicate ['prɛdɪkɪt] s (gram) Aussage f, Prädikat n || ['prɛdɪ,ket] tr (of) aussagen (über acc); (base) (on) gründen (auf acc)
predict [prɪ'dɪkt] tr voraussagen
prediction [prɪ'dɪk/ən] s Voraussage f
predispose [,pridɪs'poz] tr (to) im voraus geneigt machen (zu); (pathol) empfänglich machen (für)
predominant [prɪ'dɑmɪnənt] adj vorwiegend

reeminent [prɪˈɛmɪnənt] *adj* hervor-ragend

reempt [prɪˈɛmpt] *tr (a program)* er-setzen; *(land)* durch Vorkaufsrecht erwerben

reen [prin] *tr* putzen

refabricated [priˈfæbrɪˌketɪd] *adj* Fertig–

reface [ˈprefɪs] *s* Vorwort *n*, Vorrede *f* ‖ *tr* einleiten

refer [prɪˈfʌr] *v (pret & pp* **–ferred;** *ger* **–ferring)** *tr* bevorzugen; *(charges)* vorbringen; **I p. to wait** ich warte lieber

preferable [ˈprefərəbəl] *adj* (to) vorzu-ziehen(d) *(dat)*

preferably [ˈprefərəbli] *adv* vorzugs-weise

preferred/ stock/ *s* Vorzugsaktie *f*

prefix [ˈprifɪks] *s* Vorsilbe *f*, Präfix *n* ‖ *tr* vorsetzen

pregnancy [ˈpregnənsi] *s* Schwanger-schaft *f*; *(of animals)* Trächtigkeit *f*

pregnant [ˈpregnənt] *adj* schwanger; *(animals)* trächtig; *(fig)* inhalts-schwer

prehistoric [ˌprihɪsˈtɔrɪk] *adj* vorge-schichtlich, prähistorisch

prejudice [ˈpredʒədɪs] *s* Voreingeno-menheit *f*; *(detriment)* Schaden *m* ‖ *tr* beeinträchtigen; **p. s.o. against** j-n einnehmen gegen

pre/judiced *adj* voreingenommen

prejudicial [ˌpredʒəˈdɪʃəl] *adj* (to) schädlich (für)

prelate [ˈprelɪt] *s* Prälat *m*

preliminary [prɪˈlɪmɪˌneri] *adj* ein-leitend, Vor– ‖ *s* Vorbereitung *f*

prelude [ˈprel(j)ud] *s* (fig, mus, theat) Vorspiel *n*

premarital [prɪˈmærɪtəl] *adj* vorehelich

premature [ˌpriməˈt(j)ur] *adj* verfrüht; **p. birth** Frühgeburt *f*

premeditated [priˈmedɪˌtetɪd] *adj* vor-bedacht; *(murder)* vorsätzlich

premier [prɪˈmɪr] *s* Premier *m*

premiere [prɪˈmɪr] *s* Erstaufführung *f*

premise [ˈpremɪs] *s* Voraussetzung *f*; **on the premises** an Ort und Stelle; **the premises** das Lokal

premium [ˈprimɪˌəm] *s* Prämie *f*; **at a p.** *(in demand)* sehr gesucht; *(at a high price)* über pari

premonition [ˌpriməˈnɪʃən] *s* Vorah-nung *f*

preoccupation [priˌɑkjəˈpeʃən] *s* (with) Beschäftigtsein *n* (mit)

preoccupied [priˈɑkjəˌpaɪd] *adj* aus-schließlich beschäftigt

preparation [ˌprepəˈreʃən] *s* Vorberei-tung *f*; (med) Präparat *n*

preparatory [prɪˈpærəˌtori] *adj* vorbe-reitend; **p. to** vor *(dat)*

prepare [prɪˈper] *tr* vorbereiten; *(a meal)* zubereiten; *(a prescription)* anfertigen; *(a document)* abfassen

preparedness [prɪˈperɪdnɪs] *s* Bereit-schaft *f*; (mil) Einsatzbereitschaft *f*

pre·pay [priˈpe] *v (pret & pp* **–paid)** *tr* im voraus bezahlen

preponderant [prɪˈpɑndərənt] *adj* über-wiegend

preposition [ˌprepəˈzɪʃən] *s* Präposi-tion *f*, Verhältniswort *n*

prepossessing [ˌpripəˈzesɪŋ] *adj* ein-nehmend

preposterous [prɪˈpɑstərəs] *adj* lächer-lich

prep/ school/ [prep] *s* Vorbereitungs-schule *f*

prerecorded [ˌpririˈkɔrdɪd] *adj* vor-her aufgenommen

prerequisite [priˈrekwɪzɪt] *s* Voraus-setzung *f*, Vorbedingung *f*

prerogative [prɪˈrɑgətɪv] *s* Vorrecht *n*

presage [ˈpresɪdʒ] *s* Vorzeichen *n* ‖ [prɪˈsedʒ] *tr* ein Vorzeichen sein für

Presbyterian [ˌprezbɪˈtɪriən] *adj* presbyterianisch ‖ *s* Presbyterianer –in *mf*

prescribe [prɪˈskraɪb] *tr* vorschreiben; (med) verordnen

prescription [prɪˈskrɪpʃən] *s* Vorschrift *f*; (med) Rezept *n*, Verordnung *f*

presence [ˈprezəns] *s* Anwesenheit *f*

pres/ence of mind/ *s* Geistesgegenwart *f*

present [ˈprezənt] *adj (at this place)* anwesend; *(of the moment)* gegen-wärtig ‖ *s (gift)* Geschenk *n*; *(present time or tense)* Gegenwart *f*; **at p.** zur Zeit; **for the p.** vorläufig ‖ [prɪˈzent] *tr* bieten; *(facts)* darstel-len; *(introduce)* vorstellen; (theat) vorführen; **p. s.o. with s.th.** j-m etw verehren

presentable [prɪˈzentəbəl] *adj* presen-tabel

presentation [ˌprezənˈteʃən] *s* Vorstel-lung *f*; (theat) Aufführung *f*

pres/ent-day/ *adj* heutig, aktuell

presentiment [prɪˈzentɪmənt] *s* Ahnung *f*

presently [ˈprezəntli] *adv* gegenwärtig; *(soon)* alsbald

preservation [ˌprezərˈveʃən] *s* Erhal-tung *f*; (from) Bewahrung *f* (vor *dat*)

preservative [prɪˈzɑrvətɪv] *s* Konser-vierungsmittel *n*

preserve [prɪˈzɑrv] *s* Revier *n*; pre-serves Konserven *pl* ‖ *tr* konservie-ren; **p. from** schützen vor *(dat)*

preside [prɪˈzaɪd] *intr* (over) den Vor-sitz führen (über *acc* or bei)

presidency [ˈprezɪdənsi] *s* Präsident-schaft *f*

president [ˈprezɪdənt] *s* Präsident –in *mf*; *(of a university)* Rektor –in *mf*; *(of a board)* Vorsitzende –r *mf*

presidential [ˌprezɪˈdentʃəl] *adj* Prä-sidenten–

press [pres] *adj (agency, agent, confer-ence, gallery, report, secretary)* Presse– ‖ *s (wine press; printing press; newspapers)* Presse *f*; **go to p.** in Druck gehen ‖ *tr* drucken; *(a suit)* (auf)bügeln; *(a person)* be-drängen; *(fruit)* ausdrücken; **be pressed for** knapp sein an *(dat)*; **p. s.o. to** *(inf)* j-n dringend bitten zu *(inf)*; **p. the button** auf den Knopf drücken ‖ *intr (said of time)* drän-gen; **p. for** drängen auf *(acc)*; **p. forward** sich vorwärtsdrängen

press' box' s Pressekabine f
press' card' s Presseausweis m
press'ing adj dringend, dringlich
press' release' s Pressemitteilung f
pressure ['preʃər] s Druck m; (of work) Andrang m; (aut) Reifendruck m; **put p. on** unter Druck setzen || tr drängen
pres'sure cook'er s Schnellkochtopf m
pres'sure group' s Interessengruppe f
pressurize ['preʃəˌraɪz] tr druckfest machen
prestige [pres'tiʒ] s Prestige n
presumably [prɪ'z(j)uməbli] adv vermutlich
presume [prɪ'z(j)um] tr vermuten || intr vermuten; **p. on** pochen auf (acc)
presumption [prɪ'zʌmpʃən] s Vermutung f; (presumptuousness) Anmaßung f
presumptuous [prɪ'zʌmptʃʊ·əs] adj anmaßend
presuppose [ˌprisə'poz] tr voraussetzen
pretend [prɪ'tend] tr vorgeben; **he pretended that he was a captain** er gab sich für e-n Hauptmann aus || intr so tun, als ob
pretender [prɪ'tendər] s Quaksalber m; **p. to the throne** Thronbewerber m
pretense [prɪ'tens], ['pritəns] s Schein m; **under false pretenses** unter Vorspiegelung falscher Tatsachen; **under the p. of** unter dem Vorwand (genit)
pretentious [prɪ'tenʃəs] adj (person) anmaßend; (home) protzig
pretext ['pritekst] s Vorwand m
pretty ['prɪti] adj hübsch || adv (coll) ziemlich
pretzel ['pretsəl] s Brezel f
prevail [prɪ'vel] intr (predominate) (vor)herrschen; (triumph) (against) sich behaupten (gegen); **p. on** überreden
prevail'ing adj (fashion, view) (vor)herrschend; (situation) obwaltend
prevalence ['prevələns] s Vorherrschen n
prevalent ['prevələnt] adj vorherrschend; **be p.** herrschen
prevaricate [prɪ'værɪˌket] intr Ausflüchte machen
prevent [prɪ'vent] tr verhindern; (war, danger) abwenden; **p. s.o. from** j-n hindern an (dat); **p. s.o. from** (ger) j-n daran hindern zu (inf)
prevention [prɪ'venʃən] s Verhütung f
preventive [prɪ'ventɪv] adj vorbeugend || s Schutzmittel n
preview ['pri·ˌvju] s Vorschau f
previous ['privi·əs] adj vorhergehend, vorig; Vor-, e.g., **p. conviction** Vorstrafe f; **p. day** Vortag m; **p. record** Vorstrafenregister n
previously ['privi·əsli] adv vorher
prewar ['pri·ˌwɔr] adj Vorkriegs-
prey [pre] s Beute f, Raub m; (fig) Opfer n; **fall p. to** (& fig) zum Opfer fallen (dat) || intr—**p. on** erbeuten; (exploit) ausbeuten; **p. on s.o.'s mind** an j-s Gewissen nagen

price [praɪs] s Preis m; (st. exch.) Kurs m; **at any p.** um jeden Preis; **at the p. of** im Wert von || tr mit Preisen versehen; (inquire about the price of) nach dem Preis fragen (genit)
price' control' s Preiskontrolle f
price' fix'ing s Preisbindung f
price' freeze' s Preisstopp m
priceless ['praɪslɪs] adj unbezahlbar; (coll) sehr komisch
price' range' s Preislage f
price' rig'ging s Preistreiberei f
price' tag' s Preiszettel m, Preisschild n
price'-wage' spi'ral s Preis-Lohn-Spirale f
price' war' s Preiskrieg m
prick [prɪk] s (& fig) Stich m || tr stechen; **p. up** (ears) spitzen
prickly ['prɪkli] adj stachelig, Stech-
prick'ly heat' s Hitzepickel pl
pride [praɪd] s Stolz m; (pej) Hochmut m; **swallow one's p.** seinen Stolz in die Tasche stecken; **take p. in** stolz sein auf (acc) || tr—**p. oneself on** sich viel einbilden auf (acc)
priest [prist] s Priester m
priestess ['pristɪs] s Priesterin f
priest'hood' s Priestertum n
priestly ['pristli] adj priesterlich
prig [prɪg] s Tugendbold m
prim [prɪm] adj (primmer; primmest) spröde
primacy ['praɪməsi] s Primat m & n
primarily [praɪ'merɪli] adv vor allem
primary ['praɪˌmeri] adj primär, Haupt-; (e.g., color, school) Grund- || s (pol) Vorwahl f
primate ['praɪmet] s (zool) Primat m
prime [praɪm] adj (chief) Haupt-; (best) erstklassig || s Blüte f; (math) Primzahl f; **p. of life** Lenz m des Lebens || tr (a pump) ansaugen lassen; (ammunition) scharfmachen; (a surface for painting) grundieren; (with information) vorher informieren
prime' min'ister s Ministerpräsident m; (in England) Premierminister m
primer ['praɪmər] s Fibel f || ['praɪmər] s (for painting) Grundierfarbe f; (of an explosive) Zündsatz m; (aut) Einspritzpumpe f
prime' time' s schönste Zeit f
primeval [praɪ'mivəl] adj urweltlich, Ur-; **p. world** Urwelt f
primitive ['prɪmɪtɪv] adj primitiv || s Primitive mf, Urmensch m
primp [prɪmp] tr aufputzen || intr sich aufputzen, sich zieren
prim'rose' s Himmelschlüssel m
prince [prɪns] s Prinz m, Fürst m
Prince' Al'bert s Gehrock m
princely ['prɪnsli] adj prinzlich
princess ['prɪnsɪs] s Prinzessin f, Fürstin f
principal ['prɪnsɪpəl] adj Haupt- || s (educ) Schuldirektor -in mf; (fin) Kapitalbetrag m, Kapital n
principality [ˌprɪnsɪ'pælɪti] s Fürstentum n

principally ['prɪnsɪpəli] adv größtenteils
principle ['prɪnsɪpəl] s Grundsatz m, Prinzip n; in p. im Prinzip
print [prɪnt] s (lettering; design on cloth) Druck m; (printed dress) bedrucktes Kleid n; (phot) Abzug m; in cold p. schwarz auf weiß; out of p. vergriffen || tr drucken; (e.g., one's name) in Druckschrift schreiben; (phot) kopieren; (tex) bedrucken
print'ed mat'ter s Drucksache f
printer ['prɪntər] s Drucker m; (phot) Kopiermaschine f
prin'ter's ink' s Druckerschwärze f
print'ing s Drucken n; (of a book) Buchdruck m; (subsequent printing) Abdruck m; (phot) Kopieren n, Abziehen n
print'ing press' s Druckerpresse f
print' shop' s Druckerei f
prior ['praɪ·ər] adj vorherig; p. to vor (dat) || s (eccl) Prior m
priority [praɪ'ɔrɪti] s Priorität f
prism ['prɪzəm] s Prisma f
prison ['prɪzən] s Gefängnis n
pris'on camp' s Gefangenenlager n
prisoner ['prɪz(ə)nər] s Gefangene mf; (in a concentration camp) Häftling m; be taken p. in Gefangenschaft geraten; take p. gefangennehmen
pris'oner of war' s Kriegsgefangene mf
prissy ['prɪsi] adj zimperlich
privacy ['praɪvəsi] s Zurückgezogenheit f; disturb s.o.'s p. j-s Ruhe stören
private ['praɪvɪt] adj privat; (personal) persönlich; keep p. geheimhalten || s (mil) Gemeine mf; in p. privat(im); privates Geschlechtsteile pl
pri'vate cit'izen s Privatperson f
pri'vate eye' s (coll) Privatdetektiv m
pri'vate first' class' s Gefreite mf
privately ['praɪvɪtli] adv privat(im)
privet ['prɪvɪt] s Liguster m
privilege ['prɪvɪlɪdʒ] s Privileg n
privy ['prɪvi] adj—p. to eingeweiht in (acc) || s Abtritt m
prize [praɪz] s Preis m, Prämie f; (nav) Prise f || tr schätzen
prize' fight' s Preisboxkampf m
prize' fight'er s Berufsboxer m
prize' ring' s Boxring m
pro [pro] s (pros) (coll) Profi m; the pros and the cons das Für und Wider || prep für (acc)
probability [,prabə'bɪlɪti] s Wahrscheinlichkeit f; in all p. aller Wahrscheinlichkeit nach
probable ['prabəbəl] adj wahrscheinlich
probate ['probet] s Testamentsbestätigung f || tr bestätigen
pro'bate court' s Nachlaßgericht n
probation [pro'beʃən] s Probe f; (jur) Bewährungsfrist f; on p. auf Probe; (jur) mit Bewährung
proba'tion of'ficer s Bewährungshelfer –in mf
probe [prob] s (jur) Untersuchung f;

(mil) Sondierungsangriff m; (rok) Versuchsrakete f; (surg) Sonde f || tr (with the hands) abtasten; (fig & surg) sondieren
problem ['prabləm] s Problem n; (math) Aufgabe f
prob'lem child' s Sorgenkind n
procedure [pro'sidʒər] s Verfahren n
proceed [pro'sid] intr (go on) fortfahren; (act) verfahren; p. against (jur) vorgehen gegen; p. from kommen von; p. to (inf) darangehen zu (inf)
proceed'ing s Vorgehen n; proceedings (of a society) Sitzungsberichte pl; (jur) Verfahren f
proceeds ['prosidz] spl Erlös m
process ['prases] s Verfahren n, Prozeß m; be in p. im Gang sein; in the p. dabei || tr (raw materials) verarbeiten; (applications) bearbeiten; (persons) abfertigen; (phot) entwickeln und vervielfältigen
procession [pro'seʃən] s Prozession f
proclaim [pro'klem] tr ankündigen; (a law) bekanntmachen; p. (as) a holiday zum Feiertag erklären
proclamation [,praklə'meʃən] s Aufruf m, Proklamation f
procrastinate [pro'kræstɪ,net] intr zaudern
proctor ['praktər] s Aufsichtsführende mf || tr beaufsichtigen
procure [pro'kjʊr] tr besorgen, verschaffen; (said of a pimp) verkuppeln
procurement [pro'kjʊrmənt] s Besorgung f
procurer [pro'kjʊrər] s Kuppler m
prod [prad] s Stoß m; (stick) Stachelstock m || v (pret & pp prodded; ger prodding) tr stoßen; prod s.o. into (ger) j-n dazu anstacheln zu (inf)
prodigal ['pradɪgəl] adj verschwenderisch
prod'igal son' s verlorener Sohn m
prodigious [pro'dɪdʒəs] adj großartig
prodigy ['pradɪdʒi] s Wunderzeichen n; (talented child) Wunderkind n
produce ['prod(j)us] s (product) Erzeugnis n; (amount produced) Ertrag m; (fruits and vegetables) Bodenprodukte pl || [pro'd(j)us] tr produzieren; (manufacture) herstellen; (said of plants, trees) hervorbringen; (interest, profit) abwerfen; (proof) beibringen; (papers) vorlegen; (cin) produzieren; (theat) inszenieren || intr (bot) tragen; (econ) Gewinne abwerfen
pro'duce depart'ment s Obst- und Gemüseabteilung f
producer [pro'd(j)usər] s Hersteller m; (cin, theat) Produzent –in mf
product ['pradʌkt] s Erzeugnis n, Produkt n
production [pro'dʌkʃən] s Erzeugung f, Produktion f; (fa, lit) Werk n
productive [pro'dʌktɪv] adj produktiv
profane [pro'fen] adj profan; p. language Fluchen n || tr profanieren
profanity [pro'fænɪti] s Fluchen n; profanities Flüche pl

profess [pro'fes] *tr* gestehen
profession [pro'feʃən] *s* Beruf *m; (of faith)* Bekenntnis *n;* **by p.** von Beruf
professional [pro'feʃənəl] *adj* berufsmäßig, professionell ‖ *s (expert)* Fachmann *m;* (sport) Profi *m*
profes'sional jea'lousy *s* Brotneid *m*
professor [pro'fesər] *s* Professor –in *mf*
profes'sorship *s* Professur *f*
proffer ['prɑfər] *s* Angebot *n* ‖ *tr* anbieten
proficient [pro'fɪʃənt] *adj* tüchtig
profile ['profaɪl] *s* Profil *n; (biographical sketch)* Kurzbiographie *f*
profit ['prɑfɪt] *s* Gewinn *m;* **show a p.** e–n Gewinn abwerfen ‖ *tr* nutzen ‖ *intr* **(by)** Nutzen ziehen aus
profitable ['prɑfɪtəbəl] *adj* einträglich
profiteer [,prɑfɪ'tɪr] *s* Wucherer *m,* Schieber *m* ‖ *intr* wuchern, schieben
prof'it shar'ing *s* Gewinnbeteiligung *f*
profligate ['prɑflɪgɪt] *adj* verkommen; *(extravagant)* verschwenderisch ‖ *s* verkommener Mensch *m; (spendthrift)* Verschwender –in *mf*
profound [pro'faund] *adj (knowledge)* gründlich; *(change)* tiefgreifend
profuse [prə'fjus] *adj* überreichlich
progeny ['prɑdʒənɪ] *s (& bot)* Nachkommenschaft *f; (of animals)* Junge *pl*
progno·sis [prɑg'nosɪs] *s* (–ses [siz]) Prognose *f*
prognosticate [prɑg'nɑstɪ,ket] *tr* voraussagen
pro·gram ['progræm] *s* Programm *n; (radio or television show)* Sendung *f* ‖ *v (pret & pp* –grammed; *ger* –gramming) *tr* programmieren
progress ['prɑgres] *s* Fortschritt *m;* **be in progress** im Gang sein ‖ [prə'gres] *intr (make progress)* fortschreiten; *(develop)* sich fortentwickeln
progressive [prə'gresɪv] *adj* fortschrittlich; *(party)* Fortschritts– ‖ *s* Fortschrittler –in *mf*
prog'ress report' *s* Tätigkeitsbericht *m*
prohibit [pro'hɪbɪt] *tr* verbieten
prohibition [,pro·ə'bɪʃən] *s* Verbot *n;* (hist) Prohibition *f*
prohibitive [pro'hɪbɪtɪv] *adj (costs)* unertragbar; *(prices)* unerschwinglich
project ['prɑdʒɛkt] *s* Project *n,* Vorhaben *n* ‖ [prə'dʒɛkt] *tr (light, film)* projizieren; *(plan)* vorhaben ‖ *intr* vorspringen, vorragen
projectile [prə'dʒɛktɪl] *s (fired from a gun)* Projektil *n; (thrown object)* Wurfgeschoß *n*
projection [prə'dʒɛkʃən] *s (jutting out)* Vorsprung *m,* Vorbau *m;* (cin) Projektion *f*
projector [prə'dʒɛktər] *s* Projektor *m*
proletarian [,prolɪ'terɪ·ən] *adj* proletarisch ‖ *s* Proletarier –in *mf*
proletariat [,prolɪ'terɪ·ət] *s* Proletariat *n*
proliferate [prə'lɪfə,ret] *intr* sich stark vermehren
prolific [prə'lɪfɪk] *adj* fruchtbar
prolix [pro'lɪks] *adj* weitschweifig

prologue ['prolɔg] *s* Prolog *m*
prolong [pro'lɔŋ] *tr* verlängern
promenade [,prɑmɪ'ned] *s* Promenade *f* ‖ *intr* promenieren
promenade' deck' *s* Promenadendeck *n*
prominent ['prɑmɪnənt] *adj* hervorragend, prominent; *(chin)* vorstehend
promiscuity [,prɑmɪs'kju·ɪtɪ] *s* Promiskuität *f*
promiscuous [pro'mɪskju·əs] *adj* unterschiedslos; *(sexually)* locker
promise ['prɑmɪs] *s* Versprechen *n* ‖ *tr* versprechen
prom'ising *adj (thing)* aussichtsreich; *(person)* vielversprechend
prom'issory note' ['prɑmɪ,sorɪ] *s* Eigenwechsel *m*
promontory ['prɑmən,torɪ] *s* Landspitze *f*
promote [prə'mot] *tr (in rank)* befördern; *(a cause)* fördern; *(a pupil)* versetzen; *(wares)* werben für
promoter [prə'motər] *s* Förderer –in *mf;* (sport) Veranstalter –in *mf*
promotion [prə'moʃən] *s (in rank)* Beförderung *f; (of a cause)* Förderung *f; (of a pupil)* Versetzung *f*
prompt [prɑmpt] *adj* prompt ‖ *tr* veranlassen; (theat) soufflieren *(dat)*
prompter ['prɑmptər] *s* Souffleur *m,* Souffleuse *f*
promp'ter's box' *s* Souffleurkasten *m*
promptness ['prɑmptnɪs] *s* Pünktlichkeit *f*
promulgate [pro'mʌlget] *tr* bekanntmachen
prone [pron] *adj*—**be p. to** neigen zu; **in the p. position** auf Anschlag liegend
prong [prɔŋ] *s (of a fork)* Zinke *f; (of a deer)* Sprosse *f*
pronoun ['pronaun] *s* Fürwort *n*
pronounce [prə'nauns] *tr (enunciate)* aussprechen; **p. sentence** das Strafausmaß festsetzen; **p. s.o.** *(e.g., guilty, insane, man and wife)* erklären für
pronouncement [prə'naunsmənt] *s (announcement)* Erklärung *f; (of a sentence)* (jur) Verkündung *f*
pronunciation [prə,nʌnsɪ'eʃən] *s* Aussprache *f*
proof [pruf] *adj*—**p. against** (fig) gefeit gegen; **90 p. 45** prozentig ‖ *s* Beweis *m;* (phot) Probebild *n;* (typ) Korrekturbogen *m*
proof'read'er *s* Korrektor –in *mf*
prop [prɑp] *s* Stütze *f;* **props** (coll) Beine *pl;* (theat) Requisiten *pl* ‖ *v (pret & pp* propped; *ger* propping) *tr* stützen; **p. oneself up** sich aufstemmen; **p. up** abstützen
propaganda [,prɑpə'gændə] *s* Propaganda *f*
propagate ['prɑpə,get] *tr* fortpflanzen; (fig) propagieren ‖ *intr* sich fortpflanzen
pro·pel [prə'pel] *v (pret & pp* –pelled; *ger* –pelling) *tr* antreiben
propeller [prə'pelər] *s* (aer) Propeller *m;* (naut) Schraube *f*
propensity [prə'pensɪtɪ] *s* Neigung *f*

proper ['prɑpər] *adj* passend; (*way, time*) richtig; (*authority*) zuständig; (*strictly so-called*) selbst, e.g., Germany p. Deutschland selbst

properly ['prɑpərli] *adj* gehörig

prop'er name' *s* Eigenname *m*

property ['prɑpərti] *s* Eigentum *n*; (*land*) Grundstück *n*; (*quality*) Eigenschaft *f*

prop'erty dam'age *s* Sachschaden *m*

prop'erty tax' *s* Grundsteuer *f*

prophecy ['prɑfɪsi] *s* Prophezeiung *f*

prophe·sy ['prɑfɪˌsaɪ] *v* (*pret & pp -sied*) *tr* prophezeien

prophet ['prɑfɪt] *s* Prophet *m*

prophetess ['prɑfɪtɪs] *s* Prophetin *f*

prophylactic [ˌprɑfɪ'læktɪk] *adj* prophylaktisch ‖ *s* Prophylaktikum *n*; (*condom*) Präservativ *m*

propitiate [prə'pɪʃɪˌet] *tr* versöhnen

propitious [prə'pɪʃəs] *adj* günstig

prop'jet' *s* Flugzeug *n* mit Turboprop

proportion [prə'pɔrʃən] *s* Verhältnis *n*; in p. to im Verhältnis zu; out of p. to in keinem Verhältnis zu; proportions Proportionen *pl* ‖ *tr* bemessen; well proportioned gut proportioniert

proposal [prə'pozəl] *s* Vorschlag *m*; (*of marriage*) Heiratsantrag *m*

propose [prə'poz] *tr* vorschlagen; (*intend*) beabsichtigen; p. a toast to e-n Toast ausbringen auf (*acc*) ‖ *intr* (to) e-n Heiratsantrag machen (*dat*)

proposition [ˌprɑpə'zɪʃən] *s* Vorschlag *m*; (*log, math*) Lehrsatz *m* ‖ *tr* ansprechen

propound [prə'paund] *tr* vortragen

proprietor [prə'praɪ·ətər] *s* Inhaber *m*

proprietress [prə'praɪ·ətrɪs] *s* Inhaberin *f*

propriety [prə'praɪ·əti] *s* Anstand *m*; proprieties Anstandsformen *pl*

propulsion [prə'pʌlʃən] *s* Antrieb *m*

prorate [pro'ret] *tr* anteilmäßig verteilen

prosaic [pro'ze·ɪk] *adj* prosaisch

proscribe [pro'skraɪb] *tr* proskribieren

prose [proz] *adj* Prosa– ‖ *s* Prosa *f*

prosecute ['prɑsɪˌkjut] *tr* verfolgen

prosecutor ['prɑsɪˌkjutər] *s* Ankläger –in *mf*

proselytize ['prɑsɪləˌtaɪz] *intr* Anhänger gewinnen

prose' writ'er *s* Prosaiker –in *mf*

prosody ['prɑsədi] *s* Silbenmessung *f*

prospect ['prɑspɛkt] *s* Aussicht *f*; (*person*) Interessent –in *mf*; hold out the p. of s.th. etw in Aussicht stellen ‖ *intr* (for) schürfen (nach)

prospector ['prɑspɛktər] *s* Schürfer *m*

prospectus [prə'spɛktəs] *s* Prospekt *m*

prosper ['prɑspər] *intr* gedeihen

prosperity [prɑs'pɛrɪti] *s* Wohlstand *m*

prosperous ['prɑspərəs] *adj* wohlhabend

prostitute ['prɑstɪˌt(j)ut] *s* Prostituierte *f* ‖ *tr* prostituieren

prostrate ['prɑstret] *adj* hingestreckt; (*exhausted*) erschöpft ‖ *tr* niederwerfen; (fig) niederzwingen

prostration [prɑs'treʃən] *s* Niederwerfen *n*; (*abasement*) Demütigung *f*

protagonist [pro'tægənɪst] *s* Protagonist *m*, Hauptfigur *f*

protect [prə'tɛkt] *tr* (be)schützen; (*interests*) wahrnehmen; p. from schützen vor (*dat*)

protection [prə'tɛkʃən] *s* (from) Schutz *m* (vor *dat*)

protector [prə'tɛktər] *s* Beschützer *m*

protein ['protin] *s* Protein *n*

protest ['protest] *s* Protest *m* ‖ [pro'tɛst] *tr & intr* protestieren

Protestant ['prɑtɪstənt] *adj* protestantisch ‖ *s* Protestant –in *mf*

protocol ['protəˌkɑl] *s* Protokoll *n*

proton ['protɑn] *s* Proton *n*

protoplasm ['protəˌplæzəm] *s* Protoplasma *n*

prototype ['protəˌtaɪp] *s* Prototyp *m*

protozo·an [ˌprotə'zo·ən] *s* (-a [ə]) Einzeller *m*

protract [pro'trækt] *tr* hinziehen

protrude [pro'trud] *intr* hervorstehen

proud [praud] *adj* (of) stolz (auf *acc*)

prove [pruv] *v* (*pret* proved; *pp* proved & proven ['pruvən]) *tr* beweisen; p. a failure sich nicht bewähren; p. one's worth sich bewähren ‖ *intr*– p. right zutreffen; p. to be sich erweisen als

proverb ['prɑvərb] *s* Sprichwort *n*

proverbial [prə'vʌrbɪ·əl] *adj* sprichwörtlich

provide [prə'vaɪd] *tr* (*s.th.*) besorgen; p. s.o. with s.th. j–n mit etw versorgen ‖ *intr*– p. for (e.g., *a family*) sorgen für; (e.g., *a special case*) vorsehen; (*the future*) voraussehen

provid'ed *adj* (with) versehen (mit) ‖ *conj* vorausgesetzt, daß

Providence ['prɑvɪdəns] *s* Vorsehung *f*

providential [ˌprɑvɪ'dɛntʃəl] *adj* von der Vorsehung beschlossen

provid'ing *conj* vorausgesetzt, daß

province ['prɑvɪns] *s* (*district*) Provinz *f*; (*special field*) Ressort *n*

provision [prə'vɪʒən] *s* (*providing*) Versorgung *f*; (*stipulation*) Bestimmung *f*; make p. for Vorsorge treffen für; provisions Lebensmittelvorräte *pl* ‖ *tr* (mil) verpflegen

provisional [prə'vɪʒənəl] *adj* vorläufig

provi·so [prə'vaɪzo] *s* (-sos & -soes) Vorbehalt *m*

provocation [ˌprɑvə'keʃən] *s* Provokation *f*

provocative [prə'vɑkətɪv] *adj* aufreizend

provoke [prə'vok] *tr* (*a person*) provozieren; (e.g., *laughter*) erregen

provok'ing *adj* ärgerlich

prow [prau] *s* Bug *m*

prowess ['prau·ɪs] *s* Tapferkeit *f*

prowl [praul] *intr* herumschleichen

prowl' car' *s* Streifenwagen *m*

prowler ['praulər] *s* mutmaßlicher Einbrecher *m*

proximity [prɑk'sɪmɪti] *s* Nähe *f*

proxy ['prɑksi] *s* Stellvertreter –in *mf*; by p. in Vertretung

prude [prud] *s* prüde Person *f*

prudence ['prudəns] *s* Klugheit *f;* (*caution*) Vorsicht *f*

prudent ['prudənt] *adj* klug; (*cautious*) umsichtig

prudish ['prudɪʃ] *adj* prüde

prune [prun] *s* Zwetsche *f* ‖ *tr* stuzen

Prussia ['prʌʃɪ·ə] *s* Preußen *n*

Prussian ['prʌʃ/ən] *adj* preußisch ‖ *s* Preuße *m*, Preußin *f*

pry [praɪ] *v* (*pret & pp* **pried**) *tr*—**pry open** aufbrechen; **pry s.th. out of s.o.** etw aus j—m herauspressen ‖ *intr* herumschnüffeln; **pry into** seine Nase stecken in (*acc*)

P.S. ['pi'es] *s* (**postscript**) NS

psalm [sɑm] *s* Psalm *m*

pseudo– ['sudo] *adj* Pseudo–, falsch

pseudonym ['sudənɪm] *s* Deckname *m*

psyche ['saɪki] *s* Psyche *f*

psychiatrist [saɪ'kaɪ·ətrɪst] *s* Psychiater –in *mf*

psychiatry [saɪ'kaɪ·ətri] *s* Psychiatrie *f*

psychic ['saɪkɪk] *adj* psychisch ‖ *s* Medium *n*

psychoanalysis [ˌsaɪko·ə'næləsɪs] *s* Psychoanalyse *f*

psychoanalyze [ˌsaɪko'ænə,laɪz] *tr* psychoanalytisch behandeln

psychologic(al) [ˌsaɪko'lɑdʒɪk(əl)] *adj* psychologisch

psychologist [saɪ'kɑlədʒɪst] *s* Psychologe *m*, Psychologin *f*

psychology [saɪ'kɑlədʒi] *s* Psychologie *f*

psychopath ['saɪkə,pæθ] *s* Psychopath –in *mf*

psycho·sis [saɪ'kosɪs] *s* (**–ses** [siz]) Psychose *f*

psychotic [saɪ'kɑtɪk] *adj* psychotisch ‖ *s* Psychosekranke *mf*

pto'main poi'soning ['tomen] *s* Fleischvergiftung *f*

pub [pʌb] *s* Kneipe *f*

puberty ['pjubərti] *s* Pubertät *f*

public ['pʌblɪk] *adj* öffentlich ‖ *s* Öffentlichkeit *f*, Publikum *n*

pub'lic address' sys'tem *s* Lautsprecheranlage *f*

publication [ˌpʌblɪ'keʃən] *s* Veröffentlichung *f*

pub'lic domain' *n*—**in the p. d.** gemeinfrei

publicity [pʌb'lɪsɪti] *s* Publizität *f*

publicize ['pʌblɪ,saɪz] *tr* bekanntmachen

pub'lic opin'ion öffentliche Meinung *f*

pub'lic-opin'ion poll' *s* öffentliche Meinungsumfrage *f*

pub'lic pros'ecutor *s* Staatsanwalt *m*

pub'lic rela'tions *spl* Kontaktpflege *f*

pub'lic serv'ant *s* Staatsangestellte *mf*

pub'lic util'ity *s* öffentlicher Versorgungsbetrieb *m*

publish ['pʌblɪʃ] *tr* veröffentlichen

publisher ['pʌblɪʃ/ər] *s* Verleger –in *mf*

pub'lishing house' *s* Verlag *m*

puck [pʌk] *s* Puck *m*

pucker ['pʌkər] *tr* (*the lips*) spitzen ‖ *intr*—**p. up** den Mund spitzen

pudding ['pudɪŋ] *s* Pudding *m*

puddle ['pʌdəl] *s* Pfütze *f*, Lache *f*

pudgy ['pʌdʒi] *adj* dicklich

puerile ['pju·ərɪl] *adj* knabenhaft

puff [pʌf] *s* (*on a cigarette*) Zug *m;* (*of smoke*) Rauchwölkchen *n;* (*on sleeves*) Puff *m* ‖ *tr* (*e.g., a cigar*) paffen; **p. oneself up** sich aufblähen; **p. out** ausblasen ‖ *intr* keuchen; **p. on** (*a pipe, cigar*) paffen an (*dat*)

pugilist ['pjudʒɪlɪst] *s* Faustkämpfer *m*

pugnacious [pʌg'neʃəs] *adj* kampflustig

pug-nosed ['pʌg,nozd] *adj* stupsnasig

puke [pjuk] *s* (sl) Kotze *f* ‖ *intr* (sl) kotzen

pull [pul] *s* Ruck *m;* (*influence*) Beziehungen *pl;* (*of gravity*) Anziehungskraft *f* ‖ *tr* ziehen; (*a muscle*) zerren; (*proof*) (typ) abziehen; **p. down** (*e.g., a shade*) herunterziehen; (*a building*) niederreißen; **p. off** (coll) zuwegebringen; **p. oneself together** sich zusammennehmen; **p. out** (*weeds*) herausreißen; **p. up** (*e.g., a chair*) heranrücken ‖ *intr* (*on*) ziehen (an *dat*); **p. back** sich zurückziehen; **p. in** (*arrive*) ankommen; **p. out** (*depart*) abfahren; **p. over to the side** an den Straßenrand heranfahren; **p. through** durchkommen; **p. up** (*e.g., in a car*) vorfahren

pullet ['pulɪt] *s* Hühnchen *n*

pulley ['puli] *s* Rolle *f;* (*pulley block*) Flaschenzug *m*

pull'o'ver *s* Pullover *m*

pulmonary ['pʌlmə,neri] *adj* Lungen–

pulp [pʌlp] *s* Brei *m;* (*to make paper*) Papierbrei *m;* **beat to a p.** windelweich schlagen

pulpit ['pulpɪt] *s* Kanzel *f*

pulsate ['pʌlset] *intr* pulsieren

pulsation [pʌl'seʃən] *s* Pulsieren *n*

pulse [pʌls] *s* Puls *m;* **take s.o.'s p.** j—m den Puls fühlen

pulverize ['pʌlvə,raɪz] *tr* pulverisieren

pum'ice stone' ['pʌmɪs] *s* Bimsstein *m*

pum-mel ['pʌməl] *v* (*pret & pp* **–mel[l]ed;** *ger* **–mel[l]ing**) *tr* mit der Faust schlagen

pump [pʌmp] *s* Pumpe *f;* (*shoe*) Pump *m* ‖ *tr* pumpen; (*for information*) ausfragen; **p. up** (*a tire*) aufpumpen

pump'han'dle *s* Pumpenschwengel *m*

pumpkin ['pʌmpkɪn] *s* Kürbis *m*

pun [pʌn] *s* Wortspiel *n* ‖ *v* (*pret & pp* **punned;** *ger* **punning**) *intr* ein Wortspiel machen

punch [pʌntʃ] *s* Faustschlag *m;* (*to make holes*) Locher *m;* (*drink*) Punsch *m* ‖ *tr* mit der Faust schlagen; (*a card*) lochen; (*a punch clock*) stechen

punch' bowl' *s* Punschschüssel *f*

punch' card' *s* Lochkarte *f*

punch' clock' *s* Kontrolluhr *f*

punch-drunk' *adj* von Faustschlägen betäubt

punch'ing bag' *s* Punchingball *m*

punch' line' *s* Pointe *f*

punctilious [pʌŋk'tɪlɪ·əs] *adj* förmlich

punctual ['pʌŋktʃu·əl] *adj* pünktlich

punctuate ['pʌŋktʃu,et] *tr* interpunktieren

punctuation [‚pʌŋktʃu'eʃən] s Interpunktion f

punctua'tion mark' s Satzzeichen n

puncture ['pʌŋktʃər] s Loch n ‖ tr durchstechen; **p. a tire** e-e Reifenpanne haben

punc'ture-proof' adj pannensicher

pundit ['pʌndɪt] s Pandit m

pungent ['pʌndʒənt] adj beißend, scharf

punish ['pʌnɪʃ] tr (be)strafen

punishment ['pʌnɪʃmənt] s Strafe f, Bestrafung f; (educ) Strafarbeit f

punk [pʌŋk] adj (sl) mies; **I feel p.** mir ist mies ‖ s (sl) Rocker m

punster ['pʌnstər] s Wortspielmacher m

puny ['pjuni] adj kümmerlich, winzig

pup [pʌp] s junger Hund m

pupil ['pjupəl] s Schüler –in mf; (of the eye) Pupille f

puppet ['pʌpɪt] s Marionette f

pup'pet gov'ernment s Marionettenregierung f

puppy ['pʌpi] s Hündchen n

pup'py show' s Marionettentheater n

pup'py love' s Jugendliebe f

purchase ['pʌrtʃəs] s Kauf m; (leverage) Hebelwirkung f ‖ tr kaufen

pur'chasing pow'er s Kaufkraft f

pure [pjur] adj (& fig) rein

purgative ['pʌrgətɪv] s Abführmittel n

purgatory ['pʌrgə‚tori] s Fegefeuer n

purge [pʌrdʒ] s (pol) Säuberungsaktion f ‖ tr reinigen; (pol) säubern

puri·fy ['pjurɪ‚faɪ] v (pret & pp –fied) tr reinigen, läutern

puritan ['pjurɪtən] adj puritanisch ‖ **Puritan** s Puritaner –in mf

purity ['pjurɪti] s Reinheit f

purloin [pər'lɔɪn] tr entwenden

purple ['pʌrpəl] adj purpurn ‖ s Purpur m

purport ['pʌrport] s Sinn m ‖ [pər-'port] tr vorgeben; (imply) besagen

purpose ['pʌrpəs] s Absicht f; (goal) Zweck m; **on p.** absichtlich; **to no p.** ohne Erfolg

purposely ['pʌrpəsli] adv absichtlich

purr [pʌr] s Schnurren n ‖ intr schnurren

purse [pʌrs] s Beutel m; (handbag) Handtasche f ‖ tr—**p. one's lips** den Mund spitzen

purse' strings' spl—**hold the p.** über das Geld verfügen

pursue [pər's(j)u] tr (a person; a plan, goal) verfolgen; (studies, profession) betreiben; (pleasures) suchen

pursuit [pər's(j)ut] s Verfolgung f; **in hot p.** hart auf den Fersen

pursuit' plane' s Jäger m

purvey [pər've] tr liefern, versorgen

pus [pʌs] s Eiter m

push [puʃ] s Schub m; (mil) Offensive f ‖ tr (e.g., a cart) schieben; (jostle) stoßen; (a button) drücken auf (acc); **p. around** (coll) schlecht behandeln; **p. aside** beiseite schieben; (curtains) zurückschlagen; **p. one's way through** sich durchdrängen; **p. through** durchsetzen ‖ intr drängen

push' but'ton s Druckknopf m

push' cart' s Verkaufskarren m

push'o'ver s (snap) (coll) Kinderspiel n; (sucker) Gimpel m; (easy opponent) leicht zu besiegender Gegner m

push'-up' s (gym) Liegestütz m

pushy ['puʃi] adj zudringlich

puss [pus] s (cat) Mieze f; (face) (sl) Fresse f

pussy ['pʌsi] adj eit(e)rig ‖ ['pusi] s Mieze f

puss'y wil'low s Salweide f

put [put] v (pret & pp put; ger putting) tr (stand) stellen; (lay) legen; (set) setzen; **feel put out** ungehalten sein; **put across to** beibringen (dat); **put aside** beiseite legen; **put down** (a load) abstellen; (a rebellion) niederschlagen; (in writing) aufschreiben; **put in** (e.g., a windowpane) einsetzen; (e.g., a good word) einlegen; (time) (on) verwenden (auf acc); **put off** (a person) hinhalten; (postpone) aufschieben; **put on** (clothing) anziehen; (a hat) aufsetzen; (a ring) anstecken; (an apron) umbinden; (the brakes) betätigen; (to cook) ansetzen; (a play) aufführen; **put on an act** sich in Szene setzen; **put oneself into** sich hineindenken in (acc); **put oneself out** sich [dat] Umstände machen; **put on its feet again** (com) auf die Beine stellen; **put s.o. on to s.th.** j-n auf etw [acc] bringen; **put out** (a fire) löschen; (lights) auslöschen; (throw out) herauswerfen; (a new book) herausbringen; **put out of action** kampfunfähig machen; **put over on s.o.** j-n übers Ohr hauen; **put through** durchsetzen; (a call) (telp) herstellen; **put (s.o.) through to** (telp) j-n verbinden mit; **put to good use** gut verwenden; **put up** (erect) errichten; (bail) stellen; (for the night) unterbringen; **put up a fight** sich zur Wehr setzen; **put up to** anstiften zu; **to put it mildly** gelinde gesagt ‖ intr —**put on** sich verstellen; **put out to sea** (said of a ship) in See gehen; **put up with** sich abfinden mit

put'-on' adj vorgetäuscht ‖ s (affectation) Affektiertheit f; (parody) Jux m

put-put ['pʌt‚pʌt] s Tacktack n ‖ intr —**p. along** knattern

putrid ['pjutrɪd] adj faul(ig)

putt [pʌt] tr & intr (golf) putten

putter ['pʌtər] s (golf) Putter m ‖ intr—**p. around** herumwursteln

put·ty ['pʌti] s Kitt m ‖ v (pret & pp –tied) tr (ver)kitten

put'ty knife' s Spachtel m & f

put'-up job' s abgekartete Sache f

puzzle ['pʌzəl] s Rätsel n; (game) Geduldspiel n ‖ tr verwirren; **be puzzled** verwirrt sein; **p. out** enträtseln ‖ intr—**p. over** tüfteln an (dat)

puzzler ['pʌzlər] s Rätsel n

puz'zling adj rätselhaft

PW ['pi 'dʌbəl‚ju] s (**prisoner of war**) Kriegsgefangene mf

pygmy ['pɪgmɪ] s Pygmäe m, Pygmäin f

pylon ['paɪlən] s (entrance to Egyptian temple) Pylon m; (aer) Wendemarke f; (elec) Leitungsmast m

pyramid ['pɪrəmɪd] s Pyramide f

pyre [paɪr] s Scheiterhaufen m

Pyrenees ['pɪrɪ‚niz] spl Pyrenäen pl

pyrotechnics [‚paɪrə'tekniks] spl Feuerwerkskunst f, Pyrotechnik f

python ['paɪθən] s Pythonschlange f

pyx [pɪks] s (eccl) Pyxis f

Q

Q, q [kju] s siebzehnter Buchstabe des englischen Alphabets

quack [kwæk] s Quacksalber m, Kurpfuscher m ‖ intr schnattern

quadrangle ['kwad‚ræŋgəl] s Viereck n; (inner yard) Innenhof m, Lichthof m

quadrant ['kwadrənt] s Quadrant m

quadratic [kwad'rætɪk] adj quadratisch

quadruped ['kwadru‚ped] s Vierfüßer m

quadruple [kwad'rupəl] adj vierfach ‖ s Vierfache n ‖ tr vervierfachen ‖ intr sich vervierfachen

quadruplets [kwad'ruplɪts] spl Vierlinge pl

quaff [kwaf] tr in langen Zügen trinken

quagmire ['kwæg‚maɪr] s Morast m

quail [kwel] s Wachtel f ‖ intr verzagen

quaint [kwent] adj seltsam

quake [kwek] s Zittern n; (geol) Beben n ‖ intr zittern; (geol) beben

Quaker ['kwekər] s Quäker –in mf

qualification [‚kwalɪfɪ'keʃən] s (for) Qualifikation f (für)

quali·fy ['kwalɪ‚faɪ] v (pret & pp –fied) tr qualifizieren; (modify) einschränken ‖ intr sich qualifizieren

quality ['kwalɪtɪ] s (characteristic) Eigenschaft f; (grade) Qualität f

qualm [kwam] s Bedenken n

quandary ['kwandərɪ] s Dilemma n

quantity ['kwantɪtɪ] s Menge f, Quantität f; (math) Größe f; (pros) Silbenmaß n; buy in q. auf Vorrat kaufen

quan·tum the·ory ['kwantəm] s Quantentheorie f

quarantine ['kwɔrən‚tin] s Quarantäne f ‖ tr unter Quarantäne stellen

quar·rel ['kwɔrəl] s Streit m; pick a q. Händel suchen ‖ v (pret & pp –rel[l]ed; ger –el[l]ing) intr (over) streiten (über acc or um)

quarrelsome ['kwɔrəlsəm] adj streitsüchtig, händelsüchtig

quar·ry ['kwɔrɪ] s Steinbruch m; (hunt) Jagdbeute f ‖ v (pret & pp –ried) tr brechen

quart [kwɔrt] s Quart n

quarter ['kwɔrtər] s Viertel n; (of a city) Stadtviertel n; (of the moon) Mondviertel n; (of the sky) Himmelsrichtung f; (coin) Vierteldollar m; (econ) Quartal n; (sport) Viertelzeit f; a q. after one (ein) Viertel nach

eins; a q. of an hour e–e Viertelstunde f; a q. to eight dreiviertel acht, (ein) viertel vor acht; at close quarters im Nahkampf; from all quarters von überall; give no q. keinen Pardon geben; quarters (& mil) Unterkunft f, Quartier n ‖ tr (lodge) einquartieren; (divide into four, tear into quarters) vierteilen ‖ intr im Quartier liegen

quar'ter-deck' s Quarterdeck n

quar'ter·fi'nal s Zwischenrunde f

quar'ter-hour' s Viertelstunde f

quarterly ['kwɔrtərlɪ] adj vierteljährig; (econ) Quartals– ‖ s Vierteljahresschrift f

quar'termas'ter s Quartiermeister m

Quar'termaster Corps' s Versorgungstruppen pl

quar'ter note' s (mus) Viertelnote f

quar'ter rest' s (mus) Viertelpause f

quartet [kwɔr'tet] s Quartett n

quartz [kwɔrts] s Quarz m

quash [kwaʃ] tr niederschlagen

quatrain ['kwatren] s Vierzeiler m

quaver ['kwevər] s Zittern n; (mus) Triller m ‖ intr zittern; (mus) trillern, tremolieren

queasy ['kwizɪ] adj übel

queen [kwin] s Königin f; (cards) Dame f

queen' bee' s Bienenkönigin f

queen' dow'ager s Königinwitwe f

queenly ['kwinlɪ] adj königlich

queen' moth'er s Königinmutter f

queer [kwɪr] adj sonderbar; (homosexual) schwul ‖ s (homosexual) Schwule m

queer' duck' s (coll) Unikum n

quell [kwel] tr unterdrücken

quench [kwentʃ] tr (thirst) löschen; (a fire) (aus)löschen

que·ry ['kwɪrɪ] s Frage f ‖ v (pret & pp –ried) tr befragen; (cast doubt on) bezweifeln

quest [kwest] s Suche f; in q. of auf der Suche nach

question ['kwestʃən] s Frage f; ask (s.o.) a q. (j–m) e–e Frage stellen; be out of the q. außer Frage stehen; beyond q. außer Frage; call into q. in Frage stellen; call the q. (parl) um Abstimmung bitten; in q. betreffend; it is a q. of (ger) es handelt sich darum zu (inf); q. of time Zeitfrage f; that's an open q. darüber läßt sich streiten; there's no q. about it darüber besteht kein Zweifel ‖ tr be-

fragen; (*said of the police*) verhören; (*cast doubt on*) bezweifeln
questionable ['kwɛstʃənəbəl] *adj* fraglich, fragwürdig; (*doubtful*) zweifelhaft; (*character*) bedenklich
ques'tioning *s* Verhör *n*, Vernehmung *f*
ques'tion mark' *s* Fragezeichen *n*
questionnaire [,kwɛstʃə'nɛr] *s* Frage-
bogen *m*
queue [kju] *s* Schlange *f* ‖ *intr*—q. up
sich anstellen
quibble ['kwɪbəl] *s* Deutelei *f* ‖ *intr*
(*about*) deuteln (an *dat*)
quibbler ['kwɪblər] *s* Wortklauber *m*
quick [kwɪk] *adj* schnell, fix ‖ *s*—cut
to the q. bis ins Mark treffen
quicken ['kwɪkən] *tr* beschleunigen ‖
intr sich beschleunigen
quick'lime' *s* gebrannter ungelöschter
Kalk *m*
quick' lunch' *s* Schnellimbiß *m*
quick'sand' *s* Treibsand *m*
quick'sil'ver *s* Quecksilber *n*
quick'-tem'pered *adj* jähzornig
quick'-wit'ted *adj* scharfsinnig
quiet ['kwaɪ·ət] *adj* ruhig; (*person*)
schweigsam; (*still*) still; (*street*) un-
belebt; be q.! sei still!; keep q.
schweigen ‖ *s* Stille *f* ‖ *tr* beruhigen
‖ *intr*—q. down sich beruhigen; (*said
of excitement, etc.*) sich legen
quill [kwɪl] *s* Feder *f*, Federkiel *m*;
(*of a porcupine*) Stachel *m*
quilt [kwɪlt] *s* Steppdecke *f* ‖ *tr* steppen
quince [kwɪns] *s* Quitte *f*
quince' tree' *s* Quittenbaum *m*
quinine ['kwaɪnaɪn] *s* Chinin *n*
quintessence [kwɪn'tɛsəns] *s* Inbegriff
m
quintet [kwɪn'tɛt] *s* Quintett *n*
quintuplets [kwɪn'tʌplɛts] *spl* Fünf-
linge *pl*
quip [kwɪp] *s* witziger Seitenhieb *m* ‖
v (*pret & pp* quipped; *ger* quipping)
tr witzig sagen ‖ *intr* witzeln

quire [kwaɪr] *s* (bb) Lage *f*
quirk [kwʌrk] *s* Eigenart *f*; (*subterfuge*) Ausflucht *f*; (*sudden change*)
plötzliche Wendung *f*
quit [kwɪt] *adj* quitt; let's call it quits!
(coll) Strich drunter! ‖ *v* (*pret & pp*
quit & quitted; *ger* quitting) *tr* aufgeben; (*e.g., a gang*) abspringen von;
q. it! hören Sie damit auf! ‖ *intr*
aufhören; (*at work*) seine Stellung
aufgeben
quite [kwaɪt] *adv* recht, ganz; q. a disappointment e-e ausgesprochene Enttäuschung *f*; q. recently in jüngster
Zeit; q. the reverse genau das Gegenteil
quitter ['kwɪtər] *s* Schlappmacher *m*
quiver ['kwɪvər] *s* Zittern *n*; (*to hold
arrows*) Köcher *m* ‖ *intr* zittern
quixotic [kwɪks'ɑtɪk] *adj* überspannt
quiz [kwɪz] *s* Prüfung *f*; (*game*) Quiz
n ‖ *v* (*pret & pp* quizzed; *ger* quiz-
zing) *tr* ausfragen; q. s.o. on s.th.
j-n etw abfragen
quiz'mas'ter *s* Quizonkel *m*
quiz' show' *s* Quizshow *f*
quizzical ['kwɪzɪkəl] *adj* (*puzzled*)
verwirrt; (*strange*) seltsam; (*mocking*) spöttisch
quoit [kwɔɪt] *s* Wurfring *m*
quondam ['kwɑndæm] *adj* ehemalig
Quon'set hut' ['kwɑnsət] *s* Nissen-
hütte *f*
quorum ['kwɔrəm] *s* beschlußfähige
Anzahl *f*
quota ['kwotə] *s* Quote *f*, Anteil *m*;
(*work*) Arbeitsleistung *f*
quotation [kwo'teʃən] *s* Zitat *n*; (*price*)
Notierung *f*
quota'tion marks' *spl* Anführungszei-
chen *pl*
quote [kwot] *s* Zitat *n*; (*of prices*)
Notierung *f* ‖ *tr* zitieren; (*prices*)
notieren *interj*—q. ... unquote Beginn des Zitats! ... Ende des Zitats!
quotient ['kwoʃənt] *s* Quotient *m*

R

R, r [ɑr] *s* achtzehnter Buchstabe des
englischen Alphabets
rabbet ['ræbɪt] *s* Falz *m* ‖ *tr* falzen
rabbi ['ræbaɪ] *s* Rabbiner *m*
rabbit ['ræbɪt] *s* Kaninchen *n*
rabble ['ræbəl] *s* Pöbel *m*
rab'ble-rous'er *s* Volksaufwiegler *-in
mf*
rabid ['ræbɪd] *adj* rabiat; (*dog*) toll-
wütig
rabies ['rebiz] *s* Tollwut *f*
raccoon [ræ'kun] *s* Waschbär *m*
race [res] *s* Rasse *f*; (*contest*) Wettren-
nen *n*; (fig) Wettlauf *m* ‖ *tr* um die
Wette laufen mit; (*in a car*) um die
Wette fahren mit; (*a horse*) rennen
lassen; (*an engine*) hochjagen ‖ *intr*

rennen; (*on foot*) um die Wette laufen; (*in a car*) um die Wette fahren
race' driv'er *s* Rennfahrer *-in mf*
race' horse' *s* Rennpferd *n*
racer ['resər] *s* (*person*) Wettfahrer
-in mf; (*car*) Rennwagen *m*; (*in
speed skating*) Schnelläufer *-in mf*
race' ri'ot *s* Rassenaufruhr *m*
race' track' *s* Rennbahn *f*
racial ['reʃəl] *adj* rassisch, Rassen—
rac'ing *s* Rennsport *m*
racism ['resɪzm] *s* Rassenhaß *m*
rack [ræk] *s* (*shelf*) Regal *n*, Ablage *f*;
(*for clothes, bicycles, hats*) Ständer
m; (*for luggage*) Gepäcknetz *n*; (*for
fodder*) Futterraufe *f*; (*for torture*)
Folter *f*; (*toothed bar*) Zahnstange *f*;

go to r. and ruin völlig zugrunde gehen; put to the r. auf die Folter spannen || *tr (with pain)* quälen; r. one's brains (over) sich *[dat]* den Kopf zerbrechen (über *acc*)

racket ['rækɪt] *s (noise)* Krach *m; (illegal business)* Schiebergeschäft *n; (tennis)* Rakett *n*

racketeer [,rækɪ'tɪr] *s* Schieber –in *mf*

racketeer'ing *s* Schiebertum *n*

rack' rail'way *s* Zahnradbahn *f*

racy ['resɪ] *adj (off-color)* schlüpfrig; *(vivacious, pungent)* rassig

radar ['redɑr] *s* Radar *n*

ra'darscope *s* Radarschirm *m*

radial ['redɪəl] *adj* radial

radiance ['redɪəns] *s* Strahlung *f*

radiant ['redɪənt] *adj (with)* strahlend (vor *dat*); *(phys)* Strahlungs-

radiate ['redɪ,et] *tr & intr* ausstrahlen

radiation [,redɪ'eʃən] *s* Strahlung *f*

radia'tion belt *s* Strahlungsgürtel *m*

radia'tion treat'ment *s* Bestrahlung *f;* give r. treatment to bestrahlen

radiator ['redɪ,etər] *s* Heizkörper *m; (aut)* Kühler *m*

ra'diator cap' *s* Kühlerverschluß *m*

radical ['rædɪkəl] *adj* radikal || *s* Radikale *mf*

radically ['rædɪkəlɪ] *adv* von Grund auf

radi·o ['redɪ,o] *s (–os)* Radio *n*, Rundfunk *m;* go on the r. im Rundfunk sprechen || *tr* funken

ra'dioac'tive *adj* radioaktiv

ra'dio announc'er *s* Rundfunkansager –in *mf*

ra'dio bea'con *s* (aer) Funkfeuer *n*

ra'dio beam' *s* Funkleitstrahl *m*

ra'dio broad'cast *s* Rundfunksendung *f*

radiocar'bon dat'ing *s* Radiokarbonmethode *f*

ra'diofre'quency *s* Hochfrequenz *f*

radiogram ['redɪ,o,græm] *s* Radiogramm *n*

radiologist [,redɪ'ɑlədʒɪst] *s* Röntgenologe *m*, Röntgenologin *f*

radiology [redɪ'ɑlədʒɪ] *s* Röntgenologie *f*

ra'dio net'work *s* Rundfunknetz *n*

ra'dio op'erator *s* Funker –in *mf*

radioscopy [,redɪ'ɑskəpɪ] *s* Durchleuchtung *f*

ra'dio set' *s* Radioapparat *m*

ra'dio sta'tion *s* Rundfunkstation *f*

radish ['rædɪʃ] *s* Radieschen *n*

radium ['redɪəm] *s* Radium *n*

radi·us ['redɪ·əs] *s (–i [,aɪ] & –uses)* Halbmesser *m; (anat)* Speicher *f;* within a r. of in e–m Umkreis von

raffish ['ræfɪʃ] *adj* gemein, niedrig

raffle ['ræfəl] *s* Tombola *f* || *tr*—r. off in e–r Tombola verlosen

raft [ræft] *s* Floß *n;* a r. of (coll) ein Haufen *m*

rafter ['ræftər] *s* Dachsparren *m;* rafters Sparrenwerk *n*

rag [ræg] *s* Lumpen *m;* chew the rag (sl) quasseln

ragamuffin ['rægə,mʌfɪn] *s* Lump *m*

rag' doll' *s* Stoffpuppe *f*

rage [redʒ] *s* Wut *f;* all the r. letzter Schrei *m;* be the r. die große Mode sein; fly into a r. in Wut geraten || *intr* wüten, toben

ragged ['rægɪd] *adj* zerlumpt, lumpig

rag'man *s (–men)* Lumpenhändler *m*

ragout [ræ'gu] *s* Ragout *n*

rag'weed' *s* Ambrosiapflanze *f*

raid [red] *s* Beutezug *m; (by police)* Razzia *f; (mil)* Überfall *m* || *tr* überfallen; e–e Razzia machen auf *(acc)*

raider ['redər] *s (naut)* Kaperkreuzer *m;* raiders (mil) Kommandotruppe *f*

rail [rel] *s* Geländerstange *f; (naut)* Reling *f; (rr)* Schiene *f;* by r. per Bahn ||—r. at beschimpfen

rail'head' *s* Schienenkopf *m*

rail'ing *s* Geländer *n; (naut)* Reling *f*

rail'road' *s* Eisenbahn *f* || *tr (a bill)* durchpeitschen

rail'road cross'ing *s* Bahnübergang *m*

rail'road embank'ment *s* Bahndamm *m*

rail'road sta'tion *s* Bahnhof *m*

rail'road tie' *s* Schwelle *f*

rail'way' *adj* Eisenbahn- || *s* Eisenbahn *f*

raiment ['rement] *s* Kleidung *f*

rain [ren] *s* Regen *m;* it looks like r. es sieht nach Regen aus; r. or shine bei jedem Wetter || *tr*—r. cats and dogs Bindfäden regnen; r. out verregnen || *intr* regnen

rainbow ['ren,bo] *s* Regenbogen *m*

rain'coat' *s* Regenmantel *m*

rain'drop' *s* Regentropfen *m*

rain'fall' *s* Regenfall *m; (amount of rain)* Regenmenge *f*

rain' gut'ter *s* Dachrinne *f*

rain' pipe' *s* Fallrohr *n*

rain'proof' *adj* regenfest, regendicht

rainy ['renɪ] *adj* regnerisch; *(e.g., day, weather)* Regen-; save money for a r. day sich *[dat]* e–n Notpfennig aufsparen

rain'y sea'son *s* Regenzeit *f*

raise [rez] *s* Lohnerhöhung *f; (in poker)* Steigerung *f* || *tr (lift)* heben, erheben; *(increase)* erhöhen, steigern; *(erect)* aufstellen; *(children)* großziehen; *(a family)* ernähren; *(grain, vegetables)* anbauen; *(animals)* züchten; *(dust)* aufwirbeln; *(money, troops)* aufbringen; *(blisters)* ziehen; *(a question)* aufwerfen; *(hopes)* erwecken; *(a laugh, smile)* hervorrufen; *(the ante)* steigern; *(a siege)* aufheben; *(from the dead)* auferwecken; r. Cain (or hell) Krach schlagen; r. the arm *(before striking)* mit dem Arm ausholen; r. the price of verteuern; r. to a higher power potenzieren || *intr (in poker)* höher wetten

raisin ['rezən] *s* Rosine *f*

rake [rek] *s* Rechen *m; (person)* Wüstling *m* || *tr* rechen; *(with gunfire)* bestreichen; r. in *(money)* kassieren; r. together (or up) zusammenrechen

rake'-off' *s* (coll) Gewinnanteil *m*

rakish ['rekɪʃ] *adj (dissolute)* liederlich; *(jaunty)* schmissig

ral·ly ['rælɪ] *s (meeting)* Massenversammlung *f; (recovery)* Erholung *s* (mil) Umgruppierung *f* ‖ *v* (*pret & pp* **-lied**) *tr* (wieder) sammeln ‖ *intr* sich (wieder) sammeln; (*recover*) sich erholen

ram [ræm] *s* Schafbock *m* ‖ *v* (*pret & pp* **rammed**; *ger* **ramming**) *tr* rammen; **ram s.th. down s.o.'s throat** j-m etw aufdrängen

ramble ['ræmbəl] *intr*—**r. about** herumwandern; **r. on** daherreden

ramification [ˌræmɪfɪ'keʃən] *s* Verzweigung *f*

ramp [ræmp] *s* Rampe *f*

rampage ['ræmpedʒ] *s* Toben *n*, Wüten *n*; **go on a r.** toben, wüten

rampant ['ræmpənt] *adj*—**be r.** grassieren

rampart ['ræmpɑrt] *s* Wall *m*, Ringwall *m*

ram'rod' *s* Ladestock *m*; (*cleaning rod*) Reinigungsstock *m*

ram'shack'le *adj* baufällig

ranch [ræntʃ] *s* Ranch *f*

rancid ['rænsɪd] *adj* ranzig

random ['rændəm] *adj* zufällig, Zufalls–; **at r.** aufs Geratewohl

range [rendʒ] *s* (*row*) Reihe *f*; (*mountains*) Bergkette *f*; (*stove*) Herd *m*; (*for firing practice*) Schießplatz *m*; (*of a gun*) Schießweite *f*; (*distance*) Reichweite *f*; (*mus*) Umfang *m*; **at a r. of** in e-r Entfernung von; **at close r.** auf kurze Entfernung; **come within s.o.'s r.** j-m vor den Schuß kommen; **out of r.** außer Reichweite; (*in shooting*) außer Schußweite; **within r.** in Reichweite; (*in shooting*) in Schußweite ‖ *tr* reihen ‖ *intr*—**r. from ... to** sich bewegen zwischen (*dat*) ... und

range'find'er *s* Entfernungsmesser *m*

ranger ['rendʒər] *s* Förster *m*; **rangers** Stoßtruppen *pl*

rank [ræŋk] *adj* (*rancid*) ranzig; (*smelly*) stinkend; (*absolute*) kraß; (*excessive*) übermäßig; (*growth*) üppig ‖ *s* Rang *m*; **according to r.** standesgemäß; **person of r.** Standesperson *f* ‖ *tr* einreihen, rangieren; **be ranked as** gelten als ‖ *intr* rangieren; **r. above** stehen über (*dat*); **r. among** zählen zu; **r. below** stehen unter (*dat*); **r. with** mitzählen zu

rank' and file' *s* die breite Masse

rank'ing of'ficer *s* Rangälteste *m*

rankle ['ræŋkəl] *tr* nagen an (*dat*) ‖ *intr* nagen

ransack ['rænsæk] *tr* durchstöbern

ransom ['rænsəm] *s* Lösegeld *n* ‖ *tr* auslösen

rant [rænt] *intr* schwadronieren

rap [ræp] *s* (*on the door*) Klopfen *n*; (*blow*) Klaps *m*; **not give a rap for** husten auf (*acc*); **take the rap** den Kopf hinhalten; **there was a rap on the door** es klopfte an der Tür ‖ *v* (*pret & pp* **rapped**; *ger* **rapping**) *tr* (*strike*) schlagen; (*criticize*) tadeln ‖ *intr* (*talk freely*) offen reden; (*on*) klopfen (an *dat*)

rapacious [rə'peʃəs] *adj* raffgierig; (*animal*) raubgierig

rape [rep] *s* Vergewaltigung *f* ‖ *tr* vergewaltigen

rapid ['ræpɪd] *adj* rapid(e); (*river*) reißend ‖ **rapids** *spl* Stromschnelle *f*

rap'id-fire' *adj* Schnell–; (mil) Schnellfeuer–

rap'id trans'it *s* Nahschnellverkehr *m*

rapier ['repɪ.ər] *s* Rapier *n*

rapist ['repɪst] *s* sexueller Gewaltverbrecher *m*

rap' ses'sion *s* zwanglose Diskussion *f*

rapt [ræpt] *adj* (*attention*) gespannt; (*in thought*) vertieft

rapture ['ræptʃər] *s* Entzückung *f*; **go into raptures** in Entzücken geraten

rare [rer] *adj* selten; (culin) halbgar

rare' bird' *s* (fig) weißer Rabe *m*

rare-fy ['rerɪˌfaɪ] *v* (*pret & pp* **-fied**) *tr* verdünnen

rarely ['rerli] *adv* selten

rarity ['rerɪti] *s* Rarität *f*

rascal ['ræskəl] *s* Bengel *m*

rash [ræʃ] *adj* vorschnell, unbesonnen ‖ *s* Ausschlag *m*

rasp [ræsp] *s* (*sound*) Kratzlaut *m*; (*tool*) Raspel *f* ‖ *tr* raspeln

raspberry ['ræzˌberi] *s* Himbeere *f*

rat [ræt] *s* Ratte *f*; (*deserter*) (sl) Überläufer –in *mf*; (*informer*) (sl) Spitzel *m*; (*scoundrel*) (sl) Gauner *m*; **smell a rat** (coll) den Braten riechen ‖ *intr*—**rat on** (sl) verpetzen

ratchet ['rætʃɪt] *s* (*wheel*) Sperrad *n*; (*pawl*) Sperrklinke *f*

rate [ret] *s* Satz *m*; (*for mail, freight*) Tarif *m*; **at any r.** auf jeden Fall; **at the r. of** (*a certain speed*) mit der Geschwindigkeit von; (*a certain price*) zum Preis von; **at the r. of a dozen per week** ein Dutzend pro Woche; **at this** (or **that**) **r.** bei diesem Tempo ‖ *tr* bewerten ‖ *intr* (coll) hochgeschätzt sein

rate' of exchange' *s* Kurs *m*

rate' of in'terest *s* Zinssatz *m*

rather ['ræðər] *adv* ziemlich; **I would r. wait** ich würde lieber warten; **r. ... than lieber ... als** ‖ *interj* na ob!

rati-fy ['rætɪˌfaɪ] *v* (*pret & pp* **-fied**) *tr* ratifizieren, bestätigen

rat'ing *s* Beurteilung *f*; (mach) Leistung *f*; (mil) Dienstgrad *m*; (sport) Bewertung *f*

ra-tio ['re(ɪ)ˌo] *s* (**-tios**) Verhältnis *n*

ration ['ræʃən], ['reʃən] *s* Ration *f*; **rations** (mil) Verpflegung *f* ‖ *tr* rationieren

ra'tion card' *s* Bezugsschein *m*

ra'tioning *s* Rationierung *f*

rational ['ræʃənəl] *adj* vernünftig

rationalize ['ræʃənəˌlaɪz] *tr & intr* rationalisieren

rat' poi'son *s* Rattengift *n*

rat' race' *s* (fig) Hetzjagd *f*

rattle ['rætəl] *s* Geklapper *n*; (toy) Klapper *f*, Schnarre *f* ‖ *tr* (*confuse*) verwirren; **get s.o. rattled** j-n aus dem Konzept bringen; **r. off** herunterschnarren; **r. the dishes** mit dem Geschirr klappern ‖ *intr* klappern; (*said of a machine gun*) knattern;

(said of windows) klirren; **r. on** daherplappern

rat′tlebrain′ s Hohlkopf m

rat′tlesnake′ s Klapperschlange f

rat′tletrap′ s (coll) Kiste f, Karre f

rat′trap′ s Rattenfalle f

raucous ['rɔkəs] adj heiser

ravage ['rævɪdʒ] s Verwüstung f, Verheerung f ǁ tr verwüsten, verheeren

rave [rev] s (coll) Modeschrei m ǁ intr irrereden; **r. about** schwärmen von

raven ['revən] adj (black) rabenschwarz ǁ s Kolkrabe m, Rabe m

ravenous ['rævənəs] adj rasend

ravine [rə'vin] s Bergschlucht f

rav′ing adj (coll) toll ǁ adv—**r. mad** tobsüchtig

ravish ['rævɪʃ] tr vergewaltigen

rav′ishing adv entzückend

raw [rɔ] adj roh; (weather) naßkalt; (throat) rauh; (recruit) unausgebildet; (skin) wundgerieben; (leather) ungegerbt; (wool) ungesponnen

raw′-boned′ adj hager

raw′ deal′ s (sl) unfaire Behandlung f

raw′hide′ s Rohhaut f

raw′ mate′rial s Rohstoff m

ray [re] s Strahl m; (ichth) Rochen m; **ray of hope** Hoffnungsstrahl m

rayon ['re·ɑn] adj kunstseiden ǁ s Kunstseide f, Rayon m

raze [rez] tr abtragen; **r. to the ground** dem Erdboden gleichmachen

razor ['rezər] s Rasiermesser n; (safety razor) Rasierapparat m

ra′zor blade′ s Rasierklinge f

razz [ræz] tr (sl) aufziehen

re [ri] prep betreffs (genit)

reach [ritʃ] s Reichweite f; **beyond the r.** of s.o. für j-n unerreichbar; **out of r.** unerreichbar; **within easy r.** leicht zu erreichen; **within r.** in Reichweite ǁ tr (a goal, person, city, advanced age, an understanding) erreichen; (a certain amount) sich belaufen auf (acc); (a compromise) schließen; (an agreement) treffen; (e.g., the ceiling) heranreichen an (acc); **r. out** ausstrecken ǁ intr (extend) reichen, sich erstrecken; **r. for** greifen nach; **r. into one's pocket** in die Tasche greifen

react [rɪ'ækt] intr (to) reagieren (auf acc); **r. upon** zurückwirken auf (acc)

reaction [rɪ'ækʃən] s Reaktion f

reactionary [rɪ'ækʃən,erɪ] adj reaktionär ǁ s Reaktionär -in mf

reac′tion time′ s Reaktionszeit f

reactor [rɪ'æktər] s Reaktor m

read [rid] v (pret & pp **read** [red]) tr lesen; **r. a paper on** referieren über (acc); **r. off** verlesen; **r. over** durchlesen; **r. to** vorlesen (dat) ǁ intr lesen; (said of a passage) lauten; (said of a thermometer) zeigen; **r. up on** studieren

readable ['ridəbl] adj lesbar

reader ['ridər] s (person) Leser -in mf; (book) Lesebuch n

readily ['redɪlɪ] adv gern(e)

readiness ['redɪnɪs] s Bereitwilligkeit f; (preparedness) Bereitschaft f

read′ing s (act) Lesen n; (material) Lektüre f; (version) Lesart f; (eccl, parl) Lesung f

read′ing glass′es spl Lesebrille f

read′ing lamp′ s Leselampe f

read′ing room′ s Lesesaal m

readjustment [,ri·ə'dʒʌstmənt] s Umstellung f

read·y ['redɪ] adj (done) fertig; **be r.** (stand in readiness) in Bereitschaft stehen; **get r.** sich fertig (or bereit) machen; **get s.th. r.** etw fertigstellen; **r. for** bereit zu; **r. for take-off** startbereit; **r. for use** gebrauchsfertig; **r. to** (inf) bereit zu (inf) ǁ v (pret & pp -ied) tr fertigmachen

read′y cash′ s flüssiges Geld n

read′y-made′ adj von der Stange

read′y-made′ clothes′ spl Konfektion f

reaffirm [,ri·ə'fʌrm] tr nochmals beteuern

real ['ri·əl] adj wirklich; (genuine) echt; (friend) wahr

re′al estate′ s Immobilien pl

re′al-estate′ a′gent s Immobilienmakler -in mf

re′al-estate′ tax′ s Grundsteuer f

realist ['ri·əlɪst] s Realist -in mf

realistic [,ri·ə'lɪstɪk] adj wirklichkeitsnah, realistisch

reality [rɪ'ælɪtɪ] s Wirklichkeit f; **in r.** wirklich; **realities** (facts) Tatsachen pl

realize ['ri·ə,laɪz] tr einsehen; (a profit) erzielen; (a goal) verwirklichen; (a good) realisieren

really ['ri·əlɪ] adv wirklich; **not r.** eigentlich nicht

realm [relm] s Königreich n; (fig) Reich n, Gebiet n; **within the r. of possibility** im Rahmen des Möglichen

Realtor ['ri·əltər] s Immobilienmakler -in mf

ream [rim] s Ries n ǁ tr ausbohren

reamer ['rimər] s Reibahle f

reap [rip] tr (cut) mähen; (& fig) ernten

reaper ['ripər] s Mäher -in mf; (mach) Mähmaschine f

reappear [,ri·ə'pɪr] intr wiederauftauchen, wiedererscheinen

rearmament [rɪ'ɑrməmənt] s Wiederscheinen s

reappoint [,ri·ə'pɔɪnt] tr wieder anstellen

rear [rɪr] adj hintere, rückwärtig ǁ s Hinterseite f; (of an army) Nachhut f; (sl) Hintern m; **bring up the r.** den Schluß bilden; (mil) den Zug beschließen; **from the r.** von hinten; **to the r.** nach hinten; **to the r.,** march! kehrt, marsch! ǁ tr (children) aufziehen; (animals) züchten; (a structure, one's head) aufrichten ǁ intr sich bäumen

rear′ ad′miral s Konteradmiral m

rear′ ax′le s Hinterachse f

rear′ end′ s (sl) Hintern m

rear′ guard′ s (mil) Nachhut f

rear′ gun′ner s Heckschütze m

rearm [ri'arm] *tr* wieder aufrüsten

rearmament [ri'arməmənt] *s* Wieder-aufrüstung *f*

rearrange [,ri·ə'rendʒ] *tr* umstellen

rear' seat' *s* Hintersitz *m*

rear'-view mir'ror *s* Rückspiegel *m*

rear'-wheel drive' *s* Hinterradantrieb *m*

rear' win'dow *s* (aut) Heckfenster *n*

reason ['rizən] *s* Vernunft *f*; (*cause*) Grund *m*; **by r. of** auf Grund (*genit*); **for this r.** aus diesem Grund; **listen to r.** sich belehren lassen; **not listen to r.** sich [*dat*] nichts sagen lassen; **not without good r.** nicht umsonst ‖ *tr*—**r.** out durchdenken ‖ *intr*—**r.** with vernünftig reden mit

reasonable ['rizənəbəl] *adj* (*person*) vernünftig; (*price*) solid; (*wares*) preiswert

reassemble [,ri·ə'sembəl] *tr* (*people*) wieder versammeln; (*mach*) wieder zusammenbauen ‖ *intr* sich wieder sammeln

reassert [,ri·ə'sert] *tr* wieder behaupten

reassurance [,ri·ə'ʃurəns] *s* Beruhigung *f*

reassure [ri·ə'ʃur] *tr* beruhigen

reawaken [,ri·ə'wekən] *tr* wieder erwecken ‖ *intr* wieder erwachen

rebate ['ribet] *s* Rabatt *m*

re·bel ['rebəl] *adj* Rebellen- ‖ *s* Rebell –in *mf* ‖ [rɪ'bɛl] *v* (*pret & pp* –belled; *ger* –belling) *intr* rebellieren

rebellion [rɪ'bɛljən] *s* Aufstand *m*, Rebellion *f*

rebellious [rɪ'bɛljəs] *adj* aufständisch

rebirth ['ribʌrθ] *s* Wiedergeburt *f*

rebore [ri'bor] *tr* nachbohren

rebound [ri,baund] *s* Rückprall *m* ‖ [ri'baund] *intr* zurückprallen

rebroad·cast [ri'brɒd,kæst] *s* Wiederholungssendung *f* ‖ *v* (*pret & pp* –cast & –casted) *tr* nochmals übertragen

rebuff [rɪ'bʌf] *s* Zurückweisung *f* ‖ *tr* schroff abweisen

re·build [ri'bɪld] *v* (*pret & pp* –built) *tr* wiederaufbauen; (*mach*) überholen; (*confidence*) wiederherstellen

rebuke [rɪ'bjuk] *s* Verweis *m* ‖ *tr* verweisen

re·but [rɪ'bʌt] *v* (*pret & pp* –butted; *ger* –butting) *tr* widerlegen

rebuttal [rɪ'bʌtəl] *s* Widerlegung *f*

recall [rɪ'kɔl], ['rikɔl] *s* (*recollection*) Erinnerungsvermögen *n*; (com) Zurücknahme *f*; (dipl, pol) Abberufung *f*; **beyond r.** unwiderruflich ‖ [rɪ'kɔl] *tr* (*remember*) sich erinnern an (*dat*); (*an ambassador*) abberufen; (*workers*) zurückrufen; (mil) wiedereinberufen

recant [rɪ'kænt] *tr & intr* (öffentlich) widerrufen

re·cap ['ri,kæp] *s* Zusammenfassung *f* ‖ *v* (*pret & pp* –capped; *ger* –capping) *tr* zusammenfassen; (*a tire*) runderneuern

recapitulate [,rikə'pɪtʃə,let] *tr* zusammenfassen

recapitulation [,rikə,pɪtʃə'leʃən] *s* Rekapitulation *f*, Zusammenfassung *f*

re·cast ['ri,kæst] *s* Umguß *m* ‖ [ri'kæst] *v* (*pret & pp* –cast) *tr* umgießen; (*a sentence*) umarbeiten; (theat) neubesetzen

recede [rɪ'sid] *intr* zurückgehen; (*become more distant*) zurückweichen

reced'ing *adj* (*forehead, chin*) fliehend

receipt [rɪ'sit] *s* Quittung *f*; **acknowledge r. of** den Empfang bestätigen (*genit*); **receipts** Eingänge *pl* ‖ *tr* quittieren

receive [rɪ'siv] *tr* bekommen, erhalten; (*a guest*) empfangen; (*pay*) beziehen; (rad) empfangen

receiver [rɪ'sivər] *s* Empfänger –in *mf*; (jur) Zwangsverwalter –in *mf*; (telp) Hörer *m*

receiv'ership' *s* Zwangsverwaltung *f*

recent ['risənt] *adj* neu, jung; **in r. years** in den letzten Jahren; **of r. date** neueren Datums

recently ['risəntli] *adv* kürzlich

receptacle [rɪ'sɛptəkəl] *s* Behälter *m*; (elec) Steckdose *f*

reception [rɪ'sɛpʃən] *s* (& rad) Empfang *m*

recep'tion desk' *s* Empfang *m*

receptionist [rɪ'sɛpənɪst] *s* Empfangsdame *f*; (med) Sprechstundenhilfe *f*

receptive [rɪ'sɛptɪv] *adj* (**to**) aufgeschlossen (für)

recess [rɪ'sɛs], ['risɛs] *s* (*alcove*) Nische *f*; (*cleft*) Einschnitt *m*; (at *school*) Pause *f*; (jur) Unterbrechung *f*; (parl) Ferien *pl* ‖ [rɪ'sɛs] *tr* (*place in a recess*) versenken ‖ *intr* (*until*) sich vertagen (auf *acc*)

recession [rɪ'sɛʃən] *s* Rezession *f*, Rückgang *m*

recharge [rɪ'tʃɑrdʒ] *tr* wieder aufladen

recipe ['rɛsɪ,pi] *s* Rezept *n*

recipient [rɪ'sɪpɪ·ənt] *s* Empfänger –in *mf*

reciprocal [rɪ'sɪprəkəl] *adj* gegenseitig

reciprocate [rɪ'sɪprə,ket] *tr* sich erkenntlich zeigen für ‖ *intr* sich erkenntlich zeigen

reciprocity [,rɛsɪ'prɒsɪti] *s* Gegenseitigkeit *f*

recital [rɪ'saɪtəl] *s* Vortrag *m*

recite [rɪ'saɪt] *tr* vortragen

reckless ['rɛklɪs] *adj* (*careless of consequences*) unbekümmert; (*lacking caution*) leichtsinnig; (*negligent*) fahrlässig

reck'less driv'ing *s* rücksichtsloses Fahren *n*

reckon ['rɛkən] *tr* (*count*) rechnen; (*compute*) (coll) schätzen ‖ *intr* rechnen; (coll) schätzen; **r. on** rechnen auf (*acc*); **r. with** (*deal with*) abrechnen mit; (*take into consideration*) rechnen mit

reck'oning *s* (*accounting*) Abrechnung *f*; (*computation*) Berechnung *f*; (aer, naut) Besteck *n*

reclaim [rɪ'klem] *tr* (*demand back*) zurückfordern; (*from wastes*) rückgewinnen; (*land*) urbar machen

reclamation [‚reklə'meʃən] s (of land) Urbarmachung f

recline [rɪ'klaɪn] intr ruhen; **r. against** sich lehnen an (acc); **r. in** (a chair) sich zurücklehnen in (dat)

recluse ['reklus] s Einsiedler –in mf

recognition [‚rekəg'nɪʃən] s Wiedererkennung f; (acknowledgement) Anerkennung f; **gain r.** zur Geltung kommen

recognizable [‚rekəg'naɪzəbəl] adj erkennbar

recognize ['rekəg‚naɪz] tr (by) erkennen an (dat); **r.** as anerkennen als

recoil ['rɪkɔɪl] s (of a rifle) Rückstoß m; (arti) Rücklauf m || [rɪ'kɔɪl] intr (in fear) zurückfahren; (from, e.g., a challenge) zurückschrecken vor (dat); (said of a rifle) zurückstoßen; (arti) zurücklaufen

recoilless [rɪ'kɔɪlɪs] adj rückstoßfrei

recollect [‚rekə'lekt] tr sich erinnern an (acc)

recollection [‚rekə'lekʃən] s Erinnerung f

recommend [‚rekə'mend] tr empfehlen

recommendation [‚rekəmən'deʃən] s Empfehlung f

recompense ['rekəm‚pens] s (for) Vergütung f (für) || tr vergüten

reconcile ['rekən‚saɪl] tr (with) versöhnen (mit); **become reconciled** sich versöhnen; **r. oneself to** sich abfinden mit

reconciliation [‚rekən‚sɪlɪ'eʃən] s Versöhnung f, Aussöhnung f

recondite ['rekən‚daɪt] adj (deep) tiefgründig; (obscure) dunkel

recondition [‚rɪkən'dɪʃən] tr wiederinstandsetzen

reconnaissance [rɪ'kɑnɪsəns] s Aufklärung f

reconnoiter [‚rekə'nɔɪtər] tr erkunden || intr aufklären

reconquer [rɪ'kɑŋkər] tr zurückerobern

reconquest [rɪ'kɑŋkwest] s Zurückeroberung f

reconsider [‚rɪkən'sɪdər] tr noch einmal erwägen

reconstruct [‚rɪkən'strʌkt] tr (rebuild) wiederaufbauen; (make over) umbauen; (e.g., events of a case) rekonstruieren

record ['rekərd] adj Rekord– || s (highest achievement) Rekord m; (document) Akte f, Protokoll n; (documentary evidence) Aufzeichnung f; (mus) Schallplatte f; **have a criminal r.** vorbestraft sein; **keep a r. of** Buch führen über (acc); **make a r. of** zu Protokoll nehmen; **off the r.** inoffiziell; **on r.** bisher registriert; **set a r.** e-n Rekord aufstellen || [rɪ'kɔrd] tr (in writing) aufzeichnen; (officially) protokollieren; (on tape or disk) aufnehmen || intr Schallplatten aufnehmen

rec'ord chang'er s Plattenwechsler m

recorder [rɪ'kɔrdər] s Protokollführer –in mf; (device) Zähler m; (on tape

or disk) Aufnahmegerät; (mus) Blockflöte f

rec'ord hold'er s Rekordler –in mf

record'ing adj aufzeichnend; (on tape or disk) Aufnahme– || s Aufzeichnung f; (on tape or disk) Tonaufnahme f

record'ing sec'retary s Protokollführer –in mf

rec'ord play'er s Plattenspieler m

recount ['ri‚kaunt] s Nachzählung f || [ri'kaunt] tr (count again) nachzählen || [rɪ'kaunt] tr (relate) im einzelnen erzählen

recoup [rɪ'kup] tr (losses) wieder einbringen; (a fortune) wiedererlangen; (reimburse) entschädigen

recourse [rɪ'kors], ['rikors] s (to) Zuflucht f (zu); (jur) Regreß m; **have r. to** seine Zuflucht nehmen zu

recover [rɪ'kʌvər] tr (get back) wiedererlangen; (losses) wiedereinbringen; (e.g., a spent rocket) bergen; (one's balance) wiederfinden; (e.g., a chair) neu beziehen || intr (from) sich erholen (von)

recovery [rɪ'kʌvəri] s Wiedererlangung f, Rückgewinnung f; (of health) Genesung f; (of a rocket) Bergung f

recreation [‚rekri'eʃən] s Erholung f

recrea'tion room' s Unterhaltungsraum m

recruit [rɪ'krut] s Rekrut m || (& mil) rekrutieren; **be recruited from** sich rekrutieren aus

recruit'ing of'ficer s Werbeoffizier m

recruitment [rɪ'krutmənt] s Rekrutierung f; (mil) Rekrutenaushebung f

rectangle ['rek‚tæŋgəl] s Rechteck n

rectangular [rek'tæŋgjələr] adj rechteckig

rectifier ['rektə‚faɪ-ər] s Berichtiger m; (elec) Gleichrichter m

recti•fy ['rekti‚faɪ] v (pret & pp –fied) tr berichtigen; (elec) gleichrichten

rector ['rektər] s Rektor m

rectory ['rektəri] s Pfarrhaus n

rec•tum ['rektəm] s (–ta [tə]) Mastdarm m

recumbent [rɪ'kʌmbənt] adj liegend

recuperate [rɪ'k(j)upə‚ret] intr sich (wieder) erholen

re•cur [rɪ'kʌr] v (pret & pp –curred; ger –curring) intr wiederkehren

recurrence [rɪ'kʌrəns] s Wiederkehr f

red [red] adj (redder; reddest) rot || s Rot n, Röte f; **be in the red** in den Roten Zahlen stecken; **Red** (pol) Rote m/f; **see red** wild werden

red' ant' s rote Waldameise f

red'bird' s Kardinal m

red'blood'ed adj lebensprühend

red'breast' s Rotkehlchen n

red' cab'bage s Rotkohl m

red' car'pet s (fig) roter Teppich m

red' cent' s—**not give a r. for** keinen roten Heller geben für

red'-cheeked' adj rotbäckig

Red' Cross', **the** s das Rote Kreuz

redden ['redən] tr röten, rot machen || intr erröten, rot werden

reddish ['redɪʃ] adj rötlich

redecorate [ri'dekə‚ret] *tr* neu dekorieren

redeem [ri'dim] *tr* zurückkaufen; (*a pawned article, promise*) einlösen; **r. oneself** seine Ehre wiederherstellen

redeemable [ri'diməbəl] *adj* (fin) ablösbar, kündbar

Redeemer [ri'dimər] *s* Erlöser *m*

redemption [ri'dempʃən] *s* Rückkauf *m*, Wiedereinlösung *f*; (relig) Erlösung *f*

red'-haired' *adj* rothaarig

red'-hand'ed *adj*—**catch s.o. r.** j-n auf frischer Tat ertappen

red'head' *s* Rotkopf *m*

red' her'ring *s* Bückling *m*; (fig) Ablenkungsmanöver *n*

red'-hot' *adj* glühend heiß, rotglühend

redirect [‚ridɪ'rekt] *tr* umdirigieren

rediscover [‚ridɪs'kʌvər] *tr* wiederentdecken

red'-let'ter day' *s* Glückstag *m*

red' light' *s* rotes Licht *n*

red'-light' dis'trict *s* Bordellviertel *n*

red' man' *s* Rothaut *f*

redness ['rednɪs] *s* Röte *f*

re-do ['ri'du] *v* (*pret* **-did**; *pp* **-done**) *tr* neu machen; (*redecorate*) renovieren

redolent ['redələnt] *adj* (**with**) duftend (**nach**)

redoubt [ri'daut] *s* Redoute *f*

redound [ri'daund] *intr*—**r. to** gereichen zu

red' pep'per *s* spanischer Pfeffer *m*

redress [ri'dres] *s* Wiedergutmachung *f* ǁ *tr* wiedergutmachen

Red' Rid'inghood' *s* Rotkäppchen *n*

red'skin' *s* Rothaut *f*

red' tape' *s* Amtsschimmel *m*

reduce [ri'd(j)us] *tr* reduzieren, verringern; (*prices*) herabsetzen; (math) (ab)kürzen

reduction [ri'dʌkʃən] *s* Verminderung *f*; (*gradual reduction*) Abbau *m*; (*in prices*) Absetzung *f*; (*in weight*) Abnahme *f*

redundant [ri'dʌndənt] *adj* überflüssig

red' wine' *s* Rotwein *m*

red'wing' *s* Rotdrossel *f*

red'wood' *s* Rotholz *n*

reecho [ri'eko] *tr* wiederhallen lassen ǁ *intr* wiederhallen

reed [rid] *s* Schilf *n*; (in *mouthpiece*) Rohrblatt *n*; (*of metal*) Zunge *f*; (*pastoral pipe*) Hirtenflöte *f*

reedit [ri'edɪt] *tr* neu herausgeben

reeducate [ri'edʒʊ‚ket] *tr* umerziehen

reef [rif] *s* Riff *n*; (naut) Reff *n* ǁ *tr* (naut) reffen

reek [rik] *intr* (**of**) riechen (nach)

reel [ril] *s* (*sway*) Taumeln *n*; (*for cables*) Trommel *f*; (angl, cin) Spule *f*; (min, naut) Haspel *f* ǁ *tr* (angl, cin) spulen; (min, naut) haspeln; **r. in** (*a fish*) einholen; **r. off** abspulen; (fig) herunterrasseln ǁ *intr* taumeln

reelect [‚ri·ɪ'lekt] *tr* wiederwählen

reelection [‚ri·ɪ'lekʃən] *s* Wiederwahl *f*

reenlist [‚ri·en'lɪst] *tr* wieder anwerben ǁ *intr* sich weiterverpflichten

reenlistment [‚ri·en'lɪstmənt] *s* Weiterverpflichtung *f*

reentry [ri'entri] *s* Wiedereintritt *m*

reexamination [‚ri·eg‚zæmɪ'neʃən] *s* Nachprüfung *f*

re-fer [ri'fʌr] *v* (*pret* & *pp* **-ferred**; *ger* **-ferring**) *tr*—**r. s.o. to** j-n verweisen an (*acc*) ǁ *intr*—**r. to** hinweisen auf (*acc*); (*e.g., to an earlier correspondence*) sich beziehen auf (*acc*)

referee [‚refə'ri] *s* (box) Ringrichter *m*; (sport) Schiedsrichter *m* ǁ *tr* als Schiedsrichter fungieren bei ǁ *intr* als Schiedsrichter fungieren

reference ['refərəns] *s* (**to**) Hinweis *m* (auf *acc*); (*person or document*) Referenz *f*; **in r.** in Bezug auf (*acc*); **make r. to** hinweisen auf (*acc*)

ref'erence lib'rary *s* Handbibliothek *f*

ref'erence work' *s* Nachschlagewerk *n*

referen-dum [‚refə'rendəm] *s* (**-da** [də]) Volksentscheid *m*

referral [ri'fʌrəl] *s* (**to**) Zuweisung *f* (**an** *acc*, **auf** *acc*); **by r.** auf Empfehlung

refill ['rifɪl] *s* Nachfüllung *f*; (*for a pencil, ball-point pen*) Ersatzmine *f* ǁ [ri'fɪl] *tr* nachfüllen

refine [ri'faɪn] *tr* (metal) läutern; (*oil, sugar*) raffinieren; (fig) verfeinern

refinement [ri'faɪnmənt] *s* Läuterung *f*; (*of oil, sugar*) Raffination *f*; (fig) Verfeinerung *f*

refinery [ri'faɪnəri] *s* Raffinerie *f*

reflect [ri'flekt] *tr* (& fig) widerspiegeln ǁ (*throw back rays*) reflektieren; (**on**) nachdenken (über *acc*); **r. on** (*comment on*) sich äußern über (*acc*); (*bring reproach on*) ein schlechtes Licht werfen auf (*acc*)

reflection [ri'flekʃən] *s* (*e.g., of light*) Reflexion *f*; (*reflected image*) Spiegelbild *n*; (*thought*) Überlegung *f*; **that's no r. on you** das färbt nicht auf Sie ab

reflector [ri'flektər] *s* Reflektor *m*

reflex ['rifleks] *s* Reflex *m*

reflexive [ri'fleksɪv] *adj* (gram) reflexiv ǁ *s* Reflexivform *f*

reforestation [‚rifɔrɪs'teʃən] *s* Aufforstung *f*

reform [ri'fɔrm] *s* Reform *f* ǁ *tr* reformieren, verbessern ǁ *intr* sich bessern

reformation [‚refər'meʃən] *s* Besserung *f*; **Reformation** Reformation *f*

reformatory [ri'fɔrmə‚tori] *s* Besserungsanstalt *f*

reformer [ri'fɔrmər] *s* Reformator *m*

reform' school' *s* Besserungsanstalt *f*

refraction [ri'frækʃən] *s* Ablenkung *f*

refrain [ri'fren] *s* Kehrreim *m* ǁ *intr*—**r. from** sich enthalten (*genit*); **r. from** (*ger*) es unterlassen zu (*inf*)

refresh [ri'freʃ] *tr* erfrischen; (*the memory*) auffrischen

refresh'er course' [ri'freʃər] *s* Auffrischungskurs *m*

refresh'ing *adj* erfrischend

refreshment [rɪ'freʃmənt] s Erfrischung
f
refresh'ment stand' s Erfrischungsstand
m
refrigerant [rɪ'frɪdʒərənt] s Kühlmittel
n
refrigerate [rɪ'frɪdʒə‚ret] tr kühlen
refrigerator [rɪ'frɪdʒə‚retər] s Kühlschrank m; (walk-in type) Kühlraum
m
refrig'erator car' s (rr) Kühlwagen m
re‧fuel [ri'fjul] v (pret & pp –fuel[l]ed;
ger –fuel[l]ing) tr auftanken || intr
tanken
refuge ['refjudʒ] s Zuflucht f; take r.
in (sich) flüchten in (acc)
refugee [‚refju'dʒi] s Flüchtling m
refugee' camp' s Flüchtlingslager n
refund ['rifʌnd] s Zurückzahlung f ||
[rɪ'fʌnd] tr (pay back) zurückzahlen
|| [ri'fʌnd] tr (fund again) neu fun-
dieren
refurnish [ri'fʌrnɪʃ] tr neu möblieren
refusal [rɪ'fjuzəl] s Ablehnung f
refuse ['refjus] s Abfall m || [rɪ'fjuz]
tr ablehnen; r. to (inf) sich weigern
zu (inf)
refutation [‚refju'teʃən] s Widerlegung
f
refute [rɪ'fjut] tr widerlegen
regain [rɪ'gen] tr zurückgewinnen
regal ['rigəl] adj königlich
regale [rɪ'gel] tr (delight) ergötzen;
(entertain) reichlich bewirten
regalia [rɪ'gelɪ‧ə] spl Insignien pl
regard [rɪ'gard] s (for) Rücksicht f
(auf acc); best regards to herzlich-
ster Gruß an (acc); have little r. for
wenig achten; in every r. in jeder
Hinsicht; in (or with) r. to in Hinsicht auf (acc); in this r. in dieser
Hinsicht; without r. for ohne Rück-
sicht auf (acc) || tr betrachten; as
regards in Bezug auf (acc)
regard'ing prep hinsichtlich (genit)
regardless [rɪ'gardlɪs] adv (coll) ungeniert; r. of ungeachtet (genit)
regatta [rɪ'gætə] s Regatta f
regency ['ridʒənsi] s Regentschaft f
regenerate [rɪ'dʒenə‚ret] tr regenerieren
regent ['ridʒənt] s Regent –in mf
regicide ['redʒɪ‚saɪd] s (act) Königs-
mord m; (person) Königsmörder –in
mf
regime [re'ʒim] s Regime n
regiment ['redʒɪmənt] s (mil) Regiment
n || ['redʒɪ‚ment] tr reglementieren
regimental [‚redʒɪ'mentəl] adj Regiments–
region ['ridʒən] s Gegend f, Region f
regional ['ridʒənəl] adj regional
register ['redʒɪstər] s Register n, Ver-
zeichnis n || tr registrieren; (stu-
dents) immatrikulieren; (feelings) er-
kennen lassen || intr sich einschreiben
lassen; (at a hotel) sich eintragen
lassen
reg'istered let'ter s eingeschriebener
Brief m
reg'istered nurse' s (staatlich) geprüfte Krankenschwester f

registrar ['redʒɪ‚strar] s Registrator –in
mf
registration [‚redʒɪs'treʃən] s (e.g., of
firearms) Registrierung f; (for a
course; at a hotel) Anmeldung f; (of
a trademark) Eintragung f; (aut)
Zulassung f; (educ) Einschreibung f
registra'tion blank' s Meldeformular n
registra'tion fee' s Anmeldegebühr f
registra'tion num'ber s Registriernum-
mer f
regression [rɪ'greʃən] s Rückgang m
regret [rɪ'gret] s (over) Bedauern n
(über acc) || v (pret & pp –regretted;
ger regretting) tr bedauern; I r. to
say es tut mir leid, sagen zu müssen
regrettable [rɪ'gretəbəl] adj bedauerlich
regroup [rɪ'grup] tr umgruppieren
regular ['regjələr] adj (usual) gewöhnlich; (pulse, breathing, features, in-
tervals) regelmäßig; r. army stehen-
des Heer n; r. guy (coll) Pfundskerl
m; r. officer Berufsoffizier –in mf
regularity [‚regjə'lærɪti] s Regelmäßigkeit f
regulate ['regjə‚let] tr regeln
regulation [‚regjə'leʃən] s Regelung f;
(rule) Vorschrift f, Bestimmung f;
against regulations vorschriftswidrig
regulator ['regjə‚letər] s Regler m
rehabilitate [‚rihə'bɪlɪ‚tet] tr rehabilitieren
rehash [ri'hæʃ] tr (coll) aufwärmen
rehearsal [rɪ'hʌrsəl] s Probe f
rehearse [rɪ'hʌrs] tr & intr proben
rehire [rɪ'haɪr] tr wiedereinstellen
reign [ren] s Regierung f; (period of
rule) Regierungszeit f || intr regie-
ren; r. over herrschen über (acc)
reimburse [ri‧ɪm'bʌrs] tr (costs) rück-
erstatten; r. s.o. for s.th. j–m etw
vergüten
rein [ren] s Zügel m; give free r. to
die Zügel schießen lassen (dat) ||
tr—r. in (a horse) parieren
reincarnation [‚ri‧ɪnkar'neʃən] s Rein-
karnation f, Wiedergeburt f
rein'deer' s Rentier n
reinforce [‚ri‧ɪn'fors] tr verstärken
reinforced' concrete' s Stahlbeton m
reinforcement [‚ri‧ɪn'forsmənt] s Ver-
stärkung f; reinforcements (mil)
Verstärkungen pl
reinstate [‚ri‧ɪn'stet] tr (in) wieder-
einsetzen (in acc)
reiterate [ri'ɪtə‚ret] tr wiederholen
reject ['ridʒekt] s Ausschußware f ||
[rɪ'dʒekt] tr ablehnen, zurückweisen; (a request, appeal) abweisen
rejection [rɪ'dʒekʃən] s Ablehnung f;
(of a request, appeal) Abweisung f
rejoice [rɪ'dʒɔɪs] intr frohlocken
rejoin [rɪ'dʒɔɪn] tr (answer) erwidern;
(a group) sich wieder anschließen
(dat)
rejoinder [rɪ'dʒɔɪndər] s Erwiderung f;
(jur) Duplik f
rejuvenate [rɪ'dʒuvɪ‚net] tr verjüngen
rekindle [ri'kɪndəl] tr wieder anzünden; (fig) wieder entzünden
relapse [rɪ'læps] s (& pathol) Rückfall m

m ‖ *intr* (**into**) wieder verfallen (in *acc*)

relate [rɪˈlet] *tr* (*a story*) erzählen; (*connect*) verknüpfen; **r. s.th. to s.th.** etw auf etw [*acc*] beziehen ‖ *intr*—**r. to** in Beziehung stehen mit

relat′ed *adj* (*by blood*) verwandt; (*by marriage*) verschwägert; (*subjects*) benachbart

relation [rɪˈleʃən] *s* Beziehung *f*, Verhältnis *n*; (*relative*) Verwandte *mf*; **in r. to** in Bezug auf (*acc*); **relations** (*sex*) Verkehr *m*

rela′tionship′ *s* (*connection*) Beziehung *f*; (*kinship*) Verwandschaft *f*

relative [ˈrelətɪv] *adj* relativ, verhältnismäßig; **r. to** bezüglich (*genit*) ‖ *s* Verwandte *mf*

rel′ative clause′ *s* Relativsatz *m*

rel′ative pro′noun *s* Relativpronomen *n*

relativity [ˌreləˈtɪvɪti] *s* Relativität *f*

relax [rɪˈlæks] *tr* auflockern; (*muscles*) entspannen ‖ *intr* sich entspannen

relaxation [ˌrilækˈseʃən] *s* Entspannung *f*; **r. of tension** Entspannung *f*

relay [ˈrile] *s* Relais *n*; (sport) Staffel *f* ‖ [rɪˈle] *v* (*pret & pp* –**layed**) *tr* übermitteln; (*through relay stations*) übertragen

re′lay race′ *s* Staffellauf *m*

re′lay team′ *s* Staffel *f*

release [rɪˈlis] *s* (**from**) Entlassung *f* (aus); (*of bombs*) Abwurf *m*; (*of news*) Mitteilung *f* ‖ *tr* entlassen; (*a film, book*) freigeben; (*bombs*) abwerfen; (*energy*) freisetzen; (*brakes*) lösen; **r. the clutch** auskuppeln

relegate [ˈreliˌget] *tr* (**to**) verweisen (an *acc*); **r. to second position** auf den zweiten Platz verweisen

relent [rɪˈlent] *intr* (*let up*) nachlassen; (*yield*) sich erweichen lassen

relentless [rɪˈlentlɪs] *adj* (*tireless*) unermüdlich; (*unappeasable*) unerbittlich; (*never-ending*) unaufhörlich

relevant [ˈreləvənt] *adj* sachdienlich

reliable [rɪˈlaɪəbəl] *adj* zuverlässig

reliance [rɪˈlaɪəns] *s* Vertrauen *n*

relic [ˈrelɪk] *s* Reliquie *f*; **r. of the past** Zeuge *m* der Vergangenheit

relief [rɪˈlif] *s* Erleichterung *f*; (*for the poor*) Armenunterstützung *f*; (*replacement*) Ablösung *f*; (*sculpture*) Relief *n*; **on r.** von Sozialhilfe lebend; **bring r.** Linderung schaffen; **go on r.** stempeln gehen

relief′ map′ *s* Reliefkarte *f*

relieve [rɪˈliv] *tr* erleichtern; (*from guard duty*) ablösen; **r. oneself** seine Notdurft verrichten

religion [rɪˈlɪdʒən] *s* Religion *f*

religious [rɪˈlɪdʒəs] *adj* religiös; (*order*) geistlich

relinquish [rɪˈlɪŋkwɪʃ] *tr* aufgeben; **r. the right to s.th. to s.o.** j–m das Recht auf etw [*acc*] überlassen

relish [ˈrelɪʃ] *s* (**for**) Genuß *m* (an *acc*); (*condiment*) Würze *f* ‖ *tr* genießen

reluctance [rɪˈlʌktəns] *s* Widerstreben *n*

reluctant [rɪˈlʌktənt] *adj* widerstrebend; **be r. to do s.th.** etw ungern tun

reluctantly [rɪˈlʌktəntli] *adv* ungern

re·ly [rɪˈlaɪ] *v* (*pret & pp* –**lied**) *intr*—**r. on** sich verlassen auf (*acc*)

remain [rɪˈmen] *s*—**remains** Überreste *pl*; (*corpse*) sterbliche Reste *pl* ‖ *intr* bleiben; (*at end of letter*) verbleiben; **r. behind** zurückbleiben; **r. seated** sitzenbleiben; **r. steady** (*said of prices*) sich behaupten

remainder [rɪˈmendər] *s* Restbestand *m*, Rest *m* ‖ *tr* verramschen

remark [rɪˈmark] *s* Bemerkung *f* ‖ *tr* bemerken

remarkable [rɪˈmarkəbəl] *adj* markant, bemerkenswert

remar·ry [rɪˈmæri] *v* (*pret & pp* –**ried**) *tr* sich wiederverheiraten mit ‖ *intr* sich wiederverheiraten

reme·dy [ˈremɪdi] *s* (**for**) Heilmittel *n* (für); (fig) (**for**) Gegenmittel *n* (gegen) ‖ *v* (*pret & pp* –**died**) *tr* abhelfen (*dat*); (*damage, shortage*) abheben

remember [rɪˈmembər] *tr* sich erinnern an (*acc*); **r. me to** empfehlen Sie mich (*dat*) ‖ *intr* sich erinnern

remembrance [rɪˈmembrəns] *s* Erinnerung *f*; **in r. of** zum Andenken an (*acc*)

remind [rɪˈmaɪnd] *tr* (**of**) erinnern an (*acc*); **r. s.o. to** (*inf*) j–n mahnen zu (*inf*)

reminder [rɪˈmaɪndər] *s* (*note*) Zettel *m*; (*from a creditor*) Mahnung *f*

reminisce [ˌremɪˈnɪs] *intr* in Erinnerungen schwelgen

remiss [rɪˈmɪs] *adj* nachlässig

remission [rɪˈmɪʃən] *s* Nachlaß *m*

re·mit [rɪˈmɪt] *v* (*pret & pp* –**mitted**; *ger* –**mitting**) *tr* (*in cash*) übersenden; (*by check*) überweisen; (*forgive*) vergeben

remittance [rɪˈmɪtəns] *s* (*in cash*) Übersendung *f*; (*by check*) Überweisung *f*

remnant [ˈremnənt] *s* Rest *m*; (*of cloth*) Stoffrest *m*

remod·el [rɪˈmadəl] *v* (*pret & pp* –**el[l]ed**; *ger* –**el[l]ing**) *tr* umgestalten; (*a house*) umbauen

remonstrate [rɪˈmanstret] *intr* protestieren; **r. with s.o.** j–m Vorwürfe machen

remorse [rɪˈmɔrs] *s* Gewissensbisse *pl*

remorseful [rɪˈmɔrsfəl] *adj* reumütig

remote [rɪˈmot] *adj* fern; (*possibility*) vage; (*idea*) blaß; (*resemblance*) entfernt; (*secluded*) abgelegen

remote′ control′ *s* Fernsteuerung *f*; (telv) Fernbedienung *f*; **guide by r.** fernlenken

removable [rɪˈmuvəbəl] *adj* entfernbar

removal [rɪˈmuvəl] *s* Entfernung *f*; (*by truck*) Abfuhr *f*; (*from office*) Absetzung *f*

remove [rɪˈmuv] *tr* entfernen; (*clothes*) ablegen; (*one's hat*) abnehmen; (*dishes from the table*) abräumen; (*a stain*) entfernen; (*from office*) absetzen; (*furniture*) ausräumen

remuneration [rɪˌmjunəˈreʃən] *s* Vergütung *f*

renaissance [ˌrenəˈsɑns] *s* Renaissance *f*

rend [rend] *v* (*pret & pp* **rent** [rent]) *tr* (& *fig*) zerreißen

render [ˈrendər] *tr* (*give*) geben; (*a service*) leisten; (*honor*) erweisen; (*thanks*) abstatten; (*a verdict*) fällen; (*translate; play, e.g., on the piano*) wiedergeben; **r. harmless** unschädlich machen

rendez·vous [ˈrɑndəˌvu] *s* (**–vous** [ˌvuz]) Rendezvous *n*, Treffpunkt *m*; (*mil*) Sammelplatz *m* || *v* (*pret & pp* **–voused** [ˌvud]; *ger* **–vousing** [ˌvuˌɪŋ]) *intr* sich treffen; (*mil*) sich versammeln

rendition [renˈdɪʃən] *s* Wiedergabe *f*

renegade [ˈreniˌged] *s* Renegat –in *mf*

renege [rɪˈnɪg] *s* Renonce *f* || *intr* (*cards*) nicht bedienen; **r. on** nicht einhalten

renew [rɪˈn(j)u] *tr* erneuern; (*e.g., a passport*) verlängern lassen

renewable [rɪˈn(j)u·əbəl] *adj* erneuerbar

renewal [rɪˈn(j)u·əl] *s* Erneuerung *f*; (*e.g., of a passport*) Verlängerung *f*

renounce [rɪˈnauns] *tr* verzichten auf (*acc*)

renovate [ˈrenəˌvet] *tr* renovieren; (*fig*) erneuern

renovation [ˌrenəˈveʃən] *s* Renovierung *f*

renown [rɪˈnaun] *s* Ruhm *m*

renowned [rɪˈnaund] *adj* (**for**) berühmt (*wegen*)

rent [rent] *adj* zerrissen || *s* Miete *f*; (*tear*) Riß *m* || *tr* mieten; **r. out** vermieten

rental [ˈrentəl] *s* Miete *f*

rent'al serv'ice *s* Verleih *m*

rent'ed car' *s* Mietwagen *m*, Mietauto *n*

renter [ˈrentər] *s* Mieter –in *mf*

renunciation [rɪˌnʌnsɪˈeʃən] *s* (**of**) Verzicht *m* (auf *acc*)

reopen [riˈopən] *tr* wieder öffnen; (*a business*) wieder eröffnen; (*an argument; school year*) wieder beginnen || *intr* (*said of a shop or business*) wieder geöffnet werden; (*said of a school year*) wieder beginnen

reopening [riˈopənɪŋ] *s* (*of a business*) Wiedereröffnung *f*; (*of school*) Wiederbeginn *m*; (jur) Wiederaufnahme *f*

reorder [riˈordər] *tr* nachbestellen

reorganization [ˌriˌorgənɪˈzeʃən] *s* Reorganisation *f*, Neuordnung *f*

reorganize [riˈorgəˌnaɪz] *tr* reorganisieren; (*an administration*) umbilden

repack [riˈpæk] *tr* umpacken

repair [rɪˈper] *s* Ausbesserung *f*, Reparatur *f*; **in bad r.** in schlechtem Zustand; **keep in good r.** im Stande halten || *tr* ausbessern, reparieren || *intr* (**to**) sich begeben (nach, zu)

repair' gang' *s* Störungstrupp *m*

repair' shop' *s* Reparaturwerkstatt *f*

repaper [riˈpepər] *tr* neu tapezieren

reparation [ˌrepəˈreʃən] *s* Wiedergutmachung *f*; **reparations** Reparationen *pl*, Kriegsentschädigung *f*

repartee [ˌreparˈti] *s* schlagfertige Antwort *f*

repast [rɪˈpæst] *s* Mahl *n*

repatriate [riˈpetri ˌet] *tr* repatriieren

re·pay [riˈpe] *v* (*pret & pp* **–paid**) *tr* (*e.g., a loan*) zurückzahlen; (*a person*) entschädigen; **r. a favor** e–n Gefallen erwidern

repayment [rɪˈpemənt] *s* Rückzahlung *f*; (*reprisal*) Vergeltung *f*

repeal [rɪˈpil] *s* Aufhebung *f* || *tr* aufheben, außer Kraft setzen

repeat [rɪˈpit] *tr* wiederholen; (*a story, gossip*) weitererzählen; **r. s.th. after s.o.** j–m etw nachsagen

repeat'ed *adj* abermalig, mehrmalig

repeatedly [rɪˈpitɪdli] *adv* wiederholt

re·pel [rɪˈpel] *v* (*pret & pp* **–pelled**; *ger* **–pelling**) *tr* (*an enemy, an attack*) zurückschlagen; (*e.g., water*) abstoßen

repellent [rɪˈpelənt] *s* Bekämpfungsmittel *n*

repent [rɪˈpent] *tr* bereuen || *intr* Reue empfinden; **r. of** bereuen

repentance [rɪˈpentəns] *s* Reue *f*

repentant [rɪˈpentənt] *adj* reuig

repercussion [ˌripərˈkʌʃən] *s* Rückwirkung *f*

repertory [ˈrepərˌtori] *s* Repertoire *n*

repetition [ˌrepɪˈtɪʃən] *s* Wiederholung *f*

replace [rɪˈples] *tr* (**with**) ersetzen (durch)

replaceable [rɪˈplesəbəl] *adj* ersetzbar

replacement [rɪˈplesmənt] *s* (*act*) Ersetzen *n*; (*substitute part*) Ersatz *m*; (*person*) Ersatzmann *m*

replay [ˈriple] *s* (sport) Wiederholungsspiel *n* || [riˈple] *tr* nochmals spielen

replenish [rɪˈplenɪʃ] *tr* wieder auffüllen

replete [rɪˈplit] *adj* angefüllt

replica [ˈreplɪkə] *s* Replik *f*

re·ply [rɪˈplaɪ] *s* Erwiderung *f*; (*letter*) Antwortschreiben *n*; **in r. to your letter** in Beantwortung Ihres Schreibens || *v* (*pret & pp* **–plied**) *tr & intr* erwidern

report [rɪˈport] *s* Bericht *m*; (*rumor*) Gerücht *n*; (*e.g., of a gun*) Knall *m* || *tr* (*give an account of*) berichten; (*give notice of*) melden; **r. s.o. to the police** j–n bei der Polizei anzeigen || *intr* (**to**) sich melden (bei); **r. in** sich anmelden

report' card' *s* Zeugnis *n*

reportedly [rɪˈportɪdli] *adv* angeblich

reporter [rɪˈportər] *s* Reporter –in *mf*

repose [rɪˈpoz] *s* Ruhe *f* || *intr* ruhen

repository [rɪˈpazɪˌtori] *s* Verwahrungsort *m*; (*of information*) Fundgrube *f*

represent [ˌreprɪˈzənt] *tr* vertreten; (*depict*) darstellen

representation [ˌreprɪzenˈteʃən] *s* Vertretung *f*; (*depiction*) Darstellung *f*

representative [ˌreprɪˈzentɪtɪv] *adj* (*function*) stellvertretend; (*government*) parlamentarisch; (*typical*) (**of**) typisch (für) ‖ s Vertreter –in mf; (pol) Abgeordnete mf

repress [rɪˈpres] tr unterdrücken; (psychoanal) verdrängen

repression [rɪˈpreʃən] s Unterdrückung f; (psychoanal) Verdrängung f

reprieve [rɪˈpriv] s Strafaufschub m; (fig) Gnadenfrist f, Atempause f

reprimand [ˈreprɪˌmænd] s Verweis m; give s.o. a r. j-m e-n Verweis erteilen ‖ tr (for) zurechtweisen (wegen, für), rügen (wegen, für)

reprint [ˈriprɪnt] s Nachdruck m ‖ [riˈprɪnt] tr nachdrucken

reprisal [rɪˈpraɪzəl] s Vergeltung f; take reprisals against or on Repressalien ergreifen gegen

reproach [rɪˈprotʃ] s Vorwurf m ‖ tr (for) tadeln (wegen); r. s.o. with s.th. j-m etw vorwerfen

reproduce [ˌriprəˈd(j)us] tr reproduzieren; (copies) vervielfältigen; (an experiment) wiederholen; (a play neuaufführen; (a sound) wiedergeben; (a lost limb) regenerieren ‖ intr sich fortpflanzen

reproduction [ˌriprəˈdʌkʃən] s Reproduktion f; (making copies) Vervielfältigung f; (of sound) Wiedergabe f; (biol) Fortpflanzung f

reproductive [ˌriprəˈdʌktɪv] adj Fortpflanzungs-

reproof [rɪˈpruf] s Rüge f

reprove [rɪˈpruv] tr rügen

reptile [ˈreptaɪl] s Kriechtier n

republic [rɪˈpʌblɪk] s Republik f

republican [rɪˈpʌblɪkən] adj republikanisch ‖ s Republikaner –in mf

repudiate [rɪˈpjudɪˌet] tr (disown) verleugnen; (a charge) zurückweisen; (a debt) nicht anerkennen; (a treaty) für unverbindlich erklären; (a woman) verstoßen

repugnant [rɪˈpʌgnənt] adj widerwärtig

repulse [rɪˈpʌls] s (refusal) Zurückweisung f; (setback) Rückschlag m ‖ tr zurückweisen; (mil) zurückschlagen

repulsive [rɪˈpʌlsɪv] adj abstoßend

reputable [ˈrepjətəbəl] adj anständig

reputation [ˌrepjəˈteʃən] s Ruf m, Ansehen n; have the r. of being im Rufe stehen zu sein

repute [rɪˈpjut] s—be held in high r. hohes Ansehen genießen; bring into bad r. in üble Nachrede bringen; of r. von Ruf ‖ tr—she is reputed to be a beauty sie soll e-e Schönheit sein

reputedly [rɪˈpjutɪdli] adv angeblich

request [rɪˈkwest] s Bitte f, Gesuch n; at his r. auf seine Bitte; on r. auf Wunsch ‖ tr (a person) bitten; (a thing) bitten um, ersuchen

Requiem [ˈrekwɪˌem] s (Mass) Seelenmesse f; (chant, composition) Requiem n

require [rɪˈkwaɪr] tr erfordern; if required erforderlichenfalls

requirement [rɪˈkwaɪrmənt] s Anforderung f

requisite [ˈrekwɪzɪt] adj erforderlich ‖

s Erfordernis n; (required article) Requisit n

requisition [ˌrekwɪˈzɪʃən] s Anforderung f; (mil) Requisition f ‖ tr anfordern; (mil) beschlagnahmen

requital [rɪˈkwaɪtəl] s (retaliation) Vergeltung f; (for a kindness) Belohnung f

requite [rɪˈkwaɪt] tr vergelten; r. s.o. for a favor sich j-m für e-n Gefallen erkenntlich zeigen

re-read [riˈrid] v (pret & pp –read [red]) tr nachlesen

rerun [ˈriran] s (cin) Reprise f

resale [ˈriˌsel] s Wiederverkauf m

rescind [rɪˈsɪnd] tr (an order) rückgängig machen; (a law) aufheben

rescue [ˈreskju] s Rettung f, Bergung f ‖ tr retten, bergen

rescuer [ˈreskjuˌər] s Retter –in mf

research [rɪˈsʌrtʃ], [ˈrisʌrtʃ] s Forschung f; do r. on Forschungen betreiben über (acc) ‖ intr forschen

researcher [ˈrisʌrtʃər] s Forscher –in mf

re-sell [riˈsel] v (pret & pp –sold) tr wiederverkaufen, weiterverkaufen

resemblance [rɪˈzembləns] s (to) Ähnlichkeit f (mit); bear a close r. to s.o. große Ähnlichkeit mit j-m haben

resemble [rɪˈzembəl] tr ähneln (dat)

resent [rɪˈzent] tr—I r. your remark Ihre Bemerkung paßt mir nicht

resentful [rɪˈzentfəl] adj grollend

resentment [rɪˈzentmənt] s Groll m; feel r. toward Groll hegen gegen

reservation [ˌrezərˈveʃən] s Vorbestellung f; (Indian land) Reservation f; do you have a r.? haben Sie vorbestellt?; make reservations vorbestellen

reserve [rɪˈzʌrv] s (discretion) Zurückhaltung f; (econ, mil) Reserve f; without r. rückhaltlos ‖ tr (e.g., seats) reservieren, belegen; r. judgment mit seinem Urteil zurückhalten

reserved adj (place) belegt; (person) zurückhaltend

reserve of'ficer s Reserveoffizier m

reservist [rɪˈzʌrvɪst] s Reservist –in mf

reservoir [ˈrezərˌvwar] s Staubecken m

re-set [riˈset] v (pret & pp –set; ger –setting) tr (a gem) neu fassen; (mach) nachstellen; (typ) neu setzen

resettle [riˈsetəl] tr & intr umsiedeln

reshape [riˈʃep] tr umformen

reshuffle [riˈʃʌfəl] tr (cards) neu mischen; (pol) umgruppieren

reside [rɪˈzaɪd] intr wohnen

residence [ˈrezɪdəns] s Wohnsitz m; (for students) Studentenheim n

resident [ˈrezɪdənt] adj wohnhaft ‖ s Einwohner –in mf

residential [ˌrezɪˈdentʃəl] adj Wohn-

residue [ˈrezɪˌd(j)u] s Rest m; (chem) Rückstand m

resign [rɪˈzaɪn] tr (an office) niederlegen; r. oneself to sich ergeben in (acc) ‖ intr zurücktreten

resignation [ˌrezɪgˈneʃən] s (from an office) Rücktritt m; (submissive *state*) Ergebung *f;* **hand in one's r.** sein Entlassungsgesuch einreichen

resilience [rɪˈzɪlɪ·əns] *s* Elastizität *f;* (fig) Spannkraft *f*

resilient [rɪˈzɪlɪ·ənt] *adj* elastisch; (fig) unverwüstlich

resin [ˈrezɪn] *s* Harz *m*

resist [rɪˈzɪst] *tr* widerstehen (*dat*) || *intr* Widerstand leisten

resistance [rɪˈzɪstəns] *s* (& elec) Widerstand *m*

resole [riˈsol] *tr* neu besohlen

resolute [ˈrezə‚lut] *adj* entschlossen

resolution [‚rezəˈluʃən] *s* (*resoluteness*) Entschlossenheit *f;* (parl) Beschluß *m;* **make good resolutions** gute Vorsätze fassen

resolve [rɪˈzɑlv] *s* Vorsatz *m* || *tr* auflösen; (*a question, problem*) lösen; **r. to** (*inf*) beschließen zu (*inf*) || *intr* —**r. into** sich auflösen in (*acc*); **r. upon s.th.** sich [*dat*] etw vornehmen

resonance [ˈrezənəns] *s* Resonanz *f*

resort [rɪˈzɔrt] *s* (*refuge*) Zuflucht *f;* (*for health*) Kurort *m;* (*for vacation*) Ferienort *m,* Sommerfrische *f;* **as a last r.** als letztes Mittel || *intr*—**r. to** greifen zu

resound [rɪˈzaund] *intr* widerhallen

resource [ˈrisors] *s* Mittel *n;* **resources** (fin) Geldmittel *pl*

resourceful [rɪˈsorsfəl] *adj* findig

respect [rɪˈspekt] *s* (*esteem*) Achtung *f,* Respekt *m;* (*reference*) Hinsicht *f;* **in every r.** in jeder Hinsicht; **pay one's respects to s.o.** j-m seine Aufwartung machen; **with r. to** mit Bezug auf (*acc*) || *tr* achten

respectable [rɪˈspektəbəl] *adj* achtbar; (*e.g., firm*) angesehen

respect'ed *adj* angesehen

respectful [rɪˈspektfəl] *adj* ehrerbietig

respectfully [rɪˈspektfəli] *adv*—**r. yours** hochachtungsvoll, Ihr ... or Ihre ...

respective [rɪˈspektɪv] *adj* jeweilig

respectively [rɪˈspektɪvli] *adv* beziehungsweise

respiration [‚respɪˈreʃən] *s* Atmung *f*

respirator [ˈrespɪ‚retər] *s* Atemgerät *n*

respiratory [ˈrespɪrə‚tori] *adj* Atmungs-

respite [ˈrespɪt] *s* (*pause*) Atempause *f;* (*reprieve*) Aufschub *m;* **without r.** ohne Unterlaß

resplendent [rɪˈsplendənt] *adj* glänzend

respond [rɪˈspɑnd] *tr* antworten || *intr* (*reply*) (**to**) antworten (auf *acc*); (*react*) (**to**) ansprechen (auf *acc*)

response [rɪˈspɑns] *s* Antwort *f;* (*reaction*) Reaktion *f;* (fig) Widerhall *m;* **in r. to** als Antwort auf (*acc*)

responsibility [rɪ‚spɑnsɪˈbɪlɪti] *s* Verantwortung *f*

responsible [rɪˈspɑnsɪbəl] *adj* (*position*) verantwortlich; (*person*) verantwortungsbewußt; **be held r. for** verantwortlich gemacht werden für; **be r. for** (*be answerable for*) verantwortlich sein für; (*be to blame for*) schuld sein an (*dat*); (*be the cause of*) die Ursache sein (*genit*); (*be liable for*) haften für

responsive [rɪˈspɑnsɪv] *adj*—**be r. to** ansprechen auf (*acc*)

rest [rest] *s* (*repose*) Ruhe *f;* (*from work*) Ruhepause *f;* (*e.g., from walking*) Rast *f;* (*remainder*) Rest *m;* (*support*) Stütze *f;* (mus) Pause *f;* **all the r.** (*in number*) alle andern; (*in quantity*) alles übrige; **be at r.** (*be calm*) beruhigt sein; (*be dead*) ruhen; (*not be in motion*) sich in Ruhelage befinden; **come to r.** stehenbleiben; **put one's mind to r.** sich beruhigen; **take a r.** sich ausruhen; **the r. of the boys** die übrigen (or andern) Jungen || *tr* ruhen lassen, ausruhen; (*support, e.g., one's elbow*) stützen || *intr* sich ausruhen; **r. on** lasten auf (*dat*); (*be based on*) beruhen auf (*dat*); **r. with** liegen bei

restaurant [ˈrestərɑnt] *s* Restaurant *n*

restful [ˈrestfəl] *adj* ruhig

rest' home' *s* Erholungsheim *n*

rest'ing place' *s* Ruheplatz *m;* **final r.** letzte Ruhestätte *f*

restitution [‚restɪˈt(j)uʃən] *s* Wiedergutmachung *f;* **make r.** Genugtuung leisten

restive [ˈrestɪv] *adj* (*restless*) unruhig; (*balky*) störrisch

restless [ˈrestlɪs] *adj* ruhelos

restock [riˈstɑk] *tr* wieder auffüllen; (*waters*) wieder mit Fischen besetzen

restoration [‚restəˈreʃən] *s* (*of a work of art or building*) Restaurierung *f*

restore [rɪˈstor] *tr* (*order*) wiederherstellen; (*a painting, building*) restaurieren; (*stolen goods*) zurückerstatten; **r. to health** wiederherstellen

restrain [rɪˈstren] *tr* zurückhalten; (*feelings; a horse*) zügeln; (*e.g., trade*) einschränken; **r. s.o. from** (*ger*) j-n davon abhalten zu (*inf*)

restrain'ing or'der *s* Unterlassungsurteil *n*

restraint [rɪˈstrent] *s* Zurückhaltung *f;* (*force*) Zwang *m*

restrict [rɪˈstrɪkt] *tr* begrenzen; **r. to** beschränken auf (*acc*)

restrict'ed ar'ea *s* Sperrgebiet *n*

rest' room' *s* Abort *m,* Toilette *f*

result [rɪˈzʌlt] *s* Ergebnis *n,* Resultat *n;* (*consequence*) Folge *f;* **as a r. of** als Folge (*genit*); **without r.** ergebnislos || *intr*—**r. from** sich ergeben aus; **r. in** führen zu

result' clause' *s* Folgesatz *m*

resume [rɪˈzum] *tr* wieder aufnehmen; (*a journey*) fortsetzen

résumé [ˈrezu‚me] *s* Zusammenfassung *f*

resumption [rɪˈzʌmpʃən] *s* Wiederaufnahme *f*

resurface [riˈsʌrfɪs] *tr*—**r. the road with** die Straßendecke erneuern von || *intr* (naut & fig) wiederauftauchen

resurrect [‚rezəˈrekt] *tr* (*the dead*) wieder zum Leben erwecken; (fig) wieder aufleben lassen

resurrection [‚rezəˈrekʃən] *s* Auferstehung *f*

resuscitate [rɪˈsʌsɪ‚tet] *tr* wiederbeleben

retail ['ritel] *adj* Kleinhandels– ‖ *adv* im Kleinhandel ‖ *tr* im Kleinhandel verkaufen ‖ *intr*–r. at two dollars im Kleinverkauf zwei Dollar kosten

re'tail busi'ness *s* Kleinhandel *m*

retailer ['ritelər] *s* Kleinhändler –in *mf*

retain [rɪ'ten] *tr* (zurück)behalten; (*a lawyer*) sich [*dat*] nehmen

retainer [rɪ'tenər] *s* (hist) Gefolgsmann *m*; (jur) Honorarvorschuß *m*

retain'ing wall' *s* Stützmauer *f*

retake ['ritek] *s* (cin) Neuaufnahme *f* ‖ [ri'tek] *tr* (*a town*) zurückerobern; (cin) nochmals aufnehmen

retaliate [rɪ'tælɪ,et] *intr* (against) Vergeltung üben (an *dat*)

retaliation [rɪ,tælɪ'eʃən] *s* Vergeltung *f*

retaliatory [rɪ'tælɪ-ə,tori] *adj* Vergeltungs–

retard [rɪ'tɑrd] *tr* verzögern

retard'ed *adj* zurückgeblieben

retch [retʃ] *intr* würgen

retch'ing *s* Würgen *n*

retell [ri'tel] *tr* wiedererzählen

retention [rɪ'tenʃən] *s* Beibehaltung *f*

re-think [ri'θɪŋk] *v* (*pret & pp* -thought) *tr* umdenken

reticence ['retɪsəns] *s* Verschwiegenheit *f*

reticent ['retɪsənt] *adj* verschwiegen

retina ['retɪnə] *s* Netzhaut *f*, Retina *f*

retinue ['rett ,n(j)u] *s* Gefolge *n*

retire [rɪ'taɪr] *tr* pensionieren ‖ *intr* (*from employment*) in den Ruhestand treten; (*withdraw*) sich zurückziehen; (*go to bed*) sich zur Ruhe begeben

retired' *adj* pensioniert

retirement [rɪ'taɪrmənt] *s* Ruhestand *m*; **go into r.** in den Ruhestand treten, sich pensionieren lassen

retire'ment pay' *s* Pension *f*

retire'ment plan' *s* Pensionsplan *m*

retir'ing *adj* zurückhaltend

retort [rɪ'tɔrt] *s* schlagfertige Erwiderung *f*; (chem) Retorte *f* ‖ *tr & intr* erwidern

retouch [ri'tʌtʃ] *tr* retuschieren

retrace [ri'tres] *tr* zurückverfolgen

retract [rɪ'trækt] *tr* (*a statement*) widerrufen; (*claws; landing gear*) einziehen

retract'able land'ing gear' [rɪ'træktəbəl] *s* Verschwindfahrgestell *n*

retrain [ri'tren] *tr* umschulen

retread ['ri,tred] *s* (*aut*) runderneuerter Reifen *m* ‖ *tr* runderneuern

retreat [rɪ'trit] *s* (*quiet place*) Ruhesitz *m*; (mil) Rückzug *m*; (rel) Exerzitien *pl*; **beat a hasty r.** eilig den Rückzug antreten ‖ *intr* sich zurückziehen

retrench [rɪ'trentʃ] *tr* einschränken ‖ *intr* sich einschränken

retribution [,retrɪ'bjuʃən] *s* Vergeltung *f*

retrieval [rɪ'trivəl] *s* Wiedererlangung *f*

retrieve [rɪ'triv] *tr* wiedererlangen; (*a loss*) wettmachen; (hunt) apportieren

retriever [rɪ'trivər] *s* Apportierhund *m*

retroactive [,retro'æktɪv] *adj* (from) rückwirkend von ... an

retrogressive [,retro'gresɪv] *adj* rückläufig

retrorocket ['retro,rɑkɪt] *s* Bremsrakete *f*

retrospect ['retrə,spekt] *s*—**in r.** rückblickend

re-try [ri'traɪ] *v* (*pret & pp* -tried) *tr* (jur) nochmals verhandeln

return [rɪ'tʌrn] *s* Rückkehr *f*; (*giving back*) Rückgabe *f*; (*the way back*) Rückweg *m*; (*tax form*) Steuererklärung *f*; (*profit*) Umsatz *m*; (tennis) Rückschlag *m*; **in r.** dafür; **in r. for** als Entgelt für; **returns** (*profits*) Ertrag *m*; (*of an election*) Ergebnisse *pl* ‖ *tr* zurückgeben; (*send back*) zurücksenden; (*put back*) zurückstellen; (*thanks*) abstatten; (*a verdict*) fällen; (*a favor, love, gun fire*) erwidern; (tennis) zurückschlagen ‖ *intr* zurückkehren; **r. to** (e.g., *a topic*) zurückkommen auf (*acc*)

return' address' *s* Rückadresse *f*

return' flight' *s* Rückflug *m*

return' match' *s* Revanchepartie *f*

return' tick'et *s* Rückfahrkarte *f*; (aer) Rückflugkarte *f*

reunification [ri,junɪfɪ'keʃən] *s* (pol) Wiedervereinigung *f*

reunion [ri'junjən] *s* Treffen *n*

rev [rev] *v* (*pret & pp* revved; *ger* revving) *tr* (up) auf Touren bringen ‖ *intr* auf Touren kommen

revamp [ri'væmp] *tr* umgestalten

reveal [rɪ'vil] *tr* offenbaren

reveille [rɪ'veli] *s* Wecken *n*

rev-el [rɪ'revəl] *s* Gelage *n* ‖ *v* (*pret & pp* -el[l]ed; *ger* -el[l]ing) *intr* ein Gelage halten; **r. in** (fig) schwelgen in (*dat*)

revelation [,revə'leʃən] *s* Offenbarung *f*; **Revelations** (Bib) Offenbarung *f*

reveler ['revələr] *s* Zecher –in *mf*

revelry ['revəlri] *s* Zechgelage *n*

revenge [rɪ'vendʒ] *s* Rache *f*; **take r. on s.o. for s.th.** sich an j–m für etw rächen ‖ *tr* rächen

revengeful [rɪ'vendʒfəl] *adj* rachsüchtig

revenue ['revə,n(j)u] *s* (*yield*) Ertrag *m*; (*internal revenue*) Steueraufkommen *n*

rev'enue stamp' *s* Banderole *f*

reverberate [rɪ'vʌrbə,ret] *intr* widerhallen

revere [rɪ'vɪr] *tr* verehren

reverence ['revərəns] *s* (*respect given or received*) Ehrerbietung *f*; (*respect felt*) Ehrfurcht *f*

reverend ['revərənd] *adj* ehrwürdig; **the Reverend** ... Hochwürden ...

reverie ['revəri] *s* Träumerei *f*; **be lost in r.** in Träumen versunken sein

reversal [rɪ'vʌrsəl] *s* Umkehrung *f*; (*of opinion*) Umschwung *m*

reverse [rɪ'vʌrs] *adj* umgekehrt; (*side*) linke ‖ *s* (*back side*) Rückseite *f*; (*opposite*) Gegenteil *n*; (*setback*) Rückschlag *m*; (*of a coin*) Revers *m*;

(aut) Rückwärtsgang m ‖ tr umkehren, umdrehen; (a decision) umstoßen
‖ intr sich rückwärts bewegen

reverse' side' s Rückseite f, Kehrseite f

reversible [rɪ'vʌrsɪbəl] adj (decision)
umstoßbar; (material) zweiseitig;
(chem, phys) umkehrbar; (mach)
umsteuerbar

revert [rɪ'vʌrt] intr—r. to zurückkommen auf (acc); (jur) zurückfallen an
(acc)

review [rɪ'vju] s (of) Überblick m
(über acc); (of a lesson) Wiederholung f; (of a book) Besprechung f;
(periodical) Rundschau m; (mil) Besichtigung f; pass in r. mustern ‖ tr
(a lesson) wiederholen; (a book) besprechen; (e.g., the events of the day)
überblicken; (mil) besichtigen

reviewer [rɪ'vju·ər] s Besprecher –in
mf

revile [rɪ'vaɪl] tr schmähen

revise [rɪ'vaɪz] tr (a book) umarbeiten; (one's opinion) revidieren

revised' edi'tion s verbesserte Auflage
f

revision [rɪ'vɪʒən] s Neubearbeitung f

revival [rɪ'vaɪvəl] s Wiederbelebung f;
(rel) Erweckung f; (theat) Reprise f

reviv'al meet'ing s Erweckungsver-
sammlung f

revive [rɪ'vaɪv] tr wieder aufleben lassen; (memories) aufrühren; (a victim) wieder zu Bewußtsein bringen ‖
intr wieder aufleben

revoke [rɪ'vok] tr widerrufen

revolt [rɪ'volt] s Aufstand m ‖ tr abstoßen ‖ intr revoltieren

revolt'ing adj abstoßend

revolution [,revə'luʃən] s Revolution
f; (turn) Umdrehung f; revolutions
per minute Drehzahl f

revolutionary [,revə'luʃə,neri] adj revolutionär ‖ s Revolutionär –in mf

revolve [rɪ'valv] intr (around) sich
drehen (um)

revolver [rɪ'valvər] s Revolver m

revolv'ing adj Dreh-

revue [rɪ'vju] s (theat) Revue f

revulsion [rɪ'vʌlʃən] s Abscheu m

reward [rɪ'wɔrd] s Belohnung f ‖ tr
belohnen

reward'ing adj lohnend

re·wind [ri'waɪnd] v (pret & pp
-wound) tr (a tape, film) umspulen;
(a clock) wieder aufziehen

rewire [ri'waɪr] tr Leitungen neu legen
in (dat)

rework [rɪ'wʌrk] tr umarbeiten

re·write [ri'raɪt] v (pret -wrote; pp
-written) tr umschreiben

rhapsody ['ræpsədi] s Rhapsodie f

rheostat ['ri·ə,stæt] s Rheostat m

rhetoric ['retərɪk] s Redekunst f

rhetorical [rɪ'tɔrɪkəl] adj rhetorisch

rheumatic [ru'mætɪk] adj rheumatisch

rheumatism ['rumə,tɪzəm] s Rheumatismus m

Rhine [raɪn] s Rhein m

Rhineland ['raɪn,lænd] s Rheinland n

rhine'stone' s Rheinkiesel m

rhinoceros [raɪ'nɑsərəs] s Nashorn n

rhubarb ['rubɑrb] s Rhabarber m; (sl)
Krach m

rhyme [raɪm] s Reim m ‖ tr & intr
reimen

rhythm ['rɪðəm] s Rhythmus m

rhythmic(al) ['rɪðmɪk(əl)] adj rhythmisch

rib [rɪb] s Rippe f ‖ v (pret & pp
ribbed; ger ribbing) tr (coll) sich
lustig machen über (acc)

ribald ['rɪbəld] adj zotig

ribbon ['rɪbən] s Band n; (decoration)
Ordensband n; (for a typewriter)
Farbband n

rice [raɪs] s Reis m

rich [rɪtʃ] adj reich; (voice) volltönend; (soil) fruchtbar; (funny) (coll)
köstlich; r. in reich an (dat) ‖ riches
spl Reichtum n

rickets ['rɪkɪts] s Rachitis f

rickety ['rɪkɪti] adj (building) baufällig; (furniture) wackelig

rid [rɪd] v (pret & pp rid; ger ridding)
tr (of) befreien (von); get rid of
loswerden

riddance ['rɪdəns] s Befreiung f; good
r.! den (or die or das) wäre ich
glücklich los!

riddle ['rɪdəl] s Rätsel n

ride [raɪd] s Fahrt f; give s.o. a r. j-n
im Auto mitnehmen; take for a r.
(murder) entführen und umbringen;
(dupe) hochnehmen ‖ v (pret rode
[rod]; pp ridden ['rɪdən]) tr (a
bicycle) fahren; (a horse) reiten; (a
train, bus) fahren mit; (harass) hetzen; r. out (a storm) gut überstehen
‖ intr (e.g., a bicycle) fahren; (on a
horse) reiten; let s.th. r. sich mit etw
abfinden

rider ['raɪdər] s (on horseback) Reiter
–in mf; (on a bicycle) Radfahrer –in
mf; (in a vehicle) Fahrer –in mf;
(to a document) Zusatzklausel f

ridge [rɪdʒ] s (of a hill; of the nose)
Rücken m; (of a roof) Dachfirst m

ridge'pole' s Firstbalken m

ridicule ['rɪdɪ,kjul] s Spott m ‖ tr
verspotten

ridiculous [rɪ'dɪkjələs] adj lächerlich;
look r. lächerlich wirken

rid'ing acad'emy s Reitschule f

rid'ing boot' s Reitstiefel m

rid'ing breech'es spl Reithose f

rid'ing hab'it s Reitkostüm n

rife [raɪf] adj häufig; r. with voll von

riffraff ['rɪf,ræf] s Gesindel n

rifle ['raɪfəl] s Gewehr n ‖ tr aus-
plündern

rift [rɪft] s (& fig) Riß m

rig [rɪg] s (gear) Ausrüstung f; (horse
and carriage) Gespann n; (truck)
Laster m; (oil drilling) Bohrturm m;
(getup) (coll) Aufmachung f; (naut)
Takelung f ‖ v (pret & pp rigged;
ger rigging) tr (auf)takeln; (prices,
elections, accounts) manipulieren

rig'ging s Takelung f

right [raɪt] adj (side, glove, angle)
recht; (just) gerecht; (correct) richtig; (moment) richtig; do you have
the r. time? können Sie mir die ge-

naue Uhrzeit sagen?; **be in one's r.
mind** bei klarem Verstand sein; **it is
all r.** es ist schon gut; **it is r.? nicht
wahr?; that's r.!** eben!; **the r. thing**
das Richtige; **you are r.** Sie haben
recht ‖ *adv* direkt; *(to the right)*
rechts; **r. along** durchaus; **r. away**
sofort, gleich; **r. behind the door**
gleich hinter der Tür; **r. glad** (coll)
recht froh; **r. here** gleich hier; **r.
now** *(at the moment)* momentan;
(immediately) sofort; **r. through**
durch und durch ‖ *s* Recht *n;* (box)
Rechte *f;* **all rights reserved** alle
Rechte vorbehalten; **by rights** von
Rechts wegen; **in the r.** im Recht;
on the r. rechts, zur Rechten ‖ *tr*
aufrichten; *(an error)* berichtigen;
(a wrong) wiedergutmachen ‖ *interj*
stimmt!

righteous [ˈraɪt/əs] *adj* gerecht, recht-
schaffen; *(smug)* selbstgerecht

rightful [ˈraɪtfəl] *adj (owner)* rechtmäßig; *(claim, place)* berechtigt

right'-hand *adj* zur Rechten; *(glove)*
recht

right'-hand'ed *adj* rechtshändig

right-hander [ˈraɪtˈhændər] *s* Rechts-
händer –in *mf*

right'-hand man' *s* rechte Hand *f*

rightist [ˈraɪtɪst] *adj* rechtsstehend ‖ *s*
Rechtspolitiker –in *mf*

rightly [ˈraɪtli] *adv* richtig; *(rightfully)*
rechtmäßig

right' of way' *s (in traffic)* Vorfahrts-
recht *n;* *(across another's land)*
Grunddienstbarkeit *f*

right' wing' *s* rechter Flügel *m*

rigid [ˈrɪdʒɪd] *adj* steif, starr

rigmarole [ˈrɪgməˌrol] *s (meaningless
talk)* Geschwafel *n;* *(fuss)* Getue *n*

rigorous [ˈrɪgərəs] *adj* hart, streng

rile [raɪl] *tr* aufbringen

rill [rɪl] *s* Bächlein *n*

rim [rɪm] *s* Rand *m;* *(of eyeglasses)*
Fassung *f;* *(of a wheel)* Felge *f*

rind [raɪnd] *s* Rinde *f*

ring [rɪŋ] *s (for the fingers; for boxing; of criminals or spies; of a circus;
circle under the eyes)* Ring *m;* *(of a
bell, voice, laughter)* Klang *m;* **give
s.o. a r.** (telp) j-n anrufen; **run rings
around s.o.** j-n in die Tasche stecken
‖ *v (pret & pp ringed) tr* umringen;
r. in einschließen ‖ *v (pret rang
[ræŋ]; pp rung [rʌŋ]) tr* läuten; **r.
the bell** läuten, klingeln; **r. out** aus-
läuten; **r. up** anrufen ‖ *intr* läuten,
klingeln; **my ears are ringing** mir
klingen die Ohren; **r. for s.o.** nach
j-m klingeln; **r. out** laut schallen;
the bell is ringing es läutet

ring'ing *adj* schallend ‖ *s* Läuten *n;*
(in the ears) Klingen *n*

ring'lead'er *s* Rädelsführer *m*

ring'mas'ter *s* Zirkusdirektor *m*

ring'side' *s* Ringplatz *m*

ring'worm' *s* Scherpilzflechte *f*

rink [rɪŋk] *s* Eisbahn *f;* *(for roller-
skating)* Rollschuhbahn *f*

rinse [rɪns] *s* Spülen *n* ‖ *tr* ausspülen

riot [ˈraɪət] *s* Aufruhr *m;* **r. of colors**

Farbengemisch *n;* **run r.** sich austo-
ben; *(said of plants)* wuchern ‖ *intr*
sich zusammenrotten

ri'ot act' *s*—**read the r. to s.o.** j-m die
Leviten lesen

rioter [ˈraɪətər] *s* Aufrührer –in *mf*

rip [rɪp] *s* Riß *m* ‖ *v (pret & pp
ripped; ger ripping) tr (zer)reißen;
rip off abreißen; *(the skin)* abziehen;
(cheat) betrügen ‖ *intr* reißen

rip' cord' *s* Reißlinie *f*

ripe [raɪp] *adj* reif

ripen [ˈraɪpən] *tr (& fig)* reifen lassen
‖ *intr (& fig)* reifen

rip' off' *s* (sl) Wucher *m*

ripple [ˈrɪpəl] *s* leichte Welle *f* ‖ *intr*
leichte Wellen schlagen

rise [raɪz] *s* Aufsteigen *n;* *(in prices)*
Steigerung *f;* *(of heavenly bodies)*
Aufgang *m;* *(increase, e.g., in population)* Zunahme *f;* *(in the ground)*
Erhebung *f;* **get a r. out of s.o.** j-n
zu e-r Reaktion veranlassen; **give
r. to** veranlassen ‖ *v (pret rose
[roz]; pp risen [ˈrɪzən]) intr (said
of the sun, of a cake)* aufgehen; *(said
of a river, prices, temperature, barometer)* steigen; *(said of a road)*
ansteigen; *(get out of bed)* aufstehen;
(stand up) sich erheben; *(from the
dead)* auferstehen; *(said of anger)*
hochsteigen; **r. to the occasion** sich
der Lage gewachsen zeigen; **r. up
from the ranks** von der Pike auf
dienen

riser [ˈraɪzər] *s (of a staircase)* Fut-
terbrett *n;* **early r.** Frühaufsteher
–in *mf;* **late r.** Langschläfer –in *mf*

risk [rɪsk] *s* Risiko *n;* **run the r. of**
(ger) Gefahr laufen zu *(inf)* ‖ *tr*
wagen, aufs Spiel setzen

risky [ˈrɪski] *adj* riskant, gewagt

risque [rɪsˈke] *adj* schlüpfrig

rite [raɪt] *s* Ritus *m;* **last rites** Ster-
besakramente *pl*

ritual [ˈrɪtʃʊ.əl] *adj* rituell ‖ *s* Ritual
n

ri·val [ˈraɪvəl] *adj* rivalisierend ‖ *s*
Rivale *m,* Rivalin *f* ‖ *v (pret & pp
-val[l]ed; ger -val[l]ing) tr* rivalisieren, wetteifern mit

rivalry [ˈraɪvəlri] *s* Rivalität *f*

river [ˈrɪvər] *adj* Fluß– ‖ *s* Fluß *m*

riv'er ba'sin *s* Flußgebiet *n*

riv'erfront' *s* Flußufer *n*

riv'erside' *adj* am Flußufer gelegen ‖
s Flußufer *n*

rivet [ˈrɪvɪt] *s* Niet *m* ‖ *tr* nieten

riv'et gun' *s* Nietmaschine *f*

riv'eting *s (act)* Vernieten *n;* *(connection)* Nietnaht *f*

rivulet [ˈrɪvjəlɪt] *s* Flüßchen *n*

R.N. [ˈɑrˈen] *s (registered nurse)* staatlich geprüfte Krankenschwester *f*

roach [rotʃ] *s* (ent) Schabe *f;* (ichth)
Plötze *f*

road [rod] *s (& fig)* Weg *m;* **be (much)
on the r.** (viel) auf Reisen sein; **go
on the r.** auf Tour gehen; (theat) auf
Tournee gehen

road'bed' *s* Bahnkörper *m*

road'block' *s* Straßensperre *f*

road′ hog′ s rücksichtsloser Autofahrer m
road′ house′ s Wirtshaus n, Rasthaus n
road′ map′ s Straßenkarte f, Autokarte f
road′side′ adj Straßen– ‖ s Straßenrand m
road′side inn′ s Rasthaus n
road′sign′ s Wegweiser m
road′stead′ s Reede f
road′ test′ s (aut) Probefahrt f
road′way′ s Fahrweg m
roam [rom] tr durchstreifen ‖ intr herumstreifen
roar [ror] s Gebrüll n; (of a waterfall, sea, wind) Brausen n; (of an engine) Dröhnen n; (laughter) schallendes Gelächter n ‖ intr brüllen; (said of a waterfall, sea, wind) brausen; r. at anbrüllen; (e.g., a joke) schallend lachen über (acc); r. by vorbeibrausen; r. with brüllen vor (dat)
roast [rost] adj gebraten ‖ s Braten m ‖ tr (meat, fish) braten, rösten; (coffee, chestnuts) rösten; (a person) (coll) durch den Kakao ziehen ‖ intr braten
roast′ beef′ s Roastbeef n
roaster [′rostər] s (appliance) Röster m, Röstapparat m; (fowl) Brathuhn n
roast′ pork′ s Schweinsbraten m
rob [rɑb] v (pret & pp robbed; ger robbing) tr (a thing) rauben; (a person) (of) berauben (genit)
robber [′rɑbər] s Räuber –in mf
robbery [′rɑbəri] s Raubüberfall m
robe [rob] s Robe f; (house robe) Hausrock m ‖ tr feierlich ankleiden ‖ intr sich feierlich ankleiden
robin [′rɑbɪn] s Rotkehlchen n
robot [′robɑt] s Roboter m
robust [ro′bʌst] adj robust
rock [rɑk] adj (mus) Rock– ‖ s Fels m; (one that is thrown) Stein m; (mus) Rockmusik f; on the rocks mit Eiswürfeln; (ruined) kaputt ‖ tr schaukeln, wiegen; r. the boat (fig) die Sache ins Wanken bringen; r. to sleep in den Schlaf wiegen ‖ intr schwanken, wanken; (said of a boat) schaukeln
rock′-bot′tom adj äußerst niedrig ‖ s Tiefpunkt m
rock′ can′dy s Kandiszucker m
rock′ crys′tal s Bergkristall m
rocker [′rɑkər] s Schaukelstuhl m; go off one′s r. (coll) den Verstand verlieren
rocket [′rɑkɪt] s Rakete f
rock′et launch′er s Raketenwerfer m
rocketry [′rɑkɪtri] s Raketentechnik f
rock′et ship′ s Rakentenflugkörper m
rock′ gar′den s Steingarten m
rock′ing chair′ s Schaukelstuhl m
rock′ing horse′ s Schaukelpferd n
rock-′n′-roll [′rɑkən′rol] s Rock ′n Roll m
rock′ salt′ s Steinsalz n
rocky [′rɑki] adj felsig; (shaky) wacklig
rod [rɑd] s Stab m, Stange f; (whip)

Zuchtrute f; (of the retina; of a microorganism) Stäbchen n; (revolver) (sl) Schießeisen n; (angl) Angelrute f; (Bib) Reis n; (mach) Pleuelstange f; (surg) Absteckpfahl m
rodent [′rodənt] s Nagetier n
roe [ro] s (deer) Reh n; (ichth) Rogen m
rogue [rog] s Schuft m, Schurke m
rogues′ gal′lery s Verbrecheralbum n
roguish [′rogɪʃ] adj schurkisch
role, rôle [rol] s Rolle f
roll [rol] s Rolle f; (bread) Brötchen n; (of thunder, of a ship) Rollen n; (of drums) Wirbel m; (of fat) Wulst m; call the r. die Namen verlesen; (mil) Appell halten ‖ tr rollen; (cigarettes) drehen; (metals, roads) walzen; r. over überrollen; r. up zusammenrollen; (sleeves) zurückstreifen ‖ intr sich wälzen; be rolling in money im Geld wühlen
roll′back′ s (com) Senkung f
roll′call′ s Namensverlesung f; (mil) Appell m
roll′er bear′ing s Rollenlager n
roll′er coast′er s Berg-und-Tal-Bahn f
roll′er skate′ s Rollschuh m
roll′er-skate′ intr rollschuhlaufen
roll′er tow′el s Rollhandtuch n
roll′ing mill′ s Walzwerk n
roll′ing pin′ s Nudelholz n, Teigrolle f
roll′ing stock′ s (rr) rollendes Material n
roly-poly [′roli′poli] adj dick und rund
roman [′romən] adj (typ) Antiqua–; **Roman** römisch ‖ s (typ) Antiqua f; **Roman** Römer –in mf
Ro′man can′dle s Leuchtkugel f
Ro′man Cath′olic adj römisch-katholisch ‖ s Katholik –in mf
romance [ro′mæns] adj (ling) romanisch ‖ s Romanze f
Romanesque [‚romə′nesk] adj romanisch ‖ s das Romanische
Ro′man nose′ s Römernase f
Ro′man nu′meral s römische Ziffer f
romantic [ro′mæntɪk] adj romantisch
romanticism [ro′mæntɪ‚sɪzəm] s Romantik f
romp [rɑmp] intr umhertollen
rompers [′rɑmpərz] spl Spielanzug m
roof [ruf] s Dach n; (aut) Verdeck n; **raise the r.** (coll) Krach machen; **r. of the mouth** Gaumendach n
roofer [′rufər] s Dachdecker m
roof′ gar′den s Dachgarten m
roof′ tile′ s Dachziegel m
rook [rʊk] s (chess) Turm m; (orn) Saatkrähe f ‖ tr (coll) (out of) beschwindeln (um)
rookie [′rʊki] s (coll) Neuling m
room [rum] s Zimmer n; (space) Raum m, Platz m; **make r.** Platz machen; **r. for complaint** Anlaß m zur Klage; **take up too much r.** zu viel Platz in Anspruch nehmen ‖ intr wohnen
room′ and board′ s Kost und Quartier
room′ clerk′ s Empfangschef m
roomer [′rumər] s Mieter –in mf

room′ing house′ s Pension f
room′mate′ s Zimmergenosse m
room′ serv′ice s Bedienung f aufs Zimmer
roomy [′rumi] adj geräumig
roost [rust] s Hühnerstange f; **rule the r.** Hahn im Korb sein ‖ intr auf der Stange sitzen
rooster [′rustər] s Hahn m
root [rut] s Wurzel f; **get to the r. of s.th.** etw [dat] auf den Grund gehen; **take r.** Wurzel schlagen; (fig) sich einbürgern ‖ tr—**be rooted in** wurzeln in (dat); **rooted to the spot** festgewurzelt; **r. out** ausrotten ‖ intr —**r. about** wühlen; **r. for** zujubeln (dat)
rope [rop] s Strick m, Seil n; **know the ropes** alle Kniffe kennen ‖ tr mit e-m Seil festbinden; (a steer) mit e-m Lasso einfangen; **r. in** (coll) einwickeln; **r. off** absperren
rosary [′rozəri] s Rosenkranz m
rose [roz] adj rosenrot ‖ s Rose f
rose′bud′ s Rosenknospe f
rose′bush′ s Rosenstock m
rose′-col′ored adj rosenfarbig; (fig) rosa(rot)
rosemary [′roz‚meri] s Rosmarin m
rosin [′razin] s Harz n; (for violin bow) Kolophonium n
roster [′rastər] s Namenliste f; (educ) Stundenplan m; (mil, naut) Dienstplan m
rostrum [′rastrəm] s Rednerbühne f
rosy [′rozi] adj (& fig) rosig
rot [rat] s Fäulnis f; (sl) Quatsch m ‖ v (pret & pp **rotted**; ger **rotting**) tr faulen lassen ‖ intr verfaulen
rotate [′rotet] tr rotieren lassen; (tires) auswechseln; (agr) wechseln ‖ intr rotieren; (take turns) sich abwechseln
rotation [ro′teʃən] s Rotation f; **in r.** wechselweise; **r. of crops** Wechselwirtschaft f
rote [rot] s—**by r.** mechanisch
rotisserie [ro′tisəri] s Fleischbraterei f
rotten [′ratən] adj faul; (trick) niederträchtig; **feel r.** (sl) sich elend fühlen
rotund [ro′tʌnd] adj rundlich
rotunda [ro′tʌndə] s Rotunde f
rouge [ruʒ] s Rouge n ‖ tr schminken
rough [rʌf] adj (hands, voice, person) rauh; (piece of wood) roh; (work, guess, treatment) grob; (water, weather) stürmisch; (road) uneben; **have it r.** viel durchmachen ‖ tr— **r. in** roh entwerfen; (carp) grob bearbeiten; **r.** it primitiv leben; **r. up** grob behandeln
rough′ draft′ s Konzept n
roughen [′rʌfən] tr aufrauhen
rough′house′ s Radau m ‖ intr Radau machen
roughly [′rʌfli] adv grob; (about) etwa
rough′neck′ s (coll) Rauhbein n
roulette [ru′let] s Roulett n
round [raund] adj rund ‖ s Runde f; (of applause) Salve f; (shot) Schuß m; (of drinks) Lage f; (of a sentinel,

policeman, inspector, mailman) Rundgang m; **daily r.** Alltag m ‖ prep um (acc) herum ‖ tr (make round) runden; (a corner) herumgehen (or herumfahren) um (acc); **r. off** abrunden; (finish) vollenden; **r. up** (animals) zusammentreiben; (persons) zusammenbringen; (criminals) ausheben
round′house′ s (rr) Lokomotivschuppen m
round′-shoul′dered adj mit runden Schultern
round′ steak′ s Kugel f
round′-ta′ble adj am runden Tisch
round′ trip′ s Hin-und Rückfahrt f; (aer) Hin- und Rückflug m
round′-trip′ tick′et s Rückfahrkarte f
round′up′ s (of cattle) Zusammentreiben n; (of criminals) Aushebung f
rouse [rauz] tr (from) aufwecken (aus)
rout [raut] s völlige Niederlage f; (mil) wilde Flucht f; **put to r.** in die Flucht schlagen ‖ tr (mil) zersprengen
route [rut, raut] s Route f, Weg m ‖ tr leiten
routine [ru′tin] adj routinemäßig ‖ s Routine f; **be r.** die Regel sein
rove [rov] intr umherwandern
row [rau] s Krach m; **raise a row** (coll) Krach machen ‖ [ro] Reihe f; **in a row** hintereinander ‖ tr rudern
rowboat [′ro‚bot] s Ruderboot n
rowdy [′raudi] adj flegelhaft ‖ s Flegel m
rower [′ro·ər] s Ruderer –in mf
rowing [′ro·ɪŋ] s Rudersport m
royal [′rɔɪəl] adj königlich
royalist [′rɔɪ·əlɪst] adj königstreu ‖ s Königstreue mf
royalty [′rɔɪ·əlti] s (royal status) Königswürde f; (personage) fürstliche Persönlichkeit f; (collectively) fürstliche Persönlichkeiten pl; (author's compensation) Tantieme f; (inventor's compensation) Lizenzgebühr f
r.p.m. abbr (revolutions per minute) Drehzahl f
R.S.V.P. abbr u.A.w.g. (um Antwort wird gebeten)
rub [rʌb] s Reiben n; **there's the rub** (coll) da sitzt der Haken ‖ v (pret & pp **rubbed**; ger **rubbing**) tr reiben; **rub down** abreiben; **rub elbows with** verkehren mit; **rub in** einreiben; **rub it in** (sl) es (j-m) unter die Nase reiben; **rub out** ausradieren; (sl) umbringen; **rub s.o. the wrong way** j-m auf die Nerven gehen ‖ intr reiben; **rub against** sich reiben an (dat); **rub off on** (fig) abfärben auf (acc)
rubber [′rʌbər] adj Gummi– ‖ s Gummi m & n; (cards) Robber m; **rubbers** Gummischuhe pl
ru′ber band′ s Gummiband n
rubberize [′rʌbə‚raɪz] tr gummieren
rub′ber plant′ s Kautschukpflanze f
rub′ber stamp′ s Gummistempel m
rub′ber-stamp′ tr abstempeln; (coll) automatisch genehmigen
rubbery [′rʌbəri] adj gummiartig
rub′bing al′cohol s Franzbranntwein m

rubbish ['rʌbɪʃ] s (trash) Abfall m; (nonsense) dummes Zeug n
rubble ['rʌbəl] s Schutt m; (used in masonry) Bruchstein m
rub'down' s Abreibung f
rubric ['rubrɪk] s Rubrik f
ruby ['rubɪ] adj rubinrot || s Rubin m
ruckus ['rʌkəs] s (coll) Krawall m
rudder ['rʌdər] s (aer) Seitenruder n; (naut) Steuerruder n
ruddy ['rʌdɪ] adj rosig
rude [rud] adj grob
rudeness ['rudnɪs] s Grobheit f
rudiments ['rudɪmənts] spl Grundlagen pl
rue [ru] tr bereuen
rueful ['rufəl] adj reuig; (pitiable) kläglich; (mournful) wehmütig
ruffian ['rʌfɪ-ən] s Raufbold m
ruffle ['rʌfəl] s Rüsche f; (in water) Kräuseln n; (of a drum) gedämpfter Trommelwirbel m || tr kräuseln; (feathers, hair) sträuben
rug [rʌg] s Teppich m
rugged ['rʌgɪd] adj (country) wild; (robust) kräftig; (life) hart
ruin ['ru·ɪn] s Ruine f; (undoing) Ruin m; to go to r. zugrunde gehen; lie in ruins in Trümmern liegen; ruins (debris) Trümmer pl || tr ruinieren
rule [rul] s (reign) Herrschaft f; (regulation) Regel f; as a r. in der Regel; **become the r.** zur Regel werden || tr beherrschen; (paper) linieren; **r. out** ausschließen || intr (over) herrschen (über acc)
rule' of law' s Rechtsstaatlichkeit f
rule' of thumb' s Faustregel f; by r. über den Daumen gepeilt
ruler ['rulər] s Herrscher –in mf; (for measuring) Lineal n
rul'ing adj herrschend || s Regelung f
rum [rʌm] s Rum m
Rumania [ru'menɪ-ə] s Rumänien n
Rumanian [ru'menɪ-ən] adj rumänisch || s Rumäne m, Rumänin f; (language) Rumänisch n
rumble ['rʌmbəl] s (of thunder) Rollen n; (of a truck) Rumpeln n || intr rollen; rumpeln
ruminate ['rumɪ‚net] tr & intr wiederkäuen
rummage ['rʌmɪdʒ] intr—r. through durchsuchen
rum'mage sale' s Ramschverkauf m
rumor ['rumər] s Gerücht n || tr—it is rumored that es geht das Gerücht, daß
rump [rʌmp] s (of an animal) Hinterteil m & n; (buttocks) Gesäß n
rumple ['rʌmpəl] tr (clothes) zerknittern; (hair) zerzausen
rump' steak' s Rumpsteak n
rumpus ['rʌmpəs] s (coll) Krach m; raise a r. (coll) Krach machen
rum'pus room' s Spielzimmer n
run [rʌn] s Lauf m; (in stockings) Laufmasche f; (fin) Run m; (theat) Laufzeit f; be on the run auf der Flucht sein; in the long run auf die Dauer; run of bad luck Pechsträhne f; run of good luck Glückssträhne f ||

v (pret ran [ræn]; pp run; ger running) tr (a machine) bedienen; (a business, household) führen; (a distance) laufen; (a blockade) brechen; (a cable) verlegen; run a race um die Wette laufen; **run down** (with a car) niederfahren; (clues) nachgehen (dat); (a citation) aufspüren; (through gossip) schlechtmachen; **run off** (typ) Abzüge machen von; **run over** (with a vehicle) überfahren; (rehearse) nochmal durchgehen; **run through** (with a sword) erstechen; **run up** (bills) auflaufen lassen; (prices) in die Höhe treiben; (a flag) hissen || intr laufen, rennen; (flow) fließen; (said of buses, etc.) verkehren; (said of the nose) laufen, e.g., ihm läuft die Nase his nose is running; (said of colors) auslaufen; (said of a meeting) dauern; (said of a lease) (for) gelten (auf acc); **run across** zufällig treffen; **run after** nachlaufen (dat); **run around** herumlaufen; **run around with** sich herumtreiben mit; **run away** weglaufen; (said of a spouse) durchgehen; **run down** (said of a clock) ablaufen; **run dry** austrocknen; **run for** kandidieren für; **run high**, e.g., feelings ran high die Gemüter waren erhitzt; **run in the family** in der Familie liegen; **run into** (e.g., a tree) fahren gegen; (e.g., trouble, debt) geraten in (acc); (e.g., a friend) unerwartet treffen; **run into the thousands** in die Tausende gehen; **run low** knapp werden; **run out** (said of liquids) ausgehen; (said of supplies, time) zu Ende gehen; **run out of** ausgehen, e.g., they ran out of supplies die Vorräte gingen ihnen aus; **run over** (said of a pot) überlaufen; **run up against** stoßen auf (acc); **run up to s.o.** j–m entgegenlaufen; **run wild** verwildern
run'-around' s—give s.o. the r. j–n von Pontius zu Pilatus schicken
run'away' adj flüchtig; (horse) durchgegangen || s Ausreißer m; (horse) Durchgänger m
run'down' s kurze Zusammenfassung f
run'-down' adj (condition) heruntergekommen; (clock) abgelaufen; (battery) entladen
rung [rʌŋ] s (of a ladder) Sprosse f; (of a chair) Querleiste f
run-in' s (coll) Zusammenstoß m
runner ['rʌnər] s Läufer –in mf; (of a sled or skate) Kufe f; (of a sliding door) Laufschiene f; (rug) Läufer m; (bot) Ausläufer m; (mil) Meldegänger m
run'ner-up' s (runners-up) Zweitbeste mf; (sport) Zweite mf
run'ning adj (water) fließend; (debts, expenses, sore) laufend || s Laufen n, Lauf m; be in the r. gut im Rennen liegen; be out of the r. (out of the race) aus dem Rennen ausgeschieden sein; (not among the front runners) keine Aussichten haben

run'ning board' s Trittbrett n
run'ning start' s fliegender Start m
run'off' s (sport) Entscheidungslauf m
run'off elec'tion s entscheidende Vorwahl f
run'-of-the-mill' adj Durchschnitts-
runt [rʌnt] s Dreikäsehoch m
run'way' s Startbahn f
rupture ['rʌptʃər] s Bruch m || tr (relations) abbrechen; **be ruptured** e-n Bruch (or Riß) bekommen; **r. one-self** sich [dat] e-n Bruch zuziehen || intr platzen
rural ['rʊrəl] adj ländlich
ruse [ruz] s List f
rush [rʌʃ] adj dringend || s Eile f; (for) Ansturm m (auf acc); (bot) Binse f; **be in a r.** es eilig haben; **what's your r.?** wozu die Eile? || tr (a person) hetzen; (a defensive position) im Sturm nehmen; (work) schnell erledigen; (goods) schleunigst schicken; (e.g., to a hospital) schleunigst schaffen; **be rushed for time** sehr wenig Zeit haben; **r. through** (a bill) durchpeitschen; **r. up** (reinforcements) schnell herbeischaffen || intr eilen, sich stürzen; **r. at** zustürzen auf (acc); **r. forward** vorstürmen; **r. into** stürzen in (acc); **r. up to** zuschießen auf (acc); **the blood rushed to his head** ihm stieg das Blut in den Kopf
rush' hours' spl Hauptverkehrszeit f
rush' or'der s Eilauftrag m
russet ['rʌsɪt] adj rotbraun
Russia ['rʌʃə] s Rußland n
Russian ['rʌʃən] adj russisch || s Russe m, Russin f; (language) Russisch n
rust [rʌst] s Rost m || tr rostig machen || intr (ver)rosten
rustic ['rʌstɪk] adj (rural) ländlich; (countryish) bäuerlich || s Bauer m
rustle ['rʌsəl] s Rauschen n; (of silk) Knistern n || tr rascheln mit; (cattle) stehlen || intr rauschen; (said of silk) knistern
rust'proof' adj rostfrei
rusty ['rʌsti] adj rostig; (fig) eingerostet
rut [rʌt] s Geleise n, Spur f; (fig) alter Trott m
ruthless ['ruθlɪs] adj erbarmungslos
rye [raɪ] s (grain) Roggen m; (whiskey) Roggenwhisky m
rye' bread' s Roggenbrot n
rye' grass' s Raigras n

S

S, s [es] s neunzehnter Buchstabe des englischen Alphabets
Sabbath ['sæbəθ] s Sabbat m
sabbat'ical year' [sə'bætɪkəl] s einjähriger Urlaub m (e-s Professors)
saber ['sebər] s Säbel m
sable ['sebəl] adj schwarz || s (fur) Zobelpelz m; (zool) Zobel m
sabotage ['sæbə͵taʒ] s Sabotage f || tr sabotieren
saboteur [͵sæbə'tʌr] s Saboteur –in mf
saccharin ['sækərɪn] s Saccharin n
sachet [sæ'ʃe] s Duftkissen n
sack [sæk] s Sack m; (bed) (coll) Falle f; **hit the s.** (coll) in die Falle gehen || tr einsacken; (dismiss) (coll) an die Luft setzen; (mil) ausplündern
sack'cloth' s Sacktuch n; **in s. and ashes** in Sack und Asche
sacrament ['sækrəmənt] s Sakrament n
sacramental [͵sækrə'mentəl] adj sakramental
sacred ['sekrəd] adj heilig; **s. to** geweiht (dat)
sacrifice ['sækrɪ͵faɪs] s Opfer n; **at a s.** mit Verlust || tr opfern
sacrilege ['sækrɪlɪdʒ] s Sakrileg n
sacrilegious [͵sækrɪ'lɪdʒəs] adj frevelhaft, gotteslästerlich
sacristan ['sækrɪstən] s Sakristan m
sacristy ['sækrɪsti] s Sakristei f
sad [sæd] adj traurig; (plight) schlimm
sadden ['sædən] tr traurig machen
saddle ['sædəl] s Sattel m || tr satteln; **be saddled with** auf dem Halse haben
sad'dlebag' s Satteltasche f
sadism ['sedɪzəm] s Sadismus m
sadistic [se'dɪstɪk] adj sadistisch
sadness ['sædnɪs] s Traurigkeit f
sad' sack' s (sl) Trauerkloß m
safe [sef] adj (from) sicher (vor dat); (arrival) glücklich; **s. and sound** heil und gesund; (said of a thing) unversehrt; **to be on the s. side** vorsichtshalber || s Geldschrank m
safe'-con'duct s sicheres Geleit n
safe'-depos'it box' s Schließfach n
safe' dis'tance s Sicherheitsabstand m
safe'guard' s Schutz m || tr schützen
safe'keep'ing s sicherer Gewahrsam m
safety ['sefti] adj Sicherheits– || s Sicherheit f
safe'ty belt' s Sicherheitsgurt m
safe'ty pin' s Sicherheitsnadel f
safe'ty ra'zor s Rasierapparat m
safe'ty valve' s Sicherheitsventil n
saffron ['sæfrən] adj safrangelb || s Safran m
sag [sæg] s Senkung f || v (pret & pp sagged; ger sagging) intr sich senken; (said of a cable) durchhängen; (fig) sinken
sagacious [sə'geʃəs] adj scharfsinnig
sage [sedʒ] adj weise, klug || s Weise m; (plant) Salbei f
sage'brush' s Beifuß m
sail [sel] s Segel n; **set s. for** in See stechen nach || tr (a boat) fahren; (the sea) segeln über (acc) || intr segeln; (depart) abfahren; **s. across** übersegeln; **s. along the coast** an der

Küste entlangsegeln; **s. into** (coll) herunterputzen

sail'boat' *s* Segelboot *n*

sail'cloth' *s* Segeltuch *n*

sail'ing *s* Segelfahrt *f*; (sport) Segelsport *m*; **it will be smooth s.** (fig) es wird alles glattgehen

sail'ing ves'sel *s* Segelschiff *n*

sailor ['selər] *s* Matrose *m*

Saint [sent] *s* Heilige *mf*; **S. George** der heilige Georg, Sankt Georg

Saint' Bernard' *s* (dog) Bernhardiner *m*

sake [sek] *s*—**for her s.** ihretwegen; **for his s.** seinetwegen; **for my s.** meinetwegen; **for our s.** unsertwegen; **for their s.** ihretwegen; **for the s. of** um (genit) willen; **for your s.** deinetwegen, Ihretwegen

salable ['seləbəl] *adj* verkäuflich

salacious [sə'leʃəs] *adj* (person) geil; (writing, pictures) obszön

salad ['sæləd] *s* Salat *m*

sal'ad bowl' *s* Salatschüssel *f*

sal'ad dress'ing *s* Salatsoße *f*

sal'ad oil' *s* Salatöl *n*

salami [sə'lɑmi] *s* Salami *f*

salary ['sæləri] *s* Gehalt *n*

sale [sel] *s* Verkauf *m*; (special sale) Ausverkauf *m*; **be up for s.** zum Kauf stehen; **for s.** zu verkaufen; **sales** (com) Absatz *m*, Umsatz *m*; **put up for s.** zum Verkauf anbieten

sales' clerk' *s* Verkäufer -in *mf*

sales'girl' *s* Ladenmädchen *n*

sales'la'dy *s* Verkäuferin *f*

sales'man *s* (-men) Verkäufer *m*

sales'man·ship *s* Verkaufstüchtigkeit *f*

sales' promo'tion *s* Verkaufsförderung *f*

sales' slip' *s* Kassenzettel *m*, Bon *m*

sales' tax' *s* Umsatzsteuer *f*

saliva [sə'laɪvə] *s* Speichel *m*

sallow ['sælo] *adj* bläßlich

sal·ly ['sæli] *s* (side trip) Abstecher *m*; (mil) Ausfall *m* ‖ *v* (pret & pp -lied) *intr* (mil) ausfallen; **s. forth** sich aufmachen

salmon ['sæmən] *adj* lachsfarben ‖ *s* Lachs *m*

saloon [sə'lun] *s* Kneipe *f*; (naut) Salon *m*

salt [sɔlt] *s* Salz *n* ‖ *tr* salzen; **s. away** (coll) auf die hohe Kante legen

salt'cel'lar *s* Salzfaß *n*

salt'ed meat' *s* Salzfleisch *n*

salt' mine' *s* Salzbergwerk *n*; **back to the salt mines** zurück zur Tretmühle

salt'pe'ter *s* Salpeter *m*

salt' shak'er *s* Salzfaß *n*

salty ['sɔlti] *adj* salzig

salutary ['sæljə,teri] *adj* heilsam

salute [sə'lut] *s* Salut *m* ‖ *tr & intr* salutieren

salvage ['sælvɪdʒ] *s* (saving by ship) Bergung *f*; (property saved by ship) Bergungsgut *n*; (discarded material) Altmaterial *n* ‖ *tr* bergen; (discarded material) verwerten

salvation [sæl've/ən] *s* Heil *n*

Salva'tion Ar'my *s* Heilsarmee *f*

salve [sæv] *s* Salbe *f* ‖ *tr* (one's conscience) beschwichtigen

sal·vo ['sælvo] *s* (-vos & -voes) Salve *f*

Samaritan [sə'mærɪtən] *s* Samariter -in *mf*; **good S.** barmherziger Samariter *m*

same [sem] *adj*—**at the s. time** gleichzeitig; **it's all the s. to me** es ist mir ganz gleich; **just the s.** trotzdem; **thanks, s. to you!** danke, gleichfalls!; **the s.** derselbe

sameness ['semnɪs] *s* Eintönigkeit *f*

sample ['sæmpəl] *s* Muster *n*, Probe *f* ‖ *tr* (aus)probieren

sancti·fy ['sæŋktɪ,faɪ] *v* (pret & pp -fied) *tr* heiligen

sanctimonious [,sæŋktɪ'monɪəs] *adj* scheinheilig

sanction ['sæŋk/ən] *s* Sanktion *f* ‖ *tr* sanktionieren

sanctity ['sæŋktɪtɪ] *s* Heiligkeit *f*

sanctuary ['sæŋktʃu,eri] *s* (shrine) Heiligtum *n*; (of a church) Altarraum *m*; (asylum) Asyl *n*

sand [sænd] *s* Sand *m* ‖ *tr* mit Sandpapier abschleifen; (a road, sidewalk) mit Sand bestreuen

sandal ['sændəl] *s* Sandale *f*

san'dalwood' *s* Sandelholz *n*

sand'bag' *s* Sandsack *m*

sand'bank' *s* Sandbank *f*

sand' bar' *s* Sandbank *f*

sand'blast' *tr* sandstrahlen

sand'box' *s* Sandkasten *m*

sand' cas'tle *s* Strandburg *f*

sand' dune' *s* Sanddüne *f*

sand'glass' *s* Sanduhr *f*

sand'man *s* (-men) (fig) Sandmann *m*

sand'pa'per *s* Sandpapier *n* ‖ *tr* mit Sandpapier abschleifen

sand'stone' *s* Sandstein *m*

sand'storm' *s* Sandsturm *m*

sandwich ['sændwɪtʃ] *s* belegtes Brot *n*, Sandwich *n* ‖ *tr* (in between) einzwängen (zwischen dat)

sandy ['sændi] *adj* sandig; (color) sandfarben

sane [sen] *adj* geistig gesund; (e.g., advice) vernünftig

sanguine ['sæŋgwɪn] *adj* (about) zuversichtlich (in Bezug auf acc)

sanitarium [,sænɪ'terɪəm] *s* Heilanstalt *f*, Sanatorium *n*

sanitary ['sænɪ,teri] *adj* sanitär

san'itary nap'kin *s* Damenbinde *f*

sanitation [,sænɪ'teʃən] *s* Gesundheitswesen *n*; (in a building) sanitäre Einrichtungen *pl*

sanity ['sænɪtɪ] *s* geistige Gesundheit *f*

Santa Claus ['sæntə,klɔz] *s* der Weihnachtsmann *m*, der Nikolaus

sap [sæp] *s* Saft *m*; (coll) Schwachkopf *m* ‖ *v* (pret & pp sapped) ger sapping) *tr* (strength) erschöpfen

sapling ['sæplɪŋ] *s* junger Baum *m*

sapphire ['sæfaɪr] *s* Saphir *m*

Saracen ['særəsən] *adj* sarazenisch ‖ *s* Sarazene *m*, Sarazenin *f*

sarcasm ['sɑrkæzəm] *s* Sarkasmus *m*

sarcastic [sɑr'kæstɪk] *adj* sarkastisch

sarcophagus [sɑr'kɑfəgəs] *s* Sarkophag *m*

sardine [sɑr'din] *s* Sardine *f*; packed

in like **sardines** zusammengedrängt wie die Heringe

Sardinia [sɑr'dɪnɪ·ə] s Sardinien n

Sardinian [sɑr'dɪnɪ·ən] adj sardinisch ‖ s Sardinier –in mf; (language) Sardinisch n

sash [sæʃ] s Schärpe f; (of a window) Fensterrahmen m

sass [sæs] s (coll) Revolverschnauze f ‖ tr (coll) (off) patzig antworten (dat)

sassy ['sæsi] adj (coll) patzig

Satan ['setən] s Satan m

satanic(al) [sə'tænɪk(əl)] adj satanisch

satchel ['sætʃəl] s Handtasche f

sate [set] tr übersättigen

satellite ['sætə‚laɪt] s Satellit m

sat'ellite coun'try s Satellitenstaat m

satiate ['seʃɪ‚et] tr sättigen

satin ['sætɪn] s Seidenatlas m

satire ['sætaɪr] s Satire f

satiric(al) [sə'tɪrɪk(əl)] adj satirisch

satirize ['sætɪ‚raɪz] tr verspotten

satisfaction [‚sætɪs'fækʃən] s Befriedigung f, Genugtuung f

satisfactory [‚sætɪs'fæktəri] adj friedenstellend, genügend

satis·fy ['sætɪs‚faɪ] v (pret & pp –fied) tr (desires, needs) befriedigen; (requirements) genügen (dat); (a person) zufriedenstellen; **be satisfied with** zufrieden sein mit ‖ intr befriedigen

saturate ['sætʃə‚ret] tr (& chem) sättigen, saturieren

satura'tion bomb'ing s Bombenteppich m

satura'tion point' s Sättigungspunkt m

Saturday ['sætər‚de] s Samstag m; **on S.** am Samstag

sauce [sɔs] s Soße f; (coll) Frechheit f ‖ tr mit Soße zubereiten; (season) würzen

sauce'pan' s Stielkasserolle f

saucer ['sɔsər] s Untertasse f

saucy ['sɔsi] adj (impertinent) frech; (amusingly flippant) keß; (trim) flott

sauerkraut ['saur‚kraut] s Sauerkraut n

saunter ['sɔntər] s Schlendern n ‖ intr schlendern

sausage ['sɔsɪdʒ] s Wurst f

saute [so'te] v (pret & pp sauteed) tr sautieren

savage ['sævɪdʒ] adj wild ‖ s Wilde mf

savant ['sævənt] s Gelehrte m

save [sev] tr (rescue) retten; (money, fuel) sparen; (keep, preserve) aufheben; (trouble) ersparen; (time) gewinnen; (stamps) sammeln; **s. face** das Gesicht wahren; **s. from** bewahren vor (dat) ‖ prep außer (dat)

sav'ing adj (grace) seligmachend; (quality) ausgleichend ‖ s (of souls) Rettung f; (in) Ersparnis f (an dat); **savings** Ersparnisse pl

sav'ings account' s Sparkonto n

sav'ings bank' s Sparkasse f

sav'ings certi'ficate s Sparbon m

sav'ings depos'it s Spareinlage f

savior ['sevjər] s Retter –in mf; **Saviour** Heiland m

savor ['sevər] s Wohlgeschmack m ‖ tr auskosten ‖ intr—**s. of** (smell of) riechen nach; (taste of) schmecken nach

savory ['sevəri] adj wohlschmeckend

saw [sɔ] s Säge f; (saying) Sprichwort n ‖ tr sägen; **saw up** zersägen

saw'dust' s Sägespäne pl

saw'horse' s Sägebock m

saw'mill' s Sägemühle f

Saxon ['sæksən] adj sächsisch ‖ s Sachse m, Sachsin f

Saxony ['sæksəni] s Sachsen n

saxophone ['sæksə‚fon] s Saxophon n

say [se] s—**have a** (or **no**) **say in etw** (or nichts) zu sagen haben bei; **have one's say** (about) seine Meinung äußern (über acc) ‖ v (pret & pp **said** [sed]) tr sagen; (Mass) lesen; (a prayer) sprechen; (one's prayers) verrichten; (said of a newspaper article, etc.) besagen; **it says in the papers** in der Zeitung steht; (let's) **say** sagen wir; **no sooner said than done** gesagt, getan; **say!** (to draw attention) sag mal!; (to elicit agreement) gelt!; **say s.th. behind s.o.'s back** j–m etw nachsagen; **she is said to be clever** sie soll klug sein; **that is not to say** das will nicht sagen; **that is to say** das heißt; **they say** man sagt; **to say nothing of** ganz zu schweigen von; **you don't say so!** tatsächlich!

say'ing s Sprichwort n; **as the s. goes** wie man zu sagen pflegt; **it goes without s.** das versteht sich von selbst

say'-so' s (assertion) Behauptung f; (order) Anweisung f; (final authority) letztes Wort n

scab [skæb] s Schorf m; (sl) Streikbrecher –in mf

scabbard ['skæbərd] s Schwertscheide f

scabby ['skæbi] adj schorfig

scads [skædz] spl (sl) e–e Menge f

scaffold ['skæfəld] s Gerüst n; (for executions) Schafott n

scaf'folding s Baugerüst n

scald [skɔld] tr verbrühen; (milk) aufkochen

scale [skel] s (on fish, reptiles) Schuppe f; (pan of a balance) Waagschale f; (of a thermometer, wages) Skala f; (mus) Tonleiter f; **on a grand s.** im großen Stil; **on a large** (or **small**) **s.** in großem (or kleinem) Maßstab; **s. 1:1000** Maßstab 1:1000; **scales** Waage f; **to s.** maßstabgerecht ‖ tr erklettern; **s. down** maßstäblich verkleinern; (prices) herabsetzen

scallop ['skæləp] s Kammuschel f; (sew) Zacke f ‖ tr auszacken; (culin) überbacken

scalp [skælp] s Kopfhaut f; (Indian trophy) Skalp m ‖ tr skalpieren

scalpel ['skælpəl] s Skalpell n

scaly ['skeli] adj schuppig

scamp [skæmp] s Fratz m, Wildfang m

scamper ['skæmpər] intr herumtollen; **s. away** davonlaufen

scan [skæn] v (pret & pp scanned; ger

scanning) *tr* (*a page*) überfliegen; (*a verse*) skandieren; (*examine*) genau prüfen; (radar, telv) abtasten

scandal ['skændəl] *s* Skandal *m*

scandalize ['skændə,laɪz] *tr* schockieren

scandalmonger ['skændəl,mʌŋgər] *s* Lästermaul *n*

scandalous ['skændələs] *adj* skandalös

scan'dal sheet' *s* Sensationsblatt *n*

Scandinavia [,skændɪ'nevɪ-ə] *s* Skandinavien *n*

Scandinavian [,skændɪ'nevɪ-ən] *adj* skandinavisch || *s* Skandinavier –in *m*; (*language*) Skandinavisch *n*

scansion ['skænʃən] *s* Skandieren *n*

scant [skænt] *adj* gering; a s. two hours knapp zwei Stunden

scantily ['skæntɪlɪ] *adv*—s. clad leicht bekleidet

scanty ['skæntɪ] *adj* kärglich, knapp

scapegoat ['skep,got] *s* Sündenbock *m*

scar [skɑr] *s* Narbe *f*; (fig) Makel *m* || *v* (*pret & pp* scarred) *ger* scarring) *tr* (*e.g., a face*) entstellen; (*e.g., a tabletop*) verschrammen; (fig) beinträchtigen

scarce [skɛrs] *adj* knapp, rar; make oneself s. (coll) das Weite suchen

scarcely ['skɛrslɪ] *adv* kaum; be s. able to (*inf*) Not haben zu (*inf*)

scarcity ['skɛrsɪtɪ] *s* (of) Knappheit *f* (an *dat*), Mangel *m* (an *dat*)

scare [skɛr] *s* Schrecken *m*; be scared erschrecken; be scared stiff e-e Hundeangst haben; give s.o. a s. j-m e-n Schrecken einjagen || *tr* erschrecken; s. away verscheuchen; s. up (*money*) auftreiben || *intr* erschrecken

scare'crow' *s* Vogelscheuche *f*

scarf [skɑrf] *s* (scarfs & scarves [skɑrvz]) Schal *m*

scarlet ['skɑrlɪt] *adj* scharlachrot || *s* Scharlachrot *n*

scar'let fe'ver *s* Scharlach *m*

scarred *adj* narbig, schrammig

scary ['skɛrɪ] *adj* schreckerregend

scat [skæt] *interj* weg!

scathing ['skeðɪŋ] *adj* vernichtend

scatter ['skætər] *tr* zerstreuen || *intr* sich zerstreuen

scat'terbrain' *s* Wirrkopf *m*

scat'tered show'ers *spl* einzelne Schauer *pl*

scenari·o [sɪ'nɛrɪ·o] *s* (–os) Drehbuch *n*

scene [sin] *s* Szene *f*; be on the s. zur Stelle sein; behind the scenes hinter den Kulissen; make a s. e-e Szene machen; s. of the crime Tatort *m*

scenery ['sinərɪ] *s* Landschaft *f*; (theat) Bühnenausstattung *f*

scenic ['sinɪk] *adj* landschaftlich; (theat) szenisch

scent [sɛnt] *s* Duft *m*; (*of a dog*) Witterung *f*; (hunt) Spur *f*; have a s. duften || *tr* wittern

scepter ['sɛptər] *s* Zepter *n*

sceptic ['skɛptɪk] *s* Skeptiker –in *mf*

scepticism ['skɛptɪ,sɪzəm] *s* (*doubt*) Skepsis *f*; (*doctrine*) Skeptizismus *m*

schedule ['skɛdjʊl] *s* Plan *m*; (*for work*) Arbeitsplan *m*; (*in travel*) Fahrplan *m*; (at school) Stundenplan *m*; (*appendix to a tax return*) Einkommensteuerformular *n*; (table) Einkommensteuertabelle *f*; on s. fahrplanmäßig || *tr* ansetzen; the plane is scheduled to arrive at six nach dem Flugplan soll die Maschine um sechs Uhr ankommen

scheme [skim] *s* (*schematic*) Schema *n*; (*plan, program*) Plan *m*; (*intrigue*) Intrige *f* || *tr* planen || *intr* Ränke schmieden

schemer ['skimər] *s* Ränkeschmied *m*

schilling ['ʃɪlɪŋ] *s* (Aust) Schilling *m*

schism ['sɪzəm] *s* (fig) Spaltung *f*; (eccl) Schisma *n*

schizophrenia [,skɪtso'frinɪ·ə] *s* Schizophrenie *f*, Bewußtseinsspaltung *f*

schizophrenic [,skɪtso'frɛnɪk] *adj* schizophren

schmaltzy ['ʃmɔltsɪ] *adj* schmalzig

scholar ['skɑlər] *s* Gelehrte *m*

scholarly ['skɑlərlɪ] *adj* gelehrt

schol'arship' *s* Gelehrsamkeit *f*; (*award*)) Stipendium *n*

scholastic [skə'læstɪk] *adj* Schul-, Bildungs-; (hist) scholastisch

school [skul] *adj* (book, house, master, room, teacher, yard, year) Schul- || *s* Schule *f*; (*of a university*) Fakultät *f*; (*of fish*) Schwarm *m*; s. is over die Schule ist aus || *tr* schulen

school' age' *s* schulpflichtiges Alter *n*; of s. schulpflichtig

school'bag' *s* Schulranzen *m*

school' board' *s* Schulausschuß *m*

school'boy' *s* Schüler *m*

school'girl' *s* Schülerin *f*

school'ing *s* (*formal education*) Schulbildung *f*; (*training*) Schulung *f*

school'mate' *s* Mitschüler –in *mf*

schooner ['skunər] *s* Schoner *m*

sciatica [saɪ'ætɪkə] *s* Hüftschmerz *m*

science ['saɪ·əns] *s* Wissenschaft *f*; the sciences die Naturwissenschaften *pl*

sci'ence fic'tion *s* Science-fiction *f*

scientific [,saɪ·ən'tɪfɪk] *adj* wissenschaftlich

scientist ['saɪ·əntɪst] *s* Wissenschaftler –in *mf*

scimitar ['sɪmɪtər] *s* Türkensäbel *m*

scintillate ['sɪntɪ,let] *intr* funkeln

scion ['saɪ·ən] *s* Sprößling *m*; (bot) Pfropfreis *n*

scissors ['sɪzərz] *s & spl* Schere *f*; (*in wrestling*) Zangengriff *m*

scoff [skɔf] *s* Spott *m* || *intr* (at) spotten (über *acc*)

scold [skold] *tr & intr* schelten

scold'ing *s* Schelte *f*; get a s. Schelte bekommen

sconce [skɑns] *s* Wandleuchter *m*

scoop [skup] *s* (*ladle*) Schöpfkelle *f*; (*for sugar, flour*) Schaufel *f*; (*amount scooped*) Schlag *m*; (journ) Knüller *m* || *tr* schöpfen; s. out ausschaufeln; s. up scheffeln

scoot [skut] *intr* (coll) flitzen

scooter ['skutər] *s* Roller *m*

scope [skop] *s* (*extent*) Umfang *m*;

(*range*) Reichweite *f*; **give free s. to
the imagination** der Phatasie freien
Lauf lassen; **give s.o. free s.** j-m
freie Hand geben; **within the s. of**
im Rahmen (*genit*) or von

scorch [skɔrtʃ] *tr* versengen

scorched'-earth' pol'icy *s* Politik *f* der
verbrannten Erde

scorch'ing *adj & adv* sengend

score [skor] *s* (*of a game*) Punktzahl
f; (*final score*) Ergebnis *n*; (*notch*)
Kerbe *f*; (*mus*) Partitur *f*; **a s. of**
zwanzig; **have an odd s. to settle
with s.o.** mit j-m e-e alte Rechnung
zu begleichen haben; **keep s.** die
Punktzahl anschreiben; **know the s.**
(*coll*) auf Draht sein; **on that s.**
diesbezüglich; **what's the s.?** wie
steht das Spiel? || *tr* (*points*) erzielen;
(*goals*) schießen; (*notch*) einkerben;
(*mus*) in Partitur setzen || *intr* e-n
Punkt erzielen

score'board' *s* Anzeigetafel *f*

score'card' *s* Punktzettel *m*

score'keep'er *s* Anschreiber –in *mf*

score'sheet' *s* Spielberichtsbogen *m*

scorn [skɔrn] *s* Verachtung *f*; **laugh to
s.** auslachen || *tr* verachten

scornful ['skɔrnfəl] *adj* verächtlich

scorpion ['skɔrpɪ-ən] *s* Skorpion *m*

Scot [skɑt] *s* Schotte *m*, Schottin *f*

Scotch [skɑtʃ] *adj* schottisch; (sl) gei-
zig || *s* schottischer Whisky *m*; (*dia-
lect*) Schottisch *n* || *tr* (*a rumor*)
ausrotten; (*with a chock*) blockieren;
(*render harmless*) unschädlich machen

Scotch'man *s* (–men) Schotte *m*

Scotch' pine' *s* gemeine Kiefer *f*

Scotch' tape' *s* (trademark) durchsich-
tiger Klebstreifen *m*

scot'-free' *adj* ungestraft

Scotland ['skɑtlənd] *s* Schottland *n*

Scottish ['skɑtɪʃ] *adj* schottisch || *s*
(*dialect*) Schottisch *n*; **the S.** die
Schotten *pl*

scoundrel ['skaundrəl] *s* Lump *m*

scour [skaur] *tr* scheuern; (*the city*)
absuchen

scourge [skɑrdʒ] *s* Geißel *f* || *tr* geißeln

scout [skaut] *s* Pfadfinder *m*; (mil,
sport) Kundschafter *m* || *tr* auf-
klären || *intr* kundschaften

scout'mas'ter *s* Pfadfinderführer *m*

scowl [skaul] *s* finsterer Blick *m* || *intr*
finster blicken; **s. at** grollend ansehen

scram [skræm] *v* (*pret & pp* scrammed;
ger scramming) *intr* (coll) abhauen

scramble ['skræmbəl] *s* (*for*) Balgerei
f (um) || *tr* (*mix up*) durcheinander-
mischen; (*a message*) unverständlich
machen; **s. eggs** Rührei machen || *intr* (e.g., *over rocks*) klettern; **s. for
s.th.** sich um etw reißen; **s. to one's
feet** sich aufrappeln

scram'bled eggs' *spl* Rührei *n*

scrap [skræp] *s* (*of metal*) Schrott *m*;
(*of paper*) Fetzen *m*; (*of food*) Rest
m; (*refuse*) Abfall *m*; (*quarrel*)
(coll) Zank *m*; (*fight*) (coll) Rau-
ferei *f* || *v* (*pret & pp* scrapped; *ger*

scrapping) *tr* ausrangieren || *intr*
(*quarrel*) (coll) zanken; (*fight*) (coll)
raufen

scrap'book' *s* Einklebebuch *n*

scrape [skrep] *s* Kratzer *m*; (coll) Pat-
sche *f* || *tr* schaben; (*the skin*) ab-
scheuern; **s. off** abschaben; **s. together** (or up) zusammenkratzen

scrap' heap' *s* Schrotthaufen *m*; (*refuse
heap*) Abfallhaufen *m*

scrap' i'ron *s* Schrott *m*, Alteisen *n*

scrapper ['skræpər] *s* Zänker –in *mf*

scrappy ['skræpi] *adj* (*made of scraps*)
zusammengestoppelt; (coll) rauflustig

scratch [skrætʃ] *s* Kratzer *m*, Schramme *f*; **start from s.** wieder ganz von
vorne anfangen || *tr* kratzen; (*sport*)
streichen; **s. open** aufkratzen; **s. out**
(*a line*) ausstreichen; (*eyes*) aus-
hacken; **s. the surface of** nur streifen
|| *intr* kratzen; (*scratch oneself*) sich
kratzen

scratch' pad' *s* Notizblock *m*

scratch' pa'per *s* Schmierpapier *n*

scrawl [skrɔl] *s* Gekritzel *n* || *tr & intr*
kritzeln

scrawny ['skrɔni] *adj* spindeldürr

scream [skrim] *s* Aufschrei *m*; **he's a
s.!** er ist zum Schreien! || *tr & intr*
schreien

screech [skritʃ] *s* Kreischen *n* || *intr*
(*said of tires, brakes*) kreischen;
(*said of an owl*) schreien

screech' owl' *s* Kauz *m*

screen [skrin] *s* Wandschirm *m*; (*for a
window*) Fliegengitter *n*; (*camouflage*) Tarnung *f*; (aer) (of) Abschirmung *f* (durch); (cin) Leinwand *f*;
(nav) Geleitschutz *m*; (radar, telv)
Leinwand *f* || *tr* (*sand, gravel, coal;
applications*) durchsieben; (*appli-
cants*) überprüfen; (*a porch, windows*) mit Fliegengittern versehen;
(mil) verschleiern; **s. off** abschirmen

screen'play' *s* Filmdrama *n*; (*scenario*)
Drehbuch *n*

screen' test' *s* Probeaufnahme *f*

screw [skru] *s* Schraube *f*; **he has a s.
loose** (coll) bei ihm ist er-e Schraube
locker || *tr* schrauben; (*cheat*) (sl)
hereinlegen; (*vulg*) vögeln; **s. tight**
festschrauben; **s. up** (*courage*) aufbringen; (*bungle*) (coll) verpfuschen

screw'ball' *adj* (coll) verrückt || *s* (coll)
Wirrkopf *m*

screw'driv'er *s* Schraubenzieher *m*

screw'-on cap' *s* Schraubendeckel *m*

screwy ['skru-i] *adj* (sl) verrückt

scribble ['skribəl] *s* Gekritzel *n* || *tr
& intr* kritzeln

scribe [skraib] *s* Schreiber *m*; (Bib)
Schriftgelehrte *m*

scrimmage ['skrimidʒ] *s* (fb) Übungsspiel *n*

scrimp [skrimp] *tr* knausern mit ||
intr (on) knausern (mit)

scrimpy ['skrimpi] *adj* knapp

script [skript] *s* (*handwriting*) Handschrift *f*; (cin) Drehbuch *n*; (rad)
Textbuch *n*; (typ) Schreibschrift *f*

scriptural ['skriptʃərəl] *adj* biblisch;
s. passage Bibelstelle *f*

Scripture ['skrɪptʃər] s die Heilige Schrift; (*Bible passage*) Bibelzitat n
script'writ'er s (cin) Drehbuchautor m
scrofula ['skrɔfjələ] s Skrofeln pl
scroll [skrol] s Schriftrolle f; (archit) Schnörkel m
scroll'work' s Schnörkelverzierung f
scro·tum ['skrotəm] s (**-ta** [tə] or **-tums**) Hodensack m
scrounge [skraundʒ] tr stibitzen ‖ intr —s. **around for** herumstöbern nach
scrub [skrʌb] s Schrubben n; (*shrubs*) Buschwerk n; (sport) Ersatzmann m ‖ v (pret & pp **scrubbed**; ger **scrubbing**) tr schrubben
scrub'bing brush' s Scheuerbürste f
scrub'wom'an s (**-wom'en**) Scheuerfrau f
scruff [skrʌf] s—**s. of the neck** Genick n
scruple ['skrupəl] s Skrupel m
scrupulous ['skrupjələs] adj skrupulös
scrutinize ['skrutɪ‚naɪz] tr genau prüfen; (*a person*) mustern
scrutiny ['skrutɪni] s genaue Prüfung f
scud [skʌd] s Wolkenfetzen m
scuff [skʌf] tr (a shoe, waxed floor) abschürfen ‖ intr (*shuffle*) schlurfen
scuffle ['skʌfəl] s Rauferei f ‖ intr raufen
scuff' mark' s Schmutzfleck m
scull [skʌl] s (sport) Skull m ‖ intr (sport) skullen
scullery ['skʌləri] s Spülküche f
scul'lery maid' s Spülerin f
sculptor ['skʌlptər] s Bildhauer m
sculptress ['skʌlptrɪs] s Bildhauerin f
sculptural ['skʌlptʃərəl] adj bildhauerisch
sculpture ['skʌlptʃər] s (art) Bildhauerei f; (work of art) Skulptur f ‖ tr meißeln ‖ intr bildhauern
scum [skʌm] s (& fig) Abschaum m
scummy ['skʌmi] adj schaumig; (fig) niederträchtig
scurrilous ['skʌrɪləs] adj skurril
scur·ry ['skʌri] v (pret & pp **-ried**) intr huschen
scurvy ['skʌrvi] adj gemein ‖ s Skorbut m
scuttle ['skʌtəl] s (naut) Springluke f ‖ tr (hopes, plans) vernichten; (naut) selbst versenken
scut'tlebutt' s (coll) Latrinenparole f
scut'tling s Selbstversenkung f
scythe [saɪð] s Sense f
sea [si] s See f, Meer n; **at sea** auf See; **go to sea** zur See gehen; **heavy seas** hoher (or schwerer) Seegang m
sea'board' s Küstenstrich m
sea' breeze' s Seebrise f
sea'coast' s Seeküste f, Meeresküste f
seafarer ['si‚ferər] s Seefahrer m
seafaring ['si‚ferɪŋ] s Seefahrt f
sea'food' s Fischgerichte pl
sea'go'ing adj seetüchtig
sea' gull' s Seemöwe f, Möwe f
seal [sil] s Siegel n; (zool) Seehund m ‖ tr (a document) siegeln; (a deal, s.o.'s fate) besiegeln; (against leakage) verschließen, abdichten; **s. off** (mil) abriegeln; **s. up** abdichten

sea' legs' spl—**get one's s. seefest werden**
sea'lev'el s Meereshöhe f
seal'ing wax' s Siegellack m
seal'skin' s Seehundsfell n
seam [sim] s (groove) Fuge f; (geol) Lager n; (min) Flöz n; (sew) Naht f
sea'man s (**-men**) Seemann m; (nav) Matrose m
sea' mile' s Seemeile f
seamless ['simlɪs] adj nahtlos
sea' mon'ster s Meeresungeheuer n
seamstress ['simstrɪs] s Näherin f
seamy ['simi] adj verrufen; **s. side** (fig) Schattenseite f
séance ['se-ɑns] s Séance f
sea'plane' s Seeflugzeug n
sea'port' s Seehafen m
sea'port town' s Hafenstadt f
sea' pow'er s Seemacht f
sear [sɪr] tr versengen
search [sʌrtʃ] s Durchsuchung f; (for a person) (for) Fahndung f (nach); **in s. of** auf der Suche nach ‖ tr durchsuchen ‖ intr suchen; **s. for** suchen, fahnden nach
search'ing adj gründlich; (glance) forschend
search'light' s Scheinwerfer m
search' war'rant s Haussuchungsbefehl m
seascape ['si‚skep] s Seegemälde n
sea' shell' s Muschel f
sea'shore' s Strand m
sea'sick' adj seekrank
sea'sick'ness s Seekrankheit f
sea'side' adj Meeres-, See-
season ['sizən] s Jahreszeit f; (appropriate period) Saison f; **closed s.** (hunt) Schonzeit f; **dry s.** Trockenzeit f; **in and out of s.** jederzeit; **in s.** zur rechten Zeit; **out of s.** (game) außerhalb der Saison; (fruits, vegetables) nicht auf dem Markt; **peak s.** Hochsaison f ‖ tr (food) würzen; (wine) lagern; (wood) austrocknen lassen; (tobacco) reifen lassen; (soldiers) abhärten ‖ intr (e.g., said of wine) (ab)lagern
seasonal ['sizənəl] adj jahreszeitlich; (caused by seasons) saisonbedingt
sea'sonal work' s Saisonarbeit f
sea'soned adj erfahren; (troops) kampfgewohnt, fronterfahren
sea'soning s Würze f
sea'son's greet'ings spl Festgrüße pl
sea'son tick'et s Dauerkarte f
seat [sit] s Sitz m, Platz m; (of trousers) Gesäß n; **have a s.** Platz nehmen; **keep one's s.** sitzenbleiben ‖ tr (a person) e-n Platz anweisen (dat); (said of a room) Sitzplätze bieten für; **be seated** sich hinsetzen
seat' belt' s (aer, aut) Sicherheitsgurt m; **fasten seat belts!** bitte anschnallen!
seat' cov'er s (aut) Auto-Schonbezug m
seat'ing capac'ity s (for) Sitzgelegenheit f (für); **have a s. of** fassen
seat' of gov'ernment s Regierungssitz m
sea'wall' s Strandmauer f

sea'way s Seeweg m; (heavy sea) schwerer Seegang m
sea'weed' s Alge f, Seetang m
sea'wor'thy adj seetüchtig
secede [sɪ'sid] intr sich trennen
secession [sɪ'sɛʃən] s Sezession f
seclude [sɪ'klud] tr abschließen
seclud'ed adj abgeschieden; (life) zurückgezogen; (place) abgelegen
seclusion [sɪ'kluʒən] s Zurückgezogenheit f, Abgeschiedenheit f
second ['sɛkənd] adj zweite; be s. to none niemandem nachstehen; in the s. place zweitens; s. in command stellvertretender Kommandeur m ‖ s (unit of time) Sekunde f; (moment) Augenblick m; (in boxing or duelling) Sekundant m; George the Second Georg der Zweite; the s. (of the month) der zweite ‖ pron zweite ‖ tr unterstützen
secondary ['sɛkən,dɛri] adj sekundär, Neben– ‖ s (elec) Sekundärwicklung f; (fb) Spieler pl in der zweiten Reihe
sec'ondary school' s Oberschule
sec'ondary-school teach'er s Oberlehrer –in mf
sec'ondary sourc'es spl Sekundärliteratur f
sec'ondary tar'get s Ausweichziel n
sec'ond best' s Zweitbeste mfn
sec'ond-best' adj zweitbeste; come off s. den kürzeren ziehen
sec'ond-class' adj zweitklassig; s. ticket Fahrkarte f zweiter Klasse
sec'ond cous'in s Cousin m (or Kusine f) zweiten Grades
sec'ond fid'dle s—play s. die zweite Geige spielen
sec'ond hand' s (horol) Sekundenzeiger m
sec'ondhand' adj (car) gebraucht (information) aus zweiter Hand; (books) antiquarisch
sec'ondhand book'store s Antiquariat n
sec'ondhand deal'er s Altwarenhändler –in mf
sec'ond lieuten'ant s Leutnant m
secondly ['sɛkəndli] adv zweitens
sec'ond mate' s (naut) zweiter Offizier m
sec'ond na'ture s zweite Natur f
sec'ond-rate' adj zweitklassig
sec'ond sight' s zweites Gesicht n
sec'ond thought' s—have second thoughts Bedenken hegen; on s. bei weiterem Nachdenken
sec'ond wind' s—get one's s. wieder zu Kräften kommen
secrecy ['sikrəsi] s Heimlichkeit f
secret ['sikrɪt] adj geheim ‖ s Geheimnis n; in s. insgeheim; keep no secrets from keine Geheimnisse haben vor (dat); keep s. geheimhalten; make no s. of kein Hehl machen aus
secretary ['sɛkrə,tɛri] s (man, desk, bird) Sekretär m; (female) Sekretärin f; (in government) Minister m
sec'retary-gen'eral s Generalsekretär m
sec'retary of com'merce s Handelsminister m

sec'retary of defense' s Verteidigungsminister m
sec'retary of la'bor s Arbeitsminister m
sec'retary of state' s Außenminister m
sec'retary of the inter'ior s Innenminister m
sec'retary of the treas'ury s Finanzminister n
se'cret bal'lot s geheime Abstimmung f
secrete [sɪ'krit] tr (hide) verstecken; (physiol) absondern, ausscheiden
secretive ['sikrɪtɪv] adj verschwiegen
se'cret police' s Geheimpolizei f
se'cret serv'ice s Geheimdienst m
sect [sɛkt] s Sekte f
sectarian [sɛk'tɛri-ən] adj sektiererisch; (school) Konfessions–
section ['sɛkʃən] s (segment, part) Teil m; (of a newspaper, chapter) Abschnitt m; (of a city) Viertel n; (group) Abteilung f; (cross section; thin slice, e.g., of tissue) Schnitt m; (jur) Paragraph m; (mil) Halbzug m; (rr) Strecke f; (surg) Sektion f ‖ tr— s. off abteilen
sectional ['sɛkʃənəl] adj (view) Teil–; (pride) Lokal–
sec'tional fur'niture s Anbaumöbel n
sec'tion hand' s Schienenleger m
sector ['sɛktər] s Sektor m
secular ['sɛkjələr] adj weltlich ‖ s Weltpriester m, Weltgeistlicher m
secularism ['sɛkjələ,rɪzəm] s Weltlichkeit f, Säkularismus m
secure [sɪ'kjur] adj sicher ‖ tr (make fast) sichern; (obtain) sich [dat] beschaffen
security [sɪ'kjurɪti] s (& jur) Sicherheit f; securities Wertpapiere pl
sedan [sɪ'dæn] s Limousine f
sedan' chair' s Sänfte f
sedate [sɪ'det] adj gesetzt
sedation [sɪ'deʃən] s Beruhigung f
sedative ['sɛdətɪv] s Beruhigungsmittel n
sedentary ['sɛdən,tɛri] adj sitzend
sedge [sɛdʒ] s (bot) Segge f
sediment ['sɛdɪmənt] s Bodensatz m; (geol) Ablagerung f, Sediment n
sedition [sɪ'dɪʃən] s Aufruhr m
seditious [sɪ'dɪʃəs] adj aufrührerisch
seduce [sɪ'd(j)us] tr verführen
seducer [sɪ'd(j)usər] s Verführer –in mf
seduction [sɪ'dʌkʃən] s Verführung f
seductive [sɪ'dʌktɪv] adj verführerisch
sedulous ['sɛdʒələs] adj emsig
see [si] s (eccl) (erz)bischöflicher Stuhl m ‖ v (pret saw [sɔ]; pp seen [sin]) tr sehen; (comprehend) verstehen; (realize) einsehen; (a doctor) gehen zu; see red rasend werden; see s.o. off j-n an den Zug (aus Flugzeug) bringen; see s.o. to the door j-n zur Tür geleiten; see s.th. through etw durchstehen; that remains to be seen das wird man erst sehen ‖ intr sehen; see through (fig) durchschauen; see to sich kümmern um; see to it that sich darum kümmern,

daß; **you see** (*parenthetical*) wissen Sie

seed [sid] *s* Samen *m*; (*collective & fig*) Saat *f*; (*in fruit*) Kern *m*; (*physiol*) Samen *m*; **go to s.** in Samen schießen; **seeds** (fig) Keim *m* ‖ *tr* besäen

seed′bed′ *s* Samenbeet *n*

seed′ed rye′ bread′ *s* Kümmelbrot *n*

seedless [′sidlɪs] *adj* kernlos

seedling [′sidlɪŋ] *s* Sämling *m*

seedy [′sidi] *adj* (*person*) heruntergekommen; (*thing*) schäbig

see′ing *s* Sehen *n* ‖ *conj*—**s. that** in Anbetracht dessen, daß

See′ing Eye′ dog′ *s* Blindenhund *m*

seek [sik] *v* (*pret & pp* sought [sɔt]) *tr* suchen; **s. s.o.'s advice** j-s Rat erbitten; **s. to** (*inf*) versuchen zu (*inf*) ‖ *intr*—**s. after** suchen nach

seem [sim] *intr* scheinen ‖ *impers*—**it seems to me** es kommt mir vor

seemingly [′simɪŋli] *adv* anscheinend

seemly [′simli] *adj* schicklich

seep [sip] *intr* sickern

seepage [′sipɪdʒ] *s* Durchsickern *n*

seer [sɪr] *s* Seher *m*

seeress [′sɪrɪs] *s* Seherin *f*

see′saw′ *s* Schaukelbrett *n*, Wippe *f* ‖ *intr* wippen; (fig) schwanken

seethe [sið] *intr* sieden; **s. with** (fig) sieden vor (*dat*)

segment [′sɛgmənt] *s* Abschnitt *m*

segregate [′sɛgrɪˌget] *tr* trennen, absondern

segregation [ˌsɛgrɪ′geʃən] *s* Absonderung *f*; (*of races*) Rassentrennung *f*

seismograph [′saɪzməˌgræf] *s* Erdbebenmesser *m*, Seismograph *m*

seismology [saɪz′malədʒi] *s* Erdbebenkunde *f*, Seismologie *f*

seize [siz] *tr* anfassen; (*a criminal*) festnehmen; (*a town, fortress*) einnehmen; (*an opportunity*) ergreifen; (*power*) an sich reißen; (*confiscate*) beschlagnahmen

seizure [′siʒər] *s* Besitzergreifung *f*; (*confiscation*) Beschlagnahme *f*; (pathol) plötzlicher Anfall *m*

seldom [′sɛldəm] *adv* selten

select [sɪ′lɛkt] *adj* erlesen ‖ *tr* auslesen, auswählen

select′ed *adj* ausgesucht

selection [sɪ′lɛkʃən] *s* Auswahl *f*

selective [sɪ′lɛktɪv] *adj* Auswahl—; (rad) trennscharf

selec′tive serv′ice *s* allgemeine Wehrpflicht *f*

self [sɛlf] *s* (**selves** [sɛlvz]) Selbst *n*, Ich *n*; **be one's old s. again** wieder der alte sein; **his better s.** sein besseres Ich ‖ *pron*—**payable to s.** auf Selbst ausgestellt

self′-addressed en′velope *s* mit Anschrift versehener Freiumschlag *m*

self′-assur′ance *s* Selbstbewußtsein *n*

self′-cen′tered *adj* ichbezogen

self′-conceit′ed *adj* eingebildet

self′-con′fident *adj* selbstsicher

self′-con′scious *adj* befangen

self′-control′ *s* Selbstbeherrschung *f*

self′-decep′tion *s* Selbsttäuschung *f*

self′-defense′ *s* Selbstverteidigung *f*; **in s.** aus Notwehr

self′-deni′al *s* Selbstverleugnung *f*

self′-destruc′tion *s* Selbstvernichtung *f*

self′-determina′tion *s* Selbstbestimmung *f*

self′-dis′cipline *s* Selbstzucht *f*

self′-ed′ucated per′son *s* Autodidakt –in *mf*

self′-employed′ *adj* selbständig

self′-esteem′ *s* Selbsteinschätzung *f*

self′-ev′ident *adj* selbstverständlich

self′-explan′ator′y *adj* keiner Erklärung bedürftig

self′-gov′ernment *s* Selbstverwaltung *f*

self′-impor′tant *adj* eingebildet

self′-indul′gence *s* Genußsucht *f*

self′-in′terest *s* Eigennutz *m*

selfish [′sɛlfɪʃ] *adj* eigennützig

selfishness [′sɛlfɪnɪs] *s* Eigennutz *m*

selfless [′sɛlflɪs] *adj* selbstlos

self′-love′ *s* Selbstliebe *f*

self′-made man′ *s* Selfmademan *m*

self′-por′trait *s* Selbstbildnis *n*

self′-possessed′ *adj* selbstbeherrscht

self′-praise′ *s* Eigenlob *n*

self′-preserva′tion *s* Selbsterhaltung *f*

self′-reli′ant *adj* selbstsicher

self′-respect′ *s* Selbstachtung *f*

self′-right′eous *adj* selbstgerecht

self′-sac′rifice *s* Selbstaufopferung *f*

self′same′ *adj* ebenderselbe

self′-sat′isfied *adj* selbstzufrieden

self′-seek′ing *adj* selbstsüchtig

self′-serv′ice *adj* mit Selbstbedienung ‖ *s* Selbstbedienung *f*

self′-styled′ *adj* von eigenen Gnaden

self′-suffi′cient *adj* selbstgenügsam

self′-support′ing *adj* finanziell unabhängig

self′-taught′ *adj* autodidaktisch

self′-willed′ *adj* eigenwillig

self′-wind′ing *adj* automatisch

sell [sɛl] *v* (*pret & pp* sold [sold]) *tr* verkaufen; (*at auction*) versteigern; (*wares*) führen; **be sold on** (coll) begeistert sein von; **s. dirt cheap** verramschen; **s. s.o. on s.th.** (coll) j-n zu etw überreden; **s. out** ausverkaufen; (*betray*) verraten; **s. short** (st. exch.) in blanko verkaufen ‖ *intr* sich verkaufen; **s. for** verkauft werden für; **s. short** fixen

seller [′sɛlər] *s* Verkäufer –in *mf*; **good s.** (com) Reißer *m*

Seltzer [′sɛltsər] *s* Selterswasser *n*

selvage [′sɛlvɪdʒ] *s* (*of fabric*) Salleiste *f*; (*of a lock*) Eckplatte *f*

semantic [sɪ′mæntɪk] *adj* semantisch ‖ **semantics** *s* Wortbedeutungslehre *f*

semaphore [′sɛməˌfor] *s* Winkzeichen *n*; (rr) Semaphor *m* ‖ *intr* winken

semblance [′sɛmbləns] *s* Anschein *m*

semen [′simən] *s* Samen *m*

semicircle [′sɛmɪˌsʌrkəl] *s* Halbkreis *m*

semicolon [′sɛmɪˌkolən] *s* Strichpunkt *m*

semiconductor [ˌsɛmɪkən′dʌktər] *s* Halbleiter *m*

semiconscious [ˌsɛmɪ′kanʃəs] *adj* halbbewußt

semifinal [ˌsemɪˈfaɪnəl] *adj* Halbfinale– || *s* Halbfinale *n*, Vorschlußrunde *f*

seminar [ˈsemɪˌnɑr] *s* Seminar *n*

seminarian [ˌsemɪˈnerɪən] *s* Seminarist *m*

seminary [ˈsemɪˌnerɪ] *s* Seminar *n*

semiprecious [ˌsemɪˈpreʃəs] *adj* halbedel

Semite [ˈsemaɪt] *s* Semit –in *mf*

Semitic [sɪˈmɪtɪk] *adj* semitisch

semitrailer [ˈsemɪˌtreɪlər] *s* Schleppanhänger *m*

senate [ˈsenɪt] *s* Senat *m*

senator [ˈsenətər] *s* Senator *m*

senatorial [ˌsenəˈtorɪəl] *adj* (*of one senator*) senatorisch; (*of the senate*) Senats–

send [send] *v* (*pret & pp* sent [sent]) *tr* schicken, senden; (*rad, telv*) senden; **s. back** zurückschicken; **s. back word** zurücksagen lassen; **s. down** (*box*) niederschlagen; **s. forth** (*leaves*) treiben; **s. off** absenden; **s. on** (*forward*) weiterbefördern; **s. word that** benachrichtigen, daß || *intr* **s. for** (*e.g., free samples*) bestellen; (*e.g., a doctor*) rufen lassen

sender [ˈsendər] *s* Absender –in *mf*; (*telg*) Geber –in *mf*

send′-off′ *s* Abschiedsfeier *f*

senile [ˈsinaɪl] *adj* senil

senility [sɪˈnɪlɪtɪ] *s* Senilität *f*

senior [ˈsinjər] *adj* (*in age*) älter; (*in rank*) ranghöher; (*class*) oberste; **Mr. John Smith Senior** Herr John Smith senior || *s* Älteste *mf*; (*student*) Student –in *mf* im letzten Studienjahr

sen′ior cit′izen *s* bejahrter Mitbürger *m*

seniority [sinˈjɑrɪtɪ] *s* Dienstalter *n*

sen′ior of′ficer *s* Vorgesetzte *m*

sen′ior part′ner *s* geschäftsführender Partner *m*

sen′ior year′ *s* letztes Studienjahr *n*

sensation [senˈseʃən] *s* (*feeling*) Gefühl *n*; (*cause of interest*) Sensation *f*

sensational [senˈseʃənəl] *adj* sensationell

sensationalism [senˈseʃənəˌlɪzəm] *s* Sensationsgier *f*

sense [sens] *s* (*e.g., of sight; meaning*) Sinn *m*; (*feeling*) Gefühl *n*; (*common sense*) Verstand *m*; **be out of one's senses** von Sinnen sein; **bring s.o. to his senses** j–n zur Vernunft bringen; **in a s.** in gewissem Sinne; **in the broadest s.** im weitesten Sinne; **make s.** Sinn haben; **there's no s. to it** da steckt kein Sinn drin || *tr* spüren, fühlen

senseless [ˈsenslɪs] *adj* sinnlos; (*from a blow*) bewußtlos

sense′ of direc′tion *s* Ortssinn *m*

sense′ of du′ty *s* Pflichtgefühl *n*

sense′ of guilt′ *s* Schuldgefühl *n*

sense′ of hear′ing *s* Gehör *n*

sense′ of hon′or *s* Ehrgefühl *n*

sense′ of hu′mor *s* Humor *m*

sense′ of jus′tice *s* Gerechtigkeitsgefühl *n*

sense′ of responsibil′ity *s* Verantwortungsbewußtsein *n*

sense′ of sight′ *s* Gesichtssinn *m*

sense′ of smell′ *s* Geruchssinn *m*

sense′ of taste′ *s* Geschmackssinn *m*

sense′ of touch′ *s* Tastsinn *m*

sense′ or′gan *s* Sinnesorgan *n*

sensibility [ˌsensɪˈbɪlɪtɪ] *s* Empfindlichkeit *f*

sensible [ˈsensɪbəl] *adj* vernünftig

sensitive [ˈsensɪtɪv] *adj* (*to, e.g., cold*) empfindlich (gegen); (*touchy*) überempfindlich; **s. post** Vertrauensposten *m*; **very s.** überempfindlich

sensitize [ˈsensɪˌtaɪz] *tr* (phot) lichtempfindlich machen

sensory [ˈsensərɪ] *adj* Sinnes–

sen′sory depriva′tion *s* Reizentzug *m*

sensual [ˈsenʃʊəl] *adj* sinnlich

sensuality [ˌsenʃʊˈælɪtɪ] *s* Sinnlichkeit *f*, Sinnenlust *f*

sensuous [ˈsenʃʊəs] *adj* sinnlich

sentence [ˈsentəns] *s* (gram) Satz *m*; (jur) Urteil *n*; **pronounce s.** das Urteil verkünden || *tr* verurteilen

sentiment [ˈsentɪmənt] *s* Empfindung *f*

sentimental [ˌsentɪˈmentəl] *adj* sentimental, rührselig

sentinel [ˈsentɪnəl] *s* Posten *m*; **stand s.** Wache stehen

sentry [ˈsentrɪ] *s* Wachposten *m*

sen′try box′ *s* Schilderhaus *n*

separable [ˈsepərəbəl] *adj* trennbar

separate [ˈsepərɪt] *adj* getrennt; **under s. cover** separat || [ˈsepəˌret] *tr* trennen; (*segregate*) absondern; (*scatter*) zerstreuen; (*discharge*) entlassen; **s. into** teilen in (*acc*) || *intr* sich trennen, sich scheiden

sep′arated *adj* (*couple*) getrennt

separation [ˌsepəˈreʃən] *s* Trennung *f*

September [sepˈtembər] *s* September *m*

sep′tic tank′ [ˈseptɪk] *s* Kläranlage *f*

sepulcher [ˈsepəlkər] *s* Grabmal *n*

sequel [ˈsikwəl] *s* Fortsetzung *f*; (fig) Nachspiel *n*

sequence [ˈsikwəns] *s* Reihenfolge *f*

se′quence of tens′es *s* Zeitenfolge *f*

sequester [sɪˈkwestər] *tr* (*remove*) entfernen; (*separate*) absondern; (jur) sequestrieren

sequins [ˈsikwɪnz] *spl* Flitter *m*

ser–aph [ˈseræf] *s* (–aphs & –aphim [əfɪm]) Seraph *m*

Serb [sʌrb] *adj* serbisch || *s* Serbe *m*, Serbin *f*

Serbia [ˈsʌrbɪ·ə] *s* Serbien *n*

serenade [ˌserəˈned] *s* Ständchen *n* || *tr* ein Ständchen bringen (*dat*)

serene [sɪˈrin] *adj* heiter; (*sea*) ruhig

serenity [sɪˈrentɪ] *s* Heiterkeit *f*

serf [sʌrf] *s* Leibeigene *mf*

serfdom [ˈsʌrfdəm] *s* Leibeigenschaft *f*

serge [sʌrdʒ] *s* (tex) Serge *f*

sergeant [ˈsɑrdʒənt] *s* Feldwebel *m*

ser′geant-at-arms′ *s* (sergeants-at-arms) Ordnungsbeamter *m*

ser′geant first′ class′ *s* Oberfeldwebel *m*

ser′geant ma′jor *s* (**sergeant majors**) Hauptfeldwebel *m*

serial [′sɪrɪ·əl] *s* Fortsetzungsroman *m*, Romanfolge *f*

serialize [′sɪrɪ·ə‚laɪz] *tr* in Fortsetzungen veröffentlichen

se′rial num′ber *s* laufende Nummer *f*; (*of a product*) Fabriknummer *f*

se·ries [′sɪriz] *s* (**–ries**) Serie *f*, Reihe *f*; **in s.** reihenweise; (**elec**) hintereinandergeschaltet

serious [′sɪrɪ·əs] *adj* ernst; (*mistake*) schwerwiegend; (*illness*) gefährlich

seriously [′sɪrɪ·əsli] *adv* ernstlich; **s. wounded** schwerverwundet; **take s.** ernst nehmen

seriousness [′sɪrɪ·əsnɪs] *s* Ernst *m*

sermon [′sʌrmən] *s* Predigt *f*

sermonize [′sʌrmə‚naɪz] *intr* e–e Moralpredigt halten

serpent [′sʌrpənt] *s* Schlange *f*

serrated [′seretɪd] *adj* sägeartig

se·rum [′sɪrəm] *s* (**–rums & –ra** [rə]) Serum *n*

servant [′sʌrvənt] *s* Diener –in *mf*; (*domestic*) Hausdiener –in *mf*

serv′ant girl′ *s* Dienstmädchen *n*

serve [sʌrv] *s* (tennis) Aufschlag *m* ‖ *tr* (*a master, God*) dienen (*dat*); (*food*) servieren; (*a meal*) anrichten; (*guests*) bedienen; (*time in jail*) verbüßen; (*one's term in the service*) abdienen; (*the purpose*) erfüllen; (tennis) aufschlagen; **s. mass** (eccl) zur Messe dienen; **s. notice on s.o.** j–n vorladen; **s. up** (*food*) auftragen ‖ *intr* (**& mil**) dienen; (*at table*) servieren; **s. as** dienen als; **s. on a committe** e–m Ausschuß angehören

server [′sʌrvər] *s* (eccl) Ministrant *m*; (tennis) Aufschläger *m*

service [′sʌrvɪs] *s* (*diplomatic, secret, foreign, public, etc.*) Dienst *m*; (*in a restaurant*) Bedienung *f*; (*set of table utensils*) Besteck *n*; (*set of dishes*) Service *n*; (*assistance at a repair shop*) Service *m*; (*maintenance*) Wartung *f*; (*transportation*) Verkehr *m*; (relig) Gottesdienst *m*; (tennis) Aufschlag *m*; **at your s.** zu Ihren Diensten; **be in s.** (mach) in Betrieb sein; **be in the s.** (mil) beim Militär sein; **be of s.** behilflich sein; **do s.o. a s.** j–m e–n Dienst erweisen; **essential services** lebenswichtige Betriebe *pl*; **fit for active s.** kriegsverwendungsfähig; **see s.** Kriegsdienst tun; **the services** die Waffengattungen *pl* ‖ *tr* (mach) warten

serviceable [′sʌrvɪsəbəl] *adj* (*usable*) verwendungsfähig; (*helpful*) nützlich; (*durable*) haltbar

serv′ice club′ *s* (mil) Soldatenklub *m*

serv′ice en′trance *s* Dienstboteneingang *m*

serv′ice·man′ *s* (**–men′**) Monteur *m*; (*at a gas station*) Tankwart *m*; (mil) Soldat *m*

serv′ice rec′ord *s* Wehrpaß *m*

serv′ice sta′tion *s* Tankstelle *f*

serv′ice-station atten′dant *s* Tankwart *m*

serv′ice troops′ *spl* Versorgungstruppen *pl*

servile [′sʌrvaɪl] *adj* kriecherisch

serv′ing *s* Portion *f*; (*e.g., of a subpoena*) Zustellung *f*

serv′ing cart′ *s* Servierwagen *m*

servitude [′sʌrvɪ‚t(j)ud] *s* Knechtschaft *f*

ses′ame seed′ [′sesəmi] *s* Sesamsamen *m*

session [′seʃən] *s* Sitzung *f*, Tagung *f*; (educ) Semester *n*; **be in session** tagen

set [set] *adj* (*price, time*) festgesetzt; (*rule*) festgelegt; (*speech*) wohlüberlegt; **be all set** fix und fertig sein; **be set in one's ways** festgefahren sein ‖ *s* (*group of things belonging together*) Satz *m*, Garnitur *f*; (*of chess or checkers*) Spiel *n*; (*clique*) Sippschaft *f*; (rad, telv) Apparat *m*; (*tennis*) Satz *m*; (theat) Bühnenbild *n*; **younger set** Nachwuchs *m* ‖ *v* (*pret & pp* **set;** *ger* **setting**) *tr* (*put*) setzen; (*stand*) stellen; (*lay*) legen; (*a clock, a trap*) stellen; (*the hair*) legen; (*a record*) aufstellen; (*an example*) geben; (*a time, price*) festsetzen; (*the table*) decken; (*jewels*) (ein)fassen; (*a camera*) einstellen; (surg) einrenken; (typ) setzen; **set ahead** (*a clock*) vorstellen; **set back** (*a clock*) nachstellen; (*a patient*) zurückwerfen; **set down** niedersetzen; **set down in writing** schriftlich niederlegen; **set foot in** (or **on**) betreten; **set forth** (*explain*) erklären; **set free** freilassen; **set in order** in Ordnung bringen; **set limits to** Schranken setzen (*dat*); **set off** (*a bomb*) sprengen lassen; **set** (*s.o.*) **over** (j–n) überordnen (*dat*); **set right** wieder in Ordnung bringen; **set store by** Gewicht beimessen (*dat*); **set straight** (on) aufklären (über *acc*); **set the meeting for two** die Versammlung auf zwei Uhr ansetzen; **set up** (*at the bar*) (coll) zu e–m Gläschen einladen; (mach) montieren; (typ) (ab)setzen; **set up housekeeping** Wirtschaft führen; **set up in business** etablieren ‖ *intr* (*said of cement*) abbinden; (astr) untergehen; **set about** (*ger*) darangehen zu (*inf*); **set in** einsetzen; **set out** (for) sich auf den Weg machen (nach); **set out on** (*a trip*) antreten; **set to work** sich an die Arbeit machen

set′back′ *s* Rückschlag *m*, Schlappe *f*

set′screw′ *s* Stellschraube *f*

settee [se′ti] *s* Polsterbank *f*

setter [′setər] *s* Vorstehhund *m*

set′ting *s* (*of the sun*) Niedergang *m*; (*of a story*) Ort *m* der Handlung; (*of a gem*) Fassung *f*; (theat) Bühnenbild *n*

settle [′setəl] *tr* (*conclude*) erledigen; (*decide*) entscheiden; (*an argument*) schlichten; (*a problem*) erledigen; (*an account*) begleichen; (*one's affairs*) in Ordnung bringen; (*a creditor's claim*) befriedigen; (*a lawsuit*) durch Vergleich beilegen; (*a region*) besiedeln; (*people*) ansiedeln ‖ *intr* (*in a region*) sich niederlassen; (*said of a building*) sich senken; (*said of a ship*) absacken; (*said of dust*) sich legen; (*said of a liquid*) sich klären; (*said of suspended particles*) sich setzen; (*said of a cold*) (in) sich festsetzen (in *dat*); s. down (*in a chair*) sich niederlassen; (*calm down*) sich beruhigen; s. down to (e.g., *work*) sich machen an (*acc*); s. for sich einigen auf (*acc*); s. on sich entscheiden für; s. up (*fin*) die Verbindlichkeit vergleichen

settlement ['setəlmənt] *s* (*colony*) Siedlung *f*; (*agreement*) Abkommen *n*; (*of an argument*) Beilegung *f*; (*of accounts*) Abrechnung *f*; (*of a debt*) Begleichung *f*; reach a s. e-n Vergleich schließen

settler ['setlər] *s* Ansiedler –in *mf*

set'up' *s* Aufbau *m*, Anlage *f*

seven ['sevən] *adj & pron* sieben ‖ *s* Sieben *f*

seventeen ['sevən'tin] *adj & pron* siebzehn ‖ *s* Siebzehn *f*

seventeenth ['sevən'tinθ] *adj & pron* siebzehnte ‖ *s* (*fraction*) Siebzehntel *n*; the s. (*in dates or a series*) der Siebzehnte

seventh ['sevənθ] *adj & pron* sieb(en)te ‖ *s* (*fraction*) Sieb(en)tel *n*; the s. (*in dates or a series*) der Sieb(en)te

seventieth ['sevəntɪ‧ɪθ] *adj & pron* siebzigste ‖ *s* (*fraction*) Siebzigstel *n*

seventy ['sevənti] *adj & pron* siebzig ‖ *s* Siebzig *f*; the seventies die siebziger Jahre

sev'enty-first' *adj & pron* einundsiebzigste

sev'enty-one' *adj* einundsiebzig

sever ['sevər] *tr* (ab)trennen; (*relations*) abbrechen

several ['sevərəl] *adj & indef pron* mehrere; s. times mehrmals

severance ['sevərəns] *s* Trennung *f*; (*of relations*) Abbruch *m*

sev'erance pay' *s* (& *mil*) Abfindungsentschädigung *f*

severe [sɪ'vɪr] *adj* (*judge, winter, cold*) streng; (*blow, sentence, winter*) hart; (*illness, test*) schwer; (*criticism*) scharf

severity [sɪ'verɪti] *s* Strenge *f*; Härte *f*; Schärfe *f*

sew [so] *v* (*pret* sewed; *pp* sewed & sewn) *tr & intr* nähen

sewage ['su‧ɪdʒ] *s* Abwässer *pl*

sew'age-dispos'al plant' *s* Kläranlage *f*

sewer ['su‧ər] *s* Kanal *m* ‖ ['so‧ər] *s* Näher –in *mf*

sewerage ['su‧ərɪdʒ] *s* Kanalisation *f*

sew'er pipe' ['su‧ər] *s* Abwasserleitung *f*

sew'ing *s* Näharbeit *f*

sew'ing bas'ket *s* Nähkasten *m*

sew'ing kit' *s* Nähzeug *n*

sew'ing machine' *s* Nähmaschine *f*

sex [seks] *adj* (*crime, education, harmone*) Sexual– ‖ *s* Geschlecht *n*; (*intercourse*) Sex *m*

sex appeal' *s* Sex-Appeal *m*

sex' pot' *s* (coll) Sexbombe *f*

sextent ['sekstənt] *s* Sextant *m*

sexton ['sekstən] *s* Küster *m*

sexual ['sekʃʊ‧əl] *adj* geschlechtlich, Geschlechts–, sexuell

sex'ual in'tercourse *s* Geschlechtsverkehr *m*

sexuality [sekʃʊ'ælɪti] *s* Sexualität *f*

sexy ['seksi] *adj* sexy

shabbily ['ʃæbɪli] *adv* schäbig; (*in treatment*) stiefmütterlich

shabby ['ʃæbi] *adj* schäbig

shack [ʃæk] *s* Bretterbude *f*

shackle ['ʃækəl] *s* (naut) Schäkel *m*; shackles Fesseln *pl* ‖ *tr* fesseln

shad [ʃæd] *s* Shad *m*, Alse *f*

shade [ʃed] *s* Schatten *m*; (*for a window*) Rollo *n*; (*for a lamp*) Schirm *m*; (*hue*) Schattierung *f*; throw into the s. (fig) in den Schatten stellen ‖ *tr* beschatten; (paint) schattieren

shad'ing *s* Schattierung *f*

shadow ['ʃædo] *s* Schatten *m* ‖ *tr* (a *person*) beschatten

shad'ow box'ing *s* Schattenboxen *n*

shadowy ['ʃædo‧i] *adj* (*like a shadow*) schattenhaft; (*indistinct*) verschwommen; (*shady*) schattig

shady ['ʃedi] *adj* schattig; (coll) dunkel; s. character Dunkelmann *m*; s. deal Lumperei *f*; s. side (& fig) Schattenseite *f*

shaft [ʃæft] *s* Schaft *m*; (*of an elevator*) Schacht *m*; (*handle*) Stiel *m*; (*of a wagon*) Deichsel *f*; (*of a column*) Säulenschaft *m*; (*of a transmission*) Welle *f*

shaggy ['ʃægi] *adj* zottig, struppig

shake [ʃek] *s* Schütteln *n*; he's no great shakes mit ihm ist nicht viel los ‖ *v* (*pret* shook [ʃuk]; *pp* shaken) *tr* schütteln; s. a leg! (coll) rühr dich ein bißchen; s. before using vor Gebrauch schütteln; s. down (sl) erpressen; s. hands sich [*dat*] die Hand geben; s. hands with s.o. j–m die Hand drücken; s. off (& fig) abschütteln; s. one's head mit dem Kopf schütteln; s. out (a *rug*) ausschütteln; s. up aufschütteln; (fig) aufrütteln ‖ *intr* (with) zittern (vor *dat*), beben (vor *dat*)

shake'down' *s* (sl) Erpressung *f*

shake'down cruise' *s* Probefahrt *f*

shaker ['ʃekər] *s* (*for salt*) Streuer *m*; (*for cocktails*) Shaker *m*

shake'-up' *s* Umgruppierung *f*

shaky ['ʃeki] *adj* (& fig) wacklig

shale [ʃel] *s* Schiefer *m*

shale' oil' *s* Schieferöl *n*

shall [ʃæl] *v* (*pret* should [ʃʊd]) *aux* (to express future tense) werden, e.g., I s. go ich werde gehen; (to express obligation) sollen, e.g., s. I stay? soll ich bleiben?

shallow ['ʃælo] *adj* (*river, person*) seicht; (*water, bowl*) flach ‖ shallows *spl* Untiefe *f*

sham [ʃæm] *adj* Schein– ‖ *s* Schein *m* ‖ *v* (*pret & pp* shammed; *ger* shamming) *tr* vortäuschen

sham′ bat′tle s Scheingefecht n

shambles [′ʃæmbəlz] s Trümmerhaufen m

shame [ʃem] s Schande f; (feeling of shame) Scham f; **put s.o. to s.** (outdo s.o.) j–n in den Schatten stellen; **s. on you!** schäm dich!; **what a s.!** wie schade! || tr beschämen

shame′faced′ adj verschämt

shameful [′ʃemfəl] adj schändlich

shameless [′ʃemlɪs] adj unverschämt

shampoo [ʃæm′pu] s Shampoo n || tr shampoonieren

shamrock [′ʃæmrɑk] s Kleeblatt n

Shanghai [ʃæŋ′haɪ] s Shanghai n || **shanghai** [′ʃæŋhaɪ] tr schanghaien

shank [ʃæŋk] s Unterschenkel m; (of an anchor, column, golf club) Schaft m; (cut of meat) Schenkel m

shanty [′ʃænti] s Bude f

shan′tytown′ s Bretterbudensiedlung f

shape [ʃep] s Form f, Gestalt f; (coll) in schlechter Form; **in good s.** in gutem Zustand; **out of s.** aus der Form; **take s.** sich gestalten || tr formen, gestalten || intr—**s. up** (coll) sich zusammenfassen

shapeless [′ʃeplɪs] adj formlos

shapely [′ʃepli] adj wohlgestaltet

share [ʃɛr] s Anteil m; (st. exch.) Aktie f; **do one's s.** das Seine tun || tr teilen || intr—**s. in** teilhaben an (dat)

share′hold′er s Aktionär –in mf

shark [ʃɑrk] s Hai m, Haifisch m

sharp [ʃɑrp] adj scharf; (pointed) spitzig; (keen) pfiffig || adv pünktlich || s (mus) Kreuz n

sharpen [′ʃɑrpən] tr schärfen; (a pencil) spitzen

sharply [′ʃɑrpli] adv scharf

sharp′shoot′er s Scharfschütze m

shatter [′ʃætər] tr zersplittern; (the nerves) zerrütten; (dreams) zerstören || intr zersplittern

shat′terproof′ adj splittersicher

shave [ʃev] s—**get a s.** sich rasieren lassen || tr rasieren || intr sich rasieren

shav′ing brush′ s Rasierpinsel m

shav′ing cream′ s Rasierkrem m

shav′ing mug′ s Rasiernapf m

shawl [ʃɔl] s Schal m

she [ʃi] s Weibchen n || pers pron sie

sheaf [ʃif] s (sheaves [ʃivz]) Garbe f

shear [ʃɪr] s—**shears** Schere f || v (pret sheared; pp sheared & shorn [ʃorn]) tr scheren; **s. off** abschneiden

sheath [ʃiθ] s Scheide f

sheathe [ʃið] tr in die Scheide stecken

shed [ʃɛd] s Schuppen m || v (pret & pp shed; ger shedding) tr (leaves) abwerfen; (tears) vergießen; (hair, leaves) verlieren; (peace) verbreiten; **s. light on** (fig) Licht werfen auf (acc)

sheen [ʃin] s Glanz m

sheep [ʃip] s (sheep) Schaf n

sheep′dog′ s Schäferhund m

sheep′fold′ s Schafhürde f, Schafpferch m

sheepish [′ʃipɪʃ] adj (embarrassed) verlegen; (timid) schüchtern

sheep′skin′ s Schaffell n; (coll) Diplom n

sheep′skin coat′ s Schafpelz m

sheer [ʃɪr] adj rein; (tex) durchsichtig; **by s. force** durch bloße Gewalt || intr—**s. off** (naut) abscheren

sheet [ʃit] s (for the bed) Leintuch n; (of paper) Blatt n, Bogen m; (of metal) Blech n; (naut) Segelleine f; **come down in sheets** (fig) in Strömen regnen; **s. of ice** Glatteis n; **s. of flame** Feuermeer n

sheet′ i′ron s Eisenblech n

sheet′ mu′sic s Notenblatt n

she′-goat′ s Ziege f

sheik [ʃik] s Scheich m

shelf [ʃelf] s (shelves [ʃelvz]) Regal n; **put on the s.** (fig) auf die lange Bank schieben

shell [ʃel] s Schale f; (conch) Muschel f; (of a snail) Gehäuse n; (of a tortoise) Panzer m; (explosive) Granate f; (bullet) Patrone f || tr (eggs) schälen; (nuts) aufknacken; (mil) beschießen; **s. out money** (coll) mit dem Geld herausrücken || intr—**s. out** (coll) blechen

shel·lac [ʃə′læk] s Schellack m || v (pret & pp –lacked; ger –lacking) tr mit Schellack streichen; (sl) verdreschen

shell′fish′ s Schalentier n

shell′ hole′ s Granattrichter m

shell′ shock′ s Bombenneurose f

shelter [′ʃeltər] s Obdach n; (fig) Schutz m || tr schützen

shelve [ʃelv] tr auf ein Regal stellen; (fig) auf die lange Bank schieben

shenanigans [ʃɪ′nænɪgənz] spl Possen pl

shepherd [′ʃepərd] s Hirt m; (fig) Seelenhirt m || tr hüten

shep′herd dog′ s Schäferhund m

shepherdess [′ʃepərdɪs] s Hirtin f

sherbet [′ʃɑrbət] s Speiseeis n

sheriff [′ʃerɪf] s Sheriff m

sherry [′ʃeri] s Sherry m

shield [ʃild] s Schild m; (fig) Schutz m; (rad) Röhrenabschirmung f || tr (from) schützen (vor dat); (elec, mach) abschirmen

shift [ʃɪft] adj (worker, work) Schicht– || s Schicht f; (change) Verschiebung f; (loose-fitting dress) Kittelkleid n || tr (a meeting) verschieben; (the blame) (on) (ab)schieben (auf acc); **s. gears** umschalten || intr (said of the wind) umspringen; **s. for oneself** sich allein durchschlagen; **s. into second gear** in den zweiten Gang umschalten

shift′ key′ s Umschalttaste f

shiftless [′ʃɪftlɪs] adj träge

shifty [′ʃɪfti] adj schlau, gerissen

shimmer [′ʃɪmər] s Schimmer m || intr schimmern, flimmern

shin [ʃɪn] s Schienbein n

shin′bone′ s Schienbein n

shine [ʃaɪn] s Schein m, Glanz m || v (pret & pp shined) tr polieren; (shoes) wichsen || v (pret & pp shone [ʃon]) intr scheinen; (said of the *eyes*) leuchten; (*be outstanding*) (**in**) glänzen (**in** *dat*)

shiner ['ʃaɪnər] *s* (sl) blaues Auge *n*

shingle ['ʃɪŋgəl] *s* (*for a roof*) Schindel *f*; (*e.g., of a doctor*) Aushängeschild *n* || *tr* mit Schindeln decken

shin'ing *adj* (*eyes*) leuchtend, strahlend; (*example*) glänzend

shiny ['ʃaɪni] *adj* blank, glänzend

ship [ʃɪp] *s* Schiff *n* || *v* (*pret & pp* **shipped**; *ger* **shipping**) *tr* senden; **s. water** (*of a doctor*) Sturzsee bekommen || *intr*—**s. out** absegeln

ship'board' *s* Bord *m*; **on s.** an Bord

ship'build'er *s* Schiffbauer *m*

ship'build'ing *s* Schiffbau *m*

shipment ['ʃɪpmənt] *s* Lieferung *f*

ship'ping *s* Absendung *f*, Verladung *f*; (*ships*) Schiffe *pl*

ship'ping clerk' *s* Expedient –in *mf*

ship'ping depart'ment *s* Versandabteilung *f*

ship'shape' *adj* ordentlich

ship'wreck' *s* Schiffbruch *m* || *tr* scheitern lassen; **be s.** schiffbrüchig sein || *intr* Schiffbruch erleiden

ship'yard' *s* Werft *f*

shirk [ʃɪrk] *tr* sich drücken vor (*dat*) || *intr* (**from**) sich drücken (vor *dat*)

shirt [ʃʌrt] *s* Hemd *n*; **keep your s. on!** (sl) regen Sie sich nicht auf!

shirt'col'lar *s* Hemdkragen *m*

shirt'sleeve' *s* Hemdsärmel *m*

shirttail' *s* Hemdschoß *m*

shit [ʃɪt] *s* (vulg) Scheiße *f* || *v* (*pret & pp* **shit**) *tr & intr* (vulg) scheißen

shiver ['ʃɪvər] *s* Schauder *m* || *intr* (**at**) schaudern (vor *dat*); (**with**) zittern (vor *dat*)

shoal [ʃol] *s* Untiefe *f*

shock [ʃɑk] *s* Schock *m*; (*of hair*) Schopf *m*; (agr) Schober *m*; (elec) Schlag *m* || *tr* schockieren; (elec) e-n Schlag versetzen (*dat*)

shock' absorb'er [æb,sɔrbər] *s* Stoßdämpfer *m*

shock'ing *adj* schockierend

shock' troops' *spl* Stoßtruppen *pl*

shock' wave' *s* Stoßwelle *f*

shoddy ['ʃɑdi] *adj* schäbig

shoe [ʃu] *s* Schuh *m* || *v* (*pret & pp* **shod** [ʃɑd]) *tr* beschlagen

shoe'horn' *s* Schuhlöffel *m*

shoe'lace' *s* Schuhband *n*, Schnürsenkel *m*

shoe'mak'er *s* Schuster *m*

shoe' pol'ish *s* Schuhwichse *f*

shoe'shine' *s* Schuhputzen *n*

shoe' store' *s* Schuhladen *m*

shoe' string' *s* Schuhband *m*; **on a s.** mit ein paar Groschen

shoe'tree' *s* Schuhspanner *m*

shoo [ʃu] *tr* (**away**) wegscheuchen || *interj* sch!

shook-up ['ʃuk,ʌp] *adj* (coll) verdattert

shoot [ʃut] *s* Schößling *m* || *v* (*pret & pp* **shot** [ʃɑt]) *tr* (an)schießen, (ab)schießen; (*kill*) erschießen; (*dice*) schießen; (cin) drehen; (phot) aufnehmen; **s. down** (aer) abschießen; **s. up** (*e.g., a town*) zusammenschie-

ßen || *intr* schießen; **s. at** schießen auf (*acc*); **s. by** vorbeisausen an (*dat*); **s. up** (*in growth*) aufschießen; (*said of flames*) emporschlagen; (*said of prices*) emporschnellen

shoot'ing *s* Schießerei *f*; (*execution*) Erschießung *f*; (*of a film*) Drehen *n*

shoot'ing gal'lery *s* Schießbude *f*

shoot'ing match' *s* Preisschießen *n*

shoot'ing star' *s* Sternschnuppe *f*

shoot'ing war' *s* heißer Krieg *m*

shop [ʃɑp] *s* Laden *m*, Geschäft *n*; **talk s.** fachsimpeln || *v* (*pret & pp* **shopped**; *ger* **shopping**) *intr* einkaufen; **go shopping** einkaufen gehen; **s. around for** sich in einigen Läden umsehen nach

shop'girl' *s* Ladenmädchen *n*

shop'keep'er *s* Ladeninhaber –in *mf*

shoplifter ['ʃɑp,lɪftər] *s* Ladendieb –in *mf*

shop'lift'ing *s* Ladendiebstahl *m*

shopper ['ʃɑpər] *s* Einkäufer –in *mf*

shop'ping *s* Einkaufen *n*; (*purchases*) Einkäufe *pl*

shop'ping bag' *s* Einkaufstasche *f*

shop'ping cen'ter *s* Einkaufcenter *n*

shop'ping dis'trict *s* Geschäftsviertel *n*

shop'ping spree' *s* Einkaufsorgie *f*

shop'talk' *s* Fachsimpelei *f*

shop'win'dow *s* Schaufenster *n*

shop'worn' *adj* (fig) abgerissen

shore [ʃor] *s* Küste *f*; (*beach*) Strand *m*; (*of a river*) Ufer *n*; **go to the s.** ans Meer fahren || *tr*—**s. up** abstützen

shore' leave' *s* Landurlaub *m*

shore' line' *s* Küstenlinie *f*; (*of a river*) Uferlinie *f*

shore' patrol' *s* Küstenstreife *f*

short [ʃɔrt] *adj* kurz; (*person*) klein; (*loan*) kurzfristig; **a s. time ago** vor kurzem; **be s. of,** e.g., **I am s. of bread** das Brot geht mir aus; **be s. with s.o.** j–n kurz abfertigen; **cut s.** abbrechen; **fall s. of** zurückbleiben hinter (*dat*); **get the s. end das Nachsehen haben;** **I am three marks s.** es fehlen mir drei Mark; **in s.** kurzum; **s. of breath** außer Atem; **s. of cash** knapp bei Kasse || *s* (cin) Kurzfilm *m*; (elec) Kurzschluß *m* || *tr* (elec) kurzschließen

shortage ['ʃɔrtɪdʒ] *s* (**of**) Mangel *m* (**an** *dat*); (com) Minderbetrag *m*

short'cake' *s* Mürbekuchen *m*

short'-change' *tr* zu wenig Wechselgeld herausgeben (*dat*); (fig) betrügen

short' cir'cuit *s* Kurzschluß *m*

short'-cir'cuit *tr* kurzschließen

short'com'ing *s* Fehler *m*, Mangel *m*

short'cut' *s* Abkürzung *f*; **take a s.** den Weg abkürzen

shorten ['ʃɔrtən] *tr* abkürzen

short'ening *s* Abkürzung *f*; (culin) Backfett *n*

short'hand' *adj* stenographisch || *s* Stenographie *f*; **in s.** stenographisch; **take down in s.** stenographieren

short-lived ['ʃɔrt'laɪvd] *adj* kurzlebig

shortly ['ʃɔrtli] *adv* in kurzem; **s. after** kurz nach

short'-or'der cook' s Schnellimbißkoch m, Schnellimbißköchin f

short'-range' adj Nah-, auf kurze Sicht

shorts [ʃɔrts] s (underwear) Unterhose f; (walking shorts) kurze Hose f; (sport) Sporthose f

short'-sight'ed adj kurzsichtig

short' sto'ry s Novelle f

short'-tem'pered adj leicht aufbrausend

short'-term' adj kurzfristig

short'wave' adj Kurzwellen- || s Kurzwelle f

short'wind'ed adj kurzatmig

shot [ʃat] adj kaputt; (drunk) (sl) besoffen; my nerves are s. ich bin mit meinen Nerven ganz herunter || s Schuß m; (shooter) Schütze m; (pellets) Schrot m; (injection) Spritze f; (snapshot) Aufnahme f; (of liquor) Gläschen n; be a good s. gut schießen; s. in the arm (fig) Belebungsspritze f; s. in the dark Sprung m ins Ungewisse; take a s. at e-n Schuß abgeben auf (acc); (fig) versuchen; wild s. Schuß m ins Blaue

shot'gun' s Schrotflinte f

shot'gun wed'ding s Mußehe f

shot'-put' s (sport) Kugelstoßen n

should [ʃʊd] aux (to express softened affirmation) I s. like to know ich möchte wissen; I s. think so das will ich meinen; (to express obligation) how s. I know? wie sollte ich das wissen?; you shouldn't do that Sie sollten das nicht tun; (in conditional clauses) if it s. rain tomorrow wenn es morgen regnen sollte

shoulder ['ʃoldər] s Schulter f, Achsel f; (of a road) Bankett n; have broad shoulders e-n breiten Rücken haben || tr (a rifle) schultern; (responsibility) auf sich nehmen

shoul'der bag' s Umhängetasche f

shoul'der blade' s Schulterblatt n

shoul'der strap' s (of underwear) Trägerband n; (mil) Schulterriemen m

shout [ʃaʊt] s Schrei m, Ruf m || tr schreien, rufen; s. down (coll) niederschreien || intr schreien, rufen

shove [ʃʌv] s Stoß m; give s.o. a s. j-m e-n Stoß versetzen || tr stoßen; (e.g., furniture) rücken; s. around (coll) herumschubsen; s. forward vorschieben || intr drängeln; s. off (coll) abschieben; (naut) vom Land abstoßen

shov-el ['ʃʌvəl] s Schaufel f || v (pret & pp -el[l]ed; ger -el[l]ing) tr schaufeln

show [ʃo] s (exhibition) Ausstellung f; (outer appearance) Schau f; (spectacle) Theater n; (cin, theat) Vorstellung f; by s. of hands durch Handzeichen; make a s. of s.th. mit etw Staat machen; only for s. nur zur Schau || v (pret showed; pp shown [ʃon] & showed) tr zeigen; (prove) beweisen, nachweisen; (said of evidence, tests) ergeben; (tickets, passport, papers) vorweisen; s. around (a person) herumführen; (a thing) herumzeigen || intr zu sehen sein;

(said of a slip) vorgucken; s. off (with) großtun (mit); s. up erscheinen

show' busi'ness s Unterhaltungsindustrie f

show'case' s Schaukasten m, Vitrine f

show'down' s entscheidender Wendepunkt m; (e.g., in a western) Kraftprobe f; (cards) Aufdecken n der Karten

shower ['ʃaʊ·ər] s (rain) Schauer m; (bath) Dusche f; (shower room) Duschraum m; (of stones, arrows) Hagel m; (of bullets, sparks) Regen m; (for a bride) Party f zur Überreichung der Brautgeschenke; take a s. (sich) duschen || intr (with gifts) überschütten || intr duschen; (meteor) schauern

show'er bath' s Dusche f, Brausebad n

show' girl' s Revuegirl n

show'ing s Zeigen n; (cin) Vorführung f

show'ing off' s Großtuerei f

show'man s (-men) s Schauspieler m

show'-off' s Protz m

show'piece' s Schaustück n

show'room' s Ausstellungsraum m

show' win'dow s Schaufenster n

showy ['ʃo·i] adj prunkhaft

shrapnel ['ʃræpnəl] s Schrapnell n

shred [ʃred] s Fetzen m; (least bit) Spur f; tear to shreds in Fetzen reißen; (an argument) gründlich widerlegen || v (pret & pp shredded & shred; ger shredding) tr zerfetzen; (paper) in Streifen schneiden; (culin) schnitzeln

shredder ['ʃredər] s (of paper) Reißwolf m; (culin) Schnitzelmaschine f

shrew [ʃru] s böse Sieben f

shrewd [ʃrud] adj schlau

shriek [ʃrik] s Gekreische n, gellender Schrei m || intr kreischen

shrill [ʃrɪl] adj schrill

shrimp [ʃrɪmp] s Garnele f; (coll) Knirps m

shrine [ʃraɪn] s Heiligtum n

shrink [ʃrɪŋk] v (pret shrank [ʃræŋk] & shrunk [ʃrʌŋk]; pp shrunk & shrunken) tr einlaufen lassen || intr schrumpfen; s. back from zurückschrecken vor (dat); s. from sich scheuen vor (dat); s. up einschrumpfen

shrinkage ['ʃrɪŋkɪdʒ] s Schrumpfung f

shriv-el ['ʃrɪvəl] s (pret & pp -el[l]ed; ger -el[l]ing) intr schrumpfen; s. up zusammenschrumpfen

shriv'eled adj schrumpelig

shroud [ʃraʊd] s Leichentuch n; (fig) Hülle f; (naut) Want f || tr (in) einhüllen (in acc)

shrub [ʃrʌb] s Strauch m

shrubbery ['ʃrʌbəri] s Strauchwerk n

shrug [ʃrʌg] s Zucken n || v (pret & pp shrugged; ger shrugging) tr zucken; s. off mit e-m Achselzucken abtun; s. one's shoulders mit den Achseln zucken || intr mit den Achseln zucken

shuck [ʃʌk] tr enthülsen

shudder ['ʃʌdər] s Schau(d)er m || intr

intr (at) schau(d)ern (vor *dat*); **s. at the thought of s.th.** bei dem Gedanken an etw [*acc*] zittern

shuffle ['ʃʌfəl] *s* Schlurfen *n*; (cards) Mischen *n*; **get lost in the s.** (fig) unter den Tisch fallen ‖ *tr* (cards) mischen; (*the feet*) schleifen; ‖ *intr* die Karten mischen; (*walk*) schlurfen; **s. along** latschen

shun [ʃʌn] *v* (*pret & pp* **shunned;** *ger* **shunning**) *tr* (*a person*) meiden; (*a thing*) (ver)meiden

shunt [ʃʌnt] *s* (elec) Nebenschluß *m* ‖ *tr* (*shove aside*) beiseite schieben; (**across**) parallelschalten (zu); (rr) rangieren

shut [ʃʌt] *adj* zu ‖ (*pret & pp* **shut;** *ger* **shutting**) *tr* schließen, zumachen; **be s. down** stilliegen; **s. down** stillegen; **s. off** absperren; **s. one's eyes to** hinwegsehen über (*acc*); **s. out** aussperren; **s. s.o. up** j-m den Mund stopfen ‖ *intr* sich schließen; **s. up!** (coll) halt's Maul!

shut'down' *s* Stillegung *f*

shutter ['ʃʌtər] *s* Laden *m*; (phot) Verschluß *m*

shuttle ['ʃʌtəl] *s* Schiffchen *n* ‖ *intr* pendeln, hin- und herfahren

shut'tle bus' *s* Pendelbus *m*

shut'tlecock' *s* Federball *m*

shut'tle serv'ice *s* Pendelverkehr *m*

shut'tle train' *s* Pendelzug *m*

shy [ʃaɪ] *adj* (**shyer; shyest**) schüchtern; **be a dollar shy** e-n Dollar los sein ‖ *intr* (*said of a horse*) stutzen; **shy at** zurückscheuen vor (*dat*); **shy away from** sich scheuen vor (*dat*)

shyness ['ʃaɪnɪs] *s* Scheu *f*

shyster ['ʃaɪstər] *s* Winkeladvokat *m*

Siamese' twins' [ˌsaɪ·ə'miz] *spl* Siamesische Zwillinge *pl*

Siberia [saɪ'bɪrɪ·ə] *s* Sibirien *n*

Siberian [saɪ'bɪrɪ·ən] *adj* sibirisch ‖ *s* Sibirier –in *mf*

sibilant ['sɪbɪlənt] *s* Zischlaut *m*

siblings ['sɪblɪŋz] *spl* Geschwister *pl*

sibyl ['sɪbɪl] *s* Sibylle *f*

sic [sɪk] *adv* sic ‖ *v* (*pret & pp* **sicked;** *ger* **sicking**) *tr*—**sic 'em!** (coll) faß!; **sic the dog on s.o.** den Hund auf j-n hetzen

Sicilian [sɪ'sɪljən] *adj* sizilianisch ‖ *s* Sizilianer –in *mf*

Sicily ['sɪsɪli] *s* Sizilien *n*

sick [sɪk] *adj* krank; **be s. and tired of s.th.** etw gründlich satt haben; **be s. as a dog** sich hundeelend fühlen; **I am s. to my stomach** mir ist übel; **play s.** krankfeiern

sick' bay' *s* Schiffslazarett *n*

sick'bed' *s* Krankenbett *n*

sicken ['sɪkən] *tr* krank machen; (*disgust*) anekeln ‖ *intr* krank werden

sick'ening *adj* ekelhaft

sick' head'ache *s* Kopfschmerzen *pl* mit Übelkeit

sickle ['sɪkəl] *s* Sichel *f*

sick' leave' *s* Krankenurlaub *m*

sickly ['sɪkli] *adj* kränklich; (*smile*) erzwungen

sickness ['sɪknɪs] *s* Krankheit *f*

sick' room' *s* Krankenzimmer *n*

side [saɪd] *adj* Neben-, Seiten- ‖ *s* Seite *f*; (*of a team, government*) Partei *f*; (*edge*) Rand *m*; **at my s.** mir zur Seite; **dark s.** Schattenseite *f*; **off sides** (sport) abseits; **on the father's s.** väterlicherseits; **on the s.** (coll) nebenbei; **this s. up** Vorsicht, nicht stürzen; **to be on the safe s.** um ganz sicher zu gehen ‖ *intr*— **s. with s.o.** j-s Partei ergreifen

side' aisle' *s* Seitengang *m*; (*of a church*) Seitenschiff *n*

side' al'tar *s* Nebenaltar *m*

side'arm' *s* Seitengewehr *n*

side'board' *s* Anrichte *f*, Büffet *n*

side'burns' *spl* Koteletten *pl*

side' dish' *s* Nebengericht *n*

side' door' *s* Seitentür *f*

side' effect' *s* Nebenwirkung *f*

side' en'trance *s* Seiteneingang *m*

side' glance' *s* Seitenblick *m*

side' is'sue *s* Nebenfrage *f*

side' job' *s* Nebenverdienst *m*

side'kick' *s* (coll) Kumpel *m*

side'line' *s* (*occupation*) Nebenbeschäftigung *f*; (fb) Seitenlinie *f* ‖ *tr* (coll) an der aktiven Teilnahme hindern

side' of ba'con *s* Speckseite *f*

side' road' *s* Seitenweg *m*

side'sad'dle *adv*—**ride s.** im Damensattel reiten

side' show' *s* Nebenvorstellung *f*; (fig) Episode *f*

side'split'ting *adj* zwerchfellerschütternd

side-step' *v* (*pret & pp* **–stepped;** *ger* **–stepping**) *tr* ausweichen (*dat*)

side' street' *s* Seitenstraße *f*

side' stroke' *s* Seitenschwimmen *n*

side'track' *s* Seitengeleise *n* ‖ *tr* (& fig) auf ein Seitengeleise schieben

side' trip' *s* Abstecher *m*

side' view' *s* Seitenansicht *f*

side'walk' *s* Bürgersteig *m*, Gehsteig *m*

sideward ['saɪdwərd] *adj* nach der Seite gerichtet ‖ *adv* seitwärts

side'ways' *adv* seitlich, seitwärts

sid'ing *s* (*of a house*) Verkleidung *f*; (rr) Nebengeleise *n*

sidle ['saɪdəl] *intr*—**s. up to s.o.** sich heimlich an j-n heranmachen

siege [sidʒ] *s* Belagerung *f*; **lay s. to** belagern

siesta [si'estə] *s* Mittagsruhe *f*

sieve [sɪv] *s* Sieb *n* ‖ *tr* durchsieben

sift [sɪft] *tr* (durch)sieben; (fig) sichten; **s. out** aussieben

sigh [saɪ] *s* Seufzer *m*; **with a s.** seufzend ‖ *intr* seufzen

sight [saɪt] *s* Anblick *m*; (*faculty*) Sehvermögen *n*; (*on a weapon*) Visier *n*; **at first s.** auf den ersten Blick; **at s.** sofort; **be a s.** (coll) unmöglich aussehen; **by s.** vom Sehen; **catch s. of** erblicken; **in s.** in Sicht; **lose s. of** aus den Augen verlieren; **out of s.** außer Sicht; **s. for sore eyes** Augentrost *m*; **sights** Sehenswürdigkeiten *pl*; **s. unseen** unbesehen; **within s.** in Sehweite ‖ *tr* sichten

sight'see'ing s Besichtigung f; **go s. sich** [dat] die Sehenswürdigkeiten ansehen

sight'seeing tour' s Rundfahrt f

sightseer ['saɪt,si·ər] s Tourist –in mf

sign [saɪn] s (signboard) Schild n; (symbol, omen, signal) Zeichen n; (symptom, indication) Kennzeichen n; (trace) Spur f; (math, mus) Vorzeichen n; **s. of life** Lebenszeichen n || tr unterschreiben; **s. away** aufgeben; **s. over (to)** überschreiben (auf acc) || intr unterschreiben; **s. for** zeichnen für; **s. in** sich eintragen; **s. off** (rad) die Sendung beenden; **s. out** sich austragen; **s. up** (mil) sich anwerben lassen; **s. up for** (e.g., courses, work) sich anmelden für

sig·nal ['sɪgnəl] adj auffallend || s (by gesture) Zeichen n, Wink m; (aut, rad, rr, telv) Signal n || v (pret & pp –nal[l]ed; ger –nal[l]ing) tr signalisieren; (a person) ein Zeichen geben (dat)

sig'nal corps' s Fernmeldetruppen pl

sig'nal·man s (–men) (nav) Signalgast m; (rr) Bahnwärter m

signatory ['sɪgnə,tori] s Unterzeichner –in mf

signature ['sɪgnətʃər] s Unterschrift f

sign'board' s Aushängeschild n

signer ['saɪnər] s Unterzeichner –in mf

sig'net ring' ['sɪgnɪt] s Siegelring m

significance [sɪg'nɪfɪkəns] s Bedeutung f

significant [sɪg'nɪfɪkənt] adj bedeutsam

signi·fy ['sɪgnɪ,faɪ] v (pret & pp –fied) bedeuten, bezeichnen

sign' lan'guage s Zeichensprache f

sign' of the cross' s Kreuzzeichen n; **make the s.** sich bekreuzigen

sign'post' s Wegweiser m

silence ['saɪləns] s Ruhe f, Stille f; (reticence) Schweigen n; **in s.** schweigend || tr zum Schweigen bringen; (a conscience) beschwichtigen

silent ['saɪlənt] adj (night, partner) still; (movies) stumm; (person) schweigend; **be s.** stillschweigen; **keep s.** schweigen

silhouette [,sɪlu'et] s Schattenbild n, Silhouette f || tr silhouettieren

silicon ['sɪlɪkən] s Silizium n

silicone ['sɪlɪkon] s Silikon n

silk [sɪlk] adj seiden || s Seide f

silken ['sɪlkən] adj seiden

silk' hat' s Zylinder m

silk' mill' s Seidenfabrik f

silk' worm' s Seidenraupe f

silky ['sɪlki] adj seiden, seidenartig

sill [sɪl] s (of a window) Sims m & n; (of a door) Schwelle f

silliness ['sɪlɪnɪs] s Albernheit f

silly ['sɪli] adj albern, blöd

si·lo ['saɪlo] s (–los) Getreidesilo m; (rok) Raketenbunker m, Silo m

silt [sɪlt] s Schlick m || intr—**s. up** verschlammen

silver ['sɪlvər] adj silbern || s Silber n; (for the table) Silberzeug n; (money) Silbergeld n

sil'verfish' s Silberfischchen n

sil'ver foil' s Silberfolie f

sil'ver lin'ing s (fig) Silberstreifen m

sil'ver plate' s Silbergeschirr n

sil'ver-plat'ed adj versilbert

sil'versmith' s Silberschmied m

sil'ver spoon' s—**be born with a s. in one's mouth** ein Sonntagskind sein

sil'verware' s Silbergeschirr n

silvery ['sɪlvəri] adj silbern

similar ['sɪmɪlər] adj (to) ähnlich (dat)

similarity [,sɪmɪ'lærɪti] s Ähnlichkeit f

simile ['sɪmɪli] s Gleichnis n

simmer ['sɪmər] tr leicht kochen lassen || intr brodeln; **s. down** (coll) sich abreagieren

simper ['sɪmpər] s—selbstgefälliges Lächeln n || intr selbstgefällig lächeln

simple ['sɪmpəl] adj einfach; (truth) rein; (fact) bloß

sim'ple-mind'ed adj einfältig

simpleton ['sɪmpəltən] s Einfaltspinsel m

simpli·fy ['sɪmplɪ,faɪ] v (pret & pp –fied) tr vereinfachen

simply ['sɪmpli] adv einfach

simulate ['sɪmjə,let] tr (illness) simulieren; (e.g., a rocket flight) am Modell vorführen

sim'ulated adj unecht

simultaneous [,saɪməl'teni·əs] adj gleichzeitig, simultan

sin [sɪn] s Sünde f || v (pret & pp sinned; ger sinning) intr sündigen; **sin against** sich versündigen an (dat)

since [sɪns] adv seitdem, seither || prep seit (dat); **s. then** seither; **s. when** seit wann || conj (temporal) seit(dem); (causal) da

sincere [sɪn'sɪr] adj aufrichtig

sincerely [sɪn'sɪrli] adv aufrichtig, ehrlich; **Sincerely yours** Ihr ergebener, Ihre ergebene

sincerity [sɪn'serɪti] s Aufrichtigkeit f

sinecure ['saɪnɪ,kjur] s Sinekure f

sinew ['sɪnju] s Sehne f, Flechse f; (fig) Muskelkraft f

sinewy ['sɪnju·i] adj sehnig; (fig) kräftig, nervig

sinful ['sɪnfəl] adj sündhaft

sing [sɪŋ] v (pret sang [sæŋ] & sung [sʌŋ]; pp sung) tr & intr singen

singe [sɪndʒ] v (singeing) tr sengen; (the hair) versengen

singer ['sɪŋər] s Sänger –in mf

single ['sɪŋgəl] adj einzeln; (unmarried) ledig; **not a s. word** kein einziges Wort || tr—**s. out** herausgreifen

sin'gle bed' s Einzelbett n

sin'glebreast'ed adj einreihig

sin'gle file' s Gänsemarsch m

sin'gle-hand'ed adj einhändig

sin'gle-lane' adj einbahnig

sin'gle life' s Ledigenstand m

sin'gle-mind'ed adj zielstrebig

sin'gle room' s Einzelzimmer n

sin'gle-track' adj (& fig) eingleisig

sing'song' adj eintönig || s Singsang m

singular ['sɪŋgjələr] adj (outstanding) ausgezeichnet; (unique) einzig; (odd) seltsam || s (gram) Einzahl f

sinister ['sɪnɪstər] *adj* unheimlich

sink [sɪŋk] *s* (*in the kitchen*) Ausguß *m*; (*in the bathroom*) Waschbecken *n* || *v* (*pret* **sank** [sæŋk] & **sunk** [sʌŋk]; *pp* **sunk**) *tr* (*a ship; a post*) versenken; (*money*) investieren; (*min*) abteufen; **s. a well** e-n Brunnen bohren || *intr* sinken; (*said of a building*) sich senken; **he is sinking fast** seine Kräfte nehmen rapide ab; **s. in** (coll) einleuchten; **s. into** (*an easychair*) sich fallen lassen in (*acc*); (*poverty*) geraten in (*acc*); (*unconsciousness*) fallen in (*acc*)

sink'ing feel'ing *s* Beklommenheit *f*

sink'ing fund' *s* Schuldentilgungsfonds *m*

sinless ['sɪnlɪs] *adj* sünd(en)los

sinner ['sɪnər] *s* Sünder –in *mf*

sinuous ['sɪnjʊ-əs] *adj* gewunden

sinus ['saɪnəs] *s* Stirnhöhle *f*

sip [sɪp] *s* Schluck *m* || *v* (*pret & pp* **sipped**; *ger* **sipping**) *tr* schlürfen

siphon ['saɪfən] *s* Siphon *m*, Saugheber *m* || *tr* entleeren; **s. off** absaugen; (*profits*) abschöpfen

sir [sɪr] *s* Herr *m*; **yes sir!** jawohl!; **Dear Sir** Sehr geehrter Herr

sire [saɪr] *s* (& zool) Vater *m* || *tr* zeugen

siren ['saɪrən] *s* (& myth) Sirene *f*

sirloin ['sʌrlɔɪn] *s* Lendenbraten *m*

sissy ['sɪsɪ] *s* Schlappschwanz *m*

sister ['sɪstər] *s* Schwester *f*

sis'ter-in-law' *s* (**sisters-in-law**) Schwägerin *f*

sisterly ['sɪstərlɪ] *adj* schwesterlich

sit [sɪt] *v* (*pret & pp* **sat** [sæt]; *ger* **sitting**) *intr* sitzen; **sit down** sich (hin)setzen; **sit for a painter** e-m Maler Modell stehen; **sit in on** (*a meeting*) dabeisein bei; **sit up and beg** Männchen machen

sit'down strike' *s* Sitzstreik *m*

site [saɪt] *s* (*position, location*) Lage *f*; (*piece of ground*) Gelände *n*

sit'ting s—at one s. auf e-n Sitz

sit'ting duck' *s* wehrloses Ziel *n*

sit'ting room' *s* Gemeinschaftsraum *m*

situated ['sɪt/u‚etɪd] *adj* gelegen; **be s.** liegen

situation [‚sɪt/ʊ'e/ən] *s* Lage *f*; **s. wanted** Stelle gesucht

six [sɪks] *adj & pron* sechs *f* || *s* Sechs *f*

sixteen ['sɪks'tin] *adj & pron* sechzehn || *s* Sechzehn *f*

sixteenth ['sɪks'tinθ] *adj & pron* sechzehnte || *s* (*fraction*) Sechzehntel *n*; **the s.** (*in dates or in series*) der Sechzehnte

sixth [sɪksθ] *adj & pron* sechste || *s* (*fraction*) Sechstel *n*; **the s.** (*in dates or in series*) der Sechste

sixtieth ['sɪkstɪ-ɪθ] *adj & pron* sechzig || *s* (*fraction*) Sechzigstel *n*

sixty ['sɪkstɪ] *adj & pron* sechzig || *s* Sechzig *f*; **the sixties** die sechziger Jahre

six'ty-four dol'lar ques'tion *s* Preisfrage *f*

sizable ['saɪzəbəl] *adj* beträchtlich

size [saɪz] *s* Größe *f*; (*of a book,*

paper) Format *n* || *tr* grundieren; **s. up** einschätzen

sizzle ['sɪzəl] *s* Zischen *n* || *intr* zischen

skate [sket] *s* Schlittschuh *m* || *intr* Schlittschuh laufen

skat'ing rink' *s* Eisbahn *f*

skein [sken] *s* Strähne *f*

skeleton ['skɛlɪtən] *s* Gerippe *n*

skel'eton crew' *s* Minimalbelegschaft *f*

skel'eton key' *s* Dietrich *m*

skeptic ['skɛptɪk] *s* Zweifler –in *mf*

skeptical ['skɛptɪkəl] *adj* skeptisch

skepticism ['skɛptɪ‚sɪzəm] *s* (*doubt*) Skepsis *f*; (philos) Skeptizismus *m*

sketch [skɛt/] *s* Skizze *f*; (theat) Sketch *m* || *tr & intr* skizzieren

sketch'book' *s* Skizzenbuch *n*

sketchy ['skɛt/ɪ] *adj* skizzenhaft

skewer ['skju-ər] *s* Fleischspieß *m*

ski [ski] *s* Schi *m* || *intr* schilaufen

ski' boot' *s* Schistiefel *m*

skid [skɪd] *s* Rutschen *n*, Schleudern *n*; **go into a s.** ins Schleudern geraten || *v* (*pret & pp* **skidded**; *ger* **skidding**) *intr* rutschen, schleudern

skid'mark' *s* Bremsspur *f*

skid'proof' *adj* bremssicher

skid'row' [ro] *s* Elendsviertel *n*

skiff [skɪf] *s* Skiff *n*

ski'ing *s* Schilaufen *n*

ski'jack'et *s* Anorak *m*

ski' jump' *s* Schisprung *m*; (*chute*) Sprungschanze *f*

ski' jump'ing *s* Schispringen *n*

ski' lift' *s* Schilift *m*

skill [skɪl] *s* Fertigkeit *f*

skilled *adj* gelernt

skillet ['skɪlɪt] *s* Bratpfanne *f*

skillful ['skɪlfəl] *adj* geschickt

skim [skɪm] *v* (*pret & pp* **skimmed**; *ger* **skimming**) *tr* (*milk*) abrahmen; (*a book*) überfliegen; **s. off** abschöpfen || *intr—***s. over** the water über das Wasser streichen; **s. through** (*a book*) flüchtig durchblättern

skim' milk' *s* entrahmte Milch *f*

skimp [skɪmp] *intr* (**on**) knausern (mit)

skimpy ['skɪmpɪ] *adj* (*person*) knauserig; (*thing*) knapp, dürftig

skin [skɪn] *s* Haut *f*; (*fur*) Fell *n*; (*of fruit*) Schale *f*; **by the s. of one's teeth** mit knapper Not; **get under s.o.'s s.** j–m auf die Nerven gehen || *v* (*pret & pp* **skinned**; *ger* **skinning**) *tr* (*an animal*) enthäuten; (*a knee*) aufschürfen; (*fleece*) das Fell über die Ohren ziehen (*dat*); (*defeat*) schlagen; **s. alive** zur Sau machen

skin'-deep' *adj* oberflächlich

skin' div'er *s* Schwimmtaucher –in *mf*

skin'flint' *s* Geizhals *m*

skin' graft' *s* Hautverpflanzung *f*

skinny ['skɪnɪ] *adj* spindeldürr, mager

skin'tight' *adj* hauteng

skip [skɪp] *s* Sprung *m* || *v* (*pret & pp* **skipped**; *ger* **skipping**) *tr* (*omit*) auslassen; (*a page*) überblättern; **s. it!** Schwamm drüber!; **s. rope** Seil springen; **s. school** Schule schwänzen || *intr* springen; **s. out** abhauen

ski' pole' *s* Schistock *m*

skipper ['skɪpər] s Kapitän m

skirmish ['skɑrmɪʃ] s Scharmützel n || intr scharmützeln

skir'mish line' s (mil) Schützenlinie f

skirt [skʌrt] s Rock m || tr (border) umsäumen; (pass along) sich entlangziehen (an dat)

ski' run' s Schipiste f

skit [skɪt] s Sket(s)ch m

skittish ['skɪtɪʃ] adj (lively) lebhaft; (horse) scheu

skull [skʌl] s Schädel m

skull' and cross'bones s Totenkopf m

skull'cap' s Käppchen n

skunk [skʌŋk] s Stinktier n; (sl) Saukerl m

sky [skaɪ] s Himmel m; out of the clear blue sky wie aus heiterem Himmel; praise to the skies über den grünen Klee loben

sky'-blue' adj himmelblau

sky'div'er s Fallschirmspringer –in mf

sky'div'ing s Fallschirmspringen n

sky'lark' s Feldlerche f

sky'light' s Dachluke f

sky'line' s Horizontlinie f; (of a city) Stadtsilhouette f

sky'rock'et s Rakete f || intr in die Höhe schießen

sky'scrap'er s Wolkenkratzer m

sky'writ'ing s Himmelsschrift f

slab [slæb] s Platte f, Tafel f

slack [slæk] adj schlaff; (period) flau || s Spielraum m; slacks Herrenhose f, Damenhose f || intr—s. off nachlassen

slacken ['slækən] tr (slow down) verlangsamen; (loosen) lockern || intr nachlassen

slack'er per'lod s Flaute f

slack' sea'son s Sauregurkenzeit f

slag [slæg] s Schlacke f

slag' pile' s Schlackenhalde f

slake [slek] tr (thirst, lime) löschen

slalom ['slɑləm] s Slalom m

slam [slæm] s Knall m; (cards) Schlemm m || v (pret & pp slammed; ger slamming) tr zuknallen; s. down hinknallen || intr knallen

slander ['slændər] s Verleumdung f || tr verleumden

slanderous ['slændərəs] adj verleumderisch

slang [slæŋ] s Slang m

slant [slænt] s Schräge f; (view) Einstellung f; (personal point of view) Tendenz f || tr abschrägen; (fig) färben

slap [slæp] s Klaps m; s. in the face Ohrfeige f || v (pret & pp slapped; ger slapping) tr schlagen; (s.o.'s face) ohrfeigen; s. together zusammenhauen

slap'stick' adj Radau– || s Radaukomödie f

slash [slæʃ] s Schnittwunde f || tr aufschlitzen; (prices) drastisch herabsetzen

slat [slæt] s Stab m

slate [slet] s Schiefer m; (to write on) Schiefertafel f; (of candidates) Vorschlagsliste f || tr (a roof) mit Schiefer decken; (schedule) planen; he is slated to speak er soll sprechen

slate' roof' s Schieferdach n

slattern ['slætərn] s (slovenly woman) Schlampe f; (slut) Dirne f

slaughter ['slɔtər] s Schlachten n; (massacre) Metzelei f || tr schlachten; (massacre) niedermetzeln

slaugh'terhouse' s Schlachthaus n

Slav [slav], (slæv) adj slawisch || s (person) Slawe m, Slawin f

slave [slev] s Sklave m, Sklavin f || intr (coll) schuften; s. at a job sich mit e–r Arbeit abquälen

slave' driv'er s (fig) Leuteschinder m

slaver ['slævər] s Geifer m

slavery ['sleverɪ] s Sklaverei f

slave' trade' s Sklavenhandel m

Slavic ['slavɪk], ['slævɪk] adj slawisch

slavish ['slevɪʃ] adj slawisch

slay [sle] v (pret slew [slu]; pp slain [slen]) tr erschlagen

slayer ['sle-ər] s Totschläger –in mf

sled [sled] s Schlitten m || v (pret & pp sledded; ger sledding) intr Schlitten fahren

sledge [sledʒ] s Schlitten m

sledge' ham'mer s Vorschlaghammer m

sleek [slik] adj (hair) glatt; (cattle) fett || tr glätten

sleep [slip] s Schlaf m; get enough s. sich ausschlafen || v (pret & pp slept [slɛpt]) tr (accommodate) Schlafgelegenheiten bieten für; s. off a hangover seinen Kater ausschlafen || intr schlafen; I don't s. a wink ich habe kein Auge zugetan; s. like a log wie ein Murmeltier schlafen; s. with (a woman) schlafen mit

sleeper ['slipər] s Schläfer –in mf; (sleeping car) Schlafwagen m; (fig) überraschender Erfolg m

sleepiness ['slipɪnɪs] s Schläfrigkeit f

sleep'ing bag' s Schlafsack m

Sleep'ing Beau'ty s Dornröschen n

sleep'ing car' s Schlafwagen m

sleep'ing compart'ment s Schlafabteil n

sleep'ing pill' s Schlaftablette f

sleep'ing sick'ness s Schlafkrankheit f

sleepless ['slipləs] adj schlaflos

sleep'walk'er s Nachtwandler –in mf

sleepy ['slipi] adj schläfrig

sleep'yhead' s Schlafmütze f

sleet [slit] s Schneeregen m; (on the ground) Glatteis n || impers—it is sleeting es gibt Schneeregen, es graupelt

sleeve [sliv] s Ärmel m; (mach) Muffe f; have s.th. up one's s. etw im Schilde führen; roll up one's sleeves die Ärmel hochkrempeln

sleeveless ['slivlɪs] adj ärmellos

sleigh [sle] s Schlitten m

sleigh' bell' s Schlittenschelle f

sleigh' ride' s Schlittenfahrt f; go for a sleigh ride

sleight' of hand' [slaɪt] s Taschenspielertrick m

slender ['slendər] adj schlank; (means) gering

sleuth [sluθ] s Detektiv m

slice [slaɪs] s Scheibe f, Schnitte f;

(tennis) Schnittball *m* || *tr* aufschneiden

slicer ['slaɪsər] *s* Schneidemaschine *f*

slick [slɪk] *adj* glatt; (*talker*) raffiniert

slicker ['slɪkər] *s* Regenmantel *m*

slide [slaɪd] *s* (*slip*) Rutsch *m*; (*chute*) Rutschbahn *f*; (*of a microscope*) Objektträger *m*; (*phot*) Diapositiv *n* || *v* (*pret & pp* slid [slɪd]) *tr* schieben || *intr* rutschen; **let things s.** die Dinge laufen lassen

slide′ rule′ *s* Rechenschieber *m*

slide′ valve′ *s* Schieberventil *n*

slide′ view′er *s* Bildbetrachter *m*

slid′ing door′ *s* Schiebetür *f*

slid′ing scale′ *s* gleitende Skala *f*

slight [slaɪt] *adj* gering(fügig); (*illness*) leicht; (*petite*) zart || *tr* mißachten

slim [slɪm] *adj* schlank; (*chance*) gering || *intr*—**s. down** abnehmen

slime [slaɪm] *s* Schlamm *m*; (*e.g., of fish, snakes*) Schleim *m*

slimy ['slaɪmi] *adj* schleimig; (*muddy*) schlammig

sling [slɪŋ] *s* (*to hurl stones*) Schleuder *f*; (*for a broken arm*) Schlinge *f* || *v* (*pret & pp* slung [slʌŋ]) *tr* schleudern; **s. over the shoulders** umhängen

sling′shot′ *s* Schleuder *f*

slink [slɪŋk] *v* (*pret & pp* slunk [slʌŋk]) *intr* schleichen; **s. away** wegschleichen

slip [slɪp] *s* (*slide*) Ausrutschen *n*; (*cutting*) Ableger *m*; (*underwear*) Unterrock *m*; (*paper*) Zettel *m*; (*pillowcase*) Kissenbezug *m*; (*error*) Flüchtigkeitsfehler *m*; (*for ships*) Schlipp *m*; **give s.o. the s.** j-m entwischen; **s. of the pen** Schreibfehler *m*; **s. of the tongue** Sprechfehler *m* || *v* (*pret & pp* slipped; *ger* slipping) *tr*—**s. in** (*a remark*) einfließen lassen; (*poison*) heimlich schütten; **s. on** (*a glove*) überstreifen; (*a coat*) überziehen; (*a ring*) auf den Finger streifen; **s. s.o. money** j-m etw Geld zustecken; **s.o.'s mind** j-m entfallen || *intr* rutschen; (*e.g., out of or into a room*) schlüpfen; (*lose one's balance*) ausgleiten; **let s.** sich [*dat*] entgehen lassen; **s. by** verstreichen; **s. in** (*said of errors*) unterlaufen; **s. through one's fingers** durch die Finger gleiten; **s. out on s.o.** j-m entschlüpfen; **s. up (on)** danebenhauen (bei); **you are slipping** (coll) Sie lassen in der Leistung nach

slip′cov′er *s* Schonbezug *m*

slip′knot′ *s* Schleife *f*

slipper ['slɪpər] *s* Pantoffel *m*

slippery ['slɪpəri] *adj* glatt

slipshod ['slɪp,ʃad] *adj* schlampig; **do s. work** schludern

slip′stream′ *s* Luftschraubenstrahl *m*

slip′-up′ *s* (coll) Flüchtigkeitsfehler *m*

slit [slɪt] *s* Schlitz *m* || *v* (*pret & pp* slit; *ger* slitting) *tr* schlitzen; **s. open** aufschlitzen

slit′-eyed′ *adj* schlitzäugig

slither ['slɪðər] *intr* rutschen

slit′ trench′ *s* (mil) Splittergraben *m*

sliver ['slɪvər] *s* Splitter *m*, Span *m*

slob [slab] *s* (sl) Schmutzfink *m*

slobber ['slabər] *s* Geifer *m* || *intr* geifern

sloe [slo] *s* (bot) Schlehe *f*

sloe′-eyed′ *adj* schlitzäugig

slog [slag] *v* (*pret & pp* slogged; *ger* slogging) *intr* stapfen

slogan ['slogən] *s* Schlagwort *n*

sloop [slup] *s* Schaluppe *f*

slop [slap] *s* Spülicht *n*; (*bad food*) (sl) Fraß *m* || *v* (*pret & pp* slopped; *ger* slopping) *tr* (*hogs*) füttern; (*spill*) verschütten

slope [slop] *s* Abhang *m*; (*of a road*) Gefälle *n*; (*of a roof*) Neigung *f* || *tr* abschrägen || *intr* sich neigen; (*said of a road*) abfallen

sloppy ['slapi] *adj* schlampig; (*weather*) matschig

slosh [slaʃ] *intr* schwappen

slot [slat] *s* Schlitz *m*

sloth [sloθ] *s* Faulheit *f*, Trägheit *f*; (zool) Faultier *n*

slothful ['sloθfəl] *adj* faul, träge

slot′ machine′ *s* Spielautomat *m*

slouch [slautʃ] *s* nachlässige Haltung *f*; (*person*) Schlappschwanz *m* || *intr* in schlechter Haltung sitzen; **s. along** latschen

slouch′ hat′ *s* Schlapphut *m*

slough [slau] *s* Sumpf *m* || [slʌf] *s* (*of a snake*) abgestreifte Haut *f*; (pathol) Schorf *m* || *tr* (& fig) abstreifen || *intr* (*said of a snake*) sich häuten

Slovak ['slovak], ['slovæk] *adj* slowakisch || *s* (*person*) Sklowake *m*, Slowakin *f*; (*language*) Slowakisch *n*

slovenly ['slʌvənli] *adj* schlampig

slow [slo] *adj* langsam; (*dawdling*) bummelig; (*mentally*) schwer von Begriff; (com) flau; **be s.** (horol) nachgehen || *adv* langsam || *tr*—**s. down** verlangsamen || *intr*—**s. down** (*in driving*) langsamer fahren; (*in working*) nachlassen; **s. down** (public sign) Schritt fahren

slow′down′ *s* Bummelstreik *m*

slow′ mo′tion *s* (cin) Zeitlupe *f*; **in s.** (cin) in Zeitlupentempo

slow′-mo′tion *adj* Zeitlupen-

slow′poke′ *s* (coll) langsamer Mensch *m*

slow′-wit′ted *adj* schwer von Begriff

slug [slʌg] *s* Rohling *m*; (*drink*) Zug *m* (zool) Wegschnecke *f* || *v* (*pret & pp* slugged; *ger* slugging) *tr* (coll) hart mit der Faust treffen

sluggard ['slʌgərd] *s* Faulpelz *m*

sluggish ['slʌgɪʃ] *adj* träge

sluice [slus] *s* Schleuse *f*

sluice′ gate′ *s* Schleusentor *n*

slum [slʌm] *s* Elendsviertel *n*

slumber ['slʌmbər] *s* Schlummer *m* || *intr* schlummern

slum′ dwell′ing *s* Elendsquartier *n*

slump [slʌmp] *s* (st. exch.) Baisse *f*; **s. in sales** Absatzstockung *f* || *intr* zusammensacken; (*said of prices*) stürzen

slur [slʌr] *s* (*insult*) Verleumdung *f*; (mus) Bindezeichen *n* || *v* (*pret & pp* slurred; *ger* slurring) *tr* (*words*)

verschleifen; (mus) binden; **s. over**
hinweggehen über (acc)

slurp [slɑːp] s Schlürfen n || tr & intr
schlürfen

slush [slʌʃ] s Matsch m, Schneematsch
m

slush' fund' s Schmiergeld n

slushy ['slʌʃi] adj matschig

slut [slʌt] s Nutte f

sly [slaɪ] adj (slyer & slier; slyest &
sliest) schlau || s—on the sly im Ver-
borgenen

sly' fox' s Pfiffikus m

smack [smæk] s (blow) Klaps m;
(sound) Klatsch m; (kiss) Schmatz
m; **s. in the face** Backpfeife f || tr
klapsen; **one's lips** schmatzen ||
intr—s. of riechen nach

small [smɔl] adj klein; (difference) gering; (comfort) schlecht; (petty)
kleinlich

small' arms' spl Handwaffen pl

small' busi'ness s Kleinbetrieb m

small' cap'ital s (typ) Kapitälchen n

small' change' s Kleingeld n

small' fry' s kleine Fische pl

small' intes'tine s Dünndarm m

small'-mind'ed adj engstirnig

small' of the back' s Kreuz n

smallpox ['smɔl‚pɑks] s Pocken pl

small' print' s Kleindruck m

small' talk' s Geplauder m

small'-time' adj klein

small'-town' adj kleinstädtisch

smart [smɑrt] adj (bright) klug; (neat,
trim) schick; (car) schneidig; (pej)
überklug || s Schmerz m || intr weh
tun; (burn) brennen

smart' al'eck s [‚ælɪk] s Neunmalkluge
mf

smart'-look'ing adj schnittig

smart' set' s elegante Welt f

smash [smæʃ] s (hit) (coll) Bombe f;
(tennis) Schmetterschlag m || tr zer-
schmettern; (e.g., a window) einschlagen; (sport) schmettern; **s. up**
zerknallen || intr zerbrechen; **s. into**
krachen gegen

smash' hit' s (theat) Bombenerfolg m

smash'-up' s (aut) Zusammenstoß m

smattering ['smætərɪŋ] s (of) oberflächliche Kenntnis f (genit)

smear [smɪr] s Schmiere f; (smudge)
Schmutzfleck m; (vilification) Verun-
glimpfung f; (med) Abstrich m || tr
(spread) schmieren; (make dirty) beschmieren; (vilify) verunglimpfen;
(trounce) vollständig fertigmachen

smear' campaign' s Verleumdungsfeld-
zug m

smell [smɛl] s Geruch m; (aroma) Duft
m; (sense) Geruchssinn m || v (pret
& pp smelled & smelt [smɛlt]) tr
riechen; (danger, trouble) wittern ||
intr (of) riechen (nach)

smell'ing salts' pl Riechsalz n

smelly ['smɛli] adj übelriechend

smelt [smɛlt] s (fish) Stint m || tr
schmelzen, verhütten

smile [smaɪl] s Lächeln n || intr lä-
cheln; **s. at** anlächeln; (clandestinely)
zulächeln (dat); **s. on** lächeln (dat)

smirk [smɪrk] s Grinsen n || intr grin-
sen

smite [smaɪt] v (pret smote [smot];
pp smitten ['smɪtən] & smit [smɪt])
tr schlagen; (said of a plague) befallen; **smitten with** hingerissen von

smith [smɪθ] s Schmied m

smithy ['smɪθi] s Schmiede f

smock [smɑk] s Kittel m, Bluse f

smog [smɑg] s Smog m

smoke [smok] s Rauch m; (heavy
smoke) Qualm m; **go up in s.** (fig) in
Dunst und Rauch aufgehen || intr rau-
chen; (meat) räuchern || intr rauchen;
(said of a chimney) qualmen

smoke' bomb' s Rauchbombe f

smoked' ham' s Räucherschinken m

smoker ['smokər] s Raucher –in mf;
(sl) obszöner Film m

smoke' screen' s Rauchvorhang m

smoke'stack' s Schornstein m

smok'ing s Rauchen n; **no s.** (public
sign) Rauchen verboten

smok'ing car' s Raucherwagen m

smok'ing jack'et s Hausjacke f

smoky ['smoki] adj rauchig

smolder ['smoldər] intr (& fig) schwelen

smooch [smutʃ] intr sich abknutschen

smooth [smuð] adj (surface; talker;
landing, operation) glatt; (wine) mild
|| tr glätten; **s. away** (difficulties)
beseitigen; **s. out** glätten; **s. over** beschönigen

smooth'-faced' adj glattwangig

smooth-shaven ['smuð'ʃevən] adj glattrasiert

smooth'-talk'ing adj schönrednerisch

smoothy ['smuði] s Schönredner –in mf

smother ['smʌðər] tr ersticken; **s. with
kisses** abküssen

smudge [smʌdʒ] s Schmutzfleck m || tr
beschmutzen || intr schmutzig werden

smug [smʌg] adj (smugger; smuggest)
selbstgefällig

smuggle ['smʌgəl] tr & intr schmuggeln

smuggler ['smʌglər] s Schmuggler –in
mf

smug'gling s Schmuggel m

smut [smʌt] s Schmutz m

smutty ['smʌti] adj schmutzig, obszön

snack [snæk] s Imbiß m

snack' bar' s Imbißstube f, Snack Bar f

snaffle ['snæfəl] s Trense f

snag [snæg] s—hit a s. auf Schwierig-
keiten stoßen || v (pret & pp snagged;
ger snagging) tr hängenbleiben mit

snail [snel] s Schnecke f; **at a snail's
pace** im Schneckentempo

snake [snek] s Schlange f || intr sich
schlängeln

snake'bite' s Schlangenbiß m

snake' in the grass' s heimtückischer
Mensch m

snap [snæp] s (sound) Knacks m; (on
clothes) Druckknopf m; (of a dog)
Biß m; (liveliness) Schwung m; (easy
work) Kinderspiel n || v (pret & pp
snapped; ger snapping) tr (break)
zerreißen, entzweibrechen; (a picture) knipsen; **s. a whip** mit der

Peitsche knallen; s. back (words) hervorstoßen; (the head) zurückwerfen; s. off abbrechen; s. one's fingers mit den Fingern schnalzen; s. s.o.'s head off j-n zusammenstauchen; s. up gierig an sich reißen; (buy up) aufkaufen || intr (tear) zerreißen; (break) entzweibrechen; s. at schnappen nach; (fig) anfahren; s. out of it! komm zu dir!; s. shut zuschnappen; s. to it! mach zu!

snap′drag′on s (bot) Löwenmaul n
snap′ fas′tener s Druckknopf m
snap′ judg′ment s vorschnelles Urteil n
snap′per soup′ ['snæpər] s Schildkrötensuppe f
snappish ['snæpɪʃ] adj bissig
snappy ['snæpɪ] adj (caustic) bissig; (lively) energisch; make it s.! mach schnell!
snap′shot′ s Schnappschuß m
snare [snɛr] s Schlinge f || tr mit e-r Schlinge fangen; (fig) fangen
snare′ drum′ s Schnarrtrommel f
snarl [snɑrl] s (tangle) Verwicklung f; (sound) Knurren n || tr verwickeln; s. traffic e-e Verkehrsstockung verursachen || intr knurren
snatch [snætʃ] s—in snatches ruckweise; snatches (of conversation) Bruchstücke pl || tr schnappen; s. away from entreißen (dat); s. up schnappen
snazzy ['snæzɪ] adj (sl) schmissig
sneak [snik] s Schleicher –in mf || tr (e.g., a drink) heimlich trinken; s. in einschmuggeln || intr schleichen; s. away sich davonschleichen; s. in sich einschleichen; s. out sich herausschleichen; s. up on s.o. an j-n heranschleichen
sneaker ['snikər] s Tennisschuh m
sneaky ['snikɪ] adj heimtückisch
sneer [snɪr] s Hohnlächeln n || intr höhnisch grinsen; s. at spötteln über (acc)
sneeze [sniz] s Niesen n || tr—not to be sneezed at nicht zu verachten || intr niesen
snicker ['snɪkər] s Kichern n || intr kichern
snide′ remark′ [snaɪd] s Anzüglichkeit f
sniff [snɪf] s Schnüffeln n || tr (be)riechen; s. out ausschnüffeln || intr (at) schnüffeln (an dat)
sniffle ['snɪfəl] s Geschnüffel n; sniffles Schnupfen m || intr schniefen
snip [snɪp] s (cut) Einschnitt m; (small piece snipped off) Schnippel m || tr (pret & pp snipped; ger snipping) tr & intr schnippeln
snipe [snaɪp] intr—s. at aus dem Hinterhalt schießen auf (acc)
sniper ['snaɪpər] s Heckenschütze m
snippet ['snɪpɪt] s Schnippelchen n; (small person) Knirps m
snippy ['snɪpɪ] adj schroff, barsch
snitch [snɪtʃ] tr (coll) klauen || intr (coll) petzen; s. on (coll) verpfeifen
sniv′el ['snɪvəl] s (whining) Gewimmer n; (mucus) Nasenschleim m || v

(pret & pp –el[l]ed; ger –el[l]ing) intr (whine) wimmern; (cry with sniffling) schluchzen; (have a runny nose) e-e tropfende Nase haben
snob [snɑb] s Snob m
snob′ appeal′ s Snobappeal m
snobbery ['snɑbərɪ] s Snobismus m
snobbish ['snɑbɪʃ] adj snobistisch
snoop [snup] s (coll) Schnüffler –in mf || intr (coll) schnüffeln
snoopy ['snupɪ] adj schnüffelnd
snoot [snut] s (sl) Rüssel m; make a s. e-e Schnute ziehen
snooty ['snutɪ] adj hochnäsig
snooze [snuz] s (coll) Nickerchen n || intr (coll) ein Nickerchen machen
snore [snor] s Schnarchen n || intr schnarchen
snort [snort] s Schnauben n || tr wütend schnauben || intr prusten; (said of a horse) schnauben; (with laughter) vor Lachen prusten
snot [snɑt] s (sl) Rotz m
snotty ['snɑtɪ] adj (sl & fig) rotzig
snout [snaʊt] s Schnauze f, Rüssel m
snow [sno] s Schnee m || tr (sl) einwickeln; s. in einschneien; s. under mit Schnee bedecken || impers—it is snowing es schneit
snow′ball′ s Schneeball m || intr (fig) lawinenartig anwachsen
snow′bank′ s Schneeverwehung f
snow′bird′ s Schneefink m
snow′ blind′ness s Schneeblindheit f
snow′ blow′er s Schneefräse f
snow′bound′ adj eingeschneit
snow′-capped′ adj schneebedeckt
snow′ chain′ s (aut) Schneekette f
snow′-clad′ adj verschneit
snow′drift′ s Schneeverwehung f
snow′fall′ s Schneefall m
snow′flake′ s Schneeflocke f
snow′ flur′ry s Schneegestöber n
snow′ job′ s—give s.o. a s. (sl) j-n hereinlegen
snow′man′ s (–men) Schneemann m
snow′mobile′ s Motorschlitten m
snow′plow′ s Schneepflug m
snow′shoe′ s Schneeteller m
snow′ shov′el s Schneeschaufel f
snow′storm′ s Schneesturm m
snow′ tire′ s Winterreifen m
Snow′ White′ s Schneewittchen n
snow′-white′ adj schneeweiß
snowy ['sno·ɪ] adj schneeig
snub [snʌb] s verächtliche Behandlung f || v (pret & pp snubbed; ger snubbing) tr (ignore) schneiden; (treat contemptuously) verächtlich behandeln
snubby ['snʌbɪ] adj (nose) etwas abgestumpft; (person) abweisend
snub′-nosed′ adj stupsnasig
snuff [snʌf] s Schnupftabak m; (of a candle) Schnuppe f; up to s. (sl) auf Draht || tr—s. out (a candle) auslöschen; (suppress) unterdrücken
snuff′box′ s Schnupftabakdose f
snug [snʌg] adj (snugger; snuggest) behaglich; (fit) eng angeschmiegt; s. as a bug in a rug wie die Made im Speck

snuggle ['snʌgəl] *intr*—s. up (to) sich schmiegen (an *acc*)

so [so] *adv* (with adjectives or adverbs) so; (*thus*) so; (*for this reason*) daher; (*then*) also; **and so forth** und so weiter; **or so** etwa, e.g., **ten miles or so** etwa zehn Meilen; **so as to** (*inf*) um zu (*inf*); **so far** bisher; **so far as** soviel; **so far, so good** soweit ganz gut; **so I see!** das seh' ich!; **so long!** (coll) bis bald!; **so much** soviel; **so much the better** um so besser; **so that** damit; **so what?** na, und?

soak [sok] *s* Einweichen *n* || *tr* einweichen; (*soak through and through*) durchnässen; (*overcharge*) (sl) schröpfen; **soaked to the skin** bis auf die Haut durchnäßt || *intr* weichen

so'-and-so' *s* (*-sos*) Soundso *mf*

soap [sop] *s* Seife *f* || *tr* einseifen

soap'box der'by *s* Seifenkistenrennen *n*

soap'box or'ator *s* Straßenredner *–in mf*

soap' bub'ble *s* Seifenblase *f*

soap' dish' *s* Seifenschale *f*

soap' flakes' *spl* Seifenflocken *pl*

soap' op'era *s* (rad) rührselige Hörspielreihe *f*; (telv) rührselige Fernsehspielreihe *f*

soap' pow'der *s* Seifenpulver *n*

soap'stone' *s* Seifenstein *m*

soap'suds' *spl* Seifenlauge *f*

soapy ['sopi] *adj* seifig; (*like soap*) seifenartig

soar [sor] *intr* schweben, (auf)steigen; (*prices*) steigen

sob [sab] *s* Schluchzen *n* || *v* (*pret & pp* sobbed; *ger* sobbing) *intr* schluchzen

sober ['sobər] *adj* nüchtern || *tr* (up) ernüchtern || *intr*—s. up wieder nüchtern werden

sobriety [so'braɪ·əti] *s* Nüchternheit *f*

sob' sto'ry *s* Schmachtfetzen *m*

so'-called' *adj* sogenannt

soccer ['sakər] *s* Fußball *m*

soc'cer play'er *s* Fußballer *m*

sociable ['soʃəbəl] *adj* gesellig

social ['soʃəl] *adj* gesellschaftlich || *s* geselliges Beisammensein *n*

so'cial climb'er *s* Streber *–in mf*

socialism ['soʃə,lɪzəm] *s* Sozialismus *m*

socialist ['soʃəlɪst] *s* Sozialist *–in mf*

socialistic [,soʃə'lɪstɪk] *adj* sozialistisch

socialite ['soʃə,laɪt] *s* Prominente *mf*

socialize ['soʃə,laɪz] *intr* (with) verkehren (mit)

so'cialized med'icine *s* staatliche Gesundheitspflege *f*

so'cial reg'ister *s* Register *n* der prominenten Mitglieder der oberen Gesellschaftsklasse

so'cial sci'ence *s* Sozialwissenschaft *f*

so'cial secu'rity *s* Sozialversicherung *f*

so'cial wel'fare *s* Sozialfürsorge *f*

so'cial work'er *s* Sozialfürsorger *–in mf*

society [sə'saɪ·əti] *s* Gesellschaft *f*; (*an organization*) Verein *m*

soci'ety col'umn *s* Gesellschaftsspalte *f*

soci'ety for the preven'tion of cru'elty to an'imals *s* Tierschutzverein *m*

sociological [,sosɪ·ə'ladʒɪkəl] *adj* sozialwissenschaftlich, soziologisch

sociologist [,sosɪ'aledʒɪst] *s* Soziologe *m*, Soziologin *f*

sociology [,sosɪ'aledʒi] *s* Soziologie *f*

sock [sak] *s* Socke *f*; (sl) Faustschlag *m* || *tr*—s. it to him! gib's ihm!; **s. s.o.** j-m eine 'runterhauen

socket ['sakɪt] *s* (anat) Höhle *f*; (elec) Steckdose *f*; (mach) Muffe *f*

sock'et joint' *s* (anat) Kugelgelenk *n*

sock'et wrench' *s* Steckschlüssel *m*

sod [sad] *s* Rasenstück *n* || *v* (*pret & pp* sodded; *ger* sodding) *tr* mit Rasen bedecken

soda ['sodə] *s* (*refreshment*) Limonade *f*; (in mixed drinks) Selterswasser *n*; (chem) Soda *f & n*

so'da crack'er *s* Keks *m*

so'da wa'ter *s* Sodawasser *n*

sodium ['sodɪ·əm] *s* Natrium *n*

sofa ['sofə] *s* Sofa *n*

soft [soft] *adj* (*not hard or tough*) weich; (*not loud*) leise; (*light, music*) sanft; (*sleep, breeze*) leicht; (*effeminate*) verweichlicht; (*muscles*) schlaff; **be s.** on weich sein gegenüber (*dat*)

soft'-boiled egg' *s* weichgekochtes Ei *n*

soft' coal' *s* Braunkohle *f*

soft' drink' *s* alkoholfreies Getränk *n*

soften ['sofən] *tr* aufweichen; (*palliate*) lindern; (*water*) enthärten; **s. up** (mil) zermürben || *intr* (& fig) weich werden

soft'-heart'ed *adj* weichherzig

soft' job' *s* Druckposten *m*

soft' land'ing *s* (rok) weiche Landung *f*

soft' pal'ate *s* Hintergaumen *m*

soft'-ped'al *v* (*pret & pp* -al[l]ed; *ger* -al[l]ing) *tr* zurückhaltender vorbringen

soft'-soap' *tr* (coll) schmeicheln (*dat*)

soggy ['sagi] *adj* (*soaked*) durchnäßt; (*ground*) sumpfig

soil [sɔɪl] *s* Boden *m* || *tr* beschmutzen || *intr* schmutzen

soil' pipe' *s* Abflußrohr *n*

sojourn ['sodʒʌrn] *s* Aufenthalt *m* || *intr* sich vorübergehend aufhalten

solace ['salɪs] *s* Trost *m* || *tr* trösten

solar ['solər] *adj* Sonnen-

so'lar plex'us ['pleksəs] *s* (anat) Sonnengeflecht *n*

solder ['sadər] *s* Lötmetall *n* || *tr* löten

sol'dering i'ron *s* Lötkolben *m*

soldier ['soldʒər] *s* Soldat *m*

sole [sol] *adj* einzig, alleinig || *s* (*of a shoe, foot*) Sohle *f*; (fish) Scholle *f* || *tr* (be)sohlen

solely ['soli] *adv* einzig und allein

solemn ['saləm] *adj* feierlich; (*expression*) ernst

solemnity [sə'lemnɪti] *s* Feierlichkeit *f*

solicit [sə'lɪsɪt] *tr* (*beg for*) dringend bitten um; (*accost*) ansprechen; (*new members, customers*) werben

solicitor [sə'lɪsɪtər] *s* (com) Agent *–in mf*; (jur) Rechtsanwalt *m*

solicitous [sə'lɪsɪtəs] *adj* fürsorglich

solid ['salɪd] *adj* (*hard, firm, e.g., ice, ground*) fest; (*sturdy, e.g., person, furniture; firm, e.g., foundation, learning; financially sound*) solid(e); (*compact*) kompakt, massiv; (*durable*) dauerhaft; (*gold*) gediegen; (*meal, blow*) kräftig; (*hour*) ganz, geschlagen; (*of one color*) einfarbig; (*color*) getönt; (*of one mind*) einmütig; (*grounds, argument*) stichhaltig; (*row of houses*) geschlossen; (*clouds, fog*) dicht; (*geom*) Raum– || *s* (*geom, phys*) Körper *m*

solidarity [,salɪ'dærɪti] *s* Solidarität *f*, Verbundenheit *f*

sol'id food' *s* feste Nahrung *f*

sol'id geom'etry *s* Stereometrie *f*

solidi·fy [sə'lɪdɪ,faɪ] *v* (*pret & pp* –fied) *tr* fest werden lassen; (*fig*) konsolidieren || *intr* fest werden

solidity [sə'lɪdɪti] *s* (*state*) Festigkeit *f*; (*soundness*) Solidität *f*

solidly ['salɪdli] *adv*—**be s. behind s.o.** sich mit j–m solidarisch erklären

sol'id-state' *adj* Transistor–

soliloquy [sə'lɪləkwi] *s* Selbstgespräch *n*

solitaire ['salɪ,ter] *s* Solitär *m*

solitary ['salɪ,teri] *adj* allein; (*life*) zurückgezogen; (*exception*) einzig; (*lonely*) einsam

sol'itary confine'ment *s* Einzelhaft *f*

solitude ['salɪ,t(j)ud] *s* Einsamkeit *f*; (*lonely spot*) abgelegener Ort *m*

so·lo ['solo] *adj & adv* solo || *s* (–los) Solo *n*

so'lo flight' *s* Soloflug *m*

soloist ['solo·ɪst] *s* Solist –in *mf*

so'lo part' *s* (*mus*) Solostimme *f*

solstice ['salstɪs] *s* Sonnenwende *f*

soluble ['saljəbəl] *adj* (*fig*) (auf)lösbar; (*chem*) löslich

solution [sə'luʃən] *s* Lösung *f*

solvable ['salvəbəl] *adj* (auf)lösbar

solve [salv] *tr* (auf)lösen

solvency ['salvənsi] *s* Zahlungsfähigkeit *f*

solvent ['salvənt] *adj* zahlungsfähig; (*chem*) (auf)lösend || *s* Lösungsmittel *n*

somber ['sambər] *adj* düster, trüb(e)

some [sʌm] *indef adj* (*with singular nouns*) etwas; (*with plural nouns*) manche; (*sometimes not translated*) e.g., I am buying s. stockings ich kaufe Strümpfe; (*coll*) toll, e.g., s. girl! tolles Mädchen!; at s. time or other irgendeinmal, irgendwann; s. ... or other irgendein; s. other way sonstwie || *adv* (*with numerals*) etwa, ungefähr || *indef pron* manche; (*part of*) ein Teil *m*; s. of these people einige Leute; s. of us manche von uns

some'bod'y *indef pron* jemand, irgendwer; s. else jemand anderer || *s*—be a s. etwas Besonderes sein

some'day' *adv* e–s Tages

some'how' *adv* irgendwie; (*for some reason or other*) aus irgendeinem Grunde

some'one' *indef pron* jemand, irgendwer; s. else jemand anderer; s. else's fremd, e.g., s. else's property fremdes Eigentum

some'place' *adv* irgendwo; (*direction*) irgendwohin

somersault ['sʌmər,salt] *s* Purzelbaum *m*; (*gym*) Überschlag *m*; do a s. e–n Purzelbaum schlagen || *intr* sich überschlagen

some'thing' *indef pron* etwas; he is s. of an expert er ist e–e Art Experte; s. else etwas anderes; s. or other irgend etwas

some'time' *adv* einmal; s. today irgendwann heute

some'times' *adv* manchmal; sometimes ... sometimes ... mal ... mal ...

some'way', **some'ways'** *adv* irgendwie

some'what' *adv* etwas

some'where' *adv* irgendwo; (*direction*) irgendwohin; from s. else sonstwoher; s. else sonstwo

somnambulist [sam'næmbjəlɪst] *s* Nachtwandler –in *mf*

somnolent ['samnələnt] *adj* schläfrig

son [sʌn] *s* Sohn *m*

sonar ['sonar] *s* Sonar *n*

sonata [sə'natə] *s* Sonate *f*

song [saŋ] *s* Lied *n*; (*of birds*) Gesang *m*; for a s. (coll) um ein Spottgeld

Song' of Songs' *s* (Bib) Hohelied *n*

sonic ['sanɪk] *adj* Schall–

son'ic boom' *s* Kopfwellenknall *m*

son'-in-law' *s* (sons-in-law) Schwiegersohn *m*

sonnet ['sanɪt] *s* Sonett *n*

sonny ['sani] *s* Söhnchen *n*, Kleiner *m*

Son' of Man', **the** *s* (Bib) der Menschensohn

sonorous [sə'norəs] *adj* sonor

soon [sun] *adv* bald; as s. as sobald; as s. as possible sobald wie möglich; just as s. (*expressing preference*) genauso gern(e); no sooner said than done gesagt, getan; sooner (*expressing time*) früher, eher; (*expressing preference*) lieber, eher; sooner or later über kurz oder lang; the sooner the better je eher, je besser; too s. zu früh

soot [sʊt] *s* Ruß *m*

soothe [suð] *tr* beschwichtigen, beruhigen; have a soothing effect on beruhigend wirken auf (*acc*)

soothsayer ['suð,se·ər] *s* Wahrsager *m*

sooty ['suti] *adj* rußig

sop [sap] *s* eingetunktes Stück *n* Brot; (*something given to pacify*) Beschwichtigungsmittel *n*; (*bribe*) Schmiergeld *n*; (*spineless person*) Waschlappen *m* || *v* (*pret & pp* sopped; *ger* sopping) *tr* (*dip*) eintunken; sop up aufsaugen

sophist ['safɪst] *s* Sophist –in *mf*

sophisticated [sə'fɪstɪ,ketɪd] *adj* (*person*) weltklug; (*way of life*) verfeinert; (*highly developed*) hochentwickelt

sophistication [sə,fɪstɪ'keʃən] *s* Weltklugheit *f*

sophistry ['safɪstri] *s* Sophisterei *f*

sophomore ['safə‚mor] *s* Student –in *mf* im zweiten Studienjahr

sop'ping *adj* klatschnaß ‖ *adv*—s. wet klatschnaß

sopran·o [sə'præno] *adj* Sopran– ‖ *s* (–os) (*uppermost voice*) Sopran *m*; (*soprano part*) Sopranpartie *f*; (*singer*) Sopranist –in *mf*

sorcerer ['sɔrsərər] *s* Zauberer *m*

sorceress ['sɔrsəris] *s* Zauberin *f*

sorcery ['sɔrsəri] *s* Zauberei *f*

sordid ['sɔrdɪd] *adj* schmutzig; (*improper*) unlauter

sore [sor] *adj* wund; (*sensitive*) empfindlich; (coll) (at) bös (auf *acc*); be s. weh tun; s. spot (& fig) wunder Punkt *m* ‖ *s* Wunde *f*

sore'head' *s* (coll) Verbitterte *mf*

sorely ['sorli] *adv* sehr

soreness ['sornis] *s* Empfindlichkeit *f*

sore' throat' *s* Halsweh *n*

sorority [sə'rɔriti] *s* Studentinnenvereinigung *f*

sorrel ['sɔrəl] *adj* fuchsrot ‖ *s* Fuchs *m*; (bot) Sauerampfer *m*

sorrow ['sɔro] *s* Kummer *m* ‖ *intr* (for or over) Kummer haben (um)

sorrowful ['sɔrəfəl] *adj* betrübt

sorry ['sɔri] *adj* traurig, betrübt; (*appearance*) armselig; I am s. es tut mir leid; I am (or feel) s. for him er tut mir leid

sort [sɔrt] *s* Art *f*, Sorte *f*; all sorts of alle möglichen; nothing of the s. nichts dergleichen; out of sorts unpäßlich; s. of (coll) (with adjectives) etwas; (with verbs) irgendwie; (with nouns) so 'n, e.g., I had a s. of feeling that ich hatte so 'ne Ahnung, daß; these sorts of derartige; what s. of was für ein ‖ *tr* sortieren; s. out aussortieren; (fig) sichten

sortie ['sɔrti] *s* (from a fortress) Ausfall *m*; (aer) Einzeleinsatz *m* ‖ *intr* e–n Ausfall machen

so'-so' *adj* & *adv* soso, leidlich

sot [sat] *s* Trunkenbold *m*

soul [sol] *s* (spiritual being; inhabitant) Seele *f*; not a s. (coll) keine Seele *f*; upon my s.! meiner Seele!

sound [saund] *adj* Schall–, Ton–; (healthy) gesund; (valid) einwandfrei; (basis) tragfähig; (sleep) fest; (beating) (coll) tüchtig; (business) solid; (judgment) treffsicher ‖ *s* Laut *m*, Ton *m*; (noise) Geräusch *n*; (of one's voice) Klang *m*; (narrow body of water) Sund *m*; (phys) Schall *m*; (surg) Sonde *f* ‖ *adv*—be s. asleep fest schlafen ‖ *tr* ertönen lassen; (med) sondieren; (naut) loten; s. out (coll) j–m auf den Zahn fühlen; s. the alarm Alarm schlagen; s. the all-clear entwarnen ‖ *intr* (er)klingen, (er)tönen; (seem) klingen; (naut) loten; it sounds good to me es kommt mir gut vor; s. off (coll) sich laut beschweren

sound' bar'rier *s* Schallgrenze *f*, Schallmauer *f*

sound' effects' *spl* Klangeffekte *pl*

sound' film' *s* Tonfilm *m*

sound'ing *s* Lotung *f*; take soundings loten

sound'ing board' *s* (on an instrument) Resonanzboden *m*; (over an orchestra or speaker) Schallmuschel *f*; (board for damping sounds) Schalldämpfungsbrett *n*

soundly ['saundli] *adv* tüchtig

sound'proof' *adj* schalldicht ‖ *tr* schalldicht machen

sound' stu'dio *s* (cin) Tonatelier *n*

sound' techni'cian *s* Tontechniker *m*

sound' track' *s* (cin) Tonstreifen *m*

sound' truck' *s* Lautsprecherwagen *m*

sound' wave' *s* Schallwelle *f*

soup [sup] *s* Suppe *f*; (thick fog) (coll) Waschküche *f*; in the s. (coll) in der Patsche ‖ *tr*—s. up (aut) frisieren

soup' kitch'en *s* Volksküche *f*

soup'meat' *s* Suppenfleisch *n*

soup' plate' *s* Suppenteller *m*

soup'spoon' *s* Suppenlöffel *m*

sour [saur] *adj* (& fig) sauer ‖ *tr* säuern; (fig) verbittern ‖ *intr* säuern; (fig) versauern

source [sors] *s* Quelle *f*

source' lan'guage *s* Ausgangssprache *f*

source' mate'rial *s* Quellenmaterial *n*

sour' cher'ry *s* Weichsel *f*

sour' grapes' *spl* (fig) saure Trauben *pl*

sour' note' *s* (& fig) Mißklang *m*

sour'puss' *s* (sl) Sauertopf *m*

souse [saus] *s* (sl) Säufer –in *mf*

soused *adj* (sl) besoffen

south [sauθ] *adj* Süd–, südlich ‖ *adv* (direction) nach Süden; s. of südlich von ‖ *s* Süd(en) *m*

South' Amer'ica *s* Südamerika *n*

south'east' *adj* Südost– ‖ *adv* (direction) südöstlich; s. of südöstlich von ‖ *s* Südost(en) *m*

south'east'ern *adj* südöstlich

southerly ['sʌðərli] *adj* südlich

southern ['sʌðərn] *adj* südlich

southerner ['sʌðərnər] *s* Südländer –in *mf*; (in the U.S.A.) Südstaatler –in *mf*

south'paw' *adj* (coll) linkshändig ‖ *s* (coll) Linkshänder –in *mf*

South' Pole' *s* Südpol *m*

South' Seas' *spl* Südsee *f*

southward ['sauθwərd] *adv* südwärts

south'west' *adj* Südwest– ‖ *adv* südwestlich; s. of südwestlich von ‖ *s* Südwest(en) *m*

south'west'ern *adj* südwestlich

souvenir ['suvə‚nɪr] *s* Andenken *n*

sovereign ['savrɪn] *adj* souverän ‖ *s* Souverän *m*, Landesfürst *m*

sov'ereign rights' *spl* Hoheitsrechte *pl*

sovereignty ['savrinti] *s* Souveränität *f*

soviet ['sovi‚et] *adj* sowjetisch ‖ *s* Sowjet *m*; the Soviets die Sowjets *pl*

So'viet Rus'sia *s* Sowjetrußland *n*

So'viet Un'ion *s* Sowjetunion *f*

sow [sau] *s* Sau *f*; [so] *v* (pret sowed; pp sowed & sown) *tr* & *intr* säen

soybean ['sɔɪ‚bin] *s* Sojabohne *f*

spa [spa] *s* Bad *n*, Badekurort *m*

space [spes] *s* Raum *m*; (between ob-

jects) Zwischenraum *m*; (typ) Spatium *n*; take up s. Platz einnehmen ‖ *tr* in Abständen anordnen; (typ) spationieren

space' age' *s* Weltraumzeitalter *n*

space' bar' *s* (typ) Leertaste *f*

space' cap'sule *s* (rok) Raumkapsel *f*

space'craft' *s* Weltraumfahrzeug *n*

space' flight' *s* Raumflug *m*

space'man' *s* (-men') Raumfahrer *m*

space' probe' *s* Sonde *f*

space'ship' *s* Raumschiff *n*

space' shot' *s* Weltraumabschuß *m*

space' shut'tle *s* Raumfähre *f*

space' suit' *s* Raumanzug *m*

space' trav'el *s* Raumfahrt *f*

spacious ['speʃəs] *adj* geräumig

spade [sped] *s* Spaten *m*; (cards) Pik *n*; call a s. a s. das Kind beim richtigen Namen nennen

spade'work' *s* (fig) Pionierarbeit *f*

spaghetti [spə'gɛti] *s* Spahetti *pl*

Spain [spen] *s* Spanien *f*

span [spæn] *s* (& fig) Spanne *f*; (*of a bridge*) Joch *n*; s. of time Zeitspanne *f* ‖ *v* (*pret & pp* spanned); *ger* spanning) *tr* (e.g., the waist) umspannen; (*a river*) überbrücken; (*said of a bridge*) überspannen

spangle ['spæŋgəl] *s* Flitter *m* ‖ *tr* mit Flitter besetzen

Spaniard ['spænjərd] *s* Spanier –in *mf*

spaniel ['spænjəl] *s* Wachtelhund *m*

Spanish ['spænɪʃ] *adj* spanisch ‖ *s* Spanisch *n*; the S. die Spanier

Span'ish-Amer'ican *adj* spanisch-amerikanisch ‖ *s* Amerikaner –in *mf* mit spanischer Muttersprache

Span'ish moss' *s* Moosbärte *pl*

spank [spæŋk] *tr* (ver)hauen

spank'ing *adj* (quick) flink; (breeze) frisch ‖ *adv*—s. new funkelnagelneu ‖ *s* Schläge *m*

spar [spɑr] *s* (aer) Holm *m*; (mineral) Spat *m*; (naut) Spiere *f* ‖ *v* (*pret & pp* sparred); *ger* sparring) *intr* sparren

spare [sper] *adj* Ersatz-; (thin) mager; (time) frei; (leftover) übrig ‖ *s* (aut) Ersatzreifen *m* ‖ *tr* (a person) schonen; (time, money) erübrigen; (expense) scheuen; (do without) entbehren; have to s. übrig haben; s. s.o. s.th. j-m etw ersparen

spare' bed' *s* Gastbett *n*

spare' part' *s* Ersatzteil *n*

spare'rib' *s* Rippenspeer *n*

spare' time' *s* Freizeit *f*

spare'-time' *adj* nebenberuflich

spare' tire' *s* Ersatzreifen *m*

spar'ing *adj* sparsam; be s. with sparsam umgehen mit

spark [spɑrk] *s* Funke(n) *m* ‖ *tr* (set off) auslösen; (stimulate) anregen ‖ *intr* Funken sprühen

spark' gap' *s* Funkenstrecke *f*

sparkle ['spɑrkəl] *s* Funkeln *n* ‖ *intr* funkeln; (said of wine) moussieren

spark' plug' *s* Zündkerze *f*

spar'ring part'ner *s* Übungspartner *m*

sparrow ['spæro] *s* Spatz *m*, Sperling *m*

spar'row hawk' *s* Sperber *m*

sparse [spɑrs] *adj* spärlich

Spartan ['spɑrtən] *adj* spartanisch ‖ *s* Spartaner –in *mf*

spasm ['spæzəm] *s* Krampf *m*, Zuckung *f*

spasmodic [spæz'mɑdɪk] *adj* sprunghaft; (pathol) krampfartig

spastic ['spæstɪk] *adj* spastisch

spat [spæt] *s* (coll) Wortwechsel *m*

spatial ['speʃəl] *adj* räumlich

spatter ['spætər] *s* Spritzen *n*; (stain) Spritzfleck *m* ‖ *tr* verspritzen

spatula ['spætʃələ] *s* Spachtel *m & f*

spawn [spɔn] *s* Fischlaich *m* ‖ *tr* hervorbringen ‖ *intr* (said of fish) laichen

spay [spe] *tr* die Eierstöcke entfernen aus

speak [spik] *v* (*pret* spoke [spok]; *pp* spoken) *tr* sprechen; s. one's mind sich aussprechen ‖ *intr* (about) sprechen (über *acc*, von); generally speaking im allgemeinen; so to s. sozusagen; speaking! (telp) am Apparat!; s. to sprechen mit; (give a speech to) sprechen zu; s. up laut sprechen; (say something) den Mund aufmachen; s. up! heraus mit der Sprache!; s. up for eintreten für

speak'-eas'y *s* Flüsterkneipe *f*

speaker ['spikər] *s* Sprecher –in *mf*; (before an audience) Redner –in *mf*; (parl) Sprecher –in *mf*; (rad) Lautsprecher *m*

spear [spɪr] *s* Speer *m* ‖ *tr* durchbohren; (a piece of meat) aufspießen; (fish) mit dem Speer fangen

spear'head' *s* Speerspitze *f*; (mil) Stoßkeil *m* ‖ *tr* an der Spitze stehen von

spear'mint' *s* Krauseminze *f*

special ['speʃəl] *adj* besonder, Sonder– ‖ *s* (rr) Sonderzug *m*; today's s. Stammgericht *n*

spe'cial-deliv'ery *s* Eilzustellung *f*; (tab on envelope) Eilsendung *f*

spec'ial-deliv'ery let'ter *s* Eilbrief *m*

specialist ['speʃəlɪst] *s* Spezialist –in *mf*

specialization [,speʃəlɪ'zeʃən] *s* Spezialisierung *f*

specialize ['speʃə,laɪz] *intr* sich spezialisieren; specialized knowledge Fachkenntnisse *pl*

spe'cial of'fer *s* (com) Sonderangebot *n*

specialty ['speʃəlti] *s* Spezialität *f*; (special field) Spezialfach *n*

spe'cialty shop' *s* Spezialgeschäft *n*

specie ['spisi] *s*—in s. der Art nach

spe·cies ['spisiz] *s* (–cies) Gattung *f*

specific [spɪ'sɪfɪk] *adj* spezifisch

specification [,spesɪfɪ'keʃən] *s* Spezifizierung *f*; specifications (tech) technische Beschreibung *f*

specif'ic grav'ity *s* spezifisches Gewicht *n*

specify ['spesɪ,faɪ] *v* (*pret & pp* –fied) *tr* spezifizieren; (stipulate) bestimmen

specimen ['spesɪmən] *s* (example) Exemplar *n*; (test sample) Probe *f*

specious ['spiʃəs] *adj* Schein–

speck [spɛk] s Fleck m; (in the distance) Pünktchen n; s. of dust Stäubchen n; s. of grease Fettauge n

speckle ['spɛkəl] s Sprenkel m || tr sprenkeln

spectacle ['spɛktəkəl] s Schauspiel n, Anblick m; spectacles Brille f

spec'tacle case' s Brillenfutteral n

spectacular [spɛk'tækjələr] adj sensationell || s (cin) Monsterfilm m

spectator ['spɛktətər] s Zuschauer –in mf

specter ['spɛtər] s Gespenst n

spec•trum ['spɛktrəm] s (–tra [trə]) Spektrum n

speculate ['spɛkjə,let] intr spekulieren; s. in spekulieren in (dat); s. on Überlegungen anstellen über (acc)

speculation [,spɛkjə'leʃən] s Spekulation f

speculative ['spɛkjələtɪv] adj (com) Spekulations–; (philos) spekulativ

speculator ['spɛkjə,letər] s Spekulant –in mf

speech [spitʃ] s Sprache f; (address) Rede f; give a s. e–e Rede halten

speech' defect' s Sprachfehler m

speech' imped'iment s Sprachstörung f

speechless ['spitʃlɪs] adj sprachlos

speed [spid] s Geschwindigkeit f; (gear) Gang m; at top s. mit Höchstgeschwindigkeit; pick up s. auf Touren kommen || v (pret & pp speeded & sped [spɛd]) tr beschleunigen; s. up forcieren; s. it up (coll) ein scharfes Tempo vorlegen || intr sich rasen; (above the speed limit) (aut) zu schnell fahren

speed'boat' s Schnellboot n

speed'ing s (aut) Schnellfahren n; be arrested for s. wegen Überschreitung der Höchstgeschwindigkeit verhaftet werden; no s. (public sign) Schnellfahren verboten

speed' lim'it s Geschwindigkeitsgrenze f

speed' of light' s Lichtgeschwindigkeit f

speed' of sound' s Schallgeschwindigkeit f

speedometer [spi'dɑmɪtər] s Tachometer n; (mileage indicator) Meilenzähler m, Kilometerzähler m

speed' rec'ord s Geschwindigkeitsrekord m

speed' trap' s Autofalle f

speed'way' s (aut) Rennstrecke f

speedy ['spidi] adj schnell, schleunig; (reply) baldig

speed' zone' s Geschwindigkeitsbeschränkung f

spell [spɛl] s (short period) Zeitlang f; (attack) Anfall m; (magical influence) Bann m; be under s.o.'s s. in j–s Bann stehen; cast a s. bannen || v (pret & pp spelled & spelt [spɛlt]) tr buchstabieren; (in writing) schreiben; s. out Buchstaben für Buchstaben lesen; (fig) auseinanderklamüsern; s. trouble Schwie-

rigkeiten bedeuten || intr buchstabieren

spell'bind'er s faszinierender Redner m

spell'bound' adj gebannt

spell'ing s Schreibweise f; (orthography) Rechtschreibung f

spell'ing bee' s orthographischer Wettbewerb m

spelt [spɛlt] s Spelz m

spelunker [spɪ'lʌŋkər] s Höhlenforscher –in mf

spend [spɛnd] v (pret & pp spent [spɛnt]) tr (money) ausgeben; (time) verbringen; s. the night übernachten; s. time and effort on Zeit und Mühe verwenden auf (acc)

spend'thrift' s Verschwender –in mf

spent [spɛnt] adj (exhausted) erschöpft; (cartridge) leergeschossen

sperm [spʌrm] s Sperma n

sperm' whale' s Pottwal m

spew [spju] tr erbrechen; (fig) ausspeien || intr sich erbrechen; (fig) herausströmen

sphere [sfɪr] s Kugel f, Sphäre f; (fig) Bereich m; s. of influence Einflußsphäre f

spherical ['sfɛrɪkəl] adj sphärisch, kugelförmig

sphinx [sfɪŋks] s (sphinxes & sphinges ['sfɪndʒiz]) Sphinx f

spice [spaɪs] s Gewürz n, Würze f; (fig) Würze f || tr würzen

spick-and-span ['spɪkənd'spæn] adj blitzblank

spicy ['spaɪsi] adj würzig; (fig) pikant

spider ['spaɪdər] s Spinne f

spi'derweb' s Spinnengewebe n

spiffy ['spɪfi] adj (sl) fesch

spigot ['spɪgət] s Wasserhahn m

spike [spaɪk] s (nail) langer Nagel m; (in volleyball) Schmetterball m; (bot) Ähre f; (rr) Schwellenschraube f; (sport) Dorn m || tr (a drink) e–n Schuß Alkohol tun in (acc); (in volleyball) schmettern

spill [spɪl] s (spilling) Vergießen n; (stain) Fleck m, Klecks m; (fall) Sturz m; take a s. stürzen || v (pret & pp spilled & spilt [spɪlt]) tr verschütten; (a rider) abwerfen; s. out ausschütten; s. the beans (sl) alles ausplaudern || intr überlaufen; s. over into (fig) übergreifen auf (acc)

spill'way' s Überlauf m

spin [spɪn] s (rotation) Umdrehung f; (short ride) kurze Fahrt f; (aer) Trudeln n; go for a s. e–e Spritztour machen; go into a s. (aer) ins Trudeln kommen || v (pret & pp spun [spʌn]) ger spinning) tr (rotate) drehen; (tex) spinnen; s. out (a story) ausspinnen; s. s.o. around j–n im Kreise herumwirbeln || intr kreiseln, sich drehen; (tex) spinnen; my head is spinning mir dreht sich alles im Kopf

spinach ['spɪnɪtʃ] s Spinat m

spi'nal col'umn ['spaɪnəl] s Wirbelsäule f

spi'nal cord' s Rückenmark n

spi'nal flu'id s Rückenmarksflüssigkeit f

spindle ['spɪndəl] s Spindel f

spin'-dry' v (pret & pp -dried) tr schleudern

spin'-dry'er s Trockenschleuder m

spine [spaɪn] s Rückgrat n, Wirbelsäule f; (bb) Buchrücken m

spineless ['spaɪnlɪs] adj (& fig) rückgratlos

spinet ['spɪnɪt] s Spinett n

spinner ['spɪnər] s Spinner -in mf; (mach) Spinnmaschine f

spin'ning (rotating) sich drehend; (tex) Spinn– ‖ s (tex) Spinnen n

spin'ning wheel' s Spinnrad n

spinster ['spɪnstər] s alte Jungfer f

spi'ral ['spaɪrəl] adj spiralig ‖ s Spirale f; s. of rising prices and wages Lohn-Preis-Spirale f ‖ v (pret & pp -ral[l]ed; ger -ral[l]ing) intr sich in die Höhe schrauben

spi'ral stair'case s Wendeltreppe f

spire [spaɪr] s Spitze f

spirit ['spɪrɪt] s Geist m; (enthusiasm) Schwung m; (ghost) Geist m; in high spirits in gehobener Stimmung; in low spirits in gedrückter Stimmung; spirits Spirituosen pl; that's the right s.! das ist die richtige Einstellung! ‖ tr—s. away wegzaubern

spir'ited adj lebhaft; (horse) feurig

spiritless ['spɪrɪtlɪs] adj schwunglos

spiritual ['spɪrɪt/ʊəl] adj (incorporeal) geistig; (of the soul) seelisch; (religious) geistlich ‖ s geistliches Negerlied n

spiritualism ['spɪrɪt/ʊə‚lɪzəm] s Spiritismus m

spiritualist ['spɪrɪt/ʊəlɪst] s Spiritist -in mf

spir'itual life' s Seelenleben n

spit [spɪt] s Spucke f; (culin) Spieß m ‖ v (pret & pp spat [spæt] & spit; ger spitting) tr & intr spucken

spite [spaɪt] s Trotz m; for s. aus Trotz; in s. of trotz (genit) ‖ tr kränken; he did it to s. me er hat es mir zum Trotz getan

spiteful ['spaɪtfəl] adj gehässig

spit'fire' s (coll) Sprühteufel m

spit'ting im'age s (coll) Ebenbild n

spittoon [spɪ'tun] s Spucknapf m

splash [splæʃ] s Platschen n; (noise of falling into water) Klatschen n; make a s. (coll) Aufsehen erregen ‖ tr (a person, etc.) bespritzen; (e.g., water) spritzen ‖ intr klatschen, patschen; s. about planschen; s. down (rok) wassern ‖ interj schwaps!, platsch!

splash'down' s (rok) Wasserung f

splatter ['splætər] tr & intr kleckern

spleen [splin] s Milz f; (fig) schlechte Laune f; vent one's s. on seiner schlechten Laune Luft machen gegenüber (dat)

splendid ['splendɪd] adj prächtig, herrlich; (coll) großartig

splendor ['splendər] s Herrlichkeit f

splice [splaɪs] s Spleiß m ‖ tr (a rope) spleißen; (film) zusammenkleben

splint [splɪnt] s Schiene f; put in splints schienen

splinter ['splɪntər] s Splitter m ‖ tr (zer)splittern

splin'ter group' s Splittergruppe f

split [splɪt] adj rissig ‖ s Riß m, Spalt m; (fig) Spaltung f; (gym) Spagat m ‖ v (pret & pp split; ger splitting) tr spalten; (pants) platzen; (profits, the difference) sich teilen in (acc); s. hairs Haarspalterei treiben; s. one's sides laughing vor Lachen platzen; s. open aufbrechen ‖ intr (into) sich spalten (in acc); splitting headache rasende Kopfschmerzen pl; s. up (said of a couple) sich trennen

split' infin'itive s gespaltener Infinitiv m

split'-lev'el adj mit Zwischenstockwerk versehen

split' personal'ity s gespaltene Persönlichkeit f

split' sec'ond s Sekundenbruchteil m

splotch [splatʃ] s Klecks m ‖ tr kleckern

splotchy ['splatʃi] adj fleckig

splurge [splʌrdʒ] s—go on a s. verschwenderischen Aufwand treiben ‖ tr verschwenden ‖ intr (on) verschwenderische Ausgaben machen (für)

splutter ['splʌtər] s Geplapper n ‖ tr (words) herausprudeln; (besplatter) bespritzen ‖ intr plappern; (said, e.g., of grease) spritzen

spoil [spɔɪl] s—spoils Beute f ‖ v (pret & pp spoiled & spoilt [spɔɪlt]) tr (perishable goods; fun) verderben; (a child) verziehen, verwöhnen ‖ intr verderben, schlecht werden; spoiling for a fight zanksüchtig

spoilage ['spɔɪlɪdʒ] s Verderb m

spoil'sport' s Spielverderber -in mf

spoils' sys'tem s Futterkrippensystem n

spoke [spok] s Speiche f

spokes'man s (-men) Wortführer -in mf

sponge [spʌndʒ] s Schwamm m ‖ tr schnorren ‖ intr schnorren; s. on (coll) schmarotzen bei

sponge' cake' s Sandtorte f

sponger ['spʌndʒər] s Schmarotzer -in mf

sponge' rub'ber s Schaumgummi m & n

spongy ['spʌndʒi] adj schwammig

sponsor ['spansər] s Förderer -in mf; (of a program) Sponsor m; (of an immigrant) Bürge m, Bürgin f; (at baptism or confirmation) Pate m, Patin f ‖ tr fördern; (a program) finanziell fördern

spontaneity [spantə'ni‚ɪti] s Spontaneität f

spontaneous [span'teni‚əs] adj spontan

sponta'neous combus'tion s Selbstverbrennung f

spontaneously [span'teni‚əsli] adv von selbst, unaufgefordert

spoof [spuf] s (hoax) Jux m; (parody) (on) Parodie f (auf acc) || intr albern

spook [spuk] s (coll) Spuk m

spooky ['spuki] adj spukhaft

spool [spul] s Spule f, Rolle f

spoon [spun] s Löffel m; **wooden s.** Kochlöffel m || tr (out) löffeln

spoonerism ['spunə,rɪzəm] s Schüttelreim m

spoon′-feed′ v (pret & pp –fed) tr (fig) es leicht machen (dat)

spoonful ['spunful] s Löffel m

sporadic [spə'rædɪk] adj vereinzelt

spore [spor] s Spore f

sport [sport] adj Sport– || s Sport m; (biol) Spielart f; **a good s.** ein Pfundskerl m; **go in for sports** sporteln; **in s.** im Spaß; **make s. of** sich lustig machen über (acc); **play sports** Sport treiben; **poor s.** Spielverderber –in mf; **sports** Sport m; (sportscast) Sportbericht m || intr sich belustigen

sport′ing event′ s Sportveranstaltung f

sport′ing goods′ spl Sportwaren pl

sport′ jac′ket s Sportjacke f

sports′ car′ s Sportwagen m

sports′cast′ s Sportbericht m

sports′cast′er s Sportberichterstatter m

sports′ fan′ s Sportfreund –in mf

sport′ shirt′ s Sporthemd n

sports′man s (–men) Sportsmann m

sports′manlike adj sportlich

sports′manship′ s sportliches Verhalten n

sports′ news′ s Sportnachrichten pl

sports′wear′ s Sportkleidung f

sports′ world′ s Sportwelt f

sports′ writ′er s Sportjournalist –in mf

sporty ['sporti] adj auffallend

spot [spat] s (stain) Fleck(en) m; (place) Platz m, Ort m; (as on a leopard) Tüpfel m & n; **be on the s.** (be present) zur Stelle sein; (be in difficulty) in der Klemme sein; **hit the s.** gerade das Richtige sein; **on the s.** auf der Stelle; **put on the s.** in Verlegenheit bringen || v (pret & pp **spotted**; ger **spotting**) tr (stain) beflecken; (espy) erblicken; (points in betting) vorgeben

spot′ announce′ment s Durchsage f

spot′ cash′ s ungebundene Barmittel pl

spot′ check′ s Stichprobe f

spot′-check′ tr stichprobenweise prüfen

spotless ['spatlɪs] adj makellos

spot′light′ s Scheinwerfer m; **in the s.** (fig) im Rampenlicht der Öffentlichkeit || tr (fig) in den Vordergrund stellen

spot′ remov′er [rɪ,muvər] s Fleckputzmittel n

spotty ['spati] adj fleckig; (uneven) ungleichmäßig

spot′ weld′ing s Punktschweißung f

spouse [spaus] s Gatte m, Gattin f

spout [spaut] s (of a pot) Tülle f; (jet of water) Strahl m || tr (& fig) hervorsprudeln || intr spritzen; (coll) große Reden schwingen

sprain [spren] s Verstauchung f || tr verstauchen; **s. one's ankle** sich [dat] den Fuß vertreten

sprat [spræt] s (ichth) Sprotte f

sprawl [sprɔl] intr (out) alle viere von sich ausstrecken; (said of a city) sich weit ausbreiten

spray [spre] s (of ocean) Gischt m; (from a can) Spray n; (from a fountain) Sprühwasser n; **s. of flowers** Blütenzweig m || tr spritzen; (liquids) zerstäuben; (plants) besprühen

sprayer ['spre-ər] s Zerstäuber m; (for a garden) Gartenspritze f

spray′ gun′ s Spritzpistole f

spray′ paint′ s Spritzfarbe f

spread [spred] s (act of spreading) Ausbreitung f; (extent) Verbreitung f; (e.g., of a tree) Umfang m; (on bread) Aufstrich m; (bedspread) Bettdecke f; (large piece of land) weite Fläche f; (of a shot) Streubereich m & n; (sumptuous meal) Gelage n || v (pret & pp **spread**) tr (warmth, light, news, rumors) verbreiten; (mortar, glue) auftragen; (e.g., butter) aufstreichen; (the legs) spreizen; (manure) streuen; **s. oneself too thin** sich verzetteln; **s. out over a year** über ein Jahr verteilen || intr sich verbreiten; (said of margarine) sich aufstreichen lassen

spree [spri] s Bummel m; (carousal) Zechgelage n; **go on a buying s.** sich in e-e Kauforgie stürzen

sprig [sprɪg] s Zweiglein n

sprightly ['spraɪtli] adj lebhaft; (gait) federnd

spring [sprɪŋ] adj Frühlings– || s (of water) Quelle f; (season) Frühling m; (resilience) Sprungkraft f; (of metal) Feder f; (jump) Sprung m; **springs** (aut) Federung f || v (pret **sprang** [spræŋ] & **sprung** [sprʌŋ]; pp **sprung** [sprʌŋ]) tr (a trap) zuschnappen lassen; (a leak) bekommen; (a question) (on) plötzlich stellen (dat); (a surprise) (on) bereiten (dat); **s. the news on s.o.** j-n mit der Nachricht überraschen || intr springen; **s. back** zurückschnellen; **s. from** entspringen (dat); **s. up** aufspringen; (said of industry, towns) aus dem Boden schießen

spring′board′ s (& fig) Sprungbrett n

spring′ chic′ken s Hähnchen n; **she's no s.** (sl) sie ist nicht die Jüngste

spring′ fe′ver s Frühlingsmüdigkeit f

spring′time′ s Frühlingszeit f

spring′ wa′ter s Quellwasser n

springy ['sprɪŋi] adj federnd

sprinkle ['sprɪŋkəl] s Spritzen n; (light rain) Sprühregen m || tr (water, streets, lawns, laundry) sprengen; (e.g., sugar) streuen || intr sprühen

sprinkler ['sprɪŋklər] s (truck) Sprengwagen m; (for the lawn) Rasensprenger m; (eccl) Sprengwedel m

sprin′kling s Sprengung f; **a s. of** (e.g., sugar) ein bißchen n; (e.g., of people) ein paar

prin'kling can' *s* Gießkanne *f*

prin'kling sys'tem *s* Feuerlöschanlage *f*

print [sprɪnt] *s* Sprint *m* ‖ *intr* sprinten

printer ['sprɪntər] *s* Sprinter –in *mf*

prite [spraɪt] *s* Kobold *m*, Elfe *f*

procket ['sprɑkɪt] *s* Zahnrad *n*

sprout [spraut] *s* Sproß *m* ‖ *intr* sprießen

spruce [sprus] *adj* schmuck ‖ *s* (bot) Fichte *f* ‖ *intr*—s. up sich schmücken

spry [spraɪ] *adj* (spryer & sprier; spryest & spriest) flink

spud [spʌd] *s* (for weeding) Jäthacke *f*; (potatoe) (coll) Kartoffel *f*

spume [spjum] *s* Schaum *m*

spun' glass' *s* Glasfaser *f*

spunk [spʌŋk] *s* (coll) Mumm *m*

spunky ['spʌŋki] *adj* (coll) feurig

spur [spʌr] *s* (on riding boot; on a rooster) Sporn *m*; (of a mountain) Ausläufer *m*; (fig) Ansporn *m*; (archit) Strebe *f*; (bot) Stachel *m*; (rr) Seitengleis *n*; on the s. of the moment der Eingebung des Augenblicks folgend ‖ *v* (pret & pp spurred) *ger* spurring) *tr* die Sporen geben (dat); s. on anspornen

spurious ['spjurɪəs] *adj* unecht

spurn [spʌrn] *tr* verschmähen

spurt [spʌrt] *s* Ruck *m*; (sport) Spurt *m*; in spurts ruckweise ‖ *tr* speien ‖ *intr* herausspritzen; (sport) spurten

sputnick ['spʌtnɪk] *s* Sputnik *m*

sputter ['spʌtər] *s* Stottern *n* ‖ *tr* umherspritzen; (words) hervorsprudeln ‖ *intr* (said of a person, engine) stottern; (said of a candle, fire) flackern

sputum ['spjutəm] *s* Sputum *m*

spy [spaɪ] *s* Spion –in *mf* ‖ *v* (pret & pp spied) *tr*—spy out ausspionieren ‖ *intr* spionieren

spy'glass' *s* Fernglas *n*

spy'ing *s* Spionage *f*

spy' ring' *s* Spionageorganization *f*

squabble ['skwɑbəl] *s* Zank *m* ‖ *intr* zanken

squad [skwɑd] *s* (gym) Riege *f*; (mil) Gruppe *f*; (sport) Mannschaft *f*

squad' car' *s* Funkstreifenwagen *m*

squad' lead'er *s* (mil) Gruppenführer *m*

squadron ['skwɑdrən] *s* (aer) Staffel *f*; (nav) Geschwader *n*

squalid ['skwɑlɪd] *adj* verkommen

squall [skwɔl] *s* Bö *f*

squander ['skwɑndər] *tr* verschwenden

square [skwer] *adj* quadratisch; (mile, meter, foot) Quadrat–; (fellow; meal) anständig; (even) quitt; ten meters s. zehn Meter im Quadrat; ten s. meters zehn Quadratmeter ‖ *s* Quadrat *n*; (city block) Häuserblock *m*; (open area) Platz *m*; (of a checkerboard or chessboard) Feld *n*; (carp) Winkel *m*; (math) zweite Potenz *f* ‖ *tr* quadrieren; (a number) ins Quadrat erheben; (accounts) abrechnen ‖ *intr*—s. off in Kampfstellung gehen; s. with (agree with)

übereinstimmen mit; (be frank with) aufrichtig sein zu

square' dance' *s* Reigen *m*

square' deal' *s* reelles Geschäft *n*

square' root' *s* Quadratwurzel *f*

squash [skwɑʃ] *s* (bot) Kürbis *m* ‖ *tr* (a hat) zerdrücken; (a finger, grape) quetschen; (fig) unterdrücken ‖ *intr* zerdrückt (or zerquetscht) werden

squashy ['skwɑʃi] *adj* weich, matschig

squat [skwɑt] *adj* gedrungen, untersetzt ‖ *s* Hocken *f* ‖ *v* (pret & pp squatted; *ger* squatting) *intr* hocken; s. down sich (hin)hocken

squatter ['skwɑtər] *s* Ansiedler –in *mf* ohne Rechtstitel

squaw [skwɔ] *s* Indianerin *f*

squawk [skwɔk] *s* Geschrei *n*; (sl) Schimpferei *f* ‖ *intr* schreien; (sl) schimpfen

squeak [skwik] *s* (of a door) Quietschen *n*; (of a mouse) Pfeifen *n* ‖ *intr* quietschen; (said of a mouse) pfeifen

squeal [skwil] *s* Quieken *n* ‖ *intr* (said of a pig) quieken; (said of a mouse) pfeifen; (sl) petzen; s. for joy vor Vergnügen quietschen; s. on (sl) (a pupil) verpetzen; (to the police) verpfeifen

squealer ['skwilər] *s* (sl) Petze *f*

squeamish ['skwimɪʃ] *adj* zimperlich

squeeze [skwiz] *s* Druck *m*; s. of the hand Händedruck *m* ‖ *tr* drücken; (oranges) auspressen; s. into (e.g., a trunk) hineinquetschen; s. out auspressen; s. together zusammenpressen; (e.g., people) zusammenpferchen ‖ *intr*—s. in sich eindrängen; s. through sich durchzwängen (durch)

squelch [skwɛltʃ] *s* schlagfertige Antwort *f* ‖ *tr* niederschmettern

squid [skwɪd] *s* Tintenfisch *m*

squill [skwɪl] *s* (bot) Meerzwiebel *f*; (zool) Heuschreckenkrebs *m*

squint [skwɪnt] *s* Schielen *n* ‖ *intr* (look with eyes partly closed) blinzeln; (be cross-eyed) schielen; (look askance) (at) argwöhnisch blicken (auf acc)

squint'-eyed' *adj* schielend

squire [skwaɪr] *s* (hist) Knappe *m*; (jur) Friedensrichter *m*

squirm [skwʌrm] *intr* (through) sich winden (durch); (be restless) zappeln; s. out of sich herauswinden aus

squirrel ['skwʌrəl] *s* Eichhörnchen *n*

squirt [skwʌrt] *s* Spritzer *m*; (boy) (coll) Stöpfsel *m* ‖ *tr* (ver)spritzen ‖ *intr* spritzen; s. out herausspritzen

S/S' troops' ['ɛs'ɛs] *spl* Schutzstaffel *f*

stab [stæb] *s* Stich *m*; (wound) Stichwunde *f*; make a s. at (coll) probieren ‖ *v* (pret & pp stabbed; *ger* stabbing) *tr* stechen; (kill) erstechen; (a pig) abstechen; s. s.o. in the back j–m in den Rücken fallen

stability [stə'bɪltɪ] *s* Stabilität *f*

stabilization [ˌstebɪlɪ'zeʃən] *s* (e.g., of prices) Stabilisierung *f*; (aer) Dämpfung *f*

stabilize ['stebɪˌlaɪz] *tr* stabilisieren
stabilizer ['stebɪˌlaɪzər] *s* (aer) Flosse *f*
stab' in the back' *s* Stoß *m* aus dem Hinterhalt
stable ['stebəl] *adj* stabil ‖ *s* Stall *m* ‖ *tr* unterbringen
sta'ble boy' *s* Stalljunge *m*
stack [stæk] *s* (of papers, books) Stapel *m;* (of wheat) Schober *m;* (of a ship) Schornstein *m;* (of rifles) Pyramide *f;* stacks (libr) Bücherregale *pl* ‖ *tr* (wood, wheat) aufstapeln; (rifles) zusammensetzen; (cards) packen
stadi•um ['stedɪ-əm] *s* (-ums & -a [ə]) Stadion *n*
staff [stæf] *s* (rod) Stab *m;* (personnel) Personal *n;* (of a newspaper) Redaktion *f;* (mil) Stab *m;* (mus) Notensystem *n* ‖ *tr* mit Personal besetzen
staff' of'ficer *s* Stabsoffizier *m*
staff' ser'geant *s* Feldwebel *m*
stag [stæg] *adj* Herren- ‖ *adv*—go s. ohne Damenbegleitung sein ‖ *s* Hirsch *m*
stage [stedʒ] *s* (of a theater) Bühne *f;* (phase) Stadium *n;* (stretch) Strecke *f;* (of life) Etappe *f;* (of a rocket) Stufe *f;* (scene) Szene *f;* at this s. in diesem Stadium; by easy stages etappenweise; final stages Endstadien *pl* ‖ *tr* (a play) inszenieren; (a comeback) veranstalten
stage'coach' *s* Postkutsche *f*
stage'craft' *s* Bühnenkunst *f*
stage' direc'tion *s* Bühnenanweisung *f*
stage' door' *s* Bühneneingang *m*
stage' effect' *s* Bühnenwirkung *f*
stage' fright' *s* Lampenfieber *n*
stage' hand' *s* Bühnenarbeiter –in *mf*
stage' light'ing *s* Bühnenbeleuchtung *f*
stage' man'ager *s* Bühnenleiter –in *mf*
stage' play' *s* Bühnenstück *n*
stage' prop'erties *spl* Theaterrequisiten *pl*
stagestruck ['stedʒˌstrʌk] *adj* theaterbegeistert
stagger ['stægər] *s* Taumeln *n* ‖ *tr* (e.g., lunch hours) staffeln; (& fig) erschüttern ‖ *intr* taumeln
stag'gering *adj* taumelnd; (blow, loss) vernichtend; (news) erschütternd
stagnant ['stægnənt] *adj* (water) stillstehend; (air) schlecht; (fig) träge
stagnate ['stægnet] *intr* stagnieren
stag' par'ty *s* Herrenabend *m*
staid [sted] *adj* gesetzt
stain [sten] *s* Fleck *m;* (paint) Beize *f* ‖ *tr* beflecken; (wood) beizen
stained'-glass win'dow *s* buntes Glasfenster *n*
stainless ['stenlɪs] *adj* rostfrei
stair [stɛr] *s* Stufe *f;* stairs Treppe *f*
stair'case' *s* Treppenhaus *n*
stair'way' *s* Treppenaufgang *m*
stair'well' *s* Treppenschacht *m*
stake [stek] *s* Pfahl *m;* (bet) Einsatz *m;* be at s. auf dem Spiel stehen; die at the s. auf dem Scheiterhaufen sterben; play for high stakes viel riskieren; pull up stakes (coll) ab-

hauen ‖ *tr* (plants) mit e–m Pfahl stützen; s. off abstecken; s. out a claim (fig) e–e Forderung umreißen
stake'-out' *s* polizeiliche Überwachung *f*
stalactite [stə'læktaɪt] *s* Stalaktit *m*
stalagmite [stə'lægmaɪt] *s* Stalagmit *m*
stale [stel] *adj* (baked goods) altbacken; (e.g., beer) schal; (air) verbraucht; (joke) abgedroschen; get s. abstehen
stale'mate' *s* (fig) Sackgasse *f;* (chess) Patt *n* ‖ *tr* (fig) in e–e Sackgasse treiben; (chess) patt setzen
stalk [stɔk] *s* (of grain) Halm *m;* (of a plant) Stiel *m* ‖ *tr* beschleichen; s. game pirschen
stall [stɔl] *s* (for animals) Stall *m;* (booth) Bude *f;* (sl) Vorwand *m* ‖ *tr* (a motor) abwürgen; (a person) aufhalten ‖ *intr* ausweichen; (aut) absterben; s. for time Zeit zu gewinnen suchen
stallion ['stæljən] *s* Hengst *m*
stalwart ['stɔlwərt] *adj* stämmig; (supporter) treu
stamen ['stemən] *s* Staubfaden *m*
stamina ['stæmɪnə] *s* Ausdauer *f*
stammer ['stæmər] *s* Stammeln *n* ‖ *tr* & *intr* stammeln
stammerer ['stæmərər] *s* Stammler –in *mf*
stamp [stæmp] *s* (mark) Gepräge *n;* (device for stamping) Stempel *m;* (for postage) Briefmarke *f* ‖ *tr* (e.g., a document) stempeln; (a letter) freimachen; (the earth) stampfen; s. one's foot mit dem Fuß aufstampfen; s. out (a fire) austreten; (a rebellion) niederschlagen
stampede [stæm'pid] *s* panische Flucht *f* ‖ *tr* in die Flucht jagen ‖ *intr* in wilder Flucht davonrennen
stamped' en'velope *s* Freiumschlag *m*
stamp'ing grounds' *spl* Lieblingsplatz *m*
stamp' machine' *s* Briefmarkenautomat *m*
stamp' pad' *s* Stempelkissen *n*
stance [stæns] *s* Haltung *f,* Stellung *f*
stanch [stɔntʃ] *tr* stillen
stand [stænd] *s* (booth) Stand *m;* (platform) Tribüne *f;* (e.g., for bicycles) Ständer *m;* (view, position) Standpunkt *m;* (piece of furniture) Ständer *m;* take a s. (on) Stellung nehmen (zu); take one's s. (e.g., near the door) sich stellen; s. of timber Waldbestand *m;* stands (sport) Tribüne *f;* take the s. (jur) als Zeuge auftreten ‖ *v* (pret & pp stood [stud]) *tr* (put) stellen; (the cold, hardships) aushalten; (a person) leiden; s. a chance e–e Chance haben; s. one's ground sich behaupten; s. s.o. up j–n aufsitzen lassen; s. the test sich bewähren ‖ *intr* stehen; (have validity) gelten; she wants to know where she stands sie will wissen, wie sie daran ist; s. aside auf die Seite treten; s. at attention stillstehen; s.

back zurückstehen; **s. behind** s.o.
(fig) hinter j-m stehen; **s. by** (*in readiness*) in Bereitschaft stehen; (*a decision*) bleiben bei; (*e.g., for the latest news*) am Apparat bleiben; **s. by** s.o. j-m beistehen; **s. firm fest** bleiben; **s. for** (*champion*) eintreten für; (*tolerate*) sich [*dat*] gefallen lassen; (*mean*) bedeuten; **s. good for** gutstehen für; **s. idle** stillstehen; **s. on end** sich sträuben, *e.g.,* **my hair stood on end** mir sträubten sich die Haare; **s. on one's head** kopfstehen; **s. out** (*project*) abstehen; (*be conspicuous*) hervorstechen; **s. out against** sich abzeichnen gegen; **s. s.o. in good stead** j-m zugute kommen; **s. up** aufstehen; **s. up against** aufkommen gegen; **s. up for** (*a thing*) verfechten; || (*a person*) die Stange halten (*dat*); **s. up to** s.o. j-m die Stirn bieten; **s. up under** aushalten

standard ['stændərd] *adj* Standard-, Normal- || *s* Standard *m*; (*banner*) Banner *n*

stand'ard-bear'er *s* Bannerträger *m*
stand'ard-gauge track' *s* Normalspur *f*
standardize ['stændər‚daɪz] *tr* normen
stand'ard of liv'ing *s* Lebensstandard *m*

stand'ard time' *s* Normalzeit *f*
stand'-by' *adj* Reserve– || *s*—**on s. in Bereitschaft**

standee [stæn'di] *s* Stehplatzinhaber –in *mf*
stand'in' *s* (coll) Ersatzmann *m*; (cin, theat) Double *n*
stand'ing *adj* (army, water, rule) stehend; (*committee*) ständig; (*jump*) aus dem Stand || *s* Stehen *n*; (*social*) Stellung *f*; (*of a team*) Stand *m*; **in good s.** treu; **of long s.** langjährig
stand'ing or'der *s* (com) Dauerauftrag *m*
stand'ing room' *s* Stehplatz *m*; **s. only** nur noch Stehplätze
stand'-off' *s* Unentschieden *n*
stand-offish ['stænd'ɔfɪʃ] *adj* zurückhaltend
stand'out' *s* Blickfang *m*
stand'point' *s* Standpunkt *m*
stand'still' *s* Stillstand *m*; **come to a s.** zum Stillstand kommen
stanza ['stænzə] *s* Strophe *f*
staple ['stepəl] *adj* Haupt–, Stapel– || *s* (food) Hauptnahrungsmittel *n*; (product) Hauptprodukt *n*; (clip) Heftklammer *f* || *tr* mit Draht heften
stapler ['steplər] *s* Heftmaschine *f*
star [stɑr] *adj* Spitzen–; (astr) Stern– || *s* Stern *m*; (cin, rad, telv, theat) Star *m*; **I saw stars** (fig) Sterne tanzten mir vor den Augen || *v* (*pret & pp* starred) *ger* starring) *tr* (cin, rad, sport, telv, theat) als Star herausstellen; (typ) mit Sternchen kennzeichnen || *intr* Star sein
starboard ['stɑrbərd] *adj* Steuerbord– || *s* Steuerbord *n*
starch [stɑrtʃ] *s* Stärke *f* || *tr* stärken
starchy ['stɑrtʃi] *adj* stärkenhaltig
stare [ster] *s* starrer Blick *m* || *tr*—

s. down durch Anstarren aus der Fassung bringen || *intr* starren; **s. at** anstarren; **s. into space** ins Leere blicken, ins Blaue starren
star'fish' *s* Seestern *m*
stargazer ['stɑr‚gezər] *s* Sterngucker –in *mf*
stark [stɑrk] *adj* (landscape) kahl; (sheer) völlig || *adv* völlig
stark'-na'ked *adj* splitter(faser)nackt
starlet ['stɑrlət] *s* Sternchen *n*
star'light' *s* Sternenlicht *n*
starling ['stɑrlɪŋ] *s* (orn) Star *m*
star'lit' *adj* sternhell
Star' of Da'vid *s* David(s)stern *m*
starry ['stɑri] *adj* gestirnt; (night) sternklar; (sky) Stern–
star'ry-eyed' *adj* verträumt
Stars' and Stripes' *spl* Sternenbanner *n*
Star'-Spangled Ban'ner *s* Sternenbanner *n*
start [stɑrt] *s* Anfang *m*; (sudden springing movement) plötzliches Hochfahren *n*; (lead, advantage) Vorgabe *f*, Vorsprung *m*; (of a race) Start *m*; **give s.o. a s.** j-m auf die Beine helfen || *tr* anfangen; (a motor) anlassen; (a rumor) in die Welt setzen; (a conversation) anknüpfen; **s. a fire** ein Feuer anmachen; (said of an arsonist) e-n Brand legen || *intr* anfangen; **s. in to** (*inf*) anfangen zu (*inf*); **s. out** (*begin*) anfangen; (start walking) losgehen; **s. out on** (a trip) antreten; **to s. with** zunächst
start'ing gate' *s* Startmaschine *f*
start'ing gun' *s* Startpistole *f*; **at the s.** beim Startschuß
start'ing point' *s* Ausgangspunkt *m*
startle ['stɑrtəl] *tr* erschrecken; **be startled** zusammenfahren
starvation [stɑr've/ən] *s* Hunger *m*; **die of s.** verhungern
starva'tion di'et *s* Hungerkur *f*
starva'tion wag'es *spl* Hungerlohn *m*
starve [stɑrv] *tr* verhungern lassen; **s. out** aushungern || *intr* hungern; (coll) furchtbaren Hunger haben; **s. to death** verhungern
state [stet] *adj* staatlich, Staats–; (as opposed to federal) bundesstaatlich || *s* (condition) Zustand *m*; (government) Staat *m*; (of the U.S.A.) Bundesstaat *m* || *tr* angeben; (a rule, problem) aufstellen; **as stated above** wie oben angegeben
State' Depart'ment *s* Außenministerium *n*
stateless ['stetlɪs] *adj* staatenlos
stately ['stetli] *adj* stattlich
statement ['stetmənt] *s* Angabe *f*; (from a bank) Abrechnung *f*; (jur) Aussage *f*
state' of affairs' *s* Lage *f*
state' of emer'gency *s* Notstand *m*
state' of health' *s* Gesundheitszustand *m*
state' of mind' *s* Geisteszustand *m*
state' of war' *s* Kriegszustand *m*
state'-owned' *adj* staatseigen; (in communistic countries) volkseigen
state' police' *s* Staatspolizei *f*

state'room' s (*in a palace*) Prunkzimmer *n*; (*on a ship*) Passagierkabine *f*
states'man s (-men) Staatsmann *m*
states'manlike' *adj* staatsmännisch
states'manship' s Staatskunst *f*
static ['stætɪk] *adj* statisch ‖ s (rad) Nebengeräusche *pl*
station ['steʃən] s (*social*) Stellung *f*; (*of a bus, rail line*) Bahnhof *m*; (mil) Standort *m* ‖ *tr* aufstellen; (mil) stationieren
stationary ['steʃə͵nerɪ] *adj* stationär
sta'tion break' s Werbepause *f*
stationer ['steʃənər] s Schreibwarenhändler –in *mf*
stationery ['steʃə͵nerɪ] s Briefpapier *n*
sta'tionery store' s Schreibwarenhandlung *f*
sta'tion house' s Polizeiwache *f*
sta'tion identifica'tion s (rad) Pausenzeichen *n*
sta'tionmas'ter s Bahnhofsvorsteher *m*
sta'tions of the cross' spl Kreuzweg *m*
sta'tion wag'on s Kombiwagen *m*
statistic [stə'tɪstɪk] s Angabe *f*; statistics (*science*) Statistik *f* ‖ spl (*data*) Statistik *f*
statistical [stə'tɪstɪkəl] *adj* statistisch
statistician [͵stætɪs'tɪʃən] s Statistiker –in *mf*
statue ['stætʃu] s Statue *f*
statuesque [͵stætʃu'ɛsk] *adj* statuenhaft
stature ['stætʃər] s Gestalt *f*; (fig) Format *n*
status ['stetəs] s (*in society*) Stellung *f*; (*e.g., mental*) Stand *m*
sta'tus quo' [kwo] s Status *m* quo
sta'tus sym'bol s Statussymbol *n*
statute ['stætʃut] s Satzung *f*, Statut *n*
statutory ['stætʃu͵torɪ] *adj* statutenmäßig
staunch [stɒntʃ] *adj* unentwegt
stave [stev] s (*of a barrel*) Daube *f*; (*of a chair*) Steg *m*; (*of a ladder*) Sprosse *f*; (mus) Notensystem *n* ‖ *tr—s.* off abwenden
stay [ste] s (*visit*) Aufenthalt *m*; (prop) Stütze *f*; (*of execution*) Aufschub *m* ‖ *intr* bleiben; have to s. in (*after school*) nachsitzen müssen; s. away wegbleiben; s. behind zurückbleiben; (*in school*) sitzenbleiben
stay'-at-home' s Stubenhocker –in *mf*
stead [sted] s Statt *f*; in s.o.'s s. an j–s Statt
stead'fast' *adj* standhaft
stead·y ['stedɪ] *adj* fest, beständig; (*hands*) sicher; (*ladder*) fest; (*pace*) gleichmäßig; (*progress*) ständig; (*nerves*) stark; (*prices*) stabil; (*work*) regelmäßig; s. customer Stammkunde *m*, Stammkundin *f*; s. now! immer langsam! ‖ *v* (*pret & pp* –ied) *tr* festigen
steak [stek] s Beefsteak *n*
steal [stil] s—it's a s. (coll) das ist geschenkt ‖ *v* (*pret* stole [stol]; *pp* stolen) *tr* stehlen; (*a kiss*) rauben; s. s.o.'s thunder j–m den Wind aus den Segeln nehmen; s. the show den Vogel abschießen ‖ *intr* stehlen; s.

away wegstehlen; s. up on s.o. sich an j–n heranschleichen
stealth [stelθ] s—by s. heimlich
stealthy ['stelθɪ] *adj* verstohlen
steam [stim] s Dampf *m*; (*vapor*) Dunst *m*; (fig) Kraft *f*; full s. ahead! Volldampf voraus!; let off s. Dampf ablassen; (fig) sich [*dat*] Luft machen; put on s. (fig) Dampf dahinter machen ‖ *tr* dämpfen; (culin) dünsten; s. up beschlagen ‖ *intr* dampfen; (culin) dünsten; s. up sich beschlagen
steam' bath' s Dampfbad *n*
steam'boat' s Dampfer *m*
steam' en'gine s Dampfmaschine *f*
steamer ['stimər] s Dampfer *m*
steam' heat' s Dampfheizung *f*
steam' i'ron s Dampfbügeleisen *n*
steam' roll'er s (& fig) Dampfwalze *f* ‖ *tr* glattwalzen; (fig) niederwalzen
steam'ship' s Dampfschiff *n*
steam'ship line' s Dampfschiffahrtslinie *f*
steam' shov'el s Dampflöffelbagger *m*
steamy ['stimɪ] *adj* dampfig, dunstig
steed [stid] s Streitroß *n*
steel [stil] *adj* stählern, Stahl– ‖ s Stahl *m* ‖ *tr* stählen; s. oneself against s.th. sich gegen etw wappnen
steel' wool' s Stahlwolle *f*
steel'works' spl Stahlwerk *n*
steely ['stilɪ] *adj* (fig) stählern
steelyard ['stiljɑrd] s Schnellwaage *f*
steep [stip] *adj* steil; (*prices*) happig ‖ *tr* (*immerse*) eintauchen; (*soak*) einweichen; be steeped in (*e.g., prejudice*) durchdrungen sein von; (*be expert in*) ein Kenner sein (*genit*); s. oneself in sich versenken in (*acc*)
steeple ['stipəl] s Kirchturm *m*
stee'plechase' s Hindernisrennen *n*
steer [stɪr] s Stier *m* ‖ *tr* lenken, steuern; s. a middle course e–n Mittelweg einschlagen ‖ *intr* lenken, steuern; s. clear of vermeiden
steerage ['stɪrɪdʒ] s Zwischendeck *n*
steer'ing wheel' s Steuerrad *n*
stellar ['stelər] *adj* (*role*) Star–; (*attraction*) Haupt–; (astr) Stern(en)–
stem [stem] s (*of a plant*) Halm *m*; (*of a word*; *of a tree*) Stamm *m*; (*of a leaf, fruit*; *of a glass*; *of a smoke pipe*) Stiel *m*; (*of a watch*) Aufziehwelle *f*; (naut) Steven *m*; from s. to stern von vorn bis achtern ‖ *v* (*pret & pp* stemming; *ger* stemming) *tr* (*check*) hemmen; (*fruit*) entstielen; (*the flow*) (an)stauen; (*the blood*) stillen; (*in skiing*) stemmen ‖ *intr— s.* from (ab)stammen von
stench [stentʃ] s Gestank *m*
sten·cil ['stensɪl] s (*for printing*) Schablone *f*; (*for typing*) Matrize *f* ‖ *v* (*pret & pp* –cil[l]ed; *ger* –cil[l]ing) *tr* mittels Schablone aufmalen
stenographer [stə'nɑgrəfər] s Stenograph –in *mf*
stenography [stə'nɑgrəfɪ] s Stenographie *f*
step [step] s Schritt *m*; (*of a staircase*) Stufe *f*; (*footprint*) Fußtritt *m*;

(measure) Maßnahme *f;* **be out of s.**
nicht Schritt halten; **in. s.** im Takt;
keep in s. with the times mit der
Zeit Schritt halten; **s. by s.** schritt-
weise; **watch your s.!** Vorsicht! ‖ *v*
(pret & pp **stepped;** *ger* **stepping)**
tr—**s. down** *(elec)* heruntertransfor-
mieren; **s. off** abschreiten ‖ *intr*
schreiten, treten; **s. aside** beiseite-
treten; **s. back** zurücktreten; **s. for-**
ward vortreten; **s. on** betreten; **s.**
on it *(coll)* sich beeilen; **s. on s.o.'s**
toes *(fig)* j—m auf die Zehen treten;
s. out hinausgehen; **s. out on** *(a mar-*
riage partner) betrügen
step′broth′er *s* Stiefbruder *m*
step′child′ *s* (**–chil′dren**) Stiefkind *n*
step′daugh′ter *s* Stieftochter *f*
step′fa′ther *s* Stiefvater *m*
step′lad′der *s* Stehleiter *f*
step′moth′er *s* Stiefmutter *f*
steppe [step] *s* Steppe *f*
step′ping stone′ *s* Trittstein *m; (fig)*
Sprungbrett *n*
step′sis′ter *s* Stiefschwester *f*
step′son′ *s* Stiefsohn *m*
stere·o [ˈstɛrɪˌo] *adj* Stereo– ‖ *s* (**–os**)
(sound) Stereoton *m,* Raumton *m;*
(reproduction) Raumtonwiedergabe
f; (set) Stereoapparat *m*
stereotyped [ˈstɛrɪ·əˌtaɪpt] *adj* (& *fig)*
stereotyp
sterile [ˈstɛrɪl] *adj* keimfrei
sterility [stɛˈrɪlɪti] *s* Sterilität *f*
sterilize [ˈstɛrɪˌlaɪz] *tr* sterilisieren
sterling [ˈstɑrlɪŋ] *adj (fig)* gediegen ‖
s (currency) Sterling *m; (sterling sil-*
ver) Sterlingsilber *n; (articles of*
sterling silver) Sterlingsilberwaren *pl*
stern [stʌrn] *adj* streng; *(look)* finster
‖ *s (naut)* Heck *n*
stethoscope [ˈstɛθəˌskop] *s* Stethoskop
n
stevedore [ˈstivəˌdor] *s* Stauer *m*
stew [st(j)u] *s* Ragout *m,* Stew *n* ‖ *tr &*
intr dünsten; (& *fig)* schmoren
steward [ˈst(j)u·ərd] *s (aer, naut)*
Steward *m; (of an estate)* Gutsverwalter *m; (of a club)* Tafelmeister *m*
stewardess [ˈst(j)u·ərdɪs] *s (aer, naut)*
Stewardeß *f*
stewed′ fruit′ *s* Kompott *n*
stick [stɪk] *s* Stecken *m,* Stock *m; (for*
punishment) Prügel *pl; (of candy or*
gum) Stange *f;* **the sticks** *(coll)* die
Provinz *f* ‖ *tr (with a sharp point; into*
one's pocket) stecken; *(paste)* (**on**)
ankleben (an *acc);* **s. it out** durchhalten; **s. one's finger** sich in den
Finger stechen; **s. out** herausstrecken;
s. up *(sl)* überfallen und berauben ‖
intr (adhere) kleben; *(be stuck, be*
tight) klemmen; **nothing sticks in his**
mind *(coll)* bei ihm bleibt nichts
haften; **s. around** *(coll)* in der Nähe
bleiben; **s. by** *(coll)* bleiben bei; **s.**
close to sich heften an *(acc);* **s. out**
(said of ears) abstehen; *(be visible)*
heraushängen; **s. to** *(fig)* beharren
auf *(dat);* **s. together** zusammenhalten; *(fig)* zusammenhalten; **s. up**
for sich einsetzen für

sticker [ˈstɪkər] *s* Klebezettel *m*
stick′-in-the-mud′ *s* (coll) Schlafmütze
f
stickler [ˈstɪklər] *s* (**for**) Pedant *m (in*
dat)
stick′pin′ *s* Krawattennadel *f*
stick′-up′ *s (sl)* Raubüberfall *m*
sticky [ˈstɪki] *adj* klebrig; *(air)* schwül;
(ticklish) heikel
stiff [stɪf] *adj* steif; *(difficult)* schwer;
(drink) stark; *(opposition)* hartnäckig; *(sentence)* streng; *(bearing)*
steif; *(price)* hoch; **s. as a board**
stocksteif ‖ *s (corpse)* (sl) Leiche *f;*
big s. (sl) blöder Kerl *m*
stiffen [ˈstɪfən] *tr* versteifen ‖ *intr*
sich versteifen
stiffly [ˈstɪfli] *adv* gezwungen
stiff′-necked′ *adj* mit steifem Hals; *(fig)*
eigensinnig
stifle [ˈstaɪfəl] *tr (a yawn)* unterdrücken; *(a person)* ersticken
stig·ma [ˈstɪgmə] *s* (**–mas & mata**
[mətə]) Brandmal *n;* **stigmata** Wund-
male *pl* Christi
stigmatize [ˈstɪgməˌtaɪz] *tr* brandmarken
stile [staɪl] *s* Stiege *f*
stilet·to [stɪˈlɛto] *s* (**–os**) Stilett *n*
still [stɪl] *adj* still, ruhig ‖ *adv (up to*
this time, as yet, even) noch; *(yet,*
nevertheless) dennoch; **keep s.** still-
bleiben ‖ *s (stillness)* Stille *f; (for*
whiskey) Brennapparat *m; (cin)* Ein-
zelphotographie *f; (phot)* Standphoto
n ‖ *tr* stillen
still′born′ *adj* totgeboren
still′ life′ *s* (**still lifes & still lives**)
Stilleben *n*
stilt [stɪlt] *s* Stelze *f*
stilt′ed *adj (style)* geschraubt; *(archit)*
auf Pfeilern ruhend
stimulant [ˈstɪmjələnt] *s* Reizmittel *n;*
act as a s. anregend wirken
stimulate [ˈstɪmjəˌlet] *tr* anregen
stimulation [ˌstɪmjəˈleʃən] *s* Anregung
f
stimu·lus [ˈstɪmjələs] *s* (**–li** [ˌlaɪ])
(& *fig)* Reizmittel *n; (fig)* Ansporn
m
sting [stɪŋ] *s* Biß *m,* Stich *m; (sting-*
ing organ) Stachel *m* ‖ *v (pret & pp*
stung [stʌŋ]) *tr & intr* stechen
stingy [ˈstɪndʒi] *adj* geizig
stink [stɪŋk] *s* Gestank *m; (sl)* Krach
m ‖ *v (pret* **stank** [stæŋk]); **stunk**
[stʌŋk]) *tr*—**s. up** verstänkern ‖ *intr*
stinken
stinker [ˈstɪŋkər] *s (sl)* Stinker *m*
stinky [ˈstɪŋki] *adj* stinkend, stinkig
stint [stɪnt] *s* bestimmte Arbeit *f;* **with-**
out s. freigebig ‖ *tr* einschränken ‖
intr (on) knausern (mit)
stipend [ˈstaɪpənd] *s (salary)* Gehalt
n; (of a scholarship) Zuwendung *f*
stipple [ˈstɪpəl] *tr* punktieren
stipulate [ˈstɪpjəˌlet] *tr* bedingen; **as**
stipulated wie vertraglich festgelegt
stipulation [ˌstɪpjəˈleʃən] *s* Bedingung
f
stir [stʌr] *s (movement)* Bewegung *f;*
(unrest) Unruhe *f; (commotion, ex-*

citement) Aufsehen *n;* **create quite
a s.** großes Aufsehen erregen || *v
(pret & pp* **stirred;** *ger* **stirring**) *tr
e.g., with a spoon*) (um)rühren; *(said
of a breeze*) bewegen; *(the fire)*
schüren; **s. up** *(hatred)* entfachen;
(trouble) stiften; *(people)* aufhetzen
|| *intr* sich rühren
stir'ring *adj* erregend; *(times)* bewegt;
(speech) mitreißend; *(song)* schwung-
voll
stirrup ['stʌrəp] *s* Steigbügel *m*
stitch [stɪtʃ] *s* Stich *m;* *(in knitting)*
Masche *f;* **stitches** *(surg)* Naht *f;*
s. in the side Seitenstechen *n* || *tr*
heften; *(surg)* nähen
stock [stɑk] *s* *(supplies)* Lager *n;* *(of
a gun)* Schaft *m;* *(lineage)* Zucht *f;*
(of paper) Papierstoff *m;* *(culin)*
Fond *m;* *(st. exch.)* Aktie *f;* **in s.**
vorrätig, auf Lager; **not put much s.
in** nicht viel Wert legen auf *(acc);*
out of s. nicht (mehr) vorrätig; *(of
books)* vergriffen; **stocks** *(hist)*
Stock *m;* **take s.** den Bestand aufnehmen; **take s. of** (fig) in Betracht
ziehen || *tr* auf Lager halten; *(a
stream)* (mit Fischen) besetzen; *(a
farm)* ausstatten || *intr*—**s. up** (on)
sich eindecken (mit)
stockade [stɑ'ked] *s* Palisade *f;* (mil)
Gefängnis *n*
stock'breed'er *s* Viehzüchter –in *mf*
stock'brok'er *s* Börsenmakler –in *mf*
stock' car' *s* (aut) Serienwagen *m;*
(sport) als Rennwagen hergerichteter
Personenkraftwagen *m*
stock' com'pany *s* (com) Aktiengesellschaft *f;* (theat) Repertoiregruppe *f*
stock' div'idend *s* Aktiendividende *f*
stock' exchange' *s* Börse *f*
stock'hold'er *s* Aktionär –in *mf*
stock'ing *s* Strumpf *m*
stock' in trade' *s* Warenbestand *m;*
(fig) Rüstzeug *n*
stock'pile' *s* Vorrat *m* || *tr* aufstapeln
stock'room' *s* Lagerraum *m*
stocky ['stɑki] *adj* untersetzt
stock'yard' *s* Viehhof *m*
stodgy ['stɑdʒɪ] *adj* gezwungen
stogy ['stogi] *s* (coll) Glimmstengel *m*
stoic ['sto·ɪk] *adj* stoisch || *s* Stoiker
m
stoke [stok] *tr* *(a fire)* schüren; *(a
furnace)* heizen
stoker ['stokər] *s* Heizer *m*
stole [stol] *s* *(woman's fur piece)* Pelz-
stola *f;* (eccl) Stola *f*
stolid ['stɑlɪd] *adj* unempfindlich
stomach ['stʌmək] *s* Magen *m;* (fig)
(for) Lust *f* (zu) || *tr* *(food)* ver-
dauen; (fig) vertragen
stom'ach ache' *s* Magenschmerzen *pl*
stone [ston] *adj* steinern || *s* Stein *m;*
(of fruit) Kern *m;* (pathol) Stein *m*
|| *tr* steinigen; *(fruit)* entsteinen
stone' age' *s* Steinzeit *f*
stone'-broke' *adj* (coll) völlig abgebrannt
stone'-deaf' *adj* stocktaub
stone' ma'son *s* Steinmetz *m*
stone' quar'ry *s* Steinbruch *m*

stone's' throw' *s* Katzensprung *m*
stony ['stoni] *adj* steinig
stooge [studʒ] *s* Lakai *m*
stool [stul] *s* Schemel *m;* *(e.g., at a
bar)* Hocker *m;* *(bowel movement)*
Stuhl *m*
stool' pi'geon *s* Polizeispitzel *m*
stoop [stup] *s* Beugung *f;* *(condition
of the body)* gebeugte Körperhaltung
f; *(porch)* kleine Verande *f* || *intr*
sich bücken; *(demean oneself)* sich
erniedrigen
stoop'-shoul'dered *adj* gebeugt
stop [stɑp] *s* *(for a bus or streetcar)*
Haltestelle *f;* *(layover)* Aufenthalt
m; *(station)* Station *f;* *(of an organ)*
Register *n;* (ling) Verschlußlaut *m;*
bring to a s. zum Halten bringen;
come to a s. anhalten; **put a s. to**
ein Ende machen *(dat)* || *v (pret &
pp* **stopped;** *ger* **stopping**) *tr* *(an
activity)* aufhören mit; *(ger)* aufhören (zu *inf);* *(e.g., a thief, car)*
anhalten; *(bring to a stop with difficulty)* zum Halten bringen; *(delay,
detain)* aufhalten; *(a leak)* stopfen;
(a check) sperren; *(payment)* einstellen; *(the blood)* stillen; *(traffic)*
lahmlegen; **s. down** (phot) abblenden; **s. s.o. from** *(ger)* j-n davon-
halten zu *(inf)* || *intr (cease)* auf-
hören; *(come to a stop; break down)*
stehenbleiben; *(said of a person
stopping for a short time or of a vehicle at an unscheduled stop)* anhalten;
*(said of a vehicle at a scheduled
stop)* halten; **s. at nothing** vor nichts
zurückschrecken; **s. dead** plötzlich
stehenbleiben; **s. in** vorbeikommen;
s. off at e-n kurzen Halt machen
bei
stop'gap' *adj* Not–, Behelfs– || *s* Notbe-
helf *m*
stop'light' *s* *(on a car)* Bremslicht *n;*
(traffic light) Verkehrsampel *f*
stop'o'ver *s* Fahrtunterbrechung *f;*
(aer) Zwischenlandung *f*
stoppage ['stɑpɪdʒ] *s* *(of a pipe)* Verstopfung *f;* *(of payment, of work)*
Einstellung *f;* (pathol) Verstopfung *f*
stopper ['stɑpər] *s* Stöpsel *m;* *(made
of cork)* Korken *m*
stop' sign' *s* Haltezeichen *n*
stop'watch' *s* Stoppuhr *f*
storage ['storɪdʒ] *s* Lagerung *f*
stor'age bat'tery *s* Akkumulator *m*
stor'age charge' *s* Lagergebühr *f*
stor'age room' *s* Rumpelkammer *f;*
(com) Lagerraum *m*
stor'age tank' *s* Sammelbehälter *m*
store [stor] *s* *(small shop)* Laden *m;*
(large shop) Geschäft *n;* *(supply)*
Vorrat *m;* **be in s. for** bevorstehen
(dat); **have in s. for** bereithalten für;
set great s. by viel Wert legen auf
(acc); **s. of knowledge** Wissenschatz
m || *tr* einlagern; *(in the attic)* auf
den Speicher stellen; **s. up** auf-
speichern
store'house' *s* Lagerhaus *n;* (fig) Schätz
m, Fundgrube *f*
store'keep'er *s* Ladeninhaber –in *mf*

store'room' s Lagerraum m, Vorratsraum m

stork [stɔrk] s Storch m

storm [stɔrm] s Sturm m; (thunderstorm) Gewitter n; (fig) Sturm m; **take by s.** (& fig) im Sturm nehmen || tr (er)stürmen || intr stürmen

storm' cloud' s Gewitterwolke f

storm' door' s Doppeltür f

storm' warn'ing s Sturmwarnung f

storm' win'dow s Doppelfenster n

stormy ['stɔrmi] adj stürmisch

story ['stɔri] s Geschichte f; (floor) Stock m, Stockwerk n; **that's another s.** das ist e-e Sache für sich

sto'rybook' s Geschichtenbuch n

sto'rytell'er s Erzähler –in mf

stout [staut] adj beleibt; (heart) tapfer || s Starkbier n

stout'-heart'ed adj beherzt

stove [stov] s Ofen m, Küchenherd m

stove'pipe' s Ofenrohr n; (coll) Angströhre f

stow [sto] tr stauen; **s. away** verstauen || intr—**s. away** als blinder Passagier mitreisen

stowage ['sto·ɪdʒ] s Stauen n; (costs) Staugebühr f

stow'away' s blinder Passagier m

straddle ['strædəl] tr mit gespreizten Beinen sitzen auf (dat)

strafe [stref] tr im Tiefflug mit Bordwaffen angreifen

straggle ['strægəl] intr abschweifen

straggler ['stræglər] s Nachzügler –in mf; (mil) Versprengte m

straight [stret] adj gerade; (honest) aufrecht; (candid) offen; (hair) glatt; (story) wahr; (uninterrupted) ununterbrochen; (whiskey) unverdünnt || adv (directly) direkt; (without interruption) ununterbrochen; **give it to s.o. s.** j–m die ungeschminkte Wahrheit sagen; **go s.** (fig) seinen geraden Weg gehen; **is my hat on s.?** sitzt mein Hut richtig?; **make s. for** zuhalten auf (acc); **set the record s.** den Sachverhalt klarstellen; **s. ahead** (immer) geradeaus; **s. as an arrow** pfeilgerade; **s. from the horse's mouth** (coll) aus erster Hand; **s. home** schnurstracks nach Hause; **s. off** ohne weiteres || s (cards) Buch n

straight'away' adv geradewegs, sofort || s (sport) Gerade f

straighten ['stretən] tr gerade machen; (e.g., a tablecloth) glattziehen; **s. out** (fig) wieder in Ordnung bringen; **s. s.o.'s tie** j–m die Krawatte zurechtrücken; **s. up** (a room) aufräumen || intr gerade werden; **s. up** sich aufrichten

straight' face' s—**keep a s.** keine Miene verziehen

straight'for'ward adj aufrichtig

straight' left' s (box) linke Gerade f

straight' man' s Stichwortgeber m

straight' ra'zor s Rasiermesser n

straight' right' s (box) rechte Gerade f

straight'way' adv auf der Stelle

strain [stren] s Belastung f; (of a muscle or tendon) Zerrung f; (task re-

quiring effort) (coll) Strapaze f; (stock, family) Linie f; (trait) Erbeigenschaft f; (bot) Art f; **without s.** mühelos || tr (filter) durchseihen; (the eyes, nerves) überanstrengen; **s. oneself** (make a great effort) sich überanstrengen; (in lifting) sich überheben; **s. the truth** übertreiben || intr sich anstrengen; **s. after** sich abmühen um; **s. at** ziehen an (dat), zerren an (dat)

strained adj (smile) gezwungen; (relations) gespannt

strainer ['strenər] s Seiher m, Filter m

strait [stret] s Straße f; **financial straits** finanzielle Schwierigkeiten pl; **straits** Meerenge f

strait' jack'et s Zwangsjacke f

strait'-laced' adj sittenstreng

strand [strænd] s Strähne f; (beach) Strand m; **s. of pearls** Perlenschnur f || tr auf den Strand setzen; (fig) stranden lassen; **be stranded** in der Patsche sitzen; **get stranded** auflaufen; **leave s.o. stranded** j–n im Stich lassen

strange [strendʒ] adj (quaint) sonderbar; (foreign) fremd; **s. character** Sonderling m || adv—**s. to say** merkwürdigerweise

stranger ['strendʒər] s Fremde mf

strangle ['stræŋgəl] tr erwürgen || intr ersticken

stran'glehold' s Würgegriff m

strap [stræp] s Riemen m, Gurt m; (of metal) Band n || v (pret & pp strapped; ger strapping) tr (to) anschnallen (an acc); (a razor) abziehen

strap'ping adj stramm

stratagem ['strætədʒəm] s Kriegslist f

strategic(al) [strə'tidʒɪk(əl)] adj strategisch

strategist ['strætədʒɪst] s Stratege m

strategy ['strætədʒi] s Strategie f

stratification [,strætɪfɪ'keʃən] s Schichtung f

strati-fy ['strætɪ,faɪ] v (pret & pp –fied) tr schichten || intr Schichten bilden

stratosphere ['strætə,sfɪr] s Stratosphäre f

stra·tum ['stretəm], ['strætəm] s (–ta [tə] & –tums) Schicht f

straw [strɔ] adj (e.g., hat, man, mat) Stroh– || s Stroh n; (single stalk; for drinking) Strohhalm m; **that's the last s.!** das schlägt dem Faß den Boden aus!

straw'ber'ry s Erdbeere f

straw'berry blond' adj rotblond

straw' mat'tress s Strohsack m

straw' vote' s Probeabstimmung f

stray [stre] adj (e.g., bullet) verirrt; (cat, dog) streunend; **s. shell** (mil) Ausreißer m || s verirrtes Tier n || intr herumirren; (fig) abschweifen

streak [strik] s Streifen m; **like a s.** wie der Blitz; **s. of bad luck** Pechsträhne f; **s. of luck** Glückssträhne f; **s. of light** Lichtstreifen m || tr streifen || intr streifig werden; **s. along** vorbeisausen

streaky ['striki] *adj* gestreift; *(uneven)* (coll) ungleich(mäßig)

stream [strim] *s* Fluß *m; (of people, cars, air, blood, lava)* Strom *m; (of words)* Schwall *m; (of tears)* Flut *f; (of a liquid)* Strahl *m* ǁ *intr* (aus)-strömen

streamer ['strimər] *s (pennant)* Wimpel *m; (ribbon)* herabhängendes Band *n; (rolled crepe paper)* Papierschlange *f*

stream/line' *tr* in Stromlinienform bringen; *(fig)* reorganizieren

stream/lined' *adj* stromlinienförmig

street [strit] *s* Straße *f*

street'car' *s* Straßenbahn *f*

street' clean'er *s* Straßenkehrer –in *mf; (truck)* Straßenkehrmaschine *f*

street' fight' *s* Straßenschlacht *f*

street' light' *s* Straßenlaterne *f*

street' sign' *s* Straßenschild *n*

street' ven'dor *s* Straßenhändler –in *mf*

street'walk'er *s* Straßendirne *f*

strength [streŋθ] *s* Kraft *f; (strong point; potency of alcohol; moral or mental power)* Stärke *f;* (mil) Kopfstärke *f; bodily s.* Körperkraft *f; on the s. of* auf Grund (*genit*)

strengthen ['streŋθən] *tr* stärken; (fig) bestärken ǁ *intr* stärker werden

strenuous ['strenju-əs] *adj* anstrengend; *s. effort* Kraftanstrengung *f*

stress [stres] *s (emphasis, weight)* Nachdruck *m; (mental)* Belastung *f;* (mus, pros) Ton *m,* Betonung *f;* (phys) Beanspruchung *f,* Spannung *f* ǁ *tr* (& mus, pros) betonen

stress' ac'cent *s* Betonungsakzent *m*

stress' mark' *s* Betonungszeichen *n*

stretch [stretʃ] *s (of road)* Strecke *f; (of the limbs)* Strecken *n; (of water)* Fläche *f; (of a racetrack)* Gerade *f; (of years)* Zeitspanne *f; do a s.* (sl) brummen; *in one s.* in e–m Zug ǁ *tr (a rope)* spannen; *(one's neck)* recken; *(shoes, gloves)* ausdehnen; *(wire)* ziehen; *(strings of an instrument)* straffziehen; *s. a point* es nicht allzu genau nehmen; *s. oneself* sich strecken; *s. one's legs* sich [*dat*] die Beine vertreten; *s. out* (e.g., hands) ausstrecken ǁ *intr* sich (aus)-dehnen; *(said of a person)* sich strecken; *s. out on* sich ausstrecken auf (*dat*)

stretcher ['stretʃər] *s* Tragbahre *f*

stretch'erbear'er *s* Krankenträger *m*

strew [stru] *v (pret* strewed; *pp* strewed & strewn) *tr* (aus)streuen; *s. with* bestreuen mit

stricken ['strikən] *adj (with e.g., misfortune)* heimgesucht (von); *(with e.g., fear, grief)* ergriffen (von); *(with a disease)* befallen (von)

strict [strikt] *adj* streng; *in s. confidence* streng vertraulich

strictly ['striktli] *adv* streng; *s. speaking* genau genommen

stricture ['striktʃər] *s* (on) kritische Bemerkung *f* (über *acc*)

stride [straid] *s* Schritt *m; hit one's s.* auf Touren kommen; *make great*

strides große Fortschritte machen; *take in s.* ruhig hinnehmen ǁ *v (pret* strode [strod]; *pp* stridden ['stridən]) *intr* schreiten; *s. along* tüchtig ausschreiten

strident ['straidənt] *adj* schrill

strife [straif] *s* Streit *m,* Hader *m*

strike [straik] *s (work stoppage)* Streik *m; (blow)* Schlag *m; (discovery, e.g., of oil)* Fund *m;* (baseball) Fehlschlag *m; go on s.* in Streik treten ǁ *v (pret* & *pp* struck [strak]) *tr (a person, the hours, coins, strings of an instrument)* schlagen; *(a match)* anstreichen; *(a bargain)* abschließen; *(a note)* greifen; *(go on strike against)* bestreiken; *(a tent)* abbrechen; *(oil)* stoßen auf (*acc*); *(run into)* auffahren auf (*acc*); *(s.o. blind, dumb)* machen; *(s.o. with fear)* erfüllen; *(a blow)* versetzen; *(a pose)* einnehmen; *(seem to s.o.)* erscheinen (*dat*); *s. it rich* auf e–e Goldader stoßen; *s. fear into s.o.* j–m e–n Schrecken einjagen; *s. up (a conversation, an acquaintance)* anknüpfen; *(a song)* anstimmen ǁ *intr (said of a person or clock)* schlagen; *(said of workers)* streiken; *(said of lightning)* einschlagen; *s. home* Eindruck machen; *s. out* (& fig) fehlschlagen

strike/break'er *s* Streikbrecher –in *mf*

striker ['straikər] *s* Streikende *mf*

strik'ing *adj* auffallend; *(example)* treffend; *(workers)* streikend

strik'ing pow'er *s* Schlagkraft *f*

string [striŋ] *s* Bindfaden *m; (row, series)* Reihe *f; (of a bow)* Sehne *f; (of a musical instrument)* Saite *f; pull strings* (fig) der Drahtzieher sein; *s. of pearls* Perlenkette *f; strings* (mus) Streicher *pl; with no strings attached* ohne einschränkende Bedingungen ǁ *v (pret* & *pp* strung [straŋ]) *tr (pearls)* auf e–e Schnur (auf)reihen; *(a bow)* spannen; *s. along* hinhalten; *s. up* (coll) aufknüpfen

string' band' *s* Streichorchester *n*

string' bean' *s* grüne Bohne *f; (tall, thin person)* Bohnenstange *f*

stringed' in'strument *s* Saiteninstrument *n*

stringent ['strindʒənt] *adj* streng

string' quartet' *s* Streichquartett *n*

stringy ['striŋi] *adj (vegetables)* holzig; *(meat)* sehnig; *(hair)* zottelig

strip [strip] *s* Streifen *m* ǁ *v (pret* & *pp* stripped; *ger* stripping) *tr (off)* abziehen; *(clothes)* (off) abstreifen; *(a thread)* überdrehen; *(gears)* beschädigen; *s. down* abmontieren; *s.o. of office* j–n seines Amtes entkleiden ǁ *intr* sich ausziehen

stripe [straip] *s* Streifen *m; (elongated welt)* Striemen *m;* (mil) Tresse *f* ǁ *tr* streifen

strip' mine' *s* Tagebau *m*

stripper ['stripər] *s* Stripperin *f*

strip'tease' *s* Entkleidungsnummer *f*

stripteaser ['strip,tizər] *s* Stripperin *f*

strive [straiv] *v (pret* strove [strov];

pp **striven** ['strɪvən]) *intr* (**for**) streben (**nach**); **s. to** (*inf*) sich bemühen zu (*inf*)

stroke [strok] *s* Schlag *m*; (*caress with the hand*) Streicheln *n*; (*of a piston*) Hub *m*; (*of a pen, brush*) Strich *m*; (*of a sword*) Hieb *m*; (*in swimming*) Schwimmstoß *m*; (*of the leg*) Beinstoß *m*; (*of an oar*) Schlag *m*; (*pathol*) Schlaganfall *m*; **at a single s.** mit e-m Schlag; **at the s. of twelve** Schlag zwölf Uhr; **not do a s. of work** keinen Strich tun; **she'll have a s.** (coll) dann trifft sie der Schlag; **s. of genius** Genieblitz *m*; **s. of luck** Glücksfall *m*; **s. of the pen** mit e-m Federstrich ‖ *tr* streichen

stroll [strol] *s* Spaziergang *m* ‖ *intr* spazieren

stroller ['strolər] *s* Spaziergänger –in *mf*; (*for a baby*) Kindersportwagen *m*

strong [strɔŋ] *adj* kräftig; (*firm*) fest; (*drink, smell, light, wind, feeling*) stark; (*glasses*) scharf; (*wine*) schwer; (*suspicion*) dringend; (*memory*) gut; (*candidate*) aussichtsreich; (*argument*) triftig

strong'-arm' *adj* (*e.g., methods*) Zwangs–

strong'box' *s* Geldschrank *m*

strong'hold' *s* Feste *f*; (fig) Hochburg *f*

strong' lan'guage *s* Kraftausdrücke *pl*

strongly ['strɔŋli] *adv* nachdrücklich; **feel s. about** sich sehr einsetzen für

strong'-mind'ed *adj* willensstark

strontium ['strɑnʃɪəm] *s* Strontium *n*

strop [strɑp] *s* Streichriemen *m* ‖ *v* (*pret & pp* **stropped**; *ger* **stropping**) *tr* abziehen

strophe ['strofi] *s* Strophe *f*

structural ['strʌktʃərəl] *adj* strukturell, Bau–

structure ['strʌktʃər] *s* Struktur *f*; (*building*) Bau *m*

struggle ['strʌgəl] *s* Kampf *m* ‖ *intr* (**for**) kämpfen (**um**); **s. against** ankämpfen gegen; **s. to one's feet** sich mit Mühe erheben

strum [strʌm] *v* (*pret & pp* **strummed**; *ger* **strumming**) *tr* klimpern auf (*dat*)

strumpet ['strʌmpɪt] *s* Dirne *f*

strut [strʌt] *s* (brace) Strebebalken *m*; (*haughty walk*) stolzer Gang *m* ‖ *v* (*pret & pp* **strutted**; *ger* **strutting**) *intr* stolzieren

strychnine ['strɪknaɪn] *s* Strychnin *n*

stub [stʌb] *s* (*of a checkbook*) Abschnitt *m*; (*of a ticket*) Kontrollabschnitt *m*; (*of a candle, pencil, cigarette*) Stummel *m* ‖ *v* (*pret & pp* **stubbed**) *tr*—**s. one's toe** sich an der Zehe stoßen

stubble ['stʌbəl] *s* Stoppel *f*; (*facial hair*) Bartstoppeln *pl*

stubbly ['stʌbli] *adj* stopp(e)lig

stubborn ['stʌbərn] *adj* eigensinnig; (*e.g., resistance*) hartnäckig; (*hair*) widerspenstig

stubby ['stʌbi] *adj* kurz und dick; (*person*) untersetzt

stuc·co ['stʌko] *s* (**–coes & –cos**) Verputz *m* ‖ *tr* verputzen

stuc'co work' *s* Verputzarbeit *f*

stuck [stʌk] *adj*—**be s.** feststecken; (*said, e.g., of a lock*) klemmen; **be s. on** vernarrt sein in (*acc*); **get s.** steckenbleiben

stuck'-up' *adj* (coll) hochnäsig

stud [stʌd] *s* (*ornament*) Ziernagel *m*; (*horse*) Zuchthengst *m*; (*archit*) Wandpfosten *m* ‖ *v* (*pret & pp* **studded**; *ger* **studding**) *tr* mit Ziernägeln verzieren

stud' bolt' *s* Schraubenbolzen *m*

student ['st(j)udənt] *adj* Studenten– ‖ *s* (*in college*) Student –in *mf*; (*in grammar or high school*) Schüler –in *mf*; (*scholar*) Gelehrte *mf*

stu'dent bod'y *s* Studentenschaft *f*

stu'dent nurse' *s* Krankenpflegerin *f* in Ausbildung

stud' farm' *s* Gestüt *n*

stud'horse' *s* Zuchthengst *m*

stud'ied *adj* gesucht

studi·o ['st(j)udɪˌo] *s* (**–os**) (fa, phot) Atelier *n*; (cin, fa, phot, telv) Studio *n*

studious ['st(j)udɪ·əs] *adj* fleißig

stud·y ['stʌdi] *s* Studium *n*; (*room*) Studierzimmer *n*; (paint) Studie *f* ‖ *v* (*pret & pp* **–ied**) *tr & intr* studieren

stuff [stʌf] *s* Stoff *m*; (coll) Kram *m*; **do your s.!** (coll) schieß los!; **know one's s.** (coll) sich auskennen ‖ *tr* (*animals*) ausstopfen; (*a cushion*) polstern; (*e.g., cotton in the ears*) sich (*dat*) stopfen; (culin) füllen; **s. oneself** sich vollstopfen

stuffed' shirt' *s* steifer, eingebildeter Mensch *m*

stuff'ing *s* Polstermaterial *n*; (culin) Fülle *f*

stuffy ['stʌfi] *adj* (*room*) stickig; (*nose*) verstopft; (*person*) steif

stumble ['stʌmbəl] *intr* stolpern; (*in reading*) holpern; **s. across** stoßen auf (*acc*)

stum'bling block' *s* Stein *m* des Anstoßes

stump [stʌmp] *s* (*of an arm, tree, cigarette, pencil*) Stummel *m* ‖ *tr* (*a cigarette*) ausdrücken; (*nonplus*) verblüffen; (*a district, state*) als Wahlredner bereisen

stump' speak'er *s* Wahlredner –in *mf*

stun [stʌn] *v* (*pret & pp* **stunned**; *ger* **stunning**) *tr* betäuben

stun'ning *adj* (coll) phantastisch

stunt [stʌnt] *s* Kunststück *n*; **do stunts** Kunststücke vorführen ‖ *tr* hemmen

stunt'ed *adj* verkümmert

stunt' fly'ing *s* Kunstflug *m*

stunt' man' *s* (**men'**) Sensationsdarsteller *m*

stupe·fy ['st(j)upɪˌfaɪ] *v* (*pret & pp* **–fied**) *tr* verblüffen

stupendous [st(j)u'pendəs] *adj* erstaunlich

stupid ['st(j)upɪd] *adj* dumm, blöd

stupidity [st(j)u'pɪdɪti] *s* Dummheit *f*

stupor ['st(j)upər] *s* Stumpfsinn *m*

sturdy ['stʌrdi] *adj* (*person*) kräftig;

(thing) stabil; *(resolute)* standhaft; *(plant)* widerstandsfähig

sturgeon ['stɑːrdʒən] *s* Stör *m*

stutter ['stʌtər] *s* Stottern *n* ‖ *tr & intr* stottern

sty [staɪ] *s* Schweinestall *m;* (pathol) Gerstenkorn *n*

style [staɪl] *s* Stil *m; (manner)* Art *f; (fashion)* Mode *f; (cut of suit)* Schnitt *m;* **be in s.** in Mode sein; **go out of s.** veralten; **live in s.** auf großem Fuße leben ‖ *tr (title)* betiteln; *(e.g., clothes)* gestalten; *(hair)* nach der Mode frisieren

stylish ['staɪlɪʃ] *adj* modisch; *(person)* modisch gekleidet

stylistic [staɪ'lɪstɪk] *adj* stilistisch

stymie ['staɪmi] *tr* vereiteln

styp'tic pen'cil ['stɪptɪk] *s* Alaunstift *m*

suave [swɑv] *adj* verbindlich

sub [sʌb] *s* (naut) U-boot *n;* (sport) Ersatzspieler –in *mf*

sub'chas'er *s* U-bootjäger *m*

sub'commit'tee *s* Unterausschuß *m*

subconscious [sʌb'kɑn/əs] *adj* unterbewußt ‖ *s* Unterbewußtsein *n*

sub'con'tinent *s* Subkontinent *m*

sub'con'tract *s* Nebenvertrag *m* ‖ *tr* e–n Nebenvertrag abschließen über *(acc)*

sub'con'tractor *s* Unterlieferant –in *mf*

sub'divide', sub'divide' *tr* unterteilen ‖ *intr* sich unterteilen

sub'divi'sion *s (act)* Unterteilung *f; (unit)* Unterabteilung *f*

subdue [səb'd(j)u] *tr (an enemy)* unterwerfen; *(one who is struggling)* überwältigen; *(light, sound)* dämpfen; *(feelings, impulses)* bändigen

sub'floor' *s* Blindboden *m*

sub'head' *s* Untertitel *m*

subject ['sʌbdʒɪkt] *adj* (to) untertan *(dat);* **be s. to** *(e.g., approval, another country)* abhängig sein von; *(e.g., colds)* neigen zu; *(e.g., laws of nature, change)* unterworfen sein *(dat);* **s. to change without notice** Änderungen vorbehalten ‖ *s* Thema *n; (of a kingdom)* Untertan –in *mf;* (educ) Fach *n;* (fa) Vorwurf *m;* (gram) Satzgegenstand *m,* Subjekt *n;* (libr) Stichwort *n;* **change the s.** das Thema wechseln; **get off the s.** vom Thema abkommen ‖ [səb'dʒɛkt] *tr (& fig)* unterwerfen *(dat)*

subjection [səb'dʒɛk/ən] *s* Unterwerfung *f*

subjective [səb'dʒɛktɪv] *adj* subjektiv; **s. case** Werfall *m*

sub'ject mat'ter *s* Inhalt *m*

subjugate ['sʌdʒə,ɡet] *tr* unterjochen

subjunctive [səb'dʒʌŋktɪv] *adj* konjunktiv(isch) ‖ *s* Konjunktiv *m*

sub'lease' *s* Untermiete *f* ‖ **sub'lease'** *tr & intr (to s.o.)* untervermieten; *(from s.o.)* untermieten

sublet [səb'lɛt] *v (pret & pp* –let; *ger* –letting) *tr & intr (to s.o.)* untervermieten; *(from s.o.)* untermieten

sublimate ['sʌblɪmət] *s* (chem) Sublimat *n* ‖ ['sʌblɪ,met] *tr* sublimieren

sublime [sə'blaɪm] *adj* erhaben ‖ Erhabene *n*

submachine' **gun'** *s* Maschinenpistole *f*

sub'marine' *adj* U-boot– ‖ *s* U-boot *n*

sub'marine' **base'** *s* U-bootstützpunkt *m*

submerge [səb'mʌrdʒ] *tr & intr* untertauchen; **ready to s.** tauchklar

submersion [səb'mʌrʒən] *s* Untertauchen *n*

submission [səb'mɪ/ən] *s* (to) Unterwerfung *f* (unter *acc*); *(of a document)* Vorlage *f; (of a question)* Unterbreitung *f*

submissive [səb'mɪsɪv] *adj* unterwürfig

sub•mit [səb'mɪt] *v (pret & pp* –mitted; *ger* –mitting) *tr (a question)* unterbreiten; *(a document)* vorlegen; *(suggest)* der Ansicht sein ‖ *intr* (to) sich unterwerfen *(dat)*

subordinate [səb'ɔrdɪnɪt] *adj (lower in rank)* untergeordnet; *(secondary)* Neben– ‖ *s* Untergebene *mf* ‖ [səb'ɔrdɪ,net] *tr* (to) unterordnen *(dat)*

subor'dinate clause' *s* Nebensatz *m*

suborn [sə'bɔrn] *tr* verleiten; *(bribe)* bestechen

sub'plot' *s* Nebenhandlung *f*

subscribe [səb'skraɪb] *tr* unterschreiben; *(money)* zeichnen ‖ *intr*—**s. to** *(a newspaper)* abonnieren; *(to a series of volumes)* subskribieren; *(an idea)* billigen

subscriber [səb'skraɪbər] *s* Abonnent –in *mf*

subscription [səb'skrɪp/ən] *s* (to) Abonnement *n* (auf *acc*); *(to a series of volumes)* Subskription *f* (auf *acc*); **take out a s.** to sich abonnieren auf *(acc)*

sub'sec'tion *s* Unterabteilung *f*

subsequent ['sʌbsɪkwənt] *adj* (nach)folgend; **s. to** anschließend an *(acc)*

subsequently ['sʌbsɪkwəntli] *adv* anschließend

subservient [səb'sʌrvɪ-ənt] *adj* (to) unterwürfig (gegenüber *dat*)

subside [səb'saɪd] *intr* nachlassen; (geol) sich senken

subsidiary [səb'sɪdɪ,ɛri] *adj* Tochter– ‖ *s* Tochtergesellschaft *f*

subsidize ['sʌbsɪ,daɪz] *tr* subventionieren

subsidy ['sʌbsɪdi] *s* Subvention *f*

subsist [səb'sɪst] *intr (exist)* existieren; **s. on** leben von

subsistence [səb'sɪstəns] *s (existence)* Dasein *n; (livelihood)* Lebensunterhalt *m;* (philos) Subsistenz *f*

subsist'ence allow'ance *s* Unterhaltszuschuß *m*

sub'soil' *s* Untergrund *m*

subsonic [səb'sɑnɪk] *adj* Unterschall–

sub'spe'cies *s* Unterart *f*

substance ['sʌbstəns] *s* Substanz *f,* Stoff *m;* **in s.** im wesentlichen

substand'ard *adj* unter dem Niveau

substantial [səb'stæn/əl] *adj (sum, amount)* beträchtlich; *(difference)* wesentlich; (*meal*) kräftig; **be in s. agreement** im wesentlichen übereinstimmen

substantiate [səb'stænʃɪ,et] *tr* begründen, nachweisen

substantive ['sʌbstəntɪv] *adj* wesentlich ‖ *s* (gram) Substantiv *m*

sub'sta'tion *s* Nebenstelle *f*; (*post-office*) Zweigpostamt *n*; (elec) Umspannwerk *n*

substitute ['sʌbstɪ,t(j)ut] *s* (*person*) Stellvertreter –in *mf*; (*material*) Austauschstoff *m*; (pej) Ersatz *m*; (sport) Ersatzspieler –in *mf*; **act as a s.** für vertreten; **beware of substitutes** vor Nachamung wird gewarnt ‖ *tr*—**s. A for B** B durch A ersetzen ‖ *intr*—**s. for** einspringen für

sub'stitute teach'er *s* Aushilfslehrer –in *mf*

substitution [,sʌbstɪ't(j)uʃən] *s* Einsetzung *f*; (chem, math, ling) Substitution *f*; (sport) Auswechseln *s*

sub'stra'tum *s* (–ta [tə] & –tums) Unterlage *f*; (biol) Nährboden *m*

sub'struc'ture *s* Unterbau *m*

subsume [sʌb'sjum] *tr* unterordnen

subterfuge ['sʌbtər,fjudʒ] *s* Winkelzug *m*

subterranean [,sʌbtə'reni·ən] *adj* unterirdisch

sub'ti'tle *s* Untertitel *m*

subtle ['sʌtəl] *adj* fein; (*poison*) schleichend; (*cunning*) raffiniert

subtlety ['sʌtəlti] *s* Feinheit *f*

subtract [səb'trækt] *tr* subtrahieren

subtraction [səb'trækʃən] *s* Subtraktion *f*

suburb ['sʌbʌrb] *s* Vorstadt *f*, Vorort *m*; **the suburbs** der Stadtrand

suburban [sə'bʌrbən] *adj* Vorstadt-

suburbanite [sə'bʌrbə,naɪt] *s* Vorstadtbewohner –in *mf*

subvention [səb'venʃən] *s* Subvention *f*

subversion [səb'vʌrʒən] *s* Umsturz *m*

subversive [səb'vʌrsɪv] *adj* umstürzlerisch ‖ *s* Umstürzler –in *mf*

subver'sive activ'ity *s* Wühlarbeit *f*

subvert [səb'vʌrt] *tr* (*a government*) stürzen; (*the law*) umstoßen; (*corrupt*) (sittlich) verderben

sub'way' *s* U-Bahn *f*, Untergrundbahn *f*

succeed [sək'sid] *tr* folgen (*dat*) ‖ *intr* (*said of persons*) (**in**) Erfolg haben (mit); (*said of things*) gelingen; **I succeeded in** (*ger*) es gelang mir zu (*inf*); **not s.** mißglücken; **s. to the throne** die Thronfolge antreten

success [sək'ses] *s* Erfolg *m*; (*play, song, piece of merchandise*) Knüller *m*; **be a s.** Erfolg haben; **without s.** erfolglos

successful [sək'sesfəl] *adj* erfolgreich

succession [sək'seʃən] *s* Reihenfolge *f*; (*as heir*) Erbfolge *f*; **in s.** nacheinander; **s. to** (*e.g., an office, estate*) Übernahme *f* (*genit*)

successive [sək'sesɪv] *adj* aufeinanderfolgend

successor [sək'sesər] *s* Nachfolger –in *mf*; **s. to the throne** Thronfolger –in *mf*

succor ['sʌkər] *s* Beistand *m* ‖ *tr* beistehen (*dat*)

succotash ['sʌkə,tæʃ] *s* Gericht *n* aus Süßmais und grünen Bohnen

succulent ['sʌkjələnt] *adj* saftig

succumb [sə'kʌm] *intr* (**to**) erliegen (*dat*)

such [sʌtʃ] *adj* solch; **as s.** als solcher; **no s. thing** nichts dergleichen; **some s. thing** irgend so (et)was; **s. and s.** der und der; **s. as** wie (etwa); **s. a long time** so lange; **s. as it is** wie es nun einmal ist

suck [sʌk] *s* Saugen *n*; (*licking*) Lutschen *n* ‖ *tr* saugen; **s. in** einsaugen; (sl) reinlegen ‖ *intr* saugen; **s. on** (*e.g., candy*) lutschen

sucker ['sʌkər] *s* (coll) Gimpel *m*; (*carp*) Karpfenfisch *m* & (bot) Wurzelschößling *m*; (zool) Saugröhre *f*

suckle ['sʌkəl] *tr* stillen; (*animals*) säugen

suck'ling *s* Säugling *m*

suck'ling pig' *s* Spanferkel *n*

suction ['sʌkʃən] *s* Saugen *n*, Sog *m*

suc'tion cup' *s* Saugnapf *m*

suc'tion pump' *s* Saugpumpe *f*

sudden ['sʌdən] *adj* plötzlich, jäh; **all of a s.** (ganz) plötzlich

suddenly ['sʌdənli] *adv* plötzlich

suds [sʌdz] *spl* Seifenschaum *m*

sudsy ['sʌdzi] *adj* schaumig

sue [s(j)u] *tr* (**for**) verklagen (auf *acc*) ‖ *intr* (**for**) klagen (auf *acc*)

suede [swed] *adj* Wildleder– ‖ *s* Wildleder *n*

suet ['s(j)u·ɪt] *s* Talg *m*

suffer ['sʌfər] *tr* erleiden; (*damage*) nehmen; (*put up with*) ertragen ‖ *intr* (**from**) leiden (an *dat*)

sufferance ['sʌfərəns] *s* stillschweigende Einwilligung *f*

suf'fering *s* Leiden *n*

suffice [sə'faɪs] *intr* ausreichen

sufficient [sə'fɪʃənt] *adj* (**for**) ausreichend (für)

suffix ['sʌfɪks] *s* Nachsilbe *f*

suffocate ['sʌfə,ket] *tr* & *intr* ersticken

suffrage ['sʌfrɪdʒ] *s* Stimmrecht *n*

suffuse [sə'fjuz] *tr* übergießen

sugar ['ʃugər] *s* Zucker *m* ‖ *tr* zuckern

sug'ar beet' *s* Zuckerrübe *f*

sug'ar bowl' *s* Zuckerdose *f*

sug'ar cane' *s* Zuckerrohr *n*

sug'ar-coat' *tr* (& fig) überzuckern

sug'ar dad'dy *s* Geldonkel *m*

sug'ar ma'ple *s* Zuckerahorn *m*

sug'ar tongs' *spl* Zuckerzange *f*

sugary ['ʃugəri] *adj* zuckerig

suggest [səg'dʒest] *tr* vorschlagen; (*hint*) andeuten

suggestion [səg'dʒestʃən] *s* Vorschlag *m*

suggestive [səg'dʒestɪv] *adj* (*remark*) zweideutig; (*thought-provoking*) anregend; (*e.g., dress*) hauteng; **be s. of** erinnern an (*acc*)

suicidal [,su·ɪ'saɪdəl] *adj* selbstmörderisch

suicide ['su·ɪ,saɪd] *s* Selbstmord *m*;

(*person*) Selbstmörder –in *mf;* **commit s.** Selbstmord begehen

suit [sut] *s (men's)* Anzug *m;* (*women's*) Kostüm *n;* (cards) Farbe *f;* (jur) Prozeß *m;* **bring s.** (**against**) e–e Klage einbringen (gegen); **follow s.** Farbe bekennen; (fig) sich nach den anderen richten || *tr (please)* passen (*dat*); (*correspond to*) entsprechen (*dat*); (*said, e.g., of colors, style*) gut passen (*dat*); **be suited for** sich eignen für; **s. s.th. to** etw anpassen (*dat*); **s. yourself!** wie Sie wollen!

suitable ['sutəbəl] *adj* (**to**) geeignet (für)

suit'case' *s* Handkoffer *m*

suit' coat' *s* Sakko *m & n*

suite [swit] *s (series of rooms)* Zimmerflucht *f;* (*set of furniture*) Zimmergarnitur *f;* (mus) Suite *f*

suitor ['sutər] *s* Freier *m*

sul'fa drug' *s* Sulfonamid *n*

sulfate ['sʌlfet] *s* Sulfat *n*

sulfide ['sʌlfaɪd] *s* Sulfid *n*

sulfur ['sʌlfər] *adj* Schwefel– || *s* Schwefel *m* || *tr* einschwefeln

sulfur'ic ac'id [sʌl'f(j)ʊrɪk] *s* Schwefelsäure *f*

sul'fur mine' *s* Schwefelgrube *f*

sulk [sʌlk] *intr* trotzen

sulky ['sʌlki] *adj* trotzend, mürrisch || *s* (sport) Traberwagen *m*

sulk'y race' *s* Trabrennen *n*

sullen ['sʌlən] *adj* mißmutig

sul·ly ['sʌli] *v (pret & pp –lied) tr* besudeln

sulphur ['sʌlfər] *var of* sulfur

sultan ['sʌltən] *s* Sultan *m*

sultry ['sʌltri] *adj* schwül

sum [sʌm] *s* Summe *f*, Betrag *m;* **in sum** kurz gesagt || *v (pret & pp summed; ger summing)*—**sum up** summieren; (*summarize*) zusammenfassen; (*make a quick estimate of*) kurz abschätzen

sumac, sumach ['ʃumæk] *s* Sumach *m*

summarize ['sʌmə,raɪz] *tr* zusammenfassen

summary ['sʌməri] *adj* summarisch || *s* Zusammenfassung *f*

sum'mary court'martial *s* summarisches Militärgericht *n*

summer ['sʌmər] *s* Sommer *m*

sum'mer cot'tage *s* Sommerwohnung *f*

sum'mer resort' *s* Sommerfrische *f*

sum'mer school' *s* Sommerkurs *m*

sum'mertime' *s* Sommerzeit *f*

summery ['sʌməri] *adj* sommerlich

summit ['sʌmɪt] *s (& fig)* Gipfel *m*

sum'mit con'ference *s* Gipfelkonferenz *f*

sum'mit talks' *spl* Gipfelgespräche *pl*

summon ['sʌmən] *tr (e.g., a doctor)* kommen lassen; (*a conference*) einberufen; (jur) vorladen; **s. up** (*courage, strength*) aufbieten

summons ['sʌmənz] *s* (jur) Vorladung *f*

sumptuous ['sʌmptʃʊ·əs] *adj* üppig

sun [sʌn] *s* Sonne *f* || *v (pret & pp sunned; ger sunning) tr* sonnen; **sun oneself** sich sonnen

sun' bath' *s* Sonnenbad *n*

sun'beam' *s* Sonnenstrahl *m*

sun'burn' *s* Sonnenbrand *m*

sun'burned' *adj* sonnverbrannt

sundae ['sʌnde] *s* Eisbecher *m* mit Sirup, Nüssen, Früchten und Schlagsahne

Sunday ['sʌnde] *adj* sonntäglich; **dressed in one's S. best** sonntäglich gekleidet || *s* Sonntag *m;* **on S.** am Sonntag

Sun'day driv'er *s* Sonntagsfahrer –in *mf*

Sun'day school' *s* Sonntagsschule *f*

sunder ['sʌndər] *tr* trennen

sun'di'al *s* Sonnenuhr *f*

sun'down' *s* Sonnenuntergang *m*

sun'-drenched' *adj* sonnenüberflutet

sundries ['sʌndriz] *pl* Diverses *n*

sundry ['sʌndri] *adj* verschiedene

sun'fish' *s* Sonnenfisch *m*

sun'flow'er *s* Sonnenblume *f*

sun'glass'es *pl* Sonnenbrille *f*

sun' hel'met *s* Tropenhelm *m*

sunken ['sʌŋkən] *adj (ship)* gesunken; (*eyes; garden*) tiefliegend; (*treasure*) versunken; (*cheeks*) eingefallen; **s. rocks** blinde Klippe *f*

sun' lamp' *s* Höhensonne *f*

sun'light' *s* Sonnenlicht *n*

sunny ['sʌni] *adj* sonnig

sun'ny side' *s* Sonnenseite *f*

sun' par'lor *s* Glasveranda *f*

sun'rise' *s* Sonnenaufgang *m*

sun' roof' *s* (aut) Schiebedach *n*

sun'set' *s* Sonnenuntergang *m*

sun'shade' *s* Sonnenschirm *m;* (*awning*) Sonnendach *n;* (phot) Gegenlichtblende *f*

sun'shine' *s* Sonnenschein *m*

sun'spot' *s* Sonnenfleck *m*

sun'stroke' *s* Sonnenstich *m*

sun'tan' *s* Sonnenbräune *f*

sun'tanned' *adj* sonnengebräunt

sun' vi'sor *s* (aut) Sonnenblende *f*

sup [sʌp] *v (pret & pp supped; ger supping) intr* zu Abend essen

super ['supər] *adj (oversized)* Super–; (sl) prima || *s* (theat) Komparse *m*

su'perabun'dance *s* (**of**) Überfülle *f* (an *dat*)

su'perabun'dant *adj* überreichlich

superannuated [,supər'ænjʊ,etɪd] *adj* (*person*) pensioniert; (*thing*) veraltet

superb [sʊ'pərb] *adj* prachtvoll, herrlich

su'perbomb' *s* Superbombe *f*

su'perbomb'er *s* Riesenbomber *m*

supercilious [,supər'sɪlɪ·əs] *adj* hochnäsig

superficial [,supər'fɪʃəl] *adj* oberflächlich

superfluous [sʊ'pʌrflu·əs] *adj* überflüssig

su'perhigh'way' *s* Autobahn *f*

su'perhu'man *adj* übermenschlich

su'perimpose' *tr* darüberlegen; (elec, phys) überlagern

su'perintend' *tr* die Aufsicht führen über (*acc*), beaufsichtigen

superintendent [,supərɪn'tendənt] *s* Oberaufseher –in *mf;* (*in industry*)

Betriebsleiter –in *mf;* (*of a factory*) Werksleiter –in *mf;* (*of a building*) Hausverwalter –in *mf;* (educ) Schulinspektor –in *mf*
superior [səˈpɪrɪ·ər] *adj* (*physically*) höher; (*in rank*) übergeordnet; (*quality*) hervorragend; **s. in** überlegen an (*dat*); **s. to** überlegen (*dat*) ‖ *s* Vorgesetzte *mf*
supe′rior court′ *s* Obergericht *n*
superiority [səˌpɪrɪˈɑrɪti] *s* (**in**) Überlegenheit *f* (in *dat,* an *dat*); (mil) Übermacht *f*
superlative [sʊˈpʌrlətɪv] *adj* hervorragend; (gram) superlativisch, Superlativ– ‖ *s* (gram) Superlativ *m*
su′perman′ *s* (**–men′**) Übermensch *m*
su′permar′ket *s* Supermarkt *m*
su′pernat′ural *adj* übernatürlich ‖ *s* Übernatürliche *n*
supersede [ˌsupərˈsid] *tr* ersetzen
su′persen′sitive *adj* überempfindlich
su′person′ic *adj* Überschall–
superstition [ˌsupərˈstɪʃən] *s* Aberglaube *m;* (*superstitious idea*) abergläubische Vorstellung *f*
superstitious [ˌsupərˈstɪʃəs] *adj* abergläubisch
su′perstruc′ture *s* Überbau *m;* (*of a bridge*) Oberbau *m;* (*of a building or ship*) Aufbauten *pl*
supervise [ˈsupərˌvaɪz] *tr* beaufsichtigen
supervision [ˌsupərˈvɪʒən] *s* Beaufsichtigung *f*
supervisor [ˈsupərˌvaɪzər] *s* Vorgesetzte *mf*
su′pine posi′tion [ˈsupaɪn] *s* Rückenlage *f*
supper [ˈsʌpər] *s* Abendessen *n;* **eat s.** zu Abend essen
sup′pertime′ *s* Abendbrotzeit *f*
supplant [səˈplænt] *tr* ersetzen
supple [ˈsʌpəl] *adj* geschmeidig; (*mind*) beweglich
supplement [ˈsʌplɪmənt] *s* (*e.g., to a diet*) (**to**) Ergänzung *f* (*genit*); (*to a writing*) Anhang *m;* (*to a newspaper*) Beilage *f* ‖ [ˈsʌplɪˌment] *tr* ergänzen
supplementary [ˌsʌplɪˈmentəri] *adj* ergänzend
suppliant [ˈsʌplɪ·ənt] *adj* flehend ‖ *s* Bittsteller –in *mf*
supplicant [ˈsʌplɪkənt] *s* Bittsteller –in *mf*
supplicate [ˈsʌplɪˌket] *tr* flehen
supplication [ˌsʌplɪˈkeʃən] *s* Flehen *n*
supplier [səˈplaɪ·ər] *s* Lieferant –in *mf*
sup·ply [səˈplaɪ] *s* (*supplying*) Versorgung *f;* (*stock*) (**of**) Vorrat *m* (an *dat*); (com) Angebot *n;* **supplies** Vorräte *pl;* (*e.g., office supplies, dental supplies*) Bedarfsartikel *pl;* (mil) Nachschub *m* ‖ *v* (*pret & pp* **–plied**) *tr* (**with**) versorgen (mit); (*deliver*) liefern; (*procure*) beschaffen; (*with a truck*) zuführen; (*equip*) (**with**) versehen (mit); (*a demand*) befriedigen; (*a loss*) ausgleichen; (*missing words*) ergänzen; (mil) mit Nachschub versorgen
supply′ and demand′ *spl* Angebot *n* und Nachfrage *f*
supply′ base′ *s* Nachschubstützpunkt *m*
supply′ line′ *s* Versorgungsweg *m;* (mil) Nachschubweg *m*
support [səˈport] *adj* Hilfs– ‖ *s* (*prop, brace, stay; person*) Stütze *f;* (*of a family*) Unterhalt *m;* **in s. of** zur Unterstützung (*genit*); **without s.** (*unsubstantiated*) haltlos; (*unprovided*) unversorgt; **with the s. of** mit dem Beistand von ‖ *tr* stützen, tragen; (*back*) unterstützen; (*a family*) erhalten; (*a charge*) erhärten; (*a claim*) begründen
supporter [səˈportər] *s* (*of a family*) Ernährer –in *mf;* (*backer*) Förderer –in *mf;* (*jockstrap*) Suspensorium *n*
support′ing role′ *s* Nebenrolle *f*
suppose [səˈpoz] *tr* annehmen; **be supposed to** sollen; **I s. so** ich glaube schon; **s. it rains** gesetzt den Fall (or angenommen), es regnet; **s. we take a walk** wie wäre es, wenn wir e–n Spaziergang machten?; **what is that supposed to mean?** was soll das bedeuten? ‖ *intr* vermuten
supposed′ *adj* mutmaßlich
supposedly [səˈpozɪdli] *adv* angeblich
supposition [ˌsʌpəˈzɪʃən] *s* Annahme *f*
suppository [səˈpɑzɪˌtori] *s* Zäpfchen *n*
suppress [səˈprɛs] *tr* unterdrücken; (*news, scandal*) verheimlichen
suppression [səˈprɛʃən] *s* Unterdrükkung *f;* (*of news, truth, scandal*) Verheimlichung *f*
suppurate [ˈsʌpjəˌret] *intr* eitern
supremacy [səˈprɛməsi] *s* Oberherrschaft *f*
supreme [səˈprim] *adj* Ober–, höchste
supreme′ author′ity *s* Obergewalt *f*
Supreme′ Be′ing *s* höchstes Wesen *n*
supreme′ command′ *s* Oberkommando *n;* **have s.** den Oberbefehl führen
supreme′ command′er *s* oberster Befehlshaber *m*
Supreme′ Court′ *s* Oberster Gerichtshof *m*
surcharge [ˈsʌrˌtʃɑrdʒ] *s* (**on**) Zuschlag *m* (zu)
sure [ʃʊr] *adj* sicher, gewiß; (*shot, cure*) unfehlbar; (*shot, footing, ground, way, proof*) sicher; **are you s. you won't come?** kommen Sie wirklich nicht?; **be s. of** sicher sein (*genit*); **be s. to** (*inf*) vergiß nicht zu (*inf*); **feel s. of oneself** s–r selbst sicher sein; **for s.** sicherlich; **she is s. to come** sie wird sicher(lich) kommen; **s. enough** wirklich; **to be s.** (*parenthetically*) zwar
sure′-foot′ed *adj* trittsicher
surely [ˈʃʊrli] *adv* sicher(lich), gewiß
surety [ˈʃʊr(ɪ)ti] *s* Bürgschaft *f;* **stand s.** (**for**) bürgen (für)
surf [sʌrf] *s* Brandung *f* ‖ *intr* wellenreiten
surface [ˈsʌrfɪs] *adj* (*superficial*) oberflächlich; (*apparent rather than real*)

Schein- ‖ s Oberfläche f; (of a road) Belag m; (aer) Tragfläche f; **on the s.** oberflächlich (betrachtet) ‖ tr (a road) mit e-m Belag versehen ‖ intr auftauchen

sur'face mail' s gewöhnliche Post f

sur'face-to-air' mis'sile s Boden-Luft-Rakete f

sur'face-to-sur'face mis'sile s Boden-Boden-Rakete f

surf'board' s Wellenreiterbrett n

surf'board'ing s Wellenreiten n

surfeit ['sʌrfɪt] s Übersättigung f ‖ tr übersättigen

surfer ['sʌrfər] s Wellenreiter –in mf

surf'ing s Wellenreiten n

surge [sʌrdʒ] s (forward rush of a wave or crowd) Wogen n; (swelling wave) Woge f; (swelling sea) Wogen n; (elec) Stromstoß m ‖ intr (said of waves or a crowd) wogen; (said of emotions, blood) (up) (auf)wallen

surgeon ['sʌrdʒən] s Chirurg –in mf

surgery ['sʌrdʒəri] s Chirurgie f; (room) Operationssaal m; **undergo s.** sich e-r Operation unterziehen

surgical ['sʌrdʒɪkəl] adj chirurgisch; (resulting from surgery) Operations–

surly ['sʌrli] adj bärbeißig

surmise ['sʌrmaɪz] s Vermutung f ‖ tr & intr vermuten

surmount [sər'maunt] tr überwinden

surname ['sʌr,nem] s (family name) Zuname m; (epithet) Beiname m ‖ tr e-n Zunamen (or Beinamen) geben (dat)

surpass [sər'pæs] tr (in) übertreffen (an dat)

surplice ['sʌrplɪs] s Chorhemd n

surplus ['sʌrplʌs] adj überschüssig, Über– ‖ s (of) Überschuß m (an dat)

surprise [sər'praɪz] s Überraschungs– ‖ s Überraschung f; **take by s.** überraschen; **to my (great) s.** zu meiner (großen) Überraschung ‖ tr überraschen; **be surprised at** sich wundern über (acc); **be surprised to see how** staunen, wie; **I am surprised that** es wundert mich, daß

surpris'ing adj überraschend

surrealism [sə'riə,lɪzəm] s Surrealismus m

surrender [sə'rendər] s (e.g., of a fortress) Übergabe f; (of an army or unit) Kapitulation f; (of rights) Aufgabe f; (of a prisoner) Auslieferung f ‖ tr übergeben; (rights) aufgeben; (a prisoner) ausliefern ‖ intr sich ergeben

surren'der val'ue s (ins) Rückkaufswert m

surreptitious [,sʌrep'tɪʃəs] adj heimlich; (glance) verstohlen

surround [sə'raund] tr umgeben; (said of a crowd, police) umringen; (mil) einschließen

surround'ing adj umliegend ‖ **surroundings** spl Umgebung f

surtax ['sʌr,tæks] s Steuerzuschlag m

surveillance [sər'vel(j)əns] s Überwachung f; **keep under s.** unter Polizeiaufsicht halten

survey ['sʌrve] s (of) Überblick m (über acc); (of opinions) Umfrage f; (of land) Vermessung f; (plan or description of the survey) Lageplan m ‖ [sʌr've] tr überblicken; (a person) mustern; (land) vermessen; (people for their opinion) befragen

sur'vey course' s Einführungskurs m

survey'ing s Landvermessung f

surveyor [sər've·ər] s Landmesser m

survival [sər'vaɪvəl] s Überleben n; (after death) Weiterleben n

survive [sər'vaɪv] tr (a person) überleben; (a thing) überstehen; **be survived by** hinterlassen ‖ intr am Leben bleiben

surviv'ing adj überlebend

survivor [sər'vaɪvər] s Überlebende mf

susceptible [sə'septɪbəl] adj (impressionable) eindrucksfähig; **be s. of** zulassen; **be s. to** (disease, infection) anfällig sein für; (flattery) empfänglich sein für

suspect ['sʌspekt] adj verdächtig ‖ s Verdächtigte mf ‖ [səs'pekt] tr in Verdacht haben; (surmise) vermuten; (have a hint of) ahnen; **s. s.o. of** j-n verdächtigen (genit)

suspend [səs'pend] tr (from a job, office) suspendieren; (payment, hostilities, proceedings, a game) einstellen; (a rule) zeitweilig aufheben; (a sentence) aussetzen; (a player) sperren; (from a club) zeitweilig ausschließen; (from) hängen (an dat)

suspenders [səs'pendərz] spl Hosenträger pl

suspense [səs'pens] s Spannung f; **hang in s.** in der Schwebe sein; **keep in s.** im ungewissen lassen

suspension [səs'penʃən] s Aufhängung f; (of a sentence) Aussetzung f; (of work) Einstellung f; (e.g., of telephone service) Sperrung f; (aut) Federung f; (chem) Suspension f; **s. of driver's license** Führerscheinentzug m

suspen'sion bridge' s Hängebrücke f

suspen'sion points' spl (indicating unfinished thoughts) Gedankenpunkte pl; (indicating omission) Auslassungspunkte pl

suspicion [səs'pɪʃən] s Verdacht m; **above s.** über jeden Verdacht erhaben; **be under s.** unter Verdacht stehen; **on s. of murder** unter Mordverdacht

suspicious [səs'pɪʃəs] adj (person) verdächtig; (e.g., glance) argwöhnisch; (character) zweifelhaft

sustain [səs'ten] tr aufrechterhalten; (a loss, defeat, injury) erleiden; (a family) ernähren; (an army) verpflegen; (a motion, an objection) stattgeben (dat); (a theory, position) erhärten; (a note) dehnen

sustenance ['sʌstɪnəns] s (nourishment) Nahrung f; (means of livelihood) Unterhalt m

swab [swɑb] s (med, surg) Tupfer m;

(matter collected on a swab) Abstrich *m;* (naut) Schwabber *m* ‖ *v (pret & pp swabbed; ger swabbing) tr* (med, surg) abtupfen; (naut) schrubben

Swabia ['swebɪ-ə] *s* Schwaben *n*

Swabian ['swebɪ-ən] *adj* schwäbisch ‖ *s* Schwabe *m,* Schwäbin *f;* (dialect) Schwäbisch *n*

swad'dling clothes' ['swadlɪŋ] *spl* Windeln *pl*

swagger ['swægər] *s* (strut) Stolzieren *n;* (swaggering manner) Prahlerei *f* ‖ *intr* stolzieren; (show off) prahlen

swain [swen] *s* (lover) Liebhaber *m;* (country lad) Bauernbursche *m*

swallow ['swalo] *s* Schluck *m;* (orn) Schwalbe *f* ‖ *tr* schlucken; (fig) hinunterschlucken ‖ *intr* schlucken; **s. the wrong way** sich verschlucken

swamp [swamp] *s* Sumpf *m,* Moor *n* ‖ *tr* überfluten; (with work) überhäufen

swamp'land' *s* Moorland *n*

swampy ['swampi] *adj* sumpfig

swan [swan] *s* Schwan *m*

swan' dive' *s* Schwalbensprung *m*

swank [swæŋk], **swanky** ['swæŋki] *adj* (luxurious) schick; (ostentatious) protzig

swan's'-down' *s* Schwanendaunen *pl*

swan' song' *s* Schwanengesang *m*

swap [swap] *s* (coll) Tauschgeschäft *n* ‖ *v (pret & pp swapped; ger swapping) tr & intr* (coll) tauschen

swarm [swarm] *s* Schwarm *m;* (of children) Schar *f* ‖ *intr* schwärmen; **s. around** umschwärmen; **s. into** sich drängen in (acc); **s. with** (fig) wimmeln von

swarthy ['sworði] *adj* dunkelhäutig

swashbuckler ['swaʃ͵bʌklər] *s* Eisenfresser *m*

swastika ['swastɪkə] *s* Hakenkreuz *n*

swat [swat] *s* Schlag *m* ‖ *(pret & pp swatted; ger swatting) tr* schlagen

swath [swaθ] *s* Schwaden *m*

swathe [sweð] *tr* umwickeln, einwickeln

sway [swe] *s* Schwanken *n,* Schwingen *n;* (domination) Herrschaft *f* ‖ *tr* (e.g., tree) hin- und herbewegen; (influence) beeinflussen; (cause to vacillate) ins Wanken bringen ‖ *intr* schwanken

sway'-back' *s* Senkrücken *m*

swear [swer] *v (pret swore* [swor]; *pp sworn* [sworn]) *tr* schwören; *intr* vereidigen; **s. s.o. to secrecy** j–n auf Geheimhaltung vereidigen ‖ *intr* schwören; (coll) fluchen; **s. at** schimpfen über (acc) or auf (acc); **s. by** schwören bei; **s. off** abschwören (dat); **s. on a stack of Bibles** Stein und Bein schwören; **s. to** (a statement) beschwören; **s. to it** darauf schwören

swear'ing-in' *s* Vereidigung *f*

swear'word' *s* Fluchwort *n*

sweat [swet] *s* Schweiß *m;* **break out in s.** in Schweiß geraten ‖ *v (pret & pp sweat & sweated) tr* (blood)

schwitzen; (metal) seigern; (a horse) in Schweiß bringen; **s. off** abschwitzen; **s. out** (sl) geduldig abwarten; **s. up** durchschwitzen ‖ *intr* schwitzen

sweater ['swetər] *s* Sweater *m,* Pullover *m*

sweat'er girl' *s* vollbusiges Mädchen *n*

sweat' shirt' *s* Trainingsbluse *f*

sweat' shop' *s* (sl) Knochenmühle *f*

sweaty ['sweti] *adj* verschwitzt; (hand) schweißig

Swede [swid] *s* Schwede *m,* Schwedin *f*

Swedish ['swidɪʃ] *adj* schwedisch ‖ *s* Schwedisch *n*

sweep [swip] *s* (sweeper) Kehrer –in *mf;* (of the arm, scythe, weapon) Schwung *m;* (of an oar) Schlag *m;* (range) Reichweite *f;* (continuous stretch) ausgedehnte Strecke *f;* **in one clean s.** mit e–m Schlag; **make a clean s. of it** reinen Tisch machen ‖ *v (pret & pp swept* [swept]) *tr* kehren, fegen; (mines) räumen; (with machine-gun fire) bestreichen; (with a searchlight) absuchen; **he swept her off her feet** er hat sie im Sturm erobert; **s. clean** reinemachen ‖ *intr* kehren, fegen

sweeper ['swipər] *s* Kehrer –in *mf;* (carpet sweeper) Teppichkehrer *m*

sweep'ing *adj* weitreichend ‖ **sweepings** *spl* Kehricht *m & n*

sweep'-sec'ond *s* Zentralsekundenzeiger *m*

sweep'stakes' *s & spl* Lotterie *f;* (sport) Toto *m & n*

sweet [swit] *adj* süß; (person) lieb; (butter) ungesalzen; **be s. on** scharf sein auf (acc) ‖ **sweets** *spl* Süßigkeiten *pl*

sweet'bread' *s* Bries *n*

sweet'bri'er *s* Heckenrose *f*

sweet' corn' *s* Zuckermais *m*

sweeten ['switən] *tr* süßen; (fig) versüßen ‖ *intr* süß(er) werden

sweet'heart' *s* Liebste *mf,* Schatz *m*

sweetish ['switɪʃ] *adj* süßlich

sweet' mar'joram *s* Gartenmajoran *m*

sweet'meats' *spl* Zuckerwerk *n*

sweetness ['switnɪs] *s* Süßigkeit *f*

sweet' pea' *s* Gartenwicke *f*

sweet' pep'per *s* grüner Paprika *m*

sweet' pota'to *s* Süßkartoffel *f*

sweet'-scent'ed *adj* wohlriechend

sweet' tooth' *s*—**have a s.** gern naschen

sweet' wil'liam *s* Fleischnelke *f*

swell [swel] *adj* (coll) prima ‖ *s* (of the sea) Wellengang *m;* (of an organ) Schweller *m* ‖ *v (pret swelled; pp swelled & swollen* ['swolən]) *tr* zum Schwellen bringen; (the number) vermehren; (a musical tone) anschwellen ‖ *intr* schwellen

swell'ing *s* Schwellung *f*

swelter ['sweltər] *intr* unter der Hitze leiden

swept'-back' *(aer) adj* keilförmig

swerve [swʌrv] *s* Abweichung *f* ‖ *tr* ablenken ‖ *intr* scharf abbiegen

swift [swɪft] *adj* geschwind, rasch

swig [swɪg] *s* (coll) kräftiger Schluck

m ‖ *v* (*pret & pp* swigged; *ger* swigging) *tr* in langen Zügen trinken

swill [swɪl] *s* Spülicht *n*; (*for swine*) Schweinefutter *n*; (*deep drink*) tüchtiger Schluck *m* ‖ *tr & intr* gierig trinken

swim [swɪm] *s* Schwimmen *n*; take a s. schwimmen ‖ *v* (*pret* swam [swæm]; *pp* swum [swʌm]; *ger* swimming) *tr* (*e.g., a lake*) durchschwimmen; (*cause to swim*) schwimmen lassen; (*challenge in swimming*) um die Wette schwimmen mit ‖ *intr* schwimmen; my head is swimming mir schwindelt der Kopf

swimmer ['swɪmər] *s* Schwimmer –in *mf*

swim'ming *adj* Schwimm– ‖ *s* Schwimmen *n*; (*sport*) Schwimmsport *m*

swim'ming pool' *s* Schwimmbecken *n*

swim'ming suit' *s* Badeanzug *m*

swim'ming trunks' *spl* Badehose *f*

swindle ['swɪndəl] *s* Schwindel *m* ‖ *tr* gaunern; s. s.th. out of etw erschwindeln von

swindler ['swɪndlər] *s* Schwindler –in *mf*

swind'ling *s* Schwindelei *f*

swine [swaɪn] *s* Schwein *n*

swine'herd' *s* Schweinehirt *m*

swing [swɪŋ] *s* (*for children*) Schaukel *f*; (*swinging movement*) Hin– und Herschwingen *n*; (*box*) Schwinger *m*; (*mus*) Swing *m*; in full s. in vollem Gang; take a s. at s.o. nach j–m schlagen ‖ *v* (*pret & pp* swung [swʌŋ]) *tr* schwingen; (*children on a swing*) schaukeln; (*an election*) entscheidend beeinflussen; s. (*e.g., a car*) around herumdrehen; we'll s. it somhow (coll) wir werden es schon schaffen ‖ *intr* pendeln; (*on a swing*) schaukeln; s. around sich umdrehen; s. into action in Schwung kommen; things are swinging around here (coll) hier geht es lustig zu

swing'ing door' *s* Pendeltür *f*

swinish ['swaɪnɪʃ] *adj* schweinisch

swipe [swaɪp] *s* (coll) Hieb *m*; take a s. at (coll) schlagen nach ‖ *tr* (*hit with full force*) (coll) kräftig schlagen; (*steal*) (sl) mausen

swirl [swʌrl] *s* Wirbel *m* ‖ *tr* (*about*) herumwirbeln ‖ *intr* wirbeln; (*said of water*) Strudel bilden

swish [swɪʃ] *s* (*e.g., of a whip*) Sausen *n*; (*of a dress*) Rauschen *n* ‖ *tr* (*a whip*) sausen lassen; s. its tail mit dem Schwanz wedeln ‖ *intr* (*said of a whip*) sausen; (*said of a dress*) rauschen

Swiss [swɪs] *adj* schweizerisch ‖ *s* Schweizer –in *mf*

Swiss' cheese' *s* Schweizer Käse *m*

Swiss' franc' *s* Schweizerfranken *m*

Swiss' Guard' *s* Schweizergarde *f*

switch [swɪtʃ] *s* (*exchange*) Wechsel *m*, Umschwung *m*; (*stick*) Rute *f*; (elec) Schalter *m*; (rr) Weiche *f* ‖ *tr* wechseln; (*e.g., coats by mistake*) verwechseln; (rr) rangieren; s. off (elec, rad, telv) ausschalten; s. on

(elec, rad, telv) einschalten ‖ *intr* Plätze wechseln

switch'–blade knife' *s* feststellbares Messer *n*

switch'board' *s* Schaltbrett *n*, Zentrale *f*

switch'board op'erator *s* Telephonist –in *mf*

switch' box' *s* Schaltkasten *m*

switch'man *s* (–men) (rr) Weichensteller *m*

switch' tow'er *s* (rr) Blockstation *f*

switch'yard' *s* Rangierbahnhof *m*

Switzerland ['swɪtsərlənd] *s* die Schweiz

swiv·el ['swɪvəl] *s* Drehlager *n* ‖ *v* (*pret & pp* –el[l]ed; *ger* –el[l]ing) *tr* herumdrehen ‖ *intr* sich drehen

swiv'el chair' *s* Drehstuhl *m*

swiz'zle stick' ['swɪzəl] *s* Rührstäbchen *n*

swollen ['swolən] *adj* (an)geschwollen; (*eyes*) verquollen

swoon [swun] *s* Ohnmacht *f* ‖ *intr* ohnmächtig werden

swoop [swup] *s* Herabstoßen *n*; in one fell s. mit e–m Schlag ‖ *intr*–s. down (on) herabstoßen (auf *acc*)

sword [sord] *s* Schwert *n*; put to the s. mit dem Schwert hinrichten

sword' belt' *s* Schwertgehenk *n*

sword'fish' *s* Schwertfisch *m*

swords'man *s* (–men) Fechter *m*

sworn [sworn] *adj* (*statement*) eidlich; s. enemy Todfeind *m*

sycamore ['sɪkəmor] *s* Platane *f*

sycophant ['sɪkəfənt] *s* Sykophant *m*

syllabary ['sɪlə‚beri] *s* Silbenschrift *f*

syllabification [sɪ‚læbɪfɪ'keʃən] *s* Silbentrennung *f*

syllable ['sɪləbəl] *s* Silbe *f*

sylla·bus ['sɪləbəs] *s* (–bai [‚baɪ] & –buses) Lehrplan *m*

syllogism ['sɪlə‚dʒɪzəm] *s* Syllogismus *m*

sylvan ['sɪlvən] *adj* Wald–

symbol ['sɪmbəl] *s* Sinnbild *n*, Symbol *n*

symbolic(al) [sɪm'bɑlɪk(əl)] *adj* sinnbildlich, symbolisch

symbolism ['sɪmbə‚lɪzəm] *s* Symbolik *f*

symbolize ['sɪmbə‚laɪz] *tr* symbolisieren

symmetric(al) [sɪ'metrɪk(əl)] *adj* symmetrisch

symmetry ['sɪmɪtri] *s* Symmetrie *f*

sympathetic [‚sɪmpə'θetɪk] *adj* mitfühlend; (physiol) sympathisch

sympathize ['sɪmpə‚θaɪz] *intr*–s. with mitfühlen mit; (*be in accord with*) sympathisieren mit

sympathizer ['sɪmpə‚θaɪzər] *s* Sympathisant –in *mf*

sympathy ['sɪmpəθi] *s* Mitleid *n*; be in s. with im Einverständnis sein mit; offer one's sympathies to s.o. j–m sein Beileid bezeigen

sym'pathy card' *s* Beileidskarte *f*

sym'pathy strike' *s* Sympathiestreik *m*

symphonic [sɪm'fɑnɪk] *adj* sinfonisch

symphony ['sɪmfəni] *s* Sinfonie *f*

symposi·um [sɪm'pozɪ·əm] *s* (-a [ə] & -ums) Symposion *n*

symptom ['sɪmptəm] *s* (of) Symptom *n* (für)

symptomatic [ˌsɪmtə'mætɪk] *adj* (of) symptomatisch (für)

synagogue ['sɪnə‚gɔg] *s* Synagoge *f*

synchronize ['sɪŋkrə‚naɪz] *tr* synchronisieren

synchronous ['sɪŋkrənəs] *adj* synchron; (elec) Synchron–

syncopate ['sɪŋkə‚pet] *tr* synkopieren

syncopation [ˌsɪŋkə'peʃən] *s* Synkope *f*

syncope ['sɪŋkə‚pi] *s* Synkope *f*

syndicate ['sɪndɪkɪt] *s* Interessengemeinschaft *f*, Syndikat *n* || ['sɪndɪ‚ket] *tr* zu e–m Syndikat zusammenschließen; (*a column*) in mehreren Zeitungen zugleich veröffentlichen || *intr* ein Syndikat bilden

synod ['sɪnəd] *s* Synode *f*

synonym ['sɪnənɪm] *s* Synonym *n*

synonymous [sɪ'nɑnəməs] *adj* sinnverwandt; **s. with** gleichbedeutend mit

synop·sis [sɪ'nɑpsɪs] *s* (-ses [siz]) Zusammenfassung *f*

synoptic [sɪ'nɑptɪk] *adj* synoptisch

syntax ['sɪntæks] *s* Satzlehre *f*, Syntax *f*

synthe·sis ['sɪnθɪsɪs] *s* (-ses [‚siz]) Synthese *f*

synthesize ['sɪnθɪ‚saɪz] *tr* (& chem) zusammenfügen

synthetic [sɪn'θetɪk] *adj* künstlich, Kunst– || *s* Kunststoff *m*

syphilis ['sɪfɪlɪs] *s* Syphilis *f*

Syria ['sɪrɪ·ə] *s* Syrien *n*

Syrian ['sɪrɪ·ən] *adj* syrisch || *s* Syrer –in *mf*; (*language*) Syrisch *n*

syringe [sɪ'rɪndʒ] *s* Spritze *f* || *tr* (*inject*) einspritzen; (*wash*) ausspritzen

syrup ['sɪrəp] *s* Sirup *m*

system ['sɪstəm] *s* System *n*; (*bodily system*) Organismus *m*

systematic(al) [ˌsɪstə'mætɪk(əl)] *adj* systematisch, planmäßig

systematize ['sɪstəmə‚taɪz] *tr* systematisieren, systematisch ordnen

systole ['sɪstəli] *s* Systole *f*

T

T, t [ti] *s* zwanzigster Buchstabe des englischen Alphabets

tab [tæb] *s* (*label*) Etikett *n*; (*on file cards*) Karteireiter *m*; **keep tabs on** (coll) genau kontrollieren; **pick up the tab** (coll) die Zeche bezahlen || *v* (*pret & pp* tabbed; *ger* tabbing) *tr* (*designate*) ernennen

tabby ['tæbɪ] *s* getigerte Katze *f*

tabernacle ['tæbər‚nækəl] *s* Tabernakel *n*

table ['tebəl] *s* Tisch *m*; (*list, chart*) Tafel *f*, Tabelle *f*; (geol) Tafel *f*; **at t.** bei Tisch; **the tables have turned** das Blatt hat sich gewendet || *tr* (parl) verschieben

tab·leau ['tæblo] *s* (-leaus & leaux [loz]) Tableau *n*

ta′blecloth′ *s* Tischtuch *n*

ta′bleland′ *s* Tafelland *n*

ta′ble man′ners *spl* Tischmanieren *pl*

ta′ble of con′tents *s* Inhaltsverzeichnis *n*

ta′ble salt′ *s* Tafelsalz *n*

ta′ble set′ting *s* Gedeck *n*

ta′blespoon′ *s* Eßlöffel *m*

tablespoonful ['tebəl‚spun‚ful] *s* Eßlöffel *m*

tablet ['tæblɪt] *s* (*writing pad*) Schreibblock *m*; (med) Tablette *f*

ta′ble talk′ *s* Tischgespräch *n*

ta′ble ten′nis *s* Tischtennis *n*

ta′bletop′ *s* Tischplatte *f*

ta′bleware′ *s* Tafelgeschirr *n*

ta′ble wine′ *s* Tafelwein *m*

tabloid ['tæblɔɪd] *adj* konzentriert || *s* Bildzeitung *f*; (pej) Sensationsblatt *n*

taboo [tə'bu] *adj* tabu. || *s* Tabu *n* || *tr* für Tabu erklären

tabular ['tæbjələr] *adj* tabellarisch

tabulate ['tæbjə‚let] *tr* tabellarisieren

tabulator ['tæbjə‚letər] *s* Tabelliermaschine *f*

tacit ['tæsɪt] *adj* stillschweigend

taciturn ['tæsɪtʌrn] *adj* schweigsam

tack [tæk] *s* (*nail*) Zwecke *f*, Stift *m*; (*stitch*) Heftstich *m*; (*stickiness*) Klebrigkeit *f*; (*course of action*) Kurs *m*; (*gear for a riding horse*) Reitgeschirr *n*; (*course run obliquely to the wind*) Schlag *m*; **be on the wrong t.** (fig) auf dem Holzweg sein || *tr* (*down*) mit Zwecken befestigen; (sew) heften; **t. on** (to) anfügen (an *acc*) || *intr* (fig & naut) lavieren

tackle ['tækəl] *s* (*gear*) Ausrüstung *f*; (*for lifting*) Flaschenzug *m*; (fb) Halbstürmer *m*; (naut) Takelwerk *n* || *tr* (*a problem*) anpacken; (fb) packen

tacky ['tækɪ] *adj* klebrig; (*gaudy*) geschmacklos

tact [tækt] *s* Takt *m*, Feingefühl *n*

tactful ['tæktfəl] *adj* taktvoll

tactical ['tæktɪkəl] *adj* taktisch

tac′tical u′nit *s* Kampfeinheit *f*

tactician [tæk'tɪʃən] *s* Taktiker *m*

tactics ['tæktɪks] *spl* (& fig) Taktik *f*

tactless ['tæktlɪs] *adj* taktlos

tadpole ['tæd‚pol] *s* Kaulquappe *f*

taffeta ['tæfɪtə] *s* Taft *m*

taffy ['tæfɪ] *s* Sahnebonbon *n*

tag [tæg] *s* (*label*) Etikett *n*; (*loose end*) loses Ende *n*; (*on a shoestring*) Stift *m*; (*loop for hanging up a coat*) Aufhänger *m*; (*on a fish hook*) Glitzerschmuck *m*; (*game*) Haschen *n*; **play tag** sich haschen; **tags** (aut)

Nummernschild n ‖ v (pret & pp **tagged;** ger **tagging**) tr (mark with a tag) mit e-m Etikett versehen; (touch) haschen; (hit solidly) heftig schlagen; (give a traffic ticket to) e-n Strafzettel geben (dat) ‖ intr— **tag after** s.o. sich an j-s Sohlen heften

tag′ line′ s (e.g., of a play) Schlußworte pl; (favorite phrase) stehende Redensart f

tail [tel] s Schwanz m; (of a horse, comet) Schweif m; (of a shirt) Schoß m; (aer) Heck n; **tails** ein Frack m; (of a coin) Rückseite f; **turn t.** ausreißen; **wag its t.** mit dem Schwanz wedeln ‖ tr (coll) beschatten ‖ intr —t. **after** nachlaufen (dat); **t. off** abflauen

tail′ end′ s (e.g., of a conversation) Schlußteil n; **come in at the t. end** als letzter durchs Ziel gehen

tail′gate′ s (of a station wagon) Hecktür f; (of a truck) Ladeklappe f ‖ intr dicht hinter e-m anderen fahren

tail′ gun′ner s (aer) Heckschütze m

tail′-heav′y adj schwanzlastig

tail′light′ s (aer) Hecklicht n; (aut) Rücklicht n

tailor [′telər] s Schneider m ‖ tr & intr schneidern

tai′loring s Schneiderarbeit f

tai′lor-made suit′ s Maßanzug m

tai′lor shop′ s Schneiderei f

tail′piece′ s (appendage) Anhang m; (of a stringed instrument) Saitenhalter m; (typ) Zierleiste f

tail′ pipe′ s (aut) Auspuffrohr n

tail′skid′ s (aer) Sporn m

tail′spin′ s—**go into a t.** abtrudeln

tail′ wheel′ s (aer) Spornrad n

tail′wind′ s Rückenwind m

taint [tent] s Fleck m; (fig) Schandfleck m ‖ tr beflecken; (food) verderben

take [tek] s (income) (sl) Einnahmen pl; (loot) (sl) Beute f; (angl) Fang m; (cin) Szenenaufnahme f; **be on the t.** (sl) sich bestechen lassen ‖ v (pret **took** [tuk]; pp **taken**) tr nehmen; (in a car) mitnehmen; (bring, carry) bringen; (subtract) abziehen; (require) erfordern; (insults, criticism) hinnehmen; (bear, stand) ertragen; (with a camera) aufnehmen; (food, pills) einnehmen; (s.o.'s temperature) messen; (courage) schöpfen; (a deep breath) holen; (precautions) treffen; (responsibility) übernehmen; (an oath, test) ablegen; (inventory) aufnehmen; (a walk, trip, examination, turn, notes) machen; (the consequences) tragen; (measures) ergreifen; (a certain amount of time to travel) in Anspruch nehmen; (a step) tun; (advice) befolgen; (a game) gewinnen; (e.g., third place) belegen; (a trick) (cards) stechen; (gram) regieren; **be able to t. a lot** e-n breiten Rücken haben; **be taken in by** s.o. j-m auf den Leim gehen; **I'm not going to t. that**

das lasse ich nicht auf mir sitzen t. **along** mitnehmen; **t. aside** bei seitenehmen; **t. at one's word** beim Wort nehmen; **t. away** wegschaffen t. **away from** wegnehmen (dat); t. **back** zurücknehmen; t. (e.g., s.o.'s hat) **by mistake** verwechseln; **t. down** herunternehmen; (in writing) aufschreiben; (dictation) aufnehmen; (minutes) zu Protokoll nehmen; **t. in** (money) einnehmen; (washing) ins Haus nehmen; (as guest) beherbergen; (deceive) täuschen; (encompass) umfassen; (observe) beobachten; (sightsee) besichtigen; (sew) enger machen; **t. it out on** s.o. seinen Zorn an j-m auslassen; **t. it that** annehmen, daß; **taken** (occupied) besetzt; **t. off** (subtract) abziehen; (clothes) ausziehen; (a coat) ablegen; (gloves) abstreifen; (a hat) abnehmen; (a tire, wheel) abmontieren; (e.g., a day from work) sich (dat) freinehmen; **t.** (e.g., wares) **off** s.o.'s hands j-m abnehmen; **t. on** (hire) anstellen; (passengers) aufnehmen; **t. out** (from a container) herausnehmen; (a spot) entfernen; (a girl) ausführen; (a mortgage, loan) aufnehmen; (ins) abschließen; (libr) sich [dat] ausleihen; **t. over** übernehmen; **t.** s.o. **for** j-n halten für; **t. up** aufnehmen; (absorb) aufsaugen; (a profession) ergreifen; (room, time) wegnehmen; (a collection) veranstalten; (a skirt) kürzer machen; **t. upon oneself** auf sich nehmen; **t. up** (a matter) **with** besprechen mit ‖ intr (said of an injection) anschlagen; (said of seedlings, skin transplants) anwachsen; **how long does it t.?** wie lange dauert es?; **how long does it t. to** (inf)? wie lange braucht man, um zu (inf)?; **t. after** nachgeraten (dat); **t. off** (depart) (coll) abhauen; (from work) wegbleiben; (aer, rok) starten; (aut) abfahren; **t. over for** s.o. für j-n einspringen; **t. to** (a person) warm werden mit; (an idea) aufgreifen; **t. up with** sich abgeben mit

take′-home pay′ s Nettolohn m

take′-off′ s Karikatur f; (aer) Start m

take′-off ramp′ s (in skiing) Schanzentisch m

take′o′ver s Übernahme f

tal′cum pow′der [′tælkəm] s Federweiß n

tale [tel] s Geschichte f; **tell tales out of school** aus der Schule plaudern

tale′bear′er s Zuträger m

talent [′tælənt] s Talent n

tal′ented adj talentiert, begabt

talisman [′tælɪsmən] s Talisman m

talk [tɔk] s Gespräch n; (gossip) Geschwätz n; (lecture) Vortrag m; (speech) Rede f; **cause t.** von sich reden machen; **give a t.** on e-n Vortrag halten über (acc); **t. of the town** Stadtgespräch n ‖ tr reden; (business, politics, etc.) sprechen über (acc); **t. down** zum Schweigen bringen; (aer) heruntersprechen; **t. one-**

self **hoarse** sich heiser reden; **t. one's way out of** sich herausreden aus; **t. over** besprechen; **t. sense** vernünftig reden; **t. s.o. into** (ger) j–n überreden zu (inf); **t. up** Reklame machen für ‖ intr reden; (chat) schwätzen; **t. back** scharf erwidern; **t. big** große Töne reden; **t. dirty** Zoten reißen; **t. down to** herablassend reden zu; **talking of food à propos** Essen; **t. on** (a topic) e–n Vortrag halten über (acc); **t. to the walls** in den Wind reden

talkative ['tɔkətɪv] adj redselig

talker ['tɔkər] s Plauderer –in mf; **big t.** Schaumschläger m

talkie ['tælo] s (cin) Sprechfilm m

talk'ing-to' s Denkzettel m

tall [tɔl] adj hoch; (person) hochgewachsen; **t. story** Mordsgeschichte f

tallow ['tælo] s Talg m

tal·ly ['tæli] s (reckoning) Rechnung f; (game score) Punktzahl f ‖ v (pret & pp –lied) tr (up) berechnen ‖ intr (with) übereinstimmen (mit)

tallyho ['tæli'ho] interj hallo!

tal'ly sheet' s Zählbogen m

talon ['tælən] s Klaue f

tambourine [,tæmbə'rin] s Tamburin n

tame [tem] adj zahm; (docile) gefügig; (dull) langweilig ‖ tr zähmen; (e.g., lions) bändigen ‖ intr—**t. down** (said of a person) gesetzter werden

tamp [tæmp] tr (a tobacco pipe) stopfen; (earth, cement) stampfen; (a drill hole) zustopfen

tamper ['tæmpər] s Stampfer m ‖ intr —**t. with** sich einmischen in (acc); (machinery) herumbasteln an (dat); (documents) frisieren

tampon ['tæmpɑn] s Damenbinde f; (surg) Tampon m ‖ tr (surg) tamponieren

tan [tæn] adj gelbbraun ‖ s Sonnenbräunung f ‖ v (pret & pp tanned; ger tanning) tr (the skin) bräunen; (leather) gerben ‖ intr sich bräunen

tandem ['tændəm] adj & adv hintereinander (geordnet) ‖ s Tandem n; **in t.** hintereinander

tang [tæŋ] s Herbheit f; (sound) Geklingel n

tangent ['tændʒənt] adj—**be t. to** tangieren ‖ s Tangente f; **fly off on a t.** plötzlich vom Thema abschweifen

tangerine [,tændʒə'rin] s Mandarine f

tangible ['tændʒɪbəl] adj (& fig) greifbar

tangle ['tæŋgəl] s Verwicklung f; (twisted strands; confused jumble) Gewirr n; (conflict) Auseinandersetzung f ‖ tr verwirren; **get tangled** sich verfilzen ‖ intr sich verwirren; **t. with** sich in e–n Kampf einlassen mit

tango ['tæŋgo] s Tango m ‖ intr Tango tanzen

tangy ['tæŋi] adj herb

tank [tæŋk] s Behälter m; (of a toilet) Spülkasten m; (mil) Panzer m

tank' attack' s Panzerangriff m

tank' car' s (rr) Kesselwagen m, Tankwagen m

tanker ['tæŋkər] s (truck) Tankwagen m; (ship) Tanker m; (plane) Tankflugzeug n

tank' trap' s Panzersperre f

tank' truck' s Tankwagen m

tanned adj gebräunt

tanner ['tænər] s Gerber –in mf

tannery ['tænəri] s Gerberei f

tantalize ['tæntə,laɪz] tr quälen

tantamount ['tæntə,maunt] adj—**be t. to** gleichkommen (dat)

tantrum ['tæntrəm] s Koller m; **throw a t.** e–n Koller kriegen

tap [tæp] s (light blow) Klaps m; (on a window or door) Klopfen n; (faucet) Wasserhahn m; (in a cask) Faßhahn m; (elec) Anzapfung f; (mach) Gewindebohrer m; (surg) Punktion f; **on tap** vom Faß; **play taps** (mil) den Zapfenstreich blasen ‖ v (pret & pp tapped; ger tapping) tr (a cask, powerline, telephone) anzapfen; (fluids) abzapfen; (a person on the shoulder) antippen; (a hole) mit e–m Gewinde versehen; **tap one's foot** (to mark time) Takt treten; **tap s.o. for** (money) (coll) j–n anpumpen um; **tap s.o.'s spine** j–n punktieren; **tap the window** am Fenster klopfen ‖ intr tippen

tap' dance' s Steptanz m

tap'-dance' intr steppen

tap' dan'cer s Stepper –in mf

tape [tep] s Band n; (electron) Tonband n; (friction tape) Isolierband n; (of paper) Papierstreifen m; (med) Klebstreifen m; (sport) Zielband n ‖ tr (mit Band) umwickeln; (electron) auf Tonband aufnehmen

tape' meas'ure s Meßband n

taper ['tepər] s Wachsfaden m ‖ tr zuspitzen ‖ intr spitz zulaufen; **t. off** langsam abnehmen

tape' recor'der s Tonbandgerät n

ta'pered adj kegelförmig, Keil-

tapestry ['tæpɪstri] s Wandteppich m

tape'worm' s Bandwurm m

tapioca [,tæpɪ'okə] s Tapioka f

tappet ['tæpɪt] s (mach) Stößel m

tap'room' s Ausschank m

tap'root' s Pfahlwurzel f

tap' wa'ter s Leitungswasser n

tap' wrench' s Gewindeschneidkluppe f

tar [tar] s Teer m ‖ v (pret & pp tarred; ger tarring) tr teeren

tardy ['tardi] adj säumig

target ['targɪt] s Ziel n; (on a firing range; of ridicule) Zielscheibe f

tar'get ar'ea s Zielraum m

tar'get date' s Zieltag m

tar'get lan'guage s Zielsprache f

tar'get prac'tice s Scheibenschießen n

tariff ['tærɪf] s Tarif m

tarnish ['tarnɪʃ] tr matt (or blind) machen; (fig) beflecken ‖ intr matt (or blind) werden

tar' pa'per s Teerpappe f

tarpaulin ['tarpəlɪn] s Plane f

tar·ry ['tari] adj teerig ‖ ['tæri] v

(pret & pp **–ried**) intr verweilen; (stay) bleiben

tart [tɑrt] adj sauer; (reply) scharf || s Tortelett n

tartar ['tɑrtər] s (dent) Zahnstein m

tar'tar sauce' s pikante Soße f

task [tæsk] s Aufgabe f; **take to t.** zur Rede stellen

task' force' s Sonderverband m

task'mas'ter s Zuchtmeister m

tassel ['tæsəl] s Quaste f; (on corn) Narbenfäden pl

taste [test] s (& fig) Geschmack m; **develop a t. for** Geschmack gewinnen an (dat); **have a bad t.** schlecht || intr—**t. like** (or of) schmecken schmecken; **have bad t.** e-n schlechten Geschmack haben; **in bad t.** geschmacklos; **in good t.** geschmackvoll; **to t.** (culin) nach Gutdünken || tr schmecken; (try out) kosten; (e.g., the pepper in soup) herausschmecken; **t. blood** (fig) Blut lecken nach

taste' bud' s Geschmacksknospe f

tasteful ['testfəl] adj geschmackvoll

tasteless ['testlɪs] adj (& fig) geschmacklos

tasty ['testi] adj schmackhaft

tatter ['tætər] s Lumpen m || tr zerfetzen

tat'tered adj zerlumpt

tattle ['tætəl] intr petzen

tattler ['tætlər] s Petze f

tat'fletale' s Petze f

tattoo [tæ'tu] s Tätowierung f || tr tätowieren

taunt [tɔnt] s Stichelei f || tr sticheln gegen

taut [tɔt] adj straff, prall

tavern ['tævərn] s Schenke f

tawdry ['tɔdri] adj aufgedonnert

tawny ['tɔni] adj gelbbraun

tax [tæks] s Steuer f || tr besteuern; (fig) beanspruchen; **tax s.o. with** j-n rügen wegen

taxable ['tæksəbəl] adj steuerpflichtig

tax' assess'ment s Steuereinschätzung f

taxation [tæk'se/ən] s Besteuerung f

tax' brac'ket s Steuerklasse f

tax' collec'tor s Steuereinnehmer –in mf

tax' cut' s Steuersenkung f

tax' eva'sion s Steuerhinterziehung f

tax' exemp'tion s steuerfreier Betrag m

tax•i ['tæksi] s Taxi n; **go by t.** mit e-m Taxi fahren || v (pret & pp **–ied**) ger **–iing** & **–ying**) tr (aer) rollen lassen || intr mit e–m Taxi fahren; (aer) rollen

tax'icab' s Taxi n

tax'i danc'er s Taxigirl n

taxidermist ['tæksɪ,dʌrmɪst] s Tierpräparator –in mf

tax'i driv'er s Taxifahrer –in mf

tax'ime'ter s Taxameter m

tax'i stand' s Taxistand m

tax'pay'er s Steuerzahler –in mf

tax' rate' s Steuersatz m

tax' return' s Steuererklärung f

tea [ti] s Tee m

tea' bag' s Teebeutel m

tea' cart' s Teewagen m

teach [tit/] v (pret & pp taught [tɔt]) tr lehren; (instruct) unterrichten; **t. school** an e–r Schule unterrichten; **t. s.o. manners** j–m Manieren beibringen; **t. s.o. music** j–n in Musik unterrichten; **t. s.o. (to play) tennis** j–m das Tennisspielen beibringen || intr lehren, unterrichten

teacher ['tit/ər] s Lehrer –in mf

teach'er's pet' s Liebling m des Lehrers (or der Lehrerin)

teach'ing s Lehren n; (profession) Lehrberuf m

teach'ing aid' s Lehrmittel n

teach'ing staff' s Lehrkörper m

tea'cup' s Teetasse f

teak [tik] s Teakholz n

tea'ket'tle s Teekessel m

tea' leaves' spl Teesatz m

team [tim] s Team n; (of draught animals) Gespann n; (sport) Mannschaft f || tr (draft animals) zusammenspannen || intr—**t. up with** sich vereinigen mit

team' cap'tain s Spielführer –in mf

team'mate' s Mannschaftskamerad –in mf

teamster ['timstər] s Fuhrmann m; (trucker) Lastwagenfahrer m

team'work' s Gemeinschaftsarbeit f; (sport) Zusammenspiel n

tea'pot' s Teekanne f

tear [tɪr] s Träne f; **bring tears to the eyes** Tränen in die Augen treiben; **burst into tears** in Tränen ausbrechen || [ter] s Riß m || v (pret tore [tor]; pp torn [torn]) tr (zer)reißen; **t. apart** (meat) zerreißen; (a speech) zerpflücken; **t. away** wegreißen; **t. down** (a building) abreißen; (mach) zerlegen; (a person) sich [dat] das Maul zerreißen über (acc); **t. off** abreißen; **t. open** aufreißen; **t. oneself away** sich losreißen; **t. out** ausreißen; **t. up** (a street) aufreißen; (e.g., letter) zerreißen || intr (zer)reißen; **t. along** (at high speed) dahinsausen

teardrop ['tɪr,drɑp] s Träne f

tear' gas' [tɪr] s Tränengas n

tear-jerker ['tɪr,dʒʌrkər] s (sl) Schnulze f

tea'room' s Teestube f

tease [tiz] tr necken; (e.g., a dog) quälen; (hair) auflockern

teas'ing s Neckerei f

tea'spoon' s Teelöffel m

teaspoonful ['ti,spun,fʊl] s Teelöffel m

teat [tit] s Zitze f

technical ['tɛknɪkəl] adj technisch, Fach-

tech'nical in'stitute s technische Hochschule f

technicality [,tɛknɪ'kælɪti] s technische Einzelheit f

tech'nical school' s Technikum n

tech'nical term' s Fachausdruck m

technician [tɛk'nɪ/ən] s Techniker –in mf

technique [tɛk'nik] s Technik f

technocrat ['tɛknə͵kræt] *s* Technokrat *m*

technological [͵tɛknə'lɑdʒɪkəl] *adj* technologisch

technology [tɛk'nɑlɪdʒi] *s* Technologie *f*

ted'dy bear' ['tɛdi] *s* Teddybär *m*

tedious ['tidɪ·əs] *adj* langweilig

tee [ti] *s* (*mound*) Abschlagplatz *m*; (*wooden or plastic peg*) Aufsatz *m*; **to a tee** aufs Haar ‖ *tr*—**tee off** (sl) aufregen; **tee up** (golf) auf den Aufsatz stellen ‖ *intr*—**tee off** (golf) abschlagen

teem [tim] *intr* (**with**) wimmeln (von)

teem'ing *adj* wimmelnd; (*rain*) strömend

teen-age ['tin͵edʒ] *adj* halbwüchsig

teen-ager ['tin͵edʒər] *s* Teenager *m*

teens [tinz] *spl* Jugendalter *n* (*vom dreizehnten bis neunzehnten Lebensjahr*); **in one's t.** in den Jugendjahren

teeny ['tini] *adj* (coll) winzig

tee' shot' *s* (golf) Abschlag *m*

teeter ['titər] *s* Schaukeln *n* ‖ *intr* schaukeln

teethe [tið] *intr* zahnen

teeth'ing ring' *s* Beißring *m*

teetotaler [ti'totələr] *s* Abstinenzler –in *mf*

tele·cast ['tɛlɪ͵kæst] *s* Fernsehsendung *f* ‖ *v* (*pret & pp* **–cast & –casted**) *tr* im Fernsehen übertragen

telecommunications [͵tɛlɪkə͵mjunɪ'keʃəns] *spl* Fernmeldewesen *n*

telegram ['tɛlɪ͵græm] *s* Telegramm *n*

telegraph ['tɛlɪ͵græf] *s* Telegraph *m* ‖ *tr & intr* telegraphieren

telegrapher [tɪ'lɛgrəfər] *s* Telegraphist –in *mf*

tel'egraph pole' *s* Telegraphenstange *f*

telemeter [tɪ'lɛmɪtər] *s* Telemeter *n*

telepathy [tɪ'lɛpəθi] *s* Telepathie *f*

telephone ['tɛlɪ͵fon] *s* Telephon *n*, Fernsprecher *m*; **be on the t.** am Apparat sein; **by t.** telephonisch; **speak on the t.** with telephonieren mit ‖ *tr & intr* anrufen

tel'ephone booth' *s* Telephonzelle *f*

tel'ephone call' *s* Telephonanruf *m*

tel'ephone direc'tory *s* Teilnehmerverzeichnis *n*

tel'ephone exchange' *s* Telephonzentrale *f*

tel'ephone num'ber *s* Telephonnummer *f*

tel'ephone op'erator *s* Telephonist –in *mf*

tel'ephone receiv'er *s* Telephonhörer *m*

tel'ephoto lens' ['tɛlɪ͵foto] *s* Teleobjektiv *n*

telescope ['tɛlɪ͵skop] *s* Fernrohr *n*, Perspektiv *n* ‖ *tr* ineinanderschieben; (fig) verkürzen ‖ *intr* sich ineinanderschieben

telescopic [͵tɛlɪ'skɑpɪk] *adj* teleskopisch

telescop'ic sight' *s* Zielfernrohr *n*

Teletype ['tɛlɪ͵tarp] *s* (trademark) Fernschreiber *m* ‖ **teletype** *tr* durch Fernschreiber übermitteln ‖ *intr* fernschreiben

tel'etype'writ'er *s* Fernschreiber *m*

televiewer ['tɛlɪ͵vju·ər] *s* Fernsehteilnehmer –in *mf*

televise ['tɛlɪ͵varz] *tr* im Fernsehen übertragen (or senden)

television ['tɛlɪ͵vɪʒən] *adj* Fernseh– ‖ *s* Fernsehen *n*; **watch t.** fernsehen

tel'evision net'work *s* Fernsehnetz *n*

tel'evision screen' *s* Bildschirm *m*

tel'evision set' *s* Fernsehapparat *m*; **color t.** Farbfernsehapparat *m*

tel'evision show' *s* Fernschau *f*

telex ['tɛlɛks] *s* Fernschreiber *m*; (*message*) Telex *n* ‖ *tr* fernschreiben

tell [tɛl] *v* (*pret & pp* **told** [told]) *tr* (*the truth, a lie*) sagen; (*relate*) erzählen; (*a secret*) anvertrauen; (*let know*) Bescheid sagen (*dat*); (*inform*) bestellen; (*express*) ausdrücken; (*the reason*) angeben; (*distinguish*) auseinanderhalten; **be able to t. time** die Uhr lesen können; **t. apart** auseinanderhalten; **t. me another!** (sl) das machst du mir nicht weis!; **t. s.o. off** j–n abkanzeln; **t. s.o. that** (*assure s.o. that*) j–m versichern, daß; **t. s.o. to** (*inf*) j–m sagen, daß er (*inf*) soll; **t. s.o. where to get off** (sl) j–m e–e Zigarre verpassen; **to t. the truth** ehrlich gesagt; **you can t. by looking at her that** man sieht es ihr an, daß ‖ *intr*—**don't t. me!** na, so was!; **t. on** (*betray*) verraten; (*produce a marked effect on*) sehr mitnehmen; **you're telling me!** wem sagst du das!

teller ['tɛlər] *s* (*of a bank*) Kassierer –in *mf*; (*of votes*) Zähler –in *mf*

tell'ing *adj* (*blow*) wirksam

tell'-tale' *adj* verräterisch

temper ['tɛmpər] *s* (*anger*) Zorn *m*; (*of steel*) Härtegrad *m*; **bad t.** großer Zorn *m*; **even t.** Gleichmut *m*; **lose one's t.** in Wut geraten ‖ *tr* (**with**) mildern (durch); (*steel*) härten; (mus) temperieren

temperament ['tɛmpərəmənt] *s* Temperament *n*

temperamental [͵tɛmpərə'mɛntəl] *adj* launisch, temperamentvoll

temperance ['tɛmpərəns] *s* Mäßigkeit *f*

temperate ['tɛmpərɪt] *adj* mäßig; (*climate*) gemäßigt

Tem'perate Zone' *s* gemäßigte Zone *f*

temperature ['tɛmpərət/ər] *s* Temperatur *f*

tempest ['tɛmpɪst] *s* Sturm *m*; **a t. in a teapot** ein Sturm im Wasserglas

tempestuous [tɛm'pɛst/ʊ·əs] *adj* stürmisch

temple ['tɛmpəl] *s* Tempel *m*; (*of glasses*) Bügel *m*; (anat) Schläfe *f*

tem·po ['tɛmpo] *s* (**–pos & –pi** [pi]) Tempo *n*

temporal ['tɛmpərəl] *adj* zeitlich

temporary ['tɛmpə͵rɛri] *adj* zeitweilig; (*credit, solution*) Zwischen–

temporize ['tɛmpə͵rarz] *intr* Zeit zu gewinnen suchen

tempt [tɛmpt] *tr* versuchen; (*said of things*) reizen, locken

temptation [temp'teʃən] s Versuchung f

tempter ['tɛmptər] s Versucher m

tempt'ing adj verlockend

temptress ['tɛmptrıs] s Versucherin f

ten [ten] adj & pron zehn ‖ s Zehn f

tenable ['tɛnəbəl] adj haltbar

tenacious [tɪ'neʃəs] adj (obstinate) nartnäckig; (memory) verläßlich

tenacity [tɪ'næsɪti] s Hartnäckigkeit f

tenant ['tɛnənt] s Mieter –in mf

ten'ant farm'er s Pächter –in mf

tend [tɛnd] tr (flocks) hüten; (the sick) pflegen; (a machine) bedienen ‖ intr—t. to (attend to) sich kümmern um; (inf) dazu neigen zu (inf); t. toward(s) neigen zu

tendency ['tɛndənsi] s Tendenz f

tender ['tɛndər] adj zart ‖ s Angebot n; (nav, rr) Tender m ‖ tr anbieten

ten'derfoot' s Neuankömmling m; (boyscout) neu aufgenommener Pfadfinder m

ten'derheart'ed adj zartfühlend

ten'derloin' s Rindslendenstück n

tenderness ['tɛndərnıs] s Zartheit f

tendon ['tɛndən] s Sehne f

tendril ['tɛndrıl] s Ranke f

tenement ['tɛnɪmənt] s (dwelling) Wohnung f; (rented dwelling) Mietwohnung f

ten'ement house' s Mietskaserne f

tenet ['tɛnɪt] s Grundsatz m, Lehrsatz m

ten'fold' adj & adv zehnfach

tennis ['tɛnıs] s Tennis n

ten'nis court' s Tennisplatz m

ten'nis rack'et s Tennisschläger m

tenor ['tɛnər] s (drift, meaning; singer; voice range) Tenor m

ten'pin' s Kegel m

tense [tɛns] adj gespannt, straff; make t. spannen ‖ s (gram) Tempus n, Zeitform f

tension ['tɛnʃən] s (& elec) Spannung f; (phys) Spannkraft f

tent [tɛnt] s Zelt n

tentacle ['tɛntəkəl] s Fühler m; (bot) Tentakel m

tentative ['tɛntətıv] adj vorläufig

tenth [tɛnθ] adj & pron zehnte ‖ s (fraction) Zehntel n; the t. (in dates and in series) der Zehnte

tent' pole' s Zeltstange f

tenuous ['tɛnju·əs] adj (thin) dünn; (rarefied) verdünnt; (insignificant) unbedeutend; (weak) schwach

tenure ['tɛnjər] s (possession) Besitz m; (educ) Anstellung f auf Lebenszeit; t. of office Amtsdauer f

tepid ['tɛpıd] adj lauwarm

term [tʌrm] s (expression) Ausdruck m; (time period) Frist f; (of office) Amtszeit f; (jur) Sitzungsperiode f; (math) Glied n; (log) Begriff m; be on good terms with in guten Beziehungen stehen mit; come to terms with handelseinig werden mit; in plain terms unverblümt; in terms of im Sinne von; in terms of praise mit lobenden Worten; on easy terms zu günstigen Bedingungen; on equal terms auf gleichem Fuß; on t. (com) auf Zeit; not be on speaking terms with nicht sprechen mit; tell s.o. in no uncertain terms j–m gründlich die Meinung sagen; terms (of a contract, treaty, payment) Bedingungen pl ‖ tr bezeichnen

termagant ['tʌrməgənt] s Xanthippe f

terminal ['tʌrmınəl] adj End–; (disease) unheilbar ‖ s (aer) Flughafenempfangsgebäude n; (pole) (elec) Pol m; (rr) Kopfbahnhof m

terminate ['tʌrmı,net] tr (end) beenden; (limit) begrenzen ‖ intr enden, endigen; (gram) (in) auslauten (auf acc)

termination [,tʌrmı'neʃən] s Beendigung f; (gram) Endung f

terminology [,tʌrmı'nɑlıdʒi] s Terminologie f

term' insur'ance s Versicherung f auf Zeit

terminus ['tʌrmınəs] s (end) Endpunkt m; (boundary) Grenze f; (rr) Endstation f

termite ['tʌrmaıt] s Termite f

term' pa'per s Referat n

terrace ['tɛrəs] s Terrasse f ‖ tr abstufen, terrassieren

terra cotta ['tɛrə'kɑtə] s Terrakotta f

ter'ra-cot'ta adj Terrakotta–

terrain [tɛ'ren] s Gelände n, Terrain n

terrestrial [tə'rɛstrɪ·əl] adj irdisch

terrible ['tɛrıbəl] adj furchtbar

terribly ['tɛrıbli] adv (coll) furchtbar

terrier ['tɛrı·ər] s Terrier m

terrific [tə'rıfık] adj (frightful) fürchterlich; (intense) (coll) gewaltig; (splendid) (coll) prima

terri•fy ['tɛrı,faı] v (pret & pp –fied) tr Entsetzen einjagen (dat)

ter'rifying adj schrecklich

territorial [,tɛrı'torı·əl] adj territorial; t. waters Hoheitsgewässer pl

territory ['tɛrı,tori] s Gebiet n, Territorium n; (of a salesman) Absatzgebiet n; (pol) Hoheitsgebiet n; (sport) Spielhälfte f

terror ['tɛrər] s Schrecken m; in t. vor Schrecken

terrorism ['tɛrə,rızəm] s Terrorismus m

terrorist ['tɛrərıst] s Terrorist –in mf

terrorize ['tɛrə,raız] tr terrorisieren

ter'ror-strick'en adj schreckerfüllt

ter'ry cloth' ['tɛri] s Frottee m & n

terse [tʌrs] adj knapp

tertiary ['tʌrʃı,ɛri] adj Tertiär–

test [tɛst] s Probe f, Prüfung f; (criterion) Prüfstein m; (med) Probe f; put to the t. auf die Probe stellen ‖ tr (for) prüfen (auf acc); (chem) (for) analysieren (auf acc); t. out (coll) ausprobieren

testament ['tɛstəmənt] s Testament n

testator [tɛs'tetər] s Erblasser –in mf

test' ban' s Atomstopp m

test' case' s Probefall m; (jur) Präzedenzfall m

test'flight' s Probeflug m

testicle ['tɛstıkəl] s Hoden m

testi•fy ['tɛstı,faı] v (pret & pp –fied)

intr (against) zeugen (gegen), aussagen (gegen); **t. to** bezeugen

testimonial [ˌtestɪ'monɪ-əl] *adj* (dinner) Ehren– ‖ *s* Anerkennungsschreiben *n*

testimony ['testɪ ˌmonɪ] *s* Zeugnis *n*

test' pa'per *s* Prüfungsarbeit *f*

test' pi'lot *s* Versuchsflieger –in *mf*

test' tube' *s* Reagenzglas *n*

testy ['testi] *adj* reizbar

tetanus ['tetənəs] *s* Starrkrampf *m*

tether ['teðər] *s* Haltestrick *m*; **be at the end of one's t.** nicht mehr weiter wissen ‖ *tr* anbinden

Teuton ['t(j)utən] *s* Teutone *m*, Teutonin *f*

Teutonic [t(j)u'tɑnɪk] *adj* teutonisch

text [tekst] *s* Text *m*

text'book' *s* Lehrbuch *n*

textile ['tekstaɪl] *adj* Textil– ‖ *s* Webstoff *m*; **textiles** Textilien *pl*

textual ['tekst/ʊ-əl] *adj* textlich

texture ['tekst/ər] *s* (structure) Gefüge *n*; (of a fabric) Gewebe *n*; (of a play) Aufbau *m*

Thai [taɪ] *adj* Thai– ‖ *s* (person) Thai –in *mf*; (language) Thai *n*

Thailand ['taɪlænd] *s* Thailand *n*

Thames [temz] *s* Themse *f*

than [ðæn] *conj* als; **t. ever** denn je

thank [θæŋk] *adj* (offering) Dank– ‖ **thanks** *spl* Dank *m*; **give thanks to** danken (dat); **many thanks!** vielen Dank!; **return thanks** danksagen; **thanks a lot!** danke vielmals!; **thanks to her, I** ich verdanke es ihr, daß ich ‖ *tr* danken (dat); **t. God!** Gott sei Dank!; **t. goodness!** gottlob!; **t. you!** danke schön!; **t. you ever so much!** verbindlichsten Dank!; **you have only yourself to t. for** das hast du dir nur selbst zu verdanken

thankful ['θæŋkfəl] *adj* dankbar

thankless ['θæŋklɪs] *adj* undankbar

Thanksgiv'ing Day' *s* Danksagungstag *m*

that [ðæt] *adj* jener, der; **t. one** der da, jener ‖ *adv* (coll) so, derart ‖ *rel pron* der, welcher; (after indefinite pronouns) was ‖ *dem pron* das; **about t.** darüber; **after t.** danach; **and that's t.** und damit punktum!; **at t.** so, dabei; **by t.** dadurch; **for all t.** trotz alledem; **for t.** dafür; **from t.** daraus; **in t.** darin, daran; **on t.** darauf, drauf; **t. is** das heißt; **that's out** das kommt nicht in Frage!; **t. will do!** das reicht! ‖ *conj* daß

thatch [θæt/] *s* Dachstroh *n*

thatched' roof' *s* Strohdach *n*

thaw [θɔ] *s* Tauwetter *n* ‖ *tr & intr* (auf)tauen

the [ðə], [ði] *def art* der, die, das ‖ *adv*—so much the better um so besser; **the ... the** je ... desto, je ... um so

theater ['θi-ətər] *s* Theater *n*

the'atergo'er *s* Theaterbesucher –in *mf*

the'ater of war' *s* Kriegsschauplatz *m*

theatrical [θi'ætrɪkəl] *adj* (& fig) theatralisch

thee [ði] *pers pron* dich; **to t. dir**

theft [θeft] *s* Diebstahl *m*

their [ðer] *poss adj* ihr

theirs [ðerz] *poss pron* ihrer

them [ðem] *pron* sie; **to t.** ihnen

theme [θim] *s* Thema *n*; (essay) Aufsatz *m*; (mus) Thema *n*

theme' song' *s* Kennmelodie *f*

themselves' *intens pron* selbst, selber ‖ *reflex pron* sich

then [ðen] *adv* (next; in that case) dann; (at that time) damals; **by t.** bis dahin; **from t. on** von da an; **t. and there** auf der Stelle; **till t.** bis dahin; **what t.?** was dann?

thence [ðens] *adv* von da, von dort; (from that fact) daraus

thence'forth' *adv* von da an

theologian [ˌθi-ə'lodʒən] *s* Theologe *m*, Theologin *f*

theological [ˌθi-ə'lɑdʒɪkəl] *adj* theologisch

theology [θi'ɑlədʒi] *s* Theologie *f*

theorem ['θi-ərəm] *s* Lehrsatz *m*

theoretical [ˌθi-ə'retɪkəl] *adj* theoretisch

theorist ['θi-ərɪst] *s* Theoretiker –in *mf*

theorize ['θi-ə ˌraɪz] *intr* theoretisieren

theory ['θi-əri] *s* Theorie *f*, Lehre *f*

the'ory of relativ'ity *s* Relativitätstheorie *f*

therapeutic [ˌθerə'pjutɪk] *adj* therapeutisch ‖ **therapeutics** *s* Therapeutik *f*

therapy ['θerəpi] *s* Therapie *f*

there [ðer] *adv* (position) da; (direction) dahin; **down t.** da unten; **not be all t.** (coll) nicht ganz richtig sein; **over t.** da drüben; **t. are es gibt, es sind; t. is es gibt, es ist; t., t.!** sachte, sachte!; **up t.** da (or dort) oben

there'abouts' *adv* daherum; **ten people or t.** so ungefähr zehn Leute

there'af'ter *adv* danach

there'by' *adv* dadurch, damit

therefore ['ðer ˌfor] *adv* deshalb, darum

there'in' *adv* darin

there'of' *adv* davon

there'to' *adv* dazu

there'upon' *adv* daraufhin, danach

there'with' *adv* damit

thermal ['θʌrməl] *adj* Thermal–, Wärme–

thermodynamic [ˌθʌrmodaɪ'næmɪk] *adj* thermodynamisch ‖ **thermodynamics** *s* Thermodynamik *f*, Wärmelehre *f*

thermometer [θər'mɑmɪtər] *s* Thermometer *n*

thermonuclear [ˌθermo'n(j)uklɪ-ər] *adj* thermonuklear

ther'mos bot'tle ['θʌrməs] *s* Thermosflasche *f*

thermostat ['θʌrmə ˌstæt] *s* Thermostat *m*

thesau·rus [θɪ'sɔrəs] *s* (–ri [raɪ]) Thesaurus *m*

these [ðiz] *dem adj & pron* diese

the·sis ['θisɪs] *s* (–ses [siz]) These *f*

they [ðe] *pers pron* sie; **t. say** man sagt

thick [θɪk] *adj* dick; (dense) dicht;

(stupid) stumpfsinnig; *(lips)* wulstig; *(intimate)* (coll) dick; **t. with dust** dick bedeckt mit Staub ‖ *adv*—**be in t. with** (coll dicke Beziehungen haben mit; **come t. and fast** Schlag auf Schlag gehen; **lay it on t.** (coll) dick auftragen ‖ *s*—**in the t.** of mitten in *(dat)*; **through t. and thin** durch dick und dünn

thicken ['θɪkən] *tr* verdicken; *(make denser)* verdichten; *(a sauce)* eindicken ‖ *intr* sich verdicken; *(become denser)* sich verdichten; *(said of liquids)* sich verfestigen; *(said of a sauce)* eindicken; **the plot thickens** der Knoten schürzt sich

thicket ['θɪkɪt] *s* Dickicht *n*

thick'head' *s* (coll) Dickkopf *m*

thick'-head'ed *adj* (coll) dickköpfig

thickness ['θɪknɪs] *s* Dicke *f*

thick'-set' *adj* stämmig

thick'skinned' *adj* (coll) dickfellig

thief [θif] *s* (**thieves** [θivz]) Dieb –in *mf*

thieve [θiv] *intr* stehlen

thievery ['θivəri] *s* Dieberei *f*

thievish ['θivɪʃ] *adj* diebisch

thigh [θaɪ] *s* Schenkel *m*, Oberschenkel *m*

thighbone' *s* Oberschenkelknochen *m*

thimble ['θɪmbəl] *s* Fingerhut *m*

thin [θɪn] *adj* (**thinner; thinnest**) dünn; *(hair)* schütter; *(lean)* mager; *(excuse)* schwach; *(soup)* wäßrig ‖ *v* *(pret & pp* thinned; *ger* thinning) *tr* *(a liquid)* verdünnen; *(a forest)* lichten; **t. out** *(plants)* vereinzeln ‖ *intr (said of hair)* sich lichten; **t. out** *(said of a crowd)* sich verlaufen

thing [θɪŋ] *s* Ding *n*, Sache *f*; **among other things** unter anderem; **first t.** zu allererst; **how are things?** wie geht's?; **I'll do no such t.!** ich werde mich schön hüten; **of all things!** na sowas!; **the real t.** das Richtige; **things** *(the situation)* die Lage *f*; *(belongings)* Sachen *pl*

think [θɪŋk] *v* *(pret & pp* thought [θɔt]) *tr* denken; *(regard)* halten; *(believe)* glauben, denken; **he thinks he's clever** er hält sich für klug; **that's what you t.!** ja, denkste!; **t. better of it** sich e–s Besseren besinnen; **t. it best to** *(inf)* es für das Beste halten zu *(inf)*; **t. little of** nicht viel halten von; **t. nothing of it!** es ist nicht der Rede wert!; **t. over** sich *[dat]* überlegen; **t. up** sich *[dat]* ausdenken; **what do you t. you're doing?** was soll das? ‖ *intr* denken; **be thinking of** *(ger)* beabsichtigen zu *(inf)*; **do you t. so?** meinen Sie?; **t. about** *(call to consciousness)* denken an *(acc)*; *(reflect on)* nachdenken über *(acc)*; *(be concerned about)* bedacht sein auf *(acc)*; **t. twice before** es sich *[dat]* zweimal überlegen, bevor

thinker ['θɪŋkər] *s* Denker –in *mf*

thin'-lipped' *adj* dünnlippig

thinner ['θɪnər] *s* Verdünnungsmittel *n*

third [θɪrd] *adj & pron* dritte ‖ *s* *(fraction)* Drittel *n*; *(mus)* Terz *f*; **the third** *(in dates and in series)* der Dritte

third'-class' *adj & adv* dritter Klasse

third' degree' *s*—**give s.o. the t.** j–n e–m Folterverhör unterwerfen

third' par'ty *s* Dritter *m*, dritte Seite *f*

third'-rate' *adj* drittrangig

thirst [θʌrst] *s* (for) Durst *m* (nach); **t. for knowledge** Wissensdurst *m*; **t. for power** Herrschsucht *f* ‖ *intr* (for) dürsten (nach)

thirsty ['θʌrsti] *adj* durstig; **be t.** Durst haben

thirteen ['θʌr'tin] *adj & pron* dreizehn ‖ *s* Dreizehn *f*

thirteenth ['θʌr'tinθ] *adj & pron* dreizehnte ‖ *s* *(fraction)* Dreizehntel *n*; **the t.** *(in dates and in series)* der Dreizehnte

thirtieth ['θʌrtɪ-ɪθ] *adj & pron* dreißigste ‖ *s* *(fraction)* Dreißigstel *n*; **the t.** *(in dates and in series)* der Dreißigste

thirty ['θʌrti] *adj & pron* dreißig ‖ *s* Dreißig *f*; **the thirties** die dreißiger Jahre

thir'ty-one' *adj & pron* einunddreißig

this [ðɪs] *dem adj* dieser; **t. afternoon** heute nachmittag; **t. evening** heute abend; **t. minute** augenblicklich; **t. one** dieser ‖ *adv* (coll) so ‖ *dem pron* dieser, der; **about t.** hierüber; *(concerning this)* davon; **t. and that** dies und jenes

thistle ['θɪsəl] *s* Distel *f*

thither ['θɪðər] *adv* dorthin, hinzu

thong [θɔŋ] *s* Riemen *m*; *(sandal)* Sandale *f*

tho·rax ['θoræks] *s* (**-raxes & –races** [rə,siz]) Brustkorb *m*

thorn [θɔrn] *s* Dorn *m*; **t. in the side** Dorn *m* im Fleisch

thorny ['θɔrni] *adj* dornig; *(fig)* heikel

thorough ['θʌro] *adj* gründlich; (coll) tüchtig

thor'oughbred' *adj* reinrassig ‖ *s* Vollblut *n*; *(horse)* Vollblutpferd *n*, Rassepferd *n*

thor'oughfare' *s* Durchgang *m*; **no t.** (public sign) Durchgang verboten

thor'oughgo'ing *adj* gründlich

thoroughly ['θʌroli] *adv* gründlich

those [ðoz] *dem adj & pron* jene, die da

thou [ðau] *pers pron* du

though [ðo] *adv* immerhin ‖ *conj* obwohl

thought [θɔt] *s* Gedanke(n) *m*; **be lost in t.** in Gedanken versunken sein; **give some t. to** sich *[dat]* Gedanken machen über *(acc)*; **have second thoughts** sich *[dat]* eines Besseren besinnen; **on second t.** nach reiflicher Überlegung; **the mere t.** schon der Gedanke

thoughtful ['θɔtfəl] *adj* *(reflective)* nachdenklich; *(e.g., essay)* gedankenvoll; *(considerate)* aufmerksam; *(gift)* sinnig; **t. of** bedacht auf *(acc)*

thoughtless ['θɔtlɪs] *adj* gedankenlos

thought'-provok'ing *adj* anregend

thousand ['θauzənd] *adj & pron* tausend; **a t. times** tausendmal ‖ *s* Tausend *f*; **by the t.** zu Tausenden

thousandth ['θauzəndθ] *adj & pron* tausendste ‖ *s (fraction)* Tausendstel *n*

thrash [θræʃ] *tr (& fig)* dreschen; **t. out** *(debate)* gründlich erörten ‖ *intr* dreschen; **t. about** sich hin- und herwerfen

thrash'ing *s* Dreschen *n; (beating)* Dresche *f*

thread [θred] *s* Faden *m; (of a screw)* Gewinde *n; (of a story)* Faden *m;* **hang by a t.** an e-m Faden hängen ‖ *tr (a needle)* einfädeln; *(pearls)* aufreihen; *(mach)* Gewinde schneiden in *(acc)*

thread'bare' *adj* fadenscheinig

threat [θret] *s* Drohung *f*

threaten ['θretən] *tr* drohen *(dat)*, bedrohen; **t. so. with s.th.** j-m etw androhen ‖ *intr* drohen

three [θri] *adj & pron* drei ‖ *s* Drei *f;* **in threes** zu dritt

three' cheers' *spl* ein dreimaliges Hoch *n*

three'-dimen'sional *adj* dreidimensional

three'-en'gine *adj* dreimotorig

three'-piece' *adj (suit)* dreiteilig

three'-ply' *adj* dreischichtig

three'-point land'ing *s* Dreipunktlandung *f*

threnody ['θrenədi] *s* Klagelied *n*

thresh [θreʃ] *tr* dreschen; **t. out** *(debate)* gründlich erörten ‖ *intr* dreschen

thresh'ing floor' *s* Dreschtenne *f*

thresh'ing machine' *s* Dreschmaschine *f*

threshold ['θreʃold] *s* Türschwelle *f;* (psychol) Schwelle *f*

thrice [θraɪs] *adv* dreimal

thrift [θrɪft] *s* Sparsamkeit *f*

thrifty ['θrɪfti] *adj* sparsam

thrill [θrɪl] *s* Nervenkitzel *m* ‖ *tr* erregen, packen

thriller ['θrɪlər] *s* Thriller *m*

thrill'ing *adj* packend, spannend

thrive [θraɪv] *v (pret* thrived & throve [θrov]; *pp* thrived & thriven ['θrɪvən]) *intr* gedeihen

throat [θrot] *s* Kehle *f; (fig)* clear one's t. sich räuspern; **cut one another's t.** (fig) sich gegenseitig kaputt machen; **cut one's own t.** (fig) sich [*dat*] sein eigenes Grab schaufeln; **jump down s.o.'s t.** j-m an die Gurgel fahren; **sore t.** Halsweh *n*

throb [θrab] *s* Schlagen *n; (of a motor)* Dröhnen *n* ‖ *v (pret & pp* throbbed; *ger* throbbing) *intr* schlagen; *(said of a motor or head)* dröhnen

throes [θroz] *spl* Schmerzen *pl;* **be in the t. of death** im Todeskampf liegen

thrombosis [θrʌm'bosɪs] *s* Thrombose *f*

throne [θron] *s* Thron *m*

throng [θrɔŋ] *s* Menschenmenge *f* ‖ *tr* umdrängen; *(the streets)* sich drängen in *(acc)* ‖ *intr* (around) sich drängen (um)

throttle ['θrɑtəl] *s* Drossel(klappe) *f*

‖ *tr* drosseln; *(a person)* erwürgen ‖ *intr—***t. back** *(aut)* das Gas zurücknehmen

through [θru] *adj (traffic, train)* Durchgangs-; *(street)* durchgehend; *(finished)* fertig; *(coll)* quitt ‖ *adv—***t. and t.** durch und durch ‖ *prep* durch *(acc)*

throughout' *adv* durch und durch ‖ *prep* hindurch *(acc)* (postpositive), e.g., **t. the summer** den ganzen Sommer hindurch; **t. the world** in der ganzen Welt

throw [θro] *s* Wurf *m; (scarf)* Überwurf *m* ‖ *v (pret* threw [θru]; *pp* thrown [θron]) *tr* werfen; *(a rider)* abwerfen; *(sparks)* sprühen; *(a party, banquet)* geben; *(a game)* absichtlich verlieren; *(into confusion)* bringen; **t. away** wegwerfen; **t. down** niederwerfen; *(overturn)* umwerfen; **t. in** *(e.g., a few extras)* als Zugabe geben; **t. off** *(fig)* aus dem Gleichgewicht bringen; **t. out** hinauswerfen; *(a person)* vor die Tür setzen; *(the chest)* herausdrücken; **t. out of the game** vom Platz verweisen; **t. the book at s.o.** (fig) j-n zur Höchststrafe verurteilen; **t. up to s.o.** j-m vorwerfen ‖ *intr* werfen; **t. up** sich erbrechen

throw'away' *adj* Einweg-

throw'back' *s* (to) Rückkehr *f* (zu)

throw' rug' *s* Vorleger *m*

thrum [θrʌm] *v (pret & pp* thrummed; *ger* thrumming) *intr* (on) mit den Fingern trommeln (auf *acc*)

thrush [θrʌʃ] *s* (orn) Drossel *f*

thrust [θrʌst] *s (shove)* Stoß *m; (stab)* Hieb *m;* (aer, archit, geol, rok) Schub *m;* (mil) Vorstoß *m* ‖ *v (pret & pp* thrust) *tr* stoßen

thud [θʌd] *s* Bums *m* ‖ *v (pret & pp* thudded; *ger* thudding) *tr & intr* bumsen ‖ *interj* bums!

thug [θʌg] *s* Rocker *m*

thumb [θʌm] *s* Daumen *m;* **be all thumbs** zwei linke Hände haben; **be under s.o.'s t.** unter j-s Fuchtel stehen; **thumbs down!** pfui!; **thumbs up!** Kopf hoch! ‖ *tr (a book)* abgreifen; **t. a ride** per Anhalter fahren; **t. one's nose at s.o.** j-m e-e lange Nase machen ‖ *intr—***t. through** durchblättern

thumb' in'dex *s* Daumenindex *m*

thumb'print' *s* Daumenabdruck *m*

thumb'screw' *s* Flügelschraube *f*

thumb'tack' *s* Reißnagel *m*

thump [θʌmp] *s* Bums *m* ‖ *v tr & intr* bumsen ‖ *interj* bums!

thump'ing *adj* (coll) enorm

thunder ['θʌndər] *s* Donner *m* ‖ *tr & intr* donnern

thun'derbolt' *s* Donnerkeil *m*

thun'derclap' *s* Donnerschlag *m*

thunderous ['θʌndərəs] *adj* donnernd

thun'dershow'er *s* Gewitterregen *m*

thun'derstorm' *s* Gewitter *n*

thunderstruck ['θʌndər‚strʌk] *adj* (fig) wie vom Schlag getroffen

Thursday ['θɜrzde] *s* Donnerstag *m;* **on T.** am Donnerstag

thus [ðʌs] *adv* so; *(consequently)* also; **t. far** soweit

thwack [θwæk] *s* heftiger Schlag *m* ‖ *tr* klatschen

thwart [θwɔːt] *adj* Quer– ‖ *s* (naut) Ruderbank *f* ‖ *tr* *(plans)* durchkreuzen; *(a person)* in die Quere kommen *(dat)*

thy [ðaɪ] *poss adj* dein

thyme [taɪm] *s* Thymian *m*

thy′roid gland′ [′θaɪrɔɪd] *s* Schilddrüse *f*

thyself [ðaɪ′self] *intens pron* selbst, selber ‖ *reflex pron* dich

tiara [taɪ′erə] *s* Tiara *f*; *(lady's headdress)* Diadem *n*

tibia [′tɪbɪ·ə] *s* Schienbein *n*

tic [tɪk] *s* (pathol) Tick *m*

tick [tɪk] *s* *(of a clock)* Ticken *f*; *(mattress case)* Überzug *m*; (ent) Zecke *f*; **on t.** (coll) auf Pump ‖ *tr*—**be ticked off (at)** (sl) verärgert sein (über *acc*); **t. off** *(names, items)* abhaken; *(the minutes)* ticken ‖ *intr* ticken; **t. by** vergehen

ticker [′tɪkər] *s* *(watch)* (sl) Uhr *f*, Armbanduhr *f*; *(heart)* (sl) Herz *n*; (st. exch.) Börsentelegraph *m*

tick′er tape′ *s* Papierstreifen *m* (des Börsentelegraphen)

tick′er-tape parade′ *s* Konfettiregenparade *f*

ticket [′tɪkɪt] *s* Karte *f*; *(for travel)* Fahrkarte *f*; *(by air)* Flugkarte *f*; *(for admission)* Eintrittskarte *f*; *(in a lottery)* Los *n*; *(for a traffic violation)* Strafzettel *m*; (pol) Wahlliste *f* ‖ *tr* etikettieren; *(aut)* mit e-m Strafzettel versehen

tick′et a′gency *s* Vorverkaufsstelle *f*

tick′et a′gent *s* Fahrkartenverkäufer –in *mf*

tick′et of′fice *s* Kartenverkaufsstelle *f*

tick′et win′dow *s* Schalter *m*

tick′ing *s* Ticken *n*

tickle [′tɪkəl] *s* Kitzel *m* ‖ *tr* kitzeln ‖ *intr* jucken

ticklish [′tɪklɪʃ] *adj* kitzlig; *(touchy)* heikel

ticktock [′tɪk,tɑk] *adv*—**go t.** ticktacken machen ‖ *s* Ticken *n*

tid′al wave′ [′taɪdəl] *s* Flutwelle *f*

tidbit [′tɪd,bɪt] *s* Leckerbissen *m*

tiddlywinks [′tɪdli,wɪŋks] *s* Flohhüpfspiel *n*

tide [taɪd] *s* Gezeiten *pl*; **against the t.** (fig) gegen den Strom; **the t. is coming in** die Flut steigt; **the t. is going out** die Flut fällt ‖ *tr*—**t. s.o. over** j–n über Wasser halten

tide′land′ *s* Watt *n*

tide′wa′ter *s* Flutwasser *n*

tidings [′taɪdɪŋz] *spl* Botschaft *f*

ti·dy [′taɪdi] *adj* ordentlich; *(sum)* hübsch ‖ *v* *(pret & pp* –**died)** *tr* in Ordnung bringen; **t. up** aufräumen ‖ *intr*—**t. up** aufräumen

tie [taɪ] *adj* (sport) unentschieden ‖ *s* *(cord)* Schnur *f*; *(ribbon)* Band *n*; *(necktie)* Krawatte *f*; *(knot)* Schleife *f*; (mus) Krawatte *f*; (parl) Stimmengleichheit *f*; (rr) Schwelle *f*; (sport)

Unentschieden *n*; **end in a tie** punktgleich enden; **ties** *(e.g., of friendship)* Bande *pl* ‖ *v* (*pret & pp* **tied**; *ger* **tying**) *tr* binden; **be tied up** *(said of a person or telephone)* besetzt sein; **get tied up** *(in traffic)* steckenbleiben; **my hands are tied** mir sind die Hände gebunden; **tie in with** verknüpfen mit; **tie oneself down** sich festlegen; **tie to** festbinden an *(dat)*; **tie up** *(a wound)* verbinden; *(traffic)* lahmlegen; *(money)* fest anlegen; *(production)* stillegen; *(the telephone)* blockieren; *(a boat)* festmachen

tie′back′ *s* Gardinenhalter *m*

tie′clasp′ *s* Krawattenhalter *m*

tie′pin′ *s* Krawattennadel *f*

tier [tɪr] *s* Reihe *f*; (theat) Rang *m*

tie′rod′ *s* (aut) Zugstange *f*

tie′-up′ *s* *(of traffic)* Stockung *f*

tiger [′taɪgər] *s* Tiger *m*

ti′ger shark′ *s* Tigerhai *m*

tight [taɪt] *adj* *(firm)* fest; *(clothes)* eng; *(taut)* straff; *(scarce)* knapp; *(container)* dicht; *(drunk)* beschwipst; *(with money)* knaus(e)rig; **feel t. in the chest** sich beengt fühlen ‖ *adv* fest; **hold t.** festhalten; **sit t.** sich nicht rühren; **pull t.** strammziehen ‖ **tights** *spl* Trikot *m & n*

tighten [′taɪtən] *tr* *(a rope)* straff spannen; *(a belt)* enger schnallen; *(a jar lid)* festziehen; *(a screw)* anziehen; *(a spring)* spannen; *(a knot)* zuziehen

tight′-fist′ed *adj* knaus(e)rig

tight′-fit′ting *adj* eng anliegend

tight′-lipped′ *adj* verschlossen

tight′rope′ *s* Drahtseil *n*; **walk a t.** auf e–m festgespannten Drahtseil gehen

tight′ spot′ *s* (coll) Klemme *f*

tight′ squeeze′ *s* (coll) Zwickmühle *f*

tight′wad′ *s* Geizkragen *m*

tigress [′taɪgrɪs] *s* Tigerin *f*

tile [taɪl] *s* *(for the floor or wall)* Fliese *f*; *(for the roof)* Dachziegel *m*; *(glazed tile)* Kachel *f* ‖ *tr* *(a roof)* mit Ziegeln decken; *(a floor)* mit Fliesen auslegen; *(a bathroom)* kacheln

tile′ roof′ *s* Ziegeldach *n*

till [tɪl] *s* Kasse *f* ‖ *tr* ackern ‖ *prep* bis *(acc)*; **t. now** bisher ‖ *conj* bis

tiller [′tɪlər] *s* (naut) Pinne *f*

tilt [tɪlt] *s* Kippen *n*; **full t.** mit voller Wucht ‖ *tr* kippen; *(a bottle, the head)* neigen; **t. back** *(e.g., a chair)* zurücklehnen; **t. over** umkippen ‖ *intr* kippen; **t. over** umkippen

timber [′tɪmbər] *s* Holz *n*; *(for structural use)* Bauholz *n*; *(rafter)* Balken *m*

tim′berland′ *s* Waldland *n*

tim′ber line′ *s* Baumgrenze *f*

timbre [′tɪmbər] *s* Klangfarbe *f*

time [taɪm] *s* Zeit *f*; *(limited period)* Frist *f*; *(instance)* Mal *n*; (mus) Takt *m*; **all the t.** ständig; **all this t.** die ganze Zeit; **any number of times** x-mal; **at no t.** nie; **at one t.** einst; **at some t.** irgendwann; **at that t.**

damals; **at the present t.** derzeit; **at times** manchmal; **at what t.?** um wieviel Uhr?; **by this t.** nunmehr; **do t.** (sl) sitzen; **do you have the t.?** können Sie mir sagen, wie spät es ist?; **for a t.** e–e Zeitlang; **for the last t.** zum letzten Mal; **for the t. being** vorläufig; **give s.o. a hard t.** j–m das Leben schwer machen; **have a good t.** sich gut unterhalten; **have a hard t.** (ger) es schwer haben zu (inf); **in no t.** im Nu; **in t.** zur rechten Zeit; (in the course of time) mit der Zeit; **make good t.** Fortschritte machen; **on one's own t.** in der Freizeit; **on t.** pünktlich; (on schedule) fahrplanmäßig; (com) auf Raten; **several times** mehrmals; **take one's t.** sich [dat] Zeit lassen; **there's t. for that** das hat Zeit; **this t. tomorrow** morgen um diese Zeit; **t.!** (sport) Zeit!; **t. is up!** die Zeit ist um!; **t. of life** Lebensalter n; **times** Zeiten pl; (math) mal, e.g., **two times two** zwei mal zwei; **t. will tell** die Zeit wird es lehren; **what t. is it?** wieviel Uhr ist es? || tr (mit der Uhr) messen; **t. s.th. right** die richtige Zeit wählen für

time′ bomb′ s Zeitbombe f
time′ card′ s Stechkarte f
time′ clock′ s Stechuhr f
time′-consum′ing adj zeitraubend
time′ expo′sure s (phot) Zeitaufnahme f
time′ fuse′ s Zeitzünder m
time′-hon′ored adj altehrwürdig
time′keep′er s Zeitnehmer –in mf
time′-lag′ s Verzögerung f
timeless [′taɪmlɪs] adj zeitlos
time′ lim′it s Frist f; **set a t. on** befristen
timely [′taɪmli] adj zeitgerecht; (topic) aktuell
time′ pay′ment s Ratenzahlung f
time′piece′ s Uhr f
timer [′taɪmər] s (person) Zeitnehmer –in mf; (device) Schaltuhr f; (aut) Zündunterbrecher m; (phot) Zeitauslöser m
time′ sig′nal s Zeitzeichen n
time′ stud′y s Zeitstudien pl
time′ta′ble s Zeittabelle f; (aer) Flugplan m; (rr) Fahrplan
time′work′ s Zeitlohnarbeit f
time′-worn′ adj abgenutzt
time′ zone′ s Zeitzone f
timid [′tɪmɪd] adj ängstlich
tim′ing s genaue zeitliche Berechnung f; (aut) Zündeinstellung f
timorous [′tɪmərəs] adj furchtsam
tin [tɪn] adj Zinn– || s (element) Zinn n; (tin plate) Weißblech n
tin′ can′ s Blechdose f
tincture [′tɪŋktʃər] s Tinktur f
tinder [′tɪndər] s Zunder m
tin′derbox′ s (fig) Pulverfaß n
tin′ foil′ s Zinnfolie f
ting-a-ling [′tɪŋə‚lɪŋ] s Klingeling m
tinge [tɪndʒ] s (of color) Stich m; (fig) Spur f || v (pret **tingeing & tinging**) tr leicht färben

tingle [′tɪŋgəl] s Kribbeln n, Prickeln n || intr kribbeln, prickeln
tinker [′tɪŋkər] s (bungler) Pfuscher m || intr basteln
tinkle [′tɪŋkəl] s Klingeln n || intr klingeln
tin′ mine′ s Zinnbergwerk n
tinsel [′tɪnsəl] s Lametta f; (fig) Flitterkram m
tin′smith′ s Klempner m
tin′ sol′dier s Zinnsoldat m
tint [tɪnt] s Farbton m || tr tönen, leicht färben
tint′ed glass′ s (aut) blendungsfreies Glas n
tiny [′taɪni] adj winzig
tip [tɪp] s Spitze f; (gratuity) Trinkgeld n; (hint) Tip m; **it's on the tip of my tongue** es schwebt mir auf der Zunge || v (pret & pp **tipped**; ger **tipping**) tr schief halten; (a waiter) ein Trinkgeld geben (dat); **tip off** e–n Tip geben (dat); **tip one's hat** auf den Hut tippen || intr—**tip over** umtippen
tip′-off′ s Tip m, rechtzeitiger Wink m
tipple [′tɪpəl] s Tip & intr süffeln
tippler [′tɪplər] s Säufer –in mf
tipster [′tɪpstər] s Wettberater m
tipsy [′tɪpsi] adj beschwipst
tip′toe′ s—**on t.** auf den Zehenspitzen || v (pret & pp **–toed**; ger **–toeing**) intr auf den Zehenspitzen gehen
tip′top′ adj tipptopp
tirade [′taɪred] s Tirade f
tire [taɪr] s Reifen m || tr ermüden; **t. out** strapazieren || intr ermüden
tired adj müde; **be t. of** (ger) es satt haben zu (inf); **be t. of coffee** den Kaffee satt haben; **t. out** abgespannt
tire′ gauge′ s Reifendruckmesser m
tireless [′taɪrlɪs] adj unermüdlich
tire′ pres′sure s Reifendruck m
tiresome [′taɪrsəm] adj (tiring) ermüdend; (boring) langweilig
tissue [′tɪʃu] s Gewebe n; (thin paper) Papiertaschentuch n; **t. of lies** Lügengewebe n
tis′sue pa′per s Seidenpapier n
tit [tɪt] s (sl) Brust f; **tit for tat** wie du mir, so ich dir
Titan [′taɪtən] s Titan(e) m
titanic [taɪ′tænɪk] adj titanisch
titanium [taɪ′teni·əm] s Titan n
tithe [taɪð] s Kirchenzehnt m || tr (pay one tenth of) den Zehnten bezahlen von; (exact a tenth from) den Zehnten erheben von
Titian [′tiʃən] s tizianrot
titillate [′tɪtɪ‚let] tr & intr kitzeln, (angenehm) reizen
title [′taɪtəl] s Titel m; (to a property) Eigentumsrecht n; (claim) Rechtstitel m; (of a chapter) Überschrift f; (honor) Würde f; (aut) Kraftfahrzeugbrief m || tr titulieren
ti′tled adj ad(e)lig
ti′tle bout′ s (box) Titelkampf m
ti′tle deed′ s Eigentumsurkunde f
ti′tle hold′er s Titelverteidiger –in mf
ti′tle page′ s Titelblatt n
ti′tle role′ s Titelrolle f

titter ['tɪtər] s Gekicher n || intr kichern

titular ['tɪtələr] adj Titular-

to [tu], [tʊ] adv—to and fro hin und her || prep zu (dat); (a city, country, island) nach (dat); (as far as) bis (acc); (in order to) um ... zu (inf); (against, e.g., a wall) an (dat or acc); **a quarter to eight** viertel vor acht; **how far is it to the town?** wie weit ist es bis zur Stadt?; **to a T** haargenau

toad [tod] s Kröte f

toad'stool' s Giftpilz m

toad·y ['todi] s Schranze m & f || v (pret & pp –ied) intr (to) scharwenzeln (um)

to-and-fro ['tu·ənd'fro] adj Hin– und Her– || adv hin und her

toast [tost] s (bread; salutation) Toast m; **drink a t. to** e–n Toast ausbringen auf (acc) || tr (bread) rösten

toaster ['tostər] s Toaster m

toast'mas'ter s Toastmeister m

tobac·co [tə'bæko] s (–cos) Tabak m

tobac'co pouch' s Tabaksbeutel m

toboggan [tə'bɑgən] s Rodel m & f || intr rodeln

tocsin ['tɑksɪn] s Alarmglocke f

today [tu'de] adv heute || s—from t. on von heute an; **today's** heutig

toddle ['tɑdəl] s Watscheln n || intr watscheln

toddler ['tɑdlər] s Kleinkind n

toddy ['tɑdi] s Toddy m

to-do [tə'du] s Getue n

toe [to] s Zehe f; **be on one's toes** auf Draht sein; **step on s.o.'s toes** j–m auf die Zehen treten || v (pret & pp toed; ger toeing) tr—**toe the line** nicht aus der Reihe tanzen

toe' dance' s Spitzentanz m

toe'-in' s (aut) Spur f

toe'nail' s Zehennagel m

together [tu'gɛðər] adv zusammen; **t. with** mitsamt (dat), samt (dat)

togetherness [tu'gɛðərnɪs] s Zusammengehörigkeit f

tog'gle switch' ['tɑgəl] s (elec) Kippschalter m

togs [tɑgz] spl Klamotten pl

toil [tɔɪl] s Mühe f; **toils** Schlingen pl || intr sich mühen

toilet ['tɔɪlɪt] s (room) Toilette f; (bathroom fixture) Klosett n

toi'let ar'ticle s Toilettenartikel m

toi'let bowl' s Klosettschüssel f

toi'let pa'per s Klosettpapier n

toi'let seat' s Toilettensitz m

token ['tokən] adj (payment) symbolisch; (strike) Warn– || Zeichen n; (proof) Beweis m; **by the same t.** aus dem gleichen Grund; **as** (or **in**) **t. of** zum Beweis (genit)

tolerable ['tɑlərəbəl] adj erträglich

tolerably ['tɑlərəbli] adv leidlich

tolerance ['tɑlərəns] s Duldsamkeit f; (mach) Toleranz f

tolerant ['tɑlərənt] adj (of) duldsam (gegen), tolerant (gegen)

tolerate ['tɑlə‚ret] tr dulden

toleration [‚tɑlə'reʃən] s Duldung f

toll [tol] adj (road) gebührenpflichtig || s Wegezoll m; (at a bridge) Brückenzoll m; (of bells) Läuten n; (number of victims) Zahl f der Opfer; (fig) Tribut m; (telp) Gebühr f für ein Ferngespräch; **take a heavy t. of life** viele Menschenleben kosten || tr & intr läuten

toll' booth' s Zahlkasse f

toll' bridge' s Zollbrücke f

toll' call' s Ferngespräch n

toll' collec'tor s Zolleinnehmer –in mf

toma·to [tə'meto] s (–toes) Tomate f

toma'to juice' s Tomatensaft f

tomb [tum] s Grab n, Grabmal n

tomboy ['tɑm‚bɔɪ] s Wildfang m

tomb'stone' s Grabstein m

tomcat ['tɑm‚kæt] s Kater m

tome [tom] s Band m

tomfoolery [tɑm'fuləri] s Albernheit f

Tom'my gun' ['tɑmi] s Maschinenpistole f

tom'myrot' s Blödsinn m

tomorrow [tu'mɔro] adv morgen; **t. evening** morgen abend; **t. morning** morgen früh; **t. night** morgen abend; **t. noon** morgen mittag || s morgen; **tomorrow's** morgig

tom-tom ['tɑm‚tɑm] s Hindutrommel f

ton [tʌn] s Tonne f

tone [ton] s Ton m; (of color) Farbton m; (phot) Tönung f || tr tönen; (phot) tönen; **t. down** dämpfen || intr milder werden

tone'-control knob' s (rad) Klangregler m

tongs [tɔŋz] spl Zange f

tongue [tʌŋ] s Zunge f; (language) Sprache f; (of a shoe) Zunge f; (of a buckle) Dorn m; (of a bell) Klöppel m; (of a wagon) Deichsel f; (carp) Feder f; **hold one's t.** den Mund halten

tongue'-tied' adj zungenlahm; (fig) sprachlos

tongue' twist'er s Zungenbrecher m

tonic ['tɑnɪk] adj tonisch || s (med) Tonikum n; (mus) Tonika f

tonight [tu'naɪt] adv heute nacht; (this evening) heute abend

tonnage ['tʌnɪdʒ] s Tonnage f

tonsil ['tɑnsɪl] s Mandel f

tonsilitis [‚tɑnsɪ'laɪtɪs] s Mandelentzündung f

tonsure ['tɑnʃər] s Tonsur f

too [tu] adv (also) auch; (excessively) zu; **too bad!** Schade!

tool [tul] s (& fig) Werkzeug n || tr (with tools) bearbeiten

tool'box' s Werkzeugkasten m

tool'mak'er s Werkzeugmacher m

tool' shed' s Geräteschuppen m

toot [tut] s (aut) Hupen n || tr (a trumpet) blasen; **t. the horn** (aut) hupen || intr (aut) hupen

tooth [tuθ] s (teeth [tiθ]) Zahn m; (of a rake) Zinke f; **t. and nail** mit aller Gewalt

tooth'ache' s Zahnschmerz m, Zahnweh n

toothbrush 335 **toughen**

tooth'brush' s Zahnbürste f
tooth' decay' s Zahnfäule f
toothless ['tuθlɪs] adj zahnlos
tooth'paste' s Zahnpaste f
tooth'pick' s Zahnstocher m
tooth' pow'der s Zahnpulver n
top [tap] adj oberste; (speed, price, form) Höchst–; (team) Spitzen–; (first-class) erstklassig ‖ s Spitze f; (of a mountain) Gipfel m; (of a tree) Wipfel m; (of a car) Verdeck n; (of a box) Deckel m; (of a garment) Oberteil m & n; (of a bottle) Verschluß m; (of an object) obere Seite f; (of the water) Oberfläche f; (of a turnip) Kraut n; (toy) Kreisel m; **at the top of one's voice** aus voller Kehle; **at the top of the page** oben auf der Seite; **be tops with s.o.** (coll) bei j–m ganz groß angeschrieben sein; **from top to bottom** von oben bis unten; **on top** (& fig) obenauf; **on top of** (position) auf (dat); (direction) auf (acc); **on top of that** obendrein ‖ v (pret & pp **topped**; ger **topping**) tr (a tree) kappen; (surpass) übertreffen; **that tops everything** das übersteigt alles; **top off** (a meal, an evening) abschließen; **to top it off** zu guter Letzt
topaz ['topæz] s Topas m
top' brass' s (mil) hohe Tiere pl
top'coat' s Überzieher m
top' dog' s (coll) Erste m
top' ech'elon s Führungsspitze f
top' hat' s Zylinder m
top'-heav'y adj oberlastig
topic ['tapɪk] s Gegenstand m, Thema n
topical ['tapɪkəl] adj aktuell
top' kick' s (mil) Spieß m
topless ['taplɪs] adj Oben-ohne-
topmast ['tap ‚mest] s Toppmast m
top'most' adj oberste
top'notch' adj erstklassig
top' of the head' s Scheitel m
topography [tə'pagrəfɪ] s Topographie f
topple ['tapəl] tr & intr stürzen
topsail ['tapsəl] s Toppsegel n
top'-se'cret adj streng geheim
top' ser'geant s Hauptfeldwebel m
top'side' adv auf Deck ‖ s Oberseite f
top'soil' s Mutterboden m
topsy-turvy ['tapsɪ'tʌrvɪ] adj drunter und drüber ‖ adv—**turn t.** durcheinanderbringen
torch [tɔrtʃ] s Fackel f; (Brit) Taschenlampe f; **carry the t. for** (coll) verknallt sein in (acc)
torch'bear'er s (& fig) Fackelträger m
torch'light' s Fackelschein m
torch'light parade' s Fackelzug m
torment ['tɔrment] s Qual f ‖ [tɔr'ment] tr quälen
tormentor [tɔr'mentər] s Quäler –in mf
torn [tɔrn] adj zerrissen, rissig
torna-do [tɔr'nedo] s (–does & –dos) Tornado m, Windhose f
torpe-do [tɔr'pido] s (–does) Torpedo m ‖ tr torpedieren

torpe'do boat' s Torpedoboot n
torpe'do tube' s Ausstoßrohr n
torpid ['tɔrpɪd] adj träge
torque [tɔrk] s Drehmoment n
torrent ['tɔrənt] s Sturzbach m; (of words) Schwall m; **in torrents** stromweise
torrential [tə'rentʃəl] adj—**t. rain** Wolkenbruch m
torrid ['tɔrɪd] adj brennend
Tor'rid Zone' s heiße Zone f
tor-so ['tɔrso] s (–sos) (of a statue) Torso m; (of a human body) Rumpf m
tortoise ['tɔrtəs] s Schildkröte f
tor'toise shell' s Schildpatt n
torture ['tɔrtʃər] s Folter f, Qual f ‖ tr foltern, quälen
toss [tɔs] s Wurf m; (of the head) Zurückwerfen n; (of a ship) Schlingern n; (of a coin) Loswurf m ‖ tr (throw) werfen; (the head) zurückwerfen; (a ship) hin- und herwerfen; (a coin) hochwerfen; **t. off** (work) hinhauen; **t. s.o. for** mit j–m losen um ‖ intr (naut) schlingern; **t. for** e–e Münze hochwerfen um; **t. in bed** sich im Bett hin –und herwerfen
toss'up' s Loswurf m; **it's a t. whether** es hängt ganz vom Zufall ab, ob
tot [tat] s Knirps m
to-tal ['totəl] adj Gesamt–, total ‖ s Gesamtsumme f ‖ v (pret & pp –tal[l]ed; ger –tal[l]ing) tr (add up) zusammenrechnen; (amount to) sich belaufen auf (acc); (sl) (Wagen) ganz kaputt machen
totalitarian [to ‚tælɪ'terɪ-ən] adj totalitär
tote [tot] tr schleppen
totem ['totəm] s Totem n
totter ['tatər] intr schwanken
touch [tʌtʃ] s Berührung f; (sense of touch) Tastsinn m; (e.g., of a fever) Anflug m; (trace, small bit) Spur f; (of a pianist) Anschlag m; **get in t.** with in Verbindung treten mit; **keep in t. with** in Verbindung bleiben mit; **put in t. with** in Verbindung setzen mit; **with sure t.** mit sicherer Hand ‖ tr berühren; (fig) rühren; **he's a little touched** (coll) er hat e–n kleinen Klaps; **t. bottom** anstoßen; **t. glasses** mit den Gläsern anstoßen; **t. off** auslösen; **t. s.o. for** (coll) j–n anpumpen um; **t. up** (with cosmetics) auffrischen; (paint, phot) retuschieren ‖ intr sich berühren; **t. down** (aer) aufsetzen; **t. on** (a topic) berühren; (e.g., arrogance) grenzen an (acc)
touch' and go' s—**be t.** auf der Kippe stehen
touch'ing adj rührend, herzergreifend
touch'stone' s (fig) Prüfstein m
touch'-type' intr blindschreiben
touchy ['tʌtʃɪ] adj (spot, person) empfindlich; (situation) heikel
tough [tʌf] adj (strong) derb; (meat) zäh; (life) mühselig; (difficult) schwierig ‖ s Gassenjunge m
toughen ['tʌfən] tr zäher machen; **t.**

up *(through training)* ertüchtigen ‖ *intr* (up) zäher werden

tough′ luck′ *s* Pech *n*

tour [tur] *s (of a country)* Tour *f; (of a city)* Rundfahrt *f; (of a museum)* Führung *f; (mus, theat)* Tournee *f;* **go on t.** auf Tournee gehen ‖ *tr* besichtigen; *(a country)* bereisen ‖ *intr* auf der Reise sein; *(theat)* auf Tournee sein

tour′ guide′ *s* Reiseführer –in *mf*

tourism [′turizəm] *s* Touristik *f*

tournament [′turnəmənt] *s* Turnier *n*

tourney [′turni] *s* Turnier *n*

tourniquet [′turni‚ket] *s* Aderpresse *f*

tousle [′tauzəl] *tr* (zer)zausen

tow [to] *s*—**have in tow** im Schlepptau haben; **take in tow** ins Schlepptau nehmen ‖ *tr* schleppen; **tow away** abschleppen

toward(s) [tord(z)] *prep (with respect to)* gegenüber *(dat); (a goal, direction)* auf *(acc),* zu; *(shortly before)* gegen *(acc); (for)* für *(acc); (facing)* zugewandt *(dat)*

tow′boat′ *s* Schleppschiff *n*

tow-el [′tau‚əl] *s* Handtuch *n* ‖ *v (pret & pp* –el[l]**ed;** *ger* –el[l]**ing)** *tr* mit e–m Handtuch abtrocknen

tow′el rack′ *s* Handtuchhalter *m*

tower [′tau‚ər] *s* Turm *m;* **t. of strength** starker Hort *m* ‖ *intr* ragen; **t. over** überragen

tow′ering *adj* hochragend; *(rage)* rasend

tow′ing serv′ice *s* Schleppdienst *m*

tow′line′ *s* Schlepptau *n*

town [taun] *adj* städtisch, Stadt– ‖ *s* Stadt *f;* **in t.** in der Stadt; **out of t.** verreist; **go to t. on** Feuer und Flamme sein für

town′ coun′cil *s* Stadtrat *m*

town′ hall′ *s* Rathaus *n*

town′ house′ *s* Stadthaus *n*

town′ship′ *s* Gemeinde *f*

tow′rope′ *s* Schlepptau *n; (for a glider)* Startseil *n*

tow′ truck′ *s* Abschleppwagen *m*

toxic [′taksik] *adj* Gift–, toxisch ‖ *s* Giftstoff *m*

toy [tɔi] *adj* Spielzeug– ‖ *s* Spielzeug *n;* **toys** Spielsachen *pl; (com)* Spielwaren *pl* ‖ *intr* spielen; **toy with** *(fig)* herumspielen mit

toy′ dog′ *s* Schoßhund *m*

toy′ shop′ *s* Spielwarengeschäft *n*

toy′ sol′dier *s* Spielzeugsoldat *m*

trace [tres] *s* Spur *f; (of a harness)* Strang *m;* **without a t.** spurlos ‖ *tr (a drawing)* durchpausen; *(lines)* nachziehen; *(track)* ausfindig machen; **t. (back) to** zurückführen auf *(acc)*

tracer [′tresər] *s* Suchzettel *m*

trac′er bul′let *s* Leuchtspurgeschoß *n*

trac′ing pa′per *s* Pauspapier *n*

track [træk] *s* Spur *f; (of a foot)* Fußspur *f; (of a wheel)* Radspur *f; (chain of a tank)* Raupenkette *f; (parallel rails)* Geleise *n; (single rail)* Gleis *n,* Schiene *f; (station platform)* Bahnsteig *m; (path)* Pfad *m; (course*

for running) Laufbahn *f; (course for motor and horse racing)* Rennbahn *f; (running as a sport)* Laufen *n;* **be off the t.** *(fig)* auf dem Holzweg sein; **go off the t.** *(derail)* entgleisen; **in one's tracks** mitten auf dem Weg; **jump the t.** aus den Schienen springen ‖ *tr* verfolgen; **t. down** *(game, a criminal)* zur Strecke bringen; *(a rumor, reference)* nachgehen *(dat);* **t. up** *(a rug)* schmutzig treten

track′-and-field′ *adj* Leichtathletik–

trackless [′træklis] *adj* pfadlos; *(vehicle)* schienenlos

track′ meet′ *s* Leichtathletikwettkampf *m*

tract [trækt] *s* Strich *m; (treatise)* Traktat *n;* **t. of land** Grundstück *n*

traction [′trækʃən] *s (med)* Ziehen *n; (of the road)* Griffigkeit *f*

tractor [′træktər] *s* Traktor *m; (of a tractor-trailer)* Zugmaschine *f*

trac′tor-trail′er *s* Sattelschlepper *m* mit e–m Anhänger

trade [tred] *s* Handel *m; (calling, job)* Gewerbe *n; (exchange)* Tausch *m;* **by t.** von Beruf ‖ *tr* (aus)tauschen; **t. in** *(e.g., a used car)* in Zahlung geben ‖ *intr* Handel treiben

trade′ agree′ment *s* Handelsabkommen *n*

trade′ bar′riers *spl* Handelsschranken *pl*

trade′-in val′ue *s* Handelswert *m*

trade′mark′ *s* Warenzeichen *n*

trade′ name′ *s (of products)* Handelsbezeichnung *f; (of a firm)* Firmenname *m*

trader [′tredər] *s* Händler –in *mf*

trade′ school′ *s* Gewerbeschule *f*

trade′ se′cret *s* Geschäftsgeheimnis *n*

trades′man *s* (–men) Handelsmann *m*

trade′ un′ion *s* Gewerkschaft *f*

trade′wind′ *s* Passatwind *m*

trad′ing post′ *s* Handelsniederlassung *f*

trad′ing stamp′ *s* Rabattmarke *f*

tradition [trə′diʃən] *s* Tradition *f*

traditional [trə′diʃənəl] *adj* herkömmlich, traditionell

traf-fic [′træfik] *s* Verkehr *m; (trade)* (in) Handel *m* (in *dat*) ‖ *v (pret & pp* –ficked; *ger* –ficking) *intr*—**t. in** handeln in *(dat)*

traf′fic ac′cident *s* Verkehrsunfall *m*

traf′fic cir′cle *s* Kreisverkehr *m*

traf′fic is′land *s* Verkehrsinsel *f*

traf′fic jam′ *s* Verkehrsstockung *f*

traf′fic lane′ *s* Fahrbahn *f*

traf′fic light′ *s* Verkehrsampel *f;* **go through a t.** bei Rot durchfahren

traf′fic sign′ *s* Verkehrszeichen *n*

traf′fic tick′et *s* Strafzettel *m*

traf′fic viola′tion *s* Verkehrsdelikt *n*

tragedian [trə′dʒidi‚ən] *s* Tragiker *m*

tragedy [′trædʒɪdi] *s (& fig)* Tragödie *f*

tragic [′trædʒɪk] *adj* tragisch

trail [trel] *s (path)* Fährte *f;* **be on s.o.'s t.** j–m auf der Spur sein; **t. of smoke** Rauchfahne *f* ‖ *tr (on foot)* nachgehen *(dat); (in a vehicle)* nachfahren *(dat); (in a race)* nachhinken *(dat)* ‖ *intr (said of a robe)* schleifen

trailer ['treɪlər] *s* Anhänger *m*; *(mobile home)* Wohnwagen *m*
trail'er camp' *s* Wohnwagenparkplatz *m*
train [treɪn] *s* *(of railway cars)* Zug *m*; *(of a dress)* Schleppe *f*; *(following)* Gefolge *n*; *(of events)* Folge *f*; **go by t.** mit dem Zug fahren; **t. of thought** Gedankengang *m* ‖ *tr* ausbilden; *(for a particular job)* anlernen; *(the memory)* üben; *(plants)* am Spalier aufziehen; *(an animal)* dressieren; *(a gun)* **(on)** zielen (auf *acc*); *(sport)* trainieren ‖ *intr* üben; *(sport)* trainieren
trained *adj* geschult, ausgebildet
trainee [tre'ni] *s* Anlernling *m*
trainer ['treɪnər] *s* *(of domestic animals)* Dresseur *m*, Dresseuse *f*; *(of wild animals)* Dompteur *m*, Dompteuse *f*; *(aer)* Schulflugzeug *n*; *(sport)* Sportwart –in *mf*
train'ing *s* Ausbildung *f*; *(of animals)* Dressur *f*; *(sport)* Training *n*
train'ing school' *s* *(vocational school)* Berufsschule *f*; *(reformatory)* Erziehungsanstalt *f*
trait [tret] *s* Charakterzug *m*
traitor ['tretər] *s* Verräter –in *mf*; *(of a country)* Hochverräter –in *mf*
trajectory [trə'dʒɛktəri] *s* Flugbahn *f*
tramp [træmp] *s* Landstreicher –in *mf*; *(loose woman)* Frauenzimmer *n* ‖ *tr* trampeln; *(traverse on foot)* durchstreifen ‖ *intr* vagabundieren; **t. on** herumtrampeln auf *(dat)*
trample ['træmpəl] *s* Getrampel *n* ‖ *tr* trampeln; **t. to death** tottreten; **t. under foot** *(fig)* mit Füßen treten ‖ *intr*—**t. on** herumtrampeln auf *(dat)*; *(fig)* mit Füßen treten
trampoline ['træmpə,lin] *s* Trampolin *n*
trance [træns] *s* Trance *f*
tranquil ['træŋkwɪl] *adj* ruhig
tranquilize ['træŋkwɪ,laɪz] *tr* beruhigen
tranquilizer ['træŋkwɪ,laɪzər] *s* Beruhigungsmittel *n*
tranquillity [træn'kwɪlti] *s* Ruhe *f*
transact [træn'zækt] *tr* abwickeln
transaction [træn'zækʃən] *s* Abwicklung *f*; **transactions** *(of a society)* Sitzungsbericht *m*
transatlantic [,trænsət'læntɪk] *adj* transatlantisch
transcend [træn'sɛnd] *tr* übersteigen
transcendental [,trænsən'dɛntal] *adj* übersinnlich; *(philos)* transzendental
transcribe [træn'skraɪb] *tr* *(copy)* umschreiben; *(dictated or recorded material)* übertragen; *(mus)* transkribieren; *(phonet)* in Lautschrift wiedergeben; *(rad)* auf Band aufnehmen
transcript ['trænskrɪpt] *s* Transkript *n*
transcription [træn'skrɪpʃən] *s* Umschrift *f*; *(mus)* Transkription *f*
transept ['trænsept] *s* Querschiff *n*
trans·fer ['trænsfər] *s* *(of property)* Übertragung *f* *(of money)* Überweisung *f*; *(of an employee)* Versetzung *f*; *(of a passenger)* Umsteigen *n*; *(ticket)* Umsteigefahrschein

m ‖ [træns'fʌr], ['trænsfər] *v (pret & pp* **-ferred**; *ger* **-ferring)** *tr (property)* übertragen; *(money)* überweisen; *(to another account)* umbuchen; *(an employee)* versetzen ‖ *intr* **(to)** versetzt werden (nach, zu); *(said of a passenger)* umsteigen
transfix [træns'fɪks] *tr* durchbohren
transform [træns'fɔrm] *tr* *(a person)* verwandeln; **(into)** umwandeln (in *acc*); *(elec)* umspannen
transformer [træns'fɔrmər] *s* *(elec)* Stromwandler *m*, Transformator *m*
transfusion [træns'fjuʒən] *s* *(med)* Übertragung *f*, Transfusion *f*
transgress [træns'grɛs] *tr* überschreiten
transgression [træs'grɛʃən] *s* Vergehen *n*
transient ['trænʃənt] *adj* vorübergehend; *(fleeting)* flüchtig ‖ *s* Durchreisende *mf*
transistor [træn'sɪstər] *adj* Transistor– ‖ *s* Transistor *m*
transistorize [træn'sɪstə,raɪz] *tr* transistorisieren
transit ['trænzɪt] *s* *(astr)* Durchgang *m*; *(com)* Transit *m*; **in t.** unterwegs
transition [træn'zɪʃən] *s* Übergang *m*
transitional [træn'zɪʃənəl] *adj* Übergangs–
transitive ['trænsɪtɪv] *adj* transitiv
transitory ['trænsɪ,tori] *adj* vergänglich
translate [træns'let] *tr* übersetzen; **t. into action** in die Tat umsetzen
translation [træns'leʃən] *s* Übersetzung *f*
translator [træns'letər] *s* Übersetzer –in *mf*
transliterate [træns'lɪtə,ret] *tr* transkribieren
translucent [træns'lusənt] *adj* durchscheinend, lichtdurchlässig
transmigration [,trænsmaɪ'greʃən] *s*— **t. of the soul** Seelenwanderung *f*
transmission [træns'mɪʃən] *s* *(of a text)* Textüberlieferung *f*; *(of news, information)* Übermittlung *f*; *(aut)* Getriebe *n*; *(rad, telv)* Sendung *f*
trans·mit [træns'mɪt] *v (pret & pp* **-mitted**; *ger* **-mitting)** *tr (send forward)* übersenden; *(disease, power, light, heat)* übertragen; *(e.g., customs)* überliefern; *(by inheritance)* vererben; *(rad, telp, telv)* senden
transmitter [træns'mɪtər] *s* *(rad, telg, telv)* Sender *m*
transmutation [,trænsmʊ'teʃən] *s* Umwandlung *f*; *(biol)* Transmutation *f*; *(chem, phys)* Umwandlung *f*
transmute [træns'mjut] *tr* umwandeln
transoceanic [,trænzoʃɪ'ænɪk] *adj* überseeisch, Übersee–
transom ['trænsəm] *s* *(crosspiece)* Querbalken *m*; *(window over a door)* Oberlicht *n* mit Kreuzsprosse; *(of a boat)* Spiegel *m*
transparency [træns'perənsi] *s* Durchsichtigkeit *f*, Transparenz *f*; *(phot)* Diapositiv *n*
transparent [træns'perənt] *adj* durchsichtig, transparent

transpire [træns'paɪr] *intr* (*happen*) sich ereignen; (*leak out*) (fig) durchsickern

transplant ['træns ˌplænt] *s* (bot, surg) Verpflanzung *f* ‖ [træns'plænt] *tr* (bot, surg) verpflanzen

transport ['trænspɔrt] *s* Beförderung *f*. Transport *m*; (nav) Truppentransporter *m* ‖ [træns'pɔrt] *tr* befördern

transportation [ˌtrænspɔr'teʃən] *s* Beförderung *f*; (*public transportation*) Verkehrsmittel *n*; **do you need t.?** brauchen Sie e-e Fahrgelegenheit?

trans′port plane′ *s* Transportflugzeug *n*

transpose [træns'poz] *tr* umstellen; (math, mus) transponieren

trans-ship [træns'ʃɪp] *v* (*pret & pp* **-shipped;** *ger* **-shipping**) *tr* (com, naut) umladen

trap [træp] *s* (& fig) Falle *f*; (*snare*) Schlinge *f*; (*pit*) Fallgrube *f*; (*under a sink*) Geruchsverschluß *m*; (*mouth*) (sl) Klappe *f*; (chem) Abscheider *m*; (golf) Sandbunker *m*; **fall** (*or* **walk**) **into a t.** in die Falle gehen; **set a trap** e-e Falle stellen ‖ *v* (*pret & pp* **trapped;** *ger* **trapping**) *tr* mit e-r Falle fangen; (fig) erwischen; (mil) einfangen

trap′ door′ *s* Falltür *f*, Klapptür *f*; (theat) Versenkung *f*

trapeze [trə'piz] *s* Trapez *n*; (gym) Schwebereck *n*

trapezoid ['træpɪ ˌzɔɪd] *s* Trapéz *n*

trapper ['træpər] *s* Fallensteller *m*

trappings ['træpɪŋz] *spl* Staat *m*; (*caparison*) Staatsgeschirr *n*

trap′shoot′ing *s* Tontaubenschießen *n*

trash [træʃ] *s* Abfälle *pl*; (*junk*) Schund *m*; (*artistically inferior material*) Kitsch *m*; (*worthless people*) Gesindel *n*

trash′ can′ *s* Mülleimer *m*, Abfalleimer *m*

trashy ['træʃi] *adj* kitschig; (*literature*) Schund-

travail [trə'vel] *s* Plackerei *f*; (*labor of childbirth*) Wehen *pl*

travel ['trævəl] *s* Reisen *n*; (*trip*) Reise *f*; (*e.g., of a bullet, rocket*) Bewegung *f*; (*of moving parts*) Lauf *m*; **travels** Reiseerlebnisse *pl* ‖ *v* (*pret & pp* **-el[l]ed;** *ger* **-el[l]ing**) *tr* bereisen ‖ *intr* reisen; (*said of a vehicle or passenger*) fahren; (astr, aut, mach, phys) sich bewegen

trav′el a′gency *s* Reisebüro *n*

traveler ['trævələr] *s* Reisende *mf*

trav′eler′s check′ *s* Reisescheck *m*

trav′el fold′er *s* Reiseprospekt *m*

trav′eling bag′ *s* Reisetasche *f*

trav′eling sales′man *s* (**-men**) Geschäftsreisende *m*

travelogue ['trævə ˌlɔg] *s* Reisebericht *m*; (cin) Reisefilm *m*

traverse [trə'vʌrs] *tr* durchqueren ‖ *intr* (*said of a gun*) sich drehen

traves-ty ['trævɪsti] *s* Travestie *f* ‖ *v* (*pret & pp* **-tied**) *tr* travestieren

trawl [trɔl] *s* Schleppnetz *n* ‖ *tr* mit dem Schleppnetz fangen ‖ *intr* mit dem Schleppnetz fischen

trawler ['trɔlər] *s* Schleppnetzboot *n*

tray [tre] *s* Tablett *n*; (phot) Schale *f*

treacherous ['tretʃərəs] *adj* verräterisch; (*e.g., ice*) trügerisch

treachery ['tretʃəri] *s* Verrat *m*

tread [tred] *s* (*step*) Tritt *m*; (*imprint*) Spur *f*; (*on a tire*) Profil *n* ‖ *v* (*pret* **trod** [trɑd]; *pp* **trodden** ['trɑdən] & **trod**) *tr* betreten ‖ *intr* (on) treten (auf *acc*)

treadle ['tredəl] *s* Trittbrett *n*

tread′mill′ *s* (& fig) Tretmühle *f*

treason ['trizən] *s* Verrat *m*

treasonable ['trizənəbəl] *adj* verräterisch

treasure ['treʒər] *s* Schatz *m* ‖ *tr* sehr schätzen

treasurer ['treʒərər] *s* Schatzmeister –in *mf*

treasury ['treʒəri] *s* Schatzkammer *f*; (*chest*) Tresor *m*; (*public treasury*) Staatsschatz *m*; **Treasury** Finanzministerium *n*

treat [trit] *s* Hochgenuß *m* ‖ *tr* behandeln; (*regard*) (as) betrachten (als); **t. oneself to s.th.** sich [*dat*] etw genehmigen; **t. s.o. to s.th** j-n bewirten mit

treatise ['tritɪs] *s* Abhandlung *f*

treatment ['tritmənt] *s* Behandlung *f*

treaty ['triti] *s* Vertrag *m*

treble ['trebəl] *adj* (*threefold*) dreifach; (mus) Diskant– ‖ *s* Diskant *m*; (*voice*) Diskantstimme *f* ‖ *tr* verdreifachen ‖ *intr* sich verdreifachen

tre′ble clef′ *s* Violinschlüssel *m*

tree [tri] *s* Baum *m*

treeless ['trilɪs] *adj* baumlos

tree′top′ *s* Baumwipfel *m*

tree′ trunk′ *s* Baumstamm *m*

trellis ['trelɪs] *s* Spalier *n*; (*gazebo*) Gartenhäuschen *n*

tremble ['trembəl] *s* Zittern *n* ‖ *intr* zittern; (geol) beben; **t. all over** am ganzen Körper zittern

tremendous [trɪ'mendəs] *adj* ungeheuer

tremor ['tremər] *s* Zittern *n*; (geol) Beben *n*

trench [trentʃ] *s* Graben *m*; (mil) Schützengraben *m*

trenchant ['trentʃənt] *adj* schneidend; (*policy*) durchschlagend

trench′ war′fare *s* Stellungskrieg *m*

trend [trend] *s* Richtung *f*, Trend *m*

trespass ['trespəs] *s* unbefugtes Betreten *n*; (*sin*) Sünde *f* ‖ *intr* unbefugt fremdes Eigentum betreten; **no trespassing** (*public sign*) Betreten verboten; **t. on** unbefugt betreten

trespasser ['trespəsər] *s* Unbefugte *mf*

tress [tres] *s* Flechte *f*

trestle ['tresəl] *s* Gestell *n*; (*of a bridge*) Brückenbock *m*

trial ['traɪəl] *s* (*attempt*) Versuch *m*; (*hardship*) Beschwernis *f*; (jur) Prozeß *m*; **a week's t.** e-e Woche Probezeit; **be on t. for** vor Gericht stehen wegen; **be brought up** (*or* **come up**) **for t.** zur Verhandlung kommen; **new t.** Wiederaufnahmeverfahren *n*; **on t.** (com) auf Probe; **put on t.** vor Gericht bringen

tri′al and er′ror *s*—**by t.** durch Ausprobieren
tri′al balloon′ *s* Versuchsballon *m*
tri′al by ju′ry *s* Verhandlung *f* vor dem Schwurgericht
tri′al or′der *s* Probeauftrag *m*
tri′al run′ *s* Probelauf *m*
triangle [′traɪˌæŋgəl] *s* Dreieck *n*
triangular [traɪ′æŋgjələr] *adj* dreieckig
tribe [traɪb] *s* Stamm *m*; (pej) Sippschaft *f*
tribunal [traɪ′bjunəl] *s* Tribunal *n*
tributary [′trɪbjəˌteri] *adj* zinspflichtig ‖ *s* Nebenfluß *m*
tribute [′trɪbjut] *s* Tribut *m*, Zins *m*; **pay t. to** Anerkennung zollen (*dat*)
trice [traɪs] *s*—**in a t.** im Nu
trick [trɪk] *s* Trick *m*; (*prank*) Streich *m*; (*technique*) Kniff *m*; (*artifice*) Schlich *m*; (cards) Stich *m*; **be on to s.o.'s tricks** j-s Schliche kennen; **be up to one's old tricks** sein Unwesen treiben; **do the t.** die Sache schaffen; **play a dirty t. on s.o.** j-m e-n gemeinen Streich spielen ‖ *tr* reinlegen; **t. s.o. into** (ger) j-n durch Kniffe dazu bringen zu (*inf*)
trickery [′trɪkəri] *s* Gaunerei *f*
trickle [′trɪkəl] *s* Tröpfeln *n* ‖ *intr* tröpfeln, rieseln
trickster [′trɪkstər] *s* Gauner *m*
tricky [′trɪki] *adj* (*wily*) listig; (*touchy*) heikel; (*difficult*) verzwickt
trident [′traɪdənt] *s* Dreizack *m*
tried [traɪd] *adj* bewährt, probat
trifle [′traɪfəl] *s* Kleinigkeit *f*; **a t.** (*e.g., too big*) ein bißchen ‖ *tr*—**t. away** vertändeln ‖ *intr* tändeln
trif′ling *adj* geringfügig ‖ *s* Tändelei *f*
trigger [′trɪgər] *s* Abzug *m*; **pull the t.** abdrücken ‖ *tr* auslösen
trig′ger-hap′py *adj* schießwütig
trigonometry [ˌtrɪgə′nɑmətri] *s* Trigonometrie *f*
trill [trɪl] *s* Triller *m* ‖ *tr & intr* trillern
trillion [′trɪljən] *s* Billion *f*; (Brit) Trillion *f*
trilogy [′trɪlədʒi] *s* Trilogie *f*
trim [trɪm] *adj* (**trimmer; trimmest**) (*figure*) schick; (*well-kept*) gepflegt ‖ *s* (*e.g., of a hat*) Zierleiste *f*; (naut) Trimm *m*; **be in t.** in Form sein ‖ *v* (*pret & pp* **trimmed**; *ger* **trimming**) *tr* (*clip*) stutzen; (*decorate*) dekorieren; (*a Christmas tree*) schmücken; (*beat*) (coll) schlagen; (naut) trimmen
trim′ming *s* (*e.g., of a dress*) Besatz *m*; (*of hedges*) Stutzen *n*; **take a t.** (coll) e-e Niederlage erleiden; **trimmings** (*decorations*) Verzierungen *pl*; (*food*) Zutaten *pl*; (*scraps*) Abfälle *pl*; **with all the trimmings** (fig) mit allen Schikanen
trinity [′trɪnɪti] *s* Dreiheit *f*; **Trinity** Dreifaltigkeit *f*
trinket [′trɪŋkɪt] *s* Schmuckgegenstand *m*
tri·o [′tri-o] *s* (**-os**) (& mus) Trio *n*
trip [trɪp] *s* Reise *f*; (*on drugs*) Trip *m*; **go on** (or **take**) **a t.** e-e Reise machen ‖ *v* (*pret & pp* **tripped; ger tripping**) *tr* ein Bein stellen (*dat*); **t. up** (fig) zu Fall bringen ‖ *intr* stolpern
tripartite [traɪ′pɑrtɪt] *adj* Dreiparteien–; (*of three powers*) Dreimächte–
tripe [traɪp] *s* Kutteln *pl*; (sl) Schund *m*
trip′ham′mer *s* Schmiedehammer *m*
triple [′trɪpəl] *adj* dreifach ‖ *s* Dreifache *n* ‖ *tr* verdreifachen
triplet [′trɪplɪt] *s* (*offspring*) Drilling *m*; (mus) Triole *f*
triplicate [′trɪplɪkɪt] *adj* dreifach ‖ *s*—**in t.** in dreifacher Ausfertigung
tripod [′traɪpɑd] *s* Dreifuß *m*; (phot) Stativ *n*
triptych [′trɪptɪk] *s* Triptychon *n*
trite [traɪt] *adj* abgedroschen
triumph [′traɪəmf] *s* Triumph *m* ‖ *intr* (*over*) triumphieren (über *acc*)
triumphal [traɪ′ʌmfəl] *adj* Sieges–
triumphant [traɪ′ʌmfənt] *adj* triumphierend
trivia [′trɪvɪ·ə] *spl* Nichtigkeiten *pl*
trivial [′trɪvɪ·əl] *adj* trivial, alltäglich; (*person*) oberflächlich
triviality [ˌtrɪvɪ′ælɪti] *s* Trivialität *f*, Nebensächlichkeit *f*
Trojan [′trodʒən] *adj* trojanisch ‖ *s* Trojaner –in *mf*
troll [trol] *s* (myth) Troll *m* ‖ *tr & intr* mit der Schleppangel fischen
trolley [′trɑli] *s* Straßenbahn *f*
trollop [′trɑləp] *s* (*slovenly woman*) Schlampe *f*; (*prostitute*) Dirne *f*
trombone [′trɑmbon] *s* Posaune *f*
troop [trup] *s* Trupp *m*; (mil) Truppe *f*
trooper [′truper] *s* Kavallerist *m*; **swear like a t.** fluchen wie ein Kutscher
troop′ship′ *s* Truppentransporter *m*
trophy [′trofi] *s* Trophäe *f*; (sport) Pokal *m*
tropical [′trɑpɪkəl] *adj* Tropen–
tropics [′trɑpɪks] *spl* Tropen *pl*
trot [trɑt] *s* Trab *m* ‖ *v* (*pret & pp* **trotted**; *ger* **trotting**) *tr*—**t. out** (coll) zur Schau stellen ‖ *intr* traben
troubadour [′trubəˌdor] *s* Minnesänger *m*
trouble [′trʌbəl] *s* (*inconvenience, bother*) Mühe *f*; (*difficulty*) Schwierigkeit *f*; (*physical distress*) Leiden *n*; (*civil disorder*) Unruhe *f*; **ask for t.** das Schicksal herausfordern; **be in t.** in Schwierigkeiten sein; (*be pregnant*) schwanger sein; **cause s.o. a lot of t.** j-m viel zu schaffen machen; **get into t.** in Schwierigkeiten geraten; **go to a lot of t.** sich [*dat*] viel Mühe machen; **it was no t. at all!** gern geschehen!; **make t.** Geschichten machen; **take the t. to** (*inf*) sich der Mühe unterziehen zu (*inf*); **that's the t.** da liegt die Schwierigkeit; **what's the t.?** was ist los? ‖ *tr* (*worry*) beunruhigen; (*bother*) belästigen; (*disturb*) stören; (*said of ills*) plagen
trou′blemak′er *s* Unruhestifter –in *mf*
troubleshooter [′trʌbəlˌʃutər] *s* Stö-

rungssucher −in *mf;* (*in disputes*) Friedensstifter −in *mf*

troublesome ['trʌbəlsəm] *adj* lästig

trough [trof] *s* Trog *m;* (*of a wave*) Wellental *n*

troupe [trup] *s* Truppe *f*

trousers ['trauzərz] *spl* Hose *f*

trous·seau [tru'so] *s* (−seaux & −seaus) Brautausstattung *f*

trout [traut] *s* Forelle *f*

trowel ['trau·əl] *s* Kelle *f*

truant ['tru·ənt] *adj* schwänzend ‖ **s— play t.** die Schule schwänzen

truce [trus] *s* Waffenruhe *f*

truck [trʌk] *s* Last(kraft)wagen *m;* (*for luggage*) Gepäckwagen *m* ‖ *tr* mit Lastkraftwagen befördern

truck′driv′er *s* Lastwagenfahrer *m*

trucker ['trʌkər] *s* (*driver*) Lastwagenfahrer *m;* (*owner of a trucking firm*) Fuhrunternehmer −in *mf*

truck′ farm′ing *s* Gemüsebau *m*

truculent ['trʌkjələnt] *adj* gehässig

trudge [trʌdʒ] *intr* stapfen

true [tru] *adj* wahr; (*loyal*) (ge)treu; (*genuine*) echt; (*sign*) sicher; **come t.** sich verwirklichen; **prove t.** sich als wahr erweisen; **that's t.** das stimmt

truffle ['trʌfəl] *s* Trüffel *f*

truism ['tru·ɪzəm] *s* Binsenwahrheit *f*

truly ['truli] *adv* wirklich; **Yours t.** Hochachtungsvoll

trump [trʌmp] *s* Trumpf *m* ‖ *tr* trumpfen; **t. up** erdichten ‖ *intr* trumpfen

trumpet ['trʌmpɪt] *s* Trompete *f* ‖ *intr* (*said of an elephant*) trompeten

truncheon ['trʌntʃən] *s* Gummiknüppel *m*

trunk [trʌŋk] *s* (*chest*) Koffer *m;* (*of a tree*) Stamm *m;* (*of a living body*) Rumpf *m;* (*of an elephant*) Rüssel *m;* (*aut*) Kofferraum *m;* **trunks** (sport) Sporthose *f*

trunk′ line′ *s* Fernverkehrsweg *m*

truss [trʌs] *s* (*archit*) Tragwerk *n;* (*med*) Bruchband *n* ‖ *tr* (*archit*) stützen; (*bind*) festbinden

trust [trʌst] *s* (*in*) Vertrauen *n* (auf *acc*); (*com*) Trust *m;* (*jur*) Treuhand *f* ‖ *tr* trauen (*dat*); (*hope*) hoffen ‖ *intr*—**t. in** vertrauen auf (*acc*)

trust′ com′pany *s* Treuhandgesellschaft *f*

trustee [trʌs'ti] *s* Aufsichtsrat *m;* (*jur*) Treuhänder −in *mf*

trustee′ship *s* Treuhandverwaltung *f*

trustful ['trʌstfəl] *adj* zutraulich

trust′ fund′ *s* Treuhandfonds *m*

trust′wor′thy *adj* vertrauenswürdig

trusty ['trʌsti] *adj* treu ‖ *s* Kalfaktor *m*

truth [truθ] *s* Wahrheit *f;* **in t.** wahrlich

truthful ['truθfəl] *adj* (*person*) ehrlich; (*e.g., account*) wahrheitsgemäß

try [traɪ] *s* Versuch *m* ‖ *v* (*pret & pp* **tried**) *tr* versuchen; (*one's patience*) auf e–e harte Probe stellen; (*a case*) verhandeln; **be tried for** vor Gericht kommen wegen; **try on** anprobieren; (*a hat*) aufprobieren; **try out** erproben; (*new food*) kosten; **try s.o. for**

gegen j–n verhandeln wegen ‖ *intr* versuchen

try′ing *adj* anstrengend

try′out′ *s* (sport) Ausscheidungskampf *m*

T′-shirt′ *s* T-Shirt *n*

tub [tʌb] *s* Wanne *f;* (*boat*) Kasten *m*

tubby ['tʌbi] *adj* (coll) kugelrund

tube [t(j)ub] *s* (*pipe*) Rohr *n,* Röhre *f;* (*e.g., of toothpaste*) Tube *f;* (*of rubber*) Schlauch *m;* (rad) Röhre *f*

tuber ['t(j)ubər] *s* (bot) Knolle *f*

tubercle ['t(j)ubərkəl] *s* Tuberkel *m*

tuberculosis [t(j)u ,bʌrkjə'losɪs] *s* Lungenschwindsucht *f*

tuck [tʌk] *s* (sew) Abnäher *m* ‖ *tr* (*into one's pocket, under a mattress*) stecken; (*under one's arm*) klemmen; (*into bed*) packen; **t. in** reinstecken; **t. up** (*trousers*) hochkrempeln; (*a skirt, dress*) hochschürzen

Tuesday ['t(j)uzde] *s* Dienstag *m;* **on T.** am Dienstag

tuft [tʌft] *s* Büschel *m* & *n* ‖ *tr* (*e.g., a mattress*) durchheften

tug [tʌg] *s* (*pull*) Zug *m;* (*boat*) Schlepper *m* ‖ *v* (*pret & pp* **tugged;** *ger* **tugging**) *tr* schleppen ‖ *intr* (at) zerren (an *dat*)

tug′boat′ *s* Schleppdampfer *m*

tug′ of war′ *s* Tauziehen *n*

tuition [t(j)u'ɪʃən] *s* Schulgeld *n*

tulip ['t(j)ulɪp] *s* Tulpe *f*

tumble ['tʌmbəl] *s* (*fall*) Sturz *m;* (gym) Purzelbaum *m* ‖ *intr* (*fall*) stürzen; (gym) Saltos machen; **t. down the stairs** die Treppe herunterpurzeln

tum′ble-down′ *adj* baufällig

tumbler ['tʌmblər] *s* (*glass*) Trinkglas *n;* (*of a lock*) Zuhaltung *f;* (*acrobat*) Akrobat −in *mf*

tumor ['t(j)umər] *s* Geschwulst *f*

tumult ['t(j)umʌlt] *s* Getümmel *n*

tuna ['tunə] *s* Thunfisch *m*

tune [t(j)un] *s* Melodie *f;* **be in t.** richtig gestimmt sein; **be out of t.** falsch singen; (*said of a piano*) verstimmt sein; **change one's t.** e–n anderen Ton anschlagen ‖ *tr* stimmen; **t. up** (aut) neu einstellen ‖ *intr*— **t. in on** (rad) einstellen; **t. up** (*said of an orchestra*) stimmen

tungsten ['tʌŋstən] *s* Wolfram *n*

tunic ['t(j)unɪk] *s* Tunika *f*

tun′ing fork′ *s* Stimmgabel *f*

tun·nel ['tʌnəl] *s* Tunnel *m;* (min) Stollen *m* ‖ *v* (*pret & pp* **−nel[l]ed;** *ger* **−nel[l]ing**) *intr* e–n Tunnel bohren

turban ['tʌrbən] *s* Turban *m*

turbid ['tʌrbɪd] *adj* trüb(e)

turbine ['tʌrbɪn] *s* Turbine *f*

turboprop ['tʌrbo ,prɑp] *s* Turboprop *m*

turbulence ['tʌrbjələns] *s* Turbulenz *f*

tureen [t(j)u'rin] *s* Terrine *f*

turf [tʌrf] *s* Rasendecke *f;* (*of a gang*) (sl) Gebiet *n;* **the t.** der Turf

Turk [tʌrk] *s* Türke *m,* Türkin *f*

turkey ['tʌrki] *s* Truthahn *m;* (*female*) Truthenne *f;* **Turkey** die Türkei

Turkish ['tʌrkɪʃ] *adj* türkisch ‖ *s* Türkisch *n*

Tur'kish tow'el *s* Frottiertuch *n*

turmoil ['tʌrmɔɪl] *s* Getümmel *n*

turn [tʌrn] *s* (*rotation*) Drehung *f;* (*change of direction or condition*) Wendung *f;* (*curve*) Kurve *f;* (*by a driver*) Abbiegen *n;* (*of a century*) Wende *f;* (*of a spool*) Windung *f;* **at every t.** bei jeder Gelegenheit; **good t.** Gunst *f;* **it's his t.** er ist dran; **out of t.** außer der Reihe; **take turns** sich abwechseln ‖ *tr* drehen; (*the page*) umblättern; (*one's head*) wenden; **t. down** (*refuse*) ablehnen; (*a radio*) leiser stellen; (*a bed*) aufdecken; (*a collar*) umschlagen; (*an appeal*) (*jur*) verwerfen; **t. in** (*an application, resignation*) einreichen; (*lost articles*) abgeben; (*a person*) anzeigen; **t. into** verwandeln in (*acc*); **t. loose** frei lassen; **t. off** (*light, gas*) abdrehen; (*rad, telv*) abstellen; **t. on** (*gas, light*) andrehen; (*excite*) (coll) in Erregung versetzen; (*rad, telv*) anstellen; **t. out** produzieren; (*pockets*) umkehren; (*eject*) vor die Tür setzen; **t. over** (*property*) abtreten; (*a business*) übertragen; (*e.g., weapons*) abliefern; **t. up** (*a card, sleeve*) aufschlagen ‖ *intr* (*rotate*) sich drehen; (*in some direction*) sich wenden; **it turned out that** es stellte sich heraus, daß; **t. against** (fig) sich wenden gegen; **t. around** sich herumdrehen; **t. back** umdrehen; **t. down** (*a street*) einbiegen in (*acc*); **t. in** (*go to bed*) zu Bett gehen; **t. into** werden zu; **t. out** ausfallen; **t. out for** sich einfinden zu; **t. out for the best** sich zum Guten wenden; **t. out in force** vollzählig erscheinen; **t. out to be** sich erweisen als; **t. over** (*tip over*) umkippen; (aut) anspringen; **t. to s.o. for help** sich an j–n um Hilfe wenden; **t. towards** sich wenden gegen; **t. up** auftauchen

turn'coat' *s* Überläufer –*in* –*mf*

turn'ing point' *s* Wendepunkt *m*

turnip ['tʌrnɪp] *s* Steckrübe *f*

turn'out' *s* Beteiligung *f*

turn'o'ver *s* Umsatz *m*

turn'pike' *s* Autobahn *f*

turnstile ['tʌrn ˌstaɪl] *s* Drehkreuz *n*

turn'ta'ble *s* Plattenteller *m;* (rr) Drehscheibe *f*

turpentine ['tʌrpən ˌtaɪn] *s* Terpentin *n*

turpitude ['tʌrpɪ ˌt(j)ud] *s* Verworfenheit *f*

turquoise ['tʌrk(w)ɔɪz] *adj* türkisfarben ‖ *s* Türkis *m*

turret ['tʌrɪt] *s* Turm *m*

turtle ['tʌrtəl] *s* Schildkröte *f*

tur'tledove' *s* Turteltaube *f*

tur'tleneck' *s* Rollkragen *m*

tusk [tʌsk] *s* (*of an elephant*) Stoßzahn *m;* (*of a boar*) Hauer *m*

tussle ['tʌsəl] *s* Rauferei *f* ‖ *intr* raufen

tutor ['t(j)utər] *s* Hauslehrer –*in* –*mf*

tuxe·do [tʌk'sido] *s* (**–dos**) Smoking *m*

twang [twæŋ] *s* (*of a musical instrument*) Schwirren *n;* (*of the voice*) Näseln *n* ‖ *intr* schwirren; näseln

tweed [twid] *adj* aus Tweed ‖ *s* Tweed *m*

tweet [twit] *s* Gezwitscher *n* ‖ *intr* zwitschern

tweezers ['twizərz] *spl* Pinzette *f*

twelfth [twelfθ] *adj & pron* zwölfte ‖ *s* (*fraction*) Zwölftel *n;* **the t.** (*in dates or in series*) der Zwölfte

twelve [twelv] *adj & pron* zwölf ‖ *s* Zwölf *f*

twentieth ['twentɪ·ɪθ] *adj & pron* zwanzigste ‖ *s* (*fraction*) Zwanzigstel *n;* **the t.** (*in dates or in series*) der Zwanzigste

twenty ['twenti] *adj & pron* zwanzig ‖ *s* Zwanzig *f;* **the twenties** die zwanziger Jahre

twen'ty-one' *adj & pron* einundzwanzig

twice [twaɪs] *adv* zweimal

twiddle ['twɪdəl] *tr* müßig herumdrehen; **t. one's thumbs** Daumen drehen

twig [twɪg] *s* Zweig *m*

twilight ['twaɪ ˌlaɪt] *adj* dämmerig ‖ *s* Abenddämmerung *f*

twin [twɪn] *adj* (*brother, sister*) Zwillings–; (*double*) Doppel– ‖ *s* Zwilling *m*

twine [twaɪn] *s* (*for a package*) Bindfaden *m;* (sew) Zwirn *m* ‖ *tr*—**t. around** winden um

twin'-en'gine *adj* zweimotorig

twinge [twɪndz] *s* stechender Schmerz *m*

twinkle ['twɪŋkəl] *s* Funkeln *n;* **in a t.** im Nu ‖ *intr* funkeln

twirl [twʌrl] *s* Wirbel *m* ‖ *tr* herumwirbeln ‖ *intr* wirbeln

twist [twɪst] *s* (*turn*) Drehung *f;* (*distortion*) Verdrehung *f;* (*strand*) Flechte *f;* (*bread roll*) Zopf *m;* (*dance*) Twist *m* ‖ *tr* (*revolve*) drehen; (*wind*) winden; (*an arm, words*) verdrehen; **t. one's ankle** sich [*dat*] den Knöchel vertreten ‖ *intr* sich drehen; (*wind*) sich winden

twister ['twɪstər] *s* (coll) Windhose *f*

twit [twɪt] *s* (sl) Depp *m* ‖ *v* (*pret & pp* **twitted;** *ger* **twitting**) *tr* verspotten; (*upbraid*) rügen

twitch [twɪtʃ] *s* Zucken *n* ‖ *intr* zucken

twitter ['twɪtər] *s* Zwitschern *n* ‖ *intr* zwitschern

two [tu] *adj & pron* zwei ‖ *s* Zwei *f;* **by twos** zu zweit; **in two** entzwei; **put two and two together** Schlußfolgerungen ziehen

two'-edged' *adj* zweischneidig

two'-faced' *adj* doppelzüngig

two' hun'dred *adj & pron* zweihundert

two'-piece' *adj* (*suit*) zweiteilig

twosome ['tusəm] *s* (*of lovers*) Liebespaar *n;* (golf) Einzelspiel *n*

two'-time' *tr* untreu sein (*dat*)

two'-tone' *adj* zweifarbig

two'-way traf'fic *s* Gegenverkehr *m*

tycoon [taɪ'kun] *s* Industriekapitän *m*

type [taɪp] *s* (*kind*) Art *f;* (*of person; of manufacture*) Typ *m;* (typ) Drucktype *f,* Letter *f* ‖ *tr & intr* tippen

type′face′ s Schriftbild n
type′script′ s Maschinenschrift f
type′set′ter s Schriftsetzer –in mf
type′write′ v (pret –wrote; pp –written)
tr & intr mit der Maschine schreiben
type′writ′er s Schreibmaschine f
type′writer rib′bon s Farbband n
ty′phoid fe′ver [′taɪfɔɪd] s Typhus m
typhoon [taɪ′fun] s Taifun m
typical [′tɪpɪkəl] adj (of) typisch (für)
typi•fy [′tɪpɪ‚faɪ] v (pret & pp –fied)
tr (characterize) typisch sein für;
(exemplify) ein typisches Beispiel
sein für
typ′ing er′ror s Tippfehler m

typist [′taɪpɪst] s Maschinenschreiber
–in mf
typographic(al) [‚taɪpə′græfɪk(əl)] adj
typographisch; (error) Druck-
typography [taɪ′pɑgrəfi] s (the skill)
Buchdruckerkunst f; (the work)
Buchdruck m
tyrannical [tɪ′rænɪkəl] adj tyrannisch
tyrannize [′tɪrə‚naɪz] tr tyrannisieren
tyranny [′tɪrəni] s Tyrannei f
tyrant [′taɪrənt] s Tyrann m
ty•ro [′taɪro] s (–ros) Neuling m
Tyrol [tɪ′rol] s Tirol n
Tyrolean [tɪ′rolɪ‚ən] adj tirolerisch ‖
s Tiroler –in mf

U

U, u [ju] s einundzwanzigster Buchstabe des englischen Alphabets
ubiquitous [ju′bɪkwɪtəs] adj allgegenwärtig
udder [′ʌdər] s Euter n
ugliness [′ʌglɪnɪs] s Häßlichkeit f
ugly [′ʌgli] adj häßlich
Ukraine [ju′kren] s Ukraine f
Ukrainian [ju′krenɪ‚ən] adj ukrainisch
‖ s (person) Ukrainer –in mf; (language) Ukrainisch n
ulcer [′ʌlsər] s Geschwür n
ulcerate [′ʌlsə‚ret] intr eitern
ulte′rior mo′tive [ʌl′tɪrɪ‚ər] s Hinter-
gedanke m
ultimate [′ʌltɪmɪt] adj äußerste; (goal)
höchst; (result) End- ‖ s Letzte n
ultima•tum [‚ʌltɪ′metəm] s (–tums &
–ta [tə]) Ultimatum n
ul′trahigh fre′quency [′ʌltrə‚haɪ] s
Ultrahochfrequenz f
ultramodern [‚ʌltrə′mɑdərn] adj ultramodern
ultraviolet [‚ʌltrə′vaɪ‚əlɪt] adj ultraviolett ‖ s Ultraviolett n
ultravi′olet lamp′ s Höhensonne f
umbil′ical cord′ [ʌm′bɪlɪkəl] adj Na-
belschnur f
umbrage [′ʌmbrɪdʒ] s—take u. at Anstoß nehmen an (dat)
umbrella [ʌm′brelə] s Regenschirm m;
(aer) Abschirmung f
umlaut [′umlaut] s Umlaut m ‖ tr
umlauten
umpire [′ʌmpaɪr] s Schiedsrichter –in
mf ‖ tr als Schiedsrichter leiten ‖
intr Schiedsrichter sein
umpteen [ʌmp′tin] adj zig; u. times
zigmal
UN [′ju′ɛn] s (United Nations) UNO
f
unable [ʌn′ebəl] adj unfähig
unabridged [ʌnə′brɪdʒd] adj unge-
kürzt
unaccented [‚ʌnæk′sɛntɪd] adj unbetont
unacceptable [‚ʌnæk′sɛptɪbəl] adj un-
annehmbar
unaccountable [‚ʌnə′kauntəbəl] adj

nicht verantwortlich; (strange) seltsam
unaccounted-for [‚ʌnə′kauntɪd‚fɔr] adj
unerklärt; (acct) nicht belegt
unaccustomed [‚ʌnə′kʌstəmd] adj (to)
nicht gewöhnt (an acc)
unaffected [‚ʌnə′fɛktɪd] adj nicht affektiert; **u. by** unbeeinflusst von
unafraid [‚ʌnə′fred] adj—**be u. (of)**
sich nicht fürchten (vor dat)
unalterable [ʌn′ɔltərəbəl] adj unabän-
derlich
unanimity [‚junə′nɪmɪti] s Stimmen-
einheit f
unanimous [ju′nænɪməs] adj (persons)
einmütig; (vote) einstimmig
unannounced [‚ʌnə′naunst] adj unan-
gemeldet
unanswered [ʌn′ænsərd] adj (question)
unbeantwortet; (claim, statement)
unwiderlegt; (request) nicht erhört
unappreciative [‚ʌnə′priʃɪ‚ətɪv] adj
(of) unempfänglich (für)
unapproachable [‚ʌnə′protʃəbəl] adj
unzugänglich
unarmed [ʌn′ɑrmd] adj unbewaffnet
unasked [ʌn′æskt] adj (advice) uner-
beten; (uninvited) ungeladen
unassailable [‚ʌnə′seləbəl] adj unan-
greifbar
unassuming [‚ʌnə′s(j)umɪŋ] adj nicht
anmaßend
unattached [‚ʌnə′tæt/t] adj (to) nicht
befestigt (an dat); (person) ungebunden; (mil) zur Verfügung stehend
unattainable [‚ʌnə′tenəbəl] adj unerreichbar
unattended [‚ʌnə′tendɪd] adj unbeauf-
sichtigt
unattractive [‚ʌnə′træktɪv] adj reizlos
unauthorized [ʌn′ɔθəraɪzd] adj unbe-
rechtigt
unavailable [‚ʌnə′veləbəl] adj (person)
unabkömmlich; (thing) nicht verfügbar
unavenged [‚ʌnə′vendʒd] adj unge-
rächt
unavoidable [‚ʌnə′vɔidəbəl] adj unvermeidlich

unaware [ˌʌnəˈwɛr] *adj* (of) nicht bewußt (*genit*)

unawares [ˌʌnəˈwɛrz] *adv* (*unexpectedly*) unversehens; (*unintentionally*) versehentlich; **catch u.** überraschen

unbalanced [ʌnˈbælənst] *adj* nicht im Gleichgewicht; (fig) unausgeglichen

un·bar [ʌnˈbɑr] *v* (*pret & pp* -**barred**; *ger* -**barring**) *tr* aufriegeln

unbearable [ʌnˈbɛrəbəl] *adj* unerträglich

unbeaten [ʌnˈbitən] *adj* (& fig) ungeschlagen

unbecoming [ˌʌnbɪˈkʌmɪŋ] *adj* (*improper*) ungeziemend; (*clothing*) unkleidsam

unbelievable [ˌʌnbɪˈlivəbəl] *adj* unglaublich

unbeliever [ˌʌnbɪˈlivər] *s* Ungläubige *mf*

unbending [ʌnˈbɛndɪŋ] *adj* unbeugsam

unbiased [ʌnˈbaɪ·əst] *adj* unvoreingenommen

unbidden [ʌnˈbɪdən] *adj* ungebeten

un·bind [ʌnˈbaɪnd] *v* (*pret & pp* -**bound**) *tr* losbinden

unbleached [ʌnˈblitʃt] *adj* ungebleicht

unbolt [ʌnˈbolt] *tr* aufriegeln

unborn [ʌnˈbɔrn] *adj* ungeboren

unbosom [ʌnˈbuzəm] *tr*—u. oneself to sich offenbaren (*dat*)

unbowed [ʌnˈbaud] *adj* ungebeugt

unbreakable [ʌnˈbrekəbəl] *adj* unzerbrechlich

unbridled [ʌnˈbraɪdəld] *adj* ungezügelt

unbroken [ʌnˈbrokən] *adj* (*intact*) ungebrochen; (*line*, *series*) ununterbrochen; (*horse*) nicht zugeritten

unbuckle [ʌnˈbʌkəl] *tr* aufschnallen

unburden [ʌnˈbʌrdən] *tr* entlasten; **u. oneself** sein Herz ausschütten

unburied [ʌnˈbɛrid] *adj* unbeerdigt

unbutton [ʌnˈbʌtən] *adj* aufknöpfen

uncalled-for [ʌnˈkɔld ˌfɔr] *adj* unangebracht

uncanny [ʌnˈkæni] *adj* unheimlich

uncared-for [ʌnˈkɛrd ˌfɔr] *adj* verwahrlost

unceasing [ʌnˈsisɪŋ] *adj* unaufhörlich

unceremonious [ˌʌnsɛrɪˈmoni·əs] *adj* (*informal*) ungezwungen; (*rude*) unsanft

uncertain [ʌnˈsʌrtən] *adj* unsicher

uncertainty [ʌnˈsʌrtənti] *s* Unsicherheit *f*

unchain [ʌnˈtʃen] *tr* losketten; (fig) entfesseln

unchangeable [ʌnˈtʃendʒəbəl] *adj* unveränderlich

uncharacteristic [ˌʌnkærɪktəˈrɪstɪk] *adj* wesensfremd

uncharted [ʌnˈtʃɑrtɪd] *adj* auf keiner Karte verzeichnet

unchaste [ʌnˈtʃest] *adj* unkeusch

unchecked [ʌnˈtʃɛkt] *adj* ungehemmt

unchristian [ʌnˈkrɪstʃən] *adj* unchristlich

uncivilized [ʌnˈsɪvɪ ˌlaɪzd] *adj* unzivilisiert

unclad [ʌnˈklæd] *adj* unbekleidet

unclaimed [ʌnˈklemd] *adj* nicht abgeholt

unclasp [ʌnˈklæsp] *tr* loshaken; (*the arms, hands*) öffnen

unclassified [ʌnˈklæsɪ ˌfaɪd] *adj* nicht klassifiziert; (*not secret*) nicht geheim

uncle [ˈʌnkəl] *s* Onkel *m*

unclean [ʌnˈklin] *adj* unsauber; (relig) unrein

unclear [ʌnˈklɪr] *adj* unklar

un·clog [ʌnˈklɑg] *v* (*pret & pp* -**clogged**; *ger* -**clogging**) *tr* von e-m Hindernis befreien

uncombed [ʌnˈkomd] *adj* ungekämmt

uncomfortable [ʌnˈkʌmfərtəbəl] *adj* unbequem; **feel u.** sich nicht recht wohl fühlen

uncommitted [ˌʌnkəˈmɪtɪd] *adj* (*troops*) nicht eingesetzt; (*delegates, nations*) unentschieden

uncommon [ʌnˈkɑmən] *adj* ungewöhnlich; (*outstanding*) außergewöhnlich

uncomplaining [ˌʌnkʌmˈplenɪŋ] *adj* klaglos

uncompromising [ʌnˈkɑmprə ˌmaɪzɪŋ] *adj* unbeugsam

unconcealed [ˌʌnkənˈsild] *adj* unverholen

unconcerned [ˌʌnkənˈsʌrnd] *adj* (*about*) unbesorgt (um)

unconditional [ˌʌnkənˈdɪʃənəl] *adj* bedingungslos

unconfirmed [ˌʌnkənˈfɪrmd] *adj* unbestätigt, unverbürgt

unconquerable [ʌnˈkɑŋkərəbəl] *adj* unüberwindlich

unconquered [ʌnˈkɑŋkərd] *adj* unbezwungen

unconscious [ʌnˈkɑnʃəs] *adj* bewußtlos; (*of*) nicht bewußt (*genit*) || *s*—**the u.** das Unbewußte

unconstitutional [ˌʌnkɑnstɪˈt(j)uʃənəl] *adj* verfassungswidrig

uncontested [ˌʌnkənˈtɛstɪd] *adj* unbestritten

uncontrollable [ˌʌnkənˈtroləbəl] *adj* unkontrollierbar; (fig) unbändig

unconventional [ˌʌnkənˈvɛntʃənəl] *adj* unkonventionell

uncork [ʌnˈkɔrk] *tr* entkorken

uncouple [ʌnˈkʌpəl] *tr* abkoppeln

uncouth [ʌnˈkuθ] *adj* ungehobelt; (*appearance*) ungeschlacht

uncover [ʌnˈkʌvər] *tr* aufdecken

unctuous [ˈʌŋktʃu·əs] *adj* salbungsvoll

uncultivated [ʌnˈkʌltɪ ˌvetɪd] *adj* unbebaut

uncultured [ʌnˈkʌltʃərd] *adj* (fig) unkultiviert

uncut [ʌnˈkʌt] *adj* nicht abgeschnitten; (*gem*) ungeschliffen; (*grain*) ungemäht

undamaged [ʌnˈdæmɪdʒd] *adj* unbeschädigt, unversehrt

undaunted [ʌnˈdɔntɪd] *adj* unverzagt

undecided [ˌʌndɪˈsaɪdɪd] *adj* (*person*) unschlüssig; (*thing*) unentschieden

undefeated [ˌʌndɪˈfitɪd] *adj* unbesiegt

undefended [ˌʌndɪˈfɛndɪd] *adj* unverteidigt

undefiled [ˌʌndɪˈfaɪld] *adj* unbefleckt

undefined [ˌʌndɪˈfaɪnd] *adj* unklar

undeliverable [ˌʌndɪˈlɪvərəbəl] *adj* unbestellbar

undeniable [ˌʌndɪˈnaɪ·əbəl] *adj* un-leugbar

under [ˈʌndər] *adj* Unter– || *adv* unter–, e.g., **go u.** untergehen || *prep* unter (*position*) (*dat*); (*direction*) unter (*acc*)

un'derage' *adj* unmündig

un'der·bid' *v* (*pret & pp* –bid; *ger* –bidding) *tr* unterbieten

un'derbrush' *s* Unterholz *n*

un'dercar'riage *s* Fahrgestell *n*

un'derclothes' *spl* Unterwäsche *f*

un'dercov'er *adj* Geheim–; **u. agent** Spitzel *m*

un'dercur'rent *s* (& *fig*) Unterströmung *f*

un'dercut' *v* (*pret & pp* –cut; *ger* –cutting) *tr* unterbieten

un'derdevel'oped *adj* unterentwickelt

un'derdog' *s* (coll) Unterlegene *mf*

un'derdone' *adj* nicht durchgebraten

un'deres'timate *tr* unterschätzen

un'derexpose' *tr* (phot) unterbelichten

un'dergar'ment *s* Unterkleidung *f*

un'der·go' *v* (*pret* –went; *pp* –gone) durchmachen; (*an operation*) sich unterziehen (*dat*)

un'dergrad'uate *s* Collegestudent –in *mf*

un'derground' *adj* unterirdisch; (*fig*) Untergrund–; (*water*) Grund–; (*min*) unter Tage || **un'derground'** *s* (*secret movement*) Untergrundbewegung *f*; **go u.** untertauchen

un'dergrowth' *s* Buschholz *n*, Unterholz *n*

un'derhand' *adj* (*throw*) unter Schulterhöhe (ausgeführt)

un'derhand'ed *adj* hinterhältig

un'derline', **un'derline'** *tr* unterstreichen

underling [ˈʌndərlɪŋ] *s* Handlanger *m*

un'dermine' *tr* (& *fig*) untergraben

underneath [ˌʌndərˈniθ] *adv* unten || *s* Unterseite *f* || *prep* (*position*) unter (*dat*), unterhalb (*genit*); (*direction*) unter (*acc*)

un'dernour'ished *adj* unterernährt

un'dernour'ishment *s* Unterernährung *f*

un'derpad' *s* (*of a rug*) Unterlage *f*

un'derpaid' *adj* unterbezahlt

un'derpass' *s* Straßenunterführung *f*

un'der·pin' *v* (*pret & pp* –pinned; *ger* –pinning) *tr* untermauern

un'derplay' *tr* unterspielen

un'derpriv'ileged *adj* benachteiligt

un'derrate' *tr* unterschätzen

un'derscore' *tr* (& *fig*) unterstreichen

un'dersea' *adj* Unterwasser–

un'dersec'retar'y *s* Untersekretär –in *mf*

un'der·sell' *v* (*pret & pp* –sold; *ger* –selling) *tr* (*a person*) unterbieten; (*goods*) verschleudern

un'dershirt' *s* Unterhemd *n*

un'derside' *s* Unterseite *f*

un'dersigned' *adj* unterschrieben || **un'dersigned'** *s* Unterzeichnete *mf*

un'der·stand' *v* (*pret & pp* –stood) *tr* verstehen; **it's understood that** es ist selbstverständlich, daß; **make oneself understood** sich verständlich machen

understandable [ˌʌndərˈstændəbəl] *a* verständlich

understandably [ˌʌndərˈstændəbli] *a* begreiflicherweise

un'derstand'ing *adj* verständnisvoll (**of**) Verständnis *n* (für); (*betwee persons*) Einvernehmen *n*; (*agreement*) Übereinkommen *n*; **come to a u. with s.o.** sich mit j–m verständigen; **it is my u. that** wie ich verstehe

un'derstud'y *s* Ersatzmann *m*; (ci theat) Ersatzschauspieler –in *mf*

un'der·take' *v* (*pret* –took; *pp* –taker *tr* unternehmen

undertaker [ˈʌndərˌtekər] *s* Leichenbestatter –in *mf*

un'dertak'ing *s* Unternehmen *n*

un'dertone' *s* leise Stimme *f*; (fig Unterton *m*

un'dertow' *s* Sog *m*

un'derwa'ter *adj* Unterwasser–

un'derwear' *s* Unterwäsche *f*

un'derweight' *adj* untergewichtig

un'derworld' *s* (*of criminals*) Unterwelt *f*; (myth) Totenreich *n*

un'der·write', **un'der·write'** *v* (*pre* –wrote; *pp* –written) *tr* unterschreiben; (ins) versichern

un'derwrit'er *s* Unterzeichner –in *mf* (ins) Versicherer –in *mf*; (st. exch.) Wertpapiermakler –in *mf*; **underwriters** Emissionsfirma *f*

undeserved [ˌʌndɪˈzɑrvd] *adj* unverdient

undeservedly [ˌʌndɪˈzɑrvɪdli] *adv* unverdientermaßen

undesirable [ˌʌndɪˈzaɪrəbəl] *adj* unerwünscht || *s* Unerwünschte *mf*

undeveloped [ˌʌndɪˈvɛləpt] *adj* unentwickelt; (*land*) unerschlossen

undies [ˈʌndiz] *spl* (coll) Unterwäsche *f*)

undigested [ˌʌndɪˈdʒɛstɪd] *adj* (& *fig*) unverdaut

undignified [ʌnˈdɪɡnɪˌfaɪd] *adj* würdelos

undiluted [ˌʌndɪˈlutɪd] *adj* unverdünnt

undiminished [ˌʌndɪˈmɪnɪʃt] *adj* unvermindert

undisciplined [ʌnˈdɪsəplɪnd] *adj* undiszipliniert, zuchtlos

undisputed [ˌʌndɪsˈpjutɪd] *adj* unbestritten, unangefochten

undisturbed [ˌʌndɪsˈtʌrbd] *adj* ungestört

undivided [ˌʌndɪˈvaɪdɪd] *adj* ungeteilt

un·do' [ʌnˈdu] *v* (*pret* –did; *pp* –done) *tr* (*a knot*) aufschnüren; (*a deed*) ungeschehen machen

undo'ing *s* Ruin *m*

undone [ʌnˈdʌn] *adj* (*not done*) ungetan; (*ruined*) ruiniert; **come u.** sich lösen; **leave nothing u.** nichts unversucht lassen

undoubtedly [ʌnˈdaʊtɪdli] *adv* zweifellos

undramatic [ˌʌndrəˈmætɪk] *adj* undramatisch

undress [ʌnˈdrɛs] *s*—**in a state of u.** (*nude*) in unbekleidetem Zustand; (*in a negligee*) im Negligé || *tr* ausziehen || *intr* sich ausziehen undrinkable [ʌn'drɪŋkəbəl] adj nicht trinkbar

undue [ʌn'd(j)u] adj (inappropriate) unangemessen; (excessive) übermäßig

undulate ['ʌndjə‚let] intr wogen

undulating ['ʌndjə‚letɪŋ] adj wellenförmig

unduly [ʌn'd(j)uli] adv übermäßig

undying [ʌn'daɪ‚ɪŋ] adj unsterblich

un'earned in'come ['ʌn‚ɑrnd] s Kapitalrente f

unearth [ʌn'ʌrθ] tr ausgraben; (fig) aufstöbern

unearthly [ʌn'ʌrθli] adj unirdisch; (cry) schauerlich; at an u. hour (early) in aller Herrgottsfrühe

uneasy [ʌn'izi] adj (worried) ängstlich; (ill at ease) unbehaglich

uneatable [ʌn'itəbəl] adj ungenießbar

uneconomic(al) [‚ʌnɛkə'nɑmɪk(əl)] adj unwirtschaftlich

uneducated [ʌn'ɛdjə‚ketɪd] adj ungebildet

unemployed [‚ʌnɛm'plɔɪd] adj arbeitslos ‖ s Arbeitslose mf

unemployment [‚ʌnɛm'plɔɪmənt] s Arbeitslosigkeit f

unemploy'ment compensa'tion s Arbeitslosenunterstützung f; collect u. (sl) Stempeln gehen

unencumbered [‚ʌnən'kʌmbərd] adj unbelastet

unending [ʌn'ɛndɪŋ] adj endlos

unequal [ʌn'ikwəl] adj ungleich; u. to nicht gewachsen (dat)

unequaled [ʌn'ikwəld] adj ohnegleichen

unequivocal [‚ʌnə'kwɪvəkəl] adj eindeutig

unerring [ʌn'ɛrɪŋ] adj unfehlbar

UNESCO [ju'nɛsko] s (United Nations Educational, Scientific, and Cultural Organization) UNESCO f

unessential [‚ʌnə'sɛnʃəl] adj unwesentlich

uneven [ʌn'ivən] adj (not smooth) uneben; (unbalanced) ungleich; (not uniform) ungleichmäßig; (number) ungerade

uneventful [‚ʌnɪ'vɛntfəl] adj ereignislos

unexceptional [‚ʌnɛk'sɛpʃənəl] adj nicht außergewöhnlich

unexpected [‚ʌnɛk'spɛktɪd] adj unerwartet

unexplained [‚ʌnɛk'splɛnd] adj unerklärt

unexplored [‚ʌnɛk'splord] adj unerforscht

unexposed [‚ʌnɛk'spozd] adj (phot) unbelichtet

unfading [ʌn'fedɪŋ] adj unverwelklich

unfailing [ʌn'felɪŋ] adj unfehlbar

unfair [ʌn'fɛr] adj unfair; (competition) unlauter

unfaithful [ʌn'feθfəl] adj treulos

unfamiliar [‚ʌnfə'mɪljər] adj unbekannt

unfasten [ʌn'fæsən] tr losbinden; (e.g., a seat belt) aufschnallen

unfathomable [ʌn'fæðəməbəl] adj unergründlich

unfavorable [ʌn'fevərəbəl] adj ungünstig

unfeasible [ʌn'fizəbəl] adj unausführbar

unfeeling [ʌn'filɪŋ] adj unempfindlich

unfilled [ʌn'fɪld] adj ungefüllt; (post) unbesetzt

unfinished [ʌn'fɪnɪʃt] adj unfertig; (business) unerledigt

unfit [ʌn'fɪt] adj (for) ungeeignet (für); (not qualified) (for) untauglich (für); u. for military service wehrdienstuntauglich

unfold [ʌn'fold] tr (a chair) aufklappen; (cloth, paper) entfalten; (ideas, plans) offenbaren

unforeseeable [‚ʌnfor'si‚əbəl] adj unabsehbar

unforeseen [‚ʌnfor'sin] adj unvorhergesehen

unforgettable [‚ʌnfor'gɛtəbəl] adj unvergeßlich

unfortunate [ʌn'fortʃənɪt] adj unglücklich

unfortunately [ʌn'fortʃənɪtli] adv leider

unfounded [ʌn'faundɪd] adj unbegründet

un-freeze [ʌn'friz] v (pret –froze; pp –frozen) tr auftauen; (prices) freigeben

unfriendly [ʌn'frɛndli] adj unfreundlich

unfruitful [ʌn'frutfəl] adj unfruchtbar

unfulfilled [‚ʌnfəl'fɪld] adj unerfüllt

unfurl [ʌn'fʌrl] tr (a flag) entrollen; (sails) losmachen

unfurnished [ʌn'fʌrnɪʃt] adj unmöbliert

ungainly [ʌn'genli] adj plump

ungentlemanly [ʌn'dʒɛntəlmənli] adj unfein, unedel

ungodly [ʌn'gɑdli] adj (hour) ungehörig

ungracious [ʌn'greʃəs] adj ungnädig

ungrammatical [‚ʌngrə'mætɪkəl] adj ungrammatisch

ungrateful [ʌn'gretfəl] adj undankbar

ungrudgingly [ʌn'grʌdʒɪŋli] adv gern

unguarded [ʌn'gɑrdɪd] adj unbewacht; (moment) unbedacht

unguent ['ʌŋgwɛnt] s Salbe f

unhandy [ʌn'hændi] adj unhandlich; (person) unbeholfen

unhappy [ʌn'hæpi] adj unglücklich

unharmed [ʌn'hɑrmd] adj unversehrt

unharness [ʌn'hɑrnɪs] tr abschirren

unhealthful [ʌn'hɛlθfəl] adj ungesund

unhealthy [ʌn'hɛlθi] adj ungesund

unheard-of [ʌn'hʌrd‚ɑv] adj unerhört

unheated [ʌn'hitɪd] adj ungeheizt

unhesitating [ʌn'hɛzɪ‚tetɪŋ] adj (immediate) unverzüglich; (unswerving) unbeirrbar; (support) bereitwillig

unhinge [ʌn'hɪndʒ] tr (fig) aus den Angeln heben

unhitch [ʌn'hɪtʃ] tr (horses) ausspannen; (undo) losmachen

unholy [ʌn'holi] adj unheilig

unhook [ʌn'hʊk] tr losmachen; (a dress) aufhaken; (the receiver) abnehmen

unhoped-for [ʌn'hopt ˌfɔr] *adj* unverhofft

unhurt [ʌn'hʌrt] *adj* unbeschädigt;
(person) unversehrt

unicorn ['junɪ ˌkɔrn] *s* Einhorn *n*

unification [ˌjunɪfɪ'keʃən] *s* Vereinigung *f*

uniform ['junɪ ˌfɔrm] *adj* gleichförmig
|| *s* Uniform *f*

uniformity [ˌjunɪ'fɔrmɪtɪ] *s* Gleichförmigkeit *f*

uni·fy ['junɪ ˌfaɪ] *v* (*pret & pp* **–fied**)
tr vereinigen

unilateral [ˌjunɪ'lætərəl] *adj* einseitig

unimpaired [ˌʌnɪm'perd] *adj* unge-
schwächt

unimpeachable [ˌʌnɪm'pitʃəbəl] *adj*
unantastbar

unimportant [ˌʌnɪm'pɔrtənt] *adj* unwichtig

uninflected [ˌʌnɪn'flektɪd] *adj* (gram)
unflektiert

uninhabited [ˌʌnɪn'hæbɪtɪd] *adj* unbewohnt

uninspired [ˌʌnɪn'spaɪrd] *adj* schwunglos

unintelligible [ˌʌnɪn'telɪdʒəbəl] *adj*
unverständlich

unintentional [ˌʌnɪn'tenʃənəl] *adj* unabsichtlich

uninterested [ʌn'ɪntə ˌrestɪd] *adj* (in)
uninteressiert (an *dat*)

uninteresting [ʌn'ɪntə ˌrestɪŋ] *adj* un-
interessant

uninterrupted [ˌʌnɪntə'rʌptɪd] *adj* ununterbrochen

uninvited [ˌʌnɪn'vaɪtɪd] *adj* ungeladen

union ['junjən] *adj* Gewerkschafts– ||
s Vereinigung *f*; *(harmony)* Eintracht
f; *(of workers)* Gewerkschaft *f*; (pol)
Union *f*

unionize ['junjə ˌnaɪz] *tr* gewerkschaft-
lich organisieren || *intr* sich gewerk-
schaftlich organisieren

un'ion shop' *s* Betrieb *m*, der nur Ge-
werkschaftsmitglieder beschäftigt

unique [ju'nik] *adj* einzigartig

unison ['junɪsən] *s* Einklang *m*

unit ['junɪt] *s* (& mil) Einheit *f*

unite [ju'naɪt] *tr* vereinigen; (chem)
verbinden || *intr* sich vereinigen;
(chem) sich verbinden

Unit'ed King'dom *s* Vereinigtes Königreich *n*

Unit'ed Na'tions *spl* Vereinte Natio-
nen *pl*

Unit'ed States' *s* Vereinigte Staaten *pl*

unity ['junɪtɪ] *s* (harmony) Einigkeit *f*;
(e.g., of a nation) Einheit *f*; (fa)
Einheitlichkeit *f*

universal [ˌjunɪ'vʌrsəl] *adj* universal,
allgemein || *s* Allgemeine *n*; (philos)
Allgemeinbegriff *m*

u'niver'sal joint' *s* Kardangelenk *n*

u'niver'sal mil'itary train'ing *s* allgemeine Wehrpflicht *f*

universe ['junɪ ˌvʌrs] *s* Universum *n*

university [ˌjunɪ'vɜrsɪtɪ] *adj* Universi-
täts– || *s* Universität *f*

unjust [ʌn'dʒʌst] *adj* ungerecht

unjustified [ʌn'dʒʌstɪ ˌfaɪd] *adj* unge-
rechtfertigt

unjustly [ʌn'dʒʌstlɪ] *adv* zu Unrecht

unkempt [ʌn'kempt] *adj* ungekämmt;
(fig) verwahrlost

unkind [ʌn'kaɪnd] *adj* unfreundlich

unknown [ʌn'non] *adj* unbekannt

un'known quan'tity *s* Unbekannte *f*

Un'known Sol'dier *s* Unbekannter Soldat *m*

unlatch [ʌn'lætʃ] *tr* aufklinken

unlawful [ʌn'lɔfəl] *adj* gesetzwidrig

unleash [ʌn'liʃ] *tr* losbinden; (fig) entfesseln

unleavened [ʌn'levənd] *adj* ungesäuert

unless [ʌn'les] *conj* wenn ... nicht

unlettered [ʌn'letərd] *adj* ungebildet

unlicensed [ʌn'laɪsənst] *adj* unerlaubt

unlike [ʌn'laɪk] *adj* (unequal) ungleich;
(dissimilar) unähnlich || *prep* im Ge-
gensatz zu (dat); **be u. s.o.** anders
als jemand sein

unlikely [ʌn'laɪklɪ] *adj* unwahrscheinlich

unlimited [ʌn'lɪmɪtɪd] *adj* unbe-
schränkt

unlined [ʌn'laɪnd] *adj* (clothes) ungefüttert; (paper) unliniert; (face)
faltenlos

unload [ʌn'lod] *tr & intr* ausladen

unload'ing *s* Ausladen *n*; (naut)
Löschen *n*

unlock [ʌn'lɑk] *tr* aufsperren

unloose [ʌn'lus] *tr* lösen

unloved [ʌn'lʌvd] *adj* ungeliebt

unlucky [ʌn'lʌkɪ] *adj* unglücklich

un·make [ʌn'mek] *v* (*pret & pp* **–made**)
tr rückgängig machen; (a bed) ab-
decken

unmanageable [ʌn'mænɪdʒəbəl] *adj*
(person, animal) widerspenstig;
(thing) unhandlich

unmanly [ʌn'mænlɪ] *adj* unmännlich

unmanned [ʌn'mænd] *adj* (rok) unbemannt

unmannerly [ʌn'mænərlɪ] *adj* unmännlich

unmarketable [ʌn'mɑrkɪtəbəl] *adj*
nicht marktgängig

unmarriageable [ʌn'mærɪdʒəbəl] *adj*
nicht heiratsfähig

unmarried [ʌn'mærɪd] *adj* unverheiratet

unmask [ʌn'mæsk] *tr* (& fig) demaskie-
ren || *intr* sich demaskieren

unmatched [ʌn'mætʃt] *adj* (not
matched) ungleichartig; (unmatch-
able) unvergleichlich

unmerciful [ʌn'mʌrsɪfəl] *adj* unbarm-
herzig

unmesh [ʌn'meʃ] *tr* (mach) ausrücken

unmindful [ʌn'maɪndfəl] *adj* uneinge-
denk

unmistakable [ˌʌnmɪs'tekəbəl] *adj* un-
mißverständlich

unmitigated [ʌn'mɪtɪ ˌgetɪd] *adj* unge-
mildert; (liar) Erz–

unmixed [ʌn'mɪkst] *adj* ungemischt

unmoor [ʌn'mur] *tr* losmachen || *intr*
sich losmachen

unmoved [ʌn'muvd] *adj* (fig) ungerührt

unmuzzle [ʌn'mʌzəl] *tr* den Maulkorb
abnehmen (dat)

unnatural [ʌnˈnætʃərəl] *adj* unnatür-
lich; (*forced*) gezwungen
unnecessary [ʌnˈnesəˌseri] *adj* unnötig
unneeded [ʌnˈnidid] *adj* nutzlos
unnerve [ʌnˈnʌrv] *tr* entnerven
unnoticeable [ʌnˈnotisəbəl] *adj* unbe-
merkbar
unnoticed [ʌnˈnotist] *adj* unbemerkt
unobserved [ˌʌnəbˈzʌrvd] *adj* unbeob-
achtet
unobtainable [ˌʌnəbˈtenəbəl] *adj* nicht
erhältlich
unobtrusive [ˌʌnəbˈtrusiv] *adj* unauf-
dringlich
unoccupied [ʌnˈɑkjəˌpaɪd] *adj* (*room,
house*) leerstehend; (*seat*) unbesetzt;
(*person*) unbeschäftigt
unofficial [ˌʌnəˈfɪʃəl] *adj* inoffiziell
unopened [ʌnˈopənd] *adj* ungeöffnet
unopposed [ˌʌnəˈpozd] *adj* (*without
opposition*) widerspruchslos; (*unre-
sisted*) unbehindert
unorthodox [ʌnˈɔrθəˌdɑks] *adj* unorthodox; (relig) nicht orthodox
unpack [ʌnˈpæk] *tr* auspacken
unpalatable [ʌnˈpælətəbəl] *adj* un-
schmackhaft; (fig) widerlich
unparalleled [ʌnˈpærəˌleld] *adj* unvergleichlich
unpardonable [ʌnˈpɑrdənəbəl] *adj* un-
verzeihlich
unpatriotic [ˌʌnpetriˈɑtɪk] *adj* unpatri-
otisch
unpaved [ʌnˈpevd] *adj* ungepflastert
unperceived [ˌʌnpərˈsivd] *adj* unbemerkt
unpleasant [ʌnˈplezənt] *adj* unangenehm; (*person*) unsympathisch
unpopular [ʌnˈpɑpjələr] *adj* unbeliebt
unpopularity [ʌnˌpɑpjəˈlæriti] *s* Unbe-
liebtheit *f*
unprecedented [ʌnˈpresiˌdentid] *adj*
unerhört; (jur) ohne Präzedenzfall
unpredictable [ˌʌnprɪˈdɪktəbəl] *adj* unberechenbar; (*weather*) wechselhaft
unprejudiced [ʌnˈpredʒədɪst] *adj* unvoreingenommen
unprepared [ˌʌnprɪˈperd] *adj* unvorbereitet
unpresentable [ˌʌnprɪˈzentəbəl] *adj*
nicht präsentabel
unpretentious [ˌʌnprɪˈtenʃəs] *adj* an-
spruchslos
unprincipled [ʌnˈprɪnsɪpəld] *adj* haltlos
unproductive [ˌʌnprəˈdʌktɪv] *adj* un-
produktiv; (of) unergiebig (an *dat*)
unprofessional [ˌʌnprəˈfeʃənəl] *adj*
(*work*) unfachmännisch; (*conduct*)
berufswidrig
unprofitable [ʌnˈprɑfɪtəbəl] *adj* (*useless*) nutzlos; (fi) unrentabel
unpronounceable [ˌʌnprəˈnaunsəbəl]
adj unaussprechlich
unprotected [ˌʌnprəˈtektid] *adj* (*place*)
ungeschützt; (*person*) unbeschützt
unpropitious [ˌʌnprəˈpɪʃəs] *adj* ungünstig
unpublished [ʌnˈpʌblɪʃt] *adj* unveröf-
fentlicht
unpunished [ʌnˈpʌnɪʃt] *adj* ungestraft
unqualified [ʌnˈkwɑləˌfaɪd] *adj* un-

qualifiziert; (*full, complete*) unbedingt
unquenchable [ʌnˈkwentʃəbəl] *adj* un-
stillbar
unquestionably [ʌnˈkwestʃənəbli] *adv*
fraglos, unbezweifelbar
unquestioning [ʌnˈkwestʃənɪŋ] *adj*
(*obedience*) bedingungslos
unquiet [ʌnˈkwaɪ·ət] *adj* unruhig
unrav·el [ʌnˈrævəl] *v* (*pret & pp*
-el[l]ed; *ger* **-el[l]ing**) *tr* (a knitted
fabric) auftrennen; (fig) entwirren ‖
intr sich fasern; (fig) sich entwirren
unreachable [ʌnˈritʃəbəl] *adj* unerreichbar
unreal [ʌnˈri·əl] *adj* unwirklich
unreality [ˌʌnriˈæliti] *s* Unwirklich-
keit *f*
unreasonable [ʌnˈrizənəbəl] *adj* unver-
nünftig
unrecognizable [ʌnˈrekəgˌnaɪzəbəl] *adj*
unerkennbar
unreel [ʌnˈril] *tr* abspulen
unrefined [ˌʌnrɪˈfaɪnd] *adj* roh
unrelated [ˌʌnrɪˈletid] *adj* (**to**) ohne
Beziehung (zu)
unrelenting [ˌʌnrɪˈlentɪŋ] *adj* unerbittlich
unreliable [ˌʌnrɪˈlaɪ·əbəl] *adj* unzuverlässig; (fin) unsolid(e)
unremitting [ˌʌnrɪˈmɪtɪŋ] *adj* unablässig
unrepentant [ˌʌnrɪˈpentənt] *adj* unbußfertig
unrequited [ˌʌnrɪˈkwaɪtid] *adj* uner-
widert
unreserved [ˌʌnrɪˈzʌrvd] *adj* vorbehaltlos
unresponsive [ˌʌnrɪˈspansɪv] *adj* (**to**)
unempfänglich (für)
unrest [ʌnˈrest] *s* Unruhe *f*
unrestricted [ˌʌnrɪˈstrɪktid] *adj* unein-
geschränkt
unrewarded [ˌʌnrɪˈwɔrdid] *adj* unbe-
lohnt
unrhymed [ʌnˈraɪmd] *adj* ungereimt
un·rig [ʌnˈrɪg] *v* (*pret & pp* **-rigged;**
ger **-rigging**) *tr* abtakeln
unripe [ʌnˈraɪp] *adj* unreif
unrivaled [ʌnˈraɪvəld] *adj* unübertreff-
lich
unroll [ʌnˈrol] *tr* aufrollen; (*e.g., a
cable*) abrollen ‖ *intr* sich aufrollen;
sich abrollen
unromantic [ˌʌnroˈmæntɪk] *adj* unro-
mantisch
unruffled [ʌnˈrʌfəld] *adj* unerschüttert
unruly [ʌnˈruli] *adj* ungebärdig
unsaddle [ʌnˈsædəl] *tr* (a *horse*) ab-
satteln; (a *rider*) aus dem Sattel
werfen
unsafe [ʌnˈsef] *adj* unsicher
unsaid [ʌnˈsed] *adj* ungesagt
unsalable [ʌnˈseləbəl] *adj* unverkäuf-
lich
unsanitary [ʌnˈsænɪˌteri] *adj* unhygie-
nisch
unsalted [ʌnˈsɔltid] *adj* ungesalzen
unsatisfactory [ʌnˌsætɪsˈfæktəri] *adj*
unbefriedigend
unsatisfied [ʌnˈsætɪsˌfaɪd] *adj* unbe-
friedigt

unsavory [ʌn'sevəri] *adj* unschmack-
haft; (fig) widerlich
unscathed [ʌn'skeðd] *adj* unversehrt
unscientific [ˌʌnsaɪ·ən'tɪfɪk] *adj* un-
wissenschaftlich
unscramble [ʌn'skræmbəl] *tr* (a message) entziffern; (fig) entflechten
unscrew [ʌn'skru] *tr* aufschrauben
unscrupulous [ʌn'skrupjələs] *adj* skru-
pellos
unseal [ʌn'sil] *tr* entsiegeln; (eyes,
lips) öffnen
unseasonable [ʌn'sizənəbəl] *adj* unzei-
tig; (weather) nicht der Jahreszeit
entsprechend
unseasoned [ʌn'sizənd] *adj* ungewürzt
unseat [ʌn'sit] *tr* (a rider) aus dem
Sattel heben; (an official) aus dem
Posten verdrängen
unseemly [ʌn'simli] *adj* ungehörig
unseen [ʌn'sin] *adj* ungesehen
unselfish [ʌn'selfɪʃ] *adj* selbstlos
unsettle [ʌn'setəl] *tr* beunruhigen
unsettled [ʌn'setəld] *adj* (matter, bill)
unerledigt; (without a residence)
ohne festen Wohnsitz; (restless) unruhig; (life) unstet
unshackle [ʌn'ʃækəl] *tr* die Fesseln
abnehmen (dat)
unshakable [ʌn'ʃekəbəl] *adj* unerschütterlich
unshapely [ʌn'ʃepli] *adj* mißgestaltet
unshaven [ʌn'ʃevən] *adj* unrasiert
unsheathe [ʌn'ʃið] *tr* aus der Scheide
ziehen
unshod [ʌn'ʃɑd] *adj* unbeschuht
unsightly [ʌn'saɪtli] *adj* unansehnlich
unsinkable [ʌn'sɪŋkəbəl] *adj* nicht ver-
senkbar
unskilled [ʌn'skɪld] *adj* ungelernt; **u.
laborer** Hilfsarbeiter –in *mf*
unskillful [ʌn'skɪlfəl] *adj* ungewandt
unsnarl [ʌn'snɑrl] *tr* entwirren
unsociable [ʌn'soʃəbəl] *adj* ungesellig
unsolicited [ˌʌnsə'lɪsɪtɪd] *adj* unverlangt
unsold [ʌn'sold] *adj* unverkauft
unsophisticated [ˌʌnsə'fɪstɪˌketɪd] *adj*
unverfälscht; (naive) arglos
unsound [ʌn'saʊnd] *adj* ungesund;
(sleep) unruhig; **of u. mind** geistes-
krank
unspeakable [ʌn'spikəbəl] *adj* unsagbar
unspoiled [ʌn'spɔɪld] *adj* unverdorben
unsportsmanlike [ʌn'sportsmən ˌlaɪk]
adj unsportlich
unstable [ʌn'stebəl] *adj* unbeständig;
(e.g., ladder) wacklig; (hand) zittrig;
(market, walk) schwankend; (inconstant) unbeständig; (chem) unbeständig
unstinted [ʌn'stɪntɪd] *adj* uneinge-
schränkt
unstinting [ʌn'stɪntɪŋ] *adj* freigebig
unstitch [ʌn'stɪtʃ] *tr* auftrennen
unstressed [ʌn'strest] *adj* unbetont
unsuccessful [ˌʌnsək'sɛsfəl] *adj* erfolglos
unsuitable [ʌn'sutəbəl] *adj* ungeeignet;
(inappropriate) unangemessen
unsullied [ʌn'sʌlid] *adj* unbefleckt

unsung [ʌn'sʌŋ] *adj* unbesungen
unsuspected [ˌʌnsəs'pɛktɪd] *adj* unver-
dächtig; (not known to exist) ungeahnt
unsuspecting [ˌʌnsəs'pɛktɪŋ] *adj* arglos
unswerving [ʌn'swɑrvɪŋ] *adj* unentwegt
unsympathetic [ˌʌnsɪmpə'θɛtɪk] *adj*
teilnahmslos
unsystematic(al) [ˌʌnsɪstə'mætɪk(əl)]
adj unsystematisch
untactful [ʌn'tæktfəl] *adj* taktlos
untalented [ʌn'tæləntɪd] *adj* unbegabt
untamed [ʌn'temd] *adj* ungezähmt
untangle [ʌn'tæŋgəl] *tr* (& fig) entwirren
untenable [ʌn'tenəbəl] *adj* unhaltbar
untested [ʌn'testɪd] *adj* ungeprüft
unthankful [ʌn'θæŋkfəl] *adj* undankbar
unthinking [ʌn'θɪŋkɪŋ] *adj* gedankenlos
untidy [ʌn'taɪdi] *adj* unordentlich
un·tie [ʌn'taɪ] *v* (pret & pp –tied; ger
–tying) *tr* aufbinden; (a knot) lösen;
my shoe is untied mein Schuh ist auf-
gegangen
until [ʌn'tɪl] *prep* bis (acc); **u. further
notice** bis auf weiteres || *conj* bis
untimely [ʌn'taɪmli] *adj* frühzeitig; (at
the wrong time) unzeitgemäß
untiring [ʌn'taɪrɪŋ] *adj* unermüdlich
untold [ʌn'told] *adj* (suffering) unsäglich; (countless) zahllos
untouched [ʌn'tʌtʃt] *adj* unangetastet;
(fig) ungerührt
untoward [ʌn'tord] *adj* (unfavorable)
ungünstig; (unruly) widerspenstig
untrained [ʌn'trend] *adj* unausgebildet; (eye) ungeschult; (sport) un-
trainiert
untried [ʌn'traɪd] *adj* (unattempted)
unversucht; (untested) unerprobt;
(case) (jur) nicht verhandelt
untroubled [ʌn'trʌbəld] *adj* (mind,
times) ruhig; (peace) ungestört
untrue [ʌn'tru] *adj* unwahr; (unfaithful) un(ge)treu; (not exact) ungenau
untrustworthy [ʌn'trʌst ˌwɑrði] *adj* un-
glaubwürdig
untruth [ʌn'truθ] *s* Unwahrheit *f*
untruthful [ʌn'truθfəl] *adj* (statement)
unwahr; (person) unaufrichtig
untwist [ʌn'twɪst] *tr* aufflechten || *intr*
aufgehen
unusable [ʌn'juzəbəl] *adj* nicht verwendbar; (unconsumable) unbenutzbar
unusual [ʌn'juʒʊ·əl] *adj* ungewöhnlich
unutterable [ʌn'ʌtərəbəl] *adj* unaussprechlich
unvarnished [ʌn'vɑrnɪʃt] *adj* nicht ge-
firnißt; (truth) ungeschminkt
unveil [ʌn'vel] *tr* (a monument) enthüllen; (a face) entschleiern
unventilated [ʌn'ventɪ ˌletɪd] *adj* un-
gelüftet
unvoiced [ʌn'vɔɪst] *adj* (ling) stimmlos
unwanted [ʌn'wɑntɪd] *adj* unerwünscht
unwarranted [ʌn'wɑrəntɪd] *adj* unge-
rechtfertigt
unwary [ʌn'weri] *adj* unvorsichtig

unwavering [ʌn'wevərɪŋ] *adj* standhaft
unwelcome [ʌn'welkəm] *adj* unwillkommen
unwell [ʌn'wel] *adj* unwohl
unwept [ʌn'wept] *adj* unbeweint
unwholesome [ʌn'holsəm] *adj* schädlich; (& fig) unbekömmlich
unwieldy [ʌn'wildɪ] *adj* (*person*) schwerfällig; (*thing*) unhandlich
unwilling [ʌn'wɪlɪŋ] *adj* (*involuntary*) unfreiwillig; (*reluctant*) widerwillig; (*obstinate*) eigensinnig; **be u. to** (*inf*) nicht (*inf*) wollen
unwillingly [ʌn'wɪlɪŋlɪ] *adv* ungern
un·wind [ʌn'waɪnd] *v* (*pret & pp* **-wound**) *tr* abwickeln ‖ *intr* sich abwickeln; (fig) sich entspannen
unwise [ʌn'waɪz] *adj* unklug
unwished-for [ʌn'wɪ∫t‚fɔr] *adj* unerwünscht
unwitting [ʌn'wɪtɪŋ] *adj* unwissentlich
unworkable [ʌn'wɑrkəbəl] *adj* (*plan*) unausführbar; (*material*) nicht zu bearbeiten(d)
unworldly [ʌn'wʌrldlɪ] *adj* nicht weltlich; (*naive*) weltfremd
unworthy [ʌn'wʌrðɪ] *adj* unwürdig
un·wrap [ʌn'ræp] *v* (*pret & pp* **-wrapped**) *ger* **-wrapping**) *tr* auspacken ‖ *intr* aufgehen
unwrinkled [ʌn'rɪŋkəld] *adj* faltenlos
unwritten [ʌn'rɪtən] *adj* ungeschrieben; (*agreement*) mündlich
unyielding [ʌn'jildɪŋ] *adj* unnachgiebig
up [ʌp] *adj & adv* (*at a height*) oben; (*to a height*) hinauf; **be up** (*be out of bed; said of a shade*) aufsein; (baseball) am Schlag sein; **be up and around again** wieder auf dem Damm sein; **be up to** (*be ready for*) gewachsen sein (*dat*); (*e.g., mischief*) vorhaben; **from ten dollars and up** von zehn Dollar aufwärts; **it's up to you** es hängt von Ihnen ab; **prices are up** die Preise sind gestiegen; **up and down** (*back and forth*) auf und ab; (*from head to toe*) von oben bis unten; **up there** da oben; **up to** (*e.g., one hour*) bis zu; **up to the ears in debt** bis über die Ohren in Schulden ‖ *v* (*pret & pp* **upped**) *ger* **upping**) *tr* erhöhen ‖ *prep* (*acc*) hinauf (postpositive)
up-and-coming ['ʌpən'kʌmɪŋ] *adj* (coll) unternehmungslustig
up-and-up ['ʌpən'ʌp] *s*—**be on the u.** aufrichtig sein
upbraid' *tr* Vorwürfe machen (*dat*)
upbringing ['ʌp‚brɪŋɪŋ] *s* Erziehung *f*
update' *tr* aufs laufende bringen
up'draft' *s* Aufwind *m*
upend' *tr* hochkant stellen
up'grade' *s* Steigung *f*; **on the u.** (fig) im Aufsteigen ‖ **up'grade'** *tr* (*reclassify*) höher einstufen; (*improve*) verbessern
upheaval [ʌp'hivəl] *s* Umbruch *m*
up'hill' *adj* ansteigend; (fig) mühsam; **u. struggle** harter Kampf *m* ‖ *adv* bergauf
uphold' *v* (*pret & pp* **-held**) *tr* (*the law*) unterstützen; (*a verdict*) bestätigen

upholster [ʌp'holstər] *tr* (auf)polstern
upholsterer [ʌp'holstərər] *s* Polsterer –in *mf*
upholstery [ʌp'holstərɪ] *s* Polsterung *f*
up'keep' *s* Instandhaltung *f*; (*maintenance costs*) Instandhaltungskosten *pl*
upland ['ʌplənd] *adj* Hochlands–, Berg– ‖ **the uplands** *spl* das Hochland
up'lift' *s* (fig) Aufschwung *m*; **moral u.** moralischer Auftrieb *m* ‖ **up'lift'** *tr* (fig) geistig (or moralisch) erheben
upon [ə'pɑn] *prep* (*position*) an (*dat*), auf (*dat*); (*direction*) an (*acc*), auf (*acc*); **u. my word!** auf mein Wort!
upper ['ʌpər] *adj* obere, Ober– ‖ **uppers** *spl* Oberleder *n*
up'per-case' *adj* in Großbuchstaben gedruckt (or geschrieben)
up'per class'es *spl* Oberschicht *f*
up'percut' *s* (box) Aufwärtshaken *m*
up'per deck' *s* Oberdeck *n*
up'per hand' *s* Oberhand *f*
up'per lip' *s* Oberlippe *f*
up'permost' *adj* oberste
uppish ['ʌpɪ∫] *adj* (coll) hochnäsig
uppity ['ʌpɪtɪ] *adj* (coll) eingebildet
upraise' *tr* erheben
up'right' *adj* aufrecht; (fig) redlich ‖ *s* (fb) Torpfosten *m*
up'ris'ing *s* Aufstand *m*
up'roar' *s* Aufruhr *m*
uproarious [ʌp'rorɪ·əs] *adj* (*noisy*) lärmend; (*laughter*) schallend; (*applause*) tosend; (*very funny*) zwerchfellerschütternd
uproot' *tr* entwurzeln
ups' and downs' *spl* Auf und Ab *n*
upset' *adj* (*over*) verstimmt (über *acc*) ‖ **upset'** *s* unerwartete Niederlage *f* ‖ **up'set'** *v* (*pret & pp* **-set**) *ger* **-setting**) *tr* (*throw over*) umwerfen; (*tip over*) umkippen; (*plans*) umstoßen; (*a person*) aufregen; (*the stomach*) verderben
up'shot' *s* Ergebnis *n*
up'side down' *adv* verkehrt; **turn u.** auf den Kopf stellen
up'stage' *adv* in den (or im) Hintergrund der Bühne ‖ *tr* (coll) ausstechen
up'stairs' *adj* im oberen Stockwerk ‖ *adv* (*position*) oben; (*direction*) nach oben ‖ *s* oberes Stockwerk *n*
upstand'ing *adj* aufrecht; (*sincere*) aufrichtig
up'start' *s* Emporkömmling *m*
up'stream' *adj* weiter stromaufwärts gelegen ‖ *adv* stromaufwärts
up'stroke' *s* Aufstrich *m*; (mach) Hub *m*
up'surge' *s* Aufwallung *f*
up'sweep' *s* Hochfrisur *f*
up'swing' *s* (fig) Aufschwung *m*
upsy-daisy ['ʌpsi'dezɪ] *interj* hopsasa!
up-to-date ['ʌptə'det] *adj* (*modern*) zeitgemäß; (*with latest information*) auf dem neuesten Stand
up'-to-the-min'ute news' ['ʌptəðə'mɪnɪt] *s* Zeitfunk *m*
up'trend' *s* steigende Tendenz *f*

up'turn' s Aufschwung m

upturned' adj nach oben gebogen; **u. nose** Stupsnase f

upward ['ʌpwərd] adj nach oben gerichtet; (*tendency*) steigend || adv aufwärts

U'ral Moun'tains ['jʊrəl] spl Ural m

uranium [jʊ'reni·əm] adj Uran– || s Uran n

urban ['ʌrbən] adj städtisch, Stadt–

urbane [ʌr'ben] adj weltgewandt

urbanite ['ʌrbə‚naɪt] s Städter –in mf

urbanize ['ʌrbə‚naɪz] tr verstädtern

ur'ban renew'al s Altstadtsanierung f

urchin ['ʌrtʃɪn] s Bengel m

ure·thra [jʊ'riθrə] s (–thras & –thrae [θri]) Harnröhre f

urge [ʌrdʒ] s Drang m, Trieb m || tr drängen; **u.** on antreiben

urgency ['ʌrdʒənsɪ] s Dringlichkeit f

urgent ['ʌrdʒənt] adj dringend

urinal ['jʊrɪnəl] s (*in a toilet*) Urinbecken n; (*in a sick bed*) Urinflasche f

urinary ['jʊrɪ‚nerɪ] adj Harn–, Urin–

urinate ['jʊrɪ‚net] intr harnen

urine ['jʊrɪn] s Harn m, Urin m

urn [ʌrn] s Urne f; (*for coffee*) Kaffeemaschine f

urology [jɪ'ralədʒɪ] s Urologie f

us [ʌs] per pron uns

U.S.A. ['ju'es'e] s (**United States of America**) USA pl

usable ['juzəbəl] adj (*consumable items*) verwendbar; (*non-consumable items*) benutzbar

usage ['jusɪdʒ] s (*using*) Gebrauch m; (*treatment*) Behandlung f; (*ling*) Sprachgebrauch m; **rough u.** starke Beanspruchung f

use [jus] s (*of consumable items*) Verwendung f, Gebrauch m; (*of non-consumable items*) Benutzung f; (*application*) Anwendung f; (*advantage*) Nutzen m; (*purpose*) Zweck m; (*consumption*) Verbrauch m; **I have no use for him** ich habe nichts für ihn übrig; **in use** in Gebrauch; **it's no use** es nützt nichts; **make use of** ausnutzen; **of use** von Nutzen; **there's no use in** (*ger*) es hat keinen Zweck zu (*inf*) || [juz] tr (ge)brauchen, verwenden; (*non-consumable items*) benutzen; (*apply*) anwenden; (*e.g.,*

troops) einsetzen; **use up** verbrauchen || intr—**he used to live here** er wohnte früher hier

used [juzd] adj gebraucht; (*car*) Gebraucht–; **be u. to** gewöhnt sein an (*acc*); **be u. to** (*ger*) gewöhnt sein zu (*inf*); **get s.o. u. to** j–n gewöhnen an (*acc*); **get u. to** sich gewöhnen an (*acc*)

useful ['jusfəl] adj nützlich

usefulness ['jusfəlnɪs] s Nützlichkeit f; (*usability*) Brauchbarkeit f

useless ['juslɪs] adj nutzlos; (*not usable*) unbrauchbar

user ['juzər] s (*of gas, electric*) Verbraucher –in mf; (*e.g., of a book*) Benutzer –in f

usher ['ʌʃər] s Platzanweiser –in mf || tr—**u. in** hereinführen; (*a new era*) einleiten

U.S.S.R. ['ju'es'es'ar] s (**Union of Soviet Socialist Republics**) UdSSR f

usual ['juʒʊ·əl] adj gewöhnlich; **as u.** wie gewöhnlich

usually ['juʒʊ·əlɪ] adv gewöhnlich

usurp [ju'zʌrp] tr usurpieren

usurper [ju'zʌrpər] s Usurpator –in mf

usury ['juʒərɪ] s Wucher m

utensil [jʊ'tensɪl] s Gerät n; **utensils** Utensilien pl

uter·us ['jutərəs] s (–i [‚aɪ]) Gebärmutter f

utilitarian [‚jutɪlɪ'terɪ·ən] adj utilitaristisch, Nützlichkeits–

utility [jʊ'tɪlɪtɪ] s (*usefulness*) Nützlichkeit f; (*company*) öffentlicher Versorgungsbetrieb m; **apartment with all utilities** Wohnung f mit allem Zubehör; **utilities** Gas, Wasser, Strom pl

utilize ['jutɪ‚laɪz] tr verwerten

utmost ['ʌt‚most] adj äußerste, höchste || s—**do one's u.** sein Äußerstes tun; **to the u.** auf äußerste; **to the u. of one's power** nach besten Kräften

utopia [ju'topɪ·ə] s Utopie f

utopian [ju'topɪ·ən] adj utopisch

utter ['ʌtər] adj völlig, Erz– || tr (*a sigh*) ausstoßen; (*a sound*) hervorbringen; (*feelings*) ausdrücken; (*words*) äußern

utterance ['ʌtərəns] s Äußerung f

utterly ['ʌtərlɪ] adv ganz und gar, völlig

V

V, v [vi] s zweiundzwanzigster Buchstabe des englischen Alphabets

vacancy ['vekənsɪ] s (*emptiness*) Leere f; (*unfilled job*) freie Stelle f; **no v.** (public sign) kein freies Zimmer

vacant ['vekənt] adj frei; (*stare*) geistesabwesend; (*lot*) unbebaut

vacate [ve'ket] tr (*a home*) räumen; (*a seat*) freimachen || intr ausziehen

vacation [ve'keʃən] s Urlaub m; (*educ*)

Ferien pl; **on v.** auf Urlaub || intr Urlaub machen

vacationer [ve'keʃənər] s Urlauber –in mf

vaccinate ['væksɪ‚net] tr impfen

vaccination [‚væksɪ'neʃən] s Impfung f

vaccina'tion certi'ficate s Impfschein m

vaccine [væk'sin] s Impfstoff m

vacillate ['væsɪ‚let] *intr* schwanken

vacuous ['vækju·əs] *adj* nichtssagend

vacu·um ['vækju·əm] *s* (–ums & –a [ə]) Vakuum *n* ‖ *tr & intr* staubsaugen

vac'uum clean'er *s* Staubsauger *m*

vac'uum pump' *s* Absaugepumpe *f*

vac'uum tube' *s* Vakuumröhre *f*

vagabond ['vægə‚band] *s* Landstreicher –in *mf*

vagary ['vegəri] *s* Laune *f*

vagina [və'dʒaɪnə] *s* Scheide *f*

vagrancy ['vegrənsi] *s* Landstreicherei *f*

vagrant ['vegrənt] *adj* vagabundierend ‖ *s* Landstreicher –in *mf*

vague [veg] *adj* unbestimmt, vage

vain [ven] *adj* (proud) eitel; (pointless) vergeblich; in v. vergebens

vainglo'rious *adj* prahlerisch

valance ['væləns] *s* Quervolant *m*

vale [vel] *s* Tal *n*

valedictory [‚vælɪ'dɪktəri] *s* Abschiedsrede *f*

valence ['veləns] *s* Wertigkeit *f*

valentine ['vælən‚taɪn] *s* Valentinsgruß *m*

vale' of tears' *s* Jammertal *n*

valet ['vælɪt] *s* Kammerdiener *m*

valiant ['væljənt] *adj* tapfer

valid ['vælɪd] *adj* (law, ticket) gültig; (argument, objection) wohlbegründet; (e.g., contract) rechtsgültig; be v. gelten

validate ['vælɪ‚det] *tr* bestätigen

validation [‚vælɪ'deʃən] *s* Bestätigung *f*

validity [və'lɪdɪti] *s* Gültigkeit *f*

valise [və'lis] *s* Reisetasche *f*

valley ['væli] *s* Tal *n*

valor ['vælər] *s* Tapferkeit *f*

valorous ['vælərəs] *adj* tapfer

valuable ['vælju·əbəl] *adj* wertvoll ‖ *s* **valuables** *spl* Wertsachen *pl*

value ['vælju] *s* Wert *m* ‖ *tr* (at) schätzen (auf acc)

val'ue judg'ment *s* Werturteil *n*

valueless ['væljulɪs] *adj* wertlos

valve [vælv] *s* (anat, mach, zool) Klappe *f*; (mach, mus) Ventil *n*

vamp [væmp] *s* (coll) Vamp *m*

vampire ['væmpaɪr] *s* Vampir *m*

van [væn] *s* Möbelwagen *m*; (panel truck) Kastenwagen *m*; (fig) Avantgarde *f*; (mil) Vorhut *f*

vandal ['vændəl] *s* Vandale *m*; **Vandal** Vandale *m*

vandalism ['vændə‚lɪzəm] *s* Vandalismus *m*

vane [ven] *s* (of a windmill, fan, propeller) Flügel *m*; (in a turbine) Schaufel *f*

vanguard ['væn‚gɑrd] *s* (fig) Spitze *f*; (mil) Vorhut *f*

vanilla [və'nɪlə] *s* Vanille *f*

vanish ['vænɪʃ] *intr* (ver)schwinden; **v. into thin air** sich in blauen Dunst auflösen

van'ishing cream' *s* Tagescreme *f*

vanity ['vænɪti] *s* (arrogance) Anmaßung *f*; (emptiness) Nichtigkeit *f*; (furniture) Frisiertisch *m*

van'ity case' *s* Kosmetikköfferchen *n*

vanquish ['væŋkwɪʃ] *tr* besiegen

van'tage point' ['væntɪdʒ] *s* (advantage) günstiger Ausgangspunkt *m*; (view) Aussichtspunkt *m*

vapid ['væpɪd] *adj* schal, fad(e)

vapor ['vepər] *s* Dampf *m*, Dunst *m*

vaporize ['vepə‚raɪz] *tr & intr* verdampfen

vaporizer ['vepə‚raɪzər] *s* Inhalationsapparat *m*

va'por trail' *s* Kondensstreifen *m*

variable ['vɛrɪ·əbəl] *adj* veränderlich; (wind) aus wechselnden Richtungen ‖ *s* (math) Veränderliche *f*

variance ['vɛrɪ·əns] *s* Veränderung *f*; (difference) Abweichung *f*; (argument) Streit *m*; **be at v. with** (a person) in Zwiespalt sein mit; (a thing) in Widerspruch stehen zu

variant ['vɛrɪ·ənt] *adj* abweichend ‖ *s* Variante *f*

variation [‚vɛrɪ'eʃən] *s* Veränderung *f*; (alg, biol, mus) Variation *f*

var'icose vein' ['vɛrɪ‚kos] *s* Krampfader *f*

varied ['vɛrɪd] *adj* abwechslungsreich; (diverse) verschieden

variegated ['vɛrɪ·ə‚getɪd] *adj* (diverse) verschieden; (in color) bunt

variety [və'raɪ·əti] *s* (choice) Auswahl *f*; (difference) Verschiedenheit *f*; (sort) Art *f*; (biol) Spielart *f*; **for a v. of reasons** aus verschiedenen Gründen

vari'ety show' *s* Variétévorstellung *f*

various ['vɛrɪ·əs] *adj* verschieden; (several) mehrere

varnish ['vɑrnɪʃ] *s* Firnis *m*, Lack *m* ‖ *tr* firnissen

varsity ['vɑrsɪti] *adj* Auswahl– ‖ *s* Auswahlmannschaft *f*

var·y ['vɛri] *v* (pret & pp –ied) *tr & intr* abwechseln, variieren

vase [ves, vez] *s* Vase *f*

vaseline ['væsə‚lin] *s* (trademark) Vaseline *f*

vassal ['væsəl] *s* Lehensmann *m*

vast [væst] *adj* riesig; (majority) überwiegend; **v. amount** Unmasse *f*

vastness ['væstnɪs] *s* Unermeßlichkeit *f*

vat [væt] *s* Bottich *m*

Vatican ['vætɪkən] *adj* vatikanisch; (city) Vatikan– ‖ *s* Vatikan *m*

Vat'ican Coun'cil *s* Vatikanisches Konzil *n*

vaudeville ['vɔdvɪl] *s* Varié *n*

vaude'ville show' *s* Variétévorstellung *f*

vault [vɔlt] *s* (underground chamber) Gruft *f*; (of a bank) Tresor *m*; (archit) Gewölbe *n*; **v. of heaven** Himmelsgewölbe *n* ‖ *tr* überspringen

vaunt [vɔnt] *s* Prahlerei *f* ‖ *tr* sich rühmen (genit) ‖ *intr* sich rühmen

veal [vil] *s* Kalbfleisch *n*

veal' cut'let *s* Kalbskotelett *n*

veer [vɪr] *intr* drehen, wenden

vegetable ['vedʒɪtəbəl] *adj* pflanzlich; (garden, soup) Gemüse–; (kingdom, life, oil, dye) Pflanzen– ‖ *s* Gemüse *n*; **vegetables** Gemüse *n*

vegetarian [ˌvɛdʒɪˈterɪ·ən] *adj* vegetarisch || *s* Vegetarier –in *mf*
vegetate [ˈvɛdʒɪˌtet] *intr* vegetieren
vegetation [ˌvɛdʒɪˈteʃən] *s* Vegetation *f*
vehemence [ˈvi·ɪməns] *s* Heftigkeit *f*
vehement [ˈvi·ɪmənt] *adj* heftig
vehicle [ˈvi·ɪkəl] *s* Fahrzeug *n*
veil [vel] *s* Schleier *m* || *tr* (& fig) verschleiern
veiled *adj* verschleiert; (*threat*) verhüllt
vein [ven] *s* Vene *f;* (geol, min) Ader *f*
vellum [ˈvɛləm] *s* Velin *n*
velocity [vɪˈlɑsɪti] *s* Geschwindigkeit *f*
velvet [ˈvɛlvɪt] *adj* Samt– || *s* Samt *m*
velveteen [ˌvɛlvɪˈtin] *s* Baumwollsamt *m*
velvety [ˈvɛlvɪti] *adj* samtartig
vend [vend] *tr* verkaufen
vend′ing machine′ *s* Automat *m*
vendor [ˈvɛndər] *s* Verkäufer –in *mf*
veneer [vəˈnɪr] *s* Furnier *n;* (fig) Tünche *f* || *tr* furnieren
venerable [ˈvɛnərəbəl] *adj* ehrwürdig
venerate [ˈvɛnəˌret] *tr* verehren
veneration [ˌvɛnəˈreʃən] *s* Verehrung *f*
Venetian [vɪˈniʃən] *adj* venezianisch || *s* Venezianer –in *mf*
Vene′tian blind′ *s* Fensterjalousie *f*
vengeance [ˈvɛndʒəns] *s* Rache *f;* **take v. on** sich rächen an (*dat*); **with a v.** mit Gewalt
vengeful [ˈvɛndʒfəl] *adj* rachsüchtig
venial [ˈvinɪ·əl] *adj* (*sin*) läßlich
Venice [ˈvɛnɪs] *s* Venedig *n*
venison [ˈvɛnɪsən] *s* Wildbret *n*
venom [ˈvɛnəm] *s* Gift *n;* (fig) Geiger *m*
venomous [ˈvɛnəməs] *adj* giftig
vent [vɛnt] *s* Öffnung *f;* **give v. to** Luft machen (*dat*) || *tr* auslassen
ventilate [ˈvɛntɪˌlet] *tr* ventilieren
ventilation [ˌvɛntɪˈleʃən] *s* Ventilation *f*
ventilator [ˈvɛntɪˌletər] *s* Ventilator *m*
ventricle [ˈvɛntrɪkəl] *s* Ventrikel *m*
ventriloquist [venˈtrɪləkwɪst] *s* Bauchredner –in *mf*
venture [ˈventʃər] *s* Unternehmen *n* || *tr* wagen || *intr* (**on**) sich wagen (an *acc*); **v. out** sich hinauswagen; **v. to** (*inf*) sich vermessen zu (*inf*)
venturesome [ˈvɛntʃərsəm] *adj* (*person*) wagemutig; (*deed*) gewagt
venue [ˈvenju] *s* zuständiger Gerichtsort *m;* **change of v.** Änderung *f* des Gerichtsstandes
Venus [ˈvinəs] *s* Venus *f*
veracity [vɪˈræsɪti] *s* Wahrhaftigkeit *f*
veranda [vəˈrændə] *s* Veranda *f*
verb [vɛrb] *s* Verb *n*, Zeitwort *n*
verbal [ˈvɛrbəl] *adj* (*oral*) mündlich; (gram) verbal
verbatim [vərˈbetɪm] *adj* wortgetreu
verbiage [ˈvɛrbɪ·ɪdʒ] *s* Wortschwall *m*
verbose [vərˈbos] *adj* weitschweifig
verdant [ˈvɛrdənt] *adj* grün
verdict [ˈvɛrdɪkt] *s* Urteilsspruch *m* (der Geschworenen); **give a v.** e–n Spruch fällen
verdigris [ˈvʌrdɪˌgris] *s* Grünspan *m*
verge [vʌrdʒ] *s* (fig) Rand *m;* **on the v. of** (*ger*) nahe daran zu (*inf*) || *intr*—**v. on** grenzen an (*acc*)
verifiable [ˌvɛrɪˈfaɪ·əbəl] *adj* nachprüfbar
verification [ˌvɛrɪfɪˈkeʃən] *s* Nachprüfung *f*
veri•fy [ˈvɛrɪˌfaɪ] *v* (*pret & pp* **–fied**) *tr* nachprüfen
verily [ˈvɛrɪli] *adv* (Bib) wahrlich
veritable [ˈvɛrɪtəbəl] *adj* echt
vermilion [vərˈmɪljən] *adj* zinnoberrot
vermin [ˈvʌrmɪn] *s* (*objectionable person*) Halunke *m;* **v.** *spl* Schädlinge *pl;* (*objectionable persons*) Gesindel *n*
vermouth [vərˈmuθ] *s* Wermut *m*
vernacular [vərˈnækjələr] *adj* volkssprachlich || *s* Volkssprache *f*
ver′nal e′quinox [ˈvʌrnəl] *s* Frühlingstagundnachtgleiche *f*
versatile [ˈvʌrsətɪl] *adj* beweglich
verse [vʌrs] *s* (& Bib) Vers *m;* (*stanza*) Strophe *f*
versed [vʌrst] *adj* (**in**) bewandert in (*dat*)
versification [ˌvʌrsɪfɪˈkeʃən] *s* (*metrical structure*) Versbau *m;* (*versifying*) Verskunst *f;* (*metrical version*) Versfassung *f*
versifier [ˈvʌrsɪˌfaɪ·ər] *s* Verseschmied *m*
version [ˈvʌrʒən] *s* Version *f*
ver•so [ˈvʌrso] *s* (**–sos**) (*of a coin*) Revers *m;* (typ) Verso *n*
versus [ˈvʌrsəs] *prep* gegen (*acc*)
verte•bra [ˈvʌrtɪbrə] *s* (**–brae** [ˌbri] & **–bras**) Rückenwirbel *m*, Wirbel *m*
vertebrate [ˈvʌrtɪˌbret] *s* Wirbeltier *n*
ver•tex [ˈvʌrtɛks] *s* (**–texes** & **–tices** [tɪˌsiz]) Scheitelpunkt *m*
vertical [ˈvʌrtɪkəl] *adj* senkrecht || *s* Vertikale *f*
ver′tical hold′ *s* (telv) Vertikaleinstellung *f*
ver′tical take′off *s* Senkrechtstart *m*
vertigo [ˈvʌrtɪˌgo] *s* Schwindel *m*, Schwindelfegühl *n*
very [ˈveri] *adj*—**that v. day** an demselben Tag; **the v. thought** der bloße Gedanke; **the v. truth** die reine Wahrheit; **the v. man** genau der Mann || *adv* sehr; **the v. best** der allerbeste; **the v. same** ebenderselbe
vesicle [ˈvɛsɪkəl] *s* Bläschen *n*
vespers [ˈvɛspərz] *spl* Vesper *f*
vessel [ˈvɛsəl] *s* (*ship*) Schiff *n;* (*container*) Gefäß *n*
vest [vɛst] *s* Weste *f;* (*for women*) Leibchen *n* || *tr* (**with**) bekleiden (mit); **be vested in** zustehen (*dat*)
vest′ed in′terest *s* (*for personal benefits*) persönliches Interesse *n;* (jur) rechtmäßiges Interesse *n*
vestibule [ˈvɛstɪˌbjul] *s* Vestibül *n*
vestige [ˈvɛstɪdʒ] *s* Spur *f*
vestment [ˈvɛstmənt] *s* Gewand *n*
vest′-pock′et *adj* Westentaschen–
vestry [ˈvɛstri] *s* Sakristei *f;* (*committee*) Gemeindevertretung *f*
vetch [vɛtʃ] *s* Wicke *f*

veteran ['vetərən] *s* Veteran *m*; (sport) Senior *m*

veterinarian [,vetərɪ'nerɪ·ən] *s* Tierarzt *m*, Tierärztin *f*

veterinary ['vetərɪ,nerɪ] *adj* (college) tierärztlich; **v. medicine** Tierheilkunde *f*

ve·to ['vito] *s* (–toes) Veto *n* ‖ *tr* ein Veto einlegen gegen

vex [veks] *tr* ärgern

vexation [vek'seʃən] *s* Ärger *m*

V′-forma′tion *s* (aer) Staffelkeil *m*

via ['vi·ə] *prep* über (*acc*)

viable ['vaɪ·əbəl] *adj* lebensfähig

viaduct ['vaɪ·ə,dʌkt] *s* Viadukt *m*

vial ['vaɪ·əl] *s* Phiole *f*

viands ['vaɪ·əndz] *spl* Lebensmittel *pl*

vibrate ['vaɪbret] *intr* vibrieren; **cause to v.** in Schwingung versetzen

vibration [vaɪ'breʃən] *s* Schwingung *f*

vicar ['vɪkər] *s* Vikar *m*

vicarage ['vɪkərɪdʒ] *s* Pfarrhaus *n*

vicarious [vaɪ'kerɪ·əs] *adj* (pleasure) nachempfunden; (taking the place of another) stellvertretend; **v. experience** Ersatzbefriedigung *f*

vice [vaɪs] *s* Laster *n*

vice′-ad′miral *s* Vizeadmiral *m*

vice′-con′sul *s* Vizekonsul *m*

vice′-pres′ident *s* Vizepräsident –in *mf*

viceroy ['vaɪsrɔɪ] *s* Vizekönig *m*

vice′ squad′ *s* Sittenpolizei *f*

vice versa ['vaɪsə'vʌrsə] *adv* umgekehrt

vicinity [vɪ'sɪnɪti] *s* Umgebung *f*; **in the v. of** in der Nähe (*genit*)

vicious ['vɪʃəs] *adj* (temper) bösartig; (dog) bissig; (person, gossip) heimtückisch

vi′cious cir′cle *s* Zirkelschluß *m*

vicissitudes [vɪ'sɪsɪ,tjudz] *spl* Wechselfälle *pl*

victim ['vɪktɪm] *s* Opfer *n*; (animal) Opfertier *n*; **fall v. to** zum Opfer fallen (*dat*)

victimize ['vɪktɪ,maɪz] *tr* (make a victim of) benachteiligen; (dupe) hereinlegen

victor ['vɪktər] *s* Sieger –in *mf*

victorious [vɪk'torɪ·əs] *adj* siegreich

victory ['vɪktərɪ] *adj* Sieges– ‖ *s* Sieg *m*; (myth) Siegesgöttin *f*; **flushed with v.** siegestrunken

victuals ['vɪtəlz] *spl* Viktualien *pl*

vid′eo sig′nal ['vɪdɪ,o] *s* Bildsignal *n*

vid′eo tape′ *s* Bildband *n*

vid′eo tape′ record′er *s* Bildbandgerät *n*

vid′eo tape′ record′ing *s* Bildbandaufnahme *f*

vie [vaɪ] *v* (pret & pp **vied**; ger **vying**) *intr* (with) wetteifern (mit)

Vienna [vɪ'enə] *s* Wien *n*

Vien·nese [,vi·ə'niz] *adj* wienerisch ‖ *s* (–nese) Wiener –in *mf*

Vietnam [vɪ'et'nam] *s* Vietnam *n*

Vietnam·ese [vɪ,etnə'miz] *adj* vietnamesisch ‖ *s* (–se) Vietnamese *m*, Vietnamesin *f*

view [vju] *s* Aussicht *f*; (opinion) Ansicht *f*; **come into v.** in Sicht kommen; **in my v.** meiner Ansicht nach;

in v. of angesichts (*genit*); **with a v. to** (*ger*) in der Absicht zu (inf) ‖ *tr* betrachten; (sights) besichtigen

viewer ['vju·ər] *s* Zuschauer –in *mf*

view′find′er *s* Bildsucher *m*

view′point *s* Standpunkt *m*

vigil ['vɪdʒɪl] *s* Nachtwache *f*; **keep v.** wachen

vigilance ['vɪdʒɪləns] *s* Wachsamkeit *f*

vigilant ['vɪdʒɪlənt] *adj* wachsam

vignette [vɪn'jet] *s* Vignette *f*

vigor ['vɪgər] *s* (physical) Kraft *f*; (mental) Energie *f*; (intensity) Wucht *f*

vigorous ['vɪgərəs] *adj* (strong) kräftig; (act) energisch

vile [vaɪl] *adj* gemein; (coll) scheußlich

vileness ['vaɪlnɪs] *s* Gemeinheit *f*

vili·fy ['vɪlɪ,faɪ] *v* (pret & pp –fied) *tr* verleumden

villa ['vɪlə] *s* Villa *f*

village ['vɪlɪdʒ] *s* Dorf *n*, Ort *m*

villager ['vɪlɪdʒər] *s* Dorfbewohner –in *mf*

villain ['vɪlən] *s* Bösewicht *m*, Schurke *m*

villainous ['vɪlənəs] *adj* schurkisch

villainy ['vɪlənɪ] *s* Schurkerei *f*

vim [vɪm] *s* Mumm *m*

vindicate ['vɪndɪ,ket] *tr* rechtfertigen

vindictive [vɪn'dɪktɪv] *adj* rachsüchtig

vine [vaɪn] *s* Rebe *f*; (creeper) Ranke *f*

vinegar ['vɪnɪgər] *s* Essig *m*

vine′ grow′er [,gro·ər] *s* Winzer *m*

vineyard ['vɪnjərd] *s* Weinberg *m*

vintage ['vɪntɪdʒ] *adj* Qualitäts– ‖ *s* Weinernte *f*

vin′tage year′ *s* Weinjahr *n*

vintner ['vɪntnər] *s* Weinbauer –in *mf*

vinyl ['vaɪnɪl] *adj* Vinyl–

viola [vaɪ'olə] *s* Bratsche *f*, Viola *f*

violate ['vaɪ·ə,let] *tr* (a law) verletzen; (a promise) brechen; (the peace) stören; (a custom, shrine) entweihen; (a girl) vergewaltigen

violation [,vaɪ·ə'leʃən] *s* (of the law) Verletzung *f*; (of a shrine) Entweihung *f*; (of a girl) Vergewaltigung *f*

violence ['vaɪ·ələns] *s* Gewalt *f*

violent ['vaɪ·ələnt] *adj* (person) gewalttätig; (deed) gewaltsam; (anger, argument) heftig

violet ['vaɪ·əlɪt] *adj* violett ‖ *s* Veilchen *n*

violin [,vaɪ·ə'lɪn] *s* Geige *f*

violinist [,vaɪ·ə'lɪnɪst] *s* Geiger –in *mf*

violoncel·lo [,vaɪ·ələn'tʃelo] *s* (–los) Violoncello *n*

viper ['vaɪpər] *s* Natter *f*, Viper *f*

virgin ['vʌrdʒɪn] *adj* Jungfern–; (land) unberührt ‖ *s* Jungfrau *f*

virginity [vər'dʒɪnɪti] *s* Jungfräulichkeit *f*

virility [vɪ'rɪlɪti] *s* Zeugungskraft *f*

virology [vaɪ'rɑlədʒi] *s* Virusforschung *f*

virtual ['vʌrtʃʊ·əl] *adj* faktisch; (opt, tech) virtuell

virtue ['vʌrtʃʊ] *s* Tugend *f*; **by v. of** kraft (*genit*), vermöge (*genit*)

virtuosity [ˌvɑrtʃuˈɑsɪti] s Virtuosität f

virtuo·so [ˌvɑrtʃuˈoso] s (-sos & -si [si]) Virtuose m, Virtuosin f

virtuous [ˈvɑrtʃuˑəs] adj tugendhaft

virulence [ˈvɪrjələns] s Virulenz f

virulent [ˈvɪrjələnt] adj virulent

virus [ˈvaɪrəs] s Virus n

visa [ˈvizə] s Visum n

visage [ˈvɪzɪdʒ] s Antlitz n

viscera [ˈvɪsərə] s Eingeweide pl

viscosity [vɪsˈkɑsɪti] s Viskosität f

viscount [ˈvaɪkaunt] s Vicomte m

viscountess [ˈvaɪkauntɪs] s Vicomtesse f

viscous [ˈvɪskəs] adj zähflüssig

vise [vaɪs] s Schraubstock m

visibility [ˌvɪzɪˈbɪlɪti] s Sichtbarkeit f; (meteor) Sicht f

visible [ˈvɪzɪbəl] adj sichtbar

visibly [ˈvɪzɪbli] adv zusehends

vision [ˈvɪʒən] s (faculty) Sehvermögen n; (appearance) Vision f; of great v. von großem Weitblick

visionary [ˈvɪʒəˌnɛri] adj visionär || s Visionär –in mf

visit [ˈvɪzɪt] s Besuch m; (official) Visite f || tr besuchen; (a museum, town) besichtigen

visitation [ˌvɪzɪˈteʃən] s Visitation f; **Visitation of Our Lady** Heimsuchung f Mariä

vis'iting hours' spl Besuchszeit f

vis'iting nurse' s Fürsorgerin f

visitor [ˈvɪzɪtər] s Besucher –in mf; **have visitors** Besuch haben

visor [ˈvaɪzər] s Schirm m; (on a helmet) Visier n

vista [ˈvɪstə] s (& fig) Ausblick m

Vistula [ˈvɪstʃulə] s Weichsel f

visual [ˈvɪʒuˑəl] adj visuell

vis'ual aids' spl Anschauungsmaterial n

visualize [ˈvɪʒuˑəˌlaɪz] tr sich [dat] vorstellen

vital [ˈvaɪtəl] adj (lebens)wichtig; (signs, functions) Lebens– || **vitals** spl edle Teile pl

vitality [vaɪˈtælɪti] s Lebenskraft f

vitalize [ˈvaɪtəˌlaɪz] tr beleben

vitamin [ˈvaɪtəmɪn] s Vitamin n

vi'tamin defi'ciency s Vitaminmangel m

vitiate [ˈvɪʃiˌet] tr verderben

vitreous [ˈvɪtriˑəs] adj glasartig

vitriolic [ˌvɪtriˈɑlɪk] adj (fig) beißend; (chem) Vitriol–

vituperate [vaɪˈt(j)upəˌret] tr schelten

vivacious [vɪˈveʃəs] adj lebhaft

vivid [ˈvɪvɪd] adj lebhaft

vivi·fy [ˈvɪvɪˌfaɪ] v (pret & pp –fied) tr beleben

vivisection [ˌvɪvɪˈsɛkʃən] s Vivisektion f

vixen [ˈvɪksən] s Füchsin f

viz. abbr nämlich

vizier [vɪˈzɪr] s Vezier m, Wesir m

vocabulary [voˈkæbjəˌlɛri] s (word range) Wortschatz m; (list) Wörterverzeichnis n

vocal [ˈvokəl] adj stimmlich, Stimm–; (outspoken) redselig

voc'al cord' s Stimmband n

vocalist [ˈvokəlɪst] s Sänger –in mf

vocalize [ˈvokəˌlaɪz] tr (phonet) vokalisieren || intr singen; (phonet) in e–n Vokal verwandelt werden

vocation [voˈkeʃən] s Beruf m; (relig) Berufung f

voca'tional guid'ance [voˈkeʃənəl] s Berufsberatung f

voca'tional school' s Berufsschule f

voca'tional train'ing s Berufsausbildung f

vocative [ˈvokətɪv] s Vokativ m

vociferous [voˈsɪfərəs] adj laut

vodka [ˈvadkə] s Wodka m

vogue [vog] s (herrschende) Mode f; **be in v.** Mode sein

voice [vɔɪs] s Stimme f; **in a low v.** mit leiser Stimme || tr äußern; (phonet) stimmhaft aussprechen

voiced adj (phonet) stimmhaft

voiceless [ˈvɔɪslɪs] adj stimmlos

void [vɔɪd] adj leer; (invalid) ungültig || s Leere f || tr für ungültig erklären; (the bowels) entleeren

volatile [ˈvaletɪl] adj (explosive) jähzornig; (changeable) unbeständig; (chem) flüchtig

volcanic [valˈkænɪk] adj vulkanisch

volca·no [valˈkeno] s (-noes & -nos) Vulkan m

volition [vəˈlɪʃən] s Wollen n; **of one's own v.** aus eigenem Antrieb

volley [ˈvali] s (of gunfire) Salve f; (of stones) Hagel m; (sport) Flugschlag m

vol'leyball' s Volleyball m

volt [volt] s Volt n

voltage [ˈvoltɪdʒ] s Spannung f

voluble [ˈvaljəbəl] adj redegewandt

volume [ˈvaljəm] s (book) Band m; (of a magazine series) Jahrgang m; (of sound) Lautstärke f; (amount) Ausmaß n; (of a container) Rauminhalt m; **speak volumes** Bände sprechen; **v. of sales** Umsatz m

vol'ume control' s Lautstärkeregler m

voluminous [vəˈluminəs] adj (writer) produktiv; (of great extent or size) umfangreich

voluntary [ˈvalənˌtɛri] adj freiwillig

volunteer [ˌvalənˈtɪr] adj Freiwilligen– || s Freiwillige mf || tr freiwillig anbieten || intr (for) sich freiwillig erbieten (für, zu)

voluptuary [vəˈlʌptʃuˑəˌɛri] s Wollüstling m

voluptuous [vəˈlʌptʃuˑəs] adj wollüstig

vomit [ˈvamɪt] s Erbrechen n || tr (er)brechen; (smoke) ausstoßen; (fire) speien; (lava) auswerfen || intr sich erbrechen

voodoo [ˈvudu] adj Wudu– || s Wudu m

voracious [vəˈreʃəs] adj gefräßig

voracity [vəˈræsɪti] s Gefräßigkeit f

vor·tex [ˈvorteks] s (-texes & -tices [tɪˌsiz]) (& fig) Wirbel m

votary [ˈvotəri] s Verehrer –in mf

vote [vot] s Stimme f; (act of voting) Abstimmung f; (right to vote) Stimmrecht n; **put to a v.** zur Abstimmung bringen || *tr (approve of, e.g., money)* (for) bewilligen (für); **v. down** niederstimmen || *intr* stimmen; **v. by acclamation** durch Zuruf stimmen; **v. for** wählen; **v. on** abstimmen über (*acc*)

vote′ get′ter [,getər] *s* Wahllokomotive *f*

vote′ of con′fidence *s* Vertrauensvotum *n*

vote′ of no′ con′fidence *s* Mißvertrauensvotum *n*

voter [′votər] *s* Wähler –in *mf*

vot′ing booth′ *s* Wahlzelle *f*

vot′ing machine′ *s* Stimmenzählapparat *m*

votive [′votɪv] *adj* Votiv-, Weih-

vo′tive of′fering *s* Weihgabe *f*

vouch [vaʊtʃ] *tr* bezeugen || *intr*—**v. for** bürgen für

voucher [′vaʊtʃər] *s* Beleg *m*

vouchsafe′ *tr* gewähren

vow [vaʊ] *s* Gelübde *n;* **take a vow of** geloben || *tr* geloben; *(revenge)* schwören; **vow to** *(inf)* sich [*dat*] geloben zu (*inf*)

vowel [′vaʊ·əl] *s* Selbstlaut *m*, Vokal *m*

voyage [′vɔɪ·ɪdʒ] *s* Reise *f; (by sea)* Seereise *f* || *intr* reisen

voyager [′vɔɪ·ɪdʒər] *s* Reisende *mf; (by sea)* Seereisende *mf*

V′-shaped′ *adj* keilförmig

V′-sign′ *s* Siegeszeichen *n*

vulcanize [′vʌlkə ,naɪz] *tr* vulkanisieren

vulgar [′vʌlgər] *adj* vulgär

vulgarity [vʌl′gærɪti] *s* Gemeinheit *f*

Vul′gar Lat′in *s* Vulgärlatein *n*

Vulgate [′vʌlget] *s* Vulgata *f*

vulnerable [′vʌlnərəbəl] *adj* verwundbar; *(position)* ungeschützt; *(fig)* angreifbar; **v. to** anfällig für

vulture [′vʌltʃər] *s* Geier *m*

W

W, w [′dʌbəl ,ju] *s* dreiunzwanzigster Buchstabe des englischen Alphabets

wad [wɑd] *s (of cotton)* Bausch *m; (of money)* Bündel *n; (of papers)* Stoß *m; (of tobacco)* Priem *m*

waddle [′wɑdəl] *s* Watscheln *n* || *intr* watscheln

wade [wed] *intr* waten; **w. into** (fig) anpacken; **w. through** (fig) sich mühsam durcharbeiten durch

wafer [′wefər] *s* Oblate *f*

waffle [′wɑfəl] *s* Waffel *f*

waf′fle i′ron *s* Waffeleisen *n*

waft [wæft], [wɑft] *tr & intr* wehen

wag [wæg] *s (nod)* Nicken *n; (shake)* Schütteln *n; (of the tail)* Wedeln *n; (mischievous person)* Schalk *m* || *v (pret & pp* **wagged;** *ger* **wagging)** *tr (the tail)* wedeln mit; *(nod)* nicken mit; *(shake)* schütteln || *intr (said of a tail)* wedeln; *(said of tongues)* nicht still sein

wage [wedʒ] *adj* Lohn- || *s* Lohn *m;* **wages** Lohn *m* || *tr (war)* führen

wage′ cut′ *s* Lohnabbau *m*

wage′ freeze′ *s* Lohnstopp *m*

wager [′wedʒər] *s* Wette *f;* **lay a w.** e-e Wette eingehen || *tr & intr* wetten

waggish [′wægɪʃ] *adj* schalkhaft

wagon [′wægən] *s* Wagen *m*

wag′on load′ *s* Wagenladung *f*

waif [wef] *s (child)* verwahrlostes Kind *n; (animal)* verwahrlostes Tier *n*

wail [wel] *s* Wehklage *f* || *intr (over)* wehklagen (*über acc*)

wain·scot [′wenskət] *s* Täfelung *f* || *v (pret & pp* **–scot[t]ed;** *ger* **–scot-[t]ing)** *tr* täfeln

waist [west] *s* Taille *f;* **strip to the w.** den Oberkörper freimachen

waist′-deep′ *adj* bis an die Hüften (reichend)

waist′line′ *s* Taille *f;* **watch one's w.** auf die schlanke Linie achten

wait [wet] *s* Warten *n;* **an hour's w.** e-e Stunde Wartezeit || *intr* warten; **that can w.** das hat Zeit; **w. for** *(a person)* warten auf (*acc*); *(e.g., an answer)* abwarten; **w. on** bedienen; **w. up for** aufbleiben und warten auf (*acc*)

wait′-and-see′ pol′icy *s* Politik *f* des Abwartens

waiter [′wetər] *s* Kellner *m;* **w.!** Herr Ober!

wait′ing line′ *s* Schlange *f*

wait′ing list′ *s* Warteliste *f*

wait′ing room′ *s* Warteraum *m; (e.g., in a railroad station)* Wartesaal *m*

waitress [′wetrɪs] *s* Kellnerin *f*

waive [wev] *tr* verzichten auf (*acc*)

waiver [′wevər] *s* Verzicht *m*

wake [wek] *s (at a funeral)* Totenwache *f; (naut)* Kielwasser *n;* **in the w. of** im Gefolge (*genit*) || *v (pret* **waked &** **woke** [wok]; *pp* **waked)** *tr* wecken; **w. up** aufwecken || *intr* erwachen; **w. up** aufwachen; **w. up to** (fig) bewußt werden (*acc*)

wakeful [′wekfəl] *adj* wachsam

waken [′wekən] *tr* (auf)wecken || *intr* erwachen

walk [wɔk] *s* Spaziergang *m; (gait)* Gang *m; (path)* Spazierweg *m;* **a five-minute w. to** fünf Minuten zu Fuß zu; **from all walks of life** aus allen Ständen; **go for a w.** spazierengehen; **take for a w.** spazierenführen || *tr (a dog)* spazierenführen; *(a person)* begleiten; *(a horse)* führen; *(the streets)* ablaufen || *intr* (zu Fuß) gehen, laufen; **w. off with** klauen; **w. out on** sitzenlassen; **w. up to** zugehen auf (*acc*)

walk′-away′ *s* (coll) leichter Sieg *m*

walker ['wɔkər] s Fußgänger –in *mf*
walkie-talkie ['wɔki'tɔki] s Sprechfunkgerät *n*
walk'-in' *adj* (*closet*) begehbar
walk'ing pa'pers *spl* Laufpaß *m*
walk'ing shoes' *spl* Straßenschuhe *pl*
walk'ing stick' s Spazierstock *m*
walk'-on' s (theat) Statist –in *mf*
walk'out' s Ausstand *m*
walk'-o'ver s (sport) leichter Sieg *m*
walk'-up' s Mietwohnung *f* ohne Fahrstuhl
wall [wɔl] s Mauer *f*; (*between rooms*) Wand *f* || *tr*—w. up vermauern
wall' brack'et s Konsole *f*
wall' clock' s Wanduhr *f*
wallet ['walɪt] s Brieftasche *f*
wall'flow'er s (coll) Wandblümchen *n*
wall' map' s Wandkarte *f*
wallop ['waləp] s Puff *m*; have a w. Schlagkraft haben || *tr* verprügeln; (*defeat*) schlagen
wal'loping *adj* (sl) mordsgroß
wallow ['walo] *intr* sich wälzen; w. in (fig) schwelgen in (*dat*)
wall'pa'per s Tapete *f* || *tr* tapezieren
walnut ['wɔlnət] s Walnuß *f*; (*wood*) Walnußholz *n*; (*tree*) Walnußbaum *m*
walrus ['wɔlrəs] s Walroß *n*
waltz [wɔlts] s Walzer *m* || *intr* Walzer tanzen
wan [wan] *adj* (*wanner; wannest*) bleich; (*smile*) schwach, matt
wand [wand] s Stab *m*; (*in magic*) Zauberstab *m*
wander ['wandər] *intr* wandern; (*from a subject*) abschweifen
wanderer ['wandərər] s Wanderer –in *mf*
wan'derlust' s Wanderlust *f*
wane [wen] s—be on the w. abnehmen || *intr* abnehmen
wangle ['wæŋgəl] *tr* sich [*dat*] erschwindeln
want [wɔnt] s Bedürfnis *n*; for w. of mangels (*genit*) || *tr* wollen; wanted (*sought, desired*) gesucht
want' ad' s Kleinanzeige *f*
want'ing *adj*—be w. in ermangeln (*genit*)
war [wɔr] s Krieg *m*; at war im Kriege; go to war with e–n Krieg beginnen gegen; make war on Krieg führen gegen || *v* (*pret & pp* warred; *ger* warring) *intr* kämpfen
warble ['wɔrbəl] s Trillern *n* || *intr* trillern
war' bond' s Kriegsanleihe *f*
war' cry' s Schlachtruf *m*
ward [wɔrd] s (*in a hospital*) Station *f*; (*of a city*) Bezirk *m*; (*person under protection*) Schützling *m*; (*person under guardianship*) Mündel *n*; (*guardianship*) Vormundschaft *f* || *tr*—w. off abwehren
warden ['wɔrdən] s Gefängnisdirektor *m*
ward'robe' s Garderobe *f*
ward'room' s (nav) Offiziersmesse *f*
ware [wer] s Ware *f*
ware'house' s Lagerhaus *n*, Warenlager *n*

ware'house'man s (–men) Lagerist *m*
war'fare' s Kriegsführung *f*, Krieg *m*
war' foot'ing s Kriegsbereitschaft *f*
war'head' s Gefechtskopf *m*
war'-horse' s (coll) alter Kämpe *m*
war'like' *adj* kriegerisch
war' lord' s Kriegsherr *m*
warm [wɔrm] *adj* warm; (*friends*) intim || *tr* wärmen; w. up aufwärmen || *intr*—w. up warm werden; (sport) in Form kommen
warm'-blood'ed *adj* warmblütig
warm'front' s Warmfront *f*
warm'-heart'ed *adj* warmherzig
warmonger ['wɔr,mʌŋgər] s Kriegshetzer –in *mf*
warmth [wɔrmθ] s Wärme *f*
warm'-up' s (sport) Lockerungsübungen *pl*
warn [wɔrn] *tr* (*against*) warnen (vor *dat*)
warn'ing s Warnung *f*; let this be a w. to you lassen Sie sich das zur Warnung dienen
warn'ing shot' s Warnschuß *m*
war' of attri'tion s Zermürbungskrieg *m*
warp [wɔrp] s (*of a board*) Verziehen *n* || *tr* (*wood*) verziehen; w. s.o.'s mind *in* verschroben machen || *intr* sich verziehen
war'path' s Kriegspfad *m*
warped *adj* (*wood*) verzogen; (*mind, opinion*) verschroben
war'plane' s Kampfflugzeug *n*
warrant ['wɔrənt] s (*justification*) Rechtfertigung *f*; (*authorization*) Berechtigung *f*; w. for arrest Haftbefehl *m* || *tr* (*justify*) rechtfertigen; (*guarantee*) garantieren
war'rant of'ficer s (mil) Stabsfeldwebel *m*; (nav) Deckoffizier *m*
warranty ['wɔrənti] s Gewährleistung *f*
war'ranty serv'ice s Kundendienst *m*
warren ['wɔrən] s Kaninchengehege *n*
war'ring *adj* kriegsführend
warrior ['wɔri·ər] s Krieger *m*
Warsaw ['wɔrsɔ] s Warschau *n*
war'ship' s Kriegsschiff *n*
wart [wɔrt] s Warze *f*
war'time' *adj* Kriegs– || s Kriegszeit *f*
war'-torn' *adj* vom Krieg verwüstet
wary ['weri] *adj* vorsichtig
war' zone' s Kriegsgebiet *n*
wash [wɔʃ] *adj* Wash– || s Wäsche *f*; (aer) Luftstrudel *m*; (paint) dünner Farbüberzug *m*; do the w. die Wäsche waschen || *tr* waschen; (metal) schlämmen; (paint) tuschen; (phot) wässern; w. ashore anschwemmen; w. away wegspülen; w. off abwaschen; w. out auswaschen; (a bridge) wegreißen; w. up aufwaschen || *intr* waschen; w. ashore ans Land spülen
washable ['wɔʃəbəl] *adj* waschbar
wash'-and-wear' *adj* bügelfrei
wash'ba'sin s Waschbecken *n*
wash'bas'ket s Wäschekorb *m*
wash'board' s Waschbrett *n*
wash'bowl' s Waschbecken *n*
wash'cloth' s Waschlappen *m*

wash'day' s Waschtag m
washed'-out' adj verwaschen; (tired) schlapp
washer ['wɔʃər] s Waschmaschine f; (of rubber) Dichtungsring m; (of metal) Unterlegscheibe f
washed'-up' adj (coll) erledigt
wash'er-wom'an s (-wom'en) Waschfrau f
wash'ing s Waschen n; (clothes) Wäsche f
wash'ing machine' s Waschmaschine f
wash'out' s Auswaschung f; (failure) Pleite f; (person who fails) Versager –in mf
wash'rag' s Waschlappen m
wash'room' s Waschraum m
wash'stand' s Waschtisch m
wash'tub' s Waschtrog m
wasp [wɑsp] s Wespe f
wasp' waist' s Wespentaille f
waste [west] adj (superfluous) überflüssig; (land) öde ‖ s (of material goods, time, energy) Verschwendung f; (waste material) Müll m; (wilderness) Wildnis f; go to w. vergeudet werden ‖ tr verschwenden, vergeuden ‖ intr—w. away verfallen
waste'bas'ket s Papierkorb m
wasteful ['westfəl] adj verschwenderisch
waste'land' s Ödland n
waste'pa'per s Makulatur f
waste'pipe' s Abflußrohr n
waste'prod'uct s Abfallprodukt n
wastrel ['westrəl] s Verschwender –in mf
watch [wɑtʃ] s Uhr f; (lookout) Wache f; be on the w. for acht haben auf (acc) ‖ tr (observe) beobachten; (guard) bewachen; (oversee) aufpassen auf (acc); **w. how I do it** passen Sie auf, wie ich es mache; **w. your step!** Vorsicht, Stufe! ‖ intr (keep guard) wachen; (observe) zuschauen; **w. for** abwarten; **w. over** überwachen; **w. out!** Vorsicht!; **w. out for** ausschauen nach; (some danger) sich hüten vor (dat); **w. out for oneself** sich vorsehen
watch'band' s Uhrarmband n
watch'case' s Uhrgehäuse n
watch' crys'tal s Uhrglas n
watch'dog' s Wachhund m
watch'dog commit'tee s Überwachungsausschuß m
watchful ['wɑtʃfəl] adj wachsam
watchfulness ['wɑtʃfəlnɪs] s Wachsamkeit f
watch'mak'er s Uhrmacher –in mf
watch'man s (-men) Wächter m
watch' pock'et s Uhrtasche f
watch' strap' s Uhrarmband n
watch'tow'er s Wachturm m
watch'word' s Kennwort n, Parole f
water ['wɔtər] s Wasser n; (body of water) Gewässer n; **pass w.** Wasser lassen ‖ tr (e.g., flowers) begießen; (fields) bewässern; (animals) tränken; (the garden, streets) sprengen; **w. down** (& fig) verwässern ‖ intr (said of the eyes) tränen; **my mouth**

waters das Wasser läuft mir im Mund zusammen
wa'ter boy' s Wasserträger m
wa'ter clos'et s Wasserklosett n
wa'tercol'or s (paint) Aquarellfarbe f; (painting) Aquarell n
wa'tercourse' s Wasserlauf m
wa'tercress' s Brunnenkresse f
wa'terfall' s Wasserfall m
wa'terfront' s Hafenviertel n
wa'ter heat'er s Warmwasserbereiter m
wa'tering can' s Wasserkanne f
wa'tering place' s (for cattle) Tränke f; (for tourists) Badeort m
wa'ter lev'el s Wasserstand m
wa'terlogged' adj vollgesogen
wa'ter main' s Wasserleitung f
wa'termark' s Wasserzeichen n
wa'ter mat'tress s Wasserbett n
wa'termel'on s Wassermelone f
wa'ter me'ter s Wasserzähler m
wa'ter pipe' s Wasserrohr n
wa'ter po'lo s Wasserball m
wa'ter pow'er s Wasserkraft f
wa'terproof' adj wasserdicht ‖ tr imprägnieren
wa'ter-repel'lent adj wasserabstoßend
wa'tershed' s Wasserscheide f
wa'ter-ski' intr wasserschifahren
wa'terspout' s (orifice) Wasserspeier m; (pipe) Ablaufrohr n
wa'ter supply' s Wasserversorgung f
wa'ter ta'ble s Grundwasserspiegel m
wa'ter tank' s Wasserbehälter m
wa'tertight' adj wasserdicht; (fig) eindeutig
wa'ter wag'on s—be on the w. Abstinenzler sein
wa'terway' s Wasserstraße f
wa'ter wheel' s (for raising water) Schöpfwerk n; (water-driven) Wasserrad n
wa'ter wings' spl Schwimmkissen n
wa'terworks' s Wasserwerk n
watery ['wɔtəri] adj wäss(e)rig
watt [wɑt] s Watt n
wattage ['wɑtɪdʒ] s Wattleistung f
wattles ['wɑtəlz] spl Flechtwerk s
watt'me'ter s Wattmeter m
wave [wev] s (fig, meteor, mil, phys, rad) Welle f; **w. of the hand** Wink m mit der Hand ‖ tr (a hat, flag) schwenken; (a hand, handkerchief) winken mit; (hair) wellen; **w. one's hands about** mit den Händen herumfuchteln; **w. s.o. away** j–n abwinken ‖ intr (said of a flag) wehen; (said of grain) wogen; (with the hand) winken; **w. to** zuwinken (dat)
wave'length' s Wellenlänge f
waver ['wevər] intr schweben, wanken
wavy ['wevi] adj wellenförmig; **w. line** Wellenlinie f
wax [wæks] adj Wachs– ‖ s Wachs n ‖ tr (the floor) bohnern; (skis) wachsen ‖ intr werden; (said of the moon) zunehmen; **wax and wane** zu– und abnehmen
wax' muse'um s Wachsfigurenkabinett n
wax' pa'per s Wachspapier n
way [we] adv weit; **way ahead** weit

voraus || *s* Weg *m;* *(manner)* Art *f;* *(means)* Mittel *n;* *(condition)* Verfassung *f;* *(direction)* Richtung *f;* **across the way** gegenüber; **a long way from** weit weg von; **a long way off** weit weg; **by the way** übrigens; **by way of** über *(acc);* **by way of comparison** vergleichsweise; **get s.th. out of the way** etw aus dem Wege schaffen; **get under way** in Gang kommen; **go all the way aufs Ganze gehen;** **go one's own way** aus der Reihe tanzen; **have a way with s.o.** mit j–m umzugehen verstehen; **have in the way of** *(merchandise)* haben an *(dat);* **have it both ways** es sich *[dat]* aussuchen können; **have one's own way** seinen Willen durchsetzen; **I'm on my way!** ich komme schon!; **in a way** gewissermaßen; **in no way** keineswegs; **in the way** im Weg; **in this way** auf diese Weise; **in what way** in welcher Hinsicht; **make one's way through the crowd** sich *[dat]* e–n Weg durch die Menge bahnen; **one way or another** irgendwie; **on the way** unterwegs; **on the way out** (fig) im Begriff unmodern zu werden; **see one's way clear** bereit sein; that way auf diese Weise; *(in that direction)* in jener Richtung; **the way it looks** voraussichtlich; **way back** Rückweg *m;* **way here** Herweg *m;* **way out** Ausgang *m;* (fig) Ausweg *m;* **way there** Hinweg *m*

wayfarer ['we͵ferər] *s* Wanderer *m*

way′lay′ *v (pret & pp* –laid) *tr* auflauern *(dat)*

way′ of life′ *s* Lebensweise *f*

way′ of think′ing *s* Denkweise *f*

ways′ and means′ *spl* Mittel und Wege *pl*

way′side′ *adj* an der Straße gelegen || *s* Wegrand *m;* **fall by the w.** dem Untergang anheimfallen

wayward ['weward] *adj* ungeraten

we [wi] *pers pron* wir

weak [wik] *adj* schwach

weaken ['wikən] *tr* (ab)schwächen || *intr* schwach werden

weakling ['wiklɪŋ] *s* Schwächling *m*

weak′-mind′ed *adj* willenlos

weakness ['wiknɪs] *s* (& fig) Schwäche *f*

weak′ spot′ *s* schwache Stelle *f*

weal [wil] *s* Strieme *f,* Striemen *m*

wealth [welθ] *s* (of) Reichtum *m* (an *dat)*

wealthy ['welθi] *adj* wohlhabend

wean [win] *tr (from)* entwöhnen *(genit)*

weapon ['wepən] *s* Waffe *f*

weaponry ['wepənri] *s* Bewaffnung *f*

wear [wer] *s (use)* Gebrauch *m; (durability)* Haltbarkeit *f; (clothing)* Kleidung *f; (wearing down)* Verschleiß *m* || *v (pret wore* [wor]; *pp* **worn** [worn]*)tr* tragen; **w. down** *(a heel)* abtreten; *(a person)* zermürben; **w. out** abnützen; *(tires)* abfahren; *(a person)* erschöpfen; **w. the pants in the family** die Hosen anhaben || *intr* sich tragen; **w. off** sich abtragen; **w.**

out sich abnützen; **w. thin** *(said of clothes)* fadenscheinig werden; *(said of patience)* zu Ende gehen

wearable ['werəbəl] *adj* tragbar

wear′ and tear′ [ter] *s* Verschleiß *m;* **takes a lot of w.** strapazierfähig sein

weariness ['wɪrɪnɪs] *s* Müdigkeit *f*

wearisome ['wɪrɪsəm] *adj* mühsam

wea·ry ['wɪri] *adj* müde || *v (pret & pp* –ried) *tr* ermüden || *intr* (of) müde werden *(genit)*

weasel ['wizəl] *s* Wiesel *n* || *intr*—**w. out** sich herauswinden aus

weather ['weðər] *s* Wetter *n;* **be under the w.** unpäßlich sein; **w. permitting** bei günstiger Witterung || *tr* dem Wetter aussetzen; *(the storm)* (fig) überstehen || *intr* verwittern

weath′erbeat′en *adj* verwittert

weath′er bu′reau *s* Wetterdienst *m*

weath′er condi′tions *spl* Wetterverhältnisse *pl*

weath′er fore′cast *s* Wettervoraussage *f*

weath′erman′ *s* (–men′) Wetteransager *m*

weath′er report′ *s* Wetterbericht *m*

weath′erstrip′ping *s* Dichtungsstreifen *pl*

weath′er vane′ *s* (& fig) Wetterfahne *f*

weave [wiv] *s* Webart *f* || *v (pret* **wove** [wov] *& weaved; pp* **woven** ['wovən]) *tr* weben; *(a rug)* wirken; *(a basket)* flechten; *(a wreath)* winden; **w. one's way through traffic** sich durch den Verkehr schlängeln || *intr* weben

weaver ['wivər] *s* Weber –in *mf*

web [web] *s (of a spider)* Spinngewebe *n; (of ducks)* Schwimmhaut *f;* **web of lies** Lügengewebe *n*

web′-foot′ed *adj* schwimmfüßig

wed [wed] *v (pret & pp* **wed** *&* **wedded;** *ger* **wedding)** *tr & intr* heiraten

wed′ding *adj (cake, present, day, reception)* Hochzeits–; *(ring)* Trau– || *s* Hochzeit *f; (ceremony)* Trauung *f*

wedge [wedʒ] *s* Keil *m* || *tr*—**w. in** einkeilen

wed′lock′ *s* Ehestand *m;* **out of w.** unehelich

Wednesday ['wenzde] *s* Mittwoch *m;* **on W.** am Mittwoch

wee [wi] *adj* winzig; **a wee bit** ein klein wenig

weed [wid] *s* Unkraut *n; (marijuana)* (sl) Marihuana *n; (cigarette)* (sl) Zigarette *f;* **pull weeds** jäten || *tr* jäten; **w. out** (fig) aussondern

weed′ kill′er *s* Unkrautvertilgungsmittel *n*

week [wik] *s* Woche *f;* **a w. from today** heute in e–r Woche; **a w. ago today** heute vor acht Tagen; **for weeks** wochenlang

week′day′ *s* Wochentag *m*

week′end′ *s* Wochenende *n*

weekender ['wik͵endər] *s* Wochenendausflügler –in *mf*

weekly ['wikli] *adj* wöchentlich; *(wages)* Wochen– || *s* Wochenblatt *n*

weep [wip] *v (pret & pp* **wept** [wept]) *tr & intr* weinen

weep'ing wil'low s Trauerweide f
weevil ['wiːvəl] s Rüsselkäfer m
weft [weft] s (tex) Schußfaden m
weigh [we] tr wiegen; (ponder) wägen; (anchor) lichten || intr wiegen; **w. heavily on** schwer lasten auf (dat)
weight [wet] s Gewicht n; (burden) Last f; (influence) Einfluß m; (importance) Bedeutung f; **carry great w.** sehr ins Gewicht fallen; **lift weights** Gewichte heben; **pull one's w.** das Seine tun; **throw one's w. about** sich breitmachen
weightless ['wetlɪs] adj schwerelos
weightlessness ['wetlɪsnɪs] s Schwerelosigkeit f
weighty ['weti] adj (& fig) gewichtig
weird [wɪrd] adj unheimlich
weir-do ['wɪrdo] s (-dos) (sl) Kauz m
welcome ['welkəm] adj willkommen; (news) erfreulich; **you're w.!** bitte sehr!; **you're w. to** (inf) es steht Ihnen frei zu (inf) || s Empfang m, Willkomm m || tr empfangen; (an opportunity) mit Freude begrüßen || interj (to) willkommen! (in dat)
weld [weld] s Schweißnaht n || tr & intr schweißen
welder ['weldər] s Schweißer –in mf
weld'ing s Schweißung f, Schweißarbeit f
welfare ['wel ˌfer] s Wohlfahrt f
wel'fare work'er s Wohlfahrtspfleger –in mf
well [wel] adj gesund; **all is w.** alles ist in Ordnung; **feel w.** sich wohl fühlen || adv gut, wohl; **as w.** ebenso; **as w. as** so gut wie; (in addition to) sowohl ... als auch; **he is doing w.** es geht ihm gut; **his company is doing w.** seine Firma geht gut; **leave w. enough alone** es gut sein lassen; **w. on in years** schon bejahrt; **w. on the way** mitten auf dem Wege; (fig) auf dem besten Wege; **w. over** weit über || s Brunnen m; (hole) Bohrloch n; (source) Quelle f || intr— **w. up** hervorquellen || interj na!; (in surprise) nanu!
well'-behaved' adj artig
well'-be'ing s Wohlergehen n
well'born' adj aus guter Familie
wellbred ['wel'bred] adj wohlerzogen
well'-deserved' adj wohlverdient
well'-disposed' adj (toward) wohlgesinnt (dat)
well-done ['wel'dʌn] adj (culin) durchgebraten || interj gut gemacht!
well'-dressed' adj gut angezogen
well'-found'ed adj wohlbegründet
well'-groomed' adj gut gepflegt
well'-heeled' adj (coll) steinreich
well'-informed' adj wohlunterrichtet
well'-inten'tioned adj wohlmeinend
well-kept ['wel'kept] adj gut gepflegt; (secret) gut gehütet
well'-known' adj wohlbekannt
well'-mean'ing adj wohlmeinend
well'-nigh' adv fast
well'-off' adj wohlhabend, vermögend
well'-preserved' adj gut erhalten
well-read ['wel'red] adj belesen

well'-spent' adj (money) gut verwendet; (time) gut verbracht
well'spring' s Brunnquell m
well'-thought'-of' adj angesehen
well'-timed' adj wohl berechnet
well-to-do ['welto'du] adj wohlhabend
well-wisher ['wel ˌwɪʃər] s Gratulant –in mf
well'-worn' adj (clothes) abgetragen; (phrase, subject) abgedroschen
Welsh [welʃ] adj walisisch || s Walisisch n; **the W.** die Waliser pl || **welsh** intr—**welsh on** (a promise) brechen
Welsh' rab'bit or **rare'bit** ['rerbɪt] s geröstete Käseschnitte f
welt [welt] s Striemen m
welter ['weltər] s Durcheinander n || intr sich wälzen
wel'terweight' s Weltergewichtler m
wel'terweight divi'sion s Weltergewicht n
wench [wentʃ] s Dirne f, Weibsbild n
wend [wend] tr—**w. one's way** seinen Weg nehmen
werewolf ['wer ˌwʌlf] s Werwolf m
west [west] adj westlich || adv nach Westen || s Westen m
western ['westərn] adj westlich || s (cin) Wildwestfilm m
West' Ger'many s Westdeutschland n
West' In'dies, the ['ɪndiz] spl Westindien n
Westphalia [ˌwest'felɪ·ə] s Westfalen n
westward ['westwərd] adv westwärts
wet [wet] adj (wetter; wettest) naß; **all wet** (coll) auf dem Holzwege || v (pret & pp wet & wetted; ger wetting) tr naß machen
wet' blan'ket s (fig) Miesepeter m
wet' nurse' s Amme f
whack [wæk] s (coll) Klaps m || tr (coll) klapsen
whale [wel] s Wal(fisch) m; **have a w. of a time** sich großartig unterhalten
whaler ['welər] s Walfänger m
wharf [wɔrf] s (wharves [wɔrvz]) Kaianlage f
what [wɑt] interr adj welcher, was für ein || interr pron was; **so w.?** na und?; **w. about me?** und was geschieht mit mir?; **w. if** was geschieht, wenn; **w. is more** außerdem; **w. next?** was noch?; **w. of it?** was ist da schon dabei?; **what's new?** was gibt es Neues? **what's that to you?** was geht Sie das an? || interj was für ein
whatev'er adj welch ... auch immer; **no ... w.** überhaupt kein || pron was auch immer; **w. I have** alles, was ich habe; **w. you please** was Sie wollen
what'not' s—**and w.** und was weiß ich noch (alles)
what's-his-name' s (coll) Dingsda m
wheal [wil] s Pustel f; (welt) Striemen m
wheat [wit] s Weizen m
wheedle ['hwidəl] tr—**w. s.o. into** (ger) j-n beschwatzen zu (inf); **w. s.th. out of s.o.** j-m etw abschwatzen

wheel [wil] *s* Rad *n;* **at the w.** (aut) am Steuer || *tr* fahren || *intr* sich drehen; **w. around** sich umdrehen

wheelbarrow ['wil,bæro] *s* Schubkarre *f*

wheel'chair' *s* Krankenfahrstuhl *m*

wheeler-dealer ['wilər'dilər] *s* Drahtzieher –in *mf*

wheeze [wiz] *s* Schnaufen *n* || *intr* schnaufen

whelp [welp] *s* Welpe *m* || *tr* werfen

when [wen] *adv* wann || *conj* (*once in the past*) als; (*whenever; at a future time*) wenn

whence [wens] *adv & conj* woher

whenev'er *conj* wenn, wann immer

where [wɛr] *adv & conj* wo; (*whereto*) wohin; **from w.** woher

whereabouts ['wɛrə,bauts] *adv* wo ungefähr || *s & spl* Verbleib *m*

whereas' *conj* während, wohingegen

whereby' *conj* wodurch

where'fore' *adv & conj* weshalb

wherefrom' *adv* woher

wherein' *adv & conj* worin

whereof' *adv & conj* wovon

whereto' *adv* wohin

where'upon' *adv* worauf, wonach

wherever [wer'evər] *conj* wo auch

wherewith' *adv* womit

wherewithal ['werwið,ol] *s* Geldmittel *pl*

whet [wet] *v* (*pret & pp* **whetted;** *ger* **whetting**) *tr* wetzen, schleifen; (*the appetite*) anregen

whether ['weðər] *conj* ob

whet'stone' *s* Wetzstein *m,* Schleifstein *m*

whew [hwju] *interj* hui!; ui!

which [wɪtʃ] *interr adj* welcher || *interr pron* welcher || *rel pron* der, welcher

whichev'er *rel adj & rel pron* welcher

whiff [wɪf] *s* Geruch *m,* Nasevoll *f*

while [waɪl] *s* Weile *f* || *conj* während || *tr*—**w. away** sich [*dat*] vertreiben

whim [wɪm] *s* Laune *f,* Grille *f*

whimper ['wɪmpər] *s* Wimmern *n* || *tr & intr* wimmern

whimsical ['wɪmzɪkəl] *adj* schrullig

whine [waɪn] *s* Wimmern *n;* (*of a siren, engine, storm*) Heulen *n* || *intr* wimmern; heulen

whin-ny ['wɪni] *s* Wiehern *n* || *v* (*pret & pp* –nied) *intr* wiehern

whip [wɪp] *s* Peitsche *f* || *v* (*pret & pp* **whipped;** *ger* **whipping**) *tr* peitschen; (*egg whites*) zu Schaum schlagen; (*defeat*) schlagen; **w. out** blitzschnell ziehen; **w. up** (*a meal*) hervorzaubern; (*enthusiasm*) erregen

whip'lash' *s* Peitschenhieb *m;* (fig) Peitschenhiebeffekt *n*

whipped' cream' *s* Schlagsahne *f*

whipper-snapper ['wɪpər,snæpər] *s* Frechdachs *m*

whip'ping *s* Prügel *pl*

whip'ping boy' *s* Prügelknabe *m*

whip'ping post' *s* Schandpfahl *m*

whir [wʌr] *s* Schnurren *n* || *v* (*pret & pp* **whirred;** *ger* **whirring**) *intr* schnurren

whirl [wʌrl] *s* Wirbel *m;* **give s.th. a w.** (coll) etw ausprobieren || *tr* wirbeln || *intr* wirbeln; **my head is whirling** mir ist schwindlig

whirl'pool' *s* Strudel *m,* Wirbel *m*

whirl'wind' *s* Wirbelwind *m*

whirlybird ['wʌrli,bʌrd] *s* (coll) Hubschrauber *m*

whisk [wɪsk] *s* Wedel *m;* (culin) Schneebesen *m* || *tr* wischen; **w. away** (fig) eilends mitnehmen; **w. off** wegfegen

whisk' broom' *s* Kleiderbesen *m*

whiskers ['wɪskərz] *spl* Bart *m;* (on the cheeks) Backenbart *m;* (of a cat) Barthaare *pl*

whiskey ['wɪski] *s* Whisky *m*

whisper ['wɪspər] *s* Flüsterton *m* || *tr & intr* flüstern

whistle ['wɪsəl] *s* (*sound*) Pfiff *m;* (*device*) Trillerpfeife *f;* **wet one's.** sich [*dat*] die Nase begießen || *tr* pfeifen || *intr* pfeifen; (*said of the wind, bullet*) sausen; **w. for** (coll) vergeblich warten auf (*acc*)

whit [wɪt] *adj* weiß; **not care a w. about** sich keinen Deut kümmern um

white [waɪt] *adj* weiß; **w. as a sheet** kreidebleich || *s* Weiß *n;* (of the eye) Weiße *f*

white'caps' *spl* Schaumkronen *pl*

white'-col'lar work'er *s* Angestellte *mf*

white'fish' *s* Weißfisch *m*

white'-haired' *adj* weißhaarig

white'-hot' *adj* weißglühend

white' lie' *s* Notlüge *f*

white' meat' *s* weißes Fleisch *n*

whiten ['waɪtən] *tr* weiß machen || *intr* weiß werden

whiteness ['waɪtnɪs] *s* Weiße *f*

white' slav'ery *s* Mädchenhandel *m*

white' tie' *s* Frackschleife *f;* (formal) Frack *m*

white'wash' *s* Tünche *f;* (fig) Beschönigung *f* || *tr* tünchen; (fig) beschönigen

whither ['wɪðər] *adv* wohin

whitish ['waɪtɪʃ] *adj* weißlich

whittle ['wɪtəl] *tr* schnitzeln; **w. away** (or **down**) verringern || *intr*—**w. away at** herumschnitzeln an (*dat*); (fig) verringern

whiz(z) [wɪz] *s* Zischen *n;* (fig) Kanone *f* || *v* (*pret & pp* **whizzed;** *ger* **whizzing**) *intr* zischen; **w. by** flitzen

who [hu] *interr pron* wer; **who the devil** wer zum Teufel || *rel pron* der; **he who** wer

whoa [wo] *interj* halt!

whoev'er *rel pron* wer, wer auch immer

whole [hol] *adj* ganz || *s* Ganze *n;* **as a w.** im großen und ganzen

whole'-heart'ed *adj* ernsthaft

whole' note' *s* (mus) ganze Note *f*

whole' rest' *s* (mus) ganze Pause *f*

whole'sale' *adj* Massen–; (com) Großhandels– || *adv* en gros || *s* Großhandel *m* || *tr* en gros verkaufen || *intr* im großen handeln

wholesaler ['hol,selər] *s* Großhändler –in *mf*

wholesome ['holsəm] *adj* gesund; (*food*) zuträglich

whole'-wheat' bread' *s* Vollkornbrot *n*

wholly ['holi] *adv* ganz, völlig

whom [hum] *interr pron* wen; to w. wem || *rel pron* den, welchen; to w. dem, welchem

whomev'er *rel pron* wen auch immer; to w. wem auch immer

whoop [hup], [hwup] *s* Ausruf *m* || *tr*—w. it up Radau machen

whoop'ing cough' *s* Keuchhusten *m*

whopper ['wɑpər] *s* Mordsding *n*; (*lie*) (coll) faustdicke Lüge *f*

whop'ping *adj* (coll) enorm, Riesen-

whore [hor] *s* Hure *f* || *intr*—w. around huren

whose [huz] *interr pron* wessen || *rel pron* dessen

why [waɪ] *adv* warum; that's why deswegen; why, there you are! da sind Sie ja!; why, yes! aber ja! || *s* Warum *n*; the whys and the wherefores das Warum und Weshalb

wick [wɪk] *s* Docht *m*

wicked ['wɪkɪd] *adj* (*evil*) böse; (*roguish*) boshaft; (*vicious*) bösartig; (*unpleasant*) ekelhaft; (*cold, pain, storm, wound*) (coll) schlimm; (*fantastic*) (coll) großartig

wicker ['wɪkər] *adj* (*basket, chair*) Weiden- || *s* (*wickerwork*) Flechtwerk *n*

wide [waɪd] *adj* breit; (*selection*) reich || *adv* weit

wide'-an'gle lens' *s* Weitwinkelobjektiv *n*

wide'-awake' *adj* hellwach

wide'-eyed' *adj* mit weit aufgerissenen Augen; (*innocence*) naiv

widely ['waɪdli] *adv* weit

widen ['waɪdən] *tr* ausweiten, verbreiten || *intr* sich ausweiten

wide'-o'pen *adj* weit geöffnet

wide' screen' *s* (cin) Breitleinwand *f*

wide'spread' *adj* weitverbreitet; (*damage*) weitgehend

widow ['wɪdo] *s* Witwe *f*

widower ['wɪdo·ər] *s* Witwer *m*

wid'owhood' *s* Witwenstand *m*

width [wɪdθ] *s* Breite *f*; in w. breit

wield [wild] *tr* (*a weapon*) führen; (*power, influence*) ausüben

wife [waɪf] *s* (*wives* [waɪvz]) Frau *f*

wig [wɪg] *s* Perücke *f*

wiggle ['wɪgəl] *s* Wackeln *n* || *tr* wackeln mit

wigwag ['wɪg,wæg] *s* Winksignal *n*

wigwam ['wɪgwɑm] *s* Wigwam *m* & *n*

wild [waɪld] *adj* wild; w. about scharf auf (*acc*); go w. verwildern; grow w. (*become neglected*) verwildern; make s.o. w. (coll) j-n rasend machen || *adv*—grow w. (*grow in the wild*) wild wachsen; run w. verwildern

wild' boar' *s* Wildschwein *n*

wild' card' *s* wilde Karte *f*

wild'cat' *s* Wildkatze *f*

wild'cat strike' *s* wilder Streik *m*

wilderness ['wɪldərnɪs] *s* Wildnis *f*

wild'fire' *s*—like w. wie Lauffeuer

wild' flow'er *s* Feldblume *f*

wild'-goose' chase' *s*—go on a w. sich [*dat*] vergeblich Mühe machen

wild'life' *s* Wild *n*

wild' oats' *spl*—sow one's w. sich [*dat*] die Hörner abstoßen

wile [waɪl] *s* List *f* || *tr*—w. away sich [*dat*] vertreiben

will [wɪl] *s* Wille(n) *m*; (jur) Testament *n*; at w. nach Belieben || *tr* (*bequeath*) vermachen || *v* (*pret & cond* would [wʊd]) *aux* werden

willful ['wɪlfəl] *adj* absichtlich; (*stubborn*) eigensinnig

William ['wɪljəm] *s* Wilhelm *m*

will'ing *adj* bereitwillig; be w. to (*inf*) bereit sein zu (*inf*)

willingly ['wɪlɪŋli] *adv* gern

willingness ['wɪlɪŋnɪs] *s* Bereitwilligkeit *f*

will-o'-the-wisp ['wɪləðə'wɪsp] *s* (& fig) Irrlicht *n*

willow ['wɪlo] *s* Weide *f*

willowy ['wɪlo·i] *adj* biegsam

will' pow'er *s* Willenskraft *f*

willy-nilly ['wɪli'nɪli] *adv* wohl oder übel

wilt [wɪlt] *tr* verwelken lassen || *intr* verwelken

wilt'ed *adj* welk

wily ['waɪli] *adj* schlau, listig

wimple ['wɪmpəl] *s* Kinntuch *n*

win [wɪn] *s* Gewinn *m*; (sport) Sieg *m* || *v* (*pret & pp* won [wʌn]; *ger* winning) *tr* gewinnen; win over to one's side auf seine Seite ziehen || *intr* gewinnen, siegen

wince [wɪns] *s* Zucken *n* || *intr* zucken

winch [wɪntʃ] *s* (*windlass*) Winde *f*; (*handle*) Kurbel *f*; (min, naut) Haspel *f* & *m*

wind [wɪnd] *s* Wind *m*; break w. e-n Darmwind lassen; get w. of Wind bekommen von; take the w. out of s.o.'s sails j-m den Wind aus den Segeln nehmen; there is s.th. in the w. es liegt etw in der Luft || [waɪnd] *v* (*pret & pp* wound [waʊnd]) *tr* wickeln, winden; (*a timepiece*) aufziehen; w. up aufwickeln; (*affairs*) abwickeln; (*a speech*) abschließen || *intr* (*said of a river, road*) sich winden; w. around (*said of a plant*) sich ranken um

windbag ['wɪnd,bæg] *s* (coll) Schaumschläger *m* in *mf*

windbreak ['wɪnd,brek] *s* Windschutz *m*

windbreaker ['wɪnd,brekər] *s* Windjacke *f*

winded ['wɪndɪd] *adj* außer Atem, atemlos

windfall ['wɪnd,fɔl] *s* (*fallen fruit*) Fallobst *n*; (fig) Glücksfall *m*

wind'ing road' ['waɪndɪŋ] *s* Serpentinenstraße *f*; (public sign) kurvenreiche Straße *f*

wind'ing sheet' ['waɪndɪŋ] *s* Leichentuch *n*

wind' in'strument [wɪnd] *s* Blasinstrument *n*

windlass ['wɪndləs] *s* Winde *f*

windmill ['wɪnd,mɪl] *s* Windmühle *f*

window [ˈwɪndo] *s* Fenster *n; (of a ticket office)* Schalter *m; (for display)* Schaufenster *n*

win′dow display′ *s* Schaufensterauslage *f*

win′dow dress′er *s* Schaufensterdekorateur –in *mf*

win′dow dress′ing *s* Schaufensterdekoration *f*

win′dow en′velope *s* Fensterumschlag *m*

win′dow frame′ *s* Fensterrahmen *m*

win′dowpane′ *s* Fensterscheibe *f*

win′dow screen′ *s* Fliegengitter *n*

win′dow shade′ *s* Rollvorhang *m*, Rollo *n*

win′dow-shop′ *v (pret & pp* –shopped; *ger* –shopping) *intr* e-n Schaufensterbummel machen

win′dow shut′ter *s* Fensterladen *m*

win′dow sill′ *s* Fensterbrett *n*

windpipe [ˈwɪndˌpaɪp] *s* Luftröhre *f*

windshield [ˈwɪndˌʃild] *s* Windschutzscheibe *f*

wind′shield wash′er *s* Scheibenwäscher *m*

wind′shield wip′er *s* Scheibenwischer *m*

windsock [ˈwɪndˌsak] *s* Windsack *m*

windstorm [ˈwɪndˌstɔrm] *s* Sturm *m*

wind′ tun′nel [wɪnd] *s* Windkanal *m*

wind-up [ˈwaɪndˌʌp] *s (of affairs)* Abwicklung *f; (of a speech)* Schluß *m*

windward [ˈwɪndwərd] *adj (side)* Wind– ‖ *adv* windwärts ‖ *s* Windseite *f;* turn to w. anluven

windy [ˈwɪndi] *adj* windig; *(speech)* weitschweifig; *(person)* redselig

wine [waɪn] *s* Wein *m* ‖ *tr* mit Wein bewirten

wine′ cel′lar *s* Weinkeller *m*

wine′glass′ *s* Weinglas *n*

winegrower [ˈwaɪnˌgro·ər] *s* Weinbauer –in *mf*

wine′grow′ing *s* Weinbau *m*

wine′ list′ *s* Weinkarte *f*

wine′ press′ *s* Weinpresse *f*

winery [ˈwaɪnəri] *s* Weinkellerei *f*

wine′skin′ *s* Weinschlauch *m*

wing [wɪŋ] *s (of a bird, building, party)* Flügel *m; (unit of three squadrons)* Geschwader *n; (theat)* Kulisse *f* ‖ *tr (shoot)* in den Flügel treffen; **w. one′ way** dahinfliegen

wing′ chair′ *s* Ohrensessel *m*

wing′ nut′ *s* Flügelmutter *f*

wing′spread′ *s* Spannweite *f*

wink [wɪŋk] *s* Augenwink *m;* **quick as a w.** im Nu ‖ *intr* blinzeln; **w. at** zublinzeln *(dat); (overlook)* ein Auge zudrücken bei *(dat)*

winner [ˈwɪnər] *s* Gewinner –in *mf*, Sieger –in *mf; (e.g., winning ticket)* Treffer *m*

win′ning *adj (e.g., smile)* gewinnend; *(sport)* siegreich ‖ **winnings** *spl* Gewinn *m*

winsome [ˈwɪnsəm] *adj* reizend

winter [ˈwɪntər] *s* Winter *m* ‖ *intr* überwintern

winterize [ˈwɪntəˌraɪz] *tr* winterfest machen

wintry [ˈwɪntri] *adj* winterlich; *(fig)* frostig

wipe [waɪp] *tr* wischen; **w. clean** abwischen; **w. out** auswischen; *(e.g., a debt)* tilgen; *(destroy)* vernichten; *(fin)* ruinieren; **w. up** aufwischen

wire [waɪr] *s* Draht *m; (telg)* Telegramm *n;* **get in under the w.** es gerade noch schaffen ‖ *tr* mit Draht versehen; *(a house)* (elec) elektrische Leitungen legen in *(dat); (a message)* drahten; *(a person)* telegraphieren *(dat)*

wire′ cut′ter *s* Drahtschere *f*

wire′draw′ *v (pret* –drew; *pp* –drawn) *tr* drahtziehen

wire′ entan′glement *s* Drahtverhau *m*

wire′ gauge′ *s* Drahtlehre *f*

wire′-haired′ *adj* drahthaarig

wireless [ˈwaɪrlɪs] *adj* drahtlos

wire′ nail′ *s* Drahtnagel *m*

Wire′pho′to *s* (–tos) (trademark) Bildtelegramm *n*

wire′ record′er *s* Drahttonaufnahmegerät *n*

wire′tap′ *s* Abhören *n* ‖ *v (pret & pp* –tapped; *ger* –tapping) *tr* abhören

wir′ing *s* Leitungen *pl;* **do the w.** die elektrischen Leitungen legen

wiry [ˈwaɪri] *adj* drahtig

wisdom [ˈwɪzdəm] *s* Weisheit *f*

wis′dom tooth′ *s* Weisheitszahn *m*

wise [waɪz] *adj (person, decision)* klug; *(impertinent)* naseweis; **be w. to** sich *[dat]* klar werden über *(acc);* **put s.o. w. to** j-n einweihen in *(acc)* ‖ *s*—**in no w.** keineswegs ‖ *intr*—**w. up** endlich mal vernünftig werden

wise′a′cre *s* Neunmalkluge *f*

wise′crack′ *s* schnippische Bemerkung *f*

wise′ guy′ *s* (sl) Naseweis *m*

wisely [ˈwaɪzli] *adv* wohlweislich

wish [wɪʃ] *s* Wunsch *m* ‖ *tr* wünschen ‖ *intr*—**w. for** sich *[dat]* wünschen

wish′bone′ *s* Gabelbein *n*

wish′ful think′ing [ˈwɪʃfəl] *s* ein frommer Wunsch *m*

wishy-washy [ˈwɪʃiˌwaʃi] *adj* charakterlos; **be w.** ein Waschlappen sein

wisp [wɪsp] *s (of hair)* Strähne *f*

wistful [ˈwɪstfəl] *adj* versonnen

wit [wɪt] *s* Geist *m; (person)* geistreicher Mensch *m;* **be at one′s wits′ end** sich *[dat]* keinen Rat mehr wissen; **keep one′s wits about one** e-n klaren Kopf behalten; **live by one′s wits** sich durchschlagen

witch [wɪtʃ] *s* Hexe *f*

witch′craft′ *s* Hexerei *f*

witch′ doc′tor *s* Medizinmann *m*

witch′ ha′zel *s* Zaubernuß *f; (ointment)* Präparat *n* aus Zaubernuß

witch′ hunt′ *s* Hexenjagd *f*

with [wɪð], [wɪθ] *prep* mit *(dat); (at the house of)* bei *(dat); (because of)* vor *(dat), e.g.,* **green w. envy** grün vor Neid; *(despite)* trotz *(genit);* **not be w. it** nicht bei der Sache sein

with′draw′ *v (pret* –drew; *pp* –drawn) *tr* zurückziehen; *(money)* abheben ‖ *intr* sich zurückziehen

withdrawal [wɪð'drɔ‧əl] *s* Zurückziehung *f*; (*retraction*) Zurücknahme *f*; (*from a bank*) Abhebung *f*; (mil) Rückzug *m*

withdraw′al slip′ *s* Abhebungsformular *n*

wither ['wɪðər] *intr* verwelken

with·hold′ *v* (*pret & pp* **–held**) *tr* (*pay*) einbehalten; (*information*) (*from*) vorenthalten (*dat*)

withhold′ing tax′ *s* einbehaltene Steuer *f*

within′ *adv* drin(nen); *from w.* von innen || *prep* (*time*) binnen (*dat*), innerhalb von (*dat*); (*place*) innerhalb (*genit*); *w. walking distance* in Gehweite

without′ *adv* draußen || *prep* ohne (*acc*); *w.* (*ger*) ohne zu (*inf*), ohne daß; *w. reason* ohne allen Anlaß

with·stand′ *v* (*pret & pp* **–stood**) *tr* widerstehen (*dat*)

witness ['wɪtnɪs] *s* Zeuge *m*, Zeugin *f*; (*evidence*) Zeugnis *n*; *bear w. to* Zeugnis ablegen von; *in w. whereof* zum Zeugnis dessen; *w. for the defense* Entlastungszeuge *m*; *w. for the prosecution* Belastungszeuge *m* || *tr* (*an event*) anwesend sein bei; (*an accident, crime*) Augenzeuge sein (*genit*); (*e.g., a contract, will*) als Zeuge unterschreiben

wit′ness stand′ *s* Zeugenstand *n*

witticism ['wɪtɪˌsɪzəm] *s* Witzelei *f*

wittingly ['wɪtɪŋli] *adv* wissentlich

witty ['wɪti] *adj* geistreich, witzig

wizard ['wɪzərd] *s* Hexenmeister *m*

wizardry ['wɪzərdri] *s* (& fig) Hexerei *f*

wizend ['wɪzənd] *adj* runzelig

wobble ['wɑbəl] *intr* wackeln

wobbly ['wɑbli] *adj* wackelig

woe [wo] *s* Weh *n* || *interj*—**woe is me!** weh mir!

woebegone ['wobɪˌgɔn] *adj* jammervoll

woeful ['wofəl] *adj* jammervoll

wolf [wʊlf] *s* (**wolves** [wʊlvz]) Wolf *m*; (coll) Schürzenjäger *m*; *cry w.* blinden Alarm schlagen; *keep the w. from the door* sich über Wasser halten || *tr*—*w. down* verschlingen

wolf′pack′ *s* Wolfsrudel *n*; (nav) U-bootrudel *n*

wolfram ['wʊlfrəm] *s* (chem) Wolfram *n*; (mineral) Wolframit *n*

woman ['wʊmən] *s* (**women** ['wɪmən]) Frau *f*

wom′an doc′tor *s* Ärztin *f*

wom′anhood′ *s* Frauen *pl*; *reach w. e-e* Frau werden

womanish ['wʊmənɪʃ] *adj* weibisch

wom′ankind′ *s* Frauen *pl*

womanly ['wʊmənli] *adj* fraulich

womb [wʊm] *s* Mutterleib *m*

wom′enfolk′ *spl* Weibsvolk *n*

wom′en's dou′bles *spl* (tennis) Damendoppelspiel *n*

wom′en's sin′gles *spl* (tennis) Dameneinzelspiel *n*

wonder ['wʌndər] *s* Wunder *n* || *intr* (*be surprised*) sich wundern; (*ask*

oneself) sich fragen; (*reflect*) überlegen; *wonder at* sich verwundern über (*acc*)

wonderful ['wʌndərfəl] *adj* wunderbar

won′derland′ *s* Wunderland *n*

won′der work′er *s* Wundertäter –in *mf*

wont [wʌnt], [wɔnt] *adj*—*be w. to* (*inf*) pflegen zu (*inf*) || *s* Gepflogenheit *f*

wont′ed *adj* gewöhnlich, üblich

woo [wu] *tr* den Hof machen (*dat*)

wood [wʊd] *s* Holz *n*; *out of the woods* (fig) über den Berg; *woods* Wald *m*

wood′ al′cohol *s* Methylalkohol *m*

woodbine ['wʊdˌbaɪn] *s* Geißblatt *n*; (*Virginia creeper*) wilder Wein *m*

wood′ carv′ing *s* Holzschnitzerei *f*

wood′chuck′ *s* Murmeltier *n*

wood′cock′ *s* Holzschnepfe *f*

wood′cut′ *s* (*block*) Holzplatte *f*; (*print*) Holzschnitt *m*

wood′cut′ter *s* Holzfäller *m*

wood′ed *adj* bewaldet

wooden ['wʊdən] *adj* (& fig) hölzern

wood′ engrav′ing *s* Holzschnitt *m*

wood′en leg′ *s* Stelzbein *n*

wood′en shoe′ *s* Holzschuh *m*

woodland ['wʊdlənd] *adj* Wald– || *s* Waldland *n*

wood′man *s* (**–men**) Holzhauer *m*

woodpecker ['wʊdˌpekər] *s* Specht *m*

wood′ pi′geon *s* Ringeltaube *f*

wood′pile′ *s* Holzhaufen *m*

wood′pulp′ *s* Holzfaserstoff *m*

wood′ screw′ *s* Holzschraube *f*

wood′shed′ *s* Holzschuppen *m*

woods′man *s* (**–men**) Förster *m*; (*lumberman*) Holzhauer *m*

wood′winds′ *spl* Holzblasinstrumente *pl*

wood′work′ *s* Holzarbeit *f*; (*structure in wood*) Gebälk *n*

wood′work′er *s* Holzarbeiter –in *mf*

wood′worm′ *s* (ent) Holzwurm *m*

woody ['wʊdi] *adj* waldig; (*woodlike*) holzig

wooer ['wu‧ər] *s* Verehrer *m*

woof [wuf] *s* (*of a dog*) unterdrücktes Bellen *n*; (tex) Gewebe *n*

woofer ['wufər] *s* (rad) Tieftöner *m*

wool [wʊl] *adj* wollen || *s* Wolle *f*

woolen ['wʊlən] *adj* wollen, Woll– || **woolens** *spl* Wollwaren *pl*

woolly ['wʊli] *adj* wollig; (*e.g., thinking*) verschwommen

woozy ['wuzi] *adj* benebelt

word [wʌrd] *s* Wort *n*; *be as good as one's w.* zu seinem Wort stehen; *by w. of mouth* mündlich; *get w. from* Nachricht haben von; *give one's w.* sein Wort geben; *have a w. with* ein ernstes Wort sprechen mit; *have words* e–n Wortwechsel haben; *in a w.* mit e–m Wort; *in other words* mit anderen Worten; *in so many words* ausdrücklich; *leave w.* Bescheid hinterlassen; *not another w.!* kein Wort mehr!; *not a w. of truth in it* kein wahres Wort daran; *put in a good w. for s.o.* ein gutes Wort für j–n einlegen; *put into words* in

Worte kleiden; **put words in s.o.'s mouth** j-m Worte in den Mund legen; **send w. to s.o.** j-n benachrichtigen; **take s.o.'s w. for it** j-n beim Wort nehmen; **w. for w.** Wort für Wort || *tr* formulieren

word'-for-word' *adj* wörtlich

word'ing *s* Formulierung *f*

word' of hon'or *s* Ehrenwort *n*; **w.!** auf mein Wort!

word' or'der *s* Wortfolge *f*

wordy ['wʌrdi] *adj* wortreich

work [wʌrk] *s* Arbeit *f*; (*production, book*) Werk *n*; **be in the works** (coll) im Gang sein; **get to w.** sich an die Arbeit machen; (*travel to work*) zum Arbeitsplatz kommen; **give s.o. the works** (coll) j-n fertigmachen; **have one's w. cut out** zu tun haben; **it took a lot of w. to** (*inf*) es hat viel Arbeit gekostet zu (*inf*); **make short w. of** kurzen Prozeß machen mit; **out of w.** arbeitslos; **works** (horol) Uhrwerk *n* || *tr* (*a machine*) bedienen; (*a pedal*) treten; (*a mine*) abbauen; (*the soil*) bearbeiten; (*metal*) treiben; (*dough*) kneten; (*wonders*) wirken; **w. in** einarbeiten; **w. off** (*a debt*) abarbeiten; **w. oneself to death** sich totarbeiten; **w. one's way up** sich hocharbeiten; **w. out** (*a solution*) ausarbeiten; (*a problem*) lösen; **w. to death** abhetzen; **w. up an appetite** [*dat*] Appetit machen || *intr* arbeiten; (*function*) funktionieren; (*succeed*) klappen; **w. against** wirken gegen; **w. away at** losarbeiten auf (*acc*); **w. at** (*a trade*) ausüben; **w. both ways** für beide Fälle gelten; **w. loose** sich lockern; **w. on** (*a person*) bearbeiten; (*a patient, car*) arbeiten an (*dat*); **w. out** (sport) trainieren; **w. out well** gut ausgehen

workable ['wʌrkəbəl] *adj* brauchbar; (*plan*) durchführbar

work'bench' *s* Werkbank *f*

work'book' *s* Übungsheft *n*

work' camp' *s* Arbeitslager *n*

work' day' *s* Arbeitstag *m*

work' detail' *s* (mil) Arbeitskommando *n*

worked'-up' *adj* erregt; **get s.o. w.** j-n erregen; **get w.** sich erregen

worker ['wʌrkər] *s* Arbeiter –in *mf*

work' force' *s* Belegschaft *f*

work'horse' *s* Arbeitspferd *n*

work'ing day' *s* Arbeitstag *m*

work'ing girl' *s* Arbeiterin *f*

work'ing hours' *spl* Arbeitsstunden *pl*

work'ingman' *s* (**-men'**) Arbeiter *m*

work'ing or'der *s*—**in w.** betriebsfähig

work'ingwom'an *s* (**-wom'en**) Arbeiterin *f*; (*professionally*) berufstätige Frau *f*

work'man *s* (**-men**) Arbeiter *m*

work'manship' *s* Ausführung *f*

work'men's compensa'tion insur'ance *s* Arbeiterunfallversicherung *f*

work' of art' *s* Kunstwerk *n*

work'out' *s* Training *n*

work' per'mit *s* Arbeitsgenehmigung *f*

work'room' *s* Arbeitszimmer *n*

work' sche'dule *s* Dienstplan *m*

work'shop' *s* Werkstatt *f*

work' stop'page *s* Arbeitseinstellung *f*

world [wʌrld] *adj* Welt– || *s* Welt *f*; **a w. of** groß; **from all over the w.** aus aller Herren Ländern; **not for all the w.** nicht um die Welt; **see the w.** in der Welt herumkommen; **they are worlds apart** es liegen Welten zwischen den beiden; **think the w. of** große Stücke halten auf (*acc*); **who (where) in the w.** wer (wo) in aller Welt

world' affairs' *spl* internationale Angelegenheiten *pl*

world'-fa'mous *adj* weltberühmt

worldly ['wʌrldli] *adj* (*goods, pleasures*) irdisch; (*person*) weltlich; (*wisdom*) Welt–

world'ly-wise' *adj* weltklug

world's' fair' *s* Weltausstellung *f*

world'-shak'ing *adj* weltbewegend

world'-wide' *adj* weltweit

worm [wʌrm] *s* Wurm *m* || *tr*—**w. one's way** sich schlängeln; **w. secrets out of s.o.** j-m die Würmer aus der Nase ziehen

worm-eaten ['wʌrm,itən] *adj* (& fig) wurmstichig

wormy ['wʌrmi] *adj* wurmig

worn [worn] *adj* (*clothes*) getragen; (*tires*) abgenutzt; (*wearied*) müde

worn'-out' *adj* (*clothes*) abgetragen; (*tires*) abgenutzt; (*exhausted*) erschöpft

worrisome ['wʌrisəm] *adj* (*causing worry*) beunruhigend; (*inclined to worry*) sorgenvoll

wor·ry ['wʌri] *s* Sorge *f*; (*source of worry*) Ärger *m* || *v* (*pret* & *pp* **-ried**) *tr* beunruhigen; **be worried** besorgt sein || *intr* (*about*) sich [*dat*] Sorgen machen (um); **don't w.!** keine Sorge!

worse [wʌrs] *comp adj* schlechter, schlimmer; **be w. off** schlimmer daran sein; **he's none the w. for it** es hat ihm nichts geschadet; **what's w.** was noch schlimmer ist

worsen ['wʌrsən] *tr* verschlimmern || *intr* sich verschlimmern

wor·ship ['wʌrʃɪp] *s* Anbetung *f*; (*services*) Gottesdienst *m* || *v* (*pret* & *pp* **-ship**[p]**ed**) *ger* **-ship**[p]**ing**) *tr* (& fig) anbeten || *intr* seine Andacht verrichten

worship(p)er ['wʌrʃɪpər] *s* Anbeter –in *mf*; (*in church*) Andächtige *mf*

worst [wʌrst] *super adj* schlimmste || *super adv* am schlimmsten || *s* Schlimmste *n*; **at the w.** schlimmstenfalls; **get the w. of** den kürzeren ziehen bei; **if w. comes to w.** wenn alle Stricke reißen; **the w. is yet to come** das dicke Ende kommt noch || *tr* schlagen

worsted ['wustɪd] *adj* Kammgarn–

worth [wʌrθ] *adj* wert; **it is w.** (ger) es lohnt sich zu (*inf*); **it is w. the trouble** es ist der Mühe wert; **ten dollars' w. of meat** für zehn Dollar Fleisch; **w. seeing** sehenswert || *s* Wert *m*

worthless ['wʌrθlɪs] *adj* wertlos; (*person*) nichtsnutzig

worth'while' *adj* lohnend

worthy ['wʌrði] *adj* (of) würdig (*genit*)

would [wʊd] *aux* used to express 1) indirect statements, e.g., **he said he w. come** er sagte, er würde kommen; 2) the present conditional, e.g., **he w. do it if he could** er würde es tun, wenn er könnte; 3) past conditional, e.g., **he w. have paid, if he had had the money** er würde gezahlt haben, wenn er das Geld gehabt hätte; 4) habitual action in the past, e.g., **he w. always buy the morning paper** er kaufte immer das Morgenblatt; 5) polite requests, e.g., **w. you please pass me the butter?** würden Sie mir bitte die Butter reichen; 6) a wish, e.g., **w. that I had never seen it** wenn ich es nur nie gesehen hätte!; **w. rather** möchte lieber, e.g., **I w. rather go on foot** ich möchte lieber zu Fuß gehen

would'-be' *adj* angeblich, Möchtegern-

wound [wund] *s* Wunde *f* || *tr* verwunden

wound'ed *adj* verwundet || **the w.** *spl* die Verwundeten *pl*

wow [waʊ] *s* (coll) Bombenerfolg *m* || *tr* (coll) erstaunen || *interj* nanu!

wrack [ræk] *s*—**go to w. and ruin** untergehen, in Brüche gehen

wraith [reθ] *s* (*apparition*) Erscheinung *f*; (*spirit*) Geist *m*

wrangle ['ræŋgəl] *s* Streit *m* || *intr* streiten

wrap [ræp] *s* Überwurf *m* || *v* (*pret & pp* **wrapped**; *ger* **wrapping**) *tr* wickeln; (*a package*) einpacken; **be wrapped up in** (*e.g., thoughts*) versunken sein in (*dat*); **wrapped in darkness** in Dunkelheit gehüllt; **w. up** (*a deal*) abwickeln

wrapper ['ræpər] *s* Verpackung *f*; (*for mailing newspapers*) Streifband *n*

wrap'ping *s* Verpackung *f*

wrap'ping pa'per *s* Packpapier *n*

wrath [ræθ] *s* Zorn *m*, Wut *f*

wrathful ['ræθfəl] *adj* zornig, wütend

wreak [rik] *tr* (*vengeance*) üben; **w. havoc** schlimm hausen

wreath [riθ] *s* (wreaths [riðz]) Kranz *m*; **w. of smoke** Rauchfahne *f*

wreathe [rið] *tr* bekränzen, umwinden

wreck [rek] *s* (*of a car or train*) Unglück *n*; (*wrecked ship, car, person*) Wrack *n* || *tr* (*e.g., a car*) zertrümmern; (*a building*) in Trümmer legen; (*a marriage*) zerrütten; (fig) zum Scheitern bringen; **be wrecked** (fig & naut) scheitern

wreckage ['rekɪdʒ] *s* Wrackgut *n*; (*of an accident*) Trümmer *pl*

wrecker ['rekər] *s* Abschleppwagen *m*

wren [ren] *s* (orn) Zaunkönig *m*

wrench [rentʃ] *s* (tool) Schraubenschlüssel *m*; (*of a muscle*) Verrenkung *f* || *tr* verrenken

wrest [rest] *tr* (from) entreißen (*dat*)

wrestle ['resəl] *tr* ringen mit || *intr* ringen

wrestler ['reslər] *s* Ringer *m*; (*professional wrestler*) Catcher *m*

wrestling ['reslɪŋ] *s* Ringen *n*; (*professional wrestling*) Catchen *n*

wres'tling match' *s* Ringkampf *m*

wretch [retʃ] *s* armer Kerl *m*; (*vile person*) Schuft *m*

wretched ['retʃɪd] *adj* elend; (*terrible*) scheußlich

wriggle ['rɪgəl] *s* Krümmung *f*; (*of a worm*) schlängelnde Bewegung *f* || *tr* hin- und herbewegen; **w. one's way** sich dahinschlängeln || *intr* sich winden

wring [rɪŋ] *v* (*pret & pp* **wrung** [rʌŋ]) *tr* (*the hands*) ringen; **w. out** (*the wash*) auswinden; **w. s.o.'s neck** j-m den Hals umdrehen

wringer ['rɪŋər] *s* Wringmaschine *f*

wrinkle ['rɪŋkəl] *s* Falte *f*; **new w.** (fig) neuer Kniff *m*; **take out the wrinkles** (fig) den letzten Schliff geben || *tr* falten, runzeln; (*paper, clothes*) zerknittern || *intr* Falten werfen

wrin'kle-proof' *adj* knitterfrei

wrinkly ['rɪŋkli] *adj* faltig, runzelig

wrist [rɪst] *s* Handgelenk *n*

wrist'band' *s* Armband *n*

wrist' watch' *s* Armbanduhr *f*

writ [rɪt] *s* gerichtlicher schriftlicher Befehl *m*

write [raɪt] *v* (*pret* **wrote** [rot]; *pp* **written** ['rɪtən]) *tr* schreiben; (*compose*) verfassen; **it is written** (*in the Bible*) es steht geschrieben; **it is written all over his face** es steht ihm im Gesicht geschrieben; **w. down** aufschreiben; **w. off** abschreiben; **w. out** ausschreiben; (*a check*) ausstellen || *intr* schreiben; **w. for information** Informationen anfordern

write'-off' *s* Abschreibung *f*

writer ['raɪtər] *s* Schreiber –in *mf*; (*author*) Schriftsteller –in *mf*

writ'er's cramp' *s* Schreibkrampf *m*

write'-up' *s* Pressebericht *m*

writhe [raɪð] *intr* (in) sich krümmen (vor *dat*)

writ'ing *s* Schreiben *n*; (*handwriting*) Schrift *f*; **in w.** schriftlich; **put in w.** niederschreiben

writ'ing desk' *s* Schreibtisch *m*

writ'ing pad' *s* Schreibblock *m*

writ'ing pa'per *s* Schreibpapier *n*; (*stationery*) Briefpapier *n*

written ['rɪtən] *adj* schriftlich; (*law*) geschrieben; (*language*) Schrift-

wrong [rɔŋ] *adj* (*incorrect*) falsch; (*unjust*) unrecht; **be w.** (*be incorrect*) nicht stimmen; (*be in error*) Unrecht haben; (*said of a situation*) nicht in Ordnung sein; **be. w. with** fehlen (*dat*); **sorry, w. number!** (telp) falsch verbunden! || *s* Unrecht *n*; **be in the w.** im Unrecht sein; **do w.** ein Unrecht begehen; **do w. to s.o.** j-m ein Unrecht zufügen; **get in w. with s.o.** es sich (*dat*) mit j-m verderben || *adv* falsch, unrecht; **go w.** (*morally*) auf Abwege geraten; (*in walking*) sich verirren; (*in reckoning*) irregehen; (*in driving*) sich verfahren; (*said of plans*) schief gehen

wrongdoer ['rɔŋ‚duˌ.ər] *s* Missetäter –in *mf*

wrong'do'ing *s* Missetat *f*
wrought' i'ron [rɔt] *s* Schmiedeeisen *n*
wrought'-up' *adj* aufgebracht
wry [raɪ] *adj* schief

X

X, x [eks] *s* vierundzwanzigster Buchstabe des englischen Alphabets

xenophobia [‚zenə'fobɪ.ə] *s* Fremdenhaß *m*

Xerox ['zɪrɑks] *s* (trademark) Xerographie *f* || **xerox** *tr* ablichten

Xer'ox-cop'y *s* Ablichtung *f*

Xmas ['krɪsməs] *adj* Weihnachts- || *s* Weihnachten *pl*

x'-ray' *adj* Röntgen- || *s* (*picture*) Röntgenbild *n*; **x-rays** Röntgenstrahlen *pl* || *tr* röntgen

x'-ray ther'apy *s* Röntgentherapie *f*

xylophone ['zaɪlə‚fon] *s* Xylophon *n*

Y

Y, y [waɪ] *s* fünfundzwanzigster Buchstabe des englischen Alphabets

yacht [jɑt] *s* Jacht *f*
yacht' club' *s* Jachtklub *m*
yam [jæm] *s* Yamwurzel *f*
yank [jæŋk] *s* Ruck *m*; **Yank** Ami *m* || *tr*—**y. s.th. out** of reißen aus || *intr* —**y. on** heftig ziehen an (*dat*)
Yankee ['jæŋkɪ] *s* Yankee *m*
yap [jæp] *s* (*talk*) (sl) Geschwätz *n*; (*mouth*) (sl) Maul *n*; (*bark*) Gekläff *n* || *v* (*pret & pp* yapped; *ger* yapping) *intr* (*bark*) kläffen; (*talk*) (sl) schwätzen
yard [jɑrd] *s* (*measure*) Yard *n*; (*ground adjoining a building*) Hof *m*; (naut) Rahe *f*; (rr) Rangierbahnhof *m*
yard'arm' *s* (naut) Nock *f & n*
yard' mas'ter *s* (rr) Rangiermeister *m*
yard'stick' *s* Yardmaß *n*; (fig) Maßstab *m*
yarn [jɑrn] *s* (*thread; story*) Garn *n*; **spin yarns** (fig) Garne spinnen
yaw [jɔ] *s* (aer, rok) Schwanken *n*; (naut) Gieren *n* || *intr* (aer, rok) schwanken; (naut) gieren
yawl [jɔl] *s* (naut) Jolle *f*
yawn [jɔn] *s* Gähnen *n* || *intr* gähnen; (*said, e.g., of a gorge*) klaffen
ye [ji] *pers pron* ihr
yea [je] *s* Jastimme *f* || *adv* ja
yeah [je] *adv* ja
year [jɪr] *s* Jahr *n*; **all y. round** das ganze Jahr hindurch; **a y. from to-day** heute übers Jahr; **for years** seit Jahren; jahrelang; **in years** seit Jahren; **y. in y. out** jahraus jahrein
year'book' *s* Jahrbuch *n*
yearling ['jɪrlɪŋ] *s* Jährling *m*
yearly ['jɪrlɪ] *adj & adv* jährlich
yearn [jʌrn] *intr*—**y. for** sich sehnen nach; **y. to** (*inf*) sich danach sehnen zu (*inf*)
yearn'ing *s* Sehnsucht *f*

yeast [jist] *s* Hefe *f*
yell [jel] *s* Ruf *m*, Aufschrei *m*; (sport) Kampfruf *m* || *tr* (gellend) schreien; **y. one's lungs out** sich tot schreien || *intr* schreien; **y. at** anschreien
yellow ['jelo] *adj* gelb; (sl) feige || *s* Gelb *n* || *tr* gelb machen || *intr* vergilben
yellowish ['jelo‚ɪʃ] *adj* gelblich
yel'lowjack'et *s* Wespe *f*
yel'low jour'nalism *s* Sensationspresse *f*
yel'low streak' *s* Zug *m* von Feigheit
yelp [jelp] *s* Gekläff *n* || *intr* kläffen
yen [jen] *s* (*Japanese money*) Yen *m*; (for) brennendes Verlangen *n* (nach)
yeo-man ['jomən] *s* (-men) (nav) Verwaltungsunteroffizier *m*
yeo'man's serv'ice *s* großer Dienst *m*
yes [jes] *adv* ja; **Sir** jawohl || *s* Ja *n*; **say yes to** bejahen
yes' man' *s* Jasager *m*
yesterday ['jestar‚de] *adv* gestern; **y. morning** gestern früh || *s* Gestern *n*; **yesterday's** gestrig
yet [jet] *adv* (*still*) noch; (*however*) doch; (*already*) schon; **and yet** trotzdem, dennoch; **as yet** schon; **not yet** noch nicht || *conj* aber
yew [ju] *s* Eibe *f*
Yiddish ['jɪdɪʃ] *adj* jiddisch || *s* Jiddisch *n*
yield [jild] *s* Ertrag *m* || *tr* (*profit*) einbringen; (*interest*) tragen; (*crops*) hervorbringen; (*give up*) überlassen || *intr* (to) nachgeben (*dat*)
yo-del ['jodəl] *s* Jodler *m* || *v* (*pret & pp* -del[l]ed; *ger* -del[l]ing) *intr* jodeln
yodeler ['jodələr] *s* Jodler –in *mf*
yogurt ['jogurt] *s* Yoghurt *m & n*
yoke [jok] *s* (*part of harness; burden*) Joch *n*; **pass under the y.** sich in ein Joch fügen; **y. of oxen** Ochsengespann *n* || *tr* ins Joch spannen

yokel ['jokəl] *s* Bauerntölpel *m*

yolk [jok] *s* Dotter *m & n*

yonder ['jandər] *adv* dort drüben

yore [jor] *s*—**of y.** vormals

you [ju] *pers pron* du; (*plural form*) ihr; (*polite form*) Sie; **to you** dir; (*plural form*) euch; (*polite form*) Ihnen; **you of all people!** ausgerechnet Sie! || *indef pron* man

young [jʌŋ] *adj* (**younger** ['jʌŋgər]; **youngest** ['jʌŋgɪst]) jung; **y. for one's age** jugendlich für sein Alter || *spl* (*of animals*) Jungen *pl*; **the y.** die Jungen, die Jugend; **with y.** (*pregnant*) trächtig

young' la'dy *s* Fräulein *n*

young' man' *s* junger Mann *m*; (*boyfriend*) Freund *m*

youngster ['jʌŋstər] *s* Jugendliche *mf*

your [jur] *poss adj* dein; (*plural form*) euer; (*polite form*) Ihr

yours [jurz] *poss pron* deiner; (*plural*

form) euerer; (*polite form*) Ihrer;

your-self [jur'sɛlf] *intens pron* (**–selves** ['sɛlvz]) selbst, selber || *reflex pron* dich; (*plural form*) euch; (*polite form*) Sich; **to y.** dir; (*polite form*) Sich; **to yourselves** euch; (*polite form*) Sich

youth [juθ] *s* (**youths** [juθs], [juðz]) (*age*) Jugend *f*; (*person*) Jugendliche *mf*

youthful ['juθfəl] *adj* jugendlich

youth' hos'tel *s* Jugendherberge *f*

yowl [jaul] *s* Gejaule *n* || *tr & intr* jaulen

Yugoslav ['jugo'slav] *adj* jugoslawisch || *s* Jugoslawe *m*, Jugoslawin *f*

Yugoslavia ['jugo'slavɪə] *s* Jugoslavien *n*

yule' log' [jul] *s* Weihnachtsscheit *n*

yule'tide' *s* Weihnachtszeit *f*

Z

Z, z [zi] *s* sechsundzwanzigster Buchstabe des englischen Alphabets

zany ['zeni] *adj* närrisch || *s* Hanswurst *m*

zeal [zil] *s* Eifer *m*

zealot ['zɛlət] *s* Zelot –in *mf*

zealous ['zɛləs] *adj* eifrig

zebra ['zibrə] *s* Zebra *n*

zenith ['zinɪθ] *s* Scheitelpunkt *m*, Zenit *m*

zephyr ['zɛfər] *s* Zephir *m*

zeppelin ['zɛpəlɪn] *s* Zeppelin *m*

ze-ro ['ziro] *s* (**–ros & –roes**) Null *f* || *tr*—**z. in a rifle** Visier e–s Gewehrs justieren || *intr*—**z. in on** zielen auf (*acc*)

ze'ro hour' *s* Stunde *f* Null

zest [zɛst] *s* Würze *f*

Zeus [zus] *s* Zeus *m*

zig-zag ['zɪg͵zæg] *adj* Zickzack– || *adv* im Zickzack || *s* Zickzack *m* || (*pret & pp* **–zagged;** *ger* **–zagging**) *intr* im Zickzack fahren

zinc [zɪŋk] *s* Zink *n*

Zionism ['zaɪ͵ə͵nɪzəm] *s* Zionismus *m*

zip [zɪp] *s* (*coll*) Schmiß *m* || *v* (*pret & pp* **zipped;** *ger* **zipping**) *tr* (*convey with speed*) mit Schwung befördern; (*fasten with a zipper*) mit e–m Reißverschluß schließen || *intr* sausen; **zip by** vorbeisausen || *interj* wuppdich!

zip' code' *s* Postleitzahl *f*

zipper ['zɪpər] *s* Reißverschluß *m*

zircon ['zʌrkan] *s* Zirkon *m*

zither ['zɪθər] *s* Zither *f*

zodiac ['zodɪ͵æk] *s* Tierkreis *m*

zombie ['zɔmbi] *s* (*sl*) Depp *m*

zone [zon] *s* (& *geol*) Zone *f*; (*postal zone*) Postbezirk *m*; (*mil*) Bereich *m*

zoo [zu] *s* Zoo *m*, Tiergarten *m*

zoologic(al) [͵zo·ə'ladʒɪk(əl)] *adj* zoologisch

zoologist [zo'alədʒɪst] *s* Zoologe *m*, Zoologin *f*

zoology [zo'alədʒi] *s* Zoologie *f*

zoom [zum] *s* lautes Summen *n*; (aer) Hochreißen *n* || *intr* laut summen; **z. up** (aer) hochreißen

zoom' lens' *s* Gummilinse *f*

METRIC CONVERSIONS

Multiply:	By:	To Obtain:
acres	43,560	sq. ft.
	0.4047	hectares
	0.0015625	sq. mi.
ampere-hours	3600	coulombs
atmospheres	76.0	cm. of mercury
	33.90	ft. of water
	14.70	lbs./sq. in.
British thermal units	1054	joules
	777.5	ft.-lbs.
	252.0	gram calories
	0.0003927	horsepower-hrs.
	0.0002928	kilowatt-hrs.
B.T.U./hr.	0.2928	watts
B.T.U./min.	12.96	ft.-lbs./sec.
	0.02356	horsepower
bushels	3523.8	hectoliters
	2150.42	cu. ins.
	35.238	liters
°C + 17.78	1.8	°F
centimeters	0.3937	inches
cm-grams	980.1	cm.-dynes
chains	66	ft.
circumference	6.2832	radians
cubic centimeters	0.0610	cu. ins.
cu. feet	1728	cu. ins.
	62.43	lbs. of water
	7.481	gals. (liq.)
	0.0283	cu. m.
cu. ft./min.	62.43	lbs. water/min.
cu. ft./sec.	448.831	gals./min.
cu. inches	16.387	cu. cm.
	0.0005787	cu. ft.
cu. meters	264.2	gals. (liq.)
	35.3147	cu. ft.
	1.3079	cu. yds.
cu. yards	27	cu. ft.
	0.765	cu. m.
days	86,400	seconds
degrees/sec.	0.1667	revolutions/min.
°F − 32	0.5556	°C
faradays/sec.	96,500	amperes
feet	30.48	cm.
	0.3048	meters
	0.0001894	mi. (stat.)
	0.0001645	mi. (Brit. naut.)

Multiply:	By:	To Obtain:
ft. of water	62.43	lbs./sq. ft.
	0.4335	lbs./sq. in.
ft./min.	0.5080	cm./sec.
ft./sec.	0.6818	mi./hr.
	0.5921	knots
fluid ounces	29.573	milliliters
furlongs	660	feet
	0.125	mi.
gallons	231	cu. ins.
	8.345	lbs. of water
	8	pts.
	4	qts.
	3.785	liters
	0.003785	cu. m.
gals./min.	8.0208	cu. ft./hr.
grains	0.0648	grams
grams	980.1	dynes
	15.43	grains
	0.0353	oz. (avdp.)
	0.0022	lbs. (avdp.)
hectares	107,600	sq. ft.
	2.47	acres
hectoliters	2.838	bushels
horsepower	33,000	ft.-lbs./min.
	2545	B.T.U./hr.
	745.7	watts
	42.44	B.T.U./min.
	0.7457	kilowatts
inches	25.40	mm.
	2.540	cm.
	0.00001578	mi.
ins. of water	0.03613	lbs./sq. in.
kilograms	980,100	dynes
	2.2046	lbs. (avdp.)
kg. calories	3086	ft.-lbs.
	3.968	B.T.U.
kg. cal./min.	51.43	ft.-lbs./sec.
	0.06972	kilowatts
kilometers	3280.8	ft.
	0.621	mi.
km./hr.	0.621	mi./hr.
	0.5396	knots
kilowatts	737.6	ft.-lbs./sec.
	56.92	B.T.U./min.
	1.341	horsepower
kilowatt-hrs.	2,655,000	ft.-lbs.
	3415	B.T.U.
	1.341	horsepower-hrs.
knots	6080	ft./hr.
	1.151	stat. mi./hr.
	1	(Brit.) naut. mi./hr.
liters	61.02	cu. ins.
	2.113	pts. (liq.)
	1.057	qts. (liq.)
	0.264	gals. (liq.)
	1.816	pts. (dry)
	0.908	qts. (dry)
	0.1135	pecks
	0.0284	bushels

Multiply:	By:	To Obtain:
meters	39.37	inches
	3.2808	ft.
	1.0936	yds.
	0.0006215	mi. (stat.)
	0.0005396	mi. (Brit. naut.)
miles		
statute	5280	ft.
	1.609	km.
	0.8624	mi. (Brit. naut.)
nautical (Brit.)	6080	ft.
	1.151	mi. (stat.)
mi./hr.	1.467	ft./sec.
milligrams/liter	1	parts/million
milliliters	0.0338	fluid oz.
millimeters	0.03937	inches
ounces		
avoirdupois	28.349	grams
	0.9115	oz. (troy)
	0.0625	lbs. (avdp.)
troy	31.103	grams
	1.0971	oz. (avdp.)
pecks	8.8096	liters
pints		
liquid	473.2	cu. cm.
	28.875	cu. ins.
	0.473	liters
dry	0.550	liters
pounds		
avoirdupois	444,600	dynes
	453.6	grams
	32.17	poundals
	14.58	oz. (troy)
	1.21	lbs. (troy)
	0.4536	kg.
troy	0.373	kg.
lbs. (avdp.)/sq. in.	70.22	g./sq. cm.
	2.307	ft. of water
quarts		
liquid	57.75	cu. ins.
	32	fluid oz.
	2	pts.
	0.946	liters
dry	67.20	cu. ins.
	1.101	liters
quires	25	sheets
radians	3437.7	minutes
	57.296	degrees
reams	500	sheets
revolutions/min.	6	degrees/sec.
rods	16.5	ft.
	5.5	yds.
	5.029	meters
slugs	32.17	lbs. (mass)
square centimeters	0.155	sq. ins.
sq. feet	0.093	sq. m.
sq. inches	6.451	sq. cm.
sq. kilometers	247.1	acres
	0.3861	sq. mi.

Multiply:	By:	To Obtain:
sq. meters	10.76	sq. ft.
	1.1960	sq. yds.
sq. miles	27,878,400	sq. ft.
	640	acres
	2.5889	sq. km.
sq. yards	0.8361	sq. m.
tons		
long	2240	lbs. (avdp.)
	1.12	short tons
	1.0160	metric tons
metric	2204.6	lbs. (avdp.)
	1000	kg.
	1.1023	short tons
	0.9842	long tons
short	2000	lbs. (avdp.)
	0.9072	metric tons
	0.8929	long tons
watts	3.415	B.T.U./hr.
	0.001341	horsepower
yards	36	inches
	3	ft.
	0.9144	meters
	0.0005682	mi. (stat.)
	0.0004934	mi. (Brit. naut.)

LABELS AND ABBREVIATIONS

BEZEICHNUNGEN DER SACHGEBIETE UND ABKÜRZUNGEN

abbr abbreviation—Abkürzung
acc accusative—Akkusativ
(acct) accounting—Rechnungswesen
adj adjective—Adjektiv
(adm) administration—Verwaltung
adv adverb—Adverb
(aer) aeronautics—Luftfahrt
(agr) agriculture—Landwirtschaft
(alg) algebra—Algebra
(Am) American—amerikanisch
(anat) anatomy—Anatomie
(angl) angling—Angeln
(archeol) archeology—Archäologie
(archit) architecture—Architektur
(arith) arithmetic—Rechnen
art article—Artikel
(arti) artillery—Artillerie
(astr) astronomy—Astronomie
(atom. phys.) Atomic physics—Atomphysik
(Aust) Austrian—österreichisch
(aut) automobile—Automobile
aux auxiliary verb—Hilfsverb
(bact) bacteriology—Bakteriologie
(baseball) Baseball
(basketball) Korbball
(bb) bookbinding—Buchbinderei
(Bib) Biblical—biblisch
(billiards) Billard
(biochem) biochemistry—Biochemie
(biol) biology—Biologie
(bowling) Kegeln
(bot) botany—Botanik
(box) boxing—Boxen
(Brit) British—britisch
(cards) Kartenspiel
(carp) carpentry—Zimmerhandwerk
(checkers) Damespiel

372

chem) chemistry—Chemie
chess) Schachspiel
cin) cinematography—Kinematographie
coll) colloquial—umgangssprachlich
com) commercial—Handels-
comb.fm. combining form—Wortbildungselement
comp comparative—Komparativ
conj conjunction—Konjunktion
crew) Rudersport
culin) culinary—kulinarisch
data proc.) data processing—Datenverarbeitung
dem demonstrative—hinweisend
(dent) dentistry—Zahnheilkunde
(dial) dialectical—dialektisch
(dipl) diplomacy—Diplomatie
(eccl) ecclesiastical—kirchlich
(econ) economics—Wirtschaft
(educ) education—Schulwesen
e-e a(n)—eine
e.g. for example—zum Beispiel
(elec) electricity—Elektrizität
(electron) electronics—Elektronik
e-m to a(n)—einem
e-n a(n)—einen
(eng) engineering—Technik
(ent) entomology—Entomologie
e-r of a(n), to a(n)—einer
e-s of a(n)—eines
etw something—etwas
f feminine noun—Femininum
(fa) fine arts—schöne Künste
fem feminine—weiblich
(fencing) Fechtkunst
(fig) figurative—bildlich
(& fig) literal and figurative—buchstäblich und bildlich
(fin) finance—Finanzwesen
(fb) football, soccer—Fußball
fut future—Zukunft
genit genitive—Genitiv
(geog) geography, Geographie
(geol) geology—Geologie
(geom) geometry—Geometrie
ger gerund—Gerundium
(golf) Golf
(gram) grammar—Grammatik
(gym) gymnastics—Gymnastik
(heral) heraldry—Wappenkunde
(hist) history—Geschichte
(horol) horology—Zeitmessung
(hort) horticulture—Gartenbau
(hum) humorous—scherzhaft
(hunt) hunting—Jagdwesen
(ichth) ichthyology—Ichthyologie

imperf imperfect—Imperfekt
impers impersonal—unpersönlich
ind indicative—Indikativ
indecl indeclinable—undeklinierbar
indef indefinite—unbestimmt
(indust) industry—Industrie
inf infinitive—Infinitiv
(ins) insurance—Versicherungswesen
insep inseparable—untrennbar
intens intensive—verstärkend
interj interjection—Interjektion
interr interrogative—Frage-
intr intransitive—intransitiv
invar invariable—unveränderlich
(iron) ironical—ironisch
j-m to someone—jemandem
j-n someone—jemanden
(journ) journalism—Zeitungswesen
j-s someone's—jemand(e)s
(jur) jurisprudence—Rechtswissenschaft
(libr) library science—Bibliothekswissenschaft
(ling) linguistics—Linguistik
(lit) literary—literarisch
(log) logic—Logik
m masculine noun—Maskulinum
(mach) machinery—Maschinen
(mech) mechanics—Mechanik
(med) medicine—Medizin
(metal) metallurgy—Metallurgie
(meteor) meteorology—Meteorologie
mf masculine or feminine noun according to sex—Maskulinum
    oder Femininum je nach Geschlecht
(mil) military—Militär-
(min) mining—Bergwerkswesen
(mineral) mineralogy—Mineralogie
mod aux modal auxiliary—Modalverb
(mount) mountain climbing—Bergsteigerei
(mus) music—Musik
(myth) mythology—Mythologie
m & f masculine and feminine noun without regard to sex—
    Maskulinum oder Femininum ohne Rücksicht auf Geschlecht
(naut) nautical—nautisch
(nav) navy—Kriegsmarine
neut neuter—sächlich
(obs) obsolete—veraltet
(obstet) obstetrics—Geburtshilfe
(opt) optics—Optik
(orn) ornithology—Ornithologie
(paint) painting—Malerei
(parl) parliamentary—parlamentarisch
(pathol) pathology—Pathologie
(pej) pejorative—pejorativ
pers personal—Personal-

374

(pharm) pharmacy—Pharmazie
(philos) philosophy—Philosophie
(phonet) phonetics—Phonetik
(phot) photography—Photographie
(phys) physics—Physik
(physiol) physiology—Physiologie
pl plural—Plural
(poet) poetical—dichterisch
(pol) politics—Politik
poss possessive—besitzanzeigend
pp past participal—Partizip Perfekt
pref prefix—Präfix
prep preposition—Präposition
pres present—Gegenwart
pret preterit—Präteritum
pron pronoun—Pronomen
pros prosody—Prosodie
(Prot) Protestant—protestantisch
(psychol) psychology—Psychologie
(public sign) Hinweisschild
(rad) radio—Radio
(radar) Radar
recip reciprocal—wechselseitig
ref reflexive verb—Reflexivverb
reflex reflexive—reflexiv
rel relative—relativ
(relig) religion—Religion
(rhet) rhetoric—Rhetorik
(rok) rocketry—Raketen
(rr) railroad—Eisenbahn
s substantive—Substantiv
(sculp) sculpture—Bildhauerkunst
sep separable—trennbar
(sewing) Näherei
sg singular—Einzahl
(sl) slang—Slang
s.o. someone—jemand
s.o.'s someone's—jemand(e)s
spl substantive plural—pluralisches Substantiv
(sport) sports—Sports
(st. exch.) stock exchange—Börse
subj subjunctive—Konjunktiv
suf suffix—Suffix
super superlative—Superlativ
(surg) surgery—Chirurgie
(surv) surveying—Vermessungswesen
(tech) technical—Fachsprache
(telg) telegraphy—Telegraphie
(telp) telephone—Fernsprechwesen
(telv) television—Fernsehen
(tennis) Tennis
(tex) textiles—Textilien
(theat) theater—Theater

(theol) theology—Theologie
tr transitive—transitiv
(typ) typography—Typographie
usw. and so forth—und so weiter
v verb—Verb
var variant—Variante
(vet) veterinary medicine—Veterinärmedizin
(vulg) vulgar—vulgär
(zool) zoology—Zoologie